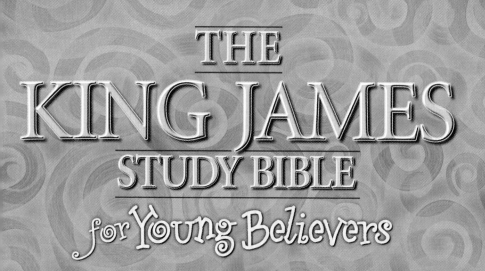

THE
KING JAMES
STUDY BIBLE
for Young Believers

✵ This Bible belongs to:

nicoleBrockett

✵ Given by:

(mom) ReginaBrockett

✵ Date:

10/16/04

✵ occasion:

just going to Christain Book
Store

The Road to Heaven

(How to Be Saved)

We are separated from God by sin.
Everyone has sinned by disobeying God.
We all fall short of the glory of God.
Read Romans 3:23.

God has taken the first step in rescuing us.
While we were still sinners, God showed His love toward
us by sending His Son Jesus to die in our place.
Read Romans 5:8.

God gives the gift of everlasting life.
Even though our sin has earned us death,
God has given us the gift of eternal life through
Jesus Christ our Lord.
Read Romans 6:23.

Believe in Jesus' death as the payment for your sins.
God loved the world so much that He gave Jesus,
His one and only Son, so that anybody who believes in
Him will not really die, but will have everlasting life.
Read John 3:16.

Just ask Jesus to be your Savior now!
If you mean it with all your heart, believing that
God has raised Him from the dead, you will be saved.
Read Romans 10:9.

My Decision Record

I _____Nicole Brockett_____ have
Name

this day _____when I was 5_____ accepted
Date

the Lord Jesus Christ as my personal Savior.

_____NicoleBrockett_____
Signature

"And this is the record, that God hath given to us eternal life, and this life is in his Son.

He that hath the Son hath life; and he that hath not the Son of God hath not life."

–1 John 5:11, 12

Certificate of Baptism

This certifies that ___Nicole Brockett___
Name

Born on the _13_ day of _Janurary_ , _93_
Month   *Year*

In _Joliet , Plainfeild_
Place of Birth

Was baptized in the name of the Father, and of the Son, and of the Holy Ghost

on the ____ day of _____ , _____.
Month   *Year*

In the sanctuary of

_____
Church Name

_____
Address

_____
Pastor

FAVORITE BIBLE VERSES FOR MY LIFE
FROM FAMILY AND FRIENDS

John 3:16 _____

_____ _____

_____ _____

_____ _____

_____ _____

_____ _____

_____ _____

_____ _____

_____ _____

_____ _____

_____

_____

FAVORITE BIBLE VERSES FOR MY LIFE FROM FAMILY AND FRIENDS

_____

_____

_____

_____

_____

_____

_____

_____

_____

_____

_____

_____

_____

_____

_____

_____

_____

_____

_____

_____

_____

_____

MY CHURCH EVENTS AND ACHIEVEMENTS

_____   _____

_____   _____

_____   _____

_____   _____

_____   _____

_____   _____

_____   _____

_____   _____

_____   _____

_____   _____

_____

_____

_____

MY CHURCH EVENTS AND ACHIEVEMENTS

_____   _____

_____   _____

_____   _____

_____   _____

_____   _____

_____   _____

_____   _____

_____   _____

_____   _____

_____

_____

_____

_____

THE
KING
JAMES
STUDY BIBLE
for Young Believers

NELSON

THOMAS NELSON BIBLES
A Division of Thomas Nelson, Inc.
www.ThomasNelson.com

Contents

How to Use This Bible

God's Word Is Good . . .

Good to read, good to keep, good to learn, good to explore, good to pray, and so much more. The Bible is God's Word to us. God uses the Bible to teach us, guide us, help us, correct us, and change us to be more like Him. Your *King James Study Bible for Young Believers* will help you begin the life-long practice of reading, memorizing, and studying God's Word. Several of the features (like the Bible reading plans and memorization charts) are interactive. That means, for example, that you are asked to answer quizzes and record your progress in reading. A ballpoint pen or pencil (no markers or roller ball pens) will work best on this Bible's paper.

Let's take a look at some of the special features this Bible has to help you get started.

Good Information

In the front of this Bible you will find a number of helpful articles that talk about how the Bible came to be, the men who wrote the books of the Bible, how you can study the Bible, where to find certain Bible topics, the importance of discipline, and more.

God's Word Is Good to Learn

Have you ever wondered when certain events in the Bible took place? "God's Word Is Good to Learn" gives you a historical time line to help you see when things in the Bible happened and what was going on in world history at that time.

God's Word Is Good to Read

Have you ever wondered just how to get started on a good Bible reading plan? This section is your answer. There are ten different reading plans to help you read through the Bible. Take a look.

God's Word Is Good to Keep

Have you always wanted to memorize more Bible verses, but just didn't know what verses to choose? The first "track," or plan, in this section asks you to learn the books of the Bible so that you can find verses easily. Then you can begin by memorizing one verse each week for one year. When you've mastered that challenge, you can move on to learning passages and chapters.

God's Word Is Good to Pray

You know you need to pray and talk with God, but sometimes you just don't know what to say, or how to do it. In this feature, you'll discover how men and women in the Bible prayed. As you read and study their prayers, you will begin to learn how

God wants us to talk with Him. You'll also be able to record your prayers and God's answers in journal pages.

God's Word Is Good to Explore

Inserted throughout your Bible, you will find a treasure chest of study helps. Family trees of famous men and women in the Bible, maps, charts, illustrations of the tabernacle furniture and priests' clothing, houses in Bible times, and more. These forty-eight pages of study materials will help you better understand the people and events in your Bible!

Illustrated Word List

Have you ever run across a Bible word you just couldn't understand? The dictionary in the back of your Bible will give you meanings for some of the more difficult words you'll discover in your Bible, and it will give you one or more Scripture references where that word can be found. This list also includes the definitions for some words that aren't actually in the Bible but that talk about Christian teachings and ideas.

Book Introductions

At the beginning of each book of the Bible, you will find a short introduction telling you about who wrote that particular book, what happens, and how it fits in the big picture of Bible events.

You'll also find:

- An illustrated, full-color time line of biblical and world history
- Color maps
- End-of-verse references and translation notes
- A concordance
- And more.

Start exploring God's Word today with *The King James Study Bible for Young Believers*. Find out for yourself that God's Word *is* good!

What is the Bible?

The Bible is God's holy word. "Bible" means "book," and your Bible is a book of books. In fact, the Bible contains sixty-six different books. Together, all these books tell the story of God's wonderful love for us. They teach us how to live the way God wants us to live. The Bible tells us about God's Son, Jesus Christ, and what His special mission was here on earth. It is a book of adventure, excitement, and mystery. It is a book you'll want to read and study over and over again.

Who is the Bible for? Most of the books in the Old Testament were written to the Jewish people (also called Israelites). They were the nation God had chosen to help bring His Son into the world.

Books in the New Testament were written to many other groups of people. Sometimes the books themselves give you a clue. For instance, Paul wrote Romans to the Christians who lived in Rome. He wrote Ephesians to the Christians at Ephesus. And he wrote Philemon to his friend, Philemon. Other New Testament books were written to all of Christ's followers. These books were passed around from church to church for everyone to read or hear read.

But wait! The Bible was written for you, too. Just as it told the Christians in the first century how to live for God, it tells you, too. God's Word, the Bible, is a personal guide for everyone who wants to follow God. It is God's love letter to each of us.

Has the Bible changed? No. It is true that the Bible was not written in English. The Old Testament was written in the Hebrew language. Most of the New Testament was written in the Greek language. And some of the New Testament was written in the language of Jesus—Aramaic.

Through the years, the Bible has been translated from those languages into other languages, including English. That means people used other languages to say exactly what the Bible said in Hebrew and Greek and Aramaic. They did not change God's meaning; they only put His meaning into our words. And that's great news for us! Now we can read and understand God's Word for ourselves.

Sections of the Bible

There are two major sections of the Bible: the Old Testament and the New Testament.

The Old Testament

This first section of the Bible begins with how God created the world. It tells the story of God's love for His people from the beginning until just before He sent His Son into the world. There are thirty-nine books in the Old Testament section of the Bible. They can be divided into even smaller sections of God's "bookshelf."

Books of Law

Genesis   Exodus   Leviticus   Numbers   Deuteronomy

The first five books of the Old Testament are usually referred to as the "Pentateuch." That just means "five books." The Jewish people called the five books the "Torah." These books are called Books of Law because they contain the many laws God gave to the Jewish people to keep them pure and holy. It was very important for them to stay pure because God would someday send His Son, Jesus, to us through this people. These were special laws for God's special people. The Books of Law begin with the creation of the world. They end with the people of Israel ready to enter the land God had promised to them.

Books of History

Joshua   Judges   Ruth   1 Samuel   2 Samuel   1 Kings
2 Kings   1 Chronicles   2 Chronicles   Ezra   Nehemiah   Esther

The next twelve books of the Old Testament tell the history of God's chosen people. This part of the story begins with Joshua. He was God's chosen leader who brought the Israelites into the Promised Land. These books tell the stories of the kings (like Saul and David and Solomon) and what happened when they obeyed God and when they didn't. These books also tell how God allowed the Israelites to be captured by other nations when they disobeyed God. Finally, these books tell how the Jewish people returned to God and to their Promised Land.

Books of Poetry

Job   Psalms   Proverbs   Ecclesiastes   Song of Solomon

These five books of the Old Testament are beautiful words of prayer and praise to God. They were written by people who loved God very much. These poems and songs were used by the Jewish people during their feasts and festivals. They used them to celebrate God's goodness to them. They also used them to praise and honor God. Today many of our songs of praise and prayer contain the words found in the books of poetry.

Books of Prophecy

Isaiah	Jeremiah	Lamentations	Ezekiel	Daniel	Hosea
Joel	Amos	Obadiah	Jonah	Micah	Nahum
Habakkuk	Zephaniah	Haggai	Zechariah	Malachi	

The last seventeen books of the Old Testament are about God's messengers, or "prophets." The books of prophecy are God's special messages to His chosen people, the Jewish people. The prophets were sent to remind the people about God's laws and how they were to live. There are five long books of prophecy by the "major" prophets. "Major" only means that their books are longer, not more important. The other twelve books of prophecy are shorter. The writers of these books are called "minor" prophets. "Minor" only means that their books are shorter, not less important.

The New Testament

This second major section of the Bible begins with the birth of Jesus Christ, the Son of God. It tells us about Jesus' teaching, how He was killed and buried, and how He came to life again. The New Testament tells us about God's church. It also tells us that Jesus will come back someday. There are twenty-seven books in the New Testament section of the Bible. They also can be divided into smaller sections of God's great library.

The Gospels

Matthew	Mark	Luke	John

The first four books of the New Testament are called the Gospels. The word "gospel" means "good news." The Gospels contain God's good news. That good news is the story of His Son, Jesus Christ, who came to save God's people from their sins. The Gospels tell about Jesus' birth, teachings, miracles (wonderful works of power and healing), death, burial, and coming back to life. It is the greatest story ever told. Even though the Gospels have the same story to tell us, each book tells the story in a slightly different way.

The History of the Church

Acts of the Apostles

The fifth book of the New Testament is the Acts of the Apostles. This book tells us how Christ's church began and how it grew. It begins with Jesus telling His followers to go and teach the whole world about Him. Then Jesus went to heaven. His followers began teaching everyone in Jerusalem about Jesus. Then they traveled to other places and started churches by telling the story of Jesus to everyone they met. In the Book of Acts, we read about the preaching of Paul. He preached in Jerusalem, all around Asia Minor and Greece, and as far as Rome, the capital of the Roman Empire. The church we read about in those pages of the Book of Acts is still alive and growing today!

The Letters

Romans	1 Corinthians	2 Corinthians	Galatians	Ephesians
Philippians	Colossians	1 Thessalonians	2 Thessalonians	1 Timothy
2 Timothy	Titus	Philemon	Hebrews	James
1 Peter	2 Peter	1 John	2 John	3 John
Jude				

The next twenty-one books of the New Testament are actually letters. The apostle Paul wrote thirteen of these letters. They were written because some believers were confused about Jesus. Sometimes they didn't understand what Jesus had taught about living as God wanted His people to live. What the letter writers had to say was so good that their advice and teachings have helped Christians for almost two thousand years.

The Book of Prophecy

Revelation

The last book of the Bible (Revelation) is a book with a special message. It was written to Christians who were facing great danger. The apostle John, who probably wrote Revelation, had a wonderful message. He told the Christians to expect hard times and trouble. But he also told them that they would be the winners in the end! Revelation tells Christians not to lose hope because they will share with Jesus in the final victory over the powers of sin, death, and evil at the end of time.

Who Wrote the Bible?

The Bible was written over a period of thousands of years by more than thirty different men. Some of them were:

Moses, one of the best-educated men of his time.

Ezra, a religious scholar.

David, a shepherd boy who grew up to be king.

Solomon, David's son, who was given special gifts of riches and wisdom by God.

Jeremiah, a shy young man who thought he was too young to be God's spokesman.

Matthew, a publican (tax collector) who was hated by his fellow men.

Luke, a doctor.

Peter, James, and **John,** three fishermen.

The apostle Paul, as well educated in his time as Moses had been hundreds of years earlier.

The other men who helped write the Bible came from backgrounds just as varied as these. The one thing they all had in common was that God through the Holy Spirit guided them in every word they wrote.

How Did the Bible Come to Be?

One of the most exciting stories of all times is the story of how the Bible came to be. It is a miracle that all of the books of the Bible have been preserved for us to read today. After all, the first book of the Bible was written more than three thousand years ago, and the last one was finished nearly two thousand years ago. Since there were no printing presses until just the last few hundred years, there was no way to make copies of the Bible except to write them by hand. You can imagine how long that would take.

The sixty-six books that make up the Bible were first collected together about three hundred years after the last book was completed. The Jewish people had used the Old Testament for years (and still use it today). Christians had been sharing the New Testament books with each other all along. The entire Bible, however, was not available until about A.D. 400.

Courageous Jewish People and Christians. God has used many courageous Jewish people and Christians during the past three thousand years to preserve His Word. In the years just before Jesus was born, several nations invaded Israel, and they all tried to destroy the Bible. One evil ruler, Antiochus IV, even passed a law in 169 B.C. saying that anyone found with a copy of the Scriptures (the Bible) would be put to death. (See the *When Did It Happen?* section of this Bible for a time line showing what was happening when Antiochus IV was in power.)

The Power of the Bible. But these enemies of God's Word did not count on one thing. They did not count on the power of God and the faith and courage He gave to people who read the Bible. Every time the enemy tried to destroy the Bible, brave men and women hid it away and saved it.

A Language People Could Not Understand. Even as recently as five hundred years ago, some kings and powerful church leaders tried to keep people from knowing what was in the Bible. They did not want people thinking for themselves about God. In those days it was easy to keep people from reading the Bible. Printing had not been invented, so the Bible had to be copied by hand. Besides, the Bible was only available in Latin, a language that few people could understand.

Sentenced to Death for Smuggling Bibles. William Tyndale was one of the first people to try to make the Bible available to people in English. His story is like an exciting spy thriller. In England it was against the law to translate the Bible into English, so he went to Germany. There, he translated the New Testament into English and began smuggling copies of it into England. He was arrested in Belgium, thrown into prison, and sentenced to death.

At Last! Bibles People Can Read. A little more than four hundred years ago, some rulers finally allowed the Bible to be translated into English. One of the translations that came into being at this point in history is the King James Version. It has been used by Christians all over the world and is still being used today. In fact, Bibles are so plentiful today that it is hard to imagine that there was ever a time when people could not read the Bible in English for themselves.

How to Study the Bible

The Bible is the greatest book ever written. In it God Himself speaks to us. It offers comfort when we are sad, guidance when we are confused, advice for our problems, correction for our sins, and hope and help for our every need.

The Bible is not simply one book. It is an entire library of books. It includes books that contain history, poetry, drama, biography, prophecy, science, and more. Little wonder, then, that all or part of the Bible has been translated into more than 1,200 languages, and every year more copies of the Bible are sold than of any other single book.

The Bible alone truly answers the greatest questions that men and women, boys and girls have asked throughout history: "Where have I come from?" "Where am I going?" "Why am I here?" "How can I know the truth?" The Bible shows us the truth about God, explains the beginning of man, points out the only way to salvation and eternal life, and explains what we can do about the problem of sin in our lives.

The great theme of the Bible is the Lord Jesus Christ and His work of redemption for us (rescuing us from sin). The Old Testament includes promises, prophecies, and symbols of Jesus Christ. In the Gospels, the Lord Jesus Christ is revealed in all of His truth and beauty. The full meaning of His life, His death, and His resurrection (rising from death) are explained in the Epistles (New Testament letters). His glorious return to earth in the future is written about in the Book of Revelation. The great purpose of the written Word of God, the Bible, is to reveal the living Word of God, the Lord Jesus Christ (read John 1:1–18).

There are seven great things that studying the Bible will do for us:

1. The Bible shows us our sins and allows us to feel God-given guilt for those sins.
2. The Bible explains how we can have our sins taken away or removed.
3. The Bible gives us strength.
4. The Bible tells us what to do and how to live.
5. The Bible helps us fight against sinning and doing wrong things.
6. The Bible helps us live the way God wants us to live.
7. The Bible tells us how to pray.

You do not need a whole library of books to study the Bible. The Bible explains itself to us. It is important, however, to have a way to study the Bible.

Devotional Bible Study

The Bible is the book God has given us so that we can know Him and do His will. The apostle Paul said, "Study to shew thyself approved unto God, a workman that needeth not to be ashamed, rightly dividing the word of truth" (2 Timothy 2:15). God has given us the Bible so we can know Him and so we can do His will. Devotional Bible study is one way to study the Bible. As you study the Bible this way, you are able to hear God's voice, find out His will for you, and discover how He wants you to live the Christian life.

For your devotional reading and study of the Bible, here are several important, practical suggestions:

1. Begin your Bible reading with prayer (see Psalm 119:18; John 16:13–15).

2. Choose your passage, read it, and take brief notes on what you read. (A good place to start would be to study the passages in the "Good to Keep" section on page 48 following the Illustrated Word List at the back of this Bible.) Keep a small notebook for your Bible study (see number 4 below).

3. Read slowly through one chapter or even just one verse at a time. After reading, ask yourself what this passage means. Then reread it.

4. It is often very helpful in finding out the true meaning of a chapter or passage to ask yourself the following questions, then write the answers in your notebook:

   a. What is the main topic of this passage?
   b. Who is being talked about in this passage? Who is speaking? About whom is he speaking? Who is doing something? What is he doing?
   c. What is the main verse of this passage?
   d. What does this passage teach me about God?
   e. Does this passage show me any sin I need to confess and stop doing?
   f. Does this passage contain any command for me to obey?
   g. Is there any promise for me to claim as my own?
   h. Is there any instruction for me to follow?

(Not all of these questions will be answered in every passage.)

5. Keep a special diary of your thoughts during your Bible study time. This can be included in your Bible study notebook or you can keep a separate personal Bible-time diary. Write down each day what God says to you as you study the Bible. Write down the sins that you confess or the commands you should obey.

6. Memorize passages of God's Word (see the "Good to Keep" section on page 48 following the Illustrated Word List at the back of this Bible). Take the time to write your memory verses on index cards with the book, chapter, and verse

reference on one side and the words of the verses on the other side. Review these verses when you have free time or as part of your Bible study time each day. When you have memorized the verses and passages listed in the "Good to Keep" section of this Bible, begin making your own lists of favorite verses, passages, and chapters. Work on learning those as well.

7. Obey the Word of God. As Paul said to Timothy in 2 Timothy 3:16: "All scripture is given by inspiration of God, and is profitable for doctrine, for reproof, for correction, for instruction in righteousness." God has given us the Bible so that we can learn to live a life that pleases Him. Therefore God says, "But be ye doers of the word, and not hearers only" (James 1:22).

As you grow older, you will find that there are many different ways to study your Bible. The Devotional Bible Study method is just one of those. The important thing to remember is that the study of God's Word helps you become a stronger, more mature Christian. During your Bible study time, always remember that the Bible is God's Word. There are no mistakes in the Bible. God has included everything in the Bible that He wants you to know regarding Himself, your salvation, and the Christian life. Never forget that you can ask your parents, teachers, or pastor to help you understand passages that you find confusing. If you get confused, do not be discouraged. Understanding the Bible is a life-long process, and God is our ultimate teacher. Be patient with yourself and trust Him to help you all along the way.

The Bible Teaches Us How to Build Christian Character The Proverbs Way

The wisest man who ever lived, King Solomon, wrote most of the Book of Proverbs. This book of the Bible is full of wisdom and good advice for believers of all ages— young, old, and in-between. If you want to learn some basic, good ideas for living in a way that pleases God, check out the Book of Proverbs. You will be glad you did . . . and so will your parents, your friends, your teachers—everyone around you. Keep reading and find out why.

What kinds of character traits does God want to see in your life? He wants you to . . .

1. Depart from evil (walk away from or stop doing wrong things).
   * Proverbs 3:7: "Be not wise in thine own eyes: fear the LORD, and depart from evil."
   * Proverbs 16:17: "The highway of the upright is to depart from evil. . . ."

2. Choose the right kind of friends.
   * Proverbs 13:20: "He that walketh with wise men shall be wise: but a companion of fools shall be destroyed."
   * Proverbs 2:20: "That thou mayest walk in the way of good men, and keep the paths of the righteous."

3. Make good decisions about what you choose to say.
   * Proverbs 6:2: "Thou art snared with the words of thy mouth. . . ."
   * Proverbs 4:24: "Put away from thee a froward mouth, and perverse lips put far from thee."

4. Be honest.
   * Proverbs 12:17: "He that speaketh truth showeth forth righteousness: but a false witness deceit."
   * Proverbs 12:22: "Lying lips are abomination to the LORD: but they that deal truly are his delight."

5. Be willing to share and give to those in need.
   * Proverbs 3:27: "Withhold not good from them to whom it is due, when it is in the power of thine hand to do it."

- Proverbs 21:13: "Whoso stoppeth his ears at the cry of the poor, he also shall cry himself, but shall not be heard."

6. Exercise self-control.
    - Proverbs 16:32: "He that is slow to anger is better than the mighty; and he that ruleth his spirit than he that taketh a city."
    - Proverbs 29:22: "An angry man stirreth up strife, and a furious man aboundeth in transgression."

7. Be diligent (work hard and do a good job).
    - Proverbs 4:23: "Keep thy heart with all diligence; for out of it are the issues of life."
    - Proverbs 10:4: "He becometh poor that dealeth with a slack hand: but the hand of the diligent maketh rich."

8. Be content, happy with what you have.
    - Proverbs 3:31: "Envy thou not the oppressor, and choose none of his ways."
    - Proverbs 23:17: "Let not thine heart envy sinners. . . ."

9. Be friendly.
    - Proverbs 18:24: "A man that hath friends must shew himself friendly. . . ."
    - Proverbs 27:10: "Thine own friend, and thy father's friend, forsake not. . . ."

10. Be obedient.
    - Proverbs 19:16: "He that keepeth the commandment keepeth his own soul. . . ."
    - Proverbs 5:7: "Hear me now therefore, O ye children, and depart not from the words of my mouth."

You can dig deeper into Proverbs and learn how Solomon wrote about being a peacemaker; being honest, humble, generous, and unselfish. Write down the references that mention these traits and also how young believers should learn how to be prudent and wise.

What kinds of character traits does God want you to avoid?

1. Lying
    - Proverbs 12:22: "Lying lips are abomination to the LORD: but they that deal truly are his delight."
    - Proverbs 19:5: "A false witness shall not be unpunished, and he that speaketh lies shall not escape."

2. Pride (thinking too highly of yourself)
    - Proverbs 16:5: "Every one that is proud in heart is an abomination to the LORD. . . ."
    - Proverbs 21:4: "An high look, and a proud heart, and the plowing of the wicked, is sin."

3. Stealing
- Proverbs 28:24: "Whoso robbeth his father or his mother . . . the same is the companion of a destroyer."
- Proverbs 21:7: "The robbery of the wicked shall destroy them. . . ."

4. Anger
- Proverbs 14:29: "He that is slow to wrath is of great understanding: but he that is hasty of spirit exalteth folly."
- Proverbs 19:19: "A man of great wrath shall suffer punishment. . . ."

5. Wrong friends
- Proverbs 24:1: "Be not thou envious against evil men, neither desire to be with them."
- Proverbs 4:14: "Enter not into the path of the wicked, and go not in the way of evil men."

6. Gossip (talking about others or telling something personal that someone else has done—not in a good way)
- Proverbs 16:28: "A froward man soweth strife: and a whisperer separateth chief friends."
- Proverbs 26:20: ". . . so where there is no talebearer, the strife ceaseth."

7. Rebellion (not being obedient to someone in authority)
- Proverbs 5:12: "How have I hated instruction, and my heart despised reproof."
- Proverbs 17:11: "An evil man seeketh only rebellion: therefore a cruel messenger shall be sent against him."

8. Improper talk
- Proverbs 6:2: "Thou art snared with the words of thy mouth, thou art taken with the words of thy mouth."
- Proverbs 13:3: "He that keepeth his mouth keepeth his life: but he that openeth wide his lips shall have destruction."
- Proverbs 14:9: "Fools make a mock at sin. . . ."

9. Laziness
- Proverbs 18:9: "He also that is slothful in his work is brother to him that is a great waster."
- Proverbs 20:13: "Love not sleep, lest thou come to poverty."

10. Greed (wanting more than you need)
- Proverbs 22:16: "He that oppresseth the poor to increase his riches, and he that giveth to the rich, shall surely come to want."
- Proverbs 15:27: "He that is greedy of gain troubleth his own house; but he that hateth gifts [bribes] shall live."

Your study in Proverbs can teach you about other character traits that will hinder your growth as a Christian. Solomon writes about Deceit, Envy, Waywardness, Uncontrolled Appetites, Foolishness, and Arrogance.

The Bible tells us that parents and other leaders in our lives are responsible for helping to shape our Christian character and that requires discipline. Becoming Christlike is a part of our daily lives. What attitude does God expect you to have toward obedience and discipline?

1. The right attitude
   * Proverbs 4:1: "Hear, ye children, the instruction of a father, and attend to know understanding."
   * Proverbs 14:16: "A wise man feareth, and departeth from evil: but the fool rageth, and is confident."
   * Proverbs 23:22: "Hearken unto thy father that begat thee, and despise not thy mother when she is old."
   * Proverbs 10:23: "It is as sport to a fool to do mischief: but a man of understanding hath wisdom."
   * Proverbs 10:17, 18: "He is in the way of life that keepeth instruction: but he that refuseth reproof erreth. He that hideth hatred with lying lips, and he that uttereth a slander, is a fool."

2. The wrong attitude
   * Proverbs 28:10: "Whoso causeth the righteous to go astray in an evil way, he shall fall himself into his own pit: but the upright shall have good things in possession."
   * Proverbs 13:13: "Whoso despiseth the word shall be destroyed: but he that feareth the commandment shall be rewarded."
   * Proverbs 28:4: "They that forsake the law praise the wicked: but such as keep the law contend with them."
   * Proverbs 28:13: "He that covereth his sins shall not prosper: but whoso confesseth and forsaketh them shall have mercy."
   * Proverbs 1:29: "For that they hated knowledge, and did not choose the fear of the LORD . . ."

What does God promise you when you obey Him and live the Proverbs way?

1. Long life
   * Proverbs 3:1, 2: "My son, forget not my law; but let thine heart keep my commandments: for length of days, and long life, and peace, shall they add to thee."
   * Proverbs 9:11: "For by me thy days shall be multiplied, and the years of thy life shall be increased."

2. Wisdom
- Proverbs 28:7: "Whoso keepeth the law is a wise son."
- Proverbs 1:23: "Turn you at my reproof: behold, I will pour out my spirit unto you, I will make known my words unto you."

3. Peace
- Proverbs 16:7: "When a man's ways please the LORD, he maketh even his enemies to be at peace with him."
- Proverbs 1:33: "But whoso hearkeneth unto me shall dwell safely, and shall be quiet from fear of evil."

4. Happiness
- Proverbs 29:18: "Where there is no vision, the people perish: but he that keepeth the law, happy is he."
- Proverbs 27:18: "Whoso keepeth the fig tree shall eat the fruit thereof: so he that waiteth on his master shall be honoured."

5. Honor
- Proverbs 13:18: "Poverty and shame shall be to him that refuseth instruction: but he that regardeth reproof shall be honoured."
- Proverbs 10:1: "The proverbs of Solomon. A wise son maketh a glad father: but a foolish son is the heaviness of his mother."

6. Blessings
- Proverbs 10:3: "The LORD will not suffer the soul of the righteous to famish. . . ."
- Proverbs 14:11: ". . . but the tabernacle of the upright shall flourish."

7. Rewards
- Proverbs 8:21: "That I may cause those that love me to inherit substance; and I will fill their treasures."
- Proverbs 13:13: "Whoso despiseth the word shall be destroyed: but he that feareth the commandment shall be rewarded."

What does God promise you when you disobey Him and do not live the Proverbs way?

1. Shortened life
- Proverbs 10:27: ". . . but the years of the wicked shall be shortened."
- Proverbs 19:16: ". . . but he that despiseth his ways shall die."

2. Shame
- Proverbs 28:7: ". . . but he that is a companion of riotous men shameth his father."
- Proverbs 11:20: "They that are of a froward heart are abomination to the LORD. . . ."

3. Destruction
- Proverbs 1:32: "For the turning away of the simple shall slay them, and the prosperity of fools shall destroy them."
- Proverbs 14:11: "The house of the wicked shall be overthrown. . . ."

Why do your parents and other adult leaders (teachers, pastors) guide and discipline you?

1. Because the Bible says they should.
   - Proverbs 22:6: "Train up a child in the way he should go: and when he is old, he will not depart from it."
   - Proverbs 23:13: "Withhold not correction from the child: for if thou beatest him with the rod, he shall not die."
   - Proverbs 19:18: "Chasten thy son while there is hope. . . ."

2. Because discipline brings you and your parents peace.
   - Proverbs 16:7: "When a man's ways please the LORD, he maketh even his enemies to be at peace with him."
   - Proverbs 29:17: "Correct thy son, and he shall give thee rest; yea, he shall give delight unto thy soul."

3. Because they love you and want to prepare you to be saved.
   - Proverbs 13:24: "He that spareth the rod hateth his son: but he that loveth him chasteneth him betimes."
   - Proverbs 23:14: "Thou shalt beat him with the rod, and shalt deliver his soul from hell."

4. Because discipline brings you wisdom.
   - Proverbs 29:15: "The rod and reproof give wisdom. . . ."
   - Proverbs 22:15: "Foolishness is bound in the heart of a child; but the rod of correction shall drive it far from him."

What kinds of guidance and discipline does God expect your parents to use?

1. Chastening (discipline, correction, or punishment)
   - Proverbs 3:11, 12: "My son, despise not the chastening of the LORD; neither be weary of his correction: for whom the LORD loveth he correcteth; even as a father the son in whom he delighteth."
   - Proverbs 19:18: "Chasten thy son while there is hope, and let not thy soul spare for his crying."
   - Proverbs 23:13, 14: "Withhold not correction from the child: for if thou beatest him with the rod, he shall not die. Thou shalt beat him with the rod, and shalt deliver his soul from hell."

2. Instruction (talking with you about what is right and wrong and how you should live)
   - Proverbs 21:11: "When the scorner is punished, the simple is made wise: and when the wise is instructed, he receiveth knowledge."
   - Proverbs 9:9: "Give instruction to a wise man and he will be yet wiser: teach a just man, and he will increase in learning."
   - Proverbs 19:20: "Hear counsel, and receive instruction, that thou mayest be wise in thy latter end."

3. Reproof (to correct your behavior with words)
   - Proverbs 6:23: "For the commandment is a lamp; and the law is light; and reproofs of instruction are the way of life."
   - Proverbs 29:15: "The rod and reproof give wisdom. . . ."

4. Example (to live the way they want you to live)
   - Proverbs 23:26: "My son, give me thine heart, and let thine eyes observe my ways."
   - Proverbs 12:18: "There is that speaketh like the piercings of a sword: but the tongue of the wise is health."

5. Rod (to use spanking with a paddle as discipline)
   - Proverbs 19:25: "Smite a scorner, and the simple will beware: and reprove one that hath understanding, and he will understand knowledge."
   - Proverbs 13:24: "He that spareth his rod hateth his son: but he that loveth him chasteneth him betimes."

6. Counsel (to give advice)
   - Proverbs 19:20: "Hear counsel, and receive instruction, that thou mayest be wise in thy latter end."
   - Proverbs 12:15: ". . . but he that hearkeneth unto counsel is wise."

Now you can see how living the Proverbs way helps you grow and mature in your Christian life. You can start living the Proverbs way today: at home, at school, wherever you go.

Fun Ways to Study the Bible with Your Friends and Family

Studying the Bible is very important. It can also be a lot of fun! The Bible is a big, thick book, it is true. But that is because it is packed full of adventure stories, mysteries, songs, and great ideas. You will not be bored studying the Bible if you use some of these fun ways.

1. *Study in a Group.* It is more fun to study with someone than to study by yourself. Call one of your friends to come over to your house for a Bible study. Another great group to study with is your Sunday school class. You learn from the Bible, and you learn from each other. It is okay to laugh and enjoy God's Word. God wants His children to be happy and to love His Word.

2. *Sing Bible Songs.* Many songs in our church songbooks have words that come from the Bible. The Book of Psalms is a whole book of songs! (As a matter of fact, "psalms" sounds like "songs"!) Try to find a song in your songbook with words that match one of the psalms in the Bible (for example, Psalm 23). You and your friends might want to sing the psalm/song together. Try to memorize Bible words by singing them. Make up your own Scripture songs or sing Scripture songs you have learned at church. Singing them is fun, and you also learn a lot.

3. *Solve Bible Puzzles.* Ask your mom or dad to help you find a book of Bible puzzles. Some books have crossword puzzles with Bible words and clues. Some have riddles and questions to make you think and search for answers. Some are word search puzzles or "Who Am I?" games to help you study.

4. *Play Bible Games.* Ask your Sunday school teacher or look in the church library for some Bible study games you can play with your friends. Invite some of your friends over to play the games with you. Perhaps you can find "Bible Baseball" or "Bible Pictionary." There are even some great Bible computer games you can enjoy with a friend or someone in your family.

5. *Make Bible Snacks.* Ask your mom to help you find recipes for foods talked about in the Bible. Then invite some of your friends over to help you make them. When your food is ready, share it with all your friends. One interesting meal for you to try to make is the Passover meal that the Jewish people have each year. Try to do everything just as they would have done it. First you will have to study your Bible. Then you can have fun doing what they did. But you might not want to follow John the Baptist's diet (Matthew 3:4; Mark 1:6)!

6. *Act Out Bible Stories.* Ask your mom or maybe even your teacher to help you and your friends put on a Bible play. Perhaps your mom would be the play director. Get your friends to choose a story from the Bible to act out. Write out the story like a play, showing which person speaks and when. Make a copy for all the players in the play and ask them to learn their lines. Next, have each person make a Bible costume (bathrobes and towels are great!). Have two or three rehearsals to put the play together. Finally, invite children and adults from your neighborhood and school to come to the play on a nonschool day. You and your friends will learn a lot about the Bible. You can also teach the story to those who come. The story of Peter's escape from prison (Acts 12:6–19) is a good one to begin with.

7. *Give a Bible Challenge.* Challenge some of your friends to a Bible memory verse contest. Ask your parents or your teacher to be the judge and buy a prize for the winner of the contest (or make one yourself). Then ask your judge to select something in the Bible for you to memorize (see the "Good to Keep" section on page 48, following the Illustrated Word List at the back of this Bible). Get all your friends together, show the prize, and have your judge announce the memory challenge work. Then have fun trying to be the first one to memorize part of the Bible. You will learn something great, too. Another idea would be to memorize a verse each week from the "Good to Keep" verses in this Bible. Use the "Good to Keep" chart to mark the ones you have learned. Get a friend to memorize the verses along with you. See who can memorize the verses first and review them together so that you will have them for life!

Where Do I Find It?

The Bible is full of information we need to know. Below, you will find a list of important topics about our Christian faith. Look for the heading in dark type and then look up the Bible verses below that heading for an explanation from God's Word about that topic.

The Bible

Inspired by God . *2 Timothy 3:16*
Holy Spirit's role
   in giving it . . . . . . *2 Peter 1:21*
Authority . . . . *John 10:35*
Free from error . . . . . *John 17:17*
Preserved . . . . . . *Jeremiah 36:27*
Truth . . . . *Psalm 119:160*

God

Nature of God . . . . *1 John 4:8*
Definition of God . . . . *John 4:24*
Wisdom of God . . . . *Proverbs 9:1*
Holiness of God . . . *Leviticus 19:2*
Trinity (Three
   Persons, one
   God) . . . . *Matthew 28:19*
God the Father . . . . *Matthew 6:9*

Christ

His Deity (He is God) . . *John 5:18*
His Humanity
   (He is a man) . . . . . . *Luke 2:52*
Son of God . . . . . *Matthew 16:16*
Rose from the
   dead . . . . *Matthew 28:6*
Ascended into heaven . . *Acts 1:9*
Prays for us . . . . . . *Hebrews 7:25*

The Holy Spirit (the Holy Ghost)

Is a Person . . . . *John 16:13*
Is God . . . . *Matthew 28:19*
Holy Spirit in
   creation . . . . *Genesis 1:2*
Comforter . . . . *John 14:16*
Fruit of the
   Spirit . . . . . *Galatians 5:22, 23*
Sins against the Holy
   Spirit . . . . . *Matthew 12:31, 32*

Mankind

Creation of man . . . *Genesis 1:27*
Soul of man . . . . *Genesis 2:7*
Made in God's
   image . . . . *Genesis 1:26*
Heart . . . . *Proverbs 4:23*
Conscience . . . . . . *Romans 2:15*
Temptation . . . . *1 John 2:16*

Sin

Personal sin . . . . . . *Romans 3:23*
Sin nature . . . . *Psalm 51:5*
Backsliding . . . . . . *Jeremiah 3:22*
Sin pollutes the
   sinner . . . . . . *1 Corinthians 5:6*

Sin (continued)

Penalty of sin . . . . . *Romans 6:23*
Living by the flesh . *Romans 8:13*

Salvation

Gospel . . . . *1 Corinthians 15:1, 2*
Being saved . . . . . *Romans 10:13*
Being reconciled
   to God . . . . *2 Corinthians 5:19*
Saving faith . . . . . . *Ephesians 2:8*
Forgiveness of sins. *Ephesians 1:7*
Assurance of being
   saved . . . . *1 John 5:13*

Angels

Angels. . . . . *Hebrews 1:4*
Ranking of
   angels . . . . *Hebrews 12:22*
Satan . . . . *Isaiah 14:12*
Demons, or devils . *1 Timothy 4:1*
Activities of
   demons . . . . . . *Ephesians 6:12*

The Purpose and Work of the Church

Purpose of the
   church . . . . . . *Matthew 28:19*
Fellowship . . . . . *Philippians 1:27*
Baptism . . . . *Romans 6:4*
Lord's Supper. . . . . *1 Corinthians
                11:23–26*
Tithing. . . . . *Malachi 3:10*
Body of
   Christ . . . . *1 Corinthians 12:27*

Last Things

Signs of Christ's
   return . . . . *Matthew 24:33*
Kingdom
   parables . . . . . *Matthew 13:52*
Antichrist . . . . *1 John 2:22*
Second Coming . . . . . *Revelation
               19:11—22:21*
Bottomless pit. *Revelation 9:1–12*
Heaven . . . . *John 14:2*

Bible Bookshelf

God's Word is divided into two Testaments, or Covenants—the Old and the New. Over a very long time, God inspired (breathed into) special people He chose to write the sixty-six books you will find here. These books tell us all about God, His creation of the world and mankind, how sin started, and God's plan for sending His Son Jesus to save us from sin and to take us to heaven to live with Him always.

Old Testament
(39 Books)

Law
Genesis
Exodus
Leviticus
Numbers
Deuteronomy

History
Joshua
Judges
Ruth
1, 2 Samuel
1, 2 Kings
1, 2 Chronicles
Ezra
Nehemiah
Esther

Poetry
Job
Psalms
Proverbs
Ecclesiastes
Song of Solomon
Lamentations

Major Prophets
Isaiah
Jeremiah
Ezekiel
Daniel

Minor Prophets
Hosea
Joel
Amos
Obadiah
Jonah
Micah
Nahum
Habakkuk
Zephaniah
Haggai
Zechariah
Malachi

Bible Bookshelf

The New Testament books tell about Jesus' birth and life, His ministry, death, and resurrection. They also explain how the church began and include letters from Paul and others to the people in those early churches. The last book of the New Testament gives John's vision of the end of the world.

New Testament (27 Books)

The Gospels

Matthew
Mark
Luke
John

Church History

Acts

Letters

Romans
1, 2 Corinthians
Galatians
Ephesians

Philippians
Colossians
1, 2 Thessalonians
1, 2 Timothy
Titus
Philemon
Hebrews
James
1, 2 Peter
1, 2, 3 John
Jude

Prophecy

Revelation

God's Word is Good to Learn: When Did It Happen?

Have you ever wondered when certain events in the Bible took place? With this "When Did It Happen?" section of your Bible, you will be able to see when some of the most familiar Bible stories happened, and how they fit with what scholars and historians know about world history.

Some events took place so long ago that we do not know their actual dates. For instance, we do not actually know the date when God created the world or the date of the Flood. But scientists and Bible scholars have made careful and detailed studies about the approximate dates of events that took place from the life of Abraham on into New Testament times.

From the Creation to the Great Flood

Genesis chapters 1—5 tell us about how the universe began. In these chapters, we learn how God created everything, including human beings. When God created Adam and Eve and placed them in the Garden of Eden, He gave them jobs to do and told them *not* to eat from a certain tree. They disobeyed God; and that disobedience allowed sin, death, and all kinds of problems to become a part of our lives.

After sin entered the world, Adam and Eve had to leave the Garden of Eden. Many years passed and people forgot to follow God. They became very wicked and violent. In Genesis chapters 6—9, we read about the flood that God had to send because of the great sin and wickedness of the people on the earth. This flood covered the whole earth, including the mountains. Of all the people on earth at that time, only Noah and his family were saved.

God Called Abram and Chose a People to Be His Own

Genesis chapters 11—13 tell the story of how God called Abram (later called Abraham) to leave his homeland in Ur of the Chaldeans and to go to a land God would show him. God spoke directly to Abraham and entered into a covenant (a binding agreement) with him, promising to bless him and his descendants forever. God also promised to give Abraham the land of Canaan as his own and to bless all the people of the earth through him. This promise foretold God's plan to send a Savior—Jesus—into the world to save us from death and from the problem of sin.

The Israelites Left Canaan and Traveled to Egypt

Genesis chapters 41—47 tell how Abraham's great-grandson, Joseph, was betrayed by his brothers and sold into slavery. Joseph remained faithful to God, and God blessed him. Joseph became a trusted official in Egypt and saved his family from starving during a great famine in the land. Joseph's father, his brothers, and their families all moved to Egypt to be near Joseph and to enjoy the plentiful food available in Egypt.

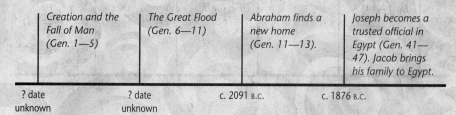

Creation and the Fall of Man (Gen. 1—5)	The Great Flood (Gen. 6—11)	Abraham finds a new home (Gen. 11—13).	Joseph becomes a trusted official in Egypt (Gen. 41—47). Jacob brings his family to Egypt.
? date unknown	? date unknown	c. 2091 B.C.	c. 1876 B.C.

Moses Led the Israelites out of Egypt

Exodus chapters 1—14 tell how Egyptian pharaohs forced the Israelites into slavery. They were made to work very hard and were often treated unkindly and unfairly. God protected baby Moses from being killed when the pharaoh (Thutmose I) commanded that all Hebrew baby boys must die. When Moses became a man, God called him to lead the Hebrew people out of Egypt (Amenhotep II was probably the pharaoh at that time). They left Egypt and traveled through the wilderness (for forty years) to Canaan, the land promised to their ancestor Abraham by God. The Book of Joshua tells how the Israelites—under Joshua's leadership—conquered the land of Canaan and began their lives in this promised land.

The Israelites Asked for a King

From the time of Joshua until the time of King Saul, Israel was ruled by a number of men and women who were called judges. Their lives and deeds are recorded in the Book of Judges. Among these judges were Deborah, Samson, and Gideon. Because they did not have a king, the nation of Israel was different from the other countries around them. In the Book of 1 Samuel, the people decided that they wanted to be like the other countries and have a king. Samuel, God's prophet at that time, sought God's will and was told to allow the people to have their way.

The first king of Israel was King Saul. Saul stopped obeying God, so God had his prophet Samuel to anoint David, a shepherd boy, as the next king. David prospered and became known as a "man after God's own heart." His son, Solomon, built the great temple in Jerusalem. King Solomon became the wisest and one of the wealthiest kings who ever lived. But he married many women, some of them from other nations that did not worship God. Solomon stopped following all of God's ways, and God told him that the kingdom would be taken away from his son because Solomon had disobeyed God's laws (1 Kings 11:9–13). (See the books of 1 Samuel and 2 Samuel; 1 Kings 1—12.)

Moses leads the Israelites out of Egypt (Ex. 1—14).	Moses dies (Deut. 34).	Joshua leads the people into the Promised Land (Josh. 1—16).	Israel is ruled by a series of men and women called judges.	Saul becomes Israel's first king (1 Sam. 11:15). He battles the Philistines throughout his reign.
c. 1446 B.C.	c. 1406 B.C.	c. 1405 B.C.	c. 1405–1050 B.C.	c. 1050 B.C.

David becomes king of Judah (2 Sam. 2:4).	David becomes king of Israel (2 Sam. 5:3).	Solomon becomes king of Israel (1 Kin. 2:12).	Solomon's temple is finished (1 Kin. 6:37, 38).	Solomon dies (1 Kin. 11:43).
c. 1010 B.C.	c. 1003 B.C.	c. 970 B.C.	c. 960 B.C.	c. 930 B.C.

The Divided Kingdom of Israel

In 1 Kings chapter 12 and the following chapters, we learn that war and disagreement split the nation of Israel into two countries . . . Judah and Israel. The northern kingdom became known as Israel, and the southern kingdom was called Judah.

Assyria Conquered the Northern Kingdom; Babylon Conquered the Southern Kingdom

The people of Israel—the northern kingdom—continued to worship idols and to disobey the laws of God. Even after the prophets—Elijah, Elisha, and others—warned them, they continued to worship foreign gods (see 2 Kings 17). As a punishment for their sins, God allowed the people of Israel to be conquered by Assyria. Many of the Israelites were taken into captivity.

The people of Judah—the southern kingdom—also continued to worship idols and disobeyed the laws of God. In 2 Kings 20, we learn that Nebuchadnezzar, king of Babylon and conqueror of Assyria, took control of Jerusalem and took many people captive.

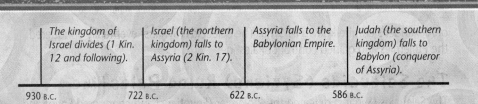

The kingdom of Israel divides (1 Kin. 12 and following).	Israel (the northern kingdom) falls to Assyria (2 Kin. 17).	Assyria falls to the Babylonian Empire.	Judah (the southern kingdom) falls to Babylon (conqueror of Assyria).
930 B.C.	722 B.C.	622 B.C.	586 B.C.

God's People Returned to Jerusalem

Cyrus the Great, king of Persia, conquered the Babylonian Empire. He allowed some of the Jewish people to return to Jerusalem and begin rebuilding the temple. The Old Testament says he was chosen by the Lord God of Israel to be the deliverer of His people. Under the rule of Artaxerxes of Persia—a later king—Ezra and Nehemiah led additional groups of Jewish people back to Jerusalem to complete work on the temple and to repair the city walls.

Between the Old and New Testaments

The Greeks Conquered the Persian Empire

Alexander the Great became the ruler in Greece in 336 B.C. He set out to expand the Greek Empire and to conquer the Persian Empire. He conquered Palestine (the area we know as the Holy Land). He also conquered Syria and Egypt. Alexander died at a young age without a son, and his generals divided the empire among themselves. His generals in Egypt and then Syria ruled Palestine.

Cyrus the Great becomes ruler of Persia.	Cyrus the Great conquers Babylon.	King Cyrus allows some Jewish people to return to Jerusalem. It takes years to rebuild the temple and the city walls (Ezra; Nehemiah).	Alexander the Great of Greece conquers all of the Persian Empire.
559 B.C.	539 B.C	538 B.C.	327 B.C

The Egyptians Ruled Palestine

After Alexander's death in 323 B.C., four generals divided the Greek Empire into four sections: two of those concern the history of God's people. The Ptolemies (Egyptians) gained control of Egypt and Palestine. The Seleucids (Syrians) ruled the northern part of Alexander's empire known as Syria. The Seleucids (Syrians) eventually conquered the Ptolemies and gained control of Palestine.

The Seleucids (Syrians) Ruled Palestine

The Seleucids (Syrians) defeated the Ptolemies (Egyptians) and conquered Egypt and Palestine. Antiochus IV took the throne and is known as one of the cruelest rulers of this era. He tried to stamp out the Hebrew faith by forbidding sacrifices to the Lord, outlawing circumcision, canceling the Sabbath and feast days, destroying copies of Scripture, forcing Jewish people to eat pork, and establishing idol worship to the Greek god Zeus in God's temple.

Alexander the Great dies. His generals divide his kingdom.	The Ptolemies (Egyptians) take control of Palestine.	The Seleucids (Syrians) conquer the Ptolemies (Egyptians) and gain control of Palestine.	Antiochus IV rules the Seleucid (Syrian) Dynasty. He is one of the cruelest rulers of the era.
323 B.C.	305 B.C	200 B.C	175–164 B.C.
Antiochus IV attacks Jerusalem and loots the temple.	Antiochus IV offers sacrifices to Zeus on the altar of the temple.	The Maccabeans lead a revolt against the Seleucids (Syrians).	The Maccabeans free Jerusalem from the Seleucids (Syrians).
169 B.C	167 B.C.	166 B.C.	164 B.C.

The Jewish People Fought for Independence

The Maccabeans (a group of Jewish people) revolted against Syrian rule. They recaptured Jerusalem, cleansed the temple, and restored worship. By 142 B.C., the Jewish people achieved independence from foreign rule and were governed by a family of Jewish leaders known as the Maccabeans or Hasmoneans until Jerusalem was conquered by Rome in 63 B.C. It is interesting to note that the Pharisees you meet in the New Testament arose during the revolt of the Maccabeans. The Pharisees saw themselves as the defenders of the Jewish religion—even against Jesus.

Rome Conquered Palestine

Julius Caesar was a brilliant general who became known as the father of the Roman Empire. Through a series of well-planned battles, Caesar was able to expand his empire throughout the known world. The power of the Roman Empire was first felt in Palestine during an invasion by the Roman general Pompey. Pompey took control of Palestine in 63 B.C. Herod the Great became the Roman governor (ruler) of Palestine and was still the ruler when Jesus Christ was born.

The New Testament

Jesus Was Born

No one knows the exact date when Jesus was born. When early Christians set up the calendar we still use today, they intended to set the date of Jesus' birth at A.D. 1. But the calendar creators made a mistake. The Jewish historian Josephus placed the death of Herod the Great in 4 B.C. Since Jesus was born during Herod's rule, the approximate date of Jesus' birth is now thought to be 5 B.C.

Maccabeans (or Hasmoneans) rule an independent Jewish state.	General Pompey the Great captures Jerusalem. Rome now rules Palestine.	Herod the Great rules as governor (king) of Judea (37–4 B.C.).	Jesus Christ is born (Matt. 1:24, 25).
142 B.C	63 B.C	37 B.C.	?5 B.C

The Life, Ministry, Death, and Resurrection of Jesus

The Gospels tell the story of Jesus' life and ministry here on earth. We learn about Jesus' earthly ancestors and His birth. We know He was presented to the Lord in the temple as an infant and that He—at age 12—talked with and amazed the priests and teachers in the temple. Later, John the Baptist, his cousin, baptized Him. At that point, Jesus began to gather His disciples and start His three-year ministry: teaching, healing, and doing the will of God. Judas Iscariot, one of His twelve disciples, betrayed Jesus to the temple authorities who wanted to kill Him. He was tried and crucified. After three days, Jesus rose from the dead; and, after appearing to His disciples many times, He ascended to heaven.

Herod the Great dies.	Jesus talks with the priests and teachers in the temple at age 12.	Pontius Pilate becomes governor of Judea. John the Baptist baptizes Jesus (Matt. 3:13–17).	Jesus is crucified and rises from the dead.
4 B.C.	A.D. 7?	A.D. 26?	A.D. 30?

Apostles and Early Church Leaders Spread the Good News of the Gospel

The Book of Acts records that a Pharisee—and persecutor of Christians—named Saul was confronted by a vision of Jesus and converted to faith in Christ on the road to

Damascus (9:1–9). God changed his name to Paul. God used Peter to introduce the gospel to the Gentiles. Paul, Timothy, Barnabas, Peter, and other church leaders and missionaries began the great missionary work of the early church, spreading the gospel to the far reaches of the Roman Empire.

The Romans Destroyed Jerusalem

In A.D 66, the Jewish people rebelled against Roman rule. In A.D. 70, the Romans defeated Jerusalem, destroyed the temple, and began to gather the temple tax as a Roman government tax. The Romans did away with the Jewish priesthood and the system of sacrifice. Jewish people were eventually forbidden to live in Jerusalem. Because Christianity had spread to all parts of the Roman Empire, the defeat of Jerusalem did not end the growth of Christianity, which eventually became the official religion of Rome.

Saul (later known as Paul) is converted on the road to Damascus (Acts 9:1–9).	Nero becomes emperor of Rome.	Jewish people rebel against Roman rule.	Paul is executed in Rome (?) (2 Tim. 4:6).	Jerusalem falls to Rome. The temple is destroyed.
A.D. 34?	A.D. 54	A.D. 66?	A.D. 67?	A.D. 70

God's Word is Good to Read

Reading the Bible allows God to teach you His ways and helps you make wise choices all through your life. If you have ever wondered where to start reading God's Word, how much to read each day, and so on . . . the Bible reading plans in this section of your Bible will help. There are two different year-long reading plans listed below. The first is organized to help you read the Bible daily but in passages and sections one month at a time. Another year-long plan shows you how to read the entire Bible one day at a time. You will find nine different monthly reading plans to get you started.

The one-Year Plan: one month at a time

For the next year, choose one of the monthly reading plans below and start getting into God's Word. Each plan gives you a daily portion of Scripture to read.

3-Month Plan: overview of the Bible

Covers the main stories of the entire Bible in just three months.

1-Month Plan: famous Bible chapters

Focuses on some of the most famous passages in the Bible. This plan includes a quiz to check your Bible knowledge.

1-Month Plan: Psalms and Proverbs

Takes you through the books of Psalms and Proverbs.

1-Month Plan: famous Men and Women of the old Testament

Includes some of the stories of the most famous men and women in the Old Testament.

1-Month Plan: Prophecies of Jesus

Shows you some of the many prophecies throughout the Old Testament about the coming Messiah . . . Jesus Christ.

1-Month Plan: The Life of Jesus

Takes you through some of the main events of Jesus' life and ministry.

1-Month Plan: The Parables of Jesus

Takes you through the parables and stories Jesus told during His earthly ministry. The quiz will add a challenge to your reading!

1-Month Plan: Famous Men and Women of the New Testament

Includes some of the stories of the most famous men and women in the New Testament.

2-Month Plan: The Life and Teachings of Paul

Includes important teachings from the apostle Paul to the early church, teachings that apply to you today!

The One-Year Plan: One day at a time

When you have completed the monthly plans above, it is time to read through the Bible in a year. With this reading plan, you will be able to read through the whole Bible—every verse—in just one year, starting with Genesis and ending with Revelation.

There are many different ways to go about reading your Bible. These are just a few plans to help you begin a life-long habit of Bible reading. Do not be discouraged if you miss a day here and there. Just start again, and keep going. Remember, the Bible is the most important book you will ever read!

3-Month Plan: overview of the Bible

Day	Reference	Read	Day	Reference	Read
1	Genesis 1:1—2:3	4/10/05	29	1 Kings 3:1–28	
2	Genesis 3:1–24		30	1 Kings 17:8–24	
3	Genesis 6:9—7:24		31	1 Kings 18:1–46	
4	Genesis 8:1—9:17		32	2 Kings 2:1–18	
5	Genesis 17:1–22		33	2 Kings 4:8–37	
6	Genesis 22:1–19		34	2 Chronicles 35:20—36:23	
7	Genesis 25:19–34				
8	Genesis 27:1—28:9		35	Esther 2:1–23	
9	Genesis 37:1–36		36	Esther 6:1—8:8	
10	Genesis 41:1–57		37	Job 1:1—2:13; 42:1–17	
11	Genesis 45:1–28				
12	Exodus 1:8—2:15		38	Psalm 23:1–6	
13	Exodus 3:1—4:17		39	Psalm 51:1–19	
14	Exodus 5:1—6:13		40	Psalm 100:1–5	
15	Exodus 12:1–42		41	Psalm 121:1–8	
16	Exodus 13:17— 14:31		42	Psalm 145:1–21	
			43	Proverbs 4:1–27	
17	Exodus 20:1–21		44	Ecclesiastes 11:9— 12:14	
18	Numbers 13:1–33				
19	Joshua 2:1–24		45	Isaiah 53:1–12	
20	Joshua 6:1–27		46	Daniel 1:1–21	
21	Judges 16:4–31		47	Daniel 3:1–30	
22	1 Samuel 1:1–28		48	Daniel 6:1–28	
23	1 Samuel 3:1–21		49	Jonah 1:1—4:11	
24	1 Samuel 10:1–27		50	Matthew 1:18— 2:23	
25	1 Samuel 16:1–13				
26	1 Samuel 17:1–58		51	Matthew 5:1–16; 6:1—7:12	
27	1 Samuel 24:1–22				
28	2 Samuel 11:1— 12:25		52	Matthew 14:13–36	
			53	Matthew 21:1–17	

3-Month Plan: overview of the Bible

Day	Reference	Read	Day	Reference	Read
54	Matthew 26:47–75		74	Acts 11:1–18	
55	Matthew 27:15–66		75	Acts 16:11–40	
56	Matthew 28:1–20		76	Romans 3:1–31	
57	Mark 1:1–20		77	Romans 8:1–39	
58	Mark 4:1–20		78	Romans 12:1–21	
59	Luke 1:26–56; 2:1–20		79	1 Corinthians 13:1–13	
60	Luke 10:25–42; 14:25–35		80	1 Corinthians 15:1–58	
61	Luke 15:1–32		81	Ephesians 2:1–22; 6:10–20	
62	Luke 22:1–23				
63	Luke 24:13–53		82	Philippians 3:1— 4:9	
64	John 1:1–18				
65	John 3:1–21		83	Colossians 3:1—4:1	
66	John 4:1–42		84	1 Thessalonians 4:1–18	
67	John 8:1–11				
68	John 11:1–44		85	Hebrews 11:1–40	
69	John 14:1–31		86	James 1:1–27	
70	Acts 1:1–11		87	James 3:1–18	
71	Acts 2:1–47		88	1 Peter 1:3–25	
72	Acts 8:26–40		89	1 John 1:1—2:17	
73	Acts 9:1–31		90	Revelation 21:1— 22:21	

1–Month Plan: Famous Chapters of the Bible

As you learn more about the Bible, you will find out that many chapters or passages of Scripture have become very popular to study, teach, and memorize. Read one chapter or passage each day for a month. Then see if you can match the biblical description on the right with the Scripture reference on the left.

Read	Day	Scripture Reference	Chapter or Passage Description	Answer
☐	1	Revelation 21	a) The Love Chapter	1. _j_
☐	2	John 13—17	b) Noah and the Great Flood	2. __
☐	3	Exodus 7—12	c) The Christmas Story in which angels appear to the shepherds	3. __
☐	4	Genesis 6—8	d) "I will lift up mine eyes unto the hills, from whence cometh my help."	4. __
☐	5	Psalm 51	e) The story of Creation	5. __
☐	6	Psalm 103	f) The giving of the Ten Commandments	6. __
☐	7	Joshua 6	g) King David's confession of sin	7. __
☐	8	Matthew 5—7	h) The Lord's Prayer	8. __
☐	9	Jonah 1; 2	i) The Beatitudes, beginning with "Blessed are the poor in spirit."	9. __
☐	10	Luke 2	j) The prophecy of a new heaven and a new earth	10. __

Read	Day	Scripture Reference	Chapter or Passage Description	Answer
☐	11	Matthew 6:9–13	k) The story of Daniel in the lions' den	11. __
☐	12	Matthew 5:3–10	l) "Bless the LORD, O my soul."	12. __
☐	13	Exodus 14	m) A description of the virtuous woman	13. __
☐	14	Acts 2	n) Jesus' story of the Good Samaritan	14. __
☐	15	Ezekiel 37:1–14	o) The story of Samson and Delilah	15. __
☐	16	The Book of Esther	p) The story of the Garden of Eden and the forbidden fruit	16. __
☐	17	Matthew 27:33–56; Mark 15:22–41; Luke 23:33–49; John 19:17–30	q) The story of the Israelites crossing the Red Sea	17. __
☐	18	1 Corinthians 13	r) The story of how the walls of Jericho fell	18. __
☐	19	Daniel 6	s) "The Lord helps those who help themselves."	19. __
☐	20	John 10:1–18	t) In the Upper Room, Jesus tells His disciples that He is going to the Father.	20. __
☐	21	Psalm 121	u) Jesus' crucifixion and death	21. __
☐	22	Judges 16	v) The story of Saul's conversion on the road to Damascus	22. __
☐	23	Acts 9:1–22	w) The Sermon on the Mount	23. __

Read	Day	Scripture Reference	Chapter or Passage Description	Answer
☐	24	Proverbs 31:10–31	x) The story of the tongues of fire at Pentecost	24. __
☐	25	Genesis 1	y) The story of how Queen Esther saved her people	25. __
☐	26	Matthew 28; Mark 16; Luke 24; John 20	z) The story of Jesus' resurrection	26. __
☐	27	Luke 10:30–37	aa) The story of the ten plagues of Egypt	27. __
☐	28	Not in the Bible!	bb) Jesus talks about the Good Shepherd.	28. __
☐	29	Exodus 20:1–17	cc) The prophecy about the valley of dry bones	29. __
☐	30	Genesis 2; 3	dd) The story of Jonah and the great fish	30. __

Turn the page for the answers to this quiz.

Answers to the quiz "Famous Chapters of the Bible"

1.	j	11.	h	21.	d
2.	t	12.	i	22.	o
3.	aa	13.	q	23.	v
4.	b	14.	x	24.	m
5.	g	15.	cc	25.	e
6.	l	16.	y	26.	z
7.	r	17.	u	27.	n
8.	w	18.	a	28.	s
9.	dd	19.	k	29.	f
10.	c	20.	bb	30.	p

1-Month Plan: Psalms and Proverbs

Day	Passage	Read
1	Psalm 1:1—10:18	☐
2	Psalm 11:1—18:50	☐
3	Psalm 19:1—26:12	☐
4	Psalm 27:1—33:22	☐
5	Psalm 34:1—37:40	☐
6	Psalm 38:1—44:26	☐
7	Psalm 45:1—51:19	☐
8	Psalm 52:1—60:12	☐
9	Psalm 61:1—68:35	☐
10	Psalm 69:1—73:28	☐
11	Psalm 74:1—78:72	☐
12	Psalm 79:1—86:17	☐
13	Psalm 87:1—91:16	☐
14	Psalm 92:1—101:8	☐
15	Psalm 102:1—105:45	☐
16	Psalm 106:1—108:13	☐
17	Psalm 109:1—116:19	☐
18	Psalm 117:1—118:29	☐
19	Psalm 119:1–176	☐
20	Psalm 120:1—135:21	☐
21	Psalm 136:1—143:12	☐
22	Psalm 144:1—Proverbs 1:19	☐
23	Proverbs 1:20—5:23	☐
24	Proverbs 6:1—9:18	☐
25	Proverbs 10:1—13:25	☐
26	Proverbs 14:1—16:33	☐
27	Proverbs 17:1—20:30	☐
28	Proverbs 21:1—23:35	☐
29	Proverbs 24:1—27:27	☐
30	Proverbs 28:1—31:31	☐

1-Month Plan: Famous Men and Women of the Old Testament

Day	Person	Passage	Read
1	Adam and Eve	Genesis 2:1—3:24	☐
2	Noah and the Flood	Genesis 6:1—9:17	☐
3	Abraham obeys God	Genesis 11:27—12:9	☐
4	Sarah becomes a mother	Genesis 18:1–15; 21:1–21	☐
5	Isaac and the sacrifice	Genesis 22:1–18	☐
6	Rebekah becomes Isaac's wife	Genesis 24:1–67	☐
7	Jacob and Rachel	Genesis 27:1—28:5; 29:1—30:24	☐
8	Joseph goes to Egypt	Genesis 37:1–36; 39:1—41:57	☐
9	Jochebed and Miriam save baby Moses	Exodus 1:8—2:10	☐
10	Moses and Aaron go before Pharaoh	Exodus 4:27—6:13; 7:1—12:42	☐
11	Joshua leads the people	Joshua 1:1–18	☐
12	Rahab saves the spies	Joshua 2:1–24; 5:13—6:27	☐
13	Deborah leads a battle	Judges 4:1–24	☐
14	Gideon and his men obey	Judges 6:1—7:22	☐
15	Delilah tricks Samson	Judges 13:2–25; 16:1–31	☐

Day	Person	Passage	Read
16	Naomi and Ruth make a journey	Ruth 1:1—4:22	☐
17	Samuel, answer to Hannah's prayer	1 Samuel 1:1–28; 3:1–21	☐
18	David and Goliath	1 Samuel 17:1–58	☐
19	David and Jonathan	1 Samuel 18:1—20:42	☐
20	Solomon asks for wisdom	1 Kings 3:3–28; 4:29–34	☐
21	Elijah and the prophets of Baal	1 Kings 18:16–40	☐
22	Elijah and the chariot of fire	2 Kings 2:9–15	☐
23	Elisha and Naaman the leper	2 Kings 5:1–27	☐
24	Josiah becomes king	2 Chronicles 34:1—35:19	☐
25	Esther is chosen to be queen	Esther 1:1—2:23	☐
26	Mordecai guides Esther	Esther 3:1—10:3	☐
27	Daniel in the king's court	Daniel 1:1—2:49	☐
28	Shadrach, Meshach, and Abed-nego in the furnace	Daniel 3:1–30	☐
29	Daniel in the lions' den	Daniel 6:1–28	☐
30	Jonah and the great fish	Jonah 1:1—2:10	☐

1–Month Plan: Prophecies of Jesus

					Day 1 Gen. 3:15; Gal. 4:4 He would be born of a woman.
Day 2 Gen. 12:3; Rom. 9:5 He would come from Abraham's family.	**Day 3** Is.40:3–5; Mal.3:1; Matt. 3:1–3; Luke1:76–78 He would have a fore-runner, someone who would come before Him, telling about Him.	**Day 4** Is. 7:14; Matt. 1:22, 23 His mother would be a virgin who obeyed God's laws, and His name would be Immanuel, or "God with Us."	**Day 5** Ps. 89:34–37; Luke 1:31–33 He would be a descendant of David and would be given the throne of King David.	**Day 6** Mic. 5:2; Matt. 2:5, 6; Luke 2:4–6 He would be born in Beth-lehem.
Day 7 Is. 60:3–9; Matt. 2:11 He would be worshiped by wise men and pre-sented with gifts at birth.	**Day 8** Jer. 31:15; Matt. 2:17,18 Israel would mourn and cry about the slaughter (murder) of many inno-cent children after His birth.	**Day 9** Hos. 11:1; Matt. 2:15 He would live in Egypt for a while.	**Day 10** Judg. 13:5; Matt. 2:23 He would be called a Nazarene.	**Day 11** Ps. 45:7; Luke 4:18, 19 He would be filled with God's Spirit.
Day 12 Ps. 78:2; Matt. 13:34, 35 He would teach in para-bles.	**Day 13** Is. 53:4, 5; Matt. 8:16, 17 He would heal many.	**Day 14** Is. 53:1; John 12:37, 38 His miracles would not be believed.	**Day 15** Is. 53:3; Matt. 26:37, 38 He would be a "man of sorrows."	**Day 16** Ps. 69:8; 118:22, 23; Is. 53:3; Zech. 13:7; Matt. 21:42; 26:31, 56; John 1:11; 7:5; 1 Pet. 2:7 He would be rejected by His own people.
Day 17 Zech. 9:9; Matt. 21:4, 5 He would make a tri-umphal (or kingly) entry into Jerusalem.	**Day 18** Zech. 9:9; Matt. 21:2–7 He would come riding upon the foal of a don-key.	**Day 19** Ps. 41:9; 55:12–14; Matt. 26:14–16; Luke 22:47 He would be betrayed by a friend.	**Day 20** Is. 50:6; Matt. 26:67; 27:26 He would be punished unjustly with whips and spat upon.	**Day 21** Ps. 22:16, 18; Matt. 27:35; John 20:27 His death would include piercing of His hands and feet and casting of lots for His clothes.
Day 22 Is. 53:12; Matt. 27:38; Mark 15:27, 28 He would be crucified between two thieves.	**Day 23** Ps. 22:15; 69:21; Matt. 27:34, 48; John 19:28–30 He would be thirsty and would be given vinegar and gall to drink.	**Day 24** Ex. 12:46; Ps. 34:20; John 19:33–36 His bones would not be broken when He died.	**Day 25** Ps. 31:5; Luke 23:46 He would commend (give) His spirit to the Father.	**Day 26** Is. 53:9; Matt. 27:57–60 He would be buried among the rich.
Day 27 Ps. 16:10; Matt. 28:2–7 He would be raised from the dead.	**Day 28** Ps. 110:1; Matt. 22:44; Heb. 10:12, 13 He would be seated at God's right hand.	**Day 29** Ps. 109:8; Acts 1:20 The one who betrayed Him (Judas Iscariot) would be replaced as one of the twelve disci-ples by another man.	**Day 30** Ps. 2:9; Is. 9:1, 2; 42:1–4; Matt. 4:13–16; 12:17–21; Rev. 2:27 He would rule the Gen-tiles and deal gently with them.	**Day 31** Ps. 110:4; Heb. 5:4–6; 7:11–28 He would become a greater high priest than Aaron.

1-Month Plan: The Life of Jesus

					Day 1
					Matt. 1:18—2:23 Jesus is born; then His parents flee with Him to Egypt to escape an evil king. Finally His family returns home.
Day 2 Matt. 4:1–11 Jesus faces very real temptations.	**Day 3** Matt. 13:54–58 People do not believe Jesus is the Messiah because of His humble family, their work, and His small hometown.	**Day 4** Matt. 23:1–39 Jesus speaks out against deceit (lying), pride, and hypocrisy (pretending to be holier or better than you are).	**Day 5** Matt. 25:31–46 Jesus will judge our hearts and our actions and how we take care of those all around us who are in need.	**Day 6** Mark 4:1–41 Jesus begins to explain the kingdom of God using stories and parables.
Day 7 Luke 2:1–52 Luke tells about Jesus' birth and how Jesus at age 12 amazed the priests and teachers in the temple.	**Day 8** Luke 4:14–37 In the synagogue at Nazareth, Jesus announces who He is and why He has come.	**Day 9** Luke 6:17–49 Jesus teaches basic truths about attitudes, true kindness, judging others, and making wise choices.	**Day 10** Luke 9:18–36 Jesus talks with His followers about who He is.	**Day 11** Luke 22:1—24:53 Jesus is betrayed, judged, crucified, buried, resurrected, and reunited with His disciples.
Day 12 John 1:1–18 John, one of Jesus' followers, describes how God became a man through Christ—full of grace and truth.	**Day 13** John 5:19–47 Jesus explains His relationship with His heavenly Father and what their relationship means for us.	**Day 14** John 6:35–51 Jesus teaches that He is the Bread of Life and tells how people can find Him.	**Day 15** John 8:12–30 Jesus announces that He is the Light of the World.	**Day 16** John 10:1–18 Jesus says that He is the Good Shepherd who seeks His Father's lost sheep.
Day 17 John 11:1—12:8 John describes Jesus' relationship with some of His friends and their deep love for each other.	**Day 18** John 14:1—15:8 Jesus explains that He is the only way to God.	**Day 19** John 21:15–25 Jesus talks about His love and purposes for Peter—the disciple who had denied Him.	**Day 20** Acts 2:22–42 Peter explains Christ to a huge crowd in Jerusalem, and 3,000 people accept Jesus as Savior and Lord.	**Day 21** Rom. 5:1–21 Paul explains how Christ sets people free from sin.
Day 22 1 Cor. 15:1–28 Paul teaches about Christ's resurrection and His victory over death.	**Day 23** Eph. 1:3–14 Paul describes Christ's work for us: before the creation of earth, now, and in eternity.	**Day 24** Phil. 2:5–16 Paul explains Jesus' choices in order to become a man and the choices we should make in following Him.	**Day 25** Col. 1:15–22 Paul states that Christ is Lord of all—yesterday, today, and tomorrow.	**Day 26** 1 Thess. 4:13—5:11 Paul explains that Jesus will return and bring earthly events to an end.
Day 27 Heb. 1:1—2:18 The author of Hebrews talks about Christ's complete and wonderful work for our salvation.	**Day 28** Heb. 4:14—5:10 Christ has experienced every kind of test or trial we will ever face.	**Day 29** Heb. 9:23—10:18 Jesus takes away sin, once and for all. Forgiveness is ours in Him.	**Day 30** 1 Pet. 1:1–12 Peter tells about our wonderful salvation in Christ.	**Day 31** Rev. 5:1–14; 22:1–21 Christ will rule heaven and earth and will welcome believers to an eternity with Him.

1-Month Plan: The Parables of Jesus

As Jesus taught His disciples and the crowds who came to see Him, He used parables that are basically earthly stories with a heavenly meaning. He would mention events or items common to His listeners' lifestyles. Read one passage each day for a month. Then see if you can match the chapter or passage to the story descriptions. (Give yourself extra points if you can find the same teaching in another Gospel.)

Read	Day	Scripture Reference	Chapter or Passage Description	Answer
☐	1	Luke 14:16–24	a) The Lost Sheep	1. <u>m</u>
☐	2	Matthew 22:1–14	b) The Lost Coin	2. __
☐	3	Luke 15:3–7	c) The Hidden Treasure	3. __
☐	4	Mark 4:30–32	d) The Pearl of Great Price	4. __
☐	5	Luke 14:25–35	e) The Lost Son	5. __
☐	6	Matthew 7:24–27	f) The Fig Tree	6. __
☐	7	Matthew 18:23–35	g) The Two Sons	7. __
☐	8	Matthew 20:1–16	h) The Wicked Husbandmen	8. __
☐	9	Luke 19:11–27	i) The Sower	9. __
☐	10	Luke 10:25–37	j) The Wheat and the Tares (weeds)	10. __
☐	11	Luke 15:8–10	k) The Mustard Seed	11. __
☐	12	Matthew 13:3–23	l) The Net	12. __
☐	13	Matthew 5:15, 16	m) The Great Supper	13. __
☐	14	Mark 13:28–32	n) The House Built upon a Rock	14. __
☐	15	Luke 18:9–14	o) The Pharisee and the Publican	15. __
☐	16	Matthew 13:44	p) The Creditor and Two Debtors	16. __

☐	17	Matthew 21:33–46	q) The King and His Son's Marriage	17. __
☐	18	Luke 7:36–50	r) The Candle under a Bushel	18. __
☐	19	Luke 11:5–13	s) The Unforgiving Servant	19. __
☐	20	Matthew 21:28–32	t) A Friend at Midnight	20. __
☐	21	Matthew 13:24–30	u) The Persistent Widow	21. __
☐	22	Matthew 25:31–46	v) The Tower	22. __
☐	23	Luke 15:11–32	w) The Good Samaritan	23. __
☐	24	Matthew 13:47–50	x) The Unjust Steward	24. __
☐	25	Luke 18:1–8	y) The Labourers in the Vineyard	25. __
☐	26	Luke 16:19–31	z) The Ten Virgins	26. __
☐	27	Luke 12:16–21	aa) The Talents	27. __
☐	28	Matthew 25:1–13	bb) The 10 Pounds	28. __
☐	29	Luke 16:1–13	cc) The Sheep and the Goats	29. __
☐	30	Matthew 25:14–30	dd) The Rich Fool	30. __
☐	31	Matthew 13:45, 46	ee) The Rich Man and Lazarus	31. __

Turn the page for the answers to this quiz.

Answers to the quiz on "The Parables of Jesus"

1. m	12. i	22. cc
2. q	13. r	23. e
3. a	14. f	24. l
4. k	15. o	25. u
5. v	16. c	26. ee
6. n	17. h	27. dd
7. s	18. p	28. z
8. y	19. t	29. x
9. bb	20. g	30. aa
10. w	21. j	31. d
11. b		

1-Month Plan: Famous Men and Women of the New Testament

Day	Person	Passage	Read
1	Elisabeth and Zacharias	Luke 1:5–25, 57–80	☐
2	Mary	Luke 1:26–56	☐
3	Joseph	Matthew 1:18–25; 2:13–23	☐
4	Wise Men (Magi)	Matthew 2:1–12	☐
5	Simeon and Anna	Luke 2:22–38	☐
6	John the Baptist	Matthew 3:1–17; Luke 3:1–22	☐
7	Matthew (Levi)	Matthew 9:9–13; Luke 5:27–32	☐
8	Nathanael	John 1:43–51	☐
9	The Twelve Disciples	Matthew 10:1–42	☐
10	James and John	Mark 1:19, 20; 10:35–45	☐
11	Peter	Mark 1:16–18; Matthew 14:22–33; 16:13–17; Luke 24:34; John 21:15–23	☐
12	Nicodemus	John 3:1–21	☐
13	Mary and Martha of Bethany	Luke 10:38–42; John 12:1–8	☐
14	Lazarus	John 11:1–45	☐
15	Rich Young Ruler	Luke 18:18–30	☐

Day	Person	Passage	Read
16	Zacchaeus	Luke 19:1–10	☐
17	Samaritan Woman	John 4:4–42	☐
18	Judas Iscariot	John 13:21–30; 18:1–14; Matthew 26:14–16, 47–56; 27:3–10	☐
19	Pilate	John 18:28—19:16; Matthew 27:11–26	☐
20	Joseph of Arimathaea	Luke 23:50–56	☐
21	Stephen	Acts 6:1—7:60	☐
22	Philip and the Ethiopian	Acts 8:26–39	☐
23	Saul/Paul	Acts 8:1–3; 9:1–31	☐
24	Cornelius	Acts 10:1–48	☐
25	Barnabas	Acts 11:19–26; 13:1–3	☐
26	Herod and Peter	Acts 12:1–19	☐
27	Silas	Acts 15:39–41; 16:16–40	☐
28	Timothy (Timotheus)	Acts 16:1–10	☐
29	Lydia	Acts 16:11–15	☐
30	Priscilla and Aquila	Acts 18:1–4, 24–28	☐

2-Month Plan: The Life and Teachings of Paul

Day	Reference	Read	Day	Reference	Read
1	Romans 1:16–32	☐	31	Galatians 6:1–10	☐
2	Romans 2:1–16	☐	32	Ephesians 1:3–14	☐
3	Romans 3:21–31	☐	33	Ephesians 1:15—2:10	☐
4	Romans 4:1–25	☐	34	Ephesians 5:1–21	☐
5	Romans 5:12–21	☐	35	Ephesians 5:22—6:9	☐
6	Romans 6:1–23	☐	36	Ephesians 6:10–20	☐
7	Romans 7:1–25	☐	37	Philippians 1:3–26	☐
8	Romans 8:18–39	☐	38	Philippians 1:27—2:18	☐
9	Romans 10:1–21	☐	39	Philippians 3:1–16	☐
10	Romans 12:1–21	☐	40	Philippians 3:17—4:9	☐
11	Romans 13:1–14	☐	41	Philippians 4:10–23	☐
12	Romans 14:1—15:6	☐	42	Colossians 1:13–23	☐
13	1 Corinthians 1:10–31	☐	43	Colossians 2:6–23	☐
14	1 Corinthians 2:1–16	☐	44	Colossians 3:1–17	☐
15	1 Corinthians 3:1–23	☐	45	Colossians 3:18—4:6	☐
16	1 Corinthians 7:1–24	☐	46	1 Thessalonians 1:1–10	☐
17	1 Corinthians 7:25–40	☐	47	1 Thessalonians 4:1–18	☐
18	1 Corinthians 9:19—10:13	☐	48	1 Thessalonians 5:1–28	☐
19	1 Corinthians 12:1–31	☐	49	2 Thessalonians 2:1–17	☐
20	1 Corinthians 13:1–13	☐	50	2 Thessalonians 3:1–15	☐
21	1 Corinthians 15:1–28	☐	51	1 Timothy 2:1–15	☐
22	2 Corinthians 1:3–14	☐	52	1 Timothy 3:1–16	☐
23	2 Corinthians 1:15—2:11	☐	53	1 Timothy 4:1–12	☐
24	2 Corinthians 4:1–18	☐	54	1 Timothy 5:1–22	☐
25	2 Corinthians 5:1—6:2	☐	55	1 Timothy 6:3–21	☐
26	2 Corinthians 6:14—7:1	☐	56	2 Timothy 1:3–18	☐
27	2 Corinthians 8:1–15	☐	57	2 Timothy 2:1—3:9	☐
28	Galatians 2:11–21	☐	58	2 Timothy 4:1–8	☐
29	Galatians 3:19—4:7	☐	59	Titus 1:1–16	☐
30	Galatians 5:1–26	☐	60	Titus 2:1—3:11	☐

The one-Year Plan: one day at a time

Day	Passage	Read	Day	Passage	Read
1	Genesis 1:1—3:24	☐	30	Exodus 31:1—33:10	☐
2	Genesis 4:1—5:32	☐	31	Exodus 33:11—36:7	☐
3	Genesis 6:1—9:19	☐	32	Exodus 36:8—38:20	☐
4	Genesis 9:20—12:9	☐	33	Exodus 38:21—40:38	☐
5	Genesis 12:10—16:16	☐	34	Leviticus 1:1—5:13	☐
6	Genesis 17:1—19:29	☐	35	Leviticus 5:14—7:38	☐
7	Genesis 19:30—22:24	☐	36	Leviticus 8:1—10:20	☐
8	Genesis 23:1—24:67	☐	37	Leviticus 11:1—13:46	☐
9	Genesis 25:1—26:35	☐	38	Leviticus 13:47—14:57	☐
10	Genesis 27:1—29:14	☐	39	Leviticus 15:1—17:16	☐
11	Genesis 29:15—31:21	☐	40	Leviticus 18:1—20:27	☐
12	Genesis 31:22—33:20	☐	41	Leviticus 21:1—23:25	☐
13	Genesis 34:1—36:30	☐	42	Leviticus 23:26—25:55	☐
14	Genesis 36:31—38:30	☐	43	Leviticus 26:1—27:34	☐
15	Genesis 39:1—41:36	☐	44	Numbers 1:1—2:34	☐
16	Genesis 41:37—43:34	☐	45	Numbers 3:1—4:33	☐
17	Genesis 44:1—45:28	☐	46	Numbers 4:34—6:27	☐
18	Genesis 46:1—48:22	☐	47	Numbers 7:1—89	☐
19	Genesis 49:1— Exodus 1:22	☐	48	Numbers 8:1—10:36	☐
			49	Numbers 11:1—13:33	☐
20	Exodus 2:1—4:31	☐	50	Numbers 14:1—15:41	☐
21	Exodus 5:1—7:25	☐	51	Numbers 16:1—18:32	☐
22	Exodus 8:1—10:20	☐	52	Numbers 19:1—21:35	☐
23	Exodus 10:21—13:16	☐	53	Numbers 22:1—24:25	☐
24	Exodus 13:17—16:36	☐	54	Numbers 25:1—26:65	☐
25	Exodus 17:1—20:26	☐	55	Numbers 27:1—29:40	☐
26	Exodus 21:1—23:13	☐	56	Numbers 30:1—31:54	☐
27	Exodus 23:14—25:40	☐	57	Numbers 32:1—33:56	☐
28	Exodus 26:1—28:43	☐	58	Numbers 34:1—36:13	☐
29	Exodus 29:1—30:38	☐	59	Deuteronomy 1:1—3:7	☐

Day	Passage	Read	Day	Passage	Read
60	Deuteronomy 3:8—5:33	☐	84	Judges 18:1—19:30	☐
61	Deuteronomy 6:1—9:6	☐	85	Judges 20:1—Ruth 1:22	☐
62	Deuteronomy 9:7—11:32	☐	86	Ruth 2:1—4:22	☐
63	Deuteronomy 12:1—14:29	☐	87	1 Samuel 1:1—3:21	☐
64	Deuteronomy 15:1—18:22	☐	88	1 Samuel 4:1—8:22	☐
65	Deuteronomy 19:1—21:23	☐	89	1 Samuel 9:1—12:25	☐
66	Deuteronomy 22:1—25:19	☐	90	1 Samuel 13:1—14:52	☐
67	Deuteronomy 26:1—28:14	☐	91	1 Samuel 15:1—16:23	☐
68	Deuteronomy 28:15—29:29	☐	92	1 Samuel 17:1—18:30	☐
69	Deuteronomy 30:1—32:47	☐	93	1 Samuel 19:1—21:15	☐
70	Deuteronomy 32:48—Joshua 2:24	☐	94	1 Samuel 22:1—24:22	☐
71	Joshua 3:1—6:27	☐	95	1 Samuel 25:1—27:12	☐
72	Joshua 7:1—9:27	☐	96	1 Samuel 28:1—31:13	☐
73	Joshua 10:1—12:24	☐	97	2 Samuel 1:1—3:21	☐
74	Joshua 13:1—15:63	☐	98	2 Samuel 3:22—6:23	☐
75	Joshua 16:1—19:31	☐	99	2 Samuel 7:1—10:19	☐
76	Joshua 19:32—21:45	☐	100	2 Samuel 11:1—13:22	☐
77	Joshua 22:1—24:33	☐	101	2 Samuel 13:23—15:37	☐
78	Judges 1:1—3:31	☐	102	2 Samuel 16:1—19:8	☐
79	Judges 4:1—6:40	☐	103	2 Samuel 19:9—21:22	☐
80	Judges 7:1—8:35	☐	104	2 Samuel 22:1—23:39	☐
81	Judges 9:1—10:18	☐	105	2 Samuel 24:1—1 Kings 2:11	☐
82	Judges 11:1—13:25	☐	106	1 Kings 2:12—4:21	☐
83	Judges 14:1—17:13	☐	107	1 Kings 4:22—7:14	☐
			108	1 Kings 7:15—8:66	☐
			109	1 Kings 9:1—11:43	☐
			110	1 Kings 12:1—13:34	☐
			111	1 Kings 14:1—16:20	☐
			112	1 Kings 16:21—18:46	☐
			113	1 Kings 19:1—21:29	☐
			114	1 Kings 22:1—2 Kings 2:25	☐

Day	Passage	Read	Day	Passage	Read
115	2 Kings 3:1—4:44	☑	140	2 Chronicles 21:1—24:27	☐
116	2 Kings 5:1—7:20	☐	141	2 Chronicles 25:1—28:27	☐
117	2 Kings 8:1—10:17	☐	142	2 Chronicles 29:1—31:21	☐
118	2 Kings 10:18—13:25	☐	143	2 Chronicles 32:1—34:33	☐
119	2 Kings 14:1—16:20	☐	144	2 Chronicles 35:1—36:23	☐
120	2 Kings 17:1—19:37	☐	145	Ezra 1:1—3:13	☐
121	2 Kings 20:1—22:20	☐	146	Ezra 4:1—7:28	☐
122	2 Kings 23:1—25:30	☐	147	Ezra 8:1—10:44	☐
123	1 Chronicles 1:1—2:2	☐	148	Nehemiah 1:1—4:23	☐
124	1 Chronicles 2:3—4:23	☐	149	Nehemiah 5:1—7:73	☐
125	1 Chronicles 4:24—5:26	☐	150	Nehemiah 8:1—10:39	☐
126	1 Chronicles 6:1—7:5	☐	151	Nehemiah 11:1—13:31	☐
127	1 Chronicles 7:6—8:40	☐	152	Esther 1:1—4:17	☐
128	1 Chronicles 9:1—11:14	☐	153	Esther 5:1—10:3	☐
129	1 Chronicles 11:15—13:14	☐	154	Job 1:1—3:26	☐
130	1 Chronicles 14:1—16:43	☐	155	Job 4:1—7:21	☐
131	1 Chronicles 17:1—20:8	☐	156	Job 8:1—10:22	☐
132	1 Chronicles 21:1—23:32	☐	157	Job 11:1—14:22	☐
133	1 Chronicles 24:1—26:32	☐	158	Job 15:1—18:21	☐
134	1 Chronicles 27:1—29:30	☐	159	Job 19:1—21:34	☐
135	2 Chronicles 1:1—4:22	☐	160	Job 22:1—25:6	☐
136	2 Chronicles 5:1—7:22	☐	161	Job 26:1—31:40	☐
137	2 Chronicles 8:1—11:23	☐	162	Job 32:1—37:24	☐
138	2 Chronicles 12:1—16:14	☐	163	Job 38:1—42:17	☐
139	2 Chronicles 17:1—20:37	☐	164	Psalm 1:1—7:17	☐
			165	Psalm 8:1—15:5	☐
			166	Psalm 16:1—19:14	☐

Day	Passage	Read	Day	Passage	Read
167	Psalm 20:1—25:22	☐	200	Proverbs 22:1—24:34	☐
168	Psalm 26:1—31:24	☐	201	Proverbs 25:1—27:27	☐
169	Psalm 32:1—35:28	☐	202	Proverbs 28:1—31:31	☐
170	Psalm 36:1—39:13	☐	203	Ecclesiastes 1:1—3:22	☐
171	Psalm 40:1—45:17	☐	204	Ecclesiastes 4:1—7:29	☐
172	Psalm 46:1—50:23	☐	205	Ecclesiastes 8:1—12:14	☐
173	Psalm 51:1—57:11	☐	206	Song 1:1—8:14	☐
174	Psalm 58:1—64:10	☐	207	Isaiah 1:1—4:6	☐
175	Psalm 65:1—68:35	☐	208	Isaiah 5:1—8:22	☐
176	Psalm 69:1—72:20	☐	209	Isaiah 9:1—12:6	☐
177	Psalm 73:1—77:20	☐	210	Isaiah 13:1—17:14	☐
178	Psalm 78:1—79:13	☐	211	Isaiah 18:1—22:25	☐
179	Psalm 80:1—85:13	☐	212	Isaiah 23:1—27:13	☐
180	Psalm 86:1—89:52	☐	213	Isaiah 28:1—30:33	☐
181	Psalm 90:1—95:11	☐	214	Isaiah 31:1—35:10	☐
182	Psalm 96:1—102:28	☐	215	Isaiah 36:1—38:22	☐
183	Psalm 103:1—105:45	☐	216	Isaiah 39:1—42:25	☐
184	Psalm 106:1—107:43	☐	217	Isaiah 43:1—45:25	☐
185	Psalm 108:1—114:8	☐	218	Isaiah 46:1—50:11	☐
186	Psalm 115:1—118:29	☐	219	Isaiah 51:1—56:12	☐
187	Psalm 119:1–88	☐	220	Isaiah 57:1—61:11	☐
188	Psalm 119:89–176	☐	221	Isaiah 62:1—66:24	☐
189	Psalm 120:1—131:3	☐	222	Jeremiah 1:1—3:25	☐
190	Psalm 132:1—138:8	☐	223	Jeremiah 4:1—5:31	☐
191	Psalm 139:1—144:15	☐	224	Jeremiah 6:1—8:22	☐
192	Psalm 145:1—150:6	☐	225	Jeremiah 9:1—11:23	☐
193	Proverbs 1:1—3:35	☐	226	Jeremiah 12:1—15:21	☐
194	Proverbs 4:1—6:35	☐	227	Jeremiah 16:1—19:15	☐
195	Proverbs 7:1—9:18	☐	228	Jeremiah 20:1—23:40	☐
196	Proverbs 10:1—12:28	☐	229	Jeremiah 24:1—26:24	☐
197	Proverbs 13:1—15:33	☐	230	Jeremiah 27:1—29:32	☐
198	Proverbs 16:1—18:24	☐	231	Jeremiah 30:1—31:40	☐
199	Proverbs 19:1—21:31	☐	232	Jeremiah 32:1—34:7	☐

Day	Passage	Read	Day	Passage	Read
233	Jeremiah 34:8—37:21	☐	266	Jonah 1:1—Micah 4:13	☐
234	Jeremiah 38:1—41:18	☐	267	Micah 5:1—	
235	Jeremiah 42:1—45:5	☐		Nahum 3:19	☐
236	Jeremiah 46:1—48:47	☐	268	Habakkuk 1:1—	
237	Jeremiah 49:1–39	☐		Zephaniah 3:20	☐
238	Jeremiah 50:1—51:64	☐	269	Haggai 1:1—	
239	Jeremiah 52:1–34	☐		Zechariah 3:10	☐
240	Lamentations 1:1—5:22	☐	270	Zechariah 4:1—10:12	☐
241	Ezekiel 1:1—5:17	☐	271	Zechariah 11:1—	
242	Ezekiel 6:1—10:22	☐		Malachi 4:6	☐
243	Ezekiel 11:1—13:23	☐	272	Matthew 1:1—2:23	☐
244	Ezekiel 14:1—16:63	☐	273	Matthew 3:1—4:25	☐
245	Ezekiel 17:1—19:14	☐	274	Matthew 5:1—7:29	☐
246	Ezekiel 20:1—21:32	☐	275	Matthew 8:1—9:38	☐
247	Ezekiel 22:1—23:49	☐	276	Matthew 10:1—11:30	☐
248	Ezekiel 24:1—27:36	☐	277	Matthew 12:1—13:58	☐
249	Ezekiel 28:1—31:18	☐	278	Matthew 14:1—15:39	☐
250	Ezekiel 32:1—34:31	☐	279	Matthew 16:1—18:35	☐
251	Ezekiel 35:1—37:28	☐	280	Matthew 19:1—20:34	☐
252	Ezekiel 38:1—40:49	☐	281	Matthew 21:1—22:46	☐
253	Ezekiel 41:1—43:27	☐	282	Matthew 23:1—24:51	☐
254	Ezekiel 44:1—46:24	☐	283	Matthew 25:1—26:46	☐
255	Ezekiel 47:1—48:35	☐	284	Matthew 27:1—28:20	☐
256	Daniel 1:1—3:30	☐	285	Mark 1:1—2:28	☐
257	Daniel 4:1—6:28	☐	286	Mark 3:1—4:41	☐
258	Daniel 7:1—9:27	☐	287	Mark 5:1—6:56	☐
259	Daniel 10:1—12:13	☐	288	Mark 7:1—8:38	☐
260	Hosea 1:1—5:15	☐	289	Mark 9:1—10:52	☐
261	Hosea 6:1—10:15	☐	290	Mark 11:1—12:44	☐
262	Hosea 11:1—14:9	☐	291	Mark 13:1—14:72	☐
263	Joel 1:1—3:21	☐	292	Mark 15:1—16:20	☐
264	Amos 1:1—4:13	☐	293	Luke 1:1–80	☐
265	Amos 5:1—Obadiah 21	☐	294	Luke 2:1–52	☐

Day	Passage	Read	Day	Passage	Read
295	Luke 3:1—4:44	☐	328	Acts 25:1—26:32	☐
296	Luke 5:1—6:49	☐	329	Acts 27:1—28:31	☐
297	Luke 7:1—8:56	☐	330	Romans 1:1—4:25	☐
298	Luke 9:1–62	☐	331	Romans 5:1—8:39	☐
299	Luke 10:1—11:54	☐	332	Romans 9:1—11:36	☐
300	Luke 12:1—13:35	☐	333	Romans 12:1—14:23	☐
301	Luke 14:1—15:32	☐	334	Romans 15:1—16:27	☐
302	Luke 16:1—17:37	☐	335	1 Corinthians 1:1—4:21	☐
303	Luke 18:1—19:48	☐	336	1 Corinthians 5:1—9:27	☐
304	Luke 20:1—21:38	☐	337	1 Corinthians 10:1—12:31	☐
305	Luke 22:1—23:25	☐			
306	Luke 23:26—24:53	☐	338	1 Corinthians 13:1—16:24	☐
307	John 1:1—2:25	☐			
308	John 3:1—4:54	☐	339	2 Corinthians 1:1—3:18	☐
309	John 5:1—6:71	☐	340	2 Corinthians 4:1—6:18	☐
310	John 7:1–53	☐	341	2 Corinthians 7:1—9:15	☐
311	John 8:1—9:41	☐	342	2 Corinthians 10:1—13:14	☐
312	John 10:1—11:44	☐			
313	John 11:45—12:50	☐	343	Galatians 1:1—3:29	☐
314	John 13:1—14:31	☐	344	Galatians 4:1—6:18	☐
315	John 15:1—17:26	☐	345	Ephesians 1:1—3:21	☐
316	John 18:1—19:42	☐	346	Ephesians 4:1—6:24	☐
317	John 20:1—21:25	☐	347	Philippians 1:1—4:23	☐
318	Acts 1:1—3:26	☐	348	Colossians 1:1—4:18	☐
319	Acts 4:1—6:15	☐	349	1 Thessalonians 1:1—5:28	☐
320	Acts 7:1—8:40	☐			
321	Acts 9:1—10:48	☐	350	2 Thessalonians 1:1—3:18	☐
322	Acts 11:1—13:12	☐			
323	Acts 13:13—14:28	☐	351	1 Timothy 1:1—6:21	☐
324	Acts 15:1—16:40	☐	352	2 Timothy 1:1—4:22	☐
325	Acts 17:1—19:41	☐	353	Titus 1:1—Philemon 25	☐
326	Acts 20:1—21:40	☐	354	Hebrews 1:1—6:20	☐
327	Acts 22:1—24:27	☐	355	Hebrews 7:1—13:25	☐

Day	Passage	Read	Day	Passage	Read
356	James 1:1—3:18	☐	361	Revelation 1:1—3:22	☐
357	James 4:1—5:19	☐	362	Revelation 4:1—9:21	☐
358	1 Peter 1:1—5:14	☐	363	Revelation 10:1—13:18	☐
359	2 Peter 1:1—3:18	☐	364	Revelation 14:1—18:24	☐
360	1 John 1:1—Jude 11	☐	365	Revelation 19:1—22:21	☐

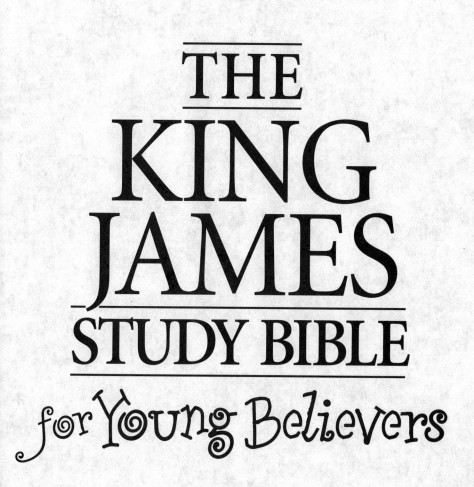

THE
KING
JAMES
STUDY BIBLE

for Young Believers

THE
HOLY BIBLE

OLD AND NEW TESTAMENTS

Authorized King James Version

TRANSLATED OUT OF THE ORIGINAL TONGUES
AND WITH PREVIOUS TRANSLATIONS
DILIGENTLY COMPARED AND REVISED

SELF-PRONOUNCING
WORDS OF CHRIST IN RED
with
Read-Along References®
and Read-Along Translations®

NELSON

THOMAS NELSON BIBLES
A Division of Thomas Nelson, Inc.
www.ThomasNelson.com

The Old Testament

The New Testament

Special Features of
Your Giant Print Reference Bible

This Bible contains the text of the Authorized King James Version, originally published in 1611.

One characteristic of this version is its use of italics, which indicate words supplied by the translators to help clarify the meaning and better convert the original language into English.

In this edition, each book of the Bible begins with a concise book introduction provided by the Publisher.

Read-Along References and Read-Along Translations are used to help you understand the text. The symbol "R" beside a word or phrase denotes a read-along reference which lists at the end of the verse other passages which have similar meanings or further bearing on the word or phrase indicated. This exciting cross-reference method of Bible study ties together the magnificent truths of Scripture.

The symbol "T" beside a word or phrase indicates a Read-Along Translation, an easy-to-understand alternate meaning at the end of the verse. Such clarifications built right into the text eliminate the need for constant referral to a Bible dictionary or to other volumes. When more than one reference or translation follows a verse, a centered point is used for division.

The Bible text is divided into meaningful paragraph units. The beginning of each paragraph is indicated by a bold verse number.

Difficult proper names are divided into syllables and accented to assist in pronunciation.

An outline star beside a verse indicates a Messianic prophecy (a prophecy concerning the Messiah, the Lord Jesus Christ) when the prophecy is made. A solid star indicates a fulfilled Messianic prophecy.

Words of Christ are printed in red.

Abbreviations

The
Old Testament

The First Book of Moses Called

GENESIS

THE first part of Genesis focuses on the beginning and spread of sin in the world and culminates in the devastating flood in the days of Noah. The second part of the book focuses on God's dealings with one man, Abraham, through whom God promises to bring salvation and blessing to the world. Abraham and his descendants learn firsthand that it is always safe to trust the Lord in times of famine and feasting, blessing and bondage. From Abraham . . . to Isaac . . . to Jacob . . . to Joseph . . . God's promises begin to come to fruition in a great nation possessing a great land.

Genesis is a Greek word meaning "origin," "source," "generation," or "beginning." The original Hebrew title *Bereshith* means "In the Beginning."

The literary structure of Genesis is clear and is built around eleven separate units, each including the word *generations* in the phrase "These are the generations" or "The book of the generations": (1) Introduction to the Genealogies (1:1—2:3); (2) Heaven and Earth (2:4—4:26); (3) Adam (5:1—6:8); (4) Noah (6:9—9:29); (5) Sons of Noah (10:1—11:9); (6) Shem (11:10—26); (7) Terah (11:27—25:11); (8) Ishmael (25:12–18); (9) Isaac (25:19—35:29); (10) Esau (36:1—37:1); (11) Jacob (37:2—50:26).

IN the beginning ᴿGod created the heaven and the earth. Ps. 8:3

2 And the earth was without form, and void; and darkness *was* upon the face of the deep. ᴿAnd the Spirit of God moved upon the face of the waters. Is. 40:13, 14

3 ᴿAnd God said, Let there be light: and there was light. Ps. 33:6, 9

4 And God saw the light, that *it was* good: and God divided the light from the darkness.

5 And God called the light Day, and the ᴿdarkness he called Night. And the evening and the morning were the first day. Ps. 19:2

6 And God said, ᴿLet there be a firmament in the midst of the waters, and let it divide the waters from the waters. Job 37:18; 2 Pet. 3:5

7 And God made the firmament, ᴿand divided the waters which *were* under the firmament from the waters which *were* ᴿabove the firmament: and it was so. Job 38:8–11; Prov. 8:27–29 · Ps. 148:4

8 And God called the ᵀfirmament Heaven. And the evening and the morning were the second day. *expanse*

9 And God said, ᴿLet the waters under the heaven be gathered together unto one place, and let the dry *land* appear: and it was so. Ps. 104:6–9; Jer. 5:22; 2 Pet. 3:5

10 And God called the dry *land* Earth; and the gathering together of the waters called he Seas: and God saw that *it was* good.

11 And God said, Let the earth ᴿbring forth grass, the herb yielding seed, *and* the ᴿfruit tree yielding fruit after his kind, whose seed *is* in itself, upon the earth: and it was so. Heb. 6:7 · Luke 6:44

12 And the earth brought forth grass, *and* herb yielding seed after his kind, and the tree yielding fruit, whose seed *was* in itself, after his kind: and God saw that *it was* good.

13 And the evening and the morning were the third day.

14 And God said, Let there be ᴿlights in the firmament of the heaven to divide the day from the night; and let them be for signs, and for ᴿseasons, and for days, and years: Deut. 4:19 · Ps. 104:19

15 And let them be for lights in the firmament of the heaven to give light upon the earth: and it was so.

16 And God made two great

lights; the ^Rgreater light to rule the day, and the ^Rlesser light to rule the night: *he made* the stars also.   Ps. 136:8 · Deut. 17:3; Ps. 8:3

17 And God set them in the firmament of the ^Rheaven to give light upon the earth,   Jer. 33:20, 25

18 And to ^Rrule over the day and over the night, and to divide the light from the darkness: and God saw that *it was* good.   Jer. 31:35

19 And the evening and the morning were the fourth day.

20 And God said, Let the waters bring forth abundantly the moving creature that hath life, and fowl *that* may fly above the earth in the open firmament of heaven.

21 And ^RGod created great ^Twhales, and every living creature that moveth, which the waters brought forth abundantly, after their kind, and every winged fowl after his kind: and God saw that *it was* good.   Ps. 104:25–28 · *sea creatures*

22 And God blessed them, saying, ^RBe fruitful, and multiply, and fill the waters in the seas, and let fowl multiply in the earth.   8:17

23 And the evening and the morning were the fifth day.

24 And God said, Let the earth bring forth the living creature after his kind, cattle, and creeping thing, and beast of the earth after his kind: and it was so.

25 And God made the beast of the earth after his kind, and cattle after their kind, and every thing that creepeth upon the earth after his kind: and God saw that *it was* good.

26 And God said, ^RLet us make man in our image, after our likeness: and let them have dominion over the fish of the sea, and over the fowl of the air, and over the cattle, and over all the earth, and over every creeping thing that creepeth upon the earth.   James 3:9

27 So God created man in his *own* image, in the image of God created he *him*; ^Rmale and female created he them.   Matt. 19:4

28 And God blessed them, and God said unto them, Be fruitful, and multiply, and replenish the earth, and ^Rsubdue it: and have dominion over the fish of the sea, and over the fowl of the air, and over every living thing that moveth upon the earth.   1 Cor. 9:27

29 And God said, Behold, I have given you every herb bearing seed, which *is* upon the face of all the earth, and every tree, in the which *is* the fruit of a tree yielding seed; to you it shall be for meat.

30 And to ^Revery beast of the earth, and to every fowl of the air, and to every thing that creepeth upon the earth, wherein *there is* life, *I have given* every green herb for meat: and it was so.   Ps. 145:15

31 And ^RGod saw every thing that he had made, and, behold, *it was* very good. And the evening and the morning were the sixth day.   [Ps. 104:24; 1 Tim. 4:4]

2 Thus the heavens and the earth were finished, and ^Rall the host of them.   Ps. 33:6

2 ^RAnd on the seventh day God ended his work which he had made; and he rested on the seventh day from all his work which he had made.   Ex. 20:9–11; Heb. 4:4, 10

3 And God ^Rblessed the seventh day, and sanctified it: because that in it he had rested from all his work which God created and made.   [Is. 58:13]

4 ^RThese *are* the generations of the heavens and of the earth when they were created, in the day that the LORD God made the earth and the heavens,   1:1; Ps. 90:1, 2

5 And every plant of the field before it was in the earth, and every herb of the field before it grew: for the LORD God had not ^Rcaused it to rain upon the earth, and *there was* not a man ^Rto till the ground.   7:4; Job 5:10 · 3:23

6 But there went up a mist from the earth, and watered the whole face of the ground.

7 And the LORD God formed man *of* the ^Rdust of the ground, and breathed into his nostrils the breath of life; and ^Rman became a living soul.   Ps. 103:14 · 1 Cor. 15:45

8 And the LORD God planted ᴿa garden eastward in ᴿEden; and there he put the man whom he had formed. Is. 51:3 · 4:16

9 And out of the ground made the LORD God to grow ᴿevery tree that is pleasant to the sight, and good for food; ᴿthe tree of life also in the midst of the garden, and the tree of knowledge of good and evil. Ezek. 31:8 · [Rev. 2:7; 22:2, 14]

10 And a river went out of Eden to water the garden; and from thence it was parted, and became into four ᵀheads. riverheads

11 The name of the first is Pi'-son: that is it which compasseth ᴿthe whole land of Hav'-i-lah, where there is gold; 25:18

12 And the gold of that land is good: ᴿthere is bdellium and the onyx stone. Num. 11:7

13 And the name of the second river is Gi'-hon: the same is it that compasseth the whole land of ᵀE-thi-o'-pi-a. Cush

14 And the name of the third river is ᴿHid'-de-kel:ᵀ that is it which goeth toward the east of Assyria. And the fourth river is Eu-phra'-tes. Dan. 10:4 · The Tigris

15 And the LORD God took the man, and put him into the garden of Eden to dress it and to keep it.

16 And the LORD God commanded the man, saying, Of every tree of the garden thou mayest freely eat:

17 But of the tree of the knowledge of good and evil, thou shalt not eat of it: for in the day that thou eatest thereof thou shalt surely ᴿdie. Rom. 5:12; 1 Cor. 15:21, 22

18 And the LORD God said, It is not good that the man should be alone; ᴿI will make him an help meet for him. 1 Cor. 11:8, 9; 1 Tim. 2:13

19 ᴿAnd out of the ground the LORD God formed every beast of the field, and every fowl of the air; and ᴿbrought them unto ᵀAdam to see what he would call them: and whatsoever Adam called every living creature, that was the name thereof. 1:20, 24 · Ps. 8:6 · the man

20 And Adam gave names to all cattle, and to the fowl of the air, and to every beast of the field; but for Adam there was not found an help meet for him.

21 And the LORD God caused a ᴿdeep sleep to fall upon Adam, and he slept: and he took one of his ribs, and closed up the flesh instead thereof; 1 Sam. 26:12

22 And the rib, which the LORD God had taken from man, made he a woman, ᴿand brought her unto the man. 3:20; 1 Tim. 2:13

23 And Adam said, This is now ᴿbone of my bones, and flesh of my flesh: she shall be called Woman, because she was taken out of Man. 29:14; Eph. 5:28–30

24 ᴿTherefore shall a man leave his father and his mother, and shall cleave unto his wife: and they shall be one flesh. Matt. 19:5

25 ᴿAnd they were both naked, the man and his wife, and were not ᴿashamed. 3:7, 10 · Is. 47:3

3 Now ᴿthe serpent was ᴿmore ᵀsubtil than any beast of the field which the LORD God had made. And he said unto the woman, Yea, hath God said, Ye shall not eat of every tree of the garden? 1 Chr. 21:1 · 2 Cor. 11:3 · cunning

2 And the woman said unto the serpent, We may eat of the fruit of the trees of the garden:

3 But of the fruit of the tree which is in the midst of the garden, God hath said, Ye shall not eat of it, neither shall ye ᴿtouch it, lest ye die. Ex. 19:12, 13; Rev. 22:14

4 ᴿAnd the serpent said unto the woman, Ye shall not surely die: John 8:44; [2 Cor. 11:3; 1 Tim. 2:14]

5 For God doth know that in the day ye eat thereof, then your eyes shall be opened, and ye shall be as ᵀgods, knowing good and evil. God

6 And when the woman ᴿsaw that the tree was good for food, and that it was pleasant to the eyes, and a tree to be desired to make one wise, she took of the fruit thereof, and did eat, and gave also unto her husband with her; and he did eat. 1 John 2:16

7 And the eyes of them both were opened, ^Rand they knew that they *were* naked; and they sewed fig leaves together, and made themselves aprons.   2:25

8 And they heard ^Rthe voice of the LORD God walking in the garden in the cool of the day: and Adam and his wife ^Rhid themselves from the presence of the LORD God amongst the trees of the garden.   Job 38:1 · Jer. 23:24

9 And the LORD God called unto Adam, and said unto him, Where *art* thou?

10 And he said, I heard thy voice in the garden, ^Rand I was afraid, because I *was* naked; and I hid myself.   Ex. 3:6; Deut. 9:19; 1 John 3:20

11 And he said, Who told thee that thou *wast* naked? Hast thou eaten of the tree, whereof I commanded thee that thou shouldest not eat?

12 And the man said, ^RThe woman whom thou gavest *to be* with me, she gave me of the tree, and I did eat.   [Prov. 28:13]

13 And the LORD God said unto the woman, What *is* this *that* thou hast done? And the woman said, ^RThe serpent ^Tbeguiled me, and I did eat.   2 Cor. 11:3; 1 Tim. 2:14 · *deceived*

14 And the LORD God said unto the serpent, Because thou hast done this, thou *art* cursed above all cattle, and above every beast of the field; upon thy belly shalt thou go, and ^Rdust shalt thou eat all the days of thy life: Is. 65:25; Mic. 7:17

☆ 15 And I will put enmity between thee and the woman, and between thy seed and her seed; ^Rit shall bruise thy head, and thou shalt bruise his heel.   Rom. 16:20

16 Unto the woman he said, I will greatly multiply thy sorrow and thy conception; ^Rin sorrow thou shalt bring forth children; ^Rand thy desire *shall be* to thy husband, and he shall rule over thee.   Is. 13:8; John 16:21 · 4:7

17 And unto Adam he said, Because thou hast hearkened unto the voice of thy wife, and hast eaten of the tree, of which I

commanded thee, saying, Thou shalt not eat of it: ^Rcursed *is* the ground for thy sake; in ^Tsorrow shalt thou eat *of* it all the days of thy life;   Rom. 8:20–22; Heb. 6:8 · *toil*

18 Thorns also and thistles shall it bring forth to thee; and thou shalt eat the herb of the field;

19 In the sweat of thy face shalt thou eat bread, till thou return unto the ground; for out of it wast thou taken: for dust thou *art*, and unto dust shalt thou return.

20 And Adam called his wife's name ^REve; because she was the mother of all living.   2 Cor. 11:3

21 Unto Adam also and to his wife did the LORD God make coats of skins, and clothed them.

22 And the LORD God said, Behold, the man is become as one of us, to know good and evil: and now, lest he put forth his hand, and take also of the tree of life, and eat, and live for ever:

23 Therefore the LORD God sent him forth from the garden of Eden, ^Rto till the ground from whence he was taken.   4:2; 9:20

24 So he drove out the man; and he placed at the east of the garden of Eden ^RCher'-u-bims, and a flaming sword which turned every way, to keep the way of the tree of life.   Ps. 104:4; Ezek. 10:1–20

4 And Adam knew Eve his wife; and she conceived, and bare ^TCain, and said, I have gotten a man from the LORD.   Lit. *Acquire*

2 And she again bare his brother ^TAbel. And Abel was a keeper of sheep, but Cain was a tiller of the ground.   Lit. *Breath* or *Nothing*

3 And in process of time it came to pass, that Cain brought of the fruit ^Rof the ground an offering unto the LORD.   Num. 18:12

4 And Abel, he also brought of ^Rthe firstlings of his flock and of the fat thereof. And the LORD had ^Rrespect unto Abel and to his offering: Num. 18:17 · Heb. 11:4

5 But unto Cain and to his offering he had not respect. And Cain was very ^Twroth, and his countenance fell.   *angry*

6 And the LORD said unto Cain, Why art thou wroth? and why is thy countenance fallen?

7 If thou doest well, shalt thou not be accepted? and if thou doest not well, sin lieth at the door. And unto thee *shall be* his desire, and thou ᵀshalt rule over him.   *should*

8 And Cain talked with Abel his brother: and it came to pass, when they were in the field, that Cain rose up against Abel his brother, and ᴿslew him.   Matt. 23:35

9 And the LORD said unto Cain, Where *is* Abel thy brother? And he said, I know not: *Am* I ᴿmy brother's keeper?   1 Cor. 8:11–13

10 And he said, What hast thou done? the voice of thy brother's blood ᴿcrieth unto me from the ground.   Heb. 12:24; Rev. 6:9, 10

11 And now *art* thou cursed from the earth, which hath opened her mouth to receive thy brother's blood from thy hand;

12 When thou tillest the ground, it shall not henceforth yield unto thee her strength; a fugitive and a vagabond shalt thou be in the earth.

13 And Cain said unto the LORD, My ᵀpunishment *is* greater than I can bear.   *iniquity*

14 Behold, thou hast driven me out this day from the face of the earth; and from thy face shall I be hid; and I shall be a fugitive and a vagabond in the earth; and it shall come to pass, ᴿ*that* every one that findeth me shall slay me.   9:6

15 And the LORD said unto him, Therefore whosoever slayeth Cain, vengeance shall be taken on him ᴿsevenfold. And the LORD set a mark upon Cain, lest any finding him should kill him.   Ps. 79:12

16 And Cain went out from the ᴿpresence of the LORD, and dwelt in the land of ᵀNod, on the east of Eden.   Jon. 1:3 · Lit. *Wandering*

17 And Cain knew his wife; and she conceived, and bare E'-noch: and he builded a city, ᴿand called the name of the city, after the name of his son, E'-noch.   Ps. 49:11

18 And unto E'-noch was born I'-rad: and I'-rad begat Me-hu'-ja-el: and Me-hu'-ja-el begat Me-thu'-sa-el: and Me-thu'-sa-el begat La'-mech.

19 And La'-mech took unto him ᴿtwo wives: the name of the one *was* A'-dah, and the name of the other Zil'-lah.   2:24; 16:3; 1 Tim. 3:2

20 And A'-dah bare Ja'-bal: he was the father of such as dwell in tents, and *of such as have* cattle.

21 And his brother's name *was* Ju'-bal: he was the father of all such as handle the harp and ᵀorgan.   *flute*

22 And Zil'-lah, she also bare Tu'-bal–cain, an ᵀinstructer of every artificer in brass and iron: and the sister of Tu'-bal–cain *was* Na'-a-mah.   Lit. *craftsman in bronze*

23 And La'-mech said unto his wives, A'-dah and Zil'-lah, Hear my voice; ye wives of La'-mech, hearken unto my speech: for I have slain a man to my wounding, and a young man to my hurt.

24 ᴿIf Cain shall be avenged sevenfold, truly La'-mech seventy and sevenfold.   v. 15

25 And Adam knew his wife again; and she bare a son, and called his name ᵀSeth: For God, *said she*, hath appointed me another seed instead of Abel, whom Cain slew.   Lit. *Appointed*

26 And to Seth, to him also there was born a son; and he called his name E'-nos: then began men to call upon the name of the LORD.

5 This *is* the book of the generations of Adam. In the day that God created man, in ᴿthe likeness of God made he him;   1:26; 9:6

2 Male and female created he them; and blessed them, and called their name Adam, in the day when they were created.

3 And Adam lived an hundred and thirty years, and begat *a son* in his own likeness, after his image; and called his name Seth:

4 And the days of Adam after he had begotten Seth were eight hundred years: ᴿand he begat sons and daughters: 1:28; 4:25

5 And all the days that Adam lived were nine hundred and thirty years: ^Rand he died.   [Heb. 9:27]

6 And Seth lived an hundred and five years, and begat E'-nos:

7 And Seth lived after he begat E'-nos eight hundred and seven years, and begat sons and daughters:

8 And all the days of Seth were nine hundred and twelve years: and he died.

9 And E'-nos lived ninety years, and begat Ca-i'-nan:

10 And E'-nos lived after he begat Ca-i'-nan eight hundred and fifteen years, and begat sons and daughters:

11 And all the days of E'-nos were nine hundred and five years: and he died.

12 And Ca-i'-nan lived seventy years, and begat Ma-ha'-la-le-el:

13 And Ca-i'-nan lived after he begat Ma-ha'-la-le-el eight hundred and forty years, and begat sons and daughters:

14 And all the days of Ca-i'-nan were nine hundred and ten years: and he died.

15 And Ma-ha'-la-le-el lived sixty and five years, and begat Ja'-red:

16 And Ma-ha'-la-le-el lived after he begat Ja'-red eight hundred and thirty years, and begat sons and daughters:

17 And all the days of Ma-ha'-la-le-el were eight hundred ninety and five years: and he died.

18 And Ja'-red lived an hundred sixty and two years, and he begat ^RE'-noch: Jude 14, 15

19 And Ja'-red lived after he begat E'-noch eight hundred years, and begat sons and daughters:

20 And all the days of Ja'-red were nine hundred sixty and two years: and he died.

21 And E'-noch lived sixty and five years, and begat Me-thu'-se-lah:

22 And E'-noch ^Rwalked with God after he begat Me-thu'-se-lah three hundred years, and begat sons and daughters: [Mic. 6:8]

23 And all the days of E'-noch were three hundred sixty and five years:

24 And ^RE'-noch walked with God: and he *was* not; for God ^Rtook him. Jude 14 · 2 Kin. 2:10; Ps. 49:15

25 And Me-thu'-se-lah lived an hundred eighty and seven years, and begat La'-mech:

26 And Me-thu'-se-lah lived after he begat La'-mech seven hundred eighty and two years, and begat sons and daughters:

27 And all the days of Me-thu'-se-lah were nine hundred sixty and nine years: and he died.

28 And La'-mech lived an hundred eighty and two years, and begat a son:

29 And he called his name ^RNoah, saying, This *same* shall comfort us concerning our work and toil of our hands, because of the ground which the LORD hath cursed. Luke 3:36; Heb. 11:7; 1 Pet. 3:20

30 And La'-mech lived after he begat Noah five hundred ninety and five years, and begat sons and daughters:

31 And all the days of La'-mech were seven hundred seventy and seven years: and he died.

32 And Noah was five hundred years old: and Noah begat ^RShem, Ham, and Ja'-pheth.   6:10; 7:13

6 And it came to pass, ^Rwhen men began to multiply on the face of the earth, and daughters were born unto them,   1:28

2 That the sons of God saw the daughters of men that they *were* fair; and they ^Rtook them wives of all which they chose.   Deut. 7:3, 4

3 And the LORD said, ^RMy spirit shall not always ^Rstrive with man, for that he also *is* flesh: yet his days shall be an hundred and twenty years.   1 Pet. 3:19 · 2 Thess. 2:7

4 There were giants in the earth in those ^Rdays; and also after that, when the sons of God came in unto the daughters of men, and they bare *children* to them, the same *became* mighty men which *were* of old, men of renown.   Num. 13:32, 33; Luke 17:27

5 And GOD saw that the wickedness of man *was* great in the earth, and *that* every ᴿimagination of the thoughts of his heart *was* only evil continually. 8:21
6 And ᴿitᵀ repented the LORD that he had made man on the earth, and it grieved him at his heart. 2 Sam. 24:16 · *the LORD was sorry*
7 And the LORD said, I will ᴿdestroy man whom I have created from the face of the earth; both man, and beast, and the creeping thing, and the fowls of the air; for it repenteth me that I have made them. Deut. 28:63; 29:20; Ps. 7:11
8 But Noah ᴿfound grace in the eyes of the LORD. Luke 1:30; Acts 7:46
9 These *are* the generations of Noah: Noah was a just man *and* ᵀperfect in his generations, *and* Noah walked with God. *blameless*
10 And Noah begat three sons, Shem, Ham, and Ja′-pheth.
11 The earth also was corrupt ᴿbefore God, and the earth was filled with violence. Rom. 2:13
12 And God looked upon the earth, and, behold, it was corrupt; for ᴿall flesh had corrupted his way upon the earth. Ps. 14:1–3
13 And God said unto Noah, ᴿThe end of all flesh is come before me; for the earth is filled with violence through them; and, behold, ᴿI will destroy them with the earth. 1 Pet. 4:7 · 2 Pet. 2:4–10
14 Make thee an ark of go′-pher wood; rooms shalt thou make in the ark, and shalt pitch it within and without with pitch.
15 And this *is the fashion* which thou shalt make it *of:* The length of the ark *shall be* three hundred ᵀcubits, the breadth of it fifty cubits, and the height of it thirty cubits. A cubit is about 18 inches.
16 A window shalt thou make ᵀto the ark, and in a cubit shalt thou finish it above; and the door of the ark shalt thou set in the side thereof; *with* lower, second, and third *stories* shalt thou make it. *for*
17 And, behold, I, even I, do bring a ᴿflood of waters upon the earth, to destroy all flesh, wherein *is* the breath of life, from under heaven; *and* every thing that *is* in the earth shall die. 2 Pet. 3:6
18 But with thee will I establish my ᴿcovenant; and thou shalt come into the ark, thou, and thy sons, and thy wife, and thy sons' wives with thee. 8:20—9:17; 17:7
19 And of every living thing of all flesh, ᴿtwo of every *sort* shalt thou bring into the ark, to keep *them* alive with thee; they shall be male and female. 7:2, 8, 9, 14–16
20 Of fowls after their kind, and of ᵀcattle after their kind, of every creeping thing of the earth after his kind, two of every *sort* ᴿshall come unto thee, to keep *them* alive. *animals* · 7:9, 15
21 And take thou unto thee of all food that is eaten, and thou shalt gather *it* to thee; and it shall be for food for thee, and for them.
22 Thus did Noah; ᴿaccording to all that God commanded him, so did he. 7:5, 9, 16

7 And the LORD said unto Noah, ᴿCome thou and all thy house into the ark; for ᴿthee have I seen righteous before me in this generation. Matt. 24:38 · Ps. 33:18
2 Of every ᴿclean beast thou shalt take to thee by sevens, the male and his female: and of beasts that *are* not clean by two, the male and his female. Lev. 11
3 Of fowls also of the air by sevens, the male and the female; to keep ᵀseed alive upon the face of all the earth. *the species*
4 For yet ᴿseven days, and I will cause it to rain upon the earth forty days and forty nights; and every living substance that I have made will I destroy from off the face of the earth. v. 10; Ex. 7:25
5 ᴿAnd Noah did according unto all that the LORD commanded him. 6:22
6 And Noah *was* six hundred years old when the flood of waters was upon the earth.
7 And Noah went in, and his sons, and his wife, and his sons' wives with him, into the ark, because of the waters of the flood.

8 Of clean beasts, and of beasts that *are* not clean, and of fowls, and of every thing that creepeth upon the earth,

9 There went in two and two unto Noah into the ark, the male and the female, as God had commanded Noah.

10 And it came to pass after seven days, that the waters of the flood were upon the earth.

11 In the six hundredth year of Noah's life, in the second month, the seventeenth day of the month, the same day were all ᴿthe fountains of the great deep broken up, and the ᴿwindows of heaven were opened.   Is. 51:10 · Ps. 78:23

12 And the rain was upon the earth forty days and forty nights.

13 In the selfsame day entered Noah, and Shem, and Ham, and Ja′-pheth, the sons of Noah, and Noah's wife, and the three wives of his sons with them, into the ark;

14 ᴿThey, and every beast after his kind, and all the cattle after their kind, and every creeping thing that creepeth upon the earth after his kind, and every fowl after his kind, every bird of every ᴿsort.   6:19 · 1:21

15 And they went in unto Noah into the ark, two and two of all flesh, wherein *is* the breath of life.

16 And they that went in, went in male and female of all flesh, ᴿas God had commanded him: and the Lᴏʀᴅ shut him in.   vv. 2, 3

17 ᴿAnd the flood was forty days upon the earth; and the waters increased, and ᵀbare up the ark, and it was lift up above the earth.   vv. 4, 12; 8:6 · *lifted*

18 And the waters prevailed, and were increased greatly upon the earth; ᴿand the ark went upon the face of the waters.   Ps. 104:26

19 And the waters prevailed exceedingly upon the earth; and all the high hills, that *were* under the whole heaven, were covered.

20 Fifteen cubits upward did the waters prevail; and the mountains were covered.

21 ᴿAnd all flesh died that moved upon ᵀthe earth, both of fowl, and of cattle, and of beast, and of every creeping thing that creepeth upon the earth, and every man: v. 4; 6:7, 13, 17 · *the land*

22 All in ᴿwhose nostrils *was* the breath of life, of all that *was* in the dry *land*, died.   2:7

23 And every living substance was destroyed which was upon the face of the ground, both man, and cattle, and the creeping things, and the fowl of the heaven; and they were destroyed from the earth: and ᴿNoah only remained *alive*, and they that *were* with him in the ark.   Luke 17:26, 27; Heb. 11:7

24 ᴿAnd the waters prevailed upon the earth an hundred and fifty days.   8:3, 4

8 And God remembered Noah, and every living thing, and all the ᵀcattle that *was* with him in the ark: and God made a wind to pass over the earth, and the waters ᵀasswaged;   *animals · subsided*

2 The fountains also of the deep and the windows of heaven were ᴿstopped, and the rain from heaven was restrained;   Deut. 11:17

3 And the waters returned from off the earth continually: and after the end ᴿof the hundred and fifty days the waters were abated.   7:24

4 And the ark rested in the seventh month, on the seventeenth day of the month, upon the mountains of Ar′-a-rat.

5 And the waters decreased continually until the tenth month: in the tenth *month*, on the first *day* of the month, were the tops of the mountains seen.

6 And it came to pass at the end of forty days, that Noah opened ᴿthe window of the ark which he had made: 6:16

7 And he sent forth a raven, which went forth to and fro, until the waters were dried up from off the earth.

8 Also he sent forth a dove from him, to see if the waters were abated from off the face of the ground;

9 But the dove found no rest for the sole of her foot, and she returned unto him into the ark, for the waters *were* on the face of the whole earth: then he put forth his hand, and took her, and pulled her in unto him into the ark.

10 And he stayed yet other seven days; and again he sent forth the dove out of the ark;

11 And the dove came in to him in the evening; and, lo, in her mouth *was* an olive leaf pluckt off: so Noah knew that the waters were abated from off the earth.

12 And he stayed yet other seven days; and sent forth the dove; which returned not again unto him any more.

13 And it came to pass in the six hundredth and first year, in the first *month*, the first *day* of the month, the waters were dried up from off the earth: and Noah removed the covering of the ark, and looked, and, behold, the face of the ground was dry.

14 And in the second month, on the seven and twentieth day of the month, was the earth dried.

15 And God spake unto Noah, saying,

16 Go forth of the ark, ᴿthou, and thy wife, and thy sons, and thy sons' wives with thee.   7:13

17 Bring forth with thee every living thing that *is* with thee, of all flesh, *both* of fowl, and of cattle, and of every creeping thing that creepeth upon the earth; that they may breed abundantly in the earth, and ᴿbe fruitful, and multiply upon the earth.   1:22, 28; 9:1, 7

18 And Noah went forth, and his sons, and his wife, and his sons' wives with him:

19 Every beast, every creeping thing, and every fowl, *and* whatsoever creepeth upon the earth, after their ᵀkinds, went forth out of the ark.   Lit. *families*

20 And Noah builded an ᴿaltar unto the LORD; and took of every clean beast, and of every clean fowl, and offered burnt offerings on the altar.   12:7; Ex. 29:18, 25

21 And the LORD smelled ᴿa sweet savour; and the LORD said in his heart, I will not again curse the ground any more for man's sake; for the ᴿimagination of man's heart *is* evil from his youth; neither will I again smite any more every thing living, as I have done.   Eph. 5:2 · Rom. 1:21; Eph. 2:1–3

22 ᴿWhile the earth remaineth, seedtime and harvest, and cold and heat, and summer and winter, and ᴿday and night shall not cease.   Is. 54:9 · Ps. 74:16; Jer. 33:20, 25

9 And God blessed Noah and his sons, and said unto them, ᴿBe fruitful, and multiply, and replenish the earth.   1:28, 29; 10:32

2 ᴿAnd the fear of you and the dread of you shall be upon every beast of the earth, and upon every fowl of the air, upon all that moveth *upon* the earth, and upon all the fishes of the sea; into your hand are they delivered.   Ps. 8:6

3 Every moving thing that liveth shall be meat for you; even as the ᴿgreen herb have I given you all things.   Col. 2:16; [1 Tim. 4:3, 4]

4 ᴿBut flesh with the life thereof, *which is* the blood thereof, shall ye not eat.   Lev. 7:26; 17:10–16

5 And surely your blood of your lives will I require; at the hand of every beast will I require it, and ᴿat the hand of man; at the hand of every man's brother will I require the life of man.   4:9, 10

6 ᴿWhoso sheddeth man's blood, by man shall his blood be shed: for in the image of God made he man.   Ex. 21:12–14; Lev. 24:17

7 And you, be ye fruitful, and multiply; bring forth abundantly in the earth, and multiply therein.

8 And God spake unto Noah, and to his sons with him, saying,

9 And I, behold, I establish ᴿmy covenant with you, and with your ᵀseed after you;   Is. 54:9 · *descendants*

10 ᴿAnd with every living creature that *is* with you, of the fowl, of the cattle, and of every beast of the earth with you; from all that go out of the ark, to every beast of the earth.   Ps. 145:9

11 And ^RI will establish my covenant with you; neither shall all flesh be cut off any more by the waters of a flood; neither shall there any more be a flood to destroy the earth.   8:21; Is. 54:9

12 And God said, This *is* the token of the covenant which I make between me and you and every living creature that *is* with you, for perpetual generations:

13 I do set ^Rmy bow in the cloud, and it shall be for a ^Ttoken of a covenant between me and the earth.   Ezek. 1:28; Rev. 4:3 · *sign*

14 And it shall come to pass, when I bring a cloud over the earth, that the ^Tbow shall be seen in the cloud: *rainbow*

15 And ^RI will remember my covenant, which *is* between me and you and every living creature of all flesh; and the waters shall no more become a flood to destroy all flesh.   Deut. 7:9; Ezek. 16:60

16 And the bow shall be in the cloud; and I will look upon it, that I may remember ^Rthe everlasting covenant between God and every living creature of all flesh that *is* upon the earth.   17:13, 19; Heb. 13:20

17 And God said unto Noah, This *is* the ^Ttoken of the covenant, which I have established between me and all flesh that *is* upon the earth.   *sign*

18 And the sons of Noah, that went forth of the ark, were Shem, and Ham, and Ja'-pheth: ^Rand Ham *is* the father of Canaan.   10:6

19 These *are* the three sons of Noah: and of them was the whole earth ^Toverspread.   *populated*

20 And Noah began *to be* ^Ran ^Thusbandman, and he planted a vineyard: Prov. 12:11; Jer. 31:24 · *farmer*

21 And he drank of the wine, and was drunken; and he was uncovered within his tent.

22 And Ham, the father of Ca-naan, saw the nakedness of his father, and told his two brethren without.

23 And Shem and Ja'-pheth took a garment, and laid *it* upon both their shoulders, and went backward, and covered the na-kedness of their father; and their faces *were* backward, and they saw not their father's nakedness.

24 And Noah awoke from his wine, and knew what his younger son had done unto him.

25 And he said, Cursed *be* Ca-naan; a ^Rservant of servants shall he be unto his brethren.   Josh. 9:23

26 And he said, ^RBlessed *be* the LORD God of Shem; and Canaan shall be his servant.   Ps. 144:15

27 God shall enlarge Ja'-pheth, ^Rand he shall dwell in the tents of Shem; and Canaan shall be his servant.   Eph. 2:13, 14; 3:6

28 And Noah lived after the flood three hundred and fifty years.

29 And all the days of Noah were nine hundred and fifty years: and he died.

10 Now these *are* the genera-tions of the sons of Noah, Shem, Ham, and Ja'-pheth: ^Rand unto them were sons born after the flood.   9:1, 7, 19

2 ^RThe sons of Ja'-pheth; Go'-mer, and Ma'-gog, and Ma'-dai, and Ja'-van, and Tu'-bal, and Me'-shech, and Ti'-ras.   1 Chr. 1:5-7

3 And the sons of Go'-mer; Ash'-ke-naz, and Ri'-phath, and To-gar'-mah.

4 And the sons of Ja'-van; E-li'-shah, and Tar'-shish, Kit'-tim, and Dod'-a-nim.

5 By these were ^Rthe isles of the Gentiles divided in their lands; every one after his tongue, after their families, in their na-tions.   11:8; Ps. 72:10; Jer. 2:10; 25:22

6 ^RAnd the sons of Ham; Cush, and Miz'-ra-im, and ^TPhut, and Canaan.   1 Chr. 1:8-16 · Or *Put*

7 And the sons of Cush; Se'-ba, and Hav'-i-lah, and Sab'-tah, and Ra'-a-mah, and Sab'-te-chah: and the sons of Ra'-a-mah; She'-ba, and De'-dan.

8 And Cush begat ^RNimrod: he began to be a mighty one in the earth.   Mic. 5:6

9 He was a mighty ^Rhunter be-fore the LORD: wherefore it is said,

Even as Nimrod the mighty hunter before the LORD.　　*Jer. 16:16*

10 ᴿAnd the beginning of his kingdom was ᴿBabel, and E'-rech, and Ac'-cad, and Cal'-neh, in the land of Shi'-nar.　　*Mic. 5:6 · 11:9*

11 Out of that land ᵀwent ᴿforth Assh'-ur, and builded Nin'-e-veh, and the city Re-ho'-both, and Ca'-lah,　　*he went to Assyria · 25:18*

12 And Re'-sen between Nin'-e-veh and Ca'-lah: the same *is* ᵀa great city.　　*the principal city*

13 And Miz'-ra-im begat Lu'-dim, and An'-a-mim, and Le'-ha-bim, and Naph'-tu-him,

14 And Path-ru'-sim, and Cas'-lu-him, (out of whom came Phi-lis'-tim,) and Caph'-to-rim.

15 And Canaan begat Si'-don his firstborn, and ᴿHeth,　　*23:3*

16 And the Jeb'-u-site, and the Am'-or-ite, and the Gir'-ga-site,

17 And the Hi'-vite, and the Ark'-ite, and the Si'-nite,

18 And the Ar'-vad-ite, and the Zem'-a-rite, and the Ha'-math-ite: and afterward were the families of the Ca'-naan-ites spread abroad.

19 And the border of the Ca'-naan-ites was from Si'-don, as thou comest to Ge'-rar, unto Ga'-za; as thou goest, unto Sodom, and Go-mor'-rah, and Ad'-mah, and Ze-bo'-im, even unto La'-sha.

20 These *are* the sons of Ham, after their families, after their tongues, in their countries, *and* in their nations.

21 Unto Shem also, the father of all the children of E'-ber, the brother of Ja'-pheth the elder, even to him were *children* born.

22 The children of Shem; E'-lam, and Assh'-ur, and Ar-phax'-ad, and Lud, and A'-ram.

23 And the children of A'-ram; Uz, and Hul, and Ge'-ther, and ᵀMash.　　*Meshech, 1 Chr. 1:17*

24 And Ar-phax'-ad begat ᴿSa'-lah; and Sa'-lah begat E'-ber.　*11:12*

25 And unto E'-ber were born two sons: the name of one *was* ᵀPe'-leg; for in his days was the

earth divided; and his brother's name *was* Jok'-tan.　　*Lit. Division*

26 And Jok'-tan begat Al-mo'-dad, and She'-leph, and Ha'-zar-ma'-veth, and Je'-rah,

27 And Ha-do'-ram, and U'-zal, and Dik'-lah,

28 And ᵀO'-bal, and A-bim'-a-el, and She'-ba,　　*Ebal, 1 Chr. 1:22*

29 And O'-phir, and Hav'-i-lah, and Jo'-bab: all these *were* the sons of Jok'-tan.

30 And their dwelling was from Me'-sha, as thou goest unto Se'-phar a mount of the east.

31 These *are* the sons of Shem, after their families, ᵀafter their tongues, in their lands, after their nations.　　*according to their languages*

32 These *are* the families of the sons of Noah, after their generations, in their nations: ᴿand by these were the nations divided in the earth after the flood.　*9:19; 11:8*

11 And the whole earth was of one ᵀlanguage, and of one speech.　　*Lit. lip*

2 And it came to pass, as they journeyed from the east, that they found a plain in the land ᴿof Shi'-nar; and they dwelt there.　*Dan. 1:2*

3 And they said one to another, ᵀGo to, let us make brick, and burn them throughly. And they had brick for stone, and ᵀslime had they for morter.　*Come · asphalt*

4 And they said, Go to, let us build us a city and a tower, whose top *may reach* unto heaven; and let us make us a name, lest we ᴿbe scattered abroad upon the face of the whole earth.　　*Deut. 4:27*

5 ᴿAnd the LORD came down to see the city and the tower, which the children of men builded.　*18:21*

6 And the LORD said, Behold, ᴿthe people *is* one, and they have all one language; and this they begin to do: and now nothing will be restrained from them, which they have imagined to do.　*9:19*

7 Go to, let us go down, and there ᴿconfound their language, that they may not understand one another's speech.　*Is. 33:19; Jer. 5:15*

8 So ᴿthe LORD scattered them

abroad from thence upon the face of all the earth: and they left off to build the city.   Deut. 32:8; Ps. 92:9

9 Therefore is the name of it called Babel; because the LORD did there confound the language of all the earth: and from thence did the LORD scatter them abroad upon the face of all the earth.

10 RThese *are* the generations of Shem: Shem *was* an hundred years old, and begat Ar-phax'-ad two years after the flood: 1 Chr. 1:17

11 And Shem lived after he begat Ar-phax'-ad five hundred years, and begat sons and daughters.

12 And Ar-phax'-ad lived five and thirty years, Rand begat Sa'-lah: Luke 3:35

13 And Ar-phax'-ad lived after he begat Sa'-lah four hundred and three years, and begat sons and daughters.

14 And Sa'-lah lived thirty years, and begat E'-ber:

15 And Sa'-lah lived after he begat E'-ber four hundred and three years, and begat sons and daughters.

16 And E'-ber lived four and thirty years, and begat Pe'-leg:

17 And E'-ber lived after he begat Pe'-leg four hundred and thirty years, and begat sons and daughters.

18 And Pe'-leg lived thirty years, and begat Re'-u:

19 And Pe'-leg lived after he begat Re'-u two hundred and nine years, and begat sons and daughters.

20 And Re'-u lived two and thirty years, and begat Se'-rug:

21 And Re'-u lived after he begat Se'-rug two hundred and seven years, and begat sons and daughters.

22 And Se'-rug lived thirty years, and begat Na'-hor:

23 And Se'-rug lived after he begat Na'-hor two hundred years, and begat sons and daughters.

24 And Na'-hor lived nine and twenty years, and begat Te'-rah:

25 And Na'-hor lived after he begat Te'-rah an hundred and

nineteen years, and begat sons and daughters.

26 And Te'-rah lived seventy years, and Rbegat Abram, Na'-hor, and Ha'-ran.   Josh. 24:2; 1 Chr. 1:26

27 Now these *are* the generations of Te'-rah: Te'-rah begat RAbram, Na'-hor, and Ha'-ran; and Ha'-ran begat Lot.   v. 31; 17:5

28 And Ha'-ran died before his father Te'-rah in the land of his nativity, in Ur of the Chal'-dees.

29 And Abram and Na'-hor took them wives: the name of Abram's wife *was* Sa'-rai; and the name of Na'-hor's wife, Mil'-cah, the daughter of Ha'-ran, the father of Mil'-cah, and the father of Is'-cah.

30 But RSa'-rai was barren; she *had* no child.   16:1, 2; Luke 1:36

31 And Te'-rah took Abram his son, and Lot the son of Ha'-ran his son's son, and Sa'-rai his daughter in law, his son Abram's wife; and they went forth with them from RUr of the Chal'-dees, to go into Rthe land of Canaan; and they came unto Ha'-ran, and dwelt there.   15:7; Neh. 9:7; Acts 7:4 · 10:19

32 And the days of Te'-rah were two hundred and five years: and Te'-rah died in Ha'-ran.

12 Now the LORD had said unto Abram, Get thee out of thy country, and from thy kindred, and from thy father's house, unto a land that I will shew thee:

2 And I will make of thee a great nation, and I will bless thee, and make thy name great; Rand thou shalt be a blessing: Gal. 3:14

3 And I will bless them that bless thee, and curse him that curseth thee: and in thee shall all families of the earth be blessed.   ☆

4 So Abram departed, as the LORD had spoken unto him; and Lot went with him: and Abram *was* seventy and five years old when he departed out of Ha'-ran.

5 And Abram took Sa'-rai his wife, and Lot his brother's son, and all their substance that they had gathered, and Rthe souls that they had gotten Rin Ha'-ran; and

they went forth to go into the land of Canaan; and into the land of Canaan they came.　　14:14 · 11:31

6 And Abram ᴿpassed through the land unto the place of ᵀSi'-chem, unto the plain of Mo'-reh. And the Ca'-naan-ite *was* then in the land.　　Heb. 11:9 · Or *Shechem*

☆ **7** And the LORD appeared unto Abram, and said, ᴿUnto thy seed will I give this land: and there builded he an altar unto the LORD, who appeared unto him.　　Gal. 3:16

8 And he removed from thence unto a mountain on the east of Beth'-el, and pitched his tent, *having* Beth'-el on the west, and Ha'-i on the east: and there he builded an altar unto the LORD, and ᴿcalled upon the name of the LORD.　　4:26; 13:4; 21:33

9 And Abram journeyed, ᴿgoing on still toward the south.　　13:1

10 And there was ᴿa famine in the land: and Abram ᴿwent down into Egypt to sojourn there; for the famine *was* ᴿgrievous in the land.　　26:1 · Ps. 105:13 · 43:1

11 And it came to pass, when he was come near to enter into Egypt, that he said unto Sa'-rai his wife, Behold now, I know that thou *art* ᴿa ᵀfair woman to look upon:　　v. 14; 26:7; 29:17 · *beautiful*

12 Therefore it shall come to pass, when the Egyptians shall see thee, that they shall say, This *is* his wife: and they ᴿwill kill me, but they will save thee alive.　　20:11

13 ᴿSay, I pray thee, thou *art* my sister: that it may be well with me for thy sake; and my soul shall live because of thee.　　20:1–18; 26:6–11

14 And it came to pass, that, when Abram was come into Egypt, the Egyptians beheld the woman that she *was* very fair.

15 The princes also of Pharaoh saw her, and commended her before Pharaoh: and the woman was taken into Pharaoh's house.

16 And he entreated Abram well for her sake: and he ᴿhad sheep, and oxen, and he asses, and menservants, and maidservants, and she asses, and camels.　　13:2

17 And the LORD ᴿplagued Pharaoh and his house with great plagues because of Sa'-rai A-bram's wife.　　20:18; 1 Chr. 16:21

18 And Pharaoh called Abram, and said, ᴿWhat *is* this *that* thou hast done unto me? why didst thou not tell me that she *was* thy wife?　　20:9, 10; 26:10

19 Why saidst thou, She *is* my sister? so I might have taken her to me to wife: now therefore behold thy wife, take *her*, and go thy way.

20 ᴿAnd Pharaoh commanded *his* men concerning him: and they sent him away, and his wife, and all that he had.　　[Prov. 21:1]

13 And Abram went up out of Egypt, he, and his wife, and all that he had, and ᴿLot with him, ᴿinto the south.　　12:4; 14:12, 16 · 12:9

2 ᴿAnd Abram *was* very rich in cattle, in silver, and in gold.　　24:35

3 And he went on his journeys ᴿfrom the south even to Beth'-el, unto the place where his tent had been at the beginning, between Beth'-el and Ha'-i;　　12:8, 9

4 Unto the place of the altar, which he had made there at the first: and there Abram ᴿcalled on the name of the LORD.　　Ps. 116:17

5 And Lot also, which went with Abram, had flocks, and herds, and tents.

6 And ᴿthe land was not able to ᵀbear them, that they might dwell together: for their substance was great, so that they could not dwell together.　　36:7 · *support*

7 And there was ᴿa strife between the herdmen of Abram's cattle and the herdmen of Lot's cattle: ᴿand the Ca'-naan-ite and the Per'-iz-zite dwelled then in the land.　　26:20 · 12:6; 15:20, 21

8 And Abram said unto Lot, ᴿLet there be no strife, I pray thee, between me and thee, and between my herdmen and thy herdmen; for we *be* brethren.　　1 Cor. 6:7

9 ᴿ*Is* not the whole land before thee? separate thyself, I pray thee, from me: if *thou wilt take* the left hand, then I will go to the right; or if *thou depart* to the right hand, then I will go to the left. 20:15; 34:10

10 And Lot lifted up his eyes, and beheld all the plain of Jordan, that it *was* well watered every where, before the LORD ^Rdestroyed Sodom and Go-mor'-rah, *even* as the garden of the LORD, like the land of Egypt, as thou comest unto Zo'-ar.   19:24

11 Then Lot chose ^Thim all the plain of Jordan; and Lot journeyed east: and they separated themselves the one from the other.   *for himself*

12 Abram dwelled in the land of Canaan, and Lot dwelled in the cities of the plain, and pitched *his* tent ^Ttoward Sodom.   *as far as*

13 But the men of Sodom ^R*were* wicked and sinners before the LORD exceedingly.   2 Pet. 2:7, 8

14 And the LORD said unto Abram, after that Lot ^Rwas separated from him, Lift up now thine eyes, and look from the place where thou art ^Rnorthward, and southward, and eastward, and westward: v. 11 · 28:14

15 For all the land which thou seest, ^Rto thee will I give it, and to thy seed for ever.   Deut. 34:4; Acts 7:5

16 And ^RI will make thy seed as the dust of the earth: so that if a man can number the dust of the earth, *then* shall thy seed also be numbered.   22:17; Ex. 32:13; Num. 23:10

17 Arise, walk through the land in the length of it and in the breadth of it; for I will give it unto thee.

18 ^RThen Abram removed *his* tent, and came and ^Rdwelt in the plain of Mam'-re, ^Rwhich *is* in He'-bron, and built there an altar unto the LORD.   26:17 · 14:13 · 23:2; 35:27

14 And it came to pass in the days of Am'-ra-phel king of Shi'-nar, A'-ri-och king of El'-la-sar, Ched-or-la'-o-mer king of E'-lam, and Ti'-dal king of nations;

2 *That these* made war with Be'-ra king of Sodom, and with Bir'-sha king of Go-mor'-rah, Shi'-nab king of Ad'-mah, and Shem-e'-ber king of Ze-boi'-im, and the king of Be'-la, which is Zo'-ar.

3 All these were joined together in the vale of Sid'-dim, ^Rwhich is the salt sea.   Num. 34:12; Deut. 3:17

4 Twelve years ^Rthey served Ched-or-la'-o-mer, and in the thirteenth year they rebelled.   9:26

5 And in the fourteenth year came Ched-or-la'-o-mer, and the kings that *were* with him, and smote ^Rthe Reph'-a-ims in Ash'-te-roth Kar-na'-im, and ^Rthe Zu'-zims in Ham, and the E'-mims in Sha'-veh Kir-i-a-tha'-im,   15:20 · Deut. 2:20

6 ^RAnd the Ho'-rites in their mount Se'-ir, unto El-pa'-ran, which *is* by the wilderness.   36:20

7 And they returned, and came to En-mish'-pat, which *is* Ka'-desh, and smote all the country of the Am'-a-lek-ites, and also the Am'-or-ites, that dwelt ^Rin Haz'-e-zon-ta'-mar.   2 Chr. 20:2

8 And there went out the king of Sodom, and the king of Go-mor'-rah, and the king of Ad'-mah, and the king of Ze-boi'-im, and the king of Be'-la (the same *is* Zo'-ar;) and they joined battle with them in the vale of Sid'-dim;

9 With Ched-or-la'-o-mer the king of E'-lam, and with Ti'-dal king of ^Tnations, and Am'-ra-phel king of Shi'-nar, and A'-ri-och king of El'-la-sar; four kings ^Twith five.   Heb. *Goyim · against*

10 And the vale of Sid'-dim *was* full of ^Rslimepits; and the kings of Sodom and Go-mor'-rah fled, and fell there; and they that remained fled ^Rto the mountain.   11:3 · 19:17, 30

11 And they took ^Rall the goods of Sodom and Go-mor'-rah, and all their ^Tvictuals, and went their way.   vv. 16, 21 · *provisions*

12 And they took Lot, Abram's ^Rbrother's son, ^Rwho dwelt in Sodom, and his goods, and departed.   11:27; 12:5 · 13:12

13 And there came one that had escaped, and told Abram the ^RHebrew; for he dwelt in the plain of Mam'-re the Am'-or-ite, brother of Esh'-col, and brother of A'-ner: ^Rand these *were* confederate with Abram.   39:14; 40:15 · v. 24; 21:27, 32

14 And ^Rwhen Abram heard that

Rhis brother was taken captive, he armed his trained *servants*, born in his own house, three hundred and eighteen, and pursued *them* unto Dan.   19:29 · v. 12; 13:8

15 And he divided himself against them, he and his servants, by night, and Rsmote them, and pursued them unto Ho'-bah, which *is* Ton the left hand of Damascus.   Is. 41:2, 3 · north

16 And he brought back all the goods, and also brought again his brother Lot, and his goods, and the women also, and the people.

17 And the king of Sodom Rwent out to meet him after his return from the Tslaughter of Ched-or-la'-o-mer, and of the kings that *were* with him, at the valley of Sha'-veh, which *is* the king's Tdale.   1 Sam. 18:6 · *defeat · valley*

18 And RMel-chiz'-e-dek king of Sa'-lem brought forth bread and wine: and he *was* the priest of the most high God.   Ps. 110:4; Heb. 7:1–10

19 And he blessed him, and said, RBlessed *be* Abram of the most high God, Rpossessor of heaven and earth: Ruth 3:10 · v. 22

20 And Rblessed be the most high God, which hath delivered thine enemies into thy hand. And he gave him tithes of all.   24:27

21 And the king of Sodom said unto Abram, Give me the persons, and take the goods to thyself.

22 And Abram said to the king of Sodom, I Rhave lift up mine hand unto the LORD, the most high God, Rthe possessor of heaven and earth,   Dan. 12:7 · v. 19

23 That RI will not *take* from a thread even to a shoelatchet, and that I will not take any thing that *is* thine, lest thou shouldest say, I have made Abram rich: 2 Kin. 5:16

24 Save only that which the young men have eaten, and the portion of the men which went with me, A'-ner, Esh'-col, and Mam'-re; let them take their portion.

15 After these things the word of the LORD came unto Abram in a vision, saying, RFear

not, Abram: I *am* thy shield, *and* thy exceeding great reward.   21:17

2 RAnd Abram said, Lord GOD, what wilt thou give me, Rseeing I go childless, and the Tsteward of my house *is* this E-li-e'-zer of Damascus?   17:18 · Acts 7:5 · *heir*

3 And Abram said, Behold, to me thou hast given no seed: and, lo, Tone born in my house is mine heir.   Lit. *a son of my house*, a servant

4 And, behold, the word of the LORD *came* unto him, saying, This shall not be thine heir; but he that Rshall come forth out of thine own bowels shall be thine heir.   Gal. 4:28

5 And he brought him forth abroad, and said, Look now toward heaven, and tell the stars, if thou be able to number them: and he said unto him, RSo shall thy seed be.   Rom. 4:18; Heb. 11:12

6 And he Rbelieved in the LORD; and he counted it to him for righteousness.   21:1; Rom. 4:3, 9, 22; Gal. 3:6

7 And he said unto him, I *am* the LORD that brought thee out of RUr of the Chal'-dees, to give thee this land to inherit it.   11:28, 31

8 And he said, Lord GOD, Rwhereby shall I know that I shall inherit it?   1 Sam. 14:9, 10; Luke 1:18

9 And he said unto him, Take me an heifer of three years old, and a she goat of three years old, and a ram of three years old, and a turtledove, and a young pigeon.

10 And he took unto him all these, and Rdivided them in the midst, and laid each piece one against another: but Rthe birds divided he not.   Jer. 34:18 · Lev. 1:17

11 And when the Tfowls came down upon the carcases, Abram drove them away.   *vultures*

12 And when the sun was going down, Ra deep sleep fell upon A-bram; and, lo, an horror of great darkness fell upon him.   2:21; 28:11

13 And he said unto Abram, Know of a surety Rthat thy seed shall be a stranger in a land *that is* not theirs, and shall serve them; and they shall afflict them four hundred years;   Ex. 1:11; Acts 7:6

14 And also that nation, whom

they shall serve, will I judge: and afterward ^Rshall they come out with great substance.　Ex. 12:36

15 And thou shalt go ^Rto thy fathers in peace; thou shalt be buried in a good old age. 25:8; 47:30

16 But in the fourth generation they shall come hither again: for the iniquity of the Am'-or-ites ^Ris not yet full.　1 Kin. 11:12; Matt. 23:32

17 And it came to pass, that, when the sun went down, and it was dark, behold a smoking ^Tfurnace, and a burning ^Tlamp that ^Rpassed between those pieces.　oven · torch · Jer. 34:18, 19

18 In the same day the LORD made a covenant with Abram, saying, ^RUnto thy seed have I given this land, from the river of Egypt unto the great river, the river Eu-phra'-tes: Num. 34:3; Acts 7:5

19 The Ken'-ites, and the Ken'-iz-zites, and the Kad'-mon-ites,

20 And the Hit'-tites, and the Per'-iz-zites, and the Reph'-a-ims,

21 And the Am'-or-ites, and the Ca'-naan-ites, and the Gir'-ga-shites, and the Jeb'-u-sites.

16 Now Sa'-rai Abram's wife ^Rbare him no children: and she had an handmaid, ^Ran E-gyptian, whose name was ^RHa'-gar.　11:30; 15:2, 3 · 12:16; 21:9 · Gal. 4:24

2 ^RAnd Sa'-rai said unto A-bram, Behold now, the LORD ^Rhath restrained me from bearing: I pray thee, go in unto my maid; it may be that I may obtain children by her. And Abram hearkened to the voice of Sa'-rai.　30:3 · 20:18

3 And Sa'-rai Abram's wife took Ha'-gar her maid the Egyptian, after Abram ^Rhad dwelt ten years in the land of Canaan, and gave her to her husband Abram to be his wife.　12:4, 5

4 And he went in unto Ha'-gar, and she conceived: and when she saw that she had conceived, her mistress was ^Rdespised in her eyes.　1 Sam. 1:6, 7; [Prov. 30:21, 23]

5 And Sa'-rai said unto Abram, My wrong be upon thee: I have given my maid into thy bosom; and when she saw that she had

conceived, I was despised in her eyes: ^Rthe LORD judge between me and thee.　31:53; Ex. 5:21

6 But Abram said unto Sa'-rai, Behold, thy maid is in thy hand; do to her as it pleaseth thee. And when Sa'-rai dealt hardly with her, ^Rshe fled from her face.　v. 9

7 And the angel of the LORD found her by a fountain of water in the wilderness, by the fountain in the way to ^RShur.　Ex. 15:22

8 And he said, Ha'-gar, Sa'-rai's maid, whence camest thou? and whither wilt thou go? And she said, I flee from the face of my mistress Sa'-rai.

9 And the angel of the LORD said unto her, Return to thy mistress, and ^Rsubmit thyself under her hands.　[Titus 2:9]

10 And the angel of the LORD said unto her, ^RI will multiply thy seed exceedingly, that it shall not be numbered for multitude.　17:20

11 And the angel of the LORD said unto her, Behold, thou art with child, and shalt bear a son, and shalt call his name ^TIsh'-ma-el; because the LORD hath heard thy affliction.　Lit. God Hears

12 And he will be a wild man; his hand will be against every man, and every man's hand against him; and he shall dwell in the presence of all his brethren.

13 And she called the name of the LORD that spake unto her, Thou God seest me: for she said, Have I also here looked after him ^Rthat seeth me?　31:42

14 Wherefore the well was called ^RBe'-er–la-hai'–roi; behold, it is ^Rbetween Ka'-desh and Be'-red.　24:62 · 14:7; Num. 13:26

15 And ^RHa'-gar bare Abram a son: and Abram called his son's name, which Ha'-gar bare, Ish'-ma-el.　Gal. 4:22

16 And Abram was fourscore and six years old, when Ha'-gar bare Ish'-ma-el to Abram.

17 And when Abram was ninety years old and nine, the LORD appeared to Abram, and said unto him, I am the Almighty

God; ^Rwalk before me, and be thou ^Rperfect.   2 Kin. 20:3 · Deut. 18:13

2 And I will make my covenant between me and thee, and will multiply thee exceedingly.

3 And Abram fell on his face: and God talked with him, saying,

4 As for me, behold, my covenant *is* with thee, and thou shalt be ^Ra father of many nations.   [Rom. 4:11, 12, 16]

5 Neither shall thy name any more be called Abram, but thy name shall be ^TAbraham; for a father of many nations have I made thee.   Lit. *Father of a Multitude*

6 And I will make thee exceeding fruitful, and I will make ^Rnations of thee, and kings shall come out of thee.   v. 16; 35:11

☆ 7 And I will establish my covenant between me and thee and thy seed after thee in their generations for an everlasting covenant, to be a God unto thee, and to ^Rthy seed after thee.   Rom. 9:8

8 And ^RI will give unto thee, and to thy seed after thee, the land wherein thou art a stranger, all the land of Canaan, for an everlasting possession; and ^RI will be their God.   Acts 7:5 · Ex. 6:7; 29:45

9 And God said unto Abraham, ^RThou shalt keep my covenant therefore, thou, and thy seed after thee in their generations.   Ex. 19:5

10 This *is* my covenant, which ye shall keep, between me and you and thy seed after thee; ^REvery man child among you shall be circumcised.   Acts 7:8

11 And ye shall circumcise the flesh of your foreskin; and it shall be ^Ra token of the covenant betwixt me and you.   [Rom. 4:11]

12 And he that is eight days old shall be circumcised among you, every man child in your generations, he that is born in the house, or bought with money of any stranger, which *is* not of thy seed.

13 He that is born in thy house, and he that is bought with thy money, must needs be circumcised: and my covenant shall be in your flesh for an everlasting covenant.

14 And the uncircumcised man child whose flesh of his foreskin is not circumcised, that soul ^Rshall be cut off from his people; he hath broken my covenant.   Ex. 4:24–26

15 And God said unto Abraham, As for Sa′-rai thy wife, thou shalt not call her name Sa′-rai, but ^TSarah *shall* her name *be*.   Lit. *Princess*

16 And I will bless her, and give thee a son also of her: yea, I will bless her, and she shall be *a mother* ^Rof nations; kings of people shall be of her.   35:11; 1 Pet. 3:6

17 Then Abraham fell upon his face, ^Rand laughed, and said in his heart, Shall *a child* be born unto him that is an hundred years old? and shall Sarah, that is ninety years old, bear?   v. 3; 18:12; 21:6

18 And Abraham ^Rsaid unto God, O that Ish′-ma-el might live before thee!   18:23

19 And God said, Sarah thy wife ☆ shall bear thee a son indeed; and thou shalt call his name Isaac: and I will establish my ^Rcovenant with him for an everlasting covenant, *and* with his seed after him.   22:16; Matt. 1:2; Luke 3:34

20 And as for Ish′-ma-el, I have heard thee: Behold, I have blessed him, and will make him fruitful, and ^Rwill multiply him exceedingly; ^Rtwelve princes shall he beget, ^Rand I will make him a great nation.   16:10 · 25:12–16 · 21:13, 18

21 But my ^Rcovenant will I establish with Isaac, ^Rwhich Sarah shall bear unto thee at this set time in the next year.   26:2–5 · 21:2

22 And he left off talking with him, and God went up from Abraham.

23 And Abraham took Ish′-ma-el his son, and all that were born in his house, and all that were bought with his money, every male among the men of Abraham's house; and circumcised the flesh of their foreskin in the selfsame day, as God had said unto him.

24 And Abraham *was* ninety years old and nine, when he was circumcised in the flesh of his foreskin.

25 And Ish'-ma-el his son *was* thirteen years old, when he was circumcised in the flesh of his foreskin.

26 In the selfsame day was Abraham circumcised, and Ish'-ma-el his son.

27 And ᴿall the men of his house, born in the house, and bought with money of the stranger, were circumcised with him. 18:19

18 And the LORD appeared unto him in the ᴿplains of Mam'-re: and he sat in the tent door in the heat of the day; 13:18

2 And he lift up his eyes and looked, and, lo, three men stood by him: ᴿand when he saw *them*, he ran to meet them from the tent door, and bowed himself toward the ground, 19:1; 1 Pet. 4:9

3 And said, My Lord, if now I have found favour in thy sight, pass not ᵀaway, I pray thee, from thy servant: *on by*

4 Let ᴿa little water, I pray you, be ᵀfetched, and wash your feet, and rest yourselves under the tree: 19:2; 24:32; 43:24 · *brought*

5 And I will fetch a morsel of bread, and ᴿcomfort ye your hearts; after that ye shall pass on: for therefore are ye come to your servant. And they said, So do, as thou hast said. Judg. 19:5; Ps. 104:15

6 And Abraham hastened into the tent unto Sarah, and said, Make ready quickly three measures of fine meal, knead *it*, and make cakes upon the hearth.

7 And Abraham ran unto the herd, and fetcht a calf tender and good, and gave *it* unto a young man; and he hasted to dress it.

8 And ᴿhe took butter, and milk, and the calf which he had ᵀdressed, and set *it* before them; and he stood by them under the tree, and they did eat. 19:3 · *prepared*

9 And they said unto him, Where *is* Sarah thy wife? And he said, Behold, ᴿin the tent. 24:67

10 And he said, I will certainly return unto thee ᴿaccording to the time of life; and, lo, ᴿSarah thy wife shall have a son. And Sarah heard *it* in the tent door, which *was* behind him. 2 Kin. 4:16 · Rom. 9:9

11 Now Abraham and Sarah *were* old *and* well stricken in age; *and* it ceased to be with Sarah ᴿafter the manner of women. 31:35

12 Therefore Sarah laughed within herself, saying, After I am waxed old shall I have pleasure, my ᴿlord being old also? 1 Pet. 3:6

13 And the LORD said unto Abraham, Wherefore did Sarah laugh, saying, Shall I of a surety bear a child, which am old?

14 ᴿIs any thing too hard for the LORD? ᴿAt the time appointed I will return unto thee, according to the time of life, and Sarah shall have a son. Matt. 19:26 · 2 Kin. 4:16

15 Then Sarah denied, saying, I laughed not; for she was afraid. And he said, Nay; but thou didst laugh.

16 And the men rose up from thence, and looked toward Sodom: and Abraham went with them to bring them on the way.

17 And the LORD said, ᴿShall I hide from Abraham that thing which I do; Ps. 25:14; Amos 3:7

18 Seeing that Abraham shall surely become a great and mighty nation, and all the nations of the earth shall be blessed in him?

19 For I know him, that he will command his children and his household after him, and they shall keep the way of the LORD, to do justice and judgment; that the LORD may bring upon Abraham that which he hath spoken of him.

20 And the LORD said, Because ᴿthe cry of Sodom and Go-mor'-rah is great, and because their sin is very grievous; 19:13; Ezek. 16:49, 50

21 ᴿI will go down now, and see whether they have done altogether according to the cry of it, which is come unto me; and if not, I will know. 11:5; Ex. 3:8; Ps. 14:2

22 And the men turned their faces from thence, ᴿand went toward Sodom: but Abraham stood yet before the LORD. 19:1

23 And Abraham drew near, and

said, ^RWilt thou also destroy the righteous with the wicked? Ex. 23:7

24 ^TPeradventure there be fifty righteous within the city: wilt thou also destroy and not spare the place for the fifty righteous that *are* therein?   *Suppose*

25 That be far from thee to do after this manner, to slay the righteous with the wicked: and ^Rthat the righteous should be as the wicked, that be far from thee: ^RShall not the Judge of all the earth do right?   Is. 3:10, 11 · Ps. 58:11

26 And the LORD said, ^RIf I find in Sodom fifty righteous within the city, then I will spare all the place for their sakes.   Ezek. 22:30

27 And Abraham answered and said, Behold now, I have taken upon me to speak unto the Lord, which *am but* dust and ashes:

28 Peradventure there shall lack five of the fifty righteous: wilt thou destroy all the city for *lack of* five? And he said, If I find there forty and five, I will not destroy *it*.

29 And he spake unto him yet again, and said, Peradventure there shall be forty found there. And he said, I will not do *it* for forty's sake.

30 And he said *unto him*, Oh let not the Lord be angry, and I will speak: Peradventure there shall thirty be found there. And he said, I will not do *it*, if I find thirty there.

31 And he said, Behold now, I have taken upon me to speak unto the Lord: Peradventure there shall be twenty found there. And he said, I will not destroy *it* for twenty's sake.

32 And he said, ^ROh let not the Lord be angry, and I will speak yet but this once: Peradventure ten shall be found there. ^RAnd he said, I will not destroy *it* for ten's sake.   Judg. 6:39 · James 5:16

33 And the LORD went his way, as soon as he had left communing with Abraham: and Abraham returned unto his place.

19 And there came two angels to Sodom at even; and ^RLot sat in the gate of Sodom: and

Lot seeing *them* rose up to meet them; and he bowed himself with his face toward the ground; 18:1–5

2 And he said, Behold now, my lords, turn in, I pray you, into your servant's house, and tarry all night, and wash your feet, and ye shall rise up early, and go on your ways. And they said, Nay; but we will abide in the street all night.

3 And he ^Tpressed upon them greatly; and they turned in unto him, and entered into his house; ^Rand he made them a feast, and did bake unleavened bread, and they did eat.   *urged them* · Ex. 23:15

4 But before they lay down, the men of the city, *even* the men of Sodom, compassed the house round, both old and young, all the people from every quarter:

5 And they called unto Lot, and said unto him, Where *are* the men which came in to thee this night? bring them out unto us, that we ^Rmay know them.   Rom. 1:24, 27

6 And ^RLot went out at the door unto them, and shut the door after him,   Judg. 19:23

7 And said, I pray you, brethren, do not so wickedly.

8 ^RBehold now, I have two daughters which have not known man; let me, I pray you, bring them out unto you, and do ye to them as *is* good in your eyes: only unto these men do nothing; ^Rfor therefore came they under the shadow of my roof. Judg. 19:24 · 18:5

9 And they said, Stand back. And they said *again*, This one *fellow* ^Rcame in to sojourn, and he will needs be a judge: now will we deal worse with thee, than with them. And they pressed sore upon the man, *even* Lot, and came near to break the door.   2 Pet. 2:7, 8

10 But the men put forth their hand, and pulled Lot into the house to them, and shut to the door.

11 And they ^Rsmote the men that *were* at the door of the house with blindness, both small and great: so that they wearied themselves to find the door.   20:17

12 And the men said unto Lot, Hast thou here any besides? son in law, and thy sons, and thy daughters, and whatsoever thou hast in the city, ^Rbring *them* out of this place: 7:1; 2 Pet. 2:7, 9

13 For we will destroy this place, because the cry of them ^Tis waxen great before the face of the LORD; and ^Rthe LORD hath sent us to destroy it.   *has grown* · Lev. 26:30–3

14 And Lot went out, and spake unto his sons in law, which married his daughters, and said, Up, get you out of this place; for the LORD will destroy this city. ^RBut he seemed as one that ^Tmocked unto his sons in law.   Ex. 9:21 · *joked*

15 And when the morning arose, then the angels hastened Lot, saying, ^RArise, take thy wife, and thy two daughters, which are here; lest thou be consumed in the iniquity of the city. Ps. 37:2; Rev. 18:4

16 And while he lingered, the men laid hold upon his hand, and upon the hand of his wife, and upon the hand of his two daughters; the ^RLORD being merciful unto him: and they brought him forth, and set him ^Twithout the city.   Ex. 34:7; Luke 18:13 · *outside*

17 And it came to pass, when they had brought them forth ^Tabroad, that he said, Escape for thy life; ^Rlook not behind thee, neither stay thou in all the plain; escape to the mountain, lest thou be consumed.   *outside* · Matt. 24:16–18

18 And Lot said unto them, Oh, ^Rnot so, my Lord: Acts 10:14

19 Behold now, thy servant hath found grace in thy sight, and thou hast magnified thy mercy, which thou hast shewed unto me in saving my life; and I cannot escape to the mountain, lest some evil take me, and I die:

20 Behold now, this city *is* near to flee unto, and it *is* a little one: Oh, let me escape thither, (*is* it not a little one?) and my soul shall live.

21 And he said unto him, See, ^RI have accepted thee concerning this thing also, that I will not over-

throw this city, for the which thou hast spoken.   Job 42:8, 9; Ps. 145:19

22 Haste thee, escape thither; for ^RI cannot do any thing till thou be come thither. Therefore the name of the city was called ^TZo'-ar.   Ex. 32:10; Deut. 9:14 · Lit. *Insignificant*

23 The sun was risen upon the earth when Lot entered into Zo'-ar.

24 Then the LORD rained upon Sodom and upon Go-mor'-rah brimstone and ^Rfire from the LORD out of heaven;   Lev. 10:2

25 And he overthrew those cities, and all the plain, and all the inhabitants of the cities, and that which grew upon the ground.

26 But his wife looked back from behind him, and she became ^Ra pillar of salt.   v. 17; Luke 17:32

27 And Abraham gat up early in the morning to the place where ^Rhe stood before the LORD: 18:22

28 And he looked toward Sodom and Go-mor'-rah, and toward all the land of the plain, and beheld, and, lo, ^Rthe smoke of the country went up as the smoke of a furnace.   Rev. 9:2; 18:9

29 And it came to pass, when God destroyed the cities of the plain, that God ^Rremembered Abraham, and sent Lot out of the midst of the overthrow, when he overthrew the cities in the which Lot dwelt.   8:1; 18:23; Deut. 7:8; 9:5, 27

30 And Lot went up out of Zo'-ar, and ^Rdwelt in the mountain, and his two daughters with him; for he feared to dwell in Zo'-ar: and he dwelt in a cave, he and his two daughters.   vv. 17, 19

31 And the firstborn said unto the younger, Our father *is* old, and *there is* not a man in the earth ^Rto come in unto us after the manner of all the earth: 38:8, 9; Deut. 25:5

32 Come, let us make our father drink wine, and we will lie with him, that we ^Rmay preserve ^Tseed of our father. [Mark 12:19] · *the lineage*

33 And they made their father drink wine that night: and the firstborn went in, and lay with her father; and he perceived not when she lay down, nor when she arose.

34 And it came to pass on the morrow, that the firstborn said unto the younger, Behold, I lay yesternight with my father: let us make him drink wine this night also; and go thou in, *and* lie with him, that we may preserve seed of our father.

35 And they made their father drink wine that night also: and the younger arose, and lay with him; and he perceived not when she lay down, nor when she arose.

36 Thus were both the daughters of Lot with child by their father.

37 And the firstborn bare a son, and called his name Moab: ᴿthe same *is* the father of the Mo'-ab-ites unto this day.   Num. 25:1; Deut. 2:9

38 And the younger, she also bare a son, and called his name Ben–am'-mi: ᴿthe same *is* the father of the children of Ammon unto this day.   Num. 21:24; Deut. 2:19

20 And Abraham journeyed from thence toward the south country, and dwelled between ᴿKa'-desh and Shur, and sojourned in Ge'-rar.   12:9; 16:7, 14

2 And Abraham said of Sarah his wife, ᴿShe *is* my sister: and A-bim'-e-lech king of Ge'-rar sent, and ᴿtook Sarah.   12:11–13; 26:7 · 12:15

3 But ᴿGod came to A-bim'-e-lech ᴿin a dream by night, and said to him, ᴿBehold, thou *art but* a dead man, for the woman which thou hast taken; for she *is* a man's wife.   Ps. 105:14 · Job 33:15 · v. 7

4 But A-bim'-e-lech had not come near her: and he said, Lord, ᴿwilt thou slay also a righteous nation?   18:23–25; Num. 16:22

5 Said he not unto me, She *is* my sister? and she, even she herself said, He *is* my brother: in the integrity of my heart and innocency of my hands have I done this.

6 And God said unto him in a dream, Yea, I know that thou didst this in the integrity of thy heart; for ᴿI also withheld thee from sinning against me: therefore suffered I thee not to touch her.   31:7

7 Now therefore restore the man *his* wife; ᴿfor he *is* a prophet, and he shall pray for thee, and thou shalt live: and if thou restore *her* not, know thou that thou shalt surely die, thou, and all that *are* thine.   1 Sam. 7:5; 2 Kin. 5:11; Job 42:8

8 Therefore A-bim'-e-lech rose early in the morning, and called all his servants, and told all these things in their ears: and the men were ᵀsore afraid.   *very*

9 Then A-bim'-e-lech called A-braham, and said unto him, What hast thou done unto us? and what have I offended thee, ᴿthat thou hast brought on me and on my kingdom a great sin? thou hast done deeds unto me that ought not to be done.   26:10; 39:9

10 And A-bim'-e-lech said unto Abraham, What sawest thou, that thou hast done this thing?

11 And Abraham said, Because I thought, Surely ᴿthe fear of God *is* not in this place; and they will slay me for my wife's sake.   42:1

12 And yet indeed *she is* my sister; she *is* the daughter of my father, but not the daughter of my mother; and she became my wife.

13 And it came to pass, when ᴿGod caused me to wander from my father's house, that I said unto her, This *is* thy kindness which thou shalt shew unto me; at every place whither we shall come, say of me, He *is* my brother.   12:1–9, 11

14 And A-bim'-e-lech ᴿtook sheep, and oxen, and menservants, and womenservants, and gave *them* unto Abraham, and restored him Sarah his wife.   12:16

15 And A-bim'-e-lech said, Behold, ᴿmy land *is* before thee: dwell where it pleaseth thee.   47:6

16 And unto Sarah he said, Behold, I have given thy brother a thousand *pieces* of silver: ᴿbehold, he *is* to thee ᴿa covering of the eyes, unto all that *are* with thee, and with all *other*: thus she was ᵀreproved.   26:11 · 24:65 · *justified*

17 So Abraham prayed unto God: and God healed A-bim'-e-lech, and his wife, and his maidservants; and they bare *children*.

18 For the LORD ^Rhad fast closed up all the wombs of the house of A-bim´-e-lech, because of Sarah Abraham's wife.   12:17

21 And the LORD ^Rvisited Sa-rah as he had said, and the LORD did unto Sarah ^Ras he had spoken.   1 Sam. 2:21 · 17:16, 19, 21

2 For Sarah ^Rconceived, and bare Abraham a son in his old age, ^Rat the set time of which God had spoken to him.   Acts 7:8 · 18:10

3 And Abraham called the name of his son that was born unto him, whom Sarah bare to him, ^RIsaac.^T   17:19, 21 · Lit. *Laughter*

4 And Abraham circumcised his son Isaac being eight days old, as God had commanded him.

5 And ^RAbraham was an hundred years old, when his son Isaac was born unto him.   17:1, 17

6 And Sarah said, ^RGod hath made me to laugh, *so that* all that hear will laugh with me.   Is. 54:1

7 And she said, Who would have said unto Abraham, that Sarah should have given children suck? ^Rfor I have born *him* a son in his old age.   18:11, 12

8 And the child grew, and was weaned: and Abraham made a great feast the *same* day that Isaac was weaned.

9 And Sarah saw the son of Ha´-gar the Egyptian, which she had born unto Abraham, ^Rmock-ing.^T   [Gal. 4:29] · *scoffing*, lit. *laughing*

10 Wherefore she said unto Abraham, ^RCast out this bond-woman and her son: for the son of this bondwoman shall not be heir with my son, *even* with Isaac. 25:6

11 And the thing was very griev-ous in Abraham's sight ^Rbecause of his son.   17:18

☆ 12 And God said unto Abraham, Let it not be grievous in thy sight because of the lad, and because of thy bondwoman; in all that Sarah hath said unto thee, hearken unto her voice; for ^Rin Isaac shall thy seed be called. [Rom. 9:7, 8]; Heb. 11:18

13 And also of the son of the bondwoman will I make ^Ra na-tion, because he *is* thy seed.   17:20

14 And Abraham rose up early in the morning, and took bread, and a ^Tbottle of water, and gave *it* unto Ha´-gar, putting *it* on her shoulder, and the ^Tchild, and ^Rsent her away: and she departed, and wandered in the wilderness of Be´-er-she´-ba.   *skin · youth* · John 8:35

15 And the water was spent in the bottle, and she ^Tcast the child under one of the shrubs.   *placed*

16 And she went, and sat her down ^Tover against *him* a good way off, as it were a bowshot: for she said, Let me not see the death of the child. And she sat over against *him,* and lift up her voice, and wept.   *opposite*

17 And ^RGod heard the voice of the lad; and the angel of God called to Ha´-gar out of heaven, and said unto her, What aileth thee, Ha´-gar? fear not; for God hath heard the voice of the lad where he *is.*   Ex. 3:7; Deut. 26:7; Ps. 6:8

18 Arise, lift up the lad, and hold him ^Tin thine hand; for I will make him a great nation.   *with*

19 And ^RGod opened her eyes, and she saw a well of water; and she went, and filled the bottle with water, and gave the lad drink.   3:7; Num. 22:31; 2 Kin. 6:17

20 And God ^Rwas with the lad; and he grew, and dwelt in the wilderness, ^Rand became an ar-cher.   28:15; 39:2, 3, 21 · 16:12

21 And he dwelt in the wilder-ness of Pa´-ran: and his mother ^Rtook him a wife out of the land of Egypt.   24:4

22 And it came to pass at that time, that ^RA-bim´-e-lech and Phi´-chol the chief captain of his host spake unto Abraham, saying, ^RGod *is* with thee in all that thou doest: 20:2, 14; 26:26 · 26:28; Is. 8:10

23 Now therefore ^Rswear unto me here by God that thou wilt not deal falsely with me, nor with my son, nor with my son's son: *but* according to the kind-ness that I have done unto thee, thou shalt do unto me, and to the land wherein thou hast sojourned.   Josh. 2:12

24 And Abraham said, I will swear.

25 And Abraham reproved A-bim'-e-lech because of a well of water, which A-bim'-e-lech's servants had violently taken away.

26 And A-bim'-e-lech said, I [T]wot not who hath done this thing: neither didst thou tell me, neither yet heard I *of it*, but to day.   *know*

27 And Abraham took sheep and oxen, and gave them unto A-bim'-e-lech; and both of them [R]made a covenant.   26:31; 31:44

28 And Abraham set seven ewe lambs of the flock by themselves.

29 And A-bim'-e-lech said unto Abraham, [R]What *mean* these seven ewe lambs which thou hast set by themselves?   33:8

30 And he said, For *these* seven ewe lambs shalt thou take of my hand, that [R]they may be a witness unto me, that I have digged this well.   31:48, 52

31 Wherefore he called that place Be'-er-she'-ba; because there they sware both of them.

32 Thus they made a covenant at Be'-er-she'-ba: then A-bim'-e-lech rose up, and Phi'-chol the chief captain of his host, and they returned into the land of the Phi-lis'-tines.

33 And *Abraham* planted a grove in Be'-er-she'-ba, and called there on the name of the LORD, [R]the everlasting God. 35:11; Ex. 15:18

34 And Abraham sojourned in the Phi-lis'-tines' land many days.

22 And it came to pass after these things, that [R]God did [T]tempt Abraham, and said unto him, Abraham: and he said, Behold, *here* I *am*.   1 Cor. 10:13 · *test*

2 And he said, Take now thy son, [R]thine only *son* Isaac, whom thou lovest, and get thee into the land of Mo-ri'-ah; and offer him there for a burnt offering upon one of the mountains which I will tell thee of.   John 3:16; 1 John 4:9

3 And Abraham rose up early in the morning, and saddled his [T]ass, and took two of his young men with him, and Isaac his son, and [T]clave the wood for the burnt offering, and rose up, and went unto the place of which God had told him.   *donkey · split*

4 Then on the third day A-braham lifted up his eyes, and saw the place afar off.

5 And Abraham said unto his young men, Abide ye here with the ass; and I and the [T]lad will go yonder and worship, and come again to you.   Lit. *young man*

6 And Abraham took the wood of the burnt offering, and [R]laid *it* upon Isaac his son; and he took the fire in his hand, and a knife; and they went both of them together.   John 19:17

7 And Isaac spake unto Abraham his father, and said, My father: and he said, Here *am* I, my son. And he said, Behold the fire and the wood: but where *is* the [T]lamb for a burnt offering? *goat*

8 And Abraham said, My son, God will provide himself a [R]lamb for a burnt offering: so they went both of them together. John 1:29, 36

9 And they came to the place which God had told him of; and Abraham built an altar there, and laid the wood in order, and bound Isaac his son, and [R]laid him on the altar upon the wood. [Heb. 11:17–19]

10 And Abraham stretched forth his hand, and took the knife to slay his son.

11 And the [R]angel of the LORD called unto him out of heaven, and said, Abraham, Abraham: and he said, Here *am* I.   16:7–11

12 And he said, Lay not thine hand upon the lad, neither do thou any thing unto him: for now I know that thou fearest God, seeing thou hast not withheld thy son, thine only *son* from me.

13 And Abraham lifted up his eyes, and looked, and behold behind *him* a ram caught in a thicket by his horns: and Abraham went and took the ram, and offered him up for a burnt offering in the stead of his son.

14 And Abraham called the

name of that place [T]Je-ho′-vah–ji′-reh: as it is said *to* this day, In the mount of the LORD it shall be seen.   Lit. *The LORD Will Provide* or *See*

15 And the angel of the LORD called unto Abraham out of heaven the second time,

16 And said, [R]By myself have I sworn, saith the LORD, for because thou hast done this thing, and hast not withheld thy son, thine only *son:*   Ps. 105:9; [Heb. 6:13, 14]

17 That in blessing I will bless thee, and in multiplying I will multiply thy seed [R]as the stars of the heaven, [R]and as the sand which *is* upon the sea shore; and thy seed shall possess the gate of his enemies;   Deut. 1:10 · 1 Kin. 4:20

☆ 18 [R]And in thy seed shall all the nations of the earth be blessed; because thou hast obeyed my voice.   [Acts 3:25, 26]; Gal. 3:8, 9, 16, 18

19 So Abraham returned unto his young men, and they rose up and went together to [R]Be′-er-she′-ba; and Abraham dwelt at Be′-er–she′-ba.   21:31

20 And it came to pass after these things, that it was told Abraham, saying, Behold, [R]Mil′-cah, she hath also born children unto thy brother Na′-hor;   24:15

21 [R]Huz his firstborn, and Buz his brother, and Kem′-u-el the father [R]of Ar′-am,   Job 1:1 · Job 32:2

22 And Che′-sed, and Ha′-zo, and Pil′-dash, and Jid′-laph, and Be-thu′-el.

23 And [R]Be-thu′-el begat [T]Rebekah: these eight Mil′-cah did bear to Na′-hor, Abraham′s brother.   24:15 · *Rebecca*, Rom. 9:10

24 And his concubine, whose name *was* Reu′-mah, she bare also Te′-bah, and Ga′-ham, and Tha′-hash, and Ma′-a-chah.

23 And Sarah was an hundred and seven and twenty years old: *these were* the years of the life of Sarah.

2 And Sarah died in [R]Kir′-jath–ar′-ba; the same *is* [R]He′-bron in the land of Canaan: and Abraham came to mourn for Sarah, and to weep for her.   35:27 · v. 19

3 And Abraham stood up from before his dead, and spake unto the sons of [R]Heth, saying,   2 Kin. 7:6

4 [R]I *am* a stranger and a sojourner with you: [R]give me a possession of a buryingplace with you, that I may bury my dead out of my sight.   Ps. 39:12 · Acts 7:5, 16

5 And the children of Heth answered Abraham, saying unto him,

6 Hear us, my lord: thou *art* [R]a mighty prince among us: in the choice of our sepulchres bury thy dead; none of us shall withhold from thee his sepulchre, but that thou mayest bury thy dead.   24:35

7 And Abraham stood up, and bowed himself to the people of the land, *even* to the children of Heth.

8 And he communed with them, saying, If it be your mind that I should bury my dead out of my sight; hear me, and intreat for me to E′-phron the son of Zo′-har,

9 That he may give me the cave of [R]Mach-pe′-lah, which he hath, which *is* in the end of his field; for as much money as it is worth he shall give it me for a possession of a buryingplace amongst you.   25:9

10 And E′-phron dwelt among the children of Heth: and E′-phron the Hit′-tite answered Abraham in the audience of the children of Heth, *even* of all that went in at the gate of his city, saying,

11 Nay, my lord, hear me: the field give I thee, and the cave that *is* therein, I give it thee; in the presence of the sons of my people give I it thee: bury thy dead.

12 And Abraham bowed down himself before the people of the land.

13 And he spake unto E′-phron in the audience of the people of the land, saying, But if thou *wilt give it,* I pray thee, hear me: I will give thee money for the field; take *it* of me, and I will bury my dead there.

14 And E′-phron answered Abraham, saying unto him,

15 My lord, hearken unto me: the land *is worth* four hundred

^Rshek'-els of silver; what *is* that betwixt me and thee? bury therefore thy dead.   Ex. 30:13; Ezek. 45:12

16 And Abraham hearkened unto E'-phron; and Abraham weighed to E'-phron the silver, which he had named in the audience of the sons of Heth, four hundred shek'-els of silver, current *money* with the merchant.

17 And ^Rthe field of E'-phron, which *was* in Mach-pe'-lah, which *was* before Mam'-re, the field, and the cave which *was* therein, and all the trees that *were* in the field, that *were* in all the borders round about, were made sure   49:29–32

18 Unto Abraham for a possession in the presence of the children of Heth, before all that went in at the gate of his city.

19 And after this, Abraham buried Sarah his wife in the cave of the field of Mach-pe'-lah before Mam'-re: the same *is* He'-bron in the land of Canaan.

20 And the field, and the cave that *is* therein, ^Rwere ^Tmade sure unto Abraham for a possession of a buryingplace by the sons of Heth.   Jer. 32:10, 11 · *deeded to*

24 And Abraham was old, *and* well stricken in age: and the LORD ^Rhad blessed Abraham in all things.   Ps. 112:3; [Gal. 3:9]

2 And Abraham said unto his eldest servant of his house, that ^Rruled over all that he had, ^RPut, I pray thee, thy hand under my thigh: v. 10; 39:4–6 · 47:29; 1 Chr. 29:24

3 And I will make thee ^Rswear by the LORD, the God of heaven, and the God of the earth, that ^Rthou shalt not take a wife unto my son of the daughters of the Ca'-naan-ites, among whom I dwell: 14:19, 22 · Deut. 7:3; 2 Cor. 6:14–17

4 But thou shalt go unto my country, and to my kindred, and take a wife unto my son Isaac.

5 And the servant said unto him, Peradventure the woman will not be willing to follow me unto this land: must I needs bring thy son again unto the land from whence thou camest?

6 And Abraham said unto him, Beware thou that thou ^Tbring not my son thither again.   *take*

7 The LORD God of heaven, which took me from my father's house, and from the land of my kindred, and which spake unto me, and that sware unto me, saying, Unto thy seed will I give this land; he shall send his angel before thee, and thou shalt take a wife unto my son from thence.

8 And if the woman will not be willing to follow thee, then ^Rthou shalt be clear from this my oath: only ^Tbring not my son thither again.   Josh. 2:17–20 · *take*

9 And the servant put his hand under the thigh of Abraham his master, and sware to him concerning that matter.

10 And the servant took ten camels of the camels of his master, and departed; for all ^Tthe goods of his master *were* in his hand: and he arose, and went to Mes-o-po-ta'-mi-a, unto ^Rthe city of Na'-hor.   Lit. *good things* · 11:31, 32

11 And he made his camels to kneel down without the city by a well of water at the time of the evening, *even* the time that women go out to draw *water*.

12 And he said, O LORD God of my master Abraham, I pray thee, ^Tsend me good speed this day, and shew kindness unto my master Abraham.   *give me success*

13 Behold, ^RI stand *here* by the well of water; and ^Rthe daughters of the men of the city come out to draw water: v. 43 · Ex. 2:16

14 And let it come to pass, that the damsel to whom I shall say, Let down thy pitcher, I pray thee, that I may drink; and she shall say, Drink, and I will give thy camels drink also: *let the same be* she *that* thou hast appointed for thy servant Isaac; and thereby shall I know that thou hast shewed kindness unto my master.

15 And it came to pass, before he had done speaking, that, behold, Rebekah came out, who was born to Be-thu'-el, son of

RMil'-cah, the wife of Na'-hor, Abraham's brother, with her pitcher upon her shoulder. 22:20, 23

16 And the damsel Rwas very fair to look upon, a virgin, neither had any man known her: and she went down to the well, and filled her pitcher, and came up. 26:7; 29:17

17 And the servant ran to meet her, and said, Let me, I pray thee, drink a little water of thy pitcher.

18 RAnd she said, Drink, my lord: and she hasted, and let down her pitcher upon her hand, and gave him drink. vv. 14, 46; [1 Pet. 3:8, 9]

19 And when she had done giving him drink, she said, I will draw water for thy camels also, until they have done drinking.

20 And she hasted, and emptied her pitcher into the trough, and ran again unto the well to draw water, and drew for all his camels.

21 And the man wondering at her held his peace, to wit whether Rthe LORD had made his journey prosperous or not.   vv. 12–14, 27, 52

22 And it came to pass, as the camels had done drinking, that the man took a golden Tearring of half a shek'-el weight, and two bracelets for her hands of ten shek'-els weight of gold;   nose ring

23 And said, Whose daughter art thou? tell me, I pray thee: is there room in thy father's house for us to lodge in?

24 And she said unto him, RI am the daughter of Be-thu'-el the son of Mil'-cah, which she bare unto Na'-hor.   v. 15; 22:23

25 She said moreover unto him, We have both straw and Tprovender enough, and room to lodge in.   food

26 And the man Rbowed down his head, and worshipped the LORD.   vv. 48, 52; Ex. 4:31

27 And he said, Blessed be the LORD God of my master Abraham, who hath not left destitute my master of Rhis mercy and his truth: I being in the way, the LORD Rled me to the house of my master's brethren. 32:10; Ps. 98:3 · vv. 21, 48

28 And the damsel ran, and told them of her mother's house these things.

29 And Rebekah had a brother, and his name was RLaban: and Laban ran out unto the man, unto the well.   29:5, 13

30 And it came to pass, when he saw the Tearring and bracelets upon his sister's hands, and when he heard the words of Rebekah his sister, saying, Thus spake the man unto me; that he came unto the man; and, behold, he stood by the camels at the well.   nose ring

31 And he said, Come in, Rthou blessed of the LORD; wherefore standest thou Twithout? for I have prepared the house, and room for the camels.   Ruth 3:10 · outside

32 And the man came into the house: and he ungirded his camels, and gave straw and provender for the camels, and water to Rwash his feet, and the men's feet that were with him.   John 13:5, 13–15

33 And there was set meat before him to eat: but he said, I will not eat, until I have told mine errand. And he said, Speak on.

34 And he said, I am Abraham's servant.

35 And the LORD Rhath blessed my master greatly; and he is become great: and he hath given him flocks, and herds, and silver, and gold, and menservants, and maidservants, and camels, and Tasses.   v. 1; 13:2 · donkeys

36 And Sarah my master's wife bare a son to my master when she was old: and Runto him hath he given all that he hath.   21:10; 25:5

37 And my master Rmade me swear, saying, Thou shalt not take a wife to my son of the daughters of the Ca'-naan-ites, in whose land I dwell: vv. 2–4

38 RBut thou shalt go unto my father's house, and to my kindred, and take a wife unto my son.   v. 4

39 RAnd I said unto my master, TPeradventure the woman will not follow me.   v. 5 · Perhaps

40 And he said unto me, The LORD, before whom I walk, will send his angel with thee, and

prosper thy way; and thou shalt take a wife for my son of my kindred, and of my father's house:

41 ^RThen shalt thou be clear from *this* my oath, when thou comest to my kindred; and if they give not thee *one*, thou shalt be clear from my oath.   v. 8

42 And I came this day unto the well, and said, ^RO LORD God of my master Abraham, if now thou do prosper my way which I go: v. 12

43 ^RBehold, I stand by the well of water; and it shall come to pass, that when the virgin cometh forth to draw *water*, and I say to her, Give me, I pray thee, a little water of thy pitcher to drink; v. 13

44 And she say to me, Both drink thou, and I will also draw for thy camels: *let* the same *be* the woman whom the LORD hath appointed out for my master's son.

45 ^RAnd before I had done speaking in mine heart, behold, Rebekah came forth with her pitcher on her shoulder; and she went down unto the well, and drew *water*: and I said unto her, Let me drink, I pray thee.   v. 15

46 And she made haste, and let down her pitcher from her *shoulder*, and said, Drink, and I will give thy camels drink also: so I drank, and she made the camels drink also.

47 And I asked her, and said, Whose daughter *art* thou? And she said, The daughter of Be-thu'-el, Na'-hor's son, whom Mil'-cah bare unto him: and I put the ^Tearring upon her face, and the bracelets upon her hands. *nose ring*

48 And I bowed down my head, and worshipped the LORD, and blessed the LORD God of my master Abraham, which had led me in the right way to take my master's brother's daughter unto his son.

49 And now if ye will ^Rdeal kindly and truly with my master, tell me: and if not, tell me; that I may turn to the right hand, or to the left.   47:29; Josh. 2:14

50 Then Laban and Be-thu'-el answered and said, ^RThe thing proceedeth from the LORD: we cannot speak unto thee bad or good.   Ps. 118:23; Matt. 21:42; Mark 12:11

51 Behold, Rebekah ^R*is* before thee, take *her*, and go, and let her be thy master's son's wife, as the LORD hath spoken.   20:15

52 And it came to pass, that, when Abraham's servant heard their words, he worshipped the LORD, *bowing himself* to the earth.

53 And the servant brought forth jewels of silver, and jewels of gold, and raiment, and gave *them* to Rebekah: he gave also to her brother and to her mother ^Rprecious things.   2 Chr. 21:3; Ezra 1:6

54 And they did eat and drink, he and the men that *were* with him, and tarried all night; and they rose up in the morning, and he said, ^RSend me away unto my master.   vv. 56, 59; 30:25

55 And her brother and her mother said, Let the damsel abide with us *a few* days, at the least ten; after that she shall go.

56 And he said unto them, Hinder me not, seeing the LORD hath prospered my way; send me away that I may go to my master.

57 And they said, We will call the damsel, and ^Tenquire at her mouth.   *ask her personally*

58 And they called Rebekah, and said unto her, Wilt thou go with this man? And she said, I will go.

59 And they sent away Rebekah their sister, and her nurse, and Abraham's servant, and his men.

60 And they blessed Rebekah, and said unto her, Thou *art* our sister, be thou ^R*the mother* of thousands of millions, and ^Rlet thy seed possess the gate of those which hate them.   17:16 · 22:17; 28:14

61 And Rebekah arose, and her damsels, and they rode upon the camels, and followed the man: and the servant took Rebekah, and went his way.

62 And Isaac came from the way of the ^Rwell La-hai'-roi; for he dwelt in the south country.   16:14

63 And Isaac went out ^Rto medi-

tate in the field at the eventide:
and he lifted up his eyes, and saw,
and, behold, the camels *were*
coming.   Josh. 1:8; Ps. 1:2; 77:12; 119:15

64 And Rebekah lifted up her
eyes, and when she saw Isaac, she
lighted off the camel.

65 For she *had* said unto the servant, What man *is* this that
walketh in the field to meet us?
And the servant *had* said, It *is* my
master: therefore she took a vail,
and covered herself.

66 And the servant told Isaac all
things that he had done.

67 And Isaac brought her into
his mother Sarah's tent, and ᴿtook
Rebekah, and she became his
wife; and he loved her: and Isaac
ᴿwas comforted after his mother's
death.   25:20; Prov. 18:22 · 23:1, 2; 38:12

25 Then again Abraham took
a wife, and her name *was*
Ke-tu'-rah.

2 And ᴿshe bare him Zim'-ran,
and Jok'-shan, and Me'-dan, and
Mid'-i-an, and Ish'-bak, and Shu'-
ah.   1 Chr. 1:32, 33

3 And Jok'-shan begat She'-ba,
and De'-dan. And the sons of De'-
dan were As-shu'-rim, and Le-tu'-
shim, and Le-um'-mim.

4 And the sons of Mid'-i-an; E'-
phah, and E'-pher, and Ha'-noch,
and A-bi'-dah, and El-da'-ah. All
these *were* the children of Ke-tu'-
rah.

5 And ᴿAbraham gave all that
he had unto Isaac.   24:35, 36

6 But unto the sons of the concubines, which Abraham had,
Abraham gave gifts, and ᴿsent
them away from Isaac his son,
while he yet lived, eastward, unto
ᴿthe east country.   21:14 · Judg. 6:3

7 And these *are* the days of the
years of Abraham's life which he
lived, an hundred threescore and
fifteen years.

8 Then Abraham gave up the
ghost, and died in a good old age,
an old man, and full of *years;* and
ᴿwas gathered to his people.   35:29

9 And his sons Isaac and Ish'-
ma-el buried him in the cave of
Mach-pe'-lah, in the field of E'-

phron the son of Zo'-har the Hit'-
tite, which *is* before Mam'-re;

10 ᴿThe field which Abraham
purchased of the sons of Heth:
ᴿthere was Abraham buried, and
Sarah his wife.   23:3-16 · 49:31

11 And it came to pass after the
death of Abraham, that God
blessed his son Isaac; and Isaac
dwelt by the well La-hai'-roi.

12 Now these *are* the ᴿgenerations of Ish'-ma-el, Abraham's
son, whom Ha'-gar the Egyptian,
Sarah's ᵀhandmaid, bare unto A-
braham: 11:10, 27; 16:15 · *maidservant*

13 And ᴿthese *are* the names of
the sons of Ish'-ma-el, by their
names, according to their generations: the firstborn of Ish'-ma-el,
Ne-ba'-joth; and Ke'-dar, and Ad'-
be-el, and Mib'-sam,   1 Chr. 1:29-31

14 And Mish'-ma, and Du'-mah,
and Mas'-sa,

15 Ha'-dar, and Te'-ma, Je'-tur,
Na'-phish, and Ked'-e-mah:

16 These *are* the sons of Ish'-
ma-el, and these *are* their names,
by their towns, and by their
ᵀcastles; twelve princes according
to their nations.   *settlements* or *camps*

17 And these *are* the years of
the life of Ish'-ma-el, an hundred
and thirty and seven years: and
he gave up the ghost and died;
and was gathered unto his people.

18 ᴿAnd they dwelt from Hav'-i-
lah unto Shur, that *is* before
Egypt, as thou goest toward Assyria: *and* he ᵀdied in the presence
of all his brethren.   20:1 · Lit. *fell*

19 And these *are* the generations of Isaac, Abraham's son:
ᴿAbraham begat Isaac: Matt. 1:2

20 And Isaac was forty years old
when he took Rebekah to wife,
ᴿthe daughter of Be-thu'-el the Syrian of Pa'-dan-a'-ram, ᴿthe sister
to Laban the Syrian.   22:23 · 24:29

21 And Isaac intreated the LORD
for his wife, because she *was* barren: ᴿand the LORD was intreated
of him, and ᴿRebekah his wife
conceived.   1 Sam. 1:17 · Rom. 9:10-13

22 And the children struggled
together within her; and she said,

If *it be* so, why *am* I thus? And she went to enquire of the LORD.

23 And the LORD said unto her, ᴿTwo nations *are* in thy womb, and two manner of people shall be separated from thy bowels; and ᴿ*the one* people shall be stronger than *the other* people; and ᴿthe elder shall serve the younger.   24:60 · 2 Sam. 8:14 · Rom. 9:12

24 And when her days to be delivered were fulfilled, behold, *there were* twins in her womb.

25 And the first came out red, all over like an hairy garment; and they called his name Esau.

26 And after that came his brother out, and ᴿhis hand took hold on Esau's heel; and ᴿhis name was called Jacob: and Isaac *was* threescore years old when she bare them.   Hos. 12:3 · 27:36

27 And the boys grew: and Esau was ᴿa cunning hunter, a man of the field; and Jacob *was* a plain man, dwelling in tents.   27:3, 5

28 And Isaac loved Esau, because he did eat of *his* venison: ᴿbut Rebekah loved Jacob.   27:6–10

29 And Jacob ᵀsod pottage: and Esau came from the field, and he *was* faint: *cooked a stew*

30 And Esau said to Jacob, Feed me, I pray thee, with that same red *pottage;* for I *am* faint: therefore was his name called E'-dom.

31 And Jacob said, Sell me this day thy birthright.

32 And Esau said, Behold, I *am* at the point to die: and what profit shall this birthright do to me?

33 And Jacob said, Swear to me this day; and he sware unto him: and ᴿhe sold his birthright unto Jacob.   Heb. 12:16

34 Then Jacob gave Esau bread and pottage of lentiles; and ᴿhe did eat and drink, and rose up, and went his way: thus Esau despised *his* birthright.   Is. 22:13

26 And there was a famine in the land, beside ᴿthe first famine that was in the days of Abraham. And Isaac went unto ᴿA-bim'-e-lech king of the Phi-lis'-tines unto Ge'-rar.   12:10 · 20:1, 2

2 And the LORD appeared unto him, and said, ᴿGo not down into Egypt; dwell in ᴿthe land which I shall tell thee of: 17:1; 18:1; 35:9 · 12:1

3 ᴿSojourn in this land, and ᴿI will be with thee, and will bless thee; for unto thee, and unto thy seed, I will give all these countries, and I will perform the oath which I sware unto Abraham thy father;   Ps. 39:12; Heb. 11:9 · 28:13, 15

4 And ᴿI will make thy seed to ☆ multiply as the stars of heaven, and will give unto thy seed all these countries; ᴿand in thy seed shall all the nations of the earth be blessed;   Ex. 32:13 · Gal. 3:8

5 ᴿBecause that Abraham obeyed my voice, and kept my charge, my commandments, my statutes, and my laws.   22:16, 18

6 And Isaac dwelt in Ge'-rar:

7 And the men of the place asked *him* of his wife; and ᴿhe said, She *is* my sister: for he feared to say, *She is* my wife; lest, *said he,* the men of the place should kill me for Rebekah; because she ᴿ*was* fair to look upon.   12:13; 20:2, 12, 13 · 12:11; 24:16

8 And it came to pass, when he had been there a long time, that A-bim'-e-lech king of the Phi-lis'-tines looked out at a window, and saw, and, behold, Isaac *was* sporting with Rebekah his wife.

9 And A-bim'-e-lech called Isaac, and said, Behold, ᵀof a surety she *is* thy wife: and how saidst thou, She *is* my sister? And Isaac said unto him, Because I said, Lest I die for her.   *obviously*

10 And A-bim'-e-lech said, What *is* this thou hast done unto us? one of the people might ᵀlightly have lien with thy wife, and ᴿthou shouldest have brought guiltiness upon us.   *soon* · 20:9

11 And A-bim'-e-lech charged all *his* people, saying, He that toucheth this man or his wife shall surely be put to death.

12 Then Isaac sowed in that land, and ᵀreceived in the same year ᴿan hundredfold: and the LORD blessed him.   *reaped* · Mark 4:8

13 And the man ᴿwaxed great, and went forward, and grew until he became very great: [Prov. 10:22]

14 For he had possession of flocks, and possession of herds, and great store of servants: and the Phi-lis′-tines ᴿenvied him. 37:11

15 For all the wells which his father's servants had digged in the days of Abraham his father, the Phi-lis′-tines had stopped them, and filled them with earth.

16 And A-bim′-e-lech said unto Isaac, Go from us; for ᴿthou art much mightier than we.   Ex. 1:9

17 And Isaac departed thence, and ᵀpitched his tent in the valley of Ge′-rar, and dwelt there. camped

18 And Isaac digged again the wells of water, which they had digged in the days of Abraham his father; for the Phi-lis′-tines had stopped them after the death of Abraham: ᴿand he called their names after the names by which his father had called them.   21:31

19 And Isaac's servants digged in the valley, and found there a well of ᵀspringing water.   running

20 And the herdmen of Ge′-rar did strive with Isaac's herdmen, saying, The water is ours: and he called the name of the well E′-sek; because they strove with him.

21 And they digged another well, and strove for that also: and he called the name of it Sit′-nah.

22 And he removed from thence, and digged another well; and for that they strove not: and he called the name of it Re-ho′-both; and he said, For now the LORD hath made room for us, and we shall be fruitful in the land.

23 And he went up from thence to Be′-er–she′-ba.

24 And the LORD appeared unto him the same night, and said, ᴿI am the God of Abraham thy father: fear not, for I am with thee, and will bless thee, and multiply thy seed for my servant Abraham's sake.   Ex. 3:6; Acts 7:32

25 And he ᴿbuilded an altar there, and ᴿcalled upon the name of the LORD, and pitched his tent there: and there Isaac's servants digged a well.   22:9; 33:20 · Ps. 116:17

26 Then A-bim′-e-lech went to him from Ge′-rar, and A-huz′-zath one of his friends, ᴿand Phi′-chol the chief captain of his army. 21:22

27 And Isaac said unto them, Wherefore come ye to me, ᴿseeing ye hate me, and have ᴿsent me away from you?   Judg. 11:7 · v. 16

28 And they said, We saw certainly that the LORD ᴿwas with thee: and we said, Let there be now an oath betwixt us, even betwixt us and thee, and let us make a covenant with thee;   21:22

29 That thou wilt do us no hurt, as we have not touched thee, and as we have done unto thee nothing but good, and have sent thee away in peace: ᴿthou art now the blessed of the LORD.   24:31; Ps. 115:15

30 ᴿAnd he made them a feast, and they did eat and drink.   19:3

31 And they rose up ᵀbetimes in the morning, and ᴿsware one to another: and Isaac sent them away, and they departed from him in peace.   early · 21:31

32 And it came to pass the same day, that Isaac's servants came, and told him concerning the well which they had digged, and said unto him, We have found water.

33 And he called it She′-bah: ᴿtherefore the name of the city is Be′-er–she′-ba unto this day.   21:31

34 ᴿAnd Esau was forty years old when he took to wife Judith the daughter of Be-e′-ri the Hit′-tite, and Bash′-e-math the daughter of E′-lon the Hit′-tite: 28:8; 36:2

35 Which ᴿwere a grief of mind unto Isaac and to Rebekah.   27:46

27 And it came to pass, that when Isaac was old, and ᴿhis eyes were dim, so that he could not see, he called Esau his eldest son, and said unto him, My son; and he said unto him, Behold, here am I.   48:10; 1 Sam. 3:2

2 And he said, Behold now, I am old, I ᴿknow not the day of my death: [Prov. 27:1; James 4:14]

3 ᴿNow therefore take, I pray

thee, thy weapons, thy quiver and thy bow, and go out to the field, and take me *some* venison;   25:28

4 And make me savoury meat, such as I love, and bring *it* to me, that I may eat; that my soul ᴿmay bless thee before I die.   49:28

5 And Rebekah heard when Isaac spake to Esau his son. And Esau went to the field to hunt *for* venison, *and* to bring *it.*

6 And Rebekah spake unto Jacob her son, saying, Behold, I heard thy father speak unto Esau thy brother, saying,

7 Bring me ᵀvenison, and make me ᵀsavoury meat, that I may eat, and bless thee before the Lᴏʀᴅ before my death.   *game · tasty food*

8 Now therefore, my son, ᴿobey my voice according to that which I command thee.   vv. 13, 43

9 Go now to the flock, and fetch me from thence two good kids of the goats; and I will make them ᴿsavoury meat for thy father, such as he loveth: v. 4

10 And thou shalt bring *it* to thy father, that he may eat, and that he ᴿmay bless thee before his death.   v. 4; 48:16

11 And Jacob said to Rebekah his mother, Behold, ᴿEsau my brother *is* a hairy man, and I *am* a smooth man: 25:25

12 My father peradventure will ᴿfeel me, and I shall seem to him as a deceiver; and I shall bring ᴿa curse upon me, and not a blessing.   vv. 21, 22 · 9:25; Deut. 27:18

13 And his mother said unto him, ᴿUpon me *be* thy curse, my son: only obey my voice, and go fetch me *them.*   1 Sam. 25:24

14 And he went, and fetched, and brought *them* to his mother: and his mother made savoury meat, such as his father loved.

15 And Rebekah took ᴿgoodlyᵀ raiment of her eldest son Esau, which *were* with her in the house, and put them upon Jacob her younger son: v. 27 · *choice clothes*

16 And she put the skins of the kids of the goats upon his hands, and upon the smooth of his neck:

17 And she gave the savoury meat and the bread, which she had prepared, into the hand of her son Jacob.

18 And he came unto his father, and said, My father: and he said, Here *am* I; who *art* thou, my son?

19 And Jacob said unto his father, I *am* Esau thy firstborn; I have done according as thou ᵀbadest me: arise, I pray thee, sit and eat of my ᵀvenison, ᴿthat thy soul may bless me.   *told · game · v. 4*

20 And Isaac said unto his son, How *is it* that thou hast found *it* so quickly, my son? And he said, Because the Lᴏʀᴅ thy God brought *it* to me.

21 And Isaac said unto Jacob, Come near, I pray thee, that I may feel thee, my son, whether thou *be* my very son Esau or not.

22 And Jacob went near unto Isaac his father; and he felt him, and said, The voice *is* Jacob's voice, but the hands *are* the hands of Esau.

23 And he ᵀdiscerned him not, because ᴿhis hands were hairy, as his brother Esau's hands: so he blessed him.   *recognized · v. 16*

24 And he said, *Art* thou my very son Esau? And he said, I *am.*

25 And he said, Bring *it* near to me, and I will eat of my son's venison, that my soul may bless thee. And he brought *it* near to him, and he did eat: and he brought him wine, and he drank.

26 And his father Isaac said unto him, Come near now, and kiss me, my son.

27 And he came near, and ᴿkissed him: and he smelled the smell of his raiment, and blessed him, and said, See, the smell of my son *is* as the smell of a field which the Lᴏʀᴅ hath blessed: 29:13

28 Therefore ᴿGod give thee of the dew of heaven, and the fatness of the earth, and plenty of ᵀcorn and wine: Heb. 11:20 · *grain*

29 ᴿLet people serve thee, and nations bow down to thee: be lord over thy brethren, and ᴿlet thy mother's sons bow down to thee:

Rcursed *be* every one that curseth thee, and blessed *be* he that blesseth thee. Is. 45:14 · 37:7, 10; 49:8 · 12:2, 3

30 And it came to pass, as soon as Isaac had made an end of blessing Jacob, and Jacob Twas yet scarce gone out from the presence of Isaac his father, that Esau his brother came in from his hunting.   *had scarcely*

31 And he also had made Tsavoury meat, and brought it unto his father, and said unto his father, Let my father arise, and Reat of his son's venison, that thy soul may bless me.   *tasty food · v. 4*

32 And Isaac his father said unto him, Who *art* thou? And he said, I *am* thy son, thy firstborn Esau.

33 And Isaac trembled very exceedingly, and said, Who? where *is* he that hath taken venison, and brought *it* me, and I have eaten of all before thou camest, and have blessed him? yea, Rand he shall be blessed. 25:23; Rom. 11:29

34 And when Esau heard the words of his father, he cried with a great and exceeding bitter cry, and said unto his father, Bless me, *even* me also, O my father.

35 And he said, Thy brother came with Tsubtilty, and hath taken away thy blessing.   *deceit*

36 And he said, RIs not he rightly named TJacob? for he hath supplanted me these two times: he took away my birthright; and, behold, now he hath taken away my blessing. And he said, Hast thou not reserved a blessing for me?   25:26, 32–34 · Lit. *Supplanter*

37 And Isaac answered and said unto Esau, Behold, I have made him thy Tlord, and all his brethren have I given to him for servants; and with corn and wine have I sustained him: and what shall I do now unto thee, my son?   *master*

38 And Esau said unto his father, Hast thou but one blessing, my father? bless me, *even* me also, O my father. And Esau lifted up his voice, Rand wept. Heb. 12:17

39 And Isaac his father answered and said unto him, Be-

hold, thy dwelling shall be the fatness of the earth, and of the dew of heaven from above;

40 And by thy sword shalt thou live, and Rshalt serve thy brother; and Rit shall come to pass when thou shalt have the dominion, that thou shalt break his yoke from off thy neck.   [Obad. 18–20] · 2 Kin. 8:20–22

41 And Esau Rhated Jacob because of the blessing wherewith his father blessed him: and Esau said in his heart, RThe days of mourning for my father are at hand; Rthen will I slay my brother Jacob.   37:4, 5, 8 · 50:2–4, 10 · Obad. 10

42 And these words of Esau her elder son were told to Rebekah: and she sent and called Jacob her younger son, and said unto him, Behold, thy brother Esau, as touching thee, doth Rcomfort himself, *purposing* to kill thee. Ps. 64:5

43 Now therefore, my son, obey my voice; and arise, flee thou to Laban my brother to Ha'-ran;

44 And Ttarry with him a Rfew days, until thy brother's fury turn away;   *stay · 31:41*

45 Until thy brother's anger turn away from thee, and he forget *that* which thou hast done to him: then I will send, and fetch thee from thence: why should I be Tdeprived also of you both in one day? *bereaved*

46 And Rebekah said to Isaac, RI am weary of my life because of the daughters of Heth: Rif Jacob take a wife of the daughters of Heth, such as these *which are* of the daughters of the land, what good shall my life do me? 28:8 · 24:3

28 And Isaac called Jacob, and Rblessed him, and charged him, and said unto him, RThou shalt not take a wife of the daughters of Canaan.   27:33 · 24:3

2 Arise, go to Pa'-dan–a'-ram, to the house of Be-thu'-el thy mother's father; and take thee a wife from thence of the daughters of RLaban thy mother's brother. 24:29

3 And God Almighty bless thee, and make thee fruitful, and multiply thee, that thou mayest be Ta multitude of people; *an assembly*

4 And give thee ^Rthe blessing of Abraham, to thee, and to thy seed with thee; that thou mayest inherit the land ^Rwherein thou art a stranger, which God gave unto Abraham. 12:2, 3; 22:17; Gal. 3:8 · 17:8

5 And Isaac sent away Jacob: and he went to Pa'-dan–a'-ram unto Laban, son of Be-thu'-el the Syrian, the brother of Rebekah, Jacob's and Esau's mother.

6 When Esau saw that Isaac had blessed Jacob, and sent him away to Pa'-dan–a'-ram, to take him a wife from thence; and that as he blessed him he gave him a charge, saying, Thou shalt not take a wife of the daughters of Canaan;

7 And that Jacob obeyed his father and his mother, and was gone to Pa'-dan–a'-ram;

8 And Esau seeing ^Rthat the daughters of Canaan pleased not Isaac his father; 24:3; 26:34, 35; 27:46

9 Then went Esau unto Ish'-ma-el, and ^Rtook unto the wives which he had ^RMa'-ha-lath the daughter of Ish'-ma-el Abraham's son, ^Rthe sister of Ne-ba'-joth, to be his wife. 26:34, 35 · 36:2, 3 · 25:13

10 And Jacob went out from Be'-er–she'-ba, and went toward ^RHa'-ran. 12:4, 5; 27:43; 2 Kin. 19:12; Acts 7:2

11 And he ^Tlighted upon a certain place, and tarried there all night, because the sun was set; and he took of the stones of that place, and ^Tput them for his pillows, and lay down in that place to sleep. came to · Lit. put it at his head

12 And he dreamed, and behold a ladder set up on the earth, and the top of it reached to heaven: and behold the angels of God ascending and descending on it.

13 And, behold, the LORD stood above it, and said, ^RI am the LORD God of Abraham thy father, and the God of Isaac: ^Rthe land whereon thou liest, to thee will I give it, and to thy seed; 26:24 · 13:15, 17; 26:3

☆ 14 And thy seed shall be as the dust of the earth, and thou shalt spread abroad to the west, and to the east, and to the north, and to

the south: and in thee and ^Rin thy seed shall all the families of the earth be blessed. Luke 3:34; Gal. 3:8

15 And, behold, I am with thee, and will keep thee in all places whither thou goest, and will bring thee again into this land; for ^RI will not leave thee, until I have done that which I have spoken to thee of. Deut. 7:9; Josh. 1:5; Heb. 13:5

16 And Jacob awaked out of his sleep, and he said, Surely the LORD is in ^Rthis place; and I knew it not. Ex. 3:5; Josh. 5:15; Ps. 139:7–12

17 And he was afraid, and said, How dreadful is this place! this is none other but the house of God, and this is the gate of heaven.

18 And Jacob rose up early in the morning, and took the stone that he had put for his pillows, and ^Rset it up for a pillar, and poured oil upon the top of it. 31:13

19 And he called the name of ^Rthat place ^TBeth'–el: but the name of that city was called Luz at the first. Judg. 1:23 · Lit. House of God

20 And Jacob vowed a vow, saying, If God will be with me, and will keep me in this way that I go, and will give me ^Rbread to eat, and raiment to put on, 1 Tim. 6:8

21 So that ^RI come again to my father's house in peace; then shall the LORD be my God: Judg. 11:31

22 And this stone, which I have set for a pillar, ^Rshall be God's house: ^Rand of all that thou shalt give me I will surely give the tenth unto thee. 35:7, 14 · 14:20; [Lev. 27:30]

29 Then Jacob went on his journey, ^Rand came into the land of the people of the east. 25:6

2 And he looked, and behold a well in the field, and, lo, there were three flocks of sheep lying by it; for out of that well they watered the flocks: and a great stone was upon the well's mouth.

3 And thither were all the flocks gathered: and they rolled the stone from the well's mouth, and watered the sheep, and put the stone again upon the well's mouth in his place.

4 And Jacob said unto them,

My brethren, whence *be* ye? And they said, Of Ha'-ran *are* we.

5 And he said unto them, Know ye ᴿLaban the son of Na'-hor? And they said, We know *him*. 24:24

6 And he said unto them, ᴿ*Is* he well? And they said, *He is* well: and, behold, Ra'-chel his daughter ᴿcometh with the sheep. 43:27 · 24:11

7 And he said, Lo, *it is* yet high day, neither *is it* time that the cattle should be gathered together: water ye the sheep, and go *and* feed *them*.

8 And they said, We cannot, until all the flocks be gathered together, and *till* they roll the stone from the well's mouth; then we water the sheep.

9 And while he yet spake with them, Ra'-chel came with her father's sheep: for she kept them.

10 And it came to pass, when Jacob saw Ra'-chel the daughter of Laban his mother's brother, and the sheep of Laban his mother's brother, that Jacob went near, and ᴿrolled the stone from the well's mouth, and watered the flock of Laban his mother's brother.   Ex. 2:17

11 And Jacob kissed Ra'-chel, and lifted up his voice, and wept.

12 And Jacob told Ra'-chel that he *was* her father's ᵀbrother, and that he *was* Rebekah's son: and she ran and told her father. *relative*

13 And it came to pass, when Laban heard the tidings of Jacob his sister's son, that ᴿhe ran to meet him, and embraced him, and kissed him, and brought him to his house. And he told Laban all these things.   24:29–31; Luke 15:20

14 And Laban said to him, ᴿSurely thou *art* my bone and my flesh. And he abode with him the space of a month.   37:27; Judg. 9:2

15 And Laban said unto Jacob, Because thou *art* my brother, shouldest thou therefore serve me for ᵀnought? tell me, ᴿwhat *shall* thy wages *be*?   *nothing* · 30:28; 31:41

16 And Laban had two daughters: the name of the elder *was* Leah, and the name of the younger *was* Ra'-chel.

17 Leah *was* ᵀtender eyed; but Ra'-chel was ᴿbeautiful and well favoured. *delicate* or *soft* · 12:11, 14; 26:7

18 And Jacob loved Ra'-chel; and said, ᴿI will serve thee seven years for Ra'-chel thy younger daughter.   31:41; 2 Sam. 3:14; Hos. 12:12

19 And Laban said, *It is* better that I give her to thee, than that I should give her to another man: abide with me.

20 And Jacob ᴿserved seven years for Ra'-chel; and they seemed unto him *but* a few days, for the love he had to her.   30:26

21 And Jacob said unto Laban, Give *me* my wife, for my days are fulfilled, that I may ᴿgo in unto her.   Judg. 15:1

22 And Laban gathered together all the men of the place, and ᴿmade a feast.   Judg. 14:10; John 2:1, 2

23 And it came to pass in the evening, that he took Leah his daughter, and brought her to him; and he went in unto her.

24 And Laban gave unto his daughter Leah ᴿZil'-pah his maid *for* an handmaid.   30:9, 10

25 And it came to pass, that in the morning, behold, it *was* Leah: and he said to Laban, What *is* this thou hast done unto me? did not I serve with thee for Ra'-chel? wherefore then hast thou ᴿbeguiled me?   27:35; 31:7; 1 Sam. 28:12

26 And Laban said, It must not be so done in our country, to give the younger before the firstborn.

27 ᴿFulfil her week, and we will give thee this also for the service which thou shalt serve with me yet seven other years.   31:41

28 And Jacob did so, and fulfilled her week: and he gave him Ra'-chel his daughter to wife also.

29 And Laban gave to Ra'-chel his daughter ᴿBil'-hah his handmaid to be her maid.   30:3–5

30 And he went in also unto Ra'-chel, and he loved also Ra'-chel more than Leah, and served with him ᴿyet seven other years.   30:26

31 And when the LORD saw that Leah *was* hated, he opened her womb: but Ra'-chel *was* barren.

32 And Leah conceived, and bare a son, and she called his name Reuben: for she said, Surely the LORD hath ^Rlooked upon my affliction; now therefore my husband will love me.   Ex. 3:7; 4:31

33 And she conceived again, and bare a son; and said, Because the LORD hath heard that I *was* ^Thated, he hath therefore given me this *son* also: and she called his name Simeon.   *unloved*

34 And she conceived again, and bare a son; and said, Now this time will my husband be ^Tjoined unto me, because I have born him three sons: therefore was his name called Levi.   *attached to*

35 And she conceived again, and bare a son: and she said, Now will I praise the LORD: therefore she called his name ^RJudah; and ^Tleft bearing.   49:8; Matt. 1:2 · *stopped*

30 And when Ra'-chel saw that she bare Jacob no children, Ra'-chel ^Renvied her sister; and said unto Jacob, Give me children, or else I die.   37:11

2 And Jacob's anger was kindled against Ra'-chel: and he said, ^R*Am* I in God's stead, who hath withheld from thee the fruit of the womb?   16:2; 1 Sam. 1:5

3 And she said, Behold my maid Bil'-hah, go in unto her; and she shall bear ^Tupon my knees, that I may also ^Thave children by her.   *to be upon* · Lit. *be built up*

4 And she gave him Bil'-hah her handmaid ^Rto^T wife: and Jacob went in unto her.   16:3, 4 · *as*

5 And Bil'-hah conceived, and bare Jacob a son.

6 And Ra'-chel said, God hath ^Rjudged ^Tme, and hath also heard my voice, and hath given me a son: therefore called she his name Dan.   Ps. 35:24; 43:1; Lam. 3:59 · *my case*

7 And Bil'-hah Ra'-chel's maid conceived again, and bare Jacob a second son.

8 And Ra'-chel said, With ^Tgreat wrestlings have I wrestled with my sister, and I have prevailed: and she called his name Naph'-ta-li.   Lit. *wrestlings of God*

9 When Leah saw that she had left bearing, she took Zil'-pah her maid, and ^Rgave her Jacob ^Tto wife.   v. 4 · *as*

10 And Zil'-pah Leah's maid bare Jacob a son.

11 And Leah said, A ^Ttroop cometh: and she called his name Gad.   *fortune*

12 And Zil'-pah Leah's maid bare Jacob a second son.

13 And Leah said, Happy am I, for the daughters ^Rwill call me blessed: and she called his name Asher.   Prov. 31:28; Luke 1:48

14 And Reuben went in the days of wheat harvest, and found mandrakes in the field, and brought them unto his mother Leah. Then Ra'-chel said to Leah, Give me, I pray thee, of thy son's mandrakes.

15 And she said unto her, ^R*Is it* a small matter that thou hast taken my husband? and wouldest thou take away my son's mandrakes also? And Ra'-chel said, Therefore he shall lie with thee to night for thy son's mandrakes.   [Num. 16:9, 13]

16 And Jacob came out of the field in the evening, and Leah went out to meet him, and said, Thou must come in unto me; for surely I have hired thee with my son's mandrakes. And he lay with her that night.

17 And God hearkened unto Leah, and she conceived, and bare Jacob the fifth son.

18 And Leah said, God hath given me my hire, because I have given my maiden to my husband: and she called his name Is'-sa-char.

19 And Leah conceived again, and bare Jacob the sixth son.

20 And Leah said, God hath endued me *with* a good ^Tdowry; now will my husband dwell with me, because I have born him six sons: and she called his name Zeb'-u-lun.   *endowment*

21 And afterwards she bare a

Rdaughter, and called her name Dinah. 34:1

22 And God Rremembered Ra'-chel, and God hearkened to her, and Ropened her womb. 19:29 · 29:31

23 And she conceived, and bare a son; and said, God hath taken away Rmy reproach: 1 Sam. 1:6; Is. 4:1

24 And she called his name Joseph; and said, RThe LORD shall add to me another son. 35:16–18

25 And it came to pass, when Ra'-chel had born Joseph, that Jacob said unto Laban, Send me away, that I may go unto mine own place, and to my country.

26 Give *me* my wives and my children, Rfor whom I have served thee, and let me go: for thou knowest my service which I have done thee. 29:18–20, 27, 30; Hos. 12:12

27 And Laban said unto him, I pray thee, if I have found favour in thine eyes, Ttarry: *for* RI have learned by experience that the LORD hath blessed me for thy sake. *stay* · 26:24; 39:3; Is. 61:9

28 And he said, RAppoint me thy wages, and I will give *it*. 29:15

29 And he said unto him, Thou knowest how I have served thee, and how thy cattle was with me.

30 For *it was* little which thou hadst before I *came*, and it is *now* increased unto a multitude; and the LORD hath blessed thee Tsince my coming: and now when shall I Rprovide for mine own house also? Lit. *at my foot* · [1 Tim. 5:8]

31 And he said, What shall I give thee? And Jacob said, Thou shalt not give me any thing: if thou wilt do this thing for me, I will again feed *and* keep thy flock.

32 I will pass through all thy flock to day, removing from thence all the speckled and spotted Tcattle, and all the brown cattle among the sheep, and the spotted and speckled among the goats: and Rof *such* shall be my hire. *sheep* · 31:8

33 So shall my Rrighteousness answer for me in time to come, when it shall come Tfor my hire before thy face: every one that *is*

not speckled and spotted among the goats, and brown among the sheep, that shall be counted stolen with me. Ps. 37:6 · *about my wages*

34 And Laban said, Behold, I would it might be according to thy word.

35 And he removed that day the he goats that were ringstrakedT and spotted, and all the she goats that were speckled and spotted, *and* every one that had *some* white in it, and all the brown among the sheep, and gave *them* into the hand of his sons. *streaked*

36 And he set three days' journey Tbetwixt himself and Jacob: and Jacob fed the rest of Laban's flocks. *between*

37 And RJacob took him rods of green poplar, and of the hazel and chesnut tree; and Tpilled white Tstrakes in them, and made the white appear which *was* in the rods. 31:9–12 · *peeled* · *strips*

38 And he set the rods which he had Tpilled before the flocks in the gutters in the watering troughs when the flocks came to drink, that they should conceive when they came to drink. *peeled*

39 And the flocks conceived before the rods, and brought forth cattle Tringstraked, speckled, and spotted. *streaked*

40 And Jacob did separate the lambs, and set the faces of the flocks toward the Tringstraked, and all the brown in the flock of Laban; and he put his own flocks by themselves, and put them not Tunto Laban's cattle. *streaked* · *with*

41 And it came to pass, whensoever the stronger Tcattle did conceive, that Jacob laid the rods before the eyes of the cattle in the gutters, that they might conceive among the rods. *livestock*

42 But when the cattle were feeble, he put *them* not in: so the feebler were Laban's, and the stronger Jacob's.

43 And the man increased exceedingly, and had much cattle, and maidservants, and menservants, and camels, and asses.

31 And he heard the words of Laban's sons, saying, Jacob hath taken away all that *was* our father's; and of *that* which *was* our father's hath he gotten all this ᴿglory.ᵀ   Ps. 49:16 · *wealth*

2 And Jacob beheld the countenance of Laban, and, behold, it *was* not toward him as before.

3 And the LORD said unto Jacob, ᴿReturn unto the land of thy fathers, and to thy kindred; and I will ᴿbe with thee.   28:15 · 46:4

4 And Jacob sent and called Ra'-chel and Leah to the field unto his flock,

5 And said unto them, I see your father's countenance, that it *is* not toward me as before; but the God of my father ᴿhath been with me.   21:22; Is. 41:10; Heb. 13:5

6 And ᴿye know that with all my ᵀpower I have served your father.   vv. 38–41; 30:29 · *might*

7 And your father hath deceived me, and changed my wages ten times; but God ᴿsuffered him not to hurt me.   Ps. 37:2

8 If he said thus, ᴿThe speckled shall be thy wages; then all the ᵀcattle bare speckled: and if he said thus, The ᵀringstraked shall be thy hire; then bare all the cattle ringstraked.   30:32 · *flocks · streaked*

9 Thus God hath ᴿtaken away the cattle of your father, and given *them* to me.   vv. 1, 16

10 And it came to pass at the time that the ᵀcattle conceived, that I lifted up mine eyes, and saw in a dream, and, behold, the rams which leaped upon the cattle *were* ᵀringstraked, speckled, and ᵀgrisled.   *flocks · streaked · gray-spotted*

11 And ᴿthe angel of God spake unto me in a dream, *saying,* Jacob: And I said, Here *am* I.   22:11

12 And he said, Lift up now thine eyes, and see, all the rams which leap upon the cattle *are* ringstraked, speckled, and grisled: for ᴿI have seen all that Laban doeth unto thee.   Ps. 139:3

13 I *am* the God of Beth'-el, ᴿwhere thou anointedst the pillar, *and* where thou vowedst a vow unto me: now arise, get thee out from this land, and return unto the land of thy kindred.   28:16–22

14 And Ra'-chel and Leah answered and said unto him, *Is there* yet any portion or inheritance for us in our father's house?

15 Are we not counted of him strangers? for ᴿhe hath sold us, and hath quite devoured also our money.   29:15, 20, 23, 27; Neh. 5:8

16 For all the riches which God hath taken from our father, that *is* ours, and our children's: now then, whatsoever God hath said unto thee, do.

17 Then Jacob rose up, and set his sons and his wives upon camels;

18 And he carried away all his cattle, and all his goods which he had gotten, the cattle of his getting, which he had gotten in Pa'-dan–a'-ram, for to go to Isaac his father in the land of ᴿCanaan.   17:8

19 And Laban went to shear his sheep: and Ra'-chel had stolen the images that *were* her father's.

20 And Jacob stole away unawares to Laban the Syrian, in that he told him not that he fled.

21 So he fled with all that he had; and he rose up, and passed over the river, and ᴿset his face *toward* the mount Gil'-e-ad.   46:28

22 And it was told Laban on the third day that Jacob was fled.

23 And he took ᴿhis brethren with him, and pursued after him seven days' journey; and they overtook him in the ᵀmount Gil'-e-ad.   13:8 · *mountains of*

24 And God ᴿcame to Laban the Syrian in a dream by night, and said unto him, Take heed that thou ᴿspeak not to Jacob either good or bad.   20:3 · 24:50

25 Then Laban overtook Jacob. Now Jacob had pitched his tent in the mount: and Laban with his brethren pitched in the mount of Gil'-e-ad.

26 And Laban said to Jacob, What hast thou done, that thou hast stolen away unawares to me,

and carried away my daughters, as captives *taken* with the sword?

27 Wherefore didst thou flee away secretly, and steal away from me; and didst not tell me, that I might have sent thee away with ᵀmirth, and with songs, with ᵀtabret, and with harp? *joy · timbrel*

28 And hast not suffered me ᴿto kiss my sons and my daughters? thou hast now done foolishly in *so* doing.   *Ruth 1:9, 14; 1 Kin. 19:20*

29 It is in the power of my hand to do you hurt: but the ᴿGod of your father spake unto me ᴿyesternight, saying, Take thou heed that thou speak not to Jacob either good or bad.   *28:13 · v. 24*

30 And now, *though* thou wouldest needs be gone, because thou sore longedst after thy father's house, *yet* wherefore hast thou ᴿstolen my gods?   *Josh. 24:2*

31 And Jacob answered and said to Laban, Because I was ᴿafraid: for I said, Peradventure thou wouldest take by force thy daughters from me.   *26:7; 32:7, 11*

32 With whomsoever thou findest thy gods, ᴿlet him not live: before our brethren discern thou what *is* thine with me, and take *it* to thee. For Jacob knew not that Ra′-chel had stolen them.   *44:9*

33 And Laban went into Jacob's tent, and into Leah's tent, and into the two maidservants' tents; but he found *them* not. Then went he out of Leah's tent, and entered into Ra′-chel's tent.

34 Now Ra′-chel had taken the images, and put them in the camel's ᵀfurniture, and sat upon them. And Laban searched all the tent, but found *them* not.   *saddle*

35 And she said to her father, Let it not displease my lord that I cannot ᴿrise up before thee; for the custom of women *is* upon me. And he searched, but found not the images.   *Ex. 20:12; Lev. 19:32*

36 And Jacob was ᵀwroth, and ᵀchode with Laban: and Jacob answered and said to Laban, What *is* my trespass? what *is* my

sin, that thou hast so hotly pursued after me?   *angry · rebuked*

37 Whereas thou hast searched all my stuff, what hast thou found of all thy household stuff? set *it* here before my brethren and thy brethren, that they may judge betwixt us both.

38 This twenty years *have* I *been* with thee; thy ewes and thy she goats have not cast their young, and the rams of thy flock have I not eaten.

39 That which was torn *of beasts* I brought not unto thee; I bare the loss of it; of my hand didst thou require it, *whether* stolen by day, or stolen by night.

40 *Thus* I was; in the day the drought consumed me, and the frost by night; and my sleep departed from mine eyes.

41 Thus have I been twenty years in thy house; I ᴿserved thee fourteen years for thy two daughters, and six years for thy ᵀcattle: and ᴿthou hast changed my wages ten times.   *29:20, 27–30 · flock · v. 7*

42 Except the God of my father, the God of Abraham, and ᴿthe fear of Isaac, had been with me, surely thou hadst sent me away now empty. ᴿGod hath seen mine affliction and the labour of my hands, and ᴿrebuked *thee* yesternight.   *Is. 8:13 · Ex. 3:7 · 1 Chr. 12:17*

43 And Laban answered and said unto Jacob, *These* daughters *are* my daughters, and *these* children *are* my children, and *these* ᵀcattle *are* my cattle, and all that thou seest *is* mine: and what can I do this day unto these my daughters, or unto their children which they have born?   *flock*

44 Now therefore come thou, let us make a ᵀcovenant, I and thou; and let it be for a witness between me and thee.   *treaty*

45 And Jacob ᴿtook a stone, and set it up *for* a pillar.   *Josh. 24:26, 27*

46 And Jacob said unto his brethren, Gather stones; and they took stones, and made an heap: and they did eat there upon the heap.

47 And Laban called it Je'-gar–sa-ha-du'-tha: but Jacob called it Gal'-e-ed.

48 And Laban said, ^RThis heap *is* a witness between me and thee this day. Therefore was the name of it called Gal'-e-ed;   Josh. 24:27

49 And ^TMiz'-pah; for he said, The LORD watch between me and thee, when we are absent one from another.   Lit. *Watch*

50 If thou shalt afflict my daughters, or if thou shalt take *other* wives beside my daughters, no man *is* with us; see, God *is* witness betwixt me and thee.

51 And Laban said to Jacob, Behold this heap, and behold *this* pillar, which I have cast betwixt me and thee;

52 This heap *be* witness, and *this* pillar *be* witness, that I will not pass ^Tover this heap to thee, and that thou shalt not pass ^Tover this heap and this pillar unto me, for harm.   *beyond*

53 The God of Abraham, and the God of Na'-hor, the God of their father, ^Rjudge betwixt us. And Jacob ^Rsware by ^Rthe fear of his father Isaac.   16:5 · 21:23 · v. 42

54 Then Jacob offered sacrifice upon the mount, and called his brethren to eat bread: and they did eat bread, and tarried all night in the mount.

55 And early in the morning Laban rose up, and kissed his sons and his daughters, and ^Rblessed them: and Laban departed, and returned unto his place.   28:1

32 And Jacob went on his way, and ^Rthe angels of God met him.   Num. 22:31; 2 Kin. 6:16, 17

2 And when Jacob saw them, he said, This *is* God's host: and he called the name of that place ^TMa-ha-na'-im.   Lit. *Double Camp*

3 And Jacob sent messengers before him to Esau his brother ^Runto the land of Se'-ir, ^Rthe country of E'-dom.   14:6 · Deut. 2:5; Josh. 24:4

4 And he commanded them, saying, ^RThus shall ye speak unto my lord Esau; Thy servant Jacob saith thus, I have sojourned with Laban, and stayed there until now: Prov. 15:1

5 And ^RI have oxen, and asses, flocks, and menservants, and womenservants: and I have sent to tell my lord, that ^RI may find grace in thy sight.   30:43 · 33:8, 15

6 And the messengers returned to Jacob, saying, We came to thy brother Esau, and also ^Rhe cometh to meet thee, and four hundred men with him.   33:1

7 Then Jacob was greatly afraid and distressed: and he divided the people that *was* with him, and the flocks, and herds, and the camels, into two bands;

8 And said, If Esau come to the one company, and ^Tsmite it, then the other company which is left shall escape.   *attack*

9 ^RAnd Jacob said, O God of my father Abraham, and God of my father Isaac, the LORD which saidst unto me, Return unto thy country, and to thy kindred, and I will deal well with thee: [Ps. 50:15]

10 I am not worthy of the least of all the mercies, and of all the truth, which thou hast shewed unto thy servant; for with my staff I passed over this Jordan; and now I am become two bands.

11 Deliver me, I pray thee, from the hand of my brother, from the hand of Esau: for I fear him, lest he will come and smite me, *and* the mother with the children.

12 And ^Rthou saidst, I will surely do thee good, and make thy seed as the ^Rsand of the sea, which cannot be numbered for multitude.   28:13–15 · 22:17

13 And he lodged there that same night; and took of that which came to his hand ^Ra present for Esau his brother;   43:11

14 Two hundred she goats, and twenty he goats, two hundred ewes, and twenty rams,

15 Thirty ^Tmilch camels with their colts, forty ^Tkine, and ten bulls, twenty ^Tshe asses, and ten foals.   *milk · cows · female donkeys*

16 And he delivered *them* into the hand of his servants, every

drove by themselves; and said unto his servants, Pass over before me, and put a space betwixt drove and drove.

17 And he commanded the foremost, saying, When Esau my brother meeteth thee, and asketh thee, saying, Whose *art* thou? and whither goest thou? and whose *are* these before thee?

18 Then thou shalt say, *They be* thy servant Jacob's; it *is* a present sent unto my lord Esau: and, behold, also he *is* behind us.

19 And so commanded he the second, and the third, and all that followed the droves, saying, On this manner shall ye speak unto Esau, when ye find him.

20 And say ye moreover, Behold, thy servant Jacob *is* behind us. For he said, I will appease him with the present that goeth before me, and afterward I will see his face; peradventure he will accept ᵀof me.   Lit. *my face*

21 So went the present over before him: and himself lodged that night in the ᵀcompany.   *camp*

22 And he rose up that night, and took his two wives, and his two womenservants, and his eleven sons, ᴿand passed over the ford Jab'-bok.   Num. 21:24; Deut. 3:16

23 And he took them, and sent them over the brook, and sent over that he had.

24 And Jacob was left alone; and there wrestled a man with him until the breaking of the day.

25 And when he saw that he prevailed not against him, he ᵀtouched the ᵀhollow of his ᵀthigh; and the hollow of Jacob's thigh was out of joint, as he wrestled with him.   struck · socket · hip

26 And ᴿhe said, Let me go, for the day breaketh. And he said, ᴿI will not let thee go, except thou bless me.   Luke 24:28 · Hos. 12:4

27 And he said unto him, What *is* thy name? And he said, Jacob.

28 And he said, Thy name shall be called no more Jacob, but ᵀIs-rael: for as a prince hast thou

power with God and with men, and hast prevailed.   *Prince with God*

29 And Jacob asked *him,* and said, Tell *me,* I pray thee, thy name. And he said, Wherefore *is* it *that* thou dost ask after my name? And he blessed him there.

30 And Jacob called the name of the place ᵀPe-ni'-el: for ᴿI have seen God face to face, and my life is preserved.   Lit. *Face of God* · Is. 6:5

31 And as he passed over Pe-nu'-el the sun rose upon him, and he ᵀhalted upon his thigh.   *limped*

32 Therefore the children of Israel eat not *of* the ᵀsinew which shrank, which *is* upon the ᵀhollow of the ᵀthigh, unto this day: because he ᵀtouched the hollow of Jacob's thigh in the sinew that shrank.   *muscle · socket · hip · struck*

33 And Jacob lifted up his eyes, and looked, and, behold, ᴿEsau came, and with him four hundred men. And he divided the children unto Leah, and unto Ra'-chel, and unto the two ᵀhandmaids.   32:6 · *maidservants*

2 And he put the handmaids and their children foremost, and Leah and her children after, and Ra'-chel and Joseph hindermost.

3 And he passed over before them, and ᴿbowed himself to the ground seven times, until he came near to his brother.   18:2; 42:6

4 ᴿAnd Esau ran to meet him, and embraced him, ᴿand fell on his neck, and kissed him: and they wept.   32:28 · 45:14, 15

5 And he lifted up his eyes, and saw the women and the children; and said, Who *are* those with thee? And he said, The children ᴿwhich God hath graciously given thy servant.   48:9; [Ps. 127:3]; Is. 8:18

6 Then the handmaidens came near, they and their children, and they bowed themselves.

7 And Leah also with her children came near, and bowed themselves: and after came Joseph near and Ra'-chel, and they bowed themselves.

8 And he said, What *meanest* thou by all this drove which I met?

And he said, *These are* to find grace in the sight of my lord.

9 And Esau said, I have enough, my brother; keep that thou hast unto thyself.

10 And Jacob said, Nay, I pray thee, if now I have found grace in thy sight, then receive my present at my hand: for therefore I ^Rhave seen thy face, as though I had seen the face of God, and thou wast pleased with me.   2 Sam. 3:13

11 Take, I pray thee, my blessing that is brought to thee; because God hath dealt graciously with me, and because I have enough. And he urged him, and he took *it*.

12 And he said, Let us take our journey, and let us go, and I will go before thee.

13 And he said unto him, My lord knoweth that the children *are* ^Ttender, and the flocks and herds with young *are* with me: and if men should overdrive them one day, all the flock will die.   *weak*

14 Let my lord, I pray thee, pass over before his servant: and I will lead on ^Tsoftly, according as the ^Tcattle that goeth before me and the children be able to endure, until I come unto my lord ^Runto Se'-ir.   *slowly · livestock · 32:3; 36:8*

15 And Esau said, Let me now leave with thee *some* of the folk that *are* with me. And he said, What needeth it? ^Rlet me find grace in the sight of my lord. 34:11

16 So Esau returned that day on his way unto Se'-ir.

17 And Jacob journeyed to Suc'-coth, and built him an house, and made ^Tbooths for his cattle: therefore the name of the place is called Suc'-coth.   *shelters*

18 And Jacob came to Sha'-lem, a city of She'-chem, which *is* in the land of Canaan, when he came from Pa'-dan–a'-ram; and pitched his tent before the city.

19 And he bought a parcel of a field, where he had spread his tent, at the hand of the children of Ha'-mor, She'-chem's father, for an hundred pieces of money.

20 And he erected there an al-tar, and ^Rcalled it ^TEl–e-lo'-he–Is'-ra-el.   35:7 · Lit. *God, the God of Israel*

34 And ^RDinah the daughter of Leah, which she bare unto Jacob, went out to see the daughters of the land.   30:21

2 And when She'-chem the son of Ha'-mor the Hi'-vite, prince of the country, saw her, he took her, and lay with her, and defiled her.

3 And his soul clave unto Di-nah the daughter of Jacob, and he loved the damsel, and spake kind-ly unto the damsel.

4 And She'-chem ^Rspake unto his father Ha'-mor, saying, Get me this damsel to wife.   Judg. 14:2

5 And Jacob heard that he had defiled Dinah his daughter: now his sons were with his cattle in the field: and Jacob ^Rheld his peace until they were come.   2 Sam. 13:22

6 And Ha'-mor the father of She'-chem went out unto Jacob to ^Tcommune with him.   *speak*

7 And the sons of Jacob came out of the field when they heard *it:* and the men were grieved, and they were very wroth, because he had wrought folly in Israel in lying with Jacob's daughter; which thing ought not to be done.

8 And Ha'-mor communed with them, saying, The soul of my son She'-chem longeth for your daughter: I pray you give her him to wife.

9 And make ye marriages with us, *and* give your daughters unto us, and take our daughters unto you.

10 And ye shall dwell with us: and the land shall be before you; dwell and trade ye therein, and get you possessions therein.

11 And She'-chem said unto her father and unto her brethren, Let me find ^Tgrace in your eyes, and what ye shall say unto me I will give.   *favour*

12 Ask me never so much dowry and gift, and I will give according as ye shall say unto me: but give me the damsel to wife.

13 And the sons of Jacob an-

swered She′-chem and Ha′-mor
his father, [R]deceitfully, and said,
because he had defiled Dinah
their sister: 31:7; Ex. 8:29
14 And they said unto them, We
cannot do this thing, to give our
sister to one that is [R]uncircum-
cised; for [R]that *were* a reproach
unto us: Ex. 12:48 · Josh. 5:2-9
15 But in this will we consent
unto you: If ye will be as we *be*,
that every male of you be circumcised;
16 Then will we give our daughters unto you, and we will take
your daughters to us, and we will
dwell with you, and we will
become one people.
17 But if ye will not hearken
unto us, to be circumcised; then
will we take our daughter, and we
will be gone.
18 And their words pleased Ha′-
mor, and She′-chem Ha′-mor's son.
19 And the young man deferred
not to do the thing, because he
had delight in Jacob's daughter:
and he *was* more honourable than
all the house of his father.
20 And Ha′-mor and She′-chem
his son came unto the [R]gate of
their city, and communed with the
men of their city, saying,   Ruth 4:1
21 These men *are* peaceable
with us; therefore let them dwell
in the land, and trade therein;
for the land, behold, *it is* large
enough for them; let us take their
daughters to us for wives, and let
us give them our daughters.
22 Only [T]herein will the men
consent unto us for to dwell with
us, to be one people, if every male
among us be circumcised, as they
are circumcised.   *on this* condition
23 *Shall* not their cattle and
their [T]substance and every [T]beast
of theirs *be* ours? only let us consent unto them, and they will
dwell with us.   property · animal
24 And unto Ha′-mor and unto
She′-chem his son hearkened all
that [R]went out of the gate of his
city; and every male was circumcised, all that went out of the gate
of his city.   23:10, 18

25 And it came to pass on the
third day, when they were sore,
that two of the sons of Jacob,
Simeon and Levi, Dinah's brethren, took each man his sword, and
came upon the city boldly, and
slew all the males.
26 And they [R]slew Ha′-mor and
She′-chem his son with the edge
of the sword, and took Dinah out
of She′-chem's house, and went
out.   49:5, 6
27 The sons of Jacob came upon
the slain, and [T]spoiled the city,
because they had defiled their sister.   *plundered*
28 They took their sheep, and
their oxen, and their asses, and
that which *was* in the city, and
that which *was* in the field,
29 And all their wealth, and all
their little ones, and their wives
took they captive, and spoiled
even all that *was* in the house.
30 And Jacob said to Simeon
and Levi, Ye have troubled me [R]to
make me [T]to stink among the
inhabitants of the land, among
the Ca′-naan-ites and the Per′-iz-
zites: and I *being* few in number,
they shall gather themselves
together against me, and slay me;
and I shall be destroyed, I and my
house.   Ex. 5:21; 2 Sam. 10:6 · *obnoxious*
31 And they said, Should he deal
with our sister as with an harlot?

35 And God said unto Jacob,
Arise, go up to Beth′-el, and
dwell there: and make there an
altar unto God, that appeared
unto thee when thou fleddest
from the face of Esau thy brother.
2 Then Jacob said unto his
household, and to all that *were*
with him, Put away the strange
gods that *are* among you, and be
clean, and change your garments:
3 And let us arise, and go up to
Beth′-el; and I will make there an
altar unto God, [R]who answered
me in the day of my distress, [R]and
was with me in the way which I
went. 32:7, 24; Ps. 107:6 · 28:15, 20; 31:3, 42
4 And they gave unto Jacob all
the [T]strange gods which *were* in

their hand, and *all their* earrings which *were* in their ears; and Jacob hid them under the oak which *was* by She'-chem.   *foreign*

5 And they journeyed: and ^Rthe terror of God was upon the cities that *were* round about them, and they did not pursue after the sons of Jacob.   Ex. 15:16; 23:27; [Deut. 2:25]

6 So Jacob came to ^RLuz, which *is* in the land of Canaan, that *is*, Beth'–el, he and all the people that *were* with him.   48:3

7 And he built there an altar, and called the place ^TEl–beth'–el: because there God appeared unto him, when he fled from the face of his brother.   *God of the House of God*

8 But ^RDeb'-o-rah Rebekah's nurse died, and she was buried ^Tbeneath Beth'–el under an oak: and the name of it was called Al'-lon–bach'-uth.   24:59 · *below*

9 And God appeared unto Jacob again, when he came out of Pa'-dan–a'-ram, and blessed him.

10 And God said unto him, Thy name *is* Jacob: thy name shall not be called any more Jacob, ^Rbut Israel shall be thy name: and he called his name Israel.   32:28

11 And God said unto him, I *am* God Almighty: be fruitful and multiply; a nation and a company of nations shall be of thee, and kings shall come out of thy loins;

12 And the ^Rland which I gave Abraham and Isaac, to thee I will give it, and to thy seed after thee will I give the land. 12:7; 13:15; 26:3, 4

13 And God ^Rwent^T up from him in the place where he talked with him.   17:22; 18:33 · *departed*

14 And Jacob ^Rset up a pillar in the place where he talked with him, *even* a pillar of stone: and he poured a drink offering thereon, and he poured oil thereon. 28:18, 19

15 And Jacob called the name of the place where God spake with him, ^RBeth'–el.   28:19

16 And they journeyed from Beth'–el; and there was but a little way to come to Eph'-rath: and Ra'-chel travailed, and she had hard labour.

17 And it came to pass, when she was in hard labour, that the midwife said unto her, Fear not; thou shalt have this son also.

18 And it came to pass, as her soul was in departing, (for she died) that she called his name ^TBen–o'-ni: but his father called him Benjamin.   Lit. *Son of My Sorrow*

19 And Ra'-chel died, and was buried in the way to ^REph'-rath, which *is* Beth'–le-hem.   Matt. 2:6

20 And Jacob set a pillar upon her grave: that *is* the pillar of Ra'-chel's grave unto this day.

21 And Israel journeyed, and spread his tent beyond ^Rthe tower of ^TE'-dar.   Mic. 4:8 · *Or Eder*

22 And it came to pass, when Israel dwelt in that land, that Reuben went and ^Rlay with Bil'-hah his father's concubine: and Israel heard *it*. Now the sons of Jacob were twelve: 49:4; 1 Chr. 5:1

23 The sons of Leah; Reuben, Jacob's firstborn, and Simeon, and Levi, and Judah, and Is'-sa-char, and Zeb'-u-lun:

24 The sons of Ra'-chel; Joseph, and Benjamin:

25 And the sons of Bil'-hah, Ra'-chel's handmaid; Dan, and Naph'-ta-li:

26 And the sons of Zil'-pah, Leah's handmaid; Gad, and Asher: these *are* the sons of Jacob, which were born to him in Pa'-dan–a'-ram.

27 And Jacob came unto Isaac his father unto ^RMam'-re, unto the ^Rcity of Ar'-bah, which *is* He'-bron, where Abraham and Isaac sojourned. 13:18; 18:1; 23:19 · Josh. 14:15

28 And the days of Isaac were an hundred and fourscore years.

29 And Isaac gave up the ghost, and died, and ^Rwas gathered unto his people, *being* old and full of days: and his sons Esau and Jacob buried him.   15:15; 25:8; 49:33

36 Now these *are* the generations of Esau, ^Rwho *is* E'-dom.   25:30

2 Esau took his wives of the daughters of Canaan; A'-dah the daughter of E'-lon the ^RHit'-tite,

and ᴿA-hol-i-ba′-mah the daughter of A′-nah the daughter of Zib′-e-on the Hi′-vite;   2 Kin. 7:6 · v. 25

3 And Bash′-e-math Ish′-ma-el's daughter, sister of Ne-ba′-joth.

4 And ᴿA′-dah bare to Esau El′-i-phaz; and Bash′-e-math bare Reu′-el;   1 Chr. 1:35

5 And A-hol-i-ba′-mah bare Je′-ush, and Ja-a′-lam, and Ko′-rah: these *are* the sons of Esau, which were born unto him in the land of Canaan.

6 And Esau took his wives, and his sons, and his daughters, and all the persons of his house, and his cattle, and all his beasts, and all his ᵀsubstance, which he had got in the land of Canaan; and went into the country from the face of his brother Jacob.   *goods*

7 For their riches were more than that they might dwell together; and ᴿthe land wherein they were strangers could not bear them because of their cattle.   17:8

8 Thus dwelt Esau in ᴿmount Se′-ir: Esau *is* E′-dom.   Deut. 2:5

9 And these *are* the generations of Esau the father of the E′-dom-ites in mount Se′-ir:

10 These *are* the names of Esau's sons; ᴿEl′-i-phaz the son of A′-dah the wife of Esau, Reu′-el the son of ᵀBash′-e-math the wife of Esau.   1 Chr. 1:35 · Heb. *Basemath*

11 And the sons of El′-i-phaz were Te′-man, Omar, Ze′-pho, and Ga′-tam, and Ke′-naz.

12 And Tim′-na was concubine to El′-i-phaz Esau's son; and she bare to El′-i-phaz ᴿAm′-a-lek: these *were* the sons of A′-dah Esau's wife.   Ex. 17:8-16; Num. 24:20

13 And these *are* the sons of Reu′-el; Na′-hath, and Ze′-rah, Sham′-mah, and Miz′-zah: these were the sons of ᵀBash′-e-math Esau's wife.   Heb. *Basemath*

14 And these were the sons of ᵀA-hol-i-ba′-mah, the daughter of A′-nah the daughter of Zib′-e-on, Esau's wife: and she bare to Esau Je′-ush, and Ja-a′-lam, and Ko′-rah.   Or *Oholibamah*

15 These *were* ᵀdukes of the sons of Esau: the sons of El′-i-phaz the firstborn *son* of Esau; duke Te′-man, duke Omar, duke Ze′-pho, duke Ke′-naz,   *chiefs*

16 Duke Ko′-rah, duke Ga′-tam, *and* duke Am′-a-lek: these *are* the dukes *that came* of El′-i-phaz in the land of E′-dom; these *were* the sons of A′-dah.

17 And these *are* the sons of Reu′-el Esau's son; duke Na′-hath, duke Ze′-rah, duke Sham′-mah, duke Miz′-zah: these *are* the dukes *that came* of Reu′-el in the land of E′-dom; these *are* the sons of Bash′-e-math Esau's wife.

18 And these *are* the sons of A-hol-i-ba′-mah Esau's wife; duke Je′-ush, duke Ja-a′-lam, duke Ko′-rah: these *were* the dukes *that came* of A-hol-i-ba′-mah the daughter of A′-nah, Esau's wife.

19 These *are* the sons of Esau, who *is* E′-dom, and these *are* their dukes.

20 ᴿThese *are* the sons of Se′-ir the Ho′-rite, who inhabited the land; Lo′-tan, and Sho′-bal, and Zib′-e-on, and A′-nah,   1 Chr. 1:38-42

21 And Di′-shon, and E′-zer, and Di′-shan: these *are* the dukes of the Ho′-rites, the children of Se′-ir in the land of E′-dom.

22 And the children of Lo′-tan were Ho′-ri and He′-mam; and Lo′-tan's sister *was* Tim′-na.

23 And the children of Sho′-bal *were* these; Al′-van, and Ma-na′-hath, and E′-bal, She′-pho, and O′-nam.

24 And these *are* the children of Zib′-e-on; both A′-jah, and A′-nah: this *was that* A′-nah that found ᴿthe mules in the wilderness, as he fed the asses of Zib′-e-on his father.   Lev. 19:19

25 And the children of A′-nah *were* these; Di′-shon, and A-hol-i-ba′-mah the daughter of A′-nah.

26 And these *are* the children of Di′-shon; Hem′-dan, and Esh′-ban, and Ith′-ran, and Che′-ran.

27 The children of E′-zer *are* these; Bil′-han, and Za′-a-van, and ᵀA′-kan.   *Jakan,* 1 Chr. 1:42

28 The children of Di′-shan *are* these; [R]Uz, and A′-ran.   Job 1:1

29 These *are* the [T]dukes *that came* of the Ho′-rites; duke Lo′-tan, duke Sho′-bal, duke Zib′-e-on, duke A′-nah,   *chiefs*

30 Duke Di′-shon, duke E′-zer, duke Di′-shan: these *are* the dukes *that came* of Ho′-ri, among their dukes in the land of Se′-ir.

31 And [R]these *are* the kings that reigned in the land of E′-dom, before there reigned any king over the children of Israel.   17:6, 16

32 And Be′-la the son of Be′-or reigned in E′-dom: and the name of his city *was* Din′-ha-bah.

33 And Be′-la died, and Jo′-bab the son of Ze′-rah of Boz′-rah reigned in his stead.

34 And Jo′-bab died, and Hu′-sham of the land of Tem′-a-ni reigned in his stead.

35 And Hu′-sham died, and Ha′-dad the son of Be′-dad, who smote Mid′-i-an in the field of Moab, reigned in his stead: and the name of his city *was* A′-vith.

36 And Ha′-dad died, and Sam′-lah of Mas-re′-kah reigned in his stead.

37 And Sam′-lah died, and Saul of [R]Re-ho′-both *by* the river reigned in his stead.   10:11

38 And Saul died, and Ba′-al-ha′-nan the son of Ach′-bor reigned in his stead.

39 And Ba′-al–ha′-nan the son of Ach′-bor died, and Ha′-dar reigned in his stead: and the name of his city *was* Pa′-u; and his wife's name *was* Me-het′-a-bel, the daughter of Ma′-tred, the daughter of Mez′-a-hab.

40 And these *are* the names of the dukes *that came* of Esau, according to their families, after their places, by their names; duke Tim′-nah, duke [T]Al′-vah, duke Je′-theth,   *Aliah,* 1 Chr. 1:51

41 Duke [T]A-hol-i-ba′-mah, duke E′-lah, duke Pi′-non,   Or *Oholibamah*

42 Duke Ke′-naz, duke Te′-man, duke Mib′-zar,

43 Duke Mag′-di-el, duke I′-ram: these *be* the dukes of E′-dom,

according to their habitations in the land of their possession: he *is* Esau the father of the E′-dom-ites.

37 And Jacob dwelt in the land wherein his father was a stranger, in the land of Canaan.

2 These *are* the generations of Jacob. Joseph, *being* seventeen years old, was feeding the flock with his brethren; and the lad *was* with the sons of Bil′-hah, and with the sons of Zil′-pah, his father's wives: and Joseph brought unto his father [R]their evil report.   35:25

3 Now Israel loved Joseph more than all his children, because he *was* the son of his old age: and he [R]made him a coat of *many* colours.   Judg. 5:30; 1 Sam. 2:19

4 And when his brethren saw that their father loved him more than all his brethren, they [R]hated him, and could not speak peaceably unto him.   1 Sam. 17:28

5 And Joseph dreamed a dream, and he told *it* his brethren: and they hated him yet the more.

6 And he said unto them, Hear, I pray you, this dream which I have dreamed:

7 For, [R]behold, we *were* binding sheaves in the field, and, lo, my sheaf arose, and also stood upright; and, behold, your sheaves stood round about, and made obeisance to my sheaf.   42:6

8 And his brethren said to him, Shalt thou indeed reign over us? or shalt thou indeed have dominion over us? And they hated him yet the more for his dreams, and for his words.

9 And he dreamed yet another dream, and told it his brethren, and said, Behold, I have dreamed a dream more; and, behold, [R]the sun and the moon and the eleven stars made obeisance to me.   46:29

10 And he told *it* to his father, and to his brethren: and his father rebuked him, and said unto him, What *is* this dream that thou hast dreamed? Shall I and thy mother and [R]thy brethren indeed come to bow down ourselves to thee to the earth?   27:29

11 And his brethren envied him; but his father ᵀobserved the saying. *kept the matter* in mind

12 And his brethren went to feed their father's flock in ᴿShe'-chem. 33:18–20

13 And Israel said unto Joseph, Do not thy brethren feed *the flock* in She'-chem? come, and I will send thee unto them. And he said to him, Here *am* I.

14 And he said to him, Go, I pray thee, see whether it be well with thy brethren, and well with the flocks; and bring me word again. So he sent him out of the vale of ᴿHe'-bron, and he came to She'-chem. 23:2, 19; 35:27; Josh. 14:14, 15

15 And a certain man found him, and, behold, *he was* wandering in the field: and the man asked him, saying, What seekest thou?

16 And he said, I seek my brethren: tell me, I pray thee, where they feed *their flocks*.

17 And the man said, They are departed hence; for I heard them say, Let us go to Do'-than. And Joseph went after his brethren, and found them in Do'-than.

18 And when they saw him afar off, even before he came near unto them, ᴿthey conspired against him to slay him. Matt. 21:38

19 And they said one to another, Behold, this dreamer cometh.

20 ᴿCome now therefore, and let us slay him, and cast him into some pit, and we will say, Some evil beast hath devoured him: and we shall see what will become of his dreams. 37:22; Prov. 1:11

21 And ᴿReuben heard *it,* and he delivered him out of their hands; and said, Let us not kill him. 42:22

22 And Reuben said unto them, Shed no blood, *but* cast him into this pit that *is* in the wilderness, and lay no hand upon him; that he might rid him out of their hands, to deliver him to his father again.

23 And it came to pass, when Joseph was come unto his brethren, that they ᴿstript Joseph out of his coat, *his* coat of *many* colours that *was* on him; Matt. 27:28

24 And they took him, and cast him into a pit: and the pit *was* empty, *there was* no water in it.

25 And they sat down to eat bread: and they lifted up their eyes and looked, and, behold, a company of ᴿIsh'-me-el-ites came from Gil'-e-ad with their camels bearing spicery and ᴿbalm and myrrh, going to carry *it* down to Egypt. vv. 28, 36; 16:11, 12; 39:1 · Jer. 8:22

26 And Judah said unto his brethren, What profit *is it* if we slay our brother, and ᴿconceal his blood? v. 20

27 Come, and let us sell him to the Ish'-me-el-ites, and let not our hand be upon him; for he *is* ᴿour brother *and* ᴿour flesh. And his brethren were content. 42:21 · 29:14

28 Then there passed by ᴿMid'-i-an-ites merchantmen; and they drew and lifted up Joseph out of the pit, and sold Joseph to the Ish'-me-el-ites for ᴿtwenty *pieces* of silver: and they brought Joseph into Egypt. v. 25; Judg. 6:1–3 · Matt. 27:9

29 And Reuben returned unto the pit; and, behold, Joseph *was* not in the pit; and he ᴿrentᵀ his clothes. v. 34; 44:13; Job 1:20 · *tore*

30 And he returned unto his brethren, and said, The ᵀchild *is* not; and I, whither shall I go? *lad*

31 And they took ᴿJoseph's coat, and killed a kid of the goats, and dipped the coat in the blood; v. 3

32 And they sent the coat of *many* colours, and they brought *it* to their father; and said, This have we found: ᵀknow now whether it *be* thy son's coat or no. *do you know*

33 And he knew it, and said, It *is* my son's coat; an ᴿevilᵀ beast hath devoured him; Joseph is without doubt rent in pieces. v. 20 · *wild*

34 And Jacob ᴿrentᵀ his clothes, and put sackcloth upon his loins, and ᴿmourned for his son many days. v. 29; 2 Sam. 3:31 · *tore* · 50:10

35 And all his sons and all his daughters ᴿrose up to comfort him; but he refused to be comforted; and he said, For ᴿI will go

down into the grave unto my son mourning. Thus his father wept for him. 2 Sam. 12:17 · 42:38; 44:29, 31

36 And [R]the Mid'-i-an-ites sold him into Egypt unto Pot'-i-phar, an officer of Pharaoh's, *and* captain of the guard. 39:1

38 And it came to pass at that time, that Judah went down from his brethren, and [R]turned in to a certain A-dul'-lam-ite, whose name *was* Hi'-rah. 2 Kin. 4:8

2 And Judah [R]saw there a daughter of a certain Ca'-naan-ite, whose name *was* [T]Shu'-ah; and he [T]took her, and went in unto her. 34:2 · Heb. *Shua;* 1 Chr. 2:3 · *married*

3 And she conceived, and bare a son; and he called his name Er.

4 And she conceived again, and bare a son; and she called his name [R]O'-nan. 46:12; Num. 26:19

5 And she yet again conceived, and bare a son; and called his name She'-lah: and he was at Che'-zib, when she bare him.

6 And Judah [R]took a wife for Er his firstborn, whose name *was* [R]Ta'-mar. 21:21 · Ruth 4:12

7 And Er, Judah's firstborn, was wicked in the sight of the LORD; and the LORD slew him.

8 And Judah said unto O'-nan, Go in unto [R]thy brother's wife, and marry her, and raise up seed to thy brother. Deut. 25:5, 6; Matt. 22:24

9 And O'-nan knew that the seed should not be his; and it came to pass, when he went in unto his brother's wife, that he spilled *it* on the ground, lest that he should give seed to his brother.

10 And the thing which he did displeased the LORD: wherefore he slew [R]him also. 46:12; Num. 26:19

11 Then said Judah to Ta'-mar his daughter in law, Remain a widow at thy father's house, till She'-lah my son be grown: for he said, Lest peradventure he die also, as his brethren *did.* And Ta'-mar went and dwelt [R]in her father's house. Lev. 22:13

12 And in process of time the daughter of Shu'-ah Judah's wife died; and Judah was comforted,

and went up unto his sheepshearers to Tim'-nath, he and his friend Hi'-rah the A-dul'-lam-ite.

13 And it was told Ta'-mar, saying, Behold thy father in law goeth up [R]to Tim'-nath to shear his sheep. Josh. 15:10, 57; Judg. 14:1

14 And she put her widow's garments off from her, and covered her with a vail, and wrapped herself, and [R]sat in an open place, which *is* by the way to Tim'-nath; for she saw [R]that She'-lah was grown, and she was not given unto him to wife. Prov. 7:12 · vv. 11, 26

15 When Judah saw her, he thought her *to be* an harlot; because she had covered her face.

16 And he turned unto her by the way, and said, Go to, I pray thee, let me come in unto thee; (for he knew not that she *was* his daughter in law.) And she said, What wilt thou give me, that thou mayest come in unto me?

17 And he said, [R]I will send *thee* a kid from the flock. And she said, Wilt thou give *me* a pledge, till thou send *it?* Judg. 15:1; Ezek. 16:33

18 And he said, What pledge shall I give thee? And she said, [R]Thy signet, and thy [T]bracelets, and thy staff that *is* in thine hand. And he gave *it* her, and came in unto her, and she conceived by him. v. 25; 41:42 · *cord*

19 And she arose, and went away, and [R]laid by her vail from her, and put on the garments of her widowhood. v. 14

20 And Judah sent the kid by the hand of his friend the A-dul'-lam-ite, to receive *his* pledge from the woman's hand: but he found her not.

21 Then he asked the men of that place, saying, Where *is* the harlot, that *was* openly by the way side? And they said, There was no harlot in this *place.*

22 And he returned to Judah, and said, I cannot find her; and also the men of the place said, *that* there was no harlot in this *place.*

23 And Judah said, Let her take

it to her, lest we be shamed: behold, I sent this kid, and thou hast not found her.

24 And it came to pass about three months after, that it was told Judah, saying, Ta′-mar thy daughter in law hath played the harlot; and also, behold, she *is* with child by whoredom. And Judah said, Bring her forth, ᴿand let her be burnt.   Lev. 20:14; 21:9; Deut. 22:21

25 When she *was* brought forth, she sent to her father in law, saying, By the man, whose these *are*, *am* I with child: and she said, ᴿDiscern, I pray thee, whose *are* these, the signet, and ᵀbracelets, and staff.   v. 18; 37:32 · *cord*

26 And Judah ᴿacknowledged *them,* and said, ᴿShe hath been more righteous than I; because that I gave her not to She′-lah my son. And he knew her again ᴿno more.   37:33 · 1 Sam. 24:17 · Job 34:31, 32

27 And it came to pass in the time of her travail, that, behold, twins *were* in her womb.

28 And it came to pass, when she travailed, that *the one* put out *his* hand: and the midwife took and bound upon his hand a scarlet thread, saying, This came out first.

29 And it came to pass, as he drew back his hand, that, behold, his brother came out: and she said, How hast thou broken forth? *this* breach *be* upon thee: therefore his name was called ᴿPha′-rez.   46:12; Ruth 4:12; 1 Chr. 2:4; Matt. 1:3

30 And afterward came out his brother, that had the scarlet thread upon his hand: and his name was called Zar′-ah.

39 And Joseph was brought down to Egypt; and ᴿPot′-i-phar, an officer of Pharaoh, captain of the guard, an Egyptian, bought him of the hands of the Ish′-me-el-ites, which had brought him down thither.   37:36; Ps. 105:17

2 And ᴿthe LORD was with Joseph, and he was a prosperous man; and he was in the house of his master the Egyptian.   Acts 7:9

3 And his master saw that the LORD *was* with him, and that the LORD ᴿmade all that he did to prosper in his hand.   Ps. 1:3

4 And Joseph ᴿfound grace in his sight, and he served him: and he made him ᴿoverseer over his house, and all *that* he had he put into his hand.   18:3; 19:19 · 24:2; 41:40

5 And it came to pass from the time *that* he had made him overseer in his house, and over all that he had, that ᴿthe LORD blessed the Egyptian's house for Joseph's sake; and the blessing of the LORD was upon all that he had in the house, and in the field.   2 Sam. 6:11

6 And he left all that he had in Joseph's hand; and he knew not ought he had, save the bread which he did eat. And Joseph ᴿwas *a* ᵀgoodly *person,* and well favoured.   29:17; 1 Sam. 16:12 · *handsome*

7 And it came to pass after these things, that his master's wife cast her eyes upon Joseph; and she said, Lie with me.

8 But he refused, and said unto his master's wife, Behold, my master ᵀwotteth not what *is* with me in the house, and he hath committed all that he hath to my hand;   *knows*

9 *There is* none greater in this house than I; neither hath he kept back any thing from me but thee, because thou *art* his wife: how then can I do this great wickedness, and ᴿsin against God? Ps. 51:4

10 And it came to pass, as she spake to Joseph day by day, that he hearkened ᴿnot unto her, to lie by her, *or* to be with her.   Prov. 1:10

11 And it came to pass about this time, that *Joseph* went into the house to do his ᵀbusiness; and *there was* none of the men of the house there within.   *work*

12 And she ᴿcaught him by his garment, saying, Lie with me: and he left his garment in her hand, and fled, and got him out. Prov. 7:13

13 And it came to pass, when she saw that he had left his garment in her hand, and was fled ᵀforth,   *outside*

14 That she called unto the men

of her house, and spake unto them, saying, See, he hath brought in an [R]Hebrew unto us to [T]mock us; he came in unto me to lie with me, and I cried with a loud voice: 14:13; 41:12 · *laugh at*

15 And it came to pass, when he heard that I lifted up my voice and cried, that he left his garment with me, and fled, and got him out.

16 And she laid up his garment by her, until his lord came home.

17 And she [R]spake unto him according to these words, saying, The Hebrew servant, which thou hast brought unto us, came in unto me to mock me: Ex. 23:1

18 And it came to pass, as I lifted up my voice and cried, that he left his garment with me, and fled out.

19 And it came to pass, when his master heard the words of his wife, which she spake unto him, saying, After this manner did thy servant to me; that his [R]wrath was kindled.   Prov. 6:34, 35

20 And Joseph's master took him, and [R]put him into the prison, a place where the king's prisoners *were* bound: and he was there in the prison.   Ps. 105:18; [1 Pet. 2:19]

21 But the LORD was with Joseph, and shewed him mercy, and [R]gave him favour in the sight of the keeper of the prison. Acts 7:9, 10

22 And the keeper of the prison [R]committed to Joseph's hand all the prisoners that *were* in the prison; and whatsoever they did there, he was the doer *of it*.   v. 4

23 The keeper of the prison [T]looked not to any thing *that was* under his hand; because [R]the LORD was with him, and *that* which he did, the LORD made *it* to prosper.   *did not look into* · vv. 2, 3

40 And it came to pass after these things, *that* the [R]butler of the king of Egypt and *his* baker had offended their lord the king of Egypt.   vv. 11, 13; Neh. 1:11

2 And Pharaoh was wroth against two *of* his officers, against the chief of the butlers, and against the chief of the bakers.

3 [R]And he put them in ward in the house of the captain of the guard, into the prison, the place where Joseph *was* bound.   41:10

4 And the captain of the guard charged Joseph with them, and he served them: and they continued [T]a season in ward.   *in custody awhile*

5 And they [R]dreamed a dream both of them, each man his dream in one night, each man according to the interpretation of his dream, the butler and the baker of the king of Egypt, which *were* bound in the prison.   37:5; 41:1

6 And Joseph came in unto them in the morning, and looked upon them, and, behold, they *were* [T]sad.   *dejected*

7 And he asked Pharaoh's officers that *were* with him in the ward of his lord's house, saying, [R]Wherefore look ye *so* sadly to day?   Neh. 2:2

8 And they said unto him, We have dreamed a dream, and *there is* no interpreter of it. And Joseph said unto them, [R]Do not interpretations *belong* to God? tell me *them*, I pray you. [41:16; Dan. 2:11–47]

9 And the chief butler told his dream to Joseph, and said to him, In my dream, behold, a vine *was* before me;

10 And in the vine *were* three branches: and it *was* as though it budded, *and* her blossoms shot forth; and the clusters thereof brought forth ripe grapes:

11 And Pharaoh's cup *was* in my hand: and I took the grapes, and pressed them into Pharaoh's cup, and I gave the cup into Pharaoh's hand.

12 And Joseph said unto him, [R]This *is* the interpretation of it: The three branches [R]*are* three days: Judg. 7:14; Dan. 2:36; 4:18, 19 · 42:17

13 Yet within three days shall Pharaoh [R]lift up thine head, and restore thee unto thy place: and thou shalt deliver Pharaoh's cup into his hand, after the former manner when thou wast his butler.   2 Kin. 25:27; Ps. 3:3; Jer. 52:31

14 But [R]think on me when it shall be well with thee, and [R]shew kindness, I pray thee, unto me, and make mention of me unto Pharaoh, and bring me out of this house:　Luke 23:42 · Josh. 2:12; 1 Kin. 2:7

15 For indeed I was [R]stolen away out of the land of the Hebrews: [R]and here also have I done nothing that they should put me into the dungeon.　37:26–28 · 39:20

16 When the chief baker saw that the interpretation was good, he said unto Joseph, I also *was* in my dream, and, behold, *I had* three white baskets on my head:

17 And in the uppermost basket *there was* of all manner of [T]bakemeats for Pharaoh; and the birds did eat them out of the basket upon my head.　*baked goods*

18 And Joseph answered and said, [R]This *is* the interpretation thereof: The three baskets *are* three days:　v. 12

19 Yet within three days shall Pharaoh lift up thy head from off thee, and shall [R]hang thee on a tree; and the birds shall eat thy flesh from off thee.　Deut. 21:22

20 And it came to pass the third day, *which was* Pharaoh's birthday, that he made a feast unto all his servants: and he lifted up the head of the chief butler and of the chief baker among his servants.

21 And he [R]restored the chief butler unto his butlership again; and [R]he gave the cup into Pharaoh's hand:　v. 13 · Neh. 2:1

22 But he [R]hanged the chief baker: as Joseph had interpreted to them.　v. 19; Deut. 21:23; Esth. 7:10

23 Yet did not the chief butler remember Joseph, but [R]forgat him.　Ps. 31:12; Is. 49:15; Amos 6:6

41 And it came to pass at the end of two full years, that [R]Pharaoh dreamed: and, behold, he stood by the river.　40:5; Judg. 7:13

2 And, behold, there came up out of the river seven well favoured [T]kine and fatfleshed; and they fed in a meadow.　*cows*

3 And, behold, seven other kine came up after them out of the river, ill favoured and leanfleshed; and stood by the *other* kine upon the [T]brink of the river.　*bank*

4 And the [T]ill favoured and leanfleshed kine did eat up the seven well favoured and fat kine. So Pharaoh awoke.　*ugly and gaunt*

5 And he slept and dreamed the second time: and, behold, seven ears of corn came up upon one stalk, [T]rank and good.　*plump*

6 And, behold, seven thin [T]ears and blasted with the east wind sprung up after them.　*heads of grain*

7 And the seven thin ears devoured the seven rank and full ears. And Pharaoh awoke, and, behold, *it was* a dream.

8 And it came to pass in the morning that his spirit was troubled; and he sent and called for all [R]the magicians of Egypt, and all the wise men thereof: and Pharaoh told them his dream; but *there was* none that could interpret them unto Pharaoh.　Ex. 7:11

9 Then spake the chief butler unto Pharaoh, saying, I do remember my faults this day:

10 Pharaoh was wroth with his servants, and put me in ward in the captain of the guard's house, *both* me and the chief baker:

11 And [R]we dreamed a dream in one night, I and he; we dreamed each man according to the interpretation of his dream.　Judg. 7:15

12 And *there was* there with us a young man, [R]an Hebrew, [R]servant to the captain of the guard; and we told him, and he [R]interpreted to us our dreams; to each man according to his dream he did interpret.　39:14; 43:32 · 37:36 · 40:12

13 And it came to pass, [R]as he interpreted to us, so it was; me he restored unto mine office, and him he hanged.　40:21, 22

14 Then Pharaoh sent and called Joseph, and they brought him hastily [R]out of the dungeon: and he shaved *himself,* and changed his raiment, and came in unto Pharaoh.　[1 Sam. 2:8]

15 And Pharaoh said unto Joseph, I have dreamed a dream,

and *there is* none that can interpret it: ^Rand I have heard say of thee, *that* thou canst understand a dream to interpret it.   Dan. 5:16

16 And Joseph answered Pharaoh, saying, ^R*It is* not in me: God shall give Pharaoh an answer of peace.   Dan. 2:30; Acts 3:12; [2 Cor. 3:5]

17 And Pharaoh said unto Joseph, In my dream, behold, I stood upon the bank of the river:

18 And, behold, there came up out of the river seven ^Tkine, fatfleshed and well favoured; and they fed in a meadow: *cows*

19 And, behold, seven other kine came up after them, poor and very ill favoured and leanfleshed, such as I never saw in all the land of Egypt for ^Tbadness: *ugliness*

20 And the lean and the ill favoured kine did eat up the first seven fat kine:

21 And when they had eaten them up, it could not be known that they had eaten them; but they *were* still ^Till favoured, as at the beginning. So I awoke.   *ugly*

22 And I saw in my dream, and, behold, seven ears came up in one stalk, full and good:

23 And, behold, seven ^Tears, withered, thin, *and* ^Tblasted with the east wind, sprung up after them: *heads · blighted*

24 And the thin ears devoured the seven good ears: and ^RI told *this* unto the magicians; but *there was* none that could declare *it* to me.   v. 8; Ex. 7:11; Is. 8:19; Dan. 4:7

25 And Joseph said unto Pharaoh, The dream of Pharaoh *is* one: ^RGod hath shewed Pharaoh what he *is* about to do.   Dan. 2:28, 29

26 The seven good kine *are* seven years; and the seven good ears *are* seven years: the dream *is* one.

27 And the seven thin and ill favoured kine that came up after them *are* seven years; and the seven empty ears blasted with the east wind shall be ^Rseven years of famine.   2 Kin. 8:1

28 ^RThis *is* the thing which I have spoken unto Pharaoh: What

God *is* about to do he sheweth unto Pharaoh.   [vv. 25, 32; Dan. 2:28]

29 Behold, there come ^Rseven years of great plenty throughout all the land of Egypt: v. 47

30 And there shall arise after them seven years of famine; and all the plenty shall be forgotten in the land of Egypt; and the famine ^Rshall consume the land;   Ps. 105:16

31 And the plenty shall not be known in the land by reason of that famine following; for it *shall be* very grievous.

32 And for that the dream was ^Tdoubled unto Pharaoh twice; *it is* because the ^Rthing *is* established by God, and God will shortly bring it to pass.   *repeated* · Num. 23:19

33 Now therefore let Pharaoh look out a man ^Tdiscreet and wise, and set him over the land of Egypt.   *discerning*

34 Let Pharaoh do *this*, and let him appoint officers over the land, and ^Rtake up the fifth part of the land of Egypt in the seven plenteous years.   [Prov. 6:6–8]

35 And let them gather all the food of those good years that come, and lay up corn under the ^Thand of Pharaoh, and let them keep food in the cities.   *authority*

36 And that food shall be for ^Tstore to the land against the seven years of famine, which shall be in the land of Egypt; that the land ^Rperish not through the famine.   *a reserve for* · 47:15, 19

37 And ^Rthe thing was good in the eyes of Pharaoh, and in the eyes of all his servants.   Ps. 105:19

38 And Pharaoh said unto his servants, Can we find *such a one* as this *is*, a man ^Rin whom the Spirit of God *is*?   Num. 27:18; Dan. 6:3

39 And Pharaoh said unto Joseph, Forasmuch as God hath shewed thee all this, *there is* none so discreet and wise as thou *art:*

40 ^RThou shalt be over my house, and according unto thy word shall all my people be ruled: only in the throne will I be greater than thou.   Ps. 105:21; Acts 7:10

41 And Pharaoh said unto Jo-

seph, See, I have ᴿset thee over all the land of Egypt.   Dan. 6:3

42 And Pharaoh took off his ring from his hand, and put it upon Joseph's hand, and ᴿarrayed him in ᵀvestures of fine linen, ᴿand put a gold chain about his neck;   Esth. 8:2, 15 · *garments* · Dan. 5:7

43 And he made him to ride in the second chariot which he had; ᴿand they cried before him, Bow the knee: and he made him *ruler* over all the land of Egypt. Esth. 6:9

44 And Pharaoh said unto Joseph, I *am* Pharaoh, and without thee shall no man lift up his hand or foot in all the land of Egypt.

45 And Pharaoh called Joseph's name Zaph'-nath-pa-a-ne'-ah; and he gave him to wife As'-e-nath the daughter of Pot-i-phe'-rah priest of On. And Joseph went out over *all* the land of Egypt.

46 And Joseph *was* thirty years old when he ᴿstood before Pharaoh king of Egypt. And Joseph went out from the presence of Pharaoh, and went throughout all the land of Egypt.   1 Sam. 16:21

47 And in the seven plenteous years the earth brought forth ᵀby handfuls.   Abundantly

48 And he gathered up all the food of the seven years, which were in the land of Egypt, and laid up the food in the cities: the food of the field, which *was* round about every city, laid he up in the same.

49 And Joseph gathered corn as the sand of the sea, very much, until he ᵀleft numbering; for *it was* without number.   *stopped*

50 ᴿAnd unto Joseph were born two sons before the years of famine came, which As'-e-nath the daughter of Pot-i-phe'-rah priest of On bare unto him.   48:5

51 And Joseph called the name of the firstborn Ma-nas'-seh: For God, *said he*, hath made me forget all my toil, and all my ᴿfather's house.   Ps. 45:10

52 And the name of the second called he E'-phra-im: For God hath caused me to be ᴿfruitful in the land of my affliction.   49:22

53 And the seven years of plenteousness, that was in the land of Egypt, were ended.

54 And the seven years of dearth began to come, according as Joseph had said: and the dearth was in all lands; but in all the land of Egypt there was bread.

55 And when all the land of Egypt was famished, the people cried to Pharaoh for bread: and Pharaoh said unto all the Egyptians, Go unto Joseph; ᴿwhat he saith to you, do.   John 2:5

56 And the famine was over all the face of the earth: And Joseph opened all the storehouses, and ᴿsold unto the Egyptians; and the famine ᵀwaxed sore in the land of Egypt.   42:6 · *became severe*

57 ᴿAnd all countries came into Egypt to Joseph for to ᴿbuy *corn;* because that the famine was *so* sore in all lands. Ezek. 29:12 · 27:28, 37

42 Now when Jacob saw that there was corn in Egypt, Jacob said unto his sons, Why do ye look one upon another?

2 And he said, Behold, I have heard that there is corn in Egypt: get you down thither, and buy for us from thence; that we may ᴿlive, and not die.   Ps. 33:18, 19; Is. 38:1

3 And Joseph's ten brethren went down to buy corn in Egypt.

4 But Benjamin, Joseph's brother, Jacob sent not with his brethren; for he said, ᴿLest peradventure mischief befall him.   v. 38

5 And the sons of Israel came to buy *corn* among those that came: for the famine was ᴿin the land of Canaan.   26:1; Acts 7:11

6 And Joseph *was* the governor ᴿover the land, *and he it was* that sold to all the people of the land: and Joseph's brethren came, and ᴿbowed down themselves before him *with* their faces to the earth. 41:41, 55 · 37:7–10; 41:43; Is. 60:14

7 And Joseph saw his brethren, and he knew them, but made himself ᵀstrange unto them, and spake roughly unto them; and he said unto them, Whence come ye?

And they said, From the land of Canaan to buy food. *a stranger*

8 And Joseph knew his brethren, but they knew not him.

9 And Joseph remembered the dreams which he dreamed of them, and said unto them, Ye *are* spies; to see the ᵀnakedness of the land ye are come. *exposed parts*

10 And they said unto him, Nay, my lord, but to buy food are thy servants come.

11 We *are* all one man's sons; we *are* ᵀtrue *men,* thy servants are no spies. *honest*

12 And he said unto them, Nay, but to see the nakedness of the land ye are come.

13 And they said, Thy servants *are* twelve brethren, the sons of one man in the land of Canaan; and, behold, the youngest *is* this day with our father, and one ᴿ*is* ᵀnot. v. 32; 44:20; Lam. 5:7 · *no more*

14 And Joseph said unto them, That *is it* that I spake unto you, saying, Ye *are* spies:

15 Hereby ye shall be proved: By the life of Pharaoh ye shall not go forth hence, except your youngest brother come hither.

16 Send one of you, and let him fetch your brother, and ye shall be kept in prison, that your words may be proved, whether *there be any* truth in you: or else by the life of Pharaoh surely ye *are* spies.

17 And he put them all together into ᵀward ᴿthree days. *prison* · 40:4

18 And Joseph said unto them the third day, This do, and live; ᴿ*for* I fear God: Ex. 1:17; Neh. 5:15

19 If ye *be* true *men,* let one of your brethren be bound in the house of your prison: go ye, carry corn for the famine of your houses:

20 But ᴿbring your youngest brother unto me; so shall your words be verified, and ye shall not die. And they did so. 43:5; 44:23

21 And they said one to another, We *are* verily guilty concerning our brother, in that we saw the anguish of his soul, when he besought us, and we would not

hear; ᴿtherefore is this distress come upon us. Prov. 21:13; Matt. 7:2

22 And Reuben answered them, saying, Spake I not unto you, saying, Do not sin against the child; and ye would not hear? therefore, behold, also his blood is ᴿrequired. Ps. 9:12; Luke 11:50, 51

23 And they knew not that Joseph understood *them;* for he spake unto them by an interpreter.

24 And he turned himself ᵀabout from them, and wept; and returned to them again, and ᵀcommuned with them, and took from them ᴿSimeon, and bound him before their eyes. *away* · *talked* · 34:25

25 Then Joseph ᴿcommanded to fill their sacks with corn, and to restore every man's money into his sack, and to give them provision for the way: and ᴿthus did he unto them. 44:1 · [Rom. 12:17, 20, 21]

26 And they laded their asses with the corn, and departed thence.

27 And as ᴿone of them opened his sack to give his ass ᵀprovender in the inn, he ᵀespied his money; for, behold, it *was* in his sack's mouth. 43:21, 22 · *feed* · *saw*

28 And he said unto his brethren, My money is restored; and, lo, *it is* even in my sack: and ᵀtheir heart failed *them,* and they were afraid, saying one to another, What *is* this *that* God hath done unto us? *their hearts sank*

29 And they came unto Jacob their father unto the land of Canaan, and told him all that befell unto them; saying,

30 The man, *who is* the lord of the land, ᴿspake ᵀroughly to us, and took us for spies of the country. v. 7 · *harshly*

31 And we said unto him, We *are* ᵀtrue *men;* we are no spies: *honest*

32 We *be* twelve brethren, sons of our father; one *is* not, and the youngest *is* this day with our father in the land of Canaan.

33 And the man, the lord of the country, said unto us, ᴿHereby shall I know that ye *are* ᵀtrue *men;* leave one of your brethren *here*

with me, and take *food for* the famine of your households, and be gone: vv. 15, 19, 20 · *honest*

34 And bring your youngest brother unto me: then shall I know that ye *are* no spies, but *that* ye *are* true *men: so* will I deliver you your brother, and ye shall Ttraffick in the land.   *trade*

35 And it came to pass as they emptied their sacks, that, behold, every man's bundle of money *was* in his sack: and when *both* they and their father saw the bundles of money, they were afraid.

36 And Jacob their father said unto them, Me have ye Rbereaved *of my children:* Joseph *is* not, and Simeon *is* not, and ye will take RBenjamin *away:* all these things are against me.   43:14 · 35:18

37 And Reuben spake unto his father, saying, Slay my two sons, if I bring him not to thee: deliver him into my hand, and I will bring him to thee again.

38 And he said, My son shall not go down with you; for his brother is dead, and he is left alone: if Tmischief befall him by the way in the which ye go, then shall ye Rbring down my gray hairs with sorrow to the grave.   *calamity* · 44:31

43 And the famine *was* Rsore^T in the land.   45:6, 11 · *severe*

2 And it came to pass, when they had eaten up the corn which they had brought out of Egypt, their father said unto them, Go Ragain, buy us a little food.   44:25

3 And Judah spake unto him, saying, The man did solemnly Tprotest unto us, saying, Ye shall not see my face, except your brother *be* with you.   Lit. *warn*

4 If thou wilt send our brother with us, we will go down and buy thee food:

5 But if thou wilt not send *him,* we will not go down: for the man said unto us, Ye shall not see my face, except your brother *be* with you.

6 And Israel said, Wherefore dealt ye *so* Till with me, *as* to tell the man whether ye had yet a brother?   *wickedly*

7 And they said, The man asked us Tstraitly of our state, and of our kindred, saying, *Is* your father yet alive? have ye *another* brother? and we told him according to the tenor of these words: could we certainly know that he would say, Bring your brother down?   *pointedly about ourselves*

8 And Judah said unto Israel his father, Send the lad with me, and we will arise and go; that we may live, and not die, both we, and thou, *and* also our little ones.

9 I will be surety for him; of my hand shalt thou require him: Rif I bring him not unto thee, and set him before thee, then let me bear the blame for ever: Philem. 18, 19

10 For except we had lingered, surely now we had returned this second time.

11 And their father Israel said unto them, If *it must be* so now, do this; take of the best fruits in the land in your vessels, and carry down the man a present, a little balm, and a little honey, spices, and myrrh, nuts, and almonds:

12 And take double money in your hand; and the money Rthat was brought again in the mouth of your sacks, carry *it* again in your hand; peradventure it *was* an oversight: vv. 21, 22; 42:25, 35

13 Take also your brother, and arise, go again unto the man:

14 And God Almighty Rgive you mercy before the man, that he may send away your other brother, and Benjamin. RIf I be bereaved *of my children,* I am bereaved.   Ps. 106:46 · 42:36; Esth. 4:16

15 And the men took that present, and they took double money in their hand, and Benjamin; and rose up, and went Rdown to Egypt, and stood before Joseph.   46:3, 6

16 And when Joseph saw Benjamin with them, he said to the ruler of his house, Bring *these* men home, and Tslay, and make ready; for *these* men shall dine with me at noon.   *slaughter an animal*

17 And the man did as Joseph ^Tbade; and the man brought the men into Joseph's house.   *ordered*

18 And the men were afraid, because they were brought into Joseph's house; and they said, Because of the money that was returned in our sacks at the first time are we brought in; that he may seek occasion against us, and fall upon us, and take us ^Tfor bondmen, and our asses.   *as slaves*

19 And they came near to the steward of Joseph's house, and they communed with him at the door of the house,

20 And said, O sir, ^Rwe came indeed down at the first time to buy food: 42:3, 10

21 And it came to pass, when we came to the ^Tinn, that we opened our sacks, and, behold, *every* man's money *was* in the mouth of his sack, our money in full weight: and we have brought it again in our hand.   *encampment*

22 And other money have we brought down in our hands to buy food: we cannot tell who put our money in our sacks.

23 And he said, Peace *be* to you, fear not: your God, and the God of your father, hath given you treasure in your sacks: I had your money. And he brought ^RSimeon out unto them.   42:24

24 And the man brought the men into Joseph's house, and ^Rgave *them* water, and they washed their feet; and he gave their asses provender.   19:2; 24:32

25 And they made ready the present against Joseph ^Tcame at noon: for they heard that they should eat bread there.   *coming*

26 And when Joseph came home, they brought him the present which *was* in their hand into the house, and ^Rbowed themselves to him to the earth.   44:14

27 And he asked them of *their* welfare, and said, *Is* your father well, the old man ^Rof whom ye spake? *Is* he yet alive?   42:11, 13

28 And they answered, Thy servant our father *is* in good health,

he *is* yet alive. And they bowed down their heads, and ^Tmade obeisance.   *prostrated themselves*

29 And he lifted up his eyes, and saw his brother Benjamin, ^Rhis mother's son, and said, *Is* this your younger brother, ^Rof whom ye spake unto me? And he said, God be gracious unto thee, my son.   35:17, 18 · 42:13

30 And Joseph made haste; for his ^Tbowels did yearn upon his brother: and he sought *where* to weep; and he entered into *his* chamber, and wept there.   *heart*

31 And he washed his face, and went out, and refrained himself, and said, ^TSet on bread.   *Serve*

32 And they ^Tset on for him by himself, and for them by themselves, and for the Egyptians, which did eat with him, by themselves: because the Egyptians might not eat bread with the Hebrews; for that *is* an abomination unto the Egyptians.   *set a place*

33 And they sat before him, the firstborn according to his ^Rbirthright, and the youngest according to his youth: and the men marvelled one at another.   Deut. 21:16, 17

34 And he took *and sent* ^Tmesses unto them from before him: but Benjamin's mess was ^Rfive times so much as any of theirs. And they drank, and were merry with him.   *servings* · 35:24; 45:22

44 And he commanded the ^Rsteward of his house, saying, ^RFill the men's sacks *with* food, as much as they can carry, and put every man's money in his sack's mouth.   43:16 · 42:25

2 And put my cup, the silver cup, in the sack's mouth of the youngest, and his ^Tcorn money. And he did according to the word that Joseph had spoken.   *grain*

3 As soon as the morning was light, the men were sent away, they and their ^Tasses.   *donkeys*

4 *And* when they were gone out of the city, *and* not *yet* far off, Joseph said unto his steward, Up, follow after the men; and when thou dost overtake them, say unto

them, Wherefore have ye ᴿreward-
ed evil for good? 1 Sam. 25:21

5 *Is* not this *it* in which my lord
drinketh, and whereby indeed he
ᵀdivineth? ye have done evil in so
doing. *practises divination*

6 And he overtook them, and
he spake unto them these same
words.

7 And they said unto him,
Wherefore saith my lord these
words? ᵀGod forbid that thy servants should do according to this
thing: *Far be it from us that*

8 Behold, ᴿthe money, which
we found in our sacks' mouths,
we brought again unto thee out of
the land of Canaan: how then
should we steal out of thy lord's
house silver or gold? 43:21

9 With whomsoever of thy servants it be found, ᴿboth let him
die, and we also will be my lord's
ᵀbondmen. 31:32 • *slaves*

10 And he said, Now also *let* it
be according unto your words: he
with whom it is found shall be my
ᵀservant; and ye shall be blameless. *slave*

11 Then they speedily took
down every man his sack to the
ground, and opened every man
his sack.

12 And he searched, *and* began
at the eldest, and ᵀleft at the
youngest: and the cup was found
in Benjamin's sack. *finished with*

13 Then they ᴿrent their clothes,
and laded every man his ass, and
returned to the city. 37:29, 34

14 And Judah and his brethren
came to Joseph's house; for he
was yet there: and they ᴿfell
before him on the ground. 37:7, 10

15 And Joseph said unto them,
What deed *is* this that ye have
done? ᵀwot ye not that such a man
as I can certainly divine? *know*

16 And Judah said, What shall
we say unto my lord? what shall
we speak? or how shall we clear
ourselves? God hath ᴿfound out
the iniquity of thy servants: behold, ᴿwe *are* my lord's servants,
both we, and *he* also with whom
the cup is found. [Num. 32:23] • v. 9

17 And he said, ᴿGod forbid that
I should do so: *but* the man in
whose hand the cup is found, he
shall be my servant; and as for
you, get you up in peace unto your
father. Prov. 17:15

18 Then Judah came near unto
him, and said, Oh my lord, let thy
servant, I pray thee, speak a word
in my lord's ears, and ᴿlet not
thine anger burn against thy servant: for thou *art* even as Pharaoh. 18:30, 32; Ex. 32:22

19 My lord asked his servants,
saying, Have ye a father, or a
brother?

20 And we said unto my lord, We
have a father, an old man, and a
child of his old age, ᵀa little one;
and his brother is dead, and he
alone is left of his mother, and his
father loveth him. *who is young*

21 And thou saidst unto thy servants, ᴿBring him down unto me,
that I may set mine eyes upon
him. 42:15, 20

22 And we said unto my lord,
The lad cannot leave his father:
for *if* he should leave his father,
his father would die.

23 And thou saidst unto thy servants, ᴿExcept your youngest brother come down with you, ye shall
see my face no more. 43:3, 5

24 And it came to pass when we
came up unto thy servant my
father, we told him the words of
my lord.

25 And ᴿour father said, Go
again, *and* buy us a little food. 43:2

26 And we said, We cannot go
down: if our youngest brother be
with us, then will we go down: for
we may not see the man's face,
except our youngest brother *be*
with us.

27 And thy servant my father
said unto us, Ye know that ᴿmy
wife bare me two *sons:* 46:19

28 And the one went out from
me, and I said, Surely he is torn in
pieces; and I saw him not since:

29 And if ye take this also from
me, and ᵀmischief befall him, ye
shall bring down my gray hairs
with sorrow to the grave. *calamity*

30 Now therefore when I come to thy servant my father, and the lad *be* not with us; seeing that his life is bound up in the lad's life;

31 It shall come to pass, when he seeth that the lad *is* not *with us,* that he will die: and thy servants shall bring down the gray hairs of thy servant our father with sorrow to the grave.

32 For thy servant became surety for the lad unto my father, saying, ᴿIf I bring him not unto thee, then I shall bear the blame to my father for ever. 43:9

33 Now therefore, I pray thee, ᴿlet thy servant ᵀabide instead of the lad ᵀa bondman to my lord; and let the lad go up with his brethren. Ex. 32:32 · *remain · as a slave*

34 For how shall I go up to my father, and the lad *be* not with me? lest peradventure I see the evil that shall come on my father.

45 Then Joseph could not refrain himself before all them that stood by him; and he cried, Cause every man to go out from me. And there stood no man with him, while Joseph made himself known unto his brethren.

2 And he ᴿwept aloud: and the Egyptians and the house of Pharaoh heard. 43:30; 46:29

3 And Joseph said unto his brethren, I *am* Joseph; doth my father yet live? And his brethren could not answer him; for they were troubled at his presence.

4 And Joseph said unto his brethren, Come near to me, I pray you. And they came near. And he said, I *am* Joseph your brother, ᴿwhom ye sold into Egypt. 39:1

5 Now therefore be not grieved, nor angry with yourselves, that ye sold me hither: ᴿfor God did send me before you to preserve life. Ps. 105:16, 17

6 For these two years *hath* the ᴿfamine *been* in the land: and yet *there are* five years, in the which *there shall* neither *be* ᵀearing nor harvest. 43:1; 47:4, 13 · *plowing*

7 And God ᴿsent me before you to preserve you a ᵀposterity in the earth, and to save your lives by a great deliverance. 50:20 · *a remnant*

8 So now *it was* not you *that* sent me hither, but ᴿGod: and he hath made me a father to Pharaoh, and lord of all his house, and a ᴿruler throughout all the land of Egypt. [Rom. 8:28] · 41:43; 42:6

9 Haste ye, and go up to my father, and say unto him, Thus saith thy son Joseph, God hath made me lord of all Egypt: come down unto me, ᵀtarry not: *delay*

10 And ᴿthou shalt dwell in the land of Go'-shen, and thou shalt be near unto me, thou, and thy children, and thy children's children, and thy flocks, and thy herds, and all that thou hast: 47:1

11 And there will I ᴿnourishᵀ thee; for yet *there are* five years of famine; lest thou, and thy household, and all that thou hast, come to poverty. 47:12 · *provide for*

12 And, behold, your eyes see, and the eyes of my brother Benjamin, that *it is* ᴿmy mouth that speaketh unto you. 42:23

13 And ye shall tell my father of all my glory in Egypt, and of all that ye have seen; and ye shall haste and ᴿbring down my father hither. 46:6–28; Acts 7:14

14 And he fell upon his brother Benjamin's neck, and wept; and Benjamin wept upon his neck.

15 Moreover he ᴿkissed all his brethren, and wept upon them: and after that his brethren talked with him. 48:10

16 And the ᵀfame thereof was heard in Pharaoh's house, saying, Joseph's brethren are come: and it pleased Pharaoh well, and his servants. *report*

17 And Pharaoh said unto Joseph, Say unto thy brethren, This do ye; lade your beasts, and go, get you unto the land of Canaan;

18 And take your father and your households, and come unto me: and I will give you the good of the land of Egypt, and ye shall eat ᴿthe ᵀfat of the land. 27:28; 47:6 · *best*

19 Now thou art commanded, this do ye; take you wagons out of

the land of Egypt for your little ones, and for your wives, and bring your father, and come.

20 Also ᵀregard not your stuff; for the good of all the land of Egypt *is* yours.   *be concerned about*

21 And the children of Israel did so: and Joseph gave them ᴿwagons,ᵀ according to the commandment of Pharaoh, and gave them provision for the way.   46:5 · *carts*

22 To all of them he gave each man ᴿchanges of ᵀraiment; but to Benjamin he gave three hundred *pieces* of silver, and ᴿfive changes of raiment.   2 Kin. 5:5 · *clothing* · 43:34

23 And to his father he sent after this *manner;* ten asses laden with the good things of Egypt, and ten she asses laden with ᵀcorn and bread and ᵀmeat for his father ᵀby the way.   *grain · food · for*

24 So he sent his brethren away, and they departed: and he said unto them, See that ye ᵀfall not out by the way.   *be not troubled*

25 And they went up out of Egypt, and came into the land of Canaan unto Jacob their father,

26 And told him, saying, Joseph *is* yet alive, and he *is* governor over all the land of Egypt. ᴿAnd Jacob's heart fainted, for he believed them not.   Ps. 126:1

27 And they told him all the words of Joseph, which he had said unto them: and when he saw the wagons which Joseph had sent to carry him, the spirit ᴿof Jacob their father revived: Is. 40:29

28 And Israel said, *It is* enough; Joseph my son *is* yet alive: I will go and see him before I die.

46 And Israel took his journey with all that he had, and came to ᴿBe'-er-she'-ba, and offered sacrifices ᴿunto the God of his father Isaac.   28:10 · 26:24, 25

2 And God spake unto Israel ᴿin the visions of the night, and said, Jacob, Jacob. And he said, Here *am* I.   15:1; 22:11; 31:11

3 And he said, I *am* God, the God of thy father: fear not to go down into Egypt; for I will there ᴿmake of thee a great nation: 12:2

4 I will go down with thee into Egypt; and I will also surely bring thee up *again:* and Joseph shall put his hand upon thine eyes.

5 And Jacob rose up from Be'-er-she'-ba: and the sons of Israel carried Jacob their father, and their little ones, and their wives, in the wagons ᴿwhich Pharaoh had sent to carry him.   45:19–21

6 And they took their cattle, and their goods, which they had gotten in the land of Canaan, and came into Egypt, ᴿJacob, and all his seed with him: Is. 52:4; Acts 7:15

7 His sons, and his sons' sons with him, his daughters, and his sons' daughters, and all his seed brought he with him into Egypt.

8 And these *are* the names of the children of Israel, which came into Egypt, Jacob and his sons: Reuben, Jacob's firstborn.

9 And the sons of Reuben; Ha'-noch, and ᵀPhal'-lu, and Hez'-ron, and Car'-mi.   *Pallu,* Num. 26:5

10 And the sons of Simeon; Jem'-u-el, and Ja'-min, and O'-had, and Ja'-chin, and Zo'-har, and Sha'-ul the son of a Ca'-naan-i-tish woman.

11 And the sons of Levi; Ger'-shon, Ko'-hath, and Me-ra'-ri.

12 And the sons of Judah; Er, and O'-nan, and She'-lah, and Pha'-rez, and Za'-rah: but Er and O'-nan died in the land of Canaan. And the sons of Pha'-rez were Hez'-ron and Ha'-mul.

13 ᴿAnd the sons of Is'-sa-char; To'-la, and Phu'-vah, and Job, and Shim'-ron.   1 Chr. 7:1

14 And the sons of Zeb'-u-lun; Se'-red, and E'-lon, and Jah'-le-el.

15 These *be* the ᴿsons of Leah, which she bare unto Jacob in Pa'-dan–a'-ram, with his daughter Dinah: all the ᵀsouls of his sons and his daughters *were* thirty and three.   35:23; 49:31 · *persons*

16 ᴿAnd the sons of Gad; Ziph'-i-on, and Hag'-gi, Shu'-ni, and Ez'-bon, E'-ri, and Ar'-o-di, and A-re'-li.   Num. 26:15

17 ᴿAnd the sons of Asher; Jim'-

nah, and Ish'-u-ah, and Is'-u-i, and
Be-ri'-ah, and Se'-rah their sister:
and the sons of Be-ri'-ah; He'-ber,
and Mal'-chi-el.   Num. 26:44–47
18 These *are* the sons of Zil'-
pah, whom Laban gave to Leah
his daughter, and these she bare
unto Jacob, *even* sixteen souls.
19 The sons of Ra'-chel Jacob's
wife; Joseph, and Benjamin.
20 ᴿAnd unto Joseph in the land
of Egypt were born Ma-nas'-seh
and E'-phra-im, which As'-e-nath
the daughter of Pot-i–phe'-rah
priest of On bare unto him.   48:1
21 ᴿAnd the sons of Benjamin
were Be'-lah, and Be'-cher, and
Ash'-bel, Ge'-ra, and Na'-a-man,
E'-hi, and Rosh, Mup'-pim, and
Hup'-pim, and Ard.   1 Chr. 7:6; 8:1
22 These *are* the sons of Ra'-
chel, which were born to Jacob:
all the souls *were* fourteen.
23 And the sons of Dan; ᵀHu'-
shim.   *Shuham*, Num. 26:42
24 ᴿAnd the sons of Naph'-ta-li;
Jah'-ze-el, and Gu'-ni, and Je'-zer,
and Shil'-lem.   Num. 26:48
25 ᴿThese *are* the sons of Bil'-
hah, ᴿwhich Laban gave unto Ra'-
chel his daughter, and she bare
these unto Jacob: all the souls
were seven.   30:5, 7 · 29:29
26 ᴿAll the souls that came with
Jacob into Egypt, which came out
of his loins, ᴿbesides Jacob's sons'
wives, all the souls *were* threescore and six;   Ex. 1:5 · 35:11
27 And the sons of Joseph,
which were born him in Egypt,
were two souls: ᴿall the souls of
the house of Jacob, which came
into Egypt, *were* threescore and
ten.   Ex. 1:5; Deut. 10:22; Acts 7:14
28 And he sent Judah before
him unto Joseph, to direct his face
unto Go'-shen; and they came
ᴿinto the land of Go'-shen.   47:1
29 And Joseph made ready his
ᴿchariot, and went up to meet
Israel his father, to Go'-shen, and
presented himself unto him; and
he ᴿfell on his neck, and wept on
his neck a good while.   41:43 · 45:14
30 And Israel said unto Joseph,
ᴿNow let me die, since I have seen

thy face, because thou *art* yet
alive.   Luke 2:29, 30
31 And Joseph said unto his
brethren, and unto his father's
house, ᴿI will go up, and ᵀshew
Pharaoh, and say unto him, My
brethren, and my father's house,
which *were* in the land of Canaan,
are come unto me;   47:1 · *tell*
32 And the men *are* ᴿshepherds,
for their ᵀtrade hath been to feed
cattle; and they have brought
their flocks, and their herds, and
all that they have.   47:3 · *occupation*
33 And it shall come to pass,
when Pharaoh shall call you, and
shall say, ᴿWhat *is* your occupation?   47:2, 3
34 That ye shall say, Thy servants' trade hath been about cattle ᴿfrom our youth even until
now, both we, *and* also our fathers: that ye may dwell in the
land of Go'-shen; for every shepherd *is* ᴿan abomination unto the
Egyptians.   34:5; 37:17 · 43:32; Ex. 8:26

47 Then Joseph came and
told Pharaoh, and said, My
father and my brethren, and their
flocks, and their herds, and all
that they have, are come out of the
land of Canaan; and, behold, they
are in ᴿthe land of Go'-shen.   50:8
2 And he took some of his
brethren, *even* five men, and presented them unto Pharaoh.
3 And Pharaoh said unto his
brethren, What *is* your occupation? And they said unto Pharaoh,
ᴿThy servants *are* shepherds, both
we, *and* also our fathers.   46:32, 34
4 They said moreover unto
Pharaoh, For to sojourn in the
land are we come; for thy servants have no pasture for their
flocks; for the famine *is* sore in
the land of Canaan: now therefore, we pray thee, let thy servants
dwell in the land of Go'-shen.
5 And Pharaoh spake unto Joseph, saying, Thy father and thy
brethren are come unto thee:
6 The land of Egypt *is* before
thee; in the best of the land make
thy father and brethren to dwell;
in the land of Go'-shen let them

dwell: and if thou knowest *any* men of activity among them, then make them rulers over my cattle.

7 And Joseph brought in Jacob his father, and set him before Pharaoh: and Jacob ^Rblessed Pharaoh.   2 Sam. 14:22; 1 Kin. 8:66; Heb. 7:7

8 And Pharaoh said unto Jacob, How old *art* thou?

9 And Jacob said unto Pharaoh, The days of the years of my pilgrimage *are* an ^Rhundred and thirty years: few and evil have the days of the years of my life been, and ^Rhave not attained unto the days of the years of the life of my fathers in the days of their pilgrimage.   v. 28 · 11:10, 11; 25:7, 8; 35:28

10 And Jacob ^Rblessed Pharaoh, and went out from before Pharaoh.   v. 7

11 And Joseph placed his father and his brethren, and gave them a possession in the land of Egypt, in the best of the land, in the land of ^RRam'-e-ses, ^Ras Pharaoh had commanded.   Ex. 1:11; 12:37 · vv. 6, 27

12 And Joseph nourished his father, and his brethren, and all his father's household, with bread, according to *their* families.

13 And *there was* no bread in all the land; for the famine *was* very sore, so that the land of Egypt and *all* the land of Canaan ^Tfainted by reason of the famine.   *languished*

14 ^RAnd Joseph gathered up all the money that was found in the land of Egypt, and in the land of Canaan, for the corn which they bought: and Joseph brought the money into Pharaoh's house.   42:6

15 And when money failed in the land of Egypt, and in the land of Canaan, all the Egyptians came unto Joseph, and said, Give us bread: for ^Rwhy should we die in thy presence? for the money faileth.   v. 19

16 And Joseph said, Give your cattle; and I will give you for your cattle, if money fail.

17 And they brought their cattle unto Joseph: and Joseph gave them bread *in exchange* for horses, and for the flocks, and for the cattle of the herds, and for the asses: and he ^Tfed them with bread for all their cattle for that year.   *supplied* or *refreshed*

18 When that year was ended, they came unto him the second year, and said unto him, We will not hide *it* from my lord, how that our money is spent; my lord also hath our herds of ^Tcattle; there is ^Tnot ought left in the sight of my lord, but our bodies, and our lands: *livestock · nothing*

19 Wherefore shall we die before thine eyes, both we and our land? buy us and our land for bread, and we and our land will be servants unto Pharaoh: and give *us* seed, that we may ^Rlive, and not die, that the land be not desolate.   43:8

20 And Joseph ^Rbought all the land of Egypt for Pharaoh; for the Egyptians sold every man his field, because the famine prevailed over them: so the land became Pharaoh's.   Jer. 32:43

21 And as for the people, he ^Tremoved them to cities from *one* end of the borders of Egypt even to the *other* end thereof.   *moved*

22 Only the land of the priests bought he not; for the priests had a portion *assigned them* of Pharaoh, and did eat their portion which Pharaoh gave them: wherefore they sold not their lands.

23 Then Joseph said unto the people, Behold, I have bought you this day and your land for Pha-raoh: lo, *here is* seed for you, and ye shall sow the land.

24 And it shall come to pass in the increase, that ye shall give the fifth *part* unto Pharaoh, and four parts shall be your own, for seed of the field, and for your food, and for them of your households, and for food for your little ones.

25 And they said, Thou hast saved our lives: let us find ^Tgrace in the sight of my lord, and we will be Pharaoh's servants.   *favour*

26 And Joseph made it a law over the land of Egypt unto this day, *that* Pharaoh should have the

fifth *part;* ^Rexcept the land of the priests only, *which* became not Pharaoh's.   v. 22

27 And Israel dwelt in the land of Egypt, in the country of Go'-shen; and they had possessions therein, and ^Rgrew, and multiplied exceedingly.   Ex. 1:7; Acts 7:17

28 And Jacob lived in the land of Egypt seventeen years: so the whole age of Jacob was an hundred forty and seven years.

29 And the time drew nigh that Israel must die: and he called his son Joseph, and said unto him, If now I have found grace in thy sight, ^Rput, I pray thee, thy hand under my thigh, and deal kindly and truly with me; ^Rbury me not, I pray thee, in Egypt: 24:2–4 · 50:25

30 But I will lie with my fathers, and thou shalt carry me out of Egypt, and ^Rbury me in their bury-ingplace. And he said, I will do as thou hast said.   50:5–13; Heb. 11:21

31 And he said, Swear unto me. And he sware unto him. And ^RIsrael bowed himself upon the bed's head.   1 Kin. 1:47; Heb. 11:21

48 And it came to pass after these things, that *one* told Joseph, Behold, thy father *is* sick: and he took with him his two sons, Ma-nas'-seh and E'-phra-im.

2 And *one* told Jacob, and said, Behold, thy son Joseph cometh unto thee: and Israel strengthened himself, and sat upon the bed.

3 And Jacob said unto Joseph, God ^RAlmighty appeared unto me at ^RLuz in the land of Canaan, and blessed me,   43:14 · 28:13, 19; 35:6, 9

4 And said unto me, Behold, I will ^Rmake thee fruitful, and multiply thee, and I will make of thee a multitude of people; and will ^Rgive this land to thy seed after thee ^R*for* an everlasting posses-sion.   46:3 · 35:12; Ex. 6:8 · 17:8

5 And now thy two sons, E'-phra-im and Ma-nas'-seh, which were born unto thee in the land of Egypt before I came unto thee into Egypt, *are* mine; as Reuben and Simeon, they shall be mine.

6 And thy ^Tissue, which thou begettest after them, shall be thine, *and* shall be called after the name of their brethren in their inheritance.   *offspring*

7 And as for me, when I came from Pa'-dan, ^RRa'-chel died ^Tby me in the land of Canaan in the way, when yet *there was* but a lit-tle way to come unto Eph'-rath: and I buried her there ^Tin the way of Eph'-rath; the same *is* Beth'–le-hem.   35:9, 16, 19, 20 · *beside · on*

8 And Israel beheld Joseph's sons, and said, Who *are* these?

9 And Joseph said unto his father, They *are* my sons, whom God hath given me in this *place.* And he said, Bring them, I pray thee, unto me, and ^RI will bless them.   27:4; 47:15

10 Now ^Rthe eyes of Israel were dim ^Tfor age, *so that* he could not see. And he brought them near unto him; and he kissed them, and embraced them.   27:1; 1 Sam. 3:2 · *with*

11 And Israel said unto Joseph, ^RI had not thought to see thy face: and, lo, God hath shewed me also thy seed.   45:26

12 And Joseph brought them out from ^Tbetween his knees, and he bowed himself with his face to the earth.   *beside*

13 And Joseph took them both, E'-phra-im in his right hand to-ward Israel's left hand, and Ma-nas'-seh in his left hand toward Israel's right hand, and brought *them* near unto him.

14 And Israel stretched out his right hand, and ^Rlaid *it* upon E'-phra-im's head, who *was* the younger, and his left hand upon Ma-nas'-seh's head, guiding his hands wittingly; for Ma-nas'-seh *was* the firstborn.   Matt. 19:15

15 And he blessed Joseph, and said, God, ^Rbefore whom my fa-thers Abraham and Isaac did walk, the God which fed me all my life long unto this day,   17:1

16 The Angel ^Rwhich redeemed me from all evil, bless the lads; and let ^Rmy name be named on them, and the name of my fathers

Abraham and Isaac; and let them grow into a multitude in the midst of the earth. 22:11, 15–18 · Acts 15:17

17 And when Joseph saw that his father ^Rlaid his right hand upon the head of E'-phra-im, it displeased him: and he held up his father's hand, to remove it from E'-phra-im's head unto Ma-nas'-seh's head. v. 14

18 And Joseph said unto his father, Not so, my father: for this *is* the firstborn; put thy right hand upon his head.

19 And his father refused, and said, ^RI know *it*, my son, I know *it*: he also shall become a people, and he also shall be great: but truly ^Rhis younger brother shall be greater than he, and his seed shall become a multitude of nations. v. 14 · Num. 1:33, 35; Deut. 33:17

20 And he blessed them that day, saying, ^RIn thee shall Israel bless, saying, God make thee as E'-phra-im and as Ma-nas'-seh: and he set E'-phra-im before Ma-nas'-seh. Ruth 4:11, 12

21 And Israel said unto Joseph, Behold, I die: but ^RGod shall be with you, and bring you again unto the land of your fathers. 50:24

22 Moreover ^RI have given to thee one portion above thy breth-ren, which I took out of the hand ^Rof the Am'-or-ite with my sword and with my bow. John 4:5 · 34:28

49 And Jacob called unto his sons, and said, Gather your-selves together, that I may tell you *that* which shall befall you ^Rin the last days. Is. 2:2; 39:6; Jer. 23:20; Heb. 1:2

2 Gather yourselves together, and hear, ye sons of Jacob; and hearken unto Israel your father.

3 Reuben, thou *art* ^Rmy first-born, my might, and the begin-ning of my strength, the excellen-cy of dignity, and the excellency of power: 29:32

4 Unstable as water, thou shalt not excel; because thou ^Rwentest up to thy father's bed; then defiledst thou *it:* he went up to my couch. 35:22; Deut. 27:20; 1 Chr. 5:1

5 Simeon and Levi *are* breth-

ren; instruments of ^Tcruelty *are in* their habitations. *violence*

6 O my soul, come not thou in-to their ^Tsecret; unto their assem-bly, mine honour, be not thou uni-ted: for in their ^Ranger they slew a man, and in their selfwill they digged down a wall. *council* · 34:26

7 Cursed *be* their anger, for *it was* fierce; and their wrath, for it was cruel: I will divide them in Jacob, and scatter them in Israel.

8 Judah, thou *art he* whom thy brethren shall praise: ^Rthy hand *shall be* ^Tin the neck of thine ene-mies; thy father's children shall bow down before thee. Ps. 18:40 · *on*

9 Judah *is* ^Ra lion's whelp: from the prey, my son, thou art gone up: he stooped down, he couched as a lion, and as an old lion; who shall rouse him up? Mic. 5:8; [Rev. 5:5]

10 ^RThe sceptre shall not depart ☆ from Judah, nor a lawgiver from between his feet, until Shi'-loh come; and unto him *shall* the gathering of the people *be*. Rev. 5:5

11 Binding his foal unto the vine, and his ass's colt unto the choice vine; he washed his gar-ments in wine, and his clothes in the blood of grapes:

12 His eyes *shall be* ^Tred with wine, and his teeth ^Twhite with milk. *darker than · whiter than*

13 Zeb'-u-lun shall dwell at the haven of the sea; and he *shall be* for an haven of ships; and his bor-der *shall be* unto Zi'-don.

14 ^RIs'-sa-char *is* a strong ass couching down between two bur-dens: 1 Chr. 12:32

15 And he saw that rest *was* good, and the land that *it was* pleasant; and bowed ^Rhis shoul-der to bear, and became a servant unto tribute. 1 Sam. 10:9

16 ^RDan shall judge his people, as one of the tribes of Israel. 30:6

17 Dan shall be a serpent by the way, an adder in the path, that biteth the horse heels, so that his rider shall fall backward.

18 ^RI have waited for thy salva-tion, O LORD. Ps. 25:5; 40:1–3; Is. 25:9

19 ^RGad, a troop shall overcome

him: but he shall overcome at the last.   30:11; Deut. 33:20; 1 Chr. 5:18

20 ^ROut of Asher his bread *shall be* ^Tfat, and he shall yield royal dainties. Deut. 33:24; Josh. 19:24–31 · *rich*

21 Naph'-ta-li *is* a hind let loose: he giveth goodly words.

22 Joseph *is* a fruitful bough, *even* a fruitful bough by a well; *whose* branches run over the wall:

23 The archers have ^Rsorely^T grieved him, and shot *at him,* and hated him: 37:4, 24; Ps. 118:13 · *bitterly*

24 But his ^Rbow abode in strength, and the arms of his hands were made strong by the hands of the mighty *God* of Jacob; (from thence *is* the shepherd, the stone of Israel:)   Ps. 37:15

25 *Even* by the God of thy father, who shall help thee; ^Rand by the Almighty, who shall bless thee with blessings of heaven above, blessings of the deep that lieth under, blessings of the breasts, and of the womb: 35:11

26 The blessings of thy father have prevailed above the blessings of my progenitors ^Runto the utmost bound of the everlasting hills: they shall be on the head of Joseph, and on the crown of the head of him that was separate from his brethren.   Deut. 33:15

27 Benjamin shall ravin *as* a wolf: in the morning he shall devour the prey, ^Rand at night he shall divide the spoil.   Zech. 14:1

28 All these *are* the twelve tribes of Israel: and this *is it* that their father spake unto them, and blessed them; every one according to his blessing he blessed them.

29 And he charged them, and said unto them, I ^Ram to be gathered unto my people: ^Rbury me with my fathers ^Rin the cave that *is* in the field of E'-phron the Hit'-tite,   35:29 · 2 Sam. 19:37 · 23:16–20; 50:13

30 In the cave that *is* in the field of Mach-pe'-lah, which *is* before Mam'-re, in the land of Canaan, which Abraham bought with the field of E'-phron the Hit'-tite for a possession of a buryingplace.

31 There they buried Abraham and Sarah his wife; there they buried Isaac and Rebekah his wife; and there I buried Leah.

32 The purchase of the field and of the cave that *is* therein *was* from the children of Heth.

33 And when Jacob had made an end of commanding his sons, he gathered up his feet into the bed, and yielded up the ghost, and was gathered unto his people.

50 And Joseph ^Rfell upon his father's face, and wept upon him, and kissed him.   46:4, 29

2 And Joseph commanded his servants the physicians to ^Rembalm his father: and the physicians embalmed Israel.   v. 26

3 And forty days were fulfilled for him; for so are fulfilled the days of those which are embalmed: and the Egyptians ^Rmourned for him threescore and ten days.   37:34; Num. 20:29; Deut. 34:8

4 And when the days of his mourning were past, Joseph spake unto ^Rthe house of Pharaoh, saying, If now I have found ^Tgrace in your eyes, speak, I pray you, in the ears of Pharaoh, saying,   Esth. 4:2 · *favour*

5 My father made me swear, saying, Lo, I die: in my grave which I have digged for me in the land of Canaan, there shalt thou bury me. Now therefore let me go up, I pray thee, and bury my father, and I will come again.

6 And Pharaoh said, Go up, and bury thy father, according as he made thee swear.

7 And Joseph went up to bury his father: and with him went up all the servants of Pharaoh, the elders of his house, and all the elders of the land of Egypt,

8 And all the house of Joseph, and his brethren, and his father's house: only their little ones, and their flocks, and their herds, they left in the land of Go'-shen.

9 And there went up with him both chariots and horsemen: and it was a very great company.

10 And they came to the thresh-

ingfloor of A'-tad, which *is* beyond Jordan, and there they
[R]mourned with a great and very
sore lamentation: [R]and he made a
mourning for his father seven
days.   Acts 8:2 · 1 Sam. 31:13; Job 2:13
11 And when the inhabitants of
the land, the Ca'-naan-ites, saw
the mourning in the floor of A'-
tad, they said, This *is* a grievous mourning to the Egyptians:
wherefore the name of it was
called [T]A'-bel-miz'-ra-im, which *is*
beyond Jordan. Lit. *Mourning of Egypt*
12 And his sons did unto him
according as he commanded
them:
13 For [R]his sons carried him into
the land of Canaan, and buried
him in the cave of the field of
Mach-pe'-lah, which Abraham
[R]bought with the field for a possession of a buryingplace of E'-
phron the Hit'-tite, before Mam'-
re.   49:29–31; Acts 7:16 · 23:16–20
14 And Joseph returned into
Egypt, he, and his brethren, and
all that went up with him to bury
his father, after he had buried his
father.
15 And when Joseph's brethren
saw that their father was dead,
[R]they said, Joseph will peradventure hate us, and will certainly
requite us all the evil which we
did unto him.   [Job 15:21]
16 And they sent a messenger
unto Joseph, saying, Thy father did
command before he died, saying,
17 So shall ye say unto Joseph,
Forgive, I pray thee now, the trespass of thy brethren, and their sin;
for they did unto thee evil: and

now, we pray thee, forgive the
trespass of the servants of the
God of thy father. And Joseph
wept when they spake unto him.
18 And his brethren also went
and [R]fell down before his face;
and they said, Behold, we *be* thy
servants.   37:7–10; 41:43; 44:14
19 And Joseph said unto them,
[R]Fear not: [R]for *am* I in the place of
God?   45:5 · 30:2; 2 Kin. 5:7
20 [R]But as for you, ye thought
evil against me; *but* [R]God meant it
unto good, to bring to pass, as *it
is* this day, to save much people
alive.   45:5, 7; Ps. 56:5 · [Acts 3:13–15]
21 Now therefore fear ye not: [R]I
will nourish you, and your little
ones. And he comforted them, and
spake kindly unto them. [Matt. 5:44]
22 And Joseph dwelt in Egypt,
he, and his father's house: and
Joseph lived an hundred and ten
years.
23 And Joseph saw E'-phra-im's
children of the third *generation:*
the children also of Ma'-chir the
son of Ma-nas'-seh [R]were brought
up upon Joseph's knees.   30:3
24 And Joseph said unto his
brethren, I die: and [R]God will
surely visit you, and bring you out
of this land unto the land [R]which
he sware to Abraham, to Isaac,
and to Jacob.   Heb. 11:22 · 26:3; 35:12
25 And Joseph took an oath of
the children of Israel, saying, God
will surely visit you, and ye shall
carry up my bones from hence.
26 So Joseph died, *being* an
hundred and ten years old: and
they embalmed him, and he was
put in a coffin in Egypt.

The Second Book of Moses Called

EXODUS

E XODUS is the record of Israel's birth as a nation. Within the protective
"womb" of Egypt, the Jewish family of seventy rapidly multiplies. At the
right time, accompanied with severe "birth pains," an infant nation, numbering between two and three million people, is brought into the world where it
is divinely protected, fed, and nurtured.

The Hebrew title, *We'elleh Shemoth*, "Now These *Are* the Names," comes from the first phrase in 1:1. Exodus begins with "Now" to show it as a continuation of Genesis. The Greek title is *Exodus*, a word meaning "exit," "departure," or "going out." The Septuagint uses this word to describe the book by its key event (see 19:1, "gone forth out"). In Luke 9:31 and in Second Peter 1:15, the word *exodus* speaks of physical death (Jesus and Peter). This embodies Exodus's theme of redemption, because redemption is accomplished only through death. The Latin title is *Liber Exodus*, "Book of Departure," taken from the Greek title.

NOW these *are* the names of the children of Israel, which came into Egypt; every man and his household came with Jacob.

2 Reuben, Simeon, Levi, and Judah,

3 Is'-sa-char, Zeb'-u-lun, and Benjamin,

4 Dan, and Naph'-ta-li, Gad, and Asher.

5 And all the souls that came out of the loins of Jacob were ᴿseventy souls: for Joseph was in Egypt *already*.   Gen. 46:26, 27

6 And Joseph died, and all his brethren, and all that generation.

7 ᴿAnd the children of Israel were fruitful, and increased abundantly, and multiplied, and waxed exceeding mighty; and the land was filled with them.   Ps. 105:24

8 Now there arose up a new king over Egypt, ᴿwhich knew not Joseph.   Acts 7:18, 19

9 And he said unto his people, Behold, the people of the children of Israel *are* more and ᴿmightier than we: Gen. 26:16

10 Come on, let us ᴿdeal wisely with them; lest they multiply, and it come to pass, that, when there falleth out any war, they join also unto our enemies, and fight against us, and so get them up out of the land.   Ps. 105:25; [Prov. 16:25]

11 Therefore they did set over them taskmasters to afflict them with their burdens. And they built for Pharaoh ᴿtreasure cities, Pi'-thom and Ra-am'-ses.   1 Kin. 9:19

12 But the more they afflicted them, the more they multiplied and grew. And they were grieved because of the children of Israel.

13 And the Egyptians made the children of Israel to ᴿserve with ᵀrigour: 5:7-19; Gen. 15:13 · harshness

14 And they ᴿmade their lives bitter with hard bondage, in morter, and in brick, and in all manner of service in the field: all their service, wherein they made them serve, *was* with rigour.   Num. 20:15

15 And the king of Egypt spake to the ᴿHebrew midwives, of which the name of the one *was* Shiph'-rah, and the name of the other Pu'-ah: 2:6

16 And he said, When ye do the office of a midwife to the Hebrew women, and see *them* upon the stools; if it *be* a ᴿson, then ye shall kill him: but if it *be* a daughter, then she shall live.   Matt. 2:16

17 But the midwives feared God, and did not ᴿas the king of Egypt commanded them, but saved the men children alive.   Dan. 3:16, 18

18 And the king of Egypt called for the midwives, and said unto them, Why have ye done this thing, and have saved the men children alive?

19 And the midwives said unto Pharaoh, Because the Hebrew women *are* not as the Egyptian women; for they ᵀ*are* lively, and are delivered ere the midwives come in unto them.   Bear quickly

20 ᴿTherefore God dealt well with the midwives: and the people multiplied, and waxed very mighty.   Eccl. 8:12; [Is. 3:10]; Heb. 6:10

21 And it came to pass, because the midwives feared God, ᴿthat he made them houses.   [Ps. 127:1]

22 And Pharaoh ᵀcharged all his people, saying, ᴿEvery son that is

born ye shall cast into the river, and every daughter ye shall save alive. *commanded · Acts 7:19*

2 And there went [R]a man of the house of Levi, and took *to wife* a daughter of Levi. *6:16–20*

2 And the woman conceived, and bare a son: and when she saw him that he *was a* goodly *child*, she hid him three months.

3 And when she could not longer hide him, she took for him an ark of bulrushes, and daubed it with slime and with pitch, and put the child therein; and she laid *it* in the flags by the river's brink.

4 [R]And his sister stood afar off, to [T]wit what would be done to him. *15:20; Num. 26:59 · know*

5 And the [R]daughter of Pharaoh came down to wash *herself* at the river; and her maidens walked along by the river's side; and when she saw the ark among the flags, she sent her maid to fetch it. *7:15; Acts 7:21*

6 And when she had opened *it*, she saw the child: and, behold, the babe wept. And she had compassion on him, and said, This *is one* of the Hebrews' children.

7 Then said his sister to Pharaoh's daughter, Shall I go and call to thee a nurse of the Hebrew women, that she may nurse the child for thee?

8 And Pharaoh's daughter said to her, Go. And the maid went and called the child's mother.

9 And Pharaoh's daughter said unto her, Take this child away, and nurse it for me, and I will give *thee* thy wages. And the woman took the child, and nursed it.

10 And the child grew, and she brought him unto Pharaoh's daughter, and he became her son. And she called his name [T]Moses: and she said, Because I drew him out of the water. *Lit. Drawn Out*

11 And it came to pass in those days, when Moses was grown, that he went out unto his brethren, and looked on their burdens: and he spied an Egyptian smiting an Hebrew, one of his brethren.

12 And he looked this way and that way, and when he saw that *there was* no man, he slew the Egyptian, and hid him in the sand.

13 And [R]when he went out the second day, behold, two men of the Hebrews [R]strove together: and he said to him that did the wrong, Wherefore smitest thou thy fellow? *Acts 7:26–28 · Prov. 25:8*

14 And he said, [R]Who made thee a prince and a judge over us? intendest thou to kill me, as thou killedst the Egyptian? And Moses [R]feared, and said, Surely this thing is known. *Gen. 19:9 · Judg. 6:27*

15 Now when Pharaoh heard this thing, he sought to slay Moses. But [R]Moses fled from the face of Pharaoh, and dwelt in the land of [R]Mid'-i-an: and he sat down by a well. *Acts 7:29 · 3:1*

16 Now the priest of Mid'-i-an had seven daughters: [R]and they came and drew *water*, and filled the [R]troughs to water their father's flock. *Gen. 24:11 · Gen. 30:38*

17 And the [R]shepherds came and drove them away: but Moses stood up and helped them, and watered their flock. *1 Sam. 25:7*

18 And when they came to Reu'-el their father, he said, How *is it that* ye are come so soon to day?

19 And they said, An Egyptian delivered us out of the hand of the shepherds, and also drew *water* enough for us, and watered the flock.

20 And he said unto his daughters, And where *is* he? why *is it that* ye have left the man? call him, that he may eat bread.

21 And Moses was content to dwell with the man: and he gave Moses Zip-po'-rah his daughter.

22 And she bare *him* a son, and he called his name Ger'-shom: for he said, I have been [R]a stranger in a strange land. *Gen. 23:4; Lev. 25:23*

23 And it came to pass in process of time, that the king of Egypt died: and the children of Israel sighed by reason of the bondage, and they cried, and [R]their

cry came up unto God by reason of the bondage.   3:7, 9; James 5:4

24 And God heard their groaning, and God remembered his Rcovenant with Abraham, with Isaac, and with Jacob.   Gen. 12:1–3

25 And God Rlooked upon the children of Israel, and God had respect unto *them*.   4:31; Luke 1:25

3 Now Moses kept the flock of RJe'-thro his father in law, Rthe priest of Mid'-i-an: and he led the flock to the backside of the desert, and came to the mountain of God, *even* to RHo'-reb.   4:18 · 2:16 · 17:6

2 And Rthe angel of the LORD appeared unto him in a flame of fire out of the midst of a bush: and he looked, and, behold, the bush burned with fire, and the bush *was* not consumed.   Luke 20:37

3 And Moses said, I will now turn aside, and see this great sight, why the bush is not burnt.

4 And when the LORD saw that he turned aside to see, God called Runto him out of the midst of the bush, and said, Moses, Moses. And he said, Here *am* I.   Deut. 33:16

5 And he said, Draw not nigh hither: put off thy shoes from off thy feet, for the place whereon thou standest *is* holy ground.

6 Moreover he said, RI *am* the God of thy father, the God of Abraham, the God of Isaac, and the God of Jacob. And Moses hid his face; for Rhe was afraid to look upon God.   Gen. 28:13 · 1 Kin. 19:13

7 And the LORD said, RI have surely seen the affliction of my people which *are* in Egypt, and have heard their cry by reason of their taskmasters; Rfor I know their sorrows;   Ps. 106:44 · Gen. 18:21

8 And I am come down to deliver them out of the hand of the Egyptians, and to bring them up out of that land unto a good land and a large, unto a land Rflowing with milk and honey; unto the place of the Ca'-naan-ites, and the Hit'-tites, and the Am'-or-ites, and the Per'-iz-zites, and the Hi'-vites, and the Jeb'-u-sites.   13:5; Jer. 11:5

9 Now therefore, behold, Rthe cry of the children of Israel is come unto me: and I have also seen the oppression wherewith the Egyptians oppress them.   2:23

10 RCome now therefore, and I will send thee unto Pharaoh, that thou mayest bring forth my people the children of Israel out of Egypt.   Gen. 15:13, 14; Acts 7:6, 7

11 And Moses said unto God, RWho *am* I, that I should go unto Pharaoh, and that I should bring forth the children of Israel out of Egypt?   4:10; 6:12; 1 Sam. 18:18

12 And he said, Certainly I will be with thee; and this *shall be* a Rtoken unto thee, that I have sent thee: When thou hast brought forth the people out of Egypt, ye shall serve God upon this mountain.   4:8; 19:3

13 And Moses said unto God, Behold, *when* I come unto the children of Israel, and shall say unto them, The God of your fathers hath sent me unto you; and they shall say to me, What *is* his name? what shall I say unto them?

14 And God said unto Moses, I AM THAT I AM: and he said, Thus shalt thou say unto the children of Israel, RI AM hath sent me unto you.   [John 8:24; Heb. 13:8; Rev. 1:8; 4:8]

15 And God said moreover unto Moses, Thus shalt thou say unto the children of Israel, The LORD God of your fathers, the God of Abraham, the God of Isaac, and the God of Jacob, hath sent me unto you: this *is* Rmy name for ever, and this *is* my memorial unto all generations.   Ps. 30:4; 102:12; 135:13

16 Go, and gather the elders of Israel together, and say unto them, The LORD God of your fathers, the God of Abraham, of Isaac, and of Jacob, appeared unto me, saying, RI have surely visited you, and *seen* that which is done to you in Egypt: Luke 1:68

17 And I have said, RI will bring you up out of the affliction of Egypt unto the land of the Ca'-naan-ites, and the Hit'-tites, and the Am'-or-ites, and the Per'-iz-

zites, and the Hi'-vites, and the Jeb'-u-sites, unto a land flowing with milk and honey. Gen. 15:13–21

18 And they shall hearken to thy voice: and thou shalt come, thou and the elders of Israel, unto the king of Egypt, and ye shall say unto him, The LORD God of the Hebrews hath ^Rmet with us: and now let us go, we beseech thee, three days' journey into the wilderness, that we may sacrifice to the LORD our God.   Num. 23:3, 4

19 And I am sure that the king of Egypt ^Rwill not let you go, no, not by a mighty hand.   5:2

20 And I will ^Rstretch out my hand, and smite Egypt with ^Rall my wonders which I will do in the midst thereof: and after that he will let you go.   6:6; 9:15 · Acts 7:36

21 And ^RI will give this people favour in the sight of the Egyptians: and it shall come to pass, that, when ye go, ye shall not go empty: 1 Kin. 8:50; Ps. 105:37; 106:46

22 But every woman shall borrow of her neighbour, and of her that sojourneth in her house, jewels of silver, and jewels of gold, and raiment: and ye shall put *them* upon your sons, and upon your daughters; and ye shall ^Tspoil the Egyptians.   *plunder*

4 And Moses answered and said, But, behold, they will not believe me, nor hearken unto my voice: for they will say, The LORD hath not appeared unto thee.

2 And the LORD said unto him, What *is* that in thine hand? And he said, A rod.

3 And he said, Cast it on the ground. And he cast it on the ground, and it became a serpent; and Moses fled from before it.

4 And the LORD said unto Moses, Put forth thine hand, and take it by the tail. And he put forth his hand, and caught it, and it became a rod in his hand:

5 That they may believe that the ^RLORD God of their fathers, the God of Abraham, the God of Isaac, and the God of Jacob, hath appeared unto thee. Gen. 28:13; 48:15

6 And the LORD said furthermore unto him, Put now thine hand into thy bosom. And he put his hand into his bosom: and when he took it out, behold, his hand *was* leprous as snow.

7 And he said, Put thine hand into thy bosom again. And he put his hand into his bosom again; and plucked it out of his bosom, and, behold, ^Rit was turned again as his *other* flesh.   Num. 12:13–15

8 And it shall come to pass, if they will not believe thee, neither hearken to the voice of the ^Rfirst sign, that they will believe the voice of the latter sign.   7:6–13

9 And it shall come to pass, if they will not believe also these two signs, neither hearken unto thy voice, that thou shalt take of the water of the ^Triver, and pour *it* upon the dry *land:* and ^Rthe water which thou takest out of the river shall become blood upon the dry *land.*   The Nile · 7:19, 20

10 And Moses said unto the LORD, O my Lord, I *am* not eloquent, neither heretofore, nor since thou hast spoken unto thy servant: but ^RI *am* slow of speech, and of a slow tongue.   6:12; Jer. 1:6

11 And the LORD said unto him, ^RWho hath made man's mouth? or who maketh the dumb, or deaf, or the seeing, or the blind? have not I the LORD?   Ps. 94:9; 146:8; Matt. 11:5

12 Now therefore go, and I will be ^Rwith thy mouth, and teach thee what thou shalt say.   Is. 50:4

13 And he said, O my Lord, ^Rsend, I pray thee, by the hand *of him whom* thou wilt send.   Jon. 1:3

14 And the anger of the LORD was kindled against Moses, and he said, *Is* not Aaron the Levite thy ^Rbrother? I know that he can speak well. And also, behold, he cometh forth to meet thee: and when he seeth thee, he will be glad in his heart.   Num. 26:59

15 And thou shalt speak unto him, and ^Rput words in his mouth: and I will be with thy mouth, and with his mouth, and will teach you what ye shall do.   Num. 23:5, 12

16 And he shall be thy spokesman unto the people: and he shall be, *even* he shall be to thee instead of a mouth, and ᴿthou shalt be to him instead of God.   7:1, 2

17 And thou shalt take this rod in thine hand, wherewith thou shalt do signs.

18 And Moses went and returned to Je'-thro his father in law, and said unto him, Let me go, I pray thee, and return unto my brethren which *are* in Egypt, and see whether they be yet alive. And Je'-thro said to Moses, ᴿGo in peace.   Gen. 43:23; Judg. 18:6

19 And the LORD said unto Moses in Mid'-i-an, Go, return into Egypt: for ᴿall the men are dead which sought thy life.   Matt. 2:20

20 And Moses took his wife and his sons, and set them upon an ass, and he returned to the land of Egypt: and Moses took ᴿthe rod of God in his hand. v. 17; 17:9; Num. 20:8

21 And the LORD said unto Moses, When thou goest to return into Egypt, see that thou do all those wonders before Pharaoh, which I have put in thine hand: but ᴿI will harden his heart, that he shall not let the people go.   7:3

22 And thou shalt say unto Pharaoh, Thus saith the LORD, Israel *is* my son, *even* my firstborn:

23 And I say unto thee, Let my son go, that he may serve me: and if thou refuse to let him go, behold, ᴿI will slay thy son, *even* thy firstborn. Ps. 105:36; 135:8; 136:10

24 And it came to pass by the way in the inn, that the LORD ᴿmet him, and sought to kill him.   3:18

25 Then Zip-po'-rah took ᴿa sharp stone, and cut off the foreskin of her son, and cast *it* at his feet, and said, Surely a bloody husband *art* thou to me. Gen. 17:14

26 So he let him go: then she said, A bloody husband *thou art*, because of the circumcision.

27 And the LORD said to Aaron, Go into the wilderness ᴿto meet Moses. And he went, and met him in ᴿthe mount of God, and kissed him.   v. 14 · 3:1; 18:5; 24:13

28 And Moses told Aaron all the words of the LORD who had sent him, and all the ᴿsigns which he had commanded him.   vv. 8, 9

29 And Moses and Aaron ᴿwent and gathered together all the elders of the children of Israel: 12:21

30 ᴿAnd Aaron spake all the words which the LORD had spoken unto Moses, and did the signs in the sight of the people. vv. 15, 16

31 And the people believed: and when they heard that the LORD had visited the children of Israel, and that he ᴿhad looked upon their affliction, then they bowed their heads and worshipped.   2:25

5 And afterward Moses and Aaron went in, and told Pharaoh, Thus saith the LORD God of Israel, Let my people go, that they may hold ᴿa feast unto me in the wilderness.   3:18; 7:16; 10:9

2 And Pharaoh said, ᴿWho *is* the LORD, that I should obey his voice to let Israel go? I know not the LORD, neither will I let Israel go.   2 Kin. 18:35; 2 Chr. 32:14; Job 21:15

3 And they said, The God of the Hebrews hath ᴿmet with us: let us go, we pray thee, three days' journey into the desert, and sacrifice unto the LORD our God; lest he fall upon us with ᴿpestilence, or with the sword.   4:24; Num. 23:3 · 9:15

4 And the king of Egypt said unto them, Wherefore do ye, Moses and Aaron, let the people from their works? get you unto your ᴿburdens. 1:11; 2:11; 6:6

5 And Pharaoh said, Behold, the people of the land now *are* ᴿmany, and ye make them rest from their burdens.   1:7, 9

6 And Pharaoh commanded the same day the ᴿtaskmasters of the people, and their officers, saying,   vv. 10, 13, 14; 1:11; 3:7

7 Ye shall no more give the people straw to make ᴿbrick, as heretofore: let them go and gather straw for themselves.   1:14

8 And the ᵀtale of the bricks, which they did make heretofore, ye shall lay upon them; ye shall not diminish *ought* thereof: for

they *be* idle; therefore they cry, saying, Let us go *and* sacrifice to our God. *quota*

9 Let there more work be laid upon the men, that they may labour therein; and let them not regard [T]vain words. *false*

10 And the taskmasters of the people went out, and their officers, and they spake to the people, saying, Thus saith Pharaoh, I will not give you straw.

11 Go ye, get you straw where ye can find it: yet not ought of your work shall be diminished.

12 So the people were scattered abroad throughout all the land of Egypt to gather stubble instead of straw.

13 And the taskmasters [T]hasted *them,* saying, Fulfil your works, *your* daily tasks, as when there was straw. *forced them to hurry*

14 And the [R]officers of the children of Israel, which Pharaoh's taskmasters had set over them, were [R]beaten, *and* demanded, Wherefore have ye not fulfilled your task in making brick both yesterday and to day, as heretofore? *v. 6 · Is. 10:24*

15 Then the officers of the children of Israel came and cried unto Pharaoh, saying, Wherefore dealest thou thus with thy servants?

16 There is no straw given unto thy servants, and they say to us, Make brick: and, behold, thy servants *are* beaten; but the fault *is* in thine own people.

17 But he said, Ye *are* idle, *ye are* idle: therefore ye say, Let us go *and* do sacrifice to the LORD.

18 Go therefore now, *and* work; for there shall no straw be given you, yet shall ye deliver the [T]tale of bricks. *quota*

19 And the officers of the children of Israel did see *that* they *were* [T]in evil *case,* after it was said, Ye shall not [T]minish *ought* from your bricks of your daily task. *in trouble · diminish any*

20 And they met Moses and Aaron, who stood in the way, as they came forth from Pharaoh:

21 [R]And they said unto them, The LORD look upon you, and judge; because ye have made our savour to be abhorred in the eyes of Pharaoh, and in the eyes of his servants, to put a sword in their hand to slay us. *6:9; 14:11; 15:24; 16:2*

22 And Moses returned unto the LORD, and said, Lord, wherefore hast thou [T]so evil entreated this people? why *is* it *that* thou hast sent me? *brought trouble on*

23 For since I came to Pharaoh to speak in thy name, he hath done evil to this people; neither hast thou delivered thy people at all.

6 Then the LORD said unto Moses, Now shalt thou see what I will do to Pharaoh: for [R]with a strong hand shall he let them go, and with a strong hand [R]shall he drive them out of his land. *3:19 · 12:31, 33, 39*

2 And God spake unto Moses, and said unto him, I *am* [T]the LORD: *Heb. YHWH*

3 And I appeared unto Abraham, unto Isaac, and unto Jacob, by *the name of* God Almighty, but by my name [T]JE-HO'-VAH was I not known to them. *Heb. YHWH*

4 [R]And I have also established my covenant with them, to give them the land of Canaan, the land of their pilgrimage, [R]wherein they were strangers. *Gen. 12:7 · Gen. 28:4*

5 And [R]I have also heard the groaning of the children of Israel, whom the Egyptians keep in bondage; and I have remembered my covenant. *[Job 34:28]; Acts 7:34*

6 Wherefore say unto the children of Israel, I *am* the LORD, and [R]I will bring you out from under the burdens of the Egyptians, and I will rid you out of their bondage, and I will [R]redeem you with a stretched out arm, and with great judgments: *Ps. 136:11 · Neh. 1:10*

7 And I will take you to me for a people, and [R]I will be to you a God: and ye shall know that I *am* the LORD your God, which bringeth you out from under the burdens of the Egyptians. *Deut. 29:13*

8 And I will bring you in unto

the land, concerning the which I did ^Rswear to give it to Abraham, to Isaac, and to Jacob; and I will give it you for an heritage: I *am* the LORD.   Gen. 15:18; 26:3; Num. 14:30

9 And Moses spake so unto the children of Israel: but they heark-ened not unto Moses for anguish of spirit, and for cruel bondage.

10 And the LORD spake unto Moses, saying,

11 Go in, speak unto Pharaoh king of Egypt, that he let the children of Israel go out of his land.

12 And Moses spake before the LORD, saying, Behold, the children of Israel have not hearkened unto me; how then shall Pharaoh hear me, ^Rwho *am* of uncircumcised lips?   v. 30; 4:10; Jer. 1:6

13 And the LORD spake unto Moses and unto Aaron, and gave them a charge unto the children of Israel, and unto Pharaoh king of Egypt, to bring the children of Israel out of the land of Egypt.

14 These *be* the heads of their fathers' houses: ^RThe sons of Reuben the firstborn of Israel; Ha'-noch, and Pal'-lu, Hez'-ron, and Car'-mi: these *be* the families of Reuben.   Num. 26:5–11; 1 Chr. 5:3

15 ^RAnd the sons of Simeon; Jem'-u-el, and Ja'-min, and O'-had, and Ja'-chin, and Zo'-har, and Sha'-ul the son of a Ca'-naan-i-tish woman: these *are* the families of Simeon.   Num. 26:12–14

16 And these *are* the names of the sons of Levi according to their generations; Ger'-shon, and Ko'-hath, and Me-ra'-ri: and the years of the life of Levi *were* an hundred thirty and seven years.

17 ^RThe sons of Ger'-shon; Lib'-ni, and Shim'-i, according to their families.   1 Chr. 6:17

18 And the sons of Ko'-hath; Am'-ram, and Iz'-har, and He'-bron, and Uz-zi'-el: and the years of the life of Ko'-hath *were* an hundred thirty and three years.

19 And ^Rthe sons of Me-ra'-ri; Ma'-ha-li and Mu'-shi: these *are*

the families of Levi according to their generations.   1 Chr. 6:19; 23:21

20 And ^RAm'-ram took him Joch'-e-bed his father's sister to wife; and she bare him Aaron and Moses: and the years of the life of Am'-ram *were* an hundred and thirty and seven years.   2:1, 2

21 And the sons of Iz'-har; Ko'-rah, and Ne'-pheg, and Zich'-ri.

22 And ^Rthe sons of Uz-zi'-el; Mish'-a-el, and El'-za-phan, and Zith'-ri.   Lev. 10:4

23 And Aaron took him E-lish'-e-ba, daughter of ^RAm-min'-a-dab, sister of Na-ash'-on, to wife; and she bare him ^RNa'-dab, and A-bi'-hu, ^RE-le-a'-zar, and Ith'-a-mar.   Ruth 4:19, 20 · Lev. 10:1 · 28:1

24 And ^Rthe sons of Ko'-rah; As'-sir, and El'-ka-nah, and A-bi'-a-saph: these *are* the families of the Kor'-hites.   Num. 26:11

25 And E-le-a'-zar Aaron's son took him *one* of the daughters of Pu'-ti-el to wife; and she bare him Phin'-e-has: these *are* the heads of the fathers of the Levites according to their families.

26 These *are* that Aaron and Moses, to whom the LORD said, Bring out the children of Israel from the land of Egypt according to their ^Rarmies.   12:17, 51; Num. 33:1

27 These *are* they which spake to Pharaoh king of Egypt, ^Rto bring out the children of Israel from Egypt: these *are* that Moses and Aaron.   v. 13; 32:7; 33:1; Ps. 77:20

28 And it came to pass on the day *when* the LORD spake unto Moses in the land of Egypt,

29 That the LORD spake unto Moses, saying, I *am* the LORD: ^Rspeak thou unto Pharaoh king of Egypt all that I say unto thee.   7:2

30 And Moses said before the LORD, Behold, ^RI *am* of uncircumcised lips, and how shall Pharaoh hearken unto me?   4:10; Jer. 1:6

7 And the LORD said unto Moses, See, I have made thee a god to Pharaoh: and Aaron thy brother shall be ^Rthy prophet.   4:15

2 Thou ^Rshalt speak all that I command thee: and Aaron thy

brother shall speak unto Pharaoh, that he send the children of Israel out of his land. Deut. 18:18

3 And I will harden Pharaoh's heart, and ᴿmultiply my ᴿsigns and my wonders in the land of Egypt. 11:9; Acts 7:36 · 4:7; Deut. 4:34

4 But Pharaoh shall not hearken unto you, that I may lay my hand upon Egypt, and bring forth mine armies, *and* my people the children of Israel, out of the land of Egypt ᴿby great judgments. 6:6

5 And the Egyptians ᴿshall know that I *am* the Lᴏʀᴅ, when I stretch forth mine hand upon Egypt, and bring out the children of Israel from among them. 8:22

6 And Moses and Aaron ᴿdid as the Lᴏʀᴅ commanded them, so did they. v. 2

7 And Moses *was* fourscore years old, and ᴿAaron fourscore and three years old, when they spake unto Pharaoh. Num. 33:39

8 And the Lᴏʀᴅ spake unto Moses and unto Aaron, saying,

9 When Pharaoh shall speak unto you, saying, ᴿShew a miracle for you: then thou shalt say unto Aaron, Take thy rod, and cast *it* before Pharaoh, *and* it shall become a serpent. Is. 7:11; John 2:18

10 And Moses and Aaron went in unto Pharaoh, and they did so ᴿas the Lᴏʀᴅ had commanded: and Aaron cast down his rod before Pharaoh, and before his servants, and it ᴿbecame a serpent. v. 9 · 4:3

11 Then Pharaoh also called the wise men and ᴿthe sorcerers: now the magicians of Egypt, they also did in like manner with their enchantments. Dan. 2:2; 2 Tim. 3:8, 9

12 For they cast down every man his rod, and they became serpents: but Aaron's rod swallowed up their rods.

13 And he hardened Pharaoh's heart, that he hearkened not unto them; as the Lᴏʀᴅ had said.

14 And the Lᴏʀᴅ said unto Moses, ᴿPharaoh's heart *is* hardened, he refuseth to let the people go. 8:15; 10:1, 20, 27

15 Get thee unto Pharaoh in the morning; lo, he goeth out unto the water; and thou shalt stand by the river's brink ᵀagainst he come; and ᴿthe rod which was turned to a serpent shalt thou take in thine hand. *to meet him* · v. 10; 4:2, 3

16 And thou shalt say unto him, ᴿThe Lᴏʀᴅ God of the Hebrews hath sent me unto thee, saying, Let my people go, ᴿthat they may ᵀserve me in the wilderness: and, behold, hitherto thou wouldest not hear. 4:22 · 3:12, 18; 4:23 · *worship*

17 Thus saith the Lᴏʀᴅ, In this thou shalt know that I *am* the Lᴏʀᴅ: behold, I will smite with the rod that *is* in mine hand upon the waters which *are* in the river, and they shall be turned to blood.

18 And the fish that *is* in the river shall die, and the river shall stink; and the Egyptians shall ᴿlotheᵀ to drink of the water of the river. v. 24 · *be weary of*

19 And the Lᴏʀᴅ spake unto Moses, Say unto Aaron, Take thy rod, and stretch out thine hand upon the waters of Egypt, upon their streams, upon their rivers, and upon their ponds, and upon all their pools of water, that they may become blood; and *that* there may be blood throughout all the land of Egypt, both in *vessels of* wood, and in *vessels of* stone.

20 And Moses and Aaron did so, as the Lᴏʀᴅ commanded; and he lifted up the rod, and smote the waters that *were* in the river, in the sight of Pharaoh, and in the sight of his servants; and all the ᴿwaters that *were* in the river were turned to blood. Ps. 78:44

21 And the fish that *was* in the river died; and the river stank, and the Egyptians ᴿcould not drink of the water of the river; and there was blood throughout all the land of Egypt. v. 18

22 And the magicians of Egypt did ᴿso with their enchantments: and Pharaoh's heart was hardened, neither did he hearken unto them; as the Lᴏʀᴅ had said. 8:7

23 And Pharaoh turned and

went into his house, neither did he set his heart to this also.

24 And all the Egyptians digged round about the river for water to drink; for they could not drink of the water of the river.

25 And seven days were fulfilled, after that the LORD had smitten the river.

8 And the LORD spake unto Moses, Go unto Pharaoh, and say unto him, Thus saith the LORD, Let my people go, ^Rthat they may serve me.   3:12, 18; 4:23; 5:1, 3

2 And if thou ^Rrefuse to let *them* go, behold, I will smite all thy borders with frogs: 7:14; 9:2

3 And the river shall bring forth frogs abundantly, which shall go up and come into thine house, and into thy bedchamber, and upon thy bed, and into the house of thy servants, and upon thy people, and into thine ovens, and into thy kneadingtroughs:

4 And the frogs shall come up both on thee, and upon thy people, and upon all thy servants.

5 And the LORD spake unto Moses, Say unto Aaron, Stretch forth thine hand with thy rod over the streams, over the rivers, and over the ponds, and cause frogs to come up upon the land of Egypt.

6 And Aaron stretched out his hand over the waters of Egypt; and ^Rthe frogs came up, and covered the land of Egypt.   Ps. 105:30

7 ^RAnd the magicians did so with their ^Tenchantments, and brought up frogs upon the land of Egypt.   7:11, 22 · *secret arts*

8 Then Pharaoh called for Moses and Aaron, and said, ^RIntreat the LORD, that he may take away the frogs from me, and from my people; and I will let the people go, that they may do sacrifice unto the LORD.   1 Kin. 13:6

9 And Moses said unto Pharaoh, Glory over me: when shall I intreat for thee, and for thy servants, and for thy people, to destroy the frogs from thee and thy houses, *that* they may remain in the river only?

10 And he said, To morrow. And he said, *Be it* according to thy word: that thou mayest know that ^R*there is* none like unto the LORD our God.   1 Chr. 17:20; Ps. 86:8; Is. 46:9

11 And the frogs shall depart from thee, and from thy houses, and from thy servants, and from thy people; they shall remain in the river only.

12 And Moses and Aaron went out from Pharaoh: and Moses ^Rcried unto the LORD because of the frogs which he had brought against Pharaoh.   9:33; 10:18; 32:11

13 And the LORD did according to the word of Moses; and the frogs died out of the houses, out of the villages, and out of the fields.

14 And they gathered them together upon heaps: and the land stank.

15 But when Pharaoh saw that there was respite, ^Rhe hardened his heart, and hearkened not unto them; as the LORD had said.   9:34

16 And the LORD said unto Moses, Say unto Aaron, Stretch out thy rod, and smite the dust of the land, that it may become lice throughout all the land of Egypt.

17 And they did so; for Aaron stretched out his hand with his rod, and smote the dust of the earth, and ^Rit became lice in man, and in beast; all the dust of the land became lice throughout all the land of Egypt.   Ps. 105:31

18 And the magicians did so with their enchantments to bring forth lice, but they ^Rcould not: so there were lice upon man, and upon beast.   Dan. 5:8; 2 Tim. 3:8, 9

19 Then the magicians said unto Pharaoh, This *is* the finger of God: and Pharaoh's heart was hardened, and he hearkened not unto them; as the LORD had said.

20 And the LORD said unto Moses, ^RRise up early in the morning, and stand before Pharaoh; lo, he cometh forth to the water; and say unto him, Thus saith the LORD, Let my people go, that they may serve me.   7:15; 9:13

21 Else, if thou wilt not let my

people go, behold, I will send swarms *of flies* upon thee, and upon thy servants, and upon thy people, and into thy houses: and the houses of the Egyptians shall be full of swarms *of flies*, and also the ground whereon they *are*.

22 And I will sever in that day the land of Go′-shen, in which my people dwell, that no swarms *of flies* shall be there; to the end thou mayest know that I *am* the LORD in the midst of the ᴿearth.   9:29

23 And I will put a division between my people and thy people: to morrow shall this ᴿsign be.   4:8

24 And the LORD did so; and ᴿthere came a grievous swarm *of flies* into the house of Pharaoh, and *into* his servants' houses, and into all the land of Egypt: the land was ᵀcorrupted by reason of the swarm *of flies*.   Ps. 105:31 · *destroyed*

25 And Pharaoh called for Moses and for Aaron, and said, Go ye, sacrifice to your God in the land.

26 And Moses said, It is not meet so to do; for we shall sacrifice the abomination of the Egyptians to the LORD our God: lo, shall we sacrifice the abomination of the Egyptians before their eyes, and will they not stone us?

27 We will go ᴿthree days' journey into the wilderness, and sacrifice to the LORD our God, as ᴿhe shall command us.   3:18; 5:3 · 3:12

28 And Pharaoh said, I will let you go, that ye may sacrifice to the LORD your God in the wilderness; only ye shall not go very far away: ᴿintreat for me.   1 Kin. 13:6

29 And Moses said, Behold, I go out from thee, and I will intreat the LORD that the swarms *of flies* may depart from Pharaoh, from his servants, and from his people, to morrow: but let not Pharaoh ᴿdeal deceitfully any more in not letting the people go to sacrifice to the LORD.   vv. 8, 15

30 And Moses went out from Pharaoh, and intreated the LORD.

31 And the LORD did according to the word of Moses; and he removed the swarms *of flies* from Pharaoh, from his servants, and from his people; there remained not one.

32 And Pharaoh ᴿhardened his heart at this time also, neither would he let the people go.   Ps. 52:2

9 Then the LORD said unto Moses, Go in unto Pharaoh, and tell him, Thus saith the LORD God of the Hebrews, Let my people go, that they may ᴿserve me.   7:16

2 For if thou ᴿrefuse to let *them* go, and wilt hold them still,   8:2

3 Behold, the ᴿhand of the LORD is upon thy cattle which *is* in the field, upon the horses, upon the asses, upon the camels, upon the oxen, and upon the sheep: *there shall be* a very ᵀgrievous murrain.   Ps. 39:10 · *severe pestilence*

4 And the LORD shall ᵀsever between the cattle of Israel and the cattle of Egypt: and there shall nothing die of all *that is* the children's of Israel.   *make a difference*

5 And the LORD appointed a set time, saying, To morrow the LORD shall do this thing in the land.

6 And the LORD did that thing on the morrow, and all the cattle of Egypt died: but of the cattle of the children of Israel died not one.

7 And Pharaoh sent, and, behold, there was not one of the cattle of the Israelites dead. And the heart of Pharaoh was hardened, and he did not let the people go.

8 And the LORD said unto Moses and unto Aaron, Take to you handfuls of ashes of the furnace, and let Moses sprinkle it toward the heaven in the sight of Pharaoh.

9 And it shall become small dust in all the land of Egypt, and shall be ᴿa boil breaking forth *with* ᵀblains upon man, and upon beast, throughout all the land of Egypt.   Deut. 28:27; Rev. 16:2 · *sores*

10 And they took ashes of the furnace, and stood before Pharaoh; and Moses sprinkled it up toward heaven; and it became a boil breaking forth *with* blains upon man, and upon beast.

11 And the magicians could not stand before Moses because of the ᴿboils; for the boil was upon the magicians, and upon all the Egyptians.　　　Job 2:7; Rev. 16:1, 2

12 And the Lᴏʀᴅ hardened the heart of Pharaoh, and he ᴿhearkened not unto them; ᴿas the Lᴏʀᴅ had spoken unto Moses.　7:13 · 4:21

13 And the Lᴏʀᴅ said unto Moses, ᴿRise up early in the morning, and stand before Pharaoh, and say unto him, Thus saith the Lᴏʀᴅ God of the Hebrews, Let my people go, that they may ᴿserve me.　　8:20 · v. 1

14 For I will at this time send all my plagues upon thine heart, and upon thy servants, and upon thy people; ᴿthat thou mayest know that *there is* none like me in all the earth.　Ps. 86:8; Is. 45:5–8; Jer. 10:6, 7

15 For now I will ᴿstretch out my hand, that I may smite thee and thy people with ᴿpestilence; and thou shalt be cut off from the earth.　　　3:20; 7:5 · 5:3

16 And in very deed for this *cause* have I raised thee up, for to ᴿshew *in* thee my power; and that my name may be declared throughout all the earth.　11:9; 14:17

17 As yet exaltest thou thyself against my people, that thou wilt not let them go?

18 Behold, to morrow about this time I will cause it to rain a very grievous hail, such as hath not been in Egypt since the foundation thereof even until now.

19 Send therefore now, *and* gather thy cattle, and all that thou hast in the field; *for upon* every man and beast which shall be found in the field, and shall not be brought home, the hail shall come down upon them, and they shall die.

20 He that feared the word of the Lᴏʀᴅ among the servants of Pharaoh made his servants and his cattle flee into the houses:

21 And he that regarded not the word of the Lᴏʀᴅ left his servants and his cattle in the field.

22 And the Lᴏʀᴅ said unto Moses, Stretch forth thine hand toward heaven, that there may be ᴿhail in all the land of Egypt, upon man, and upon beast, and upon every herb of the field, throughout the land of Egypt.　　Rev. 16:21

23 And Moses stretched forth his rod toward heaven: and ᴿthe Lᴏʀᴅ sent thunder and hail, and the fire ran along upon the ground; and the Lᴏʀᴅ rained hail upon the land of Egypt.　Rev. 8:7

24 So there was hail, and fire mingled with the hail, very grievous, such as there was none like it in all the land of Egypt since it became a nation.

25 And the ᴿhail smote throughout all the land of Egypt all that *was* in the field, both man and beast; and the hail smote every herb of the field, and brake every tree of the field.　Ps. 78:47; 105:32, 33

26 ᴿOnly in the land of Go'-shen, where the children of Israel *were*, was there no hail.　12:13; Is. 32:18, 19

27 And Pharaoh sent, and called for Moses and Aaron, and said unto them, I have sinned this time: ᴿthe Lᴏʀᴅ *is* righteous, and I and my people *are* wicked.　2 Chr. 12:6

28 ᴿIntreat the Lᴏʀᴅ (for *it is* enough) that there be no *more* mighty thunderings and hail; and I will let you go, and ye shall stay no longer.　8:8, 28; 10:17; Acts 8:24

29 And Moses said unto him, As soon as I am gone out of the city, I will ᴿspread abroad my hands unto the Lᴏʀᴅ; *and* the thunder shall cease, neither shall there be any more hail; that thou mayest know how that the ᴿearth *is* the Lᴏʀᴅ's.　Is. 1:15 · Ps. 24:1; 1 Cor. 10:26, 28

30 But as for thee and thy servants, ᴿI know that ye will not yet fear the Lᴏʀᴅ God.　8:29; [Is. 26:10]

31 And the flax and the barley was smitten: for the barley *was* in the ear, and the flax *was* bolled.

32 But the wheat and the ᵀrie were not smitten: for they *were* ᵀnot grown up.　spelt · Lit. *darkened*

33 And Moses went out of the city from Pharaoh, and ᴿspread abroad his hands unto the Lᴏʀᴅ: and the thunders and hail ceased,

and the rain was not poured upon the earth. v. 29; 8:12

34 And when Pharaoh saw that the rain and the hail and the thunders were ceased, he sinned yet more, and hardened his heart, he and his servants.

35 And ᴿthe heart of Pharaoh was hardened, neither would he let the children of Israel go; as the LORD had spoken by Moses. 4:21

10 And the LORD said unto Moses, Go in unto Pharaoh: ᴿfor I have hardened his heart, and the heart of his servants, ᴿthat I might shew these my signs before him: John 12:40; Rom. 9:18 · 7:4

2 And that ᴿthou mayest tell in the ears of thy son, and of thy son's son, what things I have wrought in Egypt, and my signs which I have done among them; that ye may ᴿknow how that I *am* the LORD. Ps. 44:1; 78:5; Joel 1:3 · 7:5, 17

3 And Moses and Aaron came in unto Pharaoh, and said unto him, Thus saith the LORD God of the Hebrews, How long wilt thou refuse to ᴿhumble thyself before me? let my people go, that they may serve me. [James 4:10; 1 Pet. 5:6]

4 Else, if thou refuse to let my people go, behold, to morrow will I bring the locusts into thy coast:

5 And they shall cover the face of the earth, that one cannot be able to see the earth: and ᴿthey shall eat the residue of that which is escaped, which remaineth unto you from the hail, and shall eat every tree which groweth for you out of the field: 9:32; Joel 1:4; 2:25

6 And they shall ᴿfill thy houses, and the houses of all thy servants, and the houses of all the Egyptians; which neither thy fathers, nor thy fathers' fathers have seen, since the day that they were upon the earth unto this day. And he turned himself, and went out from Pharaoh. 8:3, 21

7 And Pharaoh's servants said unto him, How long shall this man be ᴿa snare unto us? let the men go, that they may serve the LORD their God: knowest thou not yet that Egypt is destroyed? 23:33

8 And Moses and Aaron were brought again unto Pharaoh: and he said unto them, Go, serve the LORD your God: *but* who *are* they that shall go?

9 And Moses said, We will go with our young and with our old, with our sons and with our daughters, with our flocks and with our herds will we go; for we *must hold* a feast unto the LORD.

10 And he said unto them, Let the LORD be so with you, as I will let you go, and your little ones: look *to it*; for evil *is* before you.

11 Not so: go now ye *that are* men, and serve the LORD; for that ye did desire. And they were driven out from Pharaoh's presence.

12 And the LORD said unto Moses, ᴿStretch out thine hand over the land of Egypt for the locusts, that they may come up upon the land of Egypt, and ᴿeat every herb of the land, *even* all that the hail hath left. 7:19 · vv. 5, 15

13 And Moses stretched forth his rod over the land of Egypt, and the LORD brought an east wind upon the land all that day, and all *that* night; *and* when it was morning, the east wind brought the locusts.

14 And ᴿthe locusts went up over all the land of Egypt, and rested in all the coasts of Egypt: very grievous *were they;* ᴿbefore them there were no such locusts as they, neither after them shall be such. Ps. 78:46 · Joel 2:1–11; Rev. 9:3

15 For they ᴿcovered the face of the whole earth, so that the land was darkened; and they ᴿdid eat every herb of the land, and all the fruit of the trees which the hail had left: and there remained not any green thing in the trees, or in the herbs of the field, through all the land of Egypt. v. 5 · Ps. 105:35

16 Then Pharaoh called for Moses and Aaron in haste; and he said, I have sinned against the LORD your God, and against you.

17 Now therefore forgive, I pray

thee, my sin only this once, and ᴿintreatᵀ the LORD your God, that he may take away from me this death only.   9:28; 1 Kin. 13:6 · *pray to*

18 And he ᴿwent out from Pharaoh, and intreated the LORD.   8:30

19 And the LORD turned a mighty strong west wind, which took away the locusts, and cast them ᴿinto the Red sea; there remained not one locust in all the ᵀcoasts of Egypt.   Joel 2:20 · *territory*

20 But the LORD ᴿhardened Pharaoh's heart, so that he would not let the children of Israel go.   4:21

21 And the LORD said unto Moses, Stretch out thine hand toward heaven, that there may be darkness over the land of Egypt, even darkness *which* may be felt.

22 And Moses stretched forth his hand toward heaven; and there was a thick darkness in all the land of Egypt three days:

23 They saw not one another, neither rose any from his place for three days: ᴿbut all the children of Israel had light in their dwellings.   8:22, 23

24 And Pharaoh called unto Moses, and said, Go ye, serve the LORD; only let your flocks and your herds be stayed: let your ᴿlittle ones also go with you.   v. 10

25 And Moses said, Thou must give us also sacrifices and burnt offerings, that we may sacrifice unto the LORD our God.

26 Our ᴿcattle also shall go with us; there shall not an hoof be left behind; for thereof must we take to serve the LORD our God; and we know not with what we must serve the LORD, until we come thither.   v. 9

27 But the LORD ᴿhardened Pharaoh's heart, and he would not let them go.   vv. 1, 20; 4:21; 14:4, 8

28 And Pharaoh said unto him, ᴿGet thee from me, take heed to thyself, see my face no more; for in *that* day thou seest my face thou shalt die.   v. 11

29 And Moses said, Thou hast spoken well, ᴿI will see thy face again no more.   11:8; Heb. 11:27

11 And the LORD said unto Moses, Yet will I bring one plague *more* upon Pharaoh, and upon Egypt; afterwards he will let you go hence: ᴿwhen he shall let *you* go, he shall surely thrust you out hence altogether.   6:1; 12:39

2 Speak now in the ears of the people, and let every man ᵀborrow of his neighbour, and every woman of her neighbour, jewels of silver, and jewels of gold.   *ask*

3 ᴿAnd the LORD gave the people favour in the sight of the Egyptians. Moreover the man ᴿMoses *was* very great in the land of Egypt, in the sight of Pharaoh's servants, and in the sight of the people.   Ps. 106:46 · 2 Sam. 7:9; Esth. 9:4

4 And Moses said, Thus saith the LORD, About midnight will I go out into the midst of Egypt:

5 And ᴿall the firstborn in the land of Egypt shall die, from the firstborn of Pharaoh that sitteth upon his throne, even unto the firstborn of the maidservant that *is* behind the mill; and all the firstborn of beasts.   Ps. 78:51; Amos 4:10

6 ᴿAnd there shall be a great cry throughout all the land of Egypt, ᴿsuch as there was none like it, nor shall be like it any more.   12:30; Amos 5:17 · 10:14

7 But against any of the children of Israel shall not a dog move his tongue, against man or beast: that ye may know how that the LORD doth put a difference between the Egyptians and Israel.

8 And ᴿall these thy servants shall come down unto me, and bow down themselves unto me, saying, Get thee out, and all the people that follow thee: and after that I will go out. ᴿAnd he went out from Pharaoh in a great anger.   12:31–33 · 10:29; Heb. 11:27

9 And the LORD said unto Moses, ᴿPharaoh shall not hearken unto you; that ᴿmy wonders may be multiplied in the land of Egypt.   3:19; 7:4; 10:1 · 7:3; 9:16

10 And Moses and Aaron did all these wonders before Pharaoh: ᴿand the LORD hardened Pha-

raoh's heart, so that he would not let the children of Israel go out of his land. Is. 63:17; John 12:40; Rom. 2:5

12 And the LORD spake unto Moses and Aaron in the land of Egypt, saying,

2 ᴿThis month *shall be* unto you the beginning of months: it *shall be* the first month of the year to you. 13:4; 23:15; 34:18; Deut. 16:1

3 Speak ye unto all the congregation of Israel, saying, In the tenth *day* of this month they shall take to them every man a lamb, according to the house of *their* fathers, a lamb for an house:

4 And if the household be too little for the lamb, let him and his neighbour next unto his house take *it* according to the number of the ᵀsouls; every man according to his eating shall make your count for the lamb. *persons*

5 Your lamb shall be ᴿwithout blemish, a male of the first year: ye shall take *it* out from the sheep, or from the goats: Mal. 1:8

6 And ye shall keep it up until the ᴿfourteenth day of the same month: and the whole assembly of the congregation of Israel shall kill it in the evening. Lev. 23:5

7 And they shall take of the blood, and strike *it* on the two side posts and on the upper door post of the houses, wherein they shall eat it.

8 And they shall eat the flesh in that night, ᴿroast with fire, and unleavened bread; *and* with bitter *herbs* they shall eat it. Deut. 16:7

9 Eat not of it raw, nor sodden at all with water, but roast *with* fire; his head with his legs, and with the purtenance thereof.

10 ᴿAnd ye shall let nothing of it remain until the morning; and that which remaineth of it until the morning ye shall burn with fire. 16:19; 23:18; 34:25

11 And thus shall ye eat it; *with* your loins girded, your shoes on your feet, and your staff in your hand; and ye shall eat it in haste: ᴿit *is* the LORD's passover. vv. 13, 21

12 For I ᴿwill pass through the land of Egypt this night, and will smite all the firstborn in the land of Egypt, both man and beast; and ᴿagainst all the gods of Egypt I will execute judgment: ᴿI *am* the LORD. 11:4, 5 · Num. 33:4 · 6:2

13 And the blood shall be to you for a ᵀtoken upon the houses where ye *are:* and when I see the blood, I will pass over you, and the plague shall not be upon you to destroy *you,* when I smite the land of Egypt. *sign*

14 And this day shall be unto you ᴿfor a memorial; and ye shall keep it a ᴿfeast to the LORD throughout your generations; ye shall keep it a feast by an ordinance for ever. 13:9 · Lev. 23:4, 5

15 ᴿSeven days shall ye eat unleavened bread; even the first day ye shall put away leaven out of your houses: for whosoever eateth leavened bread from the first day until the seventh day, ᴿthat soul shall be cut off from Israel. Lev. 23:6 · Gen. 17:14; Num. 9:13

16 And in the first day *there shall be* ᴿan holy convocation, and in the seventh day there shall be an holy convocation to you; no manner of work shall be done in them, save *that* which every man must eat, that only may be done of you. Lev. 23:2, 7; 8; Num. 28:18, 25

17 And ye shall observe *the feast of* unleavened bread; for in this selfsame day have I brought your armies ᴿout of the land of Egypt: therefore shall ye observe this day in your generations by an ordinance for ever. Num. 33:1

18 ᴿIn the first *month,* on the fourteenth day of the month at even, ye shall eat unleavened bread, until the one and twentieth day of the month at even. v. 2

19 ᴿSeven days shall there be no leaven found in your houses: for whosoever eateth that which is leavened, even that soul shall be cut off from the congregation of Israel, whether he be a stranger, or born in the land. 23:15; 34:18

20 Ye shall eat nothing leav-

ened; in all your habitations shall ye eat unleavened bread.

21 Then Moses called for all the elders of Israel, and said unto them, ^RDraw out and take you a lamb according to your families, and kill the passover.   Num. 9:4

22 ^RAnd ye shall take a bunch of hyssop, and dip *it* in the blood that *is* in the bason, and ^Rstrike the lintel and the two side posts with the blood that *is* in the bason; and none of you shall go out at the door of his house until the morning.   Heb. 11:28 · v. 7

23 For the LORD will pass through to smite the Egyptians; and when he seeth the blood upon the lintel, and on the two side posts, the LORD will pass over the door, and will not suffer ^Rthe destroyer to come in unto your houses to smite *you*.   1 Cor. 10:10

24 And ye shall ^Robserve this thing for an ordinance to thee and to thy sons for ever.   13:5, 10

25 And it shall come to pass, when ye be come to the land which the LORD will give you, according as he hath promised, that ye shall keep this service.

26 ^RAnd it shall come to pass, when your children shall say unto you, What mean ye by this service?   Deut. 32:7; Josh. 4:6; Ps. 78:6

27 That ye shall say, ^RIt *is* the sacrifice of the LORD'S passover, who passed over the houses of the children of Israel in Egypt, when he smote the Egyptians, and delivered our houses. And the people ^Rbowed the head and worshipped.   v. 11 · 4:31

28 And the children of Israel went away, and ^Rdid as the LORD had commanded Moses and Aaron, so did they.   [Heb. 11:28]

29 And it came to pass, that at midnight ^Rthe LORD smote all the firstborn in the land of Egypt, from the firstborn of Pharaoh that sat on his throne unto the firstborn of the captive that *was* in the dungeon; and all the firstborn of cattle.   Num. 8:17; 33:4; Ps. 135:8; 136:10

30 And Pharaoh rose up in the night, he, and all his servants, and all the Egyptians; and there was a great cry in Egypt; for *there was* not a house where *there was* not one dead.

31 And he ^Rcalled for Moses and Aaron by night, and said, Rise up, *and* get you forth from among my people, ^Rboth ye and the children of Israel; and go, serve the LORD, as ye have said.   10:28, 29 · 8:25; 11:1

32 ^RAlso take your flocks and your herds, as ye have said, and be gone; and bless me also. 10:9, 26

33 ^RAnd the Egyptians were ^Rurgent upon the people, that they might send them out of the land in haste; for they said, We *be* all dead *men*.   10:7 · 11:8; Ps. 105:38

34 And the people took their dough before it was leavened, their ^Tkneadingtroughs being bound up in their clothes upon their shoulders.   *dough*

35 And the children of Israel did according to the word of Moses; and they ^Tborrowed of the Egyptians jewels of silver, and jewels of gold, and raiment: *asked from*

36 And the LORD gave the people favour in the sight of the Egyptians, so that they ^Tlent unto them *such things as they required.* And they ^Tspoiled the Egyptians.   *granted · plundered*

37 And the children of Israel journeyed from ^RRam'-e-ses to Suc'-coth, about six hundred thousand on foot *that were* men, beside children.   Gen. 47:11; Num. 33:3

38 And a mixed multitude went up also with them; and flocks, and herds, *even* very much cattle.

39 And they baked unleavened cakes of the dough which they brought forth out of Egypt, for it was not leavened; because ^Rthey were thrust out of Egypt, and could not tarry, neither had they prepared for themselves any victual.   vv. 31–33; 6:1; 11:1

40 Now the sojourning of the children of Israel, who dwelt in Egypt, *was* ^Rfour hundred and thirty years.   Gen. 15:13, 16; Acts 7:6

41 And it came to pass at the

end of the four hundred and thirty years, even the selfsame day it came to pass, that ᴿall the hosts of the Lᴏʀᴅ went out from the land of Egypt.   3:8, 10; 6:6; 7:4

42 It *is* ᴿa night to be much observed unto the Lᴏʀᴅ for bringing them out from the land of Egypt: this *is* that night of the Lᴏʀᴅ to be observed of all the children of Israel in their generations.   13:10

43 And the Lᴏʀᴅ said unto Moses and Aaron, This *is* ᴿthe ordinance of the passover: There shall no stranger eat thereof: Num. 9:14

44 But every man's servant that is bought for money, when thou hast ᴿcircumcised him, then shall he eat thereof.   Gen. 17:12; Lev. 22:11

45 A foreigner and an hired servant shall not eat thereof.

☆ 46 In one house shall it be eaten; thou shalt not carry forth ought of the flesh abroad out of the house; ᴿneither shall ye break a bone thereof.   Ps. 34:20; [John 19:33, 36]

47 ᴿAll the congregation of Israel shall keep it.   v. 6; Num. 9:13, 14

48 And when a stranger shall sojourn with thee, and will keep the passover to the Lᴏʀᴅ, let all his males be circumcised, and then let him come near and keep it; and he shall be as one that is born in the land: for no uncircumcised person shall eat thereof.

49 One law shall be to him that is homeborn, and unto the stranger that sojourneth among you.

50 Thus did all the children of Israel; as the Lᴏʀᴅ commanded Moses and Aaron, so did they.

51 And it came to pass the selfsame day, *that* the Lᴏʀᴅ did bring the children of Israel out of the land of Egypt by their armies.

13 And the Lᴏʀᴅ spake unto Moses, saying,

2 ᴿSanctifyᵀ unto me all the firstborn, whatsoever openeth the womb among the children of Israel, *both* of man and of beast: it *is* mine.   Lev. 27:26; Luke 2:23 · *Set apart*

3 And Moses said unto the people, ᴿRemember this day, in which ye came out from Egypt,

out of the house of bondage; for ᴿby strength of hand the Lᴏʀᴅ brought you out from this *place*: ᴿthere shall no leavened bread be eaten.   12:42; Deut. 16:3 · 3:20; 6:1 · 12:8, 19

4 ᴿThis day came ye out in the month A'-bib.   23:15; 34:18; Deut. 16:1

5 And it shall be when the Lᴏʀᴅ shall bring thee into the land of the Ca'-naan-ites, and the Hit'-tites, and the Am'-or-ites, and the Hi'-vites, and the Jeb'-u-sites, which he sware unto thy fathers to give thee, a land flowing with milk and honey, that thou shalt keep this service in this month.

6 ᴿSeven days thou shalt eat unleavened bread, and in the seventh day *shall be* a feast to the Lᴏʀᴅ.   12:15–20

7 Unleavened bread shall be eaten seven days; and there shall no leavened bread be seen with thee, neither shall there be leaven seen with thee in all thy quarters.

8 And thou shalt ᴿshew thy son in that day, saying, *This is done* because of *that which* the Lᴏʀᴅ did unto me when I came forth out of Egypt.   10:2; 12:26; Ps. 44:1

9 And it shall be for ᴿa sign unto thee upon thine hand, and for a memorial between thine eyes, that the Lᴏʀᴅ's law may be in thy mouth: for with a strong hand hath the Lᴏʀᴅ brought thee out of Egypt.   Deut. 6:8; 11:18; Matt. 23:5

10 ᴿThou shalt therefore keep this ᵀordinance in his season from year to year.   12:14, 24 · *regulation*

11 And it shall be when the Lᴏʀᴅ shall ᴿbring thee into the land of the Ca'-naan-ites, as he sware unto thee and to thy fathers, and shall give it thee,   v. 5

12 That thou shalt ᵀset apart unto the Lᴏʀᴅ all that openeth the ᵀmatrix, and every firstling that cometh of a beast which thou hast; the males *shall be* the Lᴏʀᴅ's.   Lit. *cause to pass over · womb*

13 And ᴿevery firstling of an ass thou shalt redeem with a lamb; and if thou wilt not redeem it, then thou shalt break his neck:

and all the firstborn of man among thy children ^Rshalt thou redeem.   Num. 18:15 · Num. 3:46, 47

14 ^RAnd it shall be when thy son asketh thee in time to come, saying, What *is* this? that thou shalt say unto him, ^RBy strength of hand the LORD brought us out from Egypt, from the house of bondage: Deut. 6:20; Josh. 4:6 · vv. 3, 9

15 And it came to pass, when Pharaoh would hardly let us go, that the LORD slew all the firstborn in the land of Egypt, both the firstborn of man, and the firstborn of beast: therefore I sacrifice to the LORD all that openeth the matrix, being males; but all the firstborn of my children I redeem.

16 And it shall be for a token upon thine hand, and for frontlets between thine eyes: for by strength of hand the LORD brought us forth out of Egypt.

17 And it came to pass, when Pharaoh had let the people go, that God led them not *through* the way of the land of the Phi-lis'-tines, although that *was* near; for God said, Lest peradventure the people repent when they see war, and they return to Egypt:

18 But God ^Rled the people about, *through* the way of the wilderness of the Red sea: and the children of Israel went up ^Tharnessed out of the land of Egypt.   14:2; Num. 33:6 · *in orderly ranks*

19 And Moses took the bones of ^RJoseph with him: for he had straitly sworn the children of Israel, saying, God will surely visit you; and ye shall carry up my bones away hence with you.   1:6

20 And ^Rthey took their journey from ^RSuc'-coth, and encamped in E'-tham, in the edge of the wilderness.   Num. 33:6–8 · 12:37

21 And the LORD went before them by day in a pillar of a cloud, to lead them the way; and by night in a pillar of fire, to give them light; to go by day and night:

22 He took not away the pillar of the cloud by day, nor the pillar of fire by night, *from* before the people.

14 And the LORD spake unto Moses, saying,

2 Speak unto the children of Israel, ^Rthat they turn and encamp before Pi–ha-hi'-roth, between Mig'-dol and the sea, over against Ba'-al–ze'-phon: before it shall ye encamp by the sea.   13:18

3 For Pharaoh will say of the children of Israel, ^RThey *are* entangled in the land, the wilderness hath shut them in.   Ps. 71:11

4 And I will harden Pharaoh's heart, that he shall follow after them; and I will be honoured upon Pharaoh, and upon all his host; ^Rthat the Egyptians may know that I *am* the LORD. And they did so.   v. 25; 7:5

5 And it was told the king of Egypt that the people fled: and the heart of Pharaoh and of his servants was turned against the people, and they said, Why have we done this, that we have let Israel go from serving us?

6 And he made ready his chariot, and took his people with him:

7 And he took ^Rsix hundred chosen chariots, and all the chariots of Egypt, and captains over every one of them.   15:4

8 And the LORD hardened the heart of Pharaoh king of Egypt, and he pursued after the children of Israel: and the children of Israel went out with an high hand.

9 But the ^REgyptians pursued after them, all the horses *and* chariots of Pharaoh, and his horsemen, and his army, and overtook them encamping by the sea, beside Pi–ha-hi'-roth, before Ba'-al–ze'-phon.   15:9; Josh. 24:6

10 And when Pharaoh drew nigh, the children of Israel lifted up their eyes, and, behold, the Egyptians marched after them; and they were sore afraid: and the children of Israel ^Rcried out unto the LORD.   Josh. 24:7; Neh. 9:9; Ps. 34:17

11 ^RAnd they said unto Moses,

Because *there were* no graves in Egypt, hast thou taken us away to die in the wilderness? wherefore hast thou dealt thus with us, to carry us forth out of Egypt? 5:21

12 ^R*Is* not this the word that we did tell thee in Egypt, saying, Let us alone, that we may serve the Egyptians? For *it had been* better for us to serve the Egyptians, than that we should die in the wilderness. 5:21; 6:9

13 And Moses said unto the people, Fear ye not, stand still, and see the ^Tsalvation of the LORD, which he will shew to you to day: for the Egyptians whom ye have seen to day, ye shall see them again no more for ever. *deliverance*

14 The LORD shall fight for you, and ye shall hold your peace.

15 And the LORD said unto Moses, Wherefore criest thou unto me? speak unto the children of Israel, that they go forward:

16 But ^Rlift thou up thy rod, and stretch out thine hand over the sea, and divide it: and the children of Israel shall go on dry *ground* through the midst of the sea. 4:17

17 And I, behold, I will harden the hearts of the Egyptians, and they shall follow them: and I will get me honour upon Pharaoh, and upon all his host, upon his chariots, and upon his horsemen.

18 And the Egyptians shall know that I *am* the LORD, when I have gotten me honour upon Pharaoh, upon his chariots, and upon his horsemen.

19 And the angel of God, ^Rwhich went before the camp of Israel, removed and went behind them; and the pillar of the cloud went from before their face, and stood behind them: 13:21, 22; [Is. 63:9]

20 And it came between the camp of the Egyptians and the camp of Israel; and it was a cloud and darkness *to them,* but it gave light by night *to these:* so that the one came not near the other all the night.

21 And Moses stretched out his hand over the sea; and the LORD caused the sea to go *back* by a strong east wind all that night, and made the sea dry *land,* and the waters were ^Rdivided. Ps. 74:13

22 And the children of Israel went into the midst of the sea upon the dry *ground:* and the waters *were* a wall unto them on their right hand, and on their left.

23 And the Egyptians pursued, and went in after them to the midst of the sea, *even* all Pharaoh's horses, his chariots, and his horsemen.

24 And it came to pass, that in the morning watch the LORD looked unto the host of the Egyptians through the pillar of fire and of the cloud, and troubled the host of the Egyptians,

25 And took off their chariot wheels, that they drave them heavily: so that the Egyptians said, Let us flee from the face of Israel; for the LORD ^Rfighteth for them against the Egyptians. 7:5

26 And the LORD said unto Moses, Stretch out thine hand over the sea, that the waters may come again upon the Egyptians, upon their chariots, and upon their horsemen.

27 And Moses stretched forth his hand over the sea, and the sea ^Rreturned to his strength when the morning appeared; and the Egyptians fled against it; and the LORD overthrew the Egyptians in the midst of the sea. Josh. 4:18

28 And the waters returned, and ^Rcovered the chariots, and the horsemen, *and* all the host of Pharaoh that came into the sea after them; there remained not so much as one of them. Ps. 78:53

29 But ^Rthe children of Israel walked upon dry *land* in the midst of the sea; and the waters *were* a wall unto them on their right hand, and on their left. Is. 11:15

30 Thus the LORD ^Rsaved Israel that day out of the hand of the Egyptians; and Israel saw the Egyptians dead upon the sea shore. v. 13; Ps. 106:8, 10; Is. 63:8, 11

31 And Israel saw that great work which the LORD did upon

the Egyptians: and the people feared the LORD, and [R]believed the LORD, and his servant Moses.   4:31

15 Then sang Moses and the children of Israel this song unto the LORD, and spake, saying, I will [R]sing unto the LORD, for he hath triumphed gloriously: the horse and his rider hath he thrown into the sea.   Is. 12:1–6

2 The LORD *is* my strength and song, and he is become my salvation: he *is* my God, and I will prepare him an habitation; my father's God, and I will exalt him.

3 The LORD *is* a man of [R]war: the LORD *is* his name.   Rev. 19:11

4 [R]Pharaoh's chariots and his host hath he cast into the sea: [R]his chosen captains also are drowned in the Red sea.   14:28 · 14:7

5 The depths have covered them: [R]they sank into the bottom as a stone.   v. 10; Neh. 9:11

6 [R]Thy right hand, O LORD, is become glorious in power: thy right hand, O LORD, hath dashed in pieces the enemy.   Ps. 17:7; 118:15

7 And in the greatness of thine excellency thou hast overthrown them that rose up against thee: thou sentest forth thy [R]wrath, *which* consumed them [R]as stubble.   Ps. 78:49, 50 · Deut. 4:24; Heb. 12:29

8 And with the blast of thy nostrils the waters were gathered together, the floods stood upright as an heap, *and* the depths were congealed in the heart of the sea.

9 The enemy said, I will pursue, I will overtake, I will divide the spoil; my lust shall be satisfied upon them; I will draw my sword, my hand shall destroy them.

10 Thou didst blow with thy wind, the sea covered them: they sank as lead in the mighty waters.

11 [R]Who *is* like unto thee, O LORD, among the [T]gods? who *is* like thee, glorious in holiness, fearful *in* praises, [R]doing wonders?   Deut. 3:24 · *mighty ones* · Ps. 77:11

12 Thou stretchedst out thy right hand, the earth swallowed them.

13 Thou in thy mercy hast led forth the people *which* thou hast redeemed: thou hast guided *them* in thy strength unto [R]thy holy habitation.   Deut. 12:5; Ps. 78:54

14 [R]The people shall hear, *and* be afraid: [R]sorrow shall take hold on the inhabitants of [T]Pal-es-ti'-na.   Josh. 2:9 · Ps. 48:6 · Or *Philistia*

15 Then the dukes of E'-dom shall be amazed; the mighty men of Moab, trembling shall take hold upon them; all the inhabitants of Canaan shall melt away.

16 [R]Fear and dread shall fall upon them; by the greatness of thine arm they shall be *as* still as a stone; till thy people pass over, O LORD, till the people pass over, *which* thou hast purchased.   23:27

17 Thou shalt bring them in, and [R]plant them in the [R]mountain of thine inheritance, *in* the place, O LORD, *which* thou hast made for thee to dwell in, *in* the [R]Sanctuary, O LORD, *which* thy hands have established.   Ps. 44:2 · Ps. 2:6 · Ps. 68:16

18 [R]The LORD shall reign for ever and ever.   2 Sam. 7:16; Is. 57:15

19 For the [R]horse of Pharaoh went in with his chariots and with his horsemen into the sea, and the LORD brought again the waters of the sea upon them; but the children of Israel went on dry *land* in the midst of the sea.   14:23

20 And Miriam the prophetess, the sister of Aaron, took a timbrel in her hand; and all the women went out after her [R]with timbrels and with dances.   Ps. 30:11; 150:4

21 And Miriam [R]answered them, [R]Sing ye to the LORD, for he hath triumphed gloriously; the horse and his rider hath he thrown into the sea.   1 Sam. 18:7 · v. 1

22 So Moses brought Israel from the Red sea, and they went out into the wilderness of Shur; and they went three days in the wilderness, and found no water.

23 And when they came to [R]Ma'-rah, they could not drink of the waters of Ma'-rah, for they *were* bitter: therefore the name of it was called Ma'-rah.   Num. 33:8

24 And the people ᴿmurmured against Moses, saying, What shall we drink? 14:11; 16:2; Ps. 106:13

25 And he cried unto the LORD; and the LORD shewed him a tree, *which* when he had cast into the waters, the waters were made sweet: there he made for them a statute and an ordinance, and there ᴿhe proved them, Ps. 66:10

26 And said, ᴿIf thou wilt diligently hearken to the voice of the LORD thy God, and wilt do that which is right in his sight, and wilt give ear to his commandments, and keep all his statutes, I will put none of these diseases upon thee, which I have brought upon the Egyptians: for I *am* the LORD that healeth thee. 19:5, 6

27 ᴿAnd they came to E'-lim, where *were* twelve wells of water, and threescore and ten palm trees: and they encamped there by the waters. Num. 33:9

16 And they took their journey from E'-lim, and all the congregation of the children of Israel came unto the wilderness of Sin, which *is* between E'-lim and ᴿSi'-nai, on the fifteenth day of the second month after their departing out of the land of Egypt. 12:6

2 And the whole congregation of the children of Israel ᴿmurmured against Moses and Aaron in the wilderness: 1 Cor. 10:10

3 And the children of Israel said unto them, Would to God we had died by the hand of the LORD in the land of Egypt, when we sat by the ᵀflesh pots, *and* when we did eat bread to the full; for ye have brought us forth into this wilderness, to kill this whole assembly with hunger. *pots of meat*

4 Then said the LORD unto Moses, Behold, I will rain ᴿbread from heaven for you; and the people shall go out and gather a certain rate every day, that I may prove them, whether they will walk in my law, or no. 1 Cor. 10:3

5 And it shall come to pass, that on the sixth day they shall prepare *that* which they bring in;

and ᴿit shall be twice as much as they gather daily. Lev. 25:21

6 And Moses and Aaron said unto all the children of Israel, ᴿAt even, then ye shall know that the LORD hath brought you out from the land of Egypt: 6:7

7 And in the morning, then ye shall see ᴿthe glory of the LORD; for that he heareth your murmurings against the LORD: and what *are* we, that ye murmur against us? Is. 35:2; 40:5; John 11:4, 40

8 And Moses said, *This shall be,* when the LORD shall give you in the evening flesh to eat, and in the morning bread to the full; for that the LORD heareth your murmurings which ye murmur against him: and what *are* we? your murmurings *are* not against us, but ᴿagainst the LORD. 1 Sam. 8:7

9 And Moses spake unto Aaron, Say unto all the congregation of the children of Israel, ᴿCome near before the LORD: for he hath heard your murmurings. Num. 16:16

10 And it came to pass, as Aaron spake unto the whole congregation of the children of Israel, that they looked toward the wilderness, and, behold, the glory of the LORD appeared in the cloud.

11 And the LORD spake unto Moses, saying,

12 ᴿI have heard the murmurings of the children of Israel: speak unto them, saying, At even ye shall eat flesh, and in the morning ye shall be filled with bread; and ye shall know that I *am* the LORD your God. v. 8; Num. 14:27

13 And it came to pass, that at even ᴿthe quails came up, and covered the camp: and in the morning the dew lay round about the host. Ps. 78:27–29; 105:40

14 And when the dew that lay was gone up, behold, upon the face of the wilderness *there lay* a small round thing, *as* small as the hoar frost on the ground.

15 And when the children of Israel saw *it,* they said one to another, ᵀIt *is* man'-na: for they wist not what it *was.* And Moses

said unto them, ^RThis *is* the bread which the LORD hath given you to eat.   *What is it?* · Ps. 78:24; [John 6:31, 49]

16 This *is* the thing which the LORD hath commanded, Gather of it every man ^Raccording to his eating, an o'-mer for every man, *according to* the number of your persons; take ye every man for *them* which *are* in his tents.   12:4

17 And the children of Israel did so, and gathered, some more, some less.

18 And when they did ^Tmete *it* with an o'-mer, ^Rhe that gathered much had nothing over, and he that gathered little had no lack; they gathered every man according to his eating.   *measure* · 2 Cor. 8:15

19 And Moses said, Let no man ^Rleave of it till the morning.   12:10

20 Notwithstanding they hearkened not unto Moses; but some of them left of it until the morning, and it bred worms, and stank: and Moses was wroth with them.

21 And they gathered it every morning, every man according to his eating: and when the sun waxed hot, it melted.

22 And it came to pass, *that* on the sixth day they gathered twice as much bread, two o'-mers for one *man:* and all the rulers of the congregation came and told Moses.

23 And he said unto them, This *is that* which the LORD hath said, To morrow *is* ^Rthe rest of the holy sabbath unto the LORD: bake *that* which ye will bake *to day,* and ^Tseethe that ye will ^Tseethe; and that which remaineth over lay up for you to be kept until the morning.   20:8–11; Gen. 2:3; Neh. 9:13, 14 · *boil*

24 And they laid it up till the morning, as Moses bade: and it did not ^Rstink, neither was there any worm therein.   v. 20

25 And Moses said, Eat that to day; for to day *is* a sabbath unto the LORD: to day ye shall not find it in the field.

26 ^RSix days ye shall gather it; but on the seventh day, *which is*

the sabbath, in it there shall be none.   20:9, 10

27 And it came to pass, *that* there went out *some* of the people on the seventh day for to gather, and they found none.

28 And the LORD said unto Moses, How long refuse ye to keep my commandments and my laws?

29 See, for that the LORD hath given you the sabbath, therefore he giveth you on the sixth day the bread of two days; abide ye every man in his place, let no man go out of his place on the seventh day.

30 So the people rested on the seventh day.

31 And the house of Israel called the name thereof ^TMan'-na: and it *was* like coriander seed, white; and the taste of it *was* like wafers *made* with honey. Lit. *What?*

32 And Moses said, This *is* the thing which the LORD commandeth, Fill an o'-mer of it to be kept for your generations; that they may see the bread wherewith I have fed you in the wilderness, when I brought you forth from the land of Egypt.

33 And Moses said unto Aaron, ^RTake a pot, and put an o'-mer full of man'-na therein, and lay it up before the LORD, to be kept for your generations.   Heb. 9:4; Rev. 2:17

34 As the LORD commanded Moses, so Aaron laid it up ^Rbefore the Testimony, to be kept.   25:16, 21

35 And the children of Israel did ^Reat man'-na ^Rforty years, until they came to a land inhabited; they did eat man'-na, until they came unto the borders of the land of Canaan.   Deut. 8:3, 16 · Num. 33:38

36 Now an o'-mer *is* the tenth *part* of an e'-phah.

17 And ^Rall the congregation of the children of Israel journeyed from the wilderness of ^RSin, after their journeys, according to the commandment of the LORD, and pitched in Reph'-i-dim: and *there was* no water for the people to drink.   16:1 · Num. 33:11–15

2 Wherefore the people did

chide with Moses, and said, Give us water that we may drink. And Moses said unto them, Why chide ye with me? wherefore do ye Rtempt the LORD?   [Matt. 4:7]

3 And the people thirsted there for water; and the people Rmurmured against Moses, and said, Wherefore *is* this *that* thou hast brought us up out of Egypt, to kill us and our children and our Rcattle with thirst?   16:2, 3 · 12:38

4 And Moses Rcried unto the LORD, saying, What shall I do unto this people? they be almost ready to Rstone me.   14:15 · John 8:59; 10:31

5 And the LORD said unto Moses, RGo on before the people, and take with thee of the elders of Israel; and thy rod, wherewith thou smotest the river, take in thine hand, and go.   Ezek. 2:6

6 RBehold, I will stand before thee there upon the rock in Ho'-reb; and thou shalt smite the rock, and there shall come water out of it, that the people may drink. And Moses did so in the sight of the elders of Israel.   Ps. 78:15; [1 Cor. 10:4]

7 And he called the name of the place RMas'-sah, and Mer'-i-bah, because of the chiding of the children of Israel, and because they tempted the LORD, saying, Is the LORD among us, or not? Ps. 81:7

8 Then came Am'-a-lek, and fought with Israel in Reph'-i-dim.

9 And Moses said unto Joshua, Choose us out men, and go out, fight with Am'-a-lek: to morrow I will stand on the top of the hill with Rthe rod of God in mine hand.   4:20

10 So Joshua did as Moses had said to him, and fought with Am'-a-lek: and Moses, Aaron, and Hur went up to the top of the hill.

11 And it came to pass, when Moses Rheld up his hand, that Israel prevailed: and when he let down his hand, Am'-a-lek prevailed.   [James 5:16]

12 But Moses' hands *were* heavy; and they took a stone, and put *it* under him, and he sat thereon; and Aaron and Hur stayed up his hands, the one on the one side,

and the other on the other side; and his hands were steady until the going down of the sun.

13 And Joshua discomfited Am'-a-lek and his people with the edge of the sword.

14 And the LORD said unto Moses, RWrite this *for* a memorial in a book, and rehearse *it* in the ears of Joshua: for I will utterly put out the remembrance of Am'-a-lek from under heaven.   24:4; Num. 33:2

15 And Moses built an altar, and called the name of it TJe-ho'-vah–nis'-si: Lit. *The LORD Is My Banner*

16 For he said, Because the LORD hath sworn *that* the LORD *will have* war with Am'-a-lek from generation to generation.

18 When RJe'-thro, the priest of Mid'-i-an, Moses' father in law, heard of all that God had done for Moses, and for Israel his people, *and* that the LORD had brought Israel out of Egypt;   2:16

2 Then Je'-thro, Moses' father in law, took Zip-po'-rah, Moses' wife, after he had sent her back,

3 And her Rtwo sons; of which the name of the one *was* Ger'-shom; for he said, I have been an alien in a strange land: Acts 7:29

4 And the name of the other *was* E-li-e'-zer; for the God of my father, *said he, was* mine Rhelp, and delivered me from the sword of Pharaoh: Gen. 49:25

5 And Je'-thro, Moses' father in law, came with his sons and his wife unto Moses into the wilderness, where he encamped at Rthe mount of God: 3:1, 12; 4:27; 24:13

6 And he said unto Moses, I thy father in law Je'-thro am come unto thee, and thy wife, and her two sons with her.

7 And Moses went out to meet his father in law, and did obeisance, and Rkissed him; and they asked each other of *their* welfare; and they came into the tent.   4:27

8 And Moses told his father in law all that the LORD had done unto Pharaoh and to the Egyptians for Israel's sake, *and* all the Ttravail that had come upon them

by the way, and *how* the LORD
^Rdelivered them.　　*hardship* · Ps. 81:7

9　And Je'-thro rejoiced for all
the ^Rgoodness which the LORD
had done to Israel, whom he had
delivered out of the hand of the
Egyptians.　　　　　　[Is. 63:7–14]

10　And Je'-thro said, ^RBlessed
be the LORD, who hath delivered
you out of the hand of the Egyptians, and out of the hand of Pharaoh, who hath delivered the people from under the hand of the
Egyptians.　　2 Sam. 18:28; 1 Kin. 8:56

11　Now I know that the LORD *is*
greater than all gods: for in the
thing wherein they dealt ^Rproudly
he was above them.　　　　Luke 1:51

12　And Je'-thro, Moses' father in
law, took a burnt ^Roffering and
sacrifices for God: and Aaron
came, and all the elders of Israel,
^Rto eat bread with Moses' father
in law before God.　　24:5 · Deut. 12:7

13　And it came to pass on the
morrow, that Moses ^Rsat to judge
the people: and the people stood
by Moses from the morning unto
the evening.　　Deut. 33:4, 5; Matt. 23:2

14　And when Moses' father in
law saw all that he did to the people, he said, What *is* this thing
that thou doest to the people? why
sittest thou thyself alone, and all
the people stand by thee from
morning unto even?

15　And Moses said unto his
father in law, Because the people
come unto me to enquire of God:

16　When they have ^Ra matter,
they come unto me; and I judge
between one and another, and I
do make *them* know the statutes
of God, and his laws.　　Deut. 19:17

17　And Moses' father in law said
unto him, The thing that thou
doest *is* not good.

18　Thou wilt surely wear away,
both thou, and this people that *is*
with thee: for this thing *is* too
heavy for thee; thou art not able
to perform it thyself alone.

19　Hearken now unto my voice,
I will give thee counsel, and God
shall be with thee: Be thou for
the people to ^RGod-ward, that

thou mayest ^Rbring the causes
unto God:　　4:16; 20:19 · Num. 9:8; 27:5

20　And thou shalt ^Rteach them
ordinances and laws, and shalt
shew them the way wherein they
must walk, and ^Rthe work that
they must do.　　Deut. 5:1 · Deut. 1:18

21　Moreover thou shalt provide
out of all the people able men,
such as ^Rfear God, men of truth,
hating covetousness; and place
such over them, *to be* rulers of
thousands, *and* rulers of hundreds, rulers of fifties, and rulers
of tens:　　Gen. 42:18; 2 Sam. 23:3

22　And let them judge the people at all seasons: and it shall be,
that every great matter they shall
bring unto thee, but every small
matter they shall judge: so shall it
be easier for thyself, and they
shall bear *the burden* with thee.

23　If thou shalt do this thing,
and God command thee *so*, then
thou shalt be able to endure, and
all this people shall also go to
their ^Rplace in peace.　　　　16:29

24　So Moses hearkened to the
voice of his father in law, and did
all that he had said.

25　And Moses chose able men
out of all Israel, and made them
heads over the people, rulers of
thousands, rulers of hundreds,
rulers of fifties, and rulers of
tens.

26　And they judged the people
at all seasons: the ^Rhard ^Tcauses
they brought unto Moses, but
every small matter they judged
themselves.　　Job 29:16 · *cases*

27　And Moses let his father in
law depart; and ^Rhe went his way
into his own land.　　Num. 10:29, 30

19　In the third month, when
the children of Israel were
gone forth out of the land of
Egypt, the same day came they
into the wilderness of Si'-nai.

2　For they were departed from
^RReph'-i-dim, and were come *to*
the desert of Si'-nai, and had
pitched in the wilderness; and
there Israel camped before ^Rthe
mount.　　　17:1 · 3:1, 12; 18:5

3　And ^RMoses went up unto

God, and the LORD ᴿcalled unto him out of the mountain, saying, Thus shalt thou say to the house of Jacob, and tell the children of Israel;   Acts 7:38 · 3:4

4 Ye have seen what I did unto the Egyptians, and *how* ᴿI bare you on eagles' wings, and brought you unto myself.   Is. 63:9; Rev. 12:14

5 Now therefore, if ye will obey my voice indeed, and keep my covenant, then ᴿye shall be a peculiar treasure unto me above all people: for all the earth *is* mine: Ps. 135:4; Titus 2:14; 1 Pet. 2:9

6 And ye shall be unto me a ᴿkingdom of priests, and an holy nation. These *are* the words which thou shalt speak unto the children of Israel.   [1 Pet. 2:5, 9; Rev. 1:6; 5:10]

7 And Moses came and called for the ᴿelders of the people, and ᵀlaid before their faces all these words which the LORD commanded him.   4:29, 30 · *set*

8 And ᴿall the people answered together, and said, All that the LORD hath spoken we will do. And Moses returned the words of the people unto the LORD.   4:31; 24:3, 7

9 And the LORD said unto Moses, Lo, I come unto thee ᴿin a thick cloud, ᴿthat the people may hear when I speak with thee, and believe thee for ever. And Moses told the words of the people unto the LORD.   Matt. 17:5 · John 12:29, 30

10 And the LORD said unto Moses, Go unto the people, and ᴿsanctifyᵀ them to day and to morrow, and let them wash their clothes,   Lev. 11:44, 45 · *consecrate*

11 And be ready against the third day: for the third day the LORD will come down in the sight of all the people upon mount Si'-nai.

12 And thou shalt set bounds unto the people round about, saying, Take heed to yourselves, *that* ye go *not* up into the mount, or touch the border of it: ᴿwhosoever toucheth the mount shall be surely put to death: 34:3; Heb. 12:20

13 There shall not an hand touch it, but he shall surely be stoned, or shot through; whether

it be beast or man, it shall not live: when the trumpet soundeth long, they shall come up to the mount.

14 And Moses went down from the mount unto the people, and sanctified the people; and they washed their clothes.

15 And he said unto the people, Be ready against the third day: come not ᵀat *your* wives.   *near to*

16 And it came to pass on the third day in the morning, that there were ᴿthunders and lightnings, and a thick cloud upon the mount, and the voice of the trumpet exceeding loud; so that all the people that *was* in the camp ᴿtrembled.   Heb. 12:18, 19 · Heb. 12:21

17 And Moses brought forth the people out of the camp to meet with God; and they stood at the nether part of the mount.

18 And mount Si'-nai was altogether on a smoke, because the LORD descended upon it in fire: and the smoke thereof ascended as the smoke of a furnace, and the whole mount quaked greatly.

19 And when the voice of the trumpet sounded long, and waxed louder and louder, ᴿMoses spake, and ᴿGod answered him by a voice.   Heb. 12:21 · Neh. 9:13; Ps. 81:7

20 And the LORD came down upon mount Si'-nai, on the top of the mount: and the LORD called Moses *up* to the top of the mount; and Moses went up.

21 And the LORD said unto Moses, Go down, ᵀcharge the people, lest they break through unto the LORD ᴿto gaze, and many of them perish.   *warn* · 1 Sam. 6:19

22 And let the priests also, which come near to the LORD, sanctify themselves, lest the LORD break forth upon them.

23 And Moses said unto the LORD, The people cannot come up to mount Si'-nai: for thou chargedst us, saying, Set bounds about the mount, and sanctify it.

24 And the LORD said unto him, Away, get thee down, and thou shalt come up, thou, and Aaron

with thee: but let not the priests and the people break through to come up unto the LORD, lest he break forth upon them.

25 So Moses went down unto the people, and spake unto them.

20 And God spake ᴿall these words, saying,   Deut. 5:22

2 ᴿI *am* the LORD thy God, which have brought thee out of the land of Egypt, ᴿout of the house of bondage.   Hos. 13:4 · 13:3

3 ᴿThou shalt have no other gods before me.   Deut. 6:14

4 ᴿThou shalt not make unto thee any graven image, or any likeness *of any thing* that *is* in heaven above, or that *is* in the earth beneath, or that *is* in the water under the earth: Lev. 19:4; 26:1

5 ᴿThou shalt not bow down thyself to them, nor serve them: for I the LORD thy God *am* a jealous God, visiting the iniquity of the fathers upon the children unto the third and fourth *generation* of them that hate me;   Is. 44:15, 19

6 And shewing mercy unto thousands of them that love me, and keep my commandments.

7 ᴿThou shalt not take the name of the LORD thy God in vain; for the LORD ᴿwill not hold him guiltless that taketh his name in vain. Lev. 19:12; [Matt. 5:33–37] · Mic. 6:11

8 ᴿRemember the sabbath day, to keep it holy.   Lev. 26:2; Deut. 5:12

9 ᴿSix days shalt thou labour, and do all thy work: Luke 13:14

10 But the ᴿseventh day *is* the sabbath of the LORD thy God: *in it* thou shalt not do any work, thou, nor thy son, nor thy daughter, thy manservant, nor thy maidservant, nor thy cattle, nor thy stranger that *is* within thy gates: Gen. 2:2, 3

11 For ᴿ*in* six days the LORD made heaven and earth, the sea, and all that in them *is*, and rested the seventh day: wherefore the LORD blessed the sabbath day, and hallowed it.   31:17

12 ᴿHonour thy father and thy mother: that thy days may be long upon the land which the LORD thy God giveth thee.   Matt. 15:4; Eph. 6:2

13 ᴿThou shalt not kill.   Rom. 13:9

14 ᴿThou shalt not commit adultery.   Rom. 13:9; James 2:11

15 ᴿThou shalt not steal. Lev. 19:11

16 Thou shalt not bear false witness against thy neighbour.

17 Thou shalt not covet thy neighbour's house, thou shalt not covet thy neighbour's wife, nor his manservant, nor his maidservant, nor his ox, nor his ass, nor any thing that *is* thy neighbour's.

18 And all the people saw the thunderings, and the lightnings, and the noise of the trumpet, and the mountain smoking: and when the people saw *it*, they removed, and stood afar off.

19 And they said unto Moses, ᴿSpeak thou with us, and we will hear: but let not God speak with us, lest we die.   Gal. 3:19; Heb. 12:19

20 And Moses said unto the people, ᴿFear not: ᴿfor God is come to prove you, and ᴿthat his fear may be before your faces, that ye sin not.   [Is. 41:10, 13] · [Deut. 13:3] · Is. 8:13

21 And the people stood afar off, and Moses drew near unto the thick darkness where God *was*.

22 And the LORD said unto Moses, Thus thou shalt say unto the children of Israel, Ye have seen that I have talked with you ᴿfrom heaven.   Deut. 4:36; 5:24, 26; Neh. 9:13

23 Ye shall not make ᴿwith me gods of silver, neither shall ye make unto you gods of gold.   32:1

24 An altar of earth thou shalt make unto me, and shalt sacrifice thereon thy burnt offerings, and thy peace offerings, thy sheep, and thine oxen: in all ᴿplaces where I record my name I will come unto thee, and I will bless thee.   Deut. 12:5; 16:6, 11; 2 Chr. 6:6

25 And ᴿif thou wilt make me an altar of stone, thou shalt not build it of hewn stone: for if thou ᴿlift up thy tool upon it, thou hast polluted it.   Deut. 27:5 · Josh. 8:30, 31

26 Neither shalt thou go up by steps unto mine altar, that thy ᴿnakedness be not discovered thereon.   28:42, 43

21 Now these *are* the ^Tjudgments which thou shalt ^Rset before them. *ordinances* · Deut. 4:14; 6:1

2 ^RIf thou buy an Hebrew servant, six years he shall serve: and in the seventh he shall go out free for nothing. Lev. 25:39–43; Jer. 34:14

3 If he came in by himself, he shall go out by himself: if he were married, then his wife shall go out with him.

4 If his master have given him a wife, and she have born him sons or daughters; the wife and her children shall be her master's, and he shall go out by himself.

5 ^RAnd if the servant shall plainly say, I love my master, my wife, and my children; I will not go out free: Deut. 15:16, 17

6 Then his master shall bring him unto the judges; he shall also bring him to the door, or unto the door post; and his master shall bore his ear through with an aul; and he shall serve him for ever.

7 And if a man sell his daughter to be a maidservant, she shall not go out as the menservants do.

8 If she please not her master, who hath betrothed her to himself, then shall he let her be redeemed: to sell her unto a ^Tstrange nation he shall have no power, seeing he hath dealt deceitfully with her. *foreign people*

9 And if he have betrothed her unto his son, he shall deal with her after the manner of daughters.

10 If he take him another *wife;* her food, her raiment, ^Rand her duty of marriage, shall he not diminish. [1 Cor. 7:3, 5]

11 And if he do not these three unto her, then shall she go out free without money.

12 ^RHe that smiteth a man, so that he die, shall be surely put to death. Gen. 9:6; Lev. 24:17; Num. 35:30

13 And if a man lie not in wait, but God deliver *him* into his hand; then ^RI will appoint thee a place whither he shall flee. Num. 35:11

14 But if a man come ^Tpresumptuously upon his neighbour, to slay him with guile; thou shalt take him from mine altar, that he may die. *with premeditation*

15 And he that smiteth his father, or his mother, shall be surely put to death.

16 And ^Rhe that ^Tstealeth a man, and ^Rselleth him, or if he be found in his hand, he shall surely be put to death. Deut. 24:7 · *kidnaps* · Gen. 37:28

17 And ^Rhe that curseth his father, or his mother, shall surely be put to death. Lev. 20:9; Prov. 20:20

18 And if men strive together, and one smite another with a stone, or with *his* fist, and he die not, but keepeth *his* bed:

19 If he rise again, and walk abroad upon his staff, then shall he that smote *him* be ^Tquit: only he shall pay *for* the loss of his time, and shall cause *him* to be thoroughly healed. *acquitted*

20 And if a man smite his servant, or his maid, with a rod, and he die under his hand; he shall be surely punished.

21 Notwithstanding, if he continue a day or two, he shall not be punished: for he *is* his money.

22 If men strive, and hurt a woman with child, so that ^Ther fruit depart *from her,* and yet no mischief follow: he shall be surely punished, according as the woman's husband will lay upon him; and he shall pay as the judges *determine.* *she gives birth prematurely*

23 And if *any* mischief follow, then thou shalt give life for life,

24 Eye for eye, tooth for tooth, hand for hand, foot for foot,

25 Burning for burning, wound for wound, stripe for stripe.

26 And if a man smite the eye of his servant, or the eye of his maid, that it perish; he shall let him go free for his eye's sake.

27 And if he smite out his manservant's tooth, or his maidservant's tooth; he shall let him go free for his tooth's sake.

28 If an ox gore a man or a woman, that they die: then the ox shall be surely stoned, and his flesh shall not be eaten; but the owner of the ox *shall be* quit.

29 But if the ox ^Twere wont to push with his horn in time past, and it hath been ^Ttestified to his owner, and he hath not kept him in, but that he hath killed a man or a woman; the ox shall be stoned, and his owner also shall be put to death.   *tended · made known*

30 If there be laid on him a sum of money, then he shall give for ^Rthe ransom of his life whatsoever is laid upon him.   v. 22; Num. 35:31

31 Whether he have gored a son, or have gored a daughter, according to this judgment shall it be done unto him.

32 If the ox shall push a manservant or a maidservant; he shall give unto their master ^Rthirty shek'-els of silver, and the ox shall be stoned.   Zech. 11:12, 13; Matt. 26:15

33 And if a man shall open a pit, or if a man shall dig a pit, and not cover it, and an ox or an ass fall therein;

34 The owner of the pit shall make *it* good, *and* give money unto the owner of them; and the dead *beast* shall be his.

35 And if one man's ox hurt another's, that he die; then they shall sell the live ox, and divide the money of it; and the dead ox also they shall divide.

36 Or if it be known that the ox hath used to push in time past, and his owner hath not kept him in; he shall surely pay ox for ox; and the dead shall be his own.

22 If a man shall steal an ox, or a sheep, and kill it, or sell it; he shall restore five oxen for an ox, and four sheep for a sheep.

2 If a thief be found ^Rbreaking ^Tup, and be smitten that he die, *there shall* ^Rno blood *be shed* for him. Matt. 6:19; 1 Pet. 4:15 · *in* · Num. 35:27

3 If the sun be risen upon him, *there shall be* blood *shed* for him; *for* he should make full restitution; if he have nothing, then he shall be ^Rsold for his theft.   21:2

4 If the theft be certainly ^Rfound in his hand alive, whether it be ox, or ass, or sheep; he shall ^Rrestore double.   21:16 · Prov. 6:31

5 If a man shall cause a field or vineyard to be eaten, and shall put in his beast, and shall feed in another man's field; of the best of his own field, and of the best of his own vineyard, shall he make restitution.

6 If fire break out, and catch in thorns, so that the stacks of corn, or the standing corn, or the field, be consumed *therewith;* he that kindled the fire shall surely make restitution.

7 If a man shall ^Rdeliver unto his neighbour money or stuff to keep, and it be stolen out of the man's house; if the thief be found, let him pay double.   Lev. 6:1–7

8 If the thief be not found, then the master of the house shall be brought unto the ^Rjudges, *to see* whether he have put his hand unto his neighbour's goods.   21:6, 22

9 For all manner of trespass, *whether it be* for ox, for ass, for sheep, for raiment, *or* for any manner of lost thing, which *another* challengeth to be his, the cause of both parties shall come before the judges; *and* whom the judges shall condemn, he shall pay double unto his neighbour.

10 If a man deliver unto his neighbour an ass, or an ox, or a sheep, or any beast, to keep; and it die, or be hurt, or driven away, no man seeing *it:*

11 *Then* shall an ^Roath of the LORD be between them both, that he hath not put his hand unto his neighbour's goods; and the owner of it shall accept *thereof,* and he shall not make *it* good.   Heb. 6:16

12 And ^Rif it be stolen from him, he shall make restitution unto the owner thereof.   Gen. 31:39

13 If it be torn in pieces, *then* let him bring it *for* witness, *and* he shall not make good that which was torn.

14 And if a man borrow ^T*ought* of his neighbour, and it be hurt, or die, the owner thereof *being* not with it, he shall surely make *it* good.   *anything*

15 *But* if the owner thereof *be*

with it, he shall not make *it* good: if it *be* an hired *thing*, it came for his hire.

16 And ᴿif a man entice a maid that is not betrothed, and lie with her, he shall surely endow her to be his wife. Deut. 22:28, 29

17 If her father utterly refuse to give her unto him, he shall pay money according to the ᴿdowry of virgins. Gen. 34:12; 1 Sam. 18:25

18 ᴿThou shalt not suffer a witch to live. Lev. 19:31; 20:6, 27; Deut. 18:10, 11

19 Whosoever lieth with a beast shall surely be put to death.

20 ᴿHe that sacrificeth unto *any* god, save unto the Lᴏʀᴅ only, he shall be utterly destroyed. Lev. 17:7

21 ᴿThou shalt neither vex a stranger, nor oppress him: for ye were strangers in the land of Egypt. 23:9; Deut. 10:19; Zech. 7:10

22 ᴿYe shall not afflict any widow, or fatherless child. Jer. 7:6

23 If thou afflict them in any wise, and they cry at all unto me, I will surely hear their cry;

24 And my ᴿwrath shall wax hot, and I will kill you with the sword; and ᴿyour wives shall be widows, and your children fatherless. Ps. 69:24 · Ps. 109:9

25 If thou lend money to *any* of my people *that is* poor by thee, thou shalt not be to him as an usurer, neither shalt thou lay upon him ᴿusury.ᵀ Ps. 15:5 · *interest*

26 ᴿIf thou at all take thy neighbour's raiment to pledge, thou shalt deliver it unto him by that the sun goeth down: Prov. 20:16

27 For that *is* his covering only, it *is* his raiment for his skin: wherein shall he sleep? and it shall come to pass, when he crieth unto me, that I will hear; for I *am* ᴿgracious. 34:6, 7

28 ᴿThou shalt not revile the ᵀgods, nor curse the ᴿruler of thy people. Eccl. 10:20 · *God* · Acts 23:5

29 Thou shalt not delay *to offer* the first of thy ripe fruits, and of thy liquors: ᴿthe firstborn of thy sons shalt thou give unto me. 13:2

30 ᴿLikewise shalt thou do with thine oxen, *and* with thy sheep:

ᴿseven days it shall be with his dam; on the eighth day thou shalt give it me. Deut. 15:19 · Lev. 22:27

31 And ye shall be holy men unto me: neither shall ye eat *any* flesh *that is* torn of beasts in the field; ye shall cast it to the dogs.

23 Thou shalt not raise a false report: put not thine hand with the wicked to be an ᴿunrighteous witness. Ps. 35:11; Acts 6:11

2 ᴿThou shalt not follow a multitude to *do* evil; neither shalt thou speak in a cause to decline after many to wrest *judgment:* Gen. 7:1

3 Neither shalt thou countenance a poor man in his cause.

4 ᴿIf thou meet thine enemy's ox or his ass going astray, thou shalt surely bring it back to him again. [Rom. 12:20]

5 ᴿIf thou see the ass of him that hateth thee lying under his burden, and wouldest forbear to help him, thou shalt surely help with him. Deut. 22:4

6 Thou shalt not wrest the judgment of thy poor in his cause.

7 Keep thee far from a false matter; and the innocent and righteous slay thou not: for ᴿI will not justify the wicked. Rom. 1:18

8 And ᴿthou shalt take no ᵀgift: for the gift blindeth the wise, and perverteth the words of the righteous. Prov. 15:27; 17:8; Is. 5:22, 23 · *bribe*

9 Also thou shalt not oppress a stranger: for ye know the heart of a stranger, seeing ye were strangers in the land of Egypt.

10 And ᴿsix years thou shalt sow thy land, and shalt gather in the fruits thereof: Lev. 25:1–7

11 But the seventh *year* thou shalt let it rest and lie still; that the poor of thy people may eat: and what they leave the beasts of the field shall eat. In like manner thou shalt deal with thy vineyard, *and* with thy ᵀoliveyard. *olive grove*

12 ᴿSix days thou shalt do thy work, and on the seventh day thou shalt rest: that thine ox and thine ass may rest, and the son of thy handmaid, and the stranger, may be refreshed. Luke 13:14

13 And in all *things* that I have said unto you be circumspect: and ^Rmake no mention of the name of other gods, neither let it be heard out of thy mouth.   Josh. 23:7; Ps. 16:4

14 ^RThree times thou shalt keep a feast unto me in the year.   34:22

15 ^RThou shalt keep the feast of unleavened bread: (thou shalt eat unleavened bread seven days, as I commanded thee, in the time appointed of the month A'-bib; for in it thou camest out from Egypt: ^Rand none shall appear before me empty:)   Lev. 23:6–8 · 22:29; 34:20

16 ^RAnd the feast of harvest, the firstfruits of thy labours, which thou hast sown in the field: and ^Rthe feast of ingathering, *which is* in the end of the year, when thou hast gathered in thy labours out of the field.   Num. 28:26 · Deut. 16:13

17 ^RThree times in the year all thy males shall appear before the Lord GOD.   v. 14; 34:23; Deut. 16:16

18 ^RThou shalt not offer the blood of my sacrifice with leavened bread; ^Rneither shall the fat of my sacrifice remain until the morning.   Lev. 2:11 · Lev. 7:15; Deut. 16:4

19 ^RThe first of the firstfruits of thy land thou shalt bring into the house of the LORD thy God. ^RThou shalt not seethe a kid in his mother's milk.   Deut. 26:2 · Deut. 14:21

20 ^RBehold, I send an Angel before thee, to keep thee in the way, and to bring thee into the place which I have prepared.   3:2

21 Beware of him, and obey his voice, provoke him not; for he will not pardon your transgressions: for ^Rmy name *is* in him.   Jer. 23:6

22 But if thou shalt indeed obey his voice, and do all that I speak; then ^RI will be an enemy unto thine enemies, and an adversary unto thine adversaries.   Gen. 12:3

23 ^RFor mine Angel shall go before thee, and ^Rbring thee in unto the Am'-or-ites, and the Hit'-tites, and the Per'-iz-zites, and the Ca'-naan-ites, the Hi'-vites, and the Jeb'-u-sites: and I will cut them off.   v. 20 · Josh. 24:8, 11

24 Thou shalt not bow down to their gods, nor serve them, nor do after their works: ^Rbut thou shalt utterly overthrow them, and quite break down their images. 2 Kin. 18:4

25 And ye shall ^Rserve the LORD your God, and he shall bless thy bread, and thy water; and I will take sickness away from the midst of thee.   Deut. 6:13; [Matt. 4:10]

26 ^RThere shall nothing cast their young, nor be barren, in thy land: the number of thy days I will ^Rfulfil.   Deut. 28:4; Mal. 3:11 · 1 Chr. 23:1

27 I will send ^Rmy fear before thee, and will destroy all the people to whom thou shalt come, and I will make all thine enemies turn their backs unto thee.   Josh. 2:9

28 And I will send hornets before thee, which shall drive out the Hi'-vite, the Ca'-naan-ite, and the Hit'-tite, from before thee.

29 ^RI will not drive them out from before thee in one year; lest the land become desolate, and the beast of the field multiply against thee.   Deut. 7:22

30 By little and little I will drive them out from before thee, until thou be increased, and inherit the land.

31 And I will set thy bounds from the Red sea even unto the sea of the Phi-lis'-tines, and from the desert unto the river: for I will deliver the inhabitants of the land into your hand; and thou shalt drive them out before thee.

32 ^RThou shalt make no ^Tcovenant with them, nor with their gods.   34:12, 15; Deut. 7:2 · *treaty*

33 They shall not dwell in thy land, lest they make thee sin against me: for if thou serve their gods, ^Rit will surely be a snare unto thee.   Deut. 12:30; Josh. 23:13; Judg. 2:3

24 And he said unto Moses, Come up unto the LORD, thou, and Aaron, Na'-dab, and A-bi'-hu, and seventy of the elders of Israel; and worship ye afar off.

2 And Moses alone shall come near the LORD: but they shall not come nigh; neither shall the people go up with him.

3 And Moses came and told the

people all the words of the LORD, and all the judgments: and all the people answered with one voice, and said, ^RAll the words which the LORD hath said will we do.   19:8

4 And Moses ^Rwrote all the words of the LORD, and rose up early in the morning, and builded an altar under the hill, and twelve ^Rpillars, according to the twelve tribes of Israel.   Deut. 31:9 · Gen. 28:18

5 And he sent young men of the children of Israel, which offered ^Rburnt offerings, and sacrificed peace offerings of oxen unto the LORD.   18:12; 20:24

6 And Moses ^Rtook half of the blood, and put *it* in basons; and half of the blood he sprinkled on the altar.   29:16, 20; Heb. 9:18

7 And he ^Rtook the book of the covenant, and read in the audience of the people: and they said, All that the LORD hath said will we do, and be obedient.   Heb. 9:19

8 And Moses took the blood, and sprinkled *it* on the people, and said, Behold ^Rthe blood of the covenant, which the LORD hath made with you concerning all these words.   Zech. 9:11; [Luke 22:20]

9 Then went up Moses, and Aaron, Na'-dab, and A-bi'-hu, and seventy of the elders of Israel:

10 And they saw the God of Israel: and *there was* under his feet as it were a paved work of a sapphire stone, and as it were the body of heaven in *his* clearness.

11 And upon the nobles of the children of Israel he laid not his hand: also ^Rthey saw God, and did ^Reat and drink. Judg. 13:22 · 1 Cor. 10:18

12 And the LORD said unto Moses, Come up to me into the mount, and be there: and I will give thee ^Rtables of stone, and a law, and commandments which I have written; that thou mayest teach them.   31:18; 32:15; Deut. 5:22

13 And Moses rose up, and ^Rhis minister Joshua: and Moses went up into the mount of God.   32:17

14 And he said unto the elders, Tarry ye here for us, until we come again unto you: and, behold, Aaron and ^RHur *are* with you: if any man have any matters to do, let him come unto them.   17:10, 12

15 And Moses went up into the mount, and ^Ra cloud covered the mount.   19:9; Matt. 17:5

16 And ^Rthe glory of the LORD abode upon mount Si'-nai, and the cloud covered it six days: and the seventh day he called unto Moses out of the midst of the cloud.   16:10; 33:18; Num. 14:10

17 And the sight of the glory of the LORD *was* like ^Rdevouring fire on the top of the mount in the eyes of the children of Israel.   3:2

18 And Moses went into the midst of the cloud, and gat him up into the mount: and ^RMoses was in the mount forty days and forty nights.   34:28; Deut. 9:9; 10:10

25 And the LORD spake unto Moses, saying,

2 Speak unto the children of Israel, that they bring me an offering: ^Rof every man that giveth it willingly with his heart ye shall take my offering. Ezra 2:68; Neh. 11:2

3 And this *is* the offering which ye shall take of them; gold, and silver, and brass,

4 And blue, and purple, and scarlet, and fine linen, and goats' *hair,*

5 And rams' skins dyed red, and ^Tbadgers' skins, and shit'-tim wood,   Or *dolphin*

6 ^ROil for the light, ^Rspices for anointing oil, and for sweet incense,   27:20 · 30:23

7 Onyx stones, and stones to be set in the ^Re'-phod, and in the breastplate.   28:4, 6–14

8 And let them make me a sanctuary; that ^RI may dwell among them.   1 Kin. 6:13; [Heb. 3:6]

9 According to all that I shew thee, *after* the pattern of the tabernacle, and the pattern of all the instruments thereof, even so shall ye make *it.*

10 ^RAnd they shall make an ark *of* shit'-tim wood: two cubits and a half *shall be* the length thereof, and a cubit and a half the breadth

thereof, and a cubit and a half the height thereof.   Deut. 10:3; Heb. 9:4

11 And thou shalt overlay it with pure gold, within and without shalt thou overlay it, and shalt make upon it a crown of ᴿgold round about.   37:2; Heb. 9:4

12 And thou shalt cast four rings of gold for it, and put *them* in the four corners thereof; and two rings *shall be* in the one side of it, and two rings in the other side of it.

13 And thou shalt make staves *of* shit'-tim wood, and overlay them with gold.

14 And thou shalt put the staves into the rings by the sides of the ark, that the ark may be borne with them.

15 ᴿThe staves shall be in the rings of the ark; they shall not be taken from it.   Num. 4:6; 1 Kin. 8:8

16 And thou shalt put into the ark ᴿthe testimony which I shall give thee. Deut. 31:26; 1 Kin. 8:9; Heb. 9:4

17 And ᴿthou shalt make a mercy seat *of* pure gold: two cubits and a half *shall be* the length thereof, and a cubit and a half the breadth thereof.   37:6; Heb. 9:5

18 And thou shalt make two cher'-u-bims *of* gold, *of* beaten work shalt thou make them, in the two ends of the mercy seat.

19 And make one cherub on the one end, and the other cherub on the other end: *even* of the mercy seat shall ye make the cher'-u-bims on the two ends thereof.

20 And ᴿthe cher'-u-bims shall stretch forth *their* wings on high, covering the mercy seat with their wings, and their faces *shall look* one to another; toward the mercy seat shall the faces of the cher'-u-bims be. 1 Kin. 8:7; 1 Chr. 28:18; Heb. 9:5

21 ᴿAnd thou shalt put the mercy seat above upon the ark; and in the ark thou shalt put the testimony that I shall give thee. 26:34; 40:20

22 And there I will meet with thee, and I will commune with thee from above the mercy seat, from ᴿbetween the two cher'-u-bims which *are* upon the ark of

the testimony, of all *things* which I will give thee in commandment unto the children of Israel. Ps. 80:1

23 Thou shalt also make a table *of* shit'-tim wood: two cubits *shall be* the length thereof, and a cubit the breadth thereof, and a cubit and a half the height thereof.

24 And thou shalt overlay it with pure gold, and make thereto a crown of gold round about.

25 And thou shalt make unto it a border of an hand breadth round about, and thou shalt make a golden crown to the border thereof round about.

26 And thou shalt make for it four rings of gold, and put the rings in the four corners that *are* on the four feet thereof.

27 Over against the border shall the rings be for places of the staves to bear the table.

28 And thou shalt make the staves *of* shit'-tim wood, and overlay them with gold, that the table may be borne with them.

29 And thou shalt make ᴿthe dishes thereof, and spoons thereof, and covers thereof, and bowls thereof, to cover withal: *of* pure gold shalt thou make them.   37:16

30 And thou shalt set upon the table ᴿshewbread before me always.   39:36; 40:23; Lev. 24:5–9

31 ᴿAnd thou shalt make a candlestick *of* pure gold: *of* beaten work shall the candlestick be made: his shaft, and his branches, his bowls, his knops, and his flowers, shall be of the same. Zech. 4:2

32 And six branches shall come out of the sides of it; three branches of the candlestick out of the one side, and three branches of the candlestick out of the other side:

33 ᴿThree bowls made like unto almonds, *with* a knop and a flower in one branch; and three bowls made like almonds in the other branch, *with* a knop and a flower: so in the six branches that come out of the candlestick.   37:19

34 And ᴿin the candlestick *shall be* four bowls made like unto

almonds, *with* their knops and their flowers. 37:20–22

35 And *there shall be* a knop under two branches of the same, and a knop under two branches of the same, and a knop under two branches of the same, according to the six branches that proceed out of the candlestick.

36 Their knops and their branches shall be of the same: all it *shall be* one beaten work *of* pure gold.

37 And thou shalt make the seven lamps thereof: and [R]they shall [T]light the lamps thereof, that they may [R]give light over against it. Lev. 24:3, 4 · *arrange* · Num. 8:2

38 And the tongs thereof, and the snuffdishes thereof, *shall be of* pure gold.

39 *Of* a talent of pure gold shall he make it, with all these vessels.

40 And look that thou make *them* after their pattern, which was shewed thee in the mount.

26 Moreover thou shalt make the tabernacle *with* ten curtains *of* fine twined linen, and blue, and purple, and scarlet: *with* cher'-u-bims of cunning work shalt thou make them.

2 The length of one curtain *shall be* eight and twenty cubits, and the breadth of one curtain four cubits: and every one of the curtains shall have one measure.

3 The five curtains shall be coupled together one to another; and *other* five curtains *shall be* coupled one to another.

4 And thou shalt make loops of blue upon the edge of the one curtain from the selvedge in the coupling; and likewise shalt thou make in the uttermost edge of *another* curtain, in the coupling of the second.

5 Fifty loops shalt thou make in the one curtain, and fifty loops shalt thou make in the edge of the curtain that *is* in the coupling of the second; that the loops may take hold one of another.

6 And thou shalt make fifty taches of gold, and couple the cur-

tains together with the taches: and it shall be one tabernacle.

7 And [R]thou shalt make curtains *of* goats' *hair* to be a covering upon the tabernacle: eleven curtains shalt thou make. 36:14

8 The length of one curtain *shall be* thirty cubits, and the breadth of one curtain four cubits: and the eleven curtains *shall be all* of one measure.

9 And thou shalt couple five curtains by themselves, and six curtains by themselves, and shalt double the sixth curtain in the forefront of the tabernacle.

10 And thou shalt make fifty loops on the edge of the one curtain *that is* outmost in the coupling, and fifty loops in the edge of the curtain which coupleth the second.

11 And thou shalt make fifty taches of brass, and put the taches into the loops, and couple the tent together, that it may be one.

12 And the remnant that remaineth of the curtains of the tent, the half curtain that remaineth, shall hang over the backside of the tabernacle.

13 And a cubit on the one side, and a cubit on the other side of that which remaineth in the length of the curtains of the tent, it shall hang over the sides of the tabernacle on this side and on that side, to cover it.

14 And [R]thou shalt make a covering for the tent *of* rams' skins dyed red, and a covering above *of* badgers' skins. 35:7, 23; 36:19

15 And thou shalt [R]make boards for the tabernacle *of* shit'-tim wood standing up. 36:20–34

16 Ten cubits *shall be* the length of a board, and a cubit and a half *shall be* the breadth of one board.

17 Two [T]tenons *shall there be* in one board, set in order one against another: thus shalt thou make for all the boards of the tabernacle. *projections for joining*

18 And thou shalt make the boards for the tabernacle, twenty boards on the south side southward.

19 And thou shalt make forty

sockets of silver under the twenty boards; two sockets under one board for his two tenons, and two sockets under another board for his two tenons.

20 And for the second side of the tabernacle on the north side *there shall be* twenty boards:

21 And their forty sockets *of* silver; two sockets under one board, and two sockets under another board.

22 And for the sides of the tabernacle westward thou shalt make six boards.

23 And two boards shalt thou make for the corners of the tabernacle in the two sides.

24 And they shall be ^Tcoupled together beneath, and they shall be coupled together above the head of it unto one ring: thus shall it be for them both; they shall be for the two corners.   Lit. *doubled*

25 And they shall be eight boards, and their sockets *of* silver, sixteen sockets; two sockets under one board, and two sockets under another board.

26 And thou shalt make bars *of* shit'-tim wood; five for the boards of the one side of the tabernacle,

27 And five bars for the boards of the other side of the tabernacle, and five bars for the boards of the side of the tabernacle, for the two sides westward.

28 And the ^Rmiddle bar in the midst of the boards shall reach from end to end.   36:33

29 And thou shalt overlay the boards with gold, and make their rings *of* gold *for* places for the bars: and thou shalt overlay the bars with gold.

30 And thou shalt ^Trear up the tabernacle ^Raccording to the fashion thereof which was shewed thee in the mount.   *raise* · Acts 7:44

31 And ^Rthou shalt make a vail *of* blue, and purple, and scarlet, and fine twined linen of cunning work: with cher'-u-bims shall it be made: Matt. 27:51; Heb. 9:3; 10:20

32 And thou shalt hang it upon four pillars of shit'-tim *wood* over-

laid with gold: their hooks *shall be of* gold, upon the four sockets of silver.

33 And thou shalt hang up the vail under the taches, that thou mayest bring in thither within the vail ^Rthe ark of the testimony: and the vail shall divide unto you between ^Rthe holy *place* and the most holy.   40:21 · Lev. 16:2; Heb. 9:2, 3

34 And thou shalt put the mercy seat upon the ark of the testimony in the most holy *place*.

35 And ^Rthou shalt set the table ^Twithout the vail, and the candlestick over against the table on the side of the tabernacle toward the south: and thou shalt put the table on the north side.   Heb. 9:2 · *outside*

36 And ^Rthou shalt make an hanging for the door of the tent, *of* blue, and purple, and scarlet, and fine twined linen, wrought with needlework.   36:37

37 And thou shalt make for the hanging ^Rfive pillars *of* shit'-tim *wood*, and overlay them with gold, *and* their hooks *shall be of* gold: and thou shalt cast five sockets of brass for them.   36:38

27 And thou shalt make ^Ran altar *of* shit'-tim wood, five cubits long, and five cubits broad; the altar shall be foursquare: and the height thereof *shall be* three cubits.   38:1; Ezek. 43:13

2 And thou shalt make the horns of it upon the four corners thereof: his horns shall be of the same: and thou shalt overlay it with brass.

3 And thou shalt make his pans to receive his ashes, and his shovels, and his basons, and his fleshhooks, and his firepans: all the vessels thereof thou shalt make *of* brass.

4 And thou shalt make for it a grate of network *of* brass; and upon the net shalt thou make four brasen rings in the four corners thereof.

5 And thou shalt put it under the compass of the altar beneath, that the net may be even to the midst of the altar.

6 And thou shalt make staves for the altar, staves *of* shit'-tim wood, and overlay them with brass.

7 And the staves shall be put into the rings, and the staves shall be upon the two sides of the altar, to bear it.

8 Hollow with boards shalt thou make it: ^Ras it was shewed thee in the mount, so shall they make *it*. 26:30; Acts 7:44; [Heb. 8:5]

9 And ^Rthou shalt make the court of the tabernacle: for the south side southward *there shall be* hangings for the court *of* fine twined linen of an hundred cubits long for one side: 38:9–20

10 And the twenty pillars thereof and their twenty sockets *shall be of* brass; the hooks of the pillars and their fillets *shall be of* silver.

11 And likewise for the north side in length *there shall be* hangings of an hundred *cubits* long, and his twenty pillars and their twenty sockets *of* brass; the hooks of the pillars and their fillets *of* silver.

12 And *for* the breadth of the court on the west side *shall be* hangings of fifty cubits: their pillars ten, and their sockets ten.

13 And the breadth of the court on the east side eastward *shall be* fifty cubits.

14 The hangings of one side *of the gate shall be* fifteen cubits: their pillars three, and their sockets three.

15 And on the other side *shall be* hangings fifteen *cubits:* their pillars three, and their sockets three.

16 And for the gate of the court *shall be* an hanging of twenty cubits, *of* blue, and purple, and scarlet, and fine twined linen, wrought with needlework: *and* their pillars *shall be* four, and their sockets four.

17 All the pillars round about the court *shall be* filleted with silver; their ^Rhooks *shall be of* silver, and their sockets *of* brass. 38:19

18 The length of the court *shall be* an hundred cubits, and the breadth fifty ^Tevery where, and

the height five cubits *of* fine twined linen, and their sockets *of* brass. *throughout*

19 All the vessels of the tabernacle in all the service thereof, and all the pins thereof, and all the pins of the court, *shall be of* brass.

20 And ^Rthou shalt command the children of Israel, that they bring thee pure oil olive beaten for the light, to cause the lamp to ^Tburn always. Lev. 24:1–4 · Lit. *ascend*

21 In the tabernacle of the congregation without the vail, which *is* before the testimony, Aaron and his sons shall order it from evening to morning before the LORD: ^R*it shall be* a statute for ever unto their generations on the behalf of the children of Israel. Lev. 3:17; 16:34

28 And take thou unto thee Aaron thy brother, and his sons with him, from among the children of Israel, that he may minister unto me in the priest's ^Roffice, *even* Aaron, Na'-dab and A-bi'-hu, E-le-a'-zar and Ith'-a-mar, Aaron's sons. Ps. 99:6; Heb. 5:4

2 And ^Rthou shalt make holy garments for Aaron thy brother for glory and for beauty. Lev. 8:7–9

3 And thou shalt speak unto all *that are* wise hearted, ^Rwhom I have filled with the spirit of wisdom, that they may make Aaron's garments to consecrate him, that he may minister unto me in the priest's office. Is. 11:2; Eph. 1:17

4 And these *are* the garments which they shall make; a breastplate, and an e'-phod, and a robe, and a broidered coat, a ^Tmitre, and ^Ra ^Tgirdle: and they shall make holy garments for Aaron thy brother, and his sons, that he may minister unto me in the priest's office. *turban* · Lev. 8:7 · *sash*

5 And they shall take gold, and blue, and purple, and scarlet, and fine linen.

6 And they shall make the e'-phod *of* gold, *of* blue, and *of* purple, *of* scarlet, and fine twined linen, with ^Tcunning work. *artistic*

7 It shall have the two shoulderpieces thereof joined at the

two edges thereof; and *so* it shall be joined together.

8 And the ᵀcurious girdle of the e′-phod, which *is* upon it, shall be of the same, according to the work thereof; *even of* gold, *of* blue, and purple, and scarlet, and fine twined linen.   *intricately woven*

9 And thou shalt take two onyx stones, and grave on them the names of the children of Israel:

10 Six of their names on one stone, and *the other* six names of the rest on the other stone, according to their ᴿbirth. Gen. 35:16

11 With the work of an ᴿengraver in stone, *like* the engravings of a signet, shalt thou engrave the two stones with the names of the children of Israel: thou shalt make them to be set in ᵀouches of gold.   35:35 · *settings*

12 And thou shalt put the two stones upon the shoulders of the e′-phod *for* stones of memorial unto the children of Israel: and ᴿAaron shall bear their names before the LORD upon his two shoulders for a memorial.   39:6, 7

13 And thou shalt make ouches *of* gold;

14 And two chains *of* pure gold at the ends; *of* wreathen work shalt thou make them, and fasten the wreathen chains to the ouches.

15 And ᴿthou shalt make the breastplate of judgment with cunning work; after the work of the e′-phod thou shalt make it; *of* gold, *of* blue, and *of* purple, and *of* scarlet, and *of* fine twined linen, shalt thou make it.   39:8–21

16 Foursquare it shall be *being* doubled; a span *shall be* the length thereof, and a span *shall be* the breadth thereof.

17 And thou shalt set in it settings of stones, *even* four rows of stones: *the first* row *shall be* a sardius, a topaz, and a ᵀcarbuncle: *this shall be* the first row.   *emerald*

18 And the second row *shall be* an ᵀemerald, a sapphire, and a ᵀdiamond.   *turquoise · sapphire*

19 And the third row a ᵀligure, an agate, and an amethyst.   *jacinth*

20 And the fourth row a ᵀberyl, and an ᵀonyx, and a jasper: they shall be set in gold in their inclosings.   *yellow jasper · onyx or carnelian*

21 And the stones shall be with the names of the children of Israel, twelve, according to their names, *like* the engravings of a signet; every one with his name shall they be according to the twelve tribes.

22 And thou shalt make upon the breastplate chains at the ends *of* wreathen work *of* pure gold.

23 And thou shalt make upon the breastplate two rings of gold, and shalt put the two rings on the two ends of the breastplate.

24 And thou shalt put the two wreathen *chains* of gold in the two rings *which are* on the ends of the breastplate.

25 And *the other* two ends of the two wreathen *chains* thou shalt fasten in the two ouches, and put *them* on the shoulderpieces of the e′-phod before it.

26 And thou shalt make two rings of gold, and thou shalt put them upon the two ends of the breastplate in the border thereof, which *is* in the side of the e′-phod inward.

27 And two *other* rings of gold thou shalt make, and shalt put them on the two sides of the e′-phod underneath, toward the forepart thereof, over against the *other* coupling thereof, above the curious girdle of the e′-phod.

28 And they shall bind the breastplate by the rings thereof unto the rings of the e′-phod with a lace of blue, that *it* may be above the curious girdle of the e′-phod, and that the breastplate be not loosed from the e′-phod.

29 And Aaron shall ᴿbear the names of the children of Israel in the breastplate of judgment upon his heart, when he goeth in unto the holy *place*, for a memorial before the LORD continually.   v. 12

30 And thou shalt put in the breastplate of judgment the ᵀU′-rim and the Thum′-mim; and they

shall be upon Aaron's heart, when he goeth in before the LORD: and Aaron shall bear the judgment of the children of Israel upon his heart before the LORD continually.   Lit. *Lights and the Perfections*

31 And thou shalt make the robe of the e'-phod all *of* blue.

32 And there shall be an hole in the top of it, in the midst thereof: it shall have a binding of woven work round about the hole of it, as it were the hole of an habergeon, that it be not rent.

33 And *beneath* upon the hem of it thou shalt make pomegranates *of* blue, and *of* purple, and *of* scarlet, round about the hem thereof; and bells of gold between them round about:

34 A golden bell and a pomegranate, a golden bell and a pomegranate, upon the hem of the robe round about.

35 And it shall be upon Aaron to minister: and his sound shall be heard when he goeth in unto the holy *place* before the LORD, and when he cometh out, that he die not.

36 And ᴿthou shalt make a plate *of* pure gold, and grave upon it, *like* the engravings of a signet, HOLINESS TO THE LORD.   39:30

37 And thou shalt put it on a blue lace, that it may be upon the mitre; upon the forefront of the mitre it shall be.

38 And it shall be upon Aaron's forehead, that Aaron may ᴿbear the iniquity of the holy things, which the children of Israel shall hallow in all their holy gifts; and it shall be always upon his forehead, that they may be ᴿaccepted before the LORD.   [Is. 53:11] · Is. 56:7

39 And thou shalt ᴿembroider the coat of fine linen, and thou shalt make the mitre *of* fine linen, and thou shalt make the girdle *of* needlework.   35:35; 39:27–29

40 And for Aaron's sons thou shalt make coats, and thou shalt make for them girdles, and ᵀbonnets shalt thou make for them, for glory and for ᴿbeauty.   *hats* · v. 2

41 And thou shalt put them upon Aaron thy brother, and his sons with him; and shalt anoint them, and consecrate them, and sanctify them, that they may minister unto me in the priest's office.

42 And thou shalt make them linen breeches to cover their nakedness; from the loins even unto the thighs they shall reach:

43 And they shall be upon Aaron, and upon his sons, when they come in unto the tabernacle of the congregation, or when they come near unto the altar to minister in the holy *place;* that they ᴿbear not iniquity, and die: ᴿ*it shall be* a statute for ever unto him and his seed after him.   Lev. 5:1, 17 · Lev. 17:7

29 And this *is* the thing that thou shalt do unto them to hallow them, to minister unto me in the priest's office: ᴿTake one young bullock, and two rams without blemish,   [Heb. 7:26–28]

2 And ᴿunleavened bread, and cakes unleavened tempered with oil, and wafers unleavened anointed with oil: *of* wheaten flour shalt thou make them.   Lev. 2:4; 6:19–23

3 And thou shalt put them into one basket, and bring them in the basket, with the bullock and the two rams.

4 And Aaron and his sons thou shalt bring unto the door of the tabernacle of the congregation, and shalt wash them with water.

5 ᴿAnd thou shalt take the garments, and put upon Aaron the coat, and the robe of the e'-phod, and the e'-phod, and the breastplate, and gird him with the curious girdle of the e'-phod: Lev. 8:7

6 ᴿAnd thou shalt put the mitre upon his head, and put the holy crown upon the mitre.   28:36, 37

7 Then shalt thou take the anointing ᴿoil, and pour *it* upon his head, and anoint him.   Ps. 133:2

8 And thou shalt bring his sons, and put coats upon them.

9 And thou shalt gird them with girdles, Aaron and his sons, and put the bonnets on them: and

Rthe priest's office shall be theirs for a perpetual statute: and thou shalt Rconsecrate Aaron and his sons.   Num. 3:10; 18:7; 25:13 · 28:41

10 And thou shalt cause a bullock to be brought before the tabernacle of the congregation: and RAaron and his sons shall put their hands upon the head of the bullock.   Lev. 1:4; 8:14

11 And thou shalt kill the bullock before the LORD, by the door of the tabernacle of the congregation.

12 And thou shalt take of the blood of the bullock, and put it upon the horns of the altar with thy finger, and Rpour all the blood beside the bottom of the altar. 27:2

13 And Rthou shalt take all the fat that covereth the inwards, and the caul that is above the liver, and the two kidneys, and the fat that is upon them, and burn them upon the altar.   Lev. 1:8; 3:3, 4

14 But the flesh of the bullock, and his skin, and his dung, shalt thou burn with fire Twithout the camp: it is a sin offering.   outside

15 RThou shalt also take one ram; and Aaron and his sons shall Rput their hands upon the head of the ram.   Lev. 8:18 · Lev. 1:4–9

16 And thou shalt slay the ram, and thou shalt take his blood, and Rsprinkle it round about upon the altar.   24:6; Lev. 1:5, 11

17 And thou shalt cut the ram in pieces, and wash the inwards of him, and his legs, and put them unto his pieces, and Tunto his head.   with

18 And thou shalt burn the whole ram upon the altar: it is a Rburnt offering unto the LORD: it is a sweet Tsavour, an offering made by fire unto the LORD.   20:24 · aroma

19 RAnd thou shalt take the other ram; and Aaron and his sons shall put their hands upon the head of the ram.   Lev. 8:22

20 Then shalt thou kill the ram, and take of his blood, and put it upon the tip of the right ear of Aaron, and upon the tip of the right ear of his sons, and upon the

thumb of their right hand, and upon the great toe of their right foot, and sprinkle the blood upon the altar round about.

21 And thou shalt take of the blood that is upon the altar, and of the anointing oil, and sprinkle it upon Aaron, and upon his garments, and upon his sons, and upon the garments of his sons with him: and Rhe shall be hallowed, and his garments, and his sons, and his sons' garments with him.   v. 1; 28:41; [Heb. 9:22]

22 Also thou shalt take of the ram the fat and the rump, and the fat that covereth the inwards, and the caul above the liver, and the two kidneys, and the fat that is upon them, and the right shoulder; for it is a ram of consecration:

23 RAnd one loaf of bread, and one cake of oiled bread, and one wafer out of the basket of the unleavened bread that is before the LORD: Lev. 8:26

24 And thou shalt put all in the hands of Aaron, and in the hands of his sons; and shalt Rwave them for a wave offering before the LORD.   Lev. 7:30; 10:14

25 RAnd thou shalt receive them of their hands, and burn them upon the altar for a burnt offering, for a sweet savour before the LORD: it is an offering made by fire unto the LORD.   Lev. 8:28

26 And thou shalt take Rthe breast of the ram of Aaron's consecration, and wave it for a wave offering before the LORD: and it shall be thy part.   Lev. 7:31, 34; 8:29

27 And thou shalt sanctify Rthe breast of the wave offering, and the shoulder of the heave offering, which is waved, and which is Theaved up, of the ram of the consecration, even of that which is for Aaron, and of that which is for his sons: Lev. 7:31, 34; Deut. 18:3 · raised

28 And it shall be Aaron's and his sons' by a statute for ever from the children of Israel: for it is an heave offering: and Rit shall be an heave offering from the children of Israel of the sacrifice of their

peace offerings, *even* their heave offering unto the LORD. Lev. 3:1; 7:34

29 And the holy garments of Aaron ^Rshall be his sons' after him, to be anointed therein, and to be consecrated in them. Num. 20:26

30 *And* that son that is priest in his stead shall put them on ^Rseven days, when he cometh into the tabernacle of the congregation to minister in the holy *place*. Lev. 8:35

31 And thou shalt take the ram of the consecration, and ^Rseethe his flesh in the holy place. Lev. 8:31

32 And Aaron and his sons shall eat the flesh of the ram, and the ^Rbread that *is* in the basket, *by* the door of the tabernacle of the congregation. Matt. 12:4

33 And ^Rthey shall eat those things wherewith the atonement was made, to consecrate *and* to sanctify them: ^Rbut a stranger shall not eat *thereof,* because they *are* holy. Lev. 10:14, 15 · 12:43; Lev. 22:10

34 And if ought of the flesh of the consecrations, or of the bread, remain unto the morning, then ^Rthou shalt burn the remainder with fire: it shall not be eaten, because it *is* holy. 34:25; Lev. 7:18; 8:32

35 And thus shalt thou do unto Aaron, and to his sons, according to all *things* which I have commanded thee: ^Rseven days shalt thou consecrate them. Lev. 8:33–35

36 And thou ^Rshalt offer every day a bullock *for* a sin offering for atonement: and thou shalt cleanse the altar, when thou hast made an atonement for it, and thou shalt anoint it, to sanctify it. Heb. 10:11

37 Seven days thou shalt make an atonement for the altar, and sanctify it; and it shall be an altar most holy: ^Rwhatsoever toucheth the altar shall be holy. Matt. 23:19

38 Now this *is that* which thou shalt offer upon the altar; ^Rtwo lambs of the first year ^Rday by day continually. 1 Chr. 16:40 · Dan. 12:11

39 The one lamb thou shalt offer in the morning; and the other lamb thou shalt offer at even:

40 And with the one lamb a tenth deal of flour mingled with the fourth part of an hin of beaten oil; and the fourth part of an hin of wine *for* a drink offering.

41 And the other lamb thou shalt ^Roffer ^Tat even, and shalt do thereto according to the meat offering of the morning, and according to the drink offering thereof, for a sweet savour, an offering made by fire unto the LORD. Ezra 9:4, 5; Ps. 141:2 · *at twilight*

42 *This shall be* ^Ra continual burnt offering throughout your generations *at* the door of the tabernacle of the congregation before the LORD: where I will meet you, to speak there unto thee. 30:8

43 And there I will meet with the children of Israel, and *the tabernacle* ^Rshall be sanctified by my glory. 1 Kin. 8:11; Ezek. 43:5; Hag. 2:7, 9

44 And I will sanctify the tabernacle of the congregation, and the altar: I will ^Rsanctify also both Aaron and his sons, to minister to me in the priest's office. Lev. 21:15

45 And ^RI will dwell among the children of Israel, and will be their God. [John 14:17, 23; Rev. 21:3]

46 And they shall know that ^RI *am* the LORD their God, that ^Rbrought them forth out of the land of Egypt, that I may dwell among them: I *am* the LORD their God. 16:12; 20:2; Deut. 4:35 · Lev. 11:45

30 And thou shalt make ^Ran altar to burn incense upon: *of* shit'-tim wood shalt thou make it. 37:25–29

2 A cubit *shall be* the length thereof, and a cubit the breadth thereof; foursquare shall it be: and two cubits *shall be* the height thereof: the horns thereof *shall be* of the same.

3 And thou shalt overlay it with pure gold, the top thereof, and the sides thereof round about, and the horns thereof; and thou shalt make unto it a ^Tcrown of gold round about. *moulding*

4 And two golden rings shalt thou make to it under the crown of it, by the two corners thereof, upon the two sides of it shalt thou make *it;* and they shall be

for places for the staves to bear it withal.

5 And thou shalt make the staves *of* shit'-tim wood, and overlay them with gold.

6 And thou shalt put it before the ^Rvail that *is* by the ark of the testimony, before the mercy seat that *is* over the testimony, where I will meet with thee.   26:31–35

7 And Aaron shall burn thereon ^Rsweet incense every morning: when he dresseth the lamps, he shall burn incense upon it. Luke 1:9

8 And when Aaron lighteth the lamps ^Tat even, he shall burn incense upon it, a perpetual incense before the Lord throughout your generations.   *at twilight*

9 Ye shall offer no ^Rstrange incense thereon, nor burnt sacrifice, nor meat offering; neither shall ye pour drink offering thereon.   Lev. 10:1

10 And ^RAaron shall make an atonement upon the horns of it once in a year with the blood of the sin offering of atonements: once in the year shall he make atonement upon it throughout your generations: it *is* most holy unto the Lord.   Lev. 16:3–34

11 And the Lord spake unto Moses, saying,

12 When thou takest the sum of the children of Israel after their number, then shall they give every man ^Ra ransom for his soul unto the Lord, when thou numberest them; that there be no plague among them, when *thou* numberest them.   [Matt. 20:28; 1 Pet. 1:18, 19]

13 ^RThis they shall give, every one that passeth among them that are numbered, half a shek'-el after the shek'-el of the sanctuary: (^Ra shek'-el *is* twenty ge'-rahs:) an half shek'-el *shall be* the offering of the Lord.   Matt. 17:24 · Lev. 27:25

14 Every one that passeth among them that are numbered, from twenty years old and above, shall give an ^Toffering unto the Lord.   *contribution*

15 The ^Rrich shall not give more, and the poor shall not give less

than half a shek'-el, when *they* give an offering unto the Lord, to make an atonement for your souls.   Job 34:19; Prov. 22:2; [Eph. 6:9]

16 And thou shalt take the atonement money of the children of Israel, and ^Rshalt appoint it for the service of the tabernacle of the congregation; that it may be a memorial unto the children of Israel before the Lord, to make an atonement for your souls.   38:25–31

17 And the Lord spake unto Moses, saying,

18 ^RThou shalt also make a ^Tlaver *of* brass, and his foot *also of* brass, to wash *withal:* and thou shalt ^Rput it between the tabernacle of the congregation and the altar, and thou shalt put water therein.   38:8; 1 Kin. 7:38 · *basin* · 40:30

19 For Aaron and his sons ^Rshall wash their hands and their feet thereat: Is. 52:11; John 13:8, 10; Heb. 10:22

20 When they go into the tabernacle of the congregation, they shall wash with water, that they die not; or when they come near to the altar to minister, to burn offering made by fire unto the Lord:

21 So they shall wash their hands and their feet, that they die not: and ^Rit shall be a ^Tstatute for ever to them, *even* to him and to his ^Tseed throughout their generations.   28:43 · *requirement* · *descendants*

22 Moreover the Lord spake unto Moses, saying,

23 Take thou also unto thee principal spices, of pure myrrh five hundred *shek'-els*, and of sweet cinnamon half so much, *even* two hundred and fifty *shek'-els*, and of sweet calamus two hundred and fifty *shek'-els*,

24 And of cassia five hundred *shek'-els*, after the shek'-el of the sanctuary, and of oil olive an hin:

25 And thou shalt make it an oil of holy ointment, an ointment compound after the art of the ^Tapothecary: it shall be ^Ran holy anointing oil. *perfumer* · Ps. 89:20; 133:2

26 ^RAnd thou shalt anoint the tabernacle of the congregation

therewith, and the ark of the testimony,   40:9; Lev. 8:10; Num. 7:1

27 And the table and all his vessels, and the candlestick and his vessels, and the altar of incense,

28 And the altar of burnt offering with all his vessels, and the laver and ᵀhis foot.   *its base*

29 And thou shalt sanctify them, that they may be most holy: ᴿwhatsoever toucheth them shall be holy.   29:37; Num. 4:15; Hag. 2:11–13

30 ᴿAnd thou shalt anoint Aaron and his sons, and consecrate them, that *they* may minister unto me in the priest's office.   Lev. 8:12

31 And thou shalt speak unto the children of Israel, saying, This shall be an holy anointing oil unto me throughout your generations.

32 Upon man's flesh shall it not be poured, neither shall ye make *any other* like it, after the composition of it: ᴿit *is* holy, *and* it shall be holy unto you.   vv. 25, 37

33 Whosoever compoundeth *any* like it, or whosoever putteth *any* of it upon a stranger, shall even be cut off from his people.

34 And the LORD said unto Moses, ᴿTake unto thee sweet spices, stac'-te, and on'-y-cha, and gal'-ba-num; *these* sweet spices with pure frankincense: of each shall there be a like *weight:*   25:6; 37:29

35 And thou shalt make it a perfume, a confection after the art of the ᵀapothecary, ᵀtempered together, pure *and* holy: *perfumer · salted*

36 And thou shalt beat *some* of it very small, and put of it before the testimony in the tabernacle of the congregation, ᴿwhere I will meet with thee: ᴿit shall be unto you most holy.   Lev. 16:2 · Lev. 2:3

37 And *as for* the perfume which thou shalt make, ᴿye shall not make to yourselves according to ᵀthe composition thereof: it shall be unto thee holy for the LORD.   v. 32 · Lit. *its proportion*

38 Whosoever shall make like unto that, to smell thereto, shall even be cut off from his people.

31 And the LORD spake unto Moses, saying,

2 See, I have called by name Be-zal'-e-el the son of U'-ri, the son of Hur, of the tribe of Judah:

3 And I have ᴿfilled him with the spirit of God, in wisdom, and in understanding, and in knowledge, and in all manner of workmanship,   35:31; 1 Kin. 7:14; Eph. 1:17

4 To devise ᵀcunning works, to work in gold, and in silver, and in brass,   *artistic*

5 And in cutting of stones, to set *them,* and in carving of timber, to work in all manner of workmanship.

6 And I, behold, I have given with him A-ho'-li-ab, the son of A-his'-a-mach, of the tribe of Dan: and in the hearts of all that are ᵀwise hearted I have put wisdom, that they may make all that I have commanded thee;   *gifted artisans*

7 ᴿThe tabernacle of the congregation, and ᴿthe ark of the testimony, and ᴿthe mercy seat that *is* thereupon, and all the furniture of the tabernacle,   36:8 · 37:1–5 · 37:6–9

8 And ᴿthe table and his furniture, and ᴿthe pure candlestick with all his furniture, and the altar of incense,   37:10–16 · 37:17–24

9 And ᴿthe altar of burnt offering with all his furniture, and ᴿthe laver and his foot,   38:1–7 · 38:8

10 And ᴿthe ᵀcloths of service, and the holy garments for Aaron the priest, and the garments of his sons, to minister in the priest's office,   39:1, 41 · *woven garments*

11 ᴿAnd the anointing oil, and sweet incense for the holy *place:* according to all that I have commanded thee shall they do. 30:23–38

12 And the LORD spake unto Moses, saying,

13 Speak thou also unto the children of Israel, saying, ᴿVerily my sabbaths ye shall keep: for it *is* a sign between me and you throughout your generations; that *ye* may know that I *am* the LORD that doth sanctify you.   Lev. 19:3, 30

14 Ye shall keep the sabbath therefore; for it *is* holy unto you:

every one that defileth it shall surely be put to death: for [R]whosoever doeth *any* work therein, that soul shall be cut off from among his people.　　　John 7:23

15 [R]Six days may work be done; but in the seventh *is* the sabbath of rest, holy to the LORD: whosoever doeth *any* work in the sabbath day, he shall surely be put to death.　　20:9–11; Lev. 23:3; Deut. 5:12–14

16 Wherefore the children of Israel shall keep the sabbath, to observe the sabbath throughout their generations, *for* a perpetual covenant.

17 It *is* a sign between me and the children of Israel for ever: for *in* six days the LORD made heaven and earth, and on the seventh day he rested, and was refreshed.

18 And he gave unto Moses, when he had made an end of communing with him upon mount Si′nai, [R]two tables of testimony, tables of stone, written with the finger of God.　　[Deut. 4:13; 2 Cor. 3:3]

32 And when the people saw that Moses delayed to come down out of the mount, the people gathered themselves together unto Aaron, and said unto him, Up, make us gods, which shall [R]go before us; for *as for* this Moses, the man that [R]brought us up out of the land of Egypt, we wot not what is become of him.　　13:21 · v. 8

2 And Aaron said unto them, Break off the [R]golden earrings, which *are* in the ears of your wives, of your sons, and of your daughters, and bring *them* unto me.　　11:2; 35:22; Judg. 8:24–27

3 And all the people brake off the golden earrings which *were* in their ears, and brought *them* unto Aaron.

4 [R]And he received *them* at their hand, and fashioned it with a graving tool, after he had made it a molten calf: and they said, These *be* thy gods, O Israel, which brought thee up out of the land of Egypt.　　Neh. 9:18; Ps. 106:19; Acts 7:41

5 And when Aaron saw *it*, he built an altar before it; and Aaron made proclamation, and said, To morrow *is* a feast to the LORD.

6 And they rose up early on the morrow, and offered burnt offerings, and brought peace offerings; and the people sat down to eat and to drink, and rose up to play.

7 And the LORD said unto Moses, Go, get thee down; for thy people, which thou broughtest out of the land of Egypt, [R]have corrupted *themselves:*　　Gen. 6:11, 12

8 They have turned aside quickly out of the way which [R]I commanded them: they have made them a molten calf, and have worshipped it, and have sacrificed thereunto, and said, [R]These *be* thy gods, O Israel, which have brought thee up out of the land of Egypt.　　20:3, 4; Deut. 32:17 · 1 Kin. 12:28

9 And the LORD said unto Moses, I have seen this people, and, behold, it *is* a stiffnecked people:

10 Now therefore [R]let me alone, that my wrath may wax hot against them, and that I may consume them: and I will make of thee a great nation.　　Deut. 9:14, 19

11 [R]And Moses besought the LORD his God, and said, LORD, why doth thy wrath wax hot against thy people, which thou hast brought forth out of the land of Egypt with great power, and with a mighty hand? Deut. 9:18, 26–29

12 Wherefore should the Egyptians speak, and say, For mischief did he bring them out, to slay them in the mountains, and to consume them from the face of the earth? Turn from thy fierce wrath, and [R]repent of this evil against thy people.　　v. 14

13 Remember Abraham, Isaac, and Israel, thy servants, to whom thou [R]swarest by thine own self, and saidst unto them, I will multiply your seed as the stars of heaven, and all this land that I have spoken of will I give unto your seed, and they shall inherit *it* for ever.　　Gen. 22:16–18; [Heb. 6:13]

14 And the LORD [T]repented of

the ᵀevil which he thought to do unto his people.   *relented from · harm*

15 And ᴿMoses turned, and went down from the mount, and the two tables of the testimony *were* in his hand: the tables *were* written on both their sides; on the one side and on the other *were* they written.   Deut. 9:15

16 And the ᴿtables *were* the work of God, and the writing *was* the writing of God, graven upon the tables.   31:18

17 And when Joshua heard the noise of the people as they shouted, he said unto Moses, *There is* a noise of war in the camp.

18 And he said, *It is* not the voice of *them that* shout for mastery, neither *is it* the voice of *them that* cry for being overcome: *but* the ᵀnoise of *them that* sing do I hear.   *voice*

19 And it came to pass, as soon as he came nigh unto the camp, that ᴿhe saw the calf, and the dancing: and Moses' anger waxed hot, and he cast the tables out of his hands, and brake them beneath the mount.   Deut. 9:16, 17

20 ᴿAnd he took the calf which they had made, and burnt *it* in the fire, and ground *it* to powder, and ᵀstrawed *it* upon the water, and made the children of Israel drink of *it*.   Num. 5:17, 24; Deut. 9:21 · *scattered*

21 And Moses said unto Aaron, ᴿWhat did this people unto thee, that thou hast brought so great a sin upon them?   Gen. 26:10

22 And Aaron said, Let not the anger of my lord wax hot: ᴿthou knowest the people, that they *are* set on ᵀmischief. 14:11; Deut. 9:24 · *evil*

23 For they said unto me, Make us gods, which shall go before us: for *as for* this Moses, the man that brought us up out of the land of Egypt, we ᵀwot not what is become of him.   *know*

24 And I said unto them, Whosoever hath any gold, let them break *it* off. So they gave *it* me: then I cast it into the fire, and there came out this calf.

25 And when Moses saw that the people *were* ᴿnaked; (for Aaron ᴿhad made them naked unto *their* shame among their enemies:)   33:4, 5 · 2 Chr. 28:19

26 Then Moses stood in the gate of the camp, and said, Who *is* on the Lᴏʀᴅ's side? *let him come* unto me. And all the sons of Levi gathered themselves together unto him.

27 And he said unto them, Thus saith the Lᴏʀᴅ God of Israel, Put every man his sword by his side, *and* go in and out from gate to gate throughout the camp, and slay every man his brother, and every man his companion, and every man his neighbour.

28 And the children of Levi did according to the word of Moses: and there fell of the people that day about three thousand men.

29 ᴿFor Moses had said, Consecrate yourselves to day to the Lᴏʀᴅ, even every man upon his son, and upon his brother; that he may bestow upon you a blessing this day.   1 Sam. 15:18, 22; Zech. 13:3

30 And it came to pass on the morrow, that Moses said unto the people, Ye have sinned a great sin: and now I will go up unto the Lᴏʀᴅ; peradventure I shall make an atonement for your sin.

31 And Moses returned unto the Lᴏʀᴅ, and said, Oh, this people have sinned a great sin, and have ᴿmade them gods of gold.   20:23

32 Yet now, if thou wilt forgive their sin—; and if not, ᴿblot me, I pray thee, ᴿout of thy book which thou hast written.   Is. 4:3 · Phil. 4:3

33 And the Lᴏʀᴅ said unto Moses, ᴿWhosoever hath sinned against me, him will I ᴿblot out of my book.   Lev. 23:30 · Ps. 9:5; Rev. 3:5

34 Therefore now go, lead the people unto *the place* of which I have spoken unto thee: ᴿbehold, mine Angel shall go before thee: nevertheless ᴿin the day when I ᴿvisit I will visit their sin upon them.   Josh. 5:14 · Rom. 2:5, 6 · Ps. 89:32

35 And the Lᴏʀᴅ plagued the people, because ᴿthey made the calf, which Aaron made.   Neh. 9:18

33 And the Lord said unto Moses, Depart, *and* go up hence, thou and the people which thou hast brought up out of the land of Egypt, unto the land which I sware unto Abraham, to Isaac, and to Jacob, saying, [R]Unto thy seed will I give it: Gen. 12:7

2 [R]And I will send an angel before thee; [R]and I will drive out the Ca'-naan-ite, the Am'-or-ite, and the Hit'-tite, and the Per'-iz-zite, the Hi'-vite, and the Jeb'-u-site: Josh. 5:14 · Josh. 24:11

3 [R]Unto a land flowing with milk and honey: for I will not go up in the midst of thee; for thou *art* a stiffnecked people: lest I consume thee in the way.   3:8

4 And when the people heard these evil tidings, [R]they mourned: and no man did put on him his ornaments.   Num. 14:1, 39

5 For the Lord had said unto Moses, Say unto the children of Israel, Ye *are* a stiffnecked people: I will come up into the midst of thee in a moment, and consume thee: therefore now put off thy [T]ornaments from thee, that I may know what to do unto thee. *jewels*

6 And the children of Israel stripped themselves of their ornaments by the mount Ho'-reb.

7 And Moses took the tabernacle, and pitched it without the camp, afar off from the camp, and called it the Tabernacle of the congregation. And it came to pass, *that* every one which sought the Lord went out unto the tabernacle of the congregation, which *was* without the camp.

8 And it came to pass, when Moses went out unto the tabernacle, *that* all the people rose up, and stood every man [R]*at* his tent door, and looked after Moses, until he was gone into the tabernacle.   Num. 16:27

9 And it came to pass, as Moses entered into the tabernacle, the cloudy pillar descended, and stood *at* the door of the tabernacle, and *the* [T]Lord [R]talked with Moses.   Lit. *He* · 25:22; 31:18; Ps. 99:7

10 And all the people saw the cloudy pillar stand *at* the tabernacle door: and all the people rose up and [R]worshipped, every man *in* his tent door.   4:31

11 And [R]the Lord spake unto Moses face to face, as a man speaketh unto his friend. And he turned again into the camp: but his servant Joshua, the son of Nun, a young man, departed not out of the tabernacle.   Deut. 34:10

12 And Moses said unto the Lord, See, [R]thou sayest unto me, Bring up this people: and thou hast not let me know whom thou wilt send with me. Yet thou hast said, [R]I know thee by name, and thou hast also found grace in my sight.   32:34 · John 10:14, 15; 2 Tim. 2:19

13 Now therefore, I pray thee, if I have found grace in thy sight, [R]shew me now thy way, that I may know thee, that I may find grace in thy sight: and consider that this nation *is* thy people.   Ps. 25:4; 27:11

14 And he said, [R]My presence shall go *with thee*, and I will give thee [R]rest.   Is. 63:9 · Deut. 12:10; 25:19

15 And he said unto him, [R]If thy presence go not *with me*, carry us not up hence.   v. 3

16 For wherein shall it be known here that I and thy people have found grace in thy sight? [R]*is it* not in that thou goest with us? so [R]shall we be separated, I and thy people, from all the people that *are* upon the face of the earth.   Num. 14:14 · 34:10; Deut. 4:7, 34

17 And the Lord said unto Moses, [R]I will do this thing also that thou hast spoken: for thou hast found grace in my sight, and I know thee by name.   [James 5:16]

18 And he said, I beseech thee, shew me [R]thy glory.   24:16, 17

19 And he said, I will make all my [R]goodness pass before thee, and I will proclaim the name of the Lord before thee; and will be gracious to whom I will be gracious, and will shew mercy on whom I will shew mercy.   34:6, 7

20 And he said, Thou canst not

see my face: for ᴿthere shall no man see me, and live.   [Gen. 32:30]

21 And the Lᴏʀᴅ said, Behold, *there is* a place by me, and thou shalt stand upon a rock:

22 And it shall come to pass, while my glory passeth by, that I will put thee ᴿin a clift of the rock, and will ᴿcover thee with my hand while I pass by: Is. 2:21 · Ps. 91:1, 4

23 And I will take away mine hand, and thou shalt see my back parts: but my face shall ᴿnot be seen.   v. 20; [John 1:18]

34 And the Lᴏʀᴅ said unto Moses, Hew thee two tables of stone like unto the first: and ᴿI will write upon *these* tables the words that were in the first tables, which thou brakest.   Deut. 10:2, 4

2 And be ready in the morning, and come up in the morning unto mount Si'-nai, and present thyself there to me ᴿin the top of the mount.   19:11, 18, 20

3 And no man shall ᴿcome up with thee, neither let any man be seen throughout all the mount; neither let the flocks nor herds feed before that mount.   24:9–11

4 And he hewed two tables of stone like unto the first; and Moses rose up early in the morning, and went up unto mount Si'-nai, as the Lᴏʀᴅ had commanded him, and took in his hand the two tables of stone.

5 And the Lᴏʀᴅ descended in the ᴿcloud, and stood with him there, and ᴿproclaimed the name of the Lᴏʀᴅ.   19:9 · 33:19

6 And the Lᴏʀᴅ passed by before him, and proclaimed, The Lᴏʀᴅ, The Lᴏʀᴅ God, merciful and gracious, longsuffering, and abundant in goodness and truth,

7 Keeping mercy for thousands, forgiving iniquity and transgression and sin, and that will by no means clear *the guilty;* visiting the iniquity of the fathers upon the children, and upon the children's children, unto the third and to the fourth *generation.*

8 And Moses made haste, and ᴿbowed his head toward the earth, and worshipped.   4:31

9 And he said, If now I have found grace in thy sight, O Lord, ᴿlet my Lord, I pray thee, go among us; for it *is* a ᴿstiffnecked people; and pardon our iniquity and our sin, and take us for ᴿthine inheritance.   33:12–16 · 33:3 · Ps. 33:12

10 And he said, Behold, ᴿI make a covenant: before all thy people I will ᴿdo marvels, such as have not been done in all the earth, nor in any nation: and all the people among which thou *art* shall see the work of the Lᴏʀᴅ: for it *is* ᴿa terrible thing that I will do with thee.   Deut. 5:2 · Ps. 77:14 · Ps. 145:6

11 Observe thou that which I command thee this day: behold, I drive out before thee the Am'-or-ite, and the Ca'-naan-ite, and the Hit'-tite, and the Per'-iz-zite, and the Hi'-vite, and the Jeb'-u-site.

12 ᴿTake heed to thyself, lest thou make a covenant with the inhabitants of the land whither thou goest, lest it be for a snare in the midst of thee: 23:32, 33

13 But ye shall ᴿdestroy their altars, break their images, and ᴿcut down their groves: 23:24 · Deut. 16:21

14 For thou shalt worship ᴿno other god: for the Lᴏʀᴅ, whose ᴿname *is* Jealous, *is* a ᴿjealous God: [20:3–5] · [Is. 57:15] · [Deut. 4:24]

15 Lest thou make a covenant with the inhabitants of the land, and they ᴿgo a whoring after their gods, and do sacrifice unto their gods, and *one* call thee, and thou eat of his sacrifice;   Judg. 2:17

16 And thou take of their daughters unto thy sons, and their daughters go a whoring after their gods, and make thy sons go a whoring after their gods.

17 ᴿThou shalt make thee no molten gods.   32:8; Lev. 19:4; Deut. 5:8

18 The feast of ᴿunleavened bread shalt thou keep. Seven days thou shalt eat unleavened bread, as I commanded thee, in the time of the ᴿmonth A'-bib: for in the

month A'-bib thou camest out from Egypt. 12:15, 16 · 12:2; 13:4

19 ᴿAll that openeth the ᵀmatrix *is* mine; and every firstling among thy cattle, *whether* ox or sheep, *that is male.* 13:2; 22:29 · *womb*

20 But ᴿthe firstling of an ass thou shalt redeem with a lamb: and if thou redeem *him* not, then shalt thou break his neck. All the firstborn of thy sons thou shalt redeem. And none shall appear before me ᴿempty. 13:13 · Deut. 16:16

21 ᴿSix days thou shalt work, but on the seventh day thou shalt rest: in ᵀearing time and in harvest thou shalt rest. 20:9 · *plowing*

22 And thou shalt observe the feast of weeks, of the firstfruits of wheat harvest, and the feast of ingathering at the year's end.

23 Thrice in the year shall all your men children appear before the Lord GOD, the God of Israel.

24 For I will cast out the nations before thee, and enlarge thy borders: neither shall any man desire thy land, when thou shalt go up to appear before the LORD thy God thrice in the year.

25 Thou shalt not offer the blood of my sacrifice with leaven; ᴿneither shall the sacrifice of the feast of the passover be left unto the morning. 12:10

26 ᴿThe first of the firstfruits of thy land thou shalt bring unto the house of the LORD thy God. Thou shalt not seethe a kid in his mother's milk. 23:19; Deut. 26:2

27 And the LORD said unto Moses, Write thou ᴿthese words: for after the tenor of these words I have made a covenant with thee and with Israel. 17:14; 24:4; Deut. 31:9

28 And he was there with the LORD forty days and forty nights; he did neither eat bread, nor drink water. And he wrote upon the tables the words of the covenant, the ten commandments.

29 And it came to pass, when Moses came down from mount Si'-nai with the ᴿtwo tables of testimony in Moses' hand, when he came down from the mount, that

Moses wist not that ᴿthe skin of his face shone while he talked with him. 32:15 · Matt. 17:2; 2 Cor. 3:7

30 And when Aaron and all the children of Israel saw Moses, behold, the skin of his face shone; and they were afraid to come nigh him.

31 And Moses called unto them; and Aaron and all the rulers of the congregation returned unto him: and Moses talked with them.

32 And afterward all the children of Israel came nigh: ᴿand he gave them in commandment all that the LORD had spoken with him in mount Si'-nai. 24:3

33 And *till* Moses had done speaking with them, he put ᴿa vail on his face. [2 Cor. 3:13, 14]

34 But when Moses went in before the LORD to speak with him, he took the vail off, until he came out. And he came out, and spake unto the children of Israel *that* which he was commanded.

35 And the children of Israel saw the face of Moses, that the skin of Moses' face shone: and Moses put the vail upon his face again, until he went in to speak with him.

35 And Moses gathered all the congregation of the children of Israel together, and said unto them, ᴿThese *are* the words which the LORD hath commanded, that ye should do them. 34:32

2 ᴿSix days shall work be done, but on the seventh day there shall be to you an holy day, a sabbath of rest to the LORD: whosoever doeth work therein shall be put to ᴿdeath. 20:9, 10; Lev. 23:3 · Num. 15:32–36

3 ᴿYe shall kindle no fire throughout your habitations upon the sabbath day. 12:16; 16:23

4 And Moses spake unto all the congregation of the children of Israel, saying, ᴿThis *is* the thing which the LORD commanded, saying, 25:1, 2

5 Take ye from among you an offering unto the LORD: ᴿwhosoever *is* of a willing heart, let him bring it, an offering of the LORD; gold, and silver, and brass, 25:2

6 And ᴿblue, and purple, and scarlet, and fine linen, and ᴿgoats' hair,   36:8 · 36:14

7 And rams' skins dyed red, and badgers' skins, and shit'-tim wood,

8 And oil for the light, ᴿand spices for anointing oil, and for the sweet incense,   25:6; 30:23–25

9 And onyx stones, and stones to be set for the e'-phod, and for the breastplate.

10 And ᴿevery ᵀwise hearted among you shall come, and make all that the LORD hath commanded;   31:2–6; 36:1, 2 · skilful

11 ᴿThe tabernacle, his tent, and his covering, his taches, and his boards, his bars, his pillars, and his sockets,   26:1, 2; 36:14

12 ᴿThe ark, and the staves thereof, with the mercy seat, and the vail of the covering,   25:10–22

13 The ᴿtable, and his staves, and all his vessels, ᴿand the shewbread,   25:23 · 25:30; Lev. 24:5, 6

14 The candlestick also for the light, and his furniture, and his lamps, with the oil for the light,

15 ᴿAnd the incense altar, and his staves, ᴿand the anointing oil, and the sweet incense, and the hanging for the door at the entering in of the tabernacle,   30:1 · 30:25

16 ᴿThe altar of burnt offering, with his brasen grate, his staves, and all his vessels, the laver and his foot,   27:1–8

17 ᴿThe hangings of the court, his pillars, and their sockets, and the hanging for the door of the court,   27:9–18

18 The pins of the tabernacle, and the pins of the court, and their cords,

19 ᴿThe cloths of service, to do service in the holy place, the holy garments for Aaron the priest, and the garments of his sons, to minister in the priest's office. 31:10

20 And all the congregation of the children of Israel departed from the presence of Moses.

21 And they came, every one whose heart ᵀstirred him up, and every one whom his spirit made willing, and they ᴿbrought the LORD's offering to the work of the tabernacle of the congregation, and for all his service, and for the holy garments.   Lit. lifted up · v. 24

22 And they came, both men and women, as many as were willing hearted, and brought bracelets, and earrings, and rings, and tablets, all jewels of gold: and every man that offered offered an offering of gold unto the LORD.

23 And every man, with whom was found blue, and purple, and scarlet, and fine linen, and goats' hair, and red skins of rams, and badgers' skins, brought them.

24 Every one that did offer an offering of silver and brass brought the LORD's offering: and every man, with whom was found shit'-tim wood for any work of the service, brought it.

25 And all the women that were ᴿwise hearted did spin with their hands, and brought that which they had spun, both of blue, and of purple, and of scarlet, and of fine linen.   28:3; 31:6; 36:1

26 And all the women whose heart ᵀstirred them up in wisdom spun goats' hair.   Lit. lifted them up

27 And ᴿthe rulers brought onyx stones, and stones to be set, for the e'-phod, and for the breastplate;   1 Chr. 29:6; Ezra 2:68

28 And ᴿspice, and oil for the light, and for the anointing oil, and for the sweet incense.   30:23

29 The children of Israel brought a willing offering unto the LORD, every man and woman, whose heart made them willing to bring for all manner of work, which the LORD had commanded to be made by the hand of Moses.

30 And Moses said unto the children of Israel, See, ᴿthe LORD hath called by name Be-zal'-e-el the son of U'-ri, the son of Hur, of the tribe of Judah;   31:1–6

31 And he hath filled him with the spirit of God, in wisdom, in understanding, and in knowledge, and in all manner of workmanship;

32 And to devise curious works, to work in gold, and in silver, and in brass,

33 And in the cutting of stones, to set *them*, and in carving of wood, to make any manner of ᵀcunning work.   *artistic workmanship*

34 And he hath put in his heart that he may teach, *both* he, and ᴿA-ho'-li-ab, the son of A-his'-a-mach, of the tribe of Dan.   31:6

35 Them hath he filled with wisdom of heart, to work all manner of work, of the engraver, and of the cunning workman, and of the embroiderer, in blue, and in purple, in scarlet, and in fine linen, and of the weaver, *even* of them that do any work, and of those that devise cunning work.

36 Then wrought Be-zal'-e-el and A-ho'-li-ab, and every wise hearted man, in whom the LORD put wisdom and understanding to know how to work all manner of work for the service of the sanctuary, according to all that the LORD had commanded.

2 And Moses called Be-zal'-e-el and A-ho'-li-ab, and every wise hearted man, in whose heart the LORD had put wisdom, *even* every one whose heart stirred him up to come unto the work to do it:

3 And they received of Moses all the ᴿoffering, which the children of Israel ᴿhad brought for the work of the service of the sanctuary, to make it *withal*. And they brought yet unto him free offerings every morning. 35:5 · 35:27

4 And all the wise men, that wrought all the work of the sanctuary, came every man from his work which they made;

5 And they spake unto Moses, saying, ᴿThe people bring much more than enough for the service of the work, which the LORD commanded to make. 2 Chr. 24:14; 31:6–10

6 And Moses gave commandment, and they caused it to be proclaimed throughout the camp, saying, Let neither man nor woman make any more work for the offering of the sanctuary. So the people were restrained from bringing.

7 For the stuff they had was sufficient for all the work to make it, and too ᴿmuch.   1 Kin. 8:64

8 ᴿAnd every wise hearted man among them that wrought the work of the tabernacle made ten curtains *of* fine twined linen, and blue, and purple, and scarlet: *with* cher'-u-bims of cunning work made he them.   26:1–14

9 The length of one curtain *was* twenty and eight cubits, and the breadth of one curtain four cubits: the curtains *were* all of one size.

10 And he coupled the five curtains one unto another: and *the other* five curtains he coupled one unto another.

11 And he made loops of blue on the edge of one curtain ᵀfrom the selvedge in the coupling: likewise he made in the uttermost side of *another* curtain, in the coupling of the second.   *on the selvedge of one set*

12 Fifty loops made he in one curtain, and fifty loops made he in the edge of the curtain which *was* in the coupling of the second: the loops held one *curtain* to another.

13 And he made fifty ᵀtaches of gold, and coupled the curtains one unto another with the taches: so it became one tabernacle. *clasps*

14 ᴿAnd he made curtains *of* goats' *hair* for the tent over the tabernacle: eleven curtains he made them.   26:7

15 The length of one curtain *was* thirty cubits, and four cubits *was* the breadth of one curtain: the eleven curtains *were* of one size.

16 And he coupled five curtains by themselves, and six curtains by themselves.

17 And he made fifty loops upon the uttermost edge of the curtain in the coupling, and fifty loops made he upon the edge of the curtain which coupleth the second.

18 And he made fifty taches *of* brass to couple the tent together, that it might be one.

19 ᴿAnd he made a covering for

the tent *of* rams' skins dyed red, and a covering *of* ^Tbadgers' skins above *that.*   26:14 · Or *dolphin skins*

20 ^RAnd he made boards for the tabernacle *of* shit'-tim wood, standing up.   26:15-29

21 The length of a board *was* ten cubits, and the breadth of a board one cubit and a half.

22 One board had two tenons, ^Requally distant one from another: thus did he make for all the boards of the tabernacle.   26:17

23 And he made boards for the tabernacle; twenty boards for the south side southward:

24 And forty sockets of silver he made under the twenty boards; two sockets under one board for his two tenons, and two sockets under another board for his two tenons.

25 And for the other side of the tabernacle, *which is* toward the north corner, he made twenty boards,

26 And their forty sockets of silver; two sockets under one board, and two sockets under another board.

27 And for the sides of the tabernacle westward he made six boards.

28 And two boards made he for the corners of the tabernacle in the two sides.

29 And they were ^Tcoupled beneath, and coupled together at the head thereof, to one ring: thus he did to both of them in both the corners.   *twined*

30 And there were eight boards; and their sockets *were* sixteen sockets of silver, under every board two sockets.

31 And he made bars of shit'-tim wood; five for the boards of the one side of the tabernacle,

32 And five bars for the boards of the other side of the tabernacle, and five bars for the boards of the tabernacle for the sides westward.

33 And he made the middle bar to ^Tshoot through the boards from the one end to the other.   *pass*

34 And he overlaid the boards with gold, and made their rings *of* gold *to be* places for the bars, and overlaid the bars with gold.

35 And he made a vail *of* blue, and purple, and scarlet, and fine twined linen: *with* cher'-u-bims made he it of cunning work.

36 And he made thereunto four pillars *of* shit'-tim *wood,* and overlaid them with gold: their hooks *were of* gold; and he cast for them four sockets of silver.

37 And he made an ^Rhanging for the tabernacle door *of* blue, and purple, and scarlet, and fine twined linen, of needlework;   26:36

38 And the five pillars of it with their hooks: and he overlaid their ^Tchapiters and their fillets with gold: but their five sockets *were of* brass.   *capitals*

37 And ^RBe-zal'-e-el made ^Rthe ark *of* shit'-tim wood: two cubits and a half *was* the length of it, and a cubit and a half the breadth of it, and a cubit and a half the height of it: 36:1 · 25:10-20

2 And he overlaid it with pure gold ^Twithin and without, and made a ^Tcrown of gold to it round about.   *inside* and *outside · moulding*

3 And he cast for it four rings of gold, *to be set* by the four corners of it; even two rings upon the one side of it, and two rings upon the other side of it.

4 And he made staves *of* shit'-tim wood, and overlaid them with gold.

5 And he put the staves into the rings by the sides of the ark, to bear the ark.

6 And he made the ^Rmercy seat *of* pure gold: two cubits and a half *was* the length thereof, and one cubit and a half the breadth thereof.   25:17

7 And he made two cher'-u-bims *of* gold, beaten out of one piece made he them, on the two ends of the mercy seat;

8 One cherub on the end on this side, and another cherub on the *other* end on that side: out of the mercy seat made he the cher'-u-bims on the two ends thereof.

9 ᴿAnd the cher'-u-bims spread out *their* wings on high, *and* covered with their wings over the mercy seat, with their faces one to another; *even* to the mercy seatward were the faces of the cher'-u-bims.   25:20

10 And he made ᴿthe table *of* shit'-tim wood: two cubits *was* the length thereof, and a cubit the breadth thereof, and a cubit and a half the height thereof: 25:23–29

11 And he overlaid it with pure gold, and made thereunto a crown of gold round about.

12 Also he made thereunto a border of an handbreadth round about; and made a crown of gold for the border thereof round about.

13 And he cast for it four rings of gold, and put the rings upon the four corners that *were* in the four feet thereof.

14 Over against the border were the rings, the places for the staves to bear the table.

15 And he made the staves *of* shit'-tim wood, and overlaid them with gold, to bear the table.

16 And he made the vessels which *were* upon the table, his dishes, and his spoons, and his bowls, and his covers to cover ᵀwithal, *of* pure gold.   *with them*

17 And he made the ᴿcandlestick *of* pure gold: *of* beaten work made he the candlestick; his shaft, and his branch, his bowls, his knops, and his flowers, were of the same: 25:31–39

18 And six branches going out of the sides thereof; three branches of the candlestick out of the one side thereof, and three branches of the candlestick out of the other side thereof:

19 Three bowls made after the fashion of almonds in one branch, a knop and a flower; and three bowls made like almonds in another branch, a knop and a flower: so throughout the six branches going out of the candlestick.

20 And in the candlestick *were* four bowls made like almonds, his knops, and his flowers:

21 And a knop under two branches of the same, and a knop under two branches of the same, and a knop under two branches of the same, according to the six branches going out of it.

22 Their knops and their branches were of the same: all of it *was* one beaten work *of* pure gold.

23 And he made his seven lamps, and his ᴿsnuffers, and his snuffdishes, *of* pure gold.   Num. 4:9

24 *Of* a talent of pure gold made he it, and all the vessels thereof.

25 ᴿAnd he made the incense altar *of* shit'-tim wood: the length of it *was* a cubit, and the breadth of it a cubit; *it was* foursquare; and two cubits *was* the height of it; the horns thereof were of the same.   30:1–5

26 And he overlaid it with pure gold, *both* the top of it, and the sides thereof round about, and the horns of it: also he made unto it a crown of gold round about.

27 And he made two rings of gold for it under the crown thereof, by the two corners of it, upon the two sides thereof, to be places for the staves to bear it withal.

28 And he ᴿmade the staves *of* shit'-tim wood, and overlaid them with gold.   30:5

29 And he made the holy anointing oil, and the pure incense of sweet spices, according to the work of the apothecary.

38 And ᴿhe made the altar of burnt offering *of* shit'-tim wood: five cubits *was* the length thereof, and five cubits the breadth thereof; *it was* foursquare; and three cubits the height thereof.   27:1–8

2 And he made the horns thereof on the four corners of it; the horns thereof were of the same: and he overlaid it with brass.

3 And he made all the vessels of the altar, the pots, and the shovels, and the basons, *and* the flesh-

hooks, and the firepans: all the vessels thereof made he *of* brass.

4 And he made for the altar a brasen grate of network under the compass thereof beneath unto the midst of it.

5 And he cast four rings for the four ends of the grate of brass, *to be* places for the staves.

6 And he made the staves *of* shit'-tim wood, and overlaid them with brass.

7 And he put the staves into the rings on the sides of the altar, to bear it withal; he made the altar hollow with boards.

8 And he made [R]the laver *of* brass, and the foot of it *of* brass, of the [T]lookingglasses of *the women* assembling, which assembled *at* the door of the tabernacle of the congregation.   30:18 · *mirrors*

9 And he made the court: on the south side southward the hangings of the court *were of* fine twined linen, an hundred cubits:

10 Their pillars *were* twenty, and their brasen sockets twenty; the hooks of the pillars and their fillets *were of* silver.

11 And for the north side *the hangings were* an hundred cubits, their pillars *were* twenty, and their sockets of brass twenty; the hooks of the pillars and their fillets *of* silver.

12 And for the west side *were* hangings of fifty cubits, their pillars ten, and their sockets ten; the hooks of the pillars and their fillets *of* silver.

13 And for the east side eastward fifty cubits.

14 The hangings of the one side *of the gate were* fifteen cubits; their pillars three, and their sockets three.

15 And for the other side of the court gate, on this hand and that hand, *were* hangings of fifteen cubits; their pillars three, and their sockets three.

16 All the hangings of the court round about *were* of fine twined linen.

17 And the sockets for the pillars *were of* brass; the hooks of the pillars and their fillets *of* silver; and the overlaying of their [T]chapiters *of* silver; and all the pillars of the court *were* filleted with silver.   *capitals*

18 And the hanging for the gate of the court *was* needlework, *of* blue, and purple, and scarlet, and fine twined linen: and twenty cubits *was* the length, and the height in the breadth *was* five cubits, [T]answerable to the hangings of the court.   *corresponding*

19 And their pillars *were* four, and their sockets *of* brass four; their hooks *of* silver, and the overlaying of their [T]chapiters and their fillets *of* silver.   *capitals*

20 And all the [R]pins of the tabernacle, and of the court round about, *were of* brass.   27:19

21 This is the sum of the tabernacle, *even* of [R]the tabernacle of testimony, as it was counted, according to the commandment of Moses, *for* the service of the Levites, by the hand of Ith'-a-mar, son to Aaron the priest.   Acts 7:44

22 And [R]Be-zal'-e-el the son of U'-ri, the son of Hur, of the tribe of Judah, made all that the LORD commanded Moses.   1 Chr. 2:18–20

23 And with him *was* A-ho'-li-ab, son of A-his'-a-mach, of the tribe of Dan, an engraver, and a cunning workman, and an embroiderer in blue, and in purple, and in scarlet, and fine linen.

24 All the gold that was occupied for the work in all the work of the holy *place*, even the gold of the offering, was twenty and nine talents, and seven hundred and thirty shek'-els, after [R]the shek'-el of the sanctuary.   30:13, 24; Lev. 5:15

25 And the silver of them that were numbered of the congregation *was* an hundred talents, and a thousand seven hundred and threescore and fifteen shek'-els, after the shek'-el of the sanctuary:

26 [R]A be'-kah for every man, *that is*, half a shek'-el, after the shek'-el of the sanctuary, for every one that went to be num-

bered, from twenty years old and upward, for six hundred thousand and three thousand and five hundred and fifty *men*. 30:13, 15

27 And of the hundred talents of silver were cast ᴿthe sockets of the sanctuary, and the sockets of the vail; an hundred sockets of the hundred talents, a talent for a socket. 26:19, 21, 25, 32

28 And of the thousand seven hundred seventy and five *shek'-els* he made hooks for the pillars, and overlaid their ᵀchapiters, and ᴿfilleted them. *capitals · 27:17*

29 And the brass of the offering *was* seventy talents, and two thousand and four hundred shek'-els.

30 And therewith he made the sockets to the door of the tabernacle of the congregation, and the brasen altar, and the brasen grate for it, and all the vessels of the altar,

31 And the sockets of the court round about, and the sockets of the court gate, and all the pins of the tabernacle, and all the pins of the court round about.

39 And of the ᴿblue, and purple, and scarlet, they made ᴿcloths of service, to do service in the holy *place*, and made the holy garments for Aaron; as the LORD commanded Moses. 25:4; 35:23 · 31:10

2 And he made the ᴿe'-phod *of* gold, blue, and purple, and scarlet, and fine twined linen. *Lev. 8:7*

3 And they did beat the gold into thin plates, and cut *it into* wires, to work *it* in the blue, and in the purple, and in the scarlet, and in the fine linen, *with* ᵀcunning work. *artistic designs*

4 They made shoulderpieces for it, to couple *it* together: by the two edges was it coupled together.

5 And the curious girdle of his e'-phod, that *was* upon it, *was* of the same, according to the work thereof; *of* gold, blue, and purple, and scarlet, and fine twined linen; as the LORD commanded Moses.

6 ᴿAnd they wrought onyx stones inclosed in ᵀouches of gold, graven, as signets are graven, with the names of the children of Israel. 28:9–11 · *settings*

7 And he put them on the shoulders of the e'-phod, *that they should be* stones for a ᴿmemorial to the children of Israel; as the LORD commanded Moses. 28:12, 29; Josh. 4:7

8 ᴿAnd he made the breastplate *of* cunning work, like the work of the e'-phod; *of* gold, blue, and purple, and scarlet, and fine twined linen. 28:15–30

9 It was foursquare; they made the breastplate double: a span *was* the length thereof, and a span the breadth thereof, *being* doubled.

10 ᴿAnd they set in it four rows of stones: *the first* row *was* a ᵀsardius, a topaz, and a carbuncle: this *was* the first row. 28:17 · *ruby*

11 And the second row, an emerald, a sapphire, and a diamond.

12 And the third row, a ligure, an agate, and an amethyst.

13 And the fourth row, a beryl, an onyx, and a jasper: *they were* inclosed in ᵀouches of gold in their inclosings. *settings*

14 And the stones *were* according to the names of the children of Israel, twelve, according to their names, *like* the engravings of a signet, every one with his name, according to the twelve tribes.

15 And they made upon the breastplate chains at the ends, *of* wreathen work *of* pure gold.

16 And they made two ᵀouches of gold, and two gold rings; and put the two rings in the two ends of the breastplate. *settings*

17 And they put the two wreathen chains of gold in the two rings on the ends of the breastplate.

18 And the two ends of the two wreathen chains they fastened in the two ᵀouches, and put them on the shoulderpieces of the e'-phod, before it. *settings*

19 And they made two rings of gold, and put *them* on the two ends of the breastplate, upon the

border of it, which *was* on the side of the e'-phod inward.

20 And they made two *other* golden rings, and put them on the two sides of the e'-phod underneath, toward the forepart of it, over against the *other* coupling thereof, above the ᵀcurious girdle of the e'-phod. *intricately woven band*

21 And they did bind the breastplate by his rings unto the rings of the e'-phod with a lace of blue, that it might be above the curious girdle of the e'-phod, and that the breastplate might not be loosed from the e'-phod; as the LORD commanded Moses.

22 ᴿAnd he made the ᴿrobe of the e'-phod *of* woven work, all *of* blue.   28:31–35 · 29:5; Lev. 8:7

23 And *there was* an hole in the midst of the robe, as the hole of an habergeon, *with* a band round about the hole, that it should not rend.

24 And they made upon the hems of the robe pomegranates *of* blue, and purple, and scarlet, *and* twined *linen.*

25 And they made ᴿbells *of* pure gold, and put the bells between the pomegranates upon the hem of the robe, round about between the pomegranates;   28:33

26 A bell and a pomegranate, a bell and a pomegranate, round about the hem of the robe to ᵀminister *in;* as the LORD commanded Moses.   *serve*

27 ᴿAnd they made coats *of* fine linen *of* woven work for Aaron, and for his sons,   28:39, 40

28 ᴿAnd a mitre *of* fine linen, and goodly bonnets *of* fine linen, and ᴿlinen breeches *of* fine twined linen,   Lev. 8:9; Ezek. 44:18 · Lev. 6:10

29 ᴿAnd a girdle *of* fine twined linen, and blue, and purple, and scarlet, *of* needlework; as the LORD commanded Moses.   28:39

30 And they made the plate of the holy crown *of* pure gold, and wrote upon it a writing, *like to* the engravings of a signet, ᴿHOLINESS TO THE LORD.   Zech. 14:20

31 And they tied unto it a lace of blue, to fasten *it* on high upon the mitre; as the LORD commanded Moses.

32 Thus was all the work of the tabernacle of the tent of the congregation ᴿfinished: and the children of Israel did ᴿaccording to all that the LORD commanded Moses, so did they.   40:17 · vv. 42, 43; 25:40

33 And they brought the tabernacle unto Moses, the tent, and all his furniture, his taches, his boards, his bars, and his pillars, and his sockets,

34 And the covering of rams' skins dyed red, and the covering of badgers' skins, and the vail of the covering,

35 The ark of the testimony, and the staves thereof, and the mercy seat,

36 The table, *and* all the vessels thereof, and the shewbread,

37 The pure candlestick, *with* the lamps thereof, *even with* the lamps to be set in order, and all the vessels thereof, and the oil for light,

38 And the golden altar, and the anointing oil, and the sweet incense, and the hanging for the tabernacle door,

39 The brasen altar, and his grate of brass, his staves, and all his vessels, the laver and his foot,

40 The hangings of the court, his pillars, and his sockets, and the hanging for the court gate, his cords, and his pins, and all the vessels of the service of the tabernacle, for the tent of the congregation,

41 The cloths of service to do service in the holy *place,* and the holy garments for Aaron the priest, and his sons' garments, to minister in the priest's office.

42 According to all that the LORD commanded Moses, so the children of Israel ᴿmade all the work.   35:10

43 And Moses did look upon all the work, and, behold, they had done it as the LORD had commanded, even so had they done it: and Moses ᴿblessed them.   Lev. 9:22

40 And the LORD ᴿspake unto Moses, saying,   25:1–31:18

2 On the first day of the ᴿfirst

month shalt thou set up ᴿthe tabernacle of the tent of the congregation.   12:2; 13:4 · v. 17; 26:1, 30

3 And ᴿthou shalt put therein the ark of the testimony, and cover the ark with the vail.   v. 21

4 And ᴿthou shalt bring in the table, and set in order the things that are to be set in order upon it; and thou shalt bring in the candlestick, and light the lamps thereof.   vv. 22–25

5 ᴿAnd thou shalt set the altar of gold for the incense before the ark of the testimony, and put the hanging of the door to the tabernacle.   v. 26

6 And thou shalt set the ᴿaltar of the burnt offering before the door of the tabernacle of the tent of the congregation.   39:39

7 And ᴿthou shalt set the laver between the tent of the congregation and the altar, and shalt put water therein.   v. 30; 30:18

8 And thou shalt set up the court round about, and hang up the hanging at the court gate.

9 And thou shalt take the anointing oil, and ᴿanoint the tabernacle, and all that is therein, and shalt hallow it, and all the vessels thereof: and it shall be holy.   30:26; Lev. 8:10

10 And thou shalt anoint the altar of the burnt offering, and all his vessels, and sanctify the altar: and it shall be an altar most holy.

11 And thou shalt anoint the laver and his foot, and sanctify it.

12 ᴿAnd thou shalt bring Aaron and his sons unto the door of the tabernacle of the congregation, and wash them with water.   29:4–9

13 And thou shalt put upon Aaron the holy ᴿgarments, ᴿand anoint him, and sanctify him; that he may minister unto me in the priest's office.   29:5; 39:1, 41 · Lev. 8:12

14 And thou shalt bring his sons, and clothe them with coats:

15 And thou shalt anoint them, as thou didst anoint their father, that they may minister unto me in the priest's office: for their anointing shall surely be ᴿan everlasting

priesthood throughout their generations.   29:9; Num. 25:13

16 Thus did Moses: according to all that the LORD commanded him, so did he.

17 And it came to pass in the first month in the second year, on the first day of the month, that the tabernacle was reared up.

18 And Moses reared up the tabernacle, and fastened his sockets, and set up the boards thereof, and put in the bars thereof, and reared up his pillars.

19 And he spread abroad the tent over the tabernacle, and put the covering of the tent above upon it; as the LORD commanded Moses.

20 And he took and put the testimony into the ark, and set the staves on the ark, and put the mercy seat above upon the ark:

21 And he brought the ark into the tabernacle, and ᴿset up the vail of the covering, and covered the ark of the testimony; as the LORD commanded Moses.   26:33

22 ᴿAnd he put the table in the tent of the congregation, upon the side of the tabernacle northward, without the vail.   26:35

23 And he set the bread in order upon it before the LORD; as the LORD had commanded Moses.

24 ᴿAnd he put the candlestick in the tent of the congregation, over against the table, on the side of the tabernacle southward.   26:35

25 And ᴿhe lighted the lamps before the LORD; as the LORD commanded Moses.   30:7, 8; Lev. 24:3, 4

26 ᴿAnd he put the golden altar in the tent of the congregation before the vail: v. 5; 30:1, 6

27 ᴿAnd he burnt sweet incense thereon; as the LORD commanded Moses.   30:7

28 ᴿAnd he set up the hanging at the door of the tabernacle.   26:36

29 ᴿAnd he put the altar of burnt offering by the door of the tabernacle of the tent of the congregation, and ᴿoffered upon it the burnt offering and the meat offering; as the LORD commanded Moses.   v. 6 · 29:38–42

30 [R]And he set the laver between the tent of the congregation and the altar, and put water there, to wash *withal*.　　v. 7; 30:18

31 And Moses and Aaron and his sons [R]washed their hands and their feet thereat:　30:19, 20; John 13:8

32 When they went into the tent of the congregation, and when they came near unto the altar, they washed; [R]as the LORD commanded Moses.　　30:19

33 [R]And he reared up the court round about the tabernacle and the altar, and set up the hanging of the court gate. So Moses [R]finished the work.　v. 8 · [Heb. 3:2–5]

34 [R]Then a cloud covered the tent of the congregation, and the glory of the LORD filled the tabernacle.　Num. 9:15; 2 Chr. 5:13; Is. 6:4

35 And Moses [R]was not able to enter into the tent of the congregation, because the cloud abode thereon, and the glory of the LORD filled the tabernacle.　[Lev. 16:2]

36 [R]And when the cloud was taken up from over the tabernacle, the children of Israel went onward in all their journeys:　13:21, 22

37 But if the cloud were not taken up, then they journeyed not till the day that it was taken up.

38 For the cloud of the LORD was upon the tabernacle by day, and fire was on it by night, in the sight of all the house of Israel, throughout all their journeys.

The Third Book of Moses Called

LEVITICUS

LEVITICUS is God's guidebook for His newly redeemed people, showing them how to worship, serve, and obey a holy God. Fellowship with God through sacrifice and obedience show the awesome holiness of the God of Israel. Indeed, " 'ye shall be holy: for I the LORD your God *am* holy' " (19:2).

Leviticus focuses on the worship and walk of the nation of God. In Exodus, Israel was redeemed and established as a kingdom of priests and a holy nation. Leviticus shows how God's people are to fulfill their priestly calling.

The Hebrew title is *Wayyiqra*, "And He Called." The Talmud refers to Leviticus as the "Law of the Priests," and the "Law of the Offerings." The Greek title appearing in the Septuagint is *Leuitikon*, "That Which Pertains to the Levites." From this word, the Latin Vulgate derived its name *Leviticus* which was adopted as the English title. This title is slightly misleading because the book does not deal with the Levites as a whole but more with the priests, a segment of the Levites.

AND the LORD [R]called unto Moses, and spake unto him [R]out of the tabernacle of the congregation, saying,　Ex. 19:3; 25:22 · Ex. 40:34

2 Speak unto the children of Israel, and say unto them, [R]If any man of you bring an offering unto the LORD, ye shall bring your offering of the cattle, *even* of the herd, and of the flock.　22:18, 19

3 If his offering *be* a burnt sacrifice of the herd, let him offer a male without blemish: he shall offer it of his own voluntary will at the door of the tabernacle of the congregation before the LORD.

4 And he shall put his hand upon the head of the burnt offering; and it shall be accepted for him to make atonement for him.

5 And he shall kill the [R]bullock

before the LORD: and the priests, Aaron's sons, shall bring the blood, and sprinkle the blood round about upon the altar that *is by* the door of the tabernacle of the congregation.   Mic. 6:6

6 And he shall flay the burnt offering, and cut it into his pieces.

7 And the sons of Aaron the priest shall put [R]fire upon the altar, and [R]lay the wood in order upon the fire: Mal. 1:10 · Gen. 22:9

8 And the priests, Aaron's sons, shall lay the parts, the head, and the fat, in order upon the wood that *is* on the fire which *is* upon the altar:

9 But his inwards and his legs shall he wash in water: and the priest shall burn all on the altar, *to be* a burnt sacrifice, an offering made by fire, of a [R]sweet savour unto the LORD.   Gen. 8:21; [2 Cor. 2:15]

10 And if his offering *be* of the flocks, *namely,* of the sheep, or of the goats, for a burnt sacrifice; he shall bring it a male [R]without blemish.   Ezek. 43:22; [1 Pet. 1:19]

11 [R]And he shall kill it on the side of the altar northward before the LORD: and the priests, Aaron's sons, shall sprinkle his blood round about upon the altar.   v. 5

12 And he shall cut it into his pieces, with his head and his fat: and the priest shall lay them in order on the wood that *is* on the fire which *is* upon the altar:

13 But he shall wash the inwards and the legs with water: and the priest shall bring *it* all, and burn *it* upon the altar: it *is* a burnt sacrifice, an [R]offering made by fire, of a sweet savour unto the LORD.   Num. 15:4–7; 28:12–14

14 And if the burnt sacrifice for his offering to the LORD *be* of fowls, then he shall bring his offering of [R]turtledoves, or of young pigeons.   Gen. 15:9; Luke 2:24

15 And the priest shall bring it unto the altar, and wring off his head, and burn *it* on the altar; and the blood thereof shall be wrung out at the side of the altar:

16 And he shall pluck away his crop with his feathers, and cast it [R]beside the altar on the east part, by the place of the ashes: 6:10

17 And he shall cleave it with the wings thereof, *but* [R]shall not divide *it* asunder: and the priest shall burn it upon the altar, upon the wood that *is* upon the fire: [R]it *is* a burnt sacrifice, an offering made by fire, of a sweet savour unto the LORD.   Gen. 15:10 · vv. 9, 13

2 And when any will offer a [T]meat offering unto the LORD, his offering shall be *of* fine flour; and he shall pour oil upon it, and put frankincense thereon: grain

2 And he shall bring it to Aaron's sons the priests: and he shall take thereout his handful of the flour thereof, and of the oil thereof, with all the frankincense thereof; and the priest shall burn [R]the memorial of it upon the altar, *to be* an offering made by fire, of a sweet savour unto the LORD: 2:9

3 And [R]the remnant of the meat offering *shall be* Aaron's and his [R]sons': *it is* a thing most holy of the offerings of the LORD made by fire.   7:9 · 6:6; 10:12, 13

4 And if thou bring an oblation of a meat offering baken in the oven, *it shall be* unleavened cakes of fine flour mingled with oil, or unleavened wafers [R]anointed[T] with oil.   Ex. 29:2 · spread

5 And if thy oblation *be* a meat offering *baken* in a [T]pan, it shall be *of* fine flour unleavened, mingled with oil.   flat plate or griddle

6 Thou shalt part it in pieces, and pour oil thereon: it *is* a meat offering.

7 And if thy oblation *be* a meat offering *baken* in the [R]fryingpan, it shall be made *of* fine flour with oil.   7:9

8 And thou shalt bring the meat offering that is made of these things unto the LORD: and when it is presented unto the priest, he shall bring it unto the altar.

9 And the priest shall take from the meat offering [R]a memorial thereof, and shall burn *it* upon the altar: *it is* an [R]offering

made by fire, of a sweet savour unto the LORD.	5:12; 6:15 · Ex. 29:18

10 And ᴿthat which is left of the meat offering *shall be* Aaron's and his sons': *it is* a thing most holy of the offerings of the LORD made by fire.	v. 3; 6:16

11 No meat offering, which ye shall bring unto the LORD, shall be made with ᴿleaven: for ye shall burn no leaven, nor any honey, in any offering of the LORD made by fire.	Ex. 23:18; [1 Cor. 5:8; Gal. 5:9]

12 ᴿAs for the ᵀoblation of the firstfruits, ye shall offer them unto the LORD: but they shall not be burnt on the altar for a sweet savour.	Ex. 22:29; 34:22 · *offering*

13 And every oblation of thy meat offering ᴿshalt thou season with salt; neither shalt thou suffer the salt of the covenant of thy God to be lacking from thy meat offering: with all thine offerings thou shalt offer salt. [Mark 9:49, 50; Col. 4:6]

14 And if thou offer a meat offering of thy firstfruits unto the LORD, ᴿthou shalt offer for the meat offering of thy firstfruits green ears of corn dried by the fire, *even* corn beaten out of ᴿfull ears.	23:10, 14 · 2 Kin. 4:42

15 And ᴿthou shalt put oil upon it, and lay frankincense thereon: it *is* a meat offering.	v. 1

16 And the priest shall burn ᴿthe memorial of it, *part* of the beaten corn thereof, and *part* of the oil thereof, with all the frankincense thereof: *it is* an offering made by fire unto the LORD.	v. 2

3 And if his oblation *be* a ᴿsacrifice of peace offering, if he offer *it* of the herd; whether *it be* a male or female, he shall offer it ᴿwithout blemish before the LORD.	7:11, 29 · 1:3; 22:20–24

2 And ᴿhe shall lay his hand upon the head of his offering, and kill it *at* the door of the tabernacle of the congregation: and Aaron's sons the priests shall ᴿsprinkle the blood upon the altar round about.	16:21; Ex. 29:10, 11, 16, 20 · 1:5

3 And he shall offer of the sacrifice of the peace offering an

offering made by fire unto the LORD; ᴿthe fat that covereth the inwards, and all the fat that *is* upon the inwards,	1:8; Ex. 29:13, 22

4 And the two kidneys, and the fat that *is* on them, which *is* by the flanks, and the ᵀcaul above the liver, with the kidneys, it shall he take away.	*fatty lobe attached to*

5 And Aaron's sons ᴿshall burn it on the altar upon the ᴿburnt sacrifice, which *is* upon the wood that *is* on the fire: *it is* an offering made by fire, of a sweet savour unto the LORD.	Ex. 29:13 · 2 Chr. 35:14

6 And if his offering for a sacrifice of peace offering unto the LORD *be* of the flock; male or female, ᴿhe shall offer it without blemish.	v. 1; 22:20–24

7 If he offer a lamb for his offering, then shall he ᴿoffer it before the LORD.	1 Kin. 8:62

8 And he shall lay his hand upon the head of his offering, and kill it before the tabernacle of the congregation: and Aaron's sons shall sprinkle the blood thereof round about upon the altar.

9 And he shall offer of the sacrifice of the peace offering an offering made by fire unto the LORD; the fat thereof, *and* the whole rump, it shall he take off hard by the backbone; and the fat that covereth the inwards, and all the fat that *is* upon the inwards,

10 And the two kidneys, and the fat that *is* upon them, which *is* by the flanks, and the caul above the liver, with the kidneys, it shall he take away.

11 And the priest shall burn it upon the altar: *it is* ᴿthe food of the offering made by fire unto the LORD.	Num. 28:2; [Ezek. 44:7; Mal. 1:7, 12]

12 And if his ᴿoffering *be* a goat, then ᴿhe shall offer it before the LORD.	Num. 15:6–11 · v. 1, 7

13 And he shall lay his hand upon the head of it, and kill it before the tabernacle of the congregation: and the sons of Aaron shall sprinkle the blood thereof upon the altar round about.

14 And he shall offer thereof his

offering, *even* an offering made by fire unto the LORD; the fat that covereth the inwards, and all the fat that *is* upon the inwards,

15 And the two kidneys, and the fat that *is* upon them, which *is* by the flanks, and the caul above the liver, with the kidneys, it shall he take away.

16 And the priest shall burn them upon the altar: *it is* the food of the offering made by fire for a sweet savour: ^Rall the fat *is* the LORD'S.   7:23–25; 1 Sam. 2:15; 2 Chr. 7:7

17 *It shall be* a ^Rperpetual statute for your generations throughout all your dwellings, that ye eat neither fat nor ^Rblood.   6:18 · 7:23, 26

4 And the LORD spake unto Moses, saying,

2 Speak unto the children of Israel, saying, ^RIf a soul shall sin through ignorance against any of the commandments of the LORD *concerning things* which ought not to be done, and shall do against any of them: Acts 3:17

3 If the priest that is anointed do sin according to the sin of the people; then let him bring for his sin, which he hath sinned, a young bullock without blemish unto the LORD for a sin offering.

4 And he shall bring the bullock ^Runto the door of the tabernacle of the congregation before the LORD; and shall lay his hand upon the bullock's head, and kill the bullock before the LORD.   1:3, 4

5 And the priest that is anointed ^Rshall take of the bullock's blood, and bring it to the tabernacle of the congregation: Num. 19:4

6 And the priest shall dip his finger in the blood, and sprinkle of the blood seven times before the LORD, before the ^Rvail of the sanctuary.   Ex. 40:21, 26

7 And the priest shall ^Rput *some* of the blood upon the horns of the altar of sweet incense before the LORD, which *is* in the tabernacle of the congregation; and shall pour ^Rall the blood of the bullock at the bottom of the altar of the burnt offering, which

is at the door of the tabernacle of the congregation. 8:15; 9:9 · Ex. 40:5, 6

8 And he shall take off from it all the fat of the bullock for the sin offering; the fat that covereth the inwards, and all the fat that *is* upon the inwards,

9 And the two kidneys, and the fat that *is* upon them, which *is* by the flanks, and the caul above the liver, with the kidneys, it shall he take away,

10 ^RAs it was taken off from the bullock of the sacrifice of peace offerings: and the priest shall burn them upon the altar of the burnt offering.   3:3–5

11 ^RAnd the skin of the bullock, and all his flesh, with his head, and with his legs, and his inwards, and his dung,   Ex. 29:14

12 Even the whole bullock shall he carry forth ^Twithout the camp unto a clean place, where the ashes are poured out, and ^Rburn him on the wood with fire: where the ashes are poured out shall he be burnt.   *outside* · [Heb. 13:11, 12]

13 And ^Rif the whole congregation of Israel sin through ignorance, ^Rand the thing be hid from the eyes of the assembly, and they have done *somewhat against* any of the commandments of the LORD *concerning things* which should not be done, and are guilty;   Num. 15:24–26; Josh. 7:11 · 5:2–4

14 When the sin, which they have sinned against it, is known, then the congregation shall offer a young bullock for the sin, and bring him before the tabernacle of the congregation.

15 And the elders of the congregation ^Rshall lay their hands upon the head of the bullock before the LORD: and the bullock shall be killed before the LORD.   1:3, 4

16 ^RAnd the priest that is anointed shall bring of the bullock's blood to the tabernacle of the congregation: v. 5; [Heb. 9:12–14]

17 And the priest shall dip his finger *in some* of the blood, and sprinkle *it* seven times before the LORD, *even* before the vail.

18 And he shall put *some* of the blood upon the horns of the altar which *is* before the LORD, that *is* in the tabernacle of the congregation, and shall pour out all the blood at the bottom of the altar of the burnt offering, which *is at* the door of the tabernacle of the congregation.

19 And he shall take all his fat from him, and burn *it* upon the altar.

20 And he shall do with the bullock as he did ᴿwith the bullock for a sin offering, so shall he do with this: ᴿand the priest shall make an atonement for them, and it shall be forgiven them.   v. 3 · 1:4

21 And he shall carry forth the bullock ᵀwithout the camp, and burn him as he burned the first bullock: it *is* a sin offering for the congregation.   *outside*

22 When a ruler hath sinned, and ᴿdone *somewhat* through ignorance *against* any of the commandments of the LORD his God *concerning things* which should not be done, and is guilty; vv. 2, 13

23 Or ᴿif his sin, wherein he hath sinned, come to his knowledge; he shall bring his offering, a kid of the goats, a male without blemish: v. 14; 5:4

24 And ᴿhe shall lay his hand upon the head of the goat, and kill it in the place where they kill the burnt offering before the LORD: it *is* a sin offering.   v. 4; [Is. 53:6]

25 ᴿAnd the priest shall take of the blood of the sin offering with his finger, and put *it* upon the horns of the altar of burnt offering, and shall pour out his blood at the bottom of the altar of burnt offering.   vv. 7, 18, 30, 34

26 And he shall burn all his fat upon the altar, as the fat of the sacrifice of peace offerings: and the priest shall make an atonement for him as concerning his sin, and it shall be forgiven him.

27 And ᴿif any one of the common people sin through ignorance, while he doeth *somewhat against* any of the commandments of the LORD *concerning*

things which ought not to be done, and be guilty; v. 2; Num. 15:27

28 Or ᴿif his sin, which he hath sinned, come to his knowledge: then he shall bring his offering, a kid of the goats, a female without blemish, for his sin which he hath sinned.   v. 23

29 ᴿAnd he shall lay his hand upon the head of the sin offering, and slay the sin offering in the place of the burnt offering. vv. 4, 24

30 And the priest shall take of the blood thereof with his finger, and put *it* upon the horns of the altar of burnt offering, and shall pour out all the blood thereof at the bottom of the altar.

31 And he shall take away all the fat thereof, as the fat is taken away from off the sacrifice of peace offerings; and the priest shall burn *it* upon the altar for a ᴿsweet savour unto the LORD; ᴿand the priest shall make an atonement for him, and it shall be forgiven him. Gen. 8:21; Ex. 29:18 · v. 26

32 And if he bring a lamb for a sin offering, ᴿhe shall bring it a female without blemish.   v. 28

33 And he shall ᴿlay his hand upon the head of the sin offering, and slay it for a sin offering in the place where they kill the burnt offering.   1:4; Num. 8:12

34 And the priest shall take of the blood of the sin offering with his finger, and put *it* upon the horns of the altar of burnt offering, and shall pour out all the blood thereof at the bottom of the altar:

35 And he shall take away all the fat thereof, as the fat of the lamb is taken away from the sacrifice of the peace offerings; and the priest shall burn them upon the altar, ᴿaccording to the offerings made by fire unto the LORD: ᴿand the priest shall make an atonement for his sin that he hath committed, and it shall be forgiven him.   3:5 · vv. 26, 31

5 And if a soul sin, and hear the voice of swearing, and *is* a witness, whether he hath seen or

known *of it;* if he do not utter *it,* then he shall bear his iniquity.

2 Or if a soul touch any unclean thing, whether *it be* a carcase of an unclean beast, or a carcase of unclean cattle, or the carcase of unclean creeping things, and *if* it be hidden from him; he also shall be unclean, and guilty.

3 Or if he touch ᴿthe uncleanness of man, whatsoever uncleanness *it be* that a man shall be defiled withal, and it be hid from him; when he knoweth *of it,* then he shall be guilty.   vv. 12, 13, 15

4 Or if a soul swear, pronouncing with *his* lips to do evil, or ᴿto do good, whatsoever *it be* that a man shall pronounce with an oath, and it be hid from him; when he knoweth *of it,* then he shall be guilty in one of these.   Mark 6:23

5 And it shall be, when he shall be guilty in one of these *things,* that he shall ᴿconfess that he hath sinned in that *thing:*   Ps. 32:5

6 And he shall bring his trespass offering unto the LORD for his sin which he hath sinned, a female from the flock, a lamb or a kid of the goats, for a sin offering; and the priest shall make an atonement for him concerning his sin.

7 And if he be not able to bring a lamb, then he shall bring for his trespass, which he hath committed, two ᴿturtledoves, or two young pigeons, unto the LORD; one for a sin offering, and the other for a burnt offering.   1:14

8 And he shall bring them unto the priest, who shall offer *that* which *is* for the sin offering first, and ᴿwring off his head from his neck, but shall not divide *it* ᵀasunder: 1:15–17 · *apart*

9 And he shall sprinkle of the blood of the sin offering upon the side of the altar; and the ᴿrest of the blood shall be wrung out at the bottom of the altar: it *is* a sin offering.   4:7, 18, 30, 34

10 And he shall offer the second *for* a burnt offering, according to the ᴿmanner: and the priest shall make an atonement for him for his sin which he hath sinned, and it shall be forgiven him.   1:14–17

11 But if he be ᴿnot able to bring two turtledoves, or two young pigeons, then he that sinned shall bring for his offering the tenth part of an e′-phah of fine flour for a sin offering; ᴿhe shall put no oil upon it, neither shall he put *any* frankincense thereon: for it *is* a sin offering. 14:21–32 · 2:1, 2; Num. 5:15

12 Then shall he bring it to the priest, and the priest shall take his handful of it, ᴿ*even* a ᵀmemorial thereof, and burn *it* on the altar, ᴿaccording to the offerings made by fire unto the LORD: it *is* a sin offering.   2:2 · *memorial portion* · 4:35

13 And the priest shall make an atonement for him as touching his sin that he hath sinned in one of these, and it shall be forgiven him: and *the remnant* shall be the priest's, as a meat offering.

14 And the LORD spake unto Moses, saying,

15 If a soul commit a trespass, and sin through ignorance, in the holy things of the LORD; then he shall bring for his trespass unto the LORD a ram without blemish out of the flocks, with thy estimation by shek′-els of silver, after ᴿthe shek′-el of the sanctuary, for a trespass offering: Ex. 30:13

16 And he shall make amends for the harm that he hath done in the holy thing, and ᴿshall add the fifth part thereto, and give it unto the priest: and the priest shall make an atonement for him with the ram of the trespass offering, and it shall be forgiven him.   22:14

17 And if a soul sin, and commit any of these things which are forbidden to be done by the commandments of the LORD; ᴿthough he wist *it* not, yet is he guilty, and shall bear his iniquity. 4:2, 13, 22, 27

18 ᴿAnd he shall bring a ram without blemish out of the flock, with thy estimation, for a trespass offering, unto the priest: and the priest shall make an atonement for him concerning his ignorance

wherein he erred and wist *it* not, and it shall be forgiven him. v. 15

19 It *is* a trespass offering: ᴿhe hath certainly trespassed against the LORD.   Ezra 10:2

6 And the LORD spake unto Moses, saying,

2 If a soul sin, and commit a trespass against the LORD, and ᴿlie unto his neighbour in that which was delivered him to keep, or in fellowship, or in a thing taken away by violence, or hath deceived his neighbour;   Col. 3:9

3 Or ᴿhave found that which was lost, and lieth concerning it, and ᴿsweareth falsely; in any of all these that a man doeth, sinning therein: Ex. 23:4 · Ex. 22:11; Zech. 5:4

4 Then it shall be, because he hath sinned, and is guilty, that he shall restore that which he took violently away, or the thing which he hath deceitfully gotten, or that which was delivered him to keep, or the lost thing which he found,

5 Or all that about which he hath sworn falsely; he shall even ᴿrestore it in the principal, and shall add the fifth part more thereto, *and* give it unto him to whom it appertaineth, in the day of his trespass offering. Num. 5:7, 8

6 And he shall bring his trespass offering unto the LORD, a ram without blemish out of the flock, with thy estimation, for a trespass offering, unto the priest:

7 ᴿAnd the priest shall make an atonement for him before the LORD: and it shall be forgiven him for any thing of all that he hath done in trespassing therein. 4:26

8 And the LORD spake unto Moses, saying,

9 Command Aaron and his sons, saying, This *is* the ᴿlaw of the burnt offering: It *is* the burnt offering, because of the burning upon the altar all night unto the morning, and the fire of the altar shall be burning in it. Ex. 29:38–42

10 And the priest shall put on his linen garment, and his linen breeches shall he put upon his flesh, and take up the ashes which the fire hath consumed with the burnt offering on the altar, and he shall put them beside the altar.

11 And ᴿhe shall put off his garments, and put on other garments, and carry forth the ashes ᵀwithout the camp ᴿunto a clean place.   Ezek. 44:19 · *outside* · 4:12

12 And the fire upon the altar shall be burning in it; it shall not be put out: and the priest shall burn wood on it every morning, and lay the burnt offering in order upon it; and he shall burn thereon ᴿthe fat of the peace offerings. 3:3

13 The fire shall ever be burning upon the ᴿaltar; it shall never go out.   1:7

14 And this *is* the law of the ᵀmeat offering: the sons of Aaron shall offer it before the LORD, before the altar.   *grain* or *meal*

15 And he shall take of it his handful, of the flour of the meat offering, and of the oil thereof, and all the frankincense which *is* upon the meat offering, and shall burn *it* upon the altar *for* a ᵀsweet savour, *even* the memorial of it, unto the LORD.   *pleasing aroma*

16 And the remainder thereof shall Aaron and his sons eat: with unleavened bread shall it be eaten in the holy place; in the court of the tabernacle of the congregation they shall eat it.

17 It shall not be baken with leaven. I have given it *unto them* for their ᵀportion of my offerings made by fire; it *is* most holy, as *is* the sin offering, and as the ᴿtrespass offering.   *share* · 7:7

18 All the males among the children of Aaron shall eat of it. *It shall be* a statute for ever in your generations concerning the offerings of the LORD made by fire: ᴿevery one that toucheth them shall be holy.   Num. 4:15; Hag. 2:11–13

19 And the LORD spake unto Moses, saying,

20 ᴿThis *is* the offering of Aaron and of his sons, which they shall offer unto the LORD in the day when he is anointed; the tenth

part of an ᴿe′-phah of fine flour for a meat offering perpetual, half of it in the morning, and half thereof at night.   Ex. 29:2 · Ex. 16:36

21 In a ᴿpan it shall be made with oil; *and when it is* baken, thou shalt bring it in: *and* the baken pieces of the meat offering shalt thou offer *for* a sweet savour unto the LORD.   2:5; 7:9

22 And the priest of his sons ᴿthat is anointed in his stead shall offer it: *it is* a statute for ever unto the LORD; ᴿit shall be ᵀwholly burnt.   4:3 · Ex. 29:25 · *completely*

23 For every meat offering for the priest shall be wholly burnt: it shall not be eaten.

24 And the LORD spake unto Moses, saying,

25 Speak unto Aaron and to his sons, saying, This *is* the law of the sin offering: ᴿIn the place where the burnt offering is killed shall the sin offering be killed before the LORD: it *is* most holy. 1:1, 3, 5, 11

26 ᴿThe priest that offereth it for sin shall eat it: in the holy place shall it be eaten, in the court of the tabernacle of the congregation.   [10:17, 18]; Num. 18:9, 10

27 Whatsoever shall touch the flesh thereof shall be holy: and when there is sprinkled of the blood thereof upon any garment, thou shalt wash that whereon it was sprinkled in the holy place.

28 But the earthen vessel wherein it is ᵀsodden ᴿshall be broken: and if it be sodden in a brasen pot, it shall be both scoured, and rinsed in water.   *boiled* · 11:33; 15:12

29 All the males among the priests shall eat thereof: it *is* most holy.

30 ᴿAnd no sin offering, whereof *any* of the blood is brought into the tabernacle of the congregation to reconcile *withal* in the holy *place*, shall be eaten: it shall be burnt in the fire.   [Heb. 13:11, 12]

7 Likewise ᴿthis *is* the ᵀlaw of the trespass offering: it *is* most holy.   5:14—6:7 · Heb. *torah*

2 In the place where they kill the burnt offering shall they kill the trespass offering: and the blood thereof shall he sprinkle round about upon the altar.

3 And he shall offer of it all the fat thereof; the rump, and the fat that covereth the inwards,

4 And the two kidneys, and the fat that *is* on them, which *is* by the flanks, and the caul *that is* above the liver, with the kidneys, it shall he take away:

5 And the priest shall burn them upon the altar *for* an offering made by fire unto the LORD: it *is* a trespass offering.

6 ᴿEvery male among the priests shall eat thereof: it shall be eaten in the holy place: ᴿit *is* most holy.   6:16–18, 29; Num. 18:9 · 2:3

7 As the sin offering *is*, so *is* ᴿthe trespass offering: *there is* one law for ᵀthem: the priest that maketh atonement therewith shall have *it*. 6:24–30; 14:13 · *them both*

8 And the priest that offereth any man's burnt offering, *even* the priest shall have ᵀto himself the skin of the burnt offering which he hath offered.   *for*

9 And ᴿall the meat offering that is baken in the oven, and all that is dressed in the fryingpan, and in the pan, shall be the priest's that offereth it.   Num. 18:9

10 And every meat offering, mingled with oil, and dry, shall all the sons of Aaron have, one *as much* as another.

11 And ᴿthis *is* the law of the sacrifice of peace offerings, which he shall offer unto the LORD.   3:1

12 If he offer it for a thanksgiving, then he shall offer with the sacrifice of thanksgiving unleavened cakes mingled with oil, and unleavened wafers ᴿanointed with oil, and cakes mingled with oil, of fine flour, fried.   2:4; Num. 6:15

13 Besides the cakes, he shall offer *for* his offering ᴿleavened bread with the sacrifice of thanksgiving of his peace offerings.   2:12

14 And of it he shall offer one out of the whole oblation *for* an heave offering unto the LORD, ᴿ*and* it shall be the priest's that

sprinkleth the blood of the peace offerings.   Num. 18:8, 11, 19

15 ᴿAnd the flesh of the sacrifice of his peace offerings for thanksgiving shall be eaten the same day that it is offered; he shall not leave any of it until the morning.   22:29

16 But ᴿif the sacrifice of his offering be a vow, or a voluntary offering, it shall be eaten the same day that he offereth his sacrifice: and on the morrow also the remainder of it shall be eaten: 19:5-8

17 But the remainder of the flesh of the sacrifice on the third day shall be burnt with fire.

18 And if any of the flesh of the sacrifice of his peace offerings be eaten at all on the third day, it shall not be accepted, neither shall it be ᴿimputed unto him that offereth it: it shall be an abomination, and the soul that eateth of it shall bear his iniquity.   Num. 18:27

19 And the flesh that toucheth any unclean thing shall not be eaten; it shall be burnt with fire: and as for the flesh, all that be ᵀclean shall eat thereof.   pure

20 But the soul that eateth of the flesh of the sacrifice of peace offerings, that pertain unto the ᴿLORD, having his uncleanness upon him, even that soul shall be cut off from his people.   [Heb. 2:17]

21 Moreover the soul that shall touch any unclean thing, as ᴿthe uncleanness of man, or any ᴿunclean beast, or any ᴿabominable unclean thing, and eat of the flesh of the sacrifice of peace offerings, which pertain unto the LORD, even that soul shall be cut off from his people.   5:2, 3, 5 · 11:24, 28 · Ezek. 4:14

22 And the LORD spake unto Moses, saying,

23 Speak unto the children of Israel, saying, ᴿYe shall eat no manner of fat, of ox, or of sheep, or of goat.   Deut. 14:21; Ezek. 4:14; 44:31

24 And the fat of the beast that dieth of itself, and the fat of that which is torn with beasts, may be used in any other use: but ye shall in no wise eat of it.

25 For whosoever eateth the fat of the beast, of which men offer an offering made by fire unto the LORD, even the soul that eateth it shall be cut off from his people.

26 ᴿMoreover ye shall eat no manner of blood, whether it be of fowl or of beast, in any of your dwellings.   Gen. 9:4; 1 Sam. 14:33

27 Whatsoever ᵀsoul it be that eateth any manner of blood, even that soul shall be cut off from his people.   person

28 And the LORD spake unto Moses, saying,

29 Speak unto the children of Israel, saying, ᴿHe that offereth the sacrifice of his peace offerings unto the LORD shall bring his oblation unto the LORD of the sacrifice of his peace offerings.   22:21

30 ᴿHis own hands shall bring the offerings of the LORD made by fire, the fat with the breast, it shall he bring, that the ᴿbreast may be waved for a wave offering before the LORD.   3:3, 4, 9, 14 · Ex. 29:24, 27

31 ᴿAnd the priest shall burn the fat upon the altar: but the breast shall be Aaron's and his sons'.   3:5

32 And ᴿthe right shoulder shall ye give unto the priest for an heave offering of the sacrifices of your peace offerings.   Num. 6:20

33 He among the sons of Aaron, that offereth the blood of the peace offerings, and the fat, shall have the right shoulder for his part.

34 For ᴿthe wave breast and the heave shoulder have I taken of the children of Israel from off the sacrifices of their peace offerings, and have given them unto Aaron the priest and unto his sons by a statute for ever from among the children of Israel.   Ex. 29:28; Deut. 18:3

35 This is the portion of the anointing of Aaron, and of the anointing of his sons, out of the offerings of the LORD made by fire, in the day when he presented them to minister unto the LORD in the priest's office;

36 Which the LORD commanded to be given them of the children of

Israel, ^Rin the day that he anointed them, *by* a statute for ever throughout their generations. 8:12

37 This *is* the law ^Rof the burnt offering, of the meat offering, and of the sin offering, and of the trespass offering, ^Rand of the consecrations, and of the sacrifice of the peace offerings; 6:9 · Ex. 29:1

38 Which the LORD commanded Moses in mount Si'-nai, in the day that he commanded the children of Israel ^Rto offer their oblations unto the LORD, in the wilderness of Si'-nai. 1:1, 2; Deut. 4:5

8 And the LORD spake unto Moses, saying,

2 Take Aaron and his sons with him, and the garments, and the anointing oil, and a bullock for the sin offering, and two rams, and a basket of unleavened bread;

3 And gather thou all the congregation together ^Tunto the door of the tabernacle of the ^Tcongregation. *at · meeting*

4 And Moses did as the LORD commanded him; and the assembly was gathered together unto the door of the tabernacle of the congregation.

5 And Moses said unto the congregation, This *is* the thing which the LORD commanded to be done.

6 And Moses brought Aaron and his sons, and ^Rwashed them with water. Ex. 30:20; Heb. 10:22

7 And he put upon him the coat, and girded him with the girdle, and clothed him with the robe, and put the e'-phod upon him, and he girded him with the curious girdle of the e'-phod, and bound *it* unto him therewith.

8 And he put the breastplate upon him: also he ^Rput in the breastplate the U'-rim and the Thum'-mim. Deut. 33:8; 1 Sam. 28:6

9 ^RAnd he put the mitre upon his head; also upon the mitre, *even* upon his forefront, did he put the golden plate, the holy crown; as the LORD commanded Moses. Ex. 28:36, 37; 29:6

10 ^RAnd Moses took the anointing oil, and anointed the tabernacle and all that *was* therein, and sanctified them. Ex. 30:26–29; 40:10, 11

11 And he sprinkled thereof upon the altar seven times, and anointed the altar and all his vessels, both the laver and his foot, to sanctify them.

12 And he poured of the anointing oil upon Aaron's head, and anointed him, to sanctify him.

13 ^RAnd Moses brought Aaron's sons, and put coats upon them, and girded them with girdles, and put bonnets upon them; as the LORD commanded Moses. Ex. 29:8, 9

14 ^RAnd he brought the bullock for the sin offering: and Aaron and his sons laid their hands upon the head of the bullock for the sin offering. Ex. 29:10; Ps. 66:15; Ezek. 43:19

15 And he slew *it;* and Moses took the blood, and put *it* upon the horns of the altar round about with his finger, and purified the altar, and poured the blood at the bottom of the altar, and sanctified it, to make reconciliation upon it.

16 ^RAnd he took all the fat that *was* upon the inwards, and the caul *above* the liver, and the two kidneys, and their fat, and Moses burned *it* upon the altar. Ex. 29:13

17 But the bullock, and his hide, his flesh, and his dung, he burnt with fire without the camp; as the LORD ^Rcommanded Moses. Ex. 29:14

18 ^RAnd he brought the ram for the burnt offering: and Aaron and his sons laid their hands upon the head of the ram. Ex. 29:15

19 And he killed *it;* and Moses sprinkled the blood upon the altar round about.

20 And he cut the ram into pieces; and Moses ^Rburnt the head, and the pieces, and the fat. 1:8

21 And he washed the inwards and the legs in water; and Moses burnt the whole ram upon the altar: it *was* a burnt sacrifice for a sweet savour, *and* an offering made by fire unto the LORD; as the LORD commanded Moses.

22 And he brought the other ram, the ram of consecration: and

Aaron and his sons laid their hands upon the head of the ram.

23 And he slew *it*; and Moses took of the ᴿblood of it, and put *it* upon the tip of Aaron's right ear, and upon the thumb of his right hand, and upon the great toe of his right foot.   14:14; Ex. 29:20, 21

24 And he brought Aaron's sons, and Moses put of the ᴿblood upon the tip of their right ear, and upon the thumbs of their right hands, and upon the great toes of their right feet: and Moses sprinkled the blood upon the altar round about.   [Heb. 9:13, 14, 18–23]

25 ᴿAnd he took the fat, and the rump, and all the fat that *was* upon the inwards, and the caul *above* the liver, and the two kidneys, and their fat, and the right shoulder: Ex. 29:22

26 ᴿAnd out of the basket of unleavened bread, that *was* before the LORD, he took one unleavened cake, and a cake of oiled bread, and one wafer, and put *them* on the fat, and upon the right shoulder: Ex. 29:23

27 And he put all ᴿupon Aaron's hands, and upon his sons' hands, and waved them *for* a wave offering before the LORD.   Ex. 29:24

28 And Moses took them from off their hands, and burnt *them* on the altar upon the burnt offering: they *were* consecrations for a sweet savour: it *is* an offering made by fire unto the LORD.

29 And Moses took the breast, and waved it *for* a wave offering before the LORD: *for* of the ram of consecration it was Moses' part; as the LORD commanded Moses.

30 And Moses took of the anointing oil, and of the blood which *was* upon the altar, and sprinkled *it* upon Aaron, *and* upon his garments, and upon his sons, and upon his sons' garments with him; and sanctified Aaron, *and* his garments, and his sons, and his sons' garments with him.

31 And Moses said unto Aaron and to his sons, ᴿBoil the flesh *at* the door of the tabernacle of the congregation: and there eat it with the bread that *is* in the basket of consecrations, as I commanded, saying, Aaron and his sons shall eat it.   Ex. 29:31, 32

32 ᴿAnd that which remaineth of the flesh and of the bread shall ye burn with fire.   Ex. 29:34

33 And ye shall not go out of the door of the tabernacle of the congregation *in* seven days, until the days of your consecration be at an end: for ᴿseven days shall he consecrate you.   Ex. 29:30, 35; Ezek. 43:25

34 As he hath done this day, *so* the LORD hath commanded to do, to make an atonement for you.

35 Therefore shall ye abide *at* the door of the tabernacle of the congregation day and night seven days, and ᴿkeep the charge of the LORD, that ye die not: for so I am commanded.   1 Kin. 2:3; Ezek. 48:11

36 So Aaron and his sons did all things which the LORD commanded by the hand of Moses.

9 And ᴿit came to pass on the eighth day, *that* Moses called Aaron and his sons, and the elders of Israel;   Ezek. 43:27

2 And he said unto Aaron, Take thee a young ᴿcalf for a sin offering, and a ram for a burnt offering, without blemish, and offer *them* before the LORD.   Ex. 29:21

3 And unto the children of Israel thou shalt speak, saying, Take ye a kid of the goats for a sin offering; and a calf and a lamb, *both* of the first year, without blemish, for a burnt offering;

4 Also a bullock and a ram for peace offerings, to sacrifice before the LORD; and ᴿa meat offering mingled with oil: for to day the LORD will appear unto you. 2:4

5 And they brought *that* which Moses commanded before the tabernacle of the congregation: and all the congregation drew near and stood before the LORD.

6 And Moses said, This *is* the thing which the LORD commanded that ye should do: and the glory of the LORD shall appear unto you.

7 And Moses said unto Aaron, Go unto the altar, and offer thy sin offering, and thy burnt offering, and make an atonement for thyself, and for the people: and ᴿoffer the offering of the people, and make an atonement for them; as the LORD commanded. 4:16; Heb. 5:1

8 Aaron therefore went unto the altar, and slew the calf of the sin offering, which *was* for himself.

9 And the sons of Aaron brought the blood unto him: and he dipped his finger in the blood, and put *it* upon the horns of the altar, and poured out the blood at the bottom of the altar:

10 ᴿBut the fat, and the kidneys, and the caul above the liver of the sin offering, he burnt upon the altar; as the LORD commanded Moses. 8:16; Ex. 23:18

11 ᴿAnd the flesh and the hide he burnt with fire ᵀwithout the camp. 4:11, 12; 8:17 · *outside*

12 And he slew the burnt offering; and Aaron's sons presented unto him the blood, ᴿwhich he sprinkled round about upon the altar. 1:5; 8:19

13 ᴿAnd they presented the burnt offering unto him, with the pieces thereof, and the head: and he burnt *them* upon the altar. 8:20

14 ᴿAnd he did wash the inwards and the legs, and burnt *them* upon the burnt offering on the altar. 8:21

15 ᴿAnd he brought the people's offering, and took the goat, which *was* the sin offering for the people, and slew it, and offered it for sin, as the first. [Is. 53:10; Heb. 2:17]

16 And he brought the burnt offering, and offered it ᴿaccording to the manner. 1:1–13

17 And he brought the meat offering, and took an handful thereof, and burnt *it* upon the altar, ᴿbeside the burnt sacrifice of the morning. Ex. 29:38, 39

18 He slew also the bullock and the ram *for* ᴿa sacrifice of peace offerings, which *was* for the people: and Aaron's sons presented

unto him the blood, which he sprinkled upon the altar round about, 3:1–11

19 And the fat of the bullock and of the ram, the rump, and that which covereth *the inwards,* and the kidneys, and the caul *above* the liver:

20 And they put the fat upon the breasts, ᴿand he burnt the fat upon the altar: 3:5, 16

21 And the breasts and the right shoulder Aaron waved ᴿ*for* a wave offering before the LORD; as Moses commanded. Ex. 29:24, 26, 27

22 And Aaron lifted up his hand toward the people, and ᴿblessed them, and came down from offering of the sin offering, and the burnt offering, and peace offerings. Num. 6:22–26; Deut. 21:5; Luke 24:50

23 And Moses and Aaron went into the tabernacle of the congregation, and came out, and blessed the people: and the glory of the LORD appeared unto all the people.

24 And ᴿthere came a fire out from before the LORD, and consumed upon the altar the burnt offering and the fat: *which* when all the people saw, they shouted, and fell on their faces. Judg. 6:21

10 And Na'-dab and A-bi'-hu, the sons of Aaron, took either of them his censer, and put fire therein, and put incense thereon, and offered ᴿstrange fire before the LORD, which he commanded them not. Ex. 30:9

2 And there ᴿwent out fire from the LORD, and devoured them, and they died before the LORD. Rev. 20:9

3 Then Moses said unto Aaron, This *is it* that the LORD spake, saying, I will be sanctified in them ᴿthat come nigh me, and before all the people I will be glorified. And Aaron held his peace. Ezek. 20:41

4 And Moses called Mish'-a-el and El'-za-phan, and the sons of Uz-zi'-el the uncle of Aaron, and said unto them, Come near, ᴿcarry your brethren from before the sanctuary out of the camp. Acts 5:6

5 So they went near, and car-

ried them in their coats out of the camp; as Moses had said.

6 And Moses said unto Aaron, and unto E-le-a'-zar and unto Ith'-a-mar, his sons, Uncover not your heads, neither rend your clothes; lest ye die, and ^Rlest wrath come upon all the people: but let your brethren, the whole house of Israel, bewail the burning which the LORD hath kindled.   2 Sam. 24:1

7 ^RAnd ye shall not go out from the door of the tabernacle of the congregation, lest ye die: ^Rfor the anointing oil of the LORD is upon you. And they did according to the word of Moses.   8:33; 21:12 · 8:30

8 And the LORD spake unto Aaron, saying,

9 Do not drink wine nor strong drink, thou, nor thy sons with thee, when ye go into the tabernacle of the congregation, lest ye die: it shall be a statute for ever throughout your generations:

10 And that ye may put difference between holy and unholy, and between unclean and clean;

11 And that ye may teach the children of Israel all the statutes which the LORD hath spoken unto them by the hand of Moses.

12 And Moses spake unto Aaron, and unto E-le-a'-zar and unto Ith'-a-mar, his sons that were left, Take ^Rthe meat offering that remaineth of the offerings of the LORD made by fire, and eat it without leaven beside the altar: for ^Rit is most holy: Num. 18:9 · 21:22

13 And ye shall eat it in the ^Rholy place, because it is thy due, and thy sons' due, of the sacrifices of the LORD made by fire: for ^Rso I am commanded.   Num. 18:10 · 2:3; 6:16

14 And the wave breast and heave shoulder shall ye eat in a clean place; thou, and thy sons, and thy ^Rdaughters with thee: for they be thy due, and thy sons' ^Rdue, which are given out of the sacrifices of peace offerings of the children of Israel.   22:13 · Num. 18:10

15 ^RThe heave shoulder and the wave breast shall they bring with the offerings made by fire of the

fat, to wave it for a wave offering before the LORD; and it shall be thine, and thy sons' with thee, by a statute for ever; as the LORD hath commanded.   7:29, 30, 34

16 And Moses diligently sought ^Rthe goat of the sin offering, and, behold, it was burnt: and he was angry with E-le-a'-zar and Ith'-a-mar, the sons of Aaron which were left alive, saying,   9:3, 15

17 ^RWherefore have ye not eaten the sin offering in the holy place, seeing it is most holy, and God hath given it you to bear ^Rthe iniquity of the congregation, to make atonement for them before the LORD? 6:24–30 · 22:16; Ex. 28:38; Num. 18:1

18 Behold, ^Rthe blood of it was not brought in within the holy place: ye should indeed have eaten it in the holy place, ^Ras I commanded.   6:30 · 6:26, 30

19 And Aaron said unto Moses, Behold, this day have they offered their sin offering and their burnt offering before the LORD; and such things have befallen me: and if I had eaten the sin offering to day, ^Rshould it have been accepted in the sight of the LORD? [Is. 1:11–15]

20 And when Moses heard that, he was content.

11 And the LORD spake unto Moses and to Aaron, saying unto them,

2 Speak unto the children of Israel, saying, These are the beasts which ye shall eat among all the beasts that are on the earth.

3 Whatsoever parteth the hoof, and is clovenfooted, and cheweth the cud, among the beasts, that shall ye eat.

4 Nevertheless these shall ye not eat of them that chew the cud, or of them that divide the hoof: as the camel, because he cheweth the cud, but divideth not the hoof; he is unclean unto you.

5 And the coney, because he cheweth the cud, but divideth not the hoof; he is unclean unto you.

6 And the hare, because he cheweth the cud, but divideth

not the hoof; he *is* unclean unto you.

7 And the swine, though he divide the hoof, and be cloven-footed, yet he cheweth not the cud; ^Rhe *is* unclean to you. Is. 65:4

8 Of their flesh shall ye not eat, and their carcase shall ye not touch; they *are* unclean to you.

9 ^RThese shall ye eat of all that *are* in the waters: whatsoever hath fins and scales in the waters, in the seas, and in the rivers, them shall ye eat. Deut. 14:9

10 And all that have not fins and scales in the seas, and in the rivers, of all that move in the waters, and of any living thing which *is* in the waters, they *shall be* an ^Rabomination unto you: Deut. 14:3

11 They shall be even an abomination unto you; ye shall not eat of their flesh, but ye shall have their carcases in abomination.

12 Whatsoever hath no fins nor scales in the waters, that *shall be* an abomination unto you.

13 ^RAnd these *are they which* ye shall have in abomination among the fowls; they shall not be eaten, they *are* an abomination: the eagle, and the ^Tossifrage, and the ^Tospray, Is. 66:17 · *vulture · buzzard*

14 And the ^Tvulture, and the kite after his kind; *kite, and falcon*

15 Every raven after his kind;

16 And the owl, and the night hawk, and the cuckow, and the hawk after his kind,

17 And the little owl, and the cormorant, and the great owl,

18 And the swan, and the pelican, and the gier eagle,

19 And the stork, the heron after her kind, and the lapwing, and the bat.

20 All fowls that creep, going upon *all* four, *shall be* an abomination unto you.

21 Yet these may ye eat of every flying creeping thing that goeth upon *all* four, which have legs above their feet, to leap withal upon the earth;

22 *Even* these of them ye may eat; the locust after his kind, and

the bald locust after his kind, and the beetle after his kind, and the grasshopper after his kind.

23 But all *other* flying creeping things, which have four feet, *shall be* an abomination unto you.

24 And for these ye shall be unclean: whosoever toucheth the carcase of them shall be unclean until the even.

25 And whosoever beareth *ought* of the carcase of them ^Rshall wash his clothes, and be unclean until the even. Zech. 13:1

26 *The carcases* of every beast which divideth the hoof, and *is* not clovenfooted, nor cheweth the cud, *are* unclean unto you: every one that toucheth them shall be unclean.

27 And whatsoever goeth upon his paws, among all manner of beasts that go on *all* four, those *are* unclean unto you: whoso toucheth their carcase shall be unclean until the even.

28 And he that beareth the carcase of them shall wash his clothes, and be unclean until the even: they *are* unclean unto you.

29 These also *shall be* unclean unto you among the creeping things that creep upon the earth; the weasel, and ^Rthe mouse, and the tortoise after his kind, Is. 66:17

30 And the ferret, and the chameleon, and the lizard, and the snail, and the mole.

31 These *are* unclean to you among all that creep: whosoever doth ^Rtouch them, when they be dead, shall be unclean until the even. Hag. 2:13

32 And upon whatsoever *any* of them, when they are dead, doth fall, it shall be unclean; whether *it be* any vessel of wood, or raiment, or skin, or sack, whatsoever vessel *it be*, wherein *any* work is done, ^Rit must be put into water, and it shall be unclean until the even; so it shall be cleansed. 15:12

33 And every ^Rearthen vessel, whereinto *any* of them falleth, whatsoever *is* in it shall be unclean; and ye shall break it. 6:28

34 Of all meat which may be eaten, *that* on which *such* water cometh shall be unclean: and all drink that may be drunk in every *such* vessel shall be unclean.

35 And every *thing* whereupon *any part* of their carcase falleth shall be unclean; *whether it be* oven, or ranges for pots, they shall be broken down: *for* they *are* unclean, and shall be unclean unto you.

36 Nevertheless a ^Tfountain or ^Tpit, *wherein there is* plenty of water, shall be clean: but that which toucheth their carcase shall be unclean. *spring · cistern*

37 And if *any part* of their carcase fall upon any sowing seed which is to be sown, it *shall be* clean.

38 But if *any* water be put upon the seed, and *any part* of their carcase fall thereon, it *shall be* ^Tunclean unto you. *impure*

39 And if any beast, of which ye may eat, die; he that toucheth the carcase thereof shall be ^Runclean until the even. *Hag. 2:11–13*

40 And ^Rhe that eateth of the carcase of it shall wash his clothes, and be unclean until the even: he also that beareth the carcase of it shall wash his clothes, and be unclean until the even. *22:8*

41 And every creeping thing that creepeth upon the earth *shall be* ^Tan abomination; it shall not be eaten. *detestable*

42 Whatsoever goeth upon the belly, and whatsoever goeth upon *all* four, or whatsoever hath more feet among all creeping things that creep upon the earth, them ye shall not eat; for they *are* an abomination.

43 ^RYe shall not make your selves abominable with any creeping thing that creepeth, neither shall ye make yourselves unclean with them, that ye should be defiled thereby. *20:25*

44 For I *am* the LORD your God: ye shall therefore sanctify yourselves, and ^Rye shall be holy; for I *am* holy: neither shall ye defile yourselves with any manner of creeping thing that creepeth upon the earth. *[Amos 3:3]; Matt. 5:48*

45 For I *am* the LORD that bringeth you up out of the land of Egypt, to be your God: ye shall therefore be holy, for I *am* holy.

46 This *is* the law ^Tof the beasts, and of the fowl, and of every living creature that moveth in the waters, and of every creature that creepeth upon the earth: *concerning*

47 ^RTo make a difference between the unclean and the clean, and between the beast that may be eaten and the beast that may not be eaten. *Ezek. 44:23; Mal. 3:18*

12 And the LORD spake unto Moses, saying,

2 Speak unto the children of Israel, saying, If a woman have conceived seed, and born a man child: then ^Rshe shall be unclean seven days; according to the days of the separation for her infirmity shall she be unclean. *8:33; Luke 2:22*

3 And in the ^Reighth day the flesh of his foreskin shall be circumcised. *Gen. 17:12; John 7:22, 23*

4 And she shall then continue in the blood of her purifying three and thirty days; she shall touch no hallowed thing, nor come into the sanctuary, until the days of her purifying be fulfilled.

5 But if she bear a maid child, then she shall be unclean two weeks, as in her separation: and she shall continue in the blood of her purifying threescore and six days.

6 And ^Rwhen the days of her purifying are fulfilled, for a son, or for a daughter, she shall bring a ^Rlamb of the first year for a burnt offering, and a young pigeon, or a turtledove, for a sin offering, unto the door of the tabernacle of the congregation, unto the priest: *Luke 2:22 · [John 1:29]*

7 Who shall offer it before the LORD, and make ^Tan atonement for her; and she shall be cleansed from the issue of her blood. This *is* the law for her that hath born a male or a female. *a propitiation*

8 ^RAnd if she be not able to

bring a lamb, then she shall bring two turtles, or two young pigeons; the one for the burnt offering, and the other for a sin offering: ^Rand the priest shall make an atonement for her, and she shall be ^Tclean.   5:7; Luke 2:22–24 · 4:26 · *pure*

13 And the LORD spake unto Moses and Aaron, saying,

2 When a man shall have in the skin of his flesh a rising, a scab, or bright spot, and it be in the skin of his flesh *like* the plague of leprosy; ^Rthen he shall be brought unto Aaron the priest, or unto one of his sons the priests: Luke 17:14

3 And the priest shall look on the ^Tplague in the skin of the flesh: and *when* the hair in the plague is turned white, and the plague in sight *be* deeper than the skin of his flesh, it *is* a plague of leprosy: and the priest shall look on him, and pronounce him ^Tunclean.   *sore · defiled*

4 If the bright spot *be* white in the skin of his flesh, and in sight *be* not deeper than the skin, and the hair thereof be not turned white; then the priest shall ^Tshut up *him that hath* the plague ^Rseven days: *isolate* · 14:8

5 And the priest shall look on him the seventh day: and, behold, *if* the plague in his sight be at a stay, *and* the plague spread not in the skin; then the priest shall shut him up seven days more:

6 And the priest shall look on him again the seventh day: and, behold, *if* the plague *be* somewhat dark, *and* the plague spread not in the skin, the priest shall pronounce him clean: it *is but* a scab: and he ^Rshall wash his clothes, and be clean. 11:25; 14:8; [John 13:8, 10]

7 But if the scab spread much abroad in the skin, after that he hath been seen of the priest for his cleansing, he shall be seen of the priest again:

8 And *if* the priest see that, behold, the scab spreadeth in the skin, then the priest shall pronounce him ^Tunclean: it *is* a leprosy.   *defiled*

9 When the plague of leprosy is in a man, then he shall be brought unto the priest;

10 ^RAnd the priest shall see *him*: and, behold, *if* the rising *be* white in the skin, and it have turned the hair white, and *there be* quick raw flesh in the rising; 2 Kin. 5:27

11 It *is* an old leprosy in the skin of his flesh, and the priest shall pronounce him unclean, and shall not shut him up: for he *is* unclean.

12 And if a leprosy break out abroad in the skin, and the leprosy cover all the skin of *him that hath* the plague from his head even to his foot, wheresoever the priest looketh;

13 Then the priest shall consider: and, behold, *if* the leprosy have covered all his flesh, he shall pronounce *him* clean *that hath* the plague: it is all turned ^Rwhite: he *is* clean.   Ex. 4:6

14 But when raw flesh appeareth in him, he shall be unclean.

15 And the priest shall see the raw flesh, and pronounce him to be unclean: *for* the raw flesh *is* unclean: it *is* a leprosy.

16 Or if the raw flesh turn again, and be changed unto white, he shall come unto the priest;

17 And the priest shall see him: and, behold, *if* the plague be turned into white; then the priest shall pronounce *him* clean *that hath* the plague: he *is* clean.

18 The flesh also, in which, *even* in the skin thereof, was a ^Rboil, and is healed,   Ex. 9:9; 15:26

19 And in the place of the boil there be a white rising, or a bright spot, white, and somewhat reddish, and it be shewed to the priest;

20 And if, when the priest seeth it, behold, it *be* in sight ^Tlower than the skin, and the hair thereof be turned white; the priest shall pronounce him unclean: it *is* a plague of leprosy broken out of the boil.   *deeper*

21 But if the priest look on it, and, behold, *there be* no white hairs therein, and *if* it *be* not

lower than the skin, but *be* somewhat dark; then the priest shall
^Tshut him up seven days: *isolate*
22 And if it spread much abroad
in the skin, then the priest shall
pronounce him unclean: it *is* a
^Tplague.   *infection* or *leprous sore*
23 But if the bright spot ^Tstay in
his place, *and* spread not, it *is* a
burning boil; and the priest shall
pronounce him clean.   *remains*
24 Or if there be *any* flesh, in the
skin whereof *there is* a hot burning, and the quick *flesh* that
burneth have a white bright spot,
somewhat reddish, or white;
25 Then the priest shall look
upon it: and, behold, *if* the hair in
the bright spot be turned white,
and it *be in* sight deeper than the
skin; it *is* a leprosy broken out of
the burning: wherefore the priest
shall pronounce him unclean: it *is*
the ^Tplague of leprosy.   *infection*
26 But if the priest look on it,
and, behold, *there be* no white
hair in the bright spot, and it *be*
no lower than the *other* skin, but
be somewhat dark; then the priest
shall shut him up seven days:
27 And the priest shall look
upon him the seventh day: *and* if
it be spread much abroad in the
skin, then the priest shall pronounce him unclean: it *is* the
plague of leprosy.
28 And if the bright spot stay in
his place, *and* spread not in the
skin, but it *be* somewhat dark; it *is*
a rising of the burning, and the
priest shall pronounce him clean:
for it *is* an inflammation of the
burning.
29 If a man or woman have a
plague upon the head or the
beard;
30 Then the priest shall see the
plague: and, behold, if it *be* in
sight deeper than the skin; *and*
there be in it a yellow thin hair;
then the priest shall pronounce
him unclean: it *is* a dry scall, *even*
a leprosy upon the head or beard.
31 And if the priest look on the
plague of the scall, and, behold, it
be not in sight deeper than the

skin, and *that there is* no black
hair in it; then the priest shall shut
up *him that hath* the plague of the
scall seven days:
32 And in the seventh day the
priest shall look on the plague:
and, behold, *if* the scall spread
not, and there be in it no yellow
hair, and the scall *be* not in sight
deeper than the skin;
33 He shall be shaven, but the
scall shall he not shave; and the
priest shall shut up *him that hath*
the scall seven days more:
34 And in the seventh day the
priest shall look on the scall: and,
behold, *if* the scall be not spread
in the skin, nor *be* in sight deeper
than the skin; then the priest shall
pronounce him clean: and he
shall wash his clothes, and be
clean.
35 But if the scall spread much
in the skin after his cleansing;
36 Then the priest shall look on
him: and, behold, if the scall be
spread in the skin, the priest shall
not seek for yellow hair; he *is*
unclean.
37 But if the scall be in his sight
at a stay, and *that* there is black
hair grown up therein; the scall is
healed, he *is* clean: and the priest
shall pronounce him clean.
38 If a man also or a woman
have in the skin of their flesh
bright spots, *even* white bright
spots;
39 Then the priest shall look:
and, behold, *if* the bright spots in
the skin of their flesh *be* darkish
white; it *is* a freckled spot *that*
groweth in the skin; he *is* clean.
40 And the man whose hair is
fallen off his head, he *is* bald; *yet*
is he clean.
41 And he that hath his hair fall-
en off from the part of his head
toward his face, he *is* forehead
bald: *yet is* he clean.
42 And if there be in the bald
head, or bald ^Rforehead, a white
reddish sore; it *is* a leprosy
sprung up in his bald head, or his
bald forehead.   2 Chr. 26:19
43 Then the priest shall look

upon it: and, behold, *if* the rising of the sore *be* white reddish in his bald head, or in his bald forehead, as the leprosy appeareth in the skin of the flesh;

44 He is a leprous man, he *is* unclean: the priest shall pronounce him utterly unclean; his plague *is* in his [R]head.   Is. 1:5

45 And the leper in whom the plague *is*, his clothes shall be rent, and his head bare, and he shall put a covering upon his upper lip, and shall cry, Unclean, unclean.

46 All the days wherein the plague *shall be* in him he shall be defiled; he *is* unclean: he shall dwell alone; [R]without the camp *shall* his habitation *be*.   Ps. 38:11

47 The garment also that the plague of leprosy is in, *whether it be* a woollen garment, or a linen garment;

48 Whether *it be* in the warp, or woof; of linen, or of woollen; whether in a skin, or in any thing made of [T]skin;   *leather*

49 And if the plague be greenish or reddish in the garment, or in the skin, either in the warp, or in the woof, or in any thing of [T]skin; it *is* a plague of leprosy, and shall be shewed unto the priest: *leathers*

50 And the priest shall look upon the plague, and shut up *it that hath* the plague seven days:

51 And he shall look on the plague on the seventh day: if the plague be spread in the garment, either in the warp, or in the woof, or in a skin, *or* in any work that is made of skin; the plague *is* a [T]fretting leprosy; it *is* unclean.   *active*

52 He shall therefore burn that garment, whether warp or woof, in woollen or in linen, or any thing of skin, wherein the plague is: for it *is* a fretting leprosy; it shall be burnt in the fire.

53 And if the priest shall look, and, behold, the plague be not spread in the garment, either in the warp, or in the woof, or in any thing of skin;

54 Then the priest shall command that they wash *the thing* wherein the plague *is*, and he shall shut it up seven days more:

55 And the priest shall look on the plague, after that it is washed: and, behold, *if* the plague have not changed his colour, and the plague be not spread; it *is* unclean; thou shalt burn it in the fire; it *is* fret inward, *whether* it *be* bare within or without.

56 And if the priest look, and, behold, the plague *be* somewhat dark after the washing of it; then he shall [T]rend it out of the garment, or out of the skin, or out of the warp, or out of the woof: *tear*

57 And if it appear still in the garment, either in the warp, or in the woof, or in any thing of skin; it *is* a spreading *plague:* thou shalt burn that wherein the plague *is* with fire.

58 And the garment, either warp, or woof, or whatsoever thing of skin it *be*, which thou shalt wash, if the plague be departed from them, then it shall be washed the second time, and shall be clean.

59 This *is* the law of the plague of leprosy in a garment of woollen or linen, either in the warp, or woof, or any thing of skins, to pronounce it clean, or to pronounce it unclean.

14 And the Lord spake unto Moses, saying,

2 This shall be the law of the leper in the day of his cleansing: He [R]shall be brought unto the priest: Luke 5:12, 14; 17:14

3 And the priest shall go forth out of the camp; and the priest shall look, and, behold, *if* the plague of leprosy be healed in the leper;

4 Then shall the priest command to take for him that is to be cleansed two birds alive *and* clean, and [R]cedar wood, and scarlet, and hyssop: Num. 19:6; Heb. 9:19

5 And the priest shall command that one of the birds be killed in an earthen vessel over running water:

6 As for the living bird, he shall

take it, and the cedar wood, and the scarlet, and the hyssop, and shall dip them and the living bird in the blood of the bird *that was* killed over the running water:

7   And he shall sprinkle upon him that is to be cleansed from the leprosy [R]seven times, and shall pronounce him clean, and shall let the living bird loose into the open field.   2 Kin. 5:10, 14; Ps. 51:2

8   And he that is to be cleansed shall wash his clothes, and shave off all his hair, and wash himself in water, that he may be clean: and after that he shall come into the camp, and [R]shall tarry abroad out of his tent seven days.   13:5

9   But it shall be on the [R]seventh day, that he shall shave all his hair off his head and his beard and his eyebrows, even all his hair he shall shave off: and he shall wash his clothes, also he shall wash his flesh in water, and he shall be clean.   Num. 19:19

10   And on the eighth day [R]he shall take two he lambs without blemish, and one ewe lamb of the first year without blemish, and three tenth deals of fine flour *for* a meat offering, mingled with oil, and one log of oil.   Matt. 8:4; Luke 5:14

11   And the priest that maketh *him* clean shall present the man that is to be made clean, and those things, before the LORD, *at* the door of the tabernacle of the congregation:

12   And the priest shall take one he lamb, and offer him for a trespass offering, and the log of oil, and [R]wave them *for* a wave offering before the LORD: Ex. 29:22–24, 26

13   And he shall slay the lamb [R]in the place where he shall kill the sin offering and the burnt offering, in the holy place: for [R]as the sin offering *is* the priest's, *so* is the trespass offering: [R]it *is* most holy: Ex. 29:11 · 6:24–30; 7:7 · 7:6; 21:22

14   And the priest shall take *some* of the blood of the trespass offering, and the priest shall put *it* [R]upon the tip of the right ear of him that is to be cleansed, and

upon the thumb of his right hand, and upon the great toe of his right foot: 8:23, 24; Ex. 29:20

15   And the priest shall take *some* of the log of oil, and pour *it* into the palm of his own left hand:

16   And the priest shall dip his right finger in the oil that *is* in his left hand, and shall [R]sprinkle of the oil with his finger seven times before the LORD: 4:6

17   And of the rest of the oil that *is* in his hand shall the priest put upon the tip of the right ear of him that is to be cleansed, and upon the thumb of his right hand, and upon the great toe of his right foot, upon the blood of the trespass offering:

18   And the remnant of the oil that *is* in the priest's hand he shall pour upon the head of him that is to be cleansed: [R]and the priest shall make an atonement for him before the LORD.   4:26; 5:6; [Heb. 2:17]

19   And the priest shall offer [R]the sin offering, and make an atonement for him that is to be cleansed from his uncleanness; and afterward he shall kill the burnt offering: 5:1, 6; 12:7; [2 Cor. 5:21]

20   And the priest shall offer the burnt offering and the meat offering upon the altar: and the priest shall make an atonement for him, and he shall be clean.

21   And [R]if he *be* poor, and cannot get so much; then he shall take one lamb *for* a trespass offering to be waved, to make an atonement for him, and one tenth [T]deal of fine flour mingled with oil for a meat offering, and a log of oil;   5:7, 11; 12:8; 27:8 · *ephah, measure*

22   [R]And two turtledoves, or two young pigeons, such as he is able to get; and the one shall be a sin offering, and the other a burnt offering.   12:8; 15:14, 15

23   [R]And he shall bring them on the eighth day for his cleansing unto the priest, unto the door of the tabernacle of the congregation, before the LORD.   vv. 10, 11

24   [R]And the priest shall take the lamb of the trespass offering, and

the log of oil, and the priest shall wave them *for* a wave offering before the LORD: v. 12

25 And he shall kill the lamb of the trespass offering, Rand the priest shall take *some* of the blood of the trespass offering, and put *it* upon the tip of the right ear of him that is to be cleansed, and upon the thumb of his right hand, and upon the great toe of his right foot: vv. 14, 17

26 And the priest shall pour of the oil into the palm of his own left hand:

27 And the priest shall sprinkle with his right finger *some* of the oil that *is* in his left hand seven times before the LORD:

28 And the priest shall put of the oil that *is* in his hand upon the tip of the right ear of him that is to be cleansed, and upon the thumb of his right hand, and upon the great toe of his right foot, upon the place of the blood of the trespass offering:

29 And the rest of the oil that *is* in the priest's hand he shall put upon the head of him that is to be cleansed, to make an atonement for him before the LORD.

30 And he shall offer the one of Rthe turtledoves, or of the young pigeons, such as he can get;   v. 22

31 *Even* such as he is able to get, the one *for* a sin offering, and the other *for* a burnt offering, with the meat offering: and the priest shall make an atonement for him that is to be cleansed before the LORD.

32 This *is* the law *of him* in whom *is* the plague of leprosy, Twhose hand is not able to get Rthat *which pertaineth* to his cleansing.   who cannot afford · v. 10

33 And the LORD spake unto Moses and unto Aaron, saying,

34 When ye be come into the land of Canaan, which I give to you for a possession, and I put the plague of leprosy in a house of the land of your possession;

35 And he that owneth the house shall come and tell the priest, saying, It seemeth to me

there is as it were Ra plague in the house: [Ps. 91:9, 10; Prov. 3:33; Zech. 5:4]

36 Then the priest shall command that they empty the house, before the priest go *into it* to see the plague, that all that *is* in the house be not made unclean: and afterward the priest shall go in to see the house:

37 And he shall look on the plague, and, behold, *if* the plague *be* in the walls of the house with hollow strakes, greenish or reddish, which in sight *are* Tlower than the wall;   deeper than the surface

38 Then the priest shall go out of the house to the door of the house, and Tshut up the house seven days: quarantine

39 And the priest shall come again the seventh day, and shall look: and, behold, *if* the plague be spread in the walls of the house;

40 Then the priest shall command that they take away the stones in which the plague *is*, and they shall cast them into an unclean place without the city:

41 And he shall cause the house to be scraped within round about, and they shall pour out the dust that they scrape off without the city into an unclean place:

42 And they shall take other stones, and put *them* in the place of those stones; and he shall take other morter, and shall plaister the house.

43 And if the plague come again, and break out in the house, after that he hath taken away the stones, and after he hath scraped the house, and after it is plaistered;

44 Then the priest shall come and look, and, behold, *if* the plague be spread in the house, it *is* Ra Tfretting leprosy in the house: it *is* unclean.   13:51; [Zech. 5:4] · active

45 And he shall break down the house, the stones of it, and the timber thereof, and all the morter of the house; and he shall carry *them* forth out of the city into an unclean place.

46 Moreover he that goeth into

the house all the while that it is shut up shall be ^Tunclean ^Runtil the even. *defiled* · 11:24; 15:5

47 And he that lieth in the house shall ^Rwash his clothes; and he that eateth in the house shall wash his clothes. v. 8

48 And if the priest shall come in, and look *upon it*, and, behold, the plague hath not spread in the house, after the house was plaistered: then the priest shall pronounce the house clean, because the plague is healed.

49 And ^Rhe shall take to cleanse the house two birds, and cedar wood, and scarlet, and hyssop: v. 4

50 And he shall kill the one of the birds in an earthen vessel over running water:

51 And he shall take the cedar wood, and the hyssop, and the scarlet, and the living bird, and dip them in the blood of the slain bird, and in the running water, and sprinkle the house seven times:

52 And he shall cleanse the house with the blood of the bird, and with the running water, and with the living bird, and with the cedar wood, and with the hyssop, and with the scarlet:

53 But he shall let go the living bird out of the city into the open fields, and ^Rmake an atonement for the house: and it shall be clean. v. 20

54 This *is* the law for all manner of plague of leprosy, and scall,

55 And for the ^Rleprosy of a garment, ^Rand of a house, 13:47–52 · v. 34

56 And ^Rfor a rising, and for a scab, and for a bright spot: 13:2

57 To ^Rteach when *it is* unclean, and when *it is* clean: this *is* the law of leprosy. 11:47; 20:25; Deut. 24:8

15 And the LORD spake unto Moses and to Aaron, saying,

2 Speak unto the children of Israel, and say unto them, ^RWhen any man hath a ^Trunning issue out of his flesh, *because of* his issue he *is* unclean. Num. 5:2 · *discharge*

3 And this shall be his uncleanness in his issue: whether his flesh run with his issue, or his flesh be stopped from his issue, it *is* his uncleanness.

4 Every bed, whereon he lieth that hath the issue, is ^Tunclean: and every thing, whereon he sitteth, shall be unclean. *defiled*

5 And whosoever toucheth his bed shall ^Rwash his clothes, ^Rand bathe *himself* in water, and be unclean until the even. 14:47 · 11:25

6 And he that sitteth on *any* thing whereon he sat that hath the ^Rissue shall wash his clothes, and bathe *himself* in water, and be unclean until the even. Deut. 23:10

7 And he that toucheth the flesh of him that hath the issue shall wash his clothes, and bathe *himself* in water, and be unclean until the even.

8 And if he that hath the issue ^Rspit upon him that is clean; then he shall wash his clothes, and bathe *himself* in water, and be unclean until the even. Num. 12:14

9 And what saddle soever he rideth upon that hath the issue shall be unclean.

10 And whosoever toucheth any thing that was under him shall be unclean until the even: and he that beareth *any of* those things shall wash his clothes, and bathe *himself* in water, and be unclean until the even.

11 And whomsoever he toucheth that hath the ^Tissue, and hath not rinsed his hands in water, he shall wash his clothes, and bathe *himself* in water, and be unclean until the even. *discharge*

12 And the vessel of earth, that he toucheth which hath the issue, shall be broken: and every vessel of wood shall be rinsed in water.

13 And when he that hath an issue is cleansed of his issue; then he shall number to himself seven days for his cleansing, and wash his clothes, and bathe his flesh in running water, and shall be clean.

14 And on the eighth day he shall take to him ^Rtwo turtledoves, or two young pigeons, and come before the LORD unto the door of

the tabernacle of the congregation, and give them unto the
priest: 14:22, 23, 30, 31

15 And the priest shall offer
them, ᴿthe one *for* a sin offering,
and the other *for* a burnt offering;
ᴿand the priest shall make an
atonement for him before the
LORD for his issue. 14:30, 31 · 14:19, 31

16 And ᴿif any man's seed of
copulation go out from him, then
he shall wash all his flesh in
water, and be unclean until the
even.   22:4; Deut. 23:10, 11

17 And every garment, and every skin, whereon is the seed of
copulation, shall be washed with
water, and be unclean until the
even.

18 The woman also with whom
man shall lie *with* seed of copulation, they shall *both* bathe *themselves* in water, and ᴿbe unclean
until the even.   [Ex. 19:15; 1 Sam. 21:4]

19 And ᴿif a woman have ᵀan
issue, *and* her issue in her flesh be
blood, she shall be put apart sev-
en days: and whosoever toucheth
her shall be unclean until the
even.   12:2 · *a discharge*

20 And every thing that she lieth
upon in her separation shall be
unclean: every thing also that she
sitteth upon shall be unclean.

21 And whosoever toucheth her
bed shall wash his clothes, and
bathe *himself* in water, and be
unclean until the even.

22 And whosoever toucheth any
thing that she sat upon shall wash
his clothes, and bathe *himself* in
water, and be unclean until the
even.

23 And if it *be* on *her* bed, or on
any thing whereon she sitteth,
when he toucheth it, he shall be
unclean until the even.

24 And if any man lie with her at
all, and her ᵀflowers be upon him,
he shall be unclean seven days;
and all the bed whereon he lieth
shall be unclean.   *impurity*

25 And if ᴿa woman have an
issue of her blood many days out
of the time of her separation, or if
it run beyond the time of her sep-

aration; all the days of the issue of
her uncleanness shall be as the
days of her separation: she *shall
be* unclean.   Matt. 9:20; Mark 5:25

26 Every bed whereon she lieth
all the days of her issue shall be
unto her as the bed of her separation: and whatsoever she sitteth
upon shall be unclean, as the uncleanness of her separation.

27 And whosoever toucheth
those things shall be unclean, and
shall wash his clothes, and bathe
himself in water, and be unclean
until the even.

28 But ᴿif she be cleansed of her
issue, then she shall number to
herself seven days, and after that
she shall be clean.   vv. 13–15

29 And on the eighth day she
shall take unto her two turtles, or
two young pigeons, and bring
them unto the priest, to the door
of the tabernacle of the congregation.

30 And the priest shall offer the
one *for* a sin offering, and the
other *for* a ᴿburnt offering; and
the priest shall make an atonement for her before the LORD for
the issue of her uncleanness.   5:7

31 Thus shall ye ᴿseparate the
children of Israel from their uncleanness; that they die not in
their uncleanness, when they ᴿdefile my tabernacle that *is* among
them.   [Heb. 12:15] · Ezek. 23:38; 36:17

32 ᴿThis *is* the law of him that
hath an issue, ᴿand *of him* whose
seed goeth from him, and is
defiled therewith;   v. 2 · v. 16

33 And of her that is sick ᵀof her
flowers, and of him that hath an
issue, of the man, and of the woman, and of him that lieth with
her that is unclean. *with her impurity*

16 And the LORD spake unto
Moses after the death of the
two sons of Aaron, when they
offered before the LORD, and died;

2 And the LORD said unto Moses, Speak unto Aaron thy brother, that he ᴿcome not at ᵀall times
into the holy *place* within the vail
before the mercy seat, which *is*
upon the ark; that he die not: for I

will appear in the cloud upon the mercy seat.   Ex. 30:10 · *any time*

3 Thus shall Aaron ᴿcome into the holy *place:* with a young bullock for a sin offering, and a ram for a burnt offering.   4:1–12

4 He shall put on the ᴿholy linen coat, and he shall have the linen breeches upon his flesh, and shall be girded with a linen girdle, and with the linen ᵀmitre shall he be attired: these *are* holy garments; therefore ᴿshall he wash his flesh in water, and *so* put them on.   Ezek. 44:17, 18 · *turban* · Ex. 30:20

5 And he shall take of ᴿthe congregation of the children of Israel two kids of the goats for a sin offering, and one ram for a burnt offering.   2 Chr. 29:21; Ezra 6:17

6 And Aaron shall offer his bullock of the sin offering, which *is* for himself, and ᴿmake an atonement for himself, and for his house.   9:7; [Heb. 5:3; 7:27, 28; 9:7]

7 And he shall take the two goats, and present them before the Lᴏʀᴅ *at* the door of the tabernacle of the congregation.

8 And Aaron shall cast lots upon the two goats; one lot for the Lᴏʀᴅ, and the other lot for the scapegoat.

9 And Aaron shall bring the goat upon which the Lᴏʀᴅ's lot fell, and offer him *for* a sin offering.

10 But the goat, on which the lot fell to be the scapegoat, shall be presented alive before the Lᴏʀᴅ, to make ᴿan atonement with him, *and* to let him go for a scapegoat into the wilderness.   [Is. 53:5, 6]

11 And Aaron shall bring the bullock of the sin offering, which *is* for ᴿhimself, and shall make an atonement for himself, and for his house, and shall kill the bullock of the sin offering which *is* for himself: [Heb. 7:27; 9:7]

12 And he shall take ᴿa censer full of burning coals of fire from off the altar before the Lᴏʀᴅ, and his hands full of ᴿsweet incense beaten small, and bring *it* within the vail: Is. 6:6, 7; Rev. 8:5 · Ex. 30:34–38

13 And he shall put the incense upon the fire before the Lᴏʀᴅ, that the cloud of the incense may cover the mercy seat that *is* upon the testimony, that he die not:

14 And ᴿhe shall take of the blood of the bullock, and ᴿsprinkle *it* with his finger upon the mercy seat eastward; and before the mercy seat shall he sprinkle of the blood with his finger seven times.   4:5; [Heb. 9:25; 10:4] · 4:6, 17

15 Then shall he kill the goat of the sin offering, that *is* for the people, and bring his blood ᴿwithin the vail, and do with that blood as he did with the blood of the bullock, and sprinkle it upon the mercy seat, and before the mercy seat: [Heb. 6:19; 7:27; 9:3, 7, 12]

16 And he shall make an atonement for the holy *place,* because of the uncleanness of the children of Israel, and because of their transgressions in all their sins: and so shall he do for the tabernacle of the congregation, that remaineth among them in the midst of their uncleanness.

17 And there shall be ᴿno man in the tabernacle of the congregation when he goeth in to make an atonement in the holy *place,* until he come out, and have made an atonement for himself, and for his household, and for all the congregation of Israel.   Ex. 34:3; Luke 1:10

18 And he shall go out unto the altar that *is* before the Lᴏʀᴅ, and make an atonement for ᴿit; and shall take of the blood of the bullock, and of the blood of the goat, and put *it* upon the horns of the altar round about.   Ex. 29:36

19 And he shall sprinkle of the blood upon it with his finger seven times, and cleanse it, and ᴿhallow it from the uncleanness of the children of Israel.   Ezek. 43:20

20 And when he hath made an end of ᵀreconciling the holy *place,* and the tabernacle of the congregation, and the altar, he shall bring the live goat: *atoning for*

21 And Aaron shall lay both his hands upon the head of the live goat, and confess over him all the

iniquities of the children of Israel, and all their transgressions in all their sins, ᴿputting them upon the head of the goat, and shall send *him* away by the hand of a fit man into the wilderness: [Is. 53:6]

22 And the goat shall bear upon him all their iniquities unto a land not inhabited: and he shall ᴿlet go the goat in the wilderness.   14:7

23 And Aaron shall come into the tabernacle of the congregation, ᴿand shall put off the linen garments, which he put on when he went into the holy *place*, and shall leave them there: Ezek. 42:14

24 And he shall wash his flesh with water in the holy place, and put on his garments, and come forth, and offer his burnt offering, and the burnt offering of the people, and make an atonement for himself, and for the people.

25 And the fat of the sin offering shall he burn upon the altar.

26 And he that let go the goat for the scapegoat shall wash his clothes, ᴿand bathe his flesh in water, and afterward come into the camp.   15:5

27 And the bullock *for* the sin offering, and the goat *for* the sin offering, whose blood was brought in to make atonement in the holy *place*, shall *one* carry forth without the camp; and they shall burn in the fire their skins, and their flesh, and their dung.

28 And he that burneth them shall wash his clothes, and bathe his flesh in water, and afterward he shall come into the camp.

29 And *this* shall be a statute for ever unto you: *that* in the seventh month, on the tenth *day* of the month, ye shall ᵀafflict your souls, and do no work at all, *whether it be* one of your own country, or a stranger that sojourneth among you: *humble*

30 For on that day shall *the priest* make an atonement for you, to ᴿcleanse you, *that* ye may be clean from all your sins before the LORD.   [Heb. 9:13, 14; 1 John 1:7, 9]

31 ᴿIt *shall be* a sabbath of rest unto you, and ye shall afflict your souls, by a statute for ever.   Is. 58:3

32 And the priest, whom he shall anoint, and whom he shall ᴿconsecrate to minister in the priest's office in his father's stead, shall make the atonement, and shall put on the linen clothes, *even* the holy garments: Ex. 29:29, 30

33 And he shall make an atonement for the ᵀholy sanctuary, and he shall make an atonement for the tabernacle of the congregation, and for the altar, and he shall make an atonement for the priests, and for all the people of the congregation.   *Most Holy Place*

34 ᴿAnd this shall be an everlasting statute unto you, to make an atonement for the children of Israel for all their sins ᴿonce a year. And he did as the LORD commanded Moses.   Num. 29:7 · Ex. 30:10

17 And the LORD spake unto Moses, saying,

2 Speak unto Aaron, and unto his sons, and unto all the children of Israel, and say unto them; This *is* the thing which the LORD hath commanded, saying,

3 What man soever *there be* of the house of Israel, ᴿthat killeth an ox, or lamb, or goat, in the camp, or that killeth *it* ᵀout of the camp,   Deut. 12:5, 15, 21 · *outside*

4 And bringeth it not unto the door of the tabernacle of the congregation, to offer an offering unto the LORD before the tabernacle of the LORD; blood shall be imputed unto that man; he hath shed blood; and that man shall be cut off from among his people:

5 To the end that the children of Israel may bring their sacrifices, ᴿwhich they offer in the open field, even that they may bring them unto the LORD, unto the door of the tabernacle of the congregation, unto the priest, and offer them *for* peace offerings unto the LORD. Gen. 21:33; 22:2; 31:54

6 And the priest ᴿshall sprinkle the blood upon the altar of the LORD *at* the door of the tabernacle of the congregation, and ᴿburn

the fat for a sweet savour unto the
LORD.   3:2 · Ex. 29:13, 18; Num. 18:17

7   And they shall no more offer
their sacrifices ^Runto devils, after
whom they have gone a whoring.
This shall be a statute for ever
unto them throughout their generations.   Ps. 106:37; 1 Cor. 10:20

8   And thou shalt say unto
them, Whatsoever man *there be*
of the house of Israel, or of the
strangers which sojourn among
you, ^Rthat offereth a burnt offering or sacrifice,   1:2, 3; 18:26

9   And bringeth it not unto the
door of the tabernacle of the ^Rcon-
gregation, to offer it unto the
LORD; even that man shall be cut
off from among his people.   14:23

10   ^RAnd whatsoever man *there
be* of the house of Israel, or of the
strangers that sojourn among
you, that eateth any manner of
blood; I will even set my face
against that soul that eateth
blood, and will cut him off from
among his people.   1 Sam. 14:33

11   For the ^Rlife of the flesh *is* in
the blood; and I have given it to
you upon the altar ^Rto make an
atonement for your souls: for it *is*
the blood *that* maketh an atonement for the soul.   Gen. 9:4 · Eph. 1:7

12   Therefore I said unto the children of Israel, No ^Tsoul of you
shall eat blood, neither shall any
stranger that sojourneth among
you eat blood.   *person among*

13 And whatsoever man *there
be* of the children of Israel, or of
the strangers that sojourn among
you, which hunteth and catcheth
any ^Rbeast or fowl that may be
eaten; he shall even ^Rpour out the
blood thereof, and ^Rcover it with
dust.   7:26 · Deut. 12:16, 24 · Ezek. 24:7

14 ^RFor *it is* the life of all flesh;
the blood of it *is* for the life thereof: therefore I said unto the children of Israel, Ye shall eat the
blood of no manner of flesh: for
the life of all flesh *is* the blood
thereof: whosoever eateth it shall
be cut off.   17:11; Gen. 9:4; Deut. 12:23

15 ^RAnd every soul that eateth
that which died ^T*of itself*, or that

which was torn *with beasts,*
whether it be one of your own
country, or a stranger, ^Rhe shall
both wash his clothes, and ^Rbathe
himself in water, and be unclean
until the even: then shall he be
clean.   Ex. 22:31 · *naturally* · 11:25 · 15:5

16 But if he wash *them* not, nor
bathe his flesh; then ^Rhe shall
bear his ^Tiniquity.   5:1 · *guilt*

18

And the LORD spake unto
Moses, saying,

2 Speak unto the children of
Israel, and say unto them, ^RI am
the LORD your God. Ex. 6:7; Ezek. 20:5

3 After the doings of the land
of Egypt, wherein ye dwelt, shall
ye not do: and after the doings of
the land of Canaan, whither I
bring you, shall ye not do: neither
shall ye walk in their ordinances.

4 ^RYe shall do my judgments,
and keep mine ordinances, to
walk therein: I *am* the LORD your
God.   Ezek. 20:19

5 Ye shall therefore keep my
statutes, and my judgments:
which if a man ^Tdo, he shall live
^Tin them: I *am* the LORD.   *does · by*

6 None of you shall approach
to any that is near of kin to him, to
uncover *their* nakedness: I *am* the
LORD.

7 The nakedness of thy father,
or the nakedness of thy mother,
shalt thou not uncover: she *is* thy
mother; thou shalt not uncover
her nakedness.

8 The nakedness of thy father's
wife shalt thou not uncover: it *is*
thy father's nakedness.

9 ^RThe nakedness of thy sister,
the daughter of thy father, or
daughter of thy mother, *whether
she be* born at home, or born
abroad, *even* their nakedness
thou shalt not uncover.   Deut. 27:22

10 The nakedness of thy son's
daughter, or of thy daughter's
daughter, *even* their nakedness
thou shalt not uncover: for theirs
is thine own nakedness.

11 The nakedness of thy father's
wife's daughter, begotten of thy
father, she *is* thy sister, thou shalt
not uncover her nakedness.

12 ^RThou shalt not uncover the nakedness of thy father's sister: she *is* thy father's near kinswoman.　20:19

13 Thou shalt not uncover the nakedness of thy mother's sister: for she *is* thy mother's near kinswoman.

14 ^RThou shalt not uncover the nakedness of thy father's brother, thou shalt not approach to his wife: she *is* thine aunt.　20:20

15 Thou shalt not uncover the nakedness of thy daughter in law: she *is* thy son's wife; thou shalt not uncover her nakedness.

16 Thou shalt not uncover the nakedness of thy brother's wife: it *is* thy brother's nakedness.

17 Thou shalt not uncover the nakedness of a woman and her ^Rdaughter, neither shalt thou take her son's daughter, or her daughter's daughter, to uncover her nakedness; *for* they *are* her near kinswomen: it *is* wickedness. 20:14

18 Neither shalt thou take a wife to her sister, ^Rto vex *her*, to uncover her nakedness, beside the other in her life *time*.　1 Sam. 1:6, 8

19 Also thou shalt not approach unto a woman to uncover her nakedness, as long as she is put apart for her ^Runcleanness.　15:24

20 Moreover thou shalt not lie carnally with thy neighbour's wife, to defile thyself with her.

21 And thou shalt not let any of thy seed pass through ^R*the fire* to ^RMo'-lech, neither shalt thou profane the name of thy God: I *am* the Lord.　2 Kin. 16:3 · 1 Kin. 11:7, 33

22 Thou shalt not lie with ^Rmankind, as with womankind: it *is* abomination.　20:13; Rom. 1:27

23 Neither shalt thou lie with any ^Rbeast to defile thyself therewith: neither shall any woman stand before a beast to lie down thereto: it *is* confusion.　Ex. 22:19

24 Defile not ye yourselves in any of these things: ^Rfor in all these the nations are defiled which I cast out before you:　20:23

25 And the land is defiled: therefore I do ^Rvisit the iniquity thereof

upon it, and the land itself vomiteth out her inhabitants.　Is. 26:21

26 ^RYe shall therefore keep my statutes and my judgments, and shall not commit *any* of these abominations; *neither* any of your own nation, nor any stranger that sojourneth among you:　vv. 5, 30

27 (For all these abominations have the men of the land done, which *were* before you, and the land is defiled;)

28 That ^Rthe land spue not you out also, when ye defile it, as it spued out the nations that *were* before you.　Jer. 9:19

29 For whosoever shall commit any of these abominations, even the ^Tsouls that commit *them* shall be ^Tcut off from among their people.　*persons · put to death*

30 Therefore shall ye keep mine ^Tordinance, ^Rthat ye commit not *any one* of these abominable customs, which were committed before you, and that ye defile not yourselves therein: ^RI *am* the Lord your God.　*charge* · v. 3; 22:9 · v. 2

19 And the Lord spake unto Moses, saying,

2 Speak unto all the congregation of the children of Israel, and say unto them, Ye shall be holy: for I the Lord your God *am* holy.

3 ^RYe shall ^Tfear every man his mother, and his father, and ^Rkeep my sabbaths: I *am* the Lord your God.　Eph. 6:2 · *revere* · Ex. 20:8; 31:13

4 ^RTurn ye not unto idols, nor make to yourselves molten gods: I *am* the Lord your God.　Ex. 20:4

5 And ^Rif ye offer a sacrifice of peace offerings unto the Lord, ye shall offer it at your own will. 7:16

6 It shall be eaten the same day ye offer it, and on the morrow: and if ought remain until the third day, it shall be burnt in the fire.

7 And if it be eaten at all on the third day, it *is* abominable; it shall not be accepted.

8 Therefore *every one* that eateth it shall bear his iniquity, because he hath profaned the hallowed thing of the Lord: and that

soul shall be cut off from among his people.

9 And ^Rwhen ye reap the harvest of your land, thou shalt not wholly reap the corners of thy field, neither shalt thou gather the gleanings of thy harvest.   23:22

10 And thou shalt not glean thy vineyard, neither shalt thou gather *every* grape of thy vineyard; thou shalt leave them for the poor and stranger: I *am* the LORD your God.

11 ^RYe shall not steal, neither deal falsely, ^Rneither lie one to another.   Ex. 20:15, 16 · Eph. 4:25

12 And ye shall not ^Rswear by my name falsely, neither shalt thou profane the name of thy God: I *am* the LORD.   Deut. 5:11

13 ^RThou shalt not defraud thy neighbour, neither rob *him*: the wages of him that is hired shall not abide with thee all night until the morning.   Ex. 22:7–15, 21–27

14 Thou shalt not curse the deaf, ^Rnor put a stumblingblock before the blind, but shalt fear thy God: I *am* the LORD.   Deut. 27:18

15 Ye shall do no unrighteousness in judgment: thou shalt not ^Rrespect the person of the poor, nor honour the person of the mighty: *but* in righteousness shalt thou judge thy neighbour. Deut. 1:17

16 Thou shalt not go up and down *as* a talebearer among thy people: neither shalt thou ^Rstand against the ^Tblood of thy neighbour: I *am* the LORD.   Ex. 23:7 · *life*

17 Thou shalt not hate thy brother in thine heart: thou shalt in any wise rebuke thy neighbour, and not suffer sin upon him.

18 Thou shalt not avenge, nor bear any grudge against the children of thy people, ^Rbut thou shalt love thy neighbour as thyself: I *am* the LORD.   Matt. 5:43; 19:19

19 Ye shall keep my statutes. Thou shalt not let thy cattle gender with a diverse kind: thou shalt not sow thy field with mingled seed: neither shall a garment mingled of linen and woollen come upon thee.

20 And whosoever lieth carnal-ly with a woman, that *is* a bondmaid, betrothed to an husband, and not at all redeemed, nor freedom given her; she shall be scourged; they shall not be put to death, because she was not free.

21 And he shall bring his trespass offering unto the LORD, unto the door of the tabernacle of the congregation, *even* a ram for a trespass offering.

22 And the priest shall make an atonement for him with the ram of the trespass offering before the LORD for his sin which he hath done: and the sin which he hath done shall be forgiven him.

23 And when ye shall come into the land, and shall have planted all manner of trees for food, then ye shall count the fruit thereof as ^Tuncircumcised: three years shall it be as uncircumcised unto you: it shall not be eaten of.   *unclean*

24 But in the fourth year all the fruit thereof shall be holy to praise the LORD *withal*.

25 And in the fifth year shall ye eat of the fruit thereof, that it may yield unto you the increase thereof: I *am* the LORD your God.

26 Ye shall not eat *any thing* with the blood: neither shall ye use ^Tenchantment, nor ^Tobserve times.   *practise divination · soothsaying*

27 Ye shall not round the corners of your heads, neither shalt thou mar the corners of thy beard.

28 Ye shall not ^Rmake any cuttings in your flesh for the dead, nor print any marks upon you: I *am* the LORD.   1 Kin. 18:28; Jer. 16:6

29 ^RDo not prostitute thy daughter, to cause her to be a whore; lest the land fall to whoredom, and the land become full of wickedness.   21:9; Deut. 22:21; 23:17, 18

30 Ye shall ^Tkeep my sabbaths, and ^Rreverence my sanctuary: I *am* the LORD.   *observe · 26:2; Eccl. 5:1*

31 Regard not them that have familiar spirits, neither seek after ^Rwizards, to be defiled by them: I *am* the LORD your God.   1 Sam. 28:3

32 ᴿThou shalt rise up before the hoary head, and honour the face of the old man, and fear thy God: I *am* the LORD.   Prov. 23:22; 1 Tim. 5:1

33 And if a stranger sojourn with thee in your land, ye shall not ᵀvex him.   *mistreat*

34 *But* the stranger that dwelleth with you shall be unto you as one born among you, and thou shalt love him as thyself; for ye were strangers in the land of Egypt: I *am* the LORD your God.

35 Ye shall do no ᵀunrighteousness in judgment, in meteyard, in weight, or in measure.   *injustice*

36 ᴿJust balances, just weights, a just e′-phah, and a just hin, shall ye have: I *am* the LORD your God, which brought you out of the land of Egypt.   Deut. 25:13–15; Prov. 20:10

37 ᴿTherefore shall ye observe all my statutes, and all my judgments, and do them: I *am* the LORD.   18:4, 5; Deut. 4:5, 6; 5:1; 6:25

20 And the LORD spake unto Moses, saying,

2 Again, thou shalt say to the children of Israel, Whosoever *he be* of the children of Israel, or of the strangers that sojourn in Israel, that giveth *any* of his seed unto Mo′-lech; he shall surely be put to death: the people of the land shall stone him with stones.

3 And ᴿI will set my face against that man, and will ᵀcut him off from among his people; because he hath given of his seed unto Mo′-lech, to defile my sanctuary, and to profane my holy name.   17:10 · *put him to death*

4 And if the people of the land do any ways ᵀhide their eyes from the man, when he giveth of his seed unto Mo′-lech, and kill him not: *disregard*

5 Then I will set my face against that man, and against his family, and will cut him off, and all that go a whoring after him, to commit whoredom with Mo′-lech, from among their people.

6 And ᴿthe soul that turneth after such as have familiar spirits, and after wizards, to go a whoring after them, I will even set my face against that soul, and will cut him off from among his people.   19:31

7 ᴿSanctify yourselves therefore, and be ye holy: for I *am* the LORD your God.   19:2; Heb. 12:14

8 And ye shall keep my statutes, and do them: ᴿI *am* the LORD which sanctify you.   Ezek. 37:28

9 For every one that curseth his father or his mother shall be surely put to death: he hath cursed his father or his mother; ᴿhis blood *shall be* upon him.   2 Sam. 1:16

10 And the man that committeth adultery with *another* man's wife, *even he* that committeth adultery with his neighbour's wife, the adulterer and the adulteress shall surely be put to death.

11 And the man that lieth with his father's wife hath uncovered his father's nakedness: both of them shall surely be put to death; their blood *shall be* upon them.

12 And if a man lie with his ᴿdaughter in law, both of them shall surely be put to death: they have wrought confusion; their blood *shall be* upon them.   18:15

13 ᴿIf a man also lie with mankind, as he lieth with a woman, both of them have committed an abomination: they shall surely be put to death; their blood *shall be* upon them.   18:22; Deut. 23:17

14 And if a man take a wife and her ᴿmother, it *is* wickedness: they shall be burnt with fire, both he and they; that there be no wickedness among you.   18:17

15 And if a man lie with a beast, he shall surely be put to death: and ye shall slay the beast.

16 And if a woman approach unto any beast, and lie down thereto, thou shalt kill the woman, and the beast: they shall surely be put to death; their blood *shall be* upon them.

17 And if a man shall take his ᴿsister, his father's daughter, or his mother's daughter, and see her nakedness, and she see his nakedness; it *is* a wicked thing; and they shall be cut off in the sight of their people: he hath uncovered his sister's nakedness; he shall bear his iniquity.   18:9

18 ᴿAnd if a man shall lie with a woman having her sickness, and shall uncover her nakedness; he hath ᵀdiscovered her fountain, and she hath uncovered the fountain of her blood: and both of them shall be cut off from among their people.   18:19 · Lit. *made bare*

19 And thou shalt not uncover the nakedness of thy ᴿmother's sister, nor of thy father's sister: for he uncovereth his near kin: they shall bear their iniquity.   18:12, 13

20 And if a man shall lie with his ᴿuncle's wife, he hath uncovered his uncle's nakedness: they shall bear their sin; they shall die childless.   18:14

21 And if a man shall take his ᴿbrother's wife, it *is* an unclean thing: he hath uncovered his brother's nakedness; they shall be childless.   18:16; Matt. 14:3, 4

22 Ye shall therefore keep all my ᴿstatutes, and all my judgments, and do them: that the land, whither I bring you to dwell therein, spue you not out.   18:25–28

23 ᴿAnd ye shall not walk in the manners of the nation, which I cast out before you: for they committed all these things, and therefore I abhorred them.   18:3, 24

24 But ᴿI have said unto you, Ye shall inherit their land, and I will give it unto you to possess it, a land that floweth with milk and honey: I *am* the LORD your God, ᴿwhich have separated you from *other* people.   Ex. 3:17 · 20:26; Deut. 7:6

25 ᴿYe shall therefore put difference between clean beasts and unclean, and between unclean fowls and clean: and ye shall not make your souls abominable by beast, or by fowl, or by any manner of living thing that creepeth on the ground, which I have separated from you as unclean.   10:10

26 And ye shall be holy unto me: ᴿfor I the LORD *am* holy, and have severed you from *other* people, that ye should be mine.   1 Pet. 1:16

27 ᴿA man also or woman that hath a familiar spirit, or that is a wizard, shall surely be put to death: they shall stone them with stones: their blood *shall be* upon them.   19:31; 1 Sam. 28:9

21 And the LORD said unto Moses, Speak unto the priests the sons of Aaron, and say unto them, ᴿThere shall none be defiled for the dead among his people: 19:28; Ezek. 44:25

2 But for his kin, that is near unto him, *that is,* for his mother, and for his father, and for his son, and for his daughter, and for his brother,

3 And for his sister a virgin, that is nigh unto him, which hath had no husband; for her may he be defiled.

4 *But* he shall not defile himself, *being* a chief man among his people, to profane himself.

5 ᴿThey shall not make baldness upon their head, neither shall they shave off the corner of their beard, nor make any cuttings in their flesh.   19:27; Deut. 14:1

6 They shall be ᴿholy unto their God, and not profane the name of their God: for the offerings of the LORD made by fire, *and* the bread of their God, they do offer: therefore they shall be holy.   Ex. 22:31

7 ᴿThey shall not take a wife *that is* a whore, or profane; neither shall they take a woman put away from her husband: for he *is* holy unto his God.   Ezek. 44:22

8 Thou shalt sanctify him therefore; for he offereth the bread of thy God: he shall be holy unto thee: for ᴿI the LORD, which sanctify you, *am* holy.   11:44, 45

9 And the daughter of any priest, if she profane herself by playing the whore, she profaneth her father: she shall be ᴿburnt with fire.   Deut. 22:21

10 And *he that is* the high priest among his brethren, upon whose head the anointing oil was ᴿpoured, and that is consecrated

to put on the garments, shall not [R]uncover his head, nor rend his clothes;   8:12 · 10:6, 7

11 Neither shall he go in to any dead body, nor defile himself for his father, or for his mother;

12 Neither shall he go out of the sanctuary, nor profane the sanctuary of his God; for the crown of the anointing oil of his God *is* upon him: I *am* the LORD.

13 And he shall take a wife in her virginity.

14 A widow, or a divorced woman, or profane, *or* an harlot, these shall he not take: but he shall take a virgin of his own people to wife.

15 Neither shall he profane his seed among his people: for I the LORD do sanctify him.

16 And the LORD spake unto Moses, saying,

17 Speak unto Aaron, saying, Whosoever *he be* of thy seed in their generations that hath *any* [T]blemish, let him not approach to offer the bread of his God.   *defect*

18 For whatsoever man *he be* that hath a [R]blemish, he shall not approach: a blind man, or a lame, or he that hath a flat nose, or any thing [R]superfluous,   22:19–25 · 22:23

19 Or a man that is brokenfooted, or brokenhanded,

20 Or [T]crookbackt, or a dwarf, or that hath a blemish in his eye, or be scurvy, or scabbed, or hath his stones broken;   *hunchbacked*

21 No man that hath a blemish of the seed of Aaron the priest shall come nigh to offer the offerings of the LORD made by fire: he hath a blemish; he shall not come nigh to offer the bread of his God.

22 He shall eat the bread of his God, *both* of the most holy, and of the holy.

23 Only he shall not go [T]in unto the [R]vail, nor come nigh unto the altar, because he hath a blemish; that [R]he profane not my sanctuaries: for I the LORD do sanctify them.   *near to* · 16:2 · v. 12

24 And Moses told *it* unto

Aaron, and to his sons, and unto all the children of Israel.

22 And the LORD spake unto Moses, saying,

2 Speak unto Aaron and to his sons, that they separate themselves from the holy things of the children of Israel, and that they profane not my holy name *in those things* which they [R]hallow unto me: I *am* the LORD. Num. 18:32

3 Say unto them, Whosoever *he be* of all your seed among your generations, that goeth unto the holy things, which the children of Israel hallow unto the LORD, [R]having his uncleanness upon him, that soul shall be cut off from my presence: I *am* the LORD.   7:20

4 What man soever of the seed of Aaron *is* a leper, or hath a running issue; he shall not eat of the holy things, until he be clean. And whoso toucheth any thing *that is* unclean *by* the dead, or a man whose seed goeth from him;

5 Or whosoever toucheth any creeping thing, whereby he may be made unclean, or a man of whom he may take uncleanness, whatsoever uncleanness he hath;

6 The soul which hath touched any such shall be unclean until even, and shall not eat of the holy things, unless he [R]wash his flesh with water.   15:5

7 And when the sun is down, he shall be clean, and shall afterward eat of the holy things; because [R]it *is* his food.   Num. 18:11

8 [R]That which dieth of itself, or is torn *with beasts,* he shall not eat to defile himself therewith: I *am* the LORD.   Ex. 22:31; Ezek. 44:31

9 They shall therefore keep [R]mine [T]ordinance, [R]lest they bear sin for it, and die therefore, if they profane it: I the LORD do sanctify them.   18:30 · *charge* · v. 16; Num. 18:22

10 There shall no stranger eat *of* the holy thing: a sojourner of the priest, or an hired servant, shall not eat *of* the holy thing.

11 But if the priest [R]buy *any* soul with his money, he shall eat of it,

and he that is born in his house: they shall eat of his meat. Ex. 12:44

12 If the priest's daughter also be *married* unto a stranger, she may not eat of an offering of the holy things.

13 But if the priest's daughter be a widow, or divorced, and have no child, and is returned unto her father's house, as in her youth, she shall eat of her father's meat: but there shall no stranger eat thereof.

14 And if a man eat *of* the holy thing ᵀunwittingly, then he shall put the fifth *part* thereof unto it, and shall give *it* unto the priest with the holy thing.   *unintentionally*

15 And they shall not profane the ᴿholy things of the children of Israel, which they offer unto the LORD;   Num. 18:32

16 Or ᵀsuffer them to bear the ᵀiniquity of trespass, when they eat their holy things: for I the LORD do sanctify them.   *allow · guilt*

17 And the LORD spake unto Moses, saying,

18 Speak unto Aaron, and to his sons, and unto all the children of Israel, and say unto them, ᴿWhatsoever *he be* of the house of Israel, or of the strangers in Israel, that will offer his ᵀoblation for all his vows, and for all his freewill offerings, which they will offer unto the LORD for a burnt offering;   *1:2, 3, 10 · offering for any*

19 ᴿ*Ye shall offer* at your own will a male without blemish, of the beeves, of the sheep, or of the goats.   1:3; Deut. 15:21

20 ᴿ*But* whatsoever hath a blemish, *that* shall ye not offer: for it shall not be acceptable for you.   Mal. 1:8, 14; [Eph. 5:27; Heb. 9:14]

21 And whosoever offereth a sacrifice of peace offerings unto the LORD ᴿto accomplish *his* vow, or a freewill offering in beeves or sheep, it shall be perfect to be accepted; there shall be no blemish therein.   Num. 15:3, 8; Ps. 61:8; 65:1

22 Blind, or broken, or maimed, or having ᵀa wen, or scurvy, or scabbed, ye shall not offer these unto the LORD, nor make an offer-

ing by fire of them upon the altar unto the LORD. *an ulcer or running sore*

23 Either a bullock or a lamb that hath ᵀany thing superfluous or lacking in his parts, that mayest thou offer *for* a freewill offering; but for a vow it shall not be accepted.   *a limb too long or too short*

24 Ye shall not offer unto the LORD that which is bruised, or crushed, or broken, or cut; neither shall ye make *any offering thereof* in your land.

25 Neither from a stranger's hand shall ye offer the bread of your God of any of these; because their ᴿcorruption *is* in them, *and* blemishes *be* in them: they shall not be accepted for you.   Mal. 1:14

26 And the LORD spake unto Moses, saying,

27 ᴿWhen a bullock, or a sheep, or a goat, is brought forth, then it shall be seven days ᵀunder the dam; and from the eighth day and thenceforth it shall be accepted for an offering made by fire unto the LORD.   Ex. 22:30 · *with its mother*

28 And *whether it be* cow or ewe, ye shall not kill it ᴿand her young both in one day.   Deut. 22:6, 7

29 And when ye will offer a sacrifice of thanksgiving unto the LORD, offer *it* at your own will.

30 On the same day it shall be eaten up; ye shall leave none of it until the morrow: I *am* the LORD.

31 ᴿTherefore shall ye keep my commandments, and do them: I *am* the LORD.   Num. 15:40; Deut. 4:40

32 ᴿNeither shall ye profane my holy name; but ᴿI will be hallowed among the children of Israel: I *am* the LORD which hallow you,   18:21 · 10:3; Matt. 6:9; Luke 11:2

33 ᴿThat brought you out of the land of Egypt, to be your God: I *am* the LORD.   Num. 15:40; Deut. 4:40

23 And the LORD spake unto Moses, saying,

2 Speak unto the children of Israel, and say unto them, Concerning the feasts of the LORD, which ye shall proclaim *to be* ᴿholy convocations, *even* these *are* my feasts.   Ex. 12:16

3 ᴿSix days shall work be done: but the seventh day *is* the sabbath of rest, an holy convocation; ye shall do no work *therein:* it *is* the sabbath of the Lord in all your dwellings.　　　Ex. 20:9; Luke 13:14

4 ᴿThese *are* the feasts of the Lord, *even* holy convocations, which ye shall proclaim in their seasons.　　　Ex. 23:14–16

5 ᴿIn the fourteenth *day* of the first month at even *is* the Lord's passover.　　　Ex. 12:1–28; Josh. 5:10

6 And on the fifteenth day of the same month *is* the feast of unleavened bread unto the Lord: seven days ye must eat unleavened bread.

7 ᴿIn the first day ye shall have an holy convocation: ye shall do no servile work therein.　　　Ex. 12:16

8 But ye shall offer an offering made by fire unto the Lord seven days: in the seventh day *is* an holy convocation: ye shall do no servile work *therein.*

9 And the Lord spake unto Moses, saying,

10 Speak unto the children of Israel, and say unto them, When ye be come into the land which I give unto you, and shall reap the harvest thereof, then ye shall bring a sheaf of the firstfruits of your harvest unto the priest:

11 And he shall wave the sheaf before the Lord, to be accepted for you: on the morrow after the sabbath the priest shall wave it.

12 And ye shall offer that day when ye wave the sheaf an he lamb without blemish of the first year for a burnt offering unto the Lord.

13 And the meat offering thereof *shall be* two tenth deals of fine flour mingled with oil, an offering made by fire unto the Lord *for* a sweet savour: and the drink offering thereof *shall be* of wine, the fourth *part* of an hin.

14 And ye shall eat neither bread, nor parched corn, nor green ears, until the selfsame day that ye have brought an offering unto your God: *it shall be* a statute for ever throughout your generations in all your dwellings.

15 And ye shall count unto you from the morrow after the sabbath, from the day that ye brought the sheaf of the wave offering; seven sabbaths shall be complete:

16 Even unto the morrow after the seventh sabbath shall ye number ᴿfifty days; and ye shall offer ᴿa new meat offering unto the Lord.　　　Acts 2:1 · Num. 28:26

17 Ye shall bring out of your habitations two wave loaves of two tenth deals: they shall be of fine flour; they shall be baken with leaven; *they are* ᴿthe firstfruits unto the Lord.　　　Ex. 23:16, 19

18 And ye shall offer with the bread seven lambs without blemish of the first year, and one young bullock, and two rams: they shall be *for* a burnt offering unto the Lord, with their meat offering, and their drink offerings, *even* an offering made by fire, of sweet savour unto the Lord.

19 Then ye shall sacrifice one kid of the goats for a sin offering, and two lambs of the first year for a sacrifice of ᴿpeace offerings.　3:1

20 And the priest shall wave them with the bread of the firstfruits *for* a wave offering before the Lord, with the two lambs: ᴿthey shall be holy to the Lord for the priest.　14:13; Num. 18:12; Deut. 18:4

21 And ye shall proclaim on the selfsame day, *that* it may be an holy convocation unto you: ye shall do no servile work *therein: it shall be* a statute for ever in all your dwellings throughout your generations.

22 And ᴿwhen ye reap the harvest of your land, thou shalt not make clean riddance of the corners of thy field when thou reapest, neither shalt thou gather any gleaning of thy harvest: thou shalt leave them unto the poor, and to the stranger: I *am* the Lord your God.　Deut. 24:19–22; Ruth 2:2, 15

23 And the Lord spake unto Moses, saying,

24 Speak unto the children of Israel, saying, In the ^Rseventh month, in the first *day* of the month, shall ye have a sabbath, ^Ra memorial of blowing of trumpets, an holy convocation. Num. 29:1 · 25:9

25 Ye shall do no servile work *therein:* but ye shall offer an offering made by fire unto the LORD.

26 And the LORD spake unto Moses, saying,

27 ^RAlso on the tenth *day* of this seventh month *there shall be* a day of atonement: it shall be an holy convocation unto you; and ye shall afflict your souls, and offer an offering made by fire unto the LORD. 16:1–34; 25:9; Num. 29:7

28 And ye shall do no work in that same day: for it *is* a day of atonement, ^Rto make an atonement for you before the LORD your God. 16:34

29 For whatsoever soul *it be* that shall not be ^Rafflicted in that same day, he shall be cut off from among his people. Is. 22:12; Jer. 31:9

30 And whatsoever soul *it be* that doeth any work in that same day, ^Rthe same soul will I destroy from among his people. 20:3–6

31 Ye shall do no manner of work: *it shall be* a statute for ever throughout your generations in all your dwellings.

32 It *shall be* unto you a sabbath of rest, ^Tand ye shall afflict your souls: in the ninth *day* of the month at even, from even unto even, shall ye ^Tcelebrate your sabbath.　　*humble yourselves · observe*

33 And the LORD spake unto Moses, saying,

34 Speak unto the children of Israel, saying, ^RThe fifteenth day of this seventh month *shall be* the feast of tabernacles *for* seven days unto the LORD. Ezra 3:4; John 7:2

35 On the first day *shall be* an holy convocation: ye shall do no servile work *therein*.

36 Seven days ye shall offer an offering made by fire unto the LORD: on the eighth day shall be an holy convocation unto you;

and ye shall offer an offering made by fire unto the LORD: it *is* a solemn assembly; *and* ye shall do no servile work *therein*.

37 ^RThese *are* the feasts of the LORD, which ye shall proclaim *to be* holy convocations, to offer an offering made by fire unto the LORD, a burnt offering, and a meat offering, a sacrifice, and drink offerings, every thing upon his day:　　vv. 2, 4

38 ^RBeside the sabbaths of the LORD, and beside your gifts, and beside all your vows, and beside all your freewill offerings, which ye give unto the LORD. Num. 29:39

39 Also in the fifteenth day of the seventh month, when ye have gathered in the fruit of the land, ye shall keep a feast unto the LORD seven days: on the first day *shall be* a sabbath, and on the eighth day *shall be* a sabbath.

40 And ^Rye shall take you on the first day the ^Tboughs of goodly trees, branches of palm trees, and the boughs of thick trees, and willows of the brook; and ye shall rejoice before the LORD your God seven days. Neh. 8:15 · Lit. *fruit*

41 And ye shall keep it a feast unto the LORD seven days in the year. *It shall be* a statute for ever in your generations: ye shall celebrate it in the seventh month.

42 ^RYe shall dwell in booths seven days; all that are Israelites born shall dwell in booths: [Is. 4:6]

43 That your generations may know that I made the children of Israel to dwell in booths, when I brought them out of the land of Egypt: I *am* the LORD your God.

44 And Moses ^Rdeclared unto the children of Israel the feasts of the LORD.　　v. 2

24 And the LORD spake unto Moses, saying,

2 ^RCommand the children of Israel, that they bring unto thee pure oil olive beaten for the light, to cause the lamps to burn continually. Ex. 27:20, 21

3 ^TWithout the vail of the testimony, in the tabernacle of the

congregation, shall Aaron order it from the evening unto the morning before the LORD continually: *it shall be* a statute for ever in your generations.   *Outside*

4 He shall order the lamps upon ᴿthe pure candlestick before the LORD continually. Ex. 25:31; 31:8

5 And thou shalt take fine flour, and bake twelve ᴿcakes thereof: two tenth deals shall be in one cake.   Ex. 25:30; 39:36; 40:23

6 And thou shalt set them in two rows, six on a row, upon the pure table before the LORD.

7 And thou shalt put pure frankincense upon *each* row, that it may be on the bread for a ᴿmemorial, *even* an offering made by fire unto the LORD.   2:2, 9, 16

8 ᴿEvery sabbath he shall set it in order before the LORD continually, *being taken* from the children of Israel by an everlasting covenant. Num. 4:7; 1 Chr. 9:32; 2 Chr. 2:4

9 And ᴿit shall be Aaron's and his sons'; ᴿand they shall eat it in the holy place: for it *is* most holy unto him of the offerings of the LORD made by fire by a perpetual statute.   1 Sam. 21:6; Luke 6:4 · Ex. 29:33

10 And the son of an Israelitish woman, whose father *was* an Egyptian, went out among the children of Israel: and this son of the Israelitish *woman* and a man of Israel ᵀstrove together in the camp;   *fought*

11 And the Israelitish woman's son ᴿblasphemed the name *of the* LORD, and cursed. And they ᴿbrought him unto Moses: (and his mother's name *was* Shel'-o-mith, the daughter of Dib'-ri, of the tribe of Dan:) Ex. 22:28 · Ex. 18:22

12 And they put him ᵀin ward, that the mind of the LORD might be shewed them.   *under guard*

13 And the LORD spake unto Moses, saying,

14 Bring forth him that hath cursed without the camp; and let all that heard *him* ᴿlay their hands upon his head, and let all the congregation stone him. Deut. 13:9; 17:7

15 And thou shalt speak unto the children of Israel, saying, Whosoever curseth his God ᴿshall bear his sin.   20:17; Num. 9:13

16 And he that blasphemeth the name of the LORD, he shall surely be put to death, *and* all the congregation shall certainly stone him: as well the stranger, as he that is born in the land, when he blasphemeth the name *of the* LORD, shall be put to death.

17 And he that killeth any man shall surely be put to death.

18 ᴿAnd he that killeth a beast shall make it good; beast for beast.   v. 21

19 And if a man cause a blemish in his neighbour; as he hath done, so shall it be done to him;

20 Breach for breach, eye for eye, tooth for tooth: as he hath caused a blemish in a man, so shall it be done to him *again.*

21 And he that killeth a beast, he shall restore it: and he that killeth a man, he shall be put to death.

22 Ye shall have ᴿone manner of law, as well for the stranger, as for one of your own country: for I *am* the LORD your God.   Num. 9:14; 15:15

23 And Moses spake to the children of Israel, that they should bring forth him that had cursed out of the camp, and stone him with stones. And the children of Israel did as the LORD commanded Moses.

25 And the LORD spake unto Moses in mount ᴿSi'-nai, saying,   26:46

2 Speak unto the children of Israel, and say unto them, When ye come into the land which I give you, then shall the land ᴿkeep a sabbath unto the LORD.   26:34, 35

3 Six years thou shalt sow thy field, and six years thou shalt prune thy vineyard, and gather in the fruit thereof;

4 But in the seventh year shall be a sabbath of ᴿrest unto the land, a sabbath for the LORD: thou shalt neither sow thy field, nor prune thy vineyard.   [Heb. 4:9]

5 That which groweth of its

own accord of thy harvest thou shalt not reap, neither gather the grapes of thy vine undressed: *for* it is a year of rest unto the land.

6 And the sabbath of the land shall be meat for you; for thee, and for thy servant, and for thy maid, and for thy hired servant, and for thy stranger that sojourneth with thee,

7 And for thy cattle, and for the beast that *are* in thy land, shall all the increase thereof be meat.

8 And thou shalt number seven sabbaths of years unto thee, seven times seven years; and the space of the seven sabbaths of years shall be unto thee forty and nine years.

9 Then shalt thou cause the trumpet of the jubile to sound on the tenth *day* of the seventh month, [R]in the day of atonement shall ye make the trumpet sound throughout all your land.　23:24, 27

10 And ye shall hallow the fiftieth year, and [R]proclaim liberty throughout *all* the land unto all the inhabitants thereof: it shall be a jubile unto you; and ye shall return every man unto his possession, and ye shall return every man unto his family.　Is. 61:2; 63:4

11 A jubile shall that fiftieth year be unto you: [R]ye shall not sow, neither reap that which groweth of itself in it, nor gather *the grapes* in it of thy vine undressed.　v. 5

12 For it *is* the jubile; it shall be holy unto you: ye shall eat the increase thereof out of the field.

13 [R]In the year of this jubile ye shall return every man unto his possession.　v. 10; 27:24; Num. 36:4

14 And if thou sell ought unto thy neighbour, or buyest *ought* of thy neighbour's hand, ye shall not [R]oppress one another:　19:13

15 According to the number of years after the jubile thou shalt buy of thy neighbour, *and* according to the number of years of the fruits he shall sell unto thee:

16 According to the multitude of years thou shalt increase the price thereof, and according to the few-

ness of years thou shalt diminish the price of it: for *according* to the number *of the years* of the fruits doth he sell unto thee.

17 [R]Ye shall not therefore oppress one another; but thou shalt fear thy God: for I *am* the LORD your God.　Prov. 14:31; 1 Thess. 4:6

18 [R]Wherefore ye shall do my statutes, and keep my judgments, and do them; [R]and ye shall dwell in the land in safety.　19:37 · Ps. 4:8

19 And the land shall yield her fruit, and [R]ye shall eat your fill, and dwell therein in safety.　26:5

20 And if ye shall say, What shall we eat the seventh year? behold, [R]we shall not sow, nor gather in our increase:　vv. 4, 5

21 Then I will [R]command my blessing upon you in the [R]sixth year, and it shall bring forth fruit for three years.　Deut. 28:8 · Ex. 16:29

22 [R]And ye shall sow the eighth year, and eat *yet* of [R]old fruit until the ninth year; until her fruits come in ye shall eat *of* the old *store*.　2 Kin. 19:29 · 26:10; Josh. 5:11

23 The land shall not be sold for ever: for the land *is* mine; for ye *are* [R]strangers and sojourners with me.　Ps. 39:12; Heb. 11:13; 1 Pet. 2:11

24 And in all the land of your possession ye shall grant a redemption for the land.

25 [R]If thy brother be waxen poor, and hath sold away *some* of his possession, and if [R]any of his kin come to redeem it, then shall he redeem that which his brother sold. Ruth 2:20 · Ruth 3:2, 9, 12; [Job 19:25]

26 And if the man have none to redeem it, and himself be able to redeem it;

27 Then [R]let him count the years of the sale thereof, and restore the overplus unto the man to whom he sold it; that he may return unto his possession.　vv. 50–52

28 But if he be not able to restore *it* to him, then that which is sold shall remain in the hand of him that hath bought it until the year of jubile: [R]and in the jubile it shall go out, and he shall return unto his possession.　vv. 10, 13

WHERE WAS THE GARDEN OF EDEN?

The Garden of Eden

The garden God planted in Eden was a model of what God wanted the whole world to be like. It was the most beautiful nature park you could ever imagine. Adam and Eve lived happily there with God as their personal Friend.

In the world that God planned, there would be no disease and no death. We often think sickness and dying are just natural. But those things were not part of life until Adam and Eve sinned.

Hatred and wars would not exist in the world as God made it. Instead of trying to be better than others, we would always be helping one another. Work would always be fun, not hard labor. The wild animals would be as gentle as our favorite pets because they would never need to fear us. Weeds would not grow in our fields, and there would be no hunger. Yes, living in the world God planned would be like days of heaven on earth.

Adam and Eve, however, disobeyed God and ate fruit from the Tree of the Knowledge of Good and Evil. God had told Adam and Eve to obey Him. If they didn't obey Him, they would die. Sickness, death, and all unhappiness in the world came because Adam and Eve decided to follow their own ideas rather than God's. That's how sin began.

1 Cush (Gen. 2:13) is generally identified as Ethiopia (see 2 Chr. 14:12).

2 Pison and Gihon (Gen. 2:11, 12) have not been identified, but some believe they refer to the Blue Nile and White Nile.

3 The Hiddekel (or Tigris) and the Euphrates (Gen. 2:14) were the main rivers flowing through what later became Assyria and Babylonia.

4 Havilah (Gen. 2:11) may refer to a region at the southern end of the Red Sea, either in Africa or Arabia, associated with Cush (compare Gen. 10:7).

ASIA MINOR

Euphrates

Tigris

Babylon

Jerusalem

Ur

EGYPT

Arabian Desert

Nile River

CUSH

Red Sea

SHEBA

Gulf of Aden

HAVILAH

0   300   600
Miles

N

© 1996 Thomas Nelson, Inc.

HOW OLD WERE THE PATRIARCHS?

ADAM 930 years (Gen. 5:5)

SETH 912 years (Gen. 5:8)

ENOS 905 years (Gen. 5:11)

ENOCH 365 years (Gen. 5:23)

METHUSELAH 969 years (Gen. 5:27)

LAMECH 777 years (Gen. 5:31)

NOAH 950 years (Gen. 9:29)

The Flood ⊚⊚⊚⊚⊚⊚⊚⊚⊚⊚⊚⊚⊚⊚⊚⊚ *The Flood*

SHEM 600 years (Gen. 11:10, 11)

EBER 464 years (Gen. 11:16, 17)

TERAH 205 years (Gen. 11:32)

ABRAHAM 175 years (Gen. 25:7)

ISAAC 180 years (Gen. 35:28)

JACOB 147 years (Gen. 47:28)

JOSEPH 110 years (Gen. 50:26)

The patriarchs who lived before the Flood had an average lifespan of about 900 years (Genesis 5). The ages of post-Flood patriarchs dropped rapidly and gradually leveled off (Genesis 11). Some suggest that this was because of major environmental changes brought about by the Flood.

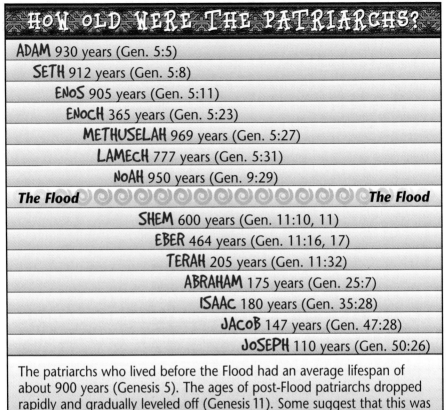

THE FAMILY OF ADAM AND EVE

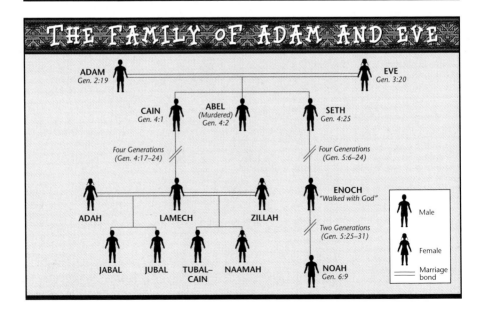

ADAM
Gen. 2:19

EVE
Gen. 3:20

CAIN
Gen. 4:1

ABEL
(Murdered)
Gen. 4:2

SETH
Gen. 4:25

Four Generations
(Gen. 4:17–24)

Four Generations
(Gen. 5:6–24)

ADAH

LAMECH

ZILLAH

ENOCH
"Walked with God"

Male

JABAL   JUBAL   TUBAL–CAIN   NAAMAH

Two Generations
(Gen. 5:25–31)

Female

NOAH
Gen. 6:9

Marriage bond

THE FAMILY OF NOAH

NOAH
Gen. 6:9

NOAH'S WIFE

SHEM
Gen. 9:18

HAM
Gen. 9:18

JAPHETH
Gen. 9:18

ARPHAXAD

CANAAN

Six Generations
(Gen. 11:14–25)

PHUT

TERAH

MIZRAIM

CUSH

ABRAM
Gen. 12:1

NIMROD
Gen. 10:8

The Canaanites
(Gen. 10:15–18)

🧍	Male
🧍	Female
—	Marriage bond

The Philistines
(Gen. 10:13)

Babylonians and Assyrians
(Gen. 10:10–11)

The coastland peoples of the Gentiles
(Gen. 10:5)

THE GREAT FLOOD

Genesis 7:1–24 describes the great Flood God sent to cover the earth.

Some people wonder if the flood really happened, but we have lots of proof that it did. Many other peoples of the world, even the Eskimos, also tell us about the ancient Flood.

Some people wonder if the Flood covered the whole world. The Bible says all the high mountains in Noah's area were covered. If the water was that high, it would have covered everything everywhere.

God told Noah to build a boat called an ark to float on top of the water. It was designed to carry Noah, his family, and two of every kind of animal God wanted to save. The ark was 450 feet long, almost as long as a city block, and 45 feet high, as tall as a five-story building.

The Flood lasted for a total of 371 days, including the time it took the waters to go down. The floodwaters came from great underground springs as well as from rain.

THE TOWER OF BABEL

Ancient peoples often built towers like the one Genesis calls the Tower of Babel. You can still see the remains of some of these towers today. Such a tower is called a ziggurat.

At the time of the Tower of Babel, after the great Flood, there was one race of people on the earth, and they all spoke the same language. Remember that these people still did not know much about astronomy (the study of the stars and other matter in space). This is why they foolishly imagined they could build a tower all the way up to the heavens.

Also, the people of Babel were sinners just like people today, and they wanted to test God's right to rule over their lives. The Tower of Babel was their way of telling God they could be just as high as He is! Sounds silly, doesn't it?

But people today still try to test God's right to rule their lives. When they break God's laws, they are telling Him, "I can do as I please!" Trying to rule our own lives is as foolish as trying to build a tower to heaven.

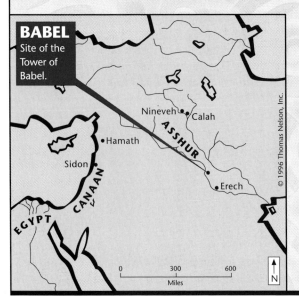

BABEL
Site of the Tower of Babel.

Nineveh • • Calah

ASSHUR

• Hamath

Sidon

CANAAN

• Erech

EGYPT

© 1996 Thomas Nelson, Inc.

0   300   600
Miles

N

THE OLD TESTAMENT WORLD

Abram is about to make a very long trip. Where is Abram when God tells him to move? (Genesis 11:31) Where does God tell him to go? (Genesis 11:31) Why? (Genesis 12:2, 3)

Abram is not alone on this trip. Who goes with him? (Genesis 12:5) Bible travelers either walked or rode camels or donkeys. Can you see the great cloud of dust stirred up by the footsteps and hoofprints as the wanderers journey northward?

The people stop first at Abram's family home. (Genesis 11:31) You will see that they do not take a shortcut across the desert. Instead, they follow the Euphrates River, which provides water for their families and flocks.

When they reach Canaan, the land God has promised them, they stop at Shechem (Genesis 12:6), Bethel, and Ai (Genesis 12:8). Find these cities on the map. What does Abram do here that pleases God?

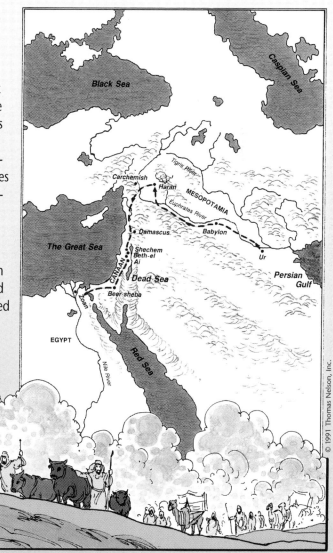

Black Sea

Caspian Sea

Tigris River

Carchemish

Haran

MESOPOTAMIA

Euphrates River

Damascus

Babylon

The Great Sea

Shechem
Beth-el
Ai

CANAAN

Dead Sea

Ur

Persian Gulf

Beer-sheba

Zoan

EGYPT

Nile River

Red Sea

© 1991 Thomas Nelson, Inc.

THE GEOGRAPHY OF CANAAN

The land of Canaan in which Lot and Abraham settled (Genesis 13:10–12) was small but had many different landscapes.

1 Dead Sea: Lowest point on earth at 1,300 feet below sea level; features several inlets but no outlets, thus resulting in increasingly salty water due to heavy evaporation, but also potentially one of the richest mineral deposits in the world.

2 Mount Carmel: A spectacular high ridge of land that juts out into the Mediterranean Sea. It had many trees in Bible times.

3 Galilee: An upland area of forests and farmland; Upper Galilee, at 3,000 feet above sea level, had many trees and few people, even in New Testament times; Lower Galilee was less hilly and enjoyed a milder climate.

4 Valley of Jezreel: A rich agricultural district and major passageway through the rugged Palestinian hills; as a crossroads for major east-west and north-south routes, Jezreel was the site of numerous battles.

5 Jordan River: Flows swiftly through the Rift Valley south to the Dead Sea; in Old Testament days, lions lived along its banks; Lot settled on the east bank, which was said to be remarkably fertile, "well watered every where...even as the garden of the LORD" (Gen. 13:10).

6 Sea of Chinnereth (Sea of Galilee): Meaning "harp-shaped," a freshwater lake fed by the Jordan River, surrounded by steep cliffs and sharply rising mountains; site of a thriving fishing industry, and thus supported a sizable population along its coast.

7 The Negev: Meaning "dry or parched," the wilderness area of southern Canaan connecting the region with Egypt to the west; known for its copper deposits.

8 The Arabah: Meaning "plain" or "desert," a hot, arid region stretching south from the Dead Sea to the Red Sea; probable site of Sodom and Gomorrah.

Gilead: A mountainous region with lots of plants and trees. It was a favorite hiding place for fugitives (people in hiding); the source for the "balm of Gilead," a sweet-smelling plant sap used as medicine.

N

GOD'S GREAT PROMISE

Sometimes you may make promises you don't keep. But God can never break any of His promises.

People who have lived a long time in the world learn that God keeps every promise He ever made. He promises us, "I will never leave thee nor forsake thee." Friends fail us. Our bodies get sick. And someday we will die. But we can still say, "Surely goodness and mercy shall follow me all the days of my life: and I will dwell in the house of the LORD for ever" (Psalm 23:6).

God made a very big promise to Abraham. First, God said He would give Abraham's people all the land of Palestine. Abraham's people still live there four thousand years later! That's the longest time any nation has lived anywhere.

Then God made a great promise that all people who trusted in Abraham's "Seed" would be blessed. The "Seed" of Abraham is Jesus who was born two thousand years after Abraham lived. So God will bless you forever if you trust in Jesus.

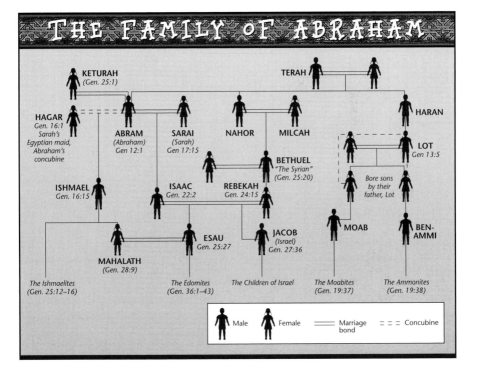

THE FAMILY OF ABRAHAM

KETURAH (Gen. 25:1)

TERAH

HARAN

HAGAR Gen. 16:1 Sarah's Egyptian maid, Abraham's concubine

ABRAM (Abraham) Gen 12:1

SARAI (Sarah) Gen 17:15

NAHOR

MILCAH

LOT Gen 13:5

BETHUEL "The Syrian" (Gen. 25:20)

ISHMAEL Gen. 16:15

ISAAC Gen. 22:2

REBEKAH Gen. 24:15

Bore sons by their father, Lot

MAHALATH (Gen. 28:9)

ESAU Gen. 25:27

JACOB (Israel) Gen. 27:36

MOAB

BEN-AMMI

The Ishmaelites (Gen. 25:12–16)

The Edomites (Gen. 36:1–43)

The Children of Israel

The Moabites (Gen. 19:37)

The Ammonites (Gen. 19:38)

Male   Female   Marriage bond   Concubine

JACOB BECOMES ISRAEL

The laws of some countries state that God has given people certain rights that should not be taken from them. As the oldest son in Isaac's family, Esau had rights to the largest share of his father's things. But he sold his rights to his younger brother Jacob for just a pot of stew!

When Jacob also tricked his father, Isaac, into giving him Esau's blessing—the blessing intended by Isaac to be for his oldest son—Esau was very angry and threatened to kill his brother. Jacob ran away to his uncle Laban in a far country. On the way, he promised his life to the Lord if He would bring him home again.

When Jacob is almost home after leaving his uncle's household (where he had lived for many years), God comes to Jacob and asks him to keep his promise and give Him his life.

Jacob struggles with God all night. In the morning, Jacob is worn out, and he has to give up. Then God gives Jacob a new name because now Jacob will be God's man. Jacob's new name is Israel and means "Prince with God."

THE FAMILY OF JACOB

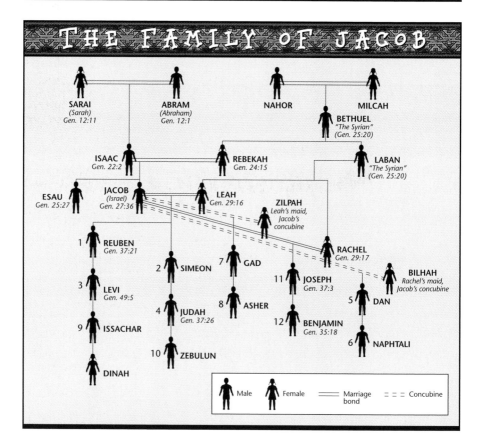

SARAI
(Sarah)
Gen. 12:11

ABRAM
(Abraham)
Gen. 12:1

NAHOR

MILCAH

BETHUEL
"The Syrian"
(Gen. 25:20)

ISAAC
Gen. 22:2

REBEKAH
Gen. 24:15

LABAN
"The Syrian"
(Gen. 25:20)

ESAU
Gen. 25:27

JACOB
(Israel)
Gen. 27:36

LEAH
Gen. 29:16

ZILPAH
Leah's maid,
Jacob's
concubine

RACHEL
Gen. 29:17

BILHAH
Rachel's maid,
Jacob's concubine

1 REUBEN
Gen. 37:21

2 SIMEON

7 GAD

11 JOSEPH
Gen. 37:3

3 LEVI
Gen. 49:5

8 ASHER

5 DAN

9 ISSACHAR

4 JUDAH
Gen. 37:26

12 BENJAMIN
Gen. 35:18

6 NAPHTALI

10 ZEBULUN

DINAH

| Male | Female | Marriage bond | Concubine |

29 And if a man sell a dwelling house in a walled city, then he may redeem it within a whole year after it is sold; *within* a full year may he redeem it.

30 And if it be not redeemed within the space of a full year, then the house that *is* in the walled city shall be established for ever to him that bought it throughout his generations: it shall not go out in the jubile.

31 But the houses of the villages which have no wall round about them shall be counted as the fields of the country: they may be redeemed, and they shall go out in the jubile.

32 Notwithstanding the cities of the Levites, *and* the houses of the cities of their possession, may the Levites redeem at any time.

33 And if a man purchase of the Levites, then the house that was sold, and the city of his possession, shall go out in *the year of* jubile: for the houses of the cities of the Levites *are* their possession among the children of Israel.

34 But ᴿthe field of the suburbs of their cities may not be ᴿsold; for it *is* their perpetual possession.   Num. 35:2-5 · Acts 4:36, 37

35 And if thy brother be waxen poor, and fallen in decay with thee; then thou shalt ᴿrelieve him: *yea, though he be* a stranger, or a sojourner; that he may live with thee.   Deut. 15:7-11; Luke 6:35; 1 John 3:17

36 Take thou no usury of him, or increase: but fear thy God; that thy brother may live with thee.

37 Thou shalt not give him thy money upon usury, nor lend him thy victuals for increase.

38 ᴿI *am* the LORD your God, which brought you forth out of the land of Egypt, to give you the land of Canaan, *and* to be your God.   11:45; 22:32, 33

39 And if thy brother *that dwelleth* by thee be waxen poor, and be sold unto thee; thou shalt not compel him to serve as a bondservant:

40 *But* as an hired servant, *and* as a sojourner, he shall be with thee, *and* shall serve thee unto the year of jubile:

41 And *then* shall he depart from thee, *both* he and his children ᴿwith him, and shall return unto his own family, and unto the possession of his fathers shall he return.   Ex. 21:3

42 For they *are* ᴿmy servants, which I brought forth out of the land of Egypt: they shall not be sold as bondmen.   v. 55; [Rom. 6:22]

43 ᴿThou shalt not rule over him with rigour; but ᴿshalt fear thy God.   Eph. 6:9; Col. 4:1 · Ex. 1:17; Mal. 3:5

44 Both thy bondmen, and thy bondmaids, which thou shalt have, *shall be* of the heathen that are round about you; of them shall ye buy bondmen and bondmaids.

45 Moreover of ᴿthe children of the strangers that do sojourn among you, of them shall ye buy, and of their families that *are* with you, which they begat in your land: and they shall be your possession.   [Is. 56:3, 6, 7]

46 And ye shall take them as an inheritance for your children after you, to inherit *them for* a possession; they shall be your bondmen for ever: but over your brethren the children of Israel, ye shall not rule one over another with rigour.

47 And if a sojourner or stranger wax rich by thee, and thy brother *that dwelleth* by him wax poor, and sell himself unto the stranger *or* sojourner by thee, or to the stock of the stranger's family:

48 After that he is sold he may be redeemed again; one of his brethren may redeem him:

49 Either his uncle, or his uncle's son, may redeem him, or *any* that is nigh of kin unto him of his family may redeem him; or if he be able, he may redeem himself.

50 And he shall reckon with him that bought him from the year that he was sold to him unto the year of jubile: and the price of his sale shall be according unto the number of years, ᴿaccording to

the time of an hired servant shall it be with him.   Job 7:1; Is. 16:14

51 If *there be* yet many years *behind*, according unto them he shall give again the price of his redemption out of the money that he was bought for.

52 And if there remain but few years unto the year of jubile, then he shall count with him, *and* according unto his years shall he give him again the price of his redemption.

53 *And* as a yearly hired servant shall he be with him: *and the other* shall not rule with rigour over him in thy sight.

54 And if he be not redeemed in these *years*, then he shall go out in the year of jubile, *both* he, and his children with him.

55 For unto me the children of Israel *are* servants; they *are* my servants whom I brought forth out of the land of Egypt: I *am* the LORD your God.

26 Ye shall make you ᴿno idols nor graven image, neither rear you up a standing image, neither shall ye set up *any* image of stone in your land, to bow down unto it: for I *am* the LORD your God.   Ex. 20:4, 5; Deut. 5:8

2 ᴿYe shall ᵀkeep my sabbaths, and reverence my sanctuary: I *am* the LORD.   19:30 · *observe*

3 ᴿIf ye walk in my statutes, and keep my commandments, and ᵀdo them;   Deut. 28:1–14 · *perform*

4 Then I will give you rain in due season, and the land shall yield her increase, and the trees of the field shall yield their fruit.

5 ᴿAnd your threshing shall reach unto the vintage, and the vintage shall reach unto the sowing time: and ye shall eat your bread to the full, and dwell in your land safely.   Deut. 11:15; Joel 2:19, 26

6 And I will give peace in the land, and ye shall lie down, and none shall make *you* afraid: and I will rid evil beasts out of the land, neither shall ᴿthe sword go through your land.   Ezek. 14:17

7 And ye shall chase your ene-mies, and they shall fall before you by the sword.

8 And ᴿfive of you shall chase an hundred, and an hundred of you shall put ten thousand to flight: and your enemies shall fall before you by the sword. Deut. 32:30

9 For I will have respect unto you, and ᴿmake you fruitful, and multiply you, and establish my covenant with you.   Ps. 107:38

10 And ye shall eat ᴿold store, and bring forth the old because of the new.   25:22

11 ᴿAnd I will set my tabernacle among you: and my soul shall not abhor you. Josh. 22:19; Ps. 76:2; Rev. 21:3

12 ᴿAnd I will walk among you, and will be your God, and ye shall be my people.   Deut. 23:14; [2 Cor. 6:16]

13 I *am* the LORD your God, which brought you forth out of the land of Egypt, that ye should not be their bondmen; and I have broken the bands of your yoke, and made you go upright.

14 But if ye will not hearken unto me, and will not do all these commandments;

15 And if ye shall despise my statutes, or if your soul abhor my judgments, so that ye will not do all my commandments, *but* that ye break my covenant:

16 I also will do this unto you; I will even appoint over you terror, consumption, and the ᵀburning ague, that shall consume the eyes, and cause sorrow of heart: and ye shall sow your seed in vain, for your enemies shall eat it.   *fever*

17 And I will set my face against you, and ye shall be slain before your enemies: they that hate you shall reign over you; and ye shall flee when none pursueth you.

18 And if ye will not yet for all this ᵀhearken unto me, then I will punish you ᴿseven times more for your sins.   *obey me* · 1 Sam. 2:5

19 And I will ᴿbreak the pride of your power; and I ᴿwill make your heaven as iron, and your earth as brass: Is. 25:11 · Deut. 28:23

20 And your ᴿstrength shall be spent in vain: for your ᴿland shall

not yield her increase, neither
shall the trees of the land yield
their fruits.   Is. 17:10, 11 · Deut. 11:17
21 And if ye walk contrary unto
me, and will not hearken unto me;
I will bring seven times more
plagues upon you according to
your sins.
22 ᴿI will also send wild beasts
among you, which shall rob you
of your children, and destroy your
cattle, and make you few in number; and ᴿyour *high* ways shall be
desolate.   Ezek. 14:21 · 2 Chr. 15:5
23 And if ye will not be re-
formed by me by these things, but
will walk contrary unto me;
24 Then will I also walk contrary unto you, and will punish
you yet seven times for your sins.
25 And ᴿI will bring a sword
upon you, that shall avenge the
quarrel of *my* covenant: and when
ye are gathered together within
your cities, ᴿI will send the pestilence among you; and ye shall be
delivered into the hand of the
enemy.   Ezek. 5:17 · 2 Sam. 24:15
26 *And* when I have broken the
staff of your bread, ten women
shall bake your bread in one
oven, and they shall deliver *you*
your bread again by weight: and
ye shall eat, and not be satisfied.
27 And if ye will not for all this
hearken unto me, but walk contrary unto me;
28 Then I will walk contrary
unto you also in fury; and I, even
I, will chastise you seven times for
your sins.
29 ᴿAnd ye shall eat the flesh of
your sons, and the flesh of your
daughters shall ye eat.   Deut. 28:53
30 And ᴿI will destroy your high
places, and cut down your images, and cast your carcases upon
the carcases of your idols, and my
soul shall abhor you.   2 Chr. 34:3
31 And I will make your cities
waste, and ᴿbring your sanctuaries unto desolation, and I will not
ᴿsmell the savour of your sweet
odours.   2 Chr. 36:19; Ps. 74:7 · Is. 1:11–15
32 ᴿAnd I will bring the land
into desolation: and your enemies

which dwell therein shall be
astonished at it.   Jer. 9:11; 18:16
33 And ᴿI will scatter you
among the heathen, and will draw
out a sword after you: and your
land shall be desolate, and your
cities waste.   Ps. 44:11; Zech. 7:14
34 Then shall the land enjoy her
sabbaths, as long as it lieth desolate, and ye *be* in your enemies'
land; *even* then shall the land rest,
and enjoy her sabbaths.
35 As long as it lieth desolate it
shall rest; because it did not rest
in your ᴿsabbaths, when ye dwelt
upon it.   25:2
36 And upon them that are left
alive of you I will send a ᴿfaint-
ness into their hearts in the lands
of their enemies; and the sound of
a shaken leaf shall chase them;
and they shall flee, as fleeing from
a sword; and they shall fall when
none pursueth.   Is. 30:17; Lam. 1:3, 6
37 And they shall fall one upon
another, as it were before a sword,
when none pursueth: and ᴿye
shall have no power to stand before your enemies.   Josh. 7:12, 13
38 And ye shall ᴿperish among
the heathen, and the land of your
enemies shall eat you up. Deut. 4:26
39 And they that are left of you
shall pine away in their iniquity in
your enemies' lands; and also in
the iniquities of their fathers shall
they pine away with them.
40 ᴿIf they shall confess their
iniquity, and the iniquity of their
fathers, with their trespass which
they trespassed against me, and
that also they have walked contrary unto me;   Luke 15:18; [1 John 1:9]
41 And *that* I also have walked
contrary unto them, and have
brought them into the land of
their enemies; if then their ᴿun-
circumcised hearts be humbled,
and they then accept of the punishment of their iniquity: Acts 7:51
42 Then will I ᴿremember my
covenant with Jacob, and also my
covenant with Isaac, and also my
covenant with Abraham will I
remember; and I will ᴿremember
the land. Ex. 2:24; Ezek. 16:60 · Ps. 136:23

43 [R]The land also shall be left of them, and shall enjoy her sabbaths, while she lieth desolate without them: and they shall accept of the punishment of their iniquity: because, even because they [R]despised my judgments, and because their soul abhorred my statutes.　　26:34, 35 · 26:15

44 And yet for all that, when they be in the land of their enemies, [R]I will not cast them away, neither will I abhor them, to destroy them utterly, and to break my covenant with them: for I *am* the LORD their God.　　[Rom. 11:1–36]

45 But I will for their sakes remember the covenant of their ancestors, [R]whom I brought forth out of the land of Egypt in the sight of the heathen, that I might be their God: I *am* the LORD.　　22:33

46 [R]These *are* the statutes and judgments and laws, which the LORD made between him and the children of Israel in mount Si'-nai by the hand of Moses.　　27:34

27 And the LORD spake unto Moses, saying,

2 Speak unto the children of Israel, and say unto them, When a man shall make a [T]singular vow, the persons *shall be* for the LORD by thy estimation.　　*extraordinary*

3 And thy estimation shall be of the male from twenty years old even unto sixty years old, even thy estimation shall be fifty shek'-els of silver, [R]after the shek'-el of the sanctuary.　　Ex. 30:13; Num. 3:47

4 And if it *be* a female, then thy estimation shall be thirty shek'-els.

5 And if *it be* from five years old even unto twenty years old, then thy estimation shall be of the male twenty shek'-els, and for the female ten shek'-els.

6 And if *it be* from a month old even unto five years old, then thy estimation shall be of the male five shek'-els of silver, and for the female thy estimation *shall be* three shek'-els of silver.

7 And if *it be* from sixty years old and above; if *it be* a male, then thy estimation shall be fifteen shek'-els, and for the female ten shek'-els.

8 But if he be poorer than thy estimation, then he shall present himself before the priest, and the priest shall value [R]him; according to his ability that vowed shall the priest value him.　　5:11; 14:21–24

9 And if *it be* a beast, whereof men bring an offering unto the LORD, all that *any man* giveth of such unto the LORD shall be holy.

10 He shall not alter it, nor change it, a good for a bad, or a bad for a good: and if he shall at all change beast for beast, then it and the exchange thereof shall be [R]holy.　　v. 33

11 And if *it be* any unclean beast, of which they do not offer a sacrifice unto the LORD, then he shall present the beast before the priest:

12 And the priest shall value it, whether it be good or bad: as thou valuest it, *who art* the priest, so shall it be.

13 [R]But if he will at all redeem it, then he shall add a fifth *part* thereof unto thy estimation.　　22:14

14 And when a man shall [T]sanctify his house *to be* holy unto the LORD, then the priest shall estimate it, whether it be good or bad: as the priest shall estimate it, so shall it stand.　　*set apart*

15 And if he that sanctified it will [T]redeem his house, then he shall add the fifth *part* of the money of thy estimation unto it, and it shall be his.　　*buy back*

16 And if a man shall [T]sanctify unto the LORD *some part* of a field of his possession, then thy estimation shall be according to the seed thereof: an ho'-mer of barley seed *shall be valued* at fifty shek'-els of silver.　　*set apart*

17 If he sanctify his field from the year of jubile, according to thy estimation it shall stand.

18 But if he sanctify his field after the jubile, then the priest shall [R]reckon unto him the money according to the years that remain, even unto the year of the

jubile, and it shall be ᵀabated from thy estimation. 25:15, 16, 28 · *deducted*

19 And if he that sanctified the field will in any wise redeem it, then he shall add the fifth *part* of the money of thy estimation unto it, and it shall be assured to him.

20 And if he will not redeem the field, or if he have sold the field to another man, it shall not be redeemed any more.

21 But the field, ᴿwhen it goeth out in the jubile, shall be holy unto the LORD, as a field devoted; ᴿthe possession thereof shall be the priest's. 25:10, 28, 31 · Ezek. 44:29

22 And if *a man* sanctify unto the LORD a field which he hath bought, which *is* not of the fields of ᴿhis possession; 25:10, 25

23 Then the priest shall reckon unto him the worth of thy estimation, *even* unto the year of the jubile: and he shall give thine estimation in that day, *as* a holy thing unto the LORD.

24 ᴿIn the year of the jubile the field shall return unto him of whom it was bought, *even* to him to whom the possession of the land *did belong.* 25:10–13, 28

25 And all thy estimations shall be according to the shek'-el of the sanctuary: ᴿtwenty ge'-rahs shall be the shek'-el. Ex. 30:13; Num. 3:47

26 Only the ᴿfirstling of the beasts, which should be the LORD'S firstling, no man shall sanctify it; whether *it be* ox, or sheep: it *is* the LORD'S. Ex. 13:2, 12

27 And if *it be* of an unclean beast, then he shall redeem *it* according to thine estimation, and ᴿshall add a fifth *part* of it thereto: or if it be not redeemed, then it shall be sold according to thy estimation. vv. 11, 12

28 Notwithstanding no devoted thing, that a man shall devote unto the LORD of all that he hath, *both* of man and beast, and of the field of his possession, shall be sold or redeemed: every devoted thing *is* most holy unto the LORD.

29 ᴿNone devoted, which shall be devoted of men, shall be redeemed; *but* shall surely be put to death. Num. 21:2

30 And all the tithe of the land, *whether* of the seed of the land, *or* of the fruit of the tree, *is* the LORD'S: *it is* holy unto the LORD.

31 And if a man will at all redeem *ought* of his tithes, he shall add thereto the fifth *part* thereof.

32 And concerning the tithe of the herd, or of the flock, *even* of whatsoever ᴿpasseth under the rod, the tenth shall be holy unto the LORD. Ezek. 20:37; Mic. 7:14

33 He shall not search whether it be good or bad, ᴿneither shall he change it: and if he change it at all, then both it and the change thereof shall be holy; it shall not be redeemed. v. 10

34 These *are* the commandments, which the LORD commanded Moses for the children of Israel in mount ᴿSi'-nai. [Heb. 12:18–29]

The Fourth Book of Moses Called

NUMBERS

NUMBERS is the book of wanderings. It takes its name from the two numberings of the Israelites—the first at Mount Sinai and the second on the plains of Moab. Most of the book, however, describes Israel's experiences as they wander in the wilderness. The lesson of Numbers is clear. While it may be necessary to pass through wilderness experiences, one does not have to live there. For Israel, an eleven-day journey became a forty-year agony.

The title of Numbers comes from the first word in the Hebrew text, *Wayyedabber,* "And He Said." Jewish writings, however, usually refer to it by the fifth Hebrew word in 1:1, *Bemidbar,* "In the Wilderness," which more nearly indicates the content of the book. The Greek title in the Septuagint is *Arithmoi,* "Numbers." The Latin Vulgate followed this title and translated it *Liber Numeri,* "Book of Numbers." These titles are based on the two numberings: the generation of Exodus (Num. 1) and the generation that grew up in the wilderness and conquered Canaan (Num. 26). Numbers has also been called the "Book of the Journeyings," the "Book of the Murmurings," and the "Fourth Book of Moses."

A ND the LORD spake unto Moses ᴿin the wilderness of Si'-nai, in the tabernacle of the congregation, on the first *day* of the second month, in the second year after they were come out of the land of Egypt, saying,　Ex. 19:1

2 Take ᵀye the sum of all the congregation of the children of Israel, after their families, by the house of their fathers, with the number of *their* names, every male by their polls;　*a census*

3 From ᴿtwenty years old and upward, all that are able to go forth to war in Israel: thou and Aaron shall number them by their armies.　Ex. 30:14; 38:26

4 And with you there shall be a man of every tribe; every one head of the house of his fathers.

5 And these *are* the names of the men that shall stand with you: of *the tribe of* Reuben; E-li'-zur the son of Shed'-e-ur.

6 Of Simeon; She-lu'-mi-el the son of Zu-ri-shad'-dai.

7 Of Judah; Nah'-shon the son of Am-min'-a-dab.

8 Of Is'-sa-char; Ne-than'-e-el the son of Zu'-ar.

9 Of Zeb'-u-lun; E-li'-ab the son of He'-lon.

10 Of the children of Joseph: of E'-phra-im; E-lish'-a-ma the son of Am-mi'-hud: of Ma-nas'-seh; Ga-ma'-li-el the son of Pe-dah'-zur.

11 Of Benjamin; Ab'-i-dan the son of Gid-e-o'-ni.

12 Of Dan; A-hi-e'-zer the son of Am-mi-shad'-dai.

13 Of Asher; Pa'-gi-el the son of Oc'-ran.

14 Of Gad; E-li'-a-saph the son of ᴿDeu'-el.ᵀ　7:42 · *Reuel,* 2:14

15 Of Naph'-ta-li; A-hi'-ra the son of E'-nan.

16 These *were* the ᵀrenowned of the congregation, princes of the tribes of their fathers, ᴿheads of thousands in Israel.　*chosen* · Jer. 5:5

17 And Moses and Aaron took these men which are ᵀexpressed ᴿby *their* names:　*designated* · Is. 43:1

18 And they assembled all the congregation together on the first *day* of the second month, and they declared their ᴿpedigrees after their families, by the house of their fathers, according to the number of the names, from twenty years old and upward, by their polls.　Ezra 2:59; Heb. 7:3

19 As the LORD commanded Moses, so he numbered them in the wilderness of Si'-nai.

20 And the ᴿchildren of Reuben, Israel's eldest son, by their generations, after their families, by the house of their fathers, according to the number of the names, by their polls, every male from twenty years old and upward, all that were able to go forth to war;　2:10

21 Those that were numbered of them, *even* of the tribe of Reuben, *were* forty and six thousand and five hundred.

22 Of the ᴿchildren of Simeon, by their generations, after their families, by the house of their fathers, those that were numbered of them, according to the number of the names, by their polls, every male from twenty years old and upward, all that were able to go forth to war;　2:12, 13; 26:12–14

23 Those that were numbered of them, *even* of the tribe of Simeon, *were* fifty and nine thousand and three hundred.

24 Of the ᴿchildren of Gad, by their generations, after their families, by the house of their fathers, according to the number of the names, from twenty years old and upward, all that were able to go forth to war;   Gen. 30:11; Josh. 4:12

25 Those that were numbered of them, *even* of the tribe of Gad, *were* forty and five thousand six hundred and fifty.

26 Of the ᴿchildren of Judah, by their generations, after their families, by the house of their fathers, according to the number of the names, from twenty years old and upward, all that were able to go forth to war;   Gen. 29:35; 2 Sam. 24:9

27 Those that were numbered of them, *even* of the tribe of Judah, *were* threescore and fourteen thousand and six hundred.

28 Of the ᴿchildren of Is'-sa-char, by their generations, after their families, by the house of their fathers, according to the number of the names, from twenty years old and upward, all that were able to go forth to war;   2:5, 6

29 Those that were numbered of them, *even* of the tribe of Is'-sa-char, *were* fifty and four thousand and four hundred.

30 Of the ᴿchildren of Zeb'-u-lun, by their generations, after their families, by the house of their fathers, according to the number of the names, from twenty years old and upward, all that were able to go forth to war;   2:7, 8

31 Those that were numbered of them, *even* of the tribe of Zeb'-u-lun, *were* fifty and seven thousand and four hundred.

32 Of the children of Joseph, *namely,* of the children of E'-phra-im, by their generations, after their families, by the house of their fathers, according to the number of the names, from twenty years old and upward, all that were able to go forth to war;

33 Those that were numbered of them, *even* of the tribe of E'-phra-im, *were* forty thousand and five hundred.

34 Of the ᴿchildren of Ma-nas'-seh, by their generations, after their families, by the house of their fathers, according to the number of the names, from twenty years old and upward, all that were able to go forth to war;   2:20

35 Those that were numbered of them, *even* of the tribe of Ma-nas'-seh, *were* thirty and two thousand and two hundred.

36 Of the ᴿchildren of Benjamin, by their generations, after their families, by the house of their fathers, according to the number of the names, from twenty years old and upward, all that were able to go forth to war;   Gen. 49:27; Rev. 7:8

37 Those that were numbered of them, *even* of the tribe of Benja-min, *were* thirty and five thousand and four hundred.

38 Of the ᴿchildren of Dan, by their generations, after their families, by the house of their fathers, according to the number of the names, from twenty years old and upward, all that were able to go forth to war;   Gen. 30:6; 46:23

39 Those that were numbered of them, *even* of the tribe of Dan, *were* threescore and two thousand and seven hundred.

40 Of the ᴿchildren of Asher, by their generations, after their families, by the house of their fathers, according to the number of the names, from twenty years old and upward, all that were able to go forth to war;   2:27, 28; 26:44–47

41 Those that were numbered of them, *even* of the tribe of Asher, *were* forty and one thousand and five hundred.

42 Of the children of Naph'-ta-li, throughout their generations, after their families, by the house of their fathers, according to the number of the names, from twenty years old and upward, all that were able to go forth to war;

43 Those that were numbered of them, *even* of the tribe of Naph'-ta-li, *were* fifty and three thousand and four hundred.

44 ᴿThese *are* those that were

numbered, which Moses and Aaron numbered, and the [T]princes of Israel, *being* twelve men: each one was for the house of his fathers.　　26:64 · *leaders*

45 So were all those that were numbered of the children of Israel, by the house of their fathers, from twenty years old and upward, all that were able to go forth to war in Israel;

46 Even all they that were numbered were [R]six hundred thousand and three thousand and five hundred and fifty.　　Heb. 11:12

47 But [R]the Levites after the tribe of their fathers were not numbered among them.　1 Chr. 21:6

48 For the LORD had spoken unto Moses, saying,

49 [R]Only thou shalt not number the tribe of Levi, neither take the sum of them among the children of Israel:　　2:33; 26:62

50 [R]But thou shalt appoint the Levites over the tabernacle of testimony, and over all the vessels thereof, and over all things that *belong* to it: they shall bear the tabernacle, and all the vessels thereof; and they shall minister unto it, [R]and shall encamp round about the tabernacle.　3:7, 8 · 3:23, 29

51 [R]And when the tabernacle setteth forward, the Levites shall take it down: and when the tabernacle is to be pitched, the Levites shall set it [R]up: [R]and the stranger that cometh nigh shall be put to death.　10:17, 21 · 10:21 · 4:15, 19, 20; 18:22

52 And the children of Israel shall pitch their tents, [R]every man by his own camp, and every man by his own standard, throughout their hosts.　　2:2, 34; 24:2

53 But the Levites shall pitch round about the tabernacle of testimony, that there be no [R]wrath upon the congregation of the children of Israel: and the Levites shall keep the charge of the tabernacle of testimony.　8:19; 16:46; 18:5

54 And the children of Israel did according to all that the LORD commanded Moses, so did they.

2 And the LORD spake unto Moses and unto Aaron, saying,

2 [R]Every man of the children of Israel shall pitch by his own standard, with the ensign of their father's house: [R]far off about the tabernacle of the congregation shall they pitch.　1:52; 24:2 · Josh. 3:4

3 And on the east side toward the rising of the sun shall they of the standard of the camp of Judah pitch throughout their armies: and [R]Nah'-shon the son of Am-min'-a-dab *shall be* captain of the children of Judah.　　Matt. 1:4

4 And his host, and those that were numbered of them, *were* threescore and fourteen thousand and six hundred.

5 And those that do [T]pitch next unto him *shall be* the tribe of Is'-sa-char: and Ne-than'-e-el the son of Zu'-ar *shall be* captain of the children of Is'-sa-char.　　*camp*

6 And his host, and those that were numbered thereof, *were* fifty and four thousand and four hundred.

7 *Then* the tribe of Zeb'-u-lun: and E-li'-ab the son of He'-lon *shall be* captain of the children of Zeb'-u-lun.

8 And his host, and those that were numbered thereof, *were* fifty and seven thousand and four hundred.

9 All that were numbered in the camp of Judah *were* an hundred thousand and fourscore thousand and six thousand and four hundred, throughout their armies. [R]These shall first [T]set forth.　　10:14 · *break camp*

10 On the [R]south side *shall be* the standard of the camp of Reuben according to their armies: and the captain of the children of Reuben *shall be* E-li'-zur the son of Shed'-e-ur.　　10:6

11 And his host, and those that were numbered thereof, *were* forty and six thousand and five hundred.

12 And those which pitch by him *shall be* the tribe of Simeon: and the captain of the children of

Simeon *shall be* She-lu'-mi-el the son of Zu-ri-shad'-dai.

13 And his host, and those that were numbered of them, *were* fifty and nine thousand and three hundred.

14 Then the tribe of Gad: and the captain of the sons of Gad *shall be* E-li'-a-saph the son of ᵀReu'-el. *Deuel,* 1:14; 7:42

15 And his host, and those that were numbered of them, *were* forty and five thousand and six hundred and fifty.

16 All that were numbered in the camp of Reuben *were* an hundred thousand and fifty and one thousand and four hundred and fifty, throughout their armies. ᴿAnd they shall set forth in the second rank. 10:18

17 ᴿThen the tabernacle of the congregation shall set forward with the ᵀcamp of the Levites ᴿin the midst of the camp: as they encamp, so shall they set forward, every man in his place by their standards. 10:17, 21 · *company* · 1:53

18 On the west side *shall be* the standard of the camp of E'-phra-im according to their armies: and the captain of the sons of E'-phra-im *shall be* E-lish'-a-ma the son of Am-mi'-hud.

19 And his host, and those that were numbered of them, *were* forty thousand and five hundred.

20 And by him *shall be* the tribe of Ma-nas'-seh: and the captain of the children of Ma-nas'-seh *shall be* Ga-ma'-li-el the son of Pe-dah'-zur.

21 And his host, and those that were numbered of them, *were* thirty and two thousand and two hundred.

22 Then the tribe of Benjamin: and the captain of the sons of Benjamin *shall be* Ab'-i-dan the son of Gid-e-o'-ni.

23 And his host, and those that were numbered of them, *were* thirty and five thousand and four hundred.

24 All that were numbered of the camp of E'-phra-im *were* an

hundred thousand and eight thousand and an hundred, throughout their armies. ᴿAnd they shall go forward in the third rank. 10:22

25 The standard of the camp of Dan *shall be* on the north side by their armies: and the captain of the children of Dan *shall be* A-hi-e'-zer the son of Am-mi-shad'-dai.

26 And his host, and those that were numbered of them, *were* threescore and two thousand and seven hundred.

27 And those that encamp by him *shall be* the tribe of Asher: and the captain of the children of Asher *shall be* Pa'-gi-el the son of Oc'-ran.

28 And his host, and those that were numbered of them, *were* forty and one thousand and five hundred.

29 Then the tribe of Naph'-ta-li: and the captain of the children of Naph'-ta-li *shall be* A-hi'-ra the son of E'-nan.

30 And his host, and those that were numbered of them, *were* fifty and three thousand and four hundred.

31 All they that were numbered in the camp of Dan *were* an hundred thousand and fifty and seven thousand and six hundred. ᴿThey shall ᵀgo hindmost with their standards. 10:25 · *break camp last*

32 These *are* those which were numbered of the children of Israel by the house of their fathers: ᴿall those that were numbered of the camps throughout their hosts *were* six hundred thousand and three thousand and five hundred and fifty. 1:46; 11:21; Ex. 38:26

33 But ᴿthe Levites were not numbered among the children of Israel; as the LORD commanded Moses. 1:47; 26:57–62

34 And the children of Israel ᴿdid according to all that the LORD commanded Moses: ᴿso they pitched by their standards, and so they set forward, every one after their families, according to the house of their fathers. 1:54 · 24:2, 5, 6

3 These also *are* the ᴿgenera-tions of Aaron and Moses in the day *that* the Lᴏʀᴅ spake with Moses in mount Si'-nai. Ex. 6:16–27

2 And these *are* the names of the sons of Aaron; Na'-dab the ᴿfirstborn, and ᴿA-bi'-hu, E-le-a'-zar, and Ith'-a-mar. Ex. 6:23 · Lev. 10:1

3 These *are* the names of the sons of Aaron, ᴿthe priests which were anointed, whom he conse-crated to minister in the priest's office. Ex. 28:41; Lev. 8

4 And Na'-dab and A-bi'-hu died before the Lᴏʀᴅ, when they offered strange fire before the Lᴏʀᴅ, in the wilderness of Si'-nai, and they had no children: and E-le-a'-zar and Ith'-a-mar minis-tered in the priest's office in the sight of Aaron their father.

5 And the Lᴏʀᴅ spake unto Moses, saying,

6 ᴿBring the tribe of Levi near, and present them before Aaron the priest, that they may minister unto him. 8:6–22; 18:1–7; Deut. 10:8

7 And they shall keep his charge, and the charge of the whole congregation before the tabernacle of the congregation, to do the service of the tabernacle.

8 And they shall keep all the instruments of the tabernacle of the congregation, and the charge of the children of Israel, to do the service of the tabernacle.

9 And ᴿthou shalt give the Le-vites unto Aaron and to his sons: they *are* wholly given unto him out of the children of Israel. 8:19

10 And thou shalt appoint Aar-on and his sons, ᴿand they shall wait on their priest's office: ᴿand the stranger that cometh nigh shall be put to death. Ex. 29:9 · 1:51

11 And the Lᴏʀᴅ spake unto Moses, saying,

12 And I, behold, ᴿI have taken the Levites from among the chil-dren of Israel instead of all the firstborn that openeth the matrix among the children of Israel: therefore the Levites shall be ᴿmine; v. 41; 8:16; 18:6 · Ex. 13:2

13 Because ᴿall the firstborn *are*

mine; ᴿfor on the day that I smote all the firstborn in the land of Egypt I hallowed unto me all the firstborn in Israel, both man and beast: mine shall they be: I *am* the Lᴏʀᴅ. Neh. 10:36; Luke 2:23 · Ex. 13:12, 15

14 And the Lᴏʀᴅ spake unto Moses in the wilderness of Si'-nai, saying,

15 Number the children of Levi after the house of their fathers, by their families: ᴿevery male from a month old and upward shalt thou number them. v. 39; 26:62

16 And Moses numbered them according to the word of the Lᴏʀᴅ, as he was commanded.

17 And these were the sons of Levi by their names; Ger'-shon, and Ko'-hath, and Me-ra'-ri.

18 And these *are* the names of the sons of Ger'-shon by their families; Lib'-ni, and Shim'-e-i.

19 And the sons of Ko'-hath by their families; Am'-ram, and Iz'-e-har, He'-bron, and Uz-zi'-el.

20 ᴿAnd the sons of Me-ra'-ri by their families; Mah'-li, and Mu'-shi. These *are* the families of the Levites according to the house of their fathers. 4:42–45; Ex. 6:19

21 Of Ger'-shon *was* the family of the Lib'-nites, and the family of the Shim'-ites: these *are* the fami-lies of the Ger'-shon-ites.

22 Those that were numbered of them, according to the number of all the males, from a month old and upward, *even* those that were numbered of them *were* seven thousand and five hun-dred.

23 ᴿThe families of the Ger'-shon-ites shall ᵀpitch behind the tabernacle westward. 1:53 · camp

24 And the chief of the house of the father of the Ger'-shon-ites *shall be* E-li'-a-saph the son of La'-el.

25 And ᴿthe charge of the sons of Ger'-shon in the tabernacle of the congregation *shall be* the tab-ernacle, and the tent, the covering thereof, and the hanging for the door of the tabernacle of the con-gregation, 4:24–26

26 And ^Rthe hangings of the court, and the curtain for the door of the court, which *is* by the tabernacle, and by the altar round about, and the cords of it for all the service thereof.   Ex. 27:9-16

27 ^RAnd of Ko'-hath *was* the family of the Am'-ram-ites, and the family of the Iz'-e-har-ites, and the family of the He'-bron-ites, and the family of the Uz-zi'-el-ites: these *are* the families of the Ko'-hath-ites.   1 Chr. 26:23

28 In the number of all the males, from a month old and upward, *were* eight thousand and six hundred, ^Tkeeping the charge of the sanctuary.   *taking care of*

29 ^RThe families of the sons of Ko'-hath shall pitch on the side of the tabernacle southward.   Ex. 6:18

30 And the chief of the house of the father of the families of the Ko'-hath-ites *shall be* E-liz'-a-phan the son of ^RUz-zi'-el.   Lev. 10:4

31 And ^Rtheir ^Tcharge *shall be* the ark, and the table, and the candlestick, and the altars, and the vessels of the sanctuary wherewith they minister, and the hanging, and all the service thereof.   4:15 • *duty*

32 And E-le-a'-zar the son of Aaron the priest *shall be* chief over the chief of the Levites, *and* have the oversight of them that keep the charge of the sanctuary.

33 Of Me-ra'-ri *was* the family of the Mah'-lites, and the family of the Mu'-shites: these *are* the families of Me-ra'-ri.

34 And those that were numbered of them, according to the number of all the males, from a month old and upward, *were* six thousand and two hundred.

35 And the chief of the house of the father of the families of Me-ra'-ri *was* Zu'-ri-el the son of Ab-i-ha'-il: *these* shall pitch on the side of the tabernacle northward.

36 And *under* the custody and charge of the sons of Me-ra'-ri *shall be* the boards of the tabernacle, and the bars thereof, and the pillars thereof, and the sockets

thereof, and all the vessels thereof, and all that serveth thereto,

37 And the pillars of the court round about, and their sockets, and their pins, and their cords.

38 ^RBut those that encamp before the tabernacle toward the east, *even* before the tabernacle of the congregation eastward, *shall be* Moses, and Aaron and his sons, ^Rkeeping the charge of the sanctuary ^Rfor the charge of the children of Israel; and ^Rthe stranger that cometh nigh shall be put to death.   1:53 • 18:5 • vv. 7, 8 • v. 10

39 All that were numbered of the Levites, which Moses and Aaron numbered at the commandment of the LORD, throughout their families, all the males from a month old and upward, *were* twenty and two thousand.

40 And the LORD said unto Moses, ^RNumber all the firstborn of the males of the children of Israel from a month old and upward, and take the number of their names.   v. 15

41 ^RAnd thou shalt take the Levites for me (I *am* the LORD) instead of all the firstborn among the children of Israel; and the cattle of the Levites instead of all the firstlings among the cattle of the children of Israel.   vv. 12, 45

42 And Moses numbered, as the LORD commanded him, all the firstborn among the children of Israel.

43 And all the firstborn males by the number of names, from a month old and upward, of those that were numbered of them, were twenty and two thousand two hundred and threescore and thirteen.

44 And the LORD spake unto Moses, saying,

45 ^RTake the Levites instead of all the firstborn among the children of Israel, and the cattle of the Levites instead of their cattle; and the Levites shall be mine: I *am* the LORD.   vv. 12, 41

46 And for those that are to be redeemed of the two hundred and

threescore and thirteen of the firstborn of the children of Israel, which are more than the Levites;

47 Thou shalt even take ᴿfive shek'-els apiece ᴿby the poll, after the shek'-el of the sanctuary shalt thou take *them:* (the shek'-el *is* twenty ge'-rahs:)   Lev. 27:6 · 1:2, 18, 20

48 And thou shalt give the money, wherewith the odd number of them is to be redeemed, unto Aaron and to his sons.

49 And Moses took the redemption money of them that were over and above them that were redeemed by the Levites:

50 Of the firstborn of the children of Israel took he the money; a thousand three hundred and threescore and five *shek'-els,* after the shek'-el of the sanctuary:

51 And Moses ᴿgave the money of them that were redeemed unto Aaron and to his sons, according to the word of the LORD, as the LORD commanded Moses.   v. 48

4 And the LORD spake unto Moses and unto Aaron, saying,

2 Take the sum of the sons of ᴿKo'-hath from among the sons of Levi, after their families, by the house of their fathers,   3:27-32

3 ᴿFrom thirty years old and upward even until fifty years old, all that enter into the host, to do the work in the tabernacle of the congregation.   1 Chr. 23:3, 24, 27

4 ᴿThis *shall be* the service of the sons of Ko'-hath in the tabernacle of the congregation, *about* ᴿthe most holy things: v. 15 · v. 19

5 And when the camp setteth forward, Aaron shall come, and his sons, and they shall take down ᴿthe covering vail, and cover the ark of testimony with it: Ex. 26:31

6 And shall put thereon the covering of badgers' skins, and shall spread over *it* a cloth wholly of ᴿblue, and shall put in ᴿthe staves thereof.   Ex. 39:1 · 1 Kin. 8:7, 8

7 And upon the ᴿtable of shewbread they shall spread a cloth of blue, and put thereon the dishes, and the spoons, and the bowls, and covers to cover withal: and

the ᴿcontinual bread shall be thereon: Ex. 25:23, 29, 30 · Lev. 24:5-9

8 And they shall spread upon them a cloth of scarlet, and cover the same with a covering of badgers' skins, and shall put in the staves thereof.

9 And they shall take a cloth of blue, and cover the ᴿcandlestick of the light, and his lamps, and his tongs, and his snuffdishes, and all the oil vessels thereof, wherewith they minister unto it: Ex. 25:31-38

10 And they shall put it and all the vessels thereof within a covering of badgers' skins, and shall put *it* upon a bar.

11 And upon ᴿthe golden altar they shall spread a cloth of blue, and cover it with a covering of badgers' skins, and shall put to the staves thereof: Ex. 30:1-5

12 And they shall take all the ᴿinstruments of ministry, wherewith they minister in the sanctuary, and put *them* in a cloth of blue, and cover them with a covering of badgers' skins, and shall put *them* on a bar: Ex. 25:9; 1 Chr. 9:29

13 And they shall take away the ashes from the altar, and spread a purple cloth thereon:

14 And they shall put upon it all the vessels thereof, wherewith they minister about it, *even* the censers, the fleshhooks, and the shovels, and the ᵀbasons, all the vessels of the altar; and they shall spread upon it a covering of badgers' skins, and put to the staves of it.   *bowls*

15 And when Aaron and his sons have made an end of covering the sanctuary, and all the vessels of the sanctuary, as the camp is to set forward; after that, ᴿthe sons of Ko'-hath shall come to bear *it:* but they shall not touch *any* holy thing, lest they die. ᴿThese *things are* the burden of the sons of Ko'-hath in the tabernacle of the congregation. 7:9 · 3:31

16 And to the office of E-le-a'-zar the son of Aaron the priest *pertaineth* ᴿthe oil for the light, and the sweet incense, and the

daily meat offering, and the anointing oil, *and* the oversight of all the tabernacle, and of all that therein *is,* in the sanctuary, and in the vessels thereof. Ex. 25:6; Lev. 24:2

17 And the Lord spake unto Moses and unto Aaron, saying,

18 Cut ye not off the tribe of the families of the Ko'-hath-ites from among the Levites:

19 But thus do unto them, that they may live, and not die, when they approach unto ᴿthe most holy things: Aaron and his sons shall go in, and ᵀappoint them every one to his service and to his burden: v. 4 · *assign*

20 ᴿBut they shall not go in to see when the holy things are covered, lest they die. 1 Sam. 6:19

21 And the Lord spake unto Moses, saying,

22 Take also the sum of the sons of ᴿGer'-shon, throughout the houses of their fathers, by their families; 3:22

23 ᴿFrom thirty years old and upward until fifty years old shalt thou number them; all that enter in to perform the service, to do the work in the tabernacle of the congregation. v. 3; 1 Chr. 23:3, 24, 27

24 This *is* the ᴿservice of the families of the Ger'-shon-ites, to serve, and for burdens: 7:7

25 ᴿAnd they shall bear the curtains of the tabernacle, and the tabernacle of the congregation, his covering, and the covering of the ᴿbadgers' skins that *is* above upon it, and the hanging for the door of the tabernacle of the congregation, 3:25, 26 · Ex. 26:14

26 And the hangings of the court, and the hanging for the door of the gate of the court, which *is* by the tabernacle and by the altar round about, and their cords, and all the instruments of their service, and all that is made for them: so shall they serve.

27 At the ᵀappointment of Aaron and his sons shall be all the service of the sons of the Ger'-shon-ites, in all their burdens, and in all

their service: and ye shall ᵀappoint unto them in charge all their burdens. *command · assign*

28 This *is* the service of the families of the sons of Ger'-shon in the tabernacle of the congregation: and their ᵀcharge *shall be* ᴿunder the hand of Ith'-a-mar the son of Aaron the priest. *duties · v. 33*

29 As for the sons of ᴿMe-ra'-ri, thou shalt number them after their families, by the house of their fathers; 3:33–37

30 ᴿFrom thirty years old and upward even unto fifty years old shalt thou number them, every one that entereth into the service, to do the work of the tabernacle of the congregation. v. 3; 8:24–26

31 And this *is* the charge of their ᴿburden, according to all their service in the tabernacle of the congregation; ᴿthe boards of the tabernacle, and the bars thereof, and the pillars thereof, and sockets thereof, 7:8 · Ex. 26:15

32 And the pillars of the court round about, and their sockets, and their pins, and their cords, with all their ᵀinstruments, and with all their service: and by name ye shall ᴿreckon the instruments of the charge of their burden. *furnishings* · Ex. 25:9; 38:21

33 This *is* the service of the families of the sons of Me-ra'-ri, according to all their service, in the tabernacle of the congregation, under the hand of Ith'-a-mar the son of Aaron the priest.

34 And Moses and Aaron and the chief of the congregation numbered the sons of the Ko'-hath-ites after their families, and after the house of their fathers,

35 From thirty ᴿyears old and upward even unto fifty years old, every one that entereth into the service, for the work in the tabernacle of the congregation: v. 47

36 And those that were numbered of them by their families were two thousand seven hundred and fifty.

37 These *were* they that were numbered of the families of the

Ko'-hath-ites, all that might do service in the tabernacle of the congregation, which Moses and Aaron did number according to the commandment of the LORD by the hand of Moses.

38 And those that were numbered of the sons of Ger'-shon, throughout their families, and by the house of their fathers,

39 From thirty years old and upward even unto fifty years old, every one that entereth into the service, for the work in the tabernacle of the congregation,

40 Even those that were numbered of them, throughout their families, by the house of their fathers, were two thousand and six hundred and thirty.

41 These *are* they that were numbered of the families of the sons of Ger'-shon, of all that might do service in the tabernacle of the congregation, whom Moses and Aaron did number according to the commandment of the LORD.

42 And those that were numbered of the families of the sons of Me-ra'-ri, throughout their families, by the house of their fathers,

43 From thirty years old and upward even unto fifty years old, every one that entereth into the service, for the work in the tabernacle of the congregation,

44 Even those that were numbered of them after their families, were three thousand and two hundred.

45 These *be* those that were numbered of the families of the sons of Me-ra'-ri, whom Moses and Aaron numbered ᴿaccording to the word of the LORD by the hand of Moses.   v. 29

46 All those that were ᴿnumbered of the Levites, whom Moses and Aaron and the chief of Israel numbered, after their families, and after the house of their fathers,   3:39; 26:57–62; 1 Chr. 23:3–23

47 ᴿFrom thirty years old and upward even unto fifty years old, every one that came to do the service of the ministry, and the service of the burden in the tabernacle of the congregation,   vv. 3, 23

48 Even those that were numbered of them, were eight thousand and five hundred and fourscore.

49 According to the commandment of the LORD they were numbered by the hand of Moses, every one according to his service, and according to his burden: thus were they numbered of him, as the LORD commanded Moses.

5 And the LORD spake unto Moses, saying,

2 Command the children of Israel, that they put out of the camp every leper, and every one that hath an ᴿissue, and whosoever is ᴿdefiled by the dead: Lev. 15:2 · 9:6

3 Both male and female shall ye put out, ᵀwithout the camp shall ye put them; that they defile not their camps, ᴿin the midst whereof I dwell.   *outside* · [2 Cor. 6:16]

4 And the children of Israel did so, and put them out without the camp: as the LORD spake unto Mo-ses, so did the children of Israel.

5 And the LORD spake unto Moses, saying,

6 Speak unto the children of Israel, ᴿWhen a man or woman shall commit any sin that men commit, ᵀto do a trespass against the LORD, and that person be guilty;   Lev. 5:14—6:7 · *acting unfaithfully*

7 Then they shall confess their sin which they have done: and he shall recompense his trespass with the principal thereof, and add unto it the fifth *part* thereof, and give *it* unto *him* against whom he hath trespassed.

8 But if the man have no kinsman to recompense the trespass unto, let the trespass be recompensed unto the LORD, *even* to the priest; beside the ram of the atonement, whereby an atonement shall be made for him.

9 And every ᴿoffering of all the holy things of the children of Israel, which they bring unto the priest, shall be his.   Lev. 6:17, 18, 26

10 And every man's hallowed things shall be his: whatsoever any man giveth the priest, it shall be ᴿhis.   Lev. 10:13

11 And the LORD spake unto Moses, saying,

12 Speak unto the children of Israel, and say unto them, If any man's wife go aside, and commit a trespass against him,

13 And a man lie with her carnally, and it be hid from the eyes of her husband, and be kept close, and she be defiled, and *there be* no witness against her, neither she be taken *with the manner;*

14 And the spirit of jealousy come upon him, and he be jealous of his wife, and she be defiled: or if the spirit of jealousy come upon him, and he be jealous of his wife, and she be not defiled:

15 Then shall the man bring his wife unto the priest, and he shall bring her offering for her, the tenth *part* of an e'-phah of barley meal; he shall pour no oil upon it, nor put frankincense thereon; for it *is* an offering of jealousy, an offering of memorial, ᴿbringing iniquity to remembrance. Heb. 10:3

16 And the priest shall bring her near, and set her before the LORD:

17 And the priest shall take holy water in an earthen vessel; and of the dust that is in the floor of the tabernacle the priest shall take, and put *it* into the water:

18 And the priest shall set the woman before the ᴿLORD, and uncover the woman's head, and put the offering of memorial in her hands, which *is* the jealousy offering: and the priest shall have in his hand the bitter water that causeth the curse: Heb. 13:4

19 And the priest shall charge her by an oath, and say unto the woman, If no man have lain with thee, and if thou hast not gone aside to uncleanness *with another* instead of thy husband, be thou free from this bitter water that causeth the curse:

20 But if thou hast gone aside *to another* instead of thy husband,

and if thou be defiled, and some man have lain with thee beside thine husband:

21 Then the priest shall ᴿcharge the woman with an oath of cursing, and the priest shall say unto the woman, ᴿThe LORD make thee a curse and an oath among thy people, when the LORD doth make thy thigh to ᵀrot, and thy belly to swell; Josh. 6:26 · Jer. 29:22 · Lit. *fall away*

22 And this water that causeth the curse ᴿshall go into thy bowels, to make *thy* belly to swell, and *thy* thigh to rot: And the woman shall say, A'-men, a'-men. Ps. 109:18

23 And the priest shall write these curses in a book, and he shall blot *them* out with the bitter water:

24 And he shall cause the woman to drink the bitter water that causeth the curse: and the water that causeth the curse shall enter into her, *and become* bitter.

25 ᴿThen the priest shall take the jealousy offering out of the woman's hand, and shall wave the offering before the LORD, and offer it upon the altar: Lev. 8:27

26 And the priest shall take an handful of the offering, ᴿ*even* the memorial thereof, and burn *it* upon the altar, and afterward shall cause the woman to drink the water.   Lev. 2:2, 9

27 And when he hath made her to drink the water, then it shall come to pass, *that,* if she be defiled, and have done trespass against her husband, that the water that causeth the ᴿcurse shall enter into her, *and become* bitter, and her belly shall swell, and her thigh shall rot: and the woman shall be a curse among her people. Is. 65:15; Jer. 24:9; 29:18, 22

28 And if the woman be not defiled, but be clean; then she shall be free, and shall conceive seed.

29 This *is* the law of jealousies, when a wife goeth aside *to another* ᴿinstead of her husband, and is defiled;   v. 19

30 Or when the spirit of jealousy

cometh upon him, and he be jealous over his wife, and shall set the woman before the LORD, and the priest shall execute upon her all this law.

31 Then shall the man be guiltless from iniquity, and this woman shall bear her iniquity.

6 And the LORD spake unto Moses, saying,

2 Speak unto the children of Israel, and say unto them, When either man or woman shall ᴿseparate *themselves* to vow a vow of a Nazarite, to separate *themselves* unto the LORD: Lev. 27:2

3 ᴿHe shall separate *himself* from wine and strong drink, and shall drink no vinegar of wine, or vinegar of strong drink, neither shall he drink any liquor of grapes, nor eat moist grapes, or dried.   Lev. 10:9; Amos 2:12; Luke 1:15

4 All the days of his separation shall he eat nothing that is made of the ᵀvine tree, from the kernels even to the husk. *grapevine*

5 All the days of the vow of his separation there shall no razor come upon his head: until the days be fulfilled, in the which he separateth *himself* unto the LORD, he shall be holy, *and* shall let the locks of the hair of his head grow.

6 All the days that he separateth *himself* unto the LORD he shall come at no dead body.

7 ᴿHe shall not make himself unclean for his father, or for his mother, for his brother, or for his sister, when they die: because the consecration of his God *is* upon his head.   9:6; Lev. 21:1, 2, 11

8 All the days of his separation he *is* holy unto the LORD.

9 And if any man die very suddenly by him, and he hath defiled the head of his consecration; then he shall ᴿshave his head in the day of his cleansing, on the seventh day shall he shave it. Lev. 14:8

10 And ᴿon the eighth day he shall bring two turtles, or two young pigeons, to the priest, to the door of the tabernacle of the congregation: Lev. 5:7; 14:22; 15:14, 29

11 And the priest shall offer the one for a sin offering, and the other for a burnt offering, and make an atonement for him, for that he sinned by the dead, and shall hallow his head that same day.

12 And he shall consecrate unto the LORD the days of his separation, and shall bring a lamb of the first year ᴿfor a trespass offering: but the days that were before shall be ᵀlost, because his separation was defiled.   Lev. 5:6 · *void*

13 And this *is* the law of the Nazarite, when the days of his separation are fulfilled: he shall be brought unto the door of the tabernacle of the congregation:

14 And he shall offer his offering unto the LORD, one he lamb of the first year without blemish for a burnt offering, and one ewe lamb of the first year without blemish ᴿfor a sin offering, and one ram without blemish for peace offerings,   Lev. 4:2, 27, 32

15 And a basket of unleavened bread, ᴿcakes of fine flour mingled with oil, and wafers of unleavened bread anointed with oil, and their meat offering, and their ᴿdrink offerings.   Lev. 2:4 · 15:5, 7, 10

16 And the priest shall bring *them* before the LORD, and shall offer his sin offering, and his burnt offering:

17 And he shall offer the ram *for* a sacrifice of peace offerings unto the LORD, with the basket of unleavened bread: the priest shall offer also his meat offering, and his drink offering.

18 ᴿAnd the Nazarite shall shave the head of his separation *at* the door of the tabernacle of the congregation, and shall take the hair of the head of his separation, and put *it* in the fire which *is* under the sacrifice of the peace offerings.   v. 9; Acts 21:23, 24

19 And the priest shall take the sodden shoulder of the ram, and one unleavened cake out of the basket, and one unleavened wafer, and shall put *them* upon the

hands of the Nazarite, after *the hair of* his separation is shaven:

20 And the priest shall wave them *for* a wave offering before the LORD: ᴿthis *is* holy for the priest, with the wave breast and heave shoulder: and after that the Nazarite may drink wine. Ex. 29:27

21 This *is* the law of the Nazarite who hath vowed, *and of* his offering unto the LORD for his separation, beside *that* that his hand shall get: according to the vow which he vowed, so he must do after the law of his separation.

22 And the LORD spake unto Moses, saying,

23 Speak unto Aaron and unto his sons, saying, On this wise ye shall bless the children of Israel, saying unto them,

24 The LORD ᴿbless thee, and ᴿkeep thee: Deut. 28:3–6 · John 7:11

25 The LORD ᴿmake his face shine upon thee, and ᴿbe gracious unto thee: Ps. 31:16 · Ex. 33:19; Mal. 1:9

26 ᴿThe LORD lift up his countenance upon thee, and ᴿgive thee peace. Ps. 4:6; 89:15 · John 14:27; Phil. 4:7

27 ᴿAnd they shall put my name upon the children of Israel; and I will bless them. 2 Sam. 7:23; Is. 43:7

7 And it came to pass on the day that Moses had fully set up the tabernacle, and had ᴿanointed it, and sanctified it, and all the instruments thereof, both the altar and all the vessels thereof, and had anointed them, and sanctified them; Lev. 8:10, 11

2 That ᴿthe princes of Israel, heads of the house of their fathers, who *were* the princes of the tribes, and were over them that were numbered, offered: 1:4

3 And they brought their offering before the LORD, six covered wagons, and twelve oxen; a wagon for two of the princes, and for each one an ox: and they brought them before the tabernacle.

4 And the LORD spake unto Moses, saying,

5 Take *it* of them, that they may be ᵀto do the service of the tabernacle of the congregation; and

thou shalt give them unto the Levites, to every man according to his service. *used for*

6 And Moses took the wagons and the oxen, and gave them unto the Levites.

7 Two wagons and four oxen he gave unto the sons of Ger'-shon, according to their service:

8 And four wagons and eight oxen he gave unto the sons of Mera'-ri, according unto their service, under the hand of Ith'-a-mar the son of Aaron the priest.

9 But unto the sons of Ko'-hath he gave none: because ᴿthe service of the sanctuary belonging unto them *was that* they should bear upon their shoulders. 4:6–15

10 And the princes offered for ᴿdedicating of the altar in the day that it was anointed, even the princes offered their offering before the altar. Deut. 20:5; 1 Kin. 8:63

11 And the LORD said unto Moses, They shall offer their offering, each prince on his day, for the dedicating of the altar.

12 And he that offered his offering the first day was ᴿNah'-shon the son of Am-min'-a-dab, of the tribe of Judah: 2:3

13 And his offering *was* one silver charger, the weight thereof *was* an hundred and thirty *shek'-els*, one silver bowl of seventy shek'-els, after ᴿthe shek'-el of the sanctuary; both of them *were* full of fine flour mingled with oil for a ᴿmeat offering: Ex. 30:13 · Lev. 2:1

14 One spoon of ten *shek'-els* of gold, full of ᴿincense: Ex. 30:34

15 ᴿOne young bullock, one ram, one lamb ᴿof the first year, for a burnt offering: Lev. 1:2 · Ex. 12:5

16 One kid of the goats for a ᴿsin offering: Lev. 4:23

17 And for ᴿa sacrifice of peace offerings, two oxen, five rams, five he goats, five lambs of the first year: this *was* the offering of Nah'-shon the son of Am-min'-a-dab. Lev. 3:1

18 On the second day Ne-than'-e-el the son of Zu'-ar, prince of Is'-sa-char, did offer:

19 He offered *for* his offering one silver ᵀcharger, the weight whereof *was* an hundred and thirty *shek'-els*, one silver bowl of seventy shek'-els, after the shek'-el of the sanctuary; both of them full of fine flour mingled with oil for a meat offering: *platter*

20 One spoon of gold of ten *shek'-els*, full of incense:

21 One young bullock, one ram, one lamb of the first year, for a burnt offering:

22 One kid of the goats for a sin offering:

23 And for a sacrifice of peace offerings, two oxen, five rams, five he goats, five lambs of the first year: this *was* the offering of Ne-than'-e-el the son of Zu'-ar.

24 On the third day E-li'-ab the son of He'-lon, prince of the children of Zeb'-u-lun, *did offer:*

25 His offering *was* one silver charger, the weight whereof *was* an hundred and thirty *shek'-els*, one silver bowl of seventy shek'-els, after the shek'-el of the sanctuary; both of them full of fine flour mingled with oil for a meat offering:

26 One golden spoon of ten *shek'-els*, full of incense:

27 One young bullock, one ram, one lamb of the first year, for a burnt offering:

28 One kid of the goats for a sin offering:

29 And for a sacrifice of peace offerings, two oxen, five rams, five he goats, five lambs of the first year: this *was* the offering of E-li'-ab the son of He'-lon.

30 On the fourth day ᴿE-li'-zur the son of Shed'-e-ur, prince of the children of Reuben, *did offer:* 1:5

31 His offering *was* one silver charger of the weight of an hundred and thirty *shek'-els*, one silver bowl of seventy shek'-els, after the shek'-el of the sanctuary; both of them full of fine flour mingled with oil for a meat offering:

32 One golden spoon of ten *shek'-els*, full of incense:

33 One young bullock, one ram, one lamb of the first year, for a burnt offering:

34 One kid of the goats for a sin offering:

35 And for a sacrifice of peace offerings, two oxen, five rams, five he goats, five lambs of the first year: this *was* the offering of E-li'-zur the son of Shed'-e-ur.

36 On the fifth day ᴿShe-lu'-mi-el the son of Zu-ri-shad'-dai, prince of the children of Simeon, *did offer:* 1:6; 2:12

37 His offering *was* one silver charger, the weight whereof *was* an hundred and thirty *shek'-els*, one silver bowl of seventy shek'-els, after the shek'-el of the sanctuary; both of them full of fine flour mingled with oil for a ᵀmeat offering: *grain* or *meal*

38 One golden spoon of ten *shek'-els*, full of incense:

39 One young bullock, one ram, one lamb of the first year, for a burnt offering:

40 One kid of the goats for a sin offering:

41 And for a sacrifice of peace offerings, two oxen, five rams, five he goats, five lambs of the first year: this *was* the offering of She-lu'-mi-el the son of Zu-ri-shad'-dai.

42 On the sixth day E-li'-a-saph the son of ᵀDeu'-el, prince of the children of Gad, *offered:* Reuel, 2:14

43 His offering *was* one silver charger of the weight of an hundred and thirty *shek'-els*, a silver bowl of seventy shek'-els, after the shek'-el of the sanctuary; both of them full of fine flour mingled with oil for a meat offering:

44 One golden spoon of ten *shek'-els*, full of incense:

45 One young bullock, one ram, one lamb of the first year, for ᴿa burnt offering: Ps. 40:6

46 One kid of the goats for a sin offering:

47 And for a sacrifice of peace offerings, two oxen, five rams, five he goats, five lambs of the first year: this *was* the offering of E-li'-a-saph the son of Deu'-el.

48 On the seventh day [R]E-lish'-a-ma the son of Am-mi'-hud, prince of the children of E'-phra-im, *offered:*   1:10; 2:18; 1 Chr. 7:26

49 His offering *was* one silver charger, the weight whereof *was* an hundred and thirty *shek'-els*, one silver bowl of seventy shek'-els, after the shek'-el of the sanctuary; both of them full of fine flour mingled with oil for a meat offering:

50 One golden spoon of ten *shek'-els*, full of incense:

51 One young bullock, one ram, one lamb of the first year, for a burnt offering:

52 One kid of the goats for a sin offering:

53 And for a sacrifice of peace offerings, two oxen, five rams, five he goats, five lambs of the first year: this *was* the offering of E-lish'-a-ma the son of Am-mi'-hud.

54 On the eighth day *offered* [R]Ga-ma'-li-el the son of Pe-dah'-zur, prince of the children of Ma-nas'-seh: 1:10; 2:20

55 His offering *was* one silver charger of the weight of an hundred and thirty *shek'-els*, one silver bowl of seventy shek'-els, after the shek'-el of the sanctuary; both of them full of fine flour mingled with oil for a meat offering:

56 One golden spoon of ten *shek'-els*, full of incense:

57 One young bullock, one ram, one lamb of the first year, for a burnt offering:

58 One kid of the goats for a sin offering:

59 And for a sacrifice of peace offerings, two oxen, five rams, five he goats, five lambs of the first year: this *was* the offering of Ga-ma'-li-el the son of Pe-dah'-zur.

60 On the ninth day Ab'-i-dan the son of Gid-e-o'-ni, prince of the children of Benjamin, *offered:*

61 His offering *was* one silver charger, the weight whereof *was* an hundred and thirty *shek'-els*, one silver bowl of seventy shek'-els, after the shek'-el of the sanctuary; both of them full of fine

flour mingled with oil for a meat offering:

62 One golden spoon of ten *shek'-els*, full of incense:

63 One young bullock, one ram, one lamb of the first year, for a burnt offering:

64 One kid of the goats for a sin offering:

65 And for a sacrifice of peace offerings, two oxen, five rams, five he goats, five lambs of the first year: this *was* the offering of Ab'-i-dan the son of Gid-e-o'-ni.

66 On the tenth day [R]A-hi-e'-zer the son of Am-mi-shad'-dai, prince of the children of Dan, *offered:*   1:12; 2:25

67 His offering *was* one silver charger, the weight whereof *was* an hundred and thirty *shek'-els*, one silver bowl of seventy shek'-els, after the shek'-el of the sanctuary; both of them full of fine flour mingled with oil for a meat offering:

68 One golden spoon of ten *shek'-els*, full of incense:

69 One young bullock, one ram, one lamb of the first year, for a burnt offering:

70 One kid of the goats for a sin offering:

71 And for a sacrifice of peace offerings, two oxen, five rams, five he goats, five lambs of the first year: this *was* the offering of A-hi-e'-zer the son of Am-mi-shad'-dai.

72 On the eleventh day [R]Pa'-gi-el the son of Oc'-ran, prince of the children of Asher, *offered:* 1:13; 2:27

73 His offering *was* one silver charger, the weight whereof *was* an hundred and thirty *shek'-els*, one silver bowl of seventy shek'-els, after the shek'-el of the sanctuary; both of them full of fine flour mingled with oil for a meat offering:

74 One golden spoon of ten *shek'-els*, full of incense:

75 One young bullock, one ram, one lamb of the first year, for a burnt offering:

76 One kid of the goats for a sin offering:

77 And for a sacrifice of peace offerings, two oxen, five rams, five he goats, five lambs of the first year: this *was* the offering of Pa'-gi-el the son of Oc'-ran.

78 On the twelfth day A-hi'-ra the son of E'-nan, prince of the children of Naph'-ta-li, *offered:*

79 His offering *was* one silver charger, the weight whereof *was* an hundred and thirty *shek'-els,* one silver bowl of seventy shek'-els, after the shek'-el of the sanctuary; both of them full of fine flour mingled with oil for a meat offering:

80 One golden spoon of ten *shek'-els,* full of incense:

81 One young bullock, one ram, one lamb of the first year, for a burnt offering:

82 One kid of the goats for a sin offering:

83 And for a sacrifice of peace offerings, two oxen, five rams, five he goats, five lambs of the first year: this *was* the offering of A-hi'-ra the son of E'-nan.

84 This *was* ^Rthe dedication of the altar, in the day when it was anointed, by the princes of Israel: twelve chargers of silver, twelve silver bowls, twelve spoons of gold: v. 10

85 Each charger of silver *weighing* an hundred and thirty *shek'-els,* each bowl seventy: all the silver vessels *weighed* two thousand and four hundred *shek'-els,* after the shek'-el of the sanctuary:

86 The golden spoons *were* twelve, full of incense, *weighing* ten *shek'-els* apiece, after the shek'-el of the sanctuary: all the gold of the spoons *was* an hundred and twenty *shek'-els.*

87 All the oxen for the burnt offering *were* twelve bullocks, the rams twelve, the lambs of the first year twelve, with their meat offering: and the kids of the goats for sin offering twelve.

88 And all the oxen for the sacrifice of the peace offerings *were* twenty and four bullocks, the rams sixty, the he goats sixty, the lambs of the first year sixty. This *was* the dedication of the altar, after that it was ^Ranointed. vv. 1, 10

89 And when Moses was gone into the tabernacle of the congregation ^Rto speak with him, then he heard the voice of one speaking unto him from off the mercy seat that *was* upon the ark of testimony, from between the two cher'-u-bims: and he spake unto him. 12:8

8 And the LORD spake unto Moses, saying,

2 Speak unto Aaron, and say unto him, When thou lightest the lamps, the seven lamps shall give light over against the candlestick.

3 And Aaron did so; he lighted the lamps thereof over against the candlestick, as the LORD commanded Moses.

4 And this work of the candlestick *was of* beaten gold, unto the shaft thereof, unto the flowers thereof, *was* beaten work: ^Raccording unto the pattern which the LORD had shewed Moses, so he made the candlestick. Acts 7:44

5 And the LORD spake unto Moses, saying,

6 Take the Levites from among the children of Israel, and cleanse them.

7 And thus shalt thou do unto them, to cleanse them: Sprinkle water of purifying upon them, and let them shave all their flesh, and let them wash their clothes, and *so* make themselves clean.

8 Then let them take a young bullock with ^Rhis meat offering, *even* fine flour mingled with oil, and another young bullock shalt thou take for a sin offering. Lev. 2:1

9 And thou shalt bring the Levites before the tabernacle of the congregation: ^Rand thou shalt gather the whole assembly of the children of Israel together: Lev. 8:3

10 And thou shalt bring the Levites before the LORD: and the children of Israel ^Rshall put their hands upon the Levites: Lev. 1:4

11 And Aaron shall offer the Levites before the LORD *for* an ^Roffering of the children of Israel,

that they may execute the service of the LORD.   18:6

12 [R]And the Levites shall lay their hands upon the heads of the bullocks: and thou shalt offer the one *for* a sin offering, and the other *for* a burnt offering, unto the LORD, to make an atonement for the Levites.   Ex. 29:10

13 And thou shalt set the Levites before Aaron, and before his sons, and offer them *for* an offering unto the LORD.

14 Thus shalt thou [R]separate the Levites from among the children of Israel: and the Levites shall be [R]mine.   16:9 · 3:12, 45; 16:9

15 And after that shall the Levites go in to do the service of the tabernacle of the congregation: and thou shalt cleanse them, and offer them *for* an offering.

16 For they *are* wholly given unto me from among the children of Israel; instead of such as open every womb, *even instead of* the firstborn of all the children of Israel, have I taken them unto me.

17 [R]For all the firstborn of the children of Israel *are* mine, *both* man and beast: on the day that I smote every firstborn in the land of Egypt I sanctified them for myself.   Ex. 12:2, 12, 13, 15; Luke 2:23

18 And I have taken the Levites [T]for all the firstborn of the children of Israel.   *instead of*

19 And [R]I have given the Levites *as* a gift to Aaron and to his sons from among the children of Israel, to do the service of the children of Israel in the tabernacle of the congregation, and to make an atonement for the children of Israel: [R]that there be no plague among the children of Israel, when the children of Israel come nigh unto the sanctuary.   3:9 · 16:46; 2 Chr. 26:16

20 And Moses, and Aaron, and all the congregation of the children of Israel, did to the Levites according unto all that the LORD commanded Moses concerning the Levites, so did the children of Israel unto them.

21 [R]And the Levites were puri-

fied, and they washed their clothes; and Aaron offered them *as* an offering before the LORD; and Aaron made an atonement for them to cleanse them.   v. 7

22 [R]And after that went the Levites in to do their service in the tabernacle of the congregation before Aaron, and before his sons: [R]as the LORD had commanded Moses concerning the Levites, so did they unto them.   v. 15 · v. 5

23 And the LORD spake unto Moses, saying,

24 This *is it* that *belongeth* unto the Levites: [R]from twenty and five years old and upward they shall go in to wait upon the service of the tabernacle of the congregation: 4:3; 1 Chr. 23:3, 24, 27

25 And from the age of fifty years they shall cease waiting upon the service *thereof*, and shall serve no more:

26 But shall minister with their brethren in the tabernacle of the congregation, to keep the charge, and shall do no service. Thus shalt thou do unto the Levites touching their charge.

9 And the LORD spake unto Moses in the wilderness of Si'-nai, in the first month of the second year after they were come out of the land of Egypt, saying,

2 Let the children of Israel also keep [R]the passover at his appointed [R]season.   Ex. 12:1–16 · [1 Cor. 5:7, 8]

3 In the fourteenth day of this month, [T]at even, ye shall keep it in his appointed season: according to all the rites of it, and according to all the ceremonies thereof, shall ye keep it.   *at twilight*

4 And Moses spake unto the children of Israel, that they should keep the passover.

5 And [R]they kept the passover on the fourteenth day of the first month at even in the wilderness of Si'-nai: according to all that the LORD commanded Moses, so did the children of Israel.   Josh. 5:10

6 And there were certain men, who were [R]defiled by the dead body of a man, that they could not

keep the passover on that day: and they came before Moses and before Aaron on that day: 5:2

7 And those men said unto him, We *are* defiled by the dead body of a man: wherefore are we kept back, that we may not offer an offering of the LORD in his appointed season among the children of Israel?

8 And Moses said unto them, Stand still, and [R]I will hear what the LORD will command concerning you.   27:5; Ex. 18:22

9 And the LORD spake unto Moses, saying,

10 Speak unto the children of Israel, saying, If any man of you or of your [T]posterity shall be unclean by reason of a dead body, or *be* in a journey afar off, yet he shall keep the passover unto the LORD.   *descendants*

11 The fourteenth day of the second month at even they shall keep it, *and* eat it with unleavened bread and bitter *herbs.*

☆ 12 [R]They shall leave none of it unto the morning, [R]nor break any bone of it: according to all the ordinances of the passover they shall keep it.   Ex. 12:10 · [John 19:36]

13 But the man that *is* clean, and is not in a journey, and forbeareth to keep the passover, even the same soul [R]shall be cut off from among his people: because he brought not the offering of the LORD in his appointed season, that man shall bear his sin.   Ex. 12:15, 47

14 And if a stranger shall sojourn among you, and will keep the passover unto the LORD; according to the ordinance of the passover, and according to the manner thereof, so shall he do: [R]ye shall have one ordinance, both for the stranger, and for him that was born in the land.   Ex. 12:49

15 And on the day that the tabernacle was reared up the cloud [R]covered the tabernacle, *namely,* the tent of the testimony: and at even there was upon the tabernacle as it were the appearance of fire, until the morning.   Is. 4:5

16 So it was alway: the cloud covered it *by day,* and the appearance of fire by night.

17 And when the cloud [R]was taken up from the tabernacle, then after that the children of Israel journeyed: and in the place where the cloud abode, there the children of Israel pitched their tents.   10:11, 12; Ex. 40:36–38; Ps. 80:1

18 At the commandment of the LORD the children of Israel journeyed, and at the commandment of the LORD they pitched: as long as the cloud abode upon the tabernacle they rested in their tents.

19 And when the cloud [T]tarried long upon the tabernacle many days, then the children of Israel [R]kept the charge of the LORD, and journeyed not.   *continued* · 1:53; 3:8

20 And *so* it was, when the cloud was a few days upon the tabernacle; according to the commandment of the LORD they abode in their tents, and according to the commandment of the LORD they journeyed.

21 And *so* it was, when the cloud abode from even unto the morning, and *that* the cloud was taken up in the morning, then they journeyed: whether *it was* by day or by night that the cloud was taken up, they journeyed.

22 Or *whether it were* two days, or a month, or a year, that the cloud tarried upon the tabernacle, remaining thereon, the children of Israel [R]abode in their tents, and journeyed not: but when it was taken up, they journeyed.   Ex. 40:36

23 At the commandment of the LORD they rested in the tents, and at the commandment of the LORD they journeyed: they [R]kept the charge of the LORD, at the commandment of the LORD by the hand of Moses.   v. 19

10 And the LORD spake unto Moses, saying,

2 Make thee two trumpets of silver; of a whole piece shalt thou make them: that thou mayest use them for the [R]calling of the

assembly, and for the journeying of the camps. Is. 1:13

3 And when [R]they shall blow with them, all the assembly shall assemble themselves to thee at the door of the tabernacle of the congregation. Jer. 4:5; Joel 2:15

4 And if they blow *but* with one *trumpet*, then the princes, *which are* [R]heads of the thousands of Israel, shall gather themselves unto thee. 1:16; 7:2; Ex. 18:21

5 When ye blow an [R]alarm, then the camps that lie on the east parts shall go forward. Joel 2:1

6 When ye blow an alarm the second time, then the camps that lie [R]on the south side shall [T]take their journey: they shall blow an alarm for their journeys. 2:10 · begin

7 But when the congregation is to be gathered together, [R]ye shall blow, but ye shall not [R]sound an alarm. v. 3 · Joel 2:1

8 [R]And the sons of Aaron, the priests, shall blow with the trumpets; and they shall be to you for an ordinance for ever throughout your generations. 1 Chr. 15:24

9 And if ye go to war in your land against the enemy that oppresseth you, then ye shall blow an alarm with the trumpets; and ye shall be remembered before the LORD your God, and ye shall be saved from your enemies.

10 Also [R]in the day of your gladness, and in your solemn days, and in the beginnings of your months, ye shall blow with the trumpets over your burnt offerings, and over the sacrifices of your peace offerings; that they may be to you for a memorial before your God: I *am* the LORD your God. 1 Chr. 15:24; 2 Chr. 5:12; Ps. 81:3

11 And it came to pass on the twentieth *day* of the second month, in the second year, that the cloud [R]was taken up from off the tabernacle of the testimony. 9:17

12 And the children of Israel took their journeys out of the [R]wilderness of Si'-nai; and the cloud rested in the [R]wilderness of Pa'-ran. Ex. 40:36 · Gen. 21:21; Deut. 1:1

13 And they first took their journey [R]according to the commandment of the LORD by the hand of Moses. vv. 5, 6

14 [R]In the first *place* went the [T]standard of the camp of the children of Judah according to their armies: and over his host *was* [R]Nah'-shon the son of Am-min'-a-dab. 2:3–9 · banner · 1:7

15 And over the host of the tribe of the children of Is'-sa-char *was* Ne-than'-e-el the son of Zu'-ar.

16 And over the host of the tribe of the children of Zeb'-u-lun *was* E-li'-ab the son of He'-lon.

17 And the tabernacle was taken down; and the sons of Ger'-shon and the sons of Me-ra'-ri set forward, bearing the tabernacle.

18 And [R]the standard of the camp of Reu'ben [T]set forward according to their armies: and over his host *was* E-li'-zur the son of Shed'-e-ur. 2:10–16 · set out

19 And over the host of the tribe of the children of Simeon *was* She-lu'-mi-el the son of Zu-ri-shad'-dai.

20 And over the host of the tribe of the children of Gad *was* E-li'-a-saph the son of Deu'-el.

21 And the Ko'-hath-ites set forward, bearing the [R]sanctuary: and *the other* did set up the tabernacle against they came. 4:4–20; 7:9

22 And the standard of the camp of the children of E'-phra-im set forward according to their armies: and over his host *was* E-lish'-a-ma the son of Am-mi'-hud.

23 And over the host of the tribe of the children of Ma-nas'-seh *was* Ga-ma'-li-el the son of Pe-dah'-zur.

24 And over the host of the tribe of the children of Benjamin *was* Ab'-i-dan the son of Gid-e-o'-ni.

25 And the standard of the camp of the children of Dan set forward, *which was* the rereward of all the camps throughout their hosts: and over his host *was* A-hi-e'-zer the son of Am-mi-shad'-dai.

26 And over the host of the tribe

of the children of Asher *was* Pa'-gi-el the son of Oc'-ran.

27 And over the host of the tribe of the children of Naph'-ta-li *was* A-hi'-ra the son of E'-nan.

28 [R]Thus [T]*were* the journeyings of the children of Israel according to their armies, when they set forward.   2:34 · *was the order of march*

29 And Moses said unto Ho'-bab, the son of Ra-gu'-el the Mid'-i-an-ite, Moses' father in law, We are journeying unto the place of which the LORD said, [R]I will give it you: come thou with us, and [R]we will do thee good: for [R]the LORD hath spoken good concerning Israel.   Ex. 6:4–8 · Judg. 1:16 · Gen. 32:12

30 And he said unto him, I will not go; but I will depart to mine own land, and to my kindred.

31 And he said, Leave us not, I pray thee; forasmuch as thou knowest how we are to encamp in the wilderness, and thou mayest be to us [R]instead of eyes.   Job 29:15

32 And it shall be, if thou go with us, yea, it shall be, that what goodness the LORD shall do unto us, the same will we do unto thee.

33 And they departed from [R]the mount of the LORD three days' journey: and the ark of the covenant of the LORD [R]went before them in the three days' journey, to search out a resting place for them.   Ex. 3:1 · Josh. 3:3–6; Ezek. 20:6

34 And [R]the cloud of the LORD *was* upon them by day, when they went out of the camp.   Ex. 13:21

35 And it came to pass, when the ark set forward, that Moses said, [R]Rise up, LORD, and let thine enemies be scattered; and let them that hate thee flee before thee.   Ps. 68:1, 2; 132:8; Is. 17:12–14

36 And when it rested, he said, Return, O LORD, unto the many thousands of Israel.

11 And [R]*when* the people complained, it displeased the LORD: and the LORD heard *it*; [R]and his anger was kindled; and the [R]fire of the LORD burnt among them, and consumed *them that*

were in the uttermost parts of the camp.   Deut. 9:22 · Ps. 78:21 · Lev. 10:2

2 And the people [R]cried unto Moses; and when Moses [R]prayed unto the LORD, the fire was quenched.   12:11, 13; 21:7 · [James 5:16]

3 And he called the name of the place [T]Tab'-e-rah: because the fire of the LORD burnt among them.   Lit. *Burning*

4 And the mixt multitude that *was* among them fell a lusting: and the children of Israel also wept again, and said, [R]Who shall give us flesh to eat?   [Ps. 78:18]

5 [R]We remember the fish, which we did eat in Egypt freely; the cucumbers, and the melons, and the leeks, and the onions, and the garlick: Ex. 16:3

6 But now [R]our [T]soul *is* dried away: *there is* nothing at all, beside this man'-na, *before* our eyes.   21:5 · *whole being is dried up*

7 And the man'-na *was* as coriander seed, and the colour thereof as the colour of bdellium.

8 *And* the people went about, and gathered *it,* and ground *it* in mills, or beat *it* in a mortar, and baked *it* in pans, and made cakes of it: and [R]the taste of it was as the taste of fresh oil.   Ex. 16:31

9 And [R]when the dew fell upon the camp in the night, the man'-na fell upon it.   Ex. 16:13, 14

10 Then Moses heard the people weep throughout their families, every man in the door of his tent: and [R]the anger of the LORD was [T]kindled greatly; Moses also was displeased.   Ps. 78:21 · *aroused*

11 [R]And Moses said unto the LORD, Wherefore hast thou afflicted thy servant? and wherefore have I not found favour in thy sight, that thou layest the burden of all this people upon me?   Ex. 5:22

12 Have I conceived all this people? have I begotten them, that thou shouldest say unto me, Carry them in thy bosom, as a [R]nursing father beareth the sucking child, unto the land which thou [R]swarest unto their fathers?   Is. 49:23 · Gen. 26:3

13 Whence should I have [T]flesh

to give unto all this people? for they weep unto me, saying, Give us flesh, that we may eat.   *meat*

14 ᴿI am not able to bear all this people alone, because *it is* too heavy for me.   Ex. 18:18; Deut. 1:12

15 And if thou deal thus with me, kill me, I pray thee, ᵀout of hand, if I have found favour in thy sight; and let me not ᴿsee my wretchedness.   *at once* · Rev. 3:17

16 And the LORD said unto Moses, Gather unto me ᴿseventy men of the elders of Israel, whom thou knowest to be the elders of the people, and ᴿofficers over them; and bring them unto the tabernacle of the congregation, that they may stand there with thee.   Ex. 18:25; 24:1, 9 · Deut. 16:18

17 And I will come down and talk with thee there: and ᴿI will take of the spirit which *is* upon thee, and will put *it* upon them; and they shall bear the burden of the people with thee, that thou bear *it* not thyself alone.   [Joel 2:28]

18 And say thou unto the people, Sanctify yourselves against to morrow, and ye shall eat ᵀflesh: for ye have wept ᴿin the ears of the LORD, saying, Who shall give us flesh to eat? for *it was* well with us in Egypt: therefore the LORD will give you flesh, and ye shall eat.   *meat* · Ex. 16:7

19 Ye shall not eat one day, nor two days, nor five days, neither ten days, nor twenty days;

20 *But* even a whole month, until it come out at your nostrils, and it be loathsome unto you: because that ye have despised the LORD which *is* among you, and have wept before him, saying, Why came we forth out of Egypt?

21 And Moses said, The people, among whom I *am, are* six hundred thousand footmen; and thou hast said, I will give them flesh, that they may eat a whole month.

22 ᴿShall the flocks and the herds be slain for them, to suffice them? or shall all the fish of the sea be gathered together for them, to suffice them?   2 Kin. 7:2

23 And the LORD said unto Moses, ᴿIs the LORD's hand waxed short? thou shalt see now whether my ᴿword shall come to pass unto thee or not.   Is. 50:2; 59:1 · 23:19

24 And Moses went out, and told the people the words of the LORD, and gathered the seventy men of the elders of the people, and set them round about the tabernacle.

25 And the LORD came down in a cloud, and spake unto him, and took of the spirit that *was* upon him, and gave *it* unto the seventy elders: and it came to pass, *that*, ᴿwhen the spirit rested upon them, ᴿthey prophesied, and did not cease.   2 Kin. 2:15 · Acts 2:17, 18

26 But there remained two *of the* men in the camp, the name of the one *was* El'-dad, and the name of the other Me'-dad: and the spirit rested upon them; and they *were* of them that were written, but ᴿwent not out unto the tabernacle: and they prophesied in the camp.   Jer. 36:5

27 And there ran a young man, and told Moses, and said, El'-dad and Me'-dad do prophesy in the camp.

28 And Joshua the son of Nun, the servant of Moses, *one* of his young men, answered and said, My lord Moses, forbid them.

29 And Moses said unto him, Enviest thou for my sake? would God that all the LORD's people were prophets, *and* that the LORD would put his spirit upon them!

30 And Moses gat him into the camp, he and the elders of Israel.

31 And there went forth a ᴿwind from the LORD, and brought quails from the sea, and let *them* fall by the camp, as it were a day's journey on this side, and as it were a day's journey on the other side, round about the camp, and as it were two cubits *high* upon the face of the earth.   Ps. 78:26–28; 105:40

32 And the people stood up all that day, and all *that* night, and all the next day, and they gathered the quails: he that gathered

least gathered ten ho'-mers: and they spread *them* all abroad for themselves round about the camp.

33 And while the ᴿflesh *was* yet between their teeth, ere it was chewed, the wrath of the LORD was kindled against the people, and the LORD smote the people with a very great plague. Ps. 106:15

34 And he called the name of that place Kib'-roth–hat-ta'-a-vah: because there they buried the people that lusted.

35 ᴿAnd the people journeyed from Kib'-roth–hat-ta'-a-vah unto Ha-ze'-roth; and abode at Ha-ze'-roth.　　33:17

12 And ᴿMiriam and Aaron spake against Moses because of the E-thi-o'-pi-an woman whom he had married: for ᴿhe had married an ᵀE-thi-o'-pi-an woman. Ex. 15:20, 21 · Ex. 2:21 · *Cushite*

2　And they said, Hath the LORD indeed spoken only by Moses? ᴿhath he not spoken also by us? And the LORD heard *it*.　　Ex. 15:20

3　(Now the man Moses *was* very meek, above all the men which *were* upon the face of the earth.)

4　ᴿAnd the LORD spake suddenly unto Moses, and unto Aaron, and unto Miriam, Come out ye three unto the tabernacle of the congregation. And they three came out.　　[Ps. 76:9]

5　ᴿAnd the LORD came down in the pillar of the cloud, and stood *in* the door of the tabernacle, and called Aaron and Miriam: and they both came forth.　Ex. 19:9; 34:5

6　And he said, Hear now my words: If there be a prophet among you, *I* the LORD will make myself known unto him in a vision, *and* will speak unto him ᴿin a dream.　Gen. 31:10; 1 Kin. 3:5, 15

7　My servant Moses *is* not so, who *is* faithful in all mine house.

8　With him will I speak mouth to mouth, even apparently, and not in dark speeches; and the similitude of the LORD shall he behold: wherefore then ᴿwere ye not afraid to speak against my servant Moses?　2 Pet. 2:10; Jude 8

9　And the anger of the LORD was kindled against them; and he departed.

10 And the cloud departed from off the tabernacle; and, ᴿbehold, Miriam *became* ᴿleprous, *white* as snow: and Aaron looked upon Miriam, and, behold, *she was* leprous.　Deut. 24:9 · Ex. 4:6; 2 Chr. 26:19, 20

11 And Aaron said unto Moses, Alas, my lord, I beseech thee, ᴿlay not the sin upon us, wherein we have done foolishly, and wherein we have sinned.　2 Sam. 19:19; 24:10

12 Let her not be ᴿas one dead, of whom the flesh is half consumed when he cometh out of his mother's womb.　Ps. 88:4

13 And Moses cried unto the LORD, saying, ᴿHeal her now, O God, I beseech thee.　Ps. 103:3

14 And the LORD said unto Moses, If her father had but ᴿspit in her face, should she not be ashamed seven days? let her be ᴿshut out from the camp seven days, and after that let her be received in *again*.　Is. 50:6 · Lev. 13:46

15 And Miriam was shut out from the camp seven days: and the people journeyed not till Miriam was brought in *again*.

16 And afterward the people removed from ᴿHa-ze'-roth, and pitched in the wilderness of Pa'-ran.　　11:35; 33:17, 18

13 And the LORD spake unto Moses, saying,

2　ᴿSend thou men, that they may search the land of Canaan, which I give unto the children of Israel: of every tribe of their fathers shall ye send a man, every one a ruler among them.　32:8

3　And Moses by the commandment of the LORD sent them ᴿfrom the wilderness of Pa'-ran: all those men *were* heads of the children of Israel.　Deut. 1:19; 9:23

4　And these *were* their names: of the tribe of Reuben, Shammu'-a the son of Zac'-cur.

5　Of the tribe of Simeon, Sha'-phat the son of Ho'-ri.

6　ᴿOf the tribe of Judah, ᴿCaleb the son of Je-phun'-neh.　34:19 · 14:6

7 Of the tribe of Is'-sa-char, I'-gal the son of Joseph.

8 Of the tribe of E'-phra-im, O-she'-a the son of Nun.

9 Of the tribe of Benjamin, Pal'-ti the son of Ra'-phu.

10 Of the tribe of Zeb'-u-lun, Gad'-di-el the son of So'-di.

11 Of the tribe of Joseph, *namely,* of the tribe of Ma-nas'-seh, Gad'-di the son of Su'-si.

12 Of the tribe of Dan, Am'-mi-el the son of Ge-mal'-li.

13 Of the tribe of Asher, Se'-thur the son of Mi'-cha-el.

14 Of the tribe of Naph'-ta-li, Nah'-bi the son of Voph'-si.

15 Of the tribe of Gad, Geu'-el the son of Ma'-chi.

16 These *are* the names of the men which Moses sent to spy out the land. And Moses called ᴿO-she'-a the son of Nun Je-hosh'-u-a.   Ex. 17:9; Deut. 32:44

17 And Moses sent them to spy out the land of Canaan, and said unto them, Get you up this *way* southward, and go up into ᴿthe mountain: Judg. 1:9

18 And see the land, what it *is*; and the people that dwelleth therein, whether they *be* strong or weak, few or many;

19 And what the land *is* that they dwell in, whether it *be* good or bad; and what cities *they be* that they dwell in, whether in tents, or in strong holds;

20 And what the land *is*, whether it *be* ᵀfat or lean, whether there be wood therein, or not. And ᴿbe ye of good courage, and bring of the fruit of the land. Now the time *was* the time of the firstripe grapes. *fertile or barren* · Deut. 31:6, 7, 23

21 So they went up, and searched the land ᴿfrom the wilderness of Zin unto Re'-hob, as men come to Ha'-math.   Josh. 15:1

22 And they ascended by the south, and came unto ᴿHe'-bron; where A-hi'-man, She'-shai, and Tal'-mai, the children of ᴿA'-nak, *were*. (Now He'-bron was built seven years before Zo'-an in Egypt.) Josh. 15:13, 14 · Josh. 11:21, 22

23 ᴿAnd they came unto the brook of Esh'-col, and cut down from thence a branch with one cluster of grapes, and they bare it between two upon a staff; and *they brought* of the pomegranates, and of the figs.   Deut. 1:24, 25

24 The place was called the brook ᵀEsh'-col, because of the cluster of grapes which the children of Israel cut down from thence.   Lit. *Cluster*

25 And they returned from searching of the land after forty days.

26 And they went and came to Moses, and to Aaron, and to all the congregation of the children of Israel, unto the wilderness of Pa'-ran, to ᴿKa'-desh; and brought back word unto them, and unto all the congregation, and shewed them the fruit of the land. Josh. 14:6

27 And they told him, and said, We came unto the land whither thou sentest us, and surely it floweth with ᴿmilk and honey; and this *is* the fruit of it.   Ex. 33:3

28 Nevertheless the ᴿpeople *be* strong that dwell in the land, and the cities *are* walled, *and* very great: and moreover we saw the children of A'-nak there. Deut. 1:28

29 ᴿThe Am'-a-lek-ites dwell in the land of the south: and the Hit'-tites, and the Jeb'-u-sites, and the Am'-or-ites, dwell in the mountains: and the Ca'-naan-ites dwell by the sea, and by the coast of Jordan.   Ex. 17:8; Judg. 6:3

30 And ᴿCaleb stilled the people before Moses, and said, Let us go up at once, and possess it; for we are well able to overcome it.   14:6

31 ᴿBut the men that went up with him said, We be not able to go up against the people; for they *are* stronger than we. 32:9; Deut. 1:28

32 And they ᴿbrought up an evil report of the land which they had searched unto the children of Israel, saying, The land, through which we have gone to search it, *is* a land that eateth up the inhabitants thereof; and ᴿall the people that we saw in it *are* men of a great stature.   Ps. 106:24 · Amos 2:9

33 And there we saw the [R]giants, the sons of A'-nak, *which come* of the giants: and we were in our own sight [R]as grasshoppers, and so we were [R]in their sight.   Josh. 11:21 · Is. 40:22 · 1 Sam. 17:42

14 And all the congregation lifted up their voice, and cried; and the people [R]wept that night.   11:4; Deut. 1:45

2 [R]And all the children of Israel murmured against Moses and against Aaron: and the whole congregation said unto them, Would God that we had died in the land of Egypt! or would God we had died in this wilderness!   1 Cor. 10:10

3 And wherefore hath the LORD brought us unto this land, to fall by the sword, that our wives and our [R]children should be a prey? were it not better for us to return into Egypt?   v. 31; Deut. 1:39

4 And they said one to another, Let us make a captain, and [R]let us return into Egypt.   Acts 7:39

5 Then Moses and Aaron fell on their faces before all the assembly of the congregation of the children of Israel.

6 And Joshua the son of Nun, and Caleb the son of Je-phun'-neh, *which were* of them that searched the land, [T]rent their clothes: *tore*

7 And they spake unto all the company of the children of Israel, saying, [R]The land, which we passed through to search it, *is* an exceeding good land.   Deut. 1:25

8 If the LORD delight in us, then he will bring us into this land, and give it us; [R]a land which floweth with milk and honey.   Ex. 3:8

9 Only rebel not ye against the LORD, [R]neither fear ye the people of the land; for [R]they *are* bread for us: their defence is departed from them, and the LORD *is* with us: fear them not.   Deut. 7:18 · 24:8

10 [R]But all the congregation bade stone them with stones. And [R]the glory of the LORD appeared in the tabernacle of the congregation before all the children of Israel.   Ex. 17:4 · Ex. 16:10; Lev. 9:23

11 And the LORD said unto Moses, How long will this people [R]provoke me? and how long will it be ere they [R]believe me, for all the signs which I have shewed among them?   Heb. 3:8 · [John 12:37]

12 I will smite them with the pestilence, and disinherit them, and will make of thee a greater nation and mightier than they.

13 And [R]Moses said unto the LORD, [R]Then the Egyptians shall hear *it*, (for thou broughtest up this people in thy might from among them;)   Ps. 106:23 · Ex. 32:12

14 And they will tell *it* to the inhabitants of this land: *for* they have heard that thou LORD *art* among this people, that thou LORD art seen face to face, and *that* thy cloud standeth over them, and *that* thou goest before them, by daytime in a pillar of a cloud, and in a pillar of fire by night.

15 Now *if* thou shalt kill *all* this people as one man, then the nations which have heard the fame of thee will speak, saying,

16 Because the LORD was not [R]able to bring this people into the land which he sware unto them, therefore he hath slain them in the wilderness.   Deut. 9:28

17 And now, I beseech thee, let the power of my LORD be great, according as thou hast spoken, saying,

18 The LORD *is* [R]longsuffering, and of great mercy, forgiving iniquity and transgression, and by no means clearing *the guilty*, visiting the iniquity of the fathers upon the children unto the third and fourth *generation*.   Ps. 103:8

19 [R]Pardon, I beseech thee, the iniquity of this people [R]according unto the greatness of thy mercy, and [R]as thou hast forgiven this people, from Egypt even until now.   Ex. 32:32; 34:9 · Ps. 51:1 · Ps. 78:38

20 And the LORD said, I have pardoned according to thy word:

21 But *as* truly *as* I live, [R]all the earth shall be filled with the glory of the LORD.   Ps. 72:19; Is. 6:3; Hab. 2:14

22 [R]Because all those men which have seen my glory, and

my miracles, which I did in Egypt and in the wilderness, and have tempted me now ᴿthese ten times, and have not hearkened to my voice;   1 Cor. 10:5; Heb. 3:17 · Gen. 31:7

23 Surely they shall not ᴿsee the land which I sware unto their fathers, neither shall any of them that provoked me see it: Heb. 3:18

24 But my servant ᴿCaleb, because he had another spirit with him, and ᴿhath followed me fully, him will I bring into the land whereinto he went; and his seed shall possess it.   Josh. 14:6, 8, 9 · 32:12

25 (Now the Am'-a-lek-ites and the Ca'-naan-ites dwelt in the valley.) To morrow turn you, and ᴿget you into the wilderness by the way of the Red sea.   21:4; Deut. 1:40

26 And the LORD spake unto Moses and unto Aaron, saying,

27 ᴿHow long *shall I bear with* this evil congregation, which murmur against me? ᴿI have heard the murmurings of the children of Israel, which they murmur against me.   Ex. 16:28 · Ex. 16:12

28 Say unto them, ᴿAs *truly as* I live, saith the LORD, as ye have spoken in mine ears, so will I do to you: Deut. 1:35; 2:14, 15; Heb. 3:16–19

29 Your carcases shall fall in this wilderness; and ᴿall that were numbered of you, according to your whole number, from twenty years old and upward, which have murmured against me,   Josh. 5:6

30 Doubtless ye shall not come into the land, *concerning* which I sware to make you dwell therein, save Caleb the son of Je-phun'-neh, and Joshua the son of Nun.

31 But your little ones, which ye said should be a prey, them will I bring in, and they shall know the land which ye have despised.

32 But *as for* you, your carcases, they shall fall in this wilderness.

33 And your children shall ᴿwander in the wilderness forty years, and bear your whoredoms, until your carcases be wasted in the wilderness.   32:13; Ps. 107:40

34 ᴿAfter the number of the days in which ye searched the land,

even forty days, each day for a year, shall ye bear your iniquities, *even* forty years, and ye shall know my breach of promise.   13:25

35 ᴿI the LORD have said, I will surely do it unto all ᴿthis evil congregation, that are gathered together against me: in this wilderness they shall be consumed, and there they shall die.   23:19 · 1 Cor. 10:5

36 And the men, which Moses sent to ᵀsearch the land, who returned, and made all the congregation to murmur against him, by bringing up a ᵀslander upon the land,   *spy out · bad report*

37 Even those men that did bring up the evil report upon the land, ᴿdied by the plague before the LORD.   [1 Cor. 10:10]; Heb. 3:17, 18

38 But Joshua the son of Nun, and Caleb the son of Je-phun'-neh, *which were* of the men that went to search the land, lived *still.*

39 And Moses told these sayings unto all the children of Israel: and the people mourned greatly.

40 And they rose up early in the morning, and gat them up into the top of the mountain, saying, Lo, we *be here,* and will go up unto the place which the LORD hath promised: for we have sinned.

41 And Moses said, Wherefore now do ye transgress the commandment of the LORD? but it shall not ᵀprosper.   *succeed*

42 Go not up, for the LORD *is* not among you; that ye be not smitten before your enemies.

43 For the Am'-a-lek-ites and the Ca'-naan-ites *are* there before you, and ye shall fall by the sword: because ye are turned away from the LORD, therefore the LORD will not be with you.

44 ᴿBut they presumed to go up unto the hill top: nevertheless the ark of the covenant of the LORD, and Moses, departed not out of the camp.   Deut. 1:43

45 Then the Am'-a-lek-ites came down, and the Ca'-naan-ites which dwelt in that hill, and smote them, and discomfited them, *even* unto ᴿHor'-mah.   21:3

15 And the LORD spake unto Moses, saying,

2 ᴿSpeak unto the children of Israel, and say unto them, When ye be come into the land ᵀof your habitations, which I give unto you,   15:18; Deut. 7:1 · *you are to inhabit*

3 And will make an offering by fire unto the LORD, a burnt offering, or a sacrifice in performing a vow, or in a freewill offering, or in your solemn feasts, to make a ᴿsweet savour unto the LORD, of the herd, or of the flock: Gen. 8:21

4 Then ᴿshall he that offereth his offering unto the LORD bring ᴿa meat offering of a tenth deal of flour mingled with the fourth *part* of an hin of oil. Lev. 2:1; 6:14 · Ex. 29:40

5 ᴿAnd the fourth *part* of an hin of wine for a drink offering shalt thou prepare with the burnt offering or sacrifice, for one ᴿlamb.   28:7, 14 · Lev. 1:10; 3:6

6 ᴿOr for a ram, thou shalt prepare *for* a meat offering two tenth deals of flour mingled with the third *part* of an hin of oil.   28:12, 14

7 And for a drink offering thou shalt offer the third *part* of an hin of wine, *for* a sweet savour unto the LORD.

8 And when thou preparest a bullock *for* a burnt offering, or *for* a sacrifice in performing a vow, or peace offerings unto the LORD:

9 Then shall he bring ᴿwith a bullock a meat offering of three tenth deals of flour mingled with half an hin of oil.   28:12, 14

10 And thou shalt bring for a drink offering half an hin of wine, *for* an offering made by fire, of a sweet savour unto the LORD.

11 ᴿThus shall it be done for one bullock, or for one ram, or for a lamb, or a kid.   28:1–31

12 According to the number that ye shall prepare, so shall ye do to every one according to their number.

13 All that are born of the country shall do these things after this manner, in offering an offering made by fire, of a sweet savour unto the LORD.

14 And if a stranger ᵀsojourn with you, or whosoever *be* among you in your generations, and will offer an offering made by fire, of a sweet savour unto the LORD; as ye do, so he shall do.   *stays temporarily*

15 ᴿOne ordinance *shall be both* for you of the congregation, and also for the stranger that sojourneth *with you,* an ordinance for ever in your generations: as ye *are,* so shall the stranger be before the LORD.   v. 29; 9:14; Ex. 12:49

16 One law and one manner shall be for you, and for the stranger that sojourneth with you.

17 And the LORD spake unto Moses, saying,

18 ᴿSpeak unto the children of Israel, and say unto them, When ye come into the land whither I bring you,   v. 2; Deut. 26:1

19 Then it shall be, that, when ye eat of ᴿthe bread of the land, ye shall offer up an heave offering unto the LORD.   Josh. 5:11, 12

20 ᴿYe shall offer up a cake of the first of your dough *for* an heave offering: as *ye do* the heave offering of the threshingfloor, so shall ye heave it.   Ex. 34:26; Lev. 23:10

21 Of the first of your dough ye shall give unto the LORD an heave offering in your generations.

22 And ᴿif ye have erred, and not observed all these commandments, which the LORD hath spoken unto Moses,   Lev. 4:2

23 *Even* all that the LORD hath commanded you by the hand of Moses, from the day that the LORD commanded *Moses,* and henceforward among your generations;

24 Then it shall be, ᴿif *ought* be committed by ignorance without the knowledge of the congregation, that all the congregation shall offer one young bullock for a burnt offering, for a sweet savour unto the LORD, with his meat offering, and his drink offering, according to the ᵀmanner, and ᴿone kid of the goats for a sin offering.   Lev. 4:13 · *ordinance* · Lev. 4:23

25 ᴿAnd the priest shall make an atonement for all the congrega-

tion of the children of Israel, and it shall be forgiven them; for it *is* ignorance: and they shall bring their offering, a sacrifice made by fire unto the LORD, and their sin offering before the LORD, for their ignorance: Lev. 4:20; [Heb. 2:17]

26 And it shall be forgiven all the congregation of the children of Israel, and the stranger that sojourneth among them; seeing all the people *were* in ignorance.

27 And ᴿif any soul sin through ignorance, then he shall bring a she goat of the first year for a sin offering. Lev. 4:27–31

28 ᴿAnd the priest shall make an atonement for the soul that sinneth ignorantly, when he sinneth by ignorance before the LORD, to make an atonement for him; and it shall be forgiven him. Lev. 4:35

29 ᴿYe shall have one law for him that sinneth through ignorance, *both for* him that is born among the children of Israel, and for the stranger that sojourneth among them. v. 15

30 But the soul that doeth *ought* presumptuously, *whether he be* born in the land, or a stranger, the same reproacheth the LORD; and that soul shall be cut off from among his people.

31 Because he hath despised the word of the LORD, and hath broken his commandment, that soul shall utterly be cut off; his iniquity *shall be* upon him.

32 And while the children of Israel were in the wilderness, they found a man that gathered sticks upon the sabbath day.

33 And they that found him gathering sticks brought him unto Moses and Aaron, and unto all the congregation.

34 And they put him ᴿin ward, because it was not declared what should be done to him. Lev. 24:12

35 And the LORD said unto Moses, ᴿThe man shall be surely put to death: all the congregation shall ᴿstone him with stones without the camp. Ex. 31:14, 15 · Lev. 24:14

36 And all the congregation brought him without the camp, and stoned him with stones, and he died; as the LORD commanded Moses.

37 And the LORD spake unto Moses, saying,

38 Speak unto the children of Israel, and bid ᴿthem that they make them fringes in the borders of their garments throughout their generations, and that they put upon the fringe of the borders a ribband of blue: Matt. 23:5

39 And it shall be unto you for a fringe, that ye may look upon it, and ᴿremember all the commandments of the LORD, and do them; and that ye ᴿseek not after your own heart and your own eyes, after which ye use ᴿto go a whoring: Ps. 103:18 · Deut. 29:19 · James 4:4

40 That ye may remember, and do all my commandments, and be ᴿholy unto your God. [Col. 1:22]

41 I *am* the LORD your God, which brought you out of the land of Egypt, to be your God: I *am* the LORD your God.

16 Now ᴿKo'-rah, the son of Iz'-har, the son of Ko'-hath, the son of Levi, and ᴿDa'-than and A-bi'-ram, the sons of E-li'-ab, and On, the son of Pe'-leth, sons of Reuben, took *men:* Ex. 6:21 · 26:9

2 And they rose up before Moses, with certain of the children of Israel, two hundred and fifty princes of the assembly, ᴿfamous in the congregation, men of renown: 1:16; 26:9

3 And ᴿthey gathered themselves together against Moses and against Aaron, and said unto them, *Ye take* too much upon you, seeing all the congregation *are* holy, every one of them, and the LORD *is* among them: wherefore then lift ye up yourselves above the congregation of the LORD? 12:2; 14:2; Ps. 106:16

4 And when Moses heard *it,* he ᴿfell upon his face: 14:5; 20:6

5 And he spake unto Ko'-rah and unto all his company, saying, Even to morrow the LORD will shew who *are* ᴿhis, and *who is*

holy; and will cause *him* to come near unto him: even *him* whom he hath chosen will he cause to come near unto him.   [2 Tim. 2:19]

6 This do; Take you censers, Ko'-rah, and all his company;

7 And put fire therein, and put incense in them before the LORD to morrow: and it shall be *that* the man whom the LORD doth choose, he *shall be* holy: ye *take* too much upon you, ye sons of Levi.

8 And Moses said unto Ko'-rah, Hear, I pray you, ye sons of Levi:

9 *Seemeth it but* [R]a small thing unto you, that the God of Israel hath separated you from the congregation of Israel, to bring you near to himself to do the service of the tabernacle of the LORD, and to stand before the congregation to minister unto them?   1 Sam. 18:23

10 And he hath brought thee near *to him,* and all thy brethren the sons of Levi with thee: and seek ye the priesthood also?

11 For which cause *both* thou and all thy company *are* gathered together against the LORD: [R]and what *is* Aaron, that ye [T]murmur against him?   Ex. 16:7, 8 · *grumble*

12 And Moses sent to call Da'-than and A-bi'-ram, the sons of E-li'-ab: which said, We will not come up:

13 *Is it* a small thing that thou hast brought us up out of a [R]land that floweth with milk and honey, to kill us in the wilderness, except thou [R]make thyself altogether a prince over us?   11:4–6 · Acts 7:27, 35

14 Moreover [R]thou hast not brought us into [R]a land that floweth with milk and honey, or given us inheritance of fields and vineyards: wilt thou put out the eyes of these men? we will not come up.   14:1–4 · Ex. 3:8; Lev. 20:24

15 And Moses was very wroth, and said unto the LORD, Respect not thou their offering: [R]I have not taken one ass from them, neither have I hurt one of them.   Acts 20:33

16 And Moses said unto Ko'-rah,

Be thou and all thy company [R]before the LORD, thou, and they, and Aaron, to morrow: 1 Sam. 12:3, 7

17 And take every man his censer, and put incense in them, and bring ye before the LORD every man his censer, two hundred and fifty censers; thou also, and Aaron, each *of you* his censer.

18 And they took every man his censer, and put fire in them, and laid incense thereon, and stood in the door of the tabernacle of the congregation with Moses and Aaron.

19 And Ko'-rah gathered all the congregation against them unto the door of the tabernacle of the congregation: and [R]the glory of the LORD appeared unto all the congregation.   Ex. 16:7, 10; Lev. 9:6, 23

20 And the LORD spake unto Moses and unto Aaron, saying,

21 Separate yourselves from among this congregation, that I may consume them in a moment.

22 And they fell upon their faces, and said, O God, [R]the God of the spirits of all flesh, shall one man sin, and wilt thou be wroth with all the congregation? Heb. 12:9

23 And the LORD spake unto Moses, saying,

24 Speak unto the congregation, saying, [T]Get you up from about the tabernacle of Ko'-rah, Da'-than, and A-bi'-ram.   *Get away from*

25 And Moses rose up and went unto Da'-than and A-bi'-ram; and the elders of Israel followed him.

26 And he spake unto the congregation, saying, [R]Depart, I pray you, from the tents of these wicked men, and touch nothing of theirs, lest ye be consumed in all their sins.   Gen. 19:12, 14, 15, 17

27 So they gat up from the tabernacle of Ko'-rah, Da'-than, and A-bi'-ram, on every side: and Da'-than and A-bi'-ram came out, and stood in the door of their tents, and their wives, and their sons, and their little [R]children.   Ex. 20:5

28 And Moses said, [R]Hereby ye shall know that the LORD hath sent me to do all these works; for

Moses unto the door of the tabernacle of the congregation: and the plague was stayed.

17 And the LORD spake unto Moses, saying,

2 Speak unto the children of Israel, and take of every one of them a rod according to the house of *their* fathers, of all their princes according to the house of their fathers twelve rods: write thou every man's name upon his rod.

3 And thou shalt write Aaron's name upon the rod of Levi: for one rod *shall be* for the head of the house of their fathers.

4 And thou shalt lay them up in the tabernacle of the congregation before the testimony, ᴿwhere I will meet with you. Ex. 25:22; 30:36

5 And it shall come to pass, *that* the man's rod, ᴿwhom I shall choose, shall blossom: and I will ᵀmake to cease from me the murmurings of the children of Israel, ᴿwhereby they murmur against you. 16:5 · *rid myself* · 16:11

6 And Moses spake unto the children of Israel, and every one of their princes gave him a rod apiece, for each prince one, according to their fathers' houses, *even* twelve rods: and the rod of Aaron *was* among their rods.

7 And Moses laid up the rods before the LORD in ᴿthe tabernacle of witness. 1:50, 51; Ex. 38:21; Acts 7:44

8 And it came to pass, that on the morrow Moses went into the tabernacle of witness; and, behold, the rod of Aaron for the house of Levi was budded, and brought forth buds, and bloomed blossoms, and yielded almonds.

9 And Moses brought out all the rods from before the LORD unto all the children of Israel: and they looked, and took every man his rod.

10 And the LORD said unto Moses, Bring ᴿAaron's rod again before the testimony, to be kept ᴿfor a token against the rebels; and thou shalt quite take away their murmurings from me, that they die not. Heb. 9:4 · Deut. 9:7, 24

11 And Moses did *so:* as the LORD commanded him, so did he.

12 And the children of Israel spake unto Moses, saying, Behold, we die, we perish, we all perish.

13 ᴿWhosoever cometh any thing near unto the tabernacle of the LORD shall die: shall we be consumed with dying? 1:51, 53; 18:4

18 And the LORD said unto Aaron, Thou and thy sons and thy father's house with thee shall ᴿbear the iniquity of the sanctuary: and thou and thy sons with thee shall bear the iniquity of your priesthood. Ex. 28:38; Lev. 10:17

2 And thy brethren also of the ᴿtribe of Levi, the tribe of thy father, bring thou with thee, that they may be ᴿjoined unto thee, and minister unto thee: but thou and thy sons with thee *shall minister* before the tabernacle of witness. 1:47; Gen. 29:34 · 3:5–10

3 And they shall keep thy charge, and the charge of all the tabernacle: ᴿonly they shall not come nigh the vessels of the sanctuary and the altar, ᴿthat neither they, nor ye also, die. 16:40 · 4:15

4 And they shall be joined unto thee, and keep the charge of the tabernacle of the congregation, for all the service of the tabernacle: ᴿand a stranger shall not come nigh unto you. 3:10

5 And ye shall keep ᴿthe charge of the sanctuary, and the charge of the altar: that there be no wrath any more upon the children of Israel. Ex. 27:21; 30:7; Lev. 24:3

6 And I, behold, I have taken your brethren the Levites from among the children of Israel: ᴿto you *they are* given *as* a gift for the LORD, to do the service of the tabernacle of the congregation. 3:9

7 Therefore thou and thy sons with thee shall keep your priest's office for every thing of the altar, and ᴿwithin the vail; and ye shall serve: I have given your priest's office *unto you as* a service of gift: and the stranger that cometh nigh shall be put to death. Heb. 9:3, 6

I have not *done them* Rof mine own mind.   John 5:36 · John 5:30

29 If these men die the common death of all men, or if they be Rvisited after the visitation of all men; *then* the LORD hath not sent me.   Ex. 20:5; Job 35:15; Is. 10:3

30 But if the LORD make Ra new thing, and the earth open her mouth, and swallow them up, with all that *appertain* unto them, and they Rgo down Tquick into the pit; then ye shall understand that these men have provoked the LORD. Job 31:3; Is. 28:21 · [Ps. 55:15] · *alive*

31 And it came to pass, as he had made an end of speaking all these words, that the ground clave asunder that *was* under them:

32 And the earth opened her mouth, and swallowed them up, and their houses, and Rall the men that *appertained* unto Ko'-rah, and all *their* goods.   1 Chr. 6:22, 37

33 They, and all that *appertained* to them, went down alive into the pit, and the earth closed upon them: and they perished from among the congregation.

34 And all Israel that *were* round about them fled at the cry of them: for they said, Lest the earth swallow us up *also*.

35 And there Rcame out a fire from the LORD, and consumed the two hundred and fifty men that offered incense.   Lev. 10:2; Ps. 106:18

36 And the LORD spake unto Moses, saying,

37 Speak unto E-le-a'-zar the son of Aaron the priest, that he take up the censers out of the burning, and scatter thou the fire yonder; for they are hallowed.

38 The censers of these Rsinners against their own souls, let them make them broad plates *for* a covering of the altar: for they offered them before the LORD, therefore they are hallowed: Rand they shall be a sign unto the children of Israel.   Prov. 20:2; Hab. 2:10 · Ezek. 14:8

39 And E-le-a'-zar the priest took the brasen censers, wherewith they that were burnt had offered; and they were made

broad *plates for* a covering of the altar:

40 *To be* a memorial unto the children of Israel, Rthat no stranger, which *is* not of the seed of Aaron, come near to offer incense before the LORD; that he be not as Ko'-rah, and as his company: as the LORD said to him by the hand of Moses.   3:10; 2 Chr. 26:18

41 But on the morrow Rall the congregation of the children of Israel Tmurmured against Moses and against Aaron, saying, Ye have killed the people of the LORD.   14:2; Ps. 106:25 · *grumbled*

42 And it came to pass, when the congregation was gathered against Moses and against Aaron, that they looked toward the tabernacle of the congregation: and, behold, the cloud covered it, and the glory of the LORD appeared.

43 And Moses and Aaron came before the tabernacle of the congregation.

44 And the LORD spake unto Moses, saying,

45 Get you up from among this congregation, that I may consume them as in a moment. And they fell upon their faces.

46 And Moses said unto Aaron, Take a censer, and put fire therein from off the altar, and put on incense, and go quickly unto the congregation, and make an atonement for them: Rfor there is wrath gone out from the LORD; the plague is begun.   18:5; Lev. 10:6

47 And Aaron took as Moses commanded, and ran into the midst of the congregation; and, behold, the plague was begun among the people: and he put on incense, and made an atonement for the people.

48 And he stood between the dead and the living; and Rthe plague was stayed.   25:8; Ps. 106:

49 Now they that died in t plague were fourteen thous and seven hundred, beside that died about the matter rah.

50 And Aaron return

8 And the LORD spake unto Aaron, Behold, I also have given thee the charge of mine heave offerings of all the hallowed things of the children of Israel; unto thee have I given them by reason of the anointing, and to thy sons, by an ordinance for ever.

9 This shall be thine of the most holy things, *reserved* from the fire: every oblation of theirs, every ᴿmeat offering of theirs, and every sin offering of theirs, and every trespass offering of theirs, which they shall render unto me, *shall be* most holy for thee and for thy sons.   Lev. 2:2, 3

10 ᴿIn the most holy *place* shalt thou eat it; every male shall eat it: it shall be holy unto thee.   Lev. 6:16

11 And this *is* thine; ᴿthe heave offering of their gift, with all the wave offerings of the children of Israel: I have given them unto thee, and to thy sons and to thy daughters with thee, by a statute for ever: every one that is clean in thy house shall eat of it.   Ex. 29:27

12 All the best of the oil, and all the best of the wine, and of the wheat, the firstfruits of them which they shall offer unto the LORD, them have I given thee.

13 *And* whatsoever is first ripe in the land, ᴿwhich they shall bring unto the LORD, shall be thine; every one that is clean in thine house shall eat *of* it. Ex. 34:26

14 ᴿEvery thing devoted in Israel shall be thine.   Lev. 27:1–33

15 Every thing that openeth the matrix in all flesh, which they bring unto the LORD, *whether it be* of men or beasts, shall be thine: nevertheless ᴿthe firstborn of man shalt thou surely redeem, and the firstling of unclean beasts shalt thou redeem.   Luke 2:22–24

16 And those that are to be redeemed from a month old shalt thou redeem, ᴿaccording to thine estimation, for the money of five shek'-els, after the shek'-el of the sanctuary, which *is* ᴿtwenty ge'-rahs.   Lev. 27:6 · Ex. 30:13

17 But the firstling of a cow, or the firstling of a sheep, or the firstling of a goat, thou shalt not redeem; they *are* holy: thou shalt sprinkle their blood upon the altar, and shalt burn their fat *for* an offering made by fire, for a sweet savour unto the LORD.

18 And the flesh of them shall be thine, as the wave breast and as the right shoulder are thine.

19 All the heave offerings of the holy things, which the children of Israel offer unto the LORD, have I given thee, and thy sons and thy daughters with thee, by a statute for ever: ᴿit *is* a covenant of salt for ever before the LORD unto thee and to thy seed with thee.   Lev. 2:13

20 And the LORD spake unto Aaron, Thou shalt have no inheritance in their land, neither shalt thou have any part among them: ᴿI *am* thy part and thine inheritance among the children of Israel.   Ps. 16:5; Ezek. 44:28

21 And, behold, ᴿI have given the children of Levi all the tenth in Israel for an inheritance, for their service which they serve, *even* the service of the tabernacle of the congregation.   [Heb. 7:4–10]

22 ᴿNeither must the children of Israel henceforth come nigh the tabernacle of the congregation, lest they bear sin, and die.   1:51

23 But the Levites shall do the service of the tabernacle of the congregation, and they shall bear their iniquity: *it shall be* a statute for ever throughout your generations, that among the children of Israel they have no inheritance.

24 But the tithes of the children of Israel, which they offer *as* an heave offering unto the LORD, I have given to the Levites to inherit: therefore I have said unto them, Among the children of Israel they shall have no inheritance.

25 And the LORD spake unto Moses, saying,

26 Thus speak unto the Levites, and say unto them, When ye take of the children of Israel the tithes which I have given you from them

for your inheritance, then ye shall offer up an heave offering of it for the LORD, [R]even a tenth *part* of the tithe.   Neh. 10:38

27 And *this* your heave offering shall be reckoned unto you, as though *it were* the corn of the [R]threshingfloor, and as the fulness of the winepress.   15:20; [2 Cor. 8:12]

28 Thus ye also shall offer an heave offering unto the LORD of all your tithes, which ye receive of the children of Israel; and ye shall give thereof the LORD's heave offering to Aaron the priest.

29 Out of all your gifts ye shall offer every heave offering of the LORD, of all the best thereof, *even* the hallowed part thereof out of it.

30 Therefore thou shalt say unto them, When ye have heaved the best thereof from it, then it shall be [T]counted unto the Levites as the increase of the threshingfloor, and as the increase of the winepress.   *reckoned or accounted*

31 And ye shall eat it in every place, ye and your households: for it *is* [R]your reward for your service in the tabernacle of the congregation.   [Luke 10:7]; 1 Cor. 9:13; [1 Tim. 5:18]

32 And ye shall bear no sin by reason of it, when ye have heaved from it the best of it: neither shall ye pollute the holy things of the children of Israel, lest ye die.

19 And the LORD spake unto Moses and unto Aaron, saying,

2 This *is* the ordinance of the law which the LORD hath commanded, saying, Speak unto the children of Israel, that they bring thee a red heifer without spot, wherein *is* no blemish, [R]*and* upon which never came yoke: Deut. 21:3

3 And ye shall give her unto E-le-a′-zar the priest, that he may bring her [R]forth without the camp, and *one* shall slay her before his face: v. 9; Lev. 4:12, 21; Heb. 13:11

4 And E-le-a′-zar the priest shall take of her blood with his finger, and sprinkle of her blood directly before the tabernacle of the congregation seven times:

5 And *one* shall burn the heifer in his sight; [R]her skin, and her flesh, and her blood, with her dung, shall he burn: Ex. 29:14

6 And the priest shall take cedar wood, and hyssop, and scarlet, and cast *it* into the midst of the burning of the heifer.

7 [R]Then the priest shall wash his clothes, and he shall bathe his flesh in water, and afterward he shall come into the camp, and the priest shall be unclean until the even.   Lev. 11:25; 15:5; 16:26, 28

8 And he that burneth her shall wash his clothes in water, and bathe his flesh in water, and shall be unclean until the even.

9 And a man *that is* clean shall gather up [R]the ashes of the heifer, and lay *them* up without the camp in a clean place, and it shall be kept for the congregation of the children of Israel [R]for a water of separation: it *is* a purification for sin.   [Heb. 9:13, 14] · vv. 13, 20, 21

10 And he that gathereth the ashes of the heifer shall wash his clothes, and be unclean until the even: and it shall be unto the children of Israel, and unto the stranger that sojourneth among them, for a statute for ever.

11 [R]He that toucheth the dead body of any man shall be unclean seven days.   Lev. 21:1, 11; Hag. 2:13

12 [R]He shall purify himself with it on the third day, and on the seventh day he shall be clean: but if he purify not himself the third day, then the seventh day he shall not be clean.   v. 19; 31:19

13 Whosoever toucheth the dead body of any man that is dead, and purifieth not himself, [R]defileth the tabernacle of the LORD; and that soul shall be cut off from Israel: because [R]the water of separation was not sprinkled upon him, he shall be unclean; [R]his uncleanness *is* yet upon him.   Lev. 15:31 · 8:7 · Lev. 7:20; 22:3

14 This *is* the law, when a man dieth in a tent: all that come into the tent, and all that *is* in the tent, shall be unclean seven days.

15 And every ^Ropen vessel, which hath no covering bound upon it, *is* unclean.   31:20; Lev. 11:32

16 And ^Rwhosoever toucheth one that is slain with a sword in the open fields, or a dead body, or a bone of a man, or a grave, shall be unclean seven days.   v. 11; 31:19

17 And for an unclean *person* they shall take of the ^Rashes of the burnt heifer of purification for sin, and running water shall be put thereto in a vessel: v. 9

18 And a clean person shall take hyssop, and dip *it* in the water, and sprinkle *it* upon the tent, and upon all the vessels, and upon the persons that were there, and upon him that touched a bone, or one slain, or one dead, or a grave:

19 And the clean *person* shall sprinkle upon the unclean on the third day, and on the seventh day: and on the seventh day he shall purify himself, and wash his clothes, and bathe himself in water, and shall be clean at even.

20 But the man that shall be unclean, and shall not purify himself, that soul shall be cut off from among the congregation, because he hath ^Rdefiled the sanctuary of the LORD: the water of separation hath not been sprinkled upon him; he *is* unclean.   v. 13

21 And it shall be a perpetual statute unto them, that he that sprinkleth the water of separation shall wash his clothes; and he that toucheth the water of separation shall be unclean until even.

22 And whatsoever the unclean *person* toucheth shall be unclean; and the soul that toucheth *it* shall be unclean until even.

20 Then came the children of Israel, *even* the whole congregation, into the desert of Zin in the first month: and the people abode in Ka'-desh; and Miriam died there, and was buried there.

2 ^RAnd there was no water for the congregation: and they gathered themselves together against Moses and against Aaron.   Ex. 17:1

3 And the people chode with Moses, and spake, saying, Would God that we had died when our brethren died before the LORD!

4 And ^Rwhy have ye brought up the congregation of the LORD into this wilderness, that we and our cattle should die there?   Ex. 17:3

5 And wherefore have ye made us to come up out of Egypt, to bring us in unto this evil place? it *is* no place of seed, or of figs, or of vines, or of pomegranates; neither *is* there any water to drink.

6 And Moses and Aaron went from the presence of the assembly unto the door of the tabernacle of the congregation, and they fell upon their faces: and the glory of the LORD appeared unto them.

7 And the LORD spake unto Moses, saying,

8 Take the rod, and gather thou the assembly together, thou, and Aaron thy brother, and speak ye unto the rock before their eyes; and it shall give forth his water, and ^Rthou shalt bring forth to them water out of the rock: so thou shalt give the congregation and their beasts drink.   [1 Cor. 10:4]

9 And Moses took the rod ^Rfrom before the LORD, as he commanded him.   17:10

10 And Moses and Aaron gathered the congregation together before the rock, and he said unto them, ^RHear now, ye rebels; must we fetch you water out of this rock?   Ps. 106:33

11 And Moses lifted up his hand, and with his rod he smote the rock twice: and ^Rthe water came out abundantly, and the congregation drank, and their beasts *also*.   Ps. 78:16; Is. 48:21

12 And the LORD spake unto Moses and Aaron, Because ^Rye believed me not, to sanctify me in the eyes of the children of Israel, therefore ye shall not bring this congregation into the land which I have given them.   27:14; Deut. 1:37

13 This *is* the water of Mer'-i-bah; because the children of Israel strove with the LORD, and he was sanctified in them.

14 And Moses sent messengers from Ka'-desh unto the king of E'-dom, Thus saith thy brother Israel, Thou knowest all the ᵀtravel that hath befallen us: *hardship*

15 How our fathers went down into Egypt, and we have dwelt in Egypt a long time; and the Egyptians vexed us, and our fathers:

16 And when we cried unto the LORD, he heard our voice, and sent an angel, and hath brought us forth out of Egypt: and, behold, we *are* in Ka'-desh, a city in the uttermost of thy border:

17 ᴿLet us pass, I pray thee, through thy country: we will not pass through the fields, or through the vineyards, neither will we drink *of* the water of the wells: we will go by the king's *high* way, we will not turn to the right hand nor to the left, until we have passed thy borders. 21:22

18 And ᴿE'-dom said unto him, Thou shalt not pass by me, lest I come out against thee with the sword. 24:18; Ps. 137:7; Obad. 10–15

19 And the children of Israel said unto him, We will go by the high way: and if I and my cattle drink of thy water, ᴿthen I will pay for it: I will only, without *doing* any thing *else,* ᵀgo through on my feet. Deut. 2:6, 28 · *pass through on foot*

20 And he said, ᴿThou shalt not go through. And E'-dom came out against him with much people, and with a strong hand. Judg. 11:17

21 Thus E'-dom ᴿrefused to give Israel passage through his border: wherefore Israel ᴿturned away from him. Deut. 2:27, 30 · Deut. 2:8

22 And the children of Israel, *even* the whole congregation, journeyed from ᴿKa'-desh, ᴿand came unto mount Hor. 33:37 · 21:4

23 And the LORD spake unto Moses and Aaron in mount Hor, by the coast of the land of E'-dom, saying,

24 Aaron shall be gathered un-to his people: for he shall not enter into the land which I have given unto the children of Israel, because ye rebelled

against my word at the water of Mer'-i-bah.

25 ᴿTake Aaron and E-le-a'-zar his son, and bring them up unto mount Hor: 33:38; Deut. 32:50

26 And strip Aaron of his garments, and put them upon E-le-a'-zar his son: and Aaron shall be gathered *unto his people,* and shall die there.

27 And Moses did as the LORD commanded: and they went up into mount Hor in the sight of all the congregation.

28 And Moses stripped Aaron of his garments, and put them upon E-le-a'-zar his son; and Aaron died there in the top of the mount: and Moses and E-le-a'-zar came down from the mount.

29 And when all the congregation saw that Aaron was dead, they mourned for Aaron thirty days, *even* all the house of Israel.

21 And *when* ᴿking A'-rad the Ca'-naan-ite, which dwelt in the south, heard tell that Israel came by the way of the spies; then he fought against Israel, and took *some* of them prisoners. 33:40

2 ᴿAnd Israel vowed a vow unto the LORD, and said, If thou wilt indeed deliver this people into my hand, then I will utterly destroy their cities. Gen. 28:20

3 And the LORD hearkened to the voice of Israel, and delivered up the Ca'-naan-ites; and they utterly destroyed them and their cities: and he called the name of the place Hor'-mah.

4 And they journeyed from mount Hor by the way of the Red sea, to ᴿcompass the land of E'-dom: and the soul of the people was much ᵀdiscouraged because of the way. Judg. 11:18 · *impatient*

5 And the people spake against God, and against Moses, Wherefore have ye brought us up out of Egypt to die in the wilderness? for *there is* no bread, neither *is there* any water; and our soul loatheth this light bread.

6 And ᴿthe LORD sent fiery ser-

pents among the people, and they bit the people; and much people of Israel died. 1 Cor. 10:9

7 Therefore the people came to Moses, and said, We have sinned, for we have spoken against the LORD, and against thee; ᴿpray unto the LORD, that he take away the serpents from us. And Moses prayed for the people. Acts 8:24

8 And the LORD said unto Moses, Make thee a ᴿfiery serpent, and set it upon a pole: and it shall come to pass, that every one that is bitten, when he looketh upon it, shall live. Is. 14:29; 30:6

9 And ᴿMoses made a serpent of brass, and put it upon a pole, and it came to pass, that if a serpent had bitten any man, when he beheld the serpent of brass, he lived. 2 Kin. 18:4; John 3:14, 15

10 And the children of Israel set forward, and pitched in O'-both.

11 And they journeyed from O'-both, and pitched at I'-je–ab'-a-rim, in the wilderness which is before Moab, toward the sunrising.

12 ᴿFrom thence they removed, and pitched in the valley of Za'-red. Deut. 2:13

13 From thence they removed, and pitched on the other side of Arnon, which is in the wilderness that cometh out of the coasts of the Am'-or-ites: for ᴿArnon is the border of Moab, between Moab and the Am'-or-ites. 22:36; Judg. 11:18

14 Wherefore it is said in the book of the wars of the LORD, What he did in the Red sea, and in the brooks of Arnon,

15 And at the stream of the brooks that goeth down to the dwelling of ᴿAr, and lieth upon the border of Moab. v. 28; Deut. 2:9, 18, 29

16 And from thence they went ᴿto Be'-er: that is the well whereof the LORD spake unto Moses, Gather the people together, and I will give them water. Judg. 9:21

17 Then Israel sang this song, Spring up, O well; sing ye unto it:

18 The princes digged the well, the nobles of the people digged it,

by the direction of the ᴿlawgiver, with their staves. And from the wilderness they went to Mat-ta'-nah: Is. 33:22

19 And from Mat-ta'-nah to Na-ha'-li-el: and from Na-ha'-li-el to Ba'-moth:

20 And from Ba'-moth in the valley, that is in the ᵀcountry of Moab, to the top of Pis'-gah, which looketh ᴿtoward ᵀJesh'-i-mon. field · 23:28 · Lit. Wasteland

21 And ᴿIsrael sent messengers unto Si'-hon king of the Am'-or-ites, saying, Deut. 2:26–37; Judg. 11:19

22 ᴿLet me pass through thy land: we will not turn into the fields, or into the vineyards; we will not drink of the waters of the well: but we will go along by the king's high way, until we be past thy borders. 20:16, 17

23 And Si'-hon would not suffer Israel to pass through his border: but Si'-hon gathered all his people together, and went out against Israel into the wilderness: ᴿand he came to Ja'-haz, and fought against Israel. Deut. 2:32; Judg. 11:20

24 And Israel smote him with the edge of the sword, and possessed his land from Arnon unto Jab'-bok, even unto the children of Ammon: for the border of the children of Ammon was strong.

25 And Israel took all these cities: and Israel ᴿdwelt in all the cities of the Am'-or-ites, in Hesh'-bon, and in all the villages thereof. Amos 2:10

26 For Hesh'-bon was the city of Si'-hon the king of the Am'-or-ites, who had fought against the former king of Moab, and taken all his land out of his hand, even unto Arnon.

27 Wherefore they that speak in ᵀproverbs say, Come into Hesh'-bon, let the city of Si'-hon be built and prepared: parables

28 For there is ᴿa fire gone out of Hesh'-bon, a flame from the city of Si'-hon: it hath consumed ᴿAr of Moab, and the lords of the high places of Arnon. Jer. 48:45, 46 · Is. 15:1

29 Woe to thee, ᴿMoab! thou art

undone, O people of ᴿChe'-mosh:
he hath given his sons that
escaped, and his daughters, into
captivity unto Si'-hon king of the
Am'-or-ites.   Jer. 48:46 · Judg. 11:24

30 We have shot at them; Hesh'-
bon is perished even unto Di'-bon,
and we have laid them waste even
unto No'-phah, which *reacheth*
unto ᴿMed'-e-ba.   Is. 15:2

31 Thus Israel dwelt in the land
of the Am'-or-ites.

32 And Moses sent to spy out
ᴿJa-a'-zer, and they took the villages thereof, and drove out the
Am'-or-ites that *were* there.   32:1, 3

33 And they turned and went up
by the way of Ba'-shan: and Og
the king of Ba'-shan went out
against them, he, and all his people, to the battle at Ed'-re-i.

34 And the LORD said unto
Moses, Fear him not: for I have
delivered him into thy hand, and
all his people, and his land; and
thou shalt do to him as thou didst
unto Si'-hon king of the Am'-or-
ites, which dwelt at Hesh'-bon.

35 ᴿSo they smote him, and his
sons, and all his people, until
there was none left him alive: and
they possessed his land.   Deut. 3:3, 4

22 And ᴿthe children of Israel
set forward, and ᵀpitched in
the plains of Moab on this side
Jordan *by* Jericho.   33:48, 49 · *camped*

2 And ᴿBa'-lak the son of Zip'-
por saw all that Israel had done to
the Am'-or-ites.   Mic. 6:5; Rev. 2:14

3 And Moab was sore afraid of
the people, because they *were*
many: and Moab was distressed
because of the children of Israel.

4 And Moab said unto the
elders of Mid'-i-an, Now shall this
company lick up all *that are*
round about us, as the ox licketh
up the grass of the field. And Ba'-
lak the son of Zip'-por *was* king of
the Mo'-ab-ites at that time.

5 He sent messengers therefore unto Ba'-laam the son of Be'-
or to ᴿPe'-thor, which *is* by the
river of the land of the children of
his people, to call him, saying,
Behold, there is a people come out

from Egypt: behold, they cover
the face of the earth, and they
abide over against me: Deut. 23:4

6 ᴿCome now therefore, I pray
thee, ᴿcurse me this people; for
they *are* too mighty for me: peradventure I shall prevail, *that* we
may smite them, and *that* I may
drive them out of the land: for I
ᵀwot that he whom thou blessest
is blessed, and he whom thou
cursest is cursed.   v. 17 · v. 12 · *know*

7 And the elders of Moab and
the elders of Mid'-i-an departed
with the ᵀrewards of divination in
their hand; and they came unto
Ba'-laam, and spake unto him the
words of Ba'-lak.   *diviner's fee*

8 And he said unto them, ᴿLodge
here this night, and I will bring you
word again, as the LORD shall speak
unto me: and the princes of Moab
abode with Ba'-laam.   v. 19

9 ᴿAnd God came unto Ba'-
laam, and said, What men *are*
these with thee?   Gen. 20:3

10 And Ba'-laam said unto God,
Ba'-lak the son of Zip'-por, king of
Moab, hath sent unto me, *saying,*

11 Behold, *there is* a people
come out of Egypt, which covereth the face of the earth: come
now, curse me them; peradventure I shall be able to overcome
them, and drive them out.

12 And God said unto Ba'-laam,
Thou shalt not go with them; thou
shalt not curse the people: for
ᴿthey *are* blessed.   23:20; [Rom. 11:28]

13 And Ba'-laam rose up in the
morning, and said unto the princes of Ba'-lak, Get you into your
land: for the LORD refuseth to give
me leave to go with you.

14 And the princes of Moab rose
up, and they went unto Ba'-lak,
and said, Ba'-laam refuseth to
come with us.

15 And Ba'-lak sent yet again
princes, more, and more ᵀhonourable than they.   *distinguished*

16 And they came to Ba'-laam,
and said to him, Thus saith Ba'-
lak the son of Zip'-por, Let nothing, I pray thee, hinder thee from
coming unto me:

17 For I will ^Rpromote thee unto very great honour, and I will do whatsoever thou sayest unto me: ^Rcome therefore, I pray thee, curse me this people. 24:11 · v. 6

18 And Ba'-laam answered and said unto the servants of Ba'-lak, If Ba'-lak would give me his house full of silver and gold, I cannot go beyond the word of the LORD my God, to do less or more.

19 Now therefore, I pray you, ^Rtarry ye also here this night, that I may know what the LORD will say unto me more. v. 8

20 ^RAnd God came unto Ba'-laam at night, and said unto him, If the men come to call thee, rise up, *and* go with them; but ^Ryet the word which I shall say unto thee, that shalt thou do. v. 9 · 23:5, 12, 16, 26

21 And Ba'-laam rose up in the morning, and saddled his ass, and went with the princes of Moab.

22 And God's anger was ^Tkindled because he went: ^Rand the angel of the LORD stood in the way ^Tfor an adversary against him. Now he was riding upon his ass, and his two servants *were* with him.   *aroused* · Ex. 4:24 · *as*

23 And ^Rthe ass saw the angel of the LORD standing in the way, and his sword drawn in his hand: and the ass turned aside out of the way, and went into the field: and Ba'-laam smote the ass, to turn her into the way. Dan. 10:7; Acts 22:9

24 But the angel of the LORD stood in a path of the vineyards, a wall *being* on this side, and a wall on that side.

25 And when the ass saw the angel of the LORD, she thrust herself unto the wall, and crushed Ba'-laam's foot against the wall: and he smote her again.

26 And the angel of the LORD went further, and stood in a narrow place, where *was* no way to turn either to the right hand or to the left.

27 And when the ass saw the angel of the LORD, she fell down under Ba'-laam: and Ba'-laam's anger was kindled, and he smote the ass with a staff.

28 And the LORD ^Ropened the mouth of the ass, and she said unto Ba'-laam, What have I done unto thee, that thou hast smitten me these three times? 2 Pet. 2:16

29 And Ba'-laam said unto the ass, Because thou hast ^Tmocked me: I would there were a sword in mine hand, ^Rfor now would I kill thee.   *abused* · [Prov. 12:10; Matt. 15:19]

30 ^RAnd the ass said unto Ba'-laam, *Am* not I thine ass, upon which thou hast ridden ever since *I was* thine unto this day? was I ever wont to do so unto thee? And he said, Nay. 2 Pet. 2:16

31 Then the LORD opened the eyes of Ba'-laam, and he saw the angel of the LORD standing in the way, and his sword drawn in his hand: and he bowed down his head, and fell flat on his face.

32 And the angel of the LORD said unto him, Wherefore hast thou smitten thine ass these three times? behold, I went out to withstand thee, because *thy* way is ^Rperverse before me: [2 Pet. 2:14, 15]

33 And the ass saw me, and turned from me these three times: unless she had turned from me, surely now also I had slain thee, and saved her alive.

34 And Ba'-laam said unto the angel of the LORD, ^RI have sinned; for I knew not that thou stoodest in the way against me: now therefore, if it displease thee, I will get me back again. 1 Sam. 15:24, 30; 26:21

35 And the angel of the LORD said unto Ba'-laam, Go with the men: ^Rbut only the word that I shall speak unto thee, that thou shalt speak. So Ba'-laam went with the princes of Ba'-lak. v. 20

36 And when Ba'-lak heard that Ba'-laam was come, he went out to meet him unto a city of Moab, ^Rwhich *is* in the border of Arnon, which *is* in the utmost coast. 21:13

37 And Ba'-lak said unto Ba'-laam, Did I not earnestly send unto thee to call thee? wherefore camest thou not unto me? am I

not able indeed [R]to promote thee to honour? v. 17; 24:11

38 And Ba'-laam said unto Ba'-lak, Lo, I am come unto thee: have I now any power at all to say any thing? the word that God putteth in my mouth, that shall I speak.

39 And Ba'-laam went with Ba'-lak, and they came unto Kir'-jath–hu'-zoth.

40 And Ba'-lak offered oxen and sheep, and sent to Ba'-laam, and to the princes that *were* with him.

41 And it came to pass on the morrow, that Ba'-lak took Ba'-laam, and brought him up into the [R]high places of Ba'-al, that thence he might see the utmost *part* of the people. 21:28; Deut. 12:2

23 And Ba'-laam said unto Ba'-lak, [R]Build me here seven altars, and prepare me here seven oxen and seven rams. v. 29

2 And Ba'-lak did as Ba'-laam had spoken; and Ba'-lak and Ba'-laam [R]offered on *every* altar a bullock and a ram. v. 14, 30

3 And Ba'-laam said unto Ba'-lak, [R]Stand by thy burnt offering, and I will go: peradventure the LORD will come [R]to meet me: and whatsoever he sheweth me I will tell thee. And he went to [T]an high place. v. 15 · vv. 4, 16 · *a desolate height*

4 [R]And God met Ba'-laam: and he said unto him, I have prepared seven altars, and I have offered upon *every* altar a bullock and a ram. v. 16

5 And the LORD [R]put a word in Ba'-laam's mouth, and said, Return unto Ba'-lak, and thus thou shalt speak. Deut. 18:18; Jer. 1:9

6 And he returned unto him and, lo, he stood by his burnt sacrifice, he, and all the princes of Moab.

7 And he took up his parable, and said, Ba'-lak the king of Moab hath brought me from A'-ram, out of the mountains of the east, *saying*, Come, curse me Jacob, and come, [R]defy Israel. 1 Sam. 17:10

8 [R]How shall I curse, *whom* God hath not cursed? or how shall I defy, *whom* the LORD hath not defied? 22:12

9 For from the top of the rocks I see him, and from the hills I behold him: lo, [R]the people shall dwell alone, and shall not be reckoned among the nations. Josh. 11:23

10 [R]Who can count the dust of Jacob, and the number of the fourth *part* of Israel? Let me die the death of the righteous, and let my last end be like his! 2 Chr. 1:9

11 And Ba'-lak said unto Ba'-laam, What hast thou done unto me? [R]I took thee to curse mine enemies, and, behold, thou hast blessed *them* altogether. 22:11

12 And he answered and said, [R]Must I not take heed to speak that which the LORD hath put in my mouth? 22:38

13 And Ba'-lak said unto him, Come, I pray thee, with me unto another place, from whence thou mayest see them: thou shalt see but the utmost part of them, and shalt not see them all: and curse me them from thence.

14 And he brought him into the field of Zo'-phim, to the top of Pis'-gah, [R]and built seven altars, and offered a bullock and a ram on *every* altar. vv. 1, 2

15 And he said unto Ba'-lak, Stand here by thy burnt offering, while I meet *the LORD* yonder.

16 And the LORD met Ba'-laam, and [R]put a word in his mouth, and said, Go again unto Ba'-lak, and say thus. v. 5; 22:35

17 And when he came to him, behold, he stood by his burnt offering, and the princes of Moab with him. And Ba'-lak said unto him, What hath the LORD spoken?

18 And he took up his parable, and said, [R]Rise up, Ba'-lak, and hear; hearken unto me, thou son of Zip'-por: Judg. 3:20

19 [R]God *is* not a man, that he should lie; neither the son of man, that he should repent: hath he [R]said, and shall he not do *it*? or hath he spoken, and shall he not make it good? James 1:17 · 1 Kin. 8:56

20 Behold, I have received *commandment* to bless: and he hath blessed; and I cannot reverse it.

21 He hath not beheld iniquity in Jacob, neither hath he seen perverseness in Israel: the Lord his God *is* with him, ^Rand the shout of a king *is* among them.   Ps. 89:15-18

22 God brought them out of Egypt; he hath as it were ^Rthe strength of an unicorn.   Deut. 33:17

23 Surely *there is* no enchantment against Jacob, neither *is there* any divination against Israel: according to this time it shall be said of Jacob and of Israel, ^RWhat hath God wrought!   Ps. 44:1

24 Behold, the people shall rise up ^Ras a great lion, and lift up himself as a young lion: ^Rhe shall not lie down until he eat *of* the prey, and drink the blood of the slain.   Gen. 49:9 · Gen. 49:27; Josh. 11:23

25 And Ba′-lak said unto Ba′-laam, Neither curse them at all, nor bless them at all.

26 But Ba′-laam answered and said unto Ba′-lak, Told not I thee, saying, ^RAll that the Lord speaketh, that I must do?   22:38

27 And Ba′-lak said unto Ba′-laam, Come, I pray thee, I will bring thee unto another place; peradventure it will please God that thou mayest curse me them from thence.

28 And Ba′-lak brought Ba′-laam unto the top of Pe′-or, that looketh ^Rtoward Jesh′-i-mon.   21:20

29 And Ba′-laam said unto Ba′-lak, Build me here seven altars, and prepare me here seven bullocks and seven rams.

30 And Ba′-lak did as Ba′-laam had said, and offered a bullock and a ram on *every* altar.

24 And when Ba′-laam saw that it pleased the Lord to bless Israel, he went not, as at ^Rother times, to seek for enchantments, but he set his face toward the wilderness.   23:3, 15

2 And Ba′-laam lifted up his eyes, and he saw Israel abiding *in his tents* according to their tribes; and ^Rthe spirit of God came upon him.   1 Sam. 10:10; 19:20, 23; 2 Chr. 15:1

3 ^RAnd he took up his parable, and said, Ba′-laam the son of Be′-

or hath said, and the man whose eyes are open hath said: 23:7, 18

4 He hath said, which heard the words of God, which saw the vision of the Almighty, ^Rfalling *into a trance,* but having his eyes open: Ezek. 1:28

5 How goodly are thy tents, O Jacob, *and* thy tabernacles, O Israel!

6 As the valleys are they spread forth, ^Ras gardens by the river's side, as the trees of lign aloes ^Rwhich the Lord hath planted, *and* as cedar trees beside the waters.   Ps. 1:3; Jer. 17:8 · Ps. 104:16

7 He shall pour the water out of his buckets, and his seed *shall be* in many waters, and his king shall be higher than A′-gag, and his kingdom shall be exalted.

8 God brought him forth out of Egypt; he hath as it were the strength of an unicorn: he shall ^Reat up the nations his enemies, and shall ^Rbreak their bones, and ^Rpierce *them* through with his arrows.   14:9 · Ps. 2:9; Jer. 50:17 · Ps. 45:5

9 ^RHe couched, he lay down as a lion, and as a great lion: who shall stir him up? Blessed *is* he that blesseth thee, and cursed *is* he that curseth thee.   23:24; Gen. 49:9

10 And Ba′-lak's anger was kindled against Ba′-laam, and he smote his hands together: and Ba′-lak said unto Ba′-laam, I called thee to curse mine enemies, and, behold, thou hast altogether blessed *them* these three times.

11 Therefore now flee thou to thy place: ^RI thought to promote thee unto great honour; but, lo, the Lord hath kept thee back from honour.   22:17, 37

12 And Ba′-laam said unto Ba′-lak, Spake I not also to thy messengers which thou sentest unto me, saying,

13 If Ba′-lak would give me his house full of silver and gold, I cannot go beyond the commandment of the Lord, to do *either* good or bad of mine own mind; *but* what the Lord saith, that will I speak?

14 And now, behold, I go unto my people: come *therefore, and* [R]I will advertise thee what this people shall do to thy people in the [R]latter days.   [Mic. 6:5] · Dan. 2:28

15 And he took up his parable, and said, Ba'-laam the son of Be'-or hath said, and the man whose eyes are open hath said:

16 He hath said, which heard the words of God, and knew the knowledge of the most High, *which* saw the vision of the Almighty, falling *into a trance,* but having his eyes open:

☆ 17 I shall see him, but not now: I shall behold him, but not nigh: there shall come [R]a Star out of Jacob, and [R]a Sceptre shall rise out of Israel, and shall smite the corners of Moab, and destroy all the children of Sheth.   Matt. 2:2 · Gen. 49:10

18 And [R]E'-dom shall be a possession, Se'-ir also shall be a possession for his enemies; and Israel shall do valiantly.   2 Sam. 8:14

19 [R]Out of Jacob shall come he that shall have dominion, and shall destroy him that remaineth of the city.   Gen. 49:10; Amos 9:11, 12

20 And when he looked on Am'-a-lek, he took up his parable, and said, Am'-a-lek *was* the first of the nations; but his latter end *shall be* that he perish for ever.

21 And he looked on the Ken'-ites, and took up his parable, and said, Strong is thy dwellingplace, and thou puttest thy nest in a rock.

22 Nevertheless the Ken'-ite shall be wasted, until Assh'-ur shall carry thee away captive.

23 And he took up his parable, and said, Alas, who shall live when God doeth this!

24 And ships *shall come* from the coast of [R]Chit'-tim, and shall afflict Assh'-ur, and shall afflict [R]E'-ber, and he also shall perish for ever.   Gen. 10:4 · Gen. 10:21, 25

25 And Ba'-laam rose up, and went and [R]returned to his place: and Ba'-lak also went his way. 31:8

25 And Israel abode in [R]Shit'-tim, and the people began to commit whoredom with the daughters of Moab.   33:49

2 And they called the people unto [R]the sacrifices of their gods: and the people did eat, and bowed down to their gods.   1 Cor. 10:20

3 And Israel joined himself unto Ba'-al–pe'-or: and [R]the anger of the LORD was [T]kindled against Israel.   Ps. 106:28, 29 · *aroused*

4 And the LORD said unto Moses, [R]Take all the heads of the people, and hang them up before the LORD against the sun, that the fierce anger of the LORD may be turned away from Israel.   Deut. 4:3

5 And Moses said unto [R]the judges of Israel, [R]Slay ye every one his men that were joined unto Ba'-al–pe'-or.   Ex. 18:21 · Deut. 13:6, 9

6 And, behold, one of the children of Israel came and brought unto his brethren a Mid'-i-an-i-tish woman in the sight of Moses, and in the sight of all the congregation of the children of Israel, [R]who *were* weeping *before* the door of the tabernacle of the congregation.   Joel 2:17

7 And when Phin'-e-has, the son of E-le-a'-zar, the son of Aaron the priest, saw *it,* he rose up from among the congregation, and took a javelin in his hand;

8 And he went after the man of Israel into the tent, and thrust both of them through, the man of Israel, and the woman through her belly. So [R]the plague was [R]stayed from the children of Israel.   Ps. 106:30 · 16:46–48

9 And [R]those that died in the plague were twenty and four thousand.   Deut. 4:3

10 And the LORD spake unto Moses, saying,

11 Phin'-e-has, the son of E-le-a'-zar, the son of Aaron the priest, hath turned my wrath away from the children of Israel, while he was zealous for my sake among them, that I consumed not the children of Israel in my jealousy.

12 Wherefore say, [R]Behold, I give unto him my [R]covenant of peace: [Mal. 2:4, 5; 3:1] · Is. 54:10

13 And he shall have it, and his seed after him, *even* the covenant of an everlasting priesthood; because he was ^Rzealous for his God, and made an atonement for the children of Israel.   Rom. 10:2

14 Now the name of the Israelite that was slain, *even* that was slain with the Mid'-i-an-i-tish woman, *was* Zim'-ri, the son of Sa'-lu, a prince of a chief house among the Simeonites.

15 And the name of the Mid'-i-an-i-tish woman that was slain *was* Coz'-bi, the daughter of ^RZur; he *was* head over a people, *and* of a chief house in Mid'-i-an.   31:8

16 And the LORD spake unto Moses, saying,

17 ^RVex^T the Mid'i-an-ites, and smite them: 31:1–3 · *Be hostile toward*

18 For they vex you with their wiles, wherewith they have beguiled you in the matter of Pe'-or, and in the matter of Coz'-bi, the daughter of a prince of Mid'-i-an, their sister, which was slain in the day of the plague for Pe'-or's sake.

26 And it came to pass after the ^Rplague, that the LORD spake unto Moses and unto E-le-a'-zar the son of Aaron the priest, saying,   25:9

2 ^RTake ^Tthe sum of all the congregation of the children of Israel, from twenty years old and upward, throughout their fathers' house, all that are able to go to war in Israel.   1:2; 14:29 · *a census*

3 And Moses and E-le-a'-zar the priest spake with them ^Rin the plains of Moab by Jordan *near* Jericho, saying,   22:1; 31:12; 33:48; 35:1

4 *Take the sum of the people*, from twenty years old and upward; as the LORD ^Rcommanded Moses and the children of Israel, which went forth out of the land of Egypt.   1:1

5 ^RReuben, the eldest son of Israel: the children of Reuben; Ha'-noch, *of whom cometh* the family of the Ha'-noch-ites: of Pal'-lu, the family of the Pal'-lu-ites: Gen. 46:8; Ex. 6:14; 1 Chr. 5:1–3

6 Of Hez'-ron, the family of the Hez'-ron-ites: of Car'-mi, the family of the Car'-mites.

7 These *are* the families of the Reu'-ben-ites: and they that were numbered of them were forty and three thousand and seven hundred and thirty.

8 And the sons of Pal'-lu; E-li'-ab.

9 And the sons of E-li'-ab; Nem'-u-el, and Da'-than, and A-bi'-ram. This *is that* Da'-than and A-bi'-ram, *which were* ^Rfamous in the congregation, who strove against Moses and against Aaron in the company of Ko'-rah, when they strove against the LORD: 1:16

10 And the earth opened her mouth, and swallowed them up together with Ko'-rah, when that company died, what time the fire devoured two hundred and fifty men: and they became a sign.

11 Notwithstanding ^Rthe children of Ko'-rah died not.   Ex. 6:24

12 The sons of Simeon after their families: of Nem'-u-el, the family of the Nem'-u-el-ites: of Ja'-min, the family of the Ja'-min-ites: of Ja'-chin, the family of the Ja'-chin-ites:

13 Of ^TZe'-rah, the family of the Zar'-hites: of Sha'-ul, the family of the Sha'-u-lites.   *Zohar*, Gen. 46:10

14 These *are* the families of the Simeonites, twenty and two thousand and two hundred.

15 The children of Gad after their families: of ^TZe'-phon, the family of the Ze'-phon-ites: of Hag'-gi, the family of the Hag'-gites: of Shu'-ni, the family of the Shu'-nites: *Ziphion*, Gen. 46:16

16 Of ^TOz'-ni, the family of the Oz'-nites: of E'-ri, the family of the E'-rites: *Ezbon*, Gen. 46:16

17 Of ^TA'-rod, the family of the Ar'-o-dites: of A-re'-li, the family of the A-re'-lites.   *Arodi*, Gen. 46:16

18 These *are* the families of the children of Gad according to those that were numbered of them, forty thousand and five hundred.

19 The sons of Judah *were* Er

and O'-nan: and Er and O'-nan died in the land of Canaan.

20 And ᴿthe sons of Judah after their families were; of She'-lah, the family of the She'-la-nites: of Pha'-rez, the family of the Phar'-zites: of Ze'-rah, the family of the Zar'-hites.   1 Chr. 2:3

21 And the sons of Pha'-rez were; of Hez'-ron, the family of the Hez'-ron-ites: of Ha'-mul, the family of the Ha'-mul-ites.

22 These *are* the families of Judah according to those that were numbered of them, three-score and sixteen thousand and five hundred.

23 *Of* the sons of Is'-sa-char after their families: *of* To'-la, the family of the To'-la-ites: of Pu'-a, the family of the Pu'-nites:

24 Of Jash'-ub, the family of the Jash'-ub-ites: of Shim'-ron, the family of the Shim'-ron-ites.

25 These *are* the families of Is'-sa-char according to those that were numbered of them, three-score and four thousand and three hundred.

26 ᴿ*Of* the sons of Zeb'-u-lun after their families: of Se'-red, the family of the Sar'-dites: of E'-lon, the family of the E'-lon-ites: of Jah'-le-el, the family of the Jah'-le-el-ites.   Gen. 46:14

27 These *are* the families of the Zeb'-u-lun-ites according to those that were numbered of them, threescore thousand and five hundred.

28 ᴿThe sons of Joseph after their families *were* Ma-nas'-seh and E'-phra-im. Gen. 46:20; Deut. 33:16

29 Of the sons of ᴿMa-nas'-seh: of Ma'-chir, the family of the Ma'-chir-ites: and Ma'-chir begat Gil'-e-ad: of Gil'-e-ad *come* the family of the Gil'-e-ad-ites.   Josh. 17:1

30 These *are* the sons of Gil'-e-ad: *of* Je-e'-zer, the family of the Je-e'-zer-ites: of He'-lek, the fami-ly of the He'-lek-ites:

31 And of As'-ri-el, the family of the As'-ri-el-ites: and *of* She'-chem, the family of the She'-chem-ites:

32 And *of* She-mi'-da, the family of the She-mi'-da-ites: and *of* He'-pher, the family of the He'-pher-ites.

33 And ᴿZe-lo'-phe-had the son of He'-pher had no sons, but daughters: and the names of the daughters of Ze-lo'-phe-had *were* Mah'-lah, and Noah, Hog'-lah, Mil'-cah, and Tir'-zah.   27:1; 36:11

34 These *are* the families of Ma-nas'-seh, and those that were numbered of them, fifty and two thousand and seven hundred.

35 These *are* the sons of E'-phra-im after their families: of Shu'-the-lah, the family of the Shu'-thal-hites: of Be'-cher, the family of the Bach'-rites: of Ta'-han, the family of the Ta'-han-ites.

36 And these *are* the sons of Shu'-the-lah: of E'-ran, the family of the E'-ran-ites.

37 These *are* the families of the sons of E'-phra-im according to those that were numbered of them, thirty and two thousand and five hundred. These *are* the sons of Joseph after their families.

38 ᴿThe sons of Benjamin after their families: of Be'-la, the family of the Be'-la-ites: of Ash'-bel, the family of the Ash'-bel-ites: of ᴿA-hi'-ram, the family of the A-hi'-ram-ites: Gen. 46:21 · 1 Chr. 8:1, 2

39 Of Shu'-pham, the family of the Shu'-pham-ites: of Hu'-pham, the family of the Hu'-pham-ites.

40 And the sons of Be'-la were Ard and Na'-a-man: ᴿ*of* Ard, the family of the Ard'-ites: *and* of Na'-a-man, the family of the Na'-a-mites.   1 Chr. 8:3

41 These *are* the sons of Benjamin after their families: and they that were numbered of them *were* forty and five thousand and six hundred.

42 These *are* the sons of Dan after their families: of Shu'-ham, the family of the Shu'-ham-ites. These *are* the families of Dan after their families.

43 All the families of the Shu'-ham-ites, according to those that were numbered of them, *were*

threescore and four thousand and four hundred.

44 ᴿOf the children of Asher after their families: of Jim'-na, the family of the Jim'-nites: of Jes'-u-i, the family of the Jes'-u-ites: of Be-ri'-ah, the family of the Be-ri'-ites. Gen. 46:17; 1 Chr. 7:30

45 Of the sons of Be-ri'-ah: of He'-ber, the family of the He'-ber-ites: of Mal'-chi-el, the family of the Mal'-chi-el-ites.

46 And the name of the daughter of Asher *was* Sarah.

47 These *are* the families of the sons of Asher according to those that were numbered of them; *who were* fifty and three thousand and four hundred.

48 *Of* the sons of Naph'-ta-li after their families: of Jah'-ze-el, the family of the Jah'-ze-el-ites: of Gu'-ni, the family of the Gu'-nites:

49 Of Je'-zer, the family of the Je'-zer-ites: of ᴿShil'-lem, the family of the Shil'-lem-ites. 1 Chr. 7:13

50 These *are* the families of Naph'-ta-li according to their families: and they that were numbered of them *were* forty and five thousand and four hundred.

51 ᴿThese *were* the numbered of the children of Israel, six hundred thousand and a thousand seven hundred and thirty. Ex. 12:37; 38:26

52 And the LORD spake unto Moses, saying,

53 ᴿUnto these the land shall be ᴿdivided for an inheritance according to the number of names. Josh. 11:23; 14:1 · 33:54

54 ᴿTo many thou shalt give the more inheritance, and to few thou shalt give the less inheritance: to every one shall his inheritance be given according to those that were numbered of him. 33:54

55 Notwithstanding the land shall be ᴿdivided by lot: according to the names of the tribes of their fathers they shall inherit. 33:54

56 According to the lot shall the possession thereof be divided between many and few.

57 ᴿAnd these *are* they that were numbered of the Levites after

their families: of Ger'-shon, the family of the Ger'-shon-ites: of Ko'-hath, the family of the Ko'-hath-ites: of Me-ra'-ri, the family of the Me-ra'-rites. Ex. 6:16–19

58 These *are* the families of the Levites: the family of the Lib'-nites, the family of the He'-bron-ites, the family of the Mah'-lites, the family of the Mu'-shites, the family of the Ko'-rath-ites. And Ko'-hath begat Am'-ram.

59 And the name of Am'-ram's wife *was* ᴿJoch'-e-bed, the daughter of Levi, whom *her mother* bare to Levi in Egypt: and she bare unto Am'-ram Aaron and Moses, and Miriam their sister. Ex. 2:1, 2

60 ᴿAnd unto Aaron was born Na'-dab, and A-bi'-hu, E-le-a'-zar, and Ith'-a-mar. 3:2

61 And ᴿNa'-dab and A-bi'-hu died, when they offered strange fire before the LORD. Lev. 10:1, 2

62 And those that were numbered of them were twenty and three thousand, all males from a month old and upward: ᴿfor they were not numbered among the children of Israel, because there was no inheritance given them among the children of Israel. 1:49

63 These *are* they that were numbered by Moses and E-le-a'-zar the priest, who numbered children of Israel ᴿin the plains of Moab by Jordan *near* Jericho. v. 3

64 ᴿBut among these there was not a man of them whom Moses and Aaron the priest numbered, when they numbered the children of Israel in the wilderness of Si'-nai. 14:29–35; Deut. 2:14–16; Heb. 3:17

65 For the LORD had said of them, They ᴿshall surely die in the wilderness. And there was not left a man of them, save Caleb the son of Je-phun'-neh, and Joshua the son of Nun. 14:26–35; [1 Cor. 10:5, 6]

27 Then came the daughters of Ze-lo'-phe-had, the son of He'-pher, the son of Gil'-e-ad, the son of Ma'-chir, the son of Manas'-seh, of the families of Ma-nas'-seh the son of Joseph: and these *are* the names of his daughters; Mah'-lah, Noah, and Hog'-lah, and Mil'-cah, and Tir'-zah.

2 And they stood before Moses, and before E-le-a'-zar the priest, and before the princes and all the congregation, *by* the door of the tabernacle of the congregation, saying,

3 Our father ^Rdied in the wilderness, and he was not in the company of them that gathered themselves together against the LORD ^Rin the company of Ko'-rah; but died in his own sin, and had no sons.   14:35; 26:64, 65 · 16:1, 2

4 Why should the name of our father be ^Rdone away from among his family, because he hath no son? ^RGive unto us *therefore* a possession among the brethren of our father.   Deut. 25:6 · Josh. 17:4

5 And Moses ^Rbrought their cause before the LORD.   Ex. 18:13–26

6 And the LORD spake unto Moses, saying,

7 The daughters of Ze-lo'-phe-had speak right: ^Rthou shalt surely give them a possession of an inheritance among their father's brethren; and thou shalt cause the inheritance of their father to pass unto them.   36:2; Josh. 17:4

8 And thou shalt speak unto the children of Israel, saying, If a man die, and have no son, then ye shall cause his inheritance to pass unto his daughter.

9 And if he have no daughter, then ye shall give his inheritance unto his brethren.

10 And if he have no brethren, then ye shall give his inheritance unto his father's brethren.

11 And if his father have no brethren, then ye shall give his inheritance unto his kinsman that is next to him of his family, and he shall possess it: and it shall be unto the children of Israel ^Ra statute of judgment, as the LORD commanded Moses.   35:29

12 And the LORD said unto Moses, ^RGet thee up into this mount Ab'-a-rim, and see the land which I have given unto the children of Israel.   Deut. 3:23–27; 32:48–52

13 And when thou hast seen it, thou also ^Rshalt be gathered unto thy people, as Aaron thy brother was gathered.   31:2; Deut. 10:6; 34:5, 6

14 For ye ^Rrebelled against my commandment in the desert of Zin, in the strife of the congregation, to sanctify me at the water before their eyes: that *is* the water of Mer'-i-bah in Ka'-desh in the wilderness of Zin.   Deut. 1:37; 32:51

15 And Moses spake unto the LORD, saying,

16 Let the LORD, ^Rthe God of the spirits of all flesh, set a man over the congregation,   16:22; Heb. 12:9

17 ^RWhich may go out before them, and which may go in before them, and which may lead them out, and which may bring them in; that the congregation of the LORD be not ^Ras sheep which have no shepherd.   Deut. 31:2 · Matt. 9:36

18 And the LORD said unto Moses, Take thee Joshua the son of Nun, a man ^Rin whom *is* the spirit, and ^Rlay thine hand upon him;   1 Sam. 16:13, 18 · Deut. 34:9

19 And set him before E-le-a'-zar the priest, and before all the congregation; and ^Rgive him a charge in their sight.   Deut. 3:28; 31:3

20 And ^Rthou shalt put *some* of thine honour upon him, that all the congregation of the children of Israel may be obedient.   11:17

21 ^RAnd he shall stand before E-le-a'-zar the priest, who shall ask *counsel* for him ^Rafter the judgment of U'-rim before the LORD: at his word shall they go out, and at his word they shall come in, *both* he, and all the children of Israel with him, even all the congregation.   Judg. 20:18 · Ex. 28:30; 1 Sam. 28:6

22 And Moses did as the LORD commanded him: and he took Joshua, and set him before E-le-a'-zar the priest, and before all the congregation:

23 And he laid his hands upon him, ^Rand gave him a charge, as the LORD commanded by the hand of Moses.   Deut. 3:28; 31:7, 8

28 And the LORD spake unto Moses, saying,

2 Command the children of Israel, and say unto them, My offering, *and* ^Rmy bread for my sacrifices made by fire, *for* a sweet savour unto me, shall ye observe to offer unto me in their due season.   Lev. 21:6, 8; [Mal. 1:7, 12]

3 And thou shalt say unto them, ^RThis *is* the offering made by fire which ye shall offer unto the LORD; two lambs of the first year without spot day by day, *for* a continual burnt offering.   Ex. 29:38

4 The one lamb shalt thou offer in the morning, and the other lamb shalt thou offer at even;

5 And ^Ra tenth *part* of an e'-phah of flour for a ^Rmeat offering, mingled with the fourth *part* of an hin of beaten oil.   Ex. 16:36 · Lev. 2:1

6 *It is* a continual burnt offering, which was ordained in mount Si'-nai for a sweet savour, a sacrifice made by fire unto the LORD.

7 And the drink offering thereof *shall be* the fourth *part* of an hin for the one lamb: ^Rin the holy *place* shalt thou cause the strong wine to be poured unto the LORD *for* a drink offering.   Ex. 29:42

8 And the other lamb shalt thou offer at even: as the ^Tmeat offering of the morning, and as the drink offering thereof, thou shalt offer *it*, a sacrifice made by fire, of a ^Tsweet savour unto the LORD.   *grain* or *meal · pleasing aroma*

9 And on the sabbath day two lambs of the first year without spot, and two tenth deals of flour *for* a meat offering, mingled with oil, and the drink offering thereof:

10 *This is* ^Rthe burnt offering of every sabbath, beside the continual burnt offering, and his drink offering.   Ezek. 46:4

11 And ^Rin the beginnings of your months ye shall offer a burnt offering unto the LORD; two young bullocks, and one ram, seven lambs of the first year without spot;   1 Sam. 20:5; 1 Chr. 23:31; 2 Chr. 2:4

12 And ^Rthree tenth deals of flour *for* a meat offering, mingled with oil, for one bullock; and two tenth deals of flour *for* a meat

offering, mingled with oil, for one ram;   15:4–12

13 And a several tenth deal of flour mingled with oil *for* a meat offering unto one lamb; *for* a burnt offering of a sweet savour, a sacrifice made by fire unto the LORD.

14 And their drink offerings shall be half an hin of wine unto a bullock, and the third *part* of an hin unto a ram, and a fourth *part* of an hin unto a lamb: this *is* the burnt offering of every month throughout the months of the year.

15 And ^Rone kid of the goats for a sin offering unto the LORD shall be offered, beside the continual burnt offering, and his drink offering.   vv. 3, 22; 15:24

16 ^RAnd in the fourteenth day of the first month *is* the passover of the LORD.   Ex. 12:1–20; Lev. 23:5–8

17 And in the fifteenth day of this month *is* the feast: seven days shall unleavened bread be eaten.

18 In the first day *shall be* an holy convocation; ye shall do no manner of servile work *therein:*

19 But ye shall offer a sacrifice made by fire *for* a burnt offering unto the LORD; two young bullocks, and one ram, and seven lambs of the first year: they shall be unto you without blemish:

20 And their meat offering *shall be of* flour mingled with oil: three tenth deals shall ye offer for a bullock, and two tenth deals for a ram;

21 A several tenth deal shalt thou offer for every lamb, throughout the seven lambs:

22 And ^Rone goat *for* a sin offering, to make ^Tan atonement for you.   v. 15 · *a propitiation*

23 Ye shall offer these beside the burnt offering in the morning, which *is* for a continual burnt offering.

24 After this manner ye shall offer daily, throughout the seven days, the meat of the sacrifice made by fire, of a sweet savour unto the LORD: it shall be offered

beside the continual burnt offering, and his drink offering.

25 And ᴿon the seventh day ye shall have an holy convocation; ye shall do no servile work.   Ex. 12:16

26 Also ᴿin the day of the firstfruits, when ye bring a new meat offering unto the LORD, after your weeks *be out,* ye shall have an holy convocation; ye shall do no servile work: Deut. 16:9–12; Acts 2:1

27 But ye shall offer the burnt offering for a sweet savour unto the LORD; ᴿtwo young bullocks, one ram, seven lambs of the first year;   Lev. 23:18, 19

28 And their ᵀmeat offering of flour mingled with oil, three tenth deals unto one bullock, two tenth deals unto one ram,   *grain* or *meal*

29 A several tenth deal unto one lamb, throughout the seven lambs;

30 *And* one kid of the goats, to make an atonement for you.

31 Ye shall offer *them* beside the continual burnt offering, and his meat offering, (ᴿthey shall be unto you without blemish) and their drink offerings.   vv. 3, 19

29 And in the seventh month, on the first *day* of the month, ye shall have an holy convocation; ye shall do no servile work: ᴿit is a day of blowing the trumpets unto you.   Ex. 23:16; 34:22; Lev. 23:23–25

2 And ye shall offer a burnt offering for a sweet savour unto the LORD; one young bullock, one ram, *and* seven lambs of the first year without blemish:

3 And their meat offering *shall be of* flour mingled with oil, three tenth deals for a bullock, *and* two tenth deals for a ram,

4 And one tenth deal for one lamb, throughout the seven lambs:

5 And one kid of the goats *for* a sin offering, to make an atonement for you:

6 Beside the burnt offering of the month, and his meat offering, and the daily burnt offering, and his meat offering, and their drink offerings, according unto their manner, for a sweet savour, a sacrifice made by fire unto the LORD.

7 And ye shall have on the tenth *day* of this seventh month an holy convocation; and ye shall ᴿafflict your souls: ye shall not do any work *therein:*   Ps. 35:13; Is. 58:5

8 But ye shall offer a burnt offering unto the LORD *for* a sweet savour; one young bullock, one ram, *and* seven lambs of the first year; ᴿthey shall be unto you without blemish: 28:19

9 And their meat offering *shall be of* flour mingled with oil, three tenth deals to a bullock, *and* two tenth deals to one ram,

10 A several tenth deal for one lamb, throughout the seven lambs:

11 One kid of the goats *for* a sin offering; beside the sin offering of atonement, and the continual burnt offering, and the meat offering of it, and their drink offerings.

12 And on the fifteenth day of the seventh month ye shall have an holy convocation; ye shall do no servile work, and ye shall keep a feast unto the LORD seven days:

13 And ᴿye shall offer a burnt offering, a sacrifice made by fire, of a sweet savour unto the LORD; thirteen young bullocks, two rams, *and* fourteen lambs of the first year; they shall be without blemish: Ezra 3:4

14 And their meat offering *shall be of* flour mingled with oil, three tenth deals unto every bullock of the thirteen bullocks, two tenth deals to each ram of the two rams,

15 And a several tenth deal to each lamb of the fourteen lambs:

16 And one kid of the goats *for* a sin offering; beside the continual burnt offering, his meat offering, and his drink offering.

17 And on the ᴿsecond day *ye shall offer* twelve young bullocks, two rams, fourteen lambs of the first year without spot: Lev. 23:36

18 And their meat offering and their drink offerings for the bullocks, for the rams, and for the lambs, *shall be* according to their number, ᴿafter the manner: 15:12

19 And one kid of the goats *for* a sin offering; beside the continual burnt offering, and the meat offering thereof, and their drink offerings.

20 And on the third day eleven bullocks, two rams, fourteen lambs of the first year without blemish;

21 And their meat offering and their drink offerings for the bullocks, for the rams, and for the lambs, *shall be* according to their number, [R]after the manner: v. 18

22 And one goat *for* a sin offering; beside the continual burnt offering, and his meat offering, and his drink offering.

23 And on the fourth day ten bullocks, two rams, *and* fourteen lambs of the first year without blemish:

24 Their meat offering and their drink offerings for the bullocks, for the rams, and for the lambs, *shall be* according to their number, after the manner:

25 And one kid of the goats *for* a sin offering; beside the continual burnt offering, his meat offering, and his drink offering.

26 And on the fifth day nine bullocks, two rams, *and* fourteen lambs of the first year without spot:

27 And their meat offering and their drink offerings for the bullocks, for the rams, and for the lambs, *shall be* according to their number, after the manner:

28 And one goat *for* a sin offering; beside the continual burnt offering, and his meat offering, and his drink offering.

29 And on the sixth day eight bullocks, two rams, *and* fourteen lambs of the first year without blemish:

30 And their meat offering and their drink offerings for the bullocks, for the rams, and for the lambs, *shall be* according to their number, after the manner:

31 And one goat *for* a sin offering; beside the continual burnt offering, his meat offering, and his drink offering.

32 And on the seventh day seven bullocks, two rams, *and* fourteen lambs of the first year without blemish:

33 And their meat offering and their drink offerings for the bullocks, for the rams, and for the lambs, *shall be* according to their number, after the manner:

34 And one goat *for* a sin offering; beside the continual burnt offering, his meat offering, and his drink offering.

35 On the eighth day ye shall have a solemn assembly: ye shall do no servile work *therein:*

36 But ye shall offer a burnt offering, a sacrifice made by fire, of a sweet savour unto the LORD: one bullock, one ram, seven lambs of the first year without blemish:

37 Their meat offering and their drink offerings for the bullock, for the ram, and for the lambs, *shall be* according to their number, after the manner:

38 And one goat *for* a sin offering; beside the continual burnt offering, and his meat offering, and his drink offering.

39 These *things* ye shall do unto the LORD in your [R]set feasts, beside your vows, and your freewill offerings, for your burnt offerings, and for your meat offerings, and for your drink offerings, and for your peace offerings.   Ezra 3:5

40 And Moses told the children of Israel according to all that the LORD commanded Moses.

30 And Moses spake unto [R]the heads of the tribes concerning the children of Israel, saying, This *is* the thing which the LORD hath commanded.   1:4, 16; 7:2

2 [R]If a man vow a vow unto the LORD, or swear an oath to bind his soul with a bond; he shall not break his word, he shall [R]do according to all that proceedeth out of his mouth.   Lev. 27:2; Matt. 14:9

3 If a woman also vow a vow unto the LORD, and bind *herself* by a bond, *being* in her father's house in her youth;

4 And her father hear her vow, and her bond wherewith she hath bound her soul, and her father shall hold his peace at her: then all her vows shall stand, and every bond wherewith she hath bound her soul shall stand.

5 But if her father ᵀdisallow her in the day that he heareth; not any of her vows, or of her bonds wherewith she hath bound her soul, shall stand: and the LORD shall forgive her, because her father disallowed her.　　　*overrule*

6 And if she had at all an husband, when she vowed, or uttered ought out of her lips, wherewith she bound her soul;

7 And her husband heard *it,* and ᵀheld his peace at her in the day that he heard *it:* then her vows shall stand, and her bonds wherewith she bound her soul shall stand.　　*made no response*

8 But if her husband ᴿdisallowedᵀ her on the day that he heard *it;* then he shall make her vow which she vowed, and that which she uttered with her lips, wherewith she bound her soul, of none effect: and the LORD shall forgive her. [Gen. 3:16] · *overruled*

9 But every vow of a widow, and of her that is divorced, wherewith they have bound their souls, shall stand against her.

10 And if she vowed in her husband's house, or bound her soul by a bond with an oath;

11 And her husband heard *it,* and held his peace at her, *and* disallowed her not: then all her vows shall stand, and every bond wherewith she bound her soul shall stand.

12 But if her husband hath utterly made them void on the day he heard *them; then* whatsoever proceeded out of her lips concerning her vows, or concerning the bond of her soul, shall not stand: her husband hath made them void; and the LORD shall forgive her.

13 Every vow, and every binding oath to afflict the soul, her husband may establish it, or her husband may make it void.

14 But if her husband altogether hold his peace at her from day to day; then he establisheth all her vows, or all her bonds, which *are* upon her: he confirmeth them, because he held his peace at her in the day that he heard *them.*

15 But if he shall any ways make them void after that he hath heard *them;* then he shall bear her ᵀiniquity.　　　　　*guilt*

16 These *are* the statutes, which the LORD commanded Moses, between a man and his wife, between the father and his daughter, *being yet* in her youth in her father's house.

31 And the LORD spake unto Moses, saying,

2 ᴿAvenge the children of Israel of the Mid′-i-an-ites: afterward shalt thou ᴿbe gathered unto thy people.　　　25:17 · 25:12, 13

3 And Moses spake unto the people, saying, Arm some of yourselves unto the war, and let them go against the Mid′-i-an-ites, and avenge the LORD of Mid′-i-an.

4 Of every tribe a thousand, throughout all the tribes of Israel, shall ye send to the war.

5 So there were delivered out of the thousands of Israel, a thousand of *every* tribe, twelve thousand armed for war.

6 And Moses sent them to the war, a thousand of *every* tribe, them and Phin′-e-has the son of E-le-a′-zar the priest, to the war, with the holy instruments, and the trumpets to blow in his hand.

7 And they warred against the Mid′-i-an-ites, as the LORD commanded Moses; and ᴿthey slew all the ᴿmales.　　Deut. 20:13 · Gen. 34:25

8 And they slew the kings of Mid′-i-an, beside the rest of them that were slain; *namely,* E′-vi, and Re′-kem, and ᴿZur, and Hur, and Re′-ba, five kings of Mid′-i-an: Ba′-laam also the son of Be′-or they slew with the sword.　25:15

9 And the children of Israel took *all* the women of Mid′-i-an

captives, and their little ones, and took the spoil of all their cattle, and all their flocks, and all their goods.

10 And they burnt all their cities wherein they dwelt, and all their goodly castles, with fire.

11 And ᴿthey took all the spoil, and all the prey, *both* of men and of beasts.   Deut. 20:14

12 And they brought the captives, and the prey, and the spoil, unto Moses, and E-le-a´-zar the priest, and unto the congregation of the children of Israel, unto the camp at the plains of Moab, which *are* by Jordan *near* Jericho.

13 And Moses, and E-le-a´-zar the priest, and all the princes of the congregation, went forth to meet them without the camp.

14 And Moses was ᵀwroth with the officers of the host, *with* the captains over thousands, and captains over hundreds, which came from the battle.   *angry*

15 And Moses said unto them, Have ye saved ᴿall the women alive?   Deut. 20:14

16 Behold, ᴿthese caused the children of Israel, through the ᴿcounsel of Ba´-laam, to commit trespass against the LORD in the matter of Pe´-or, and there was a plague among the congregation of the LORD.   25:2 · 2 Pet. 2:15; Rev. 2:14

17 Now therefore ᴿkill every male among the little ones, and kill every woman that hath known man by lying with him.   Judg. 21:11

18 But all the women children, that have not known a man by lying with him, keep alive ᴿfor yourselves.   Deut. 21:10–14

19 And ᴿdo ye abide without the camp seven days: whosoever hath killed any person, and ᴿwhosoever hath touched any slain, purify *both* yourselves and your captives on the third day, and on the seventh day.   5:2 · 19:11–22

20 And purify all *your* raiment, and all that is made of skins, and all work of goats' *hair,* and all things made of wood.

21 And E-le-a´-zar the priest said unto the men of war which went to the battle, This *is* the ᵀordinance of the law which the LORD commanded Moses;   *statute*

22 Only the gold, and the silver, the brass, the iron, the tin, and the lead,

23 Every thing that may abide the fire, ye shall make *it* go through the fire, and it shall be clean: nevertheless it shall be purified ᴿwith the water of separation: and all that abideth not the fire ye shall make go through the water.   19:9, 17

24 ᴿAnd ye shall wash your clothes on the seventh day, and ye shall be clean, and afterward ye shall come into the camp. Lev. 11:25

25 And the LORD spake unto Moses, saying,

26 Take the sum of the ᵀprey that was ᵀtaken, *both* of man and of beast, thou, and E-le-a´-zar the priest, and the chief fathers of the congregation: *plunder · captured*

27 And ᴿdivide the prey into two parts; between them that took the war upon them, who went out to battle, and between all the congregation: Josh. 22:8; 1 Sam. 30:24

28 And levy a ᵀtribute unto the LORD of the men of war which went out to battle: one soul of five hundred, *both* of the persons, and of the beeves, and of the asses, and of the sheep: *tax*

29 Take *it* of their half, and give *it* unto E-le-a´-zar the priest, *for* an heave offering of the LORD.

30 And of the children of Israel's half, thou shalt take one portion of fifty, of the persons, of the beeves, of the asses, and of the ᵀflocks, of all manner of beasts, and give them unto the Levites, ᴿwhich keep the charge of the tabernacle of the LORD.   *sheep* · 18:3, 4

31 And Moses and E-le-a´-zar the priest did as the LORD commanded Moses.

32 And the booty, *being* the rest of the prey which the men of war had caught, was six hundred thousand and seventy thousand and five thousand sheep,

33 And threescore and twelve thousand beeves,

34 And threescore and one thousand asses,

35 And thirty and two thousand persons in all, of women that had not known man by lying with him.

36 And the half, *which was* the portion of them that went out to war, was in number three hundred thousand and seven and thirty thousand and five hundred sheep:

37 And the LORD's ᵀtribute of the sheep was six hundred and threescore and fifteen.   *tax*

38 And the beeves *were* thirty and six thousand; of which the LORD's tribute *was* threescore and twelve.

39 And the asses *were* thirty thousand and five hundred; of which the LORD's tribute *was* threescore and one.

40 And the persons *were* sixteen thousand; of which the LORD's tribute *was* thirty and two persons.

41 And Moses gave the tribute, *which was* the LORD's heave offering, unto E-le-a'-zar the priest, ᴿas the LORD commanded Moses. 18:8

42 And of the children of Israel's half, which Moses divided from the men that warred,

43 (Now the half *that pertained unto* the congregation was three hundred thousand and thirty thousand *and* seven thousand and five hundred sheep,

44 And thirty and six thousand beeves,

45 And thirty thousand asses and five hundred,

46 And sixteen thousand persons;)

47 Even ᴿof the children of Israel's half, Moses took one portion of fifty, *both* of man and of beast, and gave them unto the Levites, which kept the charge of the tabernacle of the LORD; as the LORD commanded Moses.   v. 30

48 And the officers which *were* over thousands of the host, the captains of thousands, and captains of hundreds, came near unto Moses:

49 And they said unto Moses, Thy servants have taken the sum of the men of war which *are* under our ᵀcharge, and there lacketh not one man of us.   *command*

50 We have therefore brought an ᵀoblation for the LORD, what every man hath gotten, of jewels of gold, chains, and bracelets, rings, earrings, and ᵀtablets, to make an atonement for our souls before the LORD.   *offering · necklaces*

51 And Moses and E-le-a'-zar the priest took the gold of them, *even* all wrought jewels.

52 And all the gold of the offering that they offered up to the LORD, of the captains of thousands, and of the captains of hundreds, was sixteen thousand seven hundred and fifty shek'-els.

53 (*For* ᴿthe men of war had taken spoil, every man for himself.)   v. 32; Deut. 20:14

54 And Moses and E-le-a'-zar the priest took the gold of the captains of thousands and of hundreds, and brought it into the tabernacle of the congregation, ᴿ*for* a memorial for the children of Israel before the LORD.   Ex. 30:16

32 Now the children of Reuben and the children of Gad had a very great multitude of cattle: and when they saw the land of ᴿJa'-zer, and the land of Gil'-e-ad, that, behold, the place *was* a place for cattle;   Josh. 13:25

2 The children of Gad and the children of Reuben came and spake unto Moses, and to E-le-a'-zar the priest, and unto the princes of the congregation, saying,

3 At'-a-roth, and Di'-bon, and Ja'-zer, and Nim'-rah, and Hesh'-bon, and E-le-a'-leh, and She'-bam, and Ne'-bo, and Be'-on,

4 *Even* the country ᴿwhich the LORD smote before the congregation of Israel, *is* a land for cattle, and thy servants have cattle: 21:24

5 Wherefore, said they, if we

have found ᵀgrace in thy sight, let this land be given unto thy servants for a possession, *and* bring us not over Jordan.   *favour*

6 And Moses said unto the children of Gad and to the children of Reuben, Shall your brethren go to war, and shall ye sit here?

7 And wherefore discourage ye the heart of the children of Israel from going over into the land which the LORD hath given them?

8 Thus did your fathers, when I sent them from Ka′-desh–bar′-ne-a ᴿto see the land.   Deut. 1:19–25

9 For ᴿwhen they went up unto the valley of Esh′-col, and saw the land, they discouraged the heart of the children of Israel, that they should not go into the land which the LORD had given them.   13:24, 31

10 ᴿAnd the LORD's anger was kindled the same time, and he sware, saying,   14:11; Deut. 1:34–36

11 Surely none of the men that came up out of Egypt, ᴿfrom twenty years old and upward, shall see the land which I sware unto Abraham, unto Isaac, and unto Jacob; because they have not wholly followed me: Deut. 1:35

12 Save Caleb the son of Je-phun′-neh the Ken′-ez-ite, and Joshua the son of Nun: for they have wholly followed the LORD.

13 And the LORD's anger was kindled against Israel, and he made them wander in the wilderness forty years, until all the generation, that had done evil in the sight of the LORD, was consumed.

14 And, behold, ye are risen up in your fathers' stead, ᵀan increase of sinful men, to augment yet the ᴿfierce anger of the LORD toward Israel. *a brood* · 11:1; Deut. 1:34

15 For if ye turn away from after him, he will yet again leave them in the wilderness; and ye shall destroy all this people.

16 And they came near unto him, and said, We will build sheepfolds here for our cattle, and cities for our little ones:

17 But ᴿwe ourselves will go ready armed before the children

of Israel, until we have brought them unto their place: and our little ones shall dwell in the fenced cities because of the inhabitants of the land.   Josh. 4:12, 13

18 ᴿWe will not return unto our houses, until the children of Israel have ᵀinherited every man his inheritance.   Josh. 22:1–4 · *possessed*

19 For we will not inherit with them on yonder side Jordan, or forward; ᴿbecause our inheritance is fallen to us on this side Jordan eastward.   Josh. 12:1; 13:8

20 And Moses said unto them, If ye will do this thing, if ye will go armed before the LORD to war,

21 And will go all of you armed over Jordan before the LORD, until he hath driven out his enemies from before him,

22 And the land be subdued before the LORD: then afterward ye shall return, and be guiltless before the LORD, and before Israel; and this land shall be your possession before the LORD.

23 But if ye will not do so, behold, ye have sinned against the LORD: and be sure ᴿyour sin will find you out.   Is. 59:12; [Gal. 6:7]

24 ᴿBuild you cities for your little ones, and folds for your sheep; and do that which hath proceeded out of your mouth.   v. 16

25 And the children of Gad and the children of Reuben spake unto Moses, saying, Thy servants will do as my lord commandeth.

26 Our little ones, our wives, our flocks, and all our cattle, shall be there in the cities of Gil′-e-ad:

27 ᴿBut thy servants will pass over, every man armed for war, before the LORD to battle, as my lord saith.   Josh. 4:12

28 So ᴿconcerning them Moses commanded E-le-a′-zar the priest, and Joshua the son of Nun, and the chief fathers of the tribes of the children of Israel: Josh. 1:13

29 And Moses said unto them, If the children of Gad and the children of Reuben will pass with you over Jordan, every man armed to battle, before the LORD, and the

land shall be subdued before you;
then ye shall give them the land of
Gil'-e-ad for a possession:

30 But if they will not pass over
with you armed, they shall have
possessions among you in the
land of Canaan.

31 And the children of Gad and
the children of Reuben answered,
saying, As the LORD hath said
unto thy servants, so will we do.

32 We will pass over armed
before the LORD into the land of
Canaan, that the possession of
our inheritance on this side Jordan *may be* ours.

33 And Moses gave unto them,
even to the children of Gad, and to
the children of Reuben, and unto
half the tribe of Ma-nas'-seh the
son of Joseph, the kingdom of Si'-hon king of the Am'-or-ites, and
the kingdom of Og king of Ba'-shan, the land, with the cities
thereof in the coasts, *even* the
cities of the country round about.

34 And the children of Gad built
^RDi'-bon, and At'-a-roth, and ^RAr'-o-er,   33:45, 46 · Deut. 2:36

35 And At'-roth, Sho'-phan, and
Ja-a'-zer, and Jog'-be-hah,

36 And ^RBeth-nim'-rah, and
Beth-ha'-ran, ^Rfenced cities: and
folds for sheep.   v. 3 · v. 24

37 And the children of Reuben
^Rbuilt Hesh'-bon, and E-le-a'-leh,
and Kir-ja-tha'-im,   21:27

38 And ^RNe'-bo, and Ba'-al-me'-on, (their names being changed,)
and Shib'-mah: and gave other
names unto the cities which they
builded.   Is. 46:1

39 And the children of ^RMa'-chir
the son of Ma-nas'-seh went to
Gil'-e-ad, and took it, and dispossessed the Am'-or-ite which *was*
in it.   27:1; 36:1; Gen. 50:23

40 And Moses gave Gil'-e-ad
unto Ma'-chir the son of Ma-nas'-seh; and he dwelt therein.

41 And Ja'-ir the son of Ma-nas'-seh went and took the small
towns thereof, and called them
^RHa'-voth-ja'-ir. Judg. 10:4; 1 Kin. 4:13

42 And No'-bah went and took
Ke'-nath, and the villages thereof,

and called it No'-bah, after his
own name.

33 These *are* the journeys of
the children of Israel, which
went forth out of the land of
Egypt with their armies under the
hand of Moses and Aaron.

2 And Moses wrote their goings out according to their journeys by the commandment of the
LORD: and these *are* their journeys
according to their goings out.

3 And they ^Rdeparted from
Ram'-e-ses in the first month, on
the fifteenth day of the first
month; on the morrow after the
passover the children of Israel
went out with an high hand in the
sight of all the Egyptians. Ex. 12:37

4 For the Egyptians buried all
their firstborn, which the LORD
had smitten among them: ^Rupon
their gods also the LORD executed
judgments.   [Ex. 12:12; 18:11]; Is. 19:1

5 ^RAnd the children of Israel
removed from Ram'-e-ses, and
pitched in Suc'-coth.   Ex. 12:37

6 And they departed from
^RSuc'-coth, and pitched in E'-tham, which *is* in the edge of the
wilderness.   Ex. 13:20

7 And ^Rthey removed from E'-tham, and turned again unto
Pi–ha-hi'-roth, which *is* before
Ba'-al-ze'-phon: and they pitched
before Mig'-dol.   Ex. 14:1, 2, 9

8 And they departed from
before Pi–ha-hi'-roth, and passed
through the midst of the sea into
the wilderness, and went three
days' journey in the wilderness of
E'-tham, and pitched in Ma'-rah.

9 And they removed from Ma'-rah, and ^Rcame unto E'-lim: and in
E'-lim *were* twelve fountains of
water, and threescore and ten
palm trees; and they pitched
there.   Ex. 15:27

10 And they removed from E'-lim, and encamped by the Red sea.

11 And they removed from the
Red sea, and encamped in the
^Rwilderness of Sin.   Ex. 16:1

12 And they took their journey
out of the wilderness of Sin, and
encamped in Doph'-kah.

13 And they departed from Doph′-kah, and encamped in A′-lush.

14 And they removed from A′-lush, and encamped at ᴿReph′-i-dim, where was no water for the people to drink.　　Ex. 17:1; 19:2

15 And they departed from Reph′-i-dim, and pitched in the ᴿwilderness of Si′-nai.Ex. 16:1; 19:1, 2

16 And they removed from the desert of Si′-nai, and pitched ᴿat Kib′-roth–hat-ta′-a-vah.　　11:34

17 And they departed from Kib′-roth–hat-ta′-a-vah, and encamped at Ha-ze′-roth.

18 And they departed from Ha-ze′-roth, and pitched in ᴿRith′-mah.　　12:16

19 And they departed from Rith′-mah, and pitched at Rim′-mon–par′-ez.

20 And they departed from Rim′-mon–par′-ez, and pitched in Lib′-nah.

21 And they removed from Lib′-nah, and pitched at Ris′-sah.

22 And they journeyed from Ris′-sah, and pitched in Ke-hel′-a-thah.

23 And they went from Ke-hel′-a-thah, and pitched in mount Sha′-pher.

24 And they removed from mount Sha′-pher, and encamped in Har′-a-dah.

25 And they removed from Har′-a-dah, and pitched in Mak-he′-loth.

26 And they removed from Mak-he′-loth, and encamped at Ta′-hath.

27 And they departed from Ta′-hath, and pitched at Ta′-rah.

28 And they removed from Ta′-rah, and pitched in Mith′-cah.

29 And they went from Mith′-cah, and pitched in Hash-mo′-nah.

30 And they departed from Hash-mo′-nah, and ᴿencamped at Mo-se′-roth.　　Deut. 10:6

31 And they departed from Mo-se′-roth, and pitched in Bene–ja′-a-kan.

32 And they removed from ᴿBene–ja′-a-kan, and encamped at Hor–ha-gid′-gad.　　Deut. 10:6, 7

33 And they went from Hor–ha-gid′-gad, and pitched in Jot′-ba-thah.

34 And they removed from Jot′-ba-thah, and encamped at E-bro′-nah.

35 And they departed from E-bro′-nah, ᴿand encamped at E′-zi-on–ga′-ber.　　Deut. 2:8; 1 Kin. 9:26; 22:48

36 And they removed from E′-zi-on–ga′-ber, and pitched in the ᴿwilderness of Zin, which *is* Ka′-desh.　　20:1; 27:14

37 And they removed from Ka′-desh, and pitched in mount Hor, in the edge of the land of E′-dom.

38 And ᴿAaron the priest went up into mount Hor at the commandment of the LORD, and died there, in the fortieth year after the children of Israel were come out of the land of Egypt, in the first *day* of the fifth month.　　Deut. 10:6

39 And Aaron *was* an hundred and twenty and three years old when he died in mount Hor.

40 And ᴿking A′-rad the Ca′-naan-ite, which dwelt in the south in the land of Canaan, heard of the coming of the children of Israel.　　21:1

41 And they departed from mount Hor, and pitched in Zal-mo′-nah.

42 And they departed from Zal-mo′-nah, and pitched in Pu′-non.

43 And they departed from Pu′-non, and ᴿpitched in O′-both. 21:10

44 And ᴿthey departed from O′-both, and pitched in I′-je-ab′-a-rim, in the border of Moab.　　21:11

45 And they departed from I′-im, and pitched in Di′-bon–gad.

46 And they removed from Di′-bon–gad, and encamped in ᴿAl′-mon–dib-la-tha′-im.　　Ezek. 6:14

47 And they removed from Al′-mon–dib-la-tha′-im, ᴿand pitched in the mountains of Ab′-a-rim, before Ne′-bo.　　21:20; Deut. 32:49

48 And they departed from the mountains of Ab′-a-rim, and ᴿpitched in the plains of Moab by Jordan *near* Jericho. 22:1; 31:12; 35:1

49 And they pitched by Jordan, from Beth–jes′-i-moth *even* unto

^RA'-bel–shit'-tim in the plains of Moab.　25:1; Josh. 2:1

50 And the LORD spake unto Moses in the plains of Moab by Jordan, *near* Jericho, saying,

51 Speak unto the children of Israel, and say unto them, ^RWhen ye are passed over Jordan into the land of Canaan;　Deut. 9:1; Josh. 3:17

52 ^RThen ye shall drive out all the inhabitants of the land from before you, and destroy all their pictures, and destroy all their molten images, and quite pluck down all their high places: Judg. 2:2

53 And ye shall dispossess *the inhabitants of* the land, and dwell therein: for I have given you the land to ^Rpossess it.　Josh. 21:43

54 And ^Rye shall divide the land by lot for an inheritance among your families: *and* to the more ye shall give the ^Tmore inheritance, and to the fewer ye shall give the ^Tless inheritance: every man's *inheritance* shall be in the place where his lot falleth; according to the tribes of your fathers ye shall inherit.　26:53–56 · *larger* · *smaller*

55 But if ye will not drive out the inhabitants of the land from before you; then it shall come to pass, that those which ye let remain of them *shall be* ^Rpricks in your eyes, and thorns in your sides, and shall vex you in the land wherein ye dwell.　Josh. 23:13

56 Moreover it shall come to pass, *that* I shall do unto you, as I thought to do unto them.

34 And the LORD spake unto Moses, saying,

2 Command the children of Israel, and say unto them, When ye come into ^Rthe land of Canaan; (this *is* the land that shall fall unto you for an inheritance, *even* the land of Canaan with the coasts thereof:) Deut. 1:7, 8; Ps. 78:54, 55; 105:11

3 Then ^Ryour south quarter shall be from the wilderness of Zin along by the coast of E'-dom, and your south border shall be the outmost coast of ^Rthe salt sea eastward:　Josh. 15:1–3 · Gen. 14:3

4 And your border shall turn from the south ^Rto the ascent of A-krab'-bim, and pass on to Zin: and the going forth thereof shall be from the south ^Rto Ka'-desh–bar'-ne-a, and shall go on to ^RHa'-zar–ad'-dar, and pass on to Az'-mon:　Josh. 15:3 · 13:26; 32:8 · Josh. 15:3, 4

5 And the border shall ^Tfetch a compass from Az'-mon unto the river of Egypt, and the goings out of it shall be at the sea.　*turn from*

6 And *as for* the ^Rwestern border, ye shall even have the great sea for a border: this shall be your west border.　Josh. 15:12; Ezek. 47:20

7 And this shall be your north border: from the great sea ye shall point out for you mount Hor:

8 From mount Hor ye shall point out *your border* ^Runto the entrance of Ha'-math; and the goings forth of the border shall be to ^RZe'-dad:　2 Kin. 14:25 · Ezek. 47:15

9 And the border shall go on to Ziph'-ron, and the goings out of it shall be at Ha'-zar–e'-nan: this shall be your north border.

10 And ye shall point out your east border from Ha'-zar–e'-nan to She'-pham:

11 And the coast shall go down from She'-pham to Rib'-lah, on the east side of A'-in; and the border shall descend, and shall reach unto the side of the sea ^Rof Chin'-ne-reth eastward:　Josh. 11:2; Luke 5:1

12 And the border shall go down to Jordan, and the goings out of it shall be at ^Rthe salt sea: this shall be your land with the coasts thereof round about.　v. 3

13 And Moses commanded the children of Israel, saying, ^RThis *is* the land which ye shall inherit by lot, which the LORD commanded to give unto the nine tribes, and to the half tribe:　Gen. 15:18; Deut. 11:24

14 ^RFor the tribe of the children of Reuben according to the house of their fathers, and the tribe of the children of Gad according to the house of their fathers, have received *their inheritance;* and half the tribe of Ma-nas'-seh have received their inheritance:　32:33

15 The two tribes and the half

tribe have received their inheritance on this side Jordan *near* Jericho eastward, toward the sunrising.

16 And the LORD spake unto Moses, saying,

17 These *are* the names of the men which shall divide the land unto you: E-le-a′-zar the priest, and Joshua the son of Nun.

18 And ye shall take one [R]prince of every tribe, to divide the land by inheritance.   1:4, 16

19 And the names of the men *are* these: Of the tribe of Judah, Caleb the son of Je-phun′-neh.

20 And of the tribe of the children of Simeon, Shem′-u-el the son of Am-mi′-hud.

21 Of the tribe of Benjamin, E-li′-dad the son of Chis′-lon.

22 And the prince of the tribe of the children of Dan, Buk′-ki the son of Jog′-li.

23 The prince of the children of Joseph, for the tribe of the children of Ma-nas′-seh, Han′-ni-el the son of E′-phod.

24 And the prince of the tribe of the children of E′-phra-im, Kem′-u-el the son of Shiph′-tan.

25 And the prince of the tribe of the children of Zeb′-u-lun, E-liz′-a-phan the son of Par′-nach.

26 And the prince of the tribe of the children of Is′-sa-char, Pal′-ti-el the son of Az′-zan.

27 And the prince of the tribe of the children of Asher, A-hi′-hud the son of She-lo′-mi.

28 And the prince of the tribe of the children of Naph′-ta-li, Ped′-a-hel the son of Am-mi′-hud.

29 These *are they* whom the LORD commanded to divide the inheritance unto the children of Israel in the land of Canaan.

35 And the LORD spake unto Moses in [R]the plains of Moab by Jordan *near* Jericho, saying,   33:50

2 [R]Command the children of Israel, that they give unto the Levites of the inheritance of their possession cities to dwell in; and ye shall give *also* unto the Levites

[R]suburbs for the cities round about them.   Josh. 14:3, 4 · Lev. 25:22–34

3 And the cities shall they have to dwell in; and the suburbs of them shall be for their cattle, and for their goods, and for all their beasts.

4 And the suburbs of the cities, which ye shall give unto the Levites, *shall reach* from the wall of the city and outward a thousand cubits round about.

5 And ye shall measure from without the city on the east side two thousand cubits, and on the south side two thousand cubits, and on the west side two thousand cubits, and on the north side two thousand cubits; and the city *shall be* in the midst: this shall be to them the suburbs of the cities.

6 And among the cities which ye shall give unto the Levites *there shall be* [R]six cities for refuge, which ye shall appoint for the manslayer, that he may flee thither: and to them ye shall add forty and two cities.   Deut. 4:41

7 *So* all the cities which ye shall give to the Levites *shall be* forty and eight cities: them *shall ye give* with their suburbs.

8 And the cities which ye shall give *shall be* of the possession of the children of Israel: [R]from *them that have* many ye shall give many; but from *them that have* few ye shall give few: every one shall give of his cities unto the Levites according to his inheritance which he inheriteth.   26:54

9 And the LORD spake unto Moses, saying,

10 Speak unto the children of Israel, and say unto them, [R]When ye be come over Jordan into the land of Canaan;   Josh. 20:1–9

11 Then [R]ye shall appoint you cities to be cities of refuge for you; that the slayer may flee thither, which killeth any person [T]at unawares.   Deut. 19:1–13 · *accidentally*

12 [R]And they shall be unto you cities for refuge from the avenger; that the manslayer die not, until he stand before the congregation in judgment.   Deut. 19:6; Josh. 20:3, 5, 6

13 And of these cities which ye shall give ᴿsix cities shall ye have for refuge.   v. 6

14 ᴿYe shall give three cities on this side Jordan, and three cities shall ye give in the land of Canaan, *which* shall be cities of refuge.   Deut. 4:41; Josh. 20:8

15 These six cities shall be a refuge, *both* for the children of Israel, and ᴿfor the stranger, and for the sojourner among them: that every one that killeth any person unawares may flee thither.   15:16

16 And if he smite him with an instrument of iron, so that he die, he *is* a murderer: the murderer shall surely be put to death.

17 And if he smite him with throwing a stone, wherewith he may die, and he die, he *is* a murderer: the murderer shall surely be put to death.

18 Or *if* he smite him with an hand weapon of wood, wherewith he may die, and he die, he *is* a murderer: the murderer shall surely be put to death.

19 The revenger of blood himself shall slay the murderer: when he meeteth him, he shall slay him.

20 But ᴿif he thrust him of hatred, or hurl at him ᴿby laying of wait, that he die;   Gen. 4:8 · Ex. 21:14

21 Or in enmity smite him with his hand, that he die: he that smote *him* shall surely be put to death; *for* he *is* a murderer: the revenger of blood shall slay the murderer, when he meeteth him.

22 But if he thrust him suddenly ᴿwithout enmity, or have cast upon him any thing without ᵀlaying of wait,   Ex. 21:13 · *lying in wait*

23 Or with any stone, wherewith a man may die, seeing *him* not, and cast *it* upon him, that he die, and *was* not his enemy, neither sought his harm:

24 Then ᴿthe congregation shall judge between the slayer and the revenger of blood according to these judgments: v. 12; Josh. 20:6

25 And the congregation shall deliver the slayer out of the hand of the revenger of blood, and the congregation shall restore him to the city of his refuge, whither he was fled: and ᴿhe shall abide in it unto the death of the high priest, ᴿwhich was anointed with the holy oil.   Josh. 20:6 · Ex. 29:7; Lev. 4:3

26 But if the slayer shall at any time ᵀcome without the border of the city of his refuge, whither he was fled;   *go outside*

27 And the revenger of blood find him without the borders of the city of his refuge, and the revenger of blood kill the slayer; he shall not be guilty of blood:

28 Because he should have remained in the city of his refuge until the death of the high priest: but after the death of the high priest the slayer shall return into the land of his possession.

29 So these *things* shall be for ᴿa statute of judgment unto you throughout your generations in all your dwellings.   27:11

30 Whoso killeth any person, the murderer shall be put to death by the mouth of witnesses: but one witness ᵀshall not testify against any person *to cause him* to die.   *is not sufficient testimony*

31 Moreover ye shall take no satisfaction for the life of a murderer, which *is* guilty of death: but he shall be surely put to death.

32 And ye shall take no satisfaction for him that is fled to the city of his refuge, that he should come again to dwell in the land, until the death of the priest.

33 So ye shall not pollute the land wherein ye *are*: for blood it defileth the land: and the land cannot be cleansed of the blood that is shed therein, but ᴿby the blood of him that shed it.   Gen. 9:6

34 ᴿDefile not therefore the land which ye shall inhabit, wherein I dwell: for I the LORD dwell among the children of Israel.   Lev. 18:24, 25

36 And the chief fathers of the families of the ᴿchildren of Gil′-e-ad, the son of Ma′-chir,

the son of Ma-nas'-seh, of the families of the sons of Joseph, came near, and [R]spake before Moses, and before the princes, the chief fathers of the children of Israel: 26:29 · 27:1–11

2 And they said, [R]The LORD commanded my lord to give the land for an inheritance by lot to the children of Israel: and [R]my lord was commanded by the LORD to give the inheritance of Ze-lo'-phe-had our brother unto his daughters.   26:55; Josh. 17:4 · 27:1, 5–7

3 And if they be married to any of the sons of the *other* tribes of the children of Israel, then shall their inheritance be [R]taken from the inheritance of our fathers, and shall be put to the inheritance of the tribe whereunto they are received: so shall it be taken from the lot of our inheritance.   27:4

4 And when [R]the jubile of the children of Israel shall be, then shall their inheritance be put unto the inheritance of the tribe whereunto they are received: so shall their inheritance be taken away from the inheritance of the tribe of our fathers.   Lev. 25:10

5 And Moses commanded the children of Israel according to the word of the LORD, saying, The tribe of the sons of Joseph [R]hath said well.   27:7

6 This *is* the thing which the LORD doth command concerning the daughters of Ze-lo'-phe-had, saying, Let them [T]marry to whom they think best; [R]only to the fami-

ly of the tribe of their father shall they marry.   Lit. *be wives* · vv. 11, 12

7 So shall not the inheritance of the children of Israel remove from tribe to tribe: for every one of the children of Israel shall [R]keep himself to the inheritance of the tribe of his fathers. 1 Kin. 21:3

8 And [R]every daughter, that possesseth an inheritance in any tribe of the children of Israel, shall be wife unto one of the family of the tribe of her father, that the children of Israel may enjoy every man the inheritance of his fathers.   1 Chr. 23:22

9 Neither shall the inheritance remove from *one* tribe to another tribe; but every one of the tribes of the children of Israel shall keep himself to his own inheritance.

10 Even as the LORD command-ed Moses, so did the daughters of Ze-lo'-phe-had:

11 [R]For Mah'-lah, Tir'-zah, and Hog'-lah, and Mil'-cah, and Noah, the daughters of Ze-lo'-phe-had, were married unto their father's brothers' sons: 26:33; 27:1

12 *And* they were married into the families of the sons of Ma-nas'-seh the son of Joseph, and their inheritance remained in the tribe of the family of their father.

13 These *are* the command-ments and the judgments, which the LORD commanded by the hand of Moses unto the children of Israel [R]in the plains of Moab by Jordan *near* Jericho.   26:3; 33:50

The Fifth Book of Moses Called

DEUTERONOMY

DEUTERONOMY, Moses' "Upper Desert Discourse," consists of a series of farewell messages by Israel's 120-year-old leader. It is addressed to the new generation destined to possess the Land of Promise—those who survived the forty years of wilderness wandering.

Like Leviticus, Deuteronomy contains a vast amount of legal detail, but its emphasis is on the laymen rather than the priests. Moses reminds the new generation of the importance of obedience if they are to learn from the sad example of their parents.

The Hebrew title of Deuteronomy is *Haddebharim,* "The Words," taken from the opening phrase in 1:1, "These *be* the words." The parting words of Moses to the new generation are given in oral and written form so that they will endure to all generations. Deuteronomy has been called "five-fifths of the Law" since it completes the five books of Moses. The Jewish people have also called it *Mishneh Hattorah,* "Repetition of the Law," which is translated in the Septuagint as *To Deuteronomion Touto,* "This Second Law." Deuteronomy, however, is not a second law but an adaptation and expansion of much of the original law given on Mount Sinai. The English title comes from the Greek title *Deuteronomion,* "Second Law." Deuteronomy has also been appropriately called the "Book of Remembrance."

THESE *be* the words which Moses spake unto all Israel ᴿon this side Jordan in the wilderness, in the plain over against the Red *sea,* between Pa´-ran, and To´-phel, and Laban, and Ha-ze´-roth, and Diz´-a-hab.　4:44–46; Josh. 9:1, 10

2　(*There are* eleven days' *journey* from Ho´-reb by the way of mount Se´-ir ᴿunto Ka´-desh–bar´-ne-a.)　9:23; Num. 13:26; 32:8

3　And it came to pass in the fortieth year, in the eleventh month, on the first *day* of the month, *that* Moses spake unto the children of Israel, according unto all that the LORD had given him in commandment unto them;

4　ᴿAfter he had slain Si´-hon the king of the Am´-or-ites, which dwelt in Hesh´-bon, and Og the king of Ba´-shan, which dwelt at As´-ta-roth in Ed´-re-i:　Josh. 13:10

5　On this side Jordan, in the land of Moab, began Moses to declare this law, saying,

6　The LORD our God spake unto us ᴿin Ho´-reb, saying, Ye have dwelt long ᴿenough in this mount:　Ex. 3:1, 12 · Ex. 19:1, 2

7　Turn you, and take your journey, and go to the mount of the Am´-or-ites, and unto all *the places* nigh thereunto, in the plain, in the hills, and in the vale, and in the south, and by the sea side, to the land of the Ca´-naan-ites, and unto Leb´-a-non, unto the great river, the river Eu-phra´-tes.

8　Behold, I have set the land before you: go in and possess the land which the LORD sware unto your fathers, ᴿAbraham, Isaac, and Jacob, to give unto them and to their seed after them.　Gen. 12:7

9　And ᴿI spake unto you at that time, saying, I am not able to bear you myself alone:　Ex. 18:18, 24

10　The LORD your God hath multiplied you, and, behold, ᴿye *are* this day as the stars of heaven for multitude.　Gen. 15:5; 22:17; Ex. 32:13

11　(ᴿThe LORD God of your fathers make you a thousand times so many more as ye *are,* and bless you, ᴿas he hath promised you!)　2 Sam. 24:3 · Gen. 15:5

12　How can I myself alone bear your ᵀcumbrance, and your burden, and your strife?　*problems*

13　Take you wise men, and understanding, and known among your tribes, and I will make them ᵀrulers over you.　Lit. *heads*

14　And ye answered me, and said, The thing which thou hast spoken *is* good *for us* to do.

15　So I took ᴿthe chief of your tribes, wise men, and known, and ᵀmade them heads over you, captains over thousands, and captains over hundreds, and captains over fifties, and captains over tens, and officers among your tribes.　Ex. 18:25 · *appointed*

16　And I charged your judges at that time, saying, Hear *the causes* between your brethren, and ᴿjudge righteously between *every* man and his brother, and the stranger *that is* with him. John 7:24

17 Ye shall not ^Trespect persons in judgment; *but* ye shall hear the small as well as the great; ye shall not be afraid of the face of man; for the judgment *is* God's: and the cause that is too hard for you, ^Rbring *it* unto me, and I will hear it.　　*show partiality* · Ex. 18:22, 26

18 And I commanded you at that time all the things which ye should do.

19 And when we departed from Ho'-reb, ^Rwe went through all that great and terrible wilderness, which ye saw by the way of the mountain of the Am'-or-ites, as the LORD our God commanded us; and ^Rwe came to Ka'-desh–bar'-ne-a.　　Num. 10:12; Jer. 2:6 · Num. 13:26

20 And I said unto you, Ye are come unto the mountain of the Am'-or-ites, which the LORD our God doth give unto us.

21 Behold, the LORD thy God hath set the land before thee: go up *and* possess *it*, as the LORD God of thy fathers hath said unto thee; ^Rfear not, neither be discouraged.　　Josh. 1:6, 9

22 And ye came near unto me every one of you, and said, We will send men before us, and they shall search us out the land, and bring us word again by what way we must go up, and into what cities we shall come.

23 And the saying pleased me well: and ^RI took twelve men of you, one of a tribe:　　Num. 13:2, 3

24 ^RAnd they turned and went up into the mountain, and came unto the valley of Esh'-col, and searched it out.　　Num. 13:21–25

25 And they took of the fruit of the land in their hands, and brought *it* down unto us, and brought us word again, and said, *It is* a ^Rgood land which the LORD our God doth give us.　　Num. 13:27

26 ^RNotwithstanding ye would not go up, but rebelled against the commandment of the LORD your God:　　Num. 14:1–4; Ps. 106:24

27 And ye ^Rmurmured in your tents, and said, Because the LORD hated us, he hath brought us forth out of the land of Egypt, to deliver us into the hand of the Am'-or-ites, to destroy us.　　Ps. 106:25

28 Whither shall we go up? our brethren have discouraged our heart, saying, ^RThe people *is* greater and taller than we; the cities *are* great and walled up to heaven; and moreover we have seen the sons of the ^RAn'-a-kims there.　　Num. 13:28, 31–33 · Num. 13:28

29 Then I said unto you, Dread not, neither be afraid of them.

30 ^RThe LORD your God which goeth before you, he shall fight for you, according to all that he did for you in Egypt before your eyes;　　3:22; 20:4; Ex. 14:14; Neh. 4:20

31 And in the wilderness, where thou hast seen how that the LORD thy God bare thee, as a ^Rman doth bear his son, in all the way that ye went, until ye came into this place.　　32:10–12; Is. 46:3, 4; 63:9; Hos. 11:3

32 Yet in this thing ^Rye did not believe the LORD your God,　　Jude 5

33 Who went in the way before you, to search you out a place to pitch your tents *in*, in fire by night, to shew you by what way ye should go, and in a cloud by day.

34 And the LORD heard the voice of your words, and was wroth, and ^Tsware, saying,　　*took an oath*

35 ^RSurely there shall not one of these men of this evil generation see that good land, which I sware to give unto your fathers,　　Ps. 95:10

36 ^RSave Caleb the son of Je-phun'-neh; he shall see it, and to him will I give the land that he hath trodden upon, and to his children, because he hath wholly followed the LORD.　　[Josh. 14:9]

37 Also the LORD was angry with me for your sakes, saying, Thou also shalt not go in thither.

38 *But* Joshua the son of Nun, ^Rwhich standeth before thee, he shall go in thither: ^Rencourage him: for he shall cause Israel to inherit it.　　Ex. 24:13 · 31:7, 23; Josh. 11:23

39 Moreover your little ones, which ye said should be a prey,

and your children, which in that day [R]had no knowledge between good and evil, they shall go in thither, and unto them will I give it, and they shall possess it. Is. 7:15

40 But *as for* you, turn you, and take your journey into the wilderness by the way of the Red sea.

41 Then ye answered and said unto me, [R]We have sinned against the LORD, we will go up and fight, according to all that the LORD our God commanded us. And when ye had girded on every man his weapons of war, ye were ready to go up into the hill.   Num. 14:40

42 And the LORD said unto me, Say unto them, [R]Go not up, neither fight; for I *am* not among you; lest ye be [T]smitten before your enemies. Num. 14:41–43 · *defeated*

43 So I spake unto you; and ye would not hear, but [R]rebelled against the commandment of the LORD, and [R]went presumptuously up into the hill.   Num. 14:44 · 17:12, 13

44 And the Am'-or-ites, which dwelt in that mountain, came out against you, and chased you, [R]as bees do, and destroyed you in Se'-ir, *even* unto Hor'-mah.   Ps. 118:12

45 And ye returned and wept before the LORD; but the LORD would not hearken to your voice, nor give ear unto you.

46 [R]So ye abode in Ka'-desh many days, according unto the days that ye abode *there*.   2:7, 14

2 Then we turned, and took our journey into the wilderness by the way of the Red sea, as the LORD spake unto me: and we compassed mount Se'-ir many days.

2 And the LORD spake unto me, saying,

3 Ye have compassed this mountain [R]long enough: turn you northward.   vv. 7, 14

4 And command thou the people, saying, [R]Ye *are* to pass through the [T]coast of [R]your brethren the children of Esau, which dwell in Se'-ir; and they shall be afraid of you: take ye good heed unto yourselves therefore: Num. 20:14–21 · *territory* · 23:7

5 Meddle not with them; for I will not give you of their land, no, not so much as a footbreadth; because I have given mount Se'-ir unto Esau *for* a possession.

6 Ye shall buy meat of them for money, that ye may eat; and ye shall also buy water of them for money, that ye may drink.

7 For the LORD thy God hath blessed thee in all the works of thy hand: he knoweth thy walking through this great wilderness: [R]these forty years the LORD thy God *hath been* with thee; thou hast lacked nothing.   [Matt. 6:8, 32]

8 And when we passed by from our brethren the children of Esau, which dwelt in Se'-ir, through the way of the plain from [R]E'-lath, and from E'-zi-on-ga'-ber, we turned and passed by the way of the wilderness of Moab.   Judg. 11:18

9 And the LORD said unto me, Distress not the Mo'-ab-ites, neither contend with them in battle: for I will not give thee of their land *for* a possession; because I have given [R]Ar unto the children of Lot *for* a possession.   Num. 21:15

10 The E'-mims dwelt therein in times past, a people great, and many, and tall, as the An'-a-kims;

11 Which also were accounted giants, as the An'-a-kims; but the Mo'-ab-ites call them E'-mims.

12 [R]The Ho'-rims also dwelt in Se'-ir beforetime; but the children of Esau [T]succeeded them, when they had destroyed them from before them, and dwelt in their stead; as Israel did unto the land of his possession, which the LORD gave unto them.   v. 22 · *dispossessed*

13 Now rise up, *said I*, and get you over the brook Ze'-red. And we went over the brook Ze'-red.

14 And the space in which we came from Ka'-desh–bar'-ne-a, until we were come over the brook Ze'-red, *was* thirty and eight years; until all the generation of the men of war were wasted out from among the host, as the LORD sware unto them.

15 For indeed the hand of the LORD was against them, to destroy them from among the host, until they ᵀwere consumed.   *perished*

16 So it came to pass, when all the men of war were consumed and dead from among the people,

17 That the LORD spake unto me, saying,

18 Thou art to pass over through Ar, the coast of Moab, this day:

19 And *when* thou comest nigh over against the children of Ammon, distress them not, nor meddle with them: for I will not give thee of the land of the children of Ammon *any* possession; because I have given it unto the children of Lot *for* a possession.

20 (That also was accounted a land of giants: ᵀgiants dwelt therein in old time; and the Am'-mon-ites call them ᴿZam-zum'-mims;   Heb. *rephaim* · Gen. 14:5

21 ᴿA people great, and many, and tall, as the An'-a-kims; but the LORD destroyed them before them; and they succeeded them, and dwelt in their stead: v. 10

22 As he did to the children of Esau, ᴿwhich dwelt in Se'-ir, when he destroyed the Ho'-rims from before them; and they succeeded them, and dwelt in their stead even unto this day: v. 5; Gen. 36:8

23 And the A'-vims which dwelt in Ha-ze'-rim, *even* unto Az'-zah, the Caph'-to-rims, which came forth out of Caph'-tor, destroyed them, and dwelt in their stead.)

24 Rise ye up, take your journey, and ᴿpass over the river Arnon: behold, I have given into thine hand ᴿSi'-hon the Am'-or-ite, king of Hesh'-bon, and his land: begin to possess *it*, and contend with him in battle.   Num. 21:13, 14 · 1:4

25 ᴿThis day will I begin to put the dread of thee and the fear of thee upon the nations *that are* under the whole heaven, who shall hear report of thee, and shall ᴿtremble, and be in anguish because of thee.   Josh. 2:9 · Ex. 15:14–16

26 And I ᴿsent messengers out of the wilderness of Ked'-e-moth unto Si'-hon king of Hesh'-bon with words of peace, saying,   1:4

27 Let me pass through thy land: I will go along by the high way, I will neither turn unto the right hand nor to the left.

28 Thou shalt sell me meat for money, that I may eat; and give me water for money, that I may drink: ᴿonly I will pass through on my feet;   Num. 20:19

29 (ᴿAs the children of Esau which dwell in Se'-ir, and the Mo'-ab-ites which dwell in Ar, did unto me;) until I shall pass over Jordan into the land which the LORD our God giveth us.   Num. 20:18; Judg. 11:17

30 ᴿBut Si'-hon king of Hesh'-bon would not let us pass by him: for ᴿthe LORD thy God ᴿhardened his spirit, and made his heart obstinate, that he might deliver him into thy hand, as *appeareth* this day.   Num. 21:23 · Josh. 11:20 · Ex. 4:21

31 And the LORD said unto me, Behold, I have begun to ᴿgive Si'-hon and his land before thee: begin to possess, that thou mayest inherit his land.   1:3, 8

32 ᴿThen Si'-hon came out against us, he and all his people, to fight at Ja'-haz.   Num. 21:23

33 And ᴿthe LORD our God delivered him before us; and ᴿwe smote him, and his sons, and all his people.   Ex. 23:31 · Num. 21:24

34 And we took all his cities at that time, and ᴿutterly destroyed the men, and the women, and the little ones, of every city, we left none to remain: Lev. 27:28

35 Only the cattle we took for a prey unto ourselves, and the spoil of the cities which we took.

36 ᴿFrom Ar'-o-er, which *is* by the brink of the river of Arnon, and *from* the city that *is* by the river, even unto Gil'-e-ad, there was not one city too strong for us: ᴿthe LORD our God delivered all unto us: Josh. 13:9 · Ps. 44:3

37 Only unto the land of the children of Ammon thou camest not, *nor* unto any place of the river ᴿJab'-bok, nor unto the cities in the mountains, nor unto what-

soever the LORD our God forbad us.   3:16; Gen. 32:22; Num. 21:24

3 Then we turned, and went up the way to Ba'-shan: and ᴿOg the king of Ba'-shan came out against us, he and all his people, to battle at Ed'-re-i.   Num. 21:33–35

2 And the LORD said unto me, Fear him not: for I will deliver him, and all his people, and his land, into thy hand; and thou shalt do unto him as thou didst unto Si'-hon king of the Am'-or-ites, which dwelt at Hesh'-bon.

3 So the LORD our God delivered into our hands Og also, the king of Ba'-shan, and all his people: and we ᵀsmote him until none was left to him remaining. *attacked*

4 And we took all his cities at that time, there was not a city which we took not from them, threescore cities, ᴿall the region of Ar'-gob, the kingdom of Og in Ba'-shan. vv. 13, 14

5 All these cities *were* ᵀfenced with high walls, gates, and bars; beside unwalled towns a great many.   *fortified*

6 And we utterly destroyed them, as we did unto Si'-hon king ᴿof Hesh'-bon, utterly destroying the men, women, and children, of every city.   2:24, 34, 35

7 But all the cattle, and the spoil of the cities, we took for ᵀa prey to ourselves.   *booty*

8 And we took at that time out of the hand of the two kings of the Am'-or-ites the land that *was* on this side Jordan, from the river of Arnon unto mount ᴿHermon; 4:48

9 (*Which* ᴿHermon the Si-do'-ni-ans call Sir'-i-on; and the Am'-or-ites call it She'-nir;)   1 Chr. 5:23

10 ᴿAll the cities of the plain, and all Gil'-e-ad, and ᴿall Ba'-shan, unto Sal'-chah and Ed'-re-i, cities of the kingdom of Og in Ba'-shan.   4:49 · Josh. 12:5; 13:11

11 ᴿFor only Og king of Ba'-shan remained of the remnant of ᴿgiants; behold, his bedstead *was* a bedstead of iron; *is* it not in ᴿRab'-bath of the children of Ammon? nine cubits *was* the length thereof, and four cubits the breadth of it, after the cubit of a man.   Amos 2:9 · Gen. 14:5 · 2 Sam. 12:26

12 And this land, *which* we possessed at that time, from Ar'-o-er, which *is* by the river Arnon, and half mount Gil'-e-ad, and the cities thereof, gave I unto the Reu'-ben-ites and to the Gad'-ites.

13 ᴿAnd the rest of Gil'-e-ad, and all Ba'-shan, *being* the kingdom of Og, gave I unto the half tribe of Ma-nas'-seh; all the region of Ar'-gob, with all Ba'-shan, which was called the land of giants.   Josh. 13:29–31; 17:1

14 ᴿJa'-ir the son of Ma-nas'-seh took all the country of Ar'-gob unto the coasts of Gesh'-u-ri and Ma-ach'-a-thi; and called them after his own name, Ba'-shan–ha'-voth–ja'-ir, unto this day. 1 Chr. 2:22

15 And I gave ᴿGil'-e-ad unto Ma'-chir.   Num. 32:39, 40

16 And unto the Reu'-ben-ites ᴿand unto the Gad'-ites I gave from Gil'-e-ad even unto the river Arnon half the valley, and the border even unto the river Jab'-bok, *which is* the border of the children of Ammon;   2 Sam. 24:5

17 The plain also, and Jordan, and the coast *thereof,* from Chin'-ne-reth even unto the sea of the plain, *even* the salt sea, under Ash'-doth–pis'-gah eastward.

18 And I commanded you at that time, saying, The LORD your God hath given you this land to possess it: ᴿye shall pass over armed before your brethren the children of Israel, all *that are* ᵀmeet for the war.   Josh. 4:12, 13 · *men of valour*

19 But your wives, and your little ones, and your cattle, (*for* I know that ye have much cattle,) shall abide in your cities which I have given you;

20 Until the LORD have given rest unto your brethren, as well as unto you, and *until* they also possess the land which the LORD your God hath given them beyond Jordan: and *then* shall ye ᴿreturn every man unto his possession, which I have given you. Josh. 22:4

21 And I commanded Joshua at

that time, saying, Thine eyes have seen all that the LORD your God hath done unto these two kings: so shall the LORD do unto all the kingdoms whither thou passest.

22 Ye shall not fear them: for ^Rthe LORD your God he shall fight for you.   1:30; 20:4; Ex. 14:14; Neh. 4:20

23 And ^RI besought the LORD at that time, saying,   [2 Cor. 12:8, 9]

24 O Lord GOD, thou hast begun to shew thy servant ^Rthy greatness, and thy mighty hand: for ^Rwhat God is there in heaven or in earth, that can do according to thy works, and according to thy might?   5:24; 11:2 · Ps. 71:19; 86:8

25 I pray thee, let me go over, and see ^Rthe good land that is beyond Jordan, that goodly mountain, and Leb′-a-non.   4:22; Ex. 3:8

26 But the LORD ^Rwas wroth with me for your sakes, and would not hear me: and the LORD said unto me, Let it suffice thee; speak no more unto me of this matter.   1:37; 31:2; 32:51, 52; 34:4

27 Get thee up into the top of Pis′-gah, and lift up thine eyes westward, and northward, and southward, and eastward, and behold it with thine eyes: for thou shalt not go over this Jordan.

28 But ^Rcharge Joshua, and encourage him, and strengthen him: for he shall go over before this people, and he shall cause them to inherit the land which thou shalt see.   31:3, 7, 8, 23; Num. 27:18, 23

29 So we abode in ^Rthe valley over against Beth-pe′-or.   4:46; 34:6

4 Now therefore hearken, O Israel, unto ^Rthe statutes and unto the judgments, which I teach you, for to do them, that ye may live, and go in and possess the land which the LORD God of your fathers giveth you.   Lev. 19:37; 20:8

2 ^RYe shall not add unto the word which I command you, neither shall ye diminish ought from it, that ye may keep the commandments of the LORD your God which I command you.   [Josh. 1:7]

3 Your eyes have seen what the LORD did because of ^RBa′-al-pe′-

or: for all the men that followed Ba′-al-pe′-or, the LORD thy God hath destroyed them from among you.   Num. 25:1-9; Josh. 22:17; Ps. 106:28

4 But ye that ^Tdid cleave unto the LORD your God are alive every one of you this day.   held fast to

5 Behold, I have taught you statutes and judgments, even as the LORD my God commanded me, that ye should do so in the land whither ye go to possess it.

6 Keep therefore and do them; for this is ^Ryour wisdom and your understanding in the sight of the nations, which shall hear all these statutes, and say, Surely this great nation is a wise and understanding people.   Ps. 19:7; 111:10; Prov. 1:7

7 For ^Rwhat nation is there so great, who hath ^RGod so nigh unto them, as the LORD our God is in all things that we call upon him for?   [2 Sam. 7:23] · [Ps. 46:1; Is. 55:6]

8 And what nation is there so great, that hath statutes and judgments so righteous as all this law, which I set before you this day?

9 Only take heed to thyself, and ^Rkeep thy soul diligently, lest thou forget the things which thine eyes have seen, and lest they depart from thy heart all the days of thy life: but teach them thy sons, and thy sons' sons;   Prov. 4:23

10 Specially ^Rthe day that thou stoodest before the LORD thy God in Ho′-reb, when the LORD said unto me, Gather me the people together, and I will make them hear my words, that they may learn to fear me all the days that they shall live upon the earth, and that they may teach their children.   Ex. 19:9, 16, 17

11 And ye came near and stood under the mountain; and the mountain burned with fire unto the midst of heaven, with darkness, clouds, and thick darkness.

12 And the LORD spake unto you out of the midst of the fire: ye heard the voice of the words, but saw no similitude; ^Ronly ye heard a voice.   Ex. 19:17-19; 1 Kin. 19:11-18

13 ^RAnd he declared unto you

his covenant, which he commanded you to perform, *even* ten commandments; and he wrote them
upon two tables of stone.   9:9, 11
14 And ^Rthe LORD commanded
me at that time to teach you statutes and judgments, that ye might
do them in the land whither ye go
over to possess it.   Ex. 21:1
15 ^RTake ye therefore good heed
unto yourselves; for ye saw no
^Tmanner of ^Rsimilitude on the day
that the LORD spake unto you in
Ho'-reb out of the midst of the
fire: Josh. 23:11 · *form when* · Is. 40:18
16 Lest ye ^Rcorrupt *yourselves*,
and make you a graven image, the
similitude of any figure, the likeness of male or female,   9:12; 31:29
17 The likeness of any beast that
is on the earth, the likeness of any
winged fowl that flieth in the air,
18 The likeness of any thing that
creepeth on the ground, the likeness of any fish that *is* in the
waters beneath the earth:
19 And lest thou lift up thine
eyes unto heaven, and when thou
seest the sun, and the moon, and
the stars, *even* all the host of
heaven, shouldest be driven to
^Rworship them, and serve them,
which the LORD thy God hath
divided unto all nations under the
whole heaven.   [Rom. 1:25]
20 But the LORD hath taken you,
and brought you forth out of the
iron furnace, *even* out of Egypt, to
be unto him a ^Rpeople of inheritance, as *ye are* this day. [Titus 2:14]
21 Furthermore ^Rthe LORD was
angry with me for your sakes, and
sware that ^RI should not go over
Jordan, and that I should not go in
unto that good land, which the
LORD thy God giveth thee *for* an
inheritance: Num. 20:12 · Num. 27:13, 14
22 But ^RI must die in this land, ^RI
must not go over Jordan: but ye
shall go over, and possess ^Rthat
good land.   2 Pet. 1:13–15 · 3:27 · 3:25
23 Take heed unto yourselves,
lest ye forget the covenant of the
LORD your God, which he made
with you, ^Rand make you a graven
image, *or* the likeness of any

thing, which the LORD thy God
hath forbidden thee. v. 16; Ex. 20:4, 5
24 For ^Rthe LORD thy God *is* a
consuming fire, *even* ^Ra jealous
God. Is. 33:14; Heb. 12:29 · Ex. 20:5; 34:14
25 When thou shalt beget chil-
dren, and children's children, and
ye shall have remained long in the
land, and shall ^Tcorrupt *yourselves*, and make a graven image,
or the likeness of any *thing*, and
^Rshall do evil in the sight of the
LORD thy God, to provoke him to
anger: *act corruptly* · 2 Kin. 17:17
26 ^RI call heaven and earth to
witness against you this day, that
ye shall soon utterly perish from
off the land whereunto ye go over
Jordan to possess it; ye shall not
prolong *your* days upon it, but
shall utterly be destroyed. Mic. 6:2
27 And the LORD ^Rshall scatter
you among the nations, and ye
shall be left few in number among
the heathen, whither the LORD
shall lead you.   Lev. 26:33; Neh. 1:8
28 And there ye shall serve
gods, the work of men's hands,
wood and stone, which neither
see, nor hear, nor eat, nor smell.
29 But if from thence thou shalt
seek the LORD thy God, thou shalt
find *him*, if thou seek him with
all thy heart and with all thy soul.
30 When thou art in tribulation,
and all these things are come
upon thee, *even* in the ^Rlatter
days, if thou ^Rturn to the LORD thy
God, and shalt be obedient unto
his voice;   Jer. 23:20; Hos. 3:5 · Joel 2:12
31 (For the LORD thy God *is* a
merciful God;) he will not forsake
thee, neither destroy thee, nor forget the covenant of thy fathers
which he sware unto them.
32 For ^Rask now of the days that
are past, which were before thee,
since the day that God created
man upon the earth, and *ask*
^Rfrom the one side of heaven unto
the other, whether there hath
been *any such thing* as this great
thing *is*, or hath been heard like
it?   32:7; Job 8:8 · 28:64; Matt. 24:31
33 ^RDid *ever* people hear the
voice of God speaking out of the

midst of the fire, as thou hast heard, and live?   Ex. 20:22; 24:11

34 Or hath God assayed to go *and* take him a nation from the midst of *another* nation, by temptations, [R]by signs, and by wonders, and by war, and [R]by a mighty hand, and [R]by a stretched out arm, and by great terrors, according to all that the LORD your God did for you in Egypt before your eyes?   Ex. 7:3 · Ex. 13:3 · Ex. 6:6

35 Unto thee it was shewed, that thou mightest know that the LORD he *is* God; [R]*there is* none else beside him.   [Is. 43:10–12]; Mark 12:3

36 [R]Out of heaven he made thee to hear his voice, that he might instruct thee: and upon earth he shewed thee his great fire; and thou heardest his words out of the midst of the fire.   Neh. 9:13; Heb. 12:19

37 And because [R]he loved thy fathers, therefore he chose their seed after them, and brought thee out in his sight with his mighty power out of Egypt;   7:7, 8; 10:15; 33:3

38 [R]To drive out nations from before thee greater and mightier than thou *art*, to bring thee in, to give thee their land *for* an inheritance, as *it is* this day.   7:1

39 Know therefore this day, and consider *it* in thine heart, that [R]the LORD he *is* God in heaven above, and upon the earth beneath: *there is* none else.   Josh. 2:11

40 [R]Thou shalt keep therefore his statutes, and his commandments, which I command thee this day, that it may go well with thee, and with thy children after thee, and that thou mayest prolong *thy* days upon the earth, which the LORD thy God giveth thee, for ever.   5:16; 32:46, 47; Lev. 22:31

41 Then Moses [R]severed[T] three cities on this side Jordan toward the sun rising;   Josh. 20:7–9 · *set apart*

42 [R]That the slayer might flee thither, which should kill his neighbour [T]unawares, and hated him not in times past; and that fleeing unto one of these cities he might live: 19:4 · *unintentionally*

43 Namely, [R]Be'-zer in the wilderness, in the plain country, of the Reu'-ben-ites; and Ra'-moth in Gil'-e-ad, of the Gad'-ites; and Go'-lan in Ba'-shan, of the Ma-nas'-sites.   Josh. 20:8

44 And this *is* the law which Moses set before the children of Israel:

45 These *are* the testimonies, and the statutes, and the judgments, which Moses spake unto the children of Israel, after they came forth out of Egypt,

46 On this side Jordan, [R]in the valley over against Beth–pe'-or, in the land of Si'-hon king of the Am'-or-ites, who dwelt at Hesh'-bon, whom Moses and the children of Israel smote, after they were come forth out of Egypt: 3:29

47 And they possessed his land, and the land [R]of Og king of Ba'-shan, two kings of the Am'-or-ites, which *were* on this side Jordan toward the sun rising;   Num. 21:33–35

48 [R]From Ar'-o-er, which *is* by the bank of the river Arnon, even unto mount Si'-on, which *is* [R]Hermon,   2:36; 3:12 · 3:9; Ps. 133:3

49 And all the plain on this side Jordan eastward, even unto the sea of the plain, under the [R]springs of Pis'-gah.   3:17

5 And Moses called all Israel, and said unto them, Hear, O Israel, the statutes and judgments which I speak in your ears this day, that ye may learn them, and keep, and do them.

2 [R]The LORD our God made a covenant with us in Ho'-reb.   4:23

3 The LORD [R]made not this covenant with our fathers, but with us, *even* us, who *are* all of us here alive this day.   Matt. 13:17; Heb. 8:9

4 [R]The LORD talked with you face to face in the mount out of the midst of the fire,   Ex. 19:9

5 ([R]I stood between the LORD and you at that time, to shew you the word of the LORD: for [R]ye were afraid by reason of the fire, and went not up into the mount;) saying,   Ex. 20:21; Gal. 3:19 · Ex. 19:16

6 [R]I *am* the LORD thy God, which brought thee out of the

land of Egypt, from the house of bondage. Ex. 20:2–17; Lev. 26:1; Ps. 81:10

7 ᴿThou shalt have none other gods before me. Ex. 20:2, 3; Hos. 13:4

8 ᴿThou shalt not make thee *any* graven image, *or* any likeness *of any thing* that *is* in heaven above, or that *is* in the earth beneath, or that *is* in the waters beneath the earth: Ex. 20:4

9 Thou shalt not ᴿbow down thyself unto them, nor serve them: for I the Lᴏʀᴅ thy God *am* a jealous God, visiting the iniquity of the fathers upon the children unto the third and fourth *generation* of them that hate me, Ex. 34:7, 14–16

10 ᴿAnd shewing mercy unto thousands of them that love me and keep my commandments. 7:9

11 ᴿThou shalt not take the name of the Lᴏʀᴅ thy God in vain: for the Lᴏʀᴅ will not hold *him* guiltless that taketh his name in vain. Ex. 20:7; Lev. 19:12; Matt. 5:33

12 ᴿKeep the sabbath day to sanctify it, as the Lᴏʀᴅ thy God hath commanded thee. Mark 2:27

13 ᴿSix days thou shalt labour, and do all thy work: Ex. 23:12; 35:2

14 But the seventh day *is* the ᴿsabbath of the Lᴏʀᴅ thy God: *in it* thou shalt not do any work, thou, nor thy son, nor thy daughter, nor thy manservant, nor thy maidservant, nor thine ox, nor thine ass, nor any of thy cattle, nor thy stranger that *is* within thy gates; that thy manservant and thy maidservant may rest as well as thou. [Gen. 2:2]; Ex. 16:29; [Heb. 4:4]

15 ᴿAnd remember that thou wast a servant in the land of Egypt, and *that* the Lᴏʀᴅ thy God brought thee out thence ᴿthrough a mighty hand and by a stretched out arm: therefore the Lᴏʀᴅ thy God commanded thee to keep the sabbath day. 15:15 · 4:34, 37

16 ᴿHonour thy father and thy mother, as the Lᴏʀᴅ thy God hath commanded thee; ᴿthat thy days may be prolonged, and that it may go well with ᴿthee, in the land which the Lᴏʀᴅ thy God giveth thee. Ex. 20:12; Eph. 6:2, 3 · 6:2 · 4:40

17 ᴿThou shalt not kill. Ex. 20:13

18 ᴿNeither shalt thou commit adultery. Ex. 20:14; [Rom. 13:9]

19 Neither shalt thou steal.

20 Neither shalt thou bear false witness against thy neighbour.

21 Neither shalt thou desire thy neighbour's wife, neither shalt thou covet thy neighbour's house, his field, or his manservant, or his maidservant, his ox, or his ass, or any *thing* that *is* thy neighbour's.

22 These words the Lᴏʀᴅ spake unto all your assembly in the mount out of the midst of the fire, of the cloud, and of the thick darkness, with a great voice: and he added no more. And ᴿhe wrote them in two tables of stone, and delivered them unto me. Ex. 24:12

23 And it came to pass, when ye heard the voice out of the midst of the darkness, (for the mountain did burn with fire,) that ye came near unto me, *even* all the heads of your tribes, and your elders;

24 And ye said, Behold, the Lᴏʀᴅ our God hath shewed us his glory and his greatness, and ᴿwe have heard his voice out of the midst of the fire: we have seen this day that God doth talk with man, and he ᴿliveth. Ex. 19:19 · 4:33

25 Now therefore why should we die? for this great fire will consume us: ᴿif we hear the voice of the Lᴏʀᴅ our God any more, then we shall die. 18:16; Ex. 20:18, 19

26 ᴿFor who *is there of* all flesh, that hath heard the voice of the living God speaking out of the midst of the fire, as we *have*, and lived? 4:33

27 Go thou near, and hear all that the Lᴏʀᴅ our God shall say: and ᴿspeak thou unto us all that the Lᴏʀᴅ our God shall speak unto thee; and we will hear *it*, and do *it*. Ex. 20:19; Heb. 12:19

28 And the Lᴏʀᴅ heard the voice of your words, when ye spake unto me; and the Lᴏʀᴅ said unto me, I have heard the voice of the words of this people, which they have spoken unto thee: ᴿthey have well said all that they have spoken.18:17

29 ^RO that there were such an heart in them, that they would fear me, and ^Rkeep all my commandments always, ^Rthat it might be well with them, and with their children for ever! Is. 48:18 · 11:1 · 4:40

30 Go say to them, Get you into your tents again.

31 But as for thee, stand thou here by me, and I will speak unto thee all the commandments, and the statutes, and the judgments, which thou shalt teach them, that they may do *them* in the land which I give them to possess it.

32 Ye shall observe to do therefore as the LORD your God hath commanded you: ^Rye shall not turn aside to the right hand or to the left. 17:20; Josh. 1:7; 23:6; Prov. 4:27

33 Ye shall walk in ^Rall the ways which the LORD your God hath commanded you, that ye may live, ^Rand *that it may be* well with you, and *that* ye may prolong *your* days in the land which ye shall possess. Jer. 7:23; Luke 1:6 · Eph. 6:3

6 Now these *are* the commandments, the statutes, and the judgments, which the LORD your God commanded to teach you, that ye might do *them* in the land whither ye go to possess it:

2 ^RThat thou mightest fear the LORD thy God, to keep all his statutes and his commandments, which I command thee, thou, and thy son, and thy son's son, all the days of thy life; and that thy days may be prolonged. [Ps. 111:10; 128:1]

3 Hear therefore, O Israel, and observe to do *it;* that it may be well with thee, and that ye may ^Rincrease mightily, as the LORD God of thy fathers hath promised thee, in ^Rthe land that floweth with milk and honey. 7:13 · Ex. 3:8, 17

4 ^RHear, O Israel: The LORD our God *is* one LORD: [1 Cor. 8:4, 6]

5 And ^Rthou shalt love the LORD thy God with all thine heart, and with all thy soul, and with all thy might. Matt. 22:37; Luke 10:27

6 And ^Rthese words, which I command thee this day, shall be in thine heart: 11:18–20; Ps. 119:11, 98

7 And ^Rthou shalt teach them diligently unto thy children, and shalt talk of them when thou sittest in thine house, and when thou walkest by the way, and when thou liest down, and when thou risest up. 4:9; 11:19; [Eph. 6:4]

8 ^RAnd thou shalt bind them for a sign upon thine hand, and they shall be as frontlets between thine eyes. Ex. 12:14; 13:9, 16; Prov. 3:3

9 ^RAnd thou shalt write them upon the posts of thy house, and on thy gates. 11:20; Is. 57:8

10 And it shall be, when the LORD thy God shall have brought thee into the land which he sware unto thy fathers, to Abraham, to Isaac, and to Jacob, to give thee great and goodly cities, ^Rwhich thou buildedst not, Josh. 24:13

11 And houses full of all good *things,* which thou filledst not, and wells digged, which thou diggedst not, vineyards and olive trees, which thou plantedst not; ^Rwhen thou shalt have eaten and be full; 8:10; 11:15; 14:29

12 *Then* beware lest thou forget the ^RLORD, which brought thee forth out of the land of Egypt, from the house of bondage. 8:11–18

13 Thou shalt ^Rfear the LORD thy God, and serve him, and shalt swear by his name. 13:4; Matt. 4:10

14 Ye shall not go after other gods, ^Rof the gods of the people which *are* round about you; 13:7

15 (For the LORD thy God *is* a jealous God among you) lest the anger of the LORD thy God be kindled against thee, and destroy thee from off the face of the earth.

16 ^RYe shall not ^Ttempt the LORD your God, as ye tempted *him* in Mas'-sah. Matt. 4:7; Luke 4:12 · *test*

17 Ye shall ^Rdiligently keep the commandments of the LORD your God, and his testimonies, and his statutes, which he hath commanded thee. 11:22; Ps. 119:4

18 And thou ^Rshalt do *that which is* right and good in the sight of the LORD: that it may be well with thee, and that thou mayest go in and possess the

good land which the LORD sware unto thy fathers,   8:7-10; Ex. 15:26

19 [R]To cast out all thine enemies from before thee, as the LORD hath spoken.   Num. 33:52, 53

20 *And* [R]when thy son asketh thee in time to come, saying, What *mean* the testimonies, and the statutes, and the judgments, which the LORD our God hath commanded you?   Ex. 13:8, 14

21 Then thou shalt say unto thy son, We were Pharaoh's bondmen in Egypt; and the LORD brought us out of Egypt with a mighty hand:

22 And the LORD shewed signs and wonders, great and [T]sore, upon Egypt, upon Pharaoh, and upon all his household, before our eyes: *severe*

23 And he brought us out from thence, that he might bring us in, to give us the land which he [T]sware unto our fathers.   *promised*

24 And the LORD commanded us to do all these statutes, to fear the LORD our God, [R]for our good always, that he might preserve us alive, as *it is* at this day.   Jer. 32:39

25 And [R]it shall be our righteousness, if we observe to do all these commandments before the LORD our God, as he hath commanded us.   24:13; [Rom. 10:3, 5]

7 When the LORD thy God shall bring thee into the land whither thou goest to [R]possess it, and hath cast out many nations before thee, the Hit'-tites, and the Gir'-ga-shites, and the Am'-or-ites, and the Ca'naan-ites, and the Per'-iz-zites, and the Hi'-vites, and the Jeb'-u-sites, seven nations greater and mightier than thou;   6:10

2 And when the LORD thy God shall deliver [R]them before thee; thou shalt smite them, *and* utterly destroy them; thou shalt make no covenant with them, nor shew mercy unto them: Num. 31:17

3 [R]Neither shalt thou make marriages with them; thy daughter thou shalt not give unto his son, nor his daughter shalt thou take unto thy son.   1 Kin. 11:2; Ezra 9:2

4 For they will turn away thy

son from following me, that they may serve other gods: [R]so will the anger of the LORD be kindled against you, and destroy thee suddenly.   6:15

5 But thus shall ye deal with them; ye shall [R]destroy their altars, and break down their images, and cut down their groves, and burn their graven images with fire.   12:3; Ex. 23:24; 34:13

6 For thou *art* an holy people unto the LORD thy God: [R]the LORD thy God hath chosen thee to be a special people unto himself, above all people that *are* upon the face of the earth.   Amos 3:2; 1 Pet. 2:9

7 The LORD did not set his [R]love upon you, nor choose you, because ye were more in number than any people; for ye *were* [R]the fewest of all people: 4:37 · 10:22

8 But because the LORD loved you, and because he would keep the oath which he had sworn unto your fathers, hath the LORD brought you out with a mighty hand, and redeemed you out of the house of bondmen, from the hand of Pharaoh king of Egypt.

9 Know therefore that the LORD thy God, he *is* God, the faithful God, which keepeth covenant and mercy with them that love him and keep his commandments to a thousand generations;

10 And repayeth them that hate him to their face, to destroy them: he will not be [R]slack to him that hateth him, he will repay him to his face.   [2 Pet. 3:10]

11 Thou shalt therefore keep the commandments, and the statutes, and the judgments, which I command thee this day, to do them.

12 Wherefore it shall come to pass, if ye [T]hearken to these judgments, and keep, and do them, that the LORD thy God shall keep unto thee the covenant and the mercy which he sware unto thy fathers: *listen*

13 And he will [R]love thee, and bless thee, and multiply thee: he will also bless the fruit of thy womb, and the fruit of thy land,

thy corn, and thy wine, and thine oil, the increase of thy kine, and the flocks of thy sheep, in the land which he sware unto thy fathers to give thee.   Ps. 146:8; John 14:21

14 Thou shalt be blessed above all people: there shall not be male or female R barren among you, or among your cattle.   Ex. 23:26

15 And the LORD will take away from thee all sickness, and will put none of the R evil diseases of Egypt, which thou knowest, upon thee; but will lay them upon all *them* that hate thee.   Ex. 9:14; 15:26

16 And thou shalt consume all the people which the LORD thy God shall deliver thee; thine eye shall have no pity upon them: neither shalt thou serve their gods; for that *will be* a snare unto thee.

17 If thou shalt say in thine heart, These nations *are* T more than I; how can I dispossess them?   *greater*

18 Thou shalt not be afraid of them: *but* shalt well remember what the LORD thy God did unto Pharaoh, and unto all Egypt;

19 R The great temptations which thine eyes saw, and the signs, and the wonders, and the mighty hand, and the stretched out arm, whereby the LORD thy God brought thee out: so shall the LORD thy God do unto all the people of whom thou art afraid.   29:3

20 R Moreover the LORD thy God will send the hornet among them, until they that are left, and hide themselves from thee, be destroyed.   Ex. 23:28; Josh. 24:12

21 Thou shalt not be affrighted at them: for the LORD thy God *is* among you, a mighty God and T terrible.   *awesome*

22 And the LORD thy God will put out those nations before thee R by little T and little: thou mayest not T consume them at once, lest the beasts of the field increase upon thee. Ex. 23:29, 30 · *by* · *destroy*

23 But the LORD thy God shall deliver them unto thee, and shall destroy them with a mighty destruction, until they be destroyed.

24 And he shall deliver their kings into thine hand, and thou shalt destroy their name from under heaven: there shall no man be able to stand before thee, until thou have destroyed them.

25 The T graven images of their gods shall ye burn with fire: thou shalt not R desire the silver or gold *that is* on them, nor take *it* unto thee, lest thou be snared therein: for it *is* an abomination to the LORD thy God.   *carved* · Prov. 23:6

26 Neither shalt thou bring an abomination into thine house, lest thou be a cursed thing like it: *but* thou shalt utterly detest it, and thou shalt utterly abhor it; R for it *is* a cursed thing.   13:17

8 All the commandments which I command thee this day R shall ye observe to do, that ye may live, and multiply, and go in and possess the land which the LORD sware unto your fathers.   4:1

2 And thou shalt remember all the way which the LORD thy God R led thee these forty years in the wilderness, to humble thee, *and* R to prove thee, R to know what *was* in thine heart, whether thou wouldest keep his commandments, or no. 1:3 · Ex. 16:4 · [John 2:25]

3 And he humbled thee, and suffered thee to hunger, and fed thee with man'-na, which thou knewest not, neither did thy fathers know; that he might make thee know that man doth R not live by bread only, but by every *word* that proceedeth out of the mouth of the LORD doth man live. Matt. 4:4

4 R Thy raiment waxed not old upon thee, neither did thy foot swell, these forty years.   Neh. 9:21

5 R Thou shalt also consider in thine heart, that, as a man chasteneth his son, *so* the LORD thy God chasteneth thee.   Heb. 12:5-11

6 Therefore thou shalt keep the commandments of the LORD thy God, R to walk in his ways, and to fear him.   [5:33]

7 For the LORD thy God bringeth thee into a good land, R a land of brooks of water, of fountains

and depths that spring out of valleys and hills;   11:9–12; Jer. 2:7

8 A land of wheat, and barley, and vines, and fig trees, and pomegranates; a land of oil olive, and honey;

9 A land wherein thou shalt eat bread without scarceness, thou shalt not lack any *thing* in it; a land whose stones *are* iron, and out of whose hills thou mayest dig brass.

10 ᴿWhen thou hast eaten and art full, then thou shalt bless the LORD thy God for the good land which he hath given thee.   6:11, 12

11 Beware that thou forget not the LORD thy God, in not keeping his commandments, and his judgments, and his statutes, which I command thee this day:

12 ᴿLest *when* thou hast eaten and art full, and hast built goodly houses, and dwelt *therein*;   28:47

13 And *when* thy herds and thy flocks multiply, and thy silver and thy gold is multiplied, and all that thou hast is multiplied;

14 ᴿThen thine heart be lifted up, and thou forget the LORD thy God, which brought thee forth out of the land of Egypt, from the house of bondage;   1 Cor. 4:7

15 Who ᴿled thee through that great and terrible wilderness, ᴿ*wherein were* fiery serpents, and scorpions, and drought, where *there was* no water; ᴿwho brought thee forth water out of the rock of flint;   Is. 63:12–14 · Num. 21:6 · Ex. 17:6

16 Who fed thee in the wilderness with ᴿman'-na, which thy fathers knew not, that he might humble thee, and that he might prove thee, ᴿto do thee good at thy latter end;   Ex. 16:15 · [Heb. 12:11]

17 And thou say in thine heart, My power and the might of *mine* hand hath gotten me this wealth.

18 But thou shalt remember the LORD thy God: ᴿfor *it is* he that giveth thee power to get wealth, that he may establish his covenant which he sware unto thy fathers, as *it is* this day.   Prov. 10:22

19 And it shall be, if thou do at all forget the LORD thy God, and walk after other gods, and serve them, and worship them, ᴿI testify against you this day that ye shall surely perish.   4:26; 30:18

20 As the nations which the LORD destroyeth before your face, so shall ye perish; because ye would not be obedient unto the voice of the LORD your God.

9 Hear, O Israel: Thou *art* to pass over Jordan this day, to go in to possess nations greater and mightier than thyself, cities great and ᵀfenced up to heaven,   *fortified*

2 A people great and tall, the ᴿchildren of the An'-a-kims, whom thou knowest, and *of whom* thou hast heard *say*, Who can stand before the children of A'-nak!   Num. 13:22, 28, 33; Josh. 11:21, 22

3 Understand therefore this day, that the LORD thy God *is* he which ᴿgoeth over before thee; *as* a consuming fire he shall destroy them, and he shall bring them down before thy face: so shalt thou drive them out, and destroy them quickly, as the LORD hath said unto thee.   Josh. 5:14; John 10:4

4 ᴿSpeak not thou in thine heart, after that the LORD thy God hath cast them out from before thee, saying, For my righteousness the LORD hath brought me in to possess this land: but for the wickedness of these nations the LORD doth drive them out from before thee.   [Rom. 11:6, 20; 1 Cor. 4:4, 7]

5 ᴿNot for thy righteousness, or for the uprightness of thine heart, dost thou go to possess their land: but for the wickedness of these nations the LORD thy God doth drive them out from before thee, and that he may ᵀperform the ᴿword which the LORD sware unto thy fathers, Abraham, Isaac, and Jacob.   [Titus 3:5] · *fulfil* · Gen. 50:24

6 Understand therefore, that the LORD thy God giveth thee not this good land to possess it for thy righteousness; for thou *art* a ᴿstiffnecked people.   31:27; Ex. 34:9

7 Remember, *and* forget not, how thou ᴿprovokedst the LORD

thy God to wrath in the wilderness: [R]from the day that thou didst depart out of the land of Egypt, until ye came unto this place, ye have been rebellious against the LORD. Num. 14:22 · Ex. 14:11

8 Also [R]in Ho'-reb ye provoked the LORD to wrath, so that the LORD was angry with you to have destroyed you. Ex. 32:1–8; Ps. 106:19

9 [R]When I was gone up into the mount to receive the tables of stone, even the tables of the covenant which the LORD made with you, then I abode in the mount forty days and [R]forty nights, I neither did eat bread nor drink water: Ex. 24:12, 15 · Ex. 24:18

10 [R]And the LORD delivered unto me two tables of stone written with the finger of God; and on them was written according to all the words, which the LORD spake with you in the mount out of the midst of the fire [R]in the day of the assembly. 4:13; Ex. 31:18 · Ex. 19:17

11 And it came to pass at the end of forty days and forty nights, that the LORD gave me the two tables of stone, even the tables of the covenant.

12 And the LORD said unto me, [R]Arise, get thee down quickly from hence; for thy people which thou hast brought forth out of Egypt have corrupted themselves; they are [R]quickly turned aside out of the way which I commanded them; they have made them a molten image. Ex. 32:7, 8 · 31:29

13 Furthermore [R]the LORD spake unto me, saying, I have seen this people, and, behold, [R]it is a stiffnecked people: Ex. 32:9 · 9:6

14 [R]Let me alone, that I may destroy them, and blot out their name from under heaven: and I will make of thee a nation mightier and greater than they. Ex. 32:10

15 [R]So I turned and came down from the mount, and [R]the mount burned with fire: and the two tables of the covenant were in my two hands. Ex. 32:15–19 · Ex. 19:18

16 And I looked, and, behold, ye had sinned against the LORD your God, and had made you a molten calf: ye had turned aside quickly out of the way which the LORD had commanded you.

17 And I took the two tables, and cast them out of my two hands, and [R]brake them before your eyes. Ex. 32:19

18 And I fell down before the LORD, as at the first, forty days and forty nights: I did neither eat bread, nor drink water, because of all your sins which ye sinned, in doing wickedly in the sight of the LORD, to provoke him to anger.

19 [R]For I was afraid of the anger and hot displeasure, wherewith the LORD was wroth against you to destroy you. [R]But the LORD hearkened unto me at that time also. Ex. 32:10, 11; Heb. 12:21 · Ex. 32:14

20 And the LORD was very angry with Aaron to have destroyed him: and I prayed for Aaron also the same time.

21 And I took your sin, the calf which ye had made, and burnt it with fire, and stamped it, and ground it very small, even until it was as small as dust: and I cast the dust thereof into the brook that descended out of the mount.

22 And at [R]Tab'-e-rah, and at [R]Mas'-sah, and at [R]Kib'-roth–hatta'-a-vah, ye provoked the LORD to wrath. Num. 11:1, 3 · Ex. 17:7 · Num. 11:4

23 Likewise [R]when the LORD sent you from Ka'-desh–bar'-ne-a, saying, Go up and possess the land which I have given you; then ye rebelled against the commandment of the LORD your God, and ye believed him not, nor hearkened to his voice. Num. 13:3

24 [R]Ye have been rebellious against the LORD from the day that I knew you. v. 7; 31:27

25 [R]Thus I [T]fell down before the LORD forty days and forty nights, as I fell down at the first; because the LORD had said he would destroy you. v. 18 · prostrated myself

26 I prayed therefore unto the LORD, and said, O Lord GOD, destroy not thy people and [R]thine inheritance, which thou hast

redeemed through thy greatness, which thou hast brought forth out of Egypt with a mighty hand. 32:9

27 Remember thy servants, Abraham, Isaac, and Jacob; look not unto the stubbornness of this people, nor to their wickedness, nor to their sin:

28 Lest the land whence thou broughtest us out say, Because the LORD was not able to bring them into the land which he promised them, and because he hated them, he hath brought them out to slay them in the wilderness.

29 Yet they *are* thy people and thine inheritance, which thou broughtest out by thy mighty power and by thy stretched out arm.

10 At that time the LORD said unto me, ᵀHew thee two tables of stone like unto the first, and come up unto me into the mount, and make thee an ᴿark of wood.   *Cut out* · Ex. 25:10

2 And I will write on the tables the words that were in the first tables which thou brakest, and thou shalt put them in the ark.

3 And I made an ark *of* shit'-tim wood, and hewed two tables of stone like unto the first, and went up into the mount, having the two tables in mine hand.

4 And he wrote on the tables, according to the first writing, the ten commandments, ᴿwhich the LORD spake unto you in the mount out of the midst of the fire in the day of the assembly: and the LORD gave them unto me.   Ex. 20:1; 34:28

5 And I turned myself and ᴿcame down from the mount, and put the tables in the ark which I had made; and there they be, as the LORD commanded me. Ex. 34:29

6 And the children of Israel took their journey from Be-e'-roth of the children of Ja'-a-kan to Mo-se'-ra: there Aaron died, and there he was buried; and E-le-a'-zar his son ministered in the priest's office in his stead.

7 ᴿFrom thence they journeyed unto Gud'-go-dah; and from Gud'-go-dah to Jot'-bath, a land of rivers of waters.   Num. 33:32–34

8 At that time ᴿthe LORD separated the tribe of Levi, to bear the ark of the covenant of the LORD, ᴿto stand before the LORD to minister unto him, and to bless in his name, unto this day.   Num. 3:6 · 18:5

9 ᴿWherefore Levi hath no part nor inheritance with his brethren; the LORD *is* his inheritance, according as the LORD thy God promised him.   18:1, 2; Num. 18:20, 24

10 And ᴿI stayed in the mount, according to the first time, forty days and forty nights; and ᴿthe LORD hearkened unto me at that time also, *and* the LORD would not destroy thee.   Ex. 34:28 · Ex. 32:14

11 ᴿAnd the LORD said unto me, Arise, ᵀtake *thy* journey before the people, that they may go in and possess the land, which I sware unto their fathers to give unto them.   Ex. 33:1 · *begin*

12 And now, Israel, ᴿwhat doth the LORD thy God require of thee, but to fear the LORD thy God, to walk in all his ways, and to ᴿlove him, and to serve the LORD thy God with all thy heart and with all thy soul,   Mic. 6:8 · Matt. 22:37; 1 Tim. 1:5

13 To keep the commandments of the LORD, and his statutes, which I command thee this day ᴿfor thy ᵀgood? 6:24 · *benefit* or *welfare*

14 Behold, the heaven and the heaven of heavens *is* the ᴿLORD's thy God, the earth *also*, with all that therein *is*.   [Ps. 68:33; 115:16]

15 Only the LORD had a delight in thy fathers to love them, and he chose their seed after them, *even* you above all people, *as it is* this day.

16 Circumcise therefore the foreskin of your ᴿheart, and be no more ᴿstiffnecked.   Rom. 2:28, 29 · 9:6

17 For the LORD your God *is* ᴿGod of gods, and LORD of lords, a great God, a mighty, and a terrible, which regardeth not persons, nor taketh reward: Is. 44:8; Dan. 2:47

18 ᴿHe doth execute the judgment of the fatherless and widow, and loveth the stranger, in giving him food and raiment. Ps. 68:5; 146:9

19 Love ye therefore the stranger: for ye were strangers in the land of Egypt.

20 ᴿThou shalt fear the LORD thy God; him shalt thou serve, and to him shalt thou ᵀcleave, and swear by his name.　Matt. 4:10 · *hold fast*

21 He *is* thy praise, and he *is* thy God, that hath done for thee these great and ᵀterrible things, which thine eyes have seen.　*awesome*

22 Thy fathers went down into Egypt with threescore and ten persons; and now the LORD thy God hath made thee as the stars of heaven for multitude.

11 Therefore thou shalt love the LORD thy God, and keep his charge, and his statutes, and his judgments, and his commandments, alway.

2 And know ye this day: for *I speak* not with your children which have not known, and which have not seen the ᵀchastisement of the LORD your God, his greatness, his mighty hand, and his stretched out arm,　*discipline*

3 And his miracles, and his acts, which he did in the midst of Egypt unto Pharaoh the king of Egypt, and unto all his land;

4 And what he did unto the army of Egypt, unto their horses, and to their chariots; how he made the water of the Red sea to overflow them as they pursued after you, and *how* the LORD hath destroyed them unto this day;

5 And what he did unto you in the wilderness, until ye came into this place;

6 And ᴿwhat he did unto Da'-than and A-bi'-ram, the sons of E-li'-ab, the son of Reuben: how the earth opened her mouth, and swallowed them up, and their households, and their tents, and all the substance that *was* in their possession, in the midst of all Israel:　Num. 16:1–35; Ps. 106:16–18

7 But your eyes have ᴿseen all the great ᵀacts of the LORD which he did.　10:21; 29:2 · *works*

8 Therefore shall ye keep all

the commandments which I command you this day, that ye may ᴿbe strong, and go in and possess the land, whither ye go to possess it;　31:6, 7, 23; Josh. 1:6, 7

9 And ᴿthat ye may prolong *your* days in the land, ᴿwhich the LORD sware unto your fathers to give unto them and to their seed, ᴿa land that floweth with milk and honey.　5:16, 33; Prov. 10:27 · 9:5 · Ex. 3:8

10 For the land, whither thou goest in to possess it, *is* not as the land of Egypt, from whence ye came out, where thou sowedst thy seed, and wateredst *it* with thy foot, as a garden of herbs:

11 ᴿBut the land, whither ye go to possess it, *is* a land of hills and valleys, *and* drinketh water of the rain of heaven:　8:7

12 A land which the LORD thy God careth for: the eyes of the LORD thy God *are* always upon it, from the beginning of the year even unto the end of the year.

13 And it shall come to pass, if ye shall ᵀhearken diligently unto my commandments which I command you this day, to love the LORD your God, and to serve him with all your heart and with all your soul,　*obey*

14 That I will give *you* the rain of your land in his due season, the first rain and the latter rain, that thou mayest gather in thy corn, and thy wine, and thine oil.

15 ᴿAnd I will send grass in thy fields for thy cattle, that thou mayest eat and be full.　Ps. 104:1

16 Take heed to yourselves, that your heart be not deceived, and ye turn aside, and ᴿserve other gods, and worship them;　8:19

17 And *then* the LORD's wrath be kindled against you, and he ᴿshut up the heaven, that there be no rain, and that the land yield not her fruit; and *lest* ye perish quickly from off the good land which the LORD giveth you.　28:24

18 Therefore ᴿshall ye lay up these my words in your heart and in your ᴿsoul, and ᴿbind them for a sign upon your hand, that they

may be as frontlets between your eyes.   6:6–9 · Ps. 119:2, 34 · 6:8

19 ᴿAnd ye shall teach them your children, speaking of them when thou sittest in thine house, and when thou walkest by the way, when thou liest down, and when thou risest up.   6:7; Prov. 22:6

20 ᴿAnd thou shalt write them upon the door posts of thine house, and upon thy gates: 6:9

21 That your days may be multiplied, and the days of your children, in the land which the LORD sware unto your fathers to give them, as ᴿthe days of heaven upon the earth.   Ps. 72:5; 89:29; Prov. 3:2; 4:10

22 For if ye shall diligently keep all these commandments which I command you, to do them, to love the LORD your God, to walk in all his ways, and ᴿto ᵀcleave unto him;   10:20 · hold fast

23 Then will the LORD ᴿdrive out all these nations from before you, and ye shall ᴿpossess greater nations and mightier than yourselves.   4:38 · 9:1

24 Every place whereon the soles of your feet shall tread shall be yours: from the wilderness and Leb′-a-non, from the river, the river Eu-phra′-tes, even unto the uttermost sea shall your coast be.

25 There shall no man be able to stand before you: for the LORD your God shall lay the fear of you and the ᴿdread of you upon all the land that ye shall tread upon, as he hath said unto you.   Ex. 23:27

26 ᴿBehold, I set before you this day a blessing and a curse;   30:1, 15

27 ᴿA blessing, if ye obey the commandments of the LORD your God, which I command you this day: 28:1–14

28 And a ᴿcurse, if ye will not obey the commandments of the LORD your God, but turn aside out of the way which I command you this day, to go after other gods, which ye have not known.   28:15–68

29 And it shall come to pass, when the LORD thy God hath brought thee in unto the land whither thou goest to possess it, that thou shalt put the ᴿblessing upon mount Ger′-i-zim, and the curse upon mount E′-bal.   Josh. 8:33

30 Are they not on the other side Jordan, by the way where the sun goeth down, in the land of the Ca′-naan-ites, which dwell in the champaign over against Gil′-gal, beside the plains of Mo′-reh?

31 For ye shall pass over Jordan to go in to possess the land which the LORD your God giveth you, and ye shall possess it, and dwell therein.

32 And ye shall observe to do all the statutes and judgments which I set before you this day.

12 These are the statutes and judgments, which ye shall observe to do in the land, which the LORD God of thy fathers giveth thee to possess it, ᴿall the days that ye live upon the earth.   4:9, 10

2 ᴿYe shall utterly destroy all the places, wherein the nations which ye shall possess served their gods, upon the high mountains, and upon the hills, and under every green tree: Ex. 34:13

3 And ᴿye shall overthrow their altars, and break their pillars, and burn their groves with fire; and ye shall hew down the graven images of their gods, and destroy the names of them out of that place.   7:5; Num. 33:52; Judg. 2:2

4 Ye shall not do ᴿso unto the LORD your God.   v. 31

5 But unto the ᴿplace which the LORD your God shall choose out of all your tribes to put his name there, even unto his ᴿhabitation shall ye seek, and thither thou shalt come: Ex. 20:24 · 1 Sam. 2:29

6 And thither ye shall bring your burnt offerings, and your sacrifices, and your tithes, and heave offerings of your hand, and your vows, and your freewill offerings, and the firstlings of your herds and of your flocks:

7 And ᴿthere ye shall eat before the LORD your God, and ᴿye shall rejoice in all that ye put your hand unto, ye and your

households, wherein the LORD thy God hath blessed thee. 14:26 · v. 12

8 Ye shall not do after all *the things* that we do here this day, ^Revery man whatsoever *is* right in his own eyes. Judg. 17:6; 21:25

9 For ye are not as yet come to the ^Rrest and to the inheritance, which the LORD your God giveth you. 3:20; 25:19; Ps. 95:11

10 But *when* ye go over Jordan, and dwell in the land which the LORD your God giveth you to inherit, and *when* he giveth you rest from all your enemies round about, so that ye dwell in safety;

11 Then there shall be a place which the LORD your God shall choose to cause his name to dwell there; thither shall ye bring all that I command you; your burnt offerings, and your sacrifices, your tithes, and the heave offering of your hand, and all your choice ^Tvows which ye vow unto the LORD: *offerings*

12 And ^Rye shall rejoice before the LORD your God, ye, and your sons, and your daughters, and your menservants, and your maidservants, and the Levite that *is* within your gates; forasmuch as he hath no part nor inheritance with you. v. 18; 26:11

13 Take heed to thyself that thou offer not thy burnt offerings in every place that thou seest:

14 But in the place which the LORD shall choose in one of thy tribes, there thou shalt offer thy burnt offerings, and there thou shalt do all that I command thee.

15 Notwithstanding ^Rthou mayest kill and eat flesh in all thy gates, whatsoever thy soul lusteth after, according to the blessing of the LORD thy God which he hath given thee: the unclean and the clean may eat thereof, as of the roebuck, and as of the hart. v. 21

16 ^ROnly ye shall not eat the blood; ye shall pour it upon the earth as water. Gen. 9:4; Acts 15:20, 29

17 Thou mayest not eat within thy gates the tithe of thy ^Tcorn, or of thy wine, or of thy oil, or the firstlings of thy herds or of thy flock, nor any of thy vows which thou vowest, nor thy freewill offerings, or ^Theave offering of thine hand: *grain · contribution*

18 But thou must eat them before the LORD thy God in the place which the LORD thy God shall choose, thou, and thy son, and thy daughter, and thy manservant, and thy maidservant, and the Levite that *is* within thy gates: and thou shalt rejoice before the LORD thy God in all that thou puttest thine hands unto.

19 Take heed to thyself that thou forsake not the Levite as long as thou livest upon the earth.

20 When the LORD thy God shall ^Renlarge thy border, as he hath promised thee, and thou shalt say, I will eat ^Tflesh, because thy soul longeth to eat flesh; thou mayest eat flesh, whatsoever thy soul lusteth after. Gen. 15:18; Ex. 34:24 · *meat*

21 If the place which the LORD thy God hath chosen to put his name there be too far from ^Rthee, then thou shalt kill of thy herd and of thy flock, which the LORD hath given thee, as I have commanded thee, and thou shalt eat in thy gates whatsoever thy soul lusteth after. 14:24

22 Even as the ^Troebuck and the ^Thart is eaten, so thou shalt eat them: the unclean and the clean shall eat of them alike. *gazelle · deer*

23 Only be sure that thou eat not the blood: ^Rfor the blood *is* the life; and thou mayest not eat the life with the flesh. v. 16; Gen. 9:4

24 Thou shalt not eat it; thou shalt pour it upon the earth as water.

25 Thou shalt not eat it; ^Rthat it may go well with thee, and with thy children after thee, when thou shalt do *that which is* right in the sight of the LORD. 4:40; 6:18; Is. 3:10

26 Only thy holy things which thou hast, and thy vows, thou shalt take, and go unto the place which the LORD shall choose:

27 And ^Rthou shalt offer thy burnt offerings, the flesh and the

blood, upon the altar of the LORD thy God: and the blood of thy sacrifices shall be poured out upon the altar of the LORD thy God, and thou shalt eat the flesh.   Lev. 1:5, 9

28 Observe and hear all these words which I command thee, ᴿthat it may go well with thee, and with thy children after thee for ever, when thou doest *that which is* good and right in the sight of the LORD thy God.   v. 25

29 When ᴿthe LORD thy God shall cut off the nations from before thee, whither thou goest to possess them, and thou succeedest them, and dwellest in their land;   19:1; Ex. 23:23; Josh. 23:4

30 Take heed to thyself that thou be not snared by following them, after that they be destroyed from before thee; and that thou enquire not after their gods, saying, How did these nations serve their gods? even so will I do likewise.

31 ᴿThou shalt not do so unto the LORD thy God: for every abomination to the LORD, which he hateth, have they done unto their gods; for even their sons and their daughters they have burnt in the fire to their gods. Lev. 18:3, 26, 30

32 What thing soever I command you, observe to do it: ᴿthou shalt not add thereto, nor diminish from it.   Josh. 1:7; Rev. 22:18, 19

13 If there arise among you a prophet, or a ᴿdreamer of dreams, ᴿand giveth thee a sign or a wonder,   Zech. 10:2 · 2 Thess. 2:9

2 And the sign or the wonder come to pass, whereof he spake unto thee, saying, Let us go after other gods, which thou hast not known, and let us serve them;

3 Thou shalt not ᵀhearken unto the words of that prophet, or that dreamer of dreams: for the LORD your God ᴿproveth you, to know whether ye love the LORD your God with all your heart and with all your soul.   listen · 8:2, 16; Ex. 20:20

4 Ye shall ᴿwalk after the LORD your God, and fear him, and keep his commandments, and obey his voice, and ye shall serve him, and cleave unto him.   10:12, 20; 2 Kin. 23:3

5 And ᴿthat prophet, or that dreamer of dreams, shall be put to death; because he hath spoken to turn *you* away from the LORD your God, which brought you out of the land of Egypt, and redeemed you out of the house of bondage, to thrust thee out of the way which the LORD thy God commanded thee to walk in. ᴿSo shalt thou put the evil away from the midst of thee.   18:20; Jer. 14:15 · 17:5, 7; 1 Cor. 5:13

6 ᴿIf thy brother, the son of thy mother, or thy son, or thy daughter, or the wife of thy bosom, or thy friend, ᴿwhich *is* as thine own soul, entice thee secretly, saying, Let us go and serve other gods, which thou hast not known, thou, nor thy fathers;   17:2 · 1 Sam. 18:1, 3

7 *Namely,* of the gods of the people which *are* round about you, ᵀnigh unto thee, or far off from thee, from the *one* end of the earth even unto the *other* end of the earth;   *near to*

8 Thou shalt ᴿnot consent unto him, nor hearken unto him; neither shall thine eye pity him, neither shalt thou spare, neither shalt thou conceal him: Prov. 1:10

9 But thou shalt surely kill him; thine hand shall be first upon him to put him to death, and afterwards the hand of all the people.

10 And thou shalt stone him with stones, that he die; because he hath sought to thrust thee away from the LORD thy God, which brought thee out of the land of Egypt, from the house of bondage.

11 And all Israel shall hear, and ᴿfear, and shall ᵀdo no more any such wickedness as this is among you.   17:13 · *not again do*

12 ᴿIf thou shalt hear *say* in one of thy cities, which the LORD thy God hath given thee to dwell there, saying,   Judg. 20:1–48

13 *Certain* men, the children of Be'-li-al, are gone out from among you, and have ᵀwithdrawn the inhabitants of their city, saying,

Let us go and serve other gods, which ye have not known; *enticed*

14 Then shalt thou enquire, and make search, and ask diligently; and, behold, *if it be* truth, *and* the thing certain, *that* such abomination is wrought among you;

15 Thou shalt surely ᵀsmite the inhabitants of that city with the edge of the sword, destroying it utterly, and all that *is* therein, and the cattle thereof, with the edge of the sword. *strike*

16 And thou shalt gather all the spoil of it into the midst of the street thereof, and shalt burn with fire the city, and all the spoil thereof every whit, for the LORD thy God: and it shall be an heap for ever; it shall not be built again.

17 And ᴿthere shall cleave nought of the cursed thing to thine hand: that the LORD may ᴿturn from the fierceness of his anger, and shew thee mercy, and have compassion upon thee, and multiply thee, as he hath sworn unto thy fathers; Josh. 6:18 · Josh. 7:26

18 When thou shalt hearken to the voice of the LORD thy God, ᴿto keep all his commandments which I command thee this day, to do *that which is* right in the eyes of the LORD thy God. 12:25, 28, 32

14 Ye *are* ᴿthe children of the LORD your God: ᴿye shall not cut yourselves, nor make any baldness between your eyes for the dead. [Rom. 8:16] · Lev. 19:28

2 ᴿFor thou *art* an holy people unto the LORD thy God, and the LORD hath chosen thee to be a peculiar people unto himself, above all the nations that *are* upon the earth. [Rom. 12:1]

3 ᴿThou shalt not eat any abominable thing. Ezek. 4:14

4 ᴿThese *are* the beasts which ye shall eat: the ox, the sheep, and the goat, Lev. 11:2–45

5 The hart, and the roebuck, and the fallow deer, and the wild goat, and the pygarg, and the wild ox, and the chamois.

6 And every beast that parteth the hoof, and cleaveth the cleft into two claws, *and* cheweth the cud among the beasts, that ye shall eat.

7 Nevertheless these ye shall not eat of them that chew the cud, or of them that divide the cloven hoof; *as* the camel, and the hare, and the coney: for they chew the cud, but divide not the hoof; *therefore* they *are* unclean unto you.

8 And the swine, because it divideth the hoof, yet cheweth not the cud, it *is* unclean unto you: ye shall not eat of their flesh, ᴿnor touch their dead carcase. Lev. 11:26

9 ᴿThese ye shall eat of all that *are* in the waters: all that have fins and scales shall ye eat: Lev. 11:9

10 And whatsoever hath not fins and scales ye may not eat; it *is* unclean unto you.

11 *Of* all clean birds ye shall eat.

12 ᴿBut these *are they* of which ye shall not eat: the eagle, and the ossifrage, and the ospray, Lev. 11:13

13 And the glede, and the kite, and the vulture after his kind,

14 And every raven after his kind,

15 And the owl, and the night hawk, and the cuckow, and the hawk after his kind,

16 The little owl, and the great owl, and the swan,

17 And the pelican, and the gier eagle, and the cormorant,

18 And the stork, and the heron after her kind, and the lapwing, and the bat.

19 And ᴿevery creeping thing *is* unclean unto you: they shall not be eaten. Lev. 11:20

20 *But of* all clean fowls ye may eat.

21 Ye shall not eat *of* any thing that dieth of itself: thou shalt give it unto the stranger that *is* in thy gates, that he may eat it; or thou mayest sell it unto an alien: for thou *art* an holy people unto the LORD thy God. Thou shalt not seethe a kid in his mother's milk.

22 ᴿThou shalt truly tithe all the increase of thy seed, that the field bringeth forth year by year. 12:6

23 And thou shalt eat before the

LORD thy God, in the place which he shall choose to place his name there, the tithe of thy corn, of thy wine, and of thine oil, and the firstlings of thy herds and of thy flocks; that thou mayest learn to fear the LORD thy God always.

24 And if the ᵀway be too long for thee, so that thou art not able to carry it; or ᴿif the place be too far from thee, which the LORD thy God shall choose to set his name there, when the LORD thy God hath blessed thee: *journey* · 12:5, 21

25 Then shalt thou ᵀturn *it* into money, and bind up the money in thine hand, and shalt go unto the place which the LORD thy God shall choose: *exchange* it *for*

26 And thou shalt bestow that money for whatsoever ᵀthy soul lusteth after, for oxen, or for sheep, or for wine, or for strong drink, or for whatsoever thy soul desireth: and thou shalt eat there before the LORD thy God, and thou shalt ᴿrejoice, thou, and thine household,   *your heart desires* · 12:7

27 And the ᴿLevite that *is* within thy gates; thou shalt not ᵀforsake him; for he hath no part nor inheritance with thee.   12:12 · *neglect*

28 ᴿAt the end of three years thou shalt bring forth all the ᴿtithe of thine increase the same year, and shalt lay *it* up within thy gates: 26:12; Amos 4:4 · Num. 18:21–24

29 And the Levite, (because he hath no part nor inheritance with thee,) and the stranger, and the fatherless, and the widow, which *are* within thy gates, shall come, and shall eat and be satisfied; that the LORD thy God may bless thee in all the work of thine hand which thou doest.

15 At the end of ᴿ*every* seven years thou shalt make a ᵀrelease.   Lev. 25:4 · *remission of debts*

2 And this *is* the manner of the release: Every creditor that lendeth *ought* unto his neighbour shall ᵀrelease *it*; he shall not exact *it* of his neighbour, or of his brother; because it is called the LORD's release.   *cancel the debt*

3 Of a foreigner thou mayest exact *it again:* but *that* which is thine with thy brother thine hand shall release;

4 ᵀSave when there shall be no poor among you; for the LORD shall greatly ᴿbless thee in the land which the LORD thy God giveth thee *for* an inheritance to possess it: *Except* · 7:13

5 Only if thou carefully ᵀhearken unto the voice of the LORD thy God, to observe to do all these commandments which I command thee this day.   *obey*

6 For the LORD thy God blesseth thee, as he promised thee: and ᴿthou shalt lend unto many nations, but thou shalt not borrow; and thou shalt reign over many nations, but they shall not reign over thee.   28:12, 44

7 If there be among you a poor man of one of thy brethren within in any of thy ᵀgates in thy land which the LORD thy God giveth thee, ᴿthou shalt not harden thine heart, nor shut thine hand from thy poor brother: *towns* · Ex. 23:6

8 But thou shalt open thine hand wide unto him, and shalt surely lend him sufficient for his need, *in that* which he wanteth.

9 Beware that there be not a thought in thy wicked heart, saying, The seventh year, the year of release, is at hand; and thine eye be evil against thy poor brother, and thou givest him nought; and ᴿhe cry unto the LORD against thee, and it be sin unto thee.   24:15

10 Thou shalt surely give him, and thine heart shall not be grieved when thou givest unto him: because that for this thing the LORD thy God shall bless thee in all thy works, and in all that thou puttest thine hand unto.

11 For ᴿthe poor shall never cease out of the land: therefore I command thee, saying, Thou shalt open thine hand ᵀwide unto thy brother, to thy poor, and to thy needy, in thy land.   John 12:8 · *freely*

12 *And* ᴿif thy brother, an Hebrew man, or an Hebrew woman,

be [R]sold unto thee, and serve thee six years; then in the seventh year thou shalt let him go free from thee.   Ex. 21:2–6; Jer. 34:14 · Lev. 25:39–46

13 And when thou [T]sendest him out free from thee, thou shalt not let him go away empty: *set him free*

14 Thou shalt furnish him liberally out of thy flock, and out of thy floor, and out of thy winepress: *of that* wherewith the LORD thy God hath [R]blessed thee thou shalt give unto him.   Prov. 10:22

15 And thou shalt remember that thou wast a bondman in the land of Egypt, and the LORD thy God redeemed thee: therefore I command thee this thing to day.

16 And it shall be, [R]if he say unto thee, I will not go away from thee; because he loveth thee and thine house, because he is well with thee;   Ex. 21:5, 6

17 Then thou shalt take an aul, and thrust *it* through his ear unto the door, and he shall be thy servant for ever. And also unto thy maidservant thou shalt do likewise.

18 It shall not seem hard unto thee, when thou sendest him away free from thee; for he hath been worth [R]a double hired servant *to thee*, in serving thee six years: and the LORD thy God shall bless thee in all that thou doest.   Is. 16:14

19 [R]All the firstling males that come of thy herd and of thy flock thou shalt [T]sanctify unto the LORD thy God: thou shalt do no work with the firstling of thy bullock, nor shear the firstling of thy sheep.   Ex. 13:2, 12 · *set apart*

20 Thou shalt eat *it* before the LORD thy God year by year in the place which the LORD shall choose, thou and thy household.

21 [R]And if there be *any* blemish therein, *as if it be* lame, or blind, *or have* any ill blemish, thou shalt not sacrifice it unto the LORD thy God.   17:1; Lev. 22:19–25

22 Thou shalt eat it within thy gates: [R]the unclean and the clean *person shall eat it* alike, as the roebuck, and as the hart.   12:15, 16

23 Only thou shalt not eat the blood thereof; thou shalt pour it upon the ground as water.

16 Observe the [R]month of A'-bib, and keep the passover unto the LORD thy God: for [R]in the month of A'-bib the LORD thy God brought thee forth out of Egypt by night.   Ex. 12:2 · Ex. 13:4

2 Thou shalt therefore sacrifice the passover unto the LORD thy God, of the flock and the herd, in the place which the LORD shall choose to place his name there.

3 Thou shalt eat no leavened bread with it; seven days shalt thou eat unleavened bread therewith, *even* the bread of affliction; for thou camest forth out of the land of Egypt in haste: that thou mayest remember the day when thou camest forth out of the land of Egypt all the days of thy life.

4 [R]And there shall be no leavened bread seen with thee in all thy coast seven days; neither shall there *any thing* of the flesh, which thou sacrificedst the first day at even, remain all night until the [R]morning.   Ex. 13:7 · Num. 9:12

5 Thou mayest not sacrifice the passover within any of thy gates, which the LORD thy God giveth thee:

6 But at the place which the LORD thy God shall choose to place his name in, there thou shalt sacrifice the passover [R]at even, at the going down of the sun, [T]at the season that thou camest forth out of Egypt.   Ex. 12:7–10 · *at the time*

7 And thou shalt roast and eat *it* [R]in the place which the LORD thy God shall choose: and thou shalt turn in the morning, and go unto thy tents.   2 Kin. 23:23

8 Six days thou shalt eat unleavened bread: and [R]on the seventh day *shall be* a solemn assembly to the LORD thy God: thou shalt do no work *therein.*   Ex. 12:16

9 Seven weeks shalt thou number unto thee: begin to number the seven weeks from *such time as* thou beginnest *to put* the sickle to the [T]corn.   *grain*

10 And thou shalt keep the feast of weeks unto the LORD thy God with a tribute of a freewill offering of thine hand, which thou shalt give *unto the* LORD *thy God,* [R]according as the LORD thy God hath blessed thee: 1 Cor. 16:2

11 And [R]thou shalt rejoice before the LORD thy God, thou, and thy son, and thy daughter, and thy manservant, and thy maidservant, and the Levite that *is* within thy gates, and the stranger, and the fatherless, and the widow, that *are* among you, in the place which the LORD thy God hath chosen to place his name there.   v. 14

12 [R]And thou shalt remember that thou wast a [T]bondman in Egypt: and thou shalt observe and do these statutes.   15:15 · *slave*

13 [R]Thou shalt observe the feast of tabernacles seven days, after that thou hast gathered in thy corn and thy wine: Ex. 23:16

14 And [R]thou shalt rejoice in thy feast, thou, and thy son, and thy daughter, and thy manservant, and thy maidservant, and the Levite, the stranger, and the fatherless, and the widow, that *are* within thy [T]gates.   Neh. 8:9 · *towns*

15 Seven days shalt thou keep a solemn feast unto the LORD thy God in the place which the LORD shall choose: because the LORD thy God shall bless thee in all thine increase, and in all the works of thine hands, therefore thou shalt surely rejoice.

16 Three times in a year shall all thy males appear before the LORD thy God in the place which he shall choose; in the feast of unleavened bread, and in the feast of weeks, and in the feast of tabernacles: and they shall not appear before the LORD empty:

17 Every man *shall give* as he is able, [R]according to the blessing of the LORD thy God which he hath given thee.   v. 10; Lev. 14:30, 31

18 [R]Judges and officers shalt thou make thee in all thy [T]gates, which the LORD thy God giveth thee, throughout thy tribes: and

they shall judge the people with just judgment.   1:16; John 7:24 · *towns*

19 [R]Thou shalt not [T]wrest judgment; [R]thou shalt not respect persons, [R]neither take a gift: for a gift doth blind the eyes of the wise, and pervert the words of the righteous.   Ex. 23:2, 6 · *pervert* · 1:17 · Ex. 23:8

20 That which is altogether just shalt thou follow, that thou mayest [R]live, and inherit the land which the LORD thy God giveth thee.   Ezek. 18:5–9

21 [R]Thou shalt not plant thee a grove of any trees near unto the altar of the LORD thy God, which thou shalt make thee.   Ex. 34:13

22 [R]Neither shalt thou set thee up *any* [T]image; which the LORD thy God hateth.   Lev. 26:1 · *idol*

17 Thou [R]shalt not sacrifice unto the LORD thy God *any* bullock, or sheep, wherein is blemish, *or* any evilfavouredness: for that *is* an abomination unto the LORD thy God.   15:21; Mal. 1:8, 13

2 [R]If there be found among you, within any of thy gates which the LORD thy God giveth thee, man or woman, that hath wrought wickedness in the sight of the LORD thy God, [R]in transgressing his covenant,   13:6 · Josh. 7:11

3 And hath gone and served other gods, and worshipped them, either [R]the sun, or moon, or any of the host of heaven, [R]which I have not commanded;   4:19 · Jer. 7:22

4 [R]And it be told thee, and thou hast heard *of it,* and enquired diligently, and, behold, *it be* true, *and* the thing certain, *that* such abomination is wrought in Israel: 13:12

5 Then shalt thou bring forth that man or that woman, which have committed that wicked thing, unto thy gates, *even* that man or that woman, and [R]shalt stone them with stones, till they [R]die.   Lev. 24:14–16; Josh. 7:25 · 13:6–18

6 At the mouth of two witnesses, or three [R]witnesses, shall he that is worthy of death be put to death; *but* at the mouth of one witness he shall not be put to death.   Num. 35:30; Matt. 18:16; John 8:17

7 The hands of the witnesses shall be first upon him to put him to death, and afterward the hands of all the people. So thou shalt put the evil away from among you.

8 ^RIf there arise a matter too hard for thee in judgment, between blood and blood, between plea and plea, and between stroke and stroke, *being* matters of controversy within thy gates: then shalt thou arise, and get thee up into the ^Rplace which the LORD thy God shall choose;   2 Chr. 19:10 · 12:5

9 And ^Rthou shalt come unto the priests the Levites, and ^Runto the judge that shall be in those days, and enquire; ^Rand they shall shew thee the sentence of judgment: Jer. 18:18 · 19:17–19 · Ezek. 44:24

10 And thou shalt do according to the sentence, which they of that place which the LORD shall choose shall shew thee; and thou shalt observe to do according to all that they ^Tinform thee: *instruct*

11 According to the sentence of the law which they shall teach thee, and according to the judgment which they shall tell thee, thou shalt do: thou shalt not ^Tdecline from the sentence which they shall shew thee, *to* the right hand, nor *to* the left.   *turn aside*

12 And ^Rthe man that will do presumptuously, and will not ^Thearken unto the priest that standeth to minister there before the LORD thy God, or unto the judge, even that man shall die: and thou shalt put away the evil from Israel.   1:43; Num. 15:30 · *heed*

13 ^RAnd all the people shall hear, and fear, and do no more presumptuously.   13:11

14 When thou art come unto the land which the LORD thy God giveth thee, and shalt possess it, and shalt dwell therein, and shalt say, ^RI will set a king over me, like as all the nations that *are* about me;   1 Sam. 8:5, 19, 20; 10:19

15 Thou shalt in any wise set *him* king over thee, whom the LORD thy God shall choose: *one* from among thy brethren

shalt thou set king over thee: thou mayest not set a stranger over thee, which *is* not thy brother.

16 But he shall not multiply horses to himself, nor cause the people to return to Egypt, to the end that he should multiply horses: forasmuch as the LORD hath said unto you, Ye shall henceforth return no more that way.

17 Neither shall he multiply wives to himself, that his heart turn not away: neither shall he greatly multiply to himself silver and ^Rgold.   1 Kin. 10:14

18 And it shall be, when he sitteth upon the throne of his kingdom, that he shall write him a copy of this law in a book out of *that which is* ^Rbefore the priests the Levites: 31:24–26

19 And ^Rit shall be with him, and he shall read therein all the days of his life: that he may learn to fear the LORD his God, to keep all the words of this law and these statutes, to do them: Ps. 119:97, 98

20 That his heart be not lifted up above his brethren, and that he ^Rturn not aside from the commandment, *to* the right hand, or *to* the left: to the end that he may prolong *his* days in his kingdom, he, and his children, in the midst of Israel.   5:32; 1 Kin. 15:5

18 The priests the Levites, *and* all the tribe of Levi, shall have no part nor ^Rinheritance with Israel: they shall eat the offerings of the LORD made by fire, and his inheritance.   1 Cor. 9:13

2 Therefore shall they have no inheritance among their brethren: the LORD *is* their inheritance, as he hath said unto them.

3 And this shall be the priest's due from the people, from them that offer a sacrifice, whether *it be* ox or sheep; and they shall give unto the priest the shoulder, and the two cheeks, and the maw.

4 ^RThe firstfruit *also* of thy corn, of thy wine, and of thine oil, and the first of the fleece of thy sheep, shalt thou give him. Ex. 22:29

5 For ᴿthe LORD thy God hath chosen him out of all thy tribes, ᴿto stand to minister in the name of the LORD, him and his sons for ever.   Ex. 28:1 · 10:8

6 And if a Levite come from any of thy gates out of all Israel, where he ᴿsojourned, and come with all the desire of his mind ᴿunto the place which the LORD shall choose;   Num. 35:2 · 12:5; 14:23

7 Then he shall minister in the name of the LORD his God, as all his brethren the Levites do, which stand there before the LORD.

8 They shall have like ᴿportions to eat, beside that which cometh of the sale of his ᵀpatrimony.   Num. 18:21–24 · inheritance

9 When thou art come into the land which the LORD thy God giveth thee, ᴿthou shalt not learn to do after the abominations of those nations.   Lev. 18:26, 27, 30

10 There shall not be found among you any one that maketh his son or his daughter ᴿto pass through the fire, or that useth divination, or an observer of times, or an enchanter, or a witch,   12:31

11 ᴿOr a charmer, or a consulter with familiar spirits, or a wizard, or a necromancer.   Lev. 20:27

12 For all that do these things are an abomination unto the LORD: and ᴿbecause of these abominations the LORD thy God doth drive them out from before thee.   9:4; Lev. 18:24

13 Thou shalt be ᵀperfect with the LORD thy God.   blameless

14 For these nations, which thou shalt ᵀpossess, hearkened unto observers of times, and unto diviners: but as for thee, the LORD thy God hath not ᵀsuffered thee so to do. dispossess · appointed such for you

☆ 15 ᴿThe LORD thy God will raise up unto thee a Prophet from the midst of thee, of thy brethren, like unto me; unto him ye shall hearken; Matt. 21:11; Luke 7:16; Acts 3:22

16 According to all that thou desiredst of the LORD thy God in Ho′-reb ᴿin the day of the assembly, saying, Let me not hear again

the voice of the LORD my God, neither let me see this great fire any more, that I die not.   5:23–27

17 And the LORD said unto me, ᴿThey have well spoken that which they have spoken.   5:28

18 ᴿI will raise them up a Prophet from among their brethren, like unto thee, and ᴿwill put my words in his mouth; and he shall speak unto them all that I shall command him.   John 1:45 · John 17:8 ☆

19 ᴿAnd it shall come to pass, ☆ that whosoever will not hearken unto my words which he shall speak in my name, I will require it of him.   Acts 3:23; [Heb. 12:25]

20 But the prophet, which shall presume to speak a word in my name, which I have not commanded him to speak, or that shall speak in the name of other gods, even that prophet shall die.

21 And if thou say in thine heart, How shall we know the word which the LORD hath not spoken?

22 ᴿWhen a prophet speaketh in the name of the LORD, if the thing follow not, nor come to pass, that is the thing which the LORD hath not spoken, but the prophet hath spoken it presumptuously: thou shalt not be afraid of him.   Jer. 28:9

19 When the LORD thy God ᴿhath cut off the nations, whose land the LORD thy God giveth thee, and thou succeedest them, and dwellest in their cities, and in their houses;   12:29

2 ᴿThou shalt separate three cities for thee in the midst of thy land, which the LORD thy God giveth thee to possess it.   Ex. 21:13

3 Thou shalt prepare ᵀthee a way, and divide the ᵀcoasts of thy land, which the LORD thy God giveth thee to inherit, into three parts, that every slayer may flee thither.   yourselves roads · territory

4 And ᴿthis is the case of the slayer, which shall flee thither, that he may live: Whoso killeth his neighbour ignorantly, whom he hated not in time past;   4:42

5 As when a man goeth into

the wood with his neighbour to hew wood, and his hand ᵀfetcheth a stroke with the axe to cut down the tree, and the head slippeth from the ᵀhelve, and ᵀlighteth upon his neighbour, that he die; he shall flee unto one of those cities, and live: *swings · handle · strikes*

6 ᴿLest the avenger of the blood pursue the slayer, while his heart is hot, and overtake him, because the way is long, and slay him; whereas he *was* not worthy of death, inasmuch as he hated him not in time past. Num. 35:12

7 Wherefore I command thee, saying, Thou shalt separate three cities for thee.

8 And if the LORD thy God ᴿenlarge thy coast, as he hath sworn unto thy fathers, and give thee all the land which he promised to give unto thy fathers; 12:20

9 If thou shalt keep all these commandments to do them, which I command thee this day, to love the LORD thy God, and to walk ever in his ways; ᴿthen shalt thou add three cities more for thee, beside these three: Josh. 20:7-9

10 That innocent blood be not shed in thy land, which the LORD thy God giveth thee *for* an inheritance, and *so* blood be upon thee.

11 But if any man hate his neighbour, and lie in wait for him, and rise up against him, and smite him mortally that he die, and fleeth into one of these cities:

12 Then the elders of his city shall send and fetch him thence, and deliver him into the hand of the avenger of blood, that he may die.

13 ᴿThine eye shall not pity him, but thou shalt put away *the guilt* of innocent blood from Israel, that it may go well with thee. 13:8

14 Thou shalt not remove thy neighbour's landmark, which they of old time have set in thine inheritance, which thou shalt inherit in the land that the LORD thy God giveth thee to possess it.

15 ᴿOne witness shall not rise up against a man for any iniquity, or for any sin, in any sin that he sinneth: at the mouth of two witnesses, or at the mouth of three witnesses, shall the matter be established. Matt. 18:16; 1 Tim. 5:19

16 If a false witness ᴿrise up against any man to testify against him *that which is* wrong; Ex. 23:1

17 Then both the men, between whom the controversy *is*, shall stand before the LORD, ᴿbefore the priests and the judges, which shall be in those days; 17:8-11; 21:5

18 And the judges shall make diligent inquisition: and, behold, *if* the witness *be* a false witness, *and* hath testified falsely against his brother;

19 ᴿThen shall ye do unto him, as he had thought to have done unto his brother: so ᴿshalt thou put the evil away from among you. Prov. 19:5; Dan. 6:24 · 13:5; 21:21; 22:21

20 ᴿAnd those which remain shall hear, and fear, and shall henceforth commit no more any such evil among you. 17:13; 21:21

21 And thine eye shall not pity; *but* ᴿlife *shall go* for life, eye for eye, tooth for tooth, hand for hand, foot for foot. Matt. 5:38, 39

20 When thou goest out to battle against thine enemies, and seest ᴿhorses, and chariots, *and* a people more than thou, be not afraid of them: for the LORD thy God *is* ᴿwith thee, which brought thee up out of the land of Egypt. Ps. 20:7; Is. 31:1 · Ps. 23:4; Is. 41:10

2 And it shall be, when ye are come nigh unto the battle, that the priest shall approach and speak unto the people,

3 And shall say unto them, Hear, O Israel, ye approach this day unto battle against your enemies: let not your hearts faint, fear not, and do not tremble, neither be ye terrified because of them;

4 For the LORD your God *is* he that goeth with you, ᴿto fight for you against your enemies, to save you. 1:30; 3:22; Josh. 23:10

5 And the officers shall speak unto the people, saying, What

man *is there* that hath built a new house, and hath not ᴿdedicated it? let him go and return to his house, lest he die in the battle, and another man dedicate it. Neh. 12:27

6 And what man *is he* that hath planted a vineyard, and hath not *yet* eaten of it? let him *also* go and return unto his house, lest he die in the battle, and another man eat of it.

7 ᴿAnd what man *is there* that hath betrothed a wife, and hath not taken her? let him go and return unto his house, lest he die in the battle, and another man take her. 24:5

8 And the officers shall speak further unto the people, and they shall say, ᴿWhat man *is there that is* fearful and fainthearted? let him go and return unto his house, lest his brethren's heart faint as well as his heart. Judg. 7:3

9 And it shall be, when the officers have made an end of speaking unto the people, that they shall make captains of the armies to lead the people.

10 When thou comest nigh unto a city to fight against it, ᴿthen proclaim peace unto it. 2 Sam. 10:19

11 And it shall be, if it make thee answer of peace, and open unto thee, then it shall be, *that* all the people *that is* found therein shall be tributaries unto thee, and they shall serve thee.

12 And if it will make no peace with thee, but will make war against thee, then thou shalt besiege it:

13 And when the LORD thy God hath delivered it into thine hands, ᴿthou shalt smite every male thereof with the edge of the sword: Num. 31:7

14 But the women, and the little ones, and ᴿthe cattle, and all that is in the city, *even* all the spoil thereof, shalt thou take unto thyself; and thou shalt eat the spoil of thine enemies, which the LORD thy God hath given thee. Josh. 8:2

15 Thus shalt thou do unto all the cities *which are* very far off

from thee, which *are* not of the cities of these nations.

16 But ᴿof the cities of these people, which the LORD thy God doth give thee *for* an inheritance, thou shalt save alive nothing that breatheth: Num. 21:2, 3; Josh. 11:14

17 But thou shalt utterly destroy them; *namely,* the Hit'-tites, and the Am'-or-ites, the Ca'-naan-ites, and the Per'-iz-zites, the Hi'-vites, and the Jeb'-u-sites; as the LORD thy God hath commanded thee:

18 That ᴿthey teach you not to do after all their abominations, which they have done unto their gods; so should ye sin against the LORD your God. Ex. 34:12–16

19 When thou shalt besiege a city a long time, in making war against it to take it, thou shalt not destroy the trees thereof by forcing an ax against them: for thou mayest eat of them, and thou shalt not cut them down (for the tree of the field *is* man's *life*) to employ *them* in the siege:

20 Only the trees which thou knowest that they *be* not trees for ᵀmeat, thou shalt destroy and cut them down; and thou shalt build bulwarks against the city that maketh war with thee, until it be subdued. *food*

21 If *one* be found slain in the land which the LORD thy God giveth thee to possess it, lying in the field, *and* it be not known who hath slain him:

2 Then thy elders and thy judges shall come forth, and they shall measure unto the cities which *are* round about him that is slain:

3 And it shall be, *that* the city which is next unto the slain man, even the elders of that city shall take an heifer, which hath not been wrought with, *and* which hath not drawn in the yoke;

4 And the elders of that city shall bring down the heifer unto a rough valley, which is neither eared nor sown, and shall strike off the heifer's neck there in the valley:

5 And the priests the sons of Levi shall come near; for ᴿthem the LORD thy God hath chosen to minister unto him, and to bless in the name of the LORD; and by their word shall every controversy and every stroke be *tried:*　10:8

6 And all the elders of that city, *that are* next unto the slain *man*, ᴿshall wash their hands over the heifer that is beheaded in the valley:　Ps. 19:12; 26:6; Matt. 27:24

7 And they shall answer and say, Our hands have not shed this blood, neither have our eyes seen *it*.

8 Be merciful, O LORD, unto thy people Israel, whom thou hast redeemed, ᴿand lay not innocent blood unto thy people of Israel's charge. And the blood shall be forgiven them.　19:10, 13; Jon. 1:14

9 So ᴿshalt thou put away the *guilt of* innocent blood from among you, when thou shalt do *that which is* right in the sight of the LORD.　19:13

10 When thou goest forth to war against thine enemies, and the LORD thy God hath delivered them into thine hands, and thou hast taken them captive,

11 And seest among the captives a beautiful woman, and hast a desire unto her, that thou wouldest have her to thy wife;

12 Then thou shalt bring her home to thine house; and she shall ᴿshave her head, and ᵀpare her nails;　Lev. 14:8, 9; Num. 6:9 · *trim*

13 And she shall put the raiment of her captivity from off her, and shall remain in thine house, and ᴿbewailᵀ her father and her mother a full month: and after that thou shalt go in unto her, and be her husband, and she shall be thy wife.　Ps. 45:10 · *mourn*

14 And it shall be, if thou have no delight in her, then thou shalt let her go whither she will; but thou shalt not sell her at all for money, thou shalt not make merchandise of her, because thou hast ᴿhumbled her.　Gen. 34:2; Judg. 19:24

15 If a man have two wives, one beloved, ᴿand another hated, and

they have born him children, *both* the beloved and the hated; and *if* the firstborn son be hers that was hated:　Gen. 29:33

16 Then it shall be, when he maketh his sons to inherit *that* which he hath, *that* he may not make the son of the beloved firstborn before the son of the hated, *which is indeed* the firstborn:

17 But he shall acknowledge the son of the hated *for* the firstborn, by giving him a double portion of all that he hath: for he *is* the beginning of his strength; the right of the firstborn *is* his.

18 If a man have a stubborn and rebellious son, which will not obey the voice of his father, or the voice of his mother, and *that,* when they have chastened him, will not hearken unto them:

19 Then shall his father and his mother lay hold on him, and bring him out unto the elders of his city, and unto the gate of his place;

20 And they shall say unto the elders of his city, This our son *is* stubborn and rebellious, he will not obey our voice; *he is* a glutton, and a drunkard.

21 And all the men of his city shall stone him with stones, that he die: ᴿso shalt thou put evil away from among you; and all Israel shall hear, and fear.　13:5

22 And if a man have committed a sin ᴿworthy of death, and he be to be put to death, and thou hang him on a tree:　Matt. 26:66; Acts 23:29

23 ᴿHis body shall not remain all night upon the tree, but thou shalt in any wise bury him that day; (for ᴿhe that is hanged *is* accursed of God;) that ᴿthy land be not defiled, which the LORD thy God giveth thee *for* an inheritance.　John 19:31 · Lev. 18:25 · Gal. 3:13

22 Thou shalt not see thy brother's ox or his sheep go astray, and hide thyself from them: thou shalt in any case bring them again unto thy brother.

2 And if thy brother *be* not nigh unto thee, or if thou know him not, then thou shalt bring it

unto thine own house, and it shall be with thee until thy brother seek after it, and thou shalt restore it to him again.

3 In like manner shalt thou do with his ass; and so shalt thou do with his raiment; and with all lost thing of thy brother's, which he hath lost, and thou hast found, shalt thou do likewise: thou mayest not hide thyself.

4 ᴿThou shalt not see thy brother's ass or his ox fall down by the way, and hide thyself from them: thou shalt surely help him to lift *them* up again. Ex. 23:5

5 The woman shall not wear that which pertaineth unto a man, neither shall a man put on a woman's garment: for all that do so *are* ᵀabomination unto the LORD thy God. *detestable*

6 If a bird's nest chance to be before thee in the way in any tree, or on the ground, *whether they be* young ones, or eggs, and the ᵀdam sitting upon the young, or upon the eggs, thou shalt not take the dam with the young: *mother*

7 *But* thou shalt in any wise let the dam go, and take the young to thee; ᴿthat it may be well with thee, and *that* thou mayest prolong *thy* days. 4:40

8 When thou buildest a new house, then thou shalt make a battlement for thy roof, that thou bring not ᵀblood upon thine house, if any man fall from thence. *bloodguiltiness*

9 ᴿThou shalt not sow thy vineyard with ᵀdivers seeds: lest the fruit of thy seed which thou hast sown, and the fruit of thy vineyard, be defiled. Lev. 19:19 · *different*

10 Thou shalt not plow with an ox and an ass together.

11 ᴿThou shalt not wear a garment of divers sorts, *as* of woollen and linen together. Lev. 19:19

12 Thou shalt make thee ᴿfringes upon the four ᵀquarters of thy ᵀvesture, wherewith thou coverest *thyself.* Matt. 23:5 · *corners* · *clothing*

13 If any man take a wife, and go in unto her, and ᴿhate her, 24:3

14 And give occasions of speech against her, and bring up an evil name upon her, and say, I took this woman, and when I came to her, I found her not a maid:

15 Then shall the father of the damsel, and her mother, take and bring forth *the tokens of* the damsel's virginity unto the elders of the city in the gate:

16 And the damsel's father shall say unto the elders, I gave my daughter unto this man to wife, and he hateth her;

17 And, lo, he hath given occasions of speech *against her,* saying, I found not thy daughter a maid; and yet these *are the tokens of* my daughter's virginity. And they shall spread the cloth before the elders of the city.

18 And the elders of that city shall take that man and chastise him;

19 And they shall ᵀamerce him in an hundred *shek'-els* of silver, and give *them* unto the father of the damsel, because he hath brought up ᵀan evil name upon a virgin of Israel: and she shall be his wife; he may not put her away all his days. *fine · a bad*

20 But if this thing be true, *and the tokens of* virginity be not found for the damsel:

21 Then they shall bring out the damsel to the door of her father's house, and the men of her city shall stone her with stones that she die: because she hath wrought folly in Israel, to play the whore in her father's house: so shalt thou put evil away from among you.

22 If a man be found lying with a woman married to an husband, then they shall both of them die, *both* the man that lay with the woman, and the woman: so shalt thou put away evil from Israel.

23 If a damsel *that is* a virgin be ᴿbetrothed unto an husband, and a man find her in the city, and lie with her; Lev. 19:20–22; Matt. 1:18, 19

24 Then ye shall bring them both out unto the gate of that city, and ye shall stone them with

stones that they die; the damsel, because she cried not, *being* in the city; and the man, because he hath ᴿhumbled his neighbour's wife: ᴿso thou shalt put away evil from among you.   21:14 · 1 Cor. 5:2, 13

25 But if a man find a betrothed damsel in the field, and the man force her, and lie with her: then the man only that lay with her shall die:

26 But unto the damsel thou shalt do nothing; *there is* in the damsel no sin *worthy* of death: for as when a man riseth against his neighbour, and slayeth him, even so *is* this matter:

27 For he found her in the field, *and* the betrothed damsel cried, and *there was* none to save her.

28 ᴿIf a man find a damsel *that is* a virgin, which is not betrothed, and lay hold on her, and lie with her, and they be found; Ex. 22:16, 17

29 Then the man that lay with her shall give unto the damsel's father ᴿfifty *shek'-els* of silver, and she shall be his wife; because he hath humbled her, he may not put her away all his days.   Ex. 22:16, 17

30 ᴿA man shall not take his father's wife, nor discover his father's skirt.   Lev. 18:8; 20:11; 1 Cor. 5:1

23 He that is wounded in the stones, or hath his privy member cut off, shall not enter into the congregation of the LORD.

2 A bastard shall not enter into the congregation of the LORD; even to his tenth generation shall he not enter into the congregation of the LORD.

3 ᴿAn Am'-mon-ite or Mo'-ab-ite shall not enter into the congregation of the LORD; even to their tenth generation shall they not enter into the congregation of the LORD for ever: Neh. 13:1, 2

4 ᴿBecause they met you not with bread and with water in the way, when ye came forth out of Egypt; and ᴿbecause they hired against thee Ba'-laam the son of Be'-or of Pe'-thor of Mes-o-po-ta'-mi-a, to curse thee.   2:27–30 · Jude 11

5 Nevertheless the LORD thy God would not hearken unto Ba'-laam; but the LORD thy God turned the curse into a blessing unto thee, because the LORD thy God ᴿloved thee.   4:37

6 ᴿThou shalt not seek their peace nor their prosperity all thy days for ever.   Ezra 9:12

7 Thou shalt not abhor an E'-dom-ite; ᴿfor he *is* thy brother: thou shalt not abhor an Egyptian; because thou wast a stranger in his land.   Gen. 25:24–26; Obad. 10, 12

8 The children that are begotten of them shall enter into the congregation of the LORD in their third generation.

9 When the host goeth forth against thine enemies, then keep thee from every wicked thing.

10 ᴿIf there be among you any man, that is not clean by reason of uncleanness that chanceth him by night, then shall he go abroad out of the camp, he shall not come within the camp: Lev. 15:16

11 But it shall be, when evening cometh on, ᴿhe shall wash *himself* with water: and when the sun is down, he shall come into the camp *again*.   Lev. 15:5

12 Thou shalt have a place also ᵀwithout the camp, whither thou shalt go forth abroad: *outside*

13 And thou shalt have a paddle upon thy weapon; and it shall be, when thou wilt ease thyself abroad, thou shalt dig therewith, and shalt turn back and cover that which cometh from thee:

14 For the LORD thy God ᴿwalketh in the midst of thy camp, to deliver thee, and to give up thine enemies before thee; therefore shall thy camp be holy: that he see no unclean thing in thee, and turn away from thee.   7:21; Lev. 26:12

15 ᴿThou shalt not ᵀdeliver unto his master the servant which is escaped from his master unto thee: 1 Sam. 30:15 · *give back*

16 He shall dwell with thee, *even* among you, in that place which he shall choose in one of thy gates, where it liketh him best: thou shalt not oppress him.

17 There shall be no whore of the daughters of Israel, nor a sodomite of the sons of Israel.

18 Thou shalt not bring the hire of a whore, or the price of a dog, into the house of the LORD thy God for any vow: for even both these *are* Tabomination unto the LORD thy God.   *detestable*

19 Thou shalt not lend upon usury to thy brother; usury of money, usury of victuals, usury of any thing that is lent upon usury:

20 Unto a stranger thou mayest lend upon usury; but unto thy brother thou shalt not lend upon usury: that the LORD thy God may bless thee in all that thou settest thine hand to in the land whither thou goest to possess it.

21 When thou shalt vow a vow unto the LORD thy God, thou shalt not slack to pay it: for the LORD thy God will surely require it of thee; and it would be sin in thee.

22 But if thou shalt forbear to vow, it shall be no sin in thee.

23 RThat which is gone out of thy lips thou shalt keep and perform; *even* a freewill offering, according as thou hast vowed unto the LORD thy God, which thou hast promised with thy mouth.   Num. 30:2; Ps. 66:13, 14

24 When thou comest into thy neighbour's vineyard, then thou mayest eat grapes thy fill at thine own pleasure; but thou shalt not put *any* in thy vessel.

25 When thou comest into the standing corn of thy neighbour, Rthen thou mayest pluck the ears with thine hand; but thou shalt not move a sickle unto thy neighbour's standing corn.   Matt. 12:1

24 When a Rman hath taken a wife, and married her, and it come to pass that she find no favour in his eyes, because he hath found some uncleanness in her: then let him write her a bill of divorcement, and give *it* in her hand, and send her out of his house.   [Matt. 5:31; 19:7; Mark 10:4]

2 And when she is departed out of his house, she may go and be another man's *wife*.

3 And *if* the latter husband hate her, and write her a bill of divorcement, and giveth *it* in her hand, and sendeth her out of his house; or if the latter husband die, which took her *to be* his wife;

4 RHer former husband, which sent her away, may not take her again to be his wife, after that she is defiled; for that *is* abomination before the LORD: and thou shalt not cause the land to sin, which the LORD thy God giveth thee *for* an inheritance.   [Jer. 3:1]

5 RWhen a man hath taken a new wife, he shall not go out to war, neither shall he be charged with any business: *but* he shall be free at home one year, and shall Rcheer up his wife which he hath taken.   20:7 · Prov. 5:18

6 No man shall take the Tnether or the upper millstone to pledge: for he taketh *a man's* Tlife to pledge.   *lower · living in*

7 If a man be Rfound Tstealing any of his brethren of the children of Israel, and maketh merchandise of him, or selleth him; then that thief shall die; Rand thou shalt put evil away from among you.   Ex. 21:16 · *kidnapping* · 19:19

8 Take heed in Rthe plague of leprosy, that thou observe diligently, and do according to all that the priests the Levites shall teach you: as I commanded them, *so* ye shall observe to do.   Lev. 13:2

9 RRemember what the LORD thy God did Runto Miriam by the way, after that ye were come forth out of Egypt.   [1 Cor. 10:6] · Num. 12:10

10 When thou dost Rlend thy brother any thing, thou shalt not go into his house to Tfetch his pledge.   Matt. 5:42 · *get*

11 Thou shalt stand abroad, and the man to whom thou dost lend shall bring out the pledge abroad unto thee.

12 And if the man *be* poor, thou shalt not sleep with his pledge:

13 In any case thou shalt deliver him the pledge again when the sun goeth down, that he may sleep in his own raiment, and ^Rbless thee: and ^Rit shall be righteousness unto thee before the LORD thy God.   2 Tim. 1:18 · Ps. 106:31

14 Thou shalt not oppress an hired servant *that is* poor and needy, *whether he be* of thy brethren, or of thy strangers that *are* in thy land within thy gates:

15 At his day thou shalt give *him* his hire, neither shall the sun go down upon it; for he *is* poor, and setteth his heart upon it: ^Rlest he cry against thee unto the LORD, and it be sin unto thee.   James 5:4

16 The fathers shall not be put to death for the children, neither shall the children be put to death for the fathers: every man shall be put to death for his own sin.

17 Thou shalt not pervert the judgment of the stranger, *nor* of the fatherless; ^Rnor take a widow's raiment to pledge: Ex. 22:26

18 But thou shalt remember that thou wast a bondman in Egypt, and the LORD thy God redeemed thee thence: therefore I command thee to do this thing.

19 When thou cuttest down thine harvest in thy field, and hast forgot a sheaf in the field, thou shalt not go again to fetch it: it shall be for the stranger, for the fatherless, and for the widow: that the LORD thy God may bless thee in all the work of thine hands.

20 When thou beatest thine olive tree, thou shalt not go over the boughs again: it shall be for the stranger, for the fatherless, and for the widow.

21 When thou gatherest the grapes of thy vineyard, thou shalt not glean *it* afterward: it shall be for the stranger, for the fatherless, and for the widow.

22 And thou shalt remember that thou wast a bondman in the land of Egypt: therefore I command thee to do this thing.

25 If there be a ^Rcontroversy between men, and they come unto judgment, that *the judges* may judge them; then they ^Rshall justify the righteous, and condemn the wicked.   17:8–13 · Prov. 17:15

2 And it shall be, if the wicked man *be* ^Rworthy to be beaten, that the judge shall cause him to lie down, and to be beaten before his face, according to his fault, by a certain number.   Luke 12:48

3 ^RForty stripes he may give him, *and* not exceed: lest, *if* he should exceed, and beat him above these with many stripes, then thy brother should ^Rseem vile unto thee.   2 Cor. 11:24 · Job 18:3

4 Thou shalt not muzzle the ox when he treadeth out *the corn.*

5 ^RIf brethren dwell together, and one of them die, and have no child, the wife of the dead shall not marry without unto a stranger: her husband's brother shall go in unto her, and take her to him to wife, and perform the duty of an husband's brother unto her.   Matt. 22:24; Mark 12:19; Luke 20:28

6 And it shall be, *that* the firstborn which she beareth ^Rshall succeed in the name of his brother *which is* dead, that his name be not put out of Israel.   Gen. 38:9

7 And if the man like not to take his brother's wife, then let his brother's wife go up to the gate unto the elders, and say, My husband's brother refuseth to raise up unto his brother a name in Israel, he will not perform the duty of my husband's brother.

8 Then the elders of his city shall call him, and speak unto him: and *if* he stand *to it,* and say, ^RI like not to take her;   Ruth 4:6

9 Then shall his brother's wife come unto him in the presence of the elders, and ^Rloose his shoe from off his foot, and spit in his face, and shall answer and say, So shall it be done unto that man that will not ^Rbuild up his brother's house.   Ruth 4:7, 8 · Ruth 4:11

10 And his name shall be called in Israel, The house of him that hath his shoe loosed.

11 When men strive together one with another, and the wife of the one draweth near for to deliver her husband out of the hand of him that smiteth him, and putteth forth her hand, and taketh him by the secrets:

12 Then thou shalt cut off her hand, thine eye shall not pity *her*.

13 ᴿThou shalt not have in thy bag ᵀdivers weights, a great and a small.   Ezek. 45:10; Mic. 6:11 · *differing*

14 Thou shalt not have in thine house divers measures, a great and a small.

15 *But* thou shalt have a perfect and just weight, a perfect and just measure shalt thou have: ᴿthat thy days may be lengthened in the land which the LORD thy God giveth thee.   Ex. 20:12

16 For ᴿall that do such things, *and* all that do unrighteously, *are* an abomination unto the LORD thy God.   Prov. 11:1; [1 Thess. 4:6]

17 Remember what Am'-a-lek did unto thee by the way, when ye were come forth out of Egypt;

18 How he met thee by the way, and smote the hindmost of thee, *even* all *that were* feeble behind thee, when thou *wast* faint and weary; and he feared not God.

19 Therefore it shall be, when the LORD thy God hath given thee rest from all thine enemies round about, in the land which the LORD thy God giveth thee *for* an inheritance to possess it, *that* thou shalt ᴿblot out the remembrance of Am'-a-lek from under heaven; thou shalt not forget *it*.   Ex. 17:14

26 And it shall be, when thou *art* come in unto the land which the LORD thy God giveth thee *for* an inheritance, and possessest it, and dwellest therein;

2 ᴿThat thou shalt take of the first of all the fruit of the earth, which thou shalt bring of thy land that the LORD thy God giveth thee, and shalt put *it* in a basket, and shalt ᴿgo unto the place which the LORD thy God shall choose to place his name there.   Ex. 22:29 · 12:5

3 And thou shalt go unto the priest that shall be in those days, and say unto him, I ᵀprofess this day unto the LORD thy God, that I

am come unto the country which the LORD sware unto our fathers for to give us.   *declare*

4 And the priest shall take the basket out of thine hand, and set it down before the altar of the LORD thy God.

5 And thou shalt speak and say before the LORD thy God, A Syri-an ready to perish *was* my father, and he went down into Egypt, and sojourned there with a ᴿfew, and became there a nation, ᴿgreat, mighty, and populous: 10:22 · 1:10

6 And the Egyptians evil en-treated us, and afflicted us, and laid upon us hard bondage:

7 And ᴿwhen we cried unto the LORD God of our fathers, the LORD heard our voice, and looked on our affliction, and our labour, and our oppression: Ex. 2:23–25; 3:9; 4:31

8 And the LORD brought us forth out of Egypt with a mighty hand, and with an outstretched arm, and with great terribleness, and with signs, and with wonders:

9 And he hath brought us into this place, and hath given us this land, *even* ᴿa land that floweth with milk and honey.   Ex. 3:8, 17

10 And now, behold, I have brought the firstfruits of the land, which thou, O LORD, hast given me. And thou shalt set it before the LORD thy God, and worship before the LORD thy God:

11 And ᴿthou shalt rejoice in every good *thing* which the LORD thy God hath given unto thee, and unto thine house, thou, and the Levite, and the stranger that *is* among you.   12:7; 16:11; Eccl. 3:12, 13

12 When thou hast made an end of tithing all the ᴿtithes of thine increase the third year, *which is* ᴿthe year of tithing, and hast giv-en *it* unto the Levite, the stranger, the fatherless, and the widow, that they may eat within thy gates, and be filled;   Lev. 27:30; Num. 18:24 · 14:28

13 Then thou shalt say before the LORD thy God, I have brought away the hallowed things out of *mine* house, and also have given them unto the Levite, and unto the

stranger, to the fatherless, and to the widow, according to all thy commandments which thou hast commanded me: I have not transgressed thy commandments, neither have I forgotten *them:*

14 ᴿI have not eaten thereof in my mourning, neither have I taken away *ought* thereof for *any* unclean *use,* nor given *ought* thereof for the dead: *but* I have hearkened to the voice of the LORD my God, *and* have done according to all that thou hast commanded me.   Jer. 16:7; Hos. 9:4

15 ᴿLook down from thy holy habitation, from heaven, and bless thy people Israel, and the land which thou hast given us, as thou swarest unto our fathers, a land that floweth with milk and honey.   Ps. 80:14; Is. 63:15; Zech. 2:13

16 This day the LORD thy God hath commanded thee to do these statutes and judgments: thou shalt therefore keep and do them with all thine heart, and with all thy soul.

17 Thou hast ᴿavouched the LORD this day to be thy God, and to walk in his ways, and to keep his statutes, and his commandments, and his judgments, and to hearken unto his voice: Ex. 20:19

18 And the LORD hath avouched thee this day to be his ᵀpeculiar people, as he hath promised thee, and that *thou* shouldest keep all his commandments;   *special*

19 And to make thee high above all nations which he hath made, in praise, and in name, and in honour; and that thou mayest be ᴿan holy people unto the LORD thy God, as he hath spoken.   [1 Pet. 2:9]

27 And Moses with the elders of Israel commanded the people, saying, Keep all the commandments which I command you this day.

2 And it shall be on the day ᴿwhen ye shall pass over Jordan unto the land which the LORD thy God giveth thee, that thou shalt set thee up great stones, and plaister them with plaister: Josh. 4:1

3 And thou shalt write upon them all the words of this law, when thou art passed over, that thou mayest go in unto the land which the LORD thy God giveth thee, a land that floweth with milk and honey; as the LORD God of thy fathers hath promised thee.

4 Therefore it shall be when ye be gone over Jordan, *that* ye shall set up these stones, which I command you this day, ᴿin mount E'-bal, and thou shalt plaister them with plaister.   11:29; Josh. 8:30, 31

5 And there shalt thou build an altar unto the LORD thy God, an altar of stones: thou shalt not ᵀlift up *any* iron *tool* upon them.   *use*

6 Thou shalt build the altar of the LORD thy God of ᵀwhole stones: and thou shalt offer burnt offerings thereon unto the LORD thy God: *uncut*

7 And thou shalt offer peace offerings, and shalt eat there, and rejoice before the LORD thy God.

8 And thou shalt ᴿwrite upon the stones all the words of this law very plainly.   Josh. 8:32

9 And Moses and the priests the Levites spake unto all Israel, saying, Take heed, and hearken, O Israel; this day thou art become the people of the LORD thy God.

10 Thou shalt therefore obey the voice of the LORD thy God, and do his commandments and his statutes, which I command thee this day.

11 And Moses charged the people the same day, saying,

12 These shall stand ᴿupon mount Ger'-i-zim to bless the people, when ye are come over Jordan; Simeon, and Levi, and Judah, and Is'-sa-char, and Joseph, and Benjamin: Josh. 8:33; Judg. 9:7

13 And ᴿthese shall stand upon mount E'-bal to curse; Reuben, Gad, and Asher, and Zeb'-u-lun, Dan, and Naph'-ta-li. 11:29; Josh. 8:33

14 And ᴿthe Levites shall speak, and say unto all the men of Israel with a loud voice, Josh. 8:33; Dan. 9:11

15 Cursed *be* the man that maketh *any* graven or molten image, an abomination unto the LORD,

the work of the hands of the craftsman, and putteth *it* in *a* secret *place*. And all the people shall answer and say, Amen.

16 ᴿCursed *be* he that ᵀsetteth light by his father or his mother. And all the people shall say, A-men. Ex. 20:12 · *treats with contempt*

17 ᴿCursed *be* he that removeth his neighbour's landmark. And all the people shall say, Amen. 19:14

18 ᴿCursed *be* he that maketh the blind to wander out of the way. And all the people shall say, Amen. Lev. 19:14

19 ᴿCursed *be* he that perverteth the judgment of the stranger, fatherless, and widow. And all the people shall say, Amen. Ex. 22:21, 22

20 ᴿCursed *be* he that lieth with his father's wife; because he uncovereth his father's skirt. And all the people shall say, Amen. 22:30

21 ᴿCursed *be* he that lieth with any manner of beast. And all the people shall say, Amen. Ex. 22:19

22 ᴿCursed *be* he that lieth with his sister, the daughter of his father, or the daughter of his mother. And all the people shall say, Amen. Lev. 18:9

23 ᴿCursed *be* he that lieth with his mother in law. And all the people shall say, Amen. Lev. 18:17; 20:14

24 ᴿCursed *be* he that smiteth his neighbour secretly. And all the people shall say, Amen. Lev. 24:17

25 ᴿCursed *be* he that taketh reward to slay an innocent person. And all the people shall say, Amen. Ex. 23:7; Ps. 15:5; Ezek. 22:12

26 ᴿCursed *be* he that confirmeth not *all* the words of this law to do them. And all the people shall say, Amen. Jer. 11:3; Gal. 3:10

28 And it shall come to pass, if thou shalt hearken diligently unto the voice of the LORD thy God, to observe *and* to do all his commandments which I command thee this day, that the LORD thy God will set thee on high above all nations of the earth:

2 And all these blessings shall come on thee, and ᴿovertake thee,

if thou shalt hearken unto the voice of the LORD thy God. v. 15

3 ᴿBlessed *shalt* thou *be* in the city, and blessed *shalt* thou *be* ᴿin the field. Ps. 128:1, 4 · Gen. 39:5

4 Blessed *shall be* ᴿthe fruit of thy body, and the fruit of thy ground, and the fruit of thy cattle, the increase of thy kine, and the flocks of thy sheep. Gen. 22:17

5 Blessed *shall be* thy basket and thy ᵀstore. *kneading bowl*

6 Blessed *shalt* thou *be* when thou comest in, and blessed *shalt* thou *be* when thou goest out.

7 The LORD ᴿshall cause thine enemies that rise up against thee to be ᵀsmitten before thy face: they shall come out against thee one way, and flee before thee seven ways. Lev. 26:7, 8 · *defeated*

8 The LORD shall command the blessing upon thee in thy storehouses, and in all that thou ᴿsettest thine hand unto; and he shall bless thee in the land which the LORD thy God giveth thee. 15:10

9 ᴿThe LORD shall establish thee an holy people unto himself, as he hath sworn unto thee, if thou shalt keep the commandments of the LORD thy God, and walk in his ways. Ex. 19:5, 6

10 And all people of the earth shall see that thou art ᴿcalled by the name of the LORD; and they shall be afraid of thee. 2 Chr. 7:14

11 And ᴿthe LORD shall make thee plenteous in goods, in the fruit of thy body, and in the fruit of thy cattle, and in the fruit of thy ground, in the land which the LORD sware unto thy fathers to give thee. 30:9

12 The LORD shall open unto thee his good treasure, the heaven to give the rain unto thy land in his season, and ᴿto bless all the work of thine hand: and ᴿthou shalt lend unto many nations, and thou shalt not borrow. 14:29 · 15:6

13 And the LORD shall make ᴿthee the head, and not the tail; and thou shalt be above only, and thou shalt not be beneath; if that thou hearken unto the commandments of the LORD thy God, which

I command thee this day, to observe and to do *them:*   [Is. 9:14, 15]

14 And thou shalt not go aside
from any of the words which I
command thee this day, *to* the
right hand, or *to* the left, to go
after other gods to serve them.

15 But it shall come to pass, ^Rif
thou wilt not hearken unto the
voice of the LORD thy God, to
observe to do all his commandments and his statutes which I
command thee this day; that all
these curses shall come upon
thee, and overtake thee: Josh. 23:15

16 Cursed *shalt* thou *be* in the
city, and cursed *shalt* thou *be* in
the field.

17 Cursed *shall be* thy basket
and thy ^Tstore.   *kneading bowl*

18 Cursed *shall be* the ^Tfruit of
thy body, and the fruit of thy land,
the increase of thy ^Tkine, and the
flocks of thy sheep.   *offspring · cattle*

19 Cursed *shalt* thou *be* when
thou comest in, and cursed *shalt*
thou *be* when thou goest out.

20 The LORD shall send upon
thee ^Rcursing, vexation, and rebuke, in all that thou settest thine
hand unto for to do, until thou be
destroyed, and until thou perish
quickly; because of the wickedness of thy doings, whereby thou
hast forsaken me.   Mal. 2:2

21 The LORD shall make the
^Tpestilence cleave unto thee, until
he have consumed thee from off
the land, whither thou goest to
possess it.   *plague*

22 ^RThe LORD shall smite thee
with a consumption, and with a
fever, and with an inflammation,
and with an extreme burning, and
with the sword, and with ^Rblast-
ing,^T and with mildew; and they
shall pursue thee until thou perish.   Lev. 26:16 · Amos 4:9 · *scorching*

23 And ^Rthy heaven that *is* over
thy head shall be ^Tbrass, and the
earth that *is* under thee *shall be*
iron.   Lev. 26:19 · *bronze*

24 The LORD shall make the rain
of thy land powder and dust: from
heaven shall it come down upon
thee, until thou be destroyed.

25 ^RThe LORD shall cause thee to
be smitten before thine enemies:
thou shalt go out one way against
them, and flee seven ways before
them: and shalt be removed into
all the kingdoms of the earth. 32:30

26 And thy carcase shall be
meat unto all fowls of the air, and
unto the beasts of the earth, and
no man shall fray *them* away.

27 The LORD will smite thee with
^Rthe ^Tbotch of Egypt, and with the
emerods, and with the scab, and
with the itch, whereof thou canst
not be healed.   Ex. 15:26 · *boils*

28 The LORD shall smite thee
with madness, and blindness, and
^Rastonishment of heart: Jer. 4:9

29 And thou shalt grope at
noonday, as the blind gropeth in
darkness, and thou shalt not prosper in thy ways: and thou shalt be
only oppressed and spoiled evermore, and no man shall save *thee.*

30 ^RThou shalt betroth a wife,
and another man shall lie with
her: ^Rthou shalt build an house,
and thou shalt not dwell therein:
^Rthou shalt plant a vineyard, and
shalt not gather the grapes there-
of.   2 Sam. 12:11 · Zeph. 1:13 · Mic. 6:15

31 Thine ox *shall be* slain before
thine eyes, and thou shalt not eat
thereof: thine ass *shall be* violently taken away from before thy
face, and shall not be restored to
thee: thy sheep *shall be* given
unto thine enemies, and thou
shalt have none to rescue *them.*

32 Thy sons and thy daughters
shall be given unto ^Ranother people, and thine eyes shall look, and
fail *with longing* for them all the
day long: and *there shall be* no
might in thine hand.   2 Chr. 29:9

33 ^RThe fruit of thy land, and all
thy labours, shall a nation which
thou knowest not eat up; and
thou shalt be only oppressed and
crushed alway: Lev. 26:16; Jer. 5:15, 17

34 So that thou shalt be ^Tmad
for the sight of thine eyes which
thou shalt see.   *driven mad because of*

35 The LORD shall smite thee in
the knees, and in the legs, with a
sore ^Tbotch that cannot be healed,

from the sole of thy foot unto the top of thy head.   *boils*

36 The LORD shall bring thee, and thy king which thou shalt set over thee, unto a nation which neither thou nor thy fathers have known; and there shalt thou serve other gods, wood and stone.

37 And thou shalt become [R]an astonishment, a proverb, and a byword, among all nations whither the LORD shall lead thee. Jer. 24:9

38 [R]Thou shalt carry much seed out into the field, and shalt gather *but* little in; for [R]the locust shall consume it.   Hag. 1:6 · Ex. 10:4; Joel 1:4

39 Thou shalt plant vineyards, and dress *them*, but shalt neither drink *of* the [R]wine, nor gather *the grapes;* for the worms shall eat them.   Zeph. 1:13

40 Thou shalt have olive trees throughout all thy coasts, but thou shalt not anoint *thyself* with the oil; for thine [T]olive shall cast *his fruit.*   *olives shall drop off*

41 Thou shalt beget sons and daughters, but thou shalt not enjoy them; for [R]they shall go into captivity.   Lam. 1:5

42 All thy trees and fruit of thy land shall the locust consume.

43 The stranger that *is* within thee shall get up above thee very high; and thou shalt come down very low.

44 He shall lend to thee, and thou shalt not lend to him: he shall be the head, and thou shalt be the tail.

45 Moreover all these curses shall come upon thee, and shall pursue thee, and overtake thee, till thou be destroyed; because thou [T]hearkenedst not unto the voice of the LORD thy God, to keep his commandments and his statutes which he commanded thee: *did not listen*

46 And they shall be upon [R]thee for a sign and for a wonder, and upon thy seed for ever.   Ezek. 14:8

47 [R]Because thou servedst not the LORD thy God with joyfulness, and with gladness of heart, for the abundance of all *things;*   12:7

48 Therefore shalt thou serve thine enemies which the LORD shall send against thee, in [R]hunger, and in thirst, and in nakedness, and in want of all *things:* and he [R]shall put a yoke of iron upon thy neck, until he have destroyed thee.   Lam. 4:4–6 · Jer. 28:13, 14

49 The LORD shall bring a nation against thee from far, from the end of the earth, *as swift* as the eagle flieth; a nation whose tongue thou shalt not understand;

50 A nation of fierce countenance, [R]which shall not regard the person of the old, nor shew favour to the young: 2 Chr. 36:17

51 And he shall eat the fruit of thy cattle, and the fruit of thy land, until thou be destroyed: which *also* shall not leave thee *either* corn, wine, or oil, *or* the increase of thy kine, or flocks of thy sheep, until he have destroyed thee.

52 And he shall [R]besiege thee in all thy gates, until thy high and fenced walls come down, wherein thou trustedst, throughout all thy land: and he shall besiege thee in all thy gates throughout all thy land, which the LORD thy God hath given thee.   2 Kin. 25:1, 2, 4

53 And [R]thou shalt eat the fruit of thine own body, the flesh of thy sons and of thy daughters, which the LORD thy God hath given thee, in the siege, and in the straitness, wherewith thine enemies shall distress thee: Jer. 19:9; Lam. 2:20; 4:10

54 *So that* the man *that is* tender among you, and very delicate, [R]his eye shall be evil toward his brother, and toward [R]the wife of his bosom, and toward the remnant of his children which he shall leave: 15:9 · 13:6

55 So that he will not give to any of them of the flesh of his children whom he shall eat: because he hath nothing left him in the siege, and in the straitness, wherewith thine enemies shall distress thee in all thy gates.

56 The tender and delicate woman among you, which would not

adventure to set the sole of her foot upon the ground for delicateness and tenderness, her eye shall be evil toward the husband of her bosom, and toward her son, and toward her daughter,

57 And toward her young one that cometh out from between her feet, and toward her children which she shall bear: for she shall eat them for want of all *things* secretly in the siege and straitness, wherewith thine enemy shall distress thee in thy gates.

58 If thou wilt not observe to do all the words of this law that are written in this book, that thou mayest fear [R]this glorious and fearful name, THE LORD THY GOD;   Ex. 6:3

59 Then the LORD will make thy plagues [R]wonderful,[T] and the plagues of thy seed, *even* great plagues, and of long continuance, and sore sicknesses, and of long continuance.   Dan. 9:12 · *extraordinary*

60 Moreover he will bring upon thee all [R]the diseases of Egypt, which thou wast afraid of; and they shall cleave unto thee.   7:15

61 Also every sickness, and every plague, which *is* not written in the book of this law, them will the LORD bring upon thee, until thou be destroyed.

62 And ye [R]shall be left few in number, whereas ye were as the stars of heaven for multitude; because thou wouldest not obey the voice of the LORD thy God. 4:27

63 And it shall come to pass, *that* as the LORD rejoiced over you to do you good, and to multiply you; so the LORD will rejoice over you to destroy you, and to bring you to nought; and ye shall be plucked from off the land whither thou goest to possess it.

64 And the LORD [R]shall scatter thee among all people, from the one end of the earth even unto the other; and there thou shalt serve other gods, which neither thou nor thy fathers have known, *even* wood and stone.   Amos 9:9

65 And [R]among these nations shalt thou find no ease, neither shall the sole of thy foot have rest: but the LORD shall give thee there a trembling heart, and failing of eyes, and sorrow of mind: Lam. 1:3

66 And thy life shall hang in doubt before thee; and thou shalt fear day and night, and shalt have none assurance of thy life:

67 [R]In the morning thou shalt say, Would God it were even! and at even thou shalt say, Would God it were morning! for the fear of thine heart wherewith thou shalt fear, and for the sight of thine eyes which thou shalt see.   Job 7:4

68 And the LORD [R]shall bring thee into Egypt again with ships, by the way whereof I spake unto thee, [R]Thou shalt see it no more again: and there ye shall be sold unto your enemies for bondmen and bondwomen, and no man shall buy *you*.   Hos. 8:13 · 17:16

29 These *are* the words of the covenant, which the LORD commanded Moses to make with the children of Israel in the land of Moab, beside the [R]covenant which he made with them in Ho'-reb.   5:2, 3; Lev. 26:46

2 And Moses called unto all Israel, and said unto them, Ye have seen all that the LORD did before your eyes in the land of Egypt unto Pharaoh, and unto all his servants, and unto all his land;

3 The great [T]temptations which thine eyes have seen, the signs, and those great miracles: *trials*

4 Yet [R]the LORD hath not given you an heart to perceive, and eyes to see, and ears to hear, unto this day. Matt. 13:14; [Acts 28:26, 27]; Rom. 11:8

5 [R]And I have led you forty years in the wilderness: [R]your clothes are not waxen old upon you, and thy shoe is not waxen old upon thy foot.   1:3; 8:2 · 8:4

6 [R]Ye have not eaten bread, neither have ye drunk wine or strong drink: that ye might know that I *am* the LORD your God.   8:3

7 And when ye came unto this place, [R]Si'-hon the king of Hesh'-bon, and Og the king of Ba'-shan,

came out against us unto battle, and we smote them: Num. 21:23, 24

8 And we took their land, and ^Rgave it for an inheritance unto the Reu'-ben-ites, and to the Gad'-ites, and to the half tribe of Ma-nas'-seh. 3:12, 13; Num. 32:33

9 Keep therefore the words of this covenant, and do them, that ye may prosper in all that ye do.

10 Ye stand this day all of you before the LORD your God; your captains of your tribes, your elders, and your officers, *with* all the men of Israel,

11 Your little ones, your wives, and thy stranger that *is* in thy camp, from ^Rthe hewer of thy wood unto the drawer of thy water: Josh. 9:21, 23, 27

12 That thou shouldest enter into covenant with the LORD thy God, and ^Rinto his oath, which the LORD thy God maketh with thee this day: Neh. 10:29

13 That he may ^Restablish thee to day for a people unto himself, and *that* he may be unto thee a God, ^Ras he hath said unto thee, and ^Ras he hath sworn unto thy fathers, to Abraham, to Isaac, and to Jacob. 28:9 · Ex. 6:7 · Gen. 17:7, 8

14 Neither with you only do I make this covenant and this oath;

15 But with *him* that standeth here with us this day before the LORD our God, and also with *him* that *is* not here with us this day:

16 (For ye know how we have dwelt in the land of Egypt; and how we came through the nations which ye passed by;

17 And ye have seen their abom-inations, and their idols, wood and stone, silver and gold, which *were* among them:)

18 Lest there should be among you man, or woman, or family, or tribe, ^Rwhose heart turneth away this day from the LORD our God, to go *and* serve the gods of these nations; lest there should be among you a root that beareth ^Rgall and wormwood; 11:16 · 32:32

19 And it come to pass, when he heareth the words of this curse,

that he bless himself in his heart, saying, I shall have peace, though I walk ^Rin the imagination of mine heart, ^Rto add drunkenness to thirst: Jer. 3:17; 7:24 · Is. 30:1

20 The LORD will not spare him, but then the anger of the LORD and his jealousy shall smoke against that man, and all the curs-es that are written in this book shall lie upon him, and the LORD ^Rshall blot out his name from under heaven. Ex. 32:33; 2 Kin. 14:27

21 And the LORD ^Rshall separate him unto evil out of all the tribes of Israel, according to all the curs-es of the covenant that are written in this book of the law: [Matt. 24:51]

22 So that the generation to come of your children that shall rise up after you, and the stranger that shall come from a far land, shall say, when they ^Rsee the plagues of that land, and the sick-nesses which the LORD hath laid upon it; Jer. 19:8; 49:17; 50:13

23 *And that* the whole land thereof *is* brimstone, and salt, *and* burning, *that* it is not sown, nor beareth, nor any grass groweth therein, ^Rlike the overthrow of Sodom, and Go-mor'-rah, Ad'-mah, and Ze-bo'-im, which the LORD overthrew in his anger, and in his wrath: Gen. 19:24, 25; Is. 1:9

24 Even all nations shall say, Wherefore hath the LORD done thus unto this land? what *mean-eth* the heat of this great anger?

25 Then men shall say, Because they have forsaken the covenant of the LORD God of their fathers, which he made with them when he brought them forth out of the land of Egypt:

26 For they went and served other gods, and worshipped them, gods whom they knew not, and *whom* he had not given unto them:

27 And the anger of the LORD was kindled against this land, ^Rto bring upon it all the curses that are written in this book: Dan. 9:11

28 And the LORD ^Rrooted them out of their land in anger, and in wrath, and in great indignation,

and cast them into another land, as *it is* this day.   1 Kin. 14:15; Ps. 52:5

29 The secret *things belong* unto the LORD our God: but those *things which are* revealed *belong* unto us and to our children for ever, that *we* may do all the words of this law.

30 And ᴿit shall come to pass, when ᴿall these things are come upon thee, the blessing and the ᴿcurse, which I have set before thee, and thou shalt call *them* to mind among all the nations, whither the LORD thy God hath driven thee,   Lev. 26:40 · 28:2 · 28:15–45

2 And shalt ᴿreturn unto the LORD thy God, and shalt obey his voice according to all that I command thee this day, thou and thy children, with all thine heart, and with all thy soul;   Neh. 1:9; Is. 55:7

3 ᴿThat then the LORD thy God will turn thy captivity, and have compassion upon thee, and will return and gather thee from all the nations, whither the LORD thy God hath scattered thee.   Ps. 106:45

4 ᴿIf *any* of thine be driven out unto the outmost *parts* of heaven, from thence will the LORD thy God gather thee, and from thence will he fetch thee: 28:64; Neh. 1:9; Is. 62:11

5 And the LORD thy God will bring thee into the land which thy fathers possessed, and thou shalt possess it; and he will do thee good, and multiply thee above thy fathers.

6 And ᴿthe LORD thy God will circumcise thine heart, and the heart of thy seed, to love the LORD thy God with all thine heart, and with all thy soul, that thou mayest live.   10:16; Jer. 32:39; Ezek. 11:19

7 And the LORD thy God will put all these curses upon thine enemies, and on them that hate thee, which persecuted thee.

8 And thou shalt ᴿreturn and obey the voice of the LORD, and do all his commandments which I command thee this day.   Zeph. 3:20

9 ᴿAnd the LORD thy God will make thee plenteous in every work of thine hand, in the fruit of thy body, and in the fruit of thy cattle, and in the fruit of thy land, for good: for the LORD will again rejoice over thee for good, as he rejoiced over thy fathers: 28:11

10 If thou shalt hearken unto the voice of the LORD thy God, to keep his commandments and his statutes which are written in this book of the law, *and* if thou turn unto the LORD thy God with all thine heart, and with all thy soul.

11 For this commandment which I command thee this day, ᴿit *is* not hidden from thee, neither *is* it far off.   Is. 45:19

12 It *is* not in heaven, that thou shouldest say, Who shall go up for us to heaven, and bring it unto us, that we may hear it, and do it?

13 Neither *is* it beyond the sea, that thou shouldest say, Who shall go over the sea for us, and bring it unto us, that we may hear it, and do it?

14 But the word *is* very nigh unto thee, in thy mouth, and in thy heart, that thou mayest do it.

15 See, ᴿI have set before thee this day life and good, and death and evil;   vv. 1, 19

16 In that I command thee this day to love the LORD thy God, to walk in his ways, and to keep his commandments and his statutes and his judgments, that thou mayest live and multiply: and the LORD thy God shall bless thee in the land whither thou goest to possess it.

17 But if thine heart turn away, so that thou wilt not hear, but shalt be drawn away, and worship other gods, and serve them;

18 ᴿI ᵀdenounce unto you this day, that ye shall surely perish, *and that* ye shall not prolong *your* days upon the land, whither thou passest over Jordan to go to possess it.   4:26; 8:19 · announce

19 ᴿI call heaven and earth to record this day against you, *that* ᴿI have set before you life and death, blessing and cursing: therefore choose life, that both thou and thy seed may live: 4:26 · v. 15

20 That thou mayest love the LORD thy God, *and* that thou mayest obey his voice, and that thou mayest cleave unto him: for he *is* thy life, and the length of thy days: that thou mayest dwell in the land which the LORD sware unto thy fathers, to Abraham, to Isaac, and to Jacob, to give them.

31 And Moses went and spake these words unto all Israel.

2 And he said unto them, I ᴿ*am* an hundred and twenty years old this day; I can no more go out and come in: also the LORD hath said unto me, ᴿThou shalt not go over this Jordan. Ex. 7:7 · Num. 20:12

3 The LORD thy God, he will go over before thee, *and* he will destroy these nations from before thee, and thou shalt possess them: *and* ᴿJoshua, he shall go over before thee, ᴿas the LORD hath said. Num. 27:18 · Num. 27:21

4 ᴿAnd the LORD shall do unto them ᴿas he did to Si'-hon and to Og, kings of the Am'-or-ites, and unto the land of them, whom he destroyed. 3:21 · Num. 21:24, 33

5 And ᴿthe LORD shall give them up before your face, that ye may do unto them according unto all the commandments which I have commanded you. 7:2; 20:10–20

6 Be strong and of a good courage, fear not, nor be afraid of them: for the LORD thy God, he *it is* that doth go with thee; he will not fail thee, nor forsake thee.

7 And Moses called unto Joshua, and said unto him in the sight of all Israel, Be strong and of a good courage: for thou must go with this people unto the land which the LORD hath sworn unto their fathers to give them; and thou shalt cause them to inherit it.

8 And the LORD, ᴿhe *it is* that doth go before thee; ᴿhe will be with thee, he will not fail thee, neither forsake thee: fear not, neither be dismayed. Ex. 13:21 · Heb. 13:5

9 And Moses wrote this law, and delivered it unto the priests the sons of Levi, which bare the ark of the covenant of the LORD, and unto all the elders of Israel.

10 And Moses commanded them, saying, At the end of *every* seven years, in the solemnity of the ᴿyear of release, ᴿin the feast of tabernacles, 15:1, 2 · Lev. 23:34

11 When all Israel is come to appear before the LORD thy God in the place which he shall choose, thou shalt read this law before all Israel in their hearing.

12 ᴿGather the people together, men, and women, and children, and thy stranger that *is* within thy gates, that they may hear, and that they may learn, and fear the LORD your God, and observe to do all the words of this law: 4:10

13 And *that* their children, ᴿwhich have not known *any thing*, ᴿmay hear, and learn to fear the LORD your God, as long as ye live in the land whither ye go over Jordan to possess it. 11:2 · Ps. 78:6, 7

14 And the LORD said unto Moses, ᴿBehold, thy days approach that thou must die: call Joshua, and present yourselves in the tabernacle of the congregation, that I may give him a ᵀcharge. And Moses and Joshua went, and presented themselves in the tabernacle of the congregation. Num. 27:13 · *commission*

15 And ᴿthe LORD appeared in the tabernacle in a pillar of a cloud: and the pillar of the cloud stood over the door of the tabernacle. Ex. 33:9

16 And the LORD said unto Moses, Behold, thou shalt sleep with thy fathers; and this people will ᴿrise up, and go a whoring after the gods of the strangers of the land, whither they go *to be* among them, and will ᴿforsake me, and break my covenant which I have made with them. 29:22 · 32:15

17 Then my anger shall be kindled against them in that day, and I will forsake them, and I will ᴿhide my face from them, and they shall be devoured, and many evils and troubles shall befall them; so that they will say in that

day, ^RAre not these evils come upon us, because our God *is* ^Rnot among us? 32:20 · Judg. 6:13 · Num. 14:42

18 And ^RI will surely hide my face in that day for all the evils which they shall have wrought, in that they are turned unto other gods. [Is. 1:15, 16]

19 Now therefore write ye this song for you, and teach it the children of Israel: put it in their mouths, that this song may be ^Ra witness for me against the children of Israel. vv. 22, 26

20 For when I shall have brought them into the land which I sware unto their fathers, that floweth with milk and honey; and they shall have eaten and filled themselves, and ^Twaxen fat; then will they turn unto other gods, and serve them, and provoke me, and break my covenant. *grown*

21 And it shall come to pass, when many evils and troubles are befallen them, that this song shall testify against them as a witness; for it shall not be forgotten out of the mouths of their seed: for ^RI know their imagination ^Rwhich they go about, even now, before I have brought them into the land which I sware. Hos. 5:3 · Amos 5:25, 26

22 Moses therefore wrote this song the same day, and taught it the children of Israel.

23 And he gave Joshua the son of Nun a charge, and said, Be strong and of a good courage: for thou shalt bring the children of Israel into the land which I sware unto them: and I will be with thee.

24 And it came to pass, when Moses had made an end of writing the words of this law in a book, until they were finished,

25 That Moses commanded the Levites, which bare the ark of the covenant of the LORD, saying,

26 Take this book of the law, ^Rand put it in the side of the ark of the covenant of the LORD your God, that it may be there for a witness against thee. 2 Kin. 22:8

27 ^RFor I know thy rebellion, and thy ^Rstiff neck: behold, while I am yet alive with you this day, ye have been rebellious against the LORD; and how much more after my death? 9:7, 24 · 9:6, 13; Ex. 32:9

28 Gather unto me all the elders of your tribes, and your officers, that I may speak these words in their ears, ^Rand call heaven and earth to record against them. 30:19

29 For I know that after my death ye will utterly ^Rcorrupt *yourselves*, and turn aside from the way which I have commanded you; and evil will befall you in the latter days; because ye will do evil in the sight of the LORD, to provoke him to anger through the work of your hands. [Acts 20:29, 30]

30 And Moses spake in the ears of all the congregation of Israel the words of this song, until they were ended.

32 Give ear, O ye heavens, and I will speak; and hear, O earth, the words of my mouth.

2 ^RMy doctrine shall drop as the rain, my speech shall distil as the dew, as the small rain upon the tender herb, and as the showers upon the grass: Is. 55:10, 11

3 Because I will ^Tpublish the name of the LORD: ascribe ye greatness unto our God. *proclaim*

4 *He is* ^Rthe Rock, ^Rhis work *is* perfect: for all his ways *are* judgment: ^Ra God of truth and without iniquity, just and right *is* he. Ps. 18:2 · 2 Sam. 22:31 · Is. 65:16

5 They have corrupted themselves, their spot *is* not *the spot* of his children: *they are* a ^Rperverse and crooked generation. Phil. 2:15

6 Do ye thus requite the LORD, O foolish people and unwise? *is* not he thy father *that* hath ^Rbought thee? Hath he not made thee, and established thee? Ps. 74:2

7 ^RRemember the days of old, consider the years of many generations: ^Rask thy father, and he will shew thee; thy elders, and they will tell thee. Ps. 44:1 · Ps. 78:5–8

8 When the Most High ^Rdivided to the nations their inheritance, when he separated the sons of Adam, he set the bounds of the

people according to the number of the children of Israel. Acts 17:26

9 For ᴿthe LORD's portion *is* his people; Jacob *is* the lot of his inheritance. Ex. 19:5

10 He found him ᴿin a desert land, and in the waste howling wilderness; he led him about, he instructed him, he kept him as the apple of his eye. Jer. 2:6; Hos. 13:5

11 ᴿAs an eagle stirreth up her nest, fluttereth over her young, spreadeth abroad her wings, taketh them, beareth them on her wings: Is. 31:5

12 *So* the LORD alone did lead him, and *there was* no strange god with him.

13 ᴿHe made him ride on the high places of the earth, that he might eat the increase of the fields; and he made him to suck honey out of the rock, and oil out of the flinty rock; Is. 58:14

14 Butter of kine, and milk of sheep, ᴿwith fat of lambs, and rams of the breed of Ba'-shan, and goats, with the fat of kidneys of wheat; and thou didst drink the pure blood of the grape. Ps. 81:16

15 But Jesh'-u-run waxed fat, and kicked: thou art waxen fat, thou art grown thick, thou art covered *with fatness*; then he ᴿforsook God *which* ᴿmade him, and lightly esteemed the ᴿRock of his salvation. Is. 1:4 · Is. 51:13 · Ps. 95:1

16 ᴿThey provoked him to jealousy with strange *gods*, with abominations provoked they him to anger. Ps. 78:58; 1 Cor. 10:22

17 ᴿThey sacrificed unto devils, not to God; to gods whom they knew not, to new *gods* ᵀ*that* came newly up, whom your fathers feared not. Rev. 9:20 · *new arrivals*

18 Of the Rock *that* begat thee thou art unmindful, and hast forgotten God that formed thee.

19 ᴿAnd when the LORD saw *it*, he ᵀabhorred *them*, because of the provoking of his sons, and of his daughters. Judg. 2:14 · *spurned*

20 And he said, I will hide my face from them, I will see what

their end *shall be:* for they *are* a very ᵀfroward generation, children in whom *is* no faith. *perverse*

21 They have moved me to jealousy with *that which is* not God; they have provoked me to anger ᴿwith their ᵀvanities: and ᴿI will move them to jealousy with *those which are* not a people; I will provoke them to anger with a foolish nation. Ps. 31:6 · *foolish idols* · Rom. 10:19

22 For ᴿa fire is kindled in mine anger, and shall burn unto the lowest ᵀhell, and shall consume the earth with her increase, and set on fire the foundations of the mountains. Ps. 18:7, 8 · Heb. *Sheol*

23 I will heap ᵀmischiefs upon them; ᴿI will spend mine arrows upon them. *disasters* · Ps. 7:12, 13

24 *They shall be* burnt with hunger, and devoured with burning heat, and with bitter destruction: I will also send the ᴿteeth of beasts upon them, with the poison of serpents of the dust. Lev. 26:22

25 The sword without, and terror within, shall destroy both the young man and the virgin, the suckling *also* with the man of gray hairs.

26 ᴿI said, I would scatter them into corners, I would make the remembrance of them to cease from among men: Ezek. 20:23

27 Were it not that I feared the wrath of the enemy, lest their adversaries should behave themselves strangely, *and* lest they should say, Our hand *is* high, and the LORD hath not done all this.

28 For they *are* a nation void of counsel, neither *is there any* understanding in them.

29 O that they were wise, *that* they understood this, *that* they would consider their latter end!

30 How should one chase a thousand, and two put ten thousand to flight, except their Rock ᴿhad sold them, and the LORD had shut them up? Judg. 2:14; Ps. 44:12

31 For their rock *is* not as our Rock, ᴿeven our enemies themselves *being* judges. [1 Sam. 4:7, 8]

32 For their vine *is* of the vine of

Sodom, and of the fields of Go-mor'-rah: their grapes *are* grapes of gall, their clusters *are* bitter:

33 Their wine *is* [R]the poison of dragons, and the cruel [R]venom of asps.   Ps. 58:4 · Rom. 3:13

34 *Is* not this [R]laid up in store with me, *and* sealed up among my treasures?   [Jer. 2:22]

35 [R]To me *belongeth* vengeance, and recompence; their foot shall slide in *due* time: [R]for the day of their calamity *is* at hand, and the things that shall come upon them make haste.   Rom. 12:19 · 2 Pet. 2:3

36 [R]For the LORD shall judge his people, and repent himself for his servants, when he seeth that *their* power is gone, and *there is* none shut up, or left.   Ps. 135:14; Heb. 10:30

37 And he shall say, [R]Where *are* their gods, *their* rock in whom they trusted,   Judg. 10:14; Jer. 2:28

38 Which did eat the fat of their sacrifices, *and* drank the wine of their drink offerings? Let them rise up and help you, *and* be your protection.

39 See now that I, *even* I, *am* he, and *there is* no god with me: I kill, and I make alive; I wound, and I heal: neither *is there any* that can deliver out of my hand.

40 For I lift up my hand to heav-en, and say, I live for ever.

41 [R]If I whet my glittering sword, and mine hand take hold on judgment; I will render ven-geance to mine enemies, and will reward them that hate me.   Is. 1:24

42 I will make mine arrows drunk with blood, and my sword shall devour flesh; *and that* with the blood of the slain and of the captives, from the beginning of revenges upon the enemy.

☆ 43 Rejoice, O ye nations, *with* his people: for he will [R]avenge the blood of his servants, and will render vengeance to his adversa-ries, and will be merciful unto his land, *and* to his people.   Rev. 19:2

44 And Moses came and spake all the words of this song in the ears of the people, he, and [T]Ho-she'-a the son of Nun.   Joshua

45 And Moses made an end of speaking all these words to all Israel:

46 And he said unto them, [R]Set your hearts unto all the words which I testify among you this day, which ye shall command your children to observe to do, all the words of this law.   Ezek. 40:4; 44:5

47 For it *is* not a vain thing for you; because it *is* your life: and through this thing ye shall pro-long *your* days in the land, whith-er ye go over Jordan to possess it.

48 And the LORD spake unto Moses that selfsame day, saying,

49 [R]Get thee up into this moun-tain Ab'-a-rim, *unto* mount Ne'-bo, which *is* in the land of Moab, that *is* over against Jericho; and behold the land of Canaan, which I give unto the children of Israel for a possession: Num. 27:12–14

50 And die in the mount whither thou goest up, and be gathered unto thy people; as Aaron thy brother died in mount Hor, and was gathered unto his people:

51 Because [R]ye trespassed against me among the children of Israel at the waters of Mer'-i-bah–Ka'-desh, in the wilderness of Zin; because ye [R]sanctified me not in the midst of the children of Israel.   Num. 20:11–13 · Lev. 10:3

52 [R]Yet thou shalt see the land before *thee;* but thou shalt not go thither unto the land which I give the children of Israel.   Num. 27:12

33 And this *is* the blessing, wherewith Moses [R]the man of God blessed the children of Israel before his death.   Ps. 90

2 And he said, [R]The LORD came from Si'-nai, and rose up from [R]Se'-ir unto them; he shined forth from mount Pa'-ran, and he came with [R]ten thousands of saints: from his right hand *went* a fiery law for them.   Hab. 3:3 · 2:1, 4 · Rev. 5:11

3 Yea, he loved the people; all his saints *are* in thy hand: and they sat down at thy feet; *every one* shall receive of thy words.

4 [R]Moses commanded us a law,

even the inheritance of the congregation of Jacob.   John 1:17; 7:19

5   And he was ᴿking in ᴿJesh'-u-run, when the heads of the people *and* the tribes of Israel were gathered together.   Ex. 15:18 · 32:15

6   Let Reuben live, and not die; and let *not* his men be few.

7   And this *is the blessing* of Judah: and he said, Hear, LORD, the voice of Judah, and bring him unto his people: let his hands be sufficient for him; and be thou an help *to him* from his enemies.

8   And of Levi he said, ᴿ*Let* thy Thum'-mim and thy U'-rim *be* with thy holy one, whom thou didst prove at Mas'-sah, *and with* whom thou didst strive at the waters of Mer'-i-bah;   Ex. 28:30

9   Who said unto his father and to his mother, I have not seen him; neither did he acknowledge his brethren, nor knew his own children: for they have observed thy word, and kept thy covenant.

10 ᴿThey shall teach Jacob thy judgments, and Israel thy law: they shall put incense before thee, ᴿand whole burnt sacrifice upon thine altar.   Mal. 2:7 · Lev. 1:9; Ps. 51:19

11 Bless, LORD, his substance, and ᴿaccept the work of his hands: smite through the loins of them that rise against him, and of them that hate him, that they rise not again.   2 Sam. 24:23; Ezek. 20:40

12 *And* of Benjamin he said, The beloved of the LORD shall dwell in safety by him; *and the* LORD shall cover him all the day long, and he shall dwell between his shoulders.

13 And of Joseph he said, Blessed of the LORD *be* his land, for the precious things of heaven, for the ᴿdew, and for the deep that coucheth beneath,   Gen. 27:28

14 And for the precious fruits *brought forth* by the sun, and for the precious things put forth by the moon,

15 And for the chief things of ᴿthe ancient mountains, and for the precious things ᴿof the lasting hills,   Gen. 49:26 · Hab. 3:6

16 And for the precious things of the earth and fulness thereof, and *for* the good will of ᴿhim that dwelt in the bush: let *the blessing* ᴿcome upon the head of Joseph, and upon the top of the head of him *that was* separated from his brethren.   Acts 7:30–35 · Gen. 49:26

17 His glory *is like* the firstling of his bullock, and his horns *are like* the horns of unicorns: with them ᴿhe shall push the people together to the ends of the earth: and they *are* the ten thousands of E'-phra-im, and they *are* the thousands of Ma-nas'-seh.   Ps. 44:5

18 And of Zeb'u-lun he said, Rejoice, Zeb'-u-lun, in thy going out; and, Is'-sa-char, in thy tents.

19 They shall ᴿcall the people unto the mountain; there they shall offer sacrifices of righteousness: for they shall suck *of* the abundance of the seas, and *of* treasures hid in the sand.   Ex. 15:17

20 And of Gad he said, Blessed *be* he that enlargeth Gad: he dwelleth as a lion, and teareth the arm with the crown of the head.

21 And he provided the first part for himself, because there, *in* a portion of the lawgiver, *was he* seated; and ᴿhe came with the heads of the people, he executed the justice of the LORD, and his judgments with Israel.   Josh. 4:12

22 And of Dan he said, Dan *is* a lion's whelp: ᴿhe shall leap from Ba'-shan.   Gen. 49:16, 17; Josh. 19:47

23 And of Naph'-ta-li he said, O Naph'-ta-li, ᴿsatisfied with favour, and full with the blessing of the LORD: ᴿpossess thou the west and the south.   Gen. 49:21 · Josh. 19:32

24 And of Asher he said, ᴿLet Asher *be* blessed with children; let him be acceptable to his brethren, and let him ᴿdip his foot in oil.   Gen. 49:20 · Job 29:6

25 Thy shoes *shall be* ᴿiron and brass; and as thy days, *so shall* thy strength *be*.   8:9

26 *There is* none like unto the God of ᴿJesh'-u-run, *who* rideth upon the heaven in thy help, and in his excellency on the sky.   32:15

27 The eternal God *is thy* ref-

uge, and underneath *are* the everlasting arms: and [R]he shall thrust out the enemy from before thee; and shall say, Destroy *them*. 9:3–5

28 Israel then shall dwell in safety alone: [R]the fountain of Jacob *shall be* upon a land of corn and wine; also his [R]heavens shall drop down dew. Num. 23:9 · Gen. 27:28

29 Happy *art* thou, O Israel: who *is* like unto thee, O people saved by the LORD, [R]the shield of thy help, and who *is* the sword of thy excellency! And thine enemies shall be found liars unto thee; and [R]thou shalt tread upon their high places. Gen. 15:1; Ps. 115:9 · Num. 33:52

34 And Moses went up from the plains of Moab [R]unto the mountain of Ne′-bo, to the top of Pis′-gah, that *is* over against Jericho. And the LORD shewed him all the land of Gil′-e-ad, unto Dan, 32:49; Num. 27:12

2 And all Naph′-ta-li, and the land of E′-phra-im, and Ma-nas′-seh, and all the land of Judah, unto the utmost sea,

3 And the south, and the plain of the valley of Jericho, the city of palm trees, unto Zo′-ar.

4 And the LORD said unto him, [R]This *is* the land which I sware unto Abraham, unto Isaac, and unto Jacob, saying, I will give it unto thy seed: I have caused thee to see *it* with thine eyes, but thou shalt not go over thither. Gen. 12:7

5 [R]So Moses the servant of the LORD died there in the land of Moab, according to the word of the LORD. 32:50; Num. 20:12; Josh. 1:1, 2

6 And he buried him in a valley in the land of Moab, over against Beth–pe′-or: but no man knoweth of his sepulchre unto this day.

7 And Moses *was* an hundred and twenty years old when he died: [R]his eye was not dim, nor his natural force abated. Gen. 27:1; 48:10

8 And the children of Israel wept for Moses in the plains of Moab [R]thirty days: so the days of weeping *and* mourning for Moses were ended. Gen. 50:3, 10

9 And Joshua the son of Nun was full of the [R]spirit of wisdom; for [R]Moses had laid his hands upon him: and the children of Israel hearkened unto him, and did as the LORD commanded Moses. Is. 11:2 · Num. 27:18, 23

10 And there [R]arose not a prophet since in Israel like unto Moses, [R]whom the LORD knew face to face, 18:15, 18 · 5:4; Ex. 33:11

11 In all [R]the signs and the wonders, which the LORD sent him to do in the land of Egypt to Pharaoh, and to all his servants, and to all his land, 7:19

12 And in all that mighty hand, and in all the great terror which Moses shewed in the sight of all Israel.

The Book of

JOSHUA

JOSHUA, the first of the twelve historical books (Joshua–Esther), forges a link between the Pentateuch and the remainder of Israel's history. Through three major military campaigns involving more than thirty enemy armies, the people of Israel learn a crucial lesson under Joshua's capable leadership: victory comes through faith in God and obedience to His word, rather than through military might or numerical superiority.

The title of this book is appropriately named after its central figure, Joshua. His original name is *Hoshea*, "Salvation" (Num. 13:8); but Moses evidently changes it to *Yehoshua*, "Yahweh Is Salvation" (Num. 13:16). He is also called *Yeshua*, a shortened form of *Yehoshua*. This is the Hebrew equivalent of the Greek name *Iesous* (Jesus). Thus, the Greek title given to the book in the Septuagint is *Iesous Naus,* "Joshua the Son of Nun." The Latin title is *Liber Josue,* the "Book of Joshua."

His name is symbolic of the fact that although he is the leader of the Israelite nation during the conquest, the Lord is the Conqueror.

NOW after the death of Moses the servant of the LORD it came to pass, that the LORD spake unto Joshua the son of Nun, Moses' ᴿminister, saying,   Acts 7:45

2 ᴿMoses my servant is dead; now therefore arise, go over this Jordan, thou, and all this people, unto the land which I do give to them, *even* to the children of Israel.   Num. 12:7; Deut. 34:5

3 ᴿEvery place that the sole of your foot shall tread upon, that have I given unto you, as I said unto Moses.   11:23; Deut. 11:24

4 ᴿFrom the wilderness and this Leb'-a-non even unto the great river, the river Eu-phra'-tes, all the land of the Hit'-tites, and unto the great sea toward the going down of the sun, shall be your coast.   Gen. 15:18; Num. 34:3–12

5 There shall not any man be able to stand before thee all the days of thy life: as I was with Moses, *so* I will be with thee: I will not fail thee, nor forsake thee.

6 ᴿBe strong and of a good courage: for unto this people shalt thou divide for an inheritance the land, which I sware unto their fathers to give them.   Deut. 31:7, 23

7 Only be thou strong and very courageous, that thou mayest observe to do according to all the law, ᴿwhich Moses my servant commanded thee: turn not from it *to* the right hand or *to* the left, that thou mayest prosper whithersoever thou goest.   11:15; Num. 27:23

8 ᴿThis book of the law shall not depart out of thy mouth; but ᴿthou shalt meditate therein day and night, that thou mayest observe to do according to all that is written therein: for then thou shalt make thy way prosperous,

and then thou shalt have good success.   8:34; Deut. 17:18, 19 · Ps. 1:1–3

9 ᴿHave not I commanded thee? Be strong and of a good courage; ᴿbe not afraid, neither be thou dismayed: for the LORD thy God *is* with thee whithersoever thou goest.   Deut. 31:7 · Ps. 27:1

10 Then Joshua commanded the officers of the people, saying,

11 Pass through the host, and command the people, saying, Prepare you victuals; for ᴿwithin three days ye shall pass over this Jordan, to go in to possess the land, which the LORD your God giveth you to possess it.   Deut. 9:1

12 And to the Reu'-ben-ites, and to the Gad'-ites, and to half the tribe of Ma-nas'-seh, spake Joshua, saying,

13 Remember the word which Moses the servant of the LORD commanded you, saying, The LORD your God hath given you rest, and hath given you this land.

14 Your wives, your little ones, and your cattle, shall remain in the land which Moses gave you on this side Jordan; but ye shall ᵀpass before your brethren armed, all the mighty men of valour, and help them;   *cross over ahead of*

15 Until the LORD have given your brethren rest, as *he hath given* you, and they also have possessed the land which the LORD your God giveth them: ᴿthen ye shall return unto the land of your possession, and enjoy it, which Moses the LORD's servant gave you on this side Jordan toward the sunrising.   22:1–4

16 And they answered Joshua, saying, All that thou commandest us we will do, and whithersoever thou sendest us, we will go.

17 According as we hearkened

unto Moses in all things, so will we hearken unto thee: only the LORD thy God ᴿbe with thee, as he was with Moses.   1 Sam. 20:13

18 Whosoever *he be* that doth rebel against thy commandment, and will not hearken unto thy words in all that thou commandest him, he shall be put to death: only be strong and of a good courage.

2 And Joshua the son of Nun sent out of Shit'-tim two men to spy secretly, saying, Go view the land, even Jericho. And they went, and came into an harlot's house, named Ra'-hab, and lodged there.

2 And ᴿit was told the king of Jericho, saying, Behold, there came men in ᵀhither to night of the children of Israel to search out the country.   v. 22 · here

3 And the king of Jericho sent unto Ra'-hab, saying, Bring forth the men that are come to thee, which are entered into thine house: for they be come to search out all the country.

4 And the woman took the two men, and hid them, and said thus, There came men unto me, but I wist not whence they *were:*

5 And it came to pass *about the time* of shutting of the gate, when it was dark, that the men went out: whither the men went I wot not: pursue after them quickly; for ye shall overtake them.

6 But ᴿshe had brought them up to the roof of the house, and hid them with the stalks of flax, which she had laid in order upon the roof.   Ex. 1:17; 2 Sam. 17:19

7 And the men pursued after them the way to Jordan unto the fords: and as soon as they which pursued after them were gone out, they shut the gate.

8 And before they were laid down, she came up unto them upon the roof;

9 And she said unto the men, I know that the LORD hath given you the land, and that ᴿyour terror is fallen upon us, and that all the inhabitants of the land ᴿfaint because of you.   Deut. 11:25 · Ex. 15:15

10 For we have heard how the LORD ᴿdried up the water of the Red sea for you, when ye came out of Egypt; and what ye did unto the two kings of the Am'-or-ites, that *were* on the other side Jordan, Si'-hon and Og, whom ye utterly destroyed.   4:23; Ex. 14:21

11 And as soon as we had heard *these things,* ᴿour hearts did melt, neither did there remain any more courage in any man, because of you: for the LORD your God, he *is* God in heaven above, and in earth beneath.   5:1; 7:5; Is. 13:7

12 Now therefore, I pray you, ᴿswear unto me by the LORD, since I have shewed you kindness, that ye will also shew kindness unto my father's house, and ᴿgive me a true token: 1 Sam. 20:14, 15, 17 · 2:18

13 And *that* ye will save ᴿalive my father, and my mother, and my brethren, and my sisters, and all that they have, and deliver our lives from death.   6:23–25

14 And the men answered her, Our life for yours, if ye utter not this our business. And it shall be, when the LORD hath given us the land, that ᴿwe will deal kindly and truly with thee.   Judg. 1:24; [Matt. 5:7]

15 Then she let them down by a cord through the window: for her house *was* upon the town wall, and she dwelt upon the wall.

16 And she said unto them, Get you to the mountain, lest the pursuers meet you; and hide yourselves there three days, until the pursuers be returned: and afterward may ye go your way.

17 And the men said unto her, We *will be* ᴿblameless of this thine oath which thou hast made us swear.   Ex. 20:7

18 ᴿBehold, *when* we come into the land, thou shalt bind this line of scarlet thread in the window which thou didst let us down by: ᴿand thou shalt bring thy father, and thy mother, and thy brethren, and all thy father's household, home unto thee.   v. 12 · 6:23

19 And it shall be, *that* whosoever shall go out of the doors of

thy house into the street, his blood *shall be* upon his head, and we *will be* guiltless: and whosoever shall be with thee in the house, ^Rhis blood *shall be* on our head, if *any* hand be upon him.   Matt. 27:25

20 And if thou utter this our business, then we will be ^Tquit of thine oath which thou hast made us to swear.   *free from obligation to*

21 And she said, According unto your words, so *be* it. And she sent them away, and they departed: and she bound the scarlet line in the window.

22 And they went, and came unto the mountain, and abode there three days, until the pursuers were returned: and the pursuers sought *them* throughout all the way, but found *them* not.

23 So the two men returned, and descended from the mountain, and passed over, and came to Joshua the son of Nun, and told him all *things* that befell them:

24 And they said unto Joshua, Truly ^Rthe LORD hath delivered into our hands all the land; for even all the inhabitants of the country do faint because of us.   6:2; Ex. 23:31

3 And Joshua rose early in the morning; and they removed ^Rfrom ^TShit'-tim, and came to Jordan, he and all the children of Israel, and lodged there before they passed over.   2:1 · Lit. *Acacia Grove*

2 And it came to pass ^Rafter three days, that the officers went through the host;   1:10, 11

3 And they commanded the people, saying, ^RWhen ye see the ark of the covenant of the LORD your God, ^Rand the priests the Levites bearing it, then ye shall remove from your place, and go after it.   Num. 10:33 · Deut. 31:9, 25

4 ^RYet there shall be a space between you and it, about two thousand cubits by measure: come not near unto it, that ye may know the way by which ye must go: for ye have not passed *this* way ^Theretofore.   Ex. 19:12 · *before*

5 And Joshua said unto the people, ^RSanctify yourselves: for to morrow the LORD will do wonders among you.   Lev. 20:7; Joel 2:16

6 And Joshua spake unto the priests, saying, ^RTake up the ark of the covenant, and pass over before the people. And they took up the ark of the covenant, and went before the people.   Num. 4:15

7 And the LORD said unto Joshua, This day will I begin to ^Rmagnify thee in the sight of all Israel, that they may know that, ^Ras I was with Moses, *so* I will be with thee.   4:14; 1 Chr. 29:25 · 1:5, 9

8 And thou shalt command ^Rthe priests that bear the ark of the covenant, saying, When ye are come to the brink of the water of Jordan, ^Rye shall stand still in Jordan.   v. 3 · v. 17

9 And Joshua said unto the children of Israel, Come hither, and hear the words of the LORD your God.

10 And Joshua said, Hereby ye shall know that ^Rthe living God *is* among you, and *that* he will without fail ^Rdrive out from before you the Ca'-naan-ites, and the Hit'-tites, and the Hi'-vites, and the Per'-iz-zites, and the Gir'-ga-shites, and the Am'-or-ites, and the Jeb'-u-sites.   1 Thess. 1:9 · Ex. 33:2

11 Behold, the ark of the covenant of ^Rthe Lord of all the earth passeth over before you into Jordan.   v. 13; Job 41:11; Mic. 4:13; Zech. 6:5

12 Now therefore take you twelve men out of the tribes of Israel, out of every tribe a man.

13 And it shall come to pass, as soon as the soles of the feet of the priests that bear the ark of the LORD, the Lord of all the earth, shall rest in the waters of Jordan, *that* the waters of Jordan shall be cut off *from* the waters that come down from above; and they ^Rshall stand upon an heap.   Ps. 78:13; 114:3

14 And it came to pass, when the people removed from their tents, to pass over Jordan, and the priests bearing the ark of the covenant before the people;

15 And as they that bare the ark were come unto Jordan, and the

feet of the priests that bare the ark were dipped in the brim of the water, (for Jordan overfloweth all his banks all the time of harvest,)

16 That the waters which came down from above stood *and* rose up upon an heap very far from the city Adam, that *is* beside ᴿZar'-e-tan: and those that came down toward the sea of the plain, *even* the salt sea, failed, *and* were cut off: and the people passed over right against Jericho. 1 Kin. 4:12; 7:46

17 And the priests that bare the ark of the covenant of the LORD stood firm on dry ground in the midst of Jordan, ᴿand all the Is-raelites passed over on dry ground, until all the people were passed clean over Jordan. Ex. 3:8

4 And it came to pass, when all the people were clean passed ᴿover Jordan, that the LORD spake unto Joshua, saying, 3:17; Deut. 27:2

2 ᴿTake you twelve men out of the people, out of every tribe a man, 3:12

3 And command ye them, say-ing, Take you hence out of the midst of Jordan, out of the place where the priests' feet stood firm, twelve stones, and ye shall carry them over with you, and leave them in ᴿthe lodging place, where ye shall lodge this night. vv. 19, 20

4 Then Joshua called the twelve men, whom he had pre-pared of the children of Israel, out of every tribe a man:

5 And Joshua said unto them, Pass over before the ark of the LORD your God into the midst of Jordan, and take ye up every man of you a stone upon his shoulder, according unto the number of the tribes of the chil-dren of Israel:

6 That this may be ᴿa sign among you, *that* ᴿwhen your chil-dren ask *their fathers* in time to come, saying, What *mean* ye by these stones? Deut. 27:2 · Deut. 6:20

7 Then ye shall answer them, That ᴿthe waters of Jordan were cut off before the ark of the covenant of the LORD; when it

passed over Jordan, the waters of Jordan were cut off: and these stones shall be for ᴿa memorial unto the children of Israel for ever. 3:13, 16 · Ex. 12:14; Num. 16:40

8 And the children of Israel did so as Joshua commanded, and took up twelve stones out of the midst of Jordan, as the LORD spake unto Joshua, according to the number of the tribes of the children of Israel, and carried them over with them unto the place where they lodged, and laid them down there.

9 And Joshua set up twelve stones in the midst of Jordan, in the place where the feet of the priests which bare the ark of the covenant stood: and they are there unto this day.

10 For the priests which bare the ark stood in the midst of Jordan, until every thing was finished that the LORD commanded Joshua to speak unto the people, according to all that Moses commanded Joshua: and the people ᵀhasted and passed over. *hurried*

11 And it came to pass, when all the people were clean passed over, that the ᴿark of the LORD passed over, and the priests, in the presence of the people. 3:11; 6:11

12 And the children of Reuben, and the children of Gad, and half the tribe of Ma-nas'-seh, passed over armed before the children of Israel, as Moses spake unto them:

13 About forty thousand ᵀpre-pared for war passed over before the LORD unto battle, to the plains of Jericho. *equipped*

14 On that day the LORD ᴿmag-nified Joshua in the sight of all Israel; and they ᵀfeared him, as they feared Moses, all the days of his life. 3:7; 1 Chr. 29:25 · *revered*

15 And the LORD spake unto Joshua, saying,

16 Command the priests that bear the ark of the testimony, that they come up out of Jordan.

17 Joshua therefore command-ed the priests, saying, Come ye up out of Jordan.

18 And it came to pass, when the priests that bare the ark of the covenant of the LORD were come up out of the midst of Jordan, *and* the soles of the priests' feet were lifted up unto the dry land, that the waters of Jordan returned unto their place, and flowed over all his banks, as *they did* before.

19 And the people came up out of Jordan on the tenth *day* of the first month, and encamped ^Rin Gil'-gal, in the east border of Jericho.   5:9

20 And ^Rthose twelve stones, which they took out of Jordan, did Joshua pitch in Gil'-gal. Deut. 11:30

21 And he spake unto the children of Israel, saying, ^RWhen your children shall ask their fathers in time to come, saying, What *mean* these stones?   v. 6

22 Then ye shall let your children know, saying, Israel came over this Jordan on ^Rdry land. 3:17

23 For the LORD your God dried up the waters of Jordan from before you, until ye were passed over, as the LORD your God did to the Red sea, ^Rwhich he dried up from before us, until we were gone over: Ex. 14:21

24 ^RThat all the people of the earth might know the hand of the LORD, that it *is* ^Rmighty: that ye might ^Rfear the LORD your God for ever.   Ps. 106:8 · Ps. 89:13 · Ps. 76:7

5 And it came to pass, when all the kings of the Am'-or-ites, which *were* on the side of Jordan westward, and all the kings of the Ca'-naan-ites, which *were* by the sea, heard that the LORD had dried up the waters of Jordan from before the children of Israel, until we were passed over, that their heart melted, ^Rneither was there spirit in them any more, because of the children of Israel.   1 Kin. 10:5

2 At that time the LORD said unto Joshua, Make thee sharp knives, and circumcise again the children of Israel the second time.

3 And Joshua made him sharp knives, and circumcised the chil-

dren of Israel at ^Tthe hill of the foreskins.   Heb. *Gibeath-haaraloth*

4 And this *is* the cause why Joshua did circumcise: ^RAll the people that came out of Egypt, *that were* males, *even* all the men of war, died in the wilderness by the way, after they came out of Egypt.   Num. 26:64, 65; Deut. 2:14–16

5 Now all the people that came out were circumcised: but all the people *that were* born in the wilderness by the way as they came forth out of Egypt, *them* they had not circumcised.

6 For the children of Israel walked ^Rforty years in the wilderness, till all the people *that were* men of war, which came out of Egypt, were consumed, because they obeyed not the voice of the LORD: unto whom the LORD sware that ^Rhe would not shew them the land, which the LORD sware unto their fathers that he would give us, a land that floweth with milk and honey.   Num. 14:33 · Heb. 3:11

7 And their children, *whom* he raised up in their stead, them Joshua circumcised: for they were uncircumcised, because they had not circumcised them by the way.

8 And it came to pass, when they had done circumcising all the people, that they abode in their places in the camp, ^Rtill they were ^Twhole.   Gen. 34:25 · *healed*

9 And the LORD said unto Joshua, This day have I rolled away ^Rthe reproach of Egypt from off you. Wherefore the name of the place is called ^RGil'-gal^T unto this day.   Gen. 34:14 · 4:19 · Lit. *Rolling*

10 And the children of Israel encamped in Gil'-gal, and kept the passover ^Ron the fourteenth day of the month at even in the plains of Jericho.   Ex. 12:6; Num. 9:5

11 And they did eat of the ^Told corn of the land on the morrow after the passover, unleavened cakes, and ^Tparched *corn* in the selfsame day.   *produce · roasted grain*

12 And ^Rthe man'-na ceased on the morrow after they had eaten of the old corn of the land; neither

had the children of Israel man'-na any more; but they did eat of the fruit of the land of Canaan that year.   Ex. 16:35

13 And it came to pass, when Joshua was by Jericho, that he lifted up his eyes and looked, and, behold, there stood ᴿa man ᵀover against him ᴿwith his sword drawn in his hand: and Joshua went unto him, and said unto him, *Art* thou for us, or for our adversaries?   Zech. 1:8 · *opposite* · Num. 22:23

14 And he said, Nay; but *as* captain of the host of the LORD am I now come. And Joshua ᴿfell on his face to the earth, and did ᴿworship, and said unto him, What saith my lord unto his servant?   Gen. 17:3; Num. 20:6 · Ex. 34:8

15 And the captain of the LORD's host said unto Joshua, ᴿLoose thy shoe from off thy foot; for the place whereon thou standest *is* holy. And Joshua did so.   Ex. 3:5

6 Now ᴿJericho was ᵀstraitly shut up because of the children of Israel: none went out, and none came in.   2:1 · *securely*

2 And the LORD said unto Joshua, See, I have given into thine hand Jericho, and the king thereof, *and* the mighty men of valour.

3 And ye shall ᵀcompass the city, all *ye* men of war, *and* go round about the city once. Thus shalt thou do six days. *march around*

4 And seven priests shall bear before the ark seven trumpets of rams' horns: and the seventh day ye shall compass the city ᴿseven times, and the priests shall blow with the trumpets.   1 Kin. 18:43

5 And it shall come to pass, that when they make a long *blast* with the ram's horn, *and* when ye hear the sound of the trumpet, all the people shall shout with a great shout; and the wall of the city shall fall down flat, and the people shall ᵀascend up every man straight before him. Lit. *go up*

6 And Joshua the son of Nun called the priests, and said unto them, Take up the ark of the covenant, and let seven priests

bear seven trumpets of rams' horns before the ark of the LORD.

7 And he said unto the people, Pass on, and compass the city, and let him that is armed pass on before the ark of the LORD.

8 And it came to pass, when Joshua had spoken unto the people, that the seven priests bearing the seven trumpets of rams' horns passed on before the LORD, and blew with the trumpets: and the ark of the covenant of the LORD followed them.

9 And the armed men went before the priests that blew with the trumpets, ᴿand the ᵀrereward came after the ark, *the priests* going on, and blowing with the trumpets.   Num. 10:25 · *rear guard*

10 And Joshua had commanded the people, saying, Ye shall not shout, nor make any noise with your voice, neither shall *any* word proceed out of your mouth, until the day I bid you shout; then shall ye shout.

11 So the ark of the LORD compassed the city, going about *it* once: and they came into the camp, and lodged in the camp.

12 And Joshua rose early in the morning, ᴿand the priests took up the ark of the LORD.   Deut. 31:25

13 And seven priests bearing seven trumpets of rams' horns before the ark of the LORD went on continually, and blew with the trumpets: and the armed men went before them; but the rereward came after the ark of the LORD, *the priests* going on, and blowing with the trumpets.

14 And the second day they compassed the city once, and returned into the camp: so they did six days.

15 And it came to pass on the seventh day, that they rose early about the dawning of the day, and compassed the city after the same manner seven times: only on that day they compassed the city seven times.

16 And it came to pass at the seventh time, when the priests blew with the trumpets, Joshua said unto the people, Shout; for the LORD hath given you the city.

17 And the city shall be ^Raccursed, *even* it, and all that *are* therein, to the LORD: only ^RRa'-hab the harlot shall live, she and all that *are* with her in the house, because she hid the messengers that we sent.   Deut. 13:17 · Matt. 1:5

18 And ye, in any wise keep *yourselves* from the accursed thing, lest ye make *yourselves* accursed, when ye take of the accursed thing, and make the camp of Israel a curse, and trouble it.

19 But all the silver, and gold, and vessels of brass and iron, *are* ^Tconsecrated unto the LORD: they ^Tshall come into the treasury of the LORD.   *set apart · shall go*

20 So the people shouted when *the priests* blew with the trumpets: and it came to pass, when the people heard the sound of the trumpet, and the people shouted with a great shout, that ^Rthe wall fell down flat, so that the people went up into the city, every man straight before him, and they took the city.   Heb. 11:30

21 And they ^Rutterly destroyed all that *was* in the city, both man and woman, young and old, and ox, and sheep, and ass, with the edge of the sword.   Deut. 7:2; 20:16, 17

22 But Joshua had said unto the two men that had spied out the country, Go into the harlot's house, and bring out thence the woman, and all that she hath, ^Ras ye sware unto her.   2:12–19; Heb. 11:31

23 And the young men that were spies went in, and brought out Ra'-hab, ^Rand her father, and her mother, and her brethren, and all that she had; and they brought out all her kindred, and left them without the camp of Israel.   2:13

24 And they burnt the city with fire, and all that *was* therein: only the silver, and the gold, and the vessels of brass and of iron, they put into the treasury of the house of the LORD.

25 And Joshua saved Ra'-hab the harlot alive, and her father's household, and all that she had; and ^Rshe dwelleth in Israel *even* unto this day; because she hid the messengers, which Joshua sent to spy out Jericho.   [Matt. 1:5]

26 And Joshua ^Tadjured *them* at that time, saying, ^RCursed *be* the man before the LORD, that riseth up and buildeth this city Jericho: he shall lay the foundation thereof in his firstborn, and in his youngest *son* shall he set up the gates of it.   *warned* · 1 Kin. 16:34

27 So the LORD was with Joshua; and his fame was *noised* throughout all the country.

7 But the children of Israel committed a ^Rtrespass in the ^Raccursed thing: for ^RA'-chan, the son of Car'-mi, the son of Zab'-di, the son of Ze'-rah, of the tribe of Judah, took of the accursed thing: and the anger of the LORD was kindled against the children of Israel.   vv. 20, 21 · 6:17–19 · 22:20

2 And Joshua sent men from Jericho to A'-i, which *is* beside Beth–a'-ven, on the east side of Beth'–el, and spake unto them, saying, Go up and ^Tview the country. And the men went up and viewed A'-i.   *spy out*

3 And they returned to Joshua, and said unto him, Let not all the people go up; but let about two or three thousand men go up and smite A'-i; *and* make not all the people to labour thither; for they *are but* few.

4 So there went up thither of the people about three thousand men: ^Rand they fled before the men of A'-i.   Lev. 26:17; Deut. 28:25

5 And the men of A'-i smote of them about thirty and six men: for they chased *them from* before the gate *even* unto Sheb'-a-rim, and smote them in the going down: wherefore the hearts of the people melted, and became as water.

6 And Joshua ^Rrent^T his clothes, and fell to the earth upon his face before the ark of the LORD

until the eventide, he and the elders of Israel, and put dust upon their heads. Gen. 37:29, 34 · *tore*

7 And Joshua said, Alas, O Lord GOD, ^Rwherefore hast thou at all brought this people over Jordan, to deliver us into the hand of the Am'-or-ites, to destroy us? would to God we had been content, and dwelt on the other side Jordan! Ex. 17:3; Num. 21:5

8 O Lord, what shall I say, when Israel turneth their ^Tbacks before their enemies! Lit. *necks*

9 For the Ca'-naan-ites and all the inhabitants of the land shall hear *of it*, and shall environ us round, and ^Rcut off our name from the earth: and what wilt thou do unto thy great name? Deut. 32:26

10 And the LORD said unto Joshua, Get thee up; wherefore liest thou thus upon thy face?

11 Israel hath sinned, and they have also transgressed my covenant which I commanded them: ^Rfor they have even taken of the accursed thing, and have also stolen, and ^Rdissembled^T also, and they have put *it* even among their own stuff. 6:17–19 · Acts 5:1, 2 · *deceived*

12 ^RTherefore the children of Israel could not stand before their enemies, *but* turned *their* backs before their enemies, because ^Rthey were accursed: neither will I be with you any more, except ye destroy the accursed from among you. Judg. 2:14 · Deut. 7:26; [Hag. 2:13, 14]

13 Up, ^Rsanctify^T the people, and say, ^RSanctify yourselves against to morrow: for thus saith the LORD God of Israel, *There is* an accursed thing in the midst of thee, O Israel: thou canst not stand before thine enemies, until ye take away the accursed thing from among you. Ex. 19:10 · *consecrate* · 3:5

14 In the morning therefore ye shall be brought according to your tribes: and it shall be, *that* the tribe which ^Rthe LORD taketh shall come according to the families *thereof*; and the family which the LORD shall take shall come by households; and the household

which the LORD shall take shall come man by man. [Prov. 16:33]

15 And it shall be, *that* he that is taken with the accursed thing shall be burnt with fire, he and all that he hath: because he hath transgressed the covenant of the LORD, and because he ^Rhath wrought folly in Israel. Judg. 20:6

16 So Joshua rose up early in the morning, and brought Israel by their tribes; and the tribe of Judah was taken:

17 And he brought the family of Judah; and he took the family of the Zar'-hites: and he brought the family of the Zar'-hites man by man; and Zab'-di was taken:

18 And he brought his household man by man; and A'-chan, the son of Car'-mi, the son of Zab'-di, the son of Ze'-rah, of the tribe of Judah, was taken.

19 And Joshua said unto A'-chan, My son, ^Rgive, I pray thee, glory to the LORD God of Israel, and make confession unto him; and tell me now what thou hast done; hide *it* not from me. John 9:24

20 And A'-chan answered Joshua, and said, Indeed ^RI have sinned against the LORD God of Israel, and thus and thus have I done: Num. 22:34; 1 Sam. 15:24

21 When I saw among the spoils a goodly Bab-y-lo'-nish garment, and two hundred shek'-els of silver, and a wedge of gold of fifty shek'-els weight, then I ^Tcoveted them, and took them; and, behold, they *are* hid in the earth in the midst of my tent, and the silver under it. *desired*

22 So Joshua sent messengers, and they ran unto the tent; and, behold, *it was* hid in his tent, and the silver under it.

23 And they took them out of the midst of the tent, and brought them unto Joshua, and unto all the children of Israel, and laid them out before the LORD.

24 And Joshua, and all Israel with him, took A'-chan the son of Ze'-rah, and the silver, and the garment, and the wedge of gold,

and his sons, and his daughters, and his oxen, and his asses, and his sheep, and his tent, and all that he had: and they brought them unto the valley of A'-chor.

25 And Joshua said, Why hast thou troubled us? the LORD shall trouble thee this day. And all Israel stoned him with stones, and burned them with fire, after they had stoned them with stones.

26 And they ᴿraised over him a great heap of stones unto this day. So ᴿthe LORD turned from the fierceness of his anger. Wherefore the name of that place was called, ᴿThe valley of A'-chor, unto this day.   2 Sam. 18:17 · Deut. 13:17 · Is. 65:10

8 And the LORD said unto Joshua, Fear not, neither be thou dismayed: take all the people of war with thee, and arise, go up to A'-i: see, ᴿI have given into thy hand the king of A'-i, and his people, and his city, and his land: 6:2

2 And thou shalt do to A'-i and her king as thou didst unto ᴿJericho and her king: only ᴿthe spoil thereof, and the cattle thereof, shall ye take for a prey unto yourselves: lay thee an ambush for the city behind it.   6:21 · v. 27; Deut. 20:14

3 So Joshua arose, and all the people of war, to go up against A'-i: and Joshua chose out thirty thousand mighty men of valour, and sent them away by night.

4 And he commanded them, saying, Behold, ᴿye shall lie in wait against the city, even behind the city: go not very far from the city, but be ye all ready: Judg. 20:29

5 And I, and all the people that are with me, will approach unto the city: and it shall come to pass, when they come out against us, as at the first, that ᴿwe will flee before them,   7:5; Judg. 20:32

6 (For they will come out after us) till we have drawn them from the city; for they will say, They flee before us, as at the first: therefore we will flee before them.

7 Then ye shall rise up from the ambush, and seize upon the city:

for the LORD your God will deliver it into your hand.

8 And it shall be, when ye have taken the city, that ye shall set the city on fire: according to the commandment of the LORD shall ye do. See, I have commanded you.

9 Joshua therefore sent them forth: and they went to lie in ambush, and abode between Beth'-el and A'-i, on the west side of A'-i: but Joshua lodged that night among the people.

10 And Joshua rose up early in the morning, and ᵀnumbered the people, and went up, he and the elders of Israel, before the people to A'-i.   mustered

11 ᴿAnd all the people, even the people of war that were with him, went up, and drew nigh, and came before the city, and ᵀpitched on the north side of A'-i: now there was a valley between them and A'-i.   v. 5 · camped

12 And he took about five thousand men, and set them to lie in ambush between Beth'-el and A'-i, on the west side of the city.

13 And when they had set the people, even all the host that was on the north of the city, and ᵀtheir liers in wait on the west of the city, Joshua went that night into the midst of the valley.   its rear guard

14 And it came to pass, when the king of A'-i saw it, that they hasted and rose up early, and the men of the city went out against Israel to battle, he and all his people, at a time appointed, before the plain; but he wist not that there were liers in ambush against him behind the city.

15 And Joshua and all Israel ᴿmade as if they were beaten before them, and fled by the way of the wilderness.   Judg. 20:36

16 And all the people that were in A'-i were called together to pursue after them: and they pursued after Joshua, and were drawn away from the city.

17 And there was not a man left in A'-i or Beth'-el, that went not out after Israel: and they left the

city open, and pursued after Israel.

18 And the LORD said unto Joshua, Stretch out the spear that *is* in thy hand toward A'-i; for I will give it into thine hand. And Joshua stretched out the spear that *he had* in his hand toward the city.

19 And the ambush arose quickly out of their place, and they ran as soon as he had stretched out his hand: and they entered into the city, and took it, and ᵀhasted and set the city on fire.   *hurried*

20 And when the men of A'-i looked behind them, they saw, and, behold, the smoke of the city ascended up to heaven, and they had no power to flee this way or that way: and the people that fled to the wilderness turned back upon the pursuers.

21 And when Joshua and all Israel saw that the ambush had taken the city, and that the smoke of the city ascended, then they turned again, and slew the men of A'-i.

22 And the other issued out of the city against them; so they were in the midst of Israel, some on this side, and some on that side: and they ᵀsmote them, so that they ᴿlet none of them remain or escape.   *struck them down* · Deut. 7:2

23 And the king of A'-i they took alive, and brought him to Joshua.

24 And it came to pass, when Israel had made an end of slaying all the inhabitants of A'-i in the field, in the wilderness wherein they chased them, and when they were all fallen ᵀon the edge of the sword, until they were consumed, that all the Israelites returned unto A'-i, and ᵀsmote it with the edge of the sword.   *Or by · struck*

25 And *so* it was, *that* all that fell that day, both of men and women, *were* twelve thousand, *even* all the men of A'-i.

26 For Joshua drew not his hand back, wherewith he stretched out the spear, until he had ᴿutterly

destroyed all the inhabitants of A'-i.   6:21

27 ᴿOnly the cattle and the spoil of that city Israel took for a prey unto themselves, according unto the word of the LORD which he commanded Joshua.   Num. 31:22, 26

28 And Joshua burnt A'-i, and made it ᴿan heap for ever, *even* a desolation unto this day. Deut. 13:16

29 ᴿAnd the king of A'-i he hanged on a tree until eventide: ᴿand as soon as the sun was down, Joshua commanded that they should take his carcase down from the tree, and cast it at the entering of the gate of the city, and ᴿraise thereon a great heap of stones, *that remaineth* unto this day.   10:26 · Deut. 21:22, 23 · 7:26; 10:27

30 Then Joshua built an altar unto the LORD God of Israel ᴿin mount E'-bal.   Deut. 27:4–8

31 As Moses the servant of the LORD commanded the children of Israel, as it is written in the book of the law of Moses, ᴿan altar of whole stones, over which no man hath lift up *any* iron: and ᴿthey offered thereon burnt offerings unto the LORD, and sacrificed peace offerings. Deut. 27:5, 6 · Ex. 20:24

32 And ᴿhe wrote there upon the stones a copy of the law of Moses, which he wrote in the presence of the children of Israel.   Deut. 27:2, 3, 8

33 And all Israel, and their elders, and officers, and their judges, stood on this side the ark and on that side before the priests the Levites, ᴿwhich bare the ark of the covenant of the LORD, as well ᴿthe stranger, as he that was born among them; half of them over against mount Ger'-i-zim, and half of them over against mount E'-bal; as Moses the servant of the LORD had commanded before, that they should bless the people of Israel.   Deut. 31:9, 25 · Deut. 31:12

34 And afterward ᴿhe read all the words of the law, ᴿthe blessings and cursings, according to all that is written in the book of the law.   Neh. 8:3 · Deut. 28:2, 15, 45; 29:20, 21

35 There was not a word of all

that Moses commanded, which Joshua read not before all the congregation of Israel, Rwith the women, and the little ones, and the strangers that were Tconversant among them.   Ex. 12:38 · *living*

9 And it came to pass, when all the kings which *were* on this side Jordan, in the hills, and in the valleys, and in all the coasts of the great sea over against Leb'-a-non, Rthe Hit'-tite, and the Am'-or-ite, the Ca'-naan-ite, the Per'-iz-zite, the Hi'-vite, and the Jeb'-u-site, heard *thereof;*   Ex. 3:17

2 That they Rgathered themselves together, to fight with Joshua and with Israel, with one Taccord.   10:5; Ps. 83:3, 5 · *mouth*

3 And when the inhabitants of Gib'-e-on heard what Joshua had done unto Jericho and to A'-i,

4 They did work Twilily, and went and made as if they had been ambassadors, and took old sacks upon their asses, and wine bottles, old, and Trent, and Tbound up;   *craftily · torn · mended,* lit. *tied up*

5 And old shoes and Tclouted upon their feet, and old garments upon them; and all the bread of their provision was dry *and* mouldy.   *patched*

6 And they went to Joshua Runto the camp at Gil'-gal, and said unto him, and to the men of Israel, We be come from a far country: now therefore make ye a Tleague with us.   5:10 · *treaty*

7 And the men of Israel said unto the Hi'-vites, Peradventure ye dwell among us; and how shall we make a league with you?

8 And they said unto Joshua, RWe *are* thy servants. And Joshua said unto them, Who *are* ye? and from whence come ye?   Deut. 20:11

9 And they said unto him, RFrom a very far country thy servants are come because of the name of the LORD thy God: for we have heard the fame of him, and all that he did in Egypt,   Deut. 20:15

10 And Rall that he did to the two kings of the Am'-or-ites, that *were* beyond Jordan, to Si'-hon king of Hesh'-bon, and to Og king of Ba'-shan, which *was* at Ash'-ta-roth.   Num. 21:24, 33

11 Wherefore our elders and all the inhabitants of our country spake to us, saying, Take victuals with you for the journey, and go to meet them, and say unto them, We *are* your servants: therefore now make ye a Tleague with us.   *treaty*

12 This our bread we took hot *for* our provision out of our houses on the day we came forth to go unto you; but now, behold, it is dry, and it is mouldy:

13 And these bottles of wine, which we filled, *were* new; and, behold, they be Trent: and these our garments and our shoes are become old by reason of the very long journey.   *torn*

14 And the men took of their victuals, Rand asked not *counsel* at the mouth of the LORD.   Is. 30:1

15 And Joshua Rmade peace with them, and made a Tleague with them, to let them live: and the princes of the congregation sware unto them.   2 Sam. 21:2 · *treaty*

16 And it came to pass at the end of three days after they had made a league with them, that they heard that they *were* their neighbours, and *that* they dwelt among them.

17 And the children of Israel journeyed, and came unto their cities on the third day. Now their cities *were* RGib'-e-on, and Che-phi'-rah, and Be-e'-roth, and Kir'-jath–je'-a-rim.   18:25

18 And the children of Israel smote them not, because the princes of the congregation had sworn unto them by the LORD God of Israel. And all the congregation murmured against the princes.

19 But all the princes said unto all the congregation, We have sworn unto them by the LORD God of Israel: now therefore we may not touch them.

20 This we will do to them; we will even let them live, lest wrath be upon us, because of the oath which we sware unto them.

21 And the princes said unto them, Let them live; but let them be ᴿhewers of wood and drawers of water unto all the congregation; as the princes had ᴿpromised them. Deut. 29:11 · v. 15

22 And Joshua called for them, and he spake unto them, saying, Wherefore have ye beguiled us, saying, ᴿWe *are* very far from you; when ye dwell among us? vv. 6, 9

23 Now therefore ye *are* cursed, and there shall none of you be freed from being bondmen, and hewers of wood and drawers of water for the house of my God.

24 And they answered Joshua, and said, Because it was certainly told thy servants, how that the LORD thy God ᴿcommanded his servant Moses to give you all the land, and to destroy all the inhabitants of the land from before you, therefore ᴿwe were sore afraid of our lives because of you, and have done this thing. Deut. 7:1, 2 · Ex. 15:14

25 And now, behold, we *are* ᴿin thine hand: as it seemeth good and right unto thee to do unto us, do. Gen. 16:6

26 And so did he unto them, and delivered them out of the hand of the children of Israel, that they slew them not.

27 And Joshua made them that day hewers of wood and drawers of water for the congregation, and for the altar of the LORD, even unto this day, ᴿin the place which he should choose. Deut. 12:5

10 Now it came to pass, when Ad-o′-ni–ze′-dek king of Je-rusalem had ᴿheard how Joshua had taken A′-i, and had utterly destroyed it; ᴿas he had done to Jericho and her king, so he had done to A′-i and her king; and ᴿhow the inhabitants of Gib′-e-on had made peace with Israel, and were among them; 9:1 · 6:21 · 9:15

2 That they feared greatly, because Gib′-e-on *was* a great city, as one of the royal cities, and because it *was* greater than A′-i, and all the men thereof *were* mighty.

3 Wherefore Ad-o′-ni–ze′-dek king of Jerusalem sent unto Ho′-ham king of He′-bron, and unto Pi′-ram king of Jar′-muth, and unto Ja-phi′-a king of La′-chish, and unto De′-bir king of Eg′-lon, saying,

4 Come up unto me, and help me, that we may ᵀsmite Gib′-e-on: for ᴿit hath made peace with Joshua and with the children of Israel. *attack* · v. 1; 9:15

5 Therefore the five kings of the Am′-or-ites, the king of Je-rusalem, the king of He′-bron, the king of Jar′-muth, the king of La′-chish, the king of Eg′-lon, ᴿgathered themselves together, and went up, they and all their hosts, and encamped before Gib′-e-on, and made war against it. 9:2

6 And the men of Gib′-e-on sent unto Joshua to the camp ᴿto Gil′-gal, saying, Slack not thy hand from thy servants; come up to us quickly, and save us, and help us: for all the kings of the Am′-or-ites that dwell in the mountains are gathered together against us. 5:10; 9:6

7 So Joshua ascended from Gil′-gal, he, and ᴿall the people of war with him, and all the mighty men of valour. 8:1

8 And the LORD said unto Joshua, ᴿFear them not: for I have delivered them into thine hand; there shall not a man of them stand before thee. 11:6; Judg. 4:14

9 Joshua therefore came unto them suddenly, *and* went up from Gil′-gal all night.

10 And the LORD ᵀdiscomfited them before Israel, and slew them with a great slaughter at Gib′-e-on, and chased them along the way that goeth up to Beth–ho′-ron, and smote them to A-ze′-kah, and unto Mak-ke′-dah. *routed*

11 And it came to pass, as they fled from before Israel, *and* were in the going down to Beth–ho′-ron, ᴿthat the LORD cast down great stones from heaven upon them unto A-ze′-kah, and they died: *they were* more which died

with hailstones than *they* whom the children of Israel slew with the sword.   Is. 30:30; Rev. 16:21

12 Then spake Joshua to the LORD in the day when the LORD delivered up the Am'-or-ites before the children of Israel, and he said in the sight of Israel, ᴿSun, stand thou still upon Gib'-e-on; and thou, Moon, in the valley of ᴿAj'-a-lon.   Is. 28:21 · Judg. 12:12

13 And the sun stood still, and the moon stayed, until the people had avenged themselves upon their enemies. ᴿIs not this written in the book of Ja'-sher? So the sun stood still in the midst of heaven, and hasted not to go down about a whole day.   2 Sam. 1:18

14 And there was ᴿno day like that before it or after it, that the LORD hearkened unto the voice of a man: for ᴿthe LORD fought for Israel.   Is. 38:7, 8 · Ex. 14:14; Deut. 20:4

15 ᴿAnd Joshua returned, and all Israel with him, unto the camp to Gil'-gal.   v. 43

16 But these five kings fled, and hid themselves in a cave at Mak-ke'-dah.

17 And it was told Joshua, saying, The five kings are found hid in a cave at Mak-ke'-dah.

18 And Joshua said, Roll great stones upon the mouth of the cave, and set men by it for to ᵀkeep them: *guard*

19 And stay ye not, *but* pursue after your enemies, and smite the hindmost of them; suffer them not to enter into their cities: for the LORD your God hath delivered them into your hand.

20 And it came to pass, when Joshua and the children of Israel had made an end of slaying them with a very great slaughter, till they were consumed, that the rest *which* remained of them entered into ᵀfenced cities.   *fortified*

21 And all the people returned to the camp to Joshua at Mak-ke'-dah in peace: ᴿnone ᵀmoved his tongue against any of the children of Israel.   Ex. 11:7 · Lit. *sharpened*

22 Then said Joshua, Open the mouth of the cave, and bring out those five kings unto me out of the cave.

23 And they did so, and brought forth those five kings unto him out of the cave, the king of Jerusalem, the king of He'-bron, the king of Jar'-muth, the king of La'-chish, *and* the king of Eg'-lon.

24 And it came to pass, when they brought out those kings unto Joshua, that Joshua called for all the men of Israel, and said unto the captains of the men of war which went with him, Come near, put your feet upon the necks of these kings. And they came near, and ᴿput their feet upon the necks of them.   Ps. 107:40; Is. 26:5, 6; Mal. 4:3

25 And Joshua said unto them, Fear not, nor be dismayed, be strong and of good courage: for thus shall the LORD do to all your enemies against whom ye fight.

26 And afterward Joshua smote them, and slew them, and hanged them on five trees: and they ᴿwere hanging upon the trees until the evening.   8:29; 2 Sam. 21:9

27 And it came to pass at the time of the going down of the sun, *that* Joshua commanded, and they ᴿtook them down off the trees, and cast them into the cave wherein they had been hid, and laid great stones in the cave's mouth, *which remain* until this very day.   8:29; Deut. 21:22, 23

28 And that day Joshua took Mak-ke'-dah, and smote it with the edge of the sword, and the king thereof he utterly ᴿdestroyed, them, and all the souls that *were* therein; he let none remain: and he did to the king of Mak-ke'-dah ᴿas he did unto the king of Jericho.   Deut. 7:2, 16 · 6:21

29 Then Joshua passed from Mak-ke'-dah, and all Israel with him, unto ᴿLib'-nah, and fought against Lib'-nah: 15:42; 2 Kin. 8:22

30 And the LORD delivered it also, and the king thereof, into the hand of Israel; and he smote it with the edge of the sword, and all the ᵀsouls that *were* therein; he let none remain in it; but did unto the king thereof as he did unto the king of Jericho.   *people*

31 And Joshua passed from Lib′-nah, and all Israel with him, unto La′-chish, and encamped against it, and fought against it:

32 And the Lord delivered La′-chish into the hand of Israel, which took it on the second day, and smote it with the edge of the sword, and all the souls that *were* therein, according to all that he had done to Lib′-nah.

33 Then Ho′-ram king of Ge′-zer came up to help La′-chish; and Joshua smote him and his people, until he had left him none remaining.

34 And from La′-chish Joshua passed unto Eg′-lon, and all Israel with him; and they encamped against it, and fought against it:

35 And they took it on that day, and smote it with the edge of the sword, and all the souls that *were* therein he utterly destroyed that day, according to all that he had done to La′-chish.

36 And Joshua went up from Eg′-lon, and all Israel with him, unto ᴿHe′-bron; and they fought against it: Num. 13:22; Judg. 1:10, 20

37 And they took it, and smote it with the edge of the sword, and the king thereof, and all the cities thereof, and all the souls that *were* therein; he left none remaining, according to all that he had done to Eg′-lon; but destroyed it utterly, and all the souls that *were* therein.

38 And Joshua returned, and all Israel with him, to ᴿDe′-bir; and fought against it: Judg. 1:11; 1 Chr. 6:58

39 And he took it, and the king thereof, and all the cities thereof; and they smote them with the edge of the sword, and utterly destroyed all the souls that *were* therein; he left none remaining: as he had done to He′-bron, so he did to De′-bir, and to the king thereof; as he had done also to Lib′-nah, and to her king.

40 So Joshua smote all the country of the hills, and of the south, and of the vale, and of the springs, and all their kings: he left none remaining, but ᴿutterly destroyed all that breathed, as the Lord God of Israel commanded.   Deut. 20:16, 17

41 And Joshua smote them from Ka′-desh–bar′-ne-a even unto Ga′-za, and all the country of Go′-shen, even unto Gib′-e-on.

42 And all these kings and their land did Joshua take at one time, ᴿbecause the Lord God of Israel fought for Israel.   v. 14

43 And Joshua returned, and all Israel with him, unto the camp to Gil′-gal.

11 And it came to pass, when Ja′-bin king of Ha′-zor had heard *those things*, that he ᴿsent to Jo′-bab king of Ma′-don, and to the king ᴿof Shim′-ron, and to the king of Ach′-shaph,   10:3 · 19:15

2 And to the kings that *were* on the north of the mountains, and of the plains south of Chin′-ne-roth, and in the valley, and in the borders ᴿof Dor on the west,   17:11

3 *And to* the Ca′-naan-ite on the east and on the west, and *to* the ᴿAm′-or-ite, and the Hit′-tite, and the Per′-iz-zite, and the Jeb′-u-site in the mountains, ᴿand *to* the Hi′-vite under Hermon in the land of Miz′-peh.   9:1 · Deut. 7:1

4 And they went out, they and all their hosts with them, much people, ᴿeven as the sand that *is* upon the sea shore in multitude, with horses and chariots very many.   Gen. 22:17; Judg. 7:12; 1 Sam. 13:5

5 And when all these kings were met together, they came and pitched together at the waters of Me′-rom, to fight against Israel.

6 And the Lord said unto Joshua, Be not afraid because of them: for to morrow about this time will I deliver them up all slain before Israel: thou shalt ᵀhough their horses, and burn their chariots with fire.   *hamstring*

7 So Joshua came, and all the people of war with him, against them by the waters of Me′-rom suddenly; and they fell upon them.

8   And the LORD delivered them into the hand of Israel, who smote them, and chased them unto great ᴿZi'-don, and unto ᴿMis'-re-photh–ma'-im, and unto the valley of Miz'-peh eastward; and they smote them, until they left them none remaining.   Gen. 49:13 · 13:6

9   And Joshua did unto them as the LORD bade him: he ᵀhoughed their horses, and burnt their chariots with fire.   hamstrung

10 And Joshua at that time turned back, and took Ha'-zor, and ᵀsmote the king thereof with the sword: for Ha'-zor beforetime was the head of all those kingdoms.   struck

11 And they smote all the souls that were therein with the edge of the sword, ᴿutterly destroying them: there was not any left to ᴿbreathe: and he burnt Ha'-zor with fire.   Deut. 20:16 · 10:40

12 And all the cities of those kings, and all the kings of them, did Joshua take, and smote them with the edge of the sword, and he utterly destroyed them, ᴿas Moses the servant of the LORD commanded.   Num. 33:50–56; Deut. 7:2; 20:16

13 But as for the cities that stood still in their strength, Israel burned none of them, save Ha'-zor only; that did Joshua burn.

14 And all the ᴿspoil of these cities, and the cattle, the children of Israel took for a prey unto themselves; but every man they ᵀsmote with the edge of the sword, until they had destroyed them, neither left they any to breathe.   Deut. 20:14–18 · struck

15 ᴿAs the LORD commanded Moses his servant, so ᴿdid Moses command Joshua, and ᴿso did Joshua; he left nothing undone of all that the LORD commanded Moses.   Ex. 34:10–17 · Deut. 31:7, 8 · 1:7

16 So Joshua took all that land, ᴿthe hills, and all the south country, ᴿand all the land of Go'-shen, and the valley, and the plain, and the mountain of Israel, and the valley of the same;   12:8 · 10:40, 41

17 ᴿEven from the mount Ha'-lak, that goeth up to Se'-ir, even unto Ba'-al–gad in the valley of Leb'-a-non under mount Hermon: and all their kings he took, and smote them, and slew them.   12:7

18 Joshua made war a long time with all those kings.

19 There was not a city that made peace with the children of Israel, save ᴿthe Hi'-vites the inhabitants of Gib'-e-on: all other they took in battle.   9:3–7

20 For ᴿit was of the LORD to harden their hearts, that they should come against Israel in battle, that he might destroy them utterly, and that they might have no favour, but that he might destroy them, ᴿas the LORD commanded Moses.   Deut. 2:30 · Deut. 20:16

21 And at that time came Joshua, and cut off ᴿthe An'-a-kims from the mountains, from He'-bron, from De'-bir, from A'-nab, and from all the mountains of Judah, and from all the mountains of Israel: Joshua destroyed them utterly with their cities.   15:13, 14

22 There was none of the An'-a-kims left in the land of the children of Israel: only ᴿin Ga'-za, in Gath, ᴿand in Ash'-dod, there remained.   1 Sam. 17:4 · 1 Sam. 5:1; Is. 20:1

23 So Joshua took the whole land, ᴿaccording to all that the LORD said unto Moses; and Joshua gave it for an inheritance unto Israel according to their divisions by their tribes. And the land ᴿrested from war.   Ex. 33:2 · [Heb. 4:8]

12 Now these are the kings of the land, which the children of Israel smote, and possessed their land on the other side Jordan toward the rising of the sun, ᴿfrom the river Arnon ᴿunto mount Hermon, and all the plain on the east: Num. 21:24 · Deut. 3:8

2   Si'-hon king of the Am'-or-ites, who dwelt in Hesh'-bon, and ruled from Ar'-o-er, which is upon the bank of the river Arnon, and from the middle of the river, and from half Gil'-e-ad, even unto the river Jab'-bok, which is the border of the children of Ammon;

3 And from the plain to the sea of Chin'-ne-roth on the east, and unto the sea of the plain, *even* the salt sea on the east, the way to Beth–jesh'-i-moth; and from the south, under Ash'-doth–pis'-gah:

4 And the coast of Og king of Ba'-shan, *which was* of ^Rthe remnant of the giants, that dwelt at Ash'-ta-roth and at Ed'-re-i, 13:12

5 And reigned in mount Hermon, and in Sal'-cah, and in all Ba'-shan, unto the border of the Gesh'-u-rites and the Ma-ach'-a-thites, and half Gil'-e-ad, the border of Si'-hon king of Hesh'-bon.

6 ^RThem did Moses the servant of the Lord and the children of Israel smite: and Moses the servant of the Lord gave it *for* a possession unto the Reu'-ben-ites, and the Gad'-ites, and the half tribe of Ma-nas'-seh. Num. 21:24, 35

7 And these *are* the kings of the country which Joshua and the children of Israel smote on this side Jordan on the west, from Ba'-al–gad in the valley of Leb'-a-non even unto the mount Ha'-lak, that goeth up to ^RSe'-ir; which Joshua gave unto the tribes of Israel *for* a possession according to their divisions; Gen. 14:6; 32:3; Deut. 2:1, 4

8 ^RIn the mountains, and in the valleys, and in the plains, and in the springs, and in the wilderness, and in the south country; the Hit'-tites, the Am'-or-ites, and the Ca'-naan-ites, the Per'-iz-zites, the Hi'-vites, and the Jeb'-u-sites: 10:40

9 ^RThe king of Jericho, one; ^Rthe king of A'-i, which *is* beside Beth'–el, one; 6:2 · 8:29

10 ^RThe king of Jerusalem, one; the king of He'-bron, one; 10:23

11 The king of Jar'-muth, one; the king of La'-chish, one;

12 The king of Eg'-lon, one; ^Rthe king of Ge'-zer, one; 10:33

13 ^RThe king of De'-bir, one; the king of Ge'-der, one; 10:38, 39

14 The king of Hor'-mah, one; the king of A'-rad, one;

15 ^RThe king of Lib'-nah, one; the king of A-dul'-lam, one; 10:29

16 The king of Mak-ke'-dah, one; the king of Beth'–el, one;

17 The king of Tap'-pu-ah, one; the king of He'-pher, one;

18 The king of A'-phek, one; the king of La-shar'-on, one;

19 The king of Ma'-don, one; ^Rthe king of Ha'-zor, one; 11:10

20 The king of ^RShim'-ron–me'-ron, one; the king of Ach'-shaph, one; 11:1; 19:15

21 The king of Ta'-a-nach, one; the king of Me-gid'-do, one;

22 ^RThe king of Ke'-desh, one; the king of Jok'-ne-am of Carmel, one; 19:37; 20:7; 21:32

23 The king of Dor in the ^Rcoast of Dor, one; the king of ^Rthe nations of Gil'-gal, one; 11:2 · Is. 9:1

24 The king of Tir'-zah, one: ^Rall the kings thirty and one. Deut. 7:24

13 Now Joshua ^Rwas old *and* stricken in years; and the Lord said unto him, Thou art old *and* stricken in years, and there remaineth yet very much land to be possessed. 14:10; 23:1, 2

2 This *is* the land that yet remaineth: all the borders of the Phi-lis'-tines, and all Gesh'-u-ri,

3 ^RFrom Si'-hor, which *is* before Egypt, even unto the borders of Ek'-ron northward, *which* is counted to the Ca'-naan-ite: ^Rfive lords of the Phi-lis'-tines; the Ga'-zath-ites, and the Ash'-doth-ites, the Esh'-ka-lon-ites, the Git'-tites, and the Ek'-ron-ites; also the A'-vites: 1 Chr. 13:5; Jer. 2:18 · Judg. 3:3

4 From the south, all the land of the Ca'-naan-ites, and Me-a'-rah that *is* beside the Si-do'-ni-ans, ^Runto A'-phek, to the borders of ^Rthe Am'-or-ites: 12:18 · Judg. 1:34

5 And the land of ^Rthe Gib'-lites, and all Leb'-a-non, toward the sunrising, ^Rfrom Ba'-al–gad under mount Hermon unto the entering into Ha'-math. 1 Kin. 5:18 · 12:7

6 All the inhabitants of the hill country from Leb'-a-non unto Mis'-re-photh–ma'-im, *and* all the Si-do'-ni-ans, them will I drive out from before the children of Israel: only divide thou it by lot unto the

Israelites for an inheritance, as I have commanded thee.

7 Now therefore divide this land for an inheritance unto the nine tribes, and the half tribe of Ma-nas'-seh,

8 With whom the Reu'-ben-ites and the Gad'-ites have received their inheritance, ^Rwhich Moses gave them, ^Rbeyond Jordan eastward, *even* as Moses the servant of the LORD gave them; 22:4 · 12:1–6

9 From Ar'-o-er, that *is* upon the bank of the river Arnon, and the city that *is* in the midst of the river, ^Rand all the plain of Med'-e-ba unto Di'-bon; v. 16; Num. 21:30

10 And all the cities of Si'-hon king of the Am'-or-ites, which reigned in Hesh'-bon, unto the border of the children of Ammon;

11 ^RAnd Gil'-e-ad, and the border of the Gesh'-u-rites and Ma-ach'-a-thites, and all mount Hermon, and all Ba'-shan unto Sal'-cah; 12:5; Num. 32:1

12 All the kingdom of Og in Ba'-shan, which reigned in Ash'-ta-roth and in Ed'-re-i, who remained of ^Rthe remnant of the giants: ^Rfor these did Moses smite, and cast them out. 12:4 · Num. 21:24

13 Nevertheless the children of Israel expelled ^Rnot the Gesh'-u-rites, nor the Ma-ach'-a-thites: but the Gesh'-u-rites and the Ma-ach'-a-thites dwell among the Israelites until this day. v. 11

14 ^ROnly unto the tribe of Levi he gave none inheritance; the sacrifices of the LORD God of Israel made by fire *are* their inheritance, ^Ras he said unto them. 14:3, 4 · v. 33

15 ^RAnd Moses gave unto the tribe of the children of Reuben *inheritance* according to their families. vv. 15–23; Num. 34:14

16 And their coast was ^Rfrom Ar'-o-er, that *is* on the bank of the river Arnon, and the city that *is* in the midst of the river, ^Rand all the plain by Med'-e-ba; 12:2 · Num. 21:30

17 ^RHesh'-bon, and all her cities that *are* in the plain; Di'-bon, and Ba'-moth–ba'-al, and Beth–ba'-al–me'-on, Num. 21:28, 30

18 ^RAnd Ja'-ha-za, and Ked'-e-moth, and Meph'-a-ath, Num. 21:23

19 ^RAnd Kir-ja-tha'-im, and Sib'-mah, and Za'-reth–sha'-har in the mount of the valley, Num. 32:37

20 And Beth-pe'-or, and ^RAsh'-doth–pis'-gah, and Beth–jesh'-i-moth, 12:3; Deut. 3:17

21 ^RAnd all the cities of the plain, and all the kingdom of Si'-hon king of the Am'-or-ites, which reigned in Hesh'-bon, ^Rwhom Moses smote with the princes of Mid'-i-an, E'-vi, and Re'-kem, and Zur, and Hur, and Re'-ba, *which were* dukes of Si'-hon, dwelling in the country. Deut. 3:10 · Num. 21:24

22 ^RBa'-laam also the son of Be'-or, the ^Tsoothsayer, did the children of Israel slay with the sword among them that were slain by them. Num. 22:5; 31:8 · *diviner*

23 And the border of the children of Reuben was Jordan, and the border *thereof*. This *was* the inheritance of the children of Reuben after their families, the cities and the villages thereof.

24 ^RAnd Moses gave *inheritance* unto the tribe of Gad, *even* unto the children of Gad according to their families. Num. 34:14; 1 Chr. 5:11

25 And their coast was Ja'-zer, and all the cities of Gil'-e-ad, and half the land of the children of Ammon, unto Ar'-o-er that *is* before ^RRab'-bah; 2 Sam. 11:1; 12:26

26 And from Hesh'-bon unto Ra'-math–miz'-peh, and Bet'-o-nim; and from Ma-ha-na'-im unto the border of De'-bir;

27 And in the valley, Beth–a'-ram, and Beth–nim'-rah, and Suc'-coth, and Za'-phon, the rest of the kingdom of Si'-hon king of Hesh'-bon, Jordan and *his* border, *even* unto the edge ^Rof the sea of Chin'-ne-reth on the other side Jordan eastward. Num. 34:11; Deut. 3:17

28 This *is* the inheritance of the children of Gad after their families, the cities, and their villages.

29 And Moses gave *inheritance* unto the half tribe of Ma-nas'-seh: and *this* was *the possession* of the

half tribe of the children of Ma-nas'-seh by their families.

30 And their coast was from Ma-ha-na'-im, all Ba'-shan, all the kingdom of Og king of Ba'-shan, and all the towns of Ja'-ir, which *are* in Ba'-shan, threescore cities:

31 And half Gil'-e-ad, and Ash'-ta-roth, and Ed'-re-i, cities of the kingdom of Og in Ba'-shan, *were pertaining* unto the children of Ma'-chir the son of Ma-nas'-seh, *even* to the one half of the children of Ma'-chir by their families.

32 These *are the countries* which Moses did ᵀdistribute for inheritance in the plains of Moab, on the other side Jordan, by Jericho, eastward.   *apportion*

33 ᴿBut unto the tribe of Levi Moses gave not *any* inheritance: the LORD God of Israel *was* their inheritance, ᴿas he said unto them.   Deut. 18:1 · Deut. 10:9; 18:1, 2

14 And these *are the coun-tries* which the children of Israel inherited in the land of Canaan, which E-le-a'-zar the priest, and Joshua the son of Nun, and the heads of the fathers of the tribes of the children of Israel, dis-tributed for inheritance to them.

2 ᴿBy lot *was* their inheritance, as the LORD commanded by the hand of Moses, for the nine tribes, and *for* the half tribe.   Ps. 16:5

3 For Moses had given the in-heritance of two tribes and an half tribe on the other side Jor-dan: but unto the Levites he gave none inheritance among them.

4 For ᴿthe children of Joseph were two tribes, Ma-nas'-seh and E'-phra-im: therefore they gave no part unto the Levites in the land, save cities to dwell *in*, with their suburbs for their cattle and for their substance.   Gen. 41:51; 46:20

5 As the LORD commanded Mo-ses, so the children of Israel did, and they divided the land.

6 Then the children of Judah came unto Joshua in Gil'-gal: and Caleb the son of Je-phun'-neh the Ken'-ez-ite said unto him, Thou knowest ᴿthe thing that the LORD

said unto Moses the man of God concerning me and thee in Ka'-desh–bar'-ne-a.   Num. 14:24, 30

7 Forty years old *was* I when Moses the servant of the LORD ᴿsent me from Ka'-desh–bar'-ne-a to ᵀespy out the land; and I brought him word again as *it was* in mine heart.   Num. 13:6, 17; 14:6 · *spy*

8 Nevertheless ᴿmy brethren that went up with me made the heart of the people melt: but I wholly ᴿfollowed the LORD my God.   Num. 13:31, 32 · Num. 14:24

9 And Moses sware on that day, saying, ᴿSurely the land ᴿwhereon thy feet have trodden shall be thine inheritance, and thy children's for ever, because thou hast wholly followed the LORD my God.   Num. 14:23, 24 · Num. 13:22

10 And now, behold, the LORD hath kept me alive, ᴿas he said, these forty and five years, even since the LORD spake this word unto Moses, while *the children of* Israel wandered in the wilder-ness: and now, lo, I *am* this day fourscore and five years old.   5:6

11 ᴿAs yet I *am as* strong this day as *I was* in the day that Moses sent me: as my strength *was* then, even so *is* my strength now, for war, both ᴿto go out, and to come in.   Deut. 34:7 · Deut. 31:2

12 Now therefore give me this mountain, whereof the LORD spake in that day; for thou heard-est in that day how the An'-a-kims *were* there, and *that* the cities *were* great *and* fenced: ᴿif so be the LORD *will be* with me, then I shall be able to drive them out, as the LORD said.   Rom. 8:31

13 And Joshua ᴿblessed him, ᴿand gave unto Caleb the son of Je-phun'-neh He'-bron for an inheritance.   22:6 · 10:37; 15:13

14 ᴿHe'-bron therefore became the inheritance of Caleb the son of Je-phun'-neh the Ken'-ez-ite unto this day, because that he ᴿwholly followed the LORD God of Israel.   21:12 · vv. 8, 9

15 And ᴿthe name of He'-bron before *was* Kir'-jath–ar'-ba; *which*

Ar'-ba was a great man among the An'-a-kims. ^RAnd the land had rest from war.   15:13; Gen. 23:2 · 11:23

15 *This* then was the lot of the tribe of the children of Judah by their families; *even* to the border of E'-dom the ^Rwilderness of Zin southward *was* the uttermost part of the south coast.   Num. 33:36

2 And their ^Rsouth border was from the shore of the salt sea, from the bay that looketh southward: Num. 34:3, 4

3 And it went out to the south side ^Rto Ma-al'-eh–a-crab'-bim, and passed along to Zin, and ascended up on the south side unto Ka'-desh–bar'-ne-a, and passed along to Hez'-ron, and went up to A'-dar, and fetched a compass to Kar'-ka-a: Num. 34:4

4 *From thence* it passed toward Az'-mon, and went out unto the river of Egypt; and the goings out of that coast were at the sea: this shall be your south coast.

5 And the east border *was* the salt sea, *even* unto the end of Jordan. And *their* ^Rborder in the north quarter *was* from the bay of the sea at the uttermost part of Jordan: 18:15–19

6 And the border went up to ^RBeth–hog'-la, and passed along by the north of Beth–ar'-a-bah; and the border went up ^Rto the stone of Bo'-han the son of Reuben: 18:19, 21 · 18:17

7 And the border went up toward De'-bir from the valley of A'-chor, and so northward, looking toward Gil'-gal, that *is* before the going up to A-dum'-mim, which *is* on the south side of the river: and the border passed toward the waters of En–she'-mesh, and the goings out thereof were at ^REn–ro'-gel: 2 Sam. 17:17; 1 Kin. 1:9

8 And the border went up ^Rby the valley of the son of Hin'-nom unto the south side of the Jeb'-u-site; the same *is* Jerusalem: and the border went up to the top of the mountain that *lieth* before the valley of Hin'-nom westward,

which *is* at the end of the valley of the giants northward: 2 Kin. 23:10

9 And the border was drawn from the top of the hill unto ^Rthe fountain of the water of Neph'-to-ah, and went out to the cities of mount E'-phron; and the border was drawn ^Rto Ba'-al-ah, which *is* Kir'-jath–je'-a-rim: 18:15 · 1 Chr. 13:6

10 And the border compassed from Ba'-al-ah westward unto mount Se'-ir, and passed along unto the side of mount Je'-a-rim, which *is* Ches'-a-lon, on the north side, and went down to Beth–she'-mesh, and passed on to Tim'-nah:

11 And the border went out unto the side of ^REk'-ron northward: and the border was drawn to Shic'-ron, and passed along to mount Ba'-al-ah, and went out unto Jab'-neel; and the goings out of the border were at the sea.   19:43

12 And the west border *was* ^Rto the great sea, and the coast *thereof.* This *is* the coast of the children of Judah round about according to their families.   Num. 34:6, 7

13 ^RAnd unto Caleb the son of Je-phun'-neh he gave a part among the children of Judah, according to the commandment of the LORD to Joshua, *even* ^Rthe city of Ar'-ba the father of A'-nak, which *city is* He'-bron.   14:13 · 14:15

14 And Caleb drove thence ^Rthe three sons of A'-nak, She'-shai, and A-hi'-man, and Tal'-mai, the children of A'-nak.   Judg. 1:10, 20

15 And ^Rhe went up thence to the inhabitants of De'-bir: and the name of De'-bir before *was* Kir'-jath–se'-pher.   10:38; Judg. 1:11

16 ^RAnd Caleb said, He that smiteth Kir'-jath–se'-pher, and taketh it, to him will I give Ach'-sah my daughter to wife.   Judg. 1:12

17 And Oth'-ni-el the son of Ke'-naz, the brother of Caleb, took it: and he gave him ^RAch'-sah his daughter to wife.   Judg. 1:12

18 ^RAnd it came to pass, as she came *unto him,* that she moved him to ask of her father a field:

and [R]she lighted off *her* ass; and Caleb said unto her, What wouldest thou?   Judg. 1:14 · Gen. 24:64

19 Who answered, Give me a [R]blessing; for thou hast given me a south land; give me also springs of water. And he gave her the upper springs, and the [T]nether springs.   Gen. 33:11 · *lower*

20 This *is* the inheritance of the tribe of the children of Judah according to their families.

21 And the uttermost cities of the tribe of the children of Judah toward the coast of E'-dom southward were Kab'-ze-el, and [R]E'-der, and Ja'-gur,   Gen. 35:21

22 And Ki'-nah, and Di-mo'-nah, and A-da'-dah,

23 And Ke'-desh, and Ha'-zor, and Ith'-nan,

24 [R]Ziph, and Te'-lem, and Be'-a-loth,   1 Sam. 23:14

25 And Ha'-zor, Ha-dat'-tah, and Ke'-ri-oth, *and* Hez'-ron, which *is* Ha'-zor,

26 A'-mam, and She'-ma, and Mol'-a-dah,

27 And Ha'-zar–gad'-dah, and Hesh'-mon, and Beth–pa'-let,

28 And Ha'-zar–shu'-al, and Be'-er–she'-ba, and Biz-joth'-jah,

29 Ba'-al-ah, and I'-im, and A'-zem,

30 And El-to'-lad, and Che'-sil, and [R]Hor'-mah,   19:4

31 And [R]Zik'-lag, and Mad-man'-nah, and San-san'-nah,   19:5

32 And Leb'-a-oth, and Shil'-him, and A'-in, and [R]Rim'-mon: all the cities *are* twenty and nine, with their villages: Judg. 20:45, 47

33 *And* in the valley, Esh'-ta-ol, and Zo'-re-ah, and Ash'-nah,

34 And Za-no'-ah, and En–gan'-nim, Tap'-pu-ah, and E'-nam,

35 Jar'-muth, and [R]A-dul'-lam, So'-coh, and A-ze'-kah,   1 Sam. 22:1

36 And Sha-ra'-im, and Ad-i-tha'-im, and Ge-de'-rah, and Ged-e-ro-tha'-im; fourteen cities with their villages:

37 Ze'-nan, and Had'-a-shah, and Mig'-dal–gad,

38 And Dil'-e-an, and Miz'-peh, [R]and Jok'-the-el,   2 Kin. 14:7

39 [R]La'-chish, and Boz'-kath, and [R]Eg'-lon,   2 Kin. 14:19 · 10:3

40 And Cab'-bon, and [T]Lah'-mam, and Kith'-lish,   Or *Lahmas*

41 And Ge-de'-roth, Beth–da'-gon, and Na'-a-mah, and Mak-ke'-dah; sixteen cities with their villages:

42 [R]Lib'-nah, and E'-ther, and A'-shan,   21:13

43 And Jiph'-tah, and Ash'-nah, and Ne'-zib,

44 And Kei'-lah, and Ach'-zib, and Ma-re'-shah; nine cities with their villages:

45 Ek'-ron, with her towns and her villages:

46 From Ek'-ron even unto the sea, all that *lay* near [R]Ash'-dod, with their villages: 11:22

47 Ash'-dod with her towns and her villages, Ga'-za with her towns and her villages, unto the river of Egypt, and [R]the great sea, and the border *thereof:*   Num. 34:6

48 And in the mountains, Sha'-mir, and Jat'-tir, and So'-coh,

49 And Dan'-nah, and Kir'-jath–san'-nah, which *is* De'-bir,

50 And A'-nab, and Esh'-te-moh, and A'-nim,

51 [R]And Go'-shen, and Ho'-lon, and Gi'-loh; eleven cities with their villages: 10:41; 11:16

52 Arab, and Du'-mah, and E'-she-an,

53 And Ja'-num, and Beth–tap'-pu-ah, and A-phe'-kah,

54 And Hum'-tah, and [R]Kir'-jath–ar'-ba, which *is* He'-bron, and Zi'-or; nine cities with their villages: 14:15

55 [R]Ma'-on, Carmel, and Ziph, and Jut'-tah,   1 Sam. 23:24, 25

56 And Jez'-re-el, and Jok'-de-am, and Za-no'-ah,

57 Cain, Gib'-e-ah, and Tim'-nah; ten cities with their villages:

58 Hal'-hul, Beth–zur, and Ge'-dor,

59 And Ma'-a-rath, and Beth–a'-noth, and El'-te-kon; six cities with their villages:

60 Kir'-jath–ba'-al, which *is* Kir'-jath–je'-a-rim, and Rab'-bah; two cities with their villages:

61 In the wilderness, Beth–ar'-a-bah, Mid'-din, and Sec'-a-cah,

62 And Nib'-shan, and the city of Salt, and ^REn–ge'-di; six cities with their villages. 1 Sam. 23:29

63 As for the Jeb'-u-sites the inhabitants of Jerusalem, ^Rthe children of Judah could not drive them out: but the Jeb'-u-sites dwell with the children of Judah at Jerusalem unto this day. Judg. 1:8

16 And the lot of the children of Joseph fell from Jordan by Jericho, unto the water of Jericho on the east, to the wilderness that goeth up from Jeri-cho throughout mount Beth'–el,

2 And goeth out from Beth'–el to Luz, and passeth along unto the borders of Ar'-chi to At'-a-roth,

3 And goeth down westward to the coast of Japh-le'-ti, ^Runto the coast of Beth–ho'-ron the nether, and to Ge'-zer: and the goings out thereof are at the sea. 1 Kin. 9:17

4 ^RSo the children of Joseph, Ma-nas'-seh and E'-phra-im, took their ^Tinheritance. 17:14 : *possession*

5 And the border of the children of E'-phra-im according to their families was *thus:* even the border of their inheritance on the east side was ^RAt'-a-roth–ad'-dar, unto Beth–ho'-ron the upper; 18:13

6 And the border went out toward the sea to ^RMich'-me-thah on the north side; and the border went about eastward unto Ta'-a-nath–shi'-loh, and passed by it on the east to Ja-no'-hah; 17:7

7 And it went down from Ja-no'-hah to At'-a-roth, and to Na'-a-rath, and came to Jericho, and went out at Jordan.

8 The border went out from ^RTap'-pu-ah westward unto the ^Rriver Ka'-nah; and ^Tthe goings out thereof were at the sea. This *is* the inheritance of the tribe of the children of E'-phra-im by their families. 17:8 · 17:9 · *it ended at*

9 And ^Rthe separate cities for the children of E'-phra-im *were* among the inheritance of the children of Ma-nas'-seh, all the cities with their villages. 17:9

10 And they drave not out the Ca'-naan-ites that dwelt in Ge'-zer: but the Ca'-naan-ites dwell among the E'-phra-im-ites unto this day, and serve under tribute.

17 There was also a lot for the tribe of Ma-nas'-seh; for he *was* the ^Rfirstborn of Joseph; *to wit,* for ^RMa'-chir the firstborn of Ma-nas'-seh, the father of Gil'-e-ad: because he was a man of war, therefore he had Gil'-e-ad and Ba'-shan. Gen. 41:51 · Gen. 50:23

2 There was also *a lot* for ^Rthe rest of the children of Ma-nas'-seh by their families; ^Rfor the children of A'-bi-e'-zer, and for the children of He'-lek, and for the children of As'-ri-el, and for the children of She'-chem, and for the children of He'-pher, and for the children of She-mi'-da: these *were* the male children of Ma-nas'-seh the son of Joseph by their families. Num. 26:29–33 · 1 Chr. 7:18

3 But ^RZe-lo'-phe-had, the son of He'-pher, the son of Gil'-e-ad, the son of Ma'-chir, the son of Ma-nas'-seh, had no sons, but daughters: and these *are* the names of his daughters, Mah'-lah, and Noah, Hog'-lah, Mil'-cah, and Tir'-zah. Num. 26:33; 27:1; 36:2

4 And they came near before ^RE-le-a'-zar the priest, and before Joshua the son of Nun, and before the princes, saying, The LORD commanded Moses to give us an inheritance among our brethren. Therefore according to the commandment of the LORD he gave them an inheritance among the brethren of their father. 14:1

5 And there fell ten portions to Ma-nas'-seh, beside the land of Gil'-e-ad and Ba'-shan, which *were* on the other side Jordan;

6 Because the daughters of Ma-nas'-seh had an inheritance among his sons: and the rest of Ma-nas'-seh's sons had the land of Gil'-e-ad.

7 And the coast of Ma-nas'-seh was from Asher to ^RMich'-me-thah, that *lieth* before She'-chem; and the border went along on the

right hand unto the inhabitants of En–tap′-pu-ah. 16:6

8 *Now* Ma-nas′-seh had the land of Tap′-pu-ah: but ᴿTap′-pu-ah on the border of Ma-nas′-seh *belonged* to the children of E′-phra-im; 16:8

9 And the coast descended unto the ᵀriver Ka′-nah, southward of the river: ᴿthese cities of E′-phra-im *are* among the cities of Ma-nas′-seh: the coast of Ma-nas′-seh also *was* on the north side of the river, and the outgoings of it were at the sea: *brook or wadi* · 16:9

10 Southward *it was* E′-phra-im′s, and northward *it was* Ma-nas′-seh′s, and the sea is ᵀhis border; and they met together in Asher on the north, and in Is′-sa-char on the east. *its*

11 And Ma-nas′-seh had in Is′-sa-char and in Asher Beth–she′-an and her towns, and Ib′-le-am and her towns, and the inhabitants of Dor and her towns, and the inhabitants of En′–dor and her towns, and the inhabitants of Ta′-a-nach and her towns, and the inhabitants of Me-gid′-do and her towns, *even* three countries.

12 Yet ᴿthe children of Ma-nas′-seh could not drive out *the inhabitants of* those cities; but the Ca′-naan-ites would dwell in that land. Judg. 1:19, 27, 28

13 Yet it came to pass, when the children of Israel were waxen strong, that they put the Ca′-naan-ites to ᴿtribute;ᵀ but did not utterly drive them out. 16:10 · *forced labour*

14 And the children of Joseph spake unto Joshua, saying, Why hast thou given me *but* one lot and one portion to inherit, seeing I *am* ᴿa great people, forasmuch as the LORD hath blessed me hitherto? Gen. 48:19; Num. 26:34, 37

15 And Joshua answered them, If thou *be* a great people, *then* get thee up to the wood *country*, and cut down for thyself there in the land of the Per′-iz-zites and of the giants, if mount E′-phra-im be too ᵀnarrow for thee. *confined*

16 And the children of Joseph said, The hill is not enough for us: and all the Ca′-naan-ites that dwell in the land of the valley have ᴿchariots of iron, *both they* who *are* of Beth–she′-an and her towns, and *they* who *are* of the valley of Jez′-re-el. Judg. 1:19; 4:3

17 And Joshua spake unto the house of Joseph, *even* to E′-phra-im and to Ma-nas′-seh, saying, Thou *art* a great people, and hast great power: thou shalt not have one ᵀlot *only:* *allotment*

18 But the mountain shall be thine; for it *is* a wood, and thou shalt cut it down: and the outgoings of it shall be thine: for thou shalt drive out the Ca′-naan-ites, though they have iron chariots, *and* though they *be* strong.

18 And the whole congregation of the children of Israel assembled together ᴿat Shi′-loh, and set up the tabernacle of the congregation there. And the land was subdued before them. Jer. 7:12

2 And there remained among the children of Israel seven tribes, which had not yet received their inheritance.

3 And Joshua said unto the children of Israel, ᴿHow long *are* ye slack to go to possess the land, which the LORD God of your fathers hath given you? Judg. 18:9

4 Give out from among you three men for *each* tribe: and I will send them, and they shall rise, and go through the land, and ᵀdescribe it according to the inheritance of them; and they shall come *again* to me. *survey*

5 And they shall divide it into seven parts: ᴿJudah shall abide in their coast on the south, and the ᴿhouse of Joseph shall abide in their coasts on the north. 15:1 · 16:1

6 Ye shall therefore describe the land *into* seven parts, and bring *the description* hither to me, that I may cast lots for you here before the LORD our God.

7 ᴿBut the Levites have no part among you; for the priesthood of the LORD *is* their inheritance: ᴿand Gad, and Reuben, and half the

tribe of Ma-nas'-seh, have received their inheritance beyond Jordan on the east, which Moses the servant of the LORD gave them.   13:33; Num. 18:7, 20 · 13:8

8 And the men arose, and went away: and Joshua charged them that went to ^Tdescribe the land, saying, Go and walk ^Rthrough the land, and describe it, and come again to me, that I may here cast lots for you before the LORD in Shi'-loh.   *survey* · Gen. 13:17

9 And the men went and passed through the land, and described it by cities into seven parts in a book, and came *again* to Joshua to the host at Shi'-loh.

10 And Joshua cast lots for them in Shi'-loh before the LORD: and there ^RJoshua divided the land unto the children of Israel according to their divisions.   Num. 34:16-29

11 And the lot of the tribe of the children of Benjamin came up according to their families: and the coast of their lot came forth between the children of Judah and the children of Joseph.

12 ^RAnd their border on the north side was from Jordan; and the border went up to the side of Jericho on the north side, and went up through the mountains westward; and the goings out thereof were at the wilderness of Beth-a'-ven.   16:1

13 And the border went over from thence toward Luz, to the side of Luz, ^Rwhich is Beth'-el, southward: and the border descended to At'-a-roth-a'-dar, near the hill that *lieth* on the south side of the nether Beth-ho'-ron.   16:2

14 And the border was drawn *thence*, and compassed the corner of the sea southward, from the hill that *lieth* before Beth-ho'-ron southward; and ^Tthe goings out thereof were at ^RKir'-jath-ba'-al, which is Kir'-jath-je'-a-rim, a city of the children of Judah: this *was* the west quarter.   *it ended at* · 15:9

15 And the south ^Tquarter *was* from the end of Kir'-jath-je'-a-rim, and the border went out on the west, and went out to ^Rthe well of waters of Neph'-to-ah: *side* · 15:9

16 And the border came down to the end of the mountain that *lieth* before ^Rthe valley of the son of Hin'-nom, *and* which is in the valley of the ^Tgiants on the north, and descended to the valley of Hin'-nom, to the side of Jeb'-u-si on the south, and descended to ^REn-ro'-gel,   15:8 · Heb. *rephaim* · 15:7

17 And was drawn from the north, and went forth to En-she'-mesh, and went forth toward Gel'-i-loth, which is over against the going up of A-dum'-mim, and descended to ^Rthe stone of Bo'-han the son of Reuben,   15:6

18 And passed along toward the side over against ^TAr'-a-bah northward, and went down unto ^TAr'-a-bah: Or *Beth-arabah*, 15:6

19 And the border passed along to the side of Beth-hog'-lah northward: and the outgoings of the border were at the north bay of the salt sea at the south end of Jordan: this *was* the south coast.

20 And Jordan was the border of it on the east side. This *was* the inheritance of the children of Benjamin, by the coasts thereof round about, according to their families.

21 Now the cities of the tribe of the children of Benjamin according to their families were Jericho, and Beth-hog'-lah, and the valley of Ke'-ziz,

22 And Beth-ar'-a-bah, and Zem-a-ra'-im, and Beth'-el,

23 And A'-vim, and Pa'-rah, and Oph'-rah,

24 And Che'-phar-ha-am'-mo-nai, and Oph'-ni, and Ga'-ba; twelve cities with their villages:

25 ^RGib'-e-on, and Ra'-mah, and Be-e'-roth,   11:19; 21:17; 1 Kin. 3:4, 5

26 And Miz'-peh, and Che-phi'-rah, and Mo'-zah,

27 And Re'-kem, and Ir'-pe-el, and Tar'-a-lah,

28 And Ze'-lah, E'-leph, and ^RJeb'-u-si, which is Jerusalem, Gib'-e-ath, *and* Kir'-jath; fourteen cities with their villages. This is the inheritance of the children of

Benjamin according to their families.   15:8, 63

19 And the ᴿsecond lot came forth to Simeon, *even* for the tribe of the children of Simeon according to their families: ᴿand their inheritance was within the inheritance of the children of Judah.   Judg. 1:3 · v. 9

2 And ᴿthey had in their inheritance Be'-er-she'-ba, or She'-ba, and Mol'-a-dah,   1 Chr. 4:28

3 And Ha'-zar-shu'-al, and Ba'-lah, and A'-zem,

4 And El-to'-lad, and Be'-thul, and Hor'-mah,

5 And Zik'-lag, and Beth-mar'-ca-both, and Ha'-zar-su'-sah,

6 And Beth-leb'-a-oth, and Sha-ru'-hen; thirteen cities and their villages:

7 A'-in, Rem'-mon, and E'-ther, and A'-shan; four cities and their villages:

8 And all the villages that *were* round about these cities to Ba'-al-ath-be'-er, ᴿRa'-math of the south. This *is* the inheritance of the tribe of the children of Simeon according to their families.   1 Sam. 30:27

9 Out of the portion of the children of Judah *was* the inheritance of the children of Simeon: for the ᵀpart of the children of Judah was ᵀtoo much for them: ᴿtherefore the children of Simeon had their inheritance within the inheritance of them.   *portion · too large* · v. 1

10 And the third lot came up for the children of Zeb'-u-lun according to their families: and the border of their inheritance was unto Sa'-rid:

11 ᴿAnd their border went up toward the sea, and Mar'-a-lah, and reached to Dab'-ba-sheth, and reached to the river that *is* ᴿbefore Jok'-ne-am; Gen. 49:13 · 12:22

12 And turned from Sa'-rid eastward toward the sunrising unto the border of Chis'-loth-ta'-bor, and then goeth out to Dab'-e-rath, and goeth up to Ja-phi'-a,

13 And from thence passeth on along on the east to ᴿGit'-tah-he'-pher, to It'-tah-ka'-zin, and goeth

out to Rem'-mon-meth'-o-ar to Ne'-ah;   2 Kin. 14:25

14 And the border compasseth it on the north side to Han'-na-thon: and the outgoings thereof are in the valley of Jiph'-thah-el:

15 And Kat'-tath, and Na-hal'-lal, and Shim'-ron, and Id'-a-lah, and Beth'-le-hem: twelve cities with their villages.

16 This *is* the inheritance of the children of Zeb'-u-lun according to their families, these cities with their villages.

17 *And* the fourth lot came out to Is'-sa-char, for the children of Is'-sa-char according to their families.

18 And their border was toward Jez'-re-el, and Che-sul'-loth, and Shu'-nem,

19 And Haph-ra'-im, and Shi'-hon, and An-a-ha'-rath,

20 And Rab'-bith, and Kish'-i-on, and A'-bez,

21 And Re'-meth, and En-gan'-nim, and En-had'-dah, and Beth-paz'-zez;

22 And the coast reacheth to Ta'-bor, and Sha-haz'-i-mah, and ᴿBeth-she'-mesh; and the outgoings of their border were at Jordan: sixteen cities with their villages.   15:10; Judg. 1:33

23 This *is* the inheritance of the tribe of the children of Is'-sa-char according to their families, the cities and their villages.

24 And the fifth lot came out for the tribe of the children of Asher according to their families.

25 And their border was Hel'-kath, and Ha'-li, and Be'-ten, and Ach'-shaph,

26 And A-lam'-me-lech, and A'-mad, and Mi'-she-al; and reacheth to ᴿCarmel westward, and to Shi'-hor-lib'-nath;   1 Sam. 15:12; Is. 35:2

27 And turneth toward the sunrising to Beth-da'-gon, and reacheth to Zeb'-u-lun, and to the valley of Jiph'-thah-el toward the north side of Beth-e'-mek, and Ne-i'-el, and goeth out to ᴿCa'-bul on the left hand,   1 Kin. 9:13

28 And He'-bron, and Re'-hob,

and Ham'-mon, and Ka'-nah, ^R*even* unto great Zi'-don; Gen. 10:19

29 And *then* the coast turneth to Ra'-mah, and to the strong city Tyre; and the coast turneth to Ho'-sah; and the outgoings thereof are at the sea from the coast to ^RAch'-zib: Judg. 1:31

30 Um'-mah also, and A'-phek, and Re'-hob: twenty and two cities with their villages.

31 This *is* the inheritance of the tribe of the children of Asher according to their families, these cities with their villages.

32 ^RThe sixth lot came out to the children of Naph'-ta-li, *even* for the children of Naph'-ta-li according to their families. Judg. 1:33

33 And their coast was from He'-leph, from Al'-lon to Za-a-nan'-nim, and Ad'-a-mi, Ne'-keb, and Jab'-neel, unto La'-kum; and ^Tthe outgoings thereof were at Jordan: *it ended in*

34 And *then* ^Rthe coast turneth westward to Az'-noth-ta'-bor, and goeth out from thence to Huk'-kok, and reacheth to Zeb'-u-lun on the south side, and reacheth to Asher on the west side, and to Judah upon Jordan toward the sunrising. Deut. 33:23

35 And the fenced cities *are* Zid'-dim, Zer, and Ham'-math, Rak'-kath, and Chin'-ne-reth,

36 And Ad'-a-mah, and Ra'-mah, and Ha'-zor,

37 And ^RKe'-desh, and Ed'-re-i, and En-ha'-zor, 20:7

38 And I'-ron, and Mig'-dal-el, Ho'-rem, and Beth-a'-nath, and Beth-she'-mesh; nineteen cities with their villages.

39 This *is* the inheritance of the tribe of the children of Naph'-ta-li according to their families, the cities and their villages.

40 *And* the seventh lot came out for the tribe of the children of Dan according to their families.

41 And the coast of their inheritance was Zo'-rah, and ^REsh'-ta-ol, and Ir-she'-mesh, 15:33

42 And ^RSha-al-ab'-bin, and Aj'-a-lon, and Jeth'-lah, Judg. 1:35

43 And E'-lon, and Thim'-na-thah, and ^REk'-ron, 15:11; Judg. 1:18

44 And El'-te-keh, and Gib'-be-thon, and Ba'-al-ath,

45 And Je'-hud, and Ben'-e-be'-rak, and Gath–rim'-mon,

46 And Me–jar'-kon, and Rak'-kon, with the border ^Tbefore Ja'-pho. *near Joppa*

47 And the coast of the children of Dan went out *too little* for them: therefore the children of Dan went up to fight against Le'-shem, and took it, and smote it with the edge of the sword, and possessed it, and dwelt therein, and called Le'-shem, Dan, after the name of Dan their father.

48 This *is* the inheritance of the tribe of the children of Dan according to their families, these cities with their villages.

49 When they had ^Tmade an end of dividing the land for inheritance by their coasts, the children of Israel gave an inheritance to Joshua the son of Nun among them: *finished*

50 According to the word of the LORD they gave him the city which he asked, *even* ^RTim'-nath–^Rse'-rah in mount E'-phra-im: and he built the city, and dwelt therein. 24:30 · 1 Chr. 7:24

51 These *are* the inheritances, which E-le-a'-zar the priest, and Joshua the son of Nun, and the heads of the fathers of the tribes of the children of Israel, divided for an inheritance by lot ^Rin Shi'-loh before the LORD, at the door of the tabernacle of the congregation. So they made an end of dividing the country. 18:1, 10

20 The LORD also spake unto Joshua, saying,

2 Speak to the children of Israel, saying, ^RAppoint out for you cities of refuge, whereof I spake unto you by the hand of Moses: Ex. 21:13; Num. 35:6–34

3 That the slayer that killeth *any* person ^Tunawares *and* unwittingly may flee thither: and they shall be your refuge from the avenger of blood. *accidentally*

4 And when he that doth flee unto one of those cities shall stand at the entering of the gate of the city, and shall ᵀdeclare his cause in the ears of the elders of that city, they shall take him into the city unto them, and give him a place, that he may dwell among them.   *state his case*

5 ᴿAnd if the avenger of blood pursue after him, then they shall not deliver the slayer up into his hand; because he smote his neighbour unwittingly, and hated him not beforetime.   Num. 35:12

6 And he shall dwell in that city, ᴿuntil he stand before the congregation for judgment, *and* until the death of the high priest that shall be in those days: then shall the slayer return, and come unto his own city, and unto his own house, unto the city from whence he fled.   Num. 35:12, 24, 25

7 And they appointed ᴿKe'-desh in Galilee in mount Naph'-ta-li, and She'-chem in mount E'-phra-im, and Kir'-jath–ar'-ba, which *is* He'-bron, in ᴿthe mountain of Judah.   1 Chr. 6:76 · Luke 1:39

8 And on the other side Jordan by Jericho eastward, they assigned ᴿBe'-zer in the wilderness upon the plain out of the tribe of Reuben, and Ra'-moth in Gil'-e-ad out of the tribe of Gad, and Go'-lan in Ba'-shan out of the tribe of Ma-nas'-seh.   Deut. 4:43

9 These were the cities appointed for all the children of Israel, and for the stranger that sojourneth among them, that whosoever killeth *any* person ᵀat unawares might flee thither, and not die by the hand of the avenger of blood, ᴿuntil he stood before the congregation.   *accidentally* · v. 6

21 Then came near the heads of the fathers of the Levites unto E-le-a'-zar the priest, and unto Joshua the son of Nun, and unto the heads of the fathers of the tribes of the children of Israel;

2 And they spake unto them at ᴿShi'-loh in the land of Canaan,

saying, ᴿThe LORD commanded by the hand of Moses to give us cities to dwell in, with the suburbs thereof for our cattle. 18:1 · Num. 35:2

3 And the children of Israel gave unto the Levites out of their inheritance, at the commandment of the LORD, these cities and their suburbs.

4 And the lot came out for the families of the Ko'-hath-ites: and ᴿthe children of Aaron the priest, *which were* of the Levites, ᴿhad by lot out of the tribe of Judah, and out of the tribe of Simeon, and out of the tribe of Benjamin, thirteen cities.   vv. 8, 19 · 19:51

5 And ᴿthe rest of the children of Ko'-hath *had* by lot out of the families of the tribe of E'-phra-im, and out of the tribe of Dan, and out of the half tribe of Ma-nas'-seh, ten cities.   v. 20

6 And ᴿthe children of Ger'-shon *had* by lot out of the families of the tribe of Is'-sa-char, and out of the tribe of Asher, and out of the tribe of Naph'-ta-li, and out of the half tribe of Ma-nas'-seh in Ba'-shan, thirteen cities.   v. 27

7 ᴿThe children of Me-ra'-ri by their families *had* out of the tribe of Reuben, and out of the tribe of Gad, and out of the tribe of Zeb'-u-lun, twelve cities.   v. 34

8 ᴿAnd the children of Israel gave by lot unto the Levites these cities with their suburbs, ᴿas the LORD commanded by the hand of Moses.   v. 3 · Num. 35:2

9 And they gave out of the tribe of the children of Judah, and out of the tribe of the children of Simeon, these cities which are *here* mentioned by name.

10 Which the children of Aaron, *being* of the families of the Ko'-hath-ites, *who were* of the children of Levi, had: for theirs was the first lot.

11 ᴿAnd they gave them the city of Ar'-ba the father of A'-nak, which *city is* He'-bron, in the hill *country* of Judah, with the suburbs thereof round about it.   20:7

12 But ᴿthe fields of the city, and

the villages thereof, gave they to Caleb the son of Je-phun'-neh for his possession.   14:14; 1 Chr. 6:56

13 Thus ^Rthey gave to the children of Aaron the priest He'-bron with her suburbs, *to be* a city of refuge for the slayer; and Lib'-nah with her suburbs,   1 Chr. 6:57

14 And ^RJat'-tir with her suburbs, ^Rand Esh-te-mo'-a with her suburbs,   15:48 · 15:50

15 And ^RHo'-lon with her suburbs, ^Rand De'-bir with her suburbs,   1 Chr. 6:58 · 15:49

16 And ^RA'-in with her suburbs, ^Rand Jut'-tah with her suburbs, *and* ^RBeth–she'-mesh with her suburbs; nine cities out of those two tribes.   1 Chr. 6:59 · 15:55 · 15:10

17 And out of the tribe of Benjamin, ^RGib'-e-on with her suburbs, ^RGe'-ba with her suburbs, 18:25 · 18:24

18 An'-a-thoth with her suburbs, and ^RAl'-mon with her suburbs; four cities.   1 Chr. 6:60

19 All the cities of the children of Aaron, the priests, *were* thirteen cities with their suburbs.

20 ^RAnd the families of the children of Ko'-hath, the Levites which remained of the children of Ko'-hath, even they had the cities of their ^Tlot out of the tribe of E'-phra-im.   1 Chr. 6:66 · *allotment*

21 For they gave them ^RShe'-chem with her suburbs in mount E'-phra-im, *to be* a city of refuge for the slayer; and ^RGe'-zer with her suburbs,   20:7 · Judg. 1:29

22 And Kib'-za-im with her suburbs, and Beth–ho'-ron with her suburbs; four cities.

23 And out of the tribe of Dan, El'-te-keh with her suburbs, Gib'-be-thon with her suburbs,

24 ^RAi'-ja-lon with her suburbs, Gath–rim'-mon with her suburbs; four cities.   10:12

25 And out of the half tribe of Ma-nas'-seh, Ta'-nach with her suburbs, and Gath–rim'-mon with her suburbs; two cities.

26 All the cities *were* ten with their suburbs for the families of the children of Ko'-hath that remained.

27 ^RAnd unto the children of Ger'-shon, of the families of the Levites, out of the *other* half tribe of Ma-nas'-seh *they gave* ^RGo'-lan in Ba'-shan with her suburbs, *to be* a city of refuge for the slayer; and Be-esh'–te-rah with her suburbs; two cities.   v. 6; 1 Chr. 6:71 · 20:8

28 And out of the tribe of Is'-sa-char, Ki'-shon with her suburbs, Dab'-a-reh with her suburbs,

29 Jar'-muth with her suburbs, En–gan'-nim with her suburbs; four cities.

30 And out of the tribe of Asher, Mi'-shal with her suburbs, Ab'-don with her suburbs,

31 Hel'-kath with her suburbs, and Re'-hob with her suburbs; four cities.

32 And out of the tribe of Naph'-ta-li, ^RKe'-desh in Galilee with her suburbs, *to be* a city of refuge for the slayer; and Ham'-moth–dor with her suburbs, and Kar'-tan with her suburbs; three cities. 20:7

33 All the cities of the Ger'-shon-ites according to their families *were* thirteen cities with their suburbs.

34 ^RAnd unto the families of the children of Me-ra'-ri, the rest of the Levites, out of the tribe of Zeb'-u-lun, Jok'-ne-am with her suburbs, and Kar'-tah with her suburbs,   v. 7; 1 Chr. 6:77–81

35 Dim'-nah with her suburbs, Na'-ha-lal with her suburbs; four cities.

36 And out of the tribe of Reuben, ^RBe'-zer with her suburbs, and Ja'-ha-zah with her suburbs,   20:8; Deut. 4:43

37 Ked'-e-moth with her suburbs, and Meph'-a-ath with her suburbs; four cities.

38 And out of the tribe of Gad, ^RRa'-moth in Gil'-e-ad with her suburbs, *to be* a city of refuge for the slayer; and Ma-ha-na'-im with her suburbs,   20:8

39 Hesh'-bon with her suburbs, Ja'-zer with her suburbs; four cities in all.

40 So all the cities for the children of Me-ra'-ri by their families, which were remaining of the families of the Levites, were *by* their lot twelve cities.

41 ^RAll the cities of the Levites within the possession of the children of Israel *were* forty and eight cities with their suburbs. Num. 35:7

42 These cities were every one with their suburbs round about them: thus *were* all these cities.

43 And the LORD gave unto Israel ^Rall the land which he sware to give unto their fathers; and they ^Rpossessed it, and dwelt therein. Gen. 12:7; 26:3, 4 · Num. 33:53

44 ^RAnd the LORD gave them ^Rrest round about, according to all that he sware unto their fathers: and ^Rthere stood not a man of all their enemies before them; the LORD delivered all their enemies into their hand. 11:23 · 1:13 · Deut. 7:24

45 ^RThere failed not ought of any good thing which the LORD had spoken unto the house of Israel; all came to pass. [Num. 23:19]

22 Then Joshua called the Reu'-ben-ites, and the Gad'-ites, and the half tribe of Ma-nas'-seh,

2 And said unto them, Ye have kept ^Rall that Moses the servant of the LORD commanded you, and have obeyed my voice in all that I commanded you: Num. 32:20–22

3 Ye have not ^Tleft your brethren these many days unto this day, but have kept the charge of the commandment of the LORD your God. *forsaken*

4 And now the LORD your God hath given ^Rrest unto your brethren, as he promised them: therefore now return ye, and get you unto your tents, *and* unto the land of your possession, which Moses the servant of the LORD gave you on the other side Jordan. 21:44

5 But take diligent heed to do the commandment and the law, which Moses the servant of the LORD charged you, to love the LORD your God, and to walk in all his ways, and to keep his commandments, and to cleave unto him, and to serve him with all your heart and with all your soul.

6 So Joshua ^Rblessed them, and sent them away: and they went unto their tents. Gen. 47:7; Ex. 39:43

7 Now to the *one* half of the tribe of Ma-nas'-seh Moses had given *possession* in Ba'-shan: ^Rbut unto the *other* half thereof gave Joshua among their brethren on this side Jordan westward. And when Joshua sent them away also unto their tents, then he blessed them, 17:1–13

8 And he spake unto them, saying, Return with much riches unto your tents, and with very much cattle, with silver, and with gold, and with brass, and with iron, and with very much raiment: ^Rdivide the ^Tspoil of your enemies with your brethren. Num. 31:27 · *plunder*

9 And the children of Reuben and the children of Gad and the half tribe of Ma-nas'-seh returned, and departed from the children of Israel out of Shi'-loh, which *is* in the land of Canaan, to go unto ^Rthe country of Gil'-e-ad, to the land of their possession, whereof they were possessed, according to the word of the LORD by the hand of Moses. Num. 32:1

10 And when they came unto the borders of Jordan, that *are* in the land of Canaan, the children of Reuben and the children of Gad and the half tribe of Ma-nas'-seh built there an altar by Jordan, a great altar to see to.

11 And the children of Israel ^Rheard say, Behold, the children of Reuben and the children of Gad and the half tribe of Ma-nas'-seh have built an altar over against the land of Canaan, in the borders of Jordan, at the passage of the children of Israel. Judg. 20:12, 13

12 And when the children of Israel heard *of it*, ^Rthe whole congregation of the children of Israel gathered themselves together at Shi'-loh, to go up to war against them. 18:1; Judg. 20:1

13 And the children of Israel sent unto the children of Reuben,

and to the children of Gad, and to the half tribe of Ma-nas'-seh, into the land of Gil'-e-ad, Phin'-e-has the son of E-le-a'-zar the priest,

14 And with him ten princes, of each chief house a prince throughout all the tribes of Israel; and ^Reach one *was* an head of the house of their fathers among the thousands of Israel.   Num. 1:4

15 And they came unto the children of Reuben, and to the children of Gad, and to the half tribe of Ma-nas'-seh, unto the land of Gil'-e-ad, and they spake with them, saying,

16 Thus saith the whole congregation of the LORD, What trespass *is* this that ye have committed against the God of Israel, to turn away this day from following the LORD, in that ye have builded you an altar, ^Rthat ye might rebel this day against the LORD?   Lev. 17:8, 9

17 *Is* the iniquity ^Rof Pe'-or too little for us, from which we are not cleansed until this day, although there was a plague in the congregation of the LORD, Deut. 4:3

18 But that ye must turn away this day from following the LORD? and it will be, *seeing* ye rebel to day against the LORD, that to morrow he will be wroth with the whole congregation of Israel.

19 Notwithstanding, if the land of your possession *be* unclean, *then* pass ye over unto the land of the possession of the LORD, ^Rwherein the LORD's tabernacle dwelleth, and take possession among us: but rebel not against the LORD, nor rebel against us, in building you an altar beside the altar of the LORD our God.   18:1

20 ^RDid not A'-chan the son of Ze'-rah commit a trespass in the ^Taccursed thing, and wrath fell on all the congregation of Israel? and that man perished not alone in his iniquity.   7:1–26 · *devoted thing*

21 Then the children of Reuben and the children of Gad and the half tribe of Ma-nas'-seh answered, and said unto the heads of the thousands of Israel,

22 The LORD God of gods, the LORD God of gods, he ^Rknoweth, and Israel he shall know; if *it be* in rebellion, or if in transgression against the LORD, (save us not this day,)   [Job 10:7; Jer. 12:3; 2 Cor. 11:11, 31]

23 That we have built us an altar to turn from following the LORD, or if to offer thereon burnt offering or meat offering, or if to offer peace offerings thereon, let the LORD himself ^Rrequire *it;* Deut. 18:19

24 And if we have not *rather* done it for fear of *this* thing, saying, In time to come your children might speak unto our children, saying, What have ye to do with the LORD God of Israel?

25 For the LORD hath made Jordan a border between us and you, ye children of Reuben and children of Gad; ye have no part in the LORD: so shall your children make our children cease from fearing the LORD.

26 Therefore we said, Let us now prepare to build us an altar, not for burnt offering, nor for sacrifice:

27 But *that* it *may be* ^Ra witness between us, and you, and our generations after us, that we might ^Rdo the service of the LORD before him with our burnt offerings, and with our sacrifices, and with our peace offerings; that your children may not say to our children in time to come, Ye have no part in the LORD.   Gen. 31:48 · Deut. 12:5, 14

28 Therefore said we, that it shall be, when they should *so* say to us or to our generations in time to come, that we may say *again,* Behold the pattern of the altar of the LORD, which our fathers made, not for burnt offerings, nor for sacrifices; but it *is* a witness between us and you.

29 God forbid that we should rebel against the LORD, and turn this day from following the LORD, ^Rto build an altar for burnt offerings, for meat offerings, or for sacrifices, beside the altar of the LORD our God that *is* before his tabernacle.   Deut. 12:13, 14

30 And when Phin'-e-has the priest, and the princes of the congregation and heads of the thousands of Israel which *were* with him, heard the words that the children of Reuben and the children of Gad and the children of Ma-nas'-seh spake, it pleased them.

31 And Phin'-e-has the son of E-le-a'-zar the priest said unto the children of Reuben, and to the children of Gad, and to the children of Ma-nas'-seh, This day we perceive that the LORD *is* ^Ramong us, because ye have not committed this trespass against the LORD: now ye have delivered the children of Israel out of the hand of the LORD. Ex. 25:8; 2 Chr. 15:2; Zech. 8:23

32 And Phin'-e-has the son of E-le-a'-zar the priest, and the princes, returned from the children of Reuben, and from the children of Gad, out of the land of Gil'-e-ad, unto the land of Canaan, to the children of Israel, and brought them word again.

33 And the thing pleased the children of Israel; and the children of Israel ^Rblessed God, and did not intend to go up against them in battle, to destroy the land wherein the children of Reuben and Gad dwelt.   Dan. 2:19; Luke 2:28

34 And the children of Reuben and the children of Gad called the altar *Ed:* for it *shall be* a witness between us that the LORD *is* God.

23 And it came to pass a long time after that the LORD ^Rhad given rest unto Israel from all their enemies round about, that Joshua ^Rwaxed old *and* stricken in age.   21:44; 22:4 · 13:1; 24:29

2 And Joshua ^Rcalled for all Israel, *and* for their elders, and for their heads, and for their judges, and for their officers, and said unto them, I am old *and* stricken in age: Deut. 31:28

3 And ye have seen all that the LORD your God hath done unto all these nations because of you; for the ^RLORD your God *is* he that hath fought for you.   Ex. 14:14

4 Behold, I have divided unto

you by lot these nations that remain, to be an inheritance for your tribes, from Jordan, with all the nations that I have cut off, even unto the great sea westward.

5 And the LORD your God, ^Rhe shall expel them from before you, and drive them from out of your sight; and ye shall possess their land, as the LORD your God hath promised unto you.   Ex. 23:30; 33:2

6 ^RBe ye therefore very courageous to keep and to do all that is written in the book of the law of Moses, ^Rthat ye turn not aside therefrom *to* the right hand or *to* the left;   1:7 · Deut. 5:32

7 That ye ^Rcome not among these nations, these that remain among you; neither ^Rmake mention of the name of their gods, nor cause to swear *by them,* neither serve them, nor bow yourselves unto them: [Eph. 5:11] · Ps. 16:4; Jer. 5:7

8 But ^Rcleave^T unto the LORD your God, as ye have done unto this day.   Deut. 10:20 · *hold fast*

9 ^RFor the LORD hath driven out from before you great nations and strong: but *as for* you, no man hath been able to stand ^Tbefore you unto this day.   Deut. 7:24 · *against*

10 ^ROne man of you shall chase a thousand: for the LORD your God, he *it is* that fighteth for you, as he hath promised you.   Is. 30:17

11 ^RTake ^Tgood heed therefore unto yourselves, that ye love the LORD your God.   22:5 · *diligent*

12 Else if ye do in any wise go back, and cleave unto the remnant of these nations, *even* these that remain among you, and shall make marriages with them, and go in unto them, and they to you:

13 Know for a certainty that the LORD your God will no more drive out *any of* these nations from before you; ^Rbut they shall be snares and traps unto you, and scourges in your sides, and thorns in your eyes, until ye perish from off this good land which the LORD your God hath given you.   Ex. 23:33

14 And, behold, this day ^RI *am* going the way of all the earth: and

ye know in all your hearts and in all your souls, that ᴿnot one thing hath failed of all the good things which the LORD your God spake concerning you; all are come to pass unto you, *and* not one thing hath failed thereof.   1 Kin. 2:2 · 21:45

15 ᴿTherefore it shall come to pass, *that* as all good things are come upon you, which the LORD your God promised you; so shall the LORD bring upon you ᴿall evil things, until he have destroyed you from off this good land which the LORD your God hath given you.   Deut. 28:63 · Deut. 28:15–68

16 When ye have transgressed the covenant of the LORD your God, which he commanded you, and have gone and served other gods, and bowed yourselves to them; then shall the ᴿanger of the LORD be kindled against you, and ye shall perish quickly from off the good land which he hath given unto you.   Deut. 4:24–28

24 And Joshua gathered all the tribes of Israel to ᴿShe'-chem, and called for the elders of Israel, and for their heads, and for their judges, and for their officers; and they ᴿpresented themselves before God.   Gen. 35:4 · 1 Sam. 10:19

2 And Joshua said unto all the people, Thus saith the LORD God of Israel, Your fathers dwelt on the other side of the flood in old time, *even* Te'-rah, the father of Abra-ham, and the father of Na'-chor: and they served other gods.

3 And ᴿI took your father Abra-ham from the other side of the ᵀflood, and led him throughout all the land of Canaan, and mul-tiplied his seed, and gave him Isaac.   Gen. 12:1 · The Euphrates

4 And I gave unto Isaac Jacob and Esau: and I gave unto ᴿEsau mount Se'-ir, to possess it; ᴿbut Ja-cob and his children went down into Egypt.   Gen. 36:8 · Gen. 46:1, 3, 6

5 I sent Moses also and Aaron, and I plagued Egypt, according to that which I did among them: and afterward I brought you out.

6 And I ᴿbrought your fathers out of Egypt: and ye came unto the sea; and the Egyptians pur-sued after your fathers with char-iots and horsemen unto the Red sea.   Ex. 12:37, 51; 14:2–31

7 And when they cried unto the LORD, he put darkness between you and the Egyptians, and brought the sea upon them, and covered them; and ᴿyour eyes have seen what I have done in Egypt: and ye dwelt in the wilder-ness a long season.   Deut. 4:34

8 And I brought you into the land of the Am'-or-ites, which dwelt on the other side Jordan; and they fought with you: and I gave them into your hand, that ye might possess their land; and I destroyed them from before you.

9 Then ᴿBa'-lak the son of Zip'-por, king of Moab, arose and warred against Israel, and sent and called Ba'-laam the son of Be'-or to curse you: Judg. 11:25

10 ᴿBut I would not hearken un-to Ba'-laam; ᴿtherefore he blessed you still: so I delivered you out of his hand.   Deut. 23:5 · Num. 23:11; 24:10

11 And ᴿye went over Jordan, and came unto Jericho: and ᴿthe men of Jericho fought against you, the Am'-or-ites, and the Per'-iz-zites, and the Ca'-naan-ites, and the Hit'-tites, and the Gir'-ga-shites, the Hi'-vites, and the Jeb'-u-sites; and I delivered them into your hand.   3:14, 17 · 6:1; 10:1

12 And ᴿI sent the hornet before you, which drave them out from before you, *even* the two kings of the Am'-or-ites; *but* not with thy sword, nor with thy bow.   Ex. 23:28

13 And I have given you a land for which ye did not labour, and ᴿcities which ye built not, and ye dwell in them; of the vineyards and oliveyards which ye planted not do ye eat.   Deut. 6:10, 11

14 Now therefore fear the LORD, and serve him in sincerity and in truth: and put away the gods which your fathers served on the other side of the flood, and in Egypt; and serve ye the LORD.

15 And if it seem evil unto you to serve the Lord, choose you this day whom ye will serve; whether the gods which your fathers served that *were* on the other side of the flood, or the gods of the Am'-or-ites, in whose land ye dwell: but as for me and my house, we will serve the Lord.

16 And the people answered and said, God forbid that we should forsake the Lord, to serve other gods;

17 For the Lord our God, he *it is* that brought us up and our fathers out of the land of Egypt, from the house of bondage, and which did those great signs in our sight, and preserved us in all the way wherein we went, and among all the people through whom we passed:

18 And the Lord drave out from before us all the people, even the Am'-or-ites which dwelt in the land: *therefore* will we also serve the Lord; for he *is* our God.

19 And Joshua said unto the people, Ye cannot serve the Lord: for he *is* an holy God; he is a jealous God; he will not forgive your transgressions nor your sins.

20 ᴿIf ye forsake the Lord, and serve strange gods, ᴿthen he will turn and do you hurt, and consume you, after that he hath done you good.   Is. 1:28; 63:10 · Deut. 4:24–26

21 And the people said unto Joshua, Nay; but we will serve the Lord.

22 And Joshua said unto the people, Ye *are* witnesses against yourselves that ye have chosen you the Lord, to serve him. And they said, *We are* witnesses.

23 Now therefore put away, *said he*, the strange gods which *are* among you, and incline your heart unto the Lord God of Israel.

24 And the people said unto Joshua, The Lord our God will we serve, and his voice will we obey.

25 So Joshua ᴿmade a covenant with the people that day, and set them a statute and an ordinance ᴿin She'-chem.   Ex. 15:25 · v. 1

26 And Joshua wrote these words in the book of the law of God, and took a great stone, and set it up there under an oak, that *was* by the sanctuary of the Lord.

27 And Joshua said unto all the people, Behold, this stone shall be a witness unto us; for ᴿit hath heard all the words of the Lord which he spake unto us: it shall be therefore a witness unto you, lest ye deny your God.   Deut. 32:1

28 So ᴿJoshua let the people depart, every man unto his inheritance.   Judg. 2:6, 7

29 ᴿAnd it came to pass after these things, that Joshua the son of Nun, the servant of the Lord, died, *being* an hundred and ten years old.   Judg. 2:8

30 And they buried him in the border of his inheritance in ᴿTim'-nath–se'-rah, which *is* in mount E'-phra-im, on the north side of the hill of Ga'-ash.   19:50; Judg. 2:9

31 And ᴿIsrael served the Lord all the days of Joshua, and all the days of the elders that ᵀoverlived Joshua, and which had known all the works of the Lord, that he had done for Israel.   Judg. 2:7 · *outlived*

32 And the bones of Joseph, which the children of Israel brought up out of Egypt, buried they in She'-chem, in a parcel of ground which Jacob bought of the sons of Ha'-mor the father of She'-chem for an hundred pieces of silver: and it became the inheritance of the children of Joseph.

33 And ᴿE-le-a'-zar the son of Aaron died; and they buried him in a hill *that pertained to* Phin'-e-has his son, which was given him in mount E'-phra-im.   Num. 20:28

The Book of
JUDGES

THE Book of Judges stands in stark contrast to Joshua. In Joshua an obedient people conquered the land through trust in the power of God. In Judges, however, a disobedient and idolatrous people are defeated time and time again because of their rebellion against God.

In seven distinct cycles of sin to salvation, Judges shows how Israel had set aside God's law and in its place substituted "*that which was* right in his own eyes" (21:25). The recurring result of abandonment from God's law is corruption from within and oppression from without. During the nearly four centuries spanned by this book, God raises up military champions to throw off the yoke of bondage and to restore the nation to pure worship. But all too soon the "sin cycle" begins again as the nation's spiritual temperature grows steadily colder.

The Hebrew title is *Shophetim,* meaning "judges," "rulers," "deliverers," or "saviors." *Shophet* not only carries the idea of maintaining justice and settling disputes, but it is also used to mean "liberating" and "delivering." First the judges deliver the people; then they rule and administer justice. The Septuagint used the Greek equivalent of this word, *Kritai* ("Judges"). The Latin Vulgate called it *Liber Judicum,* the "Book of Judges." This book could also appropriately be titled the "Book of Failure."

NOW after the ᴿdeath of Joshua it came to pass, that the children of Israel asked the LORD, saying, Who shall go up for us against the Ca′-naan-ites first, to fight against them?   Josh. 24:29

2   And the LORD said, ᴿJudah shall go up: behold, I have delivered the land into his hand. Rev. 5:5

3   And Judah said unto Simeon his brother, Come up with me into my lot, that we may fight against the Ca′-naan-ites; and ᴿI likewise will go with thee into thy lot. So Simeon went with him.   v. 17

4   And Judah went up; and the LORD delivered the Ca′-naan-ites and the Per′-iz-zites into their hand: and they slew of them in Be′-zek ten thousand men.

5   And they found A-don′-i-be′-zek in Be′-zek: and they fought against him, and they slew the Ca′-naan-ites and the Per′-iz-zites.

6   But A-don′-i-be′-zek fled; and they pursued after him, and caught him, and cut off his thumbs and his great toes.

7   And A-don′-i-be′-zek said, Threescore and ten kings, having their thumbs and their great toes cut off, gathered *their meat* under my table: ᴿas I have done, so God hath requited me. And they brought him to Jerusalem, and there he died.   Lev. 24:19; [James 2:13]

8   Now ᴿthe children of Judah had fought against Jerusalem, and had taken it, and smitten it with the edge of the sword, and set the city on fire.   v. 21; Josh. 15:63

9   ᴿAnd afterward the children of Judah went down to fight against the Ca′-naan-ites, that dwelt in the mountain, and in the south, and in the valley.   Josh. 10:36

10   And Judah went against the Ca′-naan-ites that dwelt in ᴿHe′-bron: (now the name of He′-bron before *was* Kir′-jath-ar′-ba:) and they slew She′-shai, and A-hi′-man, and Tal′-mai.   Josh. 15:13–19

11   ᴿAnd from thence he went against the inhabitants of De′-bir: and the name of De′-bir before *was* Kir′-jath-se′-pher: Josh. 15:15

12   And Caleb said, He that smiteth Kir′-jath-se′-pher, and taketh it, to him will I give Ach′-sah my daughter ᵀto wife.   *as*

13   And Oth′-ni-el the son of Ke′-naz, ᴿCaleb's younger brother,

took it: and he gave him Ach'-sah his daughter to wife.   3:9

14 ^RAnd it came to pass, when she came *to him,* that she moved him to ask of her father a field: and she lighted from off *her* ass; and Caleb said unto her, What wilt thou?   Josh. 15:18, 19

15 And she said unto him, ^RGive me a blessing: for thou hast given me a south land; give me also springs of water. And Caleb gave her the upper springs and the nether springs.   Gen. 33:11

16 ^RAnd the children of the Ken'-ite, Moses' father in law, went up out of the city of palm trees with the children of Judah into the wilderness of Judah, which *lieth* in the south of A'-rad; and they went and dwelt among the people.   Num. 10:29-32; 1 Sam. 15:6

17 ^RAnd Judah went with Simeon his brother, and they slew the Ca'-naan-ites that inhabited Ze'-phath, and utterly destroyed it. And the name of the city was called ^RHor'-mah.   v. 3 · Josh. 19:4

18 Also Judah took Ga'-za with the coast thereof, and As'-ke-lon with the coast thereof, and Ek'-ron with the coast thereof.

19 And the LORD was with Judah; and he drave out *the inhabitants of* the mountain; but could not drive out the inhabitants of the valley, because they had ^Rchariots of iron.   4:3; Josh. 17:16, 18

20 ^RAnd they gave He'-bron unto Caleb, as Moses said: and he expelled thence the ^Rthree sons of A'-nak.   Josh. 14:9, 14 · v. 10; Josh. 15:14

21 ^RAnd the children of Benjamin did not drive out the Jeb'-u-sites that inhabited Jerusalem; but the Jeb'-u-sites dwell with the children of Benjamin in Jerusalem unto this day.   v. 8; Josh. 15:63

22 And the house of Joseph, they also went up against Beth'-el: and the LORD *was* with them.

23 And the house of Joseph ^Rsent to ^Tdescry Beth'-el. (Now the name of the city before *was* ^RLuz.)   Josh. 2:1; 7:2 · *spy out* · Gen. 28:19

24 And the spies saw a man

come forth out of the city, and they said unto him, Shew us, we pray thee, the entrance into the city, and we will shew thee mercy.

25 And when he shewed them the entrance into the city, they ^Tsmote the city with the edge of the sword; but they let go the man and all his family.   *struck*

26 And the man went into the land of the Hit'-tites, and built a city, and called the name thereof Luz: which *is* the name thereof unto this day.

27 ^RNeither did Ma-nas'-seh drive out *the inhabitants of* Beth–she'-an and her towns, nor ^RTa'-a-nach and her towns, nor the inhabitants of Dor and her towns, nor the inhabitants of Ib'-le-am and her towns, nor the inhabitants of Me-gid'-do and her towns: but the Ca'-naan-ites would dwell in that land.   Josh. 17:11–13 · Josh. 21:25

28 And it came to pass, when Israel was strong, that they put the Ca'-naan-ites to tribute, and did not utterly drive them out.

29 Neither did E'-phra-im drive out the Ca'-naan-ites that dwelt in Ge'-zer; but the Ca'-naan-ites dwelt in Ge'-zer among them.

30 Neither did Zeb'-u-lun drive out the inhabitants of Kit'-ron, nor the inhabitants of Na'-ha-lol; but the Ca'-naan-ites dwelt among them, and became tributaries.

31 ^RNeither did Asher drive out the inhabitants of Ac'-cho, nor the inhabitants of Zi'-don, nor of Ah'-lab, nor of Ach'-zib, nor of Hel'-bah, nor of A'-phik, nor of Re'-hob: Josh. 19:24–31

32 But the Asherites ^Rdwelt among the Ca'-naan-ites, the inhabitants of the land: for they did not drive them out.   Ps. 106:34, 35

33 ^RNeither did Naph'-ta-li drive out the inhabitants of Beth–she'-mesh, nor the inhabitants of Beth–a'-nath; but he dwelt among the Ca'-naan-ites, the inhabitants of the land: nevertheless the inhabitants of Beth–she'-mesh and of Beth–a'-nath became tributaries unto them.   Josh. 19:32–39

34 And the Am'-or-ites forced the children of Dan into the mountain: for they would not suffer them to come down to the valley:

35 But the Am'-or-ites would dwell in mount He'-res in Ai'-ja-lon, and in Sha-al'-bim: yet the hand of the house of Joseph ᵀprevailed, so that they became ᵀtributaries. *became stronger · forced labourers*

36 And the coast of the Am'-or-ites *was* ᴿfrom the going up to A-krab'-bim, from the rock, and upward. Num. 34:4; Josh. 15:3

2 And an angel of the LORD came up from Gil'-gal to Bo'-chim, and said, ᴿI made you to go up out of Egypt, and ᴿhave brought you unto the land which I sware unto your fathers; and I said, I will never break my covenant with you. 6:8, 9 · Deut. 1:8

2 And ye shall make no league with the inhabitants of this land; ᴿye shall throw down their altars: but ye have not obeyed my voice: why have ye done this? Deut. 12:3

3 Wherefore I also said, I will not drive them out from before you; but they shall be *as thorns* in your sides, and ᴿtheir gods shall ᵀbe a snare unto you. 3:6 · *entrap*

4 And it came to pass, when the angel of the LORD spake these words unto all the children of Israel, that the people lifted up their voice, and wept.

5 And they called the name of that place Bo'-chim: and they sacrificed there unto the LORD.

6 And when Joshua had let the people go, the children of Israel went every man unto his inheritance to possess the land.

7 ᴿAnd the people served the LORD all the days of Joshua, and all the days of the elders that outlived Joshua, who had seen all the great works of the LORD, that he did for Israel. Josh. 24:31

8 And Joshua the son of Nun, the servant of the LORD, died, *being* an hundred and ten years old.

9 ᴿAnd they buried him in the border of his inheritance in ᴿTim'-nath–he'-res, in the mount of E'-phra-im, on the north side of the hill Ga'-ash. Josh. 24:30 · Josh. 19:49, 50

10 And also all that generation were gathered unto their fathers: and there arose another generation after them, which ᴿknew not the LORD, nor yet the works which he had done for Israel. [Titus 1:16]

11 And the children of Israel did ᴿevil in the sight of the LORD, and served Ba'-a-lim: 3:7, 12; 4:1; 6:1

12 And they ᴿforsook the LORD God of their fathers, which brought them out of the land of Egypt, and followed other gods, of the gods of the people that *were* round about them, and bowed themselves unto them, and provoked the LORD to anger. 8:33; 10:6

13 And they forsook the LORD, ᴿand served Ba'-al and Ash'-ta-roth. 10:6; Ps. 106:36

14 ᴿAnd the anger of the LORD was hot against Israel, and he delivered them into the hands of spoilers that spoiled them, and ᴿhe sold them into the hands of their enemies round about, so that they could not any longer stand before their enemies. 3:8 · Is. 50:1

15 Whithersoever they went out, the hand of the LORD was against them for evil, as the LORD had said, and as the LORD had ᴿsworn unto them: and they were greatly distressed. Lev. 26:14–26; Deut. 28:15–68

16 Nevertheless the LORD raised up judges, which delivered them out of the hand of those that ᵀspoiled them. *plundered*

17 And yet they would not hearken unto their judges, but they ᴿwentᵀ a whoring after other gods, and bowed themselves unto them: they turned quickly out of the way which their fathers walked in, obeying the commandments of the LORD; *but* they did not so. Ex. 34:15 · *played the harlot with*

18 And when the LORD raised them up judges, then ᴿthe LORD was with the judge, and delivered them out of the hand of their enemies all the days of the judge: ᴿfor it repented the LORD because of

their groanings by reason of them that oppressed them and ᵀvexed them. Josh. 1:5 · Gen. 6:6 · *harassed*

19 And it came to pass, ᴿwhen the judge was dead, *that* they returned, and ᵀcorrupted *themselves* more than their fathers, in following other gods to serve them, and to bow down unto them; they ceased not from their own doings, nor from their stubborn way. 3:12 · *behaved more corruptly*

20 And the anger of the LORD was hot against Israel; and he said, Because that this people hath ᴿtransgressed my covenant which I commanded their fathers, and have not hearkened unto my voice: [Josh. 23:16]

21 I also will not henceforth drive out any from before them of the nations which Joshua ᴿleft when he died: Josh. 23:4, 5, 13

22 ᴿThat through them I may ᴿproveᵀ Israel, whether they will keep the way of the LORD to walk therein, as their fathers did keep *it*, or not. 3:1, 4 · Deut. 8:2, 16; 13:3 · *test*

23 Therefore the LORD left those nations, without driving them out hastily; neither delivered he them into the hand of Joshua.

3 Now these *are* ᴿthe nations which the LORD left, to ᵀprove Israel by them, *even* as many *of Israel* as had not known all the wars of Canaan; 1:1; 2:21, 22 · *test*

2 Only that the generations of the children of Israel might know, to teach them war, at the least such as before knew nothing thereof;

3 *Namely,* ᴿfive lords of the Phi-lis′-tines, and all the Ca′-naan-ites, and the Si-do′-ni-ans, and the Hi′-vites that dwelt in mount Leb′-a-non, from mount Ba′-al-her′-mon unto the entering in of Ha′-math. Josh. 13:3

4 And they were to ᵀprove Israel by them, to ᵀknow whether they would hearken unto the commandments of the LORD, which he commanded their fathers by the hand of Moses. *test · find out*

5 ᴿAnd the children of Israel dwelt among the Ca′-naan-ites,

Hit′-tites, and Am′-or-ites, and Per′-iz-zites, and Hi′-vites, and Jeb′-u-sites: Ps. 106:35

6 And ᴿthey took their daughters to be their wives, and gave their daughters to their sons, and served their gods. Josh. 23:12

7 And the children of Israel did evil in the sight of the LORD, and forgat the LORD their God, and served Ba′-a-lim and the groves.

8 Therefore the anger of the LORD was hot against Israel, and he ᴿsold them into the hand of Chu′-shan–rish-a-tha′-im king of Mes-o-po-ta′-mi-a: and the children of Israel served Chu′-shan–rish-a-tha′-im eight years. 2:14

9 And when the children of Israel cried unto the LORD, the LORD raised up a deliverer to the children of Israel, who delivered them, *even* Oth′-ni-el the son of Ke′-naz, Caleb's younger brother.

10 And ᴿthe spirit of the LORD came upon him, and he judged Israel, and went out to war: and the LORD delivered Chu′-shan–rish-a-tha′-im king of Mes-o-po-ta′-mi-a into his hand; and his hand prevailed against Chu′-shan–rish-a-tha′-im. Num. 27:18

11 And the land had rest forty years. And Oth′-ni-el the son of Ke′-naz died.

12 And the children of Israel did evil again in the sight of the LORD: and the LORD strengthened ᴿEg′-lon the king of Moab against Israel, because they had done evil in the sight of the LORD. 1 Sam. 12:9

13 And he gathered unto him the children of Ammon and ᴿAm′-a-lek, and went and smote Israel, and possessed ᴿthe city of palm trees. 5:14 · 1:16; Deut. 34:3; 2 Chr. 28:15

14 So the children of Israel ᴿserved Eg′-lon the king of Moab eighteen years. Deut. 28:48

15 But when the children of Israel ᴿcried unto the LORD, the LORD raised them up a deliverer, E′-hud the son of Ge′-ra, a Benjamite, a man ᴿlefthanded: and by him the children of Israel sent a

present unto Eg'-lon the king of Moab.   Ps. 78:34 · 20:16

16 But E'-hud made him a dagger which had two edges, of a cubit length; and he ^Tdid gird it under his raiment upon his right thigh.   *fastened*

17 And he brought the present unto Eg'-lon king of Moab: and Eg'-lon *was* a very fat man.

18 And when he had ^Tmade an end to offer the present, he sent away the people that ^Tbare the present.   *finished offering · carried*

19 But he himself turned again from the quarries that *were* by Gil'-gal, and said, I have a secret errand unto thee, O king: who said, Keep silence. And all that stood by him went out from him.

20 And E'-hud came unto him; and he was sitting in a summer parlour, which he had for himself alone. And E'-hud said, I have a message from God unto thee. And he arose out of *his* seat.

21 And E'-hud put forth his left hand, and took the dagger from his right thigh, and thrust it into his belly:

22 And the ^Thaft also went in after the blade; and the fat closed upon the blade, so that he could not draw the dagger out of his belly; and the dirt came out. *handle*

23 Then E'-hud went forth through the porch, and shut the doors of the parlour upon him, and locked them.

24 When he was gone out, his servants came; and when they saw that, behold, the doors of the parlour *were* locked, they said, Surely he ^Rcovereth his feet in his summer chamber.   1 Sam. 24:3

25 And they ^Ttarried till they were ^Rashamed: and, behold, he opened not the doors of the parlour; therefore they took a key, and opened *them:* and, behold, their lord *was* fallen down dead on the earth.   *waited · 2 Kin. 2:17; 8:11*

26 And E'-hud escaped while they tarried, and passed beyond the ^Tquarries, and escaped unto Se'-i-rath.   *stone images*

27 And it came to pass, when he was come, that ^Rhe blew a trumpet in the mountain of E'-phra-im, and the children of Israel went down with him from the mount, and he before them.   6:34; 1 Sam. 13:3

28 And he said unto them, Follow after me: for ^Rthe LORD hath delivered your enemies the Mo'-ab-ites into your hand. And they went down after him, and took the ^Rfords of Jordan toward Moab, and suffered not a man to pass over.   7:9, 15; 1 Sam. 17:47 · Josh. 2:7

29 And they slew of Moab at that time about ten thousand men, all lusty, and all men of valour; and there escaped not a man.

30 So Moab was ^Tsubdued that day under the hand of Israel. And ^Rthe land had rest fourscore years.   *defeated · v. 11*

31 And after him was ^RSham'-gar the son of A'-nath, which slew of the Phi-lis'-tines six hundred men with an ox goad: ^Rand he also delivered Israel.   5:6 · 2:16

4 And ^Rthe children of Israel again did evil in the sight of the LORD, when E'-hud was dead.   2:19

2 And the LORD ^Rsold them into the hand of Ja'-bin king of Canaan, that reigned in ^RHa'-zor; the captain of whose host *was* Sis'-e-ra, which dwelt in Ha-ro'-sheth of the Gentiles.   2:14 · Josh. 11:1

3 And the children of Israel cried unto the LORD: for he had nine hundred ^Rchariots of iron; and twenty years he mightily oppressed the children of Israel.   1:19

4 And Deb'-o-rah, a prophetess, the wife of Lap'-i-doth, she judged Israel at that time.

5 And she dwelt under the palm tree of Deb'-o-rah between Ra'-mah and Beth'–el in mount E'-phra-im: and the children of Israel came up to her for judgment.

6 And she sent and called Ba'-rak the son of A-bin'-o-am out of Ke'-desh–naph'-ta-li, and said unto him, Hath not the LORD God of Israel commanded, *saying,* Go and draw toward mount Ta'-bor, and take with thee ten thousand

men of the children of Naph'-ta-li and of the children of Zeb'-u-lun?

7 And I will draw unto thee to the river Ki'-shon, Sis'-e-ra, the captain of Ja'-bin's army, with his chariots and his multitude; and I will deliver him into thine hand.

8 And Ba'-rak said unto her, If thou wilt go with me, then I will go: but if thou wilt not go with me, *then* I will not go.

9 And she said, I will surely go with thee: notwithstanding the journey that thou takest shall ᵀnot be for thine honour; for the LORD shall ᴿsell Sis'-e-ra into the hand of a woman. And Deb'-o-rah arose, and went with Ba'-rak to Ke'-desh.   *be no glory for you* · 2:14

10 And Ba'-rak called ᴿZeb'-u-lun and Naph'-ta-li to Ke'-desh; and he went up with ten thousand men ᴿat his feet: and Deb'-o-rah went up with him.   5:18 · Ex. 11:8

11 Now He'-ber the Ken'-ite, *which was* of the children of Ho'-bab the father in law of Moses, had ᵀsevered himself from the Ken'-ites, and pitched his tent unto the plain of Za-a-na'-im, which *is* by Ke'-desh.   *separated*

12 And they shewed Sis'-e-ra that Ba'-rak the son of A-bin'-o-am was gone up to mount Ta'-bor.

13 And Sis'-e-ra gathered together all his chariots, *even* nine hundred chariots of iron, and all the people that *were* with him, from Ha-ro'-sheth of the Gentiles unto the river of Ki'-shon.

14 And Deb'-o-rah said unto Ba'-rak, Up; for this *is* the day in which the LORD hath delivered Sis'-e-ra into thine hand: ᴿis not the LORD gone out before thee? So Ba'-rak went down from mount Ta'-bor, and ten thousand men after him. Deut. 9:3; 2 Sam. 5:24; Ps. 68:7

15 And the LORD ᵀdiscomfited Sis'-e-ra, and all *his* chariots, and all *his* host, with the edge of the sword before Ba'-rak; so that Sis'-e-ra lighted down off *his* chariot, and fled away on his feet.   *routed*

16 But Ba'-rak pursued after the chariots, and after the host, unto Ha-ro'-sheth of the Gentiles: and all the host of Sis'-e-ra fell ᵀupon the edge of the sword; *and* there was not a man ᴿleft.   *by* · Ex. 14:28

17 Howbeit Sis'-e-ra fled away on his feet to the tent of ᴿJa'-el the wife of He'-ber the Ken'-ite: for *there was* peace between Ja'-bin the king of Ha'-zor and the house of He'-ber the Ken'-ite.   5:6

18 And Ja'-el went out to meet Sis'-e-ra, and said unto him, Turn in, my lord, turn in to me; fear not. And when he had turned in unto her into the tent, she covered him with a ᵀmantle.   *blanket* or *rug*

19 And he said unto her, Give me, I pray thee, a little water to drink; for I am thirsty. And she opened a bottle of milk, and gave him drink, and covered him.

20 Again he said unto her, Stand in the door of the tent, and it shall be, when any man doth come and enquire of thee, and say, Is there any man here? that thou shalt say, No.

21 Then Ja'-el He'-ber's wife took a nail of the tent, and took an hammer in her hand, and went softly unto him, and smote the nail into his temples, and fastened it into the ground: for he was fast asleep and weary. So he died.

22 And, behold, as Ba'-rak pursued Sis'-e-ra, Ja'-el came out to meet him, and said unto him, Come, and I will shew thee the man whom thou seekest. And when he came into her *tent*, behold, Sis'-e-ra lay dead, and the nail *was* in his temples.

23 So God subdued on that day Ja'-bin the king of Canaan before the children of Israel.

24 And the hand of the children of Israel prospered, and prevailed against Ja'-bin the king of Canaan, until they had destroyed Ja'-bin king of Canaan.

5 Then ᴿsang Deb'-o-rah and Ba'-rak the son of A-bin'-o-am on that day, saying,   4:4; Ex. 15:1

2 Praise ye the LORD for the ᴿavenging of Israel, ᴿwhen the

people willingly offered themselves.   Ps. 18:47 · 2 Chr. 17:16
3 ᴿHear, O ye kings; give ear, O
ye princes; I, *even* I, will sing unto
the LORD; I will sing *praise* to the
LORD God of Israel.   Deut. 32:1, 3
4 LORD, ᴿwhen thou wentest
out of Se′-ir, when thou marchedst
out of ᴿthe field of E′-dom, the
earth trembled, and the heavens
dropped, the clouds also dropped
water.   Deut. 33:2; Ps. 68:7 · Ps. 68:8
5 ᴿThe mountains ᵀmelted from
before the LORD, *even* ᴿthat Si′-
nai from before the LORD God of
Israel.   Ps. 97:5 · gushed · Ex. 19:18
6 In the days of ᴿSham′-gar the
son of A′-nath, in the days of ᴿJa′-
el, ᴿthe highways were unoccu-
pied, and the travellers walked
through byways.   3:31 · 4:17 · Is. 33:8
7 ᵀ*The inhabitants of* the villages ceased, they ceased in
Israel, until that I Deb′-o-rah
arose, that I arose a mother in
Israel.   *Village life ceased*
8 They chose ᴿnew gods; then
was war in the gates: was there a
shield or spear seen among forty
thousand in Israel?   Deut. 32:17
9 My heart *is* ᵀtoward the governors of Israel, that offered
themselves willingly among the
people. Bless ye the LORD.   *with*
10 Speak, ye that ride on white
ᴿasses, ye that sit in judgment,
and walk by the way.   10:4; 12:14
11 *They that are delivered* from
the noise of archers in the places
of drawing water, there shall they
ᵀrehearse the righteous acts of the
LORD, *even* the righteous acts
toward the inhabitants of his villages in Israel: then shall the people of the LORD go down to the
gates.   *recount*
12 Awake, awake, Deb′-o-rah:
awake, awake, utter a song: arise,
Ba′-rak, and lead thy captivity
captive, thou son of A-bin′-o-am.
13 Then he made him that remaineth have dominion over the
nobles among the people: the
LORD made me have dominion
over the mighty.
14 Out of E′-phra-im *was there*

a root of them against ᴿAm′-a-
lek; after thee, Benjamin, among
thy people; out of Ma′-chir came
down ᵀgovernors, and out of Zeb′-
u-lun they that handle the pen of
the writer.   3:13 · *rulers*
15 And the princes of Is′-sa-char
were with Deb′-o-rah; even Is′-sa-
char, and also Ba′-rak: he was
sent on foot into the valley. For the
divisions of Reuben *there were*
great ᵀthoughts of heart.   *resolves*
16 Why abodest thou among the
sheepfolds, to hear the ᵀbleatings
of the flocks? For the divisions of
Reuben *there were* great search-
ings of heart.   *pipings for*
17 ᴿGil′-e-ad abode beyond Jordan: and why did Dan remain
in ships? ᴿAsh′-er continued on
the sea shore, and abode in his
breaches.   Josh. 22:9 · Josh. 19:29, 31
18 ᴿZeb′-u-lun and Naph′-ta-li
were a people *that* jeoparded
their lives unto the death in the
high places of the field.   4:6, 10
19 The kings came *and* fought,
then fought the kings of Canaan
in ᴿTa′-a-nach by the waters of
Me-gid′-do; they took no ᵀgain of
money.   1:27 · *plunder of silver*
20 They fought from heaven;
the stars in their courses fought
against Sis′-e-ra.
21 ᴿThe river of Ki′-shon swept
them away, that ancient river, the
river Ki′-shon. O my soul, thou
hast trodden down strength.   4:7
22 Then were the horsehoofs
broken by the means of the pransings, the pransings of their mighty ones.
23 Curse ye Me′-roz, said the
angel of the LORD, curse ye bitterly the inhabitants thereof; because they came not to the help of
the LORD, to the help of the LORD
against the mighty.
24 Blessed above women shall
Ja′-el the wife of He′-ber the Ken′-
ite be, ᴿblessed shall she be above
women in the tent.   [Luke 1:28]
25 He asked water, *and* she gave
him milk; she brought forth butter
in a lordly dish.
26 She put her hand to the nail,

and her right hand to the workmen's hammer; and with the hammer she smote Sis'-e-ra, she smote off his head, when she had pierced and stricken through his temples.

27 At her feet he bowed, he fell, he lay down: at her feet he bowed, he fell: where he bowed, there he fell down ᴿdead.　　4:18–21

28 The mother of Sis'-e-ra looked out at a window, and cried through the lattice, Why is his chariot *so* long in coming? why tarry the wheels of his chariots?

29 Her ᵀwise ladies answered her, yea, she ᵀreturned answer to herself,　　*wisest · answers herself*

30 Have they not ᵀsped? have they *not* divided the prey; to every man a damsel *or* two; to Sis'-e-ra a prey of divers colours, a prey of divers colours of needlework, of divers colours of needlework on both sides, *meet* for the necks of *them that take* the spoil?　　*found*

31 So let all thine enemies perish, O Lᴏʀᴅ: but *let* them that love him *be* as the ᴿsun when he goeth forth in his might. And the land had rest forty years.　　Ps. 37:6; 89:36

6 And the children of Israel did ᴿevil in the sight of the Lᴏʀᴅ: and the Lᴏʀᴅ delivered them into the hand of ᴿMid'-i-an seven years.　　2:11 · Num. 22:4; 31:1–3

2 And the hand of Mid'-i-an prevailed against Israel: *and* because of the Mid'-i-an-ites the children of Israel made them the dens which *are* in the mountains, and caves, and strong holds.

3 And *so* it was, when Israel had sown, that the Mid'-i-an-ites came up, and the Am'-a-lek-ites, and the ᴿchildren of the east, even they came up against them;　　7:12

4 And they encamped against them, and ᴿdestroyed the ᵀincrease of the earth, till thou come unto Ga'-za, and left no sustenance for Israel, neither sheep, nor ox, nor ass.　　Lev. 26:16 · *produce*

5 For they came up with their cattle and their tents, and they came as grasshoppers for multi-

tude; *for* both they and their camels were ᵀwithout number: and they entered into the land to destroy it.　　*innumerable*

6 And Israel was greatly impoverished because of the Mid'-i-an-ites; and the children of Israel ᴿcried unto the Lᴏʀᴅ.　　Hos. 5:15

7 And it came to pass, when the children of Israel cried unto the Lᴏʀᴅ because of the Mid'-i-an-ites,

8 That the Lᴏʀᴅ sent a prophet unto the children of Israel, which said unto them, Thus saith the Lᴏʀᴅ God of Israel, I brought you up from Egypt, and brought you forth out of the ᴿhouse of ᵀbondage;　　Josh. 24:17 · *slavery*

9 And I delivered you out of the hand of the Egyptians, and out of the hand of all that oppressed you, and ᴿdrave them out from before you, and gave you their land;　　Ps. 44:2, 3

10 And I said unto you, I *am* the Lᴏʀᴅ your God; ᴿfear not the gods of the Am'-or-ites, in whose land ye dwell: but ye have not obeyed my ᴿvoice.　　2 Kin. 17:35, 37, 38 · 2:1, 2

11 And there came an angel of the Lᴏʀᴅ, and sat under an oak which *was* in Oph'-rah, that *pertained* unto Jo'-ash the A'-bi-ez'-rite: and his son ᴿGideon threshed wheat by the winepress, to hide *it* from the Mid'-i-an-ites.　　Heb. 11:32

12 And the ᴿangel of the Lᴏʀᴅ appeared unto him, and said unto him, The Lᴏʀᴅ *is* with thee, thou mighty man of valour.　　Luke 1:11, 28

13 And Gideon said unto him, Oh my Lord, if the Lᴏʀᴅ be with us, why then is all this befallen us? and ᴿwhere *be* all his miracles ᴿwhich our fathers told us of, saying, Did not the Lᴏʀᴅ bring us up from Egypt? but now the Lᴏʀᴅ hath forsaken us, and delivered us into the hands of the Mid'-i-an-ites.　　[Is. 59:1] · Josh. 4:6, 21; Ps. 44:1

14 And the Lᴏʀᴅ looked upon him, and said, Go in this thy might, and thou shalt save Israel from the hand of the Mid'-i-an-ites: ᴿhave not I sent thee?　　Josh. 1:9

15 And he said unto him, Oh my

Lord, wherewith shall I save Israel? behold, ^Rmy family *is* poor in Ma-nas'-seh, and I *am* the least in my father's house.   1 Sam. 9:21

16 And the LORD said unto him, ^RSurely I will be with thee, and thou shalt smite the Mid'-i-an-ites as one man.   Ex. 3:12; Josh. 1:5

17 And he said unto him, If now I have found grace in thy sight, then ^Rshew me a sign that thou talkest with me.   2 Kin. 20:8; Ps. 86:17

18 Depart not hence, I pray thee, until I come unto thee, and bring forth my present, and set *it* before thee. And he said, I will tarry until thou come again.

19 ^RAnd Gideon went in, and made ready a kid, and unleavened cakes of an e'-phah of flour: the flesh he put in a basket, and he put the broth in a pot, and brought *it* out unto him under the oak, and presented *it*.   Gen. 18:6-8

20 And the angel of God said unto him, Take the flesh and the unleavened cakes, and lay *them* upon this rock, and ^Rpour out the broth. And he did so.   1 Kin. 18:33, 34

21 Then the angel of the LORD put forth the end of the staff that *was* in his hand, and touched the flesh and the unleavened cakes; and ^Rthere rose up fire out of the rock, and consumed the flesh and the unleavened cakes. Then the angel of the LORD departed out of his sight.   Lev. 9:24

22 And when Gideon ^Rperceived that he *was* an angel of the LORD, Gideon said, Alas, O Lord GOD! for because I have seen an angel of the LORD face to face.   Gen. 32:30

23 And the LORD said unto him, ^RPeace *be* unto thee; fear not: thou shalt not die.   Dan. 10:19

24 Then Gideon built an altar there unto the LORD, and called it ^TJe-ho'-vah-sha'-lom: unto this day it *is* yet ^Rin Oph'-rah of the A'-bi-ez'-rites. Lit. *The* LORD *Is Peace* · 8:32

25 And it came to pass the same night, that the LORD said unto him, Take thy father's young bullock, even the second bullock of seven years old, and ^Rthrow down

the altar of ^RBa'-al that thy father hath, and ^Rcut down the grove that *is* by it: 2:2 · 3:7 · Deut. 7:5

26 And build an altar unto the LORD thy God upon the top of this ^Trock, in the ^Tordered place, and take the second bullock, and offer a burnt sacrifice with the wood of the grove which thou shalt cut down.   *strong hold · proper arrangement*

27 Then Gideon took ten men of his servants, and did as the LORD had said unto him: and *so* it was, because he feared his father's household, and the men of the city, that he could not do *it* by day, that he did *it* by night.

28 And when the men of the city arose early in the morning, behold, the altar of Ba'-al was cast down, and the grove was cut down that *was* by it, and the second bullock was offered upon the altar *that was* built.

29 And they said one to another, Who hath done this thing? And when they enquired and asked, they said, Gideon the son of Jo'-ash hath done this thing.

30 Then the men of the city said unto Jo'-ash, Bring out thy son, that he may die: because he hath ^Tcast down the altar of Ba'-al, and because he hath cut down the grove that *was* by it.   *torn*

31 And Jo'-ash said unto all that stood against him, Will ye ^Tplead for Ba'-al? will ye save him? he that will plead for him, let him be put to death ^Twhilst *it is yet* morning: if he *be* a god, let him plead for himself, because *one* hath cast down his altar.   *contend · by morning*

32 Therefore on that day he called him ^RJer-ub-ba'-al, saying, Let Ba'-al plead against him, because he hath thrown down his altar.   7:1; 1 Sam. 12:11; 2 Sam. 11:21

33 Then all ^Rthe Mid'-i-an-ites and the Am'-a-lek-ites and the children of the east were gathered together, and went over, and ^Tpitched in ^Rthe valley of Jez'-re-el.   v. 3 · *encamped* · Josh. 17:16; Hos. 1:5

34 But ^Rthe Spirit of the LORD came upon Gideon, and he blew

a trumpet; and A′-bi-e′-zer was gathered after him. 3:10; 1 Chr. 12:18

35 And he sent messengers throughout all Ma-nas′-seh; who also was gathered after him: and he sent messengers unto ᴿAsher, and unto ᴿZeb′-u-lun, and unto Naph′-ta-li; and they came up to meet them. 5:17; 7:23 · 4:6, 10; 5:18

36 And Gideon said unto God, If thou wilt save Israel by mine hand, as thou hast said,

37 Behold, I will put a fleece of wool in the floor; *and* if the dew be on the fleece only, and *it be* dry upon all the earth *beside,* then shall I know that thou wilt save Israel by mine hand, as thou hast said.

38 And it was so: for he rose up early on the morrow, and thrust the fleece together, and wringed the dew out of the fleece, a bowl full of water.

39 And Gideon said unto God, ᴿLet not thine anger be hot against me, and I will speak but this once: let me prove, I pray thee, but this once with the fleece; let it now be dry only upon the fleece, and upon all the ground let there be dew. Gen. 18:32

40 And God did so that night: for it was dry upon the fleece only, and there was dew on all the ground.

7 Then ᴿJer-ub-ba′-al, who *is* Gideon, and all the people that *were* with him, rose up early, and ᵀpitched beside the well of Ha′-rod: so that the ᵀhost of the Mid′-i-an-ites were on the north side of them, by the hill of Mo′-reh, in the valley. 6:32 · encamped · camp

2 And the Lᴏʀᴅ said unto Gideon, The people that *are* with thee *are* too many for me to give the Mid′-i-an-ites into their hands, lest Israel ᴿvaunt themselves against me, saying, Mine own hand hath saved me. Is. 10:13

3 Now therefore go to, proclaim in the ears of the people, saying, ᴿWhosoever *is* fearful and afraid, let him return and depart early from mount Gil′-e-ad. And there returned of the people twen-

ty and two thousand; and there remained ten thousand. Deut. 20:8

4 And the Lᴏʀᴅ said unto Gideon, The people *are* yet *too* many; bring them down unto the water, and I will try them for thee there: and it shall be, *that* of whom I say unto thee, This shall go with thee, the same shall go with thee; and of whomsoever I say unto thee, This shall not go with thee, the same shall not go.

5 So he brought down the people unto the water: and the Lᴏʀᴅ said unto Gideon, Every one that lappeth of the water with his tongue, as a dog lappeth, him shalt thou set by himself; likewise every one that boweth down upon his knees to drink.

6 And the number of them that lapped, *putting* their hand to their mouth, were three hundred men: but all the rest of the people bowed down upon their knees to drink water.

7 And the Lᴏʀᴅ said unto Gideon, ᴿBy the three hundred men that lapped will I save you, and deliver the Mid′-i-an-ites into thine hand: and let all the *other* people go every man unto his ᵀplace. 1 Sam. 14:6 · home

8 So the people took victuals in their hand, and their trumpets: and he sent all *the rest of* Israel every man unto his tent, and retained those three hundred men: and the host of Mid′-i-an was beneath him in the valley.

9 And it came to pass the same ᴿnight, that the Lᴏʀᴅ said unto him, Arise, get thee down unto the host; for I have delivered it into thine hand. 6:25; Gen. 46:2, 3

10 But if thou fear to go down, go thou with Phu′-rah thy servant down to the host:

11 And thou shalt ᴿhear what they say; and afterward shall thine hands be strengthened to go down unto the host. Then went he down with Phu′-rah his servant unto the outside of the armed men that *were* in the host. Gen. 24:14

12 And the Mid′-i-an-ites and

the Am'-a-lek-ites and Rall the children of the east lay along in the valley like grasshoppers for multitude; and their camels *were* without number, as the sand by the sea side for multitude.   6:3, 33

13 And when Gideon was come, behold, *there was* a man that told a dream unto his fellow, and said, Behold, I dreamed a dream, and, lo, a cake of barley bread tumbled into the host of Mid'-i-an, and came unto a tent, and smote it that it fell, and overturned it, that the tent lay along.

14 And his fellow answered and said, This *is* nothing else save the sword of Gideon the son of Jo'-ash, a man of Israel: *for* into his hand hath RGod delivered Mid'-i-an, and all the host.   6:14, 16

15 And it was *so*, when Gideon heard the telling of the dream, and the interpretation thereof, that he worshipped, and returned into the Thost of Israel, and said, Arise; for the LORD hath delivered into your hand the host of Mid'-i-an.   *camp*

16 And he divided the three hundred men *into* three companies, and he put a trumpet in every man's hand, with empty pitchers, and Tlamps within the pitchers.   *torches*

17 And he said unto them, Look on me, and do likewise: and, behold, when I come to the outside of the camp, it shall be *that*, as I do, so shall ye do.

18 When I blow with a trumpet, I and all that *are* with me, then blow ye the trumpets also on every side of all the camp, and say, *The sword* of the LORD, and of Gideon.

19 So Gideon, and the hundred men that *were* with him, came unto the outside of the camp in the beginning of the middle watch; and they had but newly set the watch: and they blew the trumpets, and brake the pitchers that *were* in their hands.

20 And the three companies blew the trumpets, and brake the

pitchers, and held the lamps in their left hands, and the trumpets in their right hands to blow *withal*: and they cried, The sword of the LORD, and of Gideon.

21 And they Rstood every man in his place round about the camp: and all the host ran, and cried, and fled.   Ex. 14:13, 14; 2 Chr. 20:17

22 And the three hundred blew the trumpets, and Rthe LORD set Revery man's sword against his fellow, even throughout all the host: and the host fled to Beth–shit'-tah in Zer'-e-rath, *and* to the border of A'-bel–me-ho'-lah, unto Tab'-bath.   Ps. 83:9 · 1 Sam. 14:20

23 And the men of Israel gathered themselves together out of RNaph'-ta-li, and out of Asher, and out of all Ma-nas'-seh, and pursued after the Mid'-i-an-ites.   6:35

24 And Gideon sent messengers throughout all Rmount E'-phra-im, saying, Come down against the Mid'-i-an-ites, and take before them the waters unto Beth–ba'-rah and Jordan. Then all the men of E'-phra-im gathered themselves together, and Rtook the waters unto RBeth–ba'-rah and Jordan.   3:27 · 3:28 · John 1:28

25 And they took Rtwo princes of the Mid'-i-an-ites, RO'-reb and Ze'-eb; and they slew O'-reb upon the rock O'-reb, and Ze'-eb they slew at the winepress of Ze'-eb, and pursued Mid'-i-an, and brought the heads of O'-reb and Ze'-eb to Gideon on the Rother side Jordan.   8:3 · Ps. 83:11; Is. 10:26 · 8:4

8 And Rthe men of E'-phra-im said unto him, Why hast thou served us thus, that thou calledst us not, when thou wentest to fight with the Mid'-i-an-ites? And they did chide with him sharply.   12:1

2 And he said unto them, What have I done now in comparison of you? *Is* not the gleaning of the grapes of E'-phra-im better than the vintage of RA'-bi-e'-zer?   6:11

3 RGod hath delivered into your hands the princes of Mid'-i-an, O'-reb and Ze'-eb: and what was I able to do in comparison

of you? Then their ᴿanger was ᵀabated toward him, when he had said that.   7:24, 25 · Prov. 15:1 · *subsided*

4 And Gideon came ᴿto Jordan, *and* passed over, he, and the three hundred men that *were* with him, faint, yet pursuing *them*.   7:25

5 And he said unto the men of ᴿSuc'-coth, Give, I pray you, loaves of bread unto the people that follow me; for they *be* faint, and I am pursuing after Ze'-bah and Zal-mun'-na, kings of Mid'-i-an.   Gen. 33:17; Ps. 60:6

6 And the princes of Suc'-coth said, ᴿ*Are* the hands of Ze'-bah and Zal-mun'-na now in thine hand, that we should give bread unto thine army?   v. 15; 1 Kin. 20:11

7 And Gideon said, Therefore when the LORD hath delivered Ze'-bah and Zal-mun'-na into mine hand, ᴿthen I will tear your flesh with the thorns of the wilderness and with briers.   v. 16

8 And he went up thence ᴿto Pe-nu'-el, and spake unto them likewise: and the men of Pe-nu'-el answered him as the men of Suc'-coth had answered *him*.   Gen. 32:30

9 And he spake also unto the men of Pe-nu'-el, saying, When I ᴿcome again in peace, I will break down this tower.   1 Kin. 22:27

10 Now Ze'-bah and Zal-mun'-na *were* in Kar'-kor, and their hosts with them, about fifteen thousand *men*, all that were left of ᴿall the ᵀhosts of the children of the east: for there fell ᴿan hundred and twenty thousand men that drew sword.   7:12 · *army* · 6:5

11 And Gideon went up by the way of them that dwelt in tents on the east of No'-bah and Jog'-be-hah, and smote the host: for the host was ᴿsecure.   18:27; [1 Thess. 5:3]

12 And when Ze'-bah and Zal-mun'-na fled, he pursued after them, and took the two kings of Mid'-i-an, Ze'-bah and Zal-mun'-na, and discomfited all the host.

13 And Gideon the son of Jo'-ash returned from battle before the sun *was up*,

14 And caught a young man of the men of Suc'-coth, and en-quired of him: and he described unto him the princes of Suc'-coth, and the elders thereof, *even* three-score and seventeen men.

15 And he came unto the men of Suc'-coth, and said, Behold Ze'-bah and Zal-mun'-na, with whom ye did ᴿupbraidᵀ me, saying, *Are* the hands of Ze'-bah and Zal-mun'-na now in thine hand, that we should give bread unto thy men *that are* weary?   v. 6 · *ridiculed*

16 ᴿAnd he took the elders of the city, and thorns of the wilderness and briers, and with them he taught the men of Suc'-coth.   v. 7

17 ᴿAnd he beat down the tower of ᴿPe-nu'-el, and slew the men of the city.   v. 9 · 1 Kin. 12:25

18 Then said he unto Ze'-bah and Zal-mun'-na, What manner of men *were they* whom ye slew at Ta'-bor? And they answered, As thou *art*, so *were* they; each one resembled the children of a king.

19 And he said, They *were* my brethren, *even* the sons of my mother: *as* the LORD liveth, if ye had saved them alive, I would not slay you.

20 And he said unto Je'-ther his firstborn, Up, *and* slay them. But the youth drew not his sword: for he feared, because he *was* yet a youth.

21 Then Ze'-bah and Zal-mun'-na said, Rise thou, and fall upon us: for as the man *is, so is* his strength. And Gideon arose, and slew Ze'-bah and Zal-mun'-na, and took away the ornaments that *were* on their camels' necks.

22 Then the men of Israel said unto Gideon, ᴿRule thou over us, both thou, and thy son, and thy son's son also: for thou hast ᴿde-livered us from the hand of Mid'-i-an.   [9:8] · 3:9; 9:17

23 And Gideon said unto them, I will not rule over you, neither shall my son rule over you: ᴿthe LORD shall rule over you.   1 Sam. 8:7

24 And Gideon said unto them, I would desire a request of you, that ye would give me every man the earrings of his prey. (For they had

golden earrings, Rbecause they *were* Ish'-ma-el-ites.) Gen. 37:25, 28

25 And they answered, We will willingly give *them*. And they spread a garment, and did cast therein every man the earrings of his prey.

26 And the weight of the golden earrings that he requested was a thousand and seven hundred *shek'-els* of gold; beside ornaments, and collars, and purple raiment that *was* on the kings of Mid'-i-an, and beside the chains that *were* about their camels' necks.

27 And Gideon Rmade an e'-phod thereof, and put it in his city, *even* Rin Oph'-rah: and all Israel went thither a whoring after it: which thing became a snare unto Gideon, and to his house. 17:5 · 6:11

28 Thus was Mid'-i-an subdued before the children of Israel, so that they lifted up their heads no more. RAnd the country was in quietness forty years in the days of Gideon. 5:31

29 And RJer-ub-ba'-al the son of Jo'-ash went and dwelt in his own house. 6:32; 7:1

30 And Gideon had Rthreescore and ten sons of his body begotten: for he had many wives. 9:2, 5

31 RAnd his concubine that *was* in She'-chem, she also bare him a son, whose name he called A-bim'-e-lech. 9:1

32 And Gideon the son of Jo'-ash died Rin a good old age, and was buried in the sepulchre of Jo'-ash his father, Rin Oph'-rah of the A'-bi-ez'-rites. Gen. 25:8 · v. 27; 6:24

33 And it came to pass, Ras soon as Gideon was dead, that the children of Israel turned again, and Rwent a whoring after Ba'-a-lim, Rand made Ba'-al–be'-rith their god. 2:19 · 2:17 · 9:4, 46

34 And the children of Israel Rremembered not the LORD their God, who had delivered them out of the hands of all their enemies on every side: Deut. 4:9; Ps. 78:11, 42

35 RNeither shewed they kindness to the house of Jer-ub-ba'-al, *namely*, Gideon, according to all the goodness which he had shewed unto Israel. 9:16–18

9 And A-bim'-e-lech the son of Jer-ub-ba'-al went to She'-chem unto Rhis mother's brethren, and communed with them, and with all the family of the house of his mother's father, saying, 8:31, 35

2 Speak, I pray you, in the ears of all the men of She'-chem, Whether *is* better for you, either that all the sons of Jer-ub-ba'-al, *which are* Rthreescore and ten persons, reign over you, or that one reign over you? remember also that I *am* your Rbone and your flesh. vv. 5, 18; 8:30 · Gen. 29:14

3 And his mother's brethren spake of him in the ears of all the men of She'-chem all these words: and their hearts inclined to follow A-bim'-e-lech; for they said, He *is* our Rbrother. Gen. 29:15

4 And they gave him threescore and ten *pieces* of silver out of the house of RBa'-al–be'-rith, wherewith A-bim'-e-lech hired Rvain and light persons, which followed him. 8:33 · 11:3; 2 Chr. 13:7

5 And he went unto his father's house Rat Oph'-rah, and Rslew his brethren the sons of Jer-ub-ba'-al, *being* threescore and ten persons, upon one stone: notwithstanding yet Jo'-tham the youngest son of Jer-ub-ba'-al was left; for he hid himself. 6:24 · vv. 2, 18; 8:30; 2 Kin. 11:1, 2

6 And all the men of She'-chem gathered together, and all the house of Mil'-lo, and went, and made A-bim'-e-lech king, by the plain of the pillar that *was* in She'-chem.

7 And when they told *it* to Jo'-tham, he went and stood in the top of Rmount Ger'-i-zim, and lifted up his voice, and cried, and said unto them, Hearken unto me, ye men of She'-chem, that God may hearken unto you. John 4:20

8 RThe trees went forth on *a time* to anoint a king over them; and they said unto the olive tree, Reign thou over us. 2 Kin. 14:9

9 But the olive tree said unto them, Should I leave my fatness,

Rwherewith by me they honour God and man, and go to be promoted over the trees? [John 5:23]

10 And the trees said to the fig tree, Come thou, *and* reign over us.

11 But the fig tree said unto them, Should I forsake my sweetness, and my good fruit, and go to be promoted over the trees?

12 Then said the trees unto the vine, Come thou, *and* reign over us.

13 And the vine said unto them, Should I leave my wine, which cheereth God and man, and go to be promoted over the trees?

14 Then said all the trees unto the bramble, Come thou, *and* reign over us.

15 And the bramble said unto the trees, If in truth ye anoint me king over you, *then* come *and* put your trust in my Rshadow: and if not, Rlet fire come out of the bramble, and devour the Rcedars of Leb′-a-non. Is. 30:2 · Ezek. 19:14 · Is. 2:13

16 Now therefore, if ye have done truly and sincerely, in that ye have made A-bim′-e-lech king, and if ye have dealt well with Jer-ub-ba′-al and his house, and have done unto him Raccording to the deserving of his hands; 8:35

17 (For my Rfather fought for you, and adventured his life far, and Rdelivered you out of the hand of Mid′-i-an: 7:1-25 · 8:22

18 RAnd ye are risen up against my father's house this day, and have slain his sons, threescore and ten persons, upon one stone, and have made A-bim′-e-lech, the son of his Rmaidservant, king over the men of She′-chem, because he *is* your brother;) 8:30, 35 · 8:31

19 If ye then have dealt truly and sincerely with Jer-ub-ba′-al and with his house this day, *then* Rrejoice ye in A-bim′-e-lech, and let him also rejoice in you: Is. 8:6

20 But if not, Rlet fire come out from A-bim′-e-lech, and devour the men of She′-chem, and the house of Mil′-lo; and let fire come out from the men of She′-chem,

and from the house of Mil′-lo, and devour A-bim′-e-lech. vv. 15, 45, 56

21 And Jo′-tham ran away, and fled, and went to RBe′-er, and dwelt there, for fear of A-bim′-e-lech his brother. Num. 21:16

22 When A-bim′-e-lech had reigned three years over Israel,

23 Then God sent an Revil spirit between A-bim′-e-lech and the men of She′-chem; and the men of She′-chem dealt treacherously with A-bim′-e-lech: 1 Sam. 16:14; 18:9

24 RThat the cruelty *done* to the threescore and ten sons of Jer-ub-ba′-al might come, and their Rblood be laid upon A-bim′-e-lech their brother, which slew them; and upon the men of She′-chem, which aided him in the killing of his brethren. Matt. 23:35 · Num. 35:33

25 And the men of She′-chem set Tliers in wait for him in the top of the mountains, and they robbed all that came along that way by them: and it was told A-bim′-e-lech. *men in ambush*

26 And Ga′-al the son of E′-bed came with his brethren, and went over to She′-chem: and the men of She′-chem put their confidence in him.

27 And they went out into the fields, and gathered their vineyards, and trode *the grapes*, and Tmade merry, and went into Rthe house of their god, and did eat and drink, and cursed A-bim′-e-lech. *rejoiced · v. 4*

28 And Ga′-al the son of E′-bed said, RWho *is* A-bim′-e-lech, and who *is* She′-chem, that we should serve him? *is* not *he* the son of Jer-ub-ba′-al? and Ze′-bul his officer? serve the men of RHa′-mor the father of She′-chem: for why should we serve him? 1 Sam. 25:10 · Gen. 34:2

29 And would to God this people were under my hand! then would I remove A-bim′-e-lech. And he said to A-bim′-e-lech, Increase thine army, and come out.

30 And when Ze′-bul the ruler of the city heard the words of Ga′-al the son of E′-bed, his anger was Tkindled. *aroused*

31 And he sent messengers unto A-bim'-e-lech ᵀprivily, saying, Behold, Ga'-al the son of E'-bed and his brethren be come to She'-chem; and, behold, they fortify the city against thee.   *secretly*

32 Now therefore up by night, thou and the people that *is* with thee, and lie in wait in the field:

33 And it shall be, *that* in the morning, as soon as the sun is up, thou shalt rise early, and set upon the city: and, behold, *when* he and the people that *is* with him come out against thee, then mayest thou do to them as thou shalt find occasion.

34 And A-bim'-e-lech rose up, and all the people that *were* with him, by night, and they laid wait against She'-chem in four companies.

35 And Ga'-al the son of E'-bed went out, and stood in the entering of the gate of the city: and A-bim'-e-lech rose up, and the people that *were* with him, from ᵀlying in wait.   *the ambush*

36 And when Ga'-al saw the people, he said to Ze'-bul, Behold, there come people down from the top of the mountains. And Ze'-bul said unto him, Thou seest the shadow of the mountains as *if they were* men.

37 And Ga'-al spake again and said, See there come people down by the middle of the land, and another company come along by the plain of Me-on'-e-nim.

38 Then said Ze'-bul unto him, Where *is* now thy mouth, wherewith thou ᴿsaidst, Who *is* A-bim'-e-lech, that we should serve him? *is* not this the people that thou hast despised? go out, I pray now, and fight with them.   vv. 28, 29

39 And Ga'-al went out before the men of She'-chem, and fought with A-bim'-e-lech.

40 And A-bim'-e-lech chased him, and he fled before him, and many were overthrown *and* wounded, *even* unto the ᵀentering of the gate.   *entrance*

41 And A-bim'-e-lech dwelt at A-ru'-mah: and Ze'-bul thrust out Ga'-al and his brethren, that they should not dwell in She'-chem.

42 And it came to pass on the morrow, that the people went out into the field; and they told A-bim'-e-lech.

43 And he took the people, and divided them into three companies, and ᵀlaid wait in the field, and looked, and, behold, the people *were* come forth out of the city; and he rose up against them, and smote them.   *set an ambush*

44 And A-bim'-e-lech, and the company that *was* with him, rushed forward, and stood in the entering of the gate of the city: and the two *other* companies ran upon all *the people* that *were* in the fields, and slew them.

45 And A-bim'-e-lech fought against the city all that day; and he took the city, and slew the people that *was* therein, and ᴿbeatᵀ down the city, and sowed it with salt.   Deut. 29:23; 2 Kin. 3:25 · *demolished*

46 And when all the men of the tower of She'-chem heard *that*, they entered into an hold of the house ᴿof the god Be'-rith.   8:33

47 And it was told A-bim'-e-lech, that all the men of the tower of She'-chem were gathered together.

48 And A-bim'-e-lech gat him up to mount ᴿZal'-mon, he and all the people that *were* with him; and A-bim'-e-lech took an axe in his hand, and cut down a bough from the trees, and took it, and laid *it* on his shoulder, and said unto the people that *were* with him, What ye have seen me do, make haste, *and* do as I *have done*.   Ps. 68:14

49 And all the people likewise cut down every man his bough, and followed A-bim'-e-lech, and put *them* to the ᵀhold, and set the hold on fire upon them; so that all the men of the tower of She'-chem died also, about a thousand men and women.   *fortified room*

50 Then went A-bim'-e-lech to The'-bez, and ᵀencamped against The'-bez, and took it.   *besieged*

51 But there was a strong tower within the city, and thither fled all the men and women, and all they of the city, and shut *it* to them, and ᵀgat them up to the top of the tower.   *they went up*

52 And A-bim′-e-lech came unto the tower, and fought against it, and went hard unto the door of the tower to burn it with fire.

53 And a certain woman ᴿcast a piece of a millstone upon A-bim′-e-lech's head, and ᵀall to brake his skull.   2 Sam. 11:21 · *crushed his skull*

54 Then ᴿhe called hastily unto the young man his armourbearer, and said unto him, Draw thy sword, and slay me, that men say not of me, A woman slew him. And his young man thrust him through, and he died.   1 Sam. 31:4

55 And when the men of Israel saw that A-bim′-e-lech was dead, they departed every man unto his ᵀplace.   *home*

56 Thus God rendered the wickedness of A-bim′-e-lech, which he did unto his father, in slaying his seventy brethren:

57 And all the evil of the men of She′-chem did God render upon their heads: and upon them came ᴿthe curse of Jo′-tham the son of Jer-ub-ba′-al.   v. 20

10 And after A-bim′-e-lech there ᴿarose to ᵀdefend Israel To′-la the son of Pu′-ah, the son of Dodo, a man of Is′-sa-char; and he dwelt in Sha′-mir in mount E′-phra-im.   2:16 · *save*

2 And he judged Israel twenty and three years, and died, and was buried in Sha′-mir.

3 And after him arose Ja′-ir, a Gil′-e-ad-ite, and judged Israel twenty and two years.

4 And he had thirty sons that rode on thirty ass colts, and they had thirty cities, which are called Ha′-voth–ja′-ir unto this day, which *are* in the land of Gil′-e-ad.

5 And Ja′-ir died, and was buried in Ca′-mon.

6 And the children of Israel did evil again in the sight of the LORD, and served Ba′-a-lim, and Ash′-ta-roth, and the gods of Syria, and the gods of Zi′-don, and the gods of Moab, and the gods of the children of Ammon, and the gods of the Phi-lis′-tines, and forsook the LORD, and served not him.

7 And the anger of the LORD was hot against Israel, and he ᴿsold them into the hands of the Phi-lis′-tines, and into the hands of the children of Ammon.   2:14; 4:2

8 And that year they ᵀvexed and oppressed the children of Israel: eighteen years, all the children of Israel that *were* on the other side Jordan in the ᴿland of the Am′-or-ites, which *is* in Gil′-e-ad.   *harassed*, lit. *shattered* · Num. 32:33

9 Moreover the children of Ammon passed over Jordan to fight also against Judah, and against Benjamin, and against the house of E′-phra-im; so that Israel was ᵀsore distressed.   *severely*

10 ᴿAnd the children of Israel cried unto the LORD, saying, We have sinned against thee, both because we have forsaken our God, and also served Ba′-a-lim.   6:6

11 And the LORD said unto the children of Israel, *Did* not I *deliver you* from the Egyptians, and from the Am′-or-ites, from the children of Ammon, and from the Phi-lis′-tines?

12 The Zi-do′-ni-ans also, and the Am′-a-lek-ites, and the Ma′-on-ites, ᴿdid oppress you; and ye cried to me, and I delivered you out of their hand.   Ps. 106:42, 43

13 ᴿYet ye have forsaken me, and served other gods: wherefore I will deliver you no more.   [2:12]

14 Go and ᴿcry unto the gods which ye have chosen; let them deliver you in the time of your ᵀtribulation.   Deut. 32:37, 38 · *distress*

15 And the children of Israel said unto the LORD, We have sinned: ᴿdo thou unto us whatsoever seemeth good unto thee; deliver us only, we pray thee, this day.   1 Sam. 3:18; 2 Sam. 15:26

16 ᴿAnd they put away the ᵀstrange gods from among them, and served the LORD: and ᴿhis

soul was grieved for the misery of Israel. Jer. 18:7, 8 · *foreign* · Is. 63:9

17 Then the children of Ammon were gathered together, and encamped in Gil'-e-ad. And the children of Israel assembled themselves together, and encamped in ᴿMiz'-peh. 11:11, 29; Gen. 31:49

18 And the people *and* princes of Gil'-e-ad said one to another, What man *is he* that will begin to fight against the children of Ammon? he shall ᴿbe head over all the inhabitants of Gil'-e-ad. 11:8, 11

11 Now ᴿJeph'-thah the Gil'-e-ad-ite was ᴿa mighty man of valour, and he *was* the son of an harlot: and Gil'-e-ad begat Jeph'-thah. Heb. 11:32 · 6:12; 2 Kin. 5:1

2 And Gil'-e-ad's wife bare him sons; and his wife's sons grew up, and they ᵀthrust out Jeph'-thah, and said unto him, Thou shalt ᴿnot inherit in our father's house; for thou *art* the son of a strange woman. *drove* · Gen. 21:10; Deut. 23:2

3 Then Jeph'-thah fled from his brethren, and dwelt in the land of ᴿTob: and there were gathered ᵀvain men to Jeph'-thah, and went out with him. 2 Sam. 10:6, 8 · *worthless*

4 And it came to pass in process of time, that the children of Ammon made war against Israel.

5 And it was so, that when the children of Ammon made war against Israel, the elders of Gil'-e-ad went to fetch Jeph'-thah out of the land of Tob:

6 And they said unto Jeph'-thah, Come, and be our captain, that we may fight with the children of Ammon.

7 And Jeph'-thah said unto the elders of Gil'-e-ad, ᴿDid not ye hate me, and expel me out of my father's house? and why are ye come unto me now when ye are in ᵀdistress? Gen. 26:27 · *trouble*

8 And the elders of Gil'-e-ad said unto Jeph'-thah, Therefore we ᴿturn again to thee now, that thou mayest go with us, and fight against the children of Ammon, and be our head over all the inhabitants of Gil'-e-ad. [Luke 17:4]

9 And Jeph'-thah said unto the elders of Gil'-e-ad, If ye bring me home again to fight against the children of Ammon, and the LORD deliver them before me, shall I be your head?

10 And the elders of Gil'-e-ad said unto Jeph'-thah, The LORD be witness between us, if we do not so according to thy words.

11 Then Jeph'-thah went with the elders of Gil'-e-ad, and the people made him head and captain over them: and Jeph'-thah uttered all his words ᴿbefore the LORD in Miz'-peh. 20:1; 1 Sam. 10:17

12 And Jeph'-thah sent messengers unto the king of the children of Ammon, saying, ᴿWhat hast thou to do with me, that thou art come against me to fight in my land? 2 Sam. 16:10

13 And the king of the children of Ammon answered unto the messengers of Jeph'-thah, ᴿBecause Israel took away my land, when they came up out of Egypt, from ᴿArnon even unto Jab'-bok, and unto Jordan: now therefore restore those *lands* again peaceably. Num. 21:24–26 · Josh. 13:9

14 And Jeph'-thah sent messengers again unto the king of the children of Ammon:

15 And said unto him, Thus saith Jeph'-thah, Israel took not away the land of Moab, nor the land of the children of Ammon:

16 But when Israel came up from Egypt, and walked through the wilderness unto the Red sea, and ᴿcame to Ka'-desh; Num. 13:26

17 Then Israel sent messengers unto the king of E'-dom, saying, Let me, I pray thee, pass through thy land: ᴿbut the king of E'-dom would not hearken *thereto*. And in like manner they sent unto the ᴿking of Moab: but he would not *consent:* and Israel abode in Ka'-desh. Num. 20:14–21 · Josh. 24:9

18 Then they ᴿwent along through the wilderness, and compassed the land of E'-dom, and the land of Moab, and came by the east side of the land of Moab,

and pitched on the other side of Arnon, but came not within the border of Moab: for Arnon *was* the border of Moab. Deut. 2:9, 18, 19

19 And ᴿIsrael sent messengers unto Si'-hon king of the Am'-or-ites, the king of Hesh'-bon; and Israel said unto him, ᴿLet us pass, we pray thee, through thy land into my place. Num. 21:21 · Deut. 2:27

20 ᴿBut Si'-hon trusted not Israel to pass through his coast: but Si'-hon gathered all his people together, and pitched in Ja'-haz, and fought against Israel. Num. 21:23

21 And the Lord God of Israel ᴿdelivered Si'-hon and all his people into the hand of Israel, and they ᴿsmoteᵀ them: so Israel possessed all the land of the Am'-or-ites, the inhabitants of that country. Josh. 24:8 · Num. 21:24, 25 · *defeated*

22 And they possessed ᴿall the ᵀcoasts of the Am'-or-ites, from Arnon even unto Jab'-bok, and from the wilderness even unto Jordan. Deut. 2:36, 37 · *territory*

23 So now the Lord God of Israel hath ᵀdispossessed the Am'-or-ites from before his people Israel, and shouldest thou possess it? *driven out*

24 Wilt not thou possess that which ᴿChe'-mosh thy god giveth thee to possess? So whomsoever ᴿthe Lord our God shall drive out from before us, them will we possess. 1 Kin. 11:7 · [Deut. 9:4, 5; Josh. 3:10]

25 And now *art* thou any thing better than ᴿBa'-lak the son of Zip'-por, king of Moab? did he ever strive against Israel, or did he ever fight against them, Mic. 6:5

26 While Israel dwelt in ᴿHesh'-bon and her towns, and in Ar'-o-er and her towns, and in all the cities that *be* along by the coasts of Arnon, three hundred years? why therefore did ye not recover *them* within that time? Num. 21:25, 26

27 Wherefore I have not sinned against thee, but thou doest me wrong to war against me: the Lord the Judge ᴿbe judge this day between the children of Israel and the children of Ammon. Gen. 31:53

28 Howbeit the king of the children of Ammon hearkened not unto the words of Jeph'-thah which he sent him.

29 Then ᴿthe Spirit of the Lord came upon Jeph'-thah, and he passed over Gil'-e-ad, and Ma-nas'-seh, and passed over Miz'-peh of Gil'-e-ad, and from Miz'-peh of Gil'-e-ad he passed over *unto* the children of Ammon. 3:10

30 And Jeph'-thah ᴿvowed a vow unto the Lord, and said, If thou shalt without fail deliver the children of Ammon into mine hands, Gen. 28:20; Num. 30:2; 1 Sam. 1:11

31 Then it shall be, that whatsoever cometh forth of the doors of my house to meet me, when I return in peace from the children of Ammon, ᴿshall surely be the Lord's, ᴿand I will offer it up for a burnt offering. Lev. 27:2, 3 · Ps. 66:13

32 So Jeph'-thah passed over unto the children of Ammon to fight against them; and the Lord delivered them into his hands.

33 And he smote them from Ar'-o-er, even till thou come to Min'-nith, *even* twenty cities, and unto the plain of the vineyards, with a very great slaughter. Thus the children of Ammon were subdued before the children of Israel.

34 And Jeph'-thah came to ᴿMiz'-peh unto his house, and, behold, ᴿhis daughter came out to meet him with timbrels and with dances: and she *was his* only child; beside her he had neither son nor daughter. 10:17 · Jer. 31:4

35 And it came to pass, when he saw her, that he ᴿrent his clothes, and said, Alas, my daughter! thou hast brought me very low, and thou art one of them that trouble me: for I ᴿhave opened my mouth unto the Lord, and ᴿI cannot go back. Gen. 37:29 · Eccl. 5:2–5 · Num. 30:2

36 And she said unto him, My father, *if* thou hast opened thy mouth unto the Lord, ᴿdo to me according to that which hath proceeded out of thy mouth; forasmuch as ᴿthe Lord hath taken vengeance for thee of thine ene-

mies, *even* of the children of Ammon. Num. 30:2 · 2 Sam. 18:19, 31

37 And she said unto her father, Let this thing be done for me: let me alone two months, that I may go up and down upon the mountains, and ᵀbewail my virginity, I and my ᵀfellows. *lament · companions*

38 And he said, Go. And he sent her away *for* two months: and she went with her companions, and bewailed her virginity upon the mountains.

39 And it came to pass at the end of two months, that she returned unto her father, who ᴿdid with her *according* to his vow which he had vowed: and she knew no man. And it ᵀwas a custom in Israel, *v. 31 · became*

40 *That* the daughters of Israel went yearly ᵀto lament the daughter of Jeph′-thah the Gil′-e-ad-ite four days in a year. *commemorate*

12 And ᴿthe men of E′-phra-im gathered themselves together, and went northward, and said unto Jeph′-thah, Wherefore passedst thou over to fight against the children of Ammon, and didst not call us to go with thee? we will burn thine house upon thee with fire. 8:1

2 And Jeph′-thah said unto them, I and my people were ᵀat great strife with the children of Ammon; and when I called you, ye delivered me not out of their hands. *in a great struggle*

3 And when I saw that ye delivered *me* not, I ᴿput my life in my hands, and passed over against the children of Ammon, and the LORD delivered them into my hand: wherefore then are ye come up unto me this day, to fight against me? 1 Sam. 19:5; Job 13:14

4 Then Jeph′-thah gathered together all the men of Gil′-e-ad, and fought with E′-phra-im: and the men of Gil′-e-ad smote E′-phra-im, because they said, Ye Gil′-e-ad-ites *are* fugitives of E′-phra-im among the E′-phra-im-ites, *and* among the Ma-nas′-sites.

5 And the Gil′-e-ad-ites took the passages of Jordan before the E′-phra-im-ites: and it was *so*, that when those E′-phra-im-ites which were escaped said, Let me go over; that the men of Gil′-e-ad said unto him, *Art* thou an E′-phra-im-ite? If he said, Nay;

6 Then said they unto him, Say now ᴿShib′-bo-leth: and he said Sib′-bo-leth: for he could not frame to pronounce *it* right. Then they took him, and slew him at the passages of Jordan: and there fell at that time of the E′-phra-im-ites forty and two thousand. Ps. 69:2, 15

7 And Jeph′-thah judged Israel six years. Then died Jeph′-thah the Gil′-e-ad-ite, and was buried in *one of* the cities of Gil′-e-ad.

8 And after him Ib′-zan of Beth′–le-hem judged Israel.

9 And he had thirty sons, and thirty daughters, *whom* he sent abroad, and took in thirty daughters from abroad for his sons. And he judged Israel seven years.

10 Then died Ib′-zan, and was buried at Beth′–le-hem.

11 And after him E′-lon, a Zeb′-u-lon-ite, judged Israel; and he judged Israel ten years.

12 And E′-lon the Zeb′-u-lon-ite died, and was buried in Ai′-ja-lon in the country of Zeb′-u-lun.

13 And after him Ab′-don the son of Hil′-lel, a Pir′-a-thon-ite, judged Israel.

14 And he had forty sons and thirty nephews, that ᴿrode on threescore and ten ass colts: and he judged Israel eight years. 5:10

15 And Ab′-don the son of Hil′-lel the Pir′-a-thon-ite died, and was buried in Pir′-a-thon in the land of E′-phra-im, ᴿin the mount of the Am′-a-lek-ites. 3:13, 27; 5:14

13 And the children of Israel ᴿdid evil again in the sight of the LORD; and the LORD delivered them ᴿinto the hand of the Phi-lis′-tines forty years. 2:11 · 10:7

2 And there was a certain man of ᴿZo′-rah, of the family of the Danites, whose name *was* Ma-no′-ah; and his wife *was* barren, and bare not. 16:31; Josh. 19:41

3 And the ᴿangel of the LORD appeared unto the woman, and said unto her, Behold now, thou *art* barren, and bearest not: but thou shalt conceive, and bear a son.   6:12

4 Now therefore beware, I pray thee, and ᴿdrink not wine nor strong drink, and eat not any unclean *thing:*   Num. 6:2, 3, 20; Luke 1:15

5 For, lo, thou shalt conceive, and bear a son; and no ᴿrazor shall come on his head: for the child shall be a Nazarite unto God from the womb: and he shall begin to deliver Israel out of the hand of the Phi-lis'-tines.   Num. 6:5

6 Then the woman came and told her husband, saying, ᴿA man of God came unto me, and his countenance *was* like the countenance of an angel of God, very terrible: but I ᴿasked him not whence he *was,* neither told he me his name: Gen. 32:24–30 · vv. 17, 18

7 But he said unto me, Behold, thou shalt conceive, and bear a son; and now drink no wine nor strong drink, neither eat any unclean *thing:* for the child shall be a Nazarite to God from the womb to the day of his death.

8 Then Ma-no'-ah intreated the LORD, and said, O my Lord, let the man of God which thou didst send come again unto us, and teach us what we shall do unto the child that shall be born.

9 And God ᵀhearkened to the voice of Ma-no'-ah; and the angel of God came again unto the woman as she sat in the field: but Ma-no'-ah her husband *was* not with her.   *listened*

10 And the woman made haste, and ran, and shewed her husband, and said unto him, Behold, the man hath appeared unto me, that came unto me the *other* day.

11 And Ma-no'-ah arose, and went after his wife, and came to the man, and said unto him, *Art* thou the man that spakest unto the woman? And he said, I *am.*

12 And Ma-no'-ah said, Now let

thy words come to pass. How shall we order the child, and *how* shall we do unto him?

13 And the angel of the LORD said unto Ma-no'-ah, Of all that I said unto the woman let her beware.

14 She may not eat of any *thing* that cometh of the vine, neither let her drink wine or strong drink, nor eat any unclean *thing:* all that I commanded her let her observe.

15 And Ma-no'-ah said unto the angel of the LORD, I pray thee, ᴿlet us detain thee, until we shall have made ready a kid for thee.   6:18

16 And the angel of the LORD said unto Ma-no'-ah, Though thou detain me, I will not eat of thy bread: and if thou wilt offer a burnt offering, thou must offer it unto the LORD. For Ma-no'-ah knew not that he *was* an angel of the LORD.

17 And Ma-no'-ah said unto the angel of the LORD, What *is* thy name, that when thy sayings come to pass we may do thee honour?

18 And the angel of the LORD said unto him, ᴿWhy askest thou thus after my name, seeing it *is* ᵀsecret?   Gen. 32:29 · *wonderful*

19 So Ma-no'-ah took a kid with a meat offering, and offered *it* upon a rock unto the LORD: and *the angel* did wonderously; and Ma-no'-ah and his wife looked on.

20 For it came to pass, when the flame went up toward heaven from off the altar, that the angel of the LORD ascended in the flame of the altar. And Ma-no'-ah and his wife looked on *it,* and ᴿfell on their faces to the ground.   Matt. 17:6

21 But the angel of the LORD did no more appear to Ma-no'-ah and to his wife. ᴿThen Ma-no'-ah knew that he *was* an angel of the LORD.   6:22

22 And Ma-no'-ah said unto his wife, ᴿWe shall surely die, because we have seen God.   Deut. 5:26

23 But his wife said unto him, If the LORD were pleased to kill us, he would not have received a

burnt offering and a meat offering at our hands, neither would he have shewed us all these *things*, nor would as at this time have told us *such things* as these.

24 And the woman bare a son, and called his name Samson: and ᴿthe child grew, and the LORD blessed him. 1 Sam. 3:19; Luke 1:80

25 ᴿAnd the Spirit of the LORD began to move him at times in the camp of Dan between Zo'-rah and Esh'-ta-ol. 3:10; 1 Sam. 11:6; Matt. 4:1

14 And Samson went down to Tim'-nath, and ᴿsaw a woman in Tim'-nath of the daughters of the Phi-lis'-tines. Gen. 34:2

2 And he came up, and told his father and his mother, and said, I have seen a woman in Tim'-nath of the daughters of the Phi-lis'-tines: now therefore ᴿget her for me ᵀto wife. Gen. 21:21 · *as a wife*

3 Then his father and his mother said unto him, *Is there* never a woman among the daughters of ᴿthy brethren, or among all my people, that thou goest to take a wife of the uncircumcised Phi-lis'-tines? And Samson said unto his father, Get her for me; for she pleaseth me well. Gen. 24:3, 4

4 But his father and his mother knew not that it *was* ᴿof the LORD, that he sought an occasion against the Phi-lis'-tines: for at that time the Phi-lis'-tines had dominion over Israel. 1 Kin. 12:15

5 Then went Samson down, and his father and his mother, to Tim'-nath, and came to the vineyards of Tim'-nath: and, behold, a young lion roared against him.

6 And ᴿthe Spirit of the LORD came mightily upon him, and he rent him as he would have rent a kid, and *he had* nothing in his hand: but he told not his father or his mother what he had done. 3:10

7 And he went down, and talked with the woman; and she pleased Samson well.

8 And after a time he returned to take her, and he turned aside to see the carcase of the lion: and, behold, *there was* a swarm of bees and honey in the carcase of the lion.

9 And he took thereof in his hands, and went on eating, and came to his father and mother, and gave them, and they did eat: but he told not them that he had taken the honey out of the ᴿcarcase of the lion. Lev. 11:27

10 So his father went down unto the woman; and Samson made there a feast; for so used the young men to do.

11 And it came to pass, when they saw him, that they brought thirty companions to be with him.

12 And Samson said unto them, I will now ᴿput forth a riddle unto you: if ye can certainly declare it me within the seven days of the feast, and find *it* out, then I will give you thirty sheets and thirty change of garments: 1 Kin. 10:1

13 But if ye cannot declare *it* me, then shall ye give me thirty sheets and thirty change of garments. And they said unto him, ᴿPut forth thy riddle, that we may hear it. Ezek. 17:2

14 And he said unto them, Out of the eater came forth meat, and out of the strong came forth sweetness. And they could not in three days expound the riddle.

15 And it came to pass on the seventh day, that they said unto Samson's wife, ᴿEntice thy husband, that he may declare unto us the riddle, ᴿlest we burn thee and thy father's house with fire: have ye called us to take ᵀthat we have? *is it* not *so?* 16:5 · 15:6 · *what is ours*

16 And Samson's wife wept before him, and said, ᴿThou dost but hate me, and lovest me not: thou hast put forth a riddle unto the children of my people, and hast not told *it* me. And he said unto her, Behold, I have not told *it* my father nor my mother, and shall I tell *it* thee? 16:15

17 And she wept before him the seven days, while their feast lasted: and it came to pass on the seventh day, that he told her, because she ᵀlay sore upon him: and she

THE EXODUS

It is moving day for Moses and more than 600,000 people with all their belongings! For four hundred years, God's people have been slaves in Egypt. Now, after ten awful plagues sent by God on the Egyptians, Pharaoh has agreed to let His people go.

What are the first two stops on the long journey to the Promised Land? (Exodus 12:37; 13:20) Why has God chosen this route? (Exodus 13:18) Where does God tell Moses to set up camp? (Exodus 14:2)

It looks as if God's people are trapped between the desert and the deep blue sea! Pharaoh's army is close on their heels. They must be scared to death! What great miracle takes place here? (Exodus 14:13–28) Can you imagine how the people feel when God saves them from their enemies?

Moving south, the people are hot and thirsty. What happens at Marah and Rephidim? (Exodus 15:23–25; 17:1–6) At last Moses brings the tired travelers to the base of Mount Sinai. There God speaks His laws to Moses, and Moses writes them down for the people. (Exodus 20:1–17)

THE LIFE OF MOSES

The most important moment in Moses' Life was when he went up on Mount Sinai to receive the Law from God (Exodus 19:3). But he had many other important events in his life, as well.

The Great Sea

CANAAN

9 ▲ Mt. Nebo

8

M O A B

GOSHEN

1

5

7

2

Nile River

4 Thebes

Sinai Peninsula

Mt. Sinai (?)

▲

6

M I D I A N

3

3 Moses flees to Midian after killing an Egyptian (Ex. 2:11–15). He meets Reuel (Jethro) and marries his daughter (2:16–22). After 40 years, God calls him to lead His people out of Egypt (Ex. 3:1–4:17).

4 Moses returns to Egypt, where he calls down ten plagues on the Egyptians until Pharaoh lets the Israelites leave (Ex. 5—13).

5 Moses leads the people across the Red Sea (Ex. 14).

6 God gives Moses the Law and instructions concerning the tabernacle at Mount Sinai (Ex. 19–31).

7 For 40 years Moses leads the people through the wilderness (Lev.; Num.).

8 On the plains of Moab, Moses reviews the Law and prepares a new generation of Hebrews to enter the land (Deut. 1—33).

9 Moses views Canaan from the top of Mount Nebo before dying. God buries him in an unmarked grave near Beth-peor (Deut. 34).

1 Moses is born to Hebrew slaves in Egypt, possibly in the land of Goshen (Ex. 2:1, 2; compare Gen. 47:27; Ex. 8:22).

2 When Moses is three months old, he is hidden by his mother in "the river," probably the Nile, where he is found by Pharaoh's daughter. She adopts him, and he grows up in the royal family (Ex. 2:3–10).

© 1996 Thomas Nelson, Inc.

TEN PLAGUES ON EGYPT

Pharaoh, the ruler of Egypt, refused to release the Hebrews from slavery and allow them to leave the country. So the Lord sent ten plagues (Exodus 11:1) on the Egyptians to break Pharaoh's stubborn will and demonstrate His power over the Egyptians' gods. The plagues occurred during a nine-month period.

1. The water of the Nile River is turned to *blood* (Ex. 7:14–25).

2. *Frogs* overrun the countryside (8:1–15).

3. People and animals are infested with *lice* (or insects, 8:16–19).

4. Swarms of *flies* cover the land (8:20–32).

5. *Disease* kills the livestock (9:1–7).

6. *Boils* and sores infect the Egyptians and their animals (9:8–12).

7. *Hail* destroys crops and vegetation (9:13–35).

8. Swarms of *locusts* cover the land (10:1–20).

9. Thick *darkness* covers Egypt for three days (10:21–29).

10. The Egyptian *firstborn*, both people and animals, are *destroyed* by God's death angel (11:1—12:30).

WHERE DID THEY CROSS THE RED SEA?

No one knows the exact spot at which the Israelites crossed the sea on dry ground (Exodus 14:21, 22). Several routes have been proposed.

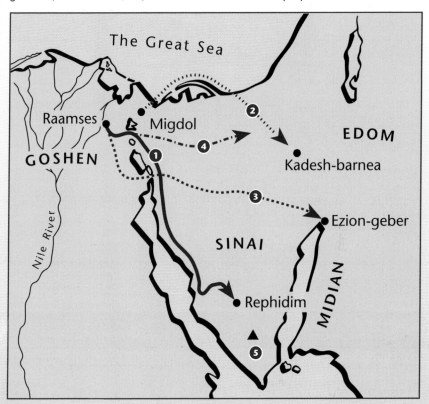

❶ The traditional route has the Hebrews crossing just north of Lake Timsah, then turning south into the Wilderness of Shur and the route for Mount Sinai, believed to be in the far south of the Sinai Peninsula.

❸ A third proposed route suggests that the Israelites crossed south of Great Bitter Lake and Little Bitter Lake. Then, instead of turning south, they would have headed directly east across the Sinai Peninsula to Ezion-geber. This was a route used by Egyptian traders, but it would have been a difficult trip for such a large group of people moving so slowly.

❷ An alternative route suggests that the people traveled north of the main highway connecting Egypt with the east, the Via Maris. The southern end of this thoroughfare was called the Way to the Land of the Philistines. The road was probably guarded by numerous Egyptian garrisons (Ex. 13:17). So the people may have traveled north from Migdol through Baal-zephon (14:2). The gulf there could have been the one called the Reed Sea (Hebrew, *Yam Suph*).

❹ A fourth possible route follows the Way to Shur east toward Kadesh-barnea.

❺ Traditional locale of Mount Sinai

THE ENCAMPMENT OF THE TRIBES OF ISRAEL

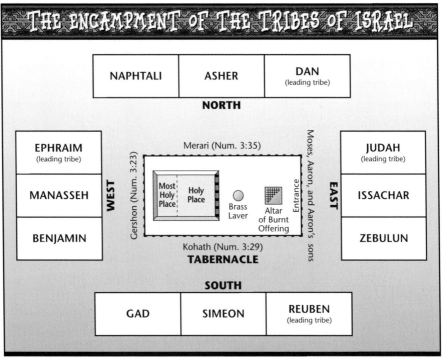

| NAPHTALI | ASHER | DAN (leading tribe) |

NORTH

EPHRAIM (leading tribe)

MANASSEH

BENJAMIN

WEST

Gershon (Num. 3:23)

Merari (Num. 3:35)

Most Holy Place | Holy Place

Brass Laver

Altar of Burnt Offering

Entrance

Kohath (Num. 3:29)

TABERNACLE

Moses, Aaron, and Aaron's sons

EAST

JUDAH (leading tribe)

ISSACHAR

ZEBULUN

SOUTH

| GAD | SIMEON | REUBEN (leading tribe) |

THE PLAN OF THE TABERNACLE

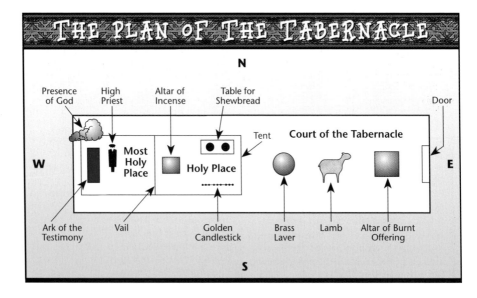

N

Presence of God

High Priest

Altar of Incense

Table for Shewbread

Door

Tent

Court of the Tabernacle

Most Holy Place

Holy Place

W

E

Ark of the Testimony

Vail

Golden Candlestick

Brass Laver

Lamb

Altar of Burnt Offering

S

THE FURNITURE OF THE TABERNACLE

Ark of the Covenant or Ark of the Testimony
(Ex. 25:10–22)
The ark was most sacred of all the furniture in the tabernacle. Here the Hebrews kept a copy of the Ten Commandments.

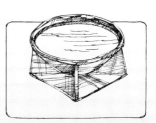

Brass Laver
(Ex. 30:17–21)
The priests would come to the laver of brass for cleansing. They must be pure to enter the presence of God.

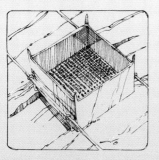

Altar of Burnt Offering
(Ex. 27:1–8)
Animal sacrifices were offered on this altar, located in the court in front of the tabernacle. The blood of the sacrifice was sprinkled on the four horns of the altar.

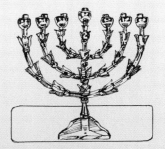

Golden Candlestick or Menorah
(Ex. 25:31–40)
The golden candlestick stood in the holy place, opposite the table of shewbread. It held seven lamps, flat bowls in which a wick lay with one end in the oil of the bowl and the lighted end hanging out.

Table of Shewbread
(Ex. 25:23–30)
Always in God's presence was the table with twelve loaves of bread representing the twelve tribes of Israel.

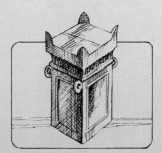

Altar of Incense
(Ex. 30:1–10)
The altar of incense inside the tabernacle was much smaller than the altar of burnt offering outside. The incense burned on the altar made a sweet-smelling aroma.

THE HIGH PRIEST'S CLOTHING

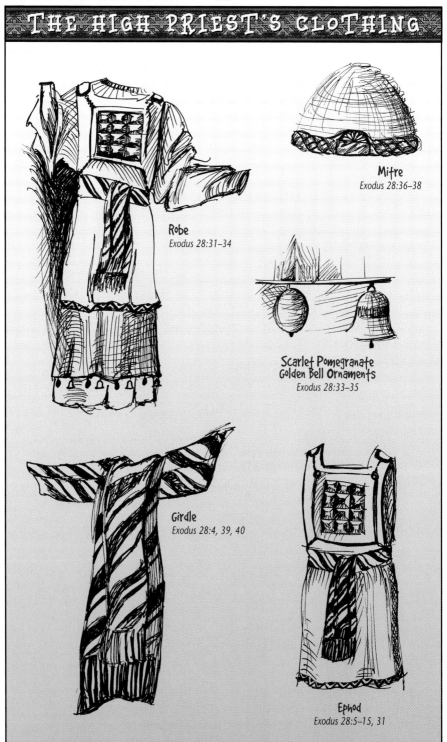

Robe
Exodus 28:31–34

Mitre
Exodus 28:36–38

Scarlet Pomegranate Golden Bell Ornaments
Exodus 28:33–35

Girdle
Exodus 28:4, 39, 40

Ephod
Exodus 28:5–15, 31

THE JOURNEY OF THE ARK FROM SINAI TO JERUSALEM

The ark of the covenant, or "ark of God" (1 Chronicles 16:1), was Israel's most holy object. The Lord's presence dwelled between the cherubim (or angels) fashioned on top of the ark (13:6). Yet the ark underwent a very hard journey during the years before David finally brought it to Jerusalem.

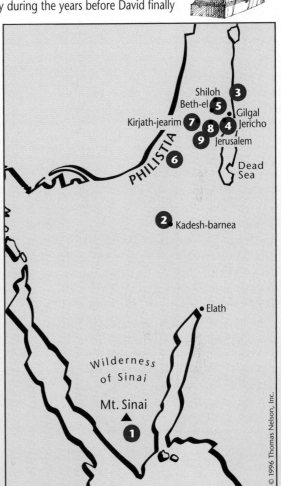

❶ The ark is constructed in the wilderness, probably at Mount Sinai, by the craftsman Bezalel, according to the Lord's instructions and under the supervision of Moses (Ex. 25:10–22; 35:30—36:2; 37:1–9).

❷ The Israelites head toward Canaan, with appointed divisions of the Levites carrying the ark (Num. 10:17). However, the people's rebellion at Kadesh-barnea results in 40 additional years of "wandering."

❸ The ark, carried by priests, leads the people across the Jordan River. While the priests stand in the riverbed, the waters are stopped up and the people cross on dry ground (Josh. 3:14–17).

❹ The ark is carried around the city of Jericho for seven days until its walls fall and the city is captured (Josh. 6).

❺ After the land of Canaan has been taken by the Israelites, the tabernacle is set up at Shiloh (Josh. 18:1; 1 Sam. 3:3). Possibly the ark is taken for a while to Beth-el (Judg. 20:26, 27).

❻ Eli's sons foolishly carry the ark into battle against the Philistines, who capture it and take it back to their own cities (1 Sam. 4:1–11). However, it causes them great trouble, and they finally send it back to the Israelites (5:1—6:12).

❼ The ark stays for 20 years at Kirjath-jearim (1 Sam. 7:1, 2).

❽ David attempts to bring the ark to Jerusalem but meets with tragedy while on the journey. The ark is left at Obed-edom's house for three months (1 Chr. 13).

❾ David finally brings the ark to Jerusalem, where it is eventually kept in the temple built by Solomon (1 Chr. 16:1; 2 Chr. 5:5–14). Years later, the Babylonians capture Jerusalem, destroying the temple (36:19). It is not known what becomes of the ark.

Map labels: Shiloh ❸, Beth-el ❺, Gilgal, Kirjath-jearim ❼, ❽ ❹ Jericho, ❾ Jerusalem, ❻, Dead Sea, PHILISTIA, ❷ Kadesh-barnea, Elath, Wilderness of Sinai, Mt. Sinai ❶

FEASTS OF ISRAEL

Name of Feast	References	Jewish Month (Modern Equivalent) and Day	Purpose
Purim (Heb. *pur*, lit. "the lot")	Esth. 9:16–32	Adar (February/March), 14 by those in villages and unwalled towns; (February/March), 15 by those in fortified cities	To commemorate the deliverance of the Jews from complete destruction through the efforts of Esther; To rejoice together and distribute food and presents
Passover (Heb. *pesah*)	Ex. 12:1–28, 43–49; Lev. 23:5; Num. 28:16; Deut. 16:1–8; Matt. 26:17–20	Nisan or Abib (March/April), 14	To commemorate Israel's deliverance from Egypt; To remind the children of Israel that God spared their firstborn (Ex. 12:27)
Feast of Unleavened Bread* (Heb. *matsot*)	Ex. 12:15–20; 13:3–10; Lev. 23:6–8; Num. 28:17–25; Deut. 16:3–8	Nisan (March/April), 15–21	To commemorate the hardships of Israel's flight from Egypt (Ex. 12:39); To symbolize consecration and devotion to God
Day of Firstfruits (Heb. *bikkurim*)	Lev 23:9–14	Nisan (March/April), 16	To dedicate and consecrate the firstfruits of the barley harvest
Feast of the Pentecost* (Harvest or Weeks; Heb. *shabuot*)	Ex. 23:16; Lev. 23:15–22; Num. 28:26–31; Deut. 16:9–12; Acts 2:1	Sivan (May/June), 6	To dedicate and consecrate the firstfruits of the wheat harvest
Day of Trumpets (Heb. *rosh hashanah*)	Lev. 23:23–25 Num. 10:10; 29:1–6	Tishri (September/October), 1, 2	To consecrate the seventh month as the sabbatical month
Day of Atonement (Heb. *yom kippur*)	Lev. 16:1–34; 23:26–32 Num. 29:7–11; Heb. 9:7	Tishri (September/October), 10	To make atonement for the sins of the priest and the people annually; To make atonement for the tabernacle of meeting
Feast of Tabernacles* (Booths or Ingathering; (Heb. *sukkot*)	Lev. 23:33–43; Num. 29:12–38; Deut. 16:13–17; Neh. 8:13–18; John 7:2	Tishri (September/October), 15–22	To commemorate God's deliverance and protection during the wilderness wandering (Lev. 23:43); To rejoice in the completion of harvest (Lev. 23:39)

*The three major feasts for which all males of Israel were required to travel to the temple in Jerusalem (Ex. 23:14–19).

told the riddle to the children of her people. *pressured him so much*

18 And the men of the city said unto him on the seventh day before the sun went down, What *is* sweeter than honey? And what *is* stronger than a lion? And he said unto them, If ye had not plowed with my heifer, ye had not found out my riddle.

19 And [R]the Spirit of the LORD came upon him, and he went down to Ash'-ke-lon, and slew thirty men of them, and took their spoil, and gave change of garments unto them which expounded the riddle. And his anger was kindled, and he went up to his father's house. 3:10; 13:25

20 But Samson's wife was *given* to his companion, whom he had used as his [T]friend. *best man*

15 But it came to pass within a while after, in the time of wheat harvest, that Samson visited his wife with a [R]kid; and he said, I will go in to my wife into the chamber. But her father would not suffer him to go in. Gen. 38:17

2 And her father said, I verily thought that thou hadst utterly [R]hated her; therefore I gave her to thy companion: *is* not her younger sister fairer than she? take her, I pray thee, instead of her. 14:20

3 And Samson said concerning them, Now shall I be more blameless than the Phi-lis'-tines, though I do them a displeasure.

4 And Samson went and caught three hundred foxes, and took [T]firebrands, and turned tail to tail, and put a firebrand in the midst between two tails. *torches*

5 And when he had set the brands on fire, he let *them* go into the standing corn of the Phi-lis'-tines, and burnt up both the shocks, and also the standing corn, with the vineyards *and* olives.

6 Then the Phi-lis'-tines said, Who hath done this? And they answered, Samson, the son in law of the Tim'-nite, because he had taken his wife, and given her to

his companion. [R]And the Phi-lis'-tines came up, and burnt her and her father with fire. 14:15

7 And Samson said unto them, Though ye have done this, yet will I be avenged of you, and after that I will cease.

8 And he smote them hip and thigh with a great slaughter: and he went down and dwelt in the top of the rock [R]E'-tam. 2 Chr. 11:6

9 Then the Phi-lis'-tines went up, and pitched in Judah, and spread themselves [R]in Le'-hi. v. 19

10 And the men of Judah said, Why are ye come up against us? And they answered, To [T]bind Samson are we come up, to do to him as he hath done to us. *imprison*

11 Then three thousand men of Judah went to the top of the rock E'-tam, and said to Samson, Knowest thou not that the Phi-lis'-tines *are* [R]rulers over us? what *is* this *that* thou hast done unto us? And he said unto them, As they did unto me, so have I done unto them. Lev. 26:25; Deut. 28:43; Ps. 106:40–42

12 And they said unto him, We are come down to bind thee, that we may deliver thee into the hand of the Phi-lis'-tines. And Samson said unto them, Swear unto me, that ye will not fall upon me yourselves.

13 And they spake unto him, saying, No; but we will bind thee fast, and deliver thee into their hand: but surely we will not kill thee. And they bound him with two [R]new cords, and brought him up from the rock. 16:11, 12

14 *And* when he came unto Le'-hi, the Phi-lis'-tines shouted against him: and [R]the Spirit of the LORD came mightily upon him, and the cords that *were* upon his arms became as flax that was burnt with fire, and his bands loosed from off his hands. 3:10; 14:6

15 And he found a new jawbone of an ass, and put forth his hand, and took it, and [R]slew a thousand men therewith. Lev. 26:8; Josh. 23:10

16 And Samson said, With the jawbone of an ass, heaps upon

heaps, with the jaw of an ass have I slain a thousand men.

17 And it came to pass, when he had made an end of speaking, that he cast away the jawbone out of his hand, and called that place Ra'-math–le'-hi.

18 And he was sore athirst, and called on the LORD, and said, ᴿThou hast given this great deliverance into the hand of thy servant: and now shall I die for thirst, and fall into the hand of the uncircumcised?   Ps. 3:7

19 But God clave an hollow place that *was* in the jaw, and there came water thereout; and when he had drunk, ᴿhis spirit came again, and he revived: wherefore he called the name thereof En–hak'-ko-re, which *is* in Le'-hi unto this day.   Gen. 45:27

20 And ᴿhe judged Israel ᴿin the days of the Phi-lis'-tines ᴿtwenty years.   10:2; 12:7–14 · 16:31 · 13:1

16 Then went Samson to Ga'-za, and saw there an harlot, and went in unto her.

2 *And it was told* the Ga'-zites, saying, Samson is come hither. And they compassed *him* in, and laid wait for him all night in the gate of the city, and were quiet all the night, saying, In the morning, when it is day, we shall kill him.

3 And Samson lay till midnight, and arose at midnight, and took the doors of the gate of the city, and the two posts, and went away with them, bar and all, and put *them* upon his shoulders, and carried them up to the top of an hill that *is* before He'-bron.

4 And it came to pass afterward, that he loved a woman in the valley of So'-rek, whose name *was* De-li'-lah.

5 And the ᴿlords of the Phi-lis'-tines came up unto her, and said unto her, Entice him, and see wherein his great strength *lieth,* and by what *means* we may prevail against him, that we may bind him to afflict him: and we will give thee every one of us eleven hundred *pieces* of silver.   Josh. 13:3

6 And De-li'-lah said to Samson, Tell me, I pray thee, wherein thy great strength *lieth,* and wherewith thou mightest be bound to afflict thee.

7 And Samson said unto her, If they bind me with seven ᵀgreen withs that were never dried, then shall I be weak, and be as another man.   *fresh bowstrings*

8 Then the lords of the Phi-lis'-tines brought up to her seven green withs which had not been dried, and she bound him with them.

9 Now *there were* men lying in wait, abiding with her in the chamber. And she said unto him, The Phi-lis'-tines *be* upon thee, Samson. And he brake the withs, as a thread of ᵀtow is broken when it toucheth the fire. So his strength was not known.   *yarn*

10 And De-li'-lah said unto Samson, Behold, thou hast mocked me, and told me lies: now tell me, I pray thee, wherewith thou mightest be bound.

11 And he said unto her, If they bind me fast with new ropes that never were occupied, then shall I be weak, and be as another man.

12 De-li'-lah therefore took new ropes, and bound him therewith, and said unto him, The Phi-lis'-tines *be* upon thee, Samson. And *there were* ᵀliers in wait abiding in the chamber. And he brake them from off his arms like a thread.   *men in hiding*

13 And De-li'-lah said unto Samson, Hitherto thou hast mocked me, and told me lies: tell me wherewith thou mightest be bound. And he said unto her, If thou weavest the seven locks of my head with the web.

14 And she fastened *it* with the pin, and said unto him, The Phi-lis'-tines *be* upon thee, Samson. And he awaked out of his sleep, and went away with the pin of the beam, and with the web.

15 And she said unto him, How canst thou say, I love thee, when thine heart *is* not with me? thou hast mocked me these three

times, and hast not told me wherein thy great strength *lieth.*

16 And it came to pass, when she pressed him daily with her words, and urged him, *so* that his soul was vexed unto death;

17 That he ^Rtold her all his heart, and said unto her, ^RThere hath not come a razor upon mine head; for I *have been* a Nazarite unto God from my mother's womb: if I be shaven, then my strength will go from me, and I shall become weak, and be like any *other* man.   [Mic. 7:5] · Num. 6:5

18 And when De-li'-lah saw that he had told her all his heart, she sent and called for the lords of the Phi-lis'-tines, saying, Come up this once, for he hath shewed me all his heart. Then the lords of the Phi-lis'-tines came up unto her, and brought money in their hand.

19 ^RAnd she made him sleep upon her knees; and she called for a man, and she caused him to shave off the seven locks of his head; and she began to afflict him, and his strength went from him.   Prov. 7:26, 27

20 And she said, The Phi-lis'-tines *be* upon thee, Samson. And he awoke out of his sleep, and said, I will go out as at other times before, and shake myself. And he ^Twist not that the LORD ^Rwas departed from him.   *knew* · Num. 14:9

21 But the Phi-lis'-tines took him, and ^Tput out his ^Reyes, and brought him down to Ga'-za, and bound him with fetters of brass; and he did grind in the prison house.   Lit. *bored out* · 2 Kin. 25:7

22 Howbeit the hair of his head began to grow again after he was shaven.

23 Then the lords of the Phi-lis'-tines gathered them together for to offer a great sacrifice unto ^RDa'-gon their god, and to rejoice: for they said, Our god hath delivered Samson our enemy into our hand.   1 Sam. 5:2

24 And when the people saw him, they ^Rpraised their god: for they said, Our god hath delivered

into our hands our enemy, and the destroyer of our country, which slew many of us.   Dan. 5:4

25 And it came to pass, when their hearts were ^Rmerry, that they said, Call for Samson, that he may ^Tmake us sport. And they called for Samson out of the prison house; and he made them sport: and they set him between the pillars.   9:27 · *perform for us*

26 And Samson said unto the lad that held him by the hand, Suffer me that I may feel the pillars whereupon the house standeth, that I may lean upon them.

27 Now the house was full of men and women; and all the lords of the Phi-lis'-tines *were* there; and *there were* upon the ^Rroof about three thousand men and women, that beheld while Samson made sport.   Deut. 22:8

28 And Samson called unto the LORD, and said, O Lord GOD, ^Rremember me, I pray thee, and strengthen me, I pray thee, only this once, O God, that I may be at once avenged of the Phi-lis'-tines for my two eyes.   Jer. 15:15

29 And Samson took hold of the two middle pillars upon which the house stood, and on which it was borne up, of the one with his right hand, and of the other with his left.

30 And Samson said, Let me die with the Phi-lis'-tines. And he bowed himself with *all his* might; and the house fell upon the lords, and upon all the people that *were* therein. So the dead which he slew at his death were more than *they* which he slew in his life.

31 Then his brethren and all the house of his father came down, and took him, and brought *him* up, and buried him between Zo'-rah and Esh'-ta-ol in the burying-place of Ma-no'-ah his father. And he judged Israel twenty years.

17 And there was a man of mount E'-phra-im, whose name *was* ^RMi'-cah.   18:2

2 And he said unto his mother, The eleven hundred *shek'-els* of silver that were taken from thee,

about which thou ᴿcursedst, and spakest of also in mine ears, behold, the silver *is* with me; I took it. And his mother said, Blessed *be thou* of the LORD, my son.   Lev. 5:1

3 And when he had restored the eleven hundred *shek'-els* of silver to his mother, his mother said, I had wholly dedicated the silver unto the LORD from my hand for my son, to ᴿmake a graven image and a molten image: now therefore I will restore it unto thee.   Ex. 20:4, 23; 34:17; Lev. 19:4

4 Yet he restored the money unto his mother; and his mother took two hundred *shek'-els* of silver, and gave them to the founder, who made thereof a graven image and a molten image: and they were in the house of Mi'-cah.

5 And the man Mi'-cah had an house of gods, and made an ᴿe'-phod, and ᴿter'-a-phim, and consecrated one of his sons, who became his priest.   18:14 · Hos. 3:4

6 ᴿIn those days *there was* no king in Israel, ᴿbut every man did *that which was* right in his own eyes.   18:1; 19:1 · 21:25; Deut. 12:8

7 And there was a young man out of Beth'–le-hem–ju'-dah of the family of Judah, who *was* a Levite, and he sojourned there.

8 And the man departed out of the city from Beth'–le-hem–ju'-dah to sojourn where he could find *a place:* and he came to mount E'-phra-im to the house of Mi'-cah, as he journeyed.

9 And Mi'-cah said unto him, Whence comest thou? And he said unto him, I *am* a Levite of Beth'–le-hem–ju'-dah, and I go to sojourn where I may find *a place.*

10 And Mi'-cah said unto him, Dwell with me, and be unto me a father and a priest, and I will give thee ten *shek'-els* of silver by the year, and a suit of apparel, and thy victuals. So the Levite went in.

11 And the Levite was content to dwell with the man; and the young man was unto him as one of his sons.

12 And Mi'-cah ᴿconsecrated the Levite; and the young man ᴿbecame his priest, and was in the house of Mi'-cah.   v. 5 · 18:30

13 Then said Mi'-cah, Now know I that the LORD will do me good, seeing I have a Levite to *my* ᴿpriest.   18:4

18 In those days *there was* no king in Israel: and in those days the tribe of the Danites sought them an inheritance to dwell in; for unto that day *all their* inheritance had not fallen unto them among the tribes of Israel.

2 And the children of Dan sent of their family five men from their coasts, men of valour, from Zo'-rah, and from Esh'-ta-ol, to spy out the land, and to search it; and they said unto them, Go, search the land: who when they came to mount E'-phra-im, to the ᴿhouse of Mi'-cah, they lodged there.   17:1

3 When they *were* by the house of Mi'-cah, they knew the voice of the young man the Levite: and they turned in thither, and said unto him, Who brought thee hither? and what makest thou in this *place?* and what hast thou here?

4 And he said unto them, Thus and thus dealeth Mi'-cah with me, and hath ᴿhired me, and I am his priest.   17:10, 12

5 And they said unto him, ᴿAsk counsel, we pray thee, ᴿof God, that we may know whether our way which we go shall be prosperous.   1 Kin. 22:5 · 1:1; 17:5; 18:14

6 And the priest said unto them, Go in peace: before the LORD *is* your way wherein ye go.

7 Then the five men departed, and came to La'-ish, and saw the people that *were* therein, ᴿhow they dwelt ᵀcareless, after the manner of the Zi-do'-ni-ans, quiet and secure; and *there was* no magistrate in the land, that might put *them* to shame in *any* thing; and they *were* far from the Zi-do'-ni-ans, and had no business with *any* man.   vv. 27–29 · *safely* or *securely*

8 And they came unto their brethren to ᴿZo'-rah and Esh'-ta-

ol: and their brethren said unto them, What *say* ye?   v. 2

9 And they said, ᴿArise, that we may go up against them: for we have seen the land, and, behold, it *is* very good: and *are* ye still? be not slothful to go, *and* to enter to possess the land.   Num. 13:30

10 When ye go, ye shall come unto a people ᴿsecure, and to a large land: for God hath given it into your hands; ᴿa place where *there is* no want of any thing that *is* in the earth.   vv. 7, 27 · Deut. 8:9

11 And there went from thence of the family of the Danites, out of Zo′-rah and out of Esh′-ta-ol, six hundred men ᵀappointed with weapons of war.   armed

12 And they went up, and pitched in ᴿKir′-jath–je′-a-rim, in Judah: wherefore they called that place ᴿMa′-ha-neh–dan unto this day: behold, *it is* behind Kir′-jath–je′-a-rim.   Josh. 15:60 · 13:25

13 And they passed thence unto mount E′-phra-im, and came unto ᴿthe house of Mi′-cah.   v. 2

14 Then answered the five men that went to spy out the country of La′-ish, and said unto their brethren, Do ye know that ᴿthere is in these houses an e′-phod, and ter′-a-phim, and a graven image, and a molten image? now therefore consider what ye have to do.   17:5

15 And they turned ᵀthitherward, and came to the house of the young man the Levite, *even* unto the house of Mi′-cah, and ᵀsaluted him.   aside there · greeted

16 And the ᴿsix hundred men appointed with their weapons of war, which *were* of the children of Dan, stood by the entering of the gate.   v. 11

17 And the five men that went to spy out the land went up, *and* came in thither, *and* took the graven image, and the e′-phod, and the ter′-a-phim, and the molten image: and the priest stood in the entering of the gate with the six hundred men *that were* appointed with weapons of war.

18 And these went into Mi′-cah's house, and fetched the carved image, the e′-phod, and the ter′-a-phim, and the molten image. Then said the priest unto them, What do ye?

19 And they said unto him, Hold thy peace, ᴿlay thine hand upon thy mouth, and go with us, ᴿand be to us a father and a priest: *is it* better for thee to be a priest unto the house of one man, or that thou be a priest unto a tribe and a family in Israel?   Job 21:5; 29:9; 40:4 · 17:10

20 And the priest's heart was glad, and he took the e′-phod, and the ter′-a-phim, and the graven image, and went in the midst of the people.

21 So they turned and departed, and put the little ones and the cattle and the carriage before them.

22 *And* when they were a good way from the house of Mi′-cah, the men that *were* in the houses near to Mi′-cah's house were gathered together, and overtook the children of Dan.

23 And they cried unto the children of Dan. And they turned their faces, and said unto Mi′-cah, What aileth thee, that thou comest with such a company?

24 And he said, Ye have ᴿtaken away my ᵀgods which I made, and the priest, and ye are gone away: and what have I more? and what *is* this *that* ye say unto me, What aileth thee?   17:5; Gen. 31:30 · idols

25 And the children of Dan said unto him, Let not thy voice be heard among us, lest ᵀangry fellows run upon thee, and thou lose thy life, with the lives of thy household.   Lit. bitter of soul

26 And the children of Dan went their way: and when Mi′-cah saw that they *were* too strong for him, he turned and went back unto his house.

27 And they took *the things* which Mi′-cah had made, and the priest which he had, and came unto La′-ish, unto a people *that were* at quiet and secure: ᴿand they ᵀsmote them with the edge of

the sword, and burnt the city with fire.   Josh. 19:47 · *struck*

28 And *there was* no deliverer, because it *was* ᴿfar from Zi'-don, and they had ᵀno business with *any* man; and it was in the valley that *lieth* ᴿby Beth–re'-hob. And they built a city, and dwelt therein.   v. 7 · *no ties* · Num. 13:21; 2 Sam. 10:6

29 And they called the name of the city Dan, after the name of Dan their father, who was born unto Israel: howbeit the name of the city *was* La'-ish at the first.

30 And the children of Dan set up the graven image: and Jonathan, the son of Ger'-shom, the son of Ma-nas'-seh, he and his sons were priests to the tribe of Dan ᴿuntil the day of the captivity of the land.   2 Kin. 15:29

31 And they set them up Mi'-cah's graven image, which he made, ᴿall the time that the house of God was in Shi'-loh.   19:18; 21:12

19 And it came to pass in those days, ᴿwhen *there was* no king in Israel, that there was a certain Levite sojourning on the side of mount E'-phra-im, who took to him a concubine out of Beth'–le-hem–ju'-dah. 17:6; 18:1; 21:25

2 And his concubine played the whore against him, and went away from him unto her father's house to Beth'–le-hem–ju'-dah, and was there four whole months.

3 And her husband arose, and went after her, to speak friendly unto her, *and* to bring her again, having his servant with him, and a couple of asses: and she brought him into her father's house: and when the father of the damsel saw him, he rejoiced to meet him.

4 And his father in law, the damsel's father, retained him; and he abode with him three days: so they did eat and drink, and lodged there.

5 And it came to pass on the fourth day, when they arose early in the morning, that he rose up to depart: and the damsel's father said unto his son in law, Comfort thine heart with a morsel of bread, and afterward go your way.

6 And they sat down, and did eat and drink both of them together: for the damsel's father had said unto the man, Be content, I pray thee, and tarry all night, and let thine heart be merry.

7 And when the man rose up to depart, his father in law urged him: therefore he lodged there again.

8 And he arose early in the morning on the fifth day to depart: and the damsel's father said, Comfort thine heart, I pray thee. And they tarried until afternoon, and they did eat both of them.

9 And when the man rose up to depart, he, and his concubine, and his servant, his father in law, the damsel's father, said unto him, Behold, now the day draweth toward evening, I pray you tarry all night: behold, the day groweth to an end, lodge here, that thine heart may be merry; and to morrow get you early on your way, that thou mayest go home.

10 But the man would not tarry that night, but he rose up and departed, and came over against ᴿJe'-bus, which *is* Jerusalem; and *there were* with him two asses saddled, his concubine also *was* with him.   Josh. 18:28; 1 Chr. 11:4, 5

11 *And* when they *were* by Je'-bus, the day was far spent; and the servant said unto his master, Come, I pray thee, and let us turn in into this city ᴿof the Jeb'-u-sites, and lodge in it.   1:21; 2 Sam. 5:6

12 And his master said unto him, We will not turn aside hither into the city of a stranger, that *is* not of the children of Israel; we will pass over to Gib'-e-ah.

13 And he said unto his servant, Come, and let us draw near to one of these places to lodge all night, in Gib'-e-ah, or in Ra'-mah.

14 And they passed on and went their way; and the sun went down upon them *when they were* by

Gib'-e-ah, which *belongeth* to Benjamin.

15 And they turned aside thither, to go in *and* to lodge in Gib'-e-ah: and when he went in, he sat him down in a street of the city: for *there was* no man that took them into his house to lodging.

16 And, behold, there came an old man from his work out of the field at even, which *was* also of mount E'-phra-im; and he sojourned in Gib'-e-ah: but the men of the place *were* Benjamites.

17 And when he had lifted up his eyes, he saw a ᵀwayfaring man in the street of the city: and the old man said, Whither goest thou? and whence comest thou? *traveller*

18 And he said unto him, We *are* passing from Beth'–le-hem–ju'-dah toward the side of mount E'-phra-im; from thence *am* I: and I went to Beth'–le-hem–ju'-dah, but I *am now* going to ᴿthe house of the LORD; and there *is* no man that receiveth me to house.   Josh. 18:1

19 Yet there is both straw and provender for our asses; and there is bread and wine also for me, and for thy handmaid, and for the young man *which is* with thy servants: *there is* no want of any thing.

20 And the old man said, ᴿPeace *be* with thee; howsoever *let* all thy wants *lie* upon me; ᴿonly lodge not in the street.   6:23 · Gen. 19:2

21 So he brought him into his house, and gave provender unto the asses: and they washed their feet, and did eat and drink.

22 *Now* as they were making their hearts merry, behold, the men of the city, certain sons of Be'-li-al, beset the house round about, *and* beat at the door, and spake to the master of the house, the old man, saying, Bring forth the man that came into thine house, that we may know him.

23 And ᴿthe man, the master of the house, went out unto them, and said unto them, Nay, my brethren, *nay*, I pray you, do not *so* wickedly; seeing that this man

is come into mine house, ᴿdo not this folly.   Gen. 19:6, 7 · Gen. 34:7

24 Behold, *here is* my daughter a maiden, and his concubine; them I will bring out now, and humble ye them, and do with them what seemeth good unto you: but unto this man do not so vile a thing.

25 But the men would not hearken to him: so the man took his concubine, and brought her forth unto them; and they knew her, and abused her all the night until the morning: and when the day began to spring, they let her go.

26 Then came the woman in the dawning of the day, and fell down at the door of the man's house where her lord *was*, till it was light.

27 And her lord rose up in the morning, and opened the doors of the house, and went out to go his way: and, behold, the woman his concubine was fallen down *at* the door of the house, and her hands *were* upon the threshold.

28 And he said unto her, Up, and let us be going. But none answered. Then the man took her *up* upon an ass, and the man rose up, and gat him unto his place.

29 And when he was come into his house, he took a knife, and laid hold on his concubine, and ᴿdivided her, *together* with her bones, into twelve pieces, and sent her into all the coasts of Israel.   20:6; 1 Sam. 11:7

30 And it was so, that all that saw it said, There was no such deed done nor seen from the day that the children of Israel came up out of the land of Egypt unto this day: consider of it, ᴿtake advice, and speak *your minds*.   20:7

20 Then ᴿall the children of Israel went out, and the congregation was gathered together as one man, from ᴿDan even to Be'-er–she'-ba, with the land of Gil'-e-ad, unto the LORD in Miz'-peh.   v. 11; 21:5; Josh. 22:12 · 18:29

2 And the chief of all the people, *even* of all the tribes of Israel, presented themselves in the

assembly of the people of God, four hundred thousand footmen Rthat drew sword.   8:10

3 (Now the children of Benjamin heard that the children of Israel were gone up to Miz'-peh.) Then said the children of Israel, Tell *us*, Thow was this wickedness?   *how did this wicked deed happen*

4 And the Levite, the husband of the woman that was slain, answered and said, RI came into Gib'-e-ah that *belongeth* to Benjamin, I and my concubine, to Tlodge.   19:15 · *spend the night*

5 RAnd the men of Gib'-e-ah rose against me, and beset the house round about upon me by night, *and* thought to have slain me: Rand my concubine have they forced, that she is dead. 19:22 · 19:25

6 And RI took my concubine, and cut her in pieces, and sent her throughout all the country of the inheritance of Israel: for they Rhave committed lewdness and folly in Israel.   19:29 · Josh. 7:15

7 Behold, ye *are* all children of Israel; Rgive here your advice and counsel.   19:30

8 And all the people arose as one man, saying, We will not any *of us* go to his tent, neither will we any *of us* turn into his house.

9 But now this *shall be* the thing which we will do to Gib'-e-ah; *we will go up* by lot against it;

10 And we will take ten men of an hundred throughout all the tribes of Israel, and an hundred of a thousand, and a thousand out of ten thousand, to Tfetch victual for the people, that they may do, when they come to Gib'-e-ah of Benjamin, according to all the Tfolly that they have wrought in Israel.   *make provisions · vileness*

11 So all the men of Israel were gathered against the city, Tknit together as one man.   *united*

12 RAnd the tribes of Israel sent men through all the tribe of Benjamin, saying, What wickedness *is* this that is done among you?   Deut. 13:14; Josh. 22:13, 16

13 Now therefore deliver *us* the men, the children of Be'-li-al, which *are* in Gib'-e-ah, that we may put them to death, and put away evil from Israel. But the children of Benjamin would not hearken to the voice of their brethren the children of Israel:

14 But the children of Benjamin gathered themselves together out of the cities unto Gib'-e-ah, to go out to battle against the children of Israel.

15 And the Rchildren of Benjamin were numbered at that time out of the cities twenty and six thousand men that drew sword, beside the inhabitants of Gib'-e-ah, which were numbered seven hundred chosen men. Num. 1:36, 37

16 Among all this people *there were* seven hundred chosen men Rlefthanded; every one could sling stones at an hair *breadth*, and not miss.   3:15; 1 Chr. 12:2

17 And the men of Israel, beside Benjamin, were numbered four hundred thousand men that drew sword: all these *were* men of war.

18 And the children of Israel arose, and went up to Tthe house of God, and Rasked counsel of God, and said, Which of us shall go up first to the battle against the children of Benjamin? And the LORD said, RJudah *shall go up* first.   Heb. *Beth-el* · Num. 27:21 · 1:1, 2

19 And the children of Israel rose up in the morning, and encamped against Gib'-e-ah.

20 And the men of Israel went out to battle against Benjamin; and the men of Israel put themselves in array to fight against them at Gib'-e-ah.

21 And Rthe children of Benjamin came forth out of Gib'-e-ah, and destroyed down to the ground of the Israelites that day twenty and two thousand men. [Gen. 49:27]

22 And the people the men of Israel encouraged themselves, and set their battle again in array in the place where they put themselves in array the first day.

23 (RAnd the children of Israel went up and wept before the LORD

until even, and asked counsel of the LORD, saying, Shall I go up again to battle against the children of Benjamin my brother? And the LORD said, Go up against him.)   vv. 26, 27

24 And the children of Israel came near against the children of Benjamin the second day.

25 And Benjamin went forth against them out of Gib'-e-ah the second day, and destroyed down to the ground of the children of Israel again eighteen thousand men; all these drew the sword.

26 Then all the children of Israel, and all the people, ᴿwent up, and came unto ᵀthe house of God, and wept, and sat there before the LORD, and fasted that day until even, and offered burnt offerings and peace offerings before the LORD.   vv. 18, 23; 21:2 · Heb. Beth-el

27 And the children of Israel enquired of the LORD, (for ᴿthe ark of the covenant of God was there in those days, Josh. 18:1; 1 Sam. 1:3; 3:3

28 ᴿAnd Phin'-e-has, the son of E-le-a'-zar, the son of Aaron, stood before it in those days,) saying, Shall I yet again go out to battle against the children of Benjamin my brother, or shall I cease? And the LORD said, Go up; for to morrow I will deliver them into thine hand.   Num. 25:7, 13; Josh. 24:33

29 And Israel ᴿset liers in wait round about Gib'-e-ah.   Josh. 8:4

30 And the children of Israel went up against the children of Benjamin on the third day, and put themselves in array against Gib'-e-ah, as at other times.

31 And the children of Benjamin went out against the people, and were drawn away from the city; and they began to smite of the people, and kill, as at other times, in the highways, of which ᴿone goeth up to the house of God, and the other to Gib'-e-ah in the field, about thirty men of Israel.   21:19

32 And the children of Benjamin said, They are smitten down before us, as at the first. But the children of Israel said, Let us flee, and

draw them from the city unto the highways.

33 And all the men of Israel rose up out of their place, and put themselves in array at Ba'-al-ta'-mar: and the ᵀliers in wait of Israel came forth out of their places, even out of the meadows of Gib'-e-ah.   men in ambush

34 And there came against Gib'-e-ah ten thousand chosen men out of all Israel, and the battle was sore: ᴿbut they knew not that ᵀevil was near them.   Josh. 8:14 · disaster

35 And the LORD smote Benjamin before Israel: and the children of Israel destroyed of the Benjamites that day twenty and five thousand and an hundred men: all these drew the sword.

36 So the children of Benjamin saw that they were smitten: ᴿfor the men of Israel gave place to the Benjamites, because they trusted unto the liers in wait which they had set beside Gib'-e-ah.   Josh. 8:15

37 ᴿAnd the liers in wait hasted, and rushed upon Gib'-e-ah; and the liers in wait drew themselves along, and smote all the city with the edge of the sword.   Josh. 8:19

38 Now there was an appointed sign between the men of Israel and the liers in wait, that they should make a great flame with smoke rise up out of the city.

39 And when the men of Israel retired in the battle, Benjamin began ᵀto smite and kill of the men of Israel about thirty persons: for they said, Surely they are smitten down before us, as in the first battle.   Lit. to strike the slain ones of

40 But when the flame began to arise up out of the city with a pillar of smoke, the Benjamites ᴿlooked behind them, and, behold, the flame of the city ascended up to heaven.   Josh. 8:20

41 And when the men of Israel turned again, the men of Benjamin were amazed: for they saw that evil was come upon them.

42 Therefore they ᵀturned their backs before the men of Israel unto the way of the wilderness;

but the battle overtook them; and them which *came* out of the cities they destroyed in the midst of them. *fled*

43 *Thus* they inclosed the Benjamites round about, *and* chased them, *and* ^Ttrode them down with ease over against Gib'-e-ah toward the ^Tsunrising. *trampled · east*

44 And there fell of Benjamin eighteen thousand men; all these *were* men of valour.

45 And they turned and fled toward the wilderness unto the rock of Rim'-mon: and they ^Tgleaned of them in the highways five thousand men; and pursued hard after them unto Gi'-dom, and slew two thousand men of them. *cut down*

46 So that all which fell that day of Benjamin were twenty and five thousand men that drew the sword; all these *were* ^Tmen of valour. *valiant warriors*

47 But six hundred men turned and fled to the wilderness unto the rock Rim'-mon, and abode in the rock Rim'-mon four months.

48 And the men of Israel ^Tturned again upon the children of Benjamin, and smote them with the edge of the sword, as well the men of *every* city, as the beast, and all that came to hand: also they set on fire all the cities that they came to. *turned back against*

21 Now ^Rthe men of Israel had sworn in Miz'-peh, saying, There shall not any of us give his daughter unto Benjamin to wife. 20:1

2 And the people came ^Rto the house of God, and abode there till even before God, and lifted up their voices, and wept sore; 20:18

3 And said, O LORD God of Israel, why is this come to pass in Israel, that there should be to day one tribe lacking in Israel?

4 And it came to pass on the morrow, that the people rose early, and ^Rbuilt there an altar, and offered burnt offerings and peace offerings. Deut. 12:5; 2 Sam. 24:25

5 And the children of Israel said, Who *is there* among all the tribes of Israel that came not up with the congregation unto the LORD? ^RFor they had made a great oath concerning him that came not up to the LORD to Miz'-peh, saying, He shall surely be put to death. 20:1–3

6 And the children of Israel ^Trepented them for Benjamin their brother, and said, There is one tribe cut off from Israel this day. *grieved*

7 How shall we do for wives for them that remain, seeing we have sworn by the LORD that we will not give them of our daughters to wives?

8 And they said, What one *is there* of the tribes of Israel that came not up to Miz'-peh to the LORD? And, behold, there came none to the camp from Ja'-besh–gil'-e-ad to the assembly.

9 For the people were ^Tnumbered, and, behold, *there were* none of the inhabitants of Ja'-besh–gil'-e-ad there. *counted*

10 And the congregation sent thither twelve thousand men of the valiantest, and commanded them, saying, ^RGo and smite the inhabitants of Ja'-besh–gil'-e-ad with the edge of the sword, with the women and the children. 5:23

11 And this *is* the thing that ye shall do, ^RYe shall utterly destroy every male, and every woman that hath lain by man. Deut. 20:13, 14

12 And they found among the inhabitants of Ja'-besh–gil'-e-ad four hundred young virgins, that had known no man by lying with any male: and they brought them unto the camp to ^RShi'-loh, which *is* in the land of Canaan. 18:31

13 And the whole congregation sent *some* to speak to the children of Benjamin ^Rthat were in the rock Rim'-mon, and to call peaceably unto them. 20:47

14 And Benjamin came again at that time; and they gave them wives which they had saved alive of the women of Ja'-besh–gil'-e-ad: and yet ^Tso they sufficed them not. *they had not found enough for them*

15 And the people [R]repented them for Benjamin, because that the LORD had made a breach in the tribes of Israel.   v. 6

16 Then the elders of the congregation said, How shall we do for wives for them that remain, seeing the women are destroyed out of Benjamin?

17 And they said, *There must be* an inheritance for them that be escaped of Benjamin, that a tribe be not destroyed out of Israel.

18 Howbeit we may not give them wives of our daughters: [R]for the children of Israel have sworn, saying, Cursed *be* he that giveth a wife to Benjamin.   v. 1; 11:35

19 Then they said, Behold, *there is* a feast of the LORD in [R]Shi'-loh yearly *in a place* which *is* on the north side of Beth'–el, on the east side of the highway that goeth up from Beth'–el to She'-chem, and on the south of Le-bo'-nah.   18:31

20 Therefore they commanded the children of Benjamin, saying, Go and lie in wait in the vineyards;

21 And see, and, behold, if the daughters of Shi'-loh come out [R]to dance in dances, then come ye out of the vineyards, and catch you every man his wife of the daughters of Shi'-loh, and go to the land of Benjamin.   11:34; Ex. 15:20

22 And it shall be, when their fathers or their brethren come unto us to complain, that we will say unto them, [T]Be favourable unto them for our sakes: because we reserved not to each man his wife in the war: for ye did not give unto them at this time, *that* ye should be guilty.   *Be kind*

23 And the children of Benjamin did so, and took *them* wives, according to their number, of them that danced, whom they caught: and they went and returned unto their inheritance, and [R]repaired[T] the cities, and dwelt in them.   20:48 · *rebuilt*

24 And the children of Israel departed thence at that time, every man to his tribe and to his family, and they went out from thence every man to his inheritance.

25 [R]In those days *there was* no king in Israel: [R]every man did *that which was* right in his own eyes.   17:6; 18:1; 19:1 · 17:6; Deut. 12:8

The Book of

RUTH

RUTH is a cameo story of love, devotion, and redemption set in the black context of the days of the judges. It is the story of a Moabite woman who forsakes her pagan heritage in order to cling to the people of Israel and to the God of Israel. Because of her *faithfulness* in a time of national *faithlessness,* God rewards her by giving her a new husband (Boaz), a son (Obed), and a privileged position in the lineage of David and Christ (she is the great-grandmother of David).

Ruth is the Hebrew title of this book. This name may be a Moabite modification of the Hebrew word *reuit,* meaning "friendship" or "association." The Septuagint entitles the book *Routh,* the Greek equivalent of the Hebrew name. The Latin title is *Ruth,* a transliteration of *Routh.*

NOW it came to pass in the days when the judges ruled, that there was a famine in the land. And a certain man of [R]Beth'– le-hem-ju'-dah went to sojourn in the country of Moab, he, and his wife, and his two sons.   Judg. 17:8

2 And the name of the man

was E-lim'-e-lech, and the name of his wife Na-o'-mi, and the name of his two sons Mah'-lon and Chil'-i-on, Eph'-rath-ites of Beth'-le-hem–ju'-dah. And they came ^Rinto the country of Moab, and continued there.   Judg. 3:30

3 And E-lim'-e-lech Na-o'-mi's husband died; and she was left, and her two sons.

4 And they took them wives of the women of Moab; the name of the one *was* Or'-pah, and the name of the other Ruth: and they dwelled there about ten years.

5 And Mah'-lon and Chil'-i-on died also both of them; and the woman was left of her two sons and her husband.

6 Then she arose with her daughters in law, that she might return from the country of Moab: for she had heard in the country of Moab how that the LORD had ^Rvisited his people in ^Rgiving them bread.   Luke 1:68 · Ps. 132:15; Matt. 6:11

7 Wherefore she went forth out of the place where she was, and her two daughters in law with her; and they went on the way to return unto the land of Judah.

8 And Na-o'-mi said unto her two daughters in law, ^RGo, return each to her mother's house: ^Rthe LORD deal kindly with you, as ye have dealt with the dead, and with me.   Josh. 24:15 · 2 Tim. 1:16–18

9 The LORD grant you that ye may find ^Rrest, each *of you* in the house of her husband. Then she kissed them; and they lifted up their voice, and wept.   3:1

10 And they said unto her, Surely we will return with thee unto thy people.

11 And Na-o'-mi said, Turn again, my daughters: why will ye go with me? *are* there yet *any more* sons in my womb, ^Rthat they may be your husbands?   Deut. 25:5

12 Turn again, my daughters, go *your way*; for I am too old to have an husband. If I should say, I have hope, *if* I should have an husband also to night, and should also bear sons;

13 Would ye tarry for them till they were grown? would ye ^Tstay for them from having husbands? nay, my daughters; for it grieveth me much for your sakes that the hand of the LORD is gone out against me.   *restrain yourselves from*

14 And they lifted up their voice, and wept again: and Or'-pah kissed her mother in law; but Ruth ^Tclave unto her.   *clung*

15 And she said, Behold, thy sister in law is gone back unto her people, and unto her gods: return thou after thy sister in law.

16 And Ruth said, ^RIntreat me not to leave thee, *or* to return from following after thee: for whither thou goest, I will go; and where thou lodgest, I will lodge: ^Rthy people *shall be* my people, and thy God my God: 2 Kin. 2:2, 4 · 2:11, 12

17 Where thou diest, will I die, and there will I be buried: ^Rthe LORD do so to me, and more also, *if ought* but death part thee and me.   1 Sam. 3:17; 2 Sam. 19:13; 2 Kin. 6:31

18 When she saw that she was stedfastly minded to go with her, then she left speaking unto her.

19 So they two went until they came to Beth'–le-hem. And it came to pass, when they were come to Beth'–le-hem, that all the city was moved about them, and they said, ^R*Is* this Na-o'-mi?   Is. 23:7

20 And she said unto them, Call me not Na-o'-mi, call me ^TMa'-ra: for the Almighty hath dealt very bitterly with me.   Lit. *Bitter*

21 I went out full, and the LORD hath brought me home again empty: why *then* call ye me ^TNa-o'-mi, seeing the LORD hath testified against me, and the Almighty hath afflicted me?   Lit. *Pleasant*

22 So Na-o'-mi returned, and Ruth the Mo'-ab-i-tess, her daughter in law, with her, which returned out of the country of Moab: and they came to Beth'–le-hem ^Rin the beginning of barley harvest.   2:23; 2 Sam. 21:9

2 And Na-o'-mi had a ^Rkinsman of her husband's, a mighty man of wealth, of the family of ^RE-

lim'-e-lech; and his name *was*
^RBo'-az.   3:2, 12 · 1:2 · 4:21
2 And Ruth the Mo'-ab-i-tess
said unto Na-o'-mi, Let me now
go to the ^Rfield, and glean ears of
corn after *him* in whose sight I
shall find grace. And she said
unto her, Go, my daughter. Lev. 19:9
3 And she went, and came, and
gleaned in the field after the
reapers: and her hap was to light
on a part of the field *belonging*
unto Bo'-az, who *was* of the kindred of E-lim'-e-lech.
4 And, behold, Bo'-az came
from ^RBeth'-le-hem, and said unto
the reapers, ^RThe LORD *be* with
you. And they answered him, The
LORD bless thee.   1:1 · Ps. 129:7, 8
5 Then said Bo'-az unto his ser-
vant that was set over the reapers,
Whose damsel *is* this?
6 And the servant that was set
over the reapers answered and
said, It *is* the Mo'-ab-i-tish damsel
^Rthat came back with Na-o'-mi out
of the country of Moab: 1:22
7 And she said, I pray you, let
me glean and gather after the
reapers among the sheaves: so
she came, and hath continued
even from the morning until now,
^Tthat she tarried a little in the
house.   *though she rested*
8 Then said Bo'-az unto Ruth,
Hearest thou not, my daughter?
Go not to glean in another field,
neither go from hence, but abide
here ^Tfast by my maidens: *close*
9 *Let* thine eyes *be* on the field
that they do reap, and go thou
after them: have I not charged the
young men that they shall not
touch thee? and when thou art
athirst, go unto the vessels, and
drink of *that* which the young
men have drawn.
10 Then she fell on her face, and
bowed herself to the ground, and
said unto him, Why have I found
^Rgrace in thine eyes, that thou
shouldest take knowledge of me,
seeing I *am* a stranger?   1 Sam. 1:18
11 And Bo'-az answered and
said unto her, It hath fully been
shewed me, ^Rall that thou hast

done unto thy mother in law since
the death of thine husband: and
how thou hast left thy father and
thy mother, and the land of thy
nativity, and art come unto a people which thou knewest not
heretofore.   1:14–18
12 ^RThe LORD recompense thy
work, and a full reward be giv-
en thee of the LORD God of Isra-
el, ^Runder whose wings thou art
come to trust.   1 Sam. 24:19 · 1:16
13 Then she said, ^RLet me find
favour in thy sight, my lord; for
that thou hast comforted me, and
for that thou hast spoken friendly
unto thine handmaid, ^Rthough I be
not like unto one of thine handmaidens.   1 Sam. 1:18 · 1 Sam. 25:41
14 And Bo'-az said unto her, At
mealtime come thou hither, and
eat of the bread, and dip thy
morsel in the vinegar. And she sat
beside the reapers: and he reached
her parched *corn*, and she did eat,
and ^Rwas sufficed, and left.   v. 18
15 And when she was risen up
to glean, Bo'-az commanded his
young men, saying, Let her glean
even among the sheaves, and
reproach her not:
16 And let fall also *some* of the
handfuls of purpose for her, and
leave *them*, that she may glean
them, and rebuke her not.
17 So she gleaned in the field
until even, and beat out that she
had gleaned: and it was about an
e'-phah of ^Rbarley.   1:22
18 And she took *it* up, and went
into the city: and her mother in
law saw what she had gleaned:
and she brought forth, and gave to
her ^Rthat she had reserved after
she was sufficed.   v. 14
19 And her mother in law said
unto her, Where hast thou
gleaned to day? and where
wroughtest thou? blessed be he
that did ^Rtake knowledge of
thee. And she shewed her mother in law with whom she had
wrought, and said, The man's
name with whom I wrought to
day *is* Bo'-az.   [Ps. 41:1]
20 And Na-o'-mi said unto her

daughter in law, Blessed *be* he of the LORD, who hath not left off his kindness to the living and to the dead. And Na-o'-mi said unto her, The man *is* near of kin unto us, one of our ^Tnext kinsmen.   *near*

21 And Ruth the Mo'-ab-i-tess said, He said unto me also, Thou shalt ^Tkeep fast by my young men, until they have ended all my harvest.   *stay close*

22 And Na-o'-mi said unto Ruth her daughter in law, *It is* good, my daughter, that thou go out with his maidens, that they meet thee not in any other field.

23 So she kept fast by the maidens of Bo'-az to glean unto the end of barley harvest and of wheat harvest; and dwelt with her mother in law.

3 Then Na-o'-mi her mother in law said unto her, My daughter, shall I not seek ^Rrest for thee, that it may be well with thee?   1:9

2 And now *is* not Bo'-az of our kindred, ^Rwith whose maidens thou wast? Behold, he winnoweth barley to night in the threshingfloor.   2:3, 8

3 Wash thyself therefore, ^Rand anoint thee, and put thy ^Traiment upon thee, and get thee down to the floor: *but* make not thyself known unto the man, until he shall have done eating and drinking.   2 Sam. 14:2 · *best garment*

4 And it shall be, when he lieth down, that thou shalt mark the place where he shall lie, and thou shalt go in, and uncover his feet, and lay thee down; and he will tell thee what thou shalt do.

5 And she said unto her, All that thou sayest unto me I will do.

6 And she went down unto the floor, and did according to all that her mother in law bade her.

7 And when Bo'-az had eaten and drunk, and ^Rhis heart was merry, he went to lie down at the end of the heap of corn: and she came softly, and uncovered his feet, and laid her down. Judg. 19:6, 9

8 And it came to pass at midnight, that the man was ^Tafraid, and turned himself: and, behold, a woman lay at his feet.   *startled*

9 And he said, Who *art* thou? And she answered, I *am* Ruth thine handmaid: spread therefore thy skirt over thine handmaid; for thou *art* a ^Tnear kinsman. *redeemer*

10 And he said, Blessed *be* thou of the LORD, my daughter: *for* thou hast shewed more kindness in the latter end than at the beginning, inasmuch as thou followedst not young men, whether poor or rich.

11 And now, my daughter, fear not; I will do to thee all that thou ^Trequirest: for all the city of my people doth know that thou *art* ^Ra virtuous woman.   *request* · Prov. 12:4

12 And now it is true that I *am* thy near kinsman: howbeit ^Rthere is a kinsman nearer than I.   4:1

13 Tarry this night, and it shall be in the morning, *that* if he will ^Rperform unto thee the part of a kinsman, well; let him do the kinsman's part: but if he will not do the part of a kinsman to thee, then will I do the part of a kinsman to thee, *as* the LORD liveth: lie down until the morning.   4:5, 10

14 And she lay at his feet until the morning: and she rose up before one could know another. And he said, Let it not be known that a woman came into the floor.

15 Also he said, Bring the ^Tvail that *thou hast* upon thee, and hold it. And when she held it, he measured six *measures* of barley, and laid *it* on her: and she went into the city.   *shawl*

16 And when she came to her mother in law, she said, ^TWho *art* thou, my daughter? And she told her all that the man had done to her.   *How are you?*

17 And she said, These six *measures* of barley gave he me; for he said to me, Go not empty unto thy mother in law.

18 Then said she, Sit still, my daughter, until thou know how the matter will fall: for the man will not be in rest, until he have finished the thing this day.

4 Then went Bo'-az up to the gate, and sat him down there: and, behold, [R]the kinsman of whom Bo'-az spake came by; unto whom he said, Ho, such a one! turn aside, sit down here. And he turned aside, and sat down. 3:12

2 And he took ten men of the elders of the city, and said, Sit ye down here. And they sat down.

3 And he said unto the kinsman, Na-o'-mi, that is come again out of the country of Moab, selleth a parcel of land, [R]which *was* our brother E-lim'-e-lech's: Lev. 25:25

4 And I thought to [T]advertise thee, saying, [R]Buy *it* before the inhabitants, and before the elders of my people. If thou wilt redeem *it,* redeem *it:* but if thou wilt not redeem *it, then* tell me, that I may know: [R]for *there is* none to redeem *it* beside thee; and I *am* after thee. And he said, I will redeem *it.* *inform* · Jer. 32:7 · Lev. 25:25

5 Then said Bo'-az, What day thou buyest the field of the hand of Na-o'-mi, thou must buy *it* also of Ruth the Mo'-ab-i-tess, the wife of the dead, to raise up the name of the dead upon his inheritance.

6 [R]And the kinsman said, I cannot redeem *it* for myself, lest I mar mine own inheritance: redeem thou my right to thyself; for I cannot redeem *it.* 3:12, 13; Job 19:14

7 Now this *was the manner* in former time in Israel concerning redeeming and concerning changing, for to confirm all things; a man plucked off his shoe, and gave *it* to his neighbour: and this *was* a testimony in Israel.

8 Therefore the kinsman said unto Bo'-az, Buy *it* for thee. So he drew off his shoe.

9 And Bo'-az said unto the elders, and *unto* all the people, Ye *are* witnesses this day, that I have bought all that *was* E-lim'-e-lech's, and all that *was* Chil'-i-on's and Mah'-lon's, of the hand of Na-o'-mi.

10 Moreover Ruth the Mo'-ab-i-tess, the wife of Mah'-lon, have I purchased to be my wife, to raise up the name of the dead upon his inheritance, [R]that the name of the dead be not cut off from among his brethren, and from the gate of his place: ye *are* witnesses this day. Deut. 25:6

11 And all the people that *were* in the gate, and the elders, said, *We are* witnesses. The LORD make the woman that is come into thine house like Ra'-chel and like Leah, which two did [R]build the house of Israel: and do thou worthily in Eph'-ra-tah, and be famous in Beth'-le-hem: Gen. 29:25–30; Deut. 25:9

12 And let thy house be like the house of Pha'-rez, [R]whom Ta'-mar bare unto Judah, of the seed which the LORD shall give thee of this young woman. Gen. 38:6–29

13 So Bo'-az [R]took Ruth, and she was his wife: and when he went in unto her, the LORD gave her conception, and she bare a son. 3:11

14 And [R]the women said unto Na-o'-mi, Blessed *be* the LORD, which hath not left thee this day without a kinsman, that his name may be famous in Israel. Luke 1:58

15 And he shall be unto thee a restorer of *thy* life, and a nourisher of thine old age: for thy daughter in law, which loveth thee, which is better to thee than seven sons, hath born him.

16 And Na-o'-mi took the child, and laid it in her bosom, and became nurse unto it.

17 [R]And the women her neighbours gave it a name, saying, There is a son born to Na-o'-mi; and they called his name O'-bed: he *is* the father of Jesse, the father of David. Luke 1:58

18 [R]Now these *are* the generations of Pha'-rez: [R]Pha'-rez begat Hez'-ron, Matt. 1:1–7 · Num. 26:20, 21

19 And Hez'-ron begat Ram, and Ram begat Am-min'-a-dab,

20 And Am-min'-a-dab begat [R]Nah'-shon, and Nah'-shon begat [R]Sal'-mon, Num. 1:7 · Matt. 1:4

21 And Sal'-mon begat Bo'-az, and Bo'-az begat O'-bed,

22 And O'-bed begat Jesse, and Jesse begat [R]David. Matt. 1:6

The First Book of

SAMUEL

THE Book of First Samuel describes the transition of leadership in Israel from judges to kings. Three characters are prominent in the book: Samuel, the last judge and first prophet; Saul, the first king of Israel; and David, the king-elect, anointed but not yet recognized as Saul's successor.

The books of First and Second Samuel were originally one book in the Hebrew Bible, known as the "Book of Samuel" or simply "Samuel." This name has been variously translated "The Name of God," "His Name Is God," "Heard of God," and "Asked of God." The Septuagint divides Samuel into two books even though it is one continuous account. This division artificially breaks up the history of David. The Greek (Septuagint) title is *Bibloi Basileion,* "Books of Kingdoms," referring to the later kingdoms of Israel and Judah. First Samuel is called *Basileion Alpha,* "First Kingdoms." Second Samuel and First and Second Kings are called "Second, Third, and Fourth Kingdoms." The Latin Vulgate originally called the books of Samuel and Kings *Libri Regum,* "Books of the Kings." Later the Latin Bible combined the Hebrew and Greek titles for the first of these books, calling it *Liber I Samuelis,* the "First Book of Samuel," or simply "First Samuel."

NOW there was a certain man of Ra-math-a'-im-zo'-phim, of mount E'-phra-im, and his name *was* ᴿEl'-ka-nah, the son of Jer'-o-ham, the son of E-li'-hu, the son of To'-hu, the son of Zuph, ᴿan Eph'-rath-ite: 1 Chr. 6:27, 33–38 · Ruth 1:2

2   And he had two wives; the name of the one *was* Hannah, and the name of the other Pe-nin'-nah: and Pe-nin'-nah had children, but Hannah had no children.

3   And this man went up out of his city yearly to worship and to sacrifice unto the LORD of hosts in Shi'-loh. And the two sons of E'-li, Hoph'-ni and Phin'-e-has, the priests of the LORD, *were* there.

4   And when the time was that El'-ka-nah offered, he gave to Pe-nin'-nah his wife, and to all her sons and her daughters, portions:

5   But unto Hannah he gave a ᵀworthy portion; for he loved Hannah: ᴿbut the LORD had shut up her womb.   double · Gen. 16:1

6   And her adversary also ᴿpro-voked her ᵀsore, for to make her fret, because the LORD had shut up her womb.   Job 24:21 · severely

7   And *as* he did so year by year, when she went up to the house of the LORD, so she pro-voked her; therefore she wept, and did not eat.

8   Then said El'-ka-nah her hus-band to her, Hannah, why weep-est thou? and why eatest thou not? and why is thy heart grieved? *am* not I ᴿbetter to thee than ten sons?   Ruth 4:15

9   So Hannah rose up after they had eaten in Shi'-loh, and after they had drunk. Now E'-li the priest sat upon a seat by a post of the ᵀtemple of the LORD.   tabernacle

10   ᴿAnd she *was* in bitterness of soul, and prayed unto the LORD, and wept ᵀsore.   Job 7:11 · greatly

11   And she vowed a vow, and said, O LORD of hosts, if thou wilt indeed look on the affliction of thine handmaid, and ᴿremember me, and not forget thine hand-maid, but wilt give unto thine handmaid a man child, then I will give him unto the LORD all the days of his life, and there shall no razor come upon his head. Gen. 8:1

12   And it came to pass, as she continued praying before the LORD, that E'-li marked her mouth.

13   Now Hannah, she spake in

her heart; only her lips moved, but her voice was not heard: therefore E′-li thought she had been drunken.

14 And E′-li said unto her, How long wilt thou be drunken? put away thy wine from thee.

15 And Hannah answered and said, No, my lord, I *am* a woman of a sorrowful spirit: I have drunk neither wine nor strong drink, but have ᴿpoured out my soul before the LORD. Job 30:16; Ps. 62:8; Lam. 2:19

16 Count not thine handmaid for a ᵀdaughter of ᴿBe′-li-al: for out of the abundance of my complaint and grief have I spoken hitherto. *wicked woman* · Deut. 13:13

17 Then E′-li answered and said, ᴿGo in peace: and the God of Israel grant *thee* thy petition that thou hast asked of him. Mark 5:34

18 And she said, ᴿLet thine handmaid find grace in thy sight. So the woman ᴿwent her way, and did eat, and her countenance was no more *sad.* Gen. 33:15 · Prov. 15:13

19 And they rose up in the morning early, and worshipped before the LORD, and returned, and came to their house to Ra′-mah: and El′-ka-nah ᴿknew Hannah his wife; and the LORD ᴿremembered her. Gen. 4:1 · Gen. 21:1

20 Wherefore it came to pass, when the time was come about after Hannah had conceived, that she bare a son, and called his name Samuel, *saying,* Because I have asked him of the LORD.

21 And the man El′-ka-nah, and all his house, ᴿwent up to offer unto the LORD the yearly sacrifice, and his vow. v. 3; Deut. 12:11

22 But Hannah went not up; for she said unto her husband, *I will not go up* until the child be weaned, and *then* I will ᴿbring him, that he may appear before the LORD, and there ᴿabide ᴿfor ever. Luke 2:22 · vv. 11, 28 · Ex. 21:6

23 And ᴿEl′-ka-nah her husband said unto her, Do what seemeth thee good; tarry until thou have weaned him; only the LORD establish his word. So the woman

abode, and gave her son suck until she weaned him. Num. 30:7, 10

24 And when she had weaned him, she ᴿtook him up with her, with three bullocks, and one e′-phah of flour, and a bottle of wine, and brought him unto ᴿthe house of the LORD in Shi′-loh: and the child *was* young. Deut. 12:5, 6 · 4:3, 4

25 And they slew a bullock, and ᴿbrought the child to E′-li. Luke 2:22

26 And she said, Oh my lord, ᴿ*as* thy soul liveth, my lord, I *am* the woman that stood by thee here, praying unto the LORD. 2 Kin. 4:30

27 For this child I prayed; and the LORD hath given me my petition which I asked of him:

28 Therefore also I have ᵀlent him to the LORD; as long as he liveth he shall be lent to the LORD. And he ᴿworshipped the LORD there. *granted* · Gen. 24:26, 52

2 And Hannah prayed, and said, My heart rejoiceth in the LORD, ᴿmine horn is exalted in the LORD: my mouth ᵀis enlarged over mine enemies; because I rejoice in thy salvation. Ps. 75:10 · *smiles at*

2 ᴿ*There is* none holy as the LORD: for *there is* none beside thee: neither *is there* any ᴿrock like our God. Ps. 86:8 · Deut. 32:4, 30, 31

3 Talk no more so exceeding proudly; ᴿlet *not* arrogancy come out of your mouth: for the LORD *is* a God of ᴿknowledge, and by him actions are weighed. Ps. 94:4 · 16:7

4 The bows of the mighty men *are* broken, and they that stumbled are girded with strength.

5 *They that were* full have hired out themselves for bread; and *they that were* hungry ceased: so that the barren hath born seven; and she that hath many children is waxed feeble.

6 ᴿThe LORD killeth, and maketh alive: he bringeth down to the grave, and bringeth up. 2 Kin. 5:7

7 The LORD ᴿmaketh poor, and maketh rich: ᴿhe bringeth low, and lifteth up. Job 1:21 · James 4:10

8 ᴿHe raiseth up the poor out of the dust, *and* lifteth up the beggar from the dunghill, ᴿto set *them*

among princes, and to make them inherit the throne of glory: [R]for the pillars of the earth *are* the LORD's, and he hath set the world upon them. Luke 1:52 · Job 36:7 · Ps. 75:3

9 He will keep the feet of his saints, and the [R]wicked shall be silent in darkness; for by strength shall no man prevail.   [Rom. 3:19]

10 The adversaries of the LORD shall be broken to pieces; out of heaven shall he thunder upon them: the LORD shall judge the ends of the earth; and he shall give strength unto his king, and exalt the horn of his anointed.

11 And El'-ka-nah went to Ra'-mah to his house. And the child did [T]minister unto the LORD before E'-li the priest.   *serve*

12 Now the sons of E'-li *were* [R]sons[T] of Be'-li-al; they knew not the LORD.   Deut. 13:13 · *worthless men*

13 And the priest's custom with the people *was, that,* when any man offered sacrifice, the priest's servant came, while the flesh was in seething, with a fleshhook of three teeth in his hand;

14 And he struck *it* into the pan, or kettle, or caldron, or pot; all that the fleshhook brought up the priest took for himself. So they did in [R]Shi'-loh unto all the Israelites that came thither.   1:3

15 Also before they [R]burnt the fat, the priest's servant came, and said to the man that sacrificed, Give flesh to roast for the priest; for he will not have [T]sodden flesh of thee, but raw. Lev. 3:3–5, 16 · *boiled*

16 And *if* any man said unto him, Let them not fail to burn the fat [T]presently, and *then* take *as much* as thy soul desireth; then he would answer him, *Nay;* but thou shalt give *it me* now: and if not, I will take *it* by force.   *first*

17 Wherefore the sin of the young men was very great before the LORD: for men [R]abhorred the offering of the LORD.   [Mal. 2:7–9]

18 [R]But Samuel ministered before the LORD, *being* a child, girded with a linen e'-phod.   v. 11; 3:1

19 Moreover his mother made him a little coat, and brought *it* to him from year to year, when she[R]came up with her husband to offer the yearly sacrifice.   1:3, 21

20 And E'-li blessed El'-ka-nah and his wife, and said, The LORD give thee seed of this woman for the [T]loan which is [R]lent[T] to the LORD. And they went unto their own home.   *gift* · 1:11, 27, 28 · *granted*

21 And the LORD visited Hannah, so that she conceived, and bare three sons and two daughters. And the child Samuel [R]grew before the LORD. Luke 1:80; 2:40

22 Now E'-li was very old, and heard all that his sons did unto all Israel; and how they lay with [R]the women that assembled *at* the door of the tabernacle of the congregation.   Ex. 38:8

23 And he said unto them, Why do ye such things? for I hear of your evil dealings by all this people.

24 Nay, my sons; for *it is* no good report that I hear: ye make the LORD's people to transgress.

25 If one man sin against another, the judge shall judge him: but if a man sin against the LORD, who shall intreat for him? Notwithstanding they hearkened not unto the voice of their father, because the LORD would slay them.

26 And the child Samuel [R]grew on, and was in favour both with the LORD, and also with men.   2:21

27 And there came a [R]man of God unto E'-li, and said unto him, Thus saith the LORD, [R]Did I plainly appear unto the house of thy father, when they were in Egypt in Pharaoh's house?   9:6 · Ex. 4:14–16

28 And did I [R]choose him out of all the tribes of Israel *to be* my priest, to offer upon mine altar, to burn incense, to wear an e'-phod before me? and [R]did I give unto the house of thy father all the offerings made by fire of the children of Israel? Num. 16:5 · Lev. 2:3, 10

29 Wherefore kick ye at my sacrifice and at mine offering, which I have commanded *in my* [R]habitation; and honourest thy sons above me, to make yourselves fat

with the chiefest of all the offerings of Israel my people?   Ps. 26:8

30 Wherefore the Lord God of Israel saith, ᴿI said indeed *that* thy house, and the house of thy father, should walk before me for ever: but now the Lord saith, Be it far from me; for them that honour me I will honour, and ᴿthey that despise me shall be lightly esteemed.   Ex. 29:9 · Ps. 91:14; Mal. 2:9–12

31 Behold, ᴿthe days come, that I will cut off thine arm, and the arm of thy father's house, that there shall not be an old man in thine house.   4:11–18; 22:18, 19; 1 Kin. 2:27, 35

32 And thou shalt see an enemy *in my* habitation, in all *the wealth* which *God* shall give Israel: and there shall not be ᴿan old man in thine house for ever.   Zech. 8:4

33 And the man of thine, *whom* I shall not cut off from mine altar, *shall be* to consume thine eyes, and to grieve thine heart: and all the increase of thine house shall die in the flower of their age.

34 And this *shall be* ᴿa sign unto thee, that shall come upon thy two sons, on Hoph'-ni and Phin'-e-has; ᴿin one day they shall die both of them.   10:7–9; 1 Kin. 13:3 · 4:11, 17

35 And ᴿI will raise me up a faithful priest, *that* shall do according to *that* which *is* in mine heart and in my mind: and I will build him a sure house; and he shall walk before ᴿmine anointed for ever.   [Heb. 2:17; 7:26–28] · Ps. 18:50

36 ᴿAnd it shall come to pass, *that* every one that is left in thine house shall come *and* ᵀcrouch to him for a piece of silver and a morsel of bread, and shall say, Put me, I pray thee, into one of the priests' offices, that I may eat a piece of bread.   1 Kin. 2:27 · bow down

3 And ᴿthe child Samuel ministered unto the Lord before E'-li. And ᴿthe word of the Lord was ᵀprecious in those days; *there was* no open vision.   2:11, 18 · Ps. 74:9 · rare

2 And it came to pass at that time, when E'-li *was* laid down in his place, and his eyes began to wax dim, *that* he could not see;

3 And ere ᴿthe lamp of God went out in the ᵀtemple of the Lord, where the ark of God *was,* and Samuel was laid down *to sleep;*   Ex. 27:20, 21 · tabernacle

4 That the Lord called Samuel: and he answered, Here *am* I.

5 And he ran unto E'-li, and said, Here *am* I; for thou calledst me. And he said, I called not; lie down again. And he went and lay down.

6 And the Lord called yet again, Samuel. And Samuel arose and went to E'-li, and said, Here *am* I; for thou didst call me. And he answered, I called not, my son; lie down again.

7 Now Samuel ᴿdid not yet know the Lord, neither was the word of the Lord yet revealed unto him.   2:12; Acts 19:2; 1 Cor. 13:11

8 And the Lord called Samuel again the third time. And he arose and went to E'-li, and said, Here *am* I; for thou didst call me. And E'-li perceived that the Lord had called the child.

9 Therefore E'-li said unto Samuel, Go, lie down: and it shall be, if he call thee, that thou shalt say, ᴿSpeak, Lord; for thy servant heareth. So Samuel went and lay down in his place.   1 Kin. 2:17

10 And the Lord came, and stood, and called as at other times, Samuel, Samuel. Then Samuel answered, Speak; for thy servant heareth.

11 And the Lord said to Samuel, Behold, I will do a thing in Israel, at which both the ears of every one that heareth it shall tingle.

12 In that day I will perform against E'-li ᴿall *things* which I have spoken concerning his house: when I begin, I will also make an end.   2:27–36; Luke 21:33

13 For I have told him that I will judge his house for ever for the iniquity which he knoweth; because his sons made themselves vile, and he restrained them not.

14 And therefore I have sworn unto the house of E'-li, that the iniquity of E'-li's house ᴿshall not

be purged with sacrifice nor offering for ever. Is. 22:14; Heb. 10:4, 26–31

15 And Samuel lay until the morning, and opened the doors of the house of the LORD. And Samuel feared to shew E'-li the vision.

16 Then E'-li called Samuel, and said, Samuel, my son. And he answered, Here *am* I.

17 And he said, What *is* the thing that *the* LORD hath said unto thee? I pray thee hide *it* not from me: ᴿGod do so to thee, and more also, if thou hide *any* thing from me of all the things that he said unto thee. Ruth 1:17

18 And Samuel told him every whit, and hid nothing from him. And he said, It *is* the LORD: let him do what seemeth him good.

19 And Samuel grew, and ᴿthe LORD was with him, ᴿand did let none of his words ᵀfall to the ground. Gen. 21:22; 28:15; 39:2 · 9:6 · *fail*

20 And all Israel ᴿfrom Dan even to Be'-er-she'-ba knew that Samuel *was* established *to be* a prophet of the LORD. Judg. 20:1

21 And the LORD appeared again in Shi'-loh: for the LORD revealed himself to Samuel in Shi'-loh by the word of the LORD.

4 And the word of Samuel came to all Israel. Now Israel went out against the Phi-lis'-tines to battle, and pitched beside ᴿEb'-en-e'-zer: and the Phi-lis'-tines pitched in A'-phek. 7:12

2 And the ᴿPhi-lis'-tines put themselves in array against Israel: and when they joined battle, Israel was ᵀsmitten before the Phi-lis'-tines: and they slew of the army in the field about four thousand men. 12:9 · *defeated*

3 And when the people were come into the camp, the elders of Israel said, Wherefore hath the LORD smitten us to day before the Phi-lis'-tines? Let us fetch the ark of the covenant of the LORD out of Shi'-loh unto us, that, when it cometh among us, it may save us out of the hand of our enemies.

4 So the people sent to Shi'-loh, that they might bring from thence the ark of the covenant of the LORD of hosts, which dwelleth *between* the cher'-u-bims: and the two sons of E'-li, Hoph'-ni and Phin'-e-has, *were* there with the ark of the covenant of God.

5 And when the ark of the covenant of the LORD came into the camp, all Israel shouted with a great shout, so that the earth rang again.

6 And when the Phi-lis'-tines heard the noise of the shout, they said, What *meaneth* the noise of this great shout in the camp of the Hebrews? And they understood that the ark of the LORD was come into the camp.

7 And the Phi-lis'-tines were afraid, for they said, God is come into the camp. And they said, Woe unto us! for there hath not been such a thing heretofore.

8 Woe unto us! who shall deliver us out of the hand of these mighty Gods? these *are* the Gods that smote the Egyptians with all the plagues in the wilderness.

9 ᴿBe strong, and ᵀquit yourselves like men, O ye Phi-lis'-tines, that ye be not servants unto the Hebrews, ᴿas they have been to you: quit yourselves like men, and fight. 1 Cor. 16:13 · *conduct* · 14:21

10 And the Phi-lis'-tines fought, and ᴿIsrael was smitten, and they fled every man into his tent: and there was a very great slaughter; for there fell of Israel thirty thousand footmen. Lev. 26:17; 2 Sam. 18:17

11 And ᴿthe ark of God was taken; and ᴿthe two sons of E'-li, Hoph'-ni and Phin'-e-has, were slain. 2:32; Ps. 78:60, 61 · 2:34; Ps. 78:64

12 And there ran a man of Benjamin out of the army, and came to Shi'-loh the same day with his clothes rent, and ᴿwith earth upon his head. Josh. 7:6

13 And when he came, lo, E'-li sat upon ᴿa seat by the wayside watching: for his heart trembled for the ark of God. And when the man came into the city, and told *it*, all the city cried out. v. 18; 1:9

14 And when E'-li heard the noise of the crying, he said, What *meaneth* the noise of this tumult? And the man came in hastily, and told E'-li.

15 Now E'-li was ninety and eight years old; and his eyes were dim, that he could not see.

16 And the man said unto E'-li, I *am* he that came out of the army, and I fled to day out of the army. And he said, ^RWhat ^Tis there done, my son?   2 Sam. 1:4 · *happened*

17 And the messenger answered and said, Israel is fled before the Phi-lis'-tines, and there hath been also a great slaughter among the people, and thy two sons also, Hoph'-ni and Phin'-e-has, are dead, and the ark of God is taken.

18 And it came to pass, when he made mention of the ark of God, that he fell from off the seat backward by the side of the gate, and his neck brake, and he died: for he was an old man, and heavy. And he had judged Israel forty years.

19 And his daughter in law, Phin'-e-has' wife, was with child, *near* to be delivered: and when she heard the tidings that the ark of God was taken, and that her father in law and her husband were dead, she bowed herself and ^Ttravailed; for her pains came upon her.   *gave birth*

20 And about the time of her death ^Rthe women that stood by her said unto her, Fear not; for thou hast born a son. But she answered not, neither did she ^Tregard *it*.   Gen. 35:16–19 · *pay attention*

21 And she named the child ^RI'–cha-bod, saying, ^RThe glory is departed from Israel: because the ark of God was taken, and because of her father in law and her husband.   14:3 · Ps. 26:8; 78:61; [Jer. 2:11]

22 And she said, The glory is departed from Israel: for the ark of God is taken.

5 And the Phi-lis'-tines took the ark of God, and brought it from Eb'-en–e'-zer unto Ash'-dod.

2 When the Phi-lis'-tines took the ark of God, they brought it into the house of ^RDa'-gon, and set it by Da'-gon.   1 Chr. 10:8–10

3 And when they of Ash'-dod arose early on the morrow, behold, Da'-gon *was* ^Rfallen upon his face to the earth before the ark of the LORD. And they took Da'-gon, and ^Rset him in his place again.   Is. 19:1; 46:1, 2 · Is. 46:7

4 And when they arose early on the morrow morning, behold, Da'-gon *was* fallen upon his face to the ground before the ark of the LORD; and ^Rthe head of Da'-gon and both the palms of his hands *were* cut off upon the threshold; only *the stump of* Da'-gon was left to him.   Jer. 50:2; Ezek. 6:4; Mic. 1:7

5 Therefore neither the priests of Da'-gon, nor any that come into Da'-gon's house, ^Rtread on the threshold of Da'-gon in Ash'-dod unto this day.   Zeph. 1:9

6 But the hand of the LORD was heavy upon them of Ash'-dod, and he ^Rdestroyed them, and smote them with emerods, *even* Ash'-dod and the coasts thereof.   6:5

7 And when the men of Ash'-dod saw that *it was* so, they said, The ark of the ^RGod of Israel shall not abide with us: for his hand is sore upon us, and upon Da'-gon our god.   6:5

8 They sent therefore and gathered all the lords of the Phi-lis'-tines unto them, and said, What shall we do with the ark of the God of Israel? And they answered, Let the ark of the God of Israel be carried about unto Gath. And they carried the ark of the God of Israel about *thither*.

9 And it was *so*, that, after they had carried it about, ^Rthe hand of the LORD was against the city with a very great destruction: and he smote the men of the city, both small and great, and they had emerods in their secret parts.   v. 11

10 Therefore they sent the ark of God to Ek'-ron. And it came to pass, as the ark of God came to Ek'-ron, that the Ek'-ron-ites cried out, saying, They have brought

about the ark of the God of Israel to us, to slay us and our people.

11 So they sent and gathered together all the lords of the Phi-lis'-tines, and said, Send away the ark of the God of Israel, and let it go again to his own place, that it slay us not, and our people: for there was a deadly destruction throughout all the city; the hand of God was very heavy there.

12 And the men that died not were smitten with the [T]emerods: and the [R]cry of the city went up to heaven.   *tumours* · 9:16; Jer. 14:2

6 And the ark of the Lord was in the country of the Phi-lis'-tines seven months.

2 And the Phi-lis'-tines [R]called for the priests and the diviners, saying, What shall we do to the ark of the Lord? tell us wherewith we shall send it to his place.   Is. 2:6

3 And they said, If ye send away the ark of the God of Israel, send it not empty; but in any wise return him a trespass offering: then ye shall be healed, and it shall be known to you why his hand is not removed from you.

4 Then said they, What *shall be* the trespass offering which we shall return to him? They answered, [R]Five golden emerods, and five golden mice, *according to* the number of the lords of the Phi-lis'-tines: for one plague *was* on you all, and on your lords.   5:6

5 Wherefore ye shall make images of your emerods, and images of your mice that [R]mar the land; and ye shall [R]give glory unto the God of Israel: peradventure he will lighten his hand from off you, and from off your gods, and from off your land.   5:6 · Josh. 7:19

6 Wherefore then do ye harden your hearts, [R]as the Egyptians and Pharaoh hardened their hearts? when he had wrought wonderfully among them, [R]did they not let the people go, and they departed? Ex. 7:13; 8:15 · Ex. 12:31

7 Now therefore make [R]a new cart, and take two milch kine, [R]on which there hath come no yoke,

and tie the kine to the cart, and bring their calves home from them: 2 Sam. 6:3 · Num. 19:2; Deut. 21:3, 4

8 And take the ark of the Lord, and lay it upon the cart; and put [R]the jewels of gold, which ye return him *for* a trespass offering, in a coffer by the side thereof; and send it away, that it may go. vv. 4, 5

9 And see, if it goeth up by the way of his own coast to [R]Beth-she'-mesh, *then* he hath done us this great evil: but if not, then we shall know that *it is* not his hand *that* smote us; it *was* a chance *that* happened to us.   Josh. 15:10

10 And the men did so; and took two [T]milch kine, and tied them to the cart, and shut up their calves at home: *milk cows*

11 And they laid the ark of the Lord upon the cart, and the [T]coffer with the mice of gold and the images of their emerods. *chest*

12 And the [T]kine took the straight way to the way of Beth-she'-mesh, *and* went along the [R]highway, lowing as they went, and turned not aside *to* the right hand or *to* the left; and the lords of the Phi-lis'-tines went after them unto the border of Beth-she'-mesh.   *cows* · Num. 20:19

13 And *they of* Beth-she'-mesh *were* reaping their [R]wheat harvest in the valley: and they lifted up their eyes, and saw the ark, and rejoiced to see *it*.   12:17

14 And the cart came into the field of Joshua, a Beth-she'-mite, and stood there, where *there was* a great stone: and they clave the wood of the cart, and offered the kine a burnt offering unto the Lord.

15 And the Levites took down the ark of the Lord, and the coffer that *was* with it, wherein the jewels of gold *were*, and put *them* on the great stone: and the men of Beth-she'-mesh offered burnt offerings and sacrificed sacrifices the same day unto the Lord.

16 And when the five lords of the Phi-lis'-tines had seen *it*, they returned to Ek'-ron the same day.

17 And these *are* the golden emerods which the Phi-lis'-tines returned *for* a trespass offering unto the LORD; for Ash'-dod one, for Ga'-za one, for As'-ke-lon one, for ᴿGath one, for Ek'-ron one;   5:8

18 And the golden mice, *according to* the number of all the cities of the Phi-lis'-tines *belonging* to the five lords, *both* of fenced cities, and of country villages, even unto the great *stone of* Abel, whereon they set down the ark of the LORD: *which stone remaineth* unto this day in the field of Joshua, the Beth–she'-mite.

19 And ᴿhe smote the men of Beth–she'-mesh, because they had looked into the ark of the LORD, even he ᴿsmote of the people fifty thousand and threescore and ten men: and the people lamented, because the LORD had smitten *many* of the people with a great slaughter.   Ex. 19:21 · 2 Sam. 6:7

20 And the men of Beth–she'-mesh said, Who is able to stand before this holy LORD God? and to whom shall he go up from us?

21 And they sent messengers to the inhabitants of ᴿKir'-jath-je'-a-rim, saying, The Phi-lis'-tines have brought again the ark of the LORD; come ye down, *and* fetch it up to you.   Josh. 9:17; 18:14; Judg. 18:12

7 And the men of ᴿKir'-jath-je'-a-rim came, and fetched up the ark of the LORD, and brought it into the house of ᴿA-bin'-a-dab in the hill, and ᴿsanctified E-le-a'-zar his son to keep the ark of the LORD.   Ps. 132:6 · 2 Sam. 6:3, 4 · Lev. 21:8

2 And it came to pass, while the ark abode in Kir'-jath-je'-a-rim, that the time was long; for it was twenty years: and all the house of Israel lamented after the LORD.

3 And Samuel spake unto all the house of Israel, saying, If ye do return unto the LORD with all your hearts, *then* put away the strange gods and Ash'-ta-roth from among you, and prepare your hearts unto the LORD, and ᴿserve him only: and he will deliver you out of the hand of the Phi-lis'-tines.   Josh. 24:14; Matt. 4:10; Luke 4:8

4 Then the children of Israel did put away Ba'-a-lim and Ash'-ta-roth, and served the LORD only.

5 And Samuel said, Gather all Israel to Miz'-peh, and ᴿI will pray for you unto the LORD.   12:17–19

6 And they gathered together to Miz'-peh, and drew water, and poured *it* out before the LORD, and fasted on that day, and said there, We have sinned against the LORD. And Samuel judged the children of Israel in Miz'-peh.

7 And when the Phi-lis'-tines heard that the children of Israel were gathered together to Miz'-peh, the lords of the Phi-lis'-tines went up against Israel. And when the children of Israel heard *it*, they were afraid of the Phi-lis'-tines.

8 And the children of Israel said to Samuel, ᴿCease not to cry unto the LORD our God for us, that he will save us out of the hand of the Phi-lis'-tines.   12:19–24; Is. 37:4

9 And Samuel took a ᴿsucking lamb, and offered *it for* a burnt offering wholly unto the LORD: and ᴿSamuel cried unto the LORD for Israel; and the LORD heard him.   Lev. 22:27 · 12:18; Ps. 99:6; Jer. 15:1

10 And as Samuel was offering up the burnt offering, the Phi-lis'-tines drew near to battle against Israel: ᴿbut the LORD thundered with a great thunder on that day upon the Phi-lis'-tines, and discomfited them; and they were smitten before Israel.   Ps. 18:13, 14

11 And the men of Israel went out of Miz'-peh, and pursued the Phi-lis'-tines, and smote them, until *they came* under Beth'–car.

12 Then Samuel ᴿtook a stone, and set *it* between Miz'-peh and Shen, and called the name of it Eb'-en-e'-zer, saying, Hitherto hath the LORD helped us.   Gen. 28:18

13 ᴿSo the Phi-lis'-tines were subdued, and they ᴿcame no more into the coast of Israel: and the hand of the LORD was against the Phi-lis'-tines all the days of Samuel.   Judg. 13:1 · 13:5

14 And the cities which the Phi-lis'-tines had taken from Israel were restored to Israel, from Ek'-ron even unto Gath; and the coasts thereof did Israel deliver out of the hands of the Phi-lis'-tines. And there was peace be-tween Israel and the Am'-or-ites.

15 And Samuel ^Rjudged Israel all the days of his life. 12:11

16 And he went from year to year in circuit to Beth'-el, and Gil'-gal, and Miz'-peh, and judged Israel in all those places.

17 And his return *was* to Ra'-mah; for there *was* his house; and there he judged Israel; and there he built an altar unto the LORD.

8 And it came to pass, when Samuel was old, that he made his sons judges over Israel.

2 Now the name of his first-born was Jo'-el; and the name of his second, A-bi'-ah: *they were* judges in Be'-er-she'-ba.

3 And his sons walked not in his ways, but turned aside ^Rafter lucre, and ^Rtook bribes, and per-verted judgment. Ex. 18:21 · Ex. 23:6–8

4 Then all the elders of Israel gathered themselves together, and came to Samuel unto Ra'-mah,

5 And said unto him, Behold, thou art old, and thy sons walk not in thy ways: now ^Rmake us a king to judge us like all the nations. Deut. 17:14, 15; Acts 13:21

6 But the thing ^Rdispleased Samuel, when they said, Give us a king to judge us. And Samuel prayed unto the LORD. 12:17

7 And the LORD said unto Sam-uel, Hearken unto the voice of the people in all that they say unto thee: for they have not rejected thee, but they have rejected me, that I should not reign over them.

8 According to all the works which they have done since the day that I brought them up out of Egypt even unto this day, where-with they have forsaken me, and served other gods, so do they also unto thee.

9 Now therefore hearken unto their voice: howbeit yet protest solemnly unto them, and ^Rshew them the manner of the king that shall reign over them. vv. 11–18

10 And Samuel told all the words of the LORD unto the people that asked of him a king.

11 And he said, This will be the manner of the king that shall reign over you: He will take your ^Rsons, and appoint *them* for him-self, for his ^Rchariots, and *to be* his horsemen; and *some* shall run before his chariots. 14:52 · 2 Sam. 15:1

12 And he will ^Rappoint him captains over thousands, and cap-tains over fifties; and *will set them* to ^Tear his ground, and to reap his harvest, and to make his instruments of war, and instru-ments of his chariots. 22:7 · plow

13 And he will take your daugh-ters *to be* confectionaries, and *to be* cooks, and *to be* bakers.

14 And he will take your fields, and your vineyards, and your oliveyards, *even* the best *of them*, and give *them* to his servants.

15 And he will take the tenth of your seed, and of your vineyards, and give to his officers, and to his servants.

16 And he will take your men-servants, and your maidservants, and your goodliest young men, and your asses, and put *them* to his work.

17 He will take the tenth of your sheep: and ye shall be his ser-vants.

18 And ye shall cry out in that day because of your king which ye shall have chosen you; and the LORD ^Rwill not hear you in that day. Prov. 1:25–28; Is. 1:15; Mic. 3:4

19 Nevertheless the people ^Rre-fused to obey the voice of Samuel; and they said, Nay; but we will have a king over us; Is. 66:4; Jer. 44:16

20 That we also may be ^Rlike all the nations; and that our king may judge us, and go out before us, and fight our battles. v. 5

21 And Samuel heard all the words of the people, and he ^Tre-hearsed them in the ears of the LORD. *repeated them in the hearing of*

22 And the LORD said to Samuel, ^RHearken unto their voice, and make them a king. And Samuel said unto the men of Israel, Go ye every man unto his city.   Hos. 13:11

9 Now there was a man of Benjamin, whose name *was* ^RKish, the son of A-bi'-el, the son of Ze'-ror, the son of Be-cho'-rath, the son of A-phi'-ah, a Benjamite, a mighty man of power.   14:51

2 And he had a son, whose name *was* Saul, a choice young man, and ^Ta goodly: and *there was* not among the children of Israel a goodlier person than he: ^Rfrom his shoulders and upward *he was* ^Thigher than any of the people.   *handsome* · 10:23 · *taller*

3 And the asses of Kish Saul's father were lost. And Kish said to Saul his son, Take now one of the servants with thee, and arise, go seek the asses.

4 And he passed through mount E'-phra-im, and passed through the land of ^RShal'-i-sha, but they found *them* not: then they passed through the land of Sha'-lim, and *there they were* not: and he passed through the land of the Benjamites, but they found *them* not.   2 Kin. 4:42

5 *And* when they were come to the land of ^RZuph, Saul said to his servant that *was* with him, Come, and let ^Rus return; lest my father leave *caring* for the asses, and take thought for us.   1:1 · 10:2

6 And he said unto him, Behold now, *there is* in this city a man of God, and *he is* an honourable man; ^Rall that he saith cometh surely to pass: now let us go thither; peradventure he can shew us our way that we should go.   3:19

7 Then said Saul to his servant, But, behold, *if* we go, ^Rwhat shall we bring the man? for the bread is spent in our vessels, and *there is* not a present to bring to the man of God: what have we?   Judg. 6:18

8 And the servant answered Saul again, and said, Behold, I have here at hand the fourth part of a shek'-el of silver: *that* will I give to the man of God, to tell us our way.

9 (Beforetime in Israel, when a man ^Rwent to enquire of God, thus he spake, Come, and let us go to the seer: for *he that is* now *called* a Prophet was beforetime called ^Ra Seer.)   Gen. 25:22 · 2 Sam. 24:11

10 Then said Saul to his servant, ^TWell said; come, let us go. So they went unto the city where the man of God *was*.   Lit. *Your word is good*

11 *And* as they went up the hill to the city, ^Rthey found young maidens going out to draw water, and said unto them, Is the seer here?   Gen. 24:11, 15; 29:8, 9; Ex. 2:16

12 And they answered them, and said, He is; behold, *he is* before you: make haste now, for he came to day to the city; for ^Rthere is a sacrifice of the people to day ^Rin the high place: 16:2 · 7:17

13 As soon as ye be come into the city, ye shall straightway find him, before he go up to the high place to eat: for the people will not eat until he come, because he doth bless the sacrifice; *and* afterwards they eat that be bidden. Now therefore get you up; for about this time ye shall find him.

14 And they went up into the city: *and* when they were come into the city, behold, Samuel came out against them, for to go up to the high place.

15 ^RNow the LORD had told Samuel in his ear a day before Saul came, saying,   15:1

16 To morrow about this time ^RI will send thee a man out of the land of Benjamin, ^Rand thou shalt anoint him *to be* captain over my people Israel, that he may save my people out of the hand of the Phi-lis'-tines: for I have looked upon my people, because their cry is come unto me.   Deut. 17:15 · 10:1

17 And when Samuel saw Saul, the LORD said unto him, ^RBehold the man whom I spake to thee of! this same shall reign over my people.   16:12; Hos. 13:11

18 Then Saul drew near to Sam-

uel in the gate, and said, Tell me, I pray thee, where the seer's house *is*.

19 And Samuel answered Saul, and said, I *am* the seer: go up before me unto the high place; for ye shall eat with me to day, and to morrow I will let thee go, and will tell thee all that *is* in thine heart.

20 And as for ^Rthine asses that were lost three days ago, set not thy mind on them; for they are found. And on whom *is* all the desire of Israel? *Is it* not on thee, and on all thy father's house?   v. 3

21 And Saul answered and said, ^R*Am* not I a Benjamite, of the ^Rsmallest of the tribes of Israel? and ^Rmy family the least of all the families of the tribe of Benjamin? wherefore then speakest thou so to me?   15:17 · Judg. 20:46–48 · Judg. 6:15

22 And Samuel took Saul and his servant, and brought them into the parlour, and made them sit in the chiefest place among them that were bidden, which *were* about thirty persons.

23 And Samuel said unto the cook, Bring the portion which I gave thee, of which I said unto thee, Set it by thee.

24 And the cook took up the shoulder, and *that* which *was* upon it, and set *it* before Saul. And *Samuel* said, Behold that which is left! set *it* before thee, *and* eat: for unto this time hath it been kept for thee since I said, I have invited the people. So Saul did eat with Samuel that day.

25 And when they were come down from the high place into the city, *Samuel* communed with Saul upon the top of the house.

26 And they arose early: and it came to pass about the spring of the day, that Samuel called Saul to the top of the house, saying, Up, that I may send thee away. And Saul arose, and they went out both of them, he and Samuel, abroad.

27 *And* as they were going down to the end of the city, Samuel said to Saul, Bid the servant pass on

before us, (and he passed on,) but stand thou still a while, that I may shew thee the word of God.

10 Then Samuel took a vial of oil, and poured *it* upon his head, and kissed him, and said, *Is it* not because ^Rthe LORD hath anointed thee *to be* captain over his inheritance? 2 Sam. 5:2; Acts 13:21

2 When thou art departed from me to day, then thou shalt find two men by ^RRa'-chel's sepulchre in the border of Benjamin at Zel'-zah; and they will say unto thee, The asses which thou wentest to seek are found: and, lo, thy father hath left the care of the asses, and sorroweth for you, saying, What shall I do for my son?   Gen. 35:16–20

3 Then shalt thou go on forward from thence, and thou shalt come to the plain of Ta'-bor, and there shall meet thee three men going up ^Rto God to Beth'–el, one carrying three kids, and another carrying three loaves of bread, and another carrying a bottle of wine: Gen. 28:22; 35:1, 3, 7

4 And they will ^Tsalute thee, and give thee two *loaves* of bread; which thou shalt receive of their hands.   *ask you about your welfare*

5 After that thou shalt come to the hill of God, ^Rwhere *is* the garrison of the Phi-lis'-tines: and it shall come to pass, when thou art come thither to the city, that thou shalt meet a company of prophets coming down from the high place with a psaltery, and a tabret, and a pipe, and a harp, before them; and they shall prophesy: 13:2, 3

6 And the Spirit of the LORD will come upon thee, and thou shalt prophesy with them, and shalt be turned into another man.

7 And let it be, when these ^Rsigns are come unto thee, *that* thou do as occasion serve thee; for ^RGod *is* with thee. Luke 2:12 · 3:19

8 And thou shalt go down before me ^Rto Gil'-gal; and, behold, I will come down unto thee, to offer burnt offerings, *and* to sacrifice sacrifices of peace offerings: ^Rseven days shalt thou tarry, till I

come to thee, and shew thee what thou shalt do.   11:14, 15; 13:8 · 13:8–10

9 And it was *so,* that when he had turned his back to go from Samuel, God [T]gave him another heart: and all those signs came to pass that day.   *changed his heart*

10 And [R]when they came thither to the hill, behold, [R]a company of prophets met him; and the Spirit of God came upon him, and he prophesied among them.   v. 5 · 19:20

11 And it came to pass, when all that knew him beforetime saw that, behold, he prophesied among the prophets, then the people said one to another, What *is* this *that* is come unto the son of Kish? [R]*Is* Saul also among the prophets?   19:24; John 7:15; Acts 4:13

12 And one of the same place answered and said, But [R]who *is* their father? Therefore it became a proverb, *Is* Saul also among the prophets?   John 5:30, 36

13 And when he had made an end of prophesying, he came to the high place.

14 And Saul's [R]uncle said unto him and to his servant, Whither went ye? And he said, To seek the asses: and when we saw that *they were* no where, we came to Samuel.   14:50

15 And Saul's uncle said, Tell me, I pray thee, what Samuel said unto you.

16 And Saul said unto his uncle, He told us plainly that the asses were [R]found. But of the matter of the kingdom, whereof Samuel spake, he told him not.   9:20

17 And Samuel called the people together [R]unto the LORD [R]to Miz'-peh;   Judg. 20:1 · 7:5, 6

18 And said unto the children of Israel, [R]Thus saith the LORD God of Israel, I brought up Israel out of Egypt, and delivered you out of the hand of the Egyptians, and out of the hand of all kingdoms, *and* of them that oppressed you: 8:8

19 [R]And ye have this day rejected your God, who himself saved you out of all your adversities and your tribulations; and ye have

said unto him, *Nay,* but set a king over us. Now therefore present yourselves before the LORD by your tribes, and by your [T]thousands.   8:7, 19; 12:12 · *clans*

20 And when Samuel had [R]caused all the tribes of Israel to come near, the tribe of Benjamin was taken.   Acts 1:24, 26

21 When he had caused the tribe of Benjamin to come near by their families, the family of Ma'-tri was taken, and Saul the son of Kish was taken: and when they sought him, he could not be found.

22 Therefore they [R]enquired of the LORD further, if the man should yet come thither. And the LORD answered, Behold, he hath hid himself among the stuff.   23:2, 4

23 And they ran and fetched him thence: and when he stood among the people, [R]he was [T]higher than any of the people from his shoulders and upward.   9:2 · *taller*

24 And Samuel said to all the people, See ye him [R]whom the LORD hath chosen, that *there is* none like him among all the people? And all the people shouted, and said, God save the king.   9:16

25 Then Samuel told the people [R]the manner of the kingdom, and wrote *it* in a book, and laid *it* up before the LORD. And Samuel sent all the people away, every man to his house.   8:11–18; Deut. 17:14–20

26 And Saul also went home [R]to Gib'-e-ah; and there went with him a band of men, whose hearts God had touched.   Judg. 20:14

27 But the [R]children[T] of Be'-li-al said, How shall this man save us? And they despised him, and brought him no presents. But he held his peace.   25:17 · *rebels*

11 Then [R]Na'-hash the Am'-mon-ite came up, and encamped against [R]Ja'-besh–gil'-e-ad: and all the men of Ja'-besh said unto Na'-hash, [R]Make a covenant with us, and we will serve thee.   12:12 · 31:11 · Ezek. 17:13

2 And Na'-hash the Am'-mon-ite answered them, On this *condition* will I make *a covenant* with you, that I may thrust out all your right eyes, and lay it *for* [R]a reproach upon all Israel.   Ps. 44:13

3 And the elders of Ja'-besh said unto him, Give us seven days' respite, that we may send messengers unto all the coasts of Israel: and then, if *there be* no man to save us, we will come out to thee.

4 Then came the messengers [R]to Gib'-e-ah of Saul, and told the tidings in the ears of the people: and [R]all the people lifted up their voices, and wept.   10:26; 15:34 · 30:4

5 And, behold, Saul came after the herd out of the field; and Saul said, What *aileth* the people that they weep? And they told him the tidings of the men of Ja'-besh.

6 [R]And the Spirit of God came upon Saul when he heard those tidings, and his anger was kindled greatly.   Judg. 3:10; 6:34; 11:29; 13:25; 14:6

7 And he took a yoke of oxen, and hewed them in pieces, and sent *them* throughout all the coasts of Israel by the hands of messengers, saying, Whosoever cometh not forth after Saul and after Samuel, so shall it be done unto his oxen. And the fear of the LORD fell on the people, and they came out with one consent.

8 And when he numbered them in [R]Be'-zek, the children [R]of Israel were three hundred thousand, and the men of Judah thirty thousand.   Judg. 1:5 · 2 Sam. 24:9

9 And they said unto the messengers that came, Thus shall ye say unto the men of Ja'-besh–gil'-e-ad, To morrow, by *that time* the sun be hot, ye shall have help. And the messengers came and shewed *it* to the men of Ja'-besh; and they were glad.

10 Therefore the men of Ja'-besh said, To morrow we will come out unto you, and ye shall do with us all that seemeth good unto you.

11 And it was *so* on the morrow, that [R]Saul put the people [R]in three companies; and they came into the midst of the host in the morning watch, and slew the Am'-mon-ites until the heat of the day: and it came to pass, that they which remained were scattered, so that two of them were not left together.   31:11 · Judg. 7:16, 20

12 And the people said unto Samuel, [R]Who *is* he that said, Shall Saul reign over us? [R]bring the men, that we may put them to death.   10:27 · Luke 19:27

13 And Saul said, There shall not a man be put to death this day: for to day [R]the LORD hath wrought salvation in Israel.   19:5

14 Then said Samuel to the people, Come, and let us go to Gil'-gal, and renew the kingdom there.

15 And all the people went to Gil'-gal; and there they made Saul king before the LORD in Gil'-gal; and [R]there they sacrificed sacrifices of peace offerings before the LORD; and there Saul and all the men of Israel rejoiced greatly.   10:8

12 And Samuel said unto all Israel, Behold, I have hearkened unto [R]your voice in all that ye said unto me, and [R]have made a king over you.   8:5, 7, 9, 20, 22 · 10:24

2 And now, behold, the king [R]walketh before you: [R]and I am old and grayheaded; and, behold, my sons *are* with you: and I have walked before you from my childhood unto this day.   8:20 · 8:1, 5

3 Behold, here I *am*: witness against me before the LORD, and before [R]his anointed: whose ox have I taken? or whose ass have I taken? or whom have I defrauded? whom have I oppressed? or of whose hand have I received *any* bribe to blind mine eyes therewith? and I will restore it you.   10:1

4 And they said, [R]Thou hast not defrauded us, nor oppressed us, neither hast thou taken [T]ought of any man's hand.   Lev. 19:13 · *anything*

5 And he said unto them, The LORD *is* witness against you, and his anointed *is* witness this day, [R]that ye have not found ought [R]in my hand. And they answered, *He is* witness.   Acts 23:9; 24:20 · Ex. 22:4

6 And Samuel said unto the people, [R]*It is* the LORD that

advanced Moses and Aaron, and that brought your fathers up out of the land of Egypt. Ex. 6:26; Mic. 6:4

7 Now therefore stand still, that I may ᴿreason with you before the LORD of all the righteous acts of the LORD, which he did to you and to your fathers. Mic. 6:1–5

8 ᴿWhen Jacob was come into Egypt, and your fathers cried unto the LORD, then the LORD ᴿsent Moses and Aaron, which brought forth your fathers out of Egypt, and made them dwell in this place. Ps. 105:23 · Ex. 3:10; 4:14–16

9 And when they forgat the LORD their God, he sold them into the hand of ᴿSis'-e-ra, captain of the host of Ha'-zor, and into the hand of the ᴿPhi-lis'-tines, and into the hand of the king of ᴿMoab, and they fought against them. Judg. 4:2 · Judg. 3:31 · Judg. 3:12–30

10 And they cried unto the LORD, and said, We have sinned, because we have forsaken the LORD, ᴿand have served Ba'-a-lim and Ash'-ta-roth: but now deliver us out of the hand of our enemies, and we will serve thee. Judg. 2:13

11 And the LORD sent ᵀJer-ub-ba'-al, and Be'-dan, and Jeph'-thah, and Samuel, and delivered you out of the hand of your enemies on every side, and ye dwelled safe. Gideon, Judg. 6:32

12 And when ye saw that Na'-hash the king of the children of Ammon came against you, ye said unto me, Nay; but a king shall reign over us: when ᴿthe LORD your God was your king. Judg. 8:23

13 Now therefore ᴿbehold the king ᴿwhom ye have chosen, and whom ye have desired! and, behold, ᴿthe LORD hath set a king over you. 10:24 · 8:5 · Hos. 13:11

14 If ye will ᴿfear the LORD, and serve him, and obey his voice, and not rebel against the commandment of the LORD then shall both ye and also the king that reigneth over you continue following the LORD your God: Josh. 24:14

15 But if ye will not obey the voice of the LORD, but ᴿrebel against the commandment of the LORD, then shall the hand of the LORD be against you, as it was against your fathers. Lev. 26:14, 15

16 Now therefore ᴿstand and see this great thing, which the LORD will do before your eyes. Ex. 14:13

17 Is it not ᴿwheat harvest to day? ᴿI will call unto the LORD, and he shall send thunder and ᴿrain; that ye may perceive and see that ᴿyour wickedness is great, which ye have done in the sight of the LORD, in asking you a king. Gen. 30:14 · 7:9, 10 · Ezra 10:9 · 8:7

18 So Samuel called unto the LORD; and the LORD sent thunder and rain that day: and ᴿall the people greatly feared the LORD and Samuel. Ex. 14:31

19 And all the people said unto Samuel, ᴿPray for thy servants unto the LORD thy God, that we die not: for we have added unto all our sins this evil, to ask us a king. Ex. 9:28; [James 5:15; 1 John 5:16]

20 And Samuel said unto the people, Fear not: ye have done all this wickedness: ᴿyet turn not aside from following the LORD, but serve the LORD with all your heart; Deut. 11:16

21 And turn ye not aside: ᴿfor then should ye go after vain things, which cannot profit nor deliver; for they are vain. 1 Cor. 8:4

22 For the LORD will not forsake his people for his great name's sake: because it hath pleased the LORD to make you his people.

23 Moreover as for me, God forbid that I should sin against the LORD ᴿin ceasing to pray for you: but I will teach you the good and the right way: Col. 1:9; 2 Tim. 1:3

24 Only fear the LORD, and serve him in truth with all your heart: for consider how ᴿgreat things he hath done for you. Deut. 10:21

25 But if ye shall still do wickedly, ᴿye shall be consumed, both ye and your king. Josh. 24:20

13 Saul reigned one year; and when he had reigned two years over Israel,

2 Saul chose him three thousand *men* of Israel; *whereof* two thousand were with Saul in Mich'-mash and in mount Beth'-el, and a thousand were with ᴿJonathan in ᴿGib'-e-ah of Benja-min: and the rest of the people he sent every man to his tent.   14:1 · 10:26

3 And Jonathan ᵀsmote ᴿthe garrison of the Phi-lis'-tines that *was* in ᴿGe'-ba, and the Phi-lis'-tines heard *of it*. And Saul blew the trumpet throughout all the land, saying, Let the Hebrews hear.   *attacked* · 10:5 · 2 Sam. 5:25

4 And all Israel heard say *that* Saul had smitten a garrison of the Phi-lis'-tines, and *that* Israel also ᵀwas had in abomination with the Phi-lis'-tines. And the people were called together after Saul to Gil'-gal.   *had become odious*

5 And the Phi-lis'-tines gathered themselves together to fight with Israel, thirty thousand chariots, and six thousand horsemen, and people ᴿas the sand which *is* on the sea shore in multitude: and they came up, and pitched in Mich'-mash, eastward from ᴿBeth-a'-ven.   Judg. 7:12 · Josh. 7:2

6 When the men of Israel saw that they were in a ᵀstrait, (for the people were distressed,) then the people ᴿdid hide themselves in caves, and in thickets, and in rocks, and in high places, and in pits.   *danger* · 14:11; Judg. 6:2

7 And *some of* the Hebrews went over Jordan to the land of Gad and Gil'-e-ad. As for Saul, he *was* yet in Gil'-gal, and all the people followed him trembling.

8 And he tarried seven days, according to the set time that Samuel *had appointed:* but Samuel came not to Gil'-gal; and the people were scattered from him.

9 And Saul said, Bring hither a burnt offering to me, and peace offerings. And he offered the burnt offering.

10 And it came to pass, that as soon as he had made an end of offering the burnt offering, behold, Samuel came; and Saul went out to meet him, that he might ᵀsalute him.   *greet, lit. bless him*

11 And Samuel said, What hast thou done? And Saul said, Because I saw that the people were scattered from me, and *that* thou camest not within the days appointed, and *that* the Phi-lis'-tines gathered themselves together at Mich'-mash;

12 Therefore said I, The Phi-lis'-tines will come down now upon me to Gil'-gal, and I have not made supplication unto the LORD: I forced myself therefore, and offered a burnt offering.

13 And Samuel said to Saul, Thou hast done foolishly: ᴿthou hast not kept the commandment of the LORD thy God, which he commanded thee: for now would the LORD have established thy kingdom upon Israel for ever.   5:11

14 But now thy kingdom shall not continue: the LORD hath sought him a man ᴿafter his own heart, and the LORD hath commanded him *to be* captain over his people, because thou hast not kept *that* which the LORD commanded thee.   Ps. 89:20; Acts 7:46; 13:22

15 And Samuel arose, and gat him up from Gil'-gal unto Gib'-e-ah of Benjamin. And Saul numbered the people *that were* present with him, ᴿabout six hundred men.   vv. 2, 6, 7; 14:2

16 And Saul, and Jonathan his son, and the people *that were* present with them, abode in Gib'-e-ah of Benjamin: but the Phi-lis'-tines encamped in Mich'-mash.

17 And the ᵀspoilers came out of the camp of the Phi-lis'-tines in three companies: one company turned unto the way *that leadeth to* ᴿOph'-rah, unto the land of Shu'-al: *raiders* · Josh. 18:23

18 And another company turned the way *to* ᴿBeth-ho'-ron: and another company turned *to* the way of the border that looketh to the valley of ᴿZe-bo'-im toward the wilderness.   Josh. 16:3 · Gen. 14:2

19 Now ᴿthere was no smith found throughout all the land of

Israel: for the Phi-lis'-tines said, Lest the Hebrews make *them* swords or spears: Judg. 5:8; Jer. 24:1

20 But all the Israelites went down to the Phi-lis'-tines, to sharpen every man his share, and his coulter, and his ax, and his mattock.

21 Yet they had a file for the mattocks, and for the coulters, and for the forks, and for the axes, and to sharpen the goads.

22 So it came to pass in the day of battle, that ^Rthere was neither sword nor spear found in the hand of any of the people that *were* with Saul and Jonathan: but with Saul and with Jonathan his son was there found. Judg. 5:8

23 ^RAnd the garrison of the Phi-lis'-tines went out to the passage of Mich'-mash. 14:1, 4

14 Now it came to pass upon a day, that Jonathan the son of Saul said unto the young man that ^Tbare his armour, Come, and let us go over to the Phi-lis'-tines' garrison, that *is* on the other side. But he told not his father. *carried*

2 And Saul tarried in the uttermost part of ^RGib'-e-ah under a pomegranate tree which *is* in Mig'-ron: and the people that *were* with him *were* about six hundred men; 13:15, 16

3 And ^RA-hi'-ah, the son of A-hi'-tub, ^RI'–cha-bod's brother, the son of Phin'-e-has, the son of E'-li, the LORD's priest in Shi'-loh, ^Rwearing an e'-phod. And the people knew not that Jonathan was gone. 22:9, 11, 20 · 4:21 · 2:28

4 And between the ^Tpassages, by which Jonathan sought to go over ^Runto the Phi-lis'-tines' garrison, *there was* a sharp rock on the one side, and a sharp rock on the other side: and the name of the one *was* Bo'-zez, and the name of the other Se'-neh. *passes* · 13:23

5 The forefront of the one *was* situate northward over against Mich'-mash, and the other southward over against Gib'-e-ah.

6 And Jonathan said to the young man that bare his armour,

Come, and let us go over unto the garrison of these ^Runcircumcised: it may be that the LORD will work for us: for *there is* no restraint to the LORD ^Rto save by many or by few. 17:26, 36; Jer. 9:25, 26 · Judg. 7:4, 7

7 And his armourbearer said unto him, Do all that *is* in thine heart: turn thee; behold, I *am* with thee according to thy heart.

8 Then said Jonathan, Behold, we will pass over unto *these* men, and we will ^Tdiscover ourselves unto them. *show*

9 If they say thus unto us, Tarry until we come to you; then we will stand still in our place, and will not go up unto them.

10 But if they say thus, Come up unto us; then we will go up: for the LORD hath delivered them into our hand: and ^Rthis *shall be* a sign unto us. Gen. 24:14; Judg. 6:36–40

11 And both of them discovered themselves unto the garrison of the Phi-lis'-tines: and the Phi-lis'-tines said, Behold, the Hebrews come forth out of the holes where they had ^Rhid themselves. v. 22; 13:6

12 And the men of the garrison answered Jonathan and his armourbearer, and said, Come up to us, and we will shew you a thing. And Jonathan said unto his armourbearer, Come up after me: for the LORD hath delivered them into the hand of Israel.

13 And Jonathan climbed up upon his hands and upon his feet, and his armourbearer after him: and they ^Rfell before Jonathan; and his armourbearer slew after him. Lev. 26:8; Josh. 23:10

14 And that first slaughter, which Jonathan and his armourbearer made, was about twenty men, within as it were an half acre of land, *which* a yoke *of oxen might plow.*

15 And there was trembling in the host, in the field, and among all the people: the garrison, and ^Rthe spoilers, they also trembled, and the earth quaked: so it was ^Ra very great trembling. 13:17 · Gen. 35:5

16 And the watchmen of Saul in Gib'-e-ah of Benjamin looked; and, behold, the multitude melted away, and they [R]went on beating down *one another*.   v. 20

17 Then said Saul unto the people that *were* with him, Number now, and see who is gone from us. And when they had numbered, behold, Jonathan and his armourbearer *were* not *there*.

18 And Saul said unto A-hi'-ah, Bring hither the ark of God. For the ark of God was at that time with the children of Israel.

19 And it came to pass, while Saul talked unto the priest, that the noise that *was* in the host of the Phi-lis'-tines went on and increased: and Saul said unto the priest, Withdraw thine hand.

20 And Saul and all the people that *were* with him assembled themselves, and they came to the battle: and, behold, [R]every man's sword was against his fellow, *and there was* a very great [T]discomfiture.   Judg. 7:22; 2 Chr. 20:23 · confusion

21 Moreover the Hebrews *that* were with the Phi-lis'-tines before that time, which went up with them into the camp *from the country* round about, even they also *turned* to be with the Israelites that *were* with Saul and Jonathan.

22 Likewise all the men of Israel which [R]had hid themselves in mount E'-phra-im, *when* they heard that the Phi-lis'-tines fled, even they also followed hard after them in the battle.   13:6

23 [R]So the LORD saved Israel that day: and the battle passed over unto Beth-a'-ven.   2 Chr. 32:22

24 And the men of Israel were distressed that day: for Saul had [R]adjured the people, saying, Cursed *be* the man that eateth *any* food until evening, that I may be avenged on mine enemies. So none of the people tasted *any* food.   Josh. 6:26

25 And all *they* of the land came to a wood; and there was [R]honey upon the ground.   Ex. 3:8; Matt. 3:4

26 And when the people were come into the wood, behold, the honey dropped; but no man put his hand to his mouth: for the people feared the oath.

27 But Jonathan heard not when his father charged the people with the oath: wherefore he put forth the end of the rod that *was* in his hand, and dipped it in an honeycomb, and put his hand to his mouth; and his [T]eyes were enlightened.   countenance brightened

28 Then answered one of the people, and said, Thy father [T]straitly charged the people with an oath, saying, Cursed *be* the man that eateth *any* food this day. And the people were faint.   strictly

29 Then said Jonathan, My father hath troubled the land: see, I pray you, how mine eyes have been enlightened, because I tasted a little of this honey.

30 How much more, if [T]haply the people had eaten freely to day of the [T]spoil of their enemies which they found? for [T]had there not been now a much greater slaughter among the Phi-lis'-tines?   only · plunder · would

31 And they [T]smote the Phi-lis'-tines that day from Mich'-mash to Ai'-ja-lon: and the people were very faint.   had driven back

32 And the people flew upon the spoil, and took sheep, and oxen, and calves, and slew *them* on the ground: and the people did eat *them* [R]with the blood.   Acts 15:20

33 Then they told Saul, saying, Behold, the people sin against the LORD, in that they eat with the blood. And he said, Ye have [T]transgressed: roll a great stone unto me this day.   dealt treacherously

34 And Saul said, Disperse yourselves among the people, and say unto them, Bring me hither every man his ox, and every man his sheep, and slay *them* here, and eat; and sin not against the LORD in eating with the blood. And all the people brought every man his ox with him that night, and slew *them* there.

35 And Saul built an altar unto the LORD: the same was the first altar that he built unto the LORD.

36 And Saul said, Let us go down after the Phi-lis'-tines by night, and spoil them until the morning light, and let us not leave a man of them. And they said, Do whatsoever seemeth good unto thee. Then said the priest, Let us draw near hither unto God.

37 And Saul asked counsel of God, Shall I go down after the Phi-lis'-tines? wilt thou deliver them into the hand of Israel? But he answered him not that day.

38 And Saul said, ^RDraw ye near hither, all the chief of the people: and know and see wherein this sin hath been this day.   Josh. 7:14

39 For, ^Ras the LORD liveth, which saveth Israel, though it be in Jonathan my son, he shall surely die. But *there was* not a man among all the people *that* answered him.   vv. 24, 44; 2 Sam. 12:5

40 Then said he unto all Israel, Be ye on one side, and I and Jonathan my son will be on the other side. And the people said unto Saul, Do what seemeth good unto thee.

41 Therefore Saul said unto the LORD God of Israel, ^RGive a perfect *lot*. ^RAnd Saul and Jonathan were taken: but the people escaped.   Acts 1:24–26 · 10:20, 21

42 And Saul said, Cast *lots* between me and Jonathan my son. And Jonathan was taken.

43 Then Saul said to Jonathan, ^RTell me what thou hast done. And Jonathan told him, and said, I did but taste a little honey with the end of the rod that *was* in mine hand, *and,* lo, I must die.   Josh. 7:19

44 And Saul answered, ^RGod do so and more also: ^Rfor thou shalt surely die, Jonathan.   25:22 · v. 39

45 And the people said unto Saul, Shall Jonathan die, who hath wrought this great salvation in Israel? God forbid: ^Ras the LORD liveth, there shall not one hair of his head fall to the ground; for he hath wrought with God this day. So the people rescued Jonathan, that he died not.   Luke 21:18

46 Then Saul went up from following the Phi-lis'-tines: and the Phi-lis'-tines went to their own place.

47 So Saul took the kingdom over Israel, and fought against all his enemies on every side, against Moab, and against the children of ^RAmmon, and against E'-dom, and against the kings of ^RZo'-bah, and against the Phi-lis'-tines: and whithersoever he turned himself, he vexed *them*.   11:1–13 · 2 Sam. 10:6

48 And he gathered an host, and ^Rsmote the Am'-a-lek-ites, and delivered Israel out of the hands of them that spoiled them.   15:3–7

49 Now ^Rthe sons of Saul were Jonathan, and Ish'-u-i, and Mel'-chi–shu'-a: and the names of his two daughters *were these*; the name of the firstborn Me'-rab, and the name of the younger ^RMi'-chal: 31:2; 1 Chr. 8:33 · 18:17–20, 27; 19:12

50 And the name of Saul's wife *was* A-hin'-o-am, the daughter of A-him'-a-az: and the name of the captain of his host *was* Abner, the son of Ner, Saul's ^Runcle.   10:14

51 ^RAnd Kish *was* the father of Saul; and Ner the father of Abner *was* the son of A-bi'-el.   9:1, 21

52 And there was sore war against the Phi-lis'-tines all the days of Saul: and when Saul saw any strong man, or any valiant man, ^Rhe took him unto him.   8:11

15

Samuel also said unto Saul, ^RThe LORD sent me to anoint thee *to be* king over his people, over Israel: now therefore hearken thou unto the voice of the words of the LORD.   9:16; 10:1

2 Thus saith the LORD of hosts, I remember *that* which Am'-a-lek did to Israel, ^Rhow he laid *wait* for him in the way, when he came up from Egypt.   Ex. 17:8, 14; Num. 24:20

3 Now go and ^Rsmite Am'-a-lek, and ^Rutterly destroy all that they have, and spare them not; but slay both man and woman, infant and suckling, ox and sheep, camel and ass.   Deut. 25:19 · Lev. 27:28

4 And Saul gathered the people together, and numbered them in Te-la′-im, two hundred thousand footmen, and ten thousand men of Judah.

5 And Saul came to a city of Am′-a-lek, and laid wait in the valley.

6 And Saul said unto the Ken′-ites, Go, depart, get you down from among the Am′-a-lek-ites, lest I destroy you with them: for ᴿye shewed kindness to all the children of Israel, when they came up out of Egypt. So the Ken′-ites departed from among the Am′-a-lek-ites.   Ex. 18:10, 19

7 ᴿAnd Saul smote the Am′-a-lek-ites from ᴿHav′-i-lah *until* thou comest to ᴿShur, that *is* over against Egypt.   14:48 · Gen. 2:11 · 27:8

8 And he took A′-gag the king of the Am′-a-lek-ites alive, and ᴿutterly destroyed all the people with the edge of the sword.   27:8, 9

9 But Saul and the people ᴿspared A′-gag, and the best of the sheep, and of the oxen, and of the fatlings, and the lambs, and all *that was* good, and would not utterly destroy them: but every thing *that was* vile and refuse, that they destroyed utterly. vv. 3, 15

10 Then came the word of the LORD unto Samuel, saying,

11 ᴿIt repenteth me that I have set up Saul *to be* king: for he is turned back from following me, and hath not performed my commandments. And it grieved Samuel; and he cried unto the LORD all night.   v. 35; Gen. 6:6, 7; 2 Sam. 24:16

12 And when Samuel rose early to meet Saul in the morning, it was told Samuel, saying, Saul came to ᴿCarmel, and, behold, he set him up a place, and is gone about, and passed on, and gone down to Gil′-gal.   25:2; Josh. 15:55

13 And Samuel came to Saul: and Saul said unto him, ᴿBlessed *be* thou of the LORD: I have performed the commandment of the LORD.   Judg. 17:2; Ruth 3:10; 2 Sam. 2:5

14 And Samuel said, What *meaneth* then this bleating of the sheep in mine ears, and the lowing of the oxen which I hear?

15 And Saul said, They have brought them from the Am′-a-lek-ites: ᴿfor the people spared the best of the sheep and of the oxen, to sacrifice unto the LORD thy God; and the rest we have utterly destroyed.   [Gen. 3:12, 13; Ex. 32:22, 23]

16 Then Samuel said unto Saul, Stay, and I will tell thee what the LORD hath said to me this night. And he said unto him, Say on.

17 And Samuel said, When thou *wast* little in thine own sight, *wast* thou not *made* the head of the tribes of Israel, and the LORD anointed thee king over Israel?

18 And the LORD sent thee on a journey, and said, Go and utterly destroy the sinners the Am′-a-lek-ites, and fight against them until they be ᵀconsumed.   *exterminated*

19 Wherefore then didst thou not obey the voice of the LORD, but didst fly upon the spoil, and didst evil in the sight of the LORD?

20 And Saul said unto Samuel, Yea, ᴿI have obeyed the voice of the LORD, and have gone the way which the LORD sent me, and have brought A′-gag the king of Am′-a-lek, and have utterly destroyed the Am′-a-lek-ites.   v. 13; [Prov. 28:13]

21 ᴿBut the people took of the ᵀspoil, sheep and oxen, the chief of the things which should have been utterly destroyed, to sacrifice unto the LORD thy God in Gil′-gal.   v. 15 · *plunder*

22 And Samuel said, Hath the LORD *as great* delight in burnt offerings and sacrifices, as in obeying the voice of the LORD? Behold, ᴿto obey *is* better than sacrifice, *and* to hearken than the fat of rams.   [Hos. 6:6; Matt. 9:13; 12:7]

23 For rebellion *is as* the sin of witchcraft, and stubbornness *is as* iniquity and idolatry. Because thou hast rejected the word of the LORD, ᴿhe hath also rejected thee from *being* king.   13:14; 16:1

24 ᴿAnd Saul said unto Samuel, I have sinned: for I have trans-

gressed the commandment of the LORD, and thy words: because I ᴿfeared the people, and obeyed their voice.   Ps. 51:4 · [Is. 51:12, 13]

25 Now therefore, I pray thee, pardon my sin, and turn again with me, that I may worship the LORD.

26 And Samuel said unto Saul, I will not return with thee: for thou hast rejected the word of the LORD, and the LORD hath rejected thee from being king over Israel.

27 And as Samuel turned about to go away, he laid hold upon the skirt of his mantle, and it rent.

28 And Samuel said unto him, The LORD hath rent the kingdom of Israel from thee this day, and hath given it to a neighbour of thine, *that is* better than thou.

29 And also the Strength of Israel ᴿwill not lie nor ᵀrepent: for he *is* not a man, that he should repent.   2 Tim. 2:13; Titus 1:2 · *relent*

30 Then he said, I have sinned: *yet* ᴿhonour me now, I pray thee, before the elders of my people, and before Israel, and turn again with me, that I may worship the LORD thy God.   [John 5:44; 12:43]

31 So Samuel ᵀturned again after Saul; and Saul worshipped the LORD.   *turned back*

32 Then said Samuel, Bring ye hither to me A'-gag the king of the Am'-a-lek-ites. And A'-gag came unto him ᵀdelicately. And A'-gag said, Surely the bitterness of death is past.   *cautiously*

33 And Samuel said, ᴿAs thy sword hath made women childless, so shall thy mother be childless among women. And Samuel hewed A'-gag in pieces before the LORD in Gil'-gal.   Num. 14:45; Judg. 1:7

34 Then Samuel went to Ra'-mah; and Saul went up to his house to ᴿGib'-e-ah of Saul.   7:17

35 And Samuel came no more to see Saul until the day of his death: nevertheless Samuel mourned for Saul: and the LORD ᵀrepented that he had made Saul king over Israel.   *regretted*

16 And the LORD said unto Samuel, How long wilt thou mourn for Saul, seeing I have rejected him from reigning over Israel? ᴿfill thine horn with oil, and go, I will send thee to ᴿJesse the Beth'-le-hem-ite: for ᴿI have provided me a king among his sons.   10:1 · Ruth 4:18–22 · Acts 13:22

2 And Samuel said, How can I go? if Saul hear *it*, he will kill me. And the LORD said, Take a heifer with thee, and say, ᴿI am come to sacrifice to the LORD.   9:12

3 And call Jesse to the sacrifice, and I will shew thee what thou shalt do: and thou shalt anoint unto me *him* whom I name unto thee.

4 And Samuel did that which the LORD spake, and came to Beth'-le-hem. And the elders of the town ᴿtrembled at his coming, and said, ᴿComest thou peaceably?   21:1 · 1 Kin. 2:13; 2 Kin. 9:22

5 And he said, Peaceably: I am come to sacrifice unto the LORD: sanctify yourselves, and come with me to the sacrifice. And he sanctified Jesse and his sons, and called them to the sacrifice.

6 And it came to pass, when they were come, that he looked on E-li'-ab, and said, Surely the LORD's anointed *is* before him.

7 But the LORD said unto Samuel, Look not on his countenance, or on the height of his stature; because I have refused him: ᴿfor *the* LORD *seeth* not as man seeth; for man ᴿlooketh on the outward appearance, but the LORD looketh on the heart.   Is. 55:8, 9 · 2 Cor. 10:7

8 Then Jesse called A-bin'-a-dab, and made him pass before Samuel. And he said, Neither hath the LORD chosen this.

9 Then Jesse made Sham'-mah to pass by. And he said, Neither hath the LORD chosen this.

10 Again, Jesse made seven of his sons to pass before Samuel. And Samuel said unto Jesse, The LORD hath not chosen these.

11 And Samuel said unto Jesse,

Are here all *thy* children? And he said, There remaineth yet the youngest, and, behold, he keepeth the ᴿsheep. And Samuel said unto Jesse, Send and ᵀfetch him: for we will not sit down till he come hither.   2 Sam. 7:8; Ps. 78:70–72 · *bring*

12 And he sent, and brought him in. Now he *was* ᴿruddy, *and* withal of a ᴿbeautiful countenance, and goodly to look to. And the LORD said, Arise, anoint him: for this *is* he.   17:42 · Ex. 2:2; Acts 7:20

13 Then Samuel took the horn of oil, and anointed him in the midst of his brethren: and ᴿthe Spirit of the LORD came upon David from that day forward. So Samuel rose up, and went to Ra'-mah.   10:6, 9, 10; Num. 27:18

14 But the Spirit of the LORD departed from Saul, and an evil spirit from the LORD troubled him.

15 And Saul's servants said unto him, Behold now, an evil spirit from God troubleth thee.

16 Let our lord now command thy servants, *which are* before thee, to seek out a man, *who is* a cunning player on an harp: and it shall come to pass, when the ᵀevil spirit from God is upon thee, that he shall ᴿplay with his hand, and thou shalt be well.   *distressing* · 18:10

17 And Saul said unto his servants, ᵀProvide me now a man that can play well, and bring *him* to me.   Lit. *Look for*

18 Then answered one of the servants, and said, Behold, I have seen a son of Jesse the Beth'–le-hem-ite, *that is* cunning in playing, and a mighty valiant man, and a man of war, and prudent in ᵀmatters, and a comely person, and the LORD *is* with him.   *speech*

19 Wherefore Saul sent messengers unto Jesse, and said, Send me David thy son, which *is* with the sheep.

20 And Jesse ᴿtook an ass *laden* with bread, and a bottle of wine, and a kid, and sent *them* by David his son unto Saul.   10:4, 27; Prov. 18:16

21 And David came to Saul, and ᴿstood before him: and he loved

him greatly; and he became his armourbearer.   Gen. 41:46; Prov. 22:29

22 And Saul sent to Jesse, saying, Let David, I pray thee, stand before me; for he hath found favour in my sight.

23 And it came to pass, when the *evil* spirit from God was upon Saul, that David took an harp, and played with his hand: so Saul was refreshed, and was well, and the evil spirit departed from him.

17 Now the Phi-lis'-tines gathered together their armies to battle, and were gathered together at Sho'-choh, which *belongeth* to Judah, and pitched between Sho'-choh and A-ze'-kah, in E'-phes–dam'-mim.

2 And Saul and the men of Israel were gathered together, and ᵀpitched by the valley of E'-lah, and set the battle in array against the Phi-lis'-tines.   *encamped*

3 And the Phi-lis'-tines stood on a mountain on the one side, and Israel stood on a mountain on the other side: and *there was* a valley between them.

4 And there went out a champion out of the camp of the Phi-lis'-tines, named ᴿGo-li'-ath, of Gath, whose height *was* six cubits and a span.   2 Sam. 21:19

5 And *he had* an helmet of brass upon his head, and he *was* armed with a coat of mail; and the weight of the coat *was* five thousand shek'-els of brass.

6 And *he had* greaves of brass upon his legs, and a target of brass between his shoulders.

7 And the staff of his spear *was* like a weaver's beam; and his spear's head *weighed* six hundred shek'-els of iron: and one bearing a shield went before him.

8 And he stood and cried unto the armies of Israel, and said unto them, Why are ye come out to set *your* battle in array? *am* not I a Phi-lis'-tine, and ye ᴿservants to Saul? choose you a man for you, and let him come down to me.   8:17

9 If he be able to fight with

me, and to kill me, then will we be your servants: but if I prevail against him, and kill him, then shall ye be our servants, and ᴿserve us.   11:1

10 And the Phi-lis'-tine said, I ᴿdefy the armies of Israel this day; give me a man, that we may fight together.   vv. 26, 36, 45; 2 Sam. 21:21

11 When Saul and all Israel heard those words of the Phi-lis'-tine, they were dismayed, and greatly afraid.

12 Now David *was* ᴿthe son of that Eph'-rath-ite of Beth'-le-hem-ju'-dah, whose name *was* Jesse; and he had eight sons: and the man went among men *for* an old man in the days of Saul.   16:1

13 And the three eldest sons of Jesse went *and* followed Saul to the battle: and the ᴿnames of his three sons that went to the battle *were* E-li'-ab the first born, and next unto him A-bin'-a-dab, and the third Sham'-mah.   1 Chr. 2:13

14 And David *was* the youngest: and the three eldest followed Saul.

15 But David went and returned from Saul ᴿto feed his father's sheep at Beth'-le-hem.   2 Sam. 7:8

16 And the Phi-lis'-tine drew near morning and evening, and presented himself forty days.

17 And Jesse said unto David his son, Take now for thy brethren an e'-phah of this parched *corn*, and these ten loaves, and run to the camp to thy brethren;

18 And carry these ten cheeses unto the captain of *their* thousand, and look how thy brethren fare, and take their pledge.

19 Now Saul, and they, and all the men of Israel, *were* in the valley of E'-lah, fighting with the Phi-lis'-tines.

20 And David rose up early in the morning, and left the sheep with a keeper, and took, and went, as Jesse had commanded him; and he came to the ᵀtrench, as the host was going forth to the fight, and shouted for the battle.   camp

21 For Israel and the Phi-lis'-tines had put the battle in array, army against army.

22 And David left his ᵀcarriage in the hand of the keeper of the carriage, and ran into the army, and came and ᵀsaluted his brethren.   *supplies · greeted*

23 And as he talked with them, behold, there came up the champion, the Phi-lis'-tine of Gath, Go-li'-ath by name, out of the armies of the Phi-lis'-tines, and spake ᴿaccording to the same words: and David heard *them*.   vv. 8–10

24 And all the men of Israel, when they saw the man, fled from him, and were sore afraid.

25 And the men of Israel said, Have ye seen this man that is come up? surely to defy Israel is he come up: and it shall be, *that* the man who killeth him, the king will enrich him with great riches, and ᴿwill give him his daughter, and make his father's house free in Israel.   Josh. 15:16

26 And David spake to the men that stood by him, saying, What shall be done to the man that killeth this Phi-lis'-tine, and taketh away the reproach from Israel? for who *is* this uncircumcised Phi-lis'-tine, that he should defy the armies of the living God?

27 And the people answered him after this manner, saying, ᴿSo shall it be done to the man that killeth him.   v. 25

28 And E-li'-ab his eldest brother heard when he spake unto the men; and E-li'-ab's anger was kindled against David, and he said, Why camest thou down hither? and with whom hast thou left those few sheep in the wilderness? I know thy pride, and the naughtiness of thine heart; for thou art come down that thou mightest see the battle.

29 And David said, What have I now done? *Is there* not a cause?

30 And he turned from him toward another, and spake after the same manner: and the people answered him again ᵀafter the former manner.   *as the first ones did*

31 And when the words were heard which David spake, they ^Trehearsed *them* before Saul: and he sent for him.   *reported*

32 And David said to Saul, ^RLet no man's heart fail because of him; thy servant will go and fight with this Phi-lis'-tine.   Deut. 20:1–4

33 And Saul said to David, Thou art not able to go against this Phi-lis'-tine to fight with him: for thou *art but* a youth, and he a man of war from his youth.

34 And David said unto Saul, Thy servant kept his father's sheep, and there came a ^Rlion, and a bear, and took a lamb out of the flock: Judg. 14:5

35 And I went out after him, and ^Tsmote him, and delivered *it* out of his mouth: and when he arose against me, I caught *him* by his beard, and smote him, and slew him.   *struck*

36 Thy servant slew both the lion and the bear: and this uncir-cumcised Phi-lis'-tine shall be as one of them, seeing he hath defied the armies of the living God.

37 David said moreover, The LORD that delivered me out of the paw of the lion, and out of the paw of the bear, he will deliver me out of the hand of this Phi-lis'-tine. And Saul said unto David, Go, and the LORD be with thee.

38 And Saul armed David with his armour, and he put an helmet of brass upon his head; also he armed him with a coat of mail.

39 And David girded his sword upon his armour, and he ^Tassayed to go; for he had not ^Tproved *it*. And David said unto Saul, I can-not go with these; for I have not proved *them*. And David put them off him.   *tried to walk · tested*

40 And he took his staff in his hand, and chose him five smooth stones out of the brook, and put them in a shepherd's bag which he had, even in a scrip; and his sling *was* in his hand: and he drew near to the Phi-lis'-tine.

41 And the Phi-lis'-tine came on and drew near unto David; and

the man that bare the shield *went* before him.

42 And when the Phi-lis'-tine looked about, and saw David, he ^Rdisdained him: for he was *but* a youth, and ^Rruddy, and of a fair countenance.   [1 Cor. 1:27, 28] · 16:12

43 And the Phi-lis'-tine said un-to David, ^RAm I a dog, that thou comest to me with ^Tstaves? And the Phi-lis'-tine cursed David by his gods.   24:14; 2 Kin. 8:13 · *sticks*

44 And the Phi-lis'-tine ^Rsaid to David, Come to me, and I will give thy flesh unto the fowls of the air, and to the beasts of the field.   v. 46

45 Then said David to the Phi-lis'-tine, Thou comest to me with a sword, and with a spear, and with a shield: ^Rbut I come to thee in the name of the LORD of hosts, the God of the armies of Israel, whom thou hast defied.   2 Sam. 22:33, 35

46 This day will the LORD deliv-er thee into mine hand; and I will smite thee, and take thine head from thee; and I will give the car-cases of the host of the Phi-lis'-tines this day unto the fowls of the air, and to the wild beasts of the earth; that all the earth may know that there is a God in Israel.

47 And all this assembly shall know that the LORD ^Rsaveth not with sword and spear: for the bat-tle *is* the LORD's, and he will give you into our hands.   14:6; Zech. 4:6

48 And it came to pass, when the Phi-lis'-tine arose, and came and drew nigh to meet David, that David hasted, and ran toward the army to meet the Phi-lis'-tine.

49 And David put his hand in his bag, and took thence a stone, and slang *it,* and smote the Phi-lis'-tine in his forehead, that the stone sunk into his forehead; and he fell upon his face to the earth.

50 So David prevailed over the Phi-lis'-tine with a sling and with a stone, and smote the Phi-lis'-tine, and slew him; but *there was* no sword in the hand of David.

51 Therefore David ran, and stood upon the Phi-lis'-tine, and took his ^Rsword, and drew it out of

the sheath thereof, and slew him, and cut off his head therewith. And when the Phi-lis'-tines saw their champion was dead, ^Rthey fled.   21:9; 2 Sam. 23:21 · Heb. 11:34

52 And the men of Israel and of Judah arose, and shouted, and pursued the Phi-lis'-tines, until thou come to the valley, and to the gates of Ek'-ron. And the wounded of the Phi-lis'-tines fell down by the way to Sha-a-ra'-im, even unto Gath, and unto Ek'-ron.

53 And the children of Israel returned from chasing after the Phi-lis'-tines, and they ^Tspoiled their tents.   *plundered*

54 And David took the head of the Phi-lis'-tine, and brought it to Jerusalem; but he put his armour in his tent.

55 And when Saul saw David go forth against the Phi-lis'-tine, he said unto Abner, the captain of the host, Abner, whose son *is* this youth? And Abner said, *As* thy soul liveth, O king, I cannot tell.

56 And the king said, Enquire thou whose son the stripling *is*.

57 And as David returned from the slaughter of the Phi-lis'-tine, Abner took him, and brought him before Saul ^Rwith the head of the Phi-lis'-tine in his hand.   v. 54

58 And Saul said to him, Whose son *art* thou, *thou* young man? And David answered, ^RI *am* the son of thy servant Jesse the Beth'–le-hem-ite.   v. 12

18 And it came to pass, when he had made an end of speaking unto Saul, that ^Rthe soul of Jonathan was knit with the soul of David, and Jonathan loved him as his own soul.   Gen. 44:30

2 And Saul took him that day, ^Rand would let him go no more home to his father's house.   17:15

3 Then Jonathan and David made a ^Rcovenant, because he loved him as his own soul.   20:8–17

4 And Jonathan stripped himself of the robe that *was* upon him, and gave it to David, and his garments, even to his sword, and to his bow, and to his girdle.

5 And David went out whithersoever Saul sent him, *and* ^Tbehaved himself wisely: and Saul set him over the men of war, and he was accepted in the sight of all the people, and also in the sight of Saul's servants.   *prospered*

6 And it came to pass as they came, when David was returned from the slaughter of the Phi-lis'-tine, that ^Rthe women came out of all cities of Israel, singing and dancing, to meet king Saul, with tabrets, with joy, and with instruments of musick.   Ps. 68:25; 149:3

7 And the women ^Ranswered *one another* as they played, and said, ^RSaul hath slain his thousands, and David his ten thousands.   Ex. 15:21 · 21:11; 29:5

8 And Saul was very wroth, and the saying displeased him; and he said, They have ascribed unto David ten thousands, and to me they have ascribed *but* thousands: and *what* can he have more but ^Rthe kingdom?   15:28

9 And Saul eyed David from that day and forward.

10 And it came to pass on the morrow, that the evil spirit from God came upon Saul, and he prophesied in the midst of the house: and David played with his hand, as at other times: and *there was* a javelin in Saul's hand.

11 And Saul ^Rcast the javelin; for he said, I will smite David even to the wall *with it*. And David ^Tavoided out of his presence twice.   19:10; 20:33 · *escaped*

12 And Saul was afraid of David, because ^Rthe LORD was with him, and was ^Rdeparted from Saul.   16:13, 18 · 16:14; 28:15

13 Therefore Saul removed him from him, and made him his captain over a thousand; and ^Rhe went out and came in before the people.   18:16; 29:6; Num. 27:17; 2 Sam. 5:2

14 And David behaved himself wisely in all his ways; and ^Rthe LORD *was* with him.   Gen. 39:2, 3, 23

15 Wherefore when Saul saw that he behaved himself very wisely, he was afraid of him.

16 But ᴿall Israel and Judah loved David, because he went out and came in before them. 1 Kin. 3:7

17 And Saul said to David, Behold my elder daughter Me´-rab, ᴿher will I give thee to wife: only be thou valiant for me, and fight the LORD's battles. For Saul said, Let not mine hand be upon him, but let the hand of the Phi-lis´-tines be upon him. 14:49; 17:25

18 And David said unto Saul, Who *am* I? and what *is* my life, *or* my father's family in Israel, that I should be son in law to the king?

19 But it came to pass at the time when Me´-rab Saul's daughter should have been given to David, that she was given unto ᴿA´-dri-el the ᴿMe-hol´-ath-ite to wife. 2 Sam. 21:8 · Judg. 7:22; 2 Sam. 21:8

20 And Mi´-chal Saul's daughter loved David: and they told Saul, and the thing pleased him.

21 And Saul said, I will give him her, that she may be a snare to him, and that ᴿthe hand of the Phi-lis´-tines may be against him. Wherefore Saul said to David, Thou shalt this day be my son in law in *the one of* the twain. v. 17

22 And Saul commanded his servants, *saying*, Commune with David secretly, and say, Behold, the king hath delight in thee, and all his servants love thee: now therefore be the king's son in law.

23 And Saul's servants spake those words in the ears of David. And David said, Seemeth it to you *a* light *thing* to be a king's son in law, seeing that I *am* a poor man, and lightly esteemed?

24 And the servants of Saul told him, saying, On this manner spake David.

25 And Saul said, Thus shall ye say to David, The king desireth not any ᴿdowry, but an hundred foreskins of the Phi-lis´-tines, to be ᴿavenged of the king's enemies. But Saul thought to make David fall by the hand of the Phi-lis´-tines. Gen. 34:12; Ex. 22:17 · 14:24

26 And when his servants told David these words, it pleased

David well to be the king's son in law: and ᴿthe days were not expired. v. 21

27 Wherefore David arose and went, he and ᴿhis men, and slew of the Phi-lis´-tines two hundred men; and ᴿDavid brought their foreskins, and they gave them in full ᵀtale to the king, that he might be the king's son in law. And Saul gave him Mi´-chal his daughter to wife. v. 13 · 2 Sam. 3:14 · count

28 And Saul saw and knew that the LORD *was* with David, and *that* Mi´-chal Saul's daughter loved him.

29 And Saul was yet the more afraid of David; and Saul became David's enemy continually.

30 Then the princes of the Phi-lis´-tines ᴿwent forth: and it came to pass, after they went forth, *that* David behaved himself more wisely than all the servants of Saul; so that his name was ᵀmuch set by. 2 Sam. 11:1 · highly esteemed

19 And Saul spake to Jona-than his son, and to all his servants, that they should kill ᴿDavid. 8:8, 9 2

2 But Jonathan Saul's son delighted much in David: and Jon-athan told David, saying, Saul my father seeketh to kill thee: now therefore, I pray thee, take heed to thyself until the morning, and abide in a secret *place,* and hide thyself:

3 And I will go out and stand beside my father in the field where thou *art,* and I will commune with my father of thee; and what I see, that I will tell thee.

4 And Jonathan spake good of David unto Saul his father, and said unto him, Let not the king ᴿsin against his servant, against David; because he hath not sinned against thee, and because his works *have been* to thee-ward very good: Gen. 42:22; Jer. 18:20

5 For he did put his life in his hand, and slew the Phi-lis´-tine, and ᴿthe LORD wrought a great salvation for all Israel: thou sawest *it,* and didst rejoice: ᴿwhere-

fore then wilt thou sin against innocent blood, to slay David without a cause?   11:13; 1 Chr. 11:14 · 20:32

6 And Saul hearkened unto the voice of Jonathan: and Saul sware, *As* the LORD liveth, he shall not be slain.

7 And Jonathan called David, and Jonathan shewed him all those things. And Jonathan brought David to Saul, and he was in his presence, ^Ras in times past.   16:21; 18:2, 10, 13

8 And there was war again: and David went out, and fought with the Phi-lis'-tines, and ^Rslew them with a great slaughter; and they fled from him.   18:27; 23:5

9 And ^Rthe evil spirit from the LORD was upon Saul, as he sat in his house with his javelin in his hand: and David played with *his* hand.   16:14; 18:10, 11

10 And Saul sought to ^Tsmite David even to the wall with the javelin; but he slipped away out of Saul's presence, and he smote the javelin into the wall: and David fled, and escaped that night.   pin

11 ^RSaul also sent messengers unto David's house, to watch him, and to slay him in the morning: and Mi'-chal David's wife told him, saying, If thou save not thy life to night, to morrow thou shalt be slain.   Judg. 16:2; Ps. 59:title

12 So Mi'-chal ^Rlet David down through a window: and he went, and fled, and escaped.   Acts 9:25

13 And Mi'-chal took an image, and laid *it* in the bed, and put a pillow of goats' *hair* for his bolster, and covered *it* with a cloth.

14 And when Saul sent messengers to take David, she said, He *is* sick.

15 And Saul sent the messengers *again* to see David, saying, Bring him up to me in the bed, that I may slay him.

16 And when the messengers were come in, behold, *there was* an image in the bed, with a pillow of goats' *hair* for his bolster.

17 And Saul said unto Mi'-chal, Why hast thou deceived me so,

and sent away mine enemy, that he is escaped? And Mi'-chal answered Saul, He said unto me, Let me go; why should I kill thee?

18 So David fled, and escaped, and came to ^RSamuel to Ra'-mah, and told him all that Saul had done to him. And he and Samuel went and dwelt in Na'-ioth.   16:13

19 And it was told Saul, saying, Behold, David *is* at Na'-ioth in Ra'-mah.

20 And Saul sent messengers to take David: ^Rand when they saw the company of the prophets prophesying, and Samuel standing *as* appointed over them, the Spirit of God was upon the messengers of Saul, and they also ^Rprophesied.   10:5, 6, 10 · Joel 2:28

21 And when it was told Saul, he sent other messengers, and they prophesied likewise. And Saul sent messengers again the third time, and they prophesied also.

22 Then went he also to Ra'-mah, and came to a great well that *is* in Se'-chu: and he asked and said, Where *are* Samuel and David? And *one* said, Behold, *they be* at Na'-ioth in Ra'-mah.

23 And he went thither to Na'-ioth in Ra'-mah: and ^Rthe Spirit of God was upon him also, and he went on, and prophesied, until he came to Na'-ioth in Ra'-mah.   10:10

24 And he stripped off his clothes also, and prophesied before Samuel in like manner, and lay down naked all that day and all that night. Wherefore they say, *Is* Saul also among the prophets?

20 And David fled from Na'-ioth in Ra'-mah, and came and said before Jonathan, What have I done? what *is* mine iniquity? and what *is* my sin before thy father, that he seeketh my life?

2 And he said unto him, God forbid; thou shalt not die: behold, my father will do nothing either great or small, but that he will shew it me: and why should my father hide this thing from me? it *is* not *so*.

3 And David sware moreover,

and said, Thy father certainly knoweth that I have found grace in thine eyes; and he saith, Let not Jonathan know this, lest he be grieved: but ᴿtruly *as* the LORD liveth, and *as* thy soul liveth, *there is* but a step between me and death.   27:1; 2 Kin. 2:6

4 Then said Jonathan unto David, Whatsoever thy soul desireth, I will even do *it* for thee.

5 And David said unto Jonathan, Behold, to morrow *is* the ᴿnew moon, and I should not fail to sit with the king ᵀat meat: but let me go, that I may ᴿhide myself in the field unto the third *day* at even. Num. 10:10; 28:11–15 · *to eat* · 19:2, 3

6 If thy father at all miss me, then say, David earnestly asked *leave* of me that he might run ᴿto Beth'–le-hem his city: for *there is* a yearly sacrifice there for all the family.   16:4; 17:12; John 7:42

7 If he say thus, *It is* well; thy servant shall have peace: but if he be very wroth, *then* be sure that ᴿevil is determined by him.   25:17

8 Therefore thou shalt ᴿdeal kindly with thy servant; for ᴿthou hast brought thy servant into a covenant of the LORD with thee: notwithstanding, ᴿif there be in me iniquity, slay me thyself; for why shouldest thou bring me to thy father? Josh. 2:14 · 18:3 · 2 Sam. 14:32

9 And Jonathan said, Far be it from thee: for if I knew certainly that evil were determined by my father to come upon thee, then would not I tell it thee?

10 Then said David to Jonathan, Who shall tell me? or what *if* thy father answer thee roughly?

11 And Jonathan said unto David, Come, and let us go out into the field. And they went out both of them into the field.

12 And Jonathan said unto David, O LORD God of Israel, when I have sounded my father about to morrow any time, *or* the third *day*, and, behold, *if there be* good toward David, and I then send not unto thee, and shew it thee;

13 ᴿThe LORD do so and much more to Jonathan: but if it please my father *to do* thee evil, then I will shew it thee, and send thee away, that thou mayest go in peace: and ᴿthe LORD be with thee, as he hath ᴿbeen with my father.   Ruth 1:17 · 17:37; 18:12 · 10:7

14 And thou shalt not only while yet I live shew me the kindness of the LORD, that I die not:

15 But *also* ᴿthou shalt not cut off thy kindness from my ᵀhouse for ever: no, not when the LORD hath cut off the enemies of David every one from the face of the earth.   24:21; 2 Sam. 9:1, 3, 7; 21:7 · *family*

16 So Jonathan made *a cov-enant* with the house of David, *saying*, ᴿLet the LORD even require *it* at the hand of David's enemies.   25:22; 31:2; 2 Sam. 4:7; 21:8

17 And Jonathan caused David to ᵀswear again, because he loved him: ᴿfor he loved him as he loved his own soul.   *vow* · 18:1

18 Then Jonathan said to David, ᴿTo morrow *is* the new moon: and thou shalt be missed, because thy seat will be empty.   vv. 5, 24

19 And *when* thou hast stayed three days, *then* thou shalt go down quickly, and come to ᴿthe place where thou didst hide thyself when the business was *in hand*, and shalt remain by the stone E'-zel.   19:2

20 And I will shoot three arrows on the side *thereof*, as though I shot at a mark.

21 And, behold, I will send a lad, *saying*, Go, find out the arrows. If I expressly say unto the lad, Behold, the arrows *are* on this side of thee, take them; then come thou: for *there is* peace to thee, and no hurt; *as* the LORD liveth.

22 But if I say thus unto the young man, Behold, the arrows *are* beyond thee; go thy way: for the LORD hath sent thee away.

23 And *as touching* ᴿthe matter which thou and I have spoken of, behold, the LORD *be* between thee and me for ever.   vv. 14, 15

24 So David hid himself in the field: and when the new moon

was come, the king sat him down to eat meat.

25 And the king sat upon his seat, as at other times, *even* upon a seat by the wall: and Jonathan arose, and Abner sat by Saul's side, and David's place was empty.

26 Nevertheless Saul spake not any thing that day: for he thought, Something hath befallen him, he *is* not clean; surely he *is* ᴿnotᵀ clean.　　　Lev. 7:20, 21; 15:5 · *unclean*

27 And it came to pass on the morrow, *which was* the second *day* of the month, that David's place was empty: and Saul said unto Jonathan his son, Wherefore cometh not the son of Jesse to meat, neither yesterday, nor to day?

28 And Jonathan ᴿanswered Saul, David earnestly asked *leave* of me *to* go to Beth'–le-hem:　v. 6

29 And he said, Let me go, I pray thee; for our family hath a sacrifice in the city; and my brother, he hath commanded me *to be there:* and now, if I have found favour in thine eyes, let me get away, I pray thee, and see my brethren. Therefore he cometh not unto the king's table.

30 Then Saul's anger was kindled against Jonathan, and he said unto him, Thou son of the perverse rebellious *woman,* do not I know that thou hast chosen the son of Jesse to thine own confusion, and unto the confusion of thy mother's nakedness?

31 For as long as the son of Jesse liveth upon the ground, thou shalt not be established, nor thy kingdom. Wherefore now send and fetch him unto me, for he ᵀshall surely die.　Lit. *is a son of death*

32 And Jonathan answered Saul his father, and said unto him, ᴿWherefore shall he be slain? what hath he done?　　Matt. 27:23

33 And Saul cast a javelin at him to smite him: ᴿwhereby Jonathan knew that it was determined of his father to slay David.　v. 7

34 So Jonathan arose from the table in fierce anger, and did eat no meat the second day of the month: for he was grieved for David, because his father had done him shame.

35 And it came to pass in the morning, that Jonathan went out into the field at the time appointed with David, and a little lad with him.

36 And he said unto his lad, Run, find out now the arrows which I shoot. *And* as the lad ran, he shot an arrow beyond him.

37 And when the lad was come to the place of the arrow which Jonathan had shot, Jonathan cried after the lad, and said, *Is* not the arrow beyond thee?

38 And Jonathan cried after the lad, Make speed, haste, ᵀstay not. And Jonathan's lad gathered up the arrows, and came to his master.　　　　　　*do not delay*

39 But the lad knew not any thing: only Jonathan and David knew the matter.

40 And Jonathan gave his ᵀartillery unto his lad, and said unto him, Go, carry *them* to the city.　　　　　　*weapons*

41 *And* as soon as the lad was gone, David arose out of *a place* toward the south, and fell on his face to the ground, and bowed himself three times: and they kissed one another, and wept one with another, until David exceeded.

42 And Jonathan said to David, Go in peace, forasmuch as we have sworn both of us in the name of the Lord, saying, The Lord be between me and thee, and be-tween my seed and thy seed for ever. And he arose and departed: and Jonathan went into the city.

21 Then came David to Nob to A-him'-e-lech the priest: and ᴿA-him'-e-lech was afraid at the meeting of David, and said unto him, Why *art* thou alone, and no man with thee?　14:3; Mark 2:26

2 And David said unto A-him'-e-lech the priest, The king hath commanded me a business, and

hath said unto me, Let no man know any thing of the business whereabout I send thee, and what I have commanded thee: and I have ᵀappointed *my* servants to such and such a place.　*directed*

3 Now therefore ᵀwhat is under thine hand? give *me* five *loaves of* bread in mine hand, or what there is present.　*what do you have on hand*

4 And the priest answered David, and said, *There is* no common bread under mine hand, but there is ᴿhallowed bread; if the young men have kept themselves at least from women.　Matt. 12:4

5 And David answered the priest, and said unto him, Of a truth women *have been* kept from us about these three days, since I came out, and the ᴿvessels of the young men are holy, and *the bread is* in a manner common, yea, though it were sanctified this day in the vessel.　1 Thess. 4:4

6 So the priest ᴿgave him hallowed *bread:* for there was no bread there but the shewbread, that was taken from before the LORD, to put hot bread in the day when it was taken away. Luke 6:3, 4

7 Now a certain man of the servants of Saul *was* there that day, detained before the LORD; and his name *was* ᴿDo'-eg, an E'-dom-ite, the chiefest of the herdmen that *belonged* to Saul.　14:47; Ps. 52:title

8 And David said unto A-him'-e-lech, And is there not here under thine hand spear or sword? for I have neither brought my sword nor my weapons with me, because the king's business required haste.

9 And the priest said, The sword of Go-li'-ath the Phi-lis'-tine, whom thou slewest in ᴿthe valley of E'-lah, behold, it *is here* wrapped in a cloth behind the e'-phod: if thou wilt take that, take *it:* for *there is* no other save that here. And David said, *There is* none like that; give it me.　17:2, 50

10 And David arose, and fled that day for fear of Saul, and went to A'-chish the king of Gath.

11 And ᴿthe servants of A'-chish said unto him, ᴿ*Is* not this David the king of the land? did they not sing one to another of him in dances, saying, Saul hath slain his thousands, and David his ten thousands?　Ps. 56:title · 18:6–8; 29:5

12 And David ᴿlaid up these words in his heart, and was ᵀsore afraid of A'-chish the king of Gath.　Luke 2:19 · *very much*

13 And ᴿhe changed his behaviour before them, and feigned himself mad in their hands, and ᵀscrabbled on the doors of the gate, and let his spittle fall down upon his beard. Ps. 34:title · *scratched*

14 Then said A'-chish unto his servants, Lo, ye see the man is ᵀmad: wherefore *then* have ye brought him to me?　*insane*

15 Have I need of mad men, that ye have brought this *fellow* to play the mad man in my presence? shall this *fellow* come into my house?

22 David therefore departed thence, and ᴿescaped ᴿto the cave A-dul'-lam: and when his brethren and all his father's house heard *it,* they went down thither to him.　Ps. 57:title · Josh. 12:15; 15:35

2 ᴿAnd every one *that was* in distress, and every one that *was* in debt, and every one *that was* discontented, gathered themselves unto him; and he became a captain over them: and there were with him about ᴿfour hundred men.　Judg. 11:3 · 25:13

3 And David went thence to Miz'-peh of ᴿMoab: and he said unto the king of Moab, Let my father and my mother, ᵀI pray thee, come forth, *and be* with you, till I know what God will do for me.　2 Sam. 8:2 · *please, come here*

4 And he brought them before the king of Moab: and they dwelt with him all the while that David was ᵀin the hold.　*strong hold*

5 And the prophet ᴿGad said unto David, Abide not in the hold; depart, and get thee into the land of Judah. Then David departed, and came into the forest of Ha'-reth. 2 Sam. 24:11; 1 Chr. 21:9; 2 Chr. 29:25

6 When Saul heard that David was discovered, and the men that *were* with him, (now Saul abode in ᴿGib′-e-ah under a ᵀtree in Ra′-mah, having his spear in his hand, and all his servants *were* standing about him;)　　*15:34 · tamarisk tree*

7 Then Saul said unto his servants that stood about him, Hear now, ye Benjamites; will the son of Jesse ᴿgive every one of you fields and vineyards, *and* make you all captains of thousands, and captains of hundreds;　　*8:14*

8 That all of you have conspired against me, and *there is* none that sheweth me that ᴿmy son hath made a league with the son of Jesse, and *there is* none of you that is sorry for me, or sheweth unto me that my son hath stirred up my servant against me, to lie in wait, as at this day?　*18:3*

9 Then answered ᴿDo′-eg the E′-dom-ite, which was set over the servants of Saul, and said, I saw the son of Jesse coming to Nob, to ᴿA-him′-e-lech the son of ᴿA-hi′-tub.　*21:7; Ps. 52:title · 21:1 · 14:3*

10 ᴿAnd he enquired of the LORD for him, and ᴿgave him victuals, and gave him the sword of Go-li′-ath the Phi-lis′-tine.　*10:22 · 21:6, 9*

11 Then the king sent to call A-him′-e-lech the priest, the son of A-hi′-tub, and all his father's house, the priests that *were* in Nob: and they came all of them to the king.

12 And Saul said, Hear now, thou son of A-hi′-tub. And he answered, Here I *am*, my lord.

13 And Saul said unto him, Why have ye conspired against me, thou and the son of Jesse, in that thou hast given him bread, and a sword, and hast enquired of God for him, that he should rise against me, to lie in wait, as at this day?

14 Then A-him′-e-lech answered the king, and said, And who *is so* faithful among all thy servants as David, which is the king's son in law, and goeth at thy bidding, and is honourable in thine house?

15 Did I then begin to enquire of God for him? be it far from me: let not the king impute *any* thing unto his servant, *nor* to all the house of my father: for thy servant knew nothing of all this, less or more.

16 And the king said, Thou shalt surely die, A-him′-e-lech, thou, and all thy father's house.

17 And the king said unto the ᵀfootmen that stood about him, Turn, and slay the priests of the LORD; because their hand also *is* with David, and because they knew when he fled, and did not shew it to me. But the servants of the king ᴿwould not put forth their hand to fall upon the priests of the LORD.　*guards · Ex. 1:17*

18 And the king said to Do′-eg, Turn thou, and fall upon the priests. And Do′-eg the E′-dom-ite turned, and he ᵀfell upon the priests, and slew on that day fourscore and five persons that did wear a linen e′-phod.　*attacked*

19 ᴿAnd Nob, the city of the priests, smote he with the edge of the sword, both men and women, children and sucklings, and oxen, and asses, and sheep, with the edge of the sword.　*Josh. 21:1–45*

20 ᴿAnd one of the sons of A-him′-e-lech the son of A-hi′-tub, named A-bi′-a-thar, ᴿescaped, and fled after David.　*23:6, 9; 30:7 · 2:33*

21 And A-bi′-a-thar shewed David that Saul had slain the LORD's priests.

22 And David said unto A-bi′-a-thar, I knew *it* that day, when Do′-eg the E′-dom-ite *was* there, that he would surely tell Saul: I have occasioned *the death* of all the persons of thy father's house.

23 Abide thou with me, fear not: ᴿfor he that seeketh my life seeketh thy life: but with me thou *shalt be* in safeguard.　*1 Kin. 2:26*

23 Then they told David, saying, Behold, the Phi-lis′-tines fight against ᴿKei′-lah, and they rob the threshingfloors.　*Josh. 15:44*

2 Therefore David ᴿenquired of the LORD, saying, Shall I go and smite these Phi-lis'-tines? And the LORD said unto David, Go, and smite the Phi-lis'-tines, and save Kei'-lah.   22:10; 28:6; 30:8; 2 Sam. 5:19, 23

3   And David's men said unto him, Behold, we be afraid here in Judah: how much more then if we come to Kei'-lah against the armies of the Phi-lis'-tines?

4   Then David enquired of the LORD yet again. And the LORD answered him and said, Arise, go down to Kei'-lah; for I will deliver the Phi-lis'-tines into thine hand.

5   So David and his men went to Kei'-lah, and Rfought with the Phi-lis'-tines, and brought away their cattle, and smote them with a great slaughter. So David saved the inhabitants of Kei'-lah.   19:8

6   And it came to pass, when A-bi'-a-thar the son of A-him'-e-lech Rfled to David to Kei'-lah, that he came down with an e'-phod in his hand.   22:20

7   And it was told Saul that David was come to Kei'-lah. And Saul said, God hath delivered him into mine hand; for he is shut in, by entering into a town that hath gates and bars.

8   And Saul called all the people together to war, to go down to Kei'-lah, to besiege David and his men.

9   And David knew that Saul secretly practised mischief a-gainst him; and Rhe said to A-bi'-a-thar the priest, Bring hither the e'-phod.   v. 6; 30:7; Num. 27:21

10   Then said David, O LORD God of Israel, thy servant hath certain-ly heard that Saul seeketh to come to Kei'-lah, Rto destroy the city for my sake.   22:19

11   Will the men of Kei'-lah deliv-er me up into his hand? will Saul come down, as thy servant hath heard? O LORD God of Israel, I beseech thee, tell thy servant. And the LORD said, He will come down.

12   Then said David, Will the men of Kei'-lah deliver me and my men into the hand of Saul? And the LORD said, They will deliver thee up.

13   Then David and his men, Rwhich were about six hundred, arose and departed out of Kei'-lah, and went whithersoever they could go. And it was told Saul that David was escaped from Kei'-lah; and he forbare to go forth.   25:13

14   And David abode in the wil-derness in strong holds, and re-mained in a mountain in the wilderness of Ziph. And Saul sought him every day, but God delivered him not into his hand.

15   And David saw that Saul was come out to seek his life: and David was in the wilderness of Ziph Tin a wood.   in Horesh

16   And Jonathan Saul's son arose, and went to David into the wood, and Tstrengthened his hand in God.   encouraged him

17   And he said unto him, Fear not: for the hand of Saul my fa-ther shall not find thee; and thou shalt be king over Israel, and I shall be next unto thee; and that also Saul my father knoweth.

18   And they two Rmade a cov-enant before the LORD: and David abode in the wood, and Jonathan went to his house.   18:3; 20:12-17, 42

19   Then Rcame up the Ziph'-ites to Saul to Gib'-e-ah, saying, Doth not David hide himself with us in strong holds in the wood, in the hill of Hach'-i-lah, which is on the south of Jesh'-i-mon?   26:1; Ps. 54:title

20   Now therefore, O king, come down according to all the desire of thy soul to come down; and Rour part shall be to deliver him into the king's hand.   Ps. 54:3

21   And Saul said, Blessed be ye of the LORD; for ye have compas-sion on me.

22   Go, I pray you, prepare yet, and know and see his place where his Thaunt is, and who hath seen him there: for it is told me that he dealeth very subtilly.   hideout

23   See therefore, and take knowledge of all the lurking places where he hideth himself, and come ye again to me with the certainty, and I will go with you: and it shall come to pass, if he be

in the land, that I will search him out throughout all the [T]thousands of Judah. *clans*

24 And they arose, and went to Ziph before Saul: but David and his men *were* in the wilderness [R]of Ma′-on, in the plain on the south of Jesh′-i-mon. 25:2; Josh. 15:55

25 Saul also and his men went to seek *him*. And they told David: wherefore he came down [T]into a rock, and abode in the wilderness of Ma′-on. And when Saul heard *that*, he pursued after David in the wilderness of Ma′-on. *to the*

26 And Saul went on this side of the mountain, and David and his men on that side of the mountain: and David made haste to get away for fear of Saul; for Saul and his men compassed David and his men round about to take them.

27 [R]But there came a messenger unto Saul, saying, Haste thee, and come; for the Phi-lis′-tines have invaded the land. 2 Kin. 19:9

28 Wherefore Saul returned from pursuing after David, and went against the Phi-lis′-tines: therefore they called that place Se′-la–ham-mah-le′-koth.

29 And David went up from thence, and dwelt in strong holds at [R]En-ge′-di. Josh. 15:62; 2 Chr. 20:2

24 And it came to pass, [R]when Saul was returned from following the Phi-lis′-tines, that it was told him, saying, Behold, David *is* in the wilderness of En-ge′-di. 23:19, 28, 29

2 Then Saul took three thousand chosen men out of all Israel, and [R]went to seek David and his men upon the rocks of the wild goats. 26:2; Ps. 38:12

3 And he came to the sheepcotes by the way, where *was* a cave; and Saul went in to cover his feet: and David and his men remained in the sides of the cave.

4 [R]And the men of David said unto him, Behold the day of which the Lord said unto thee, Behold, I will deliver thine enemy into thine hand, that thou mayest do to him as it shall seem good unto thee.

Then David arose, and cut off the skirt of Saul's robe privily. 26:8–11

5 And it came to pass afterward, that [R]David's heart smote him, because he had cut off Saul's skirt. 2 Sam. 24:10

6 And he said unto his men, [R]The Lord forbid that I should do this thing unto my master, the Lord's anointed, to stretch forth mine hand against him, seeing he *is* the anointed of the Lord. 26:11

7 So David [R]stayed his servants with these words, and suffered them not to rise against Saul. But Saul rose up out of the cave, and went on *his* way. Ps. 7:4; [Matt. 5:44]

8 David also arose afterward, and went out of the cave, and cried after Saul, saying, My lord the king. And when Saul looked behind him, David stooped with his face to the earth, and bowed himself.

9 And David said to Saul, [R]Wherefore hearest thou men's words, saying, Behold, David seeketh thy hurt? Ps. 141:6; [Prov. 17:9]

10 Behold, this day thine eyes have seen how that the Lord had delivered thee to day into mine hand in the cave: and *some* bade *me* kill thee: but *mine eye* spared thee; and I said, I will not put forth mine hand against my lord; for he *is* the Lord's anointed.

11 Moreover, my father, see, yea, see the [T]skirt of thy robe in my hand: for in that I cut off the [T]skirt of thy robe, and killed thee not, know thou and see that *there is* [R]neither evil nor transgression in mine hand, and I have not sinned against thee; yet thou [R]huntest my soul to take it. *corner* · Ps. 7:3 · 26:20

12 [R]The Lord judge between me and thee, and the Lord avenge me of thee: but mine hand shall not be upon thee. 26:10–23; Judg. 11:27

13 As saith the proverb of the ancients, Wickedness proceedeth from the wicked: but mine hand shall not be upon thee.

14 After whom is the king of Israel come out? after whom dost thou pursue? [R]after a dead dog, after [R]a flea. 17:43; 2 Sam. 9:8 · 26:20

15 ᴿThe Lᴏʀᴅ therefore be judge, and judge between me and thee, and ᴿsee, and ᴿplead my cause, and deliver me out of thine hand. v. 12 · 2 Chr. 24:22 · Ps. 35:1; Mic. 7:9

16 And it came to pass, when David had made an end of speaking these words unto Saul, that Saul said, ᴿIs this thy voice, my son David? And Saul lifted up his voice, and wept.   26:17

17 ᴿAnd he said to David, Thou art ᴿmore righteous than I: for ᴿthou hast rewarded me good, whereas I have rewarded thee evil.   26:21 · Gen. 38:26 · [Matt. 5:44]

18 And thou hast shewed this day how that thou hast dealt well with me: forasmuch as when ᴿthe Lᴏʀᴅ had delivered me into thine hand, thou killedst me not.   26:23

19 For if a man find his enemy, will he let him ᵀgo well away? wherefore the Lᴏʀᴅ reward thee good for that thou hast done unto me this day.   get away safely

20 And now, behold, ᴿI know well that thou shalt surely be king, and that the kingdom of Israel shall be established in thine hand.   23:17

21 ᴿSwear now therefore unto me by the Lᴏʀᴅ, that thou wilt not cut off my seed after me, and that thou wilt not destroy my name out of my father's house.   20:14–17

22 And David sware unto Saul. And Saul went home; but David and his men gat them up unto ᴿthe ᵀhold.   23:29 · strong hold

25 And ᴿSamuel died; and all the Israelites were gathered together, and ᴿlamented him, and buried him in his house at Ra'-mah. And David arose, and went down ᴿto the wilderness of Pa'-ran.   28:3 · Deut. 34:8 · Num. 10:12; 13:3

2 And there was a man ᴿin Ma'-on, whose ᵀpossessions were in ᴿCarmel; and the man was very great, and he had three thousand sheep, and a thousand goats: and he was shearing his sheep in Carmel.   23:24 · business · Josh. 15:55

3 Now the name of the man was Na'-bal; and the name of his wife Ab'-i-gail: and she was a woman of good understanding, and of a beautiful countenance: but the man was ᵀchurlish and evil in his doings; and he was of the house of ᴿCaleb.   harsh · 30:14

4 And David heard in the wilderness that Na'-bal did ᴿshear his sheep.   Gen. 38:13; 2 Sam. 13:23

5 And David sent out ten young men, and David said unto the young men, Get you up to Carmel, and go to Na'-bal, and greet him in my name:

6 And thus shall ye say to him that liveth in prosperity, ᴿPeace be both to thee, and peace be to thine house, and peace be unto all that thou hast.   Judg. 19:20; Luke 10:5

7 And now I have heard that thou hast shearers: now thy shepherds which were with us, we hurt them not, ᴿneither was there ought missing unto them, all the while they were in Carmel.   v. 15

8 Ask thy young men, and they will shew thee. Wherefore let the young men find favour in thine eyes: for we come in a good day: give, I pray thee, whatsoever cometh to thine hand unto thy servants, and to thy son David.

9 And when David's young men came, they spake to Na'-bal according to all those words in the name of David, and ceased.

10 And Na'-bal answered David's servants, and said, ᴿWho is David? and who is the son of Jesse? there be many servants now a days that break away every man from his master.   Judg. 9:28

11 ᴿShall I then take my bread, and my water, and my flesh that I have killed for my shearers, and give it unto men, whom I know not whence they be?   Judg. 8:6, 15

12 So David's young men turned their way, and went again, and came and told him all those sayings.

13 And David said unto his men, Gird ye on every man his sword. And they girded on every man his sword; and David also girded on his sword: and there went up after

David about four hundred men; and two hundred ^Rabode by the stuff. 30:24

14 But one of the young men told Ab'-i-gail, Na'-bal's wife, saying, Behold, David sent messengers out of the wilderness to ^Tsalute our master; and he ^Trailed on them.   greet · reviled or scolded

15 But the men *were* very good unto us, and we were not hurt, neither missed we any thing, as long as we were conversant with them, when we were in the fields:

16 They were ^Ra wall unto us both by night and day, all the while we were with them keeping the sheep.   Ex. 14:22; Job 1:10

17 Now therefore know and consider what thou wilt do; for ^Revil is determined against our master, and against all his household: for he *is such* a ^Tson of ^RBe'-li-al, that *a man* cannot speak to him.   20:7 · wicked man · Deut. 13:13

18 Then Ab'-i-gail made haste, and ^Rtook two hundred loaves, and two bottles of wine, and five sheep ready dressed, and five measures of parched *corn*, and an hundred clusters of raisins, and two hundred cakes of figs, and laid *them* on asses.   Gen. 32:13

19 And she said unto her servants, ^RGo on before me; behold, I come after you. But she told not her husband Na'-bal.   Gen. 32:16, 20

20 And it was *so, as* she rode on the ass, that she came down by the covert of the hill, and, behold, David and his men came down against her; and she met them.

21 Now David had said, Surely in vain have I kept all that this *fellow* hath in the wilderness, so that nothing was missed of all that *pertained* unto him: and he hath ^Rrequited me evil for good.   24:17

22 ^RSo and more also do God unto the enemies of David, if I leave of all that *pertain* to him by the morning light any that pisseth against the wall.   Ruth 1:17; 3:17; 20:13

23 And when Ab'-i-gail saw David, she hasted, and ^Rlighted off the ass, and fell before David on her face, and bowed herself to the ground,   Josh. 15:18; Judg. 1:14

24 And fell at his feet, and said, Upon me, my lord, *upon* me *let this* iniquity *be:* and let thine handmaid, I pray thee, speak in thine audience, and hear the words of thine handmaid.

25 Let not my lord, I pray thee, regard this man of Be'-li-al, *even* Na'-bal: for as his name *is*, so *is* he; Na'-bal *is* his name, and folly *is* with him: but I thine handmaid saw not the young men of my lord, whom thou didst send.

26 Now therefore, my lord, *as* the Lord liveth, and *as* thy soul liveth, seeing the Lord hath withholden thee from coming to *shed* blood, and from avenging thyself with thine own hand, now let thine enemies, and they that seek evil to my lord, be as Na'-bal.

27 And now this blessing which thine handmaid hath brought unto my lord, let it even be given unto the young men that follow my lord.

28 I pray thee, forgive the trespass of thine handmaid: for the Lord will certainly make my lord a sure house; because my lord ^Rfighteth the battles of the Lord, and ^Revil hath not been found in thee *all* thy days.   18:17 · 24:11; Ps. 7:3

29 Yet a man is risen to pursue thee, and to seek thy soul: but the soul of my lord shall be bound in the bundle of life with the Lord thy God; and the souls of thine enemies, them shall he sling out, *as out* of the middle of a sling.

30 And it shall come to pass, when the Lord shall have done to my lord according to all the good that he hath spoken concerning thee, and shall have appointed thee ^Rruler over Israel;   13:14; 15:28

31 That this shall be no grief unto thee, nor offence of heart unto my lord, either that thou hast shed blood causeless, or that my lord hath avenged himself: but when the Lord shall have dealt

well with my lord, then remember thine handmaid.

32 And David said to Ab'-i-gail, ^RBlessed *be* the LORD God of Israel, which sent thee this day to meet me: Ps. 72:18; 106:48; Luke 1:68

33 And blessed *be* thy advice, and blessed *be* thou, which hast ^Rkept me this day from coming to *shed* blood, and from avenging myself with mine own hand. v. 26

34 For in very deed, *as* the LORD God of Israel liveth, which hath ^Rkept me back from hurting thee, except thou hadst hasted and come to meet me, surely there had ^Rnot been left unto Na'-bal by the morning light any ^Tthat pisseth against the wall. v. 26 · v. 22 · *males*

35 So David received of her hand *that* which she had brought him, and said unto her, ^RGo up in peace to thine house; see, I have hearkened to thy voice, and have accepted thy person. Luke 7:50; 8:48

36 And Ab'-i-gail came to Na'-bal; and, behold, ^Rhe held a feast in his house, like the feast of a king; and Na'-bal's heart *was* merry within him, for he *was* very drunken: wherefore she told him nothing, less or more, until the morning light. Is. 5:11; [Hos. 4:11]

37 But it came to pass in the morning, when the wine was gone out of Na'-bal, and his wife had told him these things, that his heart died within him, and he became *as* a stone.

38 And it came to pass about ten days *after*, that the LORD ^Rsmote Na'-bal, that he died. 26:10; 2 Sam. 6:7

39 And when David heard that Na'-bal was dead, he said, Blessed *be* the LORD, that hath ^Rpleaded the cause of my reproach from the hand of Na'-bal, and hath kept his servant from evil: for the LORD hath ^Rreturned the wickedness of Na'-bal upon his own head. And David sent and ^Tcommuned with Ab'-i-gail, to take her to him to wife. Prov. 22:23 · 1 Kin. 2:44 · *proposed to*

40 And when the servants of David were come to Ab'-i-gail to Carmel, they spake unto her, say-

ing, David sent us unto thee, to take thee to him to wife.

41 And she arose, and bowed herself on *her* face to the earth, and said, Behold, *let* thine handmaid *be* a servant to wash the feet of the servants of my lord.

42 And Ab'-i-gail hasted, and arose, and rode upon an ass, with five damsels of hers that went ^Tafter her; and she went after the messengers of David, and became his wife. Lit. *at her feet*

43 David also took A-hin'-o-am of Jez'-re-el; ^Rand they were also both of them his wives. 27:3; 30:5

44 But Saul had given ^RMi'-chal his daughter, David's wife, to Phal'-ti the son of La'-ish, which *was* of Gal'-lim. 18:20; 2 Sam. 3:14

26 And the Ziph'-ites came unto Saul to Gib'-e-ah, saying, ^RDoth not David hide himself in the hill of Hach'-i-lah, *which is* before Jesh'-i-mon? 23:19; Ps. 54:title

2 Then Saul arose, and went down to the wilderness of Ziph, having three thousand chosen men of Israel with him, to seek David in the wilderness of Ziph.

3 And Saul pitched in the hill of Hach'-i-lah, which *is* before Jesh'-i-mon, by the way. But David abode in the wilderness, and he saw that Saul came after him into the wilderness.

4 David therefore sent out spies, and understood that Saul was come in very deed.

5 And David arose, and came to the place where Saul had pitched: and David beheld the place where Saul lay, and ^RAbner the son of Ner, the captain of his host: and Saul lay in the ^Ttrench, and the people pitched round about him. 14:50, 51; 17:55 · *camp*

6 Then answered David and said to A-him'-e-lech the Hit'-tite, and to A-bi'-shai ^Rthe son of Ze-ru'-iah, brother to Jo'-ab, saying, Who will go down with me to Saul to the camp? And A-bi'-shai said, I will go down with thee. 1 Chr. 2:16

7 So David and A-bi'-shai came to the people by night; and, behold, Saul lay sleeping within ᵀthe trench, and his spear stuck in the ground at his ᵀbolster: but Abner and the people lay round about him. *the camp · head*

8 Then said A-bi'-shai to David, ᴿGod hath delivered thine enemy into thine hand this day: now therefore let me smite him, I pray thee, with the spear even to the earth ᵀat once, and I will not *smite* him the second time. 24:4 · *one time*

9 And David said to A-bi'-shai, Destroy him not: for who can stretch forth his hand against the LORD's anointed, and be guiltless?

10 David said furthermore, *As* the LORD liveth, ᴿthe LORD shall smite him; or his day shall come to die; or he shall descend into battle, and perish. [Luke 18:7]

11 The LORD forbid that I should stretch forth mine hand against the LORD's anointed: but, I pray thee, take thou now the spear that *is* at his ᵀbolster, and the cruse of water, and let us go. *head*

12 So David took the spear and the cruse of water from Saul's bolster; and they gat them away, and no man saw *it,* nor knew *it,* neither awaked: for they *were* all asleep; because ᴿa deep sleep from the LORD was fallen upon them. Gen. 2:21; 15:12; Is. 29:10

13 Then David went over to the other side, and stood on the top of an hill afar off; a great space *being* between them:

14 And David cried to the people, and to Abner the son of Ner, saying, Answerest thou not, Abner? Then Abner answered and said, Who *art* thou *that* criest to the king?

15 And David said to Abner, *Art* not thou a *valiant* man? and who *is* like to thee in Israel? wherefore then hast thou not ᵀkept thy lord the king? for there came one of the people in to destroy the king thy lord. *guarded*

16 This thing *is* not good that thou hast done. *As* the LORD liveth, ye *are* worthy to die, because ye have not kept your mas-

ter, the LORD's anointed. And now see where the king's spear *is,* and the cruse of water that *was* at his ᵀbolster. *head*

17 And Saul knew David's voice, and said, ᴿ*Is* this thy voice, my son David? And David said, *It is* my voice, my lord, O king. 24:16

18 And he said, ᴿWherefore doth my lord thus pursue after his servant? for what have I done? or what evil *is* in mine hand? 24:9–14

19 Now therefore, I pray thee, let my lord the king hear the words of his servant. If the LORD have ᴿstirred thee up against me, let him accept an offering: but if *they be* the children of men, cursed *be* they before the LORD; for they have driven me out this day from abiding in the inheritance of the LORD, saying, Go, serve other gods. 2 Sam. 16:11; 24:1

20 Now therefore, let not my blood fall to the earth before the face of the LORD: for the king of Israel is come out to seek ᴿa flea, as when one doth hunt a partridge in the mountains. 24:14

21 Then said Saul, ᴿI have sinned: return, my son David: for I will no more do thee harm, because my soul was precious in thine eyes this day: behold, I have played the fool, and have erred exceedingly. 15:24; 24:17; 2 Sam. 12:13

22 And David answered and said, Behold the king's spear! and let one of the young men come over and fetch it.

23 The LORD render to every man his righteousness and his faithfulness: for the LORD delivered thee into *my* hand to day, but I would not stretch forth mine hand against the LORD's anointed.

24 And, behold, as thy life was much ᵀset by this day in mine eyes, so let my life be much set by in the eyes of the LORD, and let him deliver me out of all tribulation. *valued*

25 Then Saul said to David, Blessed *be* thou, my son David: thou shalt both do great *things,*

and also shalt still ^Rprevail. So David went on his way, and Saul returned to his place. Gen. 32:28

27 And David said in his heart, I shall now perish one day by the hand of Saul: *there is* nothing better for me than that I should speedily escape into the land of the Phi-lis'-tines; and Saul shall despair of me, to seek me any more in any coast of Israel: so shall I escape out of his hand.

2 And David arose, ^Rand he passed over with the six hundred men that *were* with him ^Runto A'-chish, the son of Ma'-och, king of Gath. 25:13 · 21:10; 1 Kin. 2:39

3 And David dwelt with A'-chish at Gath, he and his men, every man with his household, *even* David ^Rwith his two wives, A-hin'-o-am the Jez'-re-el-i-tess, and Ab'-i-gail the Car'-mel-i-tess, Na'-bal's wife. 25:42, 43

4 And it was told Saul that David was fled to Gath: and he sought no more again for him.

5 And David said unto A'-chish, If I have now found grace in thine eyes, let them give me a place in some town in the country, that I may dwell there: for why should thy servant dwell in the royal city with thee?

6 Then A'-chish gave him Zik'-lag that day: wherefore ^RZik'-lag pertaineth unto the kings of Judah unto this day. Josh. 15:31; 19:5

7 And ^Tthe time that David ^Rdwelt in the country of the Phi-lis'-tines was a full year and four months. Lit. *the number of days* · 29:3

8 And David and his men went up, and invaded the Gesh'-u-rites, and the Gez'-rites, and the Am'-a-lek-ites: for those *nations were* of old the inhabitants of the land, ^Ras thou goest to Shur, even unto the land of Egypt. Gen. 25:18; Ex. 15:22

9 And David smote the land, and left neither man nor woman alive, and took away the sheep, and the oxen, and the asses, and the camels, and the apparel, and returned, and came to A'-chish.

10 And A'-chish said, Whither have ye made a road to day? And David said, Against the south of Judah, and against the south of the Je-rah'-me-el-ites, and against the south of the Ken'-ites.

11 And David saved neither man nor woman alive, to bring *tidings* to Gath, saying, Lest they should tell on us, saying, So did David, and so *will be* his manner all the while he dwelleth in the country of the Phi-lis'-tines.

12 And A'-chish believed David, saying, He hath made his people Israel utterly to abhor him; therefore he shall be my servant for ever.

28 And ^Rit came to pass in those days, that the Phi-lis'-tines gathered their armies together for warfare, to fight with Israel. And A'-chish said unto David, Know thou assuredly, that thou shalt go out with me to battle, thou and thy men. 29:1, 2

2 And David said to A'-chish, Surely thou shalt know what thy servant can do. And A'-chish said to David, Therefore will I make thee ^Tkeeper of mine head for ever. *one of my chief guardians*

3 Now ^RSamuel was dead, and all Israel had lamented him, and buried him in ^RRa'-mah, even in his own city. And Saul had put away ^Rthose that had familiar spirits, and the wizards, out of the land. 25:1 · 1:19 · Ex. 22:18; Deut. 18:10, 11

4 And the Phi-lis'-tines gathered themselves together, and came and pitched in ^RShu'-nem: and Saul gathered all Israel together, and they pitched in ^RGil-bo'-a. Josh. 19:18; 1 Kin. 1:3 · 31:1

5 And when Saul saw the host of the Phi-lis'-tines, he was ^Rafraid, and his heart greatly trembled. Job 18:11; [Is. 57:20]

6 And when Saul enquired of the LORD, the LORD answered him not, neither by ^Rdreams, nor by U'-rim, nor by prophets. Joel 2:28

7 Then said Saul unto his servants, Seek me a woman that hath a familiar spirit, that I may go to her, and enquire of her. And his

servants said to him, Behold, *there is* a woman that hath a familiar spirit at En'–dor.

8 And Saul disguised himself, and put on other raiment, and he went, and two men with him, and they came to the woman by night: and ᴿhe said, I pray thee, divine unto me by the familiar spirit, and bring me *him* up, whom I shall name unto thee.   1 Chr. 10:13; Is. 8:19

9 And the woman said unto him, Behold, thou knowest what Saul hath done, how he hath ᴿcut off those that have familiar spirits, and the wizards, out of the land: wherefore then layest thou a snare for my life, to cause me to die?   v. 3

10 And Saul sware to her by the LORD, saying, *As* the LORD liveth, there shall no punishment happen to thee for this thing.

11 Then said the woman, Whom shall I bring up unto thee? And he said, Bring me up Samuel.

12 And when the woman saw Samuel, she cried with a loud voice: and the woman spake to Saul, saying, Why hast thou deceived me? for thou *art* Saul.

13 And the king said unto her, Be not afraid: for what sawest thou? And the woman said unto Saul, I saw ᴿgodsᵀ ascending out of the earth.   Ex. 22:28 · *a spirit*

14 And he said unto her, What form *is* he of? And she said, An old man cometh up; and he *is* covered with ᴿa mantle. And Saul perceived that it *was* Samuel, and he stooped with *his* face to the ground, and bowed himself.   15:27

15 And Samuel said to Saul, Why hast thou ᴿdisquieted me, to bring me up? And Saul answered, I am sore distressed; for the Phi-lis'-tines make war against me, and ᴿGod is departed from me, and answereth me no more, neither by prophets, nor by dreams: therefore I have called thee, that thou mayest make known unto me what I shall do.   Is. 14:9 · 16:14

16 Then said Samuel, Wherefore then dost thou ask of me, seeing

the LORD is departed from thee, and is become thine enemy?

17 And the LORD hath done to him, ᴿas he spake by me: for the LORD hath rent the kingdom out of thine hand, and given it to thy neighbour, *even* to David: 15:28

18 Because thou obeyedst not the voice of the LORD, nor executedst his fierce wrath upon ᴿAm'-a-lek, therefore hath the LORD done this thing unto thee this day. 15:3-9

19 Moreover the LORD will also deliver Israel with thee into the hand of the Phi-lis'-tines: and to morrow *shalt* thou and thy sons *be* with ᴿme: the LORD also shall deliver the host of Israel into the hand of the Phi-lis'-tines.   31:1-6

20 Then Saul fell straightway ᵀall along on the earth, and was sore afraid, because of the words of Samuel: and there was no strength in him; for he had eaten no bread all the day, nor all the night.   *full length on the ground*

21 And the woman came unto Saul, and saw that he was sore troubled, and said unto him, Behold, thine handmaid hath obeyed thy voice, and I have ᴿput my life in my hand, and have hearkened unto thy words which thou spakest unto me.   19:5; Judg. 12:3; Job 13:14

22 Now therefore, I pray thee, hearken thou also unto the voice of thine handmaid, and let me set a morsel of bread before thee; and eat, that thou mayest have strength, when thou goest on thy way.

23 But he refused, and said, I will not eat. But his servants, together with the woman, ᵀcompelled him; and he hearkened unto their voice. So he arose from the earth, and sat upon the bed.   *urged*

24 And the woman had a fat calf in the house; and she hasted, and killed it, and took flour, and kneaded *it*, and did bake unleavened bread thereof:

25 And she brought *it* before Saul, and before his servants; and they did eat. Then they rose up, and went away that night.

29 Now the Phi-lis'-tines gathered together all their armies ᴿto A'-phek: and the Is-raelites pitched by a fountain which is in Jez'-re-el. Josh. 12:18

2 And the ᴿlords of the Phi-lis'-tines passed on by hundreds, and by thousands: but ᴿDavid and his men passed on in the ᵀrereward with A'-chish. 6:4; 7:7 · 28:1, 2 · rear

3 Then said the princes of the Phi-lis'-tines, What do these Hebrews here? And A'-chish said unto the princes of the Phi-lis'-tines, Is not this David, the ser-vant of Saul the king of Israel, which hath been with me these days, or these years, and I have ᴿfound no fault in him since he fell unto me unto this day? Dan. 6:5

4 And the princes of the Phi-lis'-tines were wroth with him; and the princes of the Phi-lis'-tines said unto him, ᴿMake this fellow return, that he may go again to his place which thou hast appointed him, and let him not go down with us to ᴿbattle, lest ᴿin the battle he be an adversary to us: for wherewith should he rec-oncile himself unto his master? should it not be with the heads of these men? 27:6 · 14:21 · v. 9

5 Is not this David, ᴿof whom they sang one to another in dances, saying, ᴿSaul slew his thousands, and David his ten thousands? 21:11 · 18:7

6 Then A'-chish called David, and said unto him, Surely, as the Lᴏʀᴅ liveth, thou hast been up-right, and ᴿthy going out and thy coming in with me in the host is good in my sight: for ᴿI have not found evil in thee since the day of thy coming unto me unto this day: nevertheless the lords favour thee not. 2 Sam. 3:25; 2 Kin. 19:27 · v. 3

7 Wherefore now return, and go in peace, that thou displease not the lords of the Phi-lis'-tines.

8 And David said unto A'-chish, But what have I done? and what hast thou found in thy ser-vant so long as I have been with

thee unto this day, that I may not go fight against the enemies of my lord the king?

9 And A'-chish answered and said to David, I know that thou art good in my sight, ᴿas an an-gel of God: notwithstanding ᴿthe princes of the Phi-lis'-tines have said, He shall not go up with us to the battle. 2 Sam. 14:17, 20; 19:27 · v. 4

10 Wherefore now rise up early in the morning with thy master's servants ᴿthat are come with thee: and as soon as ye be up early in the morning, and have light, de-part. 1 Chr. 12:19, 22

11 So David and his men rose up early to depart in the morning, to return into the land of the Phi-lis'-tines. ᴿAnd the Phi-lis'-tines went up to Jez'-re-el. 2 Sam. 4:4

30 And it came to pass, when David and his men were come to ᴿZik'-lag on the third day, that the ᴿAm'-a-lek-ites had in-vaded the south, and Zik'-lag, and smitten Zik'-lag, and burned it with fire; 27:6 · 15:7; 27:8

2 And had taken the ᴿwomen captives, that were therein: they slew not any, either great or small, but carried them away, and went on their way. 27:2, 3

3 So David and his men came to the city, and, behold, it was burned with fire; and their wives, and their sons, and their daugh-ters, were taken captives.

4 Then David and the people that were with him lifted up their voice and wept, until they had no more power to weep.

5 And David's two wives were taken captives, A-hin'-o-am the Jez'-re-el-i-tess, and Ab'-i-gail the wife of Na'-bal the Car'-mel-ite.

6 And David was greatly dis-tressed; for the people spake of stoning him, because the soul of all the people was grieved, every man for his sons and for his daughters: but David encouraged himself in the Lᴏʀᴅ his God.

7 ᴿAnd David said to A-bi'-a-thar the priest, A-him'-e-lech's son, I pray thee, bring me hither

the e'-phod. And ^RA-bi'-a-thar brought thither the e'-phod to David. 23:2-9 · 23:6

8 ^RAnd David enquired at the LORD, saying, Shall I pursue after this troop? shall I overtake them? And he answered him, Pursue: for thou shalt surely overtake *them,* and without fail recover *all.* 23:2, 4

9 So David went, he and the six hundred men that *were* with him, and came to the brook Be'-sor, where those that were left behind stayed.

10 But David pursued, he and four hundred men: ^Rfor two hundred abode behind, which were so faint that they could not go over the brook Be'-sor. vv. 9, 21

11 And they found an Egyptian in the field, and brought him to David, and gave him bread, and he did eat; and they made him drink water;

12 And they gave him a piece of ^Ra cake of figs, and two clusters of raisins: and ^Rwhen he had eaten, his ^Tspirit came again to him: for he had eaten no bread, nor drunk *any* water, three days and three nights. 1 Kin. 20:7 · Judg. 15:19 · *strength*

13 And David said unto him, To whom *belongest* thou? and whence *art* thou? And he said, I *am* a young man of Egypt, servant to an Am'-a-lek-ite; and my master left me, because three days ^Tagone I fell sick. *ago*

14 We made an invasion *upon* the south of ^Rthe Cher'-e-thites, and upon *the coast* which *belongeth* to Judah, and upon the south of Caleb; and we burned Zik'-lag with fire. Ezek. 25:16

15 And David said to him, Canst thou bring me down to this company? And he said, Swear unto me by God, that thou wilt neither kill me, nor deliver me into the hands of my master, and I will bring thee down to this company.

16 And when he had brought him down, behold, *they were* spread abroad upon all the earth, ^Reating and drinking, and danc-

ing, because of all the great spoil that they had taken out of the land of the Phi-lis'-tines, and out of the land of Judah. 1 Thess. 5:3

17 And David smote them from the twilight even unto the evening of the next day: and there escaped not a man of them, save four hundred young men, which rode upon camels, and fled.

18 And David recovered all that the Am'-a-lek-ites had carried away: and David rescued his two wives.

19 And there was nothing lacking to them, neither small nor great, neither sons nor daughters, neither spoil, nor any *thing* that they had taken to them: ^RDavid recovered all. v. 8

20 And David took all the flocks and the herds, *which* they drave before those *other* cattle, and said, This *is* David's spoil.

21 And David came to the ^Rtwo hundred men, which were so ^Tfaint that they could not follow David, whom they had made also to abide at the brook Be'-sor: and they went forth to meet David, and to meet the people that *were* with him: and when David came near to the people, he ^Tsaluted them. v. 10 · *weary* · *greeted them*

22 Then answered all the wicked men and ^Tmen of Be'-li-al, of those that went with David, and said, Because they went not with us, we will not give them *ought* of the spoil that we have recovered, save to every man his wife and his children, that they may lead *them* away, and depart. *worthless men*

23 Then said David, Ye shall not do so, my brethren, with that which the LORD hath given us, who hath preserved us, and delivered the company that came against us into our hand.

24 For who will hearken unto you in this matter? but as his part *is* that goeth down to the battle, so *shall* his part *be* that tarrieth by the stuff: they shall part alike.

25 And it was *so* from that day forward, that he made it a statute

and an ordinance for Israel unto this day.

26 And when David came to Zik'-lag, he sent of the ᵀspoil unto the elders of Judah, *even* to his friends, saying, Behold a present for you of the spoil of the enemies of the LORD;   *booty*

27 To *them* which *were* in Beth'-el, and to *them* which *were* in south Ra'-moth, and to *them* which *were* in Jat'-tir,

28 And to *them* which *were* in Ar'-o-er, and to *them* which *were* in Siph'-moth, and to *them* which *were* in Esh-te-mo'-a,

29 And to *them* which *were* in Ra'-chal, and to *them* which *were* in the cities of ᴿthe Je-rah'-me-el-ites, and to *them* which *were* in the cities of the Ken'-ites,   27:10

30 And to *them* which *were* in Hor'-mah, and to *them* which *were* in Chor–a'-shan, and to *them* which *were* in A'-thach,

31 And to *them* which *were* in He'-bron, and to all the places where David himself and his men were wont to ᴿhaunt.   23:22

31 Now the Phi-lis'-tines fought against Israel: and the men of Israel fled from before the Phi-lis'-tines, and fell down slain in mount ᴿGil-bo'-a.   28:4

2 And the Phi-lis'-tines followed hard upon Saul and upon his sons; and the Phi-lis'-tines slew Jonathan, and A-bin'-a-dab, and Mel'-chi–shu'-a, Saul's sons.

3 And ᴿthe battle went sore against Saul, and the archers hit him; and he was sore wounded of the archers.   2 Sam. 1:6

4 ᴿThen said Saul unto his armourbearer, Draw thy sword, and thrust me through therewith; lest these uncircumcised come and thrust me through, and abuse

me. But his armourbearer would not; for he was sore afraid. Therefore Saul took a sword, and fell upon it.   Judg. 9:54; 1 Chr. 10:4

5 And when his armourbearer saw that Saul was dead, he fell likewise upon his sword, and died with him.

6 So Saul died, and his three sons, and his armourbearer, and all his men, that same day together.

7 And when the men of Israel that *were* on the other side of the valley, and *they* that *were* on the other side Jordan, saw that the men of Israel fled, and that Saul and his sons were dead, they forsook the cities, and fled; and the Phi-lis'-tines came and dwelt in them.

8 And it came to pass on the morrow, when the Phi-lis'-tines came to strip the slain, that they found Saul and his three sons fallen in mount Gil-bo'-a.

9 And they cut off his head, and stripped off his armour, and sent into the land of the Phi-lis'-tines round about, to ᴿpublish *it in* the house of their idols, and among the people.   2 Sam. 1:20

10 ᴿAnd they put his armour in the house of ᴿAsh'-ta-roth: and they fastened his body to the wall of ᴿBeth'–shan.   21:9 · 7:3 · Judg. 1:27

11 ᴿAnd when the inhabitants of Ja'-besh–gil'-e-ad heard of that which the Phi-lis'-tines had done to Saul;   11:1–13

12 ᴿAll the valiant men arose, and went all night, and took the body of Saul and the bodies of his sons from the wall of Beth'–shan, and came to Ja'-besh, and ᴿburnt them there.   11:1–11 · Amos 6:10

13 And they took their bones, and buried *them* under a tree at Ja'-besh, and fasted seven days.

The Second Book of

SAMUEL

THE Book of Second Samuel records the highlights of David's reign, first over the territory of Judah, and finally over the entire nation of Israel. It traces the ascension of David to the throne, his climactic sins of adultery and murder, and the shattering consequences of those sins upon his family and the nation.

See First Samuel for details on the titles of the books of Samuel. The Hebrew title for both books (originally one) is "Samuel." The Greek title for Second Samuel is *Basileion Beta*, "Second Kingdoms." The Latin title is *Liber II Samuelis*, the "Second Book of Samuel," or simply "Second Samuel."

NOW it came to pass after the death of Saul, when David was returned from the slaughter of the Am'-a-lek-ites, and David had abode two days in Zik'-lag;

2 It came even to pass on the third day, that, behold, ^Ra man came out of the camp from Saul with his clothes ^Trent, and earth upon his head: and so it was, when he came to David, that he fell to the earth, and ^Tdid obeisance.   4:10 · torn · prostrated himself

3 And David said unto him, From whence comest thou? And he said unto him, Out of the camp of Israel am I escaped.

4 And David said unto him, ^RHow went the matter? I pray thee, tell me. And he answered, That the people are fled from the battle, and many of the people also are fallen and dead; and Saul and ^RJonathan his son are dead also.   1 Sam. 4:16; 31:3 · 1 Sam. 31:2

5 And David said unto the young man that told him, How knowest thou that Saul and Jonathan his son be dead?

6 And the young man that told him said, As I happened by chance upon ^Rmount Gil-bo'-a, behold, ^RSaul leaned upon his spear; and, lo, the chariots and horsemen followed hard after him.   1 Sam. 31:1 · 1 Sam. 31:2–4

7 And when he looked behind him, he saw me, and called unto me. And I answered, Here am I.

8 And he said unto me, Who art thou? And I answered him, I am an Am'-a-lek-ite.

9 He said unto me again, Stand, I pray thee, upon me, and slay me: for ^Tanguish is come upon me, because my life is yet whole in me.   agony

10 So I stood upon him, and slew him, because I was sure that he could not live after that he was fallen: and I took the crown that was upon his head, and the bracelet that was on his arm, and have brought them hither unto my lord.

11 Then David took hold on his clothes, and ^Rrent^T them; and likewise all the men that were with him: 3:31; 13:31 · tore

12 And they ^Rmourned, and wept, and ^Rfasted until even, for Saul, and for Jonathan his son, and for the ^Rpeople of the LORD, and for the house of Israel; because they were fallen by the sword.   3:31 · 1 Sam. 31:13 · 6:21

13 And David said unto the young man that told him, Whence art thou? And he answered, I am the son of a stranger, an Am'-a-lek-ite.

14 And David said unto him, How wast thou not afraid to stretch forth thine hand to destroy the LORD's anointed?

15 And ^RDavid called one of the young men, and said, Go near, and fall upon him. And he smote him that he died.   4:10, 12

16 And David said unto him, Thy blood be upon thy head; for ^Rthy mouth hath testified against thee, saying, I have slain the LORD's anointed.   v. 10; Luke 19:22

17 And David lamented with this lamentation over Saul and over Jonathan his son:
18 (ᴿAlso he bade them teach the children of Judah *the use of* the bow: behold, *it is* written in the book of Ja′-sher.)   1 Sam. 31:3
19 The beauty of Israel is slain upon thy high places: ᴿhow are the mighty fallen!   v. 27
20 Tell *it* not in Gath, publish *it* not in the streets of As′-ke-lon; lest the daughters of the Phi-lis′-tines rejoice, lest the daughters of the uncircumcised triumph.
21 Ye mountains of Gil-bo′-a, *let there be* no dew, neither *let there be* rain, upon you, nor fields of offerings: for there the shield of the mighty is vilely cast away, the shield of Saul, *as though he had* not *been* anointed with oil.
22 From the blood of the slain, from the fat of the mighty, ᴿthe bow of Jonathan turned not back, and the sword of Saul returned not empty.   Deut. 32:42; 1 Sam. 18:4
23 Saul and Jonathan *were* lovely and pleasant in their lives, and in their ᴿdeath they were not divided: they were swifter than eagles, they were ᴿstronger than lions.   1 Sam. 31:2–4 · Judg. 14:18
24 Ye daughters of Israel, weep over Saul, who clothed you in scarlet, with *other* delights, who put on ornaments of gold upon your apparel.
25 How are the mighty fallen in the midst of the battle! O Jonathan, *thou wast* slain in thine high places.
26 I am distressed for thee, my brother Jonathan: very pleasant hast thou been unto me: ᴿthy love to me was wonderful, passing the love of women.   1 Sam. 18:1–4; 19:2
27 How are the mighty fallen, and the weapons of war perished!

2 And it came to pass after this, that David enquired of the LORD, saying, Shall I go up into any of the cities of Judah? And the LORD said unto him, Go up. And David said, Whither shall I go up? And he said, Unto ᴿHe′-bron.   v. 11

2 So David went up thither, and his two wives also, A-hin′-o-am the Jez′-re-el-i-tess, and Ab′-i-gail Na′-bal's wife the Car′-mel-ite.
3 And his men that *were* with him did David bring up, every man with his household: and they dwelt in the cities of He′-bron.
4 ᴿAnd the men of Judah came, and there they ᴿanointed David king over the house of Judah. And they told David, saying, *That* the men of Ja′-besh–gil′-e-ad *were they* that buried Saul.   v. 11; 5:5 · 5:3
5 And David sent messengers unto the men of Ja′-besh–gil′-e-ad, and said unto them, ᴿBlessed *be* ye of the LORD, that ye have shewed this kindness unto your lord, *even* unto Saul, and have buried him.   Ruth 2:20; 3:10
6 And now ᴿthe LORD shew kindness and truth unto you: and I also will ᵀrequite you this kindness, because ye have done this thing.   Ex. 34:6; 2 Tim. 1:16, 18 · *repay*
7 Therefore now let your hands be strengthened, and be ye valiant: for your master Saul is dead, and also the house of Judah have anointed me king over them.
8 But ᴿAbner the son of Ner, captain of Saul's host, took Ish–bo′-sheth the son of Saul, and brought him over to ᴿMa-ha-na′-im;   1 Sam. 14:50 · Gen. 32:2; Josh. 21:38
9 And made him king over ᴿGil′-e-ad, and over the Ash′-ur-ites, and over Jez′-re-el, and over E′-phra-im, and over Benjamin, and over all Israel.   Josh. 22:9
10 Ish–bo′-sheth Saul's son *was* forty years old when he began to reign over Israel, and reigned two years. But the house of Judah followed David.
11 And ᴿthe time that David was king in He′-bron over the house of Judah was seven years and six months.   5:5; 1 Kin. 2:11
12 And Abner the son of Ner, and the servants of Ish–bo′-sheth the son of Saul, went out from Ma-ha-na′-im to Gib′-e-on.
13 And Jo′-ab the son of Ze-ru′-iah, and the servants of David,

went out, and met together by
[R]the pool of Gib'-e-on: and they
sat down, the one on the one side
of the pool, and the other on the
other side of the pool.　　Jer. 41:12

14 And Abner said to Jo'-ab, Let
the young men now arise, and
[T]play before us. And Jo'-ab said,
Let them arise.　　compete

15 Then there arose and went
over by number twelve of Benjamin, which *pertained* to Ish–
bo'-sheth the son of Saul, and
twelve of the servants of David.

16 And they caught every one his
fellow by the head, and *thrust* his
sword in his fellow's side; so they
fell down together: wherefore that
place was called Hel'-kath–haz'-
zu-rim, which *is* in Gib'-e-on.

17 And there was a very [T]sore
battle that day; and Abner was
beaten, and the men of Israel,
before the servants of David. *fierce*

18 And there were [R]three sons
of Ze-ru'-iah there, Jo'-ab, and A-
bi'-shai, and A'-sa-hel: and A'-sa-
hel *was* [R]*as* light of foot [R]as a wild
roe.　　1 Chr. 2:16 · Hab. 3:19 · Ps. 18:33

19 And A'-sa-hel pursued after
Abner; and in going he turned not
to the right hand nor to the left
from following Abner.

20 Then Abner looked behind
him, and said, *Art* thou A'-sa-hel?
And he answered, I *am*.

21 And Abner said to him, Turn
thee aside to thy right hand or to
thy left, and lay thee hold on one
of the young men, and take thee
his armour. But A'-sa-hel would
not turn aside from following of
him.

22 And Abner said again to A'-
sa-hel, Turn thee aside from following me: wherefore should I
[T]smite thee to the ground? how
then should I hold up my face to
Jo'-ab thy brother?　　*strike you*

23 Howbeit he refused to turn
aside: wherefore Abner with the
hinder end of his spear smote him
[R]under the fifth *rib*, that the spear
came out behind him; and he fell
down there, and died in the same
place: and it came to pass, *that* as

many as came to the place where
A'-sa-hel fell down and died stood
[R]still.　　3:27; 4:6; 20:10 · 20:12

24 Jo'-ab also and A-bi'-shai
pursued after Abner: and the sun
went down when they were come
to the hill of Am'-mah, that *lieth*
before Gi'-ah by the way of the
wilderness of Gib'-e-on.

25 And the children of Benjamin gathered themselves together after Abner, and became one
[T]troop, and stood on the top of an
hill.　　*band* or *unit*

26 Then Abner called to Jo'-ab,
and said, Shall the sword devour
for ever? knowest thou not that
it will be bitterness in the latter
end? how long shall it be then, ere
thou bid the people return from
following their brethren?

27 And Jo'-ab said, *As* God
liveth, unless [R]thou hadst spoken,
surely then in the morning the
people had gone up every one
from following his brother.　　v. 14

28 So Jo'-ab blew a trumpet, and
all the people stood still, and pursued after Israel no more, neither
fought they any more.

29 And Abner and his men
walked all that night through the
plain, and passed over Jordan,
and went through all Bith'-ron,
and they came to Ma-ha-na'-im.

30 And Jo'-ab returned from following Abner: and when he had
gathered all the people together,
there lacked of David's servants
nineteen men and A'-sa-hel.

31 But the servants of David had
smitten of Benjamin, and of Abner's men, *so that* three hundred
and threescore men died.

32 And they took up A'-sa-hel,
and buried him in the sepulchre
of his father, which *was in* [R]Beth'–
le-hem. And Jo'-ab and his men
went all night, and they came to
He'-bron at break of day. 1 Sam. 20:6

3 Now there was long [R]war
between the house of Saul and
the house of David: but David
waxed stronger and stronger, and
the house of Saul waxed weaker
and weaker.　　1 Kin. 14:30; [Ps. 46:9]

2 And ^Runto David were sons born in He′-bron: and his first-born was Amnon, of A-hin′-o-am the Jez′-re-el-i-tess;   1 Chr. 3:1-4

3 And his second, Chil′-e-ab, of Ab′-i-gail the wife of Na′-bal the Car′-mel-ite; and the third, ^RAb′-sa-lom the son of Ma′-a-cah the daughter of Tal′-mai king ^Rof Ge′-shur;   15:1-10 · Josh. 13:13; 1 Sam. 27:8

4 And the fourth, Ad-o-ni′-jah the son of Hag′-gith; and the fifth, Sheph-a-ti′-ah the son of Ab′-i-tal;

5 And the sixth, Ith′-re-am, by Eg′-lah David's wife. These were born to David in He′-bron.

6 And it came to pass, while there was war between the house of Saul and the house of David, that Abner made himself strong for the house of Saul.

7 And Saul had a concubine, whose name *was* ^RRiz′-pah, the daughter of A′-iah: and Ish–bo′-sheth said to Abner, Wherefore hast thou ^Rgone in unto my father's concubine?   21:8-11 · 16:21

8 Then was Abner very wroth for the words of Ish–bo′-sheth, and said, *Am* I ^Ra dog's head, which against Judah do shew kindness this day unto the house of Saul thy father, to his brethren, and to his friends, and have not delivered thee into the hand of David, that thou chargest me to day with a fault concerning this woman?   9:8; 16:9; 1 Sam. 24:14

9 ^RSo do God to Abner, and more also, except, ^Ras the LORD hath sworn to David, even so I do to him;   Ruth 1:17 · 1 Sam. 15:28; 16:1, 12

10 To ^Ttranslate the kingdom from the house of Saul, and to set up the throne of David over Israel and over Judah, ^Rfrom Dan even to Be′-er–she′-ba.   transfer · Judg. 20:1

11 And he could not answer Abner a word again, because he feared him.

12 And Abner sent messengers to David on his behalf, saying, Whose *is* the land? saying *also*, Make thy ^Tleague with me, and, behold, my hand *shall be* with thee, to bring about all Israel unto thee.   Lit. *covenant*

13 And he said, Well; I will make a league with thee: but one thing I require of thee, that is, ^RThou shalt not see my face, except thou first bring ^RMi′-chal Saul's daughter, when thou comest to see my face.   Gen. 43:3 · 6:16; 1 Sam. 18:20; 19:11

14 And David sent messengers to ^RIsh–bo′-sheth Saul's son, saying, Deliver *me* my wife Mi′-chal, which I espoused to me ^Rfor an hundred foreskins of the Phi-lis′-tines.   2:10 · 1 Sam. 18:25-27

15 And Ish–bo′-sheth sent, and took her from *her* husband, *even* from Phal′-ti-el the son of La′-ish.

16 And her husband went with her along weeping behind her to ^RBa-hu′-rim. Then said Abner unto him, Go, return. And he returned.   16:5; 19:16

17 And Abner had communication with the elders of Israel, saying, Ye sought for David in times past *to be* king over you:

18 Now then do *it*: ^Rfor the LORD hath spoken of David, saying, By the hand of my servant David I will save my people Israel out of the hand of the Phi-lis′-tines, and out of the hand of all their enemies.   v. 9

19 And Abner also spake in the ears of ^RBenjamin: and Abner went also to speak in the ears of David in He′-bron all that seemed good to Israel, and that seemed good to the whole house of Benjamin.   1 Sam. 10:20, 21; 1 Chr. 12:29

20 So Abner came to David to He′-bron, and twenty men with him. And David made Abner and the men that *were* with him a feast.

21 And Abner said unto David, I will arise and go, and will gather all Israel unto my lord the king, that they may make a league with thee, and that thou mayest ^Rreign over all that thine heart desireth. And David sent Abner away; and he went in peace.   1 Kin. 11:37

22 And, behold, the servants of David and Jo′-ab came from *pur-*

suing a troop, and brought in a great ᵀspoil with them: but Abner *was* not with David in He'-bron; for he had sent him away, and he was gone in peace.   *booty*

23 When Jo'-ab and all the host that *was* with him were come, they told Jo'-ab, saying, Abner the son of Ner came to the king, and he hath sent him away, and he is gone in peace.

24 Then Jo'-ab came to the king, and said, What hast thou done? behold, Abner came unto thee; why *is* it *that* thou hast sent him away, and he is quite gone?

25 Thou knowest Abner the son of Ner, that he came to deceive thee, and to know ᴿthy going out and thy coming in, and to know all that thou doest.   Is. 37:28

26 And when Jo'-ab was come out from David, he sent messengers after Abner, which brought him again from the well of Si'-rah: but David knew *it* not.

27 And when Abner was returned to He'-bron, Jo'-ab ᴿtook him aside in the gate to speak with him quietly, and smote him there ᴿunder the fifth *rib*, that he died, for the blood of ᴿA'-sa-hel his brother. 20:9, 10; 1 Kin. 2:5 · 4:6 · 2:23

28 And afterward when David heard *it*, he said, I and my kingdom *are* ᵀguiltless before the LORD for ever from the blood of Abner the son of Ner: *innocent*

29 ᴿLet it rest on the head of Jo'-ab, and on all his father's house; and let there not fail from the house of Jo'-ab one ᴿthat hath an issue, or that is a leper, or that leaneth on a staff, or that falleth on the sword, or that lacketh bread.   Deut. 21:6–9 · Lev. 15:2

30 So Jo'-ab and A-bi'-shai his brother slew Abner, because he had slain their brother ᴿA'-sa-hel at Gib'-e-on in the battle.   2:23

31 And David said to Jo'-ab, and to all the people that *were* with him, Rend your clothes, and ᴿgird you with sackcloth, and mourn before Abner. And king David *himself* followed the bier. Gen. 37:34

32 And they buried Abner in He'-bron: and the king lifted up his voice, and wept at the grave of Abner; and all the people wept.

33 And the king lamented over Abner, and said, Died Abner as a ᴿfool dieth?   13:12, 13

34 Thy hands *were* not bound, nor thy feet put into fetters: as a man falleth before wicked men, *so* fellest thou. And all the people wept again over him.

35 And when all the people came to cause David to eat meat while it was yet day, David sware, saying, So do God to me, and more also, if I taste bread, or ought else, till the sun be down.

36 And all the people took notice *of it*, and it pleased them: as whatsoever the king did pleased all the people.

37 For all the people and all Israel understood that day that it was ᵀnot of the king to slay Abner the son of Ner.   *not the king's intent*

38 And the king said unto his servants, Know ye not that there is a prince and a great man fallen this day in Israel?

39 And I *am* this day weak, though anointed king; and these men the sons of Ze-ru'-iah ᴿ*be* too hard for me: ᴿthe LORD shall reward the doer of evil according to his wickedness.   19:5–7 · 2 Tim. 4:14

4 And when Saul's son heard that Abner was dead in He'-bron, his hands were feeble, and all the Israelites were troubled.

2 And Saul's son had two men *that were* captains of bands: the name of the one *was* Ba'-a-nah, and the name of the other Re'-chab, the sons of Rim'-mon a Be-e'-roth-ite, of the children of Benjamin: (for ᴿBe-e'-roth also was reckoned to Benjamin.   Josh. 18:25

3 And the Be-e'-roth-ites fled to ᴿGit'-ta-im, and were sojourners there until this day.)   Neh. 11:33

4 And ᴿJonathan, Saul's son, had a son *that was* lame of *his* feet. He was five years old when the tidings came of Saul and Jonathan ᴿout of Jez'-re-el, and

his nurse took him up, and fled: and it came to pass, as she made haste to flee, that he fell, and became lame. And his name *was* Me-phib'-o-sheth.　　9:3 · 1 Sam. 29:1

5　And the sons of Rim'-mon the Be-e'-roth-ite, Re'-chab and Ba'-a-nah, went, and came about the heat of the day to the ^Rhouse of Ish–bo'-sheth, who lay on a bed at noon.　　2:8, 9

6　And they came thither into the midst of the house, *as though* they would have fetched wheat; and they smote him ^Runder the fifth *rib*: and Re'-chab and Ba'-a-nah his brother escaped. 2:23; 20:10

7　For when they came into the house, he lay on his bed in his bedchamber, and they smote him, and slew him, and beheaded him, and took his head, and gat them away through the plain all night.

8　And they brought the head of Ish–bo'-sheth unto David to He'-bron, and said to the king, Behold the head of Ish–bo'-sheth the son of Saul thine enemy, ^Rwhich sought thy life; and the LORD hath avenged my lord the king this day of Saul, and of his seed. 1 Sam. 19:2

9　And David answered Re'-chab and Ba'-a-nah his brother, the sons of Rim'-mon the Be-e'-roth-ite, and said unto them, *As* the LORD liveth, ^Rwho hath redeemed my soul out of all adversity,　　Gen. 48:16; 1 Kin. 1:29; Ps. 31:7

10　When ^Rone told me, saying, Behold, Saul is dead, thinking to have brought good tidings, I took hold of him, and slew him in Zik'-lag, who *thought* that I would have given him a reward for his tidings:　　1:2–16

11　How much more, when wicked men have slain a righteous person in his own house upon his bed? shall I not therefore now ^Rrequire his blood of your hand, and take you away from the earth?　　[Gen. 9:5, 6; Ps. 9:12]

12　And David ^Rcommanded his young men, and they slew them, and cut off their hands and their feet, and hanged *them* up over the

pool in He'-bron. But they took the head of Ish–bo'-sheth, and buried *it* in the ^Rsepulchre of Abner in He'-bron.　　1:15 · 3:32

5　Then came all the tribes of Israel to David unto He'-bron, and spake, saying, Behold, ^Rwe *are* thy bone and thy flesh. 19:12, 13

2　Also in time past, when Saul was king over us, ^Rthou wast he that leddest out and broughtest in Israel: and the LORD said to thee, ^RThou shalt feed my people Israel, and thou shalt be a captain over Israel.　1 Sam. 18:5, 13, 16 · 1 Sam. 16:1

3　^RSo all the elders of Israel came to the king to He'-bron; ^Rand king David made a league with them in He'-bron before the LORD: and they anointed David king over Israel.　3:17 · 2:4; 3:21

4　David *was* ^Rthirty years old when he began to reign, *and* he reigned forty years.　　Luke 3:23

5　In He'-bron he reigned over Judah ^Rseven years and six months: and in Jerusalem he reigned thirty and three years over all Israel and Judah.　　2:11

6　^RAnd the king and his men went to Jerusalem unto the Jeb'-u-sites, the inhabitants of the land: which spake unto David, saying, Except thou take away the blind and the lame, thou shalt not come in hither: thinking, David cannot come in hither.　　Judg. 1:21

7　Nevertheless David took the strong hold of Zion: ^Rthe same *is* the city of David.　6:12, 16; 1 Kin. 2:10

8　And David said on that day, Whosoever getteth up to the gutter, and smiteth the Jeb'-u-sites, and the lame and the blind, *that are* hated of David's soul, ^Rhe *shall be chief and captain.* Wherefore they said, The blind and the lame shall not come into the house.　　1 Chr. 11:6–9

9　So David dwelt in the fort, and called it ^Rthe city of David. And David built round about from Mil'-lo and inward. v. 7; 1 Kin. 9:15, 24

10　And David went on, and grew great, and ^Rthe LORD God of hosts *was* with him.　1 Sam. 17:45

11 And ᴿHiram ᴿking of Tyre sent messengers to David, and cedar trees, and carpenters, and masons: and they built David an house.   1 Kin. 5:1–18 · 1 Chr. 14:1

12 And David perceived that the LORD had established him king over Israel, and that he had ᴿexalted his kingdom for his people Israel's ᴿsake.   Num. 24:7 · Is. 45:4

13 And David took *him* more concubines and wives out of Jerusalem, after he was come from He′-bron: and there were yet sons and daughters born to David.

14 And ᴿthese *be* the names of those that were born unto him in Jerusalem; Sham-mu′-ah, and Sho′-bab, and Nathan, and ᴿSolomon,   1 Chr. 3:5–8 · 12:24

15 Ib′-har also, and El-i-shu′-a, and Ne′-pheg, and Ja-phi′-a,

16 And E-lish′-a-ma, and E-li′-a-da, and E-liph′-a-let.

17 ᴿBut when the Phi-lis′-tines heard that they had anointed David king over Israel, all the Phi-lis′-tines came up to seek David; and David heard *of it*, ᴿand went down to the hold.   1 Chr. 11:16 · 23:14

18 The Phi-lis′-tines also came and spread themselves in ᴿthe valley of Reph′-a-im.   Josh. 15:8; Is. 17:5

19 And David ᴿenquired of the LORD, saying, Shall I go up to the Phi-lis′-tines? wilt thou deliver them into mine hand? And the LORD said unto David, Go up: for I will doubtless deliver the Phi-lis′-tines into thine hand. 2:1; 1 Sam. 23:2

20 And David came to ᴿBa′-al–per′-a-zim, and David smote them there, and said, The LORD hath broken forth upon mine enemies before me, as the breach of waters. Therefore he called the name of that place Ba′-al–per′-a-zim.   1 Chr. 14:11; Is. 28:21

21 And there they left their ᵀimages, and David and his men ᴿburned them.   idols · Deut. 7:5, 25

22 And the Phi-lis′-tines came up yet again, and spread themselves in the valley of Reph′-a-im.

23 And when ᴿDavid enquired

of the LORD, he said, Thou shalt not go up; *but* ᵀfetch a compass behind them, and come upon them over against the mulberry trees.   v. 19 · *circle around*

24 And let it be, when thou ᴿhearest the sound of a going in the tops of the mulberry trees, that then thou shalt bestir thyself: for then ᴿshall the LORD go out before thee, to smite the host of the Phi-lis′-tines. 2 Kin. 7:6 · Judg. 4:14

25 And David did so, as the LORD had commanded him; and smote the Phi-lis′-tines from Ge′-ba until thou come to Ga′-zer.

6 Again, David gathered together all *the* ᵀchosen *men* of Israel, thirty thousand.   *choice*

2 And ᴿDavid arose, and went with all the people that *were* with him from Ba′-a-le of Judah, to bring up from thence the ark of God, whose name is called by the name of the LORD of hosts ᴿthat dwelleth *between* the cher′-u-bims.   1 Chr. 13:5, 6 · 1 Sam. 4:4; Ps. 80:1

3 And they set the ark of God upon a new cart, and brought it out of the house of A-bin′-a-dab that *was* in Gib′-e-ah: and Uz′-zah and A-hi′-o, the sons of A-bin′-a-dab, drave the new cart.

4 And they brought it out of ᴿthe house of A-bin′-a-dab which *was* at Gib′-e-ah, accompanying the ark of God: and A-hi′-o went before the ark.   1 Sam. 7:1; 1 Chr. 13:7

5 And David and all the house of Israel ᴿplayed before the LORD on all manner of *instruments made of* fir wood, even on harps, and on psalteries, and on timbrels, and on cornets, and on cymbals.   1 Sam. 18:6, 7

6 And when they came to ᴿNa′-chon's threshingfloor, Uz′-zah put forth *his* ᴿhand to the ark of God, and took hold of it; for the oxen shook *it*.   1 Chr. 13:9 · Num. 4:15, 19, 20

7 And the anger of the LORD was kindled against Uz′-zah; and God smote him there for *his* ᵀerror; and there he died by the ark of God.   *irreverence*

8 And David was displeased,

because the LORD had made a breach upon Uz'-zah: and he called the name of the place Pe'-rez–uz'-zah to this day.

9 And David was afraid of the LORD that day, and said, How shall the ark of the LORD come to me?

10 So David would not remove the ark of the LORD unto him into the ᴿcity of David: but David carried it aside into the house of O'-bed–e'-dom the Git'-tite.   5:7

11 ᴿAnd the ark of the LORD continued in the house of O'-bed–e'-dom the Git'-tite three months: and the LORD ᴿblessed O'-bed–e'-dom, and all his household.   1 Chr. 13:14 · Gen. 30:27; 39:5

12 And it was told king David, saying, The LORD hath blessed the house of O'-bed–e'-dom, and all that *pertaineth* unto him, because of the ark of God. ᴿSo David went and brought up the ark of God from the house of O'-bed–e'-dom into the city of David with gladness.   1 Chr. 15:25—16:3

13 And it was *so*, that when ᴿthey that bare the ark of the LORD had gone six paces, he sacrificed oxen and fatlings.   15:24

14 And David ᴿdanced before the LORD with all *his* might; and David *was* girded ᴿwith a linen e'-phod.   Ps. 30:11; 149:3 · 1 Sam. 2:18, 28

15 ᴿSo David and all the house of Israel brought up the ark of the LORD with shouting, and with the sound of the trumpet.   1 Chr. 15:28

16 And as the ark of the LORD came into the city of David, ᴿMi'-chal Saul's daughter looked through a window, and saw king David leaping and dancing before the LORD; and she despised him in her heart.   3:14

17 And ᴿthey brought in the ark of the LORD, and set it in his place, in the midst of the tabernacle that David had pitched for it: and David ᴿoffered burnt offerings and peace offerings before the LORD.   1 Chr. 16:1 · 1 Kin. 8:5, 62, 63

18 And as soon as David had made an end of offering burnt offerings and peace offerings, ᴿhe

blessed the people in the name of the LORD of hosts.   1 Kin. 8:14, 15, 55

19 ᴿAnd he ᵀdealt among all the people, *even* among the whole multitude of Israel, as well to the women as men, to every one a cake of bread, and a good piece *of flesh*, and a flagon *of wine*. So all the people departed every one to his house.   1 Chr. 16:3 · distributed

20 Then David returned to bless his household. And Mi'-chal the daughter of Saul came out to meet David, and said, How glorious was the king of Israel to day, who uncovered himself to day in the eyes of the handmaids of his servants, as one of the vain fellows shamelessly uncovereth himself!

21 And David said unto Mi'-chal, *It was* before the LORD, which chose me before thy father, and before all his house, to appoint me ruler over the people of the LORD, over Israel: therefore will I play before the LORD.

22 And I will yet be more ᵀvile than thus, and will be ᵀbase in mine own sight: and of the maidservants which thou hast spoken of, of them shall I be had in honour.   undignified · humble

23 Therefore Mi'-chal the daughter of Saul had no child ᴿunto the day of her death. Is. 22:14

7 And it came to pass, when the king sat in his house, and the LORD had given him rest round about from all his enemies;

2 That the king said unto Nathan the prophet, See now, I dwell in ᴿan house of cedar, ᴿbut the ark of God dwelleth within ᴿcurtains.   5:11 · Acts 7:46 · Ex. 26:1

3 And Nathan said to the king, Go, do all that *is* in thine ᴿheart; for the LORD *is* with thee. 1 Chr. 22:7

4 And it came to pass that night, that the word of the LORD came unto Nathan, saying,

5 Go and tell my servant David, Thus saith the LORD, ᴿShalt thou build me an house for me to dwell in?   1 Kin. 5:3, 4; 8:19; 1 Chr. 22:8

6 Whereas I have not dwelt in *any* house ᴿsince the time that I

brought up the children of Israel out of Egypt, even to this day, but have walked in a tent and in a tabernacle.   Josh. 18:1; 1 Kin. 8:16

7 In all *the places* wherein I have walked with all the children of Israel spake I a word with any of the tribes of Israel, whom I commanded ᴿto feed my people Israel, saying, Why build ye not me an house of cedar?   [Acts 20:28]

8 Now therefore so shalt thou say unto my servant David, Thus saith the Lᴏʀᴅ of hosts, ᴿI took thee from the sheepcote, from following the sheep, to be ruler over my people, over Israel: 1 Sam. 16:11

9 And ᴿI was with thee whithersoever thou wentest, ᴿand have ᵀcut off all thine enemies out of thy sight, and have made thee a great name, like unto the name of the great *men* that *are* in the earth.   5:10 · 1 Sam. 31:6 · *destroyed*

10 Moreover I will appoint a place for my people Israel, and will plant them, that they may dwell in a place of their own, and move no more; neither shall the children of wickedness afflict them any more, as beforetime,

11 And as since the time that I commanded judges *to be* over my people Israel, and have caused thee to rest from all thine enemies. Also the Lᴏʀᴅ telleth thee that he will make thee an house.

☆ 12 And when thy days be fulfilled, and thou ᴿshalt sleep with thy fathers, ᴿI will set up thy seed after thee, which shall proceed out of thy bowels, and I will establish his kingdom. Acts 13:36 · Matt. 1:6

☆ 13 He shall build an house for my name, and I will stablish the throne of his kingdom for ever.

14 I will be his father, and he shall be my son. If he commit iniquity, I will chasten him with the rod of men, and with the ᵀstripes of the children of men: *strokes*

15 But my mercy shall not depart away from him, ᴿas I took *it* from Saul, whom I put away before thee.   1 Sam. 15:23, 28; 16:14

16 And ᴿthine house and thy kingdom shall be established for ever before thee: thy throne shall be established for ever.   Matt. 25:31

17 According to all these words, and according to all this vision, so did Nathan speak unto David.

18 Then went king David in, and sat before the Lᴏʀᴅ, and he said, ᴿWho *am* I, O Lord Gᴏᴅ? and what *is* my house, that thou hast brought me hitherto?   Gen. 32:10

19 And this was yet a small thing in thy sight, O Lord Gᴏᴅ; but thou hast spoken also of thy servant's house for a great while to come. ᴿAnd *is* this the manner of man, O Lord Gᴏᴅ?   [Is. 55:8, 9]

20 And what can David say more unto thee? for thou, Lord Gᴏᴅ, knowest thy servant.

21 For thy word's sake, and according to thine own heart, hast thou done all these great things, to make thy servant know *them.*

22 Wherefore thou art great, O Lᴏʀᴅ God: for *there is* none like thee, neither *is there any* God beside thee, according to all that we have heard with our ears.

23 And ᴿwhat one nation in the earth *is* like thy people, *even* like Israel, whom God went to redeem for a people to himself, and to make him a name, and to do for you great things and ᵀterrible, for thy land, before thy people, which thou redeemedst to thee from Egypt, *from* the nations and their gods?   Ps. 147:20 · *awesome*

24 For thou hast confirmed to thyself thy people Israel *to be* a people unto thee for ever: and thou, Lᴏʀᴅ, art become their God.

25 And now, O Lᴏʀᴅ God, the word that thou hast spoken concerning thy servant, and concerning his house, establish *it* for ever, and do as thou hast said.

26 And let thy name be magnified for ever, saying, The Lᴏʀᴅ of hosts *is* the God over Israel: and let the house of thy servant David be established before thee.

27 For thou, O Lᴏʀᴅ of hosts, God of Israel, hast revealed to thy

servant, saying, I will build thee an house: therefore hath thy servant found in his heart to pray this prayer unto thee.

28 And now, O Lord GOD, thou *art* that God, and ^Rthy words be true, and thou hast promised this goodness unto thy servant: Ex. 34:6

29 Therefore now let it please thee to bless the house of thy servant, that it may continue for ever before thee: for thou, O Lord GOD, hast spoken *it:* and with thy blessing let the house of thy servant be blessed ^Rfor ever.   22:51

8 And after this it came to pass, that David smote the Phi-lis'-tines, and subdued them: and David took ^TMe'-theg–am'-mah out of the hand of the Phi-lis'-tines.   Lit. *The Bridle of the Mother City*

2 And he smote Moab, and measured them with a line, casting them down to the ground; even with two lines measured he to put to death, and with one full line to keep alive. And *so* the Mo'-ab-ites became David's servants, *and* ^Rbrought gifts.   1 Sam. 10:27

3 David smote also Had-ad-e'-zer, the son of Re'-hob, king of ^RZo'-bah, as he went to recover ^Rhis border at the river Eu-phra'-tes.   1 Sam. 14:47 · Gen. 15:18

4 And David took from him a thousand *chariots,* and seven hundred horsemen, and twenty thousand footmen: and David ^Rhoughed^T all the chariot *horses,* but reserved of them *for* an hundred chariots.   Josh. 11:6, 9 · *hamstrung*

5 ^RAnd when the Syrians of Damascus came to ^Tsuccour Had-ad-e'-zer king of Zo'-bah, David slew of the Syrians two and twenty thousand men. 1 Kin. 11:23–25 · *help*

6 Then David put garrisons in Syria of Damascus: and the Syrians became servants to David, *and* brought gifts. ^RAnd the LORD preserved David whithersoever he went.   v. 14; 7:9

7 And David took ^Rthe shields of gold that were on the servants of Had-ad-e'-zer, and brought them to Jerusalem.   1 Kin. 10:16

8 And from Be'-tah, and from ^RBer'-o-thai, cities of Had-ad-e'-zer, king David took exceeding much brass.   Ezek. 47:16

9 When To'-i king of ^RHa'-math heard that David had smitten all the host of Had-ad-e'-zer, 2 Chr. 8:4

10 Then To'-i sent Jo'-ram his son unto king David, to salute him, and to bless him, because he had fought against Had-ad-e'-zer, and smitten him: for Had-ad-e'-zer had wars with To'-i. And *Jo'-ram* brought with him vessels of silver, and vessels of gold, and vessels of brass:

11 Which also king David ^Rdid dedicate unto the LORD, with the silver and gold that he had dedicated of all nations which he subdued;   1 Kin. 7:51

12 Of Syria, and of Moab, and of the children of Ammon, and of the Phi-lis'-tines, and of Am'-a-lek, and of the spoil of Had-ad-e'-zer, son of Re'-hob, king of Zo'-bah.

13 And David gat *him* a name when he returned from smiting of the Syrians in the valley of salt, *being* eighteen thousand *men.*

14 And he put garrisons in E'-dom; throughout all E'-dom put he garrisons, and ^Rall they of E'-dom became David's servants. And the LORD preserved David whithersoever he went. 1 Kin. 11:15

15 And David reigned over all Israel; and David executed judgment and justice unto all his people.

16 ^RAnd Jo'-ab the son of Ze-ru'-iah *was* over the host; and ^RJe-hosh'-a-phat the son of A-hi'-lud *was* recorder;   19:13; 20:23 · 1 Kin. 4:3

17 And Za'-dok the son of A-hi'-tub, and A-him'-e-lech the son of A-bi'-a-thar, *were* the priests; and Se-ra'-iah *was* the scribe;

18 ^RAnd Be-nai'-ah the son of Je-hoi'-a-da *was over* both the ^RCher'-e-thites and the Pel'-e-thites; and David's sons were chief rulers.   1 Kin. 1:8 · 1 Kin. 1:38

9 And David said, Is there yet any that is left of the house of

Saul, that I may ᴿshew him kindness for Jonathan's sake?　21:7

2　And *there was* of the house of Saul a servant whose name *was* Zi'-ba. And when they had called him unto David, the king said unto him, *Art* thou Zi'-ba? And he said, Thy servant *is he.*

3　And the king said, *Is* there not yet any of the house of Saul, that I may shew the kindness of God unto him? And Zi'-ba said unto the king, Jonathan hath yet a son, *which is* ᴿlame on *his* feet. 4:4

4　And the king said unto him, Where *is* he? And Zi'-ba said unto the king, Behold, he *is* in the house of ᴿMa'-chir, the son of Am'-mi-el, in Lo–de'-bar.　17:27–29

5　Then king David sent, and fetched him out of the house of Ma'-chir, the son of Am'-mi-el, from Lo–de'-bar.

6　Now when Me-phib'-o-sheth, the son of Jonathan, the son of Saul, was come unto David, he fell on his face, and ᵀdid reverence. And David said, Me-phib'-o-sheth. And he answered, Behold thy servant!　*prostrated himself*

7　And David said unto him, Fear not: for I will surely shew thee kindness for Jonathan thy father's sake, and will restore thee all the land of Saul thy father; and thou shalt eat bread at my table continually.

8　And he bowed himself, and said, What *is* thy servant, that thou shouldest look upon such ᴿa dead dog as I *am*?　16:9

9　Then the king called to Zi'-ba, Saul's servant, and said unto him, ᴿI have given unto thy master's son all that pertained to Saul and to all his house.　16:4; 19:29

10　Thou therefore, and thy sons, and thy servants, shall till the land for him, and thou shalt bring in *the fruits,* that thy master's son may have food to eat: but Me-phib'-o-sheth thy master's son ᴿshall eat bread alway at my table. Now Zi'-ba had ᴿfifteen sons and twenty servants.　19:28 · 19:17

11　Then said Zi'-ba unto the king, According to all that my lord the king hath commanded his servant, so shall thy servant do. As for Me-phib'-o-sheth, *said the king,* he shall eat at my table, as one of the king's sons.

12　And Me-phib'-o-sheth had a young son, ᴿwhose name *was* Mi'-cha. And all that dwelt in the house of Zi'-ba *were* servants unto Me-phib'-o-sheth.　1 Chr. 8:34

13　So Me-phib'-o-sheth dwelt in Jerusalem: ᴿfor he did eat continually at the king's table; and was lame on both his feet.　1 Kin. 2:7

10 And it came to pass after this, that the king of the children of Ammon died, and Ha'-nun his son reigned in his stead.

2　Then said David, I will shew kindness unto Ha'-nun the son of Na'-hash, as his father shewed kindness unto me. And David sent to comfort him by the hand of his servants for his father. And Da-vid's servants came into the land of the children of Ammon.

3　And the princes of the children of Ammon said unto Ha'-nun their lord, Thinkest thou that David doth honour thy father, that he hath sent comforters unto thee? hath not David *rather* sent his servants unto thee, to search the city, and to spy it out, and to overthrow it?

4　Wherefore Ha'-nun took Da-vid's servants, and shaved off the one half of their beards, and cut off their garments in the middle, ᴿ*even* to their buttocks, and sent them away.　Is. 20:4; 47:2

5　When they told *it* unto David, he sent to meet them, because the men were greatly ᵀashamed: and the king said, Tarry at Jericho until your beards be grown, and *then* return.　*humiliated*

6　And when the children of Ammon saw that they stank before David, the children of Ammon sent and hired ᴿthe Syrians of Beth–re'-hob, and the Syrians of Zo'-ba, twenty thousand footmen, and of king Ma'-a-cah a thousand men, and of Ish'–tob twelve thousand men.　8:3, 5

7　And when David heard of *it*, he sent Jo'-ab, and all the host of ^Rthe mighty men.　23:8

8　And the children of Ammon came out, and put the battle in array at the entering in of the gate: and ^Rthe Syrians of Zo'-ba, and of Re'-hob, and Ish'–tob, and Ma'-a-cah, *were* by themselves in the field.　v. 6

9　When Jo'-ab saw that the front of the battle was against him before and behind, he chose of all the choice *men* of Israel, and put *them* in array against the Syrians:

10　And the rest of the people he delivered into the hand of ^RA-bi'-shai his brother, that he might put *them* in array against the children of Ammon.　3:30; 1 Sam. 26:6

11　And he said, If the Syrians be too strong for me, then thou shalt help me: but if the children of Ammon be too strong for thee, then I will come and help thee.

12　^RBe of good courage, and let us ^Rplay the men for our people, and for the cities of our God: and the LORD do that which seemeth him good.　Deut. 31:6 · 1 Cor. 16:13

13　And Jo'-ab drew nigh, and the people that *were* with him, unto the battle against the Syrians: and they fled before him.

14　And when the children of Ammon saw that the Syrians were fled, then fled they also before A-bi'-shai, and entered into the city. So Jo'-ab returned from the children of Ammon, and came to ^RJerusalem.　11:1

15　And when the Syrians saw that they ^Twere smitten before Israel, they gathered themselves together.　*had been defeated*

16　And Had-ar-e'-zer sent, and brought out the Syrians that *were* beyond the river: and they came to He'-lam; and Sho'-bach the captain of the host of Had-ar-e'-zer *went* before them.

17　And when it was told David, he gathered all Israel together, and passed over Jordan, and came to He'-lam. And the Syrians set themselves in array against David, and fought with him.

18　And the Syrians fled before Israel; and David slew *the men of* seven hundred chariots of the Syrians, and forty thousand ^Rhorsemen, and ^Tsmote Sho'-bach the captain of their host, who died there.　1 Chr. 19:18 · *struck*

19　And when all the kings *that were* servants to Had-ar-e'-zer saw that they were smitten before Israel, they made peace with Israel, and ^Rserved them. So the Syrians feared to help the children of Ammon any more.　8:6

11 And it came to pass, after the year was expired, at the time when kings go forth *to battle,* that ^RDavid sent Jo'-ab, and his servants with him, and all Israel; and they destroyed the children of Ammon, and besieged ^RRab'-bah. But David tarried still at Jerusalem.　1 Chr. 20:1 · Amos 1:14

2　And it came to pass in an eveningtide, that David arose from off his bed, ^Rand walked upon the roof of the king's house: and from the roof he ^Rsaw a woman washing herself; and the woman *was* very beautiful to look upon.　1 Sam. 9:25 · Gen. 34:2; [Ex. 20:17]

3　And David sent and enquired after the woman. And *one* said, *Is* not this Bath–she'-ba, the daughter of E-li'-am, the wife ^Rof U-ri'-ah the ^RHit'-tite?　23:39 · 1 Sam. 26:6

4　And David sent messengers, and took her; and she came in unto him, and ^Rhe lay with her; for she was purified from her uncleanness: and she returned unto her house.　[Lev. 20:10; Deut. 22:22]

5　And the woman conceived, and sent and told David, and said, I *am* with child.

6　And David sent to Jo'-ab, *saying,* Send me U-ri'-ah the Hit'-tite. And Jo'-ab sent U-ri'-ah to David.

7　And when U-ri'-ah was come unto him, David ^Tdemanded *of him* how Jo'-ab did, and how the people did, and how the war prospered.　*asked*

8 And David said to U-ri′-ah, Go down to thy house, and ᴿwash thy feet. And U-ri′-ah departed out of the king's house, and there followed him ᵀa mess *of meat* from the king. Gen. 18:4 · *a gift of food*

9 But U-ri′-ah slept at the ᴿdoor of the king's house with all the servants of his lord, and went not down to his house. 1 Kin. 14:27, 28

10 And when they had told David, saying, U-ri′-ah went not down unto his house, David said unto U-ri′-ah, Camest thou not from *thy* journey? why *then* didst thou not go down unto thine house?

11 And U-ri′-ah said unto David, The ark, and Israel, and Judah, abide in tents; and my lord Jo′-ab, and the servants of my lord, are encamped in the open fields; shall I then go into mine house, to eat and to drink, and to lie with my wife? *as* thou livest, and *as* thy soul liveth, I will not do this thing.

12 And David said to U-ri′-ah, Tarry here to day also, and to morrow I will let thee depart. So U-ri′-ah abode in Jerusalem that day, and the morrow.

13 And when David had called him, he did eat and drink before him; and he made him ᴿdrunk: and at even he went out to lie on his bed ᴿwith the servants of his lord, but went not down to his house. Gen. 19:33, 35 · v. 9

14 And it came to pass in the morning, that David ᴿwrote a letter to Jo′-ab, and sent *it* by the hand of U-ri′-ah. 1 Kin. 21:8, 9

15 And he wrote in the letter, saying, Set ye U-ri′-ah in the forefront of the hottest battle, and ᵀretire ye from him, that he may ᴿbe smitten, and die. *retreat* · 12:9

16 And it came to pass, when Jo′-ab observed the city, that he assigned U-ri′-ah unto a place where he knew that valiant men *were.*

17 And the men of the city went out, and fought with Jo′-ab: and there fell *some* of the people of the servants of David; and U-ri′-ah the Hit′-tite died also.

18 Then Jo′-ab sent and told David all the things concerning the war;

19 And charged the messenger, saying, When thou hast made an end of telling the matters of the war unto the king,

20 And if so be that the king's wrath arise, and he say unto thee, Wherefore approached ye so ᵀnigh unto the city when ye did fight? knew ye not that they would shoot from the wall? *near*

21 Who smote ᴿA-bim′-e-lech the son of Je-rub′-be-sheth? did not a woman cast a piece of a millstone upon him from the wall, that he died in The′-bez? why went ye nigh the wall? then say thou, Thy servant U-ri′-ah the Hit′-tite is dead also. Judg. 9:50-54

22 So the messenger went, and came and shewed David all that Jo′-ab had sent him for.

23 And the messenger said unto David, Surely the men prevailed against us, and came out unto us into the field, and we were upon them even unto the entering of the gate.

24 And the shooters shot from off the wall upon thy servants; and *some* of the king's servants be dead, and thy servant U-ri′-ah the Hit′-tite is dead also.

25 Then David said unto the messenger, Thus shalt thou say unto Jo′-ab, Let not this thing displease thee, for the sword devoureth one as well as another: make thy battle more strong against the city, and overthrow it: and encourage thou him.

26 And when the wife of U-ri′-ah heard that U-ri′-ah her husband was dead, she mourned for her husband.

27 And when the mourning was past, David sent and fetched her to his house, and she ᴿbecame his wife, and bare him a son. But the thing that David had done ᴿdispleased the LORD. 12:9 · [Heb. 13:4]

12 And the LORD sent Nathan unto David. And he came unto him, and said unto him,

There were two men in one city; the one rich, and the other poor.

2 The rich *man* had exceeding many flocks and herds:

3 But the poor *man* had nothing, save one little ewe lamb, which he had bought and nourished up: and it grew up together with him, and with his children; it did eat of his own ᵀmeat, and drank of his own cup, and lay in his bosom, and was unto him as a daughter. *food*

4 And there came a traveller unto the rich man, and he ᵀspared to take of his own flock and of his own herd, to dress for the wayfaring man that was come unto him; but took the poor man's lamb, and ᵀdressed it for the man that was come to him. *refused · prepared*

5 And David's anger was greatly kindled against the man; and he said to Nathan, *As* the LORD liveth, the man that hath done this *thing* shall surely die:

6 And he shall restore the lamb fourfold, because he did this thing, and because he had no pity.

7 And Nathan said to David, Thou *art* the man. Thus saith the LORD God of Israel, I anointed thee king over Israel, and I delivered thee out of the hand of Saul;

8 And I gave thee thy master's house, and thy master's wives into thy bosom, and gave thee the house of Israel and of Judah; and if *that had been* too little, I would moreover have given unto thee ᵀsuch and such things. *much more*

9 Wherefore hast thou ᴿdespised the commandment of the LORD, to do evil in his sight? ᴿthou hast killed U-ri′-ah the Hit′-tite with the sword, and hast taken his wife *to be* thy wife, and hast slain him with the sword of the children of Ammon. Num. 15:31 · 11:14–1

10 Now therefore ᴿthe sword shall never depart from thine house; because thou hast despised me, and hast taken the wife of U-ri′-ah the Hit′-tite to be thy wife. 13:28; 18:14; 1 Kin. 2:25; [Amos 7:9]

11 Thus saith the LORD, Behold, I will raise up evil against thee out of thine own house, and I will ᴿtake thy wives before thine eyes, and give *them* unto thy neighbour, and he shall lie with thy wives in the sight of this sun. 16:21

12 For thou didst *it* secretly: ᴿbut I will do this thing before all Israel, and before the sun. 16:22

13 And David said unto Nathan, I have sinned against the LORD. And Nathan said unto David, The LORD also hath put away thy sin; thou shalt not die.

14 Howbeit, because by this deed thou hast given great occasion to the enemies of the LORD to blaspheme, the child also *that is* born unto thee shall surely die.

15 And Nathan departed unto his house. And the LORD struck the child that U-ri′-ah's wife bare unto David, and it was very sick.

16 David therefore ᵀbesought God for the child; and David fasted, and went in, and ᴿlay all night upon the earth. *pleaded with · 13:31*

17 And the elders of his house arose, *and went* to him, to raise him up from the earth: but he would not, neither did he eat bread with them.

18 And it came to pass on the seventh day, that the child died. And the servants of David feared to tell him that the child was dead: for they said, Behold, while the child was yet alive, we spake unto him, and he would not hearken unto our voice: how will he then ᵀvex himself, if we tell him that the child is dead? *harm*

19 But when David saw that his servants whispered, David perceived that the child was dead: therefore David said unto his servants, Is the child dead? And they said, He is dead.

20 Then David arose from the earth, and washed, and ᴿanointed *himself*, and changed his apparel, and came into the house of the LORD, and worshipped: then he came to his own house; and when

he required, they set bread before him, and he did eat. Matt. 6:17

21 Then said his servants unto him, What thing *is* this that thou hast done? thou didst fast and weep for the child, *while it was* alive; but when the child was dead, thou didst rise and eat bread.

22 And he said, While the child was yet alive, I fasted and wept: ^Rfor I said, Who can tell *whether* God will be gracious to me, that the child may live? Joel 2:14; Jon. 3:9

23 But now he is dead, wherefore should I fast? can I bring him back again? I shall go ^Rto him, but he shall not return to me. Gen. 37:35

24 And David comforted Bath–she'-ba his wife, and went in unto her, and lay with her: and ^Rshe bare a son, and ^Rhe called his name Solomon: and the LORD loved him. Matt. 1:6 · 1 Chr. 22:9

25 And he sent by the hand of Nathan the prophet; and he called his name ^TJed-i-di'-ah, because of the LORD. Lit. *Beloved of the LORD*

26 And Jo'-ab fought against ^RRab'-bah of the children of Ammon, and took the royal city. 11:1

27 And Jo'-ab sent messengers to David, and said, I have fought against Rab'-bah, and have taken the city of waters.

28 Now therefore gather the rest of the people together, and encamp against the city, and take it: lest I take the city, and it be called after my name.

29 And David gathered all the people together, and went to Rab'-bah, and fought against it, and took it.

30 ^RAnd he took their king's crown from off his head, the weight whereof *was* a talent of gold with the precious stones: and it was *set* on David's head. And he brought forth the spoil of the city in great abundance. 1 Chr. 20:2

31 And he brought forth the people that *were* therein, and put *them* under saws, and under harrows of iron, and under axes of iron, and made them ^Tpass through the brickkiln: and thus did he unto all the cities of the children of Ammon. So David and all the people returned unto Jerusalem. *cross over to*

13 And it came to pass after this, ^Rthat Ab'-sa-lom the son of David had a fair sister, whose name *was* Ta'-mar; and Amnon the son of David loved her. 3:2

2 And Amnon was so ^Tvexed, that he fell sick for his sister Ta'-mar; for she *was* a virgin; and Amnon thought it hard for him to do any thing to her. *distressed*

3 But Amnon had a friend, whose name *was* Jon'-a-dab, ^Rthe son of Shim'-e-ah David's brother: and Jon'-a-dab *was* a very ^Tsubtil man. 1 Sam. 16:9 · *crafty*

4 And he said unto him, Why *art* thou, *being* the king's son, ^Tlean from day to day? wilt thou not tell me? And Amnon said unto him, I love Ta'-mar, my brother Ab'-sa-lom's sister. *becoming thinner*

5 And Jon'-a-dab said unto him, Lay thee down on thy bed, and ^Tmake thyself sick: and when thy father cometh to see thee, say unto him, I pray thee, let my sister Ta'-mar come, and give me meat, and ^Tdress the meat in my sight, that I may see *it*, and eat *it* at her hand. *pretend to be ill · prepare the food*

6 So Amnon lay down, and made himself sick: and when the king was come to see him, Amnon said unto the king, I pray thee, let Ta'-mar my sister come, and make me a couple of cakes in my sight, that I may eat at her hand.

7 Then David sent home to Ta'-mar, saying, Go now to thy brother Amnon's house, and ^Tdress him meat. *prepare food for him*

8 So Ta'-mar went to her brother Amnon's house; and he was laid down. And she took flour, and kneaded *it*, and made cakes in his sight, and did bake the cakes.

9 And she took a pan, and poured *them* out before him; but he refused to eat. And Amnon said, ^RHave ^Tout all men from me. And they went out every man from him. Gen. 45:1 · *every one go out*

10 And Amnon said unto Ta'-mar, Bring the ᵀmeat into the ᵀchamber, that I may eat of thine hand. And Ta'-mar took the cakes which she had made, and brought *them* into the chamber to Amnon her brother.   *food · bedroom*

11 And when she had brought *them* unto him to eat, he took hold of her, and said unto her, Come lie with me, my sister.

12 And she answered him, Nay, my brother, do not force me; for no such thing ought to be done in Israel: do not thou this folly.

13 And I, whither shall I cause my shame to go? and as for thee, thou shalt be as one of the fools in Israel. Now therefore, I pray thee, speak unto the king; for he will not withhold me from thee.

14 Howbeit he would not heark-en unto her voice: but, being stronger than she, ᴿforced her, and lay with her.   Lev. 18:9

15 Then Amnon hated her ex-ceedingly; so that the hatred wherewith he hated her *was* greater than the love wherewith he had loved her. And Amnon said unto her, Arise, be gone.

16 And she said unto him, ᵀ*There is* no cause: this evil in sending me away *is* greater than the other that thou didst unto me. But he would not ᵀhearken unto her.   *No, indeed · listen*

17 Then he called his servant that ministered unto him, and said, Put now this *woman* out from me, and bolt the door after her.

18 And *she had* a garment of divers colours upon her: for with such robes were the king's daugh-ters *that were* virgins apparelled. Then his servant brought her out, and bolted the door after her.

19 And Ta'-mar put ᴿashes on her head, and rent her garment of divers colours that *was* on her, and laid her hand on her head, and went on crying. 1:2; Job 2:12; 42:6

20 And Ab'-sa-lom her brother said unto her, Hath Amnon thy brother been with thee? but hold now thy peace, my sister: he *is* thy brother; regard not this thing. So Ta'-mar remained desolate in her brother Ab'-sa-lom's house.

21 But when king David heard of all these things, he was very ᵀwroth.   *angry*

22 And Ab'-sa-lom spake unto his brother Amnon ᴿneither good nor bad: for Ab'-sa-lom hated Am-non, because he had forced his sister Ta'-mar.   Gen. 24:50; 31:24

23 And it came to pass after two full years, that Ab'-sa-lom ᴿhad sheepshearers in Ba'-al-ha'-zor, which *is* beside E'-phra-im: and Ab'-sa-lom invited all the king's sons.   Gen. 38:12, 13; 1 Sam. 25:4

24 And Ab'-sa-lom came to the king, and said, Behold now, thy servant hath sheepshearers; let the king, I beseech thee, and his servants go with thy servant.

25 And the king said to Ab'-sa-lom, Nay, my son, let us not all now go, lest we be ᵀchargeable unto thee. And he ᵀpressed him: howbeit he would not go, but blessed him.   *a burden to · urged*

26 Then said Ab'-sa-lom, If not, I pray thee, let my brother Amnon go with us. And the king said unto him, Why should he go with thee?

27 But Ab'-sa-lom ᵀpressed him, that he let Amnon and all the king's sons go with him.   *urged*

28 Now Ab'-sa-lom had com-manded his servants, saying, Mark ye now when Amnon's ᴿheart is merry with wine, and when I say unto you, Smite Am-non; then kill him, fear not: have not I commanded you? be coura-geous, and be valiant.   1 Sam. 25:36

29 And the servants of Ab'-sa-lom ᴿdid unto Amnon as Ab'-sa-lom had commanded. Then all the king's sons arose, and every man gat him up upon ᴿhis mule, and fled.   12:10 · 18:9; 1 Kin. 1:33, 38

30 And it came to pass, while they were in the way, that tidings came to David, saying, Ab'-sa-lom hath slain all the king's sons, and there is not one of them left.

31 Then the king arose, and

Rtare his garments, and lay on the earth; and all his servants stood by with their clothes rent.　1:11

32 And RJon'-a-dab, the son of Shim'-e-ah David's brother, answered and said, Let not my lord suppose *that* they have slain all the young men the king's sons; for Amnon only is dead: for by the Tappointment of Ab'-sa-lom this hath been determined from the day that he forced his sister Ta'-mar.　vv. 3–5 · *command*

33 Now therefore Rlet not my lord the king take the thing to his heart, to think that all the king's sons are dead: for Amnon only is dead.　19:19

34 RBut Ab'-sa-lom fled. And the young man that kept the watch lifted up his eyes, and looked, and, behold, there came much people by the way of the hill side behind him.　vv. 37, 38

35 And Jon'-a-dab said unto the king, Behold, the king's sons come: as thy servant said, so it is.

36 And it came to pass, as soon as he had made an end of speaking, that, behold, the king's sons came, and lifted up their voice and wept: and the king also and all his servants wept very sore.

37 But Ab'-sa-lom fled, and went to RTal'-mai, the son of Am-mi'-hud, king of Ge'-shur. And *David* mourned for his son every day. 3:3

38 So Ab'-sa-lom fled, and went to RGe'-shur, and was there three years.　14:23, 32; 15:8

39 And *the soul of* king David longed to go forth unto Ab'-sa-lom: for he was Rcomforted concerning Amnon, seeing he was dead.　12:19, 23; Gen. 38:12

14 Now Jo'-ab the son of Ze-ru'-iah perceived that the king's heart *was* RtowardT Ab'-sa-lom.　13:39 · *concerned about*

2 And Jo'-ab sent to RTe-ko'-ah, and fetched thence a wise woman, and said unto her, I pray thee, feign thyself to be a mourner, Rand put on now mourning apparel, and anoint not thyself with oil, but be as a woman that had a long time mourned for the dead:　2 Chr. 11:6; Amos 1:1 · Ruth 3:3

3 And come to the king, and speak on this manner unto him. So Jo'-ab Rput the words in her mouth.　v. 19; Ex. 4:15

4 And when the woman of Te-ko'-ah spake to the king, she Rfell on her face to the ground, and did obeisance, and said, RHelp, O king.　1 Sam. 20:41; 25:23 · 2 Kin. 6:26, 28

5 And the king said unto her, What Taileth thee? And she answered, RI *am* indeed a widow woman, and mine husband is dead.　*troubles* · [Zech. 7:10]

6 And thy handmaid had two sons, and they two Tstrove together in the field, and *there was* none to part them, but the one smote the other, and slew him.　*fought*

7 And, behold, the whole family is risen against thine handmaid, and they said, Deliver him that smote his brother, that we may kill him, Rfor the life of his brother whom he slew; and we will destroy the heir also: and so they shall quench my coal which is left, and shall not leave to my husband *neither* name nor remainder upon the earth.　Num. 35:19

8 And the king said unto the woman, Go to thine house, and I will give charge concerning thee.

9 And the woman of Te-ko'-ah said unto the king, My lord, O king, the iniquity *be* on me, and on my father's house: and the king and his throne *be* guiltless.

10 And the king said, Whosoever saith *ought* unto thee, bring him to me, and he shall not touch thee any more.

11 Then said she, I pray thee, let the king remember the LORD thy God, that thou wouldest not suffer the revengers of blood to destroy any more, lest they destroy my son. And he said, RAs the LORD liveth, there shall not one hair of thy son fall to the earth.　Matt. 10:30

12 Then the woman said, Let thine handmaid, I pray thee, speak *one* word unto my lord the king. And he said, Say on.

13 And the woman said, Wherefore then hast thou thought such a thing against ᴿthe people of God? for the king doth speak this thing as one which is ᵀfaulty, in that the king doth not fetch home again his banished.　　Judg. 20:2 · *guilty*

14 For we must needs die, and *are* as water spilt on the ground, which cannot be gathered up again; neither doth God respect *any* person: yet doth he ᴿdevise means, that his banished be not expelled from him.　　Num. 35:15

15 Now therefore that I am come to speak of this thing unto my lord the king, *it is* because the people have made me afraid: and thy handmaid said, I will now speak unto the king; it may be that the king will perform the request of his handmaid.

16 For the king will hear, to deliver his handmaid out of the hand of the man *that would* destroy me and my son together out of the ᴿinheritance of God.　　20:19

17 Then thine handmaid said, The word of my lord the king shall now be comfortable: for ᴿas an angel of God, so *is* my lord the king to ᴿdiscern good and bad: therefore the Lᴏʀᴅ thy God will be with thee.　　19:27 · 1 Kin. 3:9

18 Then the king answered and said unto the woman, Hide not from me, I pray thee, the thing that I shall ask thee. And the woman said, Let my lord the king now speak.

19 And the king said, *Is not* the hand of Jo'-ab with thee in all this? And the woman answered and said, *As* thy soul liveth, my lord the king, none can turn to the right hand or to the left from ought that my lord the king hath spoken: for thy servant Jo'-ab, he bade me, and ᴿhe put all these words in the mouth of thine handmaid:　　v. 3

20 To fetch about this form of speech hath thy servant Jo'-ab done this thing: and my lord *is* wise, ᴿaccording to the wisdom of an angel of God, to know all *things* that *are* in the earth.　　19:27

21 And the king said unto Jo'-ab, Behold now, I have done this thing: go therefore, bring the young man Ab'-sa-lom again.

22 And Jo'-ab fell to the ground on his face, and bowed himself, and ᵀthanked the king: and Jo'-ab said, To day thy servant knoweth that I have found grace in thy sight, my lord, O king, in that the king hath fulfilled the request of his servant.　　Lit. *blessed*

23 So Jo'-ab arose ᴿand went to Ge'-shur, and brought Ab'-sa-lom to Jerusalem.　　13:37, 38

24 And the king said, Let him turn to his own house, and let him ᴿnot see my face. So Ab'-sa-lom returned to his own house, and saw not the king's face.　　Gen. 43:3

25 But in all Israel there was none to be so much praised as Ab'-sa-lom for his beauty: ᴿfrom the sole of his foot even to the crown of his head there was no blemish in him.　　Deut. 28:35; Is. 1:6

26 And when he polled his head, (for it was at every year's end that he polled *it*: because *the hair* was heavy on him, therefore he polled it:) he weighed the hair of his head at two hundred shek'-els after the king's weight.

27 And ᴿunto Ab'-sa-lom there were born three sons, and one daughter, whose name *was* Ta'-mar: she was a woman of a fair countenance.　　13:1; 18:18

28 So Ab'-sa-lom dwelt two full years in Jerusalem, ᴿand saw not the king's face.　　v. 24

29 Therefore Ab'-sa-lom sent for Jo'-ab, to have sent him to the king; but he would not come to him: and when he sent again the second time, he would not come.

30 Therefore he said unto his servants, See, Jo'-ab's field is near mine, and he hath barley there; go and set it on fire. And Ab'-sa-lom's servants set the field on fire.

31 Then Jo'-ab arose, and came to Ab'-sa-lom unto *his* house, and said unto him, Wherefore have thy servants set my field on fire?

32 And Ab'-sa-lom answered

Jo'-ab, Behold, I sent unto thee, saying, Come hither, that I may send thee to the king, to say, Wherefore am I come from Ge'-shur? *it had been* good for me *to have been* there still: now therefore let me see the king's face; and ᴿif there be *any* iniquity in me, let him kill me.   1 Sam. 20:8

33 So Jo'-ab came to the king, and told him: and when he had called for Ab'-sa-lom, he came to the king, and bowed himself on his face to the ground before the king: and the king ᴿkissed Ab'-sa-lom.   Gen. 33:4; 45:15; Luke 15:20

15 And it came to pass after this, that Ab'-sa-lom prepared him chariots and horses, and fifty men to run before him.

2 And Ab'-sa-lom rose up early, and stood beside the way of the gate: and it was *so*, that when any man that had a ᵀcontroversy came to the king for judgment, then Ab'-sa-lom called unto him, and said, Of what city *art* thou? And he said, Thy servant *is* of one of the tribes of Israel.   *lawsuit*

3 And Ab'-sa-lom said unto him, See, thy matters *are* good and right; but *there is* no man *deputed* of the king to hear thee.

4 Ab'-sa-lom said moreover, Oh that I were made judge in the land, that every man which hath any suit or cause might come unto me, and I would do him justice!

5 And it was *so*, that when any man came nigh *to him* to do him obeisance, he put forth his hand, and took him, and kissed him.

6 And on this manner did Ab'-sa-lom to all Israel that came to the king for judgment: ᴿso Ab'-sa-lom stole the hearts of the men of Israel.   [Rom. 16:18]

7 And it came to pass ᴿafter forty years, that Ab'-sa-lom said unto the king, I pray thee, let me go and pay my vow, which I have vowed unto the LORD, in ᴿHe'-bron.   [Deut. 23:21] · 3:2, 3

8 ᴿFor thy servant vowed a vow while I abode at Ge'-shur in Syria, saying, If the LORD shall bring me

again indeed to Jeru-salem, then I will serve the LORD.   1 Sam. 16:2

9 And the king said unto him, Go in peace. So he arose, and went to He'-bron.

10 But Ab'-sa-lom sent spies throughout all the tribes of Israel, saying, As soon as ye hear the sound of the trumpet, then ye shall say, Ab'-sa-lom ᴿreigneth in He'-bron.   1 Kin. 1:34; 2 Kin. 9:13

11 And with Ab'-sa-lom went two hundred men out of Jeru-salem, *that were* ᴿcalled; and they ᴿwent in their simplicity, and they knew not any thing.   16:3, 5 · Gen. 20:5

12 And Ab'-sa-lom sent for A-hith'-o-phel the Gi'-lo-nite, ᴿDavid's counsellor, from his city, *even* from ᴿGi'-loh, while he offered sacrifices. And the conspiracy was strong; for the people ᴿincreased continually with Ab'-sa-lom.   Ps. 41:9 · Josh. 15:51 · Ps. 3:1

13 And there came a messenger to David, saying, ᴿThe hearts of the men of Israel are ᵀafter Ab'-sa-lom.   v. 6; Judg. 9:3 · *with*

14 And David said unto all his servants that *were* with him at Jerusalem, Arise, and let us flee; for we shall not *else* escape from Ab'-sa-lom: make speed to depart, lest he overtake us suddenly, and bring evil upon us, and smite the city with the edge of the sword.

15 And the king's servants said unto the king, Behold, thy servants *are ready to do* whatsoever my lord the king shall appoint.

16 And ᴿthe king went forth, and all his household after him. And the king left ᴿten women, *which were* concubines, to keep the house.   Ps. 3:title · 12:11; 16:21, 22

17 And the king went forth, and all the people after him, and tarried in a place that was far off.

18 And all his servants passed on beside him; and all the Cher'-e-thites, and all the Pel'-e-thites, and all the Git'-tites, six hundred men which came after him from Gath, passed on before the king.

19 Then said the king to It'-tai the Git'-tite, Wherefore goest thou

also with us? return to thy place, and abide with the king: for thou *art* a stranger, and also an exile.

20 Whereas thou camest *but* yesterday, should I this day make thee go up and down with us? seeing I go whither I may, return thou, and take back thy brethren: mercy and truth *be* with thee.

21 And It'-tai answered the king, and said, ᴿ*As* the LORD liveth, and *as* my lord the king liveth, surely in what place my lord the king shall be, whether in death or life, even there also will thy servant be. Ruth 1:16, 17

22 And David said to It'-tai, Go and pass over. And It'-tai the Git'-tite passed over, and all his men, and all the little ones that *were* with him.

23 And all the country wept with a loud voice, and all the people ᵀpassed over: the king also himself passed over the brook Kid'-ron, and all the people passed over, toward the way of the ᴿwilderness. *crossed* · v. 28; 16:2

24 And lo Za'-dok also, and all the Levites *were* with him, bearing the ᴿark of the covenant of God: and they set down the ark of God; and A-bi'-a-thar went up, until all the people had done passing out of the city. Num. 4:15; 1 Sam. 4:4

25 And the king said unto Za'-dok, Carry back the ark of God into the city: if I shall find favour in the eyes of the LORD, he ᴿwill bring me again, and shew me *both* it, and his habitation: [Ps. 43:3]

26 But if he thus say, I have no ᴿdelight in thee; behold, *here am* I, ᴿlet him do to me as seemeth good unto him. 2 Chr. 9:8; Is. 62:4 · 1 Sam. 3:18

27 The king said also unto Za'-dok the priest, *Art not* thou a seer? return into the city in peace, and your two sons with you, A-him'-a-az thy son, and Jonathan the son of A-bi'-a-thar.

28 See, ᴿI will ᵀtarry in the plain of the wilderness, until there come word from you to ᵀcertify me. 17:16; Josh. 5:10 · *wait* · *inform*

29 Za'-dok therefore and A-bi'-a-thar carried the ark of God again to Jerusalem: and they tarried there.

30 And David went up by the ascent of *mount* Olivet, and wept as he went up, and ᴿhad his head covered, and he went ᴿbarefoot: and all the people that *was* with him ᴿcovered every man his head, and they went up, weeping as they went up. Esth. 6:12 · Is. 20:2–4 · Jer. 14:3

31 And *one* told David, saying, ᴿA-hith'-o-phel *is* among the conspirators with Ab'-sa-lom. And David said, O LORD, I pray thee, ᴿturn the counsel of A-hith'-o-phel into foolishness. Ps. 55:12 · 16:23

32 And it came to pass, that *when* David was come to the top *of the mount,* where he worshipped God, behold, Hu'-shai the ᴿAr'-chite came to meet him ᴿwith his coat rent, and earth upon his head: Josh. 16:2 · 1:2

33 Unto whom David said, If thou passest on with me, then thou shalt be a burden unto me:

34 But if thou return to the city, and say unto Ab'-sa-lom, ᴿI will be thy servant, O king; *as* I *have been* thy father's servant hitherto, so *will* I now also *be* thy servant: then mayest thou for me defeat the counsel of A-hith'-o-phel. 16:19

35 And *hast thou* not there with thee Za'-dok and A-bi'-a-thar the priests? therefore it shall be, *that* what thing soever thou shalt hear out of the king's house, thou shalt tell *it* to ᴿZa'-dok and A-bi'-a-thar the priests. 17:15, 16

36 Behold, *they have* there ᴿwith them their two sons, A-him'-a-az Za'-dok's *son,* and Jonathan A-bi'-a-thar's *son;* and by them ye shall send unto me every thing that ye can hear. v. 27

37 So Hu'-shai ᴿDavid's friend came into the city, and Ab'-sa-lom came into Jerusalem. 1 Chr. 27:33

16 And when David was a little past the top *of the hill,* behold, Zi'-ba the servant of Me-phib'-o-sheth met him, with a couple of asses saddled, and upon them two hundred *loaves* of bread, and an hundred bunches of raisins, and an hundred of summer fruits, and a bottle of wine.

2 And the king said unto Zi'-ba, What meanest thou by these? And Zi'-ba said, The asses *be* for the king's household to ride on; and the bread and summer fruit for the young men to eat; and the wine, ᴿthat such as be faint in the wilderness may drink.　15:23; 17:29

3 And the king said, And where *is* thy ᴿmaster's son? ᴿAnd Zi'-ba said unto the king, Behold, he abideth at Jerusalem: for he said, To day shall the house of Israel restore ᵀme the kingdom of my father.　9:9, 10 · 19:27 · *to me*

4 Then said the king to Zi'-ba, Behold, thine *are* all that *pertained* unto Me-phib'-o-sheth. And Zi'-ba said, I humbly beseech thee *that* I may find ᵀgrace in thy sight, my lord, O king.　*favour*

5 And when king David came to ᴿBa-hu'-rim, behold, thence came out a man of the family of the house of Saul, whose name *was* ᴿShim'-e-i, the son of Ge'-ra: he came forth, and cursed still as he came.　3:16 · 19:21; 1 Kin. 2:8, 9, 44–46

6 And he cast stones at David, and at all the servants of king David: and all the people and all the mighty men *were* on his right hand and on his left.

7 And thus said Shim'-e-i when he cursed, Come out, come out, thou ᵀbloody man, and thou ᵀman of Be'-li-al:　*bloodthirsty · reprobate*

8 The LORD hath ᴿreturned upon thee all ᴿthe blood of the house of Saul, in whose stead thou hast reigned; and the LORD hath delivered the kingdom into the hand of Ab'-sa-lom thy son: and, behold, thou *art taken* in thy mischief, because thou *art* a bloody man.　Judg. 9:24, 56 · 3:28, 29

9 Then said A-bi'-shai the son of Ze-ru'-iah unto the king, Why should this dead dog curse my lord the king? let me go over, I pray thee, and take off his head.

10 And the king said, ᴿWhat have I to do with you, ye sons of Ze-ru'-iah? so let him curse, because the LORD hath said unto him, Curse David. ᴿWho shall then say, Wherefore hast thou done so?　[1 Pet. 2:23] · [Rom. 9:20]

11 And David said to A-bi'-shai, and to all his servants, Behold, ᴿmy son, which ᴿcame forth of ᵀmy bowels, seeketh my life: how much more now *may this* Benjamite *do it?* let him alone, and let him curse; for the LORD hath bidden him.　12:11 · Gen. 15:4 · *my own body*

12 It may be that the LORD will look on mine affliction, and that the LORD will requite me ᴿgood for his cursing this day.　[Rom. 8:28]

13 And as David and his men went by the way, Shim'-e-i went along on the hill's side over against him, and cursed as he went, and threw stones at him, and cast dust.

14 And the king, and all the people that *were* with him, came weary, and refreshed themselves there.

15 And ᴿAb'-sa-lom, and all the people the men of Israel, came to Jerusalem, and A-hith'-o-phel with him.　15:12, 37

16 And it came to pass, when Hu'-shai the Ar'-chite, ᴿDavid's friend, was come unto Ab'-sa-lom, that ᴿHu'-shai said unto Ab'-sa-lom, God save the king, ᵀGod save the king. 15:37 · 15:34 · *Long live the king*

17 And Ab'-sa-lom said to Hu'-shai, *Is* this thy kindness to thy friend? ᴿwhy wentest thou not with thy friend?　19:25; [Prov. 17:17]

18 And Hu'-shai said unto Ab'-sa-lom, Nay; but whom the LORD, and this people, and all the men of Israel, choose, his will I be, and with him will I abide.

19 And again, ᴿwhom should I serve? *should I* not *serve* in the presence of his son? as I have served in thy father's presence, so will I be in thy presence.　15:34

20 Then said Ab'-sa-lom to ᴿA-hith'-o-phel, Give counsel among you what we shall do.　15:12

21 And A-hith'-o-phel said unto Ab'-sa-lom, Go in unto thy fa-

ther's concubines, which he hath left to keep the house; and all Israel shall hear that thou ᴿart abhorred of thy father: then shall ᴿthe hands of all that *are* with thee be strong. Gen. 34:30 · Zech. 8:13

22 So they spread Ab'-sa-lom a tent upon the top of the house; and Ab'-sa-lom went in unto his father's concubines ᴿin the sight of all Israel. 12:11, 12

23 And the counsel of A-hith'-o-phel, which he counselled in those days, *was* as if a man had enquired at the oracle of God: so *was* all the counsel of A-hith'-o-phel ᴿboth with David and with Ab'-sa-lom. 15:12

17 Moreover A-hith'-o-phel said unto Ab'-sa-lom, Let me now choose out twelve thousand men, and I will arise and pursue after David this night:

2 And I will come upon him while he *is* ᴿweary and weak handed, and will make him afraid: and all the people that *are* with him shall flee; and I will ᴿsmite the king only: Deut. 25:18 · Zech. 13:7

3 And I will bring back all the people unto thee: the man whom thou seekest *is* as if all returned: *so* all the people shall be in peace.

4 And the saying pleased Ab'-sa-lom well, and all the ᴿelders of Israel. 5:3; 19:11

5 Then said Ab'-sa-lom, Call now Hu'-shai the Ar'-chite also, and let us hear likewise what he ᴿsaith. 15:32–34

6 And when Hu'-shai was come to Ab'-sa-lom, Ab'-sa-lom spake unto him, saying, A-hith'-o-phel hath spoken after this manner: shall we do *after* his saying? if not; speak thou.

7 And Hu'-shai said unto Ab'-sa-lom, The counsel that A-hith'-o-phel hath given *is* not good at this time.

8 For, said Hu'-shai, thou knowest thy father and his men, that they *be* mighty men, and they *be* ᵀchafed in their minds, as ᴿa bear robbed of her whelps in the field: and thy father *is* a man of

war, and will not ᵀlodge with the people. *enraged* · Hos. 13:8 · *camp*

9 Behold, he is hid now in some pit, or in some *other* place: and it will come to pass, when some of them be overthrown at the first, that whosoever heareth it will say, There is a slaughter among the people that follow Ab'-sa-lom.

10 And he also *that is* valiant, whose heart *is* as the heart of a lion, shall utterly ᴿmelt: for all Israel knoweth that thy father *is* a mighty man, and *they* which *be* with him *are* valiant men. Josh. 2:11

11 Therefore I counsel that all Israel be generally gathered unto thee, from Dan even to Be'-er–she'-ba, as the sand that *is* by the sea for multitude; and that thou go to battle in thine own person.

12 So shall we come upon him in some place where he shall be found, and we will light upon him as the dew falleth on the ground: and of him and of all the men that *are* with him there shall not be left so much as one.

13 Moreover, if he ᵀbe gotten into a city, then shall all Israel bring ropes to that city, and we will ᴿdraw it into the river, until there be not one small stone found there. *has withdrawn* · Mic. 1:6

14 And Ab'-sa-lom and all the men of Israel said, The counsel of Hu'-shai the Ar'-chite *is* better than the counsel of A-hith'-o-phel. For ᴿthe LORD had ᵀappointed to defeat the good counsel of A-hith'-o-phel, to the intent that the LORD might bring evil upon Ab'-sa-lom. 15:31, 34 · *purposed*

15 ᴿThen said Hu'-shai unto Za'-dok and to A-bi'-a-thar the priests, Thus and thus did A-hith'-o-phel counsel Ab'-sa-lom and the elders of Israel; and thus and thus have I counselled. 15:35, 36

16 Now therefore send quickly, and tell David, saying, Lodge not this night ᴿin the plains of the wilderness, but speedily ᵀpass over; lest the king be swallowed up, and all the people that *are* with him. 15:28 · *cross*

17 Now Jonathan and A-him'-a-az stayed by ᴿEn–ro'-gel; for they ᵀmight not be seen to come into the city: and a wench went and told them; and they went and told king David.   Josh. 15:7; 18:16 · dared

18 Nevertheless a lad saw them, and told Ab'-sa-lom: but they went both of them away quickly, and came to a man's house ᴿin Ba-hu'-rim, which had a well in his court; ᵀwhither they went down.   3:16; 16:5 · they went down into it

19 ᴿAnd the woman took and spread a covering over the well's mouth, and spread ground ᵀcorn thereon; and the thing was not known.   Josh. 2:4–6 · grain

20 And when Ab'-sa-lom's servants came to the woman to the house, they said, Where is A-him'-a-az and Jonathan? And ᴿthe woman said unto them, They be gone over the brook of water. And when they had sought and could not find them, they returned to Jerusalem.   [Lev. 19:11]; Josh. 2:3–5

21 And it came to pass, after they were departed, that they came up out of the well, and went and told king David, and said unto David, ᴿArise, and ᵀpass quickly over the water: for thus hath A-hith'-o-phel counselled against you.   vv. 15, 16 · cross

22 Then David arose, and all the people that were with him, and they ᵀpassed over Jordan: by the morning light there lacked not one of them that was not gone over Jordan.   crossed

23 And when A-hith'-o-phel saw that his counsel was not followed, he saddled his ass, and arose, and gat him home to his house, to his city, and put his ᴿhousehold in order, and hanged himself, and died, and was buried in the sepulchre of his father.   2 Kin. 20:1

24 Then David came to ᴿMa-ha-na'-im. And Ab'-sa-lom passed over Jordan, he and all the men of Israel with him.   Gen. 32:2; Josh. 13:26

25 And Ab'-sa-lom made ᴿAm'-a-sa captain of the host instead of Jo'-ab: which Am'-a-sa was a man's son, whose name was Ith'-ra an Israelite, that went in to ᴿAb'-i-gail the daughter of Na'-hash, sister to Ze-ru'-iah Jo'-ab's mother.   1 Kin. 2:5, 32 · 1 Chr. 2:16

26 So Israel and Ab'-sa-lom pitched in the land of Gil'-e-ad.

27 And it came to pass, when David was come to Ma-ha-na'-im, that ᴿSho'-bi the son of Na'-hash of Rab'-bah of the children of Ammon, and ᴿMa'-chir the son of Am'-mi-el of Lo–de'-bar, and ᴿBar-zil'-lai the Gil'-e-ad-ite of Ro-ge'-lim,   10:1; 12:29 · 9:4 · 19:31, 32; 1 Kin. 2:7

28 Brought beds, and basons, and earthen vessels, and wheat, and barley, and flour, and parched ᵀcorn, and beans, and lentiles, and parched ᵀpulse,   grain · seeds

29 And honey, and butter, and sheep, and cheese of ᵀkine, for David, and for the people that were with him, to eat: for they said, The people is hungry, and weary, and thirsty, ᴿin the wilderness.   the herd · 16:2, 14

18 And David numbered the people that were with him, and ᴿset captains of thousands and captains of hundreds over them.   Ex. 18:25; Num. 31:14; 1 Sam. 22:7

2 And David sent forth a third part of the people under the hand of Jo'-ab, and a third part under the hand of A-bi'-shai the son of Ze-ru'-iah, Jo'-ab's brother, and a third part under the hand of ᴿIt'-tai the Git'-tite. And the king said unto the people, I will surely go forth with you myself also. 15:19–22

3 ᴿBut the people answered, Thou shalt not go forth: for if we flee away, they will not care for us; neither if half of us die, will they care for us: but now thou art worth ten thousand of us: therefore now it is better that thou succour us out of the city.   21:17

4 And the king said unto them, What seemeth you best I will do. And the king stood by the gate side, and all the people came out by hundreds and by thousands.

5 And the king commanded Jo'-ab and A-bi'-shai and It'-tai,

saying, *Deal* gently for my sake with the young man, *even* with Ab'-sa-lom. ^RAnd all the people heard when the king gave all the captains charge concerning Ab'-sa-lom.   v. 12

6 So the people went out into the field against Israel: and the battle was in the ^Rwood of E'-phra-im;   17:26; Josh. 17:15, 18

7 Where the people of Israel were slain before the servants of David, and there was there a great slaughter that day of twenty thousand *men*.

8 For the battle was there scattered over the face of all the country: and the ^Twood devoured more people that day than the sword devoured.   *forest*

9 And Ab'-sa-lom met the servants of David. And Ab'-sa-lom rode upon a mule, and the mule went under the thick boughs of a great oak, and ^Rhis head caught hold of the oak, and he was taken up between the heaven and the earth; and the mule that *was* under him went away.   14:26

10 And a certain man saw *it*, and told Jo'-ab, and said, Behold, I saw Ab'-sa-lom hanged in an oak.

11 And Jo'-ab said unto the man that told him, And, behold, thou sawest *him*, and why didst thou not ^Tsmite him there to the ground? and I would have given thee ten *shek'-els* of silver, and a girdle.   *strike*

12 And the man said unto Jo'-ab, Though I should receive a thousand *shek'-els* of silver in mine hand, *yet* would I not put forth mine hand against the king's son: ^Rfor in our hearing the king charged thee and A-bi'-shai and It'-tai, saying, Beware that none *touch* the young man Ab'-sa-lom.   v. 5

13 Otherwise I should have ^Twrought falsehood against mine own life: for there is no matter hid from the king, and thou thyself wouldest have set thyself against *me*.   *dealt falsely*

14 Then said Jo'-ab, I may not tarry thus with thee. And he took three ^Tdarts in his hand, and thrust them through the heart of Ab'-sa-lom, while he *was* yet alive in the midst of the oak.   *spears*

15 And ten young men that bare Jo'-ab's armour ^Tcompassed about and ^Tsmote Ab'-sa-lom, and slew him.   *surrounded · struck*

16 And Jo'-ab blew the trumpet, and the people returned from pursuing after Israel: for Jo'-ab held back the people.

17 And they took Ab'-sa-lom, and cast him into a great pit in the wood, and laid a very great heap of stones upon him: and all Israel ^Rfled every one to his tent. 19:8; 20:1

18 Now Ab'-sa-lom in his lifetime had taken and reared up for himself a pillar, which *is* in ^Rthe king's dale: for he said, ^RI have no son to keep my name in remembrance: and he called the pillar after his own name: and it is called unto this day, Ab'-sa-lom's place.   Gen. 14:17 · 14:27

19 Then said ^RA-him'-a-az the son of Za'-dok, Let me now run, and bear the king tidings, how that the LORD hath ^Tavenged him of his enemies. 15:36; 17:17 · *vindicated*

20 And Jo'-ab said unto him, Thou shalt not bear tidings this day, but thou shalt bear tidings another day: but this day thou shalt bear no tidings, because the king's son is dead.

21 Then said Jo'-ab to Cu'-shi, Go tell the king what thou hast seen. And Cu'-shi bowed himself unto Jo'-ab, and ran.

22 Then said A-him'-a-az the son of Za'-dok yet again to Jo'-ab, But howsoever, let me, I pray thee, also run after Cu'-shi. And Jo'-ab said, Wherefore wilt thou run, my son, seeing that thou hast no ^Ttidings ready?   *news*

23 But howsoever, *said he*, let me run. And he said unto him, Run. Then A-him'-a-az ran by the way of the plain, and ^Toverran Cu'-shi.   *outran*

24 And David sat between the ^Rtwo gates: and the watchman went up to the roof over the gate unto the wall, and lifted up his eyes, and looked, and behold a man running alone. 13:34; Judg. 5:11

25 And the watchman cried, and told the king. And the king said, If he *be* alone, *there is* ᵀtidings in his mouth. And he came ᵀapace, and drew near. *news · rapidly*

26 And the watchman saw another man running: and the watchman called unto the ᵀporter, and said, Behold *another* man running alone. And the king said, He also bringeth tidings. *gatekeeper*

27 And the watchman said, Me thinketh the running of the foremost is like the running of A-him'-a-az the son of Za'-dok. And the king said, He *is* a good man, and cometh with good tidings.

28 And A-him'-a-az called, and said unto the king, All is well. And he fell down to the earth upon his face before the king, and said, ᴿBlessed *be* the LORD thy God, which hath delivered up the men that lifted up their hand against my lord the king. 16:12

29 And the king said, Is the young man Ab'-sa-lom safe? And A-him'-a-az answered, When Jo'-ab sent the king's servant, and *me* thy servant, I saw a great tumult, but I knew not what *it was.*

30 And the king said *unto him,* Turn aside, *and* stand here. And he turned aside, and stood still.

31 And, behold, Cu'-shi came; and Cu'-shi said, Tidings, my lord the king: for the LORD hath ᵀavenged thee this day of all them that rose up against thee. *vindicated*

32 And the king said unto Cu'-shi, *Is* the young man Ab'-sa-lom safe? And Cu'-shi answered, The enemies of my lord the king, and all that rise against thee to do *thee* ᵀhurt, be as *that* young man *is.* *harm*

33 And the king was much moved, and went up to the chamber over the gate, and wept: and as he went, thus he said, ᴿO my son Ab'-sa-lom, my son, my son

Ab'-sa-lom! would God I had died for thee, O Ab'-sa-lom, my son, ᴿmy son!   12:10 · 19:4

19 And it was told Jo'-ab, Behold, the king weepeth and mourneth for Ab'-sa-lom.

2 And the victory that day was *turned* into ᴿmourning unto all the people: for the people heard say that day how the king was grieved for his son.   Esth. 4:3

3 And the people gat them by stealth that day ᴿinto the city, as people being ashamed steal away when they flee in battle.   17:24, 27

4 But the king covered his face, and the king cried with a loud voice, ᴿO my son Ab'-sa-lom, O Ab'-sa-lom, my son, my son! 18:33

5 And ᴿJo'-ab came into the house to the king, and said, Thou hast shamed this day the faces of all thy servants, which this day have saved thy life, and the lives of thy sons and of thy daughters, and the lives of thy wives, and the lives of thy concubines;   18:14

6 In that thou lovest thine enemies, and hatest thy friends. For thou hast declared this day, that thou regardest neither princes nor servants: for this day I perceive, that if Ab'-sa-lom had lived, and all we had died this day, then it had pleased thee well.

7 Now therefore arise, go forth, and speak comfortably unto thy servants: for I swear by the LORD, if thou go not forth, there will not ᵀtarry one with thee this night: and that will be worse unto thee than all the evil that befell thee from thy youth until now.   *stay*

8 Then the king arose, and sat in the ᴿgate. And they told unto all the people, saying, Behold, the king doth sit in the gate. And all the people came before the king: for Israel had ᴿfled every man to his tent.   15:2; 18:24 · 18:17

9 And all the people were at strife throughout all the tribes of Israel, saying, The king saved us out of the hand of our ᴿenemies, and he delivered us out of the hand of the ᴿPhi-lis'-tines; and

now he is [R]fled out of the land for Ab'-sa-lom.   8:1–14 · 3:18 · 15:14

10 And Ab'-sa-lom, whom we anointed over us, is dead in battle. Now therefore why speak ye not a word of bringing the king back?

11 And king David sent to [R]Za'-dok and to A-bi'-a-thar the priests, saying, Speak unto the elders of Judah, saying, Why are ye the last to bring the king back to his house? seeing the speech of all Israel is come to the king, *even* to his house.   15:24

12 Ye *are* my brethren, ye *are* [R]my bones and my flesh: wherefore then are ye the last to bring back the king?   5:1; 1 Chr. 11:1

13 [R]And say ye to Am'-a-sa, *Art* thou not of my bone, and of my flesh? God do so to me, and more also, if thou be not captain of the host before me continually in the [T]room of Jo'-ab.   17:25 · *place*

14 And he bowed the heart of all the men of Judah, even as *the heart of* one man; so that they sent *this word* unto the king, Return thou, and all thy servants.

15 So the king returned, and came to Jordan. And Judah came to Gil'-gal, to go to meet the king, to conduct the king over Jordan.

16 And [R]Shim'-e-i the son of Ge'-ra, a Benjamite, which *was* of Ba-hu'-rim, hasted and came down with the men of Judah to meet king David.   16:5; 1 Kin. 2:8

17 And *there were* a thousand men of [R]Benjamin with him, and [R]Zi'-ba the servant of the house of Saul, and his fifteen sons and his twenty servants with him; and they went over Jordan before the king.   3:19; 1 Kin. 12:21 · 9:2, 10; 16:1, 2

18 And there went over a ferry boat to carry over the king's household, and to do what he thought good. And Shim'-e-i the son of Ge'-ra fell down before the king, as he was come over Jordan;

19 And said unto the king, [R]Let not my lord impute iniquity unto me, neither do thou remember [R]that which thy servant did per-

versely the day that my lord the king went out of Jerusalem, that the king should [R]take it to his heart.   1 Sam. 22:15 · 16:5, 6 · 13:33

20 For thy servant doth know that I have sinned: therefore, behold, I am come the first this day of all the house of Joseph to go down to meet my lord the king.

21 But A-bi'-shai the son of Ze-ru'-iah answered and said, Shall not Shim'-e-i be put to death for this, because he [R]cursed the LORD's anointed?   [1 Sam. 26:9]

22 And David said, [R]What have I to do with you, ye sons of Ze-ru'-iah, that ye should this day be adversaries unto me? shall there any man be put to death this day in Israel? for do not I know that I *am* this day king over Israel?   3:39

23 Therefore [R]the king said unto Shim'-e-i, Thou shalt not die. And the king sware unto him.   1 Kin. 2:8

24 And [R]Me-phib'-o-sheth the son of Saul came down to meet the king, and had neither dressed his feet, nor trimmed his beard, nor washed his clothes, from the day the king departed until the day he came *again* in peace.   9:6

25 And it came to pass, when he was come to Jerusalem to meet the king, that the king said unto him, [R]Wherefore wentest not thou with me, Me-phib'-o-sheth?   16:7

26 And he answered, My lord, O king, my servant deceived me: for thy servant said, I will saddle me an ass, that I may ride thereon, and go to the king; because thy servant *is* lame.

27 And [R]he hath slandered thy servant unto my lord the king; [R]but my lord the king *is* as an angel of God: do therefore *what is* good in thine eyes.   16:3, 4 · 14:17, 20

28 For all *of* my father's house were but dead men before my lord the king: [R]yet didst thou set thy servant among them that did eat at thine own table. What right therefore have I yet to cry any more unto the king?   9:7–13

29 And the king said unto him, Why speakest thou any more of

thy matters? I have said, Thou and Zi'-ba divide the land.

30 And Me-phib'-o-sheth said unto the king, Yea, let him take all, forasmuch as my lord the king is come again in peace unto his own house.

31 And ^RBar-zil'-lai the Gil'-e-ad-ite came down from Ro-ge'-lim, and went over Jordan with the king, to conduct him over Jordan.   17:27–29; 1 Kin. 2:7

32 Now Bar-zil'-lai was a very aged man, *even* fourscore years old: and ^Rhe had provided the king ^Tof sustenance while he lay at Ma-ha-na'-im; for he *was* a very great man.   17:27–29 · with supplies

33 And the king said unto Bar-zil'-lai, Come thou over with me, and I will feed thee with me in Jerusalem.

34 And Bar-zil'-lai said unto the king, How long have I to live, that I should go up with the king unto Jerusalem?

35 I *am* this day ^Rfourscore years old: *and* can I discern between good and ^Tevil? can thy servant taste what I eat or what I drink? can I hear any more the voice of singing men and singing women? wherefore then should thy servant be yet a burden unto my lord the king?   Ps. 90:10 · bad

36 Thy servant will go a little way over Jordan with the king: and why should the king recompense it me with such a reward?

37 Let thy servant, I pray thee, turn back again, that I may die in mine own city, *and be buried* by the grave of my father and of my mother. But behold thy servant Chim'-ham; let him go over with my lord the king; and do to him what shall seem good unto thee.

38 And the king answered, Chim'-ham shall go over with me, and I will do to him that which shall seem good unto thee: and whatsoever thou shalt ^Trequire of me, *that* will I do for thee.   request

39 And all the people went over Jordan. And when the king was come over, the king ^Rkissed Bar-

zil'-lai, and blessed him; and he returned unto his own place. 14:33

40 Then the king went on to Gil'-gal, and Chim'-ham went on with him: and all the people of Judah conducted the king, and also half the people of Israel.

41 And, behold, all the men of Israel came to the king, and said unto the king, Why have our brethren the men of Judah stolen thee away, and ^Rhave brought the king, and his household, and all David's men with him, over Jordan?   v. 15

42 And all the men of Judah answered the men of Israel, Because the king *is* ^Rnear of kin to us: wherefore then be ye angry for this matter? have we eaten at all of the king's *cost?* or hath he given us any gift?   v. 12

43 And the men of Israel answered the men of Judah, and said, We have ten parts in the king, and we have also more *right* in David than ye: why then did ye despise us, that our advice should not be first had in bringing back our king? And the words of the men of Judah were fiercer than the words of the men of Israel.

20 And there happened to be there a man of Be'-li-al, whose name *was* She'-ba, the son of Bich'-ri, a Benjamite: and he blew a trumpet, and said, ^RWe have no part in David, neither have we inheritance in the son of Jesse: ^Revery man to his tents, O Israel.   19:43; 1 Kin. 12:16 · 2 Chr. 10:16

2 So every man of Israel went up from after David, *and* followed She'-ba the son of Bich'-ri: but the ^Rmen of Judah clave unto their king, from Jordan even to Jerusalem.   19:14

3 And David came to his house at Jerusalem; and the king took the ten women ^Rhis concubines, whom he had left to keep the house, and put them in ^Tward, and fed them, but went not in unto them. So they were shut up unto the day of their death, living in widowhood.   15:16; 16:21, 22 · seclusion

4 Then said the king to Am'-a-sa, ᴿAssemble me the men of Judah within three days, and be thou here present.   17:25; 19:13

5 So Am'-a-sa went to assemble *the men of* Judah: but he tarried longer than the set time which he had appointed him.

6 And David said to ᴿA-bi'-shai, Now shall She'-ba the son of Bich'-ri do us more harm than *did* Ab'-sa-lom: take thou ᴿthy lord's servants, and pursue after him, lest he get him fenced cities, and escape us.   21:17 · 11:11; 1 Kin. 1:33

7 And there went out after him Jo'-ab's men, and the Cher'-e-thites, and the Pel'-e-thites, and all the mighty men: and they went out of Jerusalem, to pursue after She'-ba the son of Bich'-ri.

8 When they *were* at the great stone which *is* in Gib'-e-on, Am'-a-sa went before them. And Jo'-ab's garment that he had put on was girded unto him, and upon it a ᵀgirdle *with* a sword fastened upon his loins in the sheath thereof; and as he ᵀwent forth it fell out.   *belt · was going forward*

9 And Jo'-ab said to Am'-a-sa, *Art* thou in health, my brother? ᴿAnd Jo'-ab took Am'-a-sa by the beard with the right hand to kiss him.   Matt. 26:49; Luke 22:47

10 But Am'-a-sa took no heed to the sword that *was* in Jo'-ab's hand: so ᴿhe smote him therewith ᴿin the fifth *rib*, and shed out his bowels to the ground, and struck him not again; and he died. So Jo'-ab and A-bi'-shai his brother pursued after She'-ba the son of Bich'-ri.   3:27; 1 Kin. 2:5 · 2:23

11 And one of Jo'-ab's men stood by him, and said, He that favoureth Jo'-ab, and he that *is* for David, *let him* go after Jo'-ab.

12 And Am'-a-sa wallowed in blood in the midst of the highway. And when the man saw that all the people stood still, he removed Am'-a-sa out of the highway into the field, and cast a cloth upon him, when he saw that every one that came by him stood still.

13 When he was removed out of the highway, all the people went on after Jo'-ab, to pursue after She'-ba the son of Bich'-ri.

14 And he went through all the tribes of Israel unto Abel, and to Beth–ma'-a-chah, and all the Be'-rites: and they were gathered together, and went also after him.

15 And they came and besieged him in Abel of Beth–ma'-a-chah, and they ᴿcast up a bank against the city, and it stood in the trench: and all the people that *were* with Jo'-ab battered the wall, to throw it down.   2 Kin. 19:32; Ezek. 4:2

16 Then cried a wise woman out of the city, Hear, hear; say, I pray you, unto Jo'-ab, Come near hither, that I may speak with thee.

17 And when he was come near unto her, the woman said, *Art* thou Jo'-ab? And he answered, I *am he.* Then she said unto him, Hear the words of thine handmaid. And he answered, I do hear.

18 Then she spake, saying, They were wont to speak in old time, saying, They shall surely ask *counsel* at Abel: and so they ended *the matter.*

19 I *am one of them that are* peaceable *and* faithful in Israel: thou seekest to destroy a city and a mother in Israel: why wilt thou swallow up ᴿthe inheritance of the Lᴏʀᴅ?   14:16; 21:3; 1 Sam. 26:19

20 And Jo'-ab answered and said, Far be it, far be it from me, that I should swallow up or destroy.

21 The matter *is* not so: but a man of mount E'-phra-im, She'-ba the son of Bich'-ri by name, hath lifted up his hand against the king, *even* against David: deliver him only, and I will depart from the city. And the woman said unto Jo'-ab, Behold, his head shall be thrown to thee over the wall.

22 Then the woman went unto all the people ᴿin her wisdom. And they cut off the head of She'-ba the son of Bich'-ri, and cast *it* out to Jo'-ab. And he blew a trumpet, and they ᵀretired from the city, every man to his tent. And Jo'-ab returned to Jerusalem unto the king. v. 16; [Eccl. 9:13–16] · *withdrew*

23 Now ᴿJo'-ab *was* over all the host of Israel: and Be-nai'-ah the son of Je-hoi'-a-da *was* over the Cher'-e-thites and over the Pel'-e-thites: 8:16–18; 1 Kin. 4:3–6

24 And A-do'-ram *was* over the tribute: and ᴿJe-hosh'-a-phat the son of A-hi'-lud *was* recorder: 8:16

25 And She'-va *was* scribe: and ᴿZa'-dok and A-bi'-a-thar *were* the priests: 8:17; 1 Kin. 4:4

26 ᴿAnd I'-ra also the Ja'-ir-ite was a chief ruler about David. 8:18

21 Then there was a famine in the days of David three years, year after year; and David ᴿenquired of the LORD. And the LORD answered, *It is* for Saul, and for *his* bloody house, because he slew the Gib'-e-on-ites.   Num. 27:21

2 And the king called the Gib'-e-on-ites, and said unto them; (now the Gib'-e-on-ites *were* not of the children of Israel, but of the remnant of the Am'-or-ites; and the children of Israel had sworn unto them: and Saul sought to slay them in his zeal to the children of Israel and Judah.)

3 Wherefore David said unto the Gib'-e-on-ites, What shall I do for you? and wherewith shall I make the atonement, that ye may bless ᴿthe inheritance of the LORD?   20:19; 1 Sam. 26:19

4 And the Gib'-e-on-ites said unto him, We will have no silver nor gold of Saul, nor of his house; neither for us shalt thou kill any man in Israel. And he said, What ye shall say, *that* will I do for you.

5 And they answered the king, The man that consumed us, and that devised against us *that* we should be destroyed from remaining in any of the coasts of Israel,

6 Let seven men of his sons be delivered unto us, and we will hang them up unto the LORD in Gib'-e-ah of Saul, ᴿ*whom* the LORD did choose. And the king said, I will give *them*.   [Hos. 13:11]

7 But the king spared ᴿMe-phib'-o-sheth, the son of Jonathan the son of Saul, because of ᴿthe LORD's oath that *was* between them, between David and Jonathan the son of Saul. 4:4; 9:10 · 9:1–7

8 But the king took the two sons of Riz'-pah the daughter of A'-iah, whom she bare unto Saul, Ar-mo'-ni and Me-phib'-o-sheth; and the five sons of Mi'-chal the daughter of Saul, whom she brought up for A'-dri-el the son of Bar-zil'-lai the Me-hol'-ath-ite:

9 And he delivered them into the hands of the Gib'-e-on-ites, and they hanged them in the hill ᴿbefore the LORD: and they fell *all* seven together, and were put to death in the days of harvest, in the first *days*, in the beginning of barley harvest.   6:17

10 And ᴿRiz'-pah the daughter of A'-iah took sackcloth, and spread it for her upon the rock, ᴿfrom the beginning of harvest until water dropped upon them out of heaven, and suffered neither the birds of the air to rest on them by day, nor the beasts of the field by night. v. 8; 3:7 · Deut. 21:23

11 And it was told David what Riz'-pah the daughter of A'-iah, the concubine of Saul, had done.

12 And David went and took the bones of Saul and the bones of Jonathan his son from the men of ᴿJa'-besh–gil'-e-ad, which had stolen them from the street of Beth'–shan, where the ᴿPhi-lis'-tines had hanged them, when the Phi-lis'-tines had slain Saul in Gil-bo'-a: 1 Sam. 31:11–13 · 1 Sam. 31:8

13 And he brought up from thence the bones of Saul and the bones of Jonathan his son; and they gathered the bones of them that were hanged.

14 And the bones of Saul and Jonathan his son buried they in the country of Benjamin in ᴿZe'-lah, in the sepulchre of Kish his father: and they performed all that the king commanded. And after that ᴿGod was intreated for the land.   Josh. 18:28 · 24:25

15 Moreover the Phi-lis'-tines

had yet war again with Israel; and David went down, and his servants with him, and fought against the Phi-lis'-tines: and David waxed faint.

16 And Ish'-bi-be'-nob, which *was* of the sons of the ᴿgiant, the weight of whose spear *weighed* three hundred *shek'-els* of brass in weight, he being girded with a new *sword*, thought to have slain David.   Num. 13:22, 28; Josh. 15:14

17 But A-bi'-shai the son of Ze-ru'-iah ᵀsuccoured him, and smote the Phi-lis'-tine, and killed him. Then the men of David sware unto him, saying, ᴿThou shalt go no more out with us to battle, that thou quench not the ᴿlight of Israel.   *came to his aid* · 18:3 · 1 Kin. 11:36

18 ᴿAnd it came to pass after this, that there was again a battle with the Phi-lis'-tines at Gob: then Sib'-be-chai the Hu'-shath-ite slew Saph, which *was* of the sons of the giant.   1 Chr. 20:4–8

19 And there was again a battle in Gob with the Phi-lis'-tines, where ᴿEl-ha'-nan the son of Ja'-a-re-or'-e-gim, a Beth'-le-hem-ite, slew *the brother of* Go-li'-ath the Git'-tite, the staff of whose spear *was* like a weaver's beam.   23:24

20 And ᴿthere was yet a battle in Gath, where was a man of *great* stature, that had on every hand six fingers, and on every foot six toes, four and twenty in number; and he also was born to ᵀthe giant.   1 Chr. 20:6 · Or *Rapha*

21 And when he defied Israel, Jonathan the son of Shim'-e-ah the brother of David slew him.

22 ᴿThese four were born to ᵀthe giant in Gath, and fell by the hand of David, and by the hand of his servants.   1 Chr. 20:8 · Or *Rapha*

22 And David ᴿspake unto the LORD the words of this song, in the day *that* the LORD had ᴿde-livered him out of the hand of all his enemies, and out of the hand of Saul: Ex. 15:1; Judg. 5:1 · Ps. 18:title

2 And he ᴿsaid, The LORD *is* my rock, and my ᴿfortress, and my deliverer;   Ps. 18 · Ps. 91:2

3 The God of my rock; ᴿin him will I trust: *he is* my shield, and the ᴿhorn of my salvation, my ᴿhigh tower, and my refuge, my saviour; thou savest me from vio-lence.   Heb. 2:13 · Luke 1:69 · Prov. 18:10

4 I will call on the LORD, *who is* worthy to be praised: so shall I be saved from mine enemies.

5 When the waves of death compassed me, the floods of ungodly men made me afraid;

6 The sorrows of hell com-passed me about; the snares of death ᵀprevented me;   *confronted*

7 In my distress ᴿI called upon the LORD, and cried to my God: and he did ᴿhear my voice out of his temple, and my cry *did enter* into his ears.   Ps. 120:1 · Ps. 34:6, 15

8 Then the earth shook and trembled; ᴿthe foundations of heaven moved and shook, be-cause he was wroth.   Job 26:11

9 There went up a smoke out of his nostrils, and ᴿfire out of his mouth devoured: coals were kin-dled by it.   Ps. 97:3, 4; Heb. 12:29

10 He ᴿbowed the heavens also, and came down; and ᴿdarkness *was* under his feet.   Is. 64:1 · Ex. 20:21

11 And he rode upon a cherub, and did fly: and he was seen ᴿup-on the wings of the wind.   Ps. 104:3

12 And he made ᴿdarkness ᵀpavilions round about him, dark waters, *and* thick clouds of the skies.   Job 36:29; Ps. 97:2 · *canopies*

13 Through the brightness be-fore him were coals of fire kindled.

14 The LORD ᴿthundered from heaven, and the most High uttered his voice.   Job 37:2–5; Ps. 29:3

15 And he sent out arrows, and scattered them; lightning, and ᵀdiscomfited them.   *vanquished*

16 And the channels of the sea appeared, the foundations of the world were discovered, at the ᴿre-buking of the LORD, at the blast of the breath of his nostrils.   Ex. 15:8

17 ᴿHe sent from above, he took me; he drew me out of many waters;   Ps. 144:7; Is. 43:2

18 He delivered me from my strong enemy, *and* from them that

hated me: for they were too strong for me.

19 They [T]prevented me in the day of my calamity: but the LORD was my [R]stay. *confronted* · Is. 10:20

20 He brought me forth also into a large place: he delivered me, because he [R]delighted in me. 15:26

21 The LORD rewarded me according to my righteousness: according to the cleanness of my hands hath he recompensed me.

22 For I have [R]kept the ways of the LORD, and have not wickedly departed from my God. Ps. 119:3

23 For all his judgments *were* before me: and *as for* his statutes, I did not depart from them.

24 I was also [R]upright before him, and have kept myself from mine iniquity. [Eph. 1:4; Col. 1:21, 22]

25 Therefore the LORD hath [T]recompensed me according to my righteousness; according to my cleanness in his eye sight. *rewarded*

26 With [R]the merciful thou wilt shew thyself merciful, *and* with the upright man thou wilt shew thyself upright. [Matt. 5:7]

27 With the pure thou wilt shew thyself pure; and with the [T]froward thou wilt shew thyself [T]unsavoury. *devious* · *shrewd*

28 And the [R]afflicted people thou wilt save: but thine eyes *are* upon the haughty, *that* thou mayest bring *them* down. Ps. 72:12

29 For thou *art* my [R]lamp, O LORD: and the LORD will lighten my darkness. Ps. 119:105; 132:17

30 For by thee I have run through a troop: by my God have I leaped over a [R]wall. 5:6–8

31 *As for* God, [R]his way *is* perfect; [R]the word of the LORD *is* tried: he *is* a buckler to all them that trust in him. [Matt. 5:48] · Ps. 12:6

32 For [R]who *is* God, save the LORD? and who *is* a rock, save our God? Is. 45:5, 6

33 God *is* my [R]strength *and* power: and he [R]maketh my way [R]perfect. Ps. 27:1 · [Heb. 13:21] · Ps. 101:2, 6

34 He maketh my feet [R]like hinds' *feet*: and [R]setteth me upon my high places. Hab. 3:19 · Is. 33:16

35 He teacheth my hands to war; so that a bow of [T]steel is broken by mine arms. *bronze is bent by*

36 Thou hast also given me the shield of thy salvation: and thy gentleness hath made me great.

37 Thou hast [R]enlarged my steps under me; so that my feet did not slip. v. 20; Prov. 4:12

38 I have pursued mine enemies, and destroyed them; and turned not again until I had consumed them.

39 And I have consumed them, and wounded them, that they could not arise: yea, they are fallen [R]under my feet. Mal. 4:3

40 For thou hast [R]girded me with strength to battle: [R]them that rose up against me hast thou subdued under me. [Ps. 18:32] · [Ps. 44:5]

41 Thou hast also given me the necks of mine enemies, that I might destroy them that hate me.

42 They looked, but *there was* none to save; *even* [R]unto the LORD, but he answered them not. Is. 1:15

43 Then did I beat them as small [R]as the dust of the earth: I did stamp them [R]as the mire of the street, *and* did spread them abroad. 2 Kin. 13:7; Ps. 18:42 · Is. 10:6

44 Thou also hast delivered me from the strivings of my people, thou hast kept me *to be* head of the heathen: [R]a people *which* I knew not shall serve me. [Is. 55:5]

45 [T]Strangers shall submit themselves unto me: as soon as they hear, they shall be obedient unto me. *Foreigners*

46 Strangers shall fade away, and they shall be afraid [R]out of their close places. [Mic. 7:17]

47 The LORD liveth; and blessed *be* my rock; and exalted be the God of the rock of my salvation.

48 It *is* God that avengeth me, and that [R]bringeth down the people under me, 1 Sam. 24:12; Ps. 144:2

49 And that bringeth me forth from mine enemies: thou also hast lifted me up on high above them that rose up against me: thou hast delivered me from the [R]violent man. Ps. 140:1, 4, 11

50 Therefore I will give thanks unto thee, O LORD, among the heathen, and I will sing praises unto thy ᴿname.　Ps. 57:7; Rom. 15:9

51 *He is* the tower of salvation for his king: and sheweth mercy to his ᴿanointed, unto David, and to his seed for evermore.　Ps. 89:20

23 Now these *be* the last words of David. David the son of Jesse said, and the man *who was* raised up on high, the anointed of the God of Jacob, and the sweet psalmist of Israel, said,

2 ᴿThe Spirit of the LORD spake by me, and his word *was* in my tongue.　Matt. 22:43; [2 Pet. 1:21]

3 The God of Israel said, the Rock of Israel spake to me, He that ruleth over men *must be* just, ruling ᴿin the fear of God.　Ex. 18:21

4 And ᴿ*he shall be* as the light of the morning, *when* the sun riseth, *even* a morning without clouds; *as* the tender grass *springing* out of the earth by clear shining after rain.　Ps. 89:36; Is. 60:1

5 Although my house *be* not so with God; ᴿyet he hath made with me an everlasting covenant, ordered in all *things*, and sure: for *this is* all my salvation, and all *my* desire, although he make *it* not to grow.　7:12; Ps. 89:29; Is. 55:3

6 But *the* ᵀ*sons* of Be'-li-al *shall be* all of them as thorns thrust away, because they cannot be taken with hands:　*rebellious*

7 But the man *that* shall touch them must be ᵀfenced with iron and the staff of a spear; and they shall be utterly burned with fire in the *same* place.　*armed,* lit. *filled*

8 These *be* the names of the mighty men whom David had: The Tach'-mo-nite that sat in the seat, chief among the captains; the same *was* Ad'-i-no the Ez'-nite: *he lift up his spear* against eight hundred, whom he slew at one time.

9 And after him *was* E-le-a'-zar the son of Dodo the A-ho'-hite, *one* of the three mighty men with David, when they defied the Phi-lis'-tines *that* were there gathered

together to battle, and the men of Israel were gone away:

10 He arose, and smote the Phi-lis'-tines until his hand was weary, and his hand ᵀclave unto the sword: and the LORD wrought a great victory that day; and the people returned after him only to ᴿspoil.ᵀ　*stuck* · 1 Sam. 30:24, 25 · *plunder*

11 And after him *was* Sham'-mah the son of Ag'-e-e the Ha'-ra-rite. ᴿAnd the Phi-lis'-tines were gathered together into a troop, where was a piece of ground full of lentiles: and the people fled from the Phi-lis'-tines.　1 Chr. 11:13

12 But he stood in the midst of the ground, and defended it, and slew the Phi-lis'-tines: and the LORD wrought a great victory.

13 And ᴿthree of the thirty chief went down, and came to David in the harvest time unto ᴿthe cave of A-dul'-lam: and the troop of the Phi-lis'-tines pitched in the valley of Reph'-a-im. 1 Chr. 11:15 · 1 Sam. 22:1

14 And David *was* then in ᴿanᵀ hold, and the garrison of the Phi-lis'-tines *was* then *in* Beth'-le-hem.　1 Sam. 22:4, 5 · *the strong hold*

15 And David longed, and said, Oh that one would give me drink of the water of the well of Beth'–le-hem, which *is* by the gate!

16 And the three mighty men brake through the host of the Phi-lis'-tines, and drew water out of the well of Beth'–le-hem, that *was* by the gate, and took *it,* and brought *it* to David: nevertheless he would not drink thereof, but poured it out unto the LORD.

17 And he said, Be it far from me, O LORD, that I should do this: *is not this* ᴿthe blood of the men that went in jeopardy of their lives? therefore he would not drink it. These things did these three mighty men.　[Lev. 17:10]

18 And ᴿA-bi'-shai, the brother of Jo'-ab, the son of Ze-ru'-iah, was chief among three. And he lifted up his spear against three hundred, *and* slew *them*, and had the name among three.　21:17

19 Was he not most honourable

of three? therefore he was their captain: howbeit he attained not unto the *first* three.

20 And Be-nai'-ah the son of Je-hoi'-a-da, the son of a valiant man, of Kab'-ze-el, who had done many acts, ᴿhe slew two lionlike men of Moab: he went down also and slew a lion in the midst of a pit in time of snow: Ex. 15:15

21 And he slew an Egyptian, a goodly man: and the Egyptian had a spear in his hand; but he went down to him with a staff, and plucked the spear out of the Egyptian's hand, and slew him with his own spear.

22 These *things* did Be-nai'-ah the son of Je-hoi'-a-da, and had the name among three mighty men.

23 He was more ᵀhonourable than the thirty, but he attained not to the *first* three. And David set him ᴿover his guard. *honoured* · 8:18

24 ᴿA'-sa-hel the brother of Jo'-ab *was* one of the thirty; El-ha'-nan the son of Dodo of Beth'–le-hem, 2:18; 1 Chr. 27:7

25 ᴿSham'-mah the Ha'-rod-ite, El'-i-ka the Ha'-rod-ite, 1 Chr. 11:27

26 He'-lez the Pal'-tite, I'-ra the son of Ik'-kesh the Te-ko'-ite,

27 A-bi-e'-zer the An'-e-tho-thite, Me-bun'-nai the Hu'-shath-ite,

28 Zal'-mon the A-ho'-hite, Ma'-ha-rai the Ne-toph'-a-thite,

29 He'-leb the son of Ba'-a-nah, a Ne-toph'-a-thite, It'-tai the son of Ri'-bai out of Gib'-e-ah of the children of Benjamin,

30 Be-nai'-ah the Pir'-a-thon-ite, Hid'-dai of the brooks of Ga'-ash,

31 Ab'-i-al'-bon the Ar'-bath-ite, Az'-ma-veth the Bar-hu'-mite,

32 E-li'-ah-ba the Sha-al'-bo-nite, of the sons of Ja'-shen, Jona-than,

33 ᴿSham'-mah the Ha'-ra-rite, A-hi'-am the son of Sha'-rar the ᵀHa'-ra-rite, v. 11 · Or *Ararite*

34 E-liph'-e-let the son of A-has'-bai, the son of the Ma-ach'-a-thite, E-li'-am the son of ᴿA-hith'-o-phel the Gi'-lo-nite, 15:12

35 Hez'-rai the Car'-mel-ite, Pa'-a-rai the Ar'-bite,

36 I'-gal the son of Nathan of ᴿZo'-bah, Ba'-ni the Gad'-ite, 8:3

37 Ze'-lek the Am'-mon-ite, Na'-ha-ri the Be-e'-roth-ite, armour-bearer to Jo'-ab the son of Ze-ru'-iah,

38 ᴿI'-ra an Ith'-rite, Ga'-reb an Ith'-rite, 1 Cor. 11:28

39 ᴿU-ri'-ah the Hit'-tite: thirty and seven in all. 11:3, 6

24 And again the anger of the LORD was kindled against Israel, and he moved David against them to say, ᴿGo, number Israel and Judah. Num. 26:2

2 For the king said to Jo'-ab the captain of the host, which *was* with him, Go now through all the tribes of Israel, ᴿfrom Dan even to Be'-er–she'-ba, and number ye the people, that I may know the number of the people. Judg. 20:1

3 And Jo'-ab said unto the king, Now the LORD thy God add unto the people, how many soever they be, an hundredfold, and that the eyes of my lord the king may see *it*: but why doth my lord the king ᵀdelight in this thing? *desire*

4 Notwithstanding the king's word ᵀprevailed against Jo'-ab, and against the captains of the host. And Jo'-ab and the captains of the host went out from the presence of the king, to number the people of Israel. *overruled*

5 And they passed over Jordan, and pitched in ᴿAr'-o-er, on the right side of the city that *lieth* in the midst of the river of Gad, and toward Ja'-zer: Deut. 2:36; Josh. 13:9

6 Then they came to Gil'-e-ad, and to the land of Tah'-tim-hod'-shi; and they came to ᴿDan–ja'-an, and about to Zi'-don, Josh. 19:47

7 And came to the strong hold of ᴿTyre, and to all the cities of the ᴮHi'-vites, and of the Ca'-naan-ites: and they went out to the south of Judah, *even* to Be'-er–she'-ba. Josh. 19:29 · Josh. 11:3; Judg. 3:3

8 So when they had gone through all the land, they came to Jerusalem at the end of nine months and twenty days.

9 And Jo'-ab gave up the sum

of the number of the people unto the king: [R]and there were in Israel eight hundred thousand valiant men that drew the sword; and the men of Judah *were* five hundred thousand men.　　　1 Chr. 21:5

10 And David's heart smote him after that he had numbered the people. And David said unto the LORD, [R]I have sinned greatly in that I have done: and now, I beseech thee, O LORD, take away the iniquity of thy servant; for I have done very foolishly.　12:13

11 For when David was up in the morning, the word of the LORD came unto the prophet [R]Gad, David's seer, saying,　1 Sam. 22:5

12 Go and say unto David, Thus saith the LORD, I offer thee three *things*; choose thee one of them, that I may *do it* unto thee.

13 So Gad came to David, and told him, and said unto him, Shall seven years of famine come unto thee in thy land? or wilt thou flee three months before thine enemies, while they pursue thee? or that there be three days' pestilence in thy land? now [T]advise, and see what answer I shall return to him that sent me.　consider

14 And David said unto Gad, I am in a great strait: let us fall now into the hand of the LORD; [R]for his mercies *are* great: and let me not fall into the hand of man.　[Ps. 51:1]

15 So [R]the LORD sent a [T]pestilence upon Israel from the morning even to the time appointed: and there died of the people from Dan even to Be'-er–she'-ba seventy thousand men. 1 Chr. 21:14 · *plague*

16 And when the angel stretched out his hand upon Jerusalem to destroy it, the LORD repented him of the evil, and said to the angel that destroyed the people, It is enough: stay now thine hand. And the angel of the LORD was by the threshingplace of A-rau'-nah the Jeb'-u-site.

17 And David spake unto the LORD when he saw the angel that

smote the people, and said, Lo, [R]I have sinned, and I have done wickedly: but these sheep, what have they done? let thine hand, I pray thee, be against me, and against my father's house. Ps. 74:1

18 And Gad came that day to David, and said unto him, [R]Go up, rear an altar unto the LORD in the threshingfloor of A-rau'-nah the Jeb'-u-site.　1 Chr. 21:18

19 And David, according to the saying of Gad, went up as the LORD commanded.

20 And A-rau'-nah looked, and saw the king and his servants coming on toward him: and A-rau'-nah went out, and bowed himself before the king on his face upon the ground.

21 And A-rau'-nah said, Wherefore is my lord the king come to his servant? [R]And David said, To buy the threshingfloor of thee, to build an altar unto the LORD, that [R]the plague may be stayed from the people. Gen. 23:8–16 · Num. 16:48, 50

22 And A-rau'-nah said unto David, Let my lord the king take and offer up what *seemeth* good unto him: behold, *here be* oxen for burnt sacrifice, and threshing instruments and *other* instruments of the oxen for wood.

23 All these *things* did A-rau'-nah, *as* a king, give unto the king. And A-rau'-nah said unto the king, The LORD thy God [R]accept thee.　[Ezek. 20:40, 41]

24 And the king said unto A-rau'-nah, Nay; but I will surely buy *it* of thee at a price: neither will I offer burnt offerings unto the LORD my God of that which doth cost me nothing. So David bought the threshingfloor and the oxen for fifty shek'-els of silver.

25 And David built there an altar unto the LORD, and offered burnt offerings and peace offerings. [R]So the LORD was intreated for the land, and [R]the plague was stayed from Israel.　21:14 · v. 21

The First Book of the

KINGS

THE first half of First Kings traces the life of Solomon. Under his leadership Israel rises to the peak of her size and glory. Solomon's great accomplishments, including the unsurpassed splendor of the temple which he constructs in Jerusalem, bring him worldwide fame and respect. However, Solomon's zeal for God diminishes in his later years, as pagan wives turn his heart away from worship in the temple of God. As a result, the king with the divided heart leaves behind a divided kingdom. For the next century, the Book of First Kings traces the twin histories of two sets of kings and two nations of disobedient people who are growing indifferent to God's prophets and precepts.

Like the two books of Samuel, the two books of Kings were originally one in the Hebrew Bible. The original title was *Melechim*, "Kings," taken from the first word in 1:1, *Vehamelech*, "Now king." The Septuagint artificially divided the book of Kings in the middle of the story of Ahaziah into two books. It called the books of Samuel "First and Second Kingdoms" and the books of Kings "Third and Fourth Kingdoms." The Septuagint may have divided Samuel, Kings, and Chronicles into two books each because the Greek required a greater amount of scroll space than did the Hebrew. The Latin title for these books is *Liber Regum Tertius et Quartus*, "Third and Fourth Books of Kings."

NOW king David was old *and* stricken in years; and they covered him with clothes, but he ᵀgat no heat.   *could not get warm*

2 Wherefore his servants said unto him, Let there be sought for my lord the king a young virgin: and let her ᵀstand before the king, and let her cherish him, and let her lie in thy bosom, that my lord the king may get heat.   *serve*

3 So they sought for a fair damsel throughout all the coasts of Israel, and found ᴿAb'-i-shag a ᴿShu'-nam-mite, and brought her to the king.   2:17 · 1 Sam. 28:4

4 And the damsel *was* very fair, and cherished the king, and ministered to him: but the king knew her not.

5 Then ᴿAd-o-ni'-jah the ᵀson of Hag'-gith exalted himself, saying, I will be king: and ᴿhe prepared him chariots and horsemen, and fifty men to run before him.   2 Sam. 3:4 · *fourth son* · 2 Sam. 15:1

6 And his father had not ᵀdispleased him at any time in saying, Why hast thou done so? and he also *was a* very goodly *man;* ᴿand

his *mother* bare him after Ab'-sa-lom.   *rebuked* · 2 Sam. 3:3, 4; 1 Chr. 3:2

7 And he conferred with ᴿJo'-ab the son of Ze-ru'-iah, and with ᴿA-bi'-a-thar the priest: and ᴿthey following Ad-o-ni'-jah helped *him.*   1 Chr. 11:6 · 2 Sam. 20:25 · 2:22, 28

8 But ᴿZa'-dok the priest, and Be-na'-iah the son of Je-hoi'-a-da, and Nathan the prophet, and Shim'-e-i, and Re'-i, and the mighty men which *belonged* to David, were not with Ad-o-ni'-jah.   2:35

9 And Ad-o-ni'-jah slew sheep and oxen and fat cattle by the stone of ᵀZo'-he-leth, which *is* by ᴿEn-ro'-gel, and called all his brethren the king's sons, and all the men of Judah the king's servants: Lit. *Serpent* · Josh. 15:7; 18:16

10 But Nathan the prophet, and Be-na'-iah, and the mighty men, and ᴿSolomon his brother, he called not.   2 Sam. 12:24

11 Wherefore Nathan spake unto Bath–she'-ba the mother of Solomon, saying, Hast thou not heard that Ad-o-ni'-jah the son of ᴿHag'-gith doth reign, and David our lord knoweth *it* not?   2 Sam. 3:4

12 Now therefore come, let me, I pray thee, give thee counsel, that thou mayest save thine own life, and the life of thy son Solomon.

13 Go and get thee in unto king David, and say unto him, Didst not thou, my lord, O king, swear unto thine handmaid, saying, ᴿAssuredly Solomon thy son shall reign after me, and he shall sit upon my throne? why then doth Ad-o-ni'-jah reign?   v. 30; 1 Chr. 22:9–13

14 Behold, while thou yet talkest there with the king, I also will come in after thee, and confirm thy words.

15 And Bath–she'-ba went in unto the king into the chamber: and the king was very old; and Ab'-i-shag the Shu'-nam-mite ministered unto the king.

16 And Bath–she'-ba bowed, and did ᵀobeisance unto the king. And the king said, What ᵀwouldest thou?   homage · is your wish

17 And she said unto him, My lord, ᴿthou swarest by the LORD thy God unto thine handmaid, saying, Assuredly Solomon thy son shall reign after me, and he shall sit upon my throne.   vv. 13, 30

18 And now, behold, Ad-o-ni'-jah reigneth; and now, my lord the king, thou knowest it not:

19 ᴿAnd he hath slain oxen and fat cattle and sheep in abundance, and hath called all the sons of the king, and A-bi'-a-thar the priest, and Jo'-ab the captain of the host: but Solomon thy servant hath he not called.   vv. 7–9, 25

20 And thou, my lord, O king, the eyes of all Israel are upon thee, that thou shouldest tell them who shall sit on the throne of my lord the king after him.

21 Otherwise it shall come to pass, when my lord the king ᴿshall sleep with his fathers, that I and my son Solomon shall be counted offenders.   2:10; 2 Sam. 7:12

22 And, lo, while she yet talked with the king, Nathan the prophet also came in.

23 And they told the king, saying, Behold Nathan the prophet.

And when he was come in before the king, he bowed himself before the king with his face to the ground.

24 And Nathan said, My lord, O king, hast thou said, Ad-o-ni'-jah shall reign after me, and he shall sit upon my throne?

25 ᴿFor he is gone down this day, and hath slain oxen and fat cattle and sheep in abundance, and hath called all the king's sons, and the captains of the host, and A-bi'-a-thar the priest; and, behold, they eat and drink before him, and say, ᴿGod save king Ad-o-ni'-jah.   vv. 9, 19 · 1 Sam. 10:24

26 But me, even me thy servant, and Za'-dok the priest, and Be-na'-iah the son of Je-hoi'-a-da, and thy servant Solomon, hath he not called.

27 Is this thing done by my lord the king, and thou hast not shewed it unto thy servant, who should sit on the throne of my lord the king after him?

28 Then king David answered and said, Call me Bath–she'-ba. And she came into the king's presence, and stood before the king.

29 And the king sware, and said, ᴿAs the LORD liveth, that hath redeemed my soul out of all distress,   2 Sam. 4:9; 12:5

30 Even as I sware unto thee by the LORD God of Israel, saying, Assuredly Solomon thy son shall reign after me, and he shall sit upon my throne in my stead; even so will I certainly do this day.

31 Then Bath–she'-ba bowed with her face to the earth, and did ᵀreverence to the king, and said, ᴿLet my lord king David live for ever.   homage · Neh. 2:3; Dan. 2:4; 3:9

32 And king David said, Call me Za'-dok the priest, and Nathan the prophet, and Be-na'-iah the son of Je-hoi'-a-da. And they came before the king.

33 The king also said unto them, Take with you the servants of your lord, and cause Solomon my son to ride upon mine own mule, and bring him down to Gi'-hon:

34 And let Za'-dok the priest and Nathan the prophet ^Ranoint him there king over Israel: and blow ye with the trumpet, and say, God save king Solomon.   19:16

35 Then ye shall come up after him, that he may come and sit upon my throne; for he shall be king in my stead: and I have appointed him to be ruler over Israel and over Judah.

36 And Be-na'-iah the son of Je-hoi'-a-da answered the king, and said, A'-men: the LORD God of my lord the king say so too.

37 As the LORD hath been with my lord the king, even so be he with Solomon, and ^Rmake his throne greater than the throne of my lord king David.   v. 47

38 So Za'-dok the priest, and Nathan the prophet, ^Rand Be-na'-iah the son of Je-hoi'-a-da, and the ^RCher'-e-thites, and the Pel'-e-thites, went down, and caused Solomon to ride upon king David's mule, and brought him to Gi'-hon.   2 Sam. 8:18 · 2 Sam. 20:7

39 And Za'-dok the priest took an horn of oil out of the tabernacle, and ^Ranointed Solomon. And they blew the trumpet; ^Rand all the people said, God save king Solomon.   1 Chr. 29:22 · 1 Sam. 10:24

40 And all the people came up after him, and the people piped with pipes, and rejoiced with great joy, so that the earth ^Trent with the sound of them.   was split

41 And Ad-o-ni'-jah and all the guests that were with him heard it as they had made an end of eating. And when Jo'-ab heard the sound of the trumpet, he said, Wherefore is this noise of the city being in an uproar?

42 And while he yet spake, behold, Jonathan the son of A-bi'-a-thar the priest came: and Ad-o-ni'-jah said unto him, Come in; for thou art a ^Tvaliant man, and bringest good tidings.   prominent

43 And Jonathan answered and said to Ad-o-ni'-jah, Verily our lord king David hath made Solomon king.

44 And the king hath sent with him Za'-dok the priest, and Nathan the prophet, and Be-na'-iah the son of Je-hoi'-a-da, and the Cher'-e-thites, and the Pel'-e-thites, and they have caused him to ride upon the king's mule:

45 And Za'-dok the priest and Nathan the prophet have anointed him king in Gi'-hon: and they are come up from thence rejoicing, so that the city rang again. This is the noise that ye have heard.

46 And also Solomon ^Rsitteth on the throne of the kingdom.   2:12

47 And moreover the king's servants came to bless our lord king David, saying, ^RGod make the name of Solomon better than thy name, and make his throne greater than thy throne. And the king bowed himself upon the bed.   v. 37

48 And also thus said the king, Blessed be the LORD God of Israel, which hath ^Rgiven one to sit on my throne this day, mine eyes even seeing ^Rit.   3:6 · 2 Sam. 7:12

49 And all the guests that were with Ad-o-ni'-jah were afraid, and rose up, and went every man his way.

50 And Ad-o-ni'-jah feared because of Solomon, and arose, and went, and ^Rcaught hold on the horns of the altar.   2:28; Ex. 27:2; 30:10

51 And it was told Solomon, saying, Behold, Ad-o-ni'-jah feareth king Solomon: for, lo, he hath caught hold on the horns of the altar, saying, Let king Solomon swear unto me to day that he will not slay his servant with the sword.

52 And Solomon said, If he will shew himself a worthy man, there shall not an hair of him fall to the earth: but if wickedness shall be found in him, he shall die.

53 So king Solomon sent, and they brought him down from the altar. And he came and ^Tbowed himself to king Solomon: and Solomon said unto him, Go to thine house.   fell before

2 Now ^Rthe days of David drew nigh that he should die; and

he ^Tcharged Solomon his son, saying, Gen. 47:29; Deut. 31:14 · *commanded*

2 I go the way of all the earth: ^Rbe thou strong therefore, and shew thyself a man; 1 Chr. 22:13

3 And keep the charge of the LORD thy God, to walk in his ways, to keep his statutes, and his commandments, and his judgments, and his testimonies, as it is written in the law of Moses, that thou mayest ^Rprosper in all that thou doest, and whithersoever thou turnest thyself: [Deut. 29:9]

4 That the LORD may continue his word which he spake concerning me, saying, If thy children take heed to their way, to walk before me in truth with all their heart and with all their soul, ^Rthere shall not fail thee (said he) a man on the throne of Israel. 8:25

5 Moreover thou knowest also what Jo'-ab the son of Ze-ru'-iah ^Rdid to me, *and* what he did to the two captains of the hosts of Israel, unto Abner the son of Ner, and unto Am'-a-sa the son of Je'-ther, whom he slew, and shed the blood of war in peace, and put the blood of war upon his girdle that *was* about his loins, and in his shoes that *were* on his feet. 2 Sam. 3:39

6 Do therefore ^Raccording to thy wisdom, and let not his ^Thoar head go down to the grave in peace. v. 9; Prov. 20:26 · *gray hair*

7 But shew kindness unto the sons of ^RBar-zil'-lai the Gil'-e-ad-ite, and let them be of those that eat at thy table: for so they came to me when I fled because of Ab'-sa-lom thy brother. 2 Sam. 19:31–39

8 And, behold, *thou hast* with thee Shim'-e-i the son of Ge'-ra, a Benjamite of Ba-hu'-rim, which cursed me with a grievous curse in the day when I went to Ma-ha-na'-im: but ^Rhe came down to meet me at Jordan, and ^RI sware to him by the LORD, saying, I will not put thee to death with the sword. 2 Sam. 19:18 · 2 Sam. 19:23

9 Now therefore ^Rhold him not guiltless: for thou *art* a wise man, and knowest what thou oughtest to do unto him; but his hoar head ^Rbring thou down to the grave with blood. Ex. 20:7 · Gen. 42:38; 44:31

10 So ^RDavid slept with his fathers, and was buried in ^Rthe city of David. 1:21; Acts 2:29; 13:36 · 3:1

11 And the days that David reigned over Israel *were* forty years: seven years reigned he in He'-bron, and thirty and three years reigned he in Jerusalem.

12 ^RThen sat Solomon upon the throne of David his father; and his kingdom was ^Restablished greatly. 1:46; 1 Chr. 29:23 · v. 46; 2 Chr. 1:1

13 And Ad-o-ni'-jah the son of Hag'-gith came to Bath–she'-ba the mother of Solomon. And she said, Comest thou peaceably? And he said, Peaceably.

14 He said moreover, I have somewhat to say unto thee. And she said, Say on.

15 And he said, Thou knowest that the kingdom was mine, and *that* all Israel set their faces on me, that I should reign: howbeit the kingdom is turned about, and is become my brother's: for ^Rit was his from the LORD. [Dan. 2:21]

16 And now I ask one petition of thee, deny me not. And she said unto him, Say on.

17 And he said, Speak, I pray thee, unto Solomon the king, (for he will not say thee nay,) that he give me ^RAb'-i-shag the Shu'-nam-mite to wife. 1:3, 4

18 And Bath–she'-ba said, Well; I will speak for thee unto the king.

19 Bath–she'-ba therefore went unto king Solomon, to speak unto him for Ad-o-ni'-jah. And the king rose up to meet her, and bowed himself unto her, and sat down on his throne, and caused a seat to be set for the king's mother; ^Rand she sat on his right hand. Ps. 45:9

20 Then she said, I desire one small petition of thee; *I pray thee,* say me not nay. And the king said unto her, Ask on, my mother: for I will not say thee nay.

21 And she said, Let Ab'-i-shag the Shu'-nam-mite be given to Ad-o-ni'-jah thy brother to wife.

22 And king Solomon answered and said unto his mother, And why dost thou ask Ab'-i-shag the Shu-'nam-mite for Ad-o-ni'-jah? ask for him the kingdom also; for he *is* mine ^Relder brother; even for him, and for ^RA-bi'-a-thar the priest, and for Jo'-ab the son of Ze-ru'-iah.   v. 15; 1:6; 1 Chr. 3:2, 5 · 1:7

23 Then king Solomon sware by the Lord, saying, ^RGod do so to me, and more also, if Ad-o-ni'-jah have not spoken this word against his own life.   Ruth 1:17

24 Now therefore, *as* the Lord liveth, which hath established me, and set me on the throne of David my father, and who hath made me an house, as he ^Rpromised, Ad-o-ni'-jah shall be put to death this day.   2 Sam. 7:11, 13; 1 Chr. 22:10

25 And king Solomon sent by the hand of ^RBe-na'-iah the son of Je-hoi'-a-da; and he fell upon him that he died.   4:4; 2 Sam. 8:18

26 And unto A-bi'-a-thar the priest said the king, Get thee to ^RAn'-a-thoth, unto thine own fields; for thou *art* worthy of death: but I will not at this time put thee to death, ^Rbecause thou barest the ark of the Lord God before David my father, and because thou hast been afflicted in all wherein my father was afflicted.   Josh. 21:18; Jer. 1:1 · 1 Sam. 22:23; 23:6

27 So Solomon thrust out A-bi'-a-thar from being priest unto the Lord; that he might ^Rfulfil the word of the Lord, which he spake concerning the house of E'-li in Shi'-loh.   1 Sam. 2:31-35

28 Then tidings came to Jo'-ab: for Jo'-ab ^Rhad turned after Ad-o-ni'-jah, though he turned not after Ab'-sa-lom. And Jo'-ab fled unto the tabernacle of the Lord, and ^Rcaught^T hold on the horns of the altar.   1:7 · 1:50 · *took hold of*

29 And it was told king Solomon that Jo'-ab was fled unto the tabernacle of the Lord; and, behold, *he is* by the altar. Then Solomon sent Be-na'-iah the son of Je-hoi'-a-da, saying, Go, fall upon him.

30 And Be-na'-iah came to the tabernacle of the Lord, and said unto him, Thus saith the king, ^RCome forth. And he said, Nay; but I will die here. And Be-na'-iah brought the king word again, saying, Thus said Jo'-ab, and thus he answered me.   [Ex. 21:14]

31 And the king said unto him, ^RDo as he hath said, and fall upon him, and bury him; ^Rthat thou mayest take away the innocent blood, which Jo'-ab shed, from me, and from the house of my father.   [Ex. 21:14] · [Num. 35:33]

32 And the Lord ^Rshall return his blood upon his own head, who fell upon two men more righteous and better than he, and slew them with the sword, my father David not knowing *thereof, to wit,* Abner the son of Ner, captain of the host of Israel, and ^RAm'-a-sa the son of Je'-ther, captain of the host of Judah.   Judg. 9:24, 57 · 2 Sam. 20:9, 10

33 Their blood shall therefore return upon the head of Jo'-ab, and upon the head of his seed for ever: but upon David, and upon his seed, and upon his house, and upon his throne, shall there be peace for ever from the Lord.

34 So Be-na'-iah the son of Je-hoi'-a-da went up, and fell upon him, and slew him: and he was buried in his own house in the wilderness.

35 And the king put Be-na'-iah the son of Je-hoi'-a-da in his room over the host: and ^RZa'-dok the priest did the king put in the room of ^RA-bi'-a-thar.   4:4; 1 Sam. 2:35 · v. 27

36 And the king sent and called for ^RShim'-e-i, and said unto him, Build thee an house in Jerusalem, and dwell there, and go not forth thence any whither.   2 Sam. 16:5-13

37 For it shall be, *that* on the day thou goest out, and passest over the brook Kid'-ron, thou shalt know for certain that thou shalt surely die: ^Rthy blood shall be upon thine own head.   Lev. 20:9

38 And Shim'-e-i said unto the king, The saying *is* good: as my lord the king hath said, so will thy

servant do. And Shim'-e-i dwelt in Jerusalem many days.

39 And it came to pass at the end of three years, that two of the servants of Shim'-e-i ran away unto ᴿA'-chish son of Ma'-a-chah king of Gath. And they told Shim'-e-i, saying, Behold, thy servants *be* in Gath.   1 Sam. 27:2

40 And Shim'-e-i arose, and saddled his ass, and went to Gath to A'-chish to seek his servants: and Shim'-e-i went, and brought his servants from Gath.

41 And it was told Solomon that Shim'-e-i had gone from Jerusalem to Gath, and was come again.

42 And the king sent and called for Shim'-e-i, and said unto him, Did I not make thee to swear by the LORD, and ᵀprotested unto thee, saying, Know for a certain, on the day thou goest out, and walkest abroad any whither, that thou shalt surely die? and thou saidst unto me, The word *that* I have heard *is* good.   *warn you*

43 Why then hast thou not kept the oath of the LORD, and the commandment that I have charged thee with?

44 The king said moreover to Shim'-e-i, Thou knowest all the wickedness which thine heart is privy to, that thou didst to David my father: therefore the LORD shall ᴿreturn thy wickedness upon thine own head;   Ps. 7:16; Ezek. 17:19

45 And king Solomon *shall be* blessed, and ᴿthe throne of David shall be established before the LORD for ever.   2 Sam. 7:13; [Prov. 25:5]

46 So the king commanded Bena'-iah the son of Je-hoi'-a-da; which went out, and fell upon him, that he died. And the ᴿkingdom was established in the hand of Solomon.   v. 12; 2 Chr. 1:1

3 And ᴿSolomon made affinity with Pharaoh king of Egypt, and took Pharaoh's daughter, and brought her into the city of David, until he had made an end of building his own house, and the house of the LORD, and the wall of Jerusalem round about.   7:8; 9:24

2 ᴿOnly the people sacrificed in high places, because there was no house built unto the name of the LORD, until those days.   11:7; 22:43

3 And Solomon ᴿloved the LORD, ᴿwalking in the statutes of David his father: only he sacrificed and burnt incense in high places.   [Rom. 8:28] · [vv. 6, 14]

4 And ᴿthe king went to Gib'-e-on to sacrifice there; ᴿfor that *was* the great high place: a thousand burnt offerings did Solomon offer upon that altar.   2 Chr. 1:3 · 1 Chr. 16:39

5 In Gib'-e-on the LORD appeared to Solomon ᴿin a dream by night: and God said, Ask what I shall give thee.   Matt. 1:20; 2:13

6 And Solomon said, Thou hast shewed unto thy servant David my father great mercy, ac-cording as he ᴿwalked before thee in truth, and in righteousness, and in uprightness of heart with thee; and thou hast kept for him this great kindness, that thou hast given him a son to sit on his throne, as *it is* this day.   2:4; 9:4; 2 Kin. 20:3

7 And now, O LORD my God, thou hast made thy servant king instead of David my father: and I *am but* a ᴿlittle child: I know not *how* to go out or come in.   Jer. 1:6, 7

8 And thy servant *is* in the midst of thy people which thou hast chosen, a great people, ᴿthat cannot be numbered nor counted for multitude.   Gen. 13:6; 15:5; 22:17

9 ᴿGive therefore thy servant an understanding heart ᴿto judge thy people, that I may ᴿdiscern between good and bad: for who is able to judge this thy so great a people? [James 1:5] · Ps. 72:1 · [Heb. 5:14]

10 And the speech pleased the LORD, that Solomon had asked this thing.

11 And God said unto him, Because thou hast asked this thing, and hast ᴿnot asked for thyself long life; neither hast asked riches for thyself, nor hast asked the life of thine enemies; but hast asked for thyself understanding to discern judgment;   [James 4:3]

12 Behold, I have done accord-

ing to thy words: lo, I have given thee a wise and an understanding heart; so that there was none like thee before thee, neither after thee shall any arise like unto thee.

13 And I have also given thee that which thou hast not asked, both riches, and honour: so that there shall not be any among the kings like unto thee all thy days.

14 And if thou wilt walk in my ways, to keep my statutes and my commandments, as thy father David did walk, then I will ᴿlengthen thy days.   Ps. 91:16; Prov. 3:2

15 And Solomon ᴿawoke; and, behold, it was a dream. And he came to Jerusalem, and stood before the ark of the covenant of the LORD, and offered up burnt offerings, and offered peace offerings, and ᴿmade a feast to all his servants.   Gen. 41:7 · Dan. 5:1; Mark 6:21

16 Then came there two women, that were harlots, unto the king, and ᴿstood before him.   Num. 27:2

17 And the one woman said, O my lord, I and this woman dwell in one house; and I was delivered of a child with her in the house.

18 And it came to pass the third day after that I was delivered, that this woman was delivered also: and we were together; there was no ᵀstranger with us in the house, save we two in the house.   no one

19 And this woman's child died in the night; because she ᵀoverlaid it.   lay on him

20 And she arose at midnight, and took my son from beside me, while thine handmaid slept, and laid it in her bosom, and laid her dead child in my bosom.

21 And when I rose in the morning to give my child suck, behold, it was dead: but when I had considered it in the morning, behold, it was not my son, which I did bear.

22 And the other woman said, Nay; but the living is my son, and the dead is thy son. And this said, No; but the dead is thy son, and the living is my son. Thus they spake before the king.

23 Then said the king, The one saith, This is my son that liveth, and thy son is the dead: and the other saith, Nay; but thy son is the dead, and my son is the living.

24 And the king said, Bring me a sword. And they brought a sword before the king.

25 And the king said, Divide the living child in two, and give half to the one, and half to the other.

26 Then spake the woman whose the living child was unto the king, for ᴿher bowels yearned upon her son, and she said, O my lord, give her the living child, and in no wise slay it. But the other said, Let it be neither mine nor thine, but divide it.   Jer. 31:20

27 Then the king answered and said, Give her the living child, and in no wise slay it: she is the mother thereof.

28 And all Israel heard of the judgment which the king had judged; and they feared the king: for they saw that the wisdom of God was in him, to do judgment.

4 So king Solomon was king over all Israel.

2 And these were the princes which he had; Az-a-ri'-ah the son of Za'-dok the priest,

3 El-i-ho'-reph and A-hi'-ah, the sons of Shi'-sha, scribes; ᴿJe-hosh'-a-phat the son of A-hi'-lud, the recorder.   2 Sam. 8:16; 20:24

4 And ᴿBe-na'-iah the son of Je-hoi'-a-da was over the host: and Za'-dok and ᴿA-bi'-a-thar were the priests: 2:35 · 2:27

5 And Az-a-ri'-ah the son of Nathan was over the officers: and Za'-bud the son of Nathan was principal officer, and ᴿthe king's friend: 2 Sam. 15:37; 16:16; 1 Chr. 27:33

6 And A-hi'-shar was over the household: and ᴿAd-o-ni'-ram the son of Ab'-da was over the ᵀtribute.   5:14 · labour force

7 And Solomon had twelve officers over all Israel, which provided victuals for the king and his household: each man his month in a year made provision.

8 And these *are* their names:
[T]The son of Hur, in mount E'-
phra-im: Heb. *Ben-hur*
9 The son of De'-kar, in Ma'-
kaz, and in Sha-al'-bim, and Beth–
she'-mesh, and E'-lon–beth–ha'-
nan:
10 The son of He'-sed, in Ar'-u-
both; to him *pertained* So'-choh,
and all the land of He'-pher:
11 The son of A-bin'-a-dab, in all
the region of Dor; which had Ta'-
phath the daughter of Solomon to
wife:
12 Ba'-a-na the son of A-hi'-lud;
to *him pertained* Ta'-a-nach and
Me-gid'-do, and all Beth–she'-an,
which *is* by Zar'-ta-nah beneath
Jez'-re-el, from Beth–she'-an to
A'-bel–me-ho'-lah, *even* unto *the
place that is* beyond Jok'-ne-am:
13 The son of Ge'-ber, in Ra'-
moth–gil'-e-ad; to him *pertained*
[R]the towns of Ja'-ir the son of Ma-
nas'-seh, which *are* in Gil'-e-ad;
to him *also pertained* [R]the region
of Ar'-gob, which *is* in Ba'-shan,
threescore great cities with walls
and brasen bars: 1 Chr. 2:22 · Deut. 3:4
14 A-hin'-a-dab the son of Id'-do
[T]had Ma-ha-na'-im: *in*
15 A-him'-a-az *was* in Naph'-ta-
li; he also took Bas'-math the
daughter of Solomon to wife:
16 Ba'-a-nah the son of Hu'-shai
was in Asher and in A'-loth:
17 Je-hosh'-a-phat the son of Pa-
ru'-ah, in Is'-sa-char:
18 [R]Shim'-e-i the son of E'-lah,
in Benjamin: 1:8
19 Ge'-ber the son of U'-ri *was*
in the country of Gil'-e-ad, *in* [R]the
country of Si'-hon king of the
Am'-or-ites, and of Og king of Ba'-
shan; and *he was* the only officer
which *was* in the land. Deut. 3:8–10
20 Judah and Israel *were* many,
[R]as the sand which *is* by the sea
in multitude, eating and drinking,
and making merry. Gen. 22:17; 32:12
21 And Solomon reigned over
all kingdoms from the river unto
the land of the Phi-lis'-tines, and
unto the border of Egypt: they
brought presents, and served
Solomon all the days of his life.

22 [R]And Solomon's [T]provision
for one day was thirty measures
of fine flour, and threescore measures of meal,   Neh. 5:18 · Lit. *bread*
23 Ten fat oxen, and twenty
oxen out of the pastures, and an
hundred sheep, beside harts, and
roebucks, and fallowdeer, and fatted fowl.
24 For he had dominion over all
the *region* on this side the river,
from Tiph'-sah even to Az'-zah,
over [R]all the kings on this side the
river: and [R]he had peace on all
sides round about him. Ps. 72:11 · 5:4
25 And Judah and Israel [R]dwelt
safely, [R]every man under his vine
and under his fig tree, from Dan
even to Be'-er–she'-ba, all the
days of Solomon. [Jer. 23:6] · [Mic. 4:4]
26 And [R]Solomon had forty
thousand stalls of [R]horses for his
chariots, and twelve thousand
horsemen.   2 Chr. 1:14 · [Deut. 17:16]
27 And [R]those officers provided
victual for king Solomon, and for
all that came unto king Solomon's
table, every man in his month:
they lacked nothing.   v. 7
28 Barley also and straw for the
horses and [T]dromedaries brought
they unto the place where *the officers* were, every man according to
his charge.   *swift steeds*
29 And [R]God gave Solomon wisdom and understanding exceeding much, and largeness of heart,
even as the sand that *is* on the sea
shore.   3:12
30 And Solomon's wisdom ex-
celled the wisdom of all the children of the east country, and all
[R]the wisdom of Egypt. Is. 19:11, 12
31 For he was [R]wiser than all
men; [R]than E'-than the Ez'-ra-hite,
[R]and He'-man, and Chal'-col, and
Dar'-da, the sons of Ma'-hol: and
his fame was in all nations round
about. 3:12 · Ps. 89:title · Ps. 88:title
32 And [R]he spake three thou-
sand proverbs: and his songs
were a thousand and five. Prov. 1:1
33 And he spake of trees, from
the cedar tree that *is* in Leb'-a-
non even unto the hyssop that
springeth out of the wall: he

spake also of beasts, and of fowl, and of creeping things, and of fishes.

34 And ᴿthere came of all people to hear the wisdom of Solomon, from all kings of the earth, which had heard of his wisdom.   10:1

5 And ᴿHiram king of Tyre sent his servants unto Solomon; for he had heard that they had anointed him king in the room of his father: for Hiram was ever a lover of David.   vv. 10, 18

2 And ᴿSolomon sent to Hiram, saying,   2 Chr. 2:3

3 ᴿThou knowest how that David my father could not build an house unto the name of the LORD his God ᴿfor the wars which were about him on every side, until the LORD put them under the soles of his feet.   1 Chr. 28:2, 3 · 1 Chr. 22:8; 28:3

4 But now the LORD my God hath given me ᴿrest on every side, so that there is neither adversary nor evil occurrent.   4:24; 1 Chr. 22:9

5 And, behold, I purpose to build an house unto the name of the LORD my God, as the LORD spake unto David my father, saying, Thy son, whom I will set upon thy throne in thy room, he shall build an house unto my name.

6 Now therefore command thou that they hew me ᴿcedar trees out of Leb'-a-non; and my servants shall be with thy servants: and unto thee will I ᵀgive hire for thy servants according to all that thou shalt ᵀappoint: for thou knowest that there is not among us any that ᵀcan skill to hew timber like unto the Si-do'-ni-ans.   2 Chr. 2:8, 10 · pay wages · say · has

7 And it came to pass, when Hiram heard the words of Solomon, that he rejoiced greatly, and said, Blessed be the LORD this day, which hath given unto David a wise son over this great people.

8 And Hiram sent to Solomon, saying, I have considered the things which thou sentest to me for: and I will do all thy desire concerning timber of cedar, and concerning timber of fir.

9 My servants shall bring them down from Leb'-a-non unto the sea: and I will convey them by sea in floats unto the place that thou shalt appoint me, and will cause them to be discharged there, and thou shalt receive them: and thou shalt accomplish my desire, in giving food for my household.

10 So Hiram gave Solomon cedar trees and fir trees according to all his desire.

11 ᴿAnd Solomon gave Hiram twenty thousand ᵀmeasures of wheat for food to his household, and twenty ᵀmeasures of pure oil: thus gave Solomon to Hiram year by year.   2 Chr. 2:10 · Heb. kor

12 And the LORD gave Solomon wisdom, ᴿas he promised him: and there was peace between Hiram and Solomon; and they two made a league together.   3:12

13 And king Solomon raised a levy out of all Israel; and the levy was thirty thousand men.

14 And he sent them to Leb'-a-non, ten thousand a month ᵀby courses: a month they were in Leb'-a-non, and two months at home: and ᴿAd-o-ni'-ram was over the levy.   in shifts · 12:18

15 ᴿAnd Solomon had threescore and ten thousand that bare burdens, and fourscore thousand hewers in the mountains;   9:20–22

16 Beside the ᴿchief of Solomon's officers which were over the work, three thousand and three hundred, which ᵀruled over the people that wrought in the work.   9:23 · supervised

17 And the king commanded, and they brought great stones, costly stones, and ᴿhewed stones, to lay the foundation of the ᵀhouse.   6:7; 1 Chr. 22:2 · temple

18 And Solomon's builders and Hiram's builders did hew them, and the ᵀstonesquarers: so they prepared timber and stones to build the ᵀhouse. Or Gebalites · temple

6 And it came to pass in the four hundred and eightieth year after the children of Israel were come out of the land of

Egypt, in the fourth year of Solomon's reign over Israel, in the month Zif, which *is* the second month, that ᴿhe began to build the house of the LORD.　　　Acts 7:47

2 And ᴿthe house which king Solomon built for the LORD, the length thereof *was* threescore cubits, and the breadth thereof twenty *cubits*, and the height thereof thirty cubits.　　　Ezek. 41:1

3 And the porch before the temple of the house, twenty cubits *was* the length thereof, according to the breadth of the house; *and* ten cubits *was* the breadth thereof before the house.

4 And for the house he made windows of narrow lights.

5 And against the wall of the house he built chambers round about, *against* the walls of the house round about, *both* of the temple and of the oracle: and he made chambers round about:

6 The nethermost chamber *was* five cubits broad, and the middle *was* six cubits broad, and the third *was* seven cubits broad: for without in the wall of the house he made ᵀnarrowed rests round about, that *the beams* should not be fastened in the walls of the house.　　　*narrow ledges*

7 And ᴿthe house, when it was in building, was built of stone made ready before it was brought thither: so that there was neither hammer nor axe *nor* any tool of iron heard in the house, while it was in building. Ex. 20:25; Deut. 27:5, 6

8 The door for the middle chamber *was* in the right side of the house: and they went up with winding stairs into the middle *chamber,* and out of the middle into the third.

9 So he built the house, and finished it; and covered the house with beams and boards of cedar.

10 And *then* he built chambers against all the house, five cubits high: and they rested on the house with timber of cedar.

11 And the word of the LORD came to Solomon, saying,

12 *Concerning* this house which thou art in building, ᴿif thou wilt walk in my statutes, and execute my judgments, and keep all my commandments to walk in them; then will I perform my word with thee, ᴿwhich I spake unto David thy father:　2:4; 9:4 · [2 Sam. 7:13]

13 And ᴿI will dwell among the children of Israel, and will not forsake my people Israel.　Ex. 25:8

14 So Solomon built the house, and finished it.

15 And he built the walls of the house within with boards of ce-dar, both the floor of the house, and the walls of the cieling: *and* he covered *them* on the inside with wood, and covered the floor of the house with planks of fir.

16 And he built twenty cubits on the sides of the house, both the floor and the walls with boards of cedar: he even built *them* for it within, *even* for the oracle, *even* for the ᴿmost holy *place.*　Heb. 9:3

17 And the house, that *is,* the temple before it, was forty cubits *long.*

18 And the cedar of the house within *was* carved with ᵀknops and open flowers: all *was* cedar; there was no stone seen.　*gourds*

19 And the ᵀoracle he prepared in the house within, to set there the ark of the covenant of the LORD.　Heb. *debir;* v. 5

20 And the oracle in the forepart *was* twenty cubits in length, and twenty cubits in breadth, and twenty cubits in the height thereof: and he overlaid it with pure gold; and so covered the altar which *was* of cedar.

21 So Solomon overlaid the house within with pure gold: and he made a partition by the chains of gold before the oracle; and he overlaid it with gold.

22 And the whole house he overlaid with gold, until he had finished all the house: also ᴿthe whole altar that *was* by the oracle he overlaid with gold.　Ex. 30:1, 3, 6

23 And within the oracle he

made two cher'-u-bims *of* olive ^Ttree, *each* ten cubits high.   *wood*

24 And five cubits *was* the one wing of the cherub, and five cubits the other wing of the cherub: from the uttermost part of the one wing unto the uttermost part of the other *were* ten cubits.

25 And the other cherub *was* ten cubits: both the cher'-u-bims *were* of one measure and one size.

26 The height of the one cherub *was* ten cubits, and so *was it* of the other cherub.

27 And he set the cher'-u-bims within the inner house: and ^Rthey stretched forth the wings of the cher'-u-bims, so that the wing of the one touched the *one* wall, and the wing of the other cherub touched the other wall; and their wings touched one another in the midst of the house.   Ex. 25:20; 37:9

28 And he overlaid the cher'-u-bims with gold.

29 And he carved all the walls of the house round about with carved ^Rfigures of cher'-u-bims and palm trees and open flowers, within and without.   Ex. 36:8, 35

30 And the floor of the house he overlaid with gold, within and without.

31 And for the entering of the oracle he made doors *of* olive tree: the lintel *and* side posts *were* ^Ta fifth part *of the wall*.   Or *five-sided*

32 The two doors also *were of* olive tree; and he carved upon them carvings of cher'-u-bims and palm trees and open flowers, and overlaid *them* with gold, and spread gold upon the cher'-u-bims, and upon the palm trees.

33 So also made he for the door of the ^Ttemple posts *of* olive tree, a fourth part *of the wall*.   *sanctuary*

34 And the two doors *were of* ^Tfir tree: the ^Rtwo leaves of the one door *were* folding, and the two leaves of the other door *were* folding.   *cypress* · Ezek. 41:23–25

35 And he carved *thereon* cher'-u-bims and palm trees and open flowers: and covered *them* with gold fitted upon the carved work.

36 And he built the ^Rinner court with three rows of hewed stone, and a row of cedar beams.   7:12

37 ^RIn the fourth year was the foundation of the house of the LORD laid, in the month Zif: v. 1

38 And in the eleventh year, in the month Bul, which *is* the eighth month, was the house finished throughout all the parts thereof, and according to all the fashion of it. So was he ^Rseven years in building it.   v. 1; 5:5; 8:19; 2 Sam. 7:13

7 But Solomon was building his own house ^Rthirteen years, and he finished all his house.   3:1

2 He built also the ^Rhouse of the forest of Leb'-a-non: the length thereof *was* an hundred cubits, and the breadth thereof fifty cubits, and the height thereof thirty cubits, upon four rows of cedar pillars, with cedar beams upon the pillars.   10:17, 21; 2 Chr. 9:16

3 And *it was* ^Tcovered with cedar above upon the beams, that *lay* on forty five pillars, fifteen *in* a row.   *above the beams*

4 And *there were* windows *in* three rows, and light *was* against light *in* three ^Tranks.   *rows*

5 And all the ^Tdoors and posts *were* square, with the windows: and light *was* against light *in* three ranks.   *doorways*

6 And he made a ^Tporch of pillars; the length thereof *was* fifty cubits, and the breadth thereof thirty cubits: and the ^Tporch *was* before them: and the *other* pillars and ^Tthe thick beam *were* before them.   *hall · portico with pillars · a canopy*

7 Then he made a porch for the throne where he might judge, *even* the porch of judgment: and it *was* covered with cedar from one side of the floor to the other.

8 And his house where he dwelt *had* another court within the porch, *which* was of the like work. Solomon made also an house for Pharaoh's daughter, ^Rwhom he had taken *to* wife, like unto this ^Tporch.   3:1; 9:24 · *hall*

9 All these *were of* costly stones, according to the measures

of hewed stones, sawed with saws, within and without, even from the foundation unto the coping, and so on the outside toward the great court.

10 And the foundation *was of* costly stones, even great stones, stones of ten cubits, and stones of eight cubits.

11 And above *were* costly stones, after the measures of hewed stones, and cedars.

12 And the great court round about *was* with three rows of hewed stones, and a row of cedar beams, both for the inner court of the house of the LORD, ^Rand for the porch of the house.   John 10:23

13 And king Solomon sent and fetched Hiram out of Tyre.

14 ^RHe *was* a widow's son of the tribe of Naph'-ta-li, and ^Rhis father *was* a man of Tyre, a worker in brass: and ^Rhe was filled with wisdom, and understanding, and cunning to work all works in brass. And he came to king Solomon, and wrought all his work.   2 Chr. 2:14 · 2 Chr. 4:16 · Ex. 31:3

15 For he cast two pillars of brass, of eighteen cubits high apiece: and a line of twelve cubits did compass either of them about.

16 And he made two ^Tchapiters *of* molten brass, to set upon the tops of the pillars: the height of the one chapiter *was* five cubits, and the height of the other chapiter *was* five cubits: *capitals*

17 *And* nets of checker work, and wreaths of chain work, for the chapiters which *were* upon the top of the pillars; seven for the one chapiter, and seven for the other chapiter.

18 And he made the pillars, and two rows round about upon the one network, to cover the chapiters that *were* upon the top, with pomegranates: and so did he for the other chapiter.

19 And the chapiters that *were* upon the top of the pillars *were* of lily work in the porch, four cubits.

20 And the chapiters upon the two pillars *had pomegranates* also above, over against the belly which *was* by the network: and the pomegranates *were* ^Rtwo hundred in rows round about upon the other chapiter.   2 Chr. 3:16; 4:13

21 ^RAnd he set up the pillars in the porch of the temple: and he set up the right pillar, and called the name thereof Ja'-chin: and he set up the left pillar, and called the name thereof Bo'-az.   2 Chr. 3:17

22 And upon the top of the pillars *was* lily work: so was the work of the pillars finished.

23 And he made ^Ra molten sea, ten cubits from the one brim to the other: *it was* round all about, and his height *was* five cubits: and a line of thirty cubits did compass it round about.   2 Kin. 25:13

24 And under the brim of it round about *there were* knops compassing it, ten in a cubit, ^Rcompassing the sea round about: the knops *were* cast in two rows, when it was cast.   2 Chr. 4:3

25 It stood upon ^Rtwelve oxen, three looking toward the north, and three looking toward the west, and three looking toward the south, and three looking toward the east: and the sea *was set* above upon them, and all their hinder parts *were* inward. 2 Chr. 4:4

26 And it *was* an hand breadth thick, and the brim thereof was wrought like the brim of a cup, with flowers of lilies: it contained ^Rtwo thousand baths.   2 Chr. 4:5

27 And he made ten ^Tbases of brass; four cubits *was* the length of one base, and four cubits the breadth thereof, and three cubits the height of it.   *carts or stands*

28 And the work of the bases *was* on this *manner:* they had borders, and the borders *were* between the ledges:

29 And on the borders that *were* between the ledges *were* lions, oxen, and cher'-u-bims: and upon the ledges *there was* a base above: and beneath the lions and oxen *were* certain additions made of thin work.

30 And every base had four

brasen wheels, and plates of brass: and the four corners thereof had ᵀundersetters: under the laver *were* undersetters molten, at the side of every addition. *supports*

31 And the mouth of it within the chapiter and above *was* a cubit: but the mouth thereof *was* round *after* the work of the base, a cubit and an half: and also upon the mouth of it *were* ᵀgravings with their borders, foursquare, not round.   *engravings*

32 And under the borders *were* four wheels; and the axletrees of the wheels *were joined* to the base: and the height of a wheel *was* a cubit and half a cubit.

33 And the work of the wheels *was* like the work of a chariot wheel: their axletrees, and their naves, and their ᵀfelloes, and their spokes, *were* all molten.   *hubs*

34 And *there were* four undersetters to the four corners of one base: *and* the undersetters *were* of the very base itself.

35 And in the top of the base *was there* a round compass of half a cubit high: and on the top of the base the ledges thereof and the borders thereof *were* of the same.

36 For on the plates of the ledges thereof, and on the borders thereof, he graved cher'-u-bims, lions, and palm trees, according to the proportion of every one, and additions round about.

37 After this *manner* he made the ten bases: all of them had ᵀone casting, one measure, *and* one size.   *the same*

38 Then ᴿmade he ten lavers of brass: one laver contained forty baths: *and* every laver was four cubits: *and* upon every one of the ten bases one laver.   2 Chr. 4:6

39 And he put five bases on the right side of the house, and five on the left side of the house: and he set the sea on the right side of the house eastward over against the south.

40 ᴿAnd Hiram made the lavers, and the shovels, and the basons.

So Hiram ᵀmade an end of doing all the work that he made king Solomon for the house of the LORD: 2 Chr. 4:11—5:1 · *finished*

41 The two pillars, and the *two* bowls of the chapiters that *were* on the top of the two pillars; and the two networks, to cover the two bowls of the chapiters which *were* upon the top of the pillars;

42 And ᴿfour hundred pomegranates for the two networks, *even* two rows of pomegranates for one network, to cover the two bowls of the chapiters that *were* ᵀupon the pillars; v. 20 · *on the tops of*

43 And the ten bases, and ten lavers on the bases;

44 And one sea, and twelve oxen under the sea;

45 ᴿAnd the pots, and the shovels, and the basons: and all these vessels, which Hiram made to king Solomon for the house of the LORD, *were of* bright brass. Ex. 27:3

46 ᴿIn the plain of Jordan did the king cast them, in the clay ground between Suc'-coth and Zar'-than.   2 Chr. 4:17

47 And Solomon left all the vessels *unweighed*, because they were exceeding many: neither was the weight of the brass found ᴿout.   1 Chr. 22:3, 14

48 And Solomon made all the vessels that *pertained* unto the house of the LORD: the altar of gold, and the table of gold, whereupon the shewbread *was,*

49 And the candlesticks of pure gold, five on the right *side*, and five on the left, before the oracle, with the flowers, and the lamps, and the tongs *of* gold,

50 And the bowls, and the snuffers, and the basons, and the spoons, and the ᵀcensers *of* pure gold; and the hinges *of* gold, *both* for the doors of the inner house, the most holy *place, and* for the doors of the house, *to wit*, of the temple.   *firepans*

51 So was ended all the work that king Solomon made for the house of the LORD. And Solomon brought in the things ᴿwhich

David his father had dedicated; *even* the silver, and the gold, and the vessels, did he put among the treasures of the house of the LORD. 2 Sam. 8:11; 1 Chr. 18:11; 2 Chr. 5:1

8 Then Solomon assembled the elders of Israel, and all the heads of the tribes, the chief of the fathers of the children of Israel, unto king Solomon in Jerusalem, that they might bring up the ark of the covenant of the LORD out of the city of David, which *is* Zion.

2 And all the men of Israel assembled themselves unto king Solomon at the ᴿfeast in the month Eth'-a-nim, which *is* the seventh month. Lev. 23:34

3 And all the elders of Israel came, ᴿand the priests took up the ark. Num. 4:15; 7:9; Deut. 31:9; Josh. 3:3, 6

4 And they brought up the ark of the LORD, ᴿand the tabernacle of the congregation, and all the holy vessels that *were* in the tabernacle, even those did the priests and the Levites bring up. 3:4

5 And king Solomon, and all the congregation of Israel, that were assembled unto him, *were* with him before the ark, ᴿsacrificing sheep and oxen, that could not be told nor numbered for multitude. 2 Sam. 6:13; 2 Chr. 1:6

6 And the priests ᴿbrought in the ark of the covenant of the LORD unto his place, into the oracle of the house, to the most holy *place, even* under the wings of the cher'-u-bims. 2 Sam. 6:17

7 For the cher'-u-bims spread forth *their* two wings over the place of the ark, and the cher'-u-bims covered the ark and the staves thereof above.

8 And they ᴿdrew out the staves, that the ends of the staves were seen out in the holy *place* before the oracle; and they were not seen without: and there they are unto this day. Ex. 25:13–15; 37:4, 5

9 ᴿ*There was* nothing in the ark save the two tables of stone, which Moses put there at Ho'-reb, when the LORD made *a* covenant with the children of Israel, when

they came out of the land of Egypt. Ex. 25:21; Deut. 10:2

10 And it came to pass, when the priests were come out of the holy *place,* that the cloud ᴿfilled the house of the LORD, 2 Chr. 7:1, 2

11 So that the priests could not stand to minister because of the cloud: for the glory of the LORD had filled the house of the LORD.

12 Then spake Solomon, The LORD said that he would dwell ᴿin the thick darkness. Ps. 18:11; 97:2

13 I have surely built thee an house to dwell in, a settled place for thee to abide in for ever.

14 And the king turned his face about, and ᴿblessed all the congregation of Israel: (and all the congregation of Israel stood;) v. 55

15 And he said, Blessed *be* the LORD God of Israel, which ᴿspake with his mouth unto David my father, and hath with his hand fulfilled *it,* saying, 2 Sam. 7:2, 12, 13, 25

16 Since the day that I brought forth my people Israel out of Egypt, I chose no city out of all the tribes of Israel to build an house, that ᴿmy name might be therein; but I chose David to be over my people Israel. Deut. 12:5

17 And ᴿit was in the heart of David my father to build an house for the name of the LORD God of Israel. 2 Sam. 7:2, 3; 1 Chr. 17:1, 2

18 ᴿAnd the LORD said unto David my father, Whereas it was in thine heart to build an house unto my name, thou didst well that it was in thine heart. 2 Chr. 6:8

19 Nevertheless ᴿthou shalt not build the house; but thy son that shall come forth out of thy loins, he shall build the house unto my name. 1 Chr. 17:11, 12; 22:8–10; 2 Chr. 6:2

20 And the LORD hath performed his word that he spake, and I ᵀam risen up in the room of David my father, and sit on the throne of Israel, ᴿas the LORD promised, and have built an house for the name of the LORD God of Israel. *filled the place* · 1 Chr. 28:5, 6

21 And I have set there a place

for the ark, wherein *is* ᴿthe covenant of the LORD, which he made
with our fathers, when he brought
them out of the land of Egypt. v. 9
22 And Solomon stood before
ᴿthe altar of the LORD in the presence of all the congregation of
Israel, and ᴿspread forth his
hands toward heaven: v. 54 · Ex. 9:33
23 And he said, LORD God of
Israel, ᴿ*there is* no God like thee,
in heaven above, or on earth
beneath, ᴿwho keepest covenant
and mercy with thy servants that
ᴿwalk before thee with all their
heart: Ex. 15:11 · [Deut. 7:9] · [Gen. 17:1]
24 Who hast kept with thy ser-
vant David my father that thou
promisedst him: thou spakest also
with thy mouth, and hast fulfilled
it with thine hand, as *it is* this day.
25 Therefore now, LORD God of
Israel, keep with thy servant David my father that thou promisedst him, saying, ᴿThere shall
not fail thee a man in my sight to
sit on the throne of Israel; so that
thy children take heed to their
way, that they walk before me as
thou hast walked before me.   2:4
26 ᴿAnd now, O God of Israel, let
thy word, I pray thee, be verified,
which thou spakest unto thy servant David my father.   2 Sam. 7:25
27 But ᴿwill God indeed dwell
on the earth? behold, the heaven
and heaven of heavens cannot
contain thee; how much less this
house that I have builded? [Is. 66:1]
28 Yet ᵀhave thou respect unto
the prayer of thy servant, and to
his supplication, O LORD my God,
to hearken unto the cry and to the
prayer, which thy servant prayeth
before thee to day: *regard the prayer*
29 That thine eyes may be open
toward this house night and day,
even toward the place of which
thou hast said, My name shall be
ᴿthere: that thou mayest hearken
unto the prayer which thy servant
shall make toward this place.   9:3
30 And hearken thou to the supplication of thy servant, and of
thy people Israel, when they shall
pray toward this place: and hear

thou in heaven thy dwelling
place: and when thou hearest, forgive.
31 If any man trespass against
his neighbour, and ᴿan oath be
laid upon him to cause him to
swear, and the oath come before
thine altar in this house: Ex. 22:8–11
32 Then hear thou in heaven,
and do, and judge thy servants,
condemning the wicked, to bring
his way upon his head; and justifying the righteous, to give him
according to his righteousness.
33 ᴿWhen thy people Israel be
smitten down before the enemy,
because they have sinned against
thee, and ᴿshall turn again to thee,
and confess thy name, and pray,
and make supplication unto thee
in this house: Lev. 26:17 · Lev. 26:39, 40
34 Then hear thou in heaven,
and forgive the sin of thy people
Israel, and bring them again unto
the land which thou gavest unto
their ᴿfathers.   [Deut. 30:1–3]
35 When heaven is shut up, and
there is no rain, because they
have sinned against thee; if they
pray toward this place, and confess thy name, and turn from their
sin, when thou afflictest them:
36 Then hear thou in heaven,
and forgive the sin of thy servants, and of thy people Israel,
that thou ᴿteach them the good
way wherein they should walk,
and give rain upon thy land,
which thou hast given to thy people for an inheritance. Ps. 25:4; 27:11
37 If there be in the land famine, if there be pestilence, ᵀblast-
ing, mildew, locust, *or* if there be
caterpiller; if their enemy besiege
them in the land of their cities;
whatsoever plague, whatsoever
sickness *there be;*   *blight*
38 What prayer and supplication soever be *made* by any man,
or by all thy people Israel, which
shall know every man the plague
of his own heart, and spread forth
his hands toward this house:
39 Then hear thou in heaven thy
dwelling place, and forgive, and
do, and give to every man accord-

ing to his ways, whose heart thou knowest; (for thou, *even* thou only, [R]knowest the hearts of all the children of men;)   Acts 1:24

40 [R]That they may fear thee all the days that they live in the land which thou gavest unto our fathers.   [Ps. 130:4]

41 Moreover concerning a stranger, that *is* not of thy people Israel, but cometh out of a far country for thy name's sake;

42 (For they shall hear of thy great name, and of thy [R]strong hand, and of thy stretched out arm;) when he shall come and pray toward this house;   Ex. 13:3

43 Hear thou in heaven thy dwelling place, and do according to all that the stranger calleth to thee for: [R]that all people of the earth may know thy name, to fear thee, as *do* thy people Israel; and that they may know that this house, which I have builded, is called by thy name.   [1 Sam. 17:46]

44 If thy people go out to battle against their enemy, whithersoever thou shalt send them, and shall pray unto the LORD toward the city which thou hast chosen, and *toward* the house that I have built for thy name:

45 Then hear thou in heaven their prayer and their supplication, and maintain their cause.

46 If they sin against thee, [R](for *there is* no man that sinneth not,) and thou be angry with them, and deliver them to the enemy, so that they carry them away captives unto the land of the enemy, far or near;   Ps. 130:3; [Rom. 3:23; 1 John 1:8, 10]

47 *Yet* if they shall bethink themselves in the land whither they were carried captives, and repent, and make supplication unto thee in the land of them that carried them captives, [R]saying, We have sinned, and have done perversely, we have committed wickedness;   Ezra 9:6, 7; Ps. 106:6; Dan. 9:5

48 And *so* return unto thee with all their heart, and with all their soul, in the land of their enemies, which led them away captive, and

[R]pray unto thee toward their land, which thou gavest unto their fathers, the city which thou hast chosen, and the house which I have built for thy name: Dan. 6:10

49 Then hear thou their prayer and their supplication in heaven thy dwelling place, and maintain their [T]cause,   *justice*

50 And forgive thy people that have sinned against thee, and all their transgressions wherein they have transgressed against thee, and [R]give them compassion before them who carried them captive, that they may have compassion on them: Ps. 106:46; Acts 7:10

51 For [R]they *be* thy people, and thine inheritance, which thou broughtest forth out of Egypt, [R]from the midst of the furnace of iron: [Rom. 11:28, 29] · Deut. 4:20; Jer. 11:4

52 [R]That thine eyes may be open unto the supplication of thy servant, and unto the supplication of thy people Israel, to hearken unto them in all that they call for unto thee.   v. 29

53 For thou didst separate them from among all the people of the earth, *to be* thine inheritance, [R]as thou spakest by the hand of Moses thy servant, when thou broughtest our fathers out of Egypt, O Lord GOD.   Ex. 19:5, 6

54 And it was *so*, that when Solomon had made an end of praying all this prayer and supplication unto the LORD, he arose from before the altar of the LORD, from kneeling on his knees with his hands spread up to heaven.

55 And he stood, [R]and blessed all the congregation of Israel with a loud voice, saying,   Num. 6:23-26

56 Blessed *be* the LORD, that hath given [R]rest unto his people Israel, according to all that he promised: there hath not failed one word of all his good promise, which he promised by the hand of Moses his servant.   1 Chr. 22:18

57 The LORD our God be with us, as he was with our fathers: let him not leave us, nor forsake us:

58 That he may [R]incline our

hearts unto him, to walk in all his ways, and to keep his commandments, and his statutes, and his judgments, which he commanded our fathers. Ps. 119:36; Jer. 31:33

59 And let these my words, wherewith I have made supplication before the LORD, be nigh unto the LORD our God day and night, that he maintain the cause of his servant, and the cause of his people Israel at all times, as the matter shall require:

60 That all the people of the earth may know that the LORD *is* God, *and that there is* none else.

61 Let your heart therefore be perfect with the LORD our God, to walk in his statutes, and to keep his commandments, as at this day.

62 And Rthe king, and all Israel with him, offered sacrifice before the LORD. 2 Chr. 7:4–10

63 And Solomon offered a sacrifice of peace offerings, which he offered unto the LORD, two and twenty thousand oxen, and an hundred and twenty thousand sheep. So the king and all the children of Israel dedicated the house of the LORD.

64 RThe same day did the king hallow the middle of the court that *was* before the house of the LORD: for there he offered burnt offerings, and meat offerings, and the fat of the peace offerings: because the Rbrasen altar that *was* before the LORD *was* too little to receive the burnt offerings, and meat offerings, and the fat of the peace offerings. 2 Chr. 7:7 · 2 Chr. 4:1

65 And at that time Solomon held a feast, and all Israel with him, a great congregation, from the entering in of Ha′-math unto the river of Egypt, before the LORD our God, seven days and seven days, *even* fourteen days.

66 ROn the eighth day he sent the people away: and they blessed the king, and went unto their tents joyful and glad of heart for all the goodness that the LORD had done for David his servant, and for Israel his people. 2 Chr. 7:9

9 And Rit came to pass, when Solomon had finished the building of the house of the LORD, and the king's house, and Rall Solomon's desire which he was pleased to do, 2 Chr. 7:11 · 2 Chr. 8:6

2 That the LORD appeared to Solomon the second time, Ras he had appeared unto him at Gib′-e-on. 3:5; 11:9; 2 Chr. 1:7

3 And the LORD said unto him, RI have heard thy prayer and thy supplication, that thou hast made before me: I have hallowed this house, which thou hast built, to put my name there for ever; and mine eyes and mine heart shall be there perpetually. 2 Kin. 20:5; Ps. 10:17

4 And if thou wilt Rwalk before me, Ras David thy father walked, in integrity of heart, and in uprightness, to do according to all that I have commanded thee, *and* wilt Rkeep my statutes and my judgments: Gen. 17:1 · 11:4, 6; 15:5 · 8:61

5 Then I will establish the throne of thy kingdom upon Israel for ever, Ras I promised to David thy father, saying, There shall not fail thee a man upon the throne of Israel. 2 Sam. 7:12, 16; Matt. 1:6; 25:31

6 RBut if ye shall at all turn from following me, ye or your children, and will not keep my commandments *and* my statutes which I have set before you, but go and serve other gods, and worship them: 2 Sam. 7:14–16; Ps. 89:30

7 RThen will I cut off Israel out of the land which I have given them; and this house, which I have hallowed for my name, will I cast out of my sight; and Israel shall be a proverb and a byword among all people: [Lev. 18:24–29]

8 And Rat this house, *which* is high, every one that passeth by it shall be astonished, and shall hiss; and they shall say, Why hath the LORD done thus unto this land, and to this house? 2 Chr. 7:21

9 And they shall answer, Because they forsook the LORD their God, who brought forth their fathers out of the land of Egypt, and have taken hold upon other gods,

and have worshipped them, and served them: therefore hath the LORD brought upon them all this Revil. [Deut. 29:25–28]

10 And Rit came to pass at the end of twenty years, when Solomon had built the two houses, the house of the LORD, and the king's house, 6:37, 38; 7:1; 2 Chr. 8:1

11 R(Now Hiram the king of Tyre had furnished Solomon with cedar trees and fir trees, and with gold, according to all his desire,) that then king Solomon gave Hiram twenty cities in the land of Galilee. 5:1

12 And Hiram came out from Tyre to see the cities which Solomon had given him; and they pleased him not.

13 And he said, What cities are these which thou hast given me, my brother? And he called them the land of Ca'-bul unto this day.

14 And Hiram sent to the king sixscore talents of gold.

15 And this is the reason of Rthe levy which king Solomon raised; for to build the house of the LORD, and his own house, and RMil'-lo, and the wall of Jerusalem, and Ha'-zor, and Me-gid'-do, and Ge'-zer. 5:13 · 2 Sam. 5:9

16 For Pharaoh king of Egypt had gone up, and taken Ge'-zer, and burnt it with fire, Rand slain the Ca'-naan-ites that dwelt in the city, and given it for a present unto his daughter, Solomon's wife. Josh. 16:10; Judg. 1:29

17 And Solomon built Ge'-zer, and Beth–ho'-ron the nether,

18 And Ba'-al-ath, and Tad'-mor in the wilderness, in the land,

19 And all the cities of store that Solomon had, and cities for Rhis chariots, and cities for his horsemen, and that which Solomon desired to build in Jerusalem, and in Leb'-a-non, and in all the land of his dominion. 10:26; 2 Chr. 1:14

20 RAnd all the people that were left of the Am'-or-ites, Hit'-tites, Per'-iz-zites, Hi'-vites, and Jeb'-u-sites, which were not of the children of Israel, 2 Chr. 8:7

21 Their children Rthat were left after them in the land, whom the children of Israel also were not able utterly to destroy, upon those did Solomon levy a tribute of bondservice unto this day. Judg. 3:1

22 But of the children of Israel did Solomon Rmake no bondmen: but they were men of war, and his servants, and his princes, and his captains, and rulers of his chariots, and his horsemen. [Lev. 25:39]

23 These were the chief of the officers that were over Solomon's work, five hundred and fifty, which bare rule over the people that wrought in the work.

24 But RPharaoh's daughter came up out of the city of David unto Rher house which Solomon had built for her: Rthen did he build Mil'-lo. 3:1 · 7:8 · 11:27; 2 Chr. 32:5

25 And three times in a year did Solomon offer burnt offerings and peace offerings upon the altar which he built unto the LORD, and he burnt incense upon the altar that was before the LORD. So he finished the house.

26 And Rking Solomon made a navy of ships in RE'-zi-on-ge'-ber, which is beside E'-loth, on the shore of the Red sea, in the land of E'-dom. 2 Chr. 8:17, 18 · Num. 33:35

27 RAnd Hiram sent in the navy his servants, shipmen that had knowledge of the sea, with the servants of Solomon. 5:6, 9; 10:11

28 And they came to O'-phir, and fetched from thence gold, four hundred and twenty talents, and brought it to king Solomon.

10 And when the Rqueen of She'-ba heard of the fame of Solomon concerning the name of the LORD, she came to prove him with hard questions. Matt. 12:42

2 And she came to Jerusalem with a very great train, with camels that bare spices, and very much gold, and precious stones: and when she was come to Solomon, she communed with him of all that was in her heart.

3 And Solomon Ttold her all her questions: there was not any

thing ᵀhid from the king, which he told her not. *answered · too difficult for*

4 And when the queen of She'-ba had seen all Solomon's wisdom, and the house that he had built,

5 And the meat of his table, and the sitting of his servants, and the attendance of his ministers, and their apparel, and his cupbearers, ᴿand ᵀhis ascent by which he went up unto the house of the LORD; there was no more spirit in her. 1 Chr. 26:16 · *entryway*

6 And she said to the king, It was a true report that I heard in mine own land of thy ᵀacts and of thy wisdom. *words*

7 Howbeit I believed not the words, until I came, and mine eyes had seen *it:* and, behold, the half was not told me: thy wisdom and prosperity exceedeth the fame which I heard.

8 ᴿHappy *are* thy men, happy *are* these thy servants, which stand continually before thee, *and* that hear thy wisdom. Prov. 8:34

9 Blessed be the LORD thy God, which delighted in thee, to set thee on the throne of Israel: because the LORD loved Israel for ever, therefore made he thee king, to do judgment and justice.

10 And she gave the king an hundred and twenty talents of gold, and of spices very great store, and precious stones: there came no more such abundance of spices as these which the queen of She'-ba gave to king Solomon.

11 ᴿAnd the navy also of Hiram, that brought gold from O'-phir, brought in from O'-phir great plenty of al'-mug trees, and precious stones. 9:27, 28; Job 22:24

12 ᴿAnd the king made of the al'-mug trees pillars for the house of the LORD, and for the king's house, harps also and psalteries for singers: there came no such ᴿal'-mug trees, nor were seen unto this day. 2 Chr. 9:11 · 2 Chr. 9:10

13 And king Solomon gave unto the queen of She'-ba all her desire, whatsoever she asked, beside *that* which Solomon gave her of his royal bounty. So she turned and went to her own country, she and her servants.

14 Now the weight of gold that came to Solomon in one year was six hundred threescore and six talents of gold,

15 Beside *that he had* of the merchantmen, and of the traffick of the spice merchants, and ᴿof all the kings of Arabia, and of the governors of the country. Ps. 72:10

16 And king Solomon made two hundred targets *of* beaten gold: six hundred *shek'-els* of gold went to one target.

17 And *he made* three hundred shields *of* beaten gold; three pound of gold went to one shield: and the king put them in the house of the forest of Leb'-a-non.

18 ᴿMoreover the king made a great throne of ivory, and overlaid it with the best gold. 2 Chr. 9:17

19 The throne had six steps, and the top of the throne *was* round ᵀbehind: and *there were* ᵀstays on either side on the place of the seat, and two lions stood beside the stays. *at the back · armrests*

20 And twelve lions stood there on the one side and on the other upon the six steps: there was not the like made in any kingdom.

21 ᴿAnd all king Solomon's drinking vessels *were of* gold, and all the vessels of the house of the forest of Leb'-a-non *were of* pure gold; none *were of* silver: it was nothing accounted of in the days of Solomon. 2 Chr. 9:20

22 For the king had at sea a navy of Thar'-shish with the navy of Hiram: once in three years came the navy of Thar'-shish, bringing gold, and silver, ivory, and apes, and peacocks.

23 So ᴿking Solomon exceeded all the kings of the earth for riches and for wisdom. 3:12, 13; 4:30

24 And all the earth sought to Solomon, to hear his wisdom, which God had put in his heart.

25 And they brought every man his present, vessels of silver, and vessels of gold, and garments, and armour, and spices, horses, and mules, a rate year by year.

26 And Solomon gathered together chariots and horsemen: and he had a thousand and four hundred chariots, and twelve thousand horsemen, whom he bestowed in the cities for chariots, and with the king at Jerusalem.

27 ᴿAnd the king made silver to be in Jerusalem as stones, and cedars made he to be as the sycomore trees that are in the vale, for abundance. [Deut. 17:17]; 2 Chr. 1:15–17

28 And Solomon had horses brought out of Egypt, and linen yarn: the king's merchants received the linen yarn at a price.

29 And a chariot came up and went out of Egypt for six hundred shek'-els of silver, and an horse for an hundred and fifty: ᴿand so for all the kings of the Hit'-tites, and for the kings of Syria, did they bring them out by their means. Josh. 1:4; 2 Kin. 7:6, 7

11 But king Solomon loved ᴿmany strange women, together with the daughter of Pharaoh, women of the Mo'-ab-ites, Am'-mon-ites, E'-dom-ites, Zi-do'-ni-ans, and Hit'-tites; [Deut. 17:17]

2 Of the nations concerning which the LORD said unto the children of Israel, ᴿYe shall not go in to them, neither shall they come in unto you: for surely they will turn away your heart after their gods: Solomon ᵀclave unto these in love. Ex. 34:16; [Deut. 7:3, 4] · clung

3 And he had seven hundred wives, princesses, and three hundred concubines: and his wives turned away his heart.

4 For it came to pass, when Solomon was old, that his wives turned away his heart after other gods: and his heart was not perfect with the LORD his God, as was the heart of David his father.

5 For Solomon went after ᴿAsh'-to-reth the goddess of the Zi-do'-ni-ans, and after ᴿMil'-com

the abomination of the Am'-mon-ites. Judg. 2:13 · [Lev. 20:2–5]

6 And Solomon did evil in the sight of the LORD, and ᵀwent not fully after the LORD, as did David his father. did not fully follow

7 Then did Solomon build an high place for ᴿChe'-mosh, the abomination of Moab, in the hill that is before Jerusalem, and for Mo'-lech, the abomination of the children of Ammon. Judg. 11:24

8 And likewise did he for all his strange wives, which burnt incense and sacrificed unto their gods.

9 And the LORD was angry with Solomon, because his heart was turned from the LORD God of Israel, ᴿwhich had appeared unto him twice. 3:5; 9:2

10 And ᴿhad commanded him concerning this thing, that he should not go after other gods: but he kept not that which the LORD commanded. 6:12; 9:6, 7

11 Wherefore the LORD said unto Solomon, Forasmuch as this is done of thee, and thou hast not kept my covenant and my statutes, which I have commanded thee, ᴿI will surely rend the kingdom from thee, and will give it to thy ᴿservant. 12:15, 16 · vv. 31, 37

12 Notwithstanding in thy days I will not do it for David thy father's sake: but I will ᵀrend it out of the hand of thy son. tear

13 ᴿHowbeit I will not rend away all the kingdom; but will give ᴿone tribe to thy son ᴿfor David my servant's sake, and for Jerusalem's sake which I have chosen. Ps. 89:33 · 12:20 · 2 Sam. 7:15, 16

14 And the LORD ᴿstirred up an adversary unto Solomon, Ha'-dad the E'-dom-ite: he was of the king's seed in E'-dom. 1 Chr. 5:26

15 For it came to pass, when David was in E'-dom, and Jo'-ab the captain of the host was gone up to bury the slain, after he had smitten every male in E'-dom;

16 (For six months did Jo'-ab remain there with all Israel, until he had cut off every male in E'-dom:)

17 That Ha'-dad fled, he and certain E'-dom-ites of his father's servants with him, to go into Egypt; Ha'-dad *being* yet a little child.

18 And they arose out of Mid'-i-an, and came to Pa'-ran: and they took men with them out of Pa'-ran, and they came to Egypt, unto Pharaoh king of Egypt; which gave him an house, and ᵀappointed him victuals, and gave him land.   *apportioned food*

19 And Ha'-dad found great favour in the sight of Pharaoh, so that he gave him to wife the sister of his own wife, the sister of Tah'-pe-nes the queen.

20 And the sister of Tah'-pe-nes bare him Ge-nu'-bath his son, whom Tah'-pe-nes weaned in Pharaoh's house: and Ge-nu'-bath was in Pharaoh's household among the sons of Pharaoh.

21 ᴿAnd when Ha'-dad heard in Egypt that David slept with his fathers, and that Jo'-ab the captain of the host was dead, Ha'-dad said to Pharaoh, Let me depart, that I may go to mine own country.   2:10, 34

22 Then Pharaoh said unto him, But what hast thou lacked with me, that, behold, thou seekest to go to thine own country? And he answered, Nothing: howbeit let me go in ᵀany wise.   *anyway*

23 And God ᵀstirred him up *another* adversary, Re'-zon the son of E-li'-a-dah, which fled from his lord ᴿHad-ad-e'-zer king of Zo'-bah: *raised up* · 2 Sam. 8:3; 10:16

24 And he gathered men unto him, and became captain over a band, ᴿwhen David slew them *of* Zo'-bah: and they went to Damascus, and dwelt therein, and reigned in Damascus.   2 Sam. 8:3

25 And he was an adversary to Israel all the days of Solomon, beside the ᵀmischief that Ha'-dad *did:* and he abhorred Israel, and reigned over Syria.   *trouble*

26 And ᴿJer-o-bo'-am the son of Ne'-bat, an Eph'-rath-ite of Zer'-e-da, Solomon's servant, whose mother's name *was* Ze-ru'-ah, a widow woman, even he lifted up *his* hand against the king.   12:2

27 And this *was* the cause that he lifted up *his* hand against the king: ᴿSolomon built Mil'-lo, *and* repaired the breaches of the city of David his father.   9:15, 24

28 And the man Jer-o-bo'-am *was* a mighty man of valour: and Solomon seeing the young man that he was ᴿindustrious, he made him ruler over all the charge of the house of Joseph.   [Prov. 22:29]

29 And it came to pass at that time when Jer-o-bo'-am went out of Jerusalem, that the prophet ᴿA-hi'-jah the Shi'-lo-nite found him in the way; and he had clad himself with a new garment; and they two *were* alone in the field: 12:15

30 And A-hi'-jah caught the new garment that *was* on him, and ᴿrent it *in* twelve pieces: 1 Sam. 24:5

31 And he said to Jer-o-bo'-am, Take thee ten pieces: for thus saith the Lᴏʀᴅ, the God of Israel, Behold, I will rend the kingdom out of the hand of Solomon, and will give ten tribes to thee:

32 (But he shall have one tribe for my servant David's sake, and for Jerusalem's sake, the city which I have chosen out of all the tribes of Israel:)

33 ᴿBecause that they have forsaken me, and have worshipped Ash'-to-reth the goddess of the Zi-do'-ni-ans, Che'-mosh the god of the Mo'-ab-ites, and Mil'-com the god of the children of Ammon, and have not walked in my ways, to do *that which is* right in mine eyes, and *to keep* my statutes and my judgments, as *did* David his father.   vv. 5–8; 1 Sam. 7:3

34 Howbeit I will not take the whole kingdom out of his hand: but I will make him prince all the days of his life for David my servant's sake, whom I chose, because he kept my commandments and my statutes:

35 But I will take the kingdom out of his son's hand, and will give it unto thee, *even* ten tribes.

36 And unto his son will I give one tribe, that ^RDavid my servant may have a ^Tlight alway before me in Jerusalem, the city which I have chosen me to put my name there.   [15:4; 2 Kin. 8:19] · *lamp*

37 And I will take thee, and thou shalt reign according to all that ^Tthy soul desireth, and shalt be king over Israel.   *heart desires*

38 And it shall be, if thou wilt hearken unto all that I command thee, and wilt walk in my ways, and do *that is* right in my sight, to keep my statutes and my commandments, as David my servant did; that ^RI will be with thee, and ^Rbuild thee a sure house, as I built for David, and will give Israel unto thee.   Josh. 1:5 · 2 Sam. 7:11, 27

39 And I will for this afflict the seed of David, but not for ever.

40 Solomon sought therefore to kill Jer-o-bo'-am. And Jer-o-bo'-am arose, and fled into Egypt, unto ^RShi'-shak king of Egypt, and was in Egypt until the death of Solomon.   v. 17; 14:25; 2 Chr. 12:2–9

41 And ^Rthe rest of the acts of Solomon, and all that he did, and his wisdom, *are* they not written in the book of the acts of Solomon?   2 Chr. 9:29

42 ^RAnd the time that Solomon reigned in Jerusalem over all Israel *was* forty years.   2 Chr. 9:30

43 ^RAnd Solomon slept with his fathers, and was buried in the city of David his father: and Re-ho-bo'-am his son reigned in his ^Rstead.   2:10; 2 Chr. 9:31 · 14:21; 2 Chr. 10:1

12 And ^RRe-ho-bo'-am went to ^RShe'-chem: for all Israel were come to She'-chem to make him king.   2 Chr. 10:1 · Judg. 9:6

2 And it came to pass, when ^RJer-o-bo'-am the son of Ne'-bat, who was yet in ^REgypt, heard *of it,* (for he was fled from the presence of king Solomon, and Jer-o-bo'-am dwelt in Egypt;)   11:26 · 11:40

3 That they sent and called him. And Jer-o-bo'-am and all the congregation of Israel came, and spake unto Re-ho-bo'-am, saying,

4 Thy father made our ^Ryoke grievous: now therefore make thou the grievous service of thy father, and his heavy yoke which he put upon us, lighter, and we will serve thee.   4:7; 5:13–15

5 And he said unto them, Depart yet *for* three days, then come again to me. And the people departed.

6 And king Re-ho-bo'-am consulted with the old men, that stood before Solomon his father while he yet lived, and said, How do ye advise that I may answer this people?

7 And they spake unto him, saying, If thou wilt be a servant unto this people this day, and wilt serve them, and answer them, and speak good words to them, then they will be thy servants for ever.

8 But he forsook the counsel of the old men, which they had given him, and consulted with the young men that were grown up with him, *and* which stood before him:

9 And he said unto them, What counsel give ye that we may answer this people, who have spoken to me, saying, Make the yoke which thy father did put upon us lighter?

10 And the young men that were grown up with him spake unto him, saying, Thus shalt thou speak unto this people that spake unto thee, saying, Thy father made our yoke heavy, but make thou *it* lighter unto us; thus shalt thou say unto them, My little *finger* shall be thicker than my father's loins.

11 And now whereas my father did lade you with a heavy yoke, I will add to your yoke: my father hath chastised you with whips, but I will chastise you with scorpions.

12 So Jer-o-bo'-am and all the people came to Re-ho-bo'-am the third day, as the king had ^Tappointed, saying, Come to me again the third day.   *directed*

13 And the king answered the people ^Troughly, and ^Tforsook the

old men's ᵀcounsel that they gave
him;   *harshly · rejected · advice*
14 And spake to them after the
counsel of the young men, saying,
My father made your yoke heavy,
and I will add to your yoke: my
father *also* chastised you with
whips, but I will chastise you with
ᵀscorpions.   *scourges with points*
15 Wherefore the king heark-
ened not unto the people; for ᴿthe
ᵀcause was from the LORD, that he
might perform his saying, which
the LORD spake by A-hi'-jah the
Shi'-lo-nite unto Jer-o-bo'-am the
son of Ne'-bat.   *v. 24 · turn of affairs*
16 So when all Israel saw that
the king hearkened not unto
them, the people answered the
king, saying, What portion have
we in David? neither *have we*
inheritance in the son of Jesse: to
your tents, O Israel: now see to
thine own house, David. So Israel
departed unto their tents.
17 But ᴿ*as for* the children of
Israel which dwelt in the cities of
Judah, Re-ho-bo'-am reigned over
them.   11:13, 36; 2 Chr. 11:14–17
18 Then king Re-ho-bo'-am
ᴿsent A-do'-ram, who *was* over
the tribute; and all Israel stoned
him with stones, that he died.
Therefore king Re-ho-bo'-am
made speed to get him up to his
chariot, to flee to Jerusalem.   4:6
19 So Israel rebelled against the
house of David unto this day.
20 And it came to pass, when all
Israel heard that Jer-o-bo'-am was
come again, that they sent and
called him unto the congregation,
and made him king over all
ᴿIsrael: there was none that followed the house of David, but the
tribe of Judah only.   2 Kin. 17:21
21 And when Re-ho-bo'-am was
come to Jerusalem, he assembled
all the house of Judah, with the
tribe of Benjamin, an hundred
and fourscore thousand chosen
men, which were warriors, for to
fight against the house of Israel,
ᵀto bring the kingdom again to
Re-ho-bo'-am the son of Solomon.   *that he might restore*

22 But ᴿthe word of God came
unto She-ma'-iah the man of God,
saying,   2 Chr. 11:2; 12:5–7
23 Speak unto Re-ho-bo'-am,
the son of Solomon, king of Judah, and unto all the house of
Judah and Benjamin, and to the
remnant of the people, saying,
24 Thus saith the LORD, Ye shall
not go up, nor fight against your
brethren the children of Israel:
return every man to his house;
ᴿfor this thing is from me. They
hearkened therefore to the word
of the LORD, and ᵀreturned to
depart, according to the word of
the LORD.   *v. 15 · turned*
25 Then Jer-o-bo'-am built She'-
chem in mount E'-phra-im, and
dwelt therein; and went out from
thence, and built Pe-nu'-el.
26 And Jer-o-bo'-am said in his
heart, Now shall the kingdom
return to the house of David:
27 If this people ᴿgo up to do
sacrifice in the house of the LORD
at Jerusalem, then shall the heart
of this people turn again unto
their lord, *even* unto Re-ho-bo'-
am king of Judah, and they shall
kill me, and go again to Re-ho-
bo'-am king of Judah. [Deut. 12:5–7]
28 Whereupon the king took
counsel, and ᴿmade two calves *of*
gold, and said unto them, It is too
much for you to go up to Jerusalem: ᴿbehold thy gods, O Israel,
which brought thee up out of the
land of Egypt.   2 Kin. 10:29 · Ex. 32:4, 8
29 And he set the one in Beth'–
el, and the other put he in Dan.
30 And this thing became a sin:
for the people went *to worship*
before the one, *even* unto Dan.
31 And he made an house of
high places, ᴿand made priests of
the lowest of the people, which
were not of the sons of Levi. 13:33
32 And Jer-o-bo'-am ordained a
feast in the eighth month, on the
fifteenth day of the month, like
unto ᴿthe feast that *is* in Judah,
and he offered upon the altar. So
did he in Beth'–el, sacrificing unto
the calves that he had made: ᴿand
he placed in Beth'–el the priests of

the high places which he had made.   Lev. 23:33, 34 · Amos 7:10–13

33 So he offered upon the altar which he had made in Beth'–el the fifteenth day of the eighth month, *even* in the month which he had devised of his own heart; and ordained a feast unto the children of Israel: and he offered upon the altar, and burnt incense.

13 And, behold, there came a man of God out of Judah by the word of the LORD unto Beth'–el: ᴿand Jer-o-bo'-am stood by the altar to burn incense. 12:32

2 And he cried against the altar in the word of the LORD, and said, O altar, altar, thus saith the LORD; Behold, a child shall be born unto the house of David, ᴿJo-si'-ah by name; and upon thee shall he offer the priests of the high places that burn incense upon thee, and men's bones shall be ᴿburnt upon thee.   2 Kin. 23:15, 16 · [Lev. 26:30]

3 And he gave ᴿa sign the same day, saying, This *is* the sign which the LORD hath spoken; Behold, the altar shall be rent, and the ashes that *are* upon it shall be poured out. Is. 7:14; 38:7; John 2:18; 1 Cor. 1:22

4 And it came to pass, when king Jer-o-bo'-am heard the saying of the man of God, which had cried against the altar in Beth'–el, that he put forth his hand from the altar, saying, Lay hold on him. And his hand, which he put forth against him, dried up, so that he could not pull it in again to him.

5 The altar also was ᵀrent, and the ashes poured out from the altar, according to the sign which the man of God had given by the word of the LORD.   *split apart*

6 And the king answered and said unto the man of God, ᴿIn-treat now the face of the LORD thy God, and pray for me, that my hand may be restored me again. And the man of God besought the LORD, and the king's hand was restored him again, and became as *it was* before.   Acts 8:24

7 And the king said unto the man of God, Come home with me, and refresh thyself, and ᴿI will give thee a reward.   2 Kin. 5:15

8 And the man of God said unto the king, If thou wilt give me half thine house, I will not go in with thee, neither will I eat bread nor drink water in this place:

9 For so was it charged me by the word of the LORD, saying, ᴿEat no bread, nor drink water, nor turn again by the same way that thou camest.   [1 Cor. 5:11]

10 So he went another way, and returned not by the way that he came to Beth'–el.

11 Now there dwelt an old prophet in Beth'–el; and his sons came and told him all the works that the man of God had done that day in Beth'–el: the words which he had spoken unto the king, them they told also to their father.

12 And their father said unto them, What way went he? For his sons had seen what way the man of God went, which came from Judah.

13 And he said unto his sons, Saddle me the ass. So they saddled him the ass: and he rode thereon.

14 And went after the man of God, and found him sitting under an oak: and he said unto him, *Art* thou the man of God that camest from Judah? And he said, I *am*.

15 Then he said unto him, Come home with me, and eat bread.

16 And he said, ᴿI may not return with thee, nor go in with thee: neither will I eat bread nor drink water with thee in this place: vv. 8, 9

17 For it was said to me ᴿby the word of the LORD, Thou shalt eat no bread nor drink water there, nor turn again to go by the way that thou camest.   20:35; 1 Thess. 4:15

18 He said unto him, I *am* a prophet also as thou *art;* and an angel spake unto me by the word of the LORD, saying, Bring him back with thee into thine house, that he may eat bread and drink water. *But* he lied unto him.

19 So he went back with him, and did eat bread in his house, and drank water.

20 And it came to pass, as they sat at the table, that the word of the LORD came unto the prophet that brought him back:

21 And he cried unto the man of God that came from Judah, saying, Thus saith the LORD, Forasmuch as thou hast disobeyed the mouth of the LORD, and hast not kept the commandment which the LORD thy God commanded thee,

22 But camest back, and hast eaten bread and drunk water in the ᴿplace, of the which *the LORD* did say to thee, Eat no bread, and drink no water; thy carcase shall not come unto the sepulchre of thy fathers.   v. 9

23 And it came to pass, after he had eaten bread, and after he had drunk, that he saddled for him the ass, *to wit*, for the prophet whom he had brought back.

24 And when he was gone, a lion met him by the way, and slew him: and his carcase was cast in the way, and the ass stood by it, the lion also stood by the carcase.

25 And, behold, men passed by, and saw the carcase cast in the way, and the lion standing by the carcase: and they came and told *it* in the city where the old prophet dwelt.

26 And when the prophet that brought him back from the way heard *thereof*, he said, It *is* the man of God, who was disobedient unto the word of the LORD: therefore the LORD hath delivered him unto the lion, which hath torn him, and slain him, according to the word of the LORD, which he spake unto him.

27 And he spake to his sons, saying, Saddle me the ass. And they saddled *him*.

28 And he went and found his carcase cast in the way, and the ass and the lion standing by the carcase: the lion had not eaten the carcase, nor torn the ass.

29 And the prophet took up the carcase of the man of God, and laid it upon the ass, and brought it back: and the old prophet came to the city, to mourn and to bury him.

30 And he laid his carcase in his own ᵀgrave; and they mourned over him, *saying*, ᴿAlas, my brother!   tomb · Jer. 22:18

31 And it came to pass, after he had buried him, that he spake to his sons, saying, When I am dead, then bury me in the sepulchre wherein the man of God *is* buried; lay my bones beside his bones:

32 ᴿFor the saying which he cried by the word of the LORD against the altar in Beth′–el, and against all the houses of the high places which *are* in the cities of ᴿSa-ma′-ri-a, shall surely come to pass. 2 Kin. 23:16, 19 · John 4:5; Acts 8:14

33 ᴿAfter this thing Jer-o-bo′-am returned not from his evil way, but made again of the lowest of the people priests of the high places: whosoever would, he consecrated him, and he became *one* of the priests of the high places. 12:31, 32

34 And this thing became sin unto the house of Jer-o-bo′-am, even to cut *it* off, and to destroy *it* from off the face of the earth.

14 At that time A-bi′-jah the son of Jer-o-bo′-am fell sick.

2 And Jer-o-bo′-am said to his wife, Arise, I pray thee, and disguise thyself, that thou be not known to be the wife of Jer-o-bo′-am; and get thee to Shi′-loh: behold, there *is* A-hi′-jah the prophet, which told me that ᴿI should be king over this people. 11:29-31

3 ᴿAnd take with thee ten loaves, and ᵀcracknels, and a cruse of honey, and go to him: he shall tell thee what shall become of the child. 13:7; 2 Kin. 4:42 · *cakes*

4 And Jer-o-bo′-am′s wife did so, and arose, ᴿand went to Shi′-loh, and came to the house of A-hi′-jah. But A-hi′-jah could not see; for his eyes were ᵀset by reason of his age. 11:29 · *glazed*

5 And the LORD said unto A-hi′-

jah, Behold, the wife of Jer-o-bo'-am cometh to ask a thing of thee for her son; for he *is* sick: thus and thus shalt thou say unto her: for it shall be, when she cometh in, that she shall ᵀfeign herself *to be* another *woman*.   *pretend to be*

6 And it was *so*, when A-hi'-jah heard the sound of her feet, as she came in at the door, that he said, Come in, thou wife of Jer-o-bo'-am; why feignest thou thyself *to be* another? for I *am* sent to thee *with* ᵀheavy *tidings*.   *bad news*

7 Go, tell Jer-o-bo'-am, Thus saith the LORD God of Israel, ᴿForasmuch as I exalted thee from among the people, and made thee prince over my people Israel,   16:2

8 And ᴿrent the kingdom away from the house of David, and gave it thee: and *yet* thou hast not been as my servant David, ᴿwho kept my commandments, and who followed me with all his heart, to do *that* only *which was* right in mine eyes;   11:31 · 11:33, 38; 15:5

9 But hast done evil above all that were before thee: for thou hast gone and made thee other gods, and molten images, to provoke me to anger, and ᴿhast cast me behind thy back;   Ps. 50:17

10 Therefore, behold, ᴿI will bring ᵀevil upon the house of Jer-o-bo'-am, and ᴿwill cut off from Jer-o-bo'-am him that pisseth against the wall, *and* him that is shut up and left in Israel, and will take away the remnant of the house of Jer-o-bo'-am, as a man taketh away dung, till it be all gone.   15:29 · *disaster* · 21:21; 2 Kin. 9:8

11 ᴿHim that dieth of Jer-o-bo'-am in the city shall the dogs eat; and him that dieth in the field shall the fowls of the air eat: for the LORD hath spoken *it*.   16:4; 21:24

12 Arise thou therefore, get thee to thine own house: *and* ᴿwhen thy feet enter into the city, the child shall die.   v. 17

13 And all Israel shall mourn for him, and bury him: for he only of Jer-o-bo'-am shall come to the grave, because in him ᴿthere is found *some* good thing toward the LORD God of Israel in the house of Jer-o-bo'-am.   2 Chr. 12:12

14 ᴿMoreover the LORD shall raise him up a king over Israel, who shall cut off the house of Jer-o-bo'-am ᵀthat day: but what? even now.   15:27-29 · *this day*

15 For the LORD shall smite Israel, as a reed is shaken in the water, and he shall ᴿroot up Israel out of this good land, which he gave to their fathers, and shall scatter them beyond the river, ᴿbecause they have made their groves, provoking the LORD to anger. Ps. 52:5 · [Ex. 34:13, 14; Deut. 12:3]

16 And he shall give Israel up because of the sins of Jer-o-bo'-am, ᴿwho did sin, and who made Israel to sin.   12:30; 13:34; 15:30, 34; 16:2

17 And Jer-o-bo'-am's wife arose, and departed, and came to ᴿTir'-zah: *and* ᴿwhen she came to the threshold of the door, the child died;   15:21, 33; 16:6, 8; Song 6:4 · v. 12

18 And they buried him; and all Israel mourned for him, ᴿaccording to the word of the LORD, which he spake by the hand of his servant A-hi'-jah the prophet.   v. 13

19 And the rest of the acts of Jer-o-bo'-am, how he warred, and how he reigned, behold, they *are* written in the book of the chronicles of the kings of Israel.

20 And the days which Jer-o-bo'-am reigned *were* two and twenty years: and he slept with his fathers, and ᴿNa'-dab his son reigned in his stead.   15:25

21 And Re-ho-bo'-am the son of Solomon reigned in Judah. ᴿRe-ho-bo'-am *was* forty and one years old when he began to reign, and he reigned seventeen years in Jerusalem, the city ᴿwhich the LORD did choose out of all the tribes of Israel, to put his name there. ᴿAnd his mother's name *was* Na'-a-mah an Am'-mon-i-tess.   2 Chr. 12:13 · 11:32, 36 · v. 31

22 ᴿAnd Judah did evil in the sight of the LORD, and they ᴿprovoked him to jealousy with their sins which they had committed,

above all that their fathers had done. 2 Chr. 12:1 · Ps. 78:58; 1 Cor. 10:22

23 For they also built them high places, and images, and groves, on every high hill, and ᴿunder every green tree. Is. 57:5; Jer. 2:20

24 ᴿAnd there were also sodomites in the land: *and* they did according to all the ᴿabominations of the nations which the LORD cast out before the children of Israel. 15:12; 2 Kin. 23:7 · Deut. 20:18

25 ᴿAnd it came to pass in the fifth year of king Re-ho-bo′-am, *that* Shi′-shak king of Egypt came up against Jerusalem: 11:40

26 ᴿAnd he took away the treasures of the house of the LORD, and the treasures of the king's house; he even took away all: and he took away all the shields of gold which Solomon had made. 15:18

27 And king Re-ho-bo′-am made in their stead brasen shields, and committed *them* unto the hands of the chief of the guard, which kept the door of the king's house.

28 And it was *so*, when the king went into the house of the LORD, that the guard bare them, and brought them back into the guard chamber.

29 ᴿNow the rest of the acts of Re-ho-bo′-am, and all that he did, *are* they not written in the book of the chronicles of the kings of Judah? 2 Chr. 12:15, 16

30 And there was ᴿwar between Re-ho-bo′-am and Jer-o-bo′-am all *their* days. 12:21–24; 15:6

31 ᴿAnd Re-ho-bo′-am slept with his fathers, and was buried with his fathers in the city of David. And his mother's name *was* Na′-a-mah an Am′-mon-i-tess. And A-bi′-jam his son reigned in his stead. 2 Chr. 12:16

15 Now ᴿin the eighteenth year of king Jer-o-bo′-am the son of Ne′-bat reigned A-bi′-jam over Judah. 2 Chr. 13:1

2 Three years reigned he in Jerusalem. ᴿAnd his mother's name *was* Ma′-a-chah, the daughter of A-bish′-a-lom. 2 Chr. 11:20–22

3 And he walked in all the sins of his father, which he had done before him: and ᴿhis heart was not ᵀperfect with the LORD his God, as the heart of David his father. 11:4; Ps. 119:80 · Lit. *at peace with*

4 Nevertheless ᴿfor David's sake did the LORD his God give him a lamp in Jerusalem, to set up his son after him, and to establish Jerusalem: 2 Sam. 21:17; 2 Chr. 21:7

5 Because David ᴿdid *that which was* right in the eyes of the LORD, and turned not aside from any *thing* that he commanded him all the days of his life, ᴿsave only in the matter of U-ri′-ah the Hit′-tite. Luke 1:6 · 2 Sam. 11:3, 15–17

6 ᴿAnd there was war between Re-ho-bo′-am and Jer-o-bo′-am all the days of his life. 14:30

7 ᴿNow the rest of the acts of A-bi′-jam, and all that he did, *are* they not written in the book of the chronicles of the kings of Judah? And there was war between A-bi′-jam and Jer-o-bo′-am. 2 Chr. 13:2–22

8 ᴿAnd A-bi′-jam slept with his fathers; and they buried him in the city of David: and A′-sa his son reigned in his stead. 2 Chr. 14:1

9 And in the twentieth year of Jer-o-bo′-am king of Israel reigned A′-sa over Judah.

10 And forty and one years reigned he in Jerusalem. And his mother's name *was* Ma′-a-chah, the daughter of A-bish′-a-lom.

11 ᴿAnd A′-sa did *that which was* right in the eyes of the LORD, as *did* David his father. 2 Chr. 14:2

12 ᴿAnd he took away the sodomites out of the land, and removed all the idols that his fathers had made. 14:24; 22:46

13 And also Ma′-a-chah his mother, even her he removed from *being* queen, because she had made an idol in a grove; and A′-sa destroyed her idol, and ᴿburnt *it* by the brook Kid′-ron. Ex. 32:20

14 ᴿBut the high places were not removed: nevertheless A′-sa's ᴿheart was perfect with the LORD all his days. 3:2; 22:43 · [1 Sam. 16:7]

15 And he brought in the things which his father ᴿhad dedicated,

and the things which himself had dedicated, into the house of the LORD, silver, and gold, and vessels.   7:51

16 And there was war between A'-sa and Ba'-a-sha king of Israel all their days.

17 And ^RBa'-a-sha king of Israel went up against Judah, and built Ra'-mah, that he might not suffer any to go out or come in to A'-sa king of Judah.   2 Chr. 16:1–6

18 Then A'-sa took all the silver and the gold *that were* left in the treasures of the house of the LORD, and the treasures of the king's house, and delivered them into the hand of his servants: and king A'-sa sent them to Ben–ha'-dad, the son of Tab'-ri-mon, the son of He'-zi-on, king of Syria, that dwelt at Damascus, saying,

19 *There is* a league between me and thee, *and* between my father and thy father: behold, I have sent unto thee a present of silver and gold; come and break thy league with Ba'-a-sha king of Israel, that he may depart from me.

20 So Ben–ha'-dad hearkened unto king A'-sa, and ^Rsent the captains of the hosts which he had against the cities of Israel, and smote ^RI'-jon, and Dan, and A'-bel–beth–ma'-a-chah, and all Cin'-ne-roth, with all the land of Naph'-ta-li.   20:1 · 2 Kin. 15:29

21 And it came to pass, when Ba'-a-sha heard *thereof*, that he left off building of Ra'-mah, and dwelt in ^RTir'-zah.   14:17; 16:15–18

22 ^RThen king A'-sa made a proclamation throughout all Judah; none *was* exempted: and they took away the stones of Ra'-mah, and the timber thereof, wherewith Ba'-a-sha had builded; and king A'-sa built with them ^RGe'-ba of Benjamin, and ^RMiz'-pah.   2 Chr. 16:6 · Josh. 21:17 · Josh. 18:26

23 The rest of all the acts of A'-sa, and all his might, and all that he did, and the cities which he built, *are* they not written in the book of the chronicles of the kings of Judah? Nevertheless ^Rin the time of his old age he was diseased in his feet.   2 Chr. 16:11–14

24 And A'-sa slept with his fathers, and was buried with his fathers in the city of David his father: and ^RJe-hosh'-a-phat his son reigned in his stead.   Matt. 1:8

25 And ^RNa'-dab the son of Jer-o-bo'-am began to reign over Israel in the second year of A'-sa king of Judah, and reigned over Israel two years.   14:20

26 And he did evil in the sight of the LORD, and walked in the way of his father, and in his sin wherewith he made Israel to sin.

27 And Ba'-a-sha the son of A-hi'-jah, of the house of Is'-sa-char, conspired against him; and Ba'-a-sha smote him at Gib'-be-thon, which *belonged* to the Phi-lis'-tines; for Na'-dab and all Israel laid siege to Gib'-be-thon.

28 Even in the third year of A'-sa king of Judah did Ba'-a-sha slay him, and reigned in his stead.

29 And it came to pass, when he reigned, *that* he smote all the house of Jer-o-bo'-am; he left not to Jer-o-bo'-am any that breathed, until he had destroyed him, according unto the saying of the LORD, which he spake by his servant A-hi'-jah the Shi'-lo-nite:

30 ^RBecause of the sins of Jer-o-bo'-am which he sinned, and which he made Israel sin, by his provocation wherewith he provoked the LORD God of Israel to anger.   14:9, 16

31 Now the rest of the acts of Na'-dab, and all that he did, *are* they not written in the book of the chronicles of the kings of Israel?

32 ^RAnd there was war between A'-sa and Ba'-a-sha king of Israel all their days.   v. 16

33 In the third year of A'-sa king of Judah began Ba'-a-sha the son of A-hi'-jah to reign over all Israel in Tir'-zah, twenty and four years.

34 And he did evil in the sight of the LORD, and walked in the way of Jer-o-bo'-am, and in his sin wherewith he made Israel to sin.

16 Then the word of the LORD came to ᴿJe'-hu the son of ᴿHa-na'-ni against Ba'-a-sha, saying, *2 Chr. 19:2; 20:34 · 2 Chr. 16:7–10*

2 ᴿForasmuch as I exalted thee out of the dust, and made thee prince over my people Israel; and ᴿthou hast walked in the way of Jer-o-bo'-am, and hast made my people Israel to sin, to provoke me to anger with their sins; *14:7 · 15:34*

3 Behold, I will take away the posterity of Ba'-a-sha, and the posterity of his house; and will make thy house like the house of Jer-o-bo'-am the son of Ne'-bat.

4 ᴿHim that dieth of Ba'-a-sha in the city shall the dogs eat; and him that dieth of his in the fields shall the fowls of the air eat. *14:11*

5 Now the rest of the acts of Ba'-a-sha, and what he did, and his might, ᴿ*are* they not written in the book of the chronicles of the kings of Israel? *2 Chr. 16:11*

6 So Ba'-a-sha ᵀslept with his fathers, and was buried in ᴿTir'-zah: and E'-lah his son reigned in his stead. *rested in death · 14:17; 15:21*

7 And also by the hand of the prophet ᴿJe'-hu the son of Ha-na'-ni came the word of the LORD against Ba'-a-sha, and against his house, even for all the evil that he did in the sight of the LORD, in provoking him to anger with the work of his hands, in being like the house of Jer-o-bo'-am; and because ᴿhe killed him. *v. 1 · 15:27*

8 In the twenty and sixth year of A'-sa king of Judah began E'-lah the son of Ba'-a-sha to reign over Israel in Tir'-zah, two years.

9 ᴿAnd his servant Zim'-ri, captain of half *his* chariots, conspired against him, as he was in Tir'-zah, drinking himself drunk in the house of Ar'-za ᴿsteward of *his* house in Tir'-zah. *2 Kin. 9:30–33 · 18:3*

10 And Zim'-ri went in and ᵀsmote him, and killed him, in the twenty and seventh year of A'-sa king of Judah, and reigned in his stead. *struck*

11 And it came to pass, when he began to reign, as soon as he sat on his throne, *that* he slew all the house of Ba'-a-sha: he left him ᴿnot one ᵀthat pisseth against a wall, neither of his kinsfolks, nor of his friends. *1 Sam. 25:22 · male*

12 Thus did Zim'-ri destroy all the house of Ba'-a-sha, ᴿaccording to the word of the LORD, which he spake against Ba'-a-sha by Je'-hu the prophet, *v. 3*

13 For all the sins of Ba'-a-sha, and the sins of E'-lah his son, by which they sinned, and by which they made Israel to sin, in provoking the LORD God of Israel to anger with their ᵀvanities. *idols*

14 Now the rest of the acts of E'-lah, and all that he did, *are* they not written in the book of the chronicles of the kings of Israel?

15 In the twenty and seventh year of A'-sa king of Judah did Zim'-ri reign seven days in Tir'-zah. And the people *were* encamped ᴿagainst Gib'-be-thon, which *belonged* to the Phi-lis'-tines. *15:27*

16 And the people *that were* encamped heard say, Zim'-ri hath conspired, and hath also slain the king: wherefore all Israel made Om'-ri, the captain of the host, king over Israel that day in the camp.

17 And Om'-ri went up from Gib'-be-thon, and all Israel with him, and they besieged Tir'-zah.

18 And it came to pass, when Zim'-ri saw that the city was ᵀtaken, that he went into the palace of the king's house, and burnt the king's house ᵀover him with fire, and died, *captured · down upon himself*

19 For his sins which he sinned in doing evil in the sight of the LORD, ᴿin walking in the way of Jer-o-bo'-am, and in his sin which he did, to make Israel to sin. *15:26*

20 Now the rest of the acts of Zim'-ri, and his treason that he wrought, *are* they not written in the book of the chronicles of the kings of Israel?

21 Then were the people of Israel divided into two parts: half of the people followed Tib'-ni the

son of Gi'-nath, to make him king; and half followed Om'-ri.

22 But the people that followed Om'-ri prevailed against the people that followed Tib'-ni the son of Gi'-nath: so Tib'-ni died, and Om'-ri reigned.

23 In the thirty and first year of A'-sa king of Judah began Om'-ri to reign over Israel, twelve years: six years reigned he in Tir'-zah.

24 And he bought the hill Sama'-ri-a of She'-mer for two talents of silver, and built on the hill, and called the name of the city which he built, after the name of She'-mer, owner of the hill, ᴿSama'-ri-a.   13:32; 2 Kin. 17:24; John 4:4

25 But ᴿOm'-ri wrought evil in the eyes of the LORD, and did worse than all that *were* before him.   Mic. 6:16

26 For he ᴿwalked in all the way of Jer-o-bo'-am the son of Ne'-bat, and in his sin wherewith he made Israel to sin, to provoke the LORD God of Israel to anger with their ᴿvanities.ᵀ   v. 19 · v. 13 · *idols*

27 Now the rest of the acts of Om'-ri which he did, and his might that he shewed, *are* they not written in the book of the chronicles of the kings of Israel?

28 So Om'-ri slept with his fathers, and was buried in Sa-ma'-ri-a: and Ahab his son reigned in his stead.

29 And in the thirty and eighth year of A'-sa king of Judah began Ahab the son of Om'-ri to reign over Israel: and Ahab the son of Om'-ri reigned over Israel in Sa-ma'-ri-a twenty and two years.

30 And Ahab the son of Om'-ri did evil in the sight of the LORD above all that *were* before him.

31 And it came to pass, as if it had been a light thing for him to walk in the sins of Jer-o-bo'-am the son of Ne'-bat, ᴿthat he took to wife Jez'-e-bel the daughter of Eth'-ba-al king of the Zi-do'-nians, and went and served Ba'-al, and worshipped him.   Deut. 7:3

32 And he reared up an altar for

Ba'-al in the house of Ba'-al, which he had built in Sa-ma'-ri-a.

33 And Ahab made a grove; and Ahab ᴿdid more to provoke the LORD God of Israel to anger than all the kings of Israel that were before him.   vv. 29, 30; 14:9; 21:25

34 In his days did Hi'-el the Beth'-el-ite build Jericho: he laid the foundation thereof in A-bi'-ram his firstborn, and set up the gates thereof in his youngest *son* Se'-gub, ᴿaccording to the word of the LORD, which he spake by Joshua the son of Nun.   Josh. 6:26

17 And E-li'-jah the Tish'-bite, *who was* of the inhabitants of Gil'-e-ad, said unto Ahab, ᴿAs the LORD God of Israel liveth, before whom I stand, there shall not be dew nor rain these years, but according to my word.   18:10

2 And the word of the LORD came unto him, saying,

3 Get thee hence, and turn thee eastward, and hide thyself by the brook Che'-rith, that *is* before Jordan.

4 And it shall be, *that* thou shalt drink of the brook; and I have commanded the ᴿravens to feed thee there.   Job 38:41

5 So he went and did according unto the word of the LORD: for he went and dwelt by the brook Che'-rith, that *is* before Jordan.

6 And the ravens brought him bread and flesh in the morning, and bread and flesh in the evening; and he drank of the brook.

7 And it came to pass after a while, that the brook dried up, because there had been no rain in the land.

8 And the word of the LORD came unto him, saying,

9 Arise, get thee to ᴿZar'-e-phath, which *belongeth* to Zi'-don, and dwell there: behold, I have commanded a widow woman there to sustain thee.   Obad. 20

10 So he arose and went to Zar'-e-phath. And when he came to the gate of the city, behold, the widow woman *was* there gathering of sticks: and he called to her, and

said, Fetch me, I pray thee, a little water in a vessel, that I may drink.

11 And as she was going to fetch *it*, he called to her, and said, Bring me, I pray thee, a morsel of bread in thine hand.

12 And she said, *As* the LORD thy God liveth, I have not a cake, but an handful of meal in a barrel, and a little oil in a cruse: and, behold, I *am* gathering two sticks, that I may go in and ᵀdress it for me and my son, that we may eat it, and ᴿdie.　　*prepare* · Deut. 28:23, 24

13 And E-li′-jah said unto her, Fear not; go *and* do as thou hast said: but make me thereof a little cake first, and bring *it* unto me, and after make for thee and for thy son.

14 For thus saith the LORD God of Israel, The barrel of meal shall not waste, neither shall the cruse of oil fail, until the day *that* the LORD sendeth rain upon the earth.

15 And she went and did according to the saying of E-li′-jah: and she, and he, and her house, did eat *many* days.

16 *And* the barrel of meal wasted not, neither did the cruse of oil fail, according to the word of the LORD, which he spake by E-li′-jah.

17 And it came to pass after these things, *that* the son of the woman, the mistress of the house, fell sick; and his sickness was so ᵀsore, that there was no breath left in him.　　*severe*

18 And she said unto E-li′-jah, What have I to do with thee, O thou man of God? art thou come unto me to call my sin to remembrance, and to slay my son?

19 And he said unto her, Give me thy son. And he took him out of her ᵀbosom, and carried him up into a loft, where he abode, and laid him upon his own bed.　　*arms*

20 And he cried unto the LORD, and said, O LORD my God, hast thou also brought evil upon the widow with whom I ᵀsojourn, by slaying her son?　　*lodge*

21 And he stretched himself

upon the child three times, and cried unto the LORD, and said, O LORD my God, I pray thee, let this child's soul come into him again.

22 And the LORD heard the voice of E-li′-jah; and the soul of the child came into him again, and he ᴿrevived.　　Luke 7:14, 15; Heb. 11:35

23 And E-li′-jah took the child, and brought him down out of the chamber into the house, and delivered him unto his mother: and E-li′-jah said, See, thy son liveth.

24 And the woman said to E-li′-jah, Now by this ᴿI know that thou *art* a man of God, *and* that the word of the LORD in thy mouth *is* truth.　　John 2:11; 3:2; 16:30

18 And it came to pass *after* ᴿmany days, that the word of the LORD came to E-li′-jah in the third year, saying, Go, shew thyself unto Ahab; and I will send rain upon the earth.　　17:1; Luke 4:25

2 And E-li′-jah went to shew himself unto Ahab. And *there was* a sore famine in Sa-ma′-ri-a.

3 And Ahab called O-ba-di′-ah, which *was* ᵀthe governor of *his* house. (Now O-ba-di′-ah feared the LORD greatly:　　*in charge of*

4 For it was *so*, when Jez′-e-bel ᵀcut off the prophets of the LORD, that O-ba-di′-ah took an hundred prophets, and hid them by fifty in a cave, and fed them with bread and water.)　　*massacred*

5 And Ahab said unto O-ba-di′-ah, Go into the land, unto all fountains of water, and unto all brooks: peradventure we may find grass to save the horses and mules alive, that we lose not all the beasts.

6 So they divided the land between them to pass throughout it: Ahab went one way by himself, and O-ba-di′-ah went another way by himself.

7 And as O-ba-di′-ah was in the way, behold, E-li′-jah met him: and he ᴿknew him, and fell on his face, and said, ᵀArt thou that my lord E-li′-jah?　　2 Kin. 1:6–8 · *Is that you*

8 And he answered him, I *am*:

go, tell thy lord, Behold, E-li'-jah *is here*.

9 And he said, What have I sinned, that thou wouldest deliver thy servant into the hand of Ahab, to slay me?

10 *As* the LORD thy God liveth, there is no nation or kingdom, whither my lord hath not sent to seek thee: and when they said, *He is* not *there*; he took an oath of the kingdom and nation, that they found thee not.

11 And now thou sayest, Go, tell thy lord, Behold, E-li'-jah *is here*.

12 And it shall come to pass, *as soon as* I am gone from thee, that ^Rthe Spirit of the LORD shall carry thee whither I know not; and *so* when I come and tell Ahab, and he cannot find thee, he shall slay me: but I thy servant fear the LORD from my youth.   Acts 8:39

13 Was it not told my lord what I did when Jez'-e-bel slew the prophets of the LORD, how I hid an hundred men of the LORD's prophets by fifty in a cave, and fed them with bread and water?

14 And now thou sayest, Go, tell thy lord, Behold, E-li'-jah *is here*: and he shall slay me.

15 And E-li'-jah said, *As* the LORD of hosts liveth, before whom I stand, I will surely ^Tshew myself unto him to day.   *present*

16 So O-ba-di'-ah went to meet Ahab, and told him: and Ahab went to meet E-li'-jah.

17 And it came to pass, when Ahab saw E-li'-jah, that Ahab said unto him, *Art* thou he that ^Rtroubleth Israel?   Josh. 7:25; Acts 16:20

18 And he answered, I have not troubled Israel; but thou, and thy father's house, ^Rin that ye have forsaken the commandments of the LORD, and thou hast followed Ba'-al-im.   16:30–33; [2 Chr. 15:2]

19 Now therefore send, *and* gather to me all Israel unto mount ^RCarmel, and the prophets of Ba'-al four hundred and fifty, ^Rand the prophets of the groves four hundred, which eat at Jez'-e-bel's table.   Josh. 19:26; 2 Kin. 2:25 · 16:33

20 So Ahab sent unto all the children of Israel, and ^Rgathered the prophets together unto mount Carmel.   22:6

21 And E-li'-jah came unto all the people, and said, ^RHow long halt ye between two opinions? if the LORD *be* God, follow him: but if Ba'-al, ^R*then* follow him. And the people answered him not a word.   [Matt. 6:24] · Josh. 24:15

22 Then said E-li'-jah unto the people, ^RI, *even* I only, remain a prophet of the LORD; ^Rbut Ba'-al's prophets *are* four hundred and fifty men.   19:10, 14 · v. 19

23 Let them therefore give us two bullocks; and let them choose one bullock for themselves, and cut it in pieces, and lay *it* on wood, and put no fire *under*: and I will dress the other bullock, and lay *it* on wood, and put no fire *under*:

24 And call ye on the name of your gods, and I will call on the name of the LORD: and the God that ^Ranswereth by fire, let him be God. And all the people answered and said, It is well spoken.   v. 38

25 And E-li'-jah said unto the prophets of Ba'-al, Choose you one bullock for yourselves, and dress *it* first; for ye *are* many; and call on the name of your gods, but put no fire *under*.

26 And they took the bullock which was given them, and they dressed *it*, and called on the name of Ba'-al from morning even until noon, saying, O Ba'-al, hear us. But *there was* no voice, nor any that answered. And they leaped upon the altar which was made.

27 And it came to pass at noon, that E-li'-jah mocked them, and said, Cry aloud: for he *is* a god; either he is talking, or he is ^Tpursuing, or he is in a journey, *or* peradventure he sleepeth, and must be awaked.   *busy*

28 And they cried aloud, and cut themselves after their manner with knives and lancets, till the blood gushed out upon them.

29 And it came to pass, when

midday was past, ^Rand they prophesied until the *time* of the offering of the *evening* sacrifice, that *there was* ^Rneither voice, nor any to answer, nor any that regarded.　　　Ex. 29:39, 41 · v. 26

30 And E-li′-jah said unto all the people, Come near unto me. And all the people came near unto him. And he repaired the altar of the LORD *that was* broken down.

31 And E-li′-jah took twelve stones, according to the number of the tribes of the sons of Jacob, unto whom the word of the LORD came, saying, ^RIsrael shall be thy name:　　Gen. 32:28; 35:10; 2 Kin. 17:34

32 And with the stones he built an altar ^Rin the name of the LORD: and he made a trench about the altar, as great as would contain two measures of seed.　　[Col. 3:17]

33 And he put the wood in order, and cut the bullock in pieces, and laid *him* on the wood, and said, Fill four barrels with water, and ^Rpour *it* on the burnt sacrifice, and on the wood.　　Judg. 6:20

34 And he said, Do *it* the second time. And they did *it* the second time. And he said, Do *it* the third time. And they did *it* the third time.

35 And the water ran round about the altar; and he filled the trench also with water.

36 And it came to pass at *the time of* the offering of the *evening* sacrifice, that E-li′-jah the prophet came near, and said, LORD ^RGod of Abraham, Isaac, and of Israel, let it be known this day that thou *art* God in Israel, and *that* I *am* thy servant, and *that* I have done all these things at thy word. Gen. 28:13

37 Hear me, O LORD, hear me, that this people may know that thou *art* the LORD God, and *that* thou hast turned their heart back again.

38 Then the fire of the LORD fell, and consumed the burnt sacrifice, and the wood, and the stones, and the dust, and licked up the water that *was* in the trench.

39 And when all the people saw

it, they fell on their faces: and they said, The LORD, he *is* the God; the LORD, he *is* the God.

40 And E-li′-jah said unto them, Take the prophets of Ba′-al; let not one of them escape. And they took them: and E-li′-jah brought them down to the brook Ki′-shon, and slew them there.

41 And E-li′-jah said unto Ahab, Get thee up, eat and drink; for *there is* a sound of abundance of rain.

42 So Ahab went up to eat and to drink. And E-li′-jah went up to the top of Carmel; and he cast himself down upon the earth, and put his face between his knees,

43 And said to his servant, Go up now, look toward the sea. And he went up, and looked, and said, *There is* nothing. And he said, Go again seven times.

44 And it came to pass at the seventh time, that he said, Behold, there ariseth a little cloud out of the sea, like a man's hand. And he said, Go up, say unto Ahab, Prepare *thy chariot,* and get thee down, that the rain stop thee not.

45 And it came to pass in the mean while, that the heaven was black with clouds and wind, and there was a great rain. And Ahab rode, and went to Jez′-re-el.

46 And the hand of the LORD was on E-li′-jah; and he girded up his loins, and ran before Ahab to the entrance of Jez′-re-el.

19 And Ahab told Jez′-e-bel all that E-li′-jah had done, and withal how he had ^Rslain all the prophets with the sword. 18:40

2 Then Jez′-e-bel sent a messenger unto E-li′-jah, saying, ^RSo let the gods do *to me,* and more also, if I make not thy life as the life of one of them by to morrow about this time.　　20:10; 2 Kin. 6:31

3 And when he saw *that,* he arose, and ^Twent for his life, and came to Be′-er–she′-ba, which *belongeth* to Judah, and left his servant there.　　　　　*ran*

4 But he himself went a day's journey into the wilderness, and

came and sat down under a juniper tree: and he [R]requested for himself that he might die; and said, It is enough; now, O LORD, take away my life; for I *am* not better than my fathers.   Jon. 4:3, 8

5 And as he lay and slept under a juniper tree, behold, then an angel touched him, and said unto him, Arise *and* eat.

6 And he looked, and, behold, *there was* a cake baken on the coals, and a cruse of water at his head. And he did eat and drink, and laid him down again.

7 And the angel of the LORD came again the second time, and touched him, and said, Arise *and* eat; because the journey *is* too great for thee.

8 And he arose, and did eat and drink, and went in the strength of that meat forty days and [R]forty nights unto Ho'-reb the mount of God.   Ex. 24:18; Deut. 9:9–11, 18; Matt. 4:2

9 And he came thither unto a cave, and lodged there; and, behold, the word of the LORD *came* to him, and he said unto him, What doest thou here, E-li'-jah?

10 And he said, I have been very jealous for the LORD God of hosts: for the children of Israel have forsaken thy covenant, thrown down thine altars, and slain thy prophets with the sword; and [R]I, *even* I only, am left; and they seek my life, to take it away.   18:22; Rom. 11:3

11 And he said, Go forth, and stand upon the mount before the LORD. And, behold, the LORD passed by, and [R]a great and strong wind [T]rent the mountains, and brake in pieces the rocks before the LORD; *but* the LORD *was* not in the wind: and after the wind an earthquake; *but* the LORD *was* not in the earthquake: Ezek. 1:4 · *tore into*

12 And after the earthquake a fire; *but* the LORD *was* not in the fire: and after the fire a [T]still small voice.   *delicate whispering voice*

13 And it was *so*, when E-li'-jah heard *it*, that [R]he wrapped his face in his mantle, and went out,

and stood in the entering in of the cave. And, behold, *there came* a voice unto him, and said, What doest thou here, E-li'-jah?   Is. 6:2

14 [R]And he said, I have been very [T]jealous for the LORD God of hosts: because the children of Israel have forsaken thy covenant, thrown down thine altars, and slain thy prophets with the sword; and I, *even* I only, am left; and they seek my life, to take it away.   v. 10 · *zealous*

15 And the LORD said unto him, Go, return on thy way to the wilderness of Damascus: [R]and when thou comest, anoint Haz'-a-el *to be* king over Syria: 2 Kin. 8:8–15

16 And [R]Je'-hu the son of Nim'-shi shalt thou anoint *to be* king over Israel: and [R]E-li'-sha the son of Sha'-phat of A'-bel–me-ho'-lah shalt thou anoint *to be* prophet in thy room.   2 Kin. 9:1–10 · 2 Kin. 2:9–15

17 And it shall come to pass, *that* him that escapeth the sword of Haz'-a-el shall Je'-hu slay: and him that escapeth from the sword of Je'-hu shall E-li'-sha slay.

18 [R]Yet I have left *me* seven thousand in Israel, all the knees which have not bowed unto Ba'-al, [R]and every mouth which hath not kissed him.   Rom. 11:4 · Hos. 13:2

19 So he departed thence, and found E-li'-sha the son of Sha'-phat, who *was* plowing *with* twelve yoke *of* oxen before him, and he with the twelfth: and E-li'-jah passed by him, and cast his [R]mantle upon him.   2 Kin. 2:8, 13, 14

20 And he left the oxen, and ran after E-li'-jah, and said, [R]Let me, I pray thee, kiss my father and my mother, and *then* I will follow thee. And he said unto him, Go back again: for what have I done to thee?   [Matt. 8:21, 22]; Acts 20:37

21 And he returned back from him, and took a yoke of oxen, and slew them, and [R]boiled their flesh with the instruments of the oxen, and gave unto the people, and they did eat. Then he arose, and went after E-li'-jah, and ministered unto him.   2 Sam. 24:22

20 And ^RBen–ha′-dad the king of Syria gathered all his host together: and *there were* thirty and two kings with him, and horses, and chariots: and he went up and besieged ^RSa-ma′-ri-a, and warred against it. 15:18, 20 · 16:24

2 And he sent messengers to Ahab king of Israel into the city, and said unto him, Thus saith Ben–ha′-dad,

3 Thy silver and thy gold *is* mine; thy wives also and thy children, *even* the goodliest, *are* mine.

4 And the king of Israel answered and said, My lord, O king, according to thy saying, I *am* thine, and all that I have.

5 And the messengers came again, and said, Thus speaketh Ben–ha′-dad, saying, Although I have sent unto thee, saying, Thou shalt deliver me thy silver, and thy gold, and thy wives, and thy children;

6 Yet I will send my servants unto thee to morrow about this time, and they shall search thine house, and the houses of thy servants; and it shall be, *that* whatsoever is ^Tpleasant in thine eyes, they shall put *it* in their hand, and take *it* away. *pleasing*

7 Then the king of Israel called all the elders of the land, and said, Mark, I pray you, and see how this *man* seeketh ^Tmischief: for he sent unto me for my wives, and for my children, and for my silver, and for my gold; and I denied him not. *trouble*

8 And all the elders and all the people said unto him, Hearken not *unto him*, nor consent.

9 Wherefore he said unto the messengers of Ben–ha′-dad, Tell my lord the king, All that thou didst send for to thy servant at the first I will do: but this thing I may not do. And the messengers departed, and brought him word again.

10 And Ben–ha′-dad sent unto him, and said, ^RThe gods do so unto me, and more also, if the dust of Sa-ma′-ri-a shall suffice for handfuls for all the people that follow me. 19:2; 2 Kin. 6:31

11 And the king of Israel answered and said, Tell *him*, Let not him that girdeth on *his harness* ^Rboast himself as he that putteth it off. Prov. 27:1; [Eccl. 7:8]

12 And it came to pass, when *Ben–ha′-dad* heard this message, as he *was* drinking, he and the kings in the ^Tpavilions, that he said unto his servants, ^TSet *yourselves in array*. And they set *themselves in array* against the city. *shelters · Get ready to attack*

13 And, behold, there came a prophet unto Ahab king of Israel, saying, Thus saith the LORD, Hast thou seen all this great multitude? behold, ^RI will deliver it into thine hand this day; and thou shalt know that I *am* the LORD. v. 28

14 And Ahab said, By whom? And he said, Thus saith the LORD, *Even* by the young men of the princes of the provinces. Then he said, Who shall order the battle? And he answered, Thou.

15 Then he numbered the young men of the princes of the provinces, and they were two hundred and thirty two: and after them he numbered all the people, *even* all the children of Israel, *being* seven thousand.

16 And they went out at noon. But Ben–ha′-dad *was* ^Rdrinking himself drunk in the pavilions, he and the kings, the thirty and two kings that helped him. v. 12; 16:9

17 And the young men of the princes of the provinces went out first; and Ben–ha′-dad sent out, and they told him, saying, There are men come out of Sa-ma′-ri-a.

18 And he said, Whether they be come out for peace, take them alive; or whether they be come out for war, take them alive.

19 So these young men of the princes of the provinces came out of the city, and the army which followed them.

20 And they slew every one his man: and the Syrians fled; and Israel pursued them: and Ben–ha′-

dad the king of Syria escaped on an horse with the horsemen.

21 And the king of Israel went out, and ^Tsmote the horses and chariots, and slew the Syrians with a great slaughter. *attacked*

22 And the prophet came to the king of Israel, and said unto him, Go, strengthen thyself, and mark, and see what thou doest: for at the return of the year the king of Syria will come up against thee.

23 And the servants of the king of Syria said unto him, Their gods *are* gods of the hills; therefore they were stronger than we; but let us fight against them in the plain, and surely we shall be stronger than they.

24 And do this thing, Take the kings away, every man out of his place, and put captains in their ^Trooms: *places*

25 And ^Tnumber thee an army, like the army that ^Tthou hast lost, horse for horse, and chariot for chariot: and we will fight against them in the plain, *and* surely we shall be stronger than they. And he hearkened unto their voice, and did so. *muster · Lit. fell from you*

26 And it came to pass at the return of the year, that Ben–ha'-dad numbered the Syrians, and went up to ^RA'-phek, to fight against Israel. Josh. 13:4; 2 Kin. 13:17

27 And the children of Israel were numbered, and were all present, and went against them: and the children of Israel pitched before them like two little flocks of kids; but the Syrians filled the ^Rcountry. Judg. 6:3–5; 1 Sam. 13:5–8

28 And there came a ^Rman of God, and spake unto the king of Israel, and said, Thus saith the LORD, Because the Syrians have said, The LORD *is* God of the hills, but he *is* not God of the valleys, therefore ^Rwill I deliver all this great multitude into thine hand, and ye shall know that I *am* the LORD. 17:18 · v. 13

29 And they ^Tpitched one over against the other seven days. And *so* it was, that in the seventh day

the battle was joined: and the children of Israel slew of the Syrians an hundred thousand footmen in one day. *encamped opposite each other*

30 But the rest fled to A'-phek, into the city; and *there* a wall fell upon twenty and seven thousand of the men *that were* left. And Ben–ha'-dad fled, and came into the city, into an inner chamber.

31 And his servants said unto him, Behold now, we have heard that the kings of the house of Israel *are* merciful kings: let us, I pray thee, put sackcloth on our loins, and ropes upon our heads, and go out to the king of Israel: peradventure he will save thy life.

32 So they girded sackcloth on their loins, and *put* ropes on their heads, and came to the king of Israel, and said, Thy servant Ben–ha'-dad saith, I pray thee, let me live. And he said, *Is* he yet alive? he *is* my brother.

33 Now the men did diligently observe whether *any thing would* come from him, and did hastily catch *it:* and they said, Thy brother Ben–ha'-dad. Then he said, Go ye, bring him. Then Ben–ha'-dad came forth to him; and he caused him to come up into the chariot.

34 And *Ben–ha'-dad* said unto him, ^RThe cities, which my father took from thy father, I will restore; and thou shalt make streets for thee in Damascus, as my father made in Sa-ma'-ri-a. Then *said Ahab,* I will send thee away with this covenant. So he made a covenant with him, and sent him away. 15:20

35 And a certain man of the sons of the prophets said unto his neighbour in the word of the LORD, Smite me, I pray thee. And the man refused to smite him.

36 Then said he unto him, Because thou hast not obeyed the voice of the LORD, behold, as soon as thou art departed from me, a lion shall slay thee. And as soon as he was departed from him, a lion found him, and slew him.

37 Then he found another man,

and said, Smite me, I pray thee. And the man smote him, so that in smiting he wounded *him*.

38 So the prophet departed, and waited for the king by the way, and disguised himself with ashes upon his face.

39 And as the king passed by, he cried unto the king: and he said, Thy servant went out into the midst of the battle; and, be-hold, a man turned aside, and brought a man unto me, and said, Keep this man: if by any means he be miss-ing, then ᴿshall thy life be for his life, or else thou shalt pay a talent of silver.   2 Kin. 10:24

40 And as thy servant was busy here and there, he was gone. And the king of Israel said unto him, So *shall* thy judgment *be*; thyself hast decided *it*.

41 And he hasted, and took the ashes away from his face; and the king of Israel discerned him that he *was* of the prophets.

42 And he said unto him, Thus saith the LORD, ᴿBecause thou hast let go out of *thy* hand a man whom I appointed to utter de-struction, therefore thy life shall go for his life, and thy people for his people.   22:31-37

43 And the king of Israel went to his house ᵀheavy and displeased, and came to Sa-ma'-ri-a.   *sullen*

21 And it came to pass after these things, *that* Na'-both the Jez'-re-el-ite had a vineyard, which *was* in ᴿJez'-re-el, hard by the palace of Ahab king of Sa-ma'-ri-a.   18:45, 46; Judg. 6:33

2 And Ahab spake unto Na'-both, saying, Give me thy vine-yard, that I may have it for a gar-den of herbs, because it *is* near unto my house: and I will give thee for it a better vineyard than it; *or*, if it seem good to thee, I will give thee the worth of it in money.

3 And Na'-both said to Ahab, The LORD forbid it me, ᴿthat I should give the inheritance of my fathers unto thee.   [Lev. 25:23]

4 And Ahab came into his house heavy and displeased be-cause of the word which Na'-both the Jez'-re-el-ite had spoken to him: for he had said, I will not give thee the inheritance of my fathers. And he laid him down upon his bed, and turned away his face, and would eat no bread.

5 But ᴿJez'-e-bel his wife came to him, and said unto him, Why is thy spirit so sad, that thou eatest no bread?   19:1, 2

6 And he said unto her, Be-cause I spake unto Na'-both the Jez'-re-el-ite, and said unto him, Give me thy vineyard for money; or else, if it please thee, I will give thee *another* vineyard for it: and he answered, I will not give thee my vineyard.

7 And Jez'-e-bel his wife said unto him, Dost thou now govern the kingdom of Israel? arise, *and* eat bread, and let thine heart be merry: I will give thee the vine-yard of Na'-both the Jez'-re-el-ite.

8 So she wrote letters in Ahab's name, and sealed *them* with his seal, and sent the letters unto the elders and to the nobles that *were* in his city, dwelling with Na'-both.

9 And she wrote in the letters, saying, Proclaim a fast, and ᵀset Na'-both ᵀon high among the peo-ple: *seat · Lit. at the head*

10 And set two men, sons of Be'-li-al, before him, to bear witness against him, saying, Thou didst blaspheme God and the king. And *then* carry him out, and ᴿstone him, that he may die.   [Lev. 24:14]

11 And the men of his city, *even* the elders and the nobles who were the inhabitants in his city, did as Jez'-e-bel had sent unto them, *and* as it *was* written in the letters which she had sent unto them.

12 ᴿThey proclaimed a fast, and set Na'-both on high among the people.   Is. 58:4

13 And there came in two men, children of Be'-li-al, and sat be-fore him: and the men of Be'-li-al witnessed against him, *even* against Na'-both, in the presence

of the people, saying, Na'-both did blaspheme God and the king. ^RThen they carried him forth out of the city, and stoned him with stones, that he died.   Acts 7:58, 59

14 Then they sent to Jez'-e-bel, saying, Na'-both is stoned, and is dead.

15 And it came to pass, when Jez'-e-bel heard that Na'-both was stoned, and was dead, that Jez'-e-bel said to Ahab, Arise, take possession of the vineyard of Na'-both the Jez'-re-el-ite, which he refused to give thee for money: for Na'-both is not alive, but dead.

16 And it came to pass, when Ahab heard that Na'-both was dead, that Ahab rose up to go down to the vineyard of Na'-both the Jez'-re-el-ite, to take possession of it.

17 ^RAnd the word of the LORD came to ^RE-li'-jah the Tish'-bite, saying,   [Ps. 9:12] · 19:1

18 Arise, go down to meet Ahab king of Israel, ^Rwhich *is* in Sa-ma'-ri-a: behold, *he is* in the vineyard of Na'-both, whither he is gone down to possess it.   13:32; 2 Chr. 22:9

19 And thou shalt speak unto him, saying, Thus saith the LORD, Hast thou killed, and also taken possession? And thou shalt speak unto him, saying, Thus saith the LORD, In the place where dogs licked the blood of Na'-both shall dogs lick thy blood, even thine.

20 And Ahab said to E-li'-jah, ^RHast thou found me, O mine enemy? And he answered, I have found *thee:* because ^Rthou hast sold thyself to work evil in the sight of the LORD.   18:17 · [Rom. 7:14]

21 Behold, I will bring evil upon thee, and will take away thy ^Rposterity, and will cut off from Ahab ^Rhim that pisseth against the wall, and him that is shut up and left in Israel,   2 Kin. 10:10 · 1 Sam. 25:22

22 And will make thine house like the house of ^RJer-o-bo'-am the son of Ne'-bat, and like the house of ^RBa'-a-sha the son of A-hi'-jah, for the provocation wherewith

thou hast provoked *me* to anger, and made Israel to sin.   15:29 · 16:3

23 And ^Rof Jez'-e-bel also spake the LORD, saying, The dogs shall eat Jez'-e-bel by the wall of Jez'-re-el.   2 Kin. 9:10, 30–37

24 ^RHim that dieth of Ahab in the city the dogs shall eat; and him that dieth in the field shall the fowls of the air eat.   14:11; 16:4

25 But ^Rthere was none like unto Ahab, which did sell himself to work wickedness in the sight of the LORD, whom Jez'-e-bel his wife stirred up.   v. 20; 16:30–33

26 And he did very abominably in following idols, according to all *things* ^Ras did the Am'-or-ites, whom the LORD cast out before the children of Israel.   2 Kin. 21:11

27 And it came to pass, when Ahab heard those words, that he rent his clothes, and ^Rput sackcloth upon his flesh, and fasted, and lay in sackcloth, and went softly.   Gen. 37:34; 2 Sam. 3:31; 2 Kin. 6:30

28 And the word of the LORD came to E-li'-jah the Tish'-bite, saying,

29 Seest thou how Ahab humbleth himself before me? because he humbleth himself before me, I will not bring the evil in his days: *but* ^Rin his son's days will I bring the evil upon his house.   2 Kin. 9:25

22 And they continued three years without war between Syria and Israel.

2 And it came to pass in the third year, that ^RJe-hosh'-a-phat the king of Judah came down to the king of Israel.   15:24; 2 Chr. 18:2

3 And the king of Israel said unto his servants, Know ye that Ra'-moth in Gil'-e-ad *is* ours, and we *be* still, *and* take it not out of the hand of the king of Syria?

4 And he said unto Je-hosh'-a-phat, Wilt thou go with me to battle to Ra'-moth–gil'-e-ad? And Je-hosh'-a-phat said to the king of Israel, ^RI *am* as thou *art*, my people as thy people, my horses as thy horses.   2 Kin. 3:7

5 And Je-hosh'-a-phat said unto the king of Israel, ^REnquire, I

pray thee, ^Tat the word of the LORD to day.   2 Kin. 3:11 · *for*

6 Then the king of Israel ^Rgathered the prophets together, about four hundred men, and said unto them, Shall I go against Ra'-moth–gil'-e-ad to battle, or shall I forbear? And they said, Go up; for the LORD shall deliver *it* into the hand of the king.   18:19

7 And ^RJe-hosh'-a-phat said, *Is there* not here a prophet of the LORD besides, that we might enquire of him?   2 Kin. 3:11

8 And the king of Israel said unto Je-hosh'-a-phat, *There is* yet one man, Mi-ca'-iah the son of Im'-lah, by whom we may enquire of the LORD: but I hate him; for he doth not prophesy good concerning me, but evil. And Je-hosh'-a-phat said, Let not the king say so.

9 Then the king of Israel called an officer, and said, Hasten *hither* Mi-ca'-iah the son of Im'-lah.

10 And the king of Israel and Je-hosh'-a-phat the king of Judah sat each on his throne, having put on their robes, in a void place in the entrance of the gate of Sa-ma'-ri-a; and all the prophets prophesied before them.

11 And Zed-e-ki'-ah the son of Che-na'-a-nah made him ^Rhorns of iron: and he said, Thus saith the LORD, With these shalt thou push the Syrians, until thou have consumed them.   Zech. 1:18–21

12 And all the prophets prophesied so, saying, Go up to Ra'-moth–gil'-e-ad, and prosper: for the LORD shall deliver *it* into the king's hand.

13 And the messenger that was gone to call Mi-ca'-iah spake unto him, saying, Behold now, the words of the prophets *declare* good unto the king with one mouth: let thy word, I pray thee, be like the word of one of them, and speak *that which is* good.

14 And Mi-ca'-iah said, *As* the LORD liveth, what the LORD saith unto me, that will I speak.

15 So he came to the king. And

the king said unto him, Mi-ca'-iah, shall we go against Ra'-moth–gil'-e-ad to battle, or shall we ^Tforbear? And he answered him, Go, and prosper: for the LORD shall deliver *it* into the hand of the king.   *refrain*

16 And the king said unto him, How many times shall I ^Tadjure thee that thou tell me nothing but *that which is* true in the name of the LORD?   *make you swear*

17 And he said, I saw all Israel ^Rscattered upon the hills, as sheep that have not a shepherd: and the LORD said, These have no master: let them return every man to his house in peace. 2 Chr. 18:16; Matt. 9:36

18 And the king of Israel said unto Je-hosh'-a-phat, Did I not tell thee that he would prophesy no good concerning me, but evil?

19 And he said, Hear thou therefore the word of the LORD: ^RI saw the LORD sitting on his throne, and all the host of heaven standing by him on his right hand and on his left. Is. 6:1; Ezek. 1:26–28; Dan. 7:9

20 And the LORD said, Who shall persuade Ahab, that he may go up and fall at Ra'-moth–gil'-e-ad? And one said on this manner, and another said on that manner.

21 And there came forth a spirit, and stood before the LORD, and said, I will persuade him.

22 And the LORD said unto him, Wherewith? And he said, I will go forth, and I will be a lying spirit in the mouth of all his prophets. And he said, ^RThou shalt persuade *him,* and prevail also: go forth, and do so.   [Ezek. 14:9; 2 Thess. 2:11]

23 ^RNow therefore, behold, the LORD hath put a lying spirit in the mouth of all these thy prophets, and the LORD hath spoken evil concerning thee.   [Ezek. 14:9]

24 But Zed-e-ki'-ah the son of Che-na'-a-nah went near, and ^Rsmote Mi-ca'-iah on the cheek, and said, ^RWhich way went the Spirit of the LORD from me to speak unto thee? Jer. 20:2 · 2 Chr. 18:23

25 And Mi-ca'-iah said, Behold, thou shalt see in that day, when

thou shalt go into an ᴿinner chamber to hide thyself. 20:30

26 And the king of Israel said, Take Mi-ca'-iah, and carry him back unto Amon the governor of the city, and to Jo'-ash the king's son;

27 And say, Thus saith the king, Put this *fellow* in the ᴿprison, and feed him with bread of affliction and with water of affliction, until I come in peace. 2 Chr. 16:10; 18:25–27

28 And Mi-ca'-iah said, If thou return at all in peace, ᴿthe LORD hath not spoken by me. And he said, Hearken, O people, every one of you. Num. 16:29; Deut. 18:20–22

29 So the king of Israel and Je-hosh'-a-phat the king of Judah went up to Ra'-moth–gil'-e-ad.

30 And the king of Israel said unto Je-hosh'-a-phat, I will disguise myself, and enter into the battle; but put thou on thy robes. And the king of Israel disguised himself, and went into the battle.

31 But the king of Syria commanded his thirty and two ᴿcaptains that had rule over his chariots, saying, Fight neither with small nor great, save only with the king of Israel. 20:24; 2 Chr. 18:30

32 And it came to pass, when the captains of the chariots saw Je-hosh'-a-phat, that they said, Surely it *is* the king of Israel. And they turned aside to fight against him: and Je-hosh'-a-phat ᴿcried out. 2 Chr. 18:31

33 And it came to pass, when the captains of the chariots perceived that it *was* not the king of Israel, that they turned back from pursuing him.

34 And a *certain* man drew a bow at a venture, and smote the king of Israel between the joints of the harness: wherefore he said unto the driver of his chariot, Turn thine hand, and carry me out of the host; for I am wounded.

35 And the battle increased that day: and the king was stayed up in his chariot against the Syrians, and died at even: and the blood ran out of the wound ᵀinto the midst of the chariot. *onto the floor*

36 And there went a proclamation throughout the host about the going down of the sun, saying, Every man to his city, and every man to his own country.

37 So the king died, and was brought to Sa-ma'-ri-a; and they buried the king in Sa-ma'-ri-a.

38 And *one* washed the chariot in the pool of Sa-ma'-ri-a; and the dogs licked up his blood; and they washed his armour; according ᴿunto the word of the LORD which he spake. 21:19

39 Now the rest of the acts of Ahab, and all that he did, and the ivory house which he made, and all the cities that he built, *are* they not written in the book of the chronicles of the kings of Israel?

40 So Ahab slept with his fathers; and ᴿA-ha-zi'-ah his son reigned in his stead. 2 Kin. 1:2, 18

41 And ᴿJe-hosh'-a-phat the son of A'-sa began to reign over Judah in the fourth year of Ahab king of Israel. 2 Chr. 20:31

42 Je-hosh'-a-phat *was* thirty and five years old when he began to reign; and he reigned twenty and five years in Jerusalem. And his mother's name *was* A-zu'-bah the daughter of Shil'-hi.

43 And he walked in all the ways of A'-sa his father; he turned not aside from it, doing *that which was* right in the eyes of the LORD: nevertheless the high places were not taken away; *for* the people offered and burnt incense yet in the high places.

44 And Je-hosh'-a-phat made peace with the king of Israel.

45 Now the rest of the acts of Je-hosh'-a-phat, and his might that he shewed, and how he warred, *are* they not written ᴿin the book of the chronicles of the kings of Judah? 2 Chr. 20:34

46 ᴿAnd the remnant of the sodomites, which remained in the days of his father A'-sa, he took out of the land. Gen. 19:5; Deut. 23:17

47 *There was* then no king in E'-dom: a deputy *was* king.

48 ᴿJe-hosh'-a-phat made ships

of Thar'-shish to go to ᴿO'-phir for gold: but they went not; for the ships were broken at ᴿE'-zi-on-ge'-ber.   2 Chr. 20:35–37 · 9:28 · 9:26

49 Then said A-ha-zi'-ah the son of Ahab unto Je-hosh'-a-phat, Let my servants go with thy servants in the ships. But Je-hosh'-a-phat would not.

50 And Je-hosh'-a-phat slept with his fathers, and was buried with his fathers in the city of David his father: and Je-ho'-ram his son reigned in his stead.

51 A-ha-zi'-ah the son of Ahab

began to reign over Israel in Sa-ma'-ri-a the seventeenth year of Je-hosh'-a-phat king of Judah, and reigned two years over Israel.

52 And he did evil in the sight of the Lᴏʀᴅ, and ᴿwalked in the way of his father, and in the way of his mother, and in the way of Jer-o-bo'-am the son of Ne'-bat, who made Israel to sin: 15:26; 21:25

53 For ᴿhe served Ba'-al, and worshipped him, and provoked to anger the Lᴏʀᴅ God of Israel, ᴿaccording to all that his father had done.   Judg. 2:11 · 16:30–32

The Second Book of the
KINGS

THE Book of Second Kings continues the drama begun in First Kings—the tragic history of two nations on a collision course with captivity. The author systematically traces the reigning monarchs of Israel and Judah, first by carrying one nation's history forward, then retracing the same period for the other nation.

Nineteen consecutive evil kings rule in Israel, leading to the captivity by Assyria. The picture is somewhat brighter in Judah, where godly kings occasionally emerge to reform the evils of their predecessors. In the end, however, sin outweighs righteousness and Judah is marched off to Babylon.

THEN Moab rebelled against Israel after the death of Ahab.

2 And ᴿA-ha-zi'-ah fell down through a lattice in his upper chamber that *was* in Sa-ma'-ri-a, and was sick: and he sent messengers, and said unto them, Go, enquire of Ba'-al-ze'-bub the god of Ek'-ron whether I shall recover of this disease.   1 Kin. 22:40

3 But the angel of the Lᴏʀᴅ said to E-li'-jah the Tish'-bite, Arise, go up to meet the messengers of the king of Sa-ma'-ri-a, and say unto them, *Is it* not because *there is* not a God in Israel, *that* ye go to enquire of Ba'-al–ze'-bub the god of Ek'-ron?

4 Now therefore thus saith the Lᴏʀᴅ, Thou shalt not come down from that bed on which thou art

gone up, but shalt surely die. And E-li'-jah departed.

5 And when the messengers turned back unto ᵀhim, he said unto them, Why are ye now ᵀturned back?   Ahaziah · come back

6 And they said unto him, There came a man up to meet us, and said unto us, Go, turn again unto the king that sent you, and say unto him, Thus saith the Lᴏʀᴅ, *Is it* not because *there is* not a God in Israel, *that* thou sendest to enquire of Ba'-al–ze'-bub the god of Ek'-ron? therefore thou shalt not come down from that bed on which thou art gone up, but shalt surely die.

7 And he said unto them, What ᵀmanner of man *was he* which

came up to meet you, and told you these words?   *kind*

8 And they answered him, *He was* [R]an hairy man, and girt with a girdle of leather about his loins. And he said, It *is* E-li'-jah the Tish'-bite. Zech. 13:4; Matt. 3:4; Mark 1:6

9 Then the king sent unto him a captain of fifty with his fifty. And he went up to him: and, behold, he sat on the top of an hill. And he spake unto him, Thou man of God, the king hath said, Come down.

10 And E-li'-jah answered and said to the captain of fifty, If I *be* a man of God, then [R]let fire come down from heaven, and consume thee and thy fifty. And there came down fire from heaven, and consumed him and his fifty. Luke 9:54

11 Again also he sent unto him another captain of fifty with his fifty. And he answered and said unto him, O man of God, thus hath the king said, Come down quickly.

12 And E-li'-jah answered and said unto them, If I *be* a man of God, let fire come down from heaven, and consume thee and thy fifty. And the fire of God came down from heaven, and consumed him and his fifty.

13 And he sent again a captain of the third fifty with his fifty. And the third captain of fifty went up, and came and fell on his knees before E-li'-jah, and besought him, and said unto him, O man of God, I pray thee, let my life, and the life of these fifty thy servants, [R]be precious in thy sight. Ps. 72:14

14 Behold, there came fire down from heaven, and burnt up the two captains of the former fifties with their fifties: therefore let my life now be precious in thy sight.

15 And the angel of the LORD said unto E-li'-jah, Go down with him: be not afraid of him. And he arose, and went down with him unto the king.

16 And he said unto him, Thus saith the LORD, Forasmuch as thou hast sent messengers to enquire of

Ba'-al-ze'-bub the god of Ek'-ron, *is it* not because *there is* no God in Israel to enquire of his word? therefore thou shalt not come down off that bed on which thou art gone up, but shalt surely die.

17 So he died according to the word of the LORD which E-li'-jah had spoken. And [R]Je-ho'-ram reigned in his stead in the second year of Je-ho'-ram the son of Je-hosh'-a-phat king of Judah; because he had no son. 8:16; Matt. 1:8

18 Now the rest of the acts of A-ha-zi'-ah which he did, *are* they not written in the book of the chronicles of the kings of Israel?

2 And it came to pass, when the LORD would [R]take up E-li'-jah into heaven by a whirlwind, that E-li'-jah went with E-li'-sha from Gil'-gal. Gen. 5:24; [Heb. 11:5]

2 And E-li'-jah said unto E-li'-sha, Tarry here, I pray thee; for the LORD hath sent me to Beth'–el. And E-li'-sha said *unto him*, As the LORD liveth, and [R]*as* thy soul liveth, I will not leave thee. So they went down to Beth'–el. 4:30

3 And [R]the sons of the prophets that *were* at Beth'–el came forth to E-li'-sha, and said unto him, Knowest thou that the LORD will take away thy master from thy head to day? And he said, Yea, I know *it*; hold ye your peace. 4:1, 38

4 And E-li'-jah said unto him, E-li'-sha, tarry here, I pray thee; for the LORD hath sent me to Jericho. And he said, *As* the LORD liveth, and *as* thy soul liveth, I will not leave thee. So they came to Jericho.

5 And the sons of the prophets that *were* at Jericho came to E-li'-sha, and said unto him, Knowest thou that the LORD will take away thy master from thy head to day? And he answered, Yea, I know *it*; [T]hold ye your peace. *keep silent*

6 And E-li'-jah said unto him, Tarry, I pray thee, here; for the LORD hath sent me to Jordan. And he said, *As* the LORD liveth, and *as* thy soul liveth, I will not leave thee. And they two went on.

7 And fifty men of the sons of

the prophets went, and stood [T]to view afar off: and they two stood by Jordan.   *facing them at a distance*

8 And E-li′-jah took his mantle, and wrapped *it* together, and smote the waters, and [R]they were divided hither and thither, so that they two went over on dry ground.   Ex. 14:21, 22; Josh. 3:16

9 And it came to pass, when they were gone over, that E-li′-jah said unto E-li′-sha, Ask what I shall do for thee, before I be taken away from thee. And E-li′-sha said, I pray thee, let a double portion of thy spirit be upon me.

10 And he said, Thou hast asked a hard thing: *nevertheless,* if thou see me *when I am* taken from thee, it shall be so unto thee; but if not, it shall not be *so.*

11 And it came to pass, as they still went on, and talked, that, behold, *there appeared* [R]a chariot of fire, and horses of fire, and parted them both asunder; and E-li′-jah went up by a whirlwind into heaven.   6:17; Ps. 104:4

12 And E-li′-sha saw *it,* and he cried, [R]My father, my father, the chariot of Israel, and the horsemen thereof. And he saw him no more: and he took hold of his own clothes, and [T]rent them in two pieces.   13:14 · *tore*

13 He took up also the mantle of E-li′-jah that fell from him, and went back, and stood by the bank of Jordan;

14 And he took the mantle of E-li′-jah that fell from him, and smote the waters, and said, Where *is* the LORD God of E-li′-jah? and when he also had smitten the waters, they parted hither and thither: and E-li′-sha went over.

15 And when the sons of the prophets which *were* [R]to view at Jericho saw him, they said, The spirit of E-li′-jah doth rest on E-li′-sha. And they came to meet him, and bowed themselves to the ground before him.   v. 7

16 And they said unto him, Behold now, there be with thy servants fifty strong men; let them

go, we pray thee, and seek thy master: lest peradventure the Spirit of the LORD hath taken him up, and cast him upon some mountain, or into some valley. And he said, Ye shall not send.

17 And when they urged him till he was [R]ashamed, he said, Send. They sent therefore fifty men; and they sought three days, but found him not.   8:11

18 And when they came again to him, (for he tarried at Jericho,) he said unto them, Did I not say unto you, Go not?

19 And the men of the city said unto E-li′-sha, Behold, I pray thee, the situation of this city *is* pleasant, as my lord seeth: but the water *is* [T]naught, and the ground barren.   *bad*

20 And he said, Bring me a new cruse, and put salt therein. And they brought *it* to him.

21 And he went forth unto the spring of the waters, and [R]cast the salt in there, and said, Thus saith the LORD, I have healed these waters; there shall not be from thence any more death or barren land.   4:41; 6:6; Ex. 15:25, 26; John 9:6

22 So the waters were [R]healed unto this day, according to the saying of E-li′-sha which he spake.   Ezek. 47:8, 9

23 And he went up from thence unto Beth′-el: and as he was going up by the way, there came forth [T]little children out of the city, and mocked him, and said unto him, Go up, thou bald head; go up, thou bald head.   *youths*

24 And he turned back, and looked on them, and cursed them in the name of the LORD. And there came forth two she bears out of the wood, and tare forty and two children of them.

25 And he went from thence to [R]mount Carmel, and from thence he returned to Sa-ma′-ri-a.   4:25

3 Now [R]Je-ho′-ram the son of Ahab began to reign over Israel in Sa-ma′-ri-a the eighteenth year of Je-hosh′-a-phat king of Judah, and reigned twelve years.   1:17

2 And he wrought evil in the sight of the LORD; but not like his father, and like his mother: for he put away the image of Ba'-al that his father had made.

3 Nevertheless he cleaved unto the sins of Jer-o-bo'-am the son of Ne'-bat, which made Israel to sin; he departed not therefrom.

4 And Me'-sha king of Moab was a sheepmaster, and rendered unto the king of Israel an hundred thousand lambs, and an hundred thousand rams, with the wool.

5 But it came to pass, when ᴿAhab was dead, that the king of Moab rebelled against the king of Israel.   1:1

6 And king Je-ho'-ram went out of Sa-ma'-ri-a the same time, and ᵀnumbered all Israel. *mustered*

7 And he went and sent to Je-hosh'-a-phat the king of Judah, saying, The king of Moab hath rebelled against me: wilt thou go with me against Moab to battle? And he said, I will go up: I *am* as thou *art*, my people as thy people, *and* my horses as thy horses.

8 And he said, Which way shall we go up? And he answered, The way through the wilderness of E'-dom.

9 So the king of Israel went, and the king of Judah, and the king of E'-dom: and they fetched a compass of seven days' journey: and there was no water for the host, and for the cattle that followed them.

10 And the king of Israel said, Alas! that the LORD hath called these three kings together, to deliver them into the hand of Moab!

11 But ᴿJe-hosh'-a-phat said, *Is there* not here a prophet of the LORD, that we may enquire of the LORD by him? And one of the king of Israel's servants answered and said, Here *is* E-li'-sha the son of Sha'-phat, which poured water on the hands of E-li'-jah.   1 Kin. 22:7

12 And Je-hosh'-a-phat said, The word of the LORD is with him. So the king of Israel and Je-hosh'-a-phat and the king of E'-dom ᴿwent down to him.   2:25

13 And E-li'-sha said unto the king of Israel, What have I to do with thee? ᴿget thee to the prophets of thy father, and to the prophets of thy mother. And the king of Israel said unto him, Nay: for the LORD hath called these three kings together, to deliver them into the hand of Moab. Judg. 10:14

14 And E-li'-sha said, ᴿAs the LORD of hosts liveth, before whom I stand, surely, were it not that I regard the presence of Je-hosh'-a-phat the king of Judah, I would not look toward thee, nor see thee.   5:16; 1 Kin. 17:1

15 But now bring me a minstrel. And it came to pass, when the minstrel played, that ᴿthe hand of the LORD came upon him. Ezek. 1:3

16 And he said, Thus saith the LORD, ᴿMake this valley full of ᵀditches.   Jer. 14:3 · *water canals*

17 For thus saith the LORD, Ye shall not see wind, neither shall ye see rain; yet that valley shall be filled with water, that ye may drink, both ye, and your cattle, and your beasts.

18 And this is *but* a light thing in the sight of the LORD: he will deliver the Mo'-ab-ites also into your hand.

19 And ye shall smite every fenced city, and every choice city, and shall fell every good tree, and stop all wells of water, and ᵀmar every good piece of land with stones.   *ruin*

20 And it came to pass in the morning, when ᴿthe meat offering was offered, that, behold, there came water by the way of E'-dom, and the country was filled with water.   Ex. 29:39, 40

21 And when all the Mo'-ab-ites heard that the kings were come up to fight against them, they gathered all that were able to put on armour, ᵀand upward, and stood in the border. *and older*

22 And they rose up early in the morning, and the sun shone upon the water, and the Mo'-ab-ites saw

the water on the other side *as* red as blood:

23 And they said, This *is* blood: the kings are surely slain, and they have smitten one another: now therefore, Moab, to the spoil.

24 And when they came to the camp of Israel, the Israelites rose up and smote the Mo'-ab-ites, so that they fled before them: but they went forward smiting the Mo'-ab-ites, even in *their* country.

25 And they beat down the cities, and on every good piece of land cast every man his stone, and filled it; and they stopped all the wells of water, and felled all the good trees: only in ^RKir–har'-a-seth left they the stones thereof; howbeit the slingers ^Twent about *it,* and smote it. Is. 16:7 · *surrounded*

26 And when the king of Moab saw that the battle was too sore for him, he took with him seven hundred men that drew swords, to break through *even* unto the king of E'-dom: but they could not.

27 Then he took his eldest son that should have reigned in his stead, and offered him *for* a burnt offering upon the wall. And there was great indignation against Israel: and they departed from him, and returned to *their own* land.

4 Now there cried a certain woman of the wives of ^Rthe sons of the prophets unto E-li'-sha, saying, Thy servant my husband is dead; and thou knowest that thy servant did fear the Lord: and the creditor is come ^Rto take unto him my two sons to be bondmen. 2:3 · 1 Sam. 22:2; Matt. 18:25

2 And E-li'-sha said unto her, What shall I do for thee? tell me, what hast thou in the house? And she said, Thine handmaid hath not any thing in the house, save a pot of oil.

3 Then he said, Go, borrow thee vessels abroad of all thy neighbours, *even* empty vessels; ^Rborrow not a few. 3:16

4 And when thou art come in, thou shalt shut the door upon thee and upon thy sons, and shalt pour

out into all those vessels, and thou shalt set aside that which is full.

5 So she went from him, and shut the door upon her and upon her sons, who brought *the vessels* to her; and she poured out.

6 And it came to pass, when the vessels were full, that she said unto her son, Bring me yet a vessel. And he said unto her, *There is* not a vessel more. And the oil ^Tstayed. *ceased*

7 Then she came and told the man of God. And he said, Go, sell the oil, and pay thy debt, and live thou and thy children of the rest.

8 And it fell on a day, that E-li'-sha passed to Shu'-nem, where *was* a great woman; and she constrained him to eat bread. And *so* it was, *that* as oft as he passed by, he turned in thither to eat bread.

9 And she said unto her husband, Behold now, I perceive that this *is* an holy man of God, which passeth by us continually.

10 Let us make a little chamber, I pray thee, on the wall; and let us set for him there a bed, and a table, and a stool, and a candlestick: and it shall be, when he cometh to us, that he shall turn in thither.

11 And it fell on a day, that he came thither, and he turned into the chamber, and lay there.

12 And he said to ^RGe-ha'-zi his servant, Call this Shu'-nam-mite. And when he had called her, she stood before him. vv. 29–31; 5:20–27

13 And he said unto him, Say now unto her, Behold, thou hast been ^Tcareful for us with all this care; what *is* to be done for thee? wouldest thou be spoken for to the king, or to the captain of the host? And she answered, I dwell among mine own people. *concerned*

14 And he said, What then *is* to be done for her? And Ge-ha'-zi answered, Verily she hath no child, and her husband is old.

15 And he said, Call her. And when he had called her, she stood in the door.

16 And he said, About this sea-

son, Taccording to the time of life, thou shalt embrace a son. And she said, Nay, my lord, *thou* man of God, Rdo not lie unto thine hand- maid.   *about this time next year* · v. 28

17 And the woman conceived, and bare a son at that season that E-li′-sha had said unto her, ac- cording to the time of life.

18 And when the child was grown, it fell on a day, that he went out to his father to the reapers.

19 And he said unto his father, My head, my head. And he said to a lad, Carry him to his mother.

20 And when he had taken him, and brought him to his mother, he sat on her knees till noon, and *then* died.

21 And she went up, and laid him on the bed of the man of God, and shut *the door* upon him, and went out.

22 And she called unto her hus- band, and said, Send me, I pray thee, one of the young men, and one of the asses, that I may run to the man of God, and come again.

23 And he said, Wherefore wilt thou go to him to day? *it is* neither Rnew moon, nor sabbath. And she said, *It shall be* well.   Num. 10:10

24 Then she saddled an ass, and said to her servant, Drive, and go forward; slack not *thy* riding for me, except I bid thee.

25 So she went and came unto the man of God Rto mount Car- mel. And it came to pass, when the man of God saw her afar off, that he said to Ge-ha′-zi his ser- vant, Behold, *yonder is* that Shu′- nam-mite: 2:25

26 Run now, I pray thee, to meet her, and say unto her, *Is it* well with thee? *is it* well with thy hus- band? *is it* well with the child? And she answered, *It is* well.

27 And when she came to the man of God to the hill, she caught him by the feet: but Ge-ha′-zi came near to thrust her away. And the man of God said, Let her alone; for her soul *is* vexed within her: and the LORD hath hid *it* from me, and hath not told me.

28 Then she said, Did I desire a son of my lord? Rdid I not say, Do not deceive me?   v. 16

29 Then he said to Ge-ha′-zi, RGird up thy loins, and take my staff in thine hand, and go thy way: if thou meet any man, Rsalute him not; and if any salute thee, answer him not again: and Rlay my staff upon the face of the child.   9:1 · Luke 10:4 · 2:8, 14; Acts 19:12

30 And the mother of the child said, RAs the LORD liveth, and *as* thy soul liveth, I will not Rleave thee. And he arose, and followed her.   2:2 · 2:4

31 And Ge-ha′-zi passed on be- fore them, and laid the staff upon the face of the child; but *there was* neither voice, nor hearing. Wherefore he went again to meet him, and told him, saying, The child is Rnot awaked.   John 11:11

32 And when E-li′-sha was come into the house, behold, the child was dead, *and* laid upon his bed.

33 He Rwent in therefore, and shut the door upon them twain, and prayed unto the LORD.   v. 4

34 And he went up, and lay upon the child, and put his mouth upon his mouth, and his eyes upon his eyes, and his hands upon his hands: and Rhe stretched himself upon the child; and the flesh of the child waxed warm.   Acts 20:10

35 Then he returned, and walked in the house to and fro; and went up, Rand stretched him- self upon him: and the child sneezed seven times, and the child opened his eyes.   1 Kin. 17:21

36 And he called Ge-ha′-zi, and said, Call this Shu′-nam-mite. So he called her. And when she was come in unto him, he said, TTake up thy son.   *Pick up*

37 Then she went in, and fell at his feet, and bowed herself to the ground, and Rtook up her son, and went out.   1 Kin. 17:23; [Heb. 11:35]

38 And E-li′-sha came again to Gil′-gal: and *there was* a dearth in the land; and the sons of the prophets *were* sitting before him: and he said unto his servant, Set

on the great pot, and seethe pottage for the sons of the prophets.

39 And one went out into the field to gather herbs, and found a wild vine, and gathered thereof wild gourds his lap full, and came and shred *them* into the pot of pottage: for they knew *them* not.

40 So they poured out for the men to eat. And it came to pass, as they were eating of the pottage, that they cried out, and said, O *thou* man of God, *there is* ᴿdeath in the pot. And they could not eat *thereof.*   Ex. 10:17

41 But he said, Then bring meal. And ᴿhe cast *it* into the pot; and he said, Pour out for the people, that they may eat. And there was no harm in the pot.   2:21; Ex. 15:25

42 And there came a man from Ba'-al–shal'-i-sha, ᴿand brought the man of God bread of the firstfruits, twenty loaves of barley, and full ears of corn in the husk thereof. And he said, Give unto the people, that they may eat.   [1 Cor. 9:11]

43 And his servitor said, ᴿWhat, should I set this before an hundred men? He said again, Give the people, that they may eat: for thus saith the LORD, They shall eat, and shall leave *thereof.*   John 6:9–11

44 So he set *it* before them, and they did eat, and left *thereof,* according to the word of the LORD.

5 Now Na'-a-man, captain of the host of the king of Syria, was a great man with his master, and honourable, because by him the LORD had given deliverance unto Syria: he was also a mighty man in valour, *but he was* a leper.

2 And the Syrians had gone out by companies, and had brought away captive out of the land of Israel a little maid; and she waited on Na'-a-man's wife.

3 And she said unto her mistress, Would God my lord *were* with the prophet that *is* in Sa-ma'-ri-a! for he would ᵀrecover him of his leprosy.   *heal*

4 And ᵀone went in, and told his lord, saying, Thus and thus said the maid that *is* of the land of Israel.   *Naaman*

5 And the king of Syria said, Go to, go, and I will send a letter unto the king of Israel. And he departed, and ᴿtook with him ten talents of silver, and six thousand *pieces* of gold, and ten changes of raiment.   8:8, 9; 1 Sam. 9:8

6 And he brought the letter to the king of Israel, saying, Now when this letter is come unto thee, behold, I have *therewith* sent Na'-a-man my servant to thee, that thou mayest recover him of his leprosy.

7 And it came to pass, when the king of Israel had read the letter, that he rent his clothes, and said, *Am* I ᴿGod, to kill and to make alive, that this man doth send unto me to recover a man of his leprosy? wherefore consider, I pray you, and see how he seeketh a quarrel against me.   [Gen. 30:2]

8 And it was *so,* when E-li'-sha the man of God had heard that the king of Israel had rent his clothes, that he sent to the king, saying, Wherefore hast thou rent thy clothes? let him come now to me, and he shall know that there is a prophet in Israel.

9 So Na'-a-man came with his horses and with his chariot, and stood at the door of the house of E-li'-sha.

10 And E-li'-sha sent a messenger unto him, saying, Go and ᴿwash in Jordan seven times, and thy flesh shall come again to thee, and thou shalt be clean.   John 9:7

11 But Na'-a-man was wroth, and went away, and said, Behold, I thought, He will surely come out to me, and stand, and call on the name of the LORD his God, and ᵀstrike his hand over the place, and ᵀrecover the leper.   *wave · heal*

12 *Are* not Ab'-a-na and Phar'-par, rivers of Damascus, better than all the waters of Israel? may I not wash in them, and be clean? So he turned and went away in a rage.

13 And his ᴿservants came near, and spake unto him, and said, My

father, *if* the prophet had bid thee *do some* great thing, wouldest thou not have done *it*? how much rather then, when he saith to thee, Wash, and be clean?　1 Sam. 28:23

14 Then went he down, and dipped himself seven times in Jordan, according to the saying of the man of God: and his ^Rflesh came again like unto the flesh of a little child, and he was clean. v. 10

15 And he returned to the man of God, he and all his company, and came, and stood before him: and he said, Behold, now I know that *there is* ^Rno God in all the earth, but in Israel: now therefore, I pray thee, take ^Ra ^Tblessing of thy servant.　Dan. 2:47 · Gen. 33:11 · *gift*

16 But he said, *As* the LORD liveth, before whom I stand, ^RI will receive none. And he urged him to take *it*; but he refused.　Acts 8:18, 20

17 And Na'-a-man said, Shall there not then, I pray thee, be given to thy servant two mules' burden of earth? for thy servant will henceforth offer neither burnt offering nor sacrifice unto other gods, but unto the LORD.

18 In this thing the LORD pardon thy servant, *that* when my master goeth into the house of Rim'-mon to worship there, and ^Rhe leaneth on my hand, and I bow myself in the house of Rim'-mon: when I bow down myself in the house of Rim'-mon, the LORD pardon thy servant in this thing.　7:2, 17

19 And he said unto him, Go in peace. So he departed from him a little way.

20 But ^RGe-ha'-zi, the servant of E-li'-sha the man of God, said, Behold, my master hath spared Na'-a-man this Syrian, in not receiving at his hands that which he brought: but, *as* the LORD liveth, I will run after him, and take somewhat of him.　4:12; 8:4, 5

21 So Ge-ha'-zi followed after Na'-a-man. And when Na'-a-man saw *him* running after him, he lighted down from the chariot to meet him, and said, *Is* all well?

22 And he said, All *is* ^Rwell. My master hath sent me, saying, Behold, even now there be come to me from mount E'-phra-im two young men of the sons of the prophets: give them, I pray thee, a talent of silver, and two changes of garments.　4:26

23 And Na'-a-man said, Be content, take two talents. And he urged him, and bound two talents of silver in two bags, with two changes of garments, and laid *them* upon two of his servants; and they bare *them* before him.

24 And when he came to the tower, he took *them* from their hand, and ^Tbestowed *them* in the house: and he let the men go, and they departed.　*stored them away*

25 But he went in, and stood before his master. And E-li'-sha said unto him, Whence *comest thou*, Ge-ha'-zi? And he said, Thy servant went ^Tno whither. *nowhere*

26 And he said unto him, ^TWent not mine heart *with thee*, when the man turned again from his chariot to meet thee? *Is it* a ^Rtime to receive money, and to receive garments, and oliveyards, and vineyards, and sheep, and oxen, and menservants, and maidservants? *Did not my heart go* · [Eccl. 3:1, 6]

27 The leprosy therefore of Na'-a-man shall cleave unto thee, and unto thy seed for ever. And he went out from his presence ^Ra leper *as white* as snow.　Num. 12:10

6 And ^Rthe sons of the prophets said unto E-li'-sha, Behold now, the place where we dwell with thee is too ^Tstrait for us. 4:38 · *small*

2 Let us go, we pray thee, unto Jordan, and take thence every man a beam, and let us make us a place there, where we may dwell. And he answered, Go ye.

3 And one said, Be content, I pray thee, and go with thy servants. And he answered, I will go.

4 So he went with them. And when they came to Jordan, they cut down wood.

5 But as one was felling a beam, the ^Tax head fell into the water: and he cried, and said,

Alas, master! for it was ᴿborrowed.   Lit. *iron* · [Ex. 22:14]

6 And the man of God said, Where fell it? And he shewed him the place. And ᴿhe cut down a stick, and cast *it* in thither; and the iron did swim. 2:21; 4:41; Ex. 15:25

7 Therefore said he, Take *it* up to thee. And he put out his hand, and took it.

8 Then the ᴿking of Syria warred against Israel, and took counsel with his servants, saying, In such and such a place *shall be* my camp.   8:28, 29

9 And the man of God sent unto the king of Israel, saying, Beware that thou pass not such a place; for thither the Syrians are come down.

10 And the king of Israel sent to the place which the man of God told him and warned him of, and ᵀsaved himself there, not once nor twice.   *he was watchful*

11 Therefore the heart of the king of Syria was sore troubled for this thing; and he called his servants, and said unto them, Will ye not shew me which of us *is* for the king of Israel?

12 And one of his servants said, None, my lord, O king: but E-li′-sha, the prophet that *is* in Israel, telleth the king of Israel the words that thou speakest in thy bedchamber.

13 And he said, Go and spy where he *is*, that I may send and fetch him. And it was told him, saying, Behold, *he is* in Do′-than.

14 Therefore sent he thither horses, and chariots, and a great host: and they came by night, and compassed the city about.

15 And when the servant of the man of God was risen early, and gone forth, behold, an host compassed the city both with horses and chariots. And his servant said unto him, Alas, my master! how shall we do?

16 And he answered, Fear not: for they that *be* with us *are* more than they that *be* with them.

17 And E-li′-sha prayed, and said, Lord, I pray thee, open his eyes, that he may see. And the Lord ᴿopened the eyes of the young man; and he saw: and, behold, the mountain *was* full of ᴿhorses and chariots of fire round about E-li′-sha.   Luke 24:31 · Zech. 1:8

18 And when they came down to him, E-li′-sha prayed unto the Lord, and said, Smite this people, I pray thee, with blindness. And he smote them with blindness according to the word of E-li′-sha.

19 And E-li′-sha said unto them, This *is* not the way, neither *is* this the city: follow me, and I will bring you to the man whom ye seek. But he led them to Sa-ma′-ri-a.

20 And it came to pass, when they were come into Sa-ma′-ri-a, that E-li′-sha said, Lord, open the eyes of these *men*, that they may see. And the Lord opened their eyes, and they saw; and, behold, *they were* in the midst of Sa-ma′-ri-a.

21 And the king of Israel said unto E-li′-sha, when he saw them, My ᴿfather, shall I ᵀsmite *them*? shall I smite *them*? 2:12; 5:13; 8:9 · *kill*

22 And he answered, Thou shalt not smite *them:* wouldest thou smite those whom thou hast taken captive with thy sword and with thy bow? set bread and water before them, that they may eat and drink, and go to their master.

23 And he prepared great provision for them: and when they had eaten and drunk, he sent them away, and they went to their master. So ᴿthe bands of Syria came no more into the land of Israel. 5:2

24 And it came to pass after this, that ᴿBen–ha′-dad king of Syria gathered all his host, and went up, and besieged Sa-ma′-ri-a. 1 Kin. 20:1

25 And there was a great ᴿfamine in Sa-ma′-ri-a: and, behold, they besieged it, until an ass's head was *sold* for ᵀfourscore *pieces* of silver, and the fourth part of a cab of dove's dung for five *pieces* of silver.   4:38; 8:1 · *eighty*

26 And as the king of Israel was

passing by upon the wall, there cried a woman unto him, saying, Help, my lord, O king.

27 And he said, If the LORD do not help thee, whence shall I help thee? out of the barnfloor, or out of the winepress?

28 And the king said unto her, ^TWhat aileth thee? And she answered, This woman said unto me, Give thy son, that we may eat him to day, and we will eat my son to morrow.   *What is troubling you?*

29 So ^Rwe boiled my son, and did eat him: and I said unto her on the next day, Give thy son, that we may eat him: and she hath hid her son.   Lev. 26:27–29; Deut. 28:52–57

30 And it came to pass, when the king heard the words of the woman, that he ^Rrent^T his clothes; and he passed by upon the wall, and the people looked, and, behold, *he had* sackcloth within upon his flesh.   1 Kin. 21:27 · *tore*

31 Then he said, ^RGod do so and more also to me, if the head of E-li'-sha the son of Sha'-phat shall stand on him this day.   Ruth 1:17

32 But E-li'-sha sat in his house, and ^Rthe elders sat with him; and *the king* sent a man from before him: but ere the messenger came to him, he said to the elders, ^RSee ye how this son of ^Ra murderer hath sent to take away mine head? look, when the messenger cometh, shut the door, and hold him fast at the door: *is* not the sound of his master's feet behind him?   Ezek. 8:1 · Luke 13:32 · 1 Kin. 18:4

33 And while he yet talked with them, behold, the messenger came down unto him: and he said, Behold, this ^Tevil *is* of the LORD; ^Rwhat should I wait for the LORD any longer?   *calamity is from* · Job 2:9

7 Then E-li'-sha said, Hear ye the word of the LORD; Thus saith the LORD, To morrow about this time *shall* a measure of fine flour *be sold* for a shek'-el, and two measures of barley for a shek'-el, in the gate of Sa-ma'-ri-a.

2 ^RThen a lord on whose hand the king leaned answered the man of God, and said, Behold, ^R*if* the LORD would make windows in heaven, might this thing be? And he said, Behold, thou shalt see *it* with thine eyes, but shalt not eat thereof.   5:18 · Gen. 7:11; Mal. 3:10

3 And there were four leprous men at the entering in of the gate: and they said one to another, Why sit we here until we die?

4 If we say, We will enter into the city, then the famine *is* in the city, and we shall die there: and if we sit still here, we die also. Now therefore come, and let us ^Tfall unto the ^Rhost of the Syrians: if they save us alive, we shall live; and if they kill us, we shall but die.   *surrender* · 6:24

5 And they rose up in the twilight, to go unto the camp of the Syrians: and when they were come to the uttermost part of the camp of Syria, behold, *there was* no man there.

6 For the Lord had made the host of the Syrians ^Rto hear a noise of chariots, and a noise of horses, *even* the noise of a great host: and they said one to another, Lo, the king of Israel hath hired against us the kings of the Hit'-tites, and the kings of the Egyptians, to come upon us.   2 Sam. 5:24

7 Wherefore they ^Rarose and fled in the twilight, and left their tents, and their horses, and their asses, even the camp as it *was*, and fled for their life.   Ps. 48:4–6

8 And when these lepers came to the uttermost part of the camp, they went into one tent, and did eat and drink, and carried thence silver, and gold, and raiment, and went and hid *it*; and came again, and entered into another tent, and carried thence *also*, and went and hid *it*.

9 Then they said one to another, We ^Tdo not well: this day *is* a day of good tidings, and we hold our peace: if we tarry till the morning light, some mischief will come upon us: now therefore come, that we may go and tell the king's household.   *are not doing right*

10 So they came and called unto

the ᵀporter of the city: and they told them, saying, We came to the camp of the Syrians, and, behold, *there was* no man there, neither voice of man, but horses tied, and asses tied, and the tents as they *were.*   *gatekeepers*

11 And he called the porters; and they told *it* to the king's house within.

12 And the king arose in the night, and said unto his servants, I will now shew you what the Syrians have done to us. They know that we *be* ᴿhungry; therefore are they gone out of the camp to hide themselves in ᵀthe field, saying, When they come out of the city, we shall catch them alive, and get into the city.   6:24–29 · *ambush*

13 And one of his servants answered and said, Let *some* take, I pray thee, five of the horses that remain, which are left in the city, (behold, they *are* as all the multitude of Israel that are left in it: behold, *I say,* they *are* even as all the multitude of the Israelites that are consumed:) and let us send and see.

14 They took therefore two chariot horses; and the king sent after the host of the Syrians, saying, Go and see.

15 And they went after them unto Jordan: and, lo, all the way *was* full of garments and vessels, which the Syrians had cast away in their haste. And the messengers returned, and told the king.

16 And the people went out, and spoiled the tents of the Syrians. So a measure of fine flour was *sold* for a shek′-el, and two measures of barley for a shek′-el, according to the word of the LORD.

17 And the king appointed the lord on whose hand he leaned to have the charge of the gate: and the people trode upon him in the gate, and he died, ᴿas the man of God had said, who spake when the king came down to him.   6:32

18 And it came to pass as the man of God had spoken to the king, saying, ᴿTwo measures of barley for a shek′-el, and a measure of fine flour for a shek′-el, shall be to morrow about this time in the gate of Sa-ma′-ri-a: v. 1

19 And that lord answered the man of God, and said, Now, behold, *if* the LORD should make windows in heaven, might such a thing be? And he said, Behold, thou shalt see it with thine eyes, but shalt not eat thereof.

20 And so it fell out unto him: for the people trode upon him in the gate, and he died.

8 Then spake E-li′-sha unto the woman, whose son he had restored to life, saying, Arise, and go thou and thine household, and sojourn wheresoever thou canst sojourn: for the LORD hath called for a famine; and it shall also come upon the land seven years.

2 And the woman arose, and did after the saying of the man of God: and she went with her household, and sojourned in the land of the Phi-lis′-tines seven years.

3 And it came to pass at the seven years' end, that the woman returned out of the land of the Phi-lis′-tines: and she went forth to ᵀcry unto the king for her house and for her land.   *make an appeal*

4 And the king talked with ᴿGe-ha′-zi the servant of the man of God, saying, Tell me, I pray thee, all the great things that E-li′-sha hath done.   4:12; 5:20–27

5 And it came to pass, as he was telling the king how he had ᴿrestored a dead body to life, that, behold, the woman, whose son he had restored to life, cried to the king for her house and for her land. And Ge-ha′-zi said, My lord, O king, this *is* the woman, and this *is* her son, whom E-li′-sha restored to life.   4:35

6 And when the king asked the woman, she told him. So the king appointed unto her a certain officer, saying, Restore all that *was* her's, and all the fruits of the field since the day that she left the land, even until now.

7 And E-li'-sha came to Da-mascus; and ᴿBen-ha'-dad the king of Syria was sick; and it was told him, saying, The man of God is come hither.   6:24

8 And the king said unto ᴿHaz'-a-el, ᴿTake a present in thine hand, and go, meet the man of God, and ᴿenquire of the Lᴏʀᴅ by him, saying, Shall I recover of this disease?   1 Kin. 19:15 · 1 Kin. 14:3 · 1:2

9 So ᴿHaz'-a-el went to meet him, and took a present with him, even of every good thing of Damascus, forty camels' burden, and came and stood before him, and said, Thy son Ben–ha'-dad king of Syria hath sent me to thee, saying, Shall I recover of this disease?   1 Kin. 19:15

10 And E-li'-sha said unto him, Go, say unto him, Thou mayest certainly recover: howbeit the Lᴏʀᴅ hath shewed me that ᴿhe shall surely die.   v. 15

11 And he ᵀsettled his countenance stedfastly, until he was ashamed: and the man of God ᴿwept.   *fixed his gaze* · Luke 19:41

12 And Haz'-a-el said, Why weepeth my lord? And he answered, Because I know ᴿthe evil that thou wilt do unto the children of Israel: their strong holds wilt thou set on fire, and their young men wilt thou slay with the sword, and ᴿwilt dash their children, and rip up their women with child.   Amos 1:3, 4 · Hos. 13:16; Nah. 3:10

13 And Haz'-a-el said, But what, ᴿ*is* thy servant a dog, that he should do this great thing? And E-li'-sha answered, ᴿThe Lᴏʀᴅ hath shewed me that thou *shalt be* king over Syria.   2 Sam. 9:8 · 1 Kin. 19:15

14 So he departed from E-li'-sha, and came to his master; who said to him, What said E-li'-sha to thee? And he answered, He told me *that* thou shouldest surely recover.

15 And it came to pass on the morrow, that he took a thick cloth, and dipped *it* in water, and spread *it* on his face, so that he died: and Haz'-a-el reigned in his stead.

16 And ᴿin the fifth year of Jo'-ram the son of Ahab king of Israel, Je-hosh'-a-phat *being* then king of Judah, ᴿJe-ho'-ram the son of Je-hosh'-a-phat king of Judah began to reign.   1:17; 3:1 · 2 Chr. 21:3

17 ᴿThirty and two years old was he when he began to reign; and he reigned eight years in Jerusalem.   2 Chr. 21:5–10

18 And he walked in the way of the kings of Israel, as did the house of Ahab: for the daughter of Ahab was his wife: and he did evil in the sight of the Lᴏʀᴅ.

19 Yet the Lᴏʀᴅ would not destroy Judah for David his servant's sake, ᴿas he promised him to give him alway a light, *and* to his children.   2 Sam. 7:13; 1 Kin. 11:36

20 In his days ᴿE'-dom revolted from under the hand of Judah, ᴿand made a king over themselves.   2 Chr. 21:8–10 · 1 Kin. 22:47

21 So Jo'-ram went over to Za'-ir, and all the chariots with him: and he rose by night, and smote the E'-dom-ites which compassed him about, and the captains of the chariots: and the people fled into their tents.

22 Yet E'-dom revolted from under the hand of Judah unto this day. ᴿThen Lib'-nah revolted at the same time.   19:8; Josh. 21:13

23 And the rest of the acts of Jo'-ram, and all that he did, *are* they not written in the book of the chronicles of the kings of Judah?

24 And Jo'-ram slept with his fathers, and was buried with his fathers in the city of David: and ᴿA-ha-zi'-ah his son reigned in his stead.   2 Chr. 22:1, 7

25 In the twelfth year of Jo'-ram the son of Ahab king of Israel did A-ha-zi'-ah the son of Je-ho'-ram king of Judah begin to reign.

26 Two and twenty years old *was* A-ha-zi'-ah when he began to reign; and he reigned one year in Jerusalem. And his mother's name *was* Ath-a-li'-ah, the daughter of Om'-ri king of Israel.

27 And he walked in the way of

the house of Ahab, and did evil in the sight of the LORD, as *did* the house of Ahab: for he *was* the son in law of the house of Ahab.

28 And he went with Jo'-ram the son of Ahab to the war against Haz'-a-el king of Syria in ᴿRa'-moth–gil'-e-ad; and the Syrians wounded Jo'-ram.   1 Kin. 22:3, 29

29 And ᴿking Jo'-ram went back to be healed in Jez'-re-el of the wounds which the Syrians had given him at Ra'-mah, when he fought against Haz'-a-el king of Syria. ᴿAnd A-ha-zi'-ah the son of Je-ho'-ram king of Judah went down to see Jo'-ram the son of Ahab in Jez'-re-el, because he was sick.   9:15 · 9:16; 2 Chr. 22:6, 7

9 And E-li'-sha the prophet called one of ᴿthe children of the prophets, and said unto him, ᴿGird up thy loins, and take this box of oil in thine hand, and go to Ra'-moth–gil'-e-ad: 1 Kin. 20:35 · 4:29

2 And when thou comest thither, ᵀlook out there Je'-hu the son of Je-hosh'-a-phat the son of Nim'-shi, and go in, and make him arise up from among ᴿhis brethren, and carry him to an inner chamber;   *look there for* · vv. 5, 11

3 Then take the box of oil, and pour *it* on his head, and say, Thus saith the LORD, I have anointed thee king over Israel. Then open the door, and flee, and tarry not.

4 So the young man, *even* the young man the prophet, went to Ra'-moth–gil'-e-ad.

5 And when he came, behold, the captains of the host *were* sitting; and he said, I have an errand to thee, O captain. And Je'-hu said, Unto which of all us? And he said, To thee, O captain.

6 And he arose, and went into the house; and he poured the oil on his head, and said unto him, ᴿThus saith the LORD God of Israel, I have anointed thee king over the people of the LORD, *even* over Israel.   1 Sam. 2:7, 8; 1 Kin. 19:16

7 And thou shalt smite the house of Ahab thy master, that I may avenge the blood of my servants the prophets, and the blood of all the servants of the LORD, ᴿat the hand of Jez'-e-bel.   1 Kin. 18:4

8 For the whole house of Ahab shall perish: and ᴿI will cut off from Ahab him that pisseth against the wall, and him that is shut up and left in Israel: 10:17

9 And I will make the house of Ahab like the house of ᴿJer-o-bo'-am the son of Ne'-bat, and like the house of ᴿBa'-a-sha the son of A-hi'-jah: 1 Kin. 15:29; 21:22 · 1 Kin. 16:3, 11

10 ᴿAnd the dogs shall eat Jez'-e-bel in the ᵀportion of Jez'-re-el, and *there shall be* none to bury *her*. And he opened the door, and fled.   vv. 35, 36; 1 Kin. 21:23 · *vicinity*

11 Then Je'-hu came forth to the servants of his lord: and *one* said unto him, *Is* all well? wherefore came this mad *fellow* to thee? And he said unto them, Ye know the man, and his communication.

12 And they said, *It is* ᵀfalse; tell us now. And he said, Thus and thus spake he to me, saying, Thus saith the LORD, I have anointed thee king over Israel.   *a lie*

13 Then they hasted, and ᴿtook every man his garment, and put *it* under him on the top of the stairs, and blew with trumpets, saying, Je'-hu is king.   Mark 11:7, 8

14 So Je'-hu the son of Je-hosh'-a-phat the son of Nim'-shi conspired against ᴿJo'-ram. (Now Jo'-ram had kept Ra'-moth–gil'-e-ad, he and all Israel, because of Haz'-a-el king of Syria.   8:28

15 But ᴿking ᵀJo'-ram was returned to be healed in Jez'-re-el of the wounds which the Syrians had given him, when he fought with Haz'-a-el king of Syria.) And Je'-hu said, If it be your minds, *then* let none go forth *nor* escape out of the city to go to tell *it* in Jez'-re-el.   8:29 · *Jehoram, v. 24*

16 So Je'-hu rode in a chariot, and went to Jez'-re-el; for Jo'-ram lay there. ᴿAnd A-ha-zi'-ah king of Judah was come down to see Jo'-ram.   8:29

17 And there stood a watchman

on the tower in Jez'-re-el, and he spied the company of Je'-hu as he came, and said, I see a company. And Jo'-ram said, Take an horseman, and send to meet them, and let him say, *Is it* peace?

18 So there went one on horseback to meet him, and said, Thus saith the king, *Is it* peace? And Je'-hu said, What hast thou to do with peace? turn thee behind me. And the watchman told, saying, The messenger came to them, but he cometh not again.

19 Then he sent out a second on horseback, which came to them, and said, Thus saith the king, *Is it* peace? And Je'-hu answered, What hast thou to do with peace? turn thee behind me.

20 And the watchman told, saying, He came even unto them, and cometh not again: and the driving *is* like the driving of Je'-hu the son of Nim'-shi; for he driveth furiously.

21 And Jo'-ram said, Make ready. And his chariot was made ready. And ᴿJo'-ram king of Israel and A-ha-zi'-ah king of Judah went out, each in his chariot, and they went out against Je'-hu, and met him in the portion of Na'-both the Jez'-re-el-ite.　　1 Kin. 19:17

22 And it came to pass, when Jo'-ram saw Je'-hu, that he said, *Is it* peace, Je'-hu? And he answered, What peace, so long as the ᵀwhoredoms of thy mother Jez'-e-bel and her witchcrafts *are* so many?　　*harlotries*

23 And Jo'-ram turned his hands, and fled, and said to A-ha-zi'-ah, *There is* treachery, O A-ha-zi'-ah.

24 And Je'-hu drew a bow with his full strength, and smote Je-ho'-ram between his arms, and the arrow went out at his heart, and he sunk down in his chariot.

25 Then said *Je'-hu* to Bid'-kar his captain, Take up, *and* cast him in the portion of the field of Na'-both the Jez'-re-el-ite: for remember how that, when I and thou rode together after Ahab his fa-

ther, ᴿthe LORD laid this ᴿburden upon him;　　1 Kin. 21:19, 24–29 · Is. 13:1

26 Surely I have seen yesterday the blood of Na'-both, and the blood of his sons, saith the LORD; and I will requite thee in this ᵀplat, saith the LORD. Now therefore take *and* cast him into the plat *of ground,* according to the word of the LORD.　　*property*

27 But when A-ha-zi'-ah the king of Judah saw *this,* he fled by the way of the garden house. And Je'-hu followed after him, and said, ᵀSmite him also in the chariot. *And they did so* at the going up to Gur, which *is* by Ib'-le-am. And he fled to ᴿMe-gid'-do, and died there.　　*Shoot* · 2 Chr. 22:7, 9

28 And his servants carried him in a chariot to Jerusalem, and buried him in his sepulchre with his fathers in the city of David.

29 And in the eleventh year of Jo'-ram the son of Ahab began A-ha-zi'-ah to reign over Judah.

30 And when Je'-hu was come to Jez'-re-el, Jez'-e-bel heard *of it;* ᴿand she painted her face, and ᵀtired her head, and looked out at a window.　　Ezek. 23:40 · *adorned*

31 And as Je'-hu entered in at the gate, she said, Had Zim'-ri peace, who slew his master?

32 And he lifted up his face to the window, and said, Who *is* on my side? who? And there looked out to him two *or* three eunuchs.

33 And he said, Throw her down. So they threw her down: and *some* of her blood was sprinkled on the wall, and on the horses: and he trode her under foot.

34 And when he was come in, he did eat and drink, and said, Go, see now this cursed *woman,* and bury her: for ᴿshe *is* a king's daughter.　　[Ex. 22:28]; 1 Kin. 16:31

35 And they went to bury her: but they found no more of her than the skull, and the feet, and the palms of *her* hands.

36 Wherefore they came again, and told him. And he said, This *is* the word of the LORD, which he

spake by his servant E-li'-jah the Tish'-bite, saying, ᴿIn the portion of Jez'-re-el shall dogs eat the flesh of Jez'-e-bel: 1 Kin. 21:23

37 And the carcase of Jez'-e-bel shall be ᴿas dung upon the face of the field in the portion of Jez'-re-el; *so* that they shall not say, This *is* Jez'-e-bel.   Ps. 83:10

10 And Ahab had seventy sons in Sa-ma'-ri-a. And Je'-hu wrote letters, and sent to Sa-ma'-ri-a, unto the rulers of Jez'-re-el, to the elders, and to ᵀthem that brought up Ahab's *children,* saying,   *the guardians of*

2 Now as soon as this letter cometh to you, seeing your master's sons *are* with you, and *there are* with you chariots and horses, a fenced city also, and armour;

3 Look even out the best and meetest of your master's sons, and set *him* on his father's throne, and fight for your master's house.

4 But they were exceedingly afraid, and said, Behold, ᴿtwo kings stood not before him: how then shall we stand?   9:24, 27

5 And he that *was* over the house, and he that *was* over the city, the elders also, and the bringers up of *the children,* sent to Je'-hu, saying, We *are* thy servants, and will do all that thou shalt bid us; we will not make any king: do thou *that which is* good in thine eyes.

6 Then he wrote a letter the second time to them, saying, If ye ᵀ*be* mine, and *if* ye will hearken unto my voice, take ye the heads of the men your master's sons, and come to me to Jez'-re-el by to morrow this time. Now the king's sons, *being* seventy persons, *were* with the great men of the city, which brought them up.   *are for me*

7 And it came to pass, when the letter came to them, that they took the king's sons, and ᴿslew seventy persons, and put their heads in baskets, and sent him *them* to Jez'-re-el.   11:1; 1 Kin. 21:21

8 And there came a messenger, and told him, saying, They have brought the heads of the king's sons. And he said, Lay ye them in two heaps at the entering in of the gate until the morning.

9 And it came to pass in the morning, that he went out, and stood, and said to all the people, Ye *be* righteous: behold, I conspired against my master, and slew him: but who slew all these?

10 Know now that there shall ᴿfall unto the earth nothing of the word of the LORD, which the LORD spake concerning the house of Ahab: for the LORD hath done *that* which he spake by his servant E-li'-jah.   1 Kin. 8:56; Jer. 44:28

11 So Je'-hu slew all that remained of the house of Ahab in Jez'-re-el, and all his great men, and his kinsfolks, and his priests, until he left him none remaining.

12 And he arose and departed, and ᵀcame to Sa-ma'-ri-a. *And* as he *was* at the shearing house ᵀin the way,   *went · on*

13 Je'-hu met with the brethren of A-ha-zi'-ah king of Judah, and said, Who *are* ye? And they answered, We *are* the brethren of A-ha-zi'-ah; and we go down to salute the children of the king and the children of the queen.

14 And he said, Take them alive. And they took them alive, and slew them at the pit of the shearing house, *even* two and forty men; neither left he any of them.

15 And when he was departed thence, he lighted on Je-hon'-a-dab the son of Re'-chab *coming* to meet him: and he saluted him, and said to him, Is thine heart right, as my heart *is* with thy heart? And Je-hon'-a-dab answered, It is. If it be, give *me* thine hand. And he gave *him* his hand; and he took him up to him into the chariot.

16 And he said, Come with me, and see my zeal for the LORD. So they made him ride in his chariot.

17 And when he came to Sa-ma'-ri-a, ᴿhe slew all that remained unto Ahab in Sa-ma'-ri-a, till he had destroyed him, accord-

ing to the saying of the LORD, which he spake to E-li'-jah.   9:8

18 And Je'-hu gathered all the people together, and said unto them, Ahab served Ba'-al a little; *but* Je'-hu shall serve him much.

19 Now therefore call unto me all the ᴿprophets of Ba'-al, all his servants, and all his priests; let none be wanting: for I have a great sacrifice *to do* to Ba'-al; whosoever shall be wanting, he shall not live. But Je'-hu did *it* ᵀin subtilty, to the intent that he might destroy the worshippers of Ba'-al.   1 Kin. 18:19 · *acted deceptively*

20 And Je'-hu said, Proclaim a solemn assembly for Ba'-al. And they proclaimed *it*.

21 And Je'-hu sent through all Israel: and all the worshippers of Ba'-al came, so that there was not a man left that came not. And they came into the house of Ba'-al; and the ᴿhouse of Ba'-al was full from one end to another.   11:18; 1 Kin. 16:32

22 And he said unto him that *was* over the vestry, Bring forth vestments for all the worshippers of Ba'-al. And he brought them forth vestments.

23 And Je'-hu went, and Je-hon'-a-dab the son of Re'-chab, into the house of Ba'-al, and said unto the worshippers of Ba'-al, Search, and look that there be here with you none of the servants of the LORD, but the worshippers of Ba'-al only.

24 And when they went in to offer sacrifices and burnt offerings, Je'-hu appointed fourscore men without, and said, *If* any of the men whom I have brought into your hands escape, *he that letteth him go,* ᴿhis life *shall be* for the life of him.   1 Kin. 20:39

25 And it came to pass, as soon as he had made an end of offering the burnt offering, that Je'-hu said to the guard and to the captains, Go in, *and* slay them; let none come forth. And they smote them with the edge of the sword; and the guard and the captains cast *them* out, and went to the city of the house of Ba'-al.

26 And they brought forth the ᴿimages out of the house of Ba'-al, and burned them.   3:2; 1 Kin. 14:23

27 And they brake down the image of Ba'-al, and brake down the house of Ba'-al, and made it a draught house unto this day.

28 Thus Je'-hu destroyed Ba'-al out of Israel.

29 Howbeit *from* the sins of Jer-o-bo'-am the son of Ne'-bat, who made Israel to sin, Je'-hu departed not from after them, *to wit,* ᴿthe golden calves that *were* in Beth'–el, and that *were* in Dan. 1 Kin. 13:33

30 And the LORD said unto Je'-hu, Because thou hast done well in executing *that which is* right in mine eyes, *and* hast done unto the house of Ahab according to all that *was* in mine heart, thy children of the fourth *generation* shall sit on the throne of Israel.

31 But Je'-hu ᵀtook no heed to walk in the law of the LORD God of Israel with all his heart: for he departed not from ᴿthe sins of Jer-o-bo'-am, which made Israel to sin.   *was not careful* · 1 Kin. 14:16

32 In those days the LORD began to cut Israel short: and ᴿHaz'-a-el smote them in all the coasts of Israel;   8:12; 13:22; 1 Kin. 19:17

33 From Jordan eastward, all the land of Gil'-e-ad, the Gad'-ites, and the Reu'-ben-ites, and the Ma-nas'-sites, from ᴿAr'-o-er, which *is* by the river Arnon, even ᴿGil'-e-ad and Ba'-shan.   Deut. 2:36 · Amos 1:3–5

34 Now the rest of the acts of Je'-hu, and all that he did, and all his might, *are* they not written in the book of the chronicles of the kings of Israel?

35 And Je'-hu slept with his fathers: and they buried him in Sa-ma'-ri-a. And ᴿJe-ho'-a-haz his son reigned in his stead.   13:1

36 And the time that Je'-hu reigned over Israel in Sa-ma'-ri-a *was* twenty and eight years.

11 And when ᴿAth-a-li'-ah ᴿthe mother of A-ha-zi'-ah saw that her son was ᴿdead, she arose and destroyed all the ᵀseed royal.   2 Chr. 22:10 · 8:26 · 9:27 · *royal heirs*

2 But Je-hosh'-e-ba, the daughter of king Jo'-ram, sister of ᴿA-ha-zi'-ah, took ᵀJo'-ash the son of A-ha-zi'-ah, and stole him from among the king's sons *which were* slain; and they hid him, *even* him and his nurse, in the bedchamber from Ath-a-li'-ah, so that he was not slain.   8:25 · *Jehoash*, v. 21

3 And he was with her hid in the house of the LORD six years. And Ath-a-li'-ah did reign over the land.

4 And ᴿthe seventh year Je-hoi'-a-da sent and fetched the rulers over hundreds, with the captains and the ᵀguard, and brought them to him into the house of the LORD, and made a covenant with them, and took an oath of them in the house of the LORD, and shewed them the king's son.   12:2; 2 Chr. 23:1 · *escorts*

5 And he commanded them, saying, This *is* the thing that ye shall do; A third part of you that enter in ᴿon the sabbath shall even be keepers of the watch of the king's house;   1 Chr. 9:25

6 And a third part *shall be* at the gate of Sur; and a third part at the gate behind the guard: so shall ye keep the watch of the house, that it be not broken down.

7 And two parts of all you that go forth on the sabbath, even they shall keep the watch of the house of the LORD about the king.

8 And ye shall compass the king round about, every man with his weapons in his hand: and he that cometh within ᵀthe ranges, let him be ᵀslain: and be ye with the king as he goeth out and as he cometh in.   *range · put to death*

9 And the captains over the hundreds did according to all *things* that Je-hoi'-a-da the priest commanded: and they took every man his men that were to come in on the sabbath, with them that should go out on the sabbath, and came to Je-hoi'-a-da the priest.

10 And to the captains over hundreds did the priest give king David's spears and shields, that *were* in the temple of the LORD.

11 And the guard stood, every man with his weapons in his hand, round about the king, from the right corner of the temple to the left corner of the temple, *along* by the altar and the temple.

12 And he brought forth the king's son, and put the crown upon him, and *gave him* the ᴿtestimony; and they made him king, and anointed him; and they clapped their hands, and said, God save the king.   Ex. 25:16; 31:18

13 ᴿAnd when Ath-a-li'-ah heard the noise of the guard *and* of the people, she came to the people into the temple of the LORD.   8:26

14 And when she looked, behold, the king stood by ᴿa pillar, as the manner *was*, and the princes and the trumpeters by the king, and all the people of the land rejoiced, and blew with trumpets: and Ath-a-li'-ah ᵀrent her clothes, and cried, Treason, Treason.   23:3; 2 Chr. 34:31 · *tore*

15 But Je-hoi'-a-da the priest commanded the captains of the hundreds, the officers of the host, and said unto them, ᵀHave her forth without the ranges: and him that followeth her kill with the sword. For the priest had said, Let her not be slain in the house of the LORD.   *Take her outside*

16 And they laid hands on her; and she went by the way by the which the horses came into the king's house: and there was she slain.

17 And Je-hoi'-a-da ᴿmade a covenant between the LORD and the king and the people, that they should be the LORD's people; ᴿbetween the king also and the people.   2 Chr. 15:12–15 · 2 Sam. 5:3

18 And all the people of the land went into the house of Ba'-al, and brake it down; his altars and his images brake they in pieces thoroughly, and ᴿslew Mat'-tan the priest of Ba'-al before the altars. And the priest

appointed officers over the house of the LORD.   10:11

19 And he took the rulers over hundreds, and the captains, and the guard, and all the people of the land; and they brought down the king from the house of the LORD, and came by the way of the gate of the guard to the king's house. And he sat on the throne of the kings.

20 And all the people of the land rejoiced, and the city was in quiet: and they slew Ath-a-li'-ah with the sword *beside* the king's house.

21 Seven years old *was* Je-ho'-ash when he began to reign.

12 In the seventh year of Je'-hu ᴿJe-ho'-ashᵀ began to reign; and forty years reigned he in Jerusalem. And his mother's name *was* Zib'-i-ah of Be'-er–she'-ba.   2 Chr. 24:1 · *Joash,* 11:2

2 And Je-ho'-ash did *that which was* right in the sight of the LORD all his days wherein ᴿJe-hoi'-a-da the priest instructed him.   11:4

3 But ᴿthe high places were not taken away: the people still sacrificed and burnt incense in the high places.   14:4; 15:35; 1 Kin. 15:14

4 And Je-ho'-ash said to the priests, ᴿAll the money of the dedicated things that is brought into the house of the LORD, *even* the money of every one that passeth *the account,* the money that every man is set at, *and* all the money that ᴿcometh into any man's heart to bring into the house of the LORD,   22:4 · Ex. 35:5; 1 Chr. 29:3–9

5 Let the priests take *it* to them, every man of his acquaintance: and let them repair the breaches of the house, wheresoever any breach shall be found.

6 But it was *so, that* in the three and twentieth year of king Je-ho'-ash ᴿthe priests had not repaired the breaches of the house.   2 Chr. 24:5

7 ᴿThen king Je-ho'-ash called for Je-hoi'-a-da the priest, and the *other* priests, and said unto them,

Why repair ye not the breaches of the house? now therefore receive no *more* money of your acquaintance, but deliver it for the breaches of the house.   2 Chr. 24:6

8 And the priests consented to receive no *more* money of the people, neither to repair the breaches of the house.

9 But Je-hoi'-a-da the priest took a chest, and bored a hole in the lid of it, and set it beside the altar, on the right side as one cometh into the house of the LORD: and the priests that kept the door put ᴿtherein all the money *that was* brought into the house of the LORD.   Mark 12:41; Luke 21:1

10 And it was *so,* when they saw that *there was* much money in the chest, that the king's ᴿscribe and the high priest came up, and they put up in bags, and ᵀtold the money that was found in the house of the LORD.   19:2 · *counted*

11 And they gave the money, being ᵀtold, into the hands of them that did the work, that had the oversight of the house of the LORD: and they ᵀlaid it out to the carpenters and builders, that wrought upon the house of the LORD,   Lit. *weighed out · paid*

12 And to masons, and hewers of stone, and to buy timber and hewed stone to ᴿrepair the breaches of the house of the LORD, and for all that was laid out for the house to repair *it.*   22:5, 6

13 Howbeit ᴿthere were not made for the house of the LORD bowls of silver, snuffers, basons, trumpets, any vessels of gold, or vessels of silver, of the money *that was* brought into the house of the LORD: 2 Chr. 24:14

14 But they gave that to the workmen, and repaired therewith the house of the LORD.

15 Moreover ᴿthey reckoned not with the men, into whose hand they delivered the money to be bestowed on workmen: for they dealt faithfully.   [1 Cor. 4:2]; 2 Cor. 8:20

16 ᴿThe trespass money and sin money was not brought into the

house of the LORD: ᴿit was the priests'.   [Lev. 5:15, 18] · [Lev. 7:7]

17 Then ᴿHaz'-a-el king of Syria went up, and fought against Gath, and took it: and Haz'-a-el set his face to go up to Jerusalem.   8:12

18 And Je-ho'-ash king of Judah ᴿtook all the hallowed things that Je-hosh'-a-phat, and Je-ho'-ram, and A-ha-zi'-ah, his fathers, kings of Judah, had dedicated, and his own hallowed things, and all the gold *that was* found in the treasures of the house of the LORD, and in the king's house, and sent *it* to Haz'-a-el king of Syria: and he went away from Jerusalem.   16:8

19 And the rest of the acts of Jo'-ash, and all that he did, *are* they not written in the book of the chronicles of the kings of Judah?

20 And ᴿhis servants arose, and made a conspiracy, and slew Jo'-ash in the house of Mil'-lo, which goeth down to Sil'-la.   2 Chr. 24:25

21 For Joz'-a-char the son of Shim'-e-ath, and Je-hoz'-a-bad the son of Sho'-mer, his servants, smote him, and he died; and they buried him with his fathers in the city of David: and Am-a-zi'-ah his son reigned in his stead.

13 In the three and twentieth year of ᴿJo'-ash the son of A-ha-zi'-ah king of Judah Je-ho'-a-haz the son of Je'-hu began to reign over Israel in Sa-ma'-ri-a, *and reigned* seventeen years.   12:1

2 And he did *that which was* evil in the sight of the LORD, and followed the ᴿsins of Jer-o-bo'-am the son of Ne'-bat, which made Israel to sin; he departed not therefrom.   1 Kin. 12:26–33

3 And the anger of the LORD was kindled against Israel, and he delivered them into the hand of ᴿHaz'-a-el king of Syria, and into the hand of Ben–ha'-dad the son of Haz'-a-el, all *their* days.   8:12

4 And Je-ho'-a-haz besought the LORD, and the LORD hearkened unto him: for he saw the oppression of Israel, because the king of Syria oppressed them.

5 (And the LORD gave Israel a saviour, so that they went out from under the hand of the Syrians: and the children of Israel dwelt in their tents, as beforetime.

6 Nevertheless they departed not from the sins of the house of Jer-o-bo'-am, who made Israel sin, *but* walked therein: ᴿand there remained the grove also in Sa-ma'-ri-a.)   1 Kin. 16:33

7 Neither did he leave of the people to Je-ho'-a-haz but fifty horsemen, and ten chariots, and ten thousand footmen; for the king of Syria had destroyed them, ᴿand had made them ᴿlike the dust by threshing.   10:32 · [Amos 1:3]

8 Now the rest of the acts of Je-ho'-a-haz, and all that he did, and his might, *are* they not written in the book of the chronicles of the kings of Israel?

9 And Je-ho'-a-haz slept with his fathers; and they buried him in Sa-ma'-ri-a: and Jo'-ash his son reigned in his stead.

10 In the thirty and seventh year of Jo'-ash king of Judah began Je-ho'-ash the son of Je-ho'-a-haz to reign over Israel in Sa-ma'-ri-a, *and reigned* sixteen years.

11 And he did *that which was* evil in the sight of the LORD; he departed not from all the sins of Jer-o-bo'-am the son of Ne'-bat, who made Israel sin: *but* he walked therein.

12 ᴿAnd the rest of the acts of Jo'-ash, and all that he did, and ᴿhis might wherewith he fought against Am-a-zi'-ah king of Judah, *are* they not written in the book of the chronicles of the kings of Israel? 14:8–15 · 2 Chr. 25:17–25

13 And Jo'-ash ᴿsleptᵀ with his fathers; and Jer-o-bo'-am sat upon his throne: and Jo'-ash was buried in Sa-ma'-ri-a with the kings of Israel.   14:16 · *rested in death*

14 Now E-li'-sha was fallen sick of his sickness whereof he died. And Jo'-ash the king of Israel came down unto him, and wept over his face, and said, O my father, my father, the chariot of Israel, and the horsemen thereof.

15 And E-li'-sha said unto him, Take bow and arrows. And he took unto him bow and arrows.

16 And he said to the king of Israel, Put thine hand upon the bow. And he put his hand *upon it:* and E-li'-sha put his hands upon the king's hands.

17 And he said, Open the window eastward. And he opened *it.* Then E-li'-sha said, Shoot. And he shot. And he said, The arrow of the LORD's deliverance, and the arrow of deliverance from Syria: for thou shalt smite the Syrians in ᴿA'-phek, till thou have ᵀconsumed *them.*   1 Kin. 20:26 · destroyed

18 And he said, Take the arrows. And he took *them.* And he said unto the king of Israel, ᵀSmite upon the ground. And he smote thrice, and ᵀstayed.   *Strike · stopped*

19 And the man of God was wroth with him, and said, Thou shouldest have smitten five or six times; then hadst thou smitten Syria till thou hadst ᵀconsumed *it:* ᴿwhereas now thou shalt smite Syria *but* thrice.   *destroyed · v. 25*

20 And E-li'-sha died, and they buried him. And the ᴿbands of the Mo'-ab-ites invaded the land at the coming in of the year.   3:5; 24:2

21 And it came to pass, as they were burying a man, that, behold, they spied a band *of men;* and they cast the man into the sepulchre of E-li'-sha: and when the man was let down, and touched the bones of E-li'-sha, he revived, and stood up on his feet.

22 But ᴿHaz'-a-el king of Syria oppressed Israel all the days of Je-ho'-a-haz.   8:12, 13

23 And the LORD was ᴿgracious unto them, and had compassion on them, and had respect unto them, ᴿbecause of his covenant with Abraham, Isaac, and Jacob, and would not destroy them, neither cast he them from his presence as yet.   14:27 · Gen. 13:16, 17; 17:2–7

24 So Haz'-a-el king of Syria died; and Ben–ha'-dad his son reigned in his stead.

25 And Je-ho'-ash the son of Je-

ho'-a-haz took again out of the hand of Ben–ha'-dad the son of Haz'-a-el the cities, which he had taken out of the hand of Je-ho'-a-haz his father by war. Three times did Jo'-ash beat him, and recovered the cities of Israel.

14 In ᴿthe second year of Jo'-ash son of Je-ho'-a-haz king of Israel reigned Am-a-zi'-ah the son of Jo'-ash king of Judah. 13:10

2 He was twenty and five years old when he began to reign, and reigned twenty and nine years in Jerusalem. And his mother's name *was* Je-ho-ad'-dan of Jerusalem.

3 And he did *that which was* right in the sight of the LORD, yet not like David his father: he did according to all things ᴿas Jo'-ash his father did.   12:2

4 ᴿHowbeit the high places were not taken away: as yet the people did sacrifice and burnt incense on the high places.   12:3

5 And it came to pass, as soon as the kingdom was ᵀconfirmed in his hand, that he slew his servants ᴿwhich had slain the king his father.   *established · 12:20*

6 But the children of the murderers he slew not: according unto that which is written in the book of the law of Moses, wherein the LORD commanded, saying, The fathers shall not be put to death for the children, nor the children be put to death for the fathers; but every man shall be put to death for his own sin.

7 He slew of E'-dom in ᴿthe valley of salt ten thousand, and took Selah by war, ᴿand called the name of it Jok'-the-el unto this day.   2 Sam. 8:13; Ps. 60:title · Josh. 15:38

8 ᴿThen Am-a-zi'-ah sent messengers to Je-ho'-ash, the son of Je-ho'-a-haz son of Je'-hu, king of Israel, saying, Come, let us look one another in the face. 2 Chr. 25:17

9 And Je-ho'-ash the king of Israel sent to Am-a-zi'-ah king of Judah, saying, The thistle that *was* in Leb'-a-non sent to the cedar that *was* in Leb'-a-non, say-

ing, Give thy daughter to my son to wife: and there passed by a wild beast that *was* in Leb'-a-non, and trode down the thistle.

10 Thou hast indeed smitten E'-dom, and ᴿthine heart hath lifted thee up: glory *of this*, and tarry at home: for why shouldest thou meddle to *thy* hurt, that thou shouldest fall, *even* thou, and Judah with thee?   Deut. 8:14; [Hab. 2:4]

11 But Am-a-zi'-ah would not hear. Therefore Je-ho'-ash king of Israel went up; and he and Am-a-zi'-ah king of Judah looked one another in the face at Beth–she'-mesh, which *belongeth* to Judah.

12 And Judah was put to the worse before Israel; and they fled every man to their tents.

13 And Je-ho'-ash king of Israel took Am-a-zi'-ah king of Judah, the son of Je-ho'-ash the son of A-ha-zi'-ah, at Beth–she'-mesh, and came to Jerusalem, and brake down the wall of Jerusalem from the gate of E'-phra-im unto the corner gate, four hundred cubits.

14 And he took all ᴿthe gold and silver, and all the vessels that were found in the house of the LORD, and in the treasures of the king's house, and hostages, and returned to Sa-ma'-ri-a.   12:18; 16:8

15 Now the rest of the acts of Je-ho'-ash which he did, and his might, and how he fought with Am-a-zi'-ah king of Judah, *are* they not written in the book of the chronicles of the kings of Israel?

16 And Je-ho'-ash ᵀslept with his fathers, and was buried in Sa-ma'-ri-a with the kings of Israel; and Jer-o-bo'-am his son reigned in his stead.   *rested in death*

17 ᴿAnd Am-a-zi'-ah the son of Jo'-ash king of Judah lived after the death of Je-ho'-ash son of Je-ho'-a-haz king of Israel fifteen years.   2 Chr. 25:25–28

18 And the rest of the acts of Am-a-zi'-ah, *are* they not written in the book of the chronicles of the kings of Judah?

19 Now ᴿthey made a conspiracy against him in Jerusalem: and

he fled to ᴿLa'-chish; but they sent after him to La'-chish, and slew him there.   2 Chr. 25:27 · Josh. 10:31

20 And they brought him on horses: and he was buried at Jerusalem with his fathers in the city of David.

21 And all the people of Judah took ᵀAz-a-ri'-ah, which *was* sixteen years old, and made him king instead of his father Am-a-zi'-ah.   *Uzziah*, 2 Chr. 26:1ff; Is. 6:1

22 He built ᴿE'-lath, and restored it to Judah, after that the king slept with his fathers.   16:6

23 In the fifteenth year of Am-a-zi'-ah the son of Jo'-ash king of Judah Jer-o-bo'-am the son of Jo'-ash king of Israel began to reign in Sa-ma'-ri-a, *and reigned* forty and one years.

24 And he did *that which was* evil in the sight of the LORD: he departed not from all the sins of Jer-o-bo'-am the son of Ne'-bat, who made Israel to sin.

25 He ᴿrestored the coast of Israel from the entering of Ha'-math unto the sea of the plain, according to the word of the LORD God of Israel, which he spake by the hand of his servant Jonah, the son of A-mit'-tai, the prophet, which *was* of Gath–he'-pher.   10:32

26 For the LORD ᴿsaw the affliction of Israel, *that it was* very bitter: for ᴿ*there was* not any shut up, nor any left, nor any helper for Israel.   13:4; Ps. 106:44 · Deut. 32:36

27 ᴿAnd the LORD said not that he would blot out the name of Israel from under heaven: but he saved them by the hand of Jer-o-bo'-am the son of Jo'-ash.   [13:5, 23]

28 Now the rest of the acts of Jer-o-bo'-am, and all that he did, and his might, how he warred, and how he recovered Damascus, and Ha'-math, ᴿ*which belonged* to Judah, for Israel, *are* they not written in the book of the chronicles of the kings of Israel? 2 Chr. 8:3

29 And Jer-o-bo'-am slept with his fathers, *even* with the kings of Israel; and ᴿZach-a-ri'-ah his son reigned in his stead.   15:8

15 In the twenty and seventh year of Jer-o-bo′-am king of Israel ᴿbegan ᴿAz-a-ri′-ah son of Am-a-zi′-ah king of Judah to reign. vv. 13, 30 · 14:21; 2 Chr. 26:1, 3, 4

2 Sixteen years old was he when he began to reign, and he reigned two and fifty years in Jerusalem. And his mother's name *was* Jech-o-li′-ah of Jeru-salem.

3 And he did *that which was* right in the sight of the LORD, according to all that his father Am-a-zi′-ah had done;

4 ᴿSave that the high places were not removed: the people sacrificed and burnt incense still on the high places. v. 35; 12:3; 14:4

5 And the LORD smote the king, so that he was a leper unto the day of his death, and dwelt in a several house. And Jo′-tham the king's son *was* over the house, judging the people of the land.

6 And the rest of the acts of Az-a-ri′-ah, and all that he did, *are* they not written in the book of the chronicles of the kings of Judah?

7 So Az-a-ri′-ah slept with his fathers; and ᴿthey buried him with his fathers in the city of David: and Jo′-tham his son reigned in his stead. 2 Chr. 26:23

8 In the thirty and eighth year of Az-a-ri′-ah king of Judah did ᴿZach-a-ri′-ah the son of Jer-o-bo′-am reign over Israel in Sa-ma′-ri-a six months. 14:29

9 And he did *that which was* evil in the sight of the LORD, ᴿas his fathers had done: he departed not from the sins of Jer-o-bo′-am the son of Ne′-bat, who made Israel to sin. 14:24

10 And Shal′-lum the son of Ja′-besh conspired against him, and ᴿsmoteᵀ him ᵀbefore the people, and slew him, and reigned in his stead. Amos 7:9 · *struck · in front of*

11 And the rest of the acts of Zach-a-ri′-ah, behold, they *are* written in the book of the chronicles of the kings of Israel.

12 This *was* the ᴿword of the LORD which he spake unto Je′-hu, saying, Thy sons shall sit on the throne of Israel unto the fourth *generation.* And so it came to pass. 10:30

13 Shal′-lum the son of Ja′-besh began to reign in the nine and thirtieth year of ᵀUz-zi′-ah king of Judah; and he reigned a full month in Sa-ma′-ri-a. *Azariah,* 14:21

14 For Men′-a-hem the son of Ga′-di went up from ᴿTir′-zah, and came to Sa-ma′-ri-a, and smote Shal′-lum the son of Ja′-besh in Sa-ma′-ri-a, and slew him, and reigned in his stead. Song 6:4

15 And the rest of the acts of Shal′-lum, and his conspiracy which he made, behold, they *are* written in the book of the chronicles of the kings of Israel.

16 Then Men′-a-hem smote ᴿTiph′-sah, and all that *were* therein, and the coasts thereof from Tir′-zah: because they opened not *to him;* therefore he smote *it; and* all ᴿthe women therein that were with child he ripped up. 1 Kin. 4:24 · 8:12; Hos. 13:16

17 In the nine and thirtieth year of Az-a-ri′-ah king of Judah began Men′-a-hem the son of Ga′-di to reign over Israel, *and reigned* ten years in Sa-ma′-ri-a.

18 And he did *that which was* evil in the sight of the LORD: he departed not all his days from the sins of Jer-o-bo′-am the son of Ne′-bat, who made Israel to sin.

19 *And* ᵀPul the king of Assyria came against the land: and Men′-a-hem gave Pul a thousand talents of silver, that his hand might be with him to confirm the kingdom in his hand. *Tiglath-pileser III,* v. 29

20 And Men′-a-hem ᴿexacted the money of Israel, *even* of all the mighty men of wealth, of each man fifty shek′-els of silver, to give to the king of Assyria. So the king of Assyria turned back, and stayed not there in the land. 23:35

21 And the rest of the acts of Men′-a-hem, and all that he did, *are* they not written in the book of the chronicles of the kings of Israel?

22 And Men'-a-hem slept with his fathers; and Pek-a-hi'-ah his son reigned in his stead.

23 In the fiftieth year of Az-a-ri'-ah king of Judah Pek-a-hi'-ah the son of Men'-a-hem began to reign over Israel in Sa-ma'-ri-a, *and reigned* two years.

24 And he did *that which was* evil in the sight of the Lord: he departed not from the sins of Jer-o-bo'-am the son of Ne'-bat, who made Israel to sin.

25 But Pe'-kah the son of Rem-a-li'-ah, a captain of his, conspired against him, and smote him in Sa-ma'-ri-a, in the palace of the king's house, with Ar'-gob and A-ri'-eh, and with him fifty men of the Gil'-e-ad-ites: and he killed him, and reigned in his room.

26 And the rest of the acts of Pek-a-hi'-ah, and all that he did, behold, they *are* written in the book of the chronicles of the kings of Israel.

27 In the two and fiftieth year of Az-a-ri'-ah king of Judah ᴿPe'-kah the son of Rem-a-li'-ah began to reign over Israel in Sa-ma'-ri-a, *and reigned* twenty years.   Is. 7:1

28 And he did *that which was* evil in the sight of the Lord: he departed not from the sins of Jer-o-bo'-am the son of Ne'-bat, who made Israel to sin.

29 In the days of Pe'-kah king of Israel came Tig'-lath–pi-le'-ser king of Assyria, and took I'-jon, and A'-bel–beth–ma'-a-chah, and Ja-no'-ah, and Ke'-desh, and Ha'-zor, and Gil'-e-ad, and Galilee, all the land of Naph'-ta-li, and carried them captive to Assyria.

30 And Ho-she'-a the son of E'-lah made a conspiracy against Pe'-kah the son of Rem-a-li'-ah, and smote him, and slew him, and ᴿreigned in his stead, in the twentieth year of Jo'-tham the son of Uz-zi'-ah.   17:1; [Hos. 10:3, 7, 15]

31 And the rest of the acts of Pe'-kah, and all that he did, behold, they *are* written in the book of the chronicles of the kings of Israel.

32 In the second year of Pe'-kah the son of Rem-a-li'-ah king of Israel began Jo'-tham the son of Uz-zi'-ah king of Judah to reign.

33 Five and twenty years old was he when he began to reign, and he reigned sixteen years in Jerusalem. And his mother's name *was* ᵀJe-ru'-sha, the daughter of Za'-dok.   *Jerushah,* 2 Chr. 27:1

34 And he did *that which was* right in the sight of the Lord: he did ᴿaccording to all that his father Uz-zi'-ah had done.   vv. 3, 4

35 ᴿHowbeit the high places were not removed: the people sacrificed and burned incense still in the high places. ᴿHe built the ᵀhigher gate of the house of the Lord.   v. 4 · 2 Chr. 23:20; 27:3 · *upper*

36 Now the rest of the acts of Jo'-tham, and all that he did, *are* they not written in the book of the chronicles of the kings of Judah?

37 In those days the Lord began to send against Judah ᴿRe'-zin the king of Syria, and ᴿPe'-kah the son of Rem-a-li'-ah.   16:5-9 · vv. 26, 27

38 And Jo'-tham ᵀslept with his fathers, and was buried with his fathers in the city of David his father: and Ahaz his son reigned in his stead.   *rested in death*

16 In the seventeenth year of Pe'-kah the son of Rem-a-li'-ah Ahaz the son of Jo'-tham king of Judah began to reign.

2 Twenty years old *was* Ahaz when he began to reign, and reigned sixteen years in Jerusalem, and did not *that which was* right in the sight of the Lord his God, like David his father.

3 But he walked in the way of the kings of Israel, yea, ᴿand made his son to pass through the fire, according to the abominations of the heathen, whom the Lord cast out from before the children of Israel. Ps. 106:37, 38; Is. 1:1

4 And he sacrificed and burnt incense in the ᴿhigh places, and ᴿon the hills, and under every green tree.   15:34, 35 · 1 Kin. 14:23

5 ᴿThen Re'-zin king of Syria

and Pe'-kah son of Rem-a-li'-ah
king of Israel ᵀcame up to Jerusalem to war: and they besieged
Ahaz, but could not overcome
him.   15:37; Is. 7:1, 4 · *attacked*
6   At that time Re'-zin king of
Syria recovered E'-lath to Syria,
and drave the Jews from E'-lath:
and the Syrians came to E'-lath,
and dwelt there unto this day.
7   So Ahaz sent messengers to
Tig'-lath–pi-le'-ser king of Assyria, saying, I *am* thy servant and
thy son: come up, and save me out
of the hand of the king of Syria,
and out of the hand of the king of
Israel, which rise up against me.
8   And Ahaz ᴿtook the silver
and gold that was found in the
house of the LORD, and in the
treasures of the king's house, and
sent *it for* a present to the king of
Assyria.   12:17, 18; 2 Chr. 28:21
9   And the king of Assyria hearkened unto him: for the king of
Assyria went up against ᴿDamas-
cus, and ᴿtook it, and carried *the
people of* it captive to ᴿKir, and
slew Re'-zin.   14:28 · Amos 1:5 · Is. 22:6
10 And king Ahaz went to
Damascus to meet Tig'-lath–pi-le'-
ser king of Assyria, and saw an
altar that *was* at Damascus: and
king Ahaz sent to U-ri'-jah the
priest the fashion of the altar, and
the pattern of it, according to all
the workmanship thereof.
11 And ᴿU-ri'-jah the priest built
an altar according to all that king
Ahaz had sent from Damascus:
so U-ri'-jah the priest made *it*
ᵀagainst king Ahaz came from
Damascus.   Is. 8:2 · *before*
12 And when the king was come
from Damascus, the king saw the
altar: and the king approached to
the altar, and offered thereon.
13 And he burnt his burnt offering and his meat offering, and
poured his drink offering, and
sprinkled the blood of his peace
offerings, upon the altar.
14 And he brought also ᴿthe
brasen altar, which *was* before
the LORD, from the forefront of the
ᵀhouse, from between the altar

and the house of the LORD, and
put it on the north side of the al-
tar. Ex. 27:1, 2; 40:6, 29; 2 Chr. 4:1 · *temple*
15 And king Ahaz commanded
U-ri'-jah the priest, saying, Upon
the great altar burn the morning
burnt offering, and the evening
meat offering, and the king's
burnt sacrifice, and his meat
offering, with the burnt offering
of all the people of the land, and
their meat offering, and their
drink offerings; and sprinkle
upon it all the blood of the burnt
offering, and all the blood of the
sacrifice: and the brasen altar
shall be for me to enquire *by.*
16 Thus did U-ri'-jah the priest,
according to all that king Ahaz
commanded.
17 And king Ahaz cut off the
borders of the bases, and removed
the laver from off them; and took
down the ᵀsea from off the brasen
oxen that *were* under it, and put it
upon a pavement of stones. *bason*
18 And the covert for the sabbath that they had built in the
house, and the king's entry without, turned he from the house of
the LORD for the king of Assyria.
19 Now the rest of the acts of
Ahaz which he did, *are* they not
written in the book of the chronicles of the kings of Judah?
20 And Ahaz slept with his
fathers, and ᴿwas buried with his
fathers in the city of David: and
Hez-e-ki'-ah his son reigned in his
stead.   2 Chr. 28:27
17 In the twelfth year of Ahaz
king of Judah began Ho-
she'-a the son of E'-lah to reign in
Sa-ma'-ri-a over Israel nine years.
2   And he did *that which was*
evil in the sight of the LORD, but
not as the kings of Israel that
were before him.
3   Against him came up ᴿShal-
ma-ne'-ser king of Assyria; and
Ho-she'-a ᴿbecame his servant,
and gave him presents. 18:9–12 · 24:1
4   And the king of Assyria
found conspiracy in Ho-she'-a: for
he had sent messengers to So
king of Egypt, and brought no

present to the king of Assyria, as *he had done* year by year: therefore the king of Assyria shut him up, and bound him in prison.

5 Then ᴿthe king of Assyria came up throughout all the land, and went up to Sa-ma′-ri-a, and besieged it three years.   Hos. 13:16

6 In the ninth year of Ho-she′-a the king of Assyria took Sa-ma′-ri-a, and ᴿcarried Israel away into Assyria, and placed them in Ha′-lah and in Ha′-bor *by* the river of Go′-zan, and in the cities of the Medes.   Lev. 26:32, 33; [Deut. 28:36, 64]

7 For *so* it was, that the children of Israel had sinned against the LORD their God, which had brought them up out of the land of Egypt, from under the hand of Pharaoh king of Egypt, and had ᴿfeared other gods,   Judg. 6:10

8 And ᴿwalked in the statutes of the heathen, whom the LORD cast out from before the children of Israel, and of the kings of Israel, which they had made.   16:3

9 And the children of Israel did secretly *those* things that *were* not right against the LORD their God, and they built them high places in all their cities, ᴿfrom the tower of the watchmen to the ᵀfenced city.   18:8 · *fortified*

10 And they set them up images and groves ᴿin every high hill, and under every green tree: 16:4

11 And there they burnt incense in all the high places, as *did* the heathen whom the LORD carried away before them; and wrought wicked things to provoke the LORD to anger:

12 For they served idols, whereof the LORD had said unto them, Ye shall not do this thing.

13 Yet the LORD testified against Israel, and against Judah, by all the prophets, *and by* all the seers, saying, Turn ye from your evil ways, and keep my commandments *and* my statutes, according to all the law which I commanded your fathers, and which I sent to you by my servants the prophets.

14 Notwithstanding they would

not hear, but ᴿhardened their necks, like to the neck of their fathers, that ᴿdid not believe in the LORD their God.   Ex. 32:9 · Ps. 78:22

15 And they rejected his statutes, and his covenant that he made with their fathers, and his testimonies which he testified against them; and they followed ᵀvanity, and became vain, and went after the heathen that *were* round about them, *concerning* whom the LORD had charged them, that they should not do like them.   *idols, and became idolaters*

16 And they left all the commandments of the LORD their God, and ᴿmade them molten images, *even* two calves, and made a grove, and worshipped all the host of heaven, ᴿand served Ba′-al.   Ex. 32:8; 1 Kin. 12:28 · 1 Kin. 16:31

17 ᴿAnd they caused their sons and their daughters to pass through the fire, and used divination and enchantments, and ᴿsold themselves to do evil in the sight of the LORD, to provoke him to anger.   16:3; Ezek. 23:37 · 1 Kin. 21:20

18 Therefore the LORD was very angry with Israel, and removed them out of his sight: there was none left ᴿbut the tribe of Judah only.   1 Kin. 11:13, 32

19 Also ᴿJudah kept not the commandments of the LORD their God, but walked in the statutes of Israel which they made.   Jer. 3:8

20 And the LORD rejected all the seed of Israel, and afflicted them, and ᴿdelivered them into the hand of spoilers, until he had cast them out of his ᴿsight.   13:3; 15:29 · 24:20

21 For he rent Israel from the house of David; and they made Jer-o-bo′-am the son of Ne′-bat king: and Jer-o-bo′-am drave Israel from following the LORD, and made them sin a great sin.

22 For the children of Israel walked in all the sins of Jer-o-bo′-am which he did; they departed not from them;

23 Until the LORD removed Israel out of his sight, ᴿas he had said by all his servants the prophets. ^RSo was Israel carried away out of their own land to Assyria unto this day. 1 Kin. 14:16; Is. 8:4 · v. 6

24 ^RAnd the king of Assyria brought *men* from Babylon, and from Cu′-thah, and from ^RA′-va, and from Ha′-math, and from Seph-ar-va′-im, and placed *them* in the cities of Sa-ma′-ri-a instead of the children of Israel: and they possessed Sa-ma′-ri-a, and dwelt in the cities thereof. Ezra 4:2 · 18:34

25 And *so* it was at the beginning of their dwelling there, *that* they feared not the LORD: therefore the LORD sent lions among them, which slew *some* of them.

26 Wherefore they spake to the king of Assyria, saying, The nations which thou hast removed, and placed in the cities of Sa-ma′-ri-a, know not the ^Tmanner of the God of the land: therefore he hath sent lions among them, and, behold, they slay them, because they know not the manner of the God of the land. *rituals*

27 Then the king of Assyria commanded, saying, Carry thither one of the priests whom ye brought from thence; and let them go and dwell there, and let him teach them the manner of the God of the land.

28 Then one of the priests whom they had carried away from Sa-ma′-ri-a came and dwelt in Beth′-el, and taught them how they should fear the LORD.

29 Howbeit every nation made gods of their own, and put *them* ^Rin the houses of the high places which the Sa-mar′-i-tans had made, every nation in their cities wherein they dwelt. 1 Kin. 12:31; 13:32

30 And the men of ^RBabylon made Suc′-coth–be′-noth, and the men of Cuth made Ner′-gal, and the men of Ha′-math made Ash′-i-ma, v. 24

31 ^RAnd the A′-vites made Nib′-haz and Tar′-tak, and the Se′-phar-vites ^Rburnt their children in fire to A-dram′-me-lech and A-nam′-me-lech, the gods of Seph-ar-va′-im. Ezra 4:9 · [Deut. 12:31]

32 So they feared the LORD, and made unto themselves of the lowest of them priests of the high places, which sacrificed for them in the houses of the high places.

33 ^RThey feared the LORD, and served their own gods, after the manner of the nations whom they carried away from thence. Zeph. 1:5

34 Unto this day they do after the former manners: they fear not the LORD, neither do they after their statutes, or after their ordinances, or after the law and commandment which the LORD commanded the children of Jacob, ^Rwhom he named Israel; Gen. 32:28

35 With whom the LORD had made a covenant, and charged them, saying, ^RYe shall not fear other gods, nor ^Rbow yourselves to them, nor serve them, nor sacrifice to them: Judg. 6:10 · [Ex. 20:5]

36 But the LORD, who brought you up out of the land of Egypt with great power and ^Ra stretched out arm, him shall ye fear, and him shall ye worship, and to him shall ye do sacrifice. Ex. 6:6; 9:15

37 And the statutes, and the ordinances, and the law, and the commandment, which he wrote for you, ^Rye shall observe to do for evermore; and ye shall not fear other gods. Deut. 5:32

38 And the covenant that I have made with you ^Rye shall not forget; neither shall ye ^Tfear other gods. Deut. 4:23; 6:12 · *reverence*

39 But the LORD your God ye shall ^Tfear; and he shall deliver you out of the hand of all your enemies. *hold in awesome reverence*

40 Howbeit they did not hearken, but they did after their former manner.

41 ^RSo these nations feared the LORD, and served their graven images, both their children, and their children's children: as did their fathers, so do they unto this day. vv. 32, 33

18 Now it came to pass in the third year of ^RHo-she′-a son of E′-lah king of Israel, *that* Hez-

e-ki′-ah the son of Ahaz king of Judah began to reign.   17:1

2 Twenty and five years old was he when he began to reign; and he reigned twenty and nine years in Jerusalem. His mother's name also *was* ^RA′-bi, the daughter of Zach-a-ri′-ah.   Is. 38:5

3 And he did *that which was* right in the sight of the LORD, according to all that David his father did.

4 ^RHe removed the high places, and brake the images, and cut down the groves, and brake in pieces the ^Rbrasen serpent that Moses had made: for unto those days the children of Israel did burn incense to it: and he called it Ne-hush′-tan.   2 Chr. 31:1 · Num. 21:5–9

5 He ^Rtrusted in the LORD God of Israel; ^Rso that after him was none like him among all the kings of Judah, nor *any* that were before him.   19:10; [Job 13:15; Ps. 13:5] · 23:25

6 For he ^Rclave^T to the LORD, *and* departed not from following him, but kept his commandments, which the LORD commanded Moses.   Deut. 10:20; Josh. 23:8 · *held fast*

7 And the LORD ^Rwas with him; *and* he ^Rprospered whithersoever he went forth: and he rebelled against the king of Assyria, and served him not.   [2 Chr. 15:2] · Ps. 60:12

8 He smote the Phi-lis′-tines, *even* unto Ga′-za, and the borders thereof, ^Rfrom the tower of the watchmen to the fenced city.   17:9

9 And ^Rit came to pass in the fourth year of king Hez-e-ki′-ah, which *was* the seventh year of Ho-she′-a son of E′-lah king of Israel, *that* Shal-ma-ne′-ser king of Assyria came up against Sa-ma′-ri-a, and besieged it.   17:3

10 And at the end of three years they took it: *even* in the sixth year of Hez-e-ki′-ah, that *is* ^Rthe ninth year of Ho-she′-a king of Israel, Sa-ma′-ri-a was taken.   17:6

11 ^RAnd the king of Assyria did carry away Israel unto Assyria, and put them in Ha′-lah and in Ha′-bor *by* the river of Go′-zan, and in the cities of the Medes: 17:6

12 Because they obeyed ^Rnot the voice of the LORD their God, but transgressed his covenant, *and* all that Moses the servant of the LORD commanded, and would not hear *them,* nor do *them.*   17:7–18

13 Now ^Rin the fourteenth year of king Hez-e-ki′-ah did Sen-nach′-e-rib king of Assyria come up against all the fenced cities of Judah, and took them.   2 Chr. 32:1

14 And Hez-e-ki′-ah king of Judah sent to the king of Assyria to La′-chish, saying, I have offended; ^Treturn from me: that which thou puttest on me will I bear. And the king of Assyria appointed unto Hez-e-ki′-ah king of Judah three hundred talents of silver and thirty talents of gold.   *turn away*

15 And Hez-e-ki′-ah ^Rgave *him* all the silver that was found in the house of the LORD, and in the treasures of the king's house.   12:18

16 At that time did Hez-e-ki′-ah cut off *the gold from* the doors of the temple of the LORD, and *from* the pillars which Hez-e-ki′-ah king of Judah had overlaid, and gave it to the king of Assyria.

17 And the king of Assyria sent Tar′-tan and Rab′-sa-ris and Rab′-sha-keh from La′-chish to king Hez-e-ki′-ah with a great host against Jerusalem. And they went up and came to Jerusalem. And when they were come up, they came and stood by the ^Rconduit of the upper pool, which *is* in the highway of the fuller's field.   20:20

18 And when they had called to the king, there came out to them E-li′-a-kim the son of Hil-ki′-ah, which *was* over the household, and Sheb′-na the scribe, and Jo′-ah the son of A′-saph the recorder.

19 And Rab′-sha-keh said unto them, Speak ye now to Hez-e-ki′-ah, Thus saith the great king, the king of Assyria, What confidence *is* this wherein thou trustest?

20 Thou sayest, (but *they are but* vain words,) *I have* counsel and strength for the war. Now on whom dost thou trust, that thou rebellest against me?

21 ᴿNow, behold, thou trustest upon the staff of this bruised reed, *even* upon Egypt, on which if a man lean, it will go into his hand, and pierce it: so *is* Pharaoh king of Egypt unto all that trust on him.   Is. 30:2–7; Ezek. 29:6, 7

22 But if ye say unto me, We trust in the LORD our God: *is* not that he, whose high places and whose altars Hez-e-ki′-ah hath taken away, and hath said to Judah and Jerusalem, Ye shall worship before this altar in Jerusalem?

23 Now therefore, I pray thee, give pledges to my lord the king of Assyria, and I will deliver thee two thousand horses, if thou be able on thy part to set riders upon them.

24 How then wilt thou turn away the face of one captain of the least of my master's servants, and put thy trust on Egypt for chariots and for horsemen?

25 Am I now come up without the LORD against this place to destroy it? The LORD said to me, Go up against this land, and destroy it.

26 ᴿThen said E-li′-a-kim the son of Hil-ki′-ah, and Sheb′-na, and Jo′-ah, unto Rab′–sha-keh, Speak, I pray thee, to thy servants in the ᴿSyrian language; for we understand *it:* and talk not with us in the Jews' language in the ears of the people that *are* on the wall.   Is. 36:11—39:8 · Ezra 4:7; Dan. 2:4

27 But Rab′–sha-keh said unto them, Hath my master sent me to thy master, and to thee, to speak these words? *hath he* not *sent me* to the men which sit on the wall, that they may eat their own dung, and drink their own piss with you?

28 Then Rab′–sha-keh stood and cried with a loud voice in the ᵀJews' language, and spake, saying, Hear the word of the great king, the king of Assyria: *Hebrew*

29 Thus saith the king, ᴿLet not Hez-e-ki′-ah deceive you: for he shall not be able to deliver you out of his hand: 2 Chr. 32:15

30 Neither let Hez-e-ki′-ah make you trust in the LORD, saying, The LORD will surely deliver us, and this city shall not be delivered into the hand of the king of Assyria.

31 Hearken not to Hez-e-ki′-ah: for thus saith the king of Assyria, Make *an agreement* with me by a present, and come out to me, and *then* eat ye every man of his own ᴿvine, and every one of his fig tree, and drink ye every one the waters of his cistern: 1 Kin. 4:20, 25

32 Until I come and take you away to a land like your own land, ᴿa land of corn and wine, a land of bread and vineyards, a land of oil olive and of honey, that ye may live, and not die: and hearken not unto Hez-e-ki′-ah, when he persuadeth you, saying, The LORD will deliver us.   Deut. 8:7–9; 11:12

33 ᴿHath any of the gods of the nations delivered at all his land out of the hand of the king of Assyria?   19:12; Is. 10:10, 11

34 Where *are* the gods of ᴿHa′-math, and of Ar′-pad? where *are* the gods of Seph-ar-va′-im, He′-na, and ᴿI′-vah? have they delivered Sa-ma′-ri-a out of mine hand?   19:13 · 17:24

35 Who *are* they among all the gods of the countries, that have delivered their country out of mine hand, ᴿthat the LORD should deliver Jerusalem out of mine hand?   Dan. 3:15

36 But the people held their peace, and answered him not a word: for the king's commandment was, saying, Answer him not.

37 Then came E-li′-a-kim the son of Hil-ki′-ah, which *was* over the household, and Sheb′-na the scribe, and Jo′-ah the son of A′-saph the recorder, to Hez-e-ki′-ah with *their* clothes rent, and told him the words of Rab′–sha-keh.

19 And it came to pass, when king Hez-e-ki′-ah heard *it,* that he rent his clothes, and covered himself with sackcloth, and went into the house of the LORD.

2 And he sent E-li′-a-kim, which *was* over the household, and Sheb′-na the scribe, and the elders of the priests, covered with sackcloth, to Isaiah the prophet the son of Amoz.

3 And they said unto him, Thus saith Hez-e-ki′-ah, This day *is* a day of trouble, and of rebuke, and blasphemy: for the children are come to the birth, and *there is* not strength to ᵀbring forth.   *give birth*

4 It may be the LORD thy God will hear all the words of Rab′-sha-keh, whom the king of Assyria his master hath sent to ᴿreproach the living God; and will ᴿreprove the words which the LORD thy God hath heard: wherefore lift up *thy* prayer for the remnant that are left.   18:35 · Ps. 50:21

5 So the servants of king Hez-e-ki′-ah came to Isaiah.

6 ᴿAnd Isaiah said unto them, Thus shall ye say to your master, Thus saith the LORD, Be not ᴿafraid of the words which thou hast heard, with which the servants of the king of Assyria have blasphemed me.   Is. 37:6 · [Ps. 112:7]

7 Behold, I will send a blast upon him, and he shall hear a rumour, and shall return to his own land; and I will cause him to fall by the sword in his own land.

8 So Rab′–sha-keh returned, and found the king of Assyria warring against Lib′-nah: for he had heard that he was departed ᴿfrom La′-chish.   18:14, 17

9 And when he heard say of Tir′-ha-kah king of E-thi-o′-pi-a, Behold, he is come out to fight against thee: he sent messengers again unto Hez-e-ki′-ah, saying,

10 Thus shall ye speak to Hez-e-ki′-ah king of Judah, saying, Let not thy God ᴿin whom thou trustest deceive thee, saying, Jerusalem shall not be delivered into the hand of the king of Assyria.   18:5

11 Behold, thou hast heard what the kings of Assyria have done to all lands, by destroying them utterly: and shalt thou be delivered?

12 ᴿHave the gods of the nations delivered them which my fathers have destroyed; *as* Go′-zan, and Ha′-ran, and Re′-zeph, and the children of ᴿEden which *were* in The-la′-sar?   18:33, 34 · Ezek. 27:23

13 ᴿWhere *is* the king of Ha′-math, and the king of Ar′-pad, and the king of the city of Seph-ar-va′-im, of He′-na, and I′-vah?   18:34

14 ᴿAnd Hez-e-ki′-ah received the letter of the hand of the messengers, and read it: and Hez-e-ki′-ah went up into the house of the LORD, and spread it before the LORD.   Is. 37:14

15 And Hez-e-ki′-ah prayed before the LORD, and said, O LORD God of Israel, which dwellest *between* the cher′-u-bims, thou art the God, *even* thou alone, of all the kingdoms of the earth; thou hast made heaven and earth.

16 LORD, bow down thine ear, and hear: open, LORD, thine eyes, and see: and hear the words of Sen-nach′-e-rib, which hath sent him to reproach the living God.

17 Of a truth, LORD, the kings of Assyria have destroyed the nations and their lands,

18 And have cast their gods into the fire: for they *were* no gods, but ᴿthe work of men's hands, wood and stone: therefore they have destroyed them.   Ps. 115:4; [Acts 17:29]

19 Now therefore, O LORD our God, I beseech thee, save thou us out of his hand, ᴿthat all the kingdoms of the earth may ᴿknow that thou *art* the LORD God, *even* thou only.   Ps. 83:18 · 1 Kin. 8:42, 43

20 Then Isaiah the son of Amoz sent to Hez-e-ki′-ah, saying, Thus saith the LORD God of Israel, ᴿ*That* which thou hast prayed to me against Sen-nach′-e-rib king of Assyria I have heard.   Is. 37:21

21 This *is* the word that the LORD hath spoken concerning him; The virgin ᴿthe daughter of Zion hath despised thee, *and*

laughed thee to scorn; the daughter of Jerusalem ᴿhath shaken her head at thee.   Jer. 14:17 · Ps. 22:7, 8

22 Whom hast thou reproached and blasphemed? and against whom hast thou exalted *thy* voice, and lifted up thine eyes on high? *even* against ᴿthe Holy *One* of Israel.   Jer. 51:5

23 ᴿBy thy messengers thou hast reproached the LORD, and hast said, ᴿWith the multitude of my chariots I am come up to the height of the mountains, to the sides of Leb′-a-non, and will cut down the tall cedar trees thereof, *and* the choice fir trees thereof: and I will enter into the lodgings of his borders, *and into* the forest of his Carmel.   18:17 · Ps. 20:7

24 I have digged and drunk strange waters, and with the sole of my feet have I ᴿdried up all the rivers of besieged places.   Is. 19:6

25 Hast thou not heard long ago *how* I have done it, *and* of ancient times that I have formed it? now have I brought it to pass, that thou shouldest be to lay waste ᵀfenced cities *into* ruinous heaps.   *fortified*

26 Therefore their inhabitants were of small power, they were dismayed and confounded; they were *as* the grass of the field, and *as* the green herb, *as* ᴿthe grass on the house tops, and *as corn* blasted before it be grown up.   Ps. 129:6

27 But ᴿI know thy abode, and thy going out, and thy coming in, and thy rage against me.   Is. 37:28

28 Because thy rage against me and thy tumult is come up into mine ears, therefore ᴿI will put my hook in thy nose, and my bridle in thy lips, and I will turn thee back ᴿby the way by which thou camest.   Job 41:2; Amos 4:2 · vv. 33, 36

29 And this *shall be* a ᴿsign unto thee, Ye shall eat this year such things as grow of themselves, and in the second year that which springeth of the same; and in the third year sow ye, and reap, and plant vineyards, and eat the fruits thereof.   Ex. 3:12; Is. 7:11–14; Luke 2:12

30 ᴿAnd the remnant that is escaped of the house of Judah shall yet again take root downward, and bear fruit upward.   2 Chr. 32:22

31 For out of Jerusalem shall go forth a remnant, and they that escape out of mount Zion: ᴿthe zeal of the LORD *of hosts* shall do this.   25:26; Is. 9:7

32 Therefore thus saith the LORD concerning the king of Assyria, He shall ᴿnot come into this city, nor shoot an arrow there, nor come before it with shield, nor cast a bank against it.   Is. 8:7–10

33 By the way that he came, by the same shall he return, and shall not come into this city, saith the LORD.

34 For I will ᴿdefend this city, to save it, for mine own sake, and for my servant David's sake.   Is. 31:5

35 And ᴿit came to pass that night, that the angel of the LORD went out, and smote in the camp of the Assyrians an hundred fourscore and five thousand: and when they arose early in the morning, behold, they *were* all dead corpses.   Is. 10:12–19; 37:36

36 So Sen-nach′-e-rib king of Assyria departed, and went and returned, and dwelt at ᴿNin′-e-veh.   Gen. 10:11

37 And it came to pass, as he was worshipping in the house of Nis′-roch his god, that ᴿA-dram′-me-lech and Sha-re′-zer his sons ᴿsmote him with the sword: and they escaped into the land of Ar-me′-ni-a. And E′-sar-had′-don his son reigned in his stead.   17:31 · v. 7

20 In ᴿthose days was Hez-e-ki′-ah sick unto death. And the prophet Isaiah the son of Amoz came to him, and said unto him, Thus saith the LORD, Set thine house in order; for thou shalt die, and not live.   Is. 38:1–22

2 Then he turned his face to the wall, and prayed unto the LORD, saying,

3 I beseech thee, O LORD, ᴿremember now how I have walked before thee in truth and with a perfect heart, and have done *that which is* good in

thy sight. And Hez-e-ki'-ah wept ᵀsore.   18:3–6; Neh. 13:22 · *bitterly*

4 And it came to pass, afore Isaiah was gone out into the middle court, that the word of the LORD came to him, saying,

5 Turn again, and tell Hez-e-ki'-ah ᴿthe captain of my people, Thus saith the LORD, the God of David thy father, ᴿI have heard thy prayer, I have seen thy tears: behold, I will heal thee: on the third day thou shalt go up unto the house of the LORD. 1 Sam. 10:1 · 19:20

6 And I will add unto thy days fifteen years; and I will deliver thee and this city out of the hand of the king of Assyria; and ᴿI will defend this city for mine own sake, and for my servant David's sake.   19:34; 2 Chr. 32:21

7 And ᴿIsaiah said, Take a lump of figs. And they took and laid *it* on the boil, and he recovered.   Is. 38:21

8 And Hez-e-ki'-ah said unto Isaiah, ᴿWhat *shall be* the sign that the LORD will heal me, and that I shall go up into the house of the LORD the third day?   Judg. 6:17

9 And Isaiah said, ᴿThis sign shalt thou have of the LORD, that the LORD will do the thing that he hath spoken: shall the shadow go forward ten degrees, or go back ten degrees?   Num. 23:19; Is. 38:7, 8

10 And Hez-e-ki'-ah answered, It is ᵀa light thing for the shadow to go down ten ᵀdegrees: nay, but let the shadow return backward ten degrees.   *an easy* · Lit. *steps*

11 And Isaiah the prophet cried unto the LORD: and ᴿhe brought the shadow ten degrees backward, by which it had gone down in the dial of Ahaz.   Josh. 10:12–14

12 ᴿAt that time Be-ro'-dach–bal'-a-dan, the son of Bal'-a-dan, king of Babylon, sent letters and a present unto Hez-e-ki'-ah: for he had heard that Hez-e-ki'-ah had been sick.   8:8, 9; 2 Chr. 32:31; Is. 39:1–8

13 And ᴿHez-e-ki'-ah hearkened unto them, and shewed them all the house of his ᵀprecious things, the silver, and the gold, and the spices, and the precious ointment, and *all* the house of his armour, and all that was found in his treasures: there was nothing in his house, nor in all his dominion, that Hez-e-ki'-ah shewed them not.   16:9; 2 Chr. 32:27, 31 · *treasures*

14 Then came Isaiah the prophet unto king Hez-e-ki'-ah, and said unto him, What said these men? and from whence came they unto thee? And Hez-e-ki'-ah said, They are come from a far country, *even* from Babylon.

15 And he said, What have they seen in thine house? And Hez-e-ki'-ah answered, ᴿAll *the things* that *are* in mine house have they seen: there is nothing among my treasures that I have not shewed them.   v. 13

16 And Isaiah said unto Hez-e-ki'-ah, Hear the word of the LORD.

17 Behold, the days come, that all that *is* in thine house, and that which thy fathers have laid up in store unto this day, ᴿshall be carried into Babylon: nothing shall be left, saith the LORD.   2 Chr. 36:10

18 And of thy sons that shall issue from thee, which thou shalt beget, ᴿshall they take away; and they shall be eunuchs in the palace of the king of Babylon.   24:12

19 Then said Hez-e-ki'-ah unto Isaiah, Good *is* the word of the LORD which thou hast spoken. And he said, *Is it* not *good,* if peace and truth be in my days?

20 ᴿAnd the rest of the acts of Hez-e-ki'-ah, and all his might, and how he ᴿmade a pool, and a conduit, and brought water into the city, *are* they not written in the book of the chronicles of the kings of Judah?   2 Chr. 32:32 · Neh. 3:16

21 And ᴿHez-e-ki'-ah slept with his fathers: and Ma-nas'-seh his son reigned in his stead.   16:20

21 Ma-nas'-seh *was* twelve years old when he began to reign, and reigned fifty and five years in Jerusalem. And his mother's name *was* Heph'-zi-bah.

2 And he did *that which was* evil in the sight of the LORD, ᴿafter

the abominations of the heathen, whom the LORD cast out before the children of Israel.   16:3

3 For he built up again the high places which Hez-e-ki′-ah his father had destroyed; and he reared up altars for Ba′-al, and made a grove, as did Ahab king of Israel; and ᴿworshipped all the host of heaven, and served them. 17:16; 23:5

4 And ᴿhe built altars in the house of the LORD, of which the LORD said, ᴿIn Jerusalem will I put my name.   Jer. 7:30; 32:34 · 1 Kin. 11:13

5 And he built altars for all the host of heaven in the ᴿtwo courts of the house of the LORD.   23:12

6 ᴿAnd he made his son pass through the fire, and observed times, and used enchantments, and dealt with familiar spirits and wizards: he wrought much wickedness in the sight of the LORD, to provoke *him* to anger.   16:3; 17:17

7 And he set a graven image of the grove that he had made in the house, of which the LORD said to David, and to Solomon his son, ᴿIn this house, and in Jerusalem, which I have chosen out of all tribes of Israel, will I put my name for ever: 23:27; 2 Chr. 7:12, 16; Jer. 32:34

8 ᴿNeither will I make the feet of Israel move any more out of the land which I gave their fathers; only if they will observe to do according to all that I have commanded them, and according to all the law that my servant Moses commanded them.   2 Sam. 7:10

9 But they hearkened not: and Ma-nas′-seh ᴿseduced them to do more evil than did the nations whom the LORD destroyed before the children of Israel.   [Prov. 29:12]

10 And the LORD spake by his servants the prophets, saying,

11 Because Ma-nas′-seh king of Judah hath done these abominations, ᴿ*and* hath done wickedly above all that the ᴿAm′-or-ites did, which *were* before him, and ᴿhath made Judah also to sin with his idols: 1 Kin. 21:26 · Gen. 15:16 · v. 9

12 Therefore thus saith the LORD God of Israel, Behold, I *am* bringing *such* evil upon Jerusalem and Judah, that whosoever heareth of it, both his ears shall tingle.

13 And I will stretch over Jerusalem the line of Sa-ma′-ri-a, and the plummet of the house of Ahab: and I will wipe Jerusalem as *a man* wipeth a dish, wiping *it*, and turning *it* upside down.

14 And I will forsake the ᴿremnant of mine inheritance, and deliver them into the hand of their enemies; and they shall become a prey and a ᵀspoil to all their enemies;   Jer. 6:9 · *plunder*

15 Because they have done *that which was* evil in my sight, and have provoked me to anger, since the day their fathers came forth out of Egypt, even unto this day.

16 ᴿMoreover Ma-nas′-seh shed innocent blood very much, till he had filled Jerusalem from one end to another; beside his sin wherewith he made Judah to sin, in doing *that which was* evil in the sight of the LORD.   24:4

17 Now the rest of the acts of Ma-nas′-seh, and all that he did, and his sin that he sinned, *are* they not written in the book of the chronicles of the kings of Judah?

18 And ᴿMa-nas′-seh slept with his fathers, and was buried in the garden of his own house, in the garden of Uz′-za: and Amon his son reigned in his stead. 2 Chr. 33:20

19 Amon *was* twenty and two years old when he began to reign, and he reigned two years in Jerusalem. And his mother's name *was* Me-shul′-le-meth, the daughter of Ha′-ruz of Jot′-bah.

20 And he did *that which was* evil in the sight of the LORD, ᴿas his father Ma-nas′-seh did.   vv. 2-6

21 And he walked in all the way that his father walked in, and served the idols that his father served, and worshipped them:

22 And he ᴿforsook the LORD God of his fathers, and walked not in the way of the LORD.   1 Chr. 28:9

23 And the servants of Amon ᴿconspired against him, and slew the king in his own house.   12:20

24 And the people of the land [R]slew all them that had conspired against king Amon; and the people of the land made Jo-si'-ah his son king in his stead.   14:5

25 Now the rest of the acts of Amon which he did, *are* they not written in the book of the chronicles of the kings of Judah?

26 And he was buried in his sepulchre in the garden of Uz'-za: and Jo-si'-ah his son reigned in his stead.

22 Jo-si'-ah [R]was eight years old when he began to reign, and he reigned thirty and one years in Jerusalem. And his mother's name *was* Je-di'-dah, the daughter of A-da'-iah of Bos'-cath.   1 Kin. 13:2; 2 Chr. 34:1

2 And he did *that which was* right in the sight of the LORD, and walked in all the way of David his father, and turned not aside to the right hand or to the left.

3 [R]And it came to pass in the eighteenth year of king Jo-si'-ah, *that* the king sent Sha'-phan the son of Az-a-li'-ah, the son of Me-shul'-lam, the scribe, to the house of the LORD, saying,   2 Chr. 34:8

4 Go up to Hil-ki'-ah the high priest, that he may [T]sum the silver which is [R]brought into the house of the LORD, which [R]the keepers of the door have gathered of the people: count · 12:4 · 12:9, 10

5 And let them [R]deliver it into the hand of the doers of the work, that have the oversight of the house of the LORD: and let them give it to the doers of the work which *is* in the house of the LORD, to repair the breaches of the house,   12:11–14

6 Unto carpenters, and builders, and masons, and to buy timber and hewn stone to repair the house.

7 Howbeit [R]there was no [T]reckoning made with them of the money that was delivered into their hand, because they dealt faithfully.   12:15; [1 Cor. 4:2] · *accounting*

8 And Hil-ki'-ah the high priest said unto Sha'-phan the scribe, [R]I

have found the book of the law in the house of the LORD. And Hil-ki'-ah gave the book to Sha'-phan, and he read it.   Deut. 31:24–26

9 And Sha'-phan the scribe came to the king, and brought the king word again, and said, Thy servants have [T]gathered the money that was found in the house, and have delivered it into the hand of them that do the work, that have the oversight of the house of the LORD.   *poured out*

10 And Sha'-phan the scribe shewed the king, saying, Hil-ki'-ah the priest hath delivered me a book. And Sha'-phan read it before the king.

11 And it came to pass, when the king had heard the words of the book of the law, that he [T]rent his clothes.   *tore*

12 And the king commanded Hil-ki'-ah the priest, and [R]A-hi'-kam the son of Sha'-phan, and Ach'-bor the son of Mi-cha'-iah, and Sha'-phan the scribe, and As-a-hi'-ah a servant of the king's, saying,   25:22; Jer. 26:24

13 Go ye, enquire of the LORD for me, and for the people, and for all Judah, concerning the words of this book that is found: for great *is* the wrath of the LORD that is kindled against us, because our fathers have not hearkened unto the words of this book, to do according unto all that which is written concerning us.

14 So Hil-ki'-ah the priest, and A-hi'-kam, and Ach'-bor, and Sha'-phan, and As-a-hi'-ah, went unto Hul'-dah the prophetess, the wife of Shal'-lum the son of Tik'-vah, the son of Har'-has, keeper of the wardrobe; (now she dwelt in Jerusalem in the college;) and they [T]communed with her.   *spoke*

15 And she said unto them, Thus saith the LORD God of Israel, Tell the man that sent you to me,

16 Thus saith the LORD, Behold, [R]I will bring [T]evil upon this place, and upon the inhabitants thereof, *even* all the words of the book

which the king of Judah hath read: Deut. 29:27 · *calamity*

17 ᴿBecause they have forsaken me, and have burned incense unto other gods, that they might provoke me to anger with all the works of their hands; therefore my wrath shall be kindled against this place, and shall not be quenched. 21:22; Deut. 29:25–27

18 But to ᴿthe king of Judah which sent you to enquire of the LORD, thus shall ye say to him, Thus saith the LORD God of Israel, *As touching* the words which thou has heard; 2 Chr. 34:26

19 Because thine ᴿheart was tender, and thou hast humbled thyself before the LORD, when thou heardest what I spake against this place, and against the inhabitants thereof, that they should become a desolation and a curse, and hast rent thy clothes, and wept before me; I also have heard *thee*, saith the LORD. 1 Sam. 24:5; [Ps. 51:17]

20 Behold therefore, I will gather thee unto thy fathers, and thou ᴿshalt be gathered into thy grave in peace; and thine eyes shall not see all the evil which I will bring upon this place. And they brought the king word again. 23:30; [Ps. 37:37]

23 And ᴿthe king sent, and they gathered unto him all the elders of Judah and of Jerusalem. 2 Sam. 19:11; 2 Chr. 34:29, 30

2 And the king went up into the house of the LORD, and all the men of Judah and all the inhabitants of Jerusalem with him, and the priests, and the prophets, and all the people, both small and great: and he ᴿread in their ears all the words of the book of the covenant which was found in the house of the LORD. Deut. 31:10–13

3 And the king ᴿstood by a pillar, and made a covenant before the LORD, to walk after the LORD, and to keep his commandments and his testimonies and his statutes with all *their* heart and all *their* soul, to perform the words of this covenant that were written in this book.

And all the people stood to the covenant. 11:14

4 And the king commanded Hil-ki′-ah the high priest, and the ᴿpriests of the second order, and the keepers of the door, to bring ᴿforth out of the temple of the LORD all the vessels that were made for Ba′-al, and for the grove, and for all the host of heaven: and he burned them without Jerusalem in the fields of Kid′-ron, and carried the ashes of them unto Beth′-el. 25:18; Jer. 52:24 · 21:3–7

5 And he ᵀput down the idolatrous priests, whom the kings of Judah had ordained to burn incense in the high places in the cities of Judah, and in the places round about Jerusalem; them also that burned incense unto Ba′-al, to the sun, and to the moon, and to the planets, and to ᴿall the ᵀhost of heaven. *removed* · 21:3 · *constellations*

6 And he brought out the grove from the house of the LORD, without Jerusalem, unto the brook Kid′-ron, and burned it at the brook Kid′-ron, and stamped *it* small to powder, and cast the powder thereof upon the graves of the children of the people.

7 And he brake down the houses ᴿof the sodomites, that *were* by the house of the LORD, ᴿwhere the women wove hangings for the grove. 1 Kin. 14:24; 15:12 · Ezek. 16:16

8 And he brought all the priests out of the cities of Judah, and defiled the high places where the priests had burned incense, from ᴿGe′-ba to Be′-er-she′-ba, and brake down the high places of the gates that *were* in the entering in of the gate of Joshua the governor of the city, which *were* on a man's left hand at the gate of the city. Josh. 21:17; 1 Kin. 15:22

9 Nevertheless the priests of the high places came not up to the altar of the LORD in Jerusalem, but they did eat of the unleavened bread among their brethren.

10 And he defiled ᴿTo′-pheth, which *is* in the valley of the children of Hin′-nom, ᴿthat no man

might make his son or his daughter to ᴿpass through the fire to Mo'-lech.   Is. 30:33 · Ezek. 23:37–39 · 21:6

11 And he took away the horses that the kings of Judah had given to the sun, at the entering in of the house of the Lord, by the chamber of Na'-than–me'-lech the ᵀchamberlain, which *was* in the suburbs, and burned the chariots of the sun with fire.   *officer*

12 And the altars that *were* ᴿon the top of the upper chamber of Ahaz, which the kings of Judah had made, and the altars which ᴿMa-nas'-seh had made in the two courts of the house of the Lord, did the king beat down, and brake *them* down from thence, and cast the dust of them into the brook Kid'-ron.   Zeph. 1:5 · 21:5; 2 Chr. 33:5

13 And the high places that *were* before Jerusalem, which *were* on the right hand of the mount of corruption, which Solomon the king of Israel had builded for Ash'-to-reth the abomination of the Zi-do'-ni-ans, and for Che'-mosh the abomination of the Mo'-ab-ites, and for Mil'-com the abomination of the children of Ammon, did the king defile.

14 And he ᴿbrake in pieces the images, and cut down the groves, and filled their places with the bones of men.   [Ex. 23:24; Deut. 7:5–25]

15 Moreover the altar that *was* at Beth'-el, *and* the high place ᴿwhich Jer-o-bo'-am the son of Ne'-bat, who made Israel to sin, had made, both that altar and the high place he brake down, and burned the high place, *and* stamped *it* small to powder, and burned the grove.   1 Kin. 12:28–33

16 And as Jo-si'-ah turned himself, he spied the sepulchres that *were* there in the mount, and sent, and took the bones out of the sepulchres, and burned *them* upon the altar, and ᵀpolluted it, according to the ᴿword of the Lord which the man of God proclaimed, who proclaimed these words.   *defiled* · 1 Kin. 13:2

17 Then he said, What ᵀtitle *is*

that that I see? And the men of the city told him, *It is* the sepulchre of the man of God, which came from Judah, and proclaimed these things that thou hast done against the altar of Beth'-el.   *gravestone*

18 And he said, Let him alone; let no man move his bones. So they let his bones alone, with the bones of ᴿthe prophet that came out of Sa-ma'-ri-a.   1 Kin. 13:11, 31

19 And all the houses also of the high places that *were* ᴿin the cities of Sa-ma'-ri-a, which the kings of Israel had made to provoke *the* Lord to anger, Jo-si'-ah took away, and did to them according to all the acts that he had done in Beth'-el.   2 Chr. 34:6, 7

20 And he ᴿslew all the priests of the high places that *were* there upon the altars, and burned men's bones upon them, and returned to Jerusalem.   10:25; 11:18

21 And the king commanded all the people, saying, ᴿKeep the passover unto the Lord your God, ᴿas *it is* written in the book of this covenant.   Num. 9:5 · Ex. 12:3; Lev. 23:5

22 Surely ᴿthere was not ᵀholden such a passover from the days of the judges that judged Is-rael, nor in all the days of the kings of Israel, nor of the kings of Judah; 2 Chr. 35:18, 19 · *held*

23 But in the eighteenth year of king Jo-si'-ah, *wherein* this passover was holden to the Lord in Jerusalem.

24 Moreover the *workers with* familiar spirits, and the wizards, and the images, and the idols, and all the abominations that were spied in the land of Judah and in Jerusalem, did Jo-si'-ah put away, that he might perform the words of the law which were written in the book that Hil-ki'-ah the priest found in the house of the Lord.

25 ᴿAnd like unto him was there no king before him, that turned to the Lord with all his heart, and with all his soul, and with all his might, according to all the law of Moses; neither after him arose there *any* like him.   18:5

26 Notwithstanding the LORD turned not from the fierceness of his great wrath, wherewith his anger was kindled against Judah, ᴿbecause of all the provocations that Ma-nas′-seh had provoked him withal.   21:11, 12; 24:3, 4; Jer. 15:4

27 And the LORD said, I will remove Judah also out of my sight, as ᴿI have removed Israel, and will cast off this city Jerusalem which I have chosen, and the house of which I said, ᴿMy name shall be there.   17:18, 20; 18:11; 21:13 · 21:4, 7

28 Now the rest of the acts of Jo-si′-ah, and all that he did, *are* they not written in the book of the chronicles of the kings of Judah?

29 In his days Pha′-raoh–ne′-choh king of Egypt went up against the king of Assyria to the river Eu-phra′-tes: and king Jo-si′-ah went against him; and he slew him at ᴿMe-gid′-do, when he ᴿhad seen him.   Judg. 5:19; Zech. 12:11 · 14:8

30 ᴿAnd his servants carried him in a chariot dead from Me-gid′-do, and brought him to Jerusalem, and buried him in his own sepulchre. And ᴿthe people of the land took Je-ho′-a-haz the son of Jo-si′-ah, and anointed him, and made him king in his father′s stead.   22:20; 2 Chr. 35:24 · 2 Chr. 36:1-4

31 ᴿJe-ho′-a-haz *was* twenty and three years old when he began to reign; and he reigned three months in Jerusalem. And his mother′s name *was* ᴿHa-mu′-tal, the daughter of Jer-e-mi′-ah of Lib′-nah.   1 Chr. 3:15; Jer. 22:11 · 24:18

32 And he did *that which was* evil in the sight of the LORD, according to all that his fathers had done.

33 And Pha′-raoh–ne′-choh put him in ᵀbands ᴿat Rib′-lah in the land of Ha′-math, that he might not reign in Jerusalem; and put the land to a tribute of an hundred talents of silver, and a talent of gold.   *prison* · 25:6; Jer. 52:27

34 And ᴿPha′-raoh–ne′-choh made E-li′-a-kim the son of Jo-si′-ah king in the room of Jo-si′-ah his father, and turned his name to Je-hoi′-a-kim, and took Je-ho′-a-haz away: and he came to Egypt, and died there.   2 Chr. 36:4

35 And Je-hoi′-a-kim gave ᴿthe silver and the gold to Pharaoh; but he taxed the land to give the money according to the commandment of Pharaoh: he exacted the silver and the gold of the people of the land, of every one according to his taxation, to give *it* unto Pha′-raoh–ne′-choh.   v. 33

36 ᴿJe-hoi′-a-kim *was* twenty and five years old when he began to reign; and he reigned eleven years in Jerusalem. And his mother′s name *was* Ze-bu′-dah, the daughter of Pe-da′-iah of Ru′-mah.   2 Chr. 36:5; Jer. 22:18, 19; 26:1

37 And he did *that which was* evil in the sight of the LORD, according to all that his fathers had done.

24 In ᴿhis days Neb-u-chad-nez′-zar king of ᴿBabylon came up, and Je-hoi′-a-kim became his servant three years: then he turned and rebelled against him.   2 Chr. 36:6; Jer. 25:1, 9 · 20:14

2 ᴿAnd the LORD sent against him bands of the Chal′-dees, and bands of the Syrians, and bands of the Mo′-ab-ites, and bands of the children of Ammon, and sent them against Judah to destroy it, according to the word of the LORD, which he spake by his servants the prophets.   Jer. 25:9; 32:28

3 Surely at the commandment of the LORD came *this* upon Judah, to remove *them* out of his sight, ᴿfor the sins of Ma-nas′-seh, according to all that he did; 21:2, 11

4 ᴿAnd also for the innocent blood that he shed: for he filled Jerusalem with innocent blood; which the LORD would not pardon.   21:16

5 Now the rest of the acts of Je-hoi′-a-kim, and all that he did, *are* they not written in the book of the chronicles of the kings of Judah?

6 ᴿSo Je-hoi′-a-kim slept with his fathers: and Je-hoi′-a-chin his son reigned in his stead.   2 Chr. 36:6

7 And the king of Egypt came

not again any more out of his land: for the king of Babylon had taken from the river of Egypt unto the river Eu-phra'-tes all that pertained to the king of Egypt.

8 ᴿJe-hoi'-a-chin *was* eighteen years old when he began to reign, and he reigned in Jerusalem three months. And his mother's name *was* Ne-hush'-ta, the daughter of El-na'-than of Jerusalem. 1 Chr. 3:16

9 And he did *that which was* evil in the sight of the LORD, according to all that his father had done.

10 ᴿAt that time the servants of Neb-u-chad-nez'-zar king of Babylon came up against Jerusalem, and the city was besieged. Dan. 1:1

11 And Neb-u-chad-nez'-zar king of Babylon came against the city, and his servants did besiege it.

12 ᴿAnd Je-hoi'-a-chin the king of Judah went out to the king of Babylon, he, and his mother, and his servants, and his princes, and his officers: and the king of Babylon took him in the eighth year of his reign. Jer. 22:24–30; 24:1

13 ᴿAnd he carried out thence all the treasures of the house of the LORD, and the treasures of the king's house, and cut in pieces all the vessels of gold which Solomon king of Israel had made in the temple of the LORD, ᴿas the LORD had said. 20:17; Is. 39:6 · Jer. 20:5

14 And he carried away all Jerusalem, and all the princes, and all the mighty men of valour, ᴿ*even* ten thousand captives, and all the craftsmen and smiths: none remained, save the poorest sort of the people of the land. v. 16

15 And he carried away Je-hoi'-a-chin to Babylon, and the king's mother, and the king's wives, and his officers, and the mighty of the land, *those* carried he into captivity from Jerusalem to Babylon.

16 And all the men of might, *even* seven thousand, and craftsmen and smiths a thousand, all *that were* strong *and* ᵀapt for war, even them the king of Babylon brought captive to Babylon. fit

17 And ᴿthe king of Babylon made Mat-ta-ni'-ah ᴿhis father's brother king in his stead, and ᴿchanged his name to Zed-e-ki'-ah. Jer. 37:1 · 1 Chr. 3:15 · 2 Chr. 36:4

18 Zed-e-ki'-ah *was* twenty and one years old when he began to reign, and he reigned eleven years in Jerusalem. And his mother's name *was* Ha-mu'-tal, the daughter of Jer-e-mi'-ah of Lib'-nah.

19 ᴿAnd he did *that which was* evil in the sight of the LORD, according to all that Je-hoi'-a-kim had done. 2 Chr. 36:12

20 For ᵀthrough the anger of the LORD it came to pass in Jerusalem and Judah, until he had cast them out from his presence, ᴿthat Zed-e-ki'-ah rebelled against the king of Babylon. because of · Ezek. 17:15

25 And it came to pass in the ninth year of his reign, in the tenth month, in the tenth *day* of the month, *that* Neb-u-chad-nez'-zar king of Babylon came, he, and all his host, against Jerusalem, and pitched against it; and they built forts against it round about.

2 And the city was besieged unto the eleventh year of king Zed-e-ki'-ah.

3 And on the ninth *day* of the ᴿ*fourth* month the famine prevailed in the city, and there was no bread for the people of the land. 6:24, 25; Is. 3:1; Jer. 39:2; Lam. 4:9, 10

4 And the city was broken up, and all the men of war *fled* by night by the way of the gate between two walls, which *is* by the king's garden: (now the Chal'-dees *were* against the city round about:) and ᴿthe king went the way toward the plain. Jer. 39:4–7

5 And the army of the Chal'-dees pursued after the king, and overtook him in the plains of Jericho: and all his army were scattered from him.

6 So they took the king, and brought him up to the king of Babylon ᴿto Rib'-lah; and they gave judgment upon him. Jer. 52:9

7 And they slew the sons of Zed-e-ki'-ah before his eyes, and

Rput[T] out the eyes of Zed-e-ki'-ah, and bound him with fetters of brass, and carried him to Bab-ylon.   Jer. 39:7; Ezek. 17:16 · *blinded*

8 And in the fifth month, Ron the seventh *day* of the month, which *is* Rthe nineteenth year of king Neb-u-chad-nez'-zar king of Babylon, Rcame Neb'-u-zar–a'-dan, captain of the guard, a ser-vant of the king of Babylon, unto Jerusalem: Jer. 52:12 · 24:12 · Jer. 39:9

9 RAnd he burnt the house of the LORD, and the king's house, and all the houses of Jerusalem, and every great *man's* house burnt he with fire.   Ps. 79:1; Jer. 7:14

10 And all the army of the Chal'-dees, that *were with* the captain of the guard, brake down the walls of Jerusalem round about.

11 RNow the rest of the people *that were* left in the city, and the fugitives that fell away to the king of Babylon, with the remnant of the multitude, did Neb'-u-zar–a'-dan the captain of the guard carry away.   Is. 1:9; Jer. 5:19; 39:9

12 But the captain of the guard left of the poor of the land *to be* vinedressers and husbandmen.

13 And Rthe pillars of brass that *were* in the house of the LORD, and Rthe bases, and the brasen sea that *was* in the house of the LORD, did the Chal'-dees break in pieces, and carried the brass of them to Babylon.   Jer. 52:17 · 1 Kin. 7:27

14 And Rthe pots, and the shov-els, and the snuffers, and the spoons, and all the vessels of brass wherewith they ministered, took they away.   Ex. 27:3; 1 Kin. 7:45

15 And the firepans, and the bowls, *and* such things as *were* of gold, *in* gold, and of silver, *in* silver, the captain of the guard took away.

16 The two pillars, one sea, and the bases which Solomon had made for the house of the LORD; the brass of all these vessels was Twithout weight.   *beyond measure*

17 RThe height of the one pillar *was* eighteen cubits, and the chapiter upon it *was* brass: and the height of the chapiter three cubits; and the wreathen work, and pomegranates upon the chap-iter round about, all of brass: and like unto these had the second pil-lar with wreathen work.   Jer. 52:21

18 RAnd the captain of the guard took RSe-ra'-iah the chief priest, and Zeph-a-ni'-ah the second priest, and the three keepers of the door: Jer. 39:9–13 · 1 Chr. 6:14

19 And out of the city he took an officer that was set over the men of war, and Rfive men of them that were in the king's presence, which were found in the city, and the principal scribe of the host, which mustered the people of the land, and threescore men of the people of the land *that were* found in the city: Esth. 1:14; Jer. 52:25

20 And Neb'-u-zar–a'-dan cap-tain of the guard took these, and brought them to the king of Bab-ylon to Rib'-lah:

21 And the king of Babylon smote them, and slew them at Rib'-lah in the land of Ha'-math. RSo Judah was carried away out of their land.   Lev. 26:33; Deut. 28:36, 64

22 RAnd *as for* the people that remained in the land of Judah, whom Neb-u-chad-nez'-zar king of Babylon had left, even over them he made Ged-a-li'-ah the son of RA-hi'-kam, the son of Sha'-phan, ruler.   22:12 · Is. 1:9; Jer. 40:5

23 And when all the Rcaptains of the armies, they and their men, heard that the king of Babylon had made Ged-a-li'-ah governor, there came to Ged-a-li'-ah to Miz'-pah, even Ish'-ma-el the son of Neth-a-ni'-ah, and Jo-ha'-nan the son of Ca-re'-ah, and Se-ra'-iah the son of Tan'-hu-meth the Ne-toph'-a-thite, and Ja-az-a-ni'-ah the son of a Ma-ach'-a-thite, they and their men.   Jer. 40:7–9

24 And Ged-a-li'-ah sware to them, and to their men, and said unto them, Fear not to be the ser-vants of the Chal'-dees: dwell in the land, and serve the king of Babylon; and it shall be well with you.

25 But it came to pass in the sev-

enth month, that Ish'-ma-el the son of Neth-a-ni'-ah, the son of E-lish'-a-ma, of the seed royal, came, and ten men with him, and smote Ged-a-li'-ah, that he died, and the Jews and the Chal'-dees that were with him at Miz'-pah.

26 And all the people, both small and great, and the captains of the armies, arose, [R]and came to Egypt: for they were afraid of the Chal'-dees.   19:31; Jer. 43:4–7

27 [R]And it came to pass in the seven and thirtieth year of the captivity of Je-hoi'-a-chin king of Judah, in the twelfth month, on the seven and twentieth day of the month, that E'-vil–me-ro'-dach king of Babylon in the year that he began to reign did lift up the head of Je-hoi'-a-chin king of Judah out of prison;   Jer. 52:31–34

28 And he spake kindly to him, and set his throne above the throne of the kings that were with him in Babylon;

29 And changed his prison garments: and he did [R]eat [T]bread continually before him all the days of his life.   2 Sam. 9:7 · food

30 And his allowance was a continual allowance given him of the king, a daily rate for every day, all the days of his life.

The First Book of the
CHRONICLES

THE books of First and Second Chronicles cover the same period of Jewish history described in Second Samuel through Second Kings, but the perspective is different. These books are no mere repetition of the same material, but rather form a divine editorial on the history of God's people. While Second Samuel and First and Second Kings give a political history of Israel and Judah, First and Second Chronicles present a religious history of the Davidic dynasty of Judah. The former are written from a prophetic and moral viewpoint, and the latter from a priestly and spiritual perspective. The Book of First Chronicles begins with the royal line of David and then traces the spiritual significance of David's righteous reign.

The books of First and Second Chronicles were originally one continuous work in the Hebrew. The title was *Dibere Hayyamim*, meaning "The Words [accounts, events] of the Days." The equivalent meaning today would be "The Events of the Times." Chronicles was divided into two parts in the third-century B.C. Greek translation of the Hebrew Bible (the Septuagint). At that time it was given the name *Paraleipomenon*, "Of Things Omitted," referring to the things omitted from Samuel and Kings. Some copies add the phrase, *Basileon Iouda*, "Concerning the Kings of Judah." The first book of Chronicles was called *Paraleipomenon Primus*, "The First Book of Things Omitted." The name "Chronicles" comes from Jerome in his Latin Vulgate Bible (A.D. 385–405): *Chronicorum Liber*. He meant his title in the sense of the "Chronicles of the Whole of Sacred History."

ADAM,[R] Sheth, E'-nosh,   Gen. 2:7

2 [T]Ke'-nan, [R]Ma-ha'-la-le-el, Je'-red,   Cainan, Gen. 5:9 · Luke 3:37

3 [T]He'-noch, Me-thu'-se-lah, La'-mech,   Enoch, Gen. 4:17

4 [R]Noah, Shem, Ham, and Ja'-pheth.   Gen. 5:28—10:1

5 [R]The sons of Ja'-pheth; Go'-mer, and Ma'-gog, and Ma'-dai, and Ja'-van, and Tu'-bal, and Me'-shech, and Ti'-ras.   Gen. 10:2–4

6 And the sons of Go'-mer;
Ash-che'-naz, and Ri'-phath, and
To-gar'-mah.

7 And the sons of Ja'-van; E-li'-
shah, and ᵀTar'-shish, Kit'-tim,
and Dod'-a-nim.   Heb. *Tar-shishah*

8 The sons of Ham; Cush, and
Miz'-ra-im, Put, and Canaan.

9 And the sons of Cush; Se'-ba,
and Hav'-i-lah, and ᵀSab'-ta, and
Ra'-a-mah, and Sab'-te-cha. And
the sons of Ra'-a-mah; She'-ba,
and De'-dan.   *Sabtah,* Gen. 10:7

10 And Cush ᴿbegat Nimrod: he
began to be ᵀmighty upon the
earth.   Gen. 10:8–10, 13 · *a mighty one*

11 And Miz'-ra-im begat Lu'-
dim, and An'-a-mim, and Le'-ha-
bim, and Naph'-tu-him,

12 And Path-ru'-sim, and Cas'-
lu-him, (of whom came the Phi-
lis'-tines,) and Caph'-tho-rim.

13 And ᴿCanaan begat Zi'-don
his firstborn, and Heth,   Gen. 9:18

14 The Jeb'-u-site also, and the
Am'-or-ite, and the Gir'-ga-shite,

15 And the Hi'-vite, and the
Ark'-ite, and the Si'-nite,

16 And the Ar'-vad-ite, and the
Zem'-a-rite, and the Ha'-math-ite.

17 The sons of Shem; E'-lam,
and Assh'-ur, and Ar-phax'-ad,
and Lud, and A'-ram, and Uz, and
Hul, and Ge'-ther, and Me'-shech.

18 And Ar-phax'-ad begat She'-
lah, and She'-lah begat E'-ber.

19 And unto E'-ber were born
two sons: the name of the one *was*
Pe'-leg; because in his days the
earth was divided: and his brother's name *was* Jok'-tan.

20 And ᴿJok'-tan begat Al-mo'-
dad, and She'-leph, and Ha'-zar–
ma'-veth, and Je'-rah,   Gen. 10:26

21 Ha-do'-ram also, and U'-zal,
and Dik'-lah,

22 And ᵀE'-bal, and A-bim'-a-el,
and She'-ba,   *Obal,* Gen. 10:28

23 And O'-phir, and Hav'-i-lah,
and Jo'-bab. All these *were* the
sons of Jok'-tan.

24 Shem, Ar-phax'-ad, She'-lah,

25 E'-ber, Pe'-leg, Re'-u,

26 Se'-rug, Na'-hor, Te'-rah,

27 ᴿAbram; the same *is* Abraham.   Gen. 17:5

28 The sons of Abraham; ᴿIsaac,
and ᴿIsh'-ma-el.   Gen. 21:2 · Gen. 16:11

29 These *are* their generations:
The ᴿfirstborn of Ish'-ma-el, Ne-
ba'-ioth; then Ke'-dar, and Ad'-be-
el, and Mib'-sam,   Gen. 25:13–16

30 Mish'-ma, and Du'-mah,
Mas'-sa, Ha'-dad, and Te'-ma,

31 Je'-tur, Na'-phish, and Ked'-e-
mah. These are the sons of Ish'-
ma-el.

32 Now the sons of Ke-tu'-rah,
Abraham's concubine: she bare
Zim'-ran, and Jok'-shan, and Me'-
dan, and Mid'-i-an, and Ish'-bak,
and Shu'-ah. And the sons of Jok'-
shan; She'-ba, and De'-dan.

33 And the sons of Mid'-i-an;
E'-phah, and E'-pher, and He'-
noch, and A-bi'-da, and El-da'-ah.
All these *are* the sons of Ke-tu'-
rah.

34 And ᴿAbraham begat Isaac.
ᴿThe sons of Isaac; Esau and Is-
rael.   Gen. 21:2 · Gen. 25:9, 25, 26, 29; 32:28

35 The sons of ᴿEsau; El'-i-phaz,
Reu'-el, and Je'-ush, and Ja-a'-
lam, and Ko'-rah.   Gen. 36:10–19

36 The sons of El'-i-phaz; Te'-
man, and Omar, Ze'-phi, and Ga'-
tam, Ke'-naz, and ᴿTim'-na, and
Am'-a-lek.   Gen. 36:12

37 The sons of Reu'-el; Na'-hath,
Ze'-rah, Sham'-mah, and Miz'-zah.

38 And ᴿthe sons of Se'-ir; Lo'-
tan, and Sho'-bal, and Zib'-e-on,
and A'-nah, and Di'-shon, and E'-
zar, and Di'-shan.   Gen. 36:20–28

39 And the sons of Lo'-tan; Ho'-
ri, and Ho'-mam: and Tim'-na *was*
Lo'-tan's sister.

40 The sons of Sho'-bal; A-li'-an,
and Ma-na'-hath, and E'-bal, She'-
phi, and O'-nam. And the sons of
Zib'-e-on; A'-iah, and A'-nah.

41 The sons of A'-nah; ᴿDi'-
shon. And the sons of Di'-shon;
Am'-ram, and Esh'-ban, and Ith'-
ran, and Che'-ran.   Gen. 36:25

42 The sons of E'-zer; Bil'-han,
and Za'-van, *and* Ja'-kan. The
sons of Di'-shan; Uz, and A'-ran.

43 Now these *are* the ᴿkings that
reigned in the land of E'-dom before *any* king reigned over the
children of Israel; Be'-la the son of

Be'-or: and the name of his city *was* Din'-ha-bah.   Gen. 36:31–43

44 And when Be'-la was dead, Jo'-bab the son of Ze'-rah of Boz'-rah reigned in his stead.

45 And when Jo'-bab was dead, Hu'-sham of the land of the Te'-man-ites reigned in his stead.

46 And when Hu'-sham was dead, Ha'-dad the son of Be'-dad, which ᵀsmote Mid'-i-an in the field of Moab, reigned in his stead: and the name of his city *was* A'-vith.   *attacked*

47 And when Ha'-dad was dead, Sam'-lah of Mas-re'-kah reigned in his stead.

48 And when Sam'-lah was dead, Sha'-ul of Re-ho'-both by the river reigned in his stead.

49 And when Sha'-ul was dead, Ba'-al–ha'-nan the son of Ach'-bor reigned in his stead.

50 And when Ba'-al–ha'-nan was dead, Ha'-dad reigned in his stead: and the name of his city *was* Pa'-i; and his wife's name *was* Me-het'-a-bel, the daughter of Ma'-tred, the daughter of Mez'-a-hab.

51 Ha'-dad died also. And the dukes of E'-dom were; duke Tim'-nah, duke A-li'-ah, duke Je'-theth,

52 Duke A-hol-i-ba'-mah, duke E'-lah, duke Pi'-non,

53 Duke Ke'-naz, duke Te'-man, duke Mib'-zar,

54 Duke Mag'-di-el, duke I'-ram. These *are* the dukes of E'-dom.

2 These *are* the sons of Israel; Reuben, Simeon, Levi, and Judah, Is'-sa-char, and Zeb'-u-lun,

2 Dan, Joseph, and Benjamin, Naph'-ta-li, Gad, and Asher.

3 The sons of ᴿJudah; Er, and O'-nan, and She'-lah: *which* three were born unto him of the daughter of Shu'-a the Ca'-naan-i-tess. And Er, the firstborn of Judah, was evil in the sight of the LORD; and he slew him.   Gen. 38:3–5; 46:12

4 And ᴿTa'-mar his daughter in law ᴿbare him Pha'-rez and Ze'-rah. All the sons of Judah *were* five.   Gen. 38:6 · Matt. 1:3

5 The sons of ᴿPha'-rez; Hez'-ron, and Ha'-mul.   Gen. 46:12

6 And the sons of Ze'-rah; Zim'-ri, ᴿand E'-than, and He'-man, and Cal'-col, and Da'-ra: five of them in all.   1 Kin. 4:31

7 And the sons of ᴿCar'-mi; A'-char, the troubler of Israel, who transgressed in the thing ᴿac-cursed.ᵀ   4:1 · Josh. 6:18 · *banned*

8 And the sons of E'-than; Az-a-ri'-ah.

9 The sons also of Hez'-ron, that were born unto him; Je-rah'-me-el, and Ram, and Che-lu'-bai.

10 And Ram ᴿbegat Am-min'-a-dab; and Am-min'-a-dab begat Nah'-shon, prince of the children of Judah;   Ruth 4:19–22; Matt. 1:4

11 And Nah'-shon begat Sal'-ma, and Sal'-ma begat Bo'-az,

12 And Bo'-az begat O'-bed, and O'-bed begat Jesse,

13 And Jesse begat his firstborn E-li'-ab, and A-bin'-a-dab the second, and Shim'-ma the third,

14 Ne-than'-e-el the fourth, Rad'-dai the fifth,

15 O'-zem the sixth, David the ᴿseventh: 1 Sam. 16:10, 11; 17:12

16 Whose sisters *were* Ze-ru'-iah, and Ab'-i-gail. ᴿAnd the sons of Ze-ru'-iah; A-bi'-shai, and Jo'-ab, and A'-sa-hel, three.   2 Sam. 2:18

17 And Ab'-i-gail bare Am'-a-sa: and the father of Am'-a-sa *was* Je'-ther the Ish'-me-el-ite.

18 And Caleb the son of Hez'-ron begat *children* of A-zu'-bah *his* wife, and of Je'-ri-oth: her sons *are* these; Je'-sher, and Sho'-bab, and Ar'-don.

19 And when A-zu'-bah was dead, Caleb ᵀtook unto him Eph'-rath, which bare him Hur.   *married*

20 And Hur begat U'-ri, and U'-ri begat ᴿBe-zal'-e-el.   Ex. 31:2; 38:22

21 And afterward Hez'-ron went in to the daughter of ᴿMa'-chir the father of Gil'-e-ad, whom he mar-ried when he *was* threescore years old; and she bare him Se'-gub.   7:14; Num. 27:1; Judg. 5:14

22 And Se'-gub begat ᴿJa'-ir, who had three and twenty cities in the land of Gil'-e-ad.   Judg. 10:3

23 ᴿAnd he took Ge'-shur, and A'-ram, with the towns of Ja'-ir,

from them, with Ke'-nath, and the towns thereof, *even* threescore cities. All these *belonged to* the sons of Ma'-chir the father of Gil'-e-ad.   Num. 32:41; Deut. 3:14; Josh. 13:30

24 And after that Hez'-ron was dead in Ca'-leb–eph'-ra-tah, then A-bi'-ah Hez'-ron's wife bare him ^RAshur the father of Te-ko'-a.   4:5

25 And the sons of Je-rah'-me-el the firstborn of Hez'-ron were, Ram the firstborn, and Bu'-nah, and O'-ren, and O'-zem, *and* A-hi'-jah.

26 Je-rah'-me-el had also another wife, whose name *was* At'-a-rah; she *was* the mother of O'-nam.

27 And the sons of Ram the firstborn of Je-rah'-me-el were, Ma'-az, and Ja'-min, and E'-ker.

28 And the sons of O'-nam were, Sham'-mai, and Ja'-da. And the sons of Sham'-mai; Na'-dab, and A-bi'-shur.

29 And the name of the wife of A-bi'-shur *was* Ab-i-ha'-il, and she bare him Ah'-ban, and Mo'-lid.

30 And the sons of Na'-dab; Se'-led, and Ap'-pa-im: but Se'-led died without children.

31 And the sons of Ap'-pa-im; Ish'-i. And the sons of Ish'-i; She'-shan. And the ^Rthe children of She'-shan; Ah'-lai.   vv. 34, 35

32 And the sons of Ja'-da the brother of Sham'-mai; Je'-ther, and Jonathan: and Je'-ther died without children.

33 And the sons of Jonathan; Pe'-leth, and Za'-za. These were the sons of Je-rah'-me-el.

34 Now She'-shan had no sons, but daughters. And She'-shan had a servant, an Egyptian, whose name *was* Jar'-ha.

35 And She'-shan gave his daughter to Jar'-ha his servant to wife; and she bare him At'-tai.

36 And At'-tai begat Nathan, and Nathan begat ^RZa'-bad,   11:41

37 And Za'-bad begat Eph'-lal, and Eph'-lal begat O'-bed,

38 And O'-bed begat Je'-hu, and Je'-hu begat Az-a-ri'-ah,

39 And Az-a-ri'-ah begat He'-lez, and He'-lez begat E-le'-a-sah,

40 And E-le'-a-sah begat Sis'-a-mai, and Sis'-a-mai begat Shal'-lum,

41 And Shal'-lum begat Jek-a-mi'-ah, and Jek-a-mi'-ah begat E-lish'-a-ma.

42 Now the sons of Caleb the brother of Je-rah'-me-el *were*, Me'-sha his firstborn, which *was* the father of Ziph; and the sons of Ma-re'-shah the father of He'-bron.

43 And the sons of He'-bron; Ko'-rah, and Tap'-pu-ah, and Re'-kem, and She'-ma.

44 And She'-ma begat Ra'-ham, the father of Jor'-ko-am: and Re'-kem begat Sham'-mai.

45 And the son of Sham'-mai *was* Ma'-on: and Ma'-on *was* the father of Beth'–zur.

46 And E'-phah, Caleb's concubine, bare Ha'-ran, and Mo'-za, and Ga'-zez: and Ha'-ran begat Ga'-zez.

47 And the sons of Jah'-dai; Re'-gem, and Jo'-tham, and Ge'-sham, and Pe'-let, and E'-phah, and Sha'-aph.

48 Ma'-a-chah, Caleb's concubine, bare She'-ber, and Tir'-ha-nah.

49 She bare also Sha'-aph the father of Mad-man'-nah, She'-va the father of Mach-be'-nah, and the father of Gib'-e-a: and the daughter of Caleb *was* Ach'-sa.

50 These were the sons of Caleb the son of ^RHur, the firstborn of Eph'-ra-tah; Sho'-bal the father of ^RKir'-jath–je'-a-rim,   4:4 · Josh. 9:17

51 Sal'-ma the father of Beth'–le-hem, Ha'-reph the father of Beth–ga'-der.

52 And Sho'-bal the father of Kir'-jath–je'-a-rim had sons; Har'-o-eh, *and* half of the ^TMa-na'-heth-ites.   Heb. *Manuhoth*

53 And the families of Kir'-jath–je'-a-rim; the Ith'-rites, and the Pu'-hites, and the Shu'-math-ites, and the Mish'-ra-ites; of them came the Za'-re-ath-ites, and the Esh'-ta-ul-ites.

54 The sons of Sal'-ma; Beth'–le-hem, and the Ne-toph'-a-thites,

ᵀAt'-a-roth, the house of Jo'-ab, and half of the Ma-na'-heth-ites, the Zo'-rites. Or *Atroth-bethjoab*

55 And the families of the scribes which dwelt at Ja'-bez; the Ti'-rath-ites, the Shim'-e-ath-ites, *and* Su'-chath-ites. These *are* the ᴿKen'-ites that came of He'-math, the father of the house of ᴿRe'-chab. Judg. 1:16 · 2 Kin. 10:15; Jer. 35:2

3 Now these were the sons of David, which were born unto him in He'-bron; the firstborn Amnon, of A-hin'-o-am the Jez'-re-el-i-tess; the second Daniel, of Ab'-i-gail the Car'-mel-i-tess:

2 The third, ᴿAb'-sa-lom the son of Ma'-a-chah the daughter of Tal'-mai king of Ge'-shur: the fourth, ᴿAd-o-ni'-jah the son of Hag'-gith: 2 Sam. 13:37; 15:1 · 1 Kin. 1:5

3 The fifth, Sheph-a-ti'-ah of Ab'-i-tal: the sixth, Ith'-re-am by ᴿEg'-lah his wife. 2 Sam. 3:5

4 *These* six were born unto him in He'-bron; and there he reigned seven years and six months: and ᴿin Jerusalem he reigned thirty and three years. 2 Sam. 5:5

5 ᴿAnd these were born unto him in Jerusalem; Shim'-e-a, and Sho'-bab, and Nathan, and Solomon, four, of Bath'-shu-a the daughter of Am'-mi-el: 14:4–7

6 Ib'-har also, and E-lish'-a-ma, and E-liph'-e-let,

7 And No'-gah, and Ne'-pheg, and Ja-phi'-a,

8 And E-lish'-a-ma, and E-li'-a-da, and E-liph'-e-let, nine.

9 *These were* all the sons of David, beside the sons of the concubines, and Ta'-mar their sister.

10 And Solomon's son *was* Re-ho-bo'-am, A-bi'-a his son, A'-sa his son, Je-hosh'-a-phat his son,

11 Jo'-ram his son, A-ha-zi'-ah his son, Jo'-ash his son,

12 Am-a-zi'-ah his son, Az-a-ri'-ah his son, Jo'-tham his son,

13 Ahaz his son, Hez-e-ki'-ah his son, Ma-nas'-seh his son,

14 Amon his son, Jo-si'-ah his son.

15 And the sons of Jo-si'-ah *were*, the firstborn Jo-ha'-nan, the second Je-hoi'-a-kim, the third ᵀZed-e-ki'-ah, the fourth Shal'-lum. Mattaniah, 2 Kin. 24:17

16 And the sons of ᴿJe-hoi'-a-kim: Jec-o-ni'-ah his son, Zed-e-ki'-ah his son. Matt. 1:11

17 And the sons of Jec-o-ni'-ah; As'-sir, Sa-la'-thi-el his son,

18 Mal-chi'-ram also, and Pe-da'-iah, and She-na'-zar, Jec-a-mi'-ah, Hosh'-a-ma, and Ned-a-bi'-ah.

19 And the sons of Pe-da'-iah *were*, Ze-rub'-ba-bel, and Shim'-e-i: and the sons of Ze-rub'-ba-bel; Me-shul'-lam, and Han-a-ni'-ah, and Shel'-o-mith their sister:

20 And Ha-shu'-bah, and O'-hel, and Ber-e-chi'-ah, and Has-a-di'-ah, Ju'-shab–he'-sed, five.

21 And the sons of Han-a-ni'-ah; Pel-a-ti'-ah, and Je-sa'-iah: the sons of Re-pha'-iah, the sons of Arnan, the sons of O-ba-di'-ah, the sons of Shech-a-ni'-ah.

22 And the sons of Shech-a-ni'-ah; She-ma'-iah: and the sons of She-ma'-iah; ᴿHat'-tush, and I'-ge-al, and Ba-ri'-ah, and Ne-a-ri'-ah, and Sha'-phat, six. Ezra 8:2

23 And the sons of Ne-a-ri'-ah; E-li-o-e'-nai, and Hez-e-ki'-ah, and Az'-ri-kam, three.

24 And the sons of E-li-o-e'-nai *were*, Ho-da'-iah, and E-li'-a-shib, and Pe-la'-iah, and Ak'-kub, and Jo-ha'-nan, and Da-la'-iah, and A-na'-ni, seven.

4 The sons of Judah; ᴿPha'-rez, Hez'-ron, and Car'-mi, and Hur, and Sho'-bal. Gen. 38:29; 46:12

2 And ᵀRe-a'-iah the son of Sho'-bal begat Ja'-hath; and Ja'-hath begat A-hu'-mai, and La'-had. These *are* the families of the Zo'-rath-ites. Haroeh, 2:52

3 And these *were of* the father of E'-tam; Jez'-re-el, and Ish'-ma, and Id'-bash: and the name of their sister *was* Haz-e-lel-po'-ni:

4 And Pe-nu'-el the father of Ge'-dor, and E'-zer the father of Hu'-shah. These *are* the sons of ᴿHur, the firstborn of Eph'-ra-tah, the father of Beth'–le-hem. Ex. 31:2

5 And ᴿAshur the father of Te-

ko'-a had two wives, He'-lah and Na'-a-rah.   2:24

6 And Na'-a-rah bare him A-hu'-zam, and He'-pher, and Tem'-e-ni, and Ha-a-hash'-ta-ri. These *were* the sons of Na'-a-rah.

7 And the sons of He'-lah *were*, Ze'-reth, and Jez'-o-ar, and Eth'-nan.

8 And Coz begat A'-nub, and Zo-be'-bah, and the families of A-har'-hel the son of Ha'-rum.

9 And Ja'-bez was more honourable than his brethren: and his mother called his name ^TJa'-bez, saying, Because I bare him with sorrow.   Lit. *He Will Cause Pain*

10 And Ja'-bez called on the God of Israel, saying, Oh that thou wouldest bless me indeed, and enlarge my ^Tcoast, and that thine hand might be with me, and that thou wouldest keep *me* from evil, that it may not ^Tgrieve me! And God granted him that which he requested.   *border · cause pain*

11 And Che'-lub the brother of ^RShu'-ah begat Me'-hir, which *was* the father of Esh'-ton.   Gen. 38:1-5

12 And Esh'-ton begat Beth-ra'-pha, and Pa-se'-ah, and Te-hin'-nah the father of Ir-na'-hash. These *are* the men of Re'-chah.

13 And the sons of Ke'-naz; Oth'-ni-el, and Se-ra'-iah: and the sons of Oth'-ni-el; Ha'-thath.

14 And Me-on'-o-thai begat Oph'-rah: and Se-ra'-iah begat Jo'-ab, the father of ^Rthe valley of Char'-a-shim; for they were craftsmen.   Neh. 11:35

15 And the sons of ^RCaleb the son of Je-phun'-neh; I'-ru, E'-lah, and Na'-am: and the sons of E'-lah, even Ke'-naz.   Josh. 14:6, 14; 15:13

16 And the sons of Je-ha-le'-le-el; Ziph, and Zi'-phah, Tir'-i-a, and A-sa'-re-el.

17 And the sons of Ezra *were*, Je'-ther, and Me'-red, and E'-pher, and Ja'-lon: and she bare Miriam, and Sham'-mai, and Ish'-bah the father of Esh-te-mo'-a.

18 And his wife Je-hu-di'-jah bare Je'-red the father of Ge'-dor, and He'-ber the father of So'-cho,

and Je-ku'-thi-el the father of Za-no'-ah. And these *are* the sons of Bi-thi'-ah the daughter of Pha-raoh, which Me'-red took.

19 And the sons of *his* wife Ho-di'-ah the sister of Na'-ham, the father of Kei'-lah the Gar'-mite, and Esh-te-mo'-a the ^RMa-ach'-a-thite.   2 Kin. 25:23

20 And the sons of Shi'-mon *were*, Amnon, and Rin'-nah, Ben-ha'-nan, and Ti'-lon. And the sons of Ish'-i *were*, Zo'-heth, and Ben-zo'-heth.

21 The sons of ^RShe'-lah ^Rthe son of Judah *were*, Er the father of Le'-cah, and La'-a-dah the father of Ma-re'-shah, and the families of the house of them that wrought fine linen, of the house of Ash-be'-a,   Gen. 38:11, 14 · Gen. 46:12

22 And Jo'-kim, and the men of Cho-ze'-ba, and Jo'-ash, and Sa'-raph, who had the dominion in Moab, and Jash'-u-bi-le'-hem. And *these are* ancient things.

23 These *were* the potters, and those that dwelt among plants and hedges: there they dwelt with the king for his work.

24 The ^Rsons of Simeon *were*, Nem'-u-el, and Ja'-min, Ja'-rib, Ze'-rah, *and* Sha'-ul;   Num. 26:12-14

25 Shal'-lum his son, Mib'-sam his son, Mish'-ma his son.

26 And the sons of Mish'-ma; Ham'-u-el his son, Zac'-chur his son, Shim'-e-i his son.

27 And Shim'-e-i had sixteen sons and six daughters; but his brethren had not many children, neither did all their family multiply, like to the children of Judah.

28 And they dwelt at Be'-er-she'-ba, and Mol'-a-dah, and Ha'-zar-shu'-al,

29 And at Bil'-hah, and at E'-zem, and at To'-lad,

30 And at Be-thu'-el, and at Hor'-mah, and at Zik'-lag,

31 And at Beth-mar'-ca-both, and Ha'-zar-su'-sim, and at Beth-bir'-e-i, and at Sha-a-ra'-im. These *were* their cities unto the reign of David.

32 And their villages *were*, E'-

tam, and A'-in, Rim'-mon, and To'-chen, and A'-shan, five cities:

33 And all their villages that *were* round about the same cities, unto Ba'-al. These *were* their habitations, and their genealogy.

34 And Me-sho'-bab, and Jam'-lech, and Jo'-shah the son of Am-a-zi'-ah,

35 And Jo'-el, and Je'-hu the son of Jos-i-bi'-ah, the son of Se-ra'-iah, the son of A'-si-el,

36 And E-li-o-e'-nai, and Ja-a-ko'-bah, and Jesh-o-ha'-iah, and A-sa'-iah, and A'-di-el, and Je-sim'-i-el, and Be-na'-iah,

37 And Zi'-za the son of Shi'-phi, the son of Al'-lon, the son of Je-da'-iah, the son of Shim'-ri, the son of She-ma'-iah;

38 These mentioned by *their* names *were* ᵀprinces in their families: and the house of their fathers increased greatly.   *leaders*

39 And they went to the entrance of Ge'-dor, *even* unto the east side of the valley, to seek pasture for their flocks.

40 And they found fat pasture and good, and the land *was* wide, and quiet, and peaceable; for *they* of Ham had dwelt there of old.

41 And these written by name came in the days of Hez-e-ki'-ah king of Judah, and ᴿsmote their tents, and the habitations that were found there, and ᴿdestroyed them utterly unto this day, and dwelt in their rooms: because *there was* pasture there for their flocks.   2 Kin. 18:8 · 2 Kin. 19:11

42 And *some* of them, *even* of the sons of Simeon, five hundred men, went to mount Se'-ir, having for their captains Pel-a-ti'-ah, and Ne-a-ri'-ah, and Re-pha'-iah, and Uz-zi'-el, the sons of Ish'-i.

43 And they smote ᴿthe rest of the Am'-a-lek-ites that were escaped, and dwelt there unto this day.   Ex. 17:14; 1 Sam. 15:8; 30:17

5 Now the sons of Reuben the firstborn of Israel, (for he *was* the firstborn; but, forasmuch as he ᴿdefiled his father's bed, his birthright was given unto the sons

of Joseph the son of Israel: and the genealogy is not to be reckoned after the birthright. Gen. 35:22

2 For ᴿJudah prevailed above his brethren, and of him *came* the ᴿchief ruler; but the birthright *was* Joseph's:) Ps. 60:7; 108:8 · Matt. 2:6

3 The sons, *I say*, of ᴿReuben the firstborn of Israel *were*, Ha'-noch, and Pal'-lu, Hez'-ron, and Car'-mi. Gen. 46:9; Ex. 6:14; Num. 26:5

4 The sons of Jo'-el; She-ma'-iah his son, Gog his son, Shim'-e-i his son,

5 Mi'-cah his son, Re-a'-ia his son, Ba'-al his son,

6 Be-e'-rah his son, whom Til'-gath–pil-ne'-ser king of Assyria carried away *captive*: he *was* prince of the Reu'-ben-ites.

7 And his brethren by their families, ᴿwhen the genealogy of their generations was reckoned, *were* the chief, Je-i'-el, and Zech-a-ri'-ah,   v. 17

8 And Be'-la the son of A'-zaz, the son of She'-ma, the son of Jo'-el, who dwelt in Ar'-o-er, even unto Ne'-bo and Ba'-al–me'-on:

9 And eastward he inhabited unto the entering in of the wilderness from the river Eu-phra'-tes: because their cattle were multiplied in the land of Gil'-e-ad.

10 And in the days of Saul they made war ᴿwith the Ha'-gar-ites, who fell by their hand: and they dwelt in their tents throughout all the east *land* of Gil'-e-ad. Gen. 25:12

11 And the children of Gad dwelt over against them, in the land of Ba'-shan unto Sal'-chah:

12 Jo'-el the chief, and Sha'-pham the next, and Ja'-a-nai, and Sha'-phat in Ba'-shan.

13 And their brethren of the house of their fathers *were*, Mi'-cha-el, and Me-shul'-lam, and She'-ba, and Jo'-rai, and Ja'-chan, and Zi'-a, and He'-ber, seven.

14 These *are* the children of Ab-i-ha'-il the son of Hu'-ri, the son of Ja-ro'-ah, the son of Gil'-e-ad, the son of Mi'-cha-el, the son of Je-shish'-ai, the son of Jah'-do, the son of Buz;

15 A'-hi the son of Ab'-di-el, the son of Gu'-ni, chief of the house of their fathers.

16 And they dwelt in Gil'-e-ad in Ba'-shan, and in her towns, and in all the suburbs of ᴿShar'-on, upon their borders.   Song 2:1; Is. 35:2; 65:10

17 All these were reckoned by genealogies in the days of ᴿJo'-tham king of Judah, and in the days of ᴿJer-o-bo'-am king of Is-rael.   2 Kin. 15:5, 32 · 2 Kin. 14:16, 28

18 The sons of Reuben, and the Gad'-ites, and half the tribe of Ma-nas'-seh, of valiant men, men able to bear buckler and sword, and to shoot with bow, and skilful in war, *were* four and forty thousand seven hundred and three-score, that went out to the war.

19 And they made war with the Ha'-gar-ites, with ᴿJe'-tur, and Ne'-phish, and No'-dab.   Gen. 25:15

20 And they were helped against them, and the Ha'-gar-ites were delivered into their hand, and all that *were* with them: for they cried to God in the battle, and he was intreated of them; because they put their trust in him.

21 And they took away their cattle; of their camels fifty thousand, and of sheep two hundred and fifty thousand, and of asses two thousand, and of men an hundred thousand.

22 For there fell down many slain, because the war *was* of God. And they dwelt in their steads until the captivity.

23 And the children of the half tribe of Ma-nas'-seh dwelt in the land: they increased from Ba'-shan unto Ba'-al–her'-mon and Se'-nir, and unto mount Hermon.

24 And these *were* the heads of the house of their fathers, even E'-pher, and Ish'-i, and E-li'-el, and Az'-ri-el, and Jer-e-mi'-ah, and Hod-a-vi'-ah, and Jah'-di-el, mighty men of valour, famous men, *and* heads of the house of their fathers.

25 And they transgressed against the God of their fathers, and ᵀwent a ᴿwhoring after the gods of the people of the land, whom God destroyed before them.   *played the harlot after* · 2 Kin. 17:7

26 And the God of Israel stirred up the spirit of Pul king of As-syria, and the spirit of Til'-gath–pil-ne'-ser king of Assyria, and he carried them away, even the Reu'-ben-ites, and the Gad'-ites, and the half tribe of Ma-nas'-seh, and brought them unto Ha'-lah, and Ha'-bor, and Ha'-ra, and to the river Go'-zan, unto this day.

6 The sons of Levi; ᴿGer'-shon, Ko'-hath, and Me-ra'-ri.   Ex. 6:16

2 And the sons of Ko'-hath; Am'-ram, ᴿIz'-har, and He'-bron, and Uz-zi'-el.   vv. 18, 22

3 And the children of Am'-ram; Aaron, and Moses, and Miriam. The sons also of Aaron; ᴿNa'-dab, and A-bi'-hu, E-le-a'-zar, and Ith'-a-mar.   Lev. 10:1, 2

4 E-le-a'-zar begat Phin'-e-has, Phin'-e-has begat Ab-i-shu'-a,

5 And Ab-i-shu'-a begat Buk'-ki, and Buk'-ki begat Uz'-zi,

6 And Uz'-zi begat Zer-a-hi'-ah, and Zer-a-hi'-ah begat Me-ra'-ioth,

7 Me-ra'-ioth begat Am-a-ri'-ah, and Am-a-ri'-ah begat A-hi'-tub,

8 And ᴿA-hi'-tub begat ᴿZa'-dok, and Za'-dok begat A-him'-a-az,   2 Sam. 8:17 · 2 Sam. 15:27

9 And A-him'-a-az begat Az-a-ri'-ah, and Az-a-ri'-ah begat Jo-ha'-nan,

10 And Jo-ha'-nan begat Az-a-ri'-ah, (he *it is* that executed the priest's office in the temple that Solomon built in Jerusalem:)

11 And ᴿAz-a-ri'-ah begat ᴿAm-a-ri'-ah, and Am-a-ri'-ah begat A-hi'-tub,   Ezra 7:3 · 2 Chr. 19:11

12 And A-hi'-tub begat Za'-dok, and Za'-dok begat Shal'-lum,

13 And Shal'-lum begat Hil-ki'-ah, and Hil-ki'-ah begat Az-a-ri'-ah,

14 And Az-a-ri'-ah begat ᴿSe-ra'-iah, and Se-ra'-iah begat Je-hoz'-a-dak,   2 Kin. 25:18–21; Neh. 11:11

15 And Je-hoz'-a-dak went *into captivity,* when the LORD carried

away Judah and Jerusalem by the hand of Neb-u-chad-nez'-zar.

16 The sons of Levi; ^RGer'-shom, Ko'-hath, and Me-ra'-ri. Gen. 46:11

17 And these *be* the names of the sons of Ger'-shom; Lib'-ni, and Shim'-e-i.

18 And the sons of Ko'-hath *were*, Am'-ram, and Iz'-har, and He'-bron, and Uz-zi'-el.

19 The sons of Me-ra'-ri; Mah'-li, and Mu'-shi. And these *are* the families of the Levites according to their fathers.

20 Of Ger'-shom; Lib'-ni his son, Ja'-hath his son, ^RZim'-mah his son, v. 42

21 Jo'-ah his son, Id'-do his son, Ze'-rah his son, Je-at'-e-rai his son.

22 The sons of Ko'-hath; Am-min'-a-dab his son, ^RKo'-rah his son, As'-sir his son, Num. 16:1

23 El'-ka-nah his son, and E-bi'-a-saph his son, and As'-sir his son,

24 Ta'-hath his son, U-ri'-el his son, Uz-zi'-ah his son, and Sha'-ul his son.

25 And the sons of El'-ka-nah; Am'-a-sai, and A-hi'-moth.

26 *As for* El'-ka-nah: the sons of El'-ka-nah; Zo'-phai his son, and Na'-hath his son,

27 E-li'-ab his son, Jer'-o-ham his son, El'-ka-nah his son.

28 And the sons of Samuel; the firstborn Vash'-ni, and A-bi'-ah.

29 The sons of Me-ra'-ri; Mah'-li, Lib'-ni his son, Shim'-e-i his son, Uz'-za his son,

30 Shim'-e-a his son, Hag-gi'-ah his son, A-sa'-iah his son.

31 And these *are* ^Rthey whom David set over the service of song in the house of the Lord, after that the ark had rest. 15:16–22, 27

32 And they ministered before the dwelling place of the tabernacle of the congregation with singing, until Solomon had built the house of the Lord in Jerusalem: and *then* they waited on their office according to their order.

33 And these *are* they that waited with their children. Of the sons of the ^RKo'-hath-ites: He'-

man a singer, the son of Jo'-el, the son of Shem'-u-el, Num. 26:57

34 The son of El'-ka-nah, the son of Jer'-o-ham, the son of E-li'-el, the son of To'-ah,

35 The son of Zuph, the son of El'-ka-nah, the son of Ma'-hath, the son of Am'-a-sai,

36 The son of El'-ka-nah, the son of Jo'-el, the son of Az-a-ri'-ah, the son of Zeph-a-ni'-ah,

37 The son of Ta'-hath, the son of As'-sir, the son of ^RE-bi'-a-saph, the son of Ko'-rah, Ex. 6:24

38 The son of Iz'-har, the son of Ko'-hath, the son of Levi, the son of Israel.

39 And his brother ^RA'-saph, who stood on his right hand, *even* A'-saph the son of Ber-a-chi'-ah, the son of Shim'-e-a, 2 Chr. 5:12

40 The son of Mi'-cha-el, the son of Ba-a-se'-iah, the son of Mal-chi'-ah,

41 The son of ^REth'-ni, the son of Ze'-rah, the son of A-da'-iah, v. 21

42 The son of E'-than, the son of Zim'-mah, the son of Shim'-e-i,

43 The son of Ja'-hath, the son of Ger'-shom, the son of Levi.

44 And their brethren the sons of Me-ra'-ri *stood* on the left hand: E'-than the son of Kish'-i, the son of Ab'-di, the son of Mal'-luch,

45 The son of Hash-a-bi'-ah, the son of Am-a-zi'-ah, the son of Hil-ki'-ah,

46 The son of Am'-zi, the son of Ba'-ni, the son of Sha'-mer,

47 The son of Mah'-li, the son of Mu'-shi, the son of Me-ra'-ri, the son of Levi.

48 Their brethren also the Levites *were* appointed unto all ^Rmanner of service of the tabernacle of the house of God. 9:14–34

49 ^RBut Aaron and his sons offered ^Rupon the altar of the burnt offering, and on the altar of incense, *and were appointed* for all the work of the *place* most holy, and to make an atonement for Israel, according to all that Moses the servant of God had commanded. Ex. 28:1 · Lev. 1:8, 9

50 And these *are* the sons of Aaron; E-le-a'-zar his son, Phin'-e-has his son, A-bi-shu'-a his son,

51 Buk'-ki his son, Uz'-zi his son, Zer-a-hi'-ah his son,

52 Me-ra'-ioth his son, Am-a-ri'-ah his son, A-hi'-tub his son,

53 Za'-dok his son, A-him'-a-az his son.

54 Now these *are* their dwelling places throughout their castles in their coasts, of the sons of Aaron, of the families of the Ko'-hath-ites: for theirs was the lot.

55 And they gave them He'-bron in the land of Judah, and the suburbs thereof round about it.

56 But the fields of the city, and the villages thereof, they gave to Caleb the son of Je-phun'-neh.

57 And to the sons of Aaron they gave the cities of Judah, *namely,* He'-bron, *the city* of refuge, and Lib'-nah with her suburbs, and Jat'-tir, and Esh-te-mo'-a, with their suburbs,

58 And Hi'-len with her suburbs, De'-bir with her suburbs,

59 And ᵀA'-shan with her suburbs, and Beth–she'-mesh with her suburbs: *Ain, Josh. 21:16*

60 And out of the tribe of Benjamin; Ge'-ba with her suburbs, and ᵀAl'-e-meth with her suburbs, and An'-a-thoth with her suburbs. All their cities throughout their families *were* thirteen cities. *Almon, Josh. 21:18*

61 And unto the sons of Ko'-hath, *which were* left of the family of that tribe, *were cities given* out of the half tribe, *namely, out of* the half *tribe* of Ma-nas'-seh, ᴿby lot, ten cities. *Josh. 21:5*

62 And to the sons of Ger'-shom throughout their families out of the tribe of Is'-sa-char, and out of the tribe of Asher, and out of the tribe of Naph'-ta-li, and out of the tribe of Ma-nas'-seh in Ba'-shan, thirteen cities.

63 Unto the sons of Me-ra'-ri *were given* by lot, throughout their families, out of the tribe of Reuben, and out of the tribe of Gad, and out of the tribe of Zeb'-u-lun, ᴿtwelve cities. *Josh. 21:7, 34–40*

64 And the children of Israel gave to the Levites *these* cities with their ᵀsuburbs. *open lands*

65 And they gave by lot out of the tribe of the children of Judah, and out of the tribe of the children of Simeon, and out of the tribe of the children of Benjamin, these cities, which are called by *their* names.

66 And *the residue* of the families of the sons of Ko'-hath had cities of their ᵀcoasts out of the tribe of E'-phra-im. *territories*

67 ᴿAnd they gave unto them, *of* the cities of refuge, She'-chem in mount E'-phra-im with her suburbs; *they gave* also Ge'-zer with her suburbs, *Josh. 21:21*

68 And ᴿJok'-me-am with her suburbs, and Beth–ho'-ron with her suburbs, *Josh. 21:22*

69 And Ai'-ja-lon with her suburbs, and Gath–rim'-mon with her suburbs:

70 And out of the half tribe of Ma-nas'-seh; A'-ner with her suburbs, and Bil'-e-am with her suburbs, for the family of the remnant of the sons of Ko'-hath.

71 Unto the sons of Ger'-shom *were given* out of the family of the half tribe of Ma-nas'-seh, Go'-lan in Ba'-shan with her suburbs, and Ash'-ta-roth with her suburbs:

72 And out of the tribe of Is'-sa-char; Ke'-desh with her suburbs, Dab'-e-rath with her suburbs,

73 And Ra'-moth with her suburbs, and A'-nem with her suburbs:

74 And out of the tribe of Asher; Ma'-shal with her suburbs, and Ab'-don with her suburbs,

75 And Hu'-kok with her suburbs, and Re'-hob with her suburbs:

76 And out of the tribe of Naph'-ta-li; Ke'-desh in Galilee with her suburbs, and Ham'-mon with her suburbs, and Kir-ja-tha'-im with her suburbs.

77 Unto the rest of the children of Me-ra'-ri *were given* out of the

tribe of Zeb'-u-lun, Rim'-mon with her suburbs, Ta'-bor with her suburbs:

78 And on the other side Jordan by Jericho, on the east side of Jordan, *were given them* out of the tribe of Reuben, Be'-zer in the wilderness with her suburbs, and Jah'-zah with her suburbs,

79 Ked'-e-moth also with her suburbs, and Meph'-a-ath with her suburbs:

80 And out of the tribe of Gad; Ra'-moth in Gil'-e-ad with her suburbs, and Ma-ha-na'-im with her suburbs,

81 And Hesh'-bon with her suburbs, and Ja'-zer with her suburbs.

7 Now the sons of Is'-sa-char *were*, To'-la, and Pu'-ah, Jash'-ub, and Shim'-rom, four.

2 And the sons of To'-la; Uz'-zi, and Re-pha'-iah, and Je'-ri-el, and Jah'-mai, and Jib'-sam, and Shem'-u-el, heads of their father's house, *to wit*, of To'-la: *they were* valiant men of might in their generations; ^Rwhose number *was* in the days of David two and twenty thousand and six hundred.   27:1

3 And the sons of Uz'-zi; Iz-ra-hi'-ah: and the sons of Iz-ra-hi'-ah; Mi'-cha-el, and O-ba-di'-ah, and Jo'-el, Ish-i'-ah, five: all of them chief men.

4 And with them, by their generations, after the house of their fathers, *were* bands of soldiers for war, six and thirty thousand *men:* for they had many wives and sons.

5 And their brethren among all the families of Is'-sa-char *were* valiant men of might, reckoned in all by their genealogies fourscore and seven thousand.

6 *The sons* of ^RBenjamin; Be'-la, and Be'-cher, and Je-di'-a-el, three.   8:1; Gen. 46:21; Num. 26:38–41

7 And the sons of Be'-la; Ez'-bon, and Uz'-zi, and Uz-zi'-el, and Jer'-i-moth, and I'-ri, five; heads of the house of *their* fathers, mighty men of valour; and were reckoned by their genealogies twenty and two thousand and thirty and four.

8 And the sons of Be'-cher; Ze-mi'-ra, and Jo'-ash, and E-li-e'-zer, and E-li-o-e'-nai, and Om'-ri, and Jer'-i-moth, and A-bi'-ah, and An'-a-thoth, and A-la'-meth. All these *are* the sons of Be'-cher.

9 And the number of them, after their genealogy by their generations, heads of the house of their fathers, mighty men of valour, *was* twenty thousand and two hundred.

10 The sons also of Je-di'-a-el; Bil'-han: and the sons of Bil'-han; Je'-ush, and Benjamin, and E'-hud, and Che-na'-a-nah, and Ze'-than, and Thar'-shish, and A-hish'-a-har.

11 All these the sons of Je-di'-a-el, by the heads of their fathers, mighty men of valour, *were* seventeen thousand and two hundred *soldiers*, fit to go out for war *and* battle.

12 Shup'-pim also, and Hup'-pim, the children of Ir, *and* Hu'-shim, the sons of A'-her.

13 The sons of Naph'-ta-li; Jah'-zi-el, and Gu'-ni, and Je'-zer, and Shal'-lum, the sons of Bil'-hah.

14 The ^Rsons of Ma-nas'-seh; Ash'-ri-el, whom she bare: (*but* his concubine the A'-ram-i-tess bare ^RMa'-chir the father of Gil'-e-ad: Num. 26:29–34 · 2:21

15 And Ma'-chir took to wife *the sister* of Hup'-pim and Shup'-pim, whose sister's name *was* Ma'-a-chah;) and the name of the second *was* ^RZe-lo'-phe-had: and Ze-lo'-phe-had had daughters.   Num. 27:1

16 And Ma'-a-chah the wife of Ma'-chir bare a son, and she called his name Pe'-resh; and the name of his brother *was* She'-resh; and his sons *were* U'-lam and Ra'-kem.

17 And the sons of U'-lam; ^RBe'-dan. These *were* the sons of Gil'-e-ad, the son of Ma'-chir, the son of Ma-nas'-seh.   1 Sam. 12:11

18 And his sister Ham-mol'-e-keth bare I'-shod, and ^TA-bi-e'-zer, and Ma-ha'-lah.   *Jeezer,* Num. 26:30

19 And the sons of She-mi'-dah were, A-hi'-an, and She'-chem, and Lik'-hi, and A'-ni-am.

20 And the sons of E'-phra-im; Shu'-the-lah, and Be'-red his son, and Ta'-hath his son, and El'-a-dah his son, and Ta'-hath his son, **21** And Za'-bad his son, and Shu'-the-lah his son, and E'-zer, and E'-le-ad, whom the men of Gath *that were* born in *that* land slew, because they came down to take away their cattle. **22** And E'-phra-im their father mourned many days, and his brethren came to comfort him. **23** And when he went in to his wife, she conceived, and bare a son, and he called his name ᵀBe-ri'-ah, because it went evil with his house.   *Lit. In Tragedy* **24** (And his daughter *was* She'-rah, who built ᴿBeth–ho'-ron the nether, and the upper, and Uz'-zen–she'-rah.)   *Josh. 16:3, 5; 2 Chr. 8:5* **25** And Re'-phah *was* his son, also Re'-sheph, and Te'-lah his son, and Ta'-han his son, **26** La'-a-dan his son, Am-mi'-hud his son, E-lish'-a-ma his son, **27** ᵀNon his son, ᴿJe-hosh'-u-ah his son.   *Nun, Josh. 1:1 · Ex. 17:9; 24:13* **28** And their possessions and habitations *were*, Beth'–el and the towns thereof, and eastward Na'-a-ran, and westward Ge'-zer, with the towns thereof; She'-chem also and the towns thereof, unto Ga'-za and the towns thereof: **29** And by the borders of the children of ᴿMa-nas'-seh, Beth–she'-an and her towns, Ta'-a-nach and her towns, Me-gid'-do and her towns, Dor and her towns. In these dwelt the children of Joseph the son of Israel.   *Gen. 41:51; Josh. 17:7* **30** The sons of Asher; Im'-nah, and Is'-u-ah, and Ish'-u-ai, and Be-ri'-ah, and Se'-rah their sister. **31** And the sons of Be-ri'-ah; He'-ber, and Mal'-chi-el, who *is* the father of Bir'-za-vith. **32** And He'-ber begat Japh'-let, and Sho'-mer, and Ho'-tham, and Shu'-a their sister. **33** And the sons of Japh'-let; Pa'-sach, and Bim'-hal, and Ash'-vath. These *are* the children of Japh'-let.

34 And the sons of ᴿSha'-mer; A'-hi, and Roh'-gah, Je-hub'-bah, and A'-ram.   *v. 32* **35** And the sons of his brother He'-lem; Zo'-phah, and Im'-na, and She'-lesh, and A'-mal. **36** The sons of Zo'-phah; Su'-ah, and Har'-ne-pher, and Shu'-al, and Be'-ri, and Im'-rah, **37** Be'-zer, and Hod, and Sham'-ma, and Shil'-shah, and ᵀIth'-ran, and Be-e'-ra.   *Jether, v. 38* **38** And the sons of Je'-ther; Je-phun'-neh, and Pis'-pah, and A'-ra. **39** And the sons of Ul'-la; A'-rah, and Han'-i-el, and Re-zi'-a. **40** All these *were* the children of Asher, heads of *their* father's house, choice *and* mighty men of valour, chief of the princes. And the number throughout the genealogy of them that were apt to the war *and* to battle *was* twenty and six thousand men.

8 Now Benjamin begat ᴿBe'-la his firstborn, Ash'-bel the second, and A-har'-ah the third,   *7:6* **2** No'-hah the fourth, and Ra'-pha the fifth. **3** And the sons of Be'-la were, ᵀAd'-dar, and Ge'-ra, and A-bi'-hud,   *Ard, Num. 26:40* **4** And Ab-i-shu'-a, and Na'-a-man, and A-ho'-ah, **5** And Ge'-ra, and She-phu'-phan, and Hu'-ram. **6** And these *are* the sons of E'-hud: these are the heads of the fathers of the inhabitants of ᴿGe'-ba, and they removed them to ᴿMa-na'-hath: *6:60 · 2:52* **7** And Na'-a-man, and A-hi'-ah, and Ge'-ra, he removed them, and begat Uz'-za, and A-hi'-hud. **8** And Sha-ha-ra'-im begat *children* in the country of Moab, after he had sent them away; Hu'-shim and Ba'-a-ra *were* his wives. **9** And he begat of Ho'-desh his wife, Jo'-bab, and Zib'-i-a, and Me'-sha, and Mal'-cham, **10** And Je'-uz, and Sha-chi'-a, and Mir'-ma. These *were* his sons, heads of the fathers. **11** And of Hu'-shim he begat Ab'-i-tub, and El-pa'-al.

12 The sons of El-pa'-al; E'-ber, and Mi'-sham, and Sha'-med, who built O'-no, and Lod, with the towns thereof:

13 Be-ri'-ah also, and ᴿShe'-ma, who *were* heads of the fathers of the inhabitants of Ai'-ja-lon, who drove away the inhabitants of Gath: v. 21

14 And A-hi'-o, Sha'-shak, and Jer'-e-moth,

15 And Zeb-a-di'-ah, and A'-rad, and A'-der,

16 And Mi'-cha-el, and Is'-pah, and Jo'-ha, the sons of Be-ri'-ah;

17 And Zeb-a-di'-ah, and Me-shul'-lam, and Hez'-e-ki, and He'-ber,

18 Ish'-me-rai also, and Jez-li'-ah, and Jo'-bab, the sons of El-pa'-al;

19 And Ja'-kim, and Zich'-ri, and Zab'-di,

20 And El-i-e'-nai, and Zil'-thai, and E-li'-el,

21 And A-da'-iah, and Be-ra'-iah, and Shim'-rath, the sons of ᵀShim'-hi;   *Shema*, v. 13

22 And Ish'-pan, and He'-ber, and E-li'-el,

23 And Ab'-don, and Zich'-ri, and Ha'-nan,

24 And Han-a-ni'-ah, and E'-lam, and An-to-thi'-jah,

25 And Iph-e-de'-iah, and Pe-nu'-el, the sons of Sha'-shak;

26 And Sham'-she-rai, and She-ha-ri'-ah, and Ath-a-li'-ah,

27 And Jar-e-si'-ah, and E-li'-ah, and Zich'-ri, the sons of Jer'-o-ham.

28 These *were* heads of the fathers, by their generations, chief *men*. These dwelt in Jerusalem.

29 And at Gib'-e-on dwelt the father of Gib'-e-on; whose ᴿwife's name *was* Ma'-a-chah: 9:35–38

30 And his firstborn son Ab'-don, and Zur, and Kish, and Ba'-al, and Na'-dab,

31 And Ge'-dor, and A-hi'-o, and ᵀZa'-cher.   *Zechariah*, 9:37

32 And Mik'-loth begat ᵀShim'-e-ah. And these also dwelt with their brethren in Jerusalem, over against them.   *Shimeam*, 9:38

33 And Ner begat Kish, and Kish begat Saul, and Saul begat Jonathan, and Mal'-chi–shu'-a, and A-bin'-a-dab, and Esh–ba'-al.

34 And the son of Jonathan *was* Mer'-ib–ba'-al; and Mer'-ib–ba'-al begat ᴿMi'-cah.   2 Sam. 9:12

35 And the sons of Mi'-cah *were*, Pi'-thon, and Me'-lech, and ᵀTa-re'-a, and Ahaz.   *Tahrea*, 9:41

36 And Ahaz begat Je-ho'-a-dah; and Je-ho'-a-dah begat Al'-e-meth, and Az'-ma-veth, and Zim'-ri; and Zim'-ri begat Mo'-za,

37 And Mo'-za begat Bin'-e-a: Ra'-pha *was* his son, E-le'-a-sah his son, A'-zel his son:

38 And A'-zel had six sons, whose names *are* these, Az'-ri-kam, Boch'-e-ru, and Ish'-ma-el, and She-a-ri'-ah, and O-ba-di'-ah, and Ha'-nan. All these *were* the sons of A'-zel.

39 And the sons of E'-shek his brother *were*, U'-lam his first-born, Je'-hush the second, and E-liph'-e-let the third.

40 And the sons of U'-lam were mighty men of valour, archers, and had many sons, and sons' sons, an hundred and fifty. All these *are* of the sons of Benjamin.

9 So ᴿall Israel were reckoned by genealogies; and, behold, they *were* written in the book of the kings of Israel and Judah, *who* were carried away to Babylon for their transgression.   Ezra 2:59

2 ᴿNow the first inhabitants that *dwelt* in their possessions in their cities *were*, the Israelites, the priests, Levites, and ᴿthe Neth'-i-nims. Ezra 2:70; Neh. 7:73 · Ezra 2:43; 8:20

3 And in ᴿJerusalem dwelt the children of Judah, and of the children of Benjamin, and of the children of E'-phra-im, and Ma-nas'-seh;   Neh. 11:1, 2

4 U'-thai the son of Am-mi'-hud, the son of Om'-ri, the son of Im'-ri, the son of Ba'-ni, of the children of Pha'-rez the son of Judah.

5 And of the Shi'-lo-nites; A-sa'-iah the firstborn, and his sons.

6 And of the sons of Ze'-rah;

Jeu'-el, and their brethren, six hundred and ninety.

7 And of the sons of Benjamin; Sal'-lu the son of Me-shul'-lam, the son of Hod-a-vi'-ah, the son of Has-e-nu'-ah;

8 And Ib-ne'-iah the son of Jer'-o-ham, and E'-lah the son of Uz'-zi, the son of Mich'-ri, and Me-shul'-lam the son of Sheph-a-thi'-ah, the son of Reu'-el, the son of Ib-ni'-jah;

9 And their brethren, according to their generations, nine hundred and fifty and six. All these men were chief of the fathers in the house of their fathers.

10 ᴿAnd of the priests; Je-da'-iah, and Je-hoi'-a-rib, and Ja'-chin,   Neh. 11:10-14

11 And Az-a-ri'-ah the son of Hil-ki'-ah, the son of Me-shul'-lam, the son of Za'-dok, the son of Me-ra'-ioth, the son of A-hi'-tub, the ruler of the house of God;

12 And A-da'-iah the son of Jer'-o-ham, the son of Pash'-ur, the son of Mal-chi'-jah, and Ma-as'-i-ai the son of A'-di-el, the son of Jah'-ze-rah, the son of Me-shul'-lam, the son of Me-shil'-le-mith, the son of Im'-mer;

13 And their brethren, heads of the house of their fathers, a thousand and seven hundred and threescore; ᵀvery able men for the work of the service of the house of God.   Lit. mighty men of strength

14 And of the Levites; She-ma'-iah the son of Has'-shub, the son of Az'-ri-kam, the son of Hash-a-bi'-ah, of the sons of Me-ra'-ri;

15 And Bak-bak'-kar, He'-resh, and Ga'-lal, and Mat-ta-ni'-ah the son of Mi'-cah, the son of ᴿZich'-ri, the son of A'-saph;   Neh. 11:17

16 And O-ba-di'-ah the son of She-ma'-iah, the son of Ga'-lal, the son of Je-du'-thun, and Ber-e-chi'-ah the son of A'-sa, the son of El'-ka-nah, that dwelt in the villages of the Ne-toph'-a-thites.

17 And the porters were, Shal'-lum, and Ak'-kub, and Tal'-mon, and A-hi'-man, and their brethren: Shal'-lum was the chief;

18 Who hitherto waited in the king's gate eastward: they were porters in the companies of the children of Levi.

19 And Shal'-lum the son of Ko'-re, the son of E-bi'-a-saph, the son of Ko'-rah, and his brethren, of the house of his father, the Ko'-rah-ites, were over the work of the service, keepers of the gates of the tabernacle: and their fathers, being over the host of the LORD, were keepers of the entry.

20 And ᴿPhin'-e-has the son of E-le-a'-zar was the ruler over them in time past, and the LORD was with him.   Num. 25:6-13; 31:6

21 And ᴿZech-a-ri'-ah the son of Me-shel-e-mi'-ah was ᵀporter of the door of the tabernacle of the congregation.   26:2, 14 · gatekeeper

22 All these which were chosen to be porters in the gates were two hundred and twelve. ᴿThese were reckoned by their genealogy in their villages, whom David and Samuel ᴿthe seer did ordain in their set office.   26:1, 2 · 1 Sam. 9:9

23 So they and their children had the oversight of the gates of the house of the LORD, namely, the house of the tabernacle, by wards.

24 In four quarters were the ᵀporters, toward the east, west, north, and south.   gatekeepers

25 And their brethren, which were in their villages, were to come ᴿafter seven days from time to time with them.   2 Kin. 11:4-7

26 For these Levites, the four chief ᵀporters, were in their ᵀset office, and were over the chambers and treasuries of the house of God.   gatekeepers · trusted

27 And they lodged round about the house of God, because the ᴿcharge was upon them, and the opening thereof every morning pertained to them.   23:30-32

28 And certain of them had the charge of the ministering vessels, that they should bring them in and out ᵀby tale.   by count

29 Some of them also were appointed to oversee the vessels, and all the instruments of the

sanctuary, and the ᴿfine flour, and the wine, and the oil, and the frankincense, and the spices. 23:29

30 And *some* of the sons of the priests made ᴿthe ointment of the spices. Ex. 30:22–25

31 And Mat-ti-thi′-ah, *one* of the Levites, who *was* the firstborn of Shal′-lum the Ko′-rah-ite, had the set office ᴿover the things that were made in the pans. Lev. 2:5; 6:21

32 And *other* of their brethren, of the sons of the Ko′-hath-ites, ᴿ*were* over the shewbread, to prepare *it* every sabbath. Lev. 24:5–8

33 And these *are* ᴿthe singers, chief of the fathers of the Levites, *who remaining* in the chambers *were* free: for they were employed in *that* work day and night. 6:31

34 These chief fathers of the Levites *were* chief throughout their generations; these dwelt at Jerusalem.

35 And in Gib′-e-on dwelt the father of Gib′-e-on, Je-hi′-el, whose wife′s name *was* ᴿMa′-a-chah: 8:29–32

36 And his firstborn son Ab′-don, then Zur, and Kish, and Ba′-al, and Ner, and Na′-dab,

37 And Ge′-dor, and A-hi′-o, and Zech-a-ri′-ah, and Mik′-loth.

38 And Mik′-loth begat Shim′-e-am. And they also dwelt with their brethren at Jerusalem, over against their brethren.

39 And Ner begat Kish; and Kish begat Saul; and Saul begat Jonathan, and Mal′-chi–shu′-a, and A-bin′-a-dab, and Esh–ba′-al.

40 And the son of Jonathan *was* Mer′-ib–ba′-al: and Mer′-ib–ba′-al begat Mi′-cah.

41 And the sons of Mi′-cah *were,* Pi′-thon, and Me′-lech, and Tah-re′-a, ᴿ*and Ahaz.* 8:35

42 And Ahaz begat ᵀJa′-rah; and Ja′-rah begat Al′-e-meth, and Az′-ma-veth, and Zim′-ri; and Zim′-ri begat Mo′-za; *Jehoadah,* 8:36

43 And Mo′-za begat Bin′-e-a; and Re-pha′-iah his son, E-le′-a-sah his son, A′-zel his son.

44 And A′-zel had six sons, whose names *are* these, Az′-ri-kam, Boch′-e-ru, and Ish′-ma-el, and She-a-ri′-ah, and O-ba-di′-ah, and Ha′-nan: these *were* the sons of A′-zel.

10 Now ᴿthe Phi-lis′-tines fought against Israel; and the men of Israel fled from before the Phi-lis′-tines, and fell down slain in mount Gil-bo′-a. 1 Sam. 31:1

2 And the Phi-lis′-tines followed hard after Saul, and after his sons; and the Phi-lis′-tines slew Jonathan, and ᵀA-bin′-a-dab, and Mal′-chi–shu′-a, the sons of Saul. *Ishui,* 1 Sam. 14:49

3 And the battle ᵀwent sore against Saul, and the archers hit him, and he was wounded of the archers. *became intense against*

4 Then said Saul to his armourbearer, Draw thy sword, and thrust me through therewith; lest these uncircumcised come and abuse me. But his armourbearer would not; for he was ᵀsore afraid. So Saul took a sword, and fell upon it. *greatly*

5 And when his armourbearer saw that Saul was dead, he fell likewise on the sword, and died.

6 So Saul died, and his three sons, and all his house died together.

7 And when all the men of Israel that *were* in the valley saw that they fled, and that Saul and his sons were dead, then they forsook their cities, and fled: and the Phi-lis′-tines came and dwelt in them.

8 And it came to pass on the morrow, when the Phi-lis′-tines came to ᵀstrip the slain, that they found Saul and his sons fallen in mount Gil-bo′-a. *plunder*

9 And when they had stripped him, they took his head, and his armour, and sent into the land of the Phi-lis′-tines round about, to carry tidings unto their idols, and to the people.

10 ᴿAnd they put his armour in the house of their gods, and fastened his head in the temple of Da′-gon. 1 Sam. 31:10

11 And when all Ja′-besh–gil′-e-

ad heard all that the Phi-lis'-tines had done to Saul,

12 They arose, all the ᴿvaliant men, and took away the body of Saul, and the bodies of his sons, and brought them to ᴿJa'-besh, and buried their bones under the oak in Ja'-besh, and fasted seven days.   1 Sam. 14:52 · 2 Sam. 21:12

13 So Saul died for his transgression which he committed against the LORD, *even* against the word of the LORD, which he kept not, and also for asking *counsel* of *one that had* a familiar spirit, ᴿto enquire *of it;*   [Lev. 19:31]; 1 Sam. 28:7

14 And enquired not of the LORD: therefore he slew him, and ᴿturned the kingdom unto David the son of Jesse.   1 Sam. 15:28

11 Then ᴿall Israel gathered themselves to David unto He'-bron, saying, Behold, we *are* thy bone and thy flesh.   2 Sam. 5:1

2 And moreover in time past, even when Saul was king, thou *wast* he that leddest out and broughtest in Israel: and the LORD thy ᴿGod said unto thee, Thou shalt ᴿfeed my people Israel, and thou shalt be ruler over my people Israel.   Ps. 78:70-72 · 2 Sam. 7:7

3 Therefore came all the elders of Israel to the king to He'-bron; and David made a covenant with them in He'-bron before the LORD; and ᴿthey anointed David king over Israel, according to the word of the LORD by Samuel.   2 Sam. 5:3

4 And David and all Israel went to Jerusalem, which *is* Je'-bus; where the Jeb'-u-sites *were,* the inhabitants of the land.

5 And the inhabitants of Je'-bus said to David, Thou shalt not come hither. Nevertheless David took the castle of Zion, which *is* the city of David.

6 And David said, Whosoever ᵀsmiteth the Jeb'-u-sites first shall be chief and captain. So Jo'-ab the son of Ze-ru'-iah went first up, and ᵀwas chief.   *attacks · became*

7 And David dwelt in the ᵀcastle; therefore they called it the city of David.   *strong hold*

8 And he built the city round about, even from Mil'-lo round about: and Jo'-ab ᵀrepaired the rest of the city.   Lit. *revived*

9 So David ᴿwaxed greater and greater: for the LORD of hosts *was* with ᴿhim.   2 Sam. 3:1 · 1 Sam. 16:18

10 These also *are* the chief of the mighty men whom David had, who strengthened themselves with him in his kingdom, *and* with all Israel, to make him king, according to ᴿthe word of the LORD concerning Israel.   1 Sam. 16:1, 12

11 And this *is* the number of the mighty men whom David had; ᴿJa-sho'-be-am, an Hach'-mo-nite, the chief of the captains: he lifted up his spear against three hundred slain *by him* at one time. 27:2

12 And after him *was* E-le-a'-zar the son of ᴿDodo, the A-ho'-hite, who *was one* of the three mighties.   27:4

13 He was with David at Pas-dam'-mim, and there the Phi-lis'-tines were gathered together to battle, where was a ᵀparcel of ground full of barley; and the people fled from before the Phi-lis'-tines.   *piece* or *plot*

14 And they ᵀset themselves in the midst of *that* parcel, and delivered it, and slew the Phi-lis'-tines; and the LORD saved *them* by a great deliverance.   *stationed*

15 Now three of the thirty captains went down to the rock to David, into the cave of A-dul'-lam; and the host of the Phi-lis'-tines encamped ᴿin the valley of ᵀReph'-a-im.   14:9 · Lit. *Giants*

16 And David *was* then in the hold, and the Phi-lis'-tines' garrison *was* then at Beth'-le-hem.

17 And David longed, and said, Oh that one would give me drink of the water of the well of Beth'-le-hem, that *is* at the gate!

18 And the three brake through the host of the Phi-lis'-tines, and drew water out of the well of Beth'-le-hem, that *was* by the gate, and took *it,* and brought *it* to David: but David would not drink of it, but poured it out to the LORD,

19 And said, My God forbid it me, that I should do this thing: shall I drink the blood of these men that have put their lives in jeopardy? for with *the jeopardy of* their lives they brought it. Therefore he would not drink it. These things did these three mightiest.

20 ᴿAnd A-bi'-shai the brother of Jo'-ab, he was chief of the three: for lifting up his spear against three hundred, he slew *them,* and had a name among the three.   18:12; 2 Sam. 23:18

21 Of the three, he was more honourable than the two; for he was their captain: howbeit he attained not to the *first* three.

22 Be-na'-iah the son of Je-hoi'-a-da, the son of a valiant man of Kab'-ze-el, who had done many acts; he slew two lionlike men of Moab: also he went down and slew a lion in a pit in a snowy day.

23 And he slew an Egyptian, a man of *great* stature, five cubits high; and in the Egyptian's hand *was* a spear like a weaver's beam; and he went down to him with a staff, and plucked the spear out of the Egyptian's hand, and slew him with his own spear.

24 These *things* did Be-na'-iah the son of Je-hoi'-a-da, and had the name among the three mighties.

25 Behold, he ᵀwas honourable among the thirty, but attained not to the *first* three: and David set him over his guard.   *was honoured*

26 Also the valiant men of the armies *were,* ᴿA'-sa-hel the brother of Jo'-ab, El-ha'-nan the son of Dodo of Beth'–le-hem,   2 Sam. 23:24

27 Sham'-moth the Ha'-ro-rite, ᴿHe'-lez the Pel'-o-nite,   2 Sam. 23:26

28 ᴿI'-ra the son of Ik'-kesh the Te-ko'-ite, ᴿA'-bi-e'-zer the An'-toth-ite,   27:9 · 27:12

29 Sib'-be-cai the Hu'-shath-ite, I'-lai the A-ho'-hite,

30 ᴿMa'-ha-rai the Ne-toph'-a-thite, He'-led the son of Ba'-a-nah the Ne-toph'-a-thite,   27:13

31 I'-thai the son of Ri'-bai of Gib'-e-ah, *that pertained* to the children of Benjamin, ᴿBe-na'-iah the Pir'-a-thon-ite,   27:14

32 Hu'-rai of the brooks of Ga'-ash, A-bi'-el the Ar'-bath-ite,

33 Az'-ma-veth the Ba-ha'-rum-ite, E-li'-ah-ba the Sha-al'-bo-nite,

34 The sons of Ha'-shem the Gi'-zo-nite, Jonathan the son of Sha'-ge the Ha'-ra-rite,

35 A-hi'-am the son of Sa'-car the Ha'-ra-rite, El'-i-phal the son of Ur,

36 He'-pher the Mech'-e-rath-ite, A-hi'-jah the Pel'-o-nite,

37 Hez'-ro the Car'-mel-ite, Na'-a-rai the son of Ez'-bai,

38 Jo'-el the brother of Nathan, Mib'-har the son of Hag'-ge-ri,

39 Ze'-lek the Am'-mon-ite, Na'-ha-rai the Be'-roth-ite, the armourbearer of Jo'-ab the son of Ze-ru'-iah,

40 I'-ra the Ith'-rite, Ga'-reb the Ith'-rite,

41 ᴿU-ri'-ah the Hit'-tite, Za'-bad the son of Ah'-lai,   2 Sam. 11

42 Ad'-i-na the son of Shi'-za the Reu'-ben-ite, a captain of the Reu'-ben-ites, and thirty with him,

43 Ha'-nan the son of Ma'-a-chah, and Josh'-a-phat the Mith'-nite,

44 Uz-zi'-a the Ash'-te-rath-ite, Sha'-ma and Je-hi'-el the sons of Ho'-than the Ar'-o-er-ite,

45 Je-di'-a-el the ᵀson of Shim'-ri, and Jo'-ha his brother, the Ti'-zite,   *Or Shimrite*

46 E-li'-el the Ma'-ha-vite, and Jer'-i-bai, and Josh-a-vi'-ah, the sons of El'-na-am, and Ith'-mah the Mo'-ab-ite,

47 E-li'-el, and O'-bed, and Ja'-si-el the Me-so'-ba-ite.

12 Now ᴿthese *are* they that came to David to Zik'-lag, while he yet kept himself close because of Saul the son of Kish: and they *were* among the mighty men, helpers of the war. 1 Sam. 27:2

2 *They were* armed with bows, and could use both the right hand and ᴿthe left in *hurling* stones and *shooting* arrows out of a bow, *even* of Saul's brethren of Benjamin.   Judg. 3:15; 20:16

3 The chief *was* A-hi-e'-zer, then Jo'-ash, the sons of ^TShe-ma'-ah the Gib'-e-ath-ite; and Je'-zi-el, and Pe'-let, the sons of Az'-ma-veth; and Ber'-a-chah, and Je'-hu the An'-toth-ite,   Or Hasmaah

4 And Is-ma'-iah the Gib'-e-on-ite, a mighty man among the thir-ty, and over the thirty; and Jer-e-mi'-ah, and Ja-ha'-zi-el, and Jo-ha'-nan, and Jos'-a-bad the Ged'-e-rath-ite,

5 E-lu'-zai, and Jer'-i-moth, and Be-a-li'-ah, and Shem-a-ri'-ah, and Sheph-a-ti'-ah the Har'-u-phite,

6 El'-ka-nah, and Je-si'-ah, and A-zar'-e-el, and Jo-e'-zer, and Ja-sho'-be-am, the Kor'-hites,

7 And Jo-e'-lah, and Zeb-a-di'-ah, the sons of Jer'-o-ham of Ge'-dor.

8 And of the Gad'-ites there separated themselves unto David into the hold to the wilderness men of might, *and* men of war *fit* for the battle, that could handle shield and buckler, whose faces *were like* the faces of lions, and *were* ^Ras swift as the ^Troes upon the mountains;   2 Sam. 2:18 · *gazelles*

9 E'-zer the first, O-ba-di'-ah the second, E-li'-ab the third,

10 Mish-man'-nah the fourth, Jer-e-mi'-ah the fifth,

11 At'-tai the sixth, E-li'-el the seventh,

12 Jo-ha'-nan the eighth, El'-za-bad the ninth,

13 Jer-e-mi'-ah the tenth, Mach'-ba-nai the eleventh.

14 These *were* of the sons of Gad, captains of the host: one of the least *was* over an hundred, and the greatest over a thousand.

15 These *are* they that went over Jordan in the first month, when it had overflown all his ^Rbanks; and they put to flight all *them* of the valleys, *both* toward the east, and toward the west.   Josh. 3:15; 4:18, 19

16 And there came of the chil-dren of Benjamin and Judah to the ^Thold unto David.   *strong hold*

17 And David went out to meet them, and answered and said unto them, If ye be come peaceably unto me to help me, mine heart shall be knit unto you: but if *ye be come* to betray me to mine ene-mies, seeing *there is* no wrong in mine hands, the God of our fa-thers look *thereon*, and rebuke *it*.

18 Then the spirit came upon Am'-a-sai, *who was* chief of the captains, *and he said*, Thine *are* we, David, and on thy side, thou son of Jesse: peace, peace *be* un-to thee, and peace *be* to thine helpers; for thy God helpeth thee. Then David received them, and made them captains of the band.

19 And there fell *some* of Ma-nas'-seh to David, ^Rwhen he came with the Phi-lis'-tines against Saul to battle: but they helped them not: for the lords of the Phi-lis'-tines upon advisement sent him away, saying, ^RHe will fall to his master Saul to *the jeopardy of* our heads.   1 Sam. 29:2 · 1 Sam. 29:4

20 As he went to Zik'-lag, there fell to him of Ma-nas'-seh, Ad'-nah, and Joz'-a-bad, and Je-di'-a-el, and Mi'-cha-el, and Joz'-a-bad, and E-li'-hu, and Zil'-thai, cap-tains of the thousands that *were* of Ma-nas'-seh.

21 And they helped David against ^Rthe band *of the rovers*: for they *were* all mighty men of valour, and were captains in the host.   1 Sam. 30:1, 9, 10

22 For at *that* time day by day there came to David to help him, until *it was* a great host, ^Rlike the host of God.   Gen. 32:2; Josh. 5:13–15

23 And these *are* the numbers of the bands *that were* ready armed to the war, *and* ^Rcame to David to He'-bron, to turn the kingdom of Saul to him, according to the word of the LORD.   2 Sam. 2:1–4

24 The children of Judah that bare shield and spear *were* six thousand and eight hundred, ^Tready armed to the war.   *equipped*

25 Of the children of Simeon, mighty men of valour for the war, seven thousand and one hundred.

26 Of the children of Levi four thousand and six hundred.

27 And Je-hoi'-a-da *was* the leader of the Aaronites, and with him *were* three thousand and seven hundred;

28 And ᴿZa'-dok, a young man mighty of valour, and of his father's house twenty and two captains.   6:8, 53; 2 Sam. 8:17

29 And of the children of Benjamin, the kindred of Saul, three thousand: for hitherto ᴿthe greatest part of them had kept the ward of the house of Saul.   2 Sam. 2:8, 9

30 And of the children of E'-phra-im twenty thousand and eight hundred, mighty men of valour, famous throughout the house of their fathers.

31 And of the half tribe of Ma-nas'-seh eighteen thousand, which were expressed by name, to come and make David king.

32 And of the children of Is'-sa-char, ᴿ*which were men* that had understanding of the times, to know what Israel ought to do; the heads of them *were* two hundred; and all their brethren *were* at their commandment.   Esth. 1:13

33 Of Zeb'-u-lun, such as went forth to battle, expert in war, with all instruments of war, fifty thousand, which could keep rank: *they were* not of ᴿdouble heart. Ps. 12:2

34 And of Naph'-ta-li a thousand captains, and with them with shield and spear thirty and seven thousand.

35 And of the Danites expert in war twenty and eight thousand and six hundred.

36 And of Asher, such as went forth to battle, expert in war, forty thousand.

37 And on the other side of Jordan, of the Reu'-ben-ites, and the Gad'-ites, and of the half tribe of Ma-nas'-seh, with all manner of instruments of war for the battle, an hundred and twenty thousand.

38 All these men of war, that could keep rank, came with a ᵀperfect heart to He'-bron, to make David king over all Israel: and all the rest also of Israel were of ᴿone ᵀheart to make David king.   loyal · 2 Chr. 30:12 · mind

39 And there they were with David three days, eating and drinking: for their brethren had prepared for them.

40 Moreover they that were nigh them, *even* unto Is'-sa-char and Zeb'-u-lun and Naph'-ta-li, brought bread on asses, and on camels, and on mules, and on oxen, *and* meat, meal, cakes of figs, and bunches of raisins, and wine, and oil, and oxen, and sheep abundantly: for *there was* joy in Israel.

13 And David consulted with the ᴿcaptains of thousands and hundreds, *and* with every leader.   11:15; 12:34

2 And David said unto all the congregation of Israel, If *it seem* good unto you, and *that it be* of the LORD our God, let us send abroad unto our brethren every where, *that are* ᴿleft in all the land of Israel, and with them *also* to the priests and Levites *which are* in their cities *and* suburbs, that they may gather themselves unto us: 1 Sam. 31:1; Is. 37:4

3 And let us bring again the ark of our God to us: ᴿfor we enquired not at it in the days of Saul.   1 Sam. 7:1, 2

4 And all the congregation said that they would do so: for the thing was right in the eyes of all the people.

5 So ᴿDavid gathered all Israel together, from Shi'-hor of Egypt even unto the entering of He'-math, to bring the ark of God from Kir'-jath–je'-a-rim. 1 Sam. 7:5

6 And David went up, and all Israel, to Ba'-al-ah, *that is*, to Kir'-jath–je'-a-rim, which *belonged* to Judah, to bring up thence the ark of God the LORD, ᴿthat dwelleth *between* the cher'-u-bims, whose name is called *on it*.   Ex. 25:22

7 And they carried the ark of God in a new cart out of the house of A-bin'-a-dab: and Uz'-za and A-hi'-o drave the cart.

8 ᴿAnd David and all Israel

played before God with all *their* might, and with singing, and with harps, and with psalteries, and with timbrels, and with cymbals, and with trumpets. 　2 Sam. 6:5

9 And when they came unto the threshingfloor of Chi'-don, Uz'-za put forth his hand to hold the ark; for the oxen stumbled.

10 And the anger of the LORD was kindled against Uz'-za, and he smote him, ᴿbecause he put his hand to the ark: and there he ᴿdied before God. 15:13, 15 · Lev. 10:2

11 And David was displeased, because the LORD had made a breach upon Uz'-za: wherefore that place is called ᵀPe'-rez–uz'-za to this day. 　Lit. *Outbreak of Uzza*

12 And David was afraid of God that day, saying, How shall I bring the ark of God *home* to me?

13 So David ᵀbrought not the ark *home* to himself to the city of David, but carried it aside into the house of O'-bed–e'-dom the Git'-tite. 　*would not move*

14 ᴿAnd the ark of God remained with the family of O'-bed–e'-dom in his house three months. And the LORD blessed ᴿthe house of O'-bed–e'-dom, and all that he had. 　2 Sam. 6:11 · 26:4–8; [Gen. 30:27]

14 Now ᴿHiram king of Tyre sent messengers to David, and timber of cedars, with masons and carpenters, to build him an house. 　2 Sam. 5:11; 1 Kin. 5:1

2 And David perceived that the LORD had confirmed him king over Israel, for his kingdom was ᴿlifted up on high, because of his people Israel. 　Num. 24:7

3 And David took more wives at Jerusalem: and David begat more sons and daughters.

4 Now these *are* the names of *his* children which he had in Jerusalem; Sham-mu'-a, and Sho'-bab, Nathan, and Solomon,

5 And Ib'-har, and El-i-shu'-a, and El'-pa-let,

6 And No'-gah, and Ne'-pheg, and Ja-phi'-a,

7 And E-lish'-a-ma, and Be-e-li'-a-da, and E-liph'-a-let.

8 And when the Phi-lis'-tines heard that ᴿDavid was anointed king over all Israel, all the Phi-lis'-tines went up to seek David. And David heard *of it*, and went out against them. 　2 Sam. 5:17–21

9 And the Phi-lis'-tines came and ᵀspread themselves in the valley of Reph'-a-im. 　*made a raid*

10 And David enquired of God, saying, Shall I go up against the Phi-lis'-tines? and wilt thou deliver them into mine hand? And the LORD said unto him, Go up; for I will deliver them into thine hand.

11 So they came up to Ba'-al–per'-a-zim; and David smote them there. Then David said, God hath broken in upon mine enemies by mine hand like ᵀthe breaking forth of waters: therefore they called the name of that place Ba'-al–per'-a-zim. 　*breaking through*

12 And when they had left their gods there, David gave a commandment, and they were burned with fire.

13 ᴿAnd the Phi-lis'-tines yet again spread themselves abroad in the valley. 　2 Sam. 5:22–25

14 Therefore David enquired again of God; and God said unto him, Go not up after them; turn away from them, ᴿand come upon them ᵀover against the mulberry trees. 　2 Sam. 5:23 · *in front of the*

15 And it shall be, when thou shalt hear a sound of going in the tops of the mulberry trees, *that* then thou shalt go out to battle: for God is gone forth before thee to ᵀsmite the host of the Phi-lis'-tines. 　*strike*

16 David therefore did as God commanded him: and they ᵀsmote the host of the Phi-lis'-tines from Gib'-e-on even to Ga'-zer. 　*defeated*

17 And ᴿthe fame of David went out into all lands; and the LORD ᴿbrought the fear of him upon all nations. 　2 Chr. 26:8 · 2 Chr. 20:29

15 And *David* made him houses in the city of David, and prepared a place for the ark of God, and pitched for it a tent.

2 Then David said, None ought

to carry the ark of God but the Levites: for them hath the Lord chosen to carry the ark of God, and to minister unto him for ever.

3 And David ᴿgathered all Israel together to Jerusalem, to bring up the ark of the Lord unto his place, which he had prepared for it. Ex. 40:20, 21; 2 Sam. 6:12; 1 Kin. 8:1

4 And David assembled the children of Aaron, and the Levites:

5 Of the sons of Ko'-hath; U-ri'-el the chief, and his ᵀbrethren an hundred and twenty: kinsmen

6 Of the sons of Me-ra'-ri; A-sa'-iah the chief, and his brethren two hundred and twenty:

7 Of the sons of Ger'-shom; Jo'-el the chief, and his brethren an hundred and thirty:

8 Of the sons of ᴿE-liz'-a-phan; She-ma'-iah the chief, and his brethren two hundred: Ex. 6:22

9 Of the sons of ᴿHe'-bron; E-li'-el the chief, and his brethren fourscore: Ex. 6:18

10 Of the sons of Uz-zi'-el; Am-min'-a-dab the chief, and his brethren an hundred and twelve.

11 And David called for Za'-dok and A-bi'-a-thar the priests, and for the Levites, for U-ri'-el, A-sa'-iah, and Jo'-el, She-ma'-iah, and E-li'-el, and Am-min'-a-dab,

12 And said unto them, Ye are the chief of the fathers of the Levites: ᵀsanctify yourselves, both ye and your brethren, that ye may bring up the ark of the Lord God of Israel unto the place that I have prepared for it.   consecrate

13 For ᴿbecause ye did it not at the first, ᴿthe Lord our God made a breach upon us, for that we sought him not after the due order.   2 Sam. 6:3 · 13:7–11

14 So the priests and the Levites sanctified themselves to bring up the ark of the Lord God of Israel.

15 And the children of the Levites bare the ark of God upon their shoulders with the staves thereon, as ᴿMoses commanded according to the word of the Lord.   Ex. 25:14; Num. 4:15; 7:9

16 And David spake to the chief of the Levites to appoint their brethren to be the singers with instruments of musick, psalteries and harps and cymbals, sounding, by lifting up the voice with joy.

17 ᴿSo the Levites appointed He'-man the son of Jo'-el; and of his brethren, A'-saph the son of Ber-e-chi'-ah; and of the sons of Me-ra'-ri their brethren, E'-than the son of Kush-a'-iah;   6:33, 39, 44

18 And with them their brethren of the second degree, Zech-a-ri'-ah, Ben, and Ja-a'-zi-el, and She-mir'-a-moth, and Je-hi'-el, and Un'-ni, E-li'-ab, and Be-na'-iah, and Ma-a-se'-iah, and Mat-ti-thi'-ah, and E-liph'-e-leh, and Mik-ne'-iah, and O'-bed-e'-dom, and Je-i'-el, the porters.

19 So the singers, He'-man, A'-saph, and E'-than, were appointed to sound with cymbals of brass;

20 And Zech-a-ri'-ah, and A'-zi-el, and She-mir'-a-moth, and Je-hi'-el, and Un'-ni, and E-li'-ab, and Ma-a-se'-iah, and Be-na'-iah, with psalteries on ᴿAl'-a-moth; Ps. 46:title

21 And Mat-ti-thi'-ah, and E-liph'-e-leh, and Mik-ne'-iah, and O'-bed-e'-dom, and Je-i'-el, and Az-a-zi'-ah, with harps on the ᴿShem'-i-nith to excel.   Ps. 6:title

22 And Chen-a-ni'-ah, chief of the Levites, was for song: he instructed about the song, because he was skilful.

23 And Ber-e-chi'-ah and El'-ka-nah were doorkeepers for the ark.

24 And Sheb-a-ni'-ah, and Je-hosh'-a-phat, and Ne-than'-e-el, and Am'-a-sai, and Zech-a-ri'-ah, and Be-na'-iah, and E-li-e'-zer, the priests, did blow with the trumpets before the ark of God: and O'-bed-e'-dom and Je-hi'-ah were doorkeepers for the ark.

25 So ᴿDavid, and the elders of Israel, and the captains over thousands, went to bring up the ark of the covenant of the Lord out of the house of O'-bed-e'-dom with joy.   2 Sam. 6:12, 13; 1 Kin. 8:1

26 And it came to pass, when

God helped the Levites that bare the ark of the covenant of the LORD, that they offered seven bullocks and seven rams.

27 And David *was* clothed with a robe of fine [R]linen, and all the Levites that bare the ark, and the singers, and Chen-a-ni'-ah the master of the song with the singers: David also *had* upon him an e'-phod of linen.   1 Sam. 2:18, 28

28 [R]Thus all Israel brought up the ark of the covenant of the LORD with shouting, and with sound of the cornet, and with trumpets, and with cymbals, making a noise with psalteries and harps.   Josh. 6:20; Zech. 4:7; 1 Thess. 4:16

29 And it came to pass, *as* the ark of the covenant of the LORD came to the city of David, that Mi'-chal the daughter of Saul looking out at a window saw king David dancing and playing: and she despised him in her heart.

16 So [R]they brought the ark of God, and set it in the midst of the tent that David had pitched for it: and they offered burnt sacrifices and peace offerings before God.   15:1; 2 Sam. 6:17

2 And when David had [T]made an end of offering the burnt offerings and the peace offerings, [R]he blessed the people in the name of the LORD.   *finished* · 1 Kin. 8:14

3 And he [T]dealt to every one of Israel, both man and woman, to every one a loaf of bread, and a good piece of flesh, and a [T]flagon of *wine.*   *distributed* · Or *cake of raisins*

4 And he appointed *certain* of the Levites to minister before the ark of the LORD, and to [R]record, and to thank and praise the LORD God of Israel: Ps. 38:title; 70:title

5 A'-saph the chief, and next to him Zech-a-ri'-ah, [R]Je-i'-el, and She-mir'-a-moth, and Je-hi'-el, and Mat-ti-thi'-ah, and E-li'-ab, and Be-na'-iah, and O'-bed-e'-dom: and Je-i'-el with psalteries and with harps; but A'-saph made a sound with cymbals;   15:18

6 Be-na'-iah also and Ja-ha'-zi-el the priests with trumpets con-tinually before the ark of the covenant of God.

7 Then on that day [R]David delivered first *this psalm* to thank the LORD into the hand of A'-saph and his brethren.   2 Sam. 22:1; 23:1

8 [R]Give thanks unto the LORD, call upon his name, make known his deeds among the people.   17:19

9 Sing unto him, sing psalms unto him, talk ye of all his wondrous works.

10 Glory ye in his holy name: let the heart of them rejoice that seek the LORD.

11 Seek the LORD and his strength, seek his face continually.

12 Remember his marvellous works that he hath done, his wonders, and the judgments of his mouth;

13 O ye seed of Israel his servant, ye children of Jacob, his chosen ones.

14 He *is* the LORD our God; his judgments *are* in all the earth.

15 Be ye mindful always of his covenant; the word *which* he commanded to a thousand generations;

16 *Even of the* [R]*covenant* which he made with Abraham, and of his oath unto Isaac;   Gen. 17:2; 26:3

17 And hath confirmed the same to Jacob for a law, *and* to Israel *for* an everlasting covenant,

18 Saying, Unto thee will I give the land of Canaan, the [T]lot of your inheritance;   *allotment*

19 When ye were but few, [R]even a few, and strangers in it.   Deut. 7:7

20 And *when* they went from nation to nation, and from *one* kingdom to another people;

21 He suffered no man to do them wrong: yea, he [R]reproved kings for their sakes, Gen. 12:17; 20:3

22 *Saying,* [R]Touch not mine anointed, and do my prophets no harm.   Gen. 20:7; Ps. 105:15

23 [R]Sing unto the LORD, all the earth; shew forth from day to day his salvation.   Ps. 96:1–13

24 Declare his glory among the heathen; his marvellous works among all nations.

25 For great *is* the LORD, and greatly to be praised: he also *is* to be feared above all gods.

26 For all the gods ^Rof the people *are* idols: but the LORD made the heavens.   Lev. 19:4; [1 Cor. 8:5, 6]

27 Glory and honour *are* in his presence; strength and gladness *are* in his place.

28 Give unto the LORD, ye kindreds of the people, give unto the LORD glory and strength.

29 Give unto the LORD the glory *due* unto his name: bring an offering, and come before him: worship the LORD in the beauty of holiness.

30 ^TFear before him, all the earth: the world also shall be stable, that it be not moved.   *Tremble*

31 Let the heavens be glad, and let the earth rejoice: and let *men* say among the nations, The LORD reigneth.

32 Let the sea roar, and the fulness thereof: let the fields rejoice, and all that *is* therein.

33 Then shall the trees of the wood sing out at the presence of the LORD, because he ^Rcometh to judge the earth.   [Matt. 25:31–46]

34 ^RO give thanks unto the LORD; for *he is* good; for his mercy *endureth* for ever.   Ezra 3:11; Ps. 106:1

35 ^RAnd say ye, Save us, O God of our salvation, and gather us together, and deliver us from the heathen, that we may give thanks to thy holy name, *and* ^Tglory in thy praise.   Ps. 106:47, 48 · *triumph*

36 ^RBlessed *be* the LORD God of Israel for ever and ever. And all ^Rthe people said, A'-men, and praised the LORD.   Ps. 72:18 · Neh. 8:6

37 So he left there before the ark of the covenant of the LORD A'-saph and his brethren, to minister before the ark continually, as every day's work required:

38 And ^RO'-bed–e'-dom with their brethren, threescore and eight; O'-bed–e'-dom also the son of Je-du'-thun and Ho'-sah *to be* porters: 13:14

39 And Za'-dok the priest, and his brethren the priests, before the tabernacle of the LORD in the high place that *was* at Gib'-e-on,

40 To offer burnt offerings unto the LORD upon the altar of the burnt offering continually ^Rmorning and evening, and *to do* according to all that is written in the law of the LORD, which he commanded Israel;   [Ex. 29:38–42]

41 And with them He'-man and Je-du'-thun, and the rest that were chosen, who were expressed by name, to give thanks to the LORD, ^Rbecause his mercy *endureth* for ever;   2 Chr. 5:13; 7:3; Ezra 3:11; Jer. 33:11

42 And with them He'-man and Je-du'-thun with trumpets and cymbals for those that should make a sound, and with musical instruments of God. And the sons of Je-du'-thun *were* porters.

43 And all the people departed every man to his house: and David returned to bless his house.

17 Now it came to pass, as David sat in his house, that David said to Nathan the prophet, Lo, I dwell in an house of cedars, but the ark of the covenant of the LORD *remaineth* under curtains.

2 Then Nathan said unto David, Do all that *is* in thine heart; for God *is* with thee.

3 And it came to pass the same night, that the word of God came to Nathan, saying,

4 Go and tell David my servant, Thus saith the LORD, Thou shalt ^Rnot build me an house to dwell in: [28:2, 3]

5 For I have not dwelt in an house since the day that I brought up Israel unto this day; but have gone from tent to tent, and from one tabernacle *to another.*

6 Wheresoever I have walked with all Israel, spake I a word to any of the judges of Israel, whom I commanded to feed my people, saying, Why have ye not built me an house of cedars?

7 Now therefore thus shalt thou say unto my servant David, Thus saith the LORD of hosts, I took thee ^Rfrom the sheepcote, *even* from following the sheep,

that thou shouldest be ruler over my people Israel: 1 Sam. 16:11–13

8 And I have been with thee whithersoever thou hast walked, and have ᵀcut off all thine enemies from before thee, and have ᵀmade thee a name like the name of the great men that *are* in the earth.   *destroyed · given you prestige*

9 Also I will ordain a place for my people Israel, and will ᴿplant them, and they shall dwell in their place, and shall be moved no more; neither shall the children of wickedness waste them any more, as at the beginning,   Amos 9:14

10 And since the time that I commanded judges *to be* over my people Israel. Moreover I will subdue all thine enemies. Furthermore I tell thee that the LORD will build thee an house.

11 And it shall come to pass, when thy days be expired that thou must go *to be* with thy fathers, that I will raise up thy ᴿseed after thee, which shall be of thy sons; and I will establish his kingdom.   1 Kin. 5:5; Matt. 1:6; Luke 3:31

12 ᴿHe shall build me an house, and I will stablish his throne for ever.   1 Kin. 6:38; 2 Chr. 6:2; [Ps. 89:20–37]

13 ᴿI will be his father, and he shall be my son: and I will not take my mercy away from him, as I took *it* from *him* that was before thee: Matt. 3:17; 2 Cor. 6:18; Heb. 1:5

☆ 14 But ᴿI will settle him in mine house and in my kingdom for ever: and his throne shall be established for evermore. Ps. 89:3, 4

15 According to all these words, and according to all this vision, so did Nathan speak unto David.

16 ᴿAnd David the king came and sat before the LORD, and said, Who *am* I, O LORD God, and what *is* mine house, that thou hast brought me hitherto?   2 Sam. 7:18

17 And *yet* this was a small thing in thine eyes, O God; for thou hast *also* spoken of thy servant's house for a great while to come, and hast regarded me according to the estate of a man of high degree, O LORD God.

18 What can David *speak* more to thee for the honour of thy servant? for thou knowest thy servant.

19 O LORD, for thy servant's sake, and according to thine own heart, hast thou done all this greatness, in making known all *these* great things.

20 O LORD, *there is* none like thee, neither *is there any* God beside thee, according to all that we have heard with our ears.

21 And what one nation in the earth *is* like thy people Israel, whom God went to redeem *to be* his own people, to make thee a name of greatness and terribleness, by driving out nations from before thy people, whom thou hast redeemed out of Egypt?

22 For thy people Israel didst thou make thine own people for ever; and thou, LORD, becamest their God.

23 Therefore now, LORD, let the thing that thou hast spoken concerning thy servant and concerning his house be established for ever, and do as thou hast said.

24 Let it even be established, that thy name may be magnified for ever, saying, The LORD of hosts *is* the God of Israel, *even* a God to Israel: and *let* the house of David thy servant *be* established before thee.

25 For thou, O my God, hast told thy servant that thou wilt build him an house: therefore thy servant hath found *in his heart* to pray before thee.

26 And now, LORD, ᵀthou art God, and hast promised this goodness unto thy servant: *you alone are*

27 Now therefore ᵀlet it please thee to bless the house of thy servant, that it may be before thee for ever: for thou blessest, O LORD, and *it shall be* blessed for ever.   *you have been pleased to*

18 Now after this it came to pass, that David smote the Phi-lis'-tines, and subdued them, and took Gath and her towns out of the hand of the Phi-lis'-tines.

2 And he smote Moab; and the

Mo'-ab-ites became David's [R]servants, *and* brought gifts.   Ps. 60:8

3   And David smote [T]Had-ar-e'-zer king of Zo'-bah unto Ha'-math, as he went to stablish his dominion by the river Eu-phra'-tes.   *Hadadezer,* 2 Sam. 8:3

4   And David took from him a thousand chariots, and seven thousand horsemen, and twenty thousand footmen: David also [T]houghed all the chariot *horses,* but reserved of them an hundred chariots.   *hamstrung, crippled*

5   And when the [R]Syrians of Damascus came to help Had-ar-e'-zer king of Zo'-bah, David slew of the Syrians two and twenty thousand men.   2 Sam. 8:5, 6; 1 Kin. 11:23-25

6   Then David put *garrisons* in Syria–damascus; and the Syrians became David's servants, *and* brought gifts. Thus the LORD preserved David [T]whithersoever he went.   *wherever*

7   And David took the shields of gold that were on the servants of Had-ar-e'-zer, and brought them to Jerusalem.

8   Likewise from Tib'-hath, and from Chun, cities of Had-ar-e'-zer, brought David very much [R]brass, wherewith Solomon made the brasen sea, and the pillars, and the vessels of brass.   2 Sam. 8:8

9   Now when [T]To'-u king of Ha'-math heard how David had smitten all the host of Had-ar-e'-zer king of Zo'-bah;   *Toi,* 2 Sam. 8:9

10   He sent [T]Ha-do'-ram his son to king David, to enquire of his welfare, and to congratulate him, because he had fought against Had-ar-e'-zer, and smitten him; (for Had-ar-e'-zer had war with To'-u;) and *with him* all manner of [R]vessels of gold and silver and brass.   *Joram,* 2 Sam. 8:10 · 2 Sam. 8:10–12

11   Them also king David dedicated unto the LORD, with the silver and the gold that he brought from all *these* nations; from E'-dom, and from Moab, and from the [R]children of Ammon, and from the [R]Phi-lis'-tines, and from Am'-a-lek.   2 Sam. 10:12 · 2 Sam. 5:17–25

12   Moreover, [R]A-bi'-shai the son of Ze-ru'-iah slew of the E'-dom-ites in the valley of salt [R]eighteen thousand.   2 Sam. 23:18 · 2 Sam. 8:13

13   [R]And he put garrisons in E'-dom; and all the E'-dom-ites became David's servants. Thus the LORD preserved David whithersoever he went.   2 Sam. 8:14

14   So David reigned over all Israel, and executed judgment and justice among all his people.

15   And Jo'-ab the son of Ze-ru'-iah *was* over the host; and Je-hosh'-a-phat the son of A-hi'-lud, recorder.

16   And Za'-dok the son of A-hi'-tub, and A-bim'-e-lech the son of A-bi'-a-thar, *were* the priests; and Shav'-sha was scribe;

17   [R]And Be-na'-iah the son of Je-hoi'-a-da *was* over the Cher'-e-thites and the Pel'-e-thites; and the sons of David *were* chief about the king.   2 Sam. 8:18

19 Now it came to pass after this, that Na'-hash the king of the children of Ammon died, and his son reigned in his stead.

2   And David said, I will shew kindness unto Ha'-nun the son of Na'-hash, because his father shewed kindness to me. And David sent messengers to comfort him concerning his father. So the servants of David came into the land of the children of Ammon to Ha'-nun, to comfort him.

3   But the princes of the children of Ammon said to Ha'-nun, Thinkest thou that David doth honour thy father, that he hath sent comforters unto thee? are not his servants come unto thee for to search, and to overthrow, and to spy out the land?

4   Wherefore Ha'-nun took David's servants, and shaved them, and cut off their garments in the midst hard by their [R]buttocks, and sent them away.   Is. 20:4

5   Then there went *certain,* and told David how the men were served. And he sent to meet them: for the men were greatly ashamed. And the king said, Tarry

at Jericho until your beards be grown, and *then* return.

6 And when the children of Ammon saw that they had made themselves ᵀodious to David, Ha′-nun and the children of Ammon sent a thousand talents of silver to hire them chariots and horsemen out of Mes-o-po-ta′-mi-a, and out of Syr′-i-a–ma′-a-chah, ᴿand out of Zo′-bah.   *repulsive · 18:5, 9*

7 So they hired thirty and two thousand chariots, and the king of Ma′-a-chah and his people; who came and ᵀpitched before Med′-e-ba. And the children of Ammon gathered themselves together from their cities, and came to battle.   *encamped*

8 And when David heard *of it*, he sent Jo′-ab, and all the host of the mighty men.

9 And the children of Ammon came out, and put the battle in array before the gate of the city: and the kings that were come *were* by themselves in the field.

10 Now when Jo′-ab saw that the battle was set against him before and behind, he chose out of all the choice of Israel, and put *them* in array against the Syrians.

11 And the rest of the people he delivered unto the hand of A-bi′-shai his brother, and they set *themselves* in array against the children of Ammon.

12 And he said, If the Syrians be too strong for me, then thou shalt help me: but if the children of Ammon be too strong for thee, then I will help thee.

13 Be of good courage, and let us behave ourselves valiantly for our people, and for the cities of our God: and let the LORD do *that which is* good in his sight.

14 So Jo′-ab and the people that *were* with him drew nigh before the Syrians unto the battle; and they fled before him.

15 And when the children of Ammon saw that the Syrians were fled, they likewise fled before A-bi′-shai his brother, and

entered into the city. Then Jo′-ab came to Jerusalem.

16 And when the Syrians saw that they ᵀwere put to the worse before Israel, they sent messengers, and drew forth the Syrians that *were* beyond the river: and Sho′-phach the captain of the host of Had-ar-e′-zer *went* before them.   *had been defeated by*

17 And it was told David; and he gathered all Israel, and passed over Jordan, and came upon them, and set *the battle* in array against them. So when David had put the battle in array against the Syrians, they fought with him.

18 But the Syrians fled before Israel; and David slew of the Syrians seven thousand *men which fought in* chariots, and forty thousand footmen, and killed Sho′-phach the captain of the host.

19 And when the servants of Had-ar-e′-zer saw that they were put to the worse before Israel, they made peace with David, and became his servants: neither would the Syrians help the children of Ammon any more.

20 And it came to pass, that after the year was expired, at the time that kings go out *to battle*, Jo′-ab led forth the power of the army, and wasted the country of the children of Ammon, and came and besieged Rab′-bah. But ᴿDavid tarried at Jerusalem. And Jo′-ab smote Rab′-bah, and destroyed it.   *2 Sam. 11:2—12:25*

2 And David ᴿtook the crown of their king from off his head, and found it to weigh a talent of gold, and *there were* precious stones in it; and it was set upon David's head: and he brought also exceeding much ᵀspoil out of the city.   *2 Sam. 12:30, 31 · plunder*

3 And he brought out the people that *were* in it, and ᵀcut *them* with saws, and with harrows of iron, and with axes. Even so dealt David with all the cities of the children of Ammon. And David and all the people returned to Jerusalem.   *put them to work with*

4 And it came to pass after this, ^Rthat there arose war at Ge′-zer with the Phi-lis′-tines; at which time ^RSib′-be-chai the Hu′-shath-ite slew Sip′-pai, *that was* of the children of the giant: and they were subdued.   2 Sam. 21:18 · 11:29

5 And there was war again with the Phi-lis′-tines; and El-ha′-nan the son of Ja′-ir slew Lah′-mi the brother of Go-li′-ath the Git′-tite, whose spear staff *was* like a weaver's ^Rbeam.   11:23; 1 Sam. 17:7

6 And yet again there was war at Gath, where was a man of *great* stature, whose fingers and toes *were* four and twenty, six *on each hand,* and six *on each foot:* and he also was the son of the giant.

7 But when he defied Israel, Jonathan the son of Shim′-e-a David's brother slew him.

8 These were born unto the giant in Gath; and they fell by the hand of David, and by the hand of his servants.

21 And Satan stood up against Israel, and provoked David to number Israel.

2 And David said to Jo′-ab and to the rulers of the people, Go, number Israel from Be′-er-she′-ba even to Dan; ^Rand bring the number of them to me, that I may know *it.*   27:23, 24

3 And Jo′-ab answered, The Lord make his people an hundred times so many more as they *be:* but, my lord the king, *are* they not all my lord's servants? why then doth my lord require this thing? why will he be a cause of ^Ttrespass to Israel?   *guilt*

4 Nevertheless the king's word prevailed against Jo′-ab. Wherefore Jo′-ab departed, and went throughout all Israel, and came to Jerusalem.

5 And Jo′-ab gave the sum of the number of the people unto David. And all *they of* Israel were a thousand thousand and an hundred thousand men that drew sword: and Judah *was* four hundred threescore and ten thousand men that drew sword.

6 ^RBut Levi and Benjamin counted he not among them: for the king's ^Tword was abominable to Jo′-ab.   27:24 · *command*

7 And God was displeased with this thing; therefore he ^Tsmote Israel.   *struck*

8 And David said unto God, I have sinned greatly, because I have done this thing: ^Rbut now, I beseech thee, do away the iniquity of thy servant; for I have done very foolishly.   2 Sam. 12:13

9 And the Lord spake unto Gad, David's ^Rseer, saying,   29:29

10 Go and tell David, saying, Thus saith the Lord, I offer thee three *things:* choose thee one of them, that I may do *it* unto thee.

11 So Gad came to David, and said unto him, Thus saith the Lord, Choose thee

12 ^REither three years' famine; or three months to be destroyed before thy foes, while that the sword of thine enemies overtaketh *thee;* or else three days the sword of the Lord, even the pestilence, in the land, and the angel of the Lord destroying throughout all the ^Tcoasts of Israel. Now therefore advise thyself what word I shall bring again to him that sent me.   2 Sam. 24:13 · *territory*

13 And David said unto Gad, I am in a great strait: let me fall now into the hand of the Lord; for very great *are* his mercies: but let me not fall into the hand of man.

14 So the Lord sent ^Rpestilence upon Israel: and there fell of Israel seventy thousand men.   27:24

15 And God sent an angel unto Jerusalem to destroy it: and as he was destroying, the Lord beheld, and ^Rhe repented him of the evil, and said to the angel that destroyed, It is enough, stay now thine hand. And the angel of the Lord stood by the threshingfloor of Or′-nan the Jeb′-u-site.   Gen. 6:6

16 And David lifted up his eyes, and saw the angel of the Lord stand between the earth and the heaven, having a drawn sword in his hand stretched out over

Jerusalem. Then David and the elders *of Israel, who were* clothed in sackcloth, fell upon their faces.

17 And David said unto God, *Is it* not I *that* commanded the people to be numbered? even I it is that have sinned and done evil indeed; but *as for* these ^Rsheep, what have they done? let thine hand, I pray thee, O LORD my God, be on me, and on my father's house; but not on thy people, that they should be plagued.   Ps. 74:1

18 Then the ^Rangel of the LORD commanded Gad to say to David, that David should go up, and set up an altar unto the LORD in the threshingfloor of Or'-nan the Jeb'-u-site.   vv. 11, 12; 2 Chr. 3:1

19 And David went up at the saying of Gad, which he spake in the name of the LORD.

20 And Or'-nan turned back, and saw the angel; and his four sons with him hid themselves. Now Or'-nan was threshing wheat.

21 And as David came to Or'-nan, Or'-nan looked and saw David, and went out of the threshingfloor, and bowed himself to David with *his* face to the ground.

22 Then David said to Or'-nan, Grant me the place of *this* threshingfloor, that I may build an altar therein unto the LORD: thou shalt grant it me for the full price: that the plague may be ^Tstayed from the people.   *withdrawn*

23 And Or'-nan said unto David, Take *it* to thee, and let my lord the king do *that which is* good in his eyes: lo, I give *thee* the oxen *also* for burnt offerings, and the threshing instruments for wood, and the wheat for the ^Tmeat offering; I give it all.   *meal or grain*

24 And king David said to Or'-nan, Nay; but I will verily buy it for the full price: for I will not take *that* which *is* thine for the LORD, nor offer burnt offerings without cost.

25 So ^RDavid gave to Or'-nan for the place six hundred shek'-els of gold by weight.   2 Sam. 24:24

26 And David built there an altar unto the LORD, and offered burnt offerings and peace offerings, and called upon the LORD; and ^Rhe answered him from heaven by fire upon the altar of burnt offering.   1 Kin. 18:36–38; 2 Chr. 3:1; 7:1

27 And the LORD commanded the angel; and he put up his sword again into the sheath thereof.

28 At that time when David saw that the LORD had answered him in the threshingfloor of Or'-nan the Jeb'-u-site, then he sacrificed there.

29 ^RFor the tabernacle of the LORD, which Moses made in the wilderness, and the altar of the burnt offering, *were* at that season in the high place at ^RGib'-e-on.   1 Kin. 3:4; 2 Chr. 1:3 · 16:39

30 But David could not go before it to enquire of God: for he was afraid because of the sword of the angel of the LORD.

22 Then David said, ^RThis *is* the house of the LORD God, and this *is* the altar of the burnt offering for Israel.   21:18, 19; 2 Chr. 3:1

2 And David commanded to gather together the strangers that *were* in the land of Israel; and he set masons to hew wrought stones to build the house of God.

3 And David prepared iron in abundance for the nails for the doors of the gates, and for the joinings; and brass in abundance ^Rwithout weight;   1 Kin. 7:47

4 Also cedar trees in abundance: for the ^RZi-do'-ni-ans and they of Tyre brought much cedar wood to David.   1 Kin. 5:6–10

5 And David said, ^RSolomon my son *is* young and tender, and the house *that is* to be builded for the LORD *must be* exceeding magnifical, of fame and of glory throughout all countries: I will *therefore* now make preparation for it. So David prepared abundantly before his death.   1 Kin. 3:7

6 Then he called for Solomon his son, and ^Tcharged him to build an house for the LORD God of Israel.   *commanded*

7 And David said to Solomon, My son, as for me, ᴿit was in my mind to build an house unto the name of the LORD my God: 17:1

8 But the word of the LORD came to me, saying, Thou hast shed blood abundantly, and hast made great wars: thou shalt not build an house unto my name, because thou hast shed much blood upon the earth in my sight.

9 ᴿBehold, a son shall be born to thee, who shall be a man of rest; and I will give him rest from all his enemies round about: for his name shall be ᵀSolomon, and I will give peace and quietness unto Israel in his days.   28:5 · Lit. *Peaceful*

☆ 10 ᴿHe shall build an house for my name; and he shall be my son, and I *will be* his father; and I will establish the throne of his kingdom over Israel for ever.   17:12, 13

11 Now, my son, ᴿthe LORD be with thee; and prosper thou, and build the house of the LORD thy God, as he hath said of thee.   v. 16

12 Only the LORD give thee wisdom and understanding, and give thee charge concerning Israel, that thou mayest keep the law of the LORD thy God.

13 ᴿThen shalt thou prosper, if thou takest heed to fulfil the statutes and judgments which the LORD charged Moses with concerning Israel: be strong, and of good courage; dread not, nor be dismayed.   28:7; [Josh. 1:7, 8]

14 Now, behold, in my trouble I have prepared for the house of the LORD an hundred thousand talents of gold, and a thousand thousand talents of silver; and of brass and iron ᴿwithout weight; for it is in abundance: timber also and stone have I prepared; and thou mayest add thereto.   v. 3

15 Moreover *there are* workmen with thee in abundance, hewers and workers of stone and timber, and all manner of cunning men for every manner of work.

16 Of the gold, the silver, and the brass, and the iron, *there is* no number. Arise *therefore,* and be doing, and the LORD be with thee.

17 David also commanded all the ᴿprinces of Israel to help Solomon his son, *saying,*   28:1–6

18 *Is* not the LORD your God with you? ᴿand hath he *not* given you rest on every side? for he hath given the inhabitants of the land into mine hand; and the land is subdued before the LORD, and before his people.   2 Sam. 7:1

19 Now set your heart and your soul to seek the LORD your God; arise therefore, and build ye the sanctuary of the LORD God, to bring the ark of the covenant of the LORD, and the holy vessels of God, into the house that is to be built to the name of the LORD.

23 So when David was old and full of days, he made ᴿSolomon his son king over Israel.   28:4, 5; 1 Kin. 1:33–40

2 And he gathered together all the princes of Israel, with the priests and the Levites.

3 Now the Levites were numbered from the age of thirty years and upward: and their number by their polls, man by man, was thirty and eight thousand.

4 Of which, twenty and four thousand *were* ᵀto ᴿset forward the work of the house of the LORD; and six thousand *were* officers and judges: *to look after* · 2 Chr. 2:2, 18

5 Moreover four thousand *were* ᵀporters; and four thousand praised the LORD with the instruments which I made, *said David,* to praise *therewith.*   *gatekeepers*

6 And David divided them into ᵀcourses among the sons of Levi, *namely,* Ger'-shon, Ko'-hath, and Me-ra'-ri.   *divisions* or *groups*

7 Of the ᴿGer'-shon-ites *were,* La'-a-dan, and Shim'-e-i.   26:21

8 The sons of La'-a-dan; the chief *was* Je-hi'-el, and Ze'-tham, and Jo'-el, three.

9 The sons of Shim'-e-i; Shel'-o-mith, and Ha'-zi-el, and Ha'-ran, three. These *were* the chief of the fathers of La'-a-dan.

10 And the sons of Shim'-e-i

were, Ja'-hath, Zi'-na, and Je'-ush, and Be-ri'-ah. These four *were* the sons of Shim'-e-i.

11 And Ja'-hath was the chief, and Zi'-zah the second: but Je'-ush and Be-ri'-ah had not many sons; therefore they were ^Tin one reckoning, according to *their* father's house. *assigned as one father's*

12 ^RThe sons of Ko'-hath; Am'-ram, Iz'-har, He'-bron, and Uz-zi'-el, four. Ex. 6:18

13 The sons of Am'-ram; Aaron and Moses: and Aaron was separated, that he should sanctify the most holy things, he and his sons for ever, to burn incense before the LORD, to minister unto him, and to bless in his name for ever.

14 Now *concerning* Moses the man of God, ^Rhis sons were named of the tribe of Levi. 26:20-24

15 ^RThe sons of Moses *were,* Ger'-shom, and E-li-e'-zer. Ex. 18:3

16 Of the sons of Ger'-shom, ^RSheb'-u-el *was* the chief. 26:24

17 And the ^Tsons of E-li-e'-zer *were,* ^RRe-ha-bi'-ah the chief. And E-li-e'-zer had none other sons; but the sons of Re-ha-bi'-ah were very many. *son of Eliezer was* · 26:25

18 Of the sons of Iz'-har; ^RShel'-o-mith the chief. 24:22

19 ^ROf the sons of He'-bron; Je-ri'-ah the first, Am-a-ri'-ah the second, Ja-ha'-zi-el the third, and Jek-a-me'-am the fourth. 24:23

20 Of the sons of Uz-zi'-el; Mi'-cah the first, and Je-si'-ah the second.

21 ^RThe sons of Me-ra'-ri; Mah'-li, and Mu'-shi. The sons of Mah'-li; E-le-a'-zar, and Kish. 24:26

22 And E-le-a'-zar died, and ^Rhad no sons, but daughters: and their ^Tbrethren the sons of Kish ^Rtook them. 24:28 · *kinsmen* · Num. 36:6

23 The sons of Mu'-shi; Mah'-li, and E'-der, and Jer'-e-moth, three.

24 These *were* the sons of Levi after the house of their fathers; *even* the chief of the fathers, as they were counted by number of names ^Tby their polls, that did the work for the service of the house

of the LORD, from the age of twenty years and upward. *individually*

25 For David said, The LORD God of Israel ^Rhath given rest unto his people, that they may dwell in Jerusalem for ever: 22:18

26 And also unto the Levites; they shall no *more* ^Rcarry the tabernacle, nor any vessels of it for the service thereof. Num. 4:5, 15

27 For by the last words of David the Levites *were* numbered from twenty years old and above:

28 Because their office *was* to wait on the sons of Aaron for the service of the house of the LORD, in the courts, and in the chambers, and in the purifying of all holy things, and the work of the service of the house of God;

29 Both for the shewbread, and for the fine flour for ^Tmeat offering, and for the unleavened cakes, and for *that which is baked in* the pan, and for that which is fried, and for all manner of measure and size; *meal or grain*

30 And to stand every morning to thank and praise the LORD, and likewise at ^Teven; *evening*

31 And to offer all burnt sacrifices unto the LORD ^Rin the sabbaths, in the new moons, and on the ^Rset feasts, by number, according to the order commanded unto them, continually before the LORD: Num. 10:10 · Lev. 23:2-4

32 And that they should ^Rkeep the ^Rcharge of the tabernacle of the congregation, and the charge of the holy *place,* and the charge of the sons of Aaron their brethren, in the service of the house of the LORD. 2 Chr. 13:10, 11 · 9:27

24 Now *these are* the divisions of the sons of Aaron. ^RThe sons of Aaron; Na'-dab, and A-bi'-hu, E-le-a'-zar, and Ith'-a-mar. 6:3; Lev. 10:1-6; Num. 26:60, 61

2 But ^RNa'-dab and A-bi'-hu died before their father, and had no children: therefore E-le-a'-zar and Ith'-a-mar executed the priest's office. Num. 3:1-4; 26:61

3 And David distributed them, both Za'-dok of the sons of E-le-

a'-zar, and ᴿA-him'-e-lech of the sons of Ith'-a-mar, according to their offices in their service. 18:16

4 And there were more chief men found of the sons of E-le-a'-zar than of the sons of Ith'-a-mar; and *thus* were they divided. Among the sons of E-le-a'-zar *there were* sixteen chief men of the house of *their* fathers, and eight among the sons of Ith'-a-mar according to the house of their fathers.

5 Thus were they divided by lot, one sort with another; for the governors of the sanctuary, and governors *of the house* of God, were of the sons of E-le-a'-zar, and of the sons of Ith'-a-mar.

6 And She-ma'-iah the son of Ne-than'-e-el the scribe, *one* of the Levites, wrote them before the king, and the princes, and Za'-dok the priest, and A-him'-e-lech the son of A-bi'-a-thar, and *before* the chief of the fathers of the priests and Levites: one principal household being taken for E-le-a'-zar, and *one* taken for Ith'-a-mar.

7 Now the first lot came forth to Je-hoi'-a-rib, the second to Je-da'-iah,

8 The third to Ha'-rim, the fourth to Se-o'-rim,

9 The fifth to Mal-chi'-jah, the sixth to Mij'-a-min,

10 The seventh to Hak'-koz, the eighth to ᴿA-bi'-jah,   Luke 1:5

11 The ninth to Jesh'-u-a, the tenth to Shec-a-ni'-ah,

12 The eleventh to E-li'-a-shib, the twelfth to Ja'-kim,

13 The thirteenth to Hup'-pah, the fourteenth to Je-sheb'-e-ab,

14 The fifteenth to Bil'-gah, the sixteenth to Im'-mer,

15 The seventeenth to He'-zir, the eighteenth to Aph'-ses,

16 The nineteenth to Peth-a-hi'-ah, the twentieth to Je-hez'-e-kel,

17 The one and twentieth to Ja'-chin, the two and twentieth to Ga'-mul,

18 The three and twentieth to De-la'-iah, the four and twentieth to Ma-a-zi'-ah.

19 These *were* the ᵀorderings of them in their service ᴿto come into the house of the Lᴏʀᴅ, according to their manner, under Aaron their father, as the Lᴏʀᴅ God of Israel had commanded him.   schedules · 9:25

20 And the rest of the sons of Levi *were these:* Of the sons of Am'-ram; Shu'-ba-el: of the sons of Shu'-ba-el; Jeh-de'-iah.

21 Concerning ᴿRe-ha-bi'-ah: of the sons of Re-ha-bi'-ah, the first *was* Is-shi'-ah.   23:17

22 Of the Iz'-har-ites; Shel'-o-moth: of the sons of Shel'-o-moth; Ja'-hath.

23 And the sons *of* ᴿHe'-bron; Je-ri'-ah *the first,* Am-a-ri'-ah the second, Ja-ha'-zi-el the third, Jek-a-me'-am the fourth.   23:19; 26:31

24 *Of* the sons of Uz-zi'-el; Mi'-chah: of the sons of Mi'-chah; Sha'-mir.

25 The brother of Mi'-chah *was* Is-shi'-ah: of the sons of Is-shi'-ah; Zech-a-ri'-ah.

26 ᴿThe sons of Me-ra'-ri *were* Mah'-li and Mu'-shi: the sons of Ja-a-zi'-ah; Be'-no.   23:21; Ex. 6:19

27 The sons of Me-ra'-ri by Ja-a-zi'-ah; Be'-no, and Sho'-ham, and Zac'-cur, and Ib'-ri.

28 Of Mah'-li *came* E-le-a'-zar, ᴿwho had no sons.   23:22

29 Concerning Kish: the son of Kish *was* Je-rah'-me-el.

30 ᴿThe sons also of Mu'-shi; Mah'-li, and E'-der, and Jer'-i-moth. These *were* the sons of the Levites after the house of their fathers.   23:23

31 These likewise cast lots over against their brethren the sons of Aaron in the presence of David the king, and Za'-dok, and A-him'-e-lech, and the chief of the fathers of the priests and Levites, even the principal fathers over against their younger brethren.

25 Moreover David and the captains of the host separated to the service of the sons of ᴿA'-saph, and of He'-man, and of Je-du'-thun, who should prophesy with harps, with psalteries, and with cymbals: and the number of the workmen according to their service was: 6:30, 33, 39, 44; 2 Chr. 5:12

2 Of the sons of A'-saph; Zac'-cur, and Joseph, and Neth-a-ni'-ah, and As-a-re'-lah, the sons of A'-saph under the hands of A'-saph, which prophesied according to the order of the king.

3 Of ᴿJe-du'-thun: the sons of Je-du'-thun; Ged-a-li'-ah, and Ze'-ri, and Je-sha'-iah, Hash-a-bi'-ah, and Mat-ti-thi'-ah, six, under the hands of their father Je-du'-thun, who prophesied with a harp, to give thanks and to praise the LORD.   16:41, 42

4 Of He'-man: the sons of He'-man; Buk-ki'-ah, Mat-ta-ni'-ah, Uzzi'-el, Sheb'-u-el, and Jer'-i-moth, Han-a-ni'-ah, Ha-na'-ni, E-li'-a-thah, Gid-dal'-ti, and Ro-mam'-ti-e'-zer, Josh-bek'-a-shah, Mal'-lo-thi, Ho'-thir, and Ma-ha'-zi-oth:

5 All these were the sons of He'-man the king's seer in the words of God, to lift up the horn. And God gave to He'-man fourteen sons and three daughters.

6 All these were under the hands of their father for song in the house of the LORD, with cymbals, psalteries, and ᴿharps, for the service of the house of God, ᴿaccording to the king's order to A'-saph, Je-du'-thun, and He'-man.   15:16 · 15:19

7 So the ᴿnumber of them, with their brethren that were instructed in the songs of the LORD, even all that were cunning, was two hundred fourscore and eight. 23:5

8 And they cast lots, ward against ward, as well the small as the great, ᴿthe teacher as the scholar.   2 Chr. 23:13

9 Now the first lot came forth for A'-saph to Joseph: the second to Ged-a-li'-ah, who with his brethren and sons were twelve:

10 The third to Zac'-cur, he, his sons, and his brethren, were twelve:

11 The fourth to ᵀIz'-ri, he, his sons, and his brethren, were twelve: Zeri, v. 3

12 The fifth to Neth-a-ni'-ah, he, his sons, and his brethren, were twelve:

13 The sixth to Buk-ki'-ah, he, his sons, and his brethren, were twelve:

14 The seventh to ᵀJe-shar'-e-lah, he, his sons, and his brethren, were twelve: Asarelah, v. 2

15 The eighth to Je-sha'-iah, he, his sons, and his brethren, were twelve:

16 The ninth to Mat-ta-ni'-ah, he, his sons, and his brethren, were twelve:

17 The tenth to Shim'-e-i, he, his sons, and his brethren, were twelve:

18 The eleventh to ᵀA-zar'-e-el, he, his sons, and his brethren, were twelve: Uzziel, v. 4

19 The twelfth to Hash-a-bi'-ah, he, his sons, and his brethren, were twelve:

20 The thirteenth to ᵀShu'-ba-el, he, his sons, and his brethren, were twelve: Shebuel, v. 4

21 The fourteenth to Mat-ti-thi'-ah, he, his sons, and his brethren, were twelve:

22 The fifteenth to ᵀJer'-e-moth, he, his sons, and his brethren, were twelve: Jerimoth, v. 4

23 The sixteenth to Han-a-ni'-ah, he, his sons, and his brethren, were twelve:

24 The seventeenth to Josh-bek'-a-shah, he, his sons, and his brethren, were twelve:

25 The eighteenth to Ha-na'-ni, he, his sons, and his brethren, were twelve:

26 The nineteenth to Mal'-lo-thi, he, his sons, and his brethren, were twelve:

27 The twentieth to E-li'-a-thah, he, his sons, and his brethren, were twelve:

28 The one and twentieth to Ho'-thir, he, his sons, and his brethren, were twelve:

29 The two and twentieth to Gid-dal'-ti, he, his sons, and his brethren, were twelve:

30 The three and twentieth to Ma-ha'-zi-oth, he, his sons, and his brethren, were twelve:

31 The four and twentieth to Ro-mam'-ti-e'-zer, *he,* his sons, and his brethren, *were* twelve.

26 Concerning the divisions of the ᵀporters: Of the Kor'-hites *was* Me-shel-e-mi'-ah the son of ᴿKo'-re, of the sons of A'-saph.   *gatekeepers* · Ps. 42:title

2 And the sons of Me-shel-e-mi'-ah *were,* ᴿZech-a-ri'-ah the firstborn, Je-di'-a-el the second, Zeb-a-di'-ah the third, Jath'-ni-el the fourth,   9:21

3 E'-lam the fifth, Je-ho-ha'-nan the sixth, E-li-o-e'-nai the seventh.

4 Moreover the sons of ᴿO'-bed-e'-dom *were,* She-ma'-iah the firstborn, Je-hoz'-a-bad the second, Jo'-ah the third, and Sa'-car the fourth, and Ne-than'-e-el the fifth,   15:18, 21

5 Am'-mi-el the sixth, Is'-sa-char the seventh, Pe-ul'-thai the eighth: for God blessed him.

6 Also unto She-ma'-iah his son were sons born, that ruled throughout the house of their father: for they *were* mighty men of valour.

7 The sons of She-ma'-iah; Oth'-ni, and Re'-pha-el, and O'-bed, El'-za-bad, whose brethren *were* strong men, E-li'-hu, and Sem-a-chi'-ah.

8 All these of the sons of O'-bed-e'-dom: they and their sons and their brethren, ᴿable men for strength for the service, *were* threescore and two of O'-bed-e'-dom.   9:13

9 And Me-shel-e-mi'-ah had sons and brethren, strong men, eighteen.

10 Also ᴿHo'-sah, of the children of Me-ra'-ri, had sons; Sim'-ri the chief, (for *though* he was not the firstborn, yet his father made him the chief;)   16:38

11 Hil-ki'-ah the second, Teb-a-li'-ah the third, Zech-a-ri'-ah the fourth: all the sons and brethren of Ho'-sah *were* thirteen.

12 Among these *were* the divisions of the ᵀporters, *even* among the chief men, *having* wards one

against another, to minister in the house of the LORD.   *gatekeepers*

13 And they ᴿcast lots, as well the small as the great, according to the house of their fathers, for every gate.   24:5, 31; 25:8

14 And the lot eastward fell to Shel-e-mi'-ah. Then for Zech-a-ri'-ah his son, a wise counsellor, they cast lots; and his lot came out northward.

15 To O'-bed-e'-dom southward; and to his sons ᵀthe house of A-sup'-pim.   Or *the storehouse*

16 To Shup'-pim and Ho'-sah *the lot came forth* westward, with the gate Shal'-le-cheth, by the causeway of the going ᴿup, ward against ward.   1 Kin. 10:5

17 Eastward *were* six Levites, northward four a day, southward four a day, and toward ᵀA-sup'-pim two *and* two.   Lit. *The Storehouse*

18 At Par'-bar westward, four at the ᵀcauseway, *and* two at Par'-bar.   *highway*

19 These *are* the divisions of the porters among the sons of Ko'-re, and among the sons of Me-ra'-ri.

20 And of the Levites, A-hi'-jah *was* ᴿover the treasures of the house of God, and over the treasures of the dedicated things.   9:26

21 As concerning the sons of La'-a-dan; the sons of the Ger'-shon-ite La'-a-dan, chief fathers, *even* of La'-a-dan the Ger'-shon-ite, *were* Je-hi'-e-li.

22 The sons of Je-hi'-e-li; Ze'-tham, and Jo'-el his brother, *which were* over the treasures of the house of the LORD.

23 Of the ᴿAm'-ram-ites, *and* the Iz'-har-ites, the He'-bron-ites, *and* the Uz-zi'-el-ites: Ex. 6:18; Num. 3:19

24 And ᴿSheb'-u-el the son of Ger'-shom, the son of Moses, *was* ruler of the treasures.   23:16

25 And his brethren by E-li-e'-zer; Re-ha-bi'-ah his son, and Je-sha'-iah his son, and Jo'-ram his son, and Zich'-ri his son, and ᴿShel'-o-mith his son.   23:18

26 Which Shel'-o-mith and his brethren *were* over all the treasures of the dedicated things,

Rwhich David the king, and the chief fathers, the captains over thousands and hundreds, and the captains of the host, had dedicated.   2 Sam. 8:11

27 Out of the spoils won in battles did they dedicate to maintain the house of the LORD.

28 And all that Samuel Rthe seer, and Saul the son of Kish, and Abner the son of Ner, and Jo'-ab the son of Ze-ru'-iah, had dedicated; and whosoever had dedicated any thing, it was under the hand of Shel'-o-mith, and of his brethren.   1 Sam. 9:9

29 Of the Iz'-har-ites, Chen-a-ni'-ah and his sons were for the Routward business over Israel, for Rofficers and judges. Neh. 11:16 · 23:4

30 And of the He'-bron-ites, RHash-a-bi'-ah and his brethren, men of valour, a thousand and seven hundred, were officers among them of Israel on this side Jordan westward in all the business of the LORD, and in the service of the king.   27:17

31 Among the He'-bron-ites was RJe-ri'-jah the chief, even among the He'-bron-ites, according to the generations of his fathers. In the fortieth year of the reign of David they were sought for, and there were found among them mighty men of valour Rat Ja'-zer of Gil'-e-ad.   23:19 · Josh. 21:39

32 And his brethren, men of valour, were two thousand and seven hundred chief fathers, whom king David made rulers over the Reu'-ben-ites, the Gad'-ites, and the half tribe of Ma-nas'-seh, for every matter pertaining to God, and Raffairs of the king. 2 Chr. 19:11

27 Now the children of Israel after their number, to wit, the chief fathers and captains of thousands and hundreds, and their officers that served the king in any matter of the Tcourses, which came in and went out month by month throughout all the months of the year, of every course were twenty and four thousand.   military divisions

2 Over the first Tcourse for the first month was RJa-sho'-be-am the son of Zab'-di-el: and in his course were twenty and four thousand.   division · 11:11

3 Of the children of Pe'-rez was the chief of all the captains of the host for the first month.

4 And over the course of the second month was Do'-dai an A-ho'-hite, and of his course was Mik'-loth also the ruler: in his course likewise were twenty and four thousand.

5 The third captain of the host for the third month was RBe-na'-iah the son of Je-hoi'-a-da, a chief priest: and in his course were twenty and four thousand.   18:17

6 This is that Be-na'-iah, who was Rmighty among the thirty, and above the thirty: and in his course was Am-miz'-a-bad his son.   2 Sam. 23:20–23

7 The fourth captain for the fourth month was RA'-sa-hel the brother of Jo'-ab, and Zeb-a-di'-ah his son after him: and in his Tcourse were twenty and four thousand. 11:26; 2 Sam. 23:24 · division

8 The fifth captain for the fifth month was Sham'-huth the Iz'-ra-hite: and in his course were twenty and four thousand.

9 The sixth captain for the sixth month was RI'-ra the son of Ik'-kesh the Te-ko'-ite: and in his course were twenty and four thousand.   11:28

10 The seventh captain for the seventh month was RHe'-lez the Pel'-o-nite, of the children of E'-phra-im: and in his course were twenty and four thousand. 11:27

11 The eighth captain for the eighth month was RSib'-be-cai the Hu'-shath-ite, of the Zar'-hites: and in his course were twenty and four thousand. 11:29; 20:4; 2 Sam. 21:18

12 The ninth captain for the ninth month was RA-bi-e'-zer the An'-e-toth-ite, of the Benjamites: and in his Tcourse were twenty and four thousand. 11:28 · division

13 The tenth captain for the tenth month was RMa'-ha-rai the

Ne-toph'-a-thite, of the Zar'-hites: and in his course *were* twenty and four thousand.   11:30; 2 Sam. 23:28

14 The eleventh *captain* for the eleventh month *was* Be-na'-iah the Pir'-a-thon-ite, of the children of E'-phra-im: and in his course *were* twenty and four thousand.

15 The twelfth *captain* for the twelfth month *was* Hel'-dai the Ne-toph'-a-thite, of Oth'-ni-el: and in his course *were* twenty and four thousand.

16 Furthermore over the tribes of Israel: the ruler of the Reu'-ben-ites *was* E-li-e'-zer the son of Zich'-ri: of the Simeonites, Sheph-a-ti'-ah the son of Ma'-a-chah:

17 Of the Levites, ᴿHash-a-bi'-ah the son of Kem'-u-el: of the Aaronites, Za'-dok: 26:30

18 Of Judah, E-li'-hu, *one* of the brethren of David: of Is'-sa-char, Om'-ri the son of Mi'-cha-el:

19 Of Zeb'-u-lun, Ish-ma'-iah the son of O-ba-di'-ah: of Naph'-ta-li, Jer'-i-moth the son of Az'-ri-el:

20 Of the children of E'-phra-im, Ho-she'-a the son of Az-a-zi'-ah: of the half tribe of Ma-nas'-seh, Jo'-el the son of Pe-da'-iah:

21 Of the half *tribe* of Ma-nas'-seh in Gil'-e-ad, Id'-do the son of Zech-a-ri'-ah: of Benjamin, Ja-a'-si-el the son of Abner:

22 Of Dan, A-zar'-e-el the son of Jer'-o-ham. These *were* the princes of the tribes of Israel.

23 But David took not the number of them from twenty years old and under: because the LORD had said he would increase Israel like to the stars of the heavens.

24 Jo'-ab the son of Ze-ru'-iah began ᵀto number, but he finished not, because there fell wrath for it against Israel; neither was the number put in the account of the chronicles of king David.   *a census*

25 And over the king's treasures *was* Az'-ma-veth the son of A'-di-el: and over the storehouses in the fields, in the cities, and in the villages, and in the castles, *was* Je-hon'-a-than the son of Uz-zi'-ah:

26 And over them that did the work of the field for tillage of the ground *was* Ez'-ri the son of Che'-lub:

27 And over the vineyards *was* Shim'-e-i the Ra'-math-ite: over the ᵀincrease of the vineyards for the wine cellars *was* Zab'-di the Shiph'-mite: *produce*

28 And over the olive trees and the sycomore trees that *were* in the low plains *was* Ba'-al–ha'-nan the Ged'-e-rite: and over the cellars of oil *was* Jo'-ash:

29 And over the herds that fed in Shar'-on *was* Shit'-rai the Shar'-on-ite: and over the herds *that were* in the valleys *was* Sha'-phat the son of Ad'-lai:

30 Over the camels also *was* O'-bil the Ish'-ma-el-ite: and over the asses *was* Jeh-de'-iah the Me-ron'-o-thite:

31 And over the flocks *was* Ja'-ziz the ᴿHa'-ger-ite. All these *were* the rulers of the ᵀsubstance which *was* king David's.   5:10 · *property*

32 Also ᵀJonathan David's uncle was a counsellor, a wise man, and a ᵀscribe: and Je-hi'-el the son of Hach'-mo-ni *was* with the king's sons: Or *Jehonathan · secretary*

33 And ᴿA-hith'-o-phel *was* the king's counsellor: and ᴿHu'-shai the Ar'-chite *was* the king's companion: 2 Sam. 15:12 · 2 Sam. 15:32–37

34 And after A-hith'-o-phel *was* Je-hoi'-a-da the son of Be-na'-iah, and A-bi'-a-thar: and the general of the king's army *was* Jo'-ab.

28 And David assembled all ᴿthe princes of Israel, the princes of the tribes, and ᴿthe captains of the companies that ministered to the king by course, and the captains over the thousands, and captains over the hundreds, and ᴿthe stewards over all the substance and possession of the king, and of his sons, with the officers, and with the mighty men, and with all the valiant men, unto Jerusalem.   27:16 · 27:1, 2 · 27:25

2 Then David the king stood up upon his feet, and said, Hear me, my brethren, and my people: *As for me*, I *had* in mine heart to

build an house of rest for the ark of the covenant of the LORD, and for the footstool of our God, and had made ready for the building:

3 But God said unto me, Thou shalt not build an house for my name, because thou *hast been* a man of war, and hast shed blood.

4 Howbeit the LORD God of Israel chose me before all the house of my father to be king over Israel for ever: for he hath chosen Judah *to be* the ruler; and of the house of Judah, the house of my father; and ᴿamong the sons of my father he liked me to make *me* king over all Israel: 1 Sam. 13:14; Acts 13:22

5 And of all my sons, (for the LORD hath given me many sons,) ᴿhe hath chosen Solomon my son to sit upon the throne of the kingdom of the LORD over Israel.   22:9

6 And he said unto me, ᴿSolomon thy son, he shall build my house and my courts: for I have chosen him *to be* my son, and I will be his father.   22:9, 10; 1 Kin. 6:38

7 Moreover I will establish his kingdom for ever, if he be constant to do my commandments and my judgments, as at this day.

8 Now therefore, in the sight of all Israel the congregation of the LORD, and in the audience of our God, keep and seek for all the commandments of the LORD your God: that ye may possess this good land, and leave *it* for an inheritance for your children after you for ever.

9 And thou, Solomon my son, know thou the God of thy father, and serve him with a perfect heart and with a willing mind: for ᴿthe LORD searcheth all hearts, and understandeth all the imaginations of the thoughts: if thou seek him, he will be found of thee; but if thou forsake him, he will cast thee off for ever.   Jer. 20:12; Rev. 2:23

10 Take heed now; ᴿfor the LORD hath chosen thee to build an house for the sanctuary: be strong, and do *it*.   v. 6; 22:13

11 Then David gave to Solomon his son ᴿthe pattern of the porch, and of the houses thereof, and of the treasuries thereof, and of the upper chambers thereof, and of the inner parlours thereof, and of the place of the mercy seat,   v. 19

12 And the ᴿpattern of all that he had by the spirit, of the courts of the house of the LORD, and of all the chambers round about, of the treasuries of the house of God, and of the treasuries of the dedicated things: Ex. 25:40; Heb. 8:5

13 Also for the courses of the priests and the ᴿLevites, and for all the work of the service of the house of the LORD, and for all the vessels of service in the house of the LORD.   23:6

14 *He gave* of gold by weight for *things* of gold, for all instruments of all manner of service; *silver also* for all instruments of silver by weight, for all instruments of every kind of service:

15 Even the weight for the ᴿcandlesticks of gold, and for their lamps of gold, by weight for every candlestick, and for the lamps thereof: and for the candlesticks of silver by weight, *both* for the candlestick, and *also* for the lamps thereof, according to the use of every candlestick.   1 Kin. 7:49

16 And by weight *he gave* gold for the tables of shewbread, for every ᴿtable; and *likewise* silver for the tables of silver: 1 Kin. 7:48

17 Also pure gold for the fleshhooks, and the bowls, and the cups: and for the golden basons *he gave gold* by weight for every bason; and *likewise silver* by weight for every bason of silver:

18 And for the altar of incense refined gold by weight; and gold for the pattern of the chariot of the cher'-u-bims, that spread out *their wings*, and covered the ark of the covenant of the LORD.

19 All *this*, *said David*, the LORD made me understand in writing by *his* hand upon me, *even* all the works of this pattern.

20 And David said to Solomon his son, Be strong and of good courage, and do *it*: fear not, nor

be dismayed: for the LORD God, *even* my God, *will be* with thee; [R]he will not fail thee, nor forsake thee, until thou hast finished all the work for the service of the house of the LORD. Josh. 1:5; Heb. 13:5

21 And, behold, the courses of the priests and the Levites, *even they shall be with thee* for all the service of the house of God: and *there shall be* with thee for all manner of workmanship [R]every willing skilful man, for any manner of service: also the princes and all the people *will be* wholly at thy commandment. Ex. 35:25–35

29 Furthermore David the king said unto all the congregation, Solomon my son, whom alone God hath chosen, *is* yet young and tender, and the work *is* great: for the palace *is* not for man, but for the LORD God.

2 Now I have prepared with all my might for the house of my God the gold for *things to be made* of gold, and the silver for *things* of silver, and the brass for *things* of brass, the iron for *things* of iron, and wood for *things* of wood; [R]onyx stones, and *stones* to be set, glistering stones, and of divers colours, and all manner of precious stones, and marble stones in abundance. Is. 54:11, 12; Rev. 21:18

3 Moreover, because I have set my affection to the house of my God, I have of mine own proper good, of gold and silver, *which* I have given to the house of my God, over and above all that I have prepared for the holy house,

4 *Even* three thousand talents of gold, of the gold of [R]O'-phir, and seven thousand talents of refined silver, to overlay the walls of the houses *withal:* 1 Kin. 9:28

5 The gold for *things* of gold, and the silver for *things* of silver, and for all manner of work *to be made* by the hands of artificers. And who *then* is [R]willing to consecrate his service this day unto the LORD? 2 Chr. 29:31; [2 Cor. 8:5, 12]

6 Then [R]the chief of the fathers and princes of the tribes of Israel,

and the captains of thousands and of hundreds, with [R]the rulers of the king's work, [R]offered willingly, 27:1; 28:1 · 27:25–31 · Ex. 35:21–35

7 And gave for the service of the house of God of gold five thousand talents and ten thousand drams, and of silver ten thousand talents, and of brass eighteen thousand talents, and one hundred thousand talents of iron.

8 And they with whom *precious* stones were found gave *them* to the treasure of the house of the LORD, by the hand of [R]Je-hi'-el the Ger'-shon-ite. 23:8

9 Then the people rejoiced, for that they offered willingly, because with [T]perfect heart they [R]offered willingly to the LORD: and David the king also rejoiced with great joy. *loyal* · 2 Cor. 9:7

10 Wherefore David blessed the LORD before all the congregation: and David said, Blessed *be* thou, LORD God of Israel our father, for ever and ever.

11 Thine, O LORD, *is* the greatness, and the power, and the glory, and the victory, and the majesty: for all *that is* in the heaven and in the earth *is thine;* thine *is* the kingdom, O LORD, and thou art exalted as head above all.

12 [R]Both riches and honour *come* of thee, and thou reignest over all; and in thine hand *is* power and might; and in thine hand *it is* to make great, and to give strength unto all. Rom. 11:36

13 Now therefore, our God, we thank thee, and praise thy glorious name.

14 But who *am* I, and what *is* my people, that we should be able to offer so willingly after this sort? for all things *come* of thee, and of thine own have we given thee.

15 For [R]we *are* strangers before thee, and sojourners, as *were* all our fathers: [R]our days on the earth *are* as a shadow, and *there is* none abiding. 1 Pet. 2:11 · Ps. 90:9

16 O LORD our God, all this store that we have prepared to build

thee an house for thine holy name *cometh* of thine hand, and *is* all thine own.

17 I know also, my God, that thou Rtriest the heart, and Rhast pleasure in uprightness. As for me, in the uprightness of mine heart I have willingly offered all these things: and now have I seen with joy thy people, which are present here, to offer willingly unto thee.   [1 Sam. 16:7] · Prov. 11:20

18 O LORD God of Abraham, Isaac, and of Israel, our fathers, keep this for ever in the imagination of the thoughts of the heart of thy people, and Tprepare their heart unto thee: *fix*

19 And Rgive unto Solomon my son a perfect heart, to keep thy commandments, thy testimonies, and thy statutes, and to do all *these things*, and to build the palace, *for* the which RI have made provision.   [28:9]; Ps. 72:1 · vv. 1, 2

20 And David said to all the congregation, Now bless the LORD your God. And all the congregation blessed the LORD God of their fathers, and bowed down their heads, and worshipped the LORD, and the king.

21 And they sacrificed sacrifices unto the LORD, and offered burnt offerings unto the LORD, on the morrow after that day, *even* a thousand bullocks, a thousand rams, *and* a thousand lambs, with their drink offerings, and sacrifices in abundance for all Israel:

22 And did eat and drink before the LORD on that day with great gladness. And they made Solomon the son of David king the second time, and anointed *him* unto the LORD *to be* the chief governor, and Za´-dok *to be* priest.

23 Then Solomon sat on the throne of the LORD as king instead of David his father, and prospered; and all Israel obeyed him.

24 And all the princes, and the mighty men, and all the sons likewise of king David, RsubmittedT themselves unto Solomon the king.   Eccl. 8:2 · Lit. *gave the hand*

25 And the LORD magnified Solomon exceedingly in the sight of all Israel, and Rbestowed upon him *such* royal majesty as had not been on any king before him in Israel.   1 Kin. 3:13; 2 Chr. 1:12; Eccl. 2:9

26 Thus David the son of Jesse reigned over all Israel.

27 RAnd the time that he reigned over Israel *was* forty years; seven years reigned he in He´-bron, and thirty and three *years* reigned he in Jerusalem.   2 Sam. 5:4; 1 Kin. 2:11

28 And he Rdied in a good old age, Rfull of days, riches, and honour: and Solomon his son reigned in his Tstead.   Gen. 25:8 · 23:1 · *place*

29 Now the Tacts of David the king, first and last, behold, they *are* written in the book of Samuel the seer, and in the book of Nathan the prophet, and in the book of Gad the seer,   Lit. *words*

30 With all his reign and his might, Rand the times that went over him, and over Israel, and over all the kingdoms of the countries.   Dan. 2:21; 4:23, 25

The Second Book of the

CHRONICLES

THE Book of Second Chronicles parallels First and Second Kings but virtually ignores the northern kingdom of Israel because of its false worship and refusal to acknowledge the temple in Jerusalem. Chronicles focuses on those kings who pattern their lives and reigns after the life and reign of godly King David. It gives extended treatment to such zealous reformers as Asa, Jehoshaphat, Joash, Hezekiah, and Josiah.

The temple and temple worship, central throughout the book, befit a nation whose worship of God is central to its very survival. The book begins with Solomon's glorious temple and concludes with Cyrus's edict to rebuild the temple more than four hundred years later.

AND ^RSolomon the son of David was strengthened in his kingdom, and ^Rthe LORD his God *was* with him, and magnified him exceedingly.   1 Kin. 2:46 · Gen. 39:2

2   Then Solomon spake unto all Israel, to the captains of thousands and of hundreds, and to the judges, and to every governor in all Israel, the chief of the fathers.

3   So Solomon, and all the congregation with him, went to the high place that *was* at ^RGib'-e-on; for there was the tabernacle of the congregation of God, which Moses the servant of the LORD had made in the wilderness.   1 Kin. 3:4

4   But the ark of God had David brought up from Kir'-jath-je'-a-rim to *the place which* David had prepared for it: for he had pitched a tent for it at Jerusalem.

5   Moreover ^Rthe brasen altar, that Be-zal'-e-el the son of U'-ri, the son of Hur, had made, he put before the tabernacle of the LORD: and Solomon and the congregation sought unto it.   Ex. 27:1, 2

6   And Solomon went up thither to the brasen altar before the LORD, which *was* at the tabernacle of the congregation, and ^Roffered a thousand burnt offerings upon it.   1 Kin. 3:4

7   In that night did God appear unto Solomon, and said unto him, Ask what I shall give thee.

8   And Solomon said unto God, Thou hast shewed great mercy unto David my father, and hast made me to reign in his stead.

9   Now, O LORD God, let thy promise unto David my father be established: for thou hast made me king over a people like the dust of the earth in multitude.

10   ^RGive me now wisdom and knowledge, that I may ^Rgo out and come in before this people: for

who can judge this thy people, *that is so* great? 1 Kin. 3:9 · Num. 27:17

11   ^RAnd God said to Solomon, Because this was in thine heart, and thou hast not asked riches, wealth, or honour, nor the life of thine enemies, neither yet hast asked long life; but hast asked wisdom and knowledge for thyself, that thou mayest judge my people, over whom I have made thee king: 1 Kin. 3:11–13

12   Wisdom and knowledge *is* granted unto thee; and I will give thee riches, and wealth, and honour, such as ^Rnone of the kings have had that *have been* before thee, neither shall there any after thee have the like.   9:22; 1 Kin. 10:23

13   Then Solomon came *from his journey* to the high place that *was* at Gib'-e-on to Jerusalem, from before the tabernacle of the congregation, and reigned over Israel.

14   ^RAnd Solomon gathered chariots and horsemen: and he had a thousand and four hundred chariots, and twelve thousand horsemen, which he placed in the chariot cities, and with the king at Jerusalem.   9:25; 1 Kin. 10:26

15   And the king made silver and gold at Jerusalem *as plenteous* as stones, and cedar trees made he as the sycomore trees that *are* in the vale for abundance.

16   And Solomon had horses brought out of Egypt, and linen yarn: the king's merchants received the linen yarn at a price.

17   And they ^Tfetched up, and brought forth out of Egypt a chariot for six hundred *shek'-els* of silver, and an horse for an hundred and fifty: and so brought they out *horses* for all the kings of the Hit'-tites, and for the kings of Syria, by their means.   *acquired*

2 And Solomon ᴿdetermined to build an ᵀhouse for the name of the Lᴏʀᴅ, and an ᵀhouse for his kingdom. 1 Kin. 5:5 · *temple* · *royal house*

2 And Solomon ᵀtold out threescore and ten thousand men to bear burdens, and fourscore thousand to hew in the mountain, and three thousand and six hundred to oversee them.   *selected*

3 And Solomon sent to Hu'-ram the king of Tyre, saying, As thou didst deal with David my father, and didst send him cedars to build him an house to dwell therein, *even so deal with me.*

4 Behold, ᴿI build an house to the name of the Lᴏʀᴅ my God, to dedicate *it* to him, *and* ᴿto burn before him sweet incense, and for the continual shewbread, and for the burnt offerings morning and evening, on the ᴿsabbaths, and on the new moons, and on the solemn feasts of the Lᴏʀᴅ our God. This *is an ordinance* for ever to Israel.   v. 1 · Ex. 30:7 · Num. 28:3, 9–11

5 And the house which I build *is* great: for ᴿgreat *is* our God above all gods. Ps. 135:5; [1 Cor. 8:5, 6]

6 ᴿBut who is able to build him an house, seeing the heaven and heaven of heavens cannot contain him? who *am* I then, that I should build him an house, save only to burn sacrifice before him? Is. 66:1

7 Send me now therefore a man ᵀcunning to work in gold, and in silver, and in ᵀbrass, and in iron, and in purple, and crimson, and blue, and that can skill to grave with the cunning men that *are* with me in Judah and in Jerusalem, whom David my father did provide.   *skilful* · *bronze*

8 Send me also cedar trees, fir trees, and al'-gum trees, out of Leb'-a-non: for I know that thy servants can skill to cut timber in Leb'-a-non; and, behold, my servants *shall be* with thy servants,

9 Even to prepare me timber in abundance: for the house which I am about to build *shall be* ᵀwonderful great.   Lit. *great and wonderful*

10 ᴿAnd, behold, I will give to thy servants, the hewers that cut timber, twenty thousand ᵀmeasures of ᵀbeaten wheat, and twenty thousand measures of barley, and twenty thousand baths of wine, and twenty thousand baths of oil.   1 Kin. 5:11 · Heb. *kor* · *ground*

11 Then Hu'-ram the king of Tyre answered in writing, which he sent to Solomon, Because the Lᴏʀᴅ hath loved his people, he hath made thee king over them.

12 Hu'-ram said moreover, Blessed *be* the Lᴏʀᴅ God of Israel, ᴿthat made heaven and earth, who hath given to David the king a wise son, endued with prudence and understanding, that might build an house for the Lᴏʀᴅ, and an house for his kingdom. Rev. 10:6

13 And now I have sent a cunning man, endued with understanding, of Hu'-ram my father's,

14 ᴿThe son of a woman of the daughters of Dan, and his father *was* a man of Tyre, skilful to work in gold, and in silver, in brass, in iron, in stone, and in timber, in purple, in blue, and in fine linen, and in crimson; also to grave any manner of graving, and to find out every device which shall be put to him, with thy ᵀcunning men, and with the cunning men of my lord David thy father. 1 Kin. 7:13 · *skilful*

15 Now therefore the wheat, and the barley, the oil, and the wine, which my lord hath spoken of, let him send unto his servants:

16 ᴿAnd we will cut wood out of Leb'-a-non, as much as thou shalt need: and we will bring it to thee in ᵀflotes by sea to ᵀJop'-pa; and thou shalt carry it up to Jerusalem.   1 Kin. 5:8, 9 · *rafts* · Heb. *Japho*

17 ᴿAnd Solomon numbered all the strangers that *were* in the land of Israel, after the numbering wherewith ᴿDavid his father had numbered them; and they were found an hundred and fifty thousand and three thousand and six hundred.   8:7, 8; 1 Kin. 5:13 · 1 Chr. 22:2

18 And he set ᴿthreescore and ten thousand of them *to be* bearers of burdens, and fourscore

thousand *to be* [T]hewers in the mountain, and three thousand and six hundred overseers to set the people a work.   v. 2 · *stonecutters*

3 Then [R]Solomon began to build the house of the Lord at [R]Jerusalem in mount Mo-ri'-ah, where *the* Lord appeared unto David his father, in the place that David had prepared in the threshingfloor of [R]Or'-nan the Jeb'-u-site.   1 Kin. 6:1 · Gen. 22:2–14 · 1 Chr. 21:18

2 And he began to build in the second *day* of the second month, in the fourth year of his reign.

3 Now these *are the things* [R]wherein Solomon was instructed for the building of the house of God. The length by cubits after the first measure *was* threescore cubits, and the breadth twenty cubits.   1 Kin. 6:2; 1 Chr. 28:11–19

4 And the [R]porch that *was* in the front *of the house*, the length *of it was* according to the breadth of the house, twenty cubits, and the height *was* an hundred and twenty: and he overlaid it within with pure gold.   1 Kin. 6:3; 1 Chr. 28:11

5 And the greater [T]house he cieled with fir tree, which he overlaid with fine gold, and set thereon palm trees and chains.   *room*

6 And he [T]garnished the house with precious stones for beauty: and the gold *was* gold of Par-va'-im.   *decorated*

7 He overlaid also the house, the beams, the posts, and the walls thereof, and the doors thereof, with gold; and [T]graved cher'-u-bims on the walls.   *carved*

8 And he made the most holy house, the length whereof *was* according to the breadth of the house, twenty cubits, and the breadth thereof twenty cubits: and he overlaid it with fine gold, *amounting* to six hundred talents.

9 And the weight of the nails *was* fifty shek'-els of gold. And he overlaid the upper [R]chambers[T] with gold.   1 Chr. 28:11 · *rooms*

10 [R]And in the most holy [T]house he made two cher'-u-bims of im-age work, and overlaid them with gold.   Ex. 25:18–20; 1 Kin. 6:23–28 · *place*

11 And the wings of the cher'-u-bims *were* twenty cubits long: one wing *of the one cherub was* five cubits, reaching to the wall of the house: and the other wing *was* likewise five cubits, reaching to the wing of the other cherub.

12 And *one* wing of the other cherub *was* five cubits, reaching to the wall of the house: and the other wing *was* five cubits *also*, joining to the wing of the other cherub.

13 The wings of these cher'-u-bims spread themselves forth twenty cubits: and they stood on their feet, and their faces *were* inward.

14 And he made the [R]vail *of* blue, and purple, and crimson, and fine linen, and wrought cher'-u-bims thereon.   Matt. 27:51; Heb. 9:3

15 Also he made before the house two pillars of thirty and five cubits high, and the [T]chapiter that *was* on the top of each of them *was* five cubits.   *capital*

16 And he made chains, *as in* the oracle, and put *them* on the heads of the pillars; and made [R]an hundred pomegranates, and put *them* on the chains.   1 Kin. 7:20

17 And he reared up the pillars before the temple, one on the right hand, and the other on the left; and called the name of that on the right hand Ja'-chin, and the name of that on the left Bo'-az.

4 Moreover he made [R]an altar of brass, twenty cubits the length thereof, and twenty cubits the breadth thereof, and ten cubits the height thereof.   Ex. 27:1, 2

2 [R]Also he made a molten sea of ten cubits from brim to brim, round in compass, and five cubits the height thereof; and a line of thirty cubits did compass it round about.   Ex. 30:17–21; 1 Kin. 7:23–26

3 [R]And under it *was* the [T]similitude of oxen, which did compass it round about: ten in a cubit, compassing the sea round about. Two rows of oxen *were* cast, when it was cast.   1 Kin. 7:24–26 · *likeness*

4 It stood upon twelve oxen, three looking toward the north, and three looking toward the west, and three looking toward the south, and three looking toward the east: and the [T]sea *was* set above upon them, and all their hinder parts *were* inward.   *bason*

5 And the thickness of it *was* an handbreadth, and the brim of it like the work of the brim of a cup, with flowers of lilies; *and* it received and held [R]three thousand baths.   1 Kin. 7:26

6 He made also ten lavers, and put five on the right hand, and five on the left, to wash in them: such things as they offered for the burnt offering they washed in them; but the sea *was* for the [R]priests to wash in.   Ex. 30:19–21

7 [R]And he made ten [T]candlesticks of gold according to their form, and set *them* in the temple, five on the right hand, and five on the left.   1 Kin. 7:49 · *lampstands*

8 He made also ten tables, and placed *them* in the temple, five on the right side, and five on the left. And he made an hundred [R]basons[T] of gold.   1 Chr. 28:17 · *bowls*

9 Furthermore [R]he made the court of the priests, and the [R]great court, and doors for the court, and overlaid the doors of them with [T]brass.   1 Kin. 6:36 · 2 Kin. 21:5 · *bronze*

10 And [R]he set the sea on the right side of the east end, over against the south.   1 Kin. 7:39

11 And Hu′-ram made the pots, and the shovels, and the basons. And Hu′-ram finished the work that he was to make for king Solomon for the house of God;

12 To wit, the two pillars, and [R]the pommels, and the chapiters *which were* on the top of the two pillars, and the two wreaths to cover the two pommels of the chapiters which *were* on the top of the pillars;   1 Kin. 7:41

13 And [R]four hundred pomegranates on the two wreaths; two rows of pomegranates on each wreath, to cover the two pom-

mels of the chapiters which *were* upon the pillars.   1 Kin. 7:20

14 He made also bases, and lavers made he upon the bases;

15 One sea, and twelve oxen under it.

16 The pots also, and the shovels, and the [T]fleshhooks, and all their instruments, did [R]Hu′-ram his father make to king Solomon for the house of the LORD of bright brass.   *forks* · 2:13; 1 Kin. 7:45

17 In the plain of Jordan did the king cast them, in the clay ground between Suc′-coth and [T]Ze-red′-a-thah.   *Zarthan*, 1 Kin. 7:46

18 [R]Thus Solomon made all these vessels in great abundance: for the weight of the [T]brass could not be found out.   1 Kin. 7:47 · *bronze*

19 And [R]Solomon made all the vessels that *were for* the house of God, the golden altar also, and the tables whereon [R]the shewbread *was set*;   1 Kin. 7:48–50 · Ex. 25:30

20 Moreover the [T]candlesticks with their lamps, that they should burn after the manner before the oracle, of pure gold;   *lampstands*

21 And the flowers, and the lamps, and the tongs, *made he of* gold, *and* that [T]perfect gold;   *purest*

22 And the snuffers, and the basons, and the spoons, and the censers, of pure gold: and the entry of the house, the inner doors thereof for the most holy *place*, and the doors of the house of the temple, *were of* gold.

5 Thus all the work that Solomon made for the house of the LORD was finished: and Solomon brought in *all* the things that David his father had dedicated; and the silver, and the gold, and all the instruments, put he among the treasures of the house of God.

2 [R]Then Solomon assembled the elders of Israel, and all the heads of the tribes, the chief of the fathers of the children of Israel, unto Jerusalem, to bring up the ark of the covenant of the LORD [R]out of the city of David, which *is* Zion.   1 Kin. 8:1–9; Ps. 47:9 · 2 Sam. 6:12

3 [R]Wherefore all the men of

Israel assembled themselves unto the king in the feast which *was* in the seventh month.   1 Kin. 8:2

4   And all the elders of Israel came; and the [R]Levites took up the ark.   1 Chr. 15:2, 15

5   And they brought up the ark, and the tabernacle of the congregation, and all the holy vessels that *were* in the tabernacle, these did the priests *and* the Levites bring up.

6   Also king Solomon, and all the congregation of Israel that were assembled unto him before the ark, sacrificed sheep and oxen, which could not be [T]told nor numbered for multitude.   *counted*

7   And the priests brought in the ark of the covenant of the LORD unto his place, to the [R]oracle of the house, into the most holy *place, even* under the wings of the cher'-u-bims: 4:20

8   For the cher'-u-bims spread forth *their* wings over the place of the ark, and the cher'-u-bims covered the ark and the staves thereof above.

9   And they drew out the [R]staves *of the ark*, that the ends of the staves were seen from the ark before the oracle; but they were not seen without. And there it is unto this day.   Ex. 25:13–15

10 *There was* nothing in the ark save the two tables which Moses [R]put *therein* at Ho'-reb, when the LORD made *a covenant* with the children of Israel, when they came out of Egypt. Ex. 25:16; Heb. 9:4

11 And it came to pass, when the priests were come out of the holy *place*: (for all the priests *that were* present were sanctified, *and* did not *then* wait by course:

12 [R]Also the Levites *which were* the singers, all of them of A'-saph, of He'-man, of Je-du'-thun, with their sons and their brethren, *being* arrayed in white linen, having cymbals and psalteries and harps, stood at the east end of the altar, and with them an hundred and twenty priests sounding with trumpets:)   Ex. 32:26; 1 Chr. 25:1–7

13 It came even to pass, as the trumpeters and singers *were* as one, to make one sound to be heard in praising and thanking the LORD; and when they lifted up *their* voice with the trumpets and cymbals and instruments of musick, and praised the LORD, *saying*, [R]For *he is* good; for his mercy *endureth* for ever: that *then* the house was filled with a cloud, *even* the house of the LORD;   7:3

14 So that the priests could not stand to minister by reason of the cloud: [R]for the glory of the LORD had filled the house of God.   7:2

6 Then said Solomon, The LORD hath said that he would dwell in the thick darkness.

2   But I have built an house of habitation for thee, and a [R]place for thy dwelling for ever.   7:12

3   And the king turned his face, and [R]blessed the whole congregation of Israel: and all the congregation of Israel stood.   2 Sam. 6:18

4   And he said, Blessed *be* the LORD God of Israel, who hath with his hands fulfilled *that* which he spake with his mouth to my father David, [R]saying,   1 Chr. 17:5

5   Since the day that I brought forth my people out of the land of Egypt I chose no city among all the tribes of Israel to build an house in, that my name might be there; neither chose I any man to be a ruler over my people Israel:

6   But I have chosen Jerusalem, that my name might be there; and [R]have chosen David to be over my people Israel. 1 Sam. 16:7–13; 1 Chr. 28:4

7   Now [R]it was in the heart of David my father to build an house for the name of the LORD God of Israel.   2 Sam. 7:2; 1 Chr. 17:1; Ps. 132:1–5

8   But the LORD said to David my father, Forasmuch as it was in thine heart to build an house for my name, thou didst well in that it was in thine heart:

9   Notwithstanding thou shalt not build the house; but thy son which shall come forth out of thy loins, he shall build the house for my [R]name.   1 Chr. 28:3–6

10 The LORD therefore hath performed his word that he hath spoken; for I am risen up in the [T]room of David my father, and am [R]set on the throne of Israel, as the LORD promised, and have built the house for the name of the LORD God of Israel. *position* · 1 Kin. 2:12; 10:9

11 And in it have I put the ark, [R]wherein *is* the covenant of the LORD, that he made with the children of Israel.   5:7–10

12 [R]And he stood before the altar of the LORD in the presence of all the congregation of Israel, and spread forth his hands: 1 Kin. 8:22

13 For Solomon had made a brasen scaffold, of five cubits long, and five cubits broad, and three cubits high, and had set it in the midst of the court: and upon it he stood, and kneeled down upon his knees before all the congregation of Israel, and spread forth his hands toward heaven,

14 And said, O LORD God of Israel, [R]*there is* no God like thee in the heaven, nor in the earth; which keepest [R]covenant, and *shewest* mercy unto thy servants, that walk before thee with all their hearts: [Ex. 15:11] · [Deut. 7:9]

15 [R]Thou which hast kept with thy servant David my father that which thou hast promised him; and spakest with thy mouth, and hast fulfilled *it* with thine hand, as *it is* this day.   1 Chr. 22:9, 10

16 Now therefore, O LORD God of Israel, keep with thy servant David my father that which thou hast promised him, saying, [R]There shall not fail thee a man in my sight to sit upon the throne of Israel; [R]yet so that thy children take heed to their way to walk in my law, as thou hast walked before me.   2 Sam. 7:12, 16; 1 Kin. 2:4 · Ps. 132:12

17 Now then, O LORD God of Israel, let thy word [T]be verified, which thou hast spoken unto thy servant David.   *come true*

18 But will God in very deed dwell with men on the earth? [R]behold, heaven and the heaven of heavens cannot contain thee;

how much less this house which I have built!   [2:6; Is. 66:1; Acts 7:49]

19 Have [T]respect therefore to the prayer of thy servant, and to his supplication, O LORD my God, to hearken unto the cry and the prayer which thy servant prayeth before thee: *regard*

20 That thine eyes may be open upon this house day and night, upon the place whereof thou hast said that thou wouldest put thy name there; to hearken unto the prayer which thy servant prayeth [R]toward this place.   Ps. 5:7; Dan. 6:10

21 Hearken therefore unto the supplications of thy servant, and of thy people Israel, which they shall make toward this place: hear thou from thy dwelling place, *even* from heaven; and when thou hearest, [R]forgive.   [Is. 43:25; Mic. 7:18]

22 If a man sin against his neighbour, and an [R]oath be laid upon him to make him swear, and the oath come before thine altar in this house;   Ex. 22:8–11

23 Then hear thou from heaven, and do, and judge thy servants, by requiting the wicked, by recompensing his way upon his own head; and by justifying the righteous, by giving him according to his [R]righteousness.   [Job 34:11]

24 And if thy people Israel be put to the worse before the [R]enemy, because they have sinned against thee; and shall return and confess thy name, and pray and make supplication before thee in this house;   2 Kin. 21:14, 15

25 Then hear thou from the heavens, and forgive the sin of thy people Israel, and bring them again unto the land which thou gavest to them and to their fathers.

26 When the [R]heaven is shut up, and there is no rain, because they have sinned against thee; *yet* if they pray toward this place, and confess thy name, and turn from their sin, when thou dost afflict them;   Deut. 28:23, 24; 1 Kin. 17:1

27 Then hear thou from heaven, and forgive the sin of thy servants, and of thy people Israel,

when thou hast taught them the good way, wherein they should walk; and send rain upon thy land, which thou hast given unto thy people for an inheritance.

28 If there ᴿbe dearth in the land, if there be pestilence, if there be blasting, or mildew, locusts, or caterpillers; if their enemies besiege them in the cities of their land; whatsoever sore or whatsoever sickness *there be:* 20:9

29 *Then* what prayer *or* what supplication soever shall be made of any man, or of all thy people Israel, when every one shall know his own ᵀsore and his own grief, and shall spread forth his hands ᵀin this house: *burden · toward*

30 Then hear thou from heaven thy dwelling place, and forgive, and render unto every man according unto all his ways, whose heart thou knowest; (for thou only ᴿknowest the hearts of the children of men:)   [1 Chr. 28:9]

31 That they may fear thee, to walk in thy ways, so long as they live in the land which thou gavest unto our fathers.

32 Moreover concerning the stranger, ᴿwhich is not of thy people Israel, but is come from a far country for thy great name's sake, and thy mighty hand, and thy stretched out arm; if they come and pray in this house;   Acts 8:27

33 Then hear thou from the heavens, *even* from thy dwelling place, and do according to all that the stranger calleth to thee for; that all people of the earth may know thy name, and fear thee, as *doth* thy people Israel, and may know that this house which I have built is called by thy name.

34 If thy people go out to war against their enemies by the way that thou shalt send them, and they pray unto thee toward this city which thou hast chosen, and the house which I have built for thy name;

35 Then hear thou from the heavens their prayer and their supplication, and maintain their cause.

36 If they sin against thee, (for *there is* ᴿno man which sinneth not,) and thou be angry with them, and deliver them over before *their* enemies, and they carry them away captives unto a land far off or near;   [Rom. 3:9, 19; 5:12]

37 Yet *if* they bethink themselves in the land whither they are carried captive, and ᵀturn and pray unto thee in the land of their captivity, saying, We have sinned, we have done amiss, and have dealt wickedly;   *repent*

38 If they return to thee with all their heart and with all their soul in the land of their captivity, whither they have carried them captives, and pray toward their land, which thou gavest unto their fathers, and *toward* the ᴿcity which thou hast chosen, and toward the house which I have built for thy name: Dan. 6:10

39 Then hear thou from the heavens, *even* from thy dwelling place, their prayer and their supplications, and maintain their cause, and forgive thy people which have sinned against thee.

40 Now, my God, let, I beseech thee, thine eyes be open, and *let* thine ears *be* attent unto the prayer *that is made* in this place.

41 Now therefore arise, O LORD God, into thy resting place, thou, and the ark of thy strength: let thy priests, O LORD God, be clothed with salvation, and let thy saints ᴿrejoice in goodness.   Neh. 9:25

42 O LORD God, turn not away the face of thine anointed: ᴿremember the mercies of David thy servant.   2 Sam. 7:15; Ps. 89:49; Is. 55:3

7 Now when Solomon had made an end of praying, the fire came down from heaven, and consumed the burnt offering and the sacrifices; and the glory of the LORD filled the house.

2 ᴿAnd the priests could not enter into the house of the LORD, because the glory of the LORD had filled the LORD's house.   5:14

3 And when all the children of Israel saw how the fire came down, and the glory of the LORD upon the house, they bowed themselves with their faces to the ground upon the pavement, and worshipped, and praised the LORD, ᴿsaying, For *he is* good; for his mercy *endureth* for ever.   5:13

4 ᴿThen the king and all the people offered sacrifices before the LORD.   1 Kin. 8:62, 63

5 And king Solomon offered a sacrifice of twenty and two thousand oxen, and an hundred and twenty thousand sheep: so the king and all the people dedicated the house of God.

6 ᴿAnd the priests waited on their offices: the Levites also with instruments of musick of the LORD, which David the king had made to praise the LORD, because his mercy *endureth* for ever, when David praised by their ministry; and ᴿthe priests sounded trumpets before them, and all Israel stood.   1 Chr. 15:16 · 5:12

7 Moreover ᴿSolomon ᵀhallowed the middle of the court that *was* before the house of the LORD: for there he offered burnt offerings, and the fat of the peace offerings, because the brasen altar which Solomon had made was not able to receive the burnt offerings, and the meat offerings, and the fat.   1 Kin. 9:3 · *consecrated*

8 ᴿAlso at the same time Solomon kept the feast seven days, and all Israel with him, a very great congregation, ᴿfrom the entering in of Ha′-math unto the river of Egypt.   1 Kin. 8:65 · 1 Kin. 4:21

9 And in the eighth day they made a ᴿsolemn assembly: for they kept the dedication of the altar seven days, and the feast seven days.   Lev. 23:36

10 And on the three and twentieth day of the seventh month he sent the people away into their tents, glad and merry in heart for the goodness that the LORD had shewed unto David, and to Solomon, and to Israel his people.

11 Thus Solomon finished the house of the LORD, and the king's house: and all that came into Solomon's heart to make in the house of the LORD, and in his own house, he prosperously effected.

12 And the LORD ᴿappeared to Solomon by night, and said unto him, I have heard thy prayer, and have chosen this place to myself for an house of sacrifice.   1 Kin. 3:5

13 ᴿIf I shut up heaven that there be no rain, or if I command the locusts to devour the land, or if I send pestilence among my people;   Deut. 28:23, 24; 1 Kin. 17:1

14 If my people, which are called by my name, shall ᴿhumble themselves, and pray, and seek my face, and turn from their wicked ways; then will I hear from heaven, and will forgive their sin, and will heal their land. [James 4:10]

15 Now ᴿmine eyes shall be open, and mine ears ᵀattent unto the prayer *that is made* in this place.   6:20, 40 · *attentive*

16 For now have ᴿI chosen and sanctified this house, that my name may be there for ever: and mine eyes and mine heart shall be there perpetually.   6:6; 1 Kin. 9:3

17 ᴿAnd as for thee, if thou wilt walk before me, as David thy father walked, and do according to all that I have commanded thee, and shalt observe my statutes and my judgments;   1 Kin. 9:4

18 Then will I stablish the throne of thy kingdom, according as I have covenanted with David thy father, saying, ᴿThere shall not fail thee a man *to be* ruler in Israel.   6:16; 2 Sam. 7:12–16; 1 Kin. 2:4

19 But if ye turn away, and forsake my statutes and my commandments, which I have set before you, and shall go and serve other gods, and worship them;

20 Then will I pluck them up by the roots out of my land which I have given them; and this house, which I have sanctified for my name, will I cast out of my sight, and will make it *to be* a proverb and a byword among all nations.

21 And ᴿthis house, which is

high, shall be an [R]astonishment to every one that passeth by it; so that he shall say, Why hath the LORD done thus unto this land, and unto this house? 2 Kin. 25:9 · 29:8

22 And it shall be answered, Because they forsook the LORD God of their fathers, which brought them forth out of the land of Egypt, and laid hold on other gods, and worshipped them, and served them: therefore hath he brought all this evil upon them.

8 And it came to pass at the end of twenty years, wherein Solomon had built the house of the LORD, and his own house,

2 That the cities which [T]Hu'-ram had restored to Solomon, Solomon built them, and caused the children of Israel to dwell there.   *Hiram, 1 Kin. 7:13*

3 And Solomon went to Ha'-math–zo'-bah, and [T]prevailed against it.   *seized it*

4 And he built Tad'-mor in the wilderness, and all the store cities, which he built in Ha'-math.

5 Also he built Beth–ho'-ron the upper, and [R]Beth–ho'-ron the [T]nether, fenced cities, with walls, gates, and bars;   1 Chr. 7:24 · *lower*

6 And Ba'-al-ath, and all the store cities that Solomon had, and all the chariot cities, and the cities of the horsemen, and all that Solomon [R]desired to build in Jerusalem, and in Leb'-a-non, and throughout all the land of his dominion.   7:11

7 As for all the people *that were* left of the Hit'-tites, and the Am'-or-ites, and the Per'-iz-zites, and the Hi'-vites, and the Jeb'-u-sites, which *were* not of Israel,

8 *But* of their children, who were left after them in the land, whom the children of Israel consumed not, them did Solomon make to pay tribute until this day.

9 But of the children of Israel did Solomon make no [T]servants for his work; but they *were* men of war, and chief of his captains, and captains of his chariots and horsemen.   *slaves*

10 And these *were* the chief of king Solomon's officers, *even* [R]two hundred and fifty, that bare rule over the people.   1 Kin. 9:23

11 And Solomon [R]brought up the daughter of Pharaoh out of the city of David unto the house that he had built for her: for he said, My wife shall not dwell in the house of David king of Israel, because *the places are* holy, whereunto the ark of the LORD hath come.   1 Kin. 3:1; 7:8; 9:24; 11:1

12 Then Solomon offered burnt offerings unto the LORD on the altar of the LORD, which he had built before the porch,

13 Even after a certain rate [R]every day, offering according to the commandment of Moses, on the sabbaths, and on the new moons, and on the solemn feasts, three times in the year, *even* in the feast of unleavened bread, and in the feast of weeks, and in the feast of tabernacles.   Ex. 29:38–42; Num. 28:3

14 And he appointed, according to the order of David his father, the [R]courses of the priests to their service, and the Levites to their charges, to praise and minister before the priests, as the duty of every day required: the porters also by their courses at every gate: for so had David the man of God commanded.   1 Chr. 24:3

15 And they departed not from the commandment of the king unto the priests and Levites concerning any matter, or concerning the [R]treasures.   1 Chr. 26:20–28

16 Now all the work of Solomon was prepared unto the day of the foundation of the house of the LORD, and until it was finished. *So* the house of the LORD was [T]perfected.   *completed*

17 Then went Solomon to E'-zi-on–ge'-ber, and to E'-loth, at the sea side in the land of E'-dom.

18 [R]And Hu'-ram sent him by the hands of his servants ships, and servants that had knowledge of the sea; and they went with the servants of Solomon to O'-phir, and took thence four hundred and

fifty talents of gold, and brought *them* to king Solomon. 1 Kin. 9:27

9 And ᴿwhen the queen of She'-ba heard of the fame of Solomon, she came to prove Solomon with hard questions at Jerusalem, with a very great company, and camels that bare spices, and gold in abundance, and precious stones: and when she was come to Solomon, she commaned with him of all that was in her heart. 1 Kin. 10:1; Ps. 72:10; [Luke 11:31]

2 And Solomon ᵀtold her all her questions: and there was nothing hid from Solomon which he told her not. *answered*

3 And when the queen of She'-ba had seen the wisdom of Solomon, and the house that he had built,

4 And the meat of his table, and the sitting of his servants, and the attendance of his ministers, and their apparel; his ᴿcupbearers also, and their apparel; and his ascent by which he went up into the house of the LORD; there was no more spirit in her. Neh. 1:11

5 And she said to the king, *It was* a true report which I heard in mine own land of thine ᵀacts, and of thy wisdom: *words*

6 Howbeit I believed not their words, until I came, and mine eyes had seen *it:* and, behold, the one half of the greatness of thy wisdom was not told me: *for* thou exceedest the fame that I heard.

7 Happy *are* thy men, and happy *are* these thy servants, which stand continually before thee, and hear thy wisdom.

8 Blessed be the LORD thy God, which delighted in thee to set thee on his throne, *to be* king for the LORD thy God: because thy God ᴿloved Israel, to establish them for ever, therefore made he thee king over them, to do judgment and justice. 2:11; Deut. 7:8; [Ps. 44:3]

9 And she gave the king an hundred and twenty talents of gold, and of spices great abundance, and precious stones: neither was there any such spice as the queen of She'-ba gave king Solomon.

10 And the servants also of Hu'-ram, and the servants of Solomon, ᴿwhich brought gold from O'-phir, brought ᵀal'-gum trees and precious stones. 8:18 · *almug,* 1 Kin. 10:11

11 And the king made *of* the ᵀal'-gum trees terraces to the house of the LORD, and to the king's palace, and harps and psalteries for singers: and there were none such seen before in the land of Judah. *almug,* 1 Kin. 10:11, 12

12 And king Solomon gave to the queen of She'-ba all her desire, whatsoever she asked, beside *that* which she had brought unto the king. So she turned, and went away to her own land, she and her servants.

13 ᴿNow the weight of gold that came to Solomon in one year was six hundred and threescore and six talents of gold; 1 Kin. 10:14–29

14 Beside *that which* ᵀchapmen and merchants brought. And all the kings of Arabia and governors of the country brought gold and silver to Solomon. *traders*

15 And king Solomon made two hundred ᵀtargets *of* beaten gold: six hundred *shek'-els* of beaten gold went to one target. *large shields*

16 And three hundred shields *made he of* beaten gold: three hundred *shek'-els* of gold went to one shield. And the king put them in the ᴿhouse of the forest of Leb'-a-non. 1 Kin. 7:2

17 Moreover the king made a great throne of ivory, and overlaid it with pure gold.

18 And *there were* six steps to the throne, with a footstool of gold, *which were* fastened to the throne, and ᵀstays on each side of the sitting place, and two lions standing by the stays: *armrests*

19 And twelve lions stood there on the one side and on the other upon the six steps. There was not the like made in any kingdom.

20 And all the drinking vessels of king Solomon *were of* gold, and all the vessels of the house of the

forest of Leb'-a-non *were of* pure gold: none *were of* silver; it was *not* any thing accounted of in the days of Solomon.

21 For the king's ships went to ᴿTar'-shish with the servants of Hu'-ram: every three years once came the ships of Tar'-shish bringing gold, and silver, ivory, and apes, and peacocks.   Ps. 72:10

22 And king Solomon ᵀpassed all the kings of the earth in riches and wisdom.   *surpassed*

23 And all the kings of the earth sought the presence of Solomon, to hear his wisdom, that God had put in his heart.

24 And they brought every man his present, vessels of silver, and vessels of gold, and raiment, harness, and spices, horses, and mules, a rate year by year.

25 And Solomon ᴿhad four thousand stalls for horses and chariots, and twelve thousand horsemen; whom he bestowed in the chariot cities, and with the king at Jerusalem. Deut. 17:16; 1 Kin. 4:26; Is. 2:7

26 ᴿAnd he reigned over all the kings from the river even unto the land of the Phi-lis'-tines, and to the border of Egypt.   1 Kin. 4:21

27 ᴿAnd the king made silver in Jerusalem as stones, and cedar trees made he as the sycomore trees that *are* in the low plains in ᴿabundance.   1 Kin. 10:27 · 1:15–17

28 ᴿAnd they brought unto Solomon horses out of Egypt, and out of all lands.   1:16; 1 Kin. 10:28

29 ᴿNow the rest of the acts of Solomon, first and last, *are* they not written in the book of Nathan the prophet, and in the prophecy of ᴿA-hi'-jah the Shi'-lo-nite, and in the visions of Id'-do the seer against Jer-o-bo'-am the son of Ne'-bat?   1 Kin. 11:41 · 1 Kin. 11:29

30 ᴿAnd Solomon reigned in Jerusalem over all Israel forty years.   1 Kin. 4:21; 11:42, 43; 1 Chr. 29:28

31 And Solomon ᵀslept with his fathers, and he was buried in the city of David his father: and Re-ho-bo'-am his son reigned in his ᵀstead.   *rested in death with · place*

10 And ᴿRe-ho-bo'-am went to She'-chem: for to She'-chem were all Israel come to make him king.   1 Kin. 12:1–20

2 And it came to pass, when Jer-o-bo'-am the son of Ne'-bat, who *was* in Egypt, ᴿwhither he had fled from the presence of Solomon the king, heard *it,* that Jer-o-bo'-am returned out of Egypt.   1 Kin. 11:40

3 And they sent and called him. So Jer-o-bo'-am and all Israel came and spake to Re-ho-bo'-am, saying,

4 Thy father made our yoke grievous: now therefore ease thou somewhat the ᵀgrievous servitude of thy father, and his heavy yoke that he put upon us, and we will serve thee.   *burdensome service*

5 And he said unto them, Come again unto me after three days. And the people departed.

6 And king Re-ho-bo'-am took counsel with the old men that had stood before Solomon his father while he yet lived, saying, What counsel give ye *me* to return answer to this people?

7 And they spake unto him, saying, If thou be kind to this people, and please them, and speak good words to them, they will be thy servants for ever.

8 ᴿBut he forsook the counsel which the old men gave him, and took counsel with the young men that were brought up with him, that stood before him. 1 Kin. 12:8–11

9 And he said unto them, What advice give ye that we may return answer to this people, which have spoken to me, saying, Ease somewhat the yoke that thy father did put upon us?

10 And the young men that were brought up with him spake unto him, saying, Thus shalt thou answer the people that spake unto thee, saying, Thy father made our yoke heavy, but make thou *it* somewhat lighter for us; thus shalt thou say unto them, My little *finger* shall be thicker than my father's ᵀloins.   *waist*

11 For whereas my father put a heavy yoke upon you, I will put more to your yoke: my father chastised you with whips, but I *will chastise you* with scorpions.

12 So [R]Jer-o-bo′-am and all the people came to Re-ho-bo′-am on the third day, as the king bade, saying, Come again to me on the third day.   1 Kin. 12:12–14

13 And the king answered them roughly; and king Re-ho-bo′-am forsook the counsel of the old men,

14 And answered them after the advice of the young men, saying, My father made your yoke heavy, but I will add thereto: my father chastised you with whips, but I *will chastise you* with scorpions.

15 So the king hearkened not unto the people: for the [T]cause was of God, that the LORD might perform his word, which he spake by the hand of A-hi′-jah the Shi′-lo-nite to Jer-o-bo′-am the son of Ne′-bat.   *turn of affairs*

16 And when all Israel *saw* that the king would not hearken unto them, the people answered the king, saying, What portion have we in David? and *we have* none inheritance in the son of Jesse: every man to your tents, O Israel, *and* now, David, see to thine own house. So all Israel went to their tents.

17 But *as for* the children of Israel that dwelt in the cities of Judah, Re-ho-bo′-am reigned over them.

18 Then king Re-ho-bo′-am sent Ha-do′-ram that *was* over the tribute; and the children of Israel stoned him with stones, that he died. But king Re-ho-bo′-am made speed to get him up to *his* chariot, to flee to Jerusalem.

19 And Israel rebelled against the house of David unto this day.

11 And [R]when Re-ho-bo′-am was come to Jerusalem, he [T]gathered of the house of Judah and Benjamin an hundred and fourscore thousand chosen *men*, which were warriors, to fight against Israel, that he might bring the kingdom again to Re-ho-bo′-am.   1 Kin. 12:21–24 · *assembled from*

2 But the word of the LORD came [R]to She-ma′-iah the man of God, saying,   12:15; 1 Chr. 12:5

3 Speak unto Re-ho-bo′-am the son of Solomon, king of Judah, and to all Israel in Judah and Benjamin, saying,

4 Thus saith the LORD, Ye shall not go up, nor fight against your brethren: return every man to his house: for this thing is [T]done of me. And they obeyed the words of the LORD, and returned from going against Jer-o-bo′-am.   *from me*

5 And Re-ho-bo′-am dwelt in Jerusalem, and built cities for defence in Judah.

6 He built even Beth′–le-hem, and E′-tam, and Te-ko′-a,

7 And Beth′–zur, and [T]Sho′-co, and A-dul′-lam,   *Sochoh,* 1 Kin. 4:10

8 And Gath, and Ma-re′-shah, and Ziph,

9 And Ad-o-ra′-im, and La′-chish, and A-ze′-kah,

10 And Zo′-rah, and Ai′-ja-lon, and He′-bron, which *are* in Judah and in Benjamin fenced cities.

11 And he fortified the strong holds, and put captains in them, and store of [T]victual, and of oil and wine.   *food*

12 And in every several city *he put* shields and spears, and made them exceeding strong, having Judah and Benjamin on his side.

13 And the priests and the Levites that *were* in all Israel [T]resorted to him out of all their coasts.   *took their stand with*

14 For the Levites left their suburbs and their possession, and came to Judah and Jerusalem: for Jer-o-bo′-am and his sons had cast them off from executing the priest's office unto the LORD:

15 And he ordained him priests for the high places, and for [R]the devils, and for the calves which he had made.   [Lev. 17:7; 1 Cor. 10:20]

16 [R]And after them out of all the tribes of Israel such as set their hearts to seek the LORD God of Israel [R]came to Jerusalem, to sacrifice unto the LORD God of their fathers.   14:7 · 15:9, 10; 30:11, 18

17 So they ᴿstrengthened the kingdom of Judah, and made Re-ho-bo'-am the son of Solomon strong, three years: for three years they walked in the way of David and Solomon.   12:1, 13

18 And Re-ho-bo'-am took him Ma'-ha-lath the daughter of Jer'-i-moth the son of David to wife, *and* Ab-i-ha'-il the daughter of ᴿE-li'-ab the son of Jesse;   1 Sam. 16:6

19 Which bare him children; Je'-ush, and Sham-a-ri'-ah, and Za'-ham.

20 And after her he took Ma'-a-chah the daughter of Ab'-sa-lom; which bare him A-bi'-jah, and At'-tai, and Zi'-za, and Shel'-o-mith.

21 And Re-ho-bo'-am loved Ma'-a-chah the daughter of Ab'-sa-lom above all his wives and his concubines: (for he took eighteen wives, and threescore concubines; and begat twenty and eight sons, and threescore daughters.)

22 And Re-ho-bo'-am ᴿmade ᴿA-bi'-jah the son of Ma'-a-chah the chief, *to be* ruler among his brethren: for *he thought* to make him king.   Deut. 21:15–17 · 13:1

23 And he dealt wisely, and ᵀdispersed of all his children throughout all the countries of Judah and Benjamin, unto every ᴿfencedᵀ city: and he gave them victual in abundance. And he desired many wives.   *distributed* · v. 5 · *fortified*

12 And ᴿit came to pass, when Re-ho-bo'-am had established the kingdom, and had strengthened himself, ᴿhe forsook the law of the LORD, and all Israel with him.   11:17 · 1 Kin. 14:22–24

2 ᴿAnd it came to pass, that in the fifth year of king Re-ho-bo'-am Shi'-shak king of Egypt came up against Jerusalem, because they had transgressed against the LORD,   1 Kin. 11:40; 14:25

3 With twelve hundred chariots, and threescore thousand horsemen: and the people *were* without number that came with him out of Egypt; ᴿthe Lu'-bims, the Suk'-ki-ims, and the E-thi-o'-pi-ans.   16:8; Nah. 3:9

4 And he took the ᵀfenced cities which *pertained* to Judah, and came to Jerusalem.   *fortified*

5 Then came ᴿShe-ma'-iah the prophet to Re-ho-bo'-am, and *to* the princes of Judah, that were gathered together to Jerusalem because of Shi'-shak, and said unto them, Thus saith the LORD, Ye have forsaken me, and therefore have I also left you in the hand of Shi'-shak.   11:2

6 Whereupon the princes of Israel and the king humbled themselves; and they said, ᴿThe LORD *is* righteous.   Ex. 9:27; [Dan. 9:14]

7 And when the LORD saw that they humbled themselves, ᴿthe word of the LORD came to She-ma'-iah, saying, They have humbled themselves; *therefore* I will not destroy them, but I will grant them some deliverance; and my wrath shall not be poured out upon Jerusalem by the hand of Shi'-shak.   1 Kin. 21:28, 29

8 Nevertheless ᴿthey shall be his servants; that they may know my service, and the service of the kingdoms of the countries.   Is. 26:13

9 ᴿSo Shi'-shak king of Egypt came up against Jerusalem, and took away the treasures of the house of the LORD, and the treasures of the king's house; he took all: he carried away also the shields of gold which Solomon had ᴿmade.   1 Kin. 14:25, 26 · 9:15, 16

10 Instead of which king Re-ho-bo'-am made shields of brass, and committed *them* to the hands of the chief of the guard, that kept the entrance of the king's house.

11 And when the king entered into the house of the LORD, the guard came· and fetched them, and brought them again into the guard chamber.

12 And when he humbled himself, the wrath of the LORD turned from him, that he would not destroy *him* altogether: and also in Judah things went well.

13 So king Re-ho-bo'-am strengthened himself in Jerusa-

lem, and reigned: for ᴿRe-ho-bo'-am *was* one and forty years old when he began to reign, and he reigned seventeen years in Jeru-salem, ᴿthe city which the Lᴏʀᴅ had chosen out of all the tribes of Israel, to put his name there. And his mother's name *was* Na'-a-mah an Am'-mon-i-tess.   1 Kin. 14:21 · 6:6

14 And he did evil, because he prepared not his heart to seek the Lᴏʀᴅ.

15 Now the acts of Re-ho-bo'-am, first and last, *are* they not written in the book of She-ma'-iah the prophet, ᴿand of Id'-do the seer concerning genealogies? ᴿAnd *there were* wars between Re-ho-bo'-am and Jer-o-bo'-am continually.   9:29; 13:22 · 1 Kin. 14:30

16 And Re-ho-bo'-am slept with his fathers, and was buried in the city of David: and ᴿA-bi'-jah his son reigned in his stead.   11:20–22

13 Now ᴿin the eighteenth year of king Jer-o-bo'-am began A-bi'-jah to reign over ᴿJudah.   1 Kin. 15:1 · 1 Kin. 12:17

2 He reigned three years in Jerusalem. His mother's name also *was* Mi-cha'-iah the daughter of U-ri'-el of Gib'-e-ah. And there was war between A-bi'-jah and Je-ro-bo'-am.

3 And A-bi'-jah set the battle in ᵀarray with an army of valiant men of war, *even* four hundred thousand chosen men: Je-ro-bo'-am also set the battle in array against him with eight hundred thousand chosen men, *being* mighty men of valour.   *order*

4 And A-bi'-jah stood up upon mount ᴿZem-a-ra'-im, which *is* in mount E'-phra-im, and said, Hear me, thou Jer-o-bo'-am, and all Israel;   Josh. 18:22

5 Ought ye not to know that the Lᴏʀᴅ God of Israel ᴿgave the kingdom over Israel to David for ever, *even* to him and to his sons by a covenant of salt?   2 Sam. 7:8–16

6 Yet Jer-o-bo'-am the son of Ne'-bat, the servant of Solomon the son of David, is risen up, and hath rebelled against his lord.

7 And there are gathered unto him ᵀvain men, the ᵀchildren of Be'-li-al, and have strengthened themselves against Re-ho-bo'-am the son of Solomon, when Re-ho-bo'-am was ᴿyoung and tender-hearted, and could not withstand them.   *worthless · reprobates · 12:13*

8 And now ye think to with-stand the kingdom of the Lᴏʀᴅ in the hand of the sons of David; and ye *be* a great multitude, and *there are* with you golden calves, which Jer-o-bo'-am made you for gods.

9 ᴿHave ye not cast out the priests of the Lᴏʀᴅ, the sons of Aaron, and the Levites, and have made you priests after the man-ner of the nations of *other* lands? ᴿso that whosoever cometh to consecrate himself with a young bullock and seven rams, *the same* may be a priest of ᴿthem that are no gods. 11:13–15 · Ex. 29:29–33 · Jer. 2:11

10 But as for us, the Lᴏʀᴅ *is* our ᴿGod, and we have not forsaken him; and the priests, which minis-ter unto the Lᴏʀᴅ, *are* the sons of Aaron, and the Levites *wait* upon *their* business: Josh. 24:15

11 ᴿAnd they burn unto the Lᴏʀᴅ every morning and every evening burnt sacrifices and sweet incense: the shewbread also *set they in order* upon the pure table; and the candlestick of gold with the lamps thereof, to burn every evening: for we keep the charge of the Lᴏʀᴅ our God; but ye have forsaken him. Ex. 29:38

12 And, behold, God himself *is* with us for *our* ᴿcaptain, and his priests with sounding trumpets to cry alarm against you. O children of Israel, fight ye not against the Lᴏʀᴅ God of your fathers; for ye shall not prosper.   [Heb. 2:10]

13 But Jer-o-bo'-am caused an ambushment to come about be-hind them: so they were before Judah, and the ambushment *was* behind them.

14 And when Judah looked back, behold, the battle *was* be-fore and behind: and they ᴿcried

unto the LORD, and the priests sounded with the trumpets. 14:11

15 Then the men of Judah gave a shout: and as the men of Judah shouted, it came to pass, that God ᴿsmote Jer-o-bo'-am and all Israel before A-bi'-jah and Judah. 14:12

16 And the children of Israel fled before Judah: and God delivered them into their hand.

17 And A-bi'-jah and his people ᵀslew them with a great slaughter: so there fell down slain of Israel five hundred thousand chosen men. Lit. *struck*

18 Thus the children of Israel were brought under at that time, and the children of Judah prevailed, because they relied upon the LORD God of their fathers.

19 And A-bi'-jah pursued after Jer-o-bo'-am, and took cities from him, Beth'-el with the towns thereof, and Jesh'-a-nah with the towns thereof, and E'-phra-in with the towns thereof.

20 Neither did Jer-o-bo'-am recover strength again in the days of A-bi'-jah: and the LORD ᴿstruck him, and he died. Acts 12:23

21 But A-bi'-jah waxed mighty, and married fourteen wives, and begat twenty and two sons, and sixteen daughters.

22 And the rest of the acts of A-bi'-jah, and his ways, and his sayings, *are* written in ᴿthe story of the prophet Id'-do. 9:29

14 So A-bi'-jah slept with his fathers, and they buried him in the city of David: and A'-sa his son reigned in his stead. In his days the land was quiet ten years.

2 And A'-sa did *that which was* good and right in the eyes of the LORD his God:

3 For he took away the altars of the strange *gods,* and the high places, and brake down the images, and cut down the groves:

4 And commanded Judah to ᴿseek the LORD God of their fathers, and to ᵀdo the law and the commandment. [7:14] · *observe*

5 Also he took away out of all the cities of Judah the high places and the images: and the kingdom was quiet ᵀbefore him. *under*

6 And he built ᵀfenced cities in Judah: for the land had rest, and he had no war in those years; because the LORD had given him ᴿrest. *fortified* · 15:15

7 Therefore he said unto Judah, Let us build these cities, and make about *them* walls, and towers, gates, and bars, *while* the land *is* yet before us; because we have sought the LORD our God, we have sought *him,* and he hath given us rest on every side. So they built and prospered.

8 And A'-sa had an army *of men* that bare ᵀtargets and spears, out of Judah three hundred thousand; and out of Benjamin, that bare shields and drew ᴿbows, two hundred and fourscore thousand: all these *were* mighty men of ᴿvalour. *large shields* · 1 Chr. 12:2 · 13:3

9 ᴿAnd there came out against them Ze'-rah the E-thi-o'-pi-an with an host of a thousand thousand, and three hundred chariots; and came unto Ma-re'-shah. 16:8

10 Then A'-sa went out against him, and they set the battle in array in the valley of Zeph'-a-thah at Ma-re'-shah.

11 And A'-sa ᴿcried unto the LORD his God, and said, LORD, *it is* nothing with thee to help, whether with many, or with them that have no power: help us, O LORD our God; for we rest on thee, and in thy name we go against this multitude. O LORD, thou *art* our God; let not man prevail against thee. 13:14; Ex. 14:10; [Ps. 22:5]

12 So the LORD ᴿsmoteᵀ the E-thi-o'-pi-ans before A'-sa, and before Judah; and the E-thi-o'-pi-ans fled. 13:15 · Lit. *struck*

13 And A'-sa and the people that *were* with him pursued them unto Ge'-rar: and the E-thi-o'-pi-ans were overthrown, that they could not recover themselves; for they were destroyed before the LORD, and before his host; and they carried away very much spoil.

14 And they smote all the cities round about Ge'-rar; for ^Rthe fear of the Lord came upon them: and they ^Tspoiled all the cities; for there was exceeding much spoil in them.　Gen. 35:5; Josh. 2:9 · *plundered*

15 They smote also the tents of cattle, and carried away sheep and camels in abundance, and returned to Jerusalem.

15 And ^Rthe Spirit of God came upon Az-a-ri'-ah the son of O'-ded:　20:14; 24:20; Num. 24:2

2 And he went out to meet A'-sa, and said unto him, Hear ye me, A'-sa, and all Judah and Benjamin; ^RThe Lord *is* with you, while ye be with him; and ^Rif ye seek him, he will be found of you; but ^Rif ye forsake him, he will forsake you.　[James 4:8] · [Matt. 7:7] · 24:20

3 Now for a long season Israel *hath been* without the true God, and without a ^Rteaching priest, and without ^Rlaw.　2 Kin. 12:2 · 17:8, 9

4 But ^Rwhen they in their trouble did turn unto the Lord God of Israel, and sought him, he was found of them.　[Deut. 4:29]

5 And in those times *there was* no peace to him that went out, nor to him that came in, but great vexations *were* upon all the inhabitants of the countries.

6 ^RAnd nation was destroyed ^Tof nation, and city of city: for God did ^Tvex them with all adversity.　Matt. 24:7 · *by* · *trouble*

7 Be ye strong therefore, and let not your hands be weak: for your work shall be rewarded.

8 And when A'-sa heard these words, and the prophecy of O'-ded the prophet, he took courage, and put away the abominable idols out of all the land of Judah and Benjamin, and out of the cities which he had taken from mount E'-phra-im, and ^Trenewed the altar of the Lord, that *was* before the porch of the Lord.　*restored*

9 And he gathered all Judah and Benjamin, and the strangers with them out of E'-phra-im and Ma-nas'-seh, and out of Simeon: for they fell to him out of Israel in abundance, when they saw that the Lord his God *was* with him.

10 So they gathered themselves together at Jerusalem in the third month, in the fifteenth year of the reign of A'-sa.

11 ^RAnd they offered unto the Lord the same time, of the ^Tspoil *which* they had brought, seven hundred oxen and seven thousand sheep.　14:13–15 · *plunder*

12 And they ^Rentered into a covenant to seek the Lord God of their fathers with all their heart and with all their soul;　2 Kin. 23:3

13 ^RThat whosoever would not seek the Lord God of Israel ^Rshould be put to death, whether small or great, whether man or woman.　Ex. 22:20 · Deut. 13:5–15

14 And they sware unto the Lord with a loud voice, and with shouting, and with trumpets, and with ^Tcornets.　*rams' horns*

15 And all Judah rejoiced at the oath: for they had sworn with all their heart, and ^Rsought him with their whole desire; and he was found of them: and the Lord gave them ^Rrest round about.　v. 2 · 14:7

16 And also *concerning* ^RMa'-a-chah the mother of A'-sa the king, he removed her from *being* queen, because she had made an idol in a grove: and A'-sa cut down her idol, and stamped *it,* and burnt *it* at the brook Kid'-ron.　1 Kin. 15:2, 10

17 But ^Rthe high places were not taken away out of Israel: nevertheless the heart of A'-sa was ^Tperfect all his days.　14:3, 5 · *loyal*

18 And he brought into the house of God the things that his father had dedicated, and that he himself had dedicated, silver, and gold, and vessels.

19 And there was no *more* war unto the five and thirtieth year of the reign of A'-sa.

16 In the six and thirtieth year of the reign of A'-sa ^RBa'-a-sha king of Israel came up against Judah, and built Ra'-mah, ^Rto the intent that he might let none go out or come in to A'-sa king of Judah.　· 1 Kin. 15:17–22 · 15:9

2   Then A′-sa brought out silver and gold out of the treasures of the house of the Lord and of the king's house, and sent to Ben–ha′-dad king of Syria, that dwelt at Damascus, saying,

3   *There is* a ^Tleague between me and thee, as *there was* between my father and thy father: behold, I have sent thee silver and gold; go, break thy league with Ba′-a-sha king of Israel, that he may depart from me.   *treaty*

4   And Ben–ha′-dad hearkened unto king A′-sa, and sent the captains of his armies against the cities of Israel; and they smote I′-jon, and Dan, and A′-bel–ma′-im, and all the store cities of Naph′-ta-li.

5   And it came to pass, when Ba′-a-sha heard *it,* that he left off building of Ra′-mah, and let his work cease.

6   Then A′-sa the king took all Judah; and they carried away the stones of Ra′-mah, and the timber thereof, wherewith Ba′-a-sha was building; and he built therewith Ge′-ba and Miz-pah.

7   And at that time ^RHa-na′-ni the seer came to A′-sa king of Judah, and said unto him, ^RBecause thou hast relied on the king of Syria, and not relied on the Lord thy God, therefore is the host of the king of Syria escaped out of thine hand.   19:2 · 32:8–10

8   Were not ^Rthe E-thi-o′-pi-ans and the Lu′-bims a huge host, with very many chariots and horsemen? yet, because thou didst rely on the Lord, he delivered them into thine hand.   14:9

9   ^RFor the eyes of the Lord run to and fro throughout the whole earth, to shew himself strong in the behalf of *them* whose heart *is* perfect toward him. Herein thou hast done foolishly: therefore from henceforth thou shalt have wars.   [Prov. 5:21; Jer. 32:19]; Zech. 4:10

10   Then A′-sa was wroth with the seer, and ^Rput him in a prison house; for *he was* in a rage with him because of this *thing.* And A′-sa oppressed *some* of the people the same time.   Jer. 20:2; Matt. 14:3

11   ^RAnd, behold, the acts of A′-sa, first and last, lo, they *are* written in the book of the kings of Judah and Israel.   1 Kin. 15:23, 24

12   And A′-sa in the thirty and ninth year of his reign was diseased in his feet, until his disease *was* exceeding *great:* yet in his disease he sought not to the Lord, but to the physicians.

13   ^RAnd A′-sa slept with his fathers, and died in the one and fortieth year of his reign.   1 Kin. 15:24

14   And they buried him in his own sepulchres, which he had made for himself in the city of David, and laid him in the bed which was filled ^Rwith sweet odours and divers kinds *of spices* prepared by the apothecaries' art: and they made a very great burning for him.   Gen. 50:2; John 19:39, 40

17 And ^RJe-hosh′-a-phat his son reigned in his ^Tstead, and strengthened himself against Israel.   20:31; 1 Kin. 15:24 · *place*

2   And he placed forces in all the fenced cities of Judah, and set garrisons in the land of Judah, and in the cities of E′-phra-im, which A′-sa his father had taken.

3   And the Lord was with Je-hosh′-a-phat, because he walked in the first ways of his father David, and sought not unto Ba′-al-im;

4   But sought to the Lord God of his father, and walked in his commandments, and not after ^Rthe doings of Israel.   1 Kin. 12:28

5   Therefore the Lord stablished the kingdom in his hand; and all Judah ^Rbrought to Je-hosh′-a-phat presents; ^Rand he had riches and honour in abundance.   1 Sam. 10:27; 1 Kin. 10:25 · 18:1

6   And his heart was lifted up in the ways of the Lord: moreover ^Rhe took away the high places and groves out of Judah.   15:17; 19:3; 20:33

7   Also in the third year of his reign he sent to his princes, *even* to Ben–ha′-il, and to O-ba-di′-ah, and to Zech-a-ri′-ah, and to Ne-

than'-e-el, and to Mi-cha'-iah, ᴿto teach in the cities of Judah.　15:3

8　And with them *he sent* Levites, *even* She-ma'-iah, and Neth-a-ni'-ah, and Zeb-a-di'-ah, and A'-sa-hel, and She-mir'-a-moth, and Je-hon'-a-than, and Ad-o-ni'-jah, and To-bi'-jah, and Tob–ad-o-ni'-jah, Levites; and with them E-lish'-a-ma and Je-ho'-ram, priests.

9　ᴿAnd they taught in Judah, and *had* the book of the law of the LORD with them, and went about throughout all the cities of Judah, and taught the people.　Deut. 6:4–9

10　And ᴿthe fear of the LORD fell upon all the kingdoms of the lands that *were* round about Judah, so that they made no war against Je-hosh'-a-phat.　Gen. 35:5

11　Also *some* of the Phi-lis'-tines brought Je-hosh'-a-phat presents, and tribute silver; and the A-ra'-bi-ans brought him flocks, seven thousand and seven hundred rams, and seven thousand and seven hundred he goats.

12　And Je-hosh'-a-phat waxed great exceedingly; and he built in Judah castles, and cities of store.

13　And he had much business in the cities of Judah: and the men of war, mighty men of valour, *were* in Jerusalem.

14　And these *are* the numbers of them according to the house of their fathers: Of Judah, the captains of thousands; Ad'-nah the chief, and with him mighty men of valour three hundred thousand.

15　And next to him *was* Je-ho-ha'-nan the captain, and with him two hundred and fourscore thousand.

16　And next him *was* Am-a-si'-ah the son of Zich'-ri, who willingly offered himself unto the LORD; and with him two hundred thousand mighty men of valour.

17　And of Benjamin; E-li'-a-da a mighty man of valour, and with him armed men with bow and shield two hundred thousand.

18　And next him *was* Je-hoz'-a-bad, and with him an hundred

and fourscore thousand ready prepared for the war.

19　These waited on the king, beside ᴿ*those* whom the king put in the ᵀfenced cities throughout all Judah.　v. 2 · *fortified*

18 Now Je-hosh'-a-phat had riches and honour in abundance, and ᴿjoined affinity with Ahab.　1 Kin. 22:44; 2 Kin. 8:18

2　And after *certain* years he went down to Ahab to Sa-ma'-ri-a. And Ahab killed sheep and oxen for him in abundance, and for the people that *he had* with him, and persuaded him to go up *with him* to Ra'-moth–gil'-e-ad.

3　And Ahab king of Israel said unto Je-hosh'-a-phat king of Judah, Wilt thou go with me to Ra'-moth–gil'-e-ad? And he answered him, I *am* as thou *art*, and my people as thy people; and *we will be* with thee in the war.

4　And Je-hosh'-a-phat said unto the king of Israel, ᴿEnquire, I pray thee, at the word of the LORD to day.　1 Sam. 23:2, 4, 9; 2 Sam. 2:1

5　Therefore the king of Israel gathered together of prophets four hundred men, and said unto them, Shall we go to Ra'-moth–gil'-e-ad to battle, or shall I ᵀforbear? And they said, Go up; for God will deliver *it* into the king's hand.　*refrain*

6　But Je-hosh'-a-phat said, *Is there* not here a prophet of the LORD ᵀbesides, that we might enquire of ᴿhim?　Lit. *still* · 2 Kin. 3:11

7　And the king of Israel said unto Je-hosh'-a-phat, *There is* yet one man, by whom we may enquire of the LORD: but I hate him; for he never prophesied good unto me, but always evil: the same *is* Mi-ca'-iah the son of Im'-la. And Je-hosh'-a-phat said, Let not the king say so.

8　And the king of Israel called for one *of his* officers, and said, Fetch quickly Mi-ca'-iah the son of Im'-la.

9　And the king of Israel and Je-hosh'-a-phat king of Judah sat either of them on his throne, clothed in *their* robes, and they sat in a void place at the entering in of the gate of Sa-ma'-ri-a; and all the prophets prophesied before them.

10 And Zed-e-ki'-ah the son of Che-na'-a-nah had made him ^Rhorns of iron, and said, Thus saith the Lord, With these thou shalt push Syria until they be ^Tconsumed.   Zech. 1:18–21 · *destroyed*

11 And all the prophets prophesied so, saying, Go up to Ra'-moth–gil'-e-ad, and prosper: for the Lord shall deliver *it* into the hand of the king.

12 And the messenger that went to call Mi-ca'-iah spake to him, saying, Behold, the words of the prophets *declare* good to the king with one assent; let thy word therefore, I pray thee, be like one of theirs, and speak thou good.

13 And Mi-ca'-iah said, *As* the Lord liveth, ^Reven what my God saith, that will I speak.   1 Kin. 22:14

14 And when he was come to the king, the king said unto him, Mi-ca'-iah, shall we go to Ra'-moth–gil'-e-ad to battle, or shall I forbear? And he said, Go ye up, and prosper, and they shall be delivered into your hand.

15 And the king said to him, How many times shall I ^Tadjure thee that thou say nothing but the truth to me in the name of the Lord?   *make you swear*

16 Then he said, I did see all Israel scattered upon the mountains, as sheep that have no ^Rshepherd: and the Lord said, These have no master; let them return *therefore* every man to his house in peace.   Matt. 9:36; Mark 6:34

17 And the king of Israel said to Je-hosh'-a-phat, Did I not tell thee *that* he would not prophesy good unto me, but evil?

18 Again he said, Therefore hear the word of the Lord; I saw the Lord sitting upon his ^Rthrone, and all the host of heaven standing on his right hand and *on* his left.   Is. 6:1–5; Dan. 7:9, 10

19 And the Lord said, Who shall entice Ahab king of Israel, that he may go up and fall at Ra'-moth–gil'-e-ad? And one spake saying after this manner, and another saying after that manner.

20 Then there came out a spirit, and stood before the Lord, and said, I will entice him. And the Lord said unto him, Wherewith?

21 And he said, I will go out, and be a lying spirit in the mouth of all his prophets. And *the* Lord said, Thou shalt entice *him*, and thou shalt also prevail: go out, and do *even* so.

22 Now therefore, behold, ^Rthe Lord hath put a lying spirit in the mouth of these thy prophets, and the Lord hath ^Tspoken evil against thee. Is. 19:12 · *declared disaster*

23 Then Zed-e-ki'-ah the son of Che-na'-a-nah came near, and ^Rsmote Mi-ca'-iah upon the cheek, and said, Which way went the Spirit of the Lord from me to speak unto thee? Jer. 20:2; Mark 14:65

24 And Mi-ca'-iah said, Behold, thou shalt see on that day when thou shalt go into an inner chamber to hide thyself.

25 Then the king of Israel said, Take ye Mi-ca'-iah, and carry him back to Amon the governor of the city, and to Jo'-ash the king's son;

26 And say, Thus saith the king, ^RPut this *fellow* in the prison, and feed him with bread of affliction and with water of affliction, until I return in peace.   16:10

27 And Mi-ca'-iah said, If thou certainly return in peace, *then* hath not the Lord spoken by ^Rme. And he said, Hearken, all ye people.   Deut. 18:22

28 So the king of Israel and Je-hosh'-a-phat the king of Judah went up to Ra'-moth–gil'-e-ad.

29 And the king of Israel said unto Je-hosh'-a-phat, I will ^Rdisguise myself, and will go to the battle; but put thou on thy robes. So the king of Israel disguised himself; and they went to the battle.   35:22

30 Now the king of Syria had commanded the captains of the

chariots that *were* with him, saying, Fight ye not with small or great, save only with the king of Israel.

31 And it came to pass, when the captains of the chariots saw Je-hosh'-a-phat, that they said, It *is* the king of Israel. Therefore they ᵀcompassed about him to fight: but Je-hosh'-a-phat ᴿcried out, and the LORD helped him; and God moved them *to depart* from him.   *surrounded* · 13:14, 15

32 For it came to pass, that, when the captains of the chariots perceived that it was not the king of Israel, they turned back again from pursuing him.

33 And a *certain* man drew a bow at a venture, and smote the king of Israel between the joints of the harness: therefore he said to his chariot man, Turn thine hand, that thou mayest carry me out of the host; for I am wounded.

34 And the battle increased that day: howbeit the king of Israel stayed *himself* up in *his* chariot against the Syrians until the even: and about the time of the sun going down he died.

19 And Je-hosh'-a-phat the king of Judah returned to his house in peace to Jerusalem.

2   And Je'-hu the son of Ha-na'-ni ᴿthe seer went out to meet him, and said to king Je-hosh'-a-phat, Shouldest thou help the ungodly, and love them that hate the LORD? therefore *is* ᴿwrath upon thee from before the LORD.   20:34 · 32:25

3   Nevertheless there are ᴿgood things found in thee, in that thou hast taken away the groves out of the land, and hast ᴿprepared thine heart to seek God.   17:4, 6 · 30:19

4   And Je-hosh'-a-phat dwelt at Jerusalem: and he went out again through the people from Be'-er–she'-ba to mount E'-phra-im, and brought them back unto the LORD God of their ᴿfathers.   15:8–13

5   And he set judges in the land throughout all the ᵀfenced cities of Judah, city by city,   *fortified*

6   And said to the judges, Take

heed what ye do: for ᴿye judge not for man, but for the LORD, who *is* with you in the judgment.   Ps. 58:1

7   Wherefore now let the fear of the LORD be upon you; take heed and do *it:* for *there is* no iniquity with the LORD our God, nor ᴿrespect of persons, nor taking of gifts.   Acts 10:34; Rom. 2:11; Gal. 2:6

8   Moreover in Jerusalem did Je-hosh'-a-phat ᴿsetᵀ of the Levites, and *of* the priests, and of the chief of the fathers of Israel, for the judgment of the LORD, and for controversies, when they returned to Jerusalem.   17:8; Deut. 16:18 · *appoint*

9   And he charged them, saying, Thus shall ye do ᴿin the fear of the LORD, faithfully, and with a ᵀperfect heart.   [2 Sam. 23:3] · *loyal*

10 And what cause soever shall come to you of your brethren that dwell in their cities, between blood and blood, between law and commandment, statutes and judgments, ye shall even warn them that they trespass not against the LORD, and *so* wrath come upon you, and upon your brethren: this do, and ye shall not trespass.

11 And, behold, ᴿAm-a-ri'-ah the chief priest *is* over you in all matters of the LORD; and Zeb-a-di'-ah the son of Ish'-ma-el, the ruler of the house of Judah, for all the king's matters: also the Levites *shall be* officers before you. Deal courageously, and the LORD shall be with the good.   Ezra 7:3

20 It came to pass after this also, *that* the children of ᴿMoab, and the children of Am-mon, and with them *other* beside the Am'-mon-ites, came against Je-hosh'-a-phat to battle. 1 Chr. 18:2

2   Then there came some that told Je-hosh'-a-phat, saying, There cometh a great multitude against thee from beyond the sea on this side Syria; and, behold, they *be* in Haz'-a-zon–ta'-mar, which *is* ᴿEn-ge'-di.   Josh. 15:62

3   And Je-hosh'-a-phat feared, and set himself to ᴿseek the LORD, and ᴿproclaimed a fast throughout all Judah.   19:3 · 1 Sam. 7:6; Jon. 3:5

4 And Judah gathered themselves together, to ask ᴿhelp of the LORD: even out of all the cities of Judah they came to seek the LORD.   14:11

5 And Je-hosh′-a-phat stood in the congregation of Judah and Jerusalem, in the house of the LORD, before the new court,

6 And said, O LORD God of our fathers, *art* not thou ᴿGod in heaven? and rulest *not* thou over all the kingdoms of the heathen? and ᴿin thine hand *is there not* power and might, so that none is able to withstand thee?   Matt. 6:9 · Matt. 6:13

7 *Art* not thou our God, *who* ᴿdidst drive out the inhabitants of this land before thy people Israel, and gavest it to the seed of Abraham thy friend for ever?   Ps. 44:2

8 And they dwelt therein, and have built thee a sanctuary therein for thy name, saying,

9 ᴿIf, *when* evil cometh upon us, *as* the sword, judgment, or pestilence, or famine, we stand before this house, and in thy presence, (for thy ᴿname *is* in this house,) and cry unto thee in our affliction, then thou wilt hear and help.   6:28–30; 1 Kin. 8:33, 37 · 6:20

10 And now, behold, the children of Ammon and Moab and mount Se′-ir, whom thou wouldest not let Israel invade, when they came out of the land of Egypt, but they turned from them, and destroyed them not;

11 Behold, I *say, how* they reward us, ᴿto come to cast us out of thy possession, which thou hast given us to inherit.   Ps. 83:1–18

12 O our God, wilt thou not judge them? for we have no might against this great company that cometh against us; neither know we what to do: but ᴿour eyes *are* upon thee.   Ps. 25:15; 121:1, 2; 123:1, 2

13 And all Judah stood before the LORD, with their little ones, their wives, and their children.

14 Then upon Ja-ha′-zi-el the son of Zech-a-ri′-ah, the son of Be-na′-iah, the son of Je-i′-el, the son of Mat-ta-ni′-ah, a Levite of the sons of A′-saph, ᴿcame the Spirit of the LORD in the midst of the congregation; Num. 11:25, 26; 24:2

15 And he said, Hearken ye, all Judah, and ye inhabitants of Jerusalem, and thou king Je-hosh′-a-phat, Thus saith the LORD unto you, ᴿBe not afraid nor dismayed by reason of this great multitude; ᴿfor the battle *is* not yours, but God's.   Ex. 14:13, 14 · Zech. 14:3

16 To morrow go ye down against them: behold, they come up by the cliff of Ziz; and ye shall find them at the end of the brook, before the wilderness of Je-ru′-el.

17 ᴿYe shall not *need* to fight in this *battle:* set yourselves, stand ye *still,* and see the salvation of the LORD with you, O Judah and Jerusalem: fear not, nor be dismayed; to morrow go out against them: ᴿfor the LORD *will be* with you.   Ex. 14:13, 14 · Num. 14:9; [15:2; 32:8]

18 And Je-hosh′-a-phat ᴿbowed his head with *his* face to the ground: and all Judah and the inhabitants of Jerusalem fell before the LORD, worshipping the LORD.   7:3; 29:28; Ex. 4:31

19 And the Levites, of the children of the Ko′-hath-ites, and of the children of the Kor′-hites, stood up to praise the LORD God of Israel with a loud voice on high.

20 And they rose early in the morning, and went forth into the wilderness of Te-ko′-a: and as they went forth, Je-hosh′-a-phat stood and said, Hear me, O Judah, and ye inhabitants of Jerusalem; Believe in the LORD your God, so shall ye be established; believe his prophets, so shall ye prosper.

21 And when he had consulted with the people, he appointed singers unto the LORD, ᴿand that should praise the beauty of holiness, as they went out before the army, and to say, ᴿPraise the LORD; for his mercy *endureth* for ever. Ps. 29:2; 96:9; 110:3 · Ps. 106:1; 136:1

22 And when they began to sing and to praise, ᴿthe LORD set ambushments against the chil-

dren of Ammon, Moab, and mount Se′-ir, which were come against Judah; and they were smitten.   Judg. 7:22; 1 Sam. 14:20

23 For the children of Ammon and Moab stood up against the inhabitants of mount Se′-ir, utterly to slay and destroy *them:* and when they had made an end of the inhabitants of Se′-ir, every one helped to destroy another.

24 And when Judah came toward the watch tower in the wilderness, they looked unto the multitude, and, behold, they *were* dead bodies fallen to the earth, and none escaped.

25 And when Je-hosh′-a-phat and his people came to take away the spoil of them, they found among them in abundance both riches with the dead bodies, and precious jewels, which they stripped off for themselves, more than they could carry away: and they were three days in gathering of the spoil, it was so much.

26 And on the fourth day they assembled themselves in the valley of ᵀBer′-a-chah; for there they blessed the LORD: therefore the name of the same place was called, The valley of Ber′-a-chah, unto this day.   Lit. *Blessing*

27 Then they returned, every man of Judah and Jerusalem, and Je-hosh′-a-phat in the forefront of them, to go again to Jerusalem with joy; for the LORD had ᴿmade them to rejoice over their enemies.   Neh. 12:43

28 And they came to Jerusalem with ᵀpsalteries and harps and trumpets unto the house of the LORD.   *stringed instruments*

29 And ᴿthe fear of God was on all the kingdoms of *those* countries, when they had heard that the LORD fought against the enemies of Israel.   14:14; 17:10

30 So the realm of Je-hosh′-a-phat was quiet: for his ᴿGod gave him rest round about. 1 Kin. 22:41–43

31 ᴿAnd Je-hosh′-a-phat reigned over Judah: *he was* thirty and five years old when he began to reign,

and he reigned twenty and five years in Jerusalem. And his mother's name *was* A-zu′-bah the daughter of Shil′-hi. [1 Kin. 22:41–43]

32 And he walked in the way of ᴿA′-sa his father, and departed not from it, doing *that which was* right in the sight of the LORD. 14:2

33 Howbeit ᴿthe high places were not taken away: for as yet the people had not ᴿprepared their hearts unto the God of their fathers.   15:17; 17:6 · 12:14; 19:3

34 Now the rest of the acts of Je-hosh′-a-phat, first and last, behold, they *are* written in the book of Je′-hu the son of Ha-na′-ni, ᴿwho *is* mentioned in the book of the kings of Israel.   1 Kin. 16:1, 7

35 And after this ᴿdid Je-hosh′-a-phat king of Judah join himself with A-ha-zi′-ah king of Israel, who did very ᴿwickedly: 18:1 · [19:2]

36 And he joined himself with him ᴿto make ships to go to Tar′-shish: and they made the ships in E′-zi-on–ga′-ber.   1 Kin. 9:26; 10:22

37 Then E-li-e′-zer the son of Dod′-a-vah of Ma-re′-shah prophesied against Je-hosh′-a-phat, saying, Because thou hast joined thyself with A-ha-zi′-ah, the LORD hath broken thy works. And the ships were broken, that they were not able to go ᴿto Tar′-shish.   9:21

21 Now ᴿJe-hosh′-a-phat slept with his fathers, and was buried with his fathers in the city of David. And Je-ho′-ram his son reigned in his stead. 1 Kin. 22:50

2 And he had brethren the sons of Je-hosh′-a-phat, Az-a-ri′-ah, and Je-hi′-el, and Zech-a-ri′-ah, and Az-a-ri′-ah, and Mi′-cha-el, and Sheph-a-ti′-ah: all these *were* the sons of Je-hosh′-a-phat king of Israel.

3 And their father gave them great gifts of silver, and of gold, and of precious things, with fenced cities in Judah: but the kingdom gave he to Je-ho′-ram; because he *was* the firstborn.

4 Now when Je-ho′-ram was ᵀrisen up to the kingdom of his

father, he strengthened himself, and slew all his brethren with the sword, and *divers* also of the princes of Israel.   *established*

5 ᴿJe-ho'-ram *was* thirty and two years old when he began to reign, and he reigned eight years in Jerusalem.   2 Kin. 8:17–22

6 And he walked in the way of the kings of Israel, like as did the house of Ahab: for he had the daughter of ᴿAhab ᵀto wife: and he wrought *that which was* evil in the eyes of the LORD.   18:1 · *as a wife*

7 Howbeit the LORD would not destroy the house of David, because of the ᴿcovenant that he had made with David, and as he promised to give a light to him and to his sons for ever.   2 Sam. 7:8–17

8 ᴿIn his days the E'-dom-ites revolted from under the dominion of Judah, and made themselves a king.   25:14, 19; 2 Kin. 8:20; 14:7, 10

9 Then Je-ho'-ram went forth with his princes, and all his chariots with him: and he rose up by night, and smote the E'-dom-ites which compassed him in, and the captains of the chariots.

10 So the E'-dom-ites revolted from under the hand of Judah unto this day. The same time *also* did Lib'-nah revolt from under his hand; because he had forsaken the LORD God of his fathers.

11 Moreover he made high places in the mountains of Judah, and caused the inhabitants of Jerusalem to commit fornication, and compelled Judah *thereto*.

12 And there came a writing to him from E-li'-jah the prophet, saying, Thus saith the LORD God of David thy father, Because thou hast not walked in the ways of Je-hosh'-a-phat thy father, nor in the ways of A'-sa king of Judah,

13 But hast walked in the way of the kings of Israel, and hast made Judah and the inhabitants of Jerusalem to go a whoring, like to the whoredoms of the house of Ahab, and also hast slain thy brethren of thy father's house, *which were* better than thyself:

14 Behold, with a great plague will the LORD smite thy people, and thy children, and thy wives, and all thy goods:

15 And thou *shalt have* great sickness by disease of thy bowels, until thy bowels fall out by reason of the sickness day by day.

16 Moreover the LORD ᴿstirred up against Je-ho'-ram the spirit of the Phi-lis'-tines, and of the ᴿA-ra'-bi-ans, that *were* near the E-thi-o'-pi-ans: 1 Kin. 11:14, 23 · 17:11

17 And they came up into Judah, and brake into it, and carried away all the substance that was found in the king's house, and ᴿhis sons also, and his wives; so that there was never a son left him, save Je-ho'-a-haz, the youngest of his sons.   24:7

18 And after all this the LORD smote him ᴿin his bowels with an incurable disease.   13:20; Acts 12:23

19 And it came to pass, that in process of time, after the end of two years, his bowels fell out by reason of his sickness: so he died of sore diseases. And his people made no burning for him, like ᴿthe burning of his fathers.   16:14

20 Thirty and two years old was he when he began to reign, and he reigned in Jerusalem eight years, and departed without being desired. Howbeit they buried him in the city of David, but not in the sepulchres of the kings.

22 And the inhabitants of Jerusalem made ᴿA-ha-zi'-ah his youngest son king in his stead: for the band of men that came with the ᴿA-ra'-bi-ans to the camp had slain all the eldest. So A-ha-zi'-ah the son of Je-ho'-ram king of Judah reigned.   v. 6; 21:17 · 21:16

2 Forty and two years old *was* A-ha-zi'-ah when he began to reign, and he reigned one year in Jerusalem. His mother's name also *was* ᴿAth-a-li'-ah the ᵀdaughter of Om'-ri.   21:6 · *granddaughter*

3 He also walked in the ways of the house of Ahab: for his mother was his counsellor to do wickedly.

4 Wherefore he did evil in the

sight of the LORD like the house of Ahab: for they were his counsellors after the death of his father to his destruction.

5 He walked also after their counsel, and went with Je-ho'-ram the son of Ahab king of Israel to war against Haz'-a-el king of Syria at Ra'-moth–gil'-e-ad: and the Syrians smote Jo'-ram.

6 ᴿAnd he returned to be healed in Jez'-re-el because of the wounds which were given him at Ra'-mah, when he fought with Haz'-a-el king of Syria. And Az-a-ri'-ah the son of Je-ho'-ram king of Judah went down to see Je-ho'-ram the son of Ahab at Jez'-re-el, because he was sick.   2 Kin. 9:15

7 And the destruction of A-ha-zi'-ah ᴿwas of God by coming to Jo'-ram: for when he was come, he went out with Je-ho'-ram against Je'-hu the son of Nim'-shi, whom the LORD had anointed to cut off the house of Ahab.   10:15

8 And it came to pass, that, when Je'-hu was executing judgment upon the house of Ahab, and ᴿfound the princes of Judah, and the sons of the brethren of A-ha-zi'-ah, that ministered to A-ha-zi'-ah, he slew them.   Hos. 1:4

9 And he sought A-ha-zi'-ah: and they caught him, (for he was hid in Sa-ma'-ri-a,) and brought him to Je'-hu: and when they had slain him, they buried him: Because, said they, he is the son of Je-hosh'-a-phat, who sought the LORD with all his heart. So the house of A-ha-zi'-ah had no power to keep still the kingdom.

10 But when Ath-a-li'-ah the mother of A-ha-zi'-ah saw that her son was dead, she arose and destroyed all the ᵀseed royal of the house of Judah.   royal heirs

11 But Je-ho-shab'-e-ath, the daughter of the king, took ᴿJo'-ash the son of A-ha-zi'-ah, and stole him from among the king's sons that were ᵀslain, and put him and his nurse in a bedchamber. So Je-ho-shab'-e-ath, the daughter of king Je-ho'-ram, the wife of Je-

hoi'-a-da the priest, (for she was the sister of A-ha-zi'-ah,) hid him from Ath-a-li'-ah, so that she slew him not.   2 Kin. 12:18 · being murdered

12 And he was with them hid in the house of God six years: and Ath-a-li'-ah reigned over the land.

23 And in the seventh year ᴿJe-hoi'-a-da strengthened himself, and took the captains of hundreds, Az-a-ri'-ah the son of Jer'-o-ham, and Ish'-ma-el the son of Je-ho-ha'-nan, and Az-a-ri'-ah the son of O'-bed, and Ma-a-se'-iah the son of A-da'-iah, and E-lish'-a-phat the son of Zich'-ri, into covenant with him.   2 Kin. 12:2

2 And they went about in Judah, and gathered the Levites out of all the cities of Judah, and the chief of the fathers of Israel, and they came to Jerusalem.

3 And all the congregation made a covenant with the king in the house of God. And he said unto them, Behold, the king's son shall reign, as the LORD hath ᴿsaid of the sons of David.   6:16; 7:18; 21:7

4 This is the thing that ye shall do; A third part of you ᴿentering on the sabbath, of the priests and of the Levites, shall be ᵀporters of the doors;   1 Chr. 9:25 · keeping watch

5 And a third part shall be at the king's house; and a third part at the gate of the foundation: and all the people shall be in the courts of the house of the LORD.

6 But let none come into the house of the LORD, save the priests, and they that minister of the Levites; they shall go in, for they are holy: but all the people shall keep the watch of the LORD.

7 And the Levites shall ᵀcompass the king round about, every man with his weapons in his hand; and whosoever else cometh into the house, he shall be put to death: but be ye with the king when he cometh in, and when he goeth out.   surround the king on all sides

8 So the Levites and all Judah did according to all things that Je-hoi'-a-da the priest had commanded, and took every man his

men that were to come in on the sabbath, with them that were to go *out* on the sabbath: for Je-hoi'-a-da the priest dismissed not ᴿthe courses.   1 Chr. 24:1–31

9 Moreover Je-hoi'-a-da the priest delivered to the captains of hundreds spears, and bucklers, and ᴿshields, that *had been* king David's, which *were* in the house of God.   2 Sam. 8:7

10 And he set all the people, every man having his weapon in his hand, from the right side of the temple to the left side of the temple, along by the altar and the temple, by the king round about.

11 Then they brought out the king's son, and put upon him the crown, and *gave him* the testimony, and made him king. And Je-hoi'-a-da and his sons anointed him, and said, God save the king.

12 Now when ᴿAth-a-li'-ah heard the noise of the people running and praising the king, she came to the people into the house of the Lᴏʀᴅ: 22:10

13 And she looked, and, behold, the king stood at his pillar at the entering in, and the princes and the trumpets by the king: and all the people of the land rejoiced, and sounded with trumpets, also the singers with instruments of musick, and ᴿsuch as taught to sing praise. Then Ath-a-li'-ah rent her clothes, and said, ᴿTreason, Treason.   1 Chr. 25:8 · 2 Kin. 9:23

14 Then Je-hoi'-a-da the priest brought out the captains of hundreds that were set over the host, and said unto them, ᵀHave her forth of the ranges: and whoso followeth her, let him be slain with the sword. For the priest said, Slay her not in the house of the Lᴏʀᴅ.   *Take her outside under guard*

15 So they laid hands on her; and when she was come to the entering of the horse gate by the king's house, they slew her there.

16 And Je-hoi'-a-da made a ᴿcovenant between him, and between all the people, and between the king, that they should be the Lᴏʀᴅ's people.   15:12–15; Josh. 24:24, 25

17 Then all the people went to the ᵀhouse of Ba'-al, and brake it down, and brake his altars and his images in pieces, and ᴿslew Mat'-tan the priest of Ba'-al before the altars.   *temple* · Deut. 13:6–9; 1 Kin. 18:40

18 Also Je-hoi'-a-da appointed the offices of the house of the Lᴏʀᴅ by the hand of the priests the Levites, whom David had ᴿdistributed in the house of the Lᴏʀᴅ, to offer the burnt offerings of the Lᴏʀᴅ, as *it is* written in the ᴿlaw of Moses, with rejoicing and with singing, *as it was ordained* by David.   1 Chr. 23:6, 30, 31 · Num. 28:2

19 And he set the porters at the gates of the house of the Lᴏʀᴅ, that none *which was* unclean in any thing should enter in.

20 And he took the captains of hundreds, and the nobles, and the governors of the people, and all the people of the land, and brought down the king from the house of the Lᴏʀᴅ: and they came through the high gate into the king's house, and set the king upon the throne of the kingdom.

21 And all the people of the land rejoiced: and the city was quiet, after that they had slain Ath-a-li'-ah with the sword.

24 Jo'-ash *was* seven years old when he began to reign, and he reigned forty years in Jerusalem. His mother's name also *was* Zib'-i-ah of Be'-er–she'-ba.

2 And Jo'-ash ᴿdid *that which was* right in the sight of the Lᴏʀᴅ all the days of Je-hoi'-a-da the priest.   26:4, 5

3 And Je-hoi'-a-da took for him two wives; and he begat sons and daughters.

4 And it came to pass after this, *that* Jo'-ash was minded to repair the house of the Lᴏʀᴅ.

5 And he gathered together the priests and the Levites, and said to them, Go out unto the cities of Judah, and gather of all Israel money to repair the house of your God from year to year, and see

that ye hasten the matter. However the Levites hastened *it* not.

6 And the king called for Je-hoi'-a-da the chief, and said unto him, Why hast thou not required of the Levites to bring in out of Judah and out of Jerusalem the collection, *according to the commandment* of ᴿMoses the servant of the LORD, and of the congregation of Israel, for the ᴿtabernacle of witness?   Ex. 30:12–16 · Acts 7:44

7 For ᴿthe sons of Ath-a-li'-ah, that wicked woman, had broken up the house of God; and also all the ᴿdedicated things of the house of the LORD did they bestow upon Ba'-al-im.   21:17 · 2 Kin. 12:4

8 And at the king's commandment ᴿthey made a chest, and set it ᵀwithout at the gate of the house of the LORD.   2 Kin. 12:9 · *outside*

9 And they made a proclamation through Judah and Jerusalem, to bring in to the LORD ᴿthe collection *that* Moses the servant of God *laid* upon Israel in the wilderness.   v. 6

10 And all the princes and all the people rejoiced, and brought in, and cast into the chest, until ᵀthey had made an end. *all had given*

11 Now it came to pass, that at what time the chest was brought unto the king's office by the hand of the Levites, and ᴿwhen they saw that *there was* much money, the king's scribe and the high priest's officer came and emptied the chest, and took it, and carried it to his place again. Thus they did day by day, and gathered money in abundance.   2 Kin. 12:10

12 And the king and Je-hoi'-a-da gave it to such as did the work of the service of the house of the LORD, and hired masons and carpenters to ᴿrepair the house of the LORD, and also such as wrought iron and brass to mend the house of the LORD.   30:12

13 So the workmen wrought, and the work was perfected by them, and they set the house of God ᵀin his state, and strengthened it.   *in its original condition*

14 And when they had finished *it*, they brought the rest of the money before the king and Je-hoi'-a-da, ᴿwhereof were made vessels for the house of the LORD, *even* vessels to minister, and to offer *withal*, and spoons, and vessels of gold and silver. And they offered burnt offerings in the house of the LORD continually all the days of Je-hoi'-a-da. 2 Kin. 12:13

15 But Je-hoi'-a-da waxed old, and was full of days when he died; an hundred and thirty years old *was he* when he died.

16 And they buried him in the city of David among the kings, because he had done good in Israel, both toward God, and toward his house.

17 Now after the death of Je-hoi'-a-da came the princes of Judah, and ᵀmade obeisance to the king. Then the king hearkened unto them.   *bowed down*

18 And they left the house of the LORD God of their fathers, and served groves and idols: and wrath came upon Judah and Jerusalem for this their trespass.

19 Yet he ᴿsent prophets to them, to bring them again unto the LORD; and they testified against them: but they would not give ear.   36:15, 16; Jer. 7:25, 26; 25:4

20 And the Spirit of God came upon Zech-a-ri'-ah the son of Je-hoi'-a-da the priest, which stood above the people, and said unto them, Thus saith God, Why transgress ye the commandments of the LORD, that ye cannot prosper? because ye have forsaken the LORD, he hath also forsaken you.

21 And they conspired against him, and ᴿstoned him with stones at the commandment of the king in the court of the house of the LORD.   Matt. 23:35; Acts 7:58, 59

22 Thus Jo'-ash the king remembered not the kindness which Je-hoi'-a-da his father had done to him, but slew his son. And when he died, he said, The LORD look upon *it*, and ᴿrequire *it*.   [Gen. 9:5]

23 And it came to pass at the

end of the year, *that* ^Rthe host of Syria came up against him: and they came to Judah and Jerusalem, and destroyed all the princes of the people from among the people, and sent all the ^Tspoil of them unto the king of Damascus.   2 Kin. 12:17; Is. 7:2 · *plunder*

24 For the army of the Syrians ^Rcame with a small company of men, and the LORD ^Rdelivered a very great host into their hand, because they had forsaken the LORD God of their fathers. So they ^Rexecuted judgment against Jo'-ash.   Is. 30:17 · Lev. 26:25 · 22:8; Is. 10:5

25 And when they were departed from him, (for they left him in great diseases,) ^Rhis own servants conspired against him for the blood of the sons of Je-hoi'-a-da the priest, and slew him on his bed, and he died: and they buried him in the city of David, but they buried him not in the sepulchres of the kings.   25:3; 2 Kin. 12:20, 21

26 And these are they that conspired against him; Za'-bad the son of Shim'-e-ath an Am'-mon-i-tess, and Je-ho'-za-bad the son of Shim'-rith a Mo'-ab-i-tess.

27 Now *concerning* his sons, and the greatness of the burdens *laid* upon him, and the repairing of the house of God, behold, they *are* written in the story of the book of the kings. And Am-a-zi'-ah his son reigned in his stead.

25 Am-a-zi'-ah *was* twenty and five years old *when* he began to reign, and he reigned twenty and nine years in Jerusalem. And his mother's name *was* Je-ho-ad'-dan of Jerusalem.

2 And he did *that which was* right in the sight of the LORD, but not with a ^Tperfect heart.   *loyal*

3 ^RNow it came to pass, when the kingdom was established to him, that he slew his servants that had killed the king his father. 24:25

4 But he slew not their children, but *did* as *it is* written in the law in the book of Moses, where the LORD commanded, saying, The fathers shall not die for the

children, neither shall the children die for the fathers, but every man shall die for his own sin.

5 Moreover Am-a-zi'-ah gathered Judah together, and made them captains over thousands, and captains over hundreds, according to the houses of *their* fathers, throughout all Judah and Benjamin: and he numbered them ^Rfrom twenty years old and above, and found them three hundred thousand choice *men, able* to go forth to war, that could handle spear and shield.   Num. 1:3

6 He hired also an hundred thousand mighty men of valour out of Israel for an hundred talents of silver.

7 But there came a ^Rman of God to him, saying, O king, let not the army of Israel go with thee; for the LORD *is* not with Israel, *to wit, with* all the children of E'-phra-im.   11:2

8 But if thou wilt go, do *it,* be strong for the battle: God shall make thee fall before the enemy: for God hath ^Rpower to help, and to cast down.   14:11; 20:6

9 And Am-a-zi'-ah said to the man of God, But what shall we do for the hundred talents which I have given to the army of Israel? And the man of God answered, ^RThe LORD is able to give thee much more than this.   [Deut. 8:18]

10 Then Am-a-zi'-ah separated them, *to wit,* the army that was come to him out of E'-phra-im, to go home again: wherefore their anger was greatly kindled against Judah, and they returned home in great anger.

11 And Am-a-zi'-ah strengthened himself, and led forth his people, and went to ^Rthe valley of salt, and smote of the children of Se'-ir ten thousand.   2 Kin. 14:7

12 And *other* ten thousand *left* alive did the children of Judah carry away captive, and brought them unto the top of the rock, and cast them down from the top of the rock, that they all were ^Tbroken in pieces.   *dashed in pieces*

13 But the soldiers of the army which Am-a-zi′-ah sent back, that they should not go with him to battle, fell upon the cities of Judah, from Sa-ma′-ri-a even unto Beth–ho′-ron, and smote three thousand of them, and took much ^Tspoil.   *plunder*

14 Now it came to pass, after that Am-a-zi′-ah was come from the slaughter of the E′-dom-ites, that ^Rhe brought the gods of the children of Se′-ir, and set them up to be ^Rhis gods, and bowed down himself before them, and burned incense unto them. 28:23 · [Ex. 20:3, 5]

15 Wherefore the anger of the LORD was kindled against Am-a-zi′-ah, and he sent unto him a prophet, which said unto him, Why hast thou sought after ^Rthe gods of the people, which ^Rcould not deliver their own people out of thine hand?   [Ps. 96:5] · v. 11

16 And it came to pass, as he talked with him, that *the king* said unto him, Art thou made of the king's counsel? forbear; why shouldest thou be smitten? Then the prophet forbare, and said, I know that God hath ^Rdetermined to destroy thee, because thou hast done this, and hast not hearkened unto my counsel.   [1 Sam. 2:25]

17 Then ^RAm-a-zi′-ah king of Judah took advice, and sent to Jo′-ash, the son of Je-ho′-a-haz, the son of Je′-hu, king of Israel, saying, Come, let us see one another in the face.   2 Kin. 14:8–14

18 And Jo′-ash king of Israel sent to Am-a-zi′-ah king of Judah, saying, The thistle that *was* in Leb′-a-non sent to the cedar that *was* in Leb′-a-non, saying, Give thy daughter to my son to wife: and there passed by a wild beast that *was* in Leb′-a-non, and ^Ttrode down the thistle.   *trampled*

19 Thou sayest, Lo, thou hast smitten the E′-dom-ites; and thine heart lifteth thee up to ^Rboast: abide now at home; why shouldest thou meddle to *thine* hurt, that thou shouldest fall, *even* thou, and Judah with thee?   26:16; 32:25

20 But Am-a-zi′-ah would not hear; for it *came* of God, that he might deliver them into the hand *of their enemies*, because they sought after the gods of E′-dom.

21 So Jo′-ash the king of Israel went up; and they saw one another in the face, *both* he and Am-a-zi′-ah king of Judah, at ^RBeth–she′-mesh, which *belongeth* to Judah.   Josh. 19:38

22 And Judah was ^Tput to the worse before Israel, and they fled every man to his tent.   *defeated by*

23 And Jo′-ash the king of Israel took Am-a-zi′-ah king of Judah, the son of Jo′-ash, the son of Je-ho′-a-haz, at Beth–she′-mesh, and brought him to Jerusalem, and brake down the wall of Jerusalem from the gate of E′-phra-im to the corner gate, four hundred cubits.

24 And *he took* all the gold and the silver, and all the vessels that were found in the house of God with ^RO′-bed–e′-dom, and the treasures of the king's house, the hostages also, and returned to Sa-ma′-ri-a.   1 Chr. 26:15

25 And Am-a-zi′-ah the son of Jo′-ash king of Judah lived after the death of Jo′-ash son of Je-ho′-a-haz king of Israel fifteen years.

26 Now the rest of the acts of Am-a-zi′-ah, first and last, behold, *are* they not written in the book of the kings of Judah and Israel?

27 Now after the time that Am-a-zi′-ah did turn away from following the LORD they made a conspiracy against him in Jerusalem; and he fled to La′-chish: but they sent to La′-chish after him, and slew him there.

28 And they brought him upon horses, and buried him with his fathers in the city of Judah.

26 Then all the people of Judah took ^TUz-zi′-ah, who *was* sixteen years old, and made him king in the room of his father Am-a-zi′-ah.   *Azariah, 2 Kin. 14:21*

2 He built E′-loth, and restored it to Judah, after that the king slept with his fathers.

3   Sixteen years old *was* Uz-zi'-ah when he began to reign, and he reigned fifty and two years in Jerusalem. His mother's name also *was* Jec-o-li'-ah of Jerusalem.

4   And he did *that which was* ᴿright in the sight of the LORD, according to all that his father Am-a-zi'-ah did.   24:2

5   And he sought God in the days of Zech-a-ri'-ah, who had understanding in the visions of God: and as long as he sought the LORD, God made him to prosper.

6   And he went forth and ᴿwarred against the Phi-lis'-tines, and brake down the wall of Gath, and the wall of Jab'-neh, and the wall of Ash'-dod, and built cities ᵀabout Ash'-dod, and among the Phi-lis'-tines.   Is. 14:29 · *around, near*

7   And God helped him against ᴿthe Phi-lis'-tines, and against the A-ra'-bi-ans that dwelt in Gur–ba'-al, and the Me-hu'-nims.   21:16

8   And the Am'-mon-ites ᴿgave gifts to Uz-zi'-ah: and his name spread abroad *even* to the entering in of Egypt; for he strengthened *himself* exceedingly. 2 Sam. 8:2

9   Moreover Uz-zi'-ah built towers in Jerusalem at the ᴿcorner gate, and at the valley gate, and at the turning *of the wall*, and fortified them.   2 Kin. 14:13; Zech. 14:10

10   Also he built towers in the desert, and digged many wells: for he had much cattle, both in the low country, and in the plains: husbandmen *also*, and vine dressers in the mountains, and in Carmel: for he loved husbandry.

11   Moreover Uz-zi'-ah had an host of fighting men, that went out to war by ᵀbands, according to the number of their account by the hand of Je-i'-el the scribe and Ma-a-se'-iah the ruler, under the hand of Han-a-ni'-ah, *one* of the king's captains.   *companies*

12   The whole number of the chief of the fathers of the mighty men of valour *were* two thousand and six hundred.

13   And under their hand *was* an army, three hundred thousand and seven thousand and five hundred, that made war with mighty power, to help the king against the enemy.

14   And Uz-zi'-ah prepared for them throughout all the host shields, and spears, and helmets, and ᵀhabergeons, and bows, and slings *to cast* stones.   *body armour*

15   And he made in Jerusalem engines, invented by ᴿcunningᵀ men, to be on the towers and upon the bulwarks, to shoot arrows and great stones withal. And his name spread far abroad; for he was marvellously helped, till he was strong.   Ex. 39:3, 8 · *skilful*

16   But when he was strong, his heart was lifted up to *his* destruction: for he transgressed against the LORD his God, and went into the temple of the LORD to burn incense upon the altar of incense.

17   And ᴿAz-a-ri'-ah the priest went in after him, and with him fourscore priests of the LORD, *that were* valiant men: 1 Chr. 6:10

18   And they withstood Uz-zi'-ah the king, and said unto him, *It appertaineth* not unto thee, Uz-zi'-ah, to burn incense unto the LORD, but to the ᴿpriests the sons of Aaron, that are consecrated to burn incense: go out of the sanctuary; for thou hast trespassed; neither *shall it be* for thine honour from the LORD God.   Heb. 7:14

19   Then Uz-zi'-ah was wroth, and *had* a censer in his hand to burn incense: and while he was wroth with the priests, ᴿthe leprosy even rose up in his forehead before the priests in the house of the LORD, from beside the incense altar.   Num. 12:10; 2 Kin. 5:25–27

20   And Az-a-ri'-ah the chief priest, and all the priests, looked upon him, and, behold, he *was* leprous in his forehead, and they thrust him out from thence; yea, himself ᴿhastedᵀ also to go out, because the LORD had ᵀsmitten him.   Esth. 6:12 · *hurried · struck*

21   ᴿAnd Uz-zi'-ah the king was a leper unto the day of his death, and dwelt in ᵀa several house, *be-*

ing a leper; for he was cut off from the house of the LORD: and Jo'-tham his son *was* over the king's house, judging the people of the land. 2 Kin. 15:5 · *an isolated*

22 Now the rest of the acts of Uz-zi'-ah, first and last, did ᴿIsa-iah the prophet, the son of Amoz, write. 32:20, 32; 2 Kin. 20:1; Is. 1:1

23 ᴿSo Uz-zi'-ah slept with his fathers, and they buried him with his fathers in the field of the bur-ial which *belonged* to the kings; for they said, He *is* a leper: and Jo'-tham his son reigned in his stead. 21:20; 28:27; 2 Kin. 15:7; Is. 6:1

27 Jo'-tham *was* twenty and five years old when he be-gan to reign, and he reigned six-teen years in Jerusalem. His mo-ther's name also *was* Je-ru'-shah, the daughter of Za'-dok.

2 And he did *that which was* right in the sight of the LORD, according to all that his father Uz-zi'-ah did: howbeit he entered not into the temple of the LORD. And the people did yet corruptly.

3 He built the high gate of the house of the LORD, and on the wall of ᴿO'-phel he built much. 33:14

4 Moreover he built cities in the mountains of Judah, and in the forests he built ᵀcastles and towers. *fortresses*

5 He fought also with the king of the ᴿAm'-mon-ites, and pre-vailed against them. And the chil-dren of Ammon gave him the same year an hundred talents of silver, and ten thousand measures of wheat, and ten thousand of bar-ley. So much did the children of Ammon pay unto him, both the second year, and the third. 26:8

6 So Jo'-tham became mighty, ᴿbecause he prepared his ways before the LORD his God. 26:5

7 Now the rest of the acts of Jo'-tham, and all his wars, and his ways, lo, they *are* written in the book of the kings of Israel and Judah.

8 He was five and twenty years old when he began to reign, and reigned sixteen years in Jerusa-lem.

9 And Jo'-tham slept with his fathers, and they buried him in the city of David: and ᴿAhaz his son reigned in his stead. Is. 1:1

28 Ahaz *was* twenty years old when he began to reign, and he reigned sixteen years in Jeru-salem: but he did not *that which was* right in the sight of the LORD, like David his father:

2 For he walked in the ways of the kings of Israel, and made also molten images for Ba'-al-im.

3 Moreover he burnt incense in the valley of the son of Hin'-nom, and burnt his children in the fire, after the abominations of the hea-then whom the LORD had cast out before the children of Israel.

4 He sacrificed also and burnt incense in the high places, and on the hills, and under every green tree.

5 Wherefore the LORD his God delivered him into the hand of the king of Syria; and they smote him, and carried away a great multitude of them captives, and brought *them* to Damascus. And he was also delivered into the hand of the king of Israel, who smote him with a great slaughter.

6 For ᴿPe'-kah the son of Rem-a-li'-ah slew in Judah an hundred and twenty thousand in one day, *which were* all valiant men; be-cause they had forsaken the LORD God of their fathers. 2 Kin. 15:27

7 And Zich'-ri, a mighty man of E'-phra-im, slew Ma-a-se'-iah the king's son, and Az'-ri-kam the governor of the house, and El'-ka-nah *that was* next to the king.

8 And the children of Israel carried away captive of their ᴿbrethren two hundred thousand, women, sons, and daughters, and took also away much spoil from them, and brought the spoil to Sa-ma'-ri-a. 11:4; Deut. 28:25, 41

9 But a ᴿprophet of the LORD was there, whose name *was* O'-ded: and he went out before the host that came to Sa-ma'-ri-a, and said unto them, Behold, because the LORD God of your fathers was wroth with Judah, he hath delivered them into your hand, and ye have slain them in a rage *that* reacheth up unto heaven. 25:15

10 And now ye purpose to keep under the children of Judah and Jerusalem for bondmen and bondwomen unto you: *but are there* not with you, even with you, sins against the LORD your God?

11 Now hear me therefore, and deliver the captives again, which ye have taken captive of your brethren: ᴿfor the fierce wrath of the LORD *is* upon you. James 2:13

12 Then certain of the heads of the children of E'-phra-im, Az-a-ri'-ah the son of Jo-ha'-nan, Ber-e-chi'-ah the son of Me-shil'-le-moth, and Je-hiz-ki'-ah the son of Shal'-lum, and Am'-a-sa the son of Had'-lai, stood up against them that came from the war,

13 And said unto them, Ye shall not bring in the captives hither: for whereas we have offended against the LORD *already,* ye intend to add *more* to our sins and to our trespass: for our trespass is great, and *there* is fierce wrath against Israel.

14 So the armed men left the captives and the spoil before the princes and all the congregation.

15 And the men which were expressed by name rose up, and took the captives, and with the spoil clothed all that were naked among them, and arrayed them, and shod them, and ᴿgave them to eat and to drink, and anointed them, and carried all the feeble of them upon asses, and brought them to Jericho, the city of palm trees, to their brethren: then they returned to Sa-ma'-ri-a. [Luke 6:27]

16 ᴿAt that time did king Ahaz send unto the kings of Assyria to help him. 2 Kin. 16:7

17 For again the ᴿE'-dom-ites had come and smitten Judah, and carried away captives. Obad. 10–14

18 ᴿThe Phi-lis'-tines also had invaded the cities of the low country, and of the south of Judah, and had taken Beth–she'-mesh, and Aj'-a-lon, and Ge-de'-roth, and Sho'-cho with the villages thereof, and Tim'-nah with the villages thereof, Gim'-zo also and the villages thereof: and they dwelt there. 21:16, 17; Ezek. 16:27, 57

19 For the LORD brought Judah low because of Ahaz king of ᴿIsrael; for he ᴿmade Judah naked, and transgressed ᵀsore against the LORD. 2 Kin. 16:2 · Ex. 32:25 · *greatly*

20 And Til'-gath–pil-ne'-ser king of Assyria came unto him, and distressed him, but strengthened him not.

21 For Ahaz took away a portion *out* of the house of the LORD, and *out* of the house of the king, and of the princes, and gave *it* unto the king of Assyria: but he helped him not.

22 And in the time of his distress did he trespass yet more against the LORD: this *is that* king Ahaz.

23 For ᴿhe sacrificed unto the gods of Damascus, which ᵀsmote him: and he said, Because the gods of the kings of Syria help them, *therefore* will I sacrifice to them, that ᴿthey may help me. But they were the ruin of him, and of all Israel. 25:14 · *defeated* · Jer. 44:17, 18

24 And Ahaz gathered together the vessels of the house of God, and cut in pieces the vessels of the house of God, ᴿand shut up the doors of the house of the LORD, and he made him altars in every corner of Jerusalem. 29:3, 7

25 And in every ᵀseveral city of Judah he made high places to burn incense unto other gods, and provoked to anger the LORD God of his fathers. *single*

26 ᴿNow the rest of his acts and of all his ways, first and last, behold, they *are* written in the book of the kings of Judah and Israel. 2 Kin. 16:19, 20

27 And Ahaz slept with his fathers, and they buried him in the city, *even* in Jerusalem: but they brought him ᴿnot into the sepulchres of the kings of Israel: and

Hez-e-ki'-ah his son reigned in his stead. 21:20; 24:25

29 Hez-e-ki'-ah ᴿbegan to reign *when he was* five and twenty years old, and he reigned nine and twenty years in Jerusalem. And his mother's name *was* A-bi'-jah, the daughter ᴿof Zech-a-ri'-ah. 2 Kin. 18:1 · 26:5

2 And he did *that which was* right in the sight of the LORD, according to all that David his father had done.

3 He in the first year of his reign, in the first month, ᴿopened the doors of the house of the LORD, and repaired them. 28:24

4 And he brought in the priests and the Levites, and gathered them together into the east street,

5 And said unto them, Hear me, ye Levites, sanctify now yourselves, and ᴿsanctify the house of the LORD God of your fathers, and carry forth the filthiness out of the holy *place.* vv. 15, 34; 35:6

6 For our fathers have trespassed, and done *that which was* evil in the eyes of the LORD our God, and have forsaken him, and have ᴿturned away their faces from the habitation of the LORD, and turned *their* backs. [Is. 1:4]

7 ᴿAlso they have shut up the doors of the porch, and put out the lamps, and have not burned incense nor offered burnt offerings in the holy *place* unto the God of Israel. 28:24

8 Wherefore the ᴿwrath of the LORD was upon Judah and Jerusalem, and he hath ᴿdelivered them to trouble, to astonishment, and to ᴿhissing, as ye see with your eyes. 24:18 · 28:5 · 1 Kin. 9:8

9 For, lo, ᴿour fathers have fallen by the sword, and our sons and our daughters and our wives *are* in captivity for this. Deut. 28:25

10 Now *it is* in mine heart to make ᴿa covenant with the LORD God of Israel, that his fierce wrath may turn away from us. 15:12; 23:16

11 My sons, be not now negligent: for the LORD hath chosen you to stand before him, to serve

him, and that ye should minister unto him, and burn incense.

12 Then the Levites arose, Ma'-hath the son of Am'-a-sai, and Jo'-el the son of Az-a-ri'-ah, of the sons of the Ko'-hath-ites: and of the sons of Me-ra'-ri, Kish the son of Ab'-di, and Az-a-ri'-ah the son of Je-hal'-e-lel: and of the Ger'-shon-ites; Jo'-ah the son of Zim'-mah, and Eden the son of Jo'-ah:

13 And of the sons of E-liz'-a-phan; Shim'-ri, and Je-i'-el: and of the sons of A'-saph; Zech-a-ri'-ah, and Mat-ta-ni'-ah:

14 And of the sons of He'-man; Je-hi'-el, and Shim'-e-i: and of the sons of Je-du'-thun; She-ma'-iah, and Uz-zi'-el.

15 And they gathered their brethren, and ᴿsanctified themselves, and came, according to the commandment of the king, by the words of the LORD, ᴿto cleanse the house of the LORD. v. 5 · 1 Chr. 23:28

16 And the priests went into the inner part of the house of the LORD, to cleanse *it,* and brought out all the ᵀuncleanness that they found in the temple of the LORD into the court of the house of the LORD. And the Levites took *it,* to carry *it* out abroad into the brook ᴿKid'-ron. *debris* · 15:16; 30:14

17 Now they began on the first *day* of the first month to sanctify, and on the eighth day of the month came they to the porch of the LORD: so they sanctified the house of the LORD in eight days; and in the sixteenth day of the first month they made an end.

18 Then they went in to Hez-e-ki'-ah the king, and said, We have cleansed all the house of the LORD, and the altar of burnt offering, with all the vessels thereof, and the shewbread table, with all the vessels thereof.

19 Moreover all the vessels, which king Ahaz in his reign did ᴿcast away in his transgression, have we prepared and ᵀsanctified, and, behold, they *are* before the altar of the LORD. 28:24 · *consecrated*

20 Then Hez-e-ki'-ah the king

rose early, and gathered the rulers of the city, and went up to the house of the LORD.

21 And they brought seven bullocks, and seven rams, and seven lambs, and seven he goats, for a ᴿsin offering for the kingdom, and for the sanctuary, and for Judah. And he commanded the priests the sons of Aaron to offer *them* on the altar of the LORD.   Lev. 4:3–14

22 So they killed the bullocks, and the priests received the blood, and ᴿsprinkled *it* on the altar: likewise, when they had killed the rams, they sprinkled the blood upon the altar: they killed also the lambs, and they sprinkled the blood upon the altar.   Heb. 9:21

23 And they brought forth the he goats *for* the sin offering before the king and the congregation; and they laid their ᴿhands upon them: Lev. 4:15, 24; 8:14

24 And the priests killed them, and they made reconciliation with their blood upon the altar, to make an atonement for all Israel: for the king commanded *that* the burnt offering and the sin offering *should be made* for all Israel.

25 And he set the Levites in the house of the LORD with cymbals, with psalteries, and with harps, ᴿaccording to the commandment of David, and of Gad the king's seer, and Nathan the prophet: ᴿfor *so was* the commandment of the LORD by his prophets.   8:14 · 30:12

26 And the Levites stood with the instruments of David, and the priests with ᴿthe trumpets.   5:12

27 And Hez-e-ki'-ah commanded to offer the burnt offering upon the altar. And when the burnt offering began, the song of the LORD began *also* with the trumpets, and with the instruments *ordained* by David king of Israel.

28 And all the congregation worshipped, and the singers sang, and the trumpeters sounded: *and* all *this continued* until the burnt offering was finished.

29 And when they had made an end of offering, ᴿthe king and all that were present with him bowed themselves, and worshipped.   20:18

30 Moreover Hez-e-ki'-ah the king and the princes commanded the Levites to sing praise unto the LORD with the words of David, and of A'-saph the seer. And they sang praises with gladness, and they bowed their heads and worshipped.

31 Then Hez-e-ki'-ah answered and said, Now ye have consecrated yourselves unto the LORD, come near and bring sacrifices and ᴿthank offerings into the house of the LORD. And the congregation brought in sacrifices and thank offerings; and as many as were of a ᴿfree heart burnt offerings.   Lev. 7:12 · Ex. 35:5, 22

32 And the number of the burnt offerings, which the congregation brought, was threescore and ten bullocks, an hundred rams, *and* two hundred lambs: all these *were* for a burnt offering to the LORD.

33 And the consecrated things *were* six hundred oxen and three thousand sheep.

34 But the priests were too few, so that they could not flay all the burnt offerings: wherefore ᴿtheir brethren the Levites did help them, till the work was ended, and until the *other* priests had sanctified themselves: ᴿfor the Levites *were* more ᴿupright in heart to ᴿsanctify themselves than the priests.   35:11 · 30:3 · Ps. 7:10 · v. 5

35 And also the burnt offerings *were* in abundance, with ᴿthe fat of the peace offerings, and ᴿthe drink offerings for *every* burnt offering. So the service of the house of the LORD was set in order.   Lev. 3:16 · Num. 15:5–10

36 And Hez-e-ki'-ah rejoiced, and all the people, that God had prepared the people: for the thing was *done* suddenly.

30 And Hez-e-ki'-ah sent to all Israel and Judah, and wrote letters also to E'-phra-im and Ma-nas'-seh, that they should come to the house of the LORD at

Jerusalem, to keep the passover unto the Lord God of Israel.

2 For the king had taken counsel, and his princes, and all the congregation in Jerusalem, to keep the passover in the second ^Rmonth. vv. 13, 15; Num. 9:10, 11

3 For they could not keep it ^Rat that time, ^Rbecause the priests had not sanctified themselves sufficiently, neither had the people gathered themselves together to Jerusalem. Ex. 12:6, 18 · 19:17, 34

4 And the thing pleased the king and all the congregation.

5 So they established a decree to make proclamation throughout all Israel, from Be'-er–she'-ba even to Dan, that they should come to keep the passover unto the Lord God of Israel at Jerusalem: for they had not done *it* of a long *time in such sort* as it was written.

6 So the ^Rposts^T went with the letters from the king and his princes throughout all Israel and Judah, and according to the commandment of the king, saying, Ye children of Israel, turn again unto the Lord God of Abraham, Isaac, and Israel, and he will return to the remnant of you, that are escaped out of the hand of the kings of Assyria. Esth. 8:14; Jer. 51:31 · *runners*

7 And be not ye ^Rlike your fathers, and like your brethren, which trespassed against the Lord God of their fathers, *who* therefore ^Rgave them up to desolation, as ye see. Ezek. 20:18 · Is. 1:9

8 Now be ye not ^Rstiffnecked, as your fathers *were*, *but* yield yourselves unto the Lord, and enter into his sanctuary, which he hath sanctified for ever: and serve the Lord your God, that the fierceness of his wrath may turn away from you. Deut. 10:16; Acts 7:51

9 For if ye turn again unto the Lord, your brethren and your children *shall find* compassion before them that lead them captive, so that they shall come again into this land: for the Lord your God *is* gracious and merciful, and will

not turn away *his* face from you, if ye ^Rreturn unto him. [Is. 55:7]

10 So the ^Tposts passed from city to city through the country of E'-phra-im and Ma-nas'-seh even unto Zeb'-u-lun: but ^Rthey laughed them to scorn, and mocked them. *runners* · 36:16

11 Nevertheless ^Rdivers of Asher and Ma-nas'-seh and of Zeb'-u-lun humbled themselves, and came to Jerusalem. vv. 18, 21; 11:16

12 Also in Judah ^Rthe hand of God was to give them one heart to do the commandment of the king and of the princes, by the word of the Lord. [2 Cor. 3:5; Phil. 2:13]

13 And there assembled at Jerusalem much people to keep the feast of ^Runleavened bread in the second month, a very great congregation. Lev. 23:6; Num. 9:11

14 And they arose and took away the ^Raltars that *were* in Jerusalem, and all the altars for incense took they away, and cast *them* into the brook Kid'-ron. 28:24

15 Then they killed the passover on the fourteenth *day* of the second month: and the priests and the Levites were ^Rashamed, and sanctified themselves, and brought in the burnt offerings into the house of the Lord. 29:34

16 And they stood in their ^Rplace after their manner, according to the law of Moses the man of God: the priests sprinkled the blood, *which they received* of the hand of the Levites. 35:10, 15

17 For *there were* many in the congregation that were not sanctified: ^Rtherefore the Levites had the charge of the killing of the passovers for every one *that was* not clean, to sanctify *them* unto the Lord. 29:34

18 For a multitude of the people, *even* many of E'-phra-im, and Ma-nas'-seh, Is'-sa-char, and Zeb'-u-lun, had not cleansed themselves, ^Ryet did they eat the passover otherwise than it was written. But Hez-e-ki'-ah prayed for them, saying, The good Lord pardon every one Ex. 12:43–49; [Num. 9:10]

19 *That* ᴿprepareth his heart to seek God, the LORD God of his fathers, though *he be* not *cleansed* according to the purification of the sanctuary.   19:3

20 And the LORD hearkened to Hez-e-ki'-ah, and healed the people.

21 And the children of Israel that were present at Jerusalem kept ᴿthe feast of unleavened bread seven days with great gladness: and the Levites and the priests praised the LORD day by day, *singing* with loud instruments unto the LORD.   Ex. 12:15; 13:6

22 And Hez-e-ki'-ah spake comfortably unto all the Levites ᴿthat taught the good knowledge of the LORD: and they did eat throughout the feast seven days, offering peace offerings, and ᴿmaking confession to the LORD God of their fathers.   17:9; [Deut. 33:10] · Ezra 10:11

23 And the whole assembly took counsel to keep ᴿother seven days: and they kept *other* seven days with gladness.   1 Kin. 8:65

24 For Hez-e-ki'-ah king of Judah did give to the congregation a thousand bullocks and seven thousand sheep; and the princes gave to the congregation a thousand bullocks and ten thousand sheep: and a great number of priests sanctified themselves.

25 And all the congregation of Judah, with the priests and the Levites, and all the congregation that came out of Israel, and the strangers ᴿthat came out of the land of Israel, and that dwelt in Judah, rejoiced.   vv. 11, 18

26 So there was great joy in Jerusalem: for since the time of ᴿSolomon the son of David king of Israel *there was* not the like in Jerusalem.   7:8–10

27 Then the priests the Levites arose and blessed the people: and their voice was heard, and their prayer came *up* to his holy dwelling place, *even* unto heaven.

31 Now when all this was finished, all Israel that were present went out to the cities of Judah, and ᴿbrake the images in pieces, and cut down the groves, and threw down the high places and the altars out of all Judah and Benjamin, in E'-phra-im also and Ma-nas'-seh, until they had utterly destroyed them all. Then all the children of Israel returned, every man to his possession, into their own cities.   2 Kin. 18:4

2 And Hez-e-ki'-ah appointed ᴿthe courses of the priests and the Levites after their courses, every man according to his service, the priests and Levites for burnt offerings and for peace offerings, to minister, and to give thanks, and to praise in the gates of the tents of the LORD.   1 Chr. 23:6; 24:1

3 *He appointed* also the king's portion of his substance for the burnt offerings, *to wit*, for the morning and evening burnt offerings, and the burnt offerings for the sabbaths, and for the new moons, and for the set feasts, as *it is* written in the law of the LORD.

4 Moreover he commanded the people that dwelt in Jerusalem to give the ᴿportion of the priests and the Levites, that they might be encouraged in ᴿthe law of the LORD.   Num. 18:8; Ezek. 44:29 · Mal. 2:7

5 And as soon as the commandment came abroad, the children of Israel brought in abundance ᴿthe firstfruits of corn, wine, and oil, and honey, and of all the increase of the field; and the tithe of all *things* brought they in abundantly.   Ex. 22:29

6 And *concerning* the children of Israel and Judah, that dwelt in the cities of Judah, they also brought in the tithe of oxen and sheep, and the ᴿtithe of holy things which were consecrated unto the LORD their God, and laid *them* by heaps.   [Lev. 27:30]; Deut. 14:28

7 In the third month they began to ᵀlay the foundation of the heaps, and finished *them* in the seventh month.   *lay them in heaps*

8 And when Hez-e-ki'-ah and the princes came and saw the

heaps, they blessed the LORD, and his people Israel.

9 Then Hez-e-ki'-ah questioned with the priests and the Levites concerning the heaps.

10 And Az-a-ri'-ah the chief priest of the house of Za'-dok answered him, and said, RSince *the people* began to bring the offerings into the house of the LORD, we have had enough to eat, and have left plenty: for the LORD hath blessed his people; and that which is left *is* this great store.   [Mal. 3:10]

11 Then Hez-e-ki'-ah commanded to prepare Rchambers T in the house of the LORD; and they prepared *them,*   1 Kin. 6:5–8 · *storerooms*

12 And brought in the offerings and the tithes and the dedicated *things* faithfully: Rover which Con-o-ni'-ah the Levite *was* ruler, and Shim'-e-i his brother *was* the next.   35:9; Neh. 13:13

13 And Je-hi'-el, and Az-a-zi'-ah, and Na'-hath, and A'-sa-hel, and Jer'-i-moth, and Joz'-a-bad, and E-li'-el, and Is-ma-chi'-ah, and Ma'-hath, and Be-na'-iah, *were* overseers under the hand of Con-o-ni'-ah and Shim'-e-i his brother, at the commandment of Hez-e-ki'-ah the king, and Az-a-ri'-ah the Rruler of the house of God.   Jer. 20:1

14 And Ko'-re the son of Im'-nah the Levite, the Tporter toward the east, *was* over the Rfreewill offerings of God, to distribute the oblations of the LORD, and the most holy things.   *keeper* · 35:8; Deut. 23:23

15 And next him *were* Eden, and Mi-ni'-a-min, and Jesh'-u-a, and She-ma'-iah, Am-a-ri'-ah, and Shec-a-ni'-ah, in the cities of the priests, in *their* set office, to give to their brethren by courses, as well to the great as to the small:

16 Beside their genealogy of males, from three years old and upward, *even* unto every one that entereth into the house of the LORD, his daily portion for their service in their charges according to their Tcourses;   *divisions*

17 Both to the genealogy of the priests by the house of their fa-

thers, and the Levites from twenty years old and upward, in their charges by their courses;

18 And to the genealogy of all their little ones, their wives, and their sons, and their daughters, through all the congregation: for in their Tset office they sanctified themselves in holiness: *faithfulness*

19 Also of the sons of Aaron the priests, *which were* in the fields of the Tsuburbs of their cities, in every Tseveral city, the men that were expressed by name, to give portions to all the males among the priests, and to all that were reckoned by genealogies among the Levites.   *common lands · single*

20 And thus did Hez-e-ki'-ah throughout all Judah, and Rwrought *that which was* good and right and truth before the LORD his God.   2 Kin. 20:3; 22:2

21 And in every work that he began in the service of the house of God, and in the law, and in the commandments, to seek his God, he did *it* with all his heart, and Rprospered.   26:5; 32:30; Ps. 1:3

32 After Rthese things, and the establishment thereof, Sen-nach'-e-rib king of Assyria came, and entered into Judah, and encamped against the fenced cities, and thought to win them for himself.   2 Kin. 18:13—19:37

2 And when Hez-e-ki'-ah saw that Sen-nach'-e-rib was come, and that he was purposed to fight against Jerusalem,

3 He took counsel with his princes and his mighty men to stop the waters of the Tfountains which *were* Twithout the city: and they did help him.   *springs · outside*

4 So there was gathered much people together, who stopped all the Rfountains, T and the brook that ran through the midst of the land, saying, Why should the kings of Assyria come, and find much water?   2 Kin. 20:20 · *springs*

5 Also Rhe strengthened himself, and built up all the wall that was broken, and raised *it* up to the towers, and another wall with-

out, and repaired Mil'-lo *in* the city of David, and made darts and shields in abundance. Is. 22:9, 10

6 And he set captains of war over the people, and gathered them together to him in the street of the gate of the city, and spake comfortably to them, saying,

7 [R]Be strong and courageous, [R]be not afraid nor dismayed for the king of Assyria, nor for all the multitude that *is* with him: for [R]*there be* more with us than with him: [Deut. 31:6] · 20:15 · [Rom. 8:31]

8 With him *is* an [R]arm of flesh; but [R]with us *is* the LORD our God to help us, and to fight our battles. And the people rested themselves upon the words of Hez-e-ki'-ah king of Judah. [1 John 4:4] · [Rom. 8:31]

9 [R]After this did Sen-nach'-e-rib king of Assyria send his servants to Jerusalem, (but he *himself laid siege* against La'-chish, and all his [T]power with him,) unto Hez-e-ki'-ah king of Judah, and unto all Judah that *were* at Jerusalem, saying, 2 Kin. 18:17 · *forces*

10 [R]Thus saith Sen-nach'-e-rib king of Assyria, Whereon do ye trust, that ye abide in the siege in Jerusalem? 2 Kin. 18:19

11 Doth not Hez-e-ki'-ah persuade you to give over yourselves to die by famine and by thirst, saying, [R]The LORD our God shall deliver us out of the hand of the king of Assyria? 2 Kin. 18:30

12 Hath not the same Hez-e-ki'-ah taken away his high places and his altars, and commanded Judah and Jerusalem, saying, Ye shall worship before one altar, and burn incense upon [R]it? 31:1, 2

13 Know ye not what I and my fathers have done unto all the people of *other* lands? were the gods of the nations of those lands any ways able to deliver their lands out of mine hand?

14 Who *was there* among all the gods of those nations that my fathers utterly destroyed, that could deliver his people out of mine hand, that your God should

be able to deliver you out of mine [R]hand? [Is. 10:5–12]

15 Now therefore [R]let not Hez-e-ki'-ah deceive you, nor persuade you on this manner, neither yet believe him: for no god of any nation or kingdom was able to deliver his people out of mine hand, and out of the hand of my fathers: how much less shall your God deliver you out of mine hand? 2 Kin. 18:29

16 And his servants spake yet *more* against the LORD God, and against his servant Hez-e-ki'-ah.

17 He wrote also letters to rail on the LORD God of Israel, and to speak against him, saying, As the gods of the nations of *other* lands have not delivered their people out of mine hand, so shall not the God of Hez-e-ki'-ah deliver his people out of mine [R]hand. Dan. 3:15

18 [R]Then they cried with a loud voice in the Jews' speech unto the people of Jerusalem that *were* on the wall, to affright them, and to trouble them; that they might take the city. 2 Kin. 18:28; Ps. 59:6

19 And they spake against the God of Jerusalem, as against the gods of the people of the earth, *which were* [R]the work of the hands of man. [Ps. 96:5; 115:4–8]

20 [R]And for this *cause* Hez-e-ki'-ah the king, and the prophet Isaiah the son of Amoz, prayed and cried to heaven. 2 Kin. 19:15

21 [R]And the LORD sent an angel, which cut off all the mighty men of valour, and the leaders and captains in the camp of the king of Assyria. So he returned with shame of face to his own land. And when he was come into the house of his god, they that came forth of his own bowels slew him there with the sword. Zech. 14:3

22 Thus the LORD saved Hez-e-ki'-ah and the inhabitants of Jerusalem from the hand of Sennach'-e-rib the king of Assyria, and from the hand of all *other*, and guided them on every side.

23 And many brought gifts unto the LORD to Jerusalem, and [R]pres-

ents to Hez-e-ki'-ah king of Judah: so that he was magnified in the sight of all nations from thenceforth. 26:8; 2 Sam. 8:10; Ps. 45:12

24 In those days Hez-e-ki'-ah was sick to the death, and prayed unto the LORD: and he spake unto him, and he gave him a sign.

25 But Hez-e-ki'-ah ᴿrendered not again according to the benefit *done* unto him; for ᴿhis heart was lifted up: therefore there was wrath upon him, and upon Judah and Jerusalem. Ps. 116:12 · [Hab. 2:4]

26 ᴿNotwithstanding Hez-e-ki'-ah humbled himself for the pride of his heart, *both* he and the inhabitants of Jerusalem, so that the wrath of the LORD came not upon them ᴿin the days of Hez-e-ki'-ah. Jer. 26:18, 19 · 2 Kin. 20:19

27 And Hez-e-ki'-ah had exceeding much riches and honour: and he made himself treasuries for silver, and for gold, and for precious stones, and for spices, and for shields, and for all manner of pleasant jewels;

28 Storehouses also for the increase of corn, and wine, and oil; and stalls for all manner of beasts, and cotes for flocks.

29 Moreover he provided him cities, and possessions of flocks and herds in abundance: for ᴿGod had given him ᵀsubstance very much. 1 Chr. 29:12 · *very much property*

30 ᴿThis same Hez-e-ki'-ah also stopped the upper watercourse of Gi'-hon, and brought it straight down to the west side of the city of David. And Hez-e-ki'-ah prospered in all his works. Is. 22:9–11

31 Howbeit in *the business of* the ambassadors of the princes of Babylon, who ᴿsent unto him to enquire of the wonder that was *done* in the land, God left him, to try him, that he might know all *that was* in his heart. Is. 39:1

32 Now the rest of the acts of Hez-e-ki'-ah, and his goodness, behold, they *are* written in the vision of Isaiah the prophet, the son of Amoz, *and* in the book of the kings of Judah and Israel.

33 ᴿAnd Hez-e-ki'-ah slept with his fathers, and they buried him in the chiefest of the sepulchres of the sons of David: and all Judah and the inhabitants of Jerusalem did him ᴿhonour at his death. And Ma-nas'-seh his son reigned in his stead. 1 Kin. 1:21; 2 Kin. 20:21 · Ps. 112:6

33 Ma-nas'-seh ᴿ*was* twelve years old when he began to reign, and he reigned fifty and five years in Jerusalem: 2 Kin. 21:1–9

2 But did *that which was* evil in the sight of the LORD, like unto the ᴿabominations of the heathen, whom the LORD had cast out before the children of Israel. 28:3

3 For he built again the high places which Hez-e-ki'-ah his father had ᴿbroken down, and he reared up altars for Ba'-al-im, and ᴿmade groves, and worshipped ᴿall the host of heaven, and served them. 2 Kin. 18:4 · Deut. 16:21 · Deut. 17:3

4 Also he built altars in the house of the LORD, whereof the LORD had said, ᴿIn Jerusalem shall my name be for ever. 6:6; 7:16

5 And he built altars for all the host of heaven ᴿin the two courts of the house of the LORD. 4:9

6 ᴿAnd he caused his children to pass through the fire in the valley of the son of Hin'-nom: also he observed times, and used enchantments, and used witchcraft, and ᴿdealt with a familiar spirit, and with wizards: he wrought much evil in the sight of the LORD, to provoke him to anger. [Lev. 18:21] · [Lev. 19:31; 20:27]

7 And ᴿhe set a carved image, the idol which he had made, in the house of God, of which God had said to David and to Solomon his son, In ᴿthis house, and in Jerusalem, which I have chosen before all the tribes of Israel, will I put my name for ever: 25:14 · Ps. 132:14

8 ᴿNeither will I any more remove the foot of Israel from out of the land which I have appointed for your fathers; so that they will take heed to do all that I have commanded them, according to the whole law and the statutes

and the ordinances by the hand of Moses.   2 Sam. 7:10

9 So Ma-nas'-seh made Judah and the inhabitants of Jerusalem to err, and to do worse than the heathen, whom the Lord had destroyed before the children of Israel.

10 And the Lord spake to Ma-nas'-seh, and to his people: but they would not ᵀhearken.   obey

11 Wherefore the Lord brought upon them the captains of the host of the king of Assyria, which took Ma-nas'-seh among the thorns, and bound him with fetters, and carried him to Babylon.

12 And when he was in affliction, he besought the Lord his God, and humbled himself greatly before the God of his fathers,

13 And prayed unto him: and he was intreated of him, and heard his supplication, and brought him again to Jerusalem into his kingdom. Then Ma-nas'-seh ᴿknew that the Lord he was God. Ps. 9:16

14 Now after this he built a wall ᵀwithout the city of David, on the west side of ᴿGi'-hon, in the valley, even to the entering in at the fish gate, and compassed ᴿabout O'-phel, and raised it up a very great height, and put captains of war in all the ᵀfenced cities of Judah.   outside · 1 Kin. 1:33 · 27:3 · fortified

15 And he took away ᴿthe ᵀstrange gods, and the idol out of the house of the Lord, and all the altars that he had built in the mount of the house of the Lord, and in Jerusalem, and cast them out of the city.   vv. 3, 5, 7 · foreign

16 And he repaired the altar of the Lord, and sacrificed thereon peace offerings and thank offerings, and commanded Judah to serve the Lord God of Israel.

17 Nevertheless the people did sacrifice still in the high places, yet unto the Lord their God only.

18 Now the rest of the acts of Ma-nas'-seh, and his prayer unto his God, and the words of the seers that spake to him in the name of the Lord God of Israel,

behold, they are written in the book of the kings of Israel.

19 His prayer also, and how God was intreated of him, and all his sin, and his trespass, and the places wherein he built high places, and set up groves and graven images, before he was humbled: behold, they are written among the sayings of the seers.

20 ᴿSo Ma-nas'-seh slept with his fathers, and they buried him in his own house: and Amon his son reigned in his stead.   1 Kin. 1:21

21 ᴿAmon was two and twenty years old when he began to reign, and reigned two years in Jerusalem.   2 Kin. 21:19–24; 1 Chr. 3:14

22 But he did that which was evil in the sight of the Lord, as did Ma-nas'-seh his father: for Amon sacrificed unto all the carved images which Ma-nas'-seh his father had made, and served them;

23 And humbled not himself before the Lord, as Ma-nas'-seh his father had humbled himself; but Amon trespassed more and more.

24 ᴿAnd his servants conspired against him, and ᴿslew him in his own house.   24:25; 2 Kin. 21:23, 24 · 25:27

25 But the people of the land slew all them that had conspired against king Amon; and the people of the land made Jo-si'-ah his son king in his stead.

34 Jo-si'-ah ᴿwas eight years old when he began to reign, and he reigned in Jerusalem one and thirty years.   2 Kin. 22:1, 2

2 And he did that which was right in the sight of the Lord, and walked in the ways of David his father, and declined neither to the right hand, nor to the left.

3 For in the eighth year of his reign, while he was yet young, he began to ᴿseek after the God of David his father: and in the twelfth year he began ᴿto purge Judah and Jerusalem ᴿfrom the high places, and the groves, and the carved images, and the molten images.   15:2 · 1 Kin. 13:2 · 33:17–19, 22

4 ᴿAnd they brake down the altars of Ba'-al-im in his presence;

and the images, that *were* on high above them, he cut down; and the groves, and the carved images, and the molten images, he brake in pieces, and made dust *of them*, [R]and strowed *it* upon the graves of them that had sacrificed unto them.   Lev. 26:30; 2 Kin. 23:4 · 2 Kin. 23:6

5 And he burnt the bones of the priests upon their altars, and cleansed Judah and Jerusalem.

6 And *so did he* in the cities of Ma-nas'-seh, and E'-phra-im, and Simeon, even unto Naph'-ta-li, with their mattocks round about.

7 And when he had broken down the altars and the groves, and had [R]beaten the graven images into powder, and cut down all the idols throughout all the land of Israel, he returned to Je-rusalem.   Deut. 9:21

8 Now in the eighteenth year of his reign, when he had purged the land, and the house, he sent Sha'-phan the son of Az-a-li'-ah, and Ma-a-se'-iah the [R]governor of the city, and Jo'-ah the son of Jo'-a-haz the recorder, to repair the house of the LORD his God.   18:25

9 And when they came to Hil-ki'-ah the high priest, they deliv-ered [R]the money that was brought into the house of God, which the Levites that kept the doors had gathered of the hand of Ma-nas'-seh and E'-phra-im, and of all the [R]remnant of Israel, and of all Judah and Benjamin; and they re-turned to Jerusalem.   2 Kin. 12:4 · 30:6

10 And they put *it* in the hand of the workmen that had the over-sight of the house of the LORD, and they gave it to the workmen that wrought in the house of the LORD, to repair and [T]amend the house: *restore*

11 Even to the artificers and builders gave they *it*, to buy hewn stone, and timber for couplings, and to floor the houses which the kings of Judah had destroyed.

12 And the men did the work faithfully: and the overseers of them *were* Ja'-hath and O-ba-di'-

ah, the Levites, of the sons of Me-ra'-ri; and Zech-a-ri'-ah and Me-shul'-lam, of the sons of the Ko'-hath-ites, to set *it* forward; and *other of* the Levites, all that [T]could skill of instruments of mu-sick.   *were skilful with*

13 Also *they were* over the bear-ers of burdens, and *were* over-seers of all that wrought the work in any manner of service: and of the Levites *there were* scribes, and officers, and porters.

14 And when they brought out the money that was brought into the house of the LORD, Hil-ki'-ah the priest found a book of the law of the LORD *given* by Moses.

15 And Hil-ki'-ah answered and said to Sha'-phan the scribe, I have found the book of the law in the house of the LORD. And Hil-ki'-ah delivered the [R]book to Sha'-phan.   Deut. 31:24, 26

16 And Sha'-phan carried the book to the king, and brought the king word back again, saying, All that was committed to thy ser-vants, they do *it*.

17 And they have [T]gathered to-gether the money that was found in the house of the LORD, and have delivered it into the hand of the overseers, and to the hand of the workmen.   Lit. *poured out*

18 Then Sha'-phan the scribe told the king, saying, Hil-ki'-ah the priest hath given me a book. And Sha'-phan read it before the king.

19 And it came to pass, when the king had heard the words of the law, that he rent his clothes.

20 And the king commanded Hil-ki'-ah, and [R]A-hi'-kam the son of Sha'-phan, and Ab'-don the son of Mi'-cah, and Sha'-phan the scribe, and A-sa'-iah a servant of the king's, saying,   Jer. 26:24

21 Go, enquire of the LORD for me, and for them that are left in Israel and in Judah, concerning the words of the book that is found: for great *is* the wrath of the LORD that is poured out upon us, because our fathers have not

Rkept the word of the LORD, to do after all that is written in this book.   2 Kin. 17:15-19

22 And Hil-ki'-ah, and *they* that the king *had appointed*, went to Hul'-dah the prophetess, the wife of Shal'-lum the son of Tik'-vath, the son of Has'-rah, keeper of the wardrobe; (now she dwelt in Jerusalem in the college:) and they spake to her to that *effect*.

23 And she answered them, Thus saith the LORD God of Israel, Tell ye the man that sent you to me,

24 Thus saith the LORD, Behold, I will bring evil upon this place, and upon the inhabitants thereof, *even* all the curses that are written in the book which they have read before the king of Judah:

25 Because they have forsaken me, and have burned incense unto other gods, that they might provoke me to anger with all the works of their hands; therefore my wrath shall be poured out upon this place, and shall not be quenched.

26 And as for the king of Judah, who sent you to enquire of the LORD, so shall ye say unto him, Thus saith the LORD God of Israel *concerning* the words which thou hast heard;

27 Because thine heart was tender, and thou didst humble thyself before God, when thou heardest his words against this place, and against the inhabitants thereof, and humbledst thyself before me, and didst rend thy clothes, and weep before me; I have even heard *thee* also, saith the LORD.

28 Behold, I will gather thee to thy fathers, and thou shalt be gathered to thy grave in peace, neither shall thine eyes see all the Tevil that I will bring upon this place, and upon the inhabitants of the same. So they brought the king word again.   *calamity*

29 RThen the king sent and gathered together all the elders of Judah and Jerusalem.   2 Kin. 23:1-3

30 And the king went up into the house of the LORD, and all the men of Judah, and the inhabitants of Jerusalem, and the priests, and the Levites, and all the people, great and small: and he read in their ears all the words of the book of the covenant that was found in the house of the LORD.

31 And the king stood in his place, and made a Rcovenant before the LORD, to walk after the LORD, and to keep his commandments, and his testimonies, and his statutes, with all his heart, and with all his soul, to perform the words of the covenant which are written in this book.   23:16; 29:10

32 And he caused all that were present Tin Jerusalem and Benjamin to Tstand *to it*. And the inhabitants of Jerusalem did according to the covenant of God, the God of their fathers.   *take their stand*

33 And Jo-si'-ah took away all the Rabominations out of all the countries that *pertained* to the children of Israel, and made all that were present in Israel to serve, *even* to serve the LORD their God. *And* all his days they departed not from following the LORD, the God of their fathers.   1 Kin. 11:5

35 Moreover RJo-si'-ah kept a passover unto the LORD in Jerusalem: and they killed the passover on the fourteenth *day* of the first month.   2 Kin. 23:21, 22

2 And he set the priests in their Rcharges,T and Rencouraged them to the service of the house of the LORD,   23:18; Ezra 6:18 · *duties* · 29:5-15

3 And said unto the Levites that taught all Israel, which were holy unto the LORD, RPut the holy ark Rin the house which Solomon the son of David king of Israel did build; Rit *shall* not *be* a burden upon *your* shoulders: serve now the LORD your God, and his people Israel,   34:14 · Ex. 40:21 · 1 Chr. 23:26

4 And prepare *yourselves* by the houses of your fathers, after your courses, according to the Rwriting of David king of Israel, and according to the Rwriting of Solomon his son.   1 Chr. 23—26 · 8:14

5   And ᴿstand in the holy *place* according to the divisions of the families of the fathers of your brethren the people, and *after* the division of the families of the Levites.   Ps. 134:1

6   So kill the passover, and ᴿsanctify yourselves, and prepare your brethren, that *they* may do according to the word of the LORD by the hand of Moses.   29:5, 15

7   And Jo-si'-ah ᴿgave to the people, of the flock, lambs and kids, all for the passover offerings, for all that were present, to the number of thirty thousand, and three thousand bullocks: these *were* of the king's ᴿsubstance.ᵀ   30:24 · 31:3 · *possessions*

8   And his ᴿprinces gave willingly unto the people, to the priests, and to the Levites: Hil-ki'-ah and Zech-a-ri'-ah and Je-hi'-el, rulers of the house of God, gave unto the priests for the passover offerings two thousand and six hundred *small cattle*, and three hundred oxen.   Num. 7:2

9   ᴿCon-a-ni'-ah also, and She-ma'-iah and Ne-than'-e-el, his brethren, and Hash-a-bi'-ah and Je-i'-el and Joz'-a-bad, chief of the Levites, gave unto the Levites for passover offerings five thousand *small cattle*, and five hundred oxen.   31:12

10 So the service was prepared, and the priests ᴿstood in their place, and the ᴿLevites in their courses, according to the king's commandment.   Heb. 9:6 · 5:12; 7:6

11 And they killed the passover, and the priests ᴿsprinkled *the blood* from their hands, and the Levites ᴿflayed *them*.   29:22 · 29:34

12 And they removed the burnt offerings, that they might give according to the divisions of the families of the people, to offer unto the LORD, as *it is* written ᴿin the book of Moses. And so *did they* with the oxen.   Lev. 3:3; Ezra 6:18

13 And they ᴿroasted the passover with fire according to the ordinance: but the *other* holy *offerings* ᴿsod they in pots, and in

caldrons, and in pans, and divided *them* speedily among all the people.   Ex. 12:8, 9; Deut. 16:7 · 1 Sam. 2:13–15

14 And afterward they made ready for themselves, and for the priests: because the priests the sons of Aaron *were busied* in offering of burnt offerings and the fat until night; therefore the Levites prepared for themselves, and for the priests the sons of Aaron.

15 And the singers the sons of A'-saph *were* in their place, according to the ᴿcommandment of David, and A'-saph, and He'-man, and Je-du'-thun the king's seer; and the porters ᴿwaited at every gate; they might not depart from their service; for their brethren the Levites prepared for them.   1 Chr. 25:1–6 · 1 Chr. 9:17, 18

16 So all the service of the LORD was prepared the same day, to keep the passover, and to offer burnt offerings upon the altar of the LORD, according to the commandment of king Jo-si'-ah.

17 And the children of Israel that were present kept the passover at that time, and the feast of unleavened bread seven days.

18 And ᴿthere was no passover like to that kept in Israel from the days of Samuel the prophet; neither did all the kings of Israel keep such a passover as Jo-si'-ah kept, and the priests, and the Levites, and all Judah and Israel that were present, and the inhabitants of Jerusalem.   2 Kin. 23:22, 23

19 In the eighteenth year of the reign of Jo-si'-ah was this passover kept.

20 ᴿAfter all this, when Jo-si'-ah had prepared the temple, Ne'-cho king of Egypt came up to fight against ᴿChar'-che-mish by Eu-phra'-tes: and Jo-si'-ah went out against him.   2 Kin. 23:29 · Is. 10:9

21 But he sent ambassadors to him, saying, What have I to do with thee, thou king of Judah? *I come* not against thee this day, but against the house wherewith I have war: for God commanded

me to make haste: forbear thee from *meddling with* God, who *is* with me, that he destroy thee not.

22 Nevertheless Jo-si'-ah would not turn his face from him, but disguised himself, that he might fight with him, and hearkened not unto the words of Ne'-cho from the mouth of God, and came to fight in the valley of Me-gid'-do.

23 And the archers shot at king Jo-si'-ah; and the king said to his servants, ᵀHave me away; for I am ᵀsore wounded.   *Take · severely*

24 His servants therefore took him out of that chariot, and put him in the second chariot that he had; and they brought him to Je-rusalem, and he died, and was buried in *one of* the sepulchres of his fathers. And all Judah and Je-rusalem mourned for Jo-si'-ah.

25 And Jer-e-mi'-ah lamented for Jo-si'-ah: and ᴿall the singing men and the singing women spake of Jo-si'-ah in their lamentations to this day, ᴿand made them an ordinance in Israel: and, behold, they *are* written in the lamentations.   Matt. 9:23 · Jer. 22:20

26 Now the rest of the acts of Jo-si'-ah, and his goodness, according to *that which was* written in the law of the LORD,

27 And his deeds, first and last, behold, they *are* written in the book of the kings of Israel and Judah.

36 Then ᴿthe people of the land took Je-ho'-a-haz the son of Jo-si'-ah, and made him king in his father's stead in Je-rusalem.   2 Kin. 23:30–34

2 Je-ho'-a-haz *was* twenty and three years old when he began to reign, and he reigned three months in Jerusalem.

3 And the king of Egypt ᵀput him down at Jerusalem, and ᵀcondemned the land in an hundred talents of silver and a talent of gold.   *deposed him · imposed on*

4 And the king of Egypt made E-li'-a-kim his brother king over Judah and Jerusalem, and turned his name to Je-hoi'-a-kim. And

Ne'-cho took Je-ho'-a-haz his bro-ther, and carried him to Egypt.

5 ᴿJe-hoi'-a-kim *was* twenty and five years old when he began to reign, and he reigned eleven years in Jerusalem: and he did *that which was* evil in the sight of the LORD his God.   1 Chr. 3:15

6 ᴿAgainst him came up Neb-u-chad-nez'-zar king of Babylon, and bound him in fetters, to carry him to Babylon.   2 Kin. 24:1; Hab. 1:6

7 Neb-u-chad-nez'-zar also carried of the vessels of the house of the LORD to Babylon, and put them in his temple at Babylon.

8 Now the rest of the acts of Je-hoi'-a-kim, and his abominations which he did, and that which was found in him, behold, they *are* written in the book of the kings of Israel and Judah: and Je-hoi'-a-chin his son reigned in his stead.

9 ᴿJe-hoi'-a-chin *was* eight years old when he began to reign, and he reigned three months and ten days in Jerusalem: and he did *that which was* evil in the sight of the LORD.   2 Kin. 24:8–17

10 And when the year was expired, king Neb-u-chad-nez'-zar sent, and brought him to Bab-ylon, with the goodly vessels of the house of the LORD, and made Zed-e-ki'-ah his brother king over Judah and Jerusalem.

11 ᴿZed-e-ki'-ah *was* one and twenty years old when he began to reign, and reigned eleven years in Jerusalem.   2 Kin. 24:18–20; Jer. 52:1

12 And he did *that which was* evil in the sight of the LORD his God, *and* humbled ᴿnot himself before Jer-e-mi'-ah the prophet *speaking* from the mouth of the LORD.   Jer. 21:3–7; 44:10

13 And he also ᴿrebelled against king Neb-u-chad-nez'-zar, who had made him swear by God: but he stiffened his neck, and hard-ened his heart from turning unto the LORD God of Israel.   Jer. 52:3

14 Moreover all the chief of the priests, and the people, trans-

gressed very much after all the abominations of the heathen; and polluted the house of the LORD which he had hallowed in Jerusalem.

15 ᴿAnd the LORD God of their fathers sent to them by his messengers, rising up ᵀbetimes, and sending; because he had compassion on his people, and on his dwelling place: Jer. 7:13; 25:3, 4 · *early*

16 But they mocked the messengers of God, and despised his words, and ᴿmisused his prophets, until the ᴿwrath of the LORD arose against his people, till *there was* no remedy. Matt. 23:34 · Ps. 79:5

17 ᴿTherefore he brought upon them the king of the Chal'-dees, who ᴿslew their young men with the sword in the house of their sanctuary, and had no compassion upon young man or maiden, old man, or him that stooped for age: he gave *them* all into his hand. Ezra 9:7; Is. 3:8 · Ps. 74:20

18 And all the vessels of the house of God, great and small, and the treasures of the house of the LORD, and the treasures of the king, and of his princes; all *these* he brought to Babylon.

19 ᴿAnd they burnt the house of God, and brake down the wall of Jerusalem, and burnt all the palaces thereof with fire, and destroyed all the goodly vessels thereof. 2 Kin. 25:9; Is. 1:7, 8; Jer. 52:13

20 And them that had escaped from the sword carried he away to Babylon; where they were servants to him and his sons until the reign of the kingdom of Persia:

21 To fulfil the word of the LORD by the mouth of Jer-e-mi'-ah, until the land had enjoyed her sabbaths: *for* as long as she lay desolate she kept sabbath, to fulfil threescore and ten years.

22 Now in the first year of Cyrus king of Persia, that the word of the LORD *spoken* by the mouth of Jer-e-mi'-ah might be accomplished, the LORD stirred up the spirit of Cyrus king of Persia, that he made a proclamation throughout all his kingdom, and *put it* also in writing, saying,

23 ᴿThus saith Cyrus king of Persia, All the kingdoms of the earth hath the LORD God of heaven given me; and he hath charged me to build him an house in Jerusalem, which *is* in Judah. Who *is there* among you of all his people? The LORD his God *be* with him, and let him go up. Ezra 1:2, 3

The Book of
EZRA

Eism EZRA continues the Old Testament narrative of Second Chronicles by showing how God fulfills His promise to return His people, to the Land of Promise after seventy years of exile. Israel's "second exodus," this one from Babylon, is less impressive than the return from Egypt because only a remnant chooses to leave Babylon.

Ezra relates the story of two returns from Babylon—the first led by Zerubbabel to rebuild the temple (1—6), and the second under the leadership of Ezra to rebuild the spiritual condition of the people (7—10). Sandwiched between these two accounts is a gap of nearly six decades, during which Esther lives and rules as queen in Persia.

Ezra is the Aramaic form of the Hebrew word *ezer,* "help," and perhaps means "Yahweh helps." Ezra and Nehemiah were originally bound together as one book because Chronicles, Ezra, and Nehemiah were viewed as one continuous history. The Septuagint, a Greek-language version of the Old Testament translated in the third century B.C., calls Ezra–Nehemiah, *Esdras Deuteron,* "Second Esdras." First Esdras is the name of the apocryphal book of Esdras. The Latin title is *Liber Primus Esdrae,* "First Book of Ezra." In the Latin Bible, Ezra is called First Ezra and Nehemiah is called Second Ezra.

NOW in the first year of Cyrus king of Persia, that the word of the LORD Rby the mouth of Jere-mi'-ah might be fulfilled, the LORD stirred up the spirit of Cyrus king of Persia, Rthat he made a proclamation throughout all his kingdom, and *put it* also in writing, saying,　　2 Chr. 36:22, 23 · 5:13, 14

2　Thus saith Cyrus king of Persia, The LORD God of heaven hath given me all the kingdoms of the earth; and he hath Rcharged me to build him an house at Jerusalem, which *is* in Judah.　Is. 44:28; 45:1, 13

3　Who *is there* among you of all his people? his God be with him, and let him go up to Jerusalem, which *is* in Judah, and build the house of the LORD God of Israel, (Rhe *is* the God,) which *is* in Jerusalem.　1 Kin. 18:39; Dan. 6:26

4　And whosoever remaineth in any place where he sojourneth, let the men of his place help him with silver, and with gold, and with goods, and with beasts, beside the freewill offering for the house of God that *is* in Jerusalem.

5　Then rose up the chief of the fathers of Judah and Benjamin, and the priests, and the Levites, with all *them* whose spirit RGod had Traised, to go up to build the house of the LORD which *is* in Jerusalem.　[Phil. 2:13] · *stirred up*

6　And all they that *were* about them strengthened their hands with vessels of silver, with gold, with goods, and with beasts, and with precious things, beside all *that* was Rwillingly offered.　2:68

7　RAlso Cyrus the king brought forth the vessels of the house of the LORD, which Neb-u-chad-nez'-zar had brought forth out of Jerusalem, and had put them in the house of his gods;　5:14; Dan. 1:2; 5:2

8　Even those did Cyrus king of Persia bring forth by the hand of Mith'-re-dath the treasurer, and numbered them unto RShesh-baz'-zar, the prince of Judah.　5:14, 16

9　And this *is* the number of them: thirty chargers of gold, a thousand Tchargers of silver, nine and twenty knives,　*platters*

10　Thirty basons of gold, silver basons of a second *sort* four hundred and ten, *and* other vessels a thousand.

11　All the vessels of gold and of silver *were* five thousand and four hundred. All *these* did Shesh-baz'-zar bring up with *them* of the captivity that were brought up from Babylon unto Jerusalem.

2 Now Rthese *are* the children of the province that went up out of the captivity, of those which had been carried away, Rwhom Neb-u-chad-nez'-zar the king of Babylon had carried away unto Babylon, and came again unto Jerusalem and Judah, every one unto his city;　Neh. 7:6–73 · 2 Kin. 25:11

2　Which came with Ze-rub'-ba-bel: Jesh'-u-a, Ne-he-mi'-ah, Se-ra'-iah, Re-el-a'-iah, Mor'-de-cai, Bil'-shan, Miz'-par, Big'-vai, Re'-hum, Ba'-a-nah. The number of the men of the people of Israel:

3　The children of Pa'-rosh, two thousand an hundred seventy and two.

4　The children of Sheph-a-ti'-ah, three hundred seventy and two.

5　The children of A'-rah, seven hundred seventy and five.

6　The children of Pa'-hath–mo'-ab, of the children of Jesh'-u-a *and* Jo'-ab, two thousand eight hundred and twelve.

7　The children of E'-lam, a thousand two hundred fifty and four.

8 The children of Zat'-tu, nine hundred forty and five.

9 The children of Zac'-cai, seven hundred and threescore.

10 The children of Ba'-ni, six hundred forty and two.

11 The children of Be'-bai, six hundred twenty and three.

12 The children of Az'-gad, a thousand two hundred twenty and two.

13 The children of A-don'-i-kam, six hundred sixty and six.

14 The children of Big'-vai, two thousand fifty and six.

15 The children of A'-din, four hundred fifty and four.

16 The children of A'-ter of Hez-e-ki'-ah, ninety and eight.

17 The children of Be'-zai, three hundred twenty and three.

18 The children of Jo'-rah, an hundred and twelve.

19 The children of Ha'-shum, two hundred twenty and three.

20 The children of Gib'-bar, ninety and five.

21 The children of Beth'–le-hem, an hundred twenty and three.

22 The men of Ne-to'-phah, fifty and six.

23 The men of An'-a-thoth, an hundred twenty and eight.

24 The children of Az'-ma-veth, forty and two.

25 The children of ᵀKir'-jath–a'-rim, Che-phi'-rah, and Be-e'-roth, seven hundred and forty and three.   *Kirjath-jearim, Neh. 7:29*

26 The children of Ra'-mah and Ga'-ba, six hundred twenty and one.

27 The men of Mich'-mas, an hundred twenty and two.

28 The men of Beth'–el and A'-i, two hundred twenty and three.

29 The children of Ne'-bo, fifty and two.

30 The children of Mag'-bish, an hundred fifty and six.

31 The children of the other ᴿE'-lam, a thousand two hundred fifty and four.   2:7

32 The children of Ha'-rim, three hundred and twenty.

33 The children of Lod, Ha'-did,

and O'-no, seven hundred twenty and five.

34 The children of Jericho, three hundred forty and five.

35 The children of Se-na'-ah, three thousand and six hundred and thirty.

36 The priests: the children of ᴿJe-da'-iah, of the house of Jesh'-u-a, nine hundred seventy and three.   1 Chr. 24:7–18

37 The children of ᴿIm'-mer, a thousand fifty and two.   1 Chr. 24:14

38 The children of ᴿPash'-ur, a thousand two hundred forty and seven.   1 Chr. 9:12

39 The children of ᴿHa'-rim, a thousand and seventeen.   1 Chr. 24:8

40 The Levites: the children of Jesh'-u-a and Kad'-mi-el, of the children of Hod-a-vi'-ah, seventy and four.

41 The singers: the children of A'-saph, an hundred twenty and eight.

42 The children of the ᵀporters: the children of Shal'-lum, the children of A'-ter, the children of Tal'-mon, the children of Ak'-kub, the children of Hat'-i-ta, the children of Sho'-bai, *in* all an hundred thirty and nine.   *gatekeepers*

43 ᴿThe Neth'-i-nims: the children of Zi'-ha, the children of Ha-su'-pha, the children of Tab'-ba-oth,   7:7; 1 Chr. 9:2

44 The children of Ke'-ros, the children of Si'-a-ha, the children of Pa'-don,

45 The children of Leb'-a-nah, the children of Hag'-a-bah, the children of Ak'-kub,

46 The children of Ha'-gab, the children of Shal'-mai, the children of Ha'-nan,

47 The children of Gid'-del, the children of Ga'-har, the children of Re-a'-iah,

48 The children of Re'-zin, the children of Ne-ko'-da, the children of Gaz'-zam,

49 The children of Uz'-za, the children of Pa-se'-ah, the children of Be'-sai,

50 The children of As'-nah, the children of Me-hu'-nim, the children of Ne-phu'-sim,

51 The children of Bak´-buk, the children of Ha-ku´-pha, the children of Har´-hur,

52 The children of Baz´-luth, the children of Me-hi´-da, the children of Har´-sha,

53 The children of Bar´-kos, the children of Sis´-e-ra, the children of Tha´-mah,

54 The children of Ne-zi´-ah, the children of Hat´-i-pha.

55 The children of ᴿSolomon's servants: the children of So´-tai, the children of Soph´-e-reth, the children of Pe-ru´-da,　　1 Kin. 9:21

56 The children of Ja-a´-lah, the children of Dar´-kon, the children of Gid´-del,

57 The children of Sheph-a-ti´-ah, the children of Hat´-til, the children of Poch´-e-reth of Ze-ba´-im, the children of A´-mi.

58 All the ᴿNeth´-i-nims, and the children of ᴿSolomon's servants, *were* three hundred ninety and two.　　Josh. 9:21, 27; 1 Chr. 9:2 · 1 Kin. 9:21

59 And these *were* they which went up from Tel–me´-lah, Tel–har´-sa, Cherub, Ad´-dan, *and* Im´-mer: but they could not ᵀshew their father's house, and their ᵀseed, whether they *were* of Israel:　　*identify · genealogy*

60 The children of De-la´-iah, the children of To-bi´-ah, the children of Ne-ko´-da, six hundred fifty and two.

61 And of the children of the priests: the children of ᴿHa-ba´-iah, the children of Koz, the children of Bar-zil´-lai; which took a wife of the daughters of Bar-zil´-lai the Gil´-e-ad-ite, and was called after their name:　　Neh. 7:63

62 These sought their register *among* those that were reckoned by genealogy, but they were not found: ᴿtherefore were they, as ᵀpolluted, ᵀput from the priesthood.　　Num. 3:10 · *defiled · excluded*

63 And the Tir-sha´-tha said unto them, that they should not eat of the most holy things, till there stood up a priest with ᴿU´-rim and with Thum´-mim. Ex. 28:30

64 ᴿThe whole congregation together *was* forty and two thousand three hundred *and* threescore,　　Neh. 7:66; Is. 10:22

65 Beside their servants and their maids, of whom *there were* seven thousand three hundred thirty and seven: and *there were* among them two hundred singing men and singing women.

66 Their horses *were* seven hundred thirty and six; their mules, two hundred forty and five;

67 Their camels, four hundred thirty and five; *their* asses, six thousand seven hundred and twenty.

68 ᴿAnd *some* of the chief of the fathers, when they came to the house of the Lᴏʀᴅ which *is* at Jerusalem, offered freely for the house of God to set it up in his place:　　1:6; 3:5; Neh. 7:70

69 They gave after their ability unto the ᴿtreasure of the work threescore and one thousand drams of gold, and five thousand pound of silver, and one hundred priests' garments.　　8:25–35

70 So the priests, and the Levites, and *some* of the people, and the singers, and the porters, and the Neth´-i-nims, dwelt in their cities, and all Israel in their cities.

3 And when the seventh month was come, and the children of Israel *were* in the cities, the people gathered themselves together as one man to Jerusalem.

2 Then stood up ᵀJesh´-u-a the son of Joz´-a-dak, and his brethren the priests, and ᴿZe-rub´-ba-bel the son of She-al´-ti-el, and his brethren, and builded the altar of the God of Israel, to offer burnt offerings thereon, as *it is* ᴿwritten in the law of Moses the man of God. *Joshua*, Hag. 1:1 · 2:2 · Deut. 12:5, 6

3 And they set the altar upon ᵀhis bases; for fear *was* upon them because of the people of those countries: and they offered burnt offerings thereon unto the Lᴏʀᴅ, *even* burnt offerings morning and evening.　　*its foundations*

4 ᴿThey kept also the feast of tabernacles, ᴿas *it is* written, and *offered* the daily burnt offerings by number, according to the custom, as the duty of every day required; Lev. 23:33–43 · Ex. 23:16

5 And afterward *offered* the ᴿcontinual burnt offering, both of the new moons, and of all the set feasts of the LORD that were consecrated, and of every one that willingly offered a freewill offering unto the LORD. 1:4; 2:68; 7:15, 16

6 From the first day of the seventh month began they to offer burnt offerings unto the LORD. But the foundation of the temple of the LORD was not *yet* laid.

7 They gave money also unto the masons, and to the carpenters; and meat, and drink, and oil, unto them of Zi'-don, and to them of Tyre, to bring cedar trees from Leb'-a-non to the sea of Jop'-pa, ᴿaccording to the grant that they had of Cyrus king of Persia. 1:2; 6:3

8 Now in the second year of their coming unto the house of God at Jerusalem, in the second month, began ᴿZe-rub'-ba-bel the son of She-al'-ti-el, and Jesh'-u-a the son of Joz'-a-dak, and the remnant of their brethren the priests and the Levites, and all they that were come out of the captivity unto Jerusalem; ᴿand appointed the Levites, from twenty years old and upward, to ᵀset forward the work of the house of the LORD. v. 2; 4:3 · 1 Chr. 23:4 · *oversee*

9 Then stood Jesh'-u-a *with* his sons and his brethren, Kad'-mi-el and his sons, the sons of Judah, ᵀtogether, to set forward the workmen in the house of God: the sons of Hen'-a-dad, *with* their sons and their brethren the Levites. *as one*

10 And when the builders laid the foundation of the temple of the LORD, ᴿthey set the priests in their apparel with trumpets, and the Levites the sons of A'-saph with cymbals, to praise the LORD, after the ᴿordinance of David king of Israel. 1 Chr. 16:5, 6 · 1 Chr. 6:31; 16:4

11 And they sang together by course in praising and giving thanks unto the LORD; because *he*

is good, for his mercy *endureth* for ever toward Israel. And all the people shouted with a great shout, when they praised the LORD, because the foundation of the house of the LORD was laid.

12 But many of the priests and Levites and ᴿchief of the fathers, *who were* ancient men, that had seen the first house, when the foundation of this house was laid before their eyes, wept with a loud voice; and many shouted aloud for joy: 2:68

13 So that the people could not discern the noise of the shout of joy from the noise of the weeping of the people: for the people shouted with a loud shout, and the noise was heard afar off.

4 Now when ᴿthe ᵀadversaries of Judah and Benjamin heard that the children of the captivity builded the temple unto the LORD God of Israel; vv. 7–9 · *enemies*

2 Then they came to Ze-rub'-ba-bel, and to the chief of the fathers, and said unto them, Let us build with you: for we seek your God, as ye *do;* and we do sacrifice unto him ᴿsince the days of E'-sar-had'-don king of As'-sur, which brought us up hither. v. 10

3 But Ze-rub'-ba-bel, and Jesh'-u-a, and the rest of the chief of the fathers of Israel, said unto them, ᴿYe have nothing to do with us to build an house unto our God; but we ourselves together will build unto the LORD God of Israel, as ᴿking Cyrus the king of Persia hath commanded us. Neh. 2:20 · 1:1–4

4 Then ᴿthe people of the land ᵀweakened the hands of the people of Judah, and troubled them in building, 3:3 · *tried to discourage*

5 And hired counsellors against them, to frustrate their purpose, all the days of Cyrus king of Persia, even until the reign of ᴿDa-ri'-us king of Persia. 5:5; 6:1

6 And in the reign of A-has-u-e'-rus, in the beginning of his reign, wrote they *unto him* an accusation against the inhabitants of Judah and Jerusalem.

7 And in the days of ᴿAr-tax-erx′-es wrote Bish′-lam, Mith′-re-dath, Ta′-be-el, and the rest of their companions, unto Ar-tax-erx′-es king of Persia; and the writing of the letter *was* written in the Syrian tongue, and interpret-ed in the Syrian tongue. 7:1, 7, 21

8 Re′-hum the chancellor and Shim′-shai the scribe wrote a let-ter against Jerusalem to Ar-tax-erx′-es the king in this sort:

9 Then *wrote* Re′-hum the chancellor, and Shim′-shai the scribe, and the rest of their com-panions; ᴿthe Di′-na-ites, the A-phar′-sath-chites, the Tar′-pel-ites, the A-phar′-sites, the Ar′-che-vites, the Babylonians, the Su′-san-chites, the De-ha′-vites, *and* the E′-lam-ites, 2 Kin. 17:30, 31

10 ᴿAnd the rest of the nations whom the great and noble As-nap′-per brought over, and set in the cities of Sa-ma′-ri-a, and the rest *that are* on this side the river, and at such a time. 2 Kin. 17:24

11 This *is* the copy of the letter that they sent unto him, *even* unto Ar-tax-erx′-es the king; Thy ser-vants the men on this side the river, and at such a time.

12 Be it known unto the king, that the Jews which came up from thee to us are come unto Jerusa-lem, building the ᴿrebellious and the bad city, and have set up the ᴿwalls *thereof*, and joined the foundations. 2 Chr. 36:13 · 5:3, 9

13 Be it known now unto the king, that, if this city be builded *again, then* will they not pay ᴿtoll, tribute, and custom, and *so* thou shalt endam-age the revenue of the kings. 7:24

14 Now because we ᵀhave main-tenance from *the king's* palace, and it was not ᵀmeet for us to see the king's dishonour, therefore have we sent and ᵀcertified the king; *receive support · proper · informed*

15 That search may be made in the book of the records of thy fathers: so shalt thou find in the book of the records, and know that this city *is* a rebellious city,

and hurtful unto kings and prov-inces, and that they have moved sedition within the same of old time: for which cause was this city destroyed.

16 We certify the king that, if this city be builded *again,* and the walls thereof set up, by this means thou shalt have ᵀno portion on this side the river. *no dominion*

17 *Then* sent the king an answer unto Re′-hum the chancellor, and *to* Shim′-shai the scribe, and *to* the rest of their companions that dwell in Sa-ma′-ri-a, and *unto* the rest beyond the river, Peace, and ᵀat such a time. *so forth*

18 The letter which ye sent unto us hath been plainly read before me.

19 And I commanded, and search hath been made, and it is found that this city of old time hath made insurrection against kings, and *that* rebellion and sedition have been made therein.

20 There have been mighty kings also over Jerusalem, which have ruled over all *countries* be-yond the river; and toll, tribute, and custom, was paid unto them.

21 Give ye now commandment to cause these men to cease, and that this city be not builded, until *another* commandment shall be given from me.

22 Take heed now that ye fail not to do this: why should damage grow to the hurt of the kings?

23 Now when the copy of king Ar-tax-erx′-es′ letter *was* read before Re′-hum, and Shim′-shai the scribe, and their companions, they went up in haste to Jeru-salem unto the Jews, and made them to cease by force and power.

24 Then ceased the work of the house of God which *is* at Jeru-salem. So it ceased unto the sec-ond year of the reign of Da-ri′-us king of Persia.

5 Then the prophets, ᴿHag′-gai the prophet, and Zech-a-ri′-ah the son of Id′-do, prophesied unto the Jews that *were* in Judah and

Jerusalem in the name of the God of Israel, *even* unto them.   Hag. 1:1

2   Then rose up ᴿZe-rub'-ba-bel the son of She-al'-ti-el, and Jesh'-u-a the son of Joz'-a-dak, and began to build the house of God which *is* at Jerusalem: and ᴿwith them *were* the prophets of God helping them.   Hag. 1:12 · Hag. 2:4

3   At the same time came to them Tat'-nai, governor on this side the river, and She'-thar–boz'-nai, and their companions, and said thus unto them, Who hath commanded you to build this house, and to make up this wall?

4   ᴿThen said we unto them after this manner, What are the names of the men that ᵀmake this building?   v. 10 · *were constructing*

5   But ᴿthe eye of their God was upon the elders of the Jews, that they could not cause them to cease, till the matter came to Da-ri'-us: and then they returned ᴿanswer by letter concerning this *matter.*   7:6, 28; Ps. 33:18 · 6:6

6   The copy of the letter that Tat'-nai, governor on this side the river, and She'-thar–boz'-nai, and his companions the A-phar'-sach-ites, which *were* on this side the river, sent unto Da-ri'-us the king:

7   They sent a letter unto him, wherein was written thus; Unto Da-ri'-us the king, all peace.

8   Be it known unto the king, that we went into the province of Ju-de'-a, to the house of the great God, which is builded with great stones, and timber is laid in the walls, and this work goeth fast on, and prospereth in their hands.

9   Then asked we those elders, *and* said unto them thus, ᴿWho commanded you to build this house, and to make up these walls?   vv. 3, 4

10   We asked their names also, to ᵀcertify thee, that we might write the names of the men that *were* the chief of them.   *inform*

11   And thus they returned us answer, saying, We are the servants of the God of heaven and earth, and build the house that was builded these many years ago, which a great king of Israel builded ᴿand set up.   1 Kin. 6:1, 38

12   But after that our fathers had provoked the God of heaven unto wrath, he gave them into the hand of Neb-u-chad-nez'-zar the king of Babylon, the Chal-de'-an, who destroyed this house, and carried the people away into Babylon.

13   But in the first year of ᴿCy-rus the king of Babylon *the same* king Cyrus made a decree to build this house of God.   1:1

14   And ᴿthe vessels also of gold and silver of the house of God, which Neb-u-chad-nez'-zar took out of the temple that *was* in Je-rusalem, and brought them into the temple of Babylon, those did Cyrus the king take out of the temple of Babylon, and they were delivered unto *one,* ᴿwhose name *was* Shesh-baz'-zar, whom he had made governor;   Dan. 5:2 · Hag. 1:14

15   And said unto him, Take these vessels, go, carry them into the ᵀtemple that *is* in Jerusalem, and let the house of God be builded in his place.   *temple site*

16   Then came the same Shesh-baz'-zar, *and* ᴿlaid the foundation of the house of God which *is* in Jerusalem: and since that time even until now hath it been in building, and ᴿyet it is not finished.   3:8–10; Hag. 2:18 · 6:15

17   Now therefore, if *it seem* good to the king, ᴿlet there be search made in the king's treasure house, which *is* there at Babylon, whether it be *so,* that a decree was made of Cyrus the king to build this house of God at Jerusalem, and let the king send his pleasure to us concerning this matter.   6:1, 2

6 Then Da-ri'-us the king made a decree, ᴿand search was made in the ᵀhouse of the rolls, where the treasures were laid up in Babylon.   5:17 · *archives*

2   And there was found at Ach'-me-tha, in the palace that *is* in the province of the Medes, a roll, and therein *was* a record thus written:

THE CONQUEST

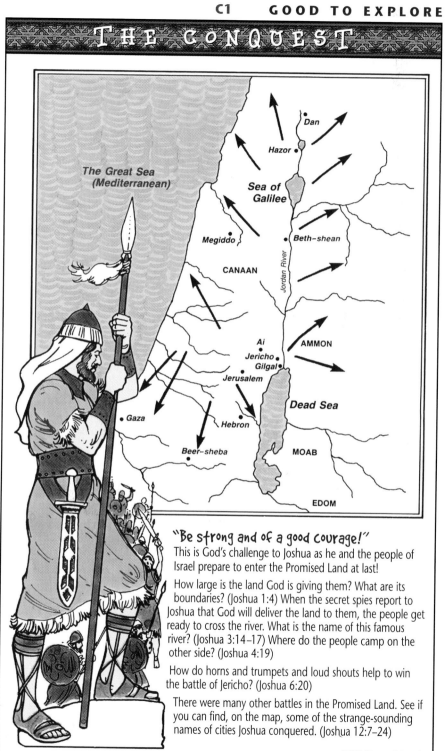

The Great Sea
(Mediterranean)

Dan

Hazor

Sea of
Galilee

Megiddo

Beth-shean

CANAAN

Jordan River

Ai
Jericho
Gilgal
Jerusalem

AMMON

Dead Sea

Gaza

Hebron

Beer-sheba

MOAB

EDOM

"Be strong and of a good courage!"

This is God's challenge to Joshua as he and the people of Israel prepare to enter the Promised Land at last!

How large is the land God is giving them? What are its boundaries? (Joshua 1:4) When the secret spies report to Joshua that God will deliver the land to them, the people get ready to cross the river. What is the name of this famous river? (Joshua 3:14–17) Where do the people camp on the other side? (Joshua 4:19)

How do horns and trumpets and loud shouts help to win the battle of Jericho? (Joshua 6:20)

There were many other battles in the Promised Land. See if you can find, on the map, some of the strange-sounding names of cities Joshua conquered. (Joshua 12:7–24)

THE PEOPLES OF THE OLD TESTAMENT

Joshua mentioned seven tribes that the Israelites found living in Canaan at the time of the conquest (Joshua 24:11). The table below summarizes who these groups were, as well as some of the other peoples mentioned in the Old Testament.

NAME	DESCRIPTION
AMALEKITES (1 Sam. 15:2, 3)	A nomadic people descended from Esau, they conducted frequent raids on the Israelites from their hideouts in the Negev and Sinai regions.
AMMONITES (1 Chr. 19:1–9)	Descendants of Lot who lived east of the Jordan near the Jabbok River and often joined Moabites and Edomites in attacking Israel.
AMORITES (Gen. 15:16)	A nomadic, savage, and cruel people living in Canaan at the time of Abraham.
ANAKIM (Deut. 9:2)	Among the earliest inhabitants of Palestine, known for their large size.
ARABS	A name rarely used in the Bible, but including many tribes living throughout the Arabian Peninsula, notably the Ishmaelites and Midianites (see next page).
ARKITES	Descendants of Canaan (Gen. 10:17), they lived in a city of Phoenicia.
ASSYRIANS (2 Kin. 17:5, 6)	A nation of Mesopotamia that dominated the Middle East between the ninth and seventh centuries B.C. and carried off the northern kingdom of Israel into captivity in 722 B.C.
BABYLONIANS (2 Chr. 36:6)	Successors to the Assyrians who dominated the Middle East in the seventh and sixth centuries B.C. and carried off the southern kingdom of Judah into captivity in 587 B.C.
CANAANITES (Josh. 3:10)	The dominant civilization of Canaan between the twenty-first and sixteenth centuries B.C., expelled by the Israelites.
EDOMITES (Gen. 36:9)	Descendants of Esau who lived between the Dead Sea and the Gulf of Aqaba and constantly feuded with the Israelites.
EGYPTIANS (Ex. 11:7)	The great civilization of Egypt ruled during the early biblical period by pharaohs, and under whom the Israelites lived for 430 years in slavery.
GIRGASHITES	Descendants of Canaan frequently listed among Canaanite tribes.
HITTITES	Descendants of Heth, the son of Canaan, they lived in the Judaean hills near Hebron.
HIVITES	Descendants of Canaan, they lived in Lebanon into the time of Solomon, who forced them into being his workers (1 Kin. 9:20).

NAME	DESCRIPTION
HORITES	Inhabitants of Edom driven out by Esau's descendants (Deut. 2:12, 22).
ISHMAELITES	Descendants of Abraham by Hagar and thus relatives of the Israelites; believed to be ancestors of the Arabs.
JEBUSITES	Descendants of Canaan and inhabitants of Jebus (Jerusalem), which was captured by David (2 Sam. 5:6, 7).
KADMONITES	An obscure tribe whose land God promised to give to Abraham's descendants (Gen. 15:19).
KENEZITES	A group of Edomites to whom the family of Caleb was related (Num. 32:12).
KENITES	A group of Midianites who may have operated metalworks southeast of the Gulf of Aqaba and many of whom lived on friendly terms with the Israelites.
MIDIANITES *(Num. 25:17)*	Five families descended from Abraham through the son of his concubine, Keturah, they lived between the Arabian Desert and the Red Sea coast and frequently attacked the Israelites.
PERIZZITES	A little-known tribe often mentioned with the Canaanite tribes, their name may mean "villagers"; seem to have preferred to live among the hills of Canaan.
PERSIANS	Successors to the Assyrians and Babylonians, they ruled a massive empire stretching from India in the east to Egypt and Macedonia in the west.
PHILISTINES *(Judg. 13:1)*	Israel's constant enemies to the southwest along the Mediterranean coast, from whose name the word *Palestine* is derived.
PHOENICIANS *(2 Chr. 9:21)*	Israel's seafaring allies during the days of David and Solomon.
REPHAIM	A group of people living throughout Canaan at the time of Abraham who, like the Anakim, were said to be giants (Deut. 2:20, 21).
SYRIANS	The peoples living north of Canaan; area composed of a number of city-states.

THE LIFE OF RUTH

1. Naomi, a Jewish woman, and Orpah and Ruth, her Moabite daughters-in-law, outlive their Jewish husbands (Ruth 1:1–5).

2. Naomi returns to Israel and Ruth insists on accompanying her (Ruth 1:6–18).

3. Probable route of Naomi and Ruth.

4. Naomi and Ruth settle in Naomi's hometown of Beth-lehem, where Ruth meets and marries Boaz (Ruth 1:19—4:13).

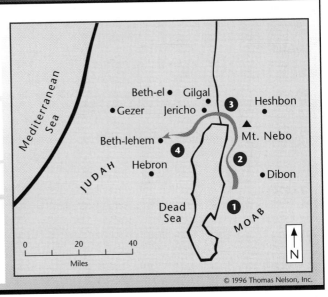

© 1996 Thomas Nelson, Inc.

THE FAMILY TREE OF RUTH

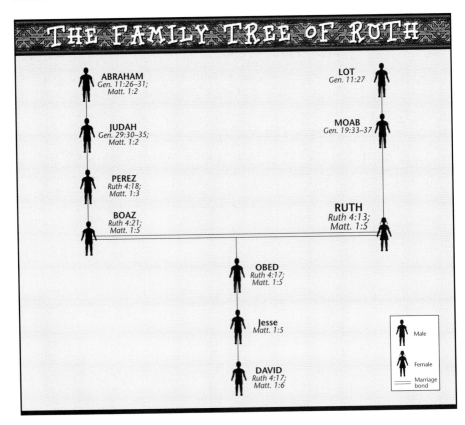

ABRAHAM
Gen. 11:26–31;
Matt. 1:2

LOT
Gen. 11:27

JUDAH
Gen. 29:30–35;
Matt. 1:2

MOAB
Gen. 19:33–37

PEREZ
Ruth 4:18;
Matt. 1:3

BOAZ
Ruth 4:21;
Matt. 1:5

RUTH
Ruth 4:13;
Matt. 1:5

OBED
Ruth 4:17;
Matt. 1:5

Jesse
Matt. 1:5

DAVID
Ruth 4:17;
Matt. 1:6

Male

Female

Marriage bond

THE LIFE OF SAMUEL

1 During a yearly trip to Shiloh, Hannah prayed for a son. She promised to dedicate the child to the Lord (1 Sam. 1:10–17).

2 Samuel was born at Ramah (1 Sam. 1:20) and lived there in his later life (7:17).

3 Samuel grew up at Shiloh under Eli's care. He served in the tabernacle and at an early age heard God's voice speaking to him as a prophet (1 Sam. 2:11; 3:1–21).

4 Every year, Samuel traveled a circuit to Beth-el, Gilgal, and Mizpah as a judge of Israel (1 Sam. 7:16, 17).

5 Samuel installed his sons, Joel and Abijah, as judges in Beer-sheba. However, they turned away from the Lord, which caused the elders of Israel to demand a king (1 Sam. 8:1–5).

6 In a private ceremony at Zuph, Samuel anointed Saul as Israel's first king (1 Sam. 9:5, 6, 27; 10:1).

7 Told by God that He had rejected Saul as king (1 Sam. 16:1), Samuel anointed David as Israel's king in a private ceremony at Beth-lehem (16:12, 13).

8 Samuel died and was buried in his home-town of Ramah (1 Sam. 25:1).

.... Samuel's circuit

Mediterranean Sea

Sea of Galilee

Jordan River

Megiddo

Zuph (?) **1** **3**
● Shiloh

Beth-el

Mizpah ●
Ramah ●
Jerusalem ● **2** **8**
● **7**
Beth-lehem

● Gaza

Dead Sea

5
●● Beer-sheba

MOAB

EDOM

0   15   30
Miles

N

4
● Gilgal

© 1996 Thomas Nelson, Inc.

SAUL'S MILITARY CAMPAIGNS

Saul's attack on the Amalekites (1 Sam. 15:3–7) was the last of his military victories. By taking King Agag prisoner and keeping the best of the enemy's possessions he won in battle (15:8, 9), he disobeyed God. He never won another battle.

❶ In his first battle after being proclaimed king, Saul liberated the people of Jabesh-gilead from Ammonite raiders (1 Sam. 11:1–11).

❷ⓐ A raid on the Philistine garrison at Geba by Saul's son Jonathan touched off war (1 Sam. 13:1–3).

❷ⓑ The Israelites gathered at Gilgal (1 Sam. 13:4), the Philistines at Michmash (13:5). Battle was joined at a nearby pass, where the Philistines were put to flight and the battle shifted to Beth-aven (14:4–23).

❷ⓒ Eventually the Philistines were pushed back to Aijalon (1 Sam. 14:31), where fighting stopped and both sides went home (14:46).

❸ Saul campaigned successfully against Moab, Ammon, and Edom to the east, the kings of Zobah in the north, the Philistines in the southwest, and the Amalekites in the south, until Israel's sovereignty was established (1 Sam. 14:47, 48).

❹ Saul defeated the Amalekites, but disobeyed God by sparing King Agag and failing to destroy all the enemy's possessions won in battle (1 Sam. 15:1–9).

❺ Saul's armies battled the Philistines in the Valley of Elah between Azekah and Sochoh (1 Sam. 17:1–3), but could not win because of the Philistine champion Goliath (17:4–11) until young David killed him (17:48–54).

❻ In his final battle, Saul was mortally wounded fighting the Philistines at Mount Gilboa (1 Sam. 28:4, 5; 31:1–3). He then took his life, and his body was disgraced by the enemy (31:4, 8–10).

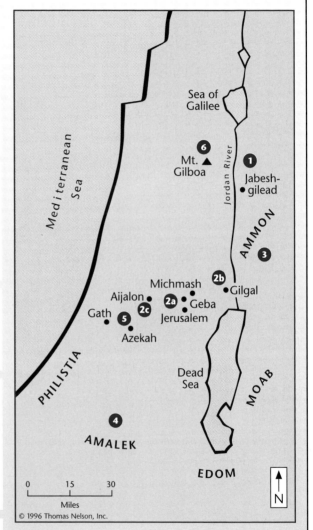

Sea of Galilee

Mt. ▲ Gilboa **❻**

❶ Jabesh-gilead

Mediterranean Sea

Jordan River

AMMON

❸

Michmash **❷ⓑ**

Gilgal

Aijalon **❷ⓒ** **❷ⓐ** Geba

Gath **❺** Jerusalem

Azekah

PHILISTIA

Dead Sea

MOAB

❹

AMALEK

EDOM

0   15   30

Miles

© 1996 Thomas Nelson, Inc.

N

THE LIFE OF DAVID

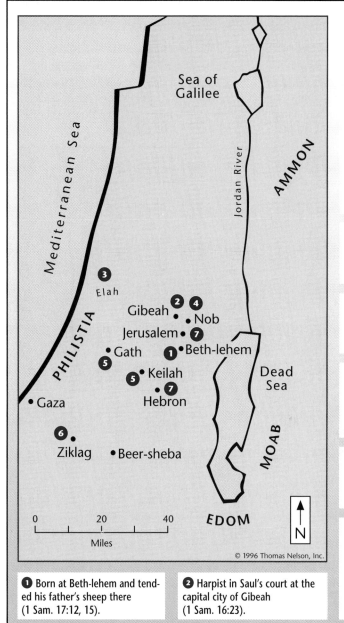

Sea of Galilee

Mediterranean Sea

Jordan River

AMMON

3
Elah

Gibeah **2** **4**
• • Nob

Jerusalem • **7**

• Gath **1** • Beth-lehem

PHILISTIA

5

5 • Keilah

• **7**
Hebron

Dead Sea

• Gaza

MOAB

6 •
Ziklag   • Beer-sheba

0   20   40   EDOM
Miles

N

© 1996 Thomas Nelson, Inc.

3 Killed Goliath in the Valley of Elah (1 Sam. 17:19, 45–50).

4 Fled from Saul and hid at Nob, where Ahimelech the priest gave him shewbread to eat. As a result, Saul had 85 priests of Nob executed (1 Sam. 21:1–9; 22:6–23).

5 Hid from Saul at Gath and Keilah (1 Sam. 21:10–15; 23:1–13).

6 Made Ziklag his headquarters during Saul's pursuit (1 Sam. 27).

7 Made Hebron his capital after becoming king of Judah (2 Sam. 2:1–4).

8 Reigned at Jerusalem as king of Israel (2 Sam. 5:1–5).

9 Won victories over the Edomites, the Moabites, the Ammonites, the Amalekites, and the Philistines (2 Sam. 8:11, 12).

1 Born at Beth-lehem and tended his father's sheep there (1 Sam. 17:12, 15).

2 Harpist in Saul's court at the capital city of Gibeah (1 Sam. 16:23).

THE CAPTURE AND RETURN OF THE ARK

The capture of the ark of the covenant by the Philistines (1 Samuel 4:11; 5:1, 2) made the people of Israel feel bad. They felt bad because the ark was the symbol of God's special promises to them as a nation, and now it was in the hands of their enemies. The people should have realized that God allowed this to happen because they had been unfaithful to Him by worshiping other gods and by not following His laws.

❶ The ark stayed with the tabernacle in Shiloh until Eli's two sons foolishly carried it into battle (Josh. 18:1; 1 Sam. 4:4).

❷ Carried into battle as a good luck charm, the ark was captured by the Philistines near Aphek (1 Sam. 4:1, 10, 11).

❸ The ark was placed in the temple of Dagon at Ashdod until the idol was toppled and the people were struck with emerods, or "tumors" (perhaps bubonic plague). Then it was sent to Gath (1 Sam. 5:1–8).

❹ At Gath, emerods, or "tumors," again struck the people, and the ark was sent to Ekron (1 Sam. 5:9, 10).

❺ After a brief stop at Ekron, where it caused more disease and death, the ark was sent on an unmanned cart back to the Israelites (1 Sam. 5:10—6:12).

❻ The cart bearing the ark stopped briefly in a field near Beth-shemesh, but was sent on after the people looked inside and were struck dead (1 Sam. 6:13–20).

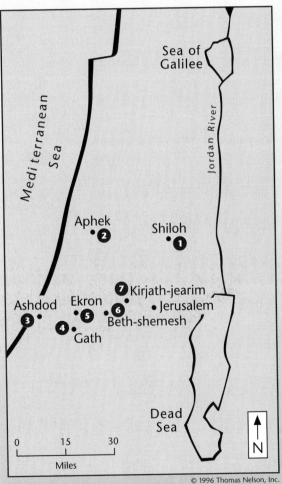

© 1996 Thomas Nelson, Inc.

❼ The ark was removed to Kirjath-jearim, where it remained for twenty years (1 Sam. 7:1, 2) until David finally relocated it to Jerusalem (2 Sam. 6).

3 In the first year of Cyrus the king *the same* Cyrus the king made a ^Rdecree *concerning* the house of God at Jerusalem, Let the house be builded, the place where they offered sacrifices, and let the foundations thereof be strongly laid; the height thereof threescore cubits, *and* the breadth thereof threescore cubits;   1:1; 5:13

4 ^R*With* three rows of great stones, and a row of new timber: and let the ^Rexpences be given out of the king's house: 1 Kin. 6:36 · 3:7

5 And also let ^Rthe golden and silver vessels of the house of God, which Neb-u-chad-nez'-zar took forth out of the temple which *is* at Jerusalem, and brought unto Babylon, be restored, and brought again unto the temple which *is* at Jerusalem, *every one* to his place, and place *them* in the house of God.   1:7, 8; 5:14

6 ^RNow *therefore*, Tat'-nai, governor beyond the river, She'-thar–boz'-nai, and your companions the A-phar'-sach-ites, which *are* beyond the river, be ye far from thence: 5:3, 6

7 Let the work of this house of God alone; let the governor of the Jews and the elders of the Jews build this house of God in his place.

8 Moreover I make a decree what ye shall do to the elders of these Jews for the building of this house of God: that of the king's goods, *even* of the tribute beyond the river, forthwith expences be given unto these men, that they be not hindered.

9 And that which they have need of, both young bullocks, and rams, and lambs, for the burnt offerings of the God of heaven, wheat, salt, wine, and oil, according to the appointment of the priests which *are* at Jerusalem, let it be given them day by day without fail:

10 That they may offer sacrifices of sweet savours unto the God of heaven, and pray for the life of the king, and of his sons.

11 Also I have made a decree, that whosoever shall alter this word, let timber be pulled down from his house, and being set up, let him be hanged thereon; ^Rand let his house be made a dunghill for this.   Dan. 2:5; 3:29

12 And the God that hath caused his ^Rname to dwell there destroy all kings and people, that shall put to their hand to alter *and* to destroy this house of God which *is* at Jerusalem. I Da-ri'-us have made a decree; let it be done with speed.   Deut. 12:5, 11; 1 Kin. 9:3

13 Then Tat'-nai, governor on this side the river, She'-thar–boz'-nai, and their companions, according to that which Da-ri'-us the king had sent, so they did speedily.

14 And the elders of the Jews builded, and they prospered through the prophesying of Hag'-gai the prophet and Zech-a-ri'-ah the son of Id'-do. And they builded, and finished *it*, according to the commandment of the God of Israel, and according to the commandment of ^RCyrus, and ^RDa-ri'-us, and ^RAr-tax-erx'-es king of Persia.   1:1; 5:13 · 4:24 · 7:1, 11; Neh. 2:1

15 And this house was finished on the third day of the month A'-dar, which was in the sixth year of the reign of Da-ri'-us the king.

16 And the children of Israel, the priests, and the Levites, and the rest of the children of the captivity, kept ^Rthe dedication of this house of God with joy,   2 Chr. 7:5

17 And ^Roffered at the dedication of this house of God an hundred bullocks, two hundred rams, four hundred lambs; and for a sin offering for all Israel, twelve he goats, according to the number of the tribes of Israel.   8:35

18 And they set the priests in their divisions, and the Levites in their courses, for the service of God, which *is* at Jerusalem; as it is written in the book of Moses.

19 And the children of the captivity kept the passover upon the fourteenth *day* of the first month.

20 For the priests and the Levites were purified together, all of them *were* pure, and killed the passover for all the children of the captivity, and for their brethren the priests, and for themselves.

21 And the children of Israel, which were come again out of captivity, and all such as had separated themselves unto them from the ᴿfilthinessᵀ of the heathen of the land, to seek the LORD God of Israel, did eat,   9:11 · *uncleanness*

22 And kept the ᴿfeast of unleavened bread seven days with joy: for the LORD had made them joyful, and ᴿturned the heart ᴿof the king of Assyria unto them, to strengthen their hands in the work of the house of God, the God of Israel.   Ex. 12:15 · 7:27 · 2 Chr. 33:11

7 Now after these things, in the reign of ᴿAr-tax-erx´-es king of Persia, Ezra the ᴿson of Se-ra´-iah, the son of Az-a-ri´-ah, the son of Hil-ki´-ah,   Neh. 2:1 · 1 Chr. 6:14

2 The son of Shal´-lum, the son of Za´-dok, the son of A-hi´-tub,

3 The son of Am-a-ri´-ah, the son of Az-a-ri´-ah, the son of Me-ra´-ioth,

4 The son of Zer-a-hi´-ah, the son of Uz´-zi, the son of Buk´-ki,

5 The son of A-bish´-u-a, the son of Phin´-e-has, the son of E-le-a´-zar, the son of Aaron the chief priest:

6 This Ezra went up from Babylon; and he *was* a ready scribe in the law of Moses, which the LORD God of Israel had given: and the king granted him all his request, ᴿaccording to the hand of the LORD his God upon him.   8:22

7 ᴿAnd there went up *some* of the children of Israel, and of the priests, and ᴿthe Levites, and the singers, and the porters, and ᴿthe Neth´-i-nims, unto Jerusalem, in the seventh year of Ar-tax-erx´-es the king.   8:1–14 · 8:15 · 2:43; 8:20

8 And he came to Jerusalem in the fifth month, which *was* in the seventh year of the king.

9 For upon the first *day* of the first month began he to go up from Babylon, and on the first *day* of the fifth month came he to Jerusalem, ᴿaccording to the good hand of his God upon him.   Neh. 2:8

10 For Ezra had prepared his heart to ᴿseek the law of the LORD, and to do *it*, and to teach in Israel statutes and judgments.   Ps. 119:45

11 Now this *is* the copy of the letter that the king Ar-tax-erx´-es gave unto Ezra the priest, the scribe, *even* a scribe of the words of the commandments of the LORD, and of his statutes to Israel.

12 Ar-tax-erx´-es, king of kings, unto Ezra the priest, a scribe of the law of the God of heaven, perfect *peace*, and at such a time.

13 I make a decree, that all they of the people of Israel, and *of* his priests and Levites, in my realm, which are minded of their own freewill to go up to Jerusalem, go with thee.

14 Forasmuch as thou art sent of the king, and of his ᴿseven counsellors, to enquire concerning Judah and Jerusalem, according to the law of thy God which *is* in thine hand;   Esth. 1:14

15 And to carry the silver and gold, which the king and his counsellors have freely offered unto the God of Israel, ᴿwhose habitation *is* in Jerusalem,   6:12

16 ᴿAnd all the silver and gold that thou canst find in all the province of Babylon, with the freewill offering of the people, and of the priests, offering willingly for the house of their God which *is* in Jerusalem: 8:25

17 That thou mayest buy speedily with this money bullocks, rams, lambs, with their ᴿmeat offerings and their drink offerings, and ᴿoffer them upon the altar of the house of your God which *is* in Jerusalem.   Num. 15:4–13 · Deut. 12:5–11

18 And whatsoever shall seem good to thee, and to thy brethren, to do with the rest of the silver and the gold, that do after the will of your God.

19 The vessels also that are given thee for the service of the

house of thy God, *those* deliver thou before the God of Jerusalem.

20 And whatsoever more shall be needful for the house of thy God, which thou shalt have occasion to bestow, bestow *it* out of the king's treasure house.

21 And I, *even* I Ar-tax-erx'-es the king, do make a decree to all the treasurers which *are* beyond the river, that whatsoever Ezra the priest, the scribe of the law of the God of heaven, shall require of you, it be done speedily,

22 Unto an hundred talents of silver, and to an hundred [T]measures of wheat, and to an hundred baths of wine, and to an hundred baths of oil, and salt without prescribing *how much*.   Lit. *kor*

23 Whatsoever is commanded by the God of heaven, let it be diligently done for the house of the God of heaven: for why should there be wrath against the realm of the king and his sons?

24 Also we certify you, that touching any of the priests and Levites, singers, [T]porters, Neth'-i-nims, or ministers of this house of God, it shall not be lawful to impose toll, tribute, or custom, upon them.   *gatekeepers*

25 And thou, Ezra, after the wisdom of thy God, that *is* in thine hand, [R]set magistrates and judges, which may judge all the people that *are* beyond the river, all such as know the laws of thy God; and [R]teach ye them that know *them* not.   Deut. 16:18 · [Mal. 2:7; Col. 1:28]

26 And whosoever will not do the law of thy God, and the law of the king, let judgment be executed speedily upon him, whether *it be* unto death, or [T]to banishment, or to confiscation of goods, or to imprisonment.   Lit. *rooting out*

27 [R]Blessed *be* the LORD God of our fathers, which hath put *such a thing* as this in the king's heart, to beautify the house of the LORD which *is* in Jerusalem: 1 Chr. 29:10

28 And hath extended mercy unto me before the king, and his counsellors, and before all the king's mighty princes. And I was strengthened as [R]the hand of the LORD my God *was* upon me, and I gathered together out of Israel chief men to go up with me.   8:18

8 These *are* now the chief of their fathers, and *this is* the genealogy of them that went up with me from Babylon, in the reign of Ar-tax-erx'-es the king.

2 Of the sons of Phin'-e-has; Ger'-shom: of the sons of Ith'-a-mar; Daniel: of the sons of David; [R]Hat'-tush.   2:68; 1 Chr. 3:22

3 Of the sons of Shech-a-ni'-ah, of the sons of [R]Pha'-rosh; Zech-a-ri'-ah: and with him were reckoned by genealogy of the males an hundred and fifty.   2:3

4 Of the sons of [R]Pa'-hath–mo'-ab; El-i-ho-e'-nai the son of Zer-a-hi'-ah, and with him two hundred males.   10:30

5 Of the sons of Shech-a-ni'-ah; the son of Ja-ha'-zi-el, and with him three hundred males.

6 Of the sons also of A'-din; E'-bed the son of Jonathan, and with him fifty males.

7 And of the sons of E'-lam; Je-sha'-iah the son of Ath-a-li'-ah, and with him seventy males.

8 And of the sons of Sheph-a-ti'-ah; Zeb-a-di'-ah the son of Mi'-cha-el, and with him fourscore males.

9 Of the sons of Jo'-ab; O-ba-di'-ah the son of Je-hi'-el, and with him two hundred and eighteen males.

10 And of the sons of Shel'-o-mith; the son of Jos-i-phi'-ah, and with him an hundred and three-score males.

11 And of the sons of [R]Be'-bai; Zech-a-ri'-ah the son of Be'-bai, and with him twenty and eight males.   10:28

12 And of the sons of Az'-gad; Jo-ha'-nan [T]the son of Hak'-ka-tan, and with him an hundred and ten males.   Or *the youngest son*

13 And of the last sons of A-don'-i-kam, whose names *are* these, E-liph'-e-let, Je-i'-el, and She-ma'-iah, and with them three-score males.

14 Of the sons also of Big'-vai; U'-thai, and ᵀZab'-bud, and with them seventy males.   Or Zakkur

15 And I gathered them together to the river that runneth to A-ha'-va; and there abode we in tents three days: and I viewed the people, and the priests, and found there none of the sons of Levi.

16 Then sent I for E-li-e'-zer, for A'-ri-el, for She-ma'-iah, and for El-na'-than, and for Ja'-rib, and for El-na'-than, and for Nathan, and for Zech-a-ri'-ah, and for ᴿMe-shul'-lam, chief men; also for Joi'-a-rib, and for El-na'-than, men of understanding.   10:15

17 And I sent them with commandment unto Id'-do the chief at the place Ca-siph'-i-a, and I told them what they should say unto Id'-do, and to his brethren the Neth'-i-nims, at the place Ca-siph'-i-a, that they should bring unto us ministers for the house of our God.

18 And by the good hand of our God upon us they ᴿbrought us a man of understanding, of the sons of Mah'-li, the son of Levi, the son of Israel; and Sher-e-bi'-ah, with his sons and his brethren, eighteen;   2 Chr. 30:22; Neh. 8:7

19 And ᴿHash-a-bi'-ah, and with him Je-sha'-iah of the sons of Me-ra'-ri, his brethren and their sons, twenty;   Neh. 12:24

20 ᴿAlso of the Neth'-i-nims, whom David and the princes had appointed for the service of the Levites, two hundred and twenty Neth'-i-nims: all of them were ᵀexpressed by name. 2:43; 7:7 · designated

21 Then I ᴿproclaimed a fast there, at the river of A-ha'-va, that we might afflict ourselves before our God, to seek of him a right way for us, and for our little ones, and for all our substance. 1 Sam. 7:6

22 For ᴿI was ashamed to require of the king a band of soldiers and horsemen to help us against the enemy in the way: because we had spoken unto the king, saying, The hand of our God is upon all them for ᴿgood that

seek him; but his power and his wrath is against all them that forsake him.   1 Cor. 9:15 · [Rom. 8:28]

23 So we fasted and besought our God for this: and he was ᴿintreated of us.   2 Chr. 33:13; Is. 19:22

24 Then I separated twelve of the chief of the priests, Sher-e-bi'-ah, Hash-a-bi'-ah, and ten of their brethren with them,

25 And weighed unto them ᴿthe silver, and the gold, and the vessels, even the offering of the house of our God, which the king, and his counsellors, and his lords, and all Israel there present, had offered: 7:15, 16

26 I even weighed unto their hand six hundred and fifty talents of silver, and silver vessels an hundred talents, and of gold an hundred talents;

27 Also twenty basons of gold, ᵀof a thousand drams; and two vessels of fine copper, precious as gold.   worth a thousand drachmas

28 And I said unto them, Ye are ᴿholy unto the LORD; the vessels are ᴿholy also; and the silver and the gold are a freewill offering unto the LORD God of your fathers.   Lev. 21:6-9 · Lev. 22:2, 3

29 Watch ye, and keep them, until ye weigh them before the chief of the priests and the Levites, and ᴿchief of the fathers of Israel, at Jerusalem, in the chambers of the house of the LORD.   4:3

30 So took the priests and the Levites the weight of the silver, and the gold, and the vessels, to bring them to Jerusalem unto the house of our God.

31 Then we departed from the river of A-ha'-va on the twelfth day of the first month, to go unto Jerusalem: and ᴿthe hand of our God was upon us, and he delivered us from the hand of the enemy, and ᵀof such as lay in wait by the way.   7:6, 9, 28 · from ambush

32 And we came to Jerusalem, and abode there three days.

33 Now on the fourth day was the silver and the gold and the vessels ᴿweighed in the house of

our God by the hand of Mer'-e-moth the son of U-ri'-ah the priest; and with him *was* E-le-a'-zar the son of Phin'-e-has; and with them *was* Joz'-a-bad the son of Jesh'-u-a, and No-a-di'-ah the son of Bin'-nu-i, Levites;   vv. 26, 30

34 By number *and* by weight of every one: and all the weight was written at that time.

35 *Also* the children of those that had been carried away, which were come out of the captivity, Roffered burnt offerings unto the God of Israel, twelve bullocks for all Israel, ninety and six rams, seventy and seven lambs, twelve he goats *for* a sin offering: all *this was* a burnt offering unto the LORD.   6:17

36 And they delivered the king's Rcommissions unto the king's lieutenants, and to the governors on this side the river: and they Tfurthered the people, and the house of God. 7:21–24 · *gave support to*

9 Now when these things were done, the princes came to me, saying, The people of Israel, and the priests, and the Levites, have not Rseparated themselves from the people of the lands, R*doing* according to their abominations, *even* of the Ca'-naan-ites, the Hit'-tites, the Per'-iz-zites, the Jeb'-u-sites, the Am'-mon-ites, the Mo'-ab-ites, the Egyptians, and the Am'-or-ites.   Neh. 9:2 · Deut. 12:30, 31

2 For they have taken of their daughters for themselves, and for their sons: so that the holy seed have mingled themselves with the people of *those* lands: yea, the hand of the princes and rulers hath been chief in this trespass.

3 And when I heard this thing, RI rent my garment and my mantle, and plucked off the hair of my head and of my beard, and sat down Rastonied.   Job 1:20 · Ps. 143:4

4 Then were assembled unto me every one that Rtrembled at the words of the God of Israel, because of the transgression of those that had been carried away;

and I sat astonied until the Reve-ning sacrifice.   10:3; Is. 66:2 · Ex. 29:39

5 And at the evening sacrifice I arose up from my Theaviness; and having Trent my garment and my mantle, I fell upon my knees, and Rspread out my hands unto the LORD my God,   *fasting · torn* · Ex. 9:29

6 And said, O my God, I am ashamed and blush to lift up my face to thee, my God: for our iniquities are increased over *our* head, and our trespass is Rgrown up unto the heavens.   Rev. 18:5

7 Since the days of our fathers *have* Rwe *been* in a great trespass unto this day; and for our iniquities Rhave we, our kings, *and* our priests, been delivered into the hand of the kings of the lands, to the sword, to captivity, and to a spoil, and to confusion of face, as *it is* this day.   Dan. 9:5, 6 · Neh. 9:30

8 And now for a little Tspace grace hath been *shewed* from the LORD our God, to leave us a remnant to escape, and to give us a Tnail in his holy place, that our God may Rlighten our eyes, and give us a little reviving in our bondage.   *while · peg* · Ps. 34:5

9 For we *were* bondmen; yet our God hath not forsaken us in our bondage, but hath extended mercy unto us in the sight of the kings of Persia, to give us a reviving, to set up the house of our God, and to repair the desolations thereof, and to give us a wall in Judah and in Jerusalem.

10 And now, O our God, what shall we say after this? for we have forsaken thy commandments,

11 Which thou hast commanded by thy servants the prophets, saying, The land, unto which ye go to possess it, is an unclean land with the Rfilthiness of the people of the lands, with their abominations, which have filled it from one end to another with their Tuncleanness.   6:21 · *impurity*

12 Now therefore give not your daughters unto their sons, neither take their daughters unto your sons, nor seek their peace or their

wealth for ever: that ye may be strong, and eat the good of the land, and leave *it* for an inheritance to your children for ever.

13 And after all that is come upon us for our evil deeds, and for our great [T]trespass, seeing that thou our God [R]hast punished us less than our iniquities *deserve*, and hast given us *such* deliverance as this;   *guilt* : [Ps. 103:10]

14 Should we again break thy commandments, and join in affinity with the people of these abominations? wouldest not thou be angry with us till thou hadst consumed *us*, so that *there should be* no remnant nor escaping?

15 O LORD God of Israel, thou *art* righteous: for we remain yet escaped, as *it is* this day: behold, we *are* before thee in our trespasses: for we cannot stand before thee because of this.

10 Now [R]when Ezra had prayed, and when he had confessed, weeping and casting himself down [R]before the house of God, there assembled unto him out of Israel a very great congregation of men and women and children: for the people wept very [R]sore.   Dan. 9:4, 20 · 2 Chr. 20:9 · Neh. 8:1–9

2 And Shech-a-ni'-ah the son of Je-hi'-el, *one* of the sons of E'-lam, answered and said unto Ezra, We have [R]trespassed against our God, and have taken strange wives of the people of the land: yet now there is hope in Israel concerning this thing. Neh. 13:23–27

3 Now therefore let us make a covenant with our God to put away all the wives, and such as are born of them, according to the counsel of my lord, and of those that [R]tremble at the commandment of our God; and let it be done according to the law.   9:4

4 Arise; for *this* matter *belongeth* unto thee: we also *will be* with thee: [R]be of good courage, and do *it.*   1 Chr. 28:10

5 Then arose Ezra, and made the chief priests, the Levites, and all Israel, [R]to swear that they should do according to this word. And they sware.   Neh. 5:12; 13:25

6 Then Ezra rose up from before the house of God, and went into the chamber of Jo-ha'-nan the son of E-li'-a-shib: and *when* he came thither, he [R]did eat no bread, nor drink water: for he mourned because of the [T]transgression of them that had been carried away.   Deut. 9:18 · *guilt*

7 And they made proclamation throughout Judah and Jerusalem unto all the children of the captivity, that they should gather themselves together unto Jerusalem;

8 And that whosoever would not come within three days, according to the counsel of the princes and the elders, all his [T]substance should be forfeited, and himself separated from the congregation of those that had been carried away.   *property*

9 Then all the men of Judah and Benjamin gathered themselves together unto Jerusalem within three days. It *was* the ninth month, on the twentieth *day* of the month; and [R]all the people sat in the street of the house of God, trembling because of *this* matter, and for the great rain. 1 Sam. 12:18

10 And Ezra the priest stood up, and said unto them, Ye have transgressed, and [T]have taken strange wives, to increase the trespass of Israel.   *have taken pagan wives*

11 Now therefore [R]make confession unto the LORD God of your fathers, and do his pleasure: and separate yourselves from the people of the land, and from the strange wives. Josh. 7:19; [Prov. 28:13]

12 Then all the congregation answered and said with a loud voice, As thou hast said, so must we do.

13 But the people *are* many, and *it is* a time of much rain, and we are not able to stand [T]without, neither *is this* a work of one day or two: for we are many that have transgressed in this thing. *outside*

14 Let now our rulers of all the congregation stand, and let all

them which have taken strange wives in our cities come at appointed times, and with them the elders of every city, and the judges thereof, until ᴿthe fierce wrath of our God for this matter be turned from us.   2 Chr. 28:11–13

15 Only Jonathan the son of A'-sa-hel and Ja-ha-zi'-ah the son of Tik'-vah were employed about this *matter:* and ᴿMe-shul'-lam and Shab'-be-thai the Levite helped them.   8:16; Neh. 3:4

16 And the children of the captivity did so. And Ezra the priest, *with* certain ᴿchief of the fathers, after the house of their fathers, and all of them by *their* names, were separated, and sat down in the first day of the tenth month to examine the matter.   4:3

17 And they made an end with all the men that had taken strange wives by the first day of the first month.

18 And among the sons of the priests there were found that had taken strange wives: *namely,* of the sons of ᴿJesh'-u-a the son of Joz'-a-dak, and his brethren; Ma-a-se'-iah, and E-li-e'-zer, and Ja'-rib, and Ged-a-li'-ah.   Zech. 3:1; 6:11

19 And they ᴿgave their hands that they would put away their wives; and *being* ᴿguilty, *they* offered a ram of the flock for their trespass.   2 Kin. 10:15 · Lev. 6:4, 6

20 And of the sons of Im'-mer; Ha-na'-ni, and Zeb-a-di'-ah.

21 And of the sons of Ha'-rim; Ma-a-se'-iah, and E-li'-jah, and She-ma'-iah, and Je-hi'-el, and Uz-zi'-ah.

22 And of the sons of Pash'-ur; E-li-o-e'-nai, Ma-a-se'-iah, Ish'-ma-el, Ne-than'-e-el, Joz'-a-bad, and El'-a-sah.

23 Also of the Levites; Joz'-a-bad, and Shim'-e-i, and Ke-la'-iah, (the same *is* Kel'-i-ta,) Peth-a-hi'-ah, Judah, and E-li-e'-zer.

24 Of the singers also; E-li'-a-shib: and of the porters; Shal'-lum, and Te'-lem, and U'-ri.

25 Moreover of Israel: of the ᴿsons of Pa'-rosh; Ra-mi'-ah, and

Je-zi'-ah, and Mal-chi'-ah, and Mi'-a-min, and E-le-a'-zar, and Mal-chi'-jah, and Be-na'-iah.   2:3

26 And of the sons of E'-lam; Mat-ta-ni'-ah, Zech-a-ri'-ah, and Je-hi'-el, and Ab'-di, and Jer'-e-moth, and E-li'-ah.

27 And of the sons of Zat'-tu; E-li-o-e'-nai, E-li'-a-shib, Mat-ta-ni'-ah, and Jer'-e-moth, and Za'-bad, and A-zi'-za.

28 Of the ᴿsons also of Be'-bai; Je-ho-ha'-nan, Han-a-ni'-ah, Zab'-bai, *and* Ath'-lai.   8:11

29 And of the sons of Ba'-ni; Me-shul'-lam, Mal'-luch, and A-da'-iah, Jash'-ub, and She'-al, and ᵀRa'-moth.   Or *Jeremoth*

30 And of the ᴿsons of Pa'-hath–mo'-ab; Ad'-na, and Che'-lal, Be-nai'-ah, Ma-a-se'-iah, Mat-ta-ni'-ah, Be-zal'-e-el, and Bin'-nu-i, and Ma-nas'-seh.   8:4

31 And *of* the sons of Ha'-rim; E-li-e'-zer, Ish-i'-jah, Mal-chi'-ah, She-ma'-iah, Shim'-e-on,

32 Benjamin, Mal'-luch, *and* Shem-a-ri'-ah.

33 Of the sons of Ha'-shum; Mat-te'-nai, Mat'-ta-thah, Za'-bad, E-liph'-e-let, Jer'-e-mai, Ma-nas'-seh, *and* Shim'-e-i.

34 Of the sons of Ba'-ni; Ma'-a-dai, Am'-ram, and U'-el,

35 Be-na'-iah, Be-de'-iah, ᵀChel'-luh,   Or *Cheluhi*

36 Va-ni'-ah, Mer'-e-moth, E-li'-a-shib,

37 Mat-ta-ni'-ah,   Mat-te'-nai, and ᵀJa'-a-sau,   Or *Jaasu*

38 And Ba'-ni, and Bin'-nu-i, Shim'-e-i,

39 And Shel-e-mi'-ah, and Na-than, and A-da'-iah,

40 Mach-na-de'-bai, Sha'-shai, Sha'-rai,

41 A-zar'-e-el, and Shel-e-mi'-ah, Shem-a-ri'-ah,

42 Shal'-lum, Am-a-ri'-ah, *and* Joseph.

43 Of the sons of Ne'-bo; Je-i'-el, Mat-ti-thi'-ah, Za'-bad, Ze-bi'-na, Ja'-dau, and Jo'-el, Be-na'-iah.

44 All these had taken strange wives: and *some* of them had wives by whom they had children.

The Book of

NEHEMIAH

NEHEMIAH, contemporary of Ezra and cupbearer to the king in the Persian palace, leads the third and last return to Jerusalem after the Babylonian exile. His concern for the welfare of Jerusalem and its inhabitants prompts him to take bold action. Granted permission to return to his homeland, Nehemiah challenges his countrymen to arise and rebuild the shattered wall of Jerusalem. In spite of opposition from without and abuse from within, the task is completed in only fifty-two days, a feat even the enemies of Israel must attribute to God's enabling. By contrast, the task of reviving and reforming the people of God within the rebuilt wall demands years of Nehemiah's godly life and leadership.

The Hebrew for Nehemiah is *Nehemyah,* "Comfort of Yahweh." The book is named after its chief character, whose name appears in the opening verse. The combined book of Ezra–Nehemiah is given the Greek title *Esdras Deuteron,* "Second Esdras" in the Septuagint, a third-century B.C. Greek-language translation of the Hebrew Old Testament. The Latin title of Nehemiah is *Liber Secundus Esdrae,* "Second Book of Ezra" (Ezra was the first). At this point, it is considered a separate book from Ezra, and is later called *Liber Nehemiae,* "Book of Nehemiah."

THE words of Ne-he-mi′-ah the son of Hach-a-li′-ah. And it came to pass in the month Chis′-leu, in the twentieth year, as I was in ᴿShu′-shan the palace, Dan. 8:2

2 That ᴿHa-na′-ni, one of my brethren, came, he and *certain* men of Judah; and I asked them concerning the Jews that had escaped, which were left of the captivity, and concerning Jerusalem. 7:2

3 And they said unto me, The remnant that are left of the captivity there in the province *are* in great affliction and reproach: ᴿthe wall of Jerusalem also ᴿ*is* broken down, and the gates thereof are burned with fire. 2:17 · 2 Kin. 25:10

4 And it came to pass, when I heard these words, that I sat down and wept, and mourned *certain* days, and fasted, and prayed before the God of heaven,

5 And said, I beseech thee, O Lᴏʀᴅ God of heaven, the great and ᴿterribleᵀ God, ᴿthat keepeth covenant and mercy for them that love him and observe his commandments: 4:14 · *awesome* · Ps. 89:2, 3

6 Let thine ear now be attentive, and thine eyes open, that thou mayest hear the prayer of thy servant, which I pray before thee now, day and night, for the children of Israel thy servants, and confess the sins of the children of Israel, which we have sinned against thee: both I and my father's house have sinned.

7 ᴿWe have dealt very corruptly against thee, and have not kept the commandments, nor the statutes, nor the judgments, which thou commandedst thy servant Moses. Ps. 106:6; Dan. 9:5

8 Remember, I beseech thee, the word that thou commandedst thy servant Moses, saying, *If* ye transgress, I will scatter you abroad among the nations:

9 ᴿBut *if* ye turn unto me, and keep my commandments, and do them; though there were of you cast out unto the uttermost part of the heaven, *yet* will I gather them from thence, and will bring them unto the place that I have chosen to set my name there. [Deut. 4:29–31]

10 ᴿNow these *are* thy servants and thy people, whom thou hast

redeemed by thy great power, and by thy strong hand. Dan. 9:15

11 O LORD, I beseech thee, ᴿlet now thine ear be attentive to the prayer of thy servant, and to the prayer of thy servants, who ᴿdesire to fear thy name: and prosper, I pray thee, thy servant this day, and grant him mercy in the sight of this man. For I was the king's cupbearer. v. 6 · Is. 26:8; [Heb. 13:18]

2 And it came to pass in the month Ni′-san, in the twentieth year of Ar-tax-erx′-es the king, *that* wine *was* before him: and I took up the wine, and gave *it* unto the king. Now I had not been *beforetime* sad in his presence.

2 Wherefore the king said unto me, Why *is* thy ᵀcountenance sad, seeing thou *art* not sick? this *is* nothing *else* but sorrow of heart. Then I was very sore afraid, *face*

3 And said unto the king, ᴿLet the king live for ever: why should not my countenance be sad, when ᴿthe city, the place of my fathers' sepulchres, *lieth* waste, and the gates thereof are consumed with ᴿfire? Dan. 2:4 · Jer. 52:12–14 · 2 Kin. 24:10

4 Then the king said unto me, For what dost thou make request? So I prayed to the God of heaven.

5 And I said unto the king, If it please the king, and if thy servant have found favour in thy sight, that thou wouldest send me unto Judah, unto the city of my fathers' sepulchres, that I may build it.

6 And the king said unto me, (the queen also sitting by him,) For how long shall thy journey be? and when wilt thou return? So it pleased the king to send me; and I set him ᴿa time. 5:14; 13:6

7 Moreover I said unto the king, If it please the king, let letters be given me to the ᴿgovernors beyond the river, that they may convey me over till I come into Judah; Ezra 7:21; 8:36

8 And a letter unto A′-saph the keeper of the king's forest, that he may give me timber to make beams for the gates of the palace which *appertained* ᴿto the house,

and for the wall of the city, and for the house that I shall enter into. And the king granted me, ᴿaccording to the good hand of my God upon me. 3:7 · Ezra 5:5; 7:6, 9, 28

9 Then I came to the governors beyond the river, and gave them the king's letters. Now the king had sent captains of the army and horsemen with me.

10 When San-bal′-lat the Hor′-o-nite, and To-bi′-ah the servant, the Am′-mon-ite, heard *of it*, it grieved them exceedingly that there was come a man to seek the welfare of the children of Israel.

11 So I ᴿcame to Jerusalem, and was there three days. Ezra 8:32

12 And I arose in the night, I and some few men with me; neither told I *any* man what my God had put in my heart to do at Jerusalem: neither *was there any* beast with me, save the beast that I rode upon.

13 And I went out by night ᴿby the gate of the valley, even before the dragon well, and to the dung port, and viewed the walls of Jerusalem, which were ᴿbroken down, and the gates thereof were consumed with fire. 3:13; 2 Chr. 26:9 · 1:3

14 Then I went on to the ᴿgate of the fountain, and to the ᴿking's pool: but *there was* no place for the beast *that was* under me to pass. 3:15 · 2 Kin. 20:20

15 Then went I up in the night by the ᴿbrook, and viewed the wall, and turned back, and entered by the gate of the valley, and so returned. 2 Sam. 15:23; Jer. 31:40

16 And the ᵀrulers knew not whither I went, or what I did; neither had I as yet told *it* to the Jews, nor to the priests, nor to the nobles, nor to the rulers, nor to the rest that did the work. *officials*

17 Then said I unto them, Ye see the distress that we *are* in, how Jerusalem *lieth* waste, and the gates thereof are burned with fire: come, and let us build up the wall of Jerusalem, that we be no more ᴿa reproach. Ps. 44:13; 79:4; Jer. 24:9

18 Then I told them of ᴿthe hand

of my God which was good upon me; as also the king's words that he had spoken unto me. And they said, Let us rise up and build. So they ᴿstrengthened their hands for *this* good *work*.   v. 8 · 2 Sam. 2:7

19 But when San-bal'-lat the Hor'-o-nite, and To-bi'-ah the servant, the Am'-mon-ite, and Ge'-shem the A-ra'-bi-an, heard *it*, they laughed us to scorn, and despised us, and said, What *is* this thing that ye do? ᴿwill ye rebel against the king?   6:6

20 Then answered I them, and said unto them, The God of heaven, he will prosper us; therefore we his servants will arise and build: ᴿbut ye have no ᵀportion, nor right, nor memorial, in Jerusalem.   6:16; Ezra 4:3 · *heritage*

3 Then E-li'-a-shib the high priest rose up with his brethren the priests, ᴿand they builded the sheep gate; they sanctified it, and set up the doors of it; ᴿeven unto the tower of Me'-ah they sanctified it, unto the tower of ᴿHa-nan'-e-el.   John 5:2 · 12:39 · Zech. 14:10

2 And next unto him builded ᴿthe men of Jericho. And next to them builded Zac'-cur the son of Im'-ri.   7:36; Ezra 2:34

3 ᴿBut the fish gate did the sons of Has-se-na'-ah build, who *also* laid the beams thereof, and ᴿset up the doors thereof, the locks thereof, and the bars thereof.   2 Chr. 33:14; Zeph. 1:10 · 6:1; 7:1

4 And next unto them repaired ᴿMer'-e-moth the son of U-ri'-jah, the son of Koz. And next unto them repaired ᴿMe-shul'-lam the son of Ber-e-chi'-ah, the son of Me-shez'-a-beel. And next unto them repaired Za'-dok the son of Ba'-a-na.   Ezra 8:33 · Ezra 10:15

5 And next unto them the Te-ko'-ites repaired; but their nobles put not their necks to ᴿthe work of their LORD.   [Judg. 5:23]

6 Moreover ᴿthe old gate repaired Je-hoi'-a-da the son of Pa-se'-ah, and Me-shul'-lam the son of Bes-o-de'-iah; they laid the beams thereof, and set up the

doors thereof, and the locks thereof, and the bars thereof.   12:39

7 And next unto them repaired Mel-a-ti'-ah the Gib'-e-on-ite, and Ja'-don the Me-ron'-o-thite, the ᴿmen of Gib'-e-on, and of Miz'-pah, unto the throne of the governor on this side the river.   7:25

8 Next unto him repaired Uz-zi'-el the son of Har-ha'-iah, of the goldsmiths. Next unto him also repaired Han-a-ni'-ah the son of *one* of the ᵀapothecaries, and they fortified Jerusalem unto the ᴿbroad wall.   *perfumers* · 12:38

9 And next unto them repaired Re-pha'-iah the son of Hur, the ruler of the half part of Jerusalem.

10 And next unto them repaired Je-da'-iah the son of Ha-ru'-maph, even over against his house. And next unto him repaired Hat'-tush the son of Hash-ab-ni'-ah.

11 Mal-chi'-jah the son of Ha'-rim, and Ha'-shub the son of Pa'-hath–mo'-ab, repaired ᵀthe other piece, ᴿand the tower of the furnaces.   *another section* · 12:38

12 And next unto him repaired Shal'-lum the son of Ha-lo'-hesh, the ruler of the half part of Je-rusalem, he and his daughters.

13 ᴿThe valley gate repaired Ha'-nun, and the inhabitants of Za-no'-ah; they built it, and set up the doors thereof, the locks thereof, and the bars thereof, and a thousand cubits on the wall unto ᴿthe dung gate.   2:13, 15 · 2:13

14 But the dung gate repaired Mal-chi'-ah the son of Re'-chab, the ruler of part of ᴿBeth–hac'-ce-rem; he built it, and set up the doors thereof, the locks thereof, and the bars thereof.   Jer. 6:1

15 But ᴿthe gate of the fountain repaired Shal'-lun the son of Col-ho'-zeh, the ruler of part of Miz'-pah; he built it, and covered it, and set up the doors thereof, the locks thereof, and the bars thereof, and the wall of the pool of ᴿSi-lo'-ah by the king's garden, and unto the stairs that go down from the city of David. 2:14 · Is. 8:6; John 9:7

16 After him repaired Ne-he-mi'-ah the son of Az'-buk, the ruler of the half part of Beth'-zur, unto *the place* over against the sepulchres of David, and to the ᴿpool that was made, and unto the house of the mighty.   Is. 7:3; 22:11

17 After him repaired the Le-vites, Re'-hum the son of Ba'-ni. Next unto him repaired Hash-a-bi'-ah, the ruler of the half part of Kei'-lah, in his part.

18 After him repaired their brethren, Ba'-vai the son of Hen'-a-dad, the ruler of the half part of Kei'-lah.

19 And next to him repaired E'-zer the son of Jesh'-u-a, the ruler of Miz'-pah, another piece over against the ᵀgoing up to the armoury at the ᴿturningᵀ *of the wall.*   ascent · 2 Chr. 26:9 · buttress

20 After him Ba'-ruch the son of Zab'-bai earnestly repaired the other piece, from the ᵀturning *of the wall* unto the door of the house of E-li'-a-shib the high priest.   buttress

21 After him repaired Mer'-e-moth the son of U-ri'-jah the son of Koz another piece, from the door of the house of E-li'-a-shib even to the end of the house of E-li'-a-shib.

22 And after him repaired the priests, the men of the plain.

23 After him repaired Benjamin and Ha'-shub over against their house. After him repaired Az-a-ri'-ah the son of Ma-a-se'-iah the son of An-a-ni'-ah by his house.

24 After him repaired ᴿBin'-nu-i the son of Hen'-a-dad another piece, from the house of Az-a-ri'-ah unto ᴿthe turning *of the wall,* even unto the corner.   Ezra 8:33 · v. 19

25 Pa'-lal the son of U'-zai, over against the turning *of the wall,* and the tower which ᵀlieth out from the king's ᵀhigh house, that *was* by the ᴿcourt of the prison. After him Pe-da'-iah the son of Pa'-rosh.   projects from · upper · Jer. 32:2

26 Moreover ᴿthe Neth'-i-nims dwelt in ᴿO'-phel, unto *the place* over against ᴿthe water gate to-ward the east, and the tower that lieth out.   11:21 · 2 Chr. 27:3 · 8:1, 3; 12:37

27 After them the Te-ko'-ites re-paired another piece, over against the great tower that lieth out, even unto the wall of O'-phel.

28 From above the ᴿhorse gate repaired the priests, every one over against his house.   2 Kin. 11:16

29 After them repaired Za'-dok the son of Im'-mer over against his house. After him repaired also She-ma'-iah the son of Shech-a-ni'-ah, the keeper of the east gate.

30 After him repaired Han-a-ni'-ah the son of Shel-e-mi'-ah, and Ha'-nun the sixth son of Za'-laph, another piece. After him repaired Me-shul'-lam the son of Ber-e-chi'-ah over against his chamber.

31 After him repaired Mal-chi'-ah the goldsmith's son unto the place of the Neth'-i-nims, and of the merchants, over against the gate Miph'-kad, and to the ᵀgoing up of the corner.   upper room of

32 And between the going up of the corner unto the ᴿsheep gate repaired the goldsmiths and the merchants.   v. 1; 12:39

4 But it came to pass, ᴿthat when San-bal'-lat heard that we builded the wall, he was wroth, and took great indigna-tion, and mocked the Jews.   2:10, 19

2 And he spake before his brethren and the army of Sa-ma'-ri-a, and said, What do these fee-ble Jews? will they fortify them-selves? will they sacrifice? will they ᵀmake an end in a day? will they revive the stones out of the heaps of the rubbish which are burned?   complete it

3 Now ᴿTo-bi'-ah the Am'-mon-ite *was* by him, and he said, Even that which they build, if a fox go up, he shall even break down their stone wall.   2:10, 19

4 ᴿHear, O our God; for we are despised: and ᴿturn their re-proach upon their own head, and give them for a prey in the land of captivity: Ps. 123:3, 4 · Ps. 79:12

5 And ᴿcover not their iniquity, and let not their sin be blotted out

from before thee: for they have provoked *thee* to anger before the builders.   Ps. 69:27, 28; 109:14, 15

6 So built we the wall; and all the wall was joined together unto the half thereof: for the people had a mind to work.

7 But it came to pass, *that* when San-bal'-lat, and To-bi'-ah, and ^Rthe A-ra'-bi-ans, and the Am'-mon-ites, and the Ash'-dod-ites, heard that the walls of Jerusalem were made up, *and* that the breaches began to be stopped, then they were very wroth,   2:19

8 And ^Rconspired all of them together to come *and* to fight against Jerusalem, and to ^Thinder it.   Ps. 83:3–5 · *create confusion*

9 Nevertheless ^Rwe made our prayer unto our God, and set a watch against them day and night, because of them.   [Ps. 50:15]

10 And Judah said, The strength of the bearers of burdens is ^Tdecayed, and *there is* much rubbish; so that we are not able to build the wall.   *failing*

11 And our adversaries said, They shall not know, neither see, till we come in the midst among them, and slay them, and cause the work to cease.

12 And it came to pass, that when the Jews which dwelt by them came, they said unto us ten times, From all places whence ye shall return unto us *they will be upon you.*

13 Therefore set I in the lower places behind the wall, *and* ^Ton the higher places, I even set the people after their families with their swords, their spears, and their bows.   *at the open places*

14 And I looked, and rose up, and said unto the nobles, and to the rulers, and to the rest of the people, ^RBe not ye afraid of them: remember the LORD, *which is* great and ^Tterrible, and fight for your brethren, your sons, and your daughters, your wives, and your houses.   Deut. 1:29 · *awesome*

15 And it came to pass, when our enemies heard that it was

known unto us, and God had brought their counsel to nought, that we returned all of us to the wall, every one unto his work.

16 And it came to pass from that time forth, *that* the half of my servants wrought in the work, and the other half of them held both the spears, the shields, and the bows, and ^Tthe habergeons; and the rulers *were* behind all the house of Judah.   *wore the armour*

17 They which builded on the wall, and they that bare burdens, with those that laded, *every one* with one of his hands wrought in the work, and with the other *hand* held a weapon.

18 For the builders, every one had his sword girded by his side, and *so* builded. And he that sounded the trumpet *was* by me.

19 And I said unto the nobles, and to the rulers, and to the rest of the people, The work *is* great and large, and we are separated upon the wall, one far from another.

20 In what place *therefore* ye hear the sound of the trumpet, resort ye thither unto us: ^Rour God shall fight for us.   Josh. 23:10

21 So we laboured in the work: and half of them held the spears from the rising of the morning till the stars appeared.

22 Likewise at the same time said I unto the people, Let every one with his servant lodge within Jerusalem, that in the night they may be a guard to us, and labour on the day.

23 So neither I, nor my brethren, nor my servants, nor the men of the guard which followed me, none of us put off our clothes, ^Tsaving *that* every one put them off for washing.   *except*

5 And there was a great cry of the people and of their wives against their brethren the Jews.

2 For there were that said, We, our sons, and our daughters, *are* many: therefore we take up ^Tcorn *for them,* that we may eat, and live.   *grain*

3 *Some* also there were that said, We have mortgaged our lands, vineyards, and houses, that we might buy [T]corn, because of the [T]dearth.   *grain · famine*

4 There were also that said, We have borrowed money for the king's [T]tribute, *and that upon* our lands and vineyards. *tax on our lands*

5 Yet now [R]our flesh *is* as the flesh of our brethren, our children as their children: and, lo, we bring into bondage our sons and our daughters to be servants, and *some* of our daughters are brought unto bondage *already*: neither *is it* in our power *to redeem them;* for other men have our lands and vineyards.   Is. 58:7

6 And I was very angry when I heard their cry and these words.

7 Then I consulted with myself, and I rebuked the nobles, and the rulers, and said unto them, [R]Ye exact usury, every one of his brother. And I set a great assembly against them.   [Ex. 22:25]

8 And I said unto them, We after our ability have redeemed our brethren the Jews, which were sold unto the heathen; and will ye even sell your brethren? or shall they be sold unto us? Then [T]held they their peace, and found nothing *to answer.*   *they were silenced*

9 Also I said, It *is* not good that ye do: ought ye not to walk in the fear of our God [R]because of the reproach of the heathen our enemies? 2 Sam. 12:14; Rom. 2:24; [1 Pet. 2:12]

10 I likewise, *and* my brethren, and my servants, might exact of them money and corn: I pray you, let us leave off this usury.

11 Restore, I pray you, to them, even this day, their lands, their vineyards, their [T]oliveyards, and their houses, also the hundredth *part* of the money, and of the corn, the wine, and the oil, that ye exact of them.   *olive groves*

12 Then said they, We will restore *them,* and will require nothing of them; so will we do as thou sayest. Then I called the priests, [R]and took an oath of them, that they should do according to this promise.   Ezra 10:5; Jer. 34:8, 9

13 Also I shook my lap, and said, So God shake out every man from his house, and from his labour, that performeth not this promise, even thus be he shaken out, and emptied. And all the congregation said, A'-men, and praised the LORD. And the people did according to this promise.

14 Moreover from the time that I was appointed to be their governor in the land of Judah, from the twentieth year [R]even unto the two and thirtieth year of Ar-tax-erx'-es the king, *that is,* twelve years, I and my brethren have not eaten the bread of the governor. 2:1; 13:6

15 But the former governors that *had been* before me were chargeable unto the people, and had taken of them bread and wine, beside forty shek'-els of silver; yea, even their servants bare rule over the people: but so did not I, because of the fear of God.

16 Yea, also I continued in the [R]work of this wall, neither bought we any land: and all my servants *were* gathered thither unto the work.   4:1; 6:1

17 Moreover *there were* at my table an hundred and fifty of the Jews and rulers, beside those that came unto us from among the heathen that *are* about us.

18 Now *that* [R]which was prepared *for me* daily *was* one ox *and* six choice sheep; also fowls were prepared for me, and once in ten days store of all sorts of wine: yet for all this [R]required not I the bread of the governor, because the bondage was heavy upon this people.   1 Kin. 4:22 · vv. 14, 15

19 [R]Think upon me, my God, for good, *according* to all that I have done for this people.   2 Kin. 20:3

6 Now it came to pass, [R]when San-bal'-lat, and To-bi'-ah, and Ge'-shem the A-ra'-bi-an, and the rest of our enemies, heard that I had builded the wall, and *that* there was no breach left therein;

(though at that time I had not set up the doors upon the gates;) 2:10

2 That San-bal'-lat and Ge'-shem sent unto me, saying, Come, let us meet together in *some one of* the villages in the plain of [R]O'-no. But they [R]thought to do me [T]mischief.   11:35 · Ps. 37:12 · *harm*

3 And I sent messengers unto them, saying, I *am* doing a great work, so that I cannot come down: why should the work cease, whilst I leave it, and come down to you?

4 Yet they sent unto me four times after this sort; and I answered them after the same manner.

5 Then sent San-bal'-lat his servant unto me in like manner the fifth time with an open letter in his hand;

6 Wherein *was* written, It is reported among the heathen, and Gash'-mu saith *it, that* thou and the Jews think to rebel: for which cause thou buildest the wall, [R]that thou mayest be their king, according to these [T]words.   2:19 · *rumours*

7 And thou hast also appointed prophets to preach of thee at Jerusalem, saying, *There is* a king in Judah: and now shall it be reported to the king according to these words. Come now therefore, and let us take counsel together.

8 Then I sent unto him, saying, There are no such things done as thou sayest, but thou feignest them out of thine own heart.

9 For they all made us afraid, saying, Their hands shall be weakened from the work, that it be not done. Now therefore, O God, strengthen my hands.

10 Afterward I came unto the house of She-ma'-iah the son of De-la'-iah the son of Me-het'-a-beel, who *was* [T]shut up; and he said, Let us meet together in the house of God, within the temple, and let us shut the doors of the temple: for they will come to slay thee; yea, in the night will they come to slay thee.   *confined*

11 And I said, Should such a man as I flee? and who *is there,*

that, *being* as I *am,* would go into the temple to save his life? I will not go in.

12 And, lo, I perceived that God had not sent him; but that [R]he pronounced this prophecy against me: for To-bi'-ah and San-bal'-lat had hired him.   Ezek. 13:22

13 Therefore *was* he hired, that I should be afraid, and do so, and sin, and *that* they might have *matter* for an evil report, that they might reproach me.

14 [R]My God, think thou upon To-bi'-ah and San-bal'-lat according to these their works, and on the prophetess No-a-di'-ah, and the rest of the prophets, that would have put me in fear.   13:29

15 So the wall was finished in the twenty and fifth *day* of *the month* E'-lul, in fifty and two days.

16 And it came to pass, that [R]when all our enemies heard *thereof,* and all the heathen that *were* about us saw *these things,* they were much cast down in their own eyes: for they perceived that this work was wrought of our God.   v. 1; 2:10, 20; 4:1, 7

17 Moreover in those days the nobles of Judah sent many letters unto To-bi'-ah, and *the letters* of To-bi'-ah came unto them.

18 For *there were* many in Judah sworn unto him, because he *was* the [R]son in law of Shech-a-ni'-ah the son of A'-rah; and his son Jo-ha'-nan had taken the daughter of [R]Me-shul'-lam the son of Ber-e-chi'-ah.   13:4, 28 · Ezra 10:15

19 Also they reported his good deeds before me, and uttered my [T]words to him. *And* To-bi'-ah sent letters to put me in fear.   *matters*

7 Now it came to pass, when the wall was built, and I had [R]set up the doors, and the porters and the singers and the Levites were appointed,   6:1, 15

2 That I gave my brother Ha-na'-ni, and Han-a-ni'-ah the ruler [R]of the palace, charge over Jerusalem: for he *was* a faithful man, and feared God above many.   2:8

3 And I said unto them, Let not the gates of Jerusalem be opened until the sun be hot; and while they ᵀstand by, let them shut the doors, and bar *them:* and appoint watches of the inhabitants of Jerusalem, every one in his watch, and every one *to be* over against his house. *stand guard*

4 Now the city *was* ᵀlarge and great: but the people *were* ᴿfew therein, and the houses *were* not builded. *broad, spacious* · Deut. 4:27

5 And my God put into mine heart to gather together the nobles, and the rulers, and the people, that they might be ᵀreckoned by genealogy. And I found a register of the genealogy of them which came up at the first, and found written therein, *registered*

6 ᴿThese *are* the children of the province, that went up out of the captivity, of those that had been carried away, whom Neb-u-chadnez'-zar the king of Babylon had carried away, and came again to Jerusalem and to Judah, every one unto his city; Ezra 2:1-70

7 Who came with Ze-rub'-babel, Jesh'-u-a, Ne-he-mi'-ah, Az-a-ri'-ah, Ra-a-mi'-ah, Na-ham'-a-ni, Mor'-de-cai, Bil'-shan, Mis'-pereth, Big'-vai, Ne'-hum, Ba'-a-nah. The number, *I say,* of the men of the people of Israel *was this;*

8 The children of Pa'-rosh, two thousand an hundred seventy and two.

9 The children of Sheph-a-ti'-ah, three hundred seventy and two.

10 The children of A'-rah, six hundred fifty and two.

11 The children of Pa'-hath-mo'-ab, of the children of Jesh'-u-a and Jo'-ab, two thousand and eight hundred *and* eighteen.

12 The children of E'-lam, a thousand two hundred fifty and four.

13 The children of Zat'-tu, eight hundred forty and five.

14 The children of Zac'-cai, seven hundred and threescore.

15 The children of Bin'-nu-i, six hundred forty and eight.

16 The children of Be'-bai, six hundred twenty and eight.

17 The children of Az'-gad, two thousand three hundred twenty and two.

18 The children of A-don'-i-kam, six hundred threescore and seven.

19 The children of Big'-vai, two thousand threescore and seven.

20 The children of A'-din, six hundred fifty and five.

21 The children of A'-ter of Hez-e-ki'-ah, ninety and eight.

22 The children of Ha'-shum, three hundred twenty and eight.

23 The children of Be'-zai, three hundred twenty and four.

24 The children of Ha'-riph, an hundred and twelve.

25 The children of Gib'-e-on, ninety and five.

26 The men of Beth'-le-hem and Ne-to'-phah, an hundred fourscore and eight.

27 The men of An'-a-thoth, an hundred twenty and eight.

28 The men of Beth-az'-maveth, forty and two.

29 The men of Kir'-jath-je'-a-rim, Che-phi'-rah, and Be-e'-roth, seven hundred forty and three.

30 The men of Ra'-mah and Ga'-ba, six hundred twenty and one.

31 The men of Mich'-mas, an hundred and twenty and two.

32 The men of Beth'-el and A'-i, an hundred twenty and three.

33 The men of the other Ne'-bo, fifty and two.

34 The children of the other ᴿE'-lam, a thousand two hundred fifty and four. v. 12

35 The children of Ha'-rim, three hundred and twenty.

36 The children of Jericho, three hundred forty and five.

37 The children of Lod, Ha'-did, and O'-no, seven hundred twenty and one.

38 The children of Se-na'-ah, three thousand nine hundred and thirty.

39 The priests: the children of ᴿJe-da'-iah, of the house of Jesh'-u-a, nine hundred seventy and three. 1 Chr. 24:7

40 The children of ᴿIm'-mer, a thousand fifty and two. 1 Chr. 9:12

41 The children of ᴿPash'-ur, a thousand two hundred forty and seven. 1 Chr. 9:12; 24:9

42 The children of ᴿHa'-rim, a thousand and seventeen. 1 Chr. 24:8

43 The Levites: the children of Jesh'-u-a, of Kad'-mi-el, *and* of the children of Ho-de'-vah, seventy and four.

44 The singers: the children of A'-saph, an hundred forty and eight.

45 The porters: the children of Shal'-lum, the children of A'-ter, the children of Tal'-mon, the children of Ak'-kub, the children of Hat'-i-ta, the children of Sho'-bai, an hundred thirty and eight.

46 The Neth'-i-nims: the children of Zi'-ha, the children of Ha-shu'-pha, the children of Tab'-ba-oth,

47 The children of Ke'-ros, the children of Si'-a, the children of Pa'-don,

48 The children of Leb'-a-na, the children of Hag'-a-ba, the children of Shal'-mai,

49 The children of Ha'-nan, the children of Gid'-del, the children of Ga'-har,

50 The children of Re-a'-iah, the children of Re'-zin, the children of Ne-ko'-da,

51 The children of Gaz'-zam, the children of Uz'-za, the children of Pha-se'-ah,

52 The children of Be'-sai, the children of Me-u'-nim, the children of Ne-phish'-e-sim,

53 The children of Bak'-buk, the children of Ha-ku'-pha, the children of Har'-hur,

54 The children of Baz'-lith, the children of Me-hi'-da, the children of Har'-sha,

55 The children of Bar'-kos, the children of Sis'-e-ra, the children of Ta'-mah,

56 The children of Ne-zi'-ah, the children of Hat'-i-pha.

57 The children of Solomon's servants: the children of So'-tai, the children of Soph'-e-reth, the children of Pe-ri'-da,

58 The children of Ja-a'-la, the children of Dar'-kon, the children of Gid'-del,

59 The children of Sheph-a-ti'-ah, the children of Hat'-til, the children of Poch'-e-reth of Ze-ba'-im, the children of Amon.

60 All the Neth'-i-nims, and the children of Solomon's servants, *were* three hundred ninety and two.

61 And these *were* they which went up *also* from Tel-me'-lah, Tel–har'-e-sha, Cherub, Ad'-don, and Im'-mer: but they ᵀcould not shew their father's house, nor their seed, whether they *were* of Israel. *could not identify their genealogies*

62 The children of De-la'-iah, the children of To-bi'-ah, the children of Ne-ko'-da, six hundred forty and two.

63 And of the priests: the children of Ha-ba'-iah, the children of Koz, the children of Bar-zil'-lai, which took *one* of the daughters of Bar-zil'-lai the Gil'-e-ad-ite to wife, and was called after their name.

64 These sought their register *among* those that were reckoned by genealogy, but it was not found: therefore were they, as ᵀpolluted, put from the priesthood. *defiled and excluded from*

65 And the ᵀTir-sha'-tha said unto them, that they should not eat of the most holy things, till there stood *up* a priest with U'-rim and Thum'-mim. *Lit. governor*

66 The whole congregation together *was* forty and two thousand three hundred and threescore,

67 Beside their manservants and their maidservants, of whom *there were* seven thousand three hundred thirty and seven: and they had two hundred forty and five singing men and singing women.

68 Their horses, seven hundred thirty and six: their mules, two hundred forty and five:

69 *Their* camels, four hundred thirty and five: six thousand seven hundred and twenty asses.

70 And some of the chief of the fathers gave unto the work. ᴿThe Tir-sha'-tha gave to the treasure a thousand ᵀdrams of gold, fifty basons, five hundred and thirty priests' garments. _8:9 · drachmas_

71 And _some_ of the chief of the fathers gave to the treasure of the work ᴿtwenty thousand ᵀdrams of gold, and two thousand and two hundred ᵀpounds of silver. _Ezra 2:69 · drachmas · minas_

72 And _that_ which the rest of the people gave _was_ twenty thousand ᵀdrams of gold, and two thousand ᵀpounds of silver, and threescore and seven priests' garments. _drachmas · minas_

73 So the priests, and the Levites, and the ᵀporters, and the singers, and _some_ of the people, and the Neth'-i-nims, and all Israel, dwelt in their cities; ᴿand when the seventh month came, the children of Israel _were_ in their cities. _gatekeepers · Ezra 3:1_

8 And all ᴿthe people gathered themselves together as one man into the street that _was_ before the water gate; and they spake unto Ezra the ᴿscribe to bring the book of the law of Moses, which the LORD had commanded to Israel. _Ezra 3:1 · Ezra 7:6_

2 And Ezra the priest brought ᴿthe law before the congregation both of men and women, and all that could hear with understanding, upon the first day of the seventh month. _v. 9; [Deut. 31:11, 12]_

3 And he ᴿread therein before the street that _was_ before the water gate from the morning until midday, before the men and the women, and those that could understand; and the ears of all the people _were attentive_ unto the book of the law. _Deut. 31:9–11_

4 And Ezra the scribe stood upon a ᵀpulpit of wood, which they had made for the purpose; and beside him stood Mat-ti-thi'-ah, and She'-ma, and A-na'-iah, and U-ri'-jah, and Hil-ki'-ah, and Ma-a-se'-iah, on his right hand; and on his left hand, Pe-da'-iah,

and Mish'-a-el, and Mal-chi'-ah, and Ha'-shum, and Hash-bad'-a-na, Zech-a-ri'-ah, _and_ Me-shul'-lam. _platform_

5 And Ezra opened the book in the sight of all people; (for he was above all the people;) and when he opened it, all the people ᴿstood up: _Judg. 3:20; 1 Kin. 8:12–14_

6 And Ezra blessed the LORD, the great God. And all the people answered, A'-men, A'-men, with ᴿlifting up their hands: and they bowed their heads, and worshipped the LORD with _their_ faces to the ground. _Ps. 28:2; 1 Tim. 2:8_

7 Also Jesh'-u-a, and Ba'-ni, and Sher-e-bi'-ah, Ja'-min, Ak'-kub, Shab'-be-thai, Ho-di'-jah, Ma-a-se'-iah, Kel'-i-ta, Az-a-ri'-ah, Joz'-a-bad, Ha'-nan, Pe-la'-iah, and the Levites, caused the people to understand the law: and the people ᴿstood in their place. _9:3_

8 So they read in the book in the law of God distinctly, and gave the sense, and caused _them_ to understand the reading.

9 ᴿAnd Ne-he-mi'-ah, which _is_ the ᵀTir-sha'-tha, and Ezra the priest the scribe, and the Levites that taught the people, said unto all the people, This day _is_ holy unto the LORD your God; mourn not, nor weep. For all the people wept, when they heard the words of the law. _7:65, 70; 10:1 · Lit. governor_

10 Then he said unto them, Go your way, eat the fat, and drink the sweet, ᴿand send portions unto them for whom nothing is prepared: for _this_ day _is_ holy unto our Lord: neither be ye sorry; for the joy of the LORD is your strength. _Esth. 9:19, 22; Rev. 11:10_

11 So the Levites stilled all the people, saying, ᵀHold your peace, for the day _is_ holy; neither be ye grieved. _Be still_

12 And all the people went their way to eat, and to drink, and to ᴿsend portions, and to make great mirth, because they had ᴿunderstood the words that were declared unto them. _v. 10 · vv. 7, 8_

13 And on the second day were

gathered together the chief of the fathers of all the people, the priests, and the Levites, unto Ezra the scribe, even to understand the words of the law.

14 And they found written in the law which the LORD had commanded by Moses, that the children of Israel should dwell in ^Rbooths in the feast of the seventh month: Lev. 23:34, 40, 42; Deut. 16:13

15 And ^Rthat they should publish and proclaim in all their cities, and ^Rin Jerusalem, saying, Go forth unto the mount, and fetch olive branches, and pine branches, and myrtle branches, and palm branches, and branches of thick trees, to make booths, as *it is* written.   Lev. 23:4 · Deut. 16:16

16 So the people went forth, and brought *them*, and made themselves booths, every one upon the ^Rroof of his house, and in their courts, and in the courts of the house of God, and in the street of the water gate, and in the street of the gate of E'-phra-im.   Deut. 22:8

17 And all the congregation of them that were come again out of the captivity made booths, and sat under the booths: for since the days of Jesh'-u-a the son of Nun unto that day had not the children of Israel done so. And there was very ^Rgreat gladness.   2 Chr. 30:21

18 Also day by day, from the first day unto the last day, he read in the book of the law of God. And they kept the feast ^Rseven days; and on the ^Reighth day *was* a solemn assembly, according unto the manner.   Lev. 23:36 · Num. 29:35

9 Now in the twenty and fourth day of ^Rthis month the children of Israel were assembled with fasting, and with sackclothes, ^Rand earth upon them.   8:2 · Job 2:12

2 And ^Rthe seed of Israel separated themselves from all strangers, and stood and ^Rconfessed their sins, and the iniquities of their fathers.   13:3, 30; Ezra 10:11 · 1:6

3 And they stood up in their place, and read in the book of the law of the LORD their God *one*

fourth part of the day; and *another* fourth part they confessed, and worshipped the LORD their God.

4 Then stood up upon the ^Tstairs, of the Levites, Jesh'-u-a, and Ba'-ni, Kad'-mi-el, Sheb-a-ni'-ah, Bun'-ni, Sher-e-bi'-ah, Ba'-ni, *and* Chen'-a-ni, and cried with a loud voice unto the LORD their God.   Lit. *ascent*

5 Then the Levites, Jesh'-u-a, and Kad'-mi-el, Ba'-ni, Hash-ab-ni'-ah, Sher-e-bi'-ah, Ho-di'-jah, Sheb-a-ni'-ah, *and* Peth-a-hi'-ah, said, Stand up *and* bless the LORD your God for ever and ever: and blessed be ^Rthy glorious name, which is exalted above all blessing and praise.   1 Chr. 29:13

6 ^RThou, *even* thou, *art* LORD alone; thou hast made heaven, the heaven of heavens, with all their host, the earth, and all *things* that *are* therein, the seas, and all that *is* therein, and thou preservest them all; and the host of heaven worshippeth thee.   [Ps. 86:10]; Is. 37:16

7 Thou *art* the LORD the God, who didst choose Abram, and broughtest him forth out of Ur of the Chal'-dees, and gavest him the name of ^RAbraham;   Gen. 17:5

8 And foundest his heart faithful before thee, and madest a cov-enant with him to give the land of the Ca'-naan-ites, the Hit'-tites, the Am'-o-rites, and the Per'-iz-zites, and the Jeb'-u-sites, and the Gir'-ga-shites, to give *it, I say,* to his seed, and hast performed thy words; for thou *art* righteous:

9 And didst see the affliction of our fathers in Egypt, and heardest their cry by the Red sea;

10 And shewedst signs and wonders upon Pharaoh, and on all his servants, and on all the people of his land: for thou knewest that they dealt proudly against them. So didst thou get thee a name, as *it is* this day.

11 ^RAnd thou didst divide the sea before them, so that they went through the midst of the sea on the dry land; and their persecu-

tors thou threwest into the deeps, [R]as a stone into the mighty waters.   Ex. 14:20–28 · Ex. 15:1, 5

12 Moreover thou [R]leddest them in the day by a cloudy pillar; and in the night by a pillar of fire, to give them light in the way wherein they should go.   Ex. 13:21, 22

13 [R]Thou camest down also upon mount Si'-nai, and spakest with them from heaven, and gavest them [R]right judgments, and true laws, good statutes and commandments: Ex. 20:1–18 · [Rom. 7:12]

14 And madest known unto them thy [R]holy sabbath, and commandedst them precepts, statutes, and laws, by the hand of Moses thy servant: Gen. 2:3; Ex. 16:23; 20:8

15 And gavest them bread from heaven for their hunger, and broughtest forth water for them out of the rock for their thirst, and promisedst them that they should go in to possess the land which thou hadst sworn to give them.

16 [R]But they and our fathers dealt proudly, and [R]hardened their necks, and hearkened not to thy commandments,   Ps. 106:6 · v. 29

17 And refused to obey, neither were mindful of thy wonders that thou didst among them; but hardened their necks, and in their rebellion appointed [R]a captain to return to their bondage: but thou *art* a God ready to pardon, [R]gracious and merciful, slow to anger, and of great kindness, and forsookest them not.   Acts 7:39 · Joel 2:13

18 Yea, [R]when they had made them a molten calf, and said, This *is* thy God that brought thee up out of Egypt, and had wrought great provocations;   Ex. 32:4–8, 31

19 Yet thou in thy manifold mercies forsookest them not in the wilderness: the [R]pillar of the cloud departed not from them by day, to lead them in the way; neither the pillar of fire by night, to shew them light, and the way wherein they should go.   1 Cor. 10:1

20 Thou gavest also thy [R]good spirit to instruct them, and withheldest not thy man'-na from their mouth, and gavest them water for their thirst.   Num. 11:17

21 Yea, forty years didst thou sustain them in the wilderness, *so that* they lacked nothing; their clothes [T]waxed not old, and their feet swelled not.   *did not wear out*

22 Moreover thou gavest them kingdoms and nations, and didst divide them into [T]corners: so thou possessed the land of [R]Si'-hon, and the land of the king of Hesh'-bon, and the land of Og king of Ba'-shan.   *districts* · Num. 21:21–35

23 [R]Their children also multipliedst thou as the stars of heaven, and broughtest them into the land, concerning which thou hadst promised to their fathers, that they should go in to possess *it.*   Gen. 15:5; 22:17; Heb. 11:12

24 So the children went in and possessed the land, and thou subduedst before them the inhabitants of the land, the Ca'-naanites, and gavest them into their hands, with their kings, and the people of the land, that they might do with them as they would.

25 And they took strong cities, and a [R]fat[T] land, and possessed [R]houses full of all goods, wells digged, vineyards, and oliveyards, and fruit trees in abundance: so they did eat, and were filled, and became fat, and delighted themselves in thy great goodness.   Num. 13:27 · *rich* · Deut. 6:11

26 Nevertheless they were disobedient, and rebelled against thee, and cast thy law behind their backs, and slew thy prophets which testified against them to turn them to thee, and they wrought great provocations.

27 [R]Therefore thou deliveredst them into the hand of their enemies, who vexed them: and in the time of their trouble, when they cried unto thee, thou [R]heardest *them* from heaven; and according to thy manifold mercies thou gavest them [T]saviours, who saved them out of the hand of their enemies.   Judg. 2:14 · Ps. 106:44 · *deliverers*

28 But after they had rest, ^Rthey did evil again before thee: therefore leftest thou them in the hand of their enemies, so that they had the dominion over them: yet when they returned, and cried unto thee, thou heardest *them* from heaven; and ^Rmany times didst thou deliver them according to thy mercies; Judg. 3:12 · Ps. 106:43

29 And testifiedst against them, that thou mightest bring them again unto thy law: yet they dealt proudly, and hearkened not unto thy commandments, but sinned against thy judgments, (^Rwhich if a man do, he shall live in them;) and withdrew the shoulder, and hardened their neck, and would not hear. Lev. 18:5; Rom. 10:5; [Gal. 3:12]

30 Yet many years didst thou forbear them, and testifiedst against them by thy spirit ^Rin thy prophets: yet would they not give ear: ^Rtherefore gavest thou them into the hand of the people of the lands. [Acts 7:51]; 1 Pet. 1:11 · Is. 5:5

31 Nevertheless for thy great mercies' sake ^Rthou didst not utterly consume them, nor forsake them; for thou *art* a gracious and merciful God. Jer. 4:27; [Rom. 11:2–5]

32 Now therefore, our God, the great, the mighty, and the ^Tterrible God, who keepest covenant and mercy, let not all the trouble seem little before thee, that hath come upon us, on our kings, on our princes, and on our priests, and on our prophets, and on our fathers, and on all thy people, since the time of the kings of Assyria unto this day. *awesome*

33 Howbeit ^Rthou *art* just in all that is brought upon us; for thou hast done right, but we have done wickedly: Ps. 119:137; [Dan. 9:14]

34 Neither have our kings, our princes, our priests, nor our fathers, kept thy law, nor hearkened unto thy commandments and thy testimonies, wherewith thou didst testify against them.

35 For they have ^Rnot served thee in their kingdom, and in thy great goodness that thou gavest

them, and in the large and ^Tfat land which thou gavest before them, neither turned they from their wicked works. Deut. 28:47 · *rich*

36 Behold, we *are* servants this day, and *for* the land that thou gavest unto our fathers to eat the fruit thereof and the good thereof, behold, we *are* servants in it:

37 And it yieldeth much increase unto the kings whom thou hast set over us because of our sins: also they have ^Rdominion over our bodies, and over our cattle, at their pleasure, and we *are* in great distress. Deut. 28:48

38 And because of all this we ^Rmake a sure *covenant*, and write *it*; and our princes, Levites, *and* priests, seal *unto it*. 2 Chr. 29:10

10 Now those that sealed *were*, Ne-he-mi′-ah, the ^TTir-sha′-tha, ^Rthe son of Hach-a-li′-ah, and Zid-ki′-jah, Lit. *governor* · 1:1

2 ^RSe-ra′-iah, Az-a-ri′-ah, Jer-e-mi′-ah, 12:1–21

3 Pash′-ur, Am-a-ri′-ah, Mal-chi′-jah,

4 Hat′-tush, Sheb-a-ni′-ah, Mal′-luch,

5 Ha′-rim, Mer′-e-moth, O-ba-di′-ah,

6 Daniel, Gin′-ne-thon, Ba′-ruch,

7 Me-shul′-lam, A-bi′-jah, Mij′-a-min,

8 Ma-a-zi′-ah, Bil′-gai, She-ma′-iah: these *were* the priests.

9 And the Levites: both Jesh′-u-a the son of Az-a-ni′-ah, Bin′-nu-i of the sons of Hen′-a-dad, Kad′-mi-el;

10 And their brethren, Sheb-a-ni′-ah, Ho-di′-jah, Kel′-i-ta, Pe-la′-iah, Ha′-nan,

11 Mi′-cha, Re′-hob, Hash-a-bi′-ah,

12 Zac′-cur, Sher-e-bi′-ah, Sheb-a-ni′-ah,

13 Ho-di′-jah, Ba′-ni, Ben′-i-nu.

14 The chief of the people; ^RPa′-rosh, Pa′-hath–mo′-ab, E′-lam, Zat′-thu, Ba′-ni, Ezra 2:3

15 Bun′-ni, Az′-gad, Be′-bai,

16 Ad-o-ni′-jah, Big′-vai, A′-din,

17 A′-ter, Hiz-ki′-jah, Az′-zur,

18 Ho-di′-jah, Ha′-shum, Be′-zai,
19 Ha′-riph, An′-a-thoth, Ne′-bai,
20 Mag′-pi-ash, Me-shul′-lam, He′-zir,
21 Me-shez′-a-beel, Za′-dok, Jad-du′-a,
22 Pel-a-ti′-ah, Ha′-nan, A-na′-iah,
23 Ho-she′-a, Han-a-ni′-ah, Ha′-shub,
24 Hal-lo′-hesh, Pil′-e-ha, Sho′-bek,
25 Re′-hum, Ha-shab′-nah, Ma-a-se′-iah,
26 And A-hi′-jah, Ha′-nan, A′-nan,
27 Mal′-luch, Ha′-rim, Ba′-a-nah.
28 ᴿAnd the rest of the people, the priests, the Levites, the porters, the singers, the Neth′-i-nims, ᴿand all they that had separated themselves from the people of the lands unto the law of God, their wives, their sons, and their daughters, every one having knowledge, and having understanding;   Ezra 2:36–43 · 13:3; Ezra 9:1
29 They clave to their brethren, their nobles, and entered into a curse, and into an oath, to walk in God's law, which was given by Moses the servant of God, and to observe and do all the commandments of the LORD our Lord, and his judgments and his statutes;
30 And that we would not give ᴿour daughters unto the people of the land, nor take their daughters for our sons: Ex. 34:16; [Ezra 9:12]
31 ᴿAnd if the people of the land bring ware or any victuals on the sabbath day to sell, that we would not buy it of them on the sabbath, or on the holy day: and that we would leave the seventh year, and the exaction of every debt. Lev. 23:3
32 Also we made ordinances for us, to charge ourselves yearly with the third ᴿpart of a shek′-el for the service of the house of our God; Ex. 38:25, 26; 2 Chr. 24:6; Matt. 17:24
33 For ᴿthe shewbread, and for the continual meat offering, and for the continual burnt offering,

of the sabbaths, of the new moons, for the set feasts, and for the holy things, and for the sin offerings to make an atonement for Israel, and for all the work of the house of our God. Lev. 24:5
34 And we cast the lots among the priests, the Levites, and the people, ᴿfor the wood offering, to bring it into the house of our God, after the houses of our fathers, at times appointed year by year, to burn upon the altar of the LORD our God, ᴿas it is written in the law: 13:31; [Is. 40:16] · Lev. 6:12
35 And to bring the firstfruits of our ground, and the firstfruits of all fruit of all trees, year by year, unto the house of the LORD:
36 Also the ᴿfirstborn of our sons, and of our cattle, as it is written in the law, and the firstlings of our herds and of our flocks, to bring to the house of our God, unto the priests that minister in the house of our God: Lev. 27:26
37 And that we should bring the firstfruits of our dough, and our offerings, and the fruit of all manner of trees, of wine and of oil, unto the priests, to the chambers of the house of our God; and ᴿthe tithes of our ground unto the Levites, that the same Levites might have the tithes in all the cities of our tillage.   Num. 18:21; Mal. 3:10
38 And the priest the son of Aaron shall be with the Levites, ᴿwhen the Levites take tithes: and the Levites shall bring up the tithe of the tithes unto the house of our God, to ᴿthe chambers, into the treasure house. Num. 18:26 · 1 Chr. 9:26
39 For the children of Israel and the children of Levi shall bring the offering of the corn, of the new wine, and the oil, unto the chambers, where are the vessels of the sanctuary, and the priests that minister, and the porters, and the singers: and we will not forsake the house of our God.

11 And the rulers of the people dwelt at Jerusalem: the rest of the people also cast lots, to bring one of ten to dwell in Jerusalem ^Rthe holy city, and nine parts *to dwell* in *other* cities. 10:18

2 And the people blessed all the men, that willingly offered themselves to dwell at Jerusalem.

3 ^RNow these *are* the chief of the province that dwelt in Jerusalem: but in the cities of Judah dwelt every one in his possession in their cities, *to wit*, Israel, the priests, and the Levites, and the Neth'-i-nims, and the children of Solomon's servants. 1 Chr. 9:2, 3

4 And ^Rat Jerusalem dwelt *certain* of the children of Judah, and of the children of Benjamin. Of the children of Judah; Ath-a-i'-ah the son of Uz-zi'-ah, the son of Zech-a-ri'-ah, the son of Am-a-ri'-ah, the son of Sheph-a-ti'-ah, the son of Ma-ha'-la-le-el, of the children of ^RPe'-rez; 1 Chr. 9:3 · Gen. 38:29

5 And Ma-a-se'-iah the son of Ba'-ruch, the son of Col-ho'-zeh, the son of Ha-za'-iah, the son of A-da'-iah, the son of Joi'-a-rib, the son of Zech-a-ri'-ah, the son of Shi-lo'-ni.

6 All the sons of Pe'-rez that dwelt at Jerusalem *were* four hundred threescore and eight valiant men.

7 And these *are* the sons of Benjamin; Sal'-lu the son of Me-shul'-lam, the son of Jo'-ed, the son of Pe-da'-iah, the son of Ko-la'-iah, the son of Ma-a-se'-iah, the son of Ith'-i-el, the son of Je-sa'-iah.

8 And after him Gab'-bai, Sal'-lai, nine hundred twenty and eight.

9 And Jo'-el the son of Zich'-ri *was* their overseer: and Judah the son of ^TSen-u'-ah *was* second over the city. Or *Hassenuah*

10 ^ROf the priests: Je-da'-iah the son of Joi'-a-rib, Ja'-chin. 1 Chr. 9:10

11 Se-ra'-iah the son of Hil-ki'-ah, the son of Me-shul'-lam, the son of Za'-dok, the son of Me-ra'-ioth, the son of A-hi'-tub, *was* the ruler of the house of God.

12 And their brethren that did the work of the house *were* eight hundred twenty and two: and A-

da'-iah the son of Jer'-o-ham, the son of Pel-a-li'-ah, the son of Am'-zi, the son of Zech-a-ri'-ah, the son of Pash'-ur, the son of Mal-chi'-ah,

13 And his brethren, chief of the fathers, two hundred forty and two: and Am'-a-shai the son of A-zar'-e-el, the son of A'-ha-sai, the son of Me-shil'-le-moth, the son of Im'-mer,

14 And their brethren, ^Tmighty men of valour, an hundred twenty and eight: and their overseer *was* Zab'-di'el, the son of *one of* the great men. *mighty warriors*

15 Also of the Levites: She-ma'-iah the son of Ha'-shub, the son of Az-ri'-kam, the son of Hash-a-bi'-ah, the son of Bun'-ni;

16 And Shab'-be-thai and Joz'-a-bad, of the chief of the Levites, *had* the oversight of ^Rthe ^Toutward business of the house of God. 1 Chr. 26:29 · *outside*

17 And Mat-ta-ni'-ah the son of Mi'-cha, the son of Zab'-di, the son of A'-saph, *was* the principal to begin the thanksgiving in prayer: and Bak-bu-ki'-ah the second among his brethren, and Ab'-da the son of Sham-mu'-a, the son of Ga'-lal, the son of Je-du'-thun.

18 All the Levites in ^Rthe holy city *were* two hundred fourscore and four. v. 1

19 Moreover the ^Tporters, Ak'-kub, Tal'-mon, and their brethren that kept the gates, *were* an hundred seventy and two. *gatekeepers*

20 And the residue of Israel, of the priests, *and* the Levites, *were* in all the cities of Judah, every one in his inheritance.

21 ^RBut the Neth'-i-nims dwelt in O'-phel: and Zi-ha and Gis'-pa *were* over the Neth'-i-nims. 3:26

22 The overseer also of the Levites at Jerusalem *was* Uz'-zi the son of Ba'-ni, the son of Hash-a-bi'-ah, the son of Mat-ta-ni'-ah, the son of Mi'-cha. Of the sons of A'-saph, the singers *were* over the business of the house of God.

23 For *it was* the king's commandment concerning them, that

a certain portion should be for the singers, due for every day.

24 And Peth-a-hi′-ah the son of Me-shez′-a-beel, of the children of ᴿZe′-rah the son of Judah, *was* at the king's hand in all matters concerning the people.   Gen. 38:30

25 And for the villages, with their fields, *some* of the children of Judah dwelt at ᴿKir′-jath–ar′-ba, and *in* the villages thereof, and at Di′-bon, and *in* the villages thereof, and at Je-kab′-ze-el, and *in* the villages thereof,   Josh. 14:15

26 And at Jesh′-u-a, and at Mol′-a-dah, and at Beth–phe′-let,

27 And at Ha′-zar–shu′-al, and at Be′-er–she′-ba, and *in* the villages thereof,

28 And at Zik′-lag, and at Me-ko′-nah, and in the villages thereof,

29 And at En–rim′-mon, and at Za′-re-ah, and at Jar′-muth,

30 Za-no′-ah, A-dul′-lam, and *in* their villages, at La′-chish, and the fields thereof, at A-ze′-kah, and *in* the villages thereof. And they dwelt from Be′-er–she′-ba unto the valley of Hin′-nom.

31 The children also of Benjamin from Ge′-ba *dwelt* at Mich′-mash, and Ai′-ja, and Beth′–el, and *in* their villages,

32 *And* at An′-a-thoth, Nob, An-a-ni′-ah,

33 Ha′-zor, Ra′-mah, Git′-ta-im,

34 Ha′-did, Ze-bo′-im, Ne-bal′-lat,

35 Lod, and O′-no, ᴿthe valley of craftsmen.   1 Chr. 4:14

36 And of the Levites *were* divisions *in* Judah, *and* in Benjamin.

12 Now these *are* the ᴿpriests and the Levites that went up with Ze-rub′-ba-bel the son of She-al′-ti-el, and Jesh′-u-a: Se-ra′-iah, Jer-e-mi′-ah, Ezra,   Ezra 2:1, 2

2 Am-a-ri′-ah, Mal′-luch, Hat′-tush,

3 Shech-a-ni′-ah,   Re′-hum, Mer′-e-moth,

4 Id′-do, Gin′-ne-tho, A-bi′-jah,

5 Mi′-a-min, Ma-a-di′-ah, Bil′-gah,

6 She-ma′-iah, and Joi′-a-rib, Je-da′-iah,

7 Sal′-lu, A′-mok, Hil-ki′-ah, Je-da′-iah. These *were* the chief of the priests and of their brethren in the days of ᴿJesh′-u-a.   Zech. 3:1

8 Moreover the Levites: Jesh′-u-a, Bin′-nu-i, Kad′-mi-el, Sher-e-bi′-ah, Judah, *and* Mat-ta-ni′-ah, ᴿwhich *was* over the thanksgiving, he and his brethren.   11:17

9 Also Bak-bu-ki′-ah and Un′-ni, their brethren, *were* over against them in the watches.

10 And Jesh′-u-a begat Joi′-a-kim, Joi′-a-kim also begat E-li′-a-shib, and E-li′-a-shib begat Joi′-a-da,

11 And Joi′-a-da begat Jona-than, and Jonathan begat Jad-du′-a.

12 And in the days of Joi′-a-kim were priests, the ᴿchief of the fathers: of Se-ra′-iah, Me-ra′-iah; of Jer-e-mi′-ah, Han-a-ni′-ah;   8:13

13 Of Ezra, Me-shul′-lam; of Am-a-ri′-ah, Je-ho-ha′-nan;

14 Of Mel′-i-cu, Jonathan; of Sheb-a-ni′-ah, Joseph;

15 Of Ha′-rim, Ad′-na; of Me-ra′-ioth, Hel′-kai;

16 Of Id′-do, Zech-a-ri′-ah; of Gin′-ne-thon, Me-shul′-lam;

17 Of A-bi′-jah, Zich′-ri; of Mi-ni′-a-min, of Mo-a-di′-ah, Pil′-tai;

18 Of Bil′-gah, Sham-mu′-a; of She-ma′-iah, Je-hon′-a-than;

19 And of Joi′-a-rib, Mat-te′-nai; of Je-da′-iah, Uz′-zi;

20 Of Sal′-lai, Kal′-lai; of A′-mok, E′-ber;

21 Of Hil-ki′-ah, Hash-a-bi′-ah; of Je-da′-iah, Ne-than′-e-el.

22 The Levites in the days of E-li′-a-shib, Joi′-a-da, and Jo-ha′-nan, and Jad-du′-a, *were* ᴿrecorded chief of the fathers: also the priests, to the reign of Da-ri′-us the Persian.   1 Chr. 24:6

23 The sons of Levi, the chief of the fathers, *were* written in the book of the ᴿchronicles, even until the days of Jo-ha′-nan the son of E-li′-a-shib.   1 Chr. 9:14–22

24 And the chief of the Levites: Hash-a-bi′-ah, Sher-e-bi′-ah, and Jesh′-u-a the son of Kad′-mi-el, with their brethren over against

them, to praise *and* to give thanks, ^Raccording to the commandment of David the man of God, ward over against ward.   Ezra 3:11

25 Mat-ta-ni'-ah, and Bak-bu-ki'-ah, O-ba-di'-ah, Me-shul'-lam, Tal'-mon, Ak'-kub, *were* ^Tporters keeping the ward at the thresholds of the gates.   *gatekeepers*

26 These *were* in the days of Joi'-a-kim the son of Jesh'-u-a, the son of Joz'-a-dak, and in the days of Ne-he-mi'-ah the governor, and of Ezra the priest, the scribe.

27 And at ^Rthe dedication of the wall of Jerusalem they sought the Levites out of all their places, to bring them to Jerusalem, to keep the dedication with gladness, both with thanksgivings, and with singing, *with* cymbals, psalteries, and with harps.   Ps. 30:title

28 And the sons of the singers gathered themselves together, both out of the plain country round about Jerusalem, and from the villages of Ne-toph'-a-thi;

29 Also from the house of Gil'-gal, and out of the fields of Ge'-ba and Az'-ma-veth: for the singers had builded them villages round about Jerusalem.

30 And the priests and the Levites ^Rpurified themselves, and purified the people, and the gates, and the wall.   13:22, 30; Ezra 6:20

31 Then I brought up the princes of Judah upon the wall, and appointed two great *companies of them that gave* thanks, *whereof* one went on the right hand upon the wall toward the dung gate:

32 And after them went Ho-sha'-iah, and half of the princes of Judah,

33 And Az-a-ri'-ah, Ezra, and Me-shul'-lam,

34 Judah, and Benjamin, and She-ma'-iah, and Jer-e-mi'-ah,

35 And *certain* of the priests' sons ^Rwith trumpets; *namely,* Zech-a-ri'-ah the son of Jonathan, the son of She-ma'-iah, the son of Mat-ta-ni'-ah, the son of Mi-cha'-iah, the son of Zac'-cur, the son of A'-saph: Num. 10:2, 8

36 And his brethren, She-ma'-iah, and A-zar'-a-el, Mil'-a-lai, Gil'-a-lai, Ma'-ai, Ne-than'-e-el, and Judah, Ha-na'-ni, with ^Rthe musical ^Rinstruments of David the man of God, and Ezra the scribe before them.   1 Chr. 23:5 · 2 Chr. 29:26

37 ^RAnd at the fountain gate, which was over against them, they went up by the stairs of the ^Rcity of David, at the going up of the wall, above the house of David, even unto ^Rthe water gate eastward.   2:14; 3:15 · 2 Sam. 5:7-9 · 3:26

38 And the other *company* of *them that gave* thanks went over against *them*, and I after them, and the half of the people upon the wall, from beyond ^Rthe tower of the furnaces even unto ^Rthe broad wall;   3:11 · 3:8

39 ^RAnd from above the gate of E'-phra-im, and above the old gate, and above the fish gate, and the tower of Ha-nan'-e-el, and the tower of Me'-ah, even unto the sheep gate: and they stood still in the prison gate.   8:16; 2 Kin. 14:13

40 So stood the two *companies of them that gave* thanks in the house of God, and I, and the half of the rulers with me:

41 And the priests; E-li'-a-kim, Ma-a-sei'-ah, Mi-ni'-a-min, Mi-cha'-iah, E-li-o-e'-nai, Zech-a-ri'-ah, *and* Han-a-ni'-ah, with trumpets;

42 And Ma-a-se'-iah, and She-ma'-iah, and E-le-a'-zar, and Uz'-zi, and Je-ho-ha'-nan, and Mal-chi'-jah, and E'-lam, and E'-zer. And the singers sang loud, with Jez-ra-hi'-ah *their* overseer.

43 Also that day they offered great sacrifices, and rejoiced: for God had made them rejoice with great joy: the wives also and the children rejoiced: so that the joy of Jerusalem was heard even ^Rafar off.   Ezra 3:13

44 ^RAnd at that time were some appointed over the chambers for the treasures, for the offerings, for the firstfruits, and for the ^Rtithes, to gather into them out of the fields of the cities the portions of

the law for the priests and Levites: for Judah rejoiced for the priests and for the Levites that waited.   2 Chr. 31:11, 12 · 10:37–39

45 And both the singers and the porters kept the ^Tward of their God, and the ward of the purification, ^Raccording to the commandment of David, *and* of Solomon his son.   *watch* · 1 Chr. 25; 26

46 For in the days of David and A′-saph of old *there were* chief of the singers, and songs of praise and thanksgiving unto God.

47 And all Israel in the days of Ze-rub′-ba-bel, and in the days of Ne-he-mi′-ah, gave the portions of the singers and the porters, ^Revery day his portion: and they sanctified *holy things* unto the Levites; and the Levites sanctified *them* unto the children of Aaron.   11:23

13 On that day ^Rthey read in the book of Moses in the audience of the people; and therein was found written, that the Am′-mon-ite and the Mo′-ab-ite should not come into the congregation of God for ever;   Is. 34:16

2 Because they met not the children of Israel with bread and with water, but ^Rhired Ba′-laam against them, that he should curse them: howbeit our God turned the curse into a blessing.   Num. 22:5

3 Now it came to pass, when they had heard the law, ^Rthat they separated from Israel all the mixed multitude.   9:2; 10:28

4 And before this, E-li′-a-shib the priest, having the oversight of the chamber of the house of our God, *was* allied unto To-bi′-ah:

5 And he had prepared for him a great chamber, ^Rwhere aforetime they laid the meat offerings, the frankincense, and the vessels, and the tithes of the corn, the new wine, and the oil, ^Rwhich was commanded *to be given* to the Levites, and the singers, and the porters; and the offerings of the priests.   12:44 · Num. 18:21, 24

6 But in all this *time* was not I at Jerusalem: for in the two and thirtieth year of Ar-tax-erx′-

es king of Babylon came I unto the king, and after certain days obtained I leave of the king:

7 And I came to Jerusalem, and understood of the evil that E-li′-a-shib did for To-bi′-ah, in ^Rpreparing him a chamber in the courts of the house of God.   vv. 1, 5

8 And it grieved me ^Tsore: therefore I cast forth all the household stuff of To-bi′-ah out of the chamber.   *bitterly*

9 Then I commanded, and they cleansed the chambers: and thither brought I again the vessels of the house of God, with the meat offering and the frankincense.

10 And I perceived that the portions of the Levites had not been given *them:* for the Levites and the singers, that did the work, were fled every one to his field.

11 Then ^Rcontended I with the rulers, and said, ^RWhy is the house of God forsaken? And I gathered them together, and set them in their place.   vv. 17, 25 · 10:39

12 ^RThen brought all Judah the tithe of the ^Tcorn and the new wine and the oil unto the ^Ttreasuries.   10:38; 12:44 · *grain* · *storehouses*

13 And I made treasurers over the treasuries, Shel-e-mi′-ah the priest, and Za′-dok the scribe, and of the Levites, Pe-da′-iah: and next to them *was* Ha′-nan the son of Zac′-cur, the son of Mat-ta-ni′-ah: for they were counted faithful, and their ^Toffice *was* to distribute unto their brethren.   *duty*

14 ^RRemember me, O my God, concerning this, and wipe not out my good deeds that I have done for the house of my God, and for the ^Toffices thereof.   5:19 · *services*

15 In those days saw I in Judah *some* treading winepresses on the sabbath, and bringing in sheaves, and lading asses; as also wine, grapes, and figs, and all *manner of* burdens, ^Rwhich they brought into Jerusalem on the sabbath day: and I testified *against them* in the day wherein they sold victuals.   10:31; [Jer. 17:21]

16 There dwelt men of Tyre also therein, which brought fish, and all manner of ware, and sold on the sabbath unto the children of Judah, and in Jerusalem.

17 Then I contended with the nobles of Judah, and said unto them, What evil thing *is* this that ye do, and profane the sabbath day?

18 Did not your fathers thus, and did not our God bring all this evil upon us, and upon this city? yet ye bring more wrath upon Israel by profaning the sabbath.

19 And it came to pass, that when the gates of Jerusalem began to be dark before the sabbath, I commanded that the gates should be shut, and charged that they should not be opened till after the sabbath: and *some* of my servants set I at the gates, *that* there should no burden be brought in on the sabbath day.

20 So the merchants and sellers of all kind of ware lodged without Jerusalem once or twice.

21 Then I testified against them, and said unto them, Why lodge ye [T]about the wall? if ye do *so* again, I will lay hands on you. From that time forth came they no *more* on the sabbath.   Lit. *before*

22 And I commanded the Levites that [R]they should cleanse themselves, and *that* they should come *and* keep the gates, to sanctify the sabbath day. Remember me, O my God, *concerning* this also, and spare me according to the greatness of thy mercy.   12:30

23 In those days also saw I Jews *that* had married wives of Ash'-dod, of Am'-mon, *and* of Moab:

24 And their children spake half in the speech of Ash'-dod, and could not speak in the Jews' language, but according to the language of each people.

25 And I [R]contended with them, and cursed them, and smote certain of them, and plucked off their hair, and made them swear by God, *saying,* Ye shall not give your daughters unto their sons, nor take their daughters unto your sons, or for yourselves.   Prov. 28:4

26 [R]Did not Solomon king of Israel sin by these things? yet among many nations was there no king like him, who was beloved of his God, and God made him king over all Israel: nevertheless even him did outlandish women cause to sin.   1 Kin. 11:1, 2

27 Shall we then hearken unto you to do all this great evil, to [R]transgress against our God in marrying strange wives?   [Ezra 10:2]

28 And *one* of the sons [R]of Joi'-a-da, the son of E-li'-a-shib the high priest, *was* son in law to San-bal'-lat the Hor'-o-nite: therefore I chased him from me.   12:10, 12

29 Remember them, O my God, because they have defiled the priesthood, and the covenant of the priesthood, and of the Levites.

30 Thus cleansed I them from all strangers, and appointed the wards of the priests and the Levites, every one in his business;

31 And for [R]the wood offering, at times appointed, and for the firstfruits. [R]Remember me, O my God, for good.   10:34 · vv. 14, 22

The Book of
ESTHER

GOD'S hand of providence and protection on behalf of His people is evident throughout the Book of Esther, though His name does not appear once. Haman's plot brings grave danger to the Jews and is countered by the courage of beautiful Esther and the counsel of her wise cousin Mordecai, resulting in a great deliverance. The Feast of Purim becomes an annual reminder of God's faithfulness on behalf of His people.

Esther's Hebrew name was *Hadassah*, "Myrtle" (2:7), but her Persian name *Ester* was derived from the Persian word for "Star" (*Stara*). The Greek title for this book is *Esther*, and the Latin title is *Hester*.

NOW it came to pass in the days of ᴿA-has-u-e′-rus, (this *is* A-has-u-e′-rus which reigned, from India even unto E-thi-o′-pi-a, *over* an hundred and seven and twenty provinces:)   Ezra 4:6; Dan. 9:1

2 *That* in those days, when the king A-has-u-e′-rus sat on the throne of his kingdom, which *was* in ᴿShu′-shan the palace,   Neh. 1:1

3 In the third year of his reign, he ᴿmade a feast unto all his princes and his servants; the power of Persia and Me′-di-a, the nobles and princes of the provinces, *being* before him: 2:18

4 When he shewed the riches of his glorious kingdom and the honour of his excellent majesty many days, *even* an hundred and fourscore days.

5 And when these days were ᵀexpired, the king made a feast unto all the people that were present in ᵀShu′-shan the palace, both unto great and small, seven days, in the court of the garden of the king's palace;   *completed* · Or *Susa*

6 *Where were* white, green, and blue, *hangings*, fastened with cords of fine linen and purple to silver rings and pillars of marble: ᴿthe beds *were of* gold and silver, upon a pavement of red, and blue, and white, and black, marble.   7:8

7 And they gave *them* drink in vessels of gold, (the vessels being diverse one from another,) and royal wine in abundance, ᴿaccording to the state of the king.   2:18

8 And the drinking *was* according to the law; none did compel: for so the king had ᵀappointed to all the officers of his house, that they should do according to every man's pleasure.   *ordered*

9 Also Vash′-ti the queen made a feast for the women *in* the royal house which *belonged* to king A-has-u-e′-rus.

10 On the seventh day, when the heart of the king was merry with wine, he commanded Me-hu′-man, Biz′-tha, ᴿHar-bo′-na, Big′-tha, and A-bag′-tha, Ze′-thar, and Car′-cas, the seven ᵀchamberlains that served in the presence of A-has-u-e′-rus the king,   7:9 · *eunuchs*

11 To bring Vash′-ti the queen before the king with the crown royal, to shew the people and the princes her beauty: for she *was* ᵀfair to look on.   *lovely to behold*

12 But the queen Vash′-ti refused to come at the king's commandment by *his* chamberlains: therefore was the king very wroth, and his anger burned in him.

13 Then the king said to the ᴿwise men, which knew the times, (for so *was* the king's manner toward all that knew law and judgment: Jer. 10:7; Dan. 2:12; Matt. 2:1

14 And the next unto him *was* Car-she′-na, She′-thar, Ad-ma′-tha, Tar′-shish, Me′-res, Mar′-se-na, *and* Me-mu′-can, the ᴿseven princes of Persia and Me′-di-a, ᴿwhich saw the king's face, *and* which sat the first in the kingdom;)   Ezra 7:14 · 2 Kin. 25:19; [Matt. 18:10]

15 What shall we do unto the queen Vash′-ti according to law, because she hath not performed the commandment of the king A-has-u-e′-rus by the chamberlains?

16 And Me-mu′-can answered before the king and the princes, Vash′-ti the queen hath not done wrong to the king only, but also to all the princes, and to all the people that *are* in all the provinces of the king A-has-u-e′-rus.

17 For *this* deed of the queen shall come abroad unto all women, so that they shall ᴿdespise

their husbands in their eyes, when it shall be reported, The king A-has-u-e′-rus commanded Vash′-ti the queen to be brought in before him, but she came not.   [Eph. 5:33]

18 *Likewise* shall the ladies of Persia and Me′-di-a say this day unto all the king's princes, which have heard of the deed of the queen. Thus *shall there arise* too much contempt and wrath.

19 If it please the king, let there go a royal commandment from him, and let it be written among the laws of the Persians and the Medes, that it be ᴿnot altered, That Vash′-ti come no more before king A-has-u-e′-rus; and let the king give her royal estate unto another that is better than she. 8:8

20 And when the king's decree which he shall make shall be published throughout all his empire, (for it is great,) all the wives shall ᴿgive to their husbands honour, both to great and small.   [Col. 3:18]

21 And the saying pleased the king and the princes; and the king did according to the word of Me-mu′-can:

22 For he sent letters into all the king's provinces, ᴿinto every province according to the writing thereof, and to every people after their language, that every man should ᴿbear rule in his own house, and that *it* should be published according to the language of every people. 3:12; 8:9 · [1 Tim. 2:12]

2 After these things, when the wrath of king A-has-u-e′-rus ᵀwas appeased, he remembered Vash′-ti, and ᴿwhat she had done, and what was decreed against her.   *had subsided* · 1:19, 20

2 Then said the king's servants that ministered unto him, Let there be fair young virgins sought for the king:

3 And let the king appoint officers in all the provinces of his kingdom, that they may gather together all the fair young virgins unto Shu′-shan the palace, to the house of the women, unto the custody of He′-ge the king's ᵀchamberlain, keeper of the women; and let their things for purification be given *them:*   *eunuch*

4 And let the maiden which pleaseth the king be queen instead of Vash′-ti. And the thing pleased the king; and he did so.

5 *Now* in Shu′-shan the palace there was a certain Jew, whose name *was* Mor′-de-cai, the son of Ja′-ir, the son of Shim′-e-i, the son of ᴿKish, a Benjamite;   1 Sam. 9:1

6 Who had been carried away from Jerusalem with the captivity which had been carried away with Jec-o-ni′-ah king of Judah, whom Neb-u-chad-nez′-zar the king of Babylon had carried away.

7 And he brought up Ha-das′-sah, that *is*, Esther, ᴿhis uncle's daughter: for she had neither father nor mother, and the maid *was* ᵀfair and beautiful; whom Mor′-de-cai, when her father and mother were dead, took for his own daughter.   v. 15 · *lovely*

8 So it came to pass, when the king's commandment and his decree was heard, and when many maidens were ᴿgathered together unto Shu′-shan the palace, to the custody of He′-gai, that Esther was brought also unto the king's house, to the custody of He′-gai, keeper of the women. v. 3

9 And the maiden pleased him, and she obtained kindness of him; and he speedily gave her her ᴿthings for purification, with such things as belonged to her, and seven maidens, *which were* meet to be given her, out of the king's house: and he preferred her and her maids unto the best *place* of the house of the women.   vv. 3, 12

10 ᴿEsther had not shewed her people nor her kindred: for Mor′-de-cai had charged her that she should not shew *it*.   v. 20

11 And Mor′-de-cai walked every day before the court of the women's house, to know how Esther did, and what should become of her.

12 Now when every maid's turn was come to go in to king A-has-

u-e′-rus, after that she had been twelve months, according to the manner of the women, (for so were the days of their purifications accomplished, *to wit*, six months with oil of myrrh, and six months with sweet odours, and with *other* things for the purifying of the women;)

13 Then thus came *every* maiden unto the king; whatsoever she desired was given her to go with her out of the house of the women unto the king's house.

14 In the evening she went, and on the morrow she returned into the second house of the women, to the custody of Sha-ash′-gaz, the king's ᵀchamberlain, which kept the concubines: she came in unto the king no more, except the king delighted in her, and that she were called by name.   *eunuch*

15 Now when the turn of Esther, ᴿthe daughter of Ab-i-ha′-il the uncle of Mor′-de-cai, who had taken her for his daughter, was come to go in unto the king, she required nothing but what He′-gai the king's chamberlain, the keeper of the women, ᵀappointed. And Esther ᴿobtained favour in the sight of all them that looked upon her.   v. 7; 9:29 · *advised* · 5:2, 8

16 So Esther was taken unto king A-has-u-e′-rus into his house royal in the tenth month, which *is* the month Te′-beth, in the seventh year of his reign.

17 And the king loved Esther above all the women, and she obtained grace and favour in his sight more than all the virgins; so that he set the royal ᴿcrown upon her head, and made her queen instead of Vash′-ti.   1:11

18 Then the king ᴿmade a great feast unto all his princes and his servants, *even* Esther's feast; and he made a release to the provinces, and gave gifts, according to the state of the king.   1:3

19 And when the virgins were gathered together the second time, then Mor′-de-cai sat in the king's gate.

20 ᴿEsther had not *yet* shewed her kindred nor her people; as Mor′-de-cai had charged her: for Esther did the commandment of Mor′-de-cai, like as when she was brought up with him.   v. 10

21 In those days, while Mor′-de-cai sat in the king's gate, two of the king's ᵀchamberlains, Big′-than and Te′-resh, of those which kept the door, were ᵀwroth, and sought to lay hand on the king A-has-u-e′-rus.   *eunuchs · furious*

22 And the thing was known to Mor′-de-cai, ᴿwho told *it* unto Esther the queen; and Esther certified the king *thereof* in Mor′-de-cai's name.   6:1, 2

23 And when ᵀinquisition was made of the matter, it was found out; therefore they were both hanged on a tree: and it was written in ᴿthe book of the chronicles before the king.   *inquiry* · 6:1

3 After these things did king A-has-u-e′-rus promote Ha′-man the son of Ham-med′-a-tha the A′-gag-ite, and ᴿadvanced him, and set his seat above all the princes that *were* with him.   5:11

2 And all the king's servants, that *were* ᴿin the king's gate, bowed, and reverenced Ha′-man: for the king had so commanded concerning him. But Mor′-de-cai ᴿbowed not, nor did *him* reverence.   2:19, 21; 5:9 · v. 5; Ps. 15:4

3 Then the king's servants, which *were* in the king's gate, said unto Mor′-de-cai, Why transgressest thou the ᴿking's commandment?   v. 2

4 Now it came to pass, when they spake daily unto him, and he hearkened not unto them, that they told Ha′-man, to see whether Mor′-de-cai's ᵀmatters would stand: for ᵀhe had told them that he *was* a Jew.   *words · Mordecai*

5 And when Ha′-man saw that Mor′-de-cai ᴿbowed not, nor did him reverence, then was Ha′-man ᴿfull of wrath.   v. 2; 5:9 · Dan. 3:19

6 And he thought scorn to lay hands on Mor′-de-cai alone; for they had shewed him the people

of Mor'-de-cai: wherefore Ha'-man sought to destroy all the Jews that *were* throughout the whole kingdom of A-has-u-e'-rus, *even* the people of Mor'-de-cai.

7 In the first month, that *is*, the month Ni'-san, in the twelfth year of king A-has-u-e'-rus, they cast Pur, that *is*, the lot, before Ha'-man from day to day, and from month to month, *to* the twelfth *month*, that *is*, the month A'-dar.

8 And Ha'-man said unto king A-has-u-e'-rus, There is a certain people scattered abroad and dispersed among the people in all the provinces of thy kingdom; and their laws *are* diverse from all people; neither keep they the king's laws: therefore it *is* not for the king's profit to suffer them.

9 If it please the king, let it be written that they may be destroyed: and I will pay ten thousand talents of silver to the hands of those that have the charge of the business, to bring *it* into the king's treasuries.

10 And the king ᴿtook ᴿhis ring from his hand, and gave it unto Ha'-man the son of Ham-med'-a-tha the A'-gag-ite, the Jews' ᴿenemy.   Gen. 41:42 · 8:2, 8 · 7:6

11 And the king said unto Ha'-man, The silver *is* given to thee, the people also, to do with them as it seemeth good to thee.

12 Then were the king's scribes called on the thirteenth day of the first month, and there was written according to all that Ha'-man had commanded unto the king's lieutenants, and to the governors that *were* over every province, and to the rulers of every people of every province according to the writing thereof, and *to* every people after their language; in the name of king A-has-u-e'-rus was it written, and sealed with the king's ring.

13 And the letters were ᴿsent by posts into all the king's provinces, to destroy, to kill, and to cause to perish, all Jews, both young and old, little children and women, ᴿin one day, *even* upon the thirteenth *day* of the twelfth month, which *is* the month A'-dar, and ᴿto *take* the spoil of them for a prey.   2 Chr. 30:6 · 8:12 · 8:11; 9:10

14 ᴿThe copy of the writing for a commandment to be given in every province was published unto all people, that they should be ready against that day.   8:13, 14

15 The ᵀposts went out, being hastened by the king's commandment, and the decree was given in Shu'-shan the palace. And the king and Ha'-man sat down to drink; but ᴿthe city Shu'-shan was perplexed.   *couriers* · 8:15; [Prov. 29:2]

4 When Mor'-de-cai perceived all that was done, Mor'-de-cai rent his clothes, and put on sackcloth with ashes, and went out into the midst of the city, and cried with a loud and a bitter cry;

2 And came even before the king's gate: for none *might* enter into the king's gate clothed with sackcloth.

3 And in every province, whithersoever the king's commandment and his decree came, *there was* great mourning among the Jews, and fasting, and weeping, and wailing; and many lay in sackcloth and ashes.

4 So Esther's maids and her ᵀchamberlains came and told *it* her. Then was the queen exceedingly grieved; and she sent raiment to clothe Mor'-de-cai, and to take away his sackcloth from him: but he received *it* not.   *eunuchs*

5 Then called Esther for Ha'-tach, *one* of the king's ᵀchamberlains, whom he had appointed to attend upon her, and gave him a commandment to Mor'-de-cai, to know what it *was*, and why it *was*.   *eunuchs*

6 So Ha'-tach went forth to Mor'-de-cai unto the street of the city, which *was* before the king's gate.

7 And Mor'-de-cai told him of all that had happened unto him, and of ᴿthe sum of the money that Ha'-man had promised to pay to

the king's treasuries for the Jews, to destroy them. 3:9

8 Also he gave him the copy of the writing of the decree that was given at Shu'-shan to destroy them, to shew *it* unto Esther, and to declare *it* unto her, and to charge her that she should go in unto the king, to make supplication unto him, and to make request before him for her people.

9 And Ha'-tach came and told Esther the words of Mor'-de-cai.

10 Again Esther spake unto Ha'-tach, and gave him commandment unto Mor'-de-cai;

11 All the king's servants, and the people of the king's provinces, do know, that whosoever, whether man or woman, shall come unto the king into the inner court, who is not called, ᴿthere is one law of his to put *him* to death, except such ᴿto whom the king shall hold out the golden sceptre, that he may live: but I have not been called to come in unto the king these thirty days. Dan. 2:9 · 5:2; 8:4

12 And they told to Mor'-de-cai Esther's words.

13 Then Mor'-de-cai commanded to answer Esther, Think not with thyself that thou shalt escape in the king's house, more than all the Jews.

14 For if thou altogether holdest thy peace at this time, *then* shall there ᵀenlargement and deliverance arise to the Jews from another place; but thou and thy father's house shall be destroyed: and who knoweth whether thou art come to the kingdom for *such* a time as this? *relief*

15 Then Esther bade *them* return Mor'-de-cai *this answer,*

16 Go, gather together all the Jews that are present in ᵀShu'-shan, and fast ye for me, and neither eat nor drink ᴿthree days, night or day: I also and my maidens will fast likewise; and so will I go in unto the king, which *is* not according to the law: ᴿand if I perish, I perish. Or *Susa* · 5:1 · Gen. 43:14

17 So Mor'-de-cai went his way,

and did according to all that Esther had commanded him.

5 Now it came to pass ᴿon the third day, that Esther put on *her* royal *apparel,* and stood in ᴿthe inner court of the king's house, over against the king's house: and the king sat upon his royal throne in the royal house, over against the gate of the house. 4:16 · 4:11; 6:4

2 And it was so, when the king saw Esther the queen standing in the court, *that* ᴿshe obtained favour in his sight: and ᴿthe king held out to Esther the golden sceptre that *was* in his hand. So Esther drew near, and touched the top of the sceptre. [Prov. 21:1] · 4:11

3 Then said the king unto her, What wilt thou, queen Esther? and what *is* thy request? ᴿit shall be even given thee to the half of the kingdom. 7:2; Mark 6:23

4 And Esther answered, If *it seem* good unto the king, let the king and Ha'-man come this day unto the banquet that I have prepared for him.

5 Then the king said, ᵀCause Ha'-man to make haste, that he may do as Esther hath said. So the king and Ha'-man came to the banquet that Esther had prepared. *Bring Haman quickly*

6 ᴿAnd the king said unto Esther at the banquet of wine, What *is* thy petition? and it shall be granted thee: and what *is* thy request? even to the half of the kingdom it shall be performed. 7:2

7 Then answered Esther, and said, My petition and my request *is;*

8 If I have found favour in the sight of the king, and if it please the king to grant my petition, and ᵀto perform my request, let the king and Ha'-man come to the ᴿbanquet that I shall prepare for them, and I will do to morrow as the king hath said. *to fulfil* · 6:14

9 Then went Ha'-man forth that day ᴿjoyful and with a glad heart: but when Ha'-man saw Mor'-de-cai in the king's gate, ᴿthat he stood not up, nor moved

for him, he was full of indignation against Mor'-de-cai. [Luke 6:25] · 3:5

10 Nevertheless Ha'-man refrained himself: and when he came home, he sent and called for his friends, and Ze'-resh his wife.

11 And Ha'-man told them of the glory of his riches, and ᴿthe multitude of his children, and all *the things* wherein the king had promoted him, and how he had ᴿadvanced him above the princes and servants of the king. 9:7–10 · 3:1

12 Ha'-man said moreover, Yea, Esther the queen did let no man come in with the king unto the banquet that she had prepared but myself; and to morrow am I invited unto her also with the king.

13 Yet all this availeth me nothing, so long as I see Mor'-de-cai the Jew sitting at the king's gate.

14 Then said Ze'-resh his wife and all his friends unto him, Let a ᴿgallows be made of fifty cubits high, and to morrow ᴿspeak thou unto the king that Mor'-de-cai may be hanged thereon: then go thou in merrily with the king unto the banquet. And the thing pleased Ha'-man; and he caused the gallows to be made.   7:9 · 6:4

6 On that night could not the king sleep, and he commanded to bring ᴿthe book of records of the chronicles; and they were read before the king.   2:23; 10:2

2 And it was found written, that Mor'-de-cai had told of Big'-tha-na and Te'-resh, two of the king's chamberlains, the keepers of the door, who sought to lay hand on the king A-has-u-e'-rus.

3 And the king said, What honour and dignity hath been done to Mor'-de-cai for this? Then said the king's servants that ministered unto him, There is nothing done for him.

4 And the king said, Who *is* in the court? Now Ha'-man was come into ᴿthe outward court of the king's house, ᴿto speak unto the king to hang Mor'-de-cai on the gallows that he had prepared for him.   5:1 · 5:14

5 And the king's servants said unto him, Behold, Ha'-man standeth in the court. And the king said, Let him come in.

6 So Ha'-man came in. And the king said unto him, What shall be done unto the man whom the king delighteth to honour? Now Ha'-man thought in his heart, To whom would the king delight to do honour more than to myself?

7 And Ha'-man answered the king, For the man whom the king delighteth to honour,

8 Let the royal apparel be brought which the king *useth* to wear, and the horse that the king rideth upon, and the crown royal which is set upon his head:

9 And let this apparel and horse be delivered to the hand of one of the king's most noble princes, that they may array the man *withal* whom the king delighteth to honour, and bring him on horseback through the street of the city, ᴿand proclaim before him, Thus shall it be done to the man whom the king delighteth to honour.   Gen. 41:43

10 Then the king said to Ha'-man, Make haste, *and* take the apparel and the horse, as thou hast said, and do even so to Mor'-de-cai the Jew, that sitteth at the king's gate: let nothing fail of all that thou hast spoken.

11 Then took Ha'-man the apparel and the horse, and arrayed Mor'-de-cai, and brought him on horseback through the street of the city, and proclaimed before him, Thus shall it be done unto the man whom the king delighteth to honour.

12 And Mor'-de-cai came again to the king's gate. But Ha'-man hasted to his house mourning, and having his head covered.

13 And Ha'-man told Ze'-resh his wife and all his friends every *thing* that had befallen him. Then said his wise men and Ze'-resh his wife unto him, If Mor'-de-cai *be* of the seed of the Jews, before whom thou hast begun to fall, thou shalt

not prevail against [R]him, but shalt surely fall before him.   Zech. 2:8

14 And while they *were* yet talking with him, came the king's chamberlains, and hasted to bring Ha'-man unto [R]the banquet that Esther had prepared.   5:8

7 So the king and Ha'-man came to banquet with Esther the queen.

2 And the king said again unto Esther on the second day [R]at the banquet of wine, What *is* thy petition, queen Esther? and it shall be granted thee: and what *is* thy request? and it shall be performed, *even* to the half of the kingdom.   5:6

3 Then Esther the queen answered and said, If I have found favour in thy sight, O king, and if it please the king, let my life be given me at my petition, and my people at my request:

4 For we are [R]sold, I and my people, to be destroyed, to be slain, and to perish. But if we had been sold for [R]bondmen and bondwomen, I had held my tongue, although the enemy could not countervail the king's damage.   3:9; 4:7 · Deut. 28:68

5 Then the king A-has-u-e'-rus answered and said unto Esther the queen, Who is he, and where is he, [T]that durst presume in his heart to do so?   *who dares to*

6 And Esther said, The adversary and [R]enemy *is* this wicked Ha'-man. Then Ha'-man [T]was afraid before the king and the queen.   3:10 · *was terrified*

7 And the king arising from the banquet of wine in his wrath *went* into the palace garden: and Ha'-man stood up to make request for his life to Esther the queen; for he saw that there was evil determined against him by the king.

8 Then the king returned out of the palace garden into the place of the banquet of wine; and Ha'-man was fallen upon [R]the bed whereon Esther *was*. Then said the king, Will he [T]force the queen also [T]before me in the house? As

the word went out of the king's mouth, they [R]covered Ha'-man's face.   1:6 · *assault* · Lit. *with me* · Job 9:24

9 And Har-bo'-nah, one of the chamberlains, said before the king, Behold also, [R]the [T]gallows fifty cubits high, which Ha'-man had made for Mor'-de-cai, who had spoken [R]good for the king, standeth in the house of Ha'-man. Then the king said, Hang him thereon.   5:14 · Lit. *tree* or *wood* · 6:2

10 So they [R]hanged Ha'-man on the gallows that he had prepared for Mor'-de-cai. Then was the king's wrath pacified.   Ps. 37:35, 36

8 On that day did the king A-has-u-e'-rus give the house of Ha'-man the Jews' enemy unto Esther the queen. And Mor'-de-cai came before the king; for Esther had told what he *was* unto her.

2 And the king took off [R]his ring, which he had taken from Ha'-man, and gave it unto Mor'-de-cai. And Esther set Mor'-de-cai over the house of Ha'-man.   3:10

3 And Esther spake yet again before the king, and fell down at his feet, and besought him with tears to put away the mischief of Ha'-man the A'-gag-ite, and his [T]device that he had devised against the Jews.   *scheme*

4 Then [R]the king held out the golden sceptre toward Esther. So Esther arose, and stood before the king,   4:11; 5:2

5 And said, If it please the king, and if I have found favour in his sight, and the thing *seem* right before the king, and I *be* pleasing in his eyes, let it be written to [T]reverse the letters devised by Ha'-man the son of Ham-med'-a-tha the A'-gag-ite, which he wrote to destroy the Jews which *are* in all the king's provinces: *revoke*

6 For how can I endure to see [R]the evil that shall come unto my people? or how can I endure to see the destruction of my kindred?   7:4; 9:1; Neh. 2:3

7 Then the king A-has-u-e'-rus said unto Esther the queen and to Mor'-de-cai the Jew, Behold, I

have given Esther the house of Ha'-man, and him they have hanged upon the gallows, because he laid his hand upon the Jews.

8 Write ye also for the Jews, ᵀas it liketh you, in the king's name, and seal *it* with the king's ring: for the writing which is written in the king's name, and sealed with the king's ring, ᴿmay no man reverse.   *as you please · 1:19*

9 ᴿThen were the king's scribes called at that time in the third month, that *is*, the month Si'-van, on the three and twentieth *day* thereof; and it was written according to all that Mor'-de-cai commanded unto the Jews, and to the lieutenants, and the deputies and rulers of the provinces which *are* ᴿfrom India unto E-thi-o'-pi-a, an hundred twenty and seven provinces, unto every province ᴿaccording to the writing thereof, and unto every people after their language, and to the Jews according to their writing, and according to their language. 3:12 · 1:1 · 1:22; 3:12

10 ᴿAnd he wrote in the king A-has-u-e'-rus' name, and sealed *it* with the king's ring, and sent letters by posts on horseback, *and* riders on mules, camels, *and* young dromedaries: 3:12, 13

11 Wherein the king granted the Jews which *were* in every city to ᴿgather themselves together, and to stand for their life, to ᴿdestroy, to slay, and to cause to perish, all the power of the people and province that would assault them, *both* little ones and women, and to *take* the spoil of them for a prey,   9:2 · 9:10, 15, 16

12 ᴿUpon one day in all the provinces of king A-has-u-e'-rus, *namely*, upon the thirteenth *day* of the twelfth month, which *is* the month A'-dar.   3:13; 9:1

13 ᴿThe copy of the writing for a commandment to be given in every province *was* published unto all people, and that the Jews should be ready against that day to avenge themselves on their enemies.   3:14, 15

14 *So* the ᵀposts that rode upon mules *and* camels went out, being hastened and pressed on by the king's commandment. And the decree was given at ᵀShu'-shan the ᵀpalace. *couriers · Or Susa · citadel*

15 And Mor'-de-cai went out from the presence of the king in royal apparel of ᵀblue and white, and with a great crown of gold, and with a garment of fine linen and purple: and the city of Shu'-shan rejoiced and was glad. *violet*

16 The Jews had light, and gladness, and joy, and honour.

17 And in every province, and in every city, whithersoever the king's commandment and his decree came, the Jews had joy and gladness, a feast and a ᵀgood day. And many of the people of the land became Jews; for the fear of the Jews fell upon them. *holiday*

9 Now in the twelfth month, that *is*, the month A'-dar, on the thirteenth day of the same, when the king's commandment and his decree drew near to be put in execution, in the day that the enemies of the Jews hoped to have power over them, (though it was turned to the contrary, that the Jews had rule over them that hated them;)

2 The Jews ᴿgathered themselves together in their cities throughout all the provinces of the king A-has-u-e'-rus, to lay hand on such as ᴿsought their hurt: and no man could withstand them; for ᴿthe fear of them fell upon all people. 8:11 · Ps. 71:13, 14 · 8:17

3 And all the rulers of the provinces, and the ᵀlieutenants, and the ᵀdeputies, and officers of the king, helped the Jews; because the fear of Mor'-de-cai fell upon them.   *satraps · governors*

4 For Mor'-de-cai *was* great in the king's house, and his fame went out throughout all the provinces: for this man Mor'-de-cai waxed greater and greater.

5 Thus the Jews smote all their enemies with the stroke of the sword, and slaughter, and de-

struction, and did what they would unto those that hated them.

6 And in ᴿShu'-shan the palace the Jews slew and destroyed five hundred men. 1:2; 3:15; 4:16

7 And Par-shan'-da-tha, and Dal'-phon, and As-pa'-tha,

8 And Por'-a-tha, and A-da'-li-a, and A-rid'-a-tha,

9 And Par-mash'-ta, and A-ri'-sai, and A-ri'-dai, and Va-jez'-a-tha,

10 The ten sons of Ha'-man the son of Ham-med'-a-tha, the enemy of the Jews, slew they; but on the spoil laid they not their hand.

11 On that day the number of those that were slain in ᵀShu'-shan the palace ᵀwas brought before the king. Or Susa · Lit. came

12 And the king said unto Esther the queen, The Jews have slain and destroyed five hundred men in Shu'-shan the palace, and the ten sons of Ha'-man; what have they done in the rest of the king's provinces? now ᴿwhat is thy petition? and it shall be granted thee: or what is thy request further? and it shall be done. 5:6; 7:2

13 Then said Esther, If it please the king, let it be granted to the Jews which are in Shu'-shan to do to morrow also ᴿaccording unto this day's decree, and let Ha'-man's ten sons ᴿbe hanged upon the gallows. v. 15; 8:11 · 2 Sam. 21:6, 9

14 And the king commanded it so to be done: and the decree was given at Shu'-shan; and they hanged Ha'-man's ten sons.

15 For the Jews that were in Shu'-shan ᴿgathered themselves together on the fourteenth day also of the month A'-dar, and slew three hundred men at Shu'-shan; ᴿbut on the ᵀprey they laid not their hand. v. 2; 8:11 · v. 10 · plunder

16 But the other Jews that were in the king's provinces ᴿgathered themselves together, and stood for their lives, and had rest from their enemies, and slew of their foes seventy and five thousand, ᴿbut they laid not their hands on the ᵀprey, v. 2 · 8:11 · plunder

17 On the thirteenth day of the month A'-dar; and on the fourteenth day of the same rested they, and made it a day of feasting and gladness.

18 But the Jews that were at Shu'-shan assembled together ᴿon the thirteenth day thereof, and on the fourteenth thereof; and on the fifteenth day of the same they rested, and made it a day of feasting and gladness. vv. 11, 15

19 Therefore the Jews of the villages, that dwelt in the unwalled towns, made the fourteenth day of the month A'-dar ᴿa day of gladness and feasting, ᴿand a good day, and of sending portions one to another. Deut. 16:11, 14 · 8:16, 17

20 And Mor'-de-cai wrote these things, and sent letters unto all the Jews that were in all the provinces of the king A-has-u-e'-rus, both nigh and far,

21 To stablish this among them, that they should keep the fourteenth day of the month A'-dar, and the fifteenth day of the same, yearly,

22 As the days wherein the Jews rested from their enemies, and the month which was turned unto them from sorrow to joy, and from mourning into a ᵀgood day: that they should make them days of feasting and joy, and of sending ᵀportions one to another, and gifts to the poor. holiday · presents

23 And the Jews undertook to do as they had begun, and as Mor'-de-cai had written unto them;

24 Because Ha'-man the son of Ham-med'-a-tha, the A'-gag-ite, the enemy of all the Jews, ᴿhad ᵀdevised against the Jews to destroy them, and had cast Pur, that is, the lot, to consume them, and to destroy them; 3:6, 7 · plotted

25 But ᴿwhen Esther came before the king, he commanded by letters that his wicked ᵀdevice, which he devised against the Jews, should ᴿreturn upon his own head, and that he and his sons should be hanged on the gallows. vv. 13, 14; 7:4–10; 8:3 · plot · 7:10

26 Wherefore they called these days Pu'-rim after the name of ᵀPur. Therefore for all the words of ᴿthis letter, and of that which they had seen concerning this matter, and which had come unto them,   Lit. Lot · v. 20
27 The Jews ordained, and took upon them, and upon their seed, and upon all such as joined themselves unto them, so as it should not fail, that they would keep these two days according to their writing, and according to their appointed time every year;
28 And that these days should be remembered and kept throughout every generation, every family, every province, and every city; and that these days of Pu'-rim should not fail from among the Jews, nor the memorial of them perish from their seed.
29 Then Esther the queen, ᴿthe daughter of Ab-i-ha'-il, and Mor'-de-cai the Jew, wrote with all authority, to confirm this ᴿsecond letter of Pu'-rim.   2:15 · vv. 20, 21; 8:10
30 And he sent the letters unto all the Jews, to ᴿthe hundred twenty and seven provinces of the kingdom of A-has-u-e'-rus, with words of peace and truth,   1:1
31 To confirm these days of Pu'-rim in their times appointed, according as Mor'-de-cai the Jew and Esther the queen had enjoined them, and as they had decreed for themselves and for their seed, the matters of ᴿthe fastings and their cry.   4:3, 16
32 And the decree of Esther confirmed these matters of Pu'-rim; and it was written in the book.

10
And the king A-has-u-e'-rus laid a tribute upon the land, and upon ᴿthe isles of the sea.   Gen. 10:5; Ps. 72:10; Is. 11:11; 24:15
2 And all the acts of his power and of his might, and the declaration of the greatness of Mor'-de-cai, whereunto the king advanced him, are they not written in the book of the ᴿchronicles of the kings of Me'-di-a and Persia?   6:1
3 For Mor'-de-cai the Jew was ᴿnext unto king A-has-u-e'-rus, and great among the Jews, and accepted of the multitude of his brethren, ᴿseeking the wealth of his people, and speaking peace to all his seed.   2 Chr. 28:7 · Ps. 122:8, 9

The Book of
JOB

JOB is perhaps the earliest book of the Bible. Set in the period of the patriarchs (Abraham, Isaac, Jacob, and Joseph), it tells the story of a man who loses everything—his wealth, his family, his health—and wrestles with the question, Why?

The book begins with a heavenly debate between God and Satan, moves through three cycles of earthly debates between Job and his friends, and concludes with a dramatic "divine diagnosis" of Job's problem. In the end, Job acknowledges the sovereignty of God in his life and receives back more than he had before his trials.

Iyyōb is the Hebrew title for this book, and the name has two possible meanings. If derived from the Hebrew word for "Persecution," it means "Persecuted One." It is more likely that it comes from the Arabic word meaning "To Come Back" or "Repent." If so, it may be defined "Repentant One." Both meanings apply to the book. The Greek title is Iob, and the Latin title is Iob.

THERE was a man in the land of Uz, whose name *was* Job; and that man was [T]perfect and upright, and one that feared God, and eschewed evil.   *blameless*

2   And there were born unto him seven sons and three daughters.

3   His [T]substance also was seven thousand sheep, and three thousand camels, and five hundred yoke of oxen, and five hundred [T]she asses, and a very great household; so that this man was the greatest of all the men of the east.   *possessions · female donkeys*

4   And his sons went and feasted *in their* houses, every one his day; and sent and called for their three sisters to eat and to drink with them.

5   And it was so, when the days of *their* feasting were gone about, that Job sent and sanctified them, and rose up early in the morning, [R]and offered burnt offerings *according* to the number of them all: for Job said, It may be that my sons have sinned, and [R]cursed God in their hearts. Thus did Job continually.   Gen. 8:20 · 1 Kin. 21:10, 13

6   Now [R]there was a day when the sons of God came to present themselves before the LORD, and Satan came also among them.   2:1

7   And the LORD said unto Satan, Whence comest thou? Then Satan answered the LORD, and said, From [R]going to and fro in the earth, and from walking up and down in it.   [1 Pet. 5:8]

8   And the LORD said unto Satan, Hast thou considered my servant Job, that *there is* none like him in the earth, a [T]perfect and an upright man, one that feareth God, and escheweth evil? *blameless*

9   Then Satan answered the LORD, and said, Doth Job fear God for [T]nought?   *nothing*

10 Hast not thou made an hedge about him, and about his house, and about all that he hath on every side? thou hast blessed the work of his hands, and his substance is increased in the land.

11 But put forth thine hand now, and touch all that he hath, and he will [R]curse thee to thy face.   Is. 8:21

12 And the LORD said unto Satan, Behold, all that he hath *is* in thy [T]power; only upon [T]himself put not forth thine hand. So Satan went forth from the presence of the LORD.   Lit. *hand · his person*

13 And there was a day [R]when his sons and his daughters *were* eating and drinking wine in their eldest brother's house: [Eccl. 9:12]

14 And there came a messenger unto Job, and said, The oxen were plowing, and the asses feeding beside them:

15 And the Sa-be'-ans fell *upon them*, and took them away; yea, they have slain the servants with the edge of the sword; and I only am escaped alone to tell thee.

16 While he *was* yet speaking, there came also another, and said, The fire of God is fallen from heaven, and hath burned up the sheep, and the servants, and [T]consumed them; and I only am escaped alone to tell thee.   *destroyed*

17 While he *was* yet speaking, there came also another, and said, The Chal-de'-ans [T]made out three bands, and fell upon the camels, and have carried them away, yea, and slain the servants with the edge of the sword; and I only am escaped alone to tell thee.   *formed*

18 While he *was* yet speaking, there came also another, and said, [R]Thy sons and thy daughters *were* eating and drinking wine in their eldest brother's house: vv. 4, 13

19 And, behold, there came a great wind from the wilderness, and [T]smote the four corners of the house, and it fell upon the young men, and they are dead; and I only am escaped alone to tell thee.   *struck*

20 Then Job arose, and [T]rent his [T]mantle, and shaved his head, and [R]fell down upon the ground, and worshipped,   *tore · robe · [1 Pet. 5:6]*

21 And said, [R]Naked came I out of my mother's womb, and naked shall I return thither: the LORD

Rgave, and the LORD hath taken away; blessed be the name of the LORD. 1 Tim. 6:7 · Eccl. 5:19; [James 1:17]

22 RIn all this Job sinned not, nor charged God foolishly. 2:10

2 Again Rthere was a day when the sons of God came to present themselves before the LORD, and Satan came also among them to present himself before the LORD. 1:6–8

2 And the LORD said unto Satan, From whence comest thou? And RSatan answered the LORD, and said, From going to and fro in the earth, and from walking up and down in it. 1:7

3 And the LORD said unto Satan, Hast thou considered my servant Job, that *there is* none like him in the earth, Ra perfect and an upright man, one that feareth God, and escheweth evil? and still he holdeth fast his integrity, although thou Tmovedst me against him, Rto destroy him without cause. 1:1, 8 · *incited* · 9:17

4 And Satan answered the LORD, and said, Skin for skin, yea, all that a man hath will he give for his life.

5 RBut Tput forth thine hand now, and touch his Rbone and his flesh, and he will curse thee to thy face. 1:11 · *stretch* · 19:20

6 RAnd the LORD said unto Satan, Behold, he *is* in thine hand; but save his life. 1:12

7 So went Satan forth from the presence of the LORD, and smote Job with sore boils Rfrom the sole of his foot unto his crown. Is. 1:6

8 And he took him a potsherd to scrape himself withal; Rand he sat down among the ashes. 42:6

9 Then said his wife unto him, Dost thou still retain thine integrity? curse God, and die.

10 But he said unto her, Thou speakest as one of the foolish women speaketh. What? Rshall we receive good at the hand of God, and shall we not Treceive evil? In all this did not Job sin with his lips. [James 5:10, 11] · *accept calamity*

11 Now when Job's three friends heard of all this evil that was come upon him, they came every one from his own place; El'-i-phaz the Te'-man-ite, and Bil'-dad the Shu'-hite, and Zo'-phar the Na'-a-ma-thite: for they had made an appointment together to come Rto mourn with him and to comfort him. Rom. 12:15

12 And when they lifted up their eyes afar off, and knew him not, they lifted up their voice, and wept; and they rent every one his mantle, and Rsprinkled dust upon their heads toward heaven. Neh. 9:1

13 So they sat down with him upon the ground Rseven days and seven nights, and none spake a word unto him: for they saw that *his* grief was very great. Ezek. 3:15

3 After this opened Job his mouth, and cursed his day.

2 And Job spake, and said,

3 RLet the day perish wherein I was born, and the night *in which* it was said, There is a man child conceived. 10:18, 19; Jer. 20:14–18

4 Let that day be darkness; let not God regard it from above, neither let the light shine upon it.

5 Let darkness and Rthe shadow of death stain it; let a cloud dwell upon it; let the blackness of the day terrify it. 10:21, 22; Jer. 13:16

6 *As for* that night, let darkness seize upon it; let it not Tbe joined unto the days of the year, let it not come into the number of the months. *be included in*

7 Lo, let that night be solitary, let no joyful voice come therein.

8 Let them curse it that curse the day, Rwho are ready to Traise up their mourning. Jer. 9:17 · *arouse*

9 Let the stars of the twilight thereof be dark; let it look for light, but *have* none; neither let it see the dawning of the day:

10 Because it shut not up the doors of my *mother's* womb, nor hid sorrow from mine eyes.

11 RWhy died I not from the womb? *why* did I *not* Tgive up the ghost when I came out of the belly? 10:18, 19 · *expire, perish*

12 ^RWhy did the knees ^Tprevent me? or why the breasts that I should suck?   Gen. 30:3 · *receive*

13 For now should I have lain still and been quiet, I should have slept: then had I been at rest,

14 With kings and counsellors of the earth, which ^Rbuilt desolate places for themselves; Is. 58:12

15 Or with princes that had gold, who filled their houses with silver:

16 Or ^Ras an hidden untimely birth I had not been; as infants *which* never saw light.   Ps. 58:8

17 There the wicked cease *from* troubling; and there the ^Tweary be at ^Rrest.   Lit. *wearied* of *strength* · 17:16

18 *There* the prisoners rest together; ^Rthey hear not the voice of the oppressor.   39:7

19 The small and great are there; and the servant *is* free from his master.

20 ^RWherefore is light given to him that is in misery, and life unto the bitter *in* soul;   Jer. 20:18

21 Which ^Rlong for death, but it *cometh* not; and dig for it more than for hid treasures;   Rev. 9:6

22 Which rejoice exceedingly, *and* are glad, when they can find the ^Rgrave?   7:15, 16

23 *Why is light given* to a man whose way is hid, ^Rand whom God hath hedged in?   19:8; Ps. 88:8

24 For my sighing cometh before I eat, and my roarings are poured out like the waters.

25 For the thing which I greatly ^Rfeared is come upon me, and that which I was afraid of is come unto me.   [9:28; 30:15]

26 I was not in safety, neither had I rest, neither was I quiet; yet trouble came.

4 Then El′-i-phaz the Te′-man-ite answered and said,

2 *If* we ^Tassay to commune with thee, wilt thou be grieved? but who can withhold himself from speaking?   *attempt a word*

3 Behold, thou hast instructed many, and thou ^Rhast strengthened the weak hands.   Is. 35:3

4 Thy words have upholden him that was falling, and thou ^Rhast strengthened the ^Tfeeble knees.   Is. 35:3 · Lit. *bending*

5 But now it is come upon thee, and thou faintest; it toucheth thee, and thou art troubled.

6 *Is* not *this* ^Rthy fear, ^Rthy confidence, thy hope, and the uprightness of thy ways?   1:1 · Prov. 3:26

7 Remember, I pray thee, who *ever* perished, being innocent? or where were the righteous cut off?

8 Even as I have seen, ^Rthey that plow iniquity, and sow wickedness, reap the same.   [Gal. 6:7]

9 By the blast of God they perish, and by the breath of his ^Tnostrils are they consumed.   *anger*

10 The roaring of the lion, and the voice of the fierce lion, and ^Rthe teeth of the young lions, are broken.   5:15; Ps. 58:6

11 ^RThe old lion perisheth for lack of prey, and the stout lion's whelps are scattered abroad. 29:17

12 Now a thing was secretly brought to me, and mine ear received a little thereof.

13 ^RIn thoughts from the visions of the night, when deep sleep falleth on men,   33:15

14 Fear came upon me, and ^Rtrembling, which made all my bones to shake.   Hab. 3:16

15 Then a spirit passed before my face; the hair of my flesh stood up:

16 It stood still, but I could not discern ^Tthe form thereof: ^Tan image *was* before mine eyes, *there was* silence, and I heard a voice, *saying,*   *its appearance · a form*

17 Shall mortal man be more just than God? shall a man be more pure than his maker?

18 Behold, he ^Rput no trust in his servants; and his angels he charged with ^Tfolly: 15:15 · *error*

19 How much less *in* them that dwell in houses of clay, whose foundation *is* in the dust, *which* are crushed before the moth?

20 They are destroyed from morning to evening: they perish for ever without any regarding *it.*

21 Doth not their excellency

which is in them go away? they die, even without wisdom.

5 Call now, if there be any that will answer thee; and to which of the saints wilt thou turn?

2 For wrath killeth the foolish man, and envy slayeth the ᵀsilly one.   *simple*

3 ᴿI have seen the foolish taking root: but suddenly I cursed his habitation.   [Ps. 37:35, 36]; Jer. 12:1-3

4 His children are ᴿfar from safety, and they are crushed in the gate, ᴿneither *is there* any to deliver *them*.   Ps. 119:155 · Ps. 109:12

5 Whose harvest the hungry eateth up, and taketh it even out of the thorns, and the robber swalloweth up their substance.

6 Although affliction cometh not forth of the dust, neither doth trouble spring out of the ground;

7 Yet man is ᴿborn unto trouble, as the sparks fly upward. 14:1

8 ᵀI would seek unto God, and unto God would I commit my cause: *But as for me I would*

9 Which doeth great things and unsearchable; marvellous things without number:

10 ᴿWho giveth rain upon the earth, and sendeth waters upon the fields: [36:27-29; 37:6-11; 38:26]

11 ᴿTo set up on high those that be low; that those which mourn may be exalted to safety.   Ps. 113:7

12 ᴿHe ᵀdisappointeth the devices of the crafty, so that their hands cannot perform *their* ᵀenterprise.   Neh. 4:15 · *frustrates · plans*

13 He taketh the wise in their own craftiness: and the counsel of the froward is carried headlong.

14 They meet with darkness in the daytime, and grope in the noonday as in the night.

15 But ᴿhe saveth the poor from the sword, from their mouth, and from the hand of the mighty.   4:10

16 So the poor hath hope, and iniquity stoppeth her mouth.

17 ᴿBehold, happy *is* the man whom God correcteth: therefore despise not thou the chastening of the Almighty: Ps. 94:12; [Heb. 12:5, 6]

18 ᴿFor he maketh sore, and bindeth up: he woundeth, and his hands make whole.   Is. 30:26; Hos. 6:1

19 ᴿHe shall deliver thee in six troubles: yea, in seven there shall no evil touch thee.   [1 Cor. 10:13]

20 ᴿIn famine he shall redeem thee from death: and in war from the power of the sword. Ps. 33:19, 20

21 ᴿThou shalt be hid from the scourge of the tongue: neither shalt thou be afraid of destruction when it cometh.   v. 15; Ps. 31:20

22 At destruction and famine thou shalt laugh: ᴿneither shalt thou be afraid of the ᴿbeasts of the earth.   Ps. 91:13; Is. 11:9; 35:9 · Hos. 2:18

23 ᴿFor thou shalt be in league with the stones of the field: and the beasts of the field shall be at peace with thee.   Ps. 91:12

24 And thou shalt know that thy tabernacle *shall be* in peace; and thou shalt visit thy habitation, and ᵀshalt not sin.   *find nothing amiss*

25 Thou shalt know also that ᴿthy seed *shall be* great, and thine offspring ᴿas the grass of the earth.   Ps. 112:2 · Ps. 72:16

26 Thou shalt come to *thy* grave in a full age, like as a shock of corn cometh in in his season.

27 Lo this, we have ᴿsearched it, so it *is*; hear it, and know thou *it* ᵀfor thy good. Ps. 111:2 · Lit. *for yourself*

6 But Job answered and said,

2 O that my grief were throughly weighed, and my calamity ᵀlaid in the balances together!   *laid with it in the balances!*

3 For now it would be heavier than the sand of the sea: therefore my words are swallowed up.

4 ᴿFor the arrows of the Almighty *are* within me, the poison whereof drinketh up my spirit: the terrors of God do set themselves in array against me.   16:13; Ps. 38:2

5 Doth the ᴿwild ass bray when he hath grass? or loweth the ox over his fodder?   39:5-8

6 Can that which is unsavoury be eaten without salt? or is there *any* taste in the white of an egg?

7 The things *that* my soul

refused to touch *are* as ^Tmy sorrowful meat.　*loathsome food to me*

8 Oh that I might have my request; and that God would grant *me* the thing that I long for!

9 Even that it would please God to destroy me; that he would let loose his hand, and ^Rcut me off!　9:21; 10:1; Num. 11:15; 1 Kin. 19:4

10 Then should I yet have comfort; yea, I would harden myself in sorrow: let him not spare; for ^RI have not concealed the words of ^Rthe Holy One.　Acts 20:20 · [Is. 57:15]

11 What *is* my strength, that I should hope? and what *is* mine end, that I should prolong my life?

12 *Is* my strength the strength of stones? or *is* my flesh of brass?

13 *Is* not my help in me? and is wisdom driven quite from me?

14 ^RTo him that is ^Tafflicted pity *should be shewed* from his friend; but he forsaketh the fear of the Almighty.　[Prov. 17:17] · *despairing*

15 My brethren have dealt deceitfully as a brook, *and* as the stream of brooks they pass away;

16 Which are blackish by reason of the ice, *and* wherein the snow is hid:

17 What time they wax warm, they vanish: when it is hot, they are consumed out of their place.

18 The paths of their way are turned aside; they go to nothing, and perish.

19 The ^Ttroops of Te′-ma looked, the ^Tcompanies of She′-ba waited for them.　*caravans · travellers*

20 They were ^Rconfounded because they had hoped; they came thither, and were ashamed.　Jer. 14:3

21 For now ^Rye are no thing; ye see *my* casting down, and ^Rare afraid.　13:4 · Ps. 38:11

22 Did I ^Tsay, Bring unto me? or, ^TGive a reward for me of your substance?　*ever say · Offer a bribe*

23 Or, Deliver me from the enemy's hand? or, Redeem me from the hand of the mighty?

24 Teach me, and I will hold my tongue: and cause me to understand wherein I have erred.

25 How forcible are right words!

but what doth your arguing ^Treprove?　*prove*

26 Do ye ^Timagine to reprove words, and the speeches of one that is desperate, *which are* as wind?　*intend to reprove my words*

27 Yea, ye overwhelm the fatherless, and ye ^Rdig^T *a pit* for your friend.　Ps. 57:6 · *undermine*

28 Now therefore ^Tbe content, look upon me; for *it is* evident unto you if I lie.　*be pleased to*

29 ^RReturn, I pray you, let it not be iniquity; yea, return again, my righteousness *is* in it.　17:10

30 Is there ^Tiniquity in my tongue? cannot my ^Ttaste discern perverse things?　*injustice · palate*

7 *Is there* not ^Ran appointed time to man upon earth? *are not* his days also like the days of an hireling?　[14:5, 13, 14]; Ps. 39:4

2 As a servant ^Tearnestly desireth the shadow, and as an hireling looketh for *the reward* of his work;　*longs for the shade,* lit. *pants*

3 So am I made to possess ^Rmonths of vanity, and wearisome nights are appointed to me.　[15:31]

4 ^RWhen I lie down, I say, When shall I arise, and the night be gone? and I am full of tossings to and fro unto the dawning of the day.　vv. 13, 14; Deut. 28:67

5 My flesh is ^Rclothed^T with worms and clods of dust; my skin is ^Tbroken, and become loathsome.　Is. 14:11 · *caked · cracked*

6 ^RMy days are swifter than a weaver's shuttle, and are spent without hope.　Is. 38:12; [James 4:14]

7 O remember that ^Rmy life *is* wind: mine eye shall no more see good.　v. 16; Ps. 78:39; 89:47

8 ^RThe eye of him that hath seen me shall see me no *more:* thine eyes *are* upon me, and ^TI *am* not.　8:18; 20:9 · *I will no longer be*

9 *As* the cloud is consumed and vanisheth away; so ^Rhe that goeth down to the grave shall come up no *more.*　2 Sam. 12:23

10 He shall return no more to his house, ^Rneither shall his place know him any more.　Ps. 103:16

11 Therefore I will not refrain

my mouth; I will speak in the anguish of my spirit; I will complain in the bitterness of my soul.

12 *Am* I a sea, or a whale, that thou settest a watch over me?

13 ^RWhen I say, My bed shall comfort me, my couch shall ease my complaint;   9:27

14 Then thou scarest me with dreams, and terrifiest me through visions:

15 So that my soul chooseth strangling, *and* death rather than my ^Tlife.   Lit. *bones*

16 ^RI loathe *it*; I would not live alway: ^Rlet me alone; for ^Rmy days *are* vanity.   10:1 · 14:6 · Ps. 62:9

17 ^RWhat *is* man, that thou shouldest magnify him? and that thou shouldest set thine heart upon him?   22:2; Ps. 8:4; 144:3; Heb. 2:6

18 And *that* thou shouldest ^Tvisit him every morning, *and* try him every moment?   *seek* or *examine*

19 How long wilt thou not depart from me, nor let me alone till I swallow down my spittle?

20 I have sinned; what shall I do unto thee, ^RO thou preserver of men? why ^Rhast thou set me as a mark against thee, so that I am a burden to myself?   Ps. 36:6 · Ps. 21:12

21 And why dost thou not pardon my transgression, and take away mine iniquity? for now shall I ^Tsleep in the dust; and thou shalt seek me in the morning, but I *shall* ^Tnot *be*.   *lie down · no longer*

8 Then answered Bil'-dad the Shu'-hite, and said,

2 How long wilt thou speak these *things*? and *how long shall* the words of thy mouth *be like* a strong wind?

3 ^RDoth God pervert judgment? or doth the Almighty pervert justice?   Gen. 18:25; [Deut. 32:4]; Rom. 3:5

4 If ^Rthy children have sinned against him, and he have cast them away ^Tfor their transgression;   1:5, 18, 19 · Lit. *in the hand of their*

5 ^RIf thou wouldest seek unto God betimes, and make thy supplication to the Almighty;   [5:17–27]

6 If thou *wert* pure and upright; surely now he would awake for thee, and make the habitation of thy righteousness prosperous.

7 Though thy beginning was small, yet thy latter end should greatly ^Rincrease.   42:12

8 For enquire, I pray thee, of the former age, and prepare thyself to the search of their fathers:

9 (For we *are but of* yesterday, and know nothing, because our days upon earth *are* a shadow:)

10 Shall not they teach thee, *and* tell thee, and utter words out of their heart?

11 Can the ^Trush grow up without ^Tmire? can the ^Tflag grow without water?   *papyrus · marsh · reeds*

12 Whilst it *is* yet in his greenness, *and* not cut down, it withereth before any *other* herb.

13 So *are* the paths of all that ^Rforget God; and the ^Rhypocrite's hope shall perish: Ps. 9:17 · Ps. 112:10

14 Whose hope shall be cut off, and whose trust *shall be* a spider's ^Tweb.   Lit. *house*

15 ^RHe shall lean upon his house, but it shall not stand: he shall hold it fast, but it shall not endure.   v. 22; 27:18; Ps. 49:11

16 He *is* green before the sun, and his branch shooteth forth in his garden.

17 His roots are wrapped about the ^Theap, *and* seeth the place of stones.   *rock heap*

18 ^RIf he destroy him from his place, then *it* shall deny him, *saying*, I have not seen thee.   7:10

19 Behold, this *is* the joy of his way, and ^Rout of the earth shall others grow.   Ps. 113:7

20 Behold, ^RGod will not cast away a ^Tperfect *man*, neither will he help the evil doers: 4:7 · *blameless*

21 Till he fill thy mouth with laughing, and thy lips with ^Trejoicing.   Lit. *shouts of joy*

22 They that hate thee shall be ^Rclothed with shame; and the dwelling place of the wicked shall come to nought.   Ps. 35:26; 109:29

9 Then Job answered and said,

2 I know *it is* so of a truth: but

how should man be ^Rjust with God?   [Hab. 2:4; Rom. 1:17; Gal. 3:11]
3 If he will contend with him, he cannot answer him ^Tone of a thousand.   *one time out of*
4 ^R*He*^T *is* wise in heart, and mighty in strength: who hath hardened *himself* against him, and hath prospered?   36:5 · God
5 Which removeth the mountains, and they know not; which overturneth them in his anger.
6 Which ^Rshaketh the earth out of her place, and the pillars thereof tremble.   Is. 2:19, 21; Heb. 12:26
7 Which commandeth the sun, and it riseth not; and sealeth up the stars.
8 ^RWhich alone spreadeth out the heavens, and treadeth upon the waves of the sea.   37:18; Gen. 1:6
9 ^RWhich maketh Arc-tu'-rus, O-ri'-on, and Ple'-ia-des, and the chambers of the south.   38:31
10 ^RWhich doeth great things past finding out; yea, and wonders without number.   5:9
11 ^RLo, he goeth by me, and I see *him* not: he passeth on also, but I perceive him not.   [23:8, 9; 35:14]
12 ^RBehold, he taketh away, who can hinder him? who will say unto him, What doest thou?   [Rom. 9:20]
13 *If* God will not withdraw his anger, ^Rthe proud helpers do stoop under him.   26:12
14 How much less ^Tshall I answer him, *and* choose out my words *to reason* with him?   *can I*
15 ^RWhom, though I were righteous, *yet* ^Twould I not answer, *but* I would make supplication to my judge.   10:15; 23:1–7 · could
16 If I had called, and he had answered me; *yet* would I not believe that he had hearkened unto my voice.
17 For he breaketh me with a tempest, and multiplieth my wounds ^Rwithout cause.   2:3
18 He will not suffer me to take my breath, but filleth me with bitterness.
19 If *I speak* of strength, lo, *he is* strong: and if of judgment, who shall set me a time *to plead?*

20 If I justify myself, mine own mouth shall condemn me: *if I say,* I *am* perfect, it shall also prove me perverse.
21 *Though* I *were* perfect, *yet* would I not know my soul: I would despise my life.
22 This *is* one *thing,* therefore I said *it,* He destroyeth the ^Tperfect and the wicked.   *blameless*
23 If the scourge slay suddenly, he will laugh at the ^Ttrial of the innocent.   *plight*
24 The earth is given into the hand of the wicked: he covereth the faces of the judges thereof; if not, where, *and* who *is* he?
25 Now ^Rmy days are swifter than a ^Tpost: they flee away, they see no good.   7:6, 7 · *runner*
26 They are passed away as the swift ships: ^Ras the eagle *that* hasteth to the prey.   39:29; Hab. 1:8
27 ^RIf I say, I will forget my complaint, I will leave off my heaviness, and comfort *myself;*   7:13
28 ^RI am afraid of all my sorrows, I know that thou wilt not hold me innocent.   Ps. 119:120
29 *If* I ^Tbe wicked, why then labour I in vain?   *shall be condemned*
30 ^RIf I wash myself with snow water, and make my hands never so clean;   [Jer. 2:22]
31 Yet shalt thou plunge me in the ^Tditch, and mine own clothes shall ^Tabhor me.   *pit · loathe*
32 For ^R*he is* not a man, as I *am, that* I should answer him, *and* we should come together in judgment.   [Is. 45:9; Jer. 49:19; Rom. 9:20]
33 ^RNeither is there any ^Tdaysman betwixt us, *that* might lay his hand upon us both. Is. 1:18 · *mediator*
34 ^RLet him take his rod away from me, and let not ^This fear terrify me: 13:20, 21; Ps. 39:10 · *dread of him*
35 *Then* would I speak, and not fear him; but *it is* not so with me.

10 My ^Rsoul is weary of my life; I will leave my complaint upon myself; I will speak in the bitterness of my soul.   Jon. 4:3
2 I will say unto God, Do not condemn me; shew me wherefore thou contendest with me.

3 *Is it* good unto thee that thou shouldest oppress, that thou shouldest despise the work of thine hands, and shine upon the counsel of the wicked?

4 Hast thou eyes of flesh? or ᴿseest thou as man seeth?   [28:24]

5 *Are* thy days as the days of man? *are* thy years as ᵀman's days,   *the days of a mighty man*

6 That thou enquirest after mine iniquity, and searchest after my sin?

7 Thou knowest that I am not wicked; and *there is* none that can deliver out of thine hand.

8 Thine hands have made me and fashioned me together round about; yet thou dost destroy me.

9 Remember, I beseech thee, ᴿthat thou hast made me as the clay; and wilt thou bring me into dust again?   33:6; Gen. 2:7

10 ᴿHast thou not poured me out as milk, and curdled me like cheese?   [Ps. 139:14–16]

11 Thou hast clothed me with skin and flesh, and hast fenced me with bones and sinews.

12 Thou hast granted me life and favour, and thy ᵀvisitation hath preserved my spirit.   *care*

13 And these *things* hast thou hid in thine heart: I know that this *is* with thee.

14 If I sin, then ᴿthou markest me, and thou wilt not acquit me from mine iniquity.   7:20; Ps. 139:1

15 If I be wicked, ᴿwoe unto me; and *if* I be righteous, *yet* will I not lift up my head. *I am* full of confusion; therefore ᴿsee thou mine affliction;   Is. 3:11 · Ps. 25:18

16 For it increaseth. ᴿThou huntest me as a fierce lion: and again thou shewest thyself marvellous upon me.   Is. 38:13; Lam. 3:10; Hos. 13:7

17 Thou renewest thy witnesses against me, and increasest thine indignation upon me; changes and war *are* against me.

18 Wherefore then hast thou brought me forth out of the womb? Oh that I had given up the ghost, and no eye had seen me!

19 I should have been as though I had not been; I should have been carried from the womb to the grave.

20 ᴿ*Are* not my days few? cease *then, and* ᴿlet me alone, that I may take comfort a little, Ps. 39:5 · 7:16, 19

21 Before I go *whence* I shall not return, *even* to the land of darkness and the shadow of death;

22 A land of darkness, as darkness *itself; and* of the shadow of death, without any order, and *where* the light *is* as darkness.

11 Then answered Zo'-phar the Na'-a-ma-thite, and said,

2 Should not the multitude of words be answered? and should a man full of talk be justified?

3 Should thy ᵀlies make men hold their peace? and when thou mockest, shall no man ᵀmake thee ashamed?   *empty talk · rebuke thee*

4 For ᴿthou hast said, My doctrine *is* pure, and I am clean in thine eyes.   6:30

5 But oh that God would speak, and open his lips against thee;

6 And that he would shew thee the secrets of wisdom, that *they are* double to that which is! Know therefore that ᴿGod exacteth of thee *less* than thine iniquity *deserveth.*   [Ezra 9:13]

7 Canst thou by searching find out God? canst thou find out the Almighty unto perfection?

8 *It is* as high as heaven; what canst thou do? deeper than ᵀhell; what canst thou know?   Heb. *Sheol*

9 The measure thereof *is* longer than the earth, and broader than the sea.

10 ᴿIf he cut off, and shut up, or gather together, then who can ᵀhinder him?   9:12; [Rev. 3:7] · *restrain*

11 For ᴿhe knoweth vain men: he seeth wickedness also; will he not then consider *it*?   [Ps. 10:14]

12 For ᴿvain man would be wise, though man be born *like* a wild ass's colt.   [Ps. 39:5]; Rom. 1:22

13 If thou ᴿprepare thine heart, and ᴿstretch out thine hands toward him;   [1 Sam. 7:3] · Ps. 88:9

14 If iniquity *be* in thine hand, put it far away, and let not wickedness dwell in thy tabernacles.

15 ᴿFor then shalt thou lift up thy face without spot; yea, thou shalt be stedfast, and shalt not fear: 22:26; Ps. 119:6; [1 John 3:21]
16 Because thou shalt ᴿforget *thy* misery, *and* remember *it* as waters *that* pass away: Is. 65:16
17 And *thine* age ᴿshall be clearer than the noonday; thou shalt shine forth, thou shalt be as the morning. Ps. 37:6; Prov. 4:18; Is. 58:8, 10
18 And thou shalt be secure, because there is hope; yea, thou shalt dig *about thee, and* ᴿthou shalt take thy rest in safety. Ps. 3:5
19 Also thou shalt lie down, and none shall make *thee* afraid; yea, many shall make suit unto thee.
20 But ᴿthe eyes of the wicked shall fail, and they shall not escape, and their hope *shall be as* the giving up of the ghost. 17:5

12 And Job answered and said,
2 No doubt but ye *are* the people, and wisdom shall die with you.
3 But I have ᵀunderstanding as well as you; I *am* not ᴿinferior to you: yea, who knoweth not such things as these? Lit. *a heart* · 13:2
4 ᴿI am *as* one mocked ᵀof his neighbour, who ᴿcalleth upon God, and he answereth him: the just upright *man is* laughed to scorn. 21:3 · *by his friends* · Ps. 91:15
5 He that is ready to slip with *his* feet *is as* a lamp despised in the thought of him that is at ease.
6 ᴿThe tabernacles of robbers prosper, and they that provoke God are secure; into whose hand God bringeth *abundantly.* [Ps. 73:12]
7 But ask now the beasts, and they shall teach thee; and the fowls of the air, and they shall tell thee:
8 Or speak to the earth, and it shall teach thee; and the fishes of the sea shall declare unto thee:
9 Who knoweth not in all these that the hand of the LORD hath wrought this?
10 ᴿIn whose hand *is* the ᵀsoul of every living thing, and the breath of all mankind. [Acts 17:28] · *life*

11 Doth not the ear try words? and the mouth taste his meat?
12 With the ᵀancient *is* wisdom; and in length of days understanding. *aged*
13 With ᵀhim *is* ᴿwisdom and strength, he hath counsel and understanding. God · 9:4; 36:5
14 Behold, ᴿhe breaketh down, and it cannot be built again: he shutteth up a man, and there can be ᵀno opening. Is. 25:2 · *no release*
15 Behold, he ᴿwithholdeth the waters, and they dry up: also he sendeth them out, and they overturn the earth. Deut. 11:17
16 With him *is* strength and wisdom: the deceived and the deceiver *are* his.
17 He leadeth counsellors away ᵀspoiled, and maketh the judges fools. *plundered*
18 He looseth the bond of kings, and girdeth their ᵀloins with a girdle. *waist with a belt*
19 He leadeth princes away ᵀspoiled, and overthroweth the mighty. *plundered*
20 ᴿHe removeth away the speech of the trusty, and taketh away the ᵀunderstanding of the aged. 32:9 · *discernment*
21 ᴿHe poureth contempt upon princes, and weakeneth the strength of the mighty. Ps. 107:40
22 He discovereth deep things out of darkness, and bringeth out to light the shadow of death.
23 ᴿHe increaseth the nations, and destroyeth them: he enlargeth the nations, and straiteneth them *again.* Is. 9:3; 26:15
24 He taketh away the ᵀheart of the chief of the people of the earth, and ᴿcauseth them to wander in a wilderness *where there is* no way. *understanding* · Ps. 107:4
25 ᴿThey grope in the dark without light, and he maketh them to stagger like *a* drunken *man.* 5:14

13 Lo, mine eye hath seen all *this*, mine ear hath heard and understood it.
2 ᴿWhat ye know, *the same* do I know also: I *am* not inferior unto you. 12:3

3 ᴿSurely I would speak to the Almighty, and I desire to reason with God. 23:3; 31:35

4 But ye *are* forgers of lies, ᴿye *are* all physicians of no value. 6:21

5 ᴿO that ye would altogether hold your peace! and it should be your wisdom. v. 13; 21:5; Prov. 17:28

6 Hear now my reasoning, and hearken to the pleadings of my lips.

7 Will ye speak wickedly for God? and talk deceitfully for him?

8 Will ye accept his person? will ye contend for God?

9 Is it good that he should search you out? or as one man mocketh another, do ye *so* mock him?

10 He will surely reprove you, if ye do secretly accept persons.

11 Shall not his ᵀexcellency make you afraid? and his dread fall upon you? Lit. exaltation

12 Your remembrances *are* like unto ashes, your ᵀbodies to bodies of clay. defences are defences of

13 ᵀHold your peace, let me alone, that I may speak, and let come on me what *will*. Be silent

14 Wherefore ᴿdo I take my flesh in my teeth, and put my life in mine hand? 18:4

15 Though he slay me, yet will I trust in him: ᴿbut I will maintain mine own ways before him. 27:5

16 He also *shall be* my salvation: for an ᴿhypocrite shall not come before him. 8:13

17 Hear diligently my speech, and my declaration with your ears.

18 Behold now, I have ᵀordered *my* cause; I know that I shall be ᴿjustified. prepared my case · [Rom. 8:34]

19 Who *is* he *that* will plead with me? for now, if I hold my tongue, I shall give up the ghost.

20 ᴿOnly do not two *things* unto me: then I will not hide myself from thee. 9:34

21 ᴿWithdraw thine hand far from me: and let not thy dread make me afraid. 9:34; Ps. 39:10

22 Then call thou, and I will ᴿanswer: or let me speak, and answer thou me. 9:16; 14:15

23 How many *are* mine iniquities and sins? make me to know my transgression and my sin.

24 ᴿWherefore hidest thou thy face, and ᴿholdest me for thine enemy? [Deut. 32:20]; Ps. 13:1 · Lam. 2:5

25 ᴿWilt thou break a leaf driven to and fro? and wilt thou pursue the dry stubble? Is. 42:3

26 For thou writest bitter things against me, and ᴿmakest me ᵀto possess the iniquities of my youth. 20:11 · inherit

27 Thou puttest my feet also in the stocks, and lookest narrowly unto all my paths; thou settest a print upon the heels of my feet.

28 And he, as a rotten thing, ᵀconsumeth, as a garment that is moth eaten. decays

14 Man *that is* born of a woman *is* of few days, and ᴿfull of trouble. 5:7; Eccl. 2:23

2 ᴿHe cometh forth like a flower, and is cut down: he fleeth also as a shadow, and continueth not. Is. 40:6; James 1:10, 11; 1 Pet. 1:24

3 And ᴿdost thou open thine eyes upon such an one, and ᴿbringest me into judgment with thee? Ps. 8:4; 144:3 · [Ps. 143:2]

4 Who can bring a clean *thing* out of an unclean? not one.

5 Seeing his days *are* determined, the number of his months *are* with thee, thou hast appointed his bounds that he cannot pass;

6 ᴿTurn from him, that he may rest, till he shall accomplish, as an hireling, his day. 7:16, 19; Ps. 39:13

7 For there is hope of a tree, if it be cut down, that it will sprout again, and that the tender branch thereof will not cease.

8 Though the root thereof ᵀwax old in the earth, and the stock thereof die in the ground; grow

9 *Yet* through the scent of water it will bud, and bring forth boughs like a plant.

10 But man dieth, and wasteth away: yea, man giveth up the ghost, and where *is* ᴿhe? 10:21, 22

11 *As* the waters ᵀfail from the sea, and the flood decayeth and drieth up: disappear

12 So man lieth down, and riseth not: ᴿtill the heavens *be* no more, they shall not awake, nor be raised out of their sleep. [Rev. 21:1]

13 O that thou wouldest hide me in the grave, that thou wouldest ᵀkeep me secret, until thy wrath be past, that thou wouldest appoint me a set time, and remember me! *conceal me*

14 If a man die, shall he live *again*? all the days of my ᵀappointed time ᴿwill I wait, till my change come. *hard service* · 13:15

15 Thou shalt call, and I will answer thee: thou wilt have a desire to the work of thine hands.

16 ᴿFor now thou numberest my steps: dost thou not watch over my sin? Ps. 139:1–3; Prov. 5:21; [Jer. 32:19]

17 ᴿMy transgression *is* sealed up in a bag, and thou sewest up mine iniquity. Deut. 32:32–34

18 And surely the mountain falling cometh to nought, and the rock is removed out of his place.

19 The waters ᵀwear the stones: thou washest away the things which grow *out* of the dust of the earth; and thou destroyest the hope of man. *wear away stones*

20 Thou prevailest for ever against him, and he passeth: thou changest his countenance, and sendest him away.

21 His sons come to honour, and ᴿhe knoweth *it* not; and they are brought low, but he perceiveth *it* not of them. Eccl. 9:5; Is. 63:16

22 But his flesh upon him shall have pain, and his soul within him shall mourn.

15 Then answered ᴿEl′-i-phaz the Te′-man-ite, and said, 4:1

2 Should a wise man utter vain knowledge, and fill ᵀhis belly with the east wind? *himself*

3 Should he reason with unprofitable talk? or with speeches wherewith he can do no good?

4 Yea, thou castest off fear, and restrainest prayer before God.

5 For thy mouth uttereth thine iniquity, and thou choosest the tongue of the crafty.

6 ᴿThine own mouth condemneth thee, and not I: yea, thine own lips testify against thee. 9:20

7 *Art* thou the first man *that* was born? ᴿor wast thou made before the hills? 38:4, 21; Ps. 90:2

8 ᴿHast thou heard the secret of God? and dost thou restrain wisdom to thyself? 29:4; Rom. 11:34

9 ᴿWhat knowest thou, that we know not? *what* understandest thou, which *is* not in us? 12:3; 13:2

10 ᴿWith us *are* both the grayheaded and very aged men, much elder than thy father. 8:8–10; 12:12

11 *Are* the consolations of God ᵀsmall with thee? is there any secret thing with thee? *too small*

12 Why doth thine heart carry thee away? and ᵀwhat do thy eyes wink at, *Or why do your eyes flash*

13 That thou turnest thy spirit against God, and lettest *such* words go out of thy mouth?

14 ᴿWhat *is* man, that he should be clean? and *he which is* born of a woman, that he should be righteous? [Eccl. 7:20; 1 John 1:8, 10]

15 ᴿBehold, ᵀhe putteth no trust in his saints; yea, the heavens are not clean in his sight. 4:18; 25:5 · God

16 How much more abominable and filthy *is* man, ᴿwhich drinketh iniquity like water? 34:7; Prov. 19:28

17 I will ᵀshew thee, hear me; and that *which* I have seen I will declare; *tell*

18 Which wise men have told ᴿfrom their fathers, and have not hid *it*: 8:8; 20:4

19 Unto whom alone the ᵀearth was given, and ᴿno stranger passed among them. *land* · Joel 3:17

20 The wicked man ᵀtravaileth with pain all *his* days, ᴿand the number of years is hidden to the oppressor. *writhes* · Ps. 90:12

21 A dreadful sound *is* in his ears: ᴿin prosperity the destroyer shall come upon him. 1 Thess. 5:3

22 He believeth not that he shall ᴿreturn out of darkness, and he is waited for of the sword. 14:10–12

23 He ᴿwandereth abroad for bread, *saying,* Where *is* it? he knoweth that the day of darkness is ready at his hand. Ps. 59:15; 109:10

24 Trouble and anguish shall make him afraid; they shall ᵀprevail against him, as a king ready to the ᵀbattle. *overpower · attack*

25 For he stretcheth out his hand against God, and ᵀstrengtheneth himself against the Almighty. *acts defiantly*

26 He runneth upon him, *even* on *his* neck, upon the thick bosses of his bucklers:

27 ᴿBecause he covereth his face with his fatness, and maketh collops of fat on *his* flanks. *Ps. 17:10*

28 And he dwelleth in desolate cities, *and* in houses which no man inhabiteth, which are ready to become ᵀheaps. *ruins*

29 He shall not be rich, neither shall his substance ᴿcontinue, neither shall he prolong the perfection thereof upon the earth. *20:28*

30 He shall not depart out of darkness; the flame shall dry up his branches, and ᴿby the breath of his mouth shall he go away. *4:9*

31 Let not him that is deceived ᴿtrust in vanity: for vanity shall be his recompence. *35:13; Is. 59:4*

32 It shall be accomplished ᴿbefore his time, and his branch shall not be green. *22:16; Ps. 55:23; Eccl. 7:17*

33 He shall shake off his unripe grape as the vine, and shall cast off his flower as the olive.

34 For the congregation of hypocrites *shall be* ᵀdesolate, and fire shall consume the ᵀtabernacles of bribery. *barren · tents*

35 ᴿThey conceive mischief, and bring forth vanity, and their belly prepareth deceit. *Ps. 7:14; Is. 59:4*

16 Then Job answered and said,

2 I have heard many such things: ᴿmiserableᵀ comforters *are* ye all. *13:4; 21:34 · troublesome*

3 Shall vain words have an end? or what ᵀemboldeneth thee that thou answerest? *provokes*

4 I also could speak as ye *do:* if your soul were in my soul's stead, I could heap up words against you, and shake mine head at you.

5 *But* I would strengthen you with my mouth, and the ᵀmoving of my lips should ᵀassuage *your* grief. *comfort from · relieve*

6 Though I speak, my grief is not asswaged: and *though* I ᵀforbear, what am I eased? *remain silent*

7 But now he hath made me ᴿweary: thou ᴿhast made desolate all my company. *7:3 · v. 20; 19:13–15*

8 And thou hast filled me with wrinkles, *which* is a ᴿwitness *against me:* and my leanness rising up in me beareth witness to my face. *10:17*

9 He teareth *me* in his wrath, who hateth me: he gnasheth upon me with his teeth; mine enemy sharpeneth his eyes upon me.

10 They have gaped upon me with their mouth; they ᴿhave smitten me upon the cheek reproachfully; they have gathered themselves together against me. *Is. 50:6*

11 God ᴿhath delivered me to the ungodly, and turned me over into the hands of the wicked. *1:15*

12 I was at ease, but he hath broken me ᴿasunder: he hath also taken *me* by my neck, and shaken me to pieces, and ᴿset me up for his ᵀmark. *9:17 · 7:20; Lam. 3:12 · target*

13 His archers ᵀcompass me round about, he cleaveth my reins asunder, and doth not spare; he poureth out my gall upon the ground. *surround me*

14 He breaketh me with ᵀbreach upon breach, he runneth upon me like a giant. *wound*

15 I have sewed sackcloth upon my skin, and ᴿdefiledᵀ my horn in the dust. *30:19; Ps. 7:5 · laid my head*

16 My face is ᵀfoul with weeping, and on my eyelids *is* the shadow of death; *flushed from*

17 Not for *any* injustice in mine hands: also my prayer *is* pure.

18 O earth, cover not thou my blood, and ᴿlet my cry have no ᵀplace. *27:9; [Ps. 66:18] · burial place*

19 Also now, behold, ᴿmy witness *is* in heaven, and my record *is* on high. *Phil. 1:8; 1 Thess. 2:5*

20 My friends scorn me: *but* mine eye poureth out *tears* unto God.

21 ᴿO that one might plead for a man with God, as a man *pleadeth* for his neighbour! [Is. 45:9; Rom. 9:20]

22 When a few years are come, then I shall ᴿgo the way *whence* I shall not return.　　10:21; Eccl. 12:5

17 My breath is corrupt, my days are extinct, ᴿthe graves *are ready* for me.　　Ps. 88:3, 4

2 *Are there* not mockers with me? and doth not mine eye continue in their ᴿprovocation?　　12:4

3 Lay down now, put me in a ᵀsurety with thee; who *is* he *that* will strike hands with me?　*pledge*

4 For thou hast hid their heart from ᴿunderstanding: therefore shalt thou not exalt *them*.　　12:20

5 He that speaketh flattery to *his* friends, even the eyes of his children shall ᴿfail.　　11:20

6 He hath made me also ᴿa byword of the people; and aforetime I was as a tabret.　　30:9

7 ᴿMine eye also is dim by reason of sorrow, and all my members *are* as a shadow.　Ps. 6:7; 31:9

8 Upright *men* shall be astonied at this, and the innocent shall stir up himself against the hypocrite.

9 The righteous also shall hold on his ᴿway, and he that hath ᴿclean hands shall be stronger and stronger.　　Prov. 4:18 · Ps. 24:4

10 But as for you all, ᴿdoᵀ ye return, and come now: for I cannot find *one* wise *man* among you.　6:29 · *please, come back again*

11 ᴿMy days are past, my purposes are broken off, *even* the ᵀthoughts of my heart.　7:6 · *desires*

12 They change the night into day: the light *is* short because of darkness.

13 If I wait, the grave *is* mine house: I have made my bed in the darkness.

14 I have said to corruption, Thou *art* my father: to the worm, *Thou art* my mother, and my sister.

15 And where *is* now my hope? as for my hope, who shall see it?

16 They shall go down to the bars of ᵀthe pit, when *our* rest together *is* in the dust.　Heb. *Sheol*

18 Then answered ᴿBil'-dad the Shu'-hite, and said,　8:1

2 How long *will it be ere* ye make an end of words? mark, and afterwards we will speak.

3 Wherefore are we counted ᴿas beasts, *and* reputed vile in your sight?　　Ps. 73:22

4 ᴿHe teareth himself in his anger: shall the earth be forsaken for thee? and shall the rock be removed out of his place?　13:14

5 Yea, ᴿthe light of the wicked shall be put out, and the spark of his fire shall not shine.　Prov. 13:9

6 The light shall be dark in his tabernacle, ᴿand his candle shall be put out with him.　21:17; Ps. 18:28

7 The steps of his strength shall be straitened, and ᴿhis own counsel shall cast him down.　15:6

8 For ᴿhe is cast into a net by his own feet, and he walketh upon a snare.　22:10; Ps. 9:15; 35:8; Is. 24:17, 18

9 The ᵀgin shall take *him* by the heel, *and* ᴿtheᵀ robber shall prevail against him.　*net* · 5:5 · *a snare*

10 The snare *is* laid for him in the ground, and a trap for him in the way.

11 ᴿTerrors shall make him afraid on every side, and shall drive him to his feet.　20:25; Jer. 6:25

12 His strength shall be hungerbitten, and ᴿdestruction *shall be* ready at his side.　　15:23

13 It shall devour the strength of his skin: *even* the firstborn of death shall devour his strength.

14 ᴿHis confidence shall be rooted out of his tabernacle, and ᵀit shall bring him to the king of terrors.　11:20 · *they parade him before*

15 ᵀIt shall dwell in his tabernacle, ᵀbecause *it is* none of his: brimstone shall be scattered upon his habitation.　*They · who are*

16 ᴿHis roots shall be dried up beneath, and above shall his branch be cut off.　　29:19

17 ᴿHis remembrance shall perish from the earth, and he shall have no name in the street.　24:20

18 ᵀHe shall be driven from light into darkness, and chased out of the world.　Or *They drive him*

19 ᴿHe shall neither have son nor ᵀnephew among his people, nor any remaining in his dwellings.　27:14, 15; Is. 14:22 · *posterity*

20 They ᵀthat come after *him* shall be astonied at his day, as they ᵀthat went before were affrighted.　*in the west · in the east*

21 Surely such *are* the dwellings of the wicked, and this *is* the place *of him that* knoweth not God.

19 Then Job answered and said,

2 How long will ye ᵀvex my soul, and break me in pieces with words?　*torment*

3 These ten times have ye reproached me: ye are not ashamed *that* ye ᵀmake yourselves strange to me.　*deal harshly with me*

4 And be it indeed *that* I have erred, mine error remaineth with myself.

5 If indeed ye will ᴿmagnify *yourselves* against me, and plead against me my reproach:　Ps. 35:26

6 Know now that ᴿGod hath overthrown me, and hath compassed me with his net.　16:11

7 Behold, I cry out of wrong, but I am not heard: I cry aloud, but *there is* no ᵀjudgment.　*justice*

8 ᴿHe hath fenced up my way that I cannot pass, and he hath set darkness in my paths.　3:23; Ps. 88:8

9 ᴿHe hath stripped me of my glory, and taken the crown *from* my head.　12:17, 19; Ps. 89:44

10 He ᵀhath destroyed me on every side, and I am gone: and mine ᴿhope hath he removed like a tree.　*breaks me down on · 17:14, 16*

11 He hath also kindled his wrath against me, and ᴿhe counteth me unto him as *one of* his enemies.　13:24; 33:10

12 His troops come together, and raise up their way against me, and encamp round about my ᵀtabernacle.　*tent*

13 He hath put my brethren far from me, and mine acquaintance are verily estranged from me.

14 My kinsfolk have failed, and my ᵀfamiliar friends have forgotten me.　*close*

15 They that dwell in mine house, and my maids, count me for a stranger: I am an alien in their sight.

16 I called my servant, and he gave *me* no answer; I intreated him with my mouth.

17 My breath is strange to my wife, though I intreated for the children's *sake* of mine own body.

18 Yea, ᴿyoung children despised me; I arose, and they spake against me.　17:6; 2 Kin. 2:23

19 ᴿAll my inward friends abhorred me: and they whom I loved are turned against me.　Ps. 55:12, 13

20 ᴿMy bone cleaveth to my skin and to my flesh, and I am escaped with the skin of my teeth.　Ps. 102:5

21 Have pity upon me, have pity upon me, O ye my friends; for the hand of God hath touched me.

22 Why do ye ᴿpersecute me as God, and are not satisfied with my flesh?　v. 6; 13:24, 25; 16:11; Ps. 69:26

23 Oh that my words were now written! oh that they were printed in a book!

24 That they were graven with an iron pen and lead in the rock for ever!

25 For I know *that* my ᵀredeemer liveth, and *that* he shall stand ᵀat the latter *day* upon the earth:　Lit. *kinsman · at last*　☆

26 And *though* after my skin *worms* destroy this *body,* yet ᴿin my flesh shall I see God:　Matt. 5:8

27 Whom I shall see for myself, and mine eyes shall behold, and not another; *though* my reins be consumed within me.

28 But ye should say, Why persecute we him, seeing the root of the matter is found in me?

29 Be ye afraid of the sword: for wrath *bringeth* the punishments of the sword, that ye may know *there is* a judgment.

20 Then answered Zo'-phar the Na'-a-ma-thite, and said,

2 Therefore do my thoughts cause me to answer, and for *this* I make haste.

3 I have heard the check of my reproach, and the spirit of my

understanding causeth me to answer.

4 Knowest thou *not* this of ^Rold, since man was placed upon earth,   8:8; 15:10

5 That the triumphing of the wicked *is* short, and the joy of the hypocrite *but* for a moment?

6 Though his excellency mount up to the heavens, and his head reach unto the clouds;

7 *Yet* he shall perish for ever like his own dung: they which have seen him shall say, Where *is* he?

8 He shall fly away ^Ras a dream, and shall not be found: yea, he shall be chased away as a vision of the night.   Ps. 73:20; 90:5

9 The eye also *which* saw him shall *see him* no more; neither shall his place any more behold him.

10 His children shall seek to please the poor, and his hands shall restore their goods.

11 His bones are full *of the sin* of his youth, ^Rwhich shall lie down with him in the dust.   21:26

12 Though wickedness be sweet in his mouth, *though* he hide it under his tongue;

13 *Though* he spare it, and forsake it not; but keep it still ^Twithin his mouth: Lit. *in his palate*

14 *Yet* his meat in his bowels ^Tis turned, *it* ^T*is* the gall of asps within him. *turns sour · becomes cobra venom*

15 He hath swallowed down riches, and he shall vomit them up again: God shall cast them out of his belly.

16 He shall suck the poison of ^Tasps: the viper's tongue shall slay him.   *cobras*

17 He shall not see ^Rthe ^Trivers, the floods, the brooks of honey and butter. Ps. 36:8; Jer. 17:8 · *streams*

18 That which he laboured for shall he restore, and shall not swallow *it* down: according to *his* substance *shall* the restitution *be,* and he shall not rejoice *therein.*

19 Because he hath oppressed *and* hath forsaken the poor;

because he hath violently ^Ttaken away an house which he builded not;   *seized*

20 Surely he shall not feel quietness in his belly, he shall not save of that which he desired.

21 There shall none of his meat be left; therefore shall no man look for his goods.

22 In the fulness of his sufficiency he shall be in straits: every hand of the ^Twicked shall come upon him.   Or *wretched* or *sufferer*

23 *When* he is about to fill his belly, *God* shall cast the fury of his wrath upon him, and shall rain *it* upon him while he is eating.

24 ^RHe shall flee from the iron weapon, *and* the bow of steel shall strike him through.   Is. 24:18

25 It is drawn, and cometh out of the body; yea, ^Rthe glittering sword cometh out of his gall: ^Rterrors *are* upon him.   16:13 · 18:11, 14

26 All darkness *shall be* hid in his secret places: ^Ra ^Tfire not blown shall consume him; it shall go ill with him that is left in his tabernacle. Ps. 21:9 · *an unfanned fire*

27 The heaven shall reveal his iniquity; and the earth shall rise up against him.

28 The increase of his house shall depart, *and his goods* shall flow away in the day of his ^Rwrath.   v. 15; 21:30

29 ^RThis *is* the portion of a wicked man from God, and the heritage appointed unto him by God.   27:13; 31:2, 3

21 But Job answered and said,

2 Hear diligently my speech, and let this be your consolations.

3 ^TSuffer me that I may speak; and after that I have spoken, ^Rmock on.   *Bear with me* · 16:10

4 As for me, *is* my complaint to man? and if *it were so,* why should not my spirit be troubled?

5 ^TMark me, and be astonished, ^Rand lay *your* hand upon *your* mouth.   *Look at me* · Judg. 18:19

6 Even when I remember I am afraid, and trembling taketh hold on my flesh.

7 ᴿWherefore do the wicked live, become old, yea, are mighty in power?   Ps. 17:10, 14; Hab. 1:13, 16

8 Their seed is established in their sight with them, and their offspring before their eyes.

9 Their houses *are* safe from fear, ᴿneither *is* the rod of God upon them.   Ps. 73:5

10 Their bull ᵀgendereth, and faileth not; their cow calveth, and casteth not her calf.   *breeds*

11 They send forth their little ones like a flock, and their children dance.

12 They take the timbrel and harp, and rejoice at the sound of the ᵀorgan.   *flute*

13 They ᴿspend their days in wealth, and in a moment go down to the ᵀgrave. v. 23; 36:11 · Heb. *Sheol*

14 ᴿTherefore they say unto God, Depart from us; for we desire not the knowledge of thy ways.   22:17

15 ᴿWhat *is* the Almighty, that we should serve him? and ᴿwhat profit should we have, if we pray unto him? 22:17; 34:9 · 35:3; Mal. 3:14

16 Lo, their good *is* not in their hand: ᴿthe counsel of the wicked is far from me. 22:18; Ps. 1:1; Prov. 1:10

17 How oft is the ᵀcandle of the wicked put out! and *how oft* cometh their destruction upon them! *God* ᴿdistributeth sorrows in his anger. *lamp* · [31:2, 3; Luke 12:46]

18 ᴿThey are as stubble before the wind, and as chaff that the storm carrieth away. Ps. 1:4; Is. 17:13

19 God layeth up ᵀhis iniquity for his children: he rewardeth him, and he shall know *it.*   *a man's*

20 His eyes shall see his destruction, and ᴿhe shall drink of the wrath of the Almighty.   Rev. 14:10

21 For what pleasure *hath* he in his house after him, when the number of his months is cut off in the midst?

22 ᴿShall *any* teach God knowledge? seeing he judgeth those that are high. [Rom. 11:34; 1 Cor. 2:16]

23 One dieth in his full strength, being wholly at ease and quiet.

24 His breasts are full of milk, and his bones are moistened with marrow.

25 And another dieth in the bitterness of his soul, and never eateth with pleasure.

26 They shall ᴿlie down alike in the dust, and the worms shall cover them.   3:13; 20:11; Eccl. 9:2

27 Behold, I know your thoughts, and the ᵀdevices *which* ye wrongfully imagine against me.   *schemes*

28 For ye say, Where *is* the house of the prince? and where *are* the dwelling places of the wicked?

29 Have ye not asked them that go by the way? and do ye not know their ᵀtokens,   *signs*

30 ᴿThat the wicked is reserved to the day of destruction? they shall be brought forth to the day of wrath. 20:29; [Prov. 16:4; 2 Pet. 2:9]

31 Who shall declare his way to his face? and who shall repay him *what* he hath done?

32 Yet shall he be brought to the grave, and ᵀshall remain in the tomb. *a vigil shall be kept over*

33 The clods of the valley shall be sweet unto him, and ᴿevery man shall ᵀdraw after him, as *there are* innumerable before him.   Heb. 9:27 · *follow*

34 How then comfort ye me in vain, seeing in your answers there remaineth ᵀfalsehood? *faithlessness*

22 Then El'-i-phaz the Te'-man-ite answered and said,

2 ᴿCan a man be profitable unto God, as he that is wise may be profitable unto himself?   35:7

3 *Is it* any pleasure to the Almighty, that thou art righteous? or *is it* gain *to him,* that thou makest thy ways ᵀperfect?   *blameless*

4 Will he reprove thee for fear of thee? will he enter with thee into judgment?

5 *Is* not thy wickedness great? and thine iniquities infinite?

6 For thou hast ᴿtaken a pledge from thy brother for nought, and stripped the naked of their clothing. [Ex. 22:26, 27]; Deut. 24:6, 10, 17

7 Thou hast not given water to

the weary to drink, and thou ᴿhast withholden bread from the hungry.   Is. 58:7; Ezek. 18:7; Matt. 25:42

8 But *as for* the mighty man, he had the earth; and the honourable man dwelt in it.

9 Thou hast sent widows away empty, and the arms of the fatherless have been ᵀbroken.   *crushed*

10 Therefore snares *are* round about thee, and sudden fear troubleth thee;

11 Or darkness, *that* thou canst not see; and abundance of ᴿwaters cover thee.   38:34; Ps. 124:5; Lam. 3:54

12 *Is* not God in the height of heaven? and behold the height of the stars, how high they are!

13 And thou sayest, How doth God know? can he judge through the ᵀdark cloud?   *thick darkness*

14 Thick clouds *are* a covering to him, that he seeth not; and he walketh in the circuit of heaven.

15 ᵀHast thou marked the old way which wicked men have trodden?   *Will you keep to the*

16 Which ᴿwere cut down out of time, whose foundation was overflown with a flood: Ps. 90:5; Is. 28:2

17 ᴿWhich said unto God, Depart from us: and what can the Almighty do for them?   21:14, 15

18 Yet he filled their houses with good *things:* but the counsel of the wicked is far from me.

19 ᴿThe righteous see *it*, and are glad: and the innocent laugh them to scorn.   Ps. 52:6; 58:10; 107:42

20 Whereas our substance is not cut down, but the remnant of them the fire consumeth.

21 Acquaint now thyself with him, and ᴿbe at peace: thereby good shall come unto thee.   Is. 27:5

22 Receive, I pray thee, the law from his mouth, and ᴿlay up his words in thine heart.   [Ps. 119:11]

23 If thou return to the Almighty, thou shalt be built up, thou shalt put away iniquity far from thy ᵀtabernacles.   *tents*

24 Then shalt thou ᴿlay up gold as the dust, and the *gold* of O'-phir as the stones of the brooks. 2 Chr. 1:15

25 Yea, the Almighty shall be

thy defence, and thou shalt have plenty of silver.

26 For then shalt thou have thy ᴿdelight in the Almighty, and shalt lift up thy face unto God.   27:10

27 ᴿThou shalt make thy prayer unto him, and he shall hear thee, and thou shalt pay thy vows. 11:13

28 Thou shalt also decree a thing, and it shall be established unto thee: and the light shall shine upon thy ways.

29 When *men* are cast down, then thou shalt say, *There is* lifting up; and ᴿhe shall save the humble person.   [Matt. 23:12; 1 Pet. 5:5]

30 He shall deliver the island of the innocent: and it is delivered by the pureness of thine hands.

23 Then Job answered and said,

2 Even to day *is* my ᴿcomplaint bitter: my stroke is heavier than my groaning.   7:11

3 ᴿOh that I knew where I might find him! *that* I might come *even* to his seat!   13:3, 18; 16:21; 31:35

4 I would order *my* cause before him, and fill my mouth with arguments.

5 I would know the words *which* he would answer me, and understand what he would say unto me.

6 ᴿWill he plead against me with *his* great power? No; but he would put *strength* in me.   Is. 57:16

7 There the righteous might dispute with him; so should I be delivered for ever from my judge.

8 ᴿBehold, I go forward, but he *is* not *there;* and backward, but I cannot perceive him: 9:11; 35:14

9 On the left hand, where he doth work, but I cannot behold *him:* he hideth himself on the right hand, that I cannot see *him:*

10 But ᴿhe knoweth the way that I take: *when* he hath tried me, I shall come forth as gold.   [Ps. 1:6]

11 ᴿMy foot hath ᵀheld his steps, his way have I kept, and not declined.   31:7; Ps. 17:5 · *held fast to*

12 Neither have I gone back from the ᴿcommandment of his lips; ᴿI have esteemed the words

of his mouth more than my necessary *food*.   6:10; 22:22 · Ps. 44:18

13 But he *is* in one *mind,* and
who can turn him? and *what* his
soul desireth, even *that* he doeth.

14 For he performeth *the thing
that is* appointed for me: and
many such *things are* with him.

15 Therefore am I troubled at
his presence: when I consider, I
am afraid of him.

16 For God ᴿmaketh my heart
ᵀsoft, and the Almighty troubleth
me: Ps. 22:14 · *weak*

17 Because I was not ᴿcut off
before the darkness, *neither* hath
he ᵀcovered the darkness from my
face.   10:18, 19 · *hidden deep darkness*

24 Why, seeing ᴿtimes are not
hidden from the Almighty,
do they that know him not see his
ᴿdays?   [Acts 1:7] · Jer. 46:10; Zeph. 1:7

2 *Some* remove the ᴿland-
marks; they violently take away
flocks, and feed *thereof.* Hos. 5:10

3 They drive away the ass of
the fatherless, they take the
widow's ox for a pledge.

4 They turn the needy out of
the way: the ᴿpoor of the earth
hide themselves together. 29:16

5 Behold, *as* wild ᵀasses in the
desert, go they forth to their work;
rising betimes for a prey: the
wilderness *yieldeth* food for them
and for *their* children. *donkeys*

6 They reap *every one* his corn
in the field: and they gather the
vintage of the wicked.

7 They ᴿcause the naked to
lodge without clothing, that *they
have* no covering in the cold. 22:6

8 They are wet with the showers of the mountains, and ᴿem-
braceᵀ the rock for want of a shelter.   Lam. 4:5 · *huddle around*

9 They pluck the fatherless
from the breast, and take a pledge
of the poor.

10 They cause *him* to go naked
without clothing, and they take
away the sheaf *from* the hungry;

11 *Which* make oil within their
walls, *and* tread *their* winepresses, and suffer thirst.

12 Men groan from out of the

city, and the soul of the wounded
crieth out: yet God layeth not folly
to *them.*

13 They are of those that rebel
against the light; they know not
the ways thereof, nor abide in the
paths thereof.

14 ᴿThe murderer rising with the
light killeth the poor and needy,
and in the night is as a thief. Ps. 10:8

15 ᴿThe eye also of the adulterer
waiteth for the twilight, ᴿsaying,
No eye shall see me: and dis-
guiseth *his* face. Prov. 7:7–10 · Ps. 10:11

16 In the dark they dig through
houses, *which* they had marked
for themselves in the daytime:
ᴿthey know not the light. [John 3:20]

17 For the morning *is* to them
even as the shadow of death: if
one know *them, they are in* the
terrors of the shadow of death.

18 He *is* swift as the waters;
their portion is cursed in the
earth: he beholdeth not the way of
the vineyards.

19 Drought and heat consume
the snow waters: *so doth* the
grave *those which* have sinned.

20 The womb shall forget him;
the worm shall feed sweetly on
him; ᴿhe shall be no more remembered; and wickedness shall be
broken as a tree. 18:17; Prov. 10:7

21 He ᵀevil entreateth the barren
that beareth not: and doeth not
good to the widow. *preys upon*

22 ᵀHe draweth also the mighty
with his power: he riseth up, and
no *man* is sure of life.   God

23 *Though* it be given him *to be*
in safety, whereon he resteth; yet
his eyes *are* upon their ways.

24 They are exalted for a little
while, ᵀbut are gone and brought
low; they are taken out of the way
as all *other,* and cut off as the tops
of the ears of corn.   *then*

25 And if *it be* not *so* now, who
will ᵀmake me a liar, and make
my speech nothing worth? *prove*

25 Then answered ᴿBil'-dad
the Shu'-hite, and said, 8:1

2 Dominion and fear *are* with
him; he maketh peace in his high
places.

3 Is there any number of his armies? and upon whom doth not ^Rhis light arise? James 1:17
4 How then can man be justified with God? or how can he be clean *that is* born of a woman?
5 Behold even to the moon, and it shineth not; yea, the stars are not pure in his ^Rsight. 15:15
6 How much less man, *that is* ^Ra ^Tworm? and the son of man, *which is* a worm? Ps. 22:6 · *a maggot*

26 But Job answered and said,
2 How hast thou helped *him that is* without power? *how* savest thou the arm *that hath* no strength?
3 How hast thou counseled *him that hath* no wisdom? and *how* hast thou plentifully declared the ^Tthing as it is? *sound advice*
4 To whom hast thou uttered words? and whose spirit came from thee?
5 Dead *things* ^Tare formed from under the waters, and the inhabitants thereof. *tremble*
6 Hell *is* naked before him, and destruction hath no covering.
7 ^RHe stretcheth out the north over the empty place, *and* hangeth the earth upon nothing. Ps. 24:2
8 ^RHe bindeth up the waters in his thick clouds; and the cloud is not rent under them. 37:11; Prov. 30:4
9 He ^Tholdeth back the face of his throne, *and* spreadeth his cloud upon it. *covers*
10 ^RHe hath compassed the waters with bounds, until the day and night come to an end. Ps. 33:7
11 The pillars of heaven tremble and are ^Tastonished at his reproof. *amazed*
12 He divideth the sea with his power, and by his understanding he smiteth through the proud.
13 By his spirit he hath garnished the heavens; his hand hath formed the crooked serpent.
14 Lo, these *are* parts of his ways: but how little a portion is heard of him? but the thunder of his power who can understand?

27 Moreover Job continued his parable, and said,

2 *As* God liveth, ^R*who* hath taken away my ^Tjudgment; and the Almighty, *who* hath vexed my soul; 34:5 · *justice*
3 ^TAll the while my breath *is* in me, and the ^Tspirit of God *is* in my nostrils; *As long as · breath of*
4 My lips shall not speak wickedness, nor my tongue utter deceit.
5 God forbid that I should justify you: till I die ^RI will not remove mine integrity from me. 2:9; 13:15
6 My righteousness I ^Rhold fast, and will not let it go: ^Rmy heart shall not reproach *me* so long as I live. 2:3; 33:9 · Acts 24:16
7 Let mine enemy be as the wicked, and he that riseth up against me as the unrighteous.
8 For what *is* the hope of the hypocrite, though he hath gained, when God taketh away his soul?
9 ^RWill God hear his cry when trouble cometh upon him? 35:12, 13
10 ^RWill he delight himself in the Almighty? will he always call upon God? 22:26, 27; [Ps. 37:4; Is. 58:14]
11 I will teach you ^Tby the hand of God: *that* which *is* with the Almighty will I not conceal. *about*
12 Behold, all ye yourselves have seen *it*; why then are ye thus altogether vain?
13 This *is* the portion of a wicked man with God, and the heritage of oppressors, *which* they shall receive of the Almighty.
14 ^RIf his children be multiplied, *it is* for the sword: and his offspring shall not be satisfied with bread. Deut. 28:41; Esth. 9:10; Hos. 9:13
15 Those that ^Tremain of him shall be buried in death: and his widows shall not weep. *survive him*
16 Though he heap up silver as the dust, and prepare raiment as the clay;
17 He may prepare *it*, but the just shall put *it* on, and the innocent shall divide the silver.
18 He buildeth his house as a moth, and ^Ras a booth *that* the keeper maketh. Is. 1:8; Lam. 2:6

19 The rich man shall lie down, but he shall not be gathered: he openeth his eyes, and he *is* not.

20 ^RTerrors take hold on him as waters, a tempest stealeth him away in the night.   18:11

21 The east wind carrieth him away, and he ^Tdeparteth: and as a storm hurleth him out of his place.   *is gone*

22 For *God* shall cast upon him, and not ^Rspare: he would fain flee out of his hand.   Jer. 13:14; Ezek. 5:11

23 *Men* shall clap their hands at him, and shall hiss him out of his place.

28 Surely there is a vein for the silver, and a place for gold *where* they ^Tfine *it*.   *refine*

2 Iron is taken out of the ^Tearth, and brass *is* molten *out of* the stone.   Lit. *dust*

3 He setteth an end to darkness, and searcheth out all perfection: the stones of darkness, and the shadow of death.

4 The flood breaketh out from the inhabitant; *even the waters* forgotten of the foot: they are dried up, they are gone away from men.

5 *As for* the earth, out of it cometh bread: and under it is turned up as it were fire.

6 The stones of it *are* the place of sapphires: and it hath dust of gold.

7 *There is* a path which no fowl knoweth, and which the vulture's eye hath not seen:

8 The lion's whelps have not trodden it, nor the fierce lion passed by it.

9 He putteth forth his hand upon the ^Trock; he overturneth the mountains by the roots.   *flint*

10 He cutteth out ^Trivers among the rocks; and his eye seeth every precious thing.   *channels through*

11 He bindeth the floods from overflowing; and *the thing that is* hid bringeth he forth to light.

12 ^RBut where shall wisdom be found? and where *is* the place of understanding?   Eccl. 7:24

13 Man knoweth not the ^Rprice^T thereof; neither is it found in the land of the living.   Prov. 3:15 · *value*

14 ^RThe ^Tdepth saith, It *is* not in me: and the sea saith, *It is* not with me.   v. 22 · *deep*

15 It ^Rcannot be gotten for gold, neither shall silver be weighed *for* the price thereof.   Prov. 3:13–15

16 It cannot be valued with the gold of O′-phir, with the precious onyx, or the sapphire.

17 The ^Rgold and the crystal cannot equal it: and the exchange of it *shall not be for* ^Tjewels of fine gold.   Prov. 8:10; 16:16 · *vessels*

18 No mention shall be made of coral, or of pearls: for the price of wisdom *is* above ^Rrubies.   Prov. 8:11

19 The topaz of E-thi-o′-pi-a shall not equal it, neither shall it be valued with pure gold.

20 ^RWhence then cometh wisdom? and where *is* the place of understanding?   [Ps. 111:10; Prov. 1:7]

21 Seeing it is hid from the eyes of all living, and ^Tkept close from the fowls of the air.   *concealed*

22 Destruction and death say, We have heard the ^Tfame thereof with our ears.   *report of it*

23 God understandeth the way thereof, and he knoweth the place thereof.

24 For he looketh to the ends of the earth, *and* ^Rseeth under the whole heaven;   [Ps. 11:4; 66:7; Prov. 15:3]

25 ^RTo make the weight for the winds; and he weigheth the waters by measure.   Ps. 135:7

26 When he ^Rmade a decree for the rain, and a way for the lightning of the thunder;   37:3; 38:25

27 Then did he see ^Tit, and declare it; he prepared it, yea, and searched it out.   *Wisdom*

28 And unto man he said, Behold, ^Rthe fear of the LORD, that *is* wisdom; and to depart from evil *is* understanding.   [Ps. 111:10; Prov. 9:10]

29 Moreover Job continued his parable, and said,

2 Oh that I were as *in* months ^Rpast, as *in* the days *when* God ^Rpreserved me;   1:1–5 · 1:10

3 When his candle shined upon

my head, *and when* by his light I
walked *through* darkness;

4 As I was in the days of my
youth, when ᴿthe secret of God
was upon my tabernacle;   15:8

5 When the Almighty *was* yet
with me, *when* my children *were*
about me;

6 When ᴿI washed my steps
with butter, and ᴿthe rock poured
me out rivers of oil;   20:17 · Ps. 81:16

7 When I went out to the gate
through the city, *when* I prepared
my seat in the street!

8 The young men saw me, and
hid themselves: and the aged
arose, *and* stood up.

9 The princes refrained talking, and ᴿlaid *their* hand on their
mouth.   21:5

10 The nobles held their peace,
and their ᴿtongue ᵀcleaved to the
roof of their mouth. Ps. 137:6 · *stuck*

11 When the ear heard *me*, then
it blessed me; and when the eye
saw *me*, it gave witness to me:

12 Because I delivered the poor
that cried, and the fatherless, and
him that had none to help him.

13 The blessing of him that was
ready to perish came upon me:
and I caused the widow's heart to
sing for joy.

14 ᴿI put on righteousness, and
it clothed me: my judgment *was*
as a robe and a diadem. [Eph. 6:14]

15 I was ᴿeyes to the blind, and
feet *was* I to the lame.   Num. 10:31

16 I *was* a father to the poor:
and ᴿthe cause *which* I knew not I
searched out.   Prov. 29:7

17 And I brake ᴿthe jaws of the
wicked, and plucked the spoil out
of his teeth.   Ps. 58:6; Prov. 30:14

18 Then I said, ᴿI shall die in my
nest, and I shall multiply *my* days
as the sand.   Ps. 30:6

19 ᴿMy root *was* spread out ᴿby
the waters, and the dew lay all
night upon my branch. 18:16 · Ps. 1:3

20 My glory *was* fresh in me,
and my ᴿbow was renewed in my
hand.   Gen. 49:24; Ps. 18:34

21 Unto me *men* gave ear, and
waited, and kept silence at my
counsel.

22 After my words they spake
not again; and my speech
dropped upon them.

23 And they waited for me as for
the rain; and they opened their
mouth wide *as* for ᴿthe ᵀlatter
rain.   [Zech. 10:1] · *spring*

24 *If* I laughed on them, they
believed *it* not; and the light of my
countenance they cast not down.

25 I chose out their way, and sat
chief, and dwelt as a king in the
army, as one *that* comforteth the
mourners.

30 But now *they that are*
younger than I have me in
derision, whose fathers I would
have disdained to have set with
the dogs of my flock.

2 Yea, whereto *might* the
strength of their hands *profit* me,
in whom old age was perished?

3 For want and famine *they
were* ᵀsolitary; fleeing into the
wilderness in former time desolate and waste.   *gaunt*

4 Who cut up mallows by the
bushes, and juniper roots *for* their
ᵀmeat.   *food*

5 They were driven forth from
among *men*, (they ᵀcried after
them as *after* a thief;)   *shouted at*

6 To dwell in the ᵀcliffs of the
ᵀvalleys, *in* caves of the earth, and
in the rocks.   *clefts · wadis*

7 Among the bushes they
brayed; under the nettles they
were gathered together.

8 *They were* children of fools,
yea, children of base men: they
were viler than the earth.

9 ᴿAnd now am I their song,
yea, I am their byword.   Ps. 69:12

10 They abhor me, they flee far
from me, and spare not ᴿto spit in
my face. 17:6; Is. 50:6; Matt. 26:67; 27:30

11 Because he hath loosed my
cord, and afflicted me, they have
also let loose the bridle before me.

12 Upon *my* right *hand* rise the
youth; they push away my feet,
and ᴿthey raise up against me the
ways of their destruction.   19:12

13 They ᵀmar my path, they ᵀset
forward my calamity, they have
no helper.   *break up · promote*

14 They came *upon me* as ^Ta wide breaking in *of waters:* in the desolation they rolled themselves *upon me.*　　　　*broad breakers*

15 Terrors are turned upon me: they pursue my ^Tsoul as the wind: and my ^Twelfare passeth away as a cloud.　　　　*honour · prosperity*

16 And now my soul is ^Rpoured out upon me; the days of affliction have taken hold upon me.　Is. 53:12

17 My bones are pierced in me in the night season: and my ^Tsinews take no rest.　　*gnawing pains*

18 By the great force *of my disease* is my garment ^Tchanged: it bindeth me about as the collar of my coat.　　　　*disfigured*

19 He hath cast me into the mire, and I am become like dust and ashes.

20 I cry unto thee, and thou dost not ^Thear me: I stand up, and thou regardest me *not.*　　Lit. *answer*

21 Thou art become cruel to me: with thy strong hand thou ^Ropposest thyself against me.　19:6, 22

22 Thou liftest me up to the wind; thou causest me to ride *upon it,* and ^Tdissolvest my substance.　　　*spoil my success*

23 For I know *that* thou wilt bring me *to* death, and *to* the house appointed for all living.

24 Howbeit he will not stretch out *his* hand to the grave, though they cry in his destruction.

25 ^RDid not I weep for him that was in trouble? was *not* my soul grieved for the poor?　Rom. 12:15

26 ^RWhen I looked for good, then evil came *unto me:* and when I waited for light, there came darkness.　3:25, 26; Jer. 8:15

27 My bowels boiled, and rested not: the days of affliction ^Tprevented me.　　　　*confront*

28 ^RI went mourning without the sun: I stood up, *and* I cried in the congregation.　v. 31; Ps. 38:6; 42:9; 43:2

29 ^RI am a brother to dragons, and a companion to owls.　Ps. 44:19

30 ^RMy skin ^Tis black upon me, and my bones are burned with heat.　Ps. 119:83; Lam. 4:8 · *grows black*

31 My harp also is *turned* to mourning, and my ^Torgan into the voice of them that weep.　*flute*

31 I made a covenant with mine eyes; why then should I ^Tthink upon a maid?　*look intently*

2 For what ^Rportion of God *is there* from above? and *what* inheritance of the Almighty from on high?　　　　20:29

3 *Is* not destruction to the wicked? and a strange *punishment* to the workers of iniquity?

4 ^RDoth not he see my ways, and count all my steps?　24:23; 28:24

5 If I have walked with vanity, or if my foot hath hasted to deceit;

6 Let me be weighed in an even balance, that God may know mine ^Rintegrity.　23:10; 27:5, 6

7 If my step hath turned out of the way, and mine heart walked after mine eyes, and if any blot hath cleaved to mine hands;

8 *Then* let me sow, and let another eat; yea, let my ^Toffspring be ^Trooted out.　*harvest · uprooted*

9 If mine heart have been deceived by a woman, or *if* I have laid wait at my neighbour's door;

10 *Then* let my wife grind unto ^Ranother, and let others bow down upon her.　2 Sam. 12:11; Jer. 8:10

11 For this *is* an heinous crime; yea, ^Rit *is* an iniquity *to be punished by* the judges.　v. 28; Gen. 38:24

12 For it *is* a fire *that* consumeth to destruction, and would root out all mine increase.

13 If I did ^Rdespise the cause of my manservant or of my maidservant, when they ^Tcontended with me;　[Deut. 24:14, 15] · *complained against*

14 What then shall I do when God riseth up? and when he visiteth, what shall I answer him?

15 ^RDid not he that made me in the womb make him? and did not one fashion us in the womb?　34:19

16 If I have withheld the poor from *their* desire, or have caused the eyes of the widow to fail;

17 Or have eaten my morsel myself alone, and the fatherless hath not eaten thereof;

18 (For from my youth he was

brought up with me, as *with* a father, and I have guided her from my mother's womb;)

19 If I have seen any perish for want of clothing, or any poor without covering;

20 If his ᵀloins have not blessed me, and *if* he were *not* warmed with the fleece of my sheep; heart

21 If I have lifted up my hand ᴿagainst the fatherless, when I saw my help in the gate: 22:9

22 *Then* let mine arm fall from my shoulder blade, and mine arm be broken from the bone.

23 For ᴿdestruction *from* God *was* a terror to me, and by reason of his ᵀhighness I could not endure.   Is. 13:6 · *magnificence*

24 If I have made gold my hope, or have said to the fine gold, *Thou art* my confidence;

25 ᴿIf I rejoiced because my wealth *was* great, and because mine hand had gotten much; 1:3, 10

26 ᴿIf I beheld the sun when it shined, or the moon walking *in* brightness; [Deut. 4:19; 17:3]; Ezek. 8:16

27 And my heart hath been secretly enticed, or my mouth hath kissed my hand:

28 This also *were* an iniquity *to be punished by* the judge: for I should have denied the God *that is* above.

29 If I rejoiced at the destruction of him that hated me, or lifted up myself when evil found him;

30 ᴿNeither have I suffered my mouth to sin by wishing a curse to his ᵀsoul.   [Matt. 5:44] · *life*

31 If the men of my tabernacle said not, Oh that we had of his flesh! we cannot be satisfied.

32 ᴿThe stranger did not lodge in the street: *but* I opened my doors to the traveller. Gen. 19:2, 3

33 If I covered my transgressions ᵀas Adam, by hiding mine iniquity in my bosom: Or *as men do*

34 Did I fear a great ᴿmultitude, or did the contempt of families terrify me, that I kept silence, *and* went not out of the door? Ex. 23:2

35 ᴿOh that one would hear me! behold, my desire *is*, ᴿ*that* the

Almighty would answer me, and *that* mine adversary had written a book. 19:7; 30:20, 24, 28 · 13:22, 24; 33:10

36 Surely I would take it upon my shoulder, *and* bind it *as* a crown to me.

37 I would declare unto him the number of my steps; as a prince would I go near unto him.

38 If my land cry against me, or that the furrows likewise thereof ᵀcomplain; Lit. *weep*

39 If ᴿI have eaten the fruits thereof without money, or ᴿhave caused the owners thereof to lose their life: [James 5:4] · 1 Kin. 21:19

40 Let thistles grow instead of wheat, and cockle instead of barley. The words of Job are ended.

32 So these three men ceased to answer Job, because he *was* righteous in his own eyes.

2 Then was kindled the wrath of E-li′-hu the son of Bar′-a-chel the Buz′-ite, of the kindred of Ram: against Job was his wrath kindled, because he ᴿjustified himself rather than God.   27:5, 6

3 Also against his three friends was his wrath kindled, because they had found no answer, and *yet* had condemned Job.

4 Now E-li′-hu had waited till Job had spoken, because they *were* elder than he.

5 When E-li′-hu saw that *there was* no answer in the mouth of *these* three men, then his wrath was kindled.

6 And E-li′-hu the son of Bar′-a-chel the Buz′-ite answered and said, I *am* young, and ye *are* very old; wherefore I was afraid, and durst not shew you mine opinion.

7 I said, ᵀDays should speak, and multitude of years should teach wisdom. Age

8 But *there is* a spirit in man: and ᴿthe ᵀinspiration of the Almighty giveth them understanding. 1 Kin. 3:12; 4:29; [Matt. 11:25] · *breath*

9 ᴿGreat men are not *always* wise: neither do the aged understand judgment. [1 Cor. 1:26]

10 Therefore I said, Hearken to me; I also will shew mine opinion.

11 Behold, I waited for your words; I gave ear to your ᵀreasons, whilst ye ᵀsearched out what to say.   *reasonings · pondered*

12 Yea, I attended unto you, and, behold, *there was* none of you that convinced Job, *or* that answered his words:

13 ᴿLest ye should say, We have found out wisdom: God thrusteth him down, not man.   [1 Cor. 1:29]

14 Now he hath not directed *his* words against me: neither will I answer him with your speeches.

15 They were amazed, they answered no more: ᵀthey left off speaking.   *words escape them*

16 When I had waited, (for they spake not, but stood still, *and* answered no more;)

17 *I said,* I will answer also my part, I also will shew mine opinion.

18 For I am full of matter, the spirit within me constraineth me.

19 Behold, my belly *is* as wine *which* hath no vent; it is ready to burst like new ᵀbottles.   *wineskins*

20 I will speak, that I may ᵀbe refreshed: I will open my lips and answer.   *be relieved*

21 Let me not, I pray you, accept any man's person, neither let me give flattering titles unto man.

22 For I know not to give flattering titles; *in so doing* my maker would soon take me ᴿaway.   27:8

33

Wherefore, Job, I pray thee, hear my speeches, and hearken to all my words.

2 Behold, now I have opened my mouth, my tongue hath spoken in my mouth.

3 My words *shall be of* the uprightness of my heart: and my lips shall utter knowledge clearly.

4 ᴿThe spirit of God hath made me, and the breath of the Almighty hath given me life.   [Gen. 2:7]

5 If thou canst answer me, set *thy words* in order before me, stand up.

6 ᴿBehold, I *am* according to thy wish in God's stead: I also am formed out of the clay.   4:19

7 ᴿBehold, my terror shall not make thee afraid, neither shall my hand be heavy upon thee.   9:34

8 Surely thou hast spoken in mine hearing, and I have heard the voice of *thy* words, *saying,*

9 ᴿI am clean without transgression, I *am* innocent; neither *is there* iniquity in me.   10:7

10 Behold, he findeth occasions against me, ᴿhe counteth me for his enemy,   13:24; 16:9

11 He putteth my feet in the stocks, he marketh all my paths.

12 Behold, *in* this thou art not ᵀjust: I will answer thee, that God is greater than man.   *right*

13 Why dost thou ᴿstrive against him? for he giveth not account of any of his matters.   40:2; [Is. 45:9]

14 For God speaketh once, yea twice, *yet man* perceiveth it not.

15 ᴿIn a dream, in a vision of the night, when deep sleep falleth upon men, in slumberings upon the bed;   [Num. 12:6]

16 Then he openeth the ears of men, and sealeth their instruction,

17 That he may ᵀwithdraw man *from his* purpose, and hide pride from man.   *turn man from his deed*

18 He keepeth back his soul from the pit, and his life from ᵀperishing by the sword. Lit. *passing*

19 ᵀHe is chastened also with pain upon his ᴿbed, and the multitude of his bones with strong *pain:*   Man · 30:17

20 So that his life abhorreth bread, and his soul dainty meat.

21 His flesh is ᵀconsumed away, that it cannot be seen; and his bones *that* were not seen stick out.   *wastes away from sight*

22 Yea, his soul draweth near unto the ᵀgrave, and his life to the destroyers.   Lit. *pit*

23 If there be a messenger with him, ᵀan interpreter, one among a thousand, to shew unto man his uprightness;   *a mediator*

24 Then he is gracious unto him, and saith, Deliver him from going down to the pit: I have found ᵀa ransom.   *an atonement*

25 His flesh shall be ᵀfresher

than a child's: he shall return to the days of his youth: *young as*

26 He shall pray unto God, and he will be ᵀfavourable unto him: and he shall see his face with joy: for he will ᵀrender unto man his righteousness.   *delight in him · restore*

27 He looketh upon men, and *if any* ᴿsay, I have sinned, and perverted *that which was* right, and it profited me not;   [1 John 1:9]

28 He will ᴿdeliver his soul from going into the pit, and his life shall see the light.   Is. 38:17

29 Lo, all these *things* worketh God oftentimes with man,

30 ᴿTo bring back his soul from the pit, to be enlightened with the light of the living.   Ps. 56:13

31 Mark well, O Job, hearken unto me: hold thy peace, and I will speak.

32 If thou hast any thing to say, answer me: speak, for I desire to justify thee.

33 If not, ᴿhearken unto me: ᵀhold thy peace, and I shall teach thee wisdom.   Ps. 34:11 · *keep silent*

34
Furthermore E-li'-hu answered and said,

2 Hear my words, O ye wise *men;* and give ear unto me, ye that have knowledge.

3 ᴿFor the ear trieth words, as the mouth tasteth meat.   6:30; 12:11

4 Let us choose to us ᵀjudgment: let us know among ourselves what *is* good.   *justice*

5 For Job hath said, ᴿI am righteous: and ᴿGod hath taken away my ᵀjudgment. 13:18; 33:9 · 27:2 · *justice*

6 ᴿShould I lie against my right? my wound *is* incurable without transgression.   6:4; 9:17

7 What man *is* like Job, *who* drinketh up scorning like water?

8 Which goeth in company with the workers of iniquity, and walketh with wicked men.

9 For ᴿhe hath said, It profiteth a man nothing that he should delight himself with God.   Mal. 3:14

10 Therefore hearken unto me, ye men of understanding: ᴿfar be it from God, *that he should do* wickedness; and *from* the Al-

mighty, *that he should commit* iniquity.   8:3; 36:23; Ps. 92:15; Rom. 9:14

11 ᴿFor the work of a man shall he render unto him, and cause every man to find according to *his* ways.   Ps. 62:12; [Matt. 16:27]; Rom. 2:6

12 Yea, surely God will not do wickedly, neither will the Almighty ᴿpervert judgment.   8:3

13 Who hath given him a charge over the earth? or who hath disposed the whole world?

14 If he set his heart upon man, *if* he ᴿgather unto himself his spirit and his breath;   12:10; Ps. 104:29

15 ᴿAll flesh shall perish together, and man shall turn again unto dust.   10:9; [Gen. 3:19]; [Eccl. 12:7]

16 If now *thou hast* understanding, hear this: hearken to the voice of my words.

17 Shall even he that hateth right govern? and wilt thou ᴿcondemn him that is most just?   40:8

18 ᴿ*Is it fit* to say to a king, *Thou art* ᵀwicked? *and* to princes, *Ye are* ungodly?   Ex. 22:28 · *worthless*

19 *How much less to him* that accepteth not the persons of princes, nor regardeth the rich more than the poor? for ᴿthey all *are* the work of his hands.   31:15

20 In a moment shall they die, and the people shall be troubled ᴿat midnight, and pass away: and the mighty shall be taken away without hand.   v. 25; 36:20; Ex. 12:29

21 ᴿFor his eyes *are* upon the ways of man, and he seeth all his goings.   31:4; Ps. 34:15; [Prov. 5:21; 15:3]

22 ᴿ*There is* no darkness, nor shadow of death, where the workers of iniquity may hide themselves.   [Ps. 139:11, 12; Amos 9:2, 3]

23 For he will not lay upon man more *than right;* that he should enter into judgment with God.

24 ᴿHe shall break in pieces mighty men without number, and set others in their stead.   [Dan. 2:21]

25 Therefore he knoweth their works, and he ᵀoverturneth *them* in the night, so that they are ᵀdestroyed.   *overthrows · crushed*

26 He striketh them as wicked men in the open sight of others;

27 Because they ^Rturned back from him, and would not consider any of his ways: 1 Sam. 15:11

28 So that they cause the cry of the poor to come unto him, and he heareth the cry of the afflicted.

29 When he giveth quietness, who then can make trouble? and when he hideth *his* face, who then can behold him? whether *it be done* against a nation, or against a man ^Tonly: *alone*

30 That the hypocrite reign not, lest the people be ensnared.

31 Surely it is meet to be said unto God, I have borne *chastisement,* I will not offend *any more:*

32 *That which* I see not teach thou me: if I have done iniquity, I will do no more.

33 *Should it be* according to thy ^Tmind? he will recompense it, whether thou refuse, or whether thou choose; and not I: therefore speak what thou knowest.   *terms*

34 Let men ^Tof understanding tell me, and let a wise man hearken unto me.   Lit. *of heart*

35 ^RJob hath spoken without knowledge, and his words *were* without wisdom.   35:16; 38:2

36 My desire *is that* Job may be tried unto the ^Tend because of *his* answers for wicked men.   *utmost*

37 For he addeth ^Rrebellion unto his sin, he clappeth *his hands* among us, and multiplieth his words against God.   7:11; 10:1

35 E-li′-hu spake moreover, and said,

2 Thinkest thou this to be right, *that* thou saidst, My righteousness *is* more than God's?

3 For ^Rthou saidst, What advantage will it be unto thee? *and,* What profit shall I have, *if I be cleansed* from my sin?   21:15; 34:9

4 I will answer thee, and ^Rthy companions with thee.   34:8

5 ^RLook unto the heavens, and see; and behold the clouds *which* are higher than thou.   Gen. 15:5

6 If thou sinnest, what doest thou ^Ragainst him? or *if* thy transgressions be multiplied, what doest thou unto him?   7:20; [Jer. 7:19]

7 ^RIf thou be righteous, what givest thou him? or what receiveth he of thine hand?   Ps. 16:2

8 Thy wickedness *may hurt* a man as thou *art;* and thy righteousness *may profit* the son of man.

9 By reason of the multitude of oppressions they make *the oppressed* to cry: they cry out by reason of the arm of the mighty.

10 But none saith, ^RWhere *is* God my maker, ^Rwho giveth songs in the night;   Is. 51:13 · 8:21; Acts 16:25

11 Who ^Rteacheth us more than the beasts of the earth, and maketh us wiser than the fowls of heaven?   Ps. 94:12; [Is. 48:17; 1 Cor. 2:13]

12 ^RThere they cry, but none giveth answer, because of the pride of evil men.   Prov. 1:28

13 ^RSurely God will not hear vanity, neither will the Almighty regard it.   [Prov. 15:29; Is. 1:15; Mic. 3:4]

14 Although thou sayest thou shalt not see him, *yet* ^Tjudgment *is* before him; therefore ^Rtrust thou in him.   *justice* · [Ps. 37:5, 6]

15 But now, because *it is* not *so,* he hath ^Rvisited in his anger; yet he knoweth *it* not in great extremity: Ps. 89:32

16 ^RTherefore doth Job open his mouth in vain; he multiplieth words without knowledge.   34:35

36 E-li′-hu also proceeded, and said,

2 ^TSuffer me a little, and I will shew thee that *I have* yet to speak on God's behalf.   *Bear with me*

3 I will fetch my knowledge from afar, and will ascribe righteousness to my Maker.

4 For truly my words *shall* not *be* false: he that is perfect in knowledge *is* with thee.

5 Behold, God *is* mighty, and despiseth not *any:* ^Rhe *is* mighty in strength *and* wisdom.   [Ps. 99:2–5]

6 He preserveth not the life of the wicked: but giveth ^Tright to the poor.   *justice to the oppressed*

7 ^RHe withdraweth not his eyes from the righteous: but with kings *are they* on the throne; yea, he doth establish them for ever, and they are exalted.   [Ps. 33:18; 34:15]

8 And ᴿif *they be* bound in ᵀfetters, *and* be holden in cords of affliction; Ps. 107:10 · *chains*

9 Then he sheweth them their work, and their transgressions that they have exceeded.

10 ᴿHe openeth also their ear to discipline, and commandeth that they return from iniquity. 33:16

11 If they obey and serve *him,* they shall ᴿspend their days in prosperity, and their years in pleasures. 21:13; [Is. 1:19, 20]

12 But if they obey not, they shall perish by the sword, and they shall die without ᴿknowledge. 4:21

13 But the hypocrites in heart ᴿheap up wrath: they cry not when he bindeth them. [Rom. 2:5]

14 ᴿThey die in youth, and their life *is* among the unclean. Ps. 55:23

15 He delivereth the poor in his affliction, and openeth their ears ᵀin oppression. *by*

16 Even so would he have removed thee out of the strait ᴿinto a broad place, where *there is* no straitness; and that which should be set on thy table *should be* full of ᴿfatness. Ps. 18:19; 31:8 · Ps. 36:8

17 But thou hast fulfilled the judgment of the ᴿwicked: judgment and justice take hold *on* thee. 22:5, 10, 11

18 Because *there is* wrath, *beware* lest he take thee away with *his* stroke: then ᴿa great ransom cannot deliver thee. Ps. 49:7

19 ᴿWill he esteem thy riches? *no,* not gold, nor all the forces of strength. [Prov. 11:4]

20 Desire not the night, when people are cut off in their place.

21 Take heed, regard not iniquity: for ᴿthis hast thou chosen rather than affliction. [Heb. 11:25]

22 Behold, God exalteth by his power: who teacheth like him?

23 ᴿWho hath ᵀenjoined him his way? or who can say, Thou hast wrought iniquity? 34:13 · *assigned him*

24 Remember that thou magnify his work, which men behold.

25 Every man may see it; man may behold *it* afar off.

26 Behold, God *is* great, and we ᴿknow *him* not, ᴿneither can the number of his years be searched out. [1 Cor. 13:12] · [Ps. 90:2]; Heb. 1:12

27 For he ᴿmaketh small the drops of water: they pour down rain according to the vapour thereof; 5:10; 37:6, 11; 38:28; Ps. 147:8

28 Which the clouds do drop *and* distil upon man abundantly.

29 Also can *any* understand the spreadings of the clouds, *or* the noise of his tabernacle?

30 Behold, he ᴿspreadeth his light upon it, and covereth the bottom of the sea. 37:3

31 For ᴿby them judgeth he the people; he ᴿgiveth meat in abundance. [Acts 14:17] · Ps. 104:14, 15

32 ᴿWith clouds he covereth the light; and commandeth it ᵀ*not to shine* by *the cloud* that cometh betwixt. Ps. 147:8 · *to strike the mark*

33 The noise thereof sheweth concerning it, the cattle also concerning ᵀthe vapour. *the rising storm*

37 At this also my heart trembleth, and ᵀis moved out of his place. *leaps from*

2 Hear attentively the ᵀnoise of his voice, and the sound *that* goeth out of his mouth. *thunder*

3 He directeth it under the whole heaven, and his ᵀlightning unto the ends of the earth. *light*

4 After it a voice roareth: he thundereth with the voice of his excellency; and he will not stay them when his voice is heard.

5 God thundereth marvellously with his voice; great things doeth he, which we cannot comprehend.

6 For ᴿhe saith to the snow, Be thou *on* the earth; likewise to the small rain, and to the great rain of his strength. Ps. 147:16, 17

7 He sealeth up the hand of every man; ᴿthat ᴿall men may know his work. Ps. 109:27 · Ps. 19:3, 4

8 Then the beasts go into dens, and remain in their places.

9 Out of the south cometh the whirlwind: and cold out of the north.

10 ᴿBy the breath of God frost is

given: and the breadth of the waters is ᵀstraitened. 38:29, 30 · *frozen*

11 Also by watering he wearieth the thick cloud: he scattereth his bright cloud:

12 And it is turned round about by his counsels: that they may ᴿdo whatsoever he commandeth them upon the face of the ᵀworld in the earth. 36:32; Ps. 148:8 · *whole earth*

13 He causeth it to come, whether for ᵀcorrection, or ᴿfor his land, or for mercy. Lit. *a rod* · 38:26, 27

14 Hearken unto this, O Job: stand still, and ᴿconsider the wondrous works of God. Ps. 111:2

15 Dost thou know when God disposed them, and caused the light of his cloud to shine?

16 ᴿDost thou know the balancings of the clouds, the wondrous works of ᴿhim which is perfect in knowledge? 36:29 · 36:4

17 How thy garments *are* warm, when he quieteth the earth by the south *wind?*

18 Hast thou with him ᴿspread out the sky, *which is* strong, *and* as a molten looking glass? Gen. 1:6

19 Teach us what we shall say unto him; *for* we cannot order *our speech* by reason of darkness.

20 Shall it be told him that I speak? If a man speak, surely he shall be swallowed up.

21 And now *men* ᵀsee not the bright light which *is* in the ᵀclouds: but the wind passeth, and cleanseth them. *cannot look at* · *skies*

22 ᵀFair weather cometh out of the north: with God *is* terrible majesty. *In golden splendour he comes*

23 *Touching* the Almighty, ᴿwe cannot find him out: *he is* excellent in power, and in judgment, and in plenty of justice: he will not afflict. [Rom. 11:33, 34; 1 Tim. 6:16]

24 Men do therefore fear him: he respecteth not any *that are* ᴿwise of heart. [Matt. 11:25]; 1 Cor. 1:26

38 Then the LORD answered Job ᴿout of the whirlwind, and said, 40:6; Ex. 19:16

2 ᴿWho *is* this that darkeneth counsel by ᴿwords without knowledge? 34:35; 42:3 · 1 Tim. 1:7

3 ᴿGird up now thy loins like a man; for I will ᵀdemand of thee, and answer thou me. 40:7 · *question*

4 ᴿWhere wast thou when I laid the foundations of the earth? declare, if thou hast understanding. 15:7; Ps. 104:5

5 Who hath laid the measures thereof, if thou knowest? or who hath stretched the line upon it?

6 Whereupon are the foundations thereof fastened? or who laid the corner stone thereof;

7 When the morning stars sang together, and all ᴿthe sons of God shouted for joy? 1:6

8 Or *who* shut up the sea with doors, when it brake forth, *as if* it had issued out of the womb?

9 When I made the cloud the garment thereof, and thick darkness a swaddlingband for it,

10 And ᴿbrakeᵀ up for it my decreed *place,* and set bars and doors, 26:10 · *I fixed my limit for it*

11 And said, Hitherto shalt thou come, but no further: and here shall thy proud waves be stayed?

12 Hast thou ᴿcommanded the morning since thy days; *and* caused the ᵀdayspring to know his place; [Ps. 74:16; 148:5] · *dawn*

13 That it might take hold of the ends of the earth, that ᴿthe wicked might be shaken out of it? 34:25

14 It is turned as clay *to* the seal; and they stand as a garment.

15 And from the wicked their ᴿlight is withholden, and the high arm shall be broken. 18:5; [Prov. 13:9]

16 Hast thou entered into the springs of the sea? or hast thou walked in the search of the depth?

17 Have ᴿthe gates of death been ᵀopened unto thee? or hast thou seen the doors of the shadow of death? Ps. 9:13 · *revealed*

18 Hast thou perceived the breadth of the earth? declare if thou knowest it all.

19 Where *is* the way *where* light dwelleth? and *as for* darkness, where *is* the place thereof,

20 That thou shouldest take it to the ᵀbound thereof, and that thou

shouldest know the paths *to* the house thereof?   *its territory*

21 Knowest thou *it,* because thou wast then born? or *because* the number of thy days *is* great?

22 Hast thou entered into ᴿthe ᵀtreasures of the snow? or hast thou seen the treasures of the hail,   Ps. 135:7 · *treasury*

23 Which I have reserved against the time of trouble, against the day of battle and war?

24 By what way is the light parted, *which* scattereth the east wind upon the earth?

25 Who ᴿhath divided a watercourse for the overflowing of waters, or a way for the ᵀlightning of thunder;   28:26 · *thunderbolt*

26 To cause it to rain on the earth, *where* no man *is; on* the wilderness, wherein *there is* no man;

27 ᴿTo satisfy the desolate and waste *ground;* and to cause the bud of the tender herb to spring forth?   Ps. 104:13, 14; 107:35

28 ᴿHath the rain a father? or who hath begotten the drops of dew?   36:27, 28; [Ps. 147:8; Jer. 14:22]

29 Out of whose womb came the ice? and the ᴿhoary frost of heaven, who hath gendered it?   [37:10]

30 The waters ᵀare hid as *with* a stone, and the face of the deep is ᴿfrozen.   *harden like stone* · [37:10]

31 Canst thou bind the sweet influences of ᴿPle′-ia-des, or loose the bands of O-ri′-on?   9:9; Amos 5:8

32 Canst thou bring forth Maz′-za-roth in his season? or canst thou guide ᵀArc-tu′-rus with his sons?   Or *The Great Bear*

33 Knowest thou the ordinances of heaven? canst thou set the dominion thereof in the earth?

34 Canst thou lift up thy voice to the clouds, that abundance of waters may cover thee?

35 Canst thou send lightnings, that they may go, and say unto thee, Here we *are?*

36 Who hath put wisdom in the ᵀinward parts? or who hath given understanding to the heart?   *mind*

37 Who can number the clouds in wisdom? or who can ᵀstay the bottles of heaven,   *pour out*

38 When the dust ᵀgroweth into hardness, and the clods cleave fast together?   *hardens into clumps*

39 ᴿWilt thou hunt the prey for the lion? or fill the appetite of the young lions,   Ps. 104:21

40 When they ᵀcouch in *their* dens, *and* ᵀabide in the covert to lie in wait?   *crouch* · *lurk in their lairs*

41 ᴿWho provideth for the raven his food? when his young ones cry unto God, they wander for lack of meat.   Ps. 147:9; [Matt. 6:26; Luke 12:24]

39 Knowest thou the time when the wild goats of the rock bring forth? *or* canst thou mark when the hinds do calve?

2 Canst thou number the months *that* they fulfil? or knowest thou the time when they bring forth?

3 They bow themselves, they bring forth their young ones, they cast out their sorrows.

4 Their young ones are ᵀin good liking, they ᵀgrow up with corn; they go forth, and return not unto them.   *healthy* · *grow strong*

5 Who hath sent out the wild ass free? or who hath loosed the bands of the ᵀwild ass?   *onager*

6 ᴿWhose house I have made the wilderness, and the barren land his dwellings.   Jer. 2:24; Hos. 8:9

7 He scorneth the ᵀmultitude of the city, neither regardeth he the ᵀcrying of the driver.   *tumult* · *shouts*

8 The range of the mountains *is* his pasture, and he searcheth after ᴿevery green thing.   Gen. 1:29

9 Will the unicorn be willing to serve thee, or abide by thy crib?

10 Canst thou bind the ᵀunicorn with ᵀhis band in the furrow? or will he harrow the valleys after thee?   *wild ox* · *ropes*

11 Wilt thou trust him, because his strength *is* great? or wilt thou leave thy labour to him?

12 Wilt thou believe him, that he will bring home thy ᵀseed, and gather *it into* thy barn?   *grain*

13 *Gavest thou* the goodly wings unto the peacocks? or

wings and feathers unto the ost-
rich?

14 Which leaveth her eggs in the
earth, and warmeth them in dust,

15 And forgetteth that the foot
may crush them, or that the wild
beast may ᵀbreak them. Lit. *trample*

16 She is ᴿhardened against her
young ones, as though *they were*
not her's: her labour is in vain
without fear;   Lam. 4:3

17 Because God hath deprived
her of wisdom, neither hath he
imparted to her understanding.

18 What time she lifteth up herself on high, she scorneth the
horse and his rider.

19 Hast thou given the horse
strength? hast thou clothed his
neck with ᵀthunder?   Or *a mane*

20 Canst thou make him ᵀafraid
as a grasshopper? the glory of his
nostrils *is* terrible.   *spring in fear*

21 He paweth in the valley, and
rejoiceth in *his* strength: he goeth
on to meet the armed men.

22 He mocketh at fear, and is
not affrighted; neither turneth he
back from the sword.

23 The quiver rattleth against
him, the glittering spear and the
ᵀshield.   *javelin*

24 He ᵀswalloweth the ground
with fierceness and rage: neither
believeth he that *it is* the sound of
the trumpet.   *devours the distance*

25 He saith among the trumpets,
Ha, ha; and he smelleth the battle
afar off, the thunder of the captains, and the shouting.

26 Doth the hawk fly by thy wisdom, *and* stretch her wings toward the south?

27 Doth the ᴿeagle mount up at
thy command, and ᴿmake her nest
on high?   Prov. 30:18, 19 · Obad. 4

28 She dwelleth and abideth on
the rock, upon the crag of the
rock, and the strong place.

29 From thence she seeketh the
prey, *and* her eyes behold afar off.

30 Her young ones also suck up
blood: and ᴿwhere the slain *are*,
there *is* she.   Matt. 24:28; Luke 17:37

40 Moreover the LORD ᴿanswered Job, and said,   38:1

2 Shall he that ᴿcontendeth
with the Almighty instruct *him*?
he that ᴿreproveth God, let him
answer it.   9:3; 10:2; 33:13 · 13:3; 23:4

3 Then Job answered the LORD,
and said,

4 Behold, I am vile; what shall I
answer thee? ᴿI will lay mine
hand upon my mouth.   29:9; Ps. 39:9

5 Once have I spoken; but I will
not answer: yea, twice; but I will
proceed no further.

6 ᴿThen answered the LORD unto Job out of the whirlwind, and
said,   38:1

7 ᴿGird up thy loins now like a
man: ᴿI will demand of thee, and
declare thou unto me.   38:3 · 42:4

8 Wilt thou also disannul my
judgment? wilt thou condemn me,
that thou mayest be righteous?

9 Hast thou an arm like God?
or canst thou thunder with ᴿa
voice like him?   37:4; [Ps. 29:3, 4]

10 Deck thyself now *with* majesty and excellency; and array
thyself with glory and beauty.

11 Cast abroad the rage of thy
wrath: and behold every one *that
is* proud, and ᵀabase him.   *humble*

12 Look on every one *that is*
ᴿproud, *and* bring him low; and
tread down the wicked in their
place.   1 Sam. 2:7; [Is. 2:12]; Dan. 4:37

13 Hide them in the dust together; *and* bind their faces in secret.

14 Then will I also confess unto
thee that thine own right hand
can save thee.

15 Behold now behemoth,
which I made with thee; he eateth
grass as an ox.

16 Lo now, his strength *is* in his
loins, and his force *is* in ᵀthe navel
of his belly.   *stomach muscles*

17 He moveth his tail like a
cedar: the sinews of his ᵀstones
are wrapped together.   *thighs*

18 His bones *are as* strong
pieces of ᵀbrass; his bones *are* like
bars of iron.   *bronze*

19 He *is* the chief of the ways
of God: he that made him can
make his sword to approach
unto him.

20 Surely the mountains ᴿbring

him forth food, where all the beasts of the field play. Ps. 104:14

21 He lieth under the ᵀshady trees, in the covert of the reed, and ᵀfens.   *lotus · marsh*

22 The shady trees cover him *with* their shadow; the willows of the brook compass him about.

23 Behold, he drinketh up a river, *and* hasteth not: he trusteth that he can draw up Jordan into his mouth.

24 He taketh it with his eyes: *his* nose pierceth through snares.

41

Canst thou draw out ᴿleviathan with an hook? or his tongue with a cord *which* thou lettest down? Ps. 74:14; 104:26; Is. 27:1

2 Canst thou ᴿput an hook into his nose? or bore his jaw through with a thorn? 2 Kin. 19:38; Is. 37:29

3 Will he make many supplications unto thee? will he speak soft *words* unto thee?

4 Will he make a covenant with thee? wilt thou take him for a servant for ever?

5 Wilt thou play with him as *with* a bird? or wilt thou bind him for thy maidens?

6 Shall the companions make a banquet of him? shall they ᵀpart him among the merchants? *divide*

7 Canst thou fill his skin with ᵀbarbed irons? or his head with fish spears? *harpoons*

8 Lay thine hand upon him, remember the battle, do no more.

9 Behold, the hope of him is in vain: shall not *one* be cast down even at the sight of him?

10 None *is* so fierce that dare stir him up: who then is able to stand before me?

11 ᴿWho hath ᵀprevented me, that I should repay *him*? ᴿ*whatsoever is* under the whole heaven is mine. [Rom. 11:35] · *preceded* · Ps. 24:1

12 I will not conceal his ᵀparts, nor his power, nor his comely proportion.   *limbs*

13 Who can discover the face of his garment? *or* who can come *to him* with his double bridle?

14 Who can open the doors of

his face? his teeth *are* terrible round about.

15 *His* scales *are his* pride, shut up together *as with* a close seal.

16 One is so near to another, that no air can come between them.

17 They are joined one to another, they stick together, that they cannot be ᵀsundered. *separated*

18 By his neesings a light doth shine, and his eyes *are* like the eyelids of the morning.

19 Out of his mouth go burning lamps, *and* sparks of fire leap out.

20 Out of his nostrils goeth smoke, as *out* of a ᵀseething pot or ᵀcaldron. *boiling · burning rushes*

21 His breath kindleth coals, and a flame goeth out of his mouth.

22 In his neck remaineth strength, and sorrow is turned into joy before him.

23 The ᵀflakes of his flesh are joined together: they are firm in themselves; they cannot be moved.   *folds*

24 His heart is as firm as a stone; yea, as hard as a piece of the ᵀnether *millstone.* *lower*

25 When he raiseth up himself, the mighty are afraid: by reason of breakings they ᵀpurify themselves.   *are beside themselves*

26 The sword of him that layeth at him cannot hold: the spear, the dart, nor the ᵀhabergeon. *Or javelin*

27 He esteemeth iron as straw, *and* brass as rotten wood.

28 The arrow cannot make him flee: slingstones are turned with him into stubble.

29 Darts are counted as ᵀstubble: he laugheth at the shaking of a spear.   *straw*

30 Sharp stones *are* under him: he spreadeth sharp pointed things upon the mire.

31 He maketh the deep to boil like a pot: he maketh the sea like a pot of ointment.

32 He maketh a path to shine after him; *one* would think the deep ᵀto be hoary. *had white hair*

33 Upon earth there is not his like, who is made without fear.

34 He beholdeth all high *things:* he *is* a king over all the children of pride.

42 Then Job answered the LORD, and said,

2 I know that thou canst do every *thing,* and *that* no thought can be withholden from thee.

3 ^RWho *is* he that hideth counsel without knowledge? therefore have I uttered that I understood not; ^Rthings too wonderful for me, which I knew not.   38:2 · Ps. 40:5; 131:1

4 Hear, I beseech thee, and I will speak: I will demand of thee, and declare thou unto me.

5 I have ^Rheard of thee by the hearing of the ear: but now mine eye seeth thee.   26:14; [Rom. 10:17]

6 Wherefore I abhor *myself,* and repent in dust and ashes.

7 And it was *so,* that after the LORD had spoken these words unto Job, the LORD said to El'-i-phaz the Te'-man-ite, My wrath is kindled against thee, and against thy two friends: for ye have not spoken of me *the thing that is* right, as my servant Job *hath.*

8 Therefore take unto you now seven bullocks and seven rams, and ^Rgo to my servant Job, and offer up for yourselves a burnt offering; and my servant Job shall pray for you: for him will I accept: lest I deal with you *after your* folly, in that ye have not spoken of me *the thing which is* right, like my servant Job.   [Matt. 5:24]

9 So El'-i-phaz the Te'-man-ite and Bil'-dad the Shu'-hite *and* Zo'-phar the Na'-a-math-ite went, and did according as the LORD commanded them: the LORD also accepted Job.

10 ^RAnd the LORD turned the captivity of Job, when he prayed for his friends: also the LORD gave Job ^Rtwice as much as he had before.   Deut. 30:3; Ps. 85:1–3 · Is. 40:2

11 Then came there unto him ^Rall his brethren, and all his sisters, and all they that had been of his acquaintance before, and did eat bread with him in his house: and they bemoaned him, and comforted him over all the ^Tevil that the LORD had brought upon him: every man also gave him a piece of money, and every one an earring of gold.   19:13 · *adversity*

12 So the LORD blessed the latter end of Job more than his beginning: for he had fourteen thousand sheep, and six thousand camels, and a thousand yoke of oxen, and a thousand she asses.

13 ^RHe had also seven sons and three daughters.   1:2

14 And he called the name of the first, Je-mi'-ma; and the name of the second, Ke-zi'-a; and the name of the third, Ker'-en-hap'-puch.

15 And in all the land were no women found *so* fair as the daughters of Job: and their father gave them inheritance among their brethren.

16 After this ^Rlived Job an hundred and forty years, and saw his sons, and his sons' sons, *even* four generations.   5:26; Prov. 3:16

17 So Job died, *being* old and ^Rfull of days.   5:26; Gen. 15:15; 25:8

The Book of
PSALMS

T HE Book of Psalms is the largest and perhaps most widely used book in the Bible. It explores the full range of human experience in a very personal and practical way. Its 150 "songs" run from the Creation through the patriarchal, theocratic, monarchical, exilic, and postexilic periods. The tremendous breadth of subject matter in the Psalms includes diverse topics, such as jubilation, war, peace, worship, judgment, messianic prophecy, praise, and lament. The Psalms were set to the accompaniment of stringed instruments and served as the temple hymnbook and devotional guide for the Jewish people.

The Book of Psalms was gradually collected and originally unnamed, perhaps due to the great variety of material. It came to be known as *Sepher Tehillim*—"Book of Praises"—because almost every psalm contains some note of praise to God. The Septuagint uses the Greek word *Psalmoi* as its title for this book, meaning "Poems Sung to the Accompaniment of Musical Instruments." It also calls it the *Psalterium* ("A Collection of Songs"), and this word is the basis for the term *Psalter*. The Latin title is *Liber Psalmorum*, "Book of Psalms."

BOOK I

PSALM 1

BLESSED ᴿ*is* the man that walketh not in the counsel of the ungodly, nor standeth in the way of sinners, nor sitteth in the seat of the scornful.   Prov. 4:14

2   But his delight *is* in the law of the LORD; ᴿand in his law doth he meditate day and night.   [Josh. 1:8]

3   And he shall be like a tree ᴿplanted by the rivers of water, that bringeth forth his fruit in his season; his leaf also shall not wither; and whatsoever he doeth shall prosper.   [92:12–14]; Jer. 17:8

4   The ungodly *are* not so: but *are* ᴿlike the chaff which the wind driveth away.   35:5; Job 21:18; Is. 17:13

5   Therefore the ungodly shall not stand in the judgment, nor sinners in the congregation of the righteous.

6   For ᴿthe LORD knoweth the way of the righteous: but the way of the ungodly shall perish.   37:18

PSALM 2

☆ **W**HY ᴿdo the ᵀheathen rage, and the people imagine a vain thing?   Acts 4:25, 26 · *Gentiles*

2   The kings of the earth set themselves, and the ᴿrulers take counsel together, against the LORD, and against his ᴿanointed, *saying*,   [Matt. 12:14; 26:3, 4] · [John 1:41]

3   ᴿLet us break their bands asunder, and cast away their cords from us.   Luke 19:14

4   He that sitteth in the heavens

ᴿshall laugh: the Lord shall have them in derision.   37:13

5   Then shall he speak unto them in his wrath, and ᵀvex them in his sore displeasure.   *distress*

6   Yet have I ᵀset my king upon my holy hill of Zi′-on.   Lit. *installed*

7   I will declare the decree: the ☆ LORD hath said unto me, ᴿThou *art* my Son; this day have I begotten thee. Luke 3:22; John 1:18; Acts 13:33

8   Ask of me, and I shall give *thee* the heathen *for* thine inheritance, and the uttermost parts of the earth *for* thy possession.

9   ᴿThou shalt break them with ☆ a rod of iron; thou shalt dash them in pieces like a potter's vessel.   Ps. 89:23; 110:5, 6; [Rev. 19:15]

10 Be wise now therefore, O ye kings: be instructed, ye judges of the earth.

11 Serve the LORD with fear, and rejoice with trembling.

12 Kiss the Son, lest he be angry, and ye perish *from* the way, when ᴿhis wrath is kindled but a little. ᴿBlessed *are* all they that put their trust in him. [Rev. 6:16, 17] · [5:11; 34:22]

PSALM 3

A Psalm of David, when he fled from Ab′-sa-lom his son.

LORD, how are they increased that trouble me! many *are* they that rise up against me.

2   Many *there be* which say of my soul, *There is* no help for him in God. Selah.

3 But thou, O LORD, *art* [R]a shield for me; my glory, and [R]the lifter up of mine head.   28:7 · 27:6

4 I cried unto the LORD with my voice, and [R]he heard me out of his [R]holy hill. Selah.   4:3; 34:4 · 2:6; 15:1

5 [R]I laid me down and slept; I awaked; for the LORD sustained me.   4:8; Lev. 26:6; Prov. 3:24

6 [R]I will not be afraid of ten thousands of people, that have set *themselves* against me round about.   23:4; 27:3

7 Arise, O LORD; save me, O my God: [R]for thou hast [T]smitten all mine enemies *upon* the cheek bone; thou hast broken the teeth of the ungodly.   Job 16:10 · *struck*

8 [R]Salvation *belongeth* unto the LORD: thy blessing *is* upon thy people. Selah.   28:8; 35:3; [Is. 43:11]

PSALM 4

To the chief Musician on Neg'-i-noth,
A Psalm of David.

HEAR me when I call, O God of my righteousness: thou hast [T]enlarged me *when I was* in distress; have mercy upon me, and hear my prayer.   *relieved*

2 O ye sons of men, how long *will ye turn* my glory into shame? *how long* will ye love vanity, *and* seek after leasing? Selah.

3 But know that [R]the LORD hath set apart him that is godly for himself: the LORD will hear when I call unto him.   [2 Tim. 2:19]

4 Stand in awe, and sin not: commune with your own heart upon your bed, and be still. Selah.

5 Offer [R]the sacrifices of righteousness, and [R]put your trust in the LORD.   51:19 · 37:3, 5; 62:8

6 *There be* many that say, Who will shew us *any* good? [R]LORD, lift thou up the light of thy countenance upon us.   80:3, 7, 19; Num. 6:26

7 Thou hast put [R]gladness in my heart, more than in the time *that* their corn and their wine increased.   97:11, 12; Is. 9:3; Acts 14:17

8 I will both lay me down in peace, and sleep: for thou, LORD, only makest me dwell in safety.

PSALM 5

To the chief Musician upon Ne'-hi-loth,
A Psalm of David.

GIVE [R]ear to my words, O LORD, consider my [T]meditation.   4:1 · Lit. *groaning*

2 Hearken unto the voice of my cry, my King, and my God: for unto thee will I pray.

3 My voice shalt thou hear in the morning, O LORD; [R]in the morning will I direct *my prayer* unto thee, and will look up.   55:1

4 For thou *art* not a God that hath pleasure in wickedness: neither shall evil dwell with thee.

5 The [R]foolish shall not [R]stand in thy sight: thou hatest all workers of iniquity.   [Hab. 1:13] · 1:5

6 Thou shalt destroy them that speak [T]leasing: the LORD will abhor the [R]bloody[T] and deceitful man.   *falsehood* · 55:23 · *bloodthirsty*

7 But as for me, I will come *into* thy house in the multitude of thy mercy: *and* in thy fear will I worship toward thy holy temple.

8 [R]Lead me, O LORD, in thy righteousness because of mine enemies; make thy way straight before my face.   25:4, 5; 27:11; 31:3

9 For *there is* no faithfulness in their mouth; their inward part *is* very wickedness; [R]their throat *is* an open sepulchre; they flatter with their tongue.   Rom. 3:13

10 Destroy thou them, O God; let them fall by their own counsels; cast them out in the multitude of their transgressions; for they have rebelled against thee.

11 But let all those that put their trust in thee rejoice: let them ever shout for joy, because thou defendest them: let them also that love thy name be joyful in thee.

12 For thou, LORD, wilt bless the righteous; with favour wilt thou compass him as *with* a shield.

PSALM 6

To the chief Musician on Neg'-i-noth upon Shem'-i-nith, A Psalm of David.

O LORD, [R]rebuke me not in thine anger, neither chasten me in thy hot displeasure. 38:1

2 Have mercy upon me, O LORD; for I *am* weak: O LORD, heal me; for my bones are vexed.

3 My soul is also sore [R]vexed: but thou, O LORD, how long? 88:3

4 Return, O LORD, deliver my soul: oh save me for thy [T]mercies' sake. *lovingkindnesses*

5 [R]For in death *there is* no remembrance of thee: in the grave who shall give thee thanks? 115:17

6 I am weary with my groaning; [T]all the night make I my bed to swim; I [T]water my couch with my tears. *Or every night · drench*

7 [R]Mine eye is consumed because of grief; it waxeth old because of all mine enemies. 31:9

8 [R]Depart from me, all ye workers of iniquity; for the LORD hath [R]heard the voice of my weeping. [Matt. 25:41] · 3:4; 28:6

9 The LORD hath heard my supplication; the LORD will receive my prayer.

10 Let all mine enemies be ashamed and [T]sore vexed: let them return *and* be ashamed suddenly. *greatly troubled*

PSALM 7

Shig-ga'-ion of David, which he sang unto the LORD, concerning the words of Cush the Benjamite.

O LORD my God, in thee do I put my trust: [R]save me from all them that persecute me, and deliver me: 31:15

2 [R]Lest he tear my soul like a lion, [R]rending *it* in pieces, while *there is* none to deliver. 57:4 · 50:22

3 O LORD my God, [R]if I have done this; if there be [R]iniquity in my hands; 2 Sam. 16:7 · 1 Sam. 24:11

4 If I have rewarded evil unto him that was at peace with me; (yea, I have delivered him that without cause is mine enemy:)

5 Let the enemy persecute my soul, and take *it*; yea, let him tread down my life upon the earth, and lay mine honour in the dust. Selah.

6 Arise, O LORD, in thine anger, [R]lift up thyself because of the rage of mine enemies: and [R]awake for me *to* the judgment *that* thou hast commanded. 94:2 · 35:23; 44:23

7 So shall the congregation of the people [T]compass thee about: for their sakes therefore return thou on high. *surround*

8 The LORD shall judge the people: [R]judge me, O LORD, [R]according to my righteousness, and according to mine integrity *that is* in me. 26:1; 35:24; 43:1 · 18:20; 35:24

9 Oh let the wickedness of the wicked come to an end; but establish the just: for the righteous God trieth the hearts and reins.

10 My defence *is* of God, which saveth the [R]upright in heart. 125:4

11 [T]God judgeth the righteous, and God is angry *with the wicked* every day. *God is a just judge*

12 If he turn not, he will [R]whet his sword; he hath bent his bow, and made it ready. Deut. 32:41

13 He hath also prepared for him the instruments of death; he [T]ordaineth his arrows [T]against the persecutors. *makes · into fiery shafts*

14 [R]Behold, he travaileth with iniquity, and hath conceived mischief, and brought forth falsehood. Job 15:35; Is. 59:4; [James 1:15]

15 He made a pit, and digged it, [R]and is fallen into the ditch *which* he made. 57:6; [Job 4:8]

16 [R]His mischief shall return upon his own head, and his violent dealing shall come down upon his own pate. 140:9; Esth. 9:25

17 I will praise the LORD according to his righteousness: and will sing praise to the name of the LORD most high.

PSALM 8

To the chief Musician upon Git'-tith, A Psalm of David.

O LORD our Lord, how [R]excellent *is* thy name in all the

earth! who ^Rhast set thy glory above the heavens. 148:13 · 113:4

2 ^ROut of the mouth of babes and sucklings hast thou ordained strength because of thine enemies, that thou mightest still the enemy and the avenger. Matt. 21:16

3 When I ^Rconsider thy heavens, the work of thy fingers, the moon and the stars, which thou hast ordained; 111:2

4 What is man, that thou art mindful of him? and the son of man, that thou visitest him?

5 For thou hast made him a little lower than the angels, and hast crowned him with glory and honour.

6 Thou madest him to have dominion over the works of thy hands; ^Rthou hast put all *things* under his feet: [Eph. 1:22; Heb. 2:8]

7 All sheep and oxen, yea, and the beasts of the field;

8 The fowl of the air, and the fish of the sea, *and whatsoever* passeth through the paths of the seas.

9 O Lord our Lord, how excellent *is* thy name in all the earth!

PSALM 9

To the chief Musician upon
Muth-lab'-ben, A Psalm of David.

I WILL praise *thee*, O Lord, with my whole heart; I will ^Tshew forth all thy marvellous works. *tell of*

2 I will be glad and ^Rrejoice in thee: I will sing praise to thy name, O thou most High. 5:11

3 When mine enemies are turned back, they shall fall and perish at thy presence.

4 For thou hast maintained my right and my cause; ^Tthou satest in the throne judging right. *you sat*

5 Thou hast rebuked the heathen, thou hast destroyed the wicked, thou hast ^Rput out their name for ever and ever. Prov. 10:7

6 O thou enemy, destructions are come to a perpetual end: and thou hast destroyed cities; their memorial is perished with them.

7 ^RBut the Lord shall endure

for ever: he hath prepared his throne for judgment. Heb. 1:11

8 And ^Rhe shall judge the world in righteousness, he shall minister judgment to the people in uprightness. [96:13; 98:9; Acts 17:31]

9 The Lord also will be a ^Rrefuge for the oppressed, a refuge in times of trouble. 46:1; 91:2

10 And they that ^Rknow thy name will put their trust in thee: for thou, Lord, hast not forsaken them that seek thee. 91:14

11 Sing praises to the Lord, which dwelleth in Zion: declare among the people his doings.

12 ^RWhen he maketh inquisition for blood, he remembereth them: he forgetteth not the cry of the humble. [72:14; Gen. 9:5]

13 Have mercy upon me, O Lord; consider my trouble *which I* suffer of them that hate me, thou that liftest me up from the gates of death:

14 That I may shew forth all thy praise in the gates of ^Tthe daughter of Zion: I will ^Rrejoice in thy salvation. Jerusalem · 13:5; 20:5; 35:9

15 ^RThe heathen are sunk down in the pit *that* they made: in the net which they hid is their own foot taken. 7:15, 16

16 The Lord is ^Rknown *by* the judgment *which* he executeth: the wicked is snared in the work of his own hands. ^RHig-ga'-ion.^T Selah. Ex. 7:5 · 92:3 · *meditation* or *song*

17 The wicked shall be turned into hell, *and* all the ^Tnations ^Rthat forget God. *Gentiles* · 50:22; Job 8:13

18 ^RFor the needy shall not alway be forgotten: ^Rthe expectation of the poor shall *not* perish for ever. 12:5 · [62:5; 71:5]; Prov. 23:18

19 Arise, O Lord; let not man prevail: let the ^Theathen be judged in thy sight. *nations* or *Gentiles*

20 Put them in fear, O Lord: *that* the nations may know themselves *to be but* men. Selah.

PSALM 10

WHY standest thou afar off, O Lord? *why* hidest thou *thyself* in times of trouble?

2   The wicked in *his* pride doth persecute the poor: ᴿlet them be taken in the devices that they have imagined.   7:16; 9:16

3   For the wicked ᴿboasteth of his heart's desire, and ᴿblesseth the covetous, *whom* the LORD abhorreth.   49:6; 94:3, 4 · Prov. 28:4

4   The wicked, through the pride of his countenance, will not seek *after God:* God *is* not in all his ᴿthoughts.   14:1; 36:1

5   His ways are always grievous; thy judgments *are* far above out of his sight: *as for* all his enemies, he puffeth at them.

6   ᴿHe hath said in his heart, I shall not be moved: for ᴿI *shall* never *be* in adversity. 49:11 · Rev. 18:7

7   His mouth is full of cursing and deceit and fraud: under his tongue *is* mischief and vanity.

8   He sitteth in the lurking places of the villages: in the secret places doth he murder the innocent: his eyes are ᵀprivily set against the poor.   *secretly*

9   He lieth in wait secretly as a lion in his den: he lieth in wait to catch the poor: he doth catch the poor, when he draweth him into his net.

10 He croucheth, *and* humbleth himself, that the poor may fall by his ᵀstrong ones.   Or *strength*

11 He hath said in his heart, God hath forgotten: he hideth his face; he will never see *it.*

12 Arise, O LORD; O God, ᴿlift up thine hand: forget not the ᴿhumble.   17:7; 94:2; Mic. 5:9 · 9:12

13 Wherefore doth the wicked contemn God? he hath said in his heart, Thou wilt not require *it.*

14 Thou hast ᴿseen *it;* for thou beholdest mischief and spite, to requite *it* with thy hand: the poor ᴿcommitteth himself unto thee; ᴿthou art the helper of the fatherless.   [11:4] · [2 Tim. 1:12] · 68:5; Hos. 14:3

15 Break thou the arm of the wicked and the evil *man:* seek out his wickedness *till* thou find none.

16 ᴿThe LORD *is* King for ever and ever: the ᵀheathen are perished out of his land.   29:10 · *nations*

17 LORD, thou hast heard the desire of the humble: thou wilt prepare their heart, thou wilt cause thine ear to hear:

18 To judge the fatherless and the oppressed, that the man of the earth may no more oppress.

PSALM 11

To the chief Musician,
A Psalm of David.

IN ᴿthe LORD put I my trust: how say ye to my soul, Flee *as* a bird to your mountain?   56:11

2   For, lo, ᴿthe wicked bend *their* bow, they make ready their arrow upon the string, that they may ᵀprivily shoot at the upright in heart. 64:3, 4 · *secretly,* lit. *in darkness*

3   ᴿIf the foundations be destroyed, what can the righteous do?   82:5; 87:1; 119:152

4   The LORD *is* in his holy temple, the LORD's ᴿthrone *is* in heaven: his eyes behold, his eyelids try, the children of men. [Is. 66:1]; Rev. 4:2

5   The LORD trieth the righteous: but the wicked and him that loveth violence his soul hateth.

6   Upon the wicked he shall rain snares, fire and brimstone, and an horrible tempest: *this shall be* the portion of their cup.

7   For the righteous LORD loveth righteousness; his countenance doth behold the upright.

PSALM 12

To the chief Musician upon
Shem′-i-nith, A Psalm of David.

HELP,ᵀ LORD; for the godly man ᴿceaseth; for the faithful fail from among the children of men.   *Save* · [Is. 57:1]; Mic. 7:2

2   ᴿThey speak vanity every one with his neighbour: *with* flattering lips *and* with a double heart do they speak.   10:7; 41:6

3   The LORD shall cut off all flattering lips, *and* the tongue that speaketh ᵀproud things: *great*

4   Who have said, With our tongue will we prevail; our lips *are* our own: who *is* lord over us?

5 For the oppression of the poor, for the sighing of the needy, now will I arise, saith the LORD; I will set *him* in safety *from him that* puffeth at him.

6 The words of the LORD *are* [R]pure words: *as* silver tried in a furnace of earth, purified seven times. 18:30; 2 Sam. 22:31; Prov. 30:5

7 Thou shalt keep them, O LORD, thou shalt preserve them from this generation for ever.

8 The wicked walk on every side, when the vilest men are exalted.

PSALM 13

To the chief Musician,
A Psalm of David.

HOW long wilt thou forget me, O LORD? for ever? [R]how long wilt thou hide thy face from me? 89:46; Job 13:24

2 How long shall I take counsel in my soul, *having* sorrow in my heart daily? how long shall mine enemy be exalted over me?

3 Consider *and* hear me, O LORD my God: lighten mine eyes, lest I sleep the *sleep of* death;

4 Lest mine enemy say, I have prevailed against him; *and* those that trouble me rejoice when I am moved.

5 But I have trusted in thy [T]mercy; my heart shall rejoice in thy salvation. *lovingkindness*

6 I will sing unto the LORD, because he hath dealt bountifully with me.

PSALM 14

To the chief Musician,
A Psalm of David.

THE [R]fool hath said in his heart, *There is* no God. They are corrupt, they have done abominable works, *there is* none that doeth good. 10:4; 53:1

2 [R]The LORD looked down from heaven upon the children of men, to see if there were any that did understand, *and* seek God. 33:13, 14

3 [R]They are all gone aside, they are *all* together become [T]filthy:

there is none that doeth good, no, not one. Rom. 3:12 · *corrupt*

4 Have all the workers of iniquity no knowledge? who eat up my people *as* they eat bread, and [R]call not upon the LORD. 79:6; Is. 64:7

5 There were they in great fear: for God *is* in the generation of the righteous.

6 Ye have shamed the counsel of the poor, because the LORD *is* his [R]refuge. 9:9; 40:17; 46:1; 142:5

7 Oh that the salvation of Israel *were come* out of Zion! when the LORD bringeth back the captivity of his people, Jacob shall rejoice, *and* Israel shall be glad.

PSALM 15

A Psalm of David.

LORD, [R]who shall abide in thy tabernacle? who shall dwell in thy holy hill? 24:3-5

2 He that walketh uprightly, and worketh righteousness, and speaketh the truth in his heart.

3 *He that* backbiteth not with his tongue, nor doeth evil to his neighbour, nor taketh up a reproach against his neighbour.

4 [R]In whose eyes a vile person is contemned; but he honoureth them that fear the LORD. *He that* [R]sweareth to *his own* hurt, and changeth not. Esth. 3:2 · Lev. 5:4

5 *He that* putteth not out his money to usury, nor taketh reward against the innocent. He that doeth these *things* [R]shall never be moved. 2 Pet. 1:10

PSALM 16

Mich'-tam of David.

PRESERVE me, O God: for in thee do I put my trust.

2 *O my soul,* thou hast said unto the LORD, Thou *art* my Lord: [R]my goodness [T]*extendeth* not to thee: Job 35:7 · *is nothing apart from thee*

3 *But* to the saints that *are* in the earth, and *to* the excellent, in [R]whom *is* all my delight. 119:63

4 Their sorrows shall be multiplied *that* hasten *after* another

god: their drink offerings of blood will I not offer, nor take up their names into my lips.

5 The Lord *is* the portion of mine inheritance and of my cup: thou ᵀmaintainest my lot. Lit. *uphold*

6 The lines are fallen unto me in pleasant *places*; yea, I have a goodly ᵀheritage.   *inheritance*

7 I will bless the Lord, who hath given me counsel: my ᵀreins also instruct me in the night seasons.   *heart*, lit. *kidneys*

8 I have set the Lord always before me: because *he is* at my right hand, I shall not be moved.

9 Therefore my heart is glad, and my glory rejoiceth: my flesh also shall rest in hope.

☆ 10 ᴿFor thou wilt not leave my soul in ᵀhell; neither wilt thou suffer thine Holy One to see corruption.   49:15; 86:13; Acts 2:31, 32 · *Sheol*

11 Thou wilt shew me the ᴿpath of life: in thy presence *is* fulness of joy; at thy right hand *there are* pleasures for evermore.   [Matt. 7:14]

PSALM 17

A Prayer of David.

HEAR the right, O Lord, attend unto my cry, give ear unto my prayer, *that goeth* not out of ᵀfeigned lips.   *deceitful*

2 Let my sentence come forth from thy presence; let thine eyes behold the things that are equal.

3 Thou hast proved mine heart; thou hast visited *me* in the night; ᴿthou hast tried me, *and* shalt find nothing; I am purposed *that* my mouth shall not transgress.   66:10

4 Concerning the works of men, by the word of thy lips I have kept *me from* the paths of the destroyer.

5 Hold up my goings in thy paths, *that* my footsteps slip not.

6 ᴿI have called upon thee, for thou wilt hear me, O God: incline thine ear unto me, *and hear* my speech.   86:7; 116:2

7 Shew thy marvellous lovingkindness, O thou that ᵀsavest by thy right hand them which put

their trust *in thee* from those that rise up *against them*.   *delivers*

8 Keep me as the ᵀapple of the eye, hide me under the shadow of thy wings,   *pupil*

9 From the wicked that oppress me, *from* my deadly enemies, *who* ᵀcompass me about.   *surround me*

10 They are inclosed in their own fat: with their mouth they ᴿspeak proudly.   [1 Sam. 2:3]

11 They have now compassed us in our steps: they have set their eyes bowing down to the earth;

12 Like as a lion *that* is greedy of his prey, and as it were a young lion lurking in secret places.

13 Arise, O Lord, ᵀdisappoint him, cast him down: deliver my soul from the wicked, ᵀ*which is* thy sword: *confront · with thy sword*

14 From men ᵀ*which are* thy hand, O Lord, from men of the world, *which have* their portion in *this* life, and whose belly thou fillest with thy ᵀhid *treasure:* they are full of children, and leave the rest of their *substance* to their babes.   *with thy hand · hidden*

15 As for me, ᴿI will behold thy face in righteousness: ᴿI shall be satisfied, when I ᴿawake, with thy likeness.   [1 John 3:2] · 16:11 · [Is. 26:19]

PSALM 18

To the chief Musician, *A Psalm* of David, the servant of the Lord, who spake unto the Lord the words of this song in the day *that* the Lord delivered him from the hand of all his enemies, and from the hand of Saul: And he said,

I ᴿWILL love thee, O Lord, my strength.   144:1

2 The Lord *is* my rock, and my fortress, and my deliverer; my God, my strength, in whom I will trust; my buckler, and the horn of my salvation, *and* my high tower.

3 I will call upon the Lord, ᴿ*who is worthy* to be praised: so shall I be saved from mine enemies.   76:4; Rev. 5:12

4 The sorrows of death com-

passed me, and the floods of ungodly men made me afraid.

5 The [T]sorrows of hell compassed me about: the snares of death prevented me. *cords of Sheol*

6 In my distress I called upon the LORD, and cried unto my God: he heard my voice [T]out of his temple, and my cry came before him, *even* into his ears. *from*

7 [R]Then the earth shook and trembled; the foundations also of the hills moved and were shaken, because he was wroth. *Acts 4:31*

8 There went up a smoke out of his nostrils, and fire out of his mouth devoured: coals were kindled by it.

9 [R]He bowed the heavens also, and came down: and darkness *was* under his feet. *144:5*

10 [R]And he rode upon a cherub, and did fly: yea, he did fly upon the wings of the wind. *80:1; 99:1*

11 He made darkness his secret place; [R]his pavilion round about him *were* dark waters *and* thick clouds of the skies. *97:2*

12 [R]At the brightness *that was* before him his thick clouds passed, hail *stones* and coals of fire. *97:3; 140:10; Hab. 3:11*

13 The LORD also thundered in the heavens, and the [T]Highest gave [R]his voice; hail *stones* and coals of fire. *Most High · [29:3–9; 104:7]*

14 [R]Yea, he sent out his arrows, and scattered them; and he shot out lightnings, and [T]discomfited them. *Is. 30:30; Hab. 3:11 · vanquished*

15 Then the channels of waters were seen, and the foundations of the world were [T]discovered at thy rebuke, O LORD, at the blast of the breath of thy nostrils. *uncovered*

16 [R]He sent from above, he took me, he drew me out of many waters. *144:7*

17 He delivered me from my strong enemy, and from them which hated me: for they were too strong for me.

18 They [T]prevented me in the day of my calamity: but the LORD was my [T]stay. *confronted · support*

19 He brought me forth also into a large place; he delivered me, because he delighted in me.

20 The LORD rewarded me according to my righteousness; according to the cleanness of my hands hath he recompensed me.

21 For I have kept the ways of the LORD, and have not wickedly departed from my God.

22 For all his judgments *were* before me, and I did not put away his statutes from me.

23 I was also upright [T]before him, and I kept myself from mine iniquity. *with*

24 [R]Therefore hath the LORD recompensed me according to my righteousness, according to the cleanness of my hands in his eyesight. *v. 20; 1 Sam. 26:23*

25 [R]With the merciful thou wilt shew thyself merciful; with an upright man thou wilt shew thyself upright; *[1 Kin. 8:32]; Matt. 5:7*

26 With the pure thou wilt shew thyself pure; and [R]with the froward thou wilt shew thyself froward. *[Lev. 26:23–28]; Prov. 3:34*

27 For thou wilt save the afflicted people; but wilt bring down [R]high looks. *[101:5]; Prov. 6:17*

28 [R]For thou wilt light my [T]candle: the LORD my God will enlighten my darkness. *1 Kin. 15:4 · lamp*

29 For by thee I have run through a troop; and by my God have I leaped over a wall.

30 *As for* God, [R]his way *is* perfect: the word of the LORD is tried: he *is* a buckler [R]to all those that trust in him. *Rev. 15:3 · [17:7]*

31 [R]For who *is* God save the LORD? or who *is* a rock save our God? *[Deut. 32:31, 39; 1 Sam. 2:2; Is. 45:5]*

32 *It is* God that [R]girdeth me with strength, and maketh my way perfect. *[91:2]*

33 [R]He maketh my feet like hinds' *feet*, and setteth me upon my high places. *2 Sam. 2:18; Hab. 3:19*

34 [R]He teacheth my hands to war, so that a bow of steel is broken by mine arms. *144:1*

35 Thou hast also given me the shield of thy salvation: and thy right hand hath [T]holden me up,

and thy gentleness hath made me great. ^{held}

36 Thou hast enlarged my ^Tsteps under me, ^Rthat my feet did not slip. ^{path · 66:9; Prov. 4:12}

37 I have pursued mine enemies, and overtaken them: neither did I turn again till they were ^Tconsumed. ^{destroyed}

38 I have wounded them that they were not able to rise: they are fallen under my feet.

39 For thou hast girded me with strength unto the battle: thou hast subdued under me those that rose up against me.

40 Thou hast also given me the necks of mine enemies; that I might destroy them that hate me.

41 They cried, but *there was* none to save *them: even* unto the LORD, but he answered them not.

42 Then did I beat them ^Tsmall as the dust before the wind: I did ^Rcast them out as the dirt in the streets. ^{as fine as · Zech. 10:5}

43 Thou hast delivered me from the strivings of the people; *and* thou hast made me the head of the heathen: a people *whom* I have not known shall serve me.

44 As soon as they hear of me, they shall obey me: the strangers shall submit themselves unto me.

45 ^RThe strangers shall fade away, and be afraid out of their ^Tclose places. ^{Mic. 7:17 · hideouts}

46 The LORD liveth; and blessed *be* my rock; and let the God of my salvation be exalted.

47 *It is* God that avengeth me, ^Rand subdueth the people under me. ^{47:3}

48 He delivereth me from mine enemies: yea, ^Rthou liftest me up above those that rise up against me: thou hast delivered me from the violent man. ^{27:6; 59:1}

49 ^RTherefore will I give thanks unto thee, O LORD, among the heathen, and sing praises unto thy name. ^{2 Sam. 22:50; Rom. 15:9}

50 ^RGreat deliverance giveth he to his king; and sheweth mercy to his anointed, to David, and to his seed for evermore. ^{2 Sam. 7:12}

PSALM 19

To the chief Musician,
A Psalm of David.

THE heavens declare the glory of God; and the firmament sheweth his handywork.

2 Day unto day uttereth speech, and night unto night ^Tsheweth knowledge. ^{reveals}

3 *There is* no speech nor language, *where* their voice is not heard.

4 ^RTheir ^Tline is gone out through all the earth, and their words to the end of the world. In them hath he set a tabernacle for the sun, ^{Rom. 10:18 · measuring line}

5 Which *is* as a bridegroom coming out of his chamber, ^R*and* rejoiceth as a strong man to run a race. ^{Eccl. 1:5}

6 His going forth *is* from the end of the heaven, and his circuit unto the ends of it: and there is nothing hid from the heat thereof.

7 The law of the LORD *is* perfect, ^Tconverting the soul: the testimony of the LORD *is* sure, making wise the simple. ^{restoring}

8 The statutes of the LORD *are* right, rejoicing the heart: the commandment of the LORD *is* pure, enlightening the eyes.

9 The fear of the LORD *is* clean, enduring for ever: the judgments of the LORD *are* true *and* righteous altogether.

10 More to be desired *are they* than ^Rgold, yea, than much fine gold: sweeter also than honey and the honeycomb. ^{119:72, 127}

11 Moreover by them is thy servant warned: *and* in keeping of them *there is* great reward.

12 Who can understand *his* errors? ^Rcleanse thou me from secret *faults.* ^[51:1, 2]

13 Keep back thy servant also from presumptuous *sins;* let them not have ^Rdominion over me: then shall I be upright, and I shall be innocent from the great transgression. ^{119:133; [Rom. 6:12–14]}

14 ^RLet the words of my mouth,

and the meditation of my heart, be acceptable in thy sight, O LORD, [T]my strength, and my [R]redeemer. 51:15 · Lit. *my rock* · 31:5; Is. 47:4

PSALM 20

To the chief Musician,
A Psalm of David.

THE LORD hear thee in the day of trouble; the name of the God of Jacob defend thee;

2 Send thee help from the sanctuary, and strengthen thee out of Zion;

3 Remember all thy offerings, and accept thy burnt sacrifice; Selah.

4 Grant thee according to thine own heart, and [R]fulfil all thy [T]counsel. 21:2 · *purpose*

5 We will rejoice in thy salvation, and in the name of our God we will set up *our* banners: the LORD fulfil all thy petitions.

6 Now know I that the LORD saveth his anointed; he will hear him from his holy heaven with the saving strength of his right hand.

7 Some *trust* in chariots, and some in [R]horses: but we will remember the name of the LORD our God. 33:16, 17; Deut. 20:1; Is. 31:1

8 They are brought down and fallen: but we are risen, and stand upright.

9 Save, LORD: let the king hear us when we call.

PSALM 21

To the chief Musician,
A Psalm of David.

THE king shall joy in thy strength, O LORD; and in thy salvation how greatly shall he rejoice!

2 Thou hast given him his heart's desire, and hast not [T]withholden the [R]request of his lips. Selah. *withheld* · 2 Sam. 7:26–29

3 For [T]thou preventest him with the blessings of goodness: thou settest a crown of pure gold on his head. *thou meetest*

4 [R]He asked life of thee, *and*

thou gavest *it* him, *even* length of days for ever and ever. 61:5, 6; 133:3

5 His glory *is* great in thy salvation: honour and majesty hast thou laid upon him.

6 For thou hast made him most blessed for ever: [R]thou hast made him exceeding glad with thy [T]countenance. 16:11; 45:7 · *presence*

7 For the king trusteth in the LORD, and through the mercy of the most High he shall not be [T]moved. *shaken*

8 Thine hand shall find out all thine enemies: thy right hand shall find out those that hate thee.

9 Thou shalt make them as a fiery oven in the time of thine anger: the LORD shall swallow them up in his wrath, and the fire shall devour them.

10 Their [T]fruit shalt thou destroy from the earth, and their [T]seed from among the children of men. *offspring · descendants*

11 For they intended evil against thee: they [T]imagined a mischievous device, *which* they are not able *to* [R]perform. *devised a plot* · 2:1–4

12 Therefore shalt thou make them turn their back, *when* thou shalt make ready *thine arrows* upon thy strings against the face of them.

13 Be thou exalted, LORD, in thine own strength: *so* will we sing and praise thy power.

PSALM 22

To the chief Musician upon Ai′-je-leth Sha′-har, A Psalm of David.

MY [R]God, my God, why hast ☆ thou forsaken me? *why art thou so* far from helping me, *and from* the words of my roaring? [Matt. 27:46; Mark 15:34]

2 O my God, I cry in the daytime, but thou hearest not; and in the night season, and am not silent.

3 But thou *art* holy, O *thou* that inhabitest the praises of Israel.

4 Our fathers trusted in thee: they trusted, and thou didst deliver them.

5 They cried unto thee, and were delivered: they trusted in thee, and were not confounded.

6 But I *am* ^Ra worm, and no man; a reproach of men, and despised of the people. Job 25:6

☆ 7 All they that see me laugh me to scorn: they shoot out the lip, they shake the head, *saying,*

☆ 8 ^RHe trusted on the LORD *that* he would deliver him: ^Rlet him deliver him, seeing he delighted in him. Matt. 27:43; Luke 23:35 · 91:14

9 ^RBut thou *art* he that took me out of the womb: thou didst make me hope *when I was* upon my mother's breasts. [71:5, 6]

10 I was cast upon thee from the womb: ^Rthou *art* my God from my mother's belly. [Is. 46:3; 49:1]; Luke 1:35

11 Be not far from me; for trouble *is* near; for *there is* none to help.

12 ^RMany bulls have compassed me: strong *bulls* of ^RBa'-shan have beset me round. 68:30 · Deut. 32:14

13 ^RThey gaped upon me *with* their mouths, *as* a ravening and a roaring lion. 35:21; Job 16:10; Lam. 2:16

14 I am poured out like water, ^Rand all my bones are out of joint: my heart is like wax; it is melted in the midst of my bowels. 31:10

15 My strength is dried up like a potsherd; and my tongue cleaveth to my jaws; and thou hast brought me into the dust of death.

☆ 16 For dogs have compassed me: the assembly of the wicked have inclosed me: ^Rthey pierced my hands and my feet. Matt. 27:35

☆ 17 I may tell all my bones: ^Rthey look *and* stare upon me. Luke 23:27

☆ 18 ^RThey part my garments among them, and cast lots upon my vesture. Mark 15:24; John 19:24

19 But be not thou far from me, O LORD: O my strength, haste thee to help me.

20 Deliver my soul from the sword; ^Rmy ^Tdarling from the power of the dog. 35:17 · *precious life*

21 Save me from the lion's mouth: for thou hast heard me from the horns of the unicorns.

☆ 22 I will declare thy name unto my brethren: in the midst of the congregation will I praise thee.

23 ^RYe that fear the LORD, praise him; all ye the ^Tseed of Jacob, glorify him; and fear him, all ye the seed of Israel. 135:19, 20 · *descendants*

24 For he hath not despised nor abhorred the affliction of the afflicted; neither hath he hid his face from him; but ^Rwhen he cried unto him, he heard. 31:22; Heb. 5:7

25 ^RMy praise *shall be* of thee in the great congregation: ^RI will pay my vows before them that fear him. 35:18; 40:9, 10 · 61:8; Eccl. 5:4

26 The meek shall eat and be satisfied: they shall praise the LORD that seek him: your heart shall live for ever.

27 All the ends of the world shall remember and turn unto the LORD: and all the kindreds of the ^Tnations shall worship before thee. *gentiles*

28 ^RFor the kingdom *is* the LORD'S: and he *is* the governor among the nations. [Zech. 14:9]

29 ^RAll *they that be* fat upon earth shall eat and worship: all they that go down to the dust shall bow before him: and none can keep alive his own soul. 17:10

30 A ^Tseed shall serve him; it shall be accounted to the Lord for a generation. *posterity*

31 They shall come, and shall declare his righteousness unto a people that shall be born, that he hath done *this.*

PSALM 23

A Psalm of David.

THE LORD *is* ^Rmy shepherd; I shall not want. 80:1; [John 10:11]

2 ^RHe maketh me to lie down in green pastures: he leadeth me beside the still waters. 65:11–13

3 He restoreth my soul: ^Rhe leadeth me in the paths of righteousness for his name's sake. 5:8

4 Yea, though I walk through the valley of ^Rthe shadow of death, I will fear no evil: ^Rfor thou *art* with me; thy rod and thy staff they comfort me. 44:19 · 16:8; [Is. 43:2]

5   Thou preparest a table before me in the presence of mine enemies: thou anointest my head with oil; my cup runneth over.

6   Surely goodness and [T]mercy shall follow me all the days of my life: and I will dwell in the house of the LORD for ever.   *lovingkindness*

PSALM 24

A Psalm of David.

THE [R]earth *is* the LORD's, and the fulness thereof; the world, and they that dwell therein.   1 Cor. 10:26, 28

2   For he hath [R]founded it upon the seas, and established it upon the [T]floods.   89:11 · Lit. *rivers*

3   [R]Who shall ascend into the hill of the LORD? or who shall stand in his holy place?   15:1–5

4   He that hath clean hands, and [R]a pure heart; who hath not lifted up his soul unto vanity, nor sworn deceitfully.   73:1; [Matt. 5:8]

5   He shall receive the blessing from the LORD, and righteousness from the God of his salvation.

6   This *is* the generation of them that [R]seek him, that seek thy face, O Jacob. Selah.   27:4, 8

7   Lift up your heads, O ye gates; and be ye lift up, ye everlasting doors; [R]and the King of glory shall come in.   Hag. 2:7; Acts 7:2

8   Who *is* this King of glory? The LORD strong and mighty, the LORD mighty in [R]battle.   Rev. 19:13–16

9   Lift up your heads, O ye gates; even lift *them* up, ye everlasting doors; and the King of glory shall come in.

10 Who is this King of glory? The LORD of hosts, he *is* the King of glory. Selah.

PSALM 25

A *Psalm* of David.

UNTO [R]thee, O LORD, do I lift up my soul.   86:4; 143:8

2   O my God, I [R]trust in thee: let me not be ashamed, let not mine enemies triumph over me.   34:8

3   Yea, let none that wait on thee be ashamed: let them be ashamed which [T]transgress without cause.   *deal treacherously*

4   [R]Shew me thy ways, O LORD; teach me thy paths.   5:8; 27:11; 86:11

5   Lead me in thy truth, and teach me: for thou *art* the God of my salvation; on thee do I wait all the day.

6   Remember, O LORD, [R]thy tender mercies and thy lovingkindnesses; for they *have been* ever of old.   103:17; 106:1

7   Remember not [R]the sins of my youth, nor my transgressions: according to thy mercy remember thou me for thy goodness' sake, O LORD.   Job 13:26; [Jer. 3:25]

8   Good and upright *is* the LORD: therefore will he teach sinners in the way.

9   The [T]meek will he guide in [T]judgment: and the meek will he teach his way.   *humble · justice*

10 All the paths of the LORD *are* mercy and truth unto such as keep his covenant and his testimonies.

11 [R]For thy name's sake, O LORD, pardon mine iniquity; for it *is* great.   31:3; 79:9; 109:21; 143:11

12 What man *is* he that feareth the LORD? him shall he teach in the way *that* he shall choose.

13 [R]His soul shall dwell at ease; and [R]his seed shall inherit the earth.   [Prov. 19:23] · 37:11; 69:36; Matt. 5:5

14 The secret of the LORD *is* with them that fear him; and he will shew them his covenant.

15 [R]Mine eyes *are* ever toward the LORD; for he shall pluck my feet out of the net.   [123:2; 141:8]

16 [R]Turn thee unto me, and have mercy upon me; for I *am* [T]desolate and afflicted.   69:16 · *lonely*

17 The troubles of my heart are enlarged: O bring thou me out of my distresses.

18 [R]Look upon mine affliction and my pain; and forgive all my sins.   31:7; 2 Sam. 16:12

19 Consider mine enemies; for they are many; and they hate me with [T]cruel hatred.   *violent*

20 O keep my soul, and deliver

me: let me not be ashamed; for I put my trust in thee.

21 Let integrity and uprightness preserve me; for I wait on thee.

22 ᴿRedeem Israel, O God, out of all his troubles.   [130:8]

PSALM 26

A Psalm of David.

JUDGE me, O Lᴏʀᴅ; for I have walked in mine integrity: I have trusted also in the Lᴏʀᴅ; *therefore* I shall not slide.

2 ᴿExamine me, O Lᴏʀᴅ, and prove me: ᵀtry my reins and my heart.   17:3; 139:23 · *test my mind*

3 For thy lovingkindness *is* before mine eyes: and ᴿI have walked in thy truth.   86:11; 2 Kin. 20:3

4 I have not ᴿsat with ᵀvain persons, neither will I go in with dissemblers.   1:1; Jer. 15:17 · *idolatrous*

5 I have ᴿhated the congregation of evildoers; and will not sit with the wicked.   31:6; 139:21

6 I will wash mine hands in innocency: so will I ᵀcompass thine altar, O Lᴏʀᴅ: *go about*

7 That I may ᵀpublish with the voice of thanksgiving, and tell of all thy wondrous works.   *proclaim*

8 Lᴏʀᴅ, ᴿI have loved the habitation of thy house, and the place where thine honour dwelleth.   27:4

9 ᴿGatherᵀ not my soul with sinners, nor my life with bloody men: 28:3 · *Do not take away*

10 In whose hands *is* ᵀmischief, and their right hand is full of ᴿbribes.   *a sinister scheme* · 1 Sam. 8:3

11 But as for me, I will walk in mine integrity: redeem me, and be merciful unto me.

12 ᴿMy foot standeth in an even place: in the congregations will I bless the Lᴏʀᴅ.   40:2

PSALM 27

A Psalm of David.

THE Lᴏʀᴅ *is* my light and my salvation; whom shall I fear? the Lᴏʀᴅ *is* the strength of my life; of whom shall I be afraid?

2 When the wicked, *even* mine ☆ enemies and my foes, came upon me to ᴿeatᵀ up my flesh, they stumbled and fell.   14:4 · *devour*

3 ᴿThough an host should encamp against me, my heart shall not fear: though war should rise against me, in this *will I be* confident.   3:6

4 ᴿOne *thing* have I desired of the Lᴏʀᴅ, that will I seek after; that I may dwell in the house of the Lᴏʀᴅ all the days of my life, to behold the beauty of the Lᴏʀᴅ, and to enquire in his temple.   65:4

5 For ᴿin the time of trouble he shall hide me in his pavilion: in the secret of his tabernacle shall he hide me; he shall ᴿset me up upon a rock.   31:20; 91:1 · 40:2

6 And now shall ᴿmine head be lifted up above mine enemies round about me: therefore will I offer in his tabernacle sacrifices of joy; I will sing, yea, I will sing praises unto the Lᴏʀᴅ.   3:3

7 Hear, O Lᴏʀᴅ, *when* I cry with my voice: have mercy also upon me, and answer me.

8 *When thou saidst,* Seek ye my face; my heart said unto thee, Thy face, Lᴏʀᴅ, will I seek.

9 ᴿHide not thy face *far* from me; put not thy servant away in anger: thou hast been my help; leave me not, neither forsake me, O God of my salvation.   69:17; 143:7

10 ᴿWhen my father and my mother forsake me, then the Lᴏʀᴅ will take me up.   Is. 49:15

11 Teach me thy way, O Lᴏʀᴅ, and lead me in a ᵀplain path, because of mine enemies.   *smooth*

12 Deliver me not over unto the ☆ will of mine enemies: for false witnesses are risen up against me, and such as breathe out cruelty.

13 *I had fainted,* unless I had believed to see the goodness of the Lᴏʀᴅ in the land of the living.

14 ᴿWait on the Lᴏʀᴅ: be of good courage, and he shall strengthen thine heart: wait, I say, on the Lᴏʀᴅ.   40:1; 62:5; 130:5; Prov. 20:22; Is. 25:9

PSALM 28

A Psalm of David.

UNTO thee will I cry, O LORD my rock; Rbe not silent to me: Rlest, *if* thou be silent to me, I become like them that go down into the pit.   35:22; 39:12 · 88:4; 143:7

2   Hear the voice of my supplications, when I cry unto thee, Rwhen I lift up my hands Rtoward thy holy Toracle. 5:7 · 138:2 · *sanctuary*

3   Draw me not away with the wicked, and with the workers of iniquity, Rwhich speak peace to their neighbours, but mischief *is* in their hearts. 12:2; 52:21; 62:4; Jer. 9:8

4   RGive them according to their deeds, and according to the wickedness of their endeavours: give them after the work of their hands; render to them their desert. [62:12]; 2 Tim. 4:14; [Rev. 18:6; 22:12]

5   Because they regard not the works of the LORD, nor the operation of his hands, he shall destroy them, and not build them up.

6   Blessed *be* the LORD, because he hath heard the voice of my supplications.

7   The LORD *is* my strength and my shield; my heart trusted in him, and I am helped: therefore my heart greatly rejoiceth; and with my song will I praise him.

8   The LORD *is* their strength, and he *is* the Rsaving strength of his anointed.   20:6

9   Save thy people, and bless thine inheritance: feed them also, and lift them up for ever.

PSALM 29

A Psalm of David.

GIVE Runto the LORD, O ye mighty, give unto the LORD glory and strength. 1 Chr. 16:28, 29

2   Give unto the LORD the glory due unto his name; worship the LORD in the beauty of holiness.

3   The voice of the LORD *is* upon the waters: Rthe God of glory thundereth: the LORD *is* upon many waters.   18:13; Acts 7:2

4   The voice of the LORD *is* powerful; the voice of the LORD *is* full of majesty.

5   The voice of the LORD breaketh Rthe cedars; yea, the LORD breaketh the cedars of Leb'-a-non.   Judg. 9:15; 1 Kin. 5:6; Is. 2:13; 14:8

6   He maketh them also to skip like a calf; Leb'-a-non and Sir'-i-on like a young Tunicorn.   *wild ox*

7   The voice of the LORD Tdivideth the flames of fire.   *hews out*

8   The voice of the LORD shaketh the wilderness; the LORD shaketh the wilderness of RKa'-desh.   Num. 13:26

9   The voice of the LORD maketh the Rhinds to calve, and Tdiscovereth the forests: and in his temple doth every one speak of *his* glory.   Job 39:1 · *strips bare*

10   The RLORD sitteth upon the flood; yea, Rthe LORD sitteth King for ever.   Gen. 6:17; Job 38:8, 25 · 10:16

11   RThe LORD will give strength unto his people; the LORD will bless his people with peace.   68:35

PSALM 30

A Psalm *and* Song *at* the dedication of the house of David.

I WILL extol thee, O LORD; for thou hast Rlifted me up, and hast not made my foes to Rrejoice over me.   28:9 · 25:2

2   O LORD my God, I cried unto thee, and thou hast healed me.

3   O LORD, Rthou hast brought up my soul from the grave: thou hast kept me alive, that I should not go down to the pit.   86:13

4   Sing unto the LORD, O ye saints of his, and give thanks at the remembrance of his holiness.

5   For his anger *endureth but* a moment; in his favour *is* life: weeping may endure for a night, but joy *cometh* in the morning.

6   And in my prosperity I said, I shall never Tbe moved.   *be shaken*

7   LORD, by thy favour thou hast made my mountain to stand strong: Rthou didst hide thy face, *and* I was troubled.   [Deut. 31:17]

8 I cried to thee, O LORD; and unto the LORD I made supplication.

9 What profit *is there* in my blood, when I go down to the ᵀpit? ᴿShall the dust praise thee? shall it declare thy truth?   *grave · [6:5]*

10 Hear, O LORD, and have mercy upon me: LORD, be thou my helper.

11 ᴿThou hast turned for me my mourning into dancing: thou hast put off my sackcloth, and girded me with gladness;   Eccl. 3:4; Is. 61:3

12 To the end that *my* glory may sing praise to thee, and not be silent. O LORD my God, I will give thanks unto thee for ever.

PSALM 31

To the chief Musician,
A Psalm of David.

IN ᴿthee, O LORD, do I put my trust; let me never be ashamed: deliver me in thy righteousness.   22:5

2 ᴿBow down thine ear to me; deliver me speedily: be thou my strong rock, for an house of defence to save me.   17:6; 71:2; 86:1

3 ᴿFor thou *art* my rock and my fortress; therefore for thy name's sake lead me, and guide me. [18:2]

4 Pull me out of the net that they have laid ᵀprivily for me: for thou *art* my strength.   *secretly*

5 ᴿInto thine hand I commit my spirit: thou hast redeemed me, O LORD God of truth.   Luke 23:46

6 I have hated them ᴿthat regard ᵀlying vanities: but I trust in the LORD.   Jon. 2:8 · *vain idols*

7 I will be glad and rejoice in thy mercy: for thou hast considered my trouble; thou hast known my soul in adversities;

8 And hast not shut me up into the hand of the enemy: ᴿthou hast set my feet in a large room.   [4:1]

9 Have mercy upon me, O LORD, for I am in trouble: ᴿmine eye is consumed with grief, *yea,* my soul and my ᵀbelly.   6:7 · *body*

10 For my life is spent with grief, and my years with sighing: my strength faileth because of mine iniquity, and my bones ᵀare consumed.   *waste away*

11 I was a reproach among all mine enemies, but especially among my neighbours, and a fear to mine acquaintance: they that did see me without fled from me.

12 ᴿI am forgotten as a dead man out of mind: I am like a broken vessel.   88:4, 5

13 ᴿFor I have heard the slander of many: fear *was* on every side: while they ᴿtook counsel together against me, they devised to take away my life.   50:20 · Matt. 27:1

14 But I trusted in thee, O LORD: I said, Thou *art* my God.

15 My times *are* in thy ᴿhand: deliver me from the hand of mine enemies, and from them that persecute me.   [Job 14:5; 24:1]

16 ᴿMake thy face to shine upon thy servant: save me for thy mercies' sake.   4:6; 80:3

17 Let me not be ashamed, O LORD; for I have called upon thee: let the wicked be ashamed, *and* let them be silent in the grave.

18 ᴿLet the lying lips be put to silence; which speak grievous things proudly and contemptuously against the righteous.   109:2

19 *Oh* how great *is* thy goodness, which thou hast laid up for them that fear thee; *which* thou hast wrought for them that trust in thee before the sons of men!

20 ᴿThou shalt hide them in the secret of thy presence from the pride of man: thou shalt keep them secretly in a pavilion from the strife of tongues.   [27:5; 32:7]

21 Blessed *be* the LORD: for ᴿhe hath shewed me his marvellous kindness in a strong city.   [17:7]

22 For I said in my haste, I am cut off from before thine eyes: nevertheless thou heardest the voice of my supplications when I cried unto thee.

23 O love the LORD, all ye his saints: *for* the LORD preserveth the faithful, and ᵀplentifully rewardeth the proud doer.   *fully repays*

24 ᴿBe of good courage, and he shall strengthen your heart, all ye that hope in the LORD.   [27:14]

PSALM 32

A Psalm of David, Mas'-chil.

BLESSED *is he whose* ᴿtransgression *is* forgiven, *whose* sin *is* covered. [85:2; 103:3]; Rom. 4:7, 8

2 Blessed *is* the man unto whom the LORD ᴿimputeth not iniquity, and in whose spirit *there is* no guile.   [2 Cor. 5:19]

3 When I kept silence, my bones waxed old through my ᵀroaring all the day long. *groaning*

4 For day and night thy ᴿhand was heavy upon me: ᵀmy moisture is turned into the drought of summer. Selah.   38:2; 39:10 · *my vitality*

5 I acknowledged my sin unto thee, and mine iniquity have I not hid. ᴿI said, I will confess my transgressions unto the LORD; and thou forgavest the iniquity of my sin. Selah.   2 Sam. 12:13; [1 John 1:9]

6 ᴿFor this shall every one that is godly ᴿpray unto thee in a time when thou mayest be found: surely in the floods of great waters they shall not come nigh unto him.   [1 Tim. 1:16] · 69:13; Is. 55:6

7 ᴿThou *art* my hiding place; thou shalt preserve me from trouble; thou shalt ᵀcompass me about with ᴿsongs of deliverance. Selah.   9:9 · *surround* · Ex. 15:1; Judg. 5:1

8 I will instruct thee and teach thee in the way which thou shalt go: I will guide thee with mine eye.

9 Be ye not as the ᴿhorse, *or* as the mule, *which* have no understanding: whose mouth must be held in with bit and bridle, lest they come near unto thee. Prov. 26:3

10 ᴿMany sorrows *shall be* to the wicked: but ᴿhe that trusteth in the LORD, mercy shall compass him about.   16:4; [Rom. 2:9] · Prov. 16:20

11 ᴿBe glad in the LORD, and rejoice, ye righteous: and shout for joy, all ye *that are* upright in heart.   64:10; 68:3; 97:12

PSALM 33

REJOICE ᴿin the LORD, O ye righteous: *for* praise is comely for the upright.   Phil. 3:1

2 Praise the LORD with harp: sing unto him with the psaltery *and* an instrument of ten strings.

3 Sing unto him a new song; play skilfully with a loud noise.

4 For the word of the LORD *is* right; and all his works *are done* in truth.

5 He loveth righteousness and ᵀjudgment: the earth is full of the goodness of the LORD.   *justice*

6 ᴿBy the word of the LORD were the heavens made; and all the host of them by the breath of his mouth.   Gen. 1:6, 7; [2 Pet. 3:5]

7 ᴿHe gathereth the waters of the sea together as an heap: he layeth up the ᵀdepth in storehouses.   Gen. 1:9; Job 26:10; 38:8 · *deep*

8 Let all the earth fear the LORD: let all the inhabitants of the world stand in awe of him.

9 For ᴿhe spake, and it was *done*; he commanded, and it stood fast.   148:5; Gen. 1:3

10 ᴿThe LORD bringeth the counsel of the heathen to nought: he maketh the devices of the people of none effect.   [2:1–3]; Is. 8:10; 19:3

11 The counsel of the LORD standeth for ever, the thoughts of his heart to all generations.

12 Blessed *is* the nation whose God *is* the LORD; *and* the people *whom* he hath ᴿchosen for his own inheritance.   [Ex. 19:5; Deut. 7:6]

13 ᴿThe LORD looketh from heaven; he beholdeth all the sons of men.   [14:2]; Job 28:24

14 From the place of his habitation he looketh upon all the inhabitants of the earth.

15 He fashioneth their hearts alike; ᴿhe considereth all their works. [2 Chr. 16:9]; Job 34:21; [Jer. 32:19]

16 ᴿThere is no king saved by the multitude of an host: a mighty man is not delivered by much strength.   44:6; 60:11; [Jer. 9:23, 24]

17 ᴿAn horse *is* a vain thing for

safety: neither shall he deliver *any* by his great strength.　[20:7]

18 [R]Behold, the eye of the LORD *is* upon them that fear him, upon them that hope in his mercy;　32:8

19 To deliver their soul from death, and [R]to keep them alive in famine.　37:19; Job. 5:20

20 Our soul waiteth for the LORD: he *is* our help and our shield.

21 For our heart shall rejoice in him, because we have trusted in his holy name.

22 Let thy mercy, O LORD, be upon us, according as we hope in thee.

PSALM 34

A Psalm of David, when he changed his behaviour before A-bim′-e-lech; who drove him away, and he departed.

I WILL [R]bless the LORD at all times: his praise *shall* continually *be* in my mouth.　[Eph. 5:20]

2 My soul shall make her boast in the LORD: the humble shall hear *thereof,* and be glad.

3 O magnify the LORD with me, and let us exalt his name together.

4 I [R]sought the LORD, and he heard me, and delivered me from all my fears.　[9:10; Matt. 7:7; Luke 11:9]

5 They looked unto him, and were [T]lightened: and their faces were not ashamed.　*radiant*

6 This poor man cried, and the LORD heard *him,* and saved him out of all his troubles.

7 The angel of the LORD encampeth round about them that fear him, and delivereth them.

8 O [R]taste and see that the LORD *is* good: blessed *is* the man *that* trusteth in him.119:103; 1 Pet. 2:3

9 O fear the LORD, ye his saints: for *there is* no [T]want to them that fear him.　*lack*

10 The young lions do lack, and suffer hunger: [R]but they that seek the LORD shall not [T]want any good *thing*.　[84:11] · *lack*

11 Come, ye children, hearken unto me: [R]I will teach you the fear of the LORD.　32:8

12 [R]What man *is he that* desireth life, *and* loveth *many* days, that he may see good? [1 Pet. 3:10–12]

13 Keep thy tongue from evil, and thy lips from speaking [R]guile.[T]　[Eph. 4:25] · *deceit*

14 Depart from evil, and do good; seek peace, and pursue it.

15 [R]The eyes of the LORD *are* upon the righteous, and his ears *are open* unto their cry.　Job 36:7

16 [R]The face of the LORD *is* against them that do evil, to cut off the remembrance of them from the earth.　Jer. 44:11; Amos 9:4

17 *The righteous* cry, and the LORD heareth, and delivereth them out of all their troubles.

18 The LORD *is* nigh [R]unto them that are of a broken heart; and saveth such as be [T]of a contrite spirit.　51:17; [Is. 57:15] · *crushed in spirit*

19 Many *are* the afflictions of the righteous: [R]but the LORD delivereth him out of them all. vv. 4, 6, 17

20 He keepeth all his bones: not one of them is broken.　☆

21 [R]Evil shall slay the wicked: and they that hate the righteous shall be desolate.　140:11; Prov. 24:16

22 The LORD [R]redeemeth the soul of his servants: and none of them that trust in him shall be desolate.　1 Kin. 1:29

PSALM 35

A Psalm of David.

P LEAD *my cause,* O LORD, with them that [T]strive with me: fight against them that fight against me.　*Contend for me*

2 Take hold of shield and [T]buckler, and stand up for mine help.　*A small shield*

3 Draw out also the spear, and stop *the way* against them that persecute me: say unto my soul, I *am* thy salvation.

4 [R]Let them be confounded and put to shame that seek after my soul: let them be [R]turned back and brought to confusion that devise my hurt.　40:14, 15; 70:2, 3 · 129:5

5 [R]Let them be as chaff before

the wind: and let the angel of the
LORD chase *them*.   83:13; Is. 29:5

6 Let their way be [R]dark and
slippery: and let the angel of the
LORD persecute them. 73:18; Jer. 23:12

7 For without cause have they
[R]hid for me their net *in* a pit,
which without cause they have
digged for my soul.   9:15

8 Let [R]destruction come upon
him at unawares; and let his net
that he hath hid catch himself:
into that very destruction let him
fall.   [55:23]; Is. 47:11; [1 Thess. 5:3]

9 And my soul shall be joyful
in the LORD: it shall rejoice in his
salvation.

10 [R]All my bones shall say,
LORD, [R]who *is* like unto thee,
which deliverest the poor from
him that is too strong for him, yea,
the poor and the needy from him
that spoileth him?   51:8 · [Mic. 7:18]

☆ 11 False witnesses did rise up;
they laid to my charge *things* that
I knew not.

12 They rewarded me evil for
good *to* the spoiling of my soul.

13 But as for me, [R]when they
were sick, my clothing *was* sackcloth: I humbled my soul with
fasting; and my prayer returned
into mine own bosom.   Job 30:25

14 I behaved myself as though
he had been my friend *or* brother:
I bowed down heavily, as one that
mourneth *for his* mother.

15 But in mine adversity they
rejoiced, and gathered themselves
together: *yea*, the abjects gathered themselves together against
me, and I knew *it* not; they did
tear *me*, and ceased not:

16 With [T]hypocritical mockers
in feasts, they gnashed upon me
with their teeth.   *ungodly*

17 Lord, how long wilt thou
[R]look on? rescue my soul from
their destructions, my darling
from the lions.   13:1; [Hab. 1:13]

18 I will give thee thanks in the
great congregation: I will praise
thee among [T]much people. *a mighty*

☆ 19 [R]Let not them that are mine
enemies wrongfully rejoice over
me: *neither* let them wink with

the eye that hate me without a
cause. 69:4; 109:3; Lam. 3:52; [John 15:25]

20 For they speak not peace: but
they devise deceitful matters
against *them that are* quiet in the
land.

21 Yea, they opened their mouth
wide against me, *and* said, Aha,
aha, our eye hath seen *it*.

22 *This* thou hast seen, O LORD:
keep not silence: O Lord, be not
far from me.

23 Stir up thyself, and awake to
my judgment, *even* unto my
cause, my God and my Lord.

24 Judge me, O LORD my God,
according to thy righteousness;
and let them not rejoice over me.

25 Let them not say in their
hearts, Ah, so would we have it:
let them not say, We have swallowed him up.

26 Let them be ashamed and
brought to confusion together
that rejoice at mine hurt: let them
be [R]clothed with shame and dishonour that magnify *themselves*
against me.   109:29

27 [R]Let them shout for joy, and
be glad, that favour my righteous
cause: yea, let them say continually, Let the LORD be magnified,
which hath pleasure in the prosperity of his servant.   Rom. 12:15

28 And my tongue shall speak
of thy righteousness *and* of thy
praise all the day long.

PSALM 36

To the chief Musician, *A Psalm* of
David, the servant of the LORD.

THE transgression of the
wicked saith within my
heart, *that* [R]*there is* no fear of
God before his eyes.   Rom. 3:18

2 For he flattereth himself in
his own eyes, [T]until his iniquity be
found to be hateful.   *when*

3 The words of his mouth *are*
iniquity and deceit: [R]he hath left
off to be wise, *and* to do good. 94:8

4 He deviseth mischief upon
his bed; he setteth himself [R]in a
way *that is* not good; he abhor-
reth not [R]evil. Is. 65:2 · [52:3; Rom. 12:9]

5 Thy mercy, O LORD, *is* in the heavens; *and* thy faithfulness *reacheth* unto the clouds.

6 Thy righteousness *is* like the great mountains; ᴿthy judgments *are* a great deep: O LORD, thou preservest man and beast.　77:19

7 How excellent *is* thy lovingkindness, O God! therefore the children of men put their trust under the shadow of thy wings.

8 ᴿThey shall be abundantly satisfied with the fatness of thy house; and thou shalt make them drink of ᴿthe river of thy pleasures.　63:5; 65:4; Is. 25:6 · 46:4; Rev. 22:1

9 ᴿFor with thee *is* the fountain of life: ᴿin thy light shall we see light.　[Jer. 2:13; John 4:10, 14] · [1 Pet. 2:9]

10 O continue thy lovingkindness unto them that know thee; and thy righteousness to the upright in heart.

11 Let not the foot of pride come against me, and let not the hand of the wicked remove me.

12 There are the workers of iniquity fallen: they are cast down, and shall not be able to rise.

PSALM 37

A Psalm of David.

FRETᴿ not thyself because of evildoers, neither be thou envious against the workers of iniquity.　73:3; [Prov. 23:17; 24:19]

2 For they shall soon be cut down ᴿlike the grass, and wither as the green herb.　92:7; James 1:11

3 Trust in the LORD, and do good; *so* shalt thou dwell in the land, and verily thou shalt be fed.

4 ᴿDelight thyself also in the LORD; and he shall give thee the desires of thine heart.　94:19; Is. 58:14

5 ᴿCommit thy way unto the LORD; trust also in him; and he shall bring *it* to pass.　[1 Pet. 5:7]

6 And he shall bring forth thy righteousness as the light, and thy ᵀjudgment as the noonday.　justice

7 Rest in the LORD, ᴿand wait patiently for him: fret not thyself because of him who ᴿprospereth in his way, because of the man

who bringeth wicked devices to pass.　40:1; 62:5; [Lam. 3:26] · [73:3–12]

8 ᴿCease from anger, and forsake wrath: ᴿfret not thyself in any wise to do evil.　[Eph. 4:26] · 73:3

9 For evildoers shall be cut off: but those that wait upon the LORD, they shall ᴿinherit the earth.　25:13

10 For ᴿyet a little while, and the wicked *shall* not *be:* yea, thou shalt diligently consider his place, and it *shall* not *be.*　[Heb. 10:36]

11 But the meek shall inherit the earth; and shall delight themselves in the abundance of peace.

12 The wicked plotteth against the just, ᴿand gnasheth upon him with his teeth.　35:16

13 ᴿThe LORD shall laugh at him: for he seeth that ᴿhis day is coming.　2:4; 59:8 · 1 Sam. 26:10; Job 18:20

14 The wicked have drawn out the sword, and have bent their bow, to cast down the poor and needy, *and* to slay such as be of upright ᵀconversation.　conduct

15 Their sword shall enter into their own heart, and their bows shall be broken.

16 ᴿA little that a righteous man hath *is* better than the riches of many wicked.　Prov. 15:16; [1 Tim. 6:6]

17 For the arms of the wicked shall be broken: but the LORD upholdeth the righteous.

18 The LORD knoweth the days of the upright: and their inheritance shall be for ever.

19 They shall not be ashamed in the evil time: and in the days of famine they shall be satisfied.

20 But the wicked shall perish, and the enemies of the LORD *shall be* as the fat of lambs: they shall ᵀconsume; into smoke shall they consume away.　vanish

21 The wicked borroweth, and payeth not again: but the righteous sheweth mercy, and giveth.

22 ᴿFor *such as be* blessed of him shall inherit the ᵀearth; and *they that be* cursed of him shall be ᵀcut off.　[Prov. 3:33] · *land · destroyed*

23 ᴿThe steps of a *good* man are ordered by the LORD: and he delighteth in his way.　40:2; 66:9; 119:5

24 Though he fall, he shall not be utterly cast down: for the LORD upholdeth *him with* his hand.

25 I have been young, and *now* am old; yet have I not seen the righteous forsaken, nor his ᵀseed begging bread.   *descendants*

26 *He is* ever merciful, and lendeth; and his seed *is* blessed.

27 Depart from evil, and do good; and dwell for evermore.

28 For the LORD loveth ᵀjudgment, and forsaketh not his saints; they are preserved for ever: but the seed of the wicked shall be cut off.   *justice*

29 ᴿThe righteous shall inherit the land, and dwell therein for ever.   v. 9; Prov. 2:21

30 ᴿThe mouth of the righteous speaketh wisdom, and his tongue talketh of judgment.   [Matt. 12:35]

31 The law of his God *is* in his heart; none of his steps shall ᵀslide.   *slip*

32 The wicked ᴿwatcheth the righteous, and seeketh to slay him.   10:8; 17:11

33 The LORD ᴿwill not leave him in his hand, nor condemn him when he is judged.   31:8; [2 Pet. 2:9]

34 ᴿWait on the LORD, and keep his way, and he shall exalt thee to inherit the land: when the wicked are cut off, thou shalt see *it*.   27:14

35 I have seen the wicked in great power, and spreading himself like a green bay tree.

36 Yet he passed away, and, lo, he *was* not: yea, I sought him, but he could not be found.

37 Mark the ᵀperfect *man*, and behold the upright: for the end of *that* man *is* peace.   *blameless*

38 ᴿBut the transgressors shall be destroyed together: the end of the wicked shall be cut off.   [1:4–6]

39 But the salvation of the righteous *is* of the LORD: *he is* their strength in the time of trouble.

40 And ᴿthe LORD shall help them, and deliver them: he shall deliver them from the wicked, and save them, ᴿbecause they trust in him.   22:4; Is. 31:5; Dan. 3:17; 6:23 · 34:22

PSALM 38

A Psalm of David,
to bring to remembrance.

O LORD, ᴿrebuke me not in thy wrath: neither chasten me in thy hot displeasure.   6:1

2 For thine arrows ᵀstick fast in me, and thy hand presseth me ᵀsore.   *pierce me deeply · down*

3 *There is* no soundness in my flesh because of thine anger; neither *is there any* ᵀrest in my bones because of my sin.   *health,* lit. *peace*

4 For mine iniquities are gone over mine head: as an heavy burden they are too heavy for me.

5 My wounds ᵀstink *and* are corrupt because of my foolishness.   *are foul* and *festering*

6 I am ᵀtroubled; I am bowed down greatly; I go mourning all the day long.   Lit. *bent down*

7 For my loins are filled with a loathsome *disease:* and *there is* no soundness in my flesh.

8 I am feeble and sore broken: I have ᵀroared by reason of the disquietness of my heart.   *groaned*

9 Lord, all my desire *is* before thee; and my ᵀgroaning is not hid from thee.   *sighing*

10 My heart panteth, my strength faileth me: as for the light of mine eyes, it also is gone from me.

11 My lovers and my friends ᴿstand aloof from my sore; and my kinsmen stand afar off.   88:18

12 They also that seek after my life lay snares *for me:* and they that seek my hurt ᵀspeak mischievous things, and imagine deceits all the day long.   *speak of destruction*

13 But I, as a deaf *man*, heard ☆ not; and *I was* as a dumb man *that* openeth not his mouth.

14 Thus I was as a man that heareth not, and in whose mouth *are* no ᵀreproofs.   *responses*

15 For ᵀin thee, O LORD, ᴿdo I hope: thou wilt hear, O Lord my God.   *I wait for thee,* O LORD · [39:7]

16 For I said, *Hear me*, lest *otherwise* they should rejoice over me: when my foot slippeth, they magnify *themselves* against me.

17 ᴿFor I *am* ready ᵀto halt, and my sorrow *is* continually before me.   51:3 · *to fall*

18 For I will declare mine iniquity; I will be sorry for my sin.

19 But mine enemies *are* ᵀlively, *and* they are strong: and they that hate me wrongfully are multiplied.   *vigorous*

20 They also ᴿthat render evil for good are mine adversaries; because I follow *the thing that good is.*   35:12

21 Forsake me not, O LORD: O my God, be not far from me.

22 Make haste to help me, O Lord my salvation.

PSALM 39

To the chief Musician, *even* to Je-du'-thun, A Psalm of David.

I SAID, I will take heed to my ways, that I sin not with my ᴿtongue: I will keep my mouth with a bridle, while the wicked is before me. Job 2:10; [James 3:5–12]

2 I was ᵀdumb with silence, I held my peace, *even* from good; and my sorrow was stirred.   *mute*

3 My heart was hot within me, while I was ᵀmusing the fire burned: *then* spake I with my tongue,   *meditating*

4 LORD, ᴿmake me to know mine end, and the measure of my days, what it *is; that* I may know how frail I *am.*   90:12; 119:84

5 Behold, thou hast made my days *as* an handbreadth; and mine age *is* as nothing before thee: verily every man at his best state *is* altogether vanity. Selah.

6 Surely every man walketh ᵀin a vain shew: surely they are disquieted in vain: he heapeth up *riches,* and knoweth not who shall gather them.   *as a shadow*

7 And now, Lord, what wait I for? my ᴿhope *is* in thee.   38:15

8 Deliver me from all my transgressions: make me not ᴿthe reproach of the foolish.   44:13; 79:4

9 I was ᵀdumb, I opened not my mouth; because thou didst *it. mute*

10 ᴿRemove thy stroke away

from me: I am consumed by the blow of thine hand. Job 9:34; 13:21

11 When thou with rebukes dost correct man for iniquity, thou makest his beauty ᴿto consume away like a moth: surely every man *is* vanity. Selah. [90:7]; Is. 50:9

12 Hear my prayer, O LORD, and give ear unto my cry; hold not thy peace at my tears: for I *am* a stranger with thee, *and* a sojourner, ᴿas all my fathers *were.* 119:19

13 ᴿO spare me, that I may recover strength, before I go hence, and be no more.   102:24

PSALM 40

To the chief Musician,
A Psalm of David.

I ᴿWAITED patiently for the LORD; and he inclined unto me, and heard my cry. 25:5; 27:1

2 He brought me up also out of an horrible pit, out of ᴿthe miry clay, and set my feet upon a rock, *and* established my goings. 69:2, 14

3 ᴿAnd he hath put a new song in my mouth, *even* praise unto our God: many shall see *it,* and fear, and shall trust in the LORD.   32:7

4 ᴿBlessed *is* that man that maketh the LORD his trust, and respecteth not the proud, nor such as turn aside to lies.   34:8; 84:12

5 ᴿMany, O LORD my God, *are* thy wonderful works *which* thou hast done, ᴿand thy thoughts *which are* to us-ward: they cannot be reckoned up in order unto thee: *if* I would declare and speak *of them,* they are more than can be numbered. Job 9:10 · 139:17; [Is. 55:8]

6 ᴿSacrifice and offering thou didst not desire; mine ears hast thou opened: burnt offering and sin offering hast thou not required.   51:16; Is. 1:11; [Jer. 6:20; 7:22, 23]

7 ᴿThen said I, Lo, I come: in the ᵀvolume of the book *it is* written of me,   [Heb. 10:5–9] · *scroll*

8 ᴿI delight to do thy will, O my God: yea, thy law *is* within my heart.   [Matt. 26:39; John 4:34]; Heb. 10:7

9 ᴿI have preached righteousness in the great congregation: lo,

ᴿI have not refrained my lips, O LORD, thou knowest. 22:22, 25 · 119:13

10 I have not hid thy righteousness within my heart; I have declared thy faithfulness and thy salvation: I have not concealed thy lovingkindness and thy truth from the great congregation.

11 Withhold not thou thy tender mercies from me, O LORD: ᴿlet thy lovingkindness and thy truth continually preserve me. 61:7; Prov. 20:28

12 For innumerable evils have ᵀcompassed me about: ᴿmine iniquities have taken hold upon me, so that I am not able to look up; they are more than the hairs of mine head: therefore my heart faileth me. *surrounded · 38:4; 65:3*

13 ᴿBe pleased, O LORD, to deliver me: O LORD, make haste to help me. 70:1

14 Let them be ashamed and confounded together that seek after my soul to destroy it; let them be driven backward and put to shame that wish me evil.

15 Let them be ᴿdesolate for a reward of their shame that say unto me, Aha, aha. 73:19

16 ᴿLet all those that seek thee rejoice and be glad in thee: let such as love thy salvation ᴿsay continually, The LORD be magnified. 70:4 · 35:27

17 But I *am* poor and needy; *yet* the Lord thinketh upon me: thou *art* my help and my deliverer; make no tarrying, O my God.

PSALM 41

To the chief Musician,
A Psalm of David.

Bᴸᴱˢˢᴱᴰ *is* he that considereth the ᵀpoor: the LORD will deliver him in time of trouble. *helpless* or *powerless*

2 The LORD will preserve him, and keep him alive; *and* he shall be blessed upon the earth: ᴿand thou wilt not deliver him unto the will of his enemies. 27:12

3 The LORD will strengthen him upon the bed of languishing: thou wilt ᵀmake all his bed in his sickness. *restore him in his sickbed*

4 I said, LORD, be merciful unto me: ᴿheal my soul; for I have sinned against thee. 6:2; 103:3; 147:3

5 Mine enemies speak evil of me, When shall he die, and his name perish?

6 And if he come to see *me*, he speaketh vanity: his heart gathereth iniquity to itself; *when* he goeth abroad, he telleth *it*.

7 All that hate me whisper together against me: against me do they ᵀdevise my hurt. *plot*

8 ᵀAn evil disease, *say they*, ᵀcleaveth fast unto him: and *now* that he lieth he shall rise up no more. *Lit. A thing of Belial · clings*

9 Yea, mine own familiar friend, in whom I trusted, ᴿwhich did eat of my bread, hath lifted up *his* heel against me. Matt. 26:14–25

10 But thou, O LORD, be merciful unto me, and raise me up, that I may ᵀrequite them. *repay*

11 By this I know that thou favourest me, because mine enemy doth not triumph over me.

12 And as for me, thou upholdest me in mine integrity, and settest me before thy face for ever.

13 Blessed *be* the LORD God of Israel from everlasting, and to everlasting. A-men', and A-men'.

BOOK II

PSALM 42

To the chief Musician, Mas'-chil,
for the sons of Ko'-rah.

Aˢ the ᵀhart panteth after the water brooks, so panteth my soul after thee, O God. *deer*

2 My soul thirsteth for God, for the ᴿliving God: when shall I come and appear before God? Rom. 9:26

3 ᴿMy tears have been my ᵀmeat day and night, while they continually say unto me, ᴿWhere is thy God? 80:5; 102:9 · *food* · 79:10

4 When I remember these *things*, ᴿI pour out my soul in me: for I had gone with the multitude,

ᴿI went with them to the house of God, with the voice of joy and praise, with a multitude that kept holyday. 1 Sam. 1:15; Job 30:16 · Is. 30:29

5 ᴿWhy art thou cast down, O my soul? and *why* art thou disquieted in me? ᴿhope thou in God: for I shall yet praise him *for* the help of his countenance. 43:5 · 71:14

6 O my God, my soul is cast down within me: therefore will I remember thee from the land of Jordan, and of the Her'-mon-ites, from ᵀthe hill Mi'-zar.   Or *Mount*

7 Deep calleth unto deep at the noise of thy ᵀwaterspouts: ᴿall thy waves and thy billows are gone over me. *waterfalls* · 88:7; Jon. 2:3

8 *Yet* the LORD will ᴿcommand his lovingkindness in the daytime, and ᴿin the night his song *shall be* with me, *and* my prayer unto the God of my life. Deut. 28:8 · Job 35:10

9 I will say unto God my rock, ᴿWhy hast thou forgotten me? why go I mourning because of the oppression of the enemy? 38:6

10 *As* with a sword in my bones, mine enemies reproach me; ᴿwhile *is* they say daily unto me, Where *is* thy God? Joel 2:17; Mic. 7:10

11 ᴿWhy art thou cast down, O my soul? and why art thou disquieted within me? hope thou in God: for I shall yet praise him, *who is* the ᵀhealth of my countenance, and my God. 43:5 · *help,* lit. *salvation*

PSALM 43

JUDGE ᴿme, O God, and ᴿplead my cause against an ungodly nation: O deliver me from the deceitful and unjust man. [35:24] · 35:1; 1 Sam. 24:15

2 For thou *art* the God of my strength: why dost thou cast me off? why go I mourning because of the oppression of the enemy?

3 ᴿO send out thy light and thy truth: let them lead me; let them bring me unto ᴿthy holy hill, and to thy ᵀtabernacles. [40:11] · 3:4 · *tents*

4 Then will I go unto the altar of God, unto God my exceeding joy: yea, upon the harp will I praise thee, O God my God.

5 ᴿWhy art thou cast down, O my soul? and why art thou disquieted within me? hope in God: for I shall yet praise him, *who is* ᵀthe health of my countenance, and my God. 42:5, 11 · *help,* lit. *salvation*

PSALM 44

To the chief Musician for the sons of Ko'-rah, Mas'-chil.

WE have heard with our ears, O God, ᴿour fathers have told us, *what* work thou didst in their days, in the times of old. [Ex. 12:26, 27; Deut. 6:20]

2 *How* thou didst drive out the heathen with thy hand, and plantedst them; *how* thou didst afflict the people, and cast them out.

3 For ᴿthey got not the land in possession by their own sword, neither did their own arm save them: but thy right hand, and thine arm, and the light of thy countenance, because thou hadst a favour unto them. Josh. 24:12

4 Thou art my King, O God: command deliverances for Jacob.

5 Through thee ᴿwill we push down our enemies: through thy name will we tread them under that rise up against us. Deut. 33:17

6 For ᴿI will not trust in my bow, neither shall my sword save me. 33:16; [1 Sam. 17:47; Hos. 1:7]

7 But thou hast saved us from our enemies, and hast put them to shame that hated us.

8 ᴿIn God we boast all the day long, and praise thy name for ever. Selah. 34:2; [Jer. 9:24]

9 But ᴿthou hast cast off, and put us to shame; and goest not forth with our armies. 60:1

10 Thou makest us to ᴿturn back from the enemy: and they which hate us spoil for themselves. 89:43

11 ᴿThou hast given us like sheep *appointed* for meat; and hast ᴿscattered us among the heathen. v. 22; Rom. 8:36 · 106:27; Ezek. 20:23

12 ᴿThou sellest thy people for nought, and dost not increase *thy wealth* by their price. Is. 52:3, 4

13 ᴿThou makest us a reproach

to our neighbours, a scorn and a derision to them that are round about us.   79:4; 80:6; Deut. 28:37

14 Thou makest us a byword among the heathen, a shaking of the head among the people.

15 My ᵀconfusion *is* continually before me, and the shame of my face hath covered me,   *dishonour*

16 For the voice of him that reproacheth and ᵀblasphemeth; ᴿby reason of the enemy and avenger.   *reviles* · 8:2

17 ᴿAll this is come upon us; yet have we not forgotten thee, neither have we dealt falsely in thy covenant.   Dan. 9:13

18 Our heart is not turned back, ᴿneither have our steps ᵀdeclined from thy way;   Job 23:11 · *departed*

19 Though thou hast sore broken us in ᴿthe place of ᵀdragons, and covered us ᴿwith the shadow of death.   Is. 34:13 · *jackals* · [23:4]

20 If we have forgotten the name of our God, or stretched out our hands to a strange god;

21 ᴿShall not God search this out? for he knoweth the secrets of the heart. [139:1, 2]; Job 31:14; [Jer. 17:10]

22 ᴿYea, for thy sake are we killed all the day long; we are counted as sheep for the slaughter.   Rom. 8:36

23 ᴿAwake, why sleepest thou, O Lord? arise, cast *us* not off for ever.   7:6

24 ᴿWherefore hidest thou thy face, *and* forgettest our affliction and our oppression?   Job 13:24

25 For ᴿour soul is bowed down to the dust: our belly cleaveth unto the ᵀearth.   119:25 · *ground*

26 Arise for our help, and redeem us for thy mercies' sake.

PSALM 45

To the chief Musician upon
Sho-shan'-nim, for the sons of Ko'-rah,
Mas'-chil, A Song of loves.

MY heart is inditing a good matter: I speak of the things which I have made touching the king: my tongue *is* the pen of a ᵀready writer.   *skilful*

2 Thou art fairer than the children of men: ᴿgrace is poured into thy lips: therefore God hath blessed thee for ever.   Luke 4:22

3 Gird thy sword upon *thy* thigh, O *most* mighty, with thy ᴿglory and thy majesty.   Jude 25

4 ᴿAnd in thy majesty ride prosperously because of truth and meekness *and* righteousness; and thy right hand shall teach thee terrible things.   Rev. 6:2

5 Thine arrows *are* sharp in the heart of the king's enemies; *whereby* the people fall under thee.

6 ᴿThy throne, O God, *is* for ☆ ever and ever: the sceptre of thy kingdom *is* a right sceptre.   [93:2]

7 Thou lovest righteousness, and hatest wickedness: therefore God, thy God, hath ᴿanointed thee with the oil of ᴿgladness above thy fellows.   2:2 · 21:6; Heb. 1:8, 9

8 All thy garments ᴿ*smell* of myrrh, and aloes, *and* cassia, out of the ivory palaces, whereby they have made thee glad.   Song 1:12, 13

9 Kings' daughters *were* among thy honourable women: upon thy right hand did stand the queen in gold of O'-phir.

10 Hearken, O daughter, and consider, and incline thine ear; ᴿforget also thine own people, and thy father's house;   Ruth 1:16, 17

11 So shall the king greatly desire thy beauty: ᴿfor he *is* thy Lord; and worship thou him. 95:6

12 And the daughter of Tyre *shall be there* with a gift; *even* ᴿthe rich among the people shall ᵀintreat thy favour.   Is. 49:23 · *seek*

13 The king's daughter *is* all glorious within: her clothing *is* ᵀof wrought gold.   *woven with gold*

14 ᴿShe shall be brought unto the king in raiment of needlework: the virgins her companions that follow her shall be brought unto thee.   Song 1:4

15 With gladness and rejoicing shall they be brought: they shall enter into the king's palace.

16 Instead of thy fathers shall be thy children, whom thou mayest make princes in all the earth.

17 ᴿI will make thy name to be remembered in all generations: therefore shall the people praise thee for ever and ever.   Mal. 1:11

PSALM 46

To the chief Musician for the sons of Ko'-rah, A Song upon Al'-a-moth.

GOD *is* our ᴿrefuge and strength, ᴿa very present help in trouble.   62:7, 8 · [145:18]
2   Therefore will not we fear, though the earth be removed, and though the mountains be carried into the midst of the sea;
3   ᴿ*Though* the waters thereof roar *and* be troubled, *though* the mountains shake with the swelling thereof. Selah.   [93:3, 4]
4   *There is* a river, the streams whereof shall make glad the city of God, the holy *place* of the tabernacles of the most High.
5   God *is* in the midst of her; she shall not be moved: God shall help her, *and that* right early.
6   ᴿThe heathen raged, the kingdoms were moved: he uttered his voice, the earth melted.   2:1, 2
7   The ᴿLORD of hosts *is* with us; the God of Jacob *is* our refuge. Selah.   Num. 14:9; 2 Chr. 13:12
8   Come, behold the works of the LORD, what desolations he hath made in the earth.
9   ᴿHe maketh wars to cease unto the end of the earth; he breaketh the bow, and cutteth the spear in sunder; ᴿhe burneth the chariot in the fire.   Is. 2:4 · Ezek. 39:9
10   Be still, and know that I *am* God: ᴿI will be exalted among the heathen, I will be exalted in the earth.   [Is. 2:11, 17]
11   The LORD of hosts *is* with us; the God of Jacob *is* our refuge. Selah.

PSALM 47

To the chief Musician,
A Psalm for the sons of Ko'-rah.

O CLAP your hands, all ye people; shout unto God with the voice of triumph.

2   For the LORD most high *is* terrible; *he is* a great ᴿKing over all the earth.   76:12; Deut. 7:21; Neh. 1:5
3   ᴿHe shall subdue the people under us, and the nations under our feet.   18:47
4   He shall choose our inheritance for us, the excellency of Jacob whom he loved. Selah.
5   ᴿGod is ᵀgone up with a shout, the LORD with the sound of a trumpet.   68:24, 25 · *ascended*
6   Sing praises to God, sing praises: sing praises unto our King, sing praises.
7   ᴿFor God *is* the King of all the earth: ᴿsing ye praises with understanding.   Zech. 14:9 · 1 Cor. 14:15
8   God reigneth over the heathen: God ᴿsitteth upon the throne of his ᴿholiness.   97:2 · 48:1
9   The princes of the people are gathered together, *even* the people of the God of Abraham: for the shields of the earth *belong* unto God: he is greatly exalted.

PSALM 48

A Song *and* Psalm for the sons of Ko'-rah.

GREAT *is* the LORD, and greatly to be praised in the ᴿcity of our God, *in* the mountain of his holiness.   87:3; Matt. 5:35
2   ᴿBeautiful for situation, the joy of the whole earth, *is* mount Zion, *on* the sides of the north, the city of the great King.   50:2
3   God is known in her palaces for a refuge.
4   For, lo, the kings were assembled, they passed by together.
5   They saw *it, and* so they marvelled; they were troubled, *and* hasted away.
6   Fear ᴿtook hold upon them there, *and* pain, as of a woman in ᵀtravail.   Ex. 15:15 · *childbirth*
7   Thou breakest the ships of Tar'-shish with an east wind.
8   As we have heard, so have we seen in the city of the LORD of hosts, in the city of our God: God will establish it for ever. Selah.

9 We have thought of ᴿthy lovingkindness, O God, in the midst of thy temple. 26:3

10 According to thy name, O God, so *is* thy praise unto the ends of the earth: thy right hand is full of righteousness. Josh. 7:9; Mal. 1:11

11 Let mount Zion rejoice, let the daughters of Judah be glad, because of thy judgments.

12 Walk about Zion, and go round about her: ᵀtell the towers thereof. *count*

13 Mark ye well her bulwarks, consider her palaces; that ye may ᴿtell *it* to the generation following. [78:5–7]

14 For this God *is* our God for ever and ever: ᴿhe will be our guide *even* unto death. Is. 58:11

PSALM 49

To the chief Musician,
A Psalm for the sons of Ko′-rah.

HEAR this, all *ye* people; give ear, all *ye* inhabitants of the world:

2 Both low and high, rich and poor, together.

3 My mouth shall speak of wisdom; and the meditation of my heart *shall be* of understanding.

4 I will incline mine ear to a ᵀparable: I will open my ᵀdark saying upon the harp. *proverb · riddle*

5 Wherefore should I fear in the days of evil, *when* the iniquity of my heels shall ᵀcompass me about? *surround*

6 They that ᴿtrust in their wealth, and boast themselves in the multitude of their riches; 52:7

7 None *of them* can by any means redeem his brother, nor give to God a ransom for him:

8 (For ᴿthe redemption of their soul *is* ᵀprecious, and it ceaseth for ever:) [Matt. 16:26] · *costly*

9 That he should still live for ever, *and* ᴿnot see corruption. 89:48

10 For he seeth *that* wise men die, likewise the fool and the ᵀbrutish person perish, and leave their wealth to others. *senseless*

11 Their inward thought *is*,

that their houses *shall continue* for ever, *and* their dwelling places to all generations; they call *their* lands after their own names.

12 Nevertheless man *being* in honour ᵀabideth not: he is like the beasts *that* perish. *does not endure*

13 This their way *is* their ᴿfolly: yet their posterity approve their sayings. Selah. [Luke 12:20]

14 Like sheep they are laid in the grave; death shall feed on them; and ᴿthe upright shall have dominion over them in the morning; and their beauty shall consume in the grave from their dwelling. [Dan. 7:18; 1 Cor. 6:2; Rev. 2:26]

15 But God will redeem my soul ☆ from the power of the grave: for he shall receive me. Selah.

16 Be not thou afraid when one is made rich, when the glory of his house is increased;

17 For when he dieth he shall carry nothing away: his glory shall not descend after him.

18 Though while he lived ᴿhe blessed his soul: and *men* will praise thee, when thou doest well to thyself. Deut. 29:19; Luke 12:19

19 He shall go to the generation of his fathers; they shall never see ᴿlight. Job 33:30

20 Man *that is* in honour, and understandeth not, ᴿis like the beasts *that* perish. Eccl. 3:19

PSALM 50

A Psalm of A′-saph.

THE ᴿmighty God, *even* the LORD, hath spoken, and called the earth from the rising of the sun unto the going down thereof. Is. 9:6

2 Out of Zion, the perfection of beauty, ᴿGod hath shined. 80:1

3 Our God shall come, and shall not keep silence: ᴿa fire shall devour before him, and it shall be very tempestuous round about him. [97:3]; Lev. 10:2; Num. 16:35

4 ᴿHe shall call to the heavens from above, and to the earth, that he may judge his people. Deut. 4:26

5 Gather my saints together unto me; those that have made a covenant with me by sacrifice.
6 And the ᴿheavens shall declare his righteousness: for ᴿGod is judge himself. Selah. [97:6] · 75:7
7 Hear, O my people, and I will speak; O Israel, and I will testify against thee: ᴿI *am* God, *even* thy God. Ex. 20:2
8 ᴿI will not reprove thee ᴿfor thy sacrifices or thy burnt offerings, *to have been* continually before me. Jer. 7:22 · Is. 1:11; [Hos. 6:6]
9 ᴿI will take no ᵀbullock out of thy house, *nor* he goats out of thy folds. 69:31 · *bull*
10 For every beast of the forest *is* mine, *and* the cattle upon a thousand hills.
11 I know all the ᵀfowls of the mountains: and the wild beasts of the field *are* mine. *birds*
12 If I were hungry, I would not tell thee: ᴿfor the world *is* mine, and the fulness thereof. 1 Cor. 10:26
13 Will I eat the flesh of bulls, or drink the blood of goats?
14 ᴿOffer unto God thanksgiving; and ᴿpay thy vows unto the most High: Heb. 13:15 · Num. 30:2
15 And ᴿcall upon me in the day of trouble: I will deliver thee, and thou shalt glorify me. [Zech. 13:9]
16 But unto the wicked God saith, What hast thou to do to declare my statutes, or *that* thou shouldest take my covenant in thy mouth?
17 ᴿSeeing thou hatest instruction, and castest my words behind thee. Neh. 9:26; Rom. 2:21
18 When thou sawest a thief, then thou ᴿconsentedst with him, and hast been ᴿpartaker with adulterers. [Rom. 1:32] · 1 Tim. 5:22
19 Thou givest thy mouth to evil, and thy tongue frameth deceit.
20 Thou sittest *and* speakest against thy brother; thou slanderest thine own mother's son.
21 These *things* hast thou done, and I kept silence; ᴿthou thoughtest that I was altogether *such an one* as thyself: *but* I will reprove thee, and ᴿset *them* in order before thine eyes. [Rom. 2:4] · [90:8]

22 Now consider this, ye that ᴿforget God, lest I tear *you* in pieces, and *there be* none to deliver. [Job 8:13]
23 Whoso offereth praise glorifieth me: and to him that ordereth *his* ᵀconversation *aright* will I shew the salvation of God. *conduct*

PSALM 51

To the chief Musician,
A Psalm of David, when Nathan the prophet came unto him, after he had gone in to Bath–she′-ba.

HAVE mercy upon me, O God, according to thy lovingkindness: according unto the multitude of thy tender mercies blot out my transgressions.
2 ᴿWash me throughly from mine iniquity, and cleanse me from my sin. [Heb. 9:14; 1 John 1:7, 9]
3 For I acknowledge my transgressions: and my sin *is* ever before me.
4 Against thee, thee only, have I sinned, and done *this* evil in thy sight: ᴿthat thou mightest be justified when thou speakest, *and* be clear when thou judgest. Rom. 3:4
5 ᴿBehold, I was shapen in iniquity; and in sin did my mother conceive me. [58:3; John 3:6; Rom. 5:12]
6 Behold, thou desirest truth in the inward parts: and in the hidden *part* thou shalt make me to know wisdom.
7 Purge me with hyssop, and I shall be clean: wash me, and I shall be whiter than snow.
8 Make me to hear joy and gladness; *that* the bones *which* thou hast broken may rejoice.
9 Hide thy face from my sins, and blot out all mine iniquities.
10 ᴿCreate in me a clean heart, O God; and renew a right spirit within me. [Ezek. 18:31; Eph. 2:10]
11 Cast me not away from thy presence; and take not thy ᴿholy spirit from me. [Luke 11:13]
12 Restore unto me the joy of thy salvation; and uphold me *with* thy ᴿfree spirit. [2 Cor. 3:17]
13 *Then* will I teach transgres-

sors thy ways; and sinners shall be converted unto thee.

14 Deliver me from bloodguiltiness, O God, thou God of my salvation: *and* my tongue shall sing aloud of thy righteousness.

15 O Lord, open thou my lips; and my mouth shall shew forth thy praise.

16 For thou desirest not sacrifice; else would I give *it:* thou delightest not in burnt offering.

17 ᴿThe sacrifices of God *are* a broken spirit: a broken and a contrite heart, O God, thou wilt not despise. 34:18; [Is. 57:15; 66:2]

18 Do good in thy good pleasure unto Zion: build thou the walls of Jerusalem.

19 Then shalt thou be pleased with ᴿthe sacrifices of righteousness, with burnt offering and whole burnt offering: then shall they offer bullocks upon thine altar. 4:5

PSALM 52

To the chief Musician, Mas'-chil, *A Psalm* of David, when Do'-eg the E'-dom-ite came and told Saul, and said unto him, David is come to the house of A-him'-e-lech.

WHY boastest thou thyself in mischief, O mighty man? the ᵀgoodness of God *endureth* continually. *lovingkindness*

2 Thy tongue ᵀdeviseth mischiefs; like a sharp rasor, working deceitfully. *plans destruction*

3 Thou lovest evil more than good; *and* lying rather than to speak righteousness. Selah.

4 Thou lovest all devouring words, O *thou* deceitful tongue.

5 God shall likewise destroy thee for ever, he shall take thee away, and pluck thee out of *thy* dwelling place, and root thee out of the land of the living. Selah.

6 The righteous also shall see, and fear, and shall laugh at him:

7 Lo, *this is* the man *that* made not God his strength; but trusted in the abundance of his riches, *and* strengthened himself in his ᵀwickedness. *destruction*

8 But I *am* ᴿlike a green olive tree in the house of God: I trust in the mercy of God for ever and ever. Jer. 11:16

9 I will praise thee for ever, because thou hast done *it:* and I will wait on thy name; for *it is* good before thy saints.

PSALM 53

To the chief Musician upon Ma'-ha-lath, Mas'-chil, *A Psalm* of David.

THE fool hath said in his heart, *There is* no God. Corrupt are they, and have done abominable iniquity: ᴿ*there is* none that doeth good. Rom. 3:10–12

2 God looked down from heaven upon the children of men, to see if there were *any* that did understand, that did seek God.

3 Every one of them is gone back: they are altogether become ᵀfilthy; *there is* none that doeth good, no, not one. *corrupt*

4 Have the workers of iniquity ᴿno knowledge? who eat up my people *as* they eat bread: they have not called upon God. Jer. 4:22

5 ᴿThere were they in great fear, *where* no fear was: for God hath scattered the bones of him that encampeth *against* thee: thou hast put *them* to shame, because God hath despised them. Lev. 26:17

6 ᴿOh that the salvation of Israel *were come* out of Zion! When God bringeth back the captivity of his people, Jacob shall rejoice, *and* Israel shall be glad. 14:7

PSALM 54

To the chief Musician on Neg'-i-noth, Mas'-chil, *A Psalm* of David, when the Ziph'-ims came and said to Saul, Doth not David hide himself with us?

SAVE me, O God, by thy name, and judge me by thy strength.

2 Hear my prayer, O God; give ear to the words of my mouth.

3 For strangers are risen up against me, and oppressors seek

after my ^Tsoul: they have not set God before them. Selah.   *life*

4 Behold, God *is* mine helper: the Lord *is* with them that ^Tuphold my soul.   *sustain*

5 He shall reward evil unto mine enemies: ^Tcut them off in thy ^Ttruth.   *destroy them · Or faithfulness*

6 I will freely sacrifice unto thee: I will praise thy name, O LORD; for *it is* good.

7 For he hath delivered me out of all trouble: ^Rand mine eye hath seen *his desire* upon mine enemies. 59:10

PSALM 55

To the chief Musician on Neg'-i-noth, Mas'-chil, *A Psalm* of David.

G IVE ear to my prayer, O God; and hide not thyself from my supplication.

2 Attend unto me, and hear me: I ^Rmourn in my complaint, and make a noise; Is. 38:14; 59:11; Ezek. 7:16

3 Because of the voice of the enemy, because of the oppression of the wicked: ^Rfor they cast iniquity upon me, and in wrath they hate me.   2 Sam. 16:7, 8

4 ^RMy heart is sore pained within me: and the terrors of death are fallen upon me.   116:3

5 Fearfulness and trembling are come upon me, and horror hath overwhelmed me.

6 And I said, Oh that I had wings like a dove! *for then* would I fly away, and be at rest.

7 Lo, *then* would I wander far off, *and* remain in the wilderness. Selah.

8 I would hasten my escape from the windy storm *and* tempest.

9 Destroy, O Lord, *and* divide their tongues: for I have seen violence and strife in the city.

10 Day and night they go about it upon the walls thereof: ^Rmischief^T also and sorrow *are* in the midst of it.   10:7 · *iniquity and trouble*

11 Wickedness *is* in the midst thereof: ^Rdeceit and guile depart not from her streets.   10:7

12 For *it was* not an enemy *that* reproached me; then I could have

borne *it*: neither *was it* he that hated me *that* did ^Rmagnify *himself* against me; then I would have hid myself from him: 35:26; 38:16

13 But *it was* thou, a man mine equal, ^Rmy ^Tguide, and mine acquaintance.   2 Sam. 15:12 · *companion*

14 We took sweet counsel together, *and* ^Rwalked unto the house of God in company.   42:4

15 Let death seize upon them, *and* let them go down ^Tquick into hell: for wickedness *is* in their dwellings, *and* among them.   *alive*

16 As for me, I will call upon God; and the LORD shall save me.

17 Evening, and morning, and at noon, will I pray, and cry aloud: and he shall hear my voice.

18 He hath delivered my soul in peace from the battle *that was* against me: for ^Rthere were many ^Twith me.   2 Chr. 32:7, 8 · *against*

19 God shall hear, and afflict them, ^Reven he that abideth of old. Selah. Because they ^Thave no changes, therefore they fear not God.   [Deut. 33:27] · *do not change*

20 He hath ^Rput forth his hands against such as ^Rbe at peace with him: he hath broken his ^Tcovenant.   Acts 12:1 · 7:4 · *treaty*

21 ^R*The words* of his mouth were smoother than butter, but war *was* in his heart: his words were softer than oil, yet *were* they drawn swords.   28:3; 57:4

22 ^RCast thy burden upon the LORD, and ^Rhe shall sustain thee: he shall never suffer the righteous to be moved.   [1 Pet. 5:7] · 37:24

23 But thou, O God, shalt bring them down into the pit of destruction: bloody and deceitful men ^Rshall not live out half their days; but I will trust in thee.   Prov. 10:27

PSALM 56

To the chief Musician upon Jo'-nath–e'-lem–re-cho'-kim, Mich'-tam of David, when the Phi-lis'-tines took him in Gath.

B E^R merciful unto me, O God: for man would swallow me up; he fighting daily oppresseth me.   57:1

2 Mine enemies would daily
^Rswallow^T me up: for *they be*
many that fight against me, O
thou most High.   57:3 · *hound me*

3 What time I am afraid, I will
trust in thee.

4 In God I will praise his word,
in God I have put my trust; ^RI will
not fear what flesh can do unto
me.   118:6; Is. 31:3; [Heb. 13:6]

5 ^TEvery day they wrest my
words: all their thoughts *are*
against me for evil. *All day they twist*

6 They gather themselves together, they hide themselves, they
mark my steps, when they ^Twait
for my soul.   *lie in wait for my life*

7 Shall they escape by iniquity? in *thine* anger cast down the
people, O God.

8 Thou ^Ttellest my wanderings:
put thou my tears into thy bottle:
are they not in thy book?   *count*

9 When I cry *unto thee,* then
shall mine enemies turn back: this
I know; for ^RGod *is* for me.   [118:6]

10 In God will I praise *his* word:
in the LORD will I praise *his* word.

11 In God have I put my trust: I
will not be afraid what man can
do unto me.

12 Thy vows *are* ^Tupon me, O
God: I will render praises unto
thee.   *are binding upon*

13 ^RFor thou hast delivered my
soul from death: *wilt* not *thou
deliver* my feet from falling, that I
may walk before God in the ^Rlight
of the living?   116:8, 9 · Job 33:30

PSALM 57

To the chief Musician, Al-tas'-chith,
Mich'-tam of David, when he fled from
Saul in the cave.

B E merciful unto me, O God,
be merciful unto me: for my
soul trusteth in thee: ^Ryea, in the
shadow of thy wings will I make
my refuge, ^Runtil *these* calamities be overpast.   Ruth 2:12 · Is. 26:20

2 I will cry unto God most high;
unto God ^Rthat performeth *all
things* for me.   [138:8]

3 ^RHe shall send from heaven,
and save me *from* the reproach of

him that would swallow me up.
Selah. God ^Rshall send forth his
mercy and his truth.   144:5, 7 · 43:3

4 My soul *is* among lions: *and* I
lie *even among* them that are set on
fire, *even* the sons of men, whose
teeth *are* spears and arrows, and
their tongue a sharp sword.

5 ^RBe thou exalted, O God,
above the heavens; *let* thy glory
be above all the earth.   108:5

6 They have prepared a net for
my steps; my soul is bowed down:
they have digged a pit before me,
into the midst whereof they are
fallen *themselves.* Selah.

7 ^RMy heart is ^Tfixed, O God,
my heart is fixed: I will sing and
give praise.   108:1–5 · *steadfast*

8 Awake up, ^Rmy glory; awake,
psaltery and harp: I *myself* will
^Tawake early.   16:9 · *awaken the dawn*

9 ^RI will praise thee, O Lord,
among the people: I will sing unto
thee among the nations.   108:3

10 ^RFor thy mercy *is* great unto
the heavens, and thy truth unto
the clouds.   103:11

11 ^RBe thou exalted, O God,
above the heavens: *let* thy glory
be above all the earth.   v. 5

PSALM 58

To the chief Musician, Al-tas'-chith,
Mich'-tam of David.

D O ye indeed speak righ-
teousness, ^TO congregation?
do ye judge uprightly, O ye sons
of men?   *ye silent ones*

2 Yea, in heart ye work wickedness; ye weigh the violence of
your hands in the earth.

3 ^RThe wicked are estranged
from the womb: they go astray as
soon as they be born, speaking
lies.   [53:3; Is. 48:8]

4 Their poison *is* like the poison of a serpent: *they are* like the
deaf adder *that* stoppeth her ear;

5 Which will not ^Rhearken to
the voice of charmers, charming
never so wisely.   Jer. 8:17

6 Break their teeth, O God, in
their mouth: break out the great
teeth of the young lions, O LORD.

7 [R]Let them melt away as waters *which* run continually: *when* he bendeth *his bow to shoot* his arrows, let them be as cut in pieces. 112:10; Is. 13:7; Ezek. 21:7

8 As a snail *which* melteth, let *every one of them* pass away: [R]*like* the [T]untimely birth of a woman, *that* they may not see the sun. Job 3:16 · *stillborn child*

9 Before your [R]pots can feel the thorns, he shall take them away [R]as with a whirlwind, both living, and in *his* wrath. 118:12 · Prov. 10:25

10 The righteous shall rejoice when he seeth the [R]vengeance: [R]he shall wash his feet in the blood of the wicked. Jer. 11:20 · 68:23

11 [R]So that a man shall say, Verily *there is* a reward for the righteous: verily he is a God that [R]judgeth in the earth. 92:1 · 50:6

PSALM 59

To the chief Musician, Al-tas′-chith, Mich′-tam of David; when Saul sent, and they watched the house to kill him.

DELIVER me from mine enemies, O my God: [T]defend me from them that rise up against me. Lit. *set me on high*

2 Deliver me from the workers of iniquity, and save me from [T]bloody men. *bloodthirsty*

3 For, lo, they lie in wait for my soul: [R]the mighty are gathered against me; not *for* my transgression, nor *for* my sin, O LORD. 56:6

4 They run and prepare themselves without *my* fault: [R]awake to help me, and behold. 35:23

5 Thou therefore, O LORD God of hosts, the God of Israel, awake to [T]visit all the [T]heathen: be not merciful to any wicked transgressors. Selah. *punish · nations*

6 [R]They return at evening: they [T]make a noise like a dog, and go round about the city. v. 14 · *growl*

7 Behold, they belch out with their mouth: [R]swords *are* in their lips: for [R]who, *say they,* doth hear? 57:4; Prov. 12:18 · 10:11; Job 22:13

8 But [R]thou, O LORD, shalt laugh at them; thou shalt have all the heathen in derision. Prov. 1:26

9 *Because of* his strength will I wait upon thee: [R]for God *is* my [T]defence. [62:2] · Lit. *strong hold*

10 The God of my mercy shall prevent me: God shall let [R]me see *my desire* upon mine enemies. 54:7

11 Slay them not, lest my people forget: scatter them by thy power; and bring them down, O Lord our shield.

12 [R]*For* the sin of their mouth *and* the words of their lips let them even be taken in their pride: and for cursing and lying *which* they speak. Prov. 12:13

13 [R]Consume *them* in wrath, consume *them,* that they *may* not *be:* and [R]let them know that God ruleth in Jacob unto the ends of the earth. Selah. 104:35 · 83:18

14 And [R]at evening let them return; *and* let them make a noise like a dog, and go round about the city. v. 6

15 Let them [R]wander up and down for [T]meat, and grudge if they be not satisfied. Job 15:23 · *food*

16 But I will sing of thy power; yea, I will sing aloud of thy mercy in the morning: for thou hast been my defence and refuge in the day of my trouble.

17 Unto thee, [R]O my strength, will I sing: for God *is* my defence, *and* the God of my mercy. 18:1

PSALM 60

To the chief Musician upon Shu′-shan–e′-duth, Mich′-tam of David, to teach; when he strove with A′-ram–na-ha-ra′-im and with A′-ram–zo′-bah, when Jo′-ab returned, and smote of E′-dom in the valley of salt twelve thousand.

O GOD, [R]thou hast cast us off, thou hast [T]scattered us, thou hast been displeased; O turn thyself to us again. 44:9 · *broken*

2 Thou hast made the earth to tremble; thou hast broken it: [R]heal the breaches thereof; for it shaketh. [2 Chr. 7:14]; Is. 30:26

3   Thou hast shewed thy people hard things: thou hast made us to drink the wine of astonishment.

4   ᴿThou hast given a banner to them that fear thee, that it may be displayed because of the truth. Selah.   20:5; Is. 5:26; 11:12; 13:2

5   ᴿThat thy beloved may be delivered; save *with* thy right hand, and hear me.   108:6–13

6   God hath ᴿspoken in his holiness; I will rejoice, I will ᴿdivide She'-chem, and mete out the valley of Suc'-coth.   89:35 · Josh. 1:6

7   Gil'-e-ad *is* mine, and Ma-nas'-seh *is* mine; ᴿE'-phra-im also *is* the strength of mine head; Judah *is* my lawgiver;   Deut. 33:17

8   ᴿMoab *is* my washpot; ᴿover E'-dom will I cast out my shoe: Phi-lis'-ti-a, triumph thou because of me.   2 Sam. 8:2 · 108:9; 2 Sam. 8:14

9   Who will bring me *into* the strong city? who will lead me into E'-dom?

10   *Wilt* not thou, O God, ᴿ*which* hadst cast us off? and *thou*, O God, *which* didst ᴿnot go out with our armies?   108:11 · Josh. 7:12

11   Give us help from trouble: ᴿfor vain *is* the help of man.   118:8

12   Through God ᴿwe shall do valiantly: for he *it is that* shall tread down our enemies. Num. 24:18

PSALM 61

To the chief Musician upon Neg'- i-nah, A *Psalm* of David.

HEAR my cry, O God; attend unto my prayer.

2   From the end of the earth will I cry unto thee, when my heart is overwhelmed: lead me to the rock *that* is higher than I.

3   For thou hast been a shelter for me, *and* ᴿa strong tower from the enemy.   Prov. 18:10

4   I will abide in thy tabernacle for ever: ᴿI will trust in the ᵀcovert of thy wings. Selah.   91:4 · shelter

5   For thou, O God, hast heard my vows: thou hast given *me* the heritage of those that fear thy name.

6   Thou wilt prolong the king's life: *and* his years as many generations.

7   He shall abide before God for ever: O prepare mercy ᴿand truth, *which* may preserve him.   40:11

8   So will I sing praise unto thy name for ever, that I may daily perform my vows.

PSALM 62

To the chief Musician, to Je-du'-thun, A Psalm of David.

TRULY ᴿmy soul waiteth upon God: from him *cometh* my salvation.   33:20

2   He only *is* my rock and my salvation; *he is* my defence; I shall not be greatly ᴿmoved.   55:22

3   How long will ye ᵀimagine mischief against a man? ye shall be slain all of you: ᴿas a ᵀbowing wall *shall ye be, and as* a tottering fence.   attack a man · Is. 30:13 · leaning

4   They only consult to cast *him* down from his ᵀexcellency: they ᴿdelight in lies: they bless with their mouth, but they curse inwardly. Selah.   high position · 28:3

5   My soul, ᵀwait thou only upon God; for my ᵀexpectation *is* from him.   wait silently · hope

6   He only *is* my rock and my salvation: *he is* my defence; I shall not be ᵀmoved.   shaken

7   ᴿIn God *is* my salvation and my glory: the rock of my strength, *and* my refuge, *is* in God. [Jer. 3:23]

8   Trust in him at all times; ye people, ᴿpour out your heart before him: God *is* a refuge for us. Selah.   42:4; 1 Sam. 1:15; Lam. 2:19

9   ᴿSurely men of low degree *are* vanity, *and* men of high degree *are* a lie: to be laid in the balance, they *are* altogether *lighter* than vanity.   39:5; Job 7:16; Is. 40:17

10   Trust not in oppression, and become not vain in robbery: ᴿif riches increase, set not your heart *upon them.*   [Luke 12:15; 1 Tim. 6:10]

11   God hath spoken once; twice have I heard this; that power *belongeth* unto God.

12   Also unto thee, O Lord, *belongeth* mercy: for ᴿthou ᵀren-

derest to every man according to his work. Rom. 2:6; 1 Cor. 3:8 · *rewardeth*

PSALM 63

A Psalm of David, when he was in the wilderness of Judah.

O GOD, thou *art* my God; ear-ly will I seek thee: ^Rmy soul thirsteth for thee, my flesh long-eth for thee in a dry and thirsty land, where no water is;   42:2

2 To see ^Rthy power and thy glory, so *as* I have seen thee in the sanctuary.   27:4

3 ^RBecause thy lovingkindness *is* better than life, my lips shall praise thee.   138:2

4 Thus will I bless thee while I live: I will ^Rlift up my hands in thy name.   28:2; 143:6

5 My soul shall be satisfied as *with* marrow and fatness; and my mouth shall praise *thee* with joy-ful lips:

6 When ^RI remember thee upon my bed, *and* meditate on thee in the *night* watches.   42:8

7 Because thou hast been my help, therefore in the shadow of thy wings will I rejoice.

8 My soul followeth ^Thard after thee: thy right hand upholdeth me.   *close behind thee*

9 But those *that* seek my soul, to destroy *it,* shall go into the lower parts of the earth.

10 They shall fall by the sword: they shall be a portion for foxes.

11 But the king shall rejoice in God; ^Revery one that sweareth by him shall glory: but the mouth of them that speak lies shall be stopped.   Deut. 6:13; [Is. 45:23; 65:16]

PSALM 64

To the chief Musician, A Psalm of David.

H EAR my voice, O God, in my prayer: preserve my life from fear of the enemy.

2 Hide me from the secret coun-sel of the wicked; from the ^Tinsurrection of the workers of iniquity: *tumult*

3 Who ^Twhet their tongue like a sword, ^R*and* bend *their bows to shoot* their arrows, *even* bitter words: *sharpen* · 58:7

4 That they may shoot in secret at the perfect: suddenly do they shoot at him, and fear not.

5 They encourage themselves *in* an evil matter: they ^Tcommune of laying snares privily; ^Rthey say, Who shall see them? *talk* · 10:11; 59:7

6 They ^Tsearch out iniquities; they accomplish a diligent search: both the inward *thought* of every one *of them,* and the heart, *is* deep.   *devise*

7 But God shall shoot at them *with* an arrow; suddenly shall they be wounded.

8 So they shall make their own tongue to fall upon themselves: all that see them shall flee away.

9 And all men shall fear, and shall ^Rdeclare the work of God; for they shall wisely consider of his doing.   Jer. 50:28; 51:10

10 ^RThe righteous shall be glad in the LORD, and shall trust in him; and all the upright in heart shall glory.   32:11; Job 22:19

PSALM 65

To the chief Musician, A Psalm *and* Song of David.

P RAISE waiteth for thee, O God in Si'-on: and unto thee shall the vow be performed.

2 O thou that hearest prayer, unto thee shall all flesh come.

3 Iniquities prevail against me: *as for* our transgressions, thou shalt ^Rpurge them away.   51:2; 79:9

4 Blessed *is the man whom* thou ^Rchoosest, and causest to ap-proach *unto thee, that* he may dwell in thy courts: we shall be satisfied with the goodness of thy house, *even* of thy holy temple. 4:3

5 *By* ^Tterrible things in righ-teousness wilt thou answer us, O God of our salvation; *who art* the confidence of all the ends of the earth, and of them that are afar off *upon* the sea: *awesome*

6 Which by his strength setteth

fast the mountains; ^R*being* girded with power: 93:1

7 Which stilleth the noise of the seas, the noise of their waves, and the tumult of the people.

8 They also that dwell in the uttermost parts are afraid at thy ^Ttokens: thou makest the outgoings of the morning and evening to ^Trejoice.   *signs · shout for joy*

9 Thou visitest the earth, and waterest it: thou greatly enrichest it ^Rwith the river of God, *which* is full of water: thou preparest them corn, when thou hast so provided for it.   46:4; 104:13; 147:8

10 Thou waterest the ridges thereof abundantly: thou settlest the furrows thereof: thou makest it soft with showers: thou blessest the ^Tspringing thereof.   *growth*

11 Thou crownest the year with thy goodness; and thy paths drop ^Tfatness.   *abundance*

12 They drop *upon* the pastures of the wilderness: and the little hills rejoice on every side.

13 The pastures are clothed with flocks; ^Rthe valleys also are covered over with corn; they shout for joy, they also sing. Is. 44:23; 55:12

PSALM 66

To the chief Musician,
A Song *or* Psalm.

MAKE ^Ra joyful ^Tnoise unto God, all ye lands: 100:1 · *shout*

2 Sing forth the honour of his name: make his praise glorious.

3 Say unto God, How ^Rterrible^T *art thou in* thy works! ^Rthrough the greatness of thy power shall thine enemies submit themselves unto thee.   65:5 · *awesome* · 18:44

4 ^RAll the earth shall worship thee, and shall sing unto thee; they shall sing *to* thy name. Selah.   117:1; Zech. 14:16

5 Come and see the works of God: *he is* terrible *in his* doing toward the children of men.

6 ^RHe turned the sea into dry *land*: ^Rthey went through the flood on foot: there did we rejoice in him.   Ex. 14:21 · Josh. 3:14–16

7 He ruleth by his power for ever; his eyes behold the nations: let not the rebellious exalt themselves. Selah.

8 O bless our God, ye people, and make the voice of his praise to be heard:

9 Which holdeth our soul ^Tin life, and suffereth not our feet to ^Tbe moved.   *among the living · slip*

10 For ^Rthou, O God, hast proved us: ^Rthou hast tried us, as silver is tried.   17:3 · [Is. 48:10; Mal. 3:3; 1 Pet. 1:7]

11 ^RThou broughtest us into the net; thou laidst affliction upon our loins.   Lam. 1:13; Ezek. 12:13

12 ^RThou hast caused men to ride over our heads; ^Rwe went through fire and through water: but thou broughtest us out into a wealthy *place*.   Is. 51:23 · Is. 43:2

13 ^RI will go into thy house with burnt offerings: ^RI will pay thee my vows, 100:4; 116:14, 17–19 · [Eccl. 5:4]

14 Which my lips have uttered, and my mouth hath spoken, when I was in trouble.

15 I will offer unto thee burnt sacrifices of fatlings, with the incense of rams: I will offer bullocks with goats. Selah.

16 Come *and* hear, all ye that fear God, and I will declare what he hath done for my soul.

17 I cried unto him with my mouth, and he was ^Textolled with my tongue.   *praised*

18 If I regard iniquity in my heart, the Lord will not hear *me*:

19 *But* verily God ^Rhath heard *me*; he hath attended to the voice of my prayer.   116:1, 2

20 Blessed *be* God, which hath not turned away my prayer, nor his mercy from me.

PSALM 67

To the chief Musician on Neg'-i-noth,
A Psalm *or* Song.

GOD be merciful unto us, and bless us; *and* ^Rcause his face to shine upon us; Selah. Num. 6:25

2 That thy way may be known upon earth, ^Rthy saving health among all nations. Is. 52:10; Titus 2:11

3 Let the people praise thee, O God; let all the people praise thee.

4 O let the nations be glad and sing for joy: for ᴿthou shalt judge the people righteously, and govern the nations upon earth. Selah.   [96:10, 13; 98:9]

5 Let the people praise thee, O God; let all the people praise thee.

6 ᴿThen shall the earth yield her increase; *and* God, *even* our own God, shall bless us. Zech. 8:12

7 God shall bless us; and all the ends of the earth shall fear him.

PSALM 68

To the chief Musician,
A Psalm *or* Song of David.

LET ᴿGod arise, let his enemies be scattered: let them also that hate him flee before him.   Num. 10:35

2 As smoke is driven away, *so* drive *them* away: ᴿas wax melteth before the fire, *so* let the wicked perish at the presence of God. 97:5

3 But ᴿlet the righteous be glad; let them rejoice before God: yea, let them exceedingly rejoice. 32:11

4 Sing unto God, sing praises to his name: ᴿextolᵀ him that rideth upon the heavens ᴿby his name JAH, and rejoice before him.   Deut. 33:26 · *praise* · [Ex. 6:3]

5 ᴿA father of the fatherless, and a judge of the widows, *is* God in his holy habitation.   [10:14, 18]

6 God setteth the solitary in families: he bringeth out those which are bound with chains: but the rebellious dwell in a dry *land*.

7 O God, ᴿwhen thou wentest forth before thy people, when thou didst march through the wilderness; Selah: Ex. 13:21

8 The earth shook, the heavens also ᵀdropped at the presence of God: *even* Si'-nai itself *was moved* at the presence of God, the God of Israel.   *dropped* rain

9 ᴿThou, O God, didst send a plentiful rain, whereby thou didst confirm thine inheritance, when it was weary.   Lev. 26:4; Job 5:10

10 Thy congregation hath dwelt therein: ᴿthou, O God, hast prepared of thy goodness for the poor.   74:19; Deut. 26:5

11 The Lord gave the word: great *was* the ᵀcompany of those that ᵀpublished *it*.   *host* · *proclaimed*

12 ᴿKings of armies did flee apace: and she that tarried at home divided the spoil.   Num. 31:8

13 ᴿThough ye have lien among the pots, ᴿ*yet shall ye be as* the wings of a dove covered with silver, and her feathers with yellow gold.   81:6 · 105:37

14 ᴿWhen the Almighty scattered kings in it, it was *white* as snow in Sal'-mon.   Josh. 10:10

15 The ᵀhill of God *is as* the hill of Ba'-shan; an high hill *as* the hill of Ba'-shan.   *mountain*

16 Why leap ye, ye high hills? ᴿ*this is* the hill *which* God desireth to dwell in; yea, the LORD will dwell *in it* for ever.   1 Kin. 9:3

17 ᴿThe chariots of God *are* twenty thousand, *even* thousands of ᵀangels: the Lord *is* among them, *as in* Si'-nai, in the holy *place*.   Deut. 33:2; Dan. 7:10 · *thousands*

18 ᴿThou hast ascended on high, ☆ thou hast led captivity captive: ᴿthou hast received gifts for men; yea, *for* the rebellious also, that the LORD God might dwell *among them*. Mark 16:19; Acts 1:9 · [Eph. 4:7–12]

19 Blessed *be* the Lord, *who* daily loadeth us *with benefits*, *even* the God of our salvation. Selah.

20 *He that is* our God *is* the God of salvation; and ᴿunto GOD the Lord *belong* the ᵀissues from death.   [Deut. 32:39] · *escapes*

21 But God shall wound the head of his enemies, *and* the hairy scalp of such an one as goeth on still in his trespasses.

22 The Lord said, I will bring ᴿagain from Ba'-shan, I will bring *my people* again ᴿfrom the depths of the sea: Amos 9:1–3 · Ex. 14:22

23 ᴿThat thy foot may be dipped in the blood of *thine* enemies, ᴿ*and* the tongue of thy dogs in the same.   58:10 · 1 Kin. 21:19; Jer. 15:3

24 They have seen thy goings, O

God; *even* the goings of my God, my King, in the sanctuary.

25 The singers went before, the players on instruments *followed* after; among *them were* the damsels playing with timbrels.

26 Bless ye God in the congregations, *even* the Lord, from ᴿthe fountain of Israel. Deut. 33:28; Is. 48:1

27 There *is* ᴿlittle Benjamin *with* their ruler, the princes of Judah *and* their council, the princes of Zeb'-u-lun, *and* the princes of Naph'-ta-li.   Judg. 5:14; 1 Sam. 9:21

28 Thy God hath ᴿcommanded thy strength: strengthen, O God, that which thou hast wrought for us.   42:8; Is. 26:12

29 Because of thy temple at Jerusalem ᴿshall kings bring presents unto thee. 1 Kin. 10:10, 25; Is. 18:7

30 Rebuke the company of spearmen, the multitude of the bulls, with the calves of the people, *till every one* submit himself with pieces of silver: scatter thou the people *that* delight in war.

31 Princes shall come out of Egypt; E-thi-o'-pi-a shall soon stretch out her hands unto God.

32 Sing unto God, ye ᴿkingdoms of the earth; O sing praises unto the Lord. Selah: [67:3, 4]

33 To him that rideth upon the heavens of heavens, *which were* of old; lo, he doth send out his voice, *and that* a mighty voice.

34 Ascribe ye strength unto God: his excellency *is* over Israel, and his strength *is* in the clouds.

35 O God, ᴿ*thou art* ᵀterrible out of thy holy places: the God of Israel *is* he that giveth strength and power unto *his* people. Blessed *be* God.   76:12 · *awesome*

PSALM 69

To the chief Musician upon
Sho-shan'-nim, A *Psalm* of David.

SAVE me, O God; for ᴿthe waters are come in unto *my* soul.   Job 22:11; Jon. 2:5

2 ᴿI sink in deep mire, where *there is* no standing: I am come into deep waters, where the floods overflow me.   40:2

3 I am weary of my crying: my throat is dried: ᴿmine eyes fail while I wait for my God. Is. 38:14

4 They that ᴿhate me without a ☆ cause are more than the hairs of mine head: they that would destroy me, *being* mine enemies wrongfully, are mighty: then I restored *that* which I ᵀtook not away.   35:19; John 15:25 · *did not steal*

5 O God, thou knowest my foolishness; and my sins are not hid from thee.

6 Let not them that wait on thee, O Lord Gᴏᴅ of hosts, be ashamed ᵀfor my sake: let not those that seek thee be ᵀconfounded for my sake, O God of Israel.   *because of me · disgraced*

7 Because for thy sake I have ☆ borne reproach; shame hath covered my face.

8 ᴿI am become a stranger unto ☆ my brethren, and an alien unto my mother's children.   Is. 53:3

9 ᴿFor the zeal of thine house ☆ hath eaten me up; and the reproaches of them that reproached thee are fallen upon me. John 2:17

10 When I wept, *and chastened* my soul with fasting, that ᵀwas to my reproach.   *became*

11 I made sackcloth also my garment; and I became a ᵀproverb to them.   *byword*

12 They that sit in the gate speak against me; and I *was* the song of the ᴿdrunkards. Job 30:9

13 But as for me, my prayer *is* unto thee, O Lᴏʀᴅ, *in* an acceptable time: O God, in the multitude of thy mercy hear me, in the truth of thy salvation.

14 Deliver me out of the mire, and let me not sink: let me be delivered from them that hate me, and out of the deep waters.

15 Let not the waterflood overflow me, neither let the deep swallow me up, and let not the pit shut her mouth upon me.

16 Hear me, O Lᴏʀᴅ; for thy lovingkindness *is* good: turn unto me

according to the multitude of thy tender mercies.

17 And hide not thy face from thy servant; for I am in trouble: hear me [T]speedily.   *quickly*

18 Draw nigh unto my soul, *and* redeem it: deliver me because of mine enemies.

19 Thou hast known [R]my reproach, and my shame, and my dishonour: mine adversaries *are* all before thee.   22:6, 7; Heb. 12:2

☆ 20 Reproach hath broken my heart; and I am full of heaviness: and I looked *for some* to take pity, but *there was* none; and for [R]comforters, but I found none.   Job 16:2

☆ 21 They gave me also gall for my meat; and in my thirst they gave me vinegar to drink.

22 Let their table become a snare before them: and *that which should have been* for *their* welfare, *let it become* a trap.

23 [R]Let their eyes be darkened, that they see not; and make their loins continually to shake. Is. 6:9, 10

24 [R]Pour out thine indignation upon them, and let thy wrathful anger take hold of them. [Jer. 10:25]

25 [R]Let their habitation be desolate; *and* let none dwell in their tents.   Matt. 23:38; Luke 13:35; Acts 1:20

26 For they persecute [R]him whom thou hast smitten; and they talk to the grief of those whom thou hast wounded.   [Is. 53:4]

27 [R]Add iniquity unto their iniquity: and let them not come into thy righteousness.   [Rom. 1:28]

28 Let them [R]be blotted out of the book of the living, and not be written with the righteous. Phil. 4:3

29 But I *am* poor and sorrowful: let thy salvation, O God, set me up on high.

30 [R]I will praise the name of God with a song, and will magnify him with thanksgiving.   [28:7]

31 [R]*This* also shall please the LORD better than an ox *or* bullock that hath horns and hoofs.   51:16

32 [R]The humble shall see *this, and* be glad: and [R]your heart shall live that seek God.   34:2 · 22:26

33 For the LORD heareth the poor, and despiseth not [R]his prisoners.   [68:6]; Eph. 3:1

34 [R]Let the heaven and earth praise him, the seas, and every thing that moveth therein.   96:11

35 [R]For God will save Zion, and will build the cities of Judah: that they may dwell there, and have it in possession.   51:18; Is. 44:26

36 The seed also of his servants shall inherit it: and they that love his name shall dwell therein.

PSALM 70

To the chief Musician, *A Psalm* of David, to bring to remembrance.

MAKE *haste,* [R]O God, to deliver me; make haste to help me, O LORD.   40:13–17

2 [R]Let them be [T]ashamed and confounded that seek after my [T]soul: let them be turned backward, and put to confusion, that desire my hurt. 35:4, 26 · *disgraced* · *life*

3 [R]Let them be turned back for a reward of their shame that say, Aha, aha.   40:15

4 Let all those that seek thee rejoice and be glad in thee: and let such as love thy salvation say continually, Let God be magnified.

5 [R]But I *am* poor and needy: make haste unto me, O God: thou *art* my help and my deliverer; O LORD, make no tarrying.   72:12, 13

PSALM 71

IN [R]thee, O LORD, do I put my trust: let me never be put to [T]confusion.   25:2, 3 · *shame*

2 [R]Deliver me in thy righteousness, and cause me to escape: [R]incline thine ear unto me, and save me.   31:1 · 17:6

3 Be thou my strong habitation, whereunto I may continually resort: thou hast given [R]commandment to save me, for thou *art* my rock and my fortress.   44:4

4 [R]Deliver me, O my God, out of the hand of the wicked, out of the hand of the unrighteous and cruel man.   140:1, 3

5 For thou *art* [R]my hope, O

Lord GOD: *thou art* my trust from my youth.   Jer. 14:8; 17:7, 13, 17; 50:7

6 ^RBy thee have I been holden up from the womb: thou art he that took me out of my mother's ^Tbowels: my praise *shall be* continually of thee.   22:9, 10 · *womb*

7 ^RI am as a wonder unto many; but thou *art* my strong refuge.   Is. 8:18; Zech. 3:8; 1 Cor. 4:9

8 Let ^Rmy mouth be filled *with* thy praise *and with* thy ^Thonour all the day.   35:28 · *glory*

9 Cast me not off in the time of old age; forsake me not when my strength faileth.

10 For mine enemies speak against me; and they that lay wait for my soul ^Rtake counsel together,   2 Sam. 17:1

11 Saying, God hath forsaken him: ^Tpersecute and take him; for *there is* none to deliver *him*. *pursue*

12 ^RO God, be not far from me: O my God, ^Rmake haste for my help.   35:22 · 70:1

13 Let them be ^Tconfounded *and* consumed that are adversaries to my soul; let them be covered *with* reproach and dishonour that seek my hurt.   *ashamed*

14 But I will hope continually, and will yet praise thee more and more.

15 My mouth shall ^Tshew forth thy righteousness *and* thy salvation all the day; for I know not the ^Tnumbers *thereof*.   *proclaim · limits*

16 I will go in the strength of the Lord GOD: I will make mention of thy righteousness, *even* of thine only.

17 O God, thou hast taught me from my ^Ryouth: and hitherto have I declared thy wondrous works.   Deut. 4:5; 6:7

18 Now also ^Rwhen I am old and greyheaded, O God, forsake me not; until I have ^Tshewed thy strength unto *this* generation, *and* thy power to every one *that* is to come.   [Is. 46:4] · *declared*

19 ^RThy righteousness also, O God, *is* very high, who hast done great things: ^RO God, who *is* like unto thee!   57:10; Deut. 3:24 · 35:10

20 ^R*Thou*, which hast shewed me great and sore troubles, ^Rshalt quicken me again, and shalt bring me up again from the depths of the earth.   60:3 · Hos. 6:1, 2

21 Thou shalt increase my greatness, and comfort me on every side.

22 I will also praise thee with the psaltery, *even* thy truth, O my God: unto thee will I sing with the harp, O thou Holy One of Israel.

23 My lips shall greatly rejoice when I sing unto thee; and my soul, which thou hast redeemed.

24 My tongue also shall talk of thy righteousness all the day long: for they are confounded, for they are brought unto shame, that seek my hurt.

PSALM 72

A Psalm for Solomon.

GIVE the king thy judgments, O God, and thy righteousness unto the king's son.

2 ^RHe shall judge thy people with righteousness, and thy poor with ^Tjudgment.   [Is. 9:7; 32:1] · *justice*

3 ^RThe mountains shall bring peace to the people, and the little hills, by righteousness.   85:10

4 ^RHe shall judge the poor of ☆ the people, he shall save the children of the needy, and shall break in pieces the oppressor.   Is. 11:4

5 They shall fear thee ^Ras long ☆ as the sun and moon endure, throughout all generations.   89:36

6 He shall come down like rain upon the mown grass: as showers *that* water the earth.

7 In his days shall the righteous flourish; ^Rand abundance of peace so long as the moon endureth.   Is. 2:4

8 ^RHe shall have dominion also from sea to sea, and from the river unto the ends of the earth. Ex. 23:31

9 ^RThey that dwell in the ☆ wilderness shall bow before him; ^Rand his enemies shall lick the dust.   74:14; Is. 23:13 · Is. 49:23; Mic. 7:17

10 ^RThe kings of Tar'-shish and of the isles shall bring presents:

the kings of She′-ba and Se′-ba shall offer gifts. 1 Kin. 10:2; 2 Chr. 9:21

11 ᴿYea, all kings shall fall down before him: all nations shall serve him.   Is. 49:23

12 For he shall deliver the needy when he crieth; the poor also, and *him* that hath no helper.

13 He shall spare the poor and needy, and shall save the souls of the needy.

14 He shall redeem their ᵀsoul from ᵀdeceit and violence: and ᴿprecious shall their blood be in his sight.   *life · oppression ·* 1 Sam. 26:21

15 And he shall live, and to him shall be given of the gold of ᴿShe′-ba: prayer also shall be made for him continually; *and* daily shall he be praised.   Is. 60:6

16 There shall be an handful of corn in the earth upon the top of the mountains; the fruit thereof shall shake like Leb′-a-non: ᴿand *they* of the city shall flourish like grass of the earth.   1 Kin. 4:20

☆ 17 His name shall endure for ever: his name shall be continued as long as the sun: and *men* shall be blessed in him: ᴿall nations shall call him blessed.   Luke 1:48

18 ᴿBlessed *be* the Lᴏʀᴅ God, the God of Israel, who only doeth wondrous things.   1 Chr. 29:10

19 And blessed *be* his glorious name for ever: ᴿand let the whole earth be filled *with* his glory; A-men′, and A-men′.   Hab. 2:14

20 The prayers of David the son of Jesse are ended.

BOOK III

PSALM 73

A Psalm of A′-saph.

TRULY God *is* good to Israel, *even* to such as are of a ᵀclean heart.   *pure*

2 But as for me, my feet were almost gone; my steps had well nigh ᴿslipped.   Job 12:5

3 ᴿFor I was envious at the foolish, *when* I saw the prosperity of the ᴿwicked.   37:1, 7 · Jer. 12:1

4 For *there are* no ᵀbands in their death: but their strength *is* firm.   *pangs* or *pain*

5 ᴿThey *are* not in trouble *as other* men; neither are they plagued like *other* men.   Job 21:9

6 Therefore pride compasseth them about as a chain; violence covereth them *as* a garment.

7 ᴿTheir eyes stand out with fatness: they have more than heart could wish.   Job 15:27; Jer. 5:28

8 ᴿThey are corrupt, and speak wickedly *concerning* oppression: they ᴿspeak loftily.   53:1 · 2 Pet. 2:18

9 They set their mouth ᴿagainst the heavens, and their tongue walketh through the earth. Rev. 13:6

10 Therefore his people return hither: ᴿand waters of a full *cup* are wrung out to them.   [75:8]

11 And they say, ᴿHow doth God know? and is there knowledge in the most High?   Job 22:13

12 Behold, these *are* the ungodly, who ᵀprosper in the world; they increase *in* riches.   *are always at ease*

13 Verily I have cleansed my heart *in* ᴿvain, and washed my hands in innocency.   Mal. 3:14

14 For all the day long have I been plagued, and chastened every morning.

15 If I say, I will speak thus; behold, I should offend *against* the generation of thy children.

16 When I thought to know this, it *was* too painful for me;

17 Until I went into the sanctuary of God; *then* understood I their ᴿend.   [37:38; 55:23]

18 Surely ᴿthou didst set them in slippery places: thou castedst them down into destruction. 35:6

19 How are they *brought* into desolation, as in a moment! they are utterly consumed with terrors.

20 As a dream when *one* awaketh; *so,* O Lord, when thou awakest, thou shalt despise their image.

21 Thus my heart was grieved, and I was pricked in my reins.

22 So foolish *was* I, and ignorant: I was *as* a beast before thee.

23 Nevertheless I *am* continually with thee: thou hast ᵀholden *me* by my right hand.   *held*

24 ᴿThou shalt guide me with thy counsel, and afterward receive me *to* glory. 32:8; 48:14; Is. 58:11

25 Whom have I in heaven *but thee?* and *there is* none upon earth *that* I desire beside thee.

26 My flesh and my heart faileth: *but* God *is* the strength of my heart, and my portion for ever.

27 For, lo, ᴿthey that are far from thee shall perish: thou hast destroyed all them that go a whoring from thee.   [119:155]

28 But *it is* good for me to ᴿdraw near to God: I have put my trust in the Lord GOD, that I may ᴿdeclare all thy works.   [Heb. 10:22] · 116:10

PSALM 74

Mas'-chil of A'-saph.

O GOD, why hast thou cast *us* off for ever? *why* doth thine anger smoke against the sheep of thy pasture?

2 Remember thy congregation, *which* thou hast purchased of old; ᵀthe rod of thine inheritance, *which* thou hast redeemed; this mount Zion, wherein thou hast dwelt.   *the tribe*

3 Lift up thy feet unto the perpetual desolations; *even* all *that* the enemy hath done wickedly in the sanctuary.

4 Thine enemies roar in the midst of thy congregations; they set up their ensigns *for* signs.

5 *A man* was famous according as he had lifted up axes upon the thick trees.

6 But now they break down the carved work thereof at once with axes and hammers.

7 They have cast fire into thy sanctuary, they have defiled *by casting down* the dwelling place of thy name to the ground.

8 ᴿThey said in their hearts, Let us destroy them together: they have burned up all the synagogues of God in the land.   83:4

9 We see not our signs: ᴿ*there is* no more any prophet: neither *is there* among us any that knoweth how long.   1 Sam. 3:1; Lam. 2:9

10 O God, how long shall the adversary reproach? shall the enemy blaspheme thy name for ever?

11 ᴿWhy withdrawest thou thy hand, even thy right hand? pluck *it* out of thy bosom.   Lam. 2:3

12 For ᴿGod *is* my King of old, working salvation in the midst of the earth.   44:4

13 ᴿThou didst divide the sea by thy strength: thou brakest the heads of the ᵀdragons in the waters.   Ex. 14:21 · *sea monsters* or *serpents*

14 Thou brakest the heads of leviathan in pieces, *and* gavest him *to be* ᵀmeat to the people inhabiting the wilderness.   *food*

15 ᴿThou didst cleave the fountain and the flood: thou driedst up mighty rivers.   105:41; Is. 48:21

16 The day *is* thine, the night also *is* thine: ᴿthou hast prepared the light and the sun.   Gen. 1:14–18

17 Thou hast ᴿset all the borders of the earth: thou hast made summer and winter.   Deut. 32:8; Acts 17:26

18 Remember this, *that* the enemy hath reproached, O LORD, and *that* the foolish people have blasphemed thy name.

19 O deliver not the ᵀsoul of thy turtledove unto the multitude *of the wicked:* forget not the congregation of thy poor for ever.   *life*

20 ᴿHave respect unto the covenant: for the dark places of the earth are full of the habitations of cruelty.   Gen. 17:7, 8; Lev. 26:44, 45

21 O let not the oppressed return ashamed: let the poor and needy praise thy name.

22 Arise, O God, plead thine own cause: remember how the foolish man ᵀreproacheth thee daily.   *reviles* or *taunts*

23 Forget not the voice of thine enemies: the tumult of those that rise up against thee increaseth continually.

PSALM 75

To the chief Musician, Al-tas'-chith, A Psalm *or* Song of A'-saph.

UNTO thee, O God, do we give thanks, *unto thee* do we give

thanks: for *that* thy name is near thy wondrous works declare.

2 When I shall ^Treceive the congregation I will judge uprightly. *choose the appointed* or *proper time*

3 The earth and all the inhabitants thereof are dissolved: I bear up the pillars of it. Selah.

4 I said unto the ^Tfools, Deal not foolishly: and to the wicked, ^RLift not up the horn: *boastful* · 94:4

5 Lift not up your horn on high: speak *not with* a stiff neck.

6 For ^Tpromotion *cometh* neither from the east, nor from the west, nor from the south. *exaltation*

7 But ^RGod *is* the judge: ^Rhe putteth down one, and setteth up another. 50:6 · 147:6; 1 Sam. 2:7; Dan. 2:21

8 For ^Rin the hand of the LORD *there is* a cup, and the wine is red; it is full of mixture; and he poureth out of the same: but the dregs thereof, all the wicked of the earth shall wring *them* out, *and* drink *them*. 60:3; Jer. 25:15; Rev. 14:10; 16:19

9 But I will declare for ever; I will sing praises to the God of Jacob.

10 All the horns of the wicked also will I cut off; *but* the horns of the righteous shall be exalted.

PSALM 76

To the chief Musician on Neg′-i-noth, A Psalm *or* Song of A′-saph.

IN ^RJudah *is* God known: his name *is* great in Israel. 48:1, 3

2 In ^TSa′-lem also is his tabernacle, and his dwelling place in Zion. *Jerusalem*

3 There brake he the arrows of the bow, the shield, and the sword, and the battle. Selah.

4 Thou *art* more glorious *and* excellent ^Rthan the mountains of prey. Ezek. 38:12

5 The stouthearted are spoiled, ^Rthey have slept their sleep: and none of the men of might have found their hands. 13:3

6 ^RAt thy rebuke, O God of Jacob, both the chariot and horse are cast into a dead sleep. Nah. 2:13

7 Thou, *even* thou, *art* to be feared: and who may stand in thy sight when once thou art angry?

8 ^RThou didst cause judgment to be heard from heaven; the earth feared, and was still, Ex. 19:9

9 When God ^Rarose to judgment, to save all the meek of the earth. Selah. [9:7–9]

10 ^RSurely the wrath of man shall praise thee: the remainder of wrath shalt thou restrain. Ex. 9:16

11 Vow, and pay unto the LORD your God: let all that be round about him bring presents unto him that ought to be feared.

12 He shall cut off the spirit of princes: ^Rhe *is* ^Tterrible to the kings of the earth. 68:35 · *awesome*

PSALM 77

To the chief Musician, to Je-du′-thun, A Psalm of A′-saph.

I CRIED unto God with my voice, *even* unto God with my voice; and he gave ear unto me.

2 In the day of my trouble I sought the Lord: my sore ran in the night, and ceased not: my soul refused to be comforted.

3 I remembered God, and was troubled: I complained, and my spirit was overwhelmed. Selah.

4 Thou ^Tholdest mine eyes waking: I am so troubled that I cannot speak. *hold my eyelids open*

5 I have considered the days of old, the years of ancient times.

6 I call to remembrance my song in the night: I commune with mine own heart: and my spirit made diligent search.

7 Will the Lord cast off for ever? and will he be favourable no more?

8 Is his mercy clean gone for ever? doth *his* ^Rpromise fail for evermore? [2 Pet. 2:8, 9]

9 Hath God forgotten to be gracious? hath he in anger shut up his tender mercies? Selah.

10 And I said, This *is* my ^Tinfirmity: *but I will remember* the

years of the right hand of the most High.   *anguish*

11 I will remember the works of the LORD: surely I will remember thy wonders of old.

12 I will meditate also of all thy work, and talk of thy doings.

13 Thy way, O God, *is* in ᵀthe ᴿsanctuary: who *is* so great a God as *our* God?   Or *holiness* · 73:17

14 Thou *art* the God that doest wonders: thou hast declared thy strength among the people.

15 Thou hast with *thine* arm redeemed thy people, the sons of Jacob and Joseph. Selah.

16 The waters saw thee, O God, the waters saw thee; they were ᴿafraid: the depths also were troubled.   Ex. 14:21; Hab. 3:8, 10

17 The clouds poured out water: the skies sent out a sound: thine arrows also went abroad.

18 The voice of thy thunder *was* in the ᵀheaven: the lightnings lightened the world: the earth trembled and shook.   *whirlwind*

19 Thy way *is* in the sea, and thy path in the great waters, and thy footsteps are not known.

20 Thou leddest thy people like a flock by the hand of Moses and Aaron.

PSALM 78

Mas'-chil of A'-saph.

GIVEᵀ ear, O my people, *to* my law: incline your ears to the words of my mouth.   *Listen*

☆ 2 I will open my mouth in a ᴿparable: I will utter dark sayings of old: Matt. 13:34, 35

3 Which we have heard and known, and our fathers have told us.

4 ᴿWe will not hide *them* from their children, ᴿshewing to the generation to come the praises of the LORD, and his strength, and his wonderful works that he hath done.   Is. 38:19; Joel 1:3 · Ex. 13:8, 14

5 For ᴿhe established a testimony in Jacob, and appointed a law in Israel, which he commanded

our fathers, that ᴿthey should make them known to their children: 147:19 · Deut. 4:9; 11:19

6 ᴿThat the generation to come might know *them, even* the children *which* should be born; *who* should arise and declare *them* to their children: 102:18

7 That they might set their hope in God, and not forget the works of God, but keep his commandments:

8 And ᴿmight not be as their fathers, ᴿa stubborn and rebellious generation; a generation ᴿthat set not their heart aright, and whose spirit was not stedfast with God.   2 Kin. 17:14 · Is. 30:9 · v. 37

9 The children of E'-phra-im, *being* armed, *and* carrying bows, turned back in the day of battle.

10 ᴿThey kept not the covenant of God, and refused to walk in his law;   2 Kin. 17:15

11 And ᴿforgat his works, and his wonders that he had shewed them.   106:13

12 ᴿMarvellous things did he in the sight of their fathers, in the land of Egypt, ᴿin the field of Zo'-an.   Ex. 7—12 · Num. 13:22; Ezek. 30:14

13 ᴿHe divided the sea, and caused them to pass through; and ᴿhe made the waters to stand as an heap.   Ex. 14:21 · Ex. 15:8

14 ᴿIn the daytime also he led them with a cloud, and all the night with a light of fire.   Ex. 13:21

15 ᴿHe clave the rocks in the wilderness, and gave *them* drink as *out of* the great depths.   Ex. 17:6

16 He brought ᴿstreams also out of the rock, and caused waters to run down like rivers.   Num. 20:8–11

17 And they sinned yet more against him by provoking the most High in the wilderness.

18 And ᴿthey ᵀtempted God in their heart by asking meat for their lust.   Ex. 16:2 · *tested*

19 ᴿYea, they spake against God; they said, Can God furnish a table in the wilderness?   Ex. 16:3

20 ᴿBehold, he smote the rock, that the waters gushed out, and the streams overflowed; can he

give bread also? can he provide flesh for his people?   Num. 20:11

21 Therefore the LORD heard *this*, and was wroth: so a fire was kindled against Jacob, and anger also came up against Israel;

22 Because they [R]believed not in God, and trusted not in his salvation: Deut. 1:32; 9:23; [Heb. 3:18]

23 Though he had commanded the clouds from above, and opened the doors of heaven,

24 [R]And had rained down manna upon them to eat, and had given them of the [T]corn of [R]heaven.   Ex. 16:4 · *bread*, lit. *grain* · John 6:31

25 Man did eat angels' food: he sent them meat to the full.

26 [R]He caused an east wind to blow in the heaven: and by his power he brought in the south wind.   Num. 11:31

27 He rained flesh also upon them as dust, and feathered fowls like as the sand of the sea:

28 And he let *it* fall in the midst of their camp, round about their [T]habitations.   *dwellings*

29 [R]So they did eat, and were well filled: for he gave them their own desire;   Num. 11:19, 20

30 They were not estranged from their lust. But while their meat *was* yet in their mouths,

31 The wrath of God came upon them, and slew the [T]fattest of them, and smote down the [T]chosen *men* of Israel.   *stoutest* · *choice*

32 For all this [R]they sinned still, and [R]believed not for his wondrous works.   Num. 14:16, 17 · vv. 11, 22

33 [R]Therefore their days did he consume in vanity, and their years in trouble.   Num. 14:29, 35

34 [R]When he slew them, then they sought him: and they returned and enquired early after God.   Num. 21:7; [Hos. 5:15]

35 And they remembered that God *was* their rock, and the high God [R]their redeemer.   Is. 41:14; 44:6

36 Nevertheless they did flatter him with their mouth, and they lied unto him with their tongues.

37 For their heart was not right

with him, neither were they [T]stedfast in his covenant.   *faithful*

38 But he, *being* full of [R]compassion, forgave *their* iniquity, and destroyed *them* not: yea, many a time [R]turned he his anger away, and [R]did not stir up all his wrath.   Ex. 34:6 · [Is. 48:9] · 1 Kin. 21:29

39 For [R]he remembered [R]that they *were but* flesh; [R]a wind that passeth away, and cometh not again.   103:14–16 · John 3:6 · [James 4:14]

40 How oft did they [R]provoke him in the wilderness, *and* grieve him in the desert!   Heb. 3:16

41 Yea, [R]they turned back and tempted God, and limited the Holy One of Israel.   Num. 14:22

42 They remembered not his hand, *nor* the day when he delivered them from the enemy.

43 How he had wrought his signs in Egypt, and his wonders in the field of Zo'-an:

44 [R]And had turned their rivers into blood; and their floods, that they could not drink.   Ex. 7:20

45 [R]He sent divers sorts of flies among them, which devoured them; and [R]frogs, which destroyed them.   Ex. 8:24 · Ex. 8:6

46 He gave also their increase unto the caterpiller, and their labour unto the [R]locust.   Ex. 10:14

47 [R]He destroyed their vines with hail, and their sycomore trees with frost.   Ex. 9:23–25

48 He gave up their [R]cattle also to the hail, and their flocks to hot thunderbolts.   Ex. 9:19

49 He cast upon them the fierceness of his anger, wrath, and indignation, and trouble, by sending evil angels *among them*.

50 He made a way to his anger; he spared not their soul from death, but gave their [T]life over to the [T]pestilence;   Or *beasts* · *plague*

51 And smote all the [R]firstborn in Egypt; [T]the chief of *their* strength in the tabernacles of Ham: Ex. 12:29, 30 · *the first of*

52 But made his own people to go forth like sheep, and guided them in the wilderness like a flock.

53 And he led them on safely, so

that they feared not: but the sea overwhelmed their enemies.

54 And he brought them to the border of his ^Rsanctuary, *even to* this mountain, ^R*which* his right hand had purchased. Ex. 15:17 · 44:3

55 ^RHe cast out the heathen also before them, and ^Rdivided them an inheritance by line, and made the tribes of Israel to dwell in their tents. 44:2 · Josh. 13:7; 19:51; 23:4

56 Yet they tempted and provoked the most high God, and kept not his testimonies:

57 But ^Rturned back, and dealt unfaithfully like their fathers: they were turned aside ^Rlike a deceitful bow. Ezek. 20:27, 28 · Hos. 7:16

58 ^RFor they provoked him to anger with their ^Rhigh places, and moved him to jealousy with their graven images. Is. 65:3 · Deut. 12:2

59 When God heard *this*, he was ^Twroth, and greatly abhorred Israel: *furious*

60 ^RSo that he forsook the tabernacle of Shi'-loh, the tent *which* he placed among men; 1 Sam. 4:11

61 ^RAnd delivered his strength into captivity, and his glory into the enemy's hand. Judg. 18:30

62 ^RHe gave his people over also unto the sword; and was wroth with his inheritance. 1 Sam. 4:10

63 The fire consumed their young men; and their maidens were not given to marriage.

64 ^RTheir priests fell by the sword; and ^Rtheir widows made no lamentation. 1 Sam. 4:17 · Job 27:15

65 Then the Lord awaked as one out of sleep, *and* ^Rlike a mighty man that shouteth by reason of wine. Is. 42:13

66 And ^Rhe smote his enemies in the hinder parts: he put them to a perpetual reproach. 1 Sam. 5:6

67 Moreover he refused the tabernacle of Joseph, and chose not the tribe of E'-phra-im:

68 But chose the tribe of Judah, the mount Zion which he loved.

69 And he built his ^Rsanctuary like high *palaces*, like the earth which he hath established for ever. 1 Kin. 6:1-38

70 ^RHe chose David also his servant, and took him from the sheepfolds: 1 Sam. 16:11, 12; 2 Sam. 7:8

71 From following the ewes great with young he brought him ^Rto feed Jacob his people, and Israel his inheritance. 2 Sam. 5:2

72 So he fed them according to the ^Rintegrity of his heart; and guided them by the skilfulness of his hands. 1 Kin. 9:4

PSALM 79

A Psalm of A'-saph.

O GOD, the heathen are come into ^Rthine inheritance; thy holy temple have they defiled; they have laid Jerusalem in heaps. 74:2

2 ^RThe dead bodies of thy servants have they given *to be* meat unto the fowls of the heaven, the flesh of thy saints unto the beasts of the earth. Deut. 28:26; Jer. 7:33; 19:7

3 Their blood have they shed like water round about Jerusalem; and *there was* none to bury *them*.

4 We are become a reproach to our ^Rneighbours, a scorn and derision to them that are round about us. 44:13; [Dan. 9:16]

5 How long, LORD? wilt thou be angry for ever? shall thy ^Rjealousy burn like fire? [Zeph. 3:8]

6 Pour out thy wrath upon the heathen that have not known thee, and upon the kingdoms that have not called upon thy name.

7 For they have devoured Jacob, and laid waste his dwelling place.

8 ^RO remember not against us former iniquities: let thy tender mercies speedily prevent us: for we are brought very low. Is. 64:9

9 Help us, O God of our salvation, for the glory of thy name: and deliver us, and purge away our sins, for thy name's sake.

10 ^RWherefore should the ^Theathen say, Where *is* their God? let him be known among the heathen in our sight *by* the revenging of

the blood of thy servants *which is* shed.   42:10 · nations or Gentiles

11 Let ᴿthe ᵀsighing of the prisoner come before thee; according to the greatness of thy power preserve thou those that are appointed to die;   102:20 · groaning

12 And render unto our neighbours sevenfold into their bosom their reproach, wherewith they have reproached thee, O Lord.

13 So we thy people and sheep of thy pasture will give thee thanks for ever: we will shew forth thy praise to all generations.

PSALM 80

To the chief Musician
upon Sho-shan'-nim–E'-duth,
A Psalm of A'-saph.

GIVE ear, O Shepherd of Israel, thou that leadest Joseph ᴿlike a flock; thou that dwellest *between* the cher'-ubims, ᴿshine forth.   77:20 · Deut. 33:2

2 Before E'-phra-im and Benjamin and Ma-nas'-seh stir up thy strength, and come *and* save us.

3 ᴿTurn us again, O God, ᴿand cause thy face to shine; and we shall be saved.   Lam. 5:21 · Num. 6:25

4 O Lord God of hosts, ᴿhow long wilt thou be angry against the prayer of thy people?   79:5

5 Thou feedest them with the bread of tears; and givest them tears to drink in great measure.

6 Thou makest us a strife unto our neighbours: and our enemies laugh among themselves.

7 ᵀTurn us again, O God of hosts, and cause thy face to shine; and we shall be saved.   Restore us

8 Thou hast brought a vine out of Egypt: ᴿthou hast cast out the heathen, and planted it.   Acts 7:45

9 Thou preparedst *room* before it, and didst cause it to take deep root, and it filled the land.

10 The hills were covered with the shadow of it, and the ᴿboughs thereof *were like* ᵀthe goodly cedars.   Lev. 23:40 · Lit. cedars of God

11 She sent out her boughs unto the sea, and her branches unto the river.

12 Why hast thou *then* ᴿbroken down her ᵀhedges, so that all they which pass by the way do pluck her?   Is. 5:5; Nah. 2:2 · walls or fences

13 The boar out of the wood doth waste it, and the wild beast of the field doth devour it.

14 Return, we beseech thee, O God of hosts: ᴿlook down from heaven, and behold, and visit this vine;   Is. 63:15

15 And the vineyard which thy right hand hath planted, and the branch *that* thou madest strong ᴿfor thyself.   [Is. 49:5]

16 *It is* burned with fire, *it is* cut down: they perish at the rebuke of thy ᵀcountenance.   presence

17 ᴿLet thy hand be upon the man of thy right hand, upon the son of man *whom* thou madest strong for thyself.   89:21

18 So will not we go back from thee: ᵀquicken us, and we will call upon thy name.   revive

19 ᵀTurn us again, O Lord God of hosts, cause thy face to shine; and we shall be saved.   Restore

PSALM 81

To the chief Musician upon Git'-tith,
A Psalm of A'-saph.

SING aloud unto God our strength: make a joyful noise unto the God of Jacob.

2 Take a psalm, and ᵀbring hither the timbrel, the pleasant harp with the psaltery.   strike

3 Blow up the trumpet in the new moon, in the time appointed, on our solemn feast day.

4 For ᴿthis *was* a statute for Israel, *and* a law of the God of Jacob.   Lev. 23:24; Num. 10:10

5 This he ordained in Joseph *for* a testimony, when he went out through the land of Egypt: ᴿ*where* I heard a language *that* I understood not.   114:1; Deut. 28:49; Jer. 5:15

6 I removed his shoulder from the burden: his hands were delivered from the ᵀpots.   baskets

7 Thou calledst in trouble, and I delivered thee; I answered thee in the secret place of thunder: I ᴿproved thee at the waters of Mer'-i-bah. Selah. Ex. 17:6, 7

8 ᴿHear, O my people, and I will testify unto thee: O Israel, if thou wilt hearken unto me; [50:7]

9 There shall no ᴿstrange god be in thee; neither shalt thou worship any strange god. [Is. 43:12]

10 I am the Lᴏʀᴅ thy God, which brought thee out of the land of Egypt: ᴿopen thy mouth wide, and I will fill it. 103:5

11 But my people would not hearken to my voice; and Israel would ᴿnone of me. Deut. 32:15

12 ᴿSo I gave them up unto their own hearts' lust: and they walked in their own counsels. [Acts 7:42]

13 ᴿOh that my people had hearkened unto me, and Israel had walked in my ways! [Is. 48:18]

14 I should soon have subdued their enemies, and turned my hand against their adversaries.

15 The haters of the Lᴏʀᴅ should have submitted themselves unto him: but their time should have endured for ever.

16 He should have fed them also with the finest of the wheat: and with honey out of the rock should I have satisfied thee.

PSALM 82
A Psalm of A'-saph.

Gᴏᴅ standeth in the congregation of the mighty; he judgeth among ᴿthe gods. 82:6

2 How long will ye judge unjustly, and ᴿaccept the persons of the wicked? Selah. [Deut. 1:17]

3 Defend the poor and fatherless: do justice to the afflicted and ᴿneedy. [Deut. 24:17; Is. 11:4; Jer. 22:16]

4 Deliver the poor and needy: ᵀrid them out of the hand of the wicked. free

5 They know not, neither will they understand; they walk on in darkness: all the ᴿfoundations of the earth are out of course. 11:3

6 I have said, ᴿYe are gods; and

all of you are children of the most High. John 10:34

7 But ye shall die like men, and fall like one of the princes.

8 Arise, O God, judge the earth: for thou shalt inherit all nations.

PSALM 83
A Song or Psalm of A'-saph.

Kᴇᴇᴘ ᴿnot thou silence, O God: hold not thy peace, and be not still, O God. 28:1

2 For, lo, ᴿthine enemies make a tumult: and they that hate thee have lifted up the head. Acts 4:25

3 They have taken crafty counsel against thy people, and consulted against thy hidden ones.

4 They have said, Come, and let us cut them off from being a nation; that the name of Israel may be no more in remembrance.

5 For they have consulted together with one ᵀconsent: they are confederate against thee: Lit. heart

6 ᴿThe tabernacles of E'-dom, and the Ish'-ma-el-ites; of Moab, and the Ha-gar-enes'; 2 Chr. 20:1

7 Ge'-bal, and Ammon, and Am'-a-lek; the Phi-lis'-tines with the inhabitants of Tyre;

8 As'-sur also is joined with them: they have holpen the children of Lot. Selah.

9 Do unto them as unto the Mid'-i-an-ites; as to Sis'-e-ra, as to Jabin, at the brook of Ki'-son:

10 Which perished at En'-dor: ᴿthey became as ᵀdung for the earth. Zeph. 1:17 · refuse on

11 Make their nobles like O'-reb, and like ᴿZe'-eb: yea, all their princes as ᴿZe'-bah, and as Zal-mun'-na: Judg. 7:25 · Judg. 8:12–21

12 Who said, Let us take to ourselves the ᵀhouses of God in possession. pastures

13 ᴿO my God, make them like a wheel; ᴿas the stubble before the wind. Is. 17:13 · 35:5; Is. 40:24; Jer. 13:24

14 As the fire burneth a wood, and as the flame ᴿsetteth the mountains on fire; Ex. 19:18

15 So ᵀpersecute them with thy

tempest, and make them afraid with thy storm.   *pursue*

16 Fill their faces with shame; that they may seek thy name, O LORD.

17 Let them be confounded and troubled for ever; yea, let them be put to shame, and perish:

18 RThat *men* may know that thou, whose Rname alone *is* JE-HO'-VAH, *art* Rthe most high over all the earth.   59:13 · Ex. 6:3 · [92:8]

PSALM 84

To the chief Musician upon Git'-tith,
A Psalm for the sons of Ko'-rah.

HOW Ramiable *are* thy taber-nacles, O LORD of hosts!   27:4

2 RMy soul longeth, yea, even fainteth for the courts of the LORD: my heart and my flesh crieth out for the living God.   42:1, 2

3 Yea, the sparrow hath found an house, and the swallow a nest for herself, where she may lay her young, *even* thine altars, O LORD of hosts, my King, and my God.

4 Blessed *are* they that dwell in thy Rhouse: they will be still prais-ing thee. Selah.   [65:4]

5 Blessed *is* the man whose strength *is* in thee; in whose heart *are* the ways *of them*.

6 *Who* passing through the val-ley of Ba'-ca make it a well; the rain also filleth the pools.

7 They go from strength to strength, *every one of them* in Zion appeareth before God.

8 O LORD God of hosts, hear my prayer: give ear, O God of Jacob. Selah.

9 Behold, RO God our shield, and look upon the face of thine anointed.   Gen. 15:1

10 For a day in thy courts *is* bet-ter than a thousand. I had rather be a doorkeeper in the house of my God, than to dwell in the tents of wickedness.

11 For the LORD God *is* Ra sun and Rshield: the LORD will give grace and glory: no good *thing* will he withhold from them that walk uprightly.   Rev. 21:23 · Gen. 15:1

12 O LORD of hosts, Rblessed *is* the man that trusteth in thee.   [2:12]

PSALM 85

To the chief Musician,
A Psalm for the sons of Ko'-rah.

LORD, thou hast been favour-able unto thy land: thou hast Rbrought back the captivity of Jacob.   Ezek. 39:25; Hos. 6:11; Joel 3:1

2 Thou hast forgiven the iniq-uity of thy people; thou hast cov-ered all their sin. Selah.

3 Thou hast taken away all thy wrath: thou hast turned *thyself* from the fierceness of thine anger.

4 RTurnT us, O God of our sal-vation, and cause thine anger toward us to cease.   80:3, 7 · *Restore*

5 RWilt thou be angry with us for ever? wilt thou draw out thine anger to all generations?   79:5

6 Wilt thou not Rrevive us again: that thy people may rejoice in thee?   Hab. 3:2

7 Shew us thy mercy, O LORD, and grant us thy salvation.

8 I will hear what God the LORD will speak: for he will speak peace unto his people, and to his saints: but let them not turn again to Tfolly.   *foolishness*

9 Surely Rhis salvation *is* nigh them that fear him; that glory may dwell in our land.   Is. 46:13

10 Mercy and truth are met together; righteousness and peace have kissed *each other*.

11 Truth shall spring out of the earth; and righteousness shall look down from heaven.

12 RYea, the LORD shall give *that which is* good; and our land shall yield her increase.   [84:11; James 1:17]

13 Righteousness shall go be-fore him; and shall set *us* in the way of his steps.

PSALM 86

A Prayer of David.

BOW down thine ear, O LORD, hear me: for I *am* poor and needy.

2   Preserve my ^Tsoul; for I *am* holy: O thou my God, save thy servant that trusteth in thee.   *life*

3   Be merciful unto me, O Lord: for I cry unto thee daily.

4   Rejoice the soul of thy servant: ^Rfor unto thee, O Lord, do I lift up my soul.   25:1; 143:8

5   For ^Rthou, Lord, *art* good, and ready to forgive; and plenteous in mercy unto all them that call upon thee.   130:7; 145:9; [Joel 2:13]

6   Give ear, O Lord, unto my prayer; and attend to the voice of my supplications.

7   In the day of my trouble I will call upon thee: for thou wilt answer me.

8   ^RAmong the gods *there is* none like unto thee, O Lord; neither *are there any works* like unto thy works.   2 Sam. 7:22; 1 Kin. 8:23

9   All nations whom thou hast made shall come and worship before thee, O Lord; and shall glorify thy name.

10   For thou *art* great, and doest wondrous things: ^Rthou *art* God alone.   Is. 37:16; Mark 12:29; 1 Cor. 8:4

11   ^RTeach me thy way, O Lord; I will walk in thy truth: unite my heart to fear thy name.   27:11; 143:8

12   I will praise thee, O Lord my God, with all my heart: and I will glorify thy name for evermore.

13   For great *is* thy mercy toward me: and thou hast delivered my soul from the lowest hell.

14   O God, the proud are risen against me, and ^Tthe assemblies of violent *men* have sought after my soul; and have not set thee before them.   *mobs*

15   But ^Rthou, O Lord, *art* a God full of compassion, and gracious, longsuffering, and plenteous in mercy and truth.   [86:5]; Ex. 34:6

16   O turn unto me, and have mercy upon me; give thy strength unto thy servant, and save the son of thine handmaid.

17   Shew me ^Ta token for good; that they which hate me may see *it,* and be ashamed: because thou, Lord, hast holpen me, and comforted me.   *a sign*

PSALM 87

A Psalm *or* Song for the sons of Ko′-rah.

HIS foundation *is* in the holy mountains.

2   ^RThe Lord loveth the gates of Zion more than all the dwellings of Jacob.   78:67, 68

3   Glorious things are spoken of thee, O city of God. Selah.

4   I will make mention of ^TRa′-hab and Babylon to them that know me: behold Phi-lis′-ti-a, and Tyre, with E-thi-o′-pi-a; this *man* was born there.   *Egypt*

5   And of Zion it shall be said, This and that man was born in her: and the highest himself shall establish her.

6   The Lord shall count, when he writeth up the people, *that* this *man* was born there. Selah.

7   As well the singers as the players on instruments *shall be there:* all my springs *are* in thee.

PSALM 88

A Song *or* Psalm for the sons of Ko′-rah, to the chief Musician upon Ma′-ha-lath Le-an′-noth, Mas′-chil of He′-man the Ez′-ra-hite.

O LORD ^RGod of my salvation, I have cried day *and* night before thee: 27:9; [Luke 18:7]

2   Let my prayer come before thee: incline thine ear unto my cry;

3   For my soul is full of troubles: and my life ^Rdraweth ^Tnigh unto the ^Tgrave.   107:18 · *near* · Or *Sheol*

4   I am counted with them that ^Rgo down into the pit: I am as a man *that hath* no strength: [28:1]

5   ^TFree among the dead, like the slain that lie in the grave, whom thou rememberest no more: and they are cut off from thy hand.   *Adrift*

6   Thou hast laid me in the lowest pit, in darkness, in the deeps.

7   Thy wrath lieth hard upon me, and thou hast afflicted *me* with all ^Rthy waves. Selah.   42:7

8   ^RThou hast put away mine

acquaintance far from me; thou hast made me an abomination unto them: ^RI *am* shut up, and I cannot come forth.   142:4 · Lam. 3:7

9 Mine eye mourneth by reason of affliction: LORD, I have called daily upon thee, I have stretched out my hands unto thee.

10 Wilt thou ^Tshew wonders to the dead? shall the dead arise *and* praise thee? Selah.   work wonders for

11 Shall thy lovingkindness be declared in the grave? *or* thy faithfulness in destruction?

12 Shall thy wonders be known in the dark? and thy righteousness in the land of forgetfulness?

13 But unto thee have I cried, O LORD; and in the morning shall my prayer prevent thee.

14 LORD, why castest thou off my soul? *why* hidest thou thy face from me?

15 I *am* afflicted and ready to die from *my* youth up: *while* I suffer thy terrors I am distracted.

16 Thy fierce wrath goeth over me; thy terrors have cut me off

17 They came round about me daily like water; they compassed me about together.

18 ^RLover and friend hast thou put far from me, *and* mine acquaintance into darkness.   31:11

PSALM 89

Mas'-chil of E'-than the Ez'-ra-hite.

I WILL sing of the mercies of the LORD for ever: with my mouth will I make known thy faithfulness to all generations.

2 For I have said, Mercy shall be built up for ever: ^Rthy faithfulness shalt thou establish in the very heavens.   [119:89, 90]

3 ^RI have made a covenant with my chosen, I have sworn unto David my servant,   1 Kin. 8:16

4 Thy seed will I establish for ever, and build up thy throne ^Rto all generations. Selah.   [Luke 1:33]

5 And ^Rthe heavens shall praise thy wonders, O LORD: thy

faithfulness also in the congregation of the saints.   [19:1]

6 ^RFor who in the heaven can be compared unto the LORD? *who* among the sons of the mighty can be likened unto the LORD?   86:8

7 ^RGod is greatly to be feared in the assembly of the saints, and to be had in reverence of all *them that are* about him.   76:7, 11

8 O LORD God of hosts, who *is* a strong LORD like unto thee? or to thy faithfulness round about thee?

9 ^RThou rulest the raging of the sea: when the waves thereof arise, thou stillest them.   65:7; 93:3, 4; 107:29

10 ^RThou hast broken Ra'-hab in pieces, as one that is slain; thou hast scattered thine enemies with thy strong arm.   87:4; Is. 30:7; 51:9

11 ^RThe heavens *are* thine, the earth also *is* thine: *as for* the world and the fulness thereof, thou hast founded them.   [Gen. 1:1]

12 The north and the south thou hast created them: ^RTa'-bor and ^RHermon shall rejoice in thy name.   Josh. 19:22 · Josh. 11:17; 12:1

13 Thou hast a mighty arm: strong is thy hand, *and* high is thy right hand.

14 Justice and judgment *are* the habitation of thy throne: mercy and truth shall go before thy face.

15 Blessed *is* the people that know the ^Rjoyful sound: they shall walk, O LORD, in the light of thy countenance.   Lev. 23:24; Num. 10:10

16 In thy name shall they rejoice all the day: and in thy righteousness shall they be exalted.

17 For thou *art* the glory of their strength: and in thy favour our horn shall be ^Rexalted.   75:10; 92:10

18 For ^Tthe LORD *is* our defence; and the Holy One of Israel *is* our king.   Or *our shield belongs to the LORD*

19 Then thou spakest in vision to thy holy one, and saidst, I have laid help upon *one that is* mighty; I have exalted *one* ^Rchosen out of the people.   1 Kin. 11:34

20 ^RI have found David my servant; with my holy oil have I anointed him: 1 Sam. 13:14; Acts 13:22

21 ^RWith whom my hand shall

be established: mine arm also shall strengthen him.   80:17

22 The enemy shall not ᵀexact upon him; nor the son of wickedness afflict him.   *outwit* or *deceive*

23 And I will beat down his foes before his face, and plague them that hate him.

24 But my faithfulness and my ᵀmercy *shall be* with him: and in my name shall his horn be exalted.   *lovingkindness*

25 I will ᴿset his hand also in the sea, and his right hand in the rivers.   72:8

26 He shall cry unto me, Thou *art* ᴿmy father, my God, and the rock of my salvation.   2 Sam. 7:14

☆ 27 Also I will make him ᴿ*my* firstborn, ᴿhigher than the kings of the earth.   [Col. 1:15, 18] · Rev. 19:16

28 My mercy will I keep for him for evermore, and my covenant shall stand fast with him.

29 His seed also will I make *to endure* for ever, ᴿand his throne as the days of heaven.   [Is. 9:7]

30 ᴿIf his children ᴿforsake my law, and walk not in my judgments;   [2 Sam. 7:14] · 119:53

31 If they ᵀbreak my statutes, and ᵀkeep not my commandments;   *profane · obey*

32 Then will I ᵀvisit their transgression with the rod, and their iniquity with stripes.   *attend to*

33 ᴿNevertheless my lovingkindness will I not utterly take from him, nor suffer my faithfulness to fail.   2 Sam. 7:14, 15

34 My covenant will I not break, nor ᴿalter the thing that is gone out of my lips.   [Num. 23:19]

35 Once have I sworn ᴿby my holiness that I will not lie unto David.   Amos 4:2; [Titus 1:2]

36 ᴿHis seed shall endure for ever, and his throne ᴿas the sun before me.   [Luke 1:33] · 72:17

37 It shall be established for ever as the moon, and *as* a faithful witness in ᵀheaven. Selah. *the sky*

38 But thou hast ᴿcast off and abhorred, thou hast been wroth with thine anointed.   [1 Chr. 28:9]

39 Thou hast made void the covenant of thy servant: ᴿthou hast profaned his crown *by casting it* to the ground.   74:7; Lam. 5:16

40 Thou hast broken down all his hedges; thou hast brought his ᵀstrong holds to ruin.   *fortresses*

41 All that pass by the way ᴿspoilᵀ him: he is a reproach to his neighbours.   80:12 · *plunder*

42 Thou hast set up the right hand of his adversaries; thou hast made all his enemies to rejoice.

43 Thou hast also turned the edge of his sword, and hast not made him to stand in the battle.

44 Thou hast made his ᵀglory to cease, and cast his throne down to the ground.   *splendour* or *brightness*

45 The days of his youth hast thou shortened: thou hast covered him with shame. Selah.

46 How long, LORD? wilt thou hide thyself for ever? shall thy wrath burn like fire?

47 Remember how short my time ᴿis: wherefore hast thou made all men in ᴿvain?   90:9 · 62:9

48 What man *is he that* liveth, and shall not see death? shall he deliver his soul from the ᵀhand of ᵀthe grave? Selah. *power of* · Or *Sheol*

49 Lord, where *are* thy former lovingkindnesses, *which* thou swarest unto David in thy truth?

50 Remember, Lord, the reproach of thy servants; ᴿ*how* I do bear in my bosom *the reproach of* all the mighty people;   69:9, 19

51 ᴿWherewith thine enemies have reproached, O LORD; wherewith they have reproached the footsteps of thine anointed.   74:10

52 Blessed *be* the LORD for evermore. A-men', and A-men'.

BOOK IV

PSALM 90

A Prayer of Moses the man of God.

LORD, ᴿthou hast been our dwelling place in all generations.   [Deut. 33:27; Ezek. 11:16]

2 ᴿBefore the mountains were brought forth, or ever thou hadst

formed the earth and the world, even from everlasting to everlasting, thou *art* God. [Prov. 8:25, 26]

3 Thou turnest man to destruction; and sayest, ^RReturn, ye children of men. Gen. 3:19; Job 34:14, 15

4 ^RFor a thousand years in thy sight *are but* as yesterday when it is past, and *as* a watch in the night. 2 Pet. 3:8

5 Thou carriest them away as with a flood; ^Rthey are *as* a sleep: in the morning *they are* like grass *which* groweth up. 73:20

6 In the morning it flourisheth, and groweth up; in the evening it is cut down, and withereth.

7 For we are consumed by thine anger, and by thy wrath are we ^Ttroubled. Lit. *terrified*

8 ^RThou hast set our iniquities before thee, our secret *sins* in the light of thy countenance. 50:21

9 For all our days are passed away in thy wrath: we spend our years as a ^Ttale *that is told.* sigh

10 The days of our years *are* threescore years and ten; and if by reason of strength *they be* fourscore years, yet *is* their strength labour and sorrow; for it is soon cut off, and we fly away.

11 Who knoweth the power of thine anger? even according to thy fear, *so is* thy wrath.

12 ^RSo teach *us* to number our days, that we may apply *our* hearts unto wisdom. 39:4

13 Return, O LORD, how long? and ^Tlet it repent thee concerning thy servants. have compassion on

14 O satisfy us early with thy mercy; ^Rthat we may rejoice and be glad all our days. 85:6

15 Make us glad according to the days *wherein* thou hast afflicted us, *and* the years *wherein* we have seen evil.

16 Let ^Rthy work appear unto thy servants, and thy glory unto their children. [Deut. 32:4]; Hab. 3:2

17 ^RAnd let the beauty of the LORD our God be upon us: and establish thou the work of our hands upon us; yea, the work of our hands establish thou it. 27:4

PSALM 91

HE ^Rthat dwelleth in the secret place of the most High shall abide ^Runder the shadow of the Almighty. 27:5; 32:7 · Is. 32:2

2 ^RI will say of the LORD, *He is* my refuge and my fortress: my God; in him will I trust. 142:5

3 Surely ^Rhe shall deliver thee from the snare of the fowler, *and* from the noisome pestilence. 124:7

4 ^RHe shall cover thee with his feathers, and under his wings shalt thou trust: his truth *shall be* thy shield and buckler. 17:8

5 ^RThou shalt not be afraid for the terror by night; *nor* for the arrow *that* flieth by day; [Is. 43:2]

6 *Nor* for the pestilence *that* walketh in darkness; *nor* for the destruction *that* ^Twasteth at noonday. lays waste

7 A thousand shall fall at thy side, and ten thousand at thy right hand; *but* it shall not come nigh thee.

8 Only ^Rwith thine eyes shalt thou behold and see the reward of the wicked. 37:34; Mal. 1:5

9 Because thou hast made the LORD, *which is* my refuge, *even* the most High, thy habitation;

10 ^RThere shall no evil befall thee, neither shall any plague come nigh thy dwelling. [Prov. 12:21]

11 ^RFor he shall give his angels charge over thee, to keep thee in all thy ways. 34:7; Matt. 4:6; Luke 4:10

12 They shall bear thee up in *their* hands, ^Rlest thou dash thy foot against a stone. Matt. 4:6

13 Thou shalt tread upon the lion and ^Tadder: the young lion and the ^Tdragon shalt thou trample under feet. cobra · serpent

14 Because he hath set his love upon me, therefore will I deliver him: I will set him on high, because he hath known my name.

15 He shall ^Rcall upon me, and I will answer him: I *will be* ^Rwith him in trouble; I will deliver him, and honour him. 50:15 · Is. 43:2

16 With long life will I satisfy him, and shew him my salvation.

PSALM 92

A Psalm or Song for the sabbath day.

*I*T is a ᴿgood *thing* to give thanks unto the LORD, and to sing praises unto thy name, O most High: 147:1

2 To ᴿshew forth thy loving-kindness in the morning, and thy faithfulness every night,   89:1

3 ᴿUpon an instrument of ten strings, and upon the psaltery; upon the harp with a solemn sound.   1 Chr. 23:5

4 For thou, LORD, hast made me glad through thy work: I will triumph in the works of thy hands.

5 ᴿO LORD, how great are thy works! *and* ᴿthy thoughts are very deep. [Rev. 15:3] · [Is. 28:29; Rom. 11:33, 34]

6 ᴿA ᵀbrutish man knoweth not; neither doth a fool understand this.   73:22 · *senseless*

7 When ᴿthe wicked spring as the grass, and when all the workers of iniquity do flourish; *it is* that they shall be destroyed for ever: Job 12:6; Jer. 12:1, 2; [Mal. 3:15]

8 ᴿBut thou, LORD, *art most* high for evermore.   [83:18]

9 For, lo, thine enemies, O LORD, for, lo, thine enemies shall perish; all the workers of iniquity shall ᴿbe scattered.   68:1

10 But my horn shalt thou exalt like *the horn of* an unicorn: I shall be anointed with fresh oil.

11 Mine eye also shall see *my desire* on mine enemies, *and* mine ears shall hear *my desire* of the wicked that rise up against me.

12 ᴿThe righteous shall flourish like the palm tree: he shall grow like a cedar in Leb'-a-non.   52:8

13 Those that be planted in the house of the LORD shall flourish in the courts of our God.

14 They shall still bring forth fruit in old age; they shall be ᵀfat and ᵀflourishing;   *plump · green*

15 To shew that the LORD *is* upright: *he is* my rock, and *there is* no unrighteousness in him.

PSALM 93

THE ᴿLORD reigneth, he is clothed with majesty; the LORD is clothed with strength, *wherewith* he hath girded himself: the world also is stablished, that it cannot be moved.   96:10

2 ᴿThy throne *is* established of old: thou *art* from everlasting. 45:6

3 The floods have ᵀlifted up, O LORD, the floods have lifted up their voice; the floods lift up their waves.   *raised up*

4 ᴿThe LORD on high *is* mightier than the noise of many waters, *yea, than* the mighty waves of the sea.   65:7

5 Thy testimonies are very sure: holiness ᵀbecometh thine house, O LORD, for ever.   *adorns*

PSALM 94

O LORD God, ᴿto whom vengeance belongeth; O God, to whom vengeance belongeth, shew thyself.   [Is. 35:4; Rom. 12:19]

2 ᵀLift up thyself, thou ᴿjudge of the earth: render a reward to the proud.   *Rise up* · [Gen. 18:25]

3 LORD, ᴿhow long shall the wicked, how long shall the wicked triumph?   [Job 20:5]

4 *How long* shall they ᴿutter *and* speak ᵀhard things? *and* all the workers of iniquity boast themselves?   31:18; Jude 15 · *insolent*

5 They break in pieces thy people, O LORD, and afflict thine heritage.

6 They slay the widow and the stranger, and murder the fatherless.

7 ᴿYet they say, The LORD shall not see, neither shall the God of Jacob regard *it*.   10:11; Job 22:13

8 Understand, ye ᵀbrutish among the people: and *ye* fools, when will ye be wise?   *senseless*

9 ᴿHe that planted the ear, shall he not hear? he that formed the eye, shall he not see?   [Ex. 4:11]

10 He that ᵀchastiseth the heathen, shall not he correct? he that teacheth man knowledge, *shall not he know?* *instructs* or *disciplines*

11 The LORD ^Rknoweth the thoughts of man, that they *are* ^Tvanity.   Job 11:11; 1 Cor. 3:20 · *futile*
12 Blessed *is* the man whom thou chastenest, O LORD, and teachest him out of thy law;
13 That thou mayest give him ^Trest from the days of adversity, until the pit be digged for the wicked.   *relief*
14 For the LORD will not ^Tcast off his people, neither will he forsake his inheritance.   *abandon*
15 But judgment shall return unto righteousness: and all the upright in heart shall follow it.
16 Who will rise up for me against the evildoers? *or* who will stand up for me against the workers of iniquity?
17 Unless the LORD *had been* my help, my soul ^Thad almost dwelt in silence.   *would soon have*
18 When I said, My foot slippeth; thy mercy, O LORD, held me up.
19 In the multitude of my ^Tthoughts within me thy comforts delight my soul.   *anxious thoughts*
20 Shall the throne of iniquity have fellowship with thee, which frameth mischief by a law?
21 They gather themselves together against the soul of the righteous, and condemn the ^Rinnocent blood.   [Prov. 17:15]; Matt. 27:4
22 But the LORD is my defence; and my God *is* the rock of my refuge.
23 And he shall bring upon them their own iniquity, and shall cut them off in their own wickedness; *yea*, the LORD our God shall ^Tcut them off.   *destroy them*

PSALM 95

O COME, let us sing unto the LORD: let us ^Tmake a joyful noise to the rock of our salvation.   *shout joyfully*
2 Let us come before his presence with thanksgiving, and make a joyful noise unto him with ^Rpsalms.   Eph. 5:19; James 5:13
3 For the LORD *is* a great God, and a great King above all gods.

4 In his hand *are* the deep places of the earth: ^Tthe strength of the hills *is* his also.   *the heights*
5 ^RThe sea *is* his, and he made it: and his hands formed the dry *land.*   Gen. 1:9, 10; Jon. 1:9
6 O come, let us worship and bow down: let ^Rus kneel before the LORD our maker.   [Phil. 2:10]
7 For he *is* our God; and ^Rwe *are* the people of his pasture, and the sheep of his hand. ^RTo day if ye will hear his voice, 79:13 · Heb. 4:7
8 Harden not your heart, as in the provocation, *and* ^Ras *in* the day of temptation in the wilderness: Ex. 17:2–7; Num. 20:13
9 When ^Ryour fathers tempted me, proved me, and ^Rsaw my work.   78:18; [1 Cor. 10:9] · Num. 14:22
10 ^RForty years long was I grieved with *this* generation, and said, It *is* a people that do err in their heart, and they have not known my ways: Acts 7:36; 13:18
11 Unto whom ^RI sware in my wrath that they should not enter into my rest.   Deut. 1:35; Heb. 4:3, 5

PSALM 96

O ^RSING unto the LORD a new song: sing unto the LORD, all the earth.   1 Chr. 16:23–33
2 Sing unto the LORD, bless his name; shew forth his salvation from day to day.
3 Declare his glory among the ^Theathen, his wonders among all people.   *nations or Gentiles*
4 For ^Rthe LORD *is* great, and ^Rgreatly to be praised: he *is* to be feared above all gods.   145:3 · 18:3
5 For ^Rall the gods of the nations *are* idols: ^Rbut the LORD made the heavens. [Jer. 10:11] · 115:15
6 Honour and majesty *are* before him: strength and ^Rbeauty *are* in his sanctuary.   29:2
7 Give unto the LORD, O ye kindreds of the people, give unto the LORD glory and strength.
8 Give unto the LORD the glory *due unto* his name: bring an offering, and come into his courts.
9 O worship the LORD ^Rin the

beauty of holiness: fear before him, all the earth. 29:2; 1 Chr. 16:29

10 Say among the heathen *that* [R]the LORD reigneth: the world also shall be established that it shall not be moved: he shall judge the people righteously. [Rev. 11:15; 19:6]

11 [R]Let the heavens rejoice, and let the earth be glad; let the sea roar, and the fulness thereof. 69:34

12 Let the field be joyful, and all that *is* therein: then shall all the trees of the wood rejoice

13 Before the LORD: for he cometh, for he cometh to judge the earth: [R]he shall judge the world with righteousness, and the people with his truth. [Rev. 19:11]

PSALM 97

THE LORD reigneth; let the earth rejoice; let the multitude of isles be glad *thereof*.

2 [R]Clouds and darkness *are* round about him: righteousness and judgment *are* the habitation of his throne. Ex. 19:9; Deut. 4:11

3 [R]A fire goeth before him, and burneth up his enemies round about. 18:8; Dan. 7:10; Hab. 3:5

4 [R]His lightnings enlightened the world: the earth saw, and trembled. Ex. 19:18

5 [R]The hills melted like wax at the presence of the LORD, at the presence of the Lord of the whole earth. 46:6; Amos 9:5; Mic. 1:4; Nah. 1:5

6 [R]The heavens declare his righteousness, and all the people see his glory. 19:1

7 [R]Confounded be all they that serve graven images, that boast themselves of idols: [R]worship him, all ye gods. [Ex. 20:4] · [Heb. 1:6]

8 Zion heard, and was glad; and the daughters of Judah rejoiced because of thy judgments, O LORD.

9 For thou, LORD, *art* [R]high above all the earth: thou art exalted far above all gods. 83:18

10 Ye that love the LORD, hate evil: [R]he preserveth the souls of his saints; he delivereth them out of the hand of the wicked. 31:23

11 [R]Light is sown for the righteous, and gladness for the upright in heart. Job 22:28; Prov. 4:18

12 [R]Rejoice in the LORD, ye righteous; and give thanks at the remembrance of his holiness. 33:1

PSALM 98

A Psalm.

O [R]SING unto the LORD a new song; for he hath [R]done marvellous things: his right hand, and his holy arm, hath gotten him the victory. 33:3; Is. 42:10 · 77:14

2 [R]The LORD hath made known his salvation: [R]his righteousness hath he openly shewed in the sight of the heathen. Is. 52:10 · Is. 62:2

3 He hath remembered his mercy and his truth toward the house of Israel: [R]all the ends of the earth have seen the salvation of our God. [Is. 49:6]; Luke 3:6

4 Make a joyful noise unto the LORD, all the earth: [T]make a loud noise, and rejoice, and sing praise. *break forth in song*

5 Sing unto the LORD with the harp; with the harp, and the [T]voice of a psalm. *sound of a song*

6 With trumpets and sound of cornet [T]make a joyful noise before the LORD, the King. *shout joyfully*

7 Let the sea roar, and the fulness thereof; the world, and they that dwell therein.

8 Let the [T]floods clap *their* hands: let the hills be joyful together *rivers*

9 Before the LORD; [R]for he cometh to judge the earth: with righteousness shall he judge the world, and the people [T]with equity. [96:10, 13] · *in uprightness*

PSALM 99

THE LORD reigneth; let the people tremble: [R]he sitteth *between* the cher'-u-bims; let the earth be moved. 80:1; Ex. 25:22

2 The LORD *is* great in Zion; and he *is* high above all the people.

3 Let them praise thy great and terrible name; *for* ᵀit *is* holy.   *he*

4 The king's strength also loveth judgment; thou dost establish equity, thou executest judgment and righteousness in Jacob.

5 Exalt ye the LORD our God, and worship at his footstool; *for* he *is* holy.

6 Moses and Aaron among his priests, and Samuel among them that ᴿcall upon his name; they called upon the LORD, and he answered them.   1 Sam. 7:9; 12:18

7 He spake unto them in the cloudy pillar: they kept his testimonies, and the ᵀordinance *that* he gave them.   *statute*

8 Thou answeredst them, O LORD our God: thou wast a God that forgavest them, though thou tookest vengeance ᵀof their inventions.   *on their evil deeds*

9 Exalt the LORD our God, and worship at his holy hill; for the LORD our God *is* holy.

PSALM 100

A Psalm of praise.

MAKE ᴿa joyful noise unto the LORD, all ye lands.   95:1

2 Serve the LORD with gladness: come before his presence with singing.

3 Know ye that the LORD he *is* God: ᴿ*it is* he *that* hath made us, and not we ourselves; ᴿ*we are* his people, and the sheep of his pasture.   139:13, 14; [Eph. 2:10] · [Is. 40:11]

4 ᴿEnter into his gates with thanksgiving, *and* into his courts with praise: be thankful unto him, *and* bless his name.   66:13; 116:17–19

5 For the LORD *is* good; ᴿhis mercy *is* everlasting; and his truth *endureth* to all generations.   136:1

PSALM 101

A Psalm of David.

I WILL sing of ᵀmercy and ᵀjudgment: unto thee, O LORD, will I sing.   *lovingkindness · justice*

2 I will behave myself wisely in a perfect way. O when wilt thou come unto me? I will walk within my house with a perfect heart.

3 I will set no wicked thing before mine eyes: ᴿI hate the work of them ᴿthat turn aside; *it* shall not cleave to me.   97:10 · Josh. 23:6

4 A ᵀfroward heart shall depart from me: I will not ᴿknow a wicked *person*.   *perverse* · [119:115]

5 Whoso privily slandereth his neighbour, him will I cut off: him that hath an high look and a proud heart will not I suffer.

6 Mine eyes *shall be* upon the faithful of the land, that they may dwell with me: he that walketh in a perfect way, he shall serve me.

7 He that worketh deceit shall not dwell within my house: he that telleth lies shall not ᵀtarry in my sight.   *continue*, lit. *be established*

8 I will ᴿearly destroy all the wicked of the land; that I may cut off all wicked doers ᴿfrom the city of the LORD.   [75:10]; Jer. 21:12 · 48:2, 8

PSALM 102

A Prayer of the afflicted, when he is overwhelmed, and poureth out his complaint before the LORD.

HEAR my prayer, O LORD, and let my cry come unto thee.

2 ᴿHide not thy face from me in the day *when* I am in trouble; incline thine ear unto me: in the day *when* I call answer me speedily.   27:9; 69:17

3 For my days are ᴿconsumed like smoke, and my bones are burned as an hearth.   James 4:14

4 My heart is ᵀsmitten, and withered like grass; so that I forget to eat my bread.   *stricken*

5 By reason of the voice of my groaning my bones ᵀcleave to my ᵀskin.   *cling · flesh*

6 I am like a pelican of the wilderness: I am like an owl of the desert.

7 I watch, and am as a sparrow alone upon the house top.

8 Mine enemies reproach me all the day; *and* they that are mad against me are sworn against me.

9 For I have eaten ashes like

bread, and mingled my drink with weeping,

10 Because of thine indignation and thy wrath: for thou hast lifted me up, and cast me down.

11 My days *are* like a shadow that declineth; and I am withered like grass.

12 But thou, O LORD, shalt endure for ever; and thy remembrance unto all generations.

13 Thou shalt arise, *and* have mercy upon Zion: for the time to favour her, yea, the set time, is come.

14 For thy servants take pleasure in her stones, and favour the dust thereof.

15 So the heathen shall fear the name of the LORD, and all the kings of the earth thy glory.

16 When the LORD shall build up Zion, he shall appear in his glory.

17 ᴿHe will regard the prayer of the destitute, and not despise their prayer.   22:24; Neh. 1:6

18 This shall be ᴿwritten for the generation to come: and ᴿthe people which shall be created shall praise the LORD.   [Rom. 15:4] · 22:31

19 For he hath ᴿlooked down from the height of his sanctuary; from heaven did the LORD behold the earth;   14:2; Deut. 26:15

20 ᴿTo hear the groaning of the prisoner; to loose those that are appointed to death;   79:11

21 To ᴿdeclare the name of the LORD in Zion, and his praise in Jerusalem;   22:22

22 ᴿWhen the people are gathered together, and the kingdoms, to serve the LORD. [Is. 2:2, 3; 49:22, 23]

23 He weakened my strength in the way; he shortened my days.

24 ᴿI said, O my God, take me not away in the midst of my days: ᴿthy years *are* throughout all generations.   [39:13]; Is. 38:10 · [90:2]

☆ 25 ᴿOf old hast thou laid the foundation of the earth: and the heavens *are* the work of thy hands.   [Gen. 1:1; Neh. 9:6; Heb. 1:10–12]

26 ᴿThey shall perish, but thou shalt endure: yea, all of them shall wax old like a garment; as a vesture shalt thou change them, and they shall be changed: Matt. 24:35

27 But thou *art* the same, and thy years shall have no end.

28 The children of thy servants shall continue, and their seed shall be established before thee.

PSALM 103

A Psalm of David.

BLESS ᴿthe LORD, O my soul: and all that is within me, *bless* his holy name.   104:1, 35

2 Bless the LORD, O my soul, and forget not all his benefits:

3 ᴿWho forgiveth all thine iniquities; who ᴿhealeth all thy diseases;   130:8; Is. 33:24 · 147:3; Jer. 17:14

4 Who redeemeth thy life from destruction; ᴿwho crowneth thee with lovingkindness and tender mercies;   [5:12]

5 Who satisfieth thy mouth with good *things; so that* thy youth is renewed like the eagle's.

6 The LORD executeth righteousness and judgment for all that are oppressed.

7 ᴿHe made known his ways unto Moses, his acts unto the children of Israel.   147:19; Ex. 33:12–17

8 ᴿThe LORD *is* merciful and gracious, slow to anger, and plenteous in mercy.   Jon. 4:2; James 5:11

9 ᴿHe will not always chide: neither will he keep *his anger* for ever.   [30:5; Is. 57:16]; Jer. 3:5; [Mic. 7:18]

10 He hath not dealt with us after our sins; nor rewarded us according to our iniquities.

11 For as the heaven is high above the earth, *so* great is his ᵀmercy toward them that fear him.   *lovingkindness*

12 As far as the east is from the west, *so* far hath he ᴿremoved our transgressions from us.   [Heb. 9:26]

13 ᴿLike as a father pitieth *his* children, *so* the LORD pitieth them that fear him.   Mal. 3:17

14 For he knoweth our frame; he remembereth that we *are* dust.

15 *As for* man, ᴿhis days *are* as

grass: as a flower of the field, so he flourisheth.   Is. 40:6–8; 1 Pet. 1:24

16 For the wind passeth over it, and it is gone; and the place thereof shall know it no more.

17 But the ᵀmercy of the LORD *is* from everlasting to everlasting upon them that fear him, and his righteousness unto children's children;   *lovingkindness*

18 ᴿTo such as keep his covenant, and to those that remember his commandments to do them.   25:10; [Deut. 7:9]

19 The LORD hath prepared his throne in the heavens; and ᴿhis kingdom ruleth over all.   [47:2]

20 Bless the LORD, ye his angels, that excel in strength, that ᴿdo his commandments, hearkening unto the voice of his word.   [Matt. 6:10]

21 Bless ye the LORD, all *ye* his hosts; ᴿye ᵀministers of his, that do his pleasure.   [Heb. 1:14] · *servants*

22 Bless the LORD, all his works in all places of his dominion: bless the LORD, O my soul.

PSALM 104

BLESS ᴿthe LORD, O my soul. O LORD my God, thou art very great; thou art clothed with honour and majesty.   103:1

2 Who coverest *thyself* with light as *with* a garment: who stretchest out the heavens like a curtain:

3 ᴿWho layeth the beams of his ᵀchambers in the waters: who maketh the clouds his chariot: who walketh upon the wings of the wind.   [Amos 9:6] · *upper chambers*

4 Who maketh his angels spirits; his ministers a flaming fire:

5 *Who* laid the foundations of the earth, *that* it should not ᵀbe removed for ever.   *shake*

6 Thou ᴿcoveredst it with the deep as *with* a garment: the waters stood above the mountains.   Gen. 1:6

7 At thy rebuke they fled; at the voice of thy thunder they hasted away.

8 They go up by the mountains;

they go down by the valleys unto the place which thou hast founded for them.

9 Thou hast set a bound that they may not pass over; that they turn not again to cover the earth.

10 He sendeth the springs into the valleys, *which* run among the hills.

11 They give drink to every beast of the field: the wild ᵀasses quench their thirst.   *donkeys*

12 By them shall the fowls of the heaven have their habitation, *which* sing among the branches.

13 He watereth the hills from his chambers: the earth is satisfied with the fruit of thy works.

14 He causeth the grass to grow for the cattle, and herb for the service of man: that he may bring forth food out of the earth;

15 And ᴿwine *that* maketh glad the heart of man, *and* oil to make *his* face to shine, and bread *which* strengtheneth man's heart.   23:5

16 The trees of the LORD are full *of sap;* the cedars of Leb'-a-non, which he hath planted;

17 Where the birds make their nests: *as for* the stork, the fir trees *are* her house.

18 The high hills *are* a refuge for the wild goats; *and* the rocks for the ᴿconies.ᵀ   Lev. 11:5 · *rock badgers*

19 ᴿHe appointed the moon for seasons: the ᴿsun knoweth his going down.   Gen. 1:14 · 19:6; Job 38:12

20 ᴿThou makest darkness, and it is night: wherein all the beasts of the forest do creep *forth.*   [74:16]

21 ᴿThe young lions roar after their prey, and seek their meat from God.   Job 38:39

22 The sun ariseth, they gather themselves together, and lay them down in their dens.

23 Man goeth forth unto ᴿhis work and to his labour until the evening.   Gen. 3:19

24 ᴿO LORD, how manifold are thy works! in wisdom hast thou made them all: the earth is full of thy ᴿriches.   40:5; Prov. 3:19 · 65:9

25 *So is* this great and wide sea, wherein *are* ᵀthings creeping in-

numerable, both small and great ᵀbeasts.   *teeming things · living creatures*

26 There go the ships: *there is* that ᴿleviathan, *whom* thou hast made to play therein.   Is. 27:1

27 ᴿThese wait all upon thee; that thou mayest give *them* their meat in due season.   136:25

28 ᵀ*That* thou givest them they gather: thou openest thine hand, they are filled with good.   What

29 Thou hidest thy face, they are troubled: ᴿthou takest away their breath, they die, and return to their dust.   Job 34:15; [Eccl. 12:7]

30 ᴿThou sendest forth thy spirit, they are created: and thou renewest the face of the earth.

31 The glory of the LORD shall endure for ever: the LORD ᴿshall rejoice in his works.   Gen. 1:31

32 He looketh on the earth, and it ᴿtrembleth: he toucheth the hills, and they smoke.   Hab. 3:10

33 I will sing unto the LORD as long as I live: I will sing praise to my God while I have my being.

34 My ᴿmeditation of him shall be sweet: I will be glad in the LORD.   19:14

35 Let ᴿthe sinners be consumed out of the earth, and let the wicked be no more. Bless thou the LORD, O my soul. ᵀPraise ye the LORD.   37:38 · Heb. *Hallelujah*

PSALM 105

O ᴿGIVE thanks unto the LORD; call upon his name: ᴿmake known his deeds among the people.   106:1; Is. 12:4 · 145:12

2 Sing unto him, sing psalms unto him: ᴿtalk ye of all his wondrous works.   119:27

3 Glory ye in his holy name: let the heart of them rejoice that seek the LORD.

4 Seek the LORD, and his strength: seek his face evermore.

5 ᴿRemember his marvellous works that he hath done; his wonders, and the judgments of his mouth;   77:11

6 O ye seed of Abraham his servant, ye children of Jacob his chosen.

7 He *is* the LORD our God: his judgments *are* in all the earth.

8 He hath ᴿremembered his covenant for ever, the word *which* he commanded to a thousand generations.   Luke 1:72

9 ᴿWhich *covenant* he made with Abraham, and his oath unto Isaac;   Luke 1:73; [Gal. 3:17]; Heb. 6:17

10 And confirmed the same unto Jacob for a law, *and* to Israel *for* an everlasting covenant:

11 Saying, ᴿUnto thee will I give the land of Canaan, the lot of your inheritance: Gen. 13:15; 15:18

12 ᴿWhen they were *but* a few men in number; yea, very few, and strangers in it.   Gen. 34:30; [Deut. 7:7]

13 When they went from one nation to another, from *one* kingdom to another people;

14 He suffered no man to do them wrong: yea, ᴿhe reproved kings for their sakes;   Gen. 12:17

15 *Saying*, Touch not mine anointed, and do my prophets no harm.

16 Moreover ᴿhe called for a famine upon the land: he brake the whole staff of bread.   Gen. 41:54

17 ᴿHe sent a man before them, *even* Joseph, *who* ᴿwas sold for a servant: [Gen. 45:5] · Acts 7:9

18 Whose feet they hurt with fetters: he was laid in iron:

19 Until the time that his word came: ᴿthe word of the LORD ᵀtried him.   Gen. 39:11–21; 41:25, 42, 43 · *tested*

20 ᴿThe king sent and loosed him; *even* the ruler of the people, and let him go free.   Gen. 41:14

21 ᴿHe made him lord of his house, and ruler of all his ᵀsubstance: Gen. 41:40–44 · *possessions*

22 To ᵀbind his princes at his pleasure; and teach his ᵀsenators wisdom.   Bind as prisoners · *elders*

23 ᴿIsrael also came into Egypt; and Jacob sojourned ᴿin the land of Ham.   Gen. 46:6; Acts 7:15 · 78:51

24 And ᴿhe increased his people greatly; and made them stronger than their enemies.   Ex. 1:7, 9

25 ᴿHe turned their heart to hate

his people, to deal ᵀsubtilly with his servants.   Ex. 1:8–10; 4:21 · *craftily*

26 He sent Moses his servant; *and* Aaron whom he had chosen.

27 They ᴿshewed his signs among them, and wonders in the land of Ham.   78:43; Ex. 7—12

28 He sent darkness, and made it dark; and they rebelled not against his word.

29 ᴿHe turned their waters into blood, and slew their fish.   78:44

30 ᴿTheir land brought forth frogs in abundance, in the chambers of their kings.   Ex. 8:6

31 ᴿHe spake, and there came divers sorts of flies, *and* lice in all their ᵀcoasts.   Ex. 8:16, 17 · *territory*

32 He gave them hail for rain, *and* flaming fire in their land.

33 ᴿHe ᵀsmote their vines also and their fig trees; and brake the trees of their coasts.   78:47 · *struck*

34 ᴿHe spake, and the locusts came, and caterpillers, and that without number,   Ex. 10:4

35 And did eat up all the ᵀherbs in their land, and devoured the fruit of their ground.   *vegetation*

36 ᴿHe smote also all the firstborn in their land, ᴿthe chief of all their strength.   135:8; 136:10 · Gen. 49:3

37 ᴿHe brought them forth also with silver and gold: and *there was* not one feeble *person* among their tribes.   Ex. 12:35, 36

38 ᴿEgypt was glad when they departed: for the fear of them fell upon them.   Ex. 12:33

39 ᴿHe spread a cloud for a covering; and fire to give light in the night.   78:14; Ex. 13:21; Neh. 9:12; Is. 4:5

40 ᴿ*The people* asked, and he brought quails, and satisfied them with the bread of heaven.   Ex. 16:12

41 ᴿHe opened the rock, and the waters gushed out; they ran in the dry places *like* a river.   [1 Cor. 10:4]

42 For he remembered ᴿhis holy promise, *and* Abraham his servant.   v. 8; Gen. 15:13, 14

43 And he brought forth his people with joy, *and* his chosen with ᵀgladness: *a joyful shout*

44 ᴿAnd gave them the lands of the heathen: and they inherited the labour of the people;   78:55

45 ᴿThat they might observe his statutes, and keep his laws. Praise ye the LORD.   [Deut. 4:1, 40]

PSALM 106

PRAISEᵀ ye the LORD. ᴿO give thanks unto the LORD; for *he is* good: for his mercy *endureth* for ever. Heb. *Hallelujah* · 1 Chr. 16:34, 41

2 Who can ᵀutter the mighty acts of the LORD? *who* can shew forth all his praise?   *express*

3 Blessed *are* they that keep ᵀjudgment, *and* he that doeth righteousness at all times.   *justice*

4 ᴿRemember me, O LORD, with the favour *that thou bearest unto* thy people: O visit me with thy salvation;   119:132

5 That I may see the good of thy chosen, that I may rejoice in the gladness of thy nation, that I may glory with thine inheritance.

6 We have sinned with our fathers, we have committed iniquity, we have done wickedly.

7 Our fathers understood not thy wonders in Egypt; they remembered not the multitude of thy mercies; but provoked *him* at the sea, *even* at the Red sea.

8 Nevertheless he saved them for his name's sake, ᴿthat he might make his mighty power to be known.   Ex. 9:16

9 ᴿHe rebuked the Red sea also, and it was dried up: so he led them through the depths, as through the wilderness.   Ex. 14:21

10 And he ᴿsaved them from the hand of him that hated *them*, and redeemed them from the hand of the enemy.   Ex. 14:30

11 ᴿAnd the waters covered their enemies: there was not one of them left.   Ex. 14:27, 28; 15:5

12 Then believed they his words; they sang his praise.

13 They soon forgat his works; they waited not for his counsel:

14 ᴿBut lusted exceedingly in the wilderness, and tempted God in the desert.   Num. 11:4; 1 Cor. 10:6

15 ᴿAnd he gave them their

request; but [R]sent leanness into their soul.　　Num. 11:31 · Is. 10:16

16 [R]They envied Moses also in the camp, *and* Aaron the saint of the LORD.　　Num. 16:1–3

17 The earth opened and swallowed up Dathan, and covered the [T]company of A-bi'-ram.　　*faction*

18 [R]And a fire was kindled in their company; the flame burned up the wicked.　　Num. 16:35, 46

19 [R]They made a calf in Ho'-reb, and worshipped the molten image.　　Ex. 32:1–4; Deut. 9:8; Acts 7:41

20 Thus [R]they changed their glory into the similitude of an ox that eateth grass.　　Jer. 2:11; Rom. 1:23

21 They forgat God their saviour, which had done great things in Egypt;

22 Wondrous works in the land of Ham, *and* [T]terrible things by the Red sea.　　*awesome*

23 [R]Therefore he said that he would destroy them, had not Moses his chosen [R]stood before him in the breach, to turn away his wrath, lest he should destroy *them.*　　Ex. 32:10; Deut. 9:19 · Ezek. 22:30

24 Yea, they despised [R]the pleasant land, they [R]believed not his word:　　Deut. 8:7; Jer. 3:19 · [Heb. 3:18, 19]

25 [R]But murmured in their tents, *and* hearkened not unto the voice of the LORD.　　Num. 14:2, 27; Deut. 1:27

26 Therefore he lifted up his hand against them, to overthrow them in the wilderness:

27 [R]To overthrow their seed also among the nations, and to scatter them in the lands.　　Lev. 26:33

28 [R]They joined themselves also unto Ba'-al–pe'-or, and ate the sacrifices of the dead.　　Num. 25:3

29 Thus they provoked *him* to anger with their inventions: and the plague brake in upon them.

30 [R]Then stood up Phin'-e-has, and executed judgment: and *so* the plague was stayed.　　Num. 25:7, 8

31 And that was counted unto him [R]for righteousness unto all generations for evermore.　　Gen. 15:6

32 [R]They angered *him* also at the waters of strife, [R]so that it

went ill with Moses for their sakes: 81:7; Num. 20:3–13 · Deut. 1:37; 3:26

33 [R]Because they provoked his spirit, so that he spake unadvisedly with his lips.　　Num. 20:3, 10

34 [R]They did not destroy the nations, concerning whom the LORD commanded them:　　Judg. 1:21

35 [R]But were mingled among the [T]heathen, and learned their works.　　Judg. 3:5, 6 · *Gentiles*

36 And they served their idols: which were a snare unto them.

37 Yea, [R]they sacrificed their sons and their daughters unto devils,　　2 Kin. 16:3; 17:17; Ezek. 16:20, 21

38 And shed innocent blood, *even* the blood of their sons and of their daughters, whom they sacrificed unto the idols of Canaan: and [R]the land was polluted with blood.　　[Num. 35:33; Jer. 3:1, 2]

39 Thus were they [R]defiled with their own works, and [R]went a whoring with their own inventions.　　Ezek. 20:18 · Judg. 2:17; Hos. 4:12

40 Therefore [R]was the wrath of the LORD kindled against his people, insomuch that he abhorred his own inheritance.　　Judg. 2:14

41 And he gave them into the hand of the heathen; and they that hated them ruled over them.

42 Their enemies also oppressed them, and they were brought into subjection under their hand.

43 [R]Many times did he deliver them; but they provoked *him* with their counsel, and were brought low for their iniquity.　　Judg. 2:16

44 Nevertheless he regarded their affliction, when [R]he heard their cry:　　Judg. 3:9; 6:7; 10:10

45 And he remembered for them his covenant, and [R]repented [R]according to the multitude of his mercies.　　Judg. 2:18 · 69:16

46 [R]He made them also to be pitied of all those that carried them captives. 1 Kin. 8:50; [2 Chr. 30:9]

47 [R]Save us, O LORD our God, and gather us from among the heathen, to give thanks unto thy holy name, *and* to triumph in thy praise.　　1 Chr. 16:35, 36

48 [R]Blessed *be* the LORD God of

Israel from everlasting to ever-lasting: and let all the people say, A-men'. Praise ye the LORD.   41:13

BOOK V

PSALM 107

O ᴿGIVE thanks unto the LORD, for *he is* good: for his mercy *endureth* for ever. Jer. 33:11

2   Let the redeemed of the LORD say *so,* whom he hath redeemed from the hand of the enemy;

3   And ᴿgathered them out of the lands, from the east, and from the west, from the north, and from the south.   Is. 43:5, 6; Jer. 29:14; 31:8–10

4   They wandered in ᴿthe wil-derness in a solitary way; they found no city to dwell in.   Josh. 5:6

5   Hungry and thirsty, their soul fainted in them.

6   ᴿThen they cried unto the LORD in their trouble, *and* he delivered them out of their dis-tresses.   50:15; [Hos. 5:15]

7   And he led them forth by the ᴿright way, that they might go to a city of habitation.   Ezra 8:21; Jer. 31:9

8   Oh that *men* would praise the LORD *for* his ᵀgoodness, and *for* his wonderful works to the chil-dren of men!   *lovingkindness*

9   For ᴿhe satisfieth the longing soul, and filleth the hungry soul with goodness.   [34:10; Luke 1:53]

10   Such as sit in darkness and in the shadow of death, *being* bound in affliction and iron;

11   Because they ᴿrebelled against the words of God, and ᵀcontemned ᴿthe counsel of the most High: Lam. 3:42 · *despised* · [73:24]

12   Therefore he brought down their heart with labour; they fell down, and *there was* ᴿnone to help.   22:11

13   Then they cried unto the LORD in their trouble, *and* he saved them out of their distresses.

14   ᴿHe brought them out of darkness and the shadow of death, and ᵀbrake their bands in sunder.   68:6 · *broke their chains in pieces*

15   Oh that *men* would praise the LORD *for* his ᵀgoodness, and *for* his wonderful works to the chil-dren of men!   *lovingkindness*

16   For he hath ᴿbroken the gates of ᵀbrass, and cut the bars of iron in sunder.   Is. 45:1, 2 · *bronze*

17   Fools ᴿbecause of their trans-gression, and because of their in-iquities, are afflicted.   [Is. 65:6, 7]

18   Their soul abhorreth all man-ner of meat; and they ᴿdraw near unto the gates of death.   Job 33:22

19   Then they cry unto the LORD in their trouble, *and* he saveth them out of their distresses.

20   ᴿHe sent his word, and healed them, and delivered *them* from their destructions.   Matt. 8:8

21   Oh that *men* would ᵀpraise the LORD *for* his goodness, and *for* his wonderful works to the chil-dren of men!   *give thanks*

22   And let them sacrifice the sacrifices of thanksgiving, and declare his works with rejoicing.

23   They that go down to the sea in ships, that do business in great waters;

24   These see the works of the LORD, and his wonders in the deep.

25   For he commandeth, and raiseth the stormy wind, which lifteth up the waves thereof.

26   They mount up to the heaven, they go down again to the depths: ᴿtheir soul is melted because of trouble.   22:14

27   They reel to and fro, and stagger like a drunken man, and are at their wit's end.

28   Then they cry unto the LORD in their trouble, and he bringeth them out of their distresses.

29   ᴿHe maketh the storm a calm, so that the waves thereof are still.   89:9; Matt. 8:26; Luke 8:24

30   Then are they glad because they be quiet; so he bringeth them unto their desired haven.

31   ᴿOh that *men* would praise the LORD *for* his goodness, and *for* his wonderful works to the chil-dren of men!   vv. 8, 15, 21

32   Let them exalt him also ᴿin

the congregation of the people, and praise him in the assembly of the elders.   22:22, 25

33 He [R]turneth rivers into a wilderness, and the watersprings into dry ground;   1 Kin. 17:1, 7; Is. 50:2

34 A [R]fruitful land into barrenness, for the wickedness of them that dwell therein.   Deut. 29:23

35 [R]He turneth the wilderness into a standing water, and dry ground into watersprings.   114:8

36 And there he maketh the hungry to dwell, that they may prepare a city for habitation;

37 And sow the fields, and plant vineyards, which may yield fruits of increase.

38 [R]He blesseth them also, so that they are multiplied greatly; and suffereth not their cattle to [R]decrease.   Gen. 12:2; 17:16, 20 · Ex. 1:7

39 Again, they are minished and brought low through oppression, affliction, and sorrow.

40 [R]He poureth contempt upon princes, and causeth them to wander in the wilderness, *where there is* no way.   Job 12:21, 24

41 Yet setteth he the poor on high from affliction, and [R]maketh *him* families like a flock.   78:52

42 [R]The righteous shall see *it*, and rejoice: and all iniquity shall stop her mouth.   Job 5:15, 16

43 [R]Whoso *is* wise, and will observe these *things*, even they shall understand the lovingkindness of the LORD.   64:9; Jer. 9:12; [Hos. 14:9]

PSALM 108

A Song *or* Psalm of David.

O [R]GOD, my heart is fixed; I will sing and give praise, even with my glory.   57:7–11

2 Awake, psaltery and harp: I *myself* will awake early.

3 I will praise thee, O LORD, among the people: and I will sing praises unto thee among the nations.

4 For thy mercy *is* great above the [T]heavens: and thy truth *reacheth* unto the clouds.   *skies*

5 [R]Be thou exalted, O God,

above the heavens: and thy glory above all the earth;   57:5, 11

6 [R]That thy beloved may be delivered: save *with* thy right hand, and answer me.   60:5–12

7 God hath spoken in his holiness; I will rejoice, I will divide She'-chem, and [T]mete out the valley of Suc'-coth.   *measure*

8 Gil'-e-ad *is* mine; Ma-nas'-seh *is* mine; E'-phra-im also *is* the [T]strength of mine head; [R]Judah *is* my lawgiver;   *helmet* · [Gen. 49:10]

9 Moab *is* my washpot; over E'-dom will I cast out my shoe; over Phi-lis'-ti-a will I triumph.

10 [R]Who will bring me into the strong city? who will lead me into E'-dom?   60:9

11 *Wilt* not *thou*, O God, *who* hast cast us off? and wilt not thou, O God, go forth with our hosts?

12 Give us help from trouble: for vain *is* the help of man.

13 [R]Through God we shall do valiantly: for he *it is that* shall tread down our enemies.   60:12

PSALM 109

To the chief Musician,
A Psalm of David.

H OLD [R]not thy peace, O God of my praise;   83:1

2 For the mouth of the wicked and the mouth of the deceitful are opened against me: they have spoken against me with a [R]lying tongue.   27:12

3 They compassed me about also with words of hatred; and fought against me [R]without a cause.   35:7; 69:4; John 15:25

4 [T]For my love they are my adversaries: but I *give myself unto* prayer.   *In return for*

5 And [R]they have rewarded me evil for good, and hatred for my love.   35:7, 12; 38:20; Prov. 17:13

6 Set thou a wicked man over him: and let [R]Satan stand at his right hand.   Zech. 3:1

7 When he shall be judged, let him be condemned: and [R]let his prayer become sin.   [Prov. 28:9]

8 Let his days be few; *and* ^Rlet another take his office.   Acts 1:20

9 Let his children be fatherless, and his wife a widow.

10 Let his children ^Tbe continually vagabonds, and beg: let them seek *their bread* also out of their desolate places.   *wander continuously*

11 ^RLet the extortioner catch all that he hath; and let the strangers spoil his labour.   Neh. 5:7; Job 5:5; 18:9

12 Let there be none to extend mercy unto him: neither let there be any to favour his fatherless children.

13 ^RLet his posterity be cut off; *and* in the generation following let their name be blotted out.   37:28

14 ^RLet the iniquity of his fathers be remembered with the LORD; and let not the sin of his mother be blotted out.   Is. 65:6

15 Let them be before the LORD continually, that he may ^Rcut^T off the memory of them from the earth.   [34:16]; Job 18:17 · *destroy*

16 Because that he remembered not to shew mercy, but persecuted the poor and needy man, that he might even slay the ^Rbroken in heart.   [34:18]

17 ^RAs he loved cursing, so let it come unto him: as he delighted not in blessing, so let it be far from him.   Prov. 14:14; [Matt. 7:2]

18 As he clothed himself with cursing like as with his garment, so let it ^Rcome into his ^Tbowels like water, and like oil into his bones.   Num. 5:22 · *body*

19 Let it be unto him as the garment *which* covereth him, and for a ^Tgirdle wherewith he is girded continually.   *belt*

20 *Let* this *be* the reward of mine ^Tadversaries from the LORD, and of them that speak evil against my ^Tsoul.   *accusers · person*

21 But do thou for me, O GOD the Lord, for thy name's sake: because thy ^Tmercy *is* good, deliver thou me.   *lovingkindness*

22 For I *am* poor and needy, and my heart is wounded within me.

23 I am gone ^Rlike the shadow when it declineth: I am tossed up and down as the locust.   102:11

24 My ^Rknees are weak through fasting; and my flesh faileth of fatness.   Heb. 12:12

25 I became also a reproach unto them: *when* they looked upon me they shaked their heads.

26 Help me, O LORD my God: O save me according to thy mercy:

27 ^RThat they may know that this *is* thy hand; *that* thou, LORD, hast done it.   Job 37:7

28 ^RLet them curse, but bless thou: when they arise, let them be ashamed; but let ^Rthy servant rejoice.   2 Sam. 6:11, 12 · Is. 65:14

29 ^RLet mine adversaries be clothed with shame, and let them cover themselves with their own confusion, as with a mantle.   35:26

30 I will greatly praise the LORD with my mouth; yea, ^RI will praise him among the multitude.   35:18

31 For ^Rhe shall stand at the right hand of the poor, to save *him* from those ^Tthat condemn his soul.   [16:8] · Lit. *judging his soul*

PSALM 110

A Psalm of David.

THE ^RLORD said unto my Lord, ☆ Sit thou at my right hand, until I make thine enemies thy footstool.   Matt. 22:44; Acts 2:34, 35

2 The LORD shall send the rod of thy strength ^Rout of Zion: ^Rrule thou in the midst of thine enemies.   [Rom. 11:26, 27] · [2:9; Dan. 7:13, 14]

3 ^RThy people *shall be* willing in the day of thy power, in the beauties of holiness from the womb of the morning: thou hast the dew of thy youth.   Judg. 5:2

4 The LORD hath sworn, and ☆ will not repent, Thou *art* a ^Rpriest for ever after the order of ^RMelchiz'-e-dek.   [Zech. 6:13] · [Heb. 5:6, 10]

5 The Lord at thy right hand shall strike through kings ^Rin the day of his wrath.   [Rom. 2:5; Rev. 6:17]

6 He shall judge among the heathen, he shall fill *the places* with the dead bodies; ^Rhe shall

wound the heads over many countries.   68:21
7　He shall drink of the brook in
the way: Rtherefore shall he lift up
the head.   [Is. 53:12]

PSALM 111

PRAISET ye the LORD. RI will
praise the LORD with *my*
whole heart, in the assembly of
the upright, and *in* the congregation.   Heb. *Hallelujah* · 35:18
2　RThe works of the LORD are
great, Rsought out of all them that
have pleasure therein.   92:5 · 143:5
3　His work *is* Rhonourable and
glorious: and his righteousness
endureth for ever.   145:4, 5
4　He hath made his wonderful
works to be remembered: Rthe
LORD *is* gracious and full of compassion.   [86:5]
5　He hath given meat unto
them that fear him: he will ever be
mindful of his covenant.
6　He hath shewed his people
the power of his works, that he
may give them the Theritage of the
heathen.   *inheritance of the nations*
7　The works of his hands *are*
Rverity and judgment; all his commandments *are* sure.   [Rev. 15:3]
8　RThey stand fast for ever and
ever, *and are* done in truth and
uprightness.   Is. 40:8; Matt. 5:18
9　RHe sent redemption unto his
people: he hath commanded his
covenant for ever: holy and rev-
erend *is* his name.   Luke 1:68
10　RThe fear of the LORD *is* the
beginning of wisdom: a good
understanding have all they that
do *his commandments:* his praise
endureth for ever.   [Prov. 1:7; 9:10]

PSALM 112

PRAISE ye the LORD. Blessed
is the man *that* feareth the
LORD, *that* Rdelighteth greatly in
his commandments.   128:1
2　RHis seed shall be mighty
upon earth: the generation of the
upright shall be blessed.   [102:28]
3　RWealth and riches *shall be* in

his house: and his righteousness
endureth for ever.   [Matt. 6:33]
4　RUnto the upright there ariseth light in the darkness: *he is*
gracious, and full of compassion,
and righteous.   97:11; Job 11:17
5　RA good man sheweth favour,
and lendeth: he will guide his
affairs with discretion.   [Luke 6:35]
6　Surely he shall not be moved
for ever: Rthe righteous shall be in
everlasting remembrance. Prov. 10:7
7　RHe shall not be afraid of evil
tidings: his heart is Tfixed, trust-
ing in the LORD. [Prov. 1:33] · *steadfast*
8　His heart *is* established, Rhe
shall not be afraid, until he see *his*
desire upon his enemies.   [27:1]
9　He hath dispersed, he hath
given to the poor; his righteousness endureth for ever; his horn
shall be exalted with honour.
10　The wicked shall see *it,* and
be grieved; he shall gnash with
his teeth, and melt away: the
desire of the wicked shall perish.

PSALM 113

PRAISE ye the LORD. Praise, O
ye servants of the LORD,
praise the name of the LORD.
2　RBlessed be the name of the
LORD from this time forth and for
evermore.   [Dan. 2:20]
3　From the rising of the sun
unto the going down of the same
the LORD's name *is* to be praised.
4　The LORD *is* Rhigh above all
nations, *and* Rhis glory above the
heavens.   97:9; 99:2 · [8:1]
5　Who *is* like unto the LORD our
God, who dwelleth on high,
6　RWho humbleth *himself* to
behold *the things that are* in
heaven, and in the earth!   [11:4]
7　RHe raiseth up the poor out of
the dust, *and* lifteth the Rneedy out
of the dunghill;   1 Sam. 2:8 · 72:12
8　That he may Rset *him* with
princes, *even* with the princes of
his people.   [Job 36:7]
9　RHe maketh the barren woman
an to keep house, *and to be* a joyful mother of children. Praise ye
the LORD.   1 Sam. 2:5; Is. 54:1

PSALM 114

WHEN ᴿIsrael went out of Egypt, the house of Jacob ᴿfrom a people of strange language;   Ex. 12:51; 13:3 · 81:5

2 ᴿJudah was his sanctuary, *and* Israel his dominion. Ex. 6:7; 19:6

3 ᴿThe sea saw *it*, and fled: Jordan was driven back.   Ex. 14:21

4 ᴿThe mountains skipped like rams, *and* the little hills like lambs.   Ex. 19:18; Judg. 5:5; Hab. 3:6

5 What *ailed* thee, O thou sea, that thou fleddest? thou Jordan, *that* thou wast driven back?

6 Ye mountains, *that* ye skipped like rams; *and* ye little hills, like lambs?

7 Tremble, thou earth, at the presence of the Lord, at the presence of the God of Jacob;

8 ᴿWhich turned the rock *into* a standing water, the flint into a fountain of waters.   Ex. 17:6

PSALM 115

NOT ᴿunto us, O Lᴏʀᴅ, not unto us, but unto thy name give glory, for thy mercy, *and* for thy truth's sake.   [Is. 48:11]

2 Wherefore should the ᵀheathen say, ᴿWhere *is* now their God?   *Gentiles* or *nations* · 42:3, 10

3 ᴿBut our God *is* in the heavens: he hath done whatsoever he hath pleased.   [1 Chr. 16:26]

4 Their idols *are* silver and gold, the work of men's hands.

5 They have mouths, but they speak not: eyes have they, but they see not:

6 They have ears, but they hear not: noses have they, but they smell not:

7 They have hands, but they handle not: feet have they, but they walk not: neither speak they through their throat.

8 ᴿThey that make them are like unto them; *so is* every one that trusteth in them.   Is. 44:9–11

9 ᴿO Israel, trust thou in the Lᴏʀᴅ: ᴿhe *is* their help and their shield.   118:2, 3 · 33:20

10 O house of Aaron, trust in the Lᴏʀᴅ: he *is* their help and their shield.

11 Ye that fear the Lᴏʀᴅ, trust in the Lᴏʀᴅ: he *is* their help and their shield.

12 The Lᴏʀᴅ hath been mindful of us: he will bless *us*; he will bless the house of Israel; he will bless the house of Aaron.

13 He will bless them that fear the Lᴏʀᴅ, *both* small and great.

14 The Lᴏʀᴅ shall ᵀincrease you more and more, you and your children.   *give you increase*

15 Ye *are* blessed of the Lᴏʀᴅ which made heaven and earth.

16 The heaven, *even* the heavens, *are* the Lᴏʀᴅ's: but the earth hath he given to the children of men.

17 ᴿThe dead praise not the Lᴏʀᴅ, neither any that go down into silence.   6:5; 88:10–12; [Is. 38:18]

18 ᴿBut we will bless the Lᴏʀᴅ from this time forth and for evermore. Praise the Lᴏʀᴅ.   113:2

PSALM 116

I ᴿLOVE the Lᴏʀᴅ, because he hath heard my voice *and* my supplications.   18:1

2 Because he hath inclined his ear unto me, therefore will I call upon *him* as long as I live.

3 ᴿThe sorrows of death compassed me, and the pains of ᵀhell gat hold upon me: I found trouble and sorrow.   18:4–6 · Or *Sheol*

4 Then called I upon the name of the Lᴏʀᴅ; O Lᴏʀᴅ, I beseech thee, deliver my soul.

5 ᴿGracious *is* the Lᴏʀᴅ, and ᴿrighteous; yea, our God *is* merciful.   [103:8] · [119:137; 145:17; Dan. 9:14]

6 The Lᴏʀᴅ preserveth the simple: I was brought low, and he ᵀhelped me.   Lit. *saved*

7 Return unto thy ᴿrest, O my soul; for the Lᴏʀᴅ hath dealt bountifully with thee.   [Matt. 11:29]

8 For thou hast delivered my soul from death, mine eyes from tears, *and* my feet from falling.

9 I will walk before the Lᴏʀᴅ ᴿin the land of the living.   27:13

10 I believed, therefore have I spoken: I was greatly afflicted:

11 ᴿI said in my haste, ᴿAll men *are* liars.   31:22 · Rom. 3:4

12 What shall I render unto the LORD *for* all his benefits toward me?

13 I will take the cup of salvation, and call upon the name of the LORD.

14 ᴿI will pay my vows unto the LORD now in the presence of all his people.   v. 18

15 Precious in the sight of the LORD *is* the death of his saints.

16 O LORD, truly ᴿI *am* thy servant; I *am* thy servant, *and* ᴿthe son of thine handmaid: thou hast loosed my bonds.   143:12 · 86:16

17 I will offer to thee ᴿthe sacrifice of thanksgiving, and will call upon the name of the LORD.   50:14

18 I will pay my vows unto the LORD now in the presence of all his people,

19 In the ᴿcourts of the LORD's house, in the midst of thee, O Jerusalem. Praise ye the LORD.   96:8

PSALM 117

O ᴿPRAISE the LORD, all ye ᵀnations: ᵀpraise him, all ye people.   Rom. 15:11 · *Gentiles · glorify*

2 For his ᵀmerciful kindness is great toward us: and ᴿthe truth of the LORD *endureth* for ever. Praise ye the LORD.   *lovingkindness* · [100:5]

PSALM 118

O ᴿGIVE thanks unto the LORD; for *he is* good: ᴿbecause his mercy *endureth* for ever.   Jer. 33:11 · 2 Chr. 5:13; 7:3; Ezra 3:11

2 ᴿLet Israel now say, that his mercy *endureth* for ever.   [115:9]

3 Let the house of Aaron now say, that his mercy *endureth* for ever.

4 Let them now that fear the LORD say, that his ᵀmercy *endureth* for ever.   *lovingkindness*

5 I called upon the LORD in distress: the LORD answered me, *and* ᴿset *me* in a large place.   18:19

6 ᴿThe LORD *is* on my side; I will not fear: what can man do unto me?   56:9; [Rom. 8:31; Heb. 13:6]

7 ᴿThe LORD taketh my part with them that help me: therefore shall ᴿI see *my desire* upon them that hate me.   54:4 · 59:10

8 ᴿIt is better to trust in the LORD than to put confidence in man.   40:4; Is. 31:1, 3; 57:13; Jer. 17:5

9 ᴿIt *is* better to trust in the LORD than to put confidence in princes.   146:3

10 All nations compassed me about: but in the name of the LORD will I destroy them.

11 They ᴿcompassedᵀ me about; yea, they compassed me about: but in the name of the LORD I will destroy them.   88:17 · *surrounded*

12 They compassed me about like bees; they are quenched as the fire of thorns: for in the name of the LORD I will destroy them.

13 Thou hast ᵀthrust sore at me that I might fall: but the LORD helped me.   *pushed at me violently*

14 The LORD *is* my strength and song, and is become my salvation.

15 The voice of rejoicing and salvation *is* in the ᵀtabernacles of the righteous: the right hand of the LORD doeth valiantly.   *tents*

16 ᴿThe right hand of the LORD is exalted: the right hand of the LORD doeth valiantly.   Ex. 15:6

17 I shall not die, but live, and declare the works of the LORD.

18 The LORD hath ᴿchastened me sore: but he hath not given me over unto death.   Jer. 31:18; 2 Cor. 6:9

19 ᴿOpen to me the gates of righteousness: I will go into them, *and* I will praise the LORD: Is. 26:2

20 This gate of the LORD, into which the righteous shall enter.

21 I will praise thee: for thou hast ᴿheardᵀ me, and art become my salvation.   116:1 · Lit. *answered*

22 ᴿThe stone *which* the builders refused is become the head *stone* of the corner.   Matt. 21:42   ☆

23 This is the LORD's doing; it *is* marvellous in our eyes.

24 This *is* the day *which* the

LORD hath made; we will rejoice and be glad in it.

25 Save now, I beseech thee, O LORD: O LORD, I beseech thee, send now prosperity.

☆ 26 ᴿBlessed *be* he that cometh in the name of the LORD: we have blessed you out of the house of the LORD.   Matt. 21:9; 23:39

27 God *is* the LORD, which hath shewed us ᴿlight: bind the sacrifice with cords, *even* unto the horns of the altar.   [1 Pet. 2:9]

28 Thou *art* my God, and I will praise thee: ᴿ*thou art* my God, I will exalt thee.   Ex. 15:2; Is. 25:1

29 O give thanks unto the LORD; for *he is* good: for his mercy *endureth* for ever.

PSALM 119

א ALEPH

BLESSED *are* the ᵀundefiled in the way, ᴿwho walk in the law of the LORD.   *blameless* · 128:1

2 Blessed *are* they that keep his testimonies, *and that* seek him with the ᴿwhole heart.   Deut. 6:5

3 ᴿThey also do no iniquity: they walk in his ways.   [1 John 3:9]

4 Thou hast commanded *us* to keep thy precepts diligently.

5 O that my ways were directed to keep thy statutes!

6 ᴿThen shall I not be ashamed, when I ᵀhave respect unto all thy commandments.   Job 22:26 · *look into*

7 I will praise thee with uprightness of heart, when I shall have learned thy righteous judgments.

8 I will keep thy statutes: O forsake me not utterly.

ב BETH

9 Wherewithal shall a young man cleanse his way? by taking heed *thereto* according to thy word.

10 With my whole heart have I sought thee: O let me not wander from thy commandments.

11 ᴿThy word have I hid in mine

heart, that I might not sin against thee.   37:31; Luke 2:19

12 Blessed *art* thou, O LORD: teach me thy statutes.

13 With my lips have I declared all the judgments of thy mouth.

14 I have rejoiced in the way of thy testimonies, as *much as* in all riches.

15 I will meditate in thy precepts, and ᵀhave respect unto thy ways.   *contemplate*

16 I will ᴿdelight myself in thy statutes: I will not forget thy word.   1:2

ג GIMEL

17 ᴿDeal bountifully with thy servant, *that* I may live, and keep thy word.   116:7

18 Open thou mine eyes, that I may behold wondrous things out of thy law.

19 ᴿI *am* a stranger in the earth: hide not thy commandments from me.   Lev. 25:23; 1 Chr. 29:15; Heb. 11:13

20 ᴿMy soul breaketh for the longing *that it hath* unto thy judgments at all times.   42:1, 2; 63:1

21 Thou hast rebuked the proud *that are* cursed, which ᵀdo err from thy commandments.   *stray*

22 ᴿRemove from me reproach and contempt; for I have kept thy testimonies.   39:8

23 Princes also did sit *and* speak against me: *but* thy servant did meditate in thy statutes.

24 Thy testimonies also *are* my delight *and* my counsellors.

ד DALETH

25 ᴿMy soul cleaveth unto the dust: ᴿquickenᵀ thou me according to thy word.   44:25 · 143:11 · *revive*

26 I have declared my ways, and thou ᵀheardest me: ᴿteach me thy statutes. Lit. *answered* · 25:4; 27:11; 86:11

27 Make me to understand the way of thy precepts: so shall I talk of thy wondrous works.

28 ᴿMy soul melteth for ᵀheaviness: strengthen thou me according unto thy word.   107:26 · *grief*

29 Remove from me the way of

lying: and grant me thy law graciously.

30 I have chosen the way of truth: thy judgments have I laid *before me*.

31 I [T]have stuck unto thy testimonies: O LORD, put me not to shame.   *cling to*

32 I will run the way of thy commandments, when thou shalt [R]enlarge my heart. Is. 60:5; 2 Cor. 6:11, 13

ה HE

33 [R]Teach me, O LORD, the way of thy statutes; and I shall keep it *unto* the end.   [Matt. 10:22; Rev. 2:26]

34 Give me understanding, and I shall keep thy law; yea, I shall observe it with *my* whole heart.

35 Make me to go in the path of thy commandments; for therein do I delight.

36 Incline my heart unto thy testimonies, and not to [R]covetousness.   [Mark 7:20–23; Heb. 13:5]

37 [R]Turn away mine eyes from beholding vanity; *and* quicken thou me in thy way.   Is. 33:15

38 [R]Stablish thy word unto thy servant, who *is devoted* to [T]thy fear.   2 Sam. 7:25 · *fearing thee*

39 Turn away my reproach which I fear: for thy judgments *are* good.

40 Behold, I have longed after thy precepts: [T]quicken me in thy righteousness.   *revive*

ו VAU

41 Let thy mercies come also unto me, O LORD, *even* thy salvation, according to thy word.

42 So shall I have wherewith to answer him that reproacheth me: for I trust in thy word.

43 And take not the word of truth utterly out of my mouth; for I have hoped in thy judgments.

44 So shall I keep thy law continually for ever and ever.

45 And I will walk at [R]liberty: for I seek thy precepts.   Prov. 4:12

46 [R]I will speak of thy testimonies also before kings, and will not be ashamed.   Matt. 10:18

47 And I will delight myself in thy commandments, which I have loved.

48 My hands also will I lift up unto thy commandments, which I have loved; and I will meditate in thy statutes.

ז ZAIN

49 Remember the word unto thy servant, upon which thou hast caused me to hope.

50 This *is* my [R]comfort in my affliction: for thy word hath quickened me.   Job 6:10; [Rom. 15:4]

51 The proud have had me greatly in derision: *yet* have I not [T]declined from thy law. *turned aside*

52 I remembered thy judgments of old, O LORD; and have comforted myself.

53 [R]Horror hath taken hold upon me because of the wicked that forsake thy law.   Ezra 9:3

54 Thy statutes have been my songsinthehouseofmypilgrimage.

55 [R]I have remembered thy name, O LORD, in the night, and have kept thy law.   63:6

56 This I had, because I kept thy precepts.

ח CHETH

57 [R]*Thou art* my portion, O LORD: I have said that I would keep thy words.   16:5; Jer. 10:16

58 I entreated thy favour with *my* whole heart: be merciful unto me according to thy word.

59 I [R]thought on my ways, and turned my feet unto thy testimonies.   Mark 14:72; Luke 15:17

60 I made haste, and delayed not to keep thy commandments.

61 The [T]bands of the wicked have [T]robbed me: *but* I have not forgotten thy law.   *cords · bound*

62 [R]At midnight I will rise to give thanks unto thee because of thy righteous judgments. Acts 16:25

63 I *am* a companion of all *them* that fear thee, and of them that keep thy precepts.

64 The earth, O LORD, is full of thy mercy: teach me thy statutes.

ט TETH

65 Thou hast dealt well with thy servant, O LORD, according unto thy word.

66 Teach me good judgment and ᴿknowledge: for I have believed thy commandments.   Phil. 1:9

67 Before I was ᴿafflicted I went astray: but now have I kept thy word.   Prov. 3:11; [Heb. 12:5–11]

68 Thou *art* ᴿgood, and doest good; teach me thy statutes.   106:1

69 The proud have forged a lie against me: *but* I will keep thy precepts with *my* whole heart.

70 Their heart is as fat as grease; *but* I delight in thy law.

71 *It is* good for me that I have been afflicted; that I might learn thy statutes.

72 ᴿThe law of thy mouth *is* better unto me than thousands of gold and silver.   19:10; Prov. 8:10, 11, 19

י JOD

73 ᴿThy hands have made me and fashioned me: give me understanding, that I may learn thy commandments.   Job 10:8; 31:15

74 ᴿThey that fear thee will be glad when they see me; because I have hoped in thy word.   34:2

75 I know, O LORD, ᴿthat thy judgments *are* ᵀright, and *that* thou in faithfulness hast afflicted me.   [Heb. 12:10] · Lit. *righteous*

76 Let, I pray thee, thy merciful kindness be for my comfort, according to thy word unto thy servant.

77 Let thy tender mercies come unto me, that I may live: for thy law *is* my delight.

78 Let the proud ᴿbe ashamed; for they dealt perversely with me without a cause: *but* I will meditate in thy precepts.   25:3

79 Let those that fear thee turn unto me, and those that have known thy testimonies.

80 Let my heart be sound in thy statutes; that I be not ashamed.

כ CAPH

81 ᴿMy soul fainteth for thy salvation: *but* I hope in thy word. 84:2

82 Mine eyes fail for thy word, saying, When wilt thou comfort me?

83 For ᴿI am become like a bottle in the smoke; *yet* do I not forget thy statutes.   Job 30:30

84 ᴿHow many *are* the days of thy servant? ᴿwhen wilt thou execute judgment on them that persecute me?   39:4 · Rev. 6:10

85 ᴿThe proud have digged pits for me, which *are* not after thy law.   35:7; Prov. 16:27; Jer. 18:22

86 All thy commandments *are* faithful: they persecute me ᴿwrongfully; help thou me.   35:19

87 They had almost ᵀconsumed me upon earth; but I forsook not thy precepts.   *made an end of me*

88 Quicken me after thy lovingkindness; so shall I keep the testimony of thy mouth.

ל LAMED

89 ᴿFor ever, O LORD, thy word is settled in heaven.   Is. 40:8; Matt. 24:35

90 Thy faithfulness *is* unto all generations: thou hast established the earth, and it ᵀabideth. Lit. *stands*

91 They continue this day according to ᴿthine ordinances: for all *are* thy servants.   Jer. 33:25

92 Unless thy law *had been* my delights, I should then have perished in mine affliction.

93 I will never forget thy precepts: for with them thou hast ᵀquickened me.   *given me life*

94 I *am* thine, save me; for I have sought thy precepts.

95 The wicked have waited for me to destroy me: *but* I will consider thy testimonies.

96 ᴿI have seen an end of all perfection: *but* thy commandment *is* exceeding broad.   Matt. 5:18

מ MEM

97 O how love I thy law! ᴿit *is* my meditation all the day.   1:2

98 Thou through thy commandments hast made me ᴿwiser than mine enemies: for they *are* ever with me.   Deut. 4:6

99 I have more understanding than all my teachers: for thy testimonies *are* my meditation.

100 [R]I understand more than the [T]ancients, because I keep thy precepts.   [Job 32:7-9] · *aged*

101 I have [T]refrained my feet from every evil way, that I might keep thy word.   *restrained*

102 I have not departed from thy judgments: for thou hast taught me.

103 [R]How sweet are thy words unto my taste! *yea, sweeter* than honey to my mouth. 19:10; Prov. 8:11

104 Through thy precepts I get understanding: therefore I hate every false way.

‫ נ‬NUN

105 [R]Thy word *is* a lamp unto my feet, and a light unto my path.

106 [R]I have sworn, and I will perform *it*, that I will keep thy righteous judgments.   Neh. 10:29

107 I am afflicted very much: [T]quicken me, O LORD, according unto thy word.   *revive*

108 Accept, I beseech thee, [R]the freewill offerings of my mouth, O LORD, and teach me thy judgments.   Hos. 14:2; Heb. 13:15

109 [R]My [T]soul *is* continually [T]in my hand: yet do I not forget thy law.   Judg. 12:3; Job 13:14 · *life* · In danger

110 [R]The wicked have laid a snare for me: yet I [T]erred not from thy precepts.   140:5 · *strayed*

111 Thy testimonies have I taken as an heritage for ever: for they *are* the rejoicing of my heart.

112 I have inclined mine heart to perform thy statutes alway, *even unto* the end.

‫ ס‬SAMECH

113 I hate [T]*vain* thoughts: but thy law do I love.   *the double-minded*

114 Thou *art* my hiding place and my shield: I hope in thy word.

115 [R]Depart from me, ye evildoers: for I will keep the commandments of my God.   6:8; Matt. 7:23

116 Uphold me according unto thy word, that I may live: and let me not be ashamed of my hope.

117 [T]Hold thou me up, and I shall be safe: and I will [T]have respect unto thy statutes continually.   *Uphold me* · *observe thy statutes*

118 Thou hast trodden down all them that [T]err from thy statutes: for their deceit *is* falsehood.   *stray*

119 Thou puttest away all the wicked of the earth *like* dross: therefore I love thy testimonies.

120 [R]My flesh trembleth for fear of thee; and I am afraid of thy judgments.   Job 4:14; Hab. 3:16

‫ ע‬AIN

121 I have done judgment and justice: leave me not to mine oppressors.

122 Be [R]surety for thy servant for good: let not the proud oppress me.   Job 17:3; Heb. 7:22

123 Mine eyes fail for thy salvation, and for [T]the word of thy righteousness.   *thy righteous word*

124 Deal with thy servant according unto thy [T]mercy, and teach me thy statutes. *lovingkindness*

125 [R]I *am* thy servant; give me understanding, that I may know thy testimonies.   116:16

126 *It is* time for *thee*, LORD, to work: *for* they have [T]made void thy law.   *regarded thy law as void*

127 [R]Therefore I love thy commandments above gold; yea, above fine gold.   19:10

128 Therefore I esteem all *thy* precepts *concerning* all *things to be* right; *and* I hate every false way.

‫ פ‬PE

129 Thy testimonies *are* wonderful: therefore doth my soul keep them.

130 The entrance of thy words giveth light; it giveth understanding unto the [R]simple.   [19:7]; Prov. 1:4

131 I opened my mouth, and [R]panted: for I longed for thy commandments.   42:1

132 [R]Look thou upon me, and be merciful unto me, [R]as thou usest to do unto those that love thy name.   106:4 · 51:1; [2 Thess. 1:6]

133 [R]Order my steps in thy word: and [R]let not any iniquity have dominion over me. 17:5 · [19:13]

134 [R]Deliver[T] me from the op-

pression of man: so will I keep thy precepts.   Luke 1:74 · *Redeem*

135 RMake thy face to shine upon thy servant; and teach me thy statutes.   4:6; Num. 6:25

136 RRivers of waters run down mine eyes, because they keep not thy law.   Jer. 14:17; Lam. 3:48; Ezek. 9:4

צ TZADDI

137 RRighteous *art* thou, O LORD, and upright *are* thy judgments.   Neh. 9:33; Jer. 12:1; Dan. 9:7, 14

138 RThy testimonies *that* thou hast commanded *are* righteous and very faithful.   [19:7–9]

139 RMy zeal hath consumed me, because mine enemies have forgotten thy words.   69:9; John 2:17

140 RThy word *is* very pure: therefore thy servant loveth it. 12:6

141 I *am* small and despised: *yet* do not I forget thy precepts.

142 Thy righteousness *is* an everlasting righteousness, and thy law *is* Rthe truth.   [19:9; John 17:17]

143 Trouble and anguish have taken hold on me: *yet* thy commandments *are* my delights.

144 The righteousness of thy testimonies *is* everlasting: give me understanding, and I shall live.

ק KOPH

145 I cried with *my* whole heart; hear me, O LORD: I will keep thy statutes.

146 I cried unto thee; save me, and I shall keep thy testimonies.

147 RI Tprevented the dawning of the morning, and cried: I hoped in thy word.   5:3 · *rose before*

148 RMine eyes prevent the *night* watches, that I might meditate in thy word.   63:1, 6

149 Hear my voice according unto thy lovingkindness: O LORD, Tquicken me according to thy Tjudgment.   *revive · justice*

150 They draw nigh that follow after mischief: they are far from thy law.

151 Thou *art* near, O LORD; and all thy commandments *are* truth.

152 Concerning thy testimonies,

I have known of old that thou hast founded them Rfor ever.   Luke 21:33

ר RESH

153 RConsider mine affliction, and deliver me: for I do not forget thy law.   Lam. 5:1

154 RPlead my cause, and deliver me: Tquicken me according to thy word.   1 Sam. 24:15; Mic. 7:9 · *revive*

155 Salvation *is* far from the wicked: for they seek not thy statutes.

156 Great *are* thy tender mercies, O LORD: quicken me according to thy judgments.

157 Many *are* my persecutors and mine enemies; *yet* do I not decline from thy testimonies.

158 I beheld the transgressors, and was Rgrieved; because they kept not thy word.   Ezek. 9:4

159 Consider how I love thy precepts: quicken me, O LORD, according to thy lovingkindness.

160 Thy word *is* true Tfrom the beginning: and every one of thy righteous judgments *endureth* for ever.   *in its entirety*

ש SCHIN

161 Princes have persecuted me without a cause: but my heart standeth in awe of thy word.

162 I rejoice at thy word, as one that findeth great Tspoil.   *treasure*

163 I hate and abhor lying: *but* thy law do I love.

164 Seven times a day do I praise thee because of thy righteous judgments.

165 RGreat peace have they which love thy law: and nothing shall offend them.   Prov. 3:2; [Is. 26:3]

166 RLORD, I have hoped for thy salvation, and done thy commandments.   Gen. 49:18

167 My soul hath kept thy testimonies;andIlovethemexceedingly.

168 I have kept thy precepts and thy testimonies: Rfor all my ways *are* before thee.   Job 24:23; Prov. 5:21

ת TAU

169 Let my cry come near before thee, O LORD: Rgive me

understanding according to thy word.   vv. 27, 144

170 Let my ^Tsupplication come before thee: deliver me according to thy word.   Prayer of supplication

171 ^RMy lips shall utter praise, when thou hast taught me thy statutes.   v. 7

172 My tongue shall speak of thy word: for all thy commandments *are* righteousness.

173 Let thine hand help me; for I have chosen thy precepts.

174 ^RI have longed for thy salvation, O LORD; and ^Rthy law *is* my delight.   v. 166 · v. 16, 24

175 Let my soul live, and it shall praise thee; and let thy judgments help me.

176 I have gone astray like a lost sheep; seek thy servant; for I do not forget thy commandments.

PSALM 120

A Song of degrees.

IN ^Rmy distress I cried unto the LORD, and he heard me.   Jon. 2:2

2 Deliver my soul, O LORD, from lying lips, *and* from a deceitful tongue.

3 What shall be given unto thee? or what shall be done unto thee, ^Tthou false tongue?   *deceitful*

4 Sharp arrows of the ^Tmighty, with coals of juniper.   *warrior*

5 Woe is me, that I sojourn in ^RMe′-sech, *that* I dwell in the tents of Ke′-dar!   Gen. 10:2; 1 Chr. 1:5

6 My soul hath long dwelt with him that hateth peace.

7 I *am for* peace: but when I speak, they *are* for war.

PSALM 121

A Song of degrees.

I ^RWILL lift up mine eyes unto the ^Thills, from whence cometh my help.   [Jer. 3:23] · *mountains*

2 ^RMy help *cometh* from the LORD, which made heaven and earth.   [124:8]

3 ^RHe will not suffer thy foot to be moved: ^Rhe that keepeth thee will not slumber. Prov. 3:23, 26 · Is. 27:3

4 Behold, he that keepeth Is-rael shall neither slumber nor sleep.

5 The LORD *is* thy ^Tkeeper: the LORD *is* ^Rthy shade ^Rupon thy right hand.   *protector* · Is. 25:4 · 16:8

6 The sun shall not smite thee by day, nor the moon by night.

7 The LORD shall ^Tpreserve thee from all evil: he shall ^Rpreserve thy soul.   Lit. *keep* · 41:2

8 The LORD shall ^Rpreserve thy going out and thy coming in from this time forth, and even for evermore.   Deut. 28:6; [Prov. 2:8; 3:6]

PSALM 122

A Song of degrees of David.

I WAS glad when they said unto me, ^RLet us go into the house of the LORD.   Zech. 8:21

2 Our feet shall stand within thy gates, O Jerusalem.

3 Jerusalem is builded as a city that is ^Rcompact together: 2 Sam. 5:9

4 Whither the tribes go up, the tribes of the LORD, unto ^Rthe testimony of Israel, to give thanks unto the name of the LORD.   Ex. 16:34

5 ^RFor there are set thrones of judgment, the thrones of the house of David.   Deut. 17:8; 2 Chr. 19:8

6 ^RPray for the peace of Jerusalem: they shall prosper that love thee.   51:18

7 Peace be within thy walls, *and* prosperity within thy palaces.

8 For my brethren and companions′ sakes, I will now say, Peace *be* within thee.

9 Because of the house of the LORD our God I will ^Rseek thy good.   Neh. 2:10; Esth. 10:3

PSALM 123

A Song of degrees.

UNTO thee ^Rlift I up mine eyes, O thou ^Rthat dwellest in the heavens.   121:1; 141:8 · 2:4; 11:4

2 Behold, as the eyes of servants *look* unto the hand of their masters, *and* as the eyes of a ^Tmaiden unto the hand of her mistress; ^Rso our eyes ^Twait upon the LORD our God, until that he have mercy upon us.   *maid* · 25:15 · Look

3 Have mercy upon us, O LORD, have mercy upon us: for we are exceedingly filled with contempt.

4 Our soul is exceedingly filled with the scorning of those that are at ease, *and* with the contempt of the proud.

PSALM 124

A Song of degrees of David.

IF *it had not been* the LORD who was on our Rside, now may Israel say;   118:6; [Rom. 8:31]

2 If *it had not been* the LORD who was on our side, when men rose up against us:

3 Then they had Rswallowed us up Tquick, when their wrath was kindled against us: 56:1, 2; 57:3 · *alive*

4 Then the waters Thad overwhelmed us, the stream had Tgone over our soul: *would have · swept over*

5 Then the proud waters had gone over our soul.

6 Blessed *be* the LORD, who hath not given us *as* a prey to their teeth.

7 ROur soul is escaped Ras a bird out of the snare of the fowlers: the snare is broken, and we are escaped.   91:3 · Hos. 9:8

8 ROur help *is* in the name of the LORD, Rwho made heaven and earth.   [121:2] · 134:3; Gen. 1:1

PSALM 125

A Song of degrees.

THEY that trust in the LORD *shall be* as mount Zion, *which* cannot be Tremoved, *but* abideth for ever.   *moved*

2 *As* the mountains Tare round about Jerusalem, so the LORD *is* round about his people from henceforth even for ever. *surround*

3 For the rod of the wicked shall not rest upon the lot of the righteous; lest the righteous put forth their hands unto iniquity.

4 Do good, O LORD, unto *those that be* good, and to *them that are* upright in their hearts.

5 As for such as turn aside unto their Rcrooked ways, the LORD shall lead them forth with

the workers of iniquity: *but* peace *shall be* upon Israel.   Is. 59:8

PSALM 126

A Song of degrees.

WHEN the LORD turned again the captivity of Zion, we were like them that dream.

2 Then was our mouth filled with laughter, and our tongue with singing: then said they among the heathen, The LORD hath done great things for them.

3 The LORD hath done great things for us; *whereof* we are glad.

4 Turn again our captivity, O LORD, as the streams in the south.

5 RThey that sow in tears shall reap in joy. Is. 35:10; Jer. 31:9; [Gal. 6:9]

6 He that goeth forth and weepeth, bearing precious seed, shall doubtless come again with Rrejoicing,T bringing his sheaves *with him.*   Is. 61:3 · *shouts of joy*

PSALM 127

A Song of degrees for Solomon.

EXCEPT the LORD build the house, they labour in vain that build it: except the LORD Tkeep the city, the watchman waketh *but* in vain.   *guard*

2 *It is* vain for you to rise up early, to sit up late, to Reat the bread of sorrows: *for* so he giveth his beloved sleep.   [Gen. 3:17, 19]

3 Lo, children *are* an heritage of the LORD: *and* Rthe fruit of the womb *is his* reward.   Is. 13:18

4 As arrows *are* in the hand of a Tmighty man; so *are* children of the youth.   *warrior*

5 RHappy *is* the man that hath his quiver full of them: Rthey shall not be ashamed, but they shall speak with the enemies in the gate.   128:2, 3 · Job 5:4; Prov. 27:11

PSALM 128

A Song of degrees.

BLESSED Ris every one that feareth the LORD; that walketh in his ways.   119:1

2 For thou shalt eat the labour of thine hands: happy *shalt* thou *be,* and *it shall be* well with thee.

3 Thy wife *shall be* as a fruitful vine by the sides of thine house: thy ᴿchildren ᴿlike olive plants round about thy table. 127:3–5 · 52:8

4 Behold, that thus shall the man be blessed that feareth the LORD.

5 ᴿThe LORD shall bless thee out of Zion: and thou shalt see the good of Jerusalem all the days of thy life. 134:3

6 Yea, thou shalt ᴿsee thy children's children, *and* ᴿpeace upon Israel. Gen. 48:11; 50:23 · 125:5

PSALM 129

A Song of degrees.

MANY a time have they ᴿafflicted me from my youth, may Israel now say: 2 Cor. 4:8, 9

2 Many a time have they afflicted me from my youth: yet they have not prevailed against me.

3 The plowers plowed upon my back: they made long their furrows.

4 The LORD *is* righteous: he hath ᵀcut asunder the cords of the wicked. *cut in pieces*

5 Let them all be confounded and turned back that hate Zion.

6 Let them be as ᴿthe grass *upon* the housetops, which withereth afore it groweth up: 37:2

7 Wherewith the mower filleth not his hand; nor he that bindeth sheaves his ᵀbosom. *armsful*

8 Neither do they which go by say, ᴿThe blessing of the LORD *be* upon you: we bless you in the name of the LORD. Ruth 2:4

PSALM 130

A Song of degrees.

OUT of the depths have I cried unto thee, O LORD.

2 Lord, hear my voice: let thine ears be attentive to the voice of my supplications.

3 If thou, LORD, shouldest mark

iniquities, O Lord, who shall ᴿstand? [Nah. 1:6; Mal. 3:2]; Rev. 6:17

4 But *there is* forgiveness with thee, that thou mayest be feared.

5 ᴿI wait for the LORD, my soul doth wait, and ᴿin his word do I hope. [27:14] · 119:81

6 My soul *waiteth* for the Lord more than they that watch for the morning: *I say, more than* they that watch for the morning.

7 ᴿLet Israel hope in the LORD: for ᴿwith the LORD *there is* mercy, and with him *is* plenteous redemption. 131:3 · [86:5, 15; Is. 55:7]

8 And ᴿhe shall redeem Israel from all his iniquities. Titus 2:14

PSALM 131

A Song of degrees of David.

LORD, my heart is not haughty, nor mine eyes lofty: ᴿneither do I exercise myself in great matters, or in things too high for me. Jer. 45:5; [Rom. 12:16]

2 Surely I have behaved and quieted myself, ᴿas a child that is weaned of his mother: my soul *is* even as a weaned child. [Matt. 18:3]

3 Let Israel hope in the LORD from henceforth and for ever.

PSALM 132

A Song of degrees.

LORD, remember David, *and* all his afflictions:

2 How he sware unto the LORD, *and* vowed unto ᴿthe mighty *God* of Jacob; Gen. 49:24; Is. 49:26; 60:16

3 Surely I will not come into the ᵀtabernacle of my house, nor go up into my bed; *chamber*

4 I will not give sleep to mine eyes, *or* slumber to mine eyelids,

5 Until I ᴿfind out a place for the LORD, an habitation for the mighty *God* of Jacob. Acts 7:46

6 Lo, we heard of it ᴿat Eph'-ra-tah: ᴿwe found it in the fields of the wood. 1 Sam. 17:12 · 1 Sam. 7:1

7 We will go into his ^Ttaber-
nacles: ^Rwe will worship at his
footstool.　　*dwelling places* · 5:7; 99:5
8 Arise, O LORD, into thy
rest; thou, and the ark of thy
strength.
9 Let thy priests ^Rbe clothed
with righteousness; and let thy
saints shout for joy.　　Job 29:14
10 For thy servant David's sake
turn not away the face of thine
^Tanointed.　*Messiah,* commissioned one
11 The LORD hath sworn *in* truth
unto David; he will not turn from
it; ^ROf the fruit of thy body will I
set upon thy throne.　　2 Sam. 7:12
12 If thy children will keep my
covenant and my testimony that I
shall teach them, their children
shall also sit upon thy throne for
evermore.
13 ^RFor the LORD hath chosen
Zion; he hath desired *it* for his
^Thabitation.　　[48:1, 2] · *dwelling place*
14 ^RThis *is* my ^Trest for ever:
here will I dwell; for I have de-
sired it.　68:16; Matt. 23:21 · *resting place*
15 ^RI will abundantly bless her
^Tprovision: I will satisfy her poor
with bread.　　147:14 · *supply of food*
16 ^RI will also clothe her priests
with salvation: and her saints
shall shout aloud for joy.　　v. 9
17 ^RThere will I make the horn
of David to bud: I have ordained a
lamp for mine anointed.　Luke 1:69
18 His enemies will I ^Rclothe
with shame: but upon himself
shall his crown flourish.　Job 8:22

PSALM 133

A Song of degrees of David.

BEHOLD, how good and how
pleasant *it is* for ^Rbrethren to
dwell together in unity!　Heb. 13:1
2 *It is* like the precious ointment upon the head, that ran
down upon the beard, *even*
Aaron's beard: that went down to
the ^Tskirts of his garments;　*edge*
3 As the dew of Hermon, *and
as the dew* that descended upon
the mountains of Zion: for ^Rthere
the LORD commanded the bless-
ing, *even* life for evermore.　42:8

PSALM 134

A Song of degrees.

BEHOLD, bless ye the LORD,
all *ye* servants of the LORD,
which by night stand in the
house of the LORD.
2 Lift up your hands *in* the
sanctuary, and bless the LORD.
3 The LORD that made heaven
and earth bless thee out of Zion.

PSALM 135

PRAISE ye the LORD. Praise ye
the name of the LORD;
^Rpraise *him,* O ye servants of the
LORD.　　　　　　　　　　113:1
2 ^RYe that stand in the house of
the LORD, in ^Rthe courts of the
house of our God,　Luke 2:37 · 116:19
3 Praise the LORD; for the LORD
is good: sing praises unto his
name; ^Rfor *it is* pleasant.　147:1
4 For ^Rthe LORD hath chosen
Jacob unto himself, *and* Israel for
his peculiar treasure.　　Mal. 3:17
5 For I know that ^Rthe LORD *is*
great, and *that* our Lord *is* above
all gods.　　　　　　　95:3; 97:9
6 ^RWhatsoever the LORD
pleased, *that* did he in heaven,
and in earth, in the seas, and all
deep places.　　　　　　115:3
7 ^RHe causeth the vapours to
ascend from the ends of the earth;
^Rhe maketh lightnings for the
rain; he bringeth the wind out of
his treasuries.　Jer. 10:13 · Job 28:25, 26
8 Who smote the firstborn of
Egypt, both of man and beast.
9 ^R*Who* sent ^Ttokens and wonders into the midst of thee, O
Egypt, upon Pharaoh, and upon
all his servants.　78:43; Ex. 7:10 · *signs*
10 ^RWho smote great nations,
and slew mighty kings;　Num. 21:24
11 Si'-hon king of the Am'-o-
rites, and Og king of Ba'-shan,
and all the kingdoms of Canaan:
12 ^RAnd gave their land *for* an
^Theritage, an heritage unto Israel
his people. 78:55; 136:21, 22 · *inheritance*
13 Thy name, O LORD, *endureth*
for ever; *and* thy memorial, O
LORD, throughout all generations.
14 ^RFor the LORD will judge his

people, and he will repent himself concerning his servants. Deut. 32:36

15 ᴿThe idols of the heathen *are* silver and gold, the work of men's hands.   [115:4–8]

16 They have mouths, but they speak not; eyes have they, but they see not;

17 They have ears, but they hear not; neither is there *any* breath in their mouths.

18 They that make them are like unto them: *so is* every one that trusteth in them.

19 ᴿBless the LORD, O house of Israel: bless the LORD, O house of Aaron: [115:9]

20 Bless the LORD, O house of Levi: ye that fear the LORD, bless the LORD.

21 Blessed be the LORD ᴿout of Zion, which dwelleth at Jerusalem. Praise ye the LORD.   134:3

PSALM 136

O ᴿGIVE thanks unto the LORD; or *he is* good: for his mercy *endureth* for ever.   106:1

2 O give thanks unto ᴿthe God of gods: for his mercy *endureth* for ever.   [Deut. 10:17]

3 O give thanks to the Lord of lords: for his mercy *endureth* for ever.

4 To him ᴿwho alone doeth great wonders: for his mercy *endureth* for ever. Deut. 6:22; Job 9:10

5 ᴿTo him that by wisdom made the heavens: for his mercy *endureth* for ever. Prov. 3:19; Jer. 51:15

6 ᴿTo him that stretched out the earth above the waters: for his mercy *endureth* for ever. Jer. 10:12

7 ᴿTo him that made great lights: for his mercy *endureth* for ever: Gen. 1:14–18

8 The sun to rule by day: for his mercy *endureth* for ever:

9 The moon and stars to rule by night: for his mercy *endureth* for ever.

10 ᴿTo him that smote Egypt in their firstborn: for his mercy *endureth* for ever: Ex. 12:29

11 ᴿAnd brought out Israel from

among them: for his mercy *endureth* for ever: Ex. 12:51; 13:3, 16

12 ᴿWith a strong hand, and with a stretched out arm: for his mercy *endureth* for ever.   Ex. 6:6

13 ᴿTo him which divided the Red sea into parts: for his mercy *endureth* for ever: Ex. 14:21

14 And made Israel to pass through the midst of it: for his mercy *endureth* for ever:

15 ᴿBut overthrew Pharaoh and his host in the Red sea: for his mercy *endureth* for ever.   Ex. 14:27

16 ᴿTo him which led his people through the wilderness: for his mercy *endureth* for ever. Ex. 13:18

17 ᴿTo him which ᵀsmote great kings: for his mercy *endureth* for ever: 135:10–12 · struck down

18 And slew famous kings: for his mercy *endureth* for ever:

19 ᴿSi'-hon king of the Am'-o-rites: for his mercy *endureth* for ever: Num. 21:21

20 ᴿAnd Og the king of Ba'-shan: for his mercy *endureth* for ever: Num. 21:33

21 ᴿAnd gave their land for an ᵀheritage: for his mercy *endureth* for ever: Josh. 12:1 · inheritance

22 *Even* an heritage unto Israel his servant: for his mercy *endureth* for ever.

23 Who ᴿremembered us in our low estate: for his mercy *endureth* for ever: 113:7; Gen. 8:1; Deut. 32:36

24 And hath ᴿredeemedᵀ us from our enemies: for his mercy *endureth* for ever.   44:7 · rescued

25 Who giveth food to all flesh: for his mercy *endureth* for ever.

26 O give thanks unto the God of heaven: for his mercy *endureth* for ever.

PSALM 137

B Y the rivers of Babylon, there we sat down, yea, we wept, when we remembered Zion.

2 We hanged our harps upon the willows in the midst thereof.

3 For there they that carried us away captive required of us a song; and they that ᴿwasted us

required of us mirth, *saying,* Sing us *one* of the songs of Zion.   79:1

4   How shall we sing the LORD's song in a ᵀstrange land?   *foreign*

5   If I forget thee, O Jerusalem, let my right hand forget *her cunning.*

6   If I do not remember thee, let my ᴿtongue cleave to the roof of my mouth; if I prefer not Jerusalem above my chief joy. Job 29:10

7   Remember, O LORD, ᴿthe children of E'-dom in the day of Jerusalem; who said, ᵀRase *it,* rase *it, even* to the foundation thereof.   Obad. 10–14 · Lit. *Make it bare*

8   O daughter of Babylon, ᴿwho art to be destroyed; happy *shall he be,* ᴿthat rewardeth thee as thou hast served us.   Is. 13:1–6 · Rev. 18:6

9   Happy *shall he be,* that taketh and ᴿdasheth thy little ones against the stones. Is. 13:16; Nah. 3:10

PSALM 138

A Psalm of David.

I WILL praise thee with my whole heart: ᴿbefore the gods will I sing praise unto thee. 119:46

2   ᴿI will worship toward thy holy temple, and praise thy name for thy lovingkindness and for thy truth: for thou hast magnified thy word above all thy name.   28:2

3   In the day when I cried thou answeredst me, *and* ᵀstrengthenedst me *with* strength in my soul.   *made me bold*

4   All the kings of the earth shall praise thee, O LORD, when they hear the words of thy mouth.

5   Yea, they shall sing ᵀin the ways of the LORD: for great *is* the glory of the LORD.   *of*

6   ᴿThough the LORD *be* high, yet ᴿhath he respect unto the lowly: but the proud he knoweth afar off. [113:4–7] · Luke 1:48; [James 4:6]

7   ᴿThough I walk in the midst of trouble, thou wilt revive me: thou shalt stretch forth thine hand against the wrath of mine enemies, and thy right hand shall save me.   [23:3, 4]

8   ᴿThe LORD will ᵀperfect *that*

which concerneth me: thy mercy, O LORD, *endureth* for ever: forsake not the works of thine own hands.   57:2; [Phil. 1:6] · *complete*

PSALM 139

To the chief Musician,
A Psalm of David.

O LORD, ᴿthou hast searched me, and known *me.*   17:3

2   Thou knowest my downsitting and mine uprising, thou understandest my thought afar off.

3   ᴿThou compassest my path and my lying down, and art acquainted *with* all my ways. Job 31:4

4   For *there is* not a word in my tongue, *but,* lo, O LORD, ᴿthou knowest it altogether.   [Heb. 4:13]

5   Thou hast ᵀbeset me behind and before, and laid thine hand upon me.   *enclosed* or *hedged*

6   ᴿSuch knowledge *is* too wonderful for me; it is high, I cannot *attain* unto it.   40:5; Job 42:3

7   ᴿWhither shall I go from thy spirit? or whither shall I flee from thy presence?   [Jer. 23:24; Amos 9:2–4]

8   If I ascend up into heaven, thou *art* there: if I make my bed in hell, behold, thou *art there.*

9   *If* I take the wings of the morning, *and* dwell in the uttermost parts of the sea;

10 Even there shall thy hand lead me, and thy right hand shall hold me.

11 If I say, Surely the darkness shall cover me; even the night shall be light about me.

12 Yea, the darkness hideth not from thee; but the night shineth as the day: the darkness and the light *are* both alike *to thee.*

13 For thou hast possessed my reins: thou hast ᵀcovered me in my mother's womb.   *weaved*

14 I will praise thee; for I am fearfully *and* wonderfully made: marvellous *are* thy works; and *that* my soul knoweth right well.

15 My substance was not hid from thee, when I was made in secret, *and* curiously wrought in the lowest parts of the earth.

16 Thine eyes did see my substance, yet being ᵀunperfect; and in thy book all *my members* were written, *which* in continuance were fashioned, when *as yet there was* none of them.   *unformed*

17 ᴿHow precious also are thy thoughts unto me, O God! how great is the sum of them!   [40:5]

18 *If* I should count them, they are more in number than the sand: when I awake, I am still with thee.

19 Surely thou wilt ᴿslay the wicked, O God: depart from me therefore, ye bloody men.   [Is. 11:4]

20 For they ᴿspeak against thee wickedly, *and* thine enemies take *thy name* in vain.   Jude 15

21 ᴿDo not I hate them, O LORD, that hate thee? and am not I grieved with those that rise up against thee?   2 Chr. 19:2

22 I hate them with perfect hatred: I count them mine enemies.

23 ᴿSearch me, O God, and know my heart: try me, and know my thoughts: 26:2; Job 31:6

24 And see if *there be any* wicked way in me, and ᴿlead me in the way everlasting.   5:8; 143:10

PSALM 140

To the chief Musician,
A Psalm of David.

DELIVER me, O LORD, from the evil man: preserve me from the violent man;

2 Which imagine mischiefs in *their* heart; ᴿcontinually are they gathered together *for* war.   56:6

3 They have sharpened their tongues like a serpent; adders' poison *is* under their lips. Selah.

4 ᴿKeep me, O LORD, from the hands of the wicked; preserve me from the violent man; who have purposed to ᵀoverthrow my goings.   71:4 · *make my steps stumble*

5 The proud have hid a ᴿsnare for me, and cords; they have spread a net by the wayside; they have set gins for me. Selah.   35:7

6 I said unto the LORD, Thou

art my God: hear the voice of my supplications, O LORD.

7 O GOD the Lord, the strength of my salvation, thou hast covered my head in the day of battle.

8 Grant not, O LORD, the desires of the wicked: further not his wicked ᵀdevice; *lest* they exalt themselves. Selah.   *scheme*

9 *As for* the head of those that compass me about, let the mischief of their own lips cover them.

10 ᴿLet burning coals fall upon them: let them be cast into the fire; into deep pits, that they rise not up again.   11:6

11 Let not ᵀan evil speaker be established in the earth: evil shall hunt the violent man to overthrow *him*.   *a slanderer*

12 I know that the LORD will ᴿmaintain the cause of the afflicted, *and* the right of the poor.   9:4

13 Surely the righteous shall give thanks unto thy name: the upright shall dwell in thy presence.

PSALM 141

A Psalm of David.

LORD, I cry unto thee: make haste unto me; give ear unto my voice, when I cry unto thee.

2 Let my prayer be set forth before thee ᴿ*as* incense; *and* ᴿthe lifting up of my hands *as* the evening sacrifice.   Luke 1:10 · [1 Tim. 2:8]

3 Set a ᵀwatch, O LORD, before my ᴿmouth; keep the door of my lips.   *guard* · [Prov. 13:3; 21:23]

4 Incline not my heart to *any* evil thing, to practise wicked works with men that work iniquity: ᴿand let me not eat of their ᵀdainties.   Prov. 23:6 · *delicacies*

5 ᴿLet the righteous smite me; *it shall be* a kindness: and let him reprove me; *it shall be* an excellent oil, *which* shall not break my head: for yet my prayer also *shall be* in their calamities.   [Gal. 6:1]

6 When their judges are overthrown ᵀin stony places, they shall hear my words; for they are sweet.   *by the sides of the cliff*

7 Our bones are scattered at

the grave's mouth, as when one
Tcutteth and cleaveth *wood* upon
the earth. *plows and breaks up the earth*
8 But mine eyes *are* unto thee,
O GOD the Lord: in thee is my
trust; leave not my soul destitute.
9 Keep me from Rthe snares
which they have laid for me, and
the Tgins of the workers of iniquity. 119:110 · *traps*
10 RLet the wicked fall into their
own nets, Twhilst that I withal
escape. 35:8 · *while I escape safely*

PSALM 142

Mas'-chil of David; A Prayer
when he was in the cave.

I CRIED unto the LORD with my
voice; with my voice unto the
LORD did I make my supplication.
2 I poured out my complaint
before him; I Tshewed before him
my trouble. *declared*
3 When my spirit was Rover-
whelmed within me, then thou
knewest my path. In the way
wherein I walked have they privily Rlaid a snare for me. 77:3 · v. 9
4 I looked on *my* right hand,
and beheld, but *there was* no man
that would Tknow me: refuge
failed me; no man cared for my
soul. *acknowledge*
5 I cried unto thee, O LORD: I
said, Thou *art* my refuge *and* my
portion in the land of the living.
6 TAttend unto my cry; for I am
brought very low: deliver me from
my persecutors; for they are
stronger than I. *Give heed*
7 Bring my soul out of prison,
that I may Rpraise thy name: the
righteous shall Tcompass me
about; for thou shalt deal bountifully with me. 34:1, 2 · *surround*

PSALM 143

A Psalm of David.

HEAR my prayer, O LORD,
give ear to my supplications:
in thy faithfulness answer me,
and in thy righteousness.
2 And enter not into judgment

with thy servant: for in thy sight
shall no man living be justified.
3 For the enemy hath persecuted my soul; he hath smitten my
life down to the ground; he hath
made me to dwell in darkness, as
those that have been long dead.
4 RTherefore is my spirit overwhelmed within me; my heart
within me is desolate. 77:3
5 RI remember the days of old; I
meditate on all thy works; I muse
on the work of thy hands. 77:5
6 I stretch forth my hands unto
thee: Rmy soul *thirsteth* after
thee, as a thirsty land. Selah. 63:1
7 Hear me speedily, O LORD:
my spirit faileth: hide not thy face
from me, Rlest I be like unto them
that go down into the pit. 28:1
8 Cause me to hear thy lovingkindness Rin the morning; for
in thee do I trust: Rcause me to
know the way wherein I should
walk; for I Rlift up my soul unto
thee. 46:5 · 5:8 · 25:1
9 Deliver me, O LORD, from
mine enemies: I flee unto thee to
hide me.
10 RTeach me to do thy will; for
thou *art* my God: Rthy spirit *is*
good; lead me into Rthe land of
uprightness. 25:4, 5 · Neh. 9:20 · Is. 26:10
11 RQuickenT me, O LORD, for
thy name's sake: for thy righteousness' sake bring my soul
out of trouble. 119:25 · *Revive*
12 And of thy mercy RcutT off
mine enemies, and destroy all
them that afflict my soul: for I *am*
thy servant. 54:5 · *put an end to*

PSALM 144

A Psalm of David.

BLESSED *be* the LORD my
Tstrength, Rwhich teacheth
my hands to war, *and* my fingers
to fight: Lit. *rock* · 18:34; 2 Sam. 22:35
2 My goodness, and my for-
tress; my high tower, and my
deliverer; my shield, and *he* in
whom I Ttrust; who subdueth my
people under me. *take refuge*
3 RLORD, what *is* man, that thou
takest knowledge of him! *or* the

son of man, that thou ᵀmakest account of him! 8:4; Heb. 2:6 · *thinketh*

4 ᴿMan is like ᵀto vanity: ᴿhis days *are* as a shadow that passeth away. 39:11 · *a breath* · Job 8:9; 14:2

5 ᴿBow thy heavens, O LORD, and come down: touch the mountains, and they shall smoke. Is. 64:1

6 ᴿCast forth lightning, and scatter them: shoot out thine arrows, and destroy them. 18:13, 14

7 Send thine hand from above; ᵀrid me, and deliver me out of great waters, from the hand of ᵀstrange children; *rescue · foreigners*

8 Whose mouth speaketh ᵀvanity, and their right hand *is* a right hand of falsehood. *empty words*

9 I will ᴿsing a new song unto thee, O God: upon a ᵀpsaltery *and* an instrument of ten strings will I sing praises unto thee. 40:3 · *harp*

10 ᴿ*It is he* that giveth ᵀsalvation unto kings: who delivereth David his servant from the hurtful sword. 18:50 · *deliverance to his kings*

11 ᵀRid me, and deliver me from the hand of ᵀstrange children, whose mouth speaketh vanity, and their right hand *is* a right hand of falsehood: *Rescue · foreigners*

12 That our sons *may be* ᴿas plants grown up in their youth; *that* our daughters *may be* as corner stones, polished *after* the similitude of a palace: 128:3

13 *That* our ᵀgarners *may be* full, affording all manner of ᵀstore: *that* our sheep may bring forth thousands and ten thousands in our streets: *barns · produce*

14 *That* our oxen *may be* ᵀstrong to labour; *that there be* no breaking in, nor going out; that *there be* no ᵀcomplaining in our streets. *well laden · outcry*

15 Happy *is that* people, that is in such a case: *yea,* happy *is that* people, whose God *is* the LORD.

PSALM 145

David's Psalm of praise.

I WILL ᵀextol thee, my God, O king; and I will bless thy name for ever and ever. *praise*

2 Every day will I bless thee; and I will praise thy name for ever and ever.

3 Great *is* the LORD, and greatly to be praised; and ᴿhis greatness *is* unsearchable. Is. 40:28

4 ᴿOne generation shall praise thy works to another, and shall declare thy mighty acts. Is. 38:19

5 I will ᵀspeak of the glorious ᵀhonour of thy majesty, and of thy wondrous works. *meditate · splendour*

6 And *men* shall speak of the might of thy ᵀterrible acts: and I will declare thy greatness. *awesome*

7 They shall ᵀabundantly utter the memory of thy great goodness, and shall sing of thy righteousness. *eagerly utter,* lit. *bubble forth*

8 ᴿThe LORD *is* gracious, and full of compassion; slow to anger, and of great mercy. 86:5, 15

9 ᴿThe LORD *is* good to all: and his tender mercies *are* over all his works. Jer. 33:11; Nah. 1:7; [Matt. 19:17]

10 ᴿAll thy works shall praise thee, O LORD; and thy saints shall bless thee. 19:1

11 They shall speak of the glory of thy kingdom, and talk of thy power;

12 To make known to the sons of men his mighty acts, and the glorious majesty of his kingdom.

13 ᴿThy kingdom *is* an everlasting kingdom, and thy dominion *endureth* throughout all generations. Dan. 2:44; 4:3; [2 Pet. 1:11]

14 The LORD upholdeth all that fall, and ᴿraiseth up all *those that be* bowed down. 146:8

15 ᴿThe eyes of all wait upon thee; and ᴿthou givest them their meat in due season. 104:27 · 136:25

16 Thou openest thine hand, ᴿand satisfiest the desire of every living thing. 104:21, 28

17 The LORD *is* righteous in all his ways, and ᵀholy in all his works. *gracious*

18 The LORD *is* nigh unto all them that call upon him, to all that call upon him ᴿin truth. [John 4:24]

19 He will fulfil the desire of them that fear him: he also will hear their cry, and will save them.

20 ᴿThe LORD preserveth all them that love him: but all the wicked will he destroy.   [31:23]
21 My mouth shall speak the praise of the LORD: and let all flesh bless his holy name for ever and ever.

PSALM 146

PRAISE ye the LORD. ᴿPraise the LORD, O my soul.   103:1
2 ᴿWhile I live will I praise the LORD: I will sing praises unto my God while I have any being. 104:33
3 ᴿPut not your trust in princes, nor in ᵀthe son of man, in whom there is no help.   [Is. 2:22] · a human
4 His breath goeth forth, he returneth to his earth; in that very day ᴿhis thoughts perish. [1 Cor. 2:6]
5 Happy is he that hath the God of Jacob for his help, whose hope is in the LORD his God:
6 Which made heaven, and earth, the sea, and all that therein is: which keepeth truth for ever:
7 Which executeth judgment for the oppressed: ᴿwhich giveth food to the hungry. ᴿThe LORD looseth the prisoners: 107:9 · Is. 61:1
8 The LORD openeth the eyes of the blind: the LORD raiseth them that are bowed down: the LORD loveth the righteous:
9 ᴿThe LORD ᵀpreserveth the strangers; he relieveth the fatherless and widow: ᴿbut the way of the wicked he turneth upside down.   68:5 · watches over · 147:6
10 ᴿThe LORD shall reign for ever, even thy God, O Zion, unto all generations. Praise ye the LORD.   10:16; Ex. 15:18; [Rev. 11:15]

PSALM 147

PRAISE ye the LORD: for ᴿit is good to sing praises unto our God; ᴿfor it is pleasant; and ᴿpraise is comely.   92:1 · 135:3 · 33:1
2 The LORD doth ᴿbuild up Jerusalem: ᴿhe gathereth together the outcasts of Israel. 102:16 · Is. 56:8
3 ᴿHe healeth the broken in heart, and bindeth up their wounds.   [51:17]; Is. 61:1; Luke 4:18
4 ᴿHe ᵀtelleth the number of

the stars; he calleth them all by their names.   Is. 40:26 · counts
5 ᴿGreat is our Lord, and of ᴿgreat power: ᴿhis understanding is infinite.   48:1 · Nah. 1:3 · Is. 40:28
6 ᴿThe LORD lifteth up the ᵀmeek: he casteth the wicked down to the ground. 146:8, 9 · humble
7 Sing unto the LORD with thanksgiving; sing praise upon the harp unto our God:
8 ᴿWho covereth the heaven with clouds, who prepareth rain for the earth, who maketh grass to grow upon the mountains.   104:13
9 ᴿHe giveth to the beast his food, and ᴿto the young ravens which cry.   Job 38:41 · [Matt. 6:26]
10 He delighteth not in the strength of the horse: he taketh not pleasure in the legs of a man.
11 The LORD taketh pleasure in them that fear him, in those that hope in his ᵀmercy.   lovingkindness
12 Praise the LORD, O Jerusalem; praise thy God, O Zion.
13 For he hath strengthened the bars of thy gates; he hath blessed thy children within thee.
14 ᴿHe maketh peace in thy borders, and ᴿfilleth thee with the finest of the wheat. Is. 54:13 · 132:15
15 ᴿHe sendeth forth his commandment upon earth: his word runneth very swiftly.   [107:20]
16 ᴿHe giveth snow like wool: he scattereth the hoarfrost like ashes.   Job 37:6
17 He casteth forth his ice ᵀlike morsels: who can stand before his cold?   as fragments of food
18 He sendeth out his word, and melteth them: he causeth his wind to blow, and the waters flow.
19 ᴿHe sheweth his word unto Jacob, ᴿhis statutes and his judgments unto Israel. Deut. 33:4 · Mal. 4:4
20 ᴿHe hath not dealt so with any nation: and as for his judgments, they have not known them. Praise ye the LORD.   [Rom. 3:1, 2]

PSALM 148

PRAISE ye the LORD. Praise ye the LORD from the heavens: praise him in the heights.

2　Praise ye him, all his angels: praise ye him, all his hosts.

3　Praise ye him, sun and moon: praise him, all ye stars of light.

4　Praise him, ^Rye heavens of heavens, and ye waters that *be* above the heavens.　　　Deut. 10:14

5　Let them praise the name of the LORD: for ^Rhe commanded, and they were created.　　Gen. 1:1, 6

6　^RHe hath also stablished them for ever and ever: he hath made a decree which shall not pass.　89:37; [Jer. 31:35, 36; 33:20, 25]

7　Praise the LORD from the earth, ye dragons, and all deeps:

8　Fire, and hail; snow, and vapours; stormy wind fulfilling his word:

9　Mountains, and all hills; fruitful trees, and all cedars:

10　Beasts, and all cattle; creeping things, and flying fowl:

11　Kings of the earth, and all people; princes, and all judges of the earth:

12　Both young men, and maidens; old men, and children:

13　Let them praise the name of the LORD: for his ^Rname alone is ^Texcellent; his glory *is* above the earth and heaven.　　8:1 · *exalted*

14　He also ^Rexalteth the horn of his people, the praise of all his saints; *even* of the children of Israel, ^Ra people near unto him. Praise ye the LORD.　75:10 · Eph. 2:17

PSALM 149

P RAISE ye the LORD. ^RSing unto the LORD a new song, *and* his praise in the congregation of saints.　　　　　33:3

2　Let Israel rejoice in him that made him: let the children of Zion be joyful in their ^RKing.　Zech. 9:9

3　^RLet them praise his name in the dance: let them sing praises unto him with the timbrel and harp.　　　81:2; Ex. 15:20

4　For the LORD taketh pleasure in his people: ^Rhe will beautify the meek with salvation.　　Is. 61:3

5　Let the saints be joyful in glory: let them ^Rsing aloud upon their beds.　　　　　Job 35:10

6　*Let* the high *praises* of God *be* in their mouth, and a twoedged sword in their hand;

7　To execute vengeance upon the ^Theathen, *and* punishments upon the people;　*nations* or *Gentiles*

8　To bind their kings with chains, and their nobles with fetters of iron;

9　^RTo execute upon them the judgment written: ^Rthis honour have all his saints. Praise ye the LORD.　Ezek. 28:26 · 148:14; 1 Cor. 6:2

PSALM 150

P RAISE ^Rye the LORD. Praise God in his sanctuary: praise him in the firmament of his power.　　　　　145:5, 6

2　Praise him for his mighty acts: praise him according to his excellent ^Rgreatness.　Deut. 3:24

3　Praise him with the sound of the ^Ttrumpet: praise him with the ^Tpsaltery and harp.　*cornet · lyre*

4　Praise him with the timbrel and dance: praise him with stringed instruments and organs.

5　Praise him upon the loud cymbals: praise him upon the high sounding cymbals.

6　Let every thing that hath breath praise the LORD. ^TPraise ye the LORD.　　Heb. *Hallelujah*

The Book of
PROVERBS

THE key word in Proverbs is *wisdom*, "the ability to live life skillfully." A godly life in an ungodly world, however, is no simple assignment. Proverbs provides God's detailed instructions for His people to deal successfully with the practical affairs of everyday life: how to relate to God, parents, children, neighbors, and government. Solomon, the principal author, uses a combination of poetry, parables, pithy questions, short stories, and wise maxims to give in strikingly memorable form the common sense and divine perspective necessary to handle life's issues.

Because Solomon, the pinnacle of Israel's wise men, was the principal contributor, the Hebrew title of this book is *Mishle Shelomoh,* "Proverbs of Solomon" (1:1). The Greek title is *Paroimiai Salomontos,* "Proverbs of Solomon." The Latin title *Liber Proverbiorum,* "Book of Proverbs," combines the words *pro* "for" and *verba* "words" to describe the way the proverbs concentrate many words into a few. The rabbinical writings called Proverbs *Sepher Hokhmah,* "Book of Wisdom."

THE Proverbs of Solomon the son of David, king of Israel;

2 To know wisdom and instruction; to ᵀperceive the words of understanding; *understand or discern*

3 To receive the instruction of wisdom, justice, and judgment, and equity;

4 To give ᵀsubtilty to the ᴿsimple, to the young man knowledge and discretion. *prudence · 9:4*

5 ᴿA wise *man* will hear, and will increase learning; and a man of understanding shall ᵀattain unto wise counsels: *9:9 · acquire*

6 To understand a proverb, and the interpretation; the words of the wise, and their dark sayings.

7 ᴿThe fear of the LORD *is* the beginning of knowledge: *but* fools despise wisdom and instruction. *Job 28:28; Ps. 111:10; [Eccl. 12:13]*

8 ᴿMy son, hear the instruction of thy father, and forsake not the law of thy mother: *4:1*

9 For they *shall be* an ornament of ᴿgrace unto thy head, and chains about thy neck. *3:22*

10 My son, if sinners entice thee, ᴿconsent thou not. *[Eph. 5:11]*

11 If they say, Come with us, let us ᴿlay wait for blood, let us lurk ᵀprivily for the innocent without cause: *12:6; Jer. 5:26 · secretly*

12 Let us swallow them up alive as the grave; and whole, ᴿas those that go down into the pit: *Ps. 28:1*

13 We shall find all precious ᵀsubstance, we shall fill our houses with ᵀspoil: *Lit. wealth · plunder*

14 Cast in thy lot among us; let us all have one purse:

15 My son, ᴿwalk not thou in the way with them; ᴿrefrain thy foot from their path: *Ps. 1:1 · Ps. 119:101*

16 ᴿFor their feet run to evil, and make haste to shed blood. *[Is. 59:7]*

17 Surely in vain the net is spread in the sight of any bird.

18 And they lay wait for their *own* blood; they lurk ᵀprivily for their *own* lives. *secretly*

19 ᴿSo *are* the ways of every one that is greedy of gain; *which* taketh away the life of the owners thereof. *15:27; [1 Tim. 6:10]*

20 Wisdom crieth without; she uttereth her voice in the streets:

21 She crieth in the chief ᵀplace of concourse, in the openings of the gates: in the city she uttereth her words, *saying,* *Lit. concourses*

22 How long, ye ᵀsimple ones, will ye love simplicity? and the scorners delight in their scorning, and fools hate knowledge? *naive*

23 Turn you at my reproof: be-

hold, [R]I will pour out my spirit unto you, I will make known my words unto you. Joel 2:28; [John 7:39]

24 Because I have called, and ye refused; I have stretched out my hand, and no man regarded;

25 But ye [R]have set at nought all my counsel, and would none of my reproof: Ps. 107:11; Luke 7:30

26 [R]I also will laugh at your calamity; I will mock when your [T]fear cometh; Ps. 2:4 · terror

27 When [R]your [T]fear cometh as [T]desolation, and your destruction cometh as a whirlwind; when distress and anguish cometh upon you. [10:24, 25] · terror · a storm

28 [R]Then shall they call upon me, but I will not answer; they shall seek me early, but they shall not find me: Ps. 18:41; Is. 1:15; Jer. 11:11

29 For that they [R]hated knowledge, and did not [R]choose the fear of the LORD: Job 21:14 · Ps. 119:173

30 [R]They [T]would none of my counsel: they despised all my reproof. v. 25; Ps. 81:11 · would have

31 Therefore [R]shall they eat of the fruit of their own way, and be filled with their own devices. 22:8

32 For [T]the turning away of the simple shall slay them, and the [T]prosperity of fools shall destroy them. the waywardness · complacency

33 But whoso hearkeneth unto me shall dwell safely, and [R]shall be quiet from fear of evil. Ps. 112:7

2 My son, if thou wilt receive my words, and [R]hide my commandments with thee; [4:21]

2 So that thou incline thine ear unto wisdom, and apply thine heart to understanding;

3 Yea, if thou criest after knowledge, and liftest up thy voice for understanding;

4 [R]If thou seekest her as silver, and searchest for her as for hid treasures; [3:14]

5 [R]Then shalt thou understand the fear of the LORD, and find the knowledge of God. [James 1:5, 6]

6 [R]For the LORD giveth wisdom: out of his mouth cometh knowledge and understanding. [Job 32:8]

7 He layeth up sound wisdom for the righteous: he is a [T]buckler to them that walk uprightly. shield

8 He keepeth the paths of judgment, and [R]preserveth the way of his saints. [1 Sam. 2:9]; Ps. 66:9

9 Then shalt thou understand righteousness, and judgment, and equity; yea, every good path.

10 When wisdom entereth into thine heart, and knowledge is pleasant unto thy soul;

11 Discretion shall preserve thee, [R]understanding shall keep thee: 4:6; 6:22

12 To deliver thee from the way of the evil man, from the man that speaketh [T]froward things; perverse

13 Who leave the paths of uprightness, to [R]walk in the ways of darkness; 4:19; Ps. 82:5

14 [R]Who rejoice to do evil, and delight in the [T]frowardness of the wicked; [Rom. 1:32] · perversity

15 Whose ways are crooked, and they froward in their paths:

16 To deliver thee from [R]the [T]strange woman, [R]even from the stranger which flattereth with her words; 5:20; 6:24; 7:5 · immoral · 5:3

17 Which forsaketh the [T]guide of her youth, and forgetteth the covenant of her God. companion

18 For [R]her house [T]inclineth unto death, and her paths unto the dead. 7:27 · sinks down

19 None that go unto her return again, neither [T]take they hold of the paths of life. do they regain

20 That thou mayest walk in the way of good men, and keep the paths of the righteous.

21 For the upright shall dwell in the [R]land, and the [T]perfect shall remain in it. Ps. 37:3 · blameless

22 But the wicked shall be cut off from the earth, and the transgressors shall be rooted out of it.

3 My son, forget not my law; [R]but let thine heart keep my commandments: Deut. 8:1

2 For length of days, and long life, and [R]peace, shall they add to thee. 4:10; Ps. 119:165

3 Let not mercy and truth forsake thee: bind them about thy

neck; ᴿwrite them upon the table of thine heart: 7:3; Jer. 17:1; [2 Cor. 3:3]

4 ᴿSo shalt thou find favour and good understanding in the sight of God and man. Rom. 14:18

5 Trust in the Lᴏʀᴅ with all thine heart; ᴿand lean not unto thine own understanding. 23:4

6 In all thy ways acknowledge him, and he shall ᵀdirect thy paths. Or *make smooth* or *straight*

7 Be not wise in thine own ᴿeyes: fear the Lᴏʀᴅ, and depart from evil. Rom. 12:16

8 It shall be health to thy navel, and marrow to thy bones.

9 ᴿHonour the Lᴏʀᴅ with thy substance, and with the firstfruits of all thine increase: [Mal. 3:10]

10 ᴿSo shall thy barns be filled with plenty, and thy presses shall burst out with new wine. Deut. 28:8

11 ᴿMy son, despise not the chastening of the Lᴏʀᴅ; neither be weary of his correction: Ps. 94:12

12 For whom the Lᴏʀᴅ loveth he correcteth; ᴿeven as a father the son *in whom* he delighteth. 13:24

13 ᴿHappy *is* the man *that* findeth wisdom, and the man *that* getteth understanding. 8:32, 34, 35

14 ᴿFor the ᵀmerchandise of it *is* better than the ᵀmerchandise of silver, and the gain thereof than fine gold. Job 28:13 · Lit. *gain* · *profit*

15 She *is* more precious than rubies: and ᴿall the things thou canst desire are not to be compared unto her. Matt. 13:44

16 ᴿLength of days *is* in her right hand; *and* in her left hand riches and honour. 8:18; [1 Tim. 4:8]

17 ᴿHer ways *are* ways of pleasantness, and all her paths *are* peace. [Matt. 11:29]

18 She *is* a tree of life to them that lay hold upon her: and happy *is every* one that retaineth her.

19 ᴿThe Lᴏʀᴅ by wisdom hath founded the earth; by understanding hath he established the heavens. 8:27; Ps. 104:24

20 By his knowledge the ᵀdepths are ᴿbroken up, and the clouds drop down the dew. *deeps* · Gen. 7:11

21 My son, let not them depart from thine eyes: keep sound wisdom and discretion:

22 So shall they be life unto thy soul, and ᵀgrace to thy neck. *favour*

23 ᴿThen shalt thou walk in thy way safely, and thy foot shall not stumble. 10:9; [Ps. 37:24; 91:11, 12]

24 When thou liest down, thou shalt not be afraid: yea, thou shalt lie down, and thy sleep shall be sweet.

25 ᴿBe not afraid of sudden fear, neither of the desolation of the wicked, when it cometh. 1 Pet. 3:14

26 For the Lᴏʀᴅ shall be thy confidence, and shall keep thy foot from being ᵀtaken. *caught*

27 ᴿWithhold not good from ᵀthem to whom it is due, when it is in the power of thine hand to do *it.* Rom. 13:7; [Gal. 6:10] · Lit. *its owners*

28 ᴿSay not unto thy neighbour, Go, and come again, and to morrow I will give; when thou hast it by thee. Lev. 19:13; Deut. 24:15

29 Devise not evil against thy neighbour, seeing he dwelleth ᵀsecurely by thee. *in safety with*

30 ᴿStrive not with a man without cause, if he have done thee no harm. 26:17; [Rom. 12:18]

31 Envy thou not the oppressor, and choose none of his ways.

32 For the ᵀfroward *is* abomination to the Lᴏʀᴅ: but his secret *is* with the righteous. *perverse person*

33 The curse of the Lᴏʀᴅ *is* in the house of the wicked: but he blesseth the habitation of the just.

34 ᴿSurely he scorneth the scorners: but he giveth grace unto the ᵀlowly. James 4:6; 1 Pet. 5:5 · *humble*

35 The wise shall inherit glory: but shame shall be ᵀthe promotion of fools. *the legacy*

4 Hear, ᴿye children, the instruction of a father, and attend to know understanding. Ps. 34:11

2 For I give you good doctrine, forsake ye not my law.

3 For I was my father's son, ᴿtender and only *beloved* in the sight of my mother. 1 Chr. 29:1

4 ᴿHe taught me also, and said unto me, Let thine heart retain my words: ᴿkeep my commandments, and live. 1 Chr. 28:9; Eph. 6:4 · 7:2

5 [R]Get wisdom, get understanding: forget *it* not; neither [T]decline from the words of my mouth.   2:2, 3 · *turn away*

6 Forsake her not, and she shall preserve thee: [R]love her, and she shall keep thee.   2 Thess. 2:10

7 [R]Wisdom *is* the principal thing; *therefore* get wisdom: and with all thy getting get understanding.   3:13, 14; Matt. 13:44

8 [R]Exalt her, and she shall promote thee: she shall bring thee to honour, when thou dost embrace her.   1 Sam. 2:30

9 She shall give to thine head [R]an ornament of grace: a crown of glory shall she deliver to thee. 3:22

10 Hear, O my son, and receive my sayings; [R]and the years of thy life shall be many.   3:2

11 I have [R]taught thee in the way of wisdom; I have led thee in right paths.   1 Sam. 12:23

12 When thou goest, [R]thy steps shall not be [T]straitened; and when thou runnest, thou shalt not stumble.   Job 18:7; Ps. 18:36 · *hindered*

13 Take [T]fast hold of instruction; let *her* not go: keep her; for she *is* thy life.   *firm*

14 [R]Enter not into the path of the wicked, and go not in the way of evil *men*.   1:15; Ps. 1:1

15 Avoid it, pass not by it, turn from it, and pass away.

16 [R]For they sleep not, except they have done mischief; and their sleep is taken away, unless they cause *some* to fall.   Ps. 36:4

17 For they eat the bread of wickedness, and drink the wine of violence.

18 [R]But the path of the just *is* as the shining light, that shineth more and more unto the perfect day.   Is. 26:7; Matt. 5:14, 45; Phil. 2:15

19 [R]The way of the wicked *is* as darkness: they know not at what they stumble.   [Is. 59:9, 10]; John 12:35

20 My son, attend to my words; incline thine ear unto my sayings.

21 Let them not depart from thine eyes; keep them in the midst of thine heart.

22 For they *are* life unto those that find them, and health to all their flesh.

23 Keep thy heart with all diligence; for out of it *are* the issues of [R]life.   [Matt. 12:34; Luke 6:45]

24 Put away from thee a [T]froward mouth, and perverse lips put far from thee.   *deceitful*

25 Let thine eyes look right on, and let thine eyelids look straight before thee.

26 Ponder the path of thy [R]feet, and let all thy ways be established.   5:21; Heb. 12:13

27 Turn not to the right hand nor to the left: remove thy foot from evil.

5 My son, attend unto my wisdom, *and* [T]bow thine ear to my understanding: *incline*

2 That thou mayest [T]regard discretion, and *that* thy lips [R]may keep knowledge.   *preserve* · Mal. 2:7

3 [R]For the lips of [T]a strange woman drop *as* an honeycomb, and her mouth *is* [R]smoother than oil: 2:16 · *an immoral* · Ps. 55:21

4 But [T]her end is bitter as wormwood, sharp as a twoedged sword.   *in the end she is bitter*

5 Her feet go down to death; [R]her steps take hold on hell.   7:27

6 Lest thou shouldest ponder the path of [T]life, her ways are [T]moveable, *that* thou canst not know *them*.   *her life* · *unstable*

7 Hear me now therefore, O ye children, and depart not from the words of my mouth.

8 Remove thy way far from her, and come not nigh the door of her house:

9 Lest thou give thine [T]honour unto others, and thy years unto the [T]cruel: *vigour* · *cruel one*

10 Lest [T]strangers be filled with thy wealth; and thy labours *be* in the house of a stranger;   *aliens*

11 And thou mourn at the last, when thy flesh and thy body are consumed,

12 And say, How have I hated instruction, and my heart despised reproof;

13 And have not obeyed the voice of my teachers, nor inclined

mine ear to them that instructed me!

14 I was [T]almost in all evil in the midst of the congregation and assembly.   *on the verge of total ruin*

15 Drink waters out of thine own cistern, and running waters out of thine own well.

16 Let thy fountains be dispersed abroad, *and* [T]rivers of waters in the streets.   *channels*

17 Let them be only thine own, and not strangers' with thee.

18 Let thy fountain be blessed: and rejoice with [R]the wife of thy youth.   Deut. 24:5; Eccl. 9:9; Mal. 2:14

19 [R]*Let her be as* the loving hind and pleasant roe; let her breasts satisfy thee at all times; and be thou [T]ravished always with her love.   Song 2:9 · *enraptured*

20 And why wilt thou, my son, be ravished with [R]a strange woman, and embrace the bosom of a stranger?   2:16

21 [R]For the ways of man *are* before the eyes of the LORD, and he pondereth all his goings.   15:3

22 [R]His own iniquities shall take the wicked himself, and he shall be holden with the cords of his sins.   Num. 32:23; Ps. 9:5; Is. 3:11

23 [R]He shall die without instruction; and in the greatness of his folly he shall go astray.   Job 4:21

6 My son, [R]if thou be surety for thy friend, *if* thou hast stricken thy hand with a stranger,   11:15

2 Thou art snared with the words of thy mouth, thou art taken with the words of thy mouth.

3 Do this now, my son, and deliver thyself, when thou art come into the hand of thy friend; go, humble thyself, and [T]make sure thy friend.   *plead with*

4 Give not sleep to thine eyes, nor slumber to thine eyelids.

5 Deliver thyself as a roe from the hand *of the hunter,* and as a bird from the hand of the fowler.

6 Go to the ant, thou sluggard; consider her ways, and be wise

7 Which having no [T]guide, overseer, or ruler,   Lit. *leader*

8 Provideth her [T]meat in the summer, *and* gathereth her food in the harvest.   Lit. *grain* or *bread*

9 [R]How long wilt thou sleep, O sluggard? when wilt thou arise out of thy sleep?   24:33, 34

10 *Yet* a little sleep, a little slumber, a little folding of the hands to sleep:

11 So shall thy poverty come as [T]one that travelleth, and thy [T]want as an armed man.   *a prowler · need*

12 A [T]naughty person, a wicked man, walketh with a froward mouth.   *worthless man,* lit. *man of Belial*

13 [R]He winketh with his eyes, he speaketh with his feet, he teacheth with his fingers;   10:10

14 [T]Frowardness *is* in his heart, he deviseth [T]mischief continually; he soweth discord.   *Perversity · evil*

15 Therefore shall his calamity come suddenly; suddenly shall he be broken without remedy.

16 These six *things* doth the LORD hate; yea, seven *are* an abomination unto [T]him: Lit. *his soul*

17 [R]A proud look, [R]a lying tongue, and [R]hands that shed innocent blood,   21:4 · 12:22 · 28:17

18 [R]An heart that deviseth wicked imaginations, feet that be swift in running to mischief,   Mark 14:1

19 [R]A false witness *that* speaketh lies, and he that soweth discord among brethren.   Ps. 27:12

20 [R]My son, keep thy father's commandment, and forsake not the law of thy mother: Eph. 6:1

21 [R]Bind them continually upon thine heart, *and* tie them about thy neck.   3:3

22 When thou goest, it shall lead thee; when thou sleepest, [R]it shall keep thee; and *when* thou awakest, it shall talk with thee.   2:11

23 [R]For the commandment *is* a lamp; and the law *is* light; and reproofs of instruction *are* the way of life: Ps. 19:8; 2 Pet. 1:19

24 [R]To keep thee from the evil woman, from the flattery of the tongue of a strange woman.   2:16

25 [R]Lust not after her beauty in thine heart; neither let her take thee with her eyelids.   Matt. 5:28

26 For [R]by means of a [T]whorish

woman *a man is brought* to a piece of bread: ^Rand the adulteress will hunt for the precious life.   29:3 · *harlot* · Gen. 39:14

27 Can a man take fire in his bosom, and his clothes not be burned?

28 Can one go upon hot coals, and his feet not be burned?

29 So he that goeth in to his neighbour's wife; whosoever toucheth her shall not be innocent.

30 *Men* do not despise a thief, if he steal to satisfy his soul when he is ^Thungry;   *starving*

31 But *if* he be found, he shall restore sevenfold; he shall give all the substance of his house.

32 *But* whoso committeth adultery with a woman ^Rlacketh understanding: he *that* doeth it destroyeth his own soul.   7:7

33 A wound and dishonour shall he get; and his reproach shall not be wiped away.

34 For ^Rjealousy *is* the rage of a man: therefore he will not spare in the day of vengeance.   27:4

35 He will not regard any ransom; neither will he rest content, though thou givest many gifts.

7 My son, keep my words, and ^Rlay^T up my commandments with thee.   2:1 · *treasure*

2 ^RKeep my commandments, and live; ^Rand my law as the apple of thine eye.   4:4; [Is. 55:3] · Zech. 2:8

3 ^RBind them upon thy fingers, write them upon the table of thine heart.   6:21; Deut. 6:8

4 Say unto wisdom, Thou *art* my sister; and call understanding *thy* ^Tkinswoman: *near kin*

5 ^RThat they may keep thee from the strange woman, from the ^Tstranger *which* flattereth with her words.   2:16; 5:3 · *seductress*

6 For at the window of my house I looked through my ^Tcasement,   *lattice*

7 And beheld among the simple ones, I discerned among the youths, a young man ^Rvoid of understanding,   [6:32; 9:4]

8 Passing through the street near her corner; and he went the way to her house,

9 ^RIn the twilight, in the evening, in the black and dark night: Job 24:15

10 And, behold, there met him a woman *with* the attire of an harlot, and ^Tsubtil of heart.   *crafty*

11 (She *is* loud and stubborn; her feet abide not in her house:

12 Now *is* she without, now in the streets, and ^Tlieth in wait at every corner.)   *lurking*

13 So she caught him, and kissed him, *and* with ^Tan impudent face said unto him,   *shameless*

14 *I have* peace offerings with me; this day have I payed my vows.

15 Therefore came I forth to meet thee, diligently to seek thy face, and I have found thee.

16 I have decked my bed with coverings of tapestry, with carved *works*, with fine linen of Egypt.

17 I have perfumed my bed with myrrh, aloes, and cinnamon.

18 Come, let us take our fill of love until the morning: let us solace ourselves with loves.

19 For the goodman *is* not at home, he is gone a long journey:

20 He hath taken a bag of money with him, *and* will come home at the day appointed.

21 With ^Rher much fair speech she caused him to yield, ^Rwith the flattering of her lips she ^Tforced him.   5:3 · Ps. 12:2 · *seduced*

22 He goeth after her ^Tstraightway, as an ox goeth to the slaughter, or as a fool to the correction of the ^Tstocks;   *immediately · chains*

23 Till a ^Tdart strike through his liver; ^Ras a bird hasteth to the snare, and knoweth not that it *is* for his life.   *arrow* · Eccl. 9:12

24 Hearken unto me now therefore, O ye children, and attend to the words of my mouth.

25 Let not thine heart ^Tdecline to her ways, go not astray in her paths.   *turn aside*

26 For she hath cast down many wounded: yea, ^Rmany strong *men* have been slain by her.   Neh. 13:26

27 [R]Her house *is* the way to [T]hell, going down to the chambers of death. [1 Cor. 6:9, 10] · Or *Sheol*

8 Doth not [R]wisdom [T]cry? and understanding put forth her voice? 1:20, 21; 9:3; [1 Cor. 1:24] · *cry out*

2 She standeth in the top of high places, by the way in the places of the paths.

3 She [T]crieth at the gates, at the entry of the city, at the [T]coming in at the doors. *cries out · entrance of*

4 Unto you, O men, I call; and my voice *is* to the sons of man.

5 O ye simple, understand [T]wisdom: and, ye fools, be ye of an understanding heart. *prudence*

6 Hear; for I will speak of excellent things; and the opening of my lips *shall be* right things.

7 For my mouth shall speak truth; and wickedness *is* an abomination to my lips.

8 All the words of my mouth *are* in righteousness; *there is* nothing [T]froward or perverse in them. *crooked*

9 They *are* all plain to him that understandeth, and right to them that find knowledge.

10 Receive my instruction, and not silver; and knowledge rather than choice gold.

11 [R]For wisdom *is* better than rubies; and all the things that may be desired are not to be compared to it. 16:16; Job 28:15; Ps. 19:10; 119:127

12 I wisdom dwell with prudence, and find out knowledge [T]of witty inventions. *and discretion*

13 [R]The fear of the LORD *is* to hate evil: pride, and arrogancy, and the evil way, and the [T]froward mouth, do I hate. 3:7; 16:6 · *perverse*

14 Counsel *is* mine, and sound wisdom: I *am* understanding; [R]I have strength. Eccl. 7:19; 9:16

15 [R]By me kings reign, and princes decree justice. Rom. 13:1

16 By me princes rule, and nobles, *even* all the judges of the earth.

17 [R]I love them that love me; and [R]those that seek me early shall find me. [John 14:21] · John 7:37

18 [R]Riches and honour *are* with me; *yea,* [T]durable riches and righteousness. 3:16; [Matt. 6:33] · *enduring*

19 My fruit *is* better than gold, yea, than fine gold; and my revenue than choice silver.

20 I [T]lead in the way of righteousness, in the midst of the paths of [T]judgment: *walk · justice*

21 That I may cause those that love me to inherit [T]substance; and I will fill their treasures. *wealth*

22 [R]The LORD possessed me in the beginning of his way, before his works of old. Job 28:26–28

23 [R]I was set up from everlasting, from the beginning, or ever the earth was. [Ps. 2:6]

24 When *there were* no depths, I was brought forth; when *there were* no fountains abounding with water.

25 [R]Before the mountains were settled, before the hills was I brought forth: Job 15:7, 8

26 While as yet he had not made the earth, nor the fields, nor the [T]highest part of the dust of the world. Lit. *beginning of the dust*

27 When he prepared the heavens, I *was* there: when he [T]set a compass upon the face of the [T]depth: *drew a circle · deep*

28 When he established the clouds above: when he strengthened the fountains of the deep:

29 [R]When he gave to the sea [T]his decree, that the waters should not [T]pass his commandment: when he appointed the foundations of the earth: Gen. 1:9, 10 · *its limit · transgress*

30 [R]Then I was by him, *as* one brought up *with him:* [R]and I was daily *his* delight, rejoicing always before him; [John 1:1–3, 18] · [Matt. 3:17]

31 Rejoicing in the habitable part of his earth; and [R]my delights *were* with the sons of men. Ps. 16:3

32 Now therefore hearken unto me, O ye children: for [R]blessed *are they that* keep my ways. Ps. 119:1, 2

33 Hear instruction, and be wise, and [T]refuse it not. *disdain*

34 [R]Blessed *is* the man that heareth me, watching daily at my gates, waiting at the posts of my doors. 3:13, 18

35 For whoso findeth me findeth life, and shall ᴿobtain favour of the LORD.　　　3:4; 12:2; [John 17:3]

36 But he that sinneth against me ᴿwrongeth his own soul: all they that hate me love death. 20:2

9 Wisdom hath ᴿbuilded her house, she hath hewn out her seven pillars: [Eph. 2:20–22; 1 Pet. 2:5]

2 She hath killed her beasts; she hath mingled her wine; she hath also furnished her table.

3 She hath sent forth her maidens: she ᵀcrieth upon the highest places of the city,　　*cries out*

4 ᴿWhoso *is* simple, let him turn in hither: *as for* him that ᵀwanteth understanding, she saith to him,　　Ps. 19:7 · *lacks*

5 ᴿCome, eat of my bread, and drink of the wine *which* I have ᵀmingled.　Is. 55:1; [John 6:27] · *mixed*

6 Forsake ᵀthe foolish, and live; and go in the way of understanding.　　*foolishness*

7 He that reproveth a scorner getteth to himself shame: and he that rebuketh a wicked *man* ᵀgetteth himself a blot.　*harms himself*

8 Reprove not a scorner, lest he hate thee: ᴿrebuke a wise man, and he will love thee.　Ps. 141:5

9 Give *instruction* to a wise *man,* and he will be yet wiser: teach a just *man,* ᴿand he will increase in learning.　[Matt. 13:12]

10 ᴿThe fear of the LORD *is* the beginning of wisdom: and the knowledge of the holy *is* understanding.　1:7; Job 28:28; Ps. 111:10

11 ᴿFor by me thy days shall be multiplied, and the years of thy life shall be increased.　3:2, 16

12 ᴿIf thou be wise, thou shalt be wise for thyself: but *if* thou scornest, thou alone shalt bear *it*.　16:26

13 ᴿA foolish woman *is* ᵀclamorous: *she is* simple, and knoweth nothing.　7:11 · *boisterous*

14 For she sitteth at the door of her house, on a seat ᴿin the high places of the city,　　v. 3

15 To call passengers who go right on their ways:

16 ᴿWhoso *is* ᵀsimple, let him turn in hither: and *as for* him that

wanteth understanding, she saith to him,　　7:7, 8 · *naive*

17 Stolen waters are sweet, and bread *eaten* in secret is pleasant.

18 But he knoweth not that the dead *are* there; *and that* her guests *are* in the depths of hell.

10 ᴿThe proverbs of Solomon. A wise son maketh a glad father: but a foolish son *is* the ᵀheaviness of his mother. 29:3 · *grief*

2 Treasures of wickedness profit nothing: ᴿbut righteousness delivereth from death.　Dan. 4:27

3 ᴿThe LORD will not suffer the soul of the righteous to famish: but he casteth away the ᵀsubstance of the wicked.　28:25 · *desire*

4 He becometh poor that dealeth *with* a slack hand: but the hand of the diligent maketh rich.

5 He that gathereth in ᴿsummer *is* a wise son: *but* he that sleepeth in harvest *is* ᴿa son that causeth shame.　6:8 · 19:26

6 Blessings *are* upon the head of the ᵀjust: but violence covereth the mouth of the wicked.　*righteous*

7 ᴿThe memory of the just *is* blessed: but the name of the wicked shall rot.　Ps. 112:6; Eccl. 8:10

8 The wise in heart will receive commandments: but a prating fool shall ᵀfall.　*be ruined*

9 He that walketh uprightly walketh surely: but he that perverteth his ways shall be known.

10 He that winketh with the eye causeth ᵀsorrow: but a ᵀprating fool shall fall.　*trouble · babbling*

11 The mouth of a righteous *man is* a well of life: but violence covereth the mouth of the wicked.

12 Hatred stirreth up strifes: but ᴿlove covereth all sins. [1 Cor. 13:4–7]

13 In the lips of him that hath understanding wisdom is found: but a rod *is* for the back of him that is void of understanding.

14 Wise *men* lay up knowledge: but ᴿthe mouth of the foolish *is* near destruction.　18:7

15 The ᴿrich man's wealth *is* his strong city: the destruction of the poor *is* their poverty.　18:11; Ps. 52:7

16 The labour of the righteous

^{T}*tendeth* to ^{R}life: the ^{T}fruit of the wicked to sin.   *leads · 6:23 · wages*

17 He *is in* the way of life that keepeth instruction: but he that refuseth reproof ^{T}erreth. *goes astray*

18 He that ^{R}hideth hatred *with* lying lips, and ^{R}he that uttereth a slander, *is* a fool. 26:24 · Ps. 15:3; 101:5

19 ^{R}In the multitude of words there wanteth not sin: but he that refraineth his lips *is* wise. Eccl. 5:3

20 The tongue of the just *is as* choice silver: the heart of the wicked *is* little worth.

21 The lips of the righteous feed many: but fools die for ^{T}want of ^{T}wisdom.   *lack · Lit. heart*

22 ^{R}The blessing of the LORD, it maketh rich, and he addeth no sorrow with it. Gen. 24:35; 26:12

23 ^{R}*It is* as sport to a fool to do mischief: but a man of understanding hath wisdom. 2:14; 15:21

24 ^{R}The fear of the wicked, it shall come upon him: but ^{R}the desire of the righteous shall be granted. 1:27; Is. 66:4 · 15:8; Matt. 5:6

25 As the whirlwind passeth, ^{R}so *is* the wicked no *more*: but ^{R}the righteous *is* an everlasting foundation. Ps. 37:9, 10 · Ps. 15:5

26 As vinegar to the teeth, and as smoke to the eyes, so *is* the sluggard to them that send him.

27 ^{R}The fear of the LORD prolongeth days: but the years of the wicked shall be shortened. 9:11

28 The hope of the righteous *shall be* gladness: but the ^{R}expectation of the wicked shall perish. Job 8:13

29 The way of the LORD *is* strength to the upright: but ^{R}destruction *shall be* to the workers of iniquity. Ps. 1:6

30 ^{R}The righteous shall never be removed: but the wicked shall not inhabit the ^{T}earth. Ps. 37:22 · *land*

31 ^{R}The mouth of the just bringeth forth wisdom: but the froward tongue shall be cut out. Ps. 37:30

32 The lips of the righteous know what is acceptable: but the mouth of the wicked *speaketh* ^{T}frowardness.   *perversity*

11 A ^{R}false balance *is* abomination to the LORD: but a just weight *is* his delight. Mic. 6:11

2 *When* pride cometh, then cometh ^{R}shame: but with the lowly *is* wisdom. 16:18; 18:12; 29:23

3 The integrity of the upright shall guide ^{R}them: but the ^{T}perverseness of ^{T}transgressors shall destroy them. 13:6 · *deceit · unfaithful*

4 ^{R}Riches profit not in the day of wrath: but righteousness delivereth from death. 10:2; Ezek. 7:1

5 The righteousness of the ^{T}perfect shall direct his way: but the wicked shall fall by his own ^{R}wickedness. *blameless · 5:22*

6 The righteousness of the upright shall deliver them: but transgressors shall be taken in *their own* ^{T}naughtiness. *lust*

7 When a wicked man dieth, *his* expectation shall perish: and the hope of unjust *men* perisheth.

8 ^{R}The righteous is delivered out of trouble, and the wicked cometh in his stead. 21:18

9 An hypocrite with *his* mouth destroyeth his neighbour: but through knowledge shall the ^{T}just be delivered. *righteous*

10 ^{R}When it goeth well with the righteous, the city rejoiceth: and when the wicked perish, *there is* shouting. 28:12

11 By the blessing of the upright the city is ^{R}exalted: but it is overthrown by the mouth of the wicked. 14:34

12 He ^{T}that is void of wisdom despiseth his neighbour: but a man of understanding holdeth his peace. *who lacks wisdom*

13 A talebearer revealeth secrets: but he that is of a faithful spirit ^{R}concealeth the matter. 19:11

14 Where no counsel *is*, the people fall: but in the multitude of counsellors *there is* safety.

15 He that is surety for a stranger shall smart *for it*: and he that hateth suretiship is sure.

16 A gracious woman retaineth honour: ^{T}and strong *men* retain riches. *but ruthless men*

17 The merciful man doeth good

to his own soul: but *he that is* cruel troubleth his own flesh.

18 The wicked worketh a deceitful work: but [R]to him that soweth righteousness *shall be* a sure reward. Hos. 10:12; [Gal. 6:8, 9]; James 3:18

19 As righteousness [T]*tendeth* to life: so he that pursueth evil *pursueth it* to his own death. *leads*

20 They that are of [T]a froward heart *are* abomination to the LORD: but *such as are* upright in *their* way *are* his delight. *a perverse*

21 [R]*Though* hand *join* in hand, the wicked shall not be unpunished: but [R]the seed of the righteous shall be delivered. 16:5 · 14:26

22 *As* a jewel of gold in a swine's snout, *so is* a fair woman which is without discretion.

23 The desire of the righteous *is* only good: *but* the expectation of the wicked [R]*is* wrath. Rom. 2:8, 9

24 There is that scattereth, and yet increaseth; and *there is* that withholdeth more than is [T]meet, but *it tendeth* to poverty. *right*

25 The liberal soul shall be made fat: and he that watereth shall be watered also himself.

26 [R]He that withholdeth corn, the people shall curse him: but blessing *shall be* upon the head of him that selleth *it*. Amos 8:5, 6

27 He that diligently seeketh good procureth favour: but [R]he that seeketh mischief, it shall come unto him. Ps. 7:15, 16; 57:6

28 He that trusteth in his riches shall fall: but [R]the righteous shall flourish as a branch. Ps. 1:3; Jer. 17:8

29 He that troubleth his own house [R]shall inherit the wind: and the fool *shall be* [R]servant to the wise of heart. Eccl. 5:16 · 14:19

30 The fruit of the righteous *is* a tree of life; and [R]he that winneth souls *is* wise. [Dan. 12:3; 1 Cor. 9:19–22]

31 [R]Behold, the righteous shall be [T]recompensed in the earth: much more the wicked and the sinner. Jer. 25:29 · *rewarded*

12 Whoso loveth instruction loveth knowledge: but he that hateth reproof *is* brutish.

2 A good *man* obtaineth favour

of the LORD: but a man of wicked devices will he condemn.

3 A man shall not be [T]established by wickedness: but the [R]root of the righteous shall not be moved. *made secure* · [10:25]

4 [R]A virtuous woman *is* a crown to her husband: but she that maketh ashamed *is* [R]as rottenness in his bones. 31:23 · 14:30

5 The thoughts of the righteous *are* right: *but* the counsels of the wicked *are* deceit.

6 [R]The words of the wicked *are* to lie in wait for blood: [R]but the mouth of the upright shall deliver them. 1:11, 18 · 14:3

7 [R]The wicked are overthrown, and *are* not: but the house of the righteous shall stand. Ps. 37:35–37

8 A man shall be [T]commended according to his wisdom: [R]but he that is of a perverse heart shall be despised. *praised* · 18:3; 1 Sam. 25:17

9 [R]*He that is* [T]despised, and hath a servant, *is* better than he that honoureth himself, and lacketh bread. 13:7 · *lightly esteemed*

10 A righteous *man* regardeth the life of his beast: but the tender mercies of the wicked *are* cruel.

11 [R]He that tilleth his land shall be satisfied with [R]bread: but he that followeth vain *persons is* void of understanding. Gen. 3:19 · 28:19

12 The wicked desireth the net of evil *men:* but the root of the righteous yieldeth *fruit.*

13 [R]The wicked is snared by the transgression of *his* lips: but the just shall come out of trouble. 18:7

14 [R]A man shall be satisfied with good by the fruit of *his* mouth: [R]and the recompence of a man's hands shall be rendered unto him. 13:2; 15:23; 18:20 · 1:31; 24:12

15 [R]The way of a fool *is* right in his own eyes: but he that hearkeneth unto counsel *is* wise. 3:7

16 [R]A fool's wrath is presently known: but a prudent *man* covereth shame. 11:13; 29:11

17 [R]*He that* speaketh truth [T]sheweth forth righteousness: but a false witness deceit. 14:5 · *declares*

18 [R]There is that speaketh like

the piercings of a sword: but the tongue of the wise *is* health.   4:22

19 The lip of truth shall be established for ever: [R]but a lying tongue *is* but for a moment.   19:9

20 Deceit *is* in the heart of them that [T]imagine evil: but to the counsellors of peace *is* joy.   *devise*

21 There shall no [R]evil happen to the just: but the wicked shall be filled with mischief.   1:33; 1 Pet. 3:13

22 [R]Lying lips *are* abomination to the LORD: but they that deal truly *are* his delight.   6:17; Rev. 22:15

23 [R]A prudent man concealeth knowledge: but the heart of fools proclaimeth foolishness.   13:16

24 The hand of the diligent shall bear rule: but the [T]slothful shall be under tribute.   *lazy*

25 [R]Heaviness in the heart of man maketh it stoop: but [R]a good word maketh it glad.   15:13 · Is. 50:4

26 The righteous *is* more excellent than his neighbour: but the way of the wicked [T]seduceth them.   *leads them astray*

27 The slothful *man* roasteth not that which he took in hunting: but the substance of a diligent man *is* precious.

28 In the way of righteousness *is* life; and *in* the pathway *thereof there is* no death.

13 A wise son *heareth* his father's instruction: but a scorner heareth not rebuke.

2 [R]A man shall eat good by the fruit of *his* mouth: but the soul of the [T]transgressors *shall* [T]eat violence.   12:14 · Lit. *unfaithful · feed on*

3 [R]He that keepeth his mouth keepeth his life: *but* he that openeth wide his lips shall have destruction.   21:23; Ps. 39:1; [James 3:2]

4 [R]The soul of the [T]sluggard desireth, and *hath* nothing: but the soul of the diligent shall be made [T]fat.   10:4 · *lazy · rich*

5 A righteous *man* hateth lying: but a wicked *man* is loathsome, and cometh to shame.

6 [R]Righteousness keepeth *him* [T]*that is* upright in the way: but wickedness overthroweth the sinner.   11:3, 5, 6 · *whose way is blameless*

7 There is [T]that maketh himself rich, yet *hath* nothing: *there is* [T]that maketh himself poor, yet *hath* great riches.   *one who*

8 The ransom of a man's life *are* his riches: but the poor heareth not rebuke.

9 The light of the righteous rejoiceth: [R]but the lamp of the wicked shall be put out.   Job 18:5, 6

10 Only by pride cometh [R]contention: but with the well advised *is* wisdom.   10:12

11 [R]Wealth *gotten* by [T]vanity shall be diminished: but he that gathereth by labour shall increase.   10:2; 20:21 · *dishonesty*

12 Hope deferred maketh the heart sick, but [R]*when* the desire cometh, *it is* a tree of life.   v. 19

13 Whoso [R]despiseth the word shall be destroyed: but he that feareth the commandment shall be rewarded.   2 Chr. 36:16; Is. 5:24

14 The law of the wise *is* a fountain of life, to depart from [R]the snares of death.   2 Sam. 22:6

15 Good understanding giveth [R]favour: but the way of transgressors *is* hard.   3:4; Ps. 111:10

16 [R]Every prudent *man* [T]dealeth with knowledge: but a fool layeth open *his* folly.   12:23 · *acts*

17 A wicked messenger falleth into [T]mischief: but [R]a faithful ambassador *is* health.   *trouble* · 25:13

18 Poverty and shame *shall be to* him that refuseth instruction: but [R]he that regardeth reproof shall be honoured.   15:5, 31, 32

19 The desire accomplished is sweet to the soul: but *it is* abomination to fools to depart from evil.

20 He that walketh with wise *men* shall be wise: but a companion of fools shall be destroyed.

21 [R]Evil pursueth sinners: but to the righteous good shall be repaid.   32:10; Is. 47:11

22 A good *man* leaveth an inheritance to his children's children: and [R]the wealth of the sinner *is* laid up for the just.   Job 27:16, 17

23 Much food *is in* the tillage of the poor: but there is *that is* destroyed for want of judgment.

24 ᴿHe that spareth his rod hateth his son: but he that loveth him chasteneth him betimes. 19:18

25 ᴿThe righteous eateth to the satisfying of his soul: but the belly of the wicked shall want. Ps. 34:10

14 Every wise woman buildeth her house: but the foolish ᵀplucketh it down with her hands. *pulls*

2 He that walketh in his uprightness feareth the LORD: ᴿbut *he that is* perverse in his ways despiseth him. [Rom. 2:4]

3 In the mouth of the foolish *is* a rod of pride: ᴿbut the lips of the wise shall preserve them. 12:6

4 Where no oxen *are*, the ᵀcrib *is* clean: but much increase *is* by the strength of the ox. *feed trough*

5 A ᴿfaithful witness will not lie: but a false witness will utter ᴿlies. Rev. 1:5; 3:14 · 6:19; 12:17; Ex. 23:1

6 A ᵀscorner seeketh wisdom, and *findeth it* not: but ᴿknowledge *is* easy unto him that understandeth. *scoffer* · 8:9; 17:24

7 Go from the presence of a foolish man, when thou perceivest not *in him* the lips of knowledge.

8 The wisdom of the prudent *is* to understand his way: but the folly of fools *is* deceit.

9 ᴿFools ᵀmake a mock at sin: but among the righteous *there is* favour. 10:23 · *mock at guilt*

10 The heart knoweth his own bitterness; and a stranger doth not intermeddle with his joy.

11 ᴿThe house of the wicked shall be overthrown: but the ᵀtabernacle of the upright shall flourish. Job 8:15 · *tent*

12 There is a way which seemeth right unto a man, but the end thereof *are* the ways of death.

13 Even in laughter the heart is sorrowful; and ᴿthe end of that mirth *is* ᵀheaviness. Eccl. 2:1, 2 · *grief*

14 The backslider in heart shall be ᴿfilled with his own ways: and a good man *shall be satisfied* from ᴿhimself. 1:31; 12:15 · 13:2; 18:20

15 The ᵀsimple believeth every word: but the prudent *man* looketh well to his going. *naive*

16 ᴿA wise *man* feareth, and departeth from evil: but the fool rageth, and is confident. Ps. 34:14

17 *He that is* soon angry dealeth foolishly: and a man of wicked ᵀdevices is hated. *intentions*

18 The simple inherit folly: but the prudent are crowned with knowledge.

19 The evil bow before the good; and the wicked at the gates of the righteous.

20 ᴿThe poor is hated even ᵀof his own neighbour: but the rich *hath* many ᴿfriends. 19:7 · *by* · 19:4

21 He that despiseth his neighbour sinneth: but he that hath mercy on the poor, happy *is* he.

22 Do they not ᵀerr that devise evil? but mercy and truth *shall be* to them that devise good. *go astray*

23 In all labour there is profit: but ᵀthe talk of the lips *tendeth* only to ᵀpenury. *idle chatter* · *poverty*

24 The crown of the wise *is* their riches: *but* the foolishness of fools *is* folly.

25 A true witness delivereth ᴿsouls: but a deceitful *witness* speaketh lies. [Ezek. 3:18–21]

26 In the fear of the LORD *is* strong confidence: and his children shall have a place of refuge.

27 ᴿThe fear of the LORD *is* a fountain of life, to depart from the snares of death. 13:14

28 In the multitude of people *is* the king's honour: but in the ᵀwant of people *is* the destruction of the prince. *lack*

29 *He that is* slow to wrath *is* of great understanding: but *he that is* hasty of spirit exalteth folly.

30 A sound heart *is* the life of the flesh: but envy ᴿthe rottenness of the bones. 12:4; Hab. 3:16

31 ᴿHe that oppresseth the poor reproacheth his Maker: but he that honoureth him hath mercy on the poor. Matt. 25:40; 1 John 3:17

32 The wicked is driven away in his wickedness: but the righteous hath hope in his death.

33 Wisdom resteth in the heart of him that hath understanding:

but [R]*that which is* in the midst of fools is made known.   12:16

34 Righteousness exalteth a [R]nation: but sin *is* a [T]reproach to any people.   11:11 · *shame* or *disgrace*

35 The king's favour *is* toward a wise servant: but his wrath is *against* him that causeth shame.

15 A [R]soft answer turneth away wrath: but [T]grievous words stir up anger.   25:15 · *harsh*

2 The tongue of the wise useth knowledge aright: but the mouth of fools poureth out foolishness.

3 [R]The eyes of the LORD *are* in every place, beholding the evil and the good.   Zech. 4:10; Heb. 4:13

4 A wholesome tongue *is* a tree of life: but perverseness therein *is* a breach in the spirit.

5 [R]A fool despiseth his father's instruction: [R]but he that regardeth reproof is prudent.   10:1 · 13:18

6 In the house of the righteous *is* much treasure: but in the revenues of the wicked is trouble.

7 The lips of the wise [T]disperse knowledge: but the heart of the foolish *doeth* not so.   *spread*

8 [R]The sacrifice of the wicked *is* an abomination to the LORD: but the prayer of the upright *is* his delight.   Is. 1:11; Jer. 6:20; Mic. 6:7

9 The way of the wicked *is* an abomination unto the LORD: but he loveth him that [R]followeth after righteousness.   21:21

10 Correction *is* grievous unto him that forsaketh the way: *and* he that hateth reproof shall die.

11 [T]Hell and [T]destruction *are* before the LORD: how much more then [R]the hearts of the children of men?   Or *Sheol* · Heb. *Abaddon* · Ps. 44:21

12 [R]A scorner loveth not one that reproveth him: neither will he go unto the wise. Amos 5:10; 2 Tim. 4:3

13 [R]A merry heart maketh a cheerful [T]countenance: but [R]by sorrow of the heart the spirit is broken.   12:25 · *face* · 17:22

14 The heart of him that hath understanding seeketh knowledge: but the mouth of fools feedeth on foolishness.

15 All the days of the afflicted *are* evil: [R]but he that is of a merry heart *hath* a continual feast.   17:22

16 [R]Better *is* little with the fear of the LORD than great treasure and trouble therewith.   1 Tim. 6:6

17 Better *is* a dinner of herbs where love is, than a [T]stalled ox and hatred therewith.   *fatted calf*

18 [R]A wrathful man stirreth up strife: but *he that is* slow to anger appeaseth [T]strife.   26:21 · *contention*

19 [R]The way of the [T]slothful *man is* as an hedge of thorns: but the way of the righteous *is* [T]made plain.   22:5 · *lazy* · *a highway*

20 [R]A wise son maketh a glad father: but a foolish man despiseth his mother.   10:1

21 Folly *is* joy to *him that is* destitute of wisdom: but a man of understanding walketh uprightly.

22 [R]Without counsel [T]purposes are disappointed: but in the multitude of counsellors they are established.   11:14 · *plans go awry*

23 A man hath joy by the answer of his mouth: and [R]a word *spoken* [T]in due season, how good *is it!*   25:11; Is. 50:4 · Lit. *in its time*

24 [R]The way of life *is* above to the wise, that he may depart from [T]hell beneath.   Phil. 3:20 · Or *Sheol*

25 [R]The LORD will destroy the house of the proud: but [R]he will establish the [T]border of the widow.   12:7; Is. 2:11 · Ps. 68:5, 6 · *boundary*

26 [R]The thoughts of the wicked *are* an abomination to the LORD: [R]but *the words* of the pure *are* pleasant words.   6:16, 18 · Ps. 37:30

27 [R]He that is greedy of gain troubleth his own house; but he that hateth gifts shall live.   Is. 5:8

28 The heart of the righteous [R]studieth[T] to answer: but the mouth of the wicked poureth out evil things.   1 Pet. 3:15 · *studies how to*

29 The LORD *is* far from the wicked: but [R]he heareth the prayer of the righteous.   [James 5:16]

30 The light of the eyes rejoiceth the heart: *and* a good report maketh the bones [T]fat.   *healthy*

31 The ear that heareth the reproof of life abideth among the wise.

32 He that refuseth instruction despiseth his own soul: but he that [T]heareth reproof getteth understanding.   *heeds*

33 [R]The fear of the LORD *is* the instruction of wisdom; and [R]before honour *is* humility.   1:7 · 18:12

16 The [R]preparations of the heart [T]in man, and the answer of the tongue, *is* from the LORD.   Jer. 10:23 · belong *to man*

2 All the ways of a man *are* clean in his own [R]eyes; but the LORD weigheth the spirits.   21:2

3 [R]Commit thy works unto the LORD, and thy thoughts shall be established.   3:6; Ps. 37:5; [1 Pet. 5:7]

4 The [R]LORD hath made all *things* for himself: yea, even the wicked for the day of evil.   Is. 43:7

5 [R]Every one *that is* proud in heart *is* an abomination to the LORD: *though* hand *join* in hand, he shall not be unpunished.   6:17

6 By mercy and truth iniquity is purged: and [R]by the fear of the LORD *men* depart from evil.   14:16

7 When a man's ways please the LORD, he maketh even his enemies to be at peace with him.

8 [R]Better *is* a little with righteousness than great revenues without [T]right.   15:16; Ps. 37:16 · *justice*

9 [R]A man's heart [T]deviseth his way: [R]but the LORD directeth his steps.   19:21 · *plans* · Ps. 37:23; Jer. 10:23

10 A divine sentence *is* in the lips of the king: his mouth transgresseth not in judgment.

11 [R]A just weight and balance *are* the LORD's: all the weights of the bag *are* his work.   Lev. 19:36

12 *It is* an abomination to kings to commit wickedness: for [R]the throne is established by righteousness.   25:5

13 [R]Righteous lips *are* the delight of kings; and they love him that speaketh right.   14:35

14 The wrath of a king *is as* messengers of death: but a wise man will [R]pacify[T] it.   25:15 · *appease*

15 In the light of the king's countenance *is* life; and his favour *is* as a cloud of the latter rain.

16 [R]How much better *is it* to get wisdom than gold! and to get understanding rather to be chosen than silver!   8:10, 11, 19

17 The highway of the upright *is* to depart from evil: he that keepeth his way preserveth his soul.

18 Pride *goeth* before destruction, and an haughty spirit before [T]a fall.   *stumbling*

19 Better *it is to be* of an humble spirit with the lowly, than to divide the spoil with the proud.

20 He that handleth a matter wisely shall find good: and whoso trusteth in the LORD, happy *is* he.

21 The wise in heart shall be called prudent: and the sweetness of the lips increaseth learning.

22 Understanding *is* a wellspring of life unto him that hath it: but the instruction of fools *is* folly.

23 The heart of the wise teacheth his mouth, and addeth learning to his lips.

24 Pleasant words *are as* an honeycomb, sweet to the soul, and health to the bones.

25 There is a way that seemeth right unto a man; but the end thereof *are* the ways of death.

26 He that laboureth laboureth for himself; for his mouth craveth it of [R]him.   [Eccl. 6:7; John 6:35]

27 [T]An ungodly man diggeth up evil: and in his lips *there is* as a burning fire.   Lit. *A man of Belial*

28 A [T]froward man soweth strife: and [R]a whisperer separateth chief friends.   *perverse* · 17:9

29 A violent man enticeth his neighbour, and leadeth him into the way *that is* not good.

30 He [T]shutteth his eyes to devise froward things: moving his lips he bringeth evil to pass. *winks*

31 [R]The [T]hoary head *is* a crown of glory, *if* it be found in the way of righteousness.   20:29 · *silvery*

32 [R]*He that is* slow to anger *is* better than the mighty; and he that ruleth his spirit than he that taketh a city.   14:29; 19:11

33 The lot is cast into the lap; but the whole [T]disposing thereof *is* of the LORD.   *decision*

17 Better *is* a dry morsel, and quietness therewith, than an house full of ᵀsacrifices *with* strife.   Or *sacrificial meals* or *feasting*

2 A wise servant shall have rule over a son that causeth shame, and shall have part of the inheritance among the brethren.

3 The ᵀfining pot *is* for silver, and the furnace for gold: but the LORD trieth the hearts.   *refining*

4 A wicked doer giveth heed to false lips; *and* a liar giveth ear to a ᵀnaughty tongue.   Lit. *destructive*

5 ᴿWhoso mocketh the poor reproacheth his Maker: *and* ᴿhe that is glad at calamities shall not be unpunished.   14:31 · 1 Cor. 13:6

6 Children's children *are* the crown of old men; and the glory of children *are* their fathers.

7 Excellent speech becometh not a fool: much less do lying lips a prince.

8 A gift *is as* a precious stone in the eyes of him that hath it: whithersoever ᵀit turneth, ᵀit prospereth.   *he*

9 ᴿHe that covereth a transgression seeketh love; but ᴿhe that repeateth a matter separateth ᵀvery friends. [10:12] · 16:28 · The best of

10 A ᴿreproof entereth more into a wise man than an hundred ᵀstripes into a fool.   [Mic. 7:9] · *blows*

11 An evil *man* seeketh only rebellion: therefore a cruel messenger shall be sent against him.

12 Let ᴿa bear robbed of her whelps meet a man, rather than a fool in his folly.   2 Sam. 17:8; Hos. 13:8

13 Whoso ᴿrewardeth evil for good, evil shall not depart from his house.   Rom. 12:17; 1 Thess. 5:15

14 The beginning of strife *is as* when one letteth out water: therefore ᴿleave off contention, before it be meddled with.   [1 Thess. 4:11]

15 ᴿHe that justifieth the wicked, and he that condemneth the just, even they both *are* abomination to the LORD.   Ex. 23:7; Is. 5:23

16 Wherefore *is there* a price in the hand of a fool to get wisdom, seeing *he hath* no heart *to it?*

17 ᴿA friend loveth at all times, and a brother is born for adversity.   18:24; Ruth 1:16

18 ᴿA man void of understanding striketh hands, *and* becometh ᵀsurety in the presence of his friend.   6:1 · *a guaranty for his friend*

19 He loveth transgression that loveth strife: *and* ᴿhe that exalteth his gate seeketh destruction.   16:18

20 He that hath a ᵀfroward heart findeth no good: and he that hath a perverse tongue falleth into ᵀmischief.   *deceitful* or *crooked* · *evil*

21 He that begetteth a ᵀfool *doeth it* to his sorrow: and the father of a fool hath no joy.   *scoffer*

22 A ᴿmerry heart doeth good *like* a medicine: but a broken spirit drieth the bones.   12:25; 15:13, 15

23 A wicked *man* taketh a ᵀgift out of the bosom to pervert the ways of judgment.   *bribe*

24 ᴿWisdom *is* before him that hath understanding; but the eyes of a fool *are* in the ends of the earth.   Eccl. 2:14

25 A ᴿfoolish son *is* a grief to his father, and bitterness to her that bare him.   10:1; 15:20; 19:13

26 Also to punish the ᵀjust *is* not good, *nor* to strike princes ᵀfor equity.   *righteous* · *for their uprightness*

27 ᴿHe that hath knowledge spareth his words: *and* a man of understanding is of an ᵀexcellent spirit.   10:19; James 1:19 · *calm*

28 Even a fool, when he holdeth his peace, is counted wise: *and* he that shutteth his lips is *esteemed* a man of understanding.

18 Through desire a man, having separated himself, seeketh *and* intermeddleth with all wisdom.

2 A fool hath no delight in understanding, but that his heart may discover ᴿitself.   Eccl. 10:3

3 When the wicked cometh, *then* cometh also contempt, and with ignominy reproach.

4 ᴿThe words of a man's mouth *are as* deep waters, *ᴿand* the wellspring of wisdom *as* a flowing brook.   10:11 · [James 3:17]

5 *It is* not good to accept the

person of the wicked, to over-throw the righteous in judgment.

6 A fool's lips enter into con-tention, and his mouth calleth for ^Tstrokes.   *blows*

7 ^RA fool's mouth *is* his de-struction, and his lips *are* the snare of his ^Rsoul. Ps. 64:8 · Eccl. 10:12

8 ^RThe words of a ^Ttalebearer *are* as wounds, and they go down into the innermost parts of the belly.   12:18 · *gossip or slanderer*

9 He also that is slothful in his work is brother to him that is a great ^Twaster.   *destroyer*

10 The name of the LORD *is* a strong ^Rtower: the righteous run-neth into it, and is safe. Ps. 18:2; 61:3

11 The rich man's wealth *is* his strong city, and as an high wall in his own ^Tconceit.   *esteem*

12 ^RBefore destruction the heart of man is haughty; and before honour *is* humility.   15:33; 16:18

13 He that answereth a matter before he heareth *it*, it *is* folly and shame unto him.

14 The spirit of a man will sus-tain his infirmity; but a ^Twounded spirit who can bear?   *broken*

15 The heart of the prudent get-teth knowledge; and the ear of the wise seeketh knowledge.

16 ^RA man's gift maketh room for him, and bringeth him before great men. Gen. 32:20, 21; 1 Sam. 25:27

17 *He that is* first in his own cause *seemeth* just; but his neigh-bour cometh and searcheth him.

18 The ^Rlot causeth contentions to cease, and ^Tparteth between the mighty.   [16:33] · *keeps apart*

19 A brother offended *is harder to be won* than a strong city: and *their* contentions *are* like the bars of a castle.

20 ^RA man's belly shall be satis-fied with the fruit of his mouth; *and* with the ^Tincrease of his lips shall he be filled. 12:14; 14:14 · *produce*

21 Death and life *are* in the power of the tongue: and they that love it shall eat the fruit thereof.

22 ^RWhoso findeth a wife find-eth a good *thing*, and obtaineth favour of the LORD.   Gen. 2:18

23 The poor useth intreaties; but the rich answereth roughly.

24 A man *that hath* friends must shew himself friendly: ^Rand there is a friend *that* sticketh closer than a brother. [John 15:14, 15]

19 Better ^R*is* the poor that walketh in his integrity, than *he that is* perverse in his lips, and is a fool.   28:6

2 Also, *that* the soul *be* without knowledge, *it is* not good; and he that hasteth with *his* feet sinneth.

3 The foolishness of man ^Tper-verteth his way: and his heart fretteth against the LORD.   *twists*

4 Wealth maketh many friends; but the poor is separated from his neighbour.

5 A ^Rfalse witness shall not be unpunished, and *he that* speaketh lies shall not escape.   Ex. 23:1

6 Many will intreat the favour of the prince: and every man *is* a friend to him that giveth gifts.

7 All the brethren of the poor do hate him: how much more do his friends go ^Rfar from him? he pursueth *them with* words, *yet* they *are* wanting *to him*.   Ps. 38:11

8 He that getteth wisdom lov-eth his own soul: he that keepeth understanding shall find good.

9 A false witness shall not be unpunished, and *he that* speaketh lies shall perish.

10 ^TDelight is not seemly for a fool; much less for a servant to have rule over princes.   *Luxury*

11 The discretion of a man de-ferreth his anger; and *it is* his glory to pass over a transgression.

12 The king's wrath *is* as the roaring of a lion; but his favour *is* ^Ras dew upon the grass.   Mic. 5:7

13 ^RA foolish son *is* the ^Tcalam-ity of his father: ^Rand the con-tentions of a wife *are* a continual dropping.   10:1 · *ruin* · 21:9, 19

14 House and riches *are* the in-heritance of fathers: and ^Ra pru-dent wife *is* from the LORD. 18:22

15 ^RSlothfulness^T casteth into a deep sleep; and an idle soul shall ^Rsuffer hunger. 6:9 · *Laziness* · 10:4

16 ^RHe that keepeth the com-

mandment keepeth his own soul; *but* he that despiseth his ways shall die.   13:13; 16:17; Luke 10:28; 11:28

17 ᴿHe that hath pity upon the poor lendeth unto the LORD; and that which he hath given will he pay him again.   Matt. 10:42; 25:40

18 ᴿChasten thy son while there is hope, and let not thy soul spare for his crying.   13:24

19 A man of great wrath shall suffer punishment: for if thou deliver *him*, yet thou must do it again.

20 Hear counsel, and receive instruction, that thou mayest be wise ᴿin thy latter end.   Ps. 37:37

21 *There are* many ᵀdevices in a man's heart; ᴿnevertheless the counsel of the LORD, that shall stand.   plans · Is. 46:10; Heb. 6:17

22 The desire of a man *is* his kindness: and a poor man *is* better than a liar.

23 ᴿThe fear of the LORD *tendeth* to life: and *he that hath it* shall abide satisfied; he shall not be visited with evil.   [1 Tim. 4:8]

24 ᴿA ᵀslothful *man* hideth his hand in *his* bosom, and will not so much as bring it to his mouth again.   15:19 · lazy

25 Smite a scorner, and the simple will beware: and ᴿreprove one that hath understanding, *and* he will understand knowledge.   9:8

26 He that wasteth *his* father, *and* chaseth away *his* mother, *is* ᴿa son that causeth shame, and bringeth reproach.   17:2

27 Cease, my son, to hear the instruction *that causeth* to err from the words of knowledge.

28 An ungodly witness scorneth judgment: and the mouth of the wicked devoureth iniquity.

29 Judgments are prepared for ᵀscorners, ᴿand ᵀstripes for the back of fools.   scoffers · 26:3 · beatings

20 Wine ᴿ*is* a mocker, strong drink *is* raging: and whosoever is deceived thereby is not wise.   Gen. 9:21; Is. 28:7; Hos. 4:11

2 The fear of a king *is* as the roaring of a lion: *whoso* provoketh him to anger sinneth *against* his own ᵀsoul.   life

3 ᴿ*It is* ᵀan honour for a man to cease from strife: but every fool will be meddling.   17:14 · honourable

4 ᴿThe sluggard will not plow ᵀby reason of the cold; ᴿ*therefore* shall he beg in harvest, and *have* nothing.   10:4 · because of winter · 19:15

5 Counsel in the heart of man *is like* deep water; but a man of understanding will draw it out.

6 Most men will proclaim every one his own goodness: but a faithful man who can find?

7 The just *man* walketh in his integrity: ᴿhis children *are* blessed after him.   Ps. 37:26

8 A king that sitteth in the throne of judgment scattereth away all evil with his eyes.

9 ᴿWho can say, I have made my heart clean, I am pure from my sin?   [Ps. 51:5; Rom. 3:9; 1 John 1:8]

10 Divers weights, *and* divers measures, both of them *are* alike abomination to the LORD.

11 Even a child is ᴿknown by his doings, whether his work *be* pure, and whether *it be* right.   Matt. 7:16

12 ᴿThe hearing ear, and the seeing eye, the LORD hath made even both of them.   Ex. 4:11; Ps. 94:9

13 ᴿLove not sleep, lest thou come to poverty; open thine eyes, *and* thou shalt be satisfied with bread.   Rom. 12:11

14 *It is* naught, *it is* naught, saith the buyer: but when he is gone his way, then he boasteth.

15 There is gold, and a multitude of rubies: but the lips of knowledge *are* a precious jewel.

16 ᴿTake his garment that is ᵀsurety *for* a stranger: and take a pledge of him for a ᵀstrange woman.   22:26 · guaranty · seductress

17 ᴿBread of deceit *is* sweet to a man; but afterwards his mouth shall be filled with gravel.   9:17

18 ᴿ*Every* purpose is established by counsel: ᴿand with good advice make war.   24:6 · Luke 14:31

19 ᴿHe that goeth about *as* a talebearer revealeth secrets: therefore meddle not with him that flattereth with his lips.   11:13

20 ᴿWhoso curseth his father or

his mother, his lamp shall be put out in obscure darkness. Matt. 15:4

21 ᴿAn inheritance *may be* gotten hastily at the beginning; ᴿbut the end thereof shall not be blessed.   28:20 · Hab. 2:6

22 ᴿSay not thou, I will recompense evil; *but* wait on the LORD, and he shall save thee. 1 Thess. 5:15

23 Divers weights *are* an abomination unto the LORD; and a false balance *is* not good.

24 Man's ᵀgoings *are* of the LORD; how can a man then understand his own way?   *steps*

25 *It is* a snare to the man *who* devoureth *that which is* holy, and after vows to make enquiry.

26 ᴿA wise king ᵀscattereth the wicked, and bringeth the wheel over them.   Ps. 101:8 · *sifts out*

27 The spirit of man *is* the ᵀcandle of the LORD, searching all the inward parts of the belly. *lamp*

28 ᴿMercy and truth preserve the king: and his throne is upholden by mercy.   21:21; Ps. 101:1

29 The glory of young men *is* their strength: and ᴿthe beauty of old men *is* the grey head.   16:31

30 The blueness of a wound cleanseth away evil: so *do* stripes the inward parts of the belly.

21 The king's heart *is* in the hand of the LORD, *as* the ᵀrivers of water: he turneth it whithersoever he will.   *channels*

2 Every way of a man *is* right in his own eyes: ᴿbut the LORD pondereth the hearts.   Luke 16:15

3 ᴿTo do justice and judgment *is* more acceptable to the LORD than sacrifice.   1 Sam. 15:22; Hos. 6:6

4 ᴿAn high look, and a proud heart, *and* the ᵀplowing of the wicked, *is* sin.   6:17 · Or *lamp*

5 ᴿThe ᵀthoughts of the diligent ᵀ*tend* only to plenteousness; but of every one *that is* hasty only to want.   10:4 · *plans* · *lead surely*

6 The getting of treasures by a lying tongue *is* a vanity tossed to and fro of them that seek death.

7 The robbery of the wicked shall destroy them; because they refuse to do ᵀjudgment.   *justice*

8 The way of man *is* froward and strange: but *as for* the pure, his work *is* right.

9 *It is* better to dwell in a corner of the housetop, than with ᴿa ᵀbrawling woman in a wide house.   19:13 · *contentious*

10 ᴿThe soul of the wicked desireth evil: his neighbour findeth no favour in his eyes. James 4:5

11 When the scorner is punished, the simple is made wise: and when the ᴿwise is instructed, he receiveth knowledge.   19:25

12 The righteous *man* wisely considereth the house of the wicked: *but God* overthroweth the wicked for *their* wickedness.

13 ᴿWhoso stoppeth his ears at the cry of the poor, he also shall cry himself, but shall not be heard. [Matt. 7:2]; James 2:13; 1 John 3:17

14 A gift in secret pacifieth anger: and a ᵀreward in the bosom strong wrath.   *bribe*

15 *It is* joy to the just to do judgment: but destruction *shall be* to the workers of iniquity.

16 The man that wandereth out of the way of understanding shall remain in the congregation of the ᴿdead.   Ps. 49:14

17 He that loveth pleasure *shall be* a poor man: he that loveth wine and oil shall not be rich.

18 The wicked *shall be* a ransom for the righteous, and the ᵀtransgressor for the upright. *unfaithful*

19 *It is* better to dwell in the wilderness, than with a contentious and an angry woman.

20 ᴿ*There is* treasure to be desired and oil in the dwelling of the wise; but a foolish man spendeth it up.   8:21; Ps. 112:3

21 ᴿHe that followeth after righteousness and mercy findeth life, righteousness, and honour.   15:9

22 A ᴿwise *man* scaleth the city of the mighty, and casteth down the strength of the confidence thereof. 2 Sam. 5:6–9; Eccl. 7:19; 9:15, 16

23 ᴿWhoso keepeth his mouth and his tongue keepeth his soul from troubles. 12:13; 13:3; [James 3:2]

24 Proud *and* haughty scorner *is* his name, who [T]dealeth in proud wrath.   *acts in arrogant pride*
25 The [R]desire of the [T]slothful killeth him; for his hands refuse to labour.   13:4 · *lazy*
26 He coveteth greedily all the day long: but the righteous [R]giveth and spareth not.   [22:9; Eph. 4:28]
27 [R]The sacrifice of the wicked *is* abomination: how much more, *when* he bringeth it with a wicked mind?   15:8; Is. 66:3; Jer. 6:20; Amos 5:22
28 A false witness shall perish: but the man that heareth speaketh [T]constantly.   *endlessly*
29 A wicked man hardeneth his face: but *as for* the upright, he [T]directeth his way.   *establishes*
30 [R]*There is* no wisdom nor understanding nor counsel against the LORD.   Acts 5:39; 1 Cor. 3:19, 20
31 The horse *is* prepared against the day of battle: but [R]safety[T] *is* of the LORD.   Ps. 3:8; Jer. 3:23 · *deliverance*

22 A [R]*good* name *is* rather to be chosen than great riches, *and* loving favour rather than silver and gold.   [10:7]; Eccl. 7:1
2 The [R]rich and poor [T]meet together: the LORD *is* the maker of them all.   29:13 · *have this in common*
3 A prudent *man* foreseeth the evil, and hideth himself: but the simple pass on, and are [R]punished.   27:12; Is. 26:20
4 By humility *and* the fear of the LORD *are* riches, and honour, and life.
5 Thorns *and* snares *are* in the way of the [T]froward: he that [T]doth keep his soul shall be far from them.   *perverse · guards*
6 [R]Train up a child in the way he should go: and when he is old, he will not depart from it.   Eph. 6:4
7 The [R]rich ruleth over the poor, and the borrower *is* servant to the lender.   18:23; James 2:6
8 He that soweth iniquity shall reap [R]vanity:[T] and the rod of his anger shall fail.   Job 4:8 · *trouble*
9 [R]He that hath a bountiful eye shall be blessed; for he giveth of his bread to the poor.   2 Cor. 9:6
10 [R]Cast out the scorner, and

contention shall go out; yea, strife and reproach shall cease.   Ps. 101:5
11 [R]He that loveth pureness of heart, *for* the grace of his lips the king *shall be* his friend.   Ps. 101:6
12 The eyes of the LORD preserve knowledge, and he overthroweth the words of the [T]transgressor.   *faithless*
13 [R]The slothful *man* saith, *There is* a lion without, I shall be slain in the streets.   26:13
14 The mouth of strange women *is* a deep pit: he that is abhorred of the LORD shall fall therein.
15 Foolishness *is* bound in the heart of a child; *but* [R]the rod of correction shall drive it far from him.   13:24; 23:13, 14
16 He that oppresseth the poor to increase his *riches, and* he that giveth to the rich, *shall* surely *come* to [T]want.   *poverty*
17 Bow down thine ear, and hear the words of the wise, and apply thine heart unto my knowledge.
18 For *it is* a pleasant thing if thou keep them within thee; they shall withal be fitted in thy lips.
19 That thy trust may be in the LORD, I have made known to thee this day, even to thee.
20 Have not I written to thee excellent things in counsels and knowledge,
21 [R]That I might make thee know the certainty of the words of truth; [R]that thou mightest answer the words of truth to them that send unto thee?   Luke 1:3, 4 · 25:13
22 Rob not the [R]poor, because he *is* poor: neither oppress the afflicted in the gate: Ex. 23:6; Zech. 7:10
23 [R]For the LORD will plead their cause, and [T]spoil the soul of those that spoiled them.   Ps. 12:5 · *plunder*
24 Make no friendship with an angry man; and with a [B]furious man thou shalt not go;   29:22
25 Lest thou learn his ways, and get a snare to thy soul.
26 [R]Be not thou *one* of them that strike hands, *or* of them that are [T]sureties for debts.   11:15 · *collateral*
27 If thou hast nothing [T]to pay,

why should he take away thy bed from under thee?   with which *to pay*

28 ^RRemove not the ancient ^Tlandmark, which thy fathers have set.   23:10 · *boundary*

29 Seest thou a man diligent in his business? he shall stand before kings; he shall not stand before ^Tmean *men.*   *obscure* or *unknown*

23 When thou sittest to eat with a ruler, consider diligently what *is* before thee:

2 And put a knife to thy throat, if thou *be* a man given to appetite.

3 Be not desirous of his dainties: for they *are* deceitful meat.

4 Labour not to be rich: ^Rcease from thine own wisdom.   Rom. 12:16

5 Wilt thou set thine eyes upon that which is not? for *riches* certainly make themselves wings; they fly away as an eagle toward heaven.

6 Eat thou not the bread of *him that hath* an evil eye, neither desire thou his dainty meats:

7 For as he thinketh in his heart, so *is* he: Eat and drink, ^Rsaith he to thee; but his heart *is* not with thee.   12:2

8 The morsel *which* thou hast eaten shalt thou vomit up, and lose thy ^Tsweet words.   *pleasant*

9 ^RSpeak not in the ears of a fool: for he will despise the wisdom of thy words.   9:8; Matt. 7:6

10 Remove not the old ^Tlandmark; and enter not into the fields of the fatherless: *boundary*

11 ^RFor their redeemer *is* mighty; he shall plead their cause with thee.   22:23

12 Apply thine heart unto instruction, and thine ears to the words of knowledge.

13 Withhold not correction from the child: for *if* thou beatest him with the rod, he shall not die.

14 Thou shalt beat him with the rod, and shalt deliver his soul from ^Thell.   Heb. *Sheol*

15 My son, if thine heart be wise, ^Tmy heart shall rejoice, even mine.   *indeed my own heart shall rejoice*

16 Yea, my reins shall rejoice, when thy lips speak right things.

17 ^RLet not thine heart envy sinners: but *be thou* in the fear of the LORD all the day long.   Ps. 37:1

18 ^RFor surely there is ^Tan end; and thine ^Texpectation shall not be cut off.   [Ps. 37:37] · *a hereafter* · *hope*

19 Hear thou, my son, and be wise, and guide thine heart in the way.

20 ^RBe not among winebibbers; among riotous eaters of flesh: 20:1

21 For the drunkard and the glutton shall come to poverty: and drowsiness shall clothe *a man* with rags.

22 ^RHearken unto thy father that begat thee, and despise not thy mother when she is old.   1:8; Eph. 6:1

23 ^RBuy the truth, and sell *it* not; *also* wisdom, and instruction, and understanding.   4:7; 18:15; [Matt. 13:44]

24 ^RThe father of the righteous shall greatly rejoice: and he that begetteth a wise *child* shall ^Thave joy of him.   10:1 · *delight in*

25 Thy father and thy mother shall be glad, and she that bare thee shall rejoice.

26 My son, give me thine heart, and let thine eyes observe my ways.

27 ^RFor a whore *is* a deep ^Tditch; and a ^Tstrange woman *is* a narrow pit.   22:14 · *pit* · *seductress*

28 ^RShe also lieth in wait as *for* a prey, and increaseth the transgressors among men.   7:12; Eccl. 7:26

29 ^RWho hath woe? who hath sorrow? who hath contentions? who hath babbling? who hath wounds without cause? who ^Rhath redness of eyes? Is. 5:11, 22 · Gen. 49:12

30 ^RThey that tarry long at the wine; they that go to seek mixed wine.   20:1; 21:17; Is. 5:11; 28:7; [Eph. 5:18]

31 Look not thou upon the wine when it is red, when it ^Tgiveth his colour in the cup, *when* it moveth itself aright.   *sparkles in the cup*

32 At the last it biteth like a serpent, and stingeth like an adder.

33 Thine eyes shall behold strange women, and thine heart shall utter perverse things.

34 Yea, thou shalt be as he that lieth down in the midst of the sea,

or as he that lieth upon the top of a mast.

35 [R]They have stricken me, *shalt thou say, and* I was not [T]sick; they have beaten me, *and* I felt *it* not: when shall [R]I awake? I will seek it yet again. 27:22; Jer. 5:3 · *hurt* · Eph. 4:19

24 Be not thou [R]envious against evil men, neither desire to be with them. Ps. 1:1; 37:1

2 For their heart [T]studieth destruction, and their lips talk of [T]mischief. *devises violence · trouble*

3 Through wisdom is an house builded; and by understanding it is established:

4 And by knowledge shall the chambers be filled with all precious and pleasant riches.

5 [R]A wise man *is* strong; yea, a man of knowledge increaseth strength. 21:22; Eccl. 9:16

6 For by wise counsel thou shalt make thy war: and in multitude of counsellors *there is* safety.

7 [R]Wisdom *is* too [T]high for a fool: he openeth not his mouth in the gate. 14:6; Ps. 10:5 · *lofty*

8 He that [R]deviseth[T] to do evil shall be called a mischievous person. 6:14; 14:22; Rom. 1:30 · *plots*

9 The [T]thought of foolishness *is* sin: and the scorner *is* an abomination to men. *planning*

10 If thou faint in the day of adversity, thy strength *is* small.

11 [R]If thou forbear to deliver *them that are* drawn unto death, and *those that are* ready to be slain; Ps. 82:4; Is. 58:6, 7; 1 John 3:16

12 If thou sayest, Behold, we knew it not; doth not [R]he that pondereth the heart consider *it?* and he that keepeth thy soul, doth *not* he know *it?* and shall *not* he render to *every* man [R]according to his works? 21:2 · Job 34:11; Ps. 62:12

13 My son, eat thou honey, because *it is* good; and the honeycomb, *which is* sweet to thy taste:

14 [R]So *shall* the knowledge of wisdom *be* unto thy soul: when thou hast found *it,* then there shall be a reward, and thy expectation shall not be cut off. Ps. 19:10

15 Lay not wait, O wicked *man,* against the dwelling of the righteous; spoil not his resting place:

16 For a just *man* falleth seven times, and riseth up again: but the wicked shall fall into mischief.

17 Rejoice not when thine enemy falleth, and let not thine heart be glad when he stumbleth:

18 Lest the LORD see *it,* and it displease him, and he turn away his wrath from him.

19 [R]Fret not thyself because of evil *men,* neither be thou envious at the wicked; Ps. 37:1

20 For there shall be no reward to the evil *man;* [T]the candle of the wicked shall be put out. *the lamp*

21 My son, fear thou the LORD and the king: *and* meddle not with them that are given to change:

22 For their calamity shall rise suddenly; and who knoweth the ruin of them both?

23 These *things* also *belong* to the wise. *It is* not good to have respect of persons in judgment.

24 [R]He that saith unto the wicked, Thou *art* righteous; him shall the people curse, nations shall abhor him: 17:15; Is. 5:23

25 But to them that rebuke *him* shall be delight, and a good blessing shall come upon them.

26 *Every man* shall kiss *his* lips that giveth a right answer.

27 [R]Prepare thy work without, and make it fit for thyself in the field; and afterwards build thine house. 27:23–27; 1 Kin. 5:17

28 [R]Be not a witness against thy neighbour without cause; and deceive *not* with thy lips. Eph. 4:25

29 [R]Say not, I will do so to him as he hath done to me: I will render to the man according to his work. [Matt. 5:39–44; Rom. 12:17–19]

30 I went by the field of the slothful, and by the vineyard of the man void of understanding;

31 And, lo, [R]it was all grown over with thorns, *and* nettles had covered [T]the face thereof, and the stone wall thereof was broken down. Gen. 3:18 · *its surface*

32 Then I saw, *and* considered *it*

well: I looked upon *it, and* received instruction.

33 [R]*Yet* a little sleep, a little slumber, a little folding of the hands to [T]sleep: 6:9, 10 · *rest*

34 So shall thy poverty come *as* [T]one that travelleth; and thy want as an armed man. *a prowler*

25 These[R] *are* also proverbs of Solomon, which the men of Hez-e-ki'-ah king of Judah copied out. 1 Kin. 4:32

2 *It is* the glory of God to conceal a thing: but the honour of kings *is* to search out a matter.

3 The heaven for height, and the earth for depth, and the heart of kings *is* unsearchable.

4 Take away the dross from the silver, and there shall come forth a vessel for the [T]finer. *refiner*

5 Take away the wicked *from* before the king, and his throne shall be established in [R]righteousness. 16:12; 20:8

6 Put not forth thyself in the presence of the king, and stand not in the place of great *men:*

7 For better *it is* that it be said unto thee, Come up hither; than that thou shouldest be put lower in the presence of the prince whom thine eyes have seen.

8 Go not forth hastily to strive, lest *thou know not* what to do in the end thereof, when thy neighbour hath put thee to shame.

9 [R]Debate thy cause with thy neighbour *himself;* and discover not a secret to another: [Matt. 18:15]

10 Lest he that heareth *it* put thee to shame, and thine infamy turn not away.

11 A word fitly [R]spoken *is like* apples of gold [T]in pictures of silver. 15:23; Is. 50:4 · *in settings*

12 *As* an earring of gold, and an ornament of fine gold, *so is* a wise reprover upon an obedient ear.

13 [R]As the cold of snow in the time of harvest, *so is* a faithful messenger to them that send him: for he refresheth the soul of his masters. 13:17

14 [R]Whoso boasteth himself of a false gift *is like* [R]clouds and wind without rain. 20:6 · Jude 12

15 By long forbearing is a prince persuaded, and a [T]soft tongue breaketh the bone. *gentle*

16 Hast thou found honey? [T]eat so much as is sufficient for thee, lest thou be filled therewith, and vomit it. *eat only as much*

17 Withdraw thy foot from thy neighbour's house; lest he be weary of thee, and *so* hate thee.

18 [R]A man that beareth false witness against his neighbour *is* a [T]maul, and a sword, and a sharp arrow. 12:18; Ps. 57:4 · *club*

19 Confidence in an unfaithful man in time of trouble *is like* a [T]broken tooth, and a foot out of joint. *bad*

20 *As* he that taketh away a garment in cold weather, *and as* vinegar upon nitre, so *is* he that singeth songs to an heavy heart.

21 If thine enemy be hungry, give him bread to eat; and if he be thirsty, give him water to drink:

22 For thou shalt heap coals of fire upon his head, [R]and the LORD shall reward thee. [Matt. 6:4, 6]

23 The north wind driveth away rain: so *doth* an angry countenance a backbiting tongue.

24 [R]*It is* better to dwell in the corner of the housetop, than with a brawling woman and in a wide house. 19:13

25 *As* cold waters to a [T]thirsty soul, so *is* [R]good news from a far country. *weary* · 15:30

26 A righteous man falling down before the wicked *is as* a [T]troubled fountain, and a [T]corrupt spring. *murky spring · polluted well*

27 *It is* not good to eat much honey: so *for men* to [T]search their own glory *is not* glory. *seek*

28 [R]He that *hath* no rule over his own spirit *is like* a city *that is* broken down, *and* without walls. 16:32

26 As snow in summer, [R]and as rain in harvest, so honour is not seemly for a fool. 1 Sam. 12:17

2 As the bird by wandering, as the swallow by flying, so the curse causeless shall not come.

3 [R]A whip for the horse, a bridle for the [T]ass, and a rod for the fool's back.   19:29; Ps. 32:9 · *donkey*

4 Answer not a fool according to his folly, lest thou also be like unto him.

5 [R]Answer a fool according to his folly, lest he be wise in his own conceit.   Matt. 16:1–4; Rom. 12:16

6 He that sendeth a message by the hand of a fool cutteth off the feet, *and* drinketh damage.

7 The legs of the lame [T]are not equal: so *is* a parable in the mouth of fools.   *hang limp*

8 As he that bindeth a stone in a sling, so *is* he that giveth honour to a fool.

9 *As* a thorn goeth up into the hand of a drunkard, so *is* a parable in the mouth of fools.

10 The great *God* that formed all *things* both rewardeth the fool, and rewardeth transgressors.

11 [R]As a dog returneth to his vomit, [R]*so* a fool [T]returneth to his folly.   2 Pet. 2:22 · Ex. 8:15 · *repeats his*

12 [R]Seest thou a man wise in his own conceit? *there is* more hope of a fool than of him.   29:20

13 The slothful *man* saith, *There is* a lion in the way; a [T]lion *is* in the [T]streets.   *fierce lion · plaza or square*

14 *As* the door turneth upon his hinges, so *doth* the slothful upon his bed.

15 The [R]slothful hideth his hand in *his* bosom; it grieveth him to bring it again to his mouth.   19:24

16 The sluggard *is* wiser in his own [T]conceit than seven men that can render a reason.   Lit. *eyes*

17 He that passeth by, *and* meddleth with strife *belonging* not to him, *is like* one that taketh a dog by the ears.

18 As a mad *man* who casteth firebrands, arrows, and death,

19 So *is* the man *that* deceiveth his neighbour, and saith, [R]Am not I [T]in sport?   Eph. 5:4 · *joking*

20 Where no wood is, *there* the fire goeth out: so where *there* is no talebearer, the strife ceaseth.

21 *As* coals *are* to burning coals, and wood to fire; so *is* a contentious man to kindle strife.

22 The words of a talebearer *are* as wounds, and they go down into the innermost parts of the belly.

23 [T]Burning lips and a wicked heart *are like* a potsherd covered with silver dross.   *Fervent*

24 He that hateth [T]dissembleth with his lips, and layeth up deceit within him;   *disguises it*

25 When he speaketh fair, believe him not: for *there are* seven abominations in his heart.

26 *Whose* hatred is covered by deceit, his wickedness shall be shewed before the *whole* congregation.

27 Whoso diggeth a pit shall fall therein: and he that rolleth a stone, it will return upon him.

28 A lying tongue hateth *those that are* afflicted by it; and a flattering mouth worketh [R]ruin.   29:5

27 Boast not thyself of to morrow; for thou knowest not what a day may bring forth.

2 Let another man praise thee, and not thine own mouth; a stranger, and not thine own lips.

3 A stone *is* heavy, and the sand weighty; but a fool's wrath *is* heavier than them both.

4 Wrath *is* cruel, and anger *is* outrageous; but [R]who *is* able to stand before envy?   6:34; 1 John 3:12

5 [R]Open rebuke *is* better than secret love.   [28:23]; Gal. 2:14

6 Faithful *are* the wounds of a friend; but the kisses of an enemy *are* [R]deceitful.   Matt. 26:49

7 The full soul loatheth an honeycomb; but to the hungry soul every bitter thing is sweet.

8 As a bird that wandereth from her nest, so *is* a man that wandereth from his place.

9 Ointment and perfume [T]rejoice the heart: so *doth* the sweetness of a man's friend by [T]hearty counsel.   *delight · Lit. counsel of the soul*

10 Thine own friend, and thy father's friend, forsake not; neither go into thy brother's house in

the day of thy calamity: *for* ^Rbetter *is* a neighbour *that is* near than a brother far off.   17:17; 18:24

11 My son, be wise, and make my heart glad, ^Rthat I may answer him that reproacheth me.   10:1

12 A prudent *man* foreseeth the evil, *and* hideth himself; *but* the simple pass on, *and* are ^Rpunished.   22:3

13 Take his garment that is ^Tsurety for a stranger, and take a pledge of him for a strange woman.   *guaranty* or *collateral*

14 He that blesseth his friend with a loud voice, rising early in the morning, it shall be counted a curse to him.

15 A ^Rcontinual dropping in a very rainy day and a contentious woman are alike.   19:13

16 Whosoever ^Thideth her hideth the wind, and the ointment of his right hand, *which* bewrayeth *itself*.   *restrains*

17 Iron sharpeneth iron; so a man sharpeneth the countenance of his friend.

18 ^RWhoso keepeth the fig tree shall eat the fruit thereof: so he that waiteth on his master shall be honoured.   Is. 36:16; 2 Tim. 2:6

19 As in water face ^Tanswereth to face, so the heart of man ^Tto man.   *reflects · reveals the man*

20 ^RHell and destruction are never full; so ^Rthe eyes of man are never satisfied.   Hab. 2:5 · Eccl. 1:8; 4:8

21 ^R*As* the ^Tfining pot for silver, and the furnace for gold; so *is* a man to his praise.   17:3 · *refining*

22 Though thou shouldest ^Tbray a fool in a mortar among wheat with a pestle, *yet* will not his foolishness depart from him.   *grind*

23 Be thou diligent to know the state of thy ^Rflocks, *and* ^Tlook well to thy herds.   24:27 · *attend to*

24 For riches *are* not for ever: and doth the crown *endure* to every generation?

25 ^RThe hay ^Tappeareth, and the tender grass sheweth itself, and herbs of the mountains are gathered.   Ps. 104:14 · *is removed*

26 The lambs *are* for thy clothing, and the goats *are* the price of the field.

27 And *thou shalt have* goats' milk enough for thy food, for the food of thy household, and *for* the maintenance for thy maidens.

28

The ^Rwicked flee when no man pursueth: but the righteous are bold as a lion.   Ps. 53:5

2 For the transgression of a land many *are* the princes thereof: but by a man of understanding *and* knowledge ^Tthe state *thereof* shall be prolonged.   Lit. *it*

3 ^RA poor man that oppresseth the poor *is like* a sweeping rain which leaveth no food.   Matt. 18:28

4 They that forsake the law praise the wicked: but such as keep the law contend with them.

5 Evil men understand not ^Tjudgment: but they that seek the LORD understand all *things*.   *justice*

6 Better *is* the poor that walketh in his ^Tuprightness, than *he that is* perverse *in his* ways, though he *be* rich.   *integrity*

7 Whoso keepeth the law *is* a ^Twise son: but he that is a companion of ^Triotous *men* shameth his father.   *discerning · gluttons*

8 He that by usury and ^Tunjust gain increaseth his ^Tsubstance, he shall gather it for him that will pity the poor.   *extortion · possessions*

9 He that turneth away his ear from hearing the law, ^Reven his prayer *shall be* abomination.   15:8

10 ^RWhoso causeth the righteous to go astray in an evil way, he shall fall himself into his own pit: but the upright shall have good *things* in possession.   Ps. 7:15

11 The rich man *is* wise in his own ^Tconceit; but the poor that hath understanding searcheth him out.   *eyes*

12 When righteous *men* do rejoice, *there is* great ^Rglory: but when the wicked rise, a man is ^Thidden.   11:10; 29:2 · Lit. *will be sought*

13 ^RHe that covereth his sins shall not prosper: but whoso confesseth and forsaketh *them* shall have mercy.   Ps. 32:3–5; 1 John 1:8–10

14 Happy *is* the man that fear-

eth alway: but he that hardeneth his heart shall fall into mischief.

15 ^RAs a roaring lion, and a ranging bear; *so is* a wicked ruler over the poor people. 19:12; 1 Pet. 5:8

16 The prince that ^Twanteth understanding *is* also a great ^Roppressor: *but* he that hateth covetousness shall prolong *his* days. *lacks* · Eccl. 10:16; Is. 3:12

17 ^RA man that doeth violence to the blood of *any* person shall flee to the pit; let no man ^Tstay him. Gen. 9:6 · *help*

18 Whoso walketh uprightly shall be saved: but *he that is* perverse *in his* ways shall fall at once.

19 ^RHe that tilleth his land shall have plenty of bread: but he that followeth after vain *persons* shall have poverty enough. 12:11; 20:13

20 A faithful man shall abound with blessings: ^Rbut he that maketh haste to be rich shall not be innocent. 13:11; 20:21; 23:4; 1 Tim. 6:9

21 To have respect of persons *is* not good: for for a piece of bread *that* man will transgress.

22 He that hasteth to be rich *hath* an evil eye, and considereth not that ^Rpoverty shall come upon him. 21:5

23 ^RHe that rebuketh a man afterwards shall find more favour than he that flattereth with the tongue. 27:5, 6

24 Whoso robbeth his father or his mother, and saith, *It is* no transgression; the same ^Ris the companion of a destroyer. 18:9

25 ^RHe that is of a proud heart stirreth up strife: ^Rbut he that putteth his trust in the LORD shall be made fat. 13:10 · 29:25; 1 Tim. 6:6

26 He that ^Rtrusteth in his own heart is a fool: but whoso walketh wisely, he shall be delivered. 3:5

27 He that giveth unto the poor shall not lack: but he that hideth his eyes shall have many a curse.

28 When the wicked rise, men hide themselves: but when they perish, the righteous increase.

29 He,^R that being often reproved hardeneth *his* neck, shall suddenly be destroyed, and that without remedy. 2 Chr. 36:16

2 When the righteous are in authority, the ^Rpeople rejoice: but when the wicked beareth rule, ^Rthe people mourn. 28:12 · Esth. 4:3

3 Whoso loveth wisdom rejoiceth his father: but he that keepeth company with harlots ^Tspendeth *his* substance. *wastes his wealth*

4 The king by judgment establisheth the land: but he that receiveth gifts overthroweth it.

5 A man that ^Rflattereth his neighbour spreadeth a net for his feet. 26:28

6 In the transgression of an evil man *there is* a snare: but the righteous doth sing and rejoice.

7 The righteous considereth the cause of the poor: *but* the wicked regardeth not to know *it.*

8 Scornful men ^Tbring a city into a ^Rsnare: but wise *men* turn away wrath. *inflame a city* · 11:11

9 *If* a wise man contendeth with a foolish man, whether he rage or laugh, *there is* no rest.

10 ^RThe bloodthirsty hate the upright: but the just seek his ^Tsoul. Gen. 4:5–8; 1 John 3:12 · *well-being*

11 A fool uttereth all his ^Rmind: but a wise *man* ^Tkeepeth it in till afterwards. 14:33 · *holds it back*

12 If a ruler hearken to lies, all his servants *are* wicked.

13 The poor and the deceitful man meet together: the LORD lighteneth both their eyes.

14 The king that faithfully judgeth the ^Rpoor, his throne shall be established for ever. Ps. 72:4; Is. 11:4

15 The rod and reproof give wisdom: but a child left *to himself* bringeth his mother to shame.

16 When the wicked are multiplied, transgression increaseth: but the righteous shall see their ^Rfall. 21:12; Ps. 37:34

17 Correct thy son, and he shall give thee rest; yea, he shall give delight unto thy soul.

18 ^RWhere *there is* no vision, the

people perish: but he that keepeth the law, happy *is* he.   Ps. 74:9

19 A servant will not be corrected by words: for though he understand he will not answer.

20 Seest thou a man *that is* hasty in his words? ^R*there is* more hope of a fool than of him.   26:12

21 He that ^Tdelicately bringeth up his servant from ^Ta child shall have him become *his* son at the ^Tlength.   *pampers · childhood · end*

22 ^RAn angry man stirreth up strife, and a furious man aboundeth in transgression.   26:21

23 ^RA man's pride shall bring him low: but honour shall uphold the humble in spirit.   Matt. 23:12

24 Whoso is partner with a thief hateth his own ^Tsoul: he heareth cursing, and bewrayeth *it* not.   *life*

25 ^RThe fear of man bringeth a snare: but whoso putteth his trust in the LORD shall be safe.   Luke 12:4

26 Many seek the ruler's ^Tfavour; but *every* man's judgment *cometh* from the LORD.   Lit. *face*

27 An unjust man *is* an abomination to the just: and *he that is* upright in the way *is* abomination to the wicked.

30 The words of A'-gur the son of Ja'-keh, *even* the prophecy: the man spake unto Ith'-i-el, even unto Ith'-i-el and U'-cal,

2 Surely I *am* more ^Tbrutish than *any* man, and have not the understanding of a man.   *stupid*

3 I neither learned wisdom, nor have the knowledge of the holy.

4 ^RWho hath ascended up into heaven, or descended? who hath gathered the wind in his fists? who hath bound the waters in a garment? who hath established all the ends of the earth? what *is* his name, and what *is* his son's name, if thou canst tell?   [John 3:13]

5 ^REvery word of God *is* pure: ^Rhe *is* a shield unto them that put their trust in him.   Ps. 12:6 · Ps. 18:30

6 ^RAdd thou not unto his words, lest he reprove thee, and thou be found a liar.   Rev. 22:18

7 Two *things* have I ^Trequired

of thee; ^Tdeny me *them* not before I die: *requested · deprive me not*

8 Remove far from me vanity and lies: give me neither poverty nor riches; ^Rfeed me with food convenient for me: Matt. 6:11

9 ^RLest I be full, and deny *thee*, and say, Who *is* the LORD? or lest I be poor, and steal, and take the name of my God *in vain*.   Hos. 13:6

10 ^TAccuse not a servant unto his master, lest he curse thee, and thou be found guilty.   Do not malign

11 *There is* a generation *that* curseth their ^Rfather, and doth not bless their mother.   Ex. 21:17

12 *There is* a generation ^R*that are* pure in their own eyes, and *yet* is not washed from their filthiness. Is. 65:5; Luke 18:11; [Titus 1:15, 16]

13 *There is* a generation, O how ^Rlofty are their eyes! and their eyelids are lifted up.   Is. 2:11; 5:15

14 *There is* a generation, whose teeth *are as* swords, and their jaw teeth *as* knives, ^Rto devour the poor from off the earth, and the needy from *among* men.   Ps. 14:4

15 The ^Thorseleach hath two daughters, *crying*, Give, give. There are three *things that* are never satisfied, *yea*, four *things* say not, *It is* enough: *leech*

16 ^RThe grave; and the barren womb; the earth *that* is not filled with water; and the fire *that* saith not, *It is* enough.   27:20; Hab. 2:5

17 ^RThe eye *that* mocketh at *his* father, and despiseth to obey *his* mother, the ravens of the valley shall pick it out, and the young eagles shall eat it.   Gen. 9:22; Lev. 20:9

18 There be three *things which* are too wonderful for me, *yea*, four which I know not:

19 The way of an eagle in the air; the way of a serpent upon a rock; the way of a ship in the ^Tmidst of the sea; and the way of a man with a ^Tmaid.   Lit. *heart · virgin*

20 Such *is* the way of an adulterous woman; she eateth, and wipeth her mouth, and saith, I have done no wickedness.

21 For three *things* the earth is

disquieted, and for four *which* it cannot bear:

22 ^RFor a servant when he reigneth; and a fool when he is filled with ^Tmeat;   Eccl. 10:7 · *food*

23 For an odious *woman* when she is married; and an handmaid that is heir to her mistress.

24 There be four *things which are* little upon the earth, but they *are* exceeding wise:

25 ^RThe ants *are* a people not strong, yet they prepare their ^Tmeat in the summer;   6:6 · *food*

26 The ^Tconies *are but* a feeble folk, yet make they their houses in the rocks;   *rock badgers* or *hyraxes*

27 The locusts have no king, yet go they forth all of them ^Tby bands;   *in ranks*

28 The ^Tspider taketh hold with her hands, and is in kings' palaces.   Or *lizard*

29 There be three *things* which go well, yea, four are ^Tcomely in going: *stately in walk*

30 A lion *which is* ^Tstrongest among beasts, and turneth not away for any;   *mighty*

31 A greyhound; an he goat also; and a king, against whom *there is* no rising up.

32 If thou hast done foolishly in lifting up thyself, or if thou hast thought evil, ^Rlay thine hand upon thy mouth.   Job 21:5; 40:4; Mic. 7:16

33 Surely the churning of milk bringeth forth butter, and the wringing of the nose bringeth forth blood: so the forcing of wrath bringeth forth strife.

31 The words of king Lem-u-el, the prophecy that his mother taught him.

2 What, my son? and what, the son of my womb? and what, ^Rthe son of my vows?   Is. 49:15

3 ^RGive not thy strength unto women, nor thy ways to that which destroyeth kings.   5:9

4 *It is* not for kings, O Lem-u-el, *it is* not for kings to drink wine; nor for princes strong drink:

5 Lest they drink, and forget the law, and pervert the judgment of any of the afflicted.

6 ^RGive strong drink unto him that is ready to perish, and wine unto those that be ^Tof heavy hearts.   Ps. 104:15 · *bitter of heart*

7 Let him drink, and forget his poverty, and remember his misery no more.

8 Open thy mouth for the dumb in the cause of all such as are appointed to destruction.

9 Open thy mouth, ^Rjudge righteously, and plead the cause of the poor and needy.   Lev. 19:15

10 Who can find a ^Tvirtuous woman? for her ^Tprice *is* far above rubies.   Lit. *wife of valour · worth*

11 The heart of her husband doth safely trust in her, so that he shall have no need of spoil.

12 She will do him good and not evil all the days of her life.

13 She seeketh wool, and flax, and worketh willingly with her hands.

14 She is like the merchants' ships; she bringeth her food from afar.

15 ^RShe riseth also while it is yet night, and ^Rgiveth meat to her household, and a portion to her maidens.   20:13; Rom. 12:11 · Luke 12:42

16 She considereth a field, and buyeth it: with the fruit of her hands she planteth a vineyard.

17 She girdeth her loins with strength, and strengtheneth her arms.

18 She perceiveth that her merchandise *is* good: her ^Tcandle goeth not out by night.   *lamp*

19 She layeth her hands to the spindle, and her hands hold the distaff.

20 ^RShe stretcheth out her hand to the poor; yea, she reacheth forth her hands to the needy.   22:9

21 She is not afraid of the snow for her household: for all her household *are* clothed with scarlet.

22 She maketh herself coverings of tapestry; her clothing *is* ^Tsilk and purple.   *fine linen*

23 ^RHer husband is known in the gates, when he sitteth among the elders of the land.   12:4

24 She maketh fine linen, and selleth *it*; and delivereth [T]girdles unto the merchant.   *sashes*

25 Strength and honour *are* her clothing; and she shall rejoice in time to come.

26 She openeth her mouth with wisdom; and in her tongue *is* the law of kindness.

27 She looketh well to the ways of her household, and eateth not the bread of idleness.

28 Her children arise up, and call her blessed; her husband *also*, and he praiseth her.

29 Many daughters have done [T]virtuously, but thou excellest them all.   *well*

30 [T]Favour *is* deceitful, and beauty *is* vain: *but* a woman *that* feareth the LORD, she shall be praised.   *Charm*

31 Give her of the fruit of her hands; and let her own works praise her in the gates.

The Book of
ECCLESIASTES

THE key word in Ecclesiastes is *vanity*, "the futile emptiness of trying to be happy apart from God." The Preacher (traditionally taken to be Solomon—1:1, 12—the wisest, richest, most influential king in Israel's history) looks at life "under the sun" (1:9) and, from the human perspective, declares it all to be empty. Power, popularity, prestige, pleasure—nothing can fill the God-shaped void in man's life but God Himself! But once seen from God's perspective, life takes on meaning and purpose, causing Solomon to exclaim, "Eat . . . drink . . . rejoice . . . do good . . . live joyfully . . . fear God . . . keep his commandments!" Skepticism and despair melt away when life is viewed as a daily gift from God.

The Hebrew title *Qoheleth* is a rare term, found only in Ecclesiastes (1:1, 2, 12; 7:27; 12:8–10). It comes from the word *qahal*, "to convoke an assembly, to assemble." Thus, it means "One Who Addresses an Assembly," "A Preacher." The Septuagint used the Greek word *Ekklesiastes* as its title for this book. Derived from the word *ekklesia*, "assembly," "congregation," "church," it simply means "Preacher." The Latin *Ecclesiastes* means "Speaker Before an Assembly."

THE words of the Preacher, the son of David, [R]king in Jerusalem.   Prov. 1:1

2 [R]Vanity[T] of vanities, saith the Preacher, vanity of vanities; all *is* vanity.   12:8 · *Futility of futilities*

3 [R]What profit hath a man of all his labour which he [T]taketh under the sun?   2:22 · *toils or labours*

4 *One* generation passeth away, and *another* generation cometh: [R]but the earth abideth for ever.   Ps. 104:5; 119:90

5 [R]The sun also ariseth, and the sun goeth down, and hasteth to his place where he arose. Ps. 19:4–6

6 [R]The wind goeth toward the south, and turneth about unto the north; it whirleth about continually, and the wind returneth again according to his circuits.   John 3:8

7 All the rivers run into the sea; yet the sea *is* not full; unto the place from whence the rivers come, thither they return again.

8 All things *are* full of labour; man cannot utter *it*: [R]the eye is

not satisfied with seeing, nor the ear filled with hearing.   Prov. 27:20

9 [R]The thing that hath been, it *is that* which shall be; and that which is done *is* that which shall be done: and *there is* no new *thing* under the sun.   3:15

10 Is there *any* thing whereof it may be said, See, this *is* new? it hath been already of old time, which was before us.

11 *There is* [R]no remembrance of former *things;* neither shall there be *any* remembrance of *things* that are to come with *those* that shall come after.   2:16

12 I the Preacher was king over Israel in Jerusalem.

13 And I [T]gave my heart to seek and search out by wisdom concerning all *things* that are done under heaven: this sore travail hath God given to the sons of man to be exercised therewith.   *set*

14 I have seen all the works that are done under the sun; and, behold, all *is* vanity and [T]vexation of spirit.   *a grasping for the wind*

15 [R]*That which is* crooked cannot be made straight: and that which is [T]wanting cannot be numbered.   7:13 · *lacking*

16 I communed with mine own heart, saying, Lo, I am come to [T]great estate, and have gotten [R]more wisdom than all *they* that have been before me in Jerusalem: yea, my heart had great experience of wisdom and knowledge.   *greatness* · 2:9; 1 Kin. 3:12, 13

17 [R]And I gave my heart to know wisdom, and to know madness and folly: I perceived that this also is vexation of spirit.   2:3

18 For in much wisdom *is* much grief: and he that increaseth knowledge increaseth sorrow.

2 I said in mine heart, Go to now, I will prove thee with mirth, therefore enjoy pleasure: and, behold, this also *is* vanity.

2 I said of laughter, *It is* mad: and of mirth, What doeth it?

3 [R]I sought in mine heart to give myself unto wine, yet acquainting mine heart with wis-

dom; and to lay hold on folly, till I might see what *was* that [R]good for the sons of men, which they should do under the heaven all the days of their life.   1:17 · [3:12, 13]

4 I made me great works; I builded me [R]houses; I planted me vineyards: 1 Kin. 7:1–12

5 I made me gardens and orchards, and I planted trees in them of all *kind of* fruits:

6 I made me pools of water, to [T]water therewith the wood that bringeth forth trees: *irrigate*

7 I got *me* [T]servants and maidens, and had servants born in my house; also I had great possessions of great and small cattle above all that were in Jerusalem before me: *male and female servants*

8 I gathered me also silver and gold, and the peculiar treasure of kings and of the provinces: I gat me men singers and women singers, and the delights of the sons of men, *as* musical instruments, and that of all sorts.

9 [R]So I was great, and increased more than all that were before me in Jerusalem: also my wisdom remained with me.   1:16

10 And whatsoever mine eyes desired I kept not from them, I withheld not my heart from any joy; for my heart rejoiced in all my labour: and [R]this was my portion of all my labour.   3:22; 5:18; 9:9

11 Then I looked on all the works that my hands had wrought, and on the labour that I had laboured to do: and, behold, all *was* [R]vanity[T] and vexation of spirit, and *there was* no profit under the sun.   1:3, 14 · *futility*

12 And I turned myself to behold wisdom, [R]and madness, and folly: for what *can* the man *do* that cometh after the king? *even* that which hath been already [R]done.   1:17; 7:25 · 1:9

13 Then I saw that wisdom [R]excelleth folly, as far as light excelleth darkness.   7:11, 14, 19; 9:18; 10:10

14 [R]The wise man's eyes *are* in his head; but the fool walketh in darkness: and I myself perceived

also that [R]one event happeneth to them all. Prov. 17:24 · 9:2, 3, 11; Ps. 49:10

15 Then said I in my heart, As it happeneth to the fool, so it happeneth even to me; and why was I then more wise? Then I said in my heart, that this also is vanity.

16 For there is no remembrance of the wise more than of the fool for ever; seeing that which now is in the days to come shall all be forgotten. And how dieth the wise man? as the fool.

17 Therefore I hated life; because the work that is wrought under the sun is grievous unto me: for all is [T]vanity and [T]vexation of spirit.   futility · a grasping for the wind

18 Yea, I hated all my labour which I had taken under the sun: because [R]I should leave it unto the man that shall be after me. Ps. 49:10

19 And who knoweth whether he shall be a wise man or a fool? yet shall he have rule over all my labour wherein I have laboured, and wherein I have shewed myself wise under the sun. This is also vanity.

20 Therefore I went about to cause my heart to despair of all the labour which I [T]took under the sun.   toiled

21 For there is a man whose labour is [T]in wisdom, and in knowledge, and [T]in equity; yet to a man that hath not laboured therein shall he leave it for [T]his portion. This also is vanity and a great evil.   with · with skill · heritage

22 [R]For what hath man of all his labour, and of the [T]vexation of his heart, wherein he hath laboured under the sun?   1:3; 3:9 · striving

23 For all his days are [R]sorrows, and his travail grief; yea, his heart taketh not rest in the night. This is also [T]vanity.   Job 5:7; 14:1 · futility

24 [R]There is nothing better for a man, than that he should eat and drink, and that he should make his soul enjoy good in his labour. This also I saw, that it was from the hand of God. Is. 56:12; Luke 12:19

25 For who can eat, or who else can [T]hasten hereunto, more than I?   have enjoyment

26 For God giveth to a man that is good in his sight [R]wisdom, and knowledge, and joy: but to the sinner he giveth travail, to gather and to heap up, that [R]he may give to him that is good before God. This also is vanity and vexation of spirit. Prov. 2:6; James 1:5 · Prov. 28:8

3 To every thing there is a season, and a [R]time to every purpose under the heaven: v. 17; 8:6

2 A time [T]to be born, and [R]a time to die; a time to plant, and a time to pluck up that which is planted; Lit. to bear · Job 14:5; Heb. 9:27

3 A time to kill, and a time to heal; a time to break down, and a time to build up;

4 A time to [R]weep, and a time to laugh; a time to mourn, and a time to dance; Rom. 12:15

5 A time to cast away stones, and a time to gather stones together; a time to embrace, and a time to refrain from embracing;

6 A time to [T]get, and a time to lose; a time to keep, and a time to cast away; gain

7 A time to [T]rend, and a time to sew; [R]a time to keep silence, and a time to speak; tear apart · Amos 5:13

8 A time to love, and a time to [R]hate; a time of war, and a time of peace. Prov. 13:5; Luke 14:26

9 [R]What profit hath he that worketh in that wherein he laboureth? 1:3

10 [R]I have seen the travail, which God hath given to the sons of men to be exercised in it. 1:13

11 He hath made every thing beautiful in his time: also he hath set the world in their heart, so that [R]no man can find out the work that God maketh from the beginning to the end. Job 5:9; Rom. 11:33

12 I know that there is no [R]good in them, but for a man to rejoice, and to do good in his life. 2:3, 24

13 And also [R]that every man should eat and drink, and enjoy the good of all his labour, it is the gift of God. 2:24

14 I know that, whatsoever God

doeth, it shall be for ever: ᴿnothing can be ᵀput to it, nor any thing taken from it: and God doeth *it,* that *men* should fear before him.   *James 1:17 · added*

15 ᴿThat which hath been is now; and that which is to be hath already been; and God requireth that which is past.   1:9

16 And moreover ᴿI saw under the sun the place of judgment, *that* wickedness *was* there; and the place of righteousness, *that* iniquity *was* there.   5:8

17 I said in mine heart, ᴿGod shall judge the righteous and the wicked: for *there is* a time there for every purpose and for every work.   [Rom. 2:6–10; 2 Cor. 5:10]

18 I said in mine heart concerning the estate of the sons of men, that God might ᵀmanifest them, and that they might see that they themselves are beasts.   *test*

19 For that which befalleth the sons of men befalleth beasts; even one thing befalleth them: as the one dieth, so dieth the other; yea, they have all one breath; so that a man hath no ᵀpreeminence above a beast: for all *is* vanity.   *advantage*

20 All go unto one place; ᴿall are of the dust, and all turn to dust again.   *Gen. 3:19; Ps. 103:14*

21 ᴿWho knoweth the spirit of man that goeth upward, and the spirit of the beast that goeth downward to the earth?   12:7

22 ᴿWherefore I perceive that *there is* nothing better, than that a man should rejoice in his own works; for ᴿthat *is* his portion: ᴿfor who shall bring him to see what shall be after him?   5:18 · 2:10 · 8:7

4 So I returned, and considered all the ᴿoppressions that are done under the sun: and behold the tears of *such as were* oppressed, and they had no comforter; and on the side of their oppressors *there was* power; but they had no comforter.   Ps. 12:5

2 ᴿWherefore I praised the dead which are already dead more than the living which are yet alive.   Job 3:17, 18

3 ᴿYea, better *is he* than both they, which hath not yet been, who hath not seen the evil work that is done under the sun.   6:3

4 Again, I ᵀconsidered all travail, and every right work, that for this a man is envied of his neighbour. This *is* also vanity and vexation of spirit.   *saw all the toil*

5 ᴿThe fool foldeth his hands together, and ᵀeateth his own flesh.   Prov. 6:10; 24:33 · *consumes*

6 ᴿBetter *is* an handful *with* quietness, than both the hands full *with* travail and vexation of spirit.   Prov. 15:16, 17; 16:8

7 Then I returned, and I saw ᵀvanity under the sun.   *futility*

8 There is one *alone,* and *there is* not a second; yea, he hath neither child nor brother: yet *is there* no end of all his labour; neither is his ᴿeye satisfied with riches; ᴿneither *saith he,* For whom do I labour, and bereave my soul of good? This *is* also vanity, yea, it *is* a sore travail.   [1 John 2:16] · Ps. 39:6

9 Two *are* better than one; because they have a good reward for their labour.

10 For if they fall, the one will lift up his ᵀfellow: but woe to him *that is* alone when he falleth; for he hath not another to help him up.   *companion*

11 Again, if two lie together, then they have heat: but how can one be warm *alone?*

12 And if one prevail against him, two shall withstand him; and a threefold cord is not quickly broken.

13 Better *is* a poor and a wise ᵀchild than an old and foolish king, who will no ᵀmore be admonished.   *youth · longer*

14 For out of prison he cometh to reign; whereas also *he that is* born in his kingdom becometh poor.

15 I considered all the living which walk under the sun, with the second ᵀchild that shall stand up in his stead.   *youth*

16 *There is* no end of all the people, *even* of all that have been

before them: they also that come after shall not rejoice in him. Surely this also *is* vanity and vexation of spirit.

5 Keep thy foot when thou goest to the house of God, and be more ready to hear, than to give the sacrifice of fools: for they consider not that they do evil.

2 Be not ᴿrash with thy mouth, and let not thine heart be hasty to utter *any* thing before God: for God *is* in heaven, and thou upon earth: therefore let thy words ᴿbe few.   Prov. 20:25 · Prov. 10:19; Matt. 6:7

3 For a dream cometh through the multitude of ᵀbusiness; and ᴿa fool's voice *is known* by multitude of words.   *effort* or *activity* · Prov. 10:19

4 When thou vowest a vow unto God, ᵀdefer not to pay it; for *he hath* no pleasure in fools: pay that which thou hast vowed. *delay*

5 ᴿBetter *is it* that thou shouldest not vow, than that thou shouldest vow and not pay. Acts 5:4

6 Suffer not thy mouth to cause thy flesh to sin; neither say thou before the angel, that it *was* an error: wherefore should God be angry at thy ᵀvoice, and destroy the work of thine hands?   *excuse*

7 For in the multitude of dreams and many words ᵀ*there are* also *divers* vanities: but ᴿfear thou God.   *futility abounds* · [12:13]

8 If thou ᴿseest the oppression of the poor, and violent perverting of judgment and justice in a province, marvel not at the matter: for ᴿ*he that is* higher than the highest regardeth; and *there be* higher than they.   3:16 · [Ps. 12:5; 82:1]

9 Moreover the profit of the earth is for all: the king *himself* is served by the field.

10 He that loveth silver shall not be satisfied with silver; nor he that loveth abundance with increase: this *is* also ᵀvanity. *futility*

11 When goods increase, they are increased that eat them: and what good *is there* to the owners thereof, saving the beholding *of* them with their eyes?

12 The sleep of a labouring man

is sweet, whether he eat little or much: but the abundance of the rich will not suffer him to sleep.

13 ᴿThere is a ᵀsore evil *which* I have seen under the sun, *namely*, riches kept for the owners thereof to their hurt.   6:1, 2 · *severe*

14 But those riches perish by ᵀevil travail: and he begetteth a son, and *there is* nothing in his hand.   *misfortune*

15 As he came forth of his mother's womb, naked shall he return to go as he came, and shall take nothing of his labour, which he may carry away in his hand.

16 And this also *is* a ᵀsore evil, *that* in all points as he came, so shall he go: and ᴿwhat profit hath he ᴿthat hath laboured for the wind?   *severe* · 1:3 · Prov. 11:29

17 All his days also he eateth in darkness, and *he hath* much sorrow and wrath with his sickness.

18 Behold *that* which I have seen: *it is* good and comely *for one* to eat and to drink, and to enjoy the good of all his labour that he taketh under the sun all the days of his life, which God giveth him: for it *is* his portion.

19 ᴿEvery man also to whom God hath given riches and wealth, and hath given him power to eat thereof, and to take his portion, and to rejoice in his labour; this *is* the ᴿgift of God.   [6:2] · 2:24; 3:13

20 For he shall not much remember the days of his life; because God ᵀanswereth *him* in the joy of his heart.   *keeps* him *busy*

6 ThereᴿR is an evil which I have seen under the sun, and it *is* common among men: 5:13

2 A man to whom God hath given riches, wealth, and honour, ᴿso that he wanteth nothing for his soul of all that he desireth, ᴿyet God giveth him not power to eat thereof, but a stranger eateth it: this *is* vanity, and it *is* an evil disease.   Ps. 17:14; 73:7 · Luke 12:20

3 If a man beget an hundred *children*, and live many years, so that the days of his years be many, and his soul be not filled with

good, and also *that* he have no burial; I say, *that* ^Ran untimely birth *is* better than he.　4:3; Ps. 58:8

4　For he cometh in with ^Tvanity, and departeth in darkness, and his name shall be covered with darkness.　*futility*

5　Moreover he hath not seen the sun, nor known *any thing*: this hath more rest than the other.

6　Yea, though he live a thousand years twice ^T*told*, yet hath he seen no good: do not all go to one ^Rplace?　*over · 2:14, 15*

7　^RAll the labour of man *is* for his mouth, and yet ^Tthe appetite is not filled.　Prov. 16:26 · Lit. *the soul*

8　For what hath the wise more than the fool? what hath the poor, that knoweth ^Tto walk before the living?　*how to walk*

9　Better *is* the ^Rsight of the eyes than the wandering of the desire: this *is* also vanity and vexation of spirit.　11:9

10　That which hath been is named ^Ralready, and it is known that it *is* man: ^Rneither may he contend with him that is mightier than he.　1:9; 3:15 · Is. 45:9; Jer. 49:19

11　Seeing there be many things that increase vanity, what *is* man the better?

12　For who knoweth what *is* good for man in *this* life, all the days of his vain life which he spendeth as ^Ra shadow? for who can tell a man what shall be after him under the sun?　James 4:14

7　A ^Rgood name *is* better than precious ointment; and the day of death than the day of one's ^Rbirth.　Prov. 15:30; 22:1 · 4:2

2　*It is* better to go to the house of mourning, than to go to the house of feasting: for that *is* the end of all men; and the living will lay *it* to his ^Rheart.　[Ps. 90:12]

3　Sorrow *is* better than laughter: ^Rfor by the sadness of the countenance the heart is made ^Tbetter.　[2 Cor. 7:10] · Lit. *well* or *good*

4　The heart of the wise *is* in the house of mourning; but the heart of fools *is* in the house of mirth.

5　^R*It is* better to hear the rebuke of the wise, than for a man to hear the song of fools.　Ps. 141:5

6　^RFor as the ^Tcrackling of thorns under a pot, so *is* the laughter of the fool: this also *is* vanity.　2:2 · Lit. *sound*

7　Surely oppression maketh a wise man mad; ^Rand a gift destroyeth the heart.　Ex. 23:8

8　Better *is* the end of a thing than the beginning thereof: *and* ^Rthe patient in spirit *is* better than the proud in spirit.　Gal. 5:22; Eph. 4:2

9　^RBe not hasty in thy spirit to be angry: for anger resteth in the bosom of fools.　Prov. 14:17; James 1:19

10　Say not thou, What is *the cause* that the former days were better than these? for thou dost not enquire wisely concerning this.

11　Wisdom *is* good with an inheritance: and by *it there is* profit ^Rto them that see the sun.　11:7

12　For wisdom *is* a ^Rdefence, *and* money *is* a defence: but the ^Texcellency of knowledge *is*, *that* wisdom giveth ^Rlife to them that have it.　9:18 · *advantage* · Prov. 3:18

13　Consider the work of God: for who can make *that* straight, which he hath made crooked?

14　^RIn the day of prosperity be joyful, but in the day of adversity consider: God also hath set the one over against the other, to the end that man should find nothing after him.　Deut. 28:47

15　All *things* have I seen in the days of my vanity: ^Rthere is a just *man* that perisheth in his righteousness, and there is a wicked *man* that prolongeth *his life* in his wickedness.　8:12–14

16　^RBe not righteous over much; ^Rneither make thyself over wise: why shouldest thou destroy thyself?　Prov. 25:16; Phil. 3:6 · Rom. 12:3

17　Be not ^Tover much wicked, neither be thou foolish: ^Rwhy shouldest thou die before thy time?　*overly* · Job 15:32; Ps. 55:23

18　*It is* good that thou shouldest take hold of this; yea, also from this withdraw not thine hand: for he that ^Rfeareth God shall come forth of them all.   3:14; 5:7; 8:12, 13

19 ^RWisdom strengtheneth the wise more than ten mighty *men* which are in the city.   Prov. 21:22

20 ^RFor *there is* not a just man upon earth, that doeth good, and sinneth not.   Rom. 3:23; 1 John 1:8

21 Also take no heed unto all words that are spoken; lest thou hear thy servant curse thee:

22 For oftentimes also thine own heart knoweth that thou thyself likewise hast cursed others.

23 All this have I ^Tproved by wisdom: ^RI said, I will be wise; but it *was* far from me. tested · Rom. 1:22

24 ^RThat which is far off, and ^Rexceeding deep, who can find it out?   Job 28:12; 1 Tim. 6:16 · Rom. 11:33

25 ^RI applied mine heart to know, and to search, and to seek out wisdom, and the reason *of things,* and to know the wickedness of folly, even of foolishness *and* madness: 1:17

26 And I find more bitter than death the woman, whose heart *is* snares and nets, *and* her hands *as* bands: whoso pleaseth God shall escape from her; but the sinner shall be taken by her.

27 Behold, this have I found, saith the preacher, *counting* one by one, to find out the account:

28 Which yet my soul seeketh, but I find not: ^Rone^T man among a thousand have I found; but a woman among all those have I not found.   Job 33:23 · one wise man

29 Lo, this only have I found, that God hath made man upright; but ^Rthey have sought out many ^Tinventions.   Gen. 3:6, 7 · schemes

8 Who *is* as the wise *man*? and who knoweth the interpretation of a thing? ^Ra man's wisdom maketh his face to shine, and the boldness of his face shall be changed.   Prov. 4:8, 9; Acts 6:15

2 I *counsel thee* to keep the king's commandment, and *that* in regard of the oath of God.

3 ^RBe not hasty to go out of his ^Tsight: stand not in an evil thing;

for he doeth whatsoever pleaseth him.   10:4 · presence

4 Where the word of a king *is, there is* power: and who may say unto him, What doest thou?

5 Whoso keepeth the commandment shall feel no evil thing: and a wise man's heart discerneth both time and judgment.

6 Because ^Rto every purpose there is time and judgment, therefore the misery of man *is* great upon him.   3:1, 17

7 ^RFor he knoweth not that which shall be: for who can tell him when it shall be?   Prov. 24:22

8 ^R*There is* no man that hath power over the spirit to retain the spirit; neither *hath he* power in the day of death: and *there is* no discharge in *that* war; neither shall wickedness deliver those that are given to it.   Ps. 49:6, 7

9 All this have I seen, and applied my heart unto every work that is done under the sun: *there is* a time wherein one man ruleth over another to his own hurt.

10 And so I saw the wicked buried, who had come and gone from the place of ^Tthe holy, and they were ^Rforgotten in the city where they had so done: this *is* also vanity.   holiness · 2:16; 9:5

11 Because sentence against an evil work is not executed speedily, therefore the heart of the sons of men is fully set in them to do evil.

12 Though a sinner do evil an hundred times, and his *days* be prolonged, yet surely I know that it shall be well with them that fear God, which fear before him:

13 But it shall not be well with the wicked, neither shall he prolong *his* days, *which are* as a shadow; because he feareth not before God.

14 There is a vanity which is done upon the earth; that there be just *men,* unto whom it ^Rhappeneth according to the work of the wicked; again, there be wicked *men,* to whom it happeneth according to the work of the

Rrighteous: I said that this also *is* vanity. Ps. 73:14 · 2:14; 7:15; 9:1–3

15 Then I commended mirth, because a man hath no better thing under the sun, than to eat, and to drink, and to be merry: for that shall abide with him of his labour the days of his life, which God giveth him under the sun.

16 When I applied mine heart to know wisdom, and to see the business that is done upon the earth: (for also *there is that* neither day nor night seeth sleep with his eyes:)

17 Then I beheld all the work of God, that Ra man cannot find out the work that is done under the sun: because though a man labour to seek *it* out, yet he shall not find *it*; yea further; though a wise *man* think to know *it*, yet shall he not be able to find *it*.   Job 5:9; Ps. 73:16

9 For all this I considered in my heart even to declare all this, Rthat the righteous, and the wise, and their works, *are* in the hand of God: no man knoweth either love or hatred *by* all *that is* before them.   8:14; Deut. 33:3; Job 12:10

2 RAll *things come* alike to all: *there is* one event to the righteous, and to the wicked; to the good and to the clean, and to the unclean; to him that sacrificeth, and to him that sacrificeth not: as *is* the good, so *is* the sinner; *and* he that sweareth, as *he* that feareth an oath.   Ps. 73:3, 12, 13; Mal. 3:15

3 This *is* an evil among all *things* that are done under the sun, that *there is* one event unto all: yea, also the heart of the sons of men is full of evil, and madness *is* in their heart while they live, and after that *they* go to the dead.

4 For to him that is joined to all the living there is hope: for a living dog is better than a dead lion.

5 For the living know that they shall die: but Rthe dead know not any thing, neither have they any more a reward; for the memory of them is forgotten.   Job 14:21; Is. 63:16

6 Also their love, and their hatred, and their envy, is now per-

ished; neither have they any more a portion for ever in any *thing* that is done under the sun.

7 Go thy way, Reat thy bread with joy, and drink thy wine with a merry heart; for God now accepteth thy works.   8:15

8 Let thy garments be always white; and let thy head lack no Tointment.   *oil*

9 Live joyfully with the wife whom thou lovest all the days of Tthe life of thy vanity, which he hath given thee under the sun, all the days of thy vanity: Rfor that *is* thy portion in *this* life, and in thy labour which thou takest under the sun.   *thy empty life* · 2:10

10 RWhatsoever thy hand findeth to do, do *it* with thy might; for *there is* no work, nor device, nor knowledge, nor wisdom, in the grave, whither thou goest.[Col. 3:17]

11 I returned, Rand saw under the sun, that the race *is* not to the swift, nor the battle to the strong, neither yet bread to the wise, nor yet riches to men of understanding, nor yet favour to men of skill; but time and Rchance happeneth to them all.   Amos 2:14, 15 · 1 Sam. 6:9

12 For Rman also knoweth not his time: as the fishes that are taken in an evil net, and as the birds that are caught in the snare; so *are* the sons of men Rsnared in an evil time, when it falleth suddenly upon them.   8:7 · 1 Thess. 5:3

13 This wisdom have I seen also under the sun, and it *seemed* great unto me:

14 RThere *was* a little city, and few men within it; and there came a great king against it, and besieged it, and built great bulwarks against it: 2 Sam. 20:16–22

15 Now there was found in it a poor wise man, and he by his wisdom delivered the city; yet no man remembered that same poor man.

16 Then said I, Wisdom *is* better than Rstrength: nevertheless the poor man's wisdom *is* despised, and his words are not heard.   7:12

17 The words of wise *men are*

heard in quiet more than the cry of him that ruleth among fools.

18 Wisdom *is* better than weapons of war: but [R]one sinner destroyeth much good.   2 Kin. 21:2–17

10 Dead flies cause the ointment of the [T]apothecary to send forth a [T]stinking savour: *so doth* a little folly him that is in reputation for wisdom *and* honour.   *perfumer · foul odour*

2 A wise man's heart *is* at his right hand; but a fool's heart at his left.

3 Yea also, when he that is a fool walketh by the way, his wisdom faileth *him,* and he [T]saith to every one *that* he *is* a fool.   *shows*

4 If the spirit of the ruler rise up against thee, [R]leave not thy [T]place; for [R]yielding pacifieth great offences.   8:3 · *post* · Prov. 25:15

5 There is an evil *which* I have seen under the sun, as an error *which* proceedeth from the ruler:

6 Folly is set in great dignity, and the rich sit in low place.

7 I have seen servants upon horses, and princes walking as servants upon the [T]earth.   *ground*

8 He that diggeth a pit shall fall into it; and whoso breaketh an hedge, a serpent shall bite him.

9 Whoso [T]removeth stones shall be hurt therewith; *and* he that [T]cleaveth wood shall be endangered thereby.   *quarries · splits*

10 If the iron be blunt, and he do not whet the edge, then must he put to more strength: but wisdom *is* profitable to direct.

11 Surely the serpent will bite [R]without enchantment; and a babbler is no better.   Ps. 58:4, 5; Jer. 8:17

12 The words of a wise man's mouth *are* gracious; but the lips of a fool will swallow up himself.

13 The beginning of the words of his mouth *is* foolishness: and the end of his talk *is* [T]mischievous madness.   *wicked*

14 [R]A fool also is full of words: a man cannot tell what shall be; and [R]what shall be after him, who can tell him?   5:3; [Prov. 15:2] · 3:22; 8:7

15 The labour of the foolish wea-

rieth every one of them, because he knoweth not how to go to the city.

16 [R]Woe to thee, O land, when thy king *is* a child, and thy princes eat in the morning!   Is. 3:4, 5; 5:11

17 Blessed *art* thou, O land, when thy king *is* the son of nobles, and thy [R]princes eat in due season, for strength, and not for drunkenness!   Prov. 31:4; Is. 5:11

18 By much slothfulness the building decayeth; and [R]through idleness of the hands the house droppeth through.   Prov. 24:30–34

19 A feast is made for laughter, and [R]wine maketh merry: but money answereth all *things.*   2:3

20 [R]Curse not the king, no not in thy thought; and curse not the rich in thy bedchamber: for a bird of the air shall carry the voice, and that which hath wings shall tell the matter.   Ex. 22:28; Acts 23:5

11 Cast thy bread [R]upon the waters: [R]for thou shalt find it after many days.   Is. 32:20 · [Heb. 6:10]

2 [R]Give a portion [R]to seven, and also to eight; [R]for thou knowest not what evil shall be upon the earth.   Ps. 112:9 · Mic. 5:5 · Eph. 5:16

3 If the clouds be full of rain, they empty *themselves* upon the earth: and if the tree fall toward the south, or toward the north, in the place where the tree falleth, there it shall be.

4 He that observeth the wind shall not sow; and he that regardeth the clouds shall not reap.

5 As [R]thou knowest not what *is* the way of the [T]spirit, *nor* how the bones *do grow* in the womb of her that is with child: even so thou knowest not the works of God who maketh all.   John 3:8 · *wind*

6 In the morning sow thy seed, and in the evening withhold not thine hand: for thou knowest not [T]whether shall prosper, either this or that, or whether they both *shall* be alike good.   *which will succeed*

7 Truly the light *is* sweet, and a pleasant *thing it is* for the eyes [R]to behold the sun: 7:11

8 But if a man live many years, *and* [R]rejoice in them all; yet let

him ᴿremember the days of darkness; for they shall be many. All that cometh *is* vanity.   9:7 · 12:1

9 Rejoice, O young man, in thy youth; and let thy heart cheer thee in the days of thy youth, ᴿand walk in the ways of thine heart, and in the sight of thine eyes: but know thou, that for all these things ᴿGod will bring thee into judgment.   Num. 15:39 · 3:17; 12:14

10 Therefore remove sorrow from thy heart, and ᴿput away evil from thy flesh: for childhood and youth *are* vanity. 2 Cor. 7:1; 2 Tim. 2:22

12 Rememberᴿ now thy Creator in the days of thy youth, while the evil days come not, nor the years draw nigh, ᴿwhen thou shalt say, I have no pleasure in them; Prov. 22:6; Lam. 3:27 · 2 Sam. 19:35

2 While the sun, or the light, or the moon, or the stars, be not darkened, nor the clouds return after the rain:

3 In the day when the keepers of the house shall tremble, and the strong men shall ᵀbow themselves, and the grinders cease because they are few, and those that look out of the windows be darkened,   stoop, lit. bend

4 And the doors shall be shut in the streets, when the sound of the grinding is low, and he shall rise up at the voice of the bird, and all ᴿthe daughters of musick shall be brought low;   2 Sam. 19:35

5 Also *when* they shall be afraid of *that which is* high, and fears *shall be* in the way, and the almond tree shall flourish, and

the grasshopper shall be a burden, and desire shall fail: because man goeth to ᴿhis ᵀlong home, and ᴿthe mourners go about the streets: Job 17:13 · eternal · Jer. 9:17

6 Or ever the silver cord be loosed, or the golden bowl be broken, or the pitcher be ᵀbroken at the fountain, or the wheel broken at the cistern.   shattered

7 ᴿThen shall the dust return to the earth as it was: ᴿand the spirit shall return unto God ᴿwho gave it. Job 34:15; Ps. 90:3 · 3:21 · Zech. 12:1

8 ᴿVanity of vanities, saith the preacher; all *is* vanity.   Ps. 62:9

9 And moreover, because the preacher was wise, he still taught the people knowledge; yea, he gave good heed, and sought out, *and* set in order many proverbs.

10 The preacher sought to find out ᵀacceptable words: and *that which was* written *was* upright, *even* words of truth.   Lit. delightful

11 The words of the wise *are* as goads, and as nails fastened *by* the masters of assemblies, *which* are given from one shepherd.

12 And further, by these, my son, be admonished: of making many books *there is* no end; and ᴿmuch study *is* a weariness of the flesh.   1:18

13 Let us hear the conclusion of the whole matter: ᴿFear God, and keep his commandments: for this *is* the whole *duty* of man.   Mic. 6:8

14 For ᴿGod shall bring every work into judgment, with every secret thing, whether *it be* good, or whether *it be* evil. 11:9; Matt. 12:36

The
SONG OF SOLOMON

THE Song of Solomon is a love song written by Solomon and abounding in metaphors and oriental imagery. Historically, it depicts the wooing and wedding of a shepherdess by King Solomon, and the joys and heartaches of wedded love.

Allegorically, it pictures Israel as God's betrothed bride (Hos. 2:19, 20), and the church as the bride of Christ. As human life finds its highest fulfillment in the love of man and woman, so spiritual life finds its highest fulfillment in the love of God for His people and Christ for His church.

The book reads like scenes in a drama with three main speakers: the bride (Shulamite), the king (Solomon), and a chorus (daughters of Jerusalem).

The Hebrew title *Shir Hashirim* comes from 1:1, "The song of songs." This is in the superlative and speaks of Solomon's most exquisite song. The Greek title *Asma Asmaton* and the Latin *Canticum Canticorum* also mean "Song of Songs" or "The Best Song." The name *Canticles* ("Songs") is derived from the Latin title. Because Solomon is mentioned in 1:1, the book is also known as the Song of Solomon.

THE ᴿsong of songs, which *is* Solomon's.   1 Kin. 4:32

2 Let him kiss me with the kisses of his mouth: ᴿfor thy love *is* better than wine.   4:10

3 Because of the ᵀsavour of thy good ointments thy name *is as* ointment poured forth, therefore do the virgins love thee.   *fragrance*

4 Draw me, we will run after thee: the king ᴿhath brought me into his chambers: we will be glad and rejoice in thee, we will remember thy love more than wine: the upright love thee.   Eph. 2:6

5 I *am* ᵀblack, but ᵀcomely, O ye daughters of Jerusalem, as the tents of Ke'-dar, as the curtains of Solomon.   *dark · lovely*

6 Look not upon me, because I *am* black, because the sun hath ᵀlooked upon me: my mother's children were angry with me; they made me the keeper of the vineyards; *but* mine own vineyard have I not kept.   *tanned me*

7 Tell me, O thou whom my soul loveth, where thou feedest, where thou makest *thy flock* to rest at noon: for why should I be as one that turneth aside by the flocks of thy companions?

8 If thou know not, ᴿO thou fairest among women, go thy way forth by the footsteps of the flock, and feed thy ᵀkids beside the shepherds' tents.   5:9 · *little goats*

9 I have compared thee, O my love, ᴿto a company of horses in Pharaoh's chariots.   2 Chr. 1:16

10 ᴿThy cheeks are comely with ᵀrows *of jewels,* thy neck with chains *of gold.* Ezek. 16:11 · *ornaments*

11 We will make thee borders of gold with studs of silver.

12 While the king *sitteth* at his table, my ᵀspikenard sendeth forth the smell thereof.   *perfume*

13 A bundle of myrrh *is* my wellbeloved unto me; he shall lie all night betwixt my breasts.

14 My beloved *is* unto me *as* a cluster of ᵀcamphire in the vineyards of En-ge'-di.   *henna* blooms

15 ᴿBehold, thou *art* fair, my love; behold, thou *art* fair; thou *hast* doves' eyes.   4:1; 5:12

16 Behold, thou *art* ᴿfair,ᵀ my beloved, yea, pleasant: also our bed *is* green.   5:10–16 · *handsome*

17 The beams of our house *are* cedar, *and* our rafters of fir.

2 I *am* the rose of Shar'-on, *and* the lily of the valleys.

2 As the lily among thorns, so *is* my love among the daughters.

3 As the apple tree among the trees of the wood, so *is* my beloved among the sons. I sat down under his ᵀshadow with great delight, and ᴿhis fruit *was* sweet to my taste.   *shade · 4:16; Rev. 22:1, 2*

4 He brought me to the ᵀbanqueting house, and his banner over me *was* love.   Lit. *house of wine*

5 ᵀStay me with ᵀflagons, comfort me with apples: for I *am* ᵀsick of love.   *Sustain · raisin cakes · lovesick*

6 ᴿHis left hand *is* under my head, and his right hand doth embrace me.   8:3

7 ᴿI charge you, O ye daughters

of Jerusalem, by the ^Troes, and by the ^Thinds of the field, that ye stir not up, nor awake *my* love, till he please.   3:5; 8:4 · *gazelles · does*

8 The voice of my beloved! behold, he cometh leaping upon the mountains, skipping upon the hills.

9 My beloved is like a ^Troe or a young ^Thart: behold, he standeth behind our wall, he looketh forth at the windows, shewing himself through the lattice.   *gazelle · stag*

10 My beloved spake, and said unto me, Rise up, my love, my fair one, and come away.

11 For, lo, the winter is past, the rain is over *and* gone;

12 The flowers appear on the earth; the time of the singing *of birds* is come, and the voice of the turtle is heard in our land;

13 The fig tree putteth forth her green figs, and the vines *with* the tender grape give a *good* smell. Arise, my love, my fair one, and come away.

14 O my dove, *that art* in the clefts of the rock, in the secret *places* of the ^Tstairs, let me see thy countenance, let me hear thy voice; for sweet *is* thy voice, and thy countenance *is* comely.   *cliff*

15 ^TTake us the foxes, the little foxes, that spoil the vines: for our vines *have* tender grapes.   *Catch*

16 ^RMy beloved *is* mine, and I *am* his: he ^Tfeedeth among the lilies.   6:3 · *feedeth* his flock

17 ^RUntil the day break, and the shadows flee away, turn, my beloved, and be thou ^Rlike a roe or a young hart upon the mountains of ^TBe'-ther.   4:6 · 8:14 · Lit. *Separation*

3 By night on my bed I sought him whom my soul loveth: I sought him, but I found him not.

2 I will rise now, and go about the city in the streets, and in the ^Tbroad ways I will seek him whom my soul loveth: I sought him, but I found him not.   *squares*

3 ^RThe watchmen that go about the city found me: *to whom I said,* Saw ye him whom my soul loveth?   5:7; Is. 21:6–8, 11, 12

4 *It was* but a little that I passed from them, but I found him whom my soul loveth: I held him, and would not let him go, until I had brought him into my ^Rmother's house, and into the ^Tchamber of her that conceived me.   8:2 · *room*

5 ^RI charge you, O ye daughters of Jerusalem, by the ^Troes, and by the ^Thinds of the field, that ye stir not up, nor awake *my* love, till he please.   2:7; 8:4 · *gazelles · does*

6 ^RWho *is* this that cometh out of the wilderness like pillars of smoke, perfumed with myrrh and frankincense, with all powders of the merchant?   8:5

7 Behold ^This bed, which *is* Solomon's; threescore valiant men *are* about it, of the valiant of Israel.   *it is Solomon's couch* or *litter*

8 They all hold swords, *being* expert in war: every man *hath* his sword upon his thigh because of fear in the night.

9 King Solomon made himself a chariot of the wood of Leb'-a-non.

10 He made the pillars thereof *of* silver, the ^Tbottom thereof *of* gold, the ^Tcovering of it *of* purple, the ^Tmidst thereof being paved *with* love, ^Tfor the daughters of Jerusalem.   *support · seat · interior · by*

11 Go forth, O ye daughters of Zion, and behold king Solomon with the crown wherewith his mother crowned him in the day of his ^Tespousals, and in the day of the gladness of his heart.   *wedding*

4 Behold, ^Rthou *art* fair, my love; behold, thou *art* fair; thou *hast* doves' eyes within thy locks: thy hair *is* as a flock of goats, that appear from mount Gil'-e-ad.   1:15

2 Thy teeth *are* like a flock *of sheep that are even* shorn, which came up from the washing; whereof every one bear twins, and none *is* barren among them.

3 Thy lips *are* like a thread of scarlet, and thy speech *is* comely: thy temples *are* like a piece of a pomegranate within thy locks.

4 ^RThy neck *is* like the tower of David builded ^Rfor an armoury, whereon there hang a thousand

ᵀbucklers, all shields of mighty men.   7:4 · Neh. 3:19 · *shields*

5 ᴿThy two breasts *are* like two ᵀyoung roes that are twins, which feed among the lilies.   7:3 · *fawns*

6 ᴿUntil the day break, and the shadows flee away, I will get me to the mountain of myrrh, and to the hill of frankincense.   2:17

7 ᴿThou *art* all fair, my love; *there is* no spot in thee.   Eph. 5:27

8 Come with me from Leb'-a-non, *my* spouse, with me from Leb'-a-non: look from the top of Am'-a-na, from the top of She'-nir ᴿand Hermon, from the lions' dens, from the mountains of the leopards. Deut. 3:9; 1 Chr. 5:23; Ezek. 27:5

9 Thou hast ᵀravished my heart, my sister, *my* spouse; thou hast ravished my heart with ᵀone of thine eyes, with one chain of thy neck.   *encouraged · one look*

10 How fair is thy love, my sister, *my* spouse! ᴿhow much better is thy love than wine! and the ᵀsmell of thine ᵀointments than all spices!   1:2, 4 · *fragrance · perfumes*

11 Thy lips, O *my* spouse, drop *as* the honeycomb: honey and milk *are* under thy tongue; and the smell of thy garments *is* ᴿlike the smell of Leb'-a-non.   Gen. 27:27

12 A garden ᵀinclosed *is* my sister, *my* spouse; a spring shut up, a fountain sealed.   *locked up*

13 Thy plants *are* an orchard of pomegranates, with pleasant fruits; camphire, with spikenard,

14 Spikenard and saffron; calamus and cinnamon, with all trees of frankincense; myrrh and aloes, with all the chief spices:

15 A fountain of gardens, a well of ᴿliving waters, and streams from Leb'-a-non. Zech. 14:8; John 4:10

16 Awake, O north wind; and come, thou south; blow upon my garden, *that* the spices thereof may flow out. ᴿLet my beloved come into his garden, and eat his pleasant ᴿfruits.   5:1 · 7:13

5 I am come into my garden, my sister, *my* spouse: I have gathered my myrrh with my spice; I have eaten my honeycomb

with my honey; I have drunk my wine with my milk: eat, O ᴿfriends; drink, yea, drink abundantly, O beloved.   Luke 15:7, 10

2 I sleep, but my heart waketh: *it is* the voice of my beloved that knocketh, *saying*, Open to me, my sister, my love, my dove, my ᵀundefiled: for my head is filled with dew, *and* my ᵀlocks with the drops of the night.   *perfect one · hair*

3 I have put off my coat; how shall I put it on? I have washed my feet; how shall I ᵀdefile them? *dirty*

4 My beloved put in his hand by the hole *of the door*, and my bowels were moved for him.

5 I rose up to open to my beloved; and my hands ᵀdropped *with* myrrh, and my fingers *with* sweet smelling myrrh, upon the handles of the lock.   *dripped*

6 I opened to my beloved; but my beloved had withdrawn himself, *and* was gone: my soul failed when he spake: ᴿI sought him, but I could not find him; I called him, but he gave me no answer.   3:1

7 ᴿThe watchmen that went about the city found me, they ᵀsmote me, they wounded me; the keepers of the walls took away my veil from me.   3:3 · *struck*

8 I charge you, O daughters of Jerusalem, if ye find my beloved, that ye tell him, that I *am* ᵀsick of love.   *lovesick*

9 What *is* thy beloved more than *another* beloved, ᴿO thou fairest among women? what *is* thy beloved more than *another* beloved, that thou dost so ᵀcharge us?   1:8; 6:1 · *adjure*

10 My beloved *is* white and ruddy, the ᵀchiefest among ten thousand.   *distinguished*

11 His head *is as* the most fine gold, his locks *are* ᵀbushy, *and* black as a raven.   *wavy*

12 His eyes *are* as *the eyes* of doves by the rivers of waters, washed with milk, *and* fitly set.

13 His cheeks *are* as a bed of spices, *as* sweet flowers: his lips *like* lilies, ᵀdropping sweet smelling myrrh.   *dripping liquid myrrh*

14 His hands *are as* gold ᵀrings set with the beryl: his ᵀbelly *is as* bright ivory overlaid *with* sapphires.

rods · body

15 His legs *are as* pillars of marble, set upon ᵀsockets of fine gold: his countenance *is* as Leb'-a-non, excellent as the cedars.

bases

16 His mouth *is* most sweet: yea, he *is* altogether lovely. This *is* my beloved, and this *is* my friend, O daughters of Jerusalem.

6 Whither is thy beloved gone, ᴿO thou fairest among women? whither is thy beloved turned aside? that we may seek him with thee.

1:8; 5:9

2 My beloved is gone down into his ᴿgarden, to the beds of spices, to feed in the gardens, and to gather lilies.

4:16; 5:1

3 ᴿI *am* my beloved's, and my beloved *is* mine: he feedeth among the lilies.

2:16; 7:10

4 Thou *art* beautiful, O my love, as Tir'-zah, ᵀcomely as Jerusalem, ᵀterrible as *an army* with banners.

lovely · awesome

5 Turn away thine eyes from me, for they have overcome me: thy hair *is* ᴿas a flock of goats that appear from Gil'-e-ad.

4:1

6 ᴿThy teeth *are* as a flock of sheep which go up from the washing, whereof every one beareth twins, and *there is* not one ᵀbarren among them.

4:2 · *bereaved*

7 As a piece of a pomegranate *are* thy temples within thy locks.

8 There are threescore queens, and fourscore concubines, and ᴿvirgins without number.

1:3

9 My dove, my ᴿundefiledᵀ is *but* one; she *is* the *only* one of her mother, she *is* the choice *one* of her that bare her. The daughters saw her, and blessed her; *yea*, the queens and the concubines, and they praised her.

2:14; 5:2 · *perfect one*

10 Who *is* she *that* looketh forth as the morning, fair as the moon, clear as the sun, *and* ᵀterrible as *an army* with banners?

awesome

11 I went down into the garden of nuts to see the fruits of the val-ley, *and* ᴿto see whether the vine flourished, *and* the pomegranates budded.

7:12

12 Or ever I was aware, my soul made me *like* the chariots of ᵀAmmi'-na-dib.

Lit. *My Noble People*

13 Return, return, O Shu'-lam-ite; return, return, that we may look upon thee. What will ye see in the Shu'-lam-ite? As it were the company of two armies.

7 How beautiful are thy feet ᵀwith shoes, O prince's daughter! the joints of thy thighs *are* like jewels, the work of the hands of a cunning workman.

in sandals

2 Thy navel *is like* a round goblet, *which* ᵀwanteth not liquor: thy belly *is like* an heap of wheat set about with lilies.

lacks no mixed wine

3 ᴿThy two breasts *are* like two young roes *that are* twins.

4:5

4 ᴿThy neck *is* as a tower of ivory; thine eyes *like* the ᵀfishpools in Hesh'-bon, by the gate of Bath-rab'-bim: thy nose *is* as the tower of Leb'-a-non which looketh toward Damascus.

4:4 · *pools*

5 Thine head upon thee *is* like Carmel, and the hair of thine head like purple; the king *is* held in the galleries.

6 How fair and how pleasant art thou, O love, for delights!

7 This thy stature is like to a palm tree, and thy breasts to clusters *of grapes*.

8 I said, I will go up to the palm tree, I will take hold of the boughs thereof: now also thy breasts shall be as clusters of the vine, and the smell of thy nose like apples;

9 And the roof of thy mouth like the best wine for my beloved, that goeth *down* ᵀsweetly, causing the lips of those that are asleep to speak.

smoothly

10 ᴿI *am* my beloved's, and ᴿhis desire *is* toward me.

6:3 · Ps. 45:11

11 Come, my beloved, let us go forth into the field; let us lodge in the villages.

12 Let us get up early to the vineyards; let us ᴿsee if the vine ᵀflourish, *whether* the tender grape appear, *and* the pomegran-

ates bud forth: there will I give thee my loves.   6:11 · *has budded*

13 The mandrakes give a ^Tsmell, and at our gates ^R*are* all manner of pleasant *fruits*, new and old, *which* I have laid up for thee, O my beloved.   *fragrance* · Matt. 13:52

8 O that thou *wert* as my brother, that sucked the breasts of my mother! *when* I should find thee without, I would kiss thee; yea, I should not be despised.

2 I would lead thee, *and* bring thee into my mother's ^Rhouse, *who* would instruct me: I would cause thee to drink of ^Rspiced wine of the juice of my pomegranate.   3:4 · Prov. 9:2

3 ^RHis left hand *should be* under my head, and his right hand should embrace me.   2:6

4 I charge you, O daughters of Jerusalem, that ye stir not up, nor awake *my* love, until he please.

5 ^RWho *is* this that cometh up from the wilderness, leaning upon her beloved? I ^Traised thee up under the apple tree: there thy mother brought thee forth: there she brought thee forth *that* bare thee.   3:6 · *awakened*

6 ^RSet me as a seal upon thine heart, as a seal upon thine arm: for love *is* strong as death; ^Rjealousy *is* cruel as the grave: the

coals thereof *are* coals of fire, *which hath* a most vehement flame.   Is. 49:16; Hag. 2:23 · Prov. 6:34, 35

7 Many waters cannot quench love, neither can the floods drown it: if a man would give all the substance of his house for love, it would utterly be contemned.

8 ^RWe have a little sister, and she hath no breasts: what shall we do for our sister in the day when she shall be spoken for? Ezek. 23:33

9 If she *be* a wall, we will build upon her a ^Tpalace of silver: and if she *be* a door, we will inclose her with boards of cedar.   *battlement*

10 I *am* a wall, and my breasts like towers: then was I in his eyes as one that found ^Tfavour. Lit. *peace*

11 Solomon had a vineyard at Ba'-al–ha'-mon; he let out the vineyard unto keepers; every one for the fruit thereof was to bring a thousand *pieces* of silver.

12 My vineyard, which *is* mine, *is* before me: thou, O Solomon, *must have* a thousand, and those that keep the fruit thereof two hundred.

13 Thou that dwellest in the gardens, the companions hearken to thy voice: cause me to hear *it*.

14 ^RMake haste, my beloved, and ^Rbe thou like to a roe or to a young hart upon the mountains of spices.   Rev. 22:17, 20 · 2:7, 9, 17

The Book of

ISAIAH

ISAIAH is like a miniature Bible. The first thirty-nine chapters (like the thirty-nine books of the Old Testament) are filled with judgment upon immoral and idolatrous men. Judah has sinned; the surrounding nations have sinned; the whole earth has sinned. Judgment must come, for God cannot allow such blatant sin to go unpunished forever. But the final twenty-seven chapters (like the twenty-seven books of the New Testament) declare a message of hope. The Messiah is coming as a Savior and a Sovereign to bear a cross and to wear a crown.

Isaiah's prophetic ministry, spanning the reigns of four kings of Judah, covers at least forty years.

Yesha 'yahu and its shortened form *Yeshaiah* mean "Yahweh Is Salvation." This name is an excellent summary of the contents of the book. The Greek form in the Septuagint is *Hesaias*, and the Latin form is *Esaias* or *Isaias*.

THE ^Rvision of Isaiah the son of Amoz, which he saw concerning Judah and Jerusalem in the ^Rdays of Uz-zi'-ah, Jo'-tham, Ahaz, *and* Hez-e-ki'-ah, kings of Judah. Num. 12:6 · 2 Chr. 26—32

2 ^RHear, O heavens, and give ear, O earth: for the LORD hath spoken, I have nourished and brought up children, and they have rebelled against me. Jer. 2:12

3 ^RThe ox knoweth his owner, and the ass his master's crib: *but* Israel ^Rdoth not know, my people doth not consider. Jer. 8:7 · Jer. 9:3, 6

4 Ah sinful nation, a people laden with iniquity, a seed of evildoers, children that are corrupters: they have forsaken the LORD, they have provoked the Holy One of Israel unto anger, they are gone away backward.

5 ^RWhy should ye be stricken any more? ye will revolt more and more: the whole head is sick, and the whole heart faint. Jer. 5:3

6 From the sole of the foot even unto the head *there is* no soundness in it; *but* wounds, and bruises, and putrifying sores: they have not been closed, neither bound up, neither ^Tmollified with ointment. *soothed*

7 Your country *is* desolate, your cities *are* burned with fire: your land, strangers devour it in your presence, and *it is* desolate, as overthrown by strangers.

8 And the daughter of Zion is left ^Ras a cottage in a vineyard, as a lodge in a garden of cucumbers, as a besieged city. Job 27:18

9 Except the LORD of hosts had left unto us a very small remnant, we should have been as ^RSodom, *and* we should have been like unto Go-mor'-rah. Gen. 19:24; Rom. 9:29

10 Hear the word of the LORD, ye rulers ^Rof Sodom; give ear unto the law of our God, ye people of Go-mor'-rah. Deut. 32:32

11 To what purpose *is* the multitude of your ^Rsacrifices unto me? saith the LORD: I am full of the burnt offerings of rams, and the fat of fed beasts; and I delight not in the blood of bullocks, or of lambs, or of he goats. [1 Sam. 15:22]

12 When ye come to appear before me, who hath required this at your hand, to tread my courts?

13 Bring no more vain oblations; incense is an abomination unto me; the new moons and sabbaths, the calling of assemblies, I cannot ^Taway with; *it is* iniquity, even the solemn meeting. *endure*

14 Your ^Rnew moons and your appointed feasts my soul hateth: they are a trouble unto me; I am weary to bear *them*. Num. 28:11

15 And when ye spread forth your hands, I will hide mine eyes from you: yea, when ye make many prayers, I will not hear: your hands are full of blood.

16 ^RWash you, make you clean; put away the evil of your doings from before mine eyes; ^Rcease to do evil; Jer. 4:14 · Rom. 12:9

17 Learn to do well; seek judgment, relieve the oppressed, judge the fatherless, plead for the widow.

18 Come now, and let us ^Rreason together, saith the LORD: though your sins be as scarlet, ^Rthey shall be as white as snow; though they be red like crimson, they shall be as wool. Mic. 6:2 · Ps. 51:7; Rev. 7:14

19 If ye be willing and obedient, ye shall eat the good of the land:

20 But if ye refuse and rebel, ye shall be devoured with the sword: ^Rfor the mouth of the LORD hath spoken *it*. 40:5; 58:14; Mic. 4:4; [Titus 1:2]

21 How is the faithful city become an harlot! it was full of ^Tjudgment; righteousness lodged in it; but now murderers. *justice*

22 ^RThy silver is become dross, thy wine mixed with water: Jer. 6:28

23 Thy princes *are* rebellious, and companions of thieves: every one loveth gifts, and followeth after rewards: they judge not the fatherless, neither doth the cause of the widow come unto them.

24 Therefore saith the Lord, the LORD of hosts, the mighty One of Israel, Ah, I will ^Tease me of mine adversaries, and avenge me of mine enemies: *be relieved of*

25 And I will turn my hand upon thee, and purely purge away thy dross, and take away all thy tin:

26 And I will restore thy judges ^Ras at the first, and thy counsellors as at the beginning: afterward ^Rthou shalt be called, The city of righteousness, the faithful city.   Jer. 33:7–11 · 33:5; Zech. 8:3

27 Zion shall be redeemed with ^Tjudgment, and her converts with righteousness.   *justice*

28 And the ^Rdestruction of the transgressors and of the sinners *shall be* together, and they that forsake the LORD shall be consumed.   [66:24]; Ps. 9:5; [2 Thess. 1:8, 9]

29 For they shall be ashamed of the oaks which ye have desired, and ye shall be confounded for the gardens that ye have chosen.

30 For ye shall be as an oak whose leaf fadeth, and as a garden that hath no water.

31 And the strong shall be as ^Ttow, and the maker of it as a spark, and they shall both burn together, and none shall ^Rquench *them.* *tinder* · 66:24; Matt. 3:12; Mark 9:43

2 The word that Isaiah the son of Amoz saw concerning Judah and Jerusalem.

☆ **2** And ^Rit shall come to pass in the last days, ^R*that* the mountain of the LORD's house shall be established in the top of the mountains, and shall be exalted above the hills; and all nations shall flow unto it.   Mic. 4:1 · Ps. 68:15

☆ **3** And many people shall go and say, ^RCome ye, and let us go up to the mountain of the LORD, to the house of the God of Jacob; and he will teach us of his ways, and we will walk in his paths: ^Rfor out of Zion shall go forth the law, and the word of the LORD from Jerusalem.   [Zech. 14:16–21] · Luke 24:47

4 And he shall judge among the nations, and shall rebuke many people: and they shall beat their swords into plowshares, and their spears into ^Tpruninghooks: nation shall not lift up sword against nation, neither shall they learn war any more.   *pruning knives*

5 O house of Jacob, come ye, and let us ^Rwalk in the light of the LORD.   Eph. 5:8

6 Therefore thou hast forsaken thy people the house of Jacob, because they be replenished from the east, and ^R*are* soothsayers like the Phi-lis'-tines, ^Rand they please themselves in the children of strangers.   Deut. 18:14 · Ps. 106:35

7 Their land also is full of silver and gold, neither *is there any* end of their treasures; their land is also full of horses, neither *is there any* end of their chariots:

8 ^RTheir land also is full of idols; they worship the work of their own hands, that which their own fingers have made: 40:19, 20

9 And the ^Tmean man boweth down, and ^Tthe great man humbleth himself: therefore forgive them not.   *people · each man*

10 ^REnter into the rock, and hide thee in the dust, for fear of the LORD, and for the glory of his majesty.   2:19, 21; Rev. 6:15, 16

11 The lofty looks of man shall be ^Rhumbled, and the haughtiness of men shall be bowed down, and the LORD alone shall be exalted ^Rin that day.   5:15; Prov. 16:5 · Hos. 2:16

12 For the day of the LORD of hosts *shall be* upon every *one that is* proud and lofty, and upon every *one that is* lifted up; and he shall be brought low:

13 And upon all ^Rthe cedars of Leb'-a-non, *that are* high and lifted up, and upon all the oaks of Ba'-shan,   14:8; Zech. 11:1, 2

14 And ^Rupon all the high mountains, and upon all the hills *that are* lifted up,   30:25

15 And upon every high tower, and upon every fenced wall,

16 ^RAnd upon all the ships of Tar'-shish, and upon all pleasant pictures.   23:1, 14; 60:9; 1 Kin. 10:22

17 And the ^Tloftiness of man shall be bowed down, and the haughtiness of men shall be made low: and the LORD alone shall be exalted in that day.   *pride*

18 And the idols ^The shall utterly abolish.   *vanish*

19 And they shall go into the ᴿholes of the rocks, and into the caves of the earth, for fear of the LORD, and for the glory of his majesty, when he ariseth to shake terribly the earth. Hos. 10:8; [Rev. 9:6]

20 In that day a man shall ᵀcast his idols of silver, and his idols of gold, which they made *each one* for himself to worship, to the moles and to the bats; *cast away*

21 To go into the clefts of the rocks, and into the tops of the ragged rocks, ᵀfor fear of the LORD, and for the glory of his majesty, when he ariseth to shake terribly the earth. *from the terror*

22 Cease ye from man, whose breath *is* in his nostrils: for wherein is he to be accounted of?

3 For, behold, the Lord, the LORD of hosts, doth take away from Jerusalem and from Judah the ᵀstay and the staff, the whole ᵀstay of bread, and the whole stay of water, *stock and the store · supply*

2 ᴿThe mighty man, and the man of war, the judge, and the prophet, and the ᵀprudent, and the ancient, 9:14, 15; Ezek. 17:12, 13 · *diviner*

3 The captain of fifty, and the honourable man, and the counsellor, and the ᵀcunning artificer, and the eloquent orator. *skilful artisan*

4 And I will give children *to be* their princes, and ᵀbabes shall rule over them. *or capricious ones*

5 And the people shall be oppressed, every one by another, and every one by his neighbour: the child shall behave himself proudly against the ancient, and the base against the honourable.

6 When a man shall take hold of his brother of the house of his father, *saying*, Thou hast clothing, be thou our ruler, and *let* this ruin *be* under thy hand:

7 In that day shall he ᵀswear, saying, I will not be an healer; for in my house *is* neither bread nor clothing: make me not a ruler of the people. *protest*

8 For ᴿJerusalem is ruined, and Judah is fallen: because their tongue and their doings *are* against the LORD, to provoke the eyes of his glory. 2 Chr. 36:16, 17

9 The shew of their countenance doth witness against them; and they declare their sin as Sodom, they hide *it* not. Woe unto their soul! for they have rewarded evil unto themselves.

10 Say ye to the righteous, that *it shall be* well *with him*: for they shall eat the fruit of their doings.

11 Woe unto the wicked! ᴿ*it shall be* ill *with him*: for the reward of his hands shall be ᵀgiven him. [Ps. 11:6; Eccl. 8:12, 13] · *done to him*

12 *As for* my people, children *are* their oppressors, and women rule over them. O my people, ᴿthey which lead thee ᵀcause *thee* to err, and destroy the way of thy paths. 9:16 · *lead thee astray*

13 The LORD standeth up ᴿto ᵀplead, and standeth to judge the people. 66:16; Hos. 4:1; Mic. 6:2 · *contend*

14 The LORD will enter into judgment with the ᵀancients of his people, and the princes thereof: for ye have eaten up ᴿthe vineyard; the spoil of the poor *is* in your houses. *elders* · Matt. 21:33

15 What mean ye *that* ye ᴿbeat my people to pieces, and grind the faces of the poor? saith the Lord GOD of hosts. Mic. 3:2, 3

16 Moreover the LORD saith, Because the daughters of Zion are ᵀhaughty, and walk with stretched forth necks and ᵀwanton eyes, walking and mincing *as* they go, and making a tinkling with their feet: *proud · seductive*

17 Therefore the LORD will smite with ᴿa scab the crown of the head of the daughters of Zion, and the LORD will ᴿdiscover their secret parts. Deut. 28:27 · Jer. 13:22

18 In that day the Lord will take away the ᵀbravery of *their* tinkling ornaments *about their feet*, and *their* cauls, and *their* round tires like the moon, *finery*

19 The chains, and the bracelets, and the ᵀmufflers, *veils*

20 The bonnets, and the ornaments of the legs, and the head-

bands, and the ᵀtablets, and the earrings,   *perfume boxes*

21 The rings, and nose jewels,

22 The changeable suits of apparel, and the mantles, and the wimples, and the crisping pins,

23 The ᵀglasses, and the fine linen, and the ᵀhoods, and the ᵀvails.   *mirrors · turbans · robes*

24 And it shall come to pass, *that* instead of sweet smell there shall be stink; and instead of a ᵀgirdle a rent; and instead of well set hair ᴿbaldness; and instead of a ᵀstomacher a girding of sackcloth; *and* burning instead of beauty.   *sash · Ezek. 27:31 · rich robe*

25 Thy men shall fall by the sword, and thy mighty in the war.

26 And her gates shall lament and mourn; and she *being* desolate shall sit upon the ground.

4 And ᴿin that day seven women shall take hold of one man, saying, We will eat our own bread, and wear our own apparel: only let us be called by thy name, to take away our reproach.   *2:11, 17*

2 In that day shall the branch of the LORD be beautiful and glorious, and the fruit of the earth *shall be* excellent and comely for them that are escaped of Israel.

3 And it shall come to pass, *that he that is* left in Zion, and *he that* remaineth in Jerusalem, ᴿshall be called holy, *even* every one that is ᴿwritten among the living in Jerusalem: *60:21 · Phil. 4:3*

4 When ᴿthe Lord shall have washed away the filth of the daughters of Zion, and shall have purged the ᵀblood of Jerusalem from the midst thereof by the spirit of judgment, and by the spirit of burning.   *Mal. 3:2, 3 · bloodshed*

5 And the LORD will create upon every dwelling place of mount Zion, and upon her assemblies, ᴿa cloud and smoke by day, and the shining of a flaming fire by night: for upon all the glory *shall be* a defence.   *Num. 9:15–23*

6 And there shall be a tabernacle for a shadow in the daytime from the heat, and ᴿfor a place of

refuge, and for a ᵀcovert from storm and from rain.   *25:4 · shelter*

5 Now will I sing to my well-beloved a song of my beloved ᴿtouching his vineyard. My well-beloved hath a vineyard in a very fruitful hill: *Mark 12:1; Luke 20:9*

2 And he fenced it, and gathered out the stones thereof, and planted it with the choicest vine, and built a tower in the midst of it, and also made a winepress therein: ᴿand he looked that it should bring forth grapes, and it brought forth wild grapes.   *Deut. 32:6*

3 And now, O inhabitants of Jerusalem, and men of Judah, ᴿjudge, I pray you, betwixt me and my vineyard.   *[Rom. 3:4]*

4 What could have been done more to my vineyard, that I have not done in ᴿit? wherefore, when I looked that it should bring forth grapes, brought it forth wild grapes?   *Jer. 2:5; Mic. 6:3; Matt. 23:37*

5 And now ᵀgo to; I will tell you what I will do to my vineyard: ᴿI will take away the hedge thereof, and it shall be eaten up; *and* break down the wall thereof, and it shall be trodden down: *come · Ps. 80:12*

6 And I will lay it ᴿwaste: it shall not be pruned, nor digged; but there shall come up briers and ᴿthorns: I will also command the clouds that they rain no rain upon it.   *2 Chr. 36:19–21 · 7:19–25; Jer. 25:11*

7 For the vineyard of the LORD of hosts *is* the house of Israel, and the men of Judah his pleasant plant: and he looked for judgment, but behold oppression; for righteousness, but behold a cry.

8 Woe unto them that join ᴿhouse to house, *that* lay field to field, till *there be* no place, that they may be placed alone in the midst of the earth!   *Jer. 22:13–17*

9 ᴿIn mine ears *said* the LORD of hosts, Of a truth many houses shall be desolate, *even* great and fair, without inhabitant.   *22:14*

10 Yea, ten acres of vineyard shall yield one ᴿbath, and the seed of an ho'-mer shall yield an e'-phah.   *Ezek. 45:11*

11 ^RWoe unto them that rise up early in the morning, *that* they may follow strong drink; that continue until night, *till* wine inflame them!   Prov. 23:29, 30; Eccl. 10:16, 17

12 And ^Rthe harp, and the viol, the tabret, and pipe, and wine, are in their feasts: but ^Rthey regard not the work of the LORD, neither consider the operation of his hands.   Amos 6:5 · Job 34:27; Ps. 28:5

13 ^RTherefore my people are gone into captivity, because *they have* no ^Rknowledge: and their honourable men *are* famished, and their multitude dried up with thirst. 2 Kin. 24:14–16 · 1:3; 27:11; Hos. 4:6

14 Therefore ^Thell hath enlarged herself, and opened her mouth without measure: and their glory, and their multitude, and their pomp, and he that rejoiceth, shall descend into it.   Or *Sheol*

15 And the mean man shall be brought down, and the mighty man shall be humbled, and the eyes of the lofty shall be humbled:

16 But the LORD of hosts shall be ^Rexalted in judgment, and God that is holy shall be ^Tsanctified in righteousness.   2:11 · *hallowed*

17 Then shall the lambs feed after their manner, and the waste places of ^Rthe fat ones shall strangers eat.   10:16

18 Woe unto them that draw iniquity with cords of vanity, and sin as it were with a cart rope:

19 ^RThat say, Let him make speed, *and* hasten his work, that we may see *it*: and let the counsel of the Holy One of Israel draw nigh and come, that we may know *it*!   Jer. 17:15; Amos 5:18

20 Woe unto them that call evil good, and good evil; that put darkness for light, and light for darkness; that put bitter for sweet, and sweet for bitter!

21 Woe unto *them that are* ^Rwise in their own eyes, and prudent in their own sight!   Rom. 1:22

22 Woe unto *them that are* mighty to drink wine, and men of strength to mingle strong drink:

23 Which ^Rjustify the wicked for reward, and take away the righteousness of the righteous from him!   1:23; Ex. 23:8; Prov. 17:15; Mic. 3:11

24 Therefore ^Ras the fire devoureth the stubble, and the flame consumeth the chaff, so ^Rtheir root shall be as rottenness, and their blossom shall go up as dust: because they have cast away the law of the LORD of hosts, and despised the word of the Holy One of Israel.   Ex. 15:7 · Job 18:16

25 Therefore is the anger of the LORD kindled against his people, and he hath stretched forth his hand against them, and hath smitten them: and the hills did tremble, and their carcases *were* torn in the midst of the streets. For all this his anger is not turned away, but his hand *is* stretched out still.

26 ^RAnd he will lift up an ensign to the nations from far, and will hiss unto them from the end of the earth: and, behold, they shall come with speed swiftly: 11:10, 12

27 None shall be weary nor stumble among them; none shall slumber nor sleep; neither ^Rshall the ^Tgirdle of their loins be loosed, nor the latchet of their shoes be broken: Dan. 5:6 · *belt on*

28 ^RWhose arrows *are* sharp, and all their bows bent, their horses' hoofs shall be counted like flint, and their wheels like a whirlwind: Jer. 5:16

29 Their roaring *shall be* like a lion, they shall roar like young lions: yea, they shall roar, and lay hold of the prey, and shall carry *it* away safe, and none shall deliver *it*.

30 And in that day they shall roar against them like the roaring of the sea: and if *one* ^Rlook unto the land, behold darkness *and* sorrow, and the light is darkened in the heavens thereof.   Joel 2:10

6 In the year that king Uz-zi'-ah died I saw also the Lord sitting upon a throne, high and lifted up, and his train filled the temple.

2 Above it stood the ser'-a-phims: each one had six wings; with twain he covered his face, and with twain he covered his feet, and with twain he did fly.

3 And one cried unto another, and said, ^RHoly, holy, holy, *is* the LORD of hosts: ^Rthe whole earth *is* full of his glory. Rev. 4:8 · Ps. 72:19

4 And the posts of the door ^Tmoved at the voice of him that ^Tcried, and the house was filled with smoke. *were shaken · cried out*

5 Then said I, Woe *is* me! for I am ^Tundone; because I *am* a man of ^Runclean lips, and I dwell in the midst of a people of unclean lips: for mine eyes have seen the King, the LORD of hosts. *destroyed* · Ex. 6:12

6 Then flew one of the ser'-a-phims unto me, having a live coal in his hand, *which* he had taken with the tongs from off the altar:

7 And he ^Rlaid *it* upon my mouth, and said, Lo, this hath touched thy lips; and thine iniquity is taken away, and thy sin ^Tpurged. Jer. 1:9 · *atoned for* or *covered*

8 Also I heard the voice of the Lord, saying, Whom shall I send, and who will go for us? Then said I, Here *am* I; send me.

☆ 9 And he said, Go, and ^Rtell this people, Hear ye indeed, but understand not; and see ye indeed, but perceive not. Luke 8:10; John 12:40

☆ 10 Make ^Rthe heart of this people fat, and make their ears heavy, and shut their eyes; ^Rlest they see with their eyes, and hear with their ears, and understand with their heart, and convert, and be healed. Acts 7:51; Rom. 10:1–4 · Jer. 5:21

11 Then said I, Lord, how long? And he answered, ^RUntil the cities be wasted without inhabitant, and the houses without man, and the land be utterly desolate, Mic. 3:12

12 ^RAnd the LORD have removed men far away, and *there be* ^Ta great forsaking in the midst of the land. 2 Kin. 25:21 · *many forsaken places*

13 But yet in it *shall be* a tenth, and *it* shall return, and shall be eaten: as a teil tree, and as an oak, whose substance *is* in them, when they cast *their leaves: so* ^Rthe holy

seed *shall be* the substance thereof. Deut. 7:6; Ezra 9:2

7 And it came to pass in the days of ^RAhaz the son of Jo'-tham, the son of Uz-zi'-ah, king of Judah, *that* Re'-zin the king of Syria, and Pe'-kah the son of Rem-a-li'-ah, king of Israel, went up toward Jerusalem to war against ^Rit, but could not prevail against it. 2 Chr. 28 · 2 Kin. 16:5, 9

2 And it was told the house of David, saying, Syria is confederate with E'-phra-im. And his heart was ^Tmoved, and the heart of his people, as the trees of the wood are moved with the wind. *shaken*

3 Then said the LORD unto Isaiah, Go forth now to meet Ahaz, thou, and She'-ar–jash'-ub thy son, at the end of the ^Tconduit of the upper pool in the highway of the fuller's field; *aqueduct*

4 And say unto him, Take heed, and be quiet; fear not, neither be fainthearted for the two tails of these smoking firebrands, for the fierce anger of Re'-zin with Syria, and of the son of Rem-a-li'-ah.

5 Because Syria, E'-phra-im, and the son of Rem-a-li'-ah, have ^Ttaken evil counsel against thee, saying, *plotted evil*

6 Let us go up against Judah, and vex it, and let us make a ^Tbreach therein for us, and set a king in the midst of it, *even* the son of Ta'-be-al: *gap in its wall*

7 Thus saith the Lord GOD, ^RIt shall not stand, neither shall it come to pass. 2 Kin. 16:5; Acts 4:25, 26

8 ^RFor the head of Syria *is* Damascus, and the head of Damascus *is* Re'-zin; and within threescore and five years shall E'-phra-im be broken, that it be not a people. 2 Sam. 8:6; 2 Kin. 17:6

9 And the head of E'-phra-im *is* Sa-ma'-ri-a, and the head of Sa-ma'-ri-a *is* Rem-a-li'-ah's son. ^RIf ye will not believe, surely ye shall not be established. 5:24; 2 Chr. 20:20

10 Moreover the LORD spake again unto Ahaz, saying,

11 ^RAsk thee a sign of the LORD

thy God; ask it either in the depth, or in the height above. Matt. 12:38

12 But Ahaz said, I will not ask, neither will I ᵀtempt the LORD. test

13 And he said, Hear ye now, O house of David; *Is it* a small thing for you to weary men, but will ye weary my God also?

☆ 14 Therefore the Lord himself shall give you a sign; ᴿBehold, a virgin shall conceive, and bear ᴿa son, and shall call his name ᴿIm-man′-u-el. Matt. 1:23 · [9:6] · 8:8, 10

15 Butter and honey shall he eat, that he may know to refuse the evil, and choose the good.

16 ᴿFor before the child shall know to refuse the evil, and choose the good, the land that thou abhorrest shall be forsaken of ᴿboth her kings. 8:4 · 2 Kin. 15:30

17 ᴿThe LORD shall bring upon thee, and upon thy people, and upon thy father's house, days that have not come, from the day that E′-phra-im departed from Judah; *even* the king of Assyria. 8:7, 8

18 And it shall come to pass in that day, *that* the LORD ᴿshall ᵀhiss for the fly that *is* in the uttermost part of the rivers of Egypt, and for the bee that *is* in the land of Assyria. 5:26 · whistle

19 And they shall come, and shall rest all of them in the desolate valleys, and in ᴿthe holes of the rocks, and upon all thorns, and upon all bushes. 2:19; Jer. 16:16

20 In the same day shall the Lord shave with a ᴿrazor that is ᴿhired, *namely,* by them beyond the river, by the king of Assyria, the head, and the hair of the feet: and it shall also consume the beard. 2 Kin. 16:7; 2 Chr. 28:20 · 10:5, 15

21 And it shall come to pass in that day, *that* a man shall nourish a young cow, and two sheep;

22 And it shall come to pass, ᵀfor the abundance of milk *that* they shall give he shall eat ᵀbutter: for butter and honey shall every one eat that is left in the land. from · curds

23 And it shall come to pass in that day, *that* every place shall be,

where there were a thousand vines at a thousand ᵀsilverlings, ᴿit shall *even* be for briers and thorns. shekels of silver · 5:6

24 With arrows and with bows shall *men* come thither; because all the land shall become briers and thorns.

25 And *on* all hills that shall be digged with the mattock, there shall not come thither the fear of briers and thorns: but it shall be for the sending forth of oxen, and for the treading of lesser cattle.

8 Moreover the LORD said unto me, Take thee a great roll, and write in it with a man's pen concerning ᵀMa′-her–shal′-al–hash′-baz. Lit. *Speed the Spoil, Hasten the Booty*

2 And I took unto me faithful witnesses to record, ᴿU-ri′-ah the priest, and Zech-a-ri′-ah the son of Je-ber-e-chi′-ah. 2 Kin. 16:10

3 And I went unto the prophetess; and she conceived, and bare a son. Then said the LORD to me, Call his name Ma′-her–shal′-al–hash′-baz.

4 ᴿFor before the child shall have knowledge to cry, My father, and my mother, the riches of Damascus and the spoil of Sa-ma′-ri-a shall be taken away before the king of Assyria. 7:16

5 The LORD spake also unto me again, saying,

6 Forasmuch as this people refuseth the waters of ᴿShi-lo′-ah that go softly, and rejoice in Re′-zin and Rem-a-li′-ah's son; John 9:7

7 Now therefore, behold, the Lord bringeth up upon them the waters of the river, strong and ᵀmany, *even* the king of Assyria, and all his glory: and he shall come up over all his channels, and go over all his banks: mighty

8 And he shall pass through Judah; he shall overflow and go over, he shall reach *even* to the neck; and the stretching out of his wings shall fill the breadth of thy land, O ᴿIm-man′-u-el. 7:14; Matt. 1:23

9 ᴿAssociateᵀ yourselves, O ye people, and ye shall be broken in pieces; and give ear, all ye of far

countries: gird yourselves, and ye shall be broken in pieces; gird yourselves, and ye shall be broken in pieces.   Joel 3:9 · *Be shattered*

10 Take counsel together, and it shall come to nought; speak the word, ^Rand it shall not stand: ^Rfor God *is* with us.   7:7; Acts 5:38 · 7:14

11 For the LORD spake thus to me with ^Ta strong hand, and instructed me that I should not walk in the way of this people, saying,   Mighty power

12 Say ye not, A confederacy, to all *them* *to* whom this people shall say, A confederacy; neither fear ye their fear, nor be afraid.

13 ^TSanctify the LORD of hosts himself; and *let* him *be* your fear, and *let* him *be* your dread.   Hallow

☆ 14 And he shall be for a sanctuary; but for ^Ra stone of stumbling and for a rock of offence to both the houses of Israel, for a ^Tgin and for a snare to the inhabitants of Jerusalem.   Luke 2:34 · *trap*

15 And many among them shall stumble, and fall, and be broken, and be snared, and be taken.

16 Bind up the testimony, seal the law among my disciples.

17 And I will wait upon the LORD, that ^Rhideth his face from the house of Jacob, and I ^Rwill look for him.   54:8; Deut. 31:17 · Hab. 2:3

☆ 18 Behold, I and the children whom the LORD hath given me *are* for signs and for wonders in Israel from the LORD of hosts, which dwelleth in mount Zion.

19 And when they shall say unto you, Seek unto them that ^Thave familiar spirits, and unto wizards ^Rthat ^Tpeep, and that mutter: should not a people seek unto their God? for the living to the dead?   *are mediums* · 29:4 · *whisper*

20 ^RTo the law and to the testimony: if they speak not according to this word, *it is* because ^R*there is* no light in them.   1:10 · Mic. 3:6

21 And they shall pass through it, ^Thardly bestead and hungry: and it shall come to pass, that when they shall be hungry, they shall fret themselves, and ^Tcurse

their king and their God, and look upward.   *hard-pressed* · *curse by*

22 And they shall look unto the earth; and behold trouble and darkness, ^Tdimness of anguish; and *they shall be* driven to darkness.   *gloom*

9 Nevertheless the dimness *shall* not *be* such as *was* in her vexation, when at the ^Rfirst he lightly ^Tafflicted the land of Zeb'-u-lun and the land of Naph'-ta-li, and afterward did more grievously afflict *her by* the way of the sea, beyond Jordan, in Galilee of the nations.   2 Kin. 15:29 · *esteemed*

2 ^RThe people that walked in darkness have seen a great light: they that dwell in the land of the shadow of death, upon them hath the light shined.   Matt. 4:16; Luke 1:79

3 Thou hast multiplied the nation, *and* not increased the joy: they joy before thee according to the joy in harvest, *and* as *men* rejoice ^Rwhen they divide the ^Tspoil.   Judg. 5:30 · *plunder*

4 For thou hast broken the yoke of his burden, and the staff of his shoulder, the rod of his oppressor, as in the day of ^RMid'-i-an.   Judg. 7:22

5 For every battle of the warrior *is* with confused noise, and garments rolled in blood; ^Rbut^T *this* shall be with burning *and* fuel of fire.   66:15 · *shall be used for burning*

6 For unto us a child is born, unto us a ^Rson is given: and the government shall be upon his shoulder: and his name shall be called Wonderful, Counsellor, The mighty God, The everlasting Father, The Prince of Peace.   Luke 2:7

7 Of the increase of *his* government and peace ^R*there shall be* no end, upon the throne of David, and upon his kingdom, to order it, and to establish it with judgment and with justice from henceforth even for ever. The zeal of the LORD of hosts will perform this.   Dan. 2:44

8 The Lord sent a word ^Tinto ^RJacob, and it hath ^Tlighted upon Israel.   *against* · Gen. 32:28 · *fallen*

9 And all the people shall

know, *even* E'-phra-im and the inhabitant of Sa-mar'-i-a, that say in the pride and ᵀstoutness of heart, *arrogance*

10 The bricks are fallen down, but we will build with hewn stones: the sycomores are cut down, but we will ᵀchange *them into* cedars. *replace them with cedars*

11 Therefore the Lᴏʀᴅ shall set up the adversaries of Re'-zin against him, and ᵀjoin his enemies together; *spur his enemies on*

12 The Syrians before, and the Phi-lis'-tines behind; and they shall devour Israel with open mouth. For all this his anger is not turned away, but his hand *is* stretched out still.

13 For the people turneth not unto him that ᵀsmiteth them, neither do they seek the Lᴏʀᴅ of hosts. *strikes*

14 Therefore the Lᴏʀᴅ will cut off from Israel head and tail, branch and rush, in one day.

15 The ancient and honourable, he *is* the head; and the prophet that teacheth lies, he *is* the tail.

16 For ᴿthe leaders of this people cause *them* to err; and *they that are* led of them *are* destroyed. *3:12; Mic. 3:1, 5, 9; Matt. 15:14*

17 Therefore the Lord ᴿshall have no joy in their young men, neither shall have mercy on their fatherless and widows: for every one *is* an hypocrite and an evildoer, and every mouth speaketh folly. ᴿFor all this his anger is not turned away, but his hand *is* stretched out still. *Ps. 147:10 · 5:25*

18 For wickedness ᴿburneth as the fire: it shall devour the briers and thorns, and shall kindle in the thickets of the forest, and they shall mount up *like* the lifting up of smoke. *Ps. 83:14; Nah. 1:10; Mal. 4:1*

19 Through the wrath of the Lᴏʀᴅ of hosts is ᴿthe land darkened, and the people shall be as the fuel of the fire: ᴿno man shall spare his brother. *8:22 · Mic. 7:2, 6*

20 And he shall snatch on the right hand, and be hungry; and he shall eat on the left hand, ᴿand

they shall not be satisfied: ᴿthey shall eat every man the flesh of his own arm: *Lev. 26:26 · Jer. 19:9*

21 Ma-nas'-seh, E'-phra-im; and E'-phra-im, Ma-nas'-seh: *and* they together *shall be* ᴿagainst Judah. ᴿFor all this his anger is not turned away, but his hand *is* stretched out still. *11:13 · vv. 12, 17*

10 Woe unto them that decree unrighteous decrees, and that write ᵀgrievousness *which* they have prescribed; *misfortune*

2 To ᵀturn aside the needy from judgment, and to take away ᵀthe right from the poor of my people, that widows may be their prey, and *that* they may rob the fatherless! *deprive · what is right*

3 And what will ye do in the day of visitation, and in the desolation *which* shall come from far? to whom will ye flee for help? and where will ye leave your glory?

4 Without me they shall bow down under the ᴿprisoners, and they shall fall under the slain. ᴿFor all this his anger is not turned away, but his hand *is* stretched out still. *24:22 · 5:25*

5 O Assyrian, ᴿthe rod of mine anger, and the staff in their hand is mine indignation. *Jer. 51:20*

6 I will send him against ᴿan hypocritical nation, and against the people of my wrath will I ᴿgive him a charge, to take the spoil, and to take the prey, and to tread them down like the mire of the streets. *9:17 · 2 Kin. 17:6; Jer. 34:22*

7 ᴿHowbeit he meaneth not so, neither doth his heart think so; but *it is* in his heart to destroy and cut off nations not a few. *Gen. 50:20*

8 For he saith, *Are* not my princes ᵀaltogether kings? *all*

9 *Is* not Cal'-no as Car'-che-mish? *is* not Ha'-math as Ar'-pad? *is* not Sa-ma'-ri-a as Damascus?

10 As my hand hath found the kingdoms of the idols, and whose graven images did excel them of Jerusalem and of Sa-ma'-ri-a;

11 Shall I not, as I have done unto Sa-ma'-ri-a and her idols, so do to Jerusalem and her idols?

12 Wherefore it shall come to pass, *that* when the Lord hath performed his whole work ^Rupon mount Zion and on Jerusalem, I will punish the fruit of the stout heart of the king of Assyria, and the glory of his high looks.   28:21

13 For he saith, By the strength of my hand I have done *it*, and by my wisdom; for I am prudent: and I have removed the bounds of the people, and have robbed their treasures, and I have put down the inhabitants like a valiant *man*:

14 And ^Rmy hand hath found as a nest the riches of the people: and as one gathereth eggs *that are* left, have I gathered all the earth; and there was none that moved the wing, or opened the mouth, or peeped.   Job 31:25

15 Shall ^Rthe ax boast itself against him that ^Theweth therewith? *or* shall the saw magnify itself against him that shaketh it? as if the rod should shake *itself* against them that lift it up, *or* as if the staff should lift up *itself, as if it were* no wood.   Jer. 51:20 · *chops*

16 Therefore shall the Lord, the Lord of hosts, send among his fat ones leanness; and under his glory he shall kindle a burning like the burning of a fire.

17 And the light of Israel shall be for a fire, and his Holy One for a flame: ^Rand it shall burn and devour his thorns and his briers in one day;   9:18

18 And shall consume the glory of his forest, and of ^Rhis fruitful field, both soul and body: and they shall be as when a standard-bearer fainteth.   2 Kin. 19:23

19 And the rest of the trees of his forest shall be few, that a child may write them.

20 And it shall come to pass in that day, *that* the remnant of Israel, and such as are escaped of the house of Jacob, ^Rshall no more again ^Tstay upon him that smote them; but shall stay upon the Lord, the Holy One of Israel, in truth.   2 Kin. 16:7 · *depend*

21 The remnant shall return, *even* the remnant of Jacob, unto the ^Rmighty God.   [9:6]

22 For though thy people Israel be as the sand of the sea, ^Ryet a remnant of them shall return: the consumption decreed shall overflow with righteousness.   6:13

23 ^RFor the Lord God of hosts shall make a consumption, even determined, in the midst of all the land.   28:22; Dan. 9:27; Rom. 9:28

24 Therefore thus saith the Lord God of hosts, O my people that dwellest in Zion, ^Rbe not afraid of the Assyrian: he shall ^Tsmite thee with a rod, and shall lift up his staff against thee, after the manner of Egypt.   7:4; 12:2 · *strike*

25 For yet a very little while, ^Rand the indignation shall cease, and mine anger in their destruction.   v. 5; 26:20; Dan. 11:36

26 And the Lord of hosts shall stir up a scourge for him according to the slaughter of ^RMid'-i-an at the rock of O'-reb: and ^Ras his rod *was* upon the sea, so shall he lift it up after the manner of Egypt.   9:4; Judg. 7:25 · Ex. 14:26, 27

27 And it shall come to pass in that day, *that* his burden shall be taken away from off thy shoulder, and his yoke from off thy neck, and the yoke shall be destroyed because of the anointing.

28 He is come to A'-iath, he is passed to Mig'-ron; at Mich'-mash he hath laid up his carriages:

29 They are gone over the passage: they have taken up their lodging at Ge'-ba; Ra'-mah is afraid; Gib'-e-ah of Saul is fled.

30 Lift up thy voice, O daughter of Gal'-lim: cause it to be heard unto La'-ish, O poor An'-a-thoth.

31 ^RMad-me'-nah is removed; the inhabitants of Ge'-bim gather themselves to flee.   Josh. 15:31

32 As yet shall he remain ^Rat Nob that day: he shall ^Rshake his hand *against* the mount of ^Rthe daughter of Zion, the hill of Jerusalem.   1 Sam. 21:1 · 13:2 · 37:22

33 Behold, the Lord, the Lord of hosts, shall lop the bough with terror: and the high ones of sta-

ture *shall be* hewn down, and the haughty shall be humbled.

34 And he shall cut down the thickets of the forest with iron, and Leb'-a-non shall fall by a mighty one.

☆ **11** And ^Rthere shall come forth a rod out of the stem of Jesse, and a Branch shall grow out of his roots: [Zech. 6:12]; Rev. 5:5

☆ 2 ^RAnd the spirit of the LORD shall rest upon him, the spirit of wisdom and understanding, the spirit of counsel and might, the spirit of knowledge and of the fear of the LORD;   Mark 1:10; Luke 3:22

3 And ^Tshall make him of quick understanding in the fear of the LORD: and he shall not judge after the sight of his eyes, neither reprove after the hearing of his ears: *his delight* shall be *in the fear*

4 But ^Rwith righteousness shall he judge the poor, and reprove with equity for the meek of the earth: and he shall smite the earth with the rod of his mouth, and with the breath of his lips shall he slay the wicked.   Rev. 19:11

5 And righteousness shall be the ^Tgirdle of his loins, and faithfulness the girdle of his reins.   *belt*

6 ^RThe wolf also shall dwell with the lamb, and the leopard shall lie down with the kid; and the calf and the young lion and the fatling together; and a little child shall lead them.   Hos. 2:18

7 And the cow and the bear shall ^Tfeed; their young ones shall lie down together: and the lion shall eat straw like the ox.   *graze*

8 And the sucking child shall play on the hole of the ^Tasp, and the weaned child shall put his hand on the cockatrice' den.   *cobra*

9 ^RThey shall not hurt nor destroy in all my holy mountain: for ^Rthe earth shall be full of the knowledge of the LORD, as the waters cover the sea.   65:25 · 45:6

☆ **10** ^RAnd in that day ^Rthere shall be a root of Jesse, which shall stand for an ensign of the people; to it shall the Gentiles seek: and his rest shall be glorious.   2:11 · v. 1

11 And it shall come to pass in that day, *that* the Lord shall set his hand again the second time to recover the remnant of his people, which shall be left, ^Rfrom Assyria, and from Egypt, and from Path'-ros, and from Cush, and from E'-lam, and from Shi'-nar, and from Ha'-math, and from the islands of the sea.   19:23–25; Hos. 11:11; Zech. 10:10

12 And he shall set up ^Tan ensign for the nations, and shall assemble the outcasts of Israel, and gather together ^Rthe dispersed of Judah from the four corners of the earth.   *a banner* · John 7:35

13 ^RThe envy also of E'-phra-im shall depart, and the adversaries of Judah shall be cut off: E'-phra-im shall not envy Judah, and Judah shall not vex E'-phra-im.   9:21

14 But they shall fly upon the shoulders of the Phi-lis'-tines toward the west; they shall spoil them of the east together: ^Rthey shall lay their hand upon E'-dom and Moab; and the children of Ammon shall obey them.   63:1

15 And the LORD ^Rshall utterly destroy the tongue of the Egyptian sea; and with his mighty wind shall he shake his hand over the river, and shall smite it in the seven streams, and make *men* go over dryshod.   50:2; Zech. 10:10, 11

16 And ^Rthere shall be an highway for the remnant of his people, which shall be left, from Assyria; ^Rlike as it was to Israel in the day that he came up out of the land of Egypt.   19:23 · Ex. 14:29

12 And ^Rin that day thou shalt say, O LORD, I will praise thee: though thou wast angry with me, thine anger is turned away, and thou comfortedst me.   2:11

2 Behold, God *is* my salvation; I will trust, and not be afraid: for the ^RLORD JE-HO'-VAH *is* my strength and *my* song; he also is become my salvation.   Ps. 118:14

3 Therefore with joy shall ye draw ^Rwater out of the wells of salvation.   [John 4:10; 14; 7:37, 38]

4 And in that day shall ye say, Praise the LORD, call upon his

name, ᴿdeclare his doings among the people, make mention that his ᴿname is exalted. Ps. 145:4–6 · Ps. 34:3

5 ᴿSing unto the LORD; for he hath done excellent things: this *is* known in all the earth.   42:10, 11

6 ᴿCry out and shout, thou inhabitant of Zion: for great *is* ᴿthe Holy One of Israel in the midst of thee.   52:9; 54:1; Zeph. 3:14, 15 · Ps. 89:18

13 The ᴿburden of Babylon, which Isaiah the son of Amoz did see.   Jer. 50; 51

2 ᴿLift ye up a banner ᴿupon the high mountain, exalt the voice unto them, ᴿshake the hand, that they may go into the gates of the nobles.   18:3 · Jer. 51:25 · 10:32

3 I have commanded my sanctified ones, I have also called my mighty ones for mine anger, *even* them that rejoice in my highness.

4 The noise of a multitude in the mountains, like as of ᵀa great people; a tumultuous noise of the kingdoms of nations gathered together: the LORD of hosts mustereth the host of the battle. *many*

5 They come from a far country, from the end of heaven, *even* the ᴿLORD, and the weapons of his indignation, to destroy the whole ᴿland.   42:13 · 24:1; 34:2

6 Howl ye; for the day of the LORD *is* at hand; it shall come as a destruction from the Almighty.

7 Therefore shall all hands ᵀbe faint, and every man's heart shall melt: *fall limp*

8 And they shall be afraid: pangs and sorrows shall take hold of them; they shall be in pain as a woman that travaileth: they shall be amazed one at another; their faces *shall be as* flames.

9 Behold, ᴿthe day of the LORD cometh, cruel both with wrath and fierce anger, to lay the land desolate: and he shall destroy the sinners thereof out of it.   Mal. 4:1

10 For the stars of heaven and the constellations thereof shall not give their light: the sun shall be ᴿdarkened in his going forth, and the moon shall not cause her light to shine.   Joel 2:31; Matt. 24:29

11 And I will ᴿpunish the world for *their* evil, and the wicked for their iniquity; ᴿand I will cause the arrogancy of the proud to cease, and will lay low the haughtiness of the terrible.   26:21 · [2:17]

12 I will make a man more ᵀprecious than fine gold; even a man than the golden wedge of O'-phir.   *rare*

13 ᴿTherefore I will shake the heavens, and the earth shall remove out of her place, in the wrath of the LORD of hosts, and in the day of his fierce anger.   34:4

14 And it shall be as the chased roe, and as a sheep that no man taketh up: they shall every man turn to his own people, and flee every one into his own land.

15 Every one that is found shall be thrust through; and every one that is ᵀjoined *unto them* shall fall by the sword.   *captured*

16 Their children also shall be dashed to pieces before their eyes; their houses shall be ᵀspoiled, and their wives ravished.   *plundered*

17 ᴿBehold, I will stir up the Medes against them, which shall not regard silver; and *as for* gold, they shall not delight in it.   21:2

18 *Their* bows also shall dash the young men to pieces; and they shall have no pity on the fruit of the womb; their eye shall not spare children.

19 And Babylon, the glory of kingdoms, the beauty of the Chal'-dees' excellency, shall be as when God overthrew ᴿSodom and Go-mor'-rah.   Gen. 19:24; Amos 4:11

20 ᴿIt shall never be inhabited, neither shall it be dwelt in from generation to generation: neither shall the A-ra'-bi-an pitch tent there; neither shall the shepherds make their fold there.   Jer. 50:3

21 But wild beasts of the desert shall lie there; and their houses shall be full of doleful creatures; and owls shall dwell there, and ᵀsatyrs shall dance there. *wild goats*

22 And the ᵀwild beasts of the islands shall cry in their desolate houses, and ᵀdragons in *their*

pleasant palaces: and her time *is* near to come, and her days shall not be prolonged.　　*hyenas · jackals*

14 For the LORD ᴿwill have mercy on Jacob, and ᴿwill yet choose Israel, and set them in their own land: ᴿand the strangers shall be joined with them, and they shall cleave to the house of Jacob.　　49:13, 15 · 41:8, 9 · 60:4, 5, 10

2 And the people shall take them, ᴿand bring them to their place: and the house of Israel shall possess them in the land of the LORD for servants and handmaids: and they shall take them captives, whose captives they were; ᴿand they shall rule over their oppressors.　　60:9; 66:20 · 60:14

3 And it shall come to pass in the day that the LORD shall give thee rest from thy sorrow, and from thy fear, and from the hard bondage wherein thou wast made to serve,

4 That thou ᴿshalt take up this proverb against the king of Babylon, and say, How hath the oppressor ceased! the ᴿgolden city ceased!　　13:19; Hab. 2:6 · Rev. 18:16

5 The LORD hath broken ᴿthe staff of the wicked, *and* the sceptre of the rulers.　　Ps. 125:3

6 He who smote the people in wrath with a continual stroke, he that ruled the nations in anger, is persecuted, *and* none hindereth.

7 The whole earth is at rest, *and* is quiet: they break forth into singing.

8 ᴿYea, the fir trees rejoice at thee, *and* the cedars of Leb'-a-non, *saying,* Since thou art laid down, no ᵀfeller is come up against us.　　Ezek. 31:16 · *woodsman*

9 ᴿHellᵀ from beneath is moved for thee to meet *thee* at thy coming: it stirreth up the dead for thee, *even* all the chief ones of the earth; it hath raised up from their thrones all the kings of the nations.　　Ezek. 32:21 · Or *Sheol*

10 All they shall ᴿspeak and say unto thee, Art thou also become weak as we? art thou become like unto us?　　Ezek. 32:21

11 Thy pomp is brought down to the grave, *and* the noise of thy viols: the worm is spread under thee, and the worms cover thee.

12 ᴿHow art thou fallen from heaven, O Lu'-ci-fer, son of the morning! *how* art thou cut down to the ground, which didst weaken the nations!　　34:4; Luke 10:18

13 For thou hast said in thine heart, ᴿI will ascend into heaven, I will exalt my throne above the stars of God: I will sit also upon the mount of the congregation, in the sides of the north:　　Matt. 11:23

14 I will ascend above the heights of the clouds; ᴿI will be like the most High.　　47:8; 2 Thess. 2:4

15 Yet thou ᴿshalt be brought down to ᵀhell, to the sides of the pit.　　Matt. 11:23; Luke 10:15 · Or *Sheol*

16 They that see thee shall ᵀnarrowly look upon thee, *and* consider thee, *saying, Is* this the man that made the earth to tremble, that did shake kingdoms;　　*gaze at*

17 *That* made the world as a wilderness, and destroyed the cities thereof; *that* opened not the house of his prisoners?

18 All the kings of the nations, *even* all of them, lie in glory, every one in his own house.

19 But thou art cast out of thy grave like an abominable branch, *and as* the ᵀraiment of those that are slain, ᵀthrust through with a sword, that go down to the stones of the pit; as a carcase trodden under feet.　　*garment · pierced*

20 Thou shalt not be joined with them in burial, because thou hast destroyed thy land, *and* slain thy people: ᴿthe seed of evildoers shall never be renowned.　　1:4; 31:2

21 Prepare slaughter for his children ᴿfor the iniquity of their fathers; that they do not rise, nor possess the land, nor fill the face of the world with cities.　　Matt. 23:35

22 For I will rise up against them, saith the LORD of hosts, and cut off from Babylon ᴿthe name, and remnant, ᴿand son, and nephew, saith the LORD.　　26:14 · 47:9

23 I will also make it a posses-

sion for the ᵀbittern, and pools of water: and I will sweep it with the ᵀbesom of destruction, saith the LORD of hosts.   *porcupine · broom*

24 The LORD of hosts hath sworn, saying, Surely as I have thought, so shall it come to pass; and as I have purposed, *so* shall it ᴿstand: 43:13

25 That I will break the ᴿAssyrian in my land, and upon my mountains tread him under foot: then shall his yoke depart from off them, and his burden depart from off their shoulders.   Mic. 5:5, 6

26 This *is* the purpose that is purposed upon the whole earth: and this *is* the hand that is stretched out upon all the nations.

27 For the LORD of hosts hath purposed, and who shall disannul *it?* and his hand *is* stretched out, and who shall turn it back?

28 In the year that ᴿking Ahaz died was this burden.   2 Kin. 16:20

29 Rejoice not thou, whole Pal-es-ti′-na, because the rod of him that smote thee is broken: for out of the serpent's root shall come forth a cockatrice, and his fruit *shall be* a fiery flying serpent.

30 And the firstborn of the poor shall feed, and the needy shall lie down in safety: and I will kill thy root with famine, and he shall slay thy remnant.

31 Howl, O gate; cry, O city; thou, whole Pal-es-ti′-na, *art* dissolved: for there shall come from the north a smoke, and none *shall be* alone in his appointed times.

32 What shall *one* then answer the messengers of the nation? That ᴿthe LORD hath founded Zi-on, and ᴿthe poor of his people shall trust in it. Ps. 87:1, 5 · Zech. 11:11

15 The ᴿburden of Moab. Because in the night Ar of Moab is laid waste, *and* brought to silence; because in the night Kir of Moab is laid waste, *and* brought to silence;   2 Kin. 3:4

2 He is gone up to Ba′-jith, and to Di′-bon, the high places, to weep: Moab shall howl over Ne′-bo, and over Med′-e-ba: ᴿon all their heads *shall be* baldness, *and* every beard cut off.   Jer. 48:37

3 In their streets they shall gird themselves with sackcloth: on the tops of their houses, and in their streets, every one shall howl, ᴿweeping abundantly.   Jer. 48:38

4 And Hesh′-bon shall cry, and E-le-a′-leh: their voice shall be heard *even* unto ᴿJa′-haz: therefore the armed soldiers of Moab shall cry out; his life shall be grievous unto him.   Jer. 48:34

5 ᴿMy heart shall cry out for Moab; his fugitives *shall flee* unto Zo′-ar, an heifer of three years old: for ᴿby the mounting up of Lu′-hith with weeping shall they go it up; for in the way of Hor-o-na′-im they shall raise up a cry of destruction.   16:11; Jer. 48:31 · Jer. 48:5

6 For the waters ᴿof Nim′-rim shall be desolate: for the hay is withered away, the grass faileth, there is no green thing.   Num. 32:36

7 Therefore the abundance they have gotten, and that which they have laid up, shall they carry away to the brook of the willows.

8 For the cry is gone round about the borders of Moab; the howling thereof unto Eg′-la-im, and the howling thereof unto Be′-er–e′-lim.

9 For the waters of Di′-mon shall be full of blood: for I will bring more upon Di′-mon, lions upon him that escapeth of Moab, and upon the remnant of the land.

16 Send ye the lamb to the ruler of the land ᴿfrom Se′-la to the wilderness, unto the mount of the daughter of Zion.   42:11

2 For it shall be, *that*, as a wandering bird cast out of the nest, *so* the daughters of Moab shall be at the fords of ᴿArnon.   Num. 21:13

3 Take counsel, execute judgment; make thy shadow as the night in the midst of the noonday; hide the outcasts; ᵀbewray not him that wandereth.   *betray*

4 Let mine outcasts dwell with thee, Moab; be thou a covert to them from the face of the spoiler: for the extortioner is at an end,

the spoiler ceaseth, the oppressors are consumed out of the land.

5 And in mercy ᴿshall the throne be established: and he shall sit upon it in truth in the tabernacle of David, judging, and seeking judgment, and hasting righteousness.   [9:6, 7; 32:1; 55:4]

6 We have heard of the ᴿpride of Moab; *he is* very proud: *even* of his haughtiness, and his pride, and his wrath: *but* his lies *shall* not *be* so. Jer. 48:29; Amos 2:1; Obad. 3, 4

7 Therefore shall Moab ᴿhowl for Moab, every one shall howl: for the foundations ᴿof Kir–har′-e-seth shall ye mourn; surely *they are* stricken.   Jer. 48:20 · Jer. 48:31

8 For the fields of Hesh′-bon languish, *and* the vine of Sib′-mah: the lords of the heathen have broken down the principal plants thereof, they are come *even* unto Ja′-zer, they wandered *through* the wilderness: her branches are stretched out, they are gone over the ᴿsea.   Jer. 48:32

9 Therefore I will bewail with the weeping of Ja′-zer the vine of Sib′-mah: I will water thee with my tears, ᴿO Hesh′-bon, and E-le-a′-leh: for the shouting for thy summer fruits and for thy harvest is fallen.   15:4

10 And ᴿgladness is taken away, and joy out of the plentiful field; and in the vineyards there shall be no singing, neither shall there be shouting: the treaders shall tread out no wine in *their* presses; I have made *their vintage* shouting to cease.   24:8; Jer. 48:33

11 Wherefore ᴿmy bowels shall sound like an harp for Moab, and mine inward parts for Kir–ha′-resh.   15:5; Jer. 48:36; Hos. 11:8; Phil. 2:1

12 And it shall come to pass, when it is seen that Moab is weary on ᴿthe high place, that he shall come to his sanctuary to pray; but he shall not prevail. 15:2

13 This *is* the word that the LORD hath spoken concerning Moab since that time.

14 But now the LORD hath spoken, saying, Within three years, as

the years of an hireling, and the glory of Moab shall be ᵀcontemned, with all that great multitude; and the remnant *shall be* very small *and* feeble.   despised

17 The ᴿburden of Damascus. Behold, Damascus is taken away from *being* a city, and it shall be a ruinous heap.   Jer. 49:23

2 The cities of ᴿAr′-o-er *are* forsaken: they shall be for flocks, which shall lie down, and none shall make *them* afraid. Num. 32:34

3 ᴿThe fortress also shall cease from E′-phra-im, and the kingdom from Damascus, and the remnant of Syria: they shall be as the glory of the children of Israel, saith the LORD of hosts.   7:16; 8:4

4 And in that day it shall come to pass, *that* the glory of Jacob shall be made thin, and the fatness of his flesh shall wax lean.

5 ᴿAnd it shall be as when the harvestman gathereth the corn, and reapeth the ears with his arm; and it shall be as he that gathereth ears in the valley of Reph′-a-im.   v. 11; Jer. 51:33; Joel 3:13; Matt. 13:30

6 ᴿYet gleaning grapes shall be left in it, as the shaking of an olive tree, two *or* three berries in the top of the uppermost bough, four *or* five in the outmost fruitful branches thereof, saith the LORD God of Israel. 24:13; Deut. 4:27; Obad. 5

7 At that day shall a man ᴿlook to his Maker, and his eyes shall ᵀhave respect to the Holy One of Israel.   10:20; Hos. 3:5; Mic. 7:7 · look to

8 And he shall not look to the altars, the work of his hands, neither shall respect *that* which his ᴿfingers have made, either the groves, or the images.   2:8; 31:7

9 In that day shall his strong cities be as a forsaken bough, and an uppermost branch, which they left because of the children of Israel: and there shall be desolation.

10 Because thou hast forgotten ᴿthe God of thy salvation, and hast not been mindful of the rock of thy strength, therefore

shalt thou plant pleasant plants, and shalt set it with strange slips: 51:13

11 In the day shalt thou make thy plant to grow, and in the morning shalt thou make thy seed to flourish: *but* the harvest *shall be* a heap in the day of grief and of desperate sorrow.

12 Woe to the multitude of many people, *which* make a noise ^Rlike the noise of the seas; and to the rushing of nations, *that* make a rushing like the rushing of mighty waters!   5:30; Ezek. 43:2; Luke 21:25

13 The nations shall rush like the rushing of many waters: but *God* shall ^Rrebuke them, and they shall flee far off, and ^Rshall be chased as the chaff of the mountains before the wind, and like a rolling thing before the whirlwind.   Ps. 9:5 · Ps. 83:13; Hos. 13:3

14 And behold at eveningtide trouble; *and* before the morning ^The *is* not. This *is* the portion of them that spoil us, and the lot of them that rob us.   *he is no more*

18 Woe to the land shadowing with wings, which *is* beyond the rivers of E-thi-o'-pi-a:

2 That sendeth ambassadors by the sea, even in vessels of bulrushes upon the waters, *saying,* Go, ye swift messengers, to a nation scattered and peeled, to a people terrible from their beginning hitherto; a nation meted out and trodden down, whose land the rivers ^Thave spoiled!   *divide*

3 All ye inhabitants of the world, and dwellers on the earth, see ye, ^Rwhen he lifteth up ^Tan ensign on the mountains; and when he bloweth a trumpet, hear ye.   5:26 · *a banner*

4 For so the LORD said unto me, I will take my rest, and I will ^Tconsider in my dwelling place like a clear heat ^Tupon herbs, *and* like a cloud of dew in the heat of harvest.   *look from · in sunshine*

5 For ^Tafore the harvest, when the bud is perfect, and the sour grape is ripening in the flower, he shall both cut off the sprigs with pruninghooks, and take away *and* cut down the branches.   *before*

6 They shall be left together unto the fowls of the mountains, and to the beasts of the earth: and the fowls shall summer upon them, and all the beasts of the earth shall winter upon them.

7 In that time ^Rshall the present be brought unto the LORD of hosts of a people scattered and peeled, and from a people terrible from their beginning hitherto; a nation meted out and trodden under foot, whose land the rivers have spoiled, to the place of the name of the LORD of hosts, the mount Zion.   Zeph. 3:10; Mal. 1:11; Acts 8:27–38

19 The ^Rburden of Egypt. Behold, the LORD ^Rrideth upon a swift cloud, and shall come into Egypt: and the idols of Egypt shall be moved at his presence, and the heart of Egypt shall melt in the midst of it.   Joel 3:19 · Ps. 18:10; Rev. 1:7

2 And I will set the Egyptians against the Egyptians: and they shall fight every one against his brother, and every one against his neighbour; city against city, *and* kingdom against kingdom.

3 And the spirit of Egypt shall fail in the midst thereof; and I will destroy the counsel thereof: and they shall ^Rseek to the idols, and to the charmers, and to them that have familiar spirits, and to the wizards.   8:19; 47:12; Dan. 2:2

4 And the Egyptians will I give over ^Rinto the hand of a cruel lord; and a fierce king shall rule over them, saith the Lord, the LORD of hosts.   20:4; Jer. 46:26; Ezek. 29:19

5 ^RAnd the waters shall fail from the sea, and the river shall be wasted and dried up.   Jer. 51:36

6 And they shall turn the rivers far away; *and* the brooks ^Rof defence shall be emptied and dried up: the reeds and ^Tflags shall wither.   2 Kin. 19:24 · *rushes*

7 The ^Tpaper reeds by the brooks, by the mouth of the brooks, and every thing sown by the brooks, shall wither, be driven away, and be no *more.*   *papyrus*

8 The fishers also shall mourn, and all they that cast ^Tangle into the brooks shall lament, and they that spread nets upon the waters shall languish.　　　*hooks*

9 Moreover they that work in fine flax, and they that weave networks, shall be confounded.

10 And they shall be broken in the purposes thereof, all that make sluices *and* ponds for fish.

11 Surely the princes of Zo'-an *are* fools, the counsel of the wise counsellors of Pharaoh is become ^Tbrutish: how say ye unto Pharaoh, I *am* the son of the wise, the son of ancient kings?　　*foolish*

12 ^RWhere *are* they? where *are* thy wise *men?* and let them tell thee now, and let them know what the LORD of hosts hath ^Rpurposed upon Egypt.　1 Cor. 1:20 · Ps. 33:11

13 The princes of Zo'-an are become fools, the princes of Noph are deceived; they have also seduced Egypt, *even they that are* the stay of the tribes thereof.

14 The LORD hath mingled ^Ra perverse spirit in the midst thereof: and they have caused Egypt to err in every work thereof, as a drunken *man* staggereth in his vomit.　　29:10; 1 Kin. 22:22

15 Neither shall there be *any* work for Egypt, which the head or tail, branch or rush, may do.

16 In that day shall Egypt ^Rbe like unto women: and it shall be afraid and fear because of the ^Tshaking of the hand of the LORD of hosts, ^Rwhich he shaketh over it.　Jer. 51:30; Nah. 3:13 · *waving* · 11:15

17 And the land of Judah shall be a terror unto Egypt, every one that maketh mention thereof shall be afraid in himself, because of the counsel of the LORD of hosts, which he hath ^Rdetermined against it.　　14:24; Dan. 4:35

18 In that day shall five cities in the land of Egypt speak the language of Canaan, and swear to the LORD of hosts; one shall be called, The city of destruction.

19 In that day shall there be an altar to the LORD in the midst of the land of Egypt, and a pillar at the border thereof to the LORD.

20 And ^Rit shall be for a sign and for a witness unto the LORD of hosts in the land of Egypt: for they shall cry unto the LORD because of the oppressors, and he shall send them a ^Rsaviour, and a ^Tgreat one, and he shall deliver them.　Josh. 4:20; 22:27 · 43:11 · *mighty*

21 And the LORD shall be known to Egypt, and the Egyptians shall ^Rknow the LORD in that day, and shall do sacrifice and oblation; yea, they shall vow a vow unto the LORD, and perform *it.*　[2:3, 4; 11:9]

22 And the LORD shall smite Egypt: he shall smite and ^Rheal *it:* and they shall return *even* to the LORD, and he shall be intreated of them, and shall heal them.　　30:26

23 In that day ^Rshall there be a highway out of Egypt to Assyria, and the Assyrian shall come into Egypt, and the Egyptian into Assyria, and the Egyptians shall serve with the Assyrians. 35:8; 49:11

24 In that day shall Israel be the third with Egypt and with Assyria, *even* a blessing in the midst of the land:

25 Whom the LORD of hosts shall bless, saying, Blessed *be* Egypt my people, and Assyria ^Rthe work of my hands, and Israel mine inheritance. Hos. 2:23; [Eph. 2:10]

20 In the year that ^RTar'-tan came unto Ash'-dod, (when Sar'-gon the king of Assyria sent him,) and fought against Ash'-dod, and took it;　　2 Kin. 18:17

2 At the same time spake the LORD by Isaiah the son of Amoz, saying, Go and loose ^Rthe sackcloth from off thy loins, and put off thy shoe from thy foot. And he did so, ^Rwalking naked and barefoot.　Zech. 13:4; Matt. 3:4 · Mic. 1:8

3 And the LORD said, Like as my servant Isaiah hath walked naked and barefoot three years ^R*for* a sign and wonder upon E-gypt and upon E-thi-o'-pi-a;　8:18

4 So shall the ^Rking of Assyria lead away the Egyptians prisoners, and the E-thi-o'-pi-ans cap-

tives, young and old, naked and barefoot, ^Reven with *their* buttocks uncovered, to the shame of Egypt.   19:4 · Jer. 13:22; Mic. 1:11

5 ^RAnd they shall be afraid and ashamed of E-thi-o′-pi-a their expectation, and of Egypt their glory.   30:3–5; 31:1; Ezek. 29:6, 7

6 And the inhabitant of this ^Tisle shall say in that day, Behold, such *is* our expectation, whither we flee for ^Rhelp to be delivered from the king of Assyria: and how shall we escape?   territory · 30:5, 7

21 The burden of the desert of the sea. As ^Rwhirlwinds in the south pass through; *so* it cometh from the desert, from a terrible land.   Zech. 9:14

2 A grievous vision is declared unto me; the treacherous dealer dealeth treacherously, and the spoiler spoileth. Go up, O E′-lam: besiege, O Me′-di-a; all the sighing thereof have I made to cease.

3 Therefore are my loins filled with pain: pangs have taken hold upon me, as the pangs of a woman that travaileth: I was bowed down at the hearing *of it*; I was dismayed at the seeing *of it.*

4 My heart ^Tpanted, fearfulness affrighted me: ^Rthe night of my ^Tpleasure hath he turned into fear unto me.   wavered · Deut. 28:67 · longing

5 Prepare the table, watch in the watchtower, eat, drink: arise, ye princes, *and* anoint the shield.

6 For thus hath the Lord said unto me, Go, set a watchman, let him declare what he seeth.

7 And he saw a chariot *with* a couple of horsemen, a chariot of ^Tasses, *and* a chariot of camels; and he hearkened diligently with ^Tmuch heed: donkeys · great care

8 And he cried, A lion: My lord, I stand continually upon the watchtower in the daytime, and I a.n set in my ward whole nights:

9 And, behold, here cometh a chariot of men, *with* a couple of horsemen. And he answered and said, ^RBabylon is fallen, is fallen; and all the graven images of her

gods he hath broken unto the ground.   Dan. 5:28, 31; Rev. 14:8; 18:2

10 ^RO my threshing, and the ^Tcorn of my floor: that which I have heard of the LORD of hosts, the God of Israel, have I declared unto you.   Jer. 51:33; Mic. 4:13 · grain

11 The burden of Du′-mah. He calleth to me out of Se′-ir, Watchman, what of the night? Watchman, what of the night?

12 The watchman said, The morning cometh, and also the night: if ye will enquire, enquire ye: return, come.

13 ^RThe burden upon Arabia. In the forest in Arabia shall ye lodge, O ye travelling companies ^Rof Ded′-a-nim.   Jer. 25:24; 49:28 · Gen. 10:7

14 The inhabitants of the land of Te′-ma brought water to him that was thirsty, they ^Tprevented with their bread him that fled.   met

15 For they fled from the swords, from the drawn sword, and from the bent bow, and from the grievousness of war.

16 For thus hath the Lord said unto me, Within a year, ^Raccording to the years of an hireling, and all the glory of ^RKe′-dar shall fail: 16:14 · Ps. 120:5; Ezek. 27:21

17 And the residue of the number of archers, the mighty men of the children of Ke′-dar, shall be diminished: for the LORD God of Israel hath spoken *it.*

22 The burden of the valley of vision. What aileth thee now, that thou art wholly gone up to the housetops?

2 Thou that art full of stirs, a tumultuous city, ^Ra joyous city: thy slain *men are* not slain with the sword, nor dead in battle. 32:13

3 All thy rulers are fled together, they are ^Tbound by the archers: all that are found in thee are bound together, *which* have fled from far.   captured

4 Therefore said I, Look away from me; ^RI will weep bitterly, labour not to comfort me, because of the ^Tspoiling of the daughter of my people.   Jer. 4:19 · plundering

5 ^RFor *it is* a day of trouble, and

of treading down, and of perplexity ^{R}by the Lord GOD of hosts in the valley of vision, breaking down the walls, and of crying to the mountains.　37:3 · Lam. 1:5; 2:2

6 ^{R}And E'-lam bare the quiver with chariots of men *and* horsemen, and ^{R}Kir uncovered the shield.　Jer. 49:35 · 15:1

7 And it shall come to pass, *that* thy choicest valleys shall be full of chariots, and the horsemen shall set themselves in array at the gate.

8 And he discovered the covering of Judah, and thou didst look in that day to the armour ^{R}of the house of the forest.　1 Kin. 7:2; 10:17

9 ^{R}Ye have seen also the breaches of the city of David, that they are many: and ye gathered together the waters of the lower pool.　2 Kin. 20:20; 2 Chr. 32:4; Neh. 3:16

10 And ye have numbered the houses of Jerusalem, and the houses have ye broken down to fortify the wall.

11 ^{R}Ye made also a ditch between the two walls for the water of the old pool: but ye have not looked unto the maker thereof, neither had respect unto him that fashioned it long ago.　Neh. 3:16

12 And in that day did the Lord GOD of hosts ^{R}call to weeping, and to mourning, and to baldness, and to girding with sackcloth:　32:11

13 And behold joy and gladness, slaying oxen, and killing sheep, eating flesh, and ^{R}drinking wine: ^{R}let us eat and drink; for to morrow we shall die.　5:11; 28:7, 8 · 56:12

14 And it was revealed in mine ears by the LORD of hosts, Surely this iniquity ^{R}shall not be purged from you till ye die, saith the Lord GOD of hosts.　1 Sam. 3:14; Ezek. 24:13

15 Thus saith the Lord GOD of hosts, Go, get thee unto this treasurer, *even* unto ^{R}Sheb'-na, which *is* over the house, *and say,*　36:3

16 What hast thou here? and whom hast thou here, that thou hast hewed thee out a sepulchre here, *as* he ^{R}that heweth him out a sepulchre on high, *and* that grav-

eth an habitation for himself in a rock?　2 Chr. 16:14; Matt. 27:60

17 Behold, the LORD will carry thee away with a mighty captivity, and will surely ^{T}cover thee.　*seize*

18 He will surely violently turn and toss thee *like* a ball into a large country: there shalt thou die, and there the ^{R}chariots of thy glory *shall be* the shame of thy lord's house.　2:7

19 And I will drive thee from thy ^{T}station, and from thy ^{T}state shall he pull thee down.　*office · position*

20 And it shall come to pass in that day, that I will call my servant E-li'-a-kim the son of Hil-ki'-ah:

21 And I will clothe him with thy robe, and strengthen him with thy ^{T}girdle, and I will commit thy ^{T}government into his hand: and he shall be a father to the inhabitants of Jerusalem, and to the house of Judah.　*belt · responsibility*

22 And the key of the house of ☆ David will I lay upon his ^{R}shoulder; so he shall ^{R}open, and none shall shut; and he shall shut, and none shall open.　9:6 · Rev. 3:7

23 And I will fasten him *as* ^{R}a nail in a sure place; and he shall be for a glorious throne to his father's house.　Ezra 9:8; Zech. 10:4

24 And they shall hang upon him all the glory of his father's house, the offspring and the issue, all vessels of small quantity, from the vessels of cups, even to all the vessels of ^{T}flagons.　*pitchers*

25 In that day, saith the LORD of hosts, shall the ^{T}nail that is fastened in the sure place be removed, and be cut down, and fall; and the burden that *was* upon it shall be cut off: for the LORD hath spoken *it.*　*peg*

23 The ^{R}burden of Tyre. Howl, ye ships of Tar'-shish; for it is laid waste, so that there is no house, no ^{T}entering in: from the land of Chit'-tim it is revealed to them.　Jer. 25:22; Zech. 9:2, 4 · *harbour*

2 Be still, ye inhabitants of the isle; thou whom the merchants of ^{T}Zi'-don, that pass over the sea, have ^{T}replenished.　Or *Sidon · filled*

3 And by great waters the
᭐seed of Si′-hor, the harvest of the
river, is her revenue; and ᴿshe is a
mart of nations.   grain · Ezek. 27:3–23

4 Be thou ashamed, O Zi′-don:
for the sea hath spoken, even the
strength of the sea, saying, I travail not, nor bring forth children,
neither do I nourish up young
men, nor bring up virgins.

5 ᴿAs at the report concerning
Egypt, so shall they be sorely
pained at the report of Tyre. 19:16

6 Pass ye over to Tar′-shish;
howl, ye inhabitants of the isle.

7 Is this your ᴿjoyous city,
whose antiquity is of ancient
days? her own feet shall carry her
afar off to sojourn.   22:2; 32:13

8 Who hath taken this counsel
against Tyre, the crowning city,
whose merchants are princes,
whose ᵀtraffickers are the honourable of the earth?   traders

9 The LORD of hosts hath purposed it, to stain the pride of
all glory, and to bring into contempt all the honourable of the
earth.

10 Pass through thy land as a
river, O daughter of Tar′-shish:
there is no more strength.

11 He stretched out his hand
over the sea, he shook the kingdoms: the LORD hath given a commandment ᴿagainst ᵀthe merchant city, to destroy the strong
holds thereof.   Zech. 9:2–4 · Canaan

12 And he said, Thou shalt no
more rejoice, O thou oppressed
virgin, daughter of Zi′-don: arise,
ᴿpass over to Chit′-tim; there also
shalt thou have no rest.   Rev. 18:22

13 Behold the land of the ᴿChal-
de′-ans; this people was not, till
the Assyrian founded it for ᴿthem
that dwell in the wilderness: they
set up the towers thereof, they
raised up the palaces thereof; and
he brought it to ruin.   47:1 · Ps. 72:9

14 Howl, ye ships of Tar′-shish:
for your strength is laid waste.

15 And it shall come to pass in
that day, that Tyre shall be forgotten seventy years, according to
the days of one king: after the end

of seventy years shall Tyre sing as
an harlot.

16 Take an harp, go about the
city, thou harlot that hast been
forgotten; make sweet melody,
sing many songs, that thou mayest be remembered.

17 And it shall come to pass
after the end of seventy years,
that the LORD will visit Tyre, and
she shall turn to her hire, and
ᴿshall commit fornication with all
the kingdoms of the world upon
the face of the earth.   Rev. 17:2

18 And her merchandise and
her hire ᴿshall be holiness to the
LORD: it shall not be treasured nor
laid up; for her merchandise shall
be for them that dwell before the
LORD, to eat sufficiently, and for
durable clothing.   Zech. 14:20, 21

24 Behold, the LORD maketh
the earth empty, and maketh
it waste, and turneth it upside
down, and scattereth abroad the
inhabitants thereof.

2 And it shall be, as with the
people, so with the ᴿpriest; as with
the servant, so with his master; as
with the maid, so with her mistress; ᴿas with the buyer, so with
the seller; as with the lender, so
with the borrower; as with the
taker of usury, so with the giver of
usury to him.   Hos. 4:9 · Ezek. 7:12, 13

3 The land shall be utterly
emptied, and utterly spoiled: for
the LORD hath spoken this word.

4 The earth mourneth and
fadeth away, the world languisheth and fadeth away, the
ᴿhaughtyᵀ people of the earth do
languish.   25:11 · proud

5 The earth also is defiled under the inhabitants thereof; because they have transgressed the
laws, changed the ordinance, broken the everlasting covenant.

6 Therefore hath the curse devoured the earth, and they that
dwell therein are desolate: therefore the inhabitants of the earth
are burned, and few men left.

7 ᴿThe new wine mourneth, the
vine languisheth, all the merry-
hearted do sigh.   16:8–10; Joel 1:10, 12

8 The mirth of tabrets ceaseth, the noise of them that rejoice endeth, the joy of the harp ceaseth.

9 They shall not drink wine with a song; strong drink shall be bitter to them that drink it.

10 The city of confusion is broken down: every house is shut up, that no man may come in.

11 *There is* a crying for wine in the streets; all joy is darkened, the mirth of the land is gone.

12 In the city is left desolation, and the gate is ᵀsmitten with destruction. *stricken*

13 When thus it shall be in the midst of the land among the people, ᴿ*there shall be* as the shaking of an olive tree, *and* as the gleaning grapes when the vintage is done. [17:5, 6; 27:12]

14 They shall lift up their voice, they shall sing for the majesty of the LORD, they shall cry aloud from the sea.

15 Wherefore ᴿglorify ye the LORD in the ᵀfires, *even* the name of the LORD God of Israel in the isles of the sea. 25:3 · *dawning light*

16 From the uttermost part of the earth have we heard songs, *even* glory to the righteous. But I said, My leanness, my leanness, woe unto me! ᴿthe treacherous dealers have dealt treacherously; yea, the treacherous dealers have dealt very treacherously. 21:2; 33:1

17 ᴿFear, and the pit, and the snare, *are* upon thee, O inhabitant of the earth. Jer. 48:43; Amos 5:19

18 And it shall come to pass, *that* he who fleeth from the noise of the fear shall fall into the pit; and he that cometh up out of the midst of the pit shall be taken in the snare: for the windows from on high are open, and the foundations of the earth do shake.

19 ᴿThe earth is utterly broken down, the earth is ᵀclean dissolved, the earth is ᵀmoved exceedingly. Jer. 4:23 · *split open · shaken*

20 The earth shall ᴿreel to and fro like a drunkard, and shall be removed like a cottage; and the transgression thereof shall be heavy upon it; and it shall fall, and not rise again. v. 1; 19:14; 28:7

21 And it shall come to pass in that day, *that* the LORD shall punish the host of the high ones *that are* on high, ᴿand the kings of the earth upon the earth. Ps. 76:12

22 And they shall be gathered together, *as* prisoners are gathered in the pit, and shall be shut up in the prison, and after many days shall they be ᵀvisited. *punished*

23 Then the moon shall be confounded, and the sun ashamed, when the LORD of hosts shall ᴿreign in ᴿmount Zion, and in Jerusalem, and before his ancients gloriously. Rev. 19:4, 6 · [Heb. 12:22]

25 O LORD, thou *art* my God; ᴿI will exalt thee, I will praise thy name; ᴿfor thou hast done wonderful *things*; ᴿ*thy* counsels of old *are* faithfulness *and* truth. Ex. 15:2 · Ps. 98:1 · Num. 23:19

2 For thou hast made ᴿof a city an heap; *of* a defenced city a ruin: a palace of strangers to be no city; it shall never be built. 21:9; 23:13

3 Therefore shall the strong people ᴿglorify thee, the city of the ᵀterrible nations shall fear thee. 24:15; Rev. 11:13 · *ruthless*

4 For thou hast been a strength to the poor, a strength to the needy in his distress, ᴿa refuge from the storm, a shadow from the heat, when the blast of the terrible ones *is* as a storm *against* the wall. 4:6

5 Thou shalt bring down the noise of strangers, as the heat in a dry place; *even* the heat with the shadow of a cloud: the ᵀbranch of the terrible ones shall be ᵀbrought low. *song · diminished*

6 And in ᴿthis mountain shall the LORD of hosts make unto all people a feast of fat things, a feast of wines on the lees, of fat things full of marrow, of wines on the lees well refined. [2:2–4; 56:7]

7 And he will destroy in this mountain the face of the covering cast over all people, and the vail that is spread over all nations.

8 He will ᴿswallow up death in

victory; and the Lord GOD will
Rwipe away tears from off all
faces; and the rebuke of his people shall he take away from off all
the earth: for the LORD hath spo-
ken *it*. [Rev. 20:14] · 30:19; Rev. 7:17; 21:4

9 And it shall be said in that
day, Lo, this *is* our God; Rwe have
waited for him, and he will save
us: this *is* the LORD; we have waited for him, we will be glad and
rejoice in his salvation. 8:17; 26:8

10 For in this mountain shall the
hand of the LORD rest, and RMoab
shall be trodden down under him,
even as straw is trodden down for
the dunghill.   Amos 2:1–3; Zeph. 2:9

11 And he shall spread forth
his hands in the midst of them,
as he that swimmeth spreadeth
forth *his hands* to swim: and he
shall bring down their Rpride
together with the spoils of their
hands.   24:4

12 And the Rfortress of the high
fort of thy walls shall he bring
down, lay low, *and* bring to the
ground, *even* to the dust. 26:5

26 In Rthat day shall this song
be sung in the land of Judah;
We have a strong city; Rsalvation
will *God* appoint *for* walls and
bulwarks.   2:11; 12:1 · 60:18

2 ROpen ye the gates, that the
righteous nation which keepeth
the truth may enter in. Ps. 118:19, 20

3 Thou wilt keep *him* in perfect
peace, *whose* mind *is* stayed *on*
thee: because he trusteth in thee.

4 Trust ye in the LORD for ever:
Rfor in the LORD JE-HO'-VAH *is*
everlasting strength: 12:2; 45:17

5 For he bringeth down them
that dwell on high; Rthe lofty city,
he layeth it low; he layeth it low,
even to the ground; he bringeth it
even to the dust.   25:11, 12

6 The foot shall Ttread it down,
even the feet of the poor, *and* the
steps of the needy.   *trample*

7 The way of the just *is* uprightness: thou, most upright, dost
weigh the path of the just.

8 Yea, Rin the way of thy judgments, O LORD, have we Rwaited
for thee; the desire of *our* soul *is*

to thy name, and to the remembrance of thee.   64:5 · 25:9; 33:2

9 With my soul have I desired
thee in the night; yea, with my
spirit within me will I seek thee
early: for when thy judgments *are*
in the earth, the inhabitants of the
world will learn righteousness.

10 RLet Tfavour be shewed to the
wicked, *yet* will he not learn righteousness: in Rthe land of uprightness will he deal unjustly, and will
not behold the majesty of the
LORD.   [Rom. 2:4] · *grace* · Ps. 143:10

11 LORD, *when* thy hand is lifted
up, Rthey will not see: *but* they
shall see, and be ashamed for
their envy at the people; yea, the
fire of thine enemies shall devour
them.   5:12; Job 34:27; Ps. 28:5

12 LORD, thou wilt Tordain peace
for us: for thou also hast wrought
all our works in us.   *establish*

13 O LORD our God, *other* lords
beside thee have had dominion
over us: *but* by thee only will we
make mention of thy name.

14 *They are* dead, they shall not
live; *they are* deceased, they shall
not rise: therefore hast thou visited and destroyed them, and made
all their memory to Rperish. 14:22

15 Thou hast Rincreased the nation, O LORD, thou hast increased
the nation: thou art glorified: thou
hadst removed *it* far *unto* all the
ends of the earth.   9:3

16 LORD, Rin trouble have they
visited thee, they Tpoured out a
prayer *when* thy chastening *was*
upon them. Hos. 5:15 · Or *whispered*

17 Like as Ra woman with child,
that draweth near the time of her
delivery, is in pain, *and* crieth out
in her pangs; so have we been in
thy sight, O LORD.   13:8; [John 16:21]

18 We have been with child, we
have been in pain, we have as it
were brought forth wind; we have
not wrought any deliverance in
the earth; neither have Rthe inhabitants of the world fallen. Ps. 17:14

19 Thy dead *men* shall live, *to-*
gether with my dead body shall
they arise. RAwake and sing, ye
that dwell in dust: for thy dew *is*

as the dew of herbs, and the earth shall cast out the dead.   Hos. 13:14

20 Come, my people, enter thou into thy chambers, and shut thy doors about thee: hide thyself as it were for a little moment, until the indignation be overpast.

21 For, behold, the LORD ᴿcometh out of his place to punish the inhabitants of the earth for their iniquity: the earth also shall disclose her blood, and shall no more cover her slain.   Mic. 1:3; [Jude 14]

27 In that day the LORD with his sore and great and strong sword shall punish le-vi′-a-than the piercing serpent, ᴶeven le-vi′-a-than that crooked serpent; and he shall slay ᴿthe dragon that *is* in the sea.   Rev. 12:9, 15 · Ezek. 29:3

2 In that day ᴿsing ye unto her, ᴿA vineyard of red wine.   5:1 · 5:7

3 I the LORD do keep it; I will water it every moment: lest *any* hurt it, I will keep it night and day.

4 Fury *is* not in me: who would set the briers *and* thorns against me in battle? I would go through them, I would burn them together.

5 Or let him take hold ᴿof my strength, *that* he may ᴿmake peace with me; *and* he shall make peace with me.   25:4 · 26:3, 12

6 He shall cause them that come of Jacob ᴿto take root: Israel shall blossom and bud, and fill the face of the world with fruit.   37:31

7 Hath he smitten him, as he smote those that smote him? *or* is he slain according to the slaughter of them that are slain by him?

8 ᴿIn measure, when it shooteth forth, thou wilt debate with it: he stayeth his rough wind in the day of the east wind.   Job 23:6; Ps. 6:1

9 By this therefore shall the iniquity of Jacob be ᵀpurged; and this *is* all the fruit to take away his sin; when he maketh all the stones of the altar as chalkstones that are beaten in sunder, the groves and images shall not stand up.   *covered*

10 Yet the defenced city *shall be* ᴿdesolate, *and* the habitation forsaken, and left like a wilderness:

there shall the calf feed, and there shall he lie down, and consume the branches thereof.   5:6, 17; 32:14

11 When the boughs thereof are withered, they shall be broken off: the women come, *and* set them on fire: for ᴿit *is* a people of no understanding: therefore he that made them will ᴿnot have mercy on them, and he that formed them will shew them no favour.   1:3 · 9:17

12 And it shall come to pass in that day, *that* the LORD shall beat off from the channel of the river unto the stream of Egypt, and ye shall be ᴿgathered one by one, O ye children of Israel.   [11:11; 56:8]

13 And it shall come to pass in that day, *that* the great trumpet shall be blown, and they shall come which were ready to perish in the land of Assyria, and the outcasts in the land of Egypt, and shall ᴿworship the LORD in the holy mount at Jerusalem.   [2:3]

28 Woe to the crown of pride, to the drunkards of E′-phra-im, whose glorious beauty *is* a fading flower, which *are* on the head of the fat valleys of them that are overcome with wine!

2 Behold, the Lord hath a mighty and strong one, ᴿ*which* as a tempest of hail *and* a destroying storm, as a flood of mighty waters overflowing, shall cast down to the earth with the hand.   30:30

3 The crown of pride, the drunkards of E′-phra-im, shall be ᵀtrodden under feet: *trampled*

4 And the glorious beauty, which *is* on the head of the fat valley, shall be a fading flower, *and* as the ᵀhasty fruit before the summer; which *when* he that looketh upon it seeth, while it is yet in his hand he eateth it up.   *firstfruit*

5 In that day shall the LORD of hosts be for a crown of glory, and for a diadem of beauty, unto the residue of his people,

6 And for a spirit of judgment to him that sitteth in judgment, and for strength to them that turn the battle to the gate.

7 But they also ᴿhave erred

through wine, and through strong drink are out of the way; the priest and the prophet have erred through strong drink, they are swallowed up of wine, they are out of the way through strong drink; they err in vision, they stumble *in* judgment.   5:11, 22

8 For all tables are full of vomit *and* filthiness, so *that there is* no place *clean.*

9 ^RWhom shall he teach knowledge? and whom shall he make to understand doctrine? *them that are* weaned from the milk, *and* drawn from the breasts.   Jer. 6:10

10 ^RFor precept *must be* upon precept, precept upon precept; line upon line, line upon line; here a little, *and* there a little: [Neh. 9:30]

11 For with ^Rstammering lips and another tongue will he speak to this people.   33:19; 1 Cor. 14:21

12 To whom he said, This *is* the rest *wherewith* ye may cause the weary to rest; and this *is* the refreshing: yet they would not hear.

13 But the word of the LORD was unto them precept upon precept, precept upon precept; line upon line, line upon line; here a little, *and* there a little; that they might go, and fall backward, and be broken, and snared, and taken.

14 Wherefore hear the word of the LORD, ye scornful men, that rule this people which *is* in Jerusalem.

15 Because ye have said, We have made a covenant with death, and with ^Thell are we at agreement; when the overflowing scourge shall pass through, it shall not come unto us: ^Rfor we have made lies our refuge, and under falsehood have we hid ourselves: Or *Sheol* · Ezek. 13:22; Amos 2:4

☆ 16 Therefore thus saith the Lord GOD, Behold, I lay in Zion for a foundation ^Ra stone, a tried stone, a precious corner *stone*, a sure foundation: he that believeth shall not make haste.   Luke 20:17; Acts 4:11

17 ^TJudgment also will I lay to the line, and righteousness to the plummet: and the hail shall sweep

away the refuge of lies, and the waters shall overflow the hiding place.   *Justice*

18 And your covenant with death shall be disannulled, and your agreement with hell shall not stand; when the overflowing scourge shall pass through, then ye shall be trodden down by it.

19 ^TFrom the time that it goeth forth it shall take you: for morning by morning shall it pass over, by day and by night: and it shall be a ^Tvexation only *to* understand the report.   *As often as · terror just*

20 For the bed is shorter than that *a man* can stretch himself *on* it: and the covering narrower than that he can wrap himself *in* it.

21 For the LORD shall rise up as *in* mount ^RPer'-a-zim, he shall be wroth as *in* the valley of Gib'-e-on, that he may do his work, his strange work; and bring to pass his act, his strange act.   2 Sam. 5:20

22 Now therefore be ye not mockers, lest your bands be made strong: for I have heard from the Lord GOD of hosts ^Ra consumption, even determined upon the whole earth.   10:22; Dan. 9:27

23 Give ye ear, and hear my voice; hearken, and hear my speech.

24 Doth the plowman plow all day to sow? doth he open and break the clods of his ground?

25 When he hath ^Tmade plain the face thereof, doth he not cast abroad the fitches, and scatter the cummin, and cast in the principal wheat and the appointed barley and the rie in their place?   *levelled*

26 For his God doth instruct him to discretion, *and* doth teach him.

27 For the ^Tfitches are not threshed with a threshing ^Tinstrument, neither is a cart wheel ^Tturned about upon the cummin; but the fitches are beaten out with a staff, and the cummin with a rod.   *black cummin is · sledge · rolled*

28 Bread ^Tcorn is bruised; because he will not ever be threshing it, nor break *it with* the wheel

of his cart, nor ^Tbruise it *with* his horsemen.   flour *must be ground · crush*

29 This also cometh forth from the LORD of hosts, ^R*which* is wonderful in counsel, *and* excellent in working.   9:6; Ps. 92:5; Jer. 32:19

29 Woe ^Rto A'-ri-el, to A'-ri-el, the city ^R*where* David dwelt! add ye year to year; let them kill sacrifices.   Ezek. 24:6, 9 · 2 Sam. 5:9

2 Yet I will distress A'-ri-el, and there shall be heaviness and sorrow: and it shall be unto me as A'-ri-el.

3 And I will camp against thee round about, and will lay siege against thee with a mount, and I will raise forts against thee.

4 And thou shalt be brought down, *and* shalt speak out of the ground, and thy speech shall be low out of the dust, and thy voice shall be, as ^Tof one that hath a familiar spirit, ^Rout of the ground, and thy speech shall whisper out of the dust.   *a medium's · 8:19*

5 Moreover the multitude of thy ^Rstrangers shall be like small dust, and the multitude of the terrible ones *shall be* ^Ras chaff that passeth away: yea, it shall be at an instant suddenly.   25:5 · 17:13

6 ^RThou shalt be visited of the LORD of hosts with thunder, and with earthquake, and great noise, with storm and tempest, and the flame of devouring fire.   28:2; 30:30

7 ^RAnd the multitude of all the nations that fight against A'-ri-el, even all that fight against her and her munition, and that distress her, shall be as a dream of a night vision.   37:36; Mic. 4:11, 12; Zech. 12:9

8 ^RIt shall even be as when an hungry *man* dreameth, and, behold, he eateth; but he awaketh, and his soul is empty: or as when a thirsty man dreameth, and, behold, he drinketh; but he awaketh, and, behold, *he is* faint, and his soul ^Thath appetite: so shall the multitude of all the nations be, that fight against mount Zion.   Ps. 73:20 · *still craves*

9 Stay yourselves, and wonder; cry ye out, and cry: they are

drunken, but not with wine; they stagger, but not with strong drink.

10 For ^Rthe LORD hath poured out upon you the spirit of deep sleep, and hath closed your eyes: the prophets and your rulers, the seers hath he covered.   Ps. 69:23

11 And the vision of all is become unto you as the words of a book ^Rthat is sealed, which *men* deliver to one that is learned, saying, Read this, I pray thee: and he saith, I cannot; for it *is* sealed: 8:16

12 And the book is delivered to him that is not learned, saying, Read this, I pray thee: and he saith, I am not learned.

13 Wherefore the Lord said, Forasmuch as this people draw near *me* with their mouth, and with their lips do honour me, but have removed their heart far from me, and their fear toward me is taught by the precept of men:

14 Therefore, behold, I will proceed to do a marvellous work among this people, *even* a marvellous work and a wonder: for the wisdom of their wise *men* shall perish, and the understanding of their prudent *men* shall be hid.

15 ^RWoe unto them that seek deep to hide their counsel from the LORD, and their works are in the dark, and they say, Who seeth us? and who knoweth us?   30:1

16 Surely your turning of things upside down shall be esteemed as the potter's clay: for shall the ^Rwork say of him that made it, He made me not? or shall the thing framed say of him that framed it, He had no understanding?   45:9

17 *Is* it not yet a very little while, and ^RLeb'-a-non shall be turned into a fruitful field, and the fruitful field shall be esteemed as a forest?   32:15

18 And ^Rin that day shall the deaf hear the words of the book, and the eyes of the blind shall see out of obscurity, and out of darkness.   35:5; Matt. 11:5; Mark 7:37

19 ^RThe meek also shall increase *their* joy in the LORD, and

☆

the poor among men shall rejoice in the Holy One of Israel. [11:4]

20 For the terrible one is brought to nought, and ^Rthe scorner is consumed, and all that watch for iniquity are cut off: 28:14

21 That make a man an offender for a word, and ^Rlay a snare for him that reproveth in the gate, and turn aside the just ^Rfor a thing of nought. Amos 5:10, 12 · Prov. 28:21

22 Therefore thus saith the LORD, ^Rwho redeemed Abraham, concerning the house of Jacob, Jacob shall not now be ^Rashamed, neither shall his face now ^Twax pale. Josh. 24:3 · 45:17 · grow

23 But when he seeth his children, ^Rthe work of mine hands, in the midst of him, they shall sanctify my name, and sanctify the Holy One of Jacob, and shall fear the God of Israel. [45:11; Eph. 2:10]

24 They also ^Rthat erred in spirit shall ^Tcome to understanding, and they that murmured shall learn doctrine. 28:7 · know understanding

30 Woe to the rebellious children, saith the LORD, ^Rthat take counsel, but not of me; and that cover with a covering, but not of my spirit, ^Rthat they may add sin to sin: 29:15 · Deut. 29:19

2 ^RThat walk to go down into Egypt, and have not asked at my mouth; to strengthen themselves in the strength of Pharaoh, and to trust in the shadow of Egypt! 31:1

3 ^RTherefore shall the strength of Pharaoh be your shame, and the trust in the shadow of Egypt your confusion. 20:5; Jer. 37:5, 7

4 For his princes were at ^RZo'-an, and his ambassadors came to Ha'-nes. 19:11

5 They were all ashamed of a people that could not profit them, nor be an help nor profit, but a shame, and also a reproach.

6 ^RThe burden of the beasts of the south: into the land of trouble and anguish, from whence come the young and old lion, ^Rthe viper and fiery flying serpent, they will carry their riches upon the shoulders of young asses, and their

treasures upon the bunches of camels, to a people that shall not profit them. 57:9; Hos. 8:9; 12:1 · 14:29

7 ^RFor the Egyptians shall help in vain, and to no purpose: therefore have I cried concerning this, Their strength is to sit still. Jer. 37:7

8 Now go, ^Rwrite it before them in a table, and note it in a book, that it may be for the time to come for ever and ever: Hab. 2:2

9 That this is a rebellious people, lying children, children that will not hear the law of the LORD:

10 Which say to the seers, See not; and to the prophets, Prophesy not unto us right things, ^Rspeak unto us smooth things, prophesy deceits: 2 Tim. 4:3, 4

11 Get you out of the way, turn aside out of the path, cause the Holy One of Israel to cease from before us.

12 Wherefore thus saith the Holy One of Israel, Because ye ^Rdespise this word, and trust in oppression and perverseness, and ^Tstay thereon: 5:24; Amos 2:4 · Or rely

13 Therefore this iniquity shall be to you ^Ras a breach ready to fall, swelling out in a high wall, whose breaking ^Rcometh suddenly at an instant. 58:12 · 29:5

14 And ^Rhe shall break it as the breaking of the potters' vessel that is broken in pieces; he shall not spare: so that there shall not be found in the bursting of it a sherd to take fire from the hearth, or to take water withal out of the ^Tpit. Ps. 2:9; Jer. 19:11 · cistern

15 For thus saith the Lord GOD, the Holy One of Israel; ^RIn returning and rest shall ye be saved; in quietness and in confidence shall be your strength: ^Rand ye would not. 7:4; 28:12; Ps. 116:7 · Matt. 23:37

16 But ye said, No; for we will flee upon horses; therefore shall ye flee: and, We will ride upon the swift; therefore shall they that pursue you be swift.

17 One thousand shall flee at the rebuke of one; at the rebuke of five shall ye flee: till ye be left as a beacon upon the top of a

mountain, and as an ensign on an hill.

18 And therefore will the LORD wait, that he may be [R]gracious unto you, and therefore will he be exalted, that he may have mercy upon you: for the LORD *is* a God of [T]judgment: blessed *are* all they that [R]wait for him.   33:2 · *justice* · 26:8

19 For the people [R]shall dwell in Zion at Jerusalem: thou shalt [R]weep no more: he will be very gracious unto thee at the voice of thy cry; when he shall hear it, he will [R]answer thee.   65:9 · 25:8 · 65:24

20 And *though* the Lord give you [R]the bread of adversity, and the water of affliction, yet shall not thy teachers be removed into a corner any more, but thine eyes shall see thy teachers: 1 Kin. 22:27

21 And thine ears shall hear a word behind thee, saying, This *is* the way, walk ye in it, when ye [R]turn to the right hand, and when ye turn to the left.   Josh. 1:7

22 [R]Ye shall defile also the covering of thy graven images of silver, and the ornament of thy molten images of gold: thou shalt cast them away as [T]a menstruous cloth; thou shalt say unto it, Get thee hence.   2:20; 31:7 · *an unclean thing*

23 [R]Then shall he give the rain of thy seed, that thou shalt sow the ground withal; and bread of the increase of the earth, and it shall be [T]fat and plenteous: in that day shall thy cattle feed in large pastures.   [Matt. 6:33]; 1 Tim. 6:8 · *rich*

24 The oxen likewise and the young asses that ear the ground shall eat clean provender, which hath been winnowed with the shovel and with the fan.

25 And there shall be upon every high mountain, and upon every high hill, rivers *and* streams of waters in the day of the great slaughter, when the towers fall.

26 Moreover [R]the light of the moon shall be as the light of the sun, and the light of the sun shall be sevenfold, as the light of seven days, in the day that the LORD bindeth up the [T]breach of his peo-

ple, and healeth the stroke of their wound. [60:19, 20; Rev. 21:23; 22:5] · *bruise*

27 Behold, the name of the LORD cometh from far, burning *with* his anger, and the burden *thereof is* heavy: his lips are full of indignation, and his tongue as a devouring fire:

28 And [R]his breath, as an overflowing stream, [R]shall reach to the midst of the neck, to sift the nations with the sieve of vanity: and *there shall be* [R]a bridle in the jaws of the people, causing *them* to err.   11:4; 2 Thess. 2:8 · 8:8 · 37:29

29 Ye shall have a song, as in the night *when* a holy [T]solemnity is kept; and gladness of heart, as when one goeth with a pipe to come into [R]the mountain of the LORD, to [T]the mighty One of Israel.   *feast* · [2:3] · Lit. *the Rock*

30 [R]And the LORD shall cause his glorious voice to be heard, and shall shew the lighting down of his arm, with the indignation of *his* anger, and *with* the flame of a devouring fire, *with* scattering, and tempest, and hailstones.   29:6

31 For [R]through the voice of the LORD shall the Assyrian be [T]beaten down, [R]*which* smote with a rod.   14:25; 37:36 · *crushed* · 10:5, 24

32 And *in* every place where the grounded staff shall pass, which the LORD shall lay upon him, *it* shall be with [T]tabrets and harps: and in battles of [R]shaking will he fight with it.   *tambourines* · 11:15

33 [R]For To'-phet *is* ordained of old; yea, for the king it is prepared; he hath made *it* deep *and* large: the pile thereof *is* fire and much wood; the breath of the LORD, like a stream of brimstone, doth kindle it.   2 Kin. 23:10; Jer. 7:31

31 Woe to them [R]that go down to Egypt for help; and [T]stay on horses, and trust in chariots, because *they are* many; and in horsemen, because they are very strong; but they look not unto the Holy One of Israel, [R]neither seek the LORD!   30:1, 2 · *rely* · Dan. 9:13

2 Yet he also *is* wise, and will bring [T]evil, and [R]will not call back

his words: but will arise against
the house of the evildoers, and
against the help of them that
work iniquity.   *disaster · Jer. 44:29*
3 Now the Egyptians *are* men,
and not God; and their horses
flesh, and not spirit. When the
LORD shall stretch out his hand,
both he that helpeth shall fall, and
he that is holpen shall fall down,
and they all shall fail together.
4 For thus hath the LORD spoken unto me, Like as the lion and
the young lion roaring on his
prey, when a multitude of shepherds is called forth against him,
he will not be afraid of their voice,
nor abase himself for the noise of
them: so shall the LORD of hosts
come down to fight for mount
Zion, and for the hill thereof.
5 ᴿAs birds flying, so will the
LORD of hosts defend Jerusalem;
defending also he will deliver *it;
and* passing over he will preserve
it.   *Deut. 32:11; Ps. 91:4*
6 ᵀTurn ye unto *him from*
whom the children of Israel have
ᴿdeeply revolted.   *Return · Hos. 9:9*
7 For in that day every man
shall ᴿcast away his idols of silver,
and his idols of gold, which your
own hands have made unto you
for ᴿa sin.   *2:20; 30:22 · 1 Kin. 12:30*
8 Then shall the Assyrian ᴿfall
with the sword, not of a mighty
man; and the sword, not of a
mean man, shall ᴿdevour him: but
he shall flee from the sword, and
his young men shall be discomfited.   *2 Kin. 19:35, 36 · 37:36*
9 ᴿAnd he shall pass over to his
strong hold for fear, and his
princes shall be afraid of the ᵀen-
sign, saith the LORD, whose fire *is*
in Zion, and his furnace in Jerusalem.   *37:37 · banner*
32 Behold, ᴿa king shall reign
in righteousness, and princ-
es shall rule in judgment.   *Ps. 45:1*
2 And a man shall be as an hiding place from the wind, and ᴿa
ᵀcovert from the tempest; as rivers
of water in a dry place, as the
shadow of a great rock in a weary
land.   *4:6 · shelter*

3 And the eyes of them that see
shall not be dim, and the ears of
them that hear shall hearken.
4 The heart also of the rash
shall understand knowledge, and
the tongue of the stammerers
shall be ready to speak plainly.
5 The ᵀvile person shall be no
more called liberal, nor the ᵀchurl
said *to be* bountiful.   *foolish · miser*
6 For the vile person will speak
villany, and his heart will work
iniquity, to practise hypocrisy, and
to utter error against the LORD, to
make empty the soul of the hungry, and he will cause the drink of
the thirsty to fail.
7 The ᵀinstruments also of the
churl *are* evil: he deviseth wicked
devices to destroy the poor with
lying words, even when the needy
speaketh right.   *schemes*
8 But the ᵀliberal deviseth liberal things; and by liberal things
shall he stand.   *generous or noble*
9 Rise up, ye women ᴿthat are
at ease; hear my voice, ye careless
daughters; give ear unto my
speech.   *47:8; Amos 6:1; Zeph. 2:15*
10 Many days and years shall ye
be troubled, ye ᵀcareless women:
for the vintage shall fail, the gathering shall not come.   *complacent*
11 Tremble, ye women that are
at ease; be troubled, ye ᵀcareless
ones: strip you, and make you
bare, and gird *sackcloth* upon
your loins.   *complacent*
12 They shall lament ᵀfor the
teats, for the pleasant fields, for
the fruitful vine.   *upon their breasts*
13 ᴿUpon the land of my people
shall come up thorns *and* briers;
yea, upon all the houses of joy *in*
ᴿthe joyous city: *7:23–25; Hos. 9:6 · 22:2*
14 Because the palaces shall be
forsaken; the multitude of the city
shall be left; the forts and towers
shall be for dens for ever, a joy of
wild asses, a pasture of flocks;
15 Until ᴿthe spirit be poured
upon us from on high, and the
wilderness be a fruitful field, and
the fruitful field be counted for a
forest.   *[11:2]; Ezek. 39:29; [Joel 2:28]*
16 Then judgment shall dwell in

the wilderness, and righteousness remain in the fruitful field.

17 ᴿAnd the work of righteousness shall be peace; and the effect of righteousness quietness and assurance for ever. 2:4; Rom. 14:17

18 And my people shall dwell in a peaceable habitation, and in sure dwellings, and in quiet ᴿresting places; 11:10; 14:3; 30:15; [Zech. 2:5]

19 ᴿWhen it shall hail, coming down on the forest; and the city shall be low in a low place. 30:30

20 Blessed *are* ye that sow beside all waters, that send forth *thither* the feet of ᴿthe ox and the ass. 30:23, 24; [Eccl. 11:1]

33 Woe to thee ᴿthat spoilest, and thou *wast* not spoiled; and dealest treacherously, and they dealt not treacherously with thee! when thou shalt cease to spoil, thou shalt be ᴿspoiled; *and* when thou shalt make an end to deal treacherously, they shall deal treacherously with thee. 21:2 ; 10:12

2 O Lᴏʀᴅ, be gracious unto us; we have waited for thee: be thou their arm every morning, our salvation also in the time of trouble.

3 At the noise of the tumult the people fled; at the lifting up of thyself the nations were scattered.

4 And your ᵀspoil shall be gathered *like* the gathering of the caterpiller: as the running to and fro of locusts shall he run upon them. *plunder*

5 ᴿThe Lᴏʀᴅ is exalted; for he dwelleth on high: he hath filled Zion with ᵀjudgment and righteousness. Ps. 97:9 · *justice*

6 And wisdom and knowledge shall be the stability of thy times, *and* strength of salvation: the fear of the Lᴏʀᴅ *is* his treasure.

7 Behold, their valiant ones shall cry without: the ambassadors of peace shall weep bitterly.

8 ᴿThe highways lie waste, the wayfaring man ceaseth: ᴿhe hath broken the covenant, he hath despised the cities, he regardeth no man. Judg. 5:6 · 2 Kin. 18:13-17

9 The earth mourneth *and* languisheth: Leb'-a-non is ashamed

and hewn down: Shar'-on is like a wilderness; and Ba'-shan and Carmel shake off *their fruits.*

10 ᴿNow will I rise, saith the Lᴏʀᴅ; now will I be exalted; now will I lift up myself. 2:19, 21; Ps. 12:5

11 Ye shall conceive chaff, ye shall bring forth stubble: your breath, *as* fire, shall devour you.

12 And the people shall be *as* the burnings of lime: ᴿ*as* thorns cut up shall they be burned in the fire. 9:18

13 Hear, ᴿye *that are* far off, what I have done; and, ye *that are* near, acknowledge my might. 49:1

14 The sinners in Zion are afraid; fearfulness hath surprised the hypocrites. Who among us shall dwell with the devouring ᴿfire? who among us shall dwell with everlasting burnings? 30:27, 30

15 He that ᴿwalketh righteously, and speaketh uprightly; he that despiseth the gain of oppressions, that shaketh his hands from holding of bribes, that stoppeth his ears from hearing of blood, and ᴿshutteth his eyes from seeing evil; 58:6-11; Ps. 15:2; 24:3, 4 · Ps. 119:37

16 He shall dwell on high: his place of defence *shall be* the ᵀmunitions of rocks: bread shall be given him; his waters *shall be* sure. *fortress*

17 Thine eyes shall see the king in his ᴿbeauty: they shall behold the land that is very far off. Ps. 27:4

18 Thine heart shall meditate terror. Where *is* the scribe? where *is* ᵀthe receiver? where *is* he that counted the towers? *he who weighs*

19 Thou shalt not see a fierce people, ᴿa people of a deeper speech than thou canst perceive; of a stammering tongue, *that* *thou canst* not understand. 28:11

20 ᴿLook upon Zion, the city of our solemnities: thine eyes shall see ᴿJerusalem a quiet habitation, a tabernacle *that* shall not be taken down; not one of the stakes thereof shall ever be removed, neither shall any of the cords thereof be broken. Ps. 48:12 · 32:18

21 But there the glorious Lᴏʀᴅ

will be unto us a place of broad rivers *and* streams; wherein shall go no galley with oars, neither shall gallant ship pass thereby.

22 For the LORD *is* our judge, the LORD *is* our lawgiver, the LORD *is* our king; he will save us.

23 Thy tacklings are loosed; they could not well strengthen their mast, they could not spread the sail: then is the prey of a great ᵀspoil divided; the lame take the prey. *plunder*

24 And the inhabitant shall not say, I am sick: ᴿthe people that dwell therein *shall be* forgiven *their* iniquity. Jer. 50:20; Mic. 7:18, 19

34 Come ᴿ near, ye nations, to hear; and hearken, ye people: let the earth hear, and all that is therein; the world, and all things that come forth of it. Ps. 49:1

2 For the indignation of the LORD *is* upon all nations, and *his* fury upon all their armies: he hath utterly destroyed them, he hath delivered them to the slaughter.

3 Their slain also shall be cast out, and ᴿtheir stink shall come up out of their carcases, and the mountains shall be melted with their blood. Joel 2:20; Amos 4:10

4 And ᴿall the host of heaven shall be dissolved, and the heavens shall be rolled together as a scroll: ᴿand all their host shall fall down, as the leaf falleth off from the vine, and as a ᴿfalling *fig* from the fig tree. 13:13 · 14:12 · Rev. 6:12–14

5 For ᴿmy sword shall be bathed in heaven: behold, it ᴿshall come down upon ᵀId-u-me′-a, and upon the people of my curse, to judgment. Ezek. 21:3–5 · 63:1 · *Edom*

6 The ᴿsword of the LORD is filled with blood, it is made ᵀfat with fatness, *and* with the blood of lambs and goats, with the fat of the kidneys of rams: for ᴿthe LORD hath a sacrifice in Boz′-rah, and a great slaughter in the land of Id-u-me′-a. 66:16 · *overflowing* · Zeph. 1:7

7 And the unicorns shall come down with them, and the bullocks with the bulls; and their land shall be soaked with blood, and their dust made fat with fatness.

8 For *it is* the day of the LORD's ᴿvengeance, *and* the year of recompences for the ᵀcontroversy of Zion. 63:4 · *cause*

9 ᴿAnd the streams thereof shall be turned into pitch, and the dust thereof into brimstone, and the land thereof shall become burning pitch. Deut. 29:23; Ps. 11:6

10 It shall not be quenched night nor day; ᴿthe smoke thereof shall go up for ever: ᴿfrom generation to generation it shall lie waste; none shall pass through it for ever and ever. Rev. 14:11; 18:18; 19:3 · 13:20–22

11 ᴿBut the cormorant and the bittern shall possess it; the owl also and the raven shall dwell in it: and he shall stretch out upon it the line of confusion, and the stones of emptiness. 14:23; Zeph. 2:14

12 They shall call the nobles thereof to the kingdom, but none *shall be* there, and all her princes shall be nothing.

13 And thorns shall come up in her palaces, nettles and brambles in the fortresses thereof: and it shall be an habitation of ᵀdragons, *and* a court for owls. *jackals*

14 The wild beasts of the desert shall also meet with the wild beasts of the island, and the satyr shall cry to his fellow; the screech owl also shall rest there, and find for herself a place of rest.

15 There shall the ᵀgreat owl make her nest, and lay, and hatch, and gather under her shadow: there shall the ᵀvultures also be gathered, every one with her mate. *arrow snake · hawks*

16 Seek ye out of ᴿthe book of the LORD, and read: no one of these shall fail, none shall want her mate: for my mouth it hath commanded, and his spirit it hath gathered them. [Mal. 3:16]

17 And he hath cast the lot for them, and his hand hath divided it unto them ᵀby line: they shall possess it for ever, from generation to generation shall they dwell therein. *with a measuring line*

35 The wilderness and the solitary place shall be glad for them; and the desert shall rejoice, and blossom as the rose.

2 ᴿIt shall blossom abundantly, and rejoice even with joy and singing: the glory of Leb'-a-non shall be given unto it, the excellency of Carmel and Shar'-on, they shall see the ᴿglory of the LORD, *and* the excellency of our God.   32:15 · 40:5

3 ᴿStrengthen ye the weak hands, and confirm the feeble knees.   Job 4:3, 4; Heb. 12:12

4 Say to them *that are* of a fearful heart, Be strong, fear not: behold, your God will come *with* ᴿvengeance, *even* God *with* a recompence; he will come and ᴿsave you.   34:8 · 33:22; Ps. 145:19

☆ 5 Then the ᴿeyes of the blind shall be opened, and the ears of the deaf shall be unstopped.   29:18

☆ 6 Then shall the lame *man* leap as an hart, and the tongue of the dumb sing: for in the wilderness shall ᴿwaters break out, and streams in the desert.   [John 7:38]

7 And the parched ground shall become a pool, and the thirsty land springs of water: in ᴿthe habitation of ᵀdragons, where each lay, *shall be* grass with reeds and rushes.   34:13 · *jackals*

8 And an ᴿhighway shall be there, and a way, and it shall be called The way of holiness; ᴿthe unclean shall not pass over it; but it *shall be* for those: the wayfaring men, though fools, shall not err *therein.*   19:23 · 52:1; 1 Pet. 1:15, 16

9 ᴿNo lion shall be there, nor *any* ravenous beast shall go up thereon, it shall not be found there; but the redeemed shall walk *there:*   Lev. 26:6; Ezek. 34:25

10 And the ᴿransomed of the LORD shall return, and come to Zion with songs and everlasting joy upon their heads: they shall obtain joy and gladness, and ᴿsorrow and sighing shall flee away.   51:11 · 30:19; 65:19; [Rev. 7:17; 21:4]

36 Now ᴿit came to pass in the fourteenth year of king Hez-

e-ki'-ah, *that* Sen-nach'-e-rib king of Assyria came up against all the defenced cities of Judah, and took them.   2 Kin. 18:13, 17; 2 Chr. 32:1

2 And the king of Assyria sent Rab'-sha-keh from La'-chish to Jerusalem unto king Hez-e-ki'-ah with a great army. And he stood by the conduit of the upper pool in the highway of the fuller's field.

3 Then came forth unto him E-li'-a-kim, Hil-ki'-ah's son, which was over the house, and ᴿSheb'-na the scribe, and Jo'-ah, A'-saph's son, the recorder.   22:15

4 And Rab'-sha-keh said unto them, Say ye now to Hez-e-ki'-ah, Thus saith the great king, the king of Assyria, What confidence *is* this wherein thou trustest?

5 I say, *sayest thou,* (but *they are but* ᵀvain words) *I have* counsel and strength for war: now on whom dost thou trust, that thou rebellest against me?   *empty*

6 Lo, thou trustest in the ᴿstaff of this broken reed, on Egypt; whereon if a man lean, it will go into his hand, and pierce it: so *is* Pharaoh king of Egypt to all that ᴿtrust in him.   Ezek. 29:6 · Ps. 146:3

7 But if thou say to me, We trust in the LORD our God: *is it* not he, whose high places and whose altars Hez-e-ki'-ah hath taken away, and said to Judah and to Jerusalem, Ye shall worship before this altar?

8 Now therefore give pledges, I pray thee, to my master the king of Assyria, and I will give thee two thousand horses, if thou be able on thy part to set riders upon them.

9 How then wilt thou turn away the face of one captain of the least of my master's servants, and put thy trust on Egypt for chariots and for horsemen?

10 And am I now come up without the LORD against this land to destroy it? the LORD said unto me, Go up against this land, and destroy it.

11 Then said E-li'-a-kim and Sheb'-na and Jo'-ah unto Rab'-

sha-keh, Speak, I pray thee, unto thy servants in the [T]Syrian language; for we understand it: and speak not to us in the Jews' language, in the ears of the people that are on the wall.   Lit. Aramaic

12 But Rab'-sha-keh said, Hath my master sent me to thy master and to thee to speak these words? hath he not sent me to the men that sit upon the wall, that they may eat their own dung, and drink their own piss with you?

13 Then Rab'-sha-keh stood, and cried with a loud voice in the Jews' language, and said, Hear ye the words of the great king, the king of Assyria.

14 Thus saith the king, Let not Hez-e-ki'-ah deceive you: for he shall not be able to deliver you.

15 Neither let Hez-e-ki'-ah make you trust in the Lord, saying, The Lord will surely deliver us: this city shall not be delivered into the hand of the king of Assyria.

16 Hearken not to Hez-e-ki'-ah: for thus saith the king of Assyria, Make an agreement with me by a present, and come out to me: [R]and eat ye every one of his vine, and every one of his fig tree, and drink ye every one the waters of his own cistern;   1 Kin. 4:25; Mic. 4:4; Zech. 3:10

17 Until I come and take you away to a land like your own land, a land of corn and wine, a land of bread and vineyards.

18 Beware lest Hez-e-ki'-ah persuade you, saying, The Lord will deliver us. Hath any of the [R]gods of the nations delivered his land out of the hand of the king of Assyria?   37:12; 2 Kin. 19:12

19 Where are the gods of Ha'-math and [T]Ar'-phad? where are the gods of Seph-ar-va'-im? and have they delivered [R]Sa-mar'-i-a out of my hand?   Or Arpad · 2 Kin. 17:6

20 Who are they among all the gods of these lands, that have delivered their land out of my hand, that the Lord should deliver Jerusalem out of my hand?

21 But they [T]held their peace, and answered him not a word: for

the king's commandment was, saying, Answer him not.   were silent

22 Then came E-li'-a-kim, the son of Hil-ki'-ah, that was over the household, and Sheb'-na the scribe, and Jo'-ah, the son of A'-saph, the recorder, to Hez-e-ki'-ah with their clothes rent, and told him the words of Rab'-sha-keh.

37 And it came to pass, when king Hez-e-ki'-ah heard it, that he rent his clothes, and covered himself with sackcloth, and went into the house of the Lord.

2 And he sent E-li'-a-kim, who was over the household, and Sheb'-na the scribe, and the elders of the priests covered with sackcloth, unto Isaiah the prophet the son of Amoz.

3 And they said unto him, Thus saith Hez-e-ki'-ah, This day is a day of [R]trouble, and of rebuke, and of [T]blasphemy: for the children are come to the birth, and there is not strength to bring forth.   22:5; 26:16; 33:2 · contempt

4 It may be the Lord thy God will hear the words of Rab'-sha-keh, whom the king of Assyria his master hath sent to reproach the living God, and will reprove the words which the Lord thy God hath heard: wherefore lift up thy prayer for the remnant that is left.

5 So the servants of king Hez-e-ki'-ah came to Isaiah.

6 And Isaiah said unto them, Thus shall ye say unto your master, Thus saith the Lord, Be not afraid of the words that thou hast heard, wherewith the servants of the king of Assyria have blasphemed me.

7 Behold, I will send a blast upon him, and he shall hear a rumour, and return to his own land; and I will cause him to fall by the sword in his own land.

8 So Rab'-sha-keh returned, and found the king of Assyria warring against Lib'-nah: for he had heard that he was departed from La'-chish.

9 And he heard say concerning Tir'-ha-kah king of E-thi-o'-pi-a,

He is come forth to make war with thee. And when he heard *it*, he sent messengers to Hez-e-ki'-ah, saying,

10 Thus shall ye speak to Hez-e-ki'-ah king of Judah, saying, Let not thy God, in whom thou trustest, deceive thee, saying, Jerusalem shall not be given into the hand of the king of Assyria.

11 Behold, thou hast heard what the kings of Assyria have done to all lands by destroying them utterly; and shalt thou be delivered?

12 Have the ᴿgods of the nations delivered them which my fathers have destroyed, *as* Go'-zan, and Ha'-ran, and Re'-zeph, and the children of Eden which *were* in Te-las'-sar?   36:18, 19

13 Where *is* the king of ᴿHa'-math, and the king of Ar'-phad, and the king of the city of Seph-ar-va'-im, He'-na, and I'-vah?   49:23

14 And Hez-e-ki'-ah received the letter from the hand of the messengers, and read it: and Hez-e-ki'-ah went up unto the house of the LORD, and spread it before the LORD.

15 And Hez-e-ki'-ah prayed unto the LORD, saying,

16 O LORD of hosts, God of Israel, that dwellest *between* the cher'-u-bims, thou *art* the God, *even* thou ᴿalone, of all the kingdoms of the earth: thou hast made heaven and earth.   43:10, 11

17 ᴿIncline thine ear, O LORD, and hear; open thine eyes, O LORD, and see: and ᴿhear all the words of Sen-nach'-e-rib, which hath sent to reproach the living God.   2 Chr. 6:40; Dan. 9:18 · Ps. 74:22

18 Of a truth, LORD, the kings of Assyria have laid waste all the nations, and their countries,

19 And have cast their gods into the fire: for they *were* ᴿno gods, but the work of men's hands, wood and stone: therefore they have destroyed them.   40:19, 20

20 Now therefore, O LORD our God, ᴿsave us from his hand, that all the kingdoms of the earth may

ᴿknow that thou *art* the LORD, *even* thou only.   33:22 · Ps. 83:18

21 Then Isaiah the son of Amoz sent unto Hez-e-ki'-ah, saying, Thus saith the LORD God of Israel, Whereas thou hast prayed to me against Sen-nach'-e-rib king of Assyria:

22 This *is* the word which the LORD hath spoken concerning him; The virgin, the daughter of Zion, hath despised thee, *and* ᵀlaughed thee to scorn; the daughter of Jerusalem hath shaken her head at thee.   *mocked thee*

23 Whom hast thou reproached and blasphemed? and against whom hast thou ᵀexalted *thy* voice, and lifted up thine eyes on high? *even* against the Holy One of Israel.   *raised*

24 By thy servants hast thou reproached the Lord, and hast said, By the multitude of my chariots am I come up to the height of the mountains, to the sides of Leb'-a-non; and I will cut down the tall cedars thereof, *and* the choice fir trees thereof: and I will enter into the height of his border, *and* the forest of his Carmel.

25 I have digged, and drunk water; and with the sole of my feet have I dried up all the rivers of the besieged places.

26 Hast thou not heard ᴿlong ago, *how* I have done it; *and* of ancient times, that I have formed it? now have I brought it to pass, that thou shouldest be to lay waste defenced cities *into* ruinous heaps.   25:1; 40:21; 45:21

27 Therefore their inhabitants ᵀ*were* of small power, they were dismayed and confounded: they were *as* the grass of the field, and *as* the green herb, *as* the grass on the housetops, and *as corn* blasted before it be grown up.   *had little*

28 But I know thy abode, and thy going out, and thy coming in, and thy rage against me.

29 Because thy rage against me, and thy tumult, is come up into mine ears, therefore will I put my hook in thy nose, and my bridle in

thy lips, and I will turn thee back by the way by which thou camest.

30 And this *shall be* a sign unto thee, Ye shall eat *this* year such as groweth of itself; and the second year that which springeth of the same: and in the third year sow ye, and reap, and plant vineyards, and eat the fruit thereof.

31 And the remnant that is escaped of the house of Judah shall again take root downward, and bear fruit upward:

32 For out of Jerusalem shall go forth a remnant, and they that escape out of mount Zion: the Rzeal of the LORD of hosts shall do this. 9:7; 59:17; Joel 2:18; Zech. 1:14

33 Therefore thus saith the LORD concerning the king of Assyria, He shall not come into this city, nor shoot an arrow there, nor come before it with shields, nor cast a bank against it.

34 By the way that he came, by the same shall he return, and shall not come into this city, saith the LORD.

35 For I will Rdefend this city to save it for mine own sake, and for my servant David's sake. 31:5; 38:6

36 Then the Rangel of the LORD went forth, and smote in the camp of the Assyrians a hundred and fourscore and five thousand: and when they arose early in the morning, behold, they *were* all dead corpses. 10:12, 33, 34; 2 Kin. 19:35

37 So Sen-nach'-e-rib king of Assyria departed, and went and returned, and dwelt at Nin'-e-veh.

38 And it came to pass, as he was worshipping in the house of Nis'-roch his god, that A-dram'-me-lech and Sha-re'-zer his sons smote him with the sword; and they escaped into the land of Ar-me'-ni-a: and RE'-sar-had'-don his son reigned in his stead. Ezra 4:2

38 In those days was Hez-e-ki'-ah sick unto death. And Isaiah the prophet the son of Amoz came unto him, and said unto him, Thus saith the LORD, RSet thine house in order: for thou shalt die, and not live. 2 Sam. 17:23

2 Then Hez-e-ki'-ah turned his face toward the wall, and prayed unto the LORD,

3 And said, Remember now, O LORD, I beseech thee, how I have walked before thee in truth and with a perfect heart, and have done *that which is* good in thy sight. And Hez-e-ki'-ah wept sore.

4 Then came the word of the LORD to Isaiah, saying,

5 Go, and say to Hez-e-ki'-ah, Thus saith the LORD, the God of David thy father, I have heard thy prayer, I have seen thy tears: behold, I will add unto thy days fifteen years.

6 And I will deliver thee and this city out of the hand of the king of Assyria: and RI will defend this city. 2 Kin. 19:35–37; 2 Chr. 32:21

7 And this *shall be* Ra sign unto thee from the LORD, that the LORD will do this thing that he hath spoken; Judg. 6:17, 21, 36–40; 2 Kin. 20:8

8 Behold, I will bring again the shadow of the degrees, which is gone down in the sun dial of Ahaz, ten degrees backward. So the sun returned ten degrees, by which degrees it was gone down.

9 The writing of Hez-e-ki'-ah king of Judah, when he had been sick, and was recovered of his sickness:

10 I said in the Tcutting off of my days, I shall go to the gates of the grave: I am deprived of the Tresidue of my years. *middle · remainder*

11 I said, I shall not see the LORD, *even* the LORD, Rin the land of the living: I shall behold man no more with the inhabitants of the world. Ps. 27:13; 116:9

12 RMine age is departed, and is removed from me as a shepherd's tent: I have cut off like a weaver my life: he Twill cut me off Twith pining sickness: from day *even* to night wilt thou make an end of me. Job 7:6 · *cuts · from the loom*

13 I reckoned till morning, *that*, as a lion, so will he break all my bones: from day *even* to night wilt thou make an end of me.

14 Like a crane *or* a swallow, so

did I chatter: ^RI did mourn as a dove: mine eyes fail *with looking* upward: O LORD, I am oppressed; undertake for me.   59:11; Nah. 2:7

15 What shall I say? He hath both spoken unto me, and himself hath done *it:* I shall ^Tgo softly all my years ^Rin the bitterness of my soul.   *walk carefully* · v. 17; Job 7:11; 10:1

16 O Lord, by these *things men* live, and in all these *things is* the life of my spirit: so wilt thou recover me, and make me to live.

17 Behold, for peace I had great bitterness: but thou hast in love to my soul *delivered it* from the pit of corruption: for thou hast cast all my sins behind thy back.

18 For ^Rthe grave cannot praise thee, death can *not* celebrate thee: they that go down into the pit cannot hope for thy truth.   Ps. 30:9

19 The living, the living, he shall praise thee, as I *do* this day: ^Rthe father to the children shall make known thy truth.   Deut. 4:9; Ps. 78:3, 4

20 The LORD *was ready* to save me: therefore we will sing my songs to the stringed instruments all the days of our life in the house of the LORD.

21 For ^RIsaiah had said, Let them take a lump of figs, and lay *it* for a plaister upon the boil, and he shall recover.   2 Kin. 20:7

22 ^RHez-e-ki'-ah also had said, What *is* the sign that I shall go up to the house of the LORD? 2 Kin. 20:8

39 At ^Rthat time Me-ro'-dach–bal'-a-dan, the son of Bal'-a-dan, king of Babylon, sent letters and a present to Hez-e-ki'-ah: for he had heard that he had been sick, and was recovered. 2 Chr. 32:31

2 ^RAnd Hez-e-ki'-ah was glad of them, and shewed them the house of his ^Tprecious things, the silver, and the gold, and the spices, and the precious ointment, and all the house of his armour, and all that was found in his treasures: there was nothing in his house, nor in all his dominion, that Hez-e-ki'-ah shewed them not. 2 Chr. 32:25, 31; Job 31:25 · *treasures*

3 Then came Isaiah the proph-et unto king Hez-e-ki'-ah, and said unto him, What said these men? and from whence came they unto thee? And Hez-e-ki'-ah said, They are come from a far country unto me, *even* from Babylon.

4 Then said he, What have they seen in thine house? And Hez-e-ki'-ah answered, All that *is* in mine house have they seen: there is nothing among my treasures that I have not shewed them.

5 Then said Isaiah to Hez-e-ki'-ah, Hear the word of the LORD of hosts:

6 Behold, the days come, ^Rthat all that *is* in thine house, and *that* which thy fathers have laid up in store until this day, shall be carried to Babylon: nothing shall be left, saith the LORD.   2 Kin. 24:13

7 And of thy sons that shall issue from thee, which thou shalt beget, shall they take away; and they shall be eunuchs in the palace of the king of Babylon.

8 Then said Hez-e-ki'-ah to Isaiah, Good *is* the word of the LORD which thou hast spoken. He said moreover, For there shall be peace and truth in my days.

40 Comfort ye, comfort ye my people, saith your God.

2 Speak ye comfortably to Je-rusalem, and cry unto her, that her warfare is ^Taccomplished, that her iniquity is pardoned: ^Rfor she hath received of the LORD's hand double for all her sins.   *ended* · 61:7

3 ^RThe voice of him that crieth in the wilderness, Prepare ye the way of the LORD, make straight in the desert a highway for our God.   Matt. 3:3; Luke 3:4–6; John 1:23

4 Every valley shall be exalted, and every mountain and hill shall be made low: ^Rand the crooked shall be made straight, and the rough places ^Tplain: 45:2 · *smooth*

5 And the glory of the LORD shall be revealed, and all flesh shall see *it* together: for the mouth of the LORD hath spoken *it.*

6 The voice said, Cry. And he said, What shall I cry? ^RAll flesh *is* grass, and all the goodliness

thereof *is* as the flower of the field: Job 14:2; James 1:10; 1 Pet. 1:24, 25

7 The grass withereth, the flower fadeth: because the ᵀspirit of the LORD bloweth upon it: surely the people *is* grass.   *breath*

8 The grass withereth, the flower fadeth: but the word of our God shall stand for ever.

9 O Zion, that bringest good tidings, get thee up into the high mountain; O Jerusalem, that bringest good tidings, lift up thy voice with strength; lift *it* up, be not afraid; say unto the cities of Judah, Behold your God!

10 Behold, the Lord GOD will come with strong *hand,* and ᴿhis arm shall rule for him: behold, ᴿhis reward *is* with him, and his work before him.   59:16, 18 · 62:11

☆ 11 He shall feed his flock like a shepherd: he shall gather the lambs with his arm, and carry *them* in his bosom, *and* shall gently lead those that are with young.

12 ᴿWho hath measured the waters in the hollow of his hand, and meted out heaven with the span, and comprehended the dust of the earth in a measure, and weighed the mountains in scales, and the hills in a balance?   Prov. 30:4

13 ᴿWho hath directed the Spirit of the LORD, or *being* his counsellor hath taught him?   Rom. 11:34

14 With whom took he counsel, and *who* instructed him, and ᴿtaught him in the path of ᵀjudgment, and taught him knowledge, and shewed to him the way of understanding?   Job 36:22, 23 · *justice*

15 Behold, the nations *are* as a drop of a bucket, and are counted as the ᵀsmall dust of the balance: behold, he ᵀtaketh up the isles as a very little thing.   *fine · lifteth*

16 And Leb'-a-non *is* not sufficient to burn, nor the beasts thereof sufficient for a burnt offering.

17 All nations before him *are* as ᴿnothing; and ᴿthey are counted to him less than nothing, and ᵀvanity.   Dan. 4:35 · Ps. 62:9 · *worthless*

18 To whom then will ye ᴿliken God? or what likeness will ye compare unto him?   46:5; Acts 17:29

19 ᴿThe workman melteth a graven image, and the goldsmith spreadeth it over with gold, and casteth silver chains.   Ps. 115:4–8

20 He that *is* so impoverished that he hath no oblation chooseth a tree *that* will not rot; he seeketh unto him a ᵀcunning workman ᴿto prepare a graven image, *that* shall not be moved.   *skilful* · 41:7; 46:7

21 ᴿHave ye not known? have ye not heard? hath it not been told you from the beginning? have ye not understood from the foundations of the earth?   37:26; Acts 14:17

22 *It is* he that sitteth upon the circle of the earth, and the inhabitants thereof *are* as grasshoppers; that stretcheth out the heavens as a curtain, and spreadeth them out as a tent to dwell in:

23 That bringeth the ᴿprinces to nothing: he maketh the judges of the earth as vanity.   34:12; Job 12:21

24 Yea, they shall not be planted; yea, they shall not be sown: yea, their stock shall not take root in the earth: and he shall also blow upon them, and they shall wither, and the whirlwind shall take them away as stubble.

25 ᴿTo whom then will ye liken me, or shall I be equal? saith the Holy One.   v. 18; [John 14:9; Col. 1:15]

26 Lift up your eyes on high, and behold who hath created these *things,* that bringeth out their host by number: ᴿhe calleth them all by names by the greatness of his might, for that *he is* strong in power; not one faileth.   Ps. 147:4

27 ᴿWhy sayest thou, O Jacob, and speakest, O Israel, My way is hid from the LORD, and my ᵀjudgment is passed over from my God?   54:7, 8 · *just claim*

28 Hast thou not known? hast thou not heard, *that* the everlasting God, the LORD, the Creator of the ends of the earth, fainteth not, neither is weary? *there is* no searching of his understanding.

29 He giveth power to the ᵀfaint;

and to *them that have* no might he increaseth strength.   *weak*

30 Even the youths shall faint and be weary, and the young men shall utterly fall:

31 But they that ^Rwait upon the Lord ^Rshall renew *their* strength; they shall mount up with wings as eagles; they shall run, and not be weary; *and* they shall walk, and not faint.   30:15; 49:23 · Ps. 103:5

41 Keep silence before me, O ^Tislands; and let the people renew *their* strength: let them come near; then let them speak: let us ^Rcome near together to judgment.   *coastlands* · 1:18

2 Who raised up the righteous *man* ^Rfrom the east, called him to his foot, ^Rgave the nations before him, and made *him* rule over kings? he gave *them* as the dust to his sword, *and* as driven stubble to his bow.   46:11 · 45:1, 13; Gen. 14:14

3 He pursued them, *and* passed safely; *even* by the way *that* he had not gone with his feet.

4 Who hath wrought and done *it*, calling the generations from the beginning? I the Lord, the first, and with the last; I *am* he.

5 The ^Tisles saw *it*, and feared; the ends of the earth were afraid, drew near, and came.   *coastlands*

6 They helped every one his neighbour; and *every one* said to his brother, Be of good courage.

7 ^RSo the carpenter encouraged the ^Rgoldsmith, *and* he that smootheth *with* the hammer him that smote the anvil, saying, It *is* ready for the sodering: and he fastened it with nails, ^R*that* it should not be moved.   44:13 · 40:19 · 40:20

8 But thou, Israel, *art* my servant, Jacob whom I have chosen, the seed of Abraham my friend.

9 *Thou* whom I have taken from the ends of the earth, and called thee from the chief men thereof, and said unto thee, Thou *art* my servant; I have chosen thee, and not cast thee away.

10 ^RFear thou not; for I *am* with thee: be not dismayed; for I *am* thy God: I will strengthen thee;

yea, I will help thee; yea, I will uphold thee with the right hand of my righteousness.   vv. 13, 14; 43:5

11 Behold, all they that were incensed against thee shall be ^Rashamed and confounded: they shall be as nothing; and they that strive with thee shall perish.   45:24

12 Thou shalt seek them, and shalt not find them, *even* them that contended with thee: they that war against thee shall be as nothing, and ^Tas a thing of nought.   *as nothing*

13 For I the Lord thy God will hold thy right hand, saying unto thee, Fear not; I will help thee.

14 Fear not, thou worm Jacob, *and* ye men of Israel; I will help thee, saith the Lord, and thy redeemer, the Holy One of Israel.

15 Behold, I will make thee a new sharp threshing instrument having teeth: thou shalt thresh the mountains, and beat *them* small, and shalt make the hills as chaff.

16 Thou shalt ^Rfan them, and the wind shall carry them away, and the whirlwind shall scatter them: and thou shalt rejoice in the Lord, *and* ^Rshalt glory in the Holy One of Israel.   Jer. 51:2 · 45:25

17 *When* the poor and needy seek water, and *there is* none, *and* their tongue faileth for thirst, I the Lord will hear them, *I* the God of Israel will not forsake them.

18 I will open ^Rrivers in high places, and fountains in the midst of the valleys: I will make the wilderness a pool of water, and the dry land springs of water.   44:3

19 I will plant in the wilderness the cedar, the ^Tshit'-tah tree, and the myrtle, and the oil tree; I will set in the ^Rdesert the ^Tfir tree, *and* the pine, and the box tree together: *acacia* · 35:1 · *cypress*

20 That they may see, and know, and consider, and understand together, that the hand of the Lord hath done this, and the Holy One of Israel hath created it.

21 Produce your cause, saith the Lord; bring forth your strong *reasons*, saith the King of Jacob.

22 ᴿLet them bring *them* forth, and shew us what shall happen: let them shew the ᴿformer things, what they *be*, that we may consider them, and know the latter end of them; or declare us things for to come. 45:21 · 43:9

23 Shew the things that are to come hereafter, that we may know that ye *are* gods: yea, do good, or do evil, that we may be dismayed, and behold *it* together.

24 Behold, ᴿye *are* of nothing, and your work of nought: an abomination *is he that* chooseth you. 44:9; Ps. 115:8; [Rom. 3:10–20]

25 I have raised up *one* from the north, and he shall come: from the rising of the sun ᴿshall he call upon my name: ᴿand he shall come upon princes as *upon* morter, and as the potter treadeth clay. Ezra 1:2 · 41:2; Jer. 50:3

26 ᴿWho hath declared from the beginning, that we may know? and beforetime, that we may say, *He is* righteous? yea, *there is* none that sheweth, yea, *there is* none that declareth, yea, *there is* none that heareth your words. 43:9

27 ᴿThe first ᴿ*shall say* to Zion, Behold, behold them: and I will give to Jerusalem one that bringeth good tidings. v. 4 · 40:9; Nah. 1:15

28 ᴿFor I beheld, and *there was* no man; even among them, and *there was* no counsellor, that, when I asked of them, could answer a word. 63:5

29 ᴿBehold, they *are* all ᵀvanity; their works *are* nothing: their molten images *are* wind and confusion. v. 24 · *worthless*

☆ **42** Behold ᴿmy servant, whom I uphold; mine elect, *in whom* my soul delighteth; ᴿI have put my spirit upon him: he shall bring forth judgment to the Gentiles. Matt. 12:18 · Matt. 3:16

2 He shall not ᵀcry, nor ᵀlift up, nor cause his voice to be heard in the street. *cry out · raise* his voice

3 A bruised reed shall he not break, and the smoking flax shall he not quench: he shall bring forth judgment unto truth.

4 He shall not fail nor be discouraged, till he have set judgment in the earth: ᴿand the isles shall wait for his law. [Gen. 49:10]

5 Thus saith God the LORD, ᴿhe that created the heavens, and stretched them out; he that spread forth the earth, and that which cometh out of it; ᴿhe that giveth breath unto the people upon it, and spirit to them that walk therein: 44:24; Zech. 12:1 · 57:16; Acts 17:25

6 ᴿI the LORD have called thee in righteousness, and will hold thine hand, and will keep thee, ᴿand give thee for a covenant of the people, for ᴿa light of the Gentiles; 43:1 · 49:8 · Luke 2:32; [Gal. 3:14]

7 ᴿTo open the blind eyes, to ☆ bring out the prisoners from the prison, *and* them that sit in darkness out of the prison house. 35:5

8 I *am* the LORD: that *is* my name: and my ᴿglory will I not give to another, neither my praise to graven images. 48:11; Ex. 20:3–5

9 Behold, the former things are come to pass, and new things do I declare: before they spring forth I tell you of them.

10 Sing unto the LORD a new song, *and* his praise from the end of the earth, ye that go down to the sea, and all that is therein; the isles, and the inhabitants thereof.

11 Let the wilderness and the cities thereof lift up *their voice*, the villages *that* Ke′-dar doth inhabit: let the inhabitants of ᵀthe rock sing, let them shout from the top of the mountains. Heb. *Sela*

12 Let them give glory unto the LORD, and declare his praise in the ᵀislands. *coastlands*

13 The LORD shall go forth as a mighty man, he shall stir up jealousy like a man of war: he shall cry, ᴿyea, roar; he shall prevail against his enemies. 31:4

14 I have long time holden my peace; I have been still, *and* refrained myself: *now* will I cry like a travailing woman; I will destroy and devour at once.

15 I will make waste mountains and hills, and dry up all their

TᵀᵀHerbs; and I will make the rivers Tislands, and I will dry up the pools.   *vegetation · coastlands*

16 And I will bring the blind by a way *that* they knew not; I will lead them in paths *that* they have not known: I will make darkness light before them, and crooked Tthings straight. These things will I do unto them, and not forsake them.   *places*

17 They shall be ᴿturned back, they shall be greatly ashamed, that trust in graven images, that say to the molten images, Ye *are* our gods.   1:29; 44:11; 45:16; Ps. 97:7

18 Hear, ye deaf; and look, ye blind, that ye may see.

19 ᴿWho *is* blind, but my servant? or deaf, as my messenger *that* I sent? who *is* blind as *he that is* perfect, and blind as the LORD's servant?   43:8; Ezek. 12:2

20 Seeing many things, ᴿbut thou observest not; opening the ears, but he heareth not.   Rom. 2:21

21 The LORD is well pleased for his righteousness' sake; he will magnify the law, and make *it* honourable.

22 But this *is* a people robbed and spoiled; *they are* all of them snared in holes, and they are hid in prison houses: they are for a prey, and none delivereth; for a spoil, and none saith, Restore.

23 Who among you will give ear to this? *who* will hearken and hear for the time to come?

24 Who gave Jacob for a spoil, and Israel to the robbers? did not the LORD, he against whom we have sinned? ᴿfor they would not walk in his ways, neither were they obedient unto his law.   65:2

25 Therefore he hath poured upon him the fury of his anger, and the strength of battle: and it hath set him on fire round about, yet he knew not; and it burned him, yet he laid *it* not to heart.

43 But now thus saith the LORD that created thee, O Jacob, and he that formed thee, O Israel, Fear not: for I have re-

deemed thee, ᴿI have called *thee* by thy name; thou *art* mine.   45:4

2 When thou passest through the waters, I *will be* with thee; and through the rivers, they shall not overflow thee: when thou ᴿwalkest through the fire, thou shalt not be burned; neither shall the flame kindle upon thee.   Dan. 3:25

3 For I *am* the LORD thy God, the Holy One of Israel, thy Saviour: ᴿI gave Egypt *for* thy ransom, E-thi-o'-pi-a and Se'-ba Tfor thee.   [Prov. 11:8; 21:18] · *in thy place*

4 Since thou wast precious in my sight, thou hast been honourable, and I have ᴿloved thee: therefore will I give men for thee, and people for thy life.   63:9

5 Fear not: for I *am* with thee: I will bring thy seed from the east, and gather thee from the west;

6 I will say to the ᴿnorth, TGive up; and to the south, Keep not back: bring my sons from far, and my daughters from the ends of the earth;   49:12 · *Give them up*

7 *Even* every one that is ᴿcalled by my name: for I have created him for my glory, I have formed him; yea, I have made him.   63:19

8 ᴿBring forth the blind people that have eyes, and the ᴿdeaf that have ears.   6:9; 42:19; Ezek. 12:2 · 29:18

9 Let all the nations be gathered together, and let the people be assembled: ᴿwho among them can declare this, and shew us former things? let them bring forth their witnesses, that they may be justified: or let them hear, and say, *It is* truth.   41:21, 22, 26

10 ᴿYe *are* my witnesses, saith the LORD, ᴿand my servant whom I have chosen: that ye may know and ᴿbelieve me, and understand that I *am* he: before me there was no God formed, neither shall there be after me.   44:8 · 55:4 · 41:4

11 I, *even* I, *am* the LORD; and beside me *there is* no saviour.

12 I have declared, and have saved, and I have shewed, when *there was* no strange *god* among you: therefore ye *are* my witnesses, saith the LORD, that I *am* God.

13 ᴿYea, before the day *was* I *am* he; and *there is* none that can deliver out of my hand: I will work, and who shall let it?   48:16

14 Thus saith the LORD, your redeemer, the Holy One of Israel; For your sake I have sent to Babylon, and have brought down all their nobles, and the Chal-de′-ans, whose cry *is* in the ships.

15 I *am* the LORD, your Holy One, the creator of Israel, your ᴿKing.   41:20, 21

16 Thus saith the LORD, which ᴿmaketh a way in the sea, and a path in the mighty waters;   51:10

17 Which ᴿbringeth forth the chariot and horse, the army and the power; they shall lie down together, they shall not rise: they are ᵀextinct, they are quenched as tow.   Ex. 14:4–9, 25 · *extinguished*

18 ᴿRemember ye not the former things, neither consider the things of old.   Jer. 16:14

19 Behold, I will do a ᴿnew thing; now it shall spring forth; shall ye not know it? ᴿI will even make a way in the wilderness, *and* rivers in the desert.   48:6 · Ps. 78:16

20 The beast of the field shall honour me, the ᵀdragons and the ᵀowls: because ᴿI give waters in the wilderness, *and* rivers in the desert, to give drink to my people, my chosen.   *jackals · ostriches ·* 48:21

21 ᴿThis people have I formed for myself; they shall ᵀshew forth my ᴿpraise.   42:12 · *declare ·* Jer. 13:11

22 But thou hast not called upon me, O Jacob; but thou ᴿhast been weary of me, O Israel.   Mic. 6:3

23 ᴿThou hast not brought me the ᵀsmall cattle of thy burnt offerings; neither hast thou honoured me with thy sacrifices. I have not caused thee to serve with an offering, nor wearied thee with incense.   Amos 5:25 · *sheep for*

24 Thou hast bought me no sweet cane with money, neither hast thou filled me with the fat of thy sacrifices: but thou hast made me to serve with thy sins, thou hast ᴿwearied me with thine iniquities.   1:14; 7:13; Ps. 95:10; Ezek. 6:9

25 I, *even* I, *am* he that ᴿblotteth out thy transgressions ᴿfor mine own sake, ᴿand will not remember thy sins.   [Acts 3:19] · Ezek. 36:22 · 1:18

26 Put me in remembrance: let us plead together: declare thou, that thou mayest be justified.

27 Thy first father hath sinned, and thy teachers have transgressed against me.

28 Therefore I have profaned the princes of the sanctuary, ᴿand have given Jacob to the curse, and Israel to reproaches.   Ps. 79:4; Jer. 24:9

44 Yet now hear, O Jacob my servant; and Israel, whom I have chosen:

2 Thus saith the LORD that made thee, and formed thee from the womb, *which* will help thee; Fear not, O Jacob, my servant; and thou, Jes′-u-run, whom I have chosen.

3 For I will pour water upon him that is thirsty, and floods upon the dry ground: I will pour my spirit upon thy seed, and my blessing upon thine offspring:

4 And they shall spring up *as* among the grass, as willows by the water courses.

5 One shall say, I *am* the LORD's; and another shall call *himself* by the name of Jacob; and another shall subscribe *with* his hand unto the LORD, and surname *himself* by the name of Israel.

6 Thus saith the LORD the King of Israel, and his redeemer the LORD of hosts; ᴿI *am* the first, and I *am* the last; and beside me *there is* no God.   41:4; [Rev. 1:8, 17; 22:13]

7 And ᴿwho, as I, shall call, and shall declare it, and set it in order for me, since I appointed the ancient people? and the things that are coming, and shall come, let them shew unto them.   41:4

8 Fear ye not, neither be afraid: have not I told thee from that time, and have declared *it*? ye *are* even my witnesses. Is there a God beside me? yea, ᴿ*there is* no God; I know not *any*.   45:5; Joel 2:27

9 They that make a graven image *are* all of them vanity; and

their delectable things shall not profit; and they *are* their own witnesses; [R]they see not, nor know; that they may be ashamed. Ps. 115:4

10 Who hath formed a god, or molten a graven image [R]*that* is profitable for nothing? Acts 19:26

11 Behold, all his fellows shall be [R]ashamed: and the workmen, they *are* of men: let them all be gathered together, let them stand up; *yet* they shall fear, *and* they shall be ashamed together. Ps. 97:7

12 [R]The smith with the tongs both worketh in the coals, and fashioneth it with hammers, and worketh it with the strength of his arms: yea, he is hungry, and his strength faileth: he drinketh no water, and is faint. 40:19; Jer. 10:3-5

13 The carpenter stretcheth out *his* rule; he marketh it out with [T]a line; he fitteth it with planes, and he marketh it out with the compass, and maketh it after the figure of a man, according to the beauty of a man; that it may remain in the house. *chalk*

14 He heweth him down cedars, and taketh the cypress and the oak, which he [T]strengtheneth for himself among the trees of the forest: he planteth an ash, and the rain doth nourish *it.* *secures*

15 Then shall it be for a man to burn: for he will take thereof, and warm himself; yea, he kindleth *it,* and baketh bread; yea, he maketh a god, and worshippeth *it;* he maketh it a graven image, and falleth down thereto.

16 He burneth [T]part thereof in the fire; with [T]part thereof he eateth flesh; he roasteth roast, and is satisfied: yea, he warmeth *himself,* and saith, Aha, I am warm, I have seen the fire: *half*

17 And the residue thereof he maketh a god, *even* his graven image: he falleth down unto it, and worshippeth *it,* and prayeth unto it, and saith, Deliver me; for thou *art* my god.

18 They have not known nor understood: for [R]he hath shut their eyes, that they cannot see;

and their hearts, that they cannot [R]understand. 2 Thess. 2:11 · Jer. 10:14

19 And none [R]considereth in his heart, neither *is there* knowledge nor understanding to say, I have burned [T]part of it in the fire; yea, also I have baked bread upon the coals thereof; I have roasted flesh, and eaten *it:* and shall I make the residue thereof an abomination? shall I fall down to [T]the stock of a tree? 46:8 · *half · a block of wood*

20 He feedeth on ashes: [R]a deceived heart hath turned him aside, that he cannot deliver his soul, nor say, *Is there* not a lie in my right hand? Rom. 1:21, 22

21 Remember these, O Jacob and Israel; for thou *art* my servant: I have formed thee; thou *art* my servant: O Israel, thou shalt not be [R]forgotten of me. 49:15

22 [R]I have blotted out, as a thick cloud, thy transgressions, and, as a cloud, thy sins: return unto me; for I have redeemed thee. 43:25

23 Sing, O ye heavens; for the LORD hath done *it:* shout, ye lower parts of the earth: break forth into singing, ye mountains, O forest, and every tree therein: for the LORD hath redeemed Jacob, and [R]glorified himself in Israel. 60:21

24 Thus saith the LORD, [R]thy redeemer, and [R]he that formed thee from the womb, I *am* the LORD that maketh all *things;* [R]that stretcheth forth the heavens alone; that spreadeth abroad the earth by myself; 43:14 · 43:1 · Job 9:8

25 That frustrateth the tokens of the liars, and maketh diviners mad; that turneth wise *men* backward, [R]and maketh their knowledge foolish; Ps. 33:10; 1 Cor. 1:20, 27

26 [R]That confirmeth the word of his servant, and performeth the counsel of his messengers; that saith to Jerusalem, Thou shalt be inhabited; and to the cities of Judah, Ye shall be built, and I will raise up the [T]decayed places thereof: Zech. 1:6; Matt. 5:18 · Lit. *waste*

27 That saith to the deep, Be dry, and I will dry up thy rivers:

28 That saith of [R]Cyrus, *He is*

my shepherd, and shall perform all my pleasure: even saying to Jerusalem, Thou shalt be built; and to the temple, Thy foundation shall be laid. 45:13; 2 Chr. 36:22; Ezra 1:1

45 Thus saith the LORD to his anointed, to ᴿCyrus, whose ᴿright hand I have holden, ᴿto subdue nations before him; and I will loose the loins of kings, to open before him the two leaved gates; and the gates shall not be shut;   44:28 · 41:13; Ps. 73:23 · Dan. 5:30

2 I will go before thee, ᴿand make the crooked places straight: ᴿI will break in pieces the gates of ᵀbrass, and cut in sunder the bars of iron: 40:4 · Ps. 107:16 · *bronze*

3 And I will give thee the treasures of darkness, and hidden riches of secret places, ᴿthat thou mayest know that I, the LORD, which ᴿcall *thee* by thy name, *am* the God of Israel.   41:23 · Ex. 33:12

4 For ᴿJacob my servant's sake, and Israel mine elect, I have even called thee by thy name: I have surnamed thee, though thou hast not known me.   44:1

5 I ᴿ*am* the LORD, and *there is* none else, *there is* no God beside me: ᴿI girded thee, though thou hast not known me: 44:8 · Ps. 18:32

6 ᴿThat they may know from the rising of the sun, and from the west, that *there is* none beside me. I *am* the LORD, and *there is* none else.   37:20; Ps. 102:15; Mal. 1:11

7 I form the light, and create darkness: I make peace, and ᴿcreate ᵀevil: I the LORD do all these *things*.   31:2; Amos 3:6 · *calamity*

8 ᴿDropᵀ down, ye heavens, from above, and let the skies pour down righteousness: let the earth open, and let them bring forth salvation, and let righteousness spring up together; I the LORD have created it.   Ps. 85:11 · *Rain down*

9 Woe unto him that striveth with ᴿhis Maker! *Let* the potsherd *strive* with the potsherds of the earth. ᴿShall the clay say to him that fashioneth it, What makest thou? or thy work, He hath no hands?   64:8 · Jer. 18:6; Rom. 9:20, 21

10 Woe unto him that saith unto *his* father, What begettest thou? or to the woman, What hast thou brought forth?

11 Thus saith the LORD, the Holy One of Israel, and his Maker, ᴿAsk me of things to come concerning ᴿmy sons, and concerning ᴿthe work of my hands command ye me.   8:19 · Jer. 31:9 · 29:23; 60:21; 64:8

12 ᴿI have made the earth, and created man upon it: I, *even* my hands, have stretched out the heavens, and ᴿall their host have I commanded.   42:5; Jer. 27:5 · Neh. 9:6

13 ᴿI have raised him up in righteousness, and I will direct all his ways: he shall ᴿbuild my city, and he shall let go my captives, not for price nor reward, saith the LORD of hosts.   41:2 · 44:28; 2 Chr. 36:22

14 Thus saith the LORD, The labour of Egypt, and merchandise of E-thi-o′-pi-a and of the Sa-be′-ans, men of stature, shall come over unto thee, and they shall be thine: they shall come after thee; ᴿin chains they shall come over, and they shall fall down unto thee, they shall make supplication unto thee, *saying*, ᴿSurely God *is* in thee; and *there is* none else, *there is* no God.   Ps. 149:8 · Jer. 16:19

15 Verily thou *art* a God ᴿthat hidest thyself, O God of Israel, the Saviour.   57:17; Ps. 44:24

16 They shall be ᴿashamed, and also confounded, all of them: they shall go to confusion together *that are* makers of idols.   44:11

17 ᴿ*But* Israel shall be saved in the LORD with an ᴿeverlasting salvation: ye shall not be ashamed nor ᴿconfounded world without end.   26:4; [Rom. 11:26] · 51:6 · 29:22

18 For thus saith the LORD ᴿthat created the heavens; God himself that formed the earth and made it; he hath established it, he created it not in vain, he formed it to be ᴿinhabited: I *am* the LORD; and *there is* none else.   42:5 · Acts 17:26

19 I have not spoken in ᴿsecret, in a dark place of the earth: I said not unto the seed of Jacob, Seek ye me in vain: ᴿI the LORD speak

righteousness, I declare things that are right. Deut. 30:11 · Ps. 19:8

20 Assemble yourselves and come; draw near together, ye *that are* escaped of the nations: they have no knowledge that set up the wood of their graven image, and pray unto a god *that* cannot save.

21 Tell ye, and bring *them* near; yea, let them take counsel together: ^Rwho hath declared this from ancient time? *who* hath told it from that time? *have* not I the LORD? and *there is* no God else beside me; a just God and a Saviour; *there is* none beside me. 43:9

22 ^TLook unto me, and be ye saved, ^Rall the ends of the earth: for I *am* God, and *there is* none else. Turn · Ps. 22:27; 65:5

☆ 23 ^RI have sworn by myself, the word is gone out of my mouth *in* righteousness, and shall not return, That unto me every ^Rknee shall bow, ^Revery tongue shall swear. 62:8 · Rom. 14:11 · Ps. 63:11

24 Surely, shall *one* say, in the LORD have I righteousness and strength: *even* to him shall *men* come; and all that are incensed against him shall be ashamed.

25 ^RIn the LORD shall all the seed of Israel be justified, and ^Rshall glory. v. 17 · 1 Cor. 1:31

46 Bel ^Rboweth down, Ne'-bo stoopeth, their idols were upon the beasts, and upon the cattle: your carriages *were* heavy loaden; ^Rthey *are* a burden to the weary *beast.* 21:9; Jer. 50:2 · Jer. 10:5

2 They stoop, they bow down together; they could not deliver the burden, ^Rbut themselves are gone into captivity. Jer. 48:7

3 Hearken unto me, O house of Jacob, and all the remnant of the house of Israel, ^Rwhich are borne *by me* from the belly, which are carried from the womb: Ps. 71:6

4 And *even* to *your* old age I *am* he; and *even* to ^Thoar hairs ^Rwill I carry *you:* I have made, and I will bear; even I will carry, and will deliver *you.* gray · Ps. 48:14

5 ^RTo whom will ye liken me,

and make *me* equal, and compare me, that we may be like? 40:18, 25

6 ^RThey lavish gold out of the bag, and weigh silver in the balance, *and* hire a goldsmith; and he maketh it a god: they fall down, yea, they worship. 40:19; 41:6; Jer. 10:4

7 ^RThey bear him upon the shoulder, they carry him, and set him in his place, and he standeth; from his place shall he not remove: yea, *one* shall cry unto him, yet can he not answer, nor save him out of his trouble. 45:20

8 Remember this, and shew yourselves men: ^Rbring *it* again to mind, O ye transgressors. 44:19

9 ^RRemember the former things of old: for I *am* God, and *there is* none else; *I am* God, and *there is* none like me, 65:17

10 Declaring the end from the beginning, and from ancient times *the things* that are not *yet* done, saying, ^RMy counsel shall stand, and I will do all my pleasure: Ps. 33:11; Acts 5:39; Heb. 6:17

11 Calling a ravenous bird from the east, the man ^Rthat executeth my counsel from a far country: yea, ^RI have spoken *it,* I will also bring it to pass; I have purposed *it,* I will also do it. 44:28 · Num. 23:19

12 Hearken unto me, ye ^Rstouthearted, that *are* far from righteousness: 48:4; Ps. 76:5; Zech. 7:11, 12

13 ^RI bring near my righteousness; it shall not be far off, and my salvation ^Rshall not tarry: and I will place salvation in Zion for Israel my glory. [Rom. 1:17] · Hab. 2:3

47 Come ^Rdown, and ^Rsit in the dust, O virgin daughter of ^RBabylon, sit on the ground: *there is* no throne, O daughter of the Chal-de'-ans: for thou shalt no more be called tender and delicate. Jer. 48:18 · 3:26 · 14:18–23; Jer. 25:12

2 ^RTake the millstones, and grind meal: uncover thy locks, make bare the leg, uncover the thigh, pass over the rivers. Ex. 11:5

3 ^RThy nakedness shall be uncovered, yea, thy shame shall be seen: I will take vengeance, and I will not meet *thee as* a man. 3:17

4 *As for* [R]our redeemer, the LORD of hosts *is* his name, the Holy One of Israel. Jer. 50:34

5 Sit thou [R]silent, and get thee into darkness, O daughter of the Chal-de′-ans: [R]for thou shalt no more be called, The lady of kingdoms. 1 Sam. 2:9 · 13:19; Rev. 17:18

6 [R]I was wroth with my people, I have polluted mine inheritance, and given them into thine hand: thou didst shew them no mercy; upon the ancient hast thou very heavily laid thy yoke. 2 Sam. 24:14

7 And thou saidst, I shall be [R]a lady for ever: *so* that thou didst not [R]lay these *things* to thy heart, [R]neither didst remember the latter end of it. Rev. 18:7 · 42:25; 46:8 · Jer. 5:31

8 Therefore hear now this, *thou that art* given to pleasures, that dwellest [T]carelessly, that sayest in thine heart, I *am,* and none else beside me; I shall not sit *as* a widow, neither shall I know the loss of children: *securely*

9 But these two *things* shall come to thee [R]in a moment in one day, the loss of children, and widowhood: they shall come upon thee in their perfection for the multitude of thy sorceries, *and* for the great abundance of thine enchantments. Ps. 73:19; 1 Thess. 5:3

10 For thou hast trusted in thy wickedness: thou hast said, None [R]seeth me. Thy wisdom and thy knowledge, it hath [T]perverted thee; and thou hast said in thine heart, I *am,* and none else beside me. 29:15; Ezek. 8:12; 9:9 · *led thee astray*

11 Therefore shall evil come upon thee; thou shalt not know from whence it riseth: and [T]mischief shall fall upon thee; thou shalt not be able to put it off: and [R]desolation shall come upon thee [R]suddenly, *which* thou shalt not know. *trouble* · Luke 17:27 · 29:5

12 Stand now with thine enchantments, and with the multitude of thy sorceries, wherein thou hast laboured from thy youth; if so be thou shalt be able to profit, if so be thou mayest prevail.

13 [R]Thou art wearied in the multitude of thy counsels. Let now [R]the astrologers, the stargazers, the monthly prognosticators, stand up, and save thee from *these things* that shall come upon thee. 57:10 · v. 9; 8:19; 44:25; Dan. 2:2, 10

14 Behold, they shall be [R]as stubble; the fire shall burn them; they shall not deliver themselves from the power of the flame: *there* shall not *be* a coal to warm at, *nor* fire to sit before it. Nah. 1:10; Mal. 4:1

15 Thus shall they be unto thee with whom thou hast laboured, *even* [R]thy merchants, from thy youth: they shall wander every one to his [T]quarter; none shall save thee. Rev. 18:11 · *own side* or *way*

48 Hear ye this, O house of Jacob, which are called by the name of Israel, and are come forth out of the waters of Judah, which swear by the name of the LORD, and make mention of the God of Israel, *but* [R]not in truth, nor in righteousness. 58:2; Jer. 5:2

2 For they call themselves [R]of the holy city, and [T]stay themselves upon the God of Israel; The LORD of hosts *is* his name. 52:1; 64:10 · *lean*

3 I have declared the former things from the beginning; and they went forth out of my mouth, and I shewed them; I did *them* suddenly, and they came to pass.

4 Because I knew that thou *art* obstinate, and thy neck *is* an iron sinew, and thy brow [T]brass; *bronze*

5 I have even from the beginning declared *it* to thee; before it came to pass I [T]shewed *it* thee: lest thou shouldest say, Mine idol hath done them, and my graven image, and my molten image, hath commanded them. *proclaimed*

6 Thou hast heard, see all this; and will not ye declare *it?* I have shewed thee new things from this time, even hidden things, and thou didst not know them.

7 They are created now, and not from the beginning; even before the day when thou heardest them not; lest thou shouldest say, Behold, I knew them.

8 Yea, thou heardest not; yea, thou knewest not; yea, from that time *that* thine ear was not opened: for I knew that thou wouldest deal very treacherously, and wast called ^Ra transgressor from the womb.   Deut. 9:7, 24; Ps. 58:3

9 ^RFor my name's sake will I defer mine anger, and for my praise will I refrain for thee, that I cut thee not off.   43:25; Ps. 79:9; 106:8

10 Behold, I have refined thee, but not with silver; I have chosen thee in the furnace of affliction.

11 For mine own sake, *even* for mine own sake, will I do *it:* for ^Rhow should *my name* be polluted? and ^RI will not give my glory unto another.   Ezek. 20:9 · 42:8

12 Hearken unto me, O Jacob and Israel, my called; I *am* he; I *am* the first, I also *am* the last.

13 ^RMine hand also hath laid the foundation of the earth, and my right hand hath spanned the heavens: *when* I call unto them, they stand up together.   Ps. 102:25

14 All ye, assemble yourselves, and hear; which among them hath declared these *things?* The LORD hath loved him: ^Rhe will do his pleasure on Babylon, and his arm *shall be on* the Chal-de'-ans.   44:28

15 I, *even* I, have spoken; yea, ^RI have called him: I have brought him, and he shall make his way prosperous.   45:1, 2

16 Come ye near unto me, hear ye this; ^RI have not spoken in secret from the beginning; from the time that it was, there *am* I: and now ^Rthe Lord GOD, and his Spirit, hath sent me.   45:19 · 61:1

17 Thus saith the LORD, thy Redeemer, the Holy One of Israel; I *am* the LORD thy God which teacheth thee to profit, ^Rwhich leadeth thee by the way *that* thou shouldest go.   49:9, 10; Ps. 32:8

18 ^RO that thou hadst hearkened to my commandments! ^Rthen had thy peace been as a river, and thy righteousness as the waves of the sea: Deut. 5:29; Ps. 81:13 · Deut. 28:1–14

19 Thy seed also had been as the sand, and the offspring of thy bowels like the gravel thereof; his name should not have been cut off nor destroyed from before me.

20 Go ye forth of Babylon, flee ye from the Chal-de'-ans, with a voice of singing declare ye, tell this, utter it *even* to the end of the earth; say ye, The LORD hath redeemed his servant Jacob.

21 And they ^Rthirsted not *when* he led them through the deserts: he ^Rcaused the waters to flow out of the rock for them: he ^Tclave the rock also, and the waters gushed out.   [41:17, 18] · Ex. 17:6; Ps. 105:41 · *split*

22 ^R*There is* no peace, saith the LORD, unto the wicked.   [57:21]

49 Listen, ^RO isles, unto me; and hearken, ye people, from far; ^RThe LORD hath called me from the womb; from the bowels of my mother hath he made mention of my name.   41:1 · Jer. 1:5

2 And he hath made ^Rmy ☆ mouth like a sharp sword; ^Rin the shadow of his hand hath he hid me, and made me ^Ra polished shaft; in his quiver hath he hid me;   11:4; Rev. 1:16; 2:12 · 51:16 · Ps. 45:5

3 And said unto me, ^RThou *art* my servant, O Israel, ^Rin whom I will be glorified.   [Zech. 3:8] · 44:23

4 Then I said, I have laboured in vain, I have spent my strength for nought, and in vain: *yet* surely my judgment *is* with the LORD, and my work with my God.

5 And now, saith the LORD that ☆ formed me from the womb *to be* his servant, to bring Jacob again to him, Though Israel ^Rbe not gathered, yet shall I be glorious in the eyes of the LORD, and my God shall be my strength.   Matt. 23:37

6 And he said, It is a light thing ☆ that thou shouldest be my servant to raise up the tribes of Jacob, and to restore the preserved of Israel: I will also give thee for a ^Rlight to the Gentiles, that thou mayest be my salvation unto the end of the earth.   42:6; 51:4; Acts 13:47; [Gal. 3:14]

7 Thus saith the LORD, the Re- ☆ deemer of Israel, *and* his Holy One, ^Rto him whom man despiseth, to him whom the nation ab-

horreth, to a servant of rulers, [R]Kings shall see and arise, princes also shall worship, because of the LORD that is faithful, *and* the Holy One of Israel, and he shall choose thee. Mark 15:29 · [52:15]

8 Thus saith the LORD, In an [R]acceptable time have I heard thee, and in a day of salvation have I helped thee: and I will preserve thee, and give thee for a covenant of the people, to establish the earth, to cause to inherit the desolate heritages; Ps. 69:13

9 That thou mayest say [R]to the prisoners, Go forth; to them that *are* in darkness, Shew yourselves. They shall feed in the ways, and their pastures *shall be* in all high places. 61:1; Zech. 9:12; Luke 4:18

10 They shall not [R]hunger nor thirst; neither shall the heat nor sun smite them: for he that hath mercy on them shall lead them, even by the springs of water shall he guide them. 33:16; 48:21; Rev. 7:16

11 [R]And I will make all my mountains a [T]way, and my highways shall be exalted. 40:4 · *road*

12 Behold, these shall come from far: and, lo, these from the north and from the west; and these from the land of Si′-nim.

13 [R]Sing, O heavens; and be joyful, O earth; and break forth into singing, O mountains: for the LORD hath comforted his people, and will have mercy upon his afflicted. 44:23

14 [R]But Zion said, The LORD hath forsaken me, and my Lord hath forgotten me. 40:27

15 [R]Can a woman forget her sucking child, that she should not have compassion on the son of her womb? yea, they may forget, yet will I not forget thee. Ps. 103:13

16 Behold, I have graven thee upon the palms of *my* hands; thy walls *are* continually before me.

17 Thy [T]children shall make haste; thy destroyers and they that made thee waste shall go [T]forth of thee. Lit. *sons · away from*

18 [R]Lift up thine eyes round about, and behold: all these gath-

er themselves together, *and* come to thee. *As* I live, saith the LORD, thou shalt surely clothe thee with them all, [R]as with an ornament, and bind them *on thee*, as a bride *doeth*. 60:4; John 4:35 · Prov. 17:6

19 For thy waste and thy desolate places, and the land of thy destruction, shall even now be too narrow by reason of the inhabitants, and they that swallowed thee up shall be far away.

20 [R]The children which thou shalt have, [R]after thou hast lost the other, shall say again in thine ears, The place *is* too [T]strait for me: give place to me that I may dwell. 60:4 · [Matt. 3:9; Rom. 11:11] · *small*

21 Then shalt thou say in thine heart, Who hath begotten me these, seeing I have lost my children, and am desolate, a captive, and [T]removing to and fro? and who hath brought up these? Behold, I was left alone; these, where *had* they *been*? *wandering*

22 [R]Thus saith the Lord GOD, Behold, I will lift up mine hand to the Gentiles, and set up my standard to the people: and they shall bring thy sons in *their* arms, and thy daughters shall be carried upon *their* shoulders. 60:4

23 [R]And kings shall be thy [T]nursing fathers, and their queens thy nursing mothers: they shall bow down to thee with *their* face toward the earth, and [R]lick up the dust of thy feet; and thou shalt know that I *am* the LORD: for they shall not be ashamed that wait for me. 52:15 · *foster fathers* · Ps. 72:9

24 [R]Shall the prey be taken from the mighty, or the lawful captive delivered? Matt. 12:29; Luke 11:21, 22

25 But thus saith the LORD, Even the captives of the mighty shall be taken away, and the prey of the terrible shall be delivered: for I will contend with him that contendeth with thee, and I will save thy children.

26 And I will [R]feed them that oppress thee with their own flesh; and they shall be drunken with their own [R]blood, as with sweet

wine: and all flesh ᴿshall know
that I the LORD *am* thy Saviour
and thy Redeemer, the mighty
One of Jacob.   9:20 · Rev. 14:20 · 60:16

50 Thus saith the LORD,
Where *is* ᴿthe bill of your
mother's divorcement, whom I
have put away? or which of my
creditors *is it* to whom I have sold
you? Behold, for your iniquities
have ye sold yourselves, and for
your transgressions is your mother put away.   Deut. 24:1; Jer. 3:8

2 Wherefore, when I came, *was
there* no man? when I called, *was
there* none to answer? Is my hand
shortened at all, that it cannot
redeem? or have I no power to
deliver? behold, at my ᴿrebuke I
dry up the sea, I make the rivers a
wilderness: their fish stinketh,
because *there is* no water, and
dieth for thirst.   Ps. 106:9; Nah. 1:4

3 ᴿI clothe the heavens with
blackness, ᴿand I make sackcloth
their covering.   Ex. 10:21 · Rev. 6:12

4 ᴿThe Lord GOD hath given me
the tongue of the learned, that I
should know how to speak a word
in season to *him that is* ᴿweary:
he wakeneth morning by morning, he wakeneth mine ear to hear
as the learned.   Ex. 4:11 · Matt. 11:28

☆ 5 The Lord GOD ᴿhath opened
mine ear, and I was not rebellious,
neither turned away back.   Ps. 40:6

☆ 6 I gave my back to the smiters,
and my cheeks to them that
plucked off the hair: I hid not my
face from shame and spitting.

☆ 7 For the Lord GOD will help
me; therefore shall I not be confounded: therefore have ᴿI set my
face like a flint, and I know that I
shall not be ashamed.   Ezek. 3:8, 9

8 *He is* near that justifieth me;
who will contend with me? let us
stand together: who *is* mine adversary? let him come near to me.

9 Behold, the Lord GOD will
help me; who *is* he *that* shall condemn me? ᴿlo, they all shall wax
old as a garment; the moth shall
eat them up.   Ps. 102:26; Heb. 1:11

10 Who *is* among you that
feareth the LORD, that obeyeth the

voice of his servant, that ᴿwalketh
in darkness, and hath no light? let
him trust in the name of the LORD,
and stay upon his God.   Ps. 23:4

11 Behold, all ye that kindle a
fire, that compass *yourselves*
about with sparks: walk in the
light of your fire, and in the
sparks *that* ye have kindled. This
shall ye have of mine hand; ye
shall lie down ᴿin sorrow.   Ps. 16:4

51 Hearken to me, ᴿye that
Tfollow after righteousness,
ye that seek the LORD: look unto
the rock *whence* ye are hewn, and
to the hole of the pit *whence* ye
are digged.   [Rom. 9:30–32] · *pursue*

2 Look unto Abraham your
father, and unto Sarah *that* bare
you: for I called him alone, and
blessed him, and increased him.

3 For the LORD shall ᴿcomfort
Zion: he will comfort all her waste
places; and he will make her
wilderness like Eden, and her
desert like the garden of the LORD;
joy and gladness shall be found
therein, thanksgiving, and the
voice of melody.   40:1; 52:9; Ps. 102:13

4 Hearken unto me, my people;
and give ear unto me, O my nation: ᴿfor a law shall Tproceed
from me, and I will make my
Tjudgment to rest ᴿfor a light of
the people.   2:3 · *go forth* · *justice* · 42:6

5 My righteousness *is* near; my
salvation is gone forth, and mine
arms shall judge the people; ᴿthe
isles shall wait upon me, and on
mine arm shall they trust.   60:9

6 ᴿLift up your eyes to the
heavens, and look upon the earth
beneath: for ᴿthe heavens shall
vanish away like smoke, ᴿand the
earth shall wax old like a garment, and they that dwell therein
shall die in like manner: but my
salvation shall be ᴿfor ever, and
my righteousness shall not be
abolished.   40:26 · 34:4 · 24:19, 20 · 45:17

7 Hearken unto me, ye that
know righteousness, the people in
whose heart *is* my law; fear ye not
the reproach of men, neither be ye
afraid of their revilings.

8 For ᴿthe moth shall eat them

up like a garment, and the worm shall eat them like wool: but my righteousness shall be for ever, and my salvation from generation to generation.   50:9

9 Awake, awake, put on strength, O arm of the LORD; awake, as in the ancient days, in the generations of old. *Art* thou not it that hath cut ᴿRa′-hab, *and* wounded the dragon?   Ps. 87:4

10 *Art* thou not it which hath ᴿdried the sea, the waters of the great deep; that hath made the depths of the sea a way for the ransomed to pass over?   63:11–13

11 Therefore ᴿthe redeemed of the LORD shall return, and come with singing unto Zion; and everlasting joy *shall be* upon their head: they shall obtain gladness and joy; *and* sorrow and mourning shall flee away.   Jer. 31:11, 12

12 I, *even* I, *am* he ᴿthat comforteth you: who *art* thou, that thou shouldest be afraid ᴿof a man *that* shall die, and of the son of man *which* shall be made ᴿ*as* grass; 2 Cor. 1:3 · 2:22 · 40:6, 7; James 1:10

13 And ᴿforgettest the LORD thy maker, ᴿthat hath stretched forth the heavens, and laid the foundations of the earth; and hast feared continually every day because of the fury of the oppressor, as if he were ready to destroy? ᴿand where *is* the fury of the oppressor?   17:10; Jer. 2:32 · Ps. 104:2 · Job 20:7

14 The captive exile hasteneth that he may be loosed, ᴿand that he should not die in the pit, nor that his bread should fail. Zech. 9:11

15 But I *am* the LORD thy God, that ᴿdivided the sea, whose waves roared: The LORD of hosts *is* his name.   Job 26:12

16 And ᴿI have put my words in thy mouth, and ᴿI have covered thee in the shadow of mine hand, ᴿthat I may plant the heavens, and lay the foundations of the earth, and say unto Zion, Thou *art* my people. 59:21; John 3:34 · Ex. 33:22 · 65:17

17 ᴿAwake, awake, stand up, O Jerusalem, which ᴿhast drunk at the hand of the LORD the cup of his fury; thou hast drunken the dregs of the cup of trembling, *and* wrung *them* out. 52:1 · 29:9; Rev. 14:10

18 *There is* none to guide her among all the sons *whom* she hath brought forth; neither *is there any* that taketh her by the hand of all the sons *that* she hath brought up.

19 ᴿThese two *things* are come unto thee; who shall be sorry for thee? desolation, and destruction, and the famine, and the sword: by whom shall I comfort thee?   47:9

20 ᴿThy sons have fainted, they lie at the head of all the streets, as ᵀa wild bull in a net: they are full of the fury of the LORD, the rebuke of thy God.   Lam. 2:11 · *an antelope*

21 Therefore hear now this, thou afflicted, and drunken, ᴿbut not with wine: Lam. 3:15

22 Thus saith thy Lord the LORD, and thy God *that* ᴿpleadeth the cause of his people, Behold, I have taken out of thine hand the cup of trembling, *even* the dregs of the cup of my fury; thou shalt no more drink it again: 3:12, 13; 49:25

23 ᴿBut I will put it into the hand of them that afflict thee; which have said to thy soul, Bow down, that we may go over: and thou hast laid thy body as the ground, and as the street, to them that went over. Jer. 25:17, 26–28; Zech. 12:2

52 Awake, awake; put on thy strength, O Zion; put on thy beautiful garments, O Jerusalem, the holy city: for henceforth there shall no more come into thee the uncircumcised and the unclean.

2 ᴿShake thyself from the dust; arise, *and* sit down, O Jerusalem: ᴿloose thyself from the bands of thy neck, O captive daughter of Zion.   3:26 · 9:4; 10:27; 14:25; Zech. 2:7

3 For thus saith the LORD, ᴿYe have sold yourselves for nought; and ye shall be redeemed ᴿwithout money.   Ps. 44:12; Jer. 15:13 · 45:13

4 For thus saith the Lord GOD, My people went down aforetime into ᴿEgypt to sojourn there; and the Assyrian oppressed them without cause.   Gen. 46:6

5 Now therefore, what have I here, saith the LORD, that my people is taken away for nought? they that rule over them make them to howl, saith the LORD; and my name continually every day *is* ^Rblasphemed. Ezek. 36:20, 23; Rom. 2:24

6 Therefore my people shall know my name: therefore *they shall know* in that day that I *am* he that doth speak: behold, *it is* I.

7 ^RHow beautiful upon the mountains are the feet of him that bringeth good tidings, that publisheth peace; that bringeth good tidings of good, that publisheth salvation; that saith unto Zion, Thy God reigneth! 40:9; 61:1; Eph. 6:15

8 Thy watchmen shall lift up the voice; with the voice together shall they sing: for they shall see eye to eye, when the LORD shall bring ^Tagain Zion.   *back*

9 Break forth into joy, sing together, ye waste places of Jerusalem: for the LORD hath comforted his people, he hath redeemed Jerusalem.

10 ^RThe LORD hath made bare his holy arm in the eyes of ^Rall the nations; and all the ends of the earth shall see the salvation of our God.   Ps. 98:1–3 · Luke 3:6

11 ^RDepart ye, depart ye, go ye out from thence, touch no unclean *thing*; go ye out of the midst of her; be ye clean, that bear the vessels of the LORD.   Jer. 50:8; 2 Cor. 6:17

12 For ye shall not go out with haste, nor go by flight: ^Rfor the LORD will go before you; ^Rand the God of Israel *will be* your ^Trereward.   Mic. 2:13 · 58:8 · *rear guard*

13 Behold, my servant shall deal prudently, he shall be exalted and extolled, and be very high.

☆ 14 As many were astonied at thee; his visage was so marred more than any man, and his form more than the sons of men:

15 So shall he sprinkle many nations; the kings shall shut their mouths at him: for *that* ^Rwhich had not been told them shall they see; and *that* which they had not heard shall they consider.   1 Pet. 1:2

53 Who hath believed our report? and to whom is the arm of the LORD revealed? ☆

2 For he shall grow up before him as a tender plant, and as a root out of a dry ground: he hath no form nor comeliness; and when we shall see him, *there is* no beauty that we should desire him.

3 ^RHe is despised and rejected ☆ of men; a man of sorrows, and acquainted with grief: and we hid as it were *our* faces from him; he was despised, and we esteemed him not.   Ps. 22:6; [Matt. 27:30, 31]

4 Surely he hath borne our ☆ griefs, and carried our sorrows: yet we did esteem him stricken, smitten of God, and afflicted.

5 But he *was* ^Rwounded for our ☆ transgressions, *he was* bruised for our iniquities: the chastisement of our peace *was* upon him; and with his stripes we are healed.   [v. 10]

6 All we like sheep have gone ☆ astray; we have turned every one to his own way; and the LORD hath laid on him the iniquity of us all.

7 He was oppressed, and he ☆ was afflicted, yet ^Rhe opened not his mouth: ^Rhe is brought as a lamb to the slaughter, and as a sheep before her shearers is dumb, so he openeth not his mouth. Luke 23:9; John 19:9 · Acts 8:32, 33

8 He was taken from prison ☆ and from judgment: and who shall declare his generation? for he was cut off out of the land of the living: for the transgression of my people was he stricken.

9 ^RAnd he made his grave with ☆ the wicked, and with the rich in his death; because he had done no violence, neither *was any* ^Rdeceit in his mouth.   Luke 23:33 · 1 Pet. 2:22

10 Yet it pleased the LORD to ☆ bruise him; he hath put *him* to grief: when thou shalt make his soul ^Ran offering for sin, he shall see *his* seed, he shall prolong *his* days, and the pleasure of the LORD shall prosper in his hand. John 1:29

11 He shall see of the travail of ☆ his soul, *and* shall be satisfied: by his knowledge shall my righteous

servant ᴿjustify many; for he shall bear their iniquities.　[Acts 13:38, 39]

☆ 12 ᴿTherefore will I divide him *a portion* with the great, and he shall divide the spoil with the strong; because he hath poured out his soul unto death: and he was ᴿnumbered with the transgressors; and he bare the sin of many, and made intercession for the transgressors. Ps. 2:8 · Mark 15:28

54 Sing, O barren, thou *that* didst not bear; break forth into singing, and cry aloud, thou *that* didst not travail with child: for more *are* the children of the desolate than the children of the married wife, saith the LORD.

2 ᴿEnlarge the place of thy tent, and let them stretch forth the curtains of thine habitations: spare not, lengthen thy cords, and strengthen thy stakes;　49:19, 20

3 For thou shalt break forth on the right hand and on the left; and thy seed shall ᴿinherit the Gentiles, and make the desolate cities to be inhabited.　14:2; 49:22, 23; 60:9

4 Fear not; for thou shalt not be ashamed: neither be thou ᵀconfounded; for thou shalt not be put to shame: for thou shalt forget the shame of thy youth, and shalt not remember the reproach of thy widowhood any more.　*disgraced*

5 For thy Maker *is* thine husband; the LORD of hosts *is* his name; and thy Redeemer the Holy One of Israel; The God of the whole earth shall he be called.

6 For the LORD ᴿhath called thee as a woman forsaken and grieved in spirit, and a wife of youth, when thou wast refused, saith thy God.　62:4

7 ᴿFor a small moment have I forsaken thee; but with great mercies will I gather thee.　2 Cor. 4:17

8 In a little wrath I hid my face from thee for a moment; ᴿbut with everlasting ᵀkindness will I have mercy on thee, saith the LORD thy Redeemer. 55:3; Jer. 31:3 · *lovingkindness*

9 For this *is as* the waters of ᴿNoah unto me: for *as* I have sworn that the waters of Noah

should no more go over the earth; so have I sworn that I would not be wroth with ᴿthee, nor rebuke thee.　Gen. 8:21; 9:11 · 12:1; Ezek. 39:29

10 For ᴿthe mountains shall depart, and the hills be removed; ᴿbut my kindness shall not depart from thee, neither shall the covenant of my peace be removed, saith the LORD that hath mercy on thee.　Ps. 46:2; Matt. 5:18 · Ps. 89:33, 34

11 O thou afflicted, tossed with tempest, *and* not comforted, behold, I will lay thy stones with ᴿfair colours, and lay thy foundations with sapphires.　Rev. 21:18, 19

12 And I will make thy windows of agates, and thy gates of carbuncles, and all thy borders of ᵀpleasant stones.　*precious*

13 And all thy children *shall be* ☆ taught of the LORD; and great *shall be* the peace of thy children.

14 In righteousness shalt thou be established: thou shalt be far from oppression; for thou shalt not fear: and from terror; for it shall not come near thee.

15 Behold, they shall surely gather together, *but* not by me: whosoever shall gather together against thee shall ᴿfall for thy sake.　41:11–16

16 Behold, I have created the smith that bloweth the coals in the fire, and that bringeth forth an ᵀinstrument for his work; and I have created the ᵀwaster to destroy.　Or *weapon* · *destroyer*

17 No weapon that is formed against thee shall ᴿprosper; and every tongue *that* shall rise against thee in judgment thou shalt condemn. This *is* the heritage of the servants of the LORD, ᴿand their righteousness *is* of me, saith the LORD. 17:12–14; 29:8 · 45:24, 25

55 Ho, ᴿevery one that thirsteth, come ye to the waters, and he that hath no money; come ye, buy, and eat; yea, come, buy wine and milk without money and without price.　[John 4:14; 7:37]

2 Wherefore do ye spend money for *that which is* not bread? and your labour for *that which*

satisfieth not? hearken diligently unto me, and eat ye *that which is* good, and let your soul delight itself in ^Tfatness.   *abundance*

3 Incline your ear, and come unto me: hear, and your soul shall live; and I will make an everlasting covenant with you, *even* the ^Rsure mercies of David. [Acts 13:34]

4 Behold, I have given him *for* a witness to the people, a leader and commander to the people.

5 Behold, thou shalt call a nation *that* thou knowest not, and nations *that* knew not thee shall run unto thee because of the LORD thy God, and for the Holy One of Israel; for he hath glorified thee.

6 ^RSeek ye the LORD while he may be found, call ye upon him while he is near: Matt. 5:25; John 7:34

7 ^RLet the wicked forsake his way, and the unrighteous man his thoughts: and let him return unto the LORD, and he will have mercy upon him; and to our God, for he will abundantly pardon.   1:16

8 For my thoughts *are* not your thoughts, neither *are* your ways my ways, saith the LORD.

9 For *as* the heavens are higher than the earth, so are my ways higher than your ways, and my thoughts than your thoughts.

10 For ^Ras the rain cometh down, and the snow from heaven, and returneth not thither, but watereth the earth, and maketh it bring forth and bud, that it may give seed to the sower, and bread to the eater: Deut. 32:2

11 ^RSo shall my word be that goeth forth out of my mouth: it shall not return unto me void, but it shall accomplish that which I please, and it shall prosper *in the thing* whereto I sent it.   Matt. 24:35

12 ^RFor ye shall go out with joy, and be led forth with peace: the mountains and the hills shall break forth before you into singing, and all the trees of the field shall clap *their* hands. 35:10

13 Instead of the thorn shall come up the fir tree, and instead of the brier shall come up the

myrtle tree: and it shall be to the LORD for a name, for an everlasting sign *that* shall not be cut off.

56 Thus saith the LORD, Keep ye judgment, and do justice: ^Rfor my salvation *is* near to come, and my righteousness to be revealed.   Matt. 3:2; 4:17; Rom. 13:11, 12

2 Blessed *is* the man *that* doeth this, and the son of man *that* layeth hold on it; ^Rthat keepeth the sabbath from polluting it, and keepeth his hand from doing any evil.   Ex. 20:8–11; Ezek. 20:12, 20

3 Neither let ^Rthe son of the stranger, that hath joined himself to the LORD, speak, saying, The LORD hath utterly separated me from his people: neither let the ^Reunuch say, Behold, I *am* a dry tree.   [Eph. 2:12–19] · Acts 8:27

4 For thus saith the LORD unto the eunuchs that keep my sabbaths, and choose *the things* that please me, and ^Ttake hold of my covenant;   *hold fast to*

5 Even unto them will I give in ^Rmine house and within my walls a place and a name better than of sons and of daughters: I will give them an everlasting name, that shall not be cut off.   1 Tim. 3:15

6 Also the sons of the stranger, that join themselves to the LORD, to serve him, and to love the name of the LORD, to be his servants, every one that keepeth the sabbath from polluting it, and taketh hold of my covenant;

7 Even them will I bring to my holy mountain, and make them joyful in my ^Rhouse of prayer: their burnt offerings and their sacrifices *shall be* ^Raccepted upon mine altar; for mine house shall be called an house of prayer for all people.   Matt. 21:13; Luke 19:46 · 60:7

8 The Lord GOD ^Rwhich gathereth the outcasts of Israel saith, ^RYet will I gather *others* to him, beside those that are gathered unto him. 11:12; 27:12 · 60:3–11; 66:18–21

9 ^RAll ye beasts of the field, come to devour, *yea*, all ye beasts in the forest.   Jer. 12:9

10 His watchmen *are* [R]blind: they are all ignorant, [R]they *are* all [T]dumb dogs, they cannot bark; sleeping, lying down, loving to slumber.   Matt. 15:14 · Phil. 3:2 · *mute*

11 Yea, *they are* greedy dogs *which* [R]can never have enough, and they *are* shepherds *that* cannot understand: they all look to their own way, every one for his gain, from his quarter. Ezek. 34:2–10

12 Come ye, *say they*, I will fetch wine, and we will fill ourselves with strong [R]drink; [R]and to-morrow shall be as this day, *and* much more abundant.   28:7 · Ps. 10:6

57 The righteous perisheth, and no man [T]layeth *it* to heart: and merciful men *are* taken away, [R]none considering that the righteous is taken away from the evil *to come*.   *takes* · 1 Kin. 14:13

2 He shall enter into peace: they shall rest in their beds, *each one* walking *in* his uprightness.

3 But draw near hither, [R]ye sons of the sorceress, the seed of the adulterer and the whore.   1:4

4 Against whom do ye [T]sport yourselves? against whom make ye a wide mouth, *and* [T]draw out the tongue? *are* ye not children of transgression, a seed of falsehood,   *ridicule?* · *stick*

5 Enflaming yourselves with idols under every green tree, slaying the children in the valleys under the clifts of the rocks?

6 Among the smooth [R]stones of the stream *is* thy portion; they, they *are* thy lot: even to them hast thou poured a drink offering, thou hast offered a meat offering. Should I receive comfort in [R]these? Jer. 3:9; Hab. 2:19 · Jer. 5:9, 29; 9:9

7 [R]Upon a lofty and high mountain hast thou set thy bed: even thither wentest thou up to offer sacrifice.   Jer. 3:6; Ezek. 16:16

8 Behind the doors also and the posts hast thou set up thy remembrance: for thou hast [T]discovered *thyself to another* than me, and art gone up; thou hast enlarged thy bed, and [T]made thee *a covenant* with them; [R]thou lov-

edst their bed where thou sawest *it*.   *uncovered* · Lit. *cut* · Ezek. 16:26

9 And [R]thou wentest to the king with ointment, and didst increase thy perfumes, and didst send thy [R]messengers far off, and didst debase *thyself even* unto [T]hell. Hos. 7:11 · Ezek. 23:16, 40 · Or *Sheol*

10 Thou art wearied in the greatness of thy way; *yet* saidst thou not, There is no hope: thou hast found the life of thine hand; therefore thou wast not grieved.

11 And of whom hast thou been afraid or feared, that thou hast lied, and hast not remembered me, nor laid *it* to thy heart? have not I held my peace even of old, and thou fearest me not?

12 I will declare thy righteousness, and thy works; for they shall not profit thee.

13 When thou [T]criest, let thy companies deliver thee; but the wind shall carry them all away; [T]vanity shall take *them*: but he that putteth his trust in me shall possess the land, and shall inherit my holy mountain;   *cry out* · *a breath*

14 And shall say, [R]Cast ye up, cast ye up, prepare the way, take up the stumblingblock out of the way of my people.   40:3; 62:10

15 For thus saith the high and lofty One that inhabiteth eternity, [R]whose name *is* Holy; [R]I dwell in the high and holy *place*, with him also *that is* of a contrite and humble spirit, to revive the spirit of the humble, and to revive the heart of the contrite ones. Luke 1:49 · Ps. 68:35

16 [R]For I will not contend for ever, neither will I be always wroth: for the spirit should fail before me, and the souls [R]which I have made.   Ps. 85:5; 103:9 · Heb. 12:9

17 For the iniquity of [R]his covetousness was I wroth, and smote him: [R]I hid me, and was wroth, [R]and he went on frowardly in the way of his heart. 2:7 · 8:17; 45:15 · 9:13

18 I have seen his ways, and [R]will heal him: I will lead him also, and restore comforts unto him and to his mourners.   Jer. 3:22

19 I create the fruit of the lips;

Peace, peace to *him that is* far off, and to *him that is* near, saith the LORD; and I will heal him.

20 ᴿBut the wicked *are* like the troubled sea, when it cannot rest, whose waters cast up mire and dirt.   Job 15:20; Prov. 4:16; Jude 13

21 ᴿ*There is* no peace, saith my God, to the wicked.   48:22

58 Cry aloud, ᵀspare not, lift up thy voice like a trumpet, and ᴿshew my people their transgression, and the house of Jacob their sins.   *do not hold back · Mic. 3:8*

2 Yet they seek me daily, and delight to know my ways, as a nation that did righteousness, and forsook not the ordinance of their God: they ask of me the ordinances of justice; they take delight in approaching to God.

3 ᴿWherefore have we fasted, *say they*, and thou seest not? *wherefore* have we afflicted our soul, and thou takest no knowledge? Behold, in the day of your fast ye find pleasure, and exact all your labours.   Mal. 3:13–18; Luke 18:12

4 ᴿBehold, ye fast for strife and debate, and to smite with the fist of wickedness: ye shall not fast as *ye do this* day, to make your voice to be heard on high.   1 Kin. 21:9

5 Is it such a fast that I have chosen? a day for a man to afflict his soul? *is it* to bow down his head as a bulrush, and ᴿto spread sackcloth and ashes *under him*? wilt thou call this a fast, and an acceptable day to the LORD?   Job 2:8

6 *Is* not this the fast that I have chosen? to ᴿloose the bands of wickedness, to undo the heavy burdens, and ᴿto let the oppressed go free, and that ye break every yoke?   Luke 4:18, 19 · Jer. 34:9

7 *Is it* not ᴿto deal thy bread to the hungry, and that thou bring the poor that are cast out to thy house? when thou seest the naked, that thou cover him; and that thou hide not thyself from thine own flesh?   Ezek. 18:7; Matt. 25:35

8 Then shall thy light break forth as the morning, and thine health shall spring forth speedily:

and thy righteousness shall go before thee; the glory of the LORD shall be thy ᵀrereward.   *rear guard*

9 Then shalt thou call, and the LORD shall answer; thou shalt cry, and he shall say, Here I *am*. If thou take away from the midst of thee the yoke, the putting forth of the finger, and speaking vanity;

10 And *if* thou draw out thy soul to the hungry, and satisfy the afflicted soul; then shall thy light rise in obscurity, and thy ᵀdarkness *be* as the noon day: Or *gloom*

11 And the LORD shall guide thee continually, and satisfy thy soul in drought, and make fat thy bones: and thou shalt be like a watered garden, and like a spring of water, whose waters fail not.

12 And *they that shall be* of thee ᴿshall build the old waste places: thou shalt raise up the foundations of many generations; and thou shalt be called, The repairer of the breach, The restorer of ᵀpaths to dwell in.   61:4 · *streets*

13 If ᴿthou turn away thy foot from the sabbath, *from* doing thy pleasure on my holy day; and call the sabbath a delight, the holy of the LORD, honourable; and shalt honour him, not doing thine own ways, nor finding thine own pleasure, nor speaking *thine own* words: Ex. 31:16, 17; 35:2, 3; Jer. 17:21–27

14 ᴿThen shalt thou delight thyself in the LORD; and I will cause thee to ᴿride upon the high places of the earth, and feed thee with the heritage of Jacob thy father: ᴿfor the mouth of the LORD hath spoken *it*.   61:10 · 33:16; Hab. 3:19 · 1:20

59 Behold, the LORD's hand is not ᴿshortened, that it cannot save; neither his ear heavy, that it cannot hear: 50:2; Jer. 32:17

2 But your iniquities have separated between you and your God, and your sins have hid *his* face from you, that he will ᴿnot hear.   1:15

3 For ᴿyour hands are defiled with blood, and your fingers with iniquity; your lips have spoken

lies, your tongue hath muttered perverseness.   Jer. 2:30, 34; Ezek. 7:23

4 None calleth for justice, nor *any* pleadeth for truth: they trust in vanity, and speak lies; ᴿthey conceive ᵀmischief, and bring forth iniquity.   33:11 · *trouble or evil*

5 They hatch ᵀcockatrice' eggs, and weave the spider's web: he that eateth of their eggs dieth, and that which is crushed ᵀbreaketh out into a viper.   *vipers'* · *hatches out*

6 ᴿTheir webs shall not become garments, neither shall they cover themselves with their works: their works *are* works of iniquity, and the act of violence *is* in their hands.   Job 8:14

7 Their feet run to evil, and they make haste to shed innocent blood: their thoughts *are* thoughts of iniquity; wasting and destruction *are* in their paths.

8 The way of ᴿpeace they know not; and *there is* no judgment in their goings: ᴿthey have made them crooked paths: whosoever goeth therein shall not know peace.   57:20, 21 · Ps. 125:5; Prov. 2:15

9 Therefore is judgment far from us, neither doth justice overtake us: ᴿwe wait for light, but behold obscurity; for brightness, *but* we walk in darkness.   Jer. 8:15

10 ᴿWe grope for the wall like the blind, and we grope as if *we had* no eyes: we stumble at noon day as in the night; *we are* in desolate places as dead *men.*   Amos 8:9

11 We roar all like bears, and ᴿmournᵀ sore like doves: we look for ᵀjudgment, but *there is* none; for salvation, *but* it is far off from us.   38:14; Ezek. 7:16 · *moan sadly* · *justice*

12 For our transgressions are multiplied before thee, and our sins testify against us: for our transgressions *are* with us; and *as for* our iniquities, we know them;

13 In transgressing and lying against the LORD, and departing away from our God, speaking oppression and revolt, conceiving and uttering ᴿfrom the heart words of falsehood.   Matt. 12:34

14 And ᵀjudgment is turned away backward, and ᵀjustice standeth afar off: for truth is fallen in the street, and equity cannot enter.   *justice* · *righteousness*

15 Yea, truth faileth; and he *that* departeth from evil maketh himself a ᴿprey: and the LORD saw *it,* and it displeased him that *there was* no judgment.   10:2; 29:21; 32:7

16 ᴿAnd he saw that *there was* no man, and ᴿwondered that *there was* no intercessor: ᴿtherefore his arm brought salvation unto him; and his righteousness, it sustained him.   Ezek. 22:30 · Mark 6:6 · 63:5

17 ᴿFor he put on righteousness as a breastplate, and an helmet of salvation upon his head; and he put on the garments of vengeance *for* clothing, and was clad with zeal as a cloke.   Eph. 6:14, 17

18 ᴿAccording to *their* deeds, accordingly he will repay, fury to his adversaries, recompence to his enemies; to the islands he will repay recompence.   63:6; Rom. 2:6

19 ᴿSo shall they fear the name of the LORD from the west, and his glory from the rising of the sun. When the enemy shall come in ᴿlike a flood, the Spirit of the LORD shall lift up a standard against him.   Mal. 1:11 · Rev. 12:15

20 And ᴿthe Redeemer shall ☆ come to Zion, and unto them that turn from transgression in Jacob, saith the LORD.   Rom. 11:26

21 ᴿAs for me, this *is* my covenant with them, saith the LORD; My spirit that *is* upon thee, and my words which I have put in thy mouth, shall not depart out of thy mouth, nor out of the mouth of thy seed, nor out of the mouth of thy seed's seed, saith the LORD, from henceforth and for ever.   [Heb. 8:10]

60 Arise, ᴿshine; for thy light is come, and the glory of the LORD is risen upon thee.   Eph. 5:14

2 For, behold, the darkness shall cover the earth, and gross darkness the people: but the LORD shall arise upon thee, and his glory shall be seen upon thee.

3 And the ᴿGentiles shall come ☆

to thy light, and kings to the brightness of thy rising.　Rev. 21:24

4 ᴿLift up thine eyes round about, and see: all they gather themselves together, ᴿthey come to thee: thy sons shall come from far, and thy daughters shall be nursed at *thy* side.　49:18 · 49:20–22

5 Then thou shalt see, and flow together, and thine heart shall fear, and be enlarged; because ᴿthe abundance of the sea shall be converted unto thee, the ᵀforces of the ᵀGentiles shall come unto thee.　[Rom. 11:25–27] · *wealth · nations*

6 The multitude of camels shall cover thee, the dromedaries of Mid'-i-an and E'-phah; all they from ᴿShe'-ba shall come: they shall bring ᴿgold and incense; and they shall shew forth the praises of the Lᴏʀᴅ.　Ps. 72:10 · Matt. 2:11

7 All the flocks of Ke'-dar shall be gathered together unto thee, the rams of Ne-bai'-oth shall minister unto thee: they shall come up with ᴿacceptance on mine altar, and ᴿI will glorify the house of my glory.　56:7 · v. 13; Hag. 2:7, 9

8 Who *are* these *that* fly as a cloud, and as the doves to their ᵀwindows?　*roosts*

9 ᴿSurely the isles shall wait for me, and the ships of Tar'-shish first, ᴿto bring thy sons from far, ᴿtheir silver and their gold with them, unto the name of the Lᴏʀᴅ thy God, and to the Holy One of Israel, ᴿbecause he hath glorified thee.　Ps. 72:10 · [Gal. 4:26] · Jer. 3:17 · 55:5

10 And ᴿthe sons of strangers shall build up thy walls, ᴿand their kings shall minister unto thee: for ᴿin my wrath I smote thee, ᴿbut in my favour have I had mercy on thee.　Zech. 6:15 · Rev. 21:24 · 57:17 · 54:7, 8

11 Therefore thy gates ᴿshall be open continually; they shall not be shut day nor night; that *men* may bring unto thee the forces of the Gentiles, and *that* their kings *may be* brought.　26:2; Rev. 21:25, 26

12 ᴿFor the nation and kingdom that will not serve thee shall perish; yea, *those* nations shall be utterly wasted.　Zech. 14:17; Matt. 21:44

13 ᴿThe glory of Leb'-a-non shall come unto thee, the fir tree, the pine tree, and the box together, to beautify the place of my sanctuary; and I will make the place of my feet glorious.　35:2

14 The sons also of them that afflicted thee shall come ᴿbending unto thee; and all they that despised thee shall bow themselves down at the soles of thy feet; and they shall call thee, The city of the Lᴏʀᴅ, ᴿThe Zion of the Holy One of Israel.　45:14 · [Heb. 12:22; Rev. 14:1]

15 Whereas thou hast been forsaken and hated, so that no man went through *thee*, I will make thee an eternal excellency, a joy of many generations.

16 Thou shalt also suck the milk of the Gentiles, ᴿand shalt suck the breast of kings: and thou shalt know that ᴿI the Lᴏʀᴅ *am* thy Saviour and thy Redeemer, the mighty One of Jacob.　49:23 · 43:3

17 For ᵀbrass I will bring gold, and for iron I will bring silver, and for wood brass, and for stones iron: I will also make thy officers peace, and ᵀthine exactors righteousness.　*bronze · thy magistrates*

18 Violence shall no more be heard in thy land, wasting nor destruction within thy borders; but thou shalt call ᴿthy walls Salvation, and thy gates Praise.　26:1

19 The ᴿsun shall be no more thy light by day; neither for brightness shall the moon give light unto thee: but the Lᴏʀᴅ shall be unto thee an everlasting light, and thy God thy glory.　Rev. 21:23

20 ᴿThy sun shall no more go down; neither shall thy moon withdraw itself: for the Lᴏʀᴅ shall be thine everlasting light, and the days of thy mourning shall be ended.　Amos 8:9

21 ᴿThy people also *shall be* all righteous: they shall inherit the land for ever, the branch of my planting, the work of my hands, that I may be glorified.　Rev. 21:27

22 ᴿA little one shall become a thousand, and a small one a

strong nation: I the Lord will hasten it in ᵀhis time. Matt. 13:31, 32 · *its*

61 The ᴿSpirit of the Lord God *is* upon me; because the Lord ᴿhath anointed me to preach good tidings unto the meek; he hath sent me ᴿto bind up the brokenhearted, to proclaim liberty to the captives, and the opening of the prison to *them that are* bound; Matt. 3:17 · Matt. 11:5 · Ps. 147:3

2 To proclaim the acceptable year of the Lord, and ᴿthe day of vengeance of our God; ᴿto comfort all that mourn; 34:8 · Matt. 5:4

3 To appoint unto them that mourn in Zion, to give unto them beauty for ashes, the oil of joy for mourning, the garment of praise for the spirit of heaviness; that they might be called trees of righteousness, the planting of the Lord, that he might be glorified.

4 And they shall ᴿbuild the old wastes, they shall raise up the former desolations, and they shall repair the waste cities, the desolations of many generations. 49:8

5 And strangers shall stand and feed your flocks, and the sons of the alien *shall be* your plowmen and your vinedressers.

6 ᴿBut ye shall be named the Priests of the Lord: *men* shall call you the Ministers of our God: ᴿye shall eat the riches of the Gentiles, and in their glory shall ye boast yourselves. Ex. 19:6 · 60:5, 11

7 ᴿFor your shame *ye shall have* double; and *for* confusion they shall rejoice in their portion: therefore in their land they shall possess the double: everlasting joy shall be unto them. Zech. 9:12

8 For I the Lord love judgment, I hate robbery for burnt offering; and I will direct their work in truth, ᴿand I will make an everlasting covenant with them. 55:3

9 And their seed shall be known among the Gentiles, and their offspring among the people: all that see them shall acknowledge them, ᴿthat they *are* the seed *which* the Lord hath blessed. 65:23

10 I will greatly rejoice in the Lord, my soul shall be joyful in my God; for ᴿhe hath clothed me with the garments of salvation, he hath covered me with the robe of righteousness, ᴿas a bridegroom decketh *himself* with ornaments, and as a bride adorneth *herself* with her jewels. Ps. 132:9, 16 · Rev. 21:2

11 For as the earth bringeth forth her bud, and as the garden causeth the things that are sown in it to spring forth; so the Lord God will cause ᴿrighteousness and ᴿpraise to spring forth before all the nations. Ps. 72:3; 85:11 · 60:18

62 For Zion's sake will I not hold my peace, and for Jerusalem's sake I will not rest, until the righteousness thereof go forth as brightness, and the salvation thereof as a lamp *that* burneth.

2 ᴿAnd the Gentiles shall see thy righteousness, and all kings thy glory: and thou shalt be called by a new name, which the mouth of the Lord shall name. 60:3

3 Thou shalt also be ᴿa crown of glory in the hand of the Lord, and a royal diadem in the hand of thy God. 28:5; Zech. 9:16; 1 Thess. 2:19

4 ᴿThou shalt no more be termed ᴿForsaken; neither shall thy land any more be termed ᴿDesolate: but thou shalt be called Heph'-zi–bah, and thy land Beu'-lah: for the Lord delighteth in thee, and thy land shall be married. Hos. 1:10; 1 Pet. 2:10 · 54:6, 7 · 54:1

5 For *as* a young man marrieth a virgin, *so* shall thy sons marry thee: and *as* the bridegroom rejoiceth over the bride, ᴿ*so* shall thy God rejoice over thee. 65:19

6 ᴿI have set watchmen upon thy walls, O Jerusalem, *which* shall never hold their peace day nor night: ye that make mention of the Lord, keep not silence, 52:8

7 And give him no rest, till he establish, and till he make Jerusalem ᴿa praise in the earth. 60:18

8 The Lord hath sworn by his right hand, and by the arm of his strength, Surely I will no more give thy corn *to be* meat for thine enemies; and the sons of the

stranger shall not drink thy wine,
for the which thou hast laboured:

9 But they that have gathered it
shall eat it, and praise the LORD;
and they that have brought it together shall drink it ᴿin the courts
of my holiness.   Deut. 12:12; 14:23, 26

10 Go through, go through the
gates; ᴿprepare ye the way of the
people; cast up, cast up the highway; gather out the stones; lift up
a standard for the people.   57:14

☆ 11 Behold, the LORD hath proclaimed unto the end of the world,
ᴿSay ye to the daughter of Zion,
Behold, thy salvation cometh;
behold, his reward *is* with him,
and his work before him.   Zech. 9:9

12 And they shall call them, The
holy people, The redeemed of the
LORD: and thou shalt be called,
Sought out, A city not forsaken.

63 Who *is* this that cometh
from E'-dom, with dyed garments from Boz'-rah? this *that is*
glorious in his apparel, travelling
in the greatness of his strength?
I that speak in righteousness,
mighty to save.

☆ 2 Wherefore ᴿ*art thou* red in
thine apparel, and thy garments
like him that treadeth in the
ᵀwinefat?   [Rev. 19:13, 15] · *winepress*

☆ 3 I have ᴿtrodden the winepress alone; and of the people
there was none with me: for I will
tread them in mine anger, and
trample them in my fury; and
their blood shall be sprinkled
upon my garments, and I will
stain all my raiment.   Rev. 14:19, 20

4 For the ᴿday of vengeance *is*
in mine heart, and the year of my
redeemed is come.   34:8; 35:4; 61:2

5 ᴿAnd I looked, and ᴿ*there
was* none to help; and I wondered
that *there was* none to uphold:
therefore mine own ᴿarm brought
salvation unto me; and my fury, it
upheld me.   41:28 · [John 16:32] · 59:16

6 And I will tread down the
people in mine anger, and make
them drunk in my fury, and I will
bring down their strength to the
earth.

7 I will mention the lovingkindnesses of the LORD, *and* the
praises of the LORD, according to
all that the LORD hath bestowed
on us, and the great goodness
toward the house of Israel, which
he hath bestowed on them according to his mercies, and according
to the multitude of his lovingkindnesses.

8 For he said, Surely they *are*
my people, children *that* will not
lie: so he was their Saviour.

9 ᴿIn all their affliction he was
afflicted, and the angel of his
presence saved them: in his love
and in his pity he redeemed them;
and he bare them, and carried
them all the days of old.   Judg. 10:16

10 But they ᴿrebelled, and vexed
his holy Spirit: therefore he was
turned to be their enemy, *and* he
fought against them.   Ex. 15:24

11 Then he ᴿremembered the
days of old, Moses, *and* his people, *saying*, Where *is* he that
brought them up out of the sea
with the shepherd of his flock?
where *is* he that put his holy Spirit
within him?   Ps. 106:44, 45

12 That led *them* by the right
hand of Moses ᴿwith his glorious
arm, ᴿdividing the water before
them, to make himself an everlasting name?   Ex. 15:6 · Ex. 14:21, 22

13 ᴿThat led them through the
deep, as an horse in the wilderness, *that* they should not stumble?   Ps. 106:9

14 As a beast goeth down into
the valley, the Spirit of the LORD
caused him to rest: so didst thou
lead thy people, ᴿto make thyself a
glorious name.   2 Sam. 7:23

15 Look down from heaven, and
behold from the habitation of thy
holiness and of thy glory: where
is thy zeal and thy strength, the
sounding of thy bowels and of thy
mercies toward me? are they restrained?

16 ᴿDoubtless thou *art* our father, though Abraham ᴿbe ignorant of us, and Israel acknowledge us not: thou, O LORD, *art* our
father, our redeemer; thy name *is*
from everlasting.   Deut. 32:6 · Job 14:21

17 O LORD, why hast thou ᴿmade us to err from thy ways, *and* hardened our heart from thy fear? Return for thy servants' sake, the tribes of thine inheritance.　6:9, 10

18 ᴿThe people of thy holiness have possessed *it* but a little while: our adversaries have trodden down thy sanctuary.　Deut. 7:6

19 We are *thine:* thou never barest rule over them; they were ᵀnot called by thy name.　*never*

64 Oh that thou wouldest rend the heavens, that thou wouldest come down, that the mountains might flow down at thy ᴿpresence,　*tear open* · Ps. 18:9

2 As *when* the ᵀmelting fire burneth, the fire causeth the waters to boil, to make thy name known to thine adversaries, *that* the nations may tremble at thy presence!　*fire burns brushwood*

3 When thou didst terrible things *which* we looked not for, thou camest down, the mountains flowed down at thy presence.

4 For since the beginning of the world ᴿ*men* have not heard, nor perceived by the ear, neither hath the eye seen, O God, beside thee, *what* he hath prepared for him that waiteth for him.　Ps. 31:19

5 Thou meetest him that rejoiceth and worketh righteousness, *those that* remember thee in thy ways: behold, thou art ᵀwroth; for we have sinned: ᴿin those is continuance, and we shall be saved.　*angry* · Mal. 3:6

6 But we are all as an unclean *thing,* and all our righteousnesses *are* as filthy rags; and we all do fade as a leaf; and our iniquities, like the wind, have taken us away.

7 And *there is* none that calleth upon thy name, that stirreth up himself to take hold of thee: for thou hast hid thy face from us, and hast ᵀconsumed us, because of our iniquities.　Lit. *caused us to melt*

8 But now, O LORD, thou *art* our father; we *are* the clay, and thou our ᴿpotter; and we all *are* the work of thy hand.　29:16; 45:9

9 Be not ᵀwroth very sore, O LORD, neither remember iniquity for ever: behold, see, we beseech thee, we *are* all thy people.　*furious*

10 Thy holy cities are a wilderness, Zion is a wilderness, Jerusalem a desolation.

11 Our holy and our beautiful ᵀhouse, where our fathers praised thee, is burned up with fire: and all ᴿour pleasant things are laid waste.　*temple* · Ezek. 24:21

12 ᴿWilt thou refrain thyself for these *things,* O LORD? ᴿwilt thou hold thy peace, and afflict us very ᵀsore?　42:14 · Ps. 83:1 · *severely*

65 I ᴿam sought of *them that* asked not *for me;* I am found of *them that* sought me not: I said, Behold me, behold me, unto a nation *that* ᴿwas not called by my name.　Rom. 9:24; 10:20 · 63:19

2 ᴿI have spread out my hands all the day unto a ᴿrebellious people, which ᴿwalketh in a way *that was* not good, after their own thoughts;　Rom. 10:21 · 1:2, 23 · 42:24

3 A people ᴿthat provoketh me to anger continually to my face; ᴿthat sacrificeth in gardens, and burneth incense upon altars of brick;　Deut. 32:21 · 1:29

4 ᴿWhich remain among the graves, and lodge in the monuments, ᴿwhich eat swine's flesh, and broth of abominable *things is in* their vessels;　Deut. 18:11 · Lev. 11:7

5 ᴿWhich say, Stand by thyself, come not near to me; for I am holier than thou. These *are* a smoke in my nose, a fire that burneth all the day.　Matt. 9:11

6 Behold, *it is* written before me: ᴿI will not keep silence, but will recompense, even recompense into their bosom,　Ps. 50:3

7 Your iniquities, and ᴿthe iniquities of your fathers together, saith the LORD, ᴿwhich have burned incense upon the mountains, ᴿand blasphemed me upon the hills: therefore will I measure their former work into their bosom.　Ex. 20:5 · Ezek. 18:6 · 57:7

8 Thus saith the LORD, As the new wine is found in the cluster, and *one* saith, Destroy it not; for

Ra blessing *is* in it: so will I do for my servants' sakes, that I may not destroy them Rall.   Joel 2:14 · 1:9

9 And I will bring forth a seed out of Jacob, and out of Judah an inheritor of my mountains: and mine elect shall inherit it, and my servants shall dwell there.

10 And RShar'-on shall be a fold of flocks, and Rthe valley of A'-chor a place for the herds to lie down in, for my people that have Rsought me.   33:9 · Hos. 2:15 · 55:6

11 But ye *are* they that forsake the LORD, that forget my holy mountain, that prepare a table for that troop, and that furnish the drink offering unto that number.

12 Therefore will I number you to the sword, and ye shall all bow down to the slaughter: Rbecause when I called, ye did not answer; when I spake, ye did not hear; but did evil before mine eyes, and did choose *that* wherein I delighted not.   41:28; 50:2; 66:4; Jer. 7:13

13 Therefore thus saith the Lord GOD, Behold, my servants shall eat, but ye shall be hungry: behold, my servants shall drink, but ye shall be thirsty: behold, my servants shall rejoice, but ye shall be ashamed:

14 Behold, my servants shall sing for joy of heart, but ye shall cry for sorrow of heart, and shall howl for vexation of spirit.

15 And ye shall leave your name Rfor a curse unto my chosen: for the Lord GOD shall slay thee, and Rcall his servants by another name: Jer. 29:22; Zech. 8:13 · [Acts 11:26]

16 RThat he who blesseth himself in the earth shall bless himself in the God of truth; and Rhe that sweareth in the earth shall swear by the God of truth; because the former troubles are forgotten, and because they are hid from mine eyes.   Ps. 72:17 · Zeph. 1:5

17 For, behold, I create Rnew heavens and a new earth: and the former shall not be remembered, nor come into mind.   51:16; Rev. 21:1

18 But be ye glad and rejoice for ever *in that* which I create: for,

behold, I create Jerusalem a rejoicing, and her people a joy.

19 And RI will rejoice in Jerusalem, and joy in my people: and the Rvoice of weeping shall be no more heard in her, nor the voice of crying. 62:4, 5 · 35:10; 51:11; Rev. 7:17; 21:4

20 There shall be no more thence an infant of days, nor an old man that hath not filled his days: for the child shall die an hundred years old; Rbut the sinner *being* an hundred years old shall be accursed.   3:11; 22:14; Eccl. 8:12, 13

21 RAnd they shall build houses, and inhabit *them*; and they shall plant vineyards, and eat the fruit of them.   Ezek. 28:26; 45:4; Hos. 11:11

22 They shall not build, and another inhabit; they shall not plant, and Ranother eat: for Ras the days of a tree *are* the days of my people, and Rmine elect shall long enjoy the work of their hands.   62:8, 9 · Ps. 92:12 · vv. 9, 15

23 They shall not labour in vain, Rnor bring forth for trouble; for Rthey *are* the seed of the blessed of the LORD, and their offspring with them.   Hos. 9:12 · 61:9; [Acts 2:39]

24 And it shall come to pass, that Rbefore they call, I will answer; and while they are yet speaking, I will Rhear.   58:9 · 30:19

25 The Rwolf and the lamb shall feed together, and the lion shall eat straw like the Tbullock: Rand dust *shall be* the serpent's meat. They shall not hurt nor destroy in all my holy mountain, saith the LORD.   11:6–9 · *ox* · Gen. 3:14; Mic. 7:17

66 Thus saith the LORD, The heaven is my throne, and the earth *is* my footstool: where *is* the house that ye build unto me? and where *is* the place of my rest?

2 For all those *things* hath mine hand made, and all those *things* Thave been, saith the LORD: Rbut to this *man* will I look, R*even* to *him that is* poor and of a contrite spirit, and trembleth at my word.   *exist* · Ps. 34:18 · Ps. 34:18; 51:17

3 RHe that killeth an ox *is as if* he slew a man; he that sacrificeth

a lamb, *as if* he ^Rcut off a dog's neck; he that offereth an oblation, *as if he offered* swine's blood; he that burneth incense, *as if* he blessed an idol. Yea, they have chosen their own ways, and their soul delighteth in their abominations.   [58:1–7; Mic. 6:7, 8] · Deut. 23:18

4 I also will choose their delusions, and will bring their fears upon them; ^Rbecause when I called, none did answer; when I spake, they did not hear: but they did evil before mine eyes, and chose *that* in which I delighted not.   65:12; Prov. 1:24; Jer. 7:13

5 Hear the word of the LORD, ye that tremble at his word; Your brethren that ^Rhated you, that cast you out for my name's sake, said, ^RLet the LORD be glorified: but he shall appear to your joy, and they shall be ashamed.   60:15 · 5:19

6 A ^Tvoice of noise from the city, a voice from the temple, a voice of the LORD that rendereth recompence to his enemies.   *sound*

7 Before she travailed, she ^Tbrought forth; before her pain came, she was delivered of a man child.   *gave birth*

8 Who hath heard such a thing? who hath seen such things? Shall the earth be made to ^Tbring forth in one day? *or* shall a nation be born at once? for as soon as Zion travailed, she brought forth her children.   *give birth*

9 Shall I bring to the ^Tbirth, and not cause ^Tto bring forth? saith the LORD: shall I cause to bring forth, and shut *the womb*? saith thy God.   *time of birth · delivery*

10 Rejoice ye with Jerusalem, and be glad with her, all ye that love her: rejoice for joy with her, all ye that mourn for her:

11 That ye may suck, and be satisfied with the breasts of her consolations; that ye may ^Tmilk out, and be delighted with the abundance of her glory.   *drink deeply*

12 For thus saith the LORD, Behold, ^RI will extend peace to her like a river, and the glory of the Gentiles like a flowing stream:

then shall ye suck, ye shall be borne upon *her* sides, and be dandled upon *her* knees.   48:18; 60:5

13 As one whom his mother comforteth, so will I ^Rcomfort you; and ye shall be comforted in Jerusalem.   51:3; [2 Cor. 1:3, 4]

14 And when ye see *this*, your heart shall rejoice, and ^Ryour bones shall flourish like ^Tan herb: and the hand of the LORD shall be known ^Ttoward his servants, and *his* indignation ^Ttoward his enemies.   Ezek. 37:1 · *grass · to*

15 ^RFor, behold, the LORD will come with fire, and with his chariots like a whirlwind, to render his anger with fury, and his rebuke with flames of fire.   9:5; [2 Thess. 1:8]

16 For by fire and by ^Rhis sword will the LORD ^Tplead with all flesh: and the slain of the LORD shall be ^Rmany.   27:1 · *judge all* · 34:6

17 ^RThey that sanctify themselves, and purify themselves in the gardens behind one *tree* in the midst, eating swine's flesh, and the abomination, and the mouse, shall be consumed together, saith the LORD.   65:3–8

18 For I *know* their works and their ^Rthoughts: it shall come, that I will ^Rgather all nations and tongues; and they shall come, and see my glory.   59:7 · 45:22–25; Jer. 3:17

19 ^RAnd I will set a sign among them, and I will send those that escape of them unto the nations, *to* Tar'-shish, Pul, and Lud, that draw the bow, *to* Tu'-bal, and Ja'-van, *to* the isles afar off, that have not heard my fame, neither have seen my glory; ^Rand they shall declare my glory among the Gentiles.   Luke 2:34 · Mal. 1:11

20 And they shall ^Rbring all your brethren ^R*for* an offering unto the LORD out of all nations upon horses, and in chariots, and in litters, and upon mules, and upon swift beasts, to my holy mountain Jerusalem, saith the LORD, as the children of Israel bring an offering in a clean vessel into the house of the LORD.   49:22 · 18:7; [Rom. 15:16]

21 And I will also take of them

for ᴿpriests *and* for Levites, saith the LORD.   Ex. 19:6; 1 Pet. 2:9; Rev. 1:6

22 For as ᴿthe new heavens and the new earth, which I will make, shall remain before me, saith the LORD, so shall your seed and your name remain.   2 Pet. 3:13; Rev. 21:1

23 And ᴿit shall come to pass, *that* from one new moon to another, and from one sabbath

to another, ᴿshall all flesh come to worship before me, saith the LORD.   Zech. 14:16 · Zech. 14:17–21

24 And they shall go forth, and look upon the carcases of the men that have transgressed against me: for their ᴿworm shall not die, neither shall their fire be quenched; and they shall be an abhorring unto all flesh.   Mark 9:44

The Book of

JEREMIAH

THE Book of Jeremiah is the prophecy of a man divinely called in his youth from the priest-city of Anathoth. A heartbroken prophet with a heart-breaking message, Jeremiah labors far more than forty years proclaiming a message of doom to the stiff-necked people of Judah. Despised and persecuted by his countrymen, Jeremiah bathes his harsh prophecies in tears of compassion. His broken heart causes him to write a broken book, which is difficult to arrange chronologically or topically. But through his sermons and signs he faithfully declares that surrender to God's will is the only way to escape calamity.

Yirmeyahu or *Yirmeyah* literally means "Yahweh Throws," perhaps in the sense of laying a foundation. It may effectively mean "Yahweh Establishes, Appoints, or Sends." The Greek form of the Hebrew name in the Septuagint is *Hieremias,* and the Latin form is *Jeremias.*

THE words of Jer-e-mi′-ah the son of Hil-ki′-ah, of the priests that *were* ᴿin An′-a-thoth in the land of Benjamin: Josh. 21:18

2 To whom the word of the LORD came in the days of Jo-si′-ah the son of Amon king of Judah, in the thirteenth year of his reign.

3 It came also in the days of Je-hoi′-a-kim the son of Jo-si′-ah king of Judah, unto the end of the eleventh year of Zed-e-ki′-ah the son of Jo-si′-ah king of Judah, unto the carrying away of Jerusalem captive in the fifth month.

4 Then the word of the LORD came unto me, saying,

5 Before I ᴿformed thee in the belly ᴿI knew thee; and before thou camest forth out of the womb I ᴿsanctified thee, *and* I

ordained thee a prophet unto the nations.   Is. 49:1, 5 · Ex. 33:12 · Gal. 1:15

6 Then said I, ᴿAh, Lord GOD! behold, I cannot speak: for I *am* a ᵀchild.   Ex. 4:10; 6:12, 30 · *youth*

7 But the LORD said unto me, Say not, I *am* a child: for thou shalt go to all that I shall send thee, and ᴿwhatsoever I command thee thou shalt speak.   Matt. 28:20

8 ᴿBe not afraid of their faces: for ᴿI *am* with thee to deliver thee, saith the LORD.   Ezek. 2:6; 3:9 · Ex. 3:12

9 Then the LORD put forth his hand, and ᴿtouched my mouth. And the LORD said unto me, Behold, I have ᴿput my words in thy mouth.   Mark 7:33–35 · Ex. 4:11–16

10 ᴿSee, I have this day set thee over the nations and over the kingdoms, to ᴿroot out, and to pull down, and to destroy, and to

throw down, to build, and to plant. 1 Kin. 19:17 · 18:7–10; Ezek. 22:18

11 Moreover the word of the LORD came unto me, saying, Jer-e-mi′-ah, what seest thou? And I said, I see a ᵀrod of an almond tree. *branch*

12 Then said the LORD unto me, Thou hast well seen: for I will hasten my word to perform it.

13 And the word of the LORD came unto me the second time, saying, What seest thou? And I said, I see ᴿa ᵀseething pot; and the face thereof *is* toward the north. Ezek. 11:3; 24:3 · *boiling*

14 Then the LORD said unto me, Out of the ᴿnorth ᵀan evil shall break forth upon all the inhabitants of the land. 6:1 · *a calamity*

15 For, lo, I will ᴿcall all the families of the kingdoms of the north, saith the LORD; and they shall come, and they shall ᴿset every one his throne at the entering of the gates of Jerusalem, and against all the walls thereof round about, and against all the cities of Judah. 6:22; 25:9 · Is. 22:7

16 And I will utter my judgments against them touching all their wickedness, ᴿwho have forsaken me, and have burned ᴿincense unto other gods, and worshipped the works of their own ᴿhands. Deut. 28:20 · Is. 65:3, 4 · Is. 37:19

17 Thou therefore gird up thy loins, and arise, and speak unto them all that I command thee: be not dismayed at their faces, lest I confound thee before them.

18 For, behold, I have made thee this day ᴿa defenced city, and an iron pillar, and brasen walls against the whole land, against the kings of Judah, against the princes thereof, against the priests thereof, and against the people of the land. 6:27; 15:20

19 And they shall fight against thee; but they shall not prevail against thee; for I *am* with thee, saith the LORD, to deliver thee.

2 Moreover the word of the LORD came to me, saying,

2 Go and cry in the ears of Jerusalem, saying, Thus saith the LORD; I remember thee, the kindness of thy youth, the love of thine espousals, when thou wentest after me in the wilderness, in a land *that was* not sown.

3 Israel *was* holiness unto the LORD, *and* the firstfruits of his increase: all that devour him shall offend; ᵀevil shall come upon them, saith the LORD. *disaster*

4 Hear ye the word of the LORD, O house of Jacob, and all the families of the house of Israel:

5 Thus saith the LORD, ᴿWhat iniquity have your fathers found in me, that they are gone far from me, and have walked after vanity, and are become vain? Is. 5:4

6 Neither said they, Where *is* the LORD that ᴿbrought us up out of the land of Egypt, that led us through the wilderness, through a land of deserts and of pits, through a land of drought, and of the shadow of death, through a land that no man passed through, and where no man dwelt? Ex. 20:2

7 And I brought you into ᴿa plentiful country, to eat the fruit thereof and the goodness thereof; but when ye entered, ye defiled my land, and made mine heritage an abomination. Num. 13:27

8 The priests said not, Where *is* the LORD? and they that handle the ᴿlaw knew me not: the pastors also transgressed against me, ᴿand the prophets prophesied by Ba′-al, and walked after *things that* do not profit. Rom. 2:20 · 23:13

9 Wherefore ᴿI will yet plead with you, saith the LORD, and with your children's children will I plead. 2:35; Ezek. 20:35, 36; Mic. 6:2

10 For pass over the isles of Chit′-tim, and see; and send unto Ke′-dar, and consider diligently, and see if there be such a thing.

11 Hath a nation changed *their* gods, which *are* ᴿyet no gods? ᴿbut my people have changed their glory for *that which* doth not profit. Is. 37:19 · Rom. 1:23

12 Be astonished, O ye heavens,

at this, and be horribly afraid, be ye very desolate, saith the LORD.

13 For my people have committed two evils; they have forsaken me the [R]fountain of living waters, *and* hewed them out cisterns, broken cisterns, that can hold no water.　　　　Ps. 36:9; [John 4:14]

14 *Is* Israel [R]a servant? *is* he a homeborn *slave?* why is he [T]spoiled?　　　[Ex. 4:22] · *plundered*

15 [R]The young lions roared upon him, *and* yelled, and they made his land waste: his cities are burned without inhabitant.　Is. 1:7

16 Also the children of Noph and [R]Ta-hap'-a-nes have broken the crown of thy head.　　　43:7-9

17 [R]Hast thou not procured this unto thyself, in that thou hast forsaken the LORD thy God, when he led thee by the way?　　　4:18

18 And now what hast thou to do in the way of Egypt, to drink the waters of [R]Si'-hor? or what hast thou to do in the way of [R]Assyria, to drink the waters of the river?　　Josh. 13:3 · Hos. 5:13

19 Thine own wickedness shall [R]correct thee, and thy backslidings shall reprove thee: know therefore and see that *it is* an evil *thing* and bitter, that thou hast forsaken the LORD thy God, and that my fear *is* not in thee, saith the Lord GOD of hosts.　　　　4:18; Hos. 5:5

20 For of old time I have broken thy yoke, *and* burst thy bands; and thou saidst, I will not transgress; when upon every high hill and under every green tree thou wanderest, playing the harlot.

21 Yet I had [R]planted thee a noble vine, wholly a right seed: how then art thou turned into [R]the degenerate plant of a strange vine unto me?　　Is. 5:2 · Deut. 32:32; Is. 5:4

22 For though thou wash thee with nitre, and take thee much sope, *yet* thine iniquity is marked before me, saith the Lord GOD.

23 [R]How canst thou say, I am not polluted, I have not gone after Ba'-a-lim? see thy way in the valley, know what thou hast done:

thou art a swift dromedary traversing her ways;　　Prov. 30:12

24 A wild ass used to the wilderness, *that* snuffeth up the wind [T]at her pleasure; in her [T]occasion who can turn her away? all they that seek her will not weary themselves; in her month they shall find her.　　*in her desire · time of mating*

25 Withhold thy foot from being unshod, and thy throat from thirst: but thou saidst, [R]There is no hope: no; for I have loved [R]strangers,[T] and after them will I go.　　　18:12 · 3:13 · *aliens*

26 As the thief is ashamed when he is found, so is the house of Israel ashamed; they, their kings, their princes, and their priests, and their [R]prophets,　　Is. 28:7

27 Saying to a [T]stock, Thou *art* my father; and to a [R]stone, Thou hast brought me forth: for they have turned *their* back unto me, and not *their* face: but in the time of their [R]trouble they will say, Arise, and save us.　*tree* · 3:9 · Is. 26:16

28 But [R]where *are* thy gods that thou hast made thee? let them arise, if they can save thee in the time of thy trouble: for *according to* the number of thy cities are thy gods, O Judah.　Deut. 32:37; Judg. 10:14

29 Wherefore will ye plead with me? ye all have transgressed against me, saith the LORD.

30 In vain have I smitten your children; they received no correction: your own sword hath [R]devoured your prophets, like a destroying lion.　Acts 7:52; 1 Thess. 2:15

31 O generation, see ye the word of the LORD. Have I been a wilderness unto Israel? a land of darkness? wherefore say my people, We are lords; [R]we will come no more unto thee?　　Deut. 32:15

32 Can a maid forget her ornaments, *or* a bride her attire? yet my people [R]have forgotten me days without number.　Ps. 106:21

33 Why [T]trimmest thou thy way to seek love? therefore hast thou also taught the wicked ones thy ways.　　　*dost thou beautify*

34 Also in thy skirts is found the

blood of the souls of the poor innocents: I have not found it by secret search, but upon all these.

35 ^RYet thou sayest, Because I am innocent, surely his anger shall turn from me. Behold, I will plead with thee, because thou sayest, I have not sinned. Mal. 2:17

36 ^RWhy gaddest thou about so much to change thy way? ^Rthou also shalt be ashamed of Egypt, ^Ras thou wast ashamed of As-syria. 31:22 · Is. 30:3 · 2 Chr. 28:16

37 Yea, thou shalt go forth from him, and thine hands upon ^Rthine head: for the LORD hath rejected thy confidences, and thou shalt not prosper in them. 2 Sam. 13:19

3 They say, If a man put away his wife, and she go from him, and become another man's, shall he return unto her again? shall not that ^Rland be greatly polluted? but thou hast played the harlot with many lovers; yet return again to me, saith the LORD. 2:7

2 Lift up thine eyes unto ^Rthe high places, and see where thou hast not been lien with. ^RIn the ways hast thou sat for them, as the A-ra′-bi-an in the wilderness; and thou hast polluted the land with thy whoredoms and with thy wickedness. Deut. 12:2 · Prov. 23:28

3 Therefore the ^Rshowers have been withholden, and there hath been no latter rain; and thou hadst a whore's forehead, thou refusedst to be ashamed. Lev. 26:19

4 Wilt thou not from this time cry unto me, My father, thou *art* ^Rthe guide of my youth? Ps. 71:17

5 Will he reserve *his anger* for ever? will he keep *it* to the end? Behold, thou hast spoken and done evil things as thou couldest.

6 The LORD said also unto me in the days of Jo-si′-ah the king, Hast thou seen *that* which ^Rbacksliding Israel hath done? she is ^Rgone up upon every high mountain and under every green tree, and there hath played the harlot. 7:24 · 2:20

7 ^RAnd I said after she had done all these *things*, Turn thou

unto me. But she returned not. And her treacherous ^Rsister Judah saw *it.* 2 Kin. 17:13 · 3:11; Ezek. 16:47, 48

8 And I saw, when for all the causes whereby backsliding Is-rael committed adultery I had put her away, and given her a bill of divorce; ^Ryet her treacherous sis-ter Judah feared not, but went and played the harlot also. Ezek. 23:11

9 And it came to pass through the lightness of her whoredom, that she ^Rdefiled the land, and committed adultery with ^Rstones and with stocks. 2:7 · Is. 57:6

10 And yet for all this her treacherous sister Judah hath not turned unto me ^Rwith her whole heart, but ^Tfeignedly, saith the LORD. 12:2; Hos. 7:14 · *in pretense*

11 And the LORD said unto me, ^RThe backsliding Israel hath justi-fied herself more than treacher-ous Judah. Ezek. 16:51, 52

12 Go and proclaim these words toward the north, and say, Return, thou backsliding Israel, saith the LORD; *and* I will not cause mine anger to fall upon you: for I *am* merciful, saith the LORD, *and* I will not keep *anger* for ever.

13 ^ROnly acknowledge thine in-iquity, that thou hast transgressed against the LORD thy God, and hast ^Rscattered thy ways to the strangers under every green tree, and ye have not obeyed my voice, saith the LORD. Lev. 26:40 · Ezek. 16:15

14 Turn, O backsliding children, saith the LORD; ^Rfor I am married unto you: and I will take you one of a city, and two of a family, and I will bring you to Zion: 31:32

15 And I will give you pastors according to mine heart, which shall ^Rfeed you with knowledge and understanding. Acts 20:28

16 And it shall come to pass, when ye be multiplied and ^Rin-creased in the land, in those days, saith the LORD, they shall say no more, The ark of the covenant of the LORD: ^Rneither shall it come to mind: neither shall they remem-ber it; neither shall they visit *it*;

THE DIVIDED KINGDOM

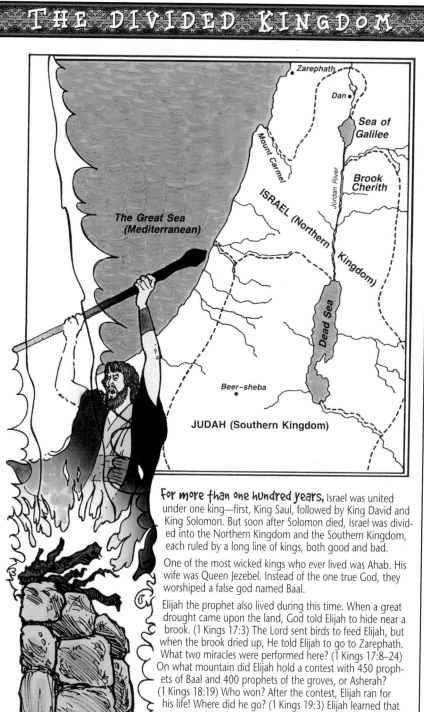

Zarephath

Dan

Sea of Galilee

Mount Carmel

Jordan River

Brook Cherith

The Great Sea (Mediterranean)

ISRAEL (Northern Kingdom)

Dead Sea

Beer-sheba

JUDAH (Southern Kingdom)

For more than one hundred years, Israel was united under one king—first, King Saul, followed by King David and King Solomon. But soon after Solomon died, Israel was divided into the Northern Kingdom and the Southern Kingdom, each ruled by a long line of kings, both good and bad.

One of the most wicked kings who ever lived was Ahab. His wife was Queen Jezebel. Instead of the one true God, they worshiped a false god named Baal.

Elijah the prophet also lived during this time. When a great drought came upon the land, God told Elijah to hide near a brook. (1 Kings 17:3) The Lord sent birds to feed Elijah, but when the brook dried up, He told Elijah to go to Zarephath. What two miracles were performed here? (1 Kings 17:8–24) On what mountain did Elijah hold a contest with 450 prophets of Baal and 400 prophets of the groves, or Asherah? (1 Kings 18:19) Who won? After the contest, Elijah ran for his life! Where did he go? (1 Kings 19:3) Elijah learned that no matter how far we may go or how serious our problems, God is always with us to care for us!

THE KINGS OF THE DIVIDED KINGDOMS

When King Solomon died in 970 B.C., the Hebrew nation was divided into northern and southern kingdoms, called Israel (northern) and Judah (southern). The kingdoms were never joined again, but continued as separate kingdoms until the Assyrians took the northern kingdom of Israel into captivity in 722 B.C. The southern kingdom of Judah survived until 587 B.C. when the Babylonians conquered it and took the people into captivity.

Here is a list of the kings of the northern kingdom, Israel, and the southern kingdom, Judah.

KINGS OF JUDAH (Southern Kingdom)			KINGS OF ISRAEL (Northern Kingdom)		
NAME	LENGTH OF REIGN	REFERENCE	NAME	LENGTH OF REIGN	REFERENCE
REHOBOAM	17 years	1 Kin. 11:42—14:31	JEROBOAM I	22 years	1 Kin. 11:26—14:20
ABIJAM	3 years	1 Kin. 14:31—15:8	NADAB	2 years	1 Kin. 15:25–28
ASA	41 years	1 Kin. 15:8–24	BAASHA	24 years	1 Kin. 15:27—16:7
JEHOSPHAPHAT	25 years	1 Kin. 22:41–50	ELAH	2 years	1 Kin. 16:6–14
JEHORAM	8 years	2 Kin. 8:16–24	ZIMRI	7 days	1 Kin. 16:9–20
AHAZIAH	1 year	2 Kin. 8:24—9:29	OMRI	12 years	1 Kin. 16:15–28
ATHALIAH (queen)	6 years	2 Kin. 11:1–20	AHAB	21 years	1 Kin. 16:28—22:40
JOASH	40 years	2 Kin. 11:1—12:21	AHAZIAH	2 years	1 Kin. 22:40–2 Kin. 1:18
AMAZIAH	29 years	2 Kin. 14:1–20	JORAM	11 years	2 Kin. 3:1—9:26
AZARIAH (Uzziah)	52 years	2 Kin. 15:1–7	JEHU	28 years	2 Kin. 9:1—10:36
JOTHAM	18 years	2 Kin. 15:32–38	JEHOAHAZ	16 years	2 Kin. 13:1–9
AHAZ	19 years	2 Kin. 16:1–20	JEHOASH	16 years	2 Kin. 13:10—14:16
HEZEKIAH	29 years	2 Kin. 18:1—20:21	JEROBOAM II	40 years	2 Kin. 14:23–29
MANASSEH	55 years	2 Kin. 21:1–18	ZACHARIAH	6 months	2 Kin. 14:29—15:12
AMON	2 years	2 Kin. 21:19–26	SHALLUM	1 month	2 Kin. 15:10–15
JOSIAH	31 years	2 Kin. 22:1—23:30	MENAHEM	10 years	2 Kin. 15:14–22
JEHOAHAZ	3 months	2 Kin. 23:31–33	PEKAHIAH	2 years	2 Kin. 15:22–26
JEHOIAKIM	11 years	2 Kin. 23:34—24:5	PEKAH	20 years	2 Kin. 15:27–31
JEHOIACHIN	3 months	2 Kin. 24:6–16	HOSHEA	9 years	2 Kin. 15:30—17:6
ZEDEKIAH	11 years	2 Kin. 24:17—25:30			

THE TIMES OF THE PROPHETS

Since the time of Moses, God used prophets to communicate His word to the Israelites. However, the prophets were used even more following the division of the kingdom into Judah and Israel (around 925 B.C.). The two prophets who spoke most often during the ninth century B.C. were Elijah and Elisha. Then in the eighth century B.C., Isaiah is the first in a series of prophets in the Old Testament. They are referred to as the Major and Minor Prophets (see the Bible Bookshelf on page 28 for the complete list of the books of prophecy).

The time line below shows the approximate dates of these prophets.

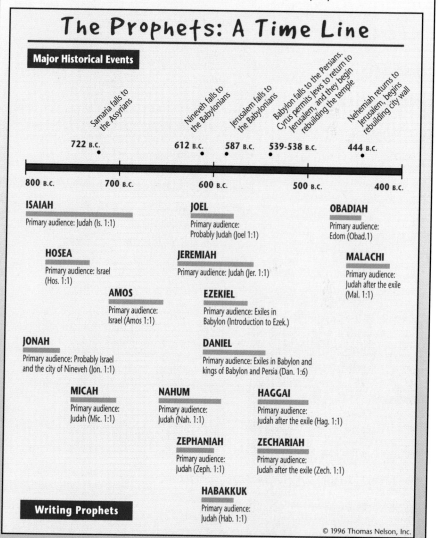

The Prophets: A Time Line

Major Historical Events

Samaria falls to the Assyrians — 722 B.C.

Nineveh falls to the Babylonians — 612 B.C.

Jerusalem falls to the Babylonians — 587 B.C.

Babylon falls to the Persians; Cyrus permits Jews to return to Jerusalem, and they begin rebuilding the temple — 539-538 B.C.

Nehemiah returns to Jerusalem, begins rebuilding city wall — 444 B.C.

800 B.C.   700 B.C.   600 B.C.   500 B.C.   400 B.C.

ISAIAH
Primary audience: Judah (Is. 1:1)

JOEL
Primary audience: Probably Judah (Joel 1:1)

OBADIAH
Primary audience: Edom (Obad.1)

HOSEA
Primary audience: Israel (Hos. 1:1)

JEREMIAH
Primary audience: Judah (Jer. 1:1)

MALACHI
Primary audience: Judah after the exile (Mal. 1:1)

AMOS
Primary audience: Israel (Amos 1:1)

EZEKIEL
Primary audience: Exiles in Babylon (Introduction to Ezek.)

JONAH
Primary audience: Probably Israel and the city of Nineveh (Jon. 1:1)

DANIEL
Primary audience: Exiles in Babylon and kings of Babylon and Persia (Dan. 1:6)

MICAH
Primary audience: Judah (Mic. 1:1)

NAHUM
Primary audience: Judah (Nah. 1:1)

HAGGAI
Primary audience: Judah after the exile (Hag. 1:1)

ZEPHANIAH
Primary audience: Judah (Zeph. 1:1)

ZECHARIAH
Primary audience: Judah after the exile (Zech. 1:1)

HABAKKUK
Primary audience: Judah (Hab. 1:1)

Writing Prophets

HOW WELL DO YOU KNOW THE PROPHETS?

See if you can match the names of the prophets on the left with the descriptions of the prophets on the right. Included are some prophets who wrote books of the Bible and some prophets who did not. (The answer key is on this page).

Prophets	Answers	Description
JONAH	B	**A.** Known as "the weeping prophet."
MIRIAM	_____	**B.** Persuaded the people of the capital city of a very strong nation to repent of their sin and ask God's forgiveness.
JEREMIAH	_____	**C.** Was imprisoned by King Ahab for predicting Israel's defeat at the hands of the Syrians (his prediction came true).
EZEKIEL	_____	**D.** Told King Josiah (the boy king) that God was going to destroy Jerusalem because of the sin and disobedience of the people. But because Josiah was sad about the sin of the people, God would not destroy Jerusalem until after he (Josiah) had died.
NOADIAH	_____	
HULDAH	_____	
HOSEA	_____	**E.** There are at least 50 instances where the New Testament quotes his writings; especially of the coming Saviour.
MICAIAH	_____	**F.** Led the people of Israel to victory over the armies of a Canaanite general.
DEBORAH	_____	**G.** Led the people of Israel in music and dance to celebrate their miraculous victory over a dreaded enemy.
ISAIAH	_____	**H.** Was taken to Babylon with the captives from Jerusalem; known for his visions of God.

I. Tried to frighten Nehemiah out of rebuilding Jerusalem's wall.

J. Married a woman—at God's command—who did not obey God and who was not faithful to her husband. This man's faithfulness and love showed the people of Israel a picture of God's relationship with them.

Answers to "How Well Do You Know the Prophets?"

Jonah, B (Jon. 1:1)
Miriam, G (Ex. 15:20, 21; see Num. 12:1)
Jeremiah, A (Jer. 1:1)
Ezekiel, H (Ezek. 1:1-3)
Noadiah, I (Neh. 6:14)
Huldah, D (2 Kin. 22:1-20)
Hosea, J (Hos. 1:1)
Micaiah, C (1 Kin. 22:8)
Deborah, F (Judg. 4:4-24)
Isaiah, E (Is. 1:1)

THE BABYLONIAN EMPIRE

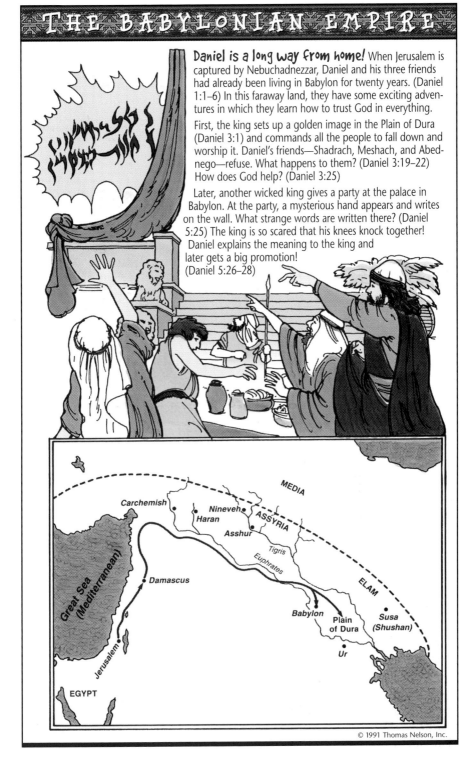

Daniel is a long way from home! When Jerusalem is captured by Nebuchadnezzar, Daniel and his three friends had already been living in Babylon for twenty years. (Daniel 1:1–6) In this faraway land, they have some exciting adventures in which they learn how to trust God in everything.

First, the king sets up a golden image in the Plain of Dura (Daniel 3:1) and commands all the people to fall down and worship it. Daniel's friends—Shadrach, Meshach, and Abednego—refuse. What happens to them? (Daniel 3:19–22) How does God help? (Daniel 3:25)

Later, another wicked king gives a party at the palace in Babylon. At the party, a mysterious hand appears and writes on the wall. What strange words are written there? (Daniel 5:25) The king is so scared that his knees knock together! Daniel explains the meaning to the king and later gets a big promotion! (Daniel 5:26–28)

© 1991 Thomas Nelson, Inc.

THE LIFE AND TIMES OF ISAIAH THE PROPHET

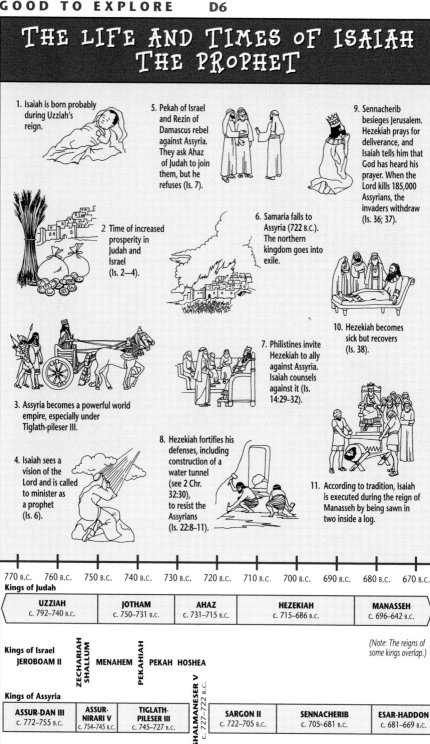

1. Isaiah is born probably during Uzziah's reign.

2. Time of increased prosperity in Judah and Israel (Is. 2—4).

3. Assyria becomes a powerful world empire, especially under Tiglath-pileser III.

4. Isaiah sees a vision of the Lord and is called to minister as a prophet (Is. 6).

5. Pekah of Israel and Rezin of Damascus rebel against Assyria. They ask Ahaz of Judah to join them, but he refuses (Is. 7).

6. Samaria falls to Assyria (722 B.C.). The northern kingdom goes into exile.

7. Philistines invite Hezekiah to ally against Assyria. Isaiah counsels against it (Is. 14:29–32).

8. Hezekiah fortifies his defenses, including construction of a water tunnel (see 2 Chr. 32:30), to resist the Assyrians (Is. 22:8–11).

9. Sennacherib besieges Jerusalem. Hezekiah prays for deliverance, and Isaiah tells him that God has heard his prayer. When the Lord kills 185,000 Assyrians, the invaders withdraw (Is. 36; 37).

10. Hezekiah becomes sick but recovers (Is. 38).

11. According to tradition, Isaiah is executed during the reign of Manasseh by being sawn in two inside a log.

770 B.C. 760 B.C. 750 B.C. 740 B.C. 730 B.C. 720 B.C. 710 B.C. 700 B.C. 690 B.C. 680 B.C. 670 B.C.

Kings of Judah

UZZIAH c. 792–740 B.C.	JOTHAM c. 750–731 B.C.	AHAZ c. 731–715 B.C.	HEZEKIAH c. 715–686 B.C.	MANASSEH c. 696–642 B.C.

Kings of Israel

JEROBOAM II   ZECHARIAH SHALLUM   MENAHEM   PEKAHIAH   PEKAH   HOSHEA

(Note: The reigns of some kings overlap.)

Kings of Assyria

SHALMANESER V c. 727–722 B.C.

ASSUR-DAN III c. 772–755 B.C.	ASSUR-NIRARI V c. 754–745 B.C.	TIGLATH-PILESER III c. 745–727 B.C.	SARGON II c. 722–705 B.C.	SENNACHERIB c. 705–681 B.C.	ESAR-HADDON c. 681–669 B.C.

© 1996 Thomas Nelson, Inc.

THE GEOGRAPHY OF JONAH

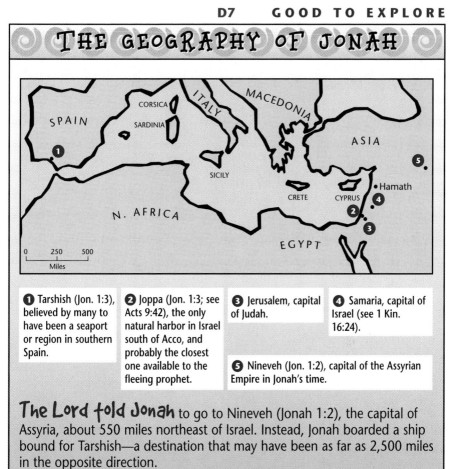

1 Tarshish (Jon. 1:3), believed by many to have been a seaport or region in southern Spain.

2 Joppa (Jon. 1:3; see Acts 9:42), the only natural harbor in Israel south of Acco, and probably the closest one available to the fleeing prophet.

3 Jerusalem, capital of Judah.

4 Samaria, capital of Israel (see 1 Kin. 16:24).

5 Nineveh (Jon. 1:2), capital of the Assyrian Empire in Jonah's time.

The Lord told Jonah to go to Nineveh (Jonah 1:2), the capital of Assyria, about 550 miles northeast of Israel. Instead, Jonah boarded a ship bound for Tarshish—a destination that may have been as far as 2,500 miles in the opposite direction.

JEWISH PEOPLE SCATTERED AMONG THE GENTILES

1 Captives from the northern kingdom were resettled by the Assyrians in the Habor River region, in the district of Nineveh, and in Media. They eventually blended into these communities. Meanwhile, the land of Israel was settled by people from other countries and religions (2 Kin. 17:24).

2 Exiles from Judah were relocated by the Babylonians to villages along the Chebar River between Babylon and Nippur. The majority remained in Babylon, establishing a Jewish community that continued into the Middle Ages.

3 Under the Seleucid Empire (third century B.C.), Jewish settlements were established throughout Mesopotamia and Asia Minor, many of which were represented at Pentecost (Acts 2:9–11). One writer of the day listed 71 cities with sizable Jewish populations. However, Jews were not always welcome among the Gentile people (16:20; 19:34). In the capital of Seleucia, 50,000 were killed in a first-century A.D. massacre.

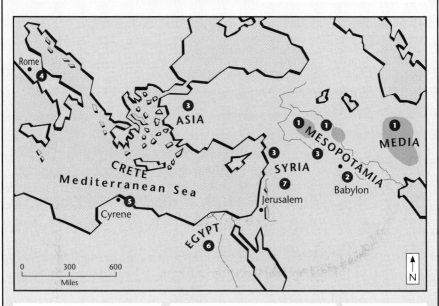

4 Substantial numbers of Jews had moved to Italy by the second century B.C. A proclamation in 139 B.C. ordered their removal from Rome, but it was ultimately unsuccessful, as were similar decrees in later years (compare Acts 18:2; 28:17).

5 Cyrene reportedly had 100,000 Jews in the first century A.D.

6 Many survivors of the Jerusalem siege (587 B.C.) fled to Egypt, settling along the Nile River in colonies that remained for centuries. Later they were joined by other immigrants from Palestine. Some of the more noteworthy settlements were at Yeb (Elephantine), Thebes, Noph (Memphis), Tahpanhes, Alexandria, and Migdol. By the first century A.D., more than one million Jews are reported to have been living in Egypt.

7 Large Jewish colonies had been established in Syria by the first century A.D.

© 1996 Thomas Nelson, Inc.

neither shall *that* be done any more. Is. 49:19 · Is. 65:17

17 At that time they shall call Jerusalem the throne of the LORD; and all the nations shall be gathered unto it, to the name of the LORD, to Jerusalem: neither shall they walk any more after the imagination of their evil heart.

18 In those days ᴿthe house of Judah shall walk with the house of Israel, and they shall come together out of the land of ᴿthe north to ᴿthe land that I have given for an inheritance unto your fathers. Is. 11:13 · 31:8 · Amos 9:15

19 But I said, How shall I put thee among the children, and give thee ᴿa pleasant land, a goodly heritage of the hosts of nations? and I said, Thou shalt call me, ᴿMy father; and shalt not turn away from me. Ps. 106:24 · Is. 63:16

20 Surely *as* a wife treacherously departeth from her ᵀhusband, so ᴿhave ye dealt treacherously with me, O house of Israel, saith the LORD. Lit. *companion* · Is. 48:8

21 A voice was heard upon ᴿthe ᵀhigh places, weeping *and* supplications of the children of Israel: for they have perverted their way, *and* they have forgotten the LORD their God. Is. 15:2 · *bare heights*

22 Return, ye backsliding children, *and* I will ᴿheal your backslidings. Behold, we come unto thee; for thou *art* the LORD our God. 30:17; 33:6; Hos. 6:1; 14:4

23 ᴿTruly in vain *is salvation hoped for* from the hills, *and from* the multitude of mountains: ᴿtruly in the LORD our God *is* the salvation of Israel. Ps. 121:1, 2 · Jon. 2:9

24 ᴿFor shame hath devoured the labour of our fathers from our youth; their flocks and their herds, their sons and their daughters. 11:13; 14:20; Hos. 9:10

25 We lie down in our shame, and our confusion covereth us: ᴿfor we have sinned against the LORD our God, we and our fathers, from our youth even unto this day, and have not obeyed the voice of the LORD our God. Ezra 9:6, 7

4 If thou wilt return, O Israel, saith the LORD, return unto me: and if thou wilt put away thine abominations out of my sight, then shalt thou not remove.

2 ᴿAnd thou shalt swear, The LORD liveth, ᴿin truth, in judgment, and in righteousness; ᴿand the nations shall bless themselves in him, and in him shall they glory. Is. 45:23 · Zech. 8:8 · 3:17

3 For thus saith the LORD to the men of Judah and Jerusalem, Break up your fallow ground, and ᴿsow not among thorns. Matt. 13:7

4 ᴿCircumcise yourselves to the LORD, and take away the foreskins of your heart, ye men of Judah and inhabitants of Jerusalem: lest my fury come forth like fire, and burn that none can quench *it*, because of the evil of your doings. Deut. 10:16; 30:6

5 Declare ye in Judah, and publish in Jerusalem; and say, ᴿBlow ye the trumpet in the land: cry, gather together, and say, Assemble yourselves, and let us go into the defenced cities. Hos. 8:1

6 Set up the standard toward Zion: retire, stay not: for I will bring ᵀevil from the ᴿnorth, and a great destruction. *disaster* · 50:17

7 ᴿThe lion is come up from his thicket, and ᴿthe destroyer of the Gentiles is on his way; he is gone forth from his place to make thy land desolate; *and* thy cities shall be laid waste, without an inhabitant. 2 Kin. 24:1; Dan. 7:4 · Ezek. 26:7–10

8 For this ᴿgird you with sackcloth, lament and howl: for the fierce anger of the LORD is not turned back from us. Is. 22:12

9 And it shall come to pass at that day, saith the LORD, *that* the heart of the king shall perish, and the heart of the princes; and the priests shall be astonished, and the prophets shall wonder.

10 Then said I, Ah, Lord GOD! surely thou hast greatly deceived this people and Jerusalem, saying, Ye shall have peace; whereas the sword reacheth unto the soul.

11 At that time shall it be said to

this people and to Jerusalem, ᴿA dry wind of the high places in the wilderness toward the daughter of my people, not to fan, nor to cleanse,   51:1; Ezek. 17:10; Hos. 13:15

12 *Even* a full wind from those *places* shall come unto me: now also ᴿwill I ᵀgive sentence against them.   1:16 · *speak judgment*

13 Behold, he shall come up as clouds, and ᴿhis chariots *shall be* as a whirlwind: ᴿhis horses are swifter than eagles. Woe unto us! for we are spoiled.   Is. 5:28 · Hos. 8:1

14 O Jerusalem, ᴿwash thine heart from wickedness, that thou mayest be saved. How long shall thy vain thoughts lodge within thee?   Prov. 1:22; Is. 1:16; James 4:8

15 For a voice declareth ᴿfrom Dan, and publisheth affliction from mount E′-phra-im.   8:16; 50:17

16 Make ye mention to the nations; behold, ᵀpublish against Jerusalem, *that* watchers come from a ᴿfar country, and give out their voice against the cities of Judah.   *proclaim* · 5:15; Is. 39:3

17 As keepers of a field, are they against her round about; because she hath been rebellious against me, saith the LORD.

18 ᴿThy way and thy doings have procured these *things* unto thee: this *is* thy wickedness, because it is bitter, because it reacheth unto thine heart.   Ps. 107:17

19 My ᴿbowels, my bowels! I am pained at my very heart; my heart maketh a noise in me; I cannot hold my peace, because thou hast heard, O my soul, the sound of the trumpet, the alarm of war.   Is. 15:5

20 ᴿDestruction upon destruction is cried; for the whole land is ᵀspoiled: suddenly are my tents ᵀspoiled, *and* my curtains in a moment.   Ps. 42:7; Ezek. 7:26 · *plundered*

21 How long shall I see the ᵀstandard, *and* hear the sound of the trumpet?   *banner*

22 For my people *is* foolish, they have not known me; they *are* ᵀsottish children, and they have none understanding: they *are*

wise to do evil, but to do good they have no knowledge.   *stupid*

23 ᴿI beheld the earth, and, lo, *it was* ᴿwithout form, and void; and the heavens, and they *had* no light.   Is. 24:19 · Gen. 1:2

24 ᴿI beheld the mountains, and, lo, they trembled, and all the hills moved lightly.   Is. 5:25; Ezek. 38:20

25 I beheld, and, lo, *there was* no man, and ᴿall the birds of the heavens were fled.   12:4; Zeph. 1:3

26 I beheld, and, lo, the fruitful place *was* a ᴿwilderness, and all the cities thereof were broken down at the presence of the LORD, *and* by his fierce anger.   9:10

27 For thus hath the LORD said, The whole land shall be desolate; ᴿyet will I not make a full end.   5:10

28 For this ᴿshall the earth mourn, and ᴿthe heavens above be black: because I have spoken *it*, I have purposed *it*, and will not ᵀrepent, neither will I turn back from it.   12:4, 11; 14:2 · Is. 5:30 · *relent*

29 The whole city shall flee for the noise of the horsemen and bowmen; they shall go into thickets, and climb up upon the rocks: every city *shall be* forsaken, and not a man dwell therein.

30 And *when* thou *art* spoiled, what wilt thou do? Though thou clothest thyself with crimson, though thou deckest thee with ornaments of gold, though thou rentest thy face with painting, in vain shalt thou make thyself fair; ᴿ*thy* lovers will despise thee, they will seek thy life.   Ezek. 23:9, 10, 22

31 For I have heard a voice as of a woman in ᵀtravail, *and* the anguish as of her that bringeth forth her first child, the voice of the daughter of Zion, *that* bewaileth herself, *that* ᴿspreadeth her hands, *saying*, Woe *is* me now! for my soul is wearied because of murderers.   *childbirth* · Is. 1:15; Lam. 1:17

5 Run ye to and fro through the streets of Jerusalem, and see now, and know, and seek in the broad places thereof, if ye can find a man, if there be *any* that executeth judgment, that seeketh the truth; and I will pardon it.

2 And ᴿthough they say, ᴿThe Lord liveth; surely they ᴿswear falsely.　　Is. 48:1; Titus 1:16 · 4:2 · 7:9

3 O Lord, *are* not thine eyes upon the truth? thou hast stricken them, but they have not grieved; thou hast consumed them, *but* ᴿthey have refused to receive correction: they have made their faces harder than a rock; they have refused to return.　　Zeph. 3:2

4 Therefore I said, Surely these *are* poor; they are foolish: for ᴿthey know not the way of the Lord, *nor* the judgment of their God.　　8:7; Is. 27:11; Hos. 4:6

5 I will get me unto the great men, and will speak unto them; for ᴿthey have known the way of the Lord, *and* the judgment of their God: but these have altogether broken the yoke, *and* burst the bonds.　　Mic. 3:1

6 Wherefore ᴿa lion out of the forest shall slay them, ᴿ*and* a wolf of the evenings shall spoil them, ᴿa leopard shall watch over their cities: every one that goeth out thence shall be torn in pieces: because their transgressions are many, *and* their backslidings are increased.　　4:7 · Zeph. 3:3 · Hos. 13:7

7 How shall I pardon thee for this? thy children have forsaken me, and ᴿsworn by *them* ᴿ*that are* no gods: when I had fed them to the full, they then committed adultery, and assembled themselves by troops in the harlots' houses.　　Josh. 23:7; Zeph. 1:5 · Gal. 4:8

8 ᴿThey were *as* fed horses in the morning: every one neighed after his neighbour's wife.　　13:27

9 Shall I not ᵀvisit for these *things*? saith the Lord: and shall not my soul be ᴿavenged on such a nation as this?　　*punish* them · 9:9

10 Go ye up upon her walls, and destroy; but make not a ᴿfull end: take away her battlements; for they *are* not the Lord's.　　4:27

11 For ᴿthe house of Israel and the house of Judah have dealt very treacherously against me, saith the Lord.　　3:6, 7, 20

12 ᴿThey have belied the Lord, and said, *It is* not he; neither shall evil come upon us; neither shall we see sword nor famine:　　4:10

13 And the prophets shall become wind, and the word *is* not in them: thus shall it be done unto them.

14 Wherefore thus saith the Lord God of hosts, Because ye speak this word, ᴿbehold, I will make my words in thy mouth fire, and this people wood, and it shall devour them.　　23:29; Hos. 6:5; Zech. 1:6

15 Lo, I will bring a ᴿnation upon you ᴿfrom far, O house of Israel, saith the Lord: it *is* a mighty nation, it *is* an ancient nation, a nation whose language thou knowest not, neither understandest what they say.　　Is. 5:26 · Is. 39:3

16 Their quiver *is* as an open sepulchre, they *are* all mighty men.

17 And they shall eat up thine ᴿharvest, and thy bread, *which* thy sons and thy daughters should eat: they shall eat up thy flocks and thine herds: they shall eat up thy vines and thy fig trees: they shall impoverish thy fenced cities, wherein thou trustedst, with the sword.　　Lev. 26:16; Deut. 28:31, 33

18 Nevertheless in those days, saith the Lord, I ᴿwill not make a full end with you.　　30:11; Amos 9:8

19 And it shall come to pass, when ye shall say, ᴿWherefore doeth the Lord our God all these *things* unto us? then shalt thou answer them, Like as ye have ᴿforsaken me, and served strange gods in your land, so ᴿshall ye serve strangers in a land *that is* not yours.　　13:22 · 1:16; 2:13 · 16:13

20 Declare this in the house of Jacob, and ᵀpublish it in Judah, saying,　　*proclaim*

21 Hear now this, O foolish people, and without understanding; which have eyes, and see not; which have ears, and hear not:

22 Fear ye not me? saith the Lord: will ye not tremble at my

presence, which have placed the sand *for* the bound of the sea by a perpetual decree, that it cannot pass it: and though the waves thereof toss themselves, yet can they not prevail; though they roar, yet can they not pass over it?

23 But this people hath a revolting and a rebellious heart; they are revolted and ᵀgone.   *departed*

24 Neither say they in their heart, Let us now fear the LORD our God, that giveth rain, both the former and the latter, in his season: he reserveth unto us the appointed weeks of the harvest.

25 ᴿYour iniquities have turned away these *things*, and your sins have withholden good *things* from you.   3:3

26 For among my people are found wicked *men*: they ᴿlay wait, as he that setteth snares; they set a trap, they catch men.   Hab. 1:15

27 As a cage is full of birds, so *are* their houses full of deceit: therefore they are become great, and ᵀwaxen rich.   *grown*

28 They are waxen ᴿfat, they shine: yea, they overpass the deeds of the wicked: they judge not ᴿthe cause, the cause of the fatherless, ᴿyet they prosper; and the right of the needy do they not judge.   Deut. 32:15 · Is. 1:23 · Ps. 73:12

29 ᴿShall I not ᵀvisit for these *things*? saith the LORD: shall not my soul be avenged on such a nation as this?   5:9; Mal. 3:5 · *punish*

30 A wonderful and horrible thing is committed in the land;

31 The prophets prophesy falsely, and the priests ᵀbear rule by their means; and my people ᴿlove *to have it* so: and what will ye do in the end thereof?   *rule* · Mic. 2:11

6 O ye children of Benjamin, gather yourselves to flee out of the midst of Jerusalem, and blow the trumpet in Te-ko'-a, and set up a sign of fire in Beth–hac'-ce-rem: ᴿfor evil appeareth out of the north, and great destruction.   4:6

2 I have likened the daughter of Zion to a ᵀcomely and delicate *woman.*   *lovely*

3 The ᴿshepherds with their flocks shall come unto her; they shall pitch *their* tents against her round about; they shall feed every one in his place.   2 Kin. 25:1–4

4 ᴿPrepare ye war against her; arise, and let us go up at noon. Woe unto us! for the day goeth away, for the shadows of the evening are stretched out.   51:27

5 Arise, and let us go by night, and let us destroy her palaces.

6 For thus hath the LORD of hosts said, Hew ye down trees, and ᵀcast a mount against Jerusalem: this *is* the city to be visited; she *is* wholly oppression in the midst of her.   *build a mound*

7 ᴿAs a fountain casteth out her waters, so she casteth out her wickedness: violence and spoil is heard in her; before me continually *is* grief and wounds.   Is. 57:20

8 Be thou instructed, O Jerusalem, lest ᴿmy soul depart from thee; lest I make thee desolate, a land not inhabited.   Hos. 9:12

9 Thus saith the LORD of hosts, They shall throughly glean the remnant of Israel as a vine: turn back thine hand as a grapegatherer into the ᵀbaskets.   *branches*

10 To whom shall I speak, and give warning, that they may hear? behold, their ᴿear *is* uncircumcised, and they cannot hearken: behold, ᴿthe word of the LORD is unto them a reproach; they have no delight in it.   [Acts 7:51] · 8:9; 20:8

11 Therefore I am full of the fury of the LORD; I am weary with holding in: I will pour it out upon the children abroad, and upon the assembly of young men together: for even the husband with the wife shall be taken, the aged with *him that is* full of days.

12 And ᴿtheir houses shall be turned ᵀunto others, *with their* fields and wives together: for I will stretch out my hand upon the inhabitants of the land, saith the LORD.   8:10; 38:22; Deut. 28:30 · *over to*

13 For from the least of them even unto the greatest of them every one *is* given to ᴿcovetous-

ness; and from the prophet even unto the ᴿpriest every one dealeth falsely. 22:17 · 5:31; 23:11; Mic. 3:5, 11

14 They have ᴿhealed also the hurt *of the daughter* of my people slightly, saying, Peace, peace; when *there is* no peace. 8:11–15

15 Were they ᴿashamed when they had committed abomination? nay, they were not at all ashamed, neither could they blush: therefore they shall fall among them that fall: at the time *that* I visit them they shall be cast down, saith the LORD. 3:3; 8:12

16 Thus saith the LORD, Stand ye in the ways, and see, and ask for the ᴿold paths, where *is* the good way, and walk therein, and ye shall find ᴿrest for your souls. But they said, We will not walk *therein.* Mal. 4:4; Luke 16:29 · Matt. 11:29

17 Also I set ᴿwatchmen over you, *saying,* Hearken to the sound of the trumpet. But they said, We will not hearken. Is. 21:11; 58:1

18 Therefore hear, ye nations, and know, O congregation, what *is* among them.

19 ᴿHear, O earth: behold, I will bring ᴿevil upon this people, *even* ᴿthe fruit of their thoughts, because they have not hearkened unto my words, nor to my law, but rejected it. Is. 1:2 · 19:3, 15 · Prov. 1:31

20 ᴿTo what purpose cometh there to me incense from She'-ba, and the sweet cane from a far country? your burnt offerings *are* not acceptable, nor your sacrifices sweet unto me. Ps. 40:6; 50:7–9

21 Therefore thus saith the LORD, Behold, I will lay stumblingblocks before this people, and the fathers and the sons together shall fall upon them; the neighbour and his friend shall perish.

22 Thus saith the LORD, Behold, a people cometh from the ᴿnorth country, and a great nation shall be raised from the ᵀsides of the earth. 1:15; 10:22; 50:41–43 · *farthest parts*

23 They shall lay hold on bow and spear; they *are* cruel, and have no mercy; their voice

ᴿroareth like the sea; and they ride upon horses, set in array as men for war against thee, O daughter of Zion. Is. 5:30

24 We have heard the fame thereof: our hands wax feeble: anguish hath taken hold of us, *and* pain, as of a woman in travail.

25 Go not forth into the field, nor walk by the way; for the sword of the enemy *and* fear *is* on every side.

26 O daughter of my people, gird *thee* with sackcloth, ᴿand wallow thyself in ashes: ᴿmake thee mourning, *as for* an only son, most bitter lamentation: for the spoiler shall suddenly come upon us. Mic. 1:10 · Amos 8:10; [Zech. 12:10]

27 I have set thee *for* ᵀa tower *and* ᴿa fortress among my people, that thou mayest know and ᵀtry their way. *an assayer* · 1:18 · *test*

28 ᴿThey *are* all grievous revolters, ᴿwalking with slanders: *they are* ᴿbrass and iron; they *are* all corrupters. 5:23 · 9:4 · Ezek. 22:18

29 The bellows are burned, the lead is consumed of the fire; the founder melteth in vain: for the wicked are not plucked away.

30 ᴿReprobate silver shall *men* call them, because the LORD hath rejected them. 7:29; Is. 1:22

7 The word that came to Jer-e-mi'-ah from the LORD, saying,

2 ᴿStand in the gate of ᵀthe LORD's house, and proclaim there this word, and say, Hear the word of the LORD, all *ye of* Judah, that enter in at these gates to worship the LORD. 17:19; 26:2 · The temple

3 Thus saith the LORD of hosts, the God of Israel, Amend your ways and your doings, and I will cause you to dwell in this place.

4 ᴿTrust ye not in lying words, saying, The temple of the LORD, The temple of the LORD, The temple of the LORD, *are* these. Mic. 3:11

5 For if ye throughly amend your ways and your doings; if ye throughly execute judgment between a man and his neighbour;

6 *If* ye oppress not the stranger, the fatherless, and the widow, and

shed not innocent blood in this place, [R]neither walk after other gods to your hurt: Deut. 6:14, 15

7 [R]Then will I cause you to dwell in this place, in [R]the land that I gave to your fathers, for ever and ever.   Deut. 4:40 · 3:18

8 Behold, ye trust in [R]lying words, that cannot profit.   14:13, 14

9 [R]Will ye steal, murder, and commit adultery, and swear falsely, and burn incense unto Ba'-al, and [R]walk after other gods whom ye know not;   Zeph. 1:5 · Ex. 20:3

10 [R]And come and stand before me in this house, [R]which is called by my name, and say, We are delivered to do all these abominations?   Ezek. 23:39 · 32:34; 34:15

11 Is [R]this house, which is called by my name, become a [R]den of robbers in your eyes? Behold, even I have seen *it*, saith the LORD.   Is. 56:7 · Matt. 21:13; Luke 19:46

12 But go ye now unto my place which *was* in Shi'-loh, where I set my name at the first, and see [R]what I did to it for the wickedness of my people Israel.   Ps. 78:60

13 And now, because ye have done all these works, saith the LORD, and I spake unto you, [R]rising up early and speaking, but ye heard not; and I called you, but ye answered not;   2 Chr. 36:15

14 Therefore will I do unto *this* house, which is called by my name, wherein ye trust, and unto the place which I gave to you and to your fathers, as I have done to [R]Shi'-loh.   1 Sam. 4:10, 11; Ps. 78:60

15 And I will cast you out of my sight, [R]as I have cast out all your brethren, [R]*even* the whole seed of E'-phra-im.   2 Kin. 17:23 · Ps. 78:67

16 Therefore [R]pray not thou for this people, neither lift up cry nor prayer for them, neither make intercession to me: for I will not hear thee.   Ex. 32:10; Deut. 9:14

17 Seest thou not what they do in the cities of Judah and in the streets of Jerusalem?

18 [R]The children gather wood, and the fathers kindle the fire, and the women knead *their* dough, to make cakes to the queen of heaven, and to [R]pour out drink offerings unto other gods, that they may provoke me to anger.   44:17 · 19:13

19 Do they provoke me to anger? saith the LORD: *do they* not *provoke* themselves to the confusion of their own faces?

20 Therefore thus saith the Lord GOD; Behold, mine anger and my fury shall be poured out upon this place, upon man, and upon beast, and upon the trees of the field, and upon the fruit of the ground; and it shall burn, and shall not be quenched.

21 Thus saith the LORD of hosts, the God of Israel; [R]Put your burnt offerings unto your sacrifices, and eat flesh.   Hos. 8:13; Amos 5:21, 22

22 For I spake not unto your fathers, nor commanded them in the day that I brought them out of the land of Egypt, concerning burnt offerings or sacrifices:

23 But this thing commanded I them, saying, [R]Obey my voice, and I will be your God, and ye shall be my people: and walk ye in all the ways that I have commanded you, that it may be well unto you.   Ex. 15:26; 16:32; Deut. 6:3

24 But they hearkened not, nor inclined their ear, but walked in the counsels *and* in the imagination of their evil heart, and went backward, and not forward.

25 Since the day that your fathers came forth out of the land of Egypt unto this day I have even [R]sent unto you all my servants the prophets, daily rising up early and sending *them*:   Luke 11:47–49

26 [R]Yet they hearkened not unto me, nor inclined their ear, but hardened their neck: they did worse than their fathers.   11:8

27 Therefore [R]thou shalt speak all these words unto them; but they will not hearken to thee: thou shalt also call unto them; but they will not answer thee.   Ezek. 2:7

28 But thou shalt say unto them, This *is* a nation that obeyeth not the voice of the LORD their God,

[R]nor receiveth [T]correction: [R]truth is perished, and is cut off from their mouth.   5:3 · *instruction* · 9:3

29 [R]Cut off thine hair, *O Jerusalem,* and cast *it* away, and take up a lamentation on high places; for the LORD hath rejected and forsaken the generation of his wrath.   Job 1:20; Is. 15:2; Mic. 1:16

30 For the children of Judah have done evil in my sight, saith the LORD: they have set their abominations in the house which is called by my name, to pollute it.

31 And they have built the high places of To'-phet, which *is* in the valley of the son of Hin'-nom, to [R]burn their sons and their daughters in the fire; which I commanded *them* not, neither came it into my heart.   2 Kin. 17:17; Ps. 106:38

32 Therefore, behold, [R]the days come, saith the LORD, that it shall no more be called To'-phet, nor the valley of the son of Hin'-nom, but the valley of slaughter: [R]for they shall bury in To'-phet, till there be no place.   19:6 · 2 Kin. 23:10

33 And the [R]carcases of this people shall be meat for the fowls of the heaven, and for the beasts of the earth; and none shall [T]fray *them* away.   9:22; Ezek. 6:5 · *frighten*

34 Then will I cause to [R]cease from the cities of Judah, and from the streets of Jerusalem, the voice of mirth, and the voice of gladness, the voice of the bridegroom, and the voice of the bride: for the land shall be desolate.   Rev. 18:23

8 At that time, saith the LORD, they shall bring out the bones of the kings of Judah, and the bones of his princes, and the bones of the priests, and the bones of the prophets, and the bones of the inhabitants of Jerusalem, out of their graves:

2 And they shall spread them before the sun, and the moon, and all the host of heaven, whom they have loved, and whom they have served, and after whom they have walked, and whom they have sought, and [R]whom they have worshipped: they shall not be

gathered, nor be buried; they shall be for dung upon the face of the earth.   2 Kin. 23:5; Zeph. 1:5; Acts 7:42

3 And death shall be chosen rather than life by all the residue of them that remain of this evil family, which remain in all the places whither I have driven them, saith the LORD of hosts.

4 Moreover thou shalt say unto them, Thus saith the LORD; Shall they fall, and not arise? shall he turn away, and not return?

5 Why *then* is this people of Jerusalem slidden back by a perpetual backsliding? they hold fast deceit, [R]they refuse to return.   5:3

6 I hearkened and heard, *but* they spake not aright: no man repented him of his wickedness, saying, What have I done? every one turned to his course, as the horse rusheth into the battle.

7 Yea, the stork in the heaven knoweth her appointed times; and the turtle and the crane and the swallow observe the time of their coming; but [R]my people know not the judgment of the LORD.   5:4; 9:3

8 How do ye say, We *are* wise, and the law of the LORD *is* with us? Lo, certainly in vain made he *it;* the pen of the scribes *is* in vain.

9 [R]The wise *men* are ashamed, they are dismayed and taken: lo, they have rejected the word of the LORD; and [R]what wisdom *is* in them?   Is. 19:11; [1 Cor. 1:27] · Is. 44:25

10 Therefore [R]will I give their wives unto others, *and* their fields to them that shall inherit *them:* for every one from the least even unto the greatest is given to [R]covetousness, from the prophet even unto the priest every one dealeth falsely.   Zeph. 1:13 · Is. 56:11

11 For they have healed the hurt of the daughter of my people slightly, saying, [R]Peace, peace; when *there is* no peace.   Ezek. 13:10

12 Were they [R]ashamed when they had committed abomination? nay, they were not at all ashamed, neither could they blush: therefore shall they fall among them that fall: in the time of their visitation they shall be cast down, saith the LORD. Ps. 52:1

13 I will surely consume them, saith the LORD: *there shall be* no grapes on the vine, nor figs on the fig tree, and the leaf shall fade; and *the things that* I have given them shall pass away from them.

14 Why do we sit still? assemble yourselves, and let us enter into the defenced cities, and let us be silent there: for the LORD our God hath put us to silence, and given us water of gall to drink, because we have sinned against the LORD.

15 We ᴿlooked for peace, but no good *came; and* for a time of health, and behold trouble! 14:19

16 The snorting of his horses was heard from Dan: the whole land trembled at the sound of the neighing of his strong ones; for they are come, and have devoured the land, and all that is in it; the city, and those that dwell therein.

17 For, behold, I will send serpents, cockatrices, among you, which *will* not *be* charmed, and they shall bite you, saith the LORD.

18 *When* I would comfort myself against sorrow, my heart *is* faint in me.

19 Behold the voice of the cry of the daughter of my people because of them that dwell in ᴿa far country: *Is* not the LORD in Zion? *is* not her king in her? Why have they provoked me to anger with their graven images, *and* with strange vanities? Is. 39:3

20 The harvest is past, the summer is ended, and we are not saved.

21 ᴿFor the hurt of the daughter of my people am I hurt; I am ᴿblack;ᵀ astonishment hath taken hold on me. 9:1 · Joel 2:6 · *mourning*

22 *Is there* no balm in Gil′-e-ad; *is there* no physician there? why then is not the health of the daughter of my people recovered?

9 Oh ᴿthat my head were waters, and mine eyes a fountain of tears, that I might weep day and night for the slain of the daughter of my people! Is. 22:4

2 Oh that I had in the wilderness a lodging place of wayfaring men; that I might leave my people, and go from them! for ᴿthey *be* all adulterers, an assembly of treacherous men. 5:7, 8; 23:10; Hos. 4:2

3 And ᴿthey bend their tongues *like* their bow *for* lies: but they are not valiant for the truth upon the earth; for they proceed from evil to evil, and they know not me, saith the LORD. Ps. 64:3; Is. 59:4

4 Take ye heed every one of his neighbour, and trust ye not in any brother: for every brother will utterly supplant, and every neighbour will walk with slanders.

5 And they will ᴿdeceive every one his neighbour, and will not speak the truth: they have taught their tongue to speak lies, *and* weary themselves to commit iniquity. Ps. 36:3, 4; Is. 59:4

6 Thine habitation *is* in the midst of deceit; through deceit they refuse to know me, saith the LORD.

7 Therefore thus saith the LORD of hosts, Behold, I will melt them, and try them; for how shall I do for the daughter of my people?

8 Their tongue *is as* an arrow shot out; it speaketh ᴿdeceit: *one* speaketh ᴿpeaceably to his neighbour with his mouth, but in heart he layeth his wait. Ps. 12:2 · Ps. 55:21

9 ᴿShall I not ᵀvisit them for these *things*? saith the LORD: shall not my soul be avenged on such a nation as this? Is. 1:24 · *punish*

10 For the mountains will I take up a weeping and wailing, and for the habitations of the wilderness a lamentation, because they are burned up, so that none can pass through *them*; neither can *men* hear the voice of the cattle; both the fowl of the heavens and the beast are fled; they are gone.

11 And I will make Jerusalem heaps, *and* a den of dragons; and I will make the cities of Judah desolate, without an inhabitant.

12 ᴿWho *is* the wise man, that may understand this? and *who is* he to whom the mouth of the

LORD hath spoken, that he may declare it, for what the land perisheth *and* is burned up like a wilderness, that none passeth through?   Ps. 107:43; Is. 42:23; Hos. 14:9

13 And the LORD saith, Because they have forsaken my law which I set before them, and have ^Rnot obeyed my voice, neither walked therein;   3:25; 7:24

14 But have walked after the imagination of their own heart, and after Ba'-a-lim, ^Rwhich their fathers taught them: 1 Pet. 1:18

15 Therefore thus saith the LORD of hosts, the God of Israel; Behold, I will feed them, *even* this people, with wormwood, and give them water of gall to drink.

16 I will ^Rscatter them also among the heathen, whom neither they nor their fathers have known: ^Rand I will send a sword after them, till I have consumed them.   Lev. 26:33; Deut. 28:64 · Lev. 26:33

17 Thus saith the LORD of hosts, Consider ye, and call for the mourning women, that they may come; and send for cunning *women*, that they may come:

18 And let them make haste, and take up a wailing for us, that ^Rour eyes may run down with tears, and our eyelids gush out with waters.   v. 1; 14:17; Is. 22:4

19 For a voice of wailing is heard out of Zion, How are we spoiled! we are greatly confounded, because we have forsaken the land, because ^Rour dwellings have cast *us* out.   Lev. 18:28

20 Yet hear the word of the LORD, O ye women, and let your ear receive the word of his mouth, and teach your daughters wailing, and every one her neighbour lamentation.

21 For death is come up into our windows, *and* is entered into our palaces, to cut off ^Rthe children from without, *and* the young men from the streets.   2 Chr. 36:17

22 Speak, Thus saith the LORD, Even the carcases of men shall fall ^Ras dung upon the open field, and as the handful after the har-

vestman, and none shall gather *them*.   Ps. 83:10; Is. 5:25

23 Thus saith the LORD, ^RLet not the wise *man* glory in his wisdom, neither let the mighty *man* glory in his might, let not the rich *man* glory in his riches: Ezek. 28:3–7

24 But let him that glorieth glory in this, that he understandeth and knoweth me, that I *am* the LORD which exercise lovingkindness, judgment, and righteousness, in the earth: for in these *things* I delight, saith the LORD.

25 Behold, the days come, saith the LORD, that ^RI will punish all *them which are* circumcised with the uncircumcised; [4:4; Rom. 2:28, 29]

26 Egypt, and Judah, and E'-dom, and the children of Ammon, and Moab, and all *that are* in the ^Rutmost corners, that dwell in the wilderness: for all *these* nations *are* uncircumcised, and all the house of Israel *are* ^Runcircumcised in the heart.   25:23 · [Rom. 2:28]

10 Hear ye the word which the LORD speaketh unto you, O house of Israel:

2 Thus saith the LORD, ^RLearn not the way of the heathen, and be not dismayed at the signs of heaven; for the heathen are dismayed at them.   [Lev. 18:3; 20:23; Deut. 12:30]

3 For the customs of the people *are* ^Tvain: for ^Rone cutteth a tree out of the forest, the work of the hands of the workman, with the ax.   *futile* · Is. 40:19; 45:20

4 They ^Tdeck it with silver and with gold; they ^Rfasten it with nails and with hammers, that it move not.   *decorate* · Is. 41:7

5 They *are* upright as the palm tree, ^Rbut speak not: they must needs be borne, because they cannot go. Be not afraid of them; for they cannot do evil, neither also *is* it in them to do good.   1 Cor. 12:2

6 Forasmuch as *there is* none ^Rlike unto thee, O LORD; thou *art* great, and thy name *is* great in might.   Ex. 15:11; Deut. 33:26; Ps. 86:8, 10

7 ^RWho would not fear thee, O King of nations? for to thee doth it appertain: forasmuch as among

all the wise *men* of the nations, and in all their kingdoms, *there is* none like unto thee.   5:22; Rev. 15:4

8 But they are altogether ^Rbrutish and foolish: the stock *is* a doctrine of vanities.   Ps. 115:8

9 Silver spread into plates is brought from Tar'-shish, and ^Rgold from U'-phaz, the work of the workman, and of the hands of the founder: blue and purple *is* their clothing: they *are* all the work of cunning *men.*   Dan. 10:5

10 But the LORD *is* the true God, he *is* ^Rthe living God, and an ^Reverlasting king: at his wrath the earth shall tremble, and the nations shall not be able to abide his indignation.   1 Tim. 6:17 · Ps. 10:16

11 Thus shall ye say unto them, ^RThe gods that have not made the heavens and the earth, *even* they shall perish from the earth, and from under these heavens.   Ps. 96:5

12 He hath made the earth by his power, he hath established the world by his wisdom, and ^Rhath stretched out the heavens by his discretion.   Job 9:8; Ps. 104:2; Is. 40:22

13 ^RWhen he uttereth his voice, *there is* a multitude of waters in the heavens, and he causeth the vapours to ascend from the ends of the earth; he maketh lightnings with rain, and bringeth forth the wind out of his treasures.   Job 38:34

14 Every man is brutish in *his* knowledge: every founder is confounded by the graven image: for his molten image *is* falsehood, and *there is* no breath in them.

15 They *are* ^Tvanity, *and* the work of errors: in the time of their visitation they shall perish.   *futile*

16 ^RThe portion of Jacob *is* not like them: for he *is* the ^Tformer of all *things;* and Israel *is* the rod of his inheritance: The LORD of hosts *is* his name.   Ps. 16:5; Lam. 3:24 · *maker*

17 ^RGather up thy wares out of the land, O inhabitant ^Tof the fortress.   6:1 · *under siege*

18 For thus saith the LORD, Behold, I will ^Rsling out the inhabitants of the land at this once, and

will distress them, ^Rthat they may find *it so.*   1 Sam. 25:29 · Ezek. 6:10

19 ^RWoe is me for my hurt! my wound is grievous: but I said, ^RTruly this *is* a grief, and ^RI must bear it.   8:21 · Ps. 77:10 · Mic. 7:9

20 ^RMy tabernacle is spoiled, and all my cords are broken: my children are gone forth of me, and they *are* not: *there is* none to stretch forth my tent any more, and to set up my curtains.   4:20

21 For the ^Tpastors are become ^Tbrutish, and have not sought the LORD: therefore they shall not prosper, and all their flocks shall be scattered.   *shepherds · dull-hearted*

22 Behold, the noise of the ^Tbruit is come, and a great commotion out of the north country, to make the cities of Judah desolate, *and* a den of ^Tdragons.   *report · jackals*

23 O LORD, I know that the ^Rway of man *is* not in himself: *it is* not in man that walketh to direct his steps.   Prov. 16:1; 20:24

24 O LORD, ^Rcorrect me, but with judgment; not in thine anger, lest thou bring me to nothing.   Ps. 6:1

25 Pour out thy fury upon the ^Theathen that know thee not, and upon the families that call not on thy name: for they have eaten up Jacob, and devoured him, and consumed him, and have made his habitation desolate.   *Gentiles*

11 The word that came to Jeremi'-ah from the LORD, saying,

2 Hear ye the words of this covenant, and speak unto the men of Judah, and to the inhabitants of Jerusalem;

3 And say thou unto them, Thus saith the LORD God of Israel; Cursed *be* the man that obeyeth not the words of this covenant,

4 Which I commanded your fathers in the day *that* I brought them forth out of the land of Egypt, from the iron furnace, saying, Obey my voice, and do them, according to all which I command you: so shall ye be my people, and I will be your God:

5 That I may perform the ^Roath

which I have sworn unto your fathers, to give them [R]a land flowing with milk and honey, as *it is* this day. Then answered I, and said, So be it, O LORD. 32:22 · Ex. 3:8

6 Then the LORD said unto me, Proclaim all these words in the cities of Judah, and in the streets of Jerusalem, saying, Hear ye the words of this covenant, [R]and do them. Deut. 17:19; [Rom. 2:13]; James 1:22

7 For I earnestly protested unto your fathers in the day *that* I brought them up out of the land of Egypt, *even* unto this day, [R]rising early and protesting, saying, Obey my voice. 35:15

8 [R]Yet they obeyed not, nor inclined their ear, but [R]walked every one in the [T]imagination of their evil heart: therefore I will bring upon them all the words of this covenant, which I commanded *them* to do; but they did *them* not. 7:26 · 13:10 · *stubbornness*

9 And the LORD said unto me, [R]A conspiracy is found among the men of Judah, and among the inhabitants of Jerusalem. Hos. 6:9

10 They are turned back to [R]the iniquities of their forefathers, which refused to hear my words; and they went after other gods to serve them: the house of Israel and the house of Judah have broken my covenant which I made with their fathers. 1 Sam. 15:11

11 Therefore thus saith the LORD, Behold, I will bring [T]evil upon them, which they shall not be able to escape; and though they shall cry unto me, I will not hearken unto them. *calamity*

12 Then shall the cities of Judah and inhabitants of Jerusalem go, and [R]cry unto the gods unto whom they offer incense: but they shall not save them at all in the time of their trouble. Deut. 32:37

13 For *according to* the number of thy [R]cities were thy gods, O Judah; and *according to* the number of the streets of Jerusalem have ye set up altars to *that* shameful thing, *even* altars to burn incense unto Ba'-al. 2:28

14 Therefore [R]pray not thou for this people, neither lift up a cry or prayer for them: for I will not hear *them* in the time that they cry unto me for their trouble. Ex. 32:10

15 [R]What hath my beloved to do in mine house, *seeing* she hath [R]wrought lewdness with many, and the holy flesh is passed from thee? when thou doest evil, then thou rejoicest. Ps. 50:16 · Ezek. 16:25

16 The LORD called thy name, [R]A green olive tree, fair, *and* of goodly fruit: with the noise of a great tumult he hath kindled fire upon it, and the branches of it are broken. Ps. 52:8; [Rom. 11:17]

17 For the LORD of hosts, [R]that planted thee, hath pronounced [T]evil against thee, for the evil of the house of Israel and of the house of Judah, which they have done against themselves to provoke me to anger in offering incense unto Ba'-al. Is. 5:2 · *doom*

18 And the LORD hath given me knowledge *of it*, and I know *it*: then thou shewedst me their doings.

19 But I *was* like a lamb *or* an ox *that* is brought to the slaughter; and I knew not that they had devised devices against me, *saying*, Let us destroy the tree with the fruit thereof, [R]and let us cut him off from [R]the land of the living, that his name may be no more remembered. Ps. 83:4 · Ps. 27:13

20 But, O LORD of hosts, that judgest righteously, that triest the reins and the heart, let me see thy vengeance on them: for unto thee have I revealed my cause.

21 Therefore thus saith the LORD of the men of [R]An'-a-thoth, that seek thy life, saying, Prophesy not in the name of the LORD, that thou die not by our hand: 1:1; 12:5, 6

22 Therefore thus saith the LORD of hosts, Behold, I will punish them: the young men shall die by the sword; their sons and their daughters shall die by famine:

23 And there shall be no remnant of them: for I will bring evil upon the men of An'-a-thoth, *even* [R]the year of their visitation. 23:12

12 Righteous ^Rart thou, O LORD, when I plead with thee: yet let me talk with thee of *thy* judgments: Wherefore doth the way of the wicked prosper? *wherefore* are all they happy that deal very treacherously?   Ezra 9:1

2 Thou hast planted them, yea, they have taken root: they grow, yea, they bring forth fruit: ^Rthou *art* near in their mouth, and far from their reins.   Is. 29:13; Mark 7:6

3 But thou, O LORD, ^Rknowest me: thou hast seen me, and tried mine heart toward thee: pull them out like sheep for the slaughter, and prepare them for ^Rthe day of slaughter.   Ps. 17:3 · 50:27; James 5:5

4 How long shall ^Rthe land mourn, and the herbs of every field wither, for the wickedness of them that dwell therein? the beasts are consumed, and the birds; because they said, He shall not see our last end.   23:10; Hos. 4:3

5 If thou hast run with the footmen, and they have wearied thee, then how canst thou contend with horses? and *if* in the land of peace, *wherein* thou trustedst, *they wearied thee*, then how wilt thou do in ^Rthe swelling of Jordan?   Josh. 3:15; 1 Chr. 12:15

6 For even ^Rthy brethren, and the house of thy father, even they have dealt treacherously with thee; yea, they have called a multitude after thee: ^Rbelieve them not, though they speak fair words unto thee.   Ps. 69:8 · Ps. 12:2; Prov. 26:25

7 I have forsaken mine house, I have left mine heritage; I have given the dearly beloved of my soul into the hand of her enemies.

8 Mine heritage is unto me as a lion in the forest; it crieth out against me: therefore have I ^Rhated it.   Hos. 9:15; Amos 6:8

9 Mine heritage *is* unto me *as* a speckled bird, the birds round about *are* against her; come ye, assemble all the beasts of the field, ^Rcome to devour.   Lev. 26:22

10 Many pastors have destroyed ^Rmy vineyard, they have ^Rtrodden my portion under foot, they have made my pleasant portion a desolate wilderness.   Ps. 80:8–16 · Is. 63:18

11 They have made it ^Rdesolate, *and being* desolate it mourneth unto me; the whole land is made desolate, because ^Rno man ^Tlayeth *it* to heart.   10:22; 22:6 · Is. 42:25 · *takes*

12 The ^Tspoilers are come upon all ^Thigh places through the wilderness: for the sword of the LORD shall devour from the *one* end of the land even to the *other* end of the land: no flesh shall have peace.   *plunderers · bare heights*

13 ^RThey have sown wheat, but shall reap thorns: they have put themselves to pain, *but* shall not profit: and they shall be ashamed of your revenues because of the fierce anger of the LORD.   Mic. 6:15

14 Thus saith the LORD against all mine evil neighbours, that ^Rtouch the inheritance which I have caused my people Israel to inherit; Behold, I will ^Rpluck them out of their land, and pluck out the house of Judah from among them.   Zech. 2:8 · Ps. 106:47; Is. 11:11–16

15 And it shall come to pass, after that I have plucked them out I will return, and have compassion on them, and will bring them again, every man to his heritage, and every man to his land.

16 And it shall come to pass, if they will diligently learn the ways of my people, ^Rto swear by my name, The LORD liveth; as they taught my people to swear by Ba'-al; then shall they be built in the midst of my people.   Zeph. 1:5

17 But if they will not ^Robey, I will utterly pluck up and destroy that nation, saith the LORD.   Is. 60:12

13 Thus saith the LORD unto me, Go and get thee a linen girdle, and put it upon thy loins, and put it not in water.

2 So I got a ^Tgirdle according to the word of the LORD, and put *it* ^Ton my loins.   *sash · around my waist*

3 And the word of the LORD came unto me the second time, saying,

4 Take the girdle that thou hast got, which *is* upon thy loins, and

arise, go to Eu-phra'-tes, and hide it there in a hole of the rock.

5 So I went, and hid it by Eu-phra'-tes, as the LORD commanded me.

6 And it came to pass after many days, that the LORD said unto me, Arise, go to Eu-phra'-tes, and take the ᵀgirdle from thence, which I commanded thee to hide there.   *sash*

7 Then I went to Eu-phra'-tes, and digged, and took the ᵀgirdle from the place where I had hid it: and, behold, the girdle was ᵀmarred, it was profitable for nothing.   *sash · ruined*

8 Then the word of the LORD came unto me, saying,

9 Thus saith the LORD, After this manner ᴿwill I mar the pride of Judah, and the great ᴿpride of Jerusalem.   Lev. 26:19 · Zeph. 3:11

10 This evil people, which ᴿrefuse to hear my words, which walk in the imagination of their heart, and walk after other gods, to serve them, and to worship them, shall even be as this girdle, which is good for nothing.   16:12

11 For as the girdle cleaveth to the loins of a man, so have I caused to cleave unto me the whole house of Israel and the whole house of Judah, saith the LORD; that they might be unto me for a people, and ᴿfor a name, and for a praise, and for a ᴿglory: but they would not hear.   33:9 · Is. 43:21

12 Therefore thou shalt speak unto them this word; Thus saith the LORD God of Israel, Every bottle shall be filled with wine: and they shall say unto thee, Do we not certainly know that every bottle shall be filled with wine?

13 Then shalt thou say unto them, Thus saith the LORD, Behold, I will fill all the inhabitants of this land, even the kings that sit upon David's throne, and the priests, and the prophets, and all the inhabitants of Jerusalem, ᴿwith drunkenness.   Ps. 60:3; 75:8

14 And I will dash them one against another, even the fathers and the sons together, saith the LORD: I will not pity, nor spare, nor have mercy, but destroy them.

15 Hear ye, and give ear; be not proud: for the LORD hath spoken.

16 ᴿGive glory to the LORD your God, before he cause darkness, and before your feet stumble upon the dark mountains, and, while ye look for light, he turn it into the shadow of death, *and* make *it* gross darkness.   Josh. 7:19

17 But if ye will not hear it, my soul shall ᴿweep in secret places for *your* pride; and mine eye shall weep sore, and run down with tears, because the LORD's flock is carried away captive.   Luke 19:41, 42

18 Say unto ᴿthe king and to the queen, Humble yourselves, sit down: for your principalities shall come down, *even* the crown of your glory.   22:26; 2 Kin. 24:12

19 The cities of the south shall be shut up, and none shall open *them:* Judah shall be carried away captive all of it, it shall be wholly carried away captive.

20 Lift up your eyes, and behold them that come from the ᴿnorth: where *is* the flock *that* was given thee, thy beautiful flock? 10:22; 46:20

21 What wilt thou say when he shall punish thee? for thou hast taught them *to be* captains, *and* as chief over thee: shall not sorrows take thee, as a woman in travail?

22 And if thou say in thine heart, ᴿWherefore come these things upon me? For the greatness of thine iniquity are ᴿthy skirts ᵀdiscovered, *and* thy heels made bare.   16:10 · Is. 47:2; Nah. 3:5 · *uncovered*

23 Can the E-thi-o'-pi-an change his skin, or the leopard his spots? *then* may ye also do good, that are accustomed to do evil.

24 Therefore will I scatter them as the stubble that passeth away by the wind of the wilderness.

25 This *is* thy lot, the portion of thy measures from me, saith the LORD; because thou hast forgotten me, and trusted in falsehood.

26 Therefore ᴿwill I discover thy

skirts upon thy face, that thy shame may appear.   Hos. 2:10

27 I have seen thine adulteries, and thy ^Rneighings, the lewdness of thy whoredom, *and* thine abominations ^Ron the hills in the fields. Woe unto thee, O Jerusalem! wilt thou not be made clean? when *shall it* once *be?*   5:7, 8 · Is. 65:7

14 The word of the Lord that came to Jer-e-mi′-ah concerning the ^Tdearth.   *droughts*

2 Judah mourneth, and the gates thereof languish; they are ^Rblack unto the ground; and the cry of Jerusalem is gone up.   8:21

3 And their nobles have sent their little ones to the waters: they came to the pits, *and* found no water; they returned with their vessels empty; they were ^Rashamed and confounded, and covered their heads.   Ps. 40:14

4 Because the ground is ^Tchapt, for there was no rain in the earth, the plowmen were ashamed, they covered their heads.   *parched*

5 Yea, the ^Thind also calved in the field, and ^Tforsook *it,* because there was no grass.   *deer · abandoned*

6 And ^Rthe wild asses did stand in the high places, they snuffed up the wind like dragons; their eyes did fail, because *there was* no grass.   2:24; Job 39:5, 6

7 O Lord, though our iniquities testify against us, do thou *it* ^Rfor thy name's sake: for our backslidings are many; we have sinned against thee.   14:21; Ps. 25:11

8 ^RO the hope of Israel, the saviour thereof in time of trouble, why shouldest thou be as a stranger in the land, and as a wayfaring man *that* turneth aside to tarry for a night?   17:13

9 Why shouldest thou be as a man astonied, as a mighty man ^R*that* cannot save? yet thou, O Lord, ^R*art* in the midst of us, and we are called by thy name; leave us not.   Is. 59:1 · Ex. 29:45; Lev. 26:11

10 Thus saith the Lord unto this people, ^RThus have they loved to wander, they have not refrained their feet, therefore the Lord doth

not accept them; ^Rhe will now remember their iniquity, and visit their sins.   2:23–25 · [44:21–23]; Hos. 8:13

11 Then said the Lord unto me, ^RPray not for this people for *their* good.   7:16; 11:14; Ex. 32:10

12 ^RWhen they fast, I will not hear their cry; and when they offer burnt offering and an oblation, I will not accept them: but ^RI will consume them by the sword, and by the famine, and by the pestilence.   Prov. 1:28; Mic. 3:4 · 9:16

13 ^RThen said I, Ah, Lord God! behold, the prophets say unto them, Ye shall not see the sword, neither shall ye have famine; but I will give you assured ^Rpeace in this place.   4:10 · 8:11; 23:17

14 Then the Lord said unto me, ^RThe prophets prophesy lies in my name: I sent them not, neither have I commanded them, neither spake unto them: they prophesy unto you a false vision and divination, and a thing of nought, and the deceit of their heart.   27:10

15 Therefore thus saith the Lord concerning the prophets that prophesy in my name, and I sent them not, ^Ryet they say, Sword and famine shall not be in this land; By sword and famine shall those prophets be consumed.   5:12

16 And the people to whom they prophesy shall be cast out in the streets of Jerusalem because of the famine and the sword; ^Rand they shall have none to bury them, them, their wives, nor their sons, nor their daughters: for I will pour their wickedness upon them.   7:32; 15:2, 3; Ps. 79:2, 3

17 Therefore thou shalt say this word unto them; Let mine eyes run down with tears night and day, and let them not cease: ^Rfor the virgin daughter of my people is broken with a great breach, with a very grievous blow.   Is. 37:22

18 If I go forth into ^Rthe field, then behold the slain with the sword! and if I enter into the city, then behold them that are sick with famine! yea, both the proph-

et and the ᴿpriest go about into a land that they know not. 6:25 · 23:11

19 Hast thou utterly rejected Judah? hath thy soul lothed Zion? why hast thou smitten us, and *there is* no healing for us? ᴿwe looked for peace, and *there is* no good; and for the time of healing, and behold trouble! 1 Thess. 5:3

20 We acknowledge, O LORD, our wickedness, *and* the iniquity of our fathers: for ᴿwe have sinned against thee. Ps. 106:6

21 Do not abhor *us*, for thy name's sake, do not disgrace the throne of thy glory: remember, break not thy covenant with us.

22 ᴿAre there *any* among the vanities of the Gentiles that can cause rain? or can the heavens give showers? *art* not thou he, O LORD our God? therefore we will wait upon thee: for thou hast made all these *things*. Zech. 10:1

15 Then said the LORD unto me, ᴿThough Moses and Samuel stood before me, *yet* my mind *could* not *be* toward this people: cast *them* out of my sight, and let them go forth. Ps. 99:6

2 And it shall come to pass, if they say unto thee, Whither shall we go forth? then thou shalt tell them, Thus saith the LORD; ᴿSuch as *are* for death, to death; and such as *are* for the sword, to the sword; and such as *are* for the famine, to the famine; and such as *are* for the captivity, to the captivity. Ezek. 5:2, 12; Zech. 11:9; [Rev. 13:10]

3 And I will ᴿappoint over them four kinds, saith the LORD: the sword to slay, and the dogs to tear, and ᴿthe fowls of the heaven, and the beasts of the earth, to devour and destroy. Ezek. 14:21 · 7:33

4 And I will cause them to be ᴿremoved into all kingdoms of the earth, because of ᴿMa-nas'-seh the son of Hez-e-ki'-ah king of Judah, for *that* which he did in Jerusalem. Deut. 28:25 · 2 Kin. 24:3, 4

5 For who shall have pity upon thee, O Jerusalem? or who shall bemoan thee? or who shall go aside to ask how thou doest?

6 ᴿThou hast forsaken me, saith the LORD, thou art ᴿgone backward: therefore will I stretch out my hand against thee, and destroy thee; ᴿI am weary with repenting. 2:13 · Is. 1:4 · 20:16; Zech. 8:14

7 And I will fan them with a fan in the gates of the land; I will bereave *them* of children, I will destroy my people, *since* they return not from their ways.

8 Their widows are increased to me above the sand of the seas: I have brought upon them against the mother of the young men a spoiler at noonday: I have caused *him* to fall upon it ᴿsuddenly, and terrors upon the city. Is. 29:5

9 She that hath borne seven languisheth: she hath given up the ghost; ᴿher sun is gone down while *it was* yet day: she hath been ashamed and confounded: and the residue of them will I deliver to the sword before their enemies, saith the LORD. Amos 8:9

10 ᴿWoe is me, my mother, that thou hast borne me a man of strife and a man of contention to the whole ᵀearth! I have neither lent on usury, nor men have lent to me on usury; *yet* every one of them doth curse me. Job 3:1 · Or *land*

11 The LORD said, Verily it shall be well with thy remnant; verily I will cause ᴿthe enemy to entreat thee *well* in the time of evil and in the time of affliction. 40:4, 5

12 Shall iron break the northern iron and the ᵀsteel? *bronze*

13 Thy substance and thy treasures will I give to the ᴿspoil without price, and *that* for all thy sins, even in all thy borders. Ps. 44:12

14 And I will make *thee* to pass with thine enemies ᴿinto a land *which* thou knowest not: for a fire is kindled in mine anger, *which* shall burn upon you. 16:13

15 O LORD, ᴿthou knowest: remember me, and visit me, and ᴿrevenge me of my persecutors; take me not away in thy longsuffering: know that for thy sake I have suffered rebuke. 12:3 · 20:12

16 Thy words were found, and I

did eat them; and thy word was unto me the joy and rejoicing of mine heart: for I am called by thy name, O Lord God of hosts.

17 ^RI sat not in the assembly of the mockers, nor rejoiced; I sat alone because of thy hand: for thou hast filled me with indignation.   Ps. 26:4, 5

18 Why is my ^Rpain perpetual, and my wound incurable, *which* refuseth to be healed? wilt thou be altogether unto me as a liar, *and as* waters *that* fail?   Job 34:6; Mic. 1:9

19 Therefore thus saith the Lord, ^RIf thou return, then will I bring thee again, *and* thou shalt stand before me: and if thou ^Rtake forth the precious from the vile, thou shalt be as my mouth: let them return unto thee; but return not thou unto them.   4:1 · 6:29

20 And I will make thee unto this people a fenced brasen wall: and they shall fight against thee, but ^Rthey shall not prevail against thee: for I *am* with thee to save thee and to deliver thee, saith the Lord.   Ps. 46:7; Is. 41:10

21 And I will deliver thee out of the hand of the wicked, and I will redeem thee out of the ^Thand of the terrible.   *grip*

16 The word of the Lord came also unto me, saying,

2 Thou shalt not take thee a wife, neither shalt thou have sons or daughters in this place.

3 For thus saith the Lord concerning the sons and concerning the daughters that are born in this place, and concerning their mothers that bare them, and concerning their fathers that begat them in this land;

4 They shall die of grievous deaths; they shall not be lamented; neither shall they be buried; *but* they shall be as dung upon the face of the earth: and they shall be consumed by the sword, and by famine; and their ^Rcarcases shall be meat for the fowls of heaven, and for the beasts of the earth.   Ps. 79:2; Is. 18:6

5 For thus saith the Lord, Enter not into the house of mourning, neither go to lament nor bemoan them: for I have taken away my peace from this people, saith the Lord, *even* lovingkindness and mercies.

6 Both the great and the small shall die in this land: they shall not be buried, ^Rneither shall *men* lament for them, nor cut themselves, nor make themselves bald for them: 22:18

7 Neither shall *men* tear *themselves* for them in mourning, to comfort them for the dead; neither shall *men* give them the cup of consolation to ^Rdrink for their father or for their mother.   Prov. 31:6

8 Thou shalt not also go into the house of feasting, to sit with them to eat and to drink.

9 For thus saith the Lord of hosts, the God of Israel; Behold, ^RI will cause to cease out of this place in your eyes, and in your days, the voice of mirth, and the voice of gladness, the voice of the bridegroom, and the voice of the bride.   Ezek. 26:13; Hos. 2:11; Rev. 18:23

10 And it shall come to pass, when thou shalt shew this people all these words, and they shall say unto thee, ^RWherefore hath the Lord pronounced all this great ^Tevil against us? or what *is* our iniquity? or what *is* our sin that we have committed against the Lord our God?   Deut. 29:24 · *disaster*

11 Then shalt thou say unto them, Because your fathers have forsaken me, saith the Lord, and have walked after other gods, and have served them, and have worshipped them, and have forsaken me, and have not kept my law;

12 And ye have done ^Rworse than your fathers; for, behold, ye walk every one after the imagination of his evil heart, that they may not hearken unto me: 7:26

13 ^RTherefore will I cast you out of this land into a land that ye know not, *neither* ye nor your fathers; and there shall ye serve other gods day and night; where I will not shew you favour.   Deut. 4:26

14 Therefore, behold, the days

come, saith the LORD, that it shall no more be said, The LORD liveth, that brought up the children of Israel out of the land of Egypt;

15 But, The LORD liveth, that brought up the children of Israel from the land of the ^Rnorth, and from all the lands whither he had driven them: and ^RI will bring them again into their land that I gave unto their fathers.   3:18 · 24:6

16 Behold, I will send for many ^Rfishers, saith the LORD, and they shall fish them; and after will I send for many hunters, and they shall hunt them from every mountain, and from every hill, and out of the holes of the rocks.   Amos 4:2

17 For mine ^Reyes *are* upon all their ways: they are not hid from my face, neither is their iniquity hid from mine eyes.   Ps. 90:8

18 And first I will ^Trecompense their iniquity and their sin double; because ^Rthey have defiled my land, they have filled mine inheritance with the carcases of their detestable and abominable ^Tthings.   *repay* · [Ezek. 43:7] · *idols*

19 O LORD, ^Rmy strength, and my fortress, and ^Rmy refuge in the day of affliction, the Gentiles shall come unto thee from the ends of the earth, and shall say, Surely our fathers have inherited lies, vanity, and *things* ^Rwherein *there* is no profit.   Is. 25:4 · 17:17 · Is. 44:10

20 Shall a man make gods unto himself, and they *are* no gods?

21 Therefore, behold, I will this once cause them to know, I will cause them to know mine hand and my might; and they shall know that my name *is* The LORD.

17 The sin of Judah *is* ^Rwritten with a ^Rpen of iron, *and* with the point of a diamond: *it is* ^Rgraven upon the table of their heart, and upon the horns of your altars;   2:22 · Job 19:24 · Is. 49:16

2 Whilst their children remember their altars and their ^Rgroves by the green trees upon the high hills.   Judg. 3:7

3 O my mountain in the field, I will give thy substance *and* all thy treasures ^Tto the spoil, *and* thy high places for sin, throughout all thy borders.   *as plunder*

4 And thou, even thyself, shalt discontinue from thine heritage that I gave thee; and I will cause thee to serve thine enemies in the land which thou knowest not: for ye have kindled a fire in mine anger, *which* shall burn for ever.

5 Thus saith the LORD; ^RCursed *be* the man that trusteth in man, and maketh ^Rflesh his arm, and whose heart departeth from the LORD.   Ps. 146:3; Is. 30:1, 2; 31:1 · Is. 31:3

6 For he shall be ^Rlike the heath in the desert, and ^Rshall not see when good cometh; but shall inhabit the parched places in the wilderness, ^R*in* a salt land and not inhabited.   48:6 · Job 20:17 · Deut. 29:23

7 ^RBlessed *is* the man that trusteth in the LORD, and whose hope the LORD is.   Ps. 2:12; Prov. 16:20

8 For he shall be as a tree planted by the waters, and *that* spreadeth out her roots by the river, and shall not see when heat cometh, but her leaf shall be green; and shall not be ^Tcareful in the year of drought, neither shall cease from yielding fruit.   *anxious*

9 The ^Rheart *is* deceitful above all *things*, and desperately wicked: who can know it?   Matt. 15:19

10 I the LORD ^Rsearch the heart, *I* try the reins, even to give every man according to his ways, *and* according to the fruit of his doings.   Ps. 139:23, 24; Prov. 17:3; Rom. 8:27

11 *As* the partridge sitteth *on eggs*, and hatcheth *them* not; *so* he that getteth riches, and not by right, ^Rshall leave them in the midst of his days, and at his end shall be ^Ra fool.   Ps. 55:23 · Luke 12:20

12 A glorious high throne from the beginning *is* the place of our sanctuary.

13 O LORD, ^Rthe hope of Israel, ^Rall that forsake thee shall be ashamed, *and* they that depart from me shall be ^Rwritten in the earth, because they have forsaken the LORD, the ^Rfountain of living waters.   14:8 · [Is. 1:28] · Luke 10:20 · 2:13

14 Heal me, O LORD, and I shall be healed; save me, and I shall be saved: for thou *art* my praise.

15 Behold, they say unto me, RWhere *is* the word of the LORD? let it come now.   Ezek. 12:22; 2 Pet. 3:4

16 As for me, RI have not hastened from *being* a pastor to follow thee: neither have I desired the woeful day; thou knowest: that which came out of my lips was *right* before thee.   1:4–12

17 Be not a terror unto me: Rthou *art* my hope in the day of Tevil.   16:19; Nah. 1:7 · *doom*

18 RLet them be confounded that persecute me, but Rlet not me be confounded: let them be dismayed, but let not me be dismayed: bring upon them the day of evil, and destroy them with double destruction.   Ps. 70:2 · Ps. 25:2

19 Thus said the LORD unto me; Go and stand in the gate of the children of the people, whereby the kings of Judah come in, and by the which they go out, and in all the gates of Jerusalem;

20 And say unto them, RHear ye the word of the LORD, ye kings of Judah, and all Judah, and all the inhabitants of Jerusalem, that enter in by these gates: Ps. 49:1, 2

21 Thus saith the LORD; RTake heed to yourselves, and bear no burden on the sabbath day, nor bring *it* in by the gates of Jerusalem;   [John 5:9–12, 17; 7:22–24]

22 Neither carry forth a burden out of your houses on the sabbath day, neither do ye any work, but hallow ye the sabbath day, as I Rcommanded your fathers.   Ex. 20:8

23 RBut they obeyed not, neither inclined their ear, but made their neck stiff, that they might not hear, nor receive instruction.   7:24

24 And it shall come to pass, Rif ye diligently hearken unto me, saith the LORD, to bring in no burden through the gates of this city on the sabbath day, but hallow the sabbath day, to do no work therein;   11:4; 26:3

25 RThen shall there enter into the gates of this city kings and princes sitting upon the throne of David, riding in chariots and on horses, they, and their princes, the men of Judah, and the inhabitants of Jerusalem: and this city shall remain for ever.   22:4

26 And they shall come from the cities of Judah, and from Rthe places about Jerusalem, and from the land of Benjamin, and from Rthe plain, and from the mountains, and from Rthe south, bringing burnt offerings, and sacrifices, and meat offerings, and incense, and bringing sacrifices of praise, unto the house of the LORD.   33:13 · Zech. 7:7 · Judg. 1:9

27 But if ye will not hearken unto me to hallow the sabbath day, and not to bear a burden, even entering in at the gates of Jerusalem on the sabbath day; then Rwill I kindle a fire in the gates thereof, and it shall devour the palaces of Jerusalem, and it shall not be quenched.   21:14

18 The word which came to Jer-e-mi'-ah from the LORD, saying,

2 Arise, and go down to the potter's house, and there I will cause thee to hear my words.

3 Then I went down to the potter's house, and, behold, he wrought a work on the wheels.

4 And the vessel that he made of clay was Tmarred in the hand of the potter: so he made it again another vessel, as seemed good to the potter to make *it*.   *ruined*

5 Then the word of the LORD came to me, saying,

6 O house of Israel, cannot I do with you as this potter? saith the LORD. Behold, as the clay *is* in the potter's hand, so *are* ye in mine hand, O house of Israel.

7 *At what* instant I shall speak concerning a nation, and concerning a kingdom, to pluck up, and to pull down, and to destroy *it*;

8 If that nation, against whom I have pronounced, turn from their evil, I will repent of the evil that I thought to do unto them.

9 And *at what* instant I shall

speak concerning a nation, and concerning a kingdom, to build and to plant *it;*

10 If it do evil in my sight, that it obey not my voice, then I will ^Trepent of the good, wherewith I said I would benefit them.   *relent*

11 Now therefore go to, speak to the men of Judah, and to the inhabitants of Jerusalem, saying, Thus saith the LORD; Behold, I frame evil against you, and devise a ^Tdevice against you: ^Rreturn ye now every one from his evil way, and make your ways and your doings good.   *plan* · 2 Kin. 17:13

12 And they said, ^RThere is no hope: but we will walk after our own devices, and we will every one do the ^Rimagination of his evil heart.   2:25; Is. 57:10 · 3:17; 23:17

13 Therefore thus saith the LORD; ^RAsk ye now among the heathen, who hath heard such things: the virgin of Israel hath done a very horrible thing.   Is. 66:8

14 Will *a man* leave the snow of Leb'-a-non *which cometh* from the rock of the field? *or* shall the cold flowing waters that come from another place be forsaken?

15 Because my people hath forgotten ^Rme, they have burned incense to ^Tvanity, and they have caused them to stumble in their ways *from* the ^Rancient paths, to walk in paths, *in* a way not cast up;   2:13, 32 · *worthless idols* · 6:16

16 To make their land desolate, *and* a perpetual hissing; every one that passeth thereby shall be astonished, and wag his head.

17 ^RI will scatter them ^Ras with an east wind before the enemy; ^RI will shew them the back, and not the face, in the day of their calamity.   13:24 · Ps. 48:7 · 2:27

18 Then said they, ^RCome, and let us devise ^Tdevices against Jer-e-mi'-ah; ^Rfor the law shall not perish from the priest, nor counsel from the wise, nor the word from the prophet. Come, and let us smite him with the tongue, and let us not give heed to any of his words. 11:19 · *plans* · Mal. 2:7; [John 7:48]

19 Give heed to me, O LORD, and ^Thearken to the voice of them that contend with me.   *listen*

20 ^RShall evil be ^Trecompensed for good? for they have digged a pit for my soul. Remember that I stood before thee to speak good for them, *and* to turn away thy wrath from them.   Ps. 109:4 · *repaid*

21 Therefore deliver up their children to the famine, and pour out their *blood* by the force of the sword; and let their wives be bereaved of their children, and *be* widows; and let their men be put to death; *let* their young men *be* slain by the sword in battle.

22 Let a cry be heard from their houses, when thou shalt bring a troop suddenly upon them: for they have digged a pit to take me, and hid snares for my feet.

23 Yet, LORD, thou knowest all their counsel against me to slay *me:* ^Rforgive not their iniquity, neither blot out their sin from thy sight, but let them be overthrown before thee; deal *thus* with them in the time of thine anger.   Neh. 4:5

19 Thus saith the LORD, Go and get a potter's earthen bottle, and *take* of the ^Tancients of the people, and of the ^Tancients of the priests;   *elders*

2 And go forth unto ^Rthe valley of the son of Hin'-nom, which *is* by the entry of the east gate, and proclaim there the words that I shall tell thee,   Josh. 15:8; 2 Kin. 23:10

3 ^RAnd say, Hear ye the word of the LORD, O kings of Judah, and inhabitants of Jerusalem; Thus saith the LORD of hosts, the God of Israel; Behold, I will bring ^Tevil upon this place, the which whosoever heareth, his ears shall ^Rtingle. 17:20 · *a catastrophe* · 1 Sam. 3:11

4 Because they ^Rhave forsaken me, and have estranged this place, and have burned incense in it unto other gods, whom neither they nor their fathers have known, nor the kings of Judah, and have filled this place with the blood of innocents;   Deut. 28:20

5 They have built also the high

places of Ba'-al, to burn their sons with fire *for* burnt offerings unto Ba'-al, ^Rwhich I commanded not, nor spake *it*, neither came *it* into my mind: 2 Kin. 17:17; Ps. 106:37, 38

6 Therefore, behold, the days come, saith the LORD, that this place shall no more be called To'-phet, nor ^RThe valley of the son of Hin'-nom, but The valley of slaughter. 7:32; Josh. 15:8

7 And I will make void the counsel of Judah and Jerusalem in this place; and I will cause them to fall by the sword before their enemies, and by the hands of them that seek their lives: and their carcases will I give to be meat for the fowls of the heaven, and for the beasts of the earth.

8 And I will make this city ^Rdesolate, and an hissing; every one that passeth thereby shall be astonished and hiss because of all the plagues thereof. 49:13; 50:13

9 And I will cause them to eat the ^Rflesh of their sons and the flesh of their daughters, and they shall eat every one the flesh of his friend in the siege and straitness, wherewith their enemies, and they that seek their lives, shall straiten them. Is. 9:20; Ezek. 5:10

10 ^RThen shalt thou break the bottle in the sight of the men that go with thee, 51:63, 64

11 And shalt say unto them, Thus saith the LORD of hosts; ^REven so will I break this people and this city, as *one* breaketh a potter's vessel, that cannot be made whole again: and they shall bury *them* in To'-phet, till *there be* no place to bury. Ps. 2:9; Rev. 2:27

12 Thus will I do unto this place, saith the LORD, and to the inhabitants thereof, and *even* make this city as To'-phet:

13 And the houses of Jerusalem, and the houses of the kings of Judah, shall be defiled ^Ras the place of To'-phet, because of all the houses upon whose ^Rroofs they have burned incense unto all the host of heaven, and ^Rhave

poured out drink offerings unto other gods. 2 Kin. 23:10 · 32:29 · 7:18

14 Then came Jer-e-mi'-ah from To'-phet, whither the LORD had sent him to prophesy; and he stood in the court of the LORD's house; and said to all the people,

15 Thus saith the LORD of hosts, the God of Israel; Behold, I will bring upon this city and upon all her towns all the ^Tevil that I have pronounced against it, because ^Rthey have hardened their necks, that they might not hear my words. *doom* · 17:23; Neh. 9:17, 29

20 Now Pash'-ur the son of Im'-mer the priest, who *was* also chief governor in the house of the LORD, heard that Jer-e-mi'-ah prophesied these things.

2 Then Pash'-ur smote Jer-e-mi'ah the prophet, and put him in the stocks that *were* in the high ^Rgate of Benjamin, which *was* by the house of the LORD. 37:13

3 And it came to pass on the morrow, that Pash'-ur brought forth Jer-e-mi'-ah out of the stocks. Then said Jer-e-mi'-ah unto him, The LORD hath not called thy name Pash'-ur, but Ma'-gor–mis'-sa-bib.

4 For thus saith the LORD, Behold, I will make thee a terror to thyself, and to all thy friends: and they shall fall by the sword of their enemies, and thine eyes shall behold *it*: and I will ^Rgive all Judah into the hand of the king of Babylon, and he shall carry them captive into Babylon, and shall slay them with the sword. 21:4-10

5 Moreover I ^Rwill deliver all the strength of this city, and all the labours thereof, and all the precious things thereof, and all the treasures of the kings of Judah will I give into the hand of their enemies, which shall spoil them, and take them, and ^Rcarry them to Babylon. 27:21, 22 · Is. 39:6

6 And thou, Pash'-ur, and all that dwell in thine house shall go into captivity: and thou shalt come to Babylon, and there thou shalt die, and shalt be buried

there, thou, and all thy friends, to whom thou hast prophesied lies.

7 O LORD, thou hast ^Tdeceived me, and I was ^Tdeceived: thou art stronger than I, and hast prevailed: I am in derision daily, every one mocketh me.   *persuaded*

8 For since I spake, I cried out, ^RI cried violence and ^Tspoil: because the word of the LORD was made a reproach unto me, and a derision, daily.   6:7 · *plunder*

9 Then I said, I will not make mention of him, nor speak any more in his name. But *his word* was in mine heart as a ^Rburning fire shut up in my bones, and I was weary with forbearing, and I could not *stay*.   Job 32:18–20; Ps. 39:3

10 ^RFor I heard the ^Tdefaming of many, fear on every side. Report, *say they*, and we will report it. All my familiars watched for my halting, *saying*, Peradventure he will be enticed, and we shall prevail against him, and we shall take our revenge on him.   Ps. 31:13 · *mocking*

11 But the LORD *is* ^Rwith me as a mighty ^Tterrible one: therefore my persecutors shall stumble, and they shall not ^Rprevail: they shall be greatly ashamed; for they shall not prosper: *their* ^Reverlasting confusion shall never be forgotten.   1:18, 19 · *awesome* · 17:18 · 23:40

12 But, O LORD of hosts, that triest the righteous, *and* seest the reins and the heart, ^Rlet me see thy vengeance on them: for unto thee have I opened my cause. 15:15

13 Sing unto the LORD, praise ye the LORD: for ^Rhe hath delivered the soul of the poor from the hand of evildoers.   Ps. 35:9, 10; 109:30, 31

14 Cursed *be* the day wherein I was born: let not the day wherein my mother bare me be blessed.

15 Cursed *be* the man who brought tidings to my father, saying, A ^Tman child is born unto thee; making him very glad.   *male*

16 And let that man be as the cities which the LORD overthrew, and ^Trepented not: and let him hear the cry in the morning, and the shouting at noontide;   *relented*

17 ^RBecause he slew me not from the womb; or that my mother might have been my grave, and her womb *to be* always great *with me*.   Job 3:10, 11

18 ^RWherefore came I forth out of the womb to see labour and sorrow, that my days should be consumed with shame?   15:10

21 The word which came unto Jer-e-mi′-ah from the LORD, when king Zed-e-ki′-ah sent unto him Pash′-ur the son of Mel-chi′-ah, and Zeph-a-ni′-ah the son of Ma-a-se′-iah the priest, saying,

2 ^REnquire, I pray thee, of the LORD for us; for Neb-u-chad-rez′-zar king of Babylon maketh war against us; if so be that the LORD will deal with us according to all his wondrous works, that he may go up from us.   Ex. 9:28; 1 Sam. 9:9

3 Then said Jer-e-mi′-ah unto them, Thus shall ye say to Zed-e-ki′-ah:

4 Thus saith the LORD God of Israel; Behold, I will turn back the weapons of war that *are* in your hands, wherewith ye fight against the king of Babylon, and *against* the Chal-de′-ans, which besiege you ^Twithout the walls, and ^RI will assemble them into the midst of this city.   *outside* · Is. 13:4; Lam. 2:5, 7

5 And I ^Rmyself will fight against you with an ^Routstretched hand and with a strong arm, even in anger, and in fury, and in great wrath.   32:24; 33:5; Is. 63:10 · Ex. 6:6

6 And I will smite the inhabitants of this city, both man and beast: they shall die of a great pestilence.

7 And afterward, saith the LORD, I will deliver Zed-e-ki′-ah king of Judah, and his servants, and the people, and such as are left in this city from the pestilence, from the sword, and from the famine, into the hand of Neb-u-chad-rez′-zar king of Babylon, and into the hand of their enemies, and into the hand of those that seek their life: and he shall smite them with the edge of the sword; he shall not spare them, neither have pity, nor have mercy.

8 And unto this people thou shalt say, Thus saith the LORD; Behold, I set before you the way of life, and the way of death.

9 He that ᴿabideth in this city shall die by the sword, and by the famine, and by the pestilence: but he that goeth out, and falleth to the Chal-de′-ans that besiege you, he shall live, and his life shall be unto him ᵀfor a prey. 38:2 · *as a prize*

10 For I have ᴿset my face against this city for evil, and not for good, saith the LORD: ᴿit shall be given into the hand of the king of Babylon, and he shall ᴿburn it with fire. Amos 9:4 · 38:3 · 2 Kin. 25:9

11 And touching the house of the king of Judah, *say*, Hear ye the word of the LORD;

12 O house of David, thus saith the LORD; ᴿExecute judgment ᴿin the morning, and deliver *him that is* spoiled out of the hand of the oppressor, lest my fury go out like fire, and burn that none can quench *it*, because of the evil of your doings. Zech. 7:9 · Zeph. 3:5

13 Behold, ᴿI *am* against thee, O inhabitant of the valley, *and* rock of the plain, saith the LORD; which say, Who shall come down against us? or who shall enter into our habitations? [23:30–32; Ezek. 13:8]

14 But I will punish you according to the ᴿfruit of your doings, saith the LORD: and I will kindle a fire in the forest thereof, and ᴿit shall devour all things round about it. Prov. 1:31; Is. 3:10, 11 · 11:16

22 Thus saith the LORD; Go down to the house of the king of Judah, and speak there this word,

2 And say, ᴿHear the word of the LORD, O king of Judah, that sittest upon the throne of David, thou, and thy servants, and thy people that enter in by these gates: 17:20

3 Thus saith the LORD; ᴿExecute ye judgment and righteousness, and deliver the spoiled out of the hand of the oppressor: and do no wrong, do no violence to the stranger, the fatherless, nor the widow, neither shed innocent blood in this place. 21:12; Matt. 23:23

4 For if ye do this thing indeed, ᴿthen shall there enter in by the gates of this house kings sitting upon the throne of David, riding in chariots and on horses, he, and his servants, and his people. 17:25

5 But if ye will not hear these words, ᴿI swear by myself, saith the LORD, that this house shall become a desolation. Matt. 23:38

6 For thus saith the LORD unto the king's house of Judah; Thou *art* Gil′-e-ad unto me, *and* the head of Leb′-a-non: *yet* surely I will make thee a wilderness, *and* cities *which* are not inhabited.

7 And I will prepare destroyers against thee, every one with his weapons: and they shall cut down ᴿthy choice cedars, ᴿand cast *them* into the fire. Is. 37:24 · 21:14

8 And many nations shall pass by this city, and they shall say every man to his neighbour, ᴿWherefore hath the LORD done thus unto this great city? 16:10

9 Then they shall answer, ᴿBecause they have forsaken the covenant of the LORD their God, and worshipped other gods, and served them. 2 Kin. 22:17; 2 Chr. 34:25

10 Weep ye not for ᴿthe dead, neither bemoan him: *but* weep sore for him ᴿthat goeth away: for he shall return no more, nor see his native country. 2 Kin. 22:20 · 14:17

11 For thus saith the LORD touching ᴿShal′-lum the son of Jo-si′-ah king of Judah, which reigned instead of Jo-si′-ah his father, which went forth out of this place; He shall not return thither any more: 1 Chr. 3:15

12 But he shall die in the place whither they have led him captive, and shall see this land no more.

13 ᴿWoe unto him that buildeth his house by unrighteousness, and his chambers by wrong; ᴿ*that* useth his neighbour's service without wages, and giveth him not for his work; 17:11 · James 5:4

14 That saith, I will build me a

wide house and large chambers, and cutteth him out windows; and *it is* cieled with cedar, and painted with vermilion.

15 Shalt thou reign, because thou ^Tclosest *thyself* in cedar? did not thy father eat and drink, and do judgment and justice, *and* then ^R*it was* well with him? *enclose · 7:23*

16 He ^Tjudged the cause of the poor and needy; then *it was* well *with him: was* not this to know me? saith the LORD. *Defended*

17 ^RBut thine eyes and thine heart *are* not but for thy covetousness, and for to shed innocent blood, and for oppression, and for violence, to do *it*. *6:13; [Luke 12:15–20]*

18 Therefore thus saith the LORD concerning Je-hoi'-a-kim the son of Jo-si'-ah king of Judah; They shall not lament for him, *saying*, Ah my brother! or, Ah sister! they shall not lament for him, *saying*, Ah lord! or, Ah his glory!

19 ^RHe shall be buried with the burial of an ass, drawn and cast forth beyond the gates of Jerusalem. *2 Chr. 36:6; Dan. 1:2*

20 Go up to Leb'-a-non, and cry; and lift up thy voice in Ba'-shan, and cry from ^Tthe passages: for all thy lovers are destroyed. *Abarim*

21 I spake unto thee in thy prosperity; *but* thou saidst, I will not hear. ^RThis *hath been* thy manner from thy youth, that thou obeyedst not my voice. *3:24, 25; 32:30*

22 The wind shall eat up all ^Rthy pastors, and thy lovers shall go into captivity: surely then shalt thou be ashamed and confounded for all thy wickedness. *23:1*

23 O inhabitant of Leb'-a-non, that makest thy nest in the cedars, how gracious shalt thou be when pangs come upon thee, ^Rthe pain as of a woman in travail! *6:24*

24 *As* I live, saith the LORD, though Co-ni'-ah the son of Je-hoi'-a-kim king of Judah were the signet upon my right hand, yet would I pluck thee thence;

25 ^RAnd I will give thee into the hand of them that seek thy life, and into the hand *of them* whose

face thou fearest, even into the hand of Neb-u-chad-rez'-zar king of Babylon, and into the hand of the Chal-de'-ans. *2 Kin. 24:15, 16*

26 And I will cast thee out, and thy mother that bare thee, into another country, where ye were not born; and there shall ye die.

27 But to the land whereunto they desire to return, thither shall they not return.

28 *Is* this man Co-ni'-ah a despised broken idol? *is he* ^Ra vessel wherein *is* no pleasure? wherefore are they cast out, he and his seed, and are cast into a land which they know not? *Ps. 31:12*

29 ^RO earth, earth, earth, hear the word of the LORD. *Is. 1:2; 34:1*

30 Thus saith the LORD, Write ye this man childless, a man *that* shall not prosper in his days: for no man of his seed shall prosper, sitting upon the throne of David, and ruling any more in Judah.

23 Woe ^Rbe unto the ^Tpastors that destroy and scatter the sheep of my pasture! saith the LORD. *10:21; Is. 56:9–12 · Lit. shepherds*

2 Therefore thus saith the LORD God of Israel against the pastors that feed my people; Ye have scattered my flock, and driven them away, and have not visited them: ^Rbehold, I will visit upon you the evil of your doings, saith the LORD. *Ex. 32:34*

3 And ^RI will gather the remnant of my flock out of all countries whither I have driven them, and will bring them again to their folds; and they shall be fruitful and increase. *32:37; Is. 11:11, 12, 16*

4 And I will set up ^Rshepherds over them which shall feed them: and they shall fear no more, nor be dismayed, neither shall they be lacking, saith the LORD. *3:15*

5 Behold, ^Rthe days come, saith the LORD, that I will raise unto David a righteous Branch, and a King shall reign and prosper, and shall execute judgment and justice in the ^Tearth. *Matt. 1:1, 6 · land* ☆

6 In his days Judah shall be saved, and Israel shall dwell safe- ☆

ly: and ^Rthis *is* his name whereby he shall be called, THE LORD OUR RIGHTEOUSNESS. Is. 45:24

7 Therefore, behold, ^Rthe days come, saith the LORD, that they shall no more say, The LORD liveth, which brought up the children of Israel out of the land of Egypt; 16:14; Is. 43:18, 19

8 But, The LORD liveth, which brought up and which led the seed of the house of Israel out of the north country, ^Rand from all countries whither I had driven them; and they shall dwell in their own ^Rland. Is. 43:5, 6 · Gen. 12:7

9 Mine heart within me is broken because of the prophets; ^Rall my bones shake; I am like a drunken man, and like a man whom wine hath overcome, because of the LORD, and because of the words of his holiness. 8:18

10 For ^Rthe land is full of adulterers; for ^Rbecause of swearing the land mourneth; the pleasant places of the wilderness are dried up, and their course is evil, and their force *is* not right. 9:2 · Hos. 4:2

11 For ^Rboth prophet and priest are profane; yea, ^Rin my house have I found their wickedness, saith the LORD. 6:13; Zeph. 3:4 · 7:30

12 ^RWherefore their way shall be unto them as slippery *ways* in the darkness: they shall be driven on, and fall therein: for I ^Rwill bring evil upon them, *even* the year of their visitation, saith the LORD. 13:16; Ps. 35:6; [Prov. 4:19] · 11:23

13 And I have seen folly in the prophets of Sa-ma′-ri-a; ^Rthey prophesied in Ba′-al, and ^Rcaused my people Israel to err. 2:8 · Is. 9:16

14 I have seen also in the prophets of Jerusalem an horrible thing: ^Rthey commit adultery, and walk in lies: they ^Rstrengthen also the hands of evildoers, that none doth return from his wickedness: they are all of them unto me as ^RSodom, and the inhabitants thereof as Go-mor′-rah. 29:23 · v. 22 · Gen. 18:20

15 Therefore thus saith the LORD of hosts concerning the prophets; Behold, I will feed them with ^Rwormwood, and make them drink the water of gall: for from the prophets of Jerusalem is profaneness gone forth into all the land. 9:15; Deut. 29:18

16 Thus saith the LORD of hosts, Hearken not unto the words of the prophets that prophesy unto you: they make you vain: they speak a vision of their own heart, *and* not out of the mouth of the LORD.

17 They say still unto them that despise me, The LORD hath said, Ye shall have peace; and they say unto every one that walketh after the imagination of his own heart, ^RNo evil shall come upon you. 5:12

18 For ^Rwho hath stood in the counsel of the LORD, and hath perceived and heard his word? who hath marked his word, and heard *it*? Job 15:8, 9; [1 Cor. 2:16]

19 Behold, a ^Rwhirlwind of the LORD is gone forth in fury, even a ^Tgrievous whirlwind: it shall fall grievously upon the head of the wicked. 25:32; 30:23; Amos 1:14 · *violent*

20 The ^Ranger of the LORD shall not return, until he have executed, and till he have performed the thoughts of his heart: ^Rin the latter days ye shall consider it perfectly. 30:24; 2 Kin. 23:26, 27 · Gen. 49:1

21 I have not sent these prophets, yet they ran: I have not spoken to them, yet they prophesied.

22 But if they had stood in my counsel, and had caused my people to hear my words, then they should have ^Rturned them from their evil way, and from the evil of their doings. 25:5

23 *Am* I a God at hand, saith the LORD, and not a God afar off?

24 Can any hide himself in secret places that I shall not see him? saith the LORD. Do not I fill heaven and earth? saith the LORD.

25 I have heard what the prophets said, that prophesy lies in my name, saying, I have dreamed, I have dreamed.

26 How long shall *this* be in the heart of the prophets that prophesy lies? yea, *they are* prophets of the deceit of their own heart;

27 Which think to cause my people to forget my name by their dreams which they tell every man to his neighbour, Ras their fathers have forgotten my name for Ba'-al.   Judg. 3:7

28 The prophet that hath a dream, let him tell a dream; and he that hath my word, let him speak my word faithfully. What *is* the chaff to the wheat? saith the LORD.

29 *Is* not my word like as a fire? saith the LORD; and like a hammer *that* breaketh the rock in pieces?

30 Therefore, behold, RI *am* against the prophets, saith the LORD, that steal my words every one from his neighbour. Deut. 18:20

31 Behold, I *am* against the prophets, saith the LORD, that use their tongues, and say, He saith.

32 Behold, I *am* against them that prophesy false dreams, saith the LORD, and do tell them, and cause my people to err by their Rlies, and by Rtheir lightness; yet I sent them not, nor commanded them: therefore they shall not Rprofit this people at all, saith the LORD.   20:6; 27:10 · Zeph. 3:4 · Lam. 2:14

33 And when this people, or the prophet, or a priest, shall ask thee, saying, What *is* the burden of the LORD? thou shalt then say unto them, What burden? I will even forsake you, saith the LORD.

34 And *as for* the prophet, and the priest, and the people, that shall say, The Tburden of the LORD, I will even Tpunish that man and his house.   *oracle · attend to*

35 Thus shall ye say every one to his neighbour, and every one to his brother, What hath the LORD answered? and, What hath the LORD spoken?

36 And the Tburden of the LORD shall ye mention no more: for every man's word shall be his Tburden; for ye have perverted the words of the living God, of the LORD of hosts our God.   *oracle*

37 Thus shalt thou say to the prophet, What hath the LORD answered thee? and, What hath the LORD spoken?

38 But since ye say, The Tburden of the LORD; therefore thus saith the LORD; Because ye say this word, The Tburden of the LORD, and I have sent unto you, saying, Ye shall not say, The Tburden of the LORD;   *oracle or prophecy*

39 Therefore, behold, I, even I, will utterly forget you, and I will forsake you, and the city that I gave you and your fathers, *and* cast *you* out of my presence:

40 And I will bring Ran everlasting reproach upon you, and a perpetual Rshame, which shall not be forgotten.   Ezek. 5:14, 15 · Mic. 3:5–7

24 The LORD shewed me, and, behold, two baskets of figs *were* set before the temple of the LORD, after that Neb-u-chad-rez'-zar Rking of Babylon had carried away captive RJec-o-ni'-ah the son of Je-hoi'-a-kim king of Judah, and the princes of Judah, with the carpenters and smiths, from Jerusalem, and had brought them to Babylon. 2 Chr. 36:10 · 22:24–28; 29:2

2 One basket *had* very good figs, *even* like the figs *that are* first ripe: and the other basket *had* very Tnaughty figs, which could not be eaten, they were so Rbad.   bad · 29:17; Is. 5:4, 7

3 Then said the LORD unto me, What seest thou, Jer-e'mi'-ah? And I said, Figs; the good figs, very good; and the Tevil, very Tevil, that cannot be eaten, they are so Tevil.   *bad*

4 Again the word of the LORD came unto me, saying,

5 Thus saith the LORD, the God of Israel; Like these good figs, so will I Tacknowledge them that are carried away captive of Judah, whom I have sent out of this place into the land of the Chal-de'-ans for *their* good.   *regard*

6 For I will set mine eyes upon them for good, and RI will bring them again to this land: and RI will build them, and not pull *them* down; and I will plant them, and not pluck *them* up. 12:15; 29:10 · 32:41

7 And I will give them an heart to know me, that I *am* the LORD:

and they shall be ^Rmy people, and I will be their God: for they shall return unto me ^Rwith their whole heart.   Zech. 8:8 · 1 Sam. 7:3; Ps. 119:2

8 And as the evil figs, which cannot be eaten, they are so evil; surely thus saith the LORD, So will I give Zed-e-ki'-ah the king of Judah, and his princes, and the ^Rresidue of Jerusalem, that remain in this land, and them that dwell in the land of Egypt: 39:9

9 And I will deliver them to ^Rbe removed into all the kingdoms of the earth for *their* hurt, *to be* a reproach and a proverb, a taunt and a curse, in all places whither I shall drive them.   Deut. 28:25, 37

10 And I will send the sword, the famine, and the pestilence, among them, till they be ^Tconsumed from off the land that I gave unto them and to their fathers.   *destroyed*

25 The word that came to Jer-e-mi'-ah concerning all the people of Judah ^Rin the fourth year of ^RJe-hoi'-a-kim the son of Jo-si'-ah king of Judah, that *was* the first year of Neb-u-chad-rez'-zar king of Babylon;   36:1 · Dan. 1:1, 2

2 The which Jer-e-mi'-ah the prophet spake unto all the people of Judah, and to all the inhabitants of Jerusalem, saying,

3 ^RFrom the thirteenth year of Jo-si'-ah the son of Amon king of Judah, even unto this day, that *is* the three and twentieth year, the word of the LORD hath come unto me, and I have spoken unto you, rising early and speaking; ^Rbut ye have not hearkened. 1:2 · 7:13; 11:7, 8

4 And the LORD hath sent unto you all his servants the prophets, ^Rrising early and sending *them;* but ye have not hearkened, nor inclined your ear to hear.   7:13, 25

5 They said, Turn ye again now every one from his evil way, and from the evil of your doings, and dwell in the land that the LORD hath given unto you and to your fathers for ever and ever:

6 And go not after other gods to serve them, and to worship them, and provoke me not to

anger with the works of your hands; and I will do you no hurt.

7 Yet ye have not hearkened unto me, saith the LORD; that ye might ^Rprovoke me to anger with the works of your hands to your own hurt.   7:19; 32:30; Deut. 32:21

8 Therefore thus saith the LORD of hosts; Because ye have not heard my words,

9 Behold, I will send and take ^Rall the families of the north, saith the LORD, and Neb-u-chad-rez'-zar the king of Babylon, ^Rmy servant, and will bring them against this land, and against the inhabitants thereof, and against all these nations round about, and will utterly destroy them, and ^Rmake them an astonishment, and an hissing, and perpetual desolations.   1:15 · 27:6; Is. 45:1 · 18:16

10 Moreover I will take from them the ^Rvoice of mirth, and the voice of gladness, the voice of the bridegroom, and the voice of the bride, the sound of the millstones, and the light of the candle.   7:34

11 And this whole land shall be a desolation, *and* an astonishment; and these nations shall serve the king of Babylon seventy ^Ryears.   2 Chr. 36:21; Dan. 9:2; Zech. 7:5

12 And it shall come to pass, ^Rwhen seventy years are accomplished, *that* I will punish the king of Babylon, and that nation, saith the LORD, for their iniquity, and the land of the Chal-de'-ans, ^Rand will make it perpetual desolations.   2 Chr. 36:21, 22; Dan. 9:2 · 50:3

13 And I will bring upon that land all my words which I have pronounced against it, *even* all that is written in this book, which Jer-e-mi'-ah hath prophesied against all the nations.

14 ^RFor many nations and great kings shall serve themselves of them also: and I will recompense them according to their deeds, and according to the works of their own hands.   50:9; 51:27, 28

15 For thus saith the LORD God of Israel unto me; Take the ^Rwine cup of this fury at my hand, and

cause all the nations, to whom I send thee, to drink it.   Rev. 14:10

16 And ^Rthey shall drink, and be moved, and be mad, because of the sword that I will send among them.   51:7; Ezek. 23:34; Nah. 3:11

17 Then took I the cup at the LORD's hand, and made all the nations to drink, unto whom the LORD had sent me:

18 *To wit*, Jerusalem, and the cities of Judah, and the kings thereof, and the princes thereof, to make them ^Ra desolation, an astonishment, an hissing, and ^Ra curse; as *it is* this day; vv. 9, 11 · 24:9

19 Pharaoh king of Egypt, and his servants, and his princes, and all his people;

20 And all the mingled people, and all the kings of ^Rthe land of Uz, and all the kings of the land of the Phi-lis'-tines, and Ash'-ke-lon, and Az'-zah, and Ek'-ron, and the remnant of Ash'-dod,   Lam. 4:21

21 ^RE'-dom, and Moab, and the children of Ammon,   49:7

22 And all the kings of ^RTy'-rus, and all the kings of Zi'-don, and the kings of the isles which *are* beyond the ^Rsea,   Zech. 9:2-4 · 49:23

23 ^RDe'-dan, and Te'-ma, and Buz, and all *that are* in the utmost corners,   49:7, 8; Is. 21:13

24 And all the kings of Arabia, and all the kings of the mingled people that dwell in the desert,

25 And all the kings of Zim'-ri, and all the kings of ^RE'-lam, and all the kings of the Medes,   49:34

26 And all the kings of the north, far and near, one with another, and all the kingdoms of the world, which *are* upon the face of the earth: and the king of She'-shach shall drink after them.

27 Therefore thou shalt say unto them, Thus saith the LORD of hosts, the God of Israel; ^RDrink ye, and ^Rbe drunken, and spue, and fall, and rise no more, because of the sword which I will send among you.   Hab. 2:16 · Is. 63:6

28 And it shall be, if they refuse to take the cup at thine hand to drink, then shalt thou say unto

them, Thus saith the LORD of hosts; Ye shall certainly drink.

29 For, lo, I begin to bring evil on the city which is called by my name, and should ye be utterly unpunished? Ye shall not be unpunished: for I will call for a sword upon all the inhabitants of the earth, saith the LORD of hosts.

30 Therefore prophesy thou against them all these words, and say unto them, The LORD shall ^Rroar from on high, and utter his voice from ^Rhis holy habitation; he shall mightily roar upon his habitation; he shall give a shout, as they that tread *the grapes*, against all the inhabitants of the earth.   Is. 42:13; Joel 3:16 · Ps. 11:4

31 A noise shall come *even* to the ends of the earth; for the LORD hath a controversy with the nations, he will plead with all flesh; he will give them *that are* wicked to the sword, saith the LORD.

32 Thus saith the LORD of hosts, Behold, ^Tevil shall go forth from nation to nation, and a great whirlwind shall be raised up from the coasts of the earth.   *disaster*

33 ^RAnd the slain of the LORD shall be at that day from *one* end of the earth even unto the *other* end of the earth: they shall not be lamented, ^Rneither gathered, nor buried; they shall be dung upon the ground. Is. 34:2, 3 · Ps. 79:3; Rev. 11:9

34 ^RHowl, ye shepherds, and cry; and wallow yourselves *in the ashes*, ye principal of the flock: for the days of your slaughter and of your dispersions are accomplished; and ye shall fall like a pleasant vessel.   4:8; 6:26; Ezek. 27:30

35 And the shepherds shall have no ^Tway to flee, nor the principal of the flock to escape.   Or *refuge*

36 A voice of the cry of the shepherds, and an howling of the ^Tprincipal of the flock, *shall be heard:* for the LORD hath ^Tspoiled their pasture.   *leaders · plundered*

37 And the ^Tpeaceable habitations are cut down because of the fierce anger of the LORD.   *peaceful*

38 He hath ^Tforsaken his covert,

as the lion: for their land is desolate because of the fierceness of the oppressor, and because of his fierce anger. *left his lair*

26 In the beginning of the reign of Je-hoi′-a-kim the son of Jo-si′-ah king of Judah came this word from the LORD, saying,

2 Thus saith the LORD; Stand in the court of the LORD's house, and speak unto all the cities of Judah, which come to worship in the LORD's house, ^Rall the words that I command thee to speak unto them; diminish not a word: 43:1

3 If so be they will hearken, and turn every man from his evil way, that I may ^Rrepent^T me of the evil, which I purpose to do unto them because of the evil of their doings. Jon. 3:9 · *relent of the calamity*

4 And thou shalt say unto them, Thus saith the LORD; ^RIf ye will not hearken to me, to walk in my law, which I have set before you, Deut. 28:15; 1 Kin. 9:6; Is. 1:20

5 To ^Thearken to the words of my servants the prophets, ^Rwhom I sent unto you, both rising up early, and sending *them*, but ye have not hearkened; *listen* · 29:19

6 Then will I make this house like ^RShi′-loh, and will make this city ^Ra curse to all the nations of the earth. Ps. 78:60 · 2 Kin. 22:19; Is. 65:15

7 So the priests and the prophets and all the people heard Jer-e-mi′-ah speaking these words in the house of the LORD.

8 Now it came to pass, when Jer-e-mi′-ah had made an end of speaking all that the LORD had commanded *him* to speak unto all the people, that the priests and the prophets and all the people ^Ttook him, saying, Thou shalt surely die. *seized*

9 Why hast thou prophesied in the name of the LORD, saying, This house shall be like Shi′-loh, and this city shall be ^Rdesolate without an inhabitant? And all the people were gathered against Jer-e-mi′-ah in ^Tthe house of the LORD. 9:11 · *The temple*

10 When the princes of Judah heard these things, then they came up from the king's house unto the house of the LORD, and sat down in the ^Tentry of the new gate of the LORD's *house*. *entrance*

11 Then spake the priests and the prophets unto the princes and to all the people, saying, This man *is* worthy to ^Rdie; for he hath prophesied against this city, as ye have heard with your ears. 38:4

12 Then spake Jer-e-mi′-ah unto all the princes and to all the people, saying, The LORD sent me to prophesy against this house and against this city all the words that ye have heard.

13 Therefore now ^Ramend your ways and your doings, and obey the voice of the LORD your God; and the LORD will repent him of the evil that he hath pronounced against you. 7:3; [Joel 2:13]; Jon. 3:8

14 As for me, behold, I *am* in your hand: do with me as seemeth good and ^Tmeet unto you. *right*

15 But know ye for certain, that if ye put me to death, ye shall surely bring innocent blood upon yourselves, and upon this city, and upon the inhabitants thereof: for of a truth the LORD hath sent me unto you to speak all these words in your ^Tears. *hearing*

16 Then said the princes and all the people unto the priests and to the prophets; This man *is* not worthy to die: for he hath spoken to us in the name of the LORD our God.

17 ^RThen rose up certain of the elders of the land, and spake to all the assembly of the people, saying, Acts 5:34

18 ^RMi′-cah the Mo′-ras-thite prophesied in the days of Hez-e-ki′-ah king of Judah, and spake to all the people of Judah, saying, Thus saith the LORD of hosts; ^RZion shall be plowed *like* a field, and Jerusalem shall become heaps, and the mountain of the house as the high places of a forest. Mic. 1:1 · Mic. 3:12

19 Did Hez-e-ki′-ah king of

Judah and all Judah put him at all to death? did he not fear the Lord, and besought the Lord, and the Lord ᴿrepented him of the evil which he had pronounced against them? Thus might we procure great evil against our souls.   18:8

20 And there was also a man that prophesied in the name of the Lord, U-ri′-jah the son of She-ma′-iah of Kir′-jath–je′-a-rim, who prophesied against this city and against this land according to all the words of Jer-e-mi′-ah:

21 And when Je-hoi′-a-kim the king, with all his mighty men, and all the princes, heard his words, the king sought to put him to death: but when U-ri′-jah heard it, he was afraid, and fled, and went into Egypt;

22 And Je-hoi′-a-kim the king sent men into Egypt, *namely*, El-na′-than the son of Ach′-bor, and *certain* men with him into Egypt.

23 And they fetched forth U-ri′-jah out of Egypt, and brought him unto Je-hoi′-a-kim the king; who slew him with the sword, and cast his dead body into the graves of the common people.

24 Nevertheless ᴿthe hand of A-hi′-kam the son of Sha′-phan was with Jer-e-mi′-ah, that they should not give him into the hand of the people to put him to death.   39:14

27 In the beginning of the reign of Je-hoi′-a-kim the son of Jo-si′-ah ᴿking of Judah came this word unto Jer-e-mi′-ah from the Lord, saying,   28:1

2 Thus saith the Lord to me; Make thee bonds and yokes, ᴿand put them upon thy neck,   28:10, 12

3 And send them to the king of E′-dom, and to the king of Moab, and to the king of the Am′-mon-ites, and to the king of ᵀTy′-rus, and to the king of ᵀZi′-don, by the hand of the messengers which come to Jerusalem unto Zed-e-ki′-ah king of Judah;   Or *Tyre* · Or *Sidon*

4 And command them to ᵀsay unto their masters, Thus saith the Lord of hosts, the God of Israel;

Thus shall ye say unto your masters;   Or go to *their masters, saying*

5 I have made the earth, the man and the beast that *are* upon the ground, by my great power and by my outstretched arm, and have given it unto whom it seemed ᵀmeet unto me.   *proper to*

6 And now have I given all these lands into the hand of Neb-u-chad-nez′-zar the king of Bab-ylon, ᴿmy servant; and ᴿthe beasts of the field have I given him also to serve him.   Ezek. 29:18, 20 · Dan. 2:38

7 ᴿAnd all nations shall serve him, and his son, and his son's son, until the very time of his land come: ᴿand then many nations and great kings shall serve them-selves of him.   2 Chr. 36:20 · 25:14

8 And it shall come to pass, *that* the nation and kingdom which will not serve the same Neb-u-chad-nez′-zar the king of Babylon, and that will not put their neck under the yoke of the king of Babylon, that nation will I punish, saith the Lord, with the sword, and with the famine, and with the pestilence, until I have consumed them by his hand.

9 Therefore hearken not ye to your prophets, nor to your divin-ers, nor to your ᵀdreamers, nor to your ᵀenchanters, nor to your sor-cerers, which speak unto you, say-ing, Ye shall not serve the king of Babylon: Lit. *dreams · soothsayers*

10 For they prophesy a ᴿlie unto you, to remove you far from your land; and that I should drive you out, and ye should perish.   23:16, 32

11 But the nations that bring their neck under the yoke of the king of Babylon, and serve him, those will I let remain still in their own land, saith the Lord; and they shall till it, and dwell therein.

12 I spake also to ᴿZed-e-ki′-ah king of Judah according to all these words, saying, Bring your necks under the yoke of the king of Babylon, and serve him and his people, and live.   28:1; 38:17

13 ᴿWhy will ye die, thou and thy people, by the sword, by the

famine, and by the pestilence, as the LORD hath spoken against the nation that will not serve the king of Babylon?   38:23; [Ezek. 18:31]

14 Therefore hearken not unto the words of the prophets that speak unto you, saying, Ye shall not serve the king of Babylon: for they prophesy a lie unto you.

15 For I have ᴿnot sent them, saith the LORD, yet they prophesy a lie in my name; that I might drive you out, and that ye might perish, ye, and the prophets that prophesy unto you.   23:21; 29:9

16 Also I spake to the priests and to all this people, saying, Thus saith the LORD; Hearken not to the words of your prophets that prophesy unto you, saying, Behold, ᴿthe vessels of the LORD's house shall now shortly be brought again from Babylon: for they prophesy a lie unto you. 28:3

17 ᵀHearken not unto them; serve the king of Babylon, and live: wherefore should this city be laid waste?   *Do not listen*

18 But if they *be* prophets, and if the word of the LORD be with them, let them now make intercession to the LORD of hosts, that the vessels which are left in the house of the LORD, and *in* the house of the king of Judah, and at Jerusalem, go not to Babylon.

19 For thus saith the LORD of hosts ᴿconcerning the pillars, and concerning the sea, and concerning the bases, and concerning the residue of the vessels that remain in this city, 1 Kin. 7:15; 2 Kin. 25:13–17

20 Which Neb-u-chad-nez'-zar king of Babylon took not, when he carried away ᴿcaptive Jec-o-ni'-ah the son of Je-hoi'-a-kim king of Judah from Jerusalem to Babylon, and all the nobles of Judah and Jerusalem; 2 Kin. 24:14, 15

21 Yea, thus saith the LORD of hosts, the God of Israel, concerning the ᴿvessels that remain *in* the house of the LORD, and *in* the house of the king of Judah and of Jerusalem;   20:5

22 They shall be ᴿcarried to Babylon, and there shall they be until the day that I ᴿvisit them, saith the LORD; then ᴿwill I bring them up, and restore them to this place. 2 Kin. 25:13 · 2 Chr. 36:21 · Ezra 1:7

28 And ᴿit came to pass the same year, in the beginning of the reign of Zed-e-ki'-ah king of Judah, in the ᴿfourth year, *and* in the fifth month, *that* Han-a-ni'-ah the son of A'-zur the prophet, which *was* of Gib'-e-on, spake unto me in the house of the LORD, in the presence of the priests and of all the people, saying, 27:1 · 51:59

2 Thus speaketh the LORD of hosts, the God of Israel, saying, I have broken ᴿthe yoke of the king of Babylon.   27:12

3 Within two full years will I bring again into this place all the vessels of the LORD's house, that Neb-u-chad-nez'-zar king of Babylon took away from this place, and carried them to Babylon:

4 And I will bring again to this place ᵀJec-o-ni'-ah the son of Je-hoi'-a-kim king of Judah, with all the ᵀcaptives of Judah, that went into Babylon, saith the LORD: for I will break the yoke of the king of Babylon. Or *Coniah* or *Jehoiachin* · *exiles*

5 Then the prophet Jer-e-mi'-ah said unto the prophet Han-a-ni'-ah in the presence of the priests, and in the presence of all the people that stood in the house of the LORD,

6 Even the prophet Jer-e-mi'-ah said, ᴿA'-men: the LORD do so: the LORD perform thy words which thou hast prophesied, to bring again the vessels of the LORD's house, and all that is carried away captive, from Babylon into this place.   11:5; 1 Kin. 1:36; Ps. 41:13

7 Nevertheless hear thou now this word that I speak in thine ears, and in the ears of all the people;

8 The prophets that have been before me and before thee of old prophesied both against many countries, and against great kingdoms, of war, and of evil, and of pestilence.

9 The prophet which prophesieth of peace, when the word of the prophet shall come to pass, *then* shall the prophet be known, that the LORD hath truly sent him.

10 Then Han-a-ni'-ah the prophet took the ^Ryoke from off the prophet Jer-e-mi'-ah's neck, and brake it.   27:2

11 And Han-a-ni'-ah spake in the presence of all the people, saying, Thus saith the LORD; Even so will I break the yoke of Neb-u-chad-nez'-zar king of Babylon ^Rfrom the neck of all nations within the space of two full years. And the prophet Jer-e-mi'-ah went his way.   27:7

12 Then the word of the LORD came unto Jer-e-mi'-ah *the prophet,* after that Han-a-ni'-ah the prophet had broken the yoke from off the neck of the prophet Jer-e-mi'-ah, saying,

13 Go and tell Han-a-ni'-ah, saying, Thus saith the LORD; Thou hast broken the yokes of wood; but thou ^Tshalt make for them yokes of iron.   *hast made in their place*

14 For thus saith the LORD of hosts, the God of Israel; ^RI have put a yoke of iron upon the neck of all these nations, that they may serve Neb-u-chad-nez'-zar king of Babylon; and they shall serve him: and ^RI have given him the beasts of the field also.   27:7, 8 · 27:6

15 Then said the prophet Jer-e-mi'-ah unto Han-a-ni'-ah the prophet, Hear now, Han-a-ni'-ah; The LORD hath not sent thee; but ^Rthou makest this people to trust in a ^Rlie.   Ezek. 13:22; Zech. 13:3 · 27:10

16 Therefore thus saith the LORD; Behold, I will cast thee from off the face of the earth: this year thou shalt ^Rdie, because thou hast taught ^Rrebellion against the LORD.   20:6 · 29:32; Deut. 13:5

17 So Han-a-ni'-ah the prophet died the same year in the seventh month.

29 Now these *are* the words of the letter that Jer-e-mi'-ah the prophet sent from Jerusalem unto the ^Tresidue of the elders

which were ^Rcarried away captives, and to the priests, and to the prophets, and to all the people whom Neb-u-chad-nez'-zar had carried away captive from Jerusalem to Babylon;   *remainder* · 27:20

2 (After that ^RJec-o-ni'-ah the king, and the queen, and the eunuchs, the princes of Judah and Jerusalem, and the carpenters, and the smiths, were departed from Jerusalem;)   2 Kin. 24:12–16

3 By the hand of El'-a-sah the son of Sha'-phan, and Gem-a-ri'-ah the son of Hil-ki'-ah, (whom Zed-e-ki'-ah king of Judah sent unto Babylon to Neb-u-chad-nez'-zar king of Babylon) saying,

4 Thus saith the LORD of hosts, the God of Israel, unto all that are carried away captives, whom I have caused to be carried away from Jerusalem unto Babylon;

5 Build ye houses, and dwell *in them;* and plant gardens, and eat the fruit of them;

6 Take ye wives, and beget sons and daughters; and take wives for your sons, and give your daughters to husbands, that they may bear sons and daughters; that ye may be increased there, and not diminished.

7 And seek the peace of the city whither I have caused you to be carried away captives, ^Rand pray unto the LORD for it: for in the peace thereof shall ye have peace.   Ezra 6:10; 1 Tim. 2:2

8 For thus saith the LORD of hosts, the God of Israel; Let not your prophets and your diviners, that *be* in the midst of you, ^Rdeceive you, neither hearken to your dreams which ye cause to be dreamed.   14:14; 23:21; 27:14, 15; Eph. 5:6

9 For they prophesy ^Rfalsely unto you in my name: I have not sent them, saith the LORD.   37:19

10 For thus saith the LORD, That after ^Rseventy years be accomplished at Babylon I will visit you, and perform my good word toward you, in causing you to ^Rreturn to this place.   25:12 · Zeph. 2:7

11 For I know the thoughts that I

think toward you, saith the LORD, thoughts of peace, and not of evil, to give you an expected end.

12 Then shall ye call upon me, and ye shall go and pray unto me, and I will hearken unto you.

13 And ᴿye shall seek me, and find *me*, when ye shall search for me with all your heart.   Deut. 30:1–3

14 And I will be found of you, saith the LORD: and I will turn away your captivity, and ᴿI will gather you from all the nations, and from all the places whither I have driven you, saith the LORD; and I will bring you again into the place whence I caused you to be carried away captive.   Is. 43:5, 6

15 Because ye have said, The LORD hath ᵀraised us up prophets in Babylon;   *raised up prophets for us*

16 *Know* that thus saith the LORD of the king that sitteth upon the throne of David, and of all the people that dwelleth in this city, *and* of your brethren that are not gone forth with you into captivity;

17 Thus saith the LORD of hosts; Behold, I will send upon them the sword, the famine, and the pestilence, and will make them like ᴿvile figs, that cannot be eaten, they are so ᵀevil.   24:3, 8–10 · *bad*

18 And I will persecute them with the sword, with the famine, and with the pestilence, and ᴿwill deliver them to be removed to all the kingdoms of the earth, to be a curse, and an astonishment, and an hissing, and a reproach, among all the nations whither I have driven them: 15:4; 2 Chr. 29:8

19 Because they have not hearkened to my words, saith the LORD, which I sent unto them by my servants the prophets, rising up early and sending *them*; but ye would not hear, saith the LORD.

20 Hear ye therefore the word of the LORD, all ye of the captivity, whom I have sent from Jerusalem to Babylon:

21 Thus saith the LORD of hosts, the God of Israel, of Ahab the son of Ko-la′-iah, and of Zed-e-ki′-ah the son of Ma-a-se′-iah, which

prophesy a ᴿlie unto you in my name; Behold, I will deliver them into the hand of Neb-u-chad-rez′-zar king of Babylon; and he shall slay them before your eyes;   14:14

22 ᴿAnd of them shall be taken up a curse by all the captivity of Judah which *are* in Babylon, saying, The LORD make thee like Zed-e-ki′-ah and like Ahab, ᴿwhom the king of Babylon roasted in the fire;   Gen. 48:20; Is. 65:15 · Dan. 3:6, 21

23 Because ᴿthey have committed villany in Israel, and have committed adultery with their neighbours′ wives, and have spoken lying words in my name, which I have not commanded them; even I ᴿknow, and *am* a witness, saith the LORD.   23:14 · [16:17]

24 *Thus* shalt thou also speak to She-ma′-iah the Ne-hel′-a-mite, saying,

25 Thus speaketh the LORD of hosts, the God of Israel, saying, Because thou hast sent letters in thy name unto all the people that *are* at Jerusalem, ᴿand to Zeph-a-ni′-ah the son of Ma-a-se′-iah the priest, and to all the priests, saying,   21:1; 2 Kin. 25:18

26 The LORD hath made thee priest in the stead of Je-hoi′-a-da the priest, that ye should be officers in the house of the LORD, for every man *that is* ᴿmad, and maketh himself a prophet, that thou shouldest ᴿput him in prison, and in the stocks.   Acts 26:24 · 20:1, 2

27 Now therefore why hast thou not reproved Jer-e-mi′-ah of An′-a-thoth, which maketh himself a prophet to you?

28 For therefore he sent unto us in Babylon, saying, This *captivity is* long: build ye houses, and dwell *in them*; and plant gardens, and eat the fruit of them.

29 And Zeph-a-ni′-ah the priest read this letter in the ears of Jer-e-mi′-ah the prophet.

30 Then came the word of the LORD unto Jer-e-mi′-ah, saying,

31 Send to all them of the captivity, saying, Thus saith the LORD concerning She-ma′-iah the Ne-

hel'-a-mite; Because that She-ma'-iah hath prophesied unto you, ^Rand I sent him not, and he caused you to trust in a lie: 28:15

32 Therefore thus saith the Lord; Behold, I will punish She-ma'-iah the Ne-hel'-a-mite, and his seed: he shall not have a man to dwell among this people; neither shall he behold the good that I will do for my people, saith the Lord; ^Rbecause he hath taught rebellion against the Lord. 28:16

30 The word that came to Jer-e-mi'-ah from the Lord, saying,

2 Thus speaketh the Lord God of Israel, saying, Write thee all the words that I have spoken unto thee in a book.

3 For, lo, the days come, saith the Lord, that ^RI will bring again the captivity of my people Israel and Judah, saith the Lord: and I will cause them to return to the land that I gave to their fathers, and they shall possess it. Zeph. 3:20

4 And these *are* the words that the Lord spake concerning Israel and concerning Judah.

5 For thus saith the Lord; We have heard a voice of trembling, of ^Tfear, and not of peace.　*dread*

6 Ask ye now, and see whether a man doth travail with child? wherefore do I see every man with his hands on his loins, ^Ras a woman in travail, and all faces are turned into paleness? 4:31; 6:24

7 ^RAlas! for that day *is* great, so that none *is* like it: it *is* even the time of Jacob's trouble; but he shall be saved out of it. Amos 5:18

8 For it shall come to pass in that day, saith the Lord of hosts, *that* I will break his yoke from off thy neck, and will burst thy bonds, and strangers shall no more serve themselves of him:

☆ 9 But they shall serve the Lord their God, and David their king, whom I will raise up unto them.

10 Therefore fear thou not, O my servant Jacob, saith the Lord; neither be dismayed, O Israel: for, lo, I will save thee from afar, and thy seed from the land of their captivity; and Jacob shall return, and shall be in rest, and be quiet, and none shall make *him* afraid.

11 For I *am* with ^Rthee, saith the Lord, to save thee: though I make a full end of all nations whither I have scattered thee, yet will I not make a full end of thee: but I will correct thee ^Rin measure, and will not leave thee altogether unpunished. [Is. 43:2–5] · Ps. 6:1; Is. 27:8

12 For thus saith the Lord, ^RThy bruise *is* incurable, *and* thy wound *is* grievous. 2 Chr. 36:16

13 *There is* none to plead thy cause, that thou mayest be bound up: ^Rthou hast no healing medicines. 8:22

14 ^RAll thy lovers have forgotten thee; they seek thee not; for I have wounded thee with the wound of an enemy, with the chastisement of a cruel one, for the multitude of thine iniquity; ^R*because* thy sins were increased. 22:20, 22 · 5:6

15 Why criest thou for thine affliction? thy sorrow *is* incurable for the multitude of thine iniquity: *because* thy sins were increased, I have done these things unto thee.

16 Therefore all they that devour thee ^Rshall be devoured; and all thine adversaries, every one of them, shall go into captivity; and they that spoil thee shall be a spoil, and all that prey upon thee will I give for a prey. Ex. 23:22

17 ^RFor I will restore health unto thee, and I will heal thee of thy wounds, saith the Lord; because they called thee an Outcast, *saying*, This *is* Zion, whom no man seeketh after. Ex. 15:26; Ps. 107:20

18 Thus saith the Lord; Behold, I will bring again the captivity of Jacob's tents, and have mercy on his dwellingplaces; and the city shall be builded upon her own heap, and the palace shall remain after the manner thereof.

19 And out of them shall proceed thanksgiving and the voice of them that make merry: and I will multiply them, and they shall

not be few; I will also glorify them, and they shall not be small.

20 Their children also shall be ᴿas aforetime, and their congregation shall be established before me; and I will punish all that oppress them.   Is. 1:26

21 And their nobles shall be of themselves, ᴿand their governor shall proceed from the midst of them; and I will cause him to draw near, and he shall approach unto me: for who *is* this that engaged his heart to approach unto me? saith the LORD. Gen. 49:10

22 And ye shall be ᴿmy people, and I will be your God.   Zech. 13:9

23 Behold, the ᴿwhirlwind of the LORD goeth forth with fury, a continuing whirlwind: it shall fall with pain upon the head of the wicked.   23:19, 20; 25:32

24 The fierce anger of the LORD shall not return, until he have done *it*, and until he have performed the intents of his heart: in the latter days ye shall consider it.

31 At ᴿthe same time, saith the LORD, ᴿwill I be the God of all the families of Israel, and they shall be my people. 30:24 · 30:22

2 Thus saith the LORD, The people *which were* left of the sword found grace in the wilderness; *even* Israel, when ᴿI went to cause him to rest.   Ps. 95:11; Is. 63:14

3 The LORD hath appeared of old unto me, *saying*, Yea, I have loved thee with ᴿan everlasting love: therefore with lovingkindness have I drawn thee. Rom. 11:28

4 Again I will build thee, and thou shalt be built, O virgin of Israel: thou shalt again be adorned with thy ᴿtabrets, and shalt go forth in the dances of them that make merry.   Ps. 149:3

5 Thou shalt yet plant vines upon the mountains of Sa-ma'-ri-a: the planters shall plant, and shall eat *them* as common things.

6 For there shall be a day, *that* the watchmen upon the mount E'-phra-im shall cry, ᴿArise ye, and let us go up to Zion unto the LORD our God.   [Is. 2:3; Mic. 4:2]

7 For thus saith the LORD: ᴿSing with gladness for Jacob, and shout among the chief of the nations: publish ye, praise ye, and say, O LORD, save thy people, the remnant of Israel.   Is. 12:5, 6

8 Behold, I will bring them from the north country, and ᴿgather them from the coasts of the earth, *and* with them the blind and the lame, the woman with child and her that travaileth with child together: a great company shall return thither.   Ezek. 20:34, 41

9 ᴿThey shall come with weeping, and with supplications will I lead them: I will cause them to walk ᴿby the rivers of waters in a straight way, wherein they shall not stumble: for I am a father to Israel, and E'-phra-im *is* my firstborn.   [50:4; Ps. 126:5] · Is. 35:8; 43:19

10 Hear the word of the LORD, O ye nations, and declare *it* in the isles afar off, and say, He that scattered Israel ᴿwill gather him, and keep him, as a shepherd *doth* his flock.   Is. 40:11; Ezek. 34:12–14

11 For ᴿthe LORD hath redeemed Jacob, and ransomed him ᴿfrom the hand of *him that was* stronger than he.   Is. 44:23; 48:20 · Is. 49:24

12 Therefore they shall come and sing in the height of Zion, and shall flow together to the goodness of the LORD, for wheat, and for wine, and for oil, and for the young of the flock and of the herd: and their soul shall be as a watered garden; and they shall not sorrow any more at all.

13 Then shall the virgin rejoice in the dance, both young men and old together: for I will turn their mourning into joy, and will comfort them, and make them rejoice from their sorrow.

14 And I will ᵀsatiate the soul of the priests with fatness, and my people shall be satisfied with my goodness, saith the LORD.   *fill*

15 Thus saith the LORD; ᴿA voice ☆ was heard in Ra'-mah, lamentation, *and* bitter weeping; Ra'-hel weeping for her children refused

to be comforted for her children, because they *were* not. Matt. 2:17, 18

16 Thus saith the LORD; Refrain thy voice from weeping, and thine eyes from tears: for thy work shall be rewarded, saith the LORD; and they shall come again from the land of the enemy.

17 And there is ^Rhope in ^Tthine end, saith the LORD, that thy children shall come again to their own border.   29:11 · *thy future*

18 I have surely heard E'-phra-im bemoaning himself *thus;* Thou hast ^Rchastised me, and I was chastised, as a bullock unaccustomed *to the yoke:* turn thou me, and I shall be turned; for thou *art* the LORD my God.   Job 5:17; Ps. 94:12

19 Surely ^Rafter that I was turned, I repented; and after that I was instructed, I smote upon *my* thigh: I was ashamed, yea, even confounded, because I did bear the reproach of my youth. Deut. 30:2

20 *Is* E'-phra-im my dear son? *is* he a pleasant child? for since I spake against him, I do earnestly remember him still: ^Rtherefore my bowels are troubled for him; I will surely have mercy upon him, saith the LORD.   Gen. 43:30; Is. 63:15

21 Set thee up ^Twaymarks, make thee high heaps: ^Rset thine heart toward the highway, *even* the way *which* thou wentest: turn again, O virgin of Israel, turn again to these thy cities.   signposts · 50:5

22 How long wilt thou ^Rgo about, O thou backsliding daughter? for the LORD hath created a new thing in the earth, A woman shall compass a man.   2:18, 23, 36

23 Thus saith the LORD of hosts, the God of Israel; As yet they shall use this speech in the land of Judah and in the cities thereof, when I shall bring again their captivity; ^RThe LORD bless thee, O habitation of justice, *and* ^Rmountain of holiness.   Is. 1:26 · [Zech. 8:3]

24 And there shall dwell in Judah itself, and in all the cities thereof together, husbandmen, and they *that* go forth with flocks.

25 For I have satiated the weary soul, and I have replenished every sorrowful soul.

26 Upon this I awaked, and beheld; and my sleep was ^Rsweet unto me.   Prov. 3:24

27 Behold, the days come, saith the LORD, that ^RI will sow the house of Israel and the house of Judah with the seed of man, and with the seed of beast. Ezek. 36:9–11

28 And it shall come to pass, *that* like as I have ^Rwatched over them, ^Rto pluck up, and to break down, and to throw down, and to destroy, and to afflict; so will I watch over them, to build, and to plant, saith the LORD.   44:27 · 18:7

29 ^RIn those days they shall say no more, The fathers have eaten a sour grape, and the children's teeth are set on edge.   Lam. 5:7

30 ^RBut every one shall die for his own iniquity: every man that eateth the sour grape, his teeth shall be set on edge.   [Gal. 6:5, 7]

31 Behold, the ^Rdays come, saith ☆ the LORD, that I will make a new covenant with the house of Israel, and with the house of Judah: 32:40

32 Not according to the covenant that I made with their fathers in the day *that* ^RI took them by the hand to bring them out of the land of Egypt; which my covenant they brake, although I was an husband unto them, saith the LORD: Deut. 1:31; Is. 63:12

33 But this *shall be* the covenant ☆ that I will make with the house of Israel; After those days, saith the LORD, I will put my law in their inward parts, and write it in their hearts; and will be their God, and they shall be my people.

34 And they shall teach no more ☆ every man his neighbour, and every man his brother, saying, Know the LORD: for ^Rthey shall all know me, from the least of them unto the greatest of them, saith the LORD: for I will forgive their iniquity, and I will remember their sin no more.   [John 6:45; 1 Cor. 2:10]

35 Thus saith the LORD, which giveth the sun for a light by day, *and* the ordinances of the moon

and of the stars for a light by night, which divideth the sea when the waves thereof roar; The LORD of hosts *is* his name:

36 ᴿIf those ordinances depart from before me, saith the LORD, *then* the seed of Israel also shall cease from being a nation before me for ever. Ps. 148:6; Is. 54:9, 10

37 Thus saith the LORD; ᴿIf heaven above can be measured, and the foundations of the earth searched out beneath, I will also ᴿcast off all the seed of Israel for all that they have done, saith the LORD. Is. 40:12 · [Rom. 11:2–5, 26, 27]

38 Behold, the days come, saith the LORD, that the city shall be built to the LORD ᴿfrom the tower of Ha-nan'-e-el unto the gate of the corner. Neh. 3:1; 12:39; Zech. 14:10

39 And the measuring line shall yet go forth over against it upon the hill Ga'-reb, and shall compass about to Go'-ath.

40 And the whole valley of the dead bodies, and of the ashes, and all the fields unto the brook of Kid'-ron, ᴿunto the corner of the horse gate toward the east, *shall be* holy unto the LORD; it shall not be plucked up, nor thrown down any more for ever. Neh. 3:28

32 The word that came to Jer-e-mi'-ah from the LORD ᴿin the tenth year of Zed-e-ki'-ah king of Judah, which *was* the eighteenth year of Neb-u-chad-rez'-zar. 39:1, 2; 2 Kin. 25:1, 2

2 For then the king of Babylon's army besieged Jerusalem: and Jer-e-mi'-ah the prophet was shut up ᴿin the court of the prison, which *was* in the king of Judah's house. 33:1; 37:21; 39:14; Neh. 3:25

3 For Zed-e-ki'-ah king of Judah had shut him up, saying, Wherefore dost thou ᴿprophesy, and say, Thus saith the LORD, ᴿBehold, I will give this city into the hand of the king of Babylon, and he shall take it; 26:8, 9 · 21:3–7

4 And Zed-e-ki'-ah king of Judah ᴿshall not escape out of the hand of the Chal-de'-ans, but shall surely be delivered into the hand of the king of Babylon, and shall speak with him mouth to mouth, and his eyes shall behold his ᴿeyes; 52:9; 2 Kin. 25:4–7 · 39:5

5 And he shall ᴿlead Zed-e-ki'-ah to Babylon, and there shall he be ᴿuntil I visit him, saith the LORD: ᴿthough ye fight with the Chal-de'-ans, ye shall not ᵀprosper. 27:22; 39:7 · 27:22 · 21:4 · *succeed*

6 And Jer-e-mi'-ah said, The word of the LORD came unto me, saying,

7 Behold, Ha-nam'-e-el the son of Shal'-lum thine uncle shall come unto thee, saying, Buy thee my field that *is* in An'-a-thoth: for the ᴿright of redemption *is* thine to buy *it*. Lev. 25:24, 25, 32; Ruth 4:4

8 So Ha-nam'-e-el mine uncle's ☆ son came to me in the court of the prison according to the word of the LORD, and said unto me, Buy my field, I pray thee, that *is* in An'-a-thoth, which *is* in the country of Benjamin: for the right of inheritance *is* thine, and the redemption *is* thine; buy *it* for thyself. Then I knew that this *was* the word of the LORD.

9 And I bought the field of Ha-nam'-e-el my uncle's son, that *was* in An'-a-thoth, and ᴿweighed him the money, *even* seventeen shek'-els of silver. Gen. 23:16; Zech. 11:12

10 And I subscribed the evidence, and sealed *it*, and took witnesses, and weighed *him* the money in the balances.

11 So I took the evidence of the purchase, *both* that which was sealed *according* to the law and custom, and that which was open:

12 And I gave the ᵀevidence of the purchase unto Ba'-ruch the son of Ne-ri'-ah, the son of Ma-a-se'-iah, in the sight of Ha-nam'-e-el mine uncle's *son*, and in the presence of the witnesses that subscribed the book of the purchase, before all the Jews that sat in the court of the prison. *deed*

13 And I charged ᴿBa'-ruch before them, saying, 36:4

14 Thus saith the LORD of hosts, the God of Israel; Take these ᵀevidences, this ᵀevidence of the

purchase, both which is sealed, and this evidence which is open; and put them in an earthen vessel, that they may ᵀcontinue many days.   *deeds · deed · last*

15 For thus saith the LORD of hosts, the God of Israel; Houses and fields and vineyards shall be ᴿpossessed again in this land.[31:5]

16 Now when I had delivered the evidence of the purchase unto Ba'-ruch the son of Ne-ri'-ah, I prayed unto the LORD, saying,

17 Ah Lord GOD! behold, thou hast made the heaven and the earth by thy great power and stretched out arm, *and* ᴿthere is nothing too hard for thee: Zech. 8:6

18 Thou shewest lovingkindness unto thousands, and recompensest the iniquity of the fathers into the bosom of their children after them: the Great, the Mighty God, the LORD of hosts, *is* his name,

19 ᴿGreat in counsel, and mighty in ᵀwork: for thine eyes *are* open upon all the ways of the sons of men: to give every one according to his ways, and according to the fruit of his doings: Is. 28:29 · *deed*

20 Which hast set signs and wonders in the land of Egypt, *even* unto this day, and in Israel, and among *other* men; and hast made thee a name, as at this day;

21 And ᴿhast brought forth thy people Israel out of the land of Egypt with signs, and with wonders, and with a strong hand, and with a stretched out arm, and with great terror;   Ex. 6:6; Ps. 136:11, 12

22 And hast given them this land, which thou didst swear to their fathers to give them, a land flowing with milk and honey;

23 And they came in, and possessed it; but ᴿthey obeyed not thy voice, neither walked in thy law; they have done nothing of all that thou commandedst them to do: therefore thou hast caused all this evil to come upon them: [Neh. 9:26]

24 Behold the ᵀmounts, they are come unto the city to take it; and the city is given into the hand of the Chal-de'-ans, that fight

against it, because of the sword, and of the famine, and of the pestilence: and what thou hast spoken is come to pass; and, behold, thou seest *it*.   *siege mounds*

25 And thou hast said unto me, O Lord GOD, Buy thee the field for money, and take witnesses; for the city is given into the hand of the Chal-de'-ans.

26 Then came the word of the LORD unto Jer-e-mi'-ah, saying,

27 Behold, I *am* the LORD, the ᴿGod of all flesh: is there any thing too hard for me? [Num. 16:22]

28 Therefore thus saith the LORD; Behold, I will give this city into the hand of the Chal-de'-ans, and into the hand of ᵀNeb-u-chad-rez'-zar king of Babylon, and he shall take it: Or *Nebuchadnezzar*

29 And the Chal-de'-ans, that fight against this city, shall come and ᴿset fire on this city, and burn it with the houses, ᴿupon whose roofs they have offered incense unto Ba'-al, and poured out drink offerings unto other gods, to provoke me to anger.   52:13 · 19:13

30 For the children of Israel and the children of Judah ᴿhave only done evil before me from their youth: for the children of Israel have only provoked me to anger with the work of their hands, saith the LORD.   Is. 63:10; Ezek. 20:28

31 For this city hath been to me *as* a provocation of mine anger and of my fury from the day that they built it even unto this day; ᴿthat I should remove it from before my face,   2 Kin. 23:27; 24:3

32 Because of all the evil of the children of Israel and of the children of Judah, which they have done to provoke me to anger, ᴿthey, their kings, their princes, their priests, and their prophets, and the men of Judah, and the inhabitants of Jerusalem. Dan. 9:8

33 And they have turned unto me the ᴿback, and not the face: though I taught them, ᴿrising up early and teaching *them*, yet they have not ᵀhearkened to receive instruction.   2:27; 7:24 · 7:13 · *listened*

34 But they ^Rset their abominations in the house, which is called by my name, to defile it. Ezek. 8:5, 6

35 And they built the high places of Ba'-al, which *are* in the valley of the son of Hin'-nom, to ^Rcause their sons and their daughters to pass through *the fire* unto Mo'-lech; which I commanded them not, neither came it into my mind, that they should do this abomination, to cause Judah to sin.   7:31; 19:5; 2 Chr. 28:2, 3; 33:6

36 And now therefore thus saith the LORD, the God of Israel, concerning this city, whereof ye say, It shall be delivered into the hand of the king of Babylon by the sword, and by the famine, and by the pestilence;

37 Behold, I will ^Rgather them out of all countries, whither I have driven them in mine anger, and in my fury, and in great wrath; and I will bring them again unto this place, and I will cause them ^Rto dwell safely: 23:3; 29:14; 31:10 · 33:16

38 And they shall be ^Rmy people, and I will be their God: [24:7]

39 And I will ^Rgive them one heart, and one way, that they may fear me for ever, for the good of them, and of their children after them: [24:7; Ezek. 11:19]

40 And ^RI will make an everlasting covenant with them, that I will not turn away from them, to do them good; but ^RI will put my fear in their hearts, that they shall not depart from me.   Ezek. 37:26 · [31:33]

41 Yea, ^RI will rejoice over them to do them good, and ^RI will plant them in this land assuredly with my whole heart and with my whole soul.   Is. 62:5 · Amos 9:15

42 For thus saith the LORD; Like as I have brought all this great ^Tevil upon this people, so will I bring upon them all the good that I have promised them.   calamity

43 And fields shall be bought in this land, ^Rwhereof ye say, It *is* desolate without man or beast; it is given into the hand of the Chal-de'-ans.   33:10

44 Men shall buy fields for money, and subscribe evidences, and seal *them*, and take witnesses in ^Rthe land of Benjamin, and in the places about Jerusalem, and in the cities of Judah, and in the cities of the mountains, and in the cities of the valley, and in the cities of the south: for ^RI will cause their captivity to return, saith the LORD.   17:26 · 33:7, 11

33 Moreover the word of the LORD came unto Jer-e-mi'-ah the second time, while he was yet ^Rshut^T up in the court of the prison, saying,   32:2, 3 · *imprisoned*

2 Thus saith the LORD the ^Rmaker thereof, the LORD that formed it, to establish it; ^Rthe LORD *is* his name;   Is. 37:26 · Ex. 15:3

3 ^RCall unto me, and I will answer thee, and shew thee great and mighty things, which thou knowest not.   Ps. 91:15; [Is. 55:6, 7]

4 For thus saith the LORD, the God of Israel, concerning the houses of this city, and concerning the houses of the kings of Judah, which are thrown down by the mounts, and by the sword;

5 They come to fight with the Chal-de'-ans, but *it is* to ^Rfill them with the dead bodies of men, whom I have slain in mine anger and in my fury, and for all whose wickedness I have hid my face from this city.   21:4–7; 32:5; 2 Kin. 23:14

6 Behold, I will bring it health and cure, and I will cure them, and will reveal unto them the abundance of peace and truth.

7 And ^RI will cause the captivity of Judah and the captivity of Israel to return, and will build them, ^Ras at the first.   30:3 · Is. 1:26

8 And I will ^Rcleanse them from all their iniquity, whereby they have sinned against me; and I will pardon all their iniquities, whereby they have sinned, and whereby they have transgressed against me.   Ps. 51:2; Is. 44:22; Zech. 13:1

9 ^RAnd it shall be to me a name of joy, a praise and an honour before all the nations of the earth, which shall hear all the good that I do unto them: and they shall

^Rfear and tremble for all the goodness and for all the prosperity that I procure unto it.   13:11 · Is. 60:5

10 Thus saith the LORD; Again there shall be heard in this place, which ye say *shall be* desolate without man and without beast, *even* in the cities of Judah, and in the streets of Jerusalem, that are desolate, without man, and without inhabitant, and without beast,

11 The voice of joy, and the voice of gladness, the voice of the bridegroom, and the voice of the bride, the voice of them that shall say, Praise the LORD of hosts: for the LORD *is* good; for his mercy *endureth* for ever: *and* of them that shall bring ^Rthe sacrifice of praise into the house of the LORD. For I will cause to return the captivity of the land, as at the first, saith the LORD.   Ps. 107:22; Heb. 13:15

12 Thus saith the LORD of hosts; ^RAgain in this place, which is desolate without man and without beast, and in all the cities thereof, shall be an habitation of shepherds causing *their* flocks to lie down.   Is. 65:10; [Zeph. 2:6, 7]

13 ^RIn the cities of the mountains, in the cities of the vale, and in the cities of the south, and in the land of Benjamin, and in the places about Jerusalem, and in the cities of Judah, shall the flocks ^Rpass again under the hands of him that telleth *them,* saith the LORD.   17:26 · Lev. 27:33; [Luke 15:4]

14 Behold, the days come, saith the LORD, that ^RI will perform that good thing which I have promised unto the house of Israel and to the house of Judah.   Is. 32:1; Hag. 2:6–9

☆ 15 In those days, and at that time, will I cause the ^RBranch of righteousness to grow up unto David; and he shall execute judgment and righteousness in the land.   Is. 4:2; 11:1; Zech. 3:8; 6:12, 13

16 In those days shall Judah be saved, and Jerusalem shall dwell safely: and this *is the name* wherewith she shall be called, The LORD our righteousness.

17 For thus saith the LORD;

David shall never ^Rwant a man to sit upon the throne of the house of Israel;   1 Kin. 2:4; Ps. 89:29; [Luke 1:32]

18 Neither shall the ^Rpriests the Levites want a man before me to offer burnt offerings, and to kindle meat offerings, and to do sacrifice continually.   Josh. 3:3

19 And the word of the LORD came unto Jer-e-mi′-ah, saying,

20 Thus saith the LORD; If ye can break my covenant of the day, and my covenant of the night, and that there should not be day and night in their season;

21 *Then* may also ^Rmy covenant be broken with David my servant, that he should not have a son to reign upon his throne; and with the Levites the priests, my ministers.   2 Sam. 23:5; 2 Chr. 7:18; Ps. 89:34

22 As the host of heaven cannot be numbered, neither the sand of the sea measured: so will I ^Rmultiply the seed of David my servant, and the ^RLevites that minister unto me.   Ezek. 36:10, 11 · Is. 66:21

23 Moreover the word of the LORD came to Jer-e-mi′-ah, saying,

24 Considerest thou not what this people have spoken, saying, The two families which the LORD hath chosen, he hath even cast them off? thus they have ^Rdespised my people, that they should be no more a nation before them.   Neh. 4:2–4; Esth. 3:6–8; Ps. 44:13, 14

25 Thus saith the LORD; If ^Rmy covenant *be* not with day and night, *and if* I have not ^Rappointed the ordinances of heaven and earth;   Gen. 8:22 · Ps. 74:16; 104:19

26 Then will I cast away the seed of Jacob, and David my servant, *so* that I will not take *any* of his seed *to be* rulers over the seed of Abraham, Isaac, and Jacob: for I will cause their captivity to return, and have mercy on them.

34 The word which came unto Jer-e-mi′-ah from the LORD, ^Rwhen Neb-u-chad-nez′-zar king of Babylon, and all his army, and ^Rall the kingdoms of the earth of his dominion, and all the people, fought against Jerusalem, and against all the cities thereof, say-ing, 39:1; 52:4 · 1:15; 25:9; Dan. 2:37, 38

2 Thus saith the LORD, the God of Israel; Go and Rspeak to Zed-e-ki'-ah king of Judah, and tell him, Thus saith the LORD; Behold, I will give this city into the hand of the king of Babylon, and he shall burn it with fire: 22:1; 2 Chr. 36:11, 12

3 And Rthou shalt not escape out of his hand, but shalt surely be taken, and delivered into his hand; and thine eyes shall behold the eyes of the king of Babylon, and he shall speak with thee Rmouth to mouth, and thou shalt go to Babylon. 52:7–11 · 2 Kin. 25:6, 7

4 Yet hear the word of the LORD, O Zed-e-ki'-ah king of Ju-dah; Thus saith the LORD of thee, Thou shalt not die by the sword:

5 But thou shalt die in peace: and with Rthe burnings of thy fathers, the former kings which were before thee, Rso shall they burn odours for thee; and they will lament thee, saying, Ah lord! for I have pronounced the word, saith the LORD. 2 Chr. 16:14 · Dan. 2:46

6 Then Jer-e-mi'-ah the prophet spake all these words unto Zed-e-ki'-ah king of Judah in Jerusalem,

7 When the king of Babylon's army fought against Jerusalem, and against all the cities of Judah that were left, against La'-chish, and against A-ze'-kah: for Rthese defenced cities remained of the cities of Judah. 2 Kin. 18:13; 19:8

8 This is the word that came unto Jer-e-mi'-ah from the LORD, after that the king Zed-e-ki'-ah had made a covenant with all the people which were at Jerusalem, to proclaim liberty unto them;

9 That every man should let his manservant, and every man his maidservant, being an Hebrew or an Hebrewess, go free; that none should serve himself of them, to wit, of a Jew his brother.

10 Now when all the princes, and all the people, which had entered into the covenant, heard that every one should let his man-servant, and every one his maid-servant, go free, that none should Tserve themselves of them any more, then they obeyed, and let them go. keep them in bondage

11 But afterward they Tturned, and caused the servants and the handmaids, whom they had let go free, to return, and brought them into subjection for servants and for handmaids. changed their minds

12 Therefore the word of the LORD came to Jer-e-mi'-ah from the LORD, saying,

13 Thus saith the LORD, the God of Israel; I made a Rcovenant with your fathers in the day that I brought them forth out of the land of Egypt, out of the house of bondmen, saying, Ex. 24:3, 7, 8

14 At the end of Rseven years let ye go every man his brother an Hebrew, which hath been sold un-to thee; and when he hath served thee six years, thou shalt let him go free from thee: but your fathers hearkened not unto me, neither inclined their ear. Deut. 15:12

15 And ye were now turned, and had done right in my sight, in pro-claiming liberty every man to his neighbour; and ye had made a covenant before me in the house which is called by my name:

16 But ye turned and Rpolluted my name, and caused every man his servant, and every man his handmaid, whom he had set at liberty at their pleasure, to return, and brought them into subjection, to be unto you for servants and for handmaids. Ex. 20:7; Lev. 19:12

17 Therefore thus saith the LORD; Ye have not hearkened unto me, in proclaiming liberty, every one to his brother, and every man to his neighbour: Rbehold, I pro-claim a liberty for you, saith the LORD, to the sword, to the pesti-lence, and to the famine; and I will make you to be removed into all the kingdoms of the earth. [Gal. 6:7]

18 And I will give the men that have transgressed my covenant, which have not performed the words of the covenant which they had made before me, when they

cut the calf in twain, and passed between the parts thereof,

19 The princes of Judah, and the princes of Jerusalem, the eunuchs, and the priests, and all the people of the land, which passed between the parts of the calf;

20 I will even ^Rgive them into the hand of their enemies, and into the hand of them that seek their life: and their ^Rdead bodies shall be for meat unto the fowls of the heaven, and to the beasts of the earth. 2 Kin. 25:19–21 · 1 Kin. 14:11; 16:4

21 And Zed-e-ki′-ah king of Judah and his princes will I give into the hand of their enemies, and into the hand of them that seek their life, and into the hand of the king of Babylon's army, ^Rwhich are gone up from you. 37:5–11; 39:4–7

22 ^RBehold, I will command, saith the LORD, and cause them to return to this city; and they shall fight against it, and take it, and burn it with fire: and ^RI will make the cities of Judah a desolation without an inhabitant. 37:8, 10 · 9:11

35 The word which came unto Jer-e-mi′-ah from the LORD in the days of Je-hoi′-a-kim the son of Jo-si′-ah king of Judah, saying,

2 Go unto the house of the ^RRe′-chab-ites, and speak unto them, and bring them into the house of the LORD, into one of ^Rthe chambers, and give them wine to drink. 1 Chr. 2:55 · 1 Chr. 9:26, 33

3 Then I took Ja-az-a-ni′-ah the son of Jer-e-mi′-ah, the son of Hab-a-zi-ni′-ah, and his brethren, and all his sons, and the whole house of the Re′-chab-ites;

4 And I brought them into the house of the LORD, into the chamber of the sons of Ha′-nan, the son of Ig-da-li′-ah, a man of God, which *was* by the chamber of the princes, which *was* above the chamber of Ma-a-se′-iah the son of Shal′-lum, ^Rthe keeper of the door: 2 Kin. 12:9; 25:18; 1 Chr. 9:18, 19

5 And I set before the sons of the house of the Re′-chab-ites pots full of wine, and cups, and I said unto them, Drink ye wine.

6 But they said, We will drink no wine: for ^RJon′-a-dab the son of Re′-chab our father commanded us, saying, Ye shall drink ^Rno wine, *neither* ye, nor your sons for ever: 2 Kin. 10:15, 23 · Ezek. 44:21

7 Neither shall ye build house, nor sow seed, nor plant vineyard, nor have *any*: but all your days ye shall dwell in tents; ^Rthat ye may live many days in the land where ye *be* strangers. Ex. 20:12; Eph. 6:2, 3

8 Thus have we ^Robeyed the voice of Jon′-a-dab the son of Re′-chab our father in all that he hath charged us, to drink no wine all our days, we, our wives, our sons, nor our daughters; [Eph. 6:1; Col. 3:20]

9 Nor to build houses for us to dwell in: neither have we vineyard, nor field, nor seed:

10 But we have dwelt in tents, and have obeyed, and done according to all that Jon′-a-dab our father commanded us.

11 But it came to pass, when Neb-u-chad-rez′-zar king of Babylon came up into the land, that we said, Come, and let us ^Rgo to Jerusalem for fear of the army of the Chal-de′-ans, and for fear of the army of the Syrians: so we dwell at Jerusalem. 4:5–7; 8:14

12 Then came the word of the LORD unto Jer-e-mi′-ah, saying,

13 Thus saith the LORD of hosts, the God of Israel; Go and tell the men of Judah and the inhabitants of Jerusalem, Will ye not ^Rreceive instruction to hearken to my words? saith the LORD. [Is. 28:9–12]

14 The words of Jon′-a-dab the son of Re′-chab, that he commanded his sons not to drink wine, are performed; for unto this day they drink none, but obey their father's commandment: notwithstanding I have spoken unto you, rising early and speaking; but ye hearkened not unto me.

15 I have sent also unto you all my ^Rservants the prophets, rising up early and sending *them*, saying, ^RReturn ye now every man from his evil way, and amend your doings, and go not after other

gods to serve them, and ye shall dwell in the land which I have given to you and to your fathers: but ye have not inclined your ear, nor hearkened unto me. 29:19 · 18:11

16 Because the sons of Jon'-a-dab the son of Re'-chab have performed the commandment of their Rfather, which he command-ed them; but this people hath not hearkened unto me:　[Heb. 12:9]

17 Therefore thus saith the LORD God of hosts, the God of Israel; Behold, I will bring upon Judah and upon all the inhabitants of Jerusalem all the Tevil that I have pronounced against them: Rbe-cause I have spoken unto them, but they have not heard; and I have called unto them, but they have not answered.　doom · Is. 65:12

18 And Jer-e-mi'-ah said unto the house of the Re'-chab-ites, Thus saith the LORD of hosts, the God of Israel; Because ye have obeyed the commandment of Jon'-a-dab your father, and kept all his precepts, and done accord-ing unto all that he hath com-manded you:

19 Therefore thus saith the LORD of hosts, the God of Israel; Jon'-a-dab the son of Re'-chab shall not want a man to Rstand before me for ever.　[Luke 21:36; Eph. 6:2, 3]

36 And it came to pass in the Rfourth year of Je-hoi'-a-kim the son of Jo-si'-ah king of Judah, that this word came unto Jer-e-mi'-ah from the LORD, saying, 45:1

2 Take thee a Rroll of a book, and Rwrite therein all the words that I have spoken unto thee against Israel, and against Judah, and against all the nations, from the day I spake unto thee, from the days of Jo-si'-ah, even into this day.　Is. 8:1; Ezek. 2:9; Zech. 5:1 · Hab. 2:2

3 It Rmay be that the house of Judah will hear all the evil which I purpose to do unto them; that they may return every man from his evil way; that I may forgive their iniquity and their sin.　26:3

4 Then Jer-e-mi'-ah called Ba'-ruch the son of Ne-ri'-ah: and Ba'-ruch wrote from the mouth of Jer-e-mi'-ah all the words of the LORD, which he had spoken unto him, upon a roll of a book.

5 And Jer-e-mi'-ah commanded Ba'-ruch, saying, I am Tshut up; I cannot go into Tthe house of the LORD:　confined · The temple

6 Therefore go thou, and read in the roll, which thou hast writ-ten from my mouth, the words of the LORD in the ears of the people in the LORD's house upon the fast-ing day: and also thou shalt read them in the ears of all Judah that come out of their cities.

7 It may be they will present their supplication before the LORD, and will Treturn every one from his evil way: for great is the anger and the fury that the LORD hath pronounced against this peo-ple.　turn

8 And Ba'-ruch the son of Ne-ri'-ah did according to all that Jer-e-mi'-ah the prophet command-ed him, reading in the book the words of the LORD in the LORD's house.

9 And it came to pass in the fifth year of Je-hoi'-a-kim the son of Jo-si'-ah king of Judah, in the ninth month, that they pro-claimed a fast before the LORD to all the people in Jerusalem, and to all the people that came from the cities of Judah unto Jerusalem.

10 Then read Ba'-ruch in the book the words of Jer-e-mi'-ah in the house of the LORD, in the chamber of Gem-a-ri'-ah the son of Sha'-phan the scribe, in the higher court, at the Rentry of the new gate of the LORD's house, in the ears of all the people.　26:10

11 When Mi-cha'-iah the son of Gem-a-ri'-ah, the son of Sha'-phan, had heard out of the book all the words of the LORD,

12 Then he went down into the king's house, into the scribe's chamber: and, lo, all the princes sat there, even RE-lish'-a-ma the scribe, and De-la'-iah the son of She-ma'-iah, and REl-na'-than the son of Ach'-bor, and Gem-a-ri'-ah

the son of Sha'-phan, and Zed-e-ki'-ah the son of Han-a-ni'-ah, and all the princes. 41:1 · 26:22

13 Then Mi-cha'-iah declared unto them all the words that he had heard, when Ba'-ruch read the book in the ᵀears of the people. *hearing*

14 Therefore all the princes sent Je-hu'-di the son of Neth-a-ni'-ah, the son of Shel-e-mi'-ah, the son of Cu'-shi, unto Ba'-ruch, saying, Take in thine hand the ᵀroll wherein thou hast read in the ᵀears of the people, and come. So Ba'-ruch the son of Ne-ri'-ah took the roll in his hand, and came unto them. *scroll · hearing*

15 And they said unto him, Sit down now, and read it in our ears. So Ba'-ruch read *it* in their ears.

16 Now it came to pass, when they had heard all the words, they ᵀwere afraid both one and other, and said unto Ba'-ruch, We will surely tell the king of all these words. *looked in fear from one to another*

17 And they asked Ba'-ruch, saying, Tell us now, How didst thou write all these words ᵀat his mouth? *Lit. from*

18 Then Ba'-ruch answered them, He pronounced all these words unto me with his mouth, and I wrote *them* with ink in the book.

19 Then said the princes unto Ba'-ruch, Go, hide thee, thou and Jer-e-mi'-ah; and let no man know where ye be.

20 And they went in to the king into the court, but they laid up the roll in the chamber of E-lish'-a-ma the scribe, and told all the words in the ears of the king.

21 So the king sent Je-hu'-di to ᵀfetch the roll: and he took it out of E-lish'-a-ma the scribe's chamber. And Je-hu'-di read it in the ears of the king, and in the ears of all the princes which stood beside the king. *bring the scroll*

22 Now the king sat in ᴿthe winterhouse in the ninth month: and *there was a fire* on the hearth burning before him. Judg. 3:20

23 And it came to pass, *that* when Je-hu'-di had read three or four leaves, he cut it with the penknife, and cast *it* into the fire that *was* on the hearth, until all the ᵀroll was consumed in the fire that *was* on the hearth. *scroll*

24 Yet they were not afraid, nor ᴿrent their garments, *neither* the king, nor any of his servants that heard all these words. Is. 36:22; 37:1

25 Nevertheless El-na'-than and De-la'-iah and Gem-a-ri'-ah had made intercession to the king that he would not burn the ᵀroll: but he would not hear them. *scroll*

26 But the king commanded Je-rah'-me-el the son of Ham'-me-lech, and Se-ra'-iah the son of Az'-ri-el, and Shel-e-mi'-ah the son of Ab'-de-el, to take Ba'-ruch the scribe and Jer-e-mi'-ah the prophet: but the LORD hid them.

27 Then the word of the LORD came to Jer-e-mi'-ah, after that the king had burned the roll, and the words which Ba'-ruch wrote at the mouth of Jer-e-mi'-ah, saying,

28 Take thee again another ᵀroll, and write in it all the former words that were in the first roll, which Je-hoi'-a-kim the king of Judah hath burned. *scroll*

29 And thou shalt say to Je-hoi'-a-kim king of Judah, Thus saith the LORD; Thou hast burned this ᵀroll, saying, ᴿWhy hast thou written therein, saying, The king of Babylon shall certainly come and destroy this land, and shall cause to ᴿcease from thence man and beast? *scroll · 32:3 · 25:9–11; 26:9*

30 Therefore thus saith the LORD of Je-hoi'-a-kim king of Judah; ᴿHe shall have none to sit upon the throne of David: and his dead body shall be ᴿcast out in the day to the heat, and in the night to the frost. 22:30 · 22:19

31 And I will punish him and his ᵀseed and his servants for their iniquity; and I will bring upon them, and upon the inhabitants of Jerusalem, and upon the men of Judah, all the ᵀevil that I have pro-

nounced against them; but they hearkened not.   *descendants · doom*

32 Then took Jer-e-mi'-ah another roll, and gave it to Ba'-ruch the scribe, the son of Ne-ri'-ah; who wrote therein from the mouth of Jer-e-mi'-ah all the words of the book which Je-hoi'-a-kim king of Judah had burned in the fire: and there were added besides unto them many ᵀlike words.   *similar*

37 And king ᴿZed-e-ki'-ah the son of Jo-si'-ah reigned instead of Co-ni'-ah the son of Je-hoi'-a-kim, whom Neb-u-chad-rez'-zar king of Babylon made king in the land of Judah.   22:24

2 ᴿBut neither he, nor his servants, nor the people of the land, did hearken unto the words of the LORD, which he spake by the prophet Jer-e-mi'-ah.   2 Kin. 24:19, 20

3 And Zed-e-ki'-ah the king sent Je-hu'-cal the son of Shel-e-mi'-ah and Zeph-a-ni'-ah the son of Ma-a-se'-iah the priest to the prophet Jer-e-mi'-ah, saying, ᴿPray now unto the LORD our God for us.   1 Kin. 13:6; Acts 8:24

4 Now Jer-e-mi'-ah came in and went out among the people: for they had not put him into prison.

5 Then ᴿPharaoh's army was come forth out of Egypt: and when the Chal-de'-ans that besieged Jerusalem heard ᵀtidings of them, they departed from Jerusalem.   v. 7; 2 Kin. 24:7; Ezek. 17:15 · *news*

6 Then came the word of the LORD unto the prophet Jer-e-mi'-ah, saying,

7 Thus saith the LORD, the God of Israel; Thus shall ye say to the king of Judah, ᴿthat sent you unto me to enquire of me; Behold, Pharaoh's army, which is come forth to help you, shall return to Egypt into their own land.   Is. 36:6

8 ᴿAnd the Chal-de'-ans shall come again, and fight against this city, and take it, and burn it with fire.   34:22; 2 Chr. 36:19

9 Thus saith the LORD; Deceive not yourselves, saying, The Chal-de'-ans shall surely depart from us: for they shall not depart.

10 ᴿFor though ye had smitten the whole army of the Chal-de'-ans that fight against you, and there remained *but* wounded men among them, *yet* should they rise up every man in his tent, and burn this city with fire.   Lev. 26:36–38

11 And it came to pass, that when the army of the Chal-de'-ans was broken up from Jerusalem for fear of Pharaoh's army,

12 Then Jer-e-mi'-ah went forth out of Jerusalem to go into the land of Benjamin, to ᵀseparate himself thence in the midst of the people.   *claim his property there among*

13 And when he was in the gate of Benjamin, a captain of the ward *was* there, whose name *was* I-ri'-jah, the son of Shel-e-mi'-ah, the son of Han-a-ni'-ah; and he ᵀtook Jer-e-mi'-ah the prophet, saying, Thou ᵀfallest away to the Chal-de'-ans.   *seized · are defecting*

14 Then said Jer-e-mi'-ah, *It is* false; I fall not away to the Chal-de'-ans. But he ᵀhearkened not to him: so I-ri'-jah took Jer-e-mi'-ah, and brought him to the princes.

15 Wherefore the princes were wroth with Jer-e-mi'-ah, and smote him, ᴿand put him in prison in the ᴿhouse of Jonathan the scribe: for they had made that the prison.   [Matt. 21:35] · 38:26; Acts 5:18

16 When Jer-e-mi'-ah was entered into the dungeon, and into the ᵀcabins, and Jer-e-mi'-ah had remained there many days;   *cells*

17 Then Zed-e-ki'-ah the king sent, and took him out: and the king asked him secretly in his house, and said, Is there *any* word from the LORD? And Jer-e-mi'-ah said, There is: for, said he, thou shalt be ᴿdelivered into the hand of the king of Babylon.   2 Kin. 25:4–7

18 Moreover Jer-e-mi'-ah said unto king Zed-e-ki'-ah, What have I offended against thee, or against thy servants, or against this people, that ye have put me in prison?

19 Where *are* now your prophets which prophesied unto you, saying, The king of Babylon shall not come against you, nor against this land?

20 Therefore hear now, I pray thee, O my lord the king: let my ᵀsupplication, I pray thee, be accepted before thee; that thou cause me not to return to the house of Jonathan the scribe, lest I die there. *petition*

21 Then Zed-e-ki'-ah the king commanded that they should commit Jer-e-mi'-ah into the court of the prison, and that they should give him daily a piece of bread out of the bakers' street, until all the bread in the city were spent. Thus Jer-e-mi'-ah remained in the court of the prison.

38 Then Sheph-a-ti'-ah the son of Mat'-tan, and Ged-a-li'-ah the son of Pash'-ur, and ᵀJu'-cal the son of Shel-e-mi'-ah, and ᴿPash'-ur the son of Mal-chi'-ah, ᴿheard the words that Jer-e-mi'-ah had spoken unto all the people, saying, *Jehucal, 37:3 · 21:1 · 21:8*

2 Thus saith the LORD, ᴿHe that remaineth in this city shall die by the sword, by the famine, and by the pestilence: but he that goeth forth to the Chal-de'-ans shall live; for he shall have his life ᵀfor a prey, and shall live. 21:9 · *as a prize*

3 Thus saith the LORD, ᴿThis city shall surely be ᴿgiven into the hand of the king of Babylon's army, which shall take it. 32:3 · 34:2

4 Therefore the princes said unto the king, We beseech thee, ᴿlet this man be put to death: for thus he ᵀweakeneth the hands of the men of war that remain in this city, and the hands of all the people, in speaking such words unto them: for this man seeketh not the ᵀwelfare of this people, but the ᵀhurt. 26:11 · Is discouraging · *good · harm*

5 Then Zed-e-ki'-ah the king said, Behold, he *is* in your hand: for the king *is* not he *that* can do *any* thing against you.

6 ᴿThen took they Jer-e-mi'-ah, and cast him into the dungeon of Mal-chi'-ah the son of ᵀHam'-me-lech, that *was* in the court of the prison: and they let down Jer-e-

mi'-ah with ᵀcords. And in the dungeon *there was* no water, but mire: so Jer-e-mi'-ah sunk in the mire. Lam. 3:55 · Lit. *the king · ropes*

7 ᴿNow when E'-bed–me'-lech the E-thi-o'-pi-an, one of the ᵀeu-nuchs which was in the king's house, heard that they had put Jer-e-mi'-ah in the dungeon; the king then sitting in the gate of Benjamin; 39:16 · *officers*

8 E'-bed–me'-lech went forth out of the king's house, and spake to the king, saying,

9 My lord the king, these men have done evil in all that they have done to Jer-e-mi'-ah the prophet, whom they have cast into the dungeon; and he is ᵀlike to die for hunger in the place where he is: for *there is* ᴿno more bread in the city. *likely · 37:21*

10 Then the king commanded E'-bed–me'-lech the E-thi-o'-pi-an, saying, Take from hence thirty men with thee, and ᵀtake up Jer-e-mi'-ah the prophet out of the dungeon, before he die. *lift*

11 So E'-bed–me'-lech took the men with him, and went into the house of the king under the treas-ury, and took thence old ᵀcast clouts and old rotten rags, and let them down by cords into the dungeon to Jer-e-mi'-ah. *clothes*

12 And E'-bed–me'-lech the E-thi-o'-pi-an said unto Jer-e-mi'-ah, Put now *these* old ᵀcast clouts and rotten rags under thine ᵀarmholes under the ᵀcords. And Jer-e-mi'-ah did so. *clothes · armpits · ropes*

13 So they drew up Jer-e-mi'-ah with cords, and took him up out of the dungeon: and Jer-e-mi'-ah remained in the court of the prison.

14 Then Zed-e-ki'-ah the king sent, and took Jer-e-mi'-ah the prophet unto him into the third entry that *is* in the house of the LORD: and the king said unto Jer-e-mi'-ah, I will ᴿask thee a thing; hide nothing from me. 21:1,2; 37:17

15 Then Jer-e-mi'-ah said unto Zed-e-ki'-ah, If I declare *it* unto thee, wilt thou not surely put me to death? and if I give thee coun-

sel, ^Twilt thou not hearken unto me?   *you will not listen to*

16 So Zed-e-ki'-ah the king sware secretly unto Jer-e-mi'-ah, saying, As the LORD liveth, that made ^Tus this soul, I will not put thee to death, neither will I give thee into the hand of these men that seek thy life.   *our very souls*

17 Then said Jer-e-mi'-ah unto Zed-e-ki'-ah, Thus saith the LORD, the God of hosts, the God of Israel; If thou wilt assuredly ^Rgo forth ^Runto the king of Babylon's princes, then thy soul shall live, and this city shall not be burned with fire; and thou shalt live, and thine house: 2 Kin. 24:12 · 39:3

18 But if thou wilt not ^Tgo forth to the king of Babylon's princes, then shall this city be given into the hand of the Chal-de'-ans, and they shall burn it with fire, and ^Rthou shalt not escape out of their hand.   *surrender* · 32:4; 34:3

19 And Zed-e-ki'-ah the king said unto Jer-e-mi'-ah, I am afraid of the Jews that ^Tare ^Rfallen to the Chal-de'-ans, lest they deliver me into their hand, and they ^Rmock me.   *have defected* · 39:9 · 1 Sam. 31:4

20 But Jer-e-mi'-ah said, They shall not deliver *thee.* Obey, I beseech thee, the voice of the LORD, which I speak unto thee: so it shall be ^Rwell unto thee, and thy soul shall live.   40:9

21 But if thou refuse to go forth, this *is* the word that the LORD hath shewed me:

22 And, behold, all the ^Rwomen that are left in the king of Judah's house *shall be* brought forth to the king of Babylon's princes, and those *women* shall say, Thy friends have set thee on, and have prevailed against thee: thy feet are sunk in the mire, *and* they are turned away back.   8:10

23 So they shall bring out all thy wives and thy children to the Chal-de'-ans: and thou shalt not escape out of their hand, but shalt be taken by the hand of the king of Babylon: and thou shalt cause this city to be burned with fire.

24 Then said Zed-e-ki'-ah unto Jer-e-mi'-ah, Let no man know of these words, and thou shalt not die.

25 But if the princes hear that I have talked with thee, and they come unto thee, and say unto thee, Declare unto us now what thou hast said unto the king, hide it not from us, and we will not put thee to death; also what the king said unto thee:

26 Then thou shalt say unto them, I presented my supplication before the king, that he would not cause me to return ^Rto Jonathan's house, to die there.   37:15

27 Then came all the princes unto Jer-e-mi'-ah, and asked him: and he told them according to all these words that the king had commanded. So they ^Tleft off speaking with him; for the matter was not perceived.   *ceased*

28 So ^RJer-e-mi'-ah abode in the court of the prison until the day that Jerusalem was taken: and he was *there* when Jerusalem was taken.   37:21; 39:14; [Ps. 23:4]

39 In the ^Rninth year of Zed-e-ki'-ah king of Judah, in the tenth month, came Neb-u-chad-rez'-zar king of Babylon and all his army against Jerusalem, and they besieged it.   Ezek. 24:1, 2

2 *And* in the ^Releventh year of Zed-e-ki'-ah, in the fourth month, the ninth *day* of the month, the city was broken up.   1:3

3 ^RAnd all the princes of the king of Babylon came in, and sat in the middle gate, *even* Ner'-gal–sha-re'-zer, Sam'-gar–ne'-bo, Sar-se'-chim, Rab'–sa-ris, Ner'-gal–sha-re'-zer, Rab'–mag, with all the residue of the princes of the king of Babylon.   1:15; 38:17

4 ^RAnd it came to pass, *that* when Zed-e-ki'-ah the king of Judah saw them, and all the men of war, then they fled, and went forth out of the city by night, by the way of the king's garden, by the gate betwixt the two walls: and he went out the way of the plain.   2 Kin. 25:4; Is. 30:16; Amos 2:14

5 But the Chal-de'-ans' army pursued after them, and ᴿovertook Zed-e-ki'-ah in the plains of Jericho: and when they had taken him, they brought him up to Neb-u-chad-nez'-zar king of Babylon to ᴿRib'-lah in the land of Ha'-math, where he gave judgment upon him. 32:4; 38:18, 23 · 2 Kin. 23:33

6 Then the king of Babylon slew the sons of Zed-e-ki'-ah in Rib'-lah before his ᴿeyes: also the king of Babylon slew all the ᴿnobles of Judah. Deut. 28:34 · 34:19–21

7 Moreover he put out Zed-e-ki'-ah's eyes, and bound him with chains, to carry him to Babylon.

8 And the Chal-de'-ans burned the king's house, and the houses of the people, with ᴿfire, and brake down the ᴿwalls of Jerusalem. 21:10 · 2 Kin. 25:10; Neh. 1:3

9 Then Neb'-u-zar–a'-dan the captain of the guard carried away captive into Babylon the remnant of the people that remained in the city, and those that fell away, that ᴿfell to him, with the rest of the people that remained. 38:19

10 But Neb'-u-zar–a'-dan the captain of the guard left of the ᴿpoor of the people, which had nothing, in the land of Judah, and gave them vineyards and fields at the same time. 40:7

11 Now Neb-u-chad-rez'-zar king of Babylon gave charge concerning Jer-e-mi'-ah to Neb'-u-zar–a'-dan the captain of the guard, saying,

12 Take him, and look well to him, and do him no ᴿharm; but do unto him ᵀeven as he shall say unto thee. 1:18, 19; 15:20, 21 · just

13 So Neb'-u-zar–a'-dan the captain of the guard sent, and Neb-u-shas'-ban, Rab'–sa-ris, and Ner'-gal–sha-re'-zer, Rab'–mag, and all the king of Babylon's princes;

14 Even they sent, ᴿand took Jer-e-mi'-ah out of the court of the prison, and committed him unto Ged-a-li'-ah the son of A-hi'-kam the son of Sha'-phan, that he should carry him home: so he dwelt among the people. 38:28

15 Now the word of the Lᴏʀᴅ came unto Jer-e-mi'-ah, while he was shut up in the court of the prison, saying,

16 Go and speak to ᴿE'-bed–me'-lech the E-thi-o'-pi-an, saying, Thus saith the Lᴏʀᴅ of hosts, the God of Israel; Behold, ᴿI will bring my words upon this city for evil, and not for good; and they shall be accomplished in that day before thee. 38:7, 12 · 21:10; [Zech. 1:6]

17 But I will deliver thee in that day, saith the Lᴏʀᴅ: and thou shalt not be given into the hand of the men of whom thou art afraid.

18 For I will surely deliver thee, and thou shalt not fall by the sword, but thy life shall be for a prey unto thee: because thou hast put thy trust in me, saith the Lᴏʀᴅ.

40 The word that came to Jer-e-mi'-ah from the Lᴏʀᴅ, ᴿafter that Neb'-u-zar–a'-dan the captain of the guard had let him go from Ra'-mah, when he had taken him being bound in chains among all that were carried away captive of Jerusalem and Judah, which were carried away captive unto Babylon. 39:9, 11

2 And the captain of the guard took Jer-e-mi'-ah, and said unto him, The Lᴏʀᴅ thy God hath pronounced this evil upon this place.

3 Now the Lᴏʀᴅ hath brought it, and done according as he hath said: ᴿbecause ye have sinned against the Lᴏʀᴅ, and have not obeyed his voice, therefore this thing is come upon you. [Rom. 2:5]

4 And now, behold, I loose thee this day from the chains which were upon thine hand. If it seem good unto thee to come with me into Babylon, come; and I will look well unto thee: but if it seem ill unto thee to come with me into Babylon, forbear: behold, ᴿall the land is before thee: whither it seemeth good and convenient for thee to go, thither go. Gen. 20:15

5 Now while he was not yet gone back, he said, Go back also to Ged-a-li'-ah the son of A-hi'-kam the son of Sha'-phan, ᴿwhom

the king of Babylon hath made governor over the cities of Judah, and dwell with him among the people: or go wheresoever it seemeth convenient unto thee to go. So the captain of the guard gave him victuals and a reward, and let him go.   2 Kin. 25:22; 41:10

6 ^RThen went Jer-e-mi'-ah unto Ged-a-li'-ah the son of A-hi'-kam to ^RMiz'-pah; and dwelt with him among the people that were left in the land.   39:14 · Judg. 20:1; 1 Sam. 7:5

7 ^RNow when all the captains of the forces which *were* in the fields, *even* they and their men, heard that the king of Babylon had made Ged-a-li'-ah the son of A-hi'-kam governor in the land, and had committed unto him men, and women, and children, and of the poor of the land, of them that were not carried away captive to Babylon;   2 Kin. 25:23, 24

8 Then they came to Ged-a-li'-ah to Miz'-pah, ^Reven Ish'-ma-el the son of Neth-a-ni'-ah, and Jo-ha'-nan and Jonathan the sons of Ka-re'-ah, and Se-ra'-iah the son of Tan'-hu-meth, and the sons of E'-phai the Ne-toph'-a-thite, and Jez-a-ni'-ah the son of a Ma-ach'-a-thite, they and their men.   41:1–10

9 And Ged-a-li'-ah the son of A-hi'-kam the son of Sha'-phan sware unto them and to their men, saying, Fear not to serve the Chal-de'-ans: dwell in the land, and serve the king of Babylon, and it shall be ^Rwell with you.   38:17–20

10 As for me, behold, I will dwell at Miz'-pah, to serve the Chal-de'-ans, which will come unto us: but ye, gather ye wine, and summer fruits, and oil, and put *them* in your vessels, and dwell in your cities that ye have taken.

11 Likewise when all the Jews that *were* in Moab, and among the Am'-mon-ites, and in E'-dom, and that *were* in all the countries, heard that the king of Babylon had left a remnant of Judah, and that he had set over them Ged-a-li'-ah the son of A-hi'-kam the son of Sha'-phan;

12 Even all the Jews ^Rreturned out of all places whither they were driven, and came to the land of Judah, to Ged-a-li'-ah, unto Miz'-pah, and gathered wine and summer fruits very much.   43:5

13 Moreover Jo-ha'-nan the son of Ka-re'-ah, and all the captains of the forces that *were* in the fields, came to Ged-a-li'-ah to Miz'-pah,

14 And said unto him, Dost thou certainly know that ^RBa'-al-is the king of the Am'-mon-ites hath sent Ish'-ma-el the son of Neth-a-ni'-ah to ^Tslay thee? But Ged-a-li'-ah the son of A-hi'-kam believed them not.   41:10 · *murder*

15 Then Jo-ha'-nan the son of Ka-re'-ah spake to Ged-a-li'-ah in Miz'-pah secretly, saying, Let me go, I pray thee, and I will ^Tslay Ish'-ma-el the son of Neth-a-ni'-ah, and no man shall know *it*: wherefore should he ^Tslay thee, that all the Jews which are gathered unto thee should be scattered, and the ^Rremnant in Judah perish?   *kill · murder* · 42:2

16 But Ged-a-li'-ah the son of A-hi'-kam said unto Jo-ha'-nan the son of Ka-re'-ah, Thou shalt not do this thing: for thou speakest falsely of Ish'-ma-el.

41 Now it came to pass in the seventh month, *that* Ish'-ma-el the son of Neth-a-ni'-ah the son of E-lish'-a-ma, of the seed royal, and the princes of the king, even ten men with him, came unto Ged-a-li'-ah the son of A-hi'-kam to Miz'-pah; and there they did eat bread together in Miz'-pah.

2 Then arose Ish'-ma-el the son of Neth-a-ni'-ah, and the ten men that were with him, and ^Rsmote Ged-a-li'-ah the son of ^RA-hi'-kam the son of Sha'-phan with the sword, and slew him, whom the king of Babylon had made governor over the land.   Ps. 41:9 · 40:5

3 Ish'-ma-el also slew all the Jews that were with him, *even* with Ged-a-li'-ah, at Miz'-pah, and the Chal-de'-ans that were found there, *and* the men of war.

4 And it came to pass the second day after he had slain Ged-a-li'-ah, and no man knew *it*,

5 That there came certain from She'-chem, from Shi'-loh, and from Sa-ma'-ri-a, *even* fourscore men, having their beards shaven, and their clothes rent, and having cut themselves, with offerings and incense in their hand, to bring *them* to the house of the Lord.

6 And Ish'-ma-el the son of Neth-a-ni'-ah went forth from Miz'-pah to meet them, weeping all along as he went: and it came to pass, as he met them, he said unto them, Come to Ged-a-li'-ah the son of A-hi'-kam.

7 And it was *so*, when they came into the midst of the city, that Ish'-ma-el the son of Neth-a-ni'-ah slew them, *and cast them* into the midst of the pit, he, and the men that *were* with him.

8 But ten men were found among them that said unto Ish'-ma-el, Slay us not: for we have treasures in the field, of wheat, and of barley, and of oil, and of honey. So he forbare, and slew them not among their brethren.

9 Now the ᵀpit wherein Ish'-ma-el had cast all the dead bodies of the men, whom he had slain because of Ged-a-li'-ah, *was* it ᴿwhich A'-sa the king had made for fear of Ba-ash'-a king of Israel: *and* Ish'-ma-el the son of Neth-a-ni'-ah filled it with *them that were* slain.   cistern · 1 Kin. 15:22

10 Then Ish'-ma-el carried away captive all the ᴿresidue of the people that *were* in Miz'-pah, *even* the king's daughters, and all the people that remained in Miz'-pah, whom Neb'-u-zar-a'-dan the captain of the guard had committed to Ged-a-li'-ah the son of A-hi'-kam: and Ish'-ma-el the son of Neth-a-ni'-ah carried them away captive, and departed to go over to the Am'-mon-ites.   40:11, 12

11 But when Jo-ha'-nan the son of Ka-re'-ah, and all the captains of the forces that *were* with him,

heard of all the evil that Ish'-ma-el the son of Neth-a-ni'-ah had done,

12 Then they took all the men, and went to fight with Ish'-ma-el the son of Neth-a-ni'-ah, and found him by ᴿthe great waters that *are* in Gib'-e-on.   2 Sam. 2:13

13 Now it came to pass, *that* when all the people which *were* with Ish'-ma-el saw Jo-ha'-nan the son of Ka-re'-ah, and all the captains of the forces that *were* with him, then they were glad.

14 So all the people that Ish'-ma-el had carried away captive from Miz'-pah cast about and returned, and went unto Jo-ha'-nan the son of Ka-re'-ah.

15 But Ish'-ma-el the son of Neth-a-ni'-ah escaped from Jo-ha'-nan with eight men, and went to the Am'-mon-ites.

16 Then took Jo-ha'-nan the son of Ka-re'-ah, and all the captains of the forces that *were* with him, all the remnant of the people whom he had recovered from Ish'-ma-el the son of Neth-a-ni'-ah, from Miz'-pah, after *that* he had slain Ged-a-li'-ah the son of A-hi'-kam, *even* mighty men of war, and the women, and the children, and the eunuchs, whom he had brought again from Gib'-e-on:

17 And they departed, and dwelt in the habitation of ᴿChim'-ham, which is by Beth'-le-hem, to go to enter into Egypt,   2 Sam. 19:37, 38

18 Because of the Chal-de'-ans: for they were afraid of them, because Ish'-ma-el the son of Neth-a-ni'-ah had ᵀslain Ged-a-li'-ah the son of A-hi'-kam, ᴿwhom the king of Babylon made governor in the land.   murdered · 40:5

42 Then all the captains of the forces, ᴿand Jo-ha'-nan the son of Ka-re'-ah, and Jez-a-ni'-ah the son of Ho-sha'-iah, and all the people from the least even unto the greatest, came near,   40:8, 13

2 And said unto Jer-e-mi'-ah the prophet, Let, we ᴿbeseech thee, our supplication be accepted before thee, and ᴿpray for us unto the Lord thy God, *even* for all this

remnant; (for we are left *but* a few of many, as thine eyes do behold us:) 15:11 · Is. 37:4; Acts 8:24; [James 5:16]

3 That the LORD thy God may shew us ᴿthe way wherein we ᵀmay walk, and the thing that we ᵀmay do.   Ezra 8:21 · *should*

4 Then Jer-e-mi'-ah the prophet said unto them, I have heard *you;* behold, I will pray unto the LORD your God according to your words; and it shall come to pass, *that* ᴿwhatsoever thing the LORD shall answer you, I will declare *it* unto you; I will ᴿkeep nothing back from you.   23:28 · Acts 20:20

5 Then they said to Jer-e-mi'-ah, ᴿThe LORD be a true and faithful witness between us, if we do not even according to all things for the which the LORD thy God shall send thee to us.   Judg. 11:10

6 Whether *it be* good, or whether *it be* evil, we will obey the voice of the LORD our God, to whom we send thee; ᴿthat it may be well with us, when we obey the voice of the LORD our God.   7:23

7 And it came to pass after ten days, that the word of the LORD came unto Jer-e-mi'-ah.

8 Then called he Jo-ha'-nan the son of Ka-re'-ah, and all the captains of the forces which *were* with him, and all the people from the least even to the greatest,

9 And said unto them, Thus saith the LORD, the God of Israel, unto whom ye sent me to present your supplication before him;

10 If ye will still abide in this land, then ᴿwill I build you, and not pull *you* down, and I will plant you, and not pluck *you* up: for I ᴿrepent me of the evil that I have done unto you. 24:6; 31:28; 33:7 · [18:8]

11 Be not afraid of the king of Babylon, of whom ye are afraid; be not afraid of him, saith the LORD: ᴿfor I *am* with you to save you, and to deliver you from his hand.   Is. 8:9, 10; 43:2, 5; Rom. 8:31

12 And ᴿI will shew mercies unto you, that he may have mercy upon you, and cause you to return to your own land. Neh. 1:11; Prov. 16:7

13 But if ye say, We will not dwell in this land, neither obey the voice of the LORD your God,

14 Saying, No; but we will go into the land of ᴿEgypt, where we shall see no war, nor hear the sound of the trumpet, nor have hunger ᵀof bread; and there will we dwell: 41:17; 43:7; Is. 31:1 · *for*

15 And now therefore hear the word of the LORD, ye remnant of Judah; Thus saith the LORD of hosts, the God of Israel; If ye ᴿwholly set ᴿyour faces to enter into Egypt, and go to sojourn there;   44:12–14; Deut. 17:16 · Luke 9:51

16 Then it shall come to pass, *that* the ᴿsword, which ye feared, shall overtake you there in the land of Egypt, and the famine, whereof ye were afraid, shall follow close after you there in Egypt; and there ye shall die.   Amos 9:1–4

17 So shall it be with all the men that set their faces to go into Egypt to sojourn there; they shall die by the sword, by the famine, and by the pestilence: and ᴿnone of them shall remain or escape from the evil that I will bring upon them.   44:14, 28

18 For thus saith the LORD of hosts, the God of Israel; As mine anger and my fury hath been ᴿpoured forth upon the inhabitants of Jerusalem; so shall my fury be poured forth upon you, when ye shall enter into Egypt: and ye shall be an ᵀexecration, and an astonishment, and a curse, and a reproach; and ye shall see this place no more.   7:20 · *oath*

19 The LORD hath said concerning you, O ye remnant of Judah; ᴿGo ye not into Egypt: know certainly that I have ᵀadmonished you this day.   Is. 30:1–7 · *warned*

20 For ye dissembled in your hearts, when ye sent me unto the LORD your God, saying, Pray for us unto the LORD our God; and according unto all that the LORD our God shall say, so declare unto us, and we will do *it.*

21 And *now* I have this day declared *it* to you; but ye have not

obeyed the voice of the LORD your God, nor any *thing* for the which he hath sent me unto you.

22 Now therefore know certainly that ᴿye shall die by the sword, by the famine, and by the pestilence, in the place whither ye desire to go *and* to sojourn.　v. 17

43 And it came to pass, *that* when Jer-e-mi′-ah had made an end of speaking unto all the people all the ᴿwords of the LORD their God, for which the LORD their God had sent him to them, *even* all these words,　42:9–18

2 ᴿThen spake Az-a-ri′-ah the son of Ho-sha′-iah, and Jo-ha′-nan the son of Ka-re′-ah, and all the proud men, saying unto Jer-e-mi′-ah, Thou speakest falsely: the LORD our God hath not sent thee to say, Go not into Egypt to sojourn there:　42:1

3 But ᴿBa′-ruch the son of Ne-ri′-ah setteth thee on against us, for to deliver us into the hand of the Chal-de′-ans, that they might put us to death, and carry us away captives into Babylon.　36:4; 45:1

4 So Jo-ha′-nan the son of Ka-re′-ah, and all the captains of the forces, and all the people, obeyed not the voice of the LORD, to ᵀdwell in the land of Judah.　*remain*

5 But Jo-ha′-nan the son of Ka-re′-ah, and all the captains of the forces, took ᴿall the remnant of Judah, that were returned from all nations, whither they had been driven, to dwell in the land of Judah;　40:11, 12

6 *Even* men, and women, and children, ᴿand the king's daughters, ᴿand every person that Neb′-u-zar–a′-dan the captain of the guard had left with Ged-a-li′-ah the son of A-hi′-kam the son of Sha′-phan, and Jer-e-mi′-ah the prophet, and Ba′-ruch the son of Ne-ri′-ah.　41:10 · 39:10; 40:7

7 ᴿSo they came into the land of Egypt: for they obeyed not the voice of the LORD: thus came they *even* to ᴿTah′-pan-hes.　42:19 · 2:16

8 Then came the ᴿword of the LORD unto Jer-e-mi′-ah in Tah′-pan-hes, saying,　44:1–30

9 Take great stones in thine hand, and hide them in the ᵀclay in the brickkiln, which *is* at the entry of Pharaoh's house in Tah′-pan-hes, in the sight of the men of Judah;　Or *mortar*

10 And say unto them, Thus saith the LORD of hosts, the God of Israel; Behold, I will send and take Neb-u-chad-rez′-zar the king of Babylon, ᴿmy servant, and will set his throne upon these stones that I have hid; and he shall spread his royal pavilion over them.　25:9; 27:6; Ezek. 29:18, 20

11 And when he cometh, he shall smite the land of Egypt, *and deliver* ᴿsuch *as are* for death to death; and such *as are* for captivity to captivity; and such *as are* for the sword to the sword.　15:2

12 And I will kindle a fire in the houses of ᴿthe gods of Egypt; and he shall burn them, and carry them away captives: and he shall array himself with the land of Egypt, as a shepherd putteth on his garment; and he shall go forth from thence in peace.　Ex. 12:12

13 He shall break also the images of Beth–she′-mesh, that *is* in the land of Egypt; and the houses of the gods of the Egyptians shall he burn with fire.

44 The word that came to Jer-e-mi′-ah concerning all the Jews which dwell in the land of Egypt, which dwell at Mig′-dol, and at Tah′-pan-hes, and at Noph, and in the country of Path′-ros, saying,

2 Thus saith the LORD of hosts, the God of Israel; Ye have seen all the ᵀevil that I have brought upon Jerusalem, and upon all the cities of Judah; and, behold, this day they *are* a desolation, and no man dwelleth therein,　*calamity*

3 Because of their wickedness which they have committed to provoke me to anger, in that they went ᴿto burn incense, *and* to ᴿserve other gods, whom they knew not, *neither* they, ye, nor your fathers.　19:4 · Deut. 13:6; 32:17

4 Howbeit ᴿI sent unto you all my servants the prophets, rising early and sending *them*, saying, Oh, do not this abominable thing that I hate. 25:4; 26:5; 29:19; Zech. 7:7

5 But they ᵀhearkened not, nor inclined their ear to turn from their wickedness, to burn no incense unto other gods. *did not listen*

6 Wherefore my fury and mine anger was poured forth, and was kindled in the cities of Judah and in the streets of Jerusalem; and they ᵀare wasted *and* desolate, as at this day. *became a ruin*

7 Therefore now thus saith the LORD, the God of hosts, the God of Israel; Wherefore commit ye *this* great evil ᴿagainst your souls, to cut off from you man and woman, child and suckling, out of Judah, to leave you none to remain; 7:19

8 In that ye ᴿprovoke me unto wrath with the works of your hands, burning incense unto other gods in the land of Egypt, whither ye be gone to dwell, that ye might cut yourselves off, and that ye might be ᴿa curse and a reproach among all the nations of the earth? 1 Cor. 10:21, 22 · 1 Kin. 9:7, 8

9 Have ye forgotten the wickedness of your fathers, and the wickedness of the kings of Judah, and the wickedness of their wives, and your own wickedness, and the wickedness of your wives, which they have committed in the land of Judah, and in the streets of Jerusalem?

10 They are not humbled *even* unto this day, neither have they feared, nor walked in my law, nor in my statutes, that I set before you and before your fathers.

11 Therefore thus saith the LORD of hosts, the God of Israel; Behold, ᴿI will set my face against you for ᵀevil, and to ᵀcut off all Judah. Amos 9:4 · *catastrophe* · *destroy*

12 And I will take the remnant of Judah, that have set their faces to go into the land of Egypt to sojourn there, and ᴿthey shall all be consumed, *and* fall in the land of Egypt; they shall *even* be con-

sumed by the sword *and* by the famine: they shall die, from the least even unto the greatest, by the sword and by the famine: and ᴿthey shall be an ᵀexecration, *and* an astonishment, and a curse, and a reproach. 42:15–17, 22 · 42:18 · *oath*

13 ᴿFor I will punish them that dwell in the land of Egypt, as I have punished Jerusalem, by the sword, by the famine, and by the pestilence: 43:11

14 So that none of the remnant of Judah, which are gone into the land of Egypt to sojourn there, shall escape or remain, that they should return into the land of Judah, to the which they have a ᴿdesire to return to dwell there: for ᴿnone shall return but such as shall escape. 22:26, 27 · [Is. 4:2; 10:20]

15 Then all the men which knew that their wives had burned incense unto other gods, and all the women that stood by, a great multitude, even all the people that dwelt in the land of Egypt, in Path′-ros, answered Jer-e-mi′-ah, saying,

16 *As for* the word that thou hast spoken unto us in the name of the LORD, ᴿwe will not ᵀhearken unto thee. 6:16 · *listen*

17 But we will certainly do ᴿwhatsoever thing goeth forth out of our own mouth, to burn incense unto the ᴿqueen of heaven, and to pour out drink offerings unto her, as we have done, we, and our fathers, our kings, and our princes, in the cities of Judah, and in the streets of Jerusalem: for *then* had we plenty of ᵀvictuals, and were well, and saw no ᵀevil. Judg. 11:36 · 7:18 · *food* · *trouble*

18 But since we left off to burn incense to the queen of heaven, and to pour out drink offerings unto her, we have wanted all *things*, and have been consumed by the sword and by the famine.

19 ᴿAndᵀ when we burned incense to the queen of heaven, and poured out drink offerings unto her, did we make her cakes to worship her, and pour out drink

offerings unto her, without our men? 7:18 · *And* the women said

20 Then Jer-e-mi'-ah said unto all the people, to the men, and to the women, and to all the people which had given him *that* answer, saying,

21 The incense that ye burned in the cities of Judah, and in the streets of Jerusalem, ye, and your fathers, your kings, and your princes, and the people of the land, did not the LORD remember them, and came it *not* into his mind?

22 So that the LORD could no longer bear, because of the evil of your doings, *and* because of the abominations which ye have committed; therefore is your land a desolation, and an astonishment, and a curse, without an inhabitant, ᴿas at this day. 25:11, 18, 38

23 Because ye have burned incense, and because ye have sinned against the LORD, and have not obeyed the voice of the LORD, nor walked in his law, nor in his statutes, nor in his testimonies; therefore this ᵀevil is happened unto you, as at this day. *calamity*

24 Moreover Jer-e-mi'-ah said unto all the people, and to all the women, Hear the word of the LORD, all Judah that *are* in the land of Egypt:

25 Thus saith the LORD of hosts, the God of Israel, saying; Ye and your wives have both spoken with your mouths, and fulfilled with your hand, saying, We will surely perform our vows that we have vowed, to burn incense to the queen of heaven, and to pour out drink offerings unto her: ye will surely accomplish your vows, and surely perform your vows.

26 Therefore hear ye the word of the LORD, all Judah that dwell in the land of Egypt; Behold, ᴿI have sworn by my great name, saith the LORD, that ᴿmy name shall no more be named in the mouth of any man of Judah in all the land of Egypt, saying, The Lord GOD liveth. Heb. 6:13 · Neh. 9:5

27 Behold, I will watch over them for ᵀevil, and not for good: and all the men of Judah that *are* in the land of Egypt ᴿshall be consumed by the sword and by the famine, until there be an end of them. *adversity* · 1:10; 31:28; Ezek. 7:6

28 Yet ᴿa small number that escape the sword shall return out of the land of Egypt into the land of Judah, and all the remnant of Judah, that are gone into the land of Egypt to sojourn there, shall know whose words shall stand, mine, or theirs. Is. 10:19; 27:12, 13

29 And this *shall be* a sign unto you, saith the LORD, that I will punish you in this place, that ye may know that my words shall surely ᴿstand against you for ᵀevil: [Ps. 33:11] · *adversity*

30 Thus saith the LORD; Behold, I will give Pha'-raoh–hoph'-ra king of Egypt into the hand of his enemies, and into the hand of them that seek his life; as I gave ᴿZed-e-ki'-ah king of Judah into the hand of Neb-u-chad-rez'-zar king of Babylon, his enemy, and that sought his life. 2 Kin. 25:4–7

45 The word that Jer-e-mi'-ah the prophet spake unto ᴿBa'-ruch the son of Ne-ri'-ah, when he had written these words in a book at the mouth of Jer-e-mi'-ah, in the fourth year of Je-hoi'-a-kim the son of Jo-si'-ah king of Judah, saying, 32:12, 16; 43:3

2 Thus saith the LORD, the God of Israel, unto thee, O Ba'-ruch;

3 Thou didst say, Woe is me now! for the LORD hath added grief to my sorrow; I fainted in my sighing, and I find no rest.

4 Thus shalt thou say unto him, The LORD saith thus; Behold, ᴿ*that* which I have built will I break down, and that which I have planted I will pluck up, even this whole land. 1:10; 11:17; 18:7–10

5 And seekest thou great things for thyself? seek *them* not: for, behold, ᴿI will bring ᵀevil upon all flesh, saith the LORD: but thy ᴿlife will I give unto thee ᵀfor a prey in all places whither thou goest. 25:26 · *adversity* · 21:9 · *as a prize*

46

The word of the LORD which came to Jer-e-mi'-ah the prophet against ᴿthe ᵀGentiles;   25:15 · *nations*

2 Against ᴿEgypt, against the army of Pha'-raoh–ne'-cho king of Egypt, which was by the river Eu-phra'-tes in Car'-che-mish, which Neb-u-chad-rez'-zar king of Babylon smote in the fourth year of Je-hoi'-a-kim the son of Jo-si'-ah king of Judah.   Ezek. 29:2—32:32

3 Order ye the buckler and shield, and draw near to battle.

4 Harness the horses; and get up, ye horsemen, and stand forth with *your* helmets; ᵀfurbish the spears, *and* ᴿput on the ᵀbrigandines.   *polish* · 51:11; Is. 21:5 · *armour*

5 Wherefore have I seen them dismayed *and* turned away back? and their mighty ones are beaten down, and are fled ᵀapace, and look not back: *for* ᴿfear *was* round about, saith the LORD. *speedily* · 49:29

6 Let not the swift flee away, nor the mighty man escape; they shall stumble, and fall toward the north by the river Eu-phra'-tes.

7 Who *is* this *that* cometh up ᴿas a flood, whose waters are moved as the rivers?   Is. 8:7, 8

8 Egypt riseth up like a flood, and *his* waters are moved like the rivers; and he saith, I will go up, *and* will cover the earth; I will destroy the city and the inhabitants thereof.

9 Come up, ye horses; and rage, ye chariots; and let the mighty men come forth; ᵀthe E-thi-o'-pi-ans and ᵀthe Lib'-y-ans, that handle the shield; and the Lyd'-i-ans, ᴿthat handle *and* bend the bow.   Heb. *Cush* · Heb. *Put* · Is. 66:19

10 For this *is* the day of the Lord GOD of hosts, a day of vengeance, that he may avenge him of his adversaries: and the sword shall devour, and it shall be ᵀsatiate and made drunk with their blood: for the Lord GOD of hosts ᴿhath a sacrifice in the north country by the river Eu-phra'-tes.   *satisfied* · Is. 34:6

11 ᴿGo up into Gil'-e-ad, and take balm, ᴿO virgin, the daughter of Egypt: in vain shalt thou use many medicines; *for* ᴿthou shalt not be cured. 8:22 · Is. 47:1 · Ezek. 30:21

12 The nations have heard of thy ᴿshame, and thy cry hath filled the land: for the mighty man hath stumbled against the mighty, *and* they are fallen both together. 2:36

13 The word that the LORD spake to Jer-e-mi'-ah the prophet, how Neb-u-chad-rez'-zar king of Babylon should come *and* ᴿsmite the land of Egypt.   Ezek. 29:1–21

14 Declare ye in Egypt, and publish in ᴿMig'-dol, and publish in Noph and in ᴿTah'-pan-hes: say ye, Stand fast, and prepare thee; for the sword shall devour ᵀround about thee.   44:1 · Ezek. 30:18 · *all around*

15 Why are thy valiant *men* swept away? they stood not, because the LORD did drive them.

16 He made many to fall, yea, ᴿone fell upon another: and they said, Arise, and ᴿlet us go again to our own people, and to the land of our nativity, from the oppressing sword.   v. 6; Lev. 26:36, 37; · 51:9

17 They did cry there, Pharaoh king of Egypt *is but* a noise; he hath passed the time appointed.

18 *As* I live, saith the King, ᴿwhose name *is* the LORD of hosts, Surely as Ta'-bor *is* among the mountains, and as Carmel by the sea, *so* shall he come. 48:15; Mal. 1:14

19 O ᴿthou daughter dwelling in Egypt, ᵀfurnish thyself ᴿto go into captivity: for Noph shall be waste and desolate without an inhabitant.   48:18 · *prepare* · Is. 20:4

20 Egypt *is like* a very fair heifer, *but* destruction cometh; it cometh ᴿout of the north. 1:14

21 Also her ᵀhired men *are* in the midst of her like fatted bullocks; for they also are turned back, *and* are fled away together: they did not stand, because ᴿthe day of their calamity was come upon them, *and* the time of their visitation.   *mercenaries* · [Ps. 37:13]

22 ᴿThe voice thereof shall go like a serpent; for they shall march with an army, and come

against her with axes, as ᵀhewers of wood. [Is. 29:4] · *those who chop*
23 They shall ᴿcut down her forest, saith the LORD, though it cannot be searched; because they are more than ᴿthe grasshoppers, and *are* innumerable. Is. 10:34 · Joel 2:25
24 The daughter of Egypt shall be ᵀconfounded; she shall be delivered into the hand of ᴿthe people of the north. *ashamed* · 1:15
25 The LORD of hosts, the God of Israel, saith; Behold, I will punish the multitude of No, and Pharaoh, and Egypt, with their gods, and their kings; even Pharaoh, and *all* them that ᴿtrust in him: Is. 30:1–5
26 ᴿAnd I will deliver them into the hand of those that seek their lives, and into the hand of Neb-u-chad-rez′-zar king of Babylon, and into the hand of his servants: and ᴿafterward it shall be inhabited, as in the days of old, saith the LORD. 44:30; Ezek. 32:11 · Ezek. 29:8–14
27 But fear not thou, O my servant Jacob, and be not dismayed, O Israel: for, behold, I will ᴿsave thee from afar off, and thy seed from the land of their captivity; and Jacob shall return, and be in rest and at ease, and none shall make *him* afraid. Is. 11:11; Mic. 7:12
28 Fear thou not, O Jacob my servant, saith the LORD: for I *am* with thee; for I will make a full end of all the nations whither I have driven thee: but I will not make a full end of thee, but correct thee in measure; yet will I not leave thee wholly unpunished.

47 The word of the LORD that came to Jer-e-mi′-ah the prophet against the Phi-lis′-tines, before that Pharaoh smote Ga′-za.
2 Thus saith the LORD; Behold, waters rise up ᴿout of the north, and shall be an overflowing flood, and shall overflow the land, and all that is therein; the city, and them that dwell therein: then the men shall cry, and all the inhabitants of the land shall howl. 1:14
3 At the ᴿnoise of the stamping of the hoofs of his strong *horses,* at the rushing of his chariots, *and*

at the rumbling of his wheels, the fathers shall not look back ᵀto *their* children for feebleness of hands; Judg. 5:22; Nah. 3:2 · *for*
4 Because of the day that cometh to spoil all the Phi-lis′-tines, *and* to cut off from Ty′-rus and Zi′-don every helper that remaineth: for the LORD will spoil the Phi-lis′-tines, ᴿthe remnant of the country of Caph′-tor. Ezek. 25:16; Amos 1:8
5 ᴿBaldness is come upon Ga′-za; ᴿAsh′-ke-lon is cut off *with* the remnant of their valley: how long wilt thou cut thyself? 48:37 · 25:20
6 O thou ᴿsword of the LORD, how long *will it be* ere thou be quiet? put up thyself into thy scabbard, rest, and be still. 12:12
7 How can ᵀit be quiet, seeing the LORD hath ᴿgiven it a charge against Ash′-ke-lon, and against the sea shore? there hath he ᴿappointed it. Lit. *you* · Is. 10:6 · Mic. 6:9

48 Against ᴿMoab thus saith the LORD of hosts, the God of Israel; Woe unto Ne′-bo! for it is spoiled: Kir-i-a-tha′-im is confounded *and* taken: Mis′-gab is confounded and dismayed. Is. 25:10
2 ᴿ*There shall be* no more praise of Moab: in ᴿHesh′-bon they have devised evil against it; come, and let us cut it off from *being* a nation. Also thou shalt be cut down, O Mad′-men; the sword shall pursue thee. Is. 16:14 · Is. 15:4
3 A voice of crying *shall be* from ᴿHor-o-na′-im, spoiling and great destruction. vv. 5, 34; Is. 15:5
4 Moab is destroyed; her little ones have caused a cry to be heard.
5 ᴿFor in the ᵀgoing up of Lu′-hith continual weeping shall go up; for in the going down of Hor-o-na′-im the enemies have heard a cry of destruction. Is. 15:5 · *ascent*
6 Flee, save your lives, and be like the heath in the wilderness.
7 For because thou hast trusted in thy works and in thy ᴿtreasures, thou shalt also be taken: and Che′-mosh shall go forth into captivity *with* his priests and his princes together. Ps. 52:7; [1 Tim. 6:17]

8 And the spoiler shall come upon every city, and no city shall escape: the valley also shall perish, and the plain shall be destroyed, as the LORD hath spoken.

9 Give wings unto Moab, that it may flee and get away: for the cities thereof shall be desolate, without any to dwell therein.

10 ᴿCursed *be* he that doeth the work of the LORD deceitfully, and cursed *be* he that keepeth back his sword from blood. 1 Kin. 20:42

11 Moab hath been at ease from his youth, and he hath settled on his lees, and hath not been emptied from vessel to vessel, neither hath he gone into captivity: therefore his taste remained in him, and his scent is not changed.

12 Therefore, behold, the days come, saith the LORD, that I will send unto him ᵀwanderers, that shall ᵀcause him to wander, and shall empty his vessels, and break their bottles. *pourers · pour him off*

13 And Moab shall be ashamed of Che'-mosh, as the house of Israel was ashamed of ᴿBeth'-el their confidence. 1 Kin. 12:29; 13:32–34

14 How say ye, We *are* mighty and strong men for the war?

15 Moab is spoiled, and gone up *out of* her cities, and his chosen young men are gone down to the slaughter, saith the King, whose name *is* the LORD of hosts.

16 The calamity of Moab *is* near ᵀto come, and his affliction hasteth fast. *at hand*

17 All ye that are ᵀabout him, bemoan him; and all ye that know his name, say, ᴿHow is the strong staff broken, *and* the beautiful rod! *around ·* Is. 9:4; 14:4, 5

18 ᴿThou daughter that dost inhabit ᴿDi'-bon, come down from *thy* glory, and sit in thirst; for the spoiler of Moab shall come upon thee, *and* he shall destroy thy strong holds. Is. 47:1 · Num. 21:30

19 O inhabitant of Ar'-o-er, stand by the way, and espy; ask him that fleeth, and her that escapeth, *and* say, What is done?

20 Moab is confounded; for it is broken down: ᴿhowl and cry; tell ye it in ᴿArnon, that Moab is spoiled, Is. 16:7 · Num. 21:13

21 And judgment is come upon the plain country; upon Ho'-lon, and upon ᵀJa'-ha-zah, and upon Meph'-a-ath, *Or Jahzah*

22 And upon Di'-bon, and upon Ne'-bo, and upon Beth–dib-la-tha'-im,

23 And upon Kir-i-a-tha'-im, and upon Beth–ga'-mul, and upon Beth–me'-on,

24 And upon ᴿKe'-ri-oth, and upon Boz'-rah, and upon all the cities of the land of Moab, far or near. v. 41; Amos 2:2

25 ᴿThe horn of Moab is cut off, and his ᴿarm is broken, saith the LORD. Zech. 1:19–21 · Ezek. 30:21

26 ᴿMake ye him drunken: for he magnified *himself* against the LORD: Moab also shall wallow in his vomit, and he also shall be in derision. 25:15

27 For was not Israel a derision unto thee? ᴿwas he found among thieves? for since thou spakest of him, thou skippedst for joy. 2:26

28 O ye that dwell in Moab, leave the cities, and ᴿdwell in the rock, and be like the dove *that* maketh her nest in the sides of the ᵀhole's mouth. Ps. 55:6, 7 · *cave's*

29 We have heard the ᴿpride of Moab, (he is exceeding proud) his loftiness, and his arrogancy, and his ᴿpride, and the haughtiness of his heart. Is. 16:6; Zeph. 2:8, 10 · 49:16

30 I know his wrath, saith the LORD; but *it shall* not *be* so; ᴿhis lies shall not so effect *it*. Is. 16:6

31 Therefore ᴿwill I howl for Moab, and I will cry out for all Moab; *mine heart* shall mourn for the men of Kir–he'-res. Is. 16:7, 11

32 ᴿO vine of Sib'-mah, I will weep for thee with the weeping of Ja'-zer: thy plants are gone over the sea, they reach *even* to the sea of Ja'-zer: the spoiler is fallen upon thy summer fruits and upon thy vintage. Is. 16:8, 9

33 And ᴿjoy and gladness is taken from the plentiful field, and from the land of Moab; and I have

caused wine to fail from the wine-presses: none shall tread with shouting; *their* shouting *shall be* no shouting.   25:10; Is. 16:10; Joel 1:12

34 From the cry of Hesh'-bon *even* unto E-le-a'-leh, *and even* unto Ja'-haz, have they uttered their voice, from Zo'-ar *even* unto Hor-o-na'-im, *as* an heifer of three years old: for the waters also of Nim'-rim shall be desolate.

35 Moreover I will cause to cease in Moab, saith the LORD, ^Rhim that offereth in the high places, and him that burneth incense to his gods.   Is. 15:2; 16:12

36 Therefore ^Rmine heart shall sound for Moab like pipes, and mine heart shall sound like pipes for the men of Kir–he'-res: because the riches *that* he hath gotten are perished.   Is. 15:5; 16:11

37 For ^Revery head *shall be* bald, and every beard clipped: upon all the hands *shall be* cuttings, and upon the loins sackcloth.   Is. 15:2, 3

38 *There shall be* lamentation generally upon all the ^Rhousetops of Moab, and in the streets thereof: for I have ^Rbroken Moab like a vessel wherein *is* no pleasure, saith the LORD.   Is. 15:3 · 22:28

39 They shall ^Thowl, *saying,* How is it broken down! how hath Moab turned the back with shame! so shall Moab be a derision and a dismaying to all them about him.   *wail*

40 For thus saith the LORD; Behold, ^Rhe shall fly as an eagle, and shall ^Rspread his wings over Moab.   Hos. 8:1; Hab. 1:8 · Is. 8:8

41 Ke'-ri-oth is taken, and the strong holds are surprised, and ^Rthe mighty men's hearts in Moab at that day shall be as the heart of a woman in her pangs.   Is. 13:8; 21:3

42 And Moab shall be destroyed ^Rfrom *being* a people, because he hath magnified *himself* against the LORD.   v. 2; Ps. 83:4

43 ^RFear, and the pit, and the snare, *shall be* upon thee, O inhabitant of Moab, saith the LORD.   Is. 24:17, 18; Lam. 3:47

44 He that fleeth from the fear shall fall into the pit; and he that getteth up out of the pit shall be ^Ttaken in the ^Rsnare: for I will bring upon it, *even* upon Moab, the year of their visitation, saith the LORD.   *caught* · 1 Kin. 19:17; Is. 24:18

45 They that fled stood under the shadow of Hesh'-bon because of the force: but a fire shall come forth out of Hesh'-bon, and a flame from the midst of Si'-hon, and shall devour the corner of Moab, and the crown of the head of the tumultuous ones.

46 Woe be unto thee, O Moab! the people of Che'-mosh perisheth: for thy sons are taken captives, and thy daughters captives.

47 Yet will I bring again the captivity of Moab ^Rin the latter days, saith the LORD. Thus far *is* the judgment of Moab.   49:6, 39

49 Concerning ^Rthe Am'-mon-ites, thus saith the LORD; Hath Israel no sons? hath he no heir? why *then* doth their king inherit ^RGad, and his people dwell in his cities?   2 Chr. 20:1 · Zeph. 2:8–11

2 Therefore, behold, the days come, saith the LORD, that I will cause an alarm of war to be heard in Rab'-bah of the Am'-mon-ites; and it shall be a desolate heap, and her ^Tdaughters shall be burned with fire: then shall Israel be heir unto them that were his heirs, saith the LORD.   *villages*

3 Howl, O Hesh'-bon, for A'-i is spoiled: cry, ye daughters of Rab'-bah, ^Rgird you with sackcloth; lament, and run to and fro by the hedges; for their king shall go into captivity, *and* his priests and his princes together.   Is. 32:11

4 Wherefore ^Rgloriest thou in the valleys, thy flowing valley, O ^Rbacksliding daughter? that trusted in her treasures, ^R*saying,* Who shall come unto me? 9:23 · 3:14 · 21:13

5 Behold, I will bring a fear upon thee, saith the Lord GOD of hosts, from all those that ^Tbe about thee; and ye shall be driven out every man right forth; and none shall gather up him that wandereth.   *are around*

6 And ^Rafterward I will bring again the captivity of the children of Ammon, saith the LORD.   48:47

7 Concerning E'-dom, thus saith the LORD of hosts; ^R*Is* wisdom no more in Te'-man? is counsel perished from the prudent? is their wisdom vanished?   Gen. 36:11

8 Flee ye, turn back, dwell ^Tdeep, O inhabitants of ^RDe'-dan; for I will bring the calamity of Esau upon him, the time *that* I will visit him.   in the depths · Is. 21:13

9 If ^Rgrapegatherers come to thee, would they not leave *some* gleaning grapes? if thieves by night, they will destroy till they have enough.   Obad. 5, 6

10 But I have made Esau bare, I have uncovered his secret places, and he shall not be able to hide himself: his seed is spoiled, and his brethren, and his neighbours, and ^Rhe *is* ^Tnot.   Is. 17:14 · *no more*

11 Leave thy fatherless children, I will preserve *them* alive; and let thy widows trust in me.

12 For thus saith the LORD; Behold, ^Rthey whose judgment *was* not to drink of the cup have assuredly drunken; and *art* thou he *that* shall altogether go unpunished? thou shalt not go unpunished, but thou shalt surely drink of it.   25:29; Obad. 16

13 For ^RI have sworn by myself, saith the LORD, that ^RBoz'-rah shall become a desolation, a reproach, a waste, and a curse; and all the cities thereof shall be perpetual wastes.   Amos 6:8 · Gen. 36:33

14 I have heard a ^Rrumour^T from the LORD, and an ambassador is sent unto the ^Theathen, *saying*, Gather ye together, and come against her, and rise up to the battle.   Obad. 1-4 · *message* · *nations*

15 For, lo, I will make thee small among the ^Theathen, *and* despised among men.   *nations*

16 Thy terribleness hath deceived thee, *and* the pride of thine heart, O thou that dwellest in the clefts of the rock, that holdest the height of the hill: though thou shouldest make thy nest as high as the eagle, I will bring thee down from thence, saith the LORD.

17 Also E'-dom shall be a desolation: ^Revery one that goeth by it shall be astonished, and shall hiss at all the plagues thereof.   Ezek. 35:7

18 ^RAs in the overthrow of Sodom and Go-mor'-rah and the neighbour *cities* thereof, saith the LORD, no man shall abide there, neither shall a son of man dwell in it.   Gen. 19:24, 25; Deut. 29:23; Zeph. 2:9

19 ^RBehold, he shall come up like a lion from the swelling of Jordan against the habitation of the strong: but I will suddenly make him run away from her: and who *is* a chosen *man, that* I may appoint over her? for who *is* like me? and who will appoint me the time? and who *is* that shepherd that will stand before me?   50:44

20 Therefore hear the counsel of the LORD, that he hath taken against E'-dom; and his purposes, that he hath purposed against the inhabitants of Te'-man: Surely the least of the flock shall draw them out: surely he shall make their habitations desolate with them.

21 ^RThe earth ^Tis moved at the noise of their fall, at the cry the noise thereof was heard in the Red sea.   50:46; Ezek. 26:15, 18 · *shakes*

22 Behold, he shall come up and fly as the eagle, and spread his wings over Boz'-rah: and at that day shall the heart of the mighty men of E'-dom be as the heart of a woman in her pangs.

23 Concerning Damascus. Ha'-math is confounded, and Ar'-pad: for they have heard evil tidings: they are fainthearted; *there is* sorrow on the sea; it cannot be quiet.

24 Damascus is waxed feeble, *and* turneth herself to flee, and fear hath seized on *her:* ^Ranguish and sorrows have taken her, as a woman in travail.   4:31; 6:24; 48:21

25 How is ^Rthe city of praise not left, the city of my joy!   33:9

26 ^RTherefore her young men shall fall in her streets, and all the men of war shall be cut off in that day, saith the LORD of hosts.   50:30

27 And I will kindle a ᴿfire in the wall of Damascus, and it shall consume the palaces of Ben–ha´-dad.   Amos 1:4

28 ᴿConcerning Ke´-dar, and concerning the kingdoms of Ha´-zor, which Neb-u-chad-rez´-zar king of Babylon shall smite, thus saith the LORD; Arise ye, go up to Ke´-dar, and spoil ᴿthe men of the east.   Gen. 25:13 · Judg. 6:3; Job 1:3

29 Their tents and their flocks shall they take away: they shall take to themselves their curtains, and all their vessels, and their camels; and they shall cry unto them, ᴿFear is on every side.   46:5

30 Flee, get you far off, dwell ᵀdeep, O ye inhabitants of Ha´-zor, saith the LORD; for Neb-u-chad-rez´-zar king of Babylon hath taken counsel against you, and hath conceived a ᵀpurpose against you.   in the depths · plan

31 Arise, get you up unto the wealthy nation, that dwelleth without care, saith the LORD, which have neither gates nor bars, which ᴿdwell alone.   Mic. 7:16

32 And their camels shall be a booty, and the multitude of their cattle a spoil: and I will ᴿscatter into all winds them that are in the utmost corners; and I will bring their calamity from all sides thereof, saith the LORD.   Ezek. 5:10

33 And Ha´-zor ᴿshall be a dwelling for dragons, and a desolation for ever: there shall no man abide there, nor any son of man dwell in it.   Zeph. 2:9, 12–15; Mal. 1:3

34 The word of the LORD that came to Jer-e-mi´-ah the prophet against ᴿE´-lam in the ᴿbeginning of the reign of Zed-e-ki´-ah king of Judah, saying,   25:25 · 28:1

35 Thus saith the LORD of hosts; Behold, I will break the bow of E´-lam, the chief of their might.

36 And upon E´-lam will I bring the four winds from the four quarters of heaven, and will scatter them toward all those winds; and there shall be no nation whither the outcasts of E´-lam shall not come.

37 For I will cause E´-lam to be dismayed before their enemies, and before them that seek their life: and I will bring ᵀevil upon them, even my fierce anger, saith the LORD; ᴿand I will send the sword after them, till I have consumed them: disaster · 9:16

38 And I will ᴿset my throne in E´-lam, and will destroy from thence the king and the princes, saith the LORD.   43:10

39 But it shall come to pass ᴿin the latter days, that I will bring again the captivity of E´-lam, saith the LORD.   48:47

50 The word that the LORD spake against Babylon and against the land of the Chal-de´-ans by Jer-e-mi´-ah the prophet.

2 Declare ye among the nations, and ᵀpublish, and ᵀset up a standard; publish, and conceal not: say, Babylon is taken, Bel is confounded, Me-ro´-dach is broken in pieces; her idols are confounded, her images are broken in pieces.   proclaim · lift up a banner

3 For out of the north there cometh up a nation against her, which shall make her land desolate, and none shall dwell therein: they shall remove, they shall depart, both man and beast.

4 In those days, and in that time, saith the LORD, the children of Israel shall come, they and the children of Judah together, ᴿgoing and weeping: they shall go, and seek the LORD their God.   [Ps. 126:5]

5 They shall ask the way to Zion with their faces thitherward, saying, Come, and let us join ourselves to the LORD in ᴿa perpetual covenant that shall not be forgotten.   31:31

6 My people hath been ᴿlost sheep: their shepherds have caused them to go astray, they have turned them away on the mountains: they have gone from mountain to hill, they have forgotten their restingplace.   1 Pet. 2:25

7 All that found them have devoured them: and their adversaries said, ᴿWe offend not, be-

cause they have sinned against the LORD, ᴿthe habitation of justice, even the LORD, the hope of their fathers. Dan. 9:16 · [Ps. 90:1; 91:1]

8 Remove out of the midst of Babylon, and go forth out of the land of the Chal-de′-ans, and be as the he goats before the flocks.

9 ᴿFor, lo, I will raise and cause to come up against Babylon an assembly of great nations from the north country: and they shall set themselves in array against her; from thence she shall be taken: their arrows shall be as of a mighty expert man; ᴿnone shall return in vain. 15:14; 51:27 · 2 Sam. 1:22

10 And Chal-de′-a shall be a spoil: ᴿall that spoil her shall be satisfied, saith the LORD. [Rev. 17:16]

11 Because ye were glad, because ye rejoiced, O ye destroyers of mine heritage, because ye are grown fat ᴿas the heifer at grass, and bellow as bulls;   Hos. 10:11

12 Your mother shall be ᵀsore confounded; she that bare you shall be ashamed: behold, the ᵀhindermost of the nations shall be a ᴿwilderness, a dry land, and a desert.   deeply ashamed · least · 51:43

13 Because of the wrath of the LORD it shall not be inhabited, ᴿbut it shall be wholly desolate: ᴿevery one that goeth by Babylon shall be ᵀastonished, and hiss at all her plagues. 25:12 · 49:17 · horrified

14 ᴿPut yourselves in array against Babylon round about: all ye that bend the bow, shoot at her, spare no arrows: for she hath sinned against the LORD.   51:2

15 Shout against her round about: she hath ᴿgiven her hand: her foundations are fallen, her walls are thrown down: for it is the vengeance of the LORD: take vengeance upon her; as she hath done, do unto her.   1 Chr. 29:24

16 Cut off the sower from Babylon, and him that handleth the sickle in the time of harvest: for fear of the oppressing sword ᴿthey shall turn every one to his people, and they shall flee every one to his own land. 51:9; Is. 13:14

17 Israel is a ᴿscattered sheep; the lions have driven him away: first the king of Assyria hath devoured him; and last this Neb-u-chad-rez′-zar king of Babylon hath broken his bones. 2 Kin. 24:10

18 Therefore thus saith the LORD of hosts, the God of Israel; Behold, I will punish the king of Babylon and his land, as I have punished the king of Assyria.

19 ᴿAnd I will bring Israel again to his habitation, and he shall feed on Carmel and Ba′-shan, and his soul shall be satisfied upon mount E′-phra-im and Gil′-e-ad. Is. 65:10

20 In those days, and in that time, saith the LORD, ᴿthe iniquity of Israel shall be sought for, and there shall be none; and the sins of Judah, and they shall not be found: for I will pardon them ᴿwhom I reserve. Num. 23:21 · Is. 1:9

21 Go up against the land of Mer-a-tha′-im, even against it, and against the inhabitants of ᴿPe′-kod: waste and utterly destroy after them, saith the LORD, and do ᴿaccording to all that I have commanded thee. Ezek. 23:23 · 2 Sam. 16:11

22 A sound of battle is in the land, and of great destruction.

23 How is ᴿthe hammer of the whole earth cut asunder and broken! how is Babylon become a desolation among the nations!   14:6

24 I have laid a snare for thee, and thou art also ᴿtaken, O Babylon, and thou wast not aware: thou art found, and also caught, because thou hast ᴿstriven against the LORD. Dan. 5:30 · [Is. 45:9]

25 The LORD hath opened his armoury, and hath brought forth ᴿthe weapons of his indignation: for this is the work of the Lord GOD of hosts in the land of the Chal-de′-ans.   Is. 13:5

26 Come against her from the utmost border, open her storehouses: cast her up as ᵀheaps, and destroy her utterly: let nothing of her be left.   ruinous heaps

27 Slay all her bullocks; let them go down to the slaughter: woe

unto them! for their day is come, the time of their visitation.

28 The voice of them that flee and escape out of the land of Babylon, Rto declare in Zion the vengeance of the LORD our God, the vengeance of his temple. 51:10

29 Call together the archers against Babylon: all ye that bend the bow, camp against it round about; let none thereof escape: Rrecompense her according to her work; according to all that she hath done, do unto her: Rfor she hath been proud against the LORD, against the Holy One of Israel. [2 Thess. 1:6]; Rev. 18:6 · [Is. 47:10]

30 RTherefore shall her young men fall in the streets, and all her men of war shall be cut off in that day, saith the LORD. Is. 13:18

31 Behold, I *am* against thee, O *thou* most proud, saith the Lord GOD most of hosts: for thy day is come, the time *that* I will visit thee.

32 And the most Rproud shall stumble and fall, and none shall raise him up: and I will kindle a fire in his cities, and it shall devour all round about him. Is. 26:5

33 Thus saith the LORD of hosts; The children of Israel and the children of Judah *were* oppressed together: and all that took them captives held them fast; they refused to let them go.

34 RTheir Redeemer *is* strong; Rthe LORD of hosts *is* his name: he shall throughly plead their Rcause, that he may give rest to the land, and disquiet the inhabitants of Babylon. 15:21 · Is. 47:4 · 32:18

35 A sword *is* upon the Chal-de′-ans, saith the LORD, and upon the inhabitants of Babylon, and Rupon her princes, and upon Rher wise *men*. Dan. 5:30 · 51:57; Is. 47:13

36 A sword *is* Rupon the liars; and they shall Tdote: a sword *is* upon her mighty men; and they shall be dismayed. Is. 44:25 · *be fools*

37 A sword *is* upon their horses, and upon their chariots, and upon all Rthe Tmingled people that *are* in the midst of her; and Rthey shall become as women: a sword

is upon her treasures; and they shall be robbed. 25:20 · *mixed* · 51:30

38 RA drought *is* upon her waters; and they shall be dried up: for it *is* the land of graven images, and they are Tmad upon *their* idols. Is. 44:27; Rev. 16:12 · *insane with*

39 Therefore the wild beasts of the desert with the wild beasts of the islands shall dwell *there*, and the owls shall dwell therein: and it shall be no more inhabited for ever; neither shall it be dwelt in from generation to generation.

40 RAs God overthrew Sodom and Go-mor′-rah and the neighbour *cities* thereof, saith the LORD; so shall no man abide there, neither shall any son of man dwell therein. Gen. 19:24, 25

41 RBehold, a people shall come from the north, and a great nation, and many kings shall be raised up from the Tcoasts of the earth. 6:22; 25:14; 51:27; Is. 13:2–5 · *ends*

42 RThey shall hold the bow and the lance: Rthey *are* cruel, and will not shew mercy: Rtheir voice shall roar like the sea, and they shall ride upon horses, *every one* put in array, like a man to the battle, against thee, O daughter of Babylon. 6:23 · Is. 13:18 · Is. 5:30

43 The king of Babylon hath Rheard the report of them, and his hands waxed feeble: anguish took hold of him, *and* pangs as of a woman in Rtravail. 51:31 · 6:24

44 Behold, he shall come up like a lion from the swelling of Jordan unto the habitation of the strong: but I will make them suddenly run away from her: and who *is* a chosen *man, that* I may appoint over her? for who *is* like me? and who will appoint me the time? and Rwho *is* that shepherd that will stand before me? Job 41:10

45 Therefore hear ye Rthe counsel of the LORD, that he hath taken against Babylon; and his Rpurposes, that he hath purposed against the land of the Chal-de′-ans: Surely the least of the flock shall draw them out: surely he

shall make *their* habitation desolate with them.　[Ps. 33:11] · 51:29

46 ᴿAt the noise of the taking of Babylon the earth ᵀis moved, and the cry is heard among the nations.　Rev. 18:9 · *trembles*

51 Thus saith the LORD; Behold, I will raise up against ᴿBabylon, and against them that dwell in the midst of them that rise up against me, ᴿa destroying wind;　Is. 47:1 · 2 Kin. 19:7

2　And will send unto Babylon fanners, that shall ᵀfan her, and shall empty her land: for in the day of trouble they shall be against her round about.　*winnow*

3　Against *him that* bendeth let the archer bend his bow, and against *him that* lifteth himself up in his ᵀbrigandine: and spare ye not her young men; ᴿdestroy ye utterly all her host.　*armour* · 50:21

4　Thus the slain shall fall in the land of the Chal-de'-ans, ᴿand *they that are* thrust through in her streets.　49:26; 50:30, 37

5　For Israel *hath* ᴿnot *been* forsaken, nor Judah of his God, of the LORD of hosts; though their land was filled with sin against the Holy One of Israel.　[Is. 54:7, 8]

6　ᴿFlee out of the midst of Babylon, and deliver every man his soul: be not cut off in her iniquity; for this *is* the time of the LORD's vengeance; he will render unto her a recompence.　Rev. 18:4

7　ᴿBabylon *hath been* a golden cup in the LORD's hand, that made all the earth drunken: the nations have drunken of her wine; therefore the nations are mad.　25:15

8　Babylon is suddenly ᴿfallen and destroyed: howl for her; ᴿtake balm for her pain, if so be she may be healed.　Rev. 14:8; 18:2 · 46:11

9　We would have healed Babylon, but she is not healed: forsake her, and let us go every one into his own country: for her judgment reacheth unto heaven, and is lifted up *even* to the skies.

10　The LORD hath ᴿbrought forth our righteousness: come, and let us declare in Zion the work of the LORD our God.　Ps. 37:6; Mic. 7:9

11　ᴿMake bright the arrows; gather the shields: ᴿthe LORD hath raised up the spirit of the kings of the Medes: for his ᵀdevice *is* against Babylon, to destroy it; because it *is* the vengeance of the LORD, the vengeance of his temple.　46:4, 9; Joel 3:9, 10 · Is. 13:17 · *plan*

12　Set up the ᵀstandard upon the walls of Babylon, make the watch strong, set up the watchmen, prepare the ambushes: for the LORD hath both devised and done that which he spake against the inhabitants of Babylon.　*banner*

13　O thou that dwellest upon many waters, abundant in treasures, thine end is come, *and* the measure of thy covetousness.

14　ᴿThe LORD of hosts hath sworn by himself, *saying,* Surely I will fill thee with men, as with caterpillers; and they shall lift up a shout against thee.　49:13; Amos 6:8

15　He hath made the earth by his power, he hath established the world by his wisdom, and ᴿhath stretched out the heaven by his understanding.　Ps. 104:2; Is. 40:22

16　When he uttereth *his* voice, *there is* a multitude of waters in the heavens; and ᴿhe causeth the vapours to ascend from the ends of the earth: he maketh lightnings with rain, and bringeth forth the wind out of his treasures.　Ps. 135:7

17　Every man is brutish by *his* knowledge; every founder is confounded by the graven image: for his molten image *is* falsehood, and *there is* no breath in them.

18　They *are* vanity, the work of errors: in the time of their ᵀvisitation they shall perish.　*punishment*

19　The portion of Jacob *is* not like them; for he *is* the ᵀformer of all things: and *Israel is* the ᵀrod of his inheritance: the LORD of hosts *is* his name.　*maker* · *tribe*

20　Thou *art* my battle ax *and* weapons of war: for with thee will I break in pieces the nations, and with thee will I destroy kingdoms;

21　And with thee will I break in

pieces the horse and his rider; and with thee will I break in pieces the chariot and his rider;

22 With thee also will I break in pieces man and woman; and with thee will I break in pieces ᴿold and young; and with thee will I break in pieces the young man and the maid; 2 Chr. 36:17; Is. 13:15, 16

23 I will also break in pieces with thee the shepherd and his flock; and with thee will I break in pieces the husbandman and his yoke of oxen; and with thee will I break in pieces ᵀcaptains and rulers. *governors*

24 ᴿAnd I will ᵀrender unto Babylon and to all the inhabitants of Chal-de′-a all their evil that they have done in Zion in your sight, saith the LORD. 50:15, 29 · *repay*

25 Behold, I *am* against thee, O destroying mountain, saith the LORD, which destroyest all the earth: and I will stretch out mine hand upon thee, and roll thee down from the rocks, and will make thee a burnt mountain.

26 And they shall not take of thee a stone for a corner, nor a stone for foundations; ᴿbut thou shalt be desolate for ever, saith the LORD. 50:26, 40

27 ᴿSet ye up a ᵀstandard in the land, blow the trumpet among the nations, prepare the nations against her, call together against her the kingdoms of A′-ra-rat, Min′-ni, and Ash′-che-naz; appoint a captain against her; cause the horses to come up as the rough caterpillers. Is. 13:2 · *banner*

28 Prepare against her the nations with the kings of the Medes, the ᵀcaptains thereof, and all the rulers thereof, and all the land of his dominion. *governors*

29 And the land shall tremble and sorrow: for every ᴿpurpose of the LORD shall be performed against Babylon, to make the land of Babylon a desolation without an inhabitant. 50:45

30 The mighty men of Babylon have forborn to fight, they have remained in *their* holds: their

might hath failed; ᴿthey became as women: they have burned her dwellingplaces; ᴿher bars are broken. Is. 19:16 · Lam. 2:9; Amos 1:5

31 ᴿOne ᵀpost shall run to meet another, and one messenger to meet another, to shew the king of Babylon that his city is taken ᵀat *one* end, 50:24 · *runner* · *on all sides*

32 And that ᴿthe passages are stopped, and the reeds they have burned with fire, and the men of war are ᵀaffrighted. 50:38 · *terrified*

33 For thus saith the LORD of hosts, the God of Israel; The daughter of Babylon *is* ᴿlike a threshingfloor, *it is* time to thresh her: yet a little while, and the time of her harvest shall come. Mic. 4:13

34 Neb-u-chad-rez′-zar the king of Babylon hath ᴿdevoured me, he hath crushed me, he hath made me an empty vessel, he hath swallowed me up like a dragon, he hath filled his belly with my delicates, he hath cast me out. 50:17

35 The violence done to me and to my flesh *be* upon Babylon, shall the inhabitant of Zion say; and my blood upon the inhabitants of Chal-de′-a, shall Jerusalem say.

36 Therefore thus saith the LORD; Behold, I will plead thy cause, and take vengeance for thee; ᴿand I will dry up her sea, and make her springs dry. 50:38

37 And Babylon shall become heaps, a dwellingplace for dragons, an astonishment, and an hissing, without an inhabitant.

38 They shall roar together like lions: they shall ᵀyell as lions' whelps. *growl*

39 In their heat I will make their feasts, and ᴿI will make them drunken, that they may rejoice, and sleep a perpetual sleep, and not wake, saith the LORD. v. 57

40 I will bring them down like lambs to the slaughter, like rams with ᵀhe goats. *male*

41 How is ᴿShe′-shach taken! and how is ᴿthe praise of the whole earth surprised! how is Babylon become an astonishment among the nations! 25:26 · Is. 13:19

42 The sea is come up upon Babylon: she is covered with the multitude of the waves thereof.

43 ᴿHer cities are a desolation, a dry land, and a wilderness, a land wherein ᴿno man dwelleth, neither doth *any* son of man pass thereby.   50:39, 40 · Is. 13:20

44 And I will punish ᴿBel in Babylon, and I will bring forth out of his mouth that which he hath swallowed up: and the nations shall not flow together any more unto him: yea, the wall of Babylon shall fall.   50:2; Is. 46:1

45 ᴿMy people, go ye out of the midst of her, and deliver ye every man his soul from the fierce anger of the LORD.   Is. 48:20; [Rev. 18:4]

46 And lest your heart faint, and ye fear for the rumour that shall be heard in the land; a rumour shall both come *one* year, and after that in *another* year *shall come* a rumour, and violence in the land, ruler against ruler.

47 Therefore, behold, the days come, that I will ᵀdo judgment upon the graven images of Babylon: and her whole land shall be confounded, and all her slain shall fall in the midst of her.   *bring*

48 Then ᴿthe heaven and the earth, and all that *is* therein, shall sing for Babylon: for the spoilers shall come unto her from the north, saith the LORD.   Rev. 18:20

49 As Babylon *hath caused* the slain of Israel to fall, so at Babylon shall fall the slain of all the earth.

50 ᴿYe that have escaped the sword, go away, stand not still: ᴿremember the LORD afar off, and let Jerusalem come into your mind.   44:28 · [Deut. 4:29–31]; Ezek. 6:9

51 We are confounded, because we have heard reproach: shame hath covered our faces: for strangers are come into the sanctuaries of the LORD's house.

52 Wherefore, behold, the days come, saith the LORD, that I will ᵀdo judgment upon her graven images: and through all her land the wounded shall groan.   *bring*

53 ᴿThough Babylon should mount up to heaven, and though she should fortify the height of her strength, *yet* from me shall spoilers come unto her, saith the LORD.   Gen. 11:4; Amos 9:2; Obad. 4

54 ᴿA sound of a cry *cometh* from Babylon, and great destruction from the land of the Chal-de'-ans: 50:22

55 Because the LORD hath ᵀspoiled Babylon, and ᵀdestroyed out of her the great voice; when her waves do roar like great waters, a noise of their voice is uttered: *plundered · silenced her*

56 Because the spoiler is come upon her, *even* upon Babylon, and her mighty men are taken, every one of their bows is broken: ᴿfor the LORD God of recompences shall surely ᵀrequite.   Ps. 94:1 · *repay*

57 And I will make drunk her princes, and her ᴿwise *men*, her captains, and her rulers, and her mighty men: and they shall sleep a perpetual sleep, and not wake, saith ᴿthe King, whose name *is* the LORD of hosts.   50:35 · 46:18; 48:15

58 Thus saith the LORD of hosts; The broad walls of Babylon shall be utterly ᴿbroken, and her high gates shall be burned with fire; and ᴿthe people shall labour in vain, and the folk in the fire, and they shall be weary.   50:15 · Hab. 2:13

59 The word which Jer-e-mi'-ah the prophet commanded Se-ra'-iah the son of ᴿNe-ri'-ah, the son of Ma-a-se'-iah, when he went with Zed-e-ki'-ah the king of Judah into Babylon in the fourth year of his reign. And *this* Se-ra'-iah *was* a quiet prince.   32:12

60 So Jer-e-mi'-ah ᴿwrote in a book all the evil that should come upon Babylon, *even* all these words that are written against Babylon.   36:2; Is. 30:8

61 And Jer-e-mi'-ah said to Se-ra'-iah, When thou comest to Babylon, and shalt see, and shalt read all these words;

62 Then shalt thou say, O LORD, thou hast spoken against this place, to cut it off, that ᴿnone shall

remain in it, neither man nor beast, but that it shall be desolate for ever.   50:3, 39; Is. 13:20; 14:22, 23;

63 And it shall be, when thou hast made an end of reading this book, ^{R}*that* thou shalt bind a stone to it, and cast it into the midst of Eu-phra'-tes: 19:10, 11

64 And thou shalt say, Thus shall Babylon sink, and shall not rise from the evil that I will bring upon her: and they shall be weary. Thus far *are* the words of Jer-e-mi'-ah.

52 Zed-e-ki'-ah *was* ^{R}one and twenty years old when he began to reign, and he reigned eleven years in Jerusalem. And his mother's name *was* Ha-mu'-tal the daughter of Jer-e-mi'-ah of ^{R}Lib'-nah.   2 Chr. 36:11 · 2 Kin. 8:22

2 And he did *that which was* evil in the eyes of the LORD, according to all that Je-hoi'-a-kim had done.

3 For through the anger of the LORD it came to pass in Jerusalem and Judah, till he had cast them out from his presence, that Zed-e-ki'-ah ^{R}rebelled against the king of Babylon.   2 Chr. 36:13

4 And it came to pass in the ^{R}ninth year of his reign, in the tenth month, in the tenth *day* of the month, *that* Neb-u-chad-rez'-zar king of Babylon came, he and all his army, against Jerusalem, and pitched against it, and built forts against it round about.   39:1

5 So the city was besieged unto the eleventh year of king Zed-e-ki'-ah.

6 And in the fourth month, in the ninth *day* of the month, the famine was ^{T}sore in the city, so that there was no ^{T}bread for the people of the land.   *severe · food*

7 Then the ^{T}city was broken up, and all the men of war fled, and went forth out of the city by night by the way of the gate between the two walls, which *was* by the king's garden; (now the Chal-de'-ans *were* by the city round about:) and they went by the way of the plain.   *city wall was broken through*

8 But the army of the Chal-de'-ans pursued after the king, and overtook Zed-e-ki'-ah in the plains of Jericho; and all his army was scattered from him.

9 ^{R}Then they took the king, and carried him up unto the king of Babylon to Rib'-lah in the land of Ha'-math; where he gave judgment upon him.   2 Kin. 25:6

10 And the king of Babylon slew the sons of Zed-e-ki'-ah before his eyes: he slew also all the princes of Judah in Rib'-lah.

11 Then he ^{R}put^T out the eyes of Zed-e-ki'-ah; and the king of Babylon bound him in chains, and carried him to Babylon, and put him in prison till the day of his death.   Ezek. 12:13 · *blinded*

12 ^{R}Now in the fifth month, in the tenth *day* of the month, ^{R}which *was* the nineteenth year of Neb-u-chad-rez'-zar king of Babylon, came Neb'-u-zar-a'-dan, captain of the guard, *which* served the king of Babylon, into Jerusalem,   2 Kin. 25:8–21 · v. 29

13 And burned the house of the LORD, and the king's house; and all the houses of Jerusalem, and all the houses of the great *men*, burned he with fire:

14 And all the army of the Chal-de'-ans, that *were* with the captain of the guard, brake down all the walls of Jerusalem round about.

15 ^{R}Then Neb'-u-zar-a'-dan the captain of the guard carried away captive *certain* of the poor of the people, and the ^{T}residue of the people that remained in the city, and those that fell away, that fell to the king of Babylon, and the rest of the multitude.   39:9 · *rest*

16 But Neb'-u-zar-a'-dan the captain of the guard left *certain* of the poor of the land for vinedressers and for husbandmen.

17 ^{R}Also the ^{R}pillars of brass that *were* in the house of the LORD, and the bases, and the brasen sea that *was* in the house of the LORD, the Chal-de'-ans

brake, and carried all the brass of them to Babylon. 27:19 · 1 Kin. 7:15, 23

18 The caldrons also, and the shovels, and the snuffers, and the bowls, and the spoons, and all the vessels of brass wherewith they ministered, took they away.

19 And the basons, and the firepans, and the bowls, and the caldrons, and the ᵀcandlesticks, and the spoons, and the cups; *that* which *was* of ᵀgold *in* gold, and *that* which *was* of ᵀsilver *in* silver, took the captain of the guard away. *lampstands · solid gold · solid silver*

20 The two pillars, one sea, and twelve brasen bulls that *were* under the bases, which king Solomon had made in the house of the LORD: the brass of all these vessels was without weight.

21 And *concerning* the ᴿpillars, the height of one pillar *was* eighteen cubits; and a fillet of twelve cubits did compass it; and the thickness thereof *was* four fingers: *it was* hollow. 1 Kin. 7:15

22 And a ᵀchapiter of brass *was* upon it; and the height of one chapiter *was* five cubits, with network and pomegranates upon the chapiters round about, all *of* ᵀbrass. The second pillar also and the pomegranates *were* like unto these. *capital of bronze · bronze*

23 And there were ninety and six pomegranates on a side; *and* ᴿall the pomegranates upon the network *were* an hundred round about. 1 Kin. 7:20

24 And ᴿthe captain of the guard took Se-ra′-iah the chief priest, ᴿand Zeph-a-ni′-ah the second priest, and the three keepers of the door: 2 Kin. 25:18 · 21:1; 29:25

25 He took also out of the city an eunuch, which had the charge of the men of war; and seven men of them that were near the king's person, which were found in the city; and the principal scribe of the host, who mustered the people of the land; and three-

score men of the people of the land, that were found in the midst of the city.

26 So Neb′-u-zar–a′-dan the captain of the guard took them, and brought them to the king of Babylon to Rib′-lah.

27 And the king of Babylon smote them, and put them to death in Rib′-lah in the land of Ha′-math. Thus Judah was carried away captive out of his own land.

28 ᴿThis *is* the people whom Neb-u-chad-rez′-zar carried away captive: ᴿin the seventh year three thousand Jews and three and twenty: 2 Kin. 24:2 · 2 Kin. 24:12

29 ᴿIn the eighteenth year of Neb-u-chad-rez′-zar he carried away captive from Jerusalem eight hundred thirty and two persons: 39:9; 2 Kin. 25:11

30 In the three and twentieth year of Neb-u-chad-rez′-zar Neb′-u-zar–a′-dan the captain of the guard carried away captive of the Jews seven hundred forty and five persons: all the persons *were* four thousand and six hundred.

31 And it came to pass in the seven and thirtieth year of the captivity of Je-hoi′-a-chin king of Judah, in the twelfth month, in the five and twentieth *day* of the month, *that* E′-vil–me-ro′-dach king of Babylon in the *first* year of his reign lifted up the head of Je-hoi′-a-chin king of Judah, and brought him forth out of prison,

32 And spake kindly unto him, and set his throne above the throne of the kings that *were* with him in Babylon,

33 And changed his prison garments: ᴿand he did continually eat bread before him all the days of his life. 2 Sam. 9:7, 13; 1 Kin. 2:7

34 And *for* his ᵀdiet, there was a continual diet given him of the king of Babylon, every day a portion until the day of his death, all the days of his life. *provisions*

The Book of
LAMENTATIONS

LAMENTATIONS describes the funeral of a city. It is a tearstained portrait of the once proud Jerusalem, now reduced to rubble by the invading Babylonian hordes. In a five-poem dirge, Jeremiah exposes his emotions. A death has occurred; Jerusalem lies barren.

Jeremiah writes his lament in acrostic or alphabetical fashion. Beginning each chapter with the first letter A (aleph) he progresses verse by verse through the Hebrew alphabet, literally weeping from A to Z. And then, in the midst of this terrible holocaust, Jeremiah triumphantly cries out, "Great is thy faithfulness" (3:23). In the face of death and destruction, with life seemingly coming apart, Jeremiah turns tragedy into a triumph of faith. God has never failed him in the past. God has promised to remain faithful in the future. In the light of the God he knows and loves, Jeremiah finds hope and comfort.

The Hebrew title of this book comes from the first word of chapters 1, 2, and 4: Ekah, "Ah, how!" Another Hebrew word Ginoth ("Elegies" or "Lamentations") has also been used as the title because it better represents the contents of the book. The Greek title Threnoi means "Dirges" or "Laments," and the Latin title Threni ("Tears" or "Lamentations") was derived from this word. The subtitle in Jerome's Vulgate reads: "Id est lamentationes Jeremiae prophetae," and this became the basis for the English title "The Lamentations of Jeremiah."

HOW doth the city sit solitary, *that was* full of people! ᴿ*how* is she become as a widow! she *that was* great among the nations, *and* ᴿprincess among the provinces, *how* is she become tributary! Is. 47:7–9 · Ezra 4:20; Jer. 31:7

2 She ᴿweepeth sore in the ᴿnight, and her tears *are* on her cheeks: among all her lovers she hath none to comfort *her*: all her friends have dealt treacherously with her, they are become her enemies. Jer. 13:17 · Job 7:3

3 Judah is gone into captivity because of affliction, and because of great servitude: she dwelleth among the heathen, she findeth no rest: all her persecutors overtook her between the straits.

4 The ᵀways of Zion do mourn, because none come to the ᵀsolemn feasts: all her gates are ᴿdesolate: her priests sigh, her virgins are afflicted, and she *is* in bitterness. *roads to · appointed* · Is. 27:10

5 Her adversaries are the chief, her enemies prosper; for the Lᴏʀᴅ hath afflicted her for the multitude of her transgressions: her ᴿchildren are gone into captivity before the enemy. Jer. 52:28

6 And from the daughter of Zion all her beauty is departed: her princes are become like ᵀharts *that* find no pasture, and they ᵀare gone without strength before the pursuer. *deer · flee*

7 Jerusalem remembered in the days of her affliction and of her miseries all her pleasant things that she had in the days of old, when her people fell into the hand of the enemy, and none did help her: the adversaries saw her, *and* did mock at her sabbaths.

8 Jerusalem hath grievously sinned; therefore she is removed: all that honoured her despise her, because ᴿthey have seen her nakedness: yea, she sigheth, and turneth backward. Jer. 13:22

9 Her filthiness *is* in her skirts; she ᴿremembereth not her last end; therefore she came down wonderfully: she had no com-

forter. O Lord, behold my affliction: for the enemy hath magnified *himself*.　　Deut. 32:29; Is. 47:7

10 The adversary hath spread
out his hand upon all her pleasant
things: for she hath seen *that* Rthe
heathen entered into her sanctuary, whom thou didst command
that Rthey should not enter into
thy congregation. Jer. 51:51 · Neh. 13:1

11 All her people sigh, Rthey
seek bread; they have given their
pleasant things for meat to relieve
the soul: see, O Lord, and consider; for I am become vile.　　Jer. 38:9

12 *Is it* nothing to you, all ye
that pass by? behold, and see if
there be any sorrow like unto my
sorrow, which is done unto me,
wherewith the Lord hath afflicted
me in the day of his fierce anger.

13 From above hath he sent fire
into my bones, and it prevaileth
against them: he hath Rspread a
net for my feet, he hath turned me
back: he hath made me desolate
and faint all the day.　　Ezek. 17:20

14 RThe yoke of my transgressions is bound by his hand: they
are Twreathed, *and* come up upon my neck: he hath made my
strength Tto fall, the Lord hath
delivered me into *their* hands,
from whom I am not able to rise
up.　　Deut. 28:48 · *woven together · fail*

15 The Lord hath Ttrodden under foot all my mighty *men* in the
midst of me: he hath called an
assembly against me to crush my
young men: Rthe Lord hath trodden the virgin, the daughter of
Judah, *as* in a winepress.　　Is. 63:3

16 For these *things* I weep; mine
eye, mine eye runneth down with
water, because the comforter that
should relieve my soul is far from
me: my children are desolate, because the enemy prevailed.

17 Zion spreadeth forth her
hands, *and there is* none to comfort her: the Lord hath commanded concerning Jacob, *that* his
adversaries *should be* round
about him: Jerusalem is as a menstruous woman among them.

18 The Lord is righteous; for I

have Rrebelled against his commandment: hear, I pray you, all
people, and behold my sorrow:
my virgins and my young men are
gone into captivity.　　1 Sam. 12:14, 15

19 I called for my lovers, *but*
they deceived me: my priests and
mine elders gave up the ghost in
the city, while they sought their
meat to relieve their souls.

20 Behold, O Lord; for I *am* in
distress: my bowels are troubled;
mine heart is turned within me;
for I have grievously rebelled:
Rabroad the sword bereaveth, at
home *there is* as death.　　Ezek. 7:15

21 They have heard that I sigh:
there is none to comfort me: all
mine enemies have heard of my
trouble; they are Rglad that thou
hast done *it*: thou wilt bring the
day *that* thou hast called, and
they shall be like unto me. Ps. 35:15

22 RLet all their wickedness
come before thee; and do unto
them, as thou hast done unto me
for all my transgressions: for my
sighs *are* many, and my heart *is*
faint.　　Ps. 109:15; 137:7, 8; Jer. 30:16

2 How hath the Lord covered
the daughter of Zion with a
Rcloud in his anger, R*and* cast
down from heaven unto the earth
the beauty of Israel, and remembered not his footstool in the day
of his anger!　　[3:44] · Matt. 11:23

2 The Lord hath swallowed up
all the habitations of Jacob, and
hath not pitied: he hath thrown
down in his wrath the strong
holds of the daughter of Judah; he
hath brought *them* down to the
ground: he hath polluted the kingdom and the princes thereof.

3 He hath cut off in *his* fierce
anger all the horn of Israel: Rhe
hath drawn back his right hand
from before the enemy, Rand he
burned against Jacob like a flaming fire, *which* devoureth round
about.　　Ps. 74:11; Jer. 21:4, 5 · Ps. 89:46

4 RHe hath bent his bow like an
enemy: he stood with his right
hand as an adversary, and slew
Rall *that were* pleasant to the eye
in the tabernacle of the daughter

of Zion: he poured out his fury like fire.   Is. 63:10 · Ezek. 24:25

5 ᴿThe Lord was as an enemy: he hath swallowed up Israel, he hath swallowed up all her palaces: he hath destroyed his strong holds, and hath increased in the daughter of Judah mourning and lamentation.   Jer. 30:14

6 And he hath violently ᴿtaken away his tabernacle, ᴿas *if it were of* a garden: he hath destroyed his places of the assembly: the LORD hath caused the solemn feasts and sabbaths to be forgotten in Zion, and hath ᴿdespised in the indignation of his anger the king and the priest.   Jer. 7:14 · Jer. 52:13 · Is. 43:28

7 The Lord hath cast off his altar, he hath abhorred his sanctuary, he hath given up into the hand of the enemy the walls of her palaces; they have made a noise in the house of the LORD, as in the day of a solemn feast.

8 The LORD hath purposed to destroy the ᴿwall of the daughter of Zion: ᴿhe hath stretched out a line, he hath not withdrawn his hand from destroying: therefore he made the rampart and the wall to lament; they languished together.   Jer. 52:14 · [2 Kin. 21:13; Amos 7:7–9]

9 Her gates are sunk into the ground; he hath destroyed and broken her bars: her king and her princes *are* among the Gentiles: the law *is* no *more;* her prophets also find no vision from the LORD.

10 The elders of the daughter of Zion ᴿsit upon the ground, *and* keep silence: they have ᴿcast up dust upon their heads; they have ᴿgirded themselves with sackcloth: the virgins of Jerusalem hang down their heads to the ground.   Is. 3:26 · Ezek. 27:30 · Is. 15:3

11 ᴿMine eyes do fail with tears, my bowels are troubled, ᴿmy liver is poured upon the earth, for the destruction of the daughter of my people; because ᴿthe children and the sucklings swoon in the streets of the city.   3:48; Ps. 6:7 · Ps. 22:14 · 4:4

12 They say to their mothers, Where *is* ᵀcorn and wine? when

they ᵀswooned as the wounded in the streets of the city, when their ᵀsoul was poured out into their mothers' bosom.   *grain · faint · life*

13 What thing shall I take to ᴿwitness for thee? what thing shall I liken to thee, O daughter of Jerusalem? what shall I equal to thee, that I may comfort thee, O virgin daughter of Zion? for thy breach *is* great like the sea: who can heal thee?   1:12; Dan. 9:12

14 Thy ᴿprophets have seen vain and foolish things for thee: and they have not ᴿdiscovered thine iniquity, to turn away thy captivity; but have seen for thee false ᴿburdens and causes of banishment.   Jer. 23:25–29 · Is. 58:1 · Jer. 23:33–36

15 All that pass by ᴿclap *their* hands at thee; they hiss and wag their head at the daughter of Jerusalem, *saying, Is* this the city that *men* call ᴿThe perfection of beauty, The joy of the whole earth?   Ezek. 25:6 · [Ps. 48:2; 50:2]

16 ᴿAll thine enemies have opened their mouth against thee: they hiss and gnash the teeth: they say, ᴿWe have swallowed *her* up: certainly this *is* the day that we looked for; we have found, ᴿwe have seen *it.*   3:46 · Jer. 51:34 · Ps. 35:21

17 The LORD hath done *that* which he had ᴿdevised; he hath fulfilled his word that he had commanded in the days of old: he hath thrown down, and hath not pitied: and he hath caused *thine* enemy to ᴿrejoice over thee, he hath set up the horn of thine adversaries.   Lev. 26:16 · Ps. 38:16

18 Their heart cried unto the Lord, O wall of the daughter of Zion, ᴿlet tears run down like a river day and night: give thyself no rest; let not the apple of thine eye cease.   1:16; Jer. 14:17

19 Arise, ᴿcry out in the night: in the beginning of the watches ᴿpour out thine heart like water before the face of the Lord: lift up thy hands toward him for the life of thy young children, that faint for hunger ᴿin the top of every street.   Ps. 119:147 · Ps. 62:8 · Is. 51:20

20 Behold, O LORD, and consider to whom thou hast done this. ᴿShall the women eat their fruit, *and* children of a span long? shall the priest and the prophet be slain in the sanctuary of the Lord? 4:10

21 The young and the old lie on the ground in the streets: my virgins and my young men are fallen by the sword; thou hast slain *them* in the day of thine anger; thou hast killed, *and* not pitied.

22 Thou hast called as in a solemn day ᴿmy terrors round about, so that in the day of the LORD's anger none escaped nor remained: those that I have swaddled and brought up hath mine enemy consumed. Is. 24:17; Jer. 6:25

3 I *am* the man *that* hath seen affliction by the rod of his wrath.

2 He hath led me, and ᵀbrought *me into* darkness, but not *into* light. made me *walk in*

3 Surely against me is he turned; he turneth his hand *against me* all the day.

4 ᴿMy flesh and my skin hath he made old; he hath ᴿbroken my bones. Job 16:8 · Ps. 51:8; Is. 38:13

5 He hath builded against me, and compassed *me* with ᵀgall and ᵀtravel. bitterness · hardship or woe

6 ᴿHe hath set me in dark places, as *they that be* dead of old. [Ps. 88:5, 6; 143:3]

7 ᴿHe hath hedged me about, that I cannot get out: he hath made my chain heavy. Job 3:23; 19:8

8 Also ᴿwhen I cry and shout, he shutteth out my prayer. Ps. 22:2

9 He hath ᵀinclosed my ways with hewn stone, he hath made my paths crooked. blocked

10 ᴿHe *was* unto me *as* a bear lying in wait, *and as* a lion in secret places. Is. 38:13

11 He hath turned aside my ways, and ᴿpulled me in pieces: he hath made me desolate. Jer. 15:3

12 He hath bent his bow, and set me as a mark for the arrow.

13 He hath caused ᴿthe arrows of his quiver to enter into my ᵀreins. Job 6:4 · loins, lit. kidneys

14 I was a ᴿderision to all my people; *and* ᴿtheir song all the day. Jer. 20:7 · v. 63; Job 30:9; Ps. 69:12

15 ᴿHe hath filled me with bitterness, he hath made me drunken with wormwood. Jer. 9:15

16 He hath also broken my teeth ᴿwith gravel stones, he hath covered me with ashes. [Prov. 20:17]

17 And thou hast removed my soul far off from peace: I forgat ᵀprosperity. Lit. good

18 ᴿAnd I said, My strength and my hope is perished from the LORD: Ps. 31:22

19 Remembering mine affliction and my misery, ᴿthe wormwood and the gall. vv. 5, 15; Jer. 9:15

20 My soul hath *them* still in remembrance, and is ᵀhumbled in me. Lit. is bowed down

21 This I recall to my mind, therefore have I ᴿhope. Ps. 130:7

22 *It is of* the LORD's mercies that we are not consumed, because his compassions fail not.

23 *They are* new every morning: great *is* thy faithfulness.

24 The LORD *is* my ᴿportion, saith my soul; therefore will I ᴿhope in him. Ps. 16:5 · Mic. 7:7

25 The LORD *is* good unto them that ᴿwait for him, to the soul *that* seeketh him. Ps. 130:6; Is. 30:18

26 *It is* good that *a man* should both hope ᴿand quietly wait for the salvation of the LORD. Is. 7:4

27 ᴿ*It is* good for a man that he bear the yoke in his youth. Ps. 94:12

28 ᴿHeᵀ sitteth alone and keepeth silence, because he hath borne *it* upon him. Jer. 15:17 · Let him sit

29 He putteth his mouth in the dust; if so be there may be hope.

30 ᴿHe giveth *his* cheek to him that smiteth him: he is filled full with reproach. Mark 14:65; Luke 22:63

31 ᴿFor the Lord will not cast off for ever: Ps. 77:7; 94:14; [Is. 54:7–10]

32 But though he cause grief, yet will he have compassion according to the multitude of his mercies.

33 For ᴿhe doth not afflict willingly nor grieve the children of men. [Is. 28:21; Ezek. 33:11; Heb. 12:10]

34 To crush under his feet all the prisoners of the earth,

35 To turn aside the ᵀright of a man before the face of the most High,   *justice* due

36 To subvert a man in his cause, the Lord approveth not.

37 Who *is* he ᴿ*that* saith, and it cometh to pass, *when* the Lord commandeth *it* not?   [Ps. 33:9–11]

38 Out of the mouth of the most High proceedeth not ᴿevil and good? [Is. 45:7]; Amos 3:6; [James 3:10, 11]

39 Wherefore doth a living man complain, ᴿa man for the punishment of his sins?   Jer. 30:15; Mic. 7:9

40 Let us search and try our ways, and turn again to the LORD.

41 ᴿLet us lift up our heart with *our* hands unto God in the heavens.   Ps. 86:4

42 ᴿWe have transgressed and have rebelled: thou hast not pardoned.   Neh. 9:26; Jer. 14:20; Dan. 9:5

43 Thou hast covered with anger, and persecuted us: thou hast slain, thou hast not pitied.

44 Thou hast covered thyself with a cloud, that *our* prayer should not pass through.

45 Thou hast made us *as* the ᴿoffscouring and refuse in the midst of the people.   1 Cor. 4:13

46 All our enemies have opened their mouths against us.

47 ᴿFear and a snare is come upon us, ᴿdesolation and destruction.   Is. 24:17, 18; Jer. 48:43, 44 · Is. 51:19

48 ᴿMine eye runneth down with rivers of water for the destruction of the daughter of my people. 2:11

49 ᴿMine eye trickleth down, and ceaseth not, without any intermission,   Ps. 77:2; Jer. 14:17

50 Till the LORD ᴿlook down, and behold from heaven.   5:1; Ps. 80:14

51 Mine eye ᵀaffecteth mine heart because of all the daughters of my city.   *brings suffering to*

52 Mine enemies chased me sore, like a bird, without cause.

53 They have cut off my life ᴿin the dungeon, and ᴿcast a stone upon me.   Jer. 37:16 · Dan. 6:17

54 Waters flowed over mine head; *then* I said, I am cut off.

55 I called upon thy name, O LORD, out of the low dungeon.

56 ᴿThou hast heard my voice: hide not thine ear at my ᵀbreathing, at my cry.   Ps. 3:4 · *sighing*

57 Thou ᴿdrewest near in the day *that* I called upon thee: thou saidst, Fear not.   James 4:8

58 O Lord, thou hast ᴿpleaded the causes of my soul; ᴿthou hast redeemed my life.   Ps. 35:1 · Ps. 71:23

59 O LORD, thou hast seen my wrong: judge thou my cause.

60 Thou hast seen all their vengeance *and* all their ᵀimaginations against me.   *schemes*

61 Thou hast heard their reproach, O LORD, *and* all their imaginations against me;

62 The lips of those that rose up against me, and their ᵀdevice against me all the day.   *whispering*

63 Behold their ᴿsitting down, and their rising up; I *am* their ᵀmusick.   Ps. 139:2 · *taunting song*

64 ᴿRender unto them a recompence, O LORD, according to the work of their hands.   Ps. 28:4

65 Give them sorrow of heart, thy curse unto them.

66 Persecute and destroy them in anger ᴿfrom under the ᴿheavens of the LORD.   Jer. 10:11 · Ps. 8:3

4 How ᵀis the gold become dim! *how* ᵀis the most fine gold changed! the stones of the sanctuary are poured out in the top of every street.   *the gold has · changed is*

2 The precious sons of Zion, comparable to fine gold, how are they esteemed ᴿas earthen pitchers, the work of the hands of the potter!   Is. 30:14; Jer. 19:11; [2 Cor. 4:7]

3 Even the sea monsters draw out the breast, they give suck to their young ones: the daughter of my people *is* become cruel, like the ostriches in the wilderness.

4 The tongue of the sucking child cleaveth to the roof of his mouth for thirst: ᴿthe young children ask bread, *and* no man breaketh *it* unto them.   Ps. 22:15

5 They that ᵀdid feed delicately are desolate in the streets: they

that were brought up in scarlet embrace dunghills. *ate delicacies*

6 For the punishment of the iniquity of the daughter of my people is greater than the punishment of the sin of Sodom, that was overthrown as in a moment, and no hands stayed on her.

7 Her ᵀNazarites were purer than snow, they were whiter than milk, they were more ruddy in body than rubies, their polishing *was* of sapphire: *Or nobles*

8 Their ᵀvisage is blacker than a coal; they are not known in the streets: their skin cleaveth to their bones; it is withered, it is become like a stick. *appearance*

9 *They that be* slain with the sword are better than *they that be* slain with hunger: for these pine away, stricken through for *want of* the fruits of the field.

10 The hands of the pitiful women have ᵀsodden their ᴿown children: they were their ᴿmeat in the destruction of the daughter of my people. *boiled · Is. 49:15 · Deut. 28:57*

11 The LORD hath accomplished his fury; he hath poured out his fierce anger, and ᴿhath kindled a fire in Zion, and it hath devoured the foundations thereof. *Jer. 21:14*

12 The kings of the earth, and all the inhabitants of the world, would not have believed that the adversary and the enemy ᵀshould have ᴿentered into the gates of Jerusalem. *could · Jer. 21:13*

13 For the sins of her prophets, *and* the iniquities of her priests, ᴿthat have shed the blood of the just in the midst of her, *Matt. 23:31*

14 They have wandered *as* blind *men* in the streets, ᴿthey have ᵀpolluted themselves with blood, ᴿso that men could not touch their garments. *Jer. 2:34 · defiled · Num. 19:16*

15 They cried unto them, Depart ye; *it is* ᴿunclean; depart, depart, touch not: when they fled away and wandered, they said among the ᵀheathen, They shall no more sojourn *there*. *Lev. 13:45, 46 · nations*

16 The anger of the LORD hath divided them; he will no more

regard them: ᴿthey respected not the persons of the priests, they favoured not the elders. *5:12*

17 As for us, our eyes as yet failed for our vain help: in our watching we have watched for a nation *that* could not save *us*.

18 ᴿThey hunt our steps, that we cannot go in our streets: our end is near, our days are fulfilled; for our end is come. *2 Kin. 25:4*

19 Our ᵀpersecutors are ᴿswifter than the eagles of the heaven: they pursued us upon the mountains, they laid wait for us in the wilderness. *pursuers · Deut. 28:49*

20 The ᴿbreath of our nostrils, the anointed of the LORD, was taken in their pits, of whom we said, Under his shadow we shall live among the heathen. *Gen. 2:7*

21 Rejoice and be glad, O daughter of ᴿE′-dom, that dwellest in the land of Uz; ᴿthe cup also shall pass through unto thee: thou shalt be drunken, and shalt make thyself naked. *Ps. 83:3–6 · Obad. 10*

22 The punishment of thine iniquity is accomplished, O daughter of Zion; he will no more carry thee away into captivity: he will visit thine iniquity, O daughter of E′-dom; he will discover thy sins.

5 Remember, ᴿO LORD, what is come upon us: consider, and behold our reproach. *Ps. 89:50*

2 Our inheritance is turned to strangers, our houses to aliens.

3 We are orphans and fatherless, our mothers *are* as widows.

4 We ᵀhave drunken our water for money; our wood is sold unto us. *must pay for the water we drink*

5 ᴿOur necks *are* under persecution: we labour, *and* have no rest. *Deut. 28:48; Jer. 28:14*

6 We have given the hand to the Egyptians, *and* to the Assyrians, to be satisfied with bread.

7 ᴿOur fathers have sinned, *and are* not; and we have borne their iniquities. *Jer. 31:29*

8 Servants have ruled over us: *there is* none that doth deliver *us* out of their hand.

9 We ᵀgat our bread with *the*

peril of our lives because of the sword of the wilderness.   *get*

10 Our skin was ᵀblack like an oven because of the ᵀterrible famine.   *hot · fever of*

11 They ᴿravished the women in Zion, *and* the maids in the cities of Judah.   Is. 13:16; Zech. 14:2

12 Princes are hanged up by their hand: the faces of elders were not ᵀhonoured.   *respected*

13 They took the young men to ᴿgrind, and the children fell under the wood.   Judg. 16:21

14 The elders have ceased from the gate, the young men from their ᴿmusick.   Is. 24:8; Jer. 7:34

15 The joy of our heart is ceased; our dance is turned into ᴿmourning.   Jer. 25:10; Amos 8:10

16 ᴿThe crown is fallen *from* our head: woe unto us, that we have sinned!   Job 19:9; Ps. 89:39; Jer. 13:18

17 For this our heart is faint; for these *things* our eyes are dim.

18 Because of the mountain of Zion, which is ᴿdesolate, the foxes walk upon it.   Is. 27:10

19 Thou, O LORD, ᴿremainest for ever; ᴿthy throne from generation to generation.   Hab. 1:12 · Ps. 45:6

20 ᴿWherefore dost thou forget us for ever, *and* forsake us so long time?   Ps. 13:1; 44:24

21 ᴿTurn thou us unto thee, O LORD, and we shall be turned; renew our days as of old.   Jer. 31:18

22 But thou hast utterly rejected us; thou art very wroth against us.

The Book of

EZEKIEL

EZEKIEL, a priest and a prophet, ministers during the darkest days of Judah's history: the seventy-year period of Babylonian captivity. Carried to Babylon before the final assault on Jerusalem, Ezekiel uses prophecies, parables, signs, and symbols to dramatize God's message to His exiled people. Though they are like dry bones in the sun, God will reassemble them and breathe life into the nation once again. Present judgment will be followed by future glory so that "ye shall know that I *am* the LORD" (6:7).

The Hebrew name *Yehezke'l* means "God Strengthens" or "Strengthened by God." Ezekiel is indeed strengthened by God for the prophetic ministry to which he is called (3:8, 9). The name occurs twice in this book and nowhere else in the Old Testament. The Greek form in the Septuagint is *Iezekiel* and the Latin form in the Vulgate is *Ezechiel.*

NOW it came to pass in the thirtieth year, in the fourth *month,* in the fifth *day* of the month, as I *was* among the captives by the river of Che'-bar, *that* ᴿthe heavens were opened, and I saw visions of God.   Matt. 3:16

2 In the fifth *day* of the month, which *was* the fifth year of king Je-hoi'-a-chin's captivity,

3 The word of the LORD came expressly unto E-ze'-ki-el the priest, the son of Bu'-zi, in the land of the Chal-de'-ans by the river Che'-bar; and the hand of the LORD was there upon him.

4 And I looked, and, behold, ᴿa whirlwind came ᴿout of the north, a great cloud, and a fire infolding itself, and a brightness *was* about it, and out of the midst thereof as the colour of amber, out of the midst of the fire.   Jer. 23:19 · Jer. 1:1

5 ᴿAlso out of the midst thereof *came* the likeness of four living creatures. And this *was* their ap-

pearance; they had ᴿthe likeness of a man. 10:15, 17, 20; Rev. 4:6–8 · 10:14

6 And every one had four faces, and every one had four wings.

7 And their feet *were* straight feet; and the sole of their feet *was* like the sole of a calf's foot: and they sparkled ᴿlike the colour of burnished brass. Dan. 10:6; Rev. 1:15

8 ᴿAnd *they had* the hands of a man under their wings on their four sides; and they four had their faces and their wings. 10:8, 21

9 Their wings ᵀ*were* joined one to another; they turned not when they went; they went every one straight ᴿforward. touched · 10:20–22

10 As for the likeness of their faces, they four had the face of a man, and the face of a lion, on the right side: and they four had the face of an ox on the left side; they four also had the face of an eagle.

11 Thus *were* their faces: and their wings *were* stretched upward; two *wings* of every one ᵀ*were* joined one to another, and two covered their bodies. touched

12 And ᴿthey went every one straight forward: whither the spirit was to go, they went; *and* they turned not when they went. 10:11

13 As for the likeness of the living creatures, their appearance *was* like burning coals of fire, *and* like the appearance of lamps: it went ᵀup and down among the living creatures; and the fire was bright, and out of the fire went forth lightning. back and forth

14 And the living creatures ran and returned ᴿas the appearance of a flash of lightning. Zech. 4:10

15 Now as I beheld the living creatures, behold ᴿone wheel upon the earth by the living creatures, with his four faces. 10:9

16 ᴿThe appearance of the wheels and their work *was* ᴿlike unto the colour of a beryl: and they four had one likeness: and their appearance and their work *was* as it were a wheel in the middle of a wheel. 10:9, 10 · Dan. 10:6

17 When they went, they went

upon their four sides: *and* they turned not when they went.

18 As for their rings, they were so high that they were dreadful; and their rings *were* ᴿfull of eyes round about them four. Rev. 4:6, 8

19 And when the living creatures went, the wheels went by them: and when the living creatures were lifted up from the earth, the wheels were lifted up.

20 Whithersoever the spirit was to go, they went, thither *was their* spirit to go; and the wheels were lifted up ᵀover against them: for the spirit of the living creature *was* in the wheels. together with

21 When those went, *these* went; and when those stood, *these* stood; and when those were lifted up from the earth, the wheels were lifted up over against them: for the spirit of the living creature *was* in the wheels.

22 And the likeness of the firmament upon the heads of the living creature *was* as the colour of the terrible crystal, stretched forth over their heads above.

23 And under the firmament *were* their wings ᵀstraight, the one toward the other: every one had two, which covered on this side, and every one had two, which covered on that side, their bodies. spread out *straight*

24 ᴿAnd when they went, I heard the noise of their wings, like the noise of great waters, as ᴿthe voice of the Almighty, the voice of speech, as the noise of an host: when they stood, they let down their wings. 10:5 · Job 37:4, 5

25 And there was a voice from the firmament that *was* over their heads, when they stood, *and* had let down their wings.

26 ᴿAnd above the firmament that *was* over their heads *was* the likeness of a throne, ᴿas the appearance of a sapphire stone: and upon the likeness of the throne *was* the likeness as the appearance of a man above upon ᴿit. 10:1 · Ex. 24:10, 16 · 8:2

27 ᴿAnd I saw as the colour of

amber, as the appearance of fire round about within it, from the appearance of his ᵀloins even upward, and from the appearance of his ᵀloins even downward, I saw as it were the appearance of fire, and it had brightness round about.　　　　8:2 · *waist and*

28 ᴿAs the appearance of the bow that is in the cloud in the day of rain, so *was* the appearance of the brightness round about. This *was* the appearance of the likeness of the glory of the LORD. And when I saw *it*, I fell upon my face, and I heard a voice of one that spake.　　[Gen. 9:13]; Rev. 4:3; 10:1

2 And he said unto me, Son of man, ᴿstand upon thy feet, and I will speak unto thee.　　Acts 9:6

2 And ᴿthe spirit entered into me when he spake unto me, and set me upon my feet, that I heard him that spake unto me.　　3:24; Dan. 8:18

3 And he said unto me, Son of man, I send thee to the children of Israel, to a rebellious nation that hath ᴿrebelled against me: ᴿthey and their fathers have transgressed against me, *even* unto this very day.　5:6; 20:8, 13, 18 · 1 Sam. 8:7, 8

4 ᴿFor *they are* impudent children and stiffhearted. I do send thee unto them; and thou shalt say unto them, Thus saith the Lord GOD.　Ps. 95:8; Is. 48:4; Jer. 5:3; 6:15

5 ᴿAnd they, whether they will hear, or whether they will forbear, (for they *are* a rebellious house,) yet shall know that there hath been a prophet among them.　3:11

6 And thou, son of man, ᴿbe not afraid of them, neither be afraid of their words, though briers and thorns *be* with thee, and thou dost dwell among scorpions: be not afraid of their words, nor be dismayed at their looks, though they *be* a rebellious house.　3:9; Is. 51:12

7 ᴿAnd thou shalt speak my words unto them, whether they will hear, or whether they will ᵀforbear: for they *are* most rebellious.　[3:10, 17]; Jer. 1:7, 17 · *refuse*

8 But thou, son of man, hear what I say unto thee; Be not thou rebellious like that rebellious house: open thy mouth, and ᴿeat that I give thee.　3:1–3; Rev. 10:9

9 And when I looked, behold, an hand *was* sent unto me; and, lo, a roll of a book *was* therein;

10 And he spread it before me; and it *was* written within and without: and *there was* written therein lamentations, and mourning, and woe.

3 Moreover he said unto me, Son of man, eat that thou findest; ᴿeat this roll, and go speak unto the house of Israel.　2:8, 9

2 So I opened my mouth, and he caused me to eat that roll.

3 And he said unto me, Son of man, cause thy belly to eat, and fill thy bowels with this roll that I give thee. Then did I ᴿeat *it*; and it was in my mouth ᴿas honey for sweetness.　Rev. 10:9 · Ps. 19:10; 119:103

4 And he said unto me, Son of man, go, get thee unto the house of Israel, and speak with my words unto them.

5 For thou *art* not sent to a people of ᵀa strange speech and of an hard language, *but* to the house of Israel;　　*unfamiliar*

6 Not to many people of a strange speech and of an hard language, whose words thou canst not understand. Surely, had I sent thee to them, they would have hearkened unto thee.

7 But the house of Israel will not hearken unto thee; ᴿfor they will not hearken unto me: ᴿfor all the house of Israel *are* impudent and hardhearted.　John 15:20, 21 · 2:4

8 Behold, I have made thy face strong against their faces, and thy forehead strong against their foreheads.

9 ᴿAs an adamant harder than flint have I made thy forehead: ᴿfear them not, neither be dismayed at their looks, though they *be* a rebellious house.　Is. 50:7 · 2:6

10 Moreover he said unto me, Son of man, all my words that I shall speak unto thee receive in thine heart, and hear with thine ears.

11 And go, get thee to them of the captivity, unto the children of thy people, and speak unto them, and tell them, ᴿThus saith the Lord GOD; whether they will hear, or whether they will forbear. 2:5, 7

12 Then ᴿthe spirit took me up, and I heard behind me a voice of a great rushing, *saying*, Blessed *be* the ᴿglory of the LORD from his place. 8:3; 1 Kin. 18:12; Acts 8:39 · 1:28; 8:4

13 *I heard* also the ᴿnoise of the wings of the living creatures that touched one another, and the noise of the wheels over against them, and a noise of a great ᵀrushing. 1:24; 10:5 · *tumult*

14 So the spirit lifted me up, and took me away, and I went in bitterness, in the ᵀheat of my spirit; but ᴿthe hand of the LORD was strong upon me. Or *anger* · 2 Kin. 3:15

15 Then I came to them of the captivity at Tel–a′-bib, that dwelt by the river of Che′-bar, and ᴿI sat where they sat, and remained there astonished among them seven days. Job 2:13; Ps. 137:1

16 And it came to pass at the end of seven days, that the word of the LORD came unto me, saying,

17 ᴿSon of man, I have made thee ᴿa watchman unto the house of Israel: therefore hear the word at my mouth, and give them warning from me. 33:7–9 · Is. 52:8

18 When I say unto the wicked, Thou shalt surely die; and thou givest him not warning, nor speakest to warn the wicked from his wicked way, to save his life; the same wicked *man* ᴿshall die in his iniquity; but his blood will I require at thine hand. [John 8:21, 24]

19 Yet if thou warn the wicked, and he turn not from his wickedness, nor from his wicked way, he shall die in his iniquity; ᴿbut thou hast delivered thy soul. 1 Tim. 4:16

20 Again, When a ᴿrighteous *man* doth turn from his righteousness, and commit iniquity, and I lay a stumblingblock before him, he shall die: because thou hast not given him warning, he shall die in his sin, and his righteousness which he hath done shall not be remembered; but his blood will I require at thine hand. Ps. 125:5

21 Nevertheless if thou warn the righteous *man*, that the righteous sin not, and he doth not sin, he shall surely live, because he ᵀis warned; also thou hast delivered thy soul. *took warning*

22 ᴿAnd the hand of the LORD was there upon me; and he said unto me, Arise, go forth ᴿinto the plain, and I will there talk with thee. 1:3 · 8:4

23 Then I arose, and went forth into the plain: and, behold, the glory of the LORD stood there, as the glory which I saw by the river of Che′-bar: and I fell on my face.

24 Then ᴿthe spirit entered into me, and set me upon my feet, and spake with me, and said unto me, Go, shut thyself within thine house. 2:2

25 But thou, O son of man, behold, ᴿthey shall put ᵀbands upon thee, and shall bind thee with them, and thou shalt not go out among them: 4:8 · *ropes*

26 And ᴿI will make thy tongue cleave to the roof of thy mouth, that thou shalt be dumb, and shalt not be to them a reprover: for they *are* a rebellious house. 24:27

27 ᴿBut when I speak with thee, I will open thy mouth, and thou shalt say unto them, Thus saith the Lord GOD; He that heareth, let him hear; and he that forbeareth, let him forbear: for they *are* a rebellious house. Ex. 4:11, 12

4 Thou also, son of man, take thee a ᵀtile, and lay it before thee, and pourtray upon it the city, *even* Jerusalem: *clay tablet*

2 And ᴿlay siege against it, and build a fort against it, and cast a mount against it; set the camp also against it, and set *battering* rams against it round about. 21:22

3 Moreover take thou unto thee an iron pan, and set it *for* a wall of iron between thee and the city: and set thy face against it, and it shall be ᴿbesieged, and thou shalt

lay siege against it. This *shall be* a sign to the house of Israel.　5:2

4 Lie thou also upon thy left side, and lay the iniquity of the house of Israel upon it: *according* to the number of the days that thou shalt lie upon it thou shalt bear their iniquity.

5 For I have laid upon thee the years of their iniquity, according to the number of the days, three hundred and ninety days: ᴿso shalt thou bear the iniquity of the house of Israel.　Num. 14:34

6 And when thou hast accomplished them, lie again on thy right side, and thou shalt bear the iniquity of the house of Judah forty days: I have appointed thee each day for a year.

7 Therefore thou shalt set thy face toward the siege of Jerusalem, and thine arm *shall be* uncovered, and thou shalt prophesy against it.

8 ᴿAnd, behold, I will ᵀlay bands upon thee, and thou shalt not turn thee from one side to another, till thou hast ended the days of thy siege.　3:25 · *constrain thee*

9 Take thou also unto thee wheat, and barley, and beans, and lentiles, and millet, and ᵀfitches, and put them in one vessel, and make thee bread thereof, *according* to the number of the days that thou shalt lie upon thy side, three hundred and ninety days shalt thou eat thereof.　*spelt*

10 And thy ᵀmeat which thou shalt eat *shall be* by weight, twenty shek'-els a day: from time to time shalt thou eat it.　*food*

11 Thou shalt drink also water by measure, the sixth part of an hin: from time to time shalt thou drink.

12 And thou shalt eat it *as* barley cakes, and thou shalt bake it with dung that cometh out of man, in their sight.

13 And the Lᴏʀᴅ said, Even thus ᴿshall the children of Israel eat their defiled bread among the Gentiles, whither I will drive them.　Dan. 1:8; Hos. 9:3

14 Then said I, Ah Lord Gᴏᴅ! behold, my soul hath not been polluted: for from my youth up even till now have I not eaten of that which dieth of itself, or is torn in pieces; neither came there abominable flesh into my mouth.

15 Then he said unto me, Lo, I have given thee cow's dung for man's dung, and thou shalt prepare thy bread ᵀtherewith.　*over it*

16 Moreover he said unto me, Son of man, behold, I will break the ᴿstaff of bread in Jerusalem: and they shall eat bread by weight, and with care; and they shall drink water by measure, and with astonishment:　Lev. 26:26; Is. 3:1

17 That they may want bread and water, and be astonied one with another, and ᴿconsume away for their iniquity.　Lev. 26:39

5 And thou, son of man, take thee a sharp knife, take thee a barber's razor, ᴿand cause *it* to pass upon thine head and upon thy beard: then take thee balances to weigh, and divide the *hair*.　44:20

2 Thou shalt burn with fire a third part in the midst of ᴿthe city, when the days of the siege are fulfilled: and thou shalt take a third part, *and* smite about it with a knife: and a third part thou shalt scatter in the wind; and I will draw out a sword after them.　4:1

3 ᴿThou shalt also take thereof a few in number, and bind them in thy ᵀskirts.　Jer. 40:6; 52:16 · *garment*

4 Then take of them again, and ᴿcast them into the midst of the fire, and burn them in the fire; *for* thereof shall a fire come forth into all the house of Israel.　Jer. 41:1, 2

5 Thus saith the Lord Gᴏᴅ; This *is* Jerusalem: I have set it in the midst of the nations and countries *that are* round about her.

6 And she hath changed my judgments into wickedness more than the nations, and my statutes more than the countries that *are* round about her: for they have refused my judgments and my statutes, they have not walked in them.

7 Therefore thus saith the Lord God; Because ye multiplied more than the nations that *are* round about you, *and* have not walked in my statutes, neither have kept my judgments, neither have done according to the judgments of the nations that *are* round about you;

8 Therefore thus saith the Lord God; Behold, I, even I, *am* against thee, and will execute judgments in the midst of thee in the sight of the nations.

9 ᴿAnd I will do in thee that which I have not done, and whereunto I will not do any more the like, because of all thine abominations.   Lam. 4:6; Dan. 9:12; Matt. 24:21

10 Therefore the fathers ᴿshall eat the sons in the midst of thee, and the sons shall eat their fathers; and I will execute judgments in thee, and the whole remnant of thee will I ᴿscatter into all the winds.   Jer. 19:9 · Ps. 44:11; Amos 9:9

11 Wherefore, *as* I live, saith the Lord God; Surely, because thou hast defiled my sanctuary with all thy ᴿdetestable things, and with all thine abominations, therefore will I also diminish *thee*; neither shall mine eye spare, neither will I have any pity.   11:21

12 A third part of thee shall die with the pestilence, and with famine shall they be consumed in the midst of thee: and a third part shall fall by the sword round about thee; and I will scatter a third part into all the winds, and I will draw out a sword after them.

13 Thus shall mine anger be accomplished, and I will cause my fury to rest upon them, and I will be comforted: ᴿand they shall know that I the Lord have spoken *it* in my zeal, when I have accomplished my fury in them.   Is. 59:17

14 Moreover I will make thee waste, and a reproach among the nations that *are* round about thee, in the sight of all that pass by.

15 So it shall be a ᴿreproach and a taunt, an ᴿinstruction and an astonishment unto the nations that *are* round about thee, when I shall execute judgments in thee in anger and in fury and in ᴿfurious rebukes. I the Lord have spoken *it*.   Ps. 79:4 · 1 Cor. 10:11 · Is. 66:15, 16

16 When I shall send upon them the evil arrows of famine, which shall be for *their* destruction, *and* which I will send to destroy you: and I will increase the famine upon you, and will break your ᴿstaff of bread: 4:16; 14:13; Lev. 26:26

17 So will I send upon you famine and ᴿevil beasts, and they shall bereave thee; and ᴿpestilence and blood shall pass through thee; and I will bring the sword upon thee. I the Lord have spoken *it*.   33:27; 34:25; Rev. 6:8 · 38:22

6 And the word of the Lord came unto me, saying,

2 Son of man, ᴿset thy face toward the mountains of Israel, and prophesy against them,   21:2

3 And say, Ye mountains of Israel, hear the word of the Lord God; Thus saith the Lord God to the mountains, and to the hills, to the rivers, and to the valleys; Behold, I, *even* I, will bring a sword upon you, and ᴿI will destroy your high places.   Lev. 26:30

4 And your altars shall be desolate, and your images shall be broken: and I will cast down your slain *men* before your idols.

5 And I will lay the dead carcases of the children of Israel before their idols; and I will scatter your bones round about your altars.

6 In all your dwellingplaces the cities shall be laid ᵀwaste, and the high places shall be desolate; that your altars may be laid waste and made desolate, and your idols may be broken and ᵀcease, and your ᵀimages may be cut down, and your works may be abolished.   *in ruins · ended · incense altars*

7 And the slain shall fall in the midst of you, and ᴿye shall know that I *am* the Lord.   7:4, 9

8 ᴿYet will I leave a remnant, that ye may have *some* that shall escape the sword among the na-

tions, when ye shall be ^Rscattered through the countries.   14:22 · 5:12

9 And they that escape of you shall remember me among the nations whither they shall be carried captives, because ^RI am broken with their whorish heart, which hath departed from me, and with their eyes, which go a whoring after their idols: and ^Rthey shall lothe themselves for the evils which they have committed in all their abominations.   Is. 7:13 · 20:43

10 And they shall know that I *am* the LORD, *and that* I have not said in vain that I would ^Tdo this evil unto them.   *bring this calamity*

11 Thus saith the Lord GOD; Smite ^Rwith thine hand, and stamp with thy foot, and say, Alas for all the evil abominations of the house of Israel! ^Rfor they shall fall by the sword, by the famine, and by the pestilence.   21:14 · 5:12

12 He that is far off shall die of the pestilence; and he that is near shall fall by the sword; and he that remaineth and is besieged shall die by the famine: thus will I accomplish my fury upon them.

13 Then shall ye know that I *am* the LORD, when their slain *men* shall be among their idols round about their altars, ^Rupon every high hill, ^Rin all the tops of the mountains, and ^Runder every green tree, and under every thick oak, the place where they did offer sweet savour to all their idols.   Jer. 2:20; 3:6 · Hos. 4:13 · Is. 57:5

14 So will I stretch out my hand upon them, and make the land desolate, yea, more desolate than the wilderness toward Dib'-lath, in all their habitations: and they shall know that I *am* the LORD.

7 Moreover the word of the LORD came unto me, saying,

2 Also, thou son of man, thus saith the Lord GOD unto the land of Israel; An end, the end is come upon the four corners of the land.

3 Now *is* the end *come* upon thee, and I will send mine anger upon thee, and will judge thee ^Raccording to thy ways, and will

^Trecompense upon thee all thine abominations. [Rom. 2:6] · *repay you for*

4 And ^Rmine eye shall not spare thee, neither will I have pity: but I will recompense thy ways upon thee, and thine abominations shall be in the midst of thee: ^Rand ye shall know that I *am* the LORD.   5:11 · 12:20

5 Thus saith the Lord GOD; An evil, an only evil, behold, is come.

6 An end is come, the end is come: it ^Twatcheth for thee; behold, it is come.   *has dawned*

7 ^RThe morning is come unto thee, O thou that dwellest in the land: the time is come, the day of trouble *is* near, and not the sounding again of the mountains.   v. 10

8 Now will I shortly ^Rpour out my fury upon thee, and accomplish mine anger upon thee: and I will judge thee according to thy ways, and will recompense thee for all thine abominations.   20:8, 21

9 And mine eye shall not spare, neither will I have pity: I will ^Trecompense thee according to thy ways and thine abominations *that* are in the midst of thee; and ye shall know that I *am* the LORD that ^Tsmiteth.   *repay,* lit. *give · strikes*

10 Behold the day, behold, it is come: ^Rthe morning is gone forth; the rod hath blossomed, pride hath budded.   v. 7

11 ^RViolence is risen up into a rod of wickedness: none of them *shall remain,* nor of their multitude, nor of any of ^Ttheirs: ^Rneither *shall there be* wailing for them.   Jer. 6:7 · Or *their wealth* · 24:16, 22

12 The time is come, the day draweth near: let not the buyer ^Rrejoice, nor the seller ^Rmourn: for wrath *is* upon all the multitude thereof.   Prov. 20:14; 1 Cor. 7:30 · Is. 24:2

13 For the seller shall not return to that which is sold, although they were yet alive: for the vision *is* touching the whole multitude thereof, *which* shall not return; neither shall any strengthen himself in the iniquity of his life.

14 They have blown the trumpet, even to make all ready; but

none goeth to the battle: for my wrath *is* upon all the multitude thereof.

15 ^RThe sword *is* without, and the pestilence and the famine within: he that *is* in the field shall die with the sword; and he that *is* in the city, famine and pestilence shall devour him.   Jer. 14:18; Lam. 1:20

16 But they that ^Rescape of them shall escape, and shall be on the mountains like doves of the valleys, all of them mourning, every one for his iniquity.   14:22; Is. 37:31

17 All ^Rhands shall be feeble, and all knees shall be weak *as* water.   Is. 13:7; Jer. 6:24; Heb. 12:12

18 They shall also ^Rgird *themselves* with sackcloth, and horror shall cover them; and shame *shall be* upon all faces, and baldness upon all their heads.   Is. 3:24; 15:2, 3

19 They shall cast their silver in the streets, and their gold shall be removed: their silver and their gold shall not be able to deliver them in the day of the wrath of the LORD: they shall not satisfy their souls, neither fill their bowels: because it ^Tis the stumbling-block of their iniquity.   *became*

20 As for the beauty of his ornament, he set it in majesty: ^Rbut they made the images of their abominations *and* of their detestable things therein: therefore have I set it far from them.   Jer. 7:30

21 And I will give it into the hands of the strangers for a prey, and to the wicked of the earth for a spoil; and they shall pollute it.

22 My face will I turn also from them, and they shall ^Tpollute my secret *place:* for the robbers shall enter into it, and defile it.   *defile*

23 Make a chain: for ^Rthe land is full of bloody crimes, and the city is full of violence.   2 Kin. 21:16

24 Wherefore I will bring the ^Rworst of the heathen, and they shall possess their houses: I will also make the pomp of the strong to cease; and their holy places shall be ^Rdefiled.   21:31; 28:7 · 24:21

25 ^TDestruction cometh; and they shall seek peace, and *there shall be* none.   Lit. *Anguish*

26 ^RMischief shall come upon mischief, and rumour shall be upon rumour; ^Rthen shall they seek a vision of the prophet; but the law shall perish from the priest, and counsel from the ancients.   Is. 47:11 · Ps. 74:9; Mic. 3:6

27 The king shall mourn, and the prince shall be clothed with desolation, and the hands of the people of the land shall be troubled: I will do unto them ^Tafter their way, and according to ^Ttheir deserts will I judge them; and they shall know that I *am* the LORD.   *according to · what they deserve*

8 And it came to pass in the sixth year, in the sixth *month,* in the fifth *day* of the month, *as* I sat in mine house, and ^Rthe elders of Judah sat before me, that ^Rthe hand of the Lord GOD fell there upon me.   14:1; 20:1; 33:31 · 1:3; 3:22

2 ^RThen I beheld, and lo a likeness as the appearance of fire: from the appearance of his loins even downward, fire; and from his loins even upward, as the appearance of brightness, ^Ras the colour of amber.   1:26, 27 · 1:4, 27

3 And he ^Rput forth the form of an hand, and took me by a lock of mine head; and ^Rthe spirit lifted me up between the earth and the heaven, and ^Rbrought me in the visions of God to Jerusalem, to the door of the inner gate, that looketh toward the north; where *was* the seat of the image of jealousy, which provoketh to jealousy.   Dan. 5:5 · 3:14; Acts 8:39 · 11:1, 24

4 And, behold, the ^Rglory of the God of Israel *was* there, according to the vision that I ^Rsaw in the plain.   3:12; 9:3 · 1:28; 3:22, 23

5 Then said he unto me, Son of man, lift up thine eyes now the way toward the north. So I lifted up mine eyes the way toward the north, and behold northward at the gate of the altar this image of jealousy in the ^Tentry.   *entrance*

6 He said furthermore unto me, Son of man, seest thou what they

do? *even* the great ^Rabominations that the house of Israel committeth here, that I should go far off from my sanctuary? but turn thee yet again, *and* thou shalt see greater abominations.   2 Kin. 23:4, 5

7 And he brought me to the door of the court; and when I looked, behold a hole in the wall.

8 Then said he unto me, Son of man, dig now in the wall: and when I had digged in the wall, behold a door.

9 And he said unto me, Go in, and behold the wicked abominations that they do here.

10 So I went in and saw; and behold every ^Rform of ^Rcreeping things, and abominable beasts, and all the idols of the house of Israel, pourtrayed upon the wall round about.   Ex. 20:4 · Rom. 1:23

11 And there stood before them seventy men of the ancients of the house of Israel, and in the midst of them stood Ja-az-a-ni'-ah the son of Sha'-phan, with every man his censer in his hand; and a thick cloud of incense went up.

12 Then said he unto me, Son of man, hast thou seen what the ancients of the house of Israel do in the dark, every man in the chambers of his imagery? for they say, The LORD seeth us not; the LORD hath forsaken the earth.

13 He said also unto me, Turn thee yet again, *and* thou shalt see greater abominations that they do.

14 Then he brought me to the door of the gate of the LORD's house which *was* toward the north; and, behold, there sat women weeping for Tam'-muz.

15 Then said he unto me, Hast thou seen *this,* O son of man? turn thee yet again, *and* thou shalt see greater abominations than these.

16 And he brought me into the inner court of the LORD's house, and, behold, at the door of the temple of the LORD, ^Rbetween the porch and the altar, *were* about five and twenty men, with their backs toward the temple of the

LORD, and their faces toward the east; and they worshipped the sun toward the east.   Joel 2:17

17 Then he said unto me, Hast thou seen *this,* O son of man? Is it a light thing to the house of Judah that they commit the abominations which they commit here? for they have ^Rfilled the land with violence, and have returned to provoke me to anger: and, lo, they put the branch to their nose.   9:9

18 ^RTherefore will I also deal in fury: mine ^Reye shall not spare, neither will I have pity: and though they ^Rcry in mine ears with a loud voice, *yet* will I not hear them.   24:13 · 5:11 · Zech. 7:13

9 He cried also in mine ^Tears with a loud voice, saying, ^TCause them that have charge over the city to draw near, even every man *with* his destroying weapon in his hand.   *hearing · Let*

2 And, behold, six men came from the way of the higher gate, which lieth toward the north, and every man a slaughter weapon in his hand; ^Rand one man among them *was* clothed with linen, with a writer's inkhorn by his side: and they went in, and stood beside the brasen altar.   10:2; Lev. 16:4; Rev. 15:6

3 And ^Rthe glory of the God of Israel was gone up from the cherub, whereupon he was, to the threshold of the house. And he called to the man clothed with linen, which *had* the writer's inkhorn by his side;   3:23; 10:4, 18

4 And the LORD said unto him, Go through the midst of the city, through the midst of Jerusalem, and set a mark upon the foreheads of the men that sigh and that cry for all the abominations that be done in the midst thereof.

5 And to the others he said in mine hearing, Go ye after him through the city, and ^Rsmite:^T ^Rlet not your eye spare, neither have ye pity: 7:9 · *kill* · 5:11

6 Slay utterly old *and* young, both maids, and little children, and women: but come not near

any man upon whom *is* the mark; and begin at my sanctuary. Then they began at the ancient men which *were* before the house.

7 And he said unto them, Defile the ᵀhouse, and fill the courts with the slain: go ye forth. And they went forth, and slew in the city.   temple

8 And it came to pass, while they were slaying them, and I was left, that I fell upon my face, and cried, and said, Ah Lord GOD! wilt thou destroy all the ᵀresidue of Israel in thy pouring out of thy fury upon Jerusalem?   remnant

9 Then said he unto me, The iniquity of the house of Israel and Judah *is* exceeding great, and ᴿthe land is full of blood, and the city full of perverseness: for they say, The LORD hath forsaken the earth, and the LORD seeth not. 2 Kin. 21:16

10 And as for me also, mine ᴿeye shall not spare, neither will I have pity, *but* ᴿI will recompense their way upon their head. Is. 65:6 · 11:21

11 And, behold, the man clothed with linen, which *had* the inkhorn by his side, reported the matter, saying, I have done as thou hast commanded me.

10 Then I looked, and, behold, in the ᴿfirmamentᵀ that was above the head of the cher'-u-bims there appeared over them as it were a sapphire stone, as the appearance of the likeness of a throne.   1:22, 26 · *expanse*

2 ᴿAnd he spake unto the man clothed with linen, and said, Go in between the wheels, *even* under the cherub, and fill thine hand with ᴿcoals of fire from between the cher'-u-bims, and ᴿscatter *them* over the city. And he went in in my sight. Dan. 10:5 · Is. 6:6 · Rev. 8:5

3 Now the cher'-u-bims stood on the right side of the house, when the man went in; and the cloud filled the inner court.

4 ᴿThen the glory of the LORD went up from the cherub, *and* stood over the threshold of the house; and ᴿthe house was filled with the cloud, and the court was full of the brightness of the LORD's ᴿglory.   1:28 · 1 Kin. 8:10 · 11:22, 23

5 And the ᴿsound of the cher'-u-bims' wings was heard *even* to the outer court, as ᴿthe voice of the Almighty God when he speaketh.   [Job 40:9; Rev. 10:3] · [Ps. 29:3]

6 And it came to pass, *that* when he had commanded the man clothed with linen, saying, Take fire from between the wheels, from between the cher'-u-bims; then he went in, and stood beside the wheels.

7 And *one* cherub stretched forth his hand from between the cher'-u-bims unto the fire that *was* between the cher'-u-bims, and took *thereof*, and put *it* into the hands of *him that was* clothed with linen: who took *it*, and went out.

8 ᴿAnd there appeared in the cher'-u-bims the form of a man's hand under their wings.   v. 21; 1:8

9 ᴿAnd when I looked, behold the four wheels by the cher'-u-bims, one wheel by one cherub, and another wheel by another cherub: and the appearance of the wheels *was* as the colour of a ᴿberyl stone.   1:15 · 1:16

10 And *as for* their appearances, they four ᵀhad one likeness, as if a wheel had been in the ᵀmidst of a wheel.   *looked alike · middle*

11 ᴿWhen they went, they went upon their four sides; they ᵀturned not as they went, but to the place whither the head looked they followed it; they ᵀturned not as they went.   1:17 · *did not turn aside*

12 And their whole body, and their backs, and their hands, and their wings, and the wheels, *were* ᴿfull of eyes round about, *even* the wheels that they four had. Rev. 4:6

13 As for the wheels, it was cried unto them in my hearing, O wheel.

14 ᴿAnd every one had four faces: the first face *was* the face of a cherub, and the second face *was* the face of a man, and the third the face of a lion, and the fourth the face of an eagle. Rev. 4:7

15 And the cher'-u-bims were lifted up. This *is* ^Rthe living creature that I saw by the river of Che'-bar.   1:3, 5

16 ^RAnd when the cher'-u-bims went, the wheels went by them: and when the cher'-u-bims lifted up their wings to mount up from the earth, the same wheels also turned not from beside them.   1:19

17 ^RWhen they stood, *these* stood; and when they were lifted up, *these* lifted up themselves *also*: for the spirit of the living creature *was* in them.   1:12, 20, 21

18 Then ^Rthe glory of the LORD ^Rdeparted from off the threshold of the house, and stood over the cher'-u-bims.   v. 4 · Hos. 9:12

19 And ^Rthe cher'-u-bims lifted up their wings, and mounted up from the earth in my sight: when they went out, the wheels also *were* beside them, and *every one* stood at the door of the ^Reast gate of the LORD's house; and the glory of the God of Israel *was* over them above.   11:22 · 11:1

20 ^RThis *is* the living creature that I saw under the God of Israel ^Rby the river of Che'-bar; and I knew that they *were* the cher'-u-bims.   1:22 · 1:1

21 ^REvery one had four faces apiece, and every one four wings; and the likeness of the hands of a man *was* under their wings.   1:6, 8

22 And ^Rthe likeness of their faces *was* the same faces which I saw by the river of Che'-bar, their appearances and ^Tthemselves: ^Rthey went every one straight forward.   1:10 · *their persons* · 1:9, 12

11 Moreover ^Rthe spirit lifted me up, and brought me unto ^Rthe east gate of the LORD's house, which looketh eastward: and behold ^Rat the door of the gate five and twenty men; among whom I saw Ja-az-a-ni'-ah the son of A'-zur, and Pel-a-ti'-ah the son of Be-na'-iah, princes of the people.   3:12, 14 · 10:19 · 8:16

2 Then said he unto me, Son of man, these *are* the men that de-

vise ^Tmischief, and give wicked counsel in this city: *iniquity*

3 Which say, *It is* not ^Rnear; let us build houses: this *city is* the caldron, and we *be* the flesh. 12:22

4 Therefore prophesy against them, prophesy, O son of man.

5 And ^Rthe Spirit of the LORD fell upon me, and said unto me, Speak; Thus saith the LORD; Thus have ye said, O house of Israel: for I know the things that come into your mind, *every one of* them.   2:2

6 Ye have multiplied your slain in this city, and ye have filled the streets thereof with the slain.

7 Therefore thus saith the Lord GOD; Your slain whom ye have laid in the midst of it, they *are* the flesh, and this *city is* the caldron: ^Rbut I will bring you forth out of the midst of it.   2 Kin. 25:18–22

8 Ye have ^Rfeared the sword; and I will bring a sword upon you, saith the Lord GOD.   Jer. 42:16

9 And I will bring you out of the midst thereof, and deliver you into the hands of strangers, and ^Rwill execute judgments among you.   5:8

10 ^RYe shall fall by the sword; I will judge you in the border of Israel; ^Rand ye shall know that I *am* the LORD.   Jer. 39:6 · Ps. 9:16

11 ^RThis *city* shall not be your caldron, neither shall ye be the flesh in the midst thereof; *but* I will judge you in the border of Israel: vv. 3, 7

12 And ye shall know that I *am* the LORD: for ye have not walked in my statutes, neither executed my judgments, but ^Rhave done after the manners of the heathen that *are* round about you. Lev. 18:3

13 And it came to pass, when I prophesied, that Pel-a-ti'-ah the son of Be-na'-iah died. Then ^Rfell I down upon my face, and cried with a loud voice, and said, Ah Lord GOD! wilt thou make a full end of the remnant of Israel?   9:8

14 Again the word of the LORD came unto me, saying,

15 Son of man, thy brethren, *even* thy ^Tbrethren, the men of thy

kindred, and all the house of Israel wholly, *are* they unto whom the inhabitants of Jerusalem have said, Get you far from the LORD: unto us is this land given in possession.   *relatives*

16 Therefore say, Thus saith the Lord GOD; Although I have cast them far off among the heathen, and although I have scattered them among the countries, ^Ryet will I be to them as a little sanctuary in the countries where they shall come. Ps. 90:1; Is. 8:14; Jer. 29:7, 11

17 Therefore say, Thus saith the Lord GOD; ^RI will even gather you from the people, and assemble you out of the countries where ye have been scattered, and I will give you the land of Israel. Jer. 24:5

18 And they shall come thither, and they shall take away all the ^Rdetestable things thereof and all the abominations thereof from thence.   37:23

19 And I will give them one heart, and I will put a new spirit within you; and I will take the stony heart out of their flesh, and will give them an heart of flesh:

20 ^RThat they may walk in my statutes, and keep mine ordinances, and do them: ^Rand they shall be my people, and I will be their God.   Ps. 105:45 · Jer. 24:7

21 But *as for them* whose heart walketh after the heart of their detestable things and their abominations, ^RI will ^Trecompense their way upon their own heads, saith the Lord GOD.   9:10 · *repay their deeds*

22 Then did the cher'-u-bims ^Rlift up their wings, and the wheels beside them; and the glory of the God of Israel *was* ^Tover them above.   1:19 · *high above them*

23 And ^Rthe glory of the LORD went up from the midst of the city, and stood ^Rupon the mountain ^Rwhich *is* on the east side of the city.   8:4; 9:3 · Zech. 14:4 · 43:2

24 Afterwards ^Rthe spirit took me up, and brought me in a vision by the Spirit of God into ^TChal-de'-a, to them of the captivity. So

the vision that I had seen went up from me.   8:3; 2 Cor. 12:2–4 · Or Babylon

25 Then I spake unto them of the captivity all the things that the LORD had shewed me.

12 The word of the LORD also came unto me, saying,

2 Son of man, thou dwellest in the midst of a rebellious house, which ^Rhave eyes to see, and see not; they have ears to hear, and hear not: for they *are* a rebellious house.   Matt. 13:13, 14; Mark 4:12; 8:18

3 Therefore, thou son of man, prepare thee stuff for removing, and remove by day in their sight; and thou shalt remove from thy place to another place in their sight: it may be they will consider, though they *be* a rebellious house.

4 Then shalt thou bring forth thy stuff by day in their sight, as stuff ^Tfor removing: and thou shalt go forth at ^Teven in their sight, as they that go forth into captivity.   *for captivity · evening*

5 Dig thou through the wall in their sight, and carry out thereby.

6 In their sight shalt thou bear *it* upon *thy* shoulders, *and* carry *it* forth in the twilight: thou shalt cover thy face, that thou see not the ground: for I have set thee *for* a sign unto the house of Israel.

7 And I did so as I was commanded: I brought forth my stuff by day, as stuff for captivity, and in the even I digged through the wall with mine hand; I brought *it* forth in the twilight, *and* I bare *it* upon *my* shoulder in their sight.

8 And in the morning came the word of the LORD unto me, saying,

9 Son of man, hath not the house of Israel, ^Rthe rebellious house, said unto thee, ^RWhat doest thou?   2:5 · 17:12; 24:19

10 Say thou unto them, Thus saith the Lord GOD; This ^Tburden *concerneth* the prince in Jerusalem, and all the house of Israel that *are* among them.   *oracle*

11 Say, ^RI *am* your sign: like as I have done, so shall it be done unto them: ^Rthey shall remove *and* go into captivity.   v. 6 · 2 Kin. 25:4, 5, 7

12 And the prince that *is* among them shall bear upon *his* shoulder in the twilight, and shall go forth: they shall dig through the wall to carry out thereby: he shall cover his face, that he see not the ground with *his* eyes.

13 My ^Rnet also will I spread upon him, and he shall be taken in my snare: and I will bring him to Babylon *to* the land of the Chal-de'-ans; yet shall he not see it, though he shall die there.   17:20

14 And ^RI will scatter toward every wind all that *are* about him to help him, and all his bands; and ^RI will draw out the sword after them.   5:10; 2 Kin. 25:4 · 5:2, 12

15 ^RAnd they shall know that I *am* the Lord, when I shall scatter them among the nations, and disperse them in the countries.   6:7

16 ^RBut I will leave a few men of them from the sword, from the famine, and from the pestilence; that they may declare all their abominations among the heathen whither they come; and they shall know that I *am* the Lord.   6:8–10

17 Moreover the word of the Lord came to me, saying,

18 Son of man, ^Reat thy bread with ^Tquaking, and drink thy water with trembling and with carefulness;   4:16; Lam. 5:9 · *shaking*

19 And say unto the people of the land, Thus saith the Lord God of the inhabitants of Jerusalem, *and* of the land of Israel; They shall eat their bread with carefulness, and drink their water with astonishment, that her land may be desolate from all that is therein, because of the violence of all them that dwell therein.

20 And the cities that are inhabited shall be laid waste, and the land shall be desolate; and ye shall know that I *am* the Lord.

21 And the word of the Lord came unto me, saying,

22 Son of man, what *is* that proverb *that* ye have in the land of Israel, saying, ^RThe days are prolonged, and every vision faileth?   v. 27; Jer. 5:12; Amos 6:3; 2 Pet. 3:4

23 Tell them therefore, Thus saith the Lord God; I will make this proverb to cease, and they shall no more use it as a proverb in Israel; but say unto them, ^RThe days are at hand, and the effect of every vision.   Ps. 37:13; Zeph. 1:14

24 For ^Rthere shall be no more any vain vision nor flattering divination within the house of Israel.   13:6; Jer. 14:13–16; Zech. 13:2–6

25 For I *am* the Lord: I will speak, and ^Rthe word that I shall speak shall come to pass; it shall be no more prolonged: for in your days, O rebellious house, will I say the word, and will perform it, saith the Lord God.   [Luke 21:33]

26 Again the word of the Lord came to me, saying,

27 ^RSon of man, behold, *they of* the house of Israel say, The vision that he seeth *is* for many days *to come*, and he prophesieth of the times *that are* far off.   v. 22

28 Therefore say unto them, Thus saith the Lord God; There shall none of my words be prolonged any more, but the word which I have spoken ^Rshall be done, saith the Lord God.   Jer. 4:7

13 And the word of the Lord came unto me, saying,

2 Son of man, prophesy ^Ragainst the prophets of Israel that prophesy, and say thou unto ^Rthem that prophesy out of their own hearts, Hear ye the word of the Lord;   Is. 28:7; Jer. 23:1–40 · 13:17

3 Thus saith the Lord God; Woe unto the foolish prophets, that follow their own spirit, and have seen ^Tnothing!   No vision

4 O Israel, thy prophets are like the foxes in the deserts.

5 Ye have not gone up into the gaps, neither made up the hedge for the house of Israel to stand in the battle in the day of the Lord.

6 ^RThey have seen vanity and lying divination, saying, The Lord saith: and the Lord hath ^Rnot sent them: and they have made *others* to hope that they would confirm the word.   Jer. 29:8 · Jer. 27:8–15

7 Have ye not seen a ^Tvain

vision, and have ye not spoken ^Ta lying divination, whereas ye say, The LORD saith *it*; albeit I have not spoken?   *futile · false*

8 Therefore thus saith the Lord GOD; Because ye have spoken vanity, and ^Tseen lies, therefore, behold, I *am* against you, saith the Lord GOD.   *envisioned*

9 And mine hand shall be upon the prophets that see vanity, and that divine lies: they shall not be in the assembly of my people, neither shall they be written in the writing of the house of Israel, ^Rneither shall they enter into the land of Israel; and ye shall know that I *am* the Lord GOD.   Jer. 20:3–6

10 Because, even because they have seduced my people, saying, ^RPeace; and *there was* no peace; and one built up a wall, and, lo, others ^Rdaubed it with untempered *morter*:   Jer. 6:14; 8:11 · 22:28

11 Say unto them which daub *it* with untempered *morter*, that it shall fall: ^Rthere shall be an overflowing shower; and ye, O great hailstones, shall fall; and a stormy wind shall rend *it*.   38:22

12 Lo, when the wall is fallen, shall it not be said unto you, Where *is* the daubing wherewith ye have ^Tdaubed *it*?   *plastered*

13 Therefore thus saith the Lord GOD; I will even rend *it* with a stormy wind in my fury; and there shall be an overflowing shower in mine anger, and great hailstones in *my* fury to consume *it*.

14 So will I break down the wall that ye have daubed with untempered *morter*, and bring it down to the ground, so that the foundation thereof shall be discovered, and it shall fall, and ye shall be consumed in the midst thereof: ^Rand ye shall know that I *am* the LORD.   vv. 9, 21, 23; 14:8

15 Thus will I accomplish my wrath upon the wall, and upon them that have daubed it with untempered *morter*, and will say unto you, The wall *is* no *more*, neither they that daubed it;

16 *To wit*, the prophets of Israel which prophesy concerning Jerusalem, and which ^Rsee visions of peace for her, and *there is* no peace, saith the Lord GOD.   Jer. 6:14

17 Likewise, thou son of man, ^Rset thy face against the daughters of thy people, which prophesy out of their own heart; and prophesy thou against them,   21:2

18 And say, Thus saith the Lord GOD; Woe to the *women* that sew pillows to all armholes, and make ^Tkerchiefs upon the head of every stature to hunt souls! Will ye ^Rhunt the souls of my people, and will ye save the souls alive *that come* unto you?   *veils* · [2 Pet. 2:14]

19 And will ye pollute me among my people for handfuls of barley and for pieces of bread, to slay the souls that should not die, and to save the souls alive that should not live, by your lying to my people that hear *your* lies?

20 Wherefore thus saith the Lord GOD; Behold, I *am* against your pillows, wherewith ye there hunt the souls ^Tto make *them* fly, and I will tear them from your arms, and will let the souls go, *even* the souls that ye hunt ^Tto make *them* fly.   *like birds*

21 Your ^Tkerchiefs also will I ^Ttear, and deliver my people out of your hand, and they shall be no more in your hand to be hunted; ^Rand ye shall know that I *am* the LORD.   *veils · tear off* · v. 9

22 Because with ^Rlies ye have made the heart of the righteous sad, whom I have not made sad; and strengthened the hands of the wicked, that he should not return from his wicked way, by promising him life: Jer. 28:15

23 Therefore ^Rye shall see no more vanity, nor divine divinations: for I will deliver my people out of your hand: and ye shall know that I *am* the LORD. Mic. 3:5, 6

14 Then ^Rcame certain of the elders of Israel unto me, and sat before me.   8:1; 20:1; 33:31

2 And the word of the LORD came unto me, saying,

3 Son of man, these men have

set up their idols in their heart, and put [R]the stumblingblock of their iniquity before their face: [R]should I be enquired of at all by them?   7:19; Zeph. 1:3 · 2 Kin. 3:13; Is. 1:15

4   Therefore speak unto them, and say unto them, Thus saith the Lord GOD; Every man of the house of Israel that setteth up his idols in his heart, and putteth the stumblingblock of his iniquity before his face, and cometh to the prophet; I the LORD will answer him that cometh according to the multitude of his idols;

5   That I may take the house of Israel in their own heart, because they are all estranged from me through their idols.

6   Therefore say unto the house of Israel, Thus saith the Lord GOD; Repent, and turn *yourselves* from your idols; and turn away your faces from all your abominations.

7   For every one of the house of Israel, or of the stranger that sojourneth in Israel, which separateth himself from me, and setteth up his idols in his heart, and putteth the stumblingblock of his iniquity before his face, and cometh to a prophet to enquire of him concerning me; I the LORD will answer him by myself:

8   And [R]I will set my face against that man, and will make him a [R]sign and a proverb, and I will cut him off from the midst of my people; and ye shall know that I *am* the LORD.   15:7 · 5:15; Num. 26:10

9   And if the prophet be deceived when he hath spoken a thing, I the LORD [R]have deceived that prophet, and I will stretch out my hand upon him, and will destroy him from the midst of my people Israel.   Is. 66:4; 2 Thess. 2:11

10   And they shall bear the punishment of their iniquity: the punishment of the prophet shall be even as the punishment of him that [T]seeketh *unto him;*   inquired of

11   That the house of Israel may go no more astray from me, neither be polluted any more with all their transgressions; but that they

may be my people, and I may be their God, saith the Lord GOD.

12   The word of the LORD came again to me, saying,

13   Son of man, when the land sinneth against me by trespassing grievously, then will I stretch out mine hand upon it, and will break the staff of the bread thereof, and will send famine upon it, and will cut off man and beast from it:

14   [R]Though these three men, Noah, Daniel, and Job, were in it, they should deliver *but* their own souls by their righteousness, saith the Lord GOD.   Jer. 15:1

15   If I cause [R]noisome[T] beasts to pass through the land, and they spoil it, so that it be desolate, that no man may pass through because of the beasts: 5:17 · *wild*

16   *Though* these three men *were* in it, *as* I live, saith the Lord GOD, they shall deliver neither sons nor daughters; they only shall be delivered, but the land shall be [R]desolate.   15:8; 33:28, 29

17   Or *if* [R]I bring a sword upon that land, and say, Sword, go through the land; so that I cut off man and beast from it: 5:12; 21:3, 4

18   Though these three men *were* in it, *as* I live, saith the Lord GOD, they shall deliver neither sons nor daughters, but they only shall be delivered themselves.

19   Or *if* I send [R]a pestilence into that land, and [R]pour out my fury upon it in blood, to cut off from it man and beast: 2 Sam. 24:15 · 7:8

20   [R]Though Noah, Daniel, and Job, *were* in it, *as* I live, saith the Lord GOD, they shall deliver neither son nor daughter; they shall *but* deliver their own souls by their righteousness.   v. 14

21   For thus saith the Lord GOD; How much more when [R]I send my four [T]sore judgments upon Jerusalem, the sword, and the famine, and the [T]noisome beast, and the pestilence, to cut off from it man and beast?   5:17; Rev. 6:8 · *severe* · *wild*

22   [R]Yet, behold, therein shall be left a remnant that shall be brought forth, *both* sons and

daughters: behold, they shall come forth unto you, and ^Rye shall see their way and their doings: and ye shall be comforted concerning the ^Tevil that I have brought upon Jerusalem, *even* concerning all that I have brought upon it. 12:16; 36:20 · 20:43 · *disaster*

23 And they shall comfort you, when ye see their ways and their doings: and ye shall know that I have not done ^Rwithout cause all that I have done in it, saith the Lord GOD. Jer. 22:8, 9

15 And the word of the LORD came unto me, saying,

2 Son of man, What is the vine tree more than any tree, *or than* a branch which is among the trees of the forest?

3 Shall wood be taken thereof to ^Tdo any work? or will *men* take a pin of it to hang any vessel thereon? *make any object*

4 Behold, it is cast into the fire for fuel; the fire devoureth both the ends of it, and the midst of it is burned. Is it meet for *any* work?

5 Behold, when it was whole, it was meet for no work: how much less shall it be meet yet for *any* work, when the fire hath devoured it, and it is burned?

6 Therefore thus saith the Lord GOD; As the vine tree among the trees of the forest, which I have given to the fire for fuel, so will I give the inhabitants of Jerusalem.

7 And I will set my face against them; ^Rthey shall go out from *one* fire, and *another* fire shall devour them; ^Rand ye shall know that I *am* the LORD, when I set my face against them. Is. 24:18 · 7:4

8 And I will make the land desolate, because they have committed a trespass, saith the Lord GOD.

16 Again the word of the LORD came unto me, saying,

2 Son of man, cause Jerusalem to know her abominations,

3 And say, Thus saith the Lord GOD unto Jerusalem; Thy birth and thy nativity *is* of the land of Canaan; thy father *was* an Am'-

or-ite, and thy mother an Hit'-tite.

4 And *as for* thy nativity, ^Rin the day thou wast born thy navel was not cut, neither wast thou washed in water to ^Tsupple *thee*; thou wast not salted at all, nor swaddled at all. Hos. 2:3 · *cleanse*

5 None eye pitied thee, to do any of these unto thee, to have compassion upon thee; but thou wast cast out in the open field, to the lothing of thy person, in the day that thou wast born.

6 And when I passed by thee, and saw thee ^Tpolluted in thine own blood, I said unto thee *when thou wast* in thy blood, Live; yea, I said unto thee *when thou wast* in thy blood, Live. *struggling*

7 ^RI have caused thee to multiply as the bud of the field, and thou hast increased and waxen great, and thou art come to excellent ornaments: *thy* breasts are fashioned, and thine hair is grown, whereas thou *wast* naked and bare. Ex. 1:7; Deut. 1:10

8 Now when I passed by thee, and looked upon thee, behold, thy time *was* the time of love; ^Rand I spread my ^Tskirt over thee, and covered thy nakedness: yea, I sware unto thee, and entered into a covenant with thee, saith the Lord GOD, and thou becamest mine. Ruth 3:9; Jer. 2:2 · *wing*

9 Then washed I thee with water; yea, I throughly washed away thy blood from thee, and I anointed thee with oil.

10 I clothed thee also with broidered ^Twork, and shod thee with badgers' skin, and I girded thee about with fine linen, and I covered thee with silk. *cloth*

11 I decked thee also with ornaments, and I ^Rput bracelets upon thy hands, ^Rand a chain on thy neck. Gen. 24:22, 47 · Gen. 41:42; Prov. 1:9

12 And I put a ^Tjewel on thy forehead, and earrings in thine ears, and a beautiful crown upon thine head. *ring in thy nose*

13 Thus wast thou decked with gold and silver; and thy raiment *was of* fine linen, and silk, and

broidered work; ^Rthou didst eat fine flour, and honey, and oil: and thou wast exceeding ^Rbeautiful, and thou didst prosper into a kingdom.   Deut. 32:13, 14 · Ps. 48:2

14 And ^Rthy renown went forth among the heathen for thy beauty: for it *was* perfect through my ^Tcomeliness, which I had put upon thee, saith the Lord GOD.   Ps. 50:2; Lam. 2:15 · *splendour*

15 ^RBut thou didst trust in thine own beauty, ^Rand playedst the harlot because of thy renown, and pouredst out thy fornications on every one that passed by; his it was.   Mic. 3:11 · Is. 1:21; Hos. 1:2

16 ^RAnd of thy garments thou didst take, and deckedst thy high places with divers colours, and playedst the harlot thereupon: *the like things* shall not come, neither shall it be *so*.   7:20; 2 Kin. 23:7; Hos. 2:8

17 Thou hast also taken thy fair jewels of my gold and of my silver, which I had given thee, and madest to thyself ^Timages of men, and didst commit whoredom with them,   *male images*

18 And tookest thy broidered garments, and coveredst them: and thou hast set mine oil and mine incense before them.

19 ^RMy ^Tmeat also which I gave thee, fine flour, and oil, and honey, *wherewith* I fed thee, thou hast even set it before them for a sweet savour: and *thus* it was, saith the Lord GOD.   Hos. 2:8 · *food*

20 Moreover thou hast taken thy sons and thy daughters, whom thou hast borne unto me, and these hast thou sacrificed unto them to be devoured. *Is this* of thy whoredoms a small matter,

21 That thou hast slain my children, and ^Tdelivered them to cause them to pass through *the* ^R*fire* for them?   *offered* · 2 Kin. 17:17

22 And in all thine abominations and thy whoredoms thou hast not remembered the days of thy ^Ryouth, ^Rwhen thou wast naked and bare, *and* wast polluted in thy blood. Jer. 2:2; Hos. 11:1 · vv. 4–6

23 And it came to pass after all thy wickedness, (woe, woe unto thee! saith the Lord GOD;)

24 *That* ^Rthou hast also built unto thee an eminent place, and ^Rhast made thee an high place in every street. 20:28, 29 · Ps. 78:58; Is. 57:7

25 Thou hast built thy high place at every head of the way, and hast made thy beauty to be abhorred, and hast opened thy feet to every one that passed by, and multiplied thy whoredoms.

26 Thou hast also committed fornication with the Egyptians thy neighbours, great of flesh; and hast increased thy whoredoms, to ^Rprovoke me to anger.   Deut. 31:20

27 Behold, therefore I have stretched out my hand ^Tover thee, and have diminished thine ordinary *food*, and delivered thee unto the will of them that hate thee, ^Rthe daughters of the Phi-lis'-tines, which are ashamed of thy lewd way. *against* · 2 Chr. 28:18; Is. 9:12

28 Thou hast played the whore also with the Assyrians, because thou wast unsatiable; yea, thou hast played the harlot with them, and yet couldest not be satisfied.

29 Thou hast moreover multiplied thy ^Tfornication in the land of Canaan ^Runto Chal-de'-a; and yet thou wast not satisfied herewith.   *acts of harlotry* · 23:14–17

30 How weak is thine heart, saith the Lord GOD, seeing thou doest all these *things*, the work of an imperious whorish woman;

31 In that ^Rthou buildest thine ^Teminent place in the head of every ^Tway, and makest thine high place in every street; and hast not been as an harlot, in that thou scornest hire; vv. 24, 39 · *shrine* · *street*

32 *But as* a wife that committeth adultery, *which* taketh strangers instead of her husband!

33 They give gifts to all whores: but ^Rthou givest thy gifts to all thy lovers, and hirest them, that they may come unto thee on every side for thy whoredom.   Hos. 8:9, 10

34 And the contrary is in thee from *other* women in thy whoredoms, whereas none followeth

thee to commit whoredoms: and in that thou givest a reward, and no reward is given unto thee, therefore thou art contrary.

35 Wherefore, O harlot, hear the word of the LORD:

36 Thus saith the Lord GOD; Because thy filthiness was poured out, and thy nakedness ᵀdiscovered through thy whoredoms with thy lovers, and with all the idols of thy abominations, and by the blood of thy children, which thou didst give unto them;   *uncovered*

37 Behold, therefore ᴿI will gather all thy lovers, with whom thou hast taken pleasure, and all *them* that thou hast loved, with all *them* that thou hast hated; I will even gather them round about against thee, and will discover thy nakedness unto them, that they may see all thy nakedness.   Lam. 1:8

38 And I will judge thee, as ᴿwomen that break wedlock and ᴿshed blood are judged; and I will give thee blood in fury and jealousy.   23:45 · Gen. 9:6; Ex. 21:12

39 And I will also give thee into their hand, and they shall throw down ᴿthine eminent place, and shall break down thy high places: ᴿthey shall strip thee also of thy clothes, and shall take thy ᵀfair jewels, and leave thee naked and bare. vv. 24, 31 · 23:26; Hos. 2:3 · *beautiful*

40 ᴿThey shall also bring up a company against thee, ᴿand they shall stone thee with stones, and thrust thee through with their swords. 23:45–47; Hab. 1:6–10 · John 8:5, 7

41 And they shall ᴿburn thine houses with fire, and execute judgments upon thee in the sight of many women: and I will cause thee to cease from playing the harlot, and thou also shalt give no hire any more. Deut. 13:16; 2 Kin. 25:9

42 So ᴿwill I make my fury toward thee to rest, and my jealousy shall depart from thee, and I will be quiet, and will be no more angry.   2 Sam. 24:25; Zech. 6:8

43 Because ᴿthou hast not remembered the days of thy youth, but hast fretted me in all these *things*; behold, therefore ᴿI also will recompense thy way upon *thine* head, saith the Lord GOD: and thou shalt not commit this lewdness above all thine abominations.   Ps. 78:42 · 9:10; 11:21; 22:31

44 Behold, every one that useth proverbs shall use *this* proverb against thee, saying, As *is* the mother, *so is* her daughter.

45 Thou *art* thy mother's daughter, that lotheth her husband and her children; and thou *art* the ᴿsister of thy sisters, which lothed their husbands and their children: your mother *was* an Hit′-tite, and your father an Am′-or-ite.   23:2–4

46 And thine elder sister *is* Sa-ma′-ri-a, she and her daughters that dwell at thy left hand: and ᴿthy younger sister, that dwelleth at thy right hand, *is* Sodom and her daughters.   Deut. 32:32; Is. 1:10

47 Yet hast thou not walked after their ways, nor done after their abominations: but, as *if that were* a very little *thing*, ᴿthou wast corrupted more than they in all thy ways.   5:6, 7; 2 Kin. 21:9

48 *As* I live, saith the Lord GOD, ᴿSodom thy sister hath not done, she nor her daughters, as thou hast done, thou and thy daughters. Lam. 4:6; Matt. 10:15; 11:24; Rev. 11:8

49 Behold, this was the iniquity of thy sister Sodom, pride, ᴿfulness of bread, and abundance of idleness was in her and in her daughters, neither did she strengthen the hand of the poor and needy.   Gen. 13:10; Is. 22:13

50 And they were haughty, and ᴿcommitted abomination before me: therefore ᴿI took them away as I saw *good.*   Gen. 19:5 · Gen. 19:24

51 Neither hath Sa-ma′-ri-a committed ᴿhalf of thy sins; but thou hast multiplied thine abominations more than they, and ᴿhast justified thy sisters in all thine abominations which thou hast done.   23:11 · Jer. 3:8–11; Matt. 12:41

52 Thou also, which hast judged thy sisters, bear thine own shame for thy sins that thou hast com-

mitted more abominable than
^Tthey: they are more righteous
than thou: yea, be thou ^Tcon-
founded also, and bear thy shame,
in that thou hast justified thy sis-
ters.   *theirs · disgraced*
53 ^RWhen I shall bring again
their captivity, the captivity of
Sodom and her daughters, and
the captivity of Sa-ma'-ri-a and
her daughters, then *will I bring
again* the captivity of thy captives
in the midst of them: [v. 60]; Is. 1:9
54 That thou mayest bear thine
own shame, and mayest be ^Tcon-
founded in all that thou hast done,
in that thou art ^Ra comfort unto
them.   *disgraced · 14:22*
55 When thy sisters, Sodom and
her daughters, shall return to
their former ^Testate, and Sa-ma'-
ri-a and her daughters shall
return to their former estate, then
thou and thy daughters shall
return to your former estate. *state*
56 For thy sister Sodom was not
mentioned by thy mouth in the
day of thy pride,
57 Before thy wickedness was
^Tdiscovered, as at the time of *thy*
^Rreproach of the daughters of
Syria, and all *that are* round
about her, the daughters of the
Phil-is'-tines, which despise thee
round about.   *uncovered · 2 Kin. 16:5*
58 ^RThou hast borne thy lewdness and thine abominations,
saith the LORD.   23:49
59 For thus saith the Lord GOD; I
will even deal with thee as thou
hast done, which hast ^Rdespised
^Rthe oath in breaking the cov-
enant.   17:13 · Deut. 29:12
60 Nevertheless I will ^Rremem-
ber my covenant with thee in the
days of thy youth, and I will establish unto thee ^Ran everlasting
covenant.   Lev. 26:42–45 · Is. 55:3
61 Then ^Rthou shalt remember
thy ways, and be ashamed, when
thou shalt receive thy sisters,
thine elder and thy younger: and I
will give them unto thee for
^Rdaughters, ^Rbut not by thy cov-
enant. 20:43; 36:31 · [Gal. 4:26] · Jer. 31:31
62 And I will establish my cov-

enant with thee; and thou shalt
know that I *am* the LORD:
63 That thou mayest ^Rremember,
and be confounded, and never
open thy mouth any more because of thy shame, when I am
pacified toward thee for all that
thou hast done, saith the Lord
GOD.   36:31, 32; Dan. 9:7, 8

17 And the word of the LORD
came unto me, saying,
2 Son of man, put forth a rid-
dle, and speak a ^Rparable unto the
house of Israel;   20:49; 24:3
3 And say, Thus saith the Lord
GOD; A great eagle with great
wings, longwinged, full of feathers, which had divers colours,
came unto Leb'-a-non, and took
the highest branch of the cedar:
4 He cropped off the top of his
young twigs, and carried it into a
land of ^Ttraffick; he set it in a city
of merchants.   *trade*
5 He took also ^Tof the seed of
the land, and planted it in ^Ra fruitful field; he placed *it* by great
waters, *and* set it ^R*as* a willow
tree.   *some of* · Deut. 8:7–9 · Is. 44:4
6 And it grew, and became a
spreading vine ^Rof low stature,
whose branches turned toward
him, and the roots thereof were
under him: so it became a vine,
and brought forth branches, and
shot forth sprigs.   v. 14
7 There was also another great
eagle with great wings and many
feathers: and, behold, this vine
did bend her roots toward him,
and shot forth her branches toward him, that he might water it
by the furrows of her plantation.
8 It was planted in a good ^Tsoil
by ^Tgreat waters, that it might
bring forth branches, and that it
might bear fruit, that it might be a
^Tgoodly vine. Lit. *field · many · majestic*
9 Say thou, Thus saith the Lord
GOD; Shall it prosper? shall he not
pull up the roots thereof, and cut
off the fruit thereof, that it wither?
it shall wither in all the leaves of
her spring, even without great
power or many people to pluck it
up by the roots thereof.

10 Yea, behold, *being* planted, shall it ᵀprosper? ᴿshall it not utterly wither, when the east wind toucheth it? it shall wither in the furrows where it grew.   *thrive* · 19:12

11 Moreover the word of the Lord came unto me, saying,

12 Say now to ᴿthe rebellious house, Know ye not what these *things mean?* tell *them,* Behold, ᴿthe king of Babylon is come to Jerusalem, and hath taken the king thereof, and the princes thereof, and led them with him to Babylon;   2:3–5; 12:9 · 2 Kin. 24:11–16

13 ᴿAnd hath taken of the king's seed, and made a covenant with him, and hath taken an oath of him: he hath also taken the mighty of the land: 2 Kin. 24:17; Jer. 37:1

14 That the kingdom might be ᴿbase, that it might not lift itself up, *but* that by keeping of his covenant it might stand.   29:14

15 But ᴿhe rebelled against him in sending his ambassadors into Egypt, ᴿthat they might give him horses and much people. Shall he prosper? shall he escape that doeth such *things?* or shall he break the covenant, and be delivered?   2 Chr. 36:13; Jer. 52:3 · Deut. 17:16

16 *As* I live, saith the Lord God, surely ᴿin the place *where* the king *dwelleth* that made him king, whose oath he despised, and whose covenant he brake, *even* with him in the midst of Babylon he shall die.   12:13; Jer. 52:11

17 Neither shall Pharaoh with *his* mighty army and great company make for him in the war, by casting up mounts, and building forts, to cut off many persons:

18 Seeing he despised the oath by breaking the covenant, when, lo, he had ᴿgiven his hand, and hath done all these *things,* he shall not escape.   1 Chr. 29:24; Lam. 5:6

19 Therefore thus saith the Lord God; *As* I live, surely mine oath that he hath despised, and my covenant that he hath broken, even it will I recompense upon his own head.

20 And I will ᴿspread my net upon him, and he shall be taken in my snare, and I will bring him to Babylon, and ᴿwill plead with him there for his trespass that he hath trespassed against me.   12:13 · 20:36

21 And ᴿall his fugitives with all his ᵀbands shall fall by the sword, and they that remain shall be ᴿscattered toward all winds: and ye shall know that I the Lord have spoken *it.*   12:14 · *troops* · 12:15; 22:15

22 Thus saith the Lord God; I will also take of the highest branch of the high cedar, and will set *it;* I will crop off from the top of his young twigs ᴿa tender one, and will plant *it* upon an high mountain and eminent: Is. 53:2

23 In the mountain of the height of Israel will I plant it: and it shall bring forth boughs, and bear fruit, and be a goodly cedar: and under it shall dwell all fowl of every wing; in the shadow of the branches thereof shall they dwell.

24 And all the trees of the field shall know that I the Lord have brought down the high tree, have exalted the low tree, have dried up the green tree, and have made the dry tree to flourish: I the Lord have spoken and have done *it.*

18 The word of the Lord came unto me again, saying,

2 What mean ye, that ye use this proverb concerning the land of Israel, saying, The fathers have eaten sour grapes, and the children's teeth are set on edge?

3 *As* I live, saith the Lord God, ye shall not have *occasion* any more to use this proverb in Israel.

4 Behold, all souls are mine; as the soul of the father, so also the soul of the son is mine: ᴿthe soul that sinneth, it shall die. [Rom. 6:23]

5 But if a man be just, and do that which is lawful and right,

6 ᴿ*And* hath not eaten upon the mountains, neither hath lifted up his eyes to the idols of the house of Israel, neither hath ᴿdefiled his neighbour's wife, neither hath come near to a menstruous woman,   22:9 · Lev. 18:20; 20:10

7 And hath not ᴿoppressed any,

but hath restored to the debtor his pledge, hath spoiled none by violence, hath given his bread to the hungry, and hath covered the naked with a garment;   Ex. 22:21

8 He *that* hath not given forth upon ᴿusury, neither hath taken any increase, *that* hath withdrawn his hand from iniquity, hath executed true judgment between man and man,   Ex. 22:25

9 Hath walked in my statutes, and hath kept my judgments, to deal truly; he *is* just, he shall surely ᴿlive, saith the Lord GOD.   20:11

10 If he beget a son *that is* a robber, ᴿa shedder of blood, and *that* doeth the like to *any* one of these *things,*   Gen. 9:6; Ex. 21:12; Num. 35:31

11 And that doeth not any of those *duties,* but even hath eaten upon the mountains, and defiled his neighbour's wife,

12 Hath oppressed the poor and needy, hath spoiled by violence, hath not restored the pledge, and hath lifted up his eyes to the idols, hath committed abomination,

13 Hath given forth upon usury, and hath taken increase: shall he then live? he shall not live: he hath done all these abominations; he shall surely die; ᴿhis blood shall be upon him.   3:18; Acts 18:6

14 Now, lo, *if* he beget a son, that seeth all his father's sins which he hath done, and considereth, and doeth not such like,

15 ᴿThat hath not eaten upon the mountains, neither hath lifted up his eyes to the idols of the house of Israel, hath not defiled his neighbour's wife,   v. 6

16 Neither hath oppressed any, hath not withholden the pledge, neither hath ᵀspoiled by violence, *but* hath given his bread to the hungry, and hath covered the naked with a garment,   *robbed*

17 *That* hath ᵀtaken off his hand from the poor, *that* hath not received usury nor increase, hath executed my judgments, hath walked in my statutes; he shall not die for the iniquity of his father, he shall surely live. *withdrawn*

18 *As for* his father, because he cruelly oppressed, ᵀspoiled his brother by violence, and did *that* which *is* not good among his people, lo, even ᴿhe shall die ᵀin his iniquity.   *robbed* · 3:18 · *for*

19 Yet say ye, Why? ᴿdoth not the son bear the ᵀiniquity of the father? When the son hath done that which is lawful and right, *and* hath kept all my statutes, and hath done them, he shall surely live.   Ex. 20:5; 2 Kin. 23:26; 24:3, 4 · *guilt*

20 The soul that sinneth, it shall die. The son shall not bear the iniquity of the father, neither shall the father bear the iniquity of the son: the righteousness of the righteous shall be upon him, ᴿand the wickedness of the wicked shall be upon him.   Rom. 2:6-9

21 But ᴿif the wicked will turn from all his sins that he hath committed, and keep all my statutes, and do that which is lawful and right, he shall surely live, he shall not die.   v. 27; 33:12, 19

22 ᴿAll his transgressions that he hath committed, they shall not be mentioned unto him: in his righteousness that he hath done he shall live.   v. 24; 33:16; Mic. 7:19

23 ᴿHave I any pleasure at all that the wicked should die? saith the Lord GOD: *and* not that he should return from his ways, and live?   Lam. 3:33; [1 Tim. 2:4; 2 Pet. 3:9]

24 But ᴿwhen the righteous turneth away from his righteousness, and committeth iniquity, *and* doeth according to all the abominations that the wicked *man* doeth, shall he live? ᴿAll his righteousness that he hath done shall not be mentioned: in his trespass that he hath trespassed, and in his sin that he hath sinned, in them shall he die.   3:20; 33:18 · [2 Pet. 2:20]

25 Yet ye say, ᴿThe way of the Lord is not equal. Hear now, O house of Israel; Is not my way equal? are not your ways unequal?   v. 29; 33:17, 20; Mal. 2:17; 3:13–15

26 ᴿWhen a righteous *man* turneth away from his righteousness, and committeth iniquity, and

dieth in them; for his iniquity that he hath done shall he die.   v. 24

27 Again, ^Rwhen the wicked *man* turneth away from his wickedness that he hath committed, and doeth that which is lawful and right, he shall ^Tsave his soul alive.   v. 21 · *preserve himself*

28 Because he ^Rconsidereth, and turneth away from all his transgressions that he hath committed, he shall surely live, he shall not die.   v. 14

29 ^RYet saith the house of Israel, The way of the Lord is not ^Tequal. O house of Israel, are not my ways equal? are not your ways ^Tunequal?   v. 25 · *fair* · *unfair*

30 ^RTherefore I will judge you, O house of Israel, every one according to his ways, saith the Lord GOD. Repent, and turn *yourselves* from all your transgressions; so iniquity shall not be your ruin. 7:3

31 Cast away from you all your transgressions, whereby ye have transgressed; and make you a new heart and a new spirit: for why will ye die, O house of Israel?

32 For ^RI have no pleasure in the death of him that dieth, saith the Lord GOD: wherefore turn *yourselves*, and live ye.   33:11; [2 Pet. 3:9]

19 Moreover ^Rtake thou up a lamentation for the princes of Israel,   26:17; 27:2

2 And say, What *is* thy mother? A lioness: she lay down among lions, she nourished her ^Twhelps among young lions.   *cubs*

3 And she brought up one of her whelps: it became a young lion, and it learned to catch the prey; it devoured men.

4 The nations also heard of him; he was ^Ttaken in their pit, and they brought him with chains unto the land of Egypt.   *trapped*

5 Now when she saw that she had waited, *and* her hope was lost, then she took ^Ranother of her ^Twhelps, *and* made him a young lion.   2 Kin. 23:34 · *cubs*

6 And he went up and down among the lions, ^Rhe became a young lion, and learned to catch the prey, *and* devoured men.   v. 3

7 And he knew ^Ttheir desolate palaces, and he laid waste their cities; and the land was desolate, and the fulness thereof, by the noise of his roaring.   Or *its widows*

8 Then the nations set against him on every side from the provinces, and spread their net over him: he was taken in their pit.

9 And they put him in ^Tward in chains, and brought him to the king of Babylon: they brought him ^Tinto holds, that his voice should no more be heard upon the mountains of Israel.   *a cage* · *in nets*

10 Thy mother *is* ^Rlike a vine in thy ^Tblood, planted by the waters: she was ^Rfruitful and full of branches by reason of many waters.   17:6 · *bloodline* · Deut. 8:7–9

11 And she had strong rods for the sceptres of them that bare rule, and her ^Rstature was exalted among the thick branches, and she appeared in her height with the multitude of her branches.   31:3

12 But she was ^Rplucked up in fury, she was cast down to the ground, and the ^Reast wind dried up her fruit: her strong rods were broken and withered; the fire consumed them.   Jer. 31:27, 28 · Hos. 13:5

13 And now she *is* planted in the wilderness, in a dry and thirsty ground.

14 ^RAnd fire is gone out of a rod of her branches, *which* hath devoured her fruit, so that she hath no strong rod *to be* a sceptre to rule. This *is* a lamentation, and shall be for a lamentation.   17:18

20 And it came to pass in the seventh year, in the fifth *month*, the tenth *day* of the month, *that* ^Rcertain of the elders of Israel came to enquire of the LORD, and sat before me.   8:1, 11, 12

2 Then came the word of the LORD unto me, saying,

3 Son of man, speak unto the elders of Israel, and say unto them, Thus saith the Lord GOD; Are ye come to enquire of me? *As*

I live, saith the Lord GOD, ^RI will not be enquired of by you. 7:26; 14:3

4 Wilt thou judge them, son of man, wilt thou judge *them?* ^Rcause them to know the abominations of their fathers: Matt. 23:32

5 And say unto them, Thus saith the Lord GOD; In the day when ^RI chose Israel, and lifted up mine hand unto the seed of the house of Jacob, and made myself ^Rknown unto them in the land of Egypt, when I lifted up mine hand unto them, saying, ^RI *am* the LORD your God; Ex. 6:6–8 · Ex. 3:8 · Ex. 20:2

6 In the day *that* I lifted up mine hand unto them, to bring them forth of the land of Egypt into a land that I had espied for them, ^Rflowing with milk and honey, which *is* ^Rthe glory of all lands: Ex. 3:8 · Dan. 8:9; Zech. 7:14

7 Then said I unto them, Cast ye away every man the abominations of his eyes, and defile not yourselves with the idols of Egypt: I *am* the LORD your God.

8 But they rebelled against me, and would not hearken unto me: they did not every man cast away the abominations of their eyes, neither did they forsake the idols of Egypt: then I said, I will ^Rpour out my fury upon them, to accomplish my anger against them in the midst of the land of Egypt. 7:8

9 ^RBut I wrought for my name's sake, that it should not be polluted before the heathen, among whom they *were,* in whose sight I made myself ^Rknown unto them, in bringing them forth out of the land of Egypt. Num. 14:13 · Josh. 2:10

10 Wherefore I ^Rcaused them to go forth out of the land of Egypt, and brought them into the wilderness. Ex. 13:18

11 And I gave them my statutes, and shewed them my judgments, ^Rwhich *if* a man do, he shall even live in them. Rom. 10:5; [Gal. 3:12]

12 Moreover also I gave them my ^Rsabbaths, to be a sign between me and them, that they might know that I *am* the LORD that sanctify them. Ex. 20:8; Neh. 9:14

13 But the house of Israel rebelled against me in the wilderness: they walked not in my statutes, and they despised my judgments, which *if* a man do, he shall even live in them; and my sabbaths they greatly polluted: then I said, I would pour out my fury upon them in the ^Rwilderness, to consume them. Num. 14:29; Ps. 106:23

14 But I wrought for my name's sake, that it should not be polluted before the heathen, in whose sight I brought them out.

15 Yet also I lifted up my hand unto them in the wilderness, that I would not bring them into the land which I had given *them,* flowing with milk and honey, which *is* the glory of all lands;

16 Because they despised my judgments, and walked not in my statutes, but polluted my sabbaths: for ^Rtheir heart went after their idols. Amos 5:25; Acts 7:42

17 ^RNevertheless mine eye spared them from destroying them, neither did I make an end of them in the wilderness. [Ps. 78:38]

18 But I said unto their children in the wilderness, Walk ye not in the statutes of your fathers, neither observe their judgments, nor defile yourselves with their idols:

19 I *am* the LORD your God; ^Rwalk in my statutes, and keep my judgments, and do them; Deut. 5:32

20 And hallow my sabbaths; and they shall be a sign between me and you, that ye may know that I *am* the LORD your God.

21 Notwithstanding ^Rthe children rebelled against me: they walked not in my statutes, neither kept my judgments to do them, ^Rwhich *if* a man do, he shall even live in them; they polluted my sabbaths: then I said, I would pour out my fury upon them, to accomplish my anger against them in the wilderness. Num. 25:1 · Lev. 18:5

22 Nevertheless I withdrew mine hand, and wrought for my name's sake, that it should not be ^Tpolluted in the sight of the hea-

then, in whose sight I brought them forth.　　　　*profaned*

23 I lifted up mine hand unto them also in the wilderness, that ᴿI would scatter them among the heathen, and disperse them through the countries;　Lev. 26:33

24 ᴿBecause they had not executed my judgments, but had despised my statutes, and had ᵀpolluted my sabbaths, and ᴿtheir eyes were after their fathers' idols.　vv. 13, 16 · *profaned* · 6:9

25 Wherefore ᴿI gave them also statutes *that were* not good, and judgments whereby they should not live;　Rom. 1:24; 2 Thess. 2:11

26 And I polluted them in their own gifts, in that they caused to pass ᴿthrough *the fire* all that openeth the womb, that I might make them desolate, to the end that they ᴿmight know that I *am* the LORD.　2 Kin. 17:17; 2 Chr. 28:3 · 6:7

27 Therefore, son of man, speak unto the house of Israel, and say unto them, Thus saith the Lord GOD; Yet in this your fathers have ᴿblasphemed me, in that they have committed a trespass against me.　Is. 65:7; Rom. 2:24

28 *For* when I had brought them into the land, *for* the which I lifted up mine hand to give it to them, then ᴿthey saw every high hill, and all the thick trees, and they offered there their sacrifices, and there they presented the provocation of their offering: there also they made their sweet savour, and poured out there their drink offerings.　Ps. 78:58; Is. 57:5-7; Jer. 3:6

29 Then I said unto them, What *is* the high place whereunto ye go? And the name thereof is called Ba'-mah unto this day.

30 Wherefore say unto the house of Israel, Thus saith the Lord GOD; Are ye polluted after the manner of your ᴿfathers? and commit ye whoredom after their ᴿabominations?　Judg. 2:19 · Jer. 7:26

31 For when ye offer your gifts, when ye make your sons to pass through the fire, ye pollute yourselves with all your idols, even

unto this day: and shall I be enquired of by you, O house of Israel? *As* I live, saith the Lord GOD, I will not be enquired of by you.

32 And that ᴿwhich cometh into your mind shall not be at all, that ye say, We will be as the ᵀheathen, as the families of the countries, to serve wood and stone.　11:5 · *Gentiles*

33 *As* I live, saith the Lord GOD, surely with a mighty hand, and ᴿwith a stretched out arm, and with fury poured out, will I rule over you:　Jer. 21:5

34 And I will bring you out from the people, and will gather you out of the countries wherein ye are scattered, with a mighty hand, and with a stretched out arm, and with fury poured out.

35 And I will bring you into the wilderness of the people, and there ᴿwill I plead with you face to face.　17:20; Jer. 2:9, 35

36 Like as I pleaded with your fathers in the wilderness of the land of Egypt, so will I plead with you, saith the Lord GOD.

37 And I will cause you to pass under the rod, and I will bring you into the bond of the covenant:

38 And ᴿI will purge out from among you the rebels, and them that transgress against me: I will bring them forth out of the country where they sojourn, and they shall not enter into the land of Israel: and ye shall know that I *am* the LORD.　Amos 9:9, 10; [Matt. 25:32]

39 As for you, O house of Israel, thus saith the Lord GOD; Go ye, serve ye every one his idols, and hereafter *also*, if ye will not hearken unto me: ᴿbut pollute ye my holy name no more with your gifts, and with your idols.　Is. 1:13-15

40 For in mine holy mountain, in the mountain of the height of Israel, saith the Lord GOD, there shall all the house of Israel, all of them in the land, serve me: there ᴿwill I accept them, and there will I require your offerings, and the firstfruits of your oblations, with all your holy things.　Zech. 8:20-22

41 I will accept you with your

Rsweet savour, when I bring you out from the people, and gather you out of the countries wherein ye have been scattered; and I will be sanctified in you before the heathen.   Eph. 5:2; Phil. 4:18

42 RAnd ye shall know that I *am* the Lord, Rwhen I shall bring you into the land of Israel, into the country *for* the which I lifted up mine hand to give it to your fathers.   36:23; 38:23 · 11:17; 34:13; 36:24

43 And there shall ye remember your ways, and all your doings, wherein ye have been defiled; and Rye shall lothe yourselves in your own sight for all your evils that ye have committed.   Lev. 26:39; Hos. 5:15

44 RAnd ye shall know that I *am* the Lord, when I have wrought with you Rfor my name's sake, not according to your wicked ways, nor according to your corrupt doings, O ye house of Israel, saith the Lord God.   24:24 · 36:22

45 Moreover the word of the Lord came unto me, saying,

46 RSon of man, set thy face toward the south, and drop *thy word* toward the south, and prophesy against the forest of the south field;   21:2; Amos 7:16

47 And say to the forest of the south, Hear the word of the Lord; Thus saith the Lord God; Behold, I will kindle a fire in thee, and it shall devour every green tree in thee, and every dry tree: the flaming flame shall not be quenched, and all faces from the south to the north shall be burned therein.

48 And all flesh shall see that I the Lord have kindled it: it shall not be quenched.

49 Then said I, Ah Lord God! they say of me, Doth he not speak Rparables?   17:2; Matt. 13:13; John 16:25

21 And the word of the Lord came unto me, saying,

2 RSon of man, set thy face toward Jerusalem, and Rdrop^T *thy word* toward the holy places, and prophesy against the land of Israel,   20:46 · Amos 7:16 · *preach*

3 And say to the land of Israel, Thus saith the Lord; Behold, I *am*

Ragainst thee, and will draw forth my sword out of his sheath, and will cut off from thee the righteous and the wicked.   Nah. 2:13

4 Seeing then that I will cut off from thee the righteous and the wicked, therefore shall my sword go forth out of his sheath against all flesh Rfrom the south to the north: 20:47; Jer. 12:12

5 That all flesh may know that I the Lord have drawn forth my sword out of his sheath: it Rshall not return any more. [Is. 45:23; 55:11]

6 RSigh therefore, thou son of man, with the breaking of *thy* loins; and with bitterness sigh before their eyes.   Is. 22:4; Luke 19:41

7 And it shall be, when they say unto thee, Wherefore sighest thou? that thou shalt answer, TFor the tidings; because it cometh: and every heart shall melt, and Rall hands shall be feeble, and every spirit shall faint, and all knees shall be weak *as* water: behold, it cometh, and shall be brought to pass, saith the Lord God.   *Because of the news* · 7:17

8 Again the word of the Lord came unto me, saying,

9 Son of man, prophesy, and say, Thus saith the Lord; Say, RA sword, a sword is sharpened, and also Tfurbished: vv. 15, 18; 5:1 · *polished*

10 It is sharpened to make a sore slaughter; it is furbished that it may glitter: should we then make mirth? it contemneth the rod of my son, *as* every tree.

11 And he hath given it to be Tfurbished, that it may be handled: this sword is sharpened, and it is Tfurbished, to give it into the hand of Rthe slayer.   *polished* · v. 19

12 Cry and howl, son of man: for it shall be upon my people, it *shall be* upon all the princes of Israel: terrors by reason of the sword shall be upon my people: smite therefore upon *thy* thigh.

13 Because *it is* Ra trial, and what if *the sword* contemn even the rod? Rit shall be no *more*, saith the Lord God. Job 9:23; 2 Cor. 8:2 · v. 27

14 Thou therefore, son of man,

prophesy, and ᴿsmite *thine* hands together, and let the sword be doubled the third time, the sword of the slain: it *is* the sword of the great *men that are* slain, which entereth into their ᴿprivy chambers. 6:11; Num. 24:10 · 1 Kin. 20:30

15 I have set the point of the sword against all their gates, that *their* heart may faint, and ᵀ*their* ruins be multiplied: ah! *it is* made bright, *it is* wrapped up for the slaughter. *many may stumble*

16 Go thee one way or other, *either* on the right hand, *or* on the left, whithersoever thy face *is* set.

17 I will also smite mine hands together, and I will cause my fury to rest: I the LORD have said *it*.

18 The word of the LORD came unto me again, saying,

19 Also, thou son of man, appoint thee two ways, ᵀthat the sword of the king of Babylon ᵀmay come: both twain shall come forth out of one land: and choose thou a place, choose *it* at the head of the way to the city. *for · to go*

20 Appoint a way, that the sword may come to ᴿRab'-bath of the Am'-mon-ites, and to Judah in Jerusalem the defenced. Deut. 3:11

21 For the king of Babylon stood at the parting of the way, at the head of the two ways, to use divination: he made *his* arrows bright, he consulted with images, he looked in the liver.

22 At his right hand was the divination for Jerusalem, to appoint captains, to open the mouth in the slaughter, to lift up the voice with shouting, ᴿto appoint *battering* rams against the gates, to cast a mount, *and* to build a fort. 4:2

23 And it shall be unto them as a false divination in their sight, to them that have sworn oaths: but he will call to remembrance the iniquity, that they may be taken.

24 Therefore thus saith the Lord GOD; Because ye have made your iniquity to be remembered, in that your transgressions are ᵀdiscovered, so that in all your doings

your sins do appear; because, *I say,* that ye are come to remembrance, ye shall be taken with the hand. *uncovered*

25 And thou, ᴿprofane wicked prince of Israel, ᴿwhose day is come, when iniquity *shall have* an end, 2 Chr. 36:13; Jer. 52:2 · v. 29

26 Thus saith the Lord GOD; Remove the diadem, and take off the crown: this *shall* not *be* the same: ᴿexalt *him that is* low, and abase *him that is* high. Luke 1:52

27 I will overturn, overturn, overturn, it: and it shall be no *more,* until he come whose right it is; and I will give it ᴿ*him.* Ps. 2:6

28 And thou, son of man, prophesy and say, Thus saith the Lord GOD concerning the Am'-mon-ites, and concerning their reproach; even say thou, The sword, the sword *is* drawn: for the slaughter *it is* furbished, to consume because of the glittering:

29 Whiles they ᴿsee vanity unto thee, whiles they divine a lie unto thee, to bring thee upon the necks of *them that are* slain, of the wicked, ᴿwhose day is come, when their iniquity *shall have* an end. 12:24; 13:6–9; 22:28 · 7:2, 3, 7

30 Shall I cause *it* to return into his sheath? I will judge thee in the place where thou wast created, ᴿin the land of thy nativity. 16:3

31 And I will ᴿpour out mine indignation upon thee, I will ᴿblow against thee in the fire of my wrath, and deliver thee into the hand of brutish men, *and* skilful to destroy. 7:8 · Ps. 18:15; Is. 30:33

32 Thou shalt be for fuel to the fire; thy blood shall be in the midst of the land; ᴿthou shalt be no *more* remembered: for I the LORD have spoken *it*. 25:10

22 Moreover the word of the LORD came unto me, saying,

2 Now, thou son of man, wilt thou judge, wilt thou judge ᴿthe bloody city? yea, thou shalt shew her all her abominations. Nah. 3:1

3 Then say thou, Thus saith the Lord GOD, The city sheddeth blood in the midst of it, that her

time may come, and maketh idols against herself to defile herself.

4   Thou art become guilty in thy blood that thou hast shed; and hast defiled thyself in thine idols which thou hast made; and thou hast caused thy days to draw near, and art come *even* unto thy years: ᴿtherefore have I made thee a reproach unto the heathen, and a mocking to all countries.   5:14

5   *Those that be* near, and *those that be* far from thee, shall mock thee, *which art* infamous *and* ᵀmuch vexed.   *full of tumult*

6   Behold, ᴿthe princes of Israel, every one were in thee to their power to shed blood.   v. 27; Is. 1:23

7   In thee have they ᵀset light by father and mother: in the midst of thee have they ᴿdealt by oppression with the stranger: in thee have they vexed the fatherless and the widow. *made light of* · Mal. 3:5

8   Thou hast despised mine holy things, and hast ᴿprofaned my sabbaths.   Lev. 19:30

9   In thee are ᴿmen that carry tales to shed blood: ᴿand in thee they eat upon the mountains: in the midst of thee they commit lewdness.   Lev. 19:16; Jer. 9:4 · 18:6, 11

10 In thee have they discovered their fathers' nakedness: in thee have they humbled her that was ᴿset apart for pollution.   18:6

11 And one hath committed abomination ᴿwith his neighbour's wife; and another ᴿhath lewdly defiled his daughter in law; and another in thee hath ᵀhumbled his sister, his father's daughter.   18:11 · Lev. 18:15 · *violated*

12 In thee ᴿhave they taken gifts to shed blood; thou hast taken usury and increase, and thou hast greedily gained of thy neighbours by extortion, and hast forgotten me, saith the Lord GOD.   Ex. 23:8

13 Behold, therefore I have ᴿsmitten mine hand at thy dishonest gain which thou hast made, and at thy blood which hath been in the midst of thee.   21:17

14 ᴿCan thine heart endure, or can thine hands be strong, in the days that I shall deal with thee? ᴿI the LORD have spoken *it*, and will do *it*.   21:7 · 17:24

15 And I will scatter thee among the heathen, and disperse thee in the countries, and will ᵀconsume thy filthiness out of thee.   *remove*

16 And thou shalt take thine inheritance in thyself in the sight of the heathen, and ᴿthou shalt know that I *am* the LORD.   Ps. 9:16

17 And the word of the LORD came unto me, saying,

18 Son of man, ᴿthe house of Israel is to me become dross: all they *are* brass, and tin, and iron, and lead, in the midst of the ᴿfurnace; they are *even* the dross of silver.   Jer. 6:28; Lam. 4:1 · Is. 48:10

19 Therefore thus saith the Lord GOD; Because ye are all become dross, behold, therefore I will gather you into the midst of Jerusalem.

20 *As* they gather silver, and brass, and iron, and lead, and tin, into the midst of the furnace, to blow the fire upon it, to ᴿmelt *it*; so will I gather *you* in mine anger and in my fury, and I will leave *you there*, and melt you.   Jer. 9:7

21 Yea, I will gather you, and blow upon you in the fire of my wrath, and ye shall be melted in the midst thereof.

22 As silver is melted in the midst of the furnace, so shall ye be melted in the midst thereof; and ye shall know that I the LORD have ᴿpoured out my fury upon you.   20:8, 33; Hos. 5:10

23 And the word of the LORD came unto me, saying,

24 Son of man, say unto her, Thou *art* the land that is ᴿnot cleansed, nor rained upon in the day of indignation. Jer. 2:30; Zeph. 3:2

25 ᴿ*There is* a conspiracy of her prophets in the midst thereof, like a roaring lion ᵀravening the prey; they have devoured ᵀsouls; they have taken the treasure and precious things; ᴿthey have made her many widows in the midst thereof.   Hos. 6:9 · *tearing* · *lives* · Mic. 3:11

26 ᴿHer priests have violated my

law, and have profaned mine holy things: they have put no difference between the holy and profane, neither have they shewed *difference* between the unclean and the clean, and have hid their eyes from my sabbaths, and I am profaned among them.   Jer. 32:32

27 Her ᴿprinces in the midst thereof *are* like wolves ᵀravening the prey, to shed blood, *and* to destroy ᵀsouls, to get dishonest gain.   Is. 1:23; Zeph. 3:3 · *tearing · lives*

28 And ᴿher prophets have daubed them with untempered *morter*, seeing vanity, and divining lies unto them, saying, Thus saith the Lord Gᴏᴅ, when the Lᴏʀᴅ hath not spoken.   13:10

29 The people of the land have used oppression, and exercised robbery, and have vexed the poor and needy: yea, they have oppressed the stranger wrongfully.

30 ᴿAnd I sought for a man among them, that should make up the hedge, and ᴿstand in the gap before me for the land, that I should not destroy it: but I found none.   Is. 59:16; 63:5 · Ps. 106:23; Jer. 15:1

31 Therefore have I poured out mine indignation upon them; I have consumed them with the fire of my wrath: ᴿtheir own way have I recompensed upon their heads, saith the Lord Gᴏᴅ.   9:10; [Rom 2:8, 9]

23 The word of the Lᴏʀᴅ came again unto me, saying,

2 Son of man, there were ᴿtwo women, the daughters of one mother: 16:44–46; Jer. 3:7, 8

3 And they committed whoredoms in Egypt; they committed whoredoms in ᴿtheir youth: there were their breasts ᵀpressed, and there they bruised the teats of their virginity.   16:22 · *embraced*

4 And the names of them *were* A-ho'-lah the elder, and A-hol'-i-bah her sister: and ᴿthey were mine, and they bare sons and daughters. Thus *were* their names; Sa-mar'-i-a *is* A-ho'-lah, and Jerusalem A-hol'-i-bah. 16:8, 20

5 And A-ho'-lah played the harlot when she was mine; and

she doted on her lovers, on ᴿthe Assyrians *her* neighbours,   16:28

6 Which *were* clothed with ᵀblue, captains and rulers, all of them desirable young men, horsemen riding upon horses.   *purple*

7 Thus she committed her whoredoms with them, with all them *that were* the chosen men of Assyria, and with all ᵀon whom she doted: with all their idols she defiled herself.   *for whom she lusted*

8 Neither left she her whoredoms *brought* ᴿfrom Egypt: for in her youth they lay with her, and they bruised the breasts of her virginity, and poured their whoredom upon her.   Ex. 32:4; 1 Kin. 12:28

9 Wherefore I have delivered her into the hand of her lovers, into the hand of the ᴿAssyrians, upon whom she doted.   2 Kin. 17:3

10 These discovered her nakedness: they took her sons and her daughters, and slew her with the sword: and she became famous among women; for they had executed judgment upon her.

11 And when her sister A-hol'-i-bah saw *this*, she was more corrupt in her inordinate love than she, and in her whoredoms more than her sister in *her* whoredoms.

12 She doted upon the Assyrians *her* neighbours, captains and rulers clothed most gorgeously, horsemen riding upon horses, all of them desirable young men.

13 Then I saw that she was defiled, *that* they *took* both one way,

14 And *that* she increased her whoredoms: for when she saw men pourtrayed upon the wall, the images of the ᴿChal-de'-ans pourtrayed with vermilion,   16:29

15 Girded with ᵀgirdles upon their loins, ᵀexceeding in dyed attire upon their heads, all of them princes to look to, after the manner of the Babylonians of Chal-de'-a, the land of their nativity: *belts · with flowing turbans upon*

16 And as soon as she saw them with her eyes, she doted upon them, and sent ᴿmessengers unto them into Chal-de'-a.   Is. 57:9

17 And the Babylonians came to her into the bed of love, and they defiled her with their whoredom, and she was polluted with them, and ᴿher mind was alienated from them.   vv. 22, 28

18 So she discovered her whoredoms, and discovered her nakedness: then my mind was alienated from her, like as my mind was alienated from her sister.

19 Yet she multiplied her whoredoms, in calling to remembrance the days of her youth, ᴿwherein she had played the harlot in the land of Egypt.   v. 2; Lev. 18:3

20 For she ᵀdoted upon their paramours, whose flesh *is as* the flesh of asses, and whose issue *is like* the issue of horses.   *lusted for*

21 Thus thou calledst to remembrance the lewdness of thy youth, in bruising thy teats by the ᴿEgyptians for the paps of thy youth.   16:26

22 Therefore, O A-hol′-i-bah, thus saith the Lord GOD; ᴿBehold, I will raise up thy lovers against thee, from whom thy mind is alienated, and I will bring them against thee on every side; 16:37-41

23 The Babylonians, and all the Chal-de′-ans, Pe′-kod, and Sho′-a, and Ko′-a, *and* ᴿall the Assyrians with them: all of them desirable young men, captains and rulers, great lords and renowned, all of them riding upon horses.   v. 12

24 And they shall come against thee with chariots, wagons, and ᵀwheels, and with ᵀan assembly of people, *which* shall set against thee buckler and shield and helmet round about: and I will set judgment before them, and they shall judge thee according to their judgments.   *war-horses · a horde*

25 And I will set my ᴿjealousy against thee, and they shall deal furiously with thee: they shall take away thy nose and thine ears; and thy remnant shall fall by the sword: they shall take thy sons and thy daughters; and thy ᵀresidue shall be devoured by the fire.   5:13; 8:17, 18; Zeph. 1:18 · *remnant*

26 ᴿThey shall also strip thee out of thy clothes, and take away thy fair jewels.   16:39; Is. 3:18-23

27 Thus will I make thy lewdness to cease from thee, and thy whoredom *brought* from the land of Egypt: so that thou shalt not lift up thine eyes unto them, nor remember Egypt any more.

28 For thus saith the Lord GOD; Behold, I will deliver thee into the hand *of them* whom thou hatest, into the hand *of them* ᴿfrom whom thy mind is alienated: v. 17

29 And they shall deal with thee hatefully, and shall take away all thy labour, and ᴿshall leave thee naked and bare: and the nakedness of thy whoredoms shall be discovered, both thy lewdness and thy whoredoms.   16:39

30 I will do these *things* unto thee, because thou hast ᴿgone a whoring after the ᵀheathen, *and* because thou art ᵀpolluted with their idols.   6:9 · *Gentiles · defiled*

31 Thou hast walked in the way of thy sister; therefore will I give her ᴿcup into thine hand.   Jer. 25:15

32 Thus saith the Lord GOD; Thou shalt drink of thy sister′s cup deep and ᵀlarge: thou shalt be laughed to scorn and ᵀhad in derision; it containeth much.   *wide · held*

33 Thou shalt be filled with drunkenness and sorrow, with the cup of ᵀastonishment and desolation, with the cup of thy sister Sama′-ri-a.   *horror*

34 Thou shalt ᴿeven drink it and suck *it* out, and thou shalt break the sherds thereof, and pluck off thine own breasts: for I have spoken *it*, saith the Lord GOD. Ps. 75:8

35 Therefore thus saith the Lord GOD; Because thou hast forgotten me, and ᴿcast me behind thy back, therefore bear thou also thy lewdness and thy whoredoms. Neh. 9:26

36 The LORD said moreover unto me; Son of man, wilt thou ᴿjudge A-ho′-lah and A-hol′-i-bah? yea, ᴿdeclare unto them their abominations;   20:4; 22:2 · Is. 58:1; Mic. 3:8

37 That they have committed adultery, and ᴿblood *is* in their

hands, and with their idols have they committed adultery, and have also caused their sons, whom they bare unto me, to pass for them through *the fire*, to devour *them*. 16:38

38 Moreover this they have done unto me: they have defiled my sanctuary in the same day, and ᴿhave profaned my sabbaths. 22:8

39 For when they had slain their children to their idols, then they came the same day into my sanctuary to profane it; and, lo, ᴿthus have they done in the midst of mine house. 2 Kin. 21:2–8

40 And furthermore, that ye have sent for men to come from far, unto whom a messenger *was* sent; and, lo, they came: for whom thou didst wash thyself, paintedst thy eyes, and ᵀdeckedst thyself with ornaments, *adorned*

41 And satest upon a stately ᴿbed, and a table prepared before it, whereupon thou hast set mine incense and mine oil. Amos 2:8; 6:4

42 And a voice of a multitude being at ease *was* with her: and with the men of the common sort *were* brought Sa-be'-ans from the wilderness, which put bracelets upon their hands, and beautiful crowns upon their heads.

43 Then said I unto *her that was* old in adulteries, Will they now commit ᵀwhoredoms with her, and she *with them*? *harlotry*

44 Yet they went in unto her, as they go in unto a woman that playeth the harlot: so went they in unto A-ho'-lah and unto A-hol'-i-bah, the lewd women.

45 And the righteous men, they shall ᴿjudge them after the manner of adulteresses, and after the manner of women that shed blood; because they *are* adulteresses, and ᴿblood *is* in their hands. 16:38 · v. 37

46 For thus saith the Lord Gᴏᴅ; I will bring up a company upon them, and will give them to be removed and ᵀspoiled. *plundered*

47 ᴿAnd the company shall stone them with stones, and dis-patch them with their swords; ᴿthey shall slay their sons and their daughters, and burn up their houses with fire. 16:40 · 24:21

48 Thus ᴿwill I cause lewdness to cease out of the land, that all women may be taught not to do after your lewdness. 22:15

49 And they shall recompense your lewdness upon you, and ye shall ᴿbear the sins of your idols: ᴿand ye shall know that I *am* the Lord Gᴏᴅ. Is. 59:18 · 20:38, 42, 44; 25:5

24 Again in the ninth year, in the tenth month, in the tenth *day* of the month, the word of the Lᴏʀᴅ came unto me, saying,

2 Son of man, write thee the name of the day, *even* of this same day: the king of Babylon ᵀset himself against Jerusalem ᴿthis same day. *laid his siege* · Jer. 39:1; 52:4

3 ᴿAnd utter a parable unto the rebellious house, and say unto them, Thus saith the Lord Gᴏᴅ; ᴿSet on a pot, set *it* on, and also pour water into it: 17:12 · Jer. 1:13

4 Gather the pieces thereof into it, *even* every good piece, the thigh, and the shoulder; fill *it* with the choice ᵀbones. *Portions*

5 Take the choice of the flock, and burn also the bones under it, *and* make it boil well, and let them seethe the bones of it therein.

6 Wherefore thus saith the Lord Gᴏᴅ; Woe to the bloody city, to the pot whose scum *is* therein, and whose scum is not gone out of it! bring it out piece by piece; let no ᴿlot fall upon it. Obad. 11; Nah. 3:10

7 For her blood is in the midst of her; she set it upon the top of a rock; she poured it not upon the ground, to cover it with dust;

8 That it might cause fury to come up to take vengeance; ᴿI have set her blood upon the top of a rock, that it should not be covered. [Matt. 7:2]

9 Therefore thus saith the Lord Gᴏᴅ; ᴿWoe to the bloody city! I will even make the pile for fire great. v. 6; Nah. 3:1; Hab. 2:12

10 Heap on wood, kindle the fire, ᵀconsume the flesh, and spice

it well, and let the bones be burned.   *cook the meat well*

11 Then set it empty upon the coals thereof, that the ᵀbrass of it may be hot, and may burn, and *that* ᴿthe filthiness of it may be molten in it, *that* the scum of it may be consumed.   *bronze · 22:15*

12 She hath wearied *herself* with lies, and her great scum went not forth out of her: her scum *shall be* in the fire.

13 In thy ᴿfilthiness *is* lewdness: because I have purged thee, and thou wast not purged, thou shalt not be purged from thy filthiness any more, till I have caused my fury to rest upon thee.   *23:36–48*

14 I the LORD have spoken *it:* it shall come to pass, and I will do *it;* I will not go back, neither will I spare, neither will I ᵀrepent; according to thy ways, and according to thy doings, shall they judge thee, saith the Lord GOD.   *relent*

15 Also the word of the LORD came unto me, saying,

16 Son of man, behold, I take away from thee the desire of thine eyes with a stroke: yet neither shalt thou mourn nor weep, neither shall thy tears run down.

17 Forbear to cry, make no mourning for the dead, bind the ᵀtire of thine head upon thee, and put on thy shoes upon thy feet, and cover not *thy* lips, and eat not the bread of men.   *turban*

18 So I spake unto the people in the morning: and at ᵀeven my wife died; and I did in the morning as I was commanded.   *evening*

19 And the people said unto me, ᴿWilt thou not tell us what these *things are* to us, that thou doest so?   *12:9; 37:18*

20 Then I answered them, The word of the LORD came unto me, saying,

21 Speak unto the house of Israel, Thus saith the Lord GOD; Behold, ᴿI will profane my sanctuary, the excellency of your strength, the desire of your eyes, and that which your soul pitieth; ᴿand your sons and your daugh-

ters whom ye have left shall fall by the sword. *7:20, 24 · Jer. 6:11; 16:3, 4*

22 And ye shall do as I have done: ye shall not cover *your* lips, nor eat the bread of men.

23 And your ᵀtires *shall be* upon your heads, and your shoes upon your feet: ye shall not mourn nor weep; but ᴿye shall pine away for your iniquities, and mourn one toward another.   *turbans · Lev. 26:39*

24 Thus ᴿE-ze′-ki-el is unto you a sign: according to all that he hath done shall ye do: and when this cometh, ye shall know that I *am* the Lord GOD.   *Luke 11:29, 30*

25 Also, thou son of man, *shall it* not *be* in the day when I take from them ᴿtheir strength, the joy of their glory, the desire of their eyes, and that whereupon they set their minds, their sons and their daughters,   *v. 21; Ps. 48:2; 50:2*

26 *That* he that escapeth in that day shall come unto thee, to cause *thee* to hear *it* with *thine* ears?

27 ᴿIn that day shall thy mouth be opened to him which is escaped, and thou shalt speak, and be no more ᵀdumb: and thou shalt be a sign unto them; and they shall know that I *am* the LORD.   *3:26; 33:22 · mute*

25

The word of the LORD came again unto me, saying,

2 Son of man, ᴿset thy face ᴿagainst the Am′-mon-ites, and prophesy against them;   *35:2 · 21:28*

3 And say unto the Am′-mon-ites, Hear the word of the Lord GOD; Thus saith the Lord GOD; ᴿBecause thou saidst, Aha, against my sanctuary, when it was profaned; and against the land of Israel, when it was desolate; and against the house of Judah, when they went into captivity; *Ps. 70:2, 3*

4 Behold, therefore I will deliver thee to the men of the east for a possession, and they shall set their ᵀpalaces in thee, and make their dwellings in thee: they shall eat thy fruit, and they shall drink thy milk.   *encampments among*

5 And I will make Rab′-bah ᴿa stable for camels, and the Am′-

mon-ites a ᵀcouchingplace for flocks: and ye shall know that I *am* the LORD.   Is. 17:2 · *resting place*

6 For thus saith the Lord GOD; Because thou hast clapped *thine* hands, and stamped with the feet, and rejoiced in heart with all thy despite against the land of Israel;

7 Behold, therefore I will ᴿstretch out mine hand upon thee, and will deliver thee ᵀfor a spoil to the ᵀheathen; and I will cut thee off from the people, and I will cause thee to perish out of the countries: I will destroy thee; and thou shalt know that I *am* the LORD.   35:3 · *plunder* · *nations*

8 Thus saith the Lord GOD; Because that ᴿMoab and Se'-ir do say, Behold, the house of Judah *is* like unto all the heathen;   Is. 15:6

9 Therefore, behold, I will open the side of Moab from the cities, from his cities *which are* on his frontiers, the glory of the country, Beth–jesh'-i-moth, Ba'-al-me'-on, and ᴿKir-i-a-tha'-im,   Jer. 48:23

10 ᴿUnto the men of the east with the Am'-mon-ites, and will give them in possession, that the Am'-mon-ites may not be remembered among the nations.   v. 4

11 And I will execute judgments upon Moab; and they shall know that I *am* the LORD.

12 Thus saith the Lord GOD; ᴿBecause that E'-dom hath dealt against the house of Judah by taking vengeance, and hath greatly offended, and revenged himself upon them;   Amos 1:11; Obad. 10–14

13 Therefore thus saith the Lord GOD; I will also stretch out mine hand upon E'-dom, and will cut off man and beast from it; and I will make it desolate from Te'-man; and they of De'-dan shall fall by the sword.

14 And ᴿI will lay my vengeance upon E'-dom by the hand of my people Israel: and they shall do in E'-dom according to mine anger and according to my fury; and they shall know my vengeance, saith the Lord GOD.   Is. 11:14

15 Thus saith the Lord GOD;

ᴿBecause the Phi-lis'-tines have dealt by revenge, and have taken vengeance with a despiteful heart, to destroy *it* for the old hatred;   Jer. 25:20; Amos 1—6

16 Therefore thus saith the Lord GOD; Behold, ᴿI will stretch out mine hand upon the Phi-lis'-tines, and I will cut off the Cher'-e-thims, ᴿand destroy the remnant of the sea coast.   Zeph. 2:4 · Jer. 47:4

17 And I will ᴿexecute great vengeance upon them with furious rebukes; ᴿand they shall know that I *am* the LORD, when I shall lay my vengeance upon them.   5:15 · Ps. 9:16

26 And it came to pass in the eleventh year, in the first *day* of the month, *that* the word of the LORD came unto me, saying,

2 Son of man, because that Ty'-rus hath said against Jerusalem, ᴿAha, she is broken *that was* the gates of the people: she is turned unto me: I shall be replenished, *now* she is laid waste: 25:3

3 Therefore thus saith the Lord GOD; Behold, I *am* against thee, O ᵀTy'-rus, and will cause many nations to come up against thee, as the sea causeth his waves to come up.   Or *Tyre*

4 And they shall destroy the walls of Ty'-rus, and break down her towers: I will also scrape her dust from her, and ᴿmake her like the top of a rock.   v. 14

5 It shall be *a place for* the spreading of nets ᴿin the midst of the sea: for I have spoken *it*, saith the Lord GOD: and it shall become a ᵀspoil to the nations. 27:32 · *plunder*

6 And her daughters which *are* in the field shall be slain by the sword; ᴿand they shall know that I *am* the LORD.   25:5

7 For thus saith the Lord GOD; Behold, I will bring upon Ty'-rus Neb-u-chad-rez'-zar king of Bab-ylon, a king of kings, from the north, with horses, and with chariots, and with horsemen, and companies, and much people.

8 He shall slay with the sword thy daughters in the field: and he

shall ^Rmake a fort against thee, and cast a mount against thee, and lift up the buckler against thee.   21:22; Jer. 52:4

9 And he shall set ^Tengines of war against thy walls, and with his axes he shall break down thy towers.   battering rams

10 By reason of the abundance of his horses their dust shall cover thee: thy walls shall shake at the noise of the horsemen, and of the ^Twheels, and of the chariots, when he shall enter into thy gates, as men enter into a city wherein is made a breach.   wagons

11 With the hoofs of his horses shall he tread down all thy streets: he shall slay thy people by the sword, and thy strong garrisons shall go down to the ground.

12 And they shall make a spoil of thy riches, and make a prey of thy merchandise: and they shall break down thy walls, and destroy thy pleasant houses: and they shall lay thy stones and thy timber and thy dust in the ^Rmidst of the water.   27:27, 32

13 ^RAnd I will cause the noise of thy songs to cease; and the sound of thy harps shall be no more heard.   Is. 14:11; 24:8; Jer. 7:34; 25:10

14 And I will make thee like the top of a rock: thou shalt be *a place* to spread nets upon; thou shalt be built no more: for I the LORD have spoken *it*, saith the Lord GOD.

15 Thus saith the Lord GOD to Ty'-rus; Shall not the isles ^Rshake at the sound of thy fall, when the wounded cry, when the slaughter is made in the midst of thee?   27:28

16 Then all the ^Rprinces of the sea shall ^Rcome down from their thrones, and lay away their robes, and put off their broidered garments: they shall clothe themselves with trembling; they shall sit upon the ground, and shall tremble at *every* moment, and be astonished at thee.   Is. 23:8 · Jon. 3:6

17 And they shall take up a lamentation for thee, and say to thee, How art thou destroyed, *that wast* inhabited of seafaring

men, the renowned city, which wast strong in the sea, she and her inhabitants, which cause their terror *to be* on all that haunt it!

18 Now shall ^Rthe isles tremble in the day of thy fall; yea, the isles that *are* in the sea shall be troubled at thy departure.   v. 15

19 For thus saith the Lord GOD; When I shall make thee a desolate city, like the cities that are not inhabited; when I shall bring up the deep upon thee, and great waters shall cover thee;

20 When I shall bring thee down ^Rwith them that descend into the pit, with the people of old time, and shall set thee in the low parts of the earth, in places desolate ^Tof old, with them that go down to the pit, that thou be not inhabited; and I shall set glory ^Rin the land of the living;   32:18 · *from antiquity* · 32:23

21 ^RI will make thee a terror, and thou *shalt be* no *more:* ^Rthough thou be sought for, yet shalt thou never be found again, saith the Lord GOD.   27:36; 28:19 · Ps. 37:10, 36

27 The word of the LORD came again unto me, saying,

2 Now, thou son of man, ^Rtake up a lamentation for Ty'-rus;   26:17

3 And say unto Ty'-rus, O thou that art situate at the entry of the sea, *which art* a merchant of the people for many isles, Thus saith the Lord GOD; O Ty'-rus, thou hast said, ^RI *am* of perfect beauty.   28:12

4 Thy borders *are* in the midst of the seas, thy builders have perfected thy beauty.

5 They have made all thy ^Tship boards of fir trees of Se'-nir: they have taken cedars from Leb'-a-non to make masts for thee.   planks

6 *Of* the ^Roaks of Ba'-shan have they made thine oars; the company of the Ash'-ur-ites have made thy benches *of* ivory, *brought* out of the isles of Chit'-tim.   Is. 2:12, 13

7 Fine linen with broidered work from Egypt was that which thou spreadest forth to be thy sail; blue and purple from the ^Tisles of E-li'-shah was that which covered thee.   coasts

8 The inhabitants of Zi'-don and Ar'-vad were thy [T]mariners: thy wise *men*, O Ty'-rus, *that* were in thee, were thy pilots.   *oarsmen*

9 The ancients of [R]Ge'-bal and the wise *men* thereof were in thee thy calkers: all the ships of the sea with their mariners were in thee to occupy thy merchandise. Ps. 83:7

10 They of Persia and of Lud and of Phut were in thine army, thy men of war: they hanged the shield and helmet in thee; they set forth thy [T]comeliness.   *splendour*

11 The men of Ar'-vad with thine army *were* upon thy walls round about, and the Gam'-ma-dims were in thy towers: they hanged their shields upon thy walls round about; they have made [R]thy beauty perfect.   v. 3

12 [R]Tar'-shish *was* thy merchant by reason of the multitude of all *kind of* riches; with silver, iron, tin, and lead, they traded in thy fairs.   38:13; Gen. 10:4; 2 Chr. 20:36

13 [R]Ja'-van, Tu'-bal, and Me'-shech, they *were* thy merchants: they traded [R]the persons of men and vessels of brass in thy market.   Gen. 10:2 · Joel 3:3–6; Rev. 18:13

14 They of the house of [R]To-gar'-mah traded in thy fairs with hors-es and horsemen and mules.   38:6

15 The men of [R]De'-dan *were* thy merchants; many isles *were* the merchandise of thine hand: they brought thee *for* a present horns of ivory and ebony.   Is. 21:13

16 Syria *was* thy merchant by reason of the multitude of the wares of thy making: they occu-pied in thy fairs with emeralds, purple, and broidered work, and fine linen, and coral, and agate.

17 Judah, and the land of Israel, they *were* thy merchants: they traded in thy market wheat of Min'-nith, and Pan'-nag, and hon-ey, and oil, and [R]balm.   Jer. 8:22

18 Damascus *was* thy merchant in the multitude of the wares of thy making, for the multitude of all riches; in the wine of Hel'-bon, and white wool.

19 Dan also and Ja'-van going to and fro [T]occupied in thy fairs: bright iron, cassia, and calamus, were in thy market.   *paid for wares*

20 De'-dan *was* thy merchant in precious clothes for chariots.

21 Arabia, and all the princes of Ke'-dar, they occupied with thee in lambs, and rams, and goats: in these *were they* thy merchants.

22 The merchants of She'-ba and Ra'-a-mah, they *were* thy merchants: they occupied in thy fairs with chief of all spices, and with all precious stones, and gold.

23 [R]Ha'-ran, and Can'-neh, and Eden, the merchants of [R]She'-ba, Assh'-ur, *and* Chil'-mad, *were* thy merchants.   Is. 37:12 · Gen. 25:3

24 These *were* thy merchants in all sorts *of things*, in blue clothes, and broidered work, and in chests of [T]rich apparel, bound with cords, and made of cedar, among thy merchandise.   *multicoloured*

25 [R]The ships of Tar'-shish did sing of thee in thy market: and thou wast replenished, and made very glorious [R]in the midst of the seas.   Ps. 48:7; Is. 2:16 · v. 4

26 Thy rowers have brought thee into [T]great waters: the east wind hath broken thee in the midst of the seas.   *many*

27 Thy [R]riches, and thy fairs, thy merchandise, thy mariners, and thy pilots, thy calkers, and the occupiers of thy merchandise, and all thy men of war, that *are* in thee, and in all thy company which *is* in the midst of thee, shall fall into the midst of the seas in the day of thy ruin.   [Prov. 11:4]

28 The suburbs shall shake at the sound of the cry of thy pilots.

29 And [R]all that handle the oar, the mariners, *and* all the pilots of the sea, shall come down from their ships, they shall stand upon the [T]land;   Rev. 18:17 · *shore*

30 And shall cause their voice to be heard against thee, and shall cry bitterly, and shall cast up dust upon their heads, they shall wal-low themselves in the ashes:

31 And they shall [R]make them-selves utterly bald for thee, and

gird them with sackcloth, and they shall weep for thee with bitterness of heart *and* bitter wailing. 29:18; Is. 15:2; Jer. 16:6

32 And in their wailing they shall ᴿtake up a lamentation for thee, and lament over thee, *saying,* ᴿWhat *city is* like Ty'-rus, like the destroyed in the midst of the sea? 26:17 · 26:4, 5; Rev. 18:18

33 ᴿWhen thy wares went forth ᵀout of the seas, thou filledst many people; thou didst enrich the kings of the earth with the multitude of thy riches and of thy merchandise. Rev. 18:19 · *by sea*

34 In the time *when* ᴿthou shalt be broken by the seas in the depths of the waters thy merchandise and all thy company in the midst of thee shall fall. 26:19

35 ᴿAll the inhabitants of the isles shall be astonished at thee, and their kings shall be sore afraid, they shall be troubled in *their* countenance. Is. 23:6

36 The merchants among the people ᴿshall hiss at thee; thou shalt be a terror, and never *shalt be* any more. Jer. 18:16; Zeph. 2:15

28 The word of the LORD came again unto me, saying,

2 Son of man, say unto the prince of Ty'-rus, Thus saith the Lord GOD; Because thine heart *is* ᴿlifted up, and ᴿthou hast said, I *am* ᵀa God, I sit *in* the seat of God, in the midst of the seas; ᴿyet thou *art* a man, and not God, though thou set thine heart as the heart of God: 31:10 · 2 Thess. 2:4 · *a god* · Is. 31:3

3 Behold, ᴿthou *art* wiser than Daniel; there is no secret that they can hide from thee: Dan. 1:20; 2:20–23

4 With thy wisdom and with thine understanding thou hast gotten thee ᴿriches, and hast gotten gold and silver into thy treasures: 27:33; Zech. 9:1–3

5 ᴿBy thy great wisdom *and* by thy traffick hast thou increased thy riches, and thine heart is lifted up because of thy riches: Ps. 62:10

6 Therefore thus saith the Lord GOD; Because thou hast set thine heart as the heart of ᵀGod; *a god*

7 Behold, therefore I will bring ᴿstrangers upon thee, the terrible of the nations: and they shall draw their swords against the beauty of thy wisdom, and they shall defile thy brightness. 26:7

8 They shall bring thee down to the ᴿpit, and thou shalt die the deaths of *them that are* slain in the midst of the seas. Is. 14:15

9 Wilt thou yet ᴿsay before him that slayeth thee, I *am* ᵀGod? but thou *shalt be* a man, and no God, in the hand of him that slayeth thee. v. 2 · *a god*

10 Thou shalt die the deaths of ᴿthe uncircumcised by the hand of strangers: for I have spoken *it,* saith the Lord GOD. 31:18; 32:19

11 Moreover the word of the LORD came unto me, saying,

12 Son of man, ᴿtake up a lamentation upon the king of Ty'-rus, and say unto him, Thus saith the Lord GOD; ᴿThou sealest up the sum, full of wisdom, and perfect in beauty. 27:2 · v. 3; 27:3

13 Thou hast been in Eden the garden of God; every precious stone *was* thy covering, the sardius, topaz, and the diamond, the beryl, the onyx, and the jasper, the sapphire, the emerald, and the carbuncle, and gold: the workmanship of ᴿthy tabrets and of thy pipes was prepared in thee in the day that thou wast created. 26:13

14 Thou *art* the anointed cherub that covereth; and I have set thee *so:* thou wast upon ᴿthe holy mountain of God; thou hast walked up and down in the midst of the stones of fire. Is. 14:13

15 Thou *wast* perfect in thy ways from the day that thou wast created, till ᴿiniquity was found in thee. [Is. 14:12]

16 By the multitude of thy ᵀmerchandise they have filled the midst of thee with violence, and thou hast sinned: therefore I will cast thee as profane out of the mountain of God: and I will destroy thee, ᴿO covering cherub, from the midst of the stones of fire. *trading* · v. 14

17 ᴿThine heart was ᵀlifted up because of thy beauty, thou hast corrupted thy wisdom by reason of thy ᵀbrightness: I will cast thee to the ground, I will lay thee before kings, that they may behold thee.   vv. 2, 5 · Proud · *splendour*

18 Thou hast defiled thy sanctuaries by the multitude of thine iniquities, by the iniquity of thy ᵀtraffick; therefore will I bring forth a fire from the midst of thee, it shall devour thee, and I will ᵀbring thee to ashes upon the earth in the sight of all them that behold thee.   *trading · turn*

19 All they that know thee among the people shall be astonished at thee: ᴿthou shalt be a ᵀterror, and never *shalt* thou *be* any ᴿmore.   26:21 · *horror* · 27:36

20 Again the word of the LORD came unto me, saying,

21 Son of man, ᴿset thy face ᴿagainst Zi′-don, and prophesy against it,   6:2; 25:2; 29:2 · Gen. 10:15

22 And say, Thus saith the Lord GOD; ᴿBehold, I *am* against thee, O Zi′-don; and I will be glorified in the midst of thee: and ᴿthey shall know that I *am* the LORD, when I shall have executed judgments in her, and shall be ᴿsanctified in her.   39:13 · Ps. 9:16 · v. 25

23 For I will send into her pestilence, and blood into her street; and the wounded shall be judged in the midst of her by the sword upon her on every side; and they shall know that I *am* the LORD.

24 And there shall be no more ᴿa pricking brier unto the house of Israel, nor *any* grieving thorn of all *that are* round about them, that ᴿdespised them; and they shall know that I *am* the Lord GOD.   Josh. 23:13; Is. 55:13 · 16:57; 25:6, 7

25 Thus saith the Lord GOD; When I shall have gathered the house of Israel from the people among whom they are scattered, and shall be sanctified in them in the sight of the heathen, then shall they dwell in their land that I have given to my servant Jacob.

26 And they shall dwell safely therein, and shall build houses, and plant vineyards; yea, they shall dwell with confidence, when I have executed judgments upon all those that despise them round about them; and they shall know that I *am* the LORD their God.

29 In the tenth year, in the tenth *month*, in the twelfth *day* of the month, the word of the LORD came unto me, saying,

2 Son of man, ᴿset thy face against Pharaoh king of Egypt, and prophesy against him, and ᴿagainst all Egypt: 28:21 · Jer. 25:19

3 Speak, and say, Thus saith the Lord GOD; ᴿBehold, I *am* against thee, Pharaoh king of Egypt, the great ᴿdragonᵀ that lieth in the midst of his rivers, ᴿwhich hath said, My river *is* mine own, and I have made *it* for myself.   Jer. 44:30 · Is. 37:1 · *monster* · 28:2

4 But ᴿI will put hooks in thy jaws, and I will cause the fish of thy rivers to stick unto thy scales, and I will bring thee up out of the midst of thy rivers, and all the fish of thy rivers shall stick unto thy scales.   38:4; 2 Kin. 19:28; Is. 37:29

5 And I will leave thee *thrown* into the wilderness, thee and all the fish of thy rivers: thou shalt fall upon the open fields; thou shalt not be brought together, nor gathered: I have given thee for meat to the beasts of the field and to the fowls of the heaven.

6 And all the inhabitants of Egypt shall know that I *am* the LORD, because they have been a ᴿstaff of reed to the house of Israel.   17:15; 2 Kin. 18:21; Is. 36:6

7 ᴿWhen they took hold of thee by thy hand, thou didst break, and ᵀrend all their shoulder: and when they leaned upon thee, thou brakest, and madest all their loins ᵀto be at a stand.   17:17 · *tear · shake*

8 Therefore thus saith the Lord GOD; Behold, I will bring ᴿa sword upon thee, and cut off man and beast out of thee.   14:17; 32:11–13

9 And the land of Egypt shall be ᴿdesolate and waste; and they shall know that I *am* the LORD:

because he hath said, The river *is* mine, and I have made *it*. 30:7, 8

10 Behold, therefore I *am* against thee, and against thy rivers, [R]and I will make the land of Egypt utterly waste *and* desolate, [R]from [T]the tower [T]of Sy-e′-ne even unto the border of E-thi-o′-pi-a. 30:12 · 30:6 · *Migdol* · to

11 [R]No foot of man shall pass through it, nor foot of beast shall pass through it, neither shall it be inhabited forty years. Jer. 43:11, 12

12 [R]And I will make the land of Egypt desolate in the midst of the countries *that are* desolate, and her cities among the cities *that are* laid waste shall be desolate forty years: and I will [R]scatter the Egyptians among the nations, and will disperse them through the countries. Jer. 25:15–19 · 30:23, 26

13 Yet thus saith the Lord God; At the [R]end of forty years will I gather the Egyptians from the people whither they were scattered: Is. 19:23; Jer. 46:26

14 And I will bring again the captivity of Egypt, and will cause them to return *into* the land of Path′-ros, into the land of their habitation; and they shall be there a [R]base[T] kingdom. 17:6, 14 · *lowly*

15 It shall be the [T]basest of the kingdoms; neither shall it exalt itself any more above the nations: for I will diminish them, that they shall no more rule over the nations. *lowliest*

16 And it shall be no more [R]the confidence of the house of Israel, which bringeth *their* iniquity to remembrance, when they shall look after them: but they shall know that I *am* the Lord God. v. 6

17 And it came to pass in the seven and twentieth year, in the first *month*, in the first *day* of the month, the word of the Lord came unto me, saying,

18 Son of man, Neb-u-chad-rez′-zar king of Babylon caused his army to serve a great service against Ty′-rus: every head *was* made bald, and every shoulder *was* peeled: yet had he no wages,

nor his army, for Ty′-rus, for the [T]service that he had served against it: *labour he had expended*

19 Therefore thus saith the Lord God; Behold, I will give the land of Egypt unto Neb-u-chad-rez′-zar king of Babylon; and he shall take her multitude, and take her spoil, and take her prey; and it shall be the wages for his army.

20 I have given him the land of Egypt *for* his labour wherewith he [R]served against it, because they wrought for me, saith the Lord God. Is. 10:6, 7; 45:1–3; Jer. 25:9

21 In that day [R]will I cause the horn of the house of Israel to bud forth, and I will give thee the opening of the mouth in the midst of them; and they shall know that I *am* the Lord. 1 Sam. 2:10; Ps. 92:10

30 The word of the Lord came again unto me, saying,

2 Son of man, prophesy and say, Thus saith the Lord God; Howl ye, Woe worth the day!

3 For [R]the day *is* near, even the day of the Lord *is* near, a cloudy day; it shall be the time of the [T]heathen. Obad. 15; Zeph. 1:7 · *Gentiles*

4 And the sword shall come upon Egypt, and great pain shall be in E-thi-o′-pi-a, when the slain shall fall in Egypt, and they [R]shall take away her [T]multitude, and [R]her foundations shall be broken down. 29:19 · *wealth* · Jer. 50:15

5 E-thi-o′-pi-a, and Lib′-y-a, and Lyd′-i-a, and all the mingled people, and Chub, and the men of the land that is in league, shall fall with them by the sword.

6 Thus saith the Lord; They also that uphold Egypt shall fall; and the pride of her power shall come down: [R]from the tower of Sy-e′-ne shall they fall in it by the sword, saith the Lord God. 29:10

7 [R]And they shall be desolate in the midst of the countries *that are* desolate, and her cities shall be in the midst of the cities *that are* [T]wasted. Jer. 25:18–26 · *laid waste*

8 And they shall know that I *am* the Lord, when I have set a fire in Egypt, and *when* all her helpers shall be destroyed.

9 In that day [R]shall messengers go forth from me in ships to make the [T]careless E-thi-o'-pi-ans afraid, and great pain shall come upon them, as in the day of Egypt: for, lo, it cometh.   Is. 18:1, 2 · *secure*

10 Thus saith the Lord GOD; [R]I will also make the multitude of Egypt to cease by the hand of Neb-u-chad-rez'-zar king of Babylon.   29:19

11 He and his people with him, [R]the [T]terrible of the nations, shall be brought to destroy the land: and they shall draw their swords against Egypt, and fill the land with the slain. 28:7; 31:12 · *most terrible*

12 And [R]I will make the rivers dry, and [R]sell the land into the hand of the wicked: and I will make the land [T]waste, and all that is therein, by the hand of strangers: I the LORD have spoken it.   Is. 19:5, 6 · Is. 19:4 · *desolate*

13 Thus saith the Lord GOD; I will also [R]destroy the idols, and I will cause *their* images to cease out of Noph; [R]and there shall be no more a prince of the land of Egypt: and I will put a fear in the land of Egypt.   Zech. 13:2 · Zech. 10:11

14 And I will make [R]Path'-ros desolate, and will set fire in [R]Zo'-an, [R]and will execute judgments in No. Is. 11:11 · Is. 19:11, 13 · Nah. 3:8–10

15 And I will pour my fury upon Sin, the strength of Egypt; and I will cut off the multitude of No.

16 And I will [R]set fire in Egypt: Sin shall have great pain, and No shall be rent asunder, and Noph *shall have* distresses daily.   v. 8

17 The young men of [T]A'-ven and of Pi–be'-seth shall fall by the sword: and these *cities* shall go into captivity.   Ancient On, Heliopolis

18 [R]At [T]Te-haph'-ne-hes also the day shall be darkened, when I shall break there the yokes of Egypt: and the [T]pomp of her strength shall cease in her: as for her, a cloud shall cover her, and her daughters shall go into captivity.   Jer. 2:16 · *Tahpanhes*, Jer. 43:7 · *pride*

19 Thus will I [R]execute judgments in Egypt: and they shall know that I *am* the LORD. [Ps. 9:16]

20 And it came to pass in the eleventh year, in the first *month*, in the seventh *day* of the month, *that* the word of the LORD came unto me, saying,

21 Son of man, I have [R]broken the arm of Pharaoh king of Egypt; and, lo, [R]it shall not be bound up to be healed, to put a roller to bind it, to make it strong to hold the sword.   Jer. 48:25 · Jer. 46:11

22 Therefore thus saith the Lord GOD; Behold, I *am* [R]against Pharaoh king of Egypt, and will [R]break his arms, the strong, and that which was broken; and I will cause the sword to fall out of his hand.   29:3; Jer. 46:25 · Ps. 37:17

23 [R]And I will scatter the Egyptians among the nations, and will disperse them through the countries.   vv. 17, 18, 26; 29:12

24 And I will strengthen the arms of the king of Babylon, and put my sword in his hand: but I will break Pharaoh's arms, and he shall groan before him with the groanings of a [T]deadly wounded *man*.   *mortally*

25 But I will strengthen the arms of the king of Babylon, and the arms of Pharaoh shall fall down; and [R]they shall know that I *am* the LORD, when I shall put my sword into the hand of the king of Babylon, and he shall stretch it out upon the land of Egypt. Ps. 9:16

26 [R]And I will scatter the Egyptians among the nations, and disperse them among the countries; and they shall know that I *am* the LORD.   29:12

31 And it came to pass in the [R]eleventh year, in the third *month*, in the first *day* of the month, *that* the word of the LORD came unto me, saying,   Jer. 52:5, 6

2 Son of man, speak unto Pharaoh king of Egypt, and to his multitude; [R]Whom art thou like in thy greatness?   v. 18

3 [R]Behold, the Assyrian *was* a cedar in Leb'-a-non with fair

branches, and with a shadowing shroud, and of an high stature; and his top was among the thick boughs. Is. 10:33, 34; Dan. 4:10, 20–23

4 [R]The waters made him great, the deep set him up on high with her rivers running round about his plants, and sent out her little rivers unto all the trees of the field. 29:3–9; Jer. 51:36

5 Therefore his height was exalted above all the trees of the field, and his boughs were multiplied, and his branches became long because of the multitude of waters, when he shot forth.

6 All the fowls of heaven made their nests in his boughs, and under his branches did all the beasts of the field bring forth their young, and under his shadow dwelt all great nations.

7 Thus was he [T]fair in his greatness, in the length of his branches: for his root [T]was by great waters. *beautiful · reached to*

8 The cedars in the [R]garden of God could not hide him: the fir trees were not like his boughs, and the chesnut trees were not like his branches; nor any tree in the garden of God was like unto him in his beauty. Gen. 2:8, 9; 13:10

9 I have made him fair by the multitude of his branches: so that all the trees of Eden, that *were* in the garden of God, envied him.

10 Therefore thus saith the Lord GOD; Because thou hast [T]lifted up thyself in height, and he hath shot up his top among the thick boughs, and [R]his heart is lifted up in his height; *increased · 2 Chr. 32:25*

11 I have therefore delivered him into the hand of the [R]mighty one of the heathen; he shall surely deal with him: I have driven him out for his wickedness. 30:10

12 And strangers, [R]the [T]terrible of the nations, have cut him off, and have left him: upon the mountains and in all the valleys his branches are fallen, and his boughs are broken by all the rivers of the land; and all the people of the earth are gone down

from his shadow, and have left him. 28:7; 30:11; 32:12 · *most terrible*

13 [R]Upon his ruin shall all the fowls of the heaven remain, and all the beasts of the field shall [T]be upon his branches: Is. 18:6 · *come to*

14 To the end that none of all the trees by the waters exalt themselves for their height, neither shoot up their top among the thick boughs, neither their trees stand up in their height, all that drink water: for they are all delivered unto death, [R]to the nether parts of the earth, in the midst of the children of men, with them that go down to the pit. 32:18

15 Thus saith the Lord GOD; In the day when he [R]went down to the grave I caused a mourning: I covered the deep for him, and I restrained the floods thereof, and the great waters were stayed: and I caused Leb'-a-non to mourn for him, and all the trees of the field [T]fainted for him. 32:22, 23 · *wilted*

16 I made the nations to shake at the sound of his fall, when I [R]cast him down to hell with them that descend into the pit: and all the trees of Eden, the choice and best of Leb'-a-non, all that drink water, shall be comforted in the nether parts of the earth. Is. 14:15

17 They also went down into hell with him unto *them that be* slain with the sword; and *they that were* his arm, *that* [R]dwelt under his shadow in the midst of the [T]heathen. Lam. 4:20 · *nations*

18 [R]To whom art thou thus like in glory and in greatness among the trees of Eden? yet shalt thou be brought down with the trees of Eden unto the [T]nether parts of the earth: thou shalt lie in the midst of the uncircumcised with *them that be* slain by the sword. This *is* Pharaoh and all his multitude, saith the Lord GOD. 32:19 · *depths*

32 And it came to pass in the twelfth year, in the [R]twelfth month, in the first *day* of the month, *that* the word of the LORD came unto me, saying, 31:1; 33:21

2 Son of man, [R]take up a lam-

entation for Pharaoh king of E-
gypt, and say unto him, ᴿThou art
like a young lion of the nations,
ᴿand thou *art* as a ᵀwhale in the
seas: and thou camest forth with
thy rivers, and troubledst the waters with thy feet, and fouledst
their rivers.　27:2 · 19:2–6 · 29:3 · *monster*

3　Thus saith the Lord GOD; I
will therefore ᴿspread out my net
over thee with a company of
many people; and they shall bring
thee up in my net.　　12:13; 17:20

4　Then ᴿwill I leave thee upon
the land, I will cast thee forth
upon the open field, and ᴿwill
cause all the fowls of the heaven
to ᵀremain upon thee, and I will
fill the beasts of the whole earth
with thee.　29:5 · Is. 18:6 · Lit. *dwell*

5　And I will lay thy ᵀflesh ᴿupon the mountains, and fill the valleys with thy height.　*carcase* · 31:12

6　I will also water with thy
blood the land wherein thou
swimmest, *even* to the mountains;
and the rivers shall be full of thee.

7　And when I shall put thee
out, I will cover the heaven, and
make the stars thereof dark; I will
cover the sun with a cloud, and
the moon shall not give her light.

8　All the bright lights of heav-
en will I make dark over thee, and
set darkness upon thy land, saith
the Lord GOD.

9　I will also ᵀvex the hearts of
many people, when I shall bring
thy destruction among the
nations, into the countries which
thou hast not known.　*trouble*

10　Yea, I will make many people
ᵀamazed at thee, and their kings
shall be horribly afraid for thee,
when I shall brandish my sword
before them; and ᴿthey shall tremble at *every* moment, every man
for his own life, in the day of thy
fall.　*astonished* · 26:16

11　ᴿFor thus saith the Lord GOD;
The sword of the king of Babylon
shall come upon thee.　Jer. 46:26

12　By the swords of the mighty
will I cause thy multitude to fall,
the terrible of the nations, all of
them: and they shall spoil the

pomp of Egypt, and all the multitude thereof shall be destroyed.

13　I will destroy also all the
beasts thereof from beside the
great waters; ᴿneither shall the
foot of man ᵀtrouble them any
more, nor the hoofs of beasts
ᵀtrouble them.　29:11 · *muddy*

14　Then will I make their waters
deep, and cause their rivers to run
like oil, saith the Lord GOD.

15　When I shall make the land
of Egypt desolate, and the country
shall be destitute of that whereof
it was full, when I shall smite all
them that dwell therein, ᴿthen
shall they know that I *am* the
LORD.　6:7; Ex. 7:5; 14:4, 18; Ps. 9:16

16　This *is* the lamentation
wherewith they shall lament
her: the daughters of the nations
shall lament her: they shall
lament for her, *even* for Egypt,
and for all her multitude, saith the
Lord GOD.

17　It came to pass also in the
twelfth year, in the fifteenth *day*
of the month, *that* the word of the
LORD came unto me, saying,

18　Son of man, wail for the multitude of Egypt, and cast them
down, *even* her, and the daughters
of the famous nations, unto the
nether parts of the earth, with
them that go down into the pit.

19　Whom dost thou pass in
beauty? ᴿgo down, and be thou
laid with the uncircumcised.　28:10

20　They shall fall in the midst of
them that are slain by the sword:
she is delivered to the sword:
draw her and all her multitudes.

21　ᴿThe strong among the
mighty shall speak to him out of
the midst of hell with them that
help him: they are gone down,
they ᵀlie uncircumcised, slain by
the sword.　Is. 1:31; 14:9, 10 · *lie with the*

22　ᴿAssh′-urᵀ *is* there and all her
company: his graves *are* about
him: all of them slain, fallen by
the sword:　31:3, 16 · *Assyria*

23　ᴿWhose graves are set in the
ᵀsides of the pit, and her company
is round about her grave: all of
them slain, fallen by the sword,

which caused terror in the land of the living.   Is. 14:15 · *recesses*

24 There *is* E'-lam and all her multitude round about her grave, all of them slain, fallen by the sword, which are gone down uncircumcised into the nether parts of the earth, which caused their terror in the land of the living; yet have they borne their shame with them that go down to the pit.

25 They have set her a bed in the midst of the slain with all her multitude: her graves *are* round about him: all of them uncircumcised, slain by the sword: though their terror was caused in the land of the living, yet have they borne their shame with them that go down to the pit: he is put in the midst of *them that be* slain.

26 There *is* ᴿMe'-shech, Tu'-bal, and all her multitude: her graves *are* round about him: all of them uncircumcised, slain by the sword, though they caused their terror in the land of the living. 39:1

27 ᴿAnd they shall not lie with the mighty *that are* fallen of the uncircumcised, which are gone down to hell with their weapons of war: and they have laid their swords under their heads, but their iniquities shall be upon their bones, though *they were* the terror of the mighty in the land of the living.   Is. 14:18, 19

28 Yea, thou shalt be broken in the midst of the uncircumcised, and shalt lie with *them that are* slain with the sword.

29 There *is* ᴿE'-dom, her kings, and all her princes, which ᵀwith their might are laid by *them that were* slain by the sword: they shall lie with the uncircumcised, and with them that go down to the pit.   25:12–14; Jer. 49:7–22 · *despite*

30 ᴿThere *be* the princes of the north, all of them, and all the Zi-do'-ni-ans, which are gone down with the slain; with their terror they are ashamed of their might; and they lie uncircumcised with *them that be* slain by the sword,

and bear their shame with them that go down to the pit.   Jer. 1:15

31 Pharaoh shall see them, and shall be ᴿcomforted over all his multitude, *even* Pharaoh and all his army slain by the sword, saith the Lord Goᴅ.   14:22; 31:16

32 For I have caused my terror in the land of the living: and he shall be laid in the midst of the uncircumcised with *them that are* slain with the sword, *even* Pharaoh and all his multitude, saith the Lord Goᴅ.

33 Again the word of the Lord came unto me, saying,

2 Son of man, speak to ᴿthe children of thy people, and say unto them, ᴿWhen I bring the sword upon a land, if the people of the land take a man of their coasts, and set him for their ᴿwatchman: 3:11 · 14:17 · Hos. 9:8

3 If when he seeth the sword come upon the land, he blow the trumpet, and warn the people;

4 Then whosoever heareth the sound of the trumpet, and taketh not warning; if the sword come, and take him away, ᴿhis blood shall be upon his own head.   18:13

5 He heard the sound of the trumpet, and took not warning; his blood shall be upon him. But he that taketh warning shall ᵀdeliver his soul.   *save his life*

6 But if the watchman see the sword come, and blow not the trumpet, and the people be not warned; if the sword come, and take *any* person from among them, he is taken away in his iniquity; but his blood will I require at the watchman's hand.

7 ᴿSo thou, O son of man, I have set thee a watchman unto the house of Israel; therefore thou shalt hear the word at my mouth, and warn them from me.   3:17–21

8 When I say unto the wicked, O wicked *man,* thou shalt surely die; if thou dost not speak to warn the wicked from his way, that wicked *man* shall die in his iniquity; but his blood will I require at thine hand.

9 Nevertheless, if thou warn the wicked of his way to turn from it; if he do not turn from his way, he shall die in his iniquity; but thou hast delivered thy soul.

10 Therefore, O thou son of man, speak unto the house of Israel; Thus ye speak, saying, If our transgressions and our sins *be* upon us, and we pine away in them, how should we then live?

11 Say unto them, *As* I live, saith the Lord GOD, I have no pleasure in the death of the wicked; but that the wicked turn from his way and live: turn ye, turn ye from your evil ways; for ^Rwhy will ye die, O house of Israel? [Acts 3:19]

12 Therefore, thou son of man, say unto the children of thy people, The ^Rrighteousness of the righteous shall not deliver him in the day of his transgression: as for the wickedness of the wicked, ^Rhe shall not fall thereby in the day that he turneth from his wickedness; neither shall the righteous be able to live for his *righteousness* in the day that he sinneth. 3:20; 18:24, 26 · v. 19; 8:21

13 When I shall say to the righteous, *that* he shall surely live; if he trust to his own righteousness, and commit iniquity, all his righteousnesses shall not be remembered; but for his iniquity that he hath committed, he shall die for it.

14 Again, ^Rwhen I say unto the wicked, Thou shalt surely die; if he turn from his sin, and do that which is lawful and right; [Is. 55:7]

15 *If* the wicked ^Rrestore the pledge, ^Rgive again that he had robbed, walk in ^Rthe statutes of life, without committing iniquity; he shall surely live, he shall not die. 18:7 · Num. 5:6, 7; Luke 19:8 · Lev. 18:5

16 ^RNone of his sins that he hath committed shall be mentioned unto him: he hath done that which is lawful and right; he shall surely live. 18:22; [Is. 1:18; 43:25]

17 ^RYet the children of thy people say, The way of the Lord is not ^Tequal: but as for them, their way is not ^Tequal. 18:25, 29 · *fair*

18 ^RWhen the righteous turneth from his righteousness, and committeth iniquity, he shall even die thereby. 18:26

19 But if the wicked turn from his wickedness, and do that which is lawful and right, he shall live thereby.

20 Yet ye say, ^RThe way of the Lord is not ^Tequal. O ye house of Israel, I will judge you every one after his ways. 18:25, 29 · *fair*

21 And it came to pass in the twelfth year ^Rof our captivity, in the tenth *month*, in the fifth *day* of the month, ^Rthat one that had escaped out of Jerusalem came unto me, saying, ^RThe city is smitten. 1:2 · 24:26 · 2 Kin. 25:4

22 Now ^Rthe hand of the LORD was upon me in the evening, afore he that was escaped came; and had ^Ropened my mouth, until he came to me in the morning; and my mouth was opened, and I was no more dumb. 1:3; 8:1; 37:1 · 24:27

23 Then the word of the LORD came unto me, saying,

24 Son of man, ^Rthey that inhabit those ^Rwastes of the land of Israel speak, saying, Abraham was one, and he inherited the land: but we *are* many; the land is given us for ^Rinheritance. 34:2 · 36:4 · 11:15

25 Wherefore say unto them, Thus saith the Lord GOD; ^RYe eat with the blood, and ^Rlift up your eyes toward your idols, and ^Rshed blood: and shall ye possess the ^Rland? Gen. 9:4 · 18:6 · 22:6, 9 · Deut. 29:28

26 Ye ^Tstand upon your sword, ye work abomination, and ye ^Rdefile every one his neighbour's wife: and shall ye possess the land? *rely* · 18:6; 22:11

27 Say thou thus unto them, Thus saith the Lord GOD; *As* I live, surely they that *are* in the wastes shall fall by the sword, and him that *is* in the open field ^Rwill I give to the beasts to be devoured, and they that *be* in the forts and ^Rin the caves shall die of the pestilence. 39:4 · Judg. 6:2; 1 Sam. 13:6; Is. 2:19

28 For I will lay the land most desolate, and the pomp of her

strength shall cease; and the mountains of Israel shall be desolate, that none shall pass through.

29 Then shall they know that I *am* the LORD, when I have laid the land most desolate because of all their abominations which they have committed.

30 Also, thou son of man, the children of thy people still are talking ^Tagainst thee by the walls and in the doors of the houses, and ^Rspeak one to another, every one to his brother, saying, Come, I pray you, and hear what is the word that cometh forth from the LORD.   *about* · 14:3; 20:3, 31; Is. 29:13

31 And they come unto thee as the people cometh, and they sit before thee *as* my people, and they hear thy words, but they will not do them: ^Rfor with their mouth they shew much love, *but* ^Rtheir heart goeth after their covetousness.   1 John 3:18 · [Matt. 13:22]

32 And, lo, thou *art* unto them as a very lovely song of one that hath a pleasant voice, and can play well on an instrument: for they hear thy words, but they do them ^Rnot. [Matt. 7:21–28; James 1:22–25]

33 ^RAnd when this cometh to pass, (lo, it will come,) then ^Rshall they know that a prophet hath been among them.   1 Sam. 3:20 · 2:5

34 And the word of the LORD came unto me, saying,

2 Son of man, prophesy against the shepherds of Israel, prophesy, and say unto them, Thus saith the Lord GOD unto the shepherds; ^RWoe *be* to the shepherds of Israel that do feed themselves! should not the shepherds feed the flocks?   Jer. 23:1; Zech. 11:17

3 ^RYe eat the fat, and ye clothe you with the wool, ye ^Rkill them that are fed: *but* ye feed not the flock.   Is. 56:11; Zech. 11:16 · Zech. 11:5

4 The diseased have ye not strengthened, neither have ye healed that which was sick, neither have ye bound up *that which was* broken, neither have ye brought again that which was driven away, neither have ye

^Rsought that which was lost; but with force and with cruelty have ye ruled them.   Matt. 9:36; Luke 15:4

5 And they were ^Rscattered, because *there is* no shepherd: ^Rand they became meat to all the beasts of the field, when they were scattered.   Matt. 9:36; Mark 6:34 · Is. 56:9

6 My sheep wandered through all the mountains, and upon every high hill: yea, my flock was scattered upon all the face of the earth, and none did search or seek *after them*.

7 Therefore, ye shepherds, hear the word of the LORD;

8 *As* I live saith the Lord GOD, surely because my flock became a prey, and my flock became meat to every beast of the field, because *there was* no shepherd, neither did my shepherds search for my flock, but the shepherds fed themselves, and fed not my flock;

9 Therefore, O ye shepherds, hear the word of the LORD;

10 Thus saith the Lord GOD; Behold, I *am* ^Ragainst the shepherds; and ^RI will require my flock at their hand, and cause them to cease from feeding the flock; neither shall the shepherds feed themselves any more; for I will ^Rdeliver my flock from their mouth, that they may not be meat for them.   Zech. 10:3 · Heb. 13:17 · 13:23

11 For thus saith the Lord GOD; Behold, I, *even* I, will both search my sheep, and seek them out.

12 As a shepherd seeketh out his flock in the day that he is among his sheep *that are* scattered; so will I seek out my sheep, and will deliver them out of all places where they have been scattered in the cloudy and dark day.

13 And I will bring them out from the people, and gather them from the countries, and will bring them to their own land, and feed them upon the mountains of Israel by the rivers, and in all the inhabited places of the country.

14 I will feed them in a good pasture, and upon the high mountains of Israel shall their fold be:

there shall they lie in a good fold, and *in* a fat pasture shall they feed upon the mountains of Israel.

15 I will feed my flock, and I will cause them to lie down, saith the Lord GOD.

16 ᴿI will seek that which was lost, and bring again that which was driven away, and will bind up *that which was* broken, and will strengthen that which was sick: but I will destroy the fat and the strong; I will feed them with judgment. [Matt. 18:11; Luke 5:32]

17 And *as for* you, O my flock, thus saith the Lord GOD; ᴿBehold, I judge between cattle and cattle, between the rams and the he goats. 20:37; Mal. 4:1; [Matt. 25:32]

18 *Seemeth it* a small thing unto you to have eaten up the good pasture, but ye must ᵀtread down with your feet the residue of your pastures? and to have drunk of the deep waters, but ye must foul the residue with your feet? *trample*

19 And *as for* my flock, they eat that which ye have ᵀtrodden with your feet; and they drink that which ye have fouled with your feet. *trampled*

20 Therefore thus saith the Lord GOD unto them; Behold, I, *even* I, will judge between the fat cattle and between the lean cattle.

21 Because ye have ᵀthrust with side and with shoulder, and ᵀpushed all the ᵀdiseased with your horns, till ye have scattered them abroad; *pushed · butted · weak*

22 Therefore will I save my flock, and they shall no more be a prey; and I will judge between ᵀcattle and cattle. *sheep and sheep*

23 And I will set up one ᴿshepherd over them, and he shall feed them, *even* my servant David; he shall feed them, and he shall be their shepherd. [John 10:11; Heb. 13:20]

24 And ᴿI the LORD will be their God, and my servant David ᴿa prince among them; I the LORD have spoken *it.* 37:25 · Is. 55:3; Hos. 3:5

25 And ᴿI will make with them a covenant of peace, and ᴿwill cause the evil beasts to cease out of the

land: and they ᴿshall dwell safely in the wilderness, and sleep in the woods. 37:26 · Is. 11:6–9 · Jer. 23:6

26 And I will make them and the places round about ᴿmy hill a blessing; and I will ᴿcause the shower to come down in his season; there shall be ᴿshowers of blessing. Is. 56:7 · Lev. 26:4 · Ps. 68:9

27 And ᴿthe tree of the field shall yield her fruit, and the earth shall yield her increase, and they shall be safe in their land, and shall know that I *am* the LORD, when I have broken the bands of their yoke, and delivered them out of the hand of those that served themselves of them. Ps. 85:12; Is. 4:2

28 And they shall no more be a prey to the heathen, neither shall the beast of the land devour them; but ᴿthey shall dwell safely, and none shall make *them* afraid. 39:26

29 And I will raise up for them a ᴿplant of renown, and they shall ᴿbe no more consumed with hunger in the land, ᴿneither bear the shame of the heathen any more. [Is. 11:1] · 36:29 · 36:3, 6, 15

30 Thus shall they know that ᴿI the LORD their God *am* with them, and *that* they, *even* the house of Israel, *are* ᴿmy people, saith the Lord GOD. v. 24 · Ps. 46:7, 11

31 And ye my flock, the flock of my pasture, *are* men, *and* I *am* your God, saith the Lord GOD.

35 Moreover the word of the LORD came unto me, saying,

2 Son of man, set thy face against ᴿmount Se′-ir, and ᴿprophesy against it, Gen. 36:8 · Amos 1:11

3 And say unto it, Thus saith the Lord GOD; Behold, O mount Se′-ir, I *am* against thee, and ᴿI will stretch out mine hand against thee, and I will make thee ᵀmost desolate. 6:14 · *a desolation and a waste*

4 I will lay thy cities waste, and thou shalt be desolate, and thou shalt know that I *am* the LORD.

5 Because thou hast had a perpetual hatred, and hast shed *the blood of* the children of Israel by

the force of the sword in the time of their calamity, in the time *that their* iniquity *had* an end:

6 Therefore, *as* I live, saith the Lord GOD, I will prepare thee unto ^Rblood, and blood shall pursue thee: ^Rsith^T thou hast not hated blood, even blood shall pursue thee.   32:6; Is. 63:1–6 · Ps. 109:17 · *since*

7 Thus will I make mount Se'-ir most desolate, and cut off from it ^Rhim that ^Tpasseth out and him that returneth.   Judg. 5:6 · *leaves*

8 And I will fill his mountains with his slain *men:* in thy hills, and in thy valleys, and in all thy ^Trivers, shall they fall that are slain with the sword.   *ravines*

9 ^RI will make thee perpetual desolations, and thy cities shall not return: ^Rand ye shall know that I *am* the LORD.   25:13 · 36:11

10 Because thou hast said, These two nations and these two countries shall be mine, and we will ^Rpossess it; whereas ^Rthe LORD was there: Ps. 83:4–12 · 48:35

11 Therefore, *as* I live, saith the Lord GOD, I will even do ^Raccording to thine anger, and according to thine envy which thou hast used out of thy hatred against them; and I will make myself known among them, when I have judged thee.   [James 2:13]

12 ^RAnd thou shalt know that I *am* the LORD, *and that* I have ^Rheard all thy blasphemies which thou hast spoken against the mountains of Israel, saying, They are laid desolate, they are given us to consume.   Ps. 9:16 · Zeph. 2:8

13 Thus with your mouth ye have boasted against me, and have multiplied your words against me: I have heard *them.*

14 Thus saith the Lord GOD; ^RWhen the whole earth rejoiceth, I will make thee desolate.   Is. 65:13

15 ^RAs thou didst rejoice at the inheritance of the house of Israel, because it was desolate, so will I do unto thee: thou shalt be desolate, O mount Se'-ir, and all Id-u-me'-a, *even* all of it: and they shall know that I *am* the LORD.   Obad. 12

36 Also, thou son of man, prophesy unto the ^Rmountains of Israel, and say, Ye mountains of Israel, hear the word of the LORD: 6:2, 3

2 Thus saith the Lord GOD; Because ^Rthe enemy hath said against you, Aha, ^Reven the ancient high places are ours in possession: 25:3; 26:2 · Is. 58:14; Hab. 3:19

3 Therefore prophesy and say, Thus saith the Lord GOD; Because they have made *you* desolate, and swallowed you up on every side, that ye might be a possession unto the residue of the heathen, ^Rand ye are taken up in the lips of ^Rtalkers, and *are* an infamy of the people: Lam. 2:15; Dan. 9:16 · Jer. 18:16

4 Therefore, ye mountains of Israel, hear the word of the Lord GOD; Thus saith the Lord GOD to the mountains, and to the hills, to the rivers, and to the valleys, to the desolate wastes, and to the cities that are forsaken, which ^Rbecame a prey and ^Rderision to the residue of the heathen that *are* round about;   34:8, 28 · Jer. 48:27

5 Therefore thus saith the Lord GOD; ^RSurely in the fire of my jealousy have I spoken against the residue of the heathen, and against all Id-u-me'-a, ^Rwhich have appointed my land into their possession with the joy of all *their* heart, with despiteful minds, to cast it out for a prey. 38:19 · 35:10, 12

6 Prophesy therefore concerning the land of Israel, and say unto the mountains, and to the hills, to the rivers, and to the valleys, Thus saith the Lord GOD; Behold, I have spoken in my jealousy and in my fury, because ye have ^Rborne the shame of the heathen: 34:29; Ps. 74:10; 123:3, 4

7 Therefore thus saith the Lord GOD; I have lifted up mine hand, Surely the heathen that *are* about you, they shall bear their shame.

8 But ye, O mountains of Israel, ye shall shoot forth your branches, and yield your fruit to my people of Israel; for they are ^Tat hand to come.   *about to*

9 For, behold, I *am* for you, and I will turn unto you, and ye shall be tilled and sown:

10 And I will multiply men upon you, all the house of Israel, *even* all of it: and the cities shall be inhabited, and ᴿthe wastes shall be builded: Is. 58:12; 61:4; Amos 9:14

11 And ᴿI will multiply upon you man and beast; and they shall increase and bring fruit: and I will settle you after your old estates, and will do better *unto you* than at your beginnings: and ye shall know that I *am* the Lᴏʀᴅ. Jer. 31:27

12 Yea, I will cause men to walk upon you, *even* my people Israel; and they shall possess thee, and thou shalt be their inheritance, and thou shalt no more henceforth bereave them *of men.*

13 Thus saith the Lord Gᴏᴅ; Because they say unto you, ᴿThou *land* devourest up men, and hast bereaved thy nations; Num. 13:32

14 Therefore thou shalt devour men no more, neither bereave thy nations any more, saith the Lord Gᴏᴅ.

15 ᴿNeither will I cause *men* to hear in thee the shame of the heathen any more, neither shalt thou bear the reproach of the people any more, neither shalt thou cause thy nations to fall any more, saith the Lord Gᴏᴅ. Is. 60:14

16 Moreover the word of the Lᴏʀᴅ came unto me, saying,

17 Son of man, when the house of Israel dwelt in their own land, ᴿthey defiled it by their own way and by their doings: their way was before me as the uncleanness of a removed woman. Lev. 18:25, 27, 28

18 Wherefore I poured my fury upon them ᴿfor the blood that they had shed upon the land, and for their idols *wherewith* they had ᵀpolluted it: 16:36, 38; 23:37 · *defiled*

19 And I scattered them among the heathen, and they were dispersed through the countries: according to their way and according to their doings I judged them.

20 And when they entered unto the heathen, whither they went, they ᴿprofaned my holy name, when they said to them, These *are* the people of the Lᴏʀᴅ, and are gone forth out of his land. 12:16

21 But I had pity for mine holy name, which the house of Israel had profaned among the ᵀheathen, whither they went. *nations*

22 Therefore say unto the house of Israel, Thus saith the Lord Gᴏᴅ; I do not *this* for your sakes, O house of Israel, ᴿbut for mine holy name's sake, which ye have profaned among the heathen, whither ye went. 20:44; Ps. 106:8

23 And I will sanctify my great name, which was profaned among the heathen, which ye have profaned in the midst of them; and the heathen shall know that I *am* the Lᴏʀᴅ, saith the Lord Gᴏᴅ, when I shall be ᴿsanctified in you before their eyes. 20:41

24 For I will take you from among the heathen, and gather you out of all countries, and will bring you into your own land.

25 ᴿThen will I sprinkle clean water upon you, and ye shall be clean: ᴿfrom all your filthiness, and from all your idols, will I cleanse you. Heb. 9:13, 19 · Jer. 33:8

26 A ᴿnew heart also will I give you, and a new spirit will I put within you: and I will take away the stony heart out of your flesh, and I will give you an heart of flesh. Ps. 51:10; Jer. 32:39; [John 3:3]

27 And I will put my ᴿspirit within you, and cause you to walk in my statutes, and ye shall keep my judgments, and do *them.* 11:19

28 ᴿAnd ye shall dwell in the land that I gave to your fathers; and ye shall be my people, and I will be your God. 28:25; 37:25

29 I will also ᴿsave you from all your uncleannesses: and I will call for the ᵀcorn, and will increase it, and lay no famine upon you. [Matt. 1:21; Rom. 11:26] · *rain*

30 ᴿAnd I will multiply the fruit of the tree, and the increase of the field, that ye shall receive no more reproach of famine among the ᵀheathen. 34:27; Lev. 26:4 · *nations*

31 Then ^Rshall ye remember your own evil ways, and your doings that *were* not good, and ^Rshall lothe yourselves in your own sight for your iniquities and for your abominations.   16:61, 63 · 6:9

32 ^RNot for your sakes do I *this*, saith the Lord God, be it known unto you: be ashamed and confounded for your own ways, O house of Israel.   Deut. 9:5

33 Thus saith the Lord God; In the day that I shall have cleansed you from all your iniquities I will also cause *you* to dwell in the cities, ^Rand the ^Twastes shall be builded.   v. 10 · *ruins*

34 And the desolate land shall be tilled, whereas it lay desolate in the sight of all that passed by.

35 And they shall say, This land that was desolate is become like the garden of ^REden; and the waste and desolate and ruined cities *are become* fenced, *and* are inhabited.   28:13; Is. 51:3; Joel 2:3

36 Then the ^Theathen that are left round about you shall know that I the Lord ^Tbuild the ruined *places, and* plant that that was desolate: I the Lord have spoken *it*, and I will do *it*.   *nations · rebuilt*

37 Thus saith the Lord God; ^RI will yet *for* this be enquired of by the house of Israel, to do *it* for them; I will increase them with men like a flock.   14:3; 20:3, 31

38 As the holy flock, as the flock of Jerusalem in her solemn feasts; so shall the ^Twaste cities be filled with flocks of men: and they shall know that I *am* the Lord.   *ruined*

37 The ^Rhand of the Lord was upon me, and carried me out in the spirit of the Lord, and set me down in the midst of the valley which *was* full of bones,   1:3

2 And caused me to pass by them round about: and, behold, *there were* very many in the open valley; and, lo, *they were* very dry.

3 And he said unto me, Son of man, can these bones live? And I answered, O Lord God, ^Rthou knowest.   [John 5:21; Rom. 4:17]

4 Again he said unto me, Prophesy upon these bones, and say unto them, O ye dry bones, hear the word of the Lord.

5 Thus saith the Lord God unto these bones; Behold, I will ^Rcause ^Tbreath to enter into you, and ye shall live: Gen. 2:7; Ps. 104:29, 30 · *spirit*

6 And I will lay sinews upon you, and will bring up flesh upon you, and cover you with skin, and put breath in you, and ye shall live; ^Rand ye shall know that I *am* the Lord.   Is. 49:23; Joel 2:27; 3:17

7 So I prophesied as I was commanded: and as I prophesied, there was a noise, and behold a shaking, and the bones came together, bone to his bone.

8 And when I beheld, lo, the sinews and the flesh came up upon them, and the skin covered them ^Tabove: but *there was* no ^Tbreath in them.   *over · spirit*

9 Then said he unto me, Prophesy unto the wind, prophesy, son of man, and say to the wind, Thus saith the Lord God; ^RCome from the four winds, O breath, and breathe upon these slain, that they may live.   [Ps. 104:30]

10 So I prophesied as he commanded me, ^Rand the breath came into them, and they lived, and stood up upon their feet, an exceeding great army.   Rev. 11:11

11 Then he said unto me, Son of man, these bones are the ^Rwhole house of Israel: behold, they say, ^ROur bones are dried, and our hope is lost: we are cut off for our parts.   Jer. 33:24 · Ps. 141:7; Is. 49:14

12 Therefore prophesy and say unto them, Thus saith the Lord God; Behold, ^RO my people, I will open your graves, and cause you to come up out of your graves, and ^Rbring you into the land of Israel.   [Dan. 12:2]; Hos. 13:14 · 36:24

13 And ye shall know that I *am* the Lord, when I have opened your graves, O my people, and brought you up out of your graves,

14 And ^Rshall put my spirit in you, and ye shall live, and I shall place you in your own land: then

shall ye know that I the LORD have spoken *it*, and performed *it*, saith the LORD.   [Joel 2:28, 29]; Zech. 12:10

15 The word of the LORD came again unto me, saying,

16 Moreover, thou son of man, ^Rtake thee one stick, and write upon it, For Judah, and for the children of Israel his companions: then take another stick, and write upon it, For Joseph, the stick of E'-phra-im, and *for* all the house of Israel his companions: Num. 17:2, 3

17 And ^Rjoin them one to another into one stick; and they shall become one in thine hand.   Is. 11:13

18 And when the children of thy people shall speak unto thee, saying, ^RWilt thou not shew us what thou *meanest* by these?   12:9; 24:19

19 ^RSay unto them, Thus saith the Lord GOD; Behold, I will take the stick of Joseph, which *is* in the hand of E'-phra-im, and the tribes of Israel his ^Tfellows, and will put them with him, *even* with the stick of Judah, and make them one stick, and they shall be one in mine hand.   Zech. 10:6 · *companions*

20 And the sticks whereon thou writest shall be in thine hand ^Rbefore their eyes.   12:3

21 And say unto them, Thus saith the Lord GOD; Behold, ^RI will take the children of Israel from among the heathen, whither they be gone, and will gather them on every side, and bring them into their own land: Is. 43:5, 6; Jer. 32:37

22 And ^RI will make them one nation in the land upon the mountains of Israel; and one king shall be king to them all: and they shall be no more two nations, neither shall they be divided into two kingdoms any more at all: Is. 11:13

23 Neither shall they defile themselves any more with their idols, nor with their detestable things, nor with any of their transgressions: but I will save them out of all their dwellingplaces, wherein they have sinned, and will cleanse them: so shall they be my people, and I will be their God.

☆ 24 And ^RDavid my servant *shall*

be king over them; and ^Rthey all shall have one shepherd: ^Rthey shall also walk in my judgments, and observe my statutes, and do them.   [Luke 1:32] · [John 10:16] · 36:27

25 ^RAnd they shall dwell in the ☆ land that I have given unto Jacob my servant, wherein your fathers have dwelt; and they shall dwell therein, *even* they, and their children, and their children's children for ever: and my servant David *shall be* their prince for ever.   36:28

26 Moreover I will make ^Ra covenant of peace with them; it shall be an everlasting covenant with them: and I will place them, and multiply them, and will set my sanctuary in the midst of them for evermore.   Ps. 89:3; Is. 55:3

27 My tabernacle also shall be with them: yea, I will be their God, and they shall be my people.

28 And the heathen shall know that I the LORD do ^Rsanctify Israel, when my sanctuary shall be in the midst of them for evermore.   20:12

38 And the word of the LORD came unto me, saying,

2 ^RSon of man, ^Rset thy face against ^RGog, the land of Ma'-gog, the chief prince of Me'-shech and Tu'-bal, and prophesy against him,   39:1 · 35:2, 3 · Rev. 20:8

3 And say, Thus saith the Lord GOD; Behold, I *am* against thee, O Gog, the ^Tchief prince of Me'-shech and Tu'-bal: *prince of Rosh*

4 And ^RI will turn thee back, and put hooks into thy jaws, and I will ^Rbring thee forth, and all thine army, horses and horsemen, all of them clothed with all sorts *of armour*, *even* a great company *with* bucklers and shields, all of them handling swords: 29:4 · Is. 43:17

5 Persia, E-thi-o'-pi-a, and Lib'-y-a with them; all of them with shield and helmet:

6 Go'-mer, and all his bands; the house of ^RTo-gar'-mah of the north quarters, and all his bands: *and* many people with thee.   27:14

7 ^RBe thou prepared, and prepare for thyself, thou, and all thy company that are assembled unto

thee, and be thou a guard unto them.   Is. 8:9, 10; Jer. 46:3, 4

8 After many days thou shalt be visited: in the latter years thou shalt come into the land *that is* brought back from the sword, ^R*and is* gathered out of many people, against the mountains of Israel, which have been always waste: but it is brought forth out of the nations, and they shall dwell safely all of them.   34:13

9 Thou shalt ascend and come ^Rlike a storm, thou shalt be ^Rlike a cloud to cover the land, thou, and all thy ^Tbands, and many people with thee.   Is. 28:2 · Jer. 4:13 · *troops*

10 Thus saith the Lord GOD; It shall also come to pass, *that* ^Tat the same time shall things come into thy mind, and thou shalt think an evil thought: *on that day*

11 And thou shalt say, I will go up to the land of unwalled villages; I will go to them that are at rest, that dwell safely, all of them dwelling without walls, and having neither bars nor gates,

12 To take ^Ta spoil, and to take ^Ta prey; to turn thine hand upon the desolate places *that are now* inhabited, ^Rand upon the people *that are* gathered out of the nations, which have gotten cattle and goods, that dwell in the midst of the land.   *plunder · booty · v. 8*

13 She'-ba, and De'-dan, and the merchants ^Rof Tar'-shish, with all ^Rthe young lions thereof, shall say unto thee, Art thou come to take a spoil? hast thou gathered thy company to take a prey? to carry away silver and gold, to take away cattle and goods, to take a great spoil?   27:12 · 19:3, 5

14 Therefore, son of man, prophesy and say unto Gog, Thus saith the Lord GOD; In that day when my people of Israel dwelleth safely, shalt thou not know *it?*

15 ^RAnd thou shalt come from thy place out of the ^Tnorth parts, thou, and many people with thee, all of them riding upon horses, a great company, and a mighty army: 39:2 · *far north*

16 And thou shalt come up against my people of Israel, as a cloud to cover the land; it shall be in the latter days, and I will bring thee against my land, that the heathen may ^Rknow me, when I shall be ^Rsanctified in thee, O Gog, before their eyes.   35:11 · 28:22

17 Thus saith the Lord GOD; *Art* thou he of whom I have spoken in old time by my servants the prophets of Israel, which prophesied in those days *many* years that I would bring thee against them?

18 And it shall come to pass at the same time when Gog shall come against the land of Israel, saith the Lord GOD, *that* my fury shall ^Tcome up in my face.   *show*

19 For in my jealousy *and* in the fire of my wrath have I spoken, ^RSurely in that day there shall be a great shaking in the land of Israel;   Joel 3:16; Hag. 2:6, 7; Rev. 16:8

20 So that the fishes of the sea, and the fowls of the heaven, and the beasts of the field, and all creeping things that creep upon the earth, and all the men that *are* upon the face of the earth, shall shake at my presence, and the mountains shall be thrown down, and the steep places shall fall, and every wall shall fall to the ground.

21 And I will call for a sword against him throughout all my mountains, saith the Lord GOD: ^Revery man's sword shall be against his brother.   Hag. 2:22

22 And I will plead against him with pestilence and with blood; and I will rain upon him, and upon his bands, and upon the many people that *are* with him, an overflowing rain, and great hailstones, fire, and brimstone.

23 Thus will I magnify myself, and ^Rsanctify myself; ^Rand I will be known in the eyes of many nations, and they shall know that I *am* the LORD.   36:23 · Ps. 9:16

39 Therefore, ^Rthou son of man, prophesy against Gog, and say, Thus saith the Lord GOD; Behold, I *am* against thee, O Gog,

Tthe chief prince of Me'-shech and Tu'-bal: 38:2, 3 · *prince of Rosh*

2 And I will Rturn thee back, and leave but the sixth part of thee, Rand will cause thee to come up from the Tnorth parts, and will bring thee upon the mountains of Israel: 38:8 · 38:15 · *far north*

3 And I will Tsmite thy bow out of thy left hand, and will cause thine arrows to fall out of thy right hand.   *knock*

4 RThou shalt fall upon the mountains of Israel, thou, and all thy bands, and the people that *is* with thee: RI will give thee unto the Travenous birds of every sort, and *to* the beasts of the field to be devoured. 38:4, 21 · 33:27 · *birds of prey*

5 Thou shalt Tfall upon the open field: for I have spoken *it*, saith the Lord GOD.   *Be slain*

6 RAnd I will send a fire on Ma'-gog, and among them that dwell Tcarelessly in Rthe isles: and they shall know that I *am* the LORD. 38:22 · *securely* · Ps. 72:10; Is. 66:19

7 RSo will I make my holy name known in the midst of my people Israel; and I will not *let them* RpolluteT my holy name any more: and the heathen shall know that I *am* the LORD, the Holy One in Israel.   v. 25 · 36:23 · *profane*

8 Behold, it is come, and it is done, saith the Lord GOD; this *is* the day whereof I have spoken.

9 And they that dwell in the cities of Israel shall go forth, and shall set on fire and burn the weapons, both the shields and the bucklers, the bows and the arrows, and the handstaves, and the spears, and they shall burn them with fire seven years:

10 So that they shall take no wood out of the field, neither cut down *any* out of the forests; for they shall burn the weapons with fire: and they shall Tspoil those that spoiled them, and Trob those that robbed them, saith the Lord GOD.   *plunder · pillage*

11 And it shall come to pass in that day, *that* I will give unto Gog a place there of graves in Israel,

the valley of the passengers on the east of the sea: and it shall stop the *noses* of the passengers: and there shall they bury Gog and all his multitude: and they shall call *it* The valley of Ha'-mon–gog.

12 And seven months shall the house of Israel be burying of them, Rthat they may cleanse the land.   vv. 14, 16; Deut. 21:23

13 Yea, all the people of the land shall bury *them;* and it shall Tbe to them a Rrenown the day that I shall be glorified, saith the Lord GOD.   *give them renown* · Zeph. 3:19, 20

14 And they shall sever out men of continual employment, passing through the land to bury with the passengers those that remain upon the face of the earth, to cleanse it: after the end of seven months shall they search.

15 And the passengers *that* pass through the land, when *any* seeth a man's bone, then shall he Tset up a sign by it, till the buriers have buried it in the valley of Ha'-mon–gog.   *build a marker*

16 And also the name of the city *shall be* Ha-mo'-nah. Thus shall they Rcleanse the land.   v. 12

17 And, thou son of man, thus saith the Lord GOD; Speak unto every feathered fowl, and to every beast of the field, Assemble yourselves, and come; gather yourselves on every side to my sacrifice that I do sacrifice for you, *even* a great sacrifice upon the mountains of Israel, that ye may eat flesh, and drink blood.

18 Ye shall eat the flesh of the mighty, and drink the blood of the princes of the earth, of rams, of lambs, and of goats, of bullocks, all of them fatlings of Ba'-shan.

19 And ye shall eat fat till ye be full, and drink blood till ye be drunken, of my sacrifice which I have sacrificed for you.

20 Thus ye shall be filled at my table with horses and chariots, with mighty men, and with all men of war, saith the Lord GOD.

21 RAnd I will set my glory among the heathen, and all the

heathen shall see my judgment that I have executed, and my hand that I have laid upon them. Ex. 9:16

22 So the house of Israel shall know that I *am* the LORD their God from that day and forward.

23 And the heathen shall know that the house of Israel went into captivity for their iniquity: because they trespassed against me, therefore ᴿhid I my face from them, and gave them into the hand of their enemies: so fell they all by the sword. Deut. 31:17; Is. 1:15

24 ᴿAccording to their uncleanness and according to their transgressions have I done unto them, and hid my face from them. 36:19

25 Therefore thus saith the Lord GOD; ᴿNow will I bring again the captivity of Jacob, and have mercy upon the ᴿwhole house of Israel, and will be jealous for my holy name; Is. 27:12, 13 · 20:40; Hos. 1:11

26 ᴿAfter that they have borne their shame, and all their trespasses whereby they have trespassed against me, when they dwelt safely in their land, and none made *them* afraid. Dan. 9:16

27 When I have brought them again from the people, and gathered them out of their enemies' lands, and ᴿam sanctified in them in the sight of many nations; 38:16

28 ᴿThen shall they know that I *am* the LORD their God, which caused them to be led into captivity among the ᵀheathen: but I have gathered them unto their own land, and have left none of them any more there. 34:30 · *nations*

29 Neither will I hide my face any more from them: for I have ᴿpoured out my spirit upon the house of Israel, saith the Lord GOD. [Joel 2:28; Zech. 12:10]; Acts 2:17

40 In the five and twentieth year of our captivity, in the beginning of the year, in the tenth *day* of the month, in the fourteenth year after that ᴿthe city was smitten, in the selfsame day the hand of the LORD was upon me, and brought me thither. 33:21

2 In the visions of God brought he me into the land of Israel, and ᴿset me upon a very high mountain, by which *was* as the frame of a city on the south. Rev. 21:10

3 And he brought me thither, and, behold, *there was* a man, whose appearance *was* like the appearance of brass, with a line of flax in his hand, and a measuring reed; and he stood in the gate.

4 And the man said unto me, ᴿSon of man, behold with thine eyes, and hear with thine ears, and set thine heart upon all that I shall shew thee; for to the intent that I might shew *them* unto thee *art* thou brought hither: ᴿdeclare all that thou seest to the house of Israel. 44:5 · 43:10

5 And behold ᴿa wall on the outside of the house round about, and in the man's hand a measuring reed of six cubits *long* by the cubit and an hand breadth: so he measured the breadth of the building, one reed; and the height, one reed. 42:20; [Is. 26:1]

6 Then came he unto the gate which looketh toward the east, and went up the stairs thereof, and measured the threshold of the gate, *which was* one reed broad; and the other threshold *of the gate, which was* one reed broad.

7 And *every* ᵀlittle chamber *was* one reed long, and one reed broad; and between the ᵀlittle chambers *were* five cubits; and the threshold of the gate by the ᵀporch of the gate within *was* one reed. *gate chamber · gate · vestibule*

8 He measured also the porch of the gate within, one reed.

9 Then measured he the porch of the gate, eight cubits; and the posts thereof, two cubits; and the porch of the gate *was* inward.

10 And the little chambers of the gate eastward *were* three on this side, and three on that side; they three *were* of one ᵀmeasure: and the posts had one measure on this side and on that side. *size*

11 And he measured the breadth of the entry of the gate, ten cubits; *and* the length of the gate, thirteen cubits.

12 The space also before the little chambers *was* one cubit *on this side,* and the space *was* one cubit on that side: and the little chambers *were* six cubits on this side, and six cubits on that side.

13 He measured then the gate from the roof of *one* ᵀlittle chamber to the roof of another: the breadth *was* five and twenty cubits, door against door.　　*gate*

14 He made also posts of threescore cubits, even unto the post of the court round about the gate.

15 And from the ᵀface of the gate of the entrance unto the ᵀface of the ᵀporch of the inner gate *were* fifty cubits.　　*front · vestibule*

16 And *there were* narrow windows to the little chambers, and to their posts within the gate round about, and likewise to the arches: and windows *were* round about inward: and upon *each* post *were* ᴿpalm trees. 1 Kin. 6:29, 32, 35; 2 Chr. 3:5

17 Then brought he me into ᴿthe outward court, and, lo, *there were* ᴿchambers, and a pavement made for the court round about: ᴿthirty chambers ᵀ*were* upon the pavement.　　Rev. 11:2 · v. 38 · 45:5 · *faced*

18 And the pavement by the side of the gates ᵀover against the length of the gates *was* the lower pavement.　　*corresponding to*

19 Then he measured the breadth from the forefront of the lower gate unto the forefront of the inner court ᵀwithout, an hundred cubits eastward and northward.　　*exterior*

20 And the gate of the outward court that looked toward the north, he measured the length thereof, and the breadth thereof.

21 And the little chambers thereof *were* three on this side and three on that side; and the posts thereof and the ᵀarches thereof were after the measure of the first gate: the length thereof *was* fifty cubits, and the breadth five and twenty cubits. Or *vestibules*

22 And their windows, and their arches, and their palm trees, *were* after the measure of the gate that looketh toward the east; and they went up unto it by seven steps; and the arches thereof *were* before them.

23 And the gate of the inner court *was* ᵀover against the gate toward the north, and toward the east; and he measured from gate to gate an hundred cubits. *opposite*

24 After that he brought me toward the south, and behold a gate ᵀtoward the south: and he measured the posts thereof and the arches thereof according to these measures.　　*facing*

25 And *there were* windows in it and in the arches thereof round about, like those windows: the length *was* fifty cubits, and the breadth five and twenty cubits.

26 And *there were* seven steps to go up to it, and the arches thereof *were* before them: and it had palm trees, one on this side, and another on that side, upon the posts thereof.

27 And *there was* a gate in the inner court ᵀtoward the south: and he measured from gate to gate toward the south an hundred cubits.　　*facing*

28 And he brought me to the inner court by the south gate: and he measured the south gate according to these measures;

29 And the ᵀlittle chambers thereof, and the posts thereof, and the arches thereof, according to these measures: and *there were* windows in it and in the arches thereof round about: *it was* fifty cubits long, and five and twenty cubits broad.　　*gate chambers*

30 And the arches round about *were* five and twenty cubits long, and five cubits broad.

31 And the arches thereof ᵀ*were* toward the utter court; and palm trees *were* upon the posts thereof: and the going up to it *had* eight steps.　　*faced*

32 And he brought me into the inner court ᵀtoward the east: and

he measured the gate according to these measures.   *facing*

33 And the ᵀlittle chambers thereof, and the posts thereof, and the arches thereof, *were* according to these measures: and *there were* windows therein and in the arches thereof round about: *it was* fifty cubits long, and five and twenty cubits broad.   *gate*

34 And the arches thereof ᵀ*were* toward the outward court; and palm trees *were* upon the posts thereof, on this side, and on that side: and the going up to it *had* eight steps.   *faced*

35 And he brought me to the north gate, and measured *it* according to these measures;

36 The ᵀlittle chambers thereof, the posts thereof, and the arches thereof, and the windows to it round about: the length *was* fifty cubits, and the breadth five and twenty cubits.   *gate*

37 And the posts thereof *were* toward the utter court; and palm trees *were* upon the posts thereof, on this side, and on that side: and the going up to it *had* eight steps.

38 And the chambers and the entries thereof *were* by the posts of the gates, where they ᴿwashed the burnt offering.   2 Chr. 4:6

39 And in the porch of the gate *were* two tables on this side, and two tables on that side, to slay thereon the burnt offering and ᴿthe sin offering and ᴿthe trespass offering.   Lev. 4:2, 3 · Lev. 5:6; 6:6; 7:1

40 And at the ᵀside without, as one goeth up to the entry of the north gate, *were* two tables; and on the other side, which *was* at the ᵀporch of the gate, *were* two tables.   *outer side · vestibule*

41 Four tables *were* on this side, and four tables on that side, by the side of the gate; eight tables, whereupon they slew *their sacrifices*.

42 And the four tables *were* of hewn stone for the burnt offering, of a cubit and an half long, and a cubit and an half broad, and one cubit high: whereupon also they

laid the instruments wherewith they ᵀslew the burnt offering and the sacrifice.   *slaughtered*

43 And within *were* hooks, an hand broad, fastened round about: and upon the tables *was* the flesh of the offering.

44 And ᵀwithout the inner gate *were* the chambers of ᴿthe singers in the inner court, which *was* at the side of the north gate; and their ᵀprospect *was* toward the south: one at the side of the east gate *having* the prospect toward the north.   *outside* · 1 Chr. 6:31, 32 · *face*

45 And he said unto me, This chamber, whose ᵀprospect *is* toward the south, *is* for the priests, ᴿtheᵀ keepers of the charge of the house.   *face* · Ps. 134:1 · *who have charge*

46 And the chamber whose prospect *is* toward the north *is* for the priests, the keepers of the charge of the altar: these *are* the sons of ᴿZa'-dok among the sons of Levi, which come near to the LORD to minister unto him.   43:19

47 So he measured the court, an hundred cubits long, and an hundred cubits broad, foursquare; and the altar *that was* before the ᵀhouse.   *Temple*

48 And he brought me to the porch of the house, and measured *each* post of the porch, five cubits on this side, and five cubits on that side: and the breadth of the gate *was* three cubits on this side, and three cubits on that side.

49 The length of the porch *was* twenty cubits, and the breadth eleven cubits; and *he brought me* by the steps whereby they went up to it: and *there were* ᴿpillars by the posts, one on this side, and another on that side.   [Rev. 3:12]

41 Afterward he ᴿbrought me to the temple, and measured the posts, six cubits broad on the one side, and six cubits broad on the other side, *which was* the breadth of the tabernacle. 40:2, 3, 17

2 And the breadth of the door *was* ten cubits; and the sides of the door *were* five cubits on the

one side, and five cubits on the other side: and he measured the length thereof, forty cubits: and the breadth, twenty cubits.

3 Then went he ᵀinward, and measured the post of the door, two cubits; and the door, six cubits; and the breadth of the door, seven cubits.   *inside*

4 So ᴿhe measured the length thereof, twenty cubits; and the breadth, twenty cubits, before the temple: and he said unto me, This *is* the most holy *place*.   1 Kin. 6:20

5 After he measured the wall of ᵀthe house, six cubits; and the breadth of *every* side chamber, four cubits, round about the house on every side.   The temple

6 ᴿAnd the side chambers *were* three, one over another, and thirty in order; and they entered into the wall which *was* of the house for the side chambers round about, that they might have hold, but they had ᴿnot hold in the wall of the house.   1 Kin. 6:5–10 · 1 Kin. 6:6, 10

7 And ᴿ*there was* an enlarging, and a winding about still upward to the side chambers: for the winding about of the house went still upward round about the house: therefore the breadth of the house ᵀ*was still* upward, and so increased *from* the lowest *chamber* to the highest by the midst.   1 Kin. 6:8 · *increased*

8 I saw also the height of the house round about: the foundations of the side chambers *were* ᴿa full reed of six great cubits.   40:5

9 The thickness of the wall, which *was* for the side chamber ᵀwithout, *was* five cubits: and *that* which *was* left ᵀ*was* the place of the side chambers ᵀthat *were* within.   *outside · by · of the temple*

10 And between the chambers *was* the ᵀwideness of twenty cubits round about the house on every side.   *width*

11 And the doors of the side chambers *were* toward *the place that was* left, one door toward the north, and another door toward the south: and the breadth of the

ᵀplace that was left *was* five cubits round about.   *terrace*

12 Now the building that *was* before the ᵀseparate place at the end toward the west *was* seventy cubits broad; and the wall of the building *was* five cubits thick round about, and the length thereof ninety cubits.   *separating courtyard*

13 So he measured the house, an ᴿhundred cubits long; and the ᵀseparate place, and the building, with the walls thereof, an hundred cubits long; 40:47 · *separating courtyard*

14 Also the ᵀbreadth of the face of the house, and of the ᵀseparate place toward the east, an hundred cubits.   *width · separating courtyard*

15 And he measured the length of the building ᵀover against the separate place which *was* behind it, and the ᴿgalleries thereof on the one side and on the other side, an hundred cubits, with the inner temple, and the porches of the court;   *facing · 42:3, 5*

16 The door posts, and the narrow windows, and the galleries round about on their three stories, over against the door, cieled with wood round about, and from the ground up to the windows, and the windows *were* covered;

17 To that above the door, even unto the inner ᵀhouse, and without, and by all the wall round about within and without, by measure.   *room, the Holy of Holies*

18 And *it was* made ᴿwith cher'-u-bims and ᴿpalm trees, so that a palm tree *was* between a cherub and a cherub; and *every* cherub had two faces;   1 Kin. 6:29 · 2 Chr. 3:5

19 ᴿSo that the face of a man *was* toward the palm tree on the one side, and the face of a young lion toward the palm tree on the other side: *it was* made through all the house round about.   1:10

20 From the ground unto above the door *were* cher'-u-bims and palm trees made, and *on* the wall of the ᵀtemple.   *sanctuary*

21 The ᴿpostsᵀ of the temple *were* squared, *and* the face of the sanctuary; the appearance *of the*

one as the appearance *of the other.*   40:9, 14, 16 · *door posts*

22 The altar of wood *was* three cubits high, and the length thereof two cubits; and the corners thereof, and the length thereof, and the walls thereof, *were* of wood: and he said unto me, This *is* the table that *is* before the LORD.

23 And the temple and the sanctuary had two doors.

24 And the doors had two leaves *apiece,* two turning leaves; two *leaves* for the one door, and two leaves for the other *door.*

25 And *there were* made on them, on the doors of the temple, cher'-u-bims and palm trees, like as *were* made upon the walls; and *there were* thick planks upon the face of the porch ᵀwithout.   *outside*

26 And *there were* narrow windows and palm trees on the one side and on the other side, on the sides of the porch, and *upon* the side chambers of the house, and ᵀthick planks.   *on the canopies*

42 Then he ᴿbrought me forth into the utter court, the way toward the north: and he brought me into ᴿthe chamber that *was* over against the separate place, and which *was* before the building toward the north.   41:1 · 41:12, 15

2 Before the length of an hundred cubits *was* the north door, and the breadth *was* fifty cubits.

3 Over against the twenty *cubits* which *were* for the inner court, and over against the ᴿpavement which *was* for the utter court, *was* ᴿgallery against gallery in three *stories.*   40:17 · 41:15, 16

4 And before the chambers *was* a walk of ten cubits breadth inward, a way of one cubit; and their doors toward the north.

5 Now the upper chambers *were* shorter: for the galleries were higher than these, than the lower, and than the middlemost of the building.

6 For they *were* in three *stories,* but had not pillars as the pillars of the courts: therefore *the* ᵀbuilding was straitened more

than the lowest and the middlemost from the ground.   Upper level

7 And the wall that *was* without over against the chambers, toward the utter court on the forepart of the chambers, the length thereof *was* fifty cubits.

8 For the length of the chambers that *were* in the utter court *was* fifty cubits: and, lo, ᵀbefore the temple *were* an ᴿhundred cubits.   *in front of* · 41:13, 14

9 And from ᵀunder these chambers *was* the ᵀentry on the east side, as one goeth into them from the utter court.   *the lower of* · *entrance*

10 The chambers *were* in the thickness of the wall of the court toward the east, over against the ᵀseparate place, and over against the building.   *separating courtyard*

11 And ᴿthe way before them *was* like the appearance of the chambers which *were* toward the north, as long as they, *and* as broad as they: and all their ᵀgoings out *were* both according to their ᵀfashions, and according to their doors.   v. 4 · *exits* · *plans*

12 And according to the doors of the chambers that *were* toward the south *was* a door in the head of the way, *even* the way directly before the wall toward the east, as one entereth into them.

13 Then said he unto me, The north chambers *and* the south chambers, which *are* before the separate place, they *be* holy chambers, where the priests that approach unto the LORD shall eat the most holy things: there shall they lay the most holy things, and ᴿthe meat offering, and the sin offering, and the trespass offering; for the place *is* holy. Lev. 2:3, 10

14 ᴿWhen the priests enter therein, then shall they not go out of the holy *place* into the utter court, but there they shall lay their garments wherein they minister; for they *are* holy; and shall put on other garments, and shall approach to *those things* which *are* for the people.   44:19

15 Now when he had made an

end of measuring the inner house, he brought me forth toward the gate whose prospect *is* toward the ^Reast, and measured it round about.   40:6; 43:1

16 He measured the east side with the measuring reed, ^Tfive hundred reeds, with the measuring reed round about.   3000 cubits

17 He measured the north side, five hundred reeds, with the measuring reed round about.

18 He measured the south side, five hundred reeds, with the measuring reed.

19 He turned about to the west side, *and* measured five hundred reeds with the measuring reed.

20 He measured it by the four sides: it had a wall round about, five hundred *reeds* long, and five hundred broad, to make a separation between the sanctuary and the ^Tprofane place.   *common*

43 Afterward he brought me to the gate, *even* the gate that looketh toward the east:

2 And, behold, the glory of the God of Israel came from the way of the east: and his voice *was* like a noise of many waters: ^Rand the earth shined with his glory.   10:4

3 And *it was* ^Raccording to the appearance of the vision which I saw, *even* according to the vision that I saw when I came ^Rto destroy the city: and the visions *were* like the vision that I saw ^Rby the river Che'-bar; and I fell upon my face.   1:4-28 · Jer. 1:10 · 1:28; 3:23

4 ^RAnd the glory of the LORD came into the house by the way of the gate whose prospect *is* toward the east.   10:19; 11:23

5 ^RSo the spirit took me up, and brought me into the inner court; and, behold, the glory of the LORD filled the house.   8:3; 2 Cor. 12:2-4

6 And I heard *him* speaking unto me out of the house; and ^Rthe man stood by me.   1:26; 40:3

7 And he said unto me, Son of man, the place of my throne, and the place of the soles of my feet, where I will dwell in the midst of the children of Israel for ever, and

my holy name, shall the house of Israel no more defile, *neither* they, nor their kings, by their whoredom, nor by the carcases of their kings in their high places.

8 In their setting of their threshold by my thresholds, and their post by my posts, and the wall between me and them, they have even defiled my holy name by their abominations that they have committed: wherefore I have consumed them in mine anger.

9 Now let them put away their ^Twhoredom, and the carcases of their kings, far from me, and I will dwell in the midst of them for ever.   *harlotry*

10 Thou son of man, ^Rshew^T the house to the house of Israel, that they may be ashamed of their iniquities: and let them measure the pattern.   40:4 · *describe the temple*

11 And if they be ashamed of all that they have done, shew them the form of the house, and the fashion thereof, and the goings out thereof, and the comings in thereof, and all the forms thereof, and all the ordinances thereof, and all the forms thereof, and all the laws thereof: and write *it* in their sight, that they may keep the whole form thereof, and all the ordinances thereof, and do them.

12 This *is* the law of the house; Upon ^Rthe top of the mountain the whole limit thereof round about *shall be* most holy. Behold, this *is* the law of the house.   40:2

13 And these *are* the measures of the ^Raltar after the cubits: The cubit *is* a cubit and an hand breadth; even the bottom *shall be* a cubit, and the breadth a cubit, and the border thereof by the edge thereof round about *shall be* a span: and this *shall be* the higher place of the altar.   Ex. 27:1-8

14 And from the ^Tbottom *upon* the ground *even* to the lower ^Tsettle *shall be* two cubits, and the breadth one cubit; and from the lesser ^Tsettle *even* to the greater ^Tsettle *shall be* four cubits, and the breadth *one* cubit.   *base · ledge*

15 So the altar *shall be* four cubits; and from the altar and upward *shall be* four horns.

16 And the altar *shall be* twelve *cubits* long, twelve broad, ^Rsquare in the four squares thereof. Ex. 27:1

17 And the ^Tsettle *shall be* fourteen *cubits* long and fourteen broad in the four ^Tsquares thereof; and the border about it *shall be* half a cubit; and the ^Tbottom thereof *shall be* a cubit about; and ^Rhis stairs shall ^Tlook toward the east.   *ledge · sides · base* · Ex. 20:26 · *face*

18 And he said unto me, Son of man, thus saith the Lord GOD; These *are* the ordinances of the altar in the day when they shall make it, to offer burnt offerings thereon, and to ^Rsprinkle blood thereon.   Lev. 1:5, 11; [Heb. 9:21, 22]

19 And thou shalt give to ^Rthe priests the Levites that be of the seed of Za'-dok, which approach unto me, to minister unto me, saith the Lord GOD, a young bullock for a sin offering.   1 Kin. 2:35

20 And thou shalt take of the blood thereof, and put *it* on the four horns of it, and on the four corners of the settle, and upon the border round about: thus shalt thou cleanse and purge it.

21 Thou shalt take the bullock also of the sin offering, and he ^Rshall burn it in the appointed place of the house, ^Rwithout the sanctuary.   Lev. 4:12 · Heb. 13:11

22 And on the second day thou shalt offer a kid of the goats without blemish for a sin offering; and they shall cleanse the altar, as they did cleanse *it* with the bullock.

23 When thou hast made an end of cleansing *it,* thou shalt offer a young bullock without blemish, and a ram out of the flock without blemish.

24 And thou shalt offer them before the LORD, and the priests shall cast salt upon them, and they shall offer them up *for* a burnt offering unto the LORD.

25 ^RSeven days shalt thou prepare every day a goat *for* a sin offering: they shall also prepare a young bullock, and a ram out of the flock, without blemish. Lev. 8:33

26 Seven days shall they purge the altar and purify it; and they shall consecrate themselves.

27 ^RAnd when these days are expired, it shall be, *that* upon the eighth day, and *so* forward, the priests shall make your burnt offerings upon the altar, and your peace offerings; and I will accept you, saith the Lord GOD.   Lev. 9:1–4

44 Then he brought me back the way of the gate of the outward sanctuary which looketh toward the east; and it *was* shut.

2 Then said the LORD unto me; This gate shall be shut, it shall not be opened, and no man shall enter in by it; ^Rbecause the LORD, the God of Israel, hath entered in by it, therefore it shall be shut. 43:2–4

3 *It is* for the ^Rprince; the prince, he shall sit in it to ^Reat bread before the LORD; he shall enter by the way of the porch of *that* gate, and shall go out by the way of the same. [1 Cor. 10:18] · 46:2, 8

4 Then brought he me the way of the north gate before the house: and I looked, and, ^Rbehold, the glory of the LORD filled the house of the LORD: ^Rand I fell upon my face.   3:23; 43:5 · 1:28; 43:3

5 And the LORD said unto me, ^RSon of man, mark well, and behold with thine eyes, and hear with thine ears all that I say unto thee concerning all the ^Rordinances of the house of the LORD, and all the laws thereof; and mark well the entering in of the house, with every going forth of the sanctuary.   Deut. 32:46 · Deut. 12:32

6 And thou shalt say to the ^Rrebellious, *even* to the house of Israel, Thus saith the Lord GOD; O ye house of Israel, let it suffice you of all your abominations,   2:5

7 In that ye have brought *into my sanctuary* strangers, ^Runcircumcised in heart, and uncircumcised in flesh, to be in my sanctuary, to pollute it, *even* my house, when ye offer my bread, the fat

and the blood, and they have broken my covenant because of all your abominations. [Acts 7:51]

8 And ye have not kept the charge of mine holy things: but ye have set keepers of my charge in my sanctuary for yourselves.

9 Thus saith the Lord GOD; ^RNo stranger, uncircumcised in heart, nor uncircumcised in flesh, shall enter into my sanctuary, of any stranger that *is* among the children of Israel.   Joel 3:17; Zech. 14:21

10 ^RAnd the Levites that are gone away far from me, when Israel went astray, which went astray away from me after their idols; they shall even bear their iniquity.   48:11; 2 Kin. 23:8

11 Yet they shall be ministers in my sanctuary, ^Rhaving charge at the gates of the house, and ministering to the house: they shall slay the burnt offering and the sacrifice for the people, and ^Rthey shall stand before them to minister unto them.   1 Chr. 26:1–19 · Num. 16:9

12 Because they ministered unto them before their idols, and caused the house of Israel to fall into iniquity; therefore have I lifted up mine hand against them, saith the Lord GOD, and they shall bear their iniquity.

13 ^RAnd they shall not come near unto me, to do the office of a priest unto me, nor to come near to any of my holy things, in the most holy *place*: but they shall ^Rbear their shame, and their abominations which they have committed.   Num. 18:3; 2 Kin. 23:9 · 32:30

14 But I will make them keepers of the charge of the house, for all the service thereof, and for all that shall be done therein.

15 ^RBut the priests the Levites, the sons of Za'-dok, that kept the charge of my sanctuary when the children of Israel went astray from me, they shall come near to me to minister unto me, and they ^Rshall stand before me to offer unto me the fat and the blood, saith the Lord GOD: 40:46 · Deut. 10:8

16 They shall ^Renter into my sanctuary, and they shall come near to ^Rmy table, to minister unto me, and they shall keep my charge.   Num. 18:5, 7, 8 · 41:22; Mal. 1:7, 12

17 And it shall come to pass, *that* when they enter in at the gates of the inner court, ^Rthey shall be clothed with linen garments; and no wool shall come upon them, whiles they minister in the gates of the inner court, and within.   Ex. 28:39–43; 39:27–29; Rev. 19:8

18 ^RThey shall have linen bonnets upon their heads, and shall have linen breeches upon their loins; they shall not gird *themselves* with any thing that causeth sweat.   Ex. 28:40; 39:28; Is. 3:20

19 And when they go forth into the utter court, *even* into the utter court to the people, ^Rthey shall put off their garments wherein they ministered, and lay them in the holy chambers, and they shall put on other garments; and they shall ^Rnot sanctify the people with their garments.   Lev. 6:10 · [Matt. 23:17]

20 ^RNeither shall they shave their heads, nor suffer their locks to grow ^Rlong; they shall only poll their heads.   Lev. 21:5 · Num. 6:5

21 ^RNeither shall any priest drink wine, when they enter into the inner court.   Lev. 10:9

22 Neither shall they take for their wives a ^Rwidow, nor her that is put away: but they shall take maidens of the seed of the house of Israel, or a widow that had a priest before.   Lev. 21:7, 13, 14

23 And ^Rthey shall teach my people *the difference* between the holy and profane, and cause them to discern between the unclean and the clean.   Hos. 4:6; Mic. 3:9–11

24 And ^Rin controversy they shall stand in judgment; *and* they shall judge it according to my judgments: and they shall keep my laws and my statutes in all mine assemblies; and they shall hallow my sabbaths.   Deut. 17:8, 9

25 And they shall come at no dead person to defile themselves: but for father, or for mother, or for son, or for daughter, for brother,

or for sister that hath had no husband, they may defile themselves.

26 And ^Rafter he is cleansed, they shall ^Treckon unto him seven days. Num. 6:10; 19:11, 13–19 · *count*

27 And in the day that he goeth into the sanctuary, ^Runto the inner court, to minister in the sanctuary, ^Rhe shall offer his sin offering, saith the Lord GOD. v. 17; · Lev. 5:3, 6

28 And it shall be unto them for an inheritance: I ^R*am* their inheritance: and ye shall give them no ^Rpossession in Israel: I *am* their possession. Josh. 13:14, 33 · 45:4

29 ^RThey shall eat the meat offering, and the sin offering, and the trespass offering; and ^Revery dedicated thing in Israel shall be theirs. Lev. 7:6 · Lev. 27:21, 28; Num. 18:14

30 And the ^Rfirst of all the firstfruits of all *things*, and every ^Toblation of all, of every *sort* of your oblations, shall be the priest's: ye shall also give unto the priest the first of your dough, that he may cause the blessing to rest in thine house. Num. 3:13 · *sacrifice*

31 The priests shall not eat of any thing that ^Tis ^Rdead of itself, or torn, whether it be fowl or beast. *died naturally* · 4:14; Lev. 22:8

45 Moreover, when ye shall ^Rdivide by lot the land for inheritance, ye shall ^Roffer an oblation unto the LORD, an holy portion of the land: the length *shall be* the length of five and twenty thousand *reeds*, and the breadth *shall be* ten thousand. This *shall be* holy in all the borders thereof round about. 47:22 · 48:8, 9

2 Of this there shall be for the sanctuary ^Rfive hundred *in length*, with five hundred *in breadth*, square round about; and fifty cubits round about for ^Tthe suburbs thereof. 42:20 · *an open space*

3 And of this measure shalt thou measure the length of five and twenty thousand, and the breadth of ten thousand: ^Rand in it shall be the sanctuary *and* the most holy *place*. 48:10

4 ^RThe holy *portion* of the land shall be for the priests the minis-

ters of the sanctuary, which shall come near to minister unto the LORD: and it shall be a place for their houses, and an holy place for the sanctuary. 48:10, 11

5 And the five and twenty thousand of length, and the ten thousand of breadth, shall also the Levites, the ministers of the house, have for themselves, for a possession for twenty chambers.

6 ^RAnd ye shall appoint the possession of the city five thousand broad, and five and twenty thousand long, ^Tover against the oblation of the holy *portion:* it shall be for the whole house of Israel. 48:15 · *adjacent to the district*

7 ^RAnd *a* portion shall be for the prince on the one side and on the other side of the oblation of the holy *portion,* and of the possession of the city, before the oblation of the holy *portion,* and before the possession of the city, from the west side westward, and from the east side eastward: and the length *shall be* over against one of the portions, from the west border unto the east border. 48:21

8 In the land shall be his possession in Israel: and ^Rmy princes shall no more oppress my people; and *the rest of* the land shall they give to the house of Israel according to their tribes. 22:27; Jer. 22:17

9 Thus saith the Lord GOD; ^RLet^T it suffice you, O princes of Israel: ^Rremove violence and spoil, and execute judgment and justice, take away your exactions from my people, saith the Lord GOD. 44:6 · *Enough* · Jer. 22:3; Zech. 8:16

10 Ye shall have just balances, and a just e'-phah, and a just bath.

11 The e'-phah and the bath shall be of one measure, that the bath may contain the tenth part of an ho'-mer, and the e'-phah the tenth part of an ho'-mer: the measure thereof shall be ^Tafter the ho'-mer. *according to*

12 And the shek'-el *shall be* twenty ge'-rahs: twenty shek'-els, five and twenty shek'-els, fifteen shek'-els, shall be your ma'-neh.

13 This *is* the oblation that ye shall offer; the sixth part of an e′-phah of an ho′-mer of wheat, and ye shall give the sixth part of an e′-phah of an ho′-mer of barley:

14 Concerning the ordinance of oil, the bath of oil, *ye shall offer* the tenth part of a bath out of the ᵀcor, *which is* an ho′-mer of ten baths; for ten baths *are* an ho′-mer:　　Or *kor*

15 And one lamb out of the flock, out of two hundred, out of the fat pastures of Israel; for a meat offering, and for a burnt offering, and for peace offerings, ᴿto make reconciliation for them, saith the Lord GOD.　　Lev. 1:4; 6:30

16 All the people of the land shall give this ᵀoblation for the prince in Israel.　　*offering*

17 And it shall be the ᴿprince's part *to give* burnt offerings, and meat offerings, and drink offerings, in the feasts, and in the new moons, and in the sabbaths, in all solemnities of the house of Israel: he shall prepare the sin offering, and the meat offering, and the burnt offering, and the peace offerings, to make reconciliation for the house of Israel.　　46:4–12

18 Thus saith the Lord GOD; In the first *month*, in the first *day* of the month, thou shalt take a young bullock without blemish, and ᴿcleanse the sanctuary:　43:22

19 ᴿAnd the priest shall take of the blood of the sin offering, and put *it* upon the posts of the house, and upon the four corners of the settle of the altar, and upon the posts of the gate of the inner court.　　43:20; Lev. 16:18–20

20 And so thou shalt do the seventh *day* of the month ᴿfor every one that erreth, and for *him that is* simple: so shall ye reconcile the house.　　Lev. 4:27; Ps. 19:12

21 ᴿIn the first *month*, in the fourteenth day of the month, ye shall have the passover, a feast of seven days; unleavened bread shall be eaten.　　Ex. 12:18; Deut. 16:1

22 And upon that day shall the prince prepare for himself and for all the people of the land ᴿa bullock *for* a sin offering.　　Lev. 4:14

23 And seven days of the feast he shall prepare a burnt offering to the LORD, seven bullocks and seven rams without blemish daily the seven days; and a kid of the goats daily *for* a sin offering.

24 And he shall prepare a meat offering of an e′-phah for a bullock, and an e′-phah for a ram, and an hin of oil for an e′-phah.

25 In the seventh *month*, in the fifteenth day of the month, shall he do the like in the ᴿfeast of the seven days, according to the sin offering, according to the burnt offering, and according to the meat offering, and according to the oil.　　Deut. 16:13; 2 Chr. 5:3; 7:8, 10

46

Thus saith the Lord GOD; The gate of the inner court that ᵀlooketh toward the east shall be shut the six ᴿworking days; but on the sabbath it shall be opened, and in the day of the new moon it shall be opened.　　*faces* · Ex. 20:9

2 ᴿAnd the prince shall enter by the way of the porch of *that* gate without, and shall stand by the post of the gate, and the priests shall prepare his burnt offering and his peace offerings, and he shall worship at the threshold of the gate: then he shall go forth; but the gate shall not be shut until the evening.　　44:3

3 Likewise the people of the land shall worship at the door of this gate before the LORD in the sabbaths and in the new moons.

4 And the burnt offering that the prince shall offer unto the LORD in the ᴿsabbath day *shall be* six lambs without blemish, and a ram without blemish.　　Num. 28:9, 10

5 ᴿAnd the meat offering *shall be* an e′-phah for a ram, and the meat offering for the lambs as he shall be able to give, and an hin of oil to an e′-phah.　　45:24; Num. 28:12

6 And in the day of the new moon *it shall be* a young bullock without blemish, and six lambs, and a ram: they shall be without blemish.

7 And he shall prepare a meat offering, an e′-phah for a bullock, and an e′-phah for a ram, and for the lambs according as his hand shall attain unto, and an hin of oil ᵀto an e′-phah.   *with every*

8 And when the prince shall enter, he shall go in by the way of the porch of *that* gate, and he shall go forth by the way thereof.

9 But when the people of the land ᴿshall come before the Lᴏʀᴅ in the solemn feasts, he that entereth in by the way of the north ᴿgate to worship shall go out by the way of the south gate; and he that entereth by the way of the south gate shall go forth by the way of the north gate: he shall not return by the way of the gate whereby he came in, but shall go forth over against it.   Ps. 84:7 · 48:31

10 And the prince in the midst of them, when they go in, shall go in; and when they go forth, shall go forth.

11 And in the feasts and in the solemnities the meat offering shall be an e′-phah to a bullock, and an e′-phah to a ram, and to the lambs as he is able to give, and an hin of oil to an e′-phah.

12 Now when the prince shall prepare a voluntary burnt offering or peace offerings voluntarily unto the Lᴏʀᴅ, ᴿone shall then open him the gate that looketh toward the east, and he shall prepare his burnt offering and his peace offerings, as he did on the sabbath day: then he shall go forth; and after his going forth *one* shall shut the gate.   44:3

13 ᴿThou shalt daily prepare a burnt offering unto the Lᴏʀᴅ *of* a lamb of the first year without blemish: thou shalt prepare it every morning. Ex. 29:38; Num. 28:3–5

14 And thou shalt prepare a meat offering for it every morning, the sixth part of an e′-phah, and the third part of an hin of oil, to temper with the fine flour; a meat offering continually by a perpetual ordinance unto the Lᴏʀᴅ.

15 Thus shall they prepare the lamb, and the meat offering, and the oil, every morning *for* a ᴿcontinual burnt offering. Num. 28:6

16 Thus saith the Lord Gᴏᴅ; If the prince give a gift unto any of his sons, the inheritance thereof shall be his sons'; it *shall be* their possession by inheritance.

17 But if he give a gift of his inheritance to one of his servants, then it shall be his to ᴿthe year of liberty; after it shall return to the prince: but his inheritance shall be his sons' for them. Lev. 25:10

18 Moreover ᴿthe prince shall not take of the people's inheritance by oppression, to thrust them out of their possession; *but* he shall give his sons inheritance out of his own possession: that my people be not scattered every man from his possession. 45:8

19 After he brought me through the entry, which *was* at the side of the gate, into the holy ᴿchambers of the priests, which looked toward the north: and, behold, there *was* a place on the two sides westward. 42:13

20 Then said he unto me, This *is* the place where the priests shall boil the trespass offering and the sin offering, where they shall bake the meat offering; that they bear *them* not out into the utter court, ᴿto sanctify the people. 44:19

21 Then he brought me forth into the utter court, and caused me to pass by the four corners of the court; and, behold, in every corner of the court *there was* a court.

22 In the four corners of the court *there were* courts joined of forty *cubits* long and thirty broad: these four corners *were* of ᵀone measure.   *the same size*

23 And *there was* a row of *building* round about in them, round about them four, and *it was* made with boiling places under the rows round about.

24 Then said he unto me, These *are* the ᵀplaces of them that boil, where the ministers of ᵀthe house

shall [R]boil the sacrifice of the people.   Kitchens · The temple · v. 20

47 Afterward he brought me again unto the door of the house; and, behold, [R]waters issued out from under the threshold of the house eastward: for the forefront of the house *stood toward* the east, and the waters came down from under from the right side of the house, at the south *side* of the altar.   Zech. 13:1

2 Then brought he me out of the way of the [T]gate northward, and led me about the way without unto the utter gate by the way that looketh [R]eastward; and, behold, there ran out waters on the right side.   *north gate* · 44:1, 2

3 And when [R]the man that had the line in his hand went forth eastward, he measured a thousand cubits, and he brought me through the waters; the waters *were* to the ancles.   40:3

4 Again he measured a thousand, and brought me through the waters; the waters *were* to the knees. Again he measured a thousand, and brought me through; the waters *were* to the [T]loins. *waist*

5 Afterward he measured a thousand; *and it was* a river that I could not [T]pass over: for the waters were risen, [T]waters to swim in, a river that could not be passed over.   *cross · waters one must swim*

6 And he said unto me, Son of man, hast thou seen *this*? Then he brought me, and caused me to return to the brink of the river.

7 Now when I had returned, behold, at the bank of the river *were* very many [R]trees on the one side and on the other.   [Is. 60:13, 21]

8 Then said he unto me, These waters issue out toward the east [T]country, and go down into the desert, and go into the sea: *which being* brought forth into the sea, the waters shall be healed.   *region*

9 And it shall come to pass, *that* every thing that liveth, which moveth, whithersoever the rivers shall come, shall live: and there shall be a very great multitude of fish, because these waters shall come thither: for they shall be healed; and every thing shall live whither the river cometh.

10 And it shall come to pass, *that* the fishers shall stand upon it from En–ge′-di even unto En–eg′-la-im; they shall be a *place* to spread forth nets; their fish shall be according to their kinds, as the fish [R]of the great sea, exceeding many.   48:28; Num. 34:3; Josh. 23:4

11 But the [T]miry places thereof and the [T]marishes thereof shall not be healed; they shall be given to salt.   *swamps · marshes*

12 And [R]by the river upon the bank thereof, on this side and on that side, shall grow all trees for meat, whose leaf shall not fade, neither shall the fruit thereof be consumed: it shall bring forth new fruit according to his months, because their waters they issued out of the sanctuary: and the fruit thereof shall be for meat, and the leaf thereof for medicine.   [Rev. 22:2]

13 Thus saith the Lord GOD; This *shall be* the border, whereby ye shall inherit the land according to the twelve tribes of Israel: Joseph *shall have two* portions.

14 And ye shall inherit it, one as well as another: *concerning* the which I [R]lifted up mine hand to give it unto your fathers: and this land shall [R]fall unto you for inheritance.   Gen. 12:7; 13:15; 15:7; 17:8 · 48:29

15 And this *shall be* the border of the land toward the north side, from the great sea, the way of Heth′-lon, as men go to Ze′-dad;

16 Ha′-math, Be-ro′-thah, Sibra′-im, which *is* between the border of Damascus and the border of Ha′-math; Ha′-zar–hat′-ti-con, which *is* by the coast of Hau′-ran.

17 And the border from the sea shall be Ha′-zar-e′-nan, the border of Damascus, and the north northward, and the border of Ha′-math. And *this is* the north side.

18 And the east side ye shall measure from Hau′-ran, and from Damascus, and from Gil′-e-ad,

and from the land of Israel *by* Jordan, from the border unto the east sea. And *this is* the east side.

19 And the south side southward, from Ta'-mar *even* to ^Rthe waters of strife *in* Ka'-desh, the river to the great sea. And *this is* the south side southward. 48:28

20 The west side also *shall be* the great sea from the border, till a man come over against Ha'-math. This *is* the west side.

21 So shall ye ^Rdivide this land unto you according to the tribes of Israel. 45:1

22 And it shall come to pass, *that* ye shall divide it by lot for an inheritance unto you, and to the strangers that sojourn among you, which shall beget children among you: and they shall be unto you as born in the country among the children of Israel; they shall have inheritance with you among the tribes of Israel.

23 And it shall come to pass, *that* in what tribe the stranger sojourneth, there shall ye give *him* his inheritance, saith the Lord God.

48 Now these *are* the names of the tribes. ^RFrom the north end to the coast of the way of Heth'-lon, as one goeth to Ha'-math, Ha'-zar-e'-nan, the border of Damascus northward, to the coast of Ha'-math; for these are his sides east *and* west; a *portion* for ^RDan. 47:15 · Josh. 19:40-48

2 And by the border of Dan, from the east side unto the west side, a *portion for* Asher.

3 And by the border of Asher, from the east side even unto the west side, a *portion for* ^RNaph'-ta-li. Josh. 19:32-39

4 And by the border of Naph'-ta-li, from the east side unto the west side, a *portion for* ^RMa-nas'-seh. Josh. 13:29-31; 17:1-11, 17, 18

5 And by the border of Ma-nas'-seh, from the east side unto the west side, a *portion for* ^RE'-phra-im. Josh. 16:5-10; 17:8-10, 14-18

6 And by the border of E'-phra-im, from the east side even unto

the west side, a *portion for* ^RReuben. Josh. 13:15-23

7 And by the border of Reuben, from the east side unto the west side, a *portion for* ^RJudah. Josh. 19:9

8 And by the border of Judah, from the east side unto the west side, shall be ^Rthe offering which ye shall offer of five and twenty thousand *reeds in* breadth, and *in* length as one of the *other* parts, from the east side unto the west side: and the sanctuary shall be in the midst of it. 45:1-6

9 The ^Toblation that ye shall offer unto the Lord *shall be* of five and twenty thousand in length, and of ten thousand in breadth. *district*

10 And for them, *even* for the priests, shall be *this* holy ^Toblation; toward the north five and twenty thousand *in length*, and toward the west ten thousand in breadth, and toward the east ten thousand in breadth, and toward the south five and twenty thousand in length: and the sanctuary of the Lord shall be in the midst thereof. *district*

11 *It shall be* for the priests that are sanctified of the sons of Za'-dok; which have kept my charge, which went not astray when the children of Israel went astray, ^Ras the Levites went astray. 44:10, 12

12 And *this* ^Toblation of the land that is ^Toffered shall be unto them a thing most ^Rholy by the border of the Levites. *district · set apart · 45:4*

13 And ^Tover against the border of the priests the ^RLevites *shall have* five and twenty thousand in length, and ten thousand in breadth: all the length *shall be* five and twenty thousand, and the breadth ten thousand. *opposite · 45:5*

14 ^RAnd they shall not sell of it, neither exchange, nor alienate the firstfruits of the land: for *it is* holy unto the Lord. Ex. 22:29; Lev. 27:10, 28

15 ^RAnd the five thousand, that are left in the breadth over against the five and twenty thousand, shall be ^Ra profane *place* for the city, for dwelling, and for sub-

urbs: and the city shall be in the midst thereof. 45:6 · 42:20

16 And these *shall be* the measures thereof; the north side four thousand and five hundred, and the south side four thousand and five hundred, and on the east side four thousand and five hundred, and the west side four thousand and five hundred.

17 And the ᵀsuburbs of the city shall be toward the north two hundred and fifty, and toward the south two hundred and fifty, and toward the east two hundred and fifty, and toward the west two hundred and fifty. *commonland*

18 And the ᵀresidue in length ᵀover against the oblation of the holy *portion shall be* ten thousand eastward, and ten thousand westward: and it shall be over against the oblation of the holy *portion;* and the increase thereof shall be for food unto them that serve the city. *rest of the · alongside the district*

19 ᴿAnd ᵀthey that serve the city shall ᵀserve it out of all the tribes of Israel. 45:6 · *the workers of · cultivate*

20 All the ᵀoblation *shall be* five and twenty thousand by five and twenty thousand: ye shall offer the holy oblation foursquare, with the possession of the city. *district*

21 ᴿAnd the residue *shall be* for the prince, on the one side and on the other of the holy oblation, and of the possession of the city, over against the five and twenty thousand of the oblation toward the east border, and westward over against the five and twenty thousand toward the west border, over against the portions for the prince: and it shall be the holy oblation; ᴿand the sanctuary of the house *shall be* in the midst thereof. v. 22; 34:24; 45:7 · vv. 8, 10

22 Moreover from the possession of the Levites, and from the possession of the city, *being* in the midst *of that* which is the prince's, between the border of Judah and the border of Benjamin, shall be for the prince.

23 As for the rest of the tribes, from the east side unto the west side, Benjamin *shall have* ᵀa *portion.* Lit. *one*

24 And by the border of Benjamin, from the east side unto the west side, ᴿSimeon *shall have* a *portion.* Josh. 19:1–9

25 And by the border of Simeon, from the east side unto the west side, Is'-sa-char a *portion.*

26 And by the border of Is'-sa-char, from the east side unto the west side, Zeb'-u-lun a *portion.*

27 And by the border of Zeb'-u-lun, from the east side unto the west side, Gad a *portion.*

28 And by the border of Gad, at the south side southward, the border shall be even from Ta'-mar *unto* ᴿthe waters of strife *in* Ka'-desh, *and* to the river toward the ᴿgreat sea. 2 Chr. 20:2 · 47:10, 15, 19, 20

29 ᴿThis *is* the land which ye shall divide by lot unto the tribes of Israel for inheritance, and these *are* their portions, saith the Lord Gᴏᴅ. 47:14, 21, 22

30 And these *are* the ᵀgoings out of the city on the north side, four thousand and five hundred measures. *exits*

31 And the gates of the city *shall be* after the names of the tribes of Israel: three gates northward; one gate of Reuben, one gate of Judah, one gate of Levi.

32 And at the east side four thousand and five hundred: and three gates; and one gate of Joseph, one gate of Benjamin, one gate of Dan.

33 And at the south side four thousand and five hundred measures: and three gates; one gate of Simeon, one gate of Is'-sa-char, one gate of Zeb'-u-lun.

34 At the west side four thousand and five hundred, *with* their three gates; one gate of Gad, one gate of Asher, one gate of Naph'-ta-li.

35 *It was* round about eighteen thousand *measures:* and the name of the city from *that* day *shall be,* ᴿThe Lᴏʀᴅ *is* there. 35:10; Joel 3:21

The Book of
DANIEL

DANIEL'S life and ministry bridge the entire seventy-year period of Babylonian captivity. Deported to Babylon at the age of sixteen, and hand-picked for government service, Daniel becomes God's prophetic mouthpiece to the gentile and Jewish world declaring God's present and eternal purpose. Nine of the twelve chapters in his book revolve around dreams, including God-given visions involving trees, animals, beasts, and images. In both his personal adventures and prophetic visions, Daniel shows God's guidance, intervention, and power in the affairs of men.

The name *Daniye'l* or *Dani'el* means "God Is My Judge," and the book is, of course, named after the author and principal character. The Greek form *Daniel* in the Septuagint is the basis for the Latin and English titles.

IN the third year of the reign of ᴿJe-hoi'-a-kim king of Judah came Neb-u-chad-nez'-zar king of Babylon unto Jerusalem, and besieged it.   2 Chr. 36:5–7; Jer. 52:12–30

2 And the Lord gave Je-hoi'-a-kim king of Judah into his hand, with ᴿpart of the vessels of the house of God: which he carried into the land of Shi'-nar to the house of his god; and he brought the vessels into the treasure house of his god.   Jer. 27:19, 20

3 And the king spake unto Ash'-pe-naz the master of his eunuchs, that he should bring ᴿ*certain* of the children of Israel, and of the king's seed, and of the princes;   2 Kin. 20:17, 18; Is. 39:7

4 ᵀChildren in whom *was* no blemish, but well favoured, and skilful in all wisdom, and cunning in knowledge, and understanding science, and such as *had* ability in them to stand in the king's palace, and ᴿwhom they might teach the learning and the tongue of the Chal-de'-ans.   *Young men* · Acts 7:22

5 And the king appointed them a daily provision of the king's meat, and of the wine which he drank: so nourishing them three years, that at the end thereof they might stand before the king.

6 Now among these were of the children of Judah, Daniel, Han-a-ni'-ah, Mish'-a-el, and Az-a-ri'-ah:

7 ᴿUnto whom the prince of the eunuchs gave names: for he gave unto Daniel *the name* of Bel-te-shaz'-zar; and to Han-a-ni'-ah, of Sha'-drach; and to Mish'-a-el, of Me'-shach; and to Az-a-ri'-ah, of A-bed'-ne-go.   Gen. 41:45; 2 Kin. 24:17

8 But Daniel purposed in his heart that he would not defile himself ᴿwith the portion of the king's meat, nor with the wine which he drank: therefore he requested of the prince of the eunuchs that he might not defile himself.   Lev. 11:47; Ezek. 4:13; Hos. 9:3

9 Now God had brought Daniel into favour and tender love with the prince of the eunuchs.

10 And the prince of the eunuchs said unto Daniel, I fear my lord the king, who hath appointed your meat and your drink: for why should he see your faces worse ᵀliking than the ᵀchildren which *are* of your ᵀsort? then shall ye make *me* endanger my head to the king.   *looking · young men · age*

11 Then said Daniel to Mel'-zar, whom the prince of the eunuchs had set over Daniel, Han-a-ni'-ah, Mish'-a-el, and Az-a-ri'-ah,

12 ᵀProve thy servants, I beseech thee, ten days; and let them give us ᵀpulse to eat, and water to drink.   *Test · vegetables*

13 Then let our countenances be looked upon before thee, and the

countenance of the children that eat of the portion of the king's meat: and as thou seest, deal with thy servants.

14 So he consented to them in this matter, and ᵀproved them ten days.   *tested*

15 And at the end of ten days their countenances appeared fairer and fatter in flesh than all the children which ᵀdid eat the portion of the king's ᵀmeat.   *food*

16 Thus Mel'-zar took away the portion of their meat, and the wine that they should drink; and gave them ᵀpulse.   *vegetables*

17 As for these four ᵀchildren, God gave them knowledge and skill in all learning and wisdom: and Daniel had understanding in all visions and dreams.   *young men*

18 Now at the end of the days that the king had said he should bring them in, then the ᵀprince of the eunuchs brought them in before Neb-u-chad-nez'-zar.   *chief*

19 And the king ᵀcommuned with them; and among them all was found none like Daniel, Han-a-ni'-ah, Mish'-a-el, and Az-a-ri'-ah: therefore stood they before the king.   *examined, lit. talked*

20 ᴿAnd in all matters of wisdom *and* understanding, that the king enquired of them, he found them ten times better than all the magicians *and* astrologers that *were* in all his realm.   *1 Kin. 10:1*

21 And Daniel continued *even* unto the first year of king Cyrus.

2 And in the second year of the reign of Neb-u-chad-nez'-zar Neb-u-chad-nez'-zar dreamed dreams, ᴿwherewith his spirit was troubled, and ᴿhis sleep ᵀbrake from him. *4:5 · 6:18; Esth. 6:1 · left him*

2 ᴿThen the king commanded to call the magicians, and the astrologers, and the sorcerers, and the Chal-de'-ans, for to shew the king his dreams. So they came and stood before the king. *Ex. 7:11*

3 And the king said unto them, I have dreamed a dream, and my spirit was troubled to ᵀknow the dream.   *Or understand*

4 Then spake the Chal-de'-ans to the king in Syr'-i-ack, ᴿO king, live for ever: tell thy servants the dream, and we will shew the interpretation. *3:9; 5:10; 6:6, 21*

5 The king answered and said to the Chal-de'-ans, The ᵀthing is gone from me: if ye will not make known unto me the dream, with the interpretation thereof, ye shall be cut in pieces, and your houses shall be made a dunghill. *decree*

6 ᴿBut if ye ᵀshew the dream, and the interpretation thereof, ye shall receive of me gifts and rewards and great honour: therefore ᵀshew me the dream, and the interpretation thereof. *5:16 · tell*

7 They answered again and said, Let the king tell his servants the dream, and we will ᵀshew the interpretation of it.   *give*

8 The king answered and said, I know of certainty that ye would gain the time, because ye see the thing is ᵀgone from me. *certain with*

9 But if ye will not make known unto me the dream, *there is but* one decree for you: for ye have prepared lying and corrupt words to speak before me, till the ᵀtime be changed: therefore tell me the dream, and I shall know that ye can ᵀshew me the interpretation thereof. *situation · give*

10 The Chal-de'-ans answered before the king, and said, There is not a man upon the earth that can shew the king's matter: therefore *there is* no king, lord, nor ruler, *that* asked such things at any magician, or astrologer, or Chal-de'-an.

11 And *it is* a rare thing that the king requireth, and there is none other that can shew it before the king, ᴿexcept the gods, whose dwelling is not with flesh. *5:11*

12 For this cause the king was angry and very furious, and commanded to destroy all the wise *men* of Babylon.

13 And the decree went forth that the wise *men* should be slain; and they sought ᴿDaniel and his fellows to be slain. *1:19, 20*

14 Then Daniel answered with counsel and ᵀwisdom to A'-ri-och the captain of the king's guard, which was gone forth to slay the wise *men* of Babylon: *understanding*

15 He answered and said to A'-ri-och the king's captain, Why *is* the decree *so* ᵀhasty from the king? Then A'-ri-och made the thing known to Daniel.　　*urgent*

16 Then Daniel went in, and desired of the king that he would give him time, and that he would shew the king the interpretation.

17 Then Daniel went to his house, and made the thing known to Han-a-ni'-ah, Mish'-a-el, and Az-a-ri'-ah, his companions:

18 ᴿThat they would desire mercies of the God of heaven concerning this secret; that Daniel and his fellows should not perish with the rest of the wise *men* of Babylon.　　[9:9; Matt. 18:19]

19 Then was the secret revealed unto Daniel ᴿin a night vision. Then Daniel blessed the God of heaven.　　Num. 12:6; Job 33:15; Amos 3:7

20 Daniel answered and said, Blessed be the name of God for ever and ever: ᴿfor wisdom and might are his:　　[Matt. 6:13; Rom. 11:33]

21 And he changeth ᴿthe times and the seasons: he removeth kings, and setteth up kings: ᴿhe giveth wisdom unto the wise, and knowledge to them that know understanding:　　7:25 · [James 1:5]

22 He revealeth the deep and secret things: he knoweth what *is* in the darkness, and ᴿthe light dwelleth with him.　　[1 John 1:5]

23 I thank thee, and praise thee, O thou God of my fathers, who hast given me wisdom and might, and hast made known unto me now what we ᴿdesired of thee: for thou hast *now* made known unto us the king's matter.　　Ps. 21:2, 4

24 Therefore Daniel went in unto A'-ri-och, whom the king had ordained to destroy the wise *men* of Babylon: he went and said thus unto him; Destroy not the wise *men* of Babylon: bring me in before the king, and I will shew unto the king the interpretation.

25 Then A'-ri-och brought in Daniel before the king in haste, and said thus unto him, I have found a man of the captives of Judah, that will make known unto the king the interpretation.

26 The king answered and said to Daniel, whose name *was* Bel-te-shaz'-zar, Art thou able to make known unto me the dream which I have seen, and the interpretation thereof?

27 Daniel answered in the presence of the king, and said, The secret which the king hath demanded cannot the wise *men*, the astrologers, the magicians, the soothsayers, shew unto the king;

28 ᴿBut there is a God in heaven that revealeth secrets, and maketh known to the king Neb-u-chad-nez'-zar ᴿwhat shall be in the latter days. Thy dream, and the visions of thy head upon thy bed, are these;　　Amos 4:13 · Mic. 4:1

29 As for thee, O king, thy thoughts came *into thy mind* upon thy bed, what should come to pass hereafter: and he that revealeth secrets maketh known to thee what shall come to pass.

30 ᴿBut as for me, this secret is not revealed to me for *any* wisdom that I have more than any living, but for *their* sakes that shall make known the interpretation to the king, ᴿand that thou mightest know the thoughts of thy heart.　　Acts 3:12 · v. 47

31 Thou, O king, sawest, and behold a great image. This great image, whose brightness *was* excellent, stood before thee; and the form thereof *was* terrible.

32 This image's head *was* of fine gold, his breast and his arms of silver, his belly and his ᵀthighs of ᵀbrass,　　*loins* or *sides* · *bronze*

33 His legs of iron, his feet part of iron and part of clay.

34 Thou sawest till that a stone was cut out ᴿwithout hands, which smote the image upon his feet *that were* of iron and clay, and brake them to pieces.　8:25

35 ᴿThen was the iron, the clay, the brass, the silver, and the gold, broken to pieces together, and became like the chaff of the summer threshingfloors; and the wind carried them away, that no place was found for them: and the stone that smote the image became a great mountain, and filled the whole earth.　7:23–27; [Rev. 16:14]

36 This *is* the dream; and we will tell the interpretation thereof before the king.

37 ᴿThou, O king, *art* a king of kings: for the God of heaven hath given thee a kingdom, power, and strength, and glory.　Ezra 7:12; Is. 47:5

38 ᴿAnd wheresoever the children of men dwell, the beasts of the field and the fowls of the heaven hath he given into thine hand, and hath made thee ruler over them all. Thou *art* this head of gold.　Ps. 50:10, 11; Jer. 27:6

39 And after thee shall arise ᴿanother kingdom inferior to thee, and another third kingdom of ᵀbrass, which shall bear rule over all the earth.　5:28, 31 · *bronze*

40 And ᴿthe fourth kingdom shall be strong as iron: forasmuch as iron breaketh in pieces and subdueth all *things:* and as iron that breaketh all these, shall it break in pieces and bruise.　7:7, 23

41 And whereas thou sawest the feet and toes, part of potters' clay, and part of iron, the kingdom shall be divided; but there shall be in it of the strength of the iron, forasmuch as thou sawest the iron mixed with ᵀmiry clay.　*ceramic*

42 And *as* the toes of the feet *were* part of iron, and part of clay, *so* the kingdom shall be partly strong, and partly ᵀbroken.　*brittle*

43 And whereas thou sawest iron mixed with miry clay, they shall mingle themselves with the seed of men: but they shall not ᵀcleave one to another, even as iron is not mixed with clay.　*adhere*

☆ 44 And in the days of these kings shall the God of heaven set up a kingdom, which shall never be destroyed: and the kingdom shall not be left to other people, ᴿ*but* it shall break in pieces and consume all these kingdoms, and it shall stand for ever.　[1 Cor. 15:24]

45 ᴿForasmuch as thou sawest that the stone was cut out of the mountain without hands, and that it brake in pieces the iron, the ᵀbrass, the clay, the silver, and the gold; the great God hath made known to the king what shall come to pass hereafter: and the dream *is* certain, and the interpretation thereof sure.　Is. 28:16 · *bronze*

46 ᴿThen the king Neb-u-chad-nez'-zar fell upon his face, and worshipped Daniel, and commanded that they should offer an oblation ᴿand sweet odours unto him.　Rev. 19:10; 22:8 · Ezra 6:10

47 The king answered unto Daniel, and said, Of a truth *it is,* that ᴿyour God *is* a God of gods, and a Lord of kings, and a revealer of secrets, seeing thou couldst reveal this secret.　3:28, 29

48 Then the king made Daniel a great man, and gave him many great gifts, and made him ruler over the whole province of Babylon, and chief of the governors over all the wise *men* of Babylon.

49 Then Daniel requested of the king, ᴿand he set Sha'-drach, Me'-shach, and A-bed'–ne-go, over the affairs of the province of Babylon: but Daniel ᴿ*sat* in the gate of the king.　1:7; 3:12 · Esth. 2:19, 21; 3:2

3 Neb-u-chad-nez'-zar the king made an image of gold, whose height *was* threescore cubits, *and* the breadth thereof six cubits: he set it up in the plain of Du'-ra, in the province of Babylon.

2 Then Neb-u-chad-nez'-zar the king sent to gather together the princes, the governors, and the captains, the judges, the treasurers, the counsellors, the sheriffs, and all the rulers of the provinces, to come to the dedication of the image which Neb-u-chad-nez'-zar the king had set up.

3 Then the princes, the gover-

nors, and captains, the judges, the treasurers, the counsellors, the sheriffs, and all the rulers of the provinces, were gathered together unto the dedication of the image that Neb-u-chad-nez′-zar the king had set up; and they stood before the image that Neb-u-chad-nez′-zar had set up.

4 Then an herald cried aloud, To you it is commanded, ᴿO people, nations, and languages,　4:1

5 *That* at what time ye hear the sound of the ᵀcornet, flute, harp, ᵀsackbut, psaltery, ᵀdulcimer, and all kinds of musick, ye fall down and worship the golden image that Neb-u-chad-nez′-zar the king hath set up:　　*horn · lyre · pipes*

6 And whoso falleth not down and worshippeth shall the same hour ᴿbe cast into the midst of a burning fiery furnace. Rev. 9:2; 13:15

7 Therefore at that time, when all the people heard the sound of the ᵀcornet, flute, harp, ᵀsackbut, psaltery, and all kinds of musick, all the people, the nations, and the languages, fell down *and* worshipped the golden image that Neb-u-chad-nez′-zar the king had set up.　　*horn · lyre*

8 Wherefore at that time certain Chal-de′-ans ᴿcame near, and accused the Jews.　Ezra 4:12–16

9 They spake and said to the king Neb-u-chad-nez′-zar, ᴿO king, live for ever.　2:4; 5:10; 6:6, 21

10 Thou, O king, hast made a decree, that every man that shall hear the sound of the ᵀcornet, flute, harp, ᵀsackbut, psaltery, and ᵀdulcimer, and all kinds of musick, shall fall down and worship the golden image:　*horn · lyre · pipes*

11 And whoso falleth not down and worshippeth, *that* he should be cast into the midst of a burning fiery furnace.

12 ᴿThere are certain Jews whom thou hast set over the affairs of the province of Babylon, Sha′-drach, Me′-shach, and A-bed′–ne-go; these men, O king, have ᴿnot regarded thee: they serve not thy gods, nor worship

the golden image which thou hast set up.　2:49 · 1:8; 6:12, 13

13 Then Neb-u-chad-nez′-zar in *his* ᴿrage and fury commanded to bring Sha′-drach, Me′-shach, and A-bed′–ne-go. Then they brought these men before the king.　2:12

14 Neb-u-chad-nez′-zar spake and said unto them, *Is it* true, O Sha′-drach, Me′-shach, and A-bed′–ne-go, do not ye serve my gods, nor worship the golden image which I have set up?

15 Now if ye be ready that at what time ye hear the sound of the cornet, flute, harp, sackbut, psaltery, and dulcimer, and all kinds of musick, ye fall down and worship the image which I have made; *well:* but if ye worship not, ye shall be cast the same hour into the midst of a burning fiery furnace; and who *is* that God that shall deliver you out of my hands?

16 Sha′-drach, Me′-shach, and A-bed′–ne-go, answered and said to the king, O Neb-u-chad-nez′-zar, ᴿwe *are* not careful to answer thee in this matter.　[Matt. 10:19]

17 If it be *so*, our ᴿGod whom we serve is able to ᴿdeliver us from the burning fiery furnace, and he will deliver *us* out of thine hand, O king.　6:19–22 · Mic. 7:7; 2 Cor. 1:10

18 But if not, be it known unto thee, O king, that we will not serve thy gods, nor ᴿworship the golden image which thou hast set up.　Job 13:15

19 Then was Neb-u-chad-nez′-zar full of fury, and the ᵀform of his visage was changed against Sha′-drach, Me′-shach, and A-bed′–ne-go: *therefore* he spake, and commanded that they should heat the furnace one seven times more than it was ᵀwont to be heated.　*expression on his face · usually*

20 And he commanded ᵀthe most mighty men that *were* in his army to bind Sha′-drach, Me′-shach, and A-bed′–ne-go, *and* to cast *them* into the burning fiery furnace.　*certain mighty men of valour*

21 Then these men were bound in their ᵀcoats, their ᵀhosen, and

their Thats, and their *other* garments, and were cast into the midst of the burning fiery furnace.   *mantles · leggings · turbans*

22 Therefore because the king's commandment was Turgent, and the furnace exceeding hot, the flame of the fire slew those men that took up Sha'-drach, Me'-shach, and A-bed'–ne-go. Or *severe*

23 And these three men, Sha'-drach, Me'-shach, and A-bed'–ne-go, fell down bound into the midst of the burning fiery furnace.

24 Then Neb-u-chad-nez'-zar the king was astonied, and rose up in haste, *and* spake, and said unto his Tcounsellors, Did not we cast three men bound into the midst of the fire? They answered and said unto the king, True, O king.   *high officials*

25 He answered and said, Lo, I see four men loose, walking in the midst of the fire, and they have no hurt; and the form of the fourth is like the Son of God.

26 Then Neb-u-chad-nez'-zar came near to the Tmouth of the burning fiery furnace, *and* spake, and said, Sha'-drach, Me'-shach, and A-bed'–ne-go, ye servants of the Rmost high God, come forth, and come *hither*. Then Sha'-drach, Me'-shach, and A-bed'–ne-go, came forth of the midst of the fire.   Lit. *door* · [4:2, 3, 17, 34, 35]

27 And the princes, governors, and captains, and the king's counsellors, being gathered together, saw these men, Rupon whose bodies the fire had no power, nor was an hair of their head singed, neither were their coats changed, nor the smell of fire had passed on them.   [Is. 43:2]; Heb. 11:34

28 *Then* Neb-u-chad-nez'-zar spake, and said, Blessed *be* the God of Sha'-drach, Me'-shach, and A-bed'–ne-go, who hath sent his angel, and delivered his servants that trusted in him, and have changed the king's word, and yielded their bodies, that they might not serve nor worship any god, except their own God.

29 RTherefore I make a decree, That every people, nation, and language, which speak any thing amiss against the God of Sha'-drach, Me'-shach, and A-bed'–ne-go, shall be cut in pieces, and their houses shall be made a dunghill: because there is no other God that can deliver after this sort.   6:26

30 Then the king Tpromoted Sha'-drach, Me'-shach, and A-bed'–ne-go, in the province of Babylon.   Lit. *caused to prosper*

4 Neb-u-chad-nez'-zar the king, Runto all people, nations, and languages, that dwell in all the earth; Peace be multiplied unto you.   3:4; 6:25; Ezra 4:17

2 I thought it good to shew the signs and wonders Rthat the high God hath wrought toward me. 3:26

3 How great *are* his signs! and how mighty *are* his wonders! his kingdom *is* Ran everlasting kingdom, and his dominion *is* from generation to generation. [2:44; 6:26]

4 I Neb-u-chad-nez'-zar was at rest in mine house, and Tflourishing in my palace: *prospering*

5 I saw a dream which made me afraid, Rand the thoughts upon my bed and the visions of my head Rtroubled me.   2:28, 29 · 2:1

6 Therefore made I a decree to bring in all the wise *men* of Babylon before me, that they might make known unto me the interpretation of the dream.

7 RThen came in the magicians, the astrologers, the Chal-de'-ans, and the soothsayers: and I told the dream before them; but they did not make known unto me the interpretation thereof.   2:2

8 But at the last Daniel came in before me, whose name *was* Bel-te-shaz'-zar, according to the name of my god, and in whom *is* the spirit of the holy gods: and before him I told the dream, *saying,*

9 O Bel-te-shaz'-zar, Rmaster of the magicians, because I know that the spirit of the holy gods *is* in thee, and no secret troubleth thee, tell me the visions of my

dream that I have seen, and the interpretation thereof.   2:48; 5:11

10 Thus *were* the visions of mine head in my bed; [T]I saw, and behold [R]a tree in the midst of the earth, and the height thereof *was* great.   *I was looking* · v. 20; Ezek. 31:3

11 The tree grew, and was strong, and the height thereof reached unto heaven, and [T]the sight thereof to the end of all the earth: *its visibility* extended

12 The leaves thereof *were* fair, and the fruit thereof much, and in it *was* meat for all: [R]the beasts of the field had shadow under it, and the fowls of the heaven dwelt in the boughs thereof, and all flesh was fed of it.   Jer. 27:6; Ezek. 17:23; 31:6

13 I saw in the visions of my head upon my bed, and, behold, a watcher and [R]an holy one came down from heaven;   Ps. 89:7; Jude 14

14 He cried aloud, and said thus, [R]Hew down the tree, and cut off his branches, shake off his leaves, and scatter his fruit: let the beasts get away from under it, and the fowls from his branches: [Matt. 3:10]

15 Nevertheless leave the stump of his roots in the earth, even with a band of iron and brass, in the tender grass of the field; and let it be wet with the dew of heaven, and *let* his portion *be* with the beasts in the grass of the earth:

16 Let his heart be changed from man's, and let a beast's heart be given unto him; and let seven [R]times pass over him.   11:13; 12:7

17 This matter *is* by the decree of the watchers, and the demand by the word of the holy ones: to the intent [R]that the living may know [R]that the most High ruleth in the kingdom of men, and [R]giveth it to whomsoever he will, and setteth up over it the basest of men.   Ps. 9:16; 83:18 · 2:21; 5:21 · 2:37; 5:18

18 This dream I king Neb-u-chad-nez'-zar have seen. Now thou, O Bel-te-shaz'-zar, declare the interpretation thereof, forasmuch as all the wise *men* of my kingdom are not able to make known unto me the interpreta-

tion: but thou *art* able; for the spirit of the holy gods *is* in thee.

19 Then Daniel, whose name *was* Bel-te-shaz'-zar, was astonied for one hour, and his thoughts [R]troubled him. The king spake, and said, Bel-te-shaz'-zar, let not the dream, or the interpretation thereof, trouble thee. Bel-te-shaz'-zar answered and said, My lord, [R]the dream *be* to them that hate thee, and the interpretation thereof to thine enemies.   8:27 · 10:16

20 [R]The tree that thou sawest, which grew, and was strong, whose height reached unto the heaven, and the sight thereof to all the earth;   vv. 10–12

21 Whose leaves *were* fair, and the fruit thereof much, and in it *was* [T]meat for all; under which the beasts of the field dwelt, and upon whose branches the fowls of the heaven had their habitation: *food*

22 It *is* thou, O king, that art grown and become strong: for thy greatness is grown, and reacheth unto heaven, [R]and thy dominion to the end of the earth.   Jer. 27:6–8

23 And whereas the king saw a watcher and an holy one coming down from heaven, and saying, Hew the tree down, and destroy it; yet leave the stump of the roots thereof in the earth, even with a band of iron and brass, in the tender grass of the field; and let it be wet with the dew of heaven, [R]and *let* his portion *be* with the beasts of the field, till seven [T]times pass over him;   5:21 · Lit. *seasons*, years

24 This *is* the interpretation, O king, and this *is* the decree of the most High, which is come upon my lord the king:

25 That they shall drive thee from men, and thy dwelling shall be with the beasts of the field, and they shall make thee to eat grass as oxen, and they shall wet thee with the dew of heaven, and seven times shall pass over thee, till thou know that the most High ruleth in the kingdom of men, and giveth it to whomsoever he will.

26 And whereas they commanded to leave the stump of the tree
roots; thy kingdom shall be ᵀsure
unto thee, after that thou shalt
have known that the ᴿheavens do
rule.   assured · Matt. 21:25; Luke 15:18

27 Wherefore, O king, let my
counsel be acceptable unto thee,
and ᴿbreak off thy sins by righteousness, and thine iniquities by
shewing mercy to the poor; if it
may be a lengthening of thy tran-
quillity.   Is. 55:7; [Rom. 2:9–11; 1 Pet. 4:8]

28 All this came upon the king
Neb-u-chad-nez′-zar.

29 At the end of twelve months
he walked ᵀin the palace of the
kingdom of Babylon.   about

30 The king ᴿspake, and said, Is
not this great Babylon, that I have
built for the house of the kingdom
by the might of my power, and for
the honour of my majesty?   5:20

31 ᴿWhile the word *was* in the
king's mouth, there fell a voice
from heaven, *saying*, O king Neb-
u-chad-nez′-zar, to thee it is spoken; The kingdom is departed
from thee.   5:5; Luke 12:20

32 And they shall drive thee
from men, and thy dwelling *shall
be* with the beasts of the field:
they shall make thee to eat grass
as oxen, and seven times shall
pass over thee, until thou know
that the most High ruleth in the
kingdom of men, and giveth it to
whomsoever he will.

33 The same hour was the thing
fulfilled upon Neb-u-chad-nez′-
zar: and he was driven from men,
and did eat grass as oxen, and his
body was wet with the dew of
heaven, till his hairs were grown
like eagles' *feathers*, and his nails
like birds' *claws*.

34 And at the end of the days I
Neb-u-chad-nez′-zar lifted up
mine eyes unto heaven, and mine
understanding returned unto me,
and I blessed the most High, and I
praised and honoured him ᴿthat
liveth for ever, whose dominion *is*
ᴿan everlasting dominion, and his
kingdom *is* from generation to
generation: [Rev. 4:10] · 7:14; [Luke 1:33]

35 And all the inhabitants of the
earth *are* reputed as nothing: and
he doeth according to his will in
the army of heaven, and *among*
the inhabitants of the earth: and
ᴿnone can stay his hand, or say
unto him, What doest thou?   6:27

36 At the same time my reason
returned unto me; and for the
glory of my kingdom, mine honour and brightness returned unto
me; and my counsellors and my
lords sought unto me; and I was
ᴿestablished in my kingdom, and
excellent majesty was ᴿadded
unto me.   2 Chr. 20:20 · [Matt. 6:33]

37 Now I Neb-u-chad-nez′-zar
ᴿpraise and extol and honour the
King of heaven, ᴿall whose works
are truth, and his ways judgment:
ᴿand those that walk in pride he is
able to abase. 2:46, 47 · [Rev. 15:3] · 5:20

5 Bel-shaz′-zar the king ᴿmade
a great feast to a thousand of
his lords, and drank wine before
the thousand.   Esth. 1:3; Is. 22:12–14

2 Bel-shaz′-zar, whiles he tasted the wine, commanded to bring
the golden and silver vessels
ᴿwhich his father Neb-u-chad-
nez′-zar had taken out of the temple which *was* in Jerusalem; that
the king, and his princes, his
wives, and his concubines, might
drink therein.   2 Kin. 24:13; 25:15

3 Then they brought the golden
vessels that were taken out of the
temple of the house of God which
was at Jerusalem; and the king,
and his princes, his wives, and his
concubines, drank in them.

4 They drank wine, ᴿand
praised the gods of gold, and of
silver, of ᵀbrass, of iron, of wood,
and of stone. Is. 42:8; Rev. 9:20 · *bronze*

5 ᴿIn the same hour came forth
fingers of a man's hand, and
wrote ᵀover against the candlestick upon the plaister of the wall
of the king's palace: and the king
saw the part of the hand that
wrote.   4:31 · *opposite the lampstand*

6 Then the king's countenance
was changed, and his thoughts
troubled him, so that the joints of
his ᵀloins were loosed, and his

Rknees Tsmote one against another. *hips* · 4:6 · *knocked*

7 RThe king cried aloud to
bring in the astrologers, the Chal-
de'-ans, and the soothsayers. *And*
the king spake, and said to the
wise *men* of Babylon, Whosoever
shall read this writing, and shew
me the interpretation thereof,
shall be clothed with scarlet, and
have a chain of gold about his
neck, and shall be the third ruler
in the kingdom. 4:6, 7

8 Then came in all the king's
wise *men:* Rbut they could not
read the writing, nor make known
to the king the interpretation
thereof. Gen. 41:8

9 Then was king Bel-shaz'-zar
greatly troubled, and his countenance was changed in him, and
his lords were Tastonied. *perplexed*

10 *Now* the queen by reason of
the words of the king and his
lords came into the banquet
house: *and* the queen spake and
said, O king, live for ever: let not
thy thoughts trouble thee, nor let
thy countenance be changed:

11 RThere is a man in thy kingdom, in whom *is* the spirit of the
holy gods; and in the days of thy
father light and understanding
and wisdom, like the wisdom of
the gods, was found in him; whom
the king Neb-u-chad-nez'-zar thy
father, the king, *I say,* thy father,
made master of the magicians,
astrologers, Chal-de'-ans, *and*
soothsayers; 2:48; 4:8, 9, 18

12 Forasmuch as an excellent
spirit, and knowledge, and understanding, interpreting of dreams,
and shewing of hard sentences,
and dissolving of doubts, were
found in the same Daniel, Rwhom
the king named Bel-te-shaz'-zar:
now let Daniel be called, and he
will shew the interpretation. 1:7; 4:8

13 Then was Daniel brought in
before the king. *And* the king
spake and said unto Daniel, *Art*
thou that Daniel, which *art* of the
children of the captivity of Judah, whom the king my Tfather
brought out of Jewry? Or *forefather*

14 I have even heard of thee,
that Rthe Tspirit of the gods *is* in
thee, and *that* light and understanding and excellent wisdom is
found in thee. 4:8, 9, 18 · *Spirit of God*

15 And now the wise *men,* the
astrologers, have been brought in
before me, that they should read
this writing, and make known
unto me the interpretation thereof: but they could not shew the
interpretation of the thing:

16 And I have heard of thee, that
thou canst make interpretations,
and dissolve doubts: now if thou
canst read the writing, and make
known to me the interpretation
thereof, thou shalt be clothed with
Tscarlet, and *have* a chain of gold
about thy neck, and shalt be the
third ruler in the kingdom. *purple*

17 Then Daniel answered and
said before the king, Let thy gifts
be to thyself, and give thy rewards
to another; yet I will read the writing unto the king, and make
known to him the interpretation.

18 O thou king, Rthe most high
God gave Neb-u-chad-nez'-zar
thy father a kingdom, and majesty, and glory, and honour: 2:37, 38

19 And for the majesty that he
gave him, Rall people, nations, and
languages, trembled and feared
before him: whom he would he
Rslew; and whom he would he
kept alive; and whom he would he
set up; and whom he would he put
down. Jer. 27:7 · 2:12, 13; 3:6

20 RBut when his heart was lifted up, and his mind hardened in
pride, he was deposed from his
kingly throne, and they took his
glory from him: Ex. 9:17; Job 15:25

21 And he was Rdriven from the
sons of men; and his heart was
made like the beasts, and his
dwelling *was* with the wild asses:
they fed him with grass like oxen,
and his body was wet with the
dew of heaven; Rtill he knew that
the most high God ruled in the
kingdom of men, and *that* he
appointeth over it whomsoever he
will. 4:32, 33 · Ps. 83:17, 18; Ezek. 17:24

22 And thou his son, O Bel-

shaz'-zar, ^Rhast not humbled thine heart, though thou knewest all this;   Ex. 10:3; 2 Chr. 33:23; 36:12

23 But hast lifted up thyself against the Lord of heaven; and they have brought the vessels of his house before thee, and thou, and thy lords, thy wives, and thy concubines, have drunk wine in them; and thou hast praised the gods of silver, and gold, of brass, iron, wood, and stone, ^Rwhich see not, nor hear, nor know: and the God in whose hand thy breath *is*, and whose *are* all thy ways, hast thou not glorified: Rom. 1:21

24 Then was the ^Tpart of the hand sent from him; and this writing was written.   Lit. *palm*, fingers

25 And this *is* the writing that was written, ME′-NE, ME′-NE, TE′-KEL, U-PHAR′-SIN.

26 This *is* the interpretation of ^Tthe thing: ME′-NE; God hath numbered thy kingdom, and finished it.   each *word*

27 TE′-KEL; ^RThou art weighed in the balances, and art found wanting.   Job 31:6; Ps. 62:9; Jer. 6:30

28 PE′-RES; Thy kingdom is divided, and given to the ^RMedes and ^RPersians.   9:1 · 6:28; Acts 2:9

29 Then commanded Bel-shaz'-zar, and they clothed Daniel with ^Tscarlet, and *put* a chain of gold about his neck, and made a proclamation concerning him, ^Rthat he should be the third ruler in the kingdom.   *purple* · vv. 7, 16

30 ^RIn that night was Bel-shaz'-zar the king of the Chal-de'-ans slain.   Jer. 51:31, 39, 57

31 ^RAnd Da-ri'-us the Me'-di-an took the kingdom, *being* about threescore and two years old.   2:39

6 It pleased Da-ri'-us to set over the kingdom an hundred and twenty princes, which should be over the whole kingdom;

2 And over these three presidents; of whom Daniel *was* first: that the princes might give accounts unto them, and the king should have no ^Tdamage.   *loss*

3 Then this Daniel ^Twas preferred above the presidents and princes, ^Rbecause an excellent spirit *was* in him; and the king thought to set him over the whole realm.   *distinguished himself* · 5:12

4 ^RThen the presidents and princes sought to find ^Toccasion against Daniel concerning the kingdom; but they could find ^Tnone occasion nor fault; forasmuch as he *was* faithful, neither was there any error or fault found in him.   Eccl. 4:4 · some *charge* · *no charge*

5 Then said these men, We shall not find any occasion against this Daniel, except we find *it* against him concerning the law of his God.

6 Then these presidents and princes assembled together to the king, and said thus unto him, ^RKing Da-ri'-us, live for ever.   v. 21

7 All the presidents of the kingdom, the governors, and the princes, the counsellors, and the captains, have ^Rconsulted together to establish a royal statute, and to make a firm decree, that whosoever shall ask a petition of any God or man for thirty days, save of thee, O king, he shall be cast into the den of lions.   Ps. 59:3

8 Now, O king, establish the decree, and sign the writing, that it be not changed, according to the ^Rlaw of the Medes and Persians, which altereth not.   vv. 12, 15

9 Wherefore king Da-ri'-us signed the ^Twriting and the decree.   *written decree*

10 Now when Daniel knew that the writing was signed, he went into his house; and his windows being open in his chamber toward Jerusalem, he kneeled upon his knees three times a day, and prayed, and gave thanks before his God, as he did aforetime.

11 Then these men assembled, and found Daniel praying and making supplication before his God.

12 ^RThen they came near, and spake before the king concerning the king's decree; Hast thou not signed a decree, that every man that shall ask *a petition* of any

God or man within thirty days, save of thee, O king, shall be cast into the den of lions? The king answered and said, The thing *is* true, ^Raccording to the law of the Medes and Persians, which altereth not.   3:8–12; Acts 16:19–21 · Esth. 1:19

13 Then answered they and said before the king, That Daniel, which *is* of the children of the captivity of Judah, ^Rregardeth not thee, O king, nor the decree that thou hast signed, but maketh his petition three times a day. Acts 5:29

14 Then the king, when he heard *these* words, was sore displeased with himself, and set *his* heart on Daniel to deliver him: and he laboured till the going down of the sun to deliver him.

15 Then these men assembled unto the king, and said unto the king, Know, O king, that ^Rthe law of the Medes and Persians *is*, That no decree nor statute which the king establisheth may be changed. vv. 8, 12; Esth. 8:8; Ps. 94:20, 21

16 Then the king commanded, and they brought Daniel, and cast *him* into the den of lions. *Now* the king spake and said unto Daniel, Thy God whom thou servest continually, he will deliver thee.

17 ^RAnd a stone was brought, and laid upon the mouth of the den; ^Rand the king sealed it with his own signet, and with the signet of his lords; that the purpose might not be changed concerning Daniel. Lam. 3:53 · Matt. 27:66

18 Then the king went to his palace, and passed the night fasting: neither were instruments of musick brought before him: ^Rand his sleep went from him. Ps. 77:4

19 Then the ^Rking arose very early in the morning, and went in haste unto the den of lions. 3:24

20 And when he came to the den, he cried with a lamentable voice unto Daniel: *and* the king spake and said to Daniel, O Daniel, servant of the living God, ^Ris thy God, whom thou servest continually, able to deliver thee from the lions? Jer. 32:17; [Luke 1:37]

21 Then said Daniel unto the king, ^RO king, live for ever. v. 6; 2:4

22 My God hath sent his angel, and hath shut the lions' mouths, that they have not hurt me: forasmuch as before him innocency was found in me; and also before thee, O king, have I done no hurt.

23 Then was the king exceeding glad for him, and commanded that they should take Daniel up out of the den. So Daniel was taken up out of the den, and no manner of hurt was found upon him, ^Rbecause he believed in his God. Heb. 11:33

24 And the king commanded, and they brought those men which had accused Daniel, and they cast *them* into the den of lions, them, their children, and their wives; and the lions had the mastery of them, and brake all their bones in pieces or ever they came at the bottom of the den.

25 Then king Da-ri'-us wrote unto all people, nations, and languages, that dwell in all the earth; Peace be multiplied unto you.

26 I make a decree, That in every dominion of my kingdom men tremble and fear before the God of Daniel: ^Rfor he *is* the living God, and stedfast for ever, and his kingdom *that* which shall not be destroyed, and his dominion *shall be even* unto the end. 4:34; Rom. 9:26

27 He delivereth and rescueth, and he worketh signs and wonders in heaven and in earth, who hath delivered Daniel from the ^Tpower of the lions. *paw,* lit. *hand*

28 So this Daniel prospered in the reign of Da-ri'-us, and in the reign of Cyrus the Persian.

7 In the first year of Bel-shaz'-zar king of Babylon ^RDaniel had a dream and ^Rvisions of his head upon his bed: then he wrote the dream, *and* told the sum of the matters. Num. 12:6; [Amos 3:7] · [2:28]

2 Daniel spake and said, I saw in my vision by night, and, behold, the four winds of the heaven strove upon the great sea.

3 And four great beasts ^Rcame

up from the sea, diverse one from another. v. 17; Rev. 13:1; 17:8

4 The first was ᴿlike a lion, and had eagle's wings: I beheld till the wings thereof were plucked, and it was lifted up from the earth, and made stand upon the feet as a man, and a ᴿman's heart was given to it. Ezek. 17:3; Hab. 1:8 · 4:16, 34

5 ᴿAnd behold another beast, a second, like to a bear, and ᵀit raised up itself on one side, and it had three ribs in the mouth of it between the teeth of it: and they said thus unto it, Arise, devour much flesh. 2:39 · it was raised up

6 After this I beheld, and lo another, like a leopard, which had upon the back of it four wings of a fowl; the beast had also ᴿfour heads; and dominion was given to it. 8:8, 22

7 After this I saw in the night visions, and behold ᴿa fourth beast, dreadful and terrible, and strong exceedingly; and it had great iron teeth: it devoured and brake in pieces, and stamped the residue with the feet of it: and it was diverse from all the beasts that were before it; ᴿand it had ten horns. 2:40 · 2:41; Rev. 12:3; 13:1

8 I considered the horns, and, behold, ᴿthere came up among them another little horn, before whom there were three of the first horns plucked up by the roots: and, behold, in this horn were eyes like the eyes of man, and a mouth speaking great things. 8:9

9 I beheld till the thrones were cast down, and the Ancient of days did sit, whose garment was white as snow, and the hair of his head like the pure wool: his throne was like the fiery flame, and his wheels as burning fire.

10 ᴿA fiery stream issued and came forth from before him: thousand thousands ministered unto him, and ten thousand times ten thousand stood before him: the judgment was set, and the books were opened. Ps. 50:3; Is. 30:33; 66:15

11 I beheld then because of the voice of the great words which the horn spake: ᴿI beheld even till the beast was slain, and his body destroyed, and given to the burning flame. [Rev. 19:20; 20:10]

12 As concerning the rest of the beasts, they had their dominion taken away: yet their lives were prolonged for a season and time.

13 I saw in the night visions, ☆ and, behold, ᴿone like the Son of man came with the clouds of heaven, and came to the Ancient of days, and they brought him near before him. [Matt. 24:30]

14 ᴿAnd there was given him do- ☆ minion, and glory, and a kingdom, that all people, nations, and languages, should serve him: his dominion is an everlasting dominion, which shall not pass away, and his kingdom that which shall not be destroyed. [Matt. 28:18]

15 I Daniel was grieved in my spirit in the midst of ᵀmy body, and the visions of my head troubled me. Lit. its sheath

16 I came near unto one of them that stood by, and asked him the truth of all this. So he told me, and ᵀmade me know the interpretation of the things. made known to me

17 These great beasts, which are four, are four kings, which shall arise out of the earth.

18 But ᴿthe saints of the most High shall take the kingdom, and possess the kingdom for ever, even for ever and ever. Is. 60:12–14

19 Then I would know the truth of the fourth beast, which was ᵀdiverse from all the others, exceeding dreadful, whose teeth were of iron, and his nails of brass; which devoured, brake in pieces, and ᵀstamped the residue with his feet; different · trampled

20 And of the ten horns that were in his head, and of the other which came up, and before whom three fell; even of that horn that had eyes, and a mouth that spake very great things, whose look was more stout than his fellows.

21 I beheld, ᴿand the same horn made war with the saints, and prevailed against them; Rev. 11:7

22 Until the Ancient of days came, ^Rand judgment was given to the saints of the most High; and the time came that the saints possessed the kingdom. [Rev. 1:6]

23 Thus he said, The fourth beast shall be ^Rthe fourth kingdom upon earth, which shall be ^Tdiverse from all kingdoms, and shall devour the whole earth, and shall ^Ttread it down, and break it in pieces. 2:40 · *different* · *trample*

24 ^RAnd the ten horns out of this kingdom *are* ten kings *that* shall arise: and another shall rise after them; and he shall be ^Tdiverse from the first, and he shall subdue three kings. Rev. 13:1; 17:12 · *different*

25 ^RAnd he shall speak *great* words against the most High, and shall wear out the saints of the most High, and think to change times and laws: and they shall be given into his hand ^Runtil a time and times and the dividing of time. 11:36; Rev. 13:1–6 · 12:7; Rev. 12:14

26 ^RBut the judgment shall sit, and they shall take away his dominion, to consume and to destroy *it* unto the end. [2:35]

27 And the ^Rkingdom and dominion, and the greatness of the kingdom under the whole heaven, shall be given to the people of the saints of the most High, whose kingdom *is* an everlasting kingdom, and all dominions shall serve and obey him. Is. 54:3; Rev. 20:4

28 Hitherto *is* the end of the matter. As for me Daniel, ^Rmy ^Tcogitations much troubled me, and my countenance changed in me: but I ^Rkept the matter in my heart. 8:27 · *thoughts* · Luke 2:19, 51

8 In the third year of the reign of king Bel-shaz'-zar a vision appeared unto me, *even unto* me Daniel, after that which appeared unto me ^Rat the first. 7:1

2 And I saw in a vision; and it came to pass, when I saw, that I *was* at ^RShu'-shan *in* the palace, which *is* in the province of E'-lam; and I saw in a vision, and I was by the river of U'-lai. Neh. 1:1; Esth. 1:2

3 Then I lifted up mine eyes, and saw, and, behold, there stood before the river a ram which had *two* horns: and the *two* horns *were* high; but one *was* ^Rhigher than the other, and the higher came up last. 7:5

4 I saw the ram pushing westward, and northward, and southward; so that no beasts might stand before him, neither *was there any* that could deliver out of his hand; ^Rbut he did according to his will, and became great. 5:19

5 And as I was considering, behold, an he goat came from the west on the face of the whole earth, and touched not the ground: and the goat *had* a notable ^Rhorn between his eyes. vv. 8, 21

6 And he came to the ram that had *two* horns, which I had seen standing before the river, and ran unto him in the fury of his power.

7 And I saw him come close unto the ram, and he was moved with ^Tcholer against him, and ^Tsmote the ram, and brake his two horns: and there was no power in the ram to stand before him, but he cast him down to the ground, and stamped upon him: and there was none that could deliver the ram out of his hand. *rage* · *attacked*

8 Therefore the he goat waxed very great: and when he was strong, the great horn was broken; and for it came up ^Rfour notable ones toward the four winds of heaven. v. 22; 7:6; 11:4

9 And out of one of them came forth a little horn, which waxed exceeding great, toward the south, and toward the east, and toward the ^Rpleasant *land.* Ps. 48:2

10 And it waxed great, *even* to ^Rthe host of heaven; and ^Rit cast down *some* of the host and of the stars to the ground, and stamped upon them. Is. 14:13; Jer. 48:26 · Rev. 12:4

11 Yea, ^Rhe magnified *himself* even to the prince of the host, and by him the daily *sacrifice* was taken away, and the place of his sanctuary was cast down. Is. 37:23

12 And an host was given *him* against the daily *sacrifice* by rea-

son of transgression, and it cast down the truth to the ground; and it ᴿpractised, and prospered. 11:36

13 Then I heard ᴿone ᵀsaint speaking, and another saint said unto that certain *saint* which spake, How long *shall be* the vision *concerning* the daily *sacrifice*, and the transgression of desolation, to give both the sanctuary and the host to be trodden under foot? 4:13, 23; 1 Pet. 1:12 · *holy one*

14 And he said unto me, Unto two thousand and three hundred ᵀdays; then shall the sanctuary be cleansed. Lit. *evening-mornings*

15 And it came to pass, when I, *even* I Daniel, had seen the vision, and sought for the meaning, then, behold, there stood before me as the appearance of a man.

16 And I heard a man's voice ᴿbetween *the banks of* U'-lai, which called, and said, ᴿGabriel, make this *man* to understand the vision. 12:6, 7 · 9:21; Luke 1:19, 26

17 So he came near where I stood: and when he came, I was afraid, and ᴿfell upon my face: but he said unto me, Understand, O son of man: for at the time of the end *shall be* the vision. Rev. 1:17

18 ᴿNow as he was speaking with me, I was in a deep sleep ᵀon my face toward the ground: ᴿbut he touched me, and set me upright. 10:9; Luke 9:32 · *with* · Ezek. 2:2

19 And he said, Behold, I will ᵀmake thee know what shall be in the ᵀlast end of the indignation: ᴿfor at the time appointed the end *shall be*. *let* · *latter time* · Hab. 2:3

20 The ram which thou sawest having *two* horns *are* the kings of Me'-di-a and Persia.

21 And the rough goat *is* the king of ᵀGre'-ci-a: and the great horn that *is* between his eyes ᴿ*is* the first king. Or *Greece* · 11:3

22 Now that being broken, whereas four stood up for it, four kingdoms shall stand up out of the nation, but not in his power.

23 And in the latter time of their kingdom, when the transgressors are come to the full, a king ᴿof

fierce countenance, and understanding ᵀdark sentences, shall stand up. Deut. 28:50 · *riddles*

24 And his power shall be mighty, ᴿbut not by his own power: and he shall destroy wonderfully, ᴿand shall prosper, and practise, ᴿand shall destroy the mighty and the holy people. Rev. 17:13 · 11:36 · 7:25

25 And ᴿthrough his policy also he shall cause craft to prosper in his hand; ᴿand he shall magnify *himself* in his heart, and by peace shall destroy many: ᴿhe shall also stand up against the Prince of princes; but he shall be broken without hand. 11:21 · 12:7 · 11:36

26 And the vision of the evening and the morning which was told *is* true: ᴿwherefore shut thou up the vision; for it *shall be* for many days. 12:4, 9; Ezek. 12:27; Rev. 22:10

27 And I Daniel fainted, and was sick *certain* days; afterward I rose up, and did the king's business; and I was astonished at the vision, but none understood *it*.

9 In the first year ᴿof Da-ri'-us the son of A-has-u-e'-rus, of the seed of the Medes, which was made king over the realm of the Chal-de'-ans; 1:21

2 In the first year of his reign I Daniel understood by books the number of the years, whereof the word of the Lᴏʀᴅ came to ᴿJer-e-mi'-ah the prophet, that he would accomplish seventy years in the desolations of Jerusalem. Jer. 29:10

3 ᴿAnd I set my face unto the Lord God, to seek by prayer and supplications, with fasting, and sackcloth, and ashes: 6:10; 10:15

4 And I prayed unto the Lᴏʀᴅ my God, and made my confession, and said, O ᴿLord, the great and ᵀdreadful God, keeping the covenant and mercy to them that love him, and to them that keep his commandments; Ex. 20:6 · *awesome*

5 We have sinned, and have committed iniquity, and have done wickedly, and have rebelled, even by departing from thy precepts and from thy judgments:

6 ᴿNeither have we hearkened

unto thy servants the prophets, which spake in thy name to our kings, our princes, and our fathers, and to all the people of the land.   2 Chr. 36:15; Jer. 44:4, 5

7 O Lord, ᴿrighteousness *belongeth* unto thee, but unto us ᵀconfusion of faces, as at this day; to the men of Judah, and to the inhabitants of Jerusalem, and unto all Israel, *that are* near, and *that are* far off, through all the countries whither thou hast driven them, because of their trespass that they have trespassed against thee.   Neh. 9:33 · *shame*

8 O Lord, to us *belongeth* ᵀconfusion of face, to our kings, to our princes, and to our fathers, because we have sinned against thee.   *shame*

9 ᴿTo the Lord our God *belong* mercies and forgivenesses, though we have rebelled against him;   [Neh. 9:17; Ps. 130:4, 7]

10 Neither have we obeyed the voice of the LORD our God, to walk in his laws, which he set before us by his servants the prophets.

11 Yea, ᴿall Israel have transgressed thy law, even by departing, that they might not obey thy voice; therefore the curse is poured upon us, and the oath that *is* written in the ᴿlaw of Moses the servant of God, because we have sinned against him.   Jer. 8:5–10

12 And he hath confirmed his words, which he spake against us, and against our judges that judged us, by bringing upon us a great evil: for under the whole heaven hath not been done as hath been done upon Jerusalem.

13 As *it is* written in the law of Moses, all this evil is come upon us: yet made we not our prayer before the LORD our God, that we might turn from our iniquities, and understand thy truth.

14 Therefore hath the LORD watched upon the evil, and brought it upon us: for ᴿthe LORD our God *is* righteous in all his works which he doeth: for we obeyed not his voice.   Neh. 9:33

15 And now, O Lord our God, ᴿthat hast brought thy people forth out of the land of Egypt with a mighty hand, and hast gotten thee ᴿrenown, as at this day; we have sinned, we have done wickedly.   Ex. 32:11; 1 Kin. 8:51 · Ex. 14:18

16 O Lord, according to all thy righteousness, I beseech thee, let thine anger and thy fury be turned away from thy city Jerusalem, thy holy mountain: because for our sins, and for the iniquities of our fathers, Jerusalem and thy people *are become* a reproach to all *that are* about us.

17 Now therefore, O our God, hear the prayer of thy servant, and his supplications, ᴿand cause thy face to shine upon thy sanctuary ᴿthat is desolate, for the Lord's sake.   Num. 6:24–26 · [John 16:24]

18 ᴿO my God, incline thine ear, and hear; open thine eyes, ᴿand behold our desolations, and the city ᴿwhich is called by thy name: for we do not present our supplications before thee for our righteousnesses, but for thy great mercies.   Is. 37:17 · Ex. 3:7 · Jer. 25:29

19 O Lord, hear; O Lord, forgive; O Lord, hearken and do; ᵀdefer not, for thine own sake, O my God: for thy city and thy people are called by thy name.   *delay*

20 And whiles I *was* speaking, and praying, and confessing my sin and the sin of my people Israel, and presenting my supplication before the LORD my God for the holy mountain of my God;

21 Yea, whiles I *was* speaking in prayer, even the man ᴿGabriel, whom I had seen in the vision at the beginning, being caused to fly swiftly, touched me about the time of the evening oblation.   Luke 1:19

22 And he informed *me,* and talked with me, and said, O Daniel, I am now come forth to give thee skill and understanding.

23 At the beginning of thy supplications the commandment came forth, and I am come to shew *thee;* for thou *art* greatly ᴿbeloved: therefore ᴿunderstand

the matter, and consider the vision. 10:11, 19 · Matt. 24:15

24 Seventy weeks are determined upon thy people and upon thy holy city, to finish the transgression, and to make an end of sins, and to make reconciliation for iniquity, ᴿand to bring in everlasting righteousness, and to seal up the vision and prophecy, and to anoint the most Holy. Rev. 14:6

☆ 25 Know therefore and understand, *that* from the going forth of the commandment to restore and to build Jerusalem unto ᴿthe Messi'-ah the Prince *shall be* seven ᵀweeks, and threescore and two weeks: the street shall be built again, and the wall, even in troublous times. Luke 2:1, 2 · Lit. *sevens*

☆ 26 And after threescore and two weeks ᴿshall Mes-si'-ah be cut off, but not for himself: and the people of the prince that shall come shall destroy the city and the sanctuary; and the end thereof *shall be* with a flood, and unto the end of the war desolations are determined. Matt. 27:50; John 19:30

27 And he shall confirm ᴿthe covenant with many for one week: and in the midst of the week he shall cause the sacrifice and the oblation to cease, and for the overspreading of abominations he shall make *it* desolate, even until the consummation, and that determined shall be poured upon the desolate. Is. 42:6

10 In the third year of Cyrus king of Persia a thing was revealed unto Daniel, whose ᴿname was called Bel-te-shaz'-zar; and the thing *was* true, but the time appointed *was* long: and he understood the thing, and had understanding of the vision. 1:7

2 In those days I Daniel was mourning three full weeks.

3 I ate no ᵀpleasant bread, neither came flesh nor wine in my mouth, neither did I anoint myself at all, till three whole weeks were fulfilled. *desirable food*

4 And in the four and twentieth day of the first month, as I was by

the side of the great river, which *is* ᵀHid'-de-kel; The Tigris

5 Then I lifted up mine eyes, and looked, and behold a certain man clothed in ᴿlinen, whose loins *were* ᴿgirded with fine gold of U'-phaz: Ezek. 9:2; 10:2 · Rev. 1:13

6 His body also *was* like the beryl, and his face as the appearance of lightning, and his eyes as lamps of fire, and his arms and his feet like in colour to polished brass, and the voice of his words like the voice of a multitude.

7 And I Daniel alone saw the vision: for the men that were with me saw not the vision; but a great ᵀquaking fell upon them, so that they fled to hide themselves. *terror*

8 Therefore I was left alone, and saw this great vision, and there remained no strength in me: for my ᵀcomeliness was turned in me into ᵀcorruption, and I retained no strength. *vigour · frailty*

9 Yet heard I the ᵀvoice of his words: and when I heard the voice of his words, then was I in a deep sleep on my face, and my face toward the ground. *sound*

10 ᴿAnd, behold, an hand touched me, which set me ᵀupon my knees and *upon* the palms of my hands. 9:21 · *trembling upon*

11 And he said unto me, O Daniel, ᴿa man greatly beloved, understand the words that I speak unto thee, and stand upright: for unto thee am I now sent. And when he had spoken this word unto me, I stood trembling. 9:23

12 Then said he unto me, ᴿFear not, Daniel: for from the first day that thou didst set thine heart to understand, and to ᵀchasten thyself before thy God, ᴿthy words were heard, and I am come for thy words. Rev. 1:17 · *humble* · Acts 10:4

13 But the prince of the kingdom of Persia withstood me one and twenty days: but, lo, ᴿMi'-cha-el, one of the chief princes, came to help me; and I remained there with the kings of Persia. Jude 9

14 Now I am come to make thee understand what shall befall thy

people ᴿin the latter days: for yet the vision *is* for *many* days.   2:28

15 And when he had spoken such words unto me, ᴿI set my face toward the ground, and I became ᵀdumb.   v. 9; 8:18 · *speechless*

16 And, behold, ᴿone like the similitude of the sons of men ᴿtouched my lips: then I opened my mouth, and spake, and said unto him that stood before me, O my lord, by the vision my sorrows are turned upon me, and I have retained no strength.   8:15 · Jer. 1:9

17 For how can the servant of this my lord talk with this my lord? for as for me, straightway there remained no strength in me, neither is there breath left in me.

18 Then there came again and touched me *one* like the appearance of a man, and he strengthened me,

19 ᴿAnd said, O man greatly beloved, ᴿfear not: peace *be* unto thee, be strong, yea, be strong. And when he had spoken unto me, I was strengthened, and said, Let my lord speak; for thou hast strengthened me.   v. 11 · Judg. 6:23

20 Then said he, Knowest thou wherefore I come unto thee? and now will I return to fight ᴿwith the prince of Persia: and when I am gone forth, lo, the prince of ᵀGre'-ci-a shall come.   v. 13 · Or *Greece*

21 But I will shew thee that which is noted in the scripture of truth: and *there is* none that holdeth with me in these things, ᴿbut Mi'-cha-el your prince.   v. 13; Jude 9

11 Also I ᴿin the first year of ᴿDa-ri'-us the Mede, *even* I, stood to confirm and to strengthen him.   9:1 · 5:31

2 And now will I shew thee the truth. Behold, there shall stand up yet three kings in Persia; and the fourth shall be far richer than *they* all: and by his strength through his riches he shall stir up all against the realm of Gre'-ci-a.

3 And ᴿa mighty king shall stand up, that shall rule with great dominion, and ᴿdo according to his will.   7:6; 8:5 · 8:4; 10:16, 36

4 And when he shall stand up, ᴿhis kingdom shall be broken, and shall be divided toward the four winds of heaven; and not to his posterity, nor according to his dominion which he ruled: for his kingdom shall be plucked up, even for others beside those.   7:2

5 And the king of the south shall be strong, ᵀand *one* of his princes; and he shall be strong above him, and have dominion; his dominion *shall be* a great dominion.   *as well as*

6 And in the end of years they shall join themselves together; for the king's daughter of the south shall come to the king of the north to make an agreement: but she shall not retain the power of the arm; neither shall he stand, nor his arm: but she shall be given up, and they that brought her, and he that begat her, and he that strengthened her in *these* times.

7 But out of a branch of her roots shall *one* stand up ᵀin his estate, which shall come with an army, and shall enter into the fortress of the king of the north, and shall deal against them, and shall prevail: *in his place*

8 And shall also carry captives into Egypt their gods, with their princes, *and* with their precious ᵀvessels of silver and of gold; and he shall continue *more* years than the king of the north.   *articles*

9 So the king of the south shall come into *his* kingdom, and shall return into his own land.

10 But his sons shall be stirred up, and shall assemble a multitude of great forces: and *one* shall certainly come, ᴿand overflow, and pass through: then shall he return, and be stirred up, *even* to his fortress.   Is. 8:8; Jer. 46:7, 8; 51:42

11 And the king of the south shall be moved with ᵀcholer, and shall come forth and fight with him, *even* with the king of the north: and he shall set forth a great multitude; but the multitude shall be given into his hand.   *rage*

12 *And* when he hath taken

away the multitude, his heart shall be ^Tlifted up; and he shall cast down *many* ten thousands: but he shall not be strengthened *by it.* Proud

13 For the king of the north shall return, and shall set forth a multitude greater than the former, and shall certainly come after certain years with a great army and with much ^Triches. *equipment*

14 And in those times there shall many stand up against the king of the south: also the robbers of thy people shall exalt themselves to establish the vision; but they shall ^Rfall. Job 9:13

15 So the king of the north shall come, and ^Rcast up a mount, and take the most fenced cities: and the arms of the south shall not withstand, neither his chosen people, neither *shall there be any* strength to withstand. Jer. 6:6

16 But he that cometh against him shall do according to his own will, and ^Rnone shall stand before him: and he shall stand in the glorious land, which by his hand shall be consumed. Josh. 1:5

17 He shall also ^Rset his face to enter with the strength of his whole kingdom, and upright ones with him; thus shall he do: and he shall give him the daughter of women, corrupting her: but she shall not stand *on his side,* neither be for him. 2 Kin. 12:17; 2 Chr. 20:3

18 After this shall he turn his face unto the ^Tisles, and shall take many: but a prince for his own behalf shall cause the reproach offered by him to cease; without his own reproach he shall cause *it* to turn upon him. *coastlands*

19 Then he shall turn his face toward the fort of his own land: but he shall ^Rstumble and fall, and not be found. Ps. 27:2; Jer. 46:6

20 Then shall stand up in his estate a raiser of taxes *in* the glory of the kingdom: but within few days he shall be destroyed, neither in anger, nor in battle.

21 And in his estate ^Rshall stand up a vile person, to whom they shall not give the honour of the kingdom: but he shall come ^Tin peaceably, and obtain the kingdom by flatteries. 7:8 · *by prosperity*

22 And with the arms of a ^Rflood shall they be ^Toverflown from before him, and shall be broken; ^Ryea, also the prince of the covenant. 9:26 · *swept away* · 8:10, 11

23 And after the league *made* with him ^Rhe shall work deceitfully: for he shall come up, and shall become strong with a ^Tsmall people. 8:25 · *small* number of

24 He shall enter peaceably even upon the fattest places of the province; and he shall do *that* which his fathers have not done, nor his fathers' fathers; he shall scatter among them the prey, and spoil, and riches: *yea,* and he shall forecast his devices against the strong holds, even for a time.

25 And he shall stir up his power and his courage against the king of the south with a great army; and the king of the south shall be stirred up to battle with a very great and mighty army; but he shall not stand: for they shall forecast devices against him.

26 Yea, they that feed of the portion of his meat shall destroy him, and his army shall overflow: and many shall fall down slain.

27 And both these kings' hearts *shall be* ^Tto do mischief, and they shall speak lies at ^Tone table; but it shall not prosper: for yet the end *shall be* at the ^Rtime appointed. *bent on evil* · *the same* · 8:19; Hab. 2:3

28 Then shall he return into his land with great riches; and his heart *shall be* against the holy covenant; and he shall do *exploits,* and return to his own land.

29 At the time appointed he shall return, and come toward the south; but it shall not be as the former, or as the latter.

30 For the ships of Chit'-tim shall come against him: therefore he shall be grieved, and return, and have indignation against the holy covenant: so shall he do; he

shall even return, and [T]have intelligence with them that forsake the holy covenant. *show regard for*

31 And arms shall stand on his part, [R]and they shall pollute the sanctuary of strength, and shall take away the daily *sacrifice*, and they shall place the abomination that maketh desolate. 8:11–13; 12:11

32 And such as do wickedly against the covenant shall he [T]corrupt by flatteries: but the people that do know their God shall be strong, and do *exploits*. *pollute*

33 And they that understand among the people shall instruct many: yet they shall fall by the sword, and by flame, by captivity, and by spoil, *many* days.

34 Now when they shall fall, they shall be [T]holpen with a little help: but many shall cleave to them with flatteries. *helped*

35 And *some* of them of understanding shall fall, [R]to try them, and to purge, and to make *them* white, *even* to the time of the end: because *it is* yet for a time appointed. 12:10; Zech. 13:9; Mal. 3:2, 3

36 And the king shall do according to his will; and he shall [R]exalt himself, and magnify himself above every god, and shall speak [T]marvellous things against the God of gods, and shall prosper till the indignation be accomplished: for that that is determined shall be done. 7:8, 25 · *unusual*

37 Neither shall he regard the [T]God of his fathers, nor the desire of women, [R]nor regard any god: for he shall magnify himself above all. *gods* · Is. 14:13; 2 Thess. 2:4

38 But in his estate shall he honour [T]the God of forces: and a god whom his fathers knew not shall he honour with gold, and silver, and with precious stones, and pleasant things. *a god of fortresses*

39 Thus shall he do in the most strong holds with a strange god, whom he shall acknowledge *and* increase with glory: and he shall cause them to rule over many, and shall divide the land for gain.

40 And at the time of the end

shall the king of the south push at him: and the king of the north shall come against him [R]like a whirlwind, with chariots, [R]and with horsemen, and with many ships; and he shall enter into the countries, and shall overflow and pass over. Is. 21:1 · Ezek. 38:4; Rev. 9:16

41 He shall enter also into the glorious land, and many *countries* shall be overthrown: but these shall escape out of his hand, [R]even E´-dom, and Moab, and the chief of the children of Ammon. Is. 11:14

42 He shall stretch forth his hand also upon the countries: and the land of [R]Egypt shall not escape. Joel 3:19

43 But he shall have power over the treasures of gold and of silver, and over all the precious things of Egypt: and the Lib´-y-ans and the E-thi-o´-pi-ans *shall* [T]be [R]at his steps. *follow at* · Ex. 11:8

44 But [T]tidings out of the east and out of the north shall trouble him: therefore he shall go forth with great fury to destroy, and utterly to make away many. *news*

45 And he shall plant the tabernacles of his palace between the seas in the glorious holy mountain; [R]yet he shall come to his end, and none shall help him. Rev. 19:20

12 And at that time shall Mi´-cha-el stand up, the great prince which standeth for the children of thy people: [R]and there shall be a time of trouble, such as never was since there was a nation *even* to that same time: and at that time thy people shall be delivered, every one that shall be found written in the book. 9:12

2 And many of them that sleep in the dust of the earth shall awake, some to everlasting life, and some to shame [R]and everlasting contempt. [Is. 66:24; Rom. 9:21]

3 And they that be wise shall shine as the brightness of the firmament; and they that turn many to righteousness [R]as the stars for ever and ever. 1 Cor. 15:41

4 But thou, O Daniel, [R]shut up the words, and seal the book, *even*

to the time of the end: many shall run to and fro, and knowledge shall be increased. Is. 8:16; Rev. 22:10

5 Then I Daniel looked, and, behold, there stood ᵀother two, the one on this side of the bank of the river, and the other on that side of the bank of the river.   *two others*

6 And *one* said to the man clothed in ᴿlinen, which *was* upon the waters of the river, ᴿHow long *shall it be to* the end of these wonders?   Ezek. 9:2 · Matt. 24:3; Mark 13:4

7 And I heard the man clothed in linen, which *was* upon the waters of the river, when he held up his right hand and his left hand unto heaven, and sware by him that liveth for ever ᴿthat *it shall be* for a time, times, and an half; and when he shall have accomplished to scatter the power of the holy people, all these *things* shall be finished.   Rev. 12:14

8 And I heard, but I understood not: then said I, O my Lord, what *shall be* the end of these *things?*

9 And he said, Go thy way, Daniel: for the words *are* closed up and sealed till the time of the end.

10 ᴿMany shall be purified, and made white, and tried; ᴿbut the wicked shall do wickedly: and none of the wicked shall understand; but the wise shall understand.   Zech. 13:9 · Is. 32:6, 7; Rev. 22:11

11 And from the time *that* the daily *sacrifice* shall be taken away, and the abomination ᵀthat maketh desolate set up, *there shall be* a thousand two hundred and ninety days.   *of desolation*

12 Blessed *is* he that waiteth, and cometh to the thousand three hundred and five and thirty days.

13 But go thou thy way till the end *be:* ᴿfor thou shalt rest, ᴿand stand in thy lot at the end of the days.   Is. 57:2; Rev. 14:13 · Ps. 1:5

The Book of
HOSEA

H OSEA, whose name means "Salvation," ministers to the northern kingdom of Israel (also called Ephraim, after its largest tribe). Outwardly, the nation is enjoying a time of prosperity and growth; but inwardly, moral corruption and spiritual adultery permeate the people. Hosea, instructed by God to marry a woman named Gomer, finds his domestic life to be an accurate and tragic dramatization of the unfaithfulness of God's people. During his half century of prophetic ministry, Hosea repeatedly echoes his threefold message: God abhors the sins of His people; judgment is certain; but God's loyal love stands firm.

The names Hosea, Joshua, and Jesus are all derived from the same Hebrew root word. The word *hoshea* means "salvation," but "Joshua" and "Jesus" include an additional idea: "Yahweh Is Salvation." As God's messenger, Hosea offers the possibility of salvation if only the nation will turn from idolatry back to God.

Israel's last king, Hoshea, has the same name as the prophet even though the English Bible spells them differently. Hosea in the Greek and Latin is *Osee.*

T HE word of the LORD that came unto Ho-se′-a, the son of Be-e′-ri, in the days of ᴿUz-zi′-ah, Jo′-tham, Ahaz, *and* Hez-e-ki′-ah, kings of Judah, and in the days of ᴿJer-o-bo′-am the son of Jo′-ash, king of Israel.   2 Chr. 26 · 2 Kin. 13:13

2 The beginning of the word of

the LORD by Ho-se'-a. And the LORD said to Ho-se'-a, ᴿGo, take unto thee a wife of whoredoms and children of whoredoms: for ᴿthe land hath committed great whoredom, *departing* from the LORD.   3:1 · Ps. 73:27; Jer. 2:13

3 So he went and took Go'-mer the daughter of Dib'-la-im; which conceived, and bare him a son.

4 And the LORD said unto him, Call his name Jez'-re-el; for yet a little *while,* ᴿand I will avenge the blood of Jez'-re-el upon the house of Je'-hu, ᴿand will cause to cease the kingdom of the house of Israel.   2 Kin. 10:11 · 2 Kin. 15:8–10; 17:6, 23

5 And it shall come to pass at that day, that I will break the bow of Israel in the valley of Jez'-re-el.

6 And she conceived again, and bare a daughter. And *God* said unto him, Call her name ᵀLo–ru'-ha-mah: ᴿfor I will no more have mercy upon the house of Israel; but I will utterly take them away.   Lit. *No Mercy* · 2 Kin. 17:6

7 ᴿBut I will have mercy upon the house of Judah, and will save them by the LORD their God, and ᴿwill not save them by bow, nor by sword, nor by battle, by horses, nor by horsemen.   Is. 30:18 · Ps. 44:3–7

8 Now when she had weaned Lo–ru'-ha-mah, she conceived, and bare a son.

9 Then said *God,* Call his name Lo–am'-mi: for ye *are* not my people, and I will not be your *God.*

10 Yet the number of the children of Israel shall be as the sand of the sea, which cannot be measured nor numbered; and it shall come to pass, *that* in the place where it was said unto them, Ye *are* not my ᴿpeople, *there* it shall be said unto them, Ye *are* the sons of the living God.   Rom. 9:26

11 Then shall the children of Judah and the children of Israel be gathered together, and appoint themselves one head, and they shall come up out of the land: for great *shall be* the day of Jez'-re-el.

2 Say ye unto your brethren, Am'-mi; and to your sisters, Ru'-ha-mah.

2 ᵀPlead with your mother, plead: for ᴿshe *is* not my wife, neither *am* I her husband: let her therefore put away her whoredoms out of her sight, and her adulteries from between her breasts;   *Bring charges against* · Is. 50:1

3 Lest ᴿI strip her naked, and set her as in the day that she was born, and make her as a wilderness, and set her like a dry land, and slay her with thirst.   Jer. 13:22

4 And I will not have mercy upon her children; for they *be* the ᴿchildren of whoredoms.   John 8:41

5 For their mother hath played the harlot: she that conceived them hath done shamefully: for she said, I will go after my lovers, ᴿthat give *me* my bread and my water, my wool and my flax, mine oil and my drink.   Ezek. 23:5

6 Therefore, behold, ᴿI will hedge up thy way with thorns, and make a wall, that she shall not find her paths.   Lam. 3:7, 9

7 And she shall follow after her lovers, but she shall not overtake them; and she shall seek them, but shall not find *them:* then shall she say, I will go and return to my ᴿfirst husband; for then *was it* better with me than now.   Is. 54:5–8

8 For she did not ᴿknow that I gave her ᵀcorn, and ᵀwine, and oil, and multiplied her silver and gold, *which* they prepared for Ba'-al.   Is. 1:3; Ezek. 16:19 · *grain* · *new wine*

9 Therefore will I return, and take away my corn in the time thereof, and my wine in the season thereof, and will ᵀrecover my wool and my ᵀflax *given* to cover her nakedness.   *take back* · *linen*

10 And now will I ᵀdiscover her lewdness in the sight of her lovers, and none shall deliver her out of mine hand.   *uncover*

11 ᴿI will also cause all her mirth to cease, her feast days, her new moons, and her sabbaths, and all her solemn feasts.   Jer. 7:34

12 And I will destroy her vines

and her fig trees, whereof she hath said, These *are* my rewards that my lovers have given me: and I will make them a forest, and the beasts of the field shall eat them.

13 And I will ^Tvisit upon her the days of Ba'-al-im, wherein she burned incense to them, and she decked herself with her earrings and her jewels, and she went after her lovers, and forgat me, saith the LORD.   *punish her for*

14 Therefore, behold, I will allure her, and bring her into the wilderness, and speak comfortably unto her.

15 And I will give her her vineyards from thence, and ^Rthe valley of A'-chor for a door of hope: and she shall sing there, as in the days of her youth, and ^Ras in the day when she came up out of the land of Egypt.   Josh. 7:26 · Ex. 15:1

16 And it shall be at that day, saith the LORD, *that* thou shalt call me ^TIsh'-i; and shalt call me no more Ba'-al-i.   Lit. *My Husband*

17 For ^RI will take away the names of Ba'-al-im out of her mouth, and they shall no more be remembered by their name. Ps. 16:4

18 And in that day will I make a ^Rcovenant for them with the beasts of the field, and with the fowls of heaven, and *with* the creeping things of the ground: and I will break the bow and the sword and the battle out of the earth, and will make them to lie down safely. Job 5:23; Is. 11:6-9

19 And I will betroth thee unto me for ever; yea, I will betroth thee unto me in righteousness, and in judgment, and in lovingkindness, and in mercies.

20 I will even betroth thee unto me in faithfulness: and ^Rthou shalt know the LORD.   [John 17:3]

21 And it shall come to pass in that day, ^RI will hear, saith the LORD, I will hear the heavens, and they shall hear the earth;   Is. 55:10

22 And the earth shall hear the corn, and the wine, and the oil; and they shall hear Jez'-re-el.

23 And I will sow her unto me in

the earth; and I will have mercy upon her that had not obtained mercy; and I ^Rwill say to *them which were* not my people, Thou *art* my people; and they shall say, *Thou art* my God.   Rom. 9:25, 26

3 Then said the LORD unto me, Go yet, love a woman beloved of *her* ^Rfriend, yet an adulteress, according to the love of the LORD toward the children of Israel, who look to other gods, and love flagons of wine.   Jer. 3:20

2 So I bought her ^Tto me for fifteen *pieces* of silver, and *for* an ho'-mer of barley, and an half ho'-mer of barley: *for myself*

3 And I said unto her, Thou shalt ^Rabide for me many days; thou shalt not play the harlot, and thou shalt not be for *another* man: so *will* I also *be* for thee. Deut. 21:13

4 For the children of Israel shall abide many days without a king, and without a prince, and without a sacrifice, and without an image, and without an e'-phod, and *without* ter'-a-phim:

5 Afterward shall the children of Israel return, and seek the LORD their God, and David their king; and shall fear the LORD and his goodness in the latter days.

4 Hear the word of the LORD, ye children of Israel: for the LORD hath a controversy with the inhabitants of the land, because *there is* no truth, nor mercy, nor knowledge of God in the land.

2 By swearing, and lying, and killing, and stealing, and committing adultery, they break out, and blood toucheth blood.

3 Therefore ^Rshall the land mourn, and ^Revery one that dwelleth therein shall ^Tlanguish, with the beasts of the field, and with the fowls of heaven; yea, the fishes of the sea also shall be taken away.   Amos 8:8 · Zeph. 1:3 · *waste away*

4 Yet let no man ^Tstrive, nor reprove another: for thy people *are* as they ^Rthat ^Tstrive with the priest.   *contend* · Deut. 17:12

5 Therefore shalt thou ^Tfall in the day, and the prophet also shall

Tfall with thee in the night, and I will destroy thy mother. *stumble*

6 RMy people are destroyed for lack of knowledge: because thou hast rejected knowledge, I will also reject thee, that thou shalt be no priest to me: seeing thou hast forgotten the law of thy God, I will also forget thy children. Is. 5:13

7 As they were increased, so they sinned against me: Rtherefore will I change their glory into shame. 1 Sam. 2:30; Mal. 2:9

8 They eat up the sin of my people, and they set their Theart on their iniquity. *Desires*

9 And there shall be, Rlike people, like priest: and I will punish them for their ways, and Treward them their doings. Is. 24:2 · *repay*

10 For Rthey shall eat, and not have enough: they shall commit whoredom, and shall not increase: because they have left off to take heed to the LORD. Mic. 6:14

11 Whoredom and wine and new wine take away the heart.

12 My people ask counsel at their stocks, and their staff declareth unto them: for the spirit of whoredoms hath caused *them* to err, and they have gone a whoring from under their God.

13 They sacrifice upon the tops of the mountains, and burn incense upon the hills, under oaks and poplars and elms, because the shadow thereof *is* good: therefore your daughters shall commit whoredom, and your spouses shall commit adultery.

14 I will not punish your daughters when they commit whoredom, nor your spouses when they commit adultery: for themselves are separated with whores, and they sacrifice with Rharlots: therefore the people *that* doth not understand shall fall. Deut. 23:18

15 Though thou, Israel, play the harlot, *yet* let not Judah offend; Rand come not ye unto Gil'-gal, neither go ye up to Beth–a'-ven, nor swear, The LORD liveth. 9:15

16 For Israel Rslideth T back as a backsliding heifer: now the LORD will feed them as a lamb in a large place. Jer. 3:6; Zech. 7:11 · *is stubborn*

17 E'-phra-im *is* joined to idols: Rlet him alone. Matt. 15:14

18 Their drink *is* Tsour: they have committed whoredom continually: Rher rulers *with* shame do love, Give ye. *rebellion* · Mic. 3:11

19 RThe wind hath bound her up in her wings, and Rthey shall be ashamed because of their sacrifices. Jer. 51:1 · Is. 1:29

5 Hear ye this, O priests; and hearken, ye house of Israel; and give ye ear, O house of the king; for Tjudgment *is* toward you, because Rye have been a snare on Miz'-pah, and a net spread upon Ta'-bor. *the judgment is yours* · 6:9

2 And the revolters are profound to make slaughter, though I *have been* a rebuker of them all.

3 I know E'-phra-im, and Israel is not hid from me: for now, O E'-phra-im, thou committest whoredom, *and* Israel is defiled.

4 They will not frame their doings to turn unto their God: for Rthe spirit of whoredoms *is* in the midst of them, and they have not known the LORD. 4:12

5 And the Rpride of Israel doth testify to his face: therefore shall Israel and E'-phra-im Tfall in their iniquity; Judah also shall Tfall with them. 7:10 · *stumble*

6 RThey shall go with their flocks and with their herds to seek the LORD; but they shall not find *him*; he hath withdrawn himself from them. Mic. 3:4; John 7:34

7 They have Rdealt treacherously against the LORD: for they have begotten Tstrange children: now shall a month devour them with their portions. Is. 48;8 · *pagan*

8 Blow ye the Tcornet in Gib'-e-ah, *and* the trumpet in Ra'-mah: cry aloud *at* Beth–a'-ven, after thee, O Benjamin. *ram's horn*

9 E'-phra-im shall be desolate in the day of rebuke: among the tribes of Israel have I made known that which shall surely be.

10 The princes of Judah were like them that remove Tthe bound:

therefore I will pour out my wrath upon them like water.   *a boundary*

11 E'-phra-im *is* ᴿoppressed *and* broken in judgment, because he willingly walked after ᴿthe commandment.   Deut. 28:33 · Mic. 6:16

12 Therefore *will* I *be* unto E'-phra-im as a moth, and to the house of Judah as rottenness.

13 When E'-phra-im saw his sickness, and Judah *saw* his wound, then went E'-phra-im ᴿto the Assyrian, and sent to king Ja'-reb: yet could he not heal you, nor cure you of your wound.   7:11; 10:6

14 For ᴿI *will be* unto E'-phra-im as a lion, and as a young lion to the house of Judah: I, *even* I, will tear and go away; I will take away, and none shall rescue *him*.   Ps. 7:2

15 I will go *and* return to my place, till they acknowledge their offence, and seek my face: in their affliction they will seek me early.

6 Come, and let us return unto the LORD: for ᴿhe hath torn, and he will heal us; he hath smitten, and he will bind us up.   Deut. 32:39

2 After two days will he revive us: in the third day he will raise us up, and we shall live in his sight.

3 ᴿThen shall we know, *if* we follow on to know the LORD: his going forth is prepared as the morning; and he shall come unto us as the rain, as the latter *and* former rain unto the earth.   Is. 54:13

4 O E'-phra-im, what shall I do unto thee? O Judah, what shall I do unto thee? for your ᵀgoodness *is* as a morning cloud, and as the early dew it goeth away.   *faithfulness*

5 Therefore have I hewed *them* by the prophets; I have slain them by ᴿthe words of my mouth: and thy judgments *are as* the light *that* goeth forth.   [Jer. 23:29]

6 For I desired mercy, and not sacrifice; and the knowledge of God more than burnt offerings.

7 But they ᵀlike men have transgressed the covenant: there have they dealt treacherously against me.   *like Adam*

8 ᴿGil'-e-ad *is* a city of them that work iniquity, *and is* polluted with blood.   12:11

9 And as troops of robbers wait for a man, *so* the company of ᴿpriests ᴿmurder in the way by consent: for they commit lewdness.   5:1 · 4:2; Jer. 7:9, 10

10 I have seen an horrible thing in the house of Israel: there *is* the whoredom of E'-phra-im, Israel is defiled.

11 Also, O Judah, he hath set an harvest for thee, when I returned the captivity of my people.

7 When I would have healed Israel, then the iniquity of E'-phra-im was discovered, and the wickedness of Sa-ma'-ri-a: for ᴿthey commit falsehood; and the thief cometh in, *and* the troop of robbers spoileth without.   5:1

2 And they consider not in their hearts *that* I remember all their wickedness: now their own doings have ᵀbeset them about; they are before my face.   *surrounded*

3 They make the king glad with their wickedness, and the princes ᴿwith their lies.   [Rom. 1:32]

4 ᴿThey *are* all adulterers, as an oven heated by the baker, *who* ceaseth from raising after he hath kneaded the dough, until it be leavened.   Jer. 9:2; 23:10

5 In the day of our king the princes have made *him* sick with bottles of ᴿwine; he stretched out his hand with scorners.   Is. 28:1, 7

6 For they have ᵀmade ready their heart like an oven, whiles they lie in wait: their baker sleepeth all the night; in the morning it burneth as a flaming fire.   *prepared*

7 They are all hot as an oven, and have devoured their judges; all their kings are fallen: ᴿ*there is* none among them that calleth unto me.   Is. 64:7

8 E'-phra-im, he hath mixed himself among the people; E'-phra-im is a cake not turned.

9 ᴿStrangers have devoured his strength, and he knoweth *it* not: yea, gray hairs are here and there upon him, yet he knoweth not.   8:7

10 And the [R]pride of Israel testifieth to his face: and [R]they do not return to the LORD their God, nor seek him for all this. 5:5 · Is. 9:13

11 [R]E'-phra-im also is like a silly dove without heart: they call to Egypt, they go to Assyria. 11:11

12 When they shall go, I will spread my net upon them; I will bring them down as the fowls of the heaven; I will chastise them, as their congregation hath heard.

13 Woe unto them! for they have fled from me: destruction unto them! because they have transgressed against me: though I have redeemed them, yet they have spoken lies against me.

14 And they have not cried unto me with their heart, when they howled upon their beds: they assemble themselves for corn and wine, *and* they rebel against me.

15 Though I have bound *and* strengthened their arms, yet do they imagine mischief against me.

16 They return, *but* not [T]to the most High: they are like a deceitful bow: their princes shall fall by the sword for the rage of their tongue: this *shall be* their derision in the land of Egypt. *upward*

8 Set the [T]trumpet to thy mouth. *He shall come* as an eagle against the house of the LORD, because they have transgressed my covenant, and trespassed against my law. *ram's horn*

2 Israel shall cry unto me, My God, [R]we know thee. Titus 1:16

3 Israel hath cast off *the thing that is* good: the enemy shall pursue him.

4 [R]They have set up kings, but not by me: they have made princes, and I knew *it* not: of their silver and their gold have they made them idols, that they may be cut off. 1 Kin. 12:20; 2 Kin. 15:23, 25

5 Thy calf, O Sa-ma'-ri-a, hath cast *thee* off; mine anger is kindled against them: how long *will it be* ere they attain to innocency?

6 For from Israel *was* it also: the workman made it; therefore it

is not God: but the calf of Sa-ma'-ri-a shall be broken in pieces.

7 For [R]they have sown the wind, and they shall reap the whirlwind: it hath no stalk: the bud shall yield no meal: if so be it yield, the [R]strangers shall swallow it up. Prov. 22:8 · 7:9

8 [R]Israel is swallowed up: now shall they be among the Gentiles [R]as a vessel wherein *is* no pleasure. 2 Kin. 17:6; Jer. 51:34 · Jer. 22:28; 25:34

9 For they are gone up to As-syria, a wild ass alone by himself: E'-phra-im hath hired lovers.

10 Yea, though they have hired among the nations, now [R]will I gather them, and they shall sorrow a little for the burden of [R]the king of princes. Ezek. 16:37 · Is. 10:8

11 Because E'-phra-im hath made many altars to sin, altars shall be unto him [T]to sin. *for sinning*

12 I have written to him the great things of my law, *but* they were counted as a strange thing.

13 [R]They sacrifice flesh *for* the sacrifices of mine offerings, and eat *it; but* the LORD accepteth them not; now will he remember their iniquity, and visit their sins: they shall return to Egypt. Zech. 7:6

14 For Israel hath forgotten his Maker, and buildeth temples; and Judah hath multiplied fenced cities: but [R]I will send a fire upon his cities, and it shall devour the palaces thereof. Jer. 17:27

9 Rejoice [R]not, O Israel, for joy, as *other* people: for thou hast gone a whoring from thy God, thou hast loved a reward upon every cornfloor. 10:5; Is. 22:12, 13

2 The [T]floor and the winepress shall not feed them, and the new wine shall fail in her. *threshingfloor*

3 They shall not dwell in the LORD's land; [R]but E'-phra-im shall return to Egypt, and they shall eat unclean *things* in Assyria. 7:16; 8:13

4 They shall not offer wine *offerings* to the LORD, [R]neither shall they be pleasing unto him: their [R]sacrifices *shall be* unto them as the bread of mourners; all that eat thereof shall be polluted:

for their bread for their soul shall not come into the house of the LORD.   Jer. 6:20 · 8:13; Amos 5:22

5 What will ye do in the ᵀsolemn day, and in the day of the feast of the LORD?   *appointed*

6 For, lo, they are gone because of destruction: Egypt shall gather them up, Mem'-phis shall bury them: the pleasant *places* for their silver, ᴿnettles shall possess them: thorns *shall be* in their ᵀtabernacles.   10:8; Is. 5:6; 7:23 · *tents*

7 The days of visitation are come, the days of recompence are come; Israel shall know *it*: the prophet *is* a fool, the spiritual man *is* mad, for the multitude of thine iniquity, and the great hatred.

8 The ᴿwatchman of E'-phra-im *was* with my God: *but* the prophet *is* a snare of a fowler in all his ways, *and* ᵀhatred in the house of his God.   Ezek. 3:17; 33:7 · *enmity*

9 They have deeply corrupted *themselves*, as in the days of ᴿGib'-e-ah: *therefore* he will remember their iniquity, he will ᵀvisit their sins.   Judg. 19:22 · *punish*

10 I found Israel like grapes in the wilderness; I saw your fathers as the ᴿfirstripe in the fig tree at her first time: *but* they went to Ba'-al-pe'-or, and separated themselves unto *that* shame; and *their* abominations were according as they loved.   Is. 28:4; Mic. 7:1

11 *As for* E'-phra-im, their glory shall fly away like a bird, from the birth, and from the womb, and from the conception.

12 Though they bring up their children, yet will I bereave them, *that there shall* not *be* a man *left*: yea, ᴿwoe also to them when I depart from them!   Deut. 31:17

13 E'-phra-im, as I saw Ty'-rus, *is* planted in a pleasant place: but E'-phra-im shall bring forth his children to the murderer.

14 Give them, O LORD: what wilt thou give? give them a miscarrying womb and dry breasts.

15 All their wickedness *is* in Gil'-gal: for there I hated them: for

the wickedness of their doings I will drive them out of mine house, I will love them no more: ᴿall their princes *are* revolters.   5:2; Is. 1:23

16 E'-phra-im is ᴿsmitten, their root is dried up, they shall bear no fruit: yea, though they bring forth, yet will I slay *even* the beloved *fruit* of their womb.   5:11

17 My God will cast them away, because they did not hearken unto him: and they shall be wanderers among the nations.

10 Israel *is* ᴿan empty vine, he bringeth forth fruit unto himself: according to the multitude of his fruit he hath increased the altars; according to the goodness of his land they have made goodly images.   Nah. 2:2

2 Their heart is ᴿdivided; now shall they be found faulty: he shall break down their altars, he shall spoil their images. [Matt. 6:24]

3 For now they shall say, We have no king, because we feared not the LORD; what then should a king do ᵀto us?   *for*

4 They have spoken words, swearing falsely in making a covenant: ᴿthus judgment springeth up as hemlock in the furrows of the field.   2 Kin. 17:3, 4; Amos 5:7

5 The inhabitants of Sa-ma'-ri-a shall fear because of the calves of Beth-a'-ven: for the people thereof shall mourn over it, and the priests thereof *that* rejoiced on it, for the ᴿglory thereof, because it is departed from it.   9:11

6 It shall be also carried unto Assyria *for* a present to king ᴿJa'-reb: E'-phra-im shall receive shame, and Israel shall be ashamed of his own counsel.   5:13

7 *As for* Sa-ma'-ri-a, her king is cut off as ᵀthe foam upon the water.   *a twig on*

8 The ᴿhigh places also of A'-ven, the sin of Israel, shall be destroyed: the thorn and the thistle shall come up on their altars; ᴿand they shall say to the mountains, Cover us; and to the hills, Fall on us.   4:15 · Luke 23:30; Rev. 6:16

9 O Israel, thou hast sinned

from the days of ᴿGib′-e-ah: there they stood: the ᴿbattle in Gib′-e-ah against the children of iniquity did not overtake them. 9:9 · Judg. 20

10 *It is* in my desire that I should chastise them; and ᴿthe people shall be gathered against them, when they shall bind themselves in their two furrows. Jer. 16:16

11 And E′-phra-im *is as* ᴿan heifer *that is* taught, *and* loveth to tread out *the corn;* but I passed over upon her fair neck: I will make E′-phra-im to ride; Judah shall plow, *and* Jacob shall break his clods. [4:16; Jer. 50:11; Mic. 4:13]

12 Sow to yourselves in righteousness, reap in mercy; ᴿbreak up your ᵀfallow ground: for *it is* time to seek the LORD, till he ᴿcome and rain righteousness upon you. Jer. 4:3 · *untilled* · 6:3

13 Ye have plowed wickedness, ye have reaped iniquity; ye have eaten the fruit of lies: because thou didst trust in thy way, in the multitude of thy mighty men.

14 Therefore shall a tumult arise among thy people, and all thy fortresses shall be ᵀspoiled, as Shal′-man ᵀspoiled Beth–ar′-bel in the day of battle: the mother was dashed in pieces upon *her* children. *plundered*

15 So shall Beth′-el do unto you because of your great wickedness: in a morning shall the king of Israel utterly be cut off.

☆ 11 When Israel *was* a child, then I loved him, and ᴿcalled my son out of Egypt. Matt. 2:15

2 *As* they called them, so they went from them: they sacrificed unto Ba′-al-im, and burned incense to graven images.

3 ᴿI taught E′-phra-im also to ᵀgo, taking them by their arms; but they knew not that ᴿI healed them. Deut. 32:10, 11 · *walk* · Ex. 15:26

4 I drew them with cords of a man, with bands of love: and I was to them as they that take off the yoke on their jaws, and I ᵀlaid meat unto them. *stooped and fed*

5 He shall not return into the land of Egypt, but the Assyrian shall be his king, because they refused to ᵀreturn. *repent*

6 And the sword shall abide on his cities, and shall consume his branches, and devour *them,* because of their own counsels.

7 And my people are bent to backsliding from me: though they called them to the most High, none at all would exalt *him.*

8 ᴿHow shall I give thee up, E′-phra-im? *how* shall I deliver thee, Israel? how shall I make thee as ᴿAd′-mah? *how* shall I set thee as Ze-bo′-im? mine heart is turned within me, my repentings are kindled together. Jer. 9:7 · Gen. 14:8

9 I will not execute the fierceness of mine anger, I will not return to destroy E′-phra-im: ᴿfor I *am* God, and not man; the Holy One in the midst of thee: and I will not enter into the city. Num. 23:19

10 They shall walk after the LORD: he shall roar like a lion: when he shall roar, then the children shall tremble from the west.

11 They shall tremble as a bird out of Egypt, ᴿand as a dove out of the land of Assyria: ᴿand I will place them in their houses, saith the LORD. Is. 11:11; 60:8 · Ezek. 28:25, 26

12 E′-phra-im compasseth me about with lies, and the house of Israel with deceit: but Judah yet ruleth with God, and is faithful with the saints.

12 E′-phra-im ᴿfeedeth on wind, and followeth after the east wind: he daily increaseth lies and desolation; ᴿand they do make a covenant with the Assyrians, and ᴿoil is carried into Egypt. Job 15:2, 3 · 8:9; 2 Kin. 17:4 · Is. 30:6

2 ᴿThe LORD hath also a controversy with Judah, and will punish Jacob according to his ways; according to his doings will he recompense him. 4:1; Mic. 6:2

3 He took his brother ᴿby the heel in the womb, and by his strength he ᴿhadᵀ power with God: Gen. 25:26 · Gen. 32:24–28 · *struggled*

4 Yea, he had power over the angel, and prevailed: he wept, and made supplication unto him: he

found him *in* ^RBeth′–el, and there he spake with us;　[Gen. 28:12–19]

5　Even the LORD God of hosts; the LORD *is* his ^Rmemorial. Ex. 3:15

6　Therefore turn thou to thy God: keep mercy and judgment, and wait on thy God continually.

7　*He is* a merchant, ^Rthe balances of deceit *are* in his hand: he loveth to oppress. Amos 8:5; Mic. 6:11

8　And E′-phra-im said, ^RYet I am become rich, I have found me out substance: *in* all my labours they shall find none iniquity in me that *were* sin.　Ps. 62:10; Rev. 3:17

9　And I *that am* the LORD thy God from the land of Egypt ^Rwill yet make thee to dwell in ^Ttabernacles, as in the days of the solemn feast.　Lev. 23:42 · *tents*

10　I have also spoken by the prophets, and I have multiplied visions, and used similitudes, by the ministry of the prophets.

11　*Is there* iniquity *in* ^RGil′-e-ad? surely they are vanity: they sacrifice bullocks in ^RGil′-gal; yea, their altars *are* as heaps in the furrows of the fields.　6:8 · 9:15

12　And Jacob ^Rfled into the country of Syria, and ^RIsrael served for a wife, and for a wife he kept *sheep*. Gen. 28:5 · Gen. 29:20, 28

13　And by a prophet the LORD brought Israel out of Egypt, and by a prophet was he preserved.

14　E′-phra-im ^Rprovoked *him* to anger most bitterly: therefore shall he leave his blood upon him, and his reproach shall his Lord return unto him.　Ezek. 18:10–13

13　When E′-phra-im spake trembling, he exalted himself in Israel; but when he offended in Ba′-al, he died.

2　And now they sin more and more, and have made them molten images of their silver, *and* idols according to their own ^Tunderstanding, all of it the work of the craftsmen: they say of them, Let the men that sacrifice kiss the calves.　*skill*

3　Therefore they shall be as the morning cloud, and as the early dew that passeth away, as the chaff *that* is driven with the whirlwind out of the floor, and as the smoke out of the chimney.

4　Yet I *am* the LORD thy God from the land of Egypt, and thou shalt know no god but me: for *there is* no saviour beside me.

5　^RI did know thee in the wilderness, ^Rin the land of great drought.　Deut. 2:7; 32:10 · Deut. 8:15

6　According to their pasture, so were they filled; they were filled, and their heart was exalted; therefore have they forgotten me.

7　Therefore ^RI will be unto them as a lion: as a leopard by the way will I observe *them:* Lam. 3:10

8　I will meet them as a bear *that is* bereaved *of her whelps,* and will ^Trend the caul of their heart, and there will I devour them like a lion: the wild beast shall tear them.　*tear open the cavity*

9　O Israel, thou hast destroyed thyself; but in me *is* thine help.

10　I will be thy king: where *is any other* that may save thee in all thy cities? and thy judges of whom ^Rthou saidst, Give me a king and princes?　1 Sam. 8:5, 6

11　^RI gave thee a king in mine anger, and took *him* away in my wrath.　1 Sam. 8:7; 10:17–24

12　^RThe iniquity of E′-phra-im *is* bound up; his sin *is* hid.　[Rom. 2:5]

13　^RThe sorrows of a travailing woman shall come upon him: he *is* an unwise son; for he should not stay long in *the place* of the breaking forth of children. Is. 13:8

14　I will ransom them from the power of ^Tthe grave; I will redeem them from death: O death, I will be thy plagues; O grave, I will be thy destruction: repentance shall be hid from mine eyes.　Heb. *Sheol*

15　Though he be fruitful among *his* brethren, ^Ran east wind shall come, the wind of the LORD shall come up from the wilderness, and his spring shall become dry, and his fountain shall be dried up: he shall spoil the treasure of all pleasant vessels. Gen. 41:6; Jer. 4:11, 12

16　Sa-ma′-ri-a shall become desolate; for she hath [R]rebelled against her God: they shall fall by the sword: their infants shall be dashed in pieces, and their women with child shall be [R]ripped [T]up.   2 Kin. 8:12 · 2 Kin. 15:16 · *open*

14 O Israel, [R]return unto the LORD thy God; for thou hast fallen by thine iniquity.   12:6

2 Take with you words, and turn to the LORD: say unto him, Take away all iniquity, and receive *us* graciously: so will we render the [R]calves of our lips. [6:6]

3 [T]Assh'-ur shall [R]not save us; we will not ride upon horses: neither will we say any more to the work of our hands, *Ye are* our gods: for in thee the fatherless findeth mercy.   Or *Assyria* · 7:11; 10:13

4 I will heal their backsliding, I will love them freely: for mine anger is turned away from him.

5 I will be as the [R]dew unto Israel: he shall grow as the lily, and cast forth his roots as Leb'-a-non.   Job 29:19; Prov. 19:12; Is. 26:19

6 His branches shall spread, and [R]his beauty shall be as the olive tree, and [R]his [T]smell as Leb'-a-non.   Ps. 52:8; 128:3 · Gen. 27:27 · *aroma*

7 [R]They that dwell under his shadow shall return; they shall revive *as* the corn, and grow as the vine: the scent thereof *shall be* as the wine of Leb'-a-non.   Dan. 4:12

8 E'-phra-im *shall say,* What have I to do any more with idols? I have heard *him,* and observed him: I *am* like a green fir tree. From me is thy fruit found.

9 Who *is* wise, and he shall understand these *things?* prudent, and he shall know them? for [R]the ways of the LORD *are* right, and the just shall walk in them: but the transgressors shall fall therein.   [Ps. 111:7, 8; Prov. 10:29]; Zeph. 3:5

The Book of

JOEL

DISASTER strikes the southern kingdom of Judah without warning. An ominous black cloud descends upon the land—the dreaded locusts. In a matter of hours, every living green thing has been stripped bare. Joel, God's spokesman during the reign of Joash (835–796 B.C.), seizes this occasion to proclaim God's message. Although the locust plague has been a terrible judgment for sin, God's future judgments during the day of the Lord will make that plague pale by comparison. In that day, God will destroy His enemies, but bring unparalleled blessing to those who faithfully obey Him.

The Hebrew name *Yo'el* means "Yahweh Is God." This name is appropriate to the theme of the book, which emphasizes God's sovereign work in history. The courses of nature and nations are in His hand. The Greek equivalent is *Ioel,* and the Latin is *Joel.*

THE word of the LORD that came to [R]Jo'-el the son of Pethu'-el.   Acts 2:16

2 Hear this, ye old men, and give ear, all ye inhabitants of the land. [R]Hath this been in your days, or even in the days of your fathers?   2:2; Jer. 30:7

3 [R]Tell ye your children of it, and *let* your children *tell* their children, and their children another generation.   Ex. 10:2; Ps. 78:4

4 [R]That which the palmerworm hath left hath the [R]locust eaten; and that which the locust hath left hath the cankerworm eaten; and that which the cankerworm hath left hath the caterpiller eaten.   2:25

5 Awake, ye drunkards, and weep; and howl, all ye drinkers of

wine, because of the new wine; for it is cut off from your mouth.

6 For a nation is come up upon my land, strong, and without number, ^Rwhose teeth *are* the teeth of a lion, and he hath the cheek teeth of a great lion. Rev. 9:8

7 He hath ^Rlaid my vine waste, and barked my fig tree: he hath made it clean bare, and cast *it* away; the branches thereof are made white. Is. 5:6; Amos 4:9

8 ^RLament like a virgin girded with sackcloth for ^Rthe husband of her youth. Is. 22:12 · Jer. 3:4

9 ^RThe meat offering and the drink offering is cut off from the house of the LORD; the priests, the LORD's ministers, mourn. Hos. 9:4

10 The field is wasted, ^Rthe land mourneth; for the corn is wasted: ^Rthe new wine is dried up, the oil languisheth. Jer. 12:11; Hos. 3:4 · Is. 24:7

11 ^RBe ye ashamed, O ye husbandmen; howl, O ye vinedressers, for the wheat and for the barley; because the harvest of the field is perished. Jer. 14:3, 4; Amos 5:16

12 ^RThe vine is dried up, and the fig tree languisheth; the pomegranate tree, the palm tree also, and the apple tree, *even* all the trees of the field, are withered: because joy is withered away from the sons of men. Hab. 3:17

13 Gird yourselves, and lament, ye priests: howl, ye ministers of the altar: come, lie all night in sackcloth, ye ministers of my God: for the meat offering and the drink offering is withholden from the house of your God.

14 Sanctify ye a fast, call a solemn assembly, gather the elders *and* all the inhabitants of the land *into* the house of the LORD your God, and cry unto the LORD,

15 Alas for the day! for ^Rthe day of the LORD *is* at hand, and as a destruction from the Almighty shall it come. Is. 13:6; Ezek. 7:2–12

16 Is not the meat cut off before our eyes, *yea,* joy and gladness from the house of our God?

17 The seed is rotten under their clods, the ^Tgarners are laid desolate, the barns are broken down; for the corn is withered. *storehouses*

18 How do ^Rthe beasts groan! the herds of cattle are perplexed, because they have no pasture; yea, the flocks of sheep are made desolate. 1 Kin. 8:5; Jer. 12:4; 14:5, 6

19 O LORD, ^Rto thee will I cry: for ^Rthe fire hath devoured the pastures of the wilderness, and the flame hath burned all the trees of the field. Mic. 7:7 · Jer. 9:10; Amos 7:4

20 The beasts of the field ^Rcry also unto thee: for ^Rthe rivers of waters are dried up, and the fire hath devoured the pastures of the wilderness. Ps. 104:21; 147:9 · 1 Kin. 17:7

2 Blow ye the ^Ttrumpet in Zion, and ^Rsound an alarm in my holy mountain: let all the inhabitants of the land tremble: for the day of the LORD cometh, for *it is* nigh at hand; *ram's horn* · Num. 10:5

2 ^RA day of darkness and of gloominess, a day of clouds and of thick darkness, as the morning spread upon the mountains: ^Ra great people and a strong; ^Rthere hath not been ever the like, neither shall be any more after it, *even* to the years of many generations. Zeph. 1:15 · 1:6 · Dan. 9:12

3 A fire devoureth before them; and behind them a flame burneth: the land *is* as ^Rthe garden of Eden before them, and behind them a desolate wilderness; yea, and nothing shall escape them. Gen. 2:8

4 The appearance of them *is* as the appearance of horses; and as horsemen, so shall they run.

5 Like the noise of chariots on the tops of mountains shall they leap, like the noise of a flame of fire that devoureth the stubble, as a strong people set in battle array.

6 Before their face the people shall be much pained: ^Rall faces shall gather blackness. Jer. 8:21

7 They shall run like mighty men; they shall climb the wall like men of war; and they shall march every one on his ways, and they shall not break their ranks:

8 Neither shall one ^Tthrust

another; they shall walk every one in his ^Tpath: and *when* they fall upon the sword, they shall not be wounded. *push · own column*

9 They shall run to and fro in the city; they shall run upon the wall, they shall climb up upon the houses; they shall enter in at the windows ^Rlike a thief. John 10:1

10 The earth shall quake before them; the heavens shall tremble: ^Rthe sun and the moon shall be dark, and the stars shall withdraw their shining: Matt. 24:29; Rev. 8:12

11 And the LORD shall utter his voice before his army: for his camp *is* very great: ^Rfor *he is* strong that executeth his word: for the ^Rday of the LORD *is* great and very terrible; and who can abide it? Rev. 18:8 · Jer. 30:7; Zeph. 1:15

12 Therefore also now, saith the LORD, ^Rturn ye *even* to me with all your heart, and with fasting, and with weeping, and with mourning: Ezek. 33:11; Hos. 12:6; 14:1

13 And rend your heart, and not your garments, and ^Tturn unto the LORD your God: for he *is* ^Rgracious and merciful, slow to anger, and of great kindness, and repenteth him of the evil. *return · [Ex. 34:6]*

14 Who knoweth *if* he will return and repent, and leave a blessing behind him; *even* ^Ra meat offering and a drink offering unto the LORD your God? 1:9, 13

15 ^RBlow the trumpet in Zion, sanctify a fast, call a solemn assembly: Num. 10:3; 2 Kin. 10:20

16 Gather the people, ^Rsanctify the congregation, assemble the elders, gather the children, and those that suck the breasts: ^Rlet the bridegroom go forth of his chamber, and the bride out of her closet. Ex. 19:10 · Ps. 19:5

17 Let the priests, the ministers of the LORD, weep between the porch and the altar, and let them say, ^RSpare thy people, O LORD, and give not thine heritage to reproach, that the heathen should rule over them: wherefore should they say among the people, Where *is* their God? Ex. 32:11, 12; [Is. 37:20]

18 Then will the LORD ^Rbe ^Tjealous for his land, and pity his people. [Is. 60:10; 63:9, 15] · *zealous*

19 Yea, the LORD will answer and say unto his people, Behold, I will send you ^Rcorn, and wine, and oil, and ye shall be satisfied therewith: and I will no more make you a reproach among the heathen: 1:10; Jer. 31:12; Hos. 2:21, 22

20 But ^RI will remove far off from you the northern *army,* and will drive him into a land barren and desolate, with his face toward the east sea, and his hinder part toward the utmost sea, and his stink shall come up, and his ill savour shall come up, because he hath done great things. Ex. 10:19

21 Fear not, O land; be glad and rejoice: for the LORD will do great things.

22 Be not afraid, ye beasts of the field: for the pastures of the wilderness do spring, for the tree beareth her fruit, the fig tree and the vine do yield their strength.

23 Be glad then, ye children of Zion, and rejoice in the LORD your God: for he hath given you the former rain moderately, and he will cause to come down for you the rain, the former rain, and the latter rain in the first *month.*

24 And the floors shall be full of wheat, and the fats shall overflow with ^Twine and oil. *new wine*

25 And I will restore to you the years ^Rthat the locust hath eaten, the cankerworm, and the caterpiller, and the palmerworm, my great army which I sent among you. vv. 2–11; 1:4–7

26 And ye shall ^Reat in plenty, and be satisfied, and praise the name of the LORD your God, that hath dealt wondrously with you: and my people shall never be ^Rashamed. Lev. 26:5; Is. 62:9 · Is. 45:17

27 And ye shall know that I *am* ^Rin the midst of Israel, and *that* ^RI *am* the LORD your God, and none else: and my people shall never be ashamed. Lev. 26:11, 12 · [Is. 45:5, 6]

28 ^RAnd it shall come to pass afterward, *that* I will pour out my

spirit upon all flesh; and your sons and your daughters shall prophesy, your old men shall dream dreams, your young men shall see visions: Acts 2:17-21

29 And also upon the servants and upon the handmaids in those days will I pour out my spirit.

30 And ᴿI will shew wonders in the heavens and in the earth, blood, and fire, and pillars of smoke. Matt. 24:29; Acts 2:19

31 ᴿThe sun shall be turned into darkness, and the moon into blood, before the great and the terrible day of the LORD come. 3:15

32 And it shall come to pass, that ᴿwhosoever shall call on the name of the LORD shall be delivered: for in mount Zion and in Jerusalem shall be deliverance, as the LORD hath said, and in ᴿthe remnant whom the LORD shall call. Rom. 10:13 · Is. 11:11; Rom. 9:27

3 For, behold, ᴿin those days, and in that time, when I shall bring again the captivity of Judah and Jerusalem, Jer. 30:3; Ezek. 38:14

2 I will also gather all nations, and will bring them down into the valley of Je-hosh'-a-phat, and will plead with them there for my people and for my heritage Israel, whom they have scattered among the nations, and parted my land.

3 And they have cast lots for my people; and have given a boy for an harlot, and sold a girl for wine, that they might drink.

4 Yea, and what have ye to do with me, O Tyre, and Zi'-don, and all the coasts of Palestine? will ye render me a recompence? and if ye recompense me, swiftly and speedily will I return your recompence upon your own head;

5 Because ye have taken my silver and my gold, and have carried into your temples my goodly pleasant things:

6 The ᵀchildren also of Judah and the ᵀchildren of Jerusalem have ye sold unto the Gre'-cians, that ye might remove them far from their border. people

7 Behold, I will raise them out of the place whither ye have sold them, and will return your recompence upon your own head:

8 And I will sell your sons and your daughters into the hand of the children of Judah, and they shall sell them to the ᴿSa-be'-ans, to a people ᴿfar off: for the LORD hath spoken it. Ezek. 23:42 · Jer. 6:20

9 Proclaim ye this among the Gentiles; Prepare war, wake up the mighty men, let all the men of war draw near; let them come up:

10 ᴿBeat your plowshares into swords, and your pruninghooks into spears: ᴿlet the weak say, I am strong. [Is. 2:4; Mic. 4:3] · Zech. 12:8

11 Assemble yourselves, and come, all ye heathen, and gather yourselves together round about: thither cause ᴿthy mighty ones to come down, O LORD. Ps. 103:20

12 Let the ᵀheathen be wakened, and come up to the valley of Je-hosh'-a-phat: for there will I sit to ᴿjudge all the ᵀheathen round about. nations · [Ps. 96:13]; Is. 2:4

13 ᴿPut ye in the sickle, for the harvest is ripe: come, get you down; for the ᴿpress is full, the fats overflow; for their wickedness is great. Rev. 14:15 · Rev. 14:19

14 Multitudes, multitudes in the valley of decision: for ᴿthe day of the LORD is near in the valley of decision. 2:1

15 The sun and the moon shall be darkened, and the stars shall withdraw their shining.

16 The LORD also shall roar out of Zion, and utter his voice from Jerusalem; and the heavens and the earth shall shake: ᴿbut the LORD will be ᵀthe hope of his people, and the strength of the children of Israel. [Is. 51:5, 6] · a shelter

17 So shall ye know that I am the LORD your God dwelling in Zion, my ᴿholy mountain: then shall Jerusalem be holy, and there shall no strangers pass through her any more. Obad. 16; Zech. 8:3

18 And it shall come to pass in that day, that the mountains shall drop down new wine, and the hills

shall flow with milk, and all the rivers of Judah shall flow with waters, and a ᴿfountain shall come forth of the house of the LORD, and shall water the valley of Shit′-tim.　　Zech. 14:8; [Rev. 22:1]

19 Egypt shall be a desolation, and E′-dom shall be a desolate wilderness, for the violence *against* the children of Judah, because they have shed innocent blood in their land.

20 But Judah shall ᵀdwell for ever, and Jerusalem from genera- tion to generation.　　*abide*

21 For I will ᴿcleanse their blood *that* I have not cleansed: for the LORD dwelleth in Zion.　　Is. 4:4

The Book of
AMOS

A MOS prophesies during a period of national optimism in Israel. Business is booming and boundaries are bulging. But below the surface, greed and injustice are festering. Hypocritical religious motions have replaced true wor- ship, creating a false sense of security and a growing callousness to God's dis- ciplining hand. Famine, drought, plagues, death, destruction—nothing can force the people to their knees.

Amos, the farmer-turned-prophet, lashes out at sin unflinchingly, trying to visualize the nearness of God's judgment and mobilize the nation to repen- tance. The nation, like a basket of rotting fruit, stands ripe for judgment because of its hypocrisy and spiritual indifference.

The name *Amos* is derived from the Hebrew root *amas*, "to lift a burden, to carry." Thus, his name means "Burden" or "Burden-Bearer." Amos lives up to the meaning of his name by bearing up under his divinely given burden of declaring judgment to rebellious Israel. The Greek and Latin titles are both transliterated in English as *Amos*.

T HE words of Amos, who was among the ᴿherdmen of Te- ko′-a, which he saw concerning Israel in the days of Uz-zi′-ah king of Judah, and in the days of ᴿJer- o-bo′-am the son of Jo′-ash king of Israel, two years before the ᴿearthquake.　　7:14 · 7:10 · Zech. 14:5

2 And he said, The LORD will ᴿroar from Zion, and utter his voice from Jerusalem; and the habitations of the shepherds shall mourn, and the top of ᴿCarmel shall wither.　　Joel 3:16 · 1 Sam. 25:2

3 Thus saith the LORD; For three transgressions of ᴿDamas- cus, and for four, I will not turn away *the punishment* thereof; because they have ᴿthreshed Gil′- e-ad with threshing instruments of iron:　　Zech. 9:1 · 2 Kin. 10:32, 33

4 ᴿBut I will send a fire into the house of Haz′-a-el, which shall devour the palaces of ᴿBen–ha′- dad.　　Jer. 49:27; 51:30 · 2 Kin. 6:24

5 I will break also the ᴿbar of Damascus, and cut off the inhabi- tant from the plain of A′-ven, and him that holdeth the sceptre from the house of Eden: and the people of Syria shall go into captivity unto Kir, saith the LORD.　　Jer. 51:30

6 Thus saith the LORD; For three transgressions of ᴿGa′-za, and for four, I will not turn away *the punishment* thereof; because they carried away captive the whole captivity, to deliver *them* up to E′-dom:　　Jer. 47:1, 5; Zeph. 2:4

7 ᴿBut I will send a fire on the wall of Ga′-za, which shall devour the palaces thereof:　　Jer. 47:1

8 And I will cut off the inhabitant from Ash'-dod, and him that holdeth the sceptre from Ash'-kelon, and I will turn mine hand against Ek'-ron: and ^Rthe remnant of the Phi-lis'-tines shall perish, saith the Lord GOD.   Zech. 9:5–7

9 Thus saith the LORD; For three transgressions of Ty'-rus, and for four, I will not turn away *the punishment* thereof; because they delivered up the whole captivity to E'-dom, and remembered not the brotherly covenant:

10 But I will send a fire on the wall of Ty'-rus, which shall devour the palaces thereof.

11 Thus saith the LORD; For three transgressions of E'-dom, and for four, I will not turn away *the punishment* thereof; because he did pursue his brother with the sword, and did cast off all pity, and his anger did tear perpetually, and he kept his wrath for ever:

12 But ^RI will send a fire upon Te'-man, which shall devour the palaces of Boz'-rah.   Obad. 9, 10

13 Thus saith the LORD; For three transgressions of ^Rthe children of Ammon, and for four, I will not turn away *the punishment* thereof; because they have ripped up the women with child of Gil'-e-ad, that they might enlarge their border: Ezek. 25:2; Zeph. 2:8, 9

14 But I will kindle a fire in the wall of ^RRab'-bah, and it shall devour the palaces thereof, ^Rwith shouting in the day of battle, with a tempest in the day of the whirlwind: 1 Chr. 20:1; Jer. 49:2 · Ezek. 21:22

15 And ^Rtheir king shall go into captivity, he and his princes together, saith the LORD.   Jer. 49:3

2 Thus saith the LORD; ^RFor three transgressions of Moab, and for four, I will not turn away *the punishment* thereof; because he burned the bones of the king of E'-dom into lime: Is. 15:1–16; Jer. 25:21

2 But I will send a fire upon Moab, and it shall devour the palaces of ^RKir'-i-oth: and Moab shall die with tumult, with shout-

ing, *and* with the sound of the trumpet: Jer. 48:24, 41

3 And I will cut off ^Rthe judge from the midst thereof, and will slay all the princes thereof with him, saith the LORD.   Jer. 48:7

4 Thus saith the LORD; For three transgressions of Judah, and for four, I will not turn away *the punishment* thereof; ^Rbecause they have despised the law of the LORD, and have not kept his commandments, and their lies caused them to err, after the which their fathers have walked: Lev. 26:14

5 ^RBut I will send a fire upon Judah, and it shall devour the palaces of Jerusalem.   Hos. 8:14

6 Thus saith the LORD; For three transgressions of Israel, and for four, I will not turn away *the punishment* thereof; because they sold the righteous for silver, and the poor for a pair of shoes;

7 That pant after the dust of the earth on the head of the poor, and ^Rturn aside the way of the meek: and a man and his father will go in unto the *same* maid, to profane my holy name: 5:12

8 And they lay *themselves* down upon clothes ^Rlaid to pledge by every altar, and they drink the wine of the condemned *in* the house of their god.   1 Cor. 8:10

9 Yet destroyed I the Am'-or-ite before them, whose height *was* like the height of the cedars, and he *was* strong as the oaks; yet I ^Rdestroyed his fruit from above, and his roots from beneath. Is. 5:24

10 Also ^RI brought you up from the land of Egypt, and ^Rled you forty years through the wilderness, to possess the land of the Am'-or-ite.   3:1; 9:7 · Deut. 2:7

11 And I raised up of your sons for ^Rprophets, and of your young men for ^RNazarites. *Is it* not even thus, O ye children of Israel? saith the LORD.   Num. 12:6 · Num. 6:2, 3

12 But ye gave the Nazarites wine to drink; and commanded the prophets, ^Rsaying, Prophesy not.   Is. 30:10; Jer. 11:21; Mic. 2:6

13 ^RBehold, I am pressed under you, as a cart is pressed *that is* full of sheaves.   Is. 1:14
14 ^RTherefore the flight shall perish from the swift, and the strong shall not strengthen his force, ^Rneither shall the mighty deliver himself: Jer. 46:6 · Ps. 33:16
15 Neither shall he stand that handleth the bow; and *he that is* swift of foot shall not deliver *himself*: neither shall he that rideth the horse deliver himself.
16 And *he that is* courageous among the mighty shall flee away naked in that day, saith the Lord.

3 Hear this word that the Lord hath spoken against you, O children of Israel, against the whole family which I brought up from the land of Egypt, saying,
2 ^RYou only have I known of all the families of the earth: ^Rtherefore I will punish you for all your iniquities. [Ps. 147:19] · Matt. 11:22
3 Can two walk together, except they be agreed?
4 Will a lion roar in the forest, when he hath no prey? will a young lion cry out of his den, if he ^Thave taken nothing?   *has caught*
5 Can a bird fall in a snare upon the earth, where no ^Tgin *is* for him? shall *one* take up a snare from the earth, and have ^Ttaken nothing at all?   *trap* or *bait* · *caught*
6 Shall a ^Ttrumpet be blown in the city, and the people not be afraid? ^Rshall there be ^Tevil in a city, and the Lord hath not done *it*?   *ram's horn* · Is. 45:7 · *calamity*
7 Surely the Lord God will do nothing, ^Tbut ^Rhe revealeth his secret unto his servants the prophets. *unless* · Dan. 9:22; [John 15:15]
8 The lion hath roared, who will not fear? the Lord God hath spoken, who can but prophesy?
9 ^TPublish in the palaces at Ash'-dod, and in the palaces in the land of Egypt, and say, Assemble yourselves upon the mountains of Sa-ma'-ri-a, and behold the great tumults in the midst thereof, and the oppressed in the midst thereof.   *Proclaim*

10 For they ^Rknow not to do right, saith the Lord, who store up violence and robbery in their palaces.   5:7; 6:12; Ps. 14:4; Jer. 4:22
11 Therefore thus saith the Lord God; An adversary *there shall be* even round about the land; and he shall bring down thy strength from thee, and thy palaces shall be ^Tspoiled.   *plundered*
12 Thus saith the Lord; As the shepherd taketh out of the mouth of the lion two legs, or a piece of an ear; so shall the children of Israel be taken out that dwell in Sa-ma'-ri-a in the corner of a bed, and in Damascus *in* a couch.
13 Hear ye, and testify in the house of Jacob, saith the Lord God, the God of hosts,
14 That in the day that I shall visit the transgressions of Israel upon him I will also visit the altars of ^RBeth'-el: and the horns of the altar shall be cut off, and fall to the ground.   2 Kin. 23:15
15 And I will smite the winter house with the summer house; and the houses of ivory shall perish, and the great houses shall have an end, saith the Lord.

4 Hear this word, ye ^Tkine of Ba'-shan, that *are* in the mountain of Sa-ma'-ri-a, which oppress the ^Rpoor, which crush the needy, which say to their masters, Bring, and let us drink.   *cows* · 2:6
2 The Lord God hath sworn by his holiness, that, lo, the days shall come upon you, that he will take you away with hooks, and your posterity with fishhooks.
3 And ^Rye shall go out at the ^Tbreaches, every *cow at that which is* before her; and ye shall cast *them* into the palace, saith the Lord. Ezek. 12:5 · *breaks* in the walls
4 ^RCome to Beth'-el, and transgress; at Gil'-gal multiply transgression; and bring your sacrifices every morning, *and* your tithes after three years: 3:14
5 ^RAnd offer a sacrifice of thanksgiving with leaven, and proclaim *and* publish ^Rthe free offerings: for this liketh you, O ye

children of Israel, saith the Lord
GOD.   Lev. 7:13 · Lev. 22:18; Deut. 12:6
6 And I also have given you
cleanness of teeth in all your
cities, and want of bread in all
your places: yet have ye not
returned unto me, saith the LORD.
7 And also I have withholden
the rain from you, when *there
were* yet three months to the harvest: and I caused it to rain upon
one city, and caused it not to rain
upon another city: one piece was
rained upon, and the piece
whereupon it rained not withered.
8 So two *or* three cities wandered unto ᵀone city, to drink
water; but they were not satisfied:
yet have ye not returned unto me,
saith the LORD.   *another*
9 I have smitten you with
blasting and mildew: when your
gardens and your vineyards and
your fig trees and your olive
trees increased, the palmerworm
devoured *them:* yet have ye
not returned unto me, saith the
LORD.
10 I have sent among you the
pestilence ᴿafter the manner of
Egypt: your young men have I
slain with the sword, and have
taken away your horses; and I
have made the stink of your
camps to come up unto your nostrils: yet have ye not returned
unto me, saith the LORD.   Ex. 9:3, 6
11 I have overthrown *some* of
you, as God overthrew ᴿSodom
and Go-mor'-rah, and ye were as
a firebrand plucked out of the
burning: yet have ye not returned
unto me, saith the LORD.   Is. 13:19
12 Therefore thus will I do unto
thee, O Israel: *and* because I will
do this unto thee, prepare to meet
thy God, O Israel.
13 For, lo, he that formeth the
mountains, and createth the wind,
ᴿand declareth unto man what *is*
his thought, that maketh the
morning darkness, ᴿand treadeth
upon the high places of the earth,
The LORD, The God of hosts, *is* his
name.   Ps. 139:2; Dan. 2:28 · Mic. 1:3

5 Hear ye this word which I
take up against you, *even* a
lamentation, O house of Israel.
2 The virgin of Israel is fallen;
she shall no more rise: she is forsaken upon her land; *there is*
none to raise her up.
3 For thus saith the Lord GOD;
The city that went out *by* a thousand shall ᵀleave an hundred, and
that which went forth *by* an hundred shall ᵀleave ten, to the house
of Israel.   *have left*
4 For thus saith the LORD unto
the house of Israel, Seek ye me,
ᴿand ye shall live: [Is. 55:3]
5 But seek not Beth'–el, nor
enter into Gil'-gal, and pass not to
Be'-er–she'-ba: for Gil'-gal shall
surely go into captivity, and
Beth'–el shall come to nought.
6 ᴿSeek the LORD, and ye shall
live; lest he break out like fire in
the house of Joseph, and devour
it, and *there be* none to quench *it*
in Beth'–el.   [Is. 55:3, 6, 7]
7 Ye who turn judgment to
wormwood, and ᵀleave off righteousness in the earth,   *abandon*
8 *Seek him* that maketh the
seven stars and O-ri'-on, and turneth the shadow of death into the
morning, and maketh the day
dark with night: that calleth for
the waters of the sea, and poureth
them out upon the face of the
earth: The LORD *is* his name:
9 That strengtheneth the
spoiled against the strong, so that
ᵀthe spoiled shall come against
the fortress.   *ruin comes upon*
10 ᴿThey hate him that rebuketh
in the gate, and they abhor him
that speaketh uprightly.   Is. 29:21
11 ᴿForasmuch therefore as
your treading *is* upon the poor,
and ye take from him burdens of
wheat: ᴿye have built houses of
hewn stone, but ye shall not dwell
in them; ye have planted pleasant
vineyards, but ye shall not drink
wine of them. 2:6 · Zeph. 1:13; Hag. 1:6
12 For I ᴿknow your manifold
transgressions and your ᵀmighty
sins: ᴿthey afflict the just, they
take a bribe, and they turn aside

the poor in the gate *from their right.*   Hos. 5:3 · *many* · Is. 1:23; 5:23

13 Therefore ᴿthe prudent shall keep silence in that time; for it *is* an evil time.   6:10

14 Seek good, and not evil, that ye may live: and so the Lᴏʀᴅ, the God of hosts, shall be with you, ᴿas ye have spoken.   Mic. 3:11

15 ᴿHate the evil, and love the good, and establish judgment in the gate: it may be that the Lᴏʀᴅ God of hosts will be gracious unto the remnant of Joseph.   Rom. 12:9

16 Therefore the Lᴏʀᴅ, the God of hosts, the Lord, saith thus; Wailing *shall be* in all streets; and they shall say in all the highways, Alas! alas! and they shall call the ᵀhusbandman to mourning, and ᴿsuch as are skilful of lamentation to wailing. *farmer* · 2 Chr. 35:25; Jer. 9:17

17 And in all vineyards *shall be* wailing: for ᴿI will pass through thee, saith the Lᴏʀᴅ.   Ex. 12:12

18 ᴿWoe unto you that desire the day of the Lᴏʀᴅ! to what end *is* it for you? the day of the Lᴏʀᴅ *is* darkness, and not light.   Is. 5:19

19 ᴿAs if a man did flee from a lion, and a bear met him; or went into the house, and leaned his hand on the wall, and a serpent bit him. Job 20:24; Is. 24:17, 18; Jer. 48:44

20 *Shall* not the day of the Lᴏʀᴅ *be* darkness, and not light? even very dark, and no brightness in it?

21 ᴿI hate, I despise your feast days, and I will not smell in your solemn assemblies.   Is. 1:11–16

22 ᴿThough ye offer me burnt offerings and your meat offerings, I will not accept *them*: neither will I regard the peace offerings of your fat beasts.   Is. 66:3; Mic. 6:6, 7

23 Take thou away from me the noise of thy songs; for I will not hear the melody of thy viols.

24 ᴿBut let judgment run down as waters, and righteousness as a mighty stream.   Jer. 22:3; Ezek. 45:9

25 ᴿHave ye offered unto me sacrifices and offerings in the wilderness forty years, O house of Israel?   Neh. 9:18–21; Acts 7:42, 43

26 But ye have borne the taber-nacle ᴿof your Mo′-loch and Chi′-un your ᵀimages, the star of your ᵀgod, which ye made to your-selves.   1 Kin. 11:33 · *idols* · *gods*

27 Therefore will I cause you to go into captivity ᴿbeyond Damas-cus, saith the Lᴏʀᴅ, ᴿwhose name *is* The God of hosts.   7:11, 17 · 4:13

6 Woe to them *that are* at ease in Zion, and trust in the moun-tain of Sa-ma′-ri-a, *which are* named chief of the nations, to whom the house of Israel came!

2 Pass ye unto ᴿCal′-neh, and see; and from thence go ye to ᴿHa′-math the great: then go down to Gath of the Phi-lis′-tines: *be they* better than these king-doms? or their border greater than your border?   Is. 10:9 · 1 Kin. 8:65

3 Ye that ᴿput far away the ᴿevil day, and cause the seat of violence to come near;   9:10 · 5:18

4 That lie upon beds of ivory, and ᵀstretch themselves upon their couches, and eat the lambs out of the flock, and the calves out of the midst of the stall;   *sprawl*

5 ᴿThat chant to the sound of the viol, *and* invent to themselves instruments of ᴿmusick, ᴿlike Da-vid;   Is. 5:12 · 5:23 · 1 Chr. 23:5

6 That ᴿdrink wine in bowls, and anoint themselves with the ᵀchief ointments: ᴿbut they are not grieved for the affliction of Jo-seph.   2:8; 4:1 · *best* · Gen. 37:25

7 Therefore now shall they go ᴿcaptive with the first that go cap-tive, and the banquet of them that stretched themselves shall be removed.   5:27

8 ᴿThe Lord Gᴏᴅ hath sworn by himself, saith the Lᴏʀᴅ the God of hosts, I abhor ᴿthe excellency of Jacob, and hate his palaces: there-fore will I deliver up the city with all that is therein.   Heb. 6:13–17 · 8:7

9 And it shall come to pass, if there remain ten men in one house, that they shall die.

10 And a man's uncle shall take him up, and he that burneth him, to bring out the bones out of the house, and shall say unto him that *is* by the sides of the house, *Is*

there yet *any* with thee? and he shall say, No. Then shall he say, RHold thy tongue: Rfor we may not make mention of the name of the LORD. 5:13 · 8:3

11 For, behold, Rthe LORD commandeth, and he will smite the great house with breaches, and the little house with clefts. Is. 55:11

12 Shall horses run upon the rock? will *one* plow *there* with oxen? for Rye have turned judgment into gall, and the fruit of righteousness into hemlock: 5:7

13 Ye which rejoice in a thing of nought, which say, Have we not taken to us horns by our own strength?

14 But, behold, I will raise up against you a nation, O house of Israel, saith the LORD the God of hosts; and they shall afflict you from the entering in of He′-math unto the river of the wilderness.

7 Thus hath the Lord GOD shewed unto me; and, behold, he formed grasshoppers in the beginning of the Tshooting up of the latter growth; and, lo, *it was* the Tlatter growth after the king's mowings. *sprouting · late crop*

2 And it came to pass, *that* when they had made an end of eating the grass of the land, then I said, O Lord GOD, forgive, I beseech thee: Rby whom shall Jacob arise? for he *is* small. Is. 51:19

3 RThe LORD repented for this: It shall not be, saith the LORD. 5:15

4 Thus hath the Lord GOD shewed unto me: and, behold, the Lord GOD called to contend by fire, and it devoured the great deep, and did eat up a part.

5 Then said I, O Lord GOD, cease, I beseech thee: by whom shall Jacob arise? for he *is* small.

6 The LORD Trepented for this: This also shall not be, saith the Lord GOD. *relented concerning this*

7 Thus he shewed me: and, behold, the Lord stood upon a wall *made* Tby a plumbline, with a plumbline in his hand. *with*

8 And the LORD said unto me, Amos, what seest thou? And I

said, A plumbline. Then said the Lord, Behold, RI will set a plumbline in the midst of my people Israel: RI will not again pass by them any more: Lam. 2:8 · Mic. 7:18

9 And the high places of Isaac shall be desolate, and the sanctuaries of Israel shall be laid waste; and I will rise against the house of Jer-o-bo′-am with the sword.

10 Then Am-a-zi′-ah the Rpriest of Beth′–el sent to RJer-o-bo′-am king of Israel, saying, Amos hath conspired against thee in the midst of the house of Israel: the land is not able to bear all his words. 1 Kin. 12:31, 32; 13:33 · 2 Kin. 14:23

11 For thus Amos saith, Jer-o-bo′-am shall die by the sword, and Israel shall surely be led away Rcaptive out of their own land. 6:7

12 Also Am-a-zi′-ah said unto Amos, O thou seer, go, flee thee away into the land of Judah, and there eat bread, and prophesy there:

13 But Rprophesy not again any more at Beth′–el: for it *is* the king's chapel, and it *is* the Tking's court. Acts 4:18 · *royal house*

14 Then answered Amos, and said to Am-a-zi′-ah, I *was* no prophet, neither *was* I a prophet's son; but I *was* an herdman, and a gatherer of sycomore fruit:

15 And the LORD took me Tas I followed the flock, and the LORD said unto me, Go, Rprophesy unto my people Israel. Lit. *from behind* · 3:8

16 Now therefore hear thou the word of the LORD: Thou sayest, Prophesy not against Israel, and Rdrop not *thy word* against the house of Isaac. Deut. 32:2; Ezek. 21:2

17 Therefore thus saith the LORD; RThy wife shall be an harlot in the city, and thy sons and thy daughters shall fall by the sword, and thy land shall be divided by line; and thou shalt die in a Rpolluted land: and Israel shall surely go into captivity forth of his land. Hos. 4:13; Zech. 14:2 · 2 Kin. 17:6

8 Thus hath the Lord GOD shewed unto me: and behold a basket of summer fruit.

2 And he said, Amos, what seest thou? And I said, A basket of summer fruit. Then said the Lord unto me, The end is come upon my people of Israel; ᴿI will not again pass by them any more. 7:8
3 And ᴿthe songs of the temple shall be ᵀhowlings in that day, saith the Lord God: *there shall be* many dead bodies in every place; ᴿthey shall cast *them* forth with silence.   5:23 · *wailing* · 6:9, 10
4 Hear this, O ye that swallow up the needy, even to make the poor of the land to fail,
5 Saying, When will the new moon be gone, that we may sell corn? and the sabbath, that we may set forth wheat, ᴿmaking the e′-phah small, and the shek′-el great, and falsifying the balances by ᴿdeceit?   Mic. 6:10, 11 · Lev. 19:35, 36
6 That we may buy the poor for ᴿsilver, and the needy for a pair of ᵀshoes; *yea*, and sell the ᵀrefuse of the wheat?   2:6 · *sandals* · *bad wheat*
7 The Lord hath sworn by the excellency of Jacob, Surely I will never forget any of their works.
8 ᴿShall not the land tremble for this, and every one mourn that dwelleth therein? and it shall rise up wholly as a flood; and it shall be cast out and drowned, ᴿas *by* the flood of Egypt.   Hos. 4:3 · 9:5
9 And it shall come to pass in that day, saith the Lord God, ᴿthat I will cause the sun to go down at noon, and I will darken the earth in the clear day: Luke 23:44
10 And I will turn your feasts into mourning, and all your songs into lamentation; ᴿand I will bring up sackcloth upon all loins, and baldness upon every head; and I will make it as the mourning of an only *son*, and the end thereof as a bitter day.   Jer. 6:26; [Zech. 12:10]
11 Behold, the days come, saith the Lord God, that I will send a famine in the land, not a famine of bread, nor a thirst for water, but of hearing the words of the Lord:
12 And they shall wander from sea to sea, and from the north even to the east, they shall run to

and fro to seek the word of the Lord, and shall not find *it*.
13 In that day shall the fair virgins and ᵀyoung men faint for thirst.   *strong young men*
14 They that swear by the sin of Samaria, and say, Thy god, O Dan, liveth; and, The manner of Be′-er–she′-ba liveth; even they shall fall, and never rise up again.
9 I saw the Lord standing upon the altar: and he said, Smite the lintel of the door, that the posts may shake: and cut them in the head, all of them; and I will slay the last of them with the sword: he that fleeth of them shall not flee away, and he that escapeth of them shall not be delivered.
2 ᴿThough they dig into ᵀhell, thence shall mine hand take them; though they climb up to heaven, thence will I bring them down: Ps. 139:8; Jer. 23:24 · Heb. *Sheol*
3 And though they hide themselves in the top of Carmel, I will search and take them out thence; and though they be hid from my sight in the bottom of the sea, thence will I command the serpent, and he shall bite them:
4 And though they go into captivity before their enemies, thence will I command the sword, and it shall slay them: and ᴿI will set mine eyes upon them for ᵀevil, and not for good.   Lev. 17:10 · *harm*
5 And the Lord God of hosts *is* he that toucheth the land, and it shall melt, ᴿand all that dwell therein shall mourn: and it shall rise up wholly like a flood; and shall be drowned, as *by* the ᵀflood of Egypt.   8:8 · *River*
6 *It is* he that buildeth his ᴿstoriesᵀ in the heaven, and hath founded his ᵀtroop in the earth; he that calleth for the waters of the sea, and poureth them out upon the face of the earth: The Lord *is* his name.   Ps. 104:3, 13 · *layers* · *strata*
7 *Are* ye not as children of the E-thi-o′-pi-ans unto me, O children of Israel? saith the Lord. Have not I brought up Israel out of the land of Egypt? and the ᴿPhi-

lis'-tines from Caph'-tor, and the Syrians from Kir?   Jer. 47:4

8 Behold, ᴿthe eyes of the Lord GOD *are* upon the sinful kingdom, and I will destroy it from off the face of the earth; saving that I will not utterly destroy the house of Jacob, saith the LORD.   Jer. 44:27

9 For, lo, I will command, and I will sift the house of Israel among all nations, like as *corn* is sifted in a sieve, yet shall not the least grain fall upon the earth.

10 All the sinners of my people shall die by the sword, ᴿwhich say, The evil shall not overtake nor prevent us.   [Is. 28:15]; Jer. 5:12

☆ 11 ᴿIn that day will I raise up the tabernacle of David that is fallen, and ᵀclose up the breaches thereof; and I will raise up his ruins, and I will build it as in the days of old: Acts 15:16–18 · *repair its damages*

12 ᴿThat they may possess the remnant of ᴿE'-dom, and of all the heathen, which are called by my name, saith the LORD that doeth this.   Obad. 19 · Num. 24:18; Is. 11:14

13 Behold, ᴿthe days come, saith the LORD, that the plowman shall overtake the reaper, and the treader of grapes him that soweth seed; ᴿand the mountains shall ᵀdrop sweet wine, and all the hills shall melt.   Lev. 26:5 · Joel 3:18 · *drip*

14 ᴿAnd I will bring again the captivity of my people of Israel, and ᴿthey shall build the waste cities, and inhabit *them;* and they shall plant vineyards, and drink the wine thereof; they shall also make gardens, and eat the fruit of them.   Ps. 53:6; Is. 60:4; Jer. 30:3 · Is. 61:4

15 And I will plant them upon their land, and ᴿthey shall no more be pulled up out of their land which I have given them, saith the LORD thy God.   Is. 60:21

The Book of
OBADIAH

A STRUGGLE that began in the womb between twin brothers, Esau and Jacob, eventuates in a struggle between their respective descendants, the Edomites and the Israelites. For the Edomites' stubborn refusal to aid Israel, first during the time of wilderness wandering (Num. 20:14–21) and later during a time of invasion, they are roundly condemned by Obadiah. This little-known prophet describes their crimes, tries their case, and pronounces their judgment: total destruction.

The Hebrew name *Obadyah* means "Worshiper of Yahweh" or "Servant of Yahweh." The Greek title in the Septuagint is *Obdiou,* and the Latin title in the Vulgate is *Abdias.*

THE vision of O-ba-di'-ah. Thus saith the Lord GOD ᴿconcerning E'-dom; We have heard a ᵀrumour from the LORD, and an ambassador is sent among the heathen, Arise ye, and let us rise up against her in battle. Is. 21:11 · *report*

2 Behold, I have made thee small among the ᵀheathen: thou art greatly despised.   *nations*

3 The pride of thine heart hath deceived thee, thou that dwellest in the clefts of the rock, whose habitation *is* high; ᴿthat saith in his heart, Who shall bring me down to the ground?   Rev. 18:7

4 ᴿThough thou exalt *thyself* as the eagle, and though thou ᴿset thy nest among the stars, thence will I bring thee down, saith the LORD.   Job 20:6 · Hab. 2:9; Mal. 1:4

5 If ᴿthieves came to thee, if robbers by night, ᵀ(how art thou cut off!) would they not have

stolen till they had enough? if the grapegatherers came to thee, would they not leave *some* grapes?   Jer. 49:9 · *Oh, how you are*

6 How ᵀare *the things* of Esau searched out! *how* are his hidden things sought up!   *Esau is*

7 All the men of thy confederacy have brought thee *even* to the border: the men that were at peace with thee have deceived thee, *and* prevailed against thee; *they that eat* thy bread have laid a wound under thee: *there is* none understanding in him.

8 ᴿShall I not in that day, saith the LORD, even destroy the wise *men* out of E′-dom, and understanding out of the mount of Esau?   [Job 5:12–14]; Is. 29:14

9 And thy mighty *men*, O Te′-man, shall be dismayed, to the end that every one of the mount of Esau may be cut off by slaughter.

10 For *thy* ᴿviolence against thy brother Jacob shame shall cover thee, and thou shalt be cut off for ever.   Gen. 27:41; Ezek. 25:12; Amos 1:11

11 In the day that thou ᴿstoodest on the other side, in the day that the strangers carried away captive his forces, and foreigners entered into his gates, and cast lots upon Jerusalem, even thou *wast* as one of them.   Ps. 83:5–8

12 But thou shouldest not have ᴿlooked on the day of thy brother in the day that he became a stranger; neither shouldest thou have rejoiced over the children of Judah in the day of their destruction; neither shouldest thou have spoken proudly in the day of distress.   Mic. 4:11; 7:10

13 Thou shouldest not have entered into the gate of my people in the day of their calamity; yea, thou shouldest not have looked on their affliction in the day of their

calamity, nor have laid *hands* on their substance in the day of their calamity;

14 Neither shouldest thou have stood in the crossway, to cut off those of his that did escape; neither shouldest thou have delivered up those of his that did remain in the day of distress.

15 ᴿFor the day of the LORD *is* near upon all the heathen: as thou hast done, it shall be done unto thee: thy reward shall return upon thine own head.   Ezek. 30:3

16 For as ye have drunk upon my holy mountain, *so* shall all the heathen drink continually, yea, they shall drink, and they shall swallow down, and they shall be as though they had not been.

17 But upon mount Zion shall be deliverance, and there shall be holiness; and the house of Jacob shall possess their possessions.

18 And the house of Jacob ᴿshall be a fire, and the house of Joseph a flame, and the house of Esau for stubble, and they shall kindle in them, and devour them; and there shall not be *any* remaining of the house of Esau; for the LORD hath spoken *it*.   Is. 5:24; 9:18, 19; Zech. 12:6

19 And *they of* the south ᴿshall possess the mount of Esau; ᴿand *they of* the plain the Phi-lis′-tines: and they shall possess the fields of E′-phra-im, and the fields of Sa-ma′-ri-a: and Benjamin *shall possess* Gil′-e-ad.   Is. 11:14 · Zeph. 2:7

20 And the captivity of this host of the children of Israel *shall possess* that of the Ca′-naan-ites, *even* ᴿunto Zar′-e-phath; and the captivity of Jerusalem, which *is* in Seph′-a-rad, shall possess the cities of the south.   Luke 4:26

21 And ᵀsaviours shall come up on mount Zion to judge the mount of Esau; and the ᴿkingdom shall be the LORD′s.   *deliverers* · [Rev. 11:15]

The Book of
JONAH

NINEVEH is northeast; Tarshish is west. When God calls Jonah to preach
repentance to the wicked Ninevites, the prophet knows that God's mercy
may follow. He turns down the assignment and heads for Tarshish instead. But
once God has dampened his spirits (by tossing him out of the boat and into the
water) and has demonstrated His protection (by moving him out of the water
and into the fish), Jonah realizes God is serious about His command. Nineveh
must hear the word of the Lord; therefore Jonah goes. Although the preaching
is a success, the preacher comes away angry and discouraged and he must
learn firsthand of God's compassion for sinful men.

    Yonah is the Hebrew word for "dove." The Septuagint hellenized this word
into *Ionas,* and the Latin Vulgate used the title *Jonas.*

NOW the word of the LORD
came unto ᴿJonah the son of
A-mit'-tai, saying,   Luke 11:29, 30, 32
2 Arise, go to Nin'-e-veh, that
ᴿgreat city, and cry against it; for
ᴿtheir wickedness is come up
before me.   Gen. 10:11, 12 · Gen. 18:20
3 But Jonah rose up to flee
unto Tar'-shish from the presence
of the LORD, and went down to
ᴿJop'-pa; and he found a ship
going to Tar'-shish: so he paid the
fare thereof, and went down into
it, to go with them unto ᴿTar'-
shish ᴿfrom the presence of the
LORD.   Acts 9:36, 43 · Is. 23:1 · Gen. 4:16
4 But ᴿthe LORD ᵀsent out a
great wind ᵀinto the sea, and there
was a mighty tempest in the sea,
so that the ship was like to be broken.   Ps. 107:25 · Lit. *hurled* · *on*
5 Then the mariners were
afraid, and cried every man unto
his god, and cast forth the ᵀwares
that *were* in the ship into the sea,
to lighten *it* of them. But Jonah
was gone down ᴿinto the sides of
the ship; and he lay, and was fast
asleep.   *cargo* · 1 Sam. 24:3
6 So the shipmaster came to
him, and said unto him, What
meanest thou, O sleeper? arise,
ᴿcall upon thy God, ᴿif so be that
God will think upon us, that we
perish not.   Ps. 107:28 · Joel 2:14
7 And they said every one to
his fellow, Come, and let us ᴿcast
lots, that we may know for whose

cause this ᵀevil *is* upon us. So they
cast lots, and the lot fell upon
Jonah.   1 Sam. 14:41, 42 · *trouble*
8 Then said they unto him, Tell
us, we pray thee, for whose cause
this evil *is* upon us; What *is* thine
occupation? and whence comest
thou? what *is* thy country? and of
what people *art* thou?
9 And he said unto them, I *am*
an Hebrew; and I fear the LORD,
the God of heaven, which hath
made the sea and the dry *land.*
10 Then were the men exceedingly afraid, and said unto him,
Why hast thou done this? For the
men knew that he fled from the
presence of the LORD, because he
had told them.
11 Then said they unto him,
What shall we do unto thee, that
the sea may be calm ᵀunto us? for
the sea ᵀwrought, and was tempestuous.   *for* · *was growing more*
12 And he said unto them, Take
me up, and cast me forth into the
sea; so shall the sea be calm unto
you: for I know that for my sake
this great tempest *is* upon you.
13 Nevertheless the men rowed
hard to bring *it* to the land;
ᴿbut they could not: for the sea
wrought, and was tempestuous
against them.   [Prov. 21:30]
14 Wherefore they cried unto
the LORD, and said, We beseech
thee, O LORD, we beseech thee, let
us not perish for this man's life,

and lay not upon us innocent blood: for thou, O LORD, ^Rhast done as it pleased thee.　Ps. 115:3

15 So they took up Jonah, and cast him forth into the sea: and the sea ceased from her raging.

16 Then the men ^Rfeared the LORD exceedingly, and offered a sacrifice unto the LORD, and made vows.　Mark 4:41; Acts 5:11

17 Now the LORD had prepared a great fish to swallow up Jonah. And Jonah was in the belly of the fish three days and three nights.

2 Then Jonah prayed unto the LORD his God out of the fish's belly,

2 And said, I ^Rcried by reason of mine affliction unto the LORD, ^Rand he heard me; out of the belly of ^Thell cried I, *and* thou heardest my voice. Ps. 120:1 · Ps. 65:2 · Heb. *Sheol*

3 ^RFor thou hadst cast me into the deep, in the midst of the seas; and the floods compassed me about: all thy billows and thy waves passed over me.　Ps. 88:6

4 Then I said, I am cast out of thy sight; yet I will look again ^Rtoward thy holy temple. 1 Kin. 8:38

5 The waters compassed me about, *even* to the soul: the depth closed me round about, the weeds were wrapped about my head.

6 I went down to the bottoms of the mountains; the earth with her bars *was* about me for ever: yet hast thou brought up my life from corruption, O LORD my God.

7 When my soul fainted within me I remembered the LORD: ^Rand my prayer came in unto thee, into thine holy temple.　2 Chr. 30:27

8 They that observe lying vanities forsake their own mercy.

9 But I will sacrifice unto thee with the voice of thanksgiving; I will pay *that* that I have vowed. ^RSalvation *is* of the LORD.　Ps. 3:8

10 And the LORD spake unto the fish, and it vomited out Jonah upon the dry *land.*

3 And the word of the LORD came unto Jonah the second time, saying,

2 Arise, go unto Nin'-e-veh, that great city, and preach unto it the preaching that I bid thee.

3 So Jonah arose, and went unto Nin'-e-veh, according to the word of the LORD. Now Nin'-e-veh was an exceeding great city of three days' journey.

4 And Jonah began to enter into the city ^Ta day's journey, and ^Rhe cried, and said, Yet forty days, and Nin'-e-veh shall be overthrown.　*on the first day's* · [Deut. 18:22]

5 So the ^Rpeople of Nin'-e-veh believed God, and proclaimed a fast, and put on sackcloth, from the greatest of them even to the least of them.　[Matt. 12:41; Luke 11:32]

6 For word came unto the king of Nin'-e-veh, and he arose from his throne, and he laid his robe from him, and covered *him* with sackcloth, and sat in ashes.

7 ^RAnd he caused *it* to be proclaimed and published through Nin'-e-veh by the decree of the king and his nobles, saying, Let neither man nor beast, herd nor flock, taste any thing: let them not feed, nor drink water:　Joel 2:15

8 But let man and beast be covered with sackcloth, and cry mightily unto God: yea, ^Rlet them turn every one from his evil way, and from ^Rthe violence that *is* in their hands.　Is. 58:6 · Is. 59:6

9 ^RWho can tell *if* God will turn and ^Trepent, and turn away from his fierce anger, that we perish not?　Joel 2:14; Amos 5:15 · *relent*

10 ^RAnd God saw their works, that they turned from their evil way; and God ^Trepented of the evil, that he had said that he would do unto them; and he did *it* not. Ex. 32:14 · *relented from the disaster*

4 But it displeased Jonah exceedingly, and he was very angry.

2 And he prayed unto the LORD, and said, I pray thee, O LORD, *was* not this my saying, when I was yet in my country? Therefore I fled before unto Tar'-shish: for I knew that thou *art* a gracious God, and merciful, slow

to anger, and of great kindness, and repentest thee of the evil.

3 ᴿTherefore now, O LORD, take, I beseech thee, my life from me; for *it is* better for me to die than to live.   1 Kin. 19:4; Job 6:8, 9

4 Then said the LORD, Doest thou well to be angry?

5 So Jonah went out of the city, and sat on the east side of the city, and there made him a ᵀbooth, and sat under it in the ᵀshadow, till he might see what would become of the city.   *shelter · shade*

6 And the LORD God prepared a gourd, and made *it* to come up over Jonah, that it might be a shadow over his head, to deliver him from his grief. So Jonah was exceeding glad of the gourd.

7 But God prepared a worm when the morning ᵀrose the next day, and it ᵀsmote the gourd that it withered.   *dawned · damaged,* lit. *struck*

8 And it came to pass, when the sun did arise, that God prepared a vehement east wind; and the sun beat upon the head of Jonah, that he fainted, and ᵀwished in himself to die, and said, *It is* better for me to die than to live.   *asked death for himself*

9 And God said to Jonah, Doest thou well to be angry for the gourd? And he said, I do well to be angry, *even* unto death.

10 Then said the LORD, Thou hast had pity on the ᵀgourd, for the which thou hast not laboured, neither madest it grow; which came up in a night, and perished in a night: *plant*

11 And should not I spare Nin′-e-veh, that great city, wherein are more than ᵀsixscore thousand persons ᴿthat cannot discern between their right hand and their left hand; and *also* much cattle?   *one hundred and twenty · Is. 7:16*

The Book of

MICAH

Micah, called from his rustic home to be a prophet, leaves his familiar surroundings to deliver a stern message of judgment to the princes and people of Jerusalem. Burdened by the abusive treatment of the poor by the rich and influential, the prophet turns his verbal rebukes upon any who would use their social or political power for personal gain. One-third of Micah's book exposes the sins of his countrymen; another third pictures the punishment God is about to send; and the final third holds out the hope of restoration once that discipline has ended. Through it all, God's righteous demands upon His people are clear: "to do justly, and to love mercy, and to walk humbly with thy God" (6:8).

The name *Michayahu* ("Who Is Like Yahweh?") is shortened to *Michaia*. In 7:18, Micah hints at his own name with the phrase "Who *is* a God like unto thee?" The Greek and Latin titles of this book are *Michaias* and *Micha*.

THE word of the LORD that came to Mi′-cah the Mo′-ras-thite in the days of Jo′-tham, Ahaz, *and* Hez-e-ki′-ah, kings of Judah, which he saw concerning Sa-mar′-i-a and Jerusalem.

2 Hear, all ye people; ᵀhearken, O earth, and all that therein is: and let the Lord GOD be witness against you, the Lord from ᴿhis holy temple.   *listen · [Ps. 11:4]*

3 For, behold, the LORD cometh forth out of his place, and will come down, and tread upon the high places of the earth.

4 And the mountains shall ᵀbe molten under him, and the valleys shall be cleft, as wax before the

fire, *and* as the waters *that are* poured down a steep place.　*melt*

5　For the transgression of Jacob *is* all this, and for the sins of the house of Israel. What *is* the transgression of Jacob? *is it* not Sa-ma′-ri-a? and what *are* the ᴿhigh places of Judah? *are they* not Jerusalem?　Deut. 32:13; Amos 4:13

6　Therefore I will make Sa-ma′-ri-a as an heap of the field, *and* as plantings of a vineyard: and I will pour down the stones thereof into the valley, and I will discover the foundations thereof.

7　And all the graven images thereof shall be beaten to pieces, and all the hires thereof shall be burned with the fire, and all the idols thereof will I lay desolate: for she gathered *it* of the hire of an harlot, and they shall return to the ᴿhire of an harlot.　Is. 23:17

8　Therefore I will wail and howl, I will go stripped and naked: ᴿI will make a wailing like the ᵀdragons, and mourning as the ᵀowls.　Ps. 102:6 · *jackals* · *ostriches*

9　For her wound *is* incurable; for ᴿit is come unto Judah; he is come unto the gate of my people, *even* to Jerusalem.　2 Kin. 18:13

10　Declare ye *it* not at Gath, weep ye not at all: in the house of Aph′-rah roll thyself in the dust.

11　Pass ye away, thou inhabitant of Sa′-phir, having thy shame naked: the inhabitant of Za′-a-nan came not forth in the mourning of Beth-e′-zel; he shall receive of you his standing.

12　For the inhabitant of Ma′-roth waited carefully for good: but evil came down from the LORD unto the gate of Jerusalem.

13　O thou inhabitant of ᴿLa′-chish, ᵀbind the chariot to the swift beast: she *is* the beginning of the sin to the daughter of Zion: for the transgressions of Israel were found in thee.　Is. 36:2 · *hitch*

14　Therefore shalt thou ᴿgive presents to Mor′-esh-eth–gath: the houses of Ach′-zib *shall be* a lie to the kings of Israel.　2 Sam. 8:2

15　Yet will I bring an heir unto

thee, O inhabitant of Ma-re′-shah: he shall come unto ᴿA-dul′-lam the glory of Israel.　2 Chr. 11:7

16　Make thee bald, and ᵀpoll thee for thy ᴿdelicate children; enlarge thy baldness as the eagle; for they are gone into captivity from thee.　*cut off your hair* · Lam. 4:5

2　Woe to them that devise iniquity, and ᵀwork evil upon their beds! when the ᴿmorning is light, they practise it, because it is in the power of their hand.　*plan* · Hos. 7:6, 7

2　And they ᴿcovet fields, and take *them* by violence; and houses, and take *them* away: so they oppress a man and his house, even a man and his heritage. Is. 5:8

3　Therefore thus saith the LORD; Behold, against this ᴿfamily do I devise an ᴿevil, from which ye shall not remove your necks; neither shall ye go haughtily: for this time *is* evil.　Amos 3:1, 2 · Amos 5:13

4　In that day shall *one* take up a ᵀparable against you, and lament with a ᵀdoleful lamentation, *and* say, We be utterly spoiled: he hath changed the portion of my people: how hath he removed *it* from me! turning away he hath divided our fields.　*proverb* · *bitter*

5　Therefore thou shalt have none that shall cast a cord by lot in the congregation of the LORD.

6　Prophesy ye not, *say they to them that* prophesy: they shall not prophesy to them, *that* they shall not take shame.

7　O *thou that art* named the house of Jacob, is the spirit of the LORD straitened? *are* these his doings? do not my words do good to him that walketh uprightly?

8　Even of late my people is risen up as an enemy: ye pull off the robe with the garment from them that pass by securely as men ᵀaverse from war.　*returning*

9　The women of my people have ye cast out from their pleasant houses; from their children have ye taken away my glory for ever.

10　Arise ye, and depart; for this *is* not *your* rest: because it is polluted, it shall destroy *you*, even with a sore destruction.

11 If a man walking in the spirit and falsehood do lie, *saying*, I will prophesy unto thee of wine and of strong drink; he shall even be the ^Rprophet of this people.   2 Tim. 4:3, 4

12 ^RI will surely assemble, O Jacob, all of thee; I will surely gather the remnant of Israel; I will put them together ^Ras the sheep of Boz'-rah, as the flock in the midst of their fold: they shall make great noise by reason of *the multitude* of men.   [4:6, 7] · Jer. 31:10

13 The breaker is come up before them: they have broken ^Tup, and have passed through the gate, and are gone out by it: and their king shall pass before them, and the LORD on the head of them.   out

3 And I said, Hear, I pray you, O heads of Jacob, and ye princes of the house of Israel; *Is it* not for you to know judgment?

2 Who hate the good, and love the evil; who ^Tpluck off their skin from off them, and their flesh from off their bones;   strip

3 Who also ^Reat the flesh of my people, and flay their skin from off them; and they break their bones, and chop them in pieces, as for the pot, and as flesh within the caldron.   Ps. 14:4; 27:2; Zeph. 3:3

4 Then ^Rshall they cry unto the LORD, but he will not hear them: he will even hide his face from them at that time, as they have behaved themselves ill in their doings.   Ps. 18:41; Prov. 1:28; Is. 1:15

5 Thus saith the LORD concerning the prophets that make my people err, that bite with their teeth, and cry, Peace; and he that putteth not into their mouths, they even prepare war against him.

6 ^RTherefore night *shall be* unto you, that ye shall not have a vision; and it shall be dark unto you, that ye shall not divine; and the sun shall go down over the prophets, and the day shall be dark over them.   Is. 8:20–22; 29:10–12

7 Then shall the seers be ashamed, and the diviners ^Tconfounded: yea, they shall all cover their lips; ^Rfor *there is* no answer ^Tof God.   embarrassed · Amos 8:11 · from

8 But truly I am full of power by the spirit of the LORD, and of judgment, and of might, ^Rto declare unto Jacob his transgression, and to Israel his sin.   Is. 58:1

9 Hear this, I pray you, ye heads of the house of Jacob, and ^Tprinces of the house of Israel, that abhor ^Tjudgment, and pervert all equity.   rulers · justice

10 ^RThey build up Zion with ^Rblood, and Jerusalem with iniquity.   Jer. 22:13, 17 · Ezek. 22:27; Hab. 2:12

11 The heads thereof judge for ^Treward, and the priests thereof teach for ^Thire, and the prophets thereof divine for money: yet will they lean upon the LORD, and say, *Is* not the LORD among us? none evil can come upon us.   a bribe · pay

12 Therefore shall Zion for your sake be plowed *as* a field, and Jerusalem shall become heaps, and the mountain of the house as the high places of the forest.

4 But ^Rin the last days it shall come to pass, *that* the mountain of the house of the LORD shall be established in the top of the mountains, and it shall be exalted above the hills; and people shall flow unto it.   Is. 2:2–4; Ezek. 17:22

2 And many nations shall come, and say, Come, and let us go up to the mountain of the LORD, and to the house of the God of Jacob; and he will teach us of his ways, and we will walk in his paths: for the law shall go forth ^Tof Zion, and the word of the LORD from Jerusalem.   out of

3 And he shall judge ^Tamong many people, and rebuke strong nations afar off; and they shall beat their swords into ^Rplowshares, and their spears into pruninghooks: nation shall not lift up a sword against nation, ^Rneither shall they learn war any more.   between · Is. 2:4; Joel 3:10 · Ps. 72:7

4 ^RBut they shall sit every man under his vine and under his fig

tree; and none shall make *them* afraid: for the mouth of the LORD of hosts hath spoken *it*.   Zech. 3:10

5 For all people will walk every one in the name of his god, and we will walk in the name of the LORD our God for ever and ever.

6 In that day, saith the LORD, ^Rwill I assemble ^Ther that halteth, ^Rand I will gather her that is driven out, and her that I have afflicted;   Ezek. 34:16 · *the lame* · Ps. 147:2

7 And I will make her that halted a remnant, and her that was cast far off a strong nation: and the LORD ^Rshall reign over them in mount Zion from henceforth, even for ever.   [Is. 9:6; Luke 1:33]

8 And thou, O tower of the flock, the strong hold of the daughter of Zion, unto thee shall it come, even the ^Tfirst dominion; the kingdom shall come to the daughter of Jerusalem.   *former*

9 Now why dost thou cry out aloud? *is there* no king in thee? is thy counsellor perished? for pangs have taken thee as a woman ^Tin travail.   *giving birth*

10 Be in pain, and labour to bring forth, O daughter of Zion, like a woman in travail: for now shalt thou go forth out of the city, and thou shalt dwell in the field, and thou shalt go *even* to ^RBabylon; there shalt thou be delivered; there the LORD shall redeem thee from the hand of thine enemies.   2 Chr. 36:20; Amos 5:27

11 ^RNow also many nations are gathered against thee, that say, Let her be defiled, and let our eye ^Rlook upon Zion.   Lam. 2:16 · Obad. 12

12 But they know not the thoughts of the LORD, neither understand they his counsel: for he shall gather them ^Ras the sheaves into the floor.   Is. 21:10

13 Arise and thresh, O daughter of Zion: for I will make thine horn iron, and I will make thy hoofs brass: and thou shalt beat in pieces many people: ^Rand I will consecrate their gain unto the LORD, and their substance unto the Lord of the whole earth. Is. 18:7

5 Now gather thyself in troops, O daughter of troops: he hath laid siege against us: they shall ^Rsmite the judge of Israel with a rod upon the cheek.   Matt. 27:30   ☆

2 But thou, ^RBeth'–le-hem Eph'-ra-tah, *though* thou be little ^Ramong the thousands of Judah, *yet* out of thee shall he come forth unto me *that is* to be ruler in Israel; whose goings forth *have been* from of old, from everlasting.   Matt. 2:6; Luke 2:4, 11 · 1 Sam. 23:23   ☆

3 Therefore will he give them up, until the time *that* ^Rshe which travaileth hath brought forth: then ^Rthe remnant of his brethren shall return unto the children of Israel.   4:10; Hos. 11:8 · 4:7; 7:18

4 And he shall stand and feed in the strength of the LORD, in the majesty of the name of the LORD his God; and they shall abide: for now ^Rshall he be great unto the ends of the earth.   [Luke 1:32]

5 And this *man* ^Rshall be the peace, when the Assyrian shall come into our land: and when he shall tread in our palaces, then shall we raise against him seven shepherds, and eight principal men.   Luke 2:14; [Eph. 2:14; Col. 1:20]

6 And they shall waste the land of Assyria with the sword, and the land of Nimrod in the entrances thereof: thus shall he deliver *us* from the Assyrian, when he cometh into our land, and when he treadeth within our borders.

7 And the remnant of Jacob shall be in the midst of many people ^Ras a dew from the LORD, as the showers upon the grass, that tarrieth not for man, nor waiteth for the sons of men. Ps. 72:6; Hos. 14:5

8 And the remnant of Jacob shall be among the Gentiles in the midst of many people as a lion among the beasts of the forest, as a young lion among the flocks of sheep: who, if he go through, both treadeth down, and teareth in pieces, and none can deliver.

9 Thine hand shall be lifted up upon thine adversaries, and all thine enemies shall be cut off.

10 And it shall come to pass in that day, saith the LORD, that I will ^Rcut off thy horses out of the midst of thee, and I will destroy thy ^Rchariots:　Zech. 9:10 · Is. 2:7; 22:18

11 And I will cut off the cities of thy land, and throw down all thy strong holds:

12 And I will cut off witchcrafts out of thine hand; and thou shalt have no *more* ^Rsoothsayers:　Is. 2:6

13 ^RThy graven images also will I cut off, and thy standing images out of the midst of thee; and thou shalt ^Rno more worship the work of thine hands.　Zech. 13:2 · Is. 2:8

14 And I will pluck up thy groves out of the midst of thee: so will I destroy thy cities.

15 And I will ^Rexecute vengeance in anger and fury upon the ^Theathen, such as they have not ^Theard.　[2 Thess. 1:8] · *nations · obeyed*

6 Hear ye now what the LORD saith; Arise, ^Tcontend thou before the mountains, and let the hills hear thy voice.　*plead your case*

2 Hear ye, O mountains, the LORD's controversy, and ye strong foundations of the earth: for ^Rthe LORD hath a controversy with his people, and he will ^Tplead with Israel.　[Is. 1:18] · *bring charges against*

3 O my people, ^Rwhat have I done unto thee? and wherein have I ^Rwearied thee? testify against me.　Jer. 2:5, 31 · Is. 43:22, 23; Mal. 1:13

4 ^RFor I brought thee up out of the land of Egypt, and redeemed thee out of the house of servants; and I sent before thee Moses, Aaron, and Miriam.　[Deut. 4:20]

5 O my people, remember now what ^RBa′-lak king of Moab consulted, and what Ba′-laam the son of Be′-or answered him from Shit′-tim unto Gil′-gal; that ye may know ^Rthe righteousness of the LORD.　Josh. 24:9 · Judg. 5:11

6 Wherewith shall I come before the LORD, *and* bow myself before the high God? shall I come before him with burnt offerings, with calves of a year old?

7 ^RWill the LORD be pleased with thousands of rams, *or* with ten thousands of rivers of oil? shall I give my firstborn *for* my transgression, the fruit of my body *for* the sin of my soul?　Is. 1:11

8 He hath shewed thee, O man, what *is* good; and what doth the LORD require of thee, but ^Rto do justly, and to love mercy, and to walk humbly with thy God?　Is. 1:17

9 The LORD's voice crieth unto the city, and *the man of* wisdom shall see thy name: hear ye the rod, and who hath appointed it.

10 Are there yet the treasures of wickedness in the house of the wicked, and the ^Tscant measure *that is* abominable?　*short*

11 Shall I count *them* pure with the wicked balances, and with the bag of deceitful weights?

12 For the rich men thereof are full of ^Rviolence, and the inhabitants thereof have spoken lies, and their tongue *is* deceitful in their mouth.　Is. 1:23; 5:7; Amos 6:3, 4

13 Therefore also will I ^Rmake *thee* sick in smiting thee, in making *thee* desolate because of thy sins.　Lev. 26:16; Ps. 107:17

14 ^RThou shalt eat, but not be satisfied; and thy casting down *shall be* in the midst of thee; and thou shalt take hold, but shalt not deliver; and *that* which thou deliverest will I give up to the sword.　Lev. 26:26

15 Thou shalt sow, but thou shalt not reap; thou shalt tread the olives, but thou shalt not anoint thee with oil; and sweet wine, but shalt not drink wine.

16 For the statutes of Om′-ri are kept, and all the works of the house of Ahab, and ye walk in their counsels; that I should make thee a desolation, and the inhabitants thereof an hissing: therefore ye shall bear the ^Rreproach of my people.　Is. 25:8

7 Woe is me! for I am as when they have gathered the summer fruits, as ^Rthe grapegleanings of the vintage: *there is* no cluster to eat: ^Rmy soul desired the firstripe fruit.　Is. 17:6 · Is. 28:4; Hos. 9:10

2 The ^Rgood *man* is perished

out of the earth: and *there is* none upright among men: they all lie in wait for blood; they hunt every man his brother with a net.   Ps. 12:1

3 That they may do evil with both hands earnestly, the prince asketh, and the judge *asketh* for a reward; and the great *man*, he uttereth his mischievous desire: so they ^Twrap it up.   *scheme together*

4 The best of them ^R*is* as a brier: the most upright *is sharper* than a thorn hedge: the day of thy watchmen *and* thy ^Tvisitation cometh; now shall be their perplexity.   Is. 55:13; Ezek. 2:6 · *punishment*

5 Trust ye ^Rnot in a friend, put ye not confidence in a guide: keep the doors of thy mouth from her that lieth in thy bosom.   Jer. 9:4

6 For ^Rthe son dishonoureth the father, the daughter riseth up against her mother, the daughter in law against her mother in law; a man's enemies *are* the men of his own house.   Matt. 10:36; John 7:5

7 Therefore I will look unto the LORD; I will ^Rwait for the God of my salvation: my God will hear me.   Ps. 130:5; Is. 25:9; Lam. 3:24, 25

8 Rejoice not against me, O mine enemy: when I fall, I shall arise; when I sit in darkness, the LORD *shall be* a light unto me.

9 ^RI will bear the indignation of the LORD, because I have sinned against him, until he plead my cause, and execute judgment for me: he will bring me forth to the light, *and* I shall behold his righteousness.   Lam. 3:39, 40; [2 Cor. 5:21]

10 Then *she that is* mine enemy shall see *it*, and ^Rshame shall cover her which said unto me, ^RWhere is the LORD thy God? mine eyes shall behold her: now shall she be trodden down as the mire of the streets.   Ps. 35:26 · Ps. 42:3

11 *In* the day that thy ^Rwalls are

to be built, *in* that day shall the decree be far removed.   Is. 54:11

12 *In* that day *also* ^Rhe shall come even to thee from Assyria, and *from* the fortified cities, and from the fortress even to the river, and from sea to sea, and *from* mountain to mountain.   [Is. 11:16]

13 Notwithstanding the land shall be desolate because of them that dwell therein, ^Rfor the fruit of their ^Tdoings.   Jer. 21:14 · *deeds*

14 Feed thy people with thy rod, the flock of thine heritage, which dwell ^Tsolitarily in ^Rthe ^Twood, in the midst of Carmel: let them feed *in* Ba'-shan and Gil'-e-ad, as in the days of old.   *alone* · Is. 37:24 · *woodland*

15 ^RAccording to the days of thy coming out of the land of Egypt will I shew unto him ^Rmarvellous *things*.   Ps. 68:22; 78:12 · Ex. 34:10

16 The nations ^Rshall see and be ^Tconfounded at all their might: ^Rthey shall lay *their* hand upon *their* mouth, their ears shall be deaf.   Is. 26:11 · *ashamed of* · Job 21:5

17 They shall lick the ^Rdust like a serpent, they shall move out of their holes like worms of the earth: ^Rthey shall be afraid of the LORD our God, and shall fear because of thee.   Ps. 72:9 · Jer. 33:9

18 Who *is* a God like unto thee, that pardoneth iniquity, and passeth by the transgression of the remnant of his heritage? he retaineth not his anger for ever, because he delighteth *in* mercy.

19 He will turn again, he will have compassion upon us; he will subdue our iniquities; and thou wilt cast all their sins into the depths of the sea.

20 Thou wilt perform the truth to Jacob, *and* the mercy to Abraham, which thou hast sworn unto our fathers from the days of old.

The Book of

NAHUM

"**F**OR unto whomsoever much is given, of him shall be much required" (Luke 12:48). Nineveh had been given the privilege of knowing the one true God. Under Jonah's preaching this great gentile city had repented, and God had graciously stayed His judgment. However, a hundred years later, Nahum proclaims the downfall of this same city. The Assyrians have forgotten their revival and have returned to their habits of violence, idolatry, and arrogance. As a result, Babylon will so destroy the city that no trace of it will remain—a prophecy fulfilled in painful detail.

The Hebrew word *nahum* ("comfort," "consolation") is a shortened form of Nehemiah ("Comfort of Yahweh"). The destruction of the capital city of Assyria is a message of comfort and consolation to Judah and all who live in fear of the cruelty of the Assyrians. The title of this book in the Greek and Latin Bibles is *Naoum* and *Nahum*.

THE burden Rof Nin'-e-veh. The book of the vision of Na'-hum the El'-kosh-ite. Jon. 1:2; Zeph. 2:13

2 God *is* Rjealous, and the LORD revengeth; the LORD Trevengeth, and *is* furious; the LORD will take vengeance on his adversaries, and he reserveth *wrath* for his enemies. Ex. 20:5; Josh. 24:19 · *avenges*

3 The LORD *is* Rslow to anger, and great in power, and will not at all acquit *the wicked:* the LORD *hath* his way in the whirlwind and in the storm, and the clouds *are* the dust of his feet. Ps. 103:8

4 RHe rebuketh the sea, and maketh it dry, and drieth up all the rivers: Ba'-shan languisheth, and Carmel, and the flower of Leb'-a-non languisheth. Matt. 8:26

5 The mountains quake at him, and the hills melt, and the earth is burned at his presence, yea, the world, and all that dwell therein.

6 Who can stand before his indignation? and Rwho can Tabide in the fierceness of his anger? his fury is poured out like fire, and the rocks are thrown down by him. Jer. 10:10; [Mal. 3:2] · *endure*

7 The LORD *is* good, a strong hold in the day of trouble; and he knoweth them that trust in him.

8 But with an overrunning flood he will make an utter end of the place thereof, and darkness shall pursue his enemies.

9 RWhat do ye imagine against the LORD? Rhe will make an utter end: affliction shall not rise up the second time. Ps. 2:1 · 1 Sam. 3:12

10 For while *they be* folden together Ras thorns, Rand while they are drunken *as* drunkards, Rthey shall be devoured as stubble fully dry. Mic. 7:4 · Is. 56:12 · Mal. 4:1

11 There is *one* come out of thee, that imagineth evil against the LORD, a wicked counsellor.

12 Thus saith the LORD; Though *they be* quiet, and likewise many, yet thus shall they be Rcut down, when he shall pass through. Though I have afflicted thee, I will afflict thee no more. [Is. 10:16–19]

13 For now will I break his yoke from off thee, and will burst thy bonds in sunder.

14 And the LORD hath given a commandment concerning thee, *that* no more of thy name be sown: out of the house of thy gods will I cut off the graven image and the molten image: I will make thy grave; for thou art Rvile. 3:6

15 Behold upon the mountains the feet of him that bringeth good tidings, that publisheth peace! O Judah, keep thy solemn feasts, perform thy vows: for the wicked shall no more pass through thee; he is utterly cut off.

2 He that dasheth in pieces is come up before thy face: Tkeep

the munition, watch the way, make *thy* loins strong, fortify *thy* power mightily. *guard the fortress*
2 For the LORD hath turned away the excellency of Jacob, as the excellency of Israel: for the emptiers have emptied them out, and marred their vine branches.
3 The shield of his mighty men is made red, the valiant men *are* in scarlet: the chariots *shall be* with flaming torches in the day of his preparation, and the fir trees shall be terribly shaken.
4 The chariots shall rage in the streets, they shall ᵀjustle one against another in the broad ᵀways: they shall seem like torches, they shall run like the lightnings. *jostle · roads*
5 He shall recount his worthies: they shall stumble in their walk; they shall make haste to the wall thereof, and the defence shall be prepared.
6 The gates of the rivers shall be opened, and the palace shall be ᵀdissolved. *melted*
7 And Huz'-zab shall be led away captive, she shall be brought up, and her maids shall lead *her* as with the voice of doves, ᵀtabering upon their breasts. *beating*
8 But Nin'-e-veh *is* of old like a pool of water: yet they shall flee away. Stand, stand, *shall they cry;* but none shall ᵀlook back. *turn*
9 Take ye the spoil of silver, take the spoil of gold: for *there is* none end of the store *and* glory out of all the pleasant furniture.
10 She is empty, and ᵀvoid, and waste: and the heart melteth, and the knees ᵀsmite together, and much pain *is* in ᵀall loins, and the faces of them all gather blackness. *desolate · shake · every side*
11 Where *is* the dwelling of the lions, and the feedingplace of the young lions, where the lion, *even* the ᵀold lion, walked, *and* the lion's ᵀwhelp, and none made *them* afraid? *lioness · cub*
12 The lion did tear in pieces enough for his whelps, and stran-

gled for his lionesses, and ᴿfilled his holes with prey, and his dens with ᵀravin. Is. 10:6; Jer. 51:34 · *torn flesh*
13 ᴿBehold, I *am* against thee, saith the LORD of hosts, and I will burn her chariots in the smoke, and the sword shall devour thy young lions: and I will cut off thy prey from the earth, and the voice of thy ᴿmessengers shall no more be heard. Jer. 21:13 · 2 Kin. 18:17–25

3 Woe to the ᴿbloody city! it *is* all full of lies *and* robbery; the prey departeth not; Ezek. 22:2, 3
2 The noise of a whip, and the noise of the rattling of the wheels, and of the ᵀpransing horses, and of the jumping chariots. *galloping*
3 The horseman ᵀlifteth up both the bright sword and the glittering spear: and *there is* a multitude of slain, and a great number of carcases; and *there is* none end of *their* corpses; they stumble upon their corpses: *charge with*
4 Because of the multitude of the whoredoms of the wellfavoured harlot, the mistress of witchcrafts, that selleth nations through her whoredoms, and families through her witchcrafts.
5 Behold, I *am* against thee, saith the LORD of hosts; and ᴿI will ᵀdiscover thy skirts ᵀupon thy face, and I will shew the nations thy nakedness, and the kingdoms thy shame. Jer. 13:26 · *lift · over*
6 And I will cast abominable filth upon thee, and make thee ᴿvile, and will set thee as ᴿa ᵀgazingstock. 1:14 · Heb. 10:33 · *spectacle*
7 And it shall come to pass, *that* all they that look upon thee ᴿshall flee from thee, and say, Nin'-e-veh is laid waste: who will bemoan her? whence shall I seek comforters for thee? Rev. 18:10
8 ᴿArt thou better than populous ᴿNo, that was situate among the rivers, *that had* the waters round about it, whose rampart *was* the sea, *and* her wall *was* from the sea? Amos 6:2 · Jer. 46:25
9 E-thi-o'-pi-a and Egypt *were* her strength, and *it was* infinite; Put and Lu'-bim were thy helpers.

10 Yet *was* she carried away, she went into captivity: [R]her young children also were dashed in pieces at the top of all the streets: and they cast lots for her honourable men, and all her great men were bound in chains. Is. 13:16

11 Thou also shalt be [R]drunken: thou shalt be hid, thou also shalt seek strength because of the enemy.   Is. 49:26; Jer. 25:27

12 All thy strong holds *shall be like* [R]fig trees with the firstripe figs: if they be shaken, they shall even fall into the mouth of the eater.   Rev. 6:12, 13

13 Behold, [R]thy people in the midst of thee *are* women: the gates of thy land shall be set wide open unto thine enemies: the fire shall devour thy bars.   Is. 19:16

14 Draw thee waters for the siege, [R]fortify thy strong holds: go into clay, and tread the morter, make strong the brickkiln.   2:1

15 There shall the fire devour thee; the sword shall cut thee off, it shall eat thee up like [R]the cankerworm: make thyself many as the cankerworm, make thyself many as the locusts.   Joel 1:4

16 Thou hast multiplied thy [R]merchants above the stars of heaven: the cankerworm spoileth, and fleeth away.   Rev. 18:3, 11–19

17 Thy [T]crowned *are* as the locusts, and thy captains as the great grasshoppers, which camp in the hedges in the cold day, *but* when the sun ariseth they flee away, and their place is not known where they *are.*   officials

18 Thy shepherds slumber, O king of Assyria: thy nobles shall dwell *in the dust:* thy people is scattered upon the mountains, and no man gathereth *them.*

19 *There is* no healing of thy bruise; thy wound is grievous: [R]all that hear the [T]bruit of thee shall clap the hands over thee: for upon whom hath not thy wickedness passed continually? Zeph. 2:15 · news

The Book of
HABAKKUK

HABAKKUK ministers during the "death throes" of the nation of Judah. Although repeatedly called to repentance, the nation stubbornly refuses to change her sinful ways. Habakkuk, knowing the hardheartedness of his countrymen, asks God how long this intolerable condition can continue. God replies that the Babylonians will be His chastening rod upon the nation—an announcement that sends the prophet to his knees. He acknowledges that the just in any generation shall live by faith (2:4), not by sight. Habakkuk concludes by praising God's wisdom even though he does not fully understand God's ways.

Habaqquq is an unusual Hebrew name derived from the verb *habaq,* "embrace." Thus his name probably means "One Who Embraces" or "Clings." At the end of his book this name becomes appropriate because Habakkuk chooses to cling firmly to God regardless of what happens to his nation (3:16–19). The Greek title in the Septuagint is *Ambakouk,* and the Latin title in Jerome's Vulgate is *Habacuc.*

THE [T]burden which Ha-bak'-kuk the prophet did see. oracle

2 O Lord, how long shall I cry, [R]and thou wilt not hear! *even* cry out unto thee *of* violence, and thou wilt not save!   Lam. 3:8

3　Why dost thou shew me iniquity, and cause *me* to behold ᵀgrievance? for ᵀspoiling and violence *are* before me: and there are *that* raise up strife and contention.　*trouble or toil · plundering*

4　Therefore the law is slacked, and judgment doth never go forth: for the wicked doth compass about the righteous; therefore wrong judgment proceedeth.

5　Behold ye among the heathen, and regard, and wonder marvellously: for *I* will work a work in your days, *which* ye will not believe, though it be told *you.*

6　For, lo, I raise up the Chal-de′-ans, *that* bitter and ᵀhasty nation, which shall march through the breadth of the land, to possess the dwellingplaces *that are* not theirs.　*impetuous*

7　They *are* terrible and dreadful: their judgment and their dignity shall proceed of themselves.

8　Their horses also are swifter than the leopards, and are more fierce than the evening wolves: and their horsemen shall spread themselves, and their horsemen shall come from far; they shall fly as the eagle *that* hasteth to eat.

9　They shall come all for violence: their faces shall sup up *as* the east wind, and they shall gather the captivity as the sand.

10　And they shall scoff at the kings, and the princes shall be a scorn unto them: they shall deride every strong hold; for they shall heap dust, and take it.

11　Then shall *his* mind change, and he shall ᵀpass over, and offend, ᴿ*imputing* this his power unto his god.　*transgress · Dan. 5:4*

12　*Art* thou not ᴿfrom everlasting, O LORD my God, mine Holy One? we shall not die. O LORD, thou hast ordained them for judgment; and, O mighty God, ᴿthou hast established them for correction.　Deut. 33:27 · Is. 10:5–7; Mal. 3:5

13　*Thou art* of purer eyes than to behold evil, and canst not look on ᵀiniquity: wherefore lookest thou upon them that deal treacherously, *and* holdest thy tongue when the wicked devoureth *the man that is* more righteous than he?　*wickedness*

14　And makest men as the fishes of the sea, as the creeping things, *that have* no ruler over them?

15　They take up all of them with ᵀthe angle, they catch them in their net, and gather them in their ᵀdrag: therefore they rejoice and are glad.　*a hook · dragnet*

16　Therefore ᴿthey sacrifice unto their net, and burn incense unto their ᵀdrag; because by them their portion *is* fat, and their meat plenteous.　Deut. 8:17 · *dragnet*

17　Shall they therefore empty their net, and not spare continually to slay the nations?

2 I will ᴿstand upon my watch, and set me upon the tower, and will watch to see what he will say unto me, and what I shall answer when I am reproved.　Is. 21:8, 11

2　And the LORD answered me, and said, ᴿWrite the vision, and make *it* plain upon tables, that he may run that readeth it.　Is. 8:1

3　For the vision *is* yet for an appointed time, but at the end it shall speak, and not lie: though it tarry, wait for it; because it will surely come, it will not tarry.

4　Behold, his soul *which* is lifted up is not upright in him: but the just shall live by his faith.

5　Yea also, because he transgresseth by wine, *he is* a proud man, neither keepeth at home, who ᴿenlargeth his desire as ᵀhell, and *is* as death, and cannot be satisfied, but gathereth unto him all nations, and heapeth unto him all people:　Is. 5:11–15 · Heb. *Sheol*

6　Shall not all these ᴿtake up a ᵀparable against him, and a taunting ᵀproverb against him, and say, Woe to him that increaseth *that which is* not his! how long? and to him that ladeth himself with thick clay!　Mic. 2:4 · *proverb · riddle*

7　Shall ᵀthey not rise up suddenly that shall bite thee, and awake that shall ᵀvex thee, and thou shalt be for ^Tbooties unto them? *your creditors · oppress · plunder*

8 Because thou hast spoiled many nations, all the remnant of the people shall spoil thee; because of men's blood, and *for* the violence of the land, of the city, and of all that dwell therein.

9 Woe to him that coveteth an evil covetousness to his house, that he may ^Rset his nest on high, that he may be delivered from the power of ^Tevil! Obad. 4 · *disaster*

10 Thou ^Thast consulted shame to thy house by cutting off many ^Tpeople, and hast sinned *against* thy soul. *gave shameful counsel · peoples*

11 For the stone shall cry out of the wall, and the beam out of the timber shall answer it.

12 Woe to him that buildeth a town with ^Tblood, and stablisheth a city by iniquity! *bloodshed*

13 Behold, *is it* not of the LORD of hosts that the people shall labour in the very fire, and the people shall weary themselves ^Tfor very vanity? *in vain*

14 For the earth shall be filled with the knowledge of the glory of the LORD, as the waters cover the sea.

15 Woe unto him that giveth his neighbour drink, that puttest thy ^Rbottle to *him*, and makest *him* drunken also, that thou mayest look on their nakedness! Hos. 7:5

16 Thou art filled with shame for glory: drink thou also, and let thy foreskin be uncovered: the cup of the LORD's right hand shall be turned unto thee, and shameful spewing *shall be* on thy glory.

17 For the violence ^Tof Leb'-a-non shall cover thee, and the ^Tspoil of beasts, *which* made them afraid, because of men's blood, and for the violence of the land, of the city, and of all that dwell therein. *Done to · plunder*

18 What profiteth the ^Tgraven image that the maker thereof hath graven it; the molten image, and a teacher of lies, that the maker of his work trusteth therein, to make ^Tdumb idols? *carved · mute*

19 Woe unto him that saith to the wood, Awake; to the ^Tdumb stone, Arise, it shall teach! Behold, it *is* laid over with gold and silver, and *there is* no breath at all in the midst of it. *silent*

20 ^RBut the LORD *is* in his holy temple: let all the earth keep silence before him. Zech. 2:13

3 A prayer of Ha-bak'-kuk the prophet upon Shig-i-o'-noth.

2 O LORD, I have heard thy speech, *and* was afraid: O LORD, revive thy work in the midst of the years, in the midst of the years make known; in wrath remember mercy.

3 God came from Te'-man, and the Holy One from mount Pa'-ran. Selah. His glory covered the heavens, and the earth was full of his praise.

4 And *his* brightness was as the light; he had horns *coming* out of his hand: and there *was* ^Tthe hiding of his power. *his power hidden*

5 Before him went the pestilence, and ^Tburning coals went forth at his feet. *fever followed at*

6 He stood, and measured the earth: he beheld, and ^Tdrove asunder the nations; ^Rand the everlasting mountains were scattered, the perpetual hills did bow: his ways *are* everlasting. *startled* · Nah. 1:5

7 I saw the tents of Cu'-shan in affliction: *and* the curtains of the land of Mid'-i-an did tremble.

8 Was the LORD displeased against the rivers? *was* thine anger against the rivers? *was* thy wrath against the sea, that thou didst ride upon thine horses *and* thy chariots of salvation?

9 Thy bow was made quite ^Tnaked, *according* to the oaths of the tribes, *even thy* word. Selah. Thou ^Tdidst cleave the earth with rivers. *bare · divided*

10 The mountains saw thee, *and* they trembled: the overflowing of the water passed by: the deep uttered his voice, *and* ^Rlifted up his hands on high. Ex. 14:22

11 The sun *and* moon stood still in their habitation: at the light of

thine arrows they went, *and* at the shining of thy glittering spear.

12 Thou didst march through the land in indignation, thou didst thresh the heathen in anger.

13 Thou wentest forth for the salvation of thy people, *even* for salvation with thine anointed; thou woundedst the head ᵀout of the house of the wicked, by ᵀdiscovering the foundation unto the neck. Selah. *from · laying bare from*

14 Thou didst strike through with ᵀhis staves the head of his villages: they came out as a whirlwind to scatter me: their rejoicing *was* as ᵀto devour the poor secretly. *his own arrows · feasting on*

15 ᴿThou didst walk through the sea with thine horses, *through* the heap of great waters. Ps. 77:19

16 When I heard, ᴿmy ᵀbelly trembled; my lips quivered at the voice: rottenness entered into my bones, and I trembled in myself, that I might rest in the day of trouble: when he cometh up unto the people, he will invade them with his troops. Ps. 119:120 · Body

17 Although the fig tree shall not blossom, neither *shall* fruit *be* in the vines; the labour of the olive shall fail, and the fields shall yield no ᵀmeat; the flock shall be cut off from the fold, and *there shall be* no herd in the stalls: *food*

18 Yet I will ᴿrejoice in the LORD, I will joy in the God of my salvation. Is. 41:16; 61:10

19 The LORD God *is* my strength, and he will make my feet like ᴿhinds' *feet*, and he will make me to ᴿwalk upon mine high places. To the chief singer on my stringed instruments. Ps. 18:33 · Deut. 32:13

The Book of

ZEPHANIAH

DURING Judah's hectic political and religious history, reform comes from time to time. Zephaniah's forceful prophecy may be a factor in the reform that occurs during Josiah's reign—a "revival" that produces outward change, but does not fully remove the inward heart of corruption which characterizes the nation. Zephaniah hammers home his message repeatedly that the day of the Lord, Judgment Day, is coming when the malignancy of sin will be dealt with. Israel and her gentile neighbors will soon experience the crushing hand of God's wrath. But after the chastening process is complete, blessing will come in the person of the Messiah, who will be the cause for praise and singing.

Tsephan-yah means "Yahweh Hides" or "Yahweh Has Hidden." Zephaniah was evidently born during the latter part of the reign of King Manasseh. His name may mean that he was "hidden" from Manasseh's atrocities. The Greek and Latin title is *Sophonias*.

THE word of the LORD which came unto Zeph-a-ni′-ah the son of Cu′-shi, the son of Ged-a-li′-ah, the son of Am-a-ri′-ah, the son of ᵀHiz-ki′-ah, in the days of Jo-si′-ah the son of Amon, king of Judah. *Hezekiah, 2 Kin. 18:1*

2 I will ᵀutterly consume all *things* from off the land, saith the LORD. Lit. *completely make an end of*

3 I will consume man and beast; I will consume the fowls of the heaven, and the fishes of the sea, and the stumblingblocks with the wicked; and I will cut off man from off the land, saith the LORD.

4 I will also stretch out mine hand upon Judah, and upon all the inhabitants of Jerusalem; and I will cut off ᵀthe remnant of Ba′-

al from this place, *and* the name of ^Rthe Chem'-a-rims with the priests; *every trace* · 2 Kin. 23:5; Hos. 10:5

5   And them ^Rthat worship the host of heaven upon the house-tops; and them that worship *and* that swear by the LORD, and that swear by Mal'-cham;   2 Kin. 23:12

6   And ^Rthem that are turned back from the LORD; and *those* that ^Rhave not sought the LORD, nor enquired for him. Is. 1:4 · Hos. 7:7

7   ^RHold thy peace at the presence of the Lord GOD: for the day of the LORD *is* at hand: for the LORD hath prepared a sacrifice, he hath bid his guests.   Zech. 2:13

8   And it shall come to pass in the day of the LORD's sacrifice, that I will ^Tpunish ^Rthe princes, and the king's children, and all such as are clothed with ^Tstrange apparel. Lit. *visit upon* · Jer. 39:6 · *foreign*

9   In the same day also will I ^Tpunish all those that ^Rleap on the threshold, which fill their masters' houses with violence and deceit.   Lit. *visit* · 1 Sam. 5:5

10 And it shall come to pass in that day, saith the LORD, *that* there shall be the noise of a cry from ^Rthe fish gate, and an howling from the second, and a great crashing from the hills.   2 Chr. 33:14

11 ^RHowl, ye inhabitants of Mak'-tesh, for all the merchant people are cut down; all they that bear silver are cut off.   James 5:1

12 And it shall come to pass at that time, *that* I will search Jerusalem with ^Tcandles, and punish the men that are settled on their lees: ^Rthat say in their heart, The LORD will not do good, neither will he do evil.   *lamps* · Ps. 94:7

13 Therefore their goods shall become a booty, and their houses a desolation: they shall also build houses, but not inhabit *them;* and they shall plant vineyards, but not drink the wine thereof.

14 ^RThe great day of the LORD *is* near, *it is* near, and hasteth greatly, *even* the voice of the day of the LORD: the mighty man shall cry there bitterly.   Jer. 30:7; Joel 2:1, 11

15 ^RThat day *is* a day of wrath, a day of trouble and distress, a day of ^Twasteness and desolation, a day of darkness and gloominess, a day of clouds and thick darkness,   Is. 22:5 · *devastation*

16 A day of the trumpet and alarm against the fenced cities, and against the high towers.

17 And I will bring distress upon men, that they shall walk like blind men, because they have sinned against the LORD: and their blood shall be poured out as dust, and their flesh as the dung.

18 ^RNeither their silver nor their gold shall be able to deliver them in the day of the LORD's wrath; but the whole land shall be devoured by the fire of his jealousy: for he shall make even a speedy ^Triddance of all them that dwell in the land.   Ezek. 7:19 · *end*

2 Gather^R yourselves together, yea, gather together, O nation not desired;   2 Chr. 20:4; Joel 1:14; 2:16

2   Before the decree ^Tbring forth, *before* the day pass as the chaff, before the fierce anger of the LORD come upon you, before the day of the LORD's anger come upon you.   *is issued*

3   ^RSeek ye the LORD, ^Rall ye meek of the earth, which have wrought his judgment; seek righteousness, seek meekness: it may be ye shall be hid in the day of the LORD's anger.   Amos 5:6 · Ps. 76:9

4   For ^RGa'-za shall be forsaken, and Ash'-ke-lon a desolation: they shall drive out Ash'-dod ^Rat the noon day, and Ek'-ron shall be rooted up. Amos 1:7, 8; Zech. 9:5 · Jer. 6:4

5   Woe unto the inhabitants of ^Rthe sea coast, the nation of the Cher'-e-thites! the word of the LORD *is* against you; O Canaan, the land of the Phi-lis'-tines, I will even destroy thee, that there shall be no inhabitant.   Ezek. 25:15–17

6   And the sea coast shall be dwellings *and* cottages for shepherds, ^Rand folds for flocks. Is. 17:2

7   And the coast shall be for ^Rthe remnant of the house of Judah; they shall feed thereupon:

in the houses of Ash'-ke-lon shall they lie down in the evening: for the LORD their God shall ^Rvisit them, and ^Rturn away their captivity.   [Mic. 5:7, 8] · Luke 1:68 · Jer. 29:14

8 ^RI have heard the reproach of Moab, and the revilings of the children of Ammon, whereby they have reproached my people, and magnified *themselves* against their border.   Jer. 48:27; Amos 2:1–3

9 Therefore *as* I live, saith the LORD of hosts, the God of Israel, Surely ^RMoab shall be as Sodom, and ^Rthe children of Ammon as Go-mor'-rah, *even* the breeding of nettles, and saltpits, and a perpetual desolation: the residue of my people shall spoil them, and the remnant of my people shall possess them.   Is. 15:1–9 · Amos 1:13

10 This shall they have ^Rfor their pride, because they have reproached and magnified *themselves* against the people of the LORD of hosts.   Is. 16:6

11 The LORD *will be* ^Tterrible unto them: for he will ^Tfamish all the gods of the earth; and *men* shall worship him, every one from his place, *even* all the isles of the heathen.   *awesome · reduce to nothing*

12 Ye E-thi-o'-pi-ans also, ye *shall be* slain by my sword.

13 And he will stretch out his hand against the north, and ^Rdestroy Assyria; and will make Nin'-e-veh a desolation, *and* dry like a wilderness.   Is. 10:5–27; 14:24–27

14 And flocks shall lie down in the midst of her, all the beasts of the nations: both the cormorant and the bittern shall lodge in the upper lintels of it; *their* voice shall sing in the windows; desolation *shall be* in the thresholds: for he shall uncover the cedar work.

15 This *is* the rejoicing city ^Rthat dwelt ^Tcarelessly, ^Rthat said in her heart, I *am,* and *there is* none beside me: how is she become a desolation, a place for beasts to lie down in! every one that passeth by her shall hiss, *and* wag his hand.   Is. 47:8 · *securely* · Rev. 18:7

3 Woe to her that is filthy and polluted, to the oppressing city!

2 She obeyed not the voice; she received not correction; she trusted not in the LORD; she drew not near to her God.

3 Her princes within her *are* roaring lions; her judges *are* ^Revening wolves; they gnaw not the bones till the morrow.   Jer. 5:6

4 Her prophets *are* light *and* treacherous persons: her priests have polluted the sanctuary, they have done violence to the law.

5 The just LORD *is* in the midst thereof; he will not do iniquity: every morning doth he bring his ^Tjudgment to light, he ^Tfaileth not; but ^Rthe unjust knoweth no shame.   *justice · never fails* · Jer. 3:3

6 I have cut off the nations: their towers are desolate; I made their streets waste, that none passeth by: their cities are destroyed, so that there is no man, that there is none inhabitant.

7 ^RI said, Surely thou wilt fear me, thou wilt receive instruction; so their dwelling should not be cut off, howsoever I punished them: but they rose early, *and* corrupted all their doings.   Jer. 8:6

8 Therefore ^Rwait ye upon me, saith the LORD, until the day that I rise up to the prey: for my determination *is* to gather the nations, that I may assemble the kingdoms, to pour upon them mine indignation, *even* all my fierce anger: for all the earth shall be devoured with the fire of my jealousy.   Prov. 20:22; Mic. 7:7; Hab. 2:3

9 For then will I ^Tturn to the people ^Ra pure language, that they may all call upon the name of the LORD, to serve him with one ^Tconsent.   *restore* · Is. 19:18; 57:19 · *accord*

10 ^RFrom beyond the rivers of E-thi-o'-pi-a my suppliants, *even* the daughter of my dispersed, shall bring mine offering.   Acts 8:27

11 In that day shalt thou not be ashamed for all thy ^Tdoings, wherein thou hast transgressed against me: for then I will take away out of the midst of thee

them that ^Rrejoice in thy pride, and thou shalt no more be haughty because of my holy mountain. *deeds* · Is. 2:12; 5:15; Matt. 3:9

12 I will also leave in the midst of thee ^Ran afflicted and poor people, and they shall trust in the name of the LORD.   Zech. 13:8, 9

13 ^RThe remnant of Israel shall not do iniquity, nor speak lies; neither shall a deceitful tongue be found in their mouth: for they shall feed and lie down, and none shall make *them* afraid. Is. 10:20–22

14 ^RSing, O daughter of Zion; shout, O Israel; be glad and rejoice with all the heart, O daughter of Jerusalem.   Is. 12:6

15 The LORD hath taken away thy judgments, he hath cast out thine enemy: ^Rthe king of Israel, *even* the LORD, ^R*is* in the midst of thee: thou shalt not see evil any more. [John 1:49] · Ezek. 48:35; [Rev. 7:15]

16 In that day ^Rit shall be said to Jerusalem, Fear thou not: *and to* Zion, ^RLet not thine hands be slack.   Is. 35:3, 4 · Job 4:3; Heb. 12:12

17 The LORD thy God in the midst of thee *is* mighty; he will save, he will rejoice over thee with joy; he will rest in his love, he will joy over thee with singing.

18 I will gather *them that are* sorrowful for the solemn assembly, *who* are of thee, *to whom* the reproach of it *was* a burden.

19 Behold, at that time I will undo all that afflict thee: and I will save ^Ther that halteth, and gather her that was driven out; and I will get them praise and fame in every land where they have been put to shame.   *the lame*

20 At that time ^Rwill I bring you *again,* even in the time that I gather you: for I will make you a name and a praise among all people of the earth, when I turn back your captivity before your eyes, saith the LORD.   Ezek. 28:25; Amos 9:14

The Book of
HAGGAI

WITH the Babylonian exile in the past, and a newly returned group of Jews back in the land, the work of rebuilding the temple can begin. However, sixteen years after the process is begun, the people have yet to finish the project, for their personal affairs have interfered with God's business. Haggai preaches a fiery series of sermonettes designed to stir up the nation to finish the temple. He calls the builders to renewed courage in the Lord, renewed holiness of life, and renewed faith in God who controls the future.

The etymology and meaning of *Haggay* is uncertain, but it is probably derived from the Hebrew word *hag,* "festival." It may also be an abbreviated form of *haggiah,* "festival of Yahweh." Thus, Haggai's name means "Festal" or "Festive," possibly because he was born on the day of a major feast, such as Tabernacles (Haggai's second message takes place during that feast, 2:1). The title in the Septuagint is *Aggaios* and in the Vulgate it is *Aggaeus.*

IN ^Rthe second year of Da-ri'-us the king, in the sixth month, in the first day of the month, came the word of the LORD by Hag'-gai the prophet unto ^RZe-rub'-ba-bel the son of She-al'-ti-el, governor of Judah, and to Joshua the son of Jos'-e-dech, the high priest, saying,   Zech. 1:1, 7 · Zech. 4:6; Matt. 1:12, 13

2 Thus speaketh the LORD of hosts, saying, This people say, The time is not come, the time that the LORD's house should be built.

3 Then came the word of the

LORD ^Rby Hag'-gai the prophet, saying,   Ezra 5:1

4 ^R*Is it* time for you, O ye, to dwell in your cieled houses, and this house *lie* waste?   2 Sam. 7:2

5 Now therefore thus saith the LORD of hosts; ^RConsider your ways.   Lam. 3:40

6 Ye have ^Rsown much, and bring in little; ye eat, but ye have not enough; ye drink, but ye are not filled with drink; ye clothe you, but there is none warm; and ^Rhe that earneth wages earneth wages *to put it* into a bag with holes.   vv. 9, 10; 2:16, 17 · Zech. 8:10

7 Thus saith the LORD of hosts; Consider your ways.

8 Go up to the mountain, and bring wood, and build the house; and I will take pleasure in it, and I will be glorified, saith the LORD.

9 ^RYe looked for much, and, lo, *it came* to little; and when ye brought *it* home, ^RI did blow upon it. Why? saith the LORD of hosts. Because of mine house that *is* waste, and ye run every man unto his own house.   2:16 · 2:17

10 Therefore the heaven over you is stayed from dew, and the earth is stayed *from* her fruit.

11 And I called for a drought upon the land, and upon the mountains, and upon the corn, and upon the new wine, and upon the oil, and upon *that* which the ground bringeth forth, and upon men, and upon cattle, and ^Rupon all the labour of the hands.   2:17

12 ^RThen Ze-rub'-ba-bel the son of She-al'-ti-el, and Joshua the son of Jos'-e-dech, the high priest, with all the remnant of the people, obeyed the voice of the LORD their God, and the words of Hag'-gai the prophet, as the LORD their God had sent him, and the people did fear before the LORD.   Ezra 5:2

13 Then spake Hag'-gai the LORD's messenger in the LORD's message unto the people, saying, I *am* with you, saith the LORD.

14 And ^Rthe LORD stirred up the spirit of Ze-rub'-ba-bel the son of She-al'-ti-el, ^Rgovernor of Judah,

and the spirit of Joshua the son of Jos'-e-dech, the high priest, and the spirit of all the remnant of the people; and they came and did work in the house of the LORD of hosts, their God,   2 Chr. 36:22 · 2:21

15 In the four and twentieth day of the sixth month, in the second year of Da-ri'-us the king.

2 In the seventh *month*, in the one and twentieth *day* of the month, came the word of the LORD by the prophet Hag'-gai, saying,

2 Speak now to Ze-rub'-ba-bel the son of She-al'-ti-el, governor of Judah, and to Joshua the son of ^TJos'- e-dech, the high priest, and to the ^Tresidue of the people, say-ing,   *Jehozadak*, 1 Chr. 6:15 · *remnant*

3 ^RWho *is* left among you that saw this house in her first glory? and how do ye see it now? ^R*is it* not in your eyes in comparison of it as nothing? Ezra 3:12, 13 · Zech. 4:10

4 Yet now be strong, O Ze-rub'-ba-bel, saith the LORD; and be strong, O Joshua, son of Jos'-e-dech, the high priest; and be strong, all ye people of the land, saith the LORD, and work: for I *am* with you, saith the LORD of hosts:

5 ^R*According to* the word that I covenanted with you when ye came out of Egypt, so ^Rmy spirit remaineth among you: fear ye not. Ex. 29:45, 46 · [Neh. 9:20]; Is. 63:11, 14

6 For thus saith the LORD of hosts; ^RYet once, it *is* a little while, and ^RI will shake the heavens, and the earth, and the sea, and the dry *land*;   Heb. 12:26 · [Joel 3:16]

7 And I will shake all nations, ^Rand the desire of all nations shall come: and I will fill this house with ^Rglory, saith the LORD of hosts.   Mal. 3:1 · Is. 60:7; Zech. 2:5

8 The silver *is* mine, and the gold *is* mine, saith the LORD of hosts.

9 The glory of this latter house shall be greater than of the former, saith the LORD of hosts: and in this place will I give ^Rpeace, saith the LORD of hosts.   Ps. 85:8, 9

10 In the four and twentieth *day* of the ninth *month*, in the second

year of Da-ri'-us, came the word of the LORD by Hag'-gai the prophet, saying,

11 Thus saith the LORD of hosts; ᴿAsk now the priests *concerning* the law, saying,   Deut. 33:10; Mal. 2:7

12 If one bear holy flesh in the skirt of his garment, and with his skirt do touch bread, or ᵀpottage, or wine, or oil, or any meat, shall it be holy? And the priests answered and said, No.   *stew*

13 Then said Hag'-gai, If *one that is* ᴿunclean by a dead body touch any of these, shall it be unclean? And the priests answered and said, It shall be unclean.   Lev. 22:4–6; Num. 19:11, 22

14 Then answered Hag'-gai, and said, ᴿSo *is* this people, and so *is* this nation before me, saith the LORD; and so *is* every work of their hands; and that which they offer there *is* unclean.   [Titus 1:15]

15 And now, I pray you, consider from this day and upward, from before a stone was laid upon a stone in the temple of the LORD:

16 Since those *days* were, when *one* came to an heap of twenty *measures*, there were *but* ten: when *one* came to the pressfat for to draw out fifty *vessels* out of the press, there were *but* twenty.

17 ᴿI smote you with blasting and with mildew and with hail ᴿin all the labours of your hands; ᴿyet

ye *turned* not to me, saith the LORD.   Amos 4:9 · 1:11 · Jer. 5:3

18 Consider now from this day and upward, from the four and twentieth day of the ninth *month*, *even* from ᴿthe day that the foundation of the LORD's temple was laid, consider *it*.   Zech. 8:9

19 ᴿIs the seed yet in the barn? yea, as yet the vine, and the fig tree, and the pomegranate, and the olive tree, hath not brought forth: from this day will I ᴿbless *you*.   Zech. 8:12 · Ps. 128:1–6; [Mal. 3:10]

20 And again the word of the LORD came unto Hag'-gai in the four and twentieth *day* of the month, saying,

21 Speak to Ze-rub'-ba-bel, governor of Judah, saying, I will shake the heavens and the earth;

22 And ᴿI will overthrow the throne of kingdoms, and I will destroy the strength of the kingdoms of the heathen; and ᴿI will overthrow the chariots, and those that ride in them; and the horses and their riders shall come down, every one by the sword of his brother.   [Dan. 2:44] · Ps. 46:9; Zech. 9:10

23 In that day, saith the LORD of hosts, will I take thee, O Ze-rub'-ba-bel, my servant, the son of She-al'-ti-el, saith the LORD, ᴿand will make thee as a signet: for ᴿI have chosen thee, saith the LORD of hosts.   Jer. 22:24 · Is. 42:1; 43:10

The Book of

ZECHARIAH

FOR a dozen years or more, the task of rebuilding the temple has been half completed. Zechariah is commissioned by God to encourage the people in their unfinished responsibility. Rather than exhorting them to action with strong words of rebuke, Zechariah seeks to encourage them to action by reminding them of the future importance of the temple. The temple must be built, for one day the Messiah's glory will inhabit it. But future blessing is contingent upon present obedience. The people are not merely building a building; they are building the future. With that as their motivation, they can enter into the building project with wholehearted zeal, for their Messiah is coming.

Zekar-yah means "Yahweh Remembers" or "Yahweh Has Remembered." This theme dominates the whole book: Israel will be blessed because Yahweh remembers the covenant He made with the fathers. The Greek and Latin version of his name is *Zacharias*.

IN the eighth month, in the second year of Da-ri'-us, came the word of the LORD unto Zech-a-ri'-ah, the son of Ber-e-chi'-ah, the son of Id'-do the prophet, saying,

2 The LORD hath been sore displeased with your fathers.

3 Therefore say thou unto them, Thus saith the LORD of hosts; Turn ye unto me, saith the LORD of hosts, and I will turn unto you, saith the LORD of hosts.

4 Be ye not as your fathers, unto whom the former prophets have cried, saying, Thus saith the LORD of hosts; Turn ye now from your evil ways, and *from* your evil doings: but they did not hear, nor hearken unto me, saith the LORD.

5 Your fathers, where *are* they? and the prophets, do they live for ever?

6 But my words and my statutes, which I commanded my servants the prophets, did they not Ttake hold of your fathers? and they returned and said, Like as the LORD of hosts thought to do unto us, according to our ways, and according to our doings, so hath he dealt with us.   *overtake*

7 Upon the four and twentieth day of the eleventh month, which *is* the month Se'-bat, in the second year of Da-ri'-us, came the word of the LORD unto Zech-a-ri'-ah, the son of Ber-e-chi'-ah, the son of Id'-do the prophet, saying,

8 I saw by night, and behold Ra man riding upon a red horse, and he stood among the myrtle trees that *were* in the bottom; and behind him *were there* red horses, speckled, and white.   Is. 55:13

9 Then said I, O Rmy lord, what *are* these? And the angel that talked with me said unto me, I will shew thee what these *be*.   4:4, 5, 13

10 And the man that stood among the myrtle trees answered and said, RThese *are they* whom the LORD hath sent to walk to and fro through the earth.   [Heb. 1:14]

11 RAnd they answered the angel of the LORD that stood among the myrtle trees, and said, We have walked to and fro through the earth, and, behold, all the earth Tsitteth still, and is at rest.   [Ps. 103:20, 21] · *is resting quietly*

12 Then the angel of the LORD answered and said, O LORD of hosts, Rhow long wilt thou not have mercy on Jerusalem and on the cities of Judah, against which thou hast had indignation these threescore and ten years? Ps. 74:10

13 And the LORD answered the angel that talked with me *with* Rgood words *and* Tcomfortable words.   Jer. 29:10 · *comforting*

14 So the angel that Tcommuned with me said unto me, Cry thou, saying, Thus saith the LORD of hosts; I am Rjealous T for Jerusalem and for Zion with a great jealousy.   *spoke* · Joel 2:18 · *zealous*

15 And I am very sore displeased with the heathen *that are* at ease: for RI was but a little Tdispleased, and they helped forward the affliction.   Is. 47:6 · *angry*

16 Therefore thus saith the LORD; I am returned to Jerusalem with mercies: my Rhouse shall be built in it, saith the LORD of hosts, and a line shall be stretched forth upon Jerusalem. Ezra 6:14, 15; Hag. 1:4

17 Cry yet, saying, Thus saith the LORD of hosts; My cities through prosperity shall yet be spread abroad; and the LORD shall yet comfort Zion, and Rshall yet choose Jerusalem.   2:12; Is. 14:1

18 Then lifted I up mine eyes, and saw, and behold four horns.

19 And I said unto the angel that talked with me, What *be* these? And he answered me, These *are*

the horns which have scattered Judah, Israel, and Jerusalem.

20 And the Lord shewed me four ᵀcarpenters.   *craftsmen*

21 Then said I, What come these to do? And he spake, saying, These *are* the ᴿhorns which have scattered Judah, so that no man did lift up his head: but these are come to ᵀfray them, to cast out the horns of the Gentiles, which lifted up *their* horn over the land of Judah to scatter it.   [Ps. 75:10] · *terrify*

2 I lifted up mine eyes again, and looked, and behold a man with a measuring line in his hand.

2 Then said I, Whither goest thou? And he said unto me, ᴿTo measure Jerusalem, to see what *is* the breadth thereof, and what *is* the length thereof.   Rev. 11:1

3 And, behold, the angel that talked with me went forth, and another angel went out to meet him,

4 And said unto him, Run, speak to this young man, saying, Jerusalem shall be inhabited *as* towns without walls for the multitude of men and cattle therein:

5 For I, saith the Lord, will be unto her ᴿa wall of fire round about, ᴿand will be the glory in the midst of her.   [Is. 26:1] · [Is. 60:19]

6 ᵀHo, ho, *come forth*, and flee from the land of the north, saith the Lord: for I have spread you abroad as the four winds of the heaven, saith the Lord.   *Up, up*

7 ᴿDeliver thyself, O Zion, that dwellest *with* the daughter of Babylon.   Is. 48:20; Jer. 51:6; [Rev. 18:4]

8 For thus saith the Lord of hosts; After the glory hath he sent me unto the nations which spoiled you: for he that toucheth you toucheth the apple of his eye.

9 For, behold, I will ᴿshake mine hand upon them, and they shall be a spoil to their servants: and ᴿye shall know that the Lord of hosts hath sent me.   Is. 19:16 · 4:9

10 ᴿSing and rejoice, O daughter of Zion: for, lo, I come, and I ᴿwill dwell in the midst of thee, saith the Lord.   Is. 12:6 · [Lev. 26:12]

11 And many nations shall be joined to the Lord in that day, and shall be my people: and I will dwell in the midst of thee, and thou shalt know that the Lord of hosts hath sent me unto thee.

12 And the Lord shall inherit Judah his portion in the holy land, and shall choose Jerusalem again.

13 ᴿBe silent, O all flesh, before the Lord: for he is raised up out of his holy habitation.   Hab. 2:20

3 And he shewed me Joshua the high priest standing before the angel of the Lord, and ᴿSatan standing at his right hand to resist him.   Job 1:6; Ps. 109:6; [Rev. 12:9, 10]

2 And the Lord said unto Satan, ᴿThe Lord rebuke thee, O Satan; even the Lord that hath chosen Jerusalem rebuke thee: ᴿ*is* not this a brand plucked out of the fire?   Mark 9:25 · Amos 4:11; Jude 23

3 Now Joshua was clothed with ᴿfilthy garments, and stood before the angel.   Ezra 9:15; Is. 64:6

4 And he answered and spake unto those that stood before him, saying, Take away the filthy garments from him. And unto him he said, Behold, I have caused thine iniquity to pass from thee, ᴿand I will clothe thee with ᵀchange of raiment.   Gen. 3:21; Is. 61:10 · *rich robes*

5 And I said, Let them set a ᵀfair ᴿmitre upon his head. So they set a fair mitre upon his head, and clothed him with garments. And the angel of the Lord stood by.   *clean turban* · Ex. 29:6

6 And the angel of the Lord protested unto Joshua, saying,

7 Thus saith the Lord of hosts; If thou wilt walk in my ways, and if thou wilt keep my charge, then thou shalt also judge my house, and shalt also keep my courts, and I will give thee places to walk among these that stand by.

8 Hear now, O Joshua the high   ☆ priest, thou, and thy fellows that sit before thee: for they *are* men wondered at: for, behold, I will bring forth ᴿmy servant the ᴿBRANCH.   Is. 42:1 · 6:12; Is. 11:1; 53:2

9 For behold the stone that I

have laid before Joshua; upon one stone *shall be* seven eyes: behold, I will engrave the ᵀgraving thereof, saith the LORD of hosts, and ᴿI will remove the iniquity of that land in one day. *inscription* · v. 4

10 ᴿIn that day, saith the LORD of hosts, shall ye call every man his neighbour ᴿunder the vine and under the fig tree. 2:11 · Mic. 4:4

4 And ᴿthe angel that talked with me came again, and waked me, ᴿas a man that is wakened out of his sleep, 2:3 · Dan. 8:18

2 And said unto me, What seest thou? And I said, I have looked, and behold ᴿa ᵀcandlestick all *of* gold, with a bowl upon the top of it, ᴿand his seven lamps thereon, and seven pipes to the seven lamps, which *are* upon the top thereof: Rev. 1:12 · *lampstand* · [Rev. 4:5]

3 ᴿAnd two olive trees by it, one upon the right *side* of the bowl, and the other upon the left *side* thereof. Rev. 11:3, 4

4 So I answered and spake to the angel that talked with me, saying, What *are* these, my lord?

5 Then the angel that talked with me answered and said unto me, Knowest thou not what these be? And I said, No, my lord.

6 Then he answered and spake unto me, saying, This *is* the word of the LORD unto ᴿZe-rub′-ba-bel, saying, ᴿNot by might, nor by power, but by my spirit, saith the LORD of hosts. Hag. 1:1 · Hag. 2:4, 5

7 Who *art* thou, ᴿO great mountain? before Ze-rub′-ba-bel *thou shalt become* a plain: and he shall bring forth the headstone *thereof with* shoutings, *crying,* Grace, grace unto it. [Matt. 21:21]

8 Moreover the word of the LORD came unto me, saying,

9 The hands of Ze-rub′-ba-bel ᴿhave laid the foundation of this house; his hands ᴿshall also finish it; and ᴿthou shalt know that the ᴿLORD of hosts hath sent me unto you. Hag. 2:18 · 6:12, 13 · 2:9, 11; 6:15 · 2:8

10 For who hath despised the day of small things? for they shall rejoice, and shall see the plummet

in the hand of Ze-rub′-ba-bel *with* those seven; they *are* the eyes of the LORD, which ᵀrun to and fro through the whole earth. *scan*

11 Then answered I, and said unto him, What *are* these ᴿtwo olive trees upon the right *side* of the ᵀcandlestick and upon the left *side* thereof? Rev. 11:4 · *lampstand*

12 And I answered again, and said unto him, What *be these* two olive branches which through the two golden pipes empty the golden *oil* out of themselves?

13 And he answered me and said, Knowest thou not what these *be?* And I said, No, my lord.

14 Then said he, These *are* the two anointed ones, ᴿthat stand by the Lord of the whole earth. 3:1–7

5 Then I turned, and lifted up mine eyes, and looked, and behold a flying ᴿroll.ᵀ Rev. 5:1 · *scroll*

2 And he said unto me, What seest thou? And I answered, I see a flying ᵀroll; the length thereof *is* twenty cubits, and the breadth thereof ten cubits. *scroll*

3 Then said he unto me, This *is* the ᴿcurse that goeth forth over the face of the whole earth: for every one that stealeth shall be ᵀcut off *as* on this side according to it; and every one that sweareth shall be cut off *as* on that side according to it. Mal. 4:6 · *purged out*

4 I will bring it forth, saith the LORD of hosts, and it shall enter into the house of the thief, and into the house of ᴿhim that sweareth falsely by my name: and it shall remain in the midst of his house, and shall consume it with the timber thereof and the stones thereof. Is. 48:1; Jer. 5:2; Mal. 3:5

5 Then the angel that talked with me went forth, and said unto me, Lift up now thine eyes, and see what *is* this that goeth forth.

6 And I said, What *is* it? And he said, This *is* ᵀan e′-phah that goeth forth. He said moreover, This *is* their resemblance through all the earth. *a basket*, a measuring container

7 And, behold, there was lifted up a ᵀtalent of lead: and this *is* a

woman that sitteth in the midst of the e'-phah.   *lead disc* or *cover*

8 And he said, This *is* wickedness. And he ᵀcast it into the midst of the ᵀe'-phah; and he cast the weight of lead upon the mouth thereof.   *thrust her down · basket*

9 Then lifted I up mine eyes, and looked, and, behold, there came out two women, and the wind *was* in their wings; for they had wings like the wings of a ᴿstork: and they lifted up the e'-phah between the earth and the heaven. Lev. 11:13, 19; Ps. 104:17; Jer. 8:7

10 Then said I to the angel that talked with me, Whither do these ᵀbear the e'-phah?   *carry the basket*

11 And he said unto me, To ᴿbuild it an house in ᴿthe land of ᵀShi'-nar: and it shall be established, and set there upon her own base. Jer. 29:5 · Dan. 1:2 · Babylon

6 And I turned, and lifted up mine eyes, and looked, and, behold, there came four chariots out from between two mountains; and the mountains *were* mountains of ᵀbrass.   *bronze*

2 ᵀIn the first chariot *were* ᴿred horses; and ᵀin the second chariot ᴿblack horses;   *With · 1:8 · Rev. 6:5*

3 And in the third chariot white horses; and in the fourth chariot grisled and bay horses.

4 Then I answered ᴿand said unto the angel that talked with me, What *are* these, my lord? 5:10

5 And the angel answered and said unto me, These *are* the four spirits of the heavens, which go forth from ᴿstanding before the Lord of all the earth. 4:14; Luke 1:19

6 The black horses which *are* therein go forth into the north country; and the white go forth after them; and the grisled go forth toward the south country.

7 And the bay went forth, and sought to go that they might ᴿwalk to and fro through the earth: and he said, Get you hence, walk to and fro through the earth. So they walked to and fro through the earth. Gen. 1:10

8 Then ᵀcried he upon me, and

spake unto me, saying, Behold, these that go toward the north country have quieted my spirit in the north country.   *he called to me*

9 And the word of the Lᴏʀᴅ came unto me, saying,

10 Take of *them of* the captivity, *even* of Hel'-dai, of To-bi'-jah, and of Je-da'-iah, which are come from Babylon, and come thou the same day, and go into the house of Jo-si'-ah the son of Zeph-a-ni'-ah;

11 Then take silver and gold, and make crowns, and set *them* upon the head of Joshua the son of Jos'-e-dech, the high priest;

12 And speak unto him, saying, Thus speaketh the Lᴏʀᴅ of hosts, saying, Behold ᴿthe man whose name *is* The BRANCH; and he shall grow up out of his place, ᴿand he shall build the temple of the Lᴏʀᴅ: John 1:45 · [Matt. 16:18]

13 Even he shall build the temple of the Lᴏʀᴅ; and he ᴿshall bear the glory, and shall sit and rule upon his throne; and ᴿhe shall be a priest upon his throne: and the counsel of peace shall be between them both. Is. 22:24 · Ps. 110:4; [Heb. 3:1]

14 And the crowns shall be to He'-lem, and to To-bi'-jah, and to Je-da'-iah, and to Hen the son of Zeph-a-ni'-ah, ᴿfor a memorial in the temple of the Lᴏʀᴅ.   Mark 14:9

15 And they *that are* far off shall come and build in the temple of the Lᴏʀᴅ, and ye shall know that the Lᴏʀᴅ of hosts hath sent me unto you. And *this* shall come to pass, if ye will diligently obey the voice of the Lᴏʀᴅ your God.

7 And it came to pass in the fourth year of king Da-ri'-us, *that* the word of the Lᴏʀᴅ came unto Zech-a-ri'-ah in the fourth *day* of the ninth month, *even* in ᵀChis'-leu;   *Or Chislev*

2 When they had sent unto ᵀthe house of God She-re'-zer and Re'-gem-me'-lech, and their men, to pray before the Lᴏʀᴅ, Heb. *Beth-el*

3 *And* to ᴿspeak unto the priests which *were* in the house of the Lᴏʀᴅ of hosts, and to the

☆

prophets, saying, Should I weep in Rthe fifth month, separating myself, as I have done these so many years? Deut. 17:9; Mal. 2:7 · 8:19

4 Then came the word of the LORD of hosts unto me, saying,

5 Speak unto all the people of the land, and to the priests, saying, When ye Rfasted and mourned in the fifth Rand seventh month, Reven those seventy years, did ye at all fast Runto me, even to me? [Is. 58:1–9] · Jer. 41:1 · 1:12 · [Rom. 14:6]

6 RAnd when ye did eat, and when ye did drink, did not ye eat for yourselves, and drink for yourselves? Deut. 12:7; 14:26; 1 Chr. 29:22

7 Should ye not hear the words which the LORD hath cried by the Rformer prophets, when Jerusalem was inhabited and in prosperity, and the cities thereof round about her, when men inhabited the south and the plain? Is. 1:16–20

8 And the word of the LORD came unto Zech-a-ri'-ah, saying,

9 Thus speaketh the LORD of hosts, saying, RExecute true judgment, and shew Tmercy and compassions every man to his brother: Is. 58:6, 7; Jer. 7:28 · lovingkindness

10 And Roppress not the widow, nor the fatherless, the stranger, nor the poor; Rand let none of you imagine evil against his brother in your heart. Ps. 72:4; Is. 1:17 · 8:16, 17

11 But they refused to hearken, and Rpulled away the shoulder, and Rstopped their ears, that they should not hear. Neh. 9:29 · Acts 7:57

12 Yea, they made their Rhearts as Tan adamant stone, Rlest they should hear the law, and the words which the LORD of hosts hath sent in his spirit by the former prophets: therefore came a great wrath from the LORD of hosts. Ezek. 11:19 · flint · Neh. 9:29, 30

13 Therefore it is come to pass, that as he cried, and they would not hear; so Rthey cried, and I would not hear, saith the LORD of hosts: Is. 1:15; Jer. 11:11; Mic. 3:4

14 But RI scattered them with a whirlwind among all the nations whom they knew not. Thus the land was desolate after them, that no man passed through nor returned: for they laid the pleasant land desolate. Lev. 26:33; Neh. 1:8

8 Again the word of the LORD of hosts came to me, saying,

2 Thus saith the LORD of hosts; I was Tjealous for Zion with great jealousy, and I was jealous for her with great Tfury. zealous · fervour

3 Thus saith the LORD; I am Rreturned unto Zion, and will Rdwell in the midst of Jerusalem: and Jerusalem Rshall be called a city of truth; and Rthe mountain of the LORD of hosts the holy mountain. 1:16 · 2:10, 11 · Is. 1:21 · [Is. 2:2, 3]

4 Thus saith the LORD of hosts; There shall yet old men and old women dwell in the streets of Jerusalem, and every man with his staff in his hand for very age.

5 And the streets of the city shall be full of boys and girls playing in the streets thereof.

6 Thus saith the LORD of hosts; If it be marvellous in the eyes of the remnant of this people in these days, Rshould it also be marvellous in mine eyes? saith the LORD of hosts. [Gen. 18:14; Luke 1:37]

7 Thus saith the LORD of hosts; Behold, RI will save my people from the east country, and from the west country; Ps. 107:3; Is. 11:11

8 And I will Rbring them, and they shall dwell in the midst of Jerusalem: and they shall be my people, and I will be their God, in truth and in righteousness. 10:10

9 Thus saith the LORD of hosts; RLet your hands be strong, ye that hear in these days these words by the mouth of the prophets, which were in Rthe day that the foundation of the house of the LORD of hosts was laid, that the temple might be built. Is. 35:4 · Hag. 2:18

10 For before these days there was no Rhire\[T] for man, nor any hire for beast; neither was there any peace to him that went out or came in because of the affliction: for I set all men every one against his neighbour. Hag. 1:6, 9 · wage

11 RBut now I will not be unto

the residue of this people as in the former days, saith the LORD of hosts. [Ps. 103:9]; Is. 12:1; Hag. 2:15–19

12 ^RFor the seed *shall be* prosperous; the vine shall give her fruit, and the ground shall give her increase, and the heavens shall give their dew; and I will cause the remnant of this people to possess all these *things*. Joel 2:22

13 And it shall come to pass, *that* as ye were ^Ra curse among the heathen, O house of Judah, and house of Israel; so will I save you, and ^Rye shall be a blessing: fear not, *but* let your hands be strong.   Jer. 42:18 · Ezek. 34:26

14 For thus saith the LORD of hosts; ^RAs I thought to punish you, when your fathers provoked me to wrath, saith the LORD of hosts, and I repented not: Jer. 31:28

15 So again have I ^Tthought in these days to do well unto Jerusalem and to the house of Judah: fear ye not.   *determined*

16 These *are* the things that ye shall do; ^RSpeak ye every man the truth to his neighbour; execute the judgment of truth and peace in your gates: Ps. 15:2; [Eph. 4:25]

17 ^RAnd let none of you imagine evil in your hearts against his neighbour; and love no false oath: for all these *are things* that I hate, saith the LORD.   Prov. 3:29; Jer. 4:14

18 And the word of the LORD of hosts came unto me, saying,

19 Thus saith the LORD of hosts; The fast of the fourth *month,* and the fast of the fifth, and the fast of the seventh, and the fast of the tenth, shall be to the house of Judah joy and gladness, and cheerful feasts; ^Rtherefore love the truth and peace.   Luke 1:74, 75

20 Thus saith the LORD of hosts; *It shall* yet *come to pass,* that there shall come ^Tpeople, and the inhabitants of many cities: *peoples*

21 And the inhabitants of one *city* shall go to another, saying, ^RLet us go speedily to pray before the LORD, and to seek the LORD of hosts: I will go also.   [Is. 2:2, 3]

22 Yea, many people and strong nations shall come to seek the LORD of hosts in Jerusalem, and to pray before the LORD.

23 Thus saith the LORD of hosts; In those days *it shall come to pass,* that ten men shall take hold out of all languages of the nations, even shall take hold of the skirt of him that is a Jew, saying, We will go with you: for we have heard *that* God *is* with you.

9 The ^Tburden of the word of the LORD in the land of Ha'-drach, and Damascus *shall be* the rest thereof: when the eyes of man, as of all the tribes of Israel, *shall be* toward the LORD.   *oracle*

2 And Ha'-math also shall border thereby; Ty'-rus, and Zi'-don, though it be very wise.

3 And Ty'-rus did build herself a strong hold, and heaped up silver as the dust, and fine gold as the mire of the streets.

4 Behold, the Lord will cast her out, and he will smite ^Rher power in the sea; and she shall be devoured with fire.   Ezek. 26:17

5 Ash'-ke-lon shall see *it,* and fear; Ga'-za also *shall see it,* and be very sorrowful, and ^REk'-ron; for her expectation shall be ashamed; and the king shall perish from Ga'-za, and Ash'-ke-lon shall not be inhabited.   Zeph. 2:4, 5

6 And a bastard shall dwell ^Rin Ash'-dod, and I will cut off the pride of the Phi-lis'-tines. Amos 1:8

7 And I will take away his blood out of his mouth, and his abominations from between his teeth: but he that remaineth, even he, *shall be* for our God, and he shall be as a ^Tgovernor in Judah, and Ek'-ron as a Jeb'-u-site.   *leader*

8 And I will encamp about mine house because of the army, because of him that passeth by, and because of him that returneth: and no oppressor shall pass through them any more: for now have I seen with mine eyes.

9 Rejoice greatly, O daughter of Zion; shout, O daughter of Jerusalem: behold, ^Rthy King cometh unto thee: he *is* just, and hav-   ☆

ing salvation; lowly, and riding upon an ass, and upon a colt the foal of an ass. Matt. 21:5; John 12:15

10 And I will cut off the chariot from E'-phra-im, and the horse from Jerusalem, and the battle bow shall be cut off: and he shall speak peace unto the heathen: and his dominion *shall be* from sea *even* to sea, and from the river *even* to the ends of the earth.

11 As for thee also, by the blood of thy covenant I have sent forth thy Rprisoners out of the pit wherein *is* no water. Is. 42:7

12 Turn you to the strong hold, Rye prisoners of hope: even to day do I declare *that* I will render double unto thee; Heb. 6:18-20

13 TWhen I have bent Judah Tfor me, filled the bow with E'-phra-im, and raised up thy sons, O Zion, against thy sons, O Greece, and made thee as the sword of a mighty man. *For · my* bow

14 And the LORD shall be seen over them, and Rhis arrow shall go forth as the lightning: and the Lord GOD shall blow the trumpet, and shall go Rwith whirlwinds of the south. Ps. 18:14; Hab. 3:11 · Is. 21:1

15 The LORD of hosts shall Rdefend them; and they shall devour, and subdue with sling stones; and they shall drink, *and* make a noise as through wine; and they shall be filled like bowls, *and* as the corners of the altar. Is. 37:35

16 And the LORD their God shall save them in that day as the flock of his people: for R*they shall be as* the stones of a crown, lifted up as an ensign upon his land. Mal. 3:17

17 For how great *is* his goodness, and how great *is* his beauty! corn shall make the young men cheerful, and new wine the maids.

10 Ask ye Rof the LORD Rrain in the time of the latter rain; so the LORD shall make bright clouds, and give them showers of rain, to every one grass in the field. [Jer. 14:22] · [Deut. 11:13, 14]

2 For the Ridols have spoken vanity, and the diviners have seen a lie, and have told false dreams; they comfort in vain: therefore they went their way as a flock, they were troubled, because *there was* no shepherd. Jer. 10:8

3 Mine anger was kindled against the Rshepherds, and I punished the goats: for the LORD of hosts Rhath visited his flock the house of Judah, and hath made them as his goodly horse in the battle. 11:17 · Luke 1:68

4 Out of him came forth the corner, out of him Rthe nail, out of him the battle bow, out of him every oppressor together. Is. 22:23

5 And they shall be as mighty men, which Rtread down *their* enemies in the mire of the streets in the battle: and they shall fight, because the LORD *is* with them, and the riders on horses shall be Tconfounded. Ps. 18:42 · *put to shame*

6 And I will strengthen the house of Judah, and I will save the house of Joseph, and RI will bring them again to place them; for I have mercy upon them: and they shall be as though I had not cast them off: for I *am* the LORD their God, and will hear them. Jer. 3:18

7 And *they* of E'-phra-im shall be like a mighty *man*, and their Rheart shall rejoice as through wine: yea, their children shall see *it*, and be glad; their heart shall rejoice in the LORD. Ps. 104:15

8 I will hiss for them, and gather them; for I have redeemed them: Rand they shall increase as they have increased. Is. 49:19

9 And RI will sow them among the people: and they shall remember me in far countries; and they shall live with their children, and turn again. Hos. 2:23

10 I will bring them again also out of the land of Egypt, and gather them out of Assyria; and I will bring them into the land of Gil'-e-ad and Leb'-a-non; and *place* shall not be found for them.

11 And he shall pass through the sea with affliction, and shall smite the waves in the sea, and all the deeps of the river shall dry up:

and ^Rthe pride of Assyria shall be brought down, and the sceptre of Egypt shall depart away.   Is. 14:25

12 And I will strengthen them in the LORD; and ^Rthey shall walk up and down in his name, saith the LORD.   Mic. 4:5

11 Open ^Rthy doors, O Leb′-a-non, that the fire may devour thy cedars.   10:10

2 Howl, fir tree; for the ^Rcedar is fallen; because the mighty are spoiled: howl, O ye oaks of Ba′-shan; ^Rfor the forest of the vintage is come down.   Ezek. 31:3 · Is. 32:19

3 *There is* a voice of the howling of the shepherds; for their glory is spoiled: a voice of the roaring of young lions; for the pride of Jordan is spoiled.

4 Thus saith the LORD my God; Feed the flock of the slaughter;

5 Whose possessors slay them, and ^Rhold themselves not guilty: and they that sell them ^Rsay, Blessed *be* the LORD; for I am rich: and their own shepherds pity them not.   [Jer. 2:3]; 50:7 · 1 Tim. 6:9

6 For I will no more pity the inhabitants of the land, saith the LORD: but, lo, I will deliver the men every one into his neighbour's hand, and into the hand of his king: and they shall ^Tsmite the land, and out of their hand I will not deliver *them*.   *attack*

7 And I will feed the flock of slaughter, *even* you, O poor of the flock. And I took unto me two staves; the one I called ^TBeauty, and the other I called ^TBands; and I fed the flock.   *Grace · Unity*

8 Three shepherds also I cut off ^Rin one month; and my soul lothed them, and their soul also abhorred me.   Hos. 5:7

9 Then said I, I will not feed you: ^Rthat that dieth, let it die; and that that is to be cut off, let it be cut off; and let the rest eat every one the flesh of another.   Jer. 15:2

10 And I took my staff, *even* Beauty, and cut it asunder, that I might break my covenant which I had made with all the people.

11 And it was broken in that day: and so ^Rthe poor of the flock that waited upon me knew that it *was* the word of the LORD.   Acts 8:32

12 And I said unto them, If ye think good, give *me* my price; and if not, forbear. So they weighed for my price thirty *pieces* of silver.   ☆

13 And the LORD said unto me, Cast it unto the ^Rpotter: a goodly price that I was prised at of them. And I took the thirty *pieces* of silver, and cast them to the potter in the house of the LORD.   Matt. 27:3–10   ☆

14 Then I cut asunder mine other staff, *even* Bands, that I might break the brotherhood between Judah and Israel.

15 And the LORD said unto me, Take unto thee yet the instruments of a foolish shepherd.

16 For, lo, I will raise up a shepherd in the land, *which* shall not visit those that be cut off, neither shall seek the young one, nor heal that that is broken, nor feed that that standeth still: but he shall eat the flesh of the fat, and tear their ^Tclaws in ^Rpieces.   *hooves · Mic. 3:1–3*

17 ^RWoe to the idol shepherd that leaveth the flock! the sword *shall be* upon his arm, and upon his right eye: his arm shall be clean dried up, and his right eye shall be utterly darkened.   Jer. 23:1

12 The ^Tburden of the word of the LORD for Israel, saith the LORD, which stretcheth forth the heavens, and layeth the foundation of the earth, and formeth the spirit of man within him.   *oracle*

2 Behold, I will make Jerusalem ^Ra cup of ^Ttrembling unto all the people round about, when they shall be in the siege both against Judah *and* against Jerusalem.   Is. 51:17 · *drunkenness or reeling*

3 ^RAnd in that day will I make Jerusalem ^Ra ^Tburdensome stone for all people: all that burden themselves with it shall be cut in pieces, though all the people of the earth be gathered together against it.   13:1 · Matt. 21:44 · *very heavy*

4 In that day, saith the LORD, ^RI will smite every horse with aston-

ishment, and his rider with madness: and I will open mine eyes upon the house of Judah, and will smite every horse of the people with blindness.   Ps. 76:6; Ezek. 38:4

5 And the governors of Judah shall say in their heart, The inhabitants of Jerusalem ᵀ*shall be* my strength in the LORD of hosts their God.

          are my strength

6 In that day will I make the governors of Judah ᴿlike an hearth of fire among the wood, and like a torch of fire in a sheaf; and they shall devour all the people round about, on the right hand and on the left: and Jerusalem shall be inhabited again in her own place, *even* in Jerusalem.   11:1

7 The LORD also shall save the tents of Judah first, that the glory of the house of David and the glory of the inhabitants of Jerusalem do not magnify *themselves* against Judah.

8 In that day shall the LORD defend the inhabitants of Jerusalem; and he that is feeble among them at that day shall be as David; and the house of David *shall be* as God, as the angel of the LORD before them.

9 And it shall come to pass in that day, *that* I will seek to ᴿdestroy all the nations that come against Jerusalem.   Hag. 2:22

☆ 10 And I will pour upon the house of David, and upon the inhabitants of Jerusalem, the spirit of grace and of supplications: and they shall ᴿlook upon me whom they have pierced, and they shall mourn for him, ᴿas one mourneth for *his* only *son,* and shall be in bitterness for him, as one that is in bitterness for *his* firstborn. John 19:34, 37; 20:27 · Jer. 6:26

11 In that day shall there be a great mourning in Jerusalem, as the mourning of Ha-dad-rim′-mon in the valley of Me-gid′-don.

12 ᴿAnd the land shall mourn, every family apart; the family of the house of David apart, and their wives apart; the family of

the house of Nathan apart, and their wives apart; [Matt. 24:30; Rev. 1:7]

13 The family of the house of Levi apart, and their wives apart; the family of Shim′-e-i apart, and their wives apart;

14 All the families that remain, every family apart, and their wives apart.

13 In that ᴿday there shall be ᴿa fountain opened to the house of David and to the inhabitants of Jerusalem for sin and for uncleanness.   Acts 10:43 · Ps. 36:9

2 And it shall come to pass in that day, saith the LORD of hosts, *that* I will ᴿcut off the names of the idols out of the land, and they shall no more be remembered: and also I will cause ᴿthe prophets and the unclean spirit to pass out of the land.   Ex. 23:13 · 2 Pet. 2:1

3 And it shall come to pass, *that* when any shall yet prophesy, then his father and his mother that begat him shall say unto him, Thou shalt ᴿnot live; for thou speakest lies in the name of the LORD: and his father and his mother that begat him shall thrust him through when he prophesieth.   Deut. 18:20

4 And it shall come to pass in that day, *that* the prophets shall be ashamed every one of his vision, when he hath prophesied; neither shall they wear ᴿa rough garment to deceive: Is. 20:2; Matt. 3:4

5 ᴿBut he shall say, I *am* no prophet, I *am* an ᵀhusbandman; for man taught me to keep cattle from my youth.   Amos 7:14 · *farmer*

6 And *one* shall say unto him, What *are* these wounds in thine hands? Then he shall answer, *Those* with which I was wounded *in* the house of my friends.

7 Awake, O sword, against my ☆ shepherd, and against the man *that is* my fellow, saith the LORD of hosts: ᴿsmite the shepherd, and the sheep shall be scattered: and I will turn mine hand upon the little ones.   Matt. 26:31, 56, 67; Mark 14:27

8 And it shall come to pass, *that* in all the land, saith the

LORD, ^Rtwo parts therein shall be cut off *and* die; ^Rbut the third shall be left therein.   Is. 6:13 · [Rom. 11:5]

9 And I will bring the third part through the fire, and will ^Rrefine them as silver is refined, and will try them as gold is tried: ^Rthey shall call on my name, and I will hear them: I will say, It *is* my people: and they shall say, The LORD *is* my God. 1 Pet. 1:6 · Ps. 50:15; Zeph. 3:9

14 Behold, ^Rthe day of the LORD cometh, and thy spoil shall be divided in the midst of thee.   [Is. 13:6, 9; Joel 2:1; Mal. 4:1]

2 For ^RI will gather all nations against Jerusalem to battle; and the city shall be taken, and the houses rifled, and the women ravished; and half of the city shall go forth into captivity, and the residue of the people shall not be cut off from the city.   Joel 3:2

3 Then shall the LORD go forth, and fight against those nations, as when he fought in the day of battle.

4 And his feet shall stand in that day ^Rupon the mount of Olives, which *is* before Jerusalem on the east, and the mount of Olives shall cleave in the midst thereof toward the east and toward the west, *and there shall be* a very great valley; and half of the mountain shall remove toward the north, and half of it toward the south.   Acts 1:9–12

5 And ye shall flee *to* the valley of the mountains; for the valley of the mountains shall reach unto A'-zal: yea, ye shall flee, like as ye fled from before the ^Rearthquake in the days of Uz-zi'-ah king of Judah: ^Rand the LORD my God shall come, *and* all the saints with thee.   Is. 29:6; Amos 1:1 · Matt. 24:30, 31

6 And it shall come to pass in that day, *that* the light shall not be clear, *nor* dark:

7 But it shall be one day ^Rwhich shall be known to the LORD, not day, nor night: but it shall come to pass, *that* at ^Revening time it shall be light.   Matt. 24:36 · Is. 30:26

8 And it shall be in that day, *that* living waters shall go out from Jerusalem; half of them toward the former sea, and half of them toward the hinder sea: in summer and in winter shall it be.

9 And the LORD shall be ^Rking over all the earth: in that day shall there be ^Rone LORD, and his name one.   [Rev. 11:15] · Deut. 6:4; [Eph. 4:5, 6]

10 All the land shall be turned as a plain from Ge'-ba to Rim'-mon south of Jerusalem: and it shall be lifted up, and ^Rinhabited in her place, from Benjamin's gate unto the place of the first gate, unto the corner gate, ^Rand *from* the tower of Ha-nan'-e-el unto the king's winepresses.   12:6 · Jer. 31:38

11 And *men* shall dwell in it, and there shall be no more utter destruction; ^Rbut Jerusalem shall be safely inhabited.   Jer. 23:6; Hos. 2:18

12 And this shall be the plague wherewith the LORD will smite all the people that have fought against Jerusalem; Their flesh shall ^Tconsume away while they stand upon their feet, and their eyes shall consume away in their holes, and their tongue shall consume away in their mouth.   *decay*

13 And it shall come to pass in that day, *that* ^Ra great tumult from the LORD shall be among them; and they shall lay hold every one on the hand of his neighbour, and his hand shall rise up against the hand of his neighbour. 1 Sam. 14:15

14 And Judah also shall fight at Jerusalem; ^Rand the wealth of all the heathen round about shall be gathered together, gold, and silver, and apparel, in great abundance.   Ezek. 39:10, 17

15 And so shall be the plague of the horse, of the mule, of the camel, and of the ass, and of all the beasts that shall be in these ^Ttents, as this plague.   *camps*

16 And it shall come to pass, *that* every one that is left of all the nations which came against Jerusalem shall even go up from year to year to worship the King, the LORD of hosts, and to keep ^Rthe feast of tabernacles.   John 7:2

17 ᴿAnd it shall be, *that* whoso will not come up of *all* the families of the earth unto Jerusalem to worship the King, the LORD of hosts, even upon them shall be no rain.   Is. 60:12

18 And if the family of ᴿEgypt go not up, and come not, ᴿthat *have* no *rain;* there shall be the plague, wherewith the LORD will smite the heathen that come not up to keep the feast of taberna-cles.   Is. 19:21 · Deut. 11:10

19 This shall be the ᵀpunish-ment of Egypt, and the punish-ment of all nations that come not up to keep the feast of taberna-cles.   Lit. *sin*

20 In that day shall there be upon the bells of the horses, HO-LINESS UNTO THE LORD; and the pots in the LORD's house shall be like the bowls before the altar.

21 Yea, every pot in Jerusalem and in Judah shall be holiness unto the LORD of hosts: and all they that sacrifice shall come and take of them, and seethe therein: and in that day there shall be no more the ᴿCa'-naan-ite in the house of the LORD of hosts. Is. 35:8

The Book of
MALACHI

MALACHI, a prophet in the days of Nehemiah, directs his message of judgment to a people plagued with corrupt priests, wicked practices, and a false sense of security in their privileged relationship with God. Using the question-and-answer method, Malachi probes deeply into their problems of hypocrisy, infidelity, mixed marriages, divorce, false worship, and arrogance. So sinful has the nation become that God's words to the people no longer have any impact. For four hundred years after Malachi's ringing condemna-tions, God remains silent. Only with the coming of John the Baptist (prophe-sied in 3:1) does God again communicate to His people through a prophet's voice.

The meaning of the name *Mal'aki* ("My Messenger") is probably a short-ened form of *Mal'akya,* "Messenger of Yahweh," and it is appropriate to the book which speaks of the coming of the "messenger of the covenant" ("mes-senger" is mentioned three times in 2:7; 3:1). The Septuagint used the title *Malachias* even though it also translated it "by the hand of his messenger." The Latin title is *Maleachi.*

THE burden of the word of the LORD to Israel by Mal'-a-chi.

2 I have loved you, saith the LORD. Yet ye say, Wherein hast thou loved us? *Was* not Esau Jacob's brother? saith the LORD: yet ᴿI loved Jacob,   Rom. 9:13

3 And I hated Esau, and ᴿlaid his mountains and his heritage waste for the ᵀdragons of the wil-derness.   Jer. 49:18 · *jackals*

4 Whereas E'-dom saith, We are impoverished, but we will return and build the desolate places; thus saith the LORD of hosts, They shall build, but I will throw down; and they shall call them, The border of wickedness, and, The people against whom the LORD hath indignation for ever.

5 And your eyes shall see, and ye shall say, ᴿThe LORD will be magnified ᵀfrom the border of Israel.   Ps. 35:27; Mic. 5:4 · *beyond*

6 A son honoureth *his* father, and a servant his master: if then I

be a father, where *is* mine honour? and if I *be* a master, where *is* my fear? saith the LORD of hosts unto you, O priests, that despise my name. And ye say, Wherein have we despised thy name?

7 Ye offer [R]polluted bread upon mine altar; and ye say, Wherein have we polluted thee? In that ye say, The [R]table of the LORD *is* contemptible.   Deut. 15:21 · Ezek. 41:22

8 And [R]if ye offer the blind for sacrifice, *is it* not evil? and if ye offer the lame and sick, *is it* not evil? offer it now unto thy governor; will he be pleased with thee, or [R]accept thy person? saith the LORD of hosts.   Lev. 22:22 · [Job 42:8]

9 And now, I pray you, beseech God that he will be gracious unto us: this hath been by your means: will he regard your persons? saith the LORD of hosts.

10 Who *is there* even among you that would shut the doors *for nought?* [R]neither do ye kindle *fire* on mine altar for nought. I have no pleasure in you, saith the LORD of hosts, neither will I accept an offering at your hand.   1 Cor. 9:13

11 For from the rising of the sun even unto the going down of the same my name *shall be* great among the Gentiles; [R]and in every place [R]incense *shall be* offered unto my name, and a pure offering: for my name *shall be* great among the heathen, saith the LORD of hosts.   1 Tim. 2:8 · Rev. 8:3

12 But ye have profaned it, in that ye say, The table of the LORD *is* polluted; and the fruit thereof, *even* his meat, *is* contemptible.

13 Ye said also, Behold, what a [R]weariness *is it!* and ye have snuffed at it, saith the LORD of hosts; and ye brought *that which was* torn, and the lame, and the sick; thus ye brought an offering: should I accept this of your hand? saith the LORD.   Is. 43:22

14 But cursed *be* the deceiver, which hath in his flock a male, and voweth, and sacrificeth unto the Lord a [R]corrupt thing: for I *am* a great King, saith the LORD of

hosts, and my name *is* dreadful among the heathen.   Lev. 22:18–20

2 And now, O ye [R]priests, this commandment *is* for you.   1:6

2 [R]If ye will not hear, and if ye will not lay *it* to heart, to give glory unto my name, saith the LORD of hosts, I will even send a curse upon you, and I will curse your blessings: yea, I have cursed them [R]already, because ye do not lay *it* to heart.   [Deut. 28:15] · 3:9

3 Behold, I will corrupt your seed, and spread dung upon your faces, *even* the dung of your solemn feasts; and *one* shall [R]take you away with it.   1 Kin. 14:10

4 And ye shall know that I have sent this commandment unto you, that my covenant might be with Levi, saith the LORD of hosts.

5 [R]My covenant was with him of life and peace; and I gave them to him [R]*for* the fear wherewith he feared me, and was afraid before my name.   Ezek. 34:25 · Deut. 33:9

6 The law of truth was in his mouth, and iniquity was not found in his lips: he walked with me in peace and equity, and did turn many away from iniquity.

7 [R]For the priest's lips should keep knowledge, and they should seek the law at his mouth: [R]for he *is* the messenger of the LORD of hosts.   Num. 27:21; Jer. 18:18 · [Gal. 4:14]

8 But ye are departed out of the way; ye [R]have caused many to stumble at the law; ye have corrupted the covenant of Levi, saith the LORD of hosts.   Jer. 18:15

9 Therefore [R]have I also made you contemptible and base before all the people, according as ye have not kept my ways, but have been partial in the law.   1 Sam. 2:30

10 [R]Have we not all one father? [R]hath not one God created us? why do we deal treacherously every man against his brother, by profaning the covenant of our fathers?   1 Cor. 8:6; [Eph. 4:6] · Job 31:15

11 Judah hath dealt treacherously, and an abomination is committed in Israel and in Jerusalem; for Judah hath [R]profaned the holi-

ness of the LORD which he loved, and hath married the daughter of a strange god.   Ezra 9:1, 2; Neh. 13:23

12 The LORD will cut off the man that doeth this, the master and the scholar, out of the tabernacles of Jacob, and him that offereth an offering unto the LORD of hosts.

13 And this have ye done again, covering the altar of the LORD with tears, with weeping, and with crying out, ᵀinsomuch that he regardeth not the offering any more, or receiveth it with good will at your hand.   Or because

14 Yet ye say, Wherefore? Because the LORD hath been witness between thee and ᴿthe wife of thy youth, against whom thou hast dealt treacherously: ᴿyet is she thy companion, and the wife of thy covenant.   3:5 · Prov. 2:17

15 And did not he make one? Yet had he the residue of the spirit. And wherefore one? That he might seek a godly seed. Therefore take heed to your spirit, and let none deal treacherously against the wife of his youth.

16 For ᴿthe LORD, the God of Israel, saith that he hateth putting away: for one covereth violence with his garment, saith the LORD of hosts: therefore take heed to your spirit, that ye deal not treacherously.   [Matt. 5:31; 19:6–8]

17 ᴿYe have wearied the LORD with your words. Yet ye say, Wherein have we wearied him? When ye say, ᴿEvery one that doeth evil is good in the sight of the LORD, and he delighteth in them; or, Where is the God of judgment?   Is. 43:22, 24 · Zeph. 1:12

☆ **3** Behold, ᴿI will send my messenger, and he shall prepare the way before me: and the Lord, whom ye seek, shall suddenly come to his temple, even the messenger of the covenant, whom ye delight in: behold, he shall come, saith the LORD of hosts.   Matt. 11:10

2 But who may abide the day of his coming? and who shall stand when he appeareth? for ᴿhe is like a refiner's fire, and like fullers' sope: Is. 4:4; Zech. 13:9; [Matt. 3:10–12]

3 And he shall sit as a refiner and purifier of silver: and he shall purify the sons of Levi, and purge them as gold and silver, that they may ᴿoffer unto the LORD an offering in righteousness.   [1 Pet. 2:5]

4 Then ᴿshall the offering of Judah and Jerusalem be pleasant unto the LORD, as in the days of old, and as in former years.   1:11

5 And I will come near to you to judgment; and I will be a swift witness against the sorcerers, and against the adulterers, ᴿand against false swearers, and against those that ᴿoppress the hireling in his wages, the widow, and the fatherless, and that turn aside the stranger from his right, and fear not me, saith the LORD of hosts.   [James 5:12] · Lev. 19:13; James 5:4

6 For I am the LORD, ᴿI change not; therefore ye sons of Jacob are not consumed.   [James 1:17]

7 Even from the days of ᴿyour fathers ye are gone away from mine ordinances, and have not kept them. Return unto me, and I will return unto you, saith the LORD of hosts. But ye said, Wherein shall we return?   Acts 7:51

8 Will a man rob God? Yet ye have robbed me. But ye say, Wherein have we robbed thee? In tithes and offerings.

9 Ye are cursed with a curse: for ye have robbed me, even this whole nation.

10 Bring ye all the tithes into the storehouse, that there may be meat in mine house, and prove me now herewith, saith the LORD of hosts, if I will not open you the windows of heaven, and pour you out a blessing, that there shall not be room enough to receive it.

11 And I will rebuke the devourer for your sakes, and he shall not destroy the fruits of your ground; neither shall your vine cast her fruit before the time in the field, saith the LORD of hosts.

12 And all nations shall call you blessed: for ye shall be ᴿa ᵀde-

lightsome land, saith the LORD of hosts.　　　　　Dan. 8:9 · *delightful*

13 ^RYour words have been ^Tstout against me, saith the LORD. Yet ye say, What have we spoken *so much* against thee?　2:17 · *harsh*

14 Ye have said, It *is* vain to serve God: and what profit *is it* that we have kept his ordinance, and that we have walked mournfully before the LORD of hosts?

15 And now we call the proud happy; yea, they that work wickedness are set up; yea, *they that* tempt God are even delivered.

16 Then they that feared the LORD spake often one to another: and the LORD hearkened, and heard *it,* and a book of remembrance was written before him for them that feared the LORD, and that thought upon his name.

17 And they shall be mine, saith the LORD of hosts, in that day when I make up my jewels; and I will spare them, as a man spareth his own son that serveth him.

18 ^RThen shall ye return, and discern between the righteous and the wicked, between him that serveth God and him that serveth him not.　　　　[Ps. 58:11]

4 For, behold, ^Rthe day cometh, that shall burn as an oven; and all the proud, yea, and all that do wickedly, shall be stubble: and the day that cometh shall burn them up, saith the LORD of hosts, that it shall leave them neither root nor branch.　Ps. 21:9; [Nah. 1:5, 6; 2 Pet. 3:7]

2 But unto you that fear my name shall the Sun of righteousness arise with healing in his wings; and ye shall go forth, and grow up as calves of the stall.

3 ^RAnd ye shall tread down the wicked; for they shall be ashes under the soles of your feet in the day that I shall do *this,* saith the LORD of hosts.　　　Mic. 7:10

4 Remember ye the ^Rlaw of Moses my servant, which I commanded unto him in Ho'-reb for all Israel, *with* ^Rthe statutes and judgments.　Ex. 20:3 · Deut. 4:10

5 Behold, I will send you ^RE-li'- jah the prophet before the coming of the great and dreadful day of the LORD:　[Matt. 11:14; 17:10–13]

6 And he shall turn the heart of the fathers to the children, and the heart of the children to their fathers, lest I come and ^Rsmite the earth with a curse.　Zech. 14:12

The
New Testament

The
New Testament

MATTHEW

MATTHEW is the gospel written by a Jew to Jews about a Jew. Matthew is the writer, his countrymen are the readers, and Jesus Christ is the subject. Matthew's design is to present Jesus as the King of the Jews, the long-awaited Messiah. Through a carefully selected series of Old Testament quotations, Matthew documents Jesus Christ's claim to be the Messiah. His genealogy, baptism, messages, and miracles all point to the same inescapable conclusion: Christ is King. Even in His death, seeming defeat is turned to victory by the Resurrection, and the message again echoes forth: the King of the Jews lives.

At an early date this gospel was given the title *Kata Matthaion*, "According to Matthew." As this title suggests, other gospel accounts were known at that time (the word "Gospel" was added later). Matthew ("Gift of the Lord") was also surnamed Levi (Mark 2:14; Luke 5:27).

THE book of the generation of Jesus Christ, the son of David, the son of Abraham.

2 Abraham begat Isaac; and Isaac begat Jacob; and Jacob begat Judas and his brethren;

3 And ᴿJudas begat Pha'-res and Za'-ra of Tha'-mar; and ᴿPha'-res begat Es'-rom; and Es'-rom begat A'-ram; Gen. 38:27 · Ruth 4:18–22

4 And A'-ram begat A-min'-a-dab; and A-min'-a-dab begat Na-as'-son; and Na-as'-son begat Sal'-mon;

5 And Sal'-mon begat ᴿBo'-oz of ᵀRa'-chab; and Bo'-oz begat O'-bed of Ruth; and O'-bed begat Jesse; Ruth 2:1; 4:1–13 · Rahab, Josh. 2:1

★ 6 And Jesse begat David the king; and ᴿDavid the king begat Solomon of her *that had been the wife* of U-ri'-as; 2 Sam. 7:12

7 And ᴿSolomon begat Ro-bo'-am; and Ro-bo'-am begat A-bi'-a; and A-bi'-a begat A'-sa; 1 Kin. 11:43

8 And A'-sa begat Jos'-a-phat; and Jos'-a-phat begat Jo'-ram; and Jo'-ram begat O-zi'-as;

9 And O-zi'-as begat Jo'-a-tham; and Jo'-a-tham begat ᴿA'-chaz; and A'-chaz begat Ez-e-ki'-as; 2 Kin. 15:38

10 And Ez-e-ki'-as begat Ma-nas'-ses; and Ma-nas'-ses begat Amon; and Amon begat Jo-si'-as;

11 And ᴿJo-si'-as begat Jech-o-ni'-as and his brethren, about the time they were ᴿcarried away to Babylon: 1 Chr. 3:15, 16 · 2 Kin. 24:14–16

12 And after they were brought to Babylon, ᴿJech-o-ni'-as begat Sa-la'-thi-el; and Sa-la'-thi-el begat Zo-rob'-a-bel; 1 Chr. 3:17

13 And Zo-rob'-a-bel begat A-bi'-ud; and A-bi'-ud begat E-li'-a-kim; and E-li'-a-kim begat A'-zor;

14 And A'-zor begat Sa'-doc; and Sa'-doc begat A'-chim; and A'-chim begat E-li'-ud;

15 And E-li'-ud begat E-le-a'-zar; and E-le-a'-zar begat Mat'-than; and Mat'-than begat Jacob;

16 And Jacob begat Joseph the husband of Mary, of whom was born Jesus, who is called Christ.

17 So all the generations from Abraham to David *are* fourteen generations; and from David until the carrying away into Babylon *are* fourteen generations; and from the carrying away into Babylon unto Christ *are* fourteen generations.

18 Now the ᴿbirth of Jesus ★ Christ was on this wise: When as his mother Mary was espoused to Joseph, before they came together, she was found with child ᴿof the Holy Ghost. Luke 1:27 · Is. 7:14

19 Then Joseph her husband, being a just *man*, and not willing ᴿto make her a publick example, was minded to put her away ᵀprivily. Deut. 24:1; John 8:4, 5 · secretly

20 But while he thought on these things, behold, the angel of the Lord appeared unto him in a dream, saying, Joseph, thou son of David, fear not to take unto thee Mary thy wife: ᴿfor that which is conceived in her is of the Holy Ghost.   Luke 1:35

21 And she shall bring forth a son, and thou shalt call his name JESUS: for ᴿhe shall save his people from their sins.   [Acts 4:12; 5:31]

22 Now all this was done, that it might be fulfilled which was spoken of the Lord by the prophet, saying,

★ 23 ᴿBehold, a virgin shall be with child, and shall bring forth a son, and they shall call his name Em-man'-u-el, which being interpreted is, God with us.   Is. 7:14

24 Then Joseph being raised from sleep did as the angel of the Lord had bidden him, and took unto him his wife:

25 And knew her not till she had brought forth her firstborn son: and he called his name JESUS.

★ 2 Now when ᴿJesus was born in Beth'-le-hem of Ju-dae'-a in the days of Herod the king, behold, there came wise men from the east to Jerusalem,   Luke 2:4–7

2 Saying, ᴿWhere is he that is born King of the Jews? for we have seen his star in the east, and are come to worship him. Luke 2:11

3 When Herod the king had heard these things, he was troubled, and all Jerusalem with him.

4 And when he had gathered all ᴿthe chief priests and scribes of the people together, ᴿhe demanded of them where Christ should be born. 2 Chr. 36:14 · Mal. 2:7

5 And they said unto him, In Beth'-le-hem of Ju-dae'-a: for thus it is written by the prophet,

★ 6 And thou Beth'-le-hem, in the land of Juda, art not the least among the princes of Juda: for out of thee shall come a Governor, that shall rule my people Israel.

7 Then Herod, when he had privily called the wise men, en-

quired of them diligently what time the ᴿstar appeared. Num. 24:17

8 And he sent them to Beth'-le-hem, and said, Go and search diligently for the young child; and when ye have found him, bring me word again, that I may come and worship him also.

9 When they had heard the king, they departed; and, lo, the star, which they saw in the east, went before them, till it came and stood over where the young child was.

10 When they saw the star, they rejoiced with exceeding great joy.

11 And when they were come into the house, they saw the young child with Mary his mother, and fell down, and worshipped him: and when they had opened their treasures, ᴿthey presented unto him gifts; gold, and frankincense, and myrrh.   Is. 60:6

12 And being warned of God ᴿin a dream that they should not return to Herod, they departed into their own country another way.   1:20; [Job 33:15, 16]

13 And when they were departed, behold, the angel of the Lord appeareth to Joseph in a dream, saying, Arise, and take the young child and his mother, and flee into Egypt, and be thou there until I bring thee word: for Herod will seek the young child to destroy him.

14 When he arose, he took the young child and his mother by night, and departed into Egypt:

15 And was there until the death ★ of Herod: that it might be fulfilled which was spoken of the Lord by the prophet, saying, ᴿOut of Egypt have I called my son.   Hos. 11:1

16 Then Herod, when he saw that he was mocked of the wise men, was exceeding wroth, and sent forth, and slew all the children that were in Beth'-le-hem, and in all the coasts thereof, from two years old and under, according to the time which he had diligently enquired of the wise men.

17 Then was fulfilled that which

was spoken by Jeremy the prophet, saying,

★ 18 ᴿIn Ra′-ma was there a voice heard, lamentation, and weeping, and great mourning, Ra′-chel weeping *for* her children, and would not be comforted, because they are not. Jer. 31:15

19 But when Herod was dead, behold, an angel of the Lord appeareth in a dream to Joseph in Egypt,

20 ᴿSaying, Arise, and take the young child and his mother, and go into the land of Israel: for they are dead which ᴿsought the young child's life. Luke 2:39 · v. 16

21 And he arose, and took the young child and his mother, and came into the land of Israel.

22 But when he heard that Ar-che-la′-us did reign in Ju-dae′-a in the room of his father Herod, he was afraid to go thither: notwithstanding, being warned of God in a dream, he turned aside ᴿinto the parts of Galilee: 3:13; Luke 2:39

★ 23 And he came and dwelt in a city called ᴿNazareth: that it might be fulfilled which was spoken by the prophets, He shall be called a Nazarene. Luke 1:26; 2:39

3 In those days came ᴿJohn the Baptist, preaching in the wilderness of Ju-dae′-a, Luke 3:2–17

2 And saying, Repent ye: for ᴿthe kingdom of heaven is at hand. 4:17; Dan. 2:44; Mal. 4:6; Mark 1:15

★ 3 For this is he that was spoken of by the prophet E-sa′-ias, saying, ᴿThe voice of one crying in the wilderness, ᴿPrepare ye the way of the Lord, make his paths straight. Is. 40:3; Luke 3:4 · Luke 1:76

4 And the same John had his raiment of camel's hair, and a leathern ᵀgirdle about his ᵀloins; and his ᵀmeat was locusts and wild honey. *belt · waist · food*

5 Then went out to him Jerusalem, and all Ju-dae′-a, and all the region round about Jordan,

6 And were baptized of him in Jordan, confessing their sins.

7 But when he saw many of the Pharisees and Sad′-du-cees come

to his baptism, he said unto them, ᴿO ᵀgeneration of vipers, who hath warned you to flee from the wrath to come? Luke 3:7–9 · *brood*

8 Bring forth therefore fruits ᵀmeet for repentance: *worthy of*

9 And think not to say within yourselves, We have Abraham to *our* father: for I say unto you, that God is able of these stones to raise up children unto Abraham.

10 And now also the ax is laid unto the root of the trees: ᴿtherefore every tree which bringeth not forth good fruit is hewn down, and cast into the fire. [Ps. 92:12–14]

11 ᴿI indeed baptize you with ☆ water unto repentance: but he that cometh after me is mightier than I, whose shoes I am not worthy to bear: ᴿhe shall baptize you with the Holy Ghost, and *with* fire: John 1:26; Acts 1:5 · [Is. 4:4; Acts 2:3, 4]

12 Whose fan *is* in his hand, and he will throughly purge his floor, and gather his wheat into the garner; but he will burn up the chaff with unquenchable fire.

13 Then cometh Jesus ᴿfrom Galilee to Jordan unto John, to be baptized of him. 2:22

14 But John forbad him, saying, I have need to be baptized of thee, and comest thou to me?

15 And Jesus answering said unto him, ᵀSuffer *it to be so* now: for thus it ᵀbecometh us to fulfil all righteousness. Then he suffered him. *Allow · is fitting for us*

16 ᴿAnd Jesus, when he was ★ baptized, went up straightway out of the water: and, lo, the heavens were opened unto him, and he saw ᴿthe Spirit of God descending like a dove, and lighting upon him: Mark 1:10 · [Is. 11:2]; John 1:32

17 And lo a voice from heaven, saying, This is my beloved Son, in whom I am well pleased.

4 Then was ᴿJesus led up of the spirit into the wilderness to be tempted of the devil. Luke 4:1

2 And when he had fasted forty days and forty nights, he was afterward ᵀan hungred. *hungry*

3 And when the tempter came

to him, he said, If thou be the Son of God, command that these stones be made bread.

4 But he answered and said, It is written, ᴿMan shall not live by bread alone, but by every word that proceedeth out of the mouth of God.   Deut. 8:3

5 Then the devil taketh him up ᴿinto the holy city, and setteth him on a pinnacle of the temple,   27:53

6 And saith unto him, If thou be the Son of God, cast thyself down: for it is written, He shall give his angels charge concerning thee: and in *their* hands they shall bear thee up, lest at any time thou dash thy foot against a stone.

7 Jesus said unto him, It is written again, ᴿThou shalt not ᵀtempt the Lord thy God.   Deut. 6:16 · *test*

8 Again, the devil taketh him up into an exceeding high mountain, and ᴿsheweth him all the kingdoms of the world, and the glory of them;   [16:26; 1 John 2:15–17]

9 And saith unto him, All these things will I give thee, if thou wilt fall down and worship me.

10 Then saith Jesus unto him, Get thee hence, Satan: for it is written, ᴿThou shalt worship the Lord thy God, and him only shalt thou serve. Deut. 6:13; 10:20; Josh. 24:14

11 Then the devil leaveth him, and, behold, ᴿangels came and ministered unto him.   26:53

12 ᴿNow when Jesus had heard that John was cast into prison, he departed into Galilee; 14:3; John 4:43

13 And leaving Nazareth, he came and dwelt in Ca-per'-na-um, which is upon the sea coast, in the borders of Zab'-u-lon and Neph'-tha-lim:

14 That it might be fulfilled which was spoken by E-sa'-ias the prophet, saying,

★ 15 ᴿThe land of Zab'-u-lon, and the land of Neph'-tha-lim, *by* the way of the sea, beyond Jordan, Galilee of the Gentiles;   Is. 9:1, 2

16 ᴿThe people which sat in darkness saw great light; and to them which sat in the region and shadow of death light ᵀis sprung up.   Is. 42:7; Luke 2:32 · *has dawned*

17 ᴿFrom that time Jesus began to preach, and to say, ᴿRepent: for the kingdom of heaven is ᵀat hand.   Mark 1:14, 15 · 3:2; 10:7 · *near*

18 And Jesus, walking by the sea of Galilee, saw two brethren, Simon ᴿcalled Peter, and Andrew his brother, casting a net into the sea: for they were fishers.   10:2

19 And he saith unto them, Follow me, and ᴿI will make you fishers of men.   Luke 5:10

20 ᴿAnd they straightway left *their* nets, and followed him. 19:27

21 ᴿAnd going on from thence, he saw other two brethren, James *the son* of Zeb'-e-dee, and John his brother, in a ship with Zeb'-e-dee their father, mending their nets; and he called them. Mark 1:19

22 And they immediately left the ship and their father, and followed him.

23 And Jesus went about all Galilee, ᴿteaching in their synagogues, and preaching ᴿthe gospel of the kingdom, and healing all manner of sickness and all manner of disease among the people.   Ps. 22:22 · [24:14]; Mark 1:14

24 And his fame went throughout all Syria: and they brought unto him all sick people that were taken with ᵀdivers diseases and torments, and those which were possessed with devils, and those which were ᵀlunatick, and those that ᵀhad the palsy; and he healed them. *various · epileptics · were paralyzed*

25 And there followed him great multitudes of people from Galilee, and *from* De-cap'-o-lis, and *from* Jerusalem, and *from* Ju-dae'-a, and *from* beyond Jordan.

5 And seeing the multitudes, ᴿhe went up into a mountain: and when he was set, his disciples came unto him: Luke 6:17; 9:28

2 And he opened his mouth, and ᴿtaught them, saying,   [7:29]

3 ᴿBlessed *are* the poor in spirit: for theirs is the kingdom of heaven. Prov. 16:19; Is. 66:2; Luke 6:20–23

4 Blessed *are* they that mourn: for they shall be comforted.

5 Blessed *are* the meek: for they shall inherit the ᵀearth. *land*

6 Blessed *are* they which do hunger and thirst after righteousness: for they shall be filled.

7 Blessed *are* the merciful: ᴿfor they shall obtain mercy. Ps. 41:1

8 Blessed *are* the pure in heart: for they shall see God.

9 Blessed *are* the peacemakers: for they shall be called the ᵀchildren of God. Lit. *sons*

10 ᴿBlessed *are* they which are persecuted for righteousness' sake: for theirs is the kingdom of heaven. [2 Cor. 4:17]; 1 Pet. 3:14

11 ᴿBlessed are ye, when *men* shall revile you, and persecute *you*, and shall say all manner of ᴿevil against you falsely, for my sake. Luke 6:22 · 1 Pet. 4:14

12 ᴿRejoice, and be exceeding glad: for great *is* your reward in heaven: for ᴿso persecuted they the prophets which were before you. Acts 5:41 · 2 Chr. 36:16; Neh. 9:26

13 Ye are the salt of the earth: but if the salt have lost his savour, ᵀwherewith shall it be salted? it is thenceforth good for nothing, but to be cast out, and to be trodden under foot of men. *by what*

14 ᴿYe are the light of the world. A city that is set on an hill cannot be hid. [Prov. 4:18; John 8:12]; Phil. 2:15

15 Neither do men light a candle, and put it under a bushel, but on a candlestick; and it giveth light unto all that are in the house.

16 Let your light so shine before men, ᴿthat they may see your good works, and glorify your Father which is in heaven. 1 Pet. 2:12

17 ᴿThink not that I am come to destroy the law, or the prophets: I am not come to destroy, but to fulfil. Rom. 10:4

18 For verily I say unto you, Till heaven and earth pass, one jot or one tittle shall in no wise pass from the law, till all be fulfilled.

19 ᴿWhosoever therefore shall break one of these least commandments, and shall teach men so, he shall be called the least in the kingdom of heaven: but whosoever shall do and teach *them*, the same shall be called great in the kingdom of heaven. [James 2:10]

20 For I say unto you, That except your righteousness shall exceed ᴿ*the righteousness* of the scribes and Pharisees, ye shall ᵀin no case enter into the kingdom of heaven. [Rom. 10:3] · *by no means*

21 Ye have heard that it was said by them of old time, ᴿThou shalt not ᵀkill; and whosoever shall ᵀkill shall be in danger of the judgment: Ex. 20:13; Deut. 5:17 · *murder*

22 But I say unto you, That whosoever is angry with his brother without a cause shall be in danger of the judgment: and whosoever shall say to his brother, ᴿRa'-ca, shall be in danger of the council: but whosoever shall say, Thou fool, shall be in danger of ᵀhell fire. [James 2:20; 3:6] · Gr. *gehenna*

23 Therefore ᴿif thou bring thy gift to the altar, and there rememberest that thy brother hath ᵀought against thee; 8:4 · *something*

24 Leave there thy gift before the altar, and go thy way; first be reconciled to thy brother, and then come and offer thy gift.

25 ᴿAgree with thine adversary quickly, ᴿwhiles thou art in the way with him; lest at any time the adversary deliver thee to the judge, and the judge deliver thee to the officer, and thou be cast into prison. [Prov. 25:8] · [Ps. 32:6]

26 Verily I say unto thee, Thou shalt by no means come out thence, till thou hast paid the uttermost ᵀfarthing. Gr. *kodrantes*

27 Ye have heard that it was said by them of old time, ᴿThou shalt not commit adultery: Ex. 20:14

28 But I say unto you, That whosoever ᴿlooketh on a woman to lust after her hath committed adultery with her already in his heart. [15:19]; Prov. 6:25; [James 1:14, 15]

29 And if thy right eye offend thee, pluck it out, and cast *it* from thee: for it is profitable for thee that one of thy members should

perish, and not *that* thy whole body should be cast into hell.

30 And if thy right hand offend thee, cut it off, and cast *it* from thee: for it is profitable for thee that one of thy members should perish, and not *that* thy whole body should be cast into hell.

31 It hath been said, [R]Whosoever shall [T]put away his wife, let him give her a [T]writing of divorcement: Deut. 24:1 · *divorce · certificate*

32 But I say unto you, That [R]whosoever shall put away his wife, saving for the cause of fornication, causeth her to commit adultery: and whosoever shall marry her that is divorced committeth adultery. [19:9]

33 Again, ye have heard that it hath been said by them of old time, Thou shalt not [T]forswear thyself, but shalt perform unto the Lord thine oaths: *swear falsely*

34 But I say unto you, [R]Swear not at all; neither by heaven; for it is [R]God's throne: 23:16 · Is. 66:1

35 Nor by the earth; for it is his footstool: neither by Jerusalem; for it is the city of the great King.

36 Neither shalt thou swear by thy head, because thou canst not make one hair white or black.

37 [R]But let your [T]communication be, Yea, yea; Nay, nay: for whatsoever is more than these cometh of evil. James 5:12 · *word*

38 Ye have heard that it hath been said, [R]An eye for an eye, and a tooth for a tooth: Ex. 21:24

39 But I say unto you, That ye resist not evil: but whosoever shall smite thee on thy right cheek, turn to him the other also.

40 And if any man will sue thee at the law, and take away thy coat, let him have *thy* cloke also.

41 And whosoever [R]shall compel thee to go a mile, go with him [T]twain. 27:32 · *two*

42 Give to him that asketh thee, and from him that would borrow of thee turn not thou away.

43 Ye have heard that it hath been said, Thou shalt love thy neighbour, and hate thine enemy.

44 But I say unto you, [R]Love your enemies, bless them that curse you, do good to them that hate you, and pray for them which despitefully use you, and persecute you; Luke 6:27; Rom. 12:14

45 That ye may be the children of your Father which is in heaven: for [R]he maketh his sun to rise on the evil and on the good, and sendeth rain on the just and on the unjust. Job 25:3; Ps. 65:9–13

46 For if ye love them which love you, what reward have ye? do not even the publicans the same?

47 And if ye [T]salute your brethren only, what do ye more *than others*? do not even the [T]publicans so? *greet · tax collectors*

48 [R]Be ye therefore perfect, even as your Father which is in heaven is perfect. James 1:4; 1 Pet. 1:15

6 Take heed that ye do not your [T]alms before men, to be seen of them: otherwise ye have no reward [T]of your Father which is in heaven. *charitable deeds · from*

2 Therefore [R]when thou doest *thine* alms, do not sound a trumpet before thee, as the hypocrites do in the synagogues and in the streets, that they may have glory of men. Verily I say unto you, They have their reward. Rom. 12:8

3 But when thou doest alms, let not thy left hand know what thy right hand doeth:

4 That thine alms may be in secret: and thy Father which seeth in secret himself [R]shall reward thee openly. Luke 14:12–14

5 And when thou prayest, thou shalt not be as the hypocrites *are*: for they love to pray standing in the synagogues and in the corners of the streets, that they may be seen of men. Verily I say unto you, They have their reward.

6 But thou, when thou prayest, [R]enter into thy closet, and when thou hast shut thy door, pray to thy Father which is in secret; and thy Father which seeth in secret shall reward thee openly. 2 Kin. 4:33

7 But when ye pray, use not vain repetitions, as the heathen

do: for they think that they shall be heard for their much speaking.

8 Be not ye therefore like unto them: for your Father ᴿknoweth what things ye have need of, before ye ask him. [Rom. 8:26, 27]

9 After this manner therefore pray ye: Our Father which art in heaven, Hallowed be thy name.

10 Thy kingdom come. ᴿThy will be done in earth, ᴿas it is in heaven.   Luke 22:42; Acts 21:14 · Ps. 103:20

11 Give us this day our ᴿdaily bread.   Prov. 30:8; Is. 33:16; Luke 11:3

12 And ᴿforgive us our debts, as we forgive our debtors.   [18:21, 22]

13 ᴿAnd lead us not into temptation, but ᴿdeliver us from evil: For thine is the kingdom, and the power, and the glory, for ever. Amen'. [2 Pet. 2:9] · John 17:15; [2 Thess. 3:3]

14 ᴿFor if ye forgive men their trespasses, your heavenly Father will also forgive you: Mark 11:25

15 But if ye forgive not men their trespasses, neither will your Father forgive your trespasses.

16 Moreover when ye fast, be not, as the hypocrites, of a sad countenance: for they disfigure their faces, that they may appear unto men to fast. Verily I say unto you, They have their reward.

17 But thou, when thou fastest, ᴿanoint thine head, and wash thy face;   Ruth 3:3; 2 Sam. 12:20; Dan. 10:3

18 That thou appear not unto men to fast, but unto thy Father which is in secret: and thy Father, which seeth in secret, shall reward thee openly.

19 Lay not up for yourselves treasures upon earth, where moth and rust doth corrupt, and where thieves break through and steal:

20 ᴿBut lay up for yourselves treasures in heaven, where neither moth nor rust doth corrupt, and where thieves do not break through nor steal: 19:21; Luke 12:33

21 For where your treasure is, there will your heart be also.

22 The ᵀlight of the body is the eye: if therefore thine eye be ᵀsingle, thy whole body shall be full of light.   lamp · Healthy

23 But if thine eye be ᵀevil, thy whole body shall be full of darkness. If therefore the light that is in thee be darkness, how great is that darkness!   Unhealthy

24 No man can serve two masters: for either he will hate the one, and love the other; or else he will hold to the one, and despise the other. ᴿYe cannot serve God and mammon.   [1 Tim. 6:17; James 4:4]

25 Therefore I say unto you, Take no thought for your life, what ye shall eat, or what ye shall drink; nor yet for your body, what ye shall put on. Is not the life more than ᵀmeat, and the body than ᵀraiment?   food · clothing

26 ᴿBehold the fowls of the air: for they sow not, neither do they reap, nor gather into barns; yet your heavenly Father feedeth them. Are ye not much better than they?   Job 38:41; Ps. 147:9; Luke 12:24

27 Which of you by ᵀtaking thought can add one cubit unto his ᵀstature?   worrying · height

28 And why take ye thought for raiment? Consider the lilies of the field, how they grow; they toil not, neither do they spin:

29 And yet I say unto you, That even Solomon in all his glory was not arrayed like one of these.

30 Wherefore, if God so clothe the grass of the field, which to day is, and to morrow is cast into the oven, shall he not much more clothe you, O ye of little faith?

31 Therefore take no thought, saying, What shall we eat? or, What shall we drink? or, Wherewithal shall we be clothed?

32 (For after all these things do the Gentiles seek:) for your heavenly Father knoweth that ye have need of all these things.

33 But ᴿseek ye first the kingdom of God, and his righteousness; and all these things shall be added unto you.   Luke 12:31

34 Take therefore no thought for the morrow: for the morrow shall take thought for the things of itself. Sufficient unto the day is the ᵀevil thereof.   trouble

7 Judge [R]not, that ye be not judged.   Rom. 14:3; [1 Cor. 4:3, 4]

2 For with what judgment ye judge, ye shall be judged: and with what measure ye mete, it shall be measured to you again.

3 And why beholdest thou the [T]mote that is in thy brother's eye, but considerest not the [T]beam that is in thine own eye?   *speck · plank*

4 Or how wilt thou say to thy brother, Let me pull out the mote out of thine eye; and, behold, a beam *is* in thine own eye?

5 Thou hypocrite, first cast out the beam out of thine own eye; and then shalt thou see clearly to cast out the mote out of thy brother's eye.

6 Give not that which is holy unto the dogs, neither cast ye your pearls before swine, lest they trample them under their feet, and turn again and rend you.

7 [R]Ask, and it shall be given you; seek, and ye shall find; knock, and it shall be opened unto you: Luke 11:9–13; 18:1–8; [John 15:7]

8 For [R]every one that asketh receiveth; and he that seeketh findeth; and to him that knocketh it shall be opened.   Jer. 29:12

9 [R]Or what man is there of you, whom if his son ask bread, will he give him a stone?   Luke 11:11

10 Or if he ask a fish, will he give him a serpent?

11 If ye then, [R]being evil, know how to give good gifts unto your children, how much more shall your Father which is in heaven give good things to them that ask him?   [Rom. 8:32; James 1:17]; 1 John 3:1

12 Therefore all things whatsoever ye would that men should do to you, do ye even so to them: for this is the law and the prophets.

13 Enter ye in at the [T]strait gate: for wide *is* the gate, and broad *is* the way, that leadeth to destruction, and many there be which go in thereat: *narrow*

14 Because strait *is* the gate, and narrow *is* the way, which leadeth unto life, and few there be that find it.

15 [R]Beware of false prophets, which come to you in sheep's clothing, but inwardly they are ravening wolves.   Mark 13:22

16 [R]Ye shall know them by their fruits. Do men gather grapes of thorns, or figs of thistles?   12:33

17 Even so [R]every good tree bringeth forth good fruit; but a corrupt tree bringeth forth [T]evil fruit.   12:33; Jer. 11:19 · *bad*

18 A good tree cannot bring forth evil fruit, neither *can* a corrupt tree bring forth good fruit.

19 [R]Every tree that bringeth not forth good fruit is hewn down, and cast into the fire.   3:10; Luke 3:9

20 Wherefore by their fruits ye shall know them.

21 Not every one that saith unto me, [R]Lord, Lord, shall enter into the kingdom of heaven; but he that doeth the will of my Father which is in heaven.   Hos. 8:2

22 Many will say to me in that day, Lord, Lord, have we [R]not prophesied in thy name? and in thy name have cast out devils? and in thy name done many wonderful works?   Num. 24:4

23 And then will I profess unto them, I never knew you: depart from me, ye that work iniquity.

24 Therefore [R]whosoever heareth these sayings of mine, and doeth them, I will liken him unto a wise man, which built his house upon [T]a rock: Luke 6:47–49 · *the*

25 And the rain descended, and the floods came, and the winds blew, and beat upon that house; and it fell not: for it was founded upon [T]a rock.   *the*

26 And every one that heareth these sayings of mine, and doeth them not, shall be likened unto a foolish man, which built his house upon the sand:

27 And the rain descended, and the floods came, and the winds blew, and beat upon that house; and it fell: and great was the fall of it.

28 And it came to pass, when Jesus had ended these sayings, [R]the people were astonished at his [T]doctrine: 13:54; John 7:46 · *teaching*

29 For he taught them as *one* having authority, and not as the scribes.

8 When he was come down from the mountain, great multitudes followed him.

2 ᴿAnd, behold, there came a leper and worshipped him, saying, Lord, if thou wilt, thou canst make me clean.   Mark 1:40–45

3 And Jesus put forth *his* hand, and touched him, saying, I will; be thou clean. And immediately his leprosy ᴿwas cleansed.   Luke 4:27

4 And Jesus saith unto him, See thou tell no man; but go thy way, shew thyself to the priest, and offer the gift that Moses ᴿcommanded, for a testimony unto them.   Lev. 14:4–32; Deut. 24:8

5 ᴿAnd when Jesus was entered into Ca-per′-na-um, there came unto him a ᴿcenturion, beseeching him,   Luke 7:1–3 · 27:54

6 And saying, Lord, my servant lieth at home ᵀsick of the palsy, grievously tormented.   *paralyzed*

7 And Jesus saith unto him, I will come and heal him.

8 The centurion answered and said, Lord, I am not worthy that thou shouldest come under my roof: but speak the word only, and my servant shall be healed.

9 For I am a man under authority, having soldiers under me: and I say to this *man*, Go, and he goeth; and to another, Come, and he cometh; and to my servant, Do this, and he doeth *it*.

10 When Jesus heard *it*, he marvelled, and said to them that followed, Verily I say unto you, I have not found so great faith, no, not in Israel.

☆ 11 And I say unto you, That ᴿmany shall come from the east and west, and shall sit down with Abraham, and Isaac, and Jacob, in the kingdom of heaven.   [Is. 2:2, 3]

12 But the ᵀchildren of the kingdom shall be cast out into outer darkness: there shall be weeping and gnashing of teeth.   Lit. *sons*

13 And Jesus said unto the centurion, Go thy way; and as thou hast believed, *so* be it done unto thee. And his servant was healed in the selfsame hour.

14 ᴿAnd when Jesus was come into Peter′s house, he saw ᴿhis wife′s mother laid, and sick of a fever.   Mark 1:29–31 · 1 Cor. 9:5

15 And he touched her hand, and the fever left her: and she arose, and ministered unto them.

16 ᴿWhen the even was come, they brought unto him many that were possessed with ᵀdevils: and he cast out the spirits with *his* word, and healed all that were sick: Mark 1:32–34; Luke 4:40, 41 · *demons*

17 That it might be fulfilled ★ which was spoken by E-sa′-ias the prophet, saying, ᴿHimself took our infirmities, and bare *our* sicknesses.   Is. 53:4; 1 Pet. 2:24

18 Now when Jesus saw great multitudes about him, he gave commandment to depart unto the other side.

19 ᴿAnd a certain scribe came, and said unto him, Master, I will follow thee whithersoever thou goest.   Luke 9:57, 58

20 And Jesus saith unto him, The foxes have holes, and the birds of the air *have* nests; but the Son of man hath not where to lay *his* head.

21 And another of his disciples said unto him, Lord, suffer me first to go and bury my father.

22 But Jesus said unto him, Follow me; and let the dead bury their dead.

23 And when he was entered into a ship, his disciples followed him.

24 And, behold, there arose a great tempest in the sea, insomuch that the ship was covered with the waves: but he was asleep.

25 And his disciples came to *him*, and awoke him, saying, Lord, save us: we perish.

26 And he saith unto them, Why are ye fearful, O ye of little faith? Then ᴿhe arose, and rebuked the winds and the sea; and there was a great calm.   Ps. 65:7; 89:9; 107:29

27 But the men marvelled, saying, What manner of man is this, that even the winds and the sea obey him!

28 ᴿAnd when he was come to the other side into the country of the Ger-ge-senes', there met him two possessed with devils, coming out of the tombs, exceeding fierce, so that no man might pass by that way.   Mark 5:1–4; Luke 8:26–33

29 And, behold, they cried out, saying, What have we to do with thee, Jesus, thou Son of God? art thou come hither to torment us before the time?

30 And there was a good way off from them an herd of many swine feeding.

31 So the ᵀdevils besought him, saying, If thou cast us out, ᵀsuffer us to go away into the herd of swine.   *demons begged · permit*

32 And he said unto them, Go. And when they were come out, they went into the herd of swine: and, behold, the whole herd of swine ran violently down a steep place into the sea, and perished in the waters.

33 And they that kept them fled, and went their ways into the city, and told every thing, and what was befallen to the ᵀpossessed of the devils.   *demon-possessed men*

34 And, behold, the whole city came out to meet Jesus: and when they saw him, ᴿthey besought *him* that he would depart out of their coasts.   Amos 7:12; Luke 5:8; Acts 16:39

9 And he entered into a ship, and passed over, ᴿand came into his own city. 4:13; 11:23; Mark 5:21

2 And, behold, they brought to him a man sick of the palsy, lying on a bed: and Jesus seeing their faith said unto the ᵀsick of the palsy; Son, be of good cheer; thy sins be forgiven thee.   *paralytic*

3 And, behold, certain of the scribes said within themselves, This *man* blasphemeth.

4 And Jesus ᴿknowing their thoughts said, Wherefore think ye evil in your hearts?   Mark 12:15

5 For ᵀwhether is easier, to say,

Thy sins be forgiven thee; or to say, Arise, and walk?   *which*

6 But that ye may know that the Son of man hath power on earth to forgive sins, (then saith he to the ᵀsick of the palsy,) Arise, take up thy bed, and go unto thine house.   *paralytic*

7 And he arose, and departed to his house.

8 But when the multitudes saw *it*, they ᴿmarvelled, and glorified God, which had given such power unto men.   8:27; John 7:15

9 ᴿAnd as Jesus passed forth from thence, he saw a man, named Matthew, sitting at the receipt of custom: and he saith unto him, Follow me. And he arose, and followed him.   Mark 2:14

10 And it came to pass, as Jesus sat at meat in the house, behold, many ᵀpublicans and sinners came and sat down with him and his disciples.   *tax collectors*

11 And when the Pharisees saw *it*, they said unto his disciples, Why eateth your Master with ᴿpublicans and sinners?   Mark 2:16

12 But when Jesus heard *that*, he said unto them, They that ᵀbe whole need not a physician, but they that are sick.   *are well*

13 But go ye and learn what *that* meaneth, ᴿI will have mercy, and not sacrifice: for I am not come to call the righteous, but sinners to repentance.   Hos. 6:6

14 Then came to him the disciples of John, saying, ᴿWhy do we and the Pharisees fast oft, but thy disciples fast not?   Luke 5:33–35; 18:12

15 And Jesus said unto them, Can ᴿthe children of the bridechamber mourn, as long as the bridegroom is with them? but the days will come, when the bridegroom shall be taken from them, and then shall they fast.   John 3:29

16 No man putteth a piece of ᵀnew cloth unto an old garment, for that which is put in to fill it up taketh from the garment, and the ᵀrent is made worse.   *unshrunk · tear*

17 Neither do men put new wine into old ᵀbottles: else the bottles

break, and the wine runneth out, and the bottles perish: but they put new wine into new bottles, and both are preserved. *wineskins*

18 While he spake these things unto them, behold, there came a certain ruler, and worshipped him, saying, My daughter is even now dead: but come and lay thy hand upon her, and she shall live.

19 And Jesus arose, and followed him, and *so did* his ᴿdisciples.   10:2–4

20 ᴿAnd, behold, a woman, which was diseased with an issue of blood twelve years, came behind *him*, and touched the hem of his garment: Mark 5:25; Luke 8:43

21 For she said within herself, If I may but touch his garment, I shall be whole.

22 But Jesus turned him about, and when he saw her, he said, Daughter, ᵀbe of good comfort; ᴿthy faith hath made thee whole. And the woman was made whole from that hour.   *take courage* · 15:28

23 And when Jesus came into the ruler's house, and saw ᴿthe minstrels and the people making a noise,   2 Chr. 35:25; Jer. 9:17; 16:6

24 He said unto them, ᴿGive place: for the maid is not dead, but sleepeth. And they laughed him to scorn.   John 11:3; Acts 20:10

25 But when the people were put ᵀforth, he went in, and ᴿtook her by the hand, and the maid arose.   *outside* · 8:3, 15; Mark 1:31

26 And the ᴿfame hereof went abroad into all that land.   4:24

27 And when Jesus departed thence, two blind men followed him, crying, and saying, *Thou* son of David, have mercy on us.

28 And when he was come into the house, the blind men came to him: and Jesus saith unto them, Believe ye that I am able to do this? They said unto him, Yea, Lord.

29 Then touched he their eyes, saying, According to your faith be it unto you.

30 And their eyes were opened; and Jesus straitly charged them, saying, See *that* no man know *it*.

31 ᴿBut they, when they were departed, spread abroad his fame in all that country.   Mark 7:36

32 As they went out, behold, they brought to him a ᵀdumb man possessed with a devil.   *mute*

33 And when the ᵀdevil was cast out, the dumb spake: and the multitudes marvelled, saying, It was never so seen in Israel.   *demon*

34 But the Pharisees said, He casteth out devils through the ᵀprince of the devils. *ruler of demons*

35 And Jesus went about all the cities and villages, ᴿteaching in their synagogues, and preaching the gospel of the kingdom, and healing every sickness and every disease among the people.   4:23

36 ᴿBut when he saw the multitudes, he was moved with compassion on them, because they ᵀfainted, and were scattered abroad, ᴿas sheep having no shepherd.   Mark 6:34 · *were weary* · Zech. 10:2

37 Then saith he unto his disciples, The harvest truly *is* plenteous, but the labourers *are* few;

38 Pray ye therefore the Lord of the harvest, that he will send forth labourers into his harvest.

10 And when he had called unto *him* his twelve disciples, he gave them power *against* unclean spirits, to cast them out, and to heal all manner of sickness and all manner of disease.

2 Now the names of the twelve apostles are these; The first, Simon, ᴿwho is called Peter, and Andrew his brother; James *the son* of Zeb'-e-dee, and John his brother;   John 1:42

3 Philip, and Bartholomew; Thomas, and Matthew the ᵀpublican; James *the son* of Al-phae'-us, and Leb-bae'-us, whose surname was Thad-dae'-us;   *tax collector*

4 ᴿSimon the Ca'-naan-ite, and Judas ᴿIs-car'-i-ot, who also betrayed him.   Acts 1:13 · John 13:2, 26

5 These twelve Jesus sent forth, and commanded them, saying, Go not into the way of the Gentiles, and into *any* city of the Sa-mar'-i-tans enter ye not:

6 But go rather to the ᴿlost sheep of the house of Israel. Is. 53:6

7 ᴿAnd as ye go, preach, saying, ᴿThe kingdom of heaven is at hand. Luke 9:2 · 3:2; Luke 10:9

8 Heal the sick, cleanse the lepers, raise the dead, cast out ᵀdevils: ᴿfreely ye have received, freely give. demons · [Acts 8:18]

9 Provide neither gold, nor silver, nor brass in your purses,

10 Nor ᵀscrip for your journey, neither two coats, neither shoes, nor yet ᵀstaves: for the workman is worthy of his meat. bag · staffs

11 ᴿAnd into whatsoever city or town ye shall enter, enquire who in it is worthy; and there abide till ye go thence. Luke 10:8

12 And when ye come into an house, ᵀsalute it. greet

13 ᴿAnd if the house be worthy, let your peace come upon it: ᴿbut if it be not worthy, let your peace return to you. Luke 10:5 · Ps. 35:13

14 ᴿAnd whosoever shall not receive you, nor hear your words, when ye depart out of that house or city, ᴿshake off the dust of your feet. Mark 6:11; Luke 9:5 · Acts 13:51

15 Verily I say unto you, ᴿIt shall be more tolerable for the land of Sodom and Go-mor'-rha in the day of judgment, than for that city. 11:22, 24

16 Behold, I send you forth as sheep in the midst of wolves: ᴿbe ye therefore wise as serpents, and harmless as doves. 2 Cor. 12:16

17 But beware of men: for they will deliver you up to the councils, and ᴿthey will scourge you in their synagogues; Acts 5:40; 22:19

18 And ᴿye shall be brought before governors and kings for my sake, for a testimony against them and the Gentiles. Acts 12:1

19 But when they deliver you up, ᵀtake no thought how or what ye shall speak: for it shall be given you in that same hour what ye shall speak. do not worry about

20 ᴿFor it is not ye that speak, but the Spirit of your Father which speaketh in you. [2 Tim. 4:17]

21 And the brother shall deliver up the brother to death, and the father the child: and the children shall rise up against their parents, and cause them to be put to death.

22 And ᴿye shall be hated of all men for my name's sake: but he that endureth to the end shall be saved. 24:9; Luke 21:17; John 15:18

23 But ᴿwhen they persecute you in this city, flee ye into another: for verily I say unto you, Ye shall not have ᴿgone over the cities of Israel, till the Son of man be come. Acts 8:1 · [24:14; Mark 13:10]

24 ᴿThe disciple is not above his ᵀmaster, nor the servant above his lord. Luke 6:40; John 15:20 · teacher

25 It is enough for the disciple that he be as his master, and the servant as his lord. If they have called the master of the house Be-el'-ze-bub, how much more shall they call them of his household?

26 Fear them not therefore: for there is nothing ᵀcovered, that shall not be revealed; and hid, that shall not be known. veiled

27 What I tell you in darkness, that ᴿspeak ye in light: and what ye hear in the ear, that preach ye upon the housetops. Luke 12:3

28 And fear not them which kill the body, but are not able to kill the soul: but rather fear him which is able to destroy both soul and body in ᵀhell. Gr. gehenna

29 Are not two ᴿsparrows sold for a farthing? and one of them shall not fall on the ground without your Father. Luke 12:6, 7

30 ᴿBut the very hairs of your head are all numbered. Acts 27:34

31 Fear ye not therefore, ye are of more value than many sparrows.

32 Whosoever therefore shall confess me before men, ᴿhim will I confess also before my Father which is in heaven. [Rev. 3:5]

33 ᴿBut whosoever shall deny me before men, him will I also deny before my Father which is in heaven. [Mark 8:38; Luke 9:26]

34 Think not that I am come to send peace on earth: I came not to send peace, but a sword.

☆ 35 For I am come to set a man at variance ᴿagainst his father, and the daughter against her mother, and the daughter in law against her mother in law.   v. 21; Mic. 7:6

36 And ᴿa man's foes *shall be* they of his own household. Ps. 41:9

37 ᴿHe that loveth father or mother more than me is not worthy of me: and he that loveth son or daughter more than me is not worthy of me.   Deut. 33:9; Luke 14:26

38 ᴿAnd he that taketh not his cross, and followeth after me, is not worthy of me.   [16:24; Mark 8:34]

39 ᴿHe that findeth his life shall lose it: and he that loseth his life for my sake shall find it.   16:25

40 He that receiveth you receiveth me, and he that receiveth me receiveth him that sent me.

41 ᴿHe that receiveth a prophet in the name of a prophet shall receive a prophet's reward; and he that receiveth a righteous man in the name of a righteous man shall receive a righteous man's reward.   1 Kin. 17:10; 2 Kin. 4:8

42 ᴿAnd whosoever shall give to drink unto one of these little ones a cup of cold *water* only in the name of a disciple, verily I say unto you, he shall in no wise lose his reward. [25:40]; Mark 9:41; Heb. 6:10

11 And it came to pass, when Jesus had ᵀmade an end of commanding his twelve disciples, he departed thence to teach and to preach in their cities.   *finished*

2 Now when John had heard ᴿin the prison the works of Christ, he sent two of his disciples,   14:3

3 And said unto him, Art thou ᴿhe that should come, or do we look for another? Dan. 9:24; John 6:14

4 Jesus answered and said unto them, Go and ᵀshew John again those things which ye do hear and see: *tell John the things*

★ 5 The blind receive their sight, and the lame walk, the lepers are cleansed, and the deaf hear, the dead are raised up, and the poor have the gospel preached to them.

6 And blessed is *he*, whosoever shall not be offended in me.

7 And as they departed, Jesus began to say unto the multitudes concerning John, What went ye out into the wilderness to see? A reed shaken with the wind?

8 But what went ye out for to see? A man clothed in soft raiment? behold, they that wear soft *clothing* are in kings' houses.

9 But what went ye out for to see? A prophet? yea, I say unto you, and more than a prophet.

10 For this is *he*, of whom it is ★ written, Behold, I send my messenger before thy face, which shall prepare thy way before thee.

11 Verily I say unto you, Among them that are born of women there hath not risen a greater than John the Baptist: notwithstanding he that is least in the kingdom of heaven is greater than he.

12 And from the days of John the Baptist until now the kingdom of heaven suffereth violence, and the violent take it by force.

13 For all the prophets and the ★ law prophesied until John.

14 And if ye will receive *it*, this is E-li'-as, which was for to come.

15 ᴿHe that hath ears to hear, let him hear.   13:9; Luke 8:8; Rev. 2:7

16 But whereunto shall I liken this generation? It is like unto children sitting in the markets, and calling unto their fellows,

17 And saying, We have piped unto you, and ye have not danced; we have mourned unto you, and ye have not lamented.

18 For John came neither eating nor drinking, and they say, He hath a ᵀdevil.   *demon*

19 The Son of man came eating and drinking, and they say, Behold a man gluttonous, and a winebibber, a friend of publicans and sinners. ᴿBut wisdom is justified ᵀof her children. Luke 7:35 · *by*

20 Then began he to ᵀupbraid the cities wherein most of his mighty works were done, because they repented not: *rebuke*

21 Woe unto thee, Cho-ra'-zin! woe unto thee, Beth-sa'-i-da! for if the mighty works, which were

done in you, had been done in Tyre and Si'-don, they would have repented long ago ᴿin sackcloth and ashes. Jon. 3:6–8

22 But I say unto you, ᴿIt shall be more tolerable for Tyre and Si'-don at the day of judgment, than for you. v. 24; 10:15

23 And thou, Ca-per'-na-um, ᴿwhich art exalted unto heaven, shalt be brought down to ᵀhell: for if the mighty works, which have been done in thee, had been done in Sodom, it would have remained until this day. Is. 14:13 · Gr. *hades*

24 But I say unto you, ᴿThat it shall be more tolerable for the land of Sodom in the day of judgment, than for thee. 10:15

25 At that time Jesus answered and said, I thank thee, O Father, Lord of heaven and earth, because thou hast hid these things from the wise and prudent, and hast revealed them unto babes.

26 Even so, Father: for so it seemed good in thy sight.

27 ᴿAll things are delivered unto me of my Father: and no man knoweth the Son, but the Father; ᴿneither knoweth any man the Father, ᵀsave the Son, and *he* to whomsoever the Son will reveal *him*. 28:18 · John 1:18; 6:46; 10:15 · *except*

28 Come unto ᴿme, all *ye* that labour and are heavy laden, and I will give you rest. [John 6:35–37]

29 Take my yoke upon you, ᴿand learn of me; for I am meek and lowly in heart: and ye shall find rest unto your souls. [John 13:15]

30 ᴿFor my yoke *is* easy, and my burden is light. [1 John 5:3]

12 At that time Jesus went on the sabbath day through the corn; and his disciples were an hungred, and began to pluck the ears of corn, and to eat.

2 But when the Pharisees saw *it*, they said unto him, Behold, thy disciples do that which is not lawful to do upon the sabbath day.

3 But he said unto them, Have ye not read ᴿwhat David did, when he was an hungred, and they that were with him; 1 Sam. 21:6

4 How he entered into the house of God, and did eat ᴿthe shewbread, which was not lawful for him to eat, neither for them which were with him, ᴿbut only for the priests? Lev. 24:5 · Lev. 8:31; 24:9

5 Or have ye not read in the ᴿlaw, how that on the sabbath days the priests in the temple profane the sabbath, and are blameless? Num. 28:9; [John 7:22]

6 But I say unto you, That in this place is ᴿone greater than the temple. [2 Chr. 6:18; Is. 66:1, 2; Mal. 3:1]

7 But if ye had known what *this* meaneth, ᴿI will have mercy, and not sacrifice, ye would not have condemned the guiltless. 9:13

8 For the Son of man is Lord even of the sabbath day.

9 ᴿAnd when he was departed thence, he went into their synagogue: Mark 3:1–6; Luke 6:6–11

10 And, behold, there was a man which had *his* hand withered. And they asked him, saying, Is it lawful to heal on the sabbath days? that they might accuse him.

11 And he said unto them, What man shall there be among you, that shall have one sheep, and if it fall into a pit on the sabbath day, will he not lay hold on it, and lift *it* out?

12 How much then is a man better than a sheep? Wherefore it is lawful to do well on the sabbath days.

13 Then saith he to the man, Stretch forth thine hand. And he stretched *it* forth; and it was restored whole, like as the other.

14 Then the Pharisees went out, and held a council against him, how they might destroy him.

15 But when Jesus knew *it*, ᴿhe withdrew himself from thence: and great multitudes followed him, and he healed them all; 10:23

16 And ᴿcharged them that they should not make him known: 17:9

17 That it might be fulfilled which was spoken by E-sa'-ias the prophet, saying,

18 ᴿBehold my servant, whom I ★

have chosen; my beloved, ^Rin whom my soul is well pleased: I will put my Spirit upon him, and he shall shew judgment to the Gentiles.   Is. 42:1–4; 49:3 · 3:17; 17:5

19 He shall not ^Tstrive, nor ^Tcry; neither shall any man hear his voice in the streets.   *quarrel · cry out*

20 A bruised reed shall he not break, and smoking flax shall he not quench, till he send forth ^Tjudgment unto victory.   *justice*

21 And in his name shall the Gentiles trust.

22 Then was brought unto him one possessed with a devil, blind, and ^Tdumb: and he healed him, insomuch that the blind and dumb both spake and saw.   *mute*

23 And all the people were amazed, and said, Is not this the ^Rson of David?   9:27; 21:9

24 ^RBut when the Pharisees heard *it*, they said, This *fellow* doth not cast out devils, but by Be-el′-ze-bub the ^Tprince of the devils.   9:34; Mark 3:22; Luke 11:15 · *ruler*

25 And Jesus ^Rknew their thoughts, and said unto them, Every kingdom divided against itself is brought to desolation; and every city or house divided against itself shall not stand: 9:4

26 And if Satan cast out Satan, he is divided against himself; how shall then his kingdom stand?

27 And if I by Be-el′-ze-bub cast out ^Tdevils, by whom do your children cast *them* out? therefore they shall be your judges.   *demons*

28 But if I cast out devils by the Spirit of God, then ^Rthe kingdom of God is come unto you. [Dan. 2:44]

29 Or else how can one enter into a strong man's house, and ^Tspoil his goods, except he first bind the strong man? and then he will ^Tspoil his house.   *plunder*

30 He that is not with me is against me; and he that gathereth not with me scattereth abroad.

31 Wherefore I say unto you, ^RAll manner of sin and blasphemy shall be forgiven unto men: ^Rbut the blasphemy *against* the Holy

Ghost shall not be forgiven unto men.   Mark 3:28–30 · Acts 7:51

32 And whosoever speaketh a word against the Son of man, it shall be forgiven him: but whosoever speaketh against the Holy Ghost, it shall not be forgiven him, neither in this ^Tworld, neither in the *world* to come.   *age*

33 Either make the tree good, and ^Rhis fruit good; or else make the tree ^Tcorrupt, and his fruit ^Tcorrupt: for the tree is known by *his* fruit.   7:16–18; Luke 6:43, 44 · *bad*

34 O generation of vipers, how can ye, being evil, speak good things? for out of the abundance of the heart the mouth speaketh.

35 A good man out of the good treasure of the heart bringeth forth good things: and an evil man out of the evil treasure bringeth forth evil things.

36 But I say unto you, That every idle word that men shall speak, they shall give account thereof in the day of judgment.

37 For by thy words thou shalt be justified, and by thy words thou shalt be condemned.

38 ^RThen certain of the scribes and of the Pharisees answered, saying, ^TMaster, we would see a sign from thee.   16:1 · Lit. *Teacher*

39 But he answered and said unto them, An evil and ^Radulterous generation seeketh after a sign; and there shall no sign be given to it, but the sign of the prophet ^RJo′-nas: Is. 57:3; Mark 8:38 · Jon. 1:17

40 For as Jo′-nas was three days and three nights in the whale's belly; so shall the Son of man be three days and three nights in the heart of the earth.

41 The men of Nin′-e-veh shall rise in judgment with this generation, and shall condemn it: because they repented at the preaching of Jo′-nas; and, behold, a greater than Jo′-nas *is* here.

42 The queen of the south shall rise up in the judgment with this generation, and shall condemn it: for she came from the uttermost parts of the earth to hear the wis-

dom of Solomon; and, behold, a greater than Solomon *is* here.

43 ^RWhen the unclean spirit is gone out of a man, he walketh through dry places, seeking rest, and findeth none.   Luke 11:24–26

44 Then he saith, I will return into my house from whence I came out; and when he is come, he findeth *it* empty, swept, and ^Tgarnished.   *put in order*

45 Then goeth he, and taketh with himself seven other spirits more wicked than himself, and they enter in and dwell there: ^Rand the last *state* of that man is worse than the first. Even so shall it be also unto this wicked generation.   Mark 5:9; Luke 11:26

46 While he yet talked to the people, behold, *his* mother and ^Rhis brethren stood without, desiring to speak with him.   Mark 6:3

47 Then one said unto him, Behold, ^Rthy mother and thy brethren stand without, desiring to speak with thee.   13:55, 56

48 But he answered and said unto him that told him, Who is my mother? and who are my brethren?

49 And he stretched forth his hand toward his disciples, and said, Behold my mother and my ^Rbrethren!   John 20:17; [Rom. 8:29]

50 For ^Rwhosoever shall do the will of my Father which is in heaven, the same is my brother, and sister, and mother.   [Gal. 5:6; 6:15]

13 The same day went Jesus out of the house, ^Rand sat by the sea side.   Mark 4:1–12; Luke 8:4–10

2 ^RAnd great multitudes were gathered together unto him, so that ^Rhe went into a ship, and sat; and the whole multitude stood on the shore.   Luke 8:4 · Luke 5:3

3 And he spake many things unto them in parables, saying, ^RBehold, a sower went forth to sow;   Luke 8:5

4 And when he sowed, some *seeds* fell by the way side, and the fowls came and devoured them up:

5 Some fell upon stony places,

where they had not much earth: and ^Tforthwith they sprung up, because they had no deepness of earth: *immediately*

6 And when the sun was up, they were scorched; and because they had no root, they withered away.

7 And some fell among thorns; and the thorns sprung up, and choked them:

8 But other fell into good ground, and brought forth fruit, some ^Ran hundredfold, some sixtyfold, some thirtyfold.   Gen. 26:12

9 ^RWho hath ears to hear, let him hear.   11:15; Mark 4:9; Rev. 2:7

10 And the disciples came, and said unto him, Why speakest thou unto them in parables?

11 He answered and said unto them, Because ^Rit is given unto you to know the mysteries of the kingdom of heaven, but to them it is not given. [11:25; 16:17]; Mark 4:10, 11

12 ^RFor whosoever hath, to him shall be given, and he shall have more abundance: but whosoever hath not, from him shall be taken away even that he hath.   25:29

13 Therefore speak I to them in parables: because they seeing see not; and hearing they hear not, neither do they understand.

14 And in them is fulfilled the prophecy of E-sa'-ias, which saith, ^RBy hearing ye shall hear, and shall not understand; and seeing ye shall see, and shall not perceive: Is. 6:9, 10; Acts 28:26, 27; Rom. 11:8

15 For this people's heart is waxed gross, and *their* ears ^Rare dull of hearing, and their eyes they have closed; lest at any time they should see with *their* eyes, and hear with *their* ears, and should understand with *their* heart, and should be converted, and I should heal them.   Zech. 7:11

16 But ^Rblessed *are* your eyes, for they see: and your ears, for they hear.   [16:17]; Luke 10:23, 24

17 For verily I say unto you, ^RThat many prophets and righteous *men* have desired to see *those things* which ye see, and

★

have not seen *them;* and to hear *those things* which ye hear, and have not heard *them.*   John 8:56

18 ᴿHear ye therefore the parable of the sower.   Luke 8:11–15

19 When any one heareth the word ᴿof the kingdom, and understandeth *it* not, then cometh the wicked *one,* and ᵀcatcheth away that which was sown in his heart. This is he which received seed by the way side.   4:23 · *snatches away*

20 But he that received the seed into stony places, the same is he that heareth the word, and ᵀanon with joy receiveth it;   *immediately*

21 Yet hath he not root in himself, but ᵀdureth for a while: for when tribulation or persecution ariseth because of the word, by and by he is offended.   *only endures*

22 ᴿHe also that received seed among the thorns is he that heareth the word; and the care of this world, and the deceitfulness of riches, choke the word, and he becometh unfruitful.   19:23

23 But he that received seed into the good ground is he that heareth the word, and understandeth *it;* which also beareth fruit, and bringeth forth, some an hundredfold, some sixty, some thirty.

24 Another parable put he forth unto them, saying, The kingdom of heaven is likened unto a man which sowed good seed in his field:

25 But while men slept, his enemy came and sowed tares among the wheat, and went his way.

26 But when the blade was sprung up, and brought forth fruit, then appeared the tares also.

27 So the servants of the householder came and said unto him, Sir, didst not thou sow good seed in thy field? from whence then hath it tares?

28 He said unto them, An enemy hath done this. The servants said unto him, Wilt thou then that we go and gather them up?

29 But he said, Nay; lest while ye gather up the tares, ye root up also the wheat with them.

30 Let both grow together until the harvest: and in the time of harvest I will say to the reapers, Gather ye together first the tares, and bind them in bundles to burn them: but ᴿgather the wheat into my barn.   3:12

31 Another parable put he forth unto them, saying, ᴿThe kingdom of heaven is like to a grain of mustard seed, which a man took, and sowed in his field: [Is. 2:2, 3; Mic. 4:1]

32 Which indeed is the least of all seeds: but when it is grown, it is the greatest among herbs, and becometh a ᴿtree, so that the birds of the air come and lodge in the branches thereof.   Ezek. 17:22–24

33 ᴿAnother parable spake he unto them; The kingdom of heaven is like unto leaven, which a woman took, and hid in three measures of meal, till the whole was leavened.   Luke 13:20, 21

34 ᴿAll these things spake Jesus unto the multitude in parables; and without a parable spake he not unto them: Mark 4:33, 34; John 10:6

35 That it might be fulfilled ★ which was spoken by the prophet, saying, ᴿI will open my mouth in parables; I will utter things which have been kept secret from the foundation of the world.   Ps. 78:2

36 Then Jesus sent the multitude away, and went into the house: and his disciples came unto him, saying, Declare unto us the parable of the tares of the field.

37 He answered and said unto them, He that soweth the good seed is the Son of man;

38 ᴿThe field is the world; the good seed are the children of the kingdom; but the tares are the children of the wicked *one;*   24:14

39 The enemy that sowed them is the devil; ᴿthe harvest is the end of the ᵀworld; and the reapers are the angels.   Joel 3:13; Rev. 14:15 · *age*

40 As therefore the tares are gathered and burned in the fire; so shall it be in the end of this ᵀworld.   *age*

41 The Son of man shall send forth his angels, [R]and they shall gather out of his kingdom all things that offend, and them which do iniquity;   18:7; 2 Pet. 2:1, 2

42 And shall cast them into a furnace of fire: there shall be wailing and gnashing of teeth.

43 Then shall the righteous shine forth as the sun in the kingdom of their Father. [R]Who hath ears to hear, let him hear.   v. 9

44 Again, the kingdom of heaven is like unto treasure hid in a field; the which when a man hath found, he hideth, and for joy thereof goeth and selleth all that he hath, and buyeth that field.

45 Again, the kingdom of heaven is like unto a merchant man, seeking [T]goodly pearls: beautiful

46 Who, when he had found [R]one pearl of great price, went and sold all that he had, and bought it.   Prov. 2:4; 3:14, 15; 8:10, 19

47 Again, the kingdom of heaven is like unto a [T]net, that was cast into the sea, and [R]gathered of every kind: dragnet · 22:9, 10

48 Which, when it was full, they drew to shore, and sat down, and gathered the good into vessels, but cast the bad away.

49 So shall it be at the end of the [T]world: the angels shall come forth, and [R]sever the wicked from among the just,   age · 25:32

50 And shall cast them into the furnace of fire: there shall be wailing and gnashing of teeth.

51 Jesus saith unto them, Have ye understood all these things? They say unto him, Yea, Lord.

52 Then said he unto them, Therefore every scribe *which is* instructed [T]unto the kingdom of heaven is like unto a man *that is* an householder, which bringeth forth out of his treasure [R]*things* new and old.   concerning · Song 7:13

53 And it came to pass, *that* when Jesus had finished these parables, he departed thence.

54 And when he was come into his own country, he taught them in their synagogue, insomuch that they were astonished, and said, Whence hath this *man* this wisdom, and *these* mighty works?

55 [R]Is not this the carpenter's son? is not his mother called Mary? and [R]his brethren, [R]James, and Jo'-ses, and Simon, and Judas?   Mark 6:3 · 12:46 · Mark 15:40

56 And his sisters, are they not all with us? Whence then hath this *man* all these things?

57 And they [R]were offended in him. But Jesus said unto them, [R]A prophet is not without honour, save in his own country, and in his own house.   11:6; Mark 6:3, 4 · Luke 4:24

58 And [R]he did not many mighty works there because of their unbelief.   Mark 6:5, 6; John 5:44, 46, 47

14 At that time [R]Herod the te'-trarch heard of the fame of Jesus,   Mark 6:14–29; Luke 9:7–9

2 And said unto his servants, This is John the Baptist; he is risen from the dead; and therefore mighty works do shew forth themselves in him.

3 [R]For Herod had laid hold on John, and bound him, and put *him* in prison for He-ro'-di-as' sake, his brother Philip's wife.   Mark 6:17

4 For John said unto him, It is not lawful for thee to have her.

5 And when he would have put him to death, he feared the multitude, [R]because they counted him as a prophet.   21:26; Luke 20:6

6 But when Herod's birthday was [T]kept, the daughter of He-ro'-di-as danced before them, and pleased Herod.   celebrated

7 Whereupon he promised with an oath to give her whatsoever she would ask.

8 And she, being [T]before instructed of her mother, said, Give me here John Baptist's head [T]in a charger.   prompted by · on a platter

9 And the king was sorry: nevertheless for the oath's sake, and them which sat with him at meat, he commanded *it* to be given *her*.

10 And he sent, and beheaded John in the prison.

11 And his head was brought [T]in a charger, and given to the

damsel: and she brought *it* to her mother.

12 And his disciples came, and took up the body, and buried it, and went and told Jesus.

13 [R]When Jesus heard *of it,* he departed thence by ship into a desert place apart: and when the people had heard *thereof,* they followed him on foot out of the cities.   Luke 9:10–17; John 6:1, 2

14 And Jesus went forth, and saw a great multitude, and was moved with compassion toward them, and he healed their sick.

15 And when it was evening, his disciples came to him, saying, This is a desert place, and the [T]time is now past; send the multitude away, that they may go into the villages, and buy themselves victuals.   *hour is already late*

16 But Jesus said unto them, They need not depart; give ye them to eat.

17 And they say unto him, We have here but five loaves, and two fishes.

18 He said, Bring them hither to me.

19 And he commanded the multitude to sit down on the grass, and took the five loaves, and the two fishes, and looking up to heaven, [R]he blessed, and brake, and gave the loaves to *his* disciples, and the disciples to the multitude.   Mark 6:41; 8:7; 14:22; Acts 27:35

20 And they did all eat, and were filled: and they took up of the fragments that remained twelve baskets full.

21 And they that had eaten were about five thousand men, beside women and children.

22 And straightway Jesus [T]constrained his disciples to get into a ship, and to go before him unto the other side, while he sent the multitudes away.   *compelled*

23 [R]And when he had sent the multitudes away, he went up into a mountain apart to pray: and when the evening was come, he was there alone.   Mark 6:46; Luke 9:28

24 But the ship was now in the midst of the sea, tossed with waves: for the wind was contrary.

25 And in the fourth watch of the night Jesus went unto them, walking on the sea.

26 And when the disciples saw him walking on the sea, they were troubled, saying, It is a spirit; and they cried out for fear.

27 But straightway Jesus spake unto them, saying, Be of good cheer; it is I; be not afraid.

28 And Peter answered him and said, Lord, if it be thou, bid me come unto thee on the water.

29 And he said, Come. And when Peter was come down out of the ship, he walked on the water, to go to Jesus.

30 But when he saw the wind [T]boisterous, he was afraid; and beginning to sink, he cried, saying, Lord, save me.   *violent*

31 And immediately Jesus stretched forth *his* hand, and caught him, and said unto him, O thou of [R]little faith, wherefore didst thou doubt?   6:30; 8:26

32 And when they were come into the ship, the wind ceased.

33 Then they that were in the ship came and worshipped him, saying, Of a truth [R]thou art the Son of God.   Acts 8:37; Rom. 1:4

34 [R]And when they were gone over, they came into the land of Gen-nes'-a-ret.   Mark 6:53; Luke 5:1

35 And when the men of that place had knowledge of him, they sent out into all that country round about, and brought unto him all that were diseased;

36 And besought him that they might only [R]touch the hem of his garment: and [R]as many as touched were made perfectly whole.   [Mark 5:24–34] · 9:20; Mark 3:10

15 Then [R]came to Jesus scribes and Pharisees, which were of Jerusalem, saying, Mark 7:1

2 [R]Why do thy disciples transgress the tradition of the elders? for they wash not their hands when they eat bread.   Mark 7:5

3 But he answered and said unto them, Why do ye also trans-

gress the commandment of God by your tradition?

4 For God commanded, saying, Honour thy father and mother: and, He that curseth father or mother, let him die the death.

5 But ye say, Whosoever shall say to *his* father or *his* mother, *It is* a gift, by whatsoever thou mightest be profited by me;

6 And honour not his father or his mother, *he shall be free.* Thus have ye made the commandment of God of none effect by your tradition.

7 *Ye* hypocrites, well did E-sa'-ias prophesy of you, saying,

★ 8 ᴿThis people draweth nigh unto me with their mouth, and honoureth me with *their* lips; but their heart is far from me. Is. 29:13

9 But in vain they do worship me, ᴿteaching *for* doctrines the commandments of men. Titus 1:14

10 ᴿAnd he called the multitude, and said unto them, Hear, and understand: Mark 7:14

11 ᴿNot that which goeth into the mouth defileth a man; but that which cometh out of the mouth, this defileth a man.   [Acts 10:15]

12 Then came his disciples, and said unto him, Knowest thou that the Pharisees were offended, after they heard this saying?

13 But he answered and said, ᴿEvery plant, which my heavenly Father hath not planted, shall be rooted up.   [1 Cor. 3:12, 13]

14 Let them alone: ᴿthey be blind leaders of the blind. And if the blind lead the blind, both shall fall into the ditch.   Is. 9:16; Mal. 2:8

15 ᴿThen answered Peter and said unto him, ᵀDeclare unto us this parable.   Mark 7:17 · *Explain*

16 And Jesus said, ᴿAre ye also yet without understanding?   16:9

17 Do not ye yet understand, that whatsoever entereth in at the mouth goeth into the belly, and is cast out into the draught?

18 But ᴿthose things which proceed out of the mouth come forth from the heart; and they defile the man.   [12:34]; Mark 7:20; [James 3:6]

19 ᴿFor out of the heart proceed evil thoughts, murders, adulteries, fornications, thefts, false witness, blasphemies: Prov. 6:14; Jer. 17:9

20 These are *the things* which defile a man: but to eat with unwashen hands defileth not a man.

21 ᴿThen Jesus went thence, and departed into the ᵀcoasts of Tyre and Si'-don.   Mark 7:24–30 · *region*

22 And, behold, a woman of Canaan came out of the same coasts, and cried unto him, saying, Have mercy on me, O Lord, *thou* son of David; my daughter is grievously vexed with a devil.

23 But he answered her not a word. And his disciples came and ᵀbesought him, saying, Send her away; for she crieth after us. *urged*

24 But he answered and said, ᴿI am not sent but unto the lost sheep of the house of Israel. 10:5, 6

25 Then came she and worshipped him, saying, Lord, help me.

26 But he answered and said, It is not ᵀmeet to take the children's bread, and to cast *it* to dogs.   *good*

27 And she said, Truth, Lord: yet the dogs eat of the crumbs which fall from their masters' table.

28 Then Jesus answered and said unto her, O woman, great *is* thy faith: be it unto thee even as thou wilt. And her daughter was made whole from that very hour.

29 And Jesus departed from thence, and came nigh unto the sea of Galilee; and went up into a mountain, and sat down there.

30 And great multitudes came unto him, having with them *those that were* lame, blind, ᵀdumb, ᵀmaimed, and many others, and cast them down at Jesus' feet; and he healed them: *mute · crippled*

31 Insomuch that the multitude wondered, when they saw the dumb to speak, the maimed to be whole, the lame to walk, and the blind to see: and they ᴿglorified the God of Israel.   Luke 5:25, 26

32 ᴿThen Jesus called his disciples *unto him,* and said, I have

compassion on the multitude, because they continue with me now three days, and have nothing to eat: and I will not send them away ᵀfasting, lest they faint in the way.   Mark 8:1–10 · *hungry*

33 And his disciples say unto him, Whence should we have so much bread in the wilderness, as to fill so great a multitude?

34 And Jesus saith unto them, How many loaves have ye? And they said, Seven, and a few little fishes.

35 And he commanded the multitude to sit down on the ground.

36 And ᴿhe took the seven loaves and the fishes, and gave thanks, and brake *them*, and gave to his disciples, and the disciples to the multitude.   14:19; 26:27

37 And they did all eat, and were filled: and they took up of the ᵀbroken *meat* that was left seven baskets full.   Fragments

38 And they that did eat were four thousand men, beside women and children.

39 ᴿAnd he sent away the multitude, and took ship, and came into the coasts of Mag'-da-la.   Mark 8:10

16 The ᴿPharisees also with the Sad'-du-cees came, and tempting desired him that he would shew them a sign from heaven.   12:38; Mark 8:11; 1 Cor. 1:22

2 He answered and said unto them, When it is evening, ye say, *It will be* fair weather: for the sky is red.

3 And in the morning, *It will be* foul weather to day: for the sky is red and ᵀlowring. O *ye* hypocrites, ye can discern the face of the sky; but can ye not *discern* the signs of the times?   *threatening*

4 ᴿA wicked and adulterous generation seeketh after a sign; and there shall no sign be given unto it, but the sign of the prophet Jo'-nas. And he left them, and departed.   Prov. 30:12; Luke 11:29; 24:46

5 And ᴿwhen his disciples were come to the other side, they had forgotten to take bread.   Mark 8:14

6 Then Jesus said unto them,

ᴿTake heed and beware of the ᵀleaven of the Pharisees and of the Sad'-du-cees.   Luke 12:1 · *yeast*

7 And they reasoned among themselves, saying, *It is* because we have taken no bread.

8 *Which* when Jesus perceived, he said unto them, O ye of little faith, why reason ye among yourselves, because ye have brought no bread?

9 ᴿDo ye not yet understand, neither remember the five loaves of the five thousand, and how many baskets ye took up?   14:15–21

10 ᴿNeither the seven loaves of the four thousand, and how many baskets ye took up?   15:32–38

11 How is it that ye do not understand that I spake *it* not to you concerning bread, that ye should beware of the ᵀleaven of the Pharisees and of the Sad'-du-cees?   *yeast*

12 Then understood they how that he bade *them* not beware of the leaven of bread, but of the ᵀdoctrine of the Pharisees and of the Sad'-du-cees.   *teaching*

13 When Jesus came into the ᵀcoasts of Caes-a-re'-a Phi-lip'-pi, he asked his disciples, saying, ᴿWhom do men say that I the Son of man am?   *region* · Luke 9:18

14 And they said, ᴿSome *say* *that thou art* John the Baptist: some, E-li'-as; and others, Jer-e-mi'-as, or one of the prophets.   14:2

15 He saith unto them, But whom say ᴿye that I am?   John 6:67

16 And Simon Peter answered and said, ᴿThou art the Christ, the Son of the living God.   John 6:69

17 And Jesus answered and said unto him, Blessed art thou, Simon Bar–jo'-na: for flesh and blood hath not revealed *it* unto thee, but my Father which is in heaven.

18 And I say also unto thee, That ᴿthou art Peter, and upon this rock I will build my church; and ᴿthe gates of hell shall not prevail against it.   John 1:42 · Ps. 9:13; 107:18

19 And I will give unto thee the keys of the kingdom of heaven: and ᴿwhatsoever thou shalt bind

on earth shall be bound in heaven: and whatsoever thou shalt loose on earth shall be loosed in heaven.   18:18; John 20:23

20 ᴿThen charged he his disciples that they should tell no man that he was Jesus the Christ.   17:9

21 From that time forth began Jesus ᴿto shew unto his disciples, how that he must go unto Jerusalem, and suffer many things of the elders and chief priests and scribes, and be killed, and be raised again the third day.   20:17

22 Then Peter ᵀtook him, and began to rebuke him, saying, Be it far from thee, Lord: this shall not be unto thee.   *took him aside*

23 But he turned, and said unto Peter, Get thee behind me, ᴿSatan: ᴿthou art an offence unto me: for thou savourest not the things that be of God, but those that be of men.   4:10 · [Rom. 8:7]

24 Then said Jesus unto his disciples, If any *man* will come after me, let him deny himself, and take up his cross, and follow me.

25 For ᴿwhosoever will save his life shall lose it: and whosoever will lose his life for my sake shall find it.   Luke 17:33; John 12:25

26 For what is a man ᴿprofited, if he shall gain the whole world, and lose his own soul? or ᴿwhat shall a man give in exchange for his soul?   Luke 12:20, 21 · Ps. 49:7, 8

☆ 27 For the Son of man shall come in the glory of his Father ᴿwith his angels; ᴿand then he shall reward every man according to his works.   Zech. 14:5 · 1 Pet. 1:17

28 Verily I say unto you, ᴿThere be some standing here, which shall not taste of death, till they see the Son of man coming in his kingdom.   Mark 9:1; Luke 9:27; Rev. 19:11

17 And ᴿafter six days Jesus taketh Peter, James, and John his brother, and bringeth them up into an high mountain apart,   Mark 9:2–8; Luke 9:28–36

2 And was transfigured before them: and his face did shine as the sun, and his ᵀraiment was white as the light.   *clothes*

3 And, behold, there appeared unto them Moses and E-li′-as talking with him.

4 Then answered Peter, and said unto Jesus, Lord, it is good for us to be here: if thou wilt, let us make here three tabernacles; one for thee, and one for Moses, and one for E-li′-as.

5 ᴿWhile he yet spake, behold, ★ a bright cloud overshadowed them: and behold a voice out of the cloud, which said, This is my beloved Son, in whom I am well pleased; hear ye him.   2 Pet. 1:17

6 And when the disciples heard *it*, they fell on their face, and were ᵀsore afraid.   *greatly*

7 And Jesus came and ᴿtouched them, and said, Arise, and be not afraid.   Dan. 8:18

8 And when they had lifted up their eyes, they saw no man, ᵀsave Jesus only.   *except*

9 And as they came down from the mountain, Jesus ᵀcharged them, saying, Tell the vision to no man, until the Son of man be risen again from the dead.   *commanded*

10 And his disciples asked him, saying, ᴿWhy then say the scribes that E-li′-as must first come?   11:14

11 And Jesus answered and said unto them, E-li′-as truly shall first come, and restore all things.

12 ᴿBut I say unto you, That E-li′-as is come already, and they knew him not, but have done unto him whatsoever they listed. Likewise shall also the Son of man suffer of them.   Mark 9:12, 13

13 ᴿThen the disciples understood that he spake unto them of John the Baptist.   11:14

14 ᴿAnd when they were come to the multitude, there came to him a *certain* man, kneeling down to him, and saying,   Mark 9:14–28

15 Lord, have mercy on my son: for he is lunatick, and sore vexed: for ofttimes he falleth into the fire, and oft into the water.

16 And I brought him to thy disciples, and they could not cure him.

17 Then Jesus answered and

said, O faithless and perverse generation, how long shall I be with you? how long shall I suffer you? bring him hither to me.

18 And Jesus ᴿrebuked the ᵀdevil; and he departed out of him: and the child was cured from that very hour.   Luke 4:41 · demon

19 Then came the disciples to Jesus ᵀapart, and said, Why could not we cast him out?   privately

20 And Jesus said unto them, Because of your unbelief: for verily I say unto you, ᴿIf ye have faith as a grain of mustard seed, ye shall say unto this mountain, Remove hence to yonder place; and it shall remove; and nothing shall be impossible unto you. Mark 11:23

21 Howbeit this kind goeth not out but by prayer and fasting.

22 ᴿAnd while they abode in Galilee, Jesus said unto them, The Son of man shall be betrayed into the hands of men: 16:21; 26:57

☆ 23 And they shall kill him, and the third day he shall be raised again. And they were exceeding ᴿsorry.   26:22; 27:50; Luke 23:46; 24:46

24 And ᴿwhen they were come to Ca-per'-na-um, they that received tribute money came to Peter, and said, Doth not your master pay tribute?   Mark 9:33

25 He saith, Yes. And when he was come into the house, Jesus ᵀprevented him, saying, What thinkest thou, Simon? of whom do the kings of the earth take custom or tribute? of their own children, or of strangers?   anticipated

26 Peter saith unto him, Of strangers. Jesus saith unto him, Then are the children free.

27 Notwithstanding, lest we should offend them, go thou to the sea, and cast an hook, and take up the fish that first cometh up; and when thou hast opened his mouth, thou shalt find a piece of money: that take, and give unto them for me and thee.

18 At ᴿthe same time came the disciples unto Jesus, saying, Who is the greatest in the kingdom of heaven?   Luke 9:46–48

2 And Jesus called a little ᴿchild unto him, and set him in the midst of them,   19:14; Mark 10:14

3 And said, Verily I say unto you, ᴿExcept ye be converted, and become as little children, ye shall not enter into the kingdom of heaven. Ps. 131:2; Mark 10:15; Luke 18:16

4 ᴿWhosoever therefore shall humble himself as this little child, the same is greatest in the kingdom of heaven.   [20:27; 23:11]

5 And ᴿwhoso shall receive one such little child in my name receiveth me.   [10:42]; Luke 9:48

6 But whoso shall ᵀoffend one of these little ones which believe in me, it were better for him that a millstone were hanged about his neck, and that he were drowned in the depth of the sea.   cause to sin

7 Woe unto the world because of offences! for ᴿit must needs be that offences come; but woe to that man by whom the offence cometh!   Luke 17:1; [1 Cor. 11:19]

8 ᴿWherefore if thy hand or thy foot offend thee, cut them off, and cast them from thee: it is better for thee to enter into life ᵀhalt or maimed, rather than having two hands or two feet to be cast into everlasting fire.   5:29, 30 · lame

9 And if thine eye ᵀoffend thee, pluck it out, and cast it from thee: it is better for thee to enter into life with one eye, rather than having two eyes to be cast into ᵀhell fire.   causes you to sin · Gr. gehenna

10 Take heed that ye despise not one of these little ones; for I say unto you, That in heaven their angels do always behold the face of my Father which is in heaven.

11 For the Son of man is come to save that which was lost.

12 How think ye? if a man have an hundred sheep, and one of them be gone astray, doth he not leave the ninety and nine, and goeth into the mountains, and seeketh that which is gone astray?

13 And if so be that he find it, verily I say unto you, he rejoiceth

more of that *sheep,* than of the ninety and nine which went not astray.

14 Even so it is not the ᴿwill of your Father which is in heaven, that one of these little ones should perish.   [1 Tim. 2:4]

15 Moreover ᴿif thy brother shall trespass against thee, go and tell him his fault between thee and him alone: if he shall hear thee, ᴿthou hast gained thy brother. 2 Thess. 3:15 · [James 5:20]; 1 Pet. 3:1

16 But if he will not hear *thee,* *then* take with thee one or two more, that in ᴿthe mouth of two or three witnesses every word may be established.   Deut. 17:6; 19:15

17 And if he shall neglect to hear them, tell *it* unto the church: but if he neglect to hear the church, let him be unto thee as an heathen man and a publican.

18 Verily I say unto you, ᴿWhatsoever ye shall bind on earth shall be bound in heaven: and whatsoever ye shall loose on earth shall be loosed in heaven.   16:19

19 Again I say unto you, That if two of you shall agree on earth as touching any thing that they shall ask, it shall be done for them of my Father which is in heaven.

20 For where two or three are gathered together in my name, there am I in the midst of them.

21 Then came Peter to him, and said, Lord, how oft shall my brother sin against me, and I forgive him? ᴿtill seven times?   Luke 17:4

22 Jesus saith unto him, I say not unto thee, Until seven times: but, Until seventy times seven.

23 Therefore is the kingdom of heaven likened unto a certain king, which would take account of his servants.

24 And when he had begun to ᵀreckon, one was brought unto him, which owed him ten thousand talents.   *settle accounts*

25 But forasmuch as he had not to pay, his lord commanded him ᴿto be sold, and his wife, and children, and all that he had, and payment to be made. Ex. 21:2; Lev. 25:39

26 The servant therefore fell down, and worshipped him, saying, Lord, have patience with me, and I will pay thee all.

27 Then the lord of that servant was moved with compassion, and ᵀloosed him, and forgave him the debt.   *released him*

28 But the same servant went out, and found one of his fellowservants, which owed him an hundred ᵀpence: and he laid hands on him, and took *him* by the throat, saying, Pay me ᵀthat thou owest.   Gr. *denarii* · *what*

29 And his fellowservant fell down at his feet, and ᵀbesought him, saying, Have patience with me, and I will pay thee all.   *begged*

30 And he would not: but went and cast him into prison, till he should pay the debt.

31 So when his fellowservants saw what was done, they were very sorry, and came and told unto their lord all that was done.

32 Then his lord, after that he had called him, said unto him, O thou wicked servant, I forgave thee ᴿall that debt, because thou ᵀdesiredst me: Luke 7:41–43 · *begged*

33 Shouldest not thou also have had compassion on thy fellowservant, even as I had pity on thee?

34 And his lord was ᵀwroth, and delivered him to the ᵀtormentors, till he should pay all that was due unto him.   *angry · torturers*

35 ᴿSo likewise shall my heavenly Father do also unto you, if ye from your hearts forgive not every one his brother their trespasses.   Prov. 21:13; James 2:13

19 And it came to pass, *that* when Jesus had finished these sayings, he departed from Galilee, and came into the ᵀcoasts of Ju-dae'-a beyond Jordan; *region*

2 ᴿAnd great multitudes followed him; and he healed them there.   12:15

3 The Pharisees also came unto him, ᵀtempting him, and saying unto him, Is it lawful for a man to ᵀput away his wife for every cause?   *testing · divorce*

4 And he answered and said unto them, Have ye not read, that he which made *them* at the beginning ᴿmade them male and female, Gen. 1:27; 5:2; [Mal. 2:15]

5 And said, ᴿFor this cause shall a man leave father and mother, and shall cleave to his wife: and they twain shall be one flesh? Gen. 2:24; Mark 10:5–9

6 Wherefore they are ᵀno more twain, but one flesh. What therefore God hath joined together, let not man put asunder. *no longer two*

7 They say unto him, ᴿWhy did Moses then command to give a writing of divorcement, and to put her away? Deut. 24:1–4

8 He saith unto them, Moses because of the ᴿhardness of your hearts suffered you to put away your wives: but from the beginning it was not so. Heb. 3:15

9 ᴿAnd I say unto you, Whosoever shall put away his wife, except *it be* for fornication, and shall marry another, committeth adultery: and whoso marrieth her which is put away doth commit adultery. [5:32]; Mark 10:11; Luke 16:18

10 His disciples say unto him, If the case of the man be so with *his* wife, it is not good to marry.

11 But he said unto them, All *men* cannot receive this saying, save *they* to whom it is given.

12 For there are some eunuchs, which were so born from *their* mother's womb: and there are some eunuchs, which were made eunuchs of men: and there be eunuchs, which have made themselves eunuchs for the kingdom of heaven's sake. He that is able to receive *it*, let him receive *it*.

13 ᴿThen were there brought unto him little children, that he should put *his* hands on them, and pray: and the disciples rebuked them. 20:31; Mark 10:13; Luke 18:15

14 But Jesus said, ᵀSuffer little children, and forbid them not, to come unto me: for of such is the kingdom of heaven. *Allow the*

15 And he laid *his* hands on them, and departed thence.

16 And, behold, one came and said unto him, ᴿGood Master, what good thing shall I do, that I may have eternal life? Luke 10:25

17 And he said unto him, Why callest thou me good? *there is* none good but one, *that is,* God: but if thou wilt enter into life, ᴿkeep the commandments. Lev. 18:5

18 He saith unto him, Which? Jesus said, Thou shalt do no murder, Thou shalt not commit adultery, Thou shalt not steal, Thou shalt not bear false witness,

19 ᴿHonour thy father and *thy* mother: and, ᴿThou shalt love thy neighbour as thyself. 15:4 · 22:39

20 The young man saith unto him, All these things have I ᴿkept from my youth up: what lack I yet? [Phil. 3:6, 7]

21 Jesus said unto him, If thou wilt be perfect, go *and* sell that thou hast, and give to the poor, and thou shalt have treasure in heaven: and come *and* follow me.

22 But when the young man heard that saying, he went away sorrowful: for he had great possessions.

23 Then said Jesus unto his disciples, Verily I say unto you, That ᴿa rich man shall hardly enter into the kingdom of heaven. [13:22]

24 And again I say unto you, It is easier for a camel to go through the eye of a needle, than for a rich man to enter into the kingdom of God.

25 When his disciples heard *it*, they were exceedingly amazed, saying, Who then can be saved?

26 But Jesus beheld *them*, and said unto them, With men this is impossible; but ᴿwith God all things are possible. Luke 1:37

27 Then answered Peter and said unto him, Behold, we have forsaken all, and followed thee; what shall we have therefore?

28 And Jesus said unto them, Verily I say unto you, That ye which have followed me, in the regeneration when the Son of man shall sit in the throne of his glory, ᴿye also shall sit upon

twelve thrones, judging the twelve tribes of Israel.   [1 Cor. 6:2; Rev. 2:26]

29 ᴿAnd every one that hath forsaken houses, or brethren, or sisters, or father, or mother, or wife, or children, or lands, for my name's sake, shall receive an hundredfold, and shall inherit everlasting life.   Luke 18:29, 30

30 But many *that are* first shall be last; and the last *shall be* first.

20 For the kingdom of heaven is like unto a man *that is* an householder, which went out early in the morning to hire labourers into his vineyard.

2 And when he had agreed with the labourers for a ᵀpenny a day, he sent them into his vineyard.   *Gr. denarius*

3 And he went out about the third hour, and saw others standing idle in the marketplace,

4 And said unto them; Go ye also into the vineyard, and whatsoever is right I will give you. And they went their way.

5 Again he went out about the sixth and ninth hour, and did likewise.

6 And about the eleventh hour he went out, and found others standing idle, and saith unto them, Why stand ye here all the day idle?

7 They say unto him, Because no man hath hired us. He saith unto them, Go ye also into the vineyard; and whatsoever is right, *that* shall ye receive.

8 So when even was come, the lord of the vineyard saith unto his steward, Call the labourers, and give them *their* ᵀhire, beginning from the last unto the first.   *wages*

9 And when they came that *were hired* about the eleventh hour, they received every man a ᵀpenny.   *Gr. denarius*

10 But when the first came, they supposed that they should have received more; and they likewise received every man a penny.

11 And when they had received *it*, they murmured against the ᵀgoodman of the house,   *landowner*

12 Saying, These last have ᵀwrought *but* one hour, and thou hast made them equal unto us, which have borne the burden and heat of the day.   *worked*

13 But he answered one of them, and said, Friend, I do thee no wrong: didst not thou agree with me for a ᵀpenny?   *Gr. denarius*

14 Take *that* thine *is*, and go thy way: I will give unto this last, even as unto thee.

15 Is it not lawful for me to do what I will with mine own? Is thine eye evil, because I am good?

16 ᴿSo the last shall be first, and the first last: ᴿfor many be called, but few chosen.   19:30 · 22:14

17 ᴿAnd Jesus going up to Jerusalem took the twelve disciples apart in the way, and said unto them,   Mark 10:32–34; Luke 18:31–33

18 ᴿBehold, we go up to Jerusalem; and the Son of man shall be betrayed unto the chief priests and unto the scribes, and they shall condemn him to death, 16:21

19 ᴿAnd shall deliver him to the Gentiles to mock, and to scourge, and to crucify *him*: and the third day he shall rise again.   John 18:28

20 Then came to him the mother of Zeb'-e-dee's children with her sons, worshipping *him,* and desiring a certain thing of him.

21 And he said unto her, ᵀWhat wilt thou? She saith unto him, Grant that these my two sons may sit, the one on thy right hand, and the other on the left, in thy kingdom.   *What do you wish*

22 But Jesus answered and said, Ye know not what ye ask. Are ye able to drink of ᴿthe cup that I shall drink of, and to be baptized with the baptism that I am baptized with? They say unto him, We are able.   Is. 51:17, 22; Jer. 49:12

23 And he saith unto them, ᴿYe shall drink indeed of my cup, and be baptized with the baptism that I am baptized with: but to sit on my right hand, and on my left, is not mine to give, but *it shall be given to them* for whom it is prepared of my Father.   [Acts 12:2]

24 And when the ten heard *it*, they were moved with indignation against the two brethren.

25 But Jesus called them *unto him*, and said, Ye know that the princes of the Gentiles ᵀexercise dominion over them, and they that are great exercise authority upon them. *lord it over*

26 But ᴿit shall not be so among you: but ᴿwhosoever will be great among you, let him be your minister; [1 Pet. 5:3] · 23:11; Mark 9:35; 10:43

27 ᴿAnd whosoever will be ᵀchief among you, let him be your ᵀservant: [18:4] · *first · slave*

☆ 28 Even as the Son of man came not to be ministered unto, but to minister, and ᴿto give his life a ransom for many. [John 11:51, 52]

29 ᴿAnd as they departed from Jericho, a great multitude followed him. Luke 18:35–43

30 And, behold, two blind men sitting by the way side, when they heard that Jesus passed by, cried out, saying, Have mercy on us, O Lord, *thou* ᴿson of David. 1:1

31 And the multitude ᴿrebuked them, because they should hold their peace: but they cried the more, saying, Have mercy on us, O Lord, *thou* son of David. 19:13

32 And Jesus stood still, and called them, and said, What will ye that I shall do unto you?

33 They say unto him, Lord, that our eyes may be opened.

34 So Jesus had ᴿcompassion *on them*, and touched their eyes: and immediately their eyes received sight, and they followed him. 9:36

21 And when they drew nigh unto Jerusalem, and were come to Beth'-pha-ge, unto ᴿthe mount of Olives, then sent Jesus two disciples, [Zech. 14:4]

2 Saying unto them, Go into the village over against you, and straightway ye shall find an ass tied, and a colt with her: loose *them*, and bring *them* unto me.

3 And if any *man* say ᵀought unto you, ye shall say, The Lord hath need of them; and straightway he will send them. *anything*

4 All this was done, that it might be fulfilled which was spoken by the prophet, saying,

5 Tell ye the daughter of Si'-on, Behold, thy King cometh unto thee, meek, and sitting upon an ass, and a colt the foal of an ass. ★

6 And the disciples went, and did as Jesus commanded them,

7 And brought the ass, and the colt, and put on them their clothes, and they set *him* thereon.

8 And a very great multitude spread their garments in the way; ᴿothers cut down branches from the trees, and ᵀstrawed *them* in the ᵀway. John 12:13 · *spread · road*

9 And the multitudes that went ★ before, and that followed, cried, saying, ᴿHo-san'-na to the son of David: Blessed *is* he that cometh in the name of the Lord; Ho-san'-na in the highest. Ps. 118:25, 26

10 ᴿAnd when he was come into Jerusalem, all the city was moved, saying, Who is this? John 2:13, 15

11 And the multitude said, This is Jesus ᴿthe prophet of Nazareth of Galilee. [Deut. 18:15, 18]; John 6:14

12 And Jesus went into the tem- ★ ple of God, and cast out all them that sold and bought in the temple, and overthrew the tables of the moneychangers, and the seats of them that sold doves,

13 And said unto them, It is written, ᴿMy house shall be called the house of prayer; but ye have made it a den of thieves. Is. 56:7

14 And the blind and the lame came to him in the temple; and he healed them.

15 And when the chief priests ★ and scribes saw the wonderful things that he did, and the children crying in the temple, and saying, Ho-san'-na to the ᴿson of David; they were ᵀsore displeased, 1:1; John 7:42 · *indignant*

16 And said unto him, Hearest thou what these say? And Jesus saith unto them, Yea; have ye never read, ᴿOut of the mouth of babes and sucklings thou hast perfected praise? Ps. 8:2

17 And he left them, and ᴿwent out of the city into Beth'-a-ny; and he lodged there. 26:6; Mark 11:1, 11, 12

18 ᴿNow in the morning as he returned into the city, he ᵀhungered. Mark 11:12–14, 20–24 · *was hungry*

19 And when he saw a fig tree ᵀin the way, he came to it, and found nothing thereon, but leaves only, and said unto it, Let no fruit grow on thee henceforward for ever. And presently the fig tree withered away. *by the road*

20 And when the disciples saw *it*, they marvelled, saying, How soon is the fig tree withered away!

21 Jesus answered and said unto them, Verily I say unto you, ᴿIf ye have faith, and doubt not, ye shall not only do this *which is done* to the fig tree, but also if ye shall say unto this mountain, Be thou removed, and be thou cast into the sea; it shall be done. 17:20

22 And ᴿall things, whatsoever ye shall ask in prayer, believing, ye shall receive. [John 15:7; James 5:16]

23 ᴿAnd when he was come into the temple, the chief priests and the elders of the people came unto him as he was teaching, and ᴿsaid, By what authority doest thou these things? and who gave thee this authority? Mark 11:27–33 · Ex. 2:14

24 And Jesus answered and said unto them, I also will ask you one thing, which if ye tell me, I in like wise will tell you by what authority I do these things.

25 The ᴿbaptism of ᴿJohn, whence was it? from heaven, or of men? And they reasoned with themselves, saying, If we shall say, From heaven; he will say unto us, Why did ye not then believe him? [John 1:29–34] · John 1:15–28

26 But if we shall say, Of men; we ᴿfear the people; for all hold John as a prophet. 14:5

27 And they answered Jesus, and said, We cannot tell. And he said unto them, Neither tell I you by what authority I do these things.

28 But what think ye? A *certain* man had two sons; and he came to the first, and said, Son, go work to day in my ᴿvineyard. 20:1

29 He answered and said, I will not: but afterward he ᵀrepented, and went. *regretted it*

30 And he came to the second, and said likewise. And he answered and said, I go, sir: and went not.

31 Whether of them twain did the will of *his* father? They say unto him, The first. Jesus saith unto them, ᴿVerily I say unto you, That the publicans and the harlots go into the kingdom of God before you. Luke 7:29, 37–50

32 For ᴿJohn came unto you in the way of righteousness, and ye believed him not: but the publicans and the harlots believed him: and ye, when ye had seen *it*, repented not afterward, that ye might believe him. Luke 3:1–12; 7:29

33 Hear another parable: There was a certain householder, ᴿwhich planted a vineyard, and hedged it round about, and digged a winepress in it, and built a tower, and let it out to husbandmen, and went into a far country: Ps. 80:9

34 And when the time of the fruit drew near, he sent his servants to the husbandmen, that they might receive the fruits of it.

35 ᴿAnd the husbandmen took his servants, and beat one, and killed another, and stoned another. [23:34, 37; Acts 7:52; 1 Thess. 2:15]

36 Again, he sent other servants more than the first: and they did unto them likewise.

37 But last of all he sent unto them his son, saying, They will ᵀreverence my son. *respect*

38 But when the husbandmen saw the son, they said among themselves, ᴿThis is the heir; come, let us kill him, and let us seize on his inheritance. [Ps. 2:8]

39 ᴿAnd they caught him, and cast *him* out of the vineyard, and slew *him*. Mark 14:46; Luke 22:54

40 When the lord therefore of the vineyard cometh, what will he do unto those husbandmen?

41 ᴿThey say unto him, ᴿHe will miserably destroy those wicked men, ᴿand will let out *his* vineyard unto other husbandmen, which shall render him the fruits in their seasons. Luke 20:16 · [Luke 21:24] · [8:11]

☆ 42 Jesus saith unto them, ᴿDid ye never read in the scriptures, The stone which the builders rejected, the same is become the head of the corner: this is the Lord's doing, and it is marvellous in our eyes? Ps. 118:22, 23; Is. 28:16

43 Therefore say I unto you, ᴿThe kingdom of God shall be taken from you, and given to a nation bringing forth the fruits thereof. [8:12]; Acts 13:46

☆ 44 And whosoever ᴿshall fall on this stone shall be broken: but on whomsoever it shall fall, it will grind him to powder. Is. 8:14, 15

45 And when the chief priests and Pharisees had heard his parables, they ᵀperceived that he spake of them. *knew*

46 But when they sought to lay hands on him, they feared the multitude, because ᴿthey took him for a prophet. Luke 7:16; John 7:40

22 And Jesus answered ᴿand spake unto them again by parables, and said, Luke 14:16

2 The kingdom of heaven is like unto a certain king, which made a marriage for his son,

3 And sent forth his servants to call them that were bidden to the wedding: and they would not come.

4 Again, he sent forth other servants, saying, Tell them which are bidden, Behold, I have prepared my dinner: ᴿmy oxen and *my* ᵀfatlings *are* killed, and all things *are* ready: come unto the marriage. Prov. 9:2 · *fattened cattle*

5 But they made light of *it*, and went their ways, one to his farm, another to his merchandise:

6 And the ᵀremnant took his servants, and entreated *them* spitefully, and slew *them*. *rest*

7 But when the king heard *thereof*, he was wroth: and he sent forth ᴿhis armies, and de-

stroyed those murderers, and burned up their city. [Dan. 9:26]

8 Then saith he to his servants, The wedding is ready, but they which were ᵀbidden were not ᴿworthy. *invited* · 10:11

9 Go ye therefore into the highways, and as many as ye shall find, ᵀbid to the marriage. *invite*

10 So those servants went out into the highways, and ᴿgathered together all as many as they found, both bad and good: and the wedding was ᵀfurnished with guests. 13:38, 47, 48; [Acts 28:28] · *filled*

11 And when the king came in to see the guests, he saw there a man ᴿwhich had not on a wedding garment: [2 Cor. 5:3; Rev. 3:4; 16:15; 19:8]

12 And he saith unto him, Friend, how camest thou in hither not having a wedding garment? And he was ᴿspeechless. [Rom. 3:19]

13 Then said the king to the servants, Bind him hand and foot, and take him away, and cast *him* into outer darkness; there shall be weeping and gnashing of teeth.

14 ᴿFor many are called, but few *are* chosen. 20:16

15 Then went the Pharisees, and took counsel how they might entangle him in *his* talk.

16 And they sent out unto him their disciples with the He-ro'-di-ans, saying, Master, we know that thou art true, and teachest the way of God in truth, neither carest thou for any *man:* for thou regardest not the person of men.

17 Tell us therefore, What thinkest thou? Is it lawful to ᵀgive tribute unto Caesar, or not? *pay taxes*

18 But Jesus ᵀperceived their wickedness, and said, Why ᵀtempt ye me, *ye* hypocrites? *knew · test*

19 Shew me the ᵀtribute money. And they brought unto him a ᵀpenny. *tax · Gr. denarius*

20 And he saith unto them, Whose *is* this image and ᵀsuperscription? *inscription*

21 They say unto him, Caesar's. Then saith he unto them, ᴿRender therefore unto Caesar the things

which are Caesar's; and unto God the things that are God's. 17:25

22 When they had heard *these words,* they marvelled, and left him, and went their way.

23 ^RThe same day came to him the Sad'-du-cees, ^Rwhich say that there is no resurrection, and asked him, Mark 12:18–27 · Acts 23:8

24 Saying, ^TMaster, ^RMoses said, If a man die, having no children, his brother shall marry his wife, and raise up ^Tseed unto his brother. *Teacher* · Deut. 25:5 · *offspring*

25 Now there were with us seven brethren: and the first, when he had married a wife, ^Tdeceased, and, having no ^Tissue, left his wife unto his brother: *died · offspring*

26 Likewise the second also, and the third, unto the seventh.

27 And last of all the woman died also.

28 Therefore in the resurrection whose wife shall she be of the seven? for they all had her.

29 Jesus answered and said unto them, Ye ^Tdo err, ^Rnot knowing the scriptures, nor the power of God. *are mistaken* · John 20:9

30 For in the resurrection they neither marry, nor are given in marriage, but ^Rare as the angels of God in heaven. [1 John 3:2]

31 But ^Tas touching the resurrection of the dead, have ye not read that which was spoken unto you by God, saying, *concerning*

32 ^RI am the God of Abraham, and the God of Isaac, and the God of Jacob? God is not the God of the dead, but of the living. Acts 7:32

33 And when the multitude heard *this,* ^Rthey were astonished at his ^Tdoctrine. 7:28 · *teaching*

34 ^RBut when the Pharisees had heard that he had put the Sad'-du-cees to silence, they were gathered together. Mark 12:28–31

35 Then one of them, *which was* a lawyer, asked *him a question,* ^Ttempting him, and saying, *testing*

36 ^TMaster, which *is* the great commandment in the law? *Teacher*

37 Jesus said unto him, ^RThou shalt love the Lord thy God with all thy heart, and with all thy soul, and with all thy mind. Deut. 6:5

38 This is the first and great commandment.

39 And the second *is* like unto it, ^RThou shalt love thy neighbour as thyself. Lev. 19:18; Mark 12:31; [Gal. 5:14]

40 ^ROn these two commandments hang all the law and the prophets. [7:12; Rom. 13:10; 1 Tim. 1:5]

41 ^RWhile the Pharisees were gathered together, Jesus asked them, Mark 12:35–37; Luke 20:41–44

42 Saying, What think ye of Christ? whose son is he? They say unto him, *The* ^Rson of David. 21:9

43 He saith unto them, How then doth David ^Tin spirit call him Lord, saying, *in the Spirit*

44 ^RThe LORD said unto my Lord, Sit thou on my right hand, till I make thine enemies thy footstool? Ps. 110:1; Acts 2:34; 1 Cor. 15:25

45 If David then call him Lord, how is he his son?

46 And no man was able to answer him a word, ^Rneither durst any *man* from that day forth ask him any more *questions.* Luke 14:6

23 Then spake Jesus to the multitude, and to his disciples,

2 Saying, The scribes and the Pharisees sit in Moses' seat:

3 All therefore whatsoever they bid you observe, *that* observe and do; but do not ye ^Tafter their works: for ^Rthey say, and do not. *according to* · [Rom. 2:19]

4 For they bind heavy burdens and grievous to be borne, and lay *them* on men's shoulders; but they *themselves* will not move them with one of their fingers.

5 But all their works they do for to ^Rbe seen of men: they make broad their phylacteries, and enlarge the borders of their garments, [6:1–6, 16–18]

6 And love the uppermost rooms at feasts, and the chief seats in the synagogues,

7 And greetings in the markets, and to be called of men, Rabbi, Rabbi.

8 But be not ye called Rabbi:

for one is your Master, *even* Christ; and all ye are brethren.

9 And call no *man* your father upon the earth: ᴿfor one is your Father, which is in heaven. 5:16, 48

10 Neither be ye called ᵀmasters: for one is your ᵀMaster, *even* Christ.   *leaders* or *teachers · Leader*

11 But he that is greatest among you shall be your servant.

12 ᴿAnd whosoever shall exalt himself shall be ᵀabased; and he that shall humble himself shall be ᵀexalted. Prov. 15:33 · *humbled · lifted up*

13 But woe unto you, scribes and Pharisees, hypocrites! for ye shut up the kingdom of heaven against men: for ye neither go in *yourselves*, neither suffer ye them that are entering to go in.

14 Woe unto you, scribes and Pharisees, hypocrites! ᴿfor ye devour widows' houses, and for a pretence make long prayer: therefore ye shall receive the greater ᵀdamnation. Mark 12:40 · *condemnation*

15 Woe unto you, scribes and Pharisees, hypocrites! for ye compass sea and land to make one proselyte, and when he is made, ye make him twofold more the child of hell than yourselves.

16 Woe unto you, ᴿye blind guides, which say, ᴿWhosoever shall swear by the temple, it is nothing; but whosoever shall swear by the gold of the temple, he is a debtor! v. 24; 15:14 · [5:33, 34]

17 Ye fools and blind: for whether is greater, the gold, ᴿor the temple that sanctifieth the gold? Ex. 30:29

18 And, Whosoever shall swear by the altar, it is nothing; but whosoever sweareth by the gift that is upon it, he is guilty.

19 Ye fools and blind: for whether *is* greater, the gift, or the altar that sanctifieth the gift?

20 Whoso therefore shall ᵀswear by the altar, sweareth by it, and by all things thereon.   *swears an oath*

21 And whoso shall swear by the temple, sweareth by it, and by ᴿhim that dwelleth therein. Ps. 26:8

22 And he that shall swear by heaven, sweareth by ᴿthe throne of God, and by him that sitteth thereon.   Ps. 11:4; Is. 66:1; Acts 7:49

23 Woe unto you, scribes and Pharisees, hypocrites! ᴿfor ye pay tithe of mint and anise and cummin, and have omitted the weightier *matters* of the law, judgment, mercy, and faith: these ought ye to have done, and not to leave the other undone.   Luke 11:42; 18:12

24 *Ye* blind guides, which strain at a gnat, and swallow a camel.

25 Woe unto you, scribes and Pharisees, hypocrites! for ye make clean the outside of the cup and of the platter, but within they are full of extortion and excess.

26 *Thou* blind Pharisee, cleanse first that *which is* within the cup and platter, that the outside of them may be clean also.

27 Woe unto you, scribes and Pharisees, hypocrites! ᴿfor ye are like unto whited sepulchres, which indeed appear beautiful outward, but are within full of dead *men's* bones, and of all uncleanness.   Luke 11:44; Acts 23:3

28 Even so ye also outwardly appear righteous unto men, but within ye are full of hypocrisy and ᵀiniquity.   *lawlessness*

29 ᴿWoe unto you, scribes and Pharisees, hypocrites! because ye build the tombs of the prophets, and ᵀgarnish the sepulchres of the righteous,   Luke 11:47, 48 · *adorn*

30 And say, If we had been in the days of our fathers, we would not have been partakers with them in the blood of the prophets.

31 Wherefore ye be witnesses unto yourselves, that ᴿye are the children of them which killed the prophets.   [Acts 7:51, 52]; 1 Thess. 2:15

32 ᴿFill ye up then the measure of your fathers.   [1 Thess. 2:16]

33 *Ye* serpents, *ye* ᵀgeneration of vipers, how can ye escape the damnation of hell? *brood* or *offspring*

34 Wherefore, behold, I send unto you prophets, and wise men, and scribes: and ᴿ*some* of them ye shall kill and crucify; and ᴿ*some*

of them shall ye scourge in your synagogues, and persecute *them* from city to city: Acts 22:19 · Acts 5:40

35 That upon you may come all the righteous blood shed upon the earth, [R]from the blood of righteous Abel unto [R]the blood of Zach-a-ri'-as son of Bar-a-chi'-as, whom ye slew between the temple and the altar. Gen. 4:8 · 2 Chr. 24:20, 21

36 Verily I say unto you, All these things shall come upon this generation.

37 O Jerusalem, Jerusalem, *thou* that killest the prophets, and stonest them which are sent unto thee, how often would I have gathered thy children together, even as a hen gathereth her chickens under *her* wings, and ye would not!

38 Behold, your house is left unto you desolate.

39 For I say unto you, Ye shall not see me henceforth, till ye shall say, [R]Blessed *is* he that cometh in the name of the Lord. Ps. 118:26

24 And [R]Jesus went out, and departed from the temple: and his disciples came to *him* for to shew him the buildings of the temple. Mark 13:1; Luke 21:5-36

2 And Jesus said unto them, See ye not all these things? verily I say unto you, There shall not be left here one stone upon another, that shall not be thrown down.

3 And as he sat upon the mount of Olives, [R]the disciples came unto him privately, saying, [R]Tell us, when shall these things be? and what *shall be* the sign of thy coming, and of the end of the [T]world? Mark 13:3 · [Luke 17:20–37] · *age*

4 And Jesus answered and said unto them, [R]Take heed that no man deceive you. [1 John 4:1–3]

5 For [R]many shall come in my name, saying, I am Christ; and shall deceive many. John 5:43

6 And ye shall hear of [R]wars and rumours of wars: see that ye be not troubled: for all *these things* must come to pass, but the end is not yet. [Rev. 6:2–4]

7 For nation shall rise against nation, and kingdom against

kingdom: and there shall be [R]famines, and pestilences, and earthquakes, in divers places. Acts 11:28

8 All these *are* the beginning of sorrows.

9 [R]Then shall they deliver you up to be afflicted, and shall kill you: and ye shall be hated of all nations for my name's sake. 10:17

10 And then shall many be offended, and shall betray one another, and shall hate one another.

11 And [R]many false prophets shall rise, and [R]shall deceive many. 2 Pet. 2:1; Rev. 19:20 · [1 Tim. 4:1]

12 And because [T]iniquity shall abound, the love of many shall [T]wax cold. *lawlessness · grow*

13 [R]But he that shall endure unto the end, the same shall be saved. 10:22; Mark 13:13

14 And this [R]gospel of the kingdom [R]shall be preached in all the world for a witness unto all nations; and then shall the end come. 4:23 · Rom. 10:18; Col. 1:6, 23

15 When ye therefore shall see the abomination of desolation, spoken of by Daniel the prophet, stand in the holy place, (whoso readeth, let him understand:)

16 Then let them which be in Ju-dae'-a flee into the mountains:

17 Let him which is on the housetop not come down to take any thing out of his house:

18 Neither let him which is in the field return back to take his clothes.

19 And [R]woe unto them that are with child, and to them that give suck in those days! Luke 23:29

20 But pray ye that your flight be not in the winter, neither on the sabbath day:

21 For [R]then shall be great tribulation, such as was not since the beginning of the world to this time, no, nor ever shall be. Dan. 9:26

22 And except those days should be shortened, there should no flesh be saved: [R]but for the elect's sake those days shall be shortened. Is. 65:8, 9; [Zech. 14:2]

23 [R]Then if any man shall say

unto you, Lo, here *is* Christ, or there; believe *it* not.   Mark 13:21

24 For ᴿthere shall arise false Christs, and false prophets, and shall shew great signs and wonders; insomuch that, ᴿif *it were* possible, they shall deceive the very elect.   John 4:48 · [John 6:37]

25 Behold, I have told you before.

26 Wherefore if they shall say unto you, Behold, he is in the desert; go not forth: behold, *he is* in the ᵀsecret chambers; believe *it* not.   *inner rooms*

27 For as the lightning cometh out of the east, and shineth even unto the west; so shall also the coming of the Son of man be.

28 ᴿFor wheresoever the carcase is, there will the eagles be gathered together.   Ezek. 39:17; Hab. 1:8

29 ᴿImmediately after the tribulation of those days ᴿshall the sun be darkened, and the moon shall not give her light, and the stars shall fall from heaven, and the powers of the heavens shall be shaken: [Dan. 7:11] · Joel 2:10, 31; 3:15

☆ 30 ᴿAnd then shall appear the sign of the Son of man in heaven: ᴿand then shall all the tribes of the earth mourn, and they shall see the Son of man coming in the clouds of heaven with power and great glory.   [Dan. 7:13, 14] · Zech. 12:12

31 And he shall send his angels with a great sound of a trumpet, and they shall gather together his elect from the four winds, from one end of heaven to the other.

32 Now learn a parable ᵀof the fig tree; When his branch is yet tender, and putteth forth leaves, ye know that summer *is* nigh: *from*

33 So likewise ye, when ye shall see all these things, know that it is near, *even* at the doors.

34 Verily I say unto you, ᴿThis generation shall not pass, till all these things be fulfilled.   [10:23]

35 ᴿHeaven and earth shall pass away, but my words shall not pass away.   [1 Pet. 1:23–25; 2 Pet. 3:10]

36 ᴿBut of that day and hour knoweth no *man*, no, not the an-

gels of heaven, ᴿbut my Father only.   Mark 13:32; Acts 1:7 · Zech. 14:7

37 But as the days of No'-e *were*, so shall also the coming of the Son of man be.

38 For as in the days that were before the flood they were eating and drinking, marrying and giving in marriage, until the day that No'-e entered into the ark,

39 And knew not until the flood came, and took them all away; so shall also the coming of the Son of man be.

40 ᴿThen shall two be in the field; the one shall be taken, and the other left.   Luke 17:34

41 Two *women shall be* grinding at the mill; the one shall be taken, and the other left.

42 ᴿWatch therefore: for ye know not what hour your Lord doth come.   Luke 21:36; 1 Thess. 5:6

43 ᴿBut know this, that if the goodman of the house had known in what watch the thief would come, he would have watched, and would not have suffered his house to be broken up.   Luke 12:39

44 ᴿTherefore be ye also ready: for in such an hour as ye think not the Son of man cometh. [1 Thess. 5:6]

45 Who then is a faithful and wise servant, whom his lord hath made ruler over his household, to give them meat in due season?

46 ᴿBlessed *is* that servant, whom his lord when he cometh shall find so doing.   Rev. 16:15

47 Verily I say unto you, That ᴿhe shall make him ruler over all his goods.   25:21, 23; Luke 22:29

48 But and if that evil servant shall say in his heart, My lord ᴿdelayeth his coming;   [2 Pet. 3:4–9]

49 And shall begin to ᵀsmite *his* fellowservants, and to eat and drink with the drunken;   *beat*

50 The lord of that servant shall come in a day when he looketh not for *him*, and in an hour that he is ᴿnot aware of,   Mark 13:32

51 And shall cut him asunder, and appoint *him* his portion with the hypocrites: there shall be weeping and gnashing of teeth.

25 Then shall the kingdom of heaven be likened unto ten virgins, which took their lamps, and went forth to meet ᴿthe bridegroom.   [Eph. 5:29, 30; Rev. 19:7; 21:2, 9]

2 ᴿAnd five of them were wise, and five *were* foolish.   13:47; 22:10

3 They that *were* foolish took their lamps, and took no oil with them:

4 But the wise took oil in their vessels with their lamps.

5 While the bridegroom ᵀtarried, ᴿthey all slumbered and slept.   *delayed* · 1 Thess. 5:6

6 And at midnight there was a cry made, Behold, the bridegroom cometh; go ye out to meet him.

7 Then all those virgins arose, and trimmed their lamps.

8 And the foolish said unto the wise, Give us of your oil; for our lamps are ᵀgone out.   *going*

9 But the wise answered, saying, *Not so*; lest there be not enough for us and you: but go ye rather to them that sell, and buy for yourselves.

10 And while they went to buy, the bridegroom came; and they that were ready went in with him to the marriage: and ᴿthe door was shut.   Luke 13:25

11 Afterward came also the other virgins, saying, ᴿLord, Lord, open to us.   [7:21–23]

12 But he answered and said, Verily I say unto you, ᴿI know you not.   [Ps. 5:5; Hab. 1:13; John 9:31]

13 ᴿWatch therefore, for ye ᴿknow neither the day nor the hour wherein the Son of man cometh.   1 Thess. 5:6 · 24:36, 42

14 ᴿFor *the kingdom of heaven is* ᴿas a man travelling into a far country, *who* called his own servants, and delivered unto them his goods.   Luke 19:12–27 · 21:33

15 And unto one he gave five talents, to another two, and to another one; to every man according to his ᵀseveral ability; and straightway took his journey.   *own*

16 Then he that had received the five talents went and traded with the same, and made *them* other five talents.

17 And likewise he that *had received* two, he also gained other two.

18 But he that had received one went and digged in the earth, and hid his lord's money.

19 After a long time the lord of those servants cometh, and ᵀreckoneth with them.   *settled accounts*

20 And so he that had received five talents came and brought other five talents, saying, Lord, thou deliveredst unto me five talents: behold, I have gained beside them five talents more.

21 His lord said unto him, Well done, *thou* good and faithful servant: thou hast been faithful over a few things, I will make thee ruler over many things: enter thou into ᴿthe joy of thy lord.   [Heb. 12:2]

22 He also that had received two talents came and said, Lord, thou deliveredst unto me two talents: behold, I have gained two other talents beside them.

23 His lord said unto him, Well done, good and faithful servant; thou hast been faithful over a few things, I will make thee ruler over many things: enter thou into the ᴿjoy of thy lord.   [John 15:10, 11]

24 Then he which had received the one talent came and said, Lord, I knew thee that thou art an hard man, reaping where thou hast not sown, and gathering where thou hast not strawed:

25 And I was afraid, and went and hid thy talent in the earth: lo, *there* thou hast *that is* thine.

26 His lord answered and said unto him, *Thou* wicked and slothful servant, thou knewest that I reap where I sowed not, and gather where I have not strawed:

27 Thou oughtest therefore to have put my money to the ᵀexchangers, and *then* at my coming I should have received mine own with ᵀusury.   *bankers · interest*

28 Take therefore the talent from him, and give *it* unto him which hath ten talents.

29 ᴿFor unto every one that hath shall be given, and he shall have abundance: but from him that hath not shall be taken away even that which he hath.   13:12; Mark 4:25

30 And cast ye the unprofitable servant ᴿinto outer darkness: there shall be weeping and gnashing of teeth.   8:12; 22:13; [Luke 13:28]

31 ᴿWhen the Son of man shall come in his glory, and all the holy angels with him, then shall he sit upon the throne of his glory: 16:27

32 And ᴿbefore him shall be gathered all nations: and ᴿhe shall separate them one from another, as a shepherd divideth *his* sheep from the goats: [Rev. 20:12] · Ezek. 20:38

33 And he shall set the ᴿsheep on his right hand, but the goats on the left.   Ps. 79:13; [John 10:11, 27, 28]

34 Then shall the King say unto them on his right hand, Come, ye blessed of my Father, inherit the kingdom ᴿprepared for you from the foundation of the world: 20:23

35 ᴿFor I was an hungred, and ye gave me meat: I was thirsty, and ye gave me drink: I was a stranger, and ye took me in: Is. 58:7

36 Naked, and ye clothed me: I was sick, and ye visited me: I was in prison, and ye came unto me.

37 Then shall the righteous answer him, saying, Lord, when saw we thee ᵀan hungred, and fed *thee?* or thirsty, and gave *thee* drink?   *hungry*

38 When saw we thee a stranger, and took *thee* in? or naked, and clothed *thee?*

39 Or when saw we thee sick, or in prison, and came unto thee?

40 And the King shall answer and say unto them, Verily I say unto you, ᴿInasmuch as ye have done *it* unto one of the least of these my brethren, ye have done *it* unto me.   Prov. 14:31; Heb. 6:10

41 Then shall he say also unto them on the left hand, ᴿDepart from me, ye cursed, into everlasting fire, prepared for ᴿthe devil and his angels: Ps. 6:8 · Jude 6

42 For I was ᵀan hungred, and ye

gave me no meat: I was thirsty, and ye gave me no drink: *hungry*

43 I was a stranger, and ye took me not in: naked, and ye clothed me not: sick, and in prison, and ye visited me not.

44 Then shall they also answer him, saying, Lord, when saw we thee ᵀan hungred, or ᵀathirst, or a stranger, or naked, or sick, or in prison, and did not minister unto thee?   *hungry · thirsty*

45 Then shall he answer them, saying, Verily I say unto you, ᴿInasmuch as ye did *it* not to one of the least of these, ye did *it* not to me.   Prov. 14:31; Zech. 2:8; Acts 9:5

46 And these shall go away into everlasting punishment: but the righteous into life eternal.

26 And it came to pass, when Jesus had finished all these sayings, he said unto his disciples,

2 ᴿYe know that after two days is *the feast of* the passover, and the Son of man is betrayed to be crucified.   27:35; Mark 14:1, 2

3 ᴿThen assembled together the chief priests, and the scribes, and the elders of the people, unto the palace of the high priest, who was called Ca'-ia-phas,   John 11:47

4 And ᵀconsulted that they might take Jesus by ᵀsubtilty, and kill *him.*   *plotted · trickery*

5 But they said, Not on the feast *day,* lest there be an uproar among the ᴿpeople.   21:26

6 Now when Jesus was in ᴿBeth'-a-ny, in the house of Simon the leper,   8:2; John 11:1, 2; 12:1–8

7 There came unto him a woman having an alabaster ᵀbox of very ᵀprecious ointment, and poured it on his head, as he sat *at meat.*   *flask · costly fragrant oil*

8 But when his disciples saw *it,* they had indignation, saying, To what purpose *is* this waste?

9 For this ointment might have been sold for much, and given to the poor.

10 When Jesus understood *it,* he said unto them, Why trouble ye the woman? for she hath wrought a good work upon me.

11 RFor ye have the poor always with you; but Rme ye have not always.   John 12:8 · [John 13:33; 14:19]

12 For in that she hath poured this ointment on my body, she did it for my Rburial.   27:60; Luke 23:53

13 Verily I say unto you, Wheresoever this gospel shall be preached in the whole world, there shall also this, that this woman hath done, be told for a memorial of her.

★ 14 RThen one of the twelve, called Judas Is-car'-i-ot, went unto the chief priests,   John 13:2, 30

15 And said unto them, RWhat will ye give me, and I will deliver him unto you? And they Tcovenanted with him for thirty pieces of silver.   27:3 · counted out to him

16 And from that time he sought opportunity to betray him.

17 Now the first day of the feast of unleavened bread the disciples came to Jesus, saying unto him, Where wilt thou that we prepare for thee to eat the passover?

18 And he said, Go into the city to such a man, and say unto him, The Master saith, My time is at hand; I will keep the passover at thy house with my disciples.

19 And the disciples did as Jesus had appointed them; and they made ready the passover.

20 RNow when the even was come, he sat down with the twelve.   Mark 14:17–21; Luke 22:14

21 And as they did eat, he said, Verily I say unto you, that one of you shall Rbetray me.   Mark 14:42

22 And they were exceeding sorrowful, and began every one of them to say unto him, Lord, is it I?

23 And he answered and said, RHe that dippeth his hand with me in the dish, the same shall betray me.   Ps. 41:9; Luke 22:21; John 13:18

24 The Son of man goeth as it is written of him: but woe unto that man by whom the Son of man is betrayed! it had been good for that man if he had not been born.

25 Then Judas, which betrayed him, answered and said, TMaster, is it I? He said unto him, Thou hast Tsaid.   Gr. Rabbi · said it

26 And as they were eating, RJesus took bread, and blessed it, and brake it, and gave it to the disciples, and said, Take, eat; Rthis is my body. 1 Cor. 11:23–25 · [1 Pet. 2:24]

27 And he took the cup, and gave thanks, and gave it to them, saying, Drink ye all of it;

28 For this is my blood of the new testament, which is shed for many for the remission of sins.

29 But RI say unto you, I will not drink henceforth of this fruit of the vine, until that day when I drink it new with you in my Father's kingdom.   Luke 22:18

30 RAnd when they had sung an hymn, they went out into the mount of Olives.   Mark 14:26–31

31 Then saith Jesus unto them, ★ RAll ye shall be offended because of me this night: for it is written, RI will smite the shepherd, and the sheep of the flock shall be scattered abroad.   John 16:32 · Zech. 13:7

32 But after I am risen again, I will go before you into Galilee.

33 Peter answered and said unto him, Though all men shall be Toffended because of thee, yet will I never be offended.   made to stumble

34 Jesus said unto him, RVerily I say unto thee, That this night, before the cock crow, thou shalt deny me thrice. Mark 14:30; Luke 22:34

35 Peter said unto him, Though I should die with thee, yet will I not deny thee. Likewise also said all the disciples.

36 RThen cometh Jesus with them unto a place called Gethsem'-a-ne, and saith unto the disciples, Sit ye here, while I go and pray Tyonder.   John 18:1 · over there

37 And he took with him Peter and Rthe two sons of Zeb'-e-dee, and began to be sorrowful and very heavy.   4:21; 17:1; Mark 5:37

38 Then saith he unto them, RMy soul is exceeding sorrowful, even unto death: Ttarry ye here, and watch with me.   John 12:27 · stay

39 And he went a little farther, and fell on his face, and prayed,

saying, ^RO my Father, if it be possible, ^Rlet this cup pass from me: nevertheless ^Rnot as I will, but as thou *wilt.*   John 12:27 · 20:22 · Ps. 40:8

40 And he cometh unto the disciples, and findeth them asleep, and saith unto Peter, What, could ye not watch with me one hour?

41 Watch and pray, that ye enter not into temptation: ^Rthe spirit indeed *is* willing, but the flesh *is* weak.   Ps. 103:14–16; [Rom. 7:15; 8:23]

42 He went away again the second time, and prayed, saying, O my Father, if this cup may not pass away from me, ^Texcept I drink it, thy will be done.   *unless*

43 And he came and found them asleep again: for their eyes were heavy.

44 And he left them, and went away again, and prayed the third time, saying the same words.

45 Then cometh he to his disciples, and saith unto them, Sleep on now, and take *your* rest: behold, the hour is at hand, and the Son of man is ^Rbetrayed into the hands of sinners.   17:22, 23

46 Rise, let us be going: behold, he is at hand that doth betray me.

47 And ^Rwhile he yet spake, lo, Judas, one of the twelve, came, and with him a great multitude with swords and staves, from the chief priests and elders of the people.   John 18:3–11; Acts 1:16

48 Now he that betrayed him gave them a sign, saying, Whomsoever I shall kiss, that same is he: ^Thold him fast.   *seize him*

49 And forthwith he came to Jesus, and said, Hail, master; ^Rand kissed him.   2 Sam. 20:9; [Prov. 27:6]

50 And Jesus said unto him, ^RFriend, wherefore art thou come? Then came they, and laid hands on Jesus, and took him.   Ps. 41:9

51 And, behold, one of them which were with Jesus stretched out *his* hand, and drew his sword, and struck a servant of the high priest's, and smote off his ear.

52 Then said Jesus unto him, Put up again thy sword into his place: for all they that take the sword shall perish with the sword.

53 Thinkest thou that I cannot now pray to my Father, and he shall presently give me more than twelve legions of angels?

54 But how then shall the scriptures be fulfilled, ^Rthat thus it must be? Is. 50:6; 53:2–11; Acts 13:29; 17:3

55 In that same hour said Jesus to the multitudes, Are ye come out as against a ^Tthief with swords and ^Tstaves for to take me? I sat daily with you teaching in the temple, and ye ^Tlaid no hold on me.   *robber · clubs · did not seize me*

56 But all this was done, that the ^Rscriptures of the prophets might be fulfilled. Then all the disciples forsook him, and fled.   Lam. 4:20

57 ^RAnd they that had laid hold on Jesus led *him* away to Ca'-ia-phas the high priest, where the scribes and the elders were assembled.   17:22; Luke 22:54

58 But ^RPeter followed him afar off unto the high priest's palace, and went in, and sat with the servants, to see the end.   John 18:15, 16

59 Now the chief priests, and elders, and all the council, sought ^Rfalse witness against Jesus, to put him to death;   Ex. 20:16; Ps. 35:11

60 But found none: yea, though ^Rmany false witnesses came, *yet* found they none. At the last came two false witnesses,   Ps. 27:12; 35:11

61 And said, This *fellow* said, I am able to destroy the temple of God, and to build it in three days.

62 And the high priest arose, and said unto him, Answerest thou nothing? what *is it which* these ^Twitness against thee? *testify*

63 But ^RJesus held his peace. And the high priest answered and said unto him, ^RI adjure thee by the living God, that thou tell us whether thou be the Christ, the Son of God.   Ps. 38:13, 14 · Lev. 5:1

64 Jesus saith unto him, Thou hast said: nevertheless I say unto you, ^RHereafter shall ye see the Son of man sitting on the right hand of power, and coming in the clouds of heaven.   Dan. 7:13; Rev. 1:7

65 ᴿThen the high priest ᵀrent his clothes, saying, He hath spoken blasphemy; what further need have we of witnesses? behold, now ye have heard his ᴿblasphemy. 2 Kin. 18:37 · *tore* · John 10:30–36

66 What think ye? They answered and said, ᴿHe is ᵀguilty of death. Lev. 24:16; John 19:7 · *deserving*

★ 67 ᴿThen did they spit in his face, and buffeted him; and ᴿothers smote *him* with the palms of their hands, 27:30 · John 19:3

68 Saying, ᴿProphesy unto us, thou Christ, Who is he that smote thee? Mark 14:65; Luke 22:64

69 ᴿNow Peter sat without in the palace: and a damsel came unto him, saying, Thou also wast with Jesus of Galilee. Mark 14:66–72

70 But he denied before *them* all, saying, I know not what thou sayest.

71 And when he was gone out ᵀinto the porch, another *maid* saw him, and said unto them that were there, This *fellow* was also with Jesus of Nazareth. *to the gateway*

72 And again he denied with an oath, I do not know the man.

73 And after a while came unto *him* they that stood by, and said to Peter, Surely thou also art *one* of them; for thy ᴿspeech bewrayeth thee. Mark 14:70; Luke 22:59; John 18:26

74 Then ᴿbegan he to curse and to swear, *saying*, I know not the man. And immediately the cock crew. Mark 14:71; Luke 22:34; John 13:38

75 And Peter remembered the word of Jesus, which said unto him, ᴿBefore the cock crow, thou shalt deny me thrice. And he went out, and wept bitterly. v. 34

27 When the morning was come, ᴿall the chief priests and elders of the people took counsel against Jesus to put him to death: Ps. 2:2; Mark 15:1; John 18:28

2 And when they had bound him, they led *him* away, and ᴿdelivered him to Pon′-tius Pilate the governor. Luke 18:32; Acts 3:13

3 ᴿThen Judas, which had betrayed him, when he saw that he was condemned, ᵀrepented himself, and brought again the thirty pieces of silver to the chief priests and elders, 26:14 · *felt remorse*

4 Saying, I have sinned in that I have betrayed the innocent blood. And they said, What *is that* to us? see thou *to that*.

5 And he cast down the pieces of silver in the temple, ᴿand departed, and went and hanged himself. 18:7; 26:24; John 17:12; Acts 1:18

6 And the chief priests took the silver pieces, and said, It is not lawful for to put them into the treasury, because it is the price of blood.

7 And they took counsel, and bought with them the potter's field, to bury strangers in.

8 Wherefore that field was called, ᴿThe field of blood, unto this day. Acts 1:19

★ 9 Then was fulfilled that which was spoken by Jeremy the prophet, saying, And they took the thirty pieces of silver, the price of him that was valued, whom they of the children of Israel did value;

10 And gave them for the potter's field, as the Lord ᴿappointedᵀ me. Jer. 32:6–9; Zech. 11:12, 13 · *directed*

11 And Jesus stood before the governor: and the governor asked him, saying, Art thou the King of the Jews? And Jesus said unto him, ᴿThou sayest. John 18:37

12 And when he was accused of the chief priests and elders, ᴿhe answered nothing. 26:63; John 19:9

13 Then said Pilate unto him, Hearest thou not how many things they witness against thee?

★ 14 And he answered him to never a word; insomuch that the governor marvelled greatly.

15 ᴿNow at *that* feast the governor was ᵀwont to release unto the people a prisoner, whom they would. Mark 15:6–15 · *accustomed*

16 And they had then a notable prisoner, called Bar-ab′-bas.

17 Therefore when they were gathered together, Pilate said unto them, Whom will ye that I release unto you? Bar-ab′-bas, or Jesus which is called Christ?

18 For he knew that for ^Renvy they had delivered him.   21:38

19 When he was set down on the judgment seat, his wife sent unto him, saying, Have thou nothing to do with that just man: for I have suffered many things this day in a dream because of him.

20 ^RBut the chief priests and elders persuaded the multitude that they should ask Bar-ab′-bas, and destroy Jesus.   John 18:40

21 The governor answered and said unto them, Whether of the twain will ye that I release unto you? They said, Bar-ab′-bas.

22 Pilate saith unto them, What shall I do then with Jesus which is called Christ? *They* all say unto him, Let him be crucified.

23 And the governor said, ^RWhy, what evil hath he done? But they cried out the more, saying, Let him be crucified.   Acts 3:13

24 When Pilate saw that he could prevail nothing, but *that* rather a tumult was made, he took water, and washed *his* hands before the multitude, saying, I am innocent of the blood of this just person: see ye *to it.*

25 Then answered all the people, and said, ^RHis blood *be* on us, and on our children.   Acts 5:28

★ 26 Then released he Bar-ab′-bas unto them: and when ^Rhe had scourged Jesus, he delivered *him* to be crucified.   20:19; John 19:1, 16

27 ^RThen the soldiers of the governor took Jesus into the common hall, and gathered unto him the whole band *of soldiers.*   John 19:2

28 And they stripped him, and put on him a scarlet robe.

29 ^RAnd when they had platted a crown of thorns, they put *it* upon his head, and a reed in his right hand: and they bowed the knee before him, and mocked him, saying, Hail, King of the Jews!   Ps. 69:19; Is. 53:3; Mark 10:34

★ 30 And ^Rthey spit upon him, and took the reed, and smote him on the head.   Is. 50:6; 52:14; Mic. 5:1

31 And after that they had mocked him, they took the robe off from him, and put on his own ^Traiment on him, ^Rand led him away to crucify *him.* *clothes* · Is. 53:7

32 ^RAnd as they came out, ^Rthey found a man of Cy-re′-ne, Simon by name: him they compelled to bear his cross. Heb. 13:12 · Mark 15:21

33 And when they were come unto a place called Gol′-go-tha, that is to say, a place of a skull,

34 ^RThey gave him vinegar to drink mingled with gall: and ★ when he had tasted *thereof,* he would not drink. Ps. 69:21

35 And they crucified him, and ★ ^Tparted his garments, casting lots: that it might be fulfilled which was spoken by the prophet, ^RThey parted my garments among them, and upon my vesture did they cast lots.   *divided* · Ps. 22:18

36 And sitting down they ^Twatched him there;   *guarded* ★

37 And set up over his head his accusation written, THIS IS JESUS THE KING OF THE JEWS.

38 ^RThen were there two ^Tthieves crucified with him, one on the right hand, and another on the left. Is. 53:9, 12; Mark 15:27 · *robbers*

39 And they that passed by ★ reviled him, wagging their heads,

40 And saying, ^RThou that destroyest the temple, and buildest *it* in three days, save thyself. ^RIf thou be the Son of God, come down from the cross.   26:61 · 26:63

41 Likewise also the chief priests mocking *him,* with the scribes and elders, said,

42 He ^Rsaved others; himself he cannot save. If he be the King of Israel, let him now come down from the cross, and we will believe him.   [18:11]; John 3:14, 15]

43 ^RHe trusted in God; let him ★ deliver him now, if he will have him: for he said, I am the Son of God.   Ps. 22:8

44 ^RThe thieves also, which were crucified with him, cast the same in his teeth. Mark 15:32; Luke 23:39–43

45 ^RNow from the sixth hour there was darkness over all the land unto the ninth hour. Amos 8:9

★ 46 And about the ninth hour Jesus cried with a loud voice, saying, E'-li, E'-li, la'-ma sa-bach'-tha-ni? that is to say, My God, my God, why hast thou forsaken me?

47 Some of them that stood there, when they heard *that*, said, This *man* calleth for E-li'-as.

48 And straightway one of them ran, and took a spunge, and filled *it* with vinegar, and put *it* on a reed, and gave him to drink.

49 The rest said, Let be, let us see whether E-li'-as will come to save him.

50 ᴿJesus, when he had cried again with a loud voice, ᴿyielded up the ghost.   John 19:30 · [John 10:18]

51 And, behold, ᴿthe veil of the temple was ᵀrent in twain from the top to the bottom; and the earth did quake, and the rocks rent;   Ex. 26:31 · *torn in two*

52 And the graves were opened; and many bodies of the saints which slept arose,

53 And came out of the graves after his resurrection, and went into the holy city, and appeared unto many.

54 Now when the centurion, and they that were with him, watching Jesus, saw the earthquake, and those things that were done, they feared greatly, saying, ᴿTruly this was the Son of God.   14:33

55 And many women were there beholding afar off, ᴿwhich followed Jesus from Galilee, ministering unto him: Luke 8:2, 3

56 Among which was Mary Mag-da-le'-ne, and Mary the mother of James and Jo'-ses, and the mother of Zeb'-e-dee's children.

★ 57 ᴿWhen the even was come, there came a rich man of Ar-i-ma-thae'-a, named Joseph, who also himself was Jesus' disciple: Is. 53:9

58 He went to Pilate, and ᵀbegged the body of Jesus. Then Pilate commanded the body to be delivered.   *asked for*

59 And when Joseph had taken the body, he wrapped it in a clean linen cloth,

60 And ᴿlaid it in his own new tomb, which he had hewn out in the rock: and he rolled a great stone to the door of the sepulchre, and departed.   26:12; Is. 53:9

61 And there was Mary Mag-da-le'-ne, and the other Mary, sitting over against the sepulchre.

62 Now the next day, that followed the day of the preparation, the chief priests and Pharisees came together unto Pilate,

63 Saying, Sir, we remember that that deceiver said, while he was yet alive, ᴿAfter three days I will rise again.   16:21; 17:23; 20:19; 26:61

64 Command therefore that the ᵀsepulchre be made sure until the third day, lest his disciples come by night, and steal him away, and say unto the people, He is risen from the dead: so the last error shall be worse than the first.   *tomb*

65 Pilate said unto them, Ye have a watch: go your way, make *it* as ᵀsure as ye can.   *secure*

66 So they went, and made the sepulchre sure, sealing the stone, and setting a ᵀwatch.   *guard*

28 In the end of the sabbath, as it began to dawn toward the first *day* of the week, came Mary Mag-da-le'-ne and the other Mary to see the sepulchre.

2 And, behold, there was a great earthquake: for ᴿthe angel of the Lord descended from heaven, and came and rolled back the stone from the door, and sat upon it.   Mark 16:5; Luke 24:4; John 20:12

3 ᴿHis countenance was like lightning, and his ᵀraiment white as snow: Dan. 7:9; Acts 1:10 · *clothing*

4 And for fear of him the ᵀkeepers did shake, and became as ᴿdead *men*.   *guards* · Rev. 1:17

5 And the angel answered and said unto the women, Fear not ye: for I know that ye seek Jesus, which was crucified.

6 He is not here: for he is risen, ᴿas he said. Come, see the place where the Lord lay.   16:21; 17:23; 20:19

7 And go quickly, and tell his disciples that he is risen from the dead; and, behold, he goeth be-

fore you into Galilee; there shall ye see him: lo, I have told you.

8 And they departed quickly from the sepulchre with fear and great joy; and did run to bring his disciples word.

9 And as they went to tell his disciples, behold, Jesus met them, saying, ᵀAll hail. And they came and held him by the feet, and worshipped him.   *Rejoice*

10 Then said Jesus unto them, Be not afraid: go tell ᴿmy brethren that they go into Galilee, and there shall they see me.   John 20:17

11 Now when they were going, behold, some of the ᵀwatch came into the city, and shewed unto the chief priests all the things that were done.   *guard*

12 And when they were assembled with the elders, and had taken counsel, they gave ᵀlarge money unto the soldiers,   *much*

13 Saying, Say ye, His disciples came by night, and stole him *away* while we slept.

14 And if this come to the governor's ears, we will persuade him, and ᵀsecure you.   *make you secure*

15 So they took the money, and did as they were taught: and this saying is commonly reported among the Jews until this day.

16 Then the eleven disciples went away into Galilee, into a mountain ᴿwhere Jesus had appointed them.   Mark 14:28; 15:41; 16:7

17 And when they saw him, they worshipped him: but some ᴿdoubted.   John 20:24–29

18 And Jesus came and spake unto them, saying, ᴿAll power is given unto me in heaven and in earth.   11:27; Acts 2:36; Rom. 14:9

19 Go ye therefore, and teach all nations, baptizing them in the name of the Father, and of the Son, and of the Holy Ghost:

20 ᴿTeaching them to observe all things whatsoever I have commanded you: and, lo, I am with you alway, *even* unto the end of the world. A-men´.   [Acts 2:42]

The Gospel According to

MARK

THE message of Mark's gospel is captured in a single verse: "For even the Son of man came not to be ministered unto, but to minister, and to give his life a ransom for many" (10:45). Chapter by chapter, the book unfolds the dual focus of Christ's life: service and sacrifice.

Mark portrays Jesus as a Servant on the move, instantly responsive to the will of the Father. By preaching, teaching, and healing, He ministers to the needs of others even to the point of death. After the Resurrection, He commissions His followers to continue His work in His power—servants following in the steps of the perfect Servant.

The ancient title for this gospel was *Kata Markon*, "According to Mark." The author is best known by his Latin name *Marcus*, but in Jewish circles he was called by his Hebrew name *John*. Acts 12:12, 25 refer to him as "John, whose surname was Mark."

THE beginning of the gospel of Jesus Christ, the Son of God;

★ 2 As it is written in the prophets, ᴿBehold, I send my messenger

before thy face, which shall prepare thy way before thee.   Mal. 3:1

3 ᴿThe voice of one crying in ★ the wilderness, Prepare ye the

way of the Lord, make his paths straight.   Is. 40:3; Luke 3:4; John 1:23

★ 4 ᴿJohn did baptize in the wilderness, and preach the baptism of repentance for the ᵀremission of sins.   Mal. 4:6; Luke 3:3 · *forgiveness*

5 And there went out unto him all the land of Ju-dae′-a, and they of Jerusalem, and were all baptized of him in the river of Jordan, confessing their sins.

6 And John was clothed with camel's hair, and with a girdle of a skin about his ᵀloins; and he did eat locusts and wild honey;   *waist*

7 And preached, saying, ᴿThere cometh one mightier than I after me, the latchet of whose shoes I am not worthy to stoop down and unloose.   Matt. 3:11; John 1:27; Acts 13:2

8 I indeed have baptized you with water: but he shall baptize you ᴿwith the Holy Ghost. [Acts 2:4]

9 ᴿAnd it came to pass in those days, that Jesus came from Nazareth of Galilee, and was baptized of John in Jordan.   Matt. 3:13–17

10 And straightway coming up out of the water, he saw the heavens opened, and the Spirit like a dove descending upon him:

11 And there came a voice from heaven, *saying*, ᴿThou art my beloved Son, in whom I am well pleased. [Ps. 2:7]; Is. 42:1; Matt. 3:17; 12:1

12 And immediately the spirit driveth him into the wilderness.

13 And he was there in the wilderness forty days, tempted of Satan; and was with the wild beasts; ᴿand the angels ministered unto him.   Matt. 4:10, 11

14 ᴿNow after that John was put in prison, Jesus came into Galilee, ᴿpreaching the gospel of the kingdom of God,   Matt. 4:12 · Matt. 4:23

15 And saying, ᴿThe time is fulfilled, and ᴿthe kingdom of God is at hand: repent ye, and believe the gospel. [Gal. 4:4]; Titus 1:3 · Matt. 3:2; 4:17

16 Now as he walked by the sea of Galilee, he saw Simon and Andrew his brother casting a net into the sea: for they were fishers.

17 And Jesus said unto them,

Come ye after me, and I will make you to become fishers of men.

18 And straightway they forsook their nets, and followed him.

19 And when he had gone a little farther thence, he saw James the son of Zeb′-e-dee, and John his brother, who also were in the ship mending their nets.

20 And straightway he called them: and they left their father Zeb′-e-dee in the ship with the hired servants, and went after him.

21 ᴿAnd they went into Ca-per′-na-um; and straightway on the sabbath day he entered into the synagogue, and taught.   Matt. 4:13

22 ᴿAnd they were astonished at his ᵀdoctrine: for he taught them as one that had authority, and not as the scribes.   Matt. 13:54 · *teaching*

23 And there was in their synagogue a man with an ᴿunclean spirit; and he cried out,   Luke 4:33

24 Saying, Let *us* alone; what have we to do with thee, thou Jesus of Nazareth? art thou come to destroy us? I know thee who thou art, the Holy One of God.

25 And Jesus ᴿrebuked him, saying, ᵀHold thy peace, and come out of him. [Luke 4:39] · Lit. *Be muzzled*

26 And when the unclean spirit had torn him, and cried with a loud voice, he came out of him.

27 And they were all amazed, insomuch that they questioned among themselves, saying, What thing is this? what new doctrine *is* this? for with authority commandeth he even the unclean spirits, and they do obey him.

28 And immediately his fame spread abroad throughout all the region round about Galilee.

29 ᴿAnd forthwith, when they were come out of the synagogue, they entered into the house of Simon and Andrew, with James and John.   Matt. 8:14, 15; Luke 4:38, 39

30 But Simon's wife's mother lay sick of a fever, and ᵀanon they tell him of her.   *at once*

31 And he came and took her by the hand, and lifted her up; and

immediately the fever left her, and she [T]ministered unto them.   *served*

32 And at even, when the sun did set, they brought unto him all that were diseased, and them that were possessed with devils.

33 And all the city was gathered together at the door.

34 And he healed many that were sick of [T]divers diseases, and cast out many devils; and suffered not the devils to speak, because they knew him.   *various*

35 And in the morning, rising up a great while before day, he went out, and departed into a [T]solitary place, and there prayed.   *deserted*

36 And Simon and they that were with him [T]followed after him.   *searched for*

37 And when they had found him, they said unto him, [R]All *men* seek for thee.   Matt. 4:25; John 3:26

38 And he said unto them, [R]Let us go into the next towns, that I may preach there also: for [R]therefore came I forth.   Luke 4:43 · [10:45]

39 And he preached in their synagogues throughout all Galilee, and [R]cast out devils.   5:8, 13; 7:29, 30

40 And there came a leper to him, beseeching him, and kneeling down to him, and saying unto him, If thou [T]wilt, thou canst make me clean.   *are willing*

41 And Jesus, moved with [R]compassion, put forth *his* hand, and touched him, and saith unto him, I will; be thou clean.   Luke 7:13

42 And as soon as he had spoken, [R]immediately the leprosy departed from him, and he was cleansed.   5:29; Matt. 15:28

43 And he straitly charged him, and forthwith sent him away;

44 And saith unto him, See thou say nothing to any man: but go thy way, shew thyself to the priest, and offer for thy cleansing those things which Moses commanded, for a testimony unto them.

45 But he went out, and began to publish *it* much, and to [T]blaze abroad the matter, insomuch that Jesus could no more openly enter into the city, but was without in desert places: and they came to him from every quarter.   *spread*

2 And again [R]he entered into Ca-per'-na-um after *some* days; and it was [T]noised that he was in the house.   Matt. 9:1 · *heard*

2 And straightway many were gathered together, insomuch that there was no room to receive *them*, no, [T]not so much as about the door: and he preached the word unto them.   *not even near*

3 And they come unto him, bringing one sick of [T]the palsy, which was borne of four.   *paralysis*

4 And when they could not come [T]nigh unto him for the [T]press, they uncovered the roof where he was: and when they had broken *it* up, they let down the bed wherein the [T]sick of the palsy lay.   *near · crowd · paralytic*

5 When Jesus saw their faith, he said unto the sick of the palsy, Son, thy sins be forgiven thee.

6 But there were certain of the scribes sitting there, and reasoning in their hearts,

7 Why doth this *man* thus speak blasphemies? [R]who can forgive sins but God only?   Is. 43:25

8 And immediately when Jesus perceived in his spirit that they so reasoned within themselves, he said unto them, Why reason ye these things in your hearts?

9 [R]Whether is it easier to say to the sick of the palsy, *Thy* sins be forgiven thee; or to say, Arise, and take up thy bed, and walk? Matt. 9:5

10 But that ye may know that the Son of man hath [T]power on earth to forgive sins, (he saith to the sick of the palsy,)   *authority*

11 I say unto thee, Arise, and take up thy bed, and go thy way into thine house.

12 And immediately he arose, took up the bed, and went forth before them all; insomuch that they were all amazed, and glorified God, saying, We never saw [T]it on this fashion.   *anything like this*

13 [R]And he went forth again by the sea side; and all the multitude

ᵀresorted unto him, and he taught them.   Matt. 9:9 · *came*

14 And as he passed by, he saw Levi the *son* of Al-phae′-us sitting at the ᵀreceipt of custom, and said unto him, Follow me. And he arose and followed him.   *tax office*

15 And it came to pass, that, as Jesus ᵀsat at meat in his house, many publicans and sinners sat also together with Jesus and his disciples: for there were many, and they followed him.   *was dining*

16 And when the scribes and Pharisees saw him eat with publicans and sinners, they said unto his disciples, How is it that he eateth and drinketh with publicans and sinners?

17 When Jesus heard *it*, he saith unto them, ᴿThey that are whole have no need of the physician, but they that are sick: I came not to call the righteous, but sinners to repentance.   Matt. 9:12, 13; 18:11

18 ᴿAnd the disciples of John and of the Pharisees used to fast: and they come and say unto him, Why do the disciples of John and of the Pharisees fast, but thy disciples fast not?   Luke 5:33–38

19 And Jesus said unto them, Can the children of the bridechamber fast, while the bridegroom is with them? *as long as* they have the bridegroom with them, they cannot fast.

20 But the days will come, when the bridegroom shall be ᴿtaken away from them, and then shall they fast in those days.   Acts 1:9

21 No man also seweth a piece of new cloth on an old garment: else the new piece that filled it up taketh away from the old, and the ᵀrent is made worse.   *tear*

22 And no man putteth new wine into old bottles: else the new wine doth burst the bottles, and the wine is spilled, and the bottles will be marred: but new wine must be put into new bottles.

23 And it came to pass, that he went through the corn fields on the sabbath day; and his disciples began, as they went, to pluck the ᵀears of corn.   *heads of grain*

24 And the Pharisees said unto him, Behold, why do they on the sabbath day that which is ᴿnot lawful?   Ex. 20:10; 31:15

25 And he said unto them, Have ye never read ᴿwhat David did, when he had need, and was ᵀan hungred, he, and they that were with him?   1 Sam. 21:1–6 · *hungry*

26 How he went into the house of God in the days of A-bi′-a-thar the high priest, and did eat the shewbread, ᴿwhich is not lawful to eat but for the priests, and gave also to them which were with him?   Ex. 29:32, 33; Lev. 24:5–9

27 And he said unto them, The sabbath was made for man, and not man for the ᴿsabbath: Ex. 23:12

28 Therefore ᴿthe Son of man is Lord also of the sabbath. Matt. 12:8

3 And ᴿhe entered again into the synagogue; and there was a man there which had a withered hand.   Matt. 12:9–14; Luke 6:6–11

2 And they ᴿwatched him, whether he would ᴿheal him on the sabbath day; that they might accuse him.   Luke 14:1 · Luke 13:14

3 And he saith unto the man which had the withered hand, ᵀStand forth.   Lit. *Arise to the middle*

4 And he saith unto them, Is it lawful to do good on the sabbath days, or to do evil? to save life, or to kill? But they held their peace.

5 And when he had looked round about on them with anger, being grieved for the ᴿhardness of their hearts, he saith unto the man, Stretch forth thine hand. And he stretched *it* out: and his hand was restored whole as the other.   Zech. 7:12

6 And the Pharisees went ★ forth, and straightway took counsel with the He-ro′-di-ans against him, how they might destroy him.

7 But Jesus withdrew himself with his disciples to the sea: and a great multitude from Galilee followed him, and from Ju-dae′-a,

8 And from Jerusalem, and

PALESTINE IN JESUS' DAY

Mediterranean Sea

Capernaum
GALILEE   Sea of
• Cana   Galilee
Nazareth
Nain •

Decapolis

SAMARIA
•
Samaria

Jordan River

PERAEA

Beth-el
•
Jericho •
Jerusalem •

Beth-lehem •

Dead Sea

JUDAEA

Jesus never traveled very far from His hometown of Nazareth in Galilee. But everywhere He went, He brought joy, peace, and healing.

In Cana, He attended a wedding where He helped the hostess when she ran out of refreshments (John 2:1–11).

In Capernaum, He invited Matthew to be His disciple (Mark 2:14), healed a soldier's paralyzed servant (Matthew 8:5–13), and healed Peter's mother-in-law of a fever (Matthew 8:14, 15).

In a boat on the Sea of Galilee, He quieted a storm and saved His disciples from capsizing in the high waves (Mark 4:35–41).

In Samaria, He healed ten lepers (Luke 17:11–19).

In Jericho, He restored the sight of a blind man (Luke 18:35–43) and went home with Zacchaeus, the tax collector (Luke 19:1–10).

"Jesus went about doing good" (see Acts 10:38).

THE LAND OF THE GOSPELS

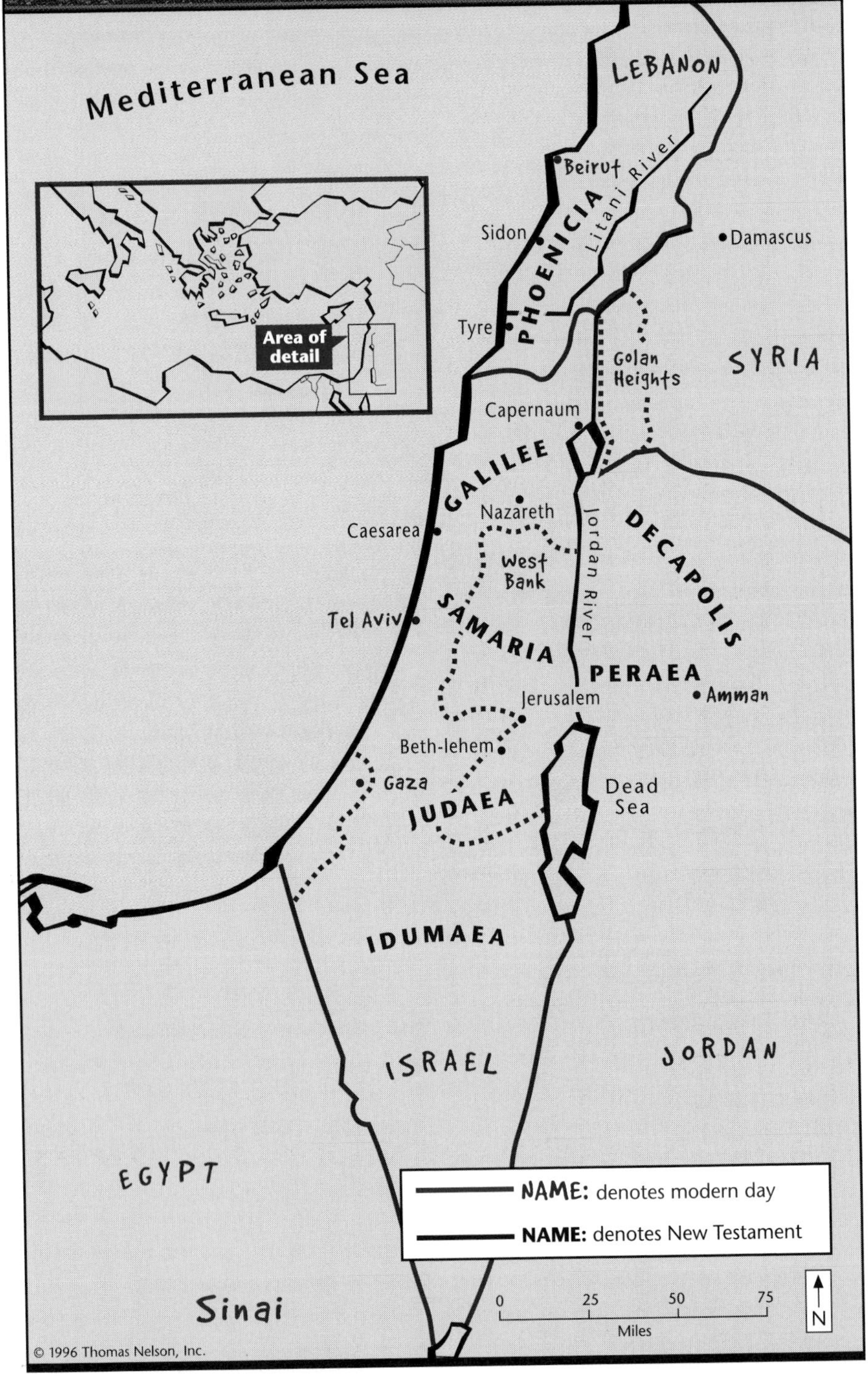

Mediterranean Sea

LEBANON

Beirut

Litani River

Sidon

•Damascus

PHOENICIA

Tyre

SYRIA

Golan
Heights

Capernaum

GALILEE

DECAPOLIS

Nazareth

Caesarea

Jordan River

West
Bank

Tel Aviv

SAMARIA

PERAEA

Jerusalem

•Amman

Beth-lehem

Gaza

Dead
Sea

JUDAEA

IDUMAEA

ISRAEL

JORDAN

EGYPT

Area of detail

NAME:	denotes modern day
NAME:	denotes New Testament

Sinai

0　　25　　50　　75
Miles

N

© 1996 Thomas Nelson, Inc.

THE LIFE OF MARY

1 Mary traveled with Joseph to Beth-lehem, and Christ was born (Luke 2:1–7).

2 The Baby Jesus was presented at the temple in Jerusalem. The prophetess Anna bore witness to the work He was sent to do in Jerusalem (Luke 2:22–38).

3 The family received the Magi in Beth-lehem (Matt. 2:1–11).

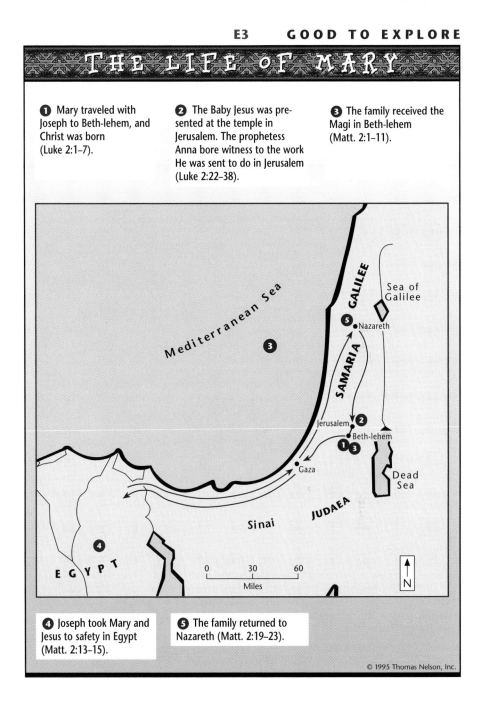

4 Joseph took Mary and Jesus to safety in Egypt (Matt. 2:13–15).

5 The family returned to Nazareth (Matt. 2:19–23).

© 1995 Thomas Nelson, Inc.

FOUR TYPES OF HOUSES

In Bible times, there were four basic kinds of houses.

Caves

During every period of Bible history, at least some people lived in caves—for example, in the limestone hills of central Israel, and in the Qumran region where the Dead Sea scrolls were discovered. Cave dwellings required little maintenance, and they were cool in the summer and warm in winter. Caves were also used as stables for livestock. According to some scholars, the stable in Beth-lehem where Jesus was born was actually a cave.

Tents

Those people who had to move their herd animals from place to place in order to find grass for the herds to eat, usually lived in tents because they were easy to move. In the days of the Old Testament patriarchs, tents were probably made from animal skins. Later they were made of goat hair fabric, which was waterproof and flexible. Some tent dwellers lived in tents for part of the year and in permanent houses during the rest of the year. Farmers, for example, might live in the city except during the growing season, when they lived in tents set up close to their fields.

Tents were still in common use in the first century A.D. The early church leaders Priscilla, Aquila, and Paul were tentmakers (Acts 18:2, 3). In fact, Paul's hometown of Tarsus was well known as a center of the tentmaking trade (see Acts 11:25).

Mud Houses

In the Canaanite city-states, there were a few large houses, but most of the people lived in small, one-room homes of mud brick built on top of one another. The mud bricks were covered with plaster, giving them a beehive appearance.

The Four-Room House

After settling in Canaan, the Israelites developed a style of house that had four rooms arranged around an open courtyard. Entrance into the home was through a door leading into the courtyard. Sometimes one or both of the long rooms flanking the courtyard were open on the side facing the courtyard, with several stone pillars supporting the roof.

These rectangular-shaped houses averaged about 900 to 1,000 square feet in area, with about one-fourth of that given to the courtyard. Many houses had second stories, almost doubling their size.

The roof was usually constructed on logs or beams laid across the top of the walls. Branches and thatch were laid on top of the beams and covered with a layer of clay. Since it was flat, the roof became a vital part of the house. An outside staircase gave easy access, and a low wall around the roof kept members of the family from falling off. In a crowded city, the roof provided needed open space. It was a place to dry fruit and grains, wash clothes, and catch a cool evening breeze on a hot night. Sometimes an extra room was added on the roof to serve as a spare bedroom (2 Kings 4:8–11).

WHAT KIND OF STORM WAS THIS?

The Sea of Galilee was no place to be caught in a storm. The kind of weather that caught Jesus and His disciples occurs there to this day. As one traveler described it:

> "The sun had scarcely set when the wind began to rush down towards the lake, and it continued all night long, with increasing violence, so that when we reached the shore the next morning the face of the lake was like a huge, boiling caldron ... .

> "We had to double-pin all the tent-ropes, and frequently were obliged to hang on with our whole weight upon them to keep the quivering tabernacle from being carried up bodily into the air.".

The reason for such gale-force winds is the surrounding landscape. The lake is 700 feet below sea level, and is fed by rivers that have cut deep ravines surrounded by flat plains that are in turn hedged in by mountains. The ravines act like wind siphons or tunnels, gathering cooler air from the mountains as it crosses the plains. When the air mass runs into the hot lake shore, violent storms are whipped up with no warning.

Several of the disciples were experienced fishermen, well acquainted with such storms. However, they had never seen winds like those that attacked their boat (Luke 8:23), for they turned to the Lord in utter terror, certain that all was lost. Yet their fear of the wind and the waves gave way to wonder and awe when Jesus turned and calmed the sea.

WHY IT STORMS OVER GALILEE

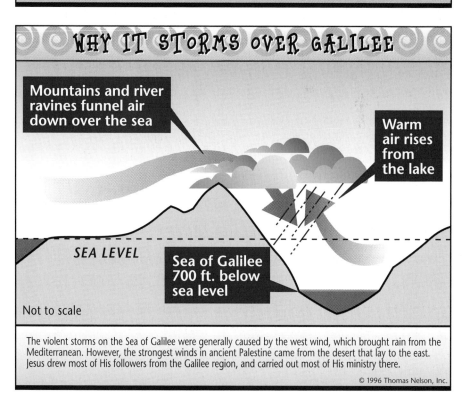

Mountains and river ravines funnel air down over the sea

Warm air rises from the lake

SEA LEVEL

Sea of Galilee 700 ft. below sea level

Not to scale

The violent storms on the Sea of Galilee were generally caused by the west wind, which brought rain from the Mediterranean. However, the strongest winds in ancient Palestine came from the desert that lay to the east. Jesus drew most of His followers from the Galilee region, and carried out most of His ministry there.

THE LIFE OF JESUS

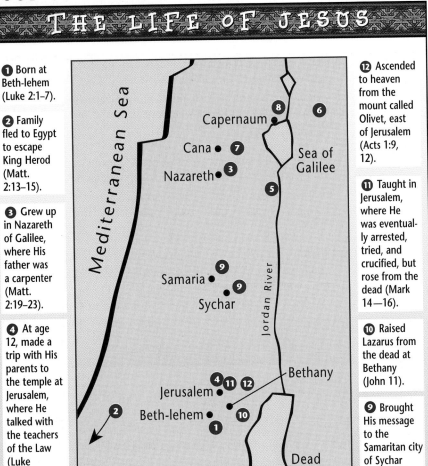

1 Born at Beth-lehem (Luke 2:1–7).

2 Family fled to Egypt to escape King Herod (Matt. 2:13–15).

3 Grew up in Nazareth of Galilee, where His father was a carpenter (Matt. 2:19–23).

4 At age 12, made a trip with His parents to the temple at Jerusalem, where He talked with the teachers of the Law (Luke 2:41–50).

5 Was baptized in the Jordan River by John the Baptist (Matt. 3:13–17; John 1:29–34).

6 Went into the wilderness for 40 days, where He was tested by Satan (Matt. 4:1–11).

7 Started His ministry in Galilee by turning water into wine at Cana (John 2:1–11), preaching in His hometown of Nazareth (Luke 4:16–30), and healing in and around Capernaum; His fame spread as far north as Syria (Matt. 4:23–25).

8 Called twelve men to follow Him as His disciples (Luke 6:12–16) and delivered the Sermon on the Mount (Matt. 5—7; Luke 6:20–49).

9 Brought His message to the Samaritan city of Sychar (John 4:1–42) and healed ten lepers of Samaria (Luke 17:11–19).

10 Raised Lazarus from the dead at Bethany (John 11).

11 Taught in Jerusalem, where He was eventually arrested, tried, and crucified, but rose from the dead (Mark 14—16).

12 Ascended to heaven from the mount called Olivet, east of Jerusalem (Acts 1:9, 12).

Map labels: Mediterranean Sea; Capernaum; Cana; Nazareth; Sea of Galilee; Samaria; Sychar; Jordan River; Jerusalem; Beth-lehem; Bethany; Dead Sea

0   15   30
Miles

N

PASSION WEEK

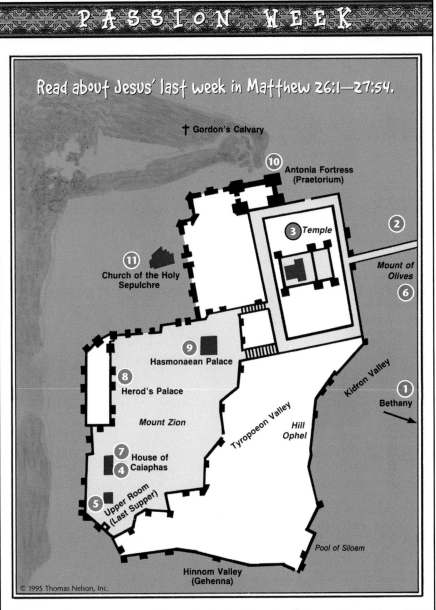

Read about Jesus' last week in Matthew 26:1—27:54.

† Gordon's Calvary

⑩ Antonia Fortress (Praetorium)

③ Temple

② Mount of Olives

⑥

⑪ Church of the Holy Sepulchre

⑨ Hasmonaean Palace

⑧ Herod's Palace

Kidron Valley

① Bethany

Mount Zion

Tyropoeon Valley

Hill Ophel

⑦
④ House of Caiaphas

⑤ Upper Room (Last Supper)

Pool of Siloam

Hinnom Valley (Gehenna)

© 1995 Thomas Nelson, Inc.

① Jesus stays with His friends—Mary, Martha, and Lazarus—in **Bethany**.

② Entering **Jerusalem** on a donkey, Jesus is greeted by happy people.

③ Going into the **temple**, Jesus drives out the money changers.

④ **House of Caiaphas** the high priest, the religious leaders plot to kill Jesus.

⑤ Jesus and His disciples celebrate the Passover in an **upper room**.

⑥ Jesus prays in the **Garden of Gethsemane**.

⑦ Jesus is arrested and taken to the **house of Caiaphas** for trial.

⑧ Jesus is moved to *Herod's palace** to appear before Pilate.

⑨ Governor Pilate sends Jesus to Herod who was probably living in the *Hasmonaean palace**.

⑩ After questioning, Herod returns Jesus to Pilate at the Praetorium in the **Fortress of Antonia**.

⑪ Jesus is sentenced to die on a cross at **Golgotha**. (The **Church of the Holy Sepulchre** is built over the traditional spot where He died.)

Some teachers think Herod and Pilate were living in these quarters during Jesus' last week on earth.

EVIDENCE FOR THE RESURRECTION— JESUS APPEARS TO MANY

Dead people don't ordinarily rise again. History stands on the fact that death is a fact, and no human can avoid it. But Jesus broke that cycle. He conquered death by rising from the grave (Mark 16:1–8) and verified His resurrection by appearing to many of His followers. Thus as Christians we can have hope in life after death, because Jesus broke the bondage of death (1 Corinthians 15:12–24, 35–58).

❶ AT THE TOMB. On early Sunday morning, Jesus appeared to Mary Magdalene, Mary the mother of James, and Salome (Matt. 28:1–10; Mark 16:1–11; Luke 24:1–12; John 20:1–18).

❷ AT JERUSALEM. Jesus appeared to Peter (Simon; Cephas) on Sunday (Luke 24:34; 1 Cor. 15:5).

❸ THE ROAD TO EMMAUS. About midday Sunday, Jesus appeared to two travelers (Luke 24:13–32).

❹ THE UPPER ROOM. Jesus appeared to the disciples on Sunday evening (Mark 16:14; Luke 24:36–43; John 20:19–25), and again one week later, when Thomas was present (John 20:26–29; 1 Cor. 15:5).

❺ THE ROAD TO DAMASCUS. Jesus confronted Saul of Tarsus in the middle of the day, an event that led to Saul's conversion (Acts 9:1–9; 1 Cor. 15:8).

❻ GALILEE. Jesus appeared to the eleven disciples in Galilee (Matt. 28:16–20; Mark 16:15–18). Later, He was seen by 500 followers, probably also in Galilee (1 Cor. 15:6).

❼ THE SEA OF GALILEE. Early one morning, Jesus appeared to seven of His disciples while they were fishing, and caused them to find a great catch of fish (John 21:1–23).

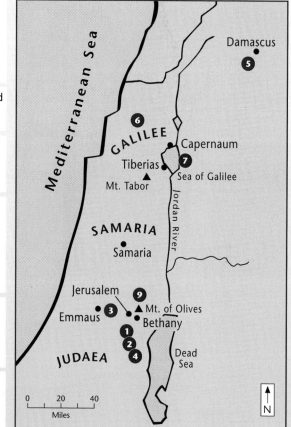

❽ LOCATION UNKNOWN. Jesus appeared to James the apostle (1 Cor. 15:7).

❾ THE MOUNT OF OLIVES. Forty days after the Resurrection, Jesus met with the eleven disciples, leading women, His brothers, and others, whom He told to take His message throughout the world. He then ascended into heaven (Luke 24:46–53; Acts 1:3–14).

from Id-u-mae'-a, and *from* beyond Jordan; and they about Tyre and Si'-don, a great multitude, when they had heard what ᴿgreat things he did, came unto him.   5:19

9   And he spake to his disciples, that a small ship should wait on him because of the multitude, lest they should ᵀthrong him.   *crush*

10 For he had healed many; insomuch that they pressed upon him for to ᴿtouch him, as many as had plagues.   Matt. 9:21; 14:36

11 ᴿAnd unclean spirits, when they saw him, fell down before him, and cried, saying, ᴿThou art the Son of God. 1:23, 24; Luke 4:41 · 5:7

12 And ᴿhe ᵀstraitly charged them that they should not make him known.   1:25, 34 · *strictly warned*

13 ᴿAnd he goeth up into a mountain, and calleth *unto him* whom he ᵀwould: and they came unto him.   Matt. 10:1; Luke 9:1 · *wanted*

14 And he ᵀordained twelve, that they should be with him, and that he might send them forth to preach,   *appointed*

15 And to have power to heal sicknesses, and to cast out devils:

16 And Simon ᴿhe ᵀsurnamed Peter;   Matt. 16:18 · *gave the name*

17 And James the *son* of Zeb'-e-dee, and John the brother of James; and he ᵀsurnamed them Bo-a-ner'-ges, which is, The sons of thunder: *gave them the name*

18 And Andrew, and Philip, and Bartholomew, and Matthew, and Thomas, and James the *son* of Al-phae'-us, and Thad-dae'-us, and Simon the Ca'-naan-ite,

19 And Judas Is-car'-i-ot, which also betrayed him: and they went into an house.

20 And the multitude cometh together again, ᴿso that they could not so much as eat bread.   6:31

21 And when his ᴿfriends heard *of it*, they went out to lay hold on him: ᴿfor they said, He is beside himself.   Matt. 13:55; John 2:12 · John 7:5

22 And the scribes which came down from Jerusalem said, ᴿHe hath Be-el'-ze-bub, and by the

prince of the devils casteth he out devils.   Luke 11:15; John 8:48, 52; 10:20

23 ᴿAnd he called them *unto him*, and said unto them in parables, How can Satan cast out Satan?   Matt. 12:25–29; Luke 11:17–22

24 And if a kingdom be divided against itself, that kingdom cannot stand.

25 And if a house be divided against itself, that house cannot stand.

26 And if Satan rise up against himself, and be divided, he cannot stand, but hath an end.

27 ᴿNo man can enter into a strong man's house, and ᵀspoil his goods, except he will first bind the strong man; and then he will ᵀspoil his house.   Matt. 12:29 · *plunder*

28 ᴿVerily I say unto you, All sins shall be forgiven unto the sons of men, and blasphemies wherewith soever they shall blaspheme: Matt. 12:31, 32; Luke 12:10

29 But he that shall blaspheme against the Holy Ghost hath never forgiveness, but is in danger of eternal ᵀdamnation: *condemnation*

30 Because they ᴿsaid, He hath an unclean spirit.   Matt. 9:34; John 7:2

31 ᴿThere came then his ᵀbrethren and his mother, and, standing ᵀwithout, sent unto him, calling him.   Luke 8:19–21 · *brothers · outside*

32 And the multitude sat about him, and they said unto him, Behold, thy mother and thy brethren without seek for thee.

33 And he answered them, saying, Who is my mother, or my ᵀbrethren?   *brothers*

34 And he looked round about on them which ᵀsat about him, and said, Behold my mother and my brethren!   *sat in a circle about*

35 For whosoever shall do the will of God, the same is my brother, and my sister, and mother.

4 And ᴿhe began again to teach by the sea side: and there was gathered unto him a great multitude, so that he entered into a ship, and sat in the sea; and the whole multitude was by the sea on the land.   Matt. 13:1–15; Luke 8:4–10

2 And he taught them many things by parables, ᴿand said unto them in his ᵀdoctrine, 12:38 · *teaching*

3 Hearken; Behold, there went out a sower to sow:

4 And it came to pass, as he sowed, some fell by the way side, and the fowls of the air came and devoured it up.

5 And some fell on stony ground, where it had not much earth; and immediately it sprang up, because it had no depth of earth:

6 But when the sun was up, it was scorched; and because it had no root, it withered away.

7 And some fell among thorns, and the thorns grew up, and choked it, and it yielded no fruit.

8 And other fell on good ground, and did yield fruit that sprang up and increased; and brought forth, some thirty, and some sixty, and some an hundred.

9 And he said unto them, He that hath ears to hear, let him hear.

10 And when he was alone, they that were about him with the twelve asked of him the parable.

11 And he said unto them, Unto you it is given to know the mystery of the kingdom of God: but unto them that are without, all *these* things are done in parables:

★ 12 ᴿThat seeing they may see, and not perceive; and hearing they may hear, and not understand; lest at any time they should be converted, and *their* sins should be forgiven them. Is. 6:9, 10

13 And he said unto them, ᵀKnow ye not this parable? and how then will ye ᵀknow all parables? *Understand*

14 The sower soweth the word.

15 And these are they by the way side, where the word is sown; but when they have heard, Satan cometh immediately, and taketh away the word that was sown in their hearts.

16 And these are they likewise which are sown on stony ground;

who, when they have heard the word, immediately receive it with gladness;

17 And have no root in themselves, and so endure but for a time: afterward, when affliction or persecution ariseth for the word's sake, immediately they are ᵀoffended.   *caused to stumble*

18 And these are they which are sown among thorns; such as hear the word,

19 And the ᴿcares of this world, and the deceitfulness of riches, and the lusts of other things entering in, choke the word, and it becometh unfruitful.   Luke 21:34

20 And these are they which are sown on good ground; such as hear the word, and receive *it*, and bring forth fruit, some thirtyfold, some sixty, and some an hundred.

21 ᴿAnd he said unto them, Is a candle brought to be put under a bushel, or under a bed? and not to be set on a candlestick?   Matt. 5:15

22 For there is nothing hid, which shall not be manifested; neither was any thing kept secret, but that it should come abroad.

23 ᴿIf any man have ears to hear, let him hear. Rev. 3:6, 13, 22; 13:9

24 And he said unto them, Take heed what ye hear: with what measure ye ᵀmete, it shall be measured to you: and unto you that hear shall more be given. *use*

25 ᴿFor he that hath, to him shall be given: and he that hath not, from him shall be taken even that which he hath.   Matt. 13:12; Luke 8:18

26 And he said, So is the kingdom of God, as if a man should cast seed ᵀinto the ground;   *upon*

27 And should sleep, and rise night and day, and the seed should spring and ᴿgrow up, he knoweth not how.   [2 Cor. 3:18]

28 For the earth bringeth forth fruit of herself; first the blade, then the ear, after that the full ᵀcorn in the ear.   *grain in the head*

29 But when the fruit ᵀis brought forth, immediately ᴿhe putteth in the sickle, because the harvest is come.   *ripens* · [13:30, 39]; Rev. 14:15

30 And he said, ᴿWhereunto shall we liken the kingdom of God? or with what comparison shall we compare it? [Acts 2:41; 4:4]
31 It is like a grain of mustard seed, which, when it is sown in the earth, is ᵀless than all the seeds that be in the earth: *smaller*
32 But when it is sown, it groweth up, and becometh greater than all herbs, and shooteth out great branches; so that the ᵀfowls of the air may lodge under ᵀthe shadow of it. *birds · its shade*
33 And with many such parables spake he the word unto them, as they were able to hear it.
34 But without a parable spake he not unto them: and when they were alone, he ᵀexpounded all things to his disciples. *explained*
35 ᴿAnd the same day, when the ᵀeven was come, he saith unto them, Let us pass over unto the other side. Matt. 8:18, 23–27 · *evening*
36 And when they had sent away the multitude, they took him even as he was in the ship. And there were also with him other little ships.
37 And there arose a great storm of wind, and the waves beat into the ship, so that it was ᵀnow full. *already filling*
38 And he was in the ᵀhinder part of the ship, asleep on a pillow: and they awake him, and say unto him, Master, ᴿcarest thou not that we perish? *stern · Ps. 44:23*
39 And he arose, and ᴿrebuked the wind, and said unto the sea, ᴿPeace, be still. And the wind ceased, and there was a great calm. Luke 4:39 · Ps. 89:9; 93:4; 104:6, 7
40 And he said unto them, Why are ye so fearful? ᴿhow is it that ye have no faith? Matt. 14:31, 32; Luke 8:25
41 And they feared exceedingly, and said one to another, What manner of man is this, that even the wind and the sea obey him?

5 And they came over unto the other side of the sea, into the country of the Gad-a-renes'.
2 And when he was come out of the ship, immediately there met

him out of the tombs a man with an ᴿunclean spirit, 1:23; 7:25
3 Who had his dwelling among the tombs; and no man could bind him, no, not with chains:
4 Because that he had been often bound with ᵀfetters and chains, and the chains had been plucked asunder by him, and the fetters broken in pieces: neither could any man tame him. *shackles*
5 And always, night and day, he was in the mountains, and in the tombs, crying, and cutting himself with stones.
6 But when he saw Jesus afar off, he ran and worshipped him,
7 And cried with a loud voice, and said, What have I to do with thee, Jesus, thou Son of the most high God? I ᵀadjure thee by God, that thou torment me not. *implore*
8 For he said unto him, ᴿCome out of the man, thou unclean spirit. 1:25; 9:25; [Acts 16:18]
9 And he asked him, What is thy name? And he answered, saying, My name is Legion: for we are many.
10 And he besought him much that he would not send them away out of the country.
11 Now there was there ᵀnigh unto the mountains a great herd of ᴿswine feeding. *near · Lev. 11:7, 8*
12 And all the ᵀdevils ᵀbesought him, saying, Send us into the swine, that we may enter into them. *demons · begged*
13 And forthwith Jesus gave them leave. And the unclean spirits went out, and entered into the swine: and the herd ran violently down a steep place into the sea, (they were about two thousand;) and were choked in the sea.
14 And they that fed the swine fled, and told it in the city, and in the country. And they went out to see what it was that was done.
15 And they come to Jesus, and see him that was ᴿpossessed with the devil, and had the legion, sitting, and clothed, and in his right mind: and they were afraid. 1:32
16 And they that saw it told

them how it befell to him that was possessed with the [T]devil, and *also* concerning the swine. *demon*

17 And they began to pray him to depart out of their coasts.

18 And when he was come into the ship, he that had been possessed with the devil prayed him that he might be with him.

19 Howbeit Jesus [T]suffered him not, but saith unto him, Go home to thy friends, and tell them how great things the Lord hath done for thee, and hath had compassion on thee. *did not permit*

20 And he departed, and began to publish in De-cap'-o-lis how great things Jesus had done for him: and all *men* did marvel.

21 [R]And when Jesus was passed over again by ship unto the other side, much people gathered unto him: and he was [T]nigh unto the sea. *Matt. 9:1; Luke 8:40 · near*

22 [R]And, behold, there cometh one of the rulers of the synagogue, Ja-i'-rus by name; and when he saw him, he fell at his feet, *Matt. 9:18–26; Luke 8:41–56; Acts 13:15*

23 And [T]besought him greatly, saying, My little daughter lieth at the point of death: *I pray thee,* come and lay thy hands on her, that she may be healed; and she shall live. *begged him earnestly*

24 And *Jesus* went with him; and [T]much people followed him, and thronged him. *a great multitude*

25 And a certain woman, [R]which had an [T]issue of blood twelve years, *Lev. 15:19, 25; Matt. 9:20 · a flow*

26 And had suffered many things of many physicians, and had spent all that she had, and was [T]nothing bettered, but rather grew worse, *no better*

27 When she had heard of Jesus, came in the [T]press behind, and [R]touched his garment. *crowd · 3:10*

28 For she said, If I may touch but his clothes, I shall be whole.

29 And straightway the fountain of her blood was dried up; and she felt in *her* body that she was healed of that [T]plague. *affliction*

30 And Jesus, immediately knowing in himself that [T]virtue had gone out of him, turned him about in the [T]press, and said, Who touched my clothes? *power · crowd*

31 And his disciples said unto him, Thou seest the multitude thronging thee, and sayest thou, Who touched me?

32 And he looked round about to see her that had done this thing.

33 But the woman [R]fearing and trembling, knowing what was done in her, came and fell down before him, and told him all the truth. *[Ps. 89:7]*

34 And he said unto her, Daughter, [R]thy faith hath made thee whole; [R]go in peace, and be whole of thy plague. *Acts 14:9 · Acts 16:36*

35 [R]While he yet spake, there came from the ruler of the synagogue's *house certain* which said, Thy daughter is dead: why troublest thou the [T]Master any further? *Luke 8:49 · Teacher*

36 As soon as Jesus heard the word that was spoken, he saith unto the ruler of the synagogue, Be not afraid, only [R]believe. *[9:23]*

37 And he suffered no man to follow him, save Peter, and James, and John the brother of James.

38 And he cometh to the house of the ruler of the synagogue, and seeth the tumult, and them that [R]wept and wailed greatly. *16:10*

39 And when he was come in, he saith unto them, Why make ye this ado, and weep? the damsel is not dead, but [R]sleepeth. *John 11:4, 11*

40 And they laughed him to scorn. [R]But when he had put them all out, he taketh the father and the mother of the damsel, and them that were with him, and entereth in where the damsel was lying. *Acts 9:40*

41 And he took the damsel by the hand, and said unto her, Tal'-i-tha cu'-mi; which is, [T]being interpreted, [T]Damsel, I say unto thee, arise. *translated · Little girl*

42 And straightway the damsel arose, and walked; for she was *of the age* of twelve years. And they

were [R]astonished with a great astonishment. 1:27; 7:37
43 And he charged them [T]straitly that no man should know it; and commanded that something should be given her to eat. *strictly*

6 And [R]he went out from thence, and came into his own country; and his disciples follow him. Matt. 13:54; Luke 4:16
2 And when the sabbath day was come, he began to teach in the synagogue: and many hearing *him* were astonished, saying, From whence hath this *man* these things? and what wisdom *is* this which is given unto him, that even such mighty works are [T]wrought by his hands? *performed*
3 Is not this the carpenter, the son of Mary, [R]the brother of James, and Jo'-ses, and of Juda, and Simon? and are not his sisters here with us? And they were offended at him. Matt. 12:46
4 But Jesus said unto them, A prophet is not without honour, but in his own country, and among his own kin, and in his own house.
5 [R]And he could there do no mighty work, save that he laid his hands upon a few sick folk, and healed *them*. Gen. 32:25; Matt. 13:58
6 And [R]he marvelled because of their unbelief. [R]And he went round about the villages, teaching. [Heb. 3:18, 19; 4:2] · Acts 10:38
7 And he called *unto him* the twelve, and began to send them forth by two and two; and gave them power over unclean spirits;
8 And commanded them that they should take nothing for *their* journey, save a staff only; no [T]scrip, no bread, no money in *their* purse: *bag*
9 But *be* shod with sandals; and not put on two [T]coats. *tunics*
10 [R]And he said unto them, In what place soever ye enter into an house, there abide till ye depart from that place. Matt. 10:11; Luke 9:4
11 [R]And whosoever shall not receive you, nor hear you, when ye depart thence, [R]shake off the dust under your feet for a testi-

mony against them. Verily I say unto you, It shall be more tolerable for Sodom and Go-mor'-rha in the day of judgment, than for that city. Matt. 10:14; Luke 10:10 · Acts 13:51
12 And they went out, and preached that men should repent.
13 And they cast out many [T]devils, [R]and anointed with oil many that were sick, and healed *them*. demons · [James 5:14]
14 [R]And king Herod heard *of him;* (for his name was spread abroad:) and he said, That John the Baptist was risen from the dead, and therefore [R]mighty works do shew forth themselves in him. Luke 9:7–9 · Luke 19:37
15 [R]Others said, That it is E-li'-as. And others said, That it is a [R]prophet, or as one of the prophets. Matt. 16:14; Luke 9:19 · Matt. 21:11
16 [R]But when Herod heard *thereof*, he said, It is John, whom I beheaded: he is risen from the dead. Matt. 14:2; Luke 3:19
17 For Herod himself had sent forth and laid hold upon John, and bound him in prison for He-ro'-di-as' sake, his brother Philip's wife: for he had married her.
18 For John had said unto Herod, [R]It is not lawful for thee to have thy brother's wife. Lev. 18:16
19 Therefore He-ro'-di-as had a quarrel against him, and would have killed him; but she could not:
20 For Herod [R]feared John, knowing that he was a just man and an [T]holy, and [T]observed him; and when he heard him, he did many things, and heard him gladly. Matt. 14:5; 21:26 · holy man · protected
21 And when a convenient day was come, that Herod on his birthday made a supper [T]to his lords, high captains, and chief estates of Galilee; for his nobles
22 And when the daughter of the said He-ro'-di-as came in, and danced, and pleased Herod and them that sat with him, the king said unto the damsel, Ask of me whatsoever [T]thou wilt, and I will give *it* thee. you want
23 And he sware unto her,

RWhatsoever thou shalt ask of me, I will give *it* thee, unto the half of my kingdom. Esth. 5:3, 6; 7:2

24 And she went forth, and said unto her mother, What shall I ask? And she said, The head of John the Baptist.

25 And she came in straightway with haste unto the king, and asked, saying, I will that thou give me Tby and by in a charger the head of John the Baptist. *at once*

26 And the king was exceeding sorry; *yet* for his oath's sake, and for their sakes which sat with him, he would not reject her.

27 And immediately the king sent an executioner, and commanded his head to be brought: and he went and beheaded him in the prison,

28 And brought his head Tin a charger, and gave it to the damsel: and the damsel gave it to her mother. *on a platter*

29 And when his disciples heard *of it,* they came and took up his corpse, and laid it in a tomb.

30 RAnd the apostles gathered themselves together unto Jesus, and told him all things, both what they had done, and what they had taught. Luke 9:10

31 RAnd he said unto them, Come ye yourselves apart into a desert place, and rest a while: for Rthere were many coming and going, and they had no leisure so much as to eat. Matt. 14:13 · 3:20

32 And they departed into a desert place by ship privately.

33 And the people saw them departing, and many Rknew him, and ran afoot thither out of all cities, and outwent them, and came together unto him. [Col. 1:6]

34 And Jesus, when he came out, saw much people, and was moved with compassion toward them, because they were as sheep not having a shepherd: and he began to teach them many things.

35 RAnd when the day was now far spent, his disciples came unto him, and said, This is a desert place, and now the time *is* far passed: Matt. 14:15; Luke 9:12

36 Send them away, that they may go into the country round about, and into the villages, and buy themselves bread: for they have nothing to eat.

37 He answered and said unto them, Give ye them to eat. And they say unto him, RShall we go and buy two hundred Tpennyworth of bread, and give them to eat? Num. 11:13, 22; 2 Kin. 4:43 · Gr. *denarii*

38 He saith unto them, How many loaves have ye? go and see. And when they knew, they say, RFive, and two fishes. Matt. 14:17

39 And he Rcommanded them to make all sit down by Tcompanies upon the green grass. 8:6 · *in groups*

40 And they sat down in ranks, by hundreds, and by fifties.

41 And when he had taken the five loaves and the two fishes, he looked up to heaven, Rand blessed, and brake the loaves, and gave *them* to his disciples to set before them; and the two fishes divided he among them all. 8:7

42 And they did all eat, and were filled.

43 And they took up twelve baskets full of the fragments, and of the fishes.

44 And they that did eat of the loaves were about five thousand men.

45 And straightway he constrained his disciples to get into the ship, and to go to the other side before unto Beth-sa′-i-da, while he sent away the people.

46 And when he had sent them away, he Rdeparted into a mountain to pray. 1:35; Luke 5:16

47 And when even was come, the ship was in the midst of the sea, and he alone on the land.

48 And he saw them toiling in rowing; for the wind was Tcontrary unto them: and about the fourth watch of the night he cometh unto them, walking upon the sea, and Rwould have passed by them. *against* · Luke 24:28

49 But when they saw him walk-

ing upon the sea, they supposed it had been a spirit, and cried out:

50 For they all saw him, and were troubled. And immediately he talked with them, and saith unto them, ᴿBe of good cheer: it is I; be not ᴿafraid. John 16:33 · Is. 41:10

51 And he went up unto them into the ship; and the wind ceased: and they were sore ᴿamazed in themselves beyond measure, and wondered. 1:27; 2:12

52 For they considered not *the miracle* of the loaves: for their ᴿheart was hardened. 3:5; Is. 63:17

53 ᴿAnd when they had passed over, they came into the land of Gen-nes′-a-ret, and ᵀdrew to the shore. John 6:24, 25 · anchored

54 And when they were come out of the ship, straightway ᵀthey knew him, The people

55 And ran through that whole region round about, and began to carry about in beds those that were sick, where they heard he was.

56 And whithersoever he entered, into villages, or cities, or country, they laid the sick in the streets, and besought him that ᴿthey might touch if it were but the ᴿborder of his garment: and as many as touched him were made whole. [Acts 19:12] · Num. 15:38, 39

7 Then ᴿcame together unto him the Pharisees, and certain of the scribes, which came from Jerusalem. Matt. 15:1–20

2 And when they saw some of his disciples eat bread with defiled, that is to say, with unwashen, hands, they found fault.

3 For the Pharisees, and all the Jews, except they wash *their* hands oft, eat not, holding the ᴿtradition of the elders. Gal. 1:14

4 And *when they come* from the market, except they wash, they eat not. And many other things there be, which they have received to hold, *as* the washing of cups, and ᵀpots, brasen vessels, and of ᵀtables. pitchers · couches

5 ᴿThen the Pharisees and scribes asked him, Why walk not thy disciples according to the tra-

dition of the elders, but eat bread with unwashen hands? Matt. 15:2

6 He answered and said unto them, Well hath E-sa′-ias prophesied of you ᴿhypocrites, as it is written, ᴿThis people honoureth me with *their* lips, but their heart is far from me. Matt. 23:13–29 · Is. 29:13 ★

7 Howbeit in vain do they worship me, teaching ᵀfor doctrines the commandments of men. as

8 For laying aside the commandment of God, ye hold the tradition of men, *as* the washing of ᵀpots and cups: and many other such like things ye do. pitchers

9 And he said unto them, Full well ye ᴿreject the commandment of God, that ye may keep your own tradition. Is. 24:5; Jer. 7:23, 24

10 For Moses said, ᴿHonour thy father and thy mother; and, Whoso curseth father or mother, let him die the death: Ex. 20:12; Deut. 5:16

11 But ye say, If a man shall say to his father or mother, *It is* ᴿCor′-ban, that is to say, a gift, by whatsoever thou mightest be profited by me; *he shall be free.* Matt. 15:5

12 And ye ᵀsuffer him no more to do ᵀought for his father or his mother; allow · anything

13 Making the word of God of none effect through your tradition, which ye have delivered: and many such like things do ye.

14 ᴿAnd when he had called all the people *unto him,* he said unto them, Hearken unto me every one *of you,* and understand: Matt. 15:10

15 There is nothing from without a man, that entering into him can defile him: but the things which come out of him, those are they that ᴿdefile the man. Is. 59:3

16 ᴿIf any man have ears to hear, let him hear. Matt. 11:15

17 ᴿAnd when he was entered into the house from the people, his disciples asked him concerning the parable. Matt. 15:15

18 And he saith unto them, Are ye so without understanding also? Do ye not perceive, that whatsoever thing from without entereth into the man, *it* cannot defile him;

19 Because it entereth not into his heart, but into the belly, and goeth out into the draught, ᵀpurging all meats? *purifying all foods*

20 And he said, ᴿThat which cometh out of the man, that defileth the man. Ps. 39:1; [James 3:6]

21 ᴿFor from within, out of the heart of men, ᴿproceed evil thoughts, adulteries, fornications, murders, Jer. 17:9 · [Gal. 5:19–21]

22 Thefts, ᴿcovetousness, wickedness, deceit, lasciviousness, an evil eye, blasphemy, ᴿpride, foolishness: Luke 12:15 · 1 John 2:16

23 All these evil things come from within, and defile the man.

24 And from thence he arose, and went into the borders of Tyre and Si'-don, and entered into an house, and would have no man know *it*: but he could not be hid.

25 For a *certain* woman, whose young daughter had an unclean spirit, heard of him, and came and ᴿfell at his feet: John 11:32; Rev. 1:17

26 The woman was a ᵀGreek, a Sy-ro-phe-ni'-cian by ᵀnation; and she ᵀbesought him that he would cast forth the devil out of her daughter. *Gentile · birth · kept begging*

27 But Jesus said unto her, Let the children first be filled: for it is not ᵀmeet to take the children's bread, and to cast *it* unto the ᵀdogs. *Lit. good · little dogs*

28 And she answered and said unto him, Yes, Lord: yet the ᵀdogs under the table eat of the children's crumbs. *little dogs*

29 And he said unto her, For this saying go thy way; the ᵀdevil is gone out of thy daughter. *demon has*

30 And when she was come to her house, she found the ᵀdevil gone out, and her daughter laid upon the bed. *demon*

31 ᴿAnd again, departing from the coasts of Tyre and Si'-don, he came unto the sea of Galilee, through the midst of the coasts of De-cap'-o-lis. Matt. 15:29; Luke 23:46

32 And ᴿthey bring unto him one that was deaf, and had an impediment in his speech; and they ᵀbeseech him to put his hand upon him. Luke 11:14 · *begged*

33 And he took him aside from the multitude, and put his fingers into his ears, and ᴿhe spit, and touched his tongue; 8:23; John 9:6

34 And looking up to heaven, he sighed, and saith unto him, Eph'-pha-tha, that is, Be opened.

35 ᴿAnd straightway his ears were opened, and the ᵀstring of his tongue was loosed, and he spake plain. Is. 35:5, 6 · *impediment*

36 And ᴿhe ᵀcharged them that they should tell no man: but the more he charged them, so much the more ᵀa great deal they published *it*; 5:43 · *commanded · widely*

37 And were ᴿbeyond measure astonished, saying, He hath done all things well: he ᴿmaketh both the deaf to hear, and the ᵀdumb to speak. 6:51; 10:26 · Matt. 12:22 · *mute*

8 In those days ᴿthe multitude being very great, and having nothing to eat, Jesus called his disciples *unto him*, and saith unto them, Matt. 15:32–39; Luke 9:12

2 I have ᴿcompassion on the multitude, because they have now been with me three days, and have nothing to eat: Matt. 9:36; 14:14

3 And if I send them away fasting to their own houses, they will faint by the way: for ᵀdivers of them came from far. *some*

4 And his disciples answered him, ᵀFrom whence can a man satisfy these *men* with bread here in the wilderness? *How*

5 ᴿAnd he asked them, How many loaves have ye? And they said, Seven. Matt. 15:34; John 6:9

6 And he commanded the ᵀpeople to sit down on the ground: and he took the seven loaves, and gave thanks, and brake, and gave to his disciples to set before *them*; and they did set *them* before the ᵀpeople. *multitude*

7 And they had a few small fishes: and ᴿhe blessed, and commanded to set them also before *them*. 6:41; Matt. 14:19

8 So they did eat, and were filled: and they took up of the

^Tbroken *meat* that was left seven baskets. Fragments
9   And they that had eaten were about four thousand: and he sent them away.
10   And ^Rstraightway he entered into a ship with his disciples, and came into the parts of Dal-ma-nu'-tha.   Matt. 15:39
11   And the Pharisees came forth, and began to question with him, seeking of him a sign from heaven, ^Ttempting him.   testing
12   And he ^Rsighed deeply in his spirit, and saith, Why doth this generation seek after a sign? veri-ly I say unto you, There shall ^Rno sign be given unto this genera-tion.   7:34 · Matt. 12:39
13   And he left them, and enter-ing into the ship again departed to the other side.
14   ^RNow *the disciples* had for-gotten to take bread, neither had they in the ship with them more than one loaf.   Matt. 16:5
15   ^RAnd he charged them, say-ing, Take heed, beware of the ^Tleaven of the Pharisees, and *of* the leaven of Herod. Luke 12:1 · yeast
16   And they reasoned among themselves, saying, *It is* because we have no bread.
17   And when Jesus knew *it*, he saith unto them, Why reason ye, because ye have no bread? ^Rper-ceive ye not yet, neither under-stand? ^Thave ye your heart yet hardened?   6:52; 16:14 · is
18   Having eyes, see ye not? and having ears, hear ye not? and do ye not remember?
19   When I brake the five loaves among five thousand, how many baskets full of fragments took ye up? They say unto him, Twelve.
20   And ^Rwhen the seven among four thousand, how many baskets full of fragments took ye up? And they said, Seven.   Matt. 15:37
21   And he said unto them, How is it that ye do not understand?
22   And he cometh to Beth-sa'-i-da; and they bring a ^Rblind man unto him, and ^Tbesought him to touch him. Matt. 9:27; John 9:1 · begged

23   And he took the blind man by the hand, and led him out of the town; and when ^Rhe had spit on his eyes, and put his hands upon him, he asked him if he saw ^Tought.   7:33 · anything
24   And he looked up, and said, I see men as trees, walking.
25   After that he put *his* hands again upon his eyes, and made him look up: and he was restored, and saw every man clearly.
26   And he sent him away to his house, saying, Neither go into the town, ^Rnor tell *it* to any in the town.   5:43; 7:36; Matt. 8:4
27   ^RAnd Jesus went out, and his disciples, into the towns of Caes-a-re'-a Phi-lip'-pi: and by the way he asked his disciples, saying unto them, Whom do men say that I am?   Matt. 16:13-16; Luke 9:18-20
28   And they answered, ^RJohn the Baptist: but some *say*, ^RE-li'-as; and others, One of the proph-ets.   Matt. 14:2 · 6:14, 15; Luke 9:7, 8
29   And he saith unto them, But whom say ye that I am? And Peter answereth and saith unto him, ^RThou art the Christ.   John 4:42; 6:69
30   And he charged them that they should tell no man of him.
31   And he began to teach them, that the Son of man must suffer many things, and be ^Rrejected of the elders, and *of* the chief priests, and scribes, and be killed, and after three days rise again.   10:33
32   And he spake that saying openly. And Peter ^Ttook him, and began to rebuke him. took him aside
33   But when he had turned about and looked on his disciples, he ^Rrebuked Peter, saying, Get thee behind me, Satan: for thou savourest not the things that be of God, but the things that be of men.   16:14; [Rev. 3:19]
34   And when he had called the people *unto him* with his disciples also, he said unto them, ^RWhoso-ever will come after me, let him deny himself, and take up his cross, and follow me.   Luke 14:27
35   For ^Rwhosoever will save his life shall lose it; but whosoever

shall lose his life for my sake and the gospel's, the same shall save it. Matt. 10:39; Luke 17:33; John 12:25

36 For what shall it profit a man, if he shall gain the whole world, and lose his own soul?

37 Or what shall a man give in exchange for his soul?

38 Whosoever therefore shall be ashamed of me and of my words in this adulterous and sinful generation; of him also shall the Son of man be ashamed, when he cometh in the glory of his Father with the holy angels.

9 And he said unto them, Verily I say unto you, That there be some of them that stand here, which shall not taste of death, till they have seen the kingdom of God come with power.

2 ᴿAnd after six days Jesus taketh *with him* Peter, and James, and John, and leadeth them up into an high mountain apart by themselves: and he was transfigured before them. Luke 9:28–36

3 And his raiment became shining, exceeding ᴿwhite as snow; so as no ᵀfuller on earth can white them. Dan. 7:9 · *launderer*

4 And there appeared unto them E-li'-as with Moses: and they were talking with Jesus.

5 And Peter answered and said to Jesus, Master, it is good for us to be here: and let us make three tabernacles; one for thee, and one for Moses, and one for E-li'-as.

6 For he ᵀwist not what to say; for they were sore afraid. *knew*

★ 7 And there was a cloud that overshadowed them: and a voice came out of the cloud, saying, This is my beloved Son: hear him.

8 And suddenly, when they had looked round about, they saw no man any more, ᵀsave Jesus only with themselves. *except*

9 ᴿAnd as they came down from the mountain, he charged them that they should tell no man what things they had seen, till the Son of man were risen from the dead. Matt. 17:9–13; Luke 24:6, 7, 46

10 And they kept that saying with themselves, questioning one with another what the rising from the dead ᵀshould mean. *meant*

11 And they asked him, saying, Why say the scribes ᴿthat E-li'-as must first come? Mal. 4:5; Matt. 17:10

12 And he answered and told ☆ them, E-li'-as verily cometh first, and restoreth all things; and ᴿhow it is written of the Son of man, that he must suffer many things, and be set at nought. Ps. 22:6; Is. 53:3

13 But I say unto you, That E-li'-as is indeed come, and they have done unto him whatsoever they listed, as it is written of him.

14 And when he came to *his* disciples, he saw a great multitude about them, and the scribes ᵀquestioning with them. *disputing*

15 And straightway all the people, when they beheld him, were greatly amazed, and running to *him* ᵀsaluted him. *greeted*

16 And he asked the scribes, What question ye with them?

17 And ᴿone of the multitude answered and said, Master, I have brought unto thee my son, which hath a ᵀdumb spirit; Luke 9:38 · *mute*

18 And wheresoever he taketh him, he ᵀteareth him: and he foameth, and gnasheth with his teeth, and pineth away: and I spake to thy disciples that they should cast him out; and they could not. *throws him down*

19 He answereth him, and saith, O ᴿfaithless generation, how long shall I be with you? how long shall I ᵀsuffer you? bring him unto me. John 4:48 · *bear with*

20 And they brought him unto him: and ᴿwhen he saw him, straightway the spirit tare him; and he fell on the ground, and wallowed foaming. 1:26; Luke 9:42

21 And he asked his father, How long is it ago since this came unto him? And he said, Of a child.

22 And ofttimes it hath cast him into the fire, and into the waters, to destroy him: but if thou canst do any thing, have compassion on us, and help us.

23 Jesus said unto him, ᴿIf thou

canst believe, all things *are* possible to him that believeth. Luke 17:6

24 And straightway the father of the child cried out, and said with tears, Lord, I believe; ᴿhelp thou mine unbelief. Luke 17:5

25 When Jesus saw that the people came running together, he rebuked the foul spirit, saying unto him, *Thou* dumb and deaf spirit, I charge thee, come out of him, and enter no more into him.

26 And *the spirit* cried, and ᵀrent him ᵀsore, and came out of him: and he was as one dead; insomuch that many said, He is dead. *convulsed · severely*

27 But Jesus took him by the hand, and lifted him up; and he arose.

28 ᴿAnd when he was come into the house, his disciples asked him privately, Why could not we cast him out? Matt. 17:19

29 And he said unto them, This kind can come forth by nothing, but by prayer and fasting.

30 And they departed thence, and passed through Galilee; and he would not that any man should know *it*.

31 For he taught his disciples, and said unto them, The Son of man is delivered into the hands of men, and they shall kill him; and after that he is killed, he shall ᴿrise the third day. 1 Cor. 15:4

32 But they understood ᴿnot that saying, and were afraid to ask him. Luke 2:50; 18:34; John 12:16

33 ᴿAnd he came to Ca-per′-na-um: and being in the house he asked them, What was it that ye disputed among yourselves by the way? Luke 9:46–48; 22:24; John 18:12; 19:7

34 But they held their peace: for by the way they had disputed among themselves, who *should be* the ᴿgreatest. Luke 22:24; 23:46; 24:46

35 And he sat down, and called the twelve, and saith unto them, ᴿIf any man desire to be first, *the same* shall be last of all, and servant of all. Matt. 23:11; Luke 22:26, 27

36 And ᴿhe took a child, and set him in the midst of them: and

when he had taken him in his arms, he said unto them, 10:13–16

37 Whosoever shall receive one of such children in my name, receiveth me: and ᴿwhosoever shall receive me, receiveth not me, but him that sent me. John 13:20

38 ᴿAnd John answered him, saying, ᵀMaster, we saw one casting out ᵀdevils in thy name, and he followeth not us: and we forbad him, because he followeth not us. Luke 9:49 · *Teacher · demons*

39 But Jesus said, Forbid him not: for there is no man which shall do a miracle in my name, that can lightly speak evil of me.

40 For ᴿhe that is not against us is on our ᵀpart. Luke 11:23 · *side*

41 ᴿFor whosoever shall give you a cup of water to drink in my name, because ye belong to Christ, verily I say unto you, he shall not lose his reward. Matt. 10:42

42 ᴿAnd whosoever shall offend one of *these* little ones that believe in me, it is better for him that a millstone were hanged about his neck, and he were cast into the sea. Luke 17:1, 2; [1 Cor. 8:12]

43 And if thy hand ᵀoffend thee, cut it off: it is better for thee to enter into life maimed, than having two hands to go into ᵀhell, into the fire that never shall be quenched: *makes you sin · Gr. gehenna*

44 Where their worm dieth not, and the fire is not quenched.

45 And if thy foot ᵀoffend thee, cut it off: it is better for thee to enter ᵀhalt into life, than having two feet to be cast into hell, into the fire that never shall be quenched: *makes you sin · lame*

46 Where their worm dieth not, and the fire is not quenched.

47 And if thine eye offend thee, pluck it out: it is better for thee to enter into the kingdom of God with one eye, than having two eyes to be cast into hell fire:

48 Where their worm dieth not, and the fire is not quenched.

49 For every one shall be salted with fire, ᴿand every sacrifice shall be salted with salt. Lev. 2:13

50 Salt *is* good: but if the salt have lost his saltness, wherewith will ye season it? ^RHave salt in yourselves, and ^Rhave peace one with another.   Col. 4;6 · Heb. 12:14

10 And he arose from thence, and cometh into the coasts of Ju-dae'-a by the farther side of Jordan: and the people resort unto him again; and, as he was wont, he taught them again.

2 And the Pharisees came to him, and asked him, Is it lawful for a man to ^Tput away *his* wife? ^Ttempting him.   *divorce · testing*

3 And he answered and said unto them, What did Moses command you?

4 And they said, Moses suffered to write a bill of divorcement, and to put *her* away.

5 And Jesus answered and said unto them, ^TFor the hardness of your heart he wrote you this precept.   *Because of*

6 But from the beginning of the creation ^RGod made them male and female.   Gen. 1:27; 5:2

7 ^RFor this cause shall a man leave his father and mother, and cleave to his wife;   Gen. 2:24

8 And they ^Ttwain shall be one flesh: so then they are no more twain, but one flesh.   *two*

9 What therefore God hath joined together, let not man ^Tput asunder.   *separate*

10 And in the house his disciples asked him again of the same *matter*.

11 And he saith unto them, ^RWhosoever shall put away his wife, and marry another, committeth adultery against her.   Ex. 20:14

12 And if a woman shall put away her husband, and be married to another, she committeth adultery.

13 And they brought young children to him, that he should touch them: and *his* disciples rebuked those that brought *them*.

14 But when Jesus saw *it*, he was much displeased, and said unto them, ^TSuffer the little children to come unto me, and forbid

them not: for ^Rof such is the kingdom of God.   *Allow* · [1 Pet. 2:2]

15 Verily I say unto you, ^RWhosoever shall not receive the kingdom of God as a little child, he shall not enter therein.   Luke 18:17

16 And he took them up in his arms, put *his* hands upon them, and blessed them.

17 And when he was gone forth into the way, there came one running, and kneeled to him, and asked him, Good Master, what shall I ^Rdo that I may inherit eternal life?   John 6:28; Acts 2:37

18 And Jesus said unto him, Why callest thou me good? *there is* none good but one, *that is,* ^RGod.   1 Sam. 2:2

19 Thou knowest the commandments, Do not commit adultery, Do not kill, Do not steal, Do not bear false witness, Defraud not, Honour thy father and mother.

20 And he answered and said unto him, Master, all these have I ^Tobserved from my youth.   *kept*

21 Then Jesus beholding him loved him, and said unto him, One thing thou lackest: go thy way, ^Rsell whatsoever thou hast, and give to the poor, and thou shalt have ^Rtreasure in heaven: and come, take up the cross, and follow me.   [Luke 12:33; 16:9] · Matt. 6:19, 20

22 And he was sad at that saying, and went away grieved: for he had great possessions.

23 And Jesus looked round about, and saith unto his disciples, How ^Thardly shall they that have riches enter into the kingdom of God!   *hard it is for those*

24 And the disciples were astonished at his words. But Jesus answereth again, and saith unto them, Children, how hard is it for them ^Rthat trust in riches to enter into the kingdom of God!   Ps. 52:7

25 It is easier for a camel to go through the eye of a needle, than for a ^Rrich man to enter into the kingdom of God.   [Matt. 13:22; 19:24]

26 And they were astonished ^Tout of measure, saying among

themselves, Who then can be saved? *beyond*

27 And Jesus looking upon them saith, With men *it is* impossible, but not with God: for with God all things are possible.

28 ᴿThen Peter began to say unto him, Lo, we have left all, and have followed thee. Luke 18:28

29 And Jesus answered and said, Verily I say unto you, There is no man that hath left house, or ᵀbrethren, or sisters, or father, or mother, or wife, or children, or ᵀlands, for my sake, and the gospel's, *brothers · Lit. fields*

30 But he shall receive an hundredfold now in this time, houses, and brethren, and sisters, and mothers, and children, and lands, with persecutions; and in the world to come eternal life.

31 ᴿBut many *that are* first shall be last; and the last first. Luke 13:30

32 ᴿAnd they were in the way going up to Jerusalem; and Jesus went before them: and they were amazed; and as they followed, they were afraid. ᴿAnd he took again the twelve, and began to tell them what things should happen unto him, Luke 18:31–33 · 8:31; 9:31

33 *Saying*, Behold, we go up to Jerusalem; and the Son of man shall be delivered unto the chief priests, and unto the scribes; and they shall condemn him to death, and shall deliver him to the Gentiles:

34 And they shall mock him, and shall ᵀscourge him, and shall spit upon him, and shall kill him: and the third day he shall rise again. *flog him* with a Roman scourge

35 And James and John, the sons of Zeb'-e-dee, come unto him, saying, Master, we would that thou shouldest do for us whatsoever we shall desire.

36 And he said unto them, What would ye that I should do for you?

37 They said unto him, Grant unto us that we may sit, one on thy right hand, and the other on thy left hand, in thy glory.

38 But Jesus said unto them, Ye know not what ye ask: can ye drink of the ᴿcup that I drink of? and be baptized with the baptism that I am baptized with? Luke 22:42

39 And they said unto him, We can. And Jesus said unto them, ᴿYe shall indeed drink of the cup that I drink of; and with the baptism that I am baptized withal shall ye be baptized: Acts 12:2

40 But to sit on my right hand and on my left hand is not mine to give; but *it shall be given to them* ᴿfor whom it is prepared.[Rom. 8:30]

41 ᴿAnd when the ten heard *it*, they began to be much displeased with James and John. Matt. 20:24

42 But Jesus called them *to him*, and saith unto them, ᴿYe know that they which are ᵀaccounted to rule over the Gentiles exercise lordship over them; and their great ones exercise authority upon them. Luke 22:25 · *considered rulers*

43 ᴿBut so shall it not be among you: but whosoever ᵀwill be great among you, shall be your minister: Luke 9:48 · *desires to be*

44 And whosoever of you ᵀwill be the chiefest, shall be servant of all. *desires to be first*

45 For even ᴿthe Son of man came not to be ministered unto, but to minister, and to give his life a ransom for many. John 13:14 ☆

46 ᴿAnd they came to Jericho: and as he went out of Jericho with his disciples and a great number of people, blind Bar-ti-mae'-us, the son of Ti-mae'-us, sat by the highway side begging. Luke 18:35–43

47 And when he heard that it was Jesus of Nazareth, he began to cry out, and say, Jesus, *thou* son of David, have mercy on me.

48 And many charged him that he should hold his peace: but he cried the more a great deal, *Thou* son of David, have mercy on me.

49 And Jesus stood still, and commanded him to be called. And they call the blind man, saying unto him, Be of good ᵀcomfort, rise; he calleth thee. *cheer*

50 And he, casting away his garment, rose, and came to Jesus.

51 And Jesus answered and said unto him, What wilt thou that I should do unto thee? The blind man said unto him, Lord, that I might receive my sight.

52 And Jesus said unto him, Go thy way; ᴿthy faith hath made thee whole. And immediately he received his sight, and followed Jesus in the way.   5:34; Matt. 9:22

11 And ᴿwhen they came nigh to Jerusalem, unto Beth'-pha-ge and Beth'-a-ny, at the mount of Olives, he sendeth forth two of his disciples,   John 2:13

2 And saith unto them, Go your way into the village ᵀover against you: and as soon as ye be entered into it, ye shall find a colt tied, whereon never man sat; loose him, and bring *him*.   *opposite*

3 And if any man say unto you, Why do ye this? say ye that the Lord hath need of him; and straightway he will send him hither.

4 And they went their way, and found the colt tied by the door without in a place where two ways met; and they loose him.

5 And certain of them that stood there said unto them, What do ye, loosing the colt?

6 And they said unto them even as Jesus had commanded: and they let them go.

★ 7 And they brought the colt to Jesus, and cast their garments on him; and he sat upon him.

8 And many spread their garments in the ᵀway: and others cut down branches off the trees, and strawed *them* in the ᵀway.   *road*

★ 9 And they that went before, and they that followed, cried, saying, Hosanna; Blessed *is* he that cometh in the name of the Lord:

10 Blessed *be* the kingdom of our father David, that cometh in the name of the Lord: ᴿHosanna in the highest.   Ps. 148:1

11 And Jesus entered into Jerusalem, and into the temple: and when he had looked round about upon all things, and now the even-

tide was come, he went out unto Beth'-a-ny with the twelve.

12 ᴿAnd on the morrow, when they were come from Beth'-a-ny, he was hungry: Matt. 21:18–22

13 ᴿAnd seeing a fig tree afar off having leaves, he came, if ᵀhaply he might find any thing thereon: and when he came to it, he found nothing but leaves; for the time of figs was not *yet*.   Matt. 21:19 · *perhaps*

14 And Jesus answered and said unto it, ᵀNo man eat fruit of thee hereafter for ever. And his disciples heard *it*.   *Let no man*

15 And they come to Jerusalem: and Jesus went into the temple, and began to cast out them that sold and bought in the temple, and overthrew the tables of the moneychangers, and the seats of them that sold ᴿdoves;   Lev. 14:22

16 And would not ᵀsuffer that any man should carry *any* ᵀvessel through the temple.   *allow · wares*

17 And he taught, saying unto them, Is it not written, ᴿMy house shall be called of all nations the house of prayer? but ye have made it a den of thieves.   Is. 56:7

18 And ᴿthe scribes and chief priests heard *it*, and sought how they might destroy him: for they feared him, because ᴿall the people was astonished at his doctrine.   Ps. 2:2; Luke 19:47 · Luke 4:32

19 And when ᵀeven was come, he went out of the city.   *evening*

20 And in the morning, as they passed by, they saw the fig tree dried up from the roots.

21 And Peter calling to remembrance saith unto him, ᵀMaster, behold, the fig tree which thou cursedst is withered away. Gr. *Rabbi*

22 And Jesus answering saith unto them, Have faith in God.

23 For verily I say unto you, That whosoever shall say unto this mountain, Be thou removed, and be thou cast into the sea; and shall not doubt in his heart, but shall believe that those things which he saith shall come to pass; he shall have whatsoever he saith.

24 Therefore I say unto you,

RWhat things soever ye desire, when ye pray, believe that ye receive *them*, and ye shall have *them*. [John 14:13; 15:7; James 1:5, 6]

25 And when ye stand praying, Rforgive, if ye have Tought against any: that your Father also which is in heaven may forgive you your trespasses. Matt. 6:14 · *anything*

26 But if ye do not forgive, neither will your Father which is in heaven forgive your trespasses.

27 And they come again to Jerusalem: Rand as he was walking in the temple, there come to him the chief priests, and the scribes, and the elders, Matt. 21:23–27

28 And say unto him, By what authority doest thou these things? and who gave thee this authority to do these things?

29 And Jesus answered and said unto them, I will also ask of you one question, and answer me, and I will tell you by what authority I do these things.

30 The Rbaptism of John, was *it* from heaven, or of men? answer me. [1:4, 5, 8]; Luke 7:29, 30

31 And they reasoned with themselves, saying, If we shall say, From heaven; he will say, Why then did ye not believe him?

32 But if we shall say, Of men; they feared the people: for Rall *men* counted John, that he was a prophet indeed. Matt. 3:5; 14:5

33 And they answered and said unto Jesus, We cannot tell. And Jesus answering saith unto them, Neither do I tell you by what authority I do these things.

12 And Rhe began to speak unto them by parables. A *certain* man planted a vineyard, and set an hedge about *it*, and digged *a place for* the winefat, and built a tower, and let it out to husbandmen, and went into a far country. Matt. 21:33–46; Luke 20:9–19

2 And at Tthe season he sent to the Thusbandmen a servant, that he might receive from the husbandmen of the fruit of the vineyard. *vintage-time* · *tenant farmers*

3 And they caught *him*, and beat him, and sent *him* away empty.

4 And again he sent unto them another servant; and at him they cast stones, and wounded *him* in the head, and sent *him* away shamefully handled.

5 And again he sent another; and him they killed, and many others; Rbeating some, and killing some. 2 Chr. 36:16

6 Having yet therefore one son, his wellbeloved, he sent him also last unto them, saying, They will Treverence my son. *respect*

7 But those husbandmen said among themselves, This is the heir; come, let us kill him, and the inheritance shall be ours.

8 And they took him, and Rkilled *him*, and cast *him* out of the vineyard. [Acts 2:23]

9 What shall therefore the Tlord of the vineyard do? he will come and destroy the Thusbandmen, and will give the vineyard unto others. *owner* · *tenant farmers*

10 And have ye not read this scripture; RThe stone which the builders rejected is become the head of the corner: Ps. 118:22, 23 ☆

11 This was the Lord's doing, and it is marvellous in our eyes?

12 RAnd they sought to lay hold on him, but feared the people: for they knew that he had spoken the parable against them: and they left him, and went their way. 11:18

13 RAnd they send unto him certain of the Pharisees and of the He-ro'-di-ans, to catch him in *his* words. Matt. 22:15–22; Luke 20:20–26

14 And when they were come, they say unto him, Master, we know that thou art true, and carest for no man: for thou regardest not the person of men, but teachest the Rway of God in truth: Is it lawful to Tgive tribute to Caesar, or not? Acts 18:26 · *pay taxes*

15 Shall we Tgive, or shall we not give? But he, knowing their Rhypocrisy, said unto them, Why Ttempt ye me? bring me a penny, that I may see *it*. *pay* · Luke 12:1 · *test*

16 And they brought *it*. And he

saith unto them, Whose *is* this image and superscription? And they said unto him, Caesar's.

17 And Jesus answering said unto them, ᵀRender to Caesar the things that are Caesar's, and to God the things that are God's. And they marvelled at him. *Pay*

18 ᴿThen come unto him the Sad'-du-cees, ᴿwhich say there is no resurrection; and they asked him, saying, Luke 20:27-38 · Acts 23:8

19 Master, ᴿMoses wrote unto us, If a man's brother die, and leave *his* wife *behind him,* and leave no children, that his brother should take his wife, and raise up seed unto his brother. Deut. 25:5

20 Now there were seven brethren: and the first took a wife, and dying left no ᵀseed. *offspring*

21 And the second took her, and died, neither left he any seed: and the third likewise.

22 And the seven had her, and left no ᵀseed: last of all the woman died also. *offspring*

23 In the resurrection therefore, when they shall rise, whose wife shall she be of them? for the seven had her to wife.

24 And Jesus answering said unto them, Do ye not therefore ᵀerr, because ye know not the scriptures, neither the power of God? *go astray*

25 For when they shall rise from the dead, they neither marry, nor are given in marriage; but are as the angels which are in heaven.

26 And ᵀas touching the dead, that they rise: have ye not read in the book of Moses, how in the bush God spake unto him, saying, ᴿI *am* the God of Abraham, and the God of Isaac, and the God of Jacob? *concerning* · Ex. 3:6, 15

27 He is not the God of the dead, but the God of the living: ye therefore do greatly err.

28 ᴿAnd one of the scribes came, and having heard them reasoning together, and perceiving that he had answered them well, asked him, Which is the first commandment of all? Matt. 22:34-40

29 And Jesus answered him, The first of all the commandments *is,* ᴿHear, O Israel; The Lord our God is one Lord: Deut. 6:4

30 And thou shalt love the Lord thy God with all thy heart, and with all thy soul, and with all thy mind, and with all thy strength: this *is* the first commandment.

31 And the second *is* like, *namely* this, ᴿThou shalt love thy neighbour as thyself. There is none other commandment greater than these. Lev. 19:18; Matt. 22:39; James 2:8

32 And the scribe said unto him, Well, Master, thou hast said the truth: for there is one God; ᴿand there is none other but he: Is. 46:9

33 And to love him with all the heart, and with all the understanding, and with all the soul, and with all the strength, and to love *his* neighbour as himself, ᴿis more than all whole burnt offerings and sacrifices. [Mic. 6:6-8]

34 And when Jesus saw that he answered ᵀdiscreetly, he said unto him, Thou art not far from the kingdom of God. ᴿAnd no man after that ᵀdurst ask him *any* question. *wisely* · Matt. 22:46 · *dared*

35 And Jesus answered and said, while he taught in the temple, How say the scribes that Christ is the son of David?

36 For David himself said ᴿby the Holy Ghost, ᴿThe Lᴏʀᴅ said to my Lord, Sit thou on my right hand, till I make thine enemies thy footstool. 2 Sam. 23:2 · Ps. 110:1 ☆

37 David therefore himself calleth him Lord; and whence is he *then* his son? And the common people heard him gladly.

38 And ᴿhe said unto them in his doctrine, ᴿBeware of the scribes, which love to go in long clothing, and ᴿlove salutations in the marketplaces, 4:2 · Matt. 23:1-7 · Luke 11:43

39 And the ᴿchiefᵀ seats in the synagogues, and the uppermost rooms at feasts: Luke 14:7 · *best*

40 ᴿWhich devour widows' houses, and for a pretence make long prayers: these shall receive greater damnation. Matt. 23:14

41 ᴿAnd Jesus sat over against the treasury, and beheld how the people cast money ᴿinto the treasury: and many that were rich cast in much.   Luke 21:1–4 · 2 Kin. 12:9

42 And there came a certain poor widow, and she threw in two mites, which make a farthing.

43 And he called *unto him* his disciples, and saith unto them, Verily I say unto you, That ᴿthis poor widow hath cast more in, than all they which have cast into the treasury: [2 Cor. 8:12]

44 For all *they* did cast in of their abundance; but she of her want did cast in all that she had, ᴿ*even* all her living.   Deut. 24:6

13 And ᴿas he went out of the temple, one of his disciples saith unto him, Master, see what manner of stones and what buildings *are here!*   Matt. 24:1; Luke 21:5–36

2 And Jesus answering said unto him, Seest thou these great buildings? ᴿthere shall not be left one stone upon another, that shall not be thrown down.   Luke 19:44

3 And as he sat upon the mount of Olives over against the temple, ᴿPeter and ᴿJames and ᴿJohn and ᴿAndrew asked him privately,   1:16 · 1:19 · 1:19 · John 1:40

4 ᴿTell us, when shall these things be? and what *shall be* the sign when all these things shall be fulfilled?   Matt. 24:3; Luke 21:7

5 And Jesus answering them began to say, ᴿTake heed lest any *man* deceive you: Jer. 29:8; 1 Thess. 2:3

6 For many shall come in my name, saying, I am *Christ;* and shall deceive many.

7 And when ye shall hear of wars and rumours of wars, be ye not troubled: for *such things* must needs be; but the end *shall* not *be* yet.

8 For nation shall rise against nation, and ᴿkingdom against kingdom: and there shall be earthquakes in ᵀdivers places, and there shall be famines and troubles: ᴿthese *are* the beginnings of sorrows.   Hag. 2:22 · *various* · Matt. 24:8

9 But ᴿtake heed to yourselves: for they shall deliver you up to councils; and in the synagogues ye shall be beaten: and ye shall be brought before rulers and kings for my sake, for a testimony against them.   Acts 12:4; [Rev. 2:10]

10 And the gospel must first be published among all nations.

11 ᴿBut when they shall lead *you,* and deliver you up, take no thought beforehand what ye shall speak, neither do ye premeditate: but whatsoever shall be given you in that hour, that speak ye: for it is not ye that speak, ᴿbut the Holy Ghost.   Luke 21:12–17 · Acts 2:4; 4:8, 31

12 Now ᴿthe brother shall betray the brother to death, and the father the son; and children shall rise up against *their* parents, and shall cause them to be put to death.   Mic. 7:6; Matt. 24:10; Luke 21:16

13 ᴿAnd ye shall be hated of all *men* for my name's sake: but he that shall endure unto the end, the same shall be saved.   John 15:21

14 But when ye shall see the abomination of desolation, ᴿspoken of by Daniel the prophet, standing where it ought not, (let him that readeth understand,) then let them that be in Ju-dae'-a flee to the mountains: Dan. 9:27

15 And let him that is on the housetop not go down into the house, neither enter *therein,* to take any thing out of his house:

16 And let him that is in the field not turn back again for to ᵀtake up his garment.   *get*

17 ᴿBut woe to them that are with child, and to them that give suck in those days!   Luke 21:23

18 And pray ye that your flight be not in the winter.

19 ᴿFor *in* those days shall be affliction, such as was not from the beginning of the creation which God created unto this time, neither shall be.   Dan. 9:26; 12:1

20 And except that the Lord had shortened those days, no flesh should be saved: but for the elect's sake, whom he hath chosen, he hath shortened the days.

21 And then if any man shall say

to you, Lo, here *is* Christ; or, lo, *he is* there; believe *him* not:

22 For false Christs and false prophets shall rise, and shall shew signs and ᴿwonders, to seduce, if *it were* possible, even the ᵀelect.   Rev. 13:13, 14 · *chosen ones*

23 But take ye heed: behold, I have foretold you all things.

24 ᴿBut in those days, after that tribulation, the sun shall be darkened, and the moon shall not give her light,   Zeph. 1:15; Matt. 24:29

25 And the stars of heaven shall fall, and the powers that are in heaven shall be ᴿshaken.   Is. 13:10

26 And then shall they see the Son of man coming in the clouds with great power and glory.

27 And then shall he send his angels, and shall gather together his elect from the four winds, from the uttermost part of the earth to the uttermost part of heaven.

28 Now learn a parable of the fig tree; When her branch is yet tender, and putteth forth leaves, ye know that summer is near:

29 So ye in like manner, when ye shall see these things come to pass, know that ᵀit is nigh, *even* at the doors.   Or *he is near*

30 Verily I say unto you, that this generation shall not pass, till all these things be done.

31 Heaven and earth shall pass away: but ᴿmy words shall not pass away.   Is. 40:8; [2 Pet. 3:7, 10, 12]

32 But of that day and *that* hour knoweth no man, no, not the angels which are in heaven, neither the Son, but the Father.

33 ᴿTake ye heed, watch and pray: for ye know not when the time is.   [Rom. 13:11]; 1 Thess. 5:6

34 ᴿ*For the Son of man is* as a man taking a far journey, who left his house, and gave authority to his servants, and to every man his work, and commanded the ᵀporter to watch.   Matt. 25:14 · *doorkeeper*

35 ᴿWatch ye therefore: for ye know not when the master of the house cometh, at ᵀeven, or at midnight, or at the cockcrowing, or in the morning: Matt. 24:42, 44 · *evening*

36 Lest coming suddenly he find you sleeping.

37 And what I say unto you I say unto all, Watch.

14 After two days was *the feast of* the passover, and of ᴿunleavened bread: and the chief priests and the scribes sought how they might take him by craft, and put *him* to death.   Ex. 12:1–27

2 But they said, Not on the feast *day*, lest there be an uproar of the people.

3 And being in Beth′-a-ny in the house of Simon the leper, as he sat at meat, there came a woman having an alabaster ᵀbox of ointment of spikenard very precious; and she brake the box, and poured *it* on his head.   *flask of oil*

4 And there were some that had indignation within themselves, and said, Why was this waste of the ointment made?

5 For it might have been sold for more than three hundred ᴿpence, and have been given to the poor. And they ᴿmurmured against her.   12:15 · John 6:61

6 And Jesus said, Let her alone; why trouble ye her? she hath wrought a ᵀgood work on me.   *beautiful deed*

7 ᴿFor ye have the poor with you always, and whensoever ye will ye may do them good: but me ye have not always.   Deut. 15:11

8 She hath done what she could: she is come aforehand to anoint my body to the burying.

9 Verily I say unto you, Wheresoever this gospel shall be ᴿpreached throughout the whole world, *this* also that she hath done shall be spoken of for a memorial of her.   Matt. 28:19, 20

10 And Judas Is-car′-i-ot, one of the twelve, went unto the chief priests, to betray him unto them.

11 And when they heard *it*, they were glad, and promised to give him money. And he sought how he might conveniently betray him.

12 ᴿAnd the first day of unleavened bread, when they killed the

passover, his disciples said unto him, Where wilt thou that we go and prepare that thou mayest eat the passover? Ex. 12:8; Matt. 26:17–19

13 And he sendeth forth two of his disciples, and saith unto them, Go ye into the city, and there shall meet you a man ᵀbearing a pitcher of water: follow him.　*carrying*

14 And wheresoever he shall go in, say ye to the ᵀgoodman of the house, The ᵀMaster saith, Where is the guestchamber, where I shall eat the passover with my disciples?　*master · Teacher*

15 And he will shew you a large upper room furnished *and* prepared: there make ready for us.

16 And his disciples went forth, and came into the city, and found as he had said unto them: and they made ready the passover.

17 ᴿAnd in the evening he cometh with the twelve.　Matt. 26:20–24

18 And as they sat and did eat, Jesus said, Verily I say unto you, ᴿOne of you which eateth with me shall betray me.　Ps. 41:9; Matt. 26:46

19 And they began to be sorrowful, and to say unto him one by one, *Is* it I? and another *said, Is* it I?

20 And he answered and said unto them, *It is* one of the twelve, that dippeth with me in the dish.

21 ᴿThe Son of man indeed goeth, as it is written of him: but woe to that man by whom the Son of man is betrayed! good were it for that man if he had never been born. Matt. 26:24; Luke 22:22; Acts 1:16–20

22 And as they did eat, Jesus took bread, and blessed, and brake *it*, and gave to them, and said, Take, eat: this is my body.

23 And he took the cup, and when he had given thanks, he gave *it* to them: and they all drank of it.

24 And he said unto them, This is my blood of the new testament, which is shed for many.

25 Verily I say unto you, I will drink no more of the fruit of the vine, until that day that I drink it new in the kingdom of God.

26 ᴿAnd when they had sung an hymn, they went out into the mount of Olives.　Matt. 26:30

27 And Jesus saith unto them, ☆ All ye shall be offended because of me this night: for it is written, ᴿI will smite the shepherd, and the sheep shall be scattered. Zech. 13:7

28 But after that I am risen, I will go before you into Galilee.

29 ᴿBut Peter said unto him, Although all shall be offended, yet *will* not I.　Matt. 26:33, 34

30 And Jesus saith unto him, Verily I say unto thee, That this day, *even* in this night, before the ᵀcock crow twice, thou shalt deny me ᵀthrice.　*rooster · three times*

31 But he spake the more vehemently, If I should die with thee, I will not deny thee in any wise. Likewise also said they all.

32 And they came to a place which was named Geth-sem′-ane: and he saith to his disciples, Sit ye here, while I shall pray.

33 And he ᴿtaketh with him Peter and James and John, and began to be sore amazed, and to be very heavy;　5:37; 9:2; 13:3

34 And saith unto them, My soul is exceeding sorrowful unto death: tarry ye here, and watch.

35 And he went forward a little, and fell on the ground, and prayed that, if it were possible, the hour might pass from him.

36 And he said, ᴿAb′-ba, Father, ★ ᴿall things *are* possible unto thee; take away this cup from me: ᴿnevertheless not what I will, but what thou wilt.　Rom. 8:15 · [Heb. 5:7] · Is. 50:5

37 And he cometh, and findeth them sleeping, and saith unto Peter, Simon, sleepest thou? couldest not thou watch one hour?

38 ᴿWatch ye and pray, lest ye enter into temptation. ᴿThe spirit truly *is* ready, but the flesh *is* weak.　Luke 21:36 · [Rom. 7:18, 21–24]

39 And again he went away, and prayed, and spake the same words.

40 And when he returned, he found them asleep again, (for their eyes were heavy,) neither wist they what to answer him.

41 And he cometh the third time, and saith unto them, Sleep on now, and take *your* rest: it is enough, ^Rthe hour is come; behold, the Son of man is betrayed into the hands of sinners. John 13:1

42 ^RRise up, let us go; lo, he that betrayeth me is at hand. Matt. 26:46

43 ^RAnd immediately, while he yet spake, cometh Judas, one of the twelve, and with him a great multitude with swords and staves, from the chief priest and the scribes and the elders. Ps. 3:1

44 And he that betrayed him had given them a ^Ttoken, saying, Whomsoever I shall ^Rkiss, that same is he; take him, and lead *him* away safely. *signal · [Prov. 27:6]*

45 And as soon as he was come, he goeth straightway to him, and saith, ^TMaster, master; and kissed him. *Gr. Rabbi, rabbi*

46 And they laid their hands on him, and took him.

47 And one of them that stood by drew a sword, and ^Tsmote a servant of the high priest, and cut off his ear. *struck the servant*

48 And Jesus answered and said unto them, Are ye come out, as against a thief, with swords and *with* ^Tstaves to take me? *clubs*

49 I was daily with you in the temple ^Rteaching, and ye took me not: but ^Rthe scriptures must be fulfilled. Matt. 21:23 · Ps. 22:6; Is. 53:7

50 ^RAnd they all forsook him, and fled. Ps. 88:8; Zech. 13:7

51 And there followed him a certain young man, having a linen cloth cast about *his* naked *body;* and the young men laid hold on him:

52 And he left the linen cloth, and fled from them naked.

53 And they led Jesus away to the high priest: and with him were assembled all the chief priests and the elders and the scribes.

54 And ^RPeter followed him ^Tafar off, even into the palace of the high priest: and he sat with the servants, and warmed himself at the fire. John 18:15 · *at a distance*

55 ^RAnd the chief priests and all the council sought for ^Twitness against Jesus to put him to death; and found none. Matt. 26:59 · *testimony*

56 For many bare ^Rfalse witness against him, but their witness agreed not together. Ps. 27:12; 35:11

57 And there arose certain, and bare false witness against him, saying, ★

58 We heard him say, ^RI will destroy this temple that is made with hands, and within three days I will build another made without hands. Matt. 26:61; John 2:19; [2 Cor. 5:1]

59 But ^Tneither so did their witness agree together. *not even then*

60 ^RAnd the high priest stood up in the midst, and asked Jesus, saying, Answerest thou nothing? what *is it which* these ^Twitness against thee? Matt. 26:62 · *testify*

61 But ^Rhe held his peace, and answered nothing. Again the high priest asked him, and said unto him, Art thou the Christ, the Son of the Blessed? Is. 53:7; John 19:9

62 And Jesus said, I am: and ye shall see the Son of man sitting on the right hand of power, and coming in the clouds of heaven.

63 Then the high priest ^Trent his clothes, and saith, What need we any further witnesses? *tore*

64 Ye have heard the ^Rblasphemy: what think ye? And they all condemned him to be ^Tguilty of death. John 10:33, 36 · *deserving*

65 And some began to ^Rspit on ★ him, and to cover his face, and to buffet him, and to say unto him, Prophesy: and the servants did strike him with the palms of their hands. Job 16:10; Is. 50:6; 52:14; Lam. 3:30

66 And as Peter was beneath in the palace, there cometh one of the maids of the high priest:

67 And when she saw Peter warming himself, she looked upon him, and said, And thou also wast with Jesus of Nazareth.

68 But he denied, saying, I know not, neither understand I what thou sayest. And he went out into the porch; and the cock crew.

69 And a maid saw him again,

and began to say to them that stood by, This is *one* of them.

70 And he denied it again. And a little after, they that stood by said again to Peter, Surely thou art *one* of them: ^Rfor thou art a Gal-i-lae'-an, and thy ^Tspeech agreeth *thereto*.   Acts 2:7 · *accent shows*

71 But he began to curse and to swear, *saying,* I know not this man of whom ye speak.

72 And the second time the ^Tcock crew. And Peter called to mind the word that Jesus said unto him, Before the cock crow twice, thou shalt deny me ^Tthrice. And when he thought thereon, he wept.   *rooster crowed · three times*

★ **15** And ^Rstraightway in the morning the chief priests held a consultation with the elders and scribes and the whole council, and bound Jesus, and carried *him* away, and delivered *him* to Pilate.   Ps. 2:2; Matt. 27:1

2 ^RAnd Pilate asked him, Art thou the King of the Jews? And he answering said unto him, Thou sayest *it*.   Matt. 27:11–14; Luke 23:2, 3

★ 3 And the chief priests accused him of many things: but he ^Ranswered nothing.   Is. 53:7; John 19:9

4 ^RAnd Pilate asked him again, saying, Answerest thou nothing? behold how many things they witness against thee.   Matt. 27:13

5 But Jesus yet answered nothing; so that Pilate marvelled.

6 Now at *that* feast he released unto them one prisoner, whomsoever they ^Tdesired.   *requested*

7 And there was *one* named Bar-ab'-bas, *which lay* bound with them that had made insurrection with him, who had committed murder in the insurrection.

8 And the multitude crying aloud began to desire *him to do* as he had ever done unto them.

9 But Pilate answered them, saying, Will ye that I release unto you the King of the Jews?

10 For he knew that the chief priests had delivered him ^Tfor envy.   *because of*

11 But the chief priests moved the people, that he should rather release Bar-ab'-bas unto them.

12 And Pilate answered and said again unto them, What will ye then that I shall do *unto him* whom ye call the ^RKing of the Jews?   Ps. 2:6; [Is. 9:7]; Jer. 23:5; Mic. 5:2

13 And they cried out again, Crucify him.

14 Then Pilate said unto them, Why, ^Rwhat evil hath he done? And they cried out the more exceedingly, Crucify him.   Is. 53:9

15 ^RAnd *so* Pilate, willing to content the people, released Bar-ab'-bas unto them, and delivered Jesus, when he had scourged *him*, to be ^Rcrucified.   Is. 50:6 · [Is. 53:8]

16 ^RAnd the soldiers led him away into the hall, called Prae-to'-ri-um; and they call together the whole ^Tband. Matt. 27:27–31 · Lit. *cohort*

17 And they clothed him with purple, and platted a crown of thorns, and put it about his *head*,

18 And began to salute him, Hail, King of the Jews!

19 And they ^Rsmote him on the ★ head with a reed, and did spit upon him, and bowing *their* knees worshipped him.   [Is. 53:5]; Mic. 5:1

20 And when they had ^Rmocked him, they took off the purple from him, and put his own clothes on him, and led him out to crucify him.   Ps. 35:16; 69:19; Is. 53:3; Matt. 20:19

21 ^RAnd they compel one Simon a Cy-re'-ni-an, who passed by, coming out of the country, the father of Alexander and Rufus, to bear his cross.   Matt. 27:32; Luke 23:26

22 And they bring him unto the place Gol'-go-tha, which is, being interpreted, The place of a skull.

23 ^RAnd they gave him to drink wine mingled with myrrh: but he received *it* not.   Ps. 69:21; Matt. 27:34

24 And when they had crucified him, ^Rthey parted his garments, casting lots upon them, what every man should take.   Ps. 22:18

25 And ^Rit was the third hour, and they crucified him.   Luke 23:44

26 And the superscription of his

accusation was written over, THE KING OF THE JEWS.

★ 27 And with him they crucify two thieves; the one on his right hand, and the other on his left.

★ 28 And the scripture was fulfilled, which saith, And he was numbered with the transgressors.

★ 29 And ᴿthey that passed by railed on him, wagging their heads, and saying, Ah, thou that destroyest the temple, and buildest *it* in three days, Ps. 69:7

30 Save thyself, and come down from the cross.

★ 31 Likewise also the chief priests ᴿmocking said among themselves with the scribes, He saved ᴿothers; himself he cannot save. Luke 18:32 · Luke 7:14, 15

32 Let Christ the King of Israel descend now from the cross, that we may see and believe. And ᴿthey that were crucified with him reviled him. Amos 8:9; Matt. 27:44

33 And ᴿwhen the sixth hour was come, there was darkness over the whole land until the ninth hour. Luke 23:44–49

★ 34 And at the ninth hour Jesus cried with a loud voice, saying, E-lo′-i, E-lo′-i, la′-ma sa-bach′-tha-ni? which is, ᵀbeing interpreted, ᴿMy God, my God, why hast thou forsaken me? *translated* · Ps. 22:1

35 And some of them that stood by, when they heard *it*, said, Behold, he calleth E-li′-as.

★ 36 And ᴿone ran and filled a spunge full of vinegar, and put *it* on a reed, and ᴿgave him to drink, saying, Let alone; let us see whether E-li′-as will come to take him down. John 19:29 · Ps. 69:21

37 And Jesus cried with a loud voice, and gave up the ghost.

38 And ᴿthe veil of the temple was ᵀrent in twain from the top to the bottom. Ex. 26:31–33 · *torn in two*

39 And when the centurion, which stood over against him, saw that he so cried out, and gave up the ghost, he said, Truly this man was the Son of God.

40 There were also women look-

ing on afar off: among whom was Mary Mag-da-le′-ne, and Mary the mother of James the less and of Jo′-ses, and Sa-lo′-me;

41 (Who also, when he was in Galilee, ᴿfollowed him, and ministered unto him;) and many other women which came up with him unto Jerusalem. Luke 8:2, 3

42 ᴿAnd now when the even was come, because it was the preparation, that is, the day before the sabbath, John 19:38–42

43 Joseph of Ar-i-ma-thae′-a, an ᵀhonourable counsellor, which also waited for the kingdom of God, came, and went in boldly unto Pilate, and craved the body of Jesus. *prominent council member*

44 And Pilate marvelled if he were already dead: and calling *unto him* the centurion, he asked him whether he had been ᵀany while dead. *a long time*

45 And when he ᵀknew *it* of the ★ centurion, he gave the body to Joseph. *learned*

46 ᴿAnd he bought fine linen, and took him down, and wrapped him in the linen, and laid him in a sepulchre which was hewn out of a rock, and rolled a stone unto the door of the sepulchre. Is. 53:9

47 And Mary Mag-da-le′-ne and Mary *the mother* of Jo′-ses beheld where he was laid.

16 And ᴿwhen the sabbath was past, Mary Mag-da-le′-ne, and Mary the *mother* of James, and Sa-lo′-me, had bought sweet spices, that they might come and anoint him. John 20:1–8

2 ᴿAnd very early in the morning the first *day* of the week, they came unto the sepulchre at the rising of the sun. Luke 24:1; John 20:1

3 And they said among themselves, Who shall roll us away the stone from the door of the sepulchre?

4 And when they looked, they saw that the stone was rolled away: for it was very ᵀgreat. *large*

5 ᴿAnd entering into the sepulchre, they saw a young man sitting on the right side, clothed in a

long white garment; and they
were affrighted.   Luke 24:3
★ 6 ᴿAnd he saith unto them, Be
not affrighted: Ye seek Jesus of
Nazareth, which was crucified: he
is risen; he is not here: behold the
place where they laid him. Ps. 16:10
★ 7 But go your way, tell his disciples and Peter that he goeth
before you into Galilee: there
shall ye see him, ᴿas he said unto
you.   14:28; Matt. 26:32; 28:16, 17
8 And they went out quickly,
and fled from the sepulchre; for
they trembled and were amazed:
neither said they any thing to any
man; for they were afraid.
9 Now when *Jesus* was risen
early the first *day* of the week, he
appeared first to Mary Mag-da-
le´-ne, ᴿout of whom he had cast
seven ᵀdevils.   Luke 8:2 · *demons*
10 ᴿ*And* she went and told them
that had been with him, as they
mourned and wept.   Luke 24:10
11 And they, when they had
heard that he was alive, and had
been seen of her, believed not.
12 After that he appeared in
another form ᴿunto two of them,
as they walked, and went into the
country.   Luke 24:13–35
13 And they went and told *it*

unto the ᵀresidue: neither believed
they them.   *rest*
14 ᴿAfterward he appeared unto
the eleven as they sat at meat, and
upbraided them with their unbelief and hardness of heart, because they believed not them
which had seen him after he was
risen.   John 20:19, 26; 1 Cor. 15:5
15 And he said unto them, Go ye
into all the world, and preach the
gospel to every creature.
16 He that believeth and is baptized shall be saved; but he that
believeth not shall be damned.
17 And these signs shall follow
them that believe; In my name
shall they cast out devils; they
shall speak with new tongues;
18 They shall take up serpents;
and if they drink any deadly
thing, it shall not hurt them; ᴿthey
shall lay hands on the sick, and
they shall recover.   James 5:14
19 So then after the Lord had ★
spoken unto them, he was ᴿre-
ceived up into heaven, and sat on
the right hand of God. Acts 1:2, 9–11
20 And they went forth, and
preached every where, the Lord
working with *them*, ᴿand confirming the word with signs following. A-men´. Acts 5:12; [1 Cor. 2:4, 5]

The Gospel According to

LUKE

L UKE, a physician, writes with the compassion and warmth of a family doctor as he carefully documents the perfect humanity of the Son of Man,
Jesus Christ. Luke emphasizes Jesus' ancestry, birth, and early life before
moving carefully and chronologically through His earthly ministry. Growing
belief and growing opposition develop side by side. Those who believe are
challenged to count the cost of discipleship. Those who oppose will not be satisfied until the Son of Man hangs lifeless on a cross. But the Resurrection
insures that His purpose will be fulfilled: "to seek and to save that which was
lost" (19:10).
    Kata Loukan, "According to Luke," is the ancient title that was added to
this gospel at a very early date. The Greek name *Luke* appears only three
times in the New Testament (Col. 4:14; 2 Tim. 4:11; Philem. 24).

FORASMUCH as many have taken in hand to set forth in order a [T]declaration of those things which are most surely believed among us, *narrative*

2 Even as they [R]delivered them unto us, which from the beginning were eyewitnesses, and ministers of the word; Acts 1:3; 10:39; Heb. 2:3

3 It seemed good to me also, having had perfect understanding of all things from [T]the very first, to write unto thee in order, most excellent The-oph'-i-lus, Or *above*

4 [R]That thou mightest know the certainty of those things, wherein thou hast been instructed. [John 20:31]

5 THERE was [R]in the days of Herod, the king of Ju-dae'-a, a certain priest named Zach-a-ri'-as, [R]of the course of A-bi'-a: and his [R]wife *was* of the daughters of Aaron, and her name *was* Elisabeth. Matt. 2:1 · 1 Chr. 24:1, 10 · Lev. 21:13

6 And they were both righteous before God, walking in all the commandments and ordinances of the Lord blameless.

7 And they had no child, because that Elisabeth was barren, and they both were *now* well [T]stricken in years. *advanced*

8 And it came to pass, that, while he [T]executed the priest's office before God in the order of his [T]course, *served as priest · division*

9 According to the custom of the priest's office, his lot was [R]to burn incense when he went into the temple of the Lord. Ex. 30:7, 8

10 [R]And the whole multitude of the people were praying without at the time of incense. Lev. 16:17

11 And there appeared unto him an angel of the Lord standing on the right side of [R]the altar of incense. Ex. 30:1

12 And when Zach-a-ri'-as saw *him*, [R]he was troubled, and fear fell upon him. Judg. 6:22; Dan. 10:8

13 But the angel said unto him, Fear not, Zach-a-ri'-as: for thy prayer is heard; and thy wife Elisabeth shall bear thee a son,

and [R]thou shalt call his name John. vv. 57, 60, 63

14 And thou shalt have joy and gladness; and [R]many shall rejoice at his birth. v. 58

15 For he shall be great in the sight of the Lord, and [R]shall drink neither wine nor strong drink; and he shall be filled with the Holy Ghost, [R]even from his mother's womb. Judg. 13:4 · Jer. 1:5

16 And many of the [T]children of Israel shall he turn to the Lord their God. Lit. *sons*

17 [R]And he shall go before him ☆ in the spirit and power of E-li'-as, to turn the hearts of the fathers to the children, and the disobedient to the wisdom of the just; to make ready a people prepared for the Lord. Mal. 4:5, 6; Matt. 3:2; 11:14; Mark 1:4

18 And Zach-a-ri'-as said unto the angel, Whereby shall I know this? for I am an old man, and my wife well stricken in years.

19 And the angel answering said unto him, I am Gabriel, that stand in the presence of God; and am sent to speak unto thee, and to shew thee these glad [R]tidings. 2:10

20 And, behold, thou shalt be dumb, and not able to speak, until the day that these things shall be performed, because thou believest not my words, which shall be fulfilled in their [T]season. *own time*

21 And the people waited for Zach-a-ri'-as, and marvelled that he tarried so long in the temple.

22 And when he came out, he could not speak unto them: and they perceived that he had seen a vision in the temple: for he beckoned unto them, and remained speechless.

23 And it came to pass, that, as soon as [R]the days of his ministration were accomplished, he departed to his own house. 2 Kin. 11:5

24 And after those days his wife Elisabeth conceived, and hid herself five months, saying,

25 Thus hath the Lord dealt with me in the days wherein he looked on *me*, to [R]take away my reproach among men. Gen. 30:23; Is. 4:1; 54:1, 4

26 And in the sixth month the angel Gabriel was sent from God unto a city of Galilee, named Naz-areth,

★ 27 To a virgin Respoused to a man whose name was Joseph, of the house of David; and the vir-gin's name *was* Mary. 2:4, 5

28 And the angel came in unto her, and said, RHail,T *thou that art* highly favoured, Rthe Lord *is* with thee: blessed *art* thou among women. Dan. 9:23 · *Rejoice* · Judg. 6:12

29 And when she saw *him,* Rshe was troubled at his saying, and cast in her mind what manner of salutation this should be. v. 12

30 And the angel said unto her, Fear not, Mary: for thou hast found Rfavour with God. 2:52

★ 31 RAnd, behold, thou shalt con-ceive in thy womb, and bring forth a son, and Rshalt call his name JESUS. Is. 7:14 · 2:21

32 He shall be great, and shall be called the Son of the Highest: and the Lord God shall give unto him the Rthrone of his father Da-vid: 2 Sam. 7:14–17; Acts 2:33; 7:55

☆ 33 And he shall reign over the house of Jacob for ever; and of his kingdom there shall be no end.

34 Then said Mary unto the angel, How shall this be, seeing I Tknow not a man? *am a virgin*

35 And the angel answered and said unto her, RThe Holy Ghost shall come upon thee, and the power of the Highest shall over-shadow thee: therefore also that holy thing which shall be born of thee shall be called Rthe Son of God. Matt. 1:20 · Ps. 2:7; Matt. 3:17; 14:33

36 And, behold, thy Tcousin Elis-abeth, she hath also conceived a son in her old age: and this is the sixth month with her, who was called barren. *relative*

37 For Rwith God nothing shall be impossible. Gen. 18:14; Jer. 32:17

38 And Mary said, Behold the handmaid of the Lord; be it unto me according to thy word. And the angel departed from her.

39 And Mary arose in those days, and went into the hill country with haste, into a city of Juda;

40 And entered into the house of Zach-a-ri'-as, and Tsaluted Elisa-beth. *greeted*

41 And it came to pass, that, when Elisabeth heard the salu-tation of Mary, the babe leaped in her womb; and Elisabeth was filled with the Holy Ghost:

42 And she spake out with a loud voice, and said, RBlessed *art* thou among women, and blessed *is* the fruit of thy womb. Judg. 5:24

43 And Twhence *is* this to me, that the mother of my Lord should come to me? *why*

44 For, lo, as soon as the voice of thy salutation sounded in mine ears, the babe leaped in my womb for joy.

45 And blessed *is* she that be-lieved: for there shall be a per-formance of those things which were told her from the Lord.

46 And Mary said, RMy soul doth magnify the Lord, Ps. 34:2, 3

47 And my spirit hath Rrejoiced in God my Saviour. Ps. 35:9; Hab. 3:18

48 For he hath regarded the low estate of his handmaiden: for, behold, from henceforth all gen-erations shall call me blessed.

49 For he that is mighty Rhath done to me great things; and holy *is* his name. Ps. 71:19; 126:2, 3

50 And Rhis mercy *is* on them that fear him from generation to generation. Gen. 17:7; Ex. 20:6; 34:6, 7

51 RHe hath shewed strength with his arm; he hath scattered the proud in the imagination of their hearts. Ps. 98:1; 118:15; Is. 40:10

52 He hath put down the mighty from *their* Tseats, and exalted them of low degree. *thrones*

53 He hath Rfilled the hungry with good things; and the rich he hath sent empty away. [Matt. 5:6]

54 He hath Tholpen his Rservant Israel, Rin remembrance of *his* mercy; *helped* · Is. 41:8 · Ps. 98:3

55 RAs he spake to our fathers, to Abraham, and to his Rseed for ever. Gen. 17:19; Ps. 132:11 · Gen. 17:7

56 And Mary abode with her

about three months, and returned to her own house.

57 Now Elisabeth's full time came that she should be delivered; and she brought forth a son.

58 And her neighbours and her cousins heard how the Lord had shewed great mercy upon her; and they rejoiced with her.

59 And it came to pass, that ᴿon the eighth day they came to circumcise the child; and they called him Zach-a-ri'-as, after the name of his father.   Gen. 17:12; Lev. 12:3

60 And his mother answered and said, ᴿNot *so*; but he shall be called John.   vv. 13, 63

61 And they said unto her, There is none of thy kindred that is called by this name.

62 And they made signs to his father, how he would have him called.

63 And he asked for a writing table, and wrote, saying, His name is John. And they marvelled all.

64 And his mouth was opened immediately, and his tongue *loosed,* and he spake, and praised God.

65 And fear came on all that dwelt round about them: and all these sayings were ᵀnoised abroad throughout all the hill country of Ju-dae'-a.   *discussed*

66 And all they that heard *them* laid *them* up in their hearts, saying, What manner of child shall this be! And ᴿthe hand of the Lord was with him.   Gen. 39:2; Acts 11:21

67 And his father Zach-a-ri'-as ᴿwas filled with the Holy Ghost, and prophesied, saying,   Joel 2:28

68 ᴿBlessed *be* the Lord God of Israel; for he hath visited and redeemed his people,   1 Kin. 1:48

69 ᴿAnd hath raised up an horn of salvation for us in the house of his servant David;   2 Sam. 22:3

70 As he spake by the mouth of his holy prophets, which have been since the world began:

71 That we should be saved from our enemies, and from the hand of all that hate us;

72 ᴿTo perform the mercy *prom-*

ised to our fathers, and to remember his holy covenant;   Lev. 26:42

73 ᴿThe oath which he sware to our father Abraham,   Gen. 12:3

74 That he would grant unto us, that we being delivered out of the hand of our enemies might ᴿserve him without fear,   [Heb. 9:14]

75 ᴿIn holiness and righteousness before him, all the days of our life.   Jer. 32:39; [2 Thess. 2:13]

76 And thou, child, shalt be called the prophet of the Highest: for thou shalt go before the face of the Lord to prepare his ways;

77 To give ᴿknowledge of salvation unto his people by the remission of their sins,   [Jer. 31:34]

78 Through the tender mercy of our God; whereby the dayspring from on high hath visited us,

79 ᴿTo give light to them that sit ☆ in darkness and *in* the shadow of death, to guide our feet into the way of peace.   Is. 9:2; Matt. 4:16

80 And ᴿthe child grew, and waxed strong in spirit, and ᴿwas in the deserts till the day of his shewing unto Israel.   2:40 · Matt. 3:1

2 And it came to pass in those days, that there went out a decree from Caesar Augustus, that all the world should be taxed.

2 (*And* this ᵀtaxing was first made when Cy-re'-ni-us was governor of Syria.)   *registration, census*

3 And all went to be taxed, every one into his own city.

4 And Joseph also went up ★ from Galilee, out of the city of Nazareth, into Ju-dae'-a, unto the city of David, which is called Beth'-le-hem; (because he was of the house and lineage of David:)

5 To be taxed with Mary ᴿhis ᵀespoused wife, being great with child.   [Matt. 1:18] · *betrothed*

6 And so it was, that, while they were there, the days were ᵀaccomplished that she should be delivered.   *completed*

7 And ᴿshe brought forth her firstborn son, and wrapped him in swaddling clothes, and laid him in a manger; because there was no room for them in the inn.   Matt. 1:25

8　And there were in the same country shepherds abiding in the field, keeping watch over their flock by night.

9　And, lo, the angel of the Lord came upon them, and the glory of the Lord shone round about them: and they were sore afraid.

10　And the angel said unto them, Fear not: for, behold, I bring you good tidings of great joy, which shall be to all people.

★ 11　^RFor unto you is born this day in the city of David a Saviour, which is Christ the Lord.　Is. 9:6

12　And this *shall be* a sign unto you; Ye shall find the babe wrapped in swaddling clothes, lying in a manger.

13　^RAnd suddenly there was with the angel a multitude of the heavenly host praising God, and saying,　Ps. 148:2; Dan. 7:10; Rev. 5:11

14　^RGlory to God in the highest, and on earth ^Rpeace, good will toward men.　Matt. 21:9 · Is. 57:19

15　And it came to pass, as the angels were gone away from them into heaven, the shepherds said one to another, Let us now go even unto Beth'-le-hem, and see this thing which is come to pass, which the Lord hath made known unto us.

16　And they came with haste, and found Mary, and Joseph, and the babe lying in a manger.

17　And when they had seen *it*, they made known abroad the saying which was told them concerning this child.

18　And all they that heard *it* wondered at those things which were told them by the shepherds.

19　^RBut Mary kept all these things, and pondered *them* in her heart.　1:66; Gen. 37:11

20　And the shepherds returned, glorifying and praising God for all the things that they had heard and seen, as it was told unto them.

21　And when eight days were accomplished for the circumcising of the child, his name was called JESUS, which was so named of the angel ^Rbefore he was conceived in the womb.　1:31

22　And when ^Rthe days of her purification according to the law of Moses were accomplished, they brought him to Jerusalem, to present *him* to the Lord;　Lev. 12:2–8

23　(^RAs it is written in the law of the Lord, Every male that openeth the womb shall be called holy to the Lord;)　Ex. 22:29; Lev. 27:26

24　And to offer a sacrifice according to that which is said in the law of the Lord, A pair of turtledoves, or two young pigeons.

25　And, behold, there was a man in Jerusalem, whose name *was* Simeon; and the same man *was* just and devout, ^Rwaiting for the consolation of Israel: and the Holy Ghost was upon him.　Is. 40:1

26　And it was revealed unto him by the Holy Ghost, that he should not ^Rsee death, before he had seen the Lord's Christ.　Ps. 89:48; [Heb. 11:5]

27　And he came ^Rby the Spirit into the temple: and when the parents brought in the child Jesus, to do for him after the custom of the law,　Matt. 4:1

28　Then took he him up in his arms, and blessed God, and said,

29　Lord, ^Rnow lettest thou thy servant depart in peace, according to thy word:　Gen. 46:30; [Phil. 1:23]

30　For mine eyes ^Rhave seen thy salvation,　Ps. 119:166, 174; [Is. 52:10]

31　Which thou hast prepared before the face of all people;

32　^RA light to lighten the Gentiles, and the glory of thy people Israel.　Is. 9:2; 42:6; 49:6; 60:1–3; Matt. 4:16　★

33　And Joseph and his mother marvelled at those things which were spoken of him.

34　And Simeon blessed them, ☆ and said unto Mary his mother, Behold, this *child* is set for the ^Rfall and rising again of many in Israel; and for a sign which shall be spoken against;　Is. 8:14; Hos. 14:9

35　(Yea, ^Ra sword shall pierce through thy own soul also,) that the thoughts of many hearts may be revealed.　Ps. 42:10; John 19:25

36　And there was one Anna, a prophetess, the daughter of Phan'-u-el, of the tribe of ^RA'-ser:

she was of a great age, and had lived with an husband seven years from her virginity; Josh. 19:24
37 And she *was* a widow of about fourscore and four years, which departed not from the temple, but served *God* with fastings and prayers night and day.
38 And she coming in that instant gave thanks likewise unto the Lord, and spake of him to all them that ᴿlooked for redemption in Jerusalem.   24:21; Mark 15:43
39 And when they had performed all things according to the law of the Lord, they returned into Galilee, to their own city Nazareth.
40 ᴿAnd the child grew, and ᵀwaxed strong in spirit, filled with wisdom: and the grace of God was upon him.   v. 52; 1:80 · *became*
41 Now his parents went to ᴿJerusalem ᴿevery year at the feast of the passover.   John 4:20 · Ex. 23:15, 17
42 And when he was twelve years old, they went up to Jerusalem ᵀafter the ᴿcustom of the feast.   *according to* · Ex. 23:14, 15
43 And when they had fulfilled the ᴿdays, as they returned, the child Jesus ᵀtarried behind in Jerusalem; and Joseph and his mother knew not of *it.* Ex. 12:15 · *lingered*
44 But they, supposing him to have been in the company, went a day's journey; and they sought him among *their* ᵀkinsfolk and acquaintance.   *relatives*
45 And when they found him not, they turned back again to Jerusalem, seeking him.
46 And it came to pass, that after three days they found him in the temple, sitting in the midst of the doctors, both hearing them, and asking them questions.
47 And ᴿall that heard him were astonished at his understanding and answers.   Matt. 7:28; 13:54; 22:33
48 And when they saw him, they were amazed: and his mother said unto him, Son, why hast thou ᵀthus dealt with us? behold, thy father and I have sought thee ᵀsorrowing.   *done this to us · anxiously*

49 And he said unto them, How is it that ye sought me? ᵀwist ye not that I must be ᴿabout my Father's business?   *knew* · John 9:4
50 And they understood not the saying which he spake unto them.
51 And he went down with them, and came to Nazareth, and was subject unto them: but his mother ᴿkept all these sayings in her heart.   Dan. 7:28
52 And Jesus increased in wisdom and stature, ᴿand in favour with God and man.   1 Sam. 2:26

3 Now in the fifteenth year of the reign of Ti-be'-ri-us Caesar, ᴿPon'-tius Pilate being governor of Ju-dae'-a, and Herod being te'-trarch of Galilee, and his brother Philip te'-trarch of It-u-rae'-a and of the region of Trach-o-ni'-tis, and Ly-sa'-ni-as the te'-trarch of Ab-i-le'-ne,   Matt. 27:2
2 An'-nas and Ca'-ia-phas being the high priests, the word of God came unto John the son of Zach-a-ri'-as in the wilderness.
3 ᴿAnd he came into all the country about Jordan, preaching the baptism of repentance ᴿfor the remission of sins;   Matt. 3:1 · 1:77
4 As it is written in the book of ★ the words of E-sa'-ias the prophet, saying, ᴿThe voice of one crying in the wilderness, Prepare ye the way of the Lord, make his paths straight.   Is. 40:3–5; Matt. 3:3; Mark 1:3
5 Every valley shall be filled, and every mountain and hill shall be brought low; and the ᵀcrooked shall be made straight, and the rough ways *shall be* made smooth;   *crooked places*
6 And ᴿall flesh shall see the salvation of God.   Ps. 98:2; Is. 52:10
7 Then said he to the multitude that came forth to be baptized of him, O ᵀgeneration of vipers, who hath warned you to flee from the wrath to come?   *brood* or *offspring*
8 Bring forth therefore fruits ᴿworthy of repentance, and begin not to say within yourselves, We have Abraham ᵀto *our* father: for I

say unto you, That God is able of these stones to raise up children unto Abraham.   [2 Cor. 7:9–11] · *as*

9 And now also the axe is laid unto the root of the trees: ^Revery tree therefore which bringeth not forth good fruit is hewn down, and cast into the fire.   Matt. 7:19

10 And the people asked him, saying, What shall we do then?

11 He answereth and saith unto them, ^RHe that hath two coats, let him impart to him that hath none; and he that hath meat, ^Rlet him do likewise.   11:41; James 2:15, 16 · Is. 58:7

12 Then ^Rcame also publicans to be baptized, and said unto him, Master, what shall we do?   7:29

13 And he said unto them, ^RExact^T no more than that which is appointed you.   19:8 · *Collect*

14 And the soldiers likewise demanded of him, saying, And what shall we do? And he said unto them, Do violence to no man, neither accuse *any* falsely; and be content with your wages.

15 And as the people were in expectation, and all men ^Tmused in their hearts of John, whether he were the Christ, or not; *reasoned*

16 John answered, saying unto *them* all, I indeed baptize you with water; but one mightier than I cometh, the latchet of whose shoes I am not worthy to unloose: he shall ^Rbaptize you with the Holy Ghost and with fire: John 7:39

17 Whose fan *is* in his hand, and he will throughly purge his floor, and will gather the wheat into his ^Tgarner; but the chaff he will burn with fire unquenchable.   *barn*

18 And many other ^Tthings in his exhortation preached he unto the people.   *exhortations he preached*

19 ^RBut Herod the te'-trarch, being ^Treproved by him for He-ro'-di-as his brother Philip's wife, and for all the evils which Herod had done,   Matt. 14:3 · *rebuked*

20 Added yet this above all, that he shut up John in prison.

21 Now when all the people were baptized, ^Rit came to pass, that Jesus also being baptized,

and praying, the heaven was opened,   Matt. 3:13–17; John 1:32

22 And the Holy Ghost descend-ed in a bodily shape like a dove upon him, and a voice came from heaven, which said, Thou art my beloved Son; in thee I am ^Rwell pleased.   Ps. 2:7; Mark 1:11; 2 Pet. 1:17

23 And Jesus himself began to be about thirty years of age, be-ing (as was supposed) ^Rthe son of Joseph, which was the son of He'-li,   Matt. 13:55; John 6:42

24 Which was *the son* of Mat'-that, which was *the son* of Levi, which was *the son* of Mel'-chi, which was *the son* of Jan'-na, which was *the son* of Joseph,

25 Which was *the son* of Mat-ta-thi'-as, which was *the son* of Amos, which was *the son* of Na'-um, which was *the son* of Es'-li, which was *the son* of Nag'-ge,

26 Which was *the son* of Ma'-ath, which was *the son* of Mat-ta-thi'-as, which was *the son* of Sem'-e-i, which was *the son* of Joseph, which was *the son* of Juda,

27 Which was *the son* of Jo-an'-na, which was *the son* of Rhe'-sa, which was *the son* of Zo-rob'-a-bel, which was *the son* of Sa-la'-thi-el, which was *the son* of Ne'-ri,

28 Which was *the son* of Mel'-chi, which was *the son* of Ad'-di, which was *the son* of Co'-sam, which was *the son* of El-mo'-dam, which was *the son* of Er,

29 Which was *the son* of Jo'-se, which was *the son* of E-li-e'-zer, which was *the son* of Jo'-rim, which was *the son* of Mat'-that, which was *the son* of Levi,

30 Which was *the son* of Sim-eon, which was *the son* of Juda, which was *the son* of Joseph, which was *the son* of Jo'-nan, which was *the son* of E-li'-a-kim,

31 Which was *the son* of Me'-le-a, which was *the son* of Me'-nan, which was *the son* of Mat'-ta-tha, which was *the son* of Nathan, which was *the son* of David,   ★

32 Which was *the son* of Jesse, which was *the son* of O'-bed,

★ which was *the son* of Bo'-oz, which was *the son* of Sal'-mon, which was *the son* of Na-as'-son,

33 Which was *the son* of A-min'-a-dab, which was *the son* of A'-ram, which was *the son* of Es'-rom, which was *the son* of Pha'-res, which was *the son* of Juda,

34 Which was *the son* of Jacob, which was *the son* of Isaac, which was *the son* of Abraham, ᴿwhich was *the son* of Tha'-ra, which was *the son* of Na'-chor,   Gen. 11:24, 26–30

35 Which was *the son* of Sa'-ruch, which was *the son* of Ra'-gau, which was *the son* of Pha'-lec, which was *the son* of He'-ber, which was *the son* of Sa'-la,

36 Which was *the son* of Ca-i'-nan, which was *the son* of Ar-phax'-ad, which was *the son* of Sem, which was *the son* of No'-e, which was *the son* of La'-mech,

37 Which was *the son* of Ma-thu'-sa-la, which was *the son* of E'-noch, which was *the son* of Ja'-red, which was *the son* of Ma-le'-le-el, which was *the son* of Ca-i'-nan,

38 Which was *the son* of E'-nos, which was *the son* of Seth, which was *the son* of Adam, ᴿwhich was *the son* of God.   Gen. 5:1, 2

4 And Jesus being full of the Holy Ghost returned from Jordan, and ᴿwas led by the Spirit into the wilderness,   2:27; Ezek. 3:12

2 Being forty days ᵀtempted of the devil. And ᴿin those days he did eat nothing: and when they were ended, he afterward hungered.   *tested by* · Ex. 34:28; 1 Kin. 19:8

3 And the devil said unto him, If thou be the ᴿSon of God, command this stone that it be made bread.   Mark 3:11; John 20:31

4 And Jesus answered him, saying, It is written, ᴿThat man shall not live by bread alone, but by every word of God.   Deut. 8:3

5 And the devil, taking him up into an high mountain, shewed unto him all the kingdoms of the world in a moment of time.

6 And the devil said unto him, All this ᵀpower will I give thee, and the glory of them: for that is delivered unto me; and to whomsoever I will I give it.   *authority*

7 If thou therefore wilt worship me, all shall be thine.

8 And Jesus answered and said unto him, Get thee behind me, Satan: for it is written, Thou shalt worship the Lord thy God, and him only shalt thou serve.

9 And he brought him to Jerusalem, and set him on a pinnacle of the temple, and said unto him, If thou be the Son of God, cast thyself down from hence:

10 For it is written, ᴿHe shall give his angels charge over thee, to keep thee: Ps. 91:11, 12

11 And in *their* hands they shall bear thee up, lest at any time thou dash thy foot against a stone.

12 And Jesus answering said unto him, It is said, Thou shalt not ᵀtempt the Lord thy God.   *test*

13 And when the devil had ended all the temptation, he departed from him for a season.

14 ᴿAnd Jesus returned ᴿin the power of the Spirit into Galilee: and there went out ᵀa fame of him through all the region round about.   Matt. 4:12 · John 4:43 · *news*

15 And he taught in their synagogues, being glorified of all.

16 And he came to Nazareth, where he had been brought up: and, as his custom was, he went into the synagogue on the sabbath day, and stood up for to read.

17 And there was delivered unto him the book of the prophet E-sa'-ias. And when he had opened the book, he found the ᴿplace where it was written,   Is. 61:1, 2

18 The Spirit of the Lord *is* upon ★ me, because he hath anointed me to preach the gospel to the poor; he hath sent me to heal the brokenhearted, to preach deliverance to the captives, and recovering of sight to the blind, to set at liberty them that are bruised,

19 To preach the acceptable year of the Lord.

20 And he closed the book, and he gave *it* again to the ^Tminister, and sat down. And the eyes of all them that were in the synagogue were fastened on him.   *attendant*

21 And he began to say unto them, This day is this scripture ^Rfulfilled in your ears.   Acts 13:29

22 And all bare him witness, and ^Rwondered at the gracious words which proceeded out of his mouth. And they said, ^RIs not this Joseph's son?   Mark 6:2 · John 6:42

23 And he said unto them, Ye will surely say unto me this proverb, Physician, heal thyself: whatsoever we have heard done in ^RCa-per'-na-um, do also here in ^Rthy country.   Matt. 4:13 · Matt. 13:54

24 And he said,Verily I say unto you, No ^Rprophet is accepted in his own country.   Mark 6:4; John 4:44

25 But I tell you of a truth, many widows were in Israel in the days of E-li'-as, when the heaven was shut up three years and six months, when great famine was throughout all the land;

26 But unto none of them was E-li'-as sent, save unto ^TSa-rep'-ta, *a city* of Si'-don, unto a woman *that was* a widow.   *Zarephath,* 1 Kin. 17:9

27 ^RAnd many lepers were in Israel in the time of El-i-se'-us the prophet; and none of them was cleansed, saving Na'-a-man the Syrian.   2 Kin. 5:1–14

28 And all they in the synagogue, when they heard these things, were filled with wrath,

29 ^RAnd rose up, and thrust him out of the city, and led him unto the brow of the hill whereon their city was built, that they might cast him down headlong.   17:25; John 8:37

30 But he passing through the midst of them went his way,

31 And came down to Ca-per'-na-um, a city of Galilee, and taught them on the sabbath days.

32 And they were astonished at his ^Tdoctrine: ^Rfor his word was with power.   *teaching* · [John 6:63; 7:46]

33 ^RAnd in the synagogue there was a man, which had a spirit of an unclean ^Tdevil, and cried out with a loud voice,   Mark 1:23 · *demon*

34 Saying, Let *us* alone; what have we to do with thee, *thou* Jesus of Nazareth? art thou come to destroy us? I know thee who thou art; the Holy One of God.

35 And Jesus rebuked him, saying, ^THold thy peace, and come out of him. And when the ^Tdevil had thrown him in the midst, he came out of him, and hurt him not.   Lit. *Be muzzled* · *demon*

36 And they were all amazed, and spake among themselves, saying, What a word *is* this! for with authority and power he commandeth the unclean spirits, and they come out.

37 And the ^Tfame of him went out into every place of the country round about.   *report about him*

38 And he arose out of the synagogue, and entered into Si-mon's house. And Simon's wife's mother was taken with a great fever; and they besought him for her.

39 And he stood over her, and ^Rrebuked the fever; and it left her: and immediately she arose and ^Tministered unto them.   8:24 · *served*

40 ^RNow when the sun was setting, all they that had any sick with divers diseases brought them unto him; and he laid his hands on every one of them, and healed them.   Matt. 8:16, 17; Mark 1:32–34

41 And devils also came out of many, crying out, and saying, Thou art Christ the Son of God. And ^Rhe rebuking *them* suffered them not to speak: for they knew that he was Christ. Mark 1:25, 34; 3:11

42 ^RAnd when it was day, he departed and went into a desert place: and the people sought him, and came unto him, and ^Tstayed him, that he should not depart from them.   9:10 · *tried to restrain him*

43 And he said unto them, I must ^Rpreach the kingdom of God to other cities also: for therefore am I sent.   Mark 1:14; [John 9:4]

44 ^RAnd he preached in the synagogues of Galilee.   Matt. 4:23; 9:35

5 And it came to pass, that, as the people pressed upon him to hear the word of God, he stood by the lake of Gen-nes'-a-ret,

2 And saw two ships standing by the lake: but the fishermen were gone out of them, and were washing *their* nets.

3 And he entered into one of the ships, which was Simon's, and prayed him that he would thrust out a little from the land. And he ᴿsat down, and taught the ᵀpeople out of the ship. John 8:2 · *multitudes*

4 Now when he had left speaking, he said unto Simon, Launch out into the deep, and let down your nets for a ᵀdraught. *catch*

5 And Simon answering said unto him, Master, we have toiled all the night, and have taken nothing: nevertheless ᴿat thy word I will let down the net. Ps. 33:9

6 And when they had this done, they ᵀinclosed a great multitude of fishes: and their net ᵀbrake. *caught · was breaking*

7 And they beckoned unto *their* partners, which were in the other ship, that they should come and help them. And they came, and filled both the ships, so that they began to sink.

8 When Simon Peter saw *it*, he fell down at Jesus' knees, saying, ᴿDepart from me; for I am a sinful man, O Lord. 2 Sam. 6:9; 1 Kin. 17:18

9 For he was ᴿastonished, and all that were with him, at the ᵀdraught of the fishes which they had taken: Mark 5:42; 10:24, 26 · *catch*

10 And so *was* also James, and John, the sons of Zeb'-e-dee, which were partners with Simon. And Jesus said unto Simon, Fear not; ᴿfrom henceforth thou shalt catch men. Matt. 4:19; Mark 1:17

11 And when they had brought their ships to land, ᴿthey forsook all, and followed him. Matt. 4:20

12 And it came to pass, when he was in a certain city, behold a man full of leprosy: who seeing Jesus fell on *his* face, and besought him, saying, Lord, if thou wilt, thou canst make me clean.

13 And he put forth *his* hand, and touched him, saying, I will: be thou clean. And ᴿimmediately the leprosy departed from him. 8:44

14 ᴿAnd he charged him to tell no man: but go, and shew thyself to the priest, and offer for thy cleansing, ᴿaccording as Moses commanded, for a testimony unto them. Matt. 8:4 · Lev. 13:1–3; 14:2–32

15 But so much the more went there a ᴿfame abroad of him: ᴿand great multitudes came together to hear, and to be healed by him of their infirmities. Mark 1:45 · Matt. 4:25

16 And he withdrew himself into the wilderness, and prayed.

17 And it came to pass on a certain day, as he was teaching, that there were Pharisees and ᵀdoctors of the law sitting by, which were come out of every town of Galilee, and Ju-dae'-a, and Jerusalem: and the power of the Lord was *present* to heal them. *teachers*

18 And, behold, men brought in a bed a man which was ᵀtaken with a palsy: and they sought *means* to bring him in, and to lay *him* before him. *paralyzed*

19 And when they could not find by what *way* they might bring him in because of the multitude, they went upon the housetop, and let him down through the tiling with *his* ᵀcouch into the midst ᴿbefore Jesus. *bed* · Matt. 15:30

20 And when he saw their faith, he said unto him, Man, thy sins are forgiven thee.

21 And the scribes and the Pharisees began to reason, saying, Who is this which speaketh blasphemies? ᴿWho can forgive sins, but God alone? Ps. 32:5; Is. 43:25

22 But when Jesus ᴿperceived their thoughts, he answering said unto them, What reason ye in your hearts? 9:47; John 2:25

23 Whether is easier, to say, Thy sins be forgiven thee; or to say, Rise up and walk?

24 But that ye may know that the Son of man hath power upon earth to forgive sins, (he said unto the sick of the palsy,) ᴿI say unto

thee, Arise, and take up thy couch, and go into thine house. Mark 2:11

25 And immediately he rose up before them, and took up that whereon he lay, and departed to his own house, glorifying God.

26 And they were all amazed, and they ᴿglorified God, and were filled with fear, saying, We have seen strange things to day.1:65; 7:16

27 And after these things he went forth, and saw a ᵀpublican, named Levi, sitting at the ᵀreceipt of custom: and he said unto him, Follow me.   *tax collector · tax office*

28 And he left all, rose up, and ᴿfollowed him.   Matt. 4:22; 19:27

29 ᴿAnd Levi made him a great feast in his own house: and ᴿthere was a great company of publicans and of others that sat down with them.   Matt. 9:9, 10; Mark 2:15 · 15:1

30 But their scribes and Pharisees murmured against his disciples, saying, Why do ye eat and drink with publicans and sinners?

31 And Jesus answering said unto them, They that are ᵀwhole need not a physician; but they that are sick.   *healthy*

32 I came not to call the righteous, but sinners to repentance.

33 And they said unto him, ᴿWhy do the disciples of John fast often, and make prayers, and likewise *the disciples* of the Pharisees; but thine eat and drink?   7:33

34 And he said unto them, Can ye make the children of the bridechamber fast, while the ᴿbridegroom is with them?   John 3:29

35 But the days will come, when the bridegroom shall be taken away from them, and then shall they fast in those days.

36 ᴿAnd he spake also a parable unto them; No man putteth a piece of a new garment upon an old; if otherwise, then both the new maketh a rent, and the piece that was *taken* out of the new agreeth not with the old. Matt. 9:16

37 And no man putteth new wine into old ᵀbottles; else the new wine will burst the bottles, and be spilled, and the bottles shall ᵀperish.   *wineskins · be ruined*

38 But new wine must be put into new ᵀbottles; and both are preserved.   *wineskins*

39 No man also having drunk old *wine* straightway desireth new: for he saith, The old is better.

6 And it came to pass on the second sabbath after the first, that he went through the ᵀcorn fields; and his disciples plucked the ears of corn, and did eat, rubbing *them* in *their* hands.   *grain*

2 And certain of the Pharisees said unto them, Why do ye that ᴿwhich is not lawful to do on the sabbath days?   Ex. 20:10

3 And Jesus answering them said, Have ye not read so much as this, ᴿwhat David did, when himself was an hungred, and they which were with him;   1 Sam. 21:6

4 How he went into the house of God, and did take and eat the shewbread, and gave also to them that were with him; ᴿwhich it is not lawful to eat but for the priests alone?   Lev. 24:9

5 And he said unto them, That the Son of man is Lord also of the sabbath.

6 ᴿAnd it came to pass also on another sabbath, that he entered into the synagogue and taught: and there was a man whose right hand was withered.   Matt. 12:9–14

7 And the scribes and Pharisees watched him, whether he would ᴿheal on the sabbath day; that they might find an ᴿaccusation against him.   13:14; 14:1–6 · 20:20

8 But he ᴿknew their thoughts, and said to the man which had the withered hand, Rise up, and stand forth in the midst. And he arose and stood forth. Matt. 9:4; John 2:24, 25

9 Then said Jesus unto them, I will ask you one thing; ᴿIs it lawful on the sabbath days to do good, or to do evil? to save life, or to destroy *it*?   John 7:23

10 And looking round about upon them all, he said unto the man, Stretch forth thy hand. And

he did so: and his hand was restored whole as the other.

11 And they were filled with ᵀmadness; and ᵀcommuned one with another what they might do to Jesus.   *rage · discussed*

12 And it came to pass in those days, that he went out into a mountain to pray, and continued all night in ᴿprayer to God.   9:18

13 And when it was day, he called *unto him* his disciples: ᴿand of them he chose twelve, whom also he named apostles;   John 6:70

14 Simon, (ᴿwhom he also named Peter,) and Andrew his brother, James and John, Philip and Bartholomew,   John 1:42

15 Matthew and Thomas, James the *son* of Al-phae'-us, and Simon called ᵀZe-lo'-tes,   *the Zealot*

16 And Judas *the brother* of James, and ᴿJudas Is-car'-i-ot, which also was the traitor.   22:3-6

17 And he came down with them, and stood in the plain, and the company of his disciples, and a great multitude of people out of all Ju-dae'-a and Jerusalem, and from the sea coast of Tyre and Si'-don, which came to hear him, and to be healed of their diseases:

18 And they that were ᵀvexed with unclean spirits: and they were healed.   *tormented*

19 And the whole multitude sought to ᴿtouch him: for there went ᵀvirtue out of him, and healed *them* all.   8:44-47 · power

20 And he lifted up his eyes on his disciples, and said, ᴿBlessed *be ye* poor: for yours is the kingdom of God.   Matt. 5:3-12; [James 2:5]

21 ᴿBlessed *are ye* that hunger now: for ye shall be filled. Blessed *are ye* that weep now: for ye shall ᴿlaugh. Is. 55:1; 65:13; Matt. 5:6 · Ps. 126:5

22 ᴿBlessed are ye, when men shall hate you, and when they shall separate you *from their company*, and shall reproach *you*, and cast out your name as evil, for the Son of man's sake.   1 Pet. 2:19

23 Rejoice ye in that day, and leap for joy: for, behold, your reward *is* great in heaven: for ᴿin

the like manner did their fathers unto the prophets.   Acts 7:51

24 ᴿBut woe unto you ᴿthat are rich! for ᴿye have received your consolation.   Amos 6:1 · 12:21 · 16:25

25 Woe unto you that are full! for ye shall hunger. Woe unto you that laugh now! for ye shall mourn and ᴿweep.   James 4:9

26 Woe unto you, when all men shall speak well of you! for so did their fathers to the false prophets.

27 ᴿBut I say unto you which hear, Love your enemies, do good to them which hate you,   Matt. 5:44

28 ᴿBless them that curse you, and ᴿpray for them which despitefully use you.   Rom. 12:14 · Acts 7:60

29 ᴿAnd unto him that smiteth thee on the *one* cheek offer also the other; ᴿand him that taketh away thy cloke forbid not *to take* thy coat also. Matt. 5:39-42 · [1 Cor. 6:7]

30 ᴿGive to every man that asketh of thee; and of him that taketh away thy goods ask *them* not again.   Deut. 15:7, 8; Matt. 5:42

31 ᴿAnd as ye would that men should do to you, do ye also to them likewise.   Matt. 7:12

32 ᴿFor if ye love them which love you, what ᵀthank have ye? for sinners also love those that love them.   Matt. 5:45 · credit

33 And if ye do good to them which do good to you, what ᵀthank have ye? for sinners also do even the same.   credit

34 ᴿAnd if ye lend *to them* of whom ye hope to receive, what ᵀthank have ye? for sinners also lend to sinners, to receive as much again.   Matt. 5:42 · credit

35 But ᴿlove ye your enemies, and do good, and lend, hoping for nothing again; and your reward shall be great, and ᴿye shall be the children of the Highest: for he is kind unto the unthankful and *to* the evil.   [Rom. 13:10] · Matt. 5:46

36 Be ye therefore merciful, as your Father also is merciful.

37 ᴿJudge not, and ye shall not be judged: condemn not, and ye shall not be condemned: forgive, and ye shall be forgiven: Matt. 7:1-5

38 Give, and it shall be given unto you; good measure, pressed down, and shaken together, and running over, shall men give into your bosom. For with the same measure that ye mete withal it shall be measured to you again.

39 And he spake a parable unto them, ^RCan the blind lead the blind? shall they not both fall into the ditch?   Matt. 15:14; 23:16; Rom. 2:19

40 The disciple is not above his master: but every one that is perfect shall be as his master.

41 And why beholdest thou the ^Tmote that is in thy brother's eye, but perceivest not the ^Tbeam that is in thine own eye?   speck · plank

42 Either how canst thou say to thy brother, Brother, let me pull out the ^Tmote that is in thine eye, when thou thyself beholdest not the ^Tbeam that is in thine own eye? Thou hypocrite, cast out first the beam out of thine own eye, and then shalt thou see clearly to pull out the mote that is in thy brother's eye.   speck · plank

43 ^RFor a good tree bringeth not forth ^Tcorrupt fruit; neither doth a ^Tcorrupt tree bring forth good fruit.   Matt. 7:16–18, 20 · bad

44 For every tree is known by his own fruit. For of thorns men do not gather figs, nor of a bramble bush gather they grapes.

45 ^RA good man out of the good treasure of his heart bringeth forth that which is good; and an evil man out of the evil treasure of his heart bringeth forth that which is evil: for of the abundance of the heart his mouth speaketh.   Matt. 12:35

46 ^RAnd why call ye me, Lord, Lord, and do not the things which I say?   Mal. 1:6; Matt. 7:21; 25:11

47 ^RWhosoever cometh to me, and heareth my sayings, and doeth them, I will shew you to whom he is like: Matt. 7:24–27

48 He is like a man which built an house, and digged deep, and laid the foundation on a rock: and when the flood arose, the stream beat vehemently upon that house,

and could not shake it: for it was founded upon a rock.

49 But he that heareth, and doeth not, is like a man that without a foundation built an house upon the earth; against which the stream did beat vehemently, and immediately it fell; and the ruin of that house was great.

7 Now when he had ended all his sayings in the ^Taudience of the people, he ^Rentered into Caper'-na-um.   hearing · Matt. 8:5–13

2 And a certain centurion's servant, who was dear unto him, was sick, and ready to die.

3 And when he heard of Jesus, he sent unto him the elders of the Jews, beseeching him that he would come and heal his servant.

4 And when they came to Jesus, they besought him ^Tinstantly, saying, That he was worthy for whom he should do this: earnestly

5 For he loveth our nation, and he hath built us a synagogue.

6 Then Jesus went with them. And when he was now not far from the house, the centurion sent friends to him, saying unto him, Lord, trouble not thyself: for I am not worthy that thou shouldest enter under my roof:

7 Wherefore neither thought I myself worthy to come unto thee: but ^Rsay in a word, and my servant shall be healed.   Ps. 33:9; 107:20

8 For I also am a man set under authority, having under me soldiers, and I say unto one, Go, and he goeth; and to another, Come, and he cometh; and to my servant, Do this, and he doeth it.

9 When Jesus heard these things, he marvelled at him, and turned him about, and said unto the people that followed him, I say unto you, I have not found so great faith, no, not in Israel.

10 And they that were sent, returning to the house, found the servant ^Twhole that had been sick.   healthy

11 And it came to pass the day after, that he went into a city called Na'-in; and many of his dis-

ciples went with him, ᵀand much people. *a large crowd*

12 Now when he came ᵀnigh to the gate of the city, behold, there was a dead man carried out, the only son of his mother, and she was a widow: and much people of the city was with her. *near*

13 And when the Lord saw her, he had ᴿcompassion on her, and said unto her, Weep not. John 11:35

14 And he came and touched the bier: and they that bare *him* stood still. And he said, Young man, I say unto thee, ᴿArise. 8:54

15 And he that was dead ᴿsat up, and began to speak. And he delivered him to his mother. Matt. 11:5

16 ᴿAnd there came a fear on all: and they ᴿglorified God, saying, ᴿThat a great prophet is risen up among us; and, That God hath visited his people. 1:65 · 5:26 · 24:19

17 And this rumour of him went forth throughout all Ju-dae'-a, and throughout all the region round about.

18 And the disciples of John shewed him of all these things.

19 And John calling *unto him* two of his disciples sent *them* to Jesus, saying, Art thou he that should ᴿcome? or look we for another? [Mic. 5:2; Zech. 9:9; Mal. 3:1–3]

20 When the men were come unto him, they said, John Baptist hath sent us unto thee, saying, Art thou ᵀhe that should come? or look we for another? *the coming one*

21 And in that same hour he cured many of *their* infirmities and ᵀplagues, and of evil spirits; and unto many *that were* blind he gave sight. *afflictions*

★ 22 ᴿThen Jesus answering said unto them, Go your way, and tell John what things ye have seen and heard; how that the blind see, the lame walk, the lepers are cleansed, the deaf hear, the dead are raised, ᴿto the poor the gospel is preached. Matt. 11:4 · [4:18; Is. 61:1–3]

23 And blessed is *he*, whosoever shall not be offended in me.

24 ᴿAnd when the messengers of John were departed, he began to speak unto the people concerning John, What went ye out into the wilderness for to see? A reed shaken with the wind? Matt. 11:7

25 But what went ye out for to see? A man clothed in soft raiment? Behold, they which are gorgeously apparelled, and live delicately, are in kings' courts.

26 But what went ye out for to see? A prophet? Yea, I say unto you, and much more than a prophet.

27 This is *he*, of whom it is written, Behold, I send my messenger before thy face, which shall prepare thy way before thee. ★

28 For I say unto you, Among those that are born of women there is not a ᴿgreater prophet than John the Baptist: but he that is least in the kingdom of God is greater than he. [1:15]

29 And all the people that heard *him*, and the publicans, justified God, ᴿbeing baptized with the baptism of John. 3:12; Matt. 3:5

30 But the Pharisees and ᵀlawyers rejected the counsel of God against themselves, being not baptized of him. *experts in the law*

31 And the Lord said, ᴿWhereunto then shall I liken the men of this generation? and to what are they like? Matt. 11:16

32 They are like unto children sitting in the marketplace, and calling one to another, and saying, We have ᵀpiped unto you, and ye have not danced; we have mourned to you, and ye have not wept. *played the flute for you*

33 For ᴿJohn the Baptist came ᴿneither eating bread nor drinking wine; and ye say, He hath a devil. Matt. 3:1 · 1:15; [Matt. 3:4]

34 The Son of man is come ᴿeating and drinking; and ye say, Behold a gluttonous man, and a winebibber, a friend of ᵀpublicans and sinners! 15:2 · *tax collectors*

35 ᴿBut wisdom is justified of all her children. Matt. 11:19

36 And one of the Pharisees desired him that he would eat with him. And he went into the

Pharisee's house, and sat down to meat.

37 And, behold, a woman in the city, which was a sinner, when she knew that *Jesus* sat at meat in the Pharisee's house, brought an alabaster ᵀbox of ointment,   *flask*

38 And stood at his feet behind *him* weeping, and began to wash his feet with tears, and did wipe *them* with the hairs of her head, and kissed his feet, and anointed *them* with the ointment.

39 Now when the Pharisee which had bidden him saw *it*, he spake within himself, saying, This man, if he were a prophet, would have known who and what manner of woman *this is* that toucheth him: for she is a sinner.

40 And Jesus answering said unto him, Simon, I have somewhat to say unto thee. And he saith, ᵀMaster, say on.   *Teacher*

41 There was a certain creditor which had two debtors: the one owed five hundred ᴿpence, and the other fifty.   Matt. 18:28; Mark 6:37

42 And when they had nothing to pay, he ᵀfrankly forgave them both. Tell me therefore, which of them will love him most?   *freely*

43 Simon answered and said, I suppose that *he*, to whom he forgave most. And he said unto him, Thou hast rightly judged.

44 And he turned to the woman, and said unto Simon, Seest thou this woman? I entered into thine house, thou gavest me no water for my feet: but she hath washed my feet with tears, and wiped *them* with the hairs of her head.

45 Thou gavest me no kiss: but this woman since the time I came in hath not ceased to kiss my feet.

46 My head with oil thou didst not anoint: but this woman hath anointed my feet with ointment.

47 ᴿWherefore I say unto thee, Her sins, which are many, are forgiven; for she loved much: but to whom little is forgiven, *the same* loveth little.   [1 Tim. 1:14]

48 And he said unto her, ᴿThy sins are forgiven.   Matt. 9:2; Mark 2:5

49 And they that sat at meat with him began to say within themselves, ᴿWho is this that forgiveth sins also?   Matt. 9:3; [Mark 2:7]

50 And he said to the woman, ᴿThy faith hath saved thee; go in peace.   Matt. 9:22; Mark 5:34; 10:52

8 And it came to pass afterward, that he went throughout every city and village, preaching and ᵀshewing the glad tidings of the kingdom of God: and the twelve *were* with him,   *proclaiming*

2 And ᴿcertain women, which had been healed of evil spirits and infirmities, Mary called Mag-da-le′-ne, ᴿout of whom went seven devils,   Mark 15:40, 41 · Mark 16:9

3 And Jo-an′-na the wife of Chu′-za Herod's steward, and Susanna, and many others, which ᵀministered unto him of their ᵀsubstance.   *provided · possessions*

4 ᴿAnd when much people were gathered together, and were come to him out of every city, he spake by a parable: Matt. 13:2–9

5 A sower went out to sow his seed: and as he sowed, some fell by the way side; and it was ᵀtrodden down, and the fowls of the air devoured it.   *trampled*

6 And some fell upon a rock; and as soon as it was sprung up, it withered away, because it lacked moisture.

7 And some fell among thorns; and the thorns sprang up with it, and choked it.

8 And other fell on good ground, and sprang up, and bare fruit an hundredfold. And when he had said these things, he cried, ᴿHe that hath ears to hear, let him hear.   14:35; Matt. 11:15; Mark 7:16

9 ᴿAnd his disciples asked him, saying, What might this parable ᵀbe?   Matt. 13:10–23; Mark 4:10–20 · *mean*

10 And he said, Unto you it is   ★ given to know the mysteries of the kingdom of God: but to others in parables; ᴿthat seeing they might not see, and hearing they might not understand.   Is. 6:9; Acts 28:26

11 Now the parable is this: The seed is the ᴿword of God.   5:1; 11:28

12 Those by the way side are they that hear; then cometh the devil, and taketh away the word out of their hearts, lest they should believe and be saved.

13 They on the rock *are they*, which, when they hear, receive the word with joy; and these have no root, which for a while believe, and in time of ^Ttemptation fall away.   *testing*

14 And that which fell among thorns are they, which, when they have heard, go forth, and are choked with cares and riches and pleasures of *this* life, and bring no fruit to perfection.

15 But that on the good ground are they, which in an honest and good heart, having heard the word, keep *it*, and bring forth fruit with ^Rpatience.   [Rom. 2:7; James 5:7, 8]

16 ^RNo man, when he hath lighted a ^Tcandle, covereth it with a vessel, or putteth *it* under a bed; but setteth *it* on a ^Tcandlestick, that they which enter in may see the light.   Matt. 5:15 · *lamp · lampstand*

17 For nothing is secret, that shall not be made manifest; neither *any thing* hid, that shall not be known and come abroad.

18 Take heed therefore how ye hear: ^Rfor whosoever hath, to him shall be given; and whosoever hath not, from him shall be taken even that which he seemeth to ^Rhave.   Matt. 25:29 · Matt. 13:12

19 Then came to him *his* mother and his brethren, and could not come at him for the press.

20 And it was told him *by certain* which said, Thy mother and thy brethren stand ^Twithout, desiring to see thee.   *outside*

21 And he answered and said unto them, My mother and my brethren are these which hear the word of God, and do it.

22 Now it came to pass on a certain day, that he went into a ship with his disciples: and he said unto them, Let us go over unto the other side of the lake. And they launched forth.

23 But as they sailed he fell asleep: and there came down a storm of wind on the lake; and they were ^Tfilled *with water*, and were in jeopardy.   *filling*

24 And they came to him, and awoke him, saying, Master, master, we perish. Then he arose, and rebuked the wind and the raging of the water: and they ceased, and there was a calm.

25 And he said unto them, ^RWhere is your faith? And they being afraid ^Twondered, saying one to another, ^RWhat manner of man is this! for he commandeth even the winds and water, and they obey him.   9:41 · *marvelled* · 4:36

26 And they arrived at the country of the Gad-a-renes', which is ^Tover against Galilee.   *opposite*

27 And when he went forth to land, there met him out of the city a certain man, which had ^Tdevils long time, and ^Tware no clothes, neither abode in *any* house, but in the tombs.   *demons · wore*

28 When he saw Jesus, he ^Rcried out, and fell down before him, and with a loud voice said, What have I to do with thee, Jesus, *thou* Son of God most high? I ^Tbeseech thee, torment me not. Mark 1:26 · *beg*

29 (For he had commanded the unclean spirit to come out of the man. For oftentimes it had ^Tcaught him: and he was kept bound with chains and ^Tin fetters; and he brake the bands, and was driven of the ^Tdevil into the wilderness.)   *seized · shackles · demon*

30 And Jesus asked him, saying, What is thy name? And he said, Legion: because many ^Tdevils were entered into him.   *demons*

31 And they besought him that he would not command them to go out ^Rinto the deep.   Rom. 10:7

32 And there was there an herd of many ^Rswine feeding on the mountain: and they ^Tbesought him that he would ^Tsuffer them to enter into them. And he suffered them. Lev. 11:7; Deut. 14:8 · *begged · allow*

33 Then went the ^Tdevils out of the man, and entered into the swine: and the herd ran violently

down a steep place into the lake, and ᵀwere choked. *demons · drowned*

34 When they that fed *them* saw what was done, they fled, and went and told *it* in the city and in the country.

35 Then they went out to see what was done; and came to Jesus, and found the man, out of whom the devils were departed, sitting at the ᴿfeet of Jesus, clothed, and in his right mind: and they were afraid. Matt. 28:9; Mark 7:25

36 They also which saw *it* told them by what means he that was possessed of the devils was healed.

37 ᴿThen the whole multitude of the country of the Gad-a-renes' round about ᴿbesought him to ᴿdepart from them; for they were taken with great fear: and he went up into the ship, and returned back again. Matt. 8:34 · 4:34 · Acts 16:39

38 Now ᴿthe man out of whom the devils were departed ᵀbesought him that he might be with him: but Jesus sent him away, saying, Mark 5:18–20 · *begged*

39 Return to thine own house, and shew how great things God hath done unto thee. And he went his way, and published throughout the whole city how great things Jesus had done unto him.

40 And it came to pass, that, when Jesus was returned, the people *gladly* received him: for they were all waiting for him.

41 ᴿAnd, behold, there came a man named Ja-i'-rus, and he was a ruler of the synagogue: and he fell down at Jesus' feet, and besought him that he would come into his house: Matt. 9:18–26

42 For he had one only daughter, about twelve years of age, and she lay ᴿa dying. But as he went the people thronged him. 7:2

43 ᴿAnd a woman having an ᴿissue of blood twelve years, which had spent all her living upon physicians, neither could be healed of any, Matt. 9:20 · 15:19–22

44 Came behind *him*, and touched the border of his gar-

ment: and immediately her ᵀissue of blood ᵀstanched. *flow · stopped*

45 And Jesus said, Who touched me? When all denied, Peter and they that were with him said, Master, the multitude throng thee and press *thee*, and sayest thou, Who touched me?

46 And Jesus said, Somebody hath touched me: for I perceive that virtue is gone out of me.

47 And when the woman saw that she was not hid, she came trembling, and falling down before him, she declared unto him before all the people for what cause she had touched him, and how she was healed immediately.

48 And he said unto her, Daughter, be of good ᵀcomfort: ᴿthy faith hath made thee ᵀwhole; ᴿgo in peace. *cheer · 7:50 · well · John 8:11*

49 ᴿWhile he yet spake, there cometh one from the ruler of the synagogue's *house*, saying to him, Thy daughter is dead; trouble not the ᵀMaster. Mark 5:35 · *Teacher*

50 But when Jesus heard *it*, he answered him, saying, Fear not: ᴿbelieve only, and she shall be made whole. [Mark 11:22–24]

51 And when he came into the house, he ᵀsuffered no man to go in, save Peter, and James, and John, and the father and the mother of the maiden. *permitted*

52 And all wept, and bewailed her: but he said, Weep not; she is not dead, but sleepeth.

53 And they laughed him to scorn, knowing that she was dead.

54 And he put them all out, and took her by the hand, and called, saying, Maid, ᴿarise. 7:14; John 11:43

55 And her spirit came again, and she arose straightway: and he commanded to give her meat.

56 And her parents were astonished: but ᴿhe charged them that they should tell no man what was done. Matt. 8:4; 9:30; Mark 5:43

9 Then he called his twelve disciples together, and gave them power and authority over all devils, and to cure diseases.

2 And ᴿhe sent them to preach the kingdom of God, and to heal the sick.   Matt. 10:7, 8; Mark 6:12

3 ᴿAnd he said unto them, Take nothing for your journey, neither ᵀstaves, nor ᵀscrip, neither bread, neither money; neither have two coats apiece.   Mark 6:8–11 · staffs · bag

4 ᴿAnd whatsoever house ye enter into, there abide, and thence depart.   Matt. 10:11; Mark 6:10

5 ᴿAnd whosoever will not receive you, when ye go out of that city, ᴿshake off the very dust from your feet for a testimony against them.   Matt. 10:14 · 10:11; Acts 13:51

6 ᴿAnd they departed, and went through the towns, preaching the gospel, and healing every where.   8:1; Mark 6:12

7 ᴿNow Herod the te'-trarch heard of all that was done by him: and he was perplexed, because that it was said of some, that John was risen from the dead;   Mark 6:14

8 And of some, that E-li'-as had appeared; and of others, that one of the old prophets was risen again.

9 And Herod said, John have I beheaded: but who is this, of whom I hear such things? ᴿAnd he ᵀdesired to see him.   23:8 · sought

10 ᴿAnd the apostles, when they were returned, told him all that they had done. And he took them, and went aside privately into a desert place belonging to the city called Beth-sa'-i-da.   Mark 6:30

11 And the ᵀpeople, when they knew it, followed him: and he received them, and spake unto them of the kingdom of God, and healed them that had need of healing.   multitudes

12 ᴿAnd when the day began to wear away, then came the twelve, and said unto him, Send the multitude away, that they may go into the towns and country round about, and lodge, and get ᵀvictuals: for we are here in a desert place.   Matt. 14:15; Mark 6:35 · provisions

13 But he said unto them, Give ye them to eat. And they said, We have no more but five loaves and two fishes; except we should go and buy meat for all this people.

14 For they were about five thousand men. And he said to his disciples, Make them sit down by fifties in a ᵀcompany.   group

15 And they did so, and made them all sit down.

16 Then he took the five loaves and the two fishes, and looking up to heaven, he ᴿblessed them, and brake, and gave to the disciples to set before the multitude.   24:30

17 And they did eat, and were all ᵀfilled: and there was taken up of fragments that remained to them twelve baskets.   satisfied

18 ᴿAnd it came to pass, as he was alone praying, his disciples were with him: and he asked them, saying, Whom say the people that I am?   Matt. 16:13–16

19 They answering said, ᴿJohn the Baptist; but some say, E-li'-as; and others say, that one of the old prophets is risen again.   Matt. 14:2

20 He said unto them, But whom say ye that I am? Peter answering said, The Christ of God.

21 And he ᵀstraitly charged them, and commanded them to tell no man that thing;   strictly

22 Saying, ᴿThe Son of man must suffer many things, and be rejected of the elders and chief priests and scribes, and be slain, and be raised the third day.   23:46

23 ᴿAnd he said to them all, If any man will come after me, let him deny himself, and take up his cross daily, and follow me.   14:27

24 ᴿFor whosoever will save his life shall lose it: but whosoever will lose his life for my sake, the same shall save it.   Matt. 10:39

25 For what is a man ᵀadvantaged, if he gain the whole world, and ᵀlose himself, or ᵀbe cast away?   benefited · is destroyed · lost

26 For whosoever shall be ashamed of me and of my words, of him shall the Son of man be ᴿashamed, when he shall come in his own glory, and in his Father's, and of the holy angels.   Matt. 10:33

27 ᴿBut I tell you of a truth, there

be some standing here, which shall not taste of death, till they see the kingdom of God. Matt. 16:28

28 ᴿAnd it came to pass about an eight days after these sayings, he took Peter and John and James, and went up into a mountain to pray. Matt. 17:1–8; Mark 9:2–8

29 And as he prayed, the fashion of his countenance was altered, and his ᵀraiment *was* white *and* ᵀglistering. *robe · glistening*

30 And, behold, there talked with him two men, which were ᴿMoses and E-li'-as: Heb. 11:23–29

31 Who appeared in glory, and spake of his decease which he should accomplish at Jerusalem.

32 But Peter and they that were with him ᴿwere heavy with sleep: and when they were awake, they saw his glory, and the two men that stood with him. Dan. 8:18; 10:9

33 And it came to pass, as they departed from him, Peter said unto Jesus, Master, it is good for us to be here: and let us make three tabernacles; one for thee, and one for Moses, and one for E-li'-as: not knowing what he said.

34 While he thus spake, there came a cloud, and overshadowed them: and they feared as they entered into the ᴿcloud. Acts 1:9

35 And there came a voice out of the cloud, saying, This is my beloved Son: ᴿhear him. Acts 3:22

36 And when the voice was past, Jesus was found alone. ᴿAnd they kept *it* ᵀclose, and told no man in those days any of those things which they had seen. Mark 9:9 · *quiet*

37 ᴿAnd it came to pass, that on the next day, when they were come down from the hill, much people met him. Matt. 17:14–18

38 And, behold, a man of the company cried out, saying, Master, I beseech thee, look upon my son: for he is mine only child.

39 And, lo, a spirit taketh him, and he suddenly crieth out; and it ᵀteareth him that he foameth again, and bruising him hardly departeth from him. *convulses*

40 And I ᵀbesought thy disciples to cast him out; and they could not. *implored*

41 And Jesus answering said, O ᵀfaithless and perverse generation, how long shall I be with you, and ᵀsuffer you? Bring thy son hither. *unbelieving · bear with*

42 And as he was yet a coming, the ᵀdevil threw him down, and ᵀtare *him*. And Jesus rebuked the unclean spirit, and healed the child, and delivered him again to his father. *demon · convulsed*

43 And they were all amazed at the ᵀmighty power of God. But while they wondered every one at all things which Jesus did, he said unto his disciples, *majesty*

44 ᴿLet these sayings sink down into your ears: for the Son of man shall be delivered into the hands of men. 22:54; John 18:12

45 ᴿBut they understood not this saying, and it was hid from them, ᵀthat they perceived it not: and they feared to ask him of that saying. 2:50; 18:34; Mark 9:32 · *so that*

46 ᴿThen there arose a ᵀreasoning among them, which of them should be greatest. 22:24 · *dispute*

47 And Jesus, perceiving the thought of their heart, took a ᴿchild, and set him by him, 18:17

48 And said unto them, Whosoever shall receive this child in my name receiveth me: and whosoever shall receive me receiveth him that sent me: ᴿfor he that is least among you all, the same shall be great. 1 Cor. 15:9

49 ᴿAnd John answered and said, Master, we saw one casting out ᵀdevils in thy name; and we forbad him, because he followeth not with us. Mark 9:38–40 · *demons*

50 And Jesus said unto him, Forbid *him* not: for ᴿhe that is not against us is for us. Matt. 12:30

51 And it came to pass, when the time was come that ᴿhe should be received up, he stedfastly set his face to go to Jerusalem, Is. 50:7

52 And sent messengers before his face: and they went, and entered into a village of the Sa-mar'-i-tans, to make ready for him.

53 And they did not receive him, because his face was as though he would go to Jerusalem.

54 And when his disciples James and John saw *this,* they said, Lord, wilt thou that we command fire to come down from heaven, and consume them, even as ᴿE-li'-as did? 2 Kin. 1:10, 12

55 But he turned, and rebuked them, and said,Ye know not what manner of spirit ye are of.

56 For ᴿthe Son of man is not come to destroy men's lives, but to save *them.* And they went to another village. 19:10; John 3:17; 12:47

57 ᴿAnd it came to pass, that, as they went in the way, a certain *man* said unto him, Lord, I will follow thee whithersoever thou goest. Matt. 8:19–22

58 And Jesus said unto him, Foxes have holes, and birds of the air *have* nests; but the Son of man hath not where to lay *his* head.

59 ᴿAnd he said unto another, Follow me. But he said, Lord, ᵀsuffer me first to go and bury my father. Matt. 8:21, 22 · *allow*

60 Jesus said unto him, Let the dead bury their dead: but go thou and preach the kingdom of God.

61 And another also said, Lord, ᴿI will follow thee; but let me first go bid them farewell, which are at home at my house. 1 Kin. 19:20

62 And Jesus said unto him, No man, having put his hand to the plough, and looking back, is ᴿfit for the kingdom of God. 2 Tim. 4:10

10 After these things the Lord appointed other seventy also, and ᴿsent them two ᵀand two before his face into every city and place, whither he himself would come. Matt. 10:1; Mark 6:7 · *by*

2 Therefore said he unto them, ᴿThe harvest truly *is* great, but the labourers *are* few: pray ye therefore the Lord of the harvest, that he would send forth labourers into his harvest. Matt. 9:37, 38

3 Go your ways: ᴿbehold, I send you forth as lambs among wolves. Matt. 10:16

4 Carry neither purse, nor ᵀscrip, nor shoes: and ᵀsalute no man by the way. *bag · greet*

5 ᴿAnd into whatsoever house ye enter, first say, Peace *be* to this house. 1 Sam. 25:6; Matt. 10:12

6 And if the son of peace be there, your peace shall rest upon it: if not, it shall turn to you again.

7 ᴿAnd in the same house remain, eating and drinking such things as they give: for the labourer is worthy of his hire. Go not from house to house. Matt. 10:11

8 And into whatsoever city ye enter, and they receive you, eat such things as are set before you:

9 ᴿAnd heal the sick that are therein, and say unto them, ᴿThe kingdom of God is come nigh unto you. Mark 3:15 · Matt. 3:2; 10:7

10 But into whatsoever city ye enter, and they receive you not, go your ways out into the streets of the same, and say,

11 ᴿEven the very dust of your city, which ᵀcleaveth on us, we do wipe off against you: notwithstanding be ye sure of this, that the kingdom of God is come nigh unto you. Matt. 10:14 · *clings to*

12 But I say unto you, that it shall be more tolerable in that day for Sodom, than for that city.

13 Woe unto thee, Cho-ra'-zin! woe unto thee, Beth-sa'-i-da! ᴿfor if the mighty works had been done in Tyre and Si'-don, which have been done in you, they had a great while ago repented, sitting in sackcloth and ashes. Ezek. 3:6

14 But it shall be more tolerable for Tyre and Si'-don at the judgment, than for you.

15 And thou, Ca-per'-na-um, which art exalted to heaven, shalt be thrust down to ᵀhell. Gr. *hades*

16 ᴿHe that heareth you heareth me; and ᴿhe that despiseth you despiseth me; ᴿand he that despiseth me despiseth him that sent me. Gal. 4:14 · 1 Thess. 4:8 · John 5:23

17 And ᴿthe seventy returned again with joy, saying, Lord, even the devils are subject unto us through thy name. v. 1

18 And he said unto them, ᴿI

beheld Satan as lightning fall from heaven.   Rev. 9:1; 12:8, 9

19 Behold, ^RI give unto you power to tread on serpents and scorpions, and over all the power of the enemy: and nothing shall by any means hurt you.   Mark 16:18

20 Notwithstanding in this rejoice not, that the spirits are subject unto you; but rather rejoice, because ^Ryour names are written in heaven.   Ps. 69:28; Is. 4:3; Heb. 12:23

21 ^RIn that hour Jesus rejoiced in spirit, and said, I thank thee, O Father, Lord of heaven and earth, that thou hast hid these things from the wise and prudent, and hast revealed them unto babes: even so, Father; for so it seemed good in thy sight.   Matt. 11:25–27

22 ^RAll things are delivered to me of my Father: and no man knoweth who the Son is, but the Father; and who the Father is, but the Son, and he to whom the Son will reveal him.   Matt. 28:18; John 3:35

23 And he ^Tturned him unto his disciples, and said privately, Blessed are the eyes which see the things that ye see: turned to

24 For I tell you, that many prophets and kings have desired to see those things which ye see, and have not seen them; and to hear those things which ye hear, and have not heard them.

25 And, behold, a certain lawyer stood up, and ^Ttempted him, saying, Master, what shall I do to inherit eternal life?   tested

26 He said unto him, What is written in the law? how readest thou?

27 And he answering said, ^RThou shalt love the Lord thy God with all thy heart, and with all thy soul, and with all thy strength, and with all thy mind; and thy neighbour as thyself.   Deut. 6:5

28 And he said unto him, Thou hast answered right: this do, and ^Rthou shalt live.   Lev. 18:5; Matt. 19:17

29 But he, ^Twilling to ^Rjustify himself, said unto Jesus, And who is my neighbour?   wanting · 16:15

30 And Jesus answering said, A certain man went down from Jerusalem to Jericho, and fell among ^Tthieves, which stripped him of his ^Traiment, and wounded him, and departed, leaving him half dead.   robbers · clothing

31 And by chance there came down a certain priest that way: and when he saw him, ^Rhe passed by on the other side.   Ps. 38:11

32 And likewise a Levite, when he was at the place, came and looked on him, and passed by on the other side.

33 But a certain ^RSa-mar'-i-tan, as he journeyed, came where he was: and when he saw him, he had compassion on him,   John 4:9

34 And went to him, and ^Tbound up his wounds, pouring in oil and wine, and set him on his own beast, and brought him to an inn, and took care of him.   bandaged

35 And on the morrow when he departed, he took out two ^Rpence, and gave them to the host, and said unto him, Take care of him; and whatsoever thou spendest more, when I come again, I will repay thee.   Matt. 20:2

36 Which now of these three, thinkest thou, was neighbour unto him that fell among the thieves?

37 And he said, He that shewed mercy on him. Then said Jesus unto him, ^RGo, and do thou likewise.   Prov. 14:21; [Matt. 9:13; 12:7]

38 Now it came to pass, as they went, that he entered into a certain village: and a certain woman named ^RMartha received him into her house.   John 11:1; 12:2, 3

39 And she had a sister called Mary, which also ^Rsat at Jesus' feet, and heard his word.   8:35

40 But Martha was ^Tcumbered about much serving, and came to him, and said, Lord, dost thou not care that my sister hath left me to serve alone? ^Tbid her therefore that she help me.   distracted with · tell

41 And Jesus answered and said unto her, Martha, Martha, thou art ^Tcareful and troubled about many things: worried

42 But ^Rone thing is needful: and

Mary hath chosen that good part, which shall not be taken away from her.   [Ps. 27:4; John 6:27]

11 And it came to pass, that, as he was praying in a certain place, when he ceased, one of his disciples said unto him, Lord, teach us to pray, as John also taught his disciples.

2   And he said unto them, When ye pray, say, ᴿOur Father which art in heaven, Hallowed be thy name. Thy kingdom come. Thy will be done, as in heaven, so in earth.   Matt. 6:9–13

3   Give us day by day our daily bread.

4   And ᴿforgive us our sins; for we also forgive every one that is indebted to us. And lead us not into temptation; but deliver us from ᵀevil.   [Eph. 4:32] · *the evil* one

5   And he said unto them, Which of you shall have a friend, and shall go unto him at midnight, and say unto him, Friend, lend me three loaves;

6   For a friend of mine in his journey is come to me, and I have nothing to set before him?

7   And he from within shall answer and say, Trouble me not: the door is now shut, and my children are with me in bed; I cannot rise and give thee.

8   I say unto you, ᴿThough he will not rise and give him, because he is his friend, yet because of his ᵀimportunity he will rise and give him as many as he needeth.   [18:1–5] · *persistence*

9   ᴿAnd I say unto you, Ask, and it shall be given you; seek, and ye shall find; knock, and it shall be opened unto you.   James 1:5, 6

10   For every one that asketh receiveth; and he that seeketh findeth; and to him that knocketh it shall be opened.

11   ᴿIf a son shall ask bread of any of you that is a father, will he give him a stone? or if *he ask* a fish, will he for a fish give him a serpent?   Matt. 7:9

12   Or if he shall ask an egg, will he ᵀoffer him a scorpion?   *give*

13   If ye then, being evil, know how to give good gifts unto your children: how much more shall *your* heavenly Father give the Holy Spirit to them that ask him?

14   And he was casting out a devil, and it was ᵀdumb. And it came to pass, when the devil was gone out, the ᵀdumb spake; and the people wondered.   *mute*

15   But some of them said, He casteth out devils through Be-el'-ze-bub the chief of the devils.

16   And others, ᵀtempting *him*, ᴿsought of him a sign from heaven.   *testing* · Matt. 12:38; 16:1; Mark 8:11

17   But ᴿhe, knowing their thoughts, said unto them, Every kingdom divided against itself is brought to desolation; and a house *divided* against a house falleth.   Matt. 9:4; John 2:25

18   If Satan also be divided against himself, how shall his kingdom stand? because ye say that I cast out ᵀdevils through Be-el'-ze-bub.   *demons*

19   And if I by Be-el'-ze-bub cast out ᵀdevils, by whom do your sons cast *them* out? therefore shall they be your judges.   *demons*

20   But if I ᴿwith the finger of God cast out devils, no doubt the kingdom of God is come upon you.   Ex. 8:19

21   ᴿWhen a strong man armed ᵀkeepeth his palace, his goods are in peace: Matt. 12:29; Mark 3:27 · *guards*

22   But when a stronger than he shall come upon him, and overcome him, he taketh from him all his armour wherein he trusted, and divideth his ᵀspoils.   *plunder*

23   ᴿHe that is not with me is against me: and he that gathereth not with me scattereth.   Matt. 12:30

24   ᴿWhen the unclean spirit is gone out of a man, he walketh through dry places, seeking rest; and finding none, he saith, I will return unto my house whence I came out.   Matt. 12:43–45; Acts 5:16; 8:7

25   And when he cometh, he findeth *it* swept and garnished.

26   Then goeth he, and taketh *to him* seven other spirits more

wicked than himself; and they enter in, and dwell there: and ᴿthe last *state* of that man is worse than the first.　　John 5:14; [Heb. 6:4–6]

27 And it came to pass, as he spake these things, a certain woman of the company lifted up her voice, and said unto him, Blessed *is* the womb that bare thee, and the ᵀpaps which thou hast sucked. *breasts which nursed thee*

28 But he said, Yea ᴿrather, blessed *are* they that hear the word of God, and keep it.　　[8:21]

29 ᴿAnd when the people were gathered thick together, he began to say, This is an evil generation: they seek a sign; and there shall no sign be given it, but the sign of Jo′-nas the prophet.　Matt. 12:38–42

30 For as ᴿJo′-nas was a sign unto the Nin′-e-vites, so shall also the Son of man be to this generation.　Jon. 1:17; 2:10; 3:3–10; Acts 10:40

31 ᴿThe queen of the south shall rise up in the judgment with the men of this generation, and condemn them: for she came from the utmost parts of the earth to hear the wisdom of Solomon; and, behold, a greater than Solomon *is* here.　1 Kin. 10:1–9; 2 Chr. 9:1–8

32 The men of Nin′-e-ve shall rise up in the judgment with this generation, and shall condemn it: for they repented at the preaching of ᴿJo′-nas; and, behold, a greater than Jo′-nas *is* here.　Jon. 3:5

33 ᴿNo man, when he hath lighted a candle, putteth *it* in a secret place, neither under a bushel, but on a candlestick, that they which come in may see the light.　8:16

34 The light of the body is the eye: therefore when thine eye is single, thy whole body also is full of light; but when *thine eye* is evil, thy body also *is* full of darkness.

35 Take heed therefore that the light which is in thee be not darkness.

36 If thy whole body therefore *be* full of light, having no part dark, the whole shall be full of light, as when the bright shining of a candle doth give thee light.

37 And as he spake, a certain Pharisee ᵀbesought him to dine with him: and he went in, and sat down ᵀto meat.　*asked · at the table*

38 And when the Pharisee saw *it*, he marvelled that he had not first washed before dinner.

39 And the Lord said unto him, Now do ye Pharisees make clean the outside of the cup and the platter; but your inward part is full of ravening and wickedness.

40 *Ye* fools, did not he that made that which is without make that which is within also?

41 ᴿBut rather give alms of such things as ye have; and, behold, all things are clean unto you.　Is. 58:7

42 But woe unto you, Pharisees! for ye tithe mint and rue and all manner of herbs, and pass over judgment and the love of God: these ought ye to have done, and not to leave the other undone.

43 ᴿWoe unto you, Pharisees! for ye love the uppermost seats in the synagogues, and greetings in the markets.　14:7; 20:46; Matt. 23:6

44 Woe unto you, scribes and Pharisees, hypocrites! for ye are as graves which ᵀappear not, and the men that walk over *them* are not aware *of them*.　*are not seen*

45 Then answered one of the ᵀlawyers, and said unto him, Master, thus saying thou reproachest us also.　*experts in the law*

46 And he said, Woe unto you also, *ye* lawyers! ᴿfor ye ᵀlade men with burdens ᵀgrievous to be borne, and ye yourselves touch not the burdens with one of your fingers. Matt. 23:4 · *load · heavy to bear*

47 Woe unto you! for ye build the sepulchres of the prophets, and your fathers killed them.

48 Truly ye bear witness that ye ᵀallow the deeds of your fathers: for they indeed killed them, and ye build their sepulchres.　*approve*

49 Therefore also said the wisdom of God, ᴿI will send them prophets and apostles, and *some* of them they shall slay and persecute:　Prov. 1:20; Matt. 23:34

50 That the blood of all the

prophets, which was shed from the foundation of the world, may be required of this generation;

51 ᴿFrom the blood of Abel unto ᴿthe blood of Zach-a-ri'-as, which perished between the altar and the temple: verily I say unto you, It shall be required of this generation.   Gen. 4:8 · 2 Chr. 24:20, 21

52 ᴿWoe unto you, lawyers! for ye have taken away the key of knowledge: ye entered not in yourselves, and them that were entering in ye hindered. Matt. 23:13

53 And as he said these things unto them, the scribes and the Pharisees began to ᵀurge *him* vehemently, and to provoke him to speak of many things: *assail*

54 Laying wait for him, and ᴿseeking to catch something out of his mouth, that they might accuse him.   Mark 12:13

12 In the mean time, when there were gathered together an innumerable multitude of people, insomuch that they trode one upon another, he began to say unto his disciples first of all, Beware ye of the leaven of the Pharisees, which is hypocrisy.

2 ᴿFor there is nothing covered, that shall not be revealed; neither hid, that shall not be known.   8:17

3 Therefore whatsoever ye have spoken in darkness shall be heard in the light; and that which ye have spoken in the ear in ᵀclosets shall be proclaimed upon the housetops.   *inner rooms*

4 ᴿAnd I say unto you my friends, Be not afraid of them that kill the body, and after that have no more that they can do.   Jer. 1:8

5 But I will forewarn you whom ye shall fear: Fear him, which after he hath killed hath power to cast into ᵀhell; yea, I say unto you, Fear him.   Gr. *gehenna*

6 Are not five sparrows sold for two farthings, and not one of them is forgotten before God?

7 But even the very hairs of your head are all numbered. Fear not therefore: ye are of more value than many sparrows.

8 ᴿAlso I say unto you, Whosoever shall confess me before men, him shall the Son of man also confess before the angels of God: 1 Sam. 2:30; Matt. 10:32; [Mark 8:38]

9 But he that ᴿdenieth me before men shall be denied before the angels of God.   Matt. 10:33

10 And ᴿwhosoever shall speak a word against the Son of man, it shall be forgiven him: but unto him that blasphemeth against the Holy Ghost it shall not be forgiven.   [Matt. 12:31, 32; 1 John 5:16]

11 And when they bring you unto the synagogues, and *unto* magistrates, and powers, take ye no thought how or what thing ye shall answer, or what ye shall say:

12 For the Holy Ghost shall ᴿteach you in the same hour what ye ought to say.   [John 14:26]

13 And one of the ᵀcompany said unto him, ᵀMaster, speak to my brother, that he divide the inheritance with me. *crowd · Teacher*

14 And he said unto him, ᴿMan, who made me a judge or a divider over you?   [John 18:36]

15 And he said unto them, ᴿTake heed, and beware of covetousness: for a man's life consisteth not in the abundance of the things which he possesseth.   [1 Tim. 6:6–10]

16 And he spake a parable unto them, saying, The ground of a certain rich man brought forth plentifully:

17 And he thought within himself, saying, What shall I do, because I have no room where to ᵀbestow my fruits?   *store my crops*

18 And he said, This will I do: I will pull down my barns, and build greater; and there will I ᵀbestow all my ᵀfruits and my goods.   *store · crops*

19 And I will say to my soul, Soul, thou hast much goods laid up for many years; take thine ease, eat, drink, *and* be merry.

20 But God said unto him, *Thou* fool, this night thy soul shall be required of thee: ᴿthen whose shall those things be, which thou hast provided?   Ps. 39:6; Jer. 17:11

21 So *is* he that layeth up treasure for himself, [R]and is not rich toward God.   [Matt. 6:20; James 2:5]
22 And he said unto his disciples, Therefore I say unto you, Take no thought for your life, what ye shall eat; neither for the body, what ye shall put on.
23 The life is more than [T]meat, and the body *is more* than [T]raiment.   *food · clothing*
24 Consider the ravens: for they neither sow nor reap; which neither have storehouse nor barn; and [R]God feedeth them: how much more are ye better than the fowls?   Job 38:41; Ps. 147:9
25 And which of you [T]with taking thought can add to his stature one cubit?   *by worrying*
26 If ye then be not able to do that thing which is least, why take ye thought for the rest?
27 Consider the lilies how they grow: they toil not, they spin not; and yet I say unto you, that Solomon in all his glory was not [T]arrayed like one of these.   *clothed*
28 If then God so clothe the grass, which is to day in the field, and to morrow is cast into the oven; how much more *will he clothe* you, O ye of little faith?
29 And seek not ye what ye shall eat, or what ye shall drink, neither be ye of doubtful mind.
30 For all these things do the nations of the world seek after: and your Father knoweth that ye have need of these things.
31 [R]But rather seek ye the kingdom of God; and all these things shall be added unto you.   Matt. 6:33
32 Fear not, little flock; for [R]it is your Father's good pleasure to give you the kingdom.   Zech. 13:7
33 Sell that ye have, and give alms; provide yourselves bags which [T]wax not old, a treasure in the heavens that faileth not, where no thief approacheth, neither moth corrupteth.   *do not grow*
34 For where your treasure is, there will your heart be also.
35 Let your loins be girded about, and *your* lights burning;

36 And ye yourselves like unto men that wait for their lord, when he will return from the wedding; that when he cometh and knocketh, they may open unto him immediately.
37 [R]Blessed *are* those servants, whom the [T]lord when he cometh shall find watching: verily I say unto you, that he shall gird himself, and make them to sit down to [T]meat, and will come forth and serve them.   Matt. 24:46 · *master · eat*
38 And if he shall come in the second watch, or come in the third watch, and find *them* so, blessed are those servants.
39 And this know, that if the [T]goodman of the house had known what hour the thief would come, he would have watched, and not have suffered his house to be broken [T]through.   *master · into*
40 [R]Be ye therefore ready also: for the Son of man cometh at an hour when ye think not.   Matt. 24:44
41 Then Peter said unto him, Lord, speakest thou this parable unto us, or even to [T]all?   *all people*
42 And the Lord said, [R]Who then is that faithful and wise steward, whom *his* lord shall make ruler over his household, to give *them their* portion of meat in due season?   Matt. 24:45, 46; 25:21
43 Blessed *is* that servant, whom his [T]lord when he cometh shall find so doing.   *master*
44 [R]Of a truth I say unto you, that he will make him ruler over all that he hath.   Matt. 24:47; 25:21
45 [R]But and if that servant say in his heart, My lord delayeth his coming; and shall begin to beat the menservants and maidens, and to eat and drink, and to be drunken;   Matt. 24:48; 2 Pet. 3:3, 4
46 The lord of that servant will come in a day when he looketh not for *him*, and at an hour when he is not aware, and will cut him in sunder, and will appoint him his portion with the unbelievers.
47 And [R]that servant, which knew his lord's will, and prepared not *himself*, neither did according

to his will, shall be beaten with many *stripes.* Num. 15:30; Deut. 25:2

48 ᴿBut he that knew not, and did commit things worthy of stripes, shall be beaten with few *stripes.* For unto whomsoever much is given, of him shall be much required: and to whom men have committed much, of him they will ask the more. Num. 15:29

49 I am come to send fire on the earth; and ᵀwhat will I, if it be already kindled? *how I wish it were*

50 But I have a baptism to be baptized with; and how am I straitened till it be accomplished!

51 Suppose ye that I am come to give peace on earth? I tell you, Nay; ᴿbut rather division: John 7:43

52 ᴿFor from henceforth there shall be five in one house divided, three against two, and two against three. Matt. 10:35; Mark 13:12

53 The father shall be divided against the son, and the son against the father; the mother against the daughter, and the daughter against the mother; the mother in law against her daughter in law, and the daughter in law against her mother in law.

54 And he said also to the ᵀpeople, ᴿWhen ye see a cloud rise out of the west, straightway ye say, There cometh a shower; and so it is. *multitudes* · Matt. 16:2, 3

55 And when *ye see* the south wind blow, ye say, There will be heat; and it cometh to pass.

56 *Ye* hypocrites, ye can discern the face of the sky and of the earth; but how is it that ye do not discern ᴿthis time? 19:41–44

57 Yea, and why even of yourselves judge ye not what is right?

58 ᴿWhen thou goest with thine adversary to the magistrate, *as thou art* in the way, give diligence that thou mayest be delivered from him; lest he hale thee to the judge, and the judge deliver thee to the officer, and the officer cast thee into prison. Matt. 5:25, 26

59 I tell thee, thou shalt not depart thence, till thou hast paid the very last mite.

13 There were present at that season some that told him of the Gal-i-lae'-ans, whose blood Pilate had ᵀmingled with their sacrifices. *mixed*

2 And Jesus answering said unto them, Suppose ye that these Gal-i-lae'-ans were sinners ᵀabove all the Gal-i-lae'-ans, because they suffered such things? *more than*

3 I tell you, Nay: but, except ye repent, ye shall all likewise perish.

4 Or those eighteen, upon whom the tower in Si-lo'-am fell, and slew them, think ye that they were ᵀsinners above all men that dwelt in Jerusalem? *debtors*

5 I tell you, Nay: but, except ye repent, ye shall all likewise perish.

6 He spake also this parable; ᴿA certain *man* had a fig tree planted in his vineyard; and he came and sought fruit thereon, and found none. Is. 5:2; Matt. 21:19

7 Then said he unto the ᵀdresser of his vineyard, Behold, these three years I come seeking fruit on this fig tree, and find none: cut it down; why ᵀcumbereth it the ground? *keeper* · *does it use up* or *waste*

8 And he answering said unto him, ᵀLord, let it alone this year also, till I shall dig about it, and ᵀdung *it:* *Master* · *fertilize*

9 And if it bear fruit, *well:* and if not, *then* after that thou shalt ᴿcut it down. [John 15:2]

10 And he was teaching in one of the synagogues on the sabbath.

11 And, behold, there was a woman which had a spirit of infirmity eighteen years, and was ᵀbowed together, and could in no wise ᵀlift up *herself.* *bent over* · *raise*

12 And when Jesus saw her, he called *her to him,* and said unto her, Woman, thou art loosed from thine ᴿinfirmity. 7:21; 8:2

13 And he laid *his* hands on her: and immediately she was made straight, and glorified God.

14 And the ruler of the synagogue answered with indignation, because that Jesus had healed on

the sabbath day, and said unto the people, There are six days in which men ought to work: in them therefore come and be healed, and ᴿnot on the sabbath day. 14:3

15 The Lord then answered him, and said, *Thou* hypocrite, ᴿdoth not each one of you on the sabbath loose his ox or *his* ass from the stall, and lead *him* away to watering?   14:5; [Matt. 7:5; 23:13]

16 And ought not this woman, ᴿbeing a daughter of Abraham, whom Satan hath bound, lo, these eighteen years, be loosed from this bond on the sabbath day? 19:9

17 And when he had said these things, all his adversaries were ashamed: and all the people rejoiced for all the glorious things that were ᴿdone by him.   Mark 5:19

18 Then said he, Unto what is the kingdom of God like? and whereunto shall I resemble it?

19 It is like a grain of mustard seed, which a man took, and cast into his garden; and it grew, and ᵀwaxed a great tree; and the fowls of the air ᵀlodged in the branches of it.   *became · nested*

20 And again he said, Whereunto shall I liken the kingdom of God?

21 It is like ᵀleaven, which a woman took and hid in three ᴿmeasures of meal, till the whole was leavened.   *yeast* · Matt. 13:33

22 And he went through the cities and villages, teaching, and journeying toward Jerusalem.

23 Then said one unto him, Lord, are there few that be saved? And he said unto them,

24 ᴿStrive to enter in at the ᵀstrait gate: for many, I say unto you, will seek to enter in, and shall not be able. [Matt. 7:13] · *narrow*

25 ᴿWhen once the master of the house is risen up, and ᴿhath shut to the door, and ye begin to stand without, and to knock at the door, saying, ᴿLord, Lord, open unto us; and he shall answer and say unto you, ᴿI know you not whence ye are: Is. 55:6 · Rev. 22:11 · 6:46 · Matt. 7:23

26 Then shall ye begin to say, We

have eaten and drunk in thy presence, and thou hast taught in our streets.

27 ᴿBut he shall say, I tell you, I know you not whence ye are; ᴿdepart from me, all *ye* workers of iniquity.   [Matt. 7:23; 25:41] · Titus 1:16

28 ᴿThere shall be weeping and gnashing of teeth, when ye shall see Abraham, and Isaac, and Jacob, and all the prophets, in the kingdom of God, and you *yourselves* thrust out.   Matt. 24:51

29 And they shall come from the east, and *from* the west, and from the north, and *from* the south, and shall sit down in the kingdom of God.

30 ᴿAnd, behold, there are last which shall be first, and there are first which shall be last. Mark 10:31

31 The same day there came certain of the Pharisees, saying unto him, Get thee out, and depart hence: for Herod will kill thee.

32 And he said unto them, Go ye, and tell that fox, Behold, I cast out devils, and I do cures to day and to morrow, and the third *day* ᴿI shall be perfected. 24:46; Acts 10:40

33 Nevertheless I must walk to day, and to morrow, and the *day* following: for it cannot be that a prophet perish out of Jerusalem.

34 ᴿO Jerusalem, Jerusalem, which killest the prophets, and stonest them that are sent unto thee; how often would I have gathered thy children together, as a hen *doth gather* her brood under *her* wings, and ye would not!   Matt. 23:37–39

35 Behold, your house is left ☆ unto you desolate: and verily I say unto you, Ye shall not see me, until *the time* come when ye shall say, ᴿBlessed *is* he that cometh in the name of the Lord.   Ps. 118:26

14 And it came to pass, as he went into the house of one of the chief Pharisees to eat bread on the sabbath day, that they ᵀwatched him.   *closely watched*

2 And, behold, there was a certain man before him which had the dropsy.

3 And Jesus answering spake unto the lawyers and Pharisees, saying, RIs it lawful to heal on the sabbath day?   Matt. 12:10

4 And they Theld their peace. And he took *him*, and healed him, and let him go;   *kept silent*

5 And answered them, saying, RWhich of you shall have an ass or an ox fallen into a pit, and will not straightway pull him out on the sabbath day? [Ex. 23:5; Deut. 22:4]

6 And they could not answer him again to these things.

7 And he put forth a parable to those which were Tbidden, when he Tmarked how they chose out the Tchief rooms; saying unto them,   *invited · noted · best places*

8 When thou art bidden of any *man* to a Twedding, sit not down in the Thighest room; lest a more honourable man than thou be bidden of him;   *wedding feast · best place*

9 And he that Tbade thee and him come and say to thee, Give this man place; and thou begin with shame to take the lowest Troom.   *invited · place*

10 RBut when thou art bidden, go and sit down in the lowest room; that when he that Tbade thee cometh, he may say unto thee, Friend, go up higher: then shalt thou have Tworship in the presence of them that sit at meat with thee.   Prov. 25:6, 7 · *invited · glory*

11 RFor whosoever exalteth himself shall be Tabased; and he that humbleth himself shall be exalted.   James 4:6; [1 Pet. 5:5] · *humbled*

12 Then said he also to him that Tbade him, When thou makest a dinner or a supper, call not thy friends, nor thy brethren, neither thy kinsmen, nor *thy* rich neighbours; lest they also Tbid thee again, and a recompence be made thee.   *invited · invite you back*

13 But when thou makest a feast, call Rthe poor, the maimed, the lame, the blind: Neh. 8:10, 12

14 And thou shalt be blessed; for they cannot Trecompense thee: for thou shalt be recompensed at the resurrection of the just.   *repay*

15 And when one of them that sat at meat with him heard these things, he said unto him, RBlessed *is* he that shall eat bread in the kingdom of God.   Rev. 19:9

16 RThen said he unto him, A certain man made a great supper, and bade many: Matt. 22:2–14

17 And Rsent his servant at supper time to say to them that were bidden, Come; for all things are now ready.   Prov. 9:2, 5

18 And they all with one Tconsent began to make excuse. The first said unto him, I have bought a piece of ground, and I must needs go and see it: I pray thee have me excused.   *Accord*

19 And another said, I have bought five yoke of oxen, and I go to Tprove them: I pray thee have me excused.   *test*

20 And another said, I have married a wife, and therefore I cannot come.

21 So that servant came, and shewed his lord these things. Then the master of the house being angry said to his servant, Go out quickly into the streets and lanes of the city, and bring in hither the poor, and the maimed, and the Thalt, and the blind.   *lame*

22 And the servant said, Lord, it is done as thou hast commanded, and yet there is room.

23 And the lord said unto the servant, Go out into the highways and hedges, and compel *them* to come in, that my house may be filled.

24 For I say unto you, That none of those men which were bidden shall taste of my supper.

25 And there went great multitudes with him: and he turned, and said unto them,

26 If any *man* come to me, and hate not his father, and mother, and wife, and children, and brethren, and sisters, yea, and his own life also, he cannot be my disciple.

27 And Rwhosoever doth not bear his cross, and come after me, cannot be my disciple.   Matt. 16:24

28 For Rwhich of you, intend-

ing to build a tower, sitteth not down first, and counteth the cost, whether he have *sufficient* to finish *it*?　　　Prov. 24:27

29 Lest [T]haply, after he hath laid the foundation, and is not able to finish *it*, all that behold *it* begin to mock him,　　*perhaps*

30 Saying, This man began to build, and was not able to finish.

31 Or what king, going to make war against another king, sitteth not down first, and [T]consulteth whether he be able with ten thousand to meet him that cometh against him with twenty thousand?　　*considers*

32 Or else, while the other is yet a great way off, he sendeth [T]an ambassage, and [T]desireth conditions of peace.　　*a delegation · asks for*

33 So likewise, whosoever he be of you that forsaketh not all that he hath, he cannot be my disciple.

34 [R]Salt *is* good: but if the salt have lost his savour, wherewith shall it be seasoned?　　Matt. 5:13

35 It is neither fit for the land, nor yet for the [T]dunghill; *but* men cast it out. He that hath ears to hear, let him hear.　　*rubbish heap*

15 Then [R]drew near unto him all the publicans and sinners for to hear him.　　[Matt. 9:10–15]

2 And the Pharisees and scribes murmured, saying, This man receiveth sinners, [R]and eateth with them.　　Acts 11:3; Gal. 2:12

3 And he spake this parable unto them, saying,

4 [R]What man of you, having an hundred sheep, if he lose one of them, doth not leave the ninety and nine in the wilderness, and go after that which is lost, until he find it?　　Matt. 18:12–14; 1 Pet. 2:25

5 And when he hath found *it*, he layeth *it* on his shoulders, rejoicing.

6 And when he cometh home, he calleth together *his* friends and neighbours, saying unto them, Rejoice with me; for I have found my sheep [R]which was lost.　　[19:10]

7 I say unto you, that likewise joy shall be in heaven over one sinner that repenteth, more than over ninety and nine just persons, which need no repentance.

8 Either what woman having ten pieces of silver, if she lose one piece, doth not light a [T]candle, and sweep the house, and seek diligently till she find *it*?　　*lamp*

9 And when she hath found *it*, she calleth *her* friends and *her* neighbours together, saying, Rejoice with me; for I have found the piece which I had lost.

10 Likewise, I say unto you, there is joy in the presence of the angels of God over one sinner that repenteth.

11 And he said, A certain man had two sons:

12 And the younger of them said to *his* father, Father, give me the portion of goods that falleth *to me*. And he divided unto them [R]*his* [T]living.　　Mark 12:44 · *livelihood*

13 And not many days after the younger son gathered all together, and took his journey into a far country, and there wasted his substance with riotous living.

14 And when he had spent all, there arose a mighty famine in that land; and he began to be in want.

15 And he went and joined himself to a citizen of that country; and he sent him into his fields to feed swine.

16 And he would [T]fain have filled his belly with the [T]husks that the swine did eat: and no man gave unto him.　　*gladly · carob pods*

17 And when he came to himself, he said, How many hired servants of my father's have bread enough and to spare, and I perish with hunger!

18 I will arise and go to my father, and will say unto him, Father, [R]I have sinned against heaven, and before thee,　　Ex. 9:27

19 And am no [T]more worthy to be called thy son: make me as one of thy hired servants.　　*longer*

20 And he arose, and came to his father. But when he was yet a great way off, his father saw him,

and had compassion, and ran, and fell on his neck, and kissed him.

21 And the son said unto him, Father, I have sinned against heaven, ᴿand in thy sight, and am no more worthy to be called thy son.   Ps. 51:4

22 But the father said to his servants, Bring forth the best robe, and put *it* on him; and put a ring on his hand, and ᵀshoes on *his* feet: *sandals*

23 And bring hither the fatted calf, and kill *it;* and let us eat, and be merry:

24 ᴿFor this my son was dead, and is alive again; he was lost, and is found. And they began to be merry.   Matt. 8:22; Rom. 11:15

25 Now his elder son was in the field: and as he came and drew nigh to the house, he heard music and dancing.

26 And he called one of the servants, and asked what these things meant.

27 And he said unto him, Thy brother is come; and thy father hath killed the fatted calf, because he hath received him safe and sound.

28 And he was angry, and would not go in: therefore came his father out, and intreated him.

29 And he answering said to *his* father, Lo, these many years do I serve thee, neither transgressed I at any time thy commandment: and yet thou never gavest me a ᵀkid, that I might make merry with my friends: *young goat*

30 But as soon as this thy son was come, which hath devoured thy living with harlots, thou hast killed for him the fatted calf.

31 And he said unto him, Son, thou art ever with me, and all that I have is thine.

32 It was meet that we should make merry, and be glad: for this thy brother was dead, and is alive again; and was lost, and is found.

16 And he said also unto his disciples, There was a certain rich man, which had a steward; and the same was accused

unto him that he had wasted his goods.

2 And he called him, and said unto him, How is it that I hear this of thee? give an ᴿaccount of thy stewardship; for thou mayest be no longer steward.   [1 Pet. 4:5, 6]

3 Then the steward said within himself, What shall I do? for my ᵀlord taketh away from me the stewardship: I cannot dig; to beg I am ashamed.   *master*

4 I am resolved what to do, that, when I am put out of the stewardship, they may receive me into their houses.

5 So he called every one of his lord's debtors *unto him,* and said unto the first, How much owest thou unto my lord?

6 And he said, An hundred measures of oil. And he said unto him, Take thy bill, and sit down quickly, and write fifty.

7 Then said he to another, And how much owest thou? And he said, An hundred measures of wheat. And he said unto him, Take thy bill, and write ᵀfourscore.   *eighty*

8 And the lord commended the unjust steward, because he had done wisely: for the children of this world are in their generation wiser than the children of light.

9 And I say unto you, Make to yourselves friends of the mammon of unrighteousness; that, when ye fail, they may receive you into everlasting habitations.

10 ᴿHe that is faithful in that which is least is faithful also in much: and he that is unjust in the least is unjust also in much.   19:17

11 If therefore ye have not been faithful in the unrighteous ᵀmammon, who will commit to your trust the true *riches?*   *wealth*

12 And if ye have not been faithful in that which is another man's, who shall give you that which is your ᴿown?   [1 Pet. 1:3, 4]

13 ᴿNo servant can serve two masters: for either he will hate the one, and love the other; or else he will hold to the one, and despise

the other. Ye cannot serve God and ᵀmammon.   Gal. 1:10 · *wealth*

14 And the Pharisees also, who were covetous, heard all these things: and they derided him.

15 And he said unto them, Ye are they which justify yourselves ᴿbefore men; but God knoweth your hearts: for that which is highly esteemed among men is abomination in the sight of God. [Matt. 6:2, 5]

16 The law and the prophets *were* until John: since that time the kingdom of God is preached, and every man presseth into it.

17 ᴿAnd it is easier for heaven and earth to pass, than one tittle of the law to fail. Matt. 5:18; 1 Pet. 1:25

18 Whosoever ᵀputteth away his wife, and marrieth another, committeth adultery: and whosoever marrieth her that is ᵀput away from *her* husband committeth adultery.   *divorces · divorced*

19 There was a certain rich man, which was clothed in purple and fine linen, and ᵀfared sumptuously every day: *lived in luxury*

20 And there was a certain beggar named Laz'-a-rus, which was laid at his gate, full of sores,

21 And desiring to be fed with the crumbs which fell from the rich man's table: moreover the dogs came and licked his sores.

22 And it came to pass, that the beggar died, and was carried by the angels into ᴿAbraham's bosom: the rich man also died, and was buried;   Matt. 8:11

23 And in ᵀhell he lift up his eyes, being in torments, and seeth Abraham afar off, and Laz'-a-rus in his bosom.   Gr. *hades*

24 And he cried and said, Father Abraham, have mercy on me, and send Laz'-a-rus, that he may dip the tip of his finger in water, and ᴿcool my tongue; for I am tormented in this flame.   Zech. 14:12

25 But Abraham said, Son, ᴿremember that thou in thy lifetime receivedst thy good things, and likewise Laz'-a-rus evil things: but now he is comforted, and thou art tormented.   James 5:5

26 And beside all this, between us and you there is a great gulf fixed: so that they which would pass from hence to you cannot; neither can they pass to us, that *would come* from thence.

27 Then he said, I pray thee therefore, father, that thou wouldest send him to my father's house:

28 For I have five brethren; that he may testify unto them, lest they also come into this place of torment.

29 Abraham saith unto him, ᴿThey have Moses and the prophets; let them hear them.   Acts 15:21

30 And he said, Nay, father Abraham: but if one went unto them from the dead, they will repent.

31 And he said unto him, ᴿIf they hear not Moses and the prophets, ᴿneither will they be persuaded, though one rose from the dead.   [John 5:46] · John 12:10, 11

17 Then said he unto the disciples, ᴿIt is impossible but that ᵀoffences will come: but woe *unto him,* through whom they come!   [1 Cor. 11:19] · *stumbling blocks*

2 It were better for him that a millstone were hanged about his neck, and he cast into the sea, than that he should offend one of these little ones.

3 Take heed to yourselves: ᴿIf thy brother trespass against thee, ᴿrebuke him; and if he repent, forgive him.   [Matt. 18:15, 21] · Lev. 19:17

4 And if he trespass against thee seven times in a day, and seven times in a day turn again to thee, saying, I repent; thou shalt forgive him.

5 And the apostles said unto the Lord, Increase our faith.

6 ᴿAnd the Lord said, If ye had faith as a grain of mustard seed, ye might say unto this sycamine tree, Be thou plucked up by the root, and be thou planted in the sea; and it should obey you.   13:19

7 But which of you, having a servant plowing or feeding cattle, will say unto him by and by, when

he is come from the field, Go and sit down to meat?

8 And will not rather say unto him, Make ready wherewith I may sup, and gird thyself, ^Rand serve me, till I have eaten and drunken; and afterward thou shalt eat and drink?   [12:37]

9 Doth he thank that servant because he did the things that were commanded him? I ^Ttrow not.   *think*

10 So likewise ye, when ye shall have done all those things which are commanded you, say, We are ^Runprofitable servants: we have done that which was our duty to do.   Ps. 16:2; Matt. 25:30; Rom. 3:12; 11:35

11 And it came to pass, ^Ras he went to Jerusalem, that he passed through the midst of Sa-ma′-ri-a and Galilee.   9:51, 52; John 4:4

12 And as he entered into a certain village, there met him ten men that were lepers, ^Rwhich stood afar off: Lev. 13:46; Num. 5:2

13 And they lifted up *their* voices, and said, Jesus, Master, have mercy on us.

14 And when he saw *them*, he said unto them, ^RGo shew yourselves unto the priests. And it came to pass, that, as they went, they were cleansed.   5:14; Matt. 8:4

15 And one of them, when he saw that he was healed, turned back, and with a loud voice ^Rglorified God,   5:25; 18:43

16 And fell down on *his* face at his feet, giving him thanks: and he was a ^RSa-mar′-i-tan.   John 4:9

17 And Jesus answering said, Were there not ten cleansed? but where *are* the nine?

18 There are not found that returned to give glory to God, save this stranger.

19 ^RAnd he said unto him, Arise, go thy way: thy faith hath made thee whole.   7:50; 8:48; 18:42

20 And when he was ^Tdemanded of the Pharisees, when the kingdom of God should come, he answered them and said, The kingdom of God cometh not with observation: *asked by*

21 Neither shall they say, Lo here! or, lo there! for, behold, the kingdom of God is within you.

22 And he said unto the disciples, ^RThe days will come, when ye shall desire to see one of the days of the Son of man, and ye shall not see *it*.   5:35; [John 17:12]

23 ^RAnd they shall say to you, See here; or, see there: go not after *them*, nor follow *them*.   [21:8]

24 For as the lightning, that lighteneth out of the one *part* under heaven, shineth unto the other *part* under heaven; so shall also the Son of man be in his day.

25 ^RBut first must he suffer many things, and be ^Rrejected of this generation.   Mark 8:31; 9:31 · 9:22

26 And as it was in the days of ^RNo′-e, so shall it be also in the days of the Son of man.   1 Pet. 3:20

27 They did eat, they drank, they married wives, they were given in marriage, until the day that No′-e entered into the ark, and the flood came, and destroyed them all.

28 Likewise also as it was in the days of Lot; they did eat, they drank, they bought, they sold, they planted, they builded;

29 But ^Rthe same day that Lot went out of Sodom it rained fire and brimstone from heaven, and destroyed *them* all.   Gen. 19:16, 24, 29

30 Even thus shall it be in the day when the Son of man ^Ris revealed.   [2 Thess. 1:7]; 1 Pet. 1:7; 4:13

31 In that day, he ^Rwhich shall be upon the housetop, and his stuff in the house, let him not come down to take it away: and he that is in the field, let him likewise not return back.   Mark 13:15

32 Remember Lot's wife.

33 ^RWhosoever shall seek to save his life shall lose it; and whosoever shall lose his life shall preserve it.   Mark 8:35; John 12:25

34 ^RI tell you, in that night there shall be two *men* in one bed; the one shall be taken, and the other shall be left.   Matt. 24:40, 41

35 Two *women* shall be grinding together; the one shall be taken, and the other left.

36 Two *men* shall be in the field; the one shall be taken, and the other left.

37 And they answered and said unto him, Where, Lord? And he said unto them, Wheresoever the body *is*, thither will the ᵀeagles be gathered together.   *vultures*

18 And he spake a parable unto them *to this end*, that men ought ᴿalways to pray, and not to ᵀfaint;   1 Thess. 5:17 · *lose heart*

2 Saying, There was in a city a judge, which feared not God, neither ᵀregarded man: *respected*

3 And there was a widow in that city; and she came unto him, saying, ᵀAvenge me of mine adversary.   *Vindicate me against*

4 And he would not for a while: but afterward he said within himself, Though I fear not God, nor regard man;

5 ᴿYet because this widow troubleth me, I will ᵀavenge her, lest by her continual coming she weary me.   11:8 · *vindicate*

6 And the Lord said, Hear what the unjust judge saith.

7 And ᴿshall not God ᵀavenge his own elect, which cry day and night unto him, though he bear long with them?   Rev. 6:10 · *vindicate*

8 I tell you ᴿthat he will avenge them speedily. Nevertheless when the Son of man cometh, shall he find faith on the earth?   Heb. 10:37

9 And he spake this parable unto certain ᴿwhich trusted in themselves that they were righteous, and despised others: 10:29

10 Two men went up into the temple to pray; the one a Pharisee, and the other a publican.

11 The Pharisee ᴿstood and prayed thus with himself, ᴿGod, I thank thee, that I am not as other men *are*, extortioners, unjust, adulterers, or even as this publican.   Ps. 135:2 · Is. 1:15

12 I fast twice in the week, I give tithes of all that I possess.

13 And the publican, standing afar off, would not lift up so much as *his* eyes unto heaven, but smote upon his breast, saying, God be merciful to me a sinner.

14 I tell you, this man went down to his house justified *rather* than the other: ᴿfor every one that exalteth himself shall be abased; and he that humbleth himself shall be exalted.   14:11; Matt. 23:12

15 ᴿAnd they brought unto him also infants, that he would touch them: but when *his* disciples saw *it*, they rebuked them. Mark 10:13–16

16 But Jesus called them *unto him*, and said, ᵀSuffer little children to come unto me, and forbid them not: for ᴿof such is the kingdom of God. *Allow* · Matt. 18:3; 1 Pet. 2:2

17 ᴿVerily I say unto you, Whosoever shall not receive the kingdom of God as a little child shall in no wise enter therein.   Mark 10:15

18 And a certain ruler asked him, saying, Good Master, what shall I do to inherit eternal life?

19 And Jesus said unto him, Why callest thou me good? none *is* good, save one, *that is*, God.

20 Thou knowest the commandments, ᴿDo not commit adultery, Do not kill, Do not steal, Do not bear false witness, Honour thy father and thy mother.   Ex. 20:12–16

21 And he said, All ᴿthese have I kept from my youth up.   Phil. 3:6

22 Now when Jesus heard these things, he said unto him, Yet lackest thou one thing: sell all that thou hast, and distribute unto the poor, and thou shalt have treasure in heaven: and come, follow me.

23 And when he heard this, he was very sorrowful: for he was very rich.

24 And when Jesus saw that he was very sorrowful, he said, How hardly shall they that have riches enter into the kingdom of God!

25 For it is easier for a camel to go through a needle's eye, than for a rich man to enter into the kingdom of God.

26 And they that heard *it* said, Who then can be saved?

27 And he said, ᴿThe things which are impossible with men are possible with God.   Matt. 19:26

28 Then Peter said, Lo, we have left all, and followed thee.

29 And he said unto them, Verily I say unto you, There is no man that hath left house, or parents, or brethren, or wife, or children, for the kingdom of God's sake,

30 ᴿWho shall not receive manifold more in this present time, and in the ᵀworld to come life everlasting. Job 42:10 · *age*

31 ᴿThen he took *unto him* the twelve, and said unto them, Behold, we go up to Jerusalem, and all things that are written by the prophets concerning the Son of man shall be accomplished. 9:51

32 For ᴿhe shall be delivered unto the Gentiles, and shall be mocked, and spitefully entreated, and spitted on: 23:1; John 18:28

33 And they shall scourge *him,* and put him to death: and the third day he shall rise again.

34 ᴿAnd they understood none of these things: and this saying was hid from them, neither knew they the things which were spoken. 2:50; 9:45; [John 10:6; 12:16]

35 ᴿAnd it came to pass, that as he was come nigh unto Jericho, a certain blind man sat by the way side begging: Matt. 20:29–34

36 And hearing the multitude pass by, he asked what it meant.

37 And they told him, that Jesus of Nazareth passeth by.

38 And he cried, saying, Jesus, *thou* ᴿson of David, have mercy on me. Matt. 9:27

39 And they which went before rebuked him, that he should ᵀhold his peace: but he cried so much the more, *Thou* son of David, have mercy on me. *be quiet*

40 And Jesus ᵀstood, and commanded him to be brought unto him: and when he was come near, he asked him, *stood still*

41 Saying, What wilt thou that I shall do unto thee? And he said, Lord, that I may receive my sight.

42 And Jesus said unto him, Receive thy sight: ᴿthy faith hath saved thee. 17:19

43 And immediately he received his sight, and followed him, ᴿglorifying God: and all the people, when they saw *it,* gave praise unto God. 5:26; Acts 4:21; 11:18

19 And *Jesus* entered and passed through Jericho.

2 And, behold, *there was* a man named Zac-chae'-us, which was the chief among the publicans, and he was rich.

3 And he sought to ᴿsee Jesus who he was; and could not ᵀfor the press, because he was little of stature. John 12:21 · *because of the crowd*

4 And he ran before, and climbed up into a sycomore tree to see him: for he was to pass that *way.*

5 And when Jesus came to the place, he looked up, and saw him, and said unto him, Zac-chae'-us, make haste, and come down; for to day I must abide at thy house.

6 And he ᵀmade haste, and came down, and received him joyfully. *hurried*

7 And when they saw *it,* they all ᵀmurmured, saying, ᴿThat he was gone to be guest with a man that is a sinner. *grumbled* · 5:30; 15:2

8 And Zac-chae'-us stood, and said unto the Lord; Behold, Lord, the half of my goods I give to the poor; and if I have taken any thing from any man by false accusation, ᴿI restore *him* fourfold. Lev. 6:5

9 And Jesus said unto him, This day is salvation come to this house, forsomuch as ᴿhe also is a son of Abraham. 3:8; 13:16; [Rom. 4:16]

10 ᴿFor the Son of man is come to seek and to save that which was lost. Matt. 18:11; [Rom. 5:8]

11 And as they heard these things, he added and spake a parable, because he was nigh to Jerusalem, and because they thought that the kingdom of God should immediately appear.

12 ᴿHe said therefore, A certain nobleman went into a far country to receive for himself a kingdom, and to return. Mark 13:34

13 And he called his ten servants, and delivered them ten

pounds, and said unto them,
^TOccupy till I come.　　　*Do business*

14 ^RBut his citizens hated him,
and sent a message after him, saying, We will not have this *man* to
reign over us.　　　　　[John 1:11]

15 And it came to pass, that
when he was returned, having
received the kingdom, then he
commanded these servants to be
called unto him, to whom he had
given the money, that he might
know how much every man had
gained by trading.

16 Then came the first, saying,
Lord, thy pound hath gained ten
pounds.

17 And he said unto him, ^RWell,^T
thou good servant: because thou
hast been ^Rfaithful in a very little,
have thou authority over ten
cities.　　*Matt. 25:21, 23 · Well done · 16:10*

18 And the second came, saying,
Lord, thy pound hath gained five
pounds.

19 And he said likewise to him,
Be thou also over five cities.

20 And another came, saying,
Lord, behold, *here is* thy pound,
which I have kept laid up in a
^Tnapkin:　　　　　*handkerchief*

21 ^RFor I feared thee, because
thou art an austere man: ^Tthou
takest up that thou layedst not
down, and reapest that thou didst
not sow.　　　*Matt. 25:24 · you collect*

22 And he saith unto him, ^ROut
of thine own mouth will I judge
thee, *thou* wicked servant. ^RThou
knewest that I was an austere
man, taking up that I laid not
down, and reaping that I did not
sow:　　　*2 Sam. 1:16 · Matt. 25:26*

23 Wherefore then gavest not
thou my money into the bank,
that at my coming I might have
required mine own with usury?

24 And he said unto them that
stood by, Take from him the
pound, and give *it* to him that
hath ten pounds.

25 (And they said unto him,
^TLord, he hath ten pounds.) *Master*

26 For I say unto you, ^RThat unto
every one which hath shall be
given; and from him that hath not,

even that he hath shall be taken
away from him. *Matt. 13:12; Mark 4:25*

27 But those mine enemies,
which would not that I should
reign over them, bring hither, and
slay *them* before me.

28 And when he had thus spo-
ken, ^Rhe went ^Tbefore, ascending
up to Jerusalem. *Mark 10:32 · on ahead*

29 ^RAnd it came to pass, when
he was come nigh to Beth'-pha-ge
and Beth'-a-ny, at the mount
called *the mount* of Olives, he
sent two of his disciples, *Matt. 21:1*

30 Saying, Go ye into the village
over against *you;* in the which
at your entering ye shall find a
colt tied, whereon yet never
man sat: loose him, and bring *him*
hither.

31 And if any man ask you, Why
do ye loose *him?* thus shall ye say
unto him, Because the Lord hath
need of him.

32 And they that were sent went
their way, and found even ^Ras he
had said unto them.　　　　22:13

33 And as they were loosing the
colt, the owners thereof said unto
them, Why loose ye the colt?

34 And they said, The Lord hath
need of him.

35 And they brought him to
Jesus: ^Rand they ^Tcast their gar-
ments upon the colt, and they set
Jesus thereon.　　*Mark 11:7 · spread*

36 And as he went, they spread
their clothes ^Tin the way. *on the road*

37 And when he was come
^Tnigh, even now at the descent of
the mount of Olives, the whole
multitude of the disciples began
to rejoice and praise God with a
loud voice for all the mighty
works that they had seen;　　*near*

38 Saying, ^RBlessed *be* the King ★
that cometh in the name of the
Lord: ^Rpeace in heaven, and glory
in the highest.　　　13:35 · [Eph. 2:14]

39 And some of the Pharisees
from among the multitude said
unto him, ^TMaster, rebuke thy disciples.　　　　　　　　*Teacher*

40 And he answered and said
unto them, I tell you that, if these
should ^Thold their peace, ^Rthe

stones would immediately cry out. *keep silent* · Hab. 2:11

41 And when he was come near, he beheld the city, and ᴿwept over it, Is. 53:3; John 11:35

42 Saying, If thou hadst known, even thou, at least in this ᴿthy day, the things *which belong* unto thy peace! but now they are hid from thine eyes. Ps. 95:7, 8; Heb. 3:13

43 For the days shall come upon thee, that thine enemies shall ᴿcast a trench about thee, and compass thee round, and keep thee in on every side, Is. 29:3, 4

44 And ᴿshall lay thee even with the ground, and thy children within thee; and they shall not leave in thee one stone upon another; because thou knewest not the time of thy visitation. 1 Kin. 9:7, 8

45 ᴿAnd he went into the temple, and began to cast out them that sold therein, and them that bought; Mal. 3:1; Matt. 21:12, 13

46 Saying unto them, ᴿIt is written, My house is the house of prayer: but ye have made it a ᴿden of thieves. Is. 56:7 · Jer. 7:11

47 And he taught daily in the temple. But the chief priests and the scribes and the chief of the people sought to destroy him,

48 And could not find what they might do: for all the people were very attentive to ᴿhear him. 21:38

20 And ᴿit came to pass, *that* on one of those days, as he taught the people in the temple, and preached the gospel, the chief priests and the scribes came upon *him* with the elders, Matt. 21:23–27

2 And spake unto him, saying, Tell us, by what authority doest thou these things? or who is he that gave thee this authority?

3 And he answered and said unto them, I will also ask you one thing; and answer me:

4 The ᴿbaptism of John, was it from heaven, or of men? John 1:26

5 And they reasoned with themselves, saying, If we shall say, From heaven; he will say, Why then believed ye him not?

6 But and if we say, Of men; all the people will stone us: ᴿfor they be persuaded that John was a prophet. Matt. 14:5; 21:26; Mark 6:20

7 And they answered, that they could not tell whence *it was*.

8 And Jesus said unto them, Neither tell I you by what authority I do these things.

9 Then began he to speak to the people this parable; A certain man planted a vineyard, and let it forth to husbandmen, and went into a far country for a long time.

10 And at the season he ᴿsent a servant to the husbandmen, that they should give him of the fruit of the vineyard: but the husbandmen beat him, and sent *him* away empty. 2 Kin. 17:13, 14; 2 Chr. 36:15, 16

11 And again he sent another servant: and they beat him also, and ᵀentreated *him* shamefully, and sent *him* away empty. *treated*

12 And again he sent a third: and they wounded him also, and cast *him* out.

13 Then said the lord of the vineyard, What shall I do? I will send my beloved son: it may be they will ᵀreverence *him* when they see him. *respect*

14 But when the husbandmen saw him, they reasoned among themselves, saying, This is the heir: come, let us kill him, that the inheritance may be ours.

15 So they cast him out of the vineyard, and killed *him*. What therefore shall the ᵀlord of the vineyard do unto them? *owner*

16 He shall come and destroy these husbandmen, and shall give the vineyard to ᴿothers. And when they heard *it*, they said, God forbid. Rom. 11:1, 11; 1 Cor. 6:15; Gal. 2:17

17 And he beheld them, and ☆ said, What is this then that is written, ᴿThe stone which the builders rejected, the same is become the head of the corner? Ps. 118:22

18 Whosoever shall fall upon ☆ that stone shall be ᴿbroken; but on whomsoever it shall fall, it will grind him to powder. Is. 8:14, 15

19 And the chief priests and the scribes the same hour sought to lay hands on him; and they feared the people: for they perceived that he had spoken this parable against them.

20 ᴿAnd they watched *him,* and sent forth spies, which should feign themselves just men, that they might take hold of his words, that so they might deliver him unto the power and authority of the governor. Matt. 22:15

21 And they asked him, saying, Master, we know that thou sayest and teachest rightly, neither acceptest thou the person *of any,* but teachest the way of God truly:

22 Is it lawful for us to ᵀgive tribute unto Caesar, or no? *pay taxes*

23 But he perceived their craftiness, and said unto them, Why ᵀtempt ye me? *test*

24 Shew me a ᵀpenny. Whose image and ᵀsuperscription hath it? They answered and said, Caesar's. Gr. *denarius · inscription*

25 And he said unto them, ᴿRender therefore unto Caesar the things which be Caesar's, and unto God the things which be God's. Matt. 17:24–27; Rom. 13:7

26 And they could not take hold of his words before the people: and they marvelled at his answer, and held their peace.

27 ᴿThen came to *him* certain of the Sad'-du-cees, which deny that there is any resurrection; and they asked him, Matt. 22:23–33

28 Saying, ᵀMaster, Moses wrote unto us, If any man's brother die, having a wife, and he die without children, that his brother should take his wife, and raise up ᵀseed unto his brother. *Teacher · offspring*

29 There were therefore seven brethren: and the first took a wife, and died without children.

30 And the second took her to wife, and he died childless.

31 And the third took her; and in like manner the seven also: and they left no children, and died.

32 Last of all the woman died also.

33 Therefore in the resurrection whose wife of them is she? for seven had her to wife.

34 And Jesus answering said unto them, The ᵀchildren of this world marry, and are given in marriage: *sons of this age*

35 But they which shall be ᴿaccounted worthy to obtain that ᵀworld, and the resurrection from the dead, neither marry, nor are given in marriage: Phil. 3:11 · *age*

36 Neither can they die any more: for ᴿthey are equal unto the angels; and are the children of God, ᴿbeing the children of the resurrection. [1 John 3:2] · Rom. 8:23

37 Now that the dead are raised, even Moses shewed at the bush, when he calleth the Lord ᴿthe God of Abraham, and the God of Isaac, and the God of Jacob. Ex. 3:1–6, 15

38 For he is not a God of the dead, but of the living: for ᴿall live unto him. [Rom. 6:10, 11; Heb. 11:16]

39 Then certain of the scribes answering said, ᵀMaster, thou hast ᵀwell said. *Teacher · spoken well*

40 And after that they ᵀdurst not ask him any *question at all. dared*

41 And he said unto them, ᴿHow say they that Christ is David's son? Matt. 22:41–46; Mark 12:35–37

42 And David himself saith in the book of Psalms, ᴿThe Lᴏʀᴅ said unto my Lord, Sit thou on my right hand, Ps. 110:1; Acts 2:34, 35

43 Till I make thine enemies thy footstool.

44 David therefore calleth him Lord, how is he then his son?

45 ᴿThen in the ᵀaudience of all the people he said unto his disciples, Matt. 23:1–7; Mark 12:38–40 · *hearing*

46 ᴿBeware of the scribes, which desire to walk in long robes, and ᴿlove greetings in the markets, and the highest seats in the synagogues, and the chief rooms at feasts; Matt. 23:5 · 11:43; 14:7

47 Which devour widows' houses, and for a ᴿshew make long prayers: the same shall receive greater damnation. [Matt. 6:5, 6]

21 And he looked up, and saw the rich men casting their gifts into the treasury.

☆

2　And he saw also a certain [R]poor widow casting in thither two [R]mites.　[2 Cor. 6:10] · Mark 12:42

3　And he said, Of a truth I say unto you, that this poor widow hath cast in more than they all:

4　For all these have of their abundance cast in unto the offerings of God: but she of her [T]penury hath cast in all the [T]living that she had.　*poverty · livelihood*

5　And as some spake of the temple, how it was adorned with goodly stones and gifts, he said,

6　*As for* these things which ye behold, the days will come, in the which [R]there shall not be left one stone upon another, that shall not be thrown down. Lam. 2:6–9; Mic. 3:12

7　And they asked him, saying, [T]Master, but when shall these things be? and what sign *will there be* when these things shall come to pass?　*Teacher*

8　And he said, [R]Take heed that ye be not deceived: for many shall come in my name, saying, I am *Christ;* and the time draweth near: go ye not therefore after them.　Matt. 24:4; Mark 13:5; 2 Thess. 2:3

9　But when ye shall hear of [R]wars and commotions, be not terrified: for these things must first come to pass; but the end *is* not by and by.　Rev. 6:4

10　Then said he unto them, Nation shall rise against nation, and kingdom against kingdom:

11　And great [R]earthquakes shall be in [T]divers places, and famines, and pestilences; and fearful sights and great signs shall there be from heaven.　Rev. 6:12 · *various*

12　But before all these, they shall lay their hands on you, and persecute *you,* delivering *you* up to the synagogues, and into prisons, being brought before kings and rulers for my name's sake.

13　And [R]it shall turn to you for a testimony. [Phil. 1:12–14, 28; 2 Thess. 1:5]

14　[R]Settle *it* therefore in your hearts, not to meditate before what ye shall answer:　Matt. 10:19

15　For I will give you a mouth and wisdom, [R]which all your adversaries shall not be able to [T]gainsay nor resist.　Acts 6:10 · *refute*

16　[R]And ye shall be betrayed both by parents, and brethren, and kinsfolks, and friends; and [R]some of you shall they cause to be put to death.　Mic. 7:6 · Acts 7:59

17　And [R]ye shall be hated of all *men* for my name's sake. Matt. 10:22

18　[R]But there shall not an hair of your head perish.　12:7; Matt. 10:30

19　In your patience possess ye your souls.

20　[R]And when ye shall see Jerusalem compassed with armies, then know that the desolation thereof is nigh.　Matt. 24:15; Mark 13:14

21　Then let them which are in Ju-dae'-a flee to the mountains; and let them which are in the midst of it depart out; and let not them that are in the [T]countries enter thereinto.　*country*

22　For these be the days of vengeance, that [R]all things which are written may be fulfilled. Is. 63:4

23　[R]But woe unto them that are with child, and to them that give suck, in those days! for there shall be great distress in the land, and wrath upon this people.　Matt. 24:19

24　And they shall fall by the edge of the sword, and shall be led away captive into all nations: and Jerusalem shall be trodden down of the Gentiles, [R]until the times of the Gentiles be fulfilled.　[Dan. 9:27]

25　And there shall be signs in the sun, and in the moon, and in the stars; and upon the earth distress of nations, with perplexity; the sea and the waves roaring;

26　Men's hearts failing them for fear, and for looking after those things which are coming on the earth: [R]for the powers of heaven shall be shaken.　Matt. 24:29

27　And then shall they see the ☆ Son of man coming in a cloud with power and great glory.

28　And when these things begin to come to pass, then look up, and lift up your heads; for your redemption draweth [T]nigh.　*near*

29　[R]And he spake to them a

parable; Behold the fig tree, and all the trees;   Matt. 24:32; Mark 13:28

30 When they now shoot forth, ye see and know of your own selves that summer is now ᵀnigh at hand.   *near*

31 So likewise ye, when ye see these things come to pass, know ye that the kingdom of God is ᵀnigh at hand.   *near*

32 Verily I say unto you, This generation shall not pass away, till all be fulfilled.

33 ᴿHeaven and earth shall pass away: but my ᴿwords shall not pass away.   Is. 51:6 · 16:17; Is. 40:8

34 And ᴿtake heed to yourselves, lest at any time your hearts be overcharged with surfeiting, and drunkenness, and ᴿcares of this life, and so that day come upon you unawares.   12:40, 45 · 8:14

35 For ᴿas a snare shall it come on all them that dwell on the face of the whole earth.   Rev. 3:3; 16:15

36 ᴿWatch ye therefore, and ᴿpray always, that ye may be accounted ᴿworthy to escape all these things that shall come to pass, and to stand before the Son of man.   Mark 13:33 · 18:1 · 20:35

37 ᴿAnd in the day time he was teaching in the temple; and ᴿat night he went out, and abode in the mount that is called *the mount* of Olives.   John 8:1, 2 · 22:39

38 And all the people came early in the morning to him in the temple, for to hear him.

22 Now the feast of unleavened bread drew nigh, which is called the Passover.

2 And ᴿthe chief priests and scribes sought how they might kill him; for they feared the people.   Ps. 2:2; John 11:47; Acts 4:27

3 Then entered Satan into Judas surnamed Is-car′-i-ot, being of the number of the twelve.

4 And he went his way, and ᵀcommuned with the chief priests and captains, how he might betray him unto them.   *conferred*

5 And they were glad, and covenanted to give him money.

6 And he promised, and sought

opportunity to ᴿbetray him unto them in the absence of the multitude.   Ps. 41:9

7 ᴿThen came the day of unleavened bread, when the passover must be killed.   Matt. 26:17–19

8 And he sent Peter and John, saying, Go and prepare us the passover, that we may eat.

9 And they said unto him, Where wilt thou that we prepare?

10 And he said unto them, Behold, when ye are entered into the city, there shall a man meet you, bearing a pitcher of water; follow him into the house where he entereth in.

11 And ye shall say unto the ᵀgoodman of the house, The ᵀMaster saith unto thee, Where is the guestchamber, where I shall eat the passover with my disciples?   *master · Teacher*

12 And he shall shew you a large upper room furnished: there make ready.

13 And they went, and ᴿfound as he had said unto them: and they made ready the passover.   19:32

14 ᴿAnd when the hour was come, he sat down, and the twelve apostles with him.   Matt. 26:20

15 And he said unto them, With desire I have desired to eat this passover with you before I suffer:

16 For I say unto you, I will not any more eat thereof, until it be fulfilled in the kingdom of God.

17 And he took the cup, and gave thanks, and said, Take this, and divide *it* among yourselves:

18 For I say unto you, I will not drink of the fruit of the vine, until the kingdom of God shall come.

19 And he took bread, and gave thanks, and brake *it*, and gave unto them, saying, This is my body which is given for you: this do in remembrance of me.

20 Likewise also the cup after supper, saying, This cup *is* the new ᵀtestament in my blood, which is shed for you.   *covenant*

21 ᴿBut, behold, the hand of him that betrayeth me *is* with me on the table.   Matt. 26:21, 23; Mark 14:18

22 ᴿAnd truly the Son of man goeth, ᴿas it was determined: but woe unto that man by whom he is betrayed! Matt. 26:24 · John 17:12

23 And they began to enquire among themselves, which of them it was that should do this thing.

24 ᴿAnd there was also a ᵀstrife among them, which of them should be ᵀaccounted the greatest. Mark 9:34 · rivalry · considered

25 ᴿAnd he said unto them, The kings of the Gentiles exercise lordship over them; and they that exercise authority upon them are called benefactors. Mark 10:42-45

26 But ye *shall* not *be* so: but he that is greatest among you, let him be as the younger; and he that is chief, as he that doth serve.

27 ᴿFor whether *is* greater, he that sitteth at meat, or he that serveth? *is* not he that sitteth at meat? but ᴿI am among you as he that serveth. [12:37] · Matt. 20:28

28 Ye are they which have continued with me in ᴿmy ᵀtemptations. [Heb. 2:18; 4:15] · trials

29 And ᴿI appoint unto you a kingdom, as my Father hath appointed unto me; Matt. 24:47

30 That ᴿye may eat and drink at my table in my kingdom, ᴿand sit on thrones judging the twelve tribes of Israel. [Matt. 8:11] · Ps. 49:14

31 And the Lord said, Simon, Simon, behold, ᴿSatan hath desired *to have* you, that he may ᴿsift *you* as wheat: 1 Pet. 5:8 · Amos 9:9

32 But ᴿI have prayed for thee, that thy faith fail not: and when thou art converted, strengthen thy brethren. [John 17:9, 11, 15]

33 And he said unto him, Lord, I am ready to go with thee, both into prison, and to death.

34 ᴿAnd he said, I tell thee, Peter, the cock shall not crow this day, before that thou shalt thrice deny that thou knowest me. v. 61

35 ᴿAnd he said unto them, When I sent you without purse, and ᵀscrip, and shoes, lacked ye any thing? And they said, Nothing. Matt. 10:9; Mark 6:8 · bag

36 Then said he unto them, But now, he that hath a purse, let him take *it*, and likewise *his* ᵀscrip: and he that hath no sword, let him sell his garment, and buy one. bag

37 For I say unto you, that this ☆ that is written must yet be ᵀaccomplished in me, ᴿAnd he was reckoned among the transgressors: for the things concerning me have an end. fulfilled · Is. 53:12

38 And they said, Lord, behold, here *are* two swords. And he said unto them, It is enough.

39 And he came out, and ᴿwent, as he was ᵀwont, to the mount of Olives; and his disciples also followed him. 21:37 · accustomed

40 And when he was at the place, he said unto them, Pray that ye enter not into temptation.

41 And he was withdrawn from them about a stone's ᵀcast, and kneeled down, and prayed, throw

42 Saying, Father, if thou be ★ willing, remove this cup from me: nevertheless ᴿnot my will, but thine, be done. Is. 50:5; John 4:34; 5:30

43 And there appeared ᴿan angel unto him from heaven, strengthening him. Matt. 4:11

44 ᴿAnd being in an agony he prayed more earnestly: and his sweat was as it were great drops of blood falling down to the ground. John 12:27; [Heb. 5:7]

45 And when he rose up from prayer, and was come to his disciples, he found them sleeping for sorrow,

46 And said unto them, Why ᴿsleep ye? rise and pray, lest ye enter into temptation. 9:32

47 And while he yet spake, ★ behold a multitude, and he that was called Judas, one of the twelve, went before them, and drew near unto Jesus to kiss him.

48 But Jesus said unto him, Judas, betrayest thou the Son of man with a ᴿkiss? [Prov. 27:6]

49 When they which were about him saw what would follow, they said unto him, Lord, shall we ᵀsmite with the sword? strike

50 And ᴿone of them ᵀsmote the

servant of the high priest, and cut off his right ear.   Matt. 26:51 · *struck*

51 And Jesus answered and said, Suffer ye thus far. And he touched his ear, and healed him.

52 Then Jesus said unto the chief priests, and captains of the temple, and the elders, which were come to him, Be ye come out, as against a thief, with swords and ^Tstaves?   *clubs*

53 When I was daily with you in the temple, ye stretched forth no hands against me: but this is your hour, and the power of darkness.

54 ^RThen took they him, and led *him*, and brought him into the high priest's house. And Peter followed afar off.   Matt. 26:57; Acts 8:32

55 ^RAnd when they had kindled a fire in the midst of the hall, and were set down together, Peter sat down among them. John 18:15, 17, 18

56 But a certain maid beheld him as he sat by the fire, and earnestly looked upon him, and said, This man was also with him.

57 And he denied him, saying, Woman, I know him not.

58 ^RAnd after a little while another saw him, and said, Thou art also of them. And Peter said, Man, I am not.   Matt. 26:71; Mark 14:69

59 ^RAnd about the space of one hour after another confidently affirmed, saying, Of a truth this *fellow* also was with him: for he is a ^RGal-i-lae'-an.   John 18:26 · Acts 1:11

60 And Peter said, Man, I know not what thou sayest. And immediately, while he yet spake, ^Tthe cock crew.   *a rooster crowed*

61 And the Lord turned, and looked upon Peter. And Peter remembered the word of the Lord, how he had said unto him, ^RBefore the cock crow, thou shalt deny me thrice.   Matt. 26:34, 75

62 And Peter went out, and wept bitterly.

63 And the men that held Jesus mocked him, and smote *him*.

64 And when they had blindfolded him, they ^Rstruck him on the face, and asked him, saying,

Prophesy, who is it that ^Tsmote thee?   Zech. 13:7 · *struck*

65 And many other things blasphemously spake they against him.   ★

66 ^RAnd as soon as it was day, ^Rthe elders of the people and the chief priests and the scribes came together, and led him into their council, saying,   Mark 15:1 · Ps. 2:2

67 Art thou the Christ? tell us. And he said unto them, If I tell you, ye will ^Rnot believe: 20:5–7

68 And if I also ask *you*, ye will not answer me, nor let *me* go.

69 ^RHereafter shall the Son of man sit on the right hand of the power of God. Acts 2:33; 7:55; Heb. 1:3

70 Then said they all, Art thou then the Son of God? And he said unto them, ^RYe say that I am.   1:35

71 ^RAnd they said, What need we any further witness? for we ourselves have heard of his own mouth. Matt. 26:65; Mark 14:63; John 19:7

23 And ^Rthe whole multitude of them arose, and led him unto ^RPilate.   John 18:28 · 3:1; 13:1

2 And they began to ^Raccuse him, saying, We found this *fellow* ^Rperverting the nation, and ^Rforbidding to give tribute to Caesar, saying that he himself is Christ a King.   Acts 24:2 · Acts 17:7 · Matt. 17:27

3 ^RAnd Pilate asked him, saying, Art thou the King of the Jews? And he answered him and said, Thou sayest *it*.   Matt. 27:11

4 Then said Pilate to the chief priests and *to* the people, ^RI find no fault in this man.   Matt. 27:19

5 And they were the more fierce, saying, He stirreth up the people, teaching throughout all ^TJewry, beginning from ^RGalilee to this place.   *Judea* · John 7:41

6 When Pilate heard of Galilee, he asked whether the man were a Gal-i-lae'-an.

7 And as soon as he knew that he belonged unto ^RHerod's jurisdiction, he sent him to Herod, who himself also was at Jerusalem at that time.   Matt. 14:1; Mark 6:14

8 And when Herod saw Jesus, ^Rhe was exceeding glad: for he

was desirous to see him of a long *season*, because ᴿhe had heard many things of him; and he hoped to have seen some miracle done by him.   9:9 · Matt. 14:1; Mark 6:14

★ 9 Then he questioned with him in many words; but he answered him ᴿnothing.   Is. 53:7; Matt. 27:12, 14

10 And the chief priests and scribes stood and vehemently accused him.

11 ᴿAnd Herod with his men of war set him at nought, and mocked *him,* and arrayed him in a gorgeous robe, and sent him again to Pilate.   Is. 53:3

12 And the same day ᴿPilate and Herod were made friends together: for before they were at enmity between themselves.   Acts 4:26, 27

13 And Pilate, when he had called together the chief priests and the rulers and the people,

14 Said unto them, ᴿYe have brought this man unto me, as one that perverteth the people: and, behold, ᴿI, having examined *him* before you, have found no fault in this man touching those things whereof ye accuse him: vv. 1, 2 · v. 4

15 No, nor yet Herod: for I sent you to him; and, lo, nothing worthy of death is done ᵀunto him. *by*

16 ᴿI will therefore chastise him, and release *him.* Matt. 27:26; John 19:1

17 ᴿ(For of necessity he must release one unto them at the feast.) Matt. 27:15; Mark 15:6; John 18:39

18 And they cried out all at once, saying, Away with this *man,* and release unto us Bar-ab´-bas:

19 (Who for a certain ᵀsedition made in the city, and for murder, was cast into prison.) *insurrection*

20 Pilate therefore, willing to release Jesus, spake again to them.

21 But they cried, saying, Crucify *him,* crucify him.

22 And he said unto them the third time, Why, what evil hath he done? I have found no cause of death in him: I will therefore chastise him, and let *him* go.

23 And they were ᵀinstant with loud voices, requiring that he might be crucified. And the voices

of them and of the chief priests prevailed.   *insistent*

24 And Pilate gave sentence that it should be as they required.

25 ᴿAnd he released unto them him that for sedition and murder was cast into prison, whom they had ᵀdesired; but he delivered Jesus to their will. Is. 53:8 · *requested*

26 ᴿAnd as they led him away, they laid hold upon one Simon, a Cy-re´-ni-an, coming out of the country, and on him they laid the cross, that he might bear *it* after Jesus. Matt. 27:32; Mark 15:21; John 19:17

27 And there followed him a great ᵀcompany of people, and of women, which also bewailed and lamented him.   *multitude*

28 But Jesus turning unto them said, Daughters of Jerusalem, weep not for me, but weep for yourselves, and for your children.

29 For, behold, the days are coming, in the which they shall say, Blessed *are* the barren, and the wombs that never bare, and the paps which never gave suck.

30 Then shall they begin ᴿto say to the mountains, Fall on us; and to the hills, Cover us. Rev. 6:16, 17

31 ᴿFor if they do these things in a green tree, what shall be done in the dry? Ezek. 20:47; 21:3, 4; 1 Pet. 4:17

32 And there were also two oth- ★ ers, ᵀmalefactors, led with him to be put to death.   *criminals*

33 And when they were come to the place, which is called Calvary, there they crucified him, and the malefactors, one on the right hand, and the other on the left.

34 Then said Jesus, Father, ᴿforgive them; for they know not what they do. And they parted his raiment, and cast lots. Acts 7:60

35 And the people stood behold- ★ ing. And the rulers also with them derided *him,* saying, He saved others; let him save himself, if he be Christ, the chosen of God.

36 And the soldiers also mocked ★ him, coming to him, and offering him ᴿvinegar,ᵀ Ps. 69:21 · *sour wine*

37 And saying, If thou be the king of the Jews, save thyself.

38 ^RAnd a superscription also was written over him in letters of Greek, and Latin, and Hebrew, THIS IS THE KING OF THE JEWS.   Matt. 27:37; John 19:19

39 ^RAnd one of the malefactors which were hanged railed on him, saying, If thou be Christ, save thyself and us.   Matt. 27:44; Mark 15:32

40 But the other answering rebuked him, saying, Dost not thou fear God, seeing thou art in the same condemnation?

41 And we indeed justly; for we receive the due reward of our deeds: but this man hath done ^Rnothing amiss.   [2 Cor. 5:21; Heb. 7:26]

42 And he said unto Jesus, Lord, remember me when thou comest into thy kingdom.

43 And Jesus said unto him, Verily I say unto thee, to day shalt thou be with me in paradise.

★ 44 ^RAnd it was about the sixth hour, and there was a darkness over all the earth until the ninth hour.   Amos 8:9; Mark 15:33–41

45 And the sun was darkened, and ^Rthe veil of the temple was rent in the midst.   Matt. 27:51

46 And when Jesus had cried with a loud voice, he said, Father, into thy hands I commend my spirit: and having said thus, he ^Tgave up the ghost.   *breathed his last*

47 ^RNow when the centurion saw what was done, he glorified God, saying, Certainly this was a righteous man.   Matt. 27:54; Mark 15:39

48 And all the people that came together to that sight, beholding the things which were done, smote their breasts, and returned.

49 ^RAnd all his acquaintance, and the women that followed him from Galilee, stood afar off, beholding these things.   Ps. 38:11

50 ^RAnd, behold, *there was* a man named Joseph, a ^Tcounsellor; *and he was* a good man, and a just: Matt. 27:57–61 · *council member*

51 (The same had not consented to the counsel and deed of them;) he was of Ar-i-ma-thae'-a, a city of the Jews: ^Rwho also himself waited for the kingdom of God.   2:25, 38

52 This *man* went unto Pilate, and begged the body of Jesus.

★ 53 ^RAnd he took it down, and wrapped it in linen, and laid it in a sepulchre that was hewn in stone, wherein never man before was laid.   Is. 53:9; Matt. 27:59; Mark 15:46

54 And that day was the preparation, and the sabbath drew on.

55 And the women also, ^Rwhich came with him from Galilee, followed after, and ^Rbeheld the sepulchre, and how his body was laid.   8:2 · Mark 15:47

56 And they returned, and prepared spices and ointments; and rested the sabbath day ^Raccording to the commandment.   Deut. 5:14

24 Now ^Rupon the first *day* of the week, very early in the morning, they came unto the ^Tsepulchre, bringing the spices which they had prepared, and certain *others* with them.   Mark 16:1–8 · *tomb*

2 And they found the stone rolled away from the sepulchre.

3 ^RAnd they entered in, and found not the body of the Lord Jesus.   Mark 16:5

4 And it came to pass, as they were much perplexed thereabout, ^Rbehold, two men stood by them in shining garments: John 20:12

5 And as they were afraid, and bowed down *their* faces to the earth, they said unto them, Why seek ye the living among the dead?

6 He is not here, but is risen: remember how he spake unto you when he was yet in Galilee,

7 Saying, The Son of man must be ^Rdelivered into the hands of sinful men, and be crucified, and the third day rise again.   18:31–33

8 And ^Rthey remembered his words,   9:22, 44; John 2:19–22

9 And returned from the sepulchre, and told all these things unto the eleven, and to all the rest.

10 It was Mary Mag-da-le'-ne, and ^RJo-an'-na, and Mary *the mother* of James, and other *women that were* with them, which told these things unto the apostles.   8:3

11 [R]And their words seemed to them as idle tales, and they believed them not.　　　v. 25

12 Then arose Peter, and ran unto the sepulchre; and stooping down, he beheld the linen clothes laid by themselves, and departed, wondering in himself at that which was come to pass.

13 [R]And, behold, two of them went that same day to a village called Em-ma'-us, which was from Jerusalem about threescore [T]furlongs.　　Mark 16:12 · Gr. stadia

14 And they talked together of all these things which had happened.

15 And it came to pass, that, while they communed together and reasoned, Jesus himself drew near, and went with them.

16 But their eyes were holden that they should not know him.

17 And he said unto them, What manner of communications are these that ye have one to another, as ye walk, and are sad?

18 And the one of them, whose name was Cle'-o-pas, answering said unto him, Art thou only a stranger in Jerusalem, and hast not known the things which are come to pass there in these days?

19 And he said unto them, What things? And they said unto him, Concerning Jesus of Nazareth, [R]which was a prophet [R]mighty in deed and word before God and all the people:　　7:16; John 3:2 · Acts 7:22

20 [R]And how the chief priests and our rulers delivered him to be condemned to death, and have crucified him.　　23:1; Acts 13:27, 28

21 But we trusted [R]that it had been he which should have redeemed Israel: and beside all this, to day is the third day since these things were done. 1:68; 2:38; [Acts 1:6]

22 Yea, and [R]certain women also of our company made us astonished, which were early at the sepulchre;　　Matt. 28:8; Mark 16:10

23 And when they found not his body, they came, saying, that they had also seen a vision of angels, which said that he was alive.

24 And [R]certain of them which were with us went to the sepulchre, and found it even so as the women had said: but him they saw not.　　v. 12

25 Then he said unto them, O fools, and slow of heart to believe all that the prophets have spoken:

26 [R]Ought not Christ to have suffered these things, and to enter into his glory? Acts 17:2, 3; [Heb. 2:9, 10]

27 And beginning at Moses and all the prophets, he expounded unto them in all the scriptures the things concerning himself.

28 And they drew [T]nigh unto the village, whither they went: and [R]he made as though he would have gone further.　　near · Mark 6:48

29 But [R]they constrained him, saying, [R]Abide with us: for it is toward evening, and the day is far spent. And he went in to tarry with them.　　Acts 16:15 · [John 14:23]

30 And it came to pass, as [R]he sat at meat with them, he took bread, and blessed it, and brake, and gave to them.　　Matt. 14:19

31 And their eyes were opened, and they knew him; and he vanished out of their sight.

32 And they said one to another, Did not our heart burn within us, while he talked with us by the way, and while he opened to us the scriptures?

33 And they rose up the same hour, and returned to Jerusalem, and found the eleven gathered together, and them that were with them,

34 Saying, The Lord is risen indeed, and [R]hath appeared to Simon.　　1 Cor. 15:5

35 And they told what things were done in the way, and how he was known of them in breaking of bread.

36 [R]And as they thus spake, Jesus himself stood in the midst of them, and saith unto them, Peace be unto you.　　Mark 16:14

37 But they were terrified and affrighted, and supposed that they had seen [R]a spirit.　　Mark 6:49

38 And he said unto them, Why

are ye troubled? and why do thoughts arise in your hearts?

39 Behold my hands and my feet, that it is I myself: ᴿhandle me, and see; for a spirit hath not flesh and bones, as ye see me have.   John 20:20, 27; 1 John 1:1

40 And when he had thus spoken, he shewed them *his* hands and *his* feet.

41 And while they yet believed not ᴿfor joy, and wondered, he said unto them, ᴿHave ye here any ᵀmeat?   Gen. 45:26 · John 21:5 · *food*

42 And they gave him a piece of a broiled fish, and of an honeycomb.

43 ᴿAnd he took *it*, and did eat before them.   Acts 10:39–41

44 And he said unto them, ᴿThese *are* the words which I spake unto you, while I was yet with you, that all things must be fulfilled, which were written in the law of Moses, and *in* the prophets, and *in* the psalms, concerning me.   9:22; 18:31

45 Then ᴿopened he their understanding, that they might understand the scriptures,   Acts 16:14

46 And said unto them, ᴿThus it is written, and thus it behoved Christ to suffer, and to rise from the dead the third day: Ps. 22

47 And that repentance and remission of sins should be preached in his name among all nations, beginning at Jerusalem.

48 And ᴿye are witnesses of these things.   [Acts 1:8]; 1 Pet. 5:1

49 ᴿAnd, behold, I send the promise of my Father upon you: but tarry ye in the city of Jerusalem, until ye be endued with power from on high. Is. 44:3; Acts 2:4

50 And he led them out as far as to Beth'-a-ny, and he lifted up his hands, and blessed them.

51 ᴿAnd it came to pass, while ★ he blessed them, he was parted from them, and carried up into heaven. Ps. 68:18; Mark 16:19; Acts 1:9–11

52 ᴿAnd they worshipped him, and returned to Jerusalem with great joy: Matt. 28:9

53 And were continually ᴿin the temple, praising and blessing God. A-men'.   Acts 2:46

The Gospel According to

JOHN

JUST as a coin has two sides, both valid, so Jesus Christ has two natures, both valid. Luke presents Christ in His humanity as the Son of Man; John portrays Him in His deity as the Son of God. John's purpose is crystal clear: to set forth Christ in His deity in order to spark believing faith in his readers. John's gospel is topical, not primarily chronological, and it revolves around seven miracles and seven "I am" statements of Christ.

Following an extended eyewitness description of the Upper Room meal and discourse, John records events leading up to the Resurrection, the final climactic proof that Jesus is who He claims to be—the Son of God.

The title of the Fourth Gospel follows the same format as the titles of the synoptic Gospels: *Kata Ioannen,* "According to John." As with the others, the word "Gospel" was added later. *Ioannes* is derived from the Hebrew name *Johanan,* "Yahweh Has Been Gracious."

IN the beginning ^Rwas the Word, and the Word was with God, and the Word was God.   1 John 1:1

2 ^RThe same was in the beginning with God.   Gen. 1:1

3 ^RAll things were made by him; and without him was not any thing made that was made. Ps. 33:6

4 ^RIn him was life; and the life was the light of men.   [1 John 5:11]

5 And ^Rthe light shineth in darkness; and the darkness comprehended it not.   [3:19]

6 There was a man sent from God, whose name *was* John.

7 The same came for a ^Rwitness, to bear witness of the Light, that all *men* through him might ^Rbelieve.   3:25–36; 5:33–35 · [3:16]

8 He was not that Light, but *was sent* to bear witness of that ^RLight.   Is. 9:2; 49:6

9 ^R*That* was the true Light, which lighteth every man that cometh into the world.   Is. 49:6

10 He was in the world, and the world was made by him, and ^Rthe world knew him not.   Col. 1:16

★ 11 ^RHe came unto his own, and his own received him not.   Is. 53:3

12 But as many as received him, to them gave he power to become the sons of God, *even* to them that believe on his name:

13 Which were born, not of blood, nor of the will of the flesh, nor of the will of man, but of God.

14 And the Word was made flesh, and dwelt among us, (and we beheld his glory, the glory as of the only begotten of the Father,) full of grace and truth.

15 John bare witness of him, and cried, saying, This was he of whom I spake, ^RHe that cometh after me is preferred before me: for he was before me.   [Matt. 3:11]

16 And of his fulness have all we received, and grace for grace.

17 For the law was given by Moses, *but* grace and ^Rtruth came by Jesus Christ.   [8:32; 14:6; 18:37]

18 No man hath seen God at any time; the only begotten Son, which is in the bosom of the Father, he hath declared *him*.

19 And this is ^Rthe record of John, when the Jews sent priests and Levites from Jerusalem to ask him, Who art thou?   5:33

20 And ^Rhe confessed, and denied not; but confessed, I am not the Christ.   Luke 3:15; Acts 13:25

21 And they asked him, What then? Art thou E-li′-as? And he saith, I am not. Art thou that prophet? And he answered, No.

22 Then said they unto him, Who art thou? that we may give an answer to them that sent us. What sayest thou of thyself?

23 He said, ^RI *am* the voice of ★ one crying in the wilderness, Make straight the way of the Lord, as ^Rsaid the prophet E-sa′-ias.   Matt. 3:3 · Is. 40:3; Mal. 3:1

24 And they which were sent were of the Pharisees.

25 And they asked him, and said unto him, Why baptizest thou then, if thou be not that Christ, nor E-li′-as, neither that prophet?

26 John answered them, saying, ^RI baptize with water: ^Rbut there standeth one among you, whom ye know not; Matt. 3:11 · 4:10; 8:19; 9:30

27 ^RHe it is, who coming after me is preferred before me, whose shoe's latchet I am not worthy to unloose.   [3:31]; Acts 19:4; [Col. 1:17]

28 These things were done in Beth-ab′-a-ra beyond Jordan, where John was baptizing.

29 The next day John seeth Jesus coming unto him, and saith, Behold the Lamb of God, which taketh away the sin of the world.

30 This is he of whom I said, After me cometh a man which ^Tis preferred before me: for he was before me.   *ranks higher than I*

31 And I knew him not: but that he should be made manifest to Israel, ^Rtherefore am I come baptizing with water.   Mal. 3:1; Matt. 3:6

32 ^RAnd John bare record, saying, I saw the Spirit descending from heaven like a dove, and it abode upon him.   Is. 42:1; 61:1

33 And I knew him not: but he ★ that sent me to baptize with water, the same said unto me,

Upon whom thou shalt see the Spirit descending, and remaining on him, the same is he which baptizeth with the Holy Ghost.

34 And I saw, and bare record that this is the [R]Son of God. 11:27

35 Again the next day after John stood, and two of his disciples;

36 And looking upon Jesus as he walked, he saith, [R]Behold the Lamb of God! v. 29

37 And the two disciples heard him speak, and they [R]followed Jesus. Matt. 4:20, 22

38 Then Jesus turned, and saw them following, and saith unto them, What seek ye? They said unto him, Rabbi, (which is to say, being interpreted, Master,) where [T]dwellest thou? *are you staying*

39 He saith unto them, Come and see. They came and saw where he dwelt, and [T]abode with him that day: for it was about the tenth hour. *remained*

40 One of the two which heard John *speak*, and followed him, was [R]Andrew, Simon Peter's brother. 6:8; 12:22; Matt. 4:18; Mark 1:29; 13:3

41 He first findeth his own brother Simon, and saith unto him, We have found the Mes-si'-as, which is, being interpreted, the [T]Christ. Lit. *Anointed One*

42 And he brought him to Jesus. And when Jesus beheld him, he said, Thou art Simon the son of Jona: [R]thou shalt be called Ce'-phas, which is by interpretation, [T]A stone. Matt. 16:18 · *Peter*

43 The day following Jesus would go forth into Galilee, and findeth [R]Philip, and saith unto him, Follow me. 6:5; 12:21, 22; 14:8, 9

44 Now Philip was of Beth-sa'-i-da, the city of Andrew and Peter.

45 Philip findeth [R]Na-than'-a-el, and saith unto him, We have found him, of whom [R]Moses in the law, and the prophets, did write, Jesus of Nazareth, the son of Joseph. 21:2 · [Gen. 3:15; Deut. 18:18]

46 And Na-than'-a-el said unto him, Can there any good thing come out of Nazareth? Philip saith unto him, Come and see.

47 Jesus saw Na-than'-a-el coming to him, and saith of him, Behold [R]an Israelite indeed, in whom is no [T]guile! Ps. 32:2; 73:1 · *deceit*

48 Na-than'-a-el saith unto him, [T]Whence knowest thou me? Jesus answered and said unto him, Before that Philip called thee, when thou wast under the fig tree, I saw thee. *How*

49 Na-than'-a-el answered and saith unto him, Rabbi, [R]thou art the Son of God; thou art [R]the King of Israel. Ps. 2:7; Matt. 14:33 · Matt. 21:5

50 Jesus answered and said unto him, Because I said unto thee, I saw thee under the fig tree, believest thou? thou shalt see greater things than these.

51 And he saith unto him, Verily, verily, I say unto you, Hereafter ye shall see heaven open, and the angels of God ascending and descending upon the Son of man.

2 And the third day there was a [R]marriage in [R]Cana of Galilee; and the [R]mother of Jesus was there: [Heb. 13:4] · Josh. 19:28 · 19:25

2 And both Jesus was called, and his disciples, to the marriage.

3 And when they wanted wine, the mother of Jesus saith unto him, They have no wine.

4 Jesus saith unto her, Woman, what have I to do with thee? [R]mine hour is not yet come. 8:20

5 His mother saith unto the servants, Whatsoever he saith unto you, do *it*.

6 And there were set there six waterpots of stone, [R]after the manner of the purifying of the Jews, containing two or three firkins apiece. 3:25; Matt. 15:2

7 Jesus saith unto them, Fill the waterpots with water. And they filled them up to the brim.

8 And he saith unto them, Draw out now, and [T]bear unto the [T]governor of the feast. And they bare *it*. *take* it · *master*

9 When the [T]ruler of the feast had tasted [R]the water that was made wine, and knew not whence it was: (but the servants which

drew the water knew;) the [T]governor of the feast called the bridegroom, *master* · 4:46

10 And saith unto him, Every man at the beginning doth set forth good wine; and when men have well drunk, then that which is [T]worse: *but* thou hast kept the good wine until now. *inferior*

11 This [R]beginning of miracles did Jesus in Cana of Galilee, and manifested forth his glory; and his disciples believed on him. 4:54

12 After this he went down to [R]Ca-per'-na-um, he, and his mother, and his brethren, and his disciples: and they continued there not many days. 4:46

13 [R]And the Jews' passover was at hand, and Jesus went up to Jerusalem, 5:1; 6:4; 11:55; Ex. 12:14

★ 14 [R]And found in the temple those that sold oxen and sheep and doves, and the changers of money sitting: Mal. 3:1; Matt. 21:12

15 And when he had made a [T]scourge of small cords, he drove them all out of the temple, and the sheep, and the oxen; and poured out the changers' money, and overthrew the tables; *whip*

16 And said unto them that sold doves, Take these things hence; make not [R]my Father's house an house of merchandise. Luke 2:49

★ 17 And his disciples remembered that it was written, [R]The zeal of thine house hath eaten me up. Ps. 69:9

18 Then answered the Jews and said unto him, [R]What sign shewest thou unto us, seeing that thou doest these things? Matt. 12:38

19 Jesus answered and said unto them, Destroy this temple, and in three days I will raise it up.

20 Then said the Jews, Forty and six years was this temple in building, and wilt thou [T]rear it up in three days? *raise*

21 But he spake [R]of the temple of his body. [Col. 2:9; Heb. 8:2]

22 When therefore he was risen from the dead, [R]his disciples remembered that he had said this unto them; and they believed the

scripture, and the word which Jesus had said. v. 17; 12:16; 14:26

23 Now when he was in Jerusalem at the passover, in the feast *day*, many believed in his name, when they saw [R]the [T]miracles which he did. [5:36; Acts 2:22] · *signs*

24 But Jesus did not commit himself unto them, because he [R]knew all *men*, 16:30; Matt. 9:4

25 And needed not that any should testify of man: for [R]he knew what was in man. 6:64; 16:30

3 There was a man of the Pharisees, named Nic-o-de'-mus, a ruler of the Jews:

2 The same came to Jesus by night, and said unto him, Rabbi, we know that thou art a teacher come from God: for no man can do these [T]miracles that thou doest, except God be with him. *signs*

3 Jesus answered and said unto him, Verily, verily, I say unto thee, [R]Except a man be born [T]again, he cannot see the kingdom of God. [1:13] · Or *from above*

4 Nic-o-de'-mus saith unto him, How can a man be born when he is old? can he enter the second time into his mother's womb, and be born?

5 Jesus answered, Verily, verily, I say unto thee, [R]Except a man be born of water and *of* the Spirit, he cannot enter into the kingdom of God. Mark 16:16; [Acts 2:38]

6 That which is born of the flesh is [R]flesh; and that which is born of the Spirit is spirit. 1:13

7 Marvel not that I said unto thee, Ye must be born again.

8 [R]The wind bloweth where it [T]listeth, and thou hearest the sound thereof, but canst not tell whence it cometh, and whither it goeth: so is every one that is born of the Spirit. 1 Cor. 2:11 · *wishes*

9 Nic-o-de'-mus answered and said unto him, [R]How can these things be? 6:52, 60

10 Jesus answered and said unto him, Art thou a [T]master of Israel, and knowest not these things? *teacher*

11 Verily, verily, I say unto thee,

We speak that we do know, and testify that we have seen; and ^Rye receive not our witness.   v. 32; 8:14

12 If I have told you earthly things, and ye believe not, how shall ye believe, if I tell you of heavenly things?

13 And ^Rno man hath ascended up to heaven, but he that came down from heaven, *even* the Son of man which is in heaven. Eph. 4:9

14 And as Moses lifted up the serpent in the wilderness, even so must the Son of man be lifted up:

15 That whosoever ^Rbelieveth in him should not perish, but ^Rhave eternal life.   6:47 · v. 36

16 ^RFor God so loved the world, that he gave his only begotten ^RSon, that whosoever believeth in him should not perish, but have everlasting life.   Rom. 5:8 · [Is. 9:6]

17 ^RFor God sent not his Son into the world to condemn the world; but that the world through him might be saved.   1 John 4:14

18 ^RHe that believeth on him is not condemned: but he that believeth not is condemned already, because he hath not believed in the name of the only begotten Son of God.   5:24; 6:40, 47; 20:31; Rom. 8:1

19 And this is the condemnation, ^Rthat light is come into the world, and men loved darkness rather than light, because their deeds were evil.   [1:4, 9–11]

20 For ^Revery one that doeth evil hateth the light, neither cometh to the light, lest his deeds should be reproved.   Job 24:13; Eph. 5:11, 13

21 But he that doeth truth cometh to the light, that his deeds may be made manifest, that they are ^Rwrought in God.   [15:4, 5]; 1 Cor. 15:10

22 After these things came Jesus and his disciples into the land of Ju-dae′-a; and there he tarried with them, ^Rand baptized.   4:1, 2

23 And John also was baptizing in Ae′-non near to ^RSa′-lim, because there was much water there: ^Rand they came, and were baptized.   1 Sam. 9:4 · Matt. 3:5, 6

24 For ^RJohn was not yet cast into prison.   Matt. 4:12; 14:3; Mark 6:17

25 Then there arose a question between *some* of John's disciples and the Jews about purifying.

26 And they came unto John, and said unto him, Rabbi, he that was with thee beyond Jordan, ^Rto whom thou barest witness, behold, the same baptizeth, and all *men* come to him.   1:7, 15, 27, 34

27 John answered and said, ^RA man can receive nothing, except it be given him from heaven.   Heb. 5:4

28 Ye yourselves bear me witness, that I said, ^RI am not the Christ, but ^Rthat I am sent before him.   1:19–27 · Mal. 3:1; Mark 1:2

29 ^RHe that hath the bride is the bridegroom: but ^Rthe friend of the bridegroom, which standeth and heareth him, rejoiceth greatly because of the bridegroom's voice: this my joy therefore is fulfilled.   Matt. 22:2; [Eph. 5:25, 27] · Song 5:1

30 ^RHe must increase, but I *must* decrease.   [Is. 9:7]

31 ^RHe that cometh from above is above all: he that is of the earth is earthly, and speaketh of the earth: ^Rhe that cometh from heaven is above all.   v. 13 · 6:33; 1 Cor. 15:47

32 And ^Rwhat he hath seen and heard, that he testifieth; and no man receiveth his testimony.   v. 11

33 He that hath received his testimony ^Rhath ^Tset to his seal that God is true.   1 John 5:10 · *certified*

34 ^RFor he whom God hath sent ★ speaketh the words of God: for God giveth not the Spirit ^Rby measure *unto him*.   7:16 · 1:16

35 ^RThe Father loveth the Son, and hath given all things into his hand.   Matt. 11:27; Luke 10:22; [Heb. 2:8]

36 ^RHe that believeth on the Son hath everlasting life: and he that believeth not the Son shall not see life; but the wrath of God abideth on him.   6:47; Rom. 1:17; 1 John 5:10

4 When therefore the Lord knew how the Pharisees had heard that Jesus made and baptized more disciples than John,

2 (Though Jesus himself baptized not, but his disciples,)

3 He left Ju-dae′-a, and departed again into Galilee.

4 And he ^Tmust needs go through Sa-ma'-ri-a.   *needed to go*

5 Then cometh he to a city of Sa-ma'-ri-a, which is called Sy'-char, near to the parcel of ground that ^RJacob ^Rgave to his son Jo-seph.   Gen. 33:19 · Gen. 48:22; Josh. 4:12

6 Now Jacob's well was there. Jesus therefore, being wearied with *his* journey, sat thus on the well: *and* it was about the sixth hour.

7 There cometh a woman of Sa-ma'-ri-a to draw water: Jesus saith unto her, Give me to drink.

8 (For his disciples were gone away unto the city to buy meat.)

9 Then saith the woman of Sa-ma'-ri-a unto him, How is it that thou, being a Jew, askest drink of me, which am a woman of Sa-ma'-ri-a? for the Jews have no dealings with the Sa-mar'-i-tans.

10 Jesus answered and said unto her, If thou knewest the ^Rgift of God, and who it is that saith to thee, Give me to drink; thou wouldest have asked of him, and he would have given thee ^Rliving water.   [Rom. 5:15] · 7:38; Is. 12:3

11 The woman saith unto him, Sir, thou hast nothing to draw with, and the well is deep: from whence then hast thou that living water?

12 Art thou greater than our father Jacob, which gave us the well, and drank thereof himself, and his children, and his cattle?

13 Jesus answered and said unto her, Whosoever drinketh of this water shall thirst again:

14 But ^Rwhosoever drinketh of the water that I shall give him shall never thirst; but the water that I shall give him ^Rshall be in him a well of water springing up into everlasting life.   [6:35] · 7:37, 38

15 The woman saith unto him, Sir, give me this water, that I thirst not, neither come hither to draw.

16 Jesus saith unto her, Go, call thy husband, and come hither.

17 The woman answered and said, I have no husband. Jesus said unto her, Thou hast well said, I have no husband:

18 For thou hast had five husbands; and he whom thou now hast is not thy husband: in that saidst thou truly.

19 The woman saith unto him, Sir, ^RI perceive that thou art a prophet.   6:14; 7:40; 9:17

20 Our fathers worshipped in this mountain; and ye say, that in ^RJerusalem is the place where men ought to worship.   2 Chr. 7:12

21 Jesus saith unto her, Woman, believe me, the hour cometh, ^Rwhen ye shall neither in this mountain, nor yet at Jerusalem, worship the Father.   1 Tim. 2:8

22 Ye worship ye know not what: we know what we worship: for salvation is of the Jews.

23 But the hour cometh, and now is, when the true worshippers shall worship the Father in spirit ^Rand in truth: for the Father seeketh such to worship him. [1:17]

24 ^RGod *is* a Spirit: and they that worship him must worship *him* in spirit and in truth.   2 Cor. 3:17

25 The woman saith unto him, I know that Mes-si'-as cometh, which is called Christ: when he is come, he will tell us all things.

26 Jesus saith unto her, ^RI that speak unto thee am *he*.   Dan. 9:25

27 And upon this came his disciples, and marvelled that he talked with ^Tthe woman: yet no man said, What seekest thou? or, Why talkest thou with her?   Lit. *a*

28 The woman then left her waterpot, and went her way into the city, and saith to the men,

29 Come, see a man, which told me all things that ever I did: ^Tis not this the Christ?   *could this be*

30 Then they went out of the city, and came unto him.

31 In the mean while his disciples ^Tprayed him, saying, ^TMaster, eat.   *urged* · Gr. *Rabbi*

32 But he said unto them, I have meat to eat that ye know not of.

33 Therefore said the disciples one to another, Hath any man brought him *ought* to eat?

34 Jesus saith unto them, My meat is to do the will of him that sent me, and to finish his work.

35 Say not ye, There are yet four months, and *then* cometh ^Rharvest? behold, I say unto you, Lift up your eyes, and look on the fields; ^Rfor they are white already to harvest.   Gen. 8:22 · Matt. 9:37

36 And he that reapeth receiveth wages, and gathereth fruit unto life eternal: that ^Rboth he that soweth and he that reapeth may rejoice together.   1 Thess. 2:19

37 And herein is that saying true, ^ROne soweth, and another reapeth.   1 Cor. 3:5–9

38 I sent you to reap that whereon ye bestowed no labour: ^Rother men laboured, and ye are entered into their labours.   [1 Pet. 1:12]

39 And many of the Sa-mar'-i-tans of that city believed on him ^Rfor the saying of the woman, which testified, He told me all that ever I did.   v. 29

40 So when the Sa-mar'-i-tans were come unto him, they ^Tbesought him that he would ^Ttarry with them: and he ^Tabode there two days.   *urged · stay · stayed*

41 And many more believed because of his own ^Rword;   [6:63]

42 And said unto the woman, Now we believe, not because of thy saying: for ^Rwe have heard *him* ourselves, and know that this is indeed the Christ, the Saviour of the world.   17:8; 1 John 4:14

43 Now after two days he departed thence, and went into Galilee.

44 For ^RJesus himself testified, that a prophet hath no honour in his own country.   Mark 6:4; Luke 4:24

45 Then when he was come into Galilee, the Gal-i-lae'-ans received him, ^Rhaving seen all the things that he did at Jerusalem at the feast: ^Rfor they also went unto the feast.   2:13, 23; 3:2 · Deut. 16:16

46 So Jesus came again into Cana of Galilee, ^Rwhere he made the water wine. And there was a certain nobleman, whose son was sick at Ca-per'-na-um.   2:1, 11

47 When he heard that Jesus was come out of Ju-dae'-a into Galilee, he went unto him, and besought him that he would come down, and heal his son: for he was at the point of death.

48 Then said Jesus unto him, ^RExcept ye see signs and wonders, ye will not believe.   6:30

49 The nobleman saith unto him, Sir, come down ^Tere my child die.   *before my child dies*

50 Jesus saith unto him, Go thy way; thy son liveth. And the man believed the word that Jesus had spoken unto him, and he went his way.

51 And as he was now going down, his servants met him, and told *him*, saying, Thy son liveth.

52 Then enquired he of them the hour when he began to ^Tamend. And they said unto him, Yesterday at the seventh hour the fever left him.   *get better*

53 So the father knew that *it was* at the same hour, in the which Jesus said unto him, Thy son liveth: and himself believed, and his whole ^Thouse.   *household*

54 This *is* again the second ^Tmiracle *that* Jesus did, when he was come out of Ju-dae'-a into Galilee.   *sign*

5 After ^Rthis there was a feast of the Jews; and Jesus ^Rwent up to Jerusalem.   Lev. 23:2 · 2:13

2 Now there is at Jerusalem ^Rby the sheep ^T*market* a pool, which is called in the Hebrew tongue Be-thes'-da, having five porches.   Neh. 3:1, 32; 12:39 · Gate

3 In these lay a great multitude of ^Timpotent folk, of blind, ^Thalt, withered, waiting for the moving of the water.   *sick people · lame*

4 For an angel went down at a certain ^Tseason into the pool, and troubled the water: whosoever then first after the troubling of the water stepped in was made whole of whatsoever disease he had. *time*

5 And a certain man was there, which had an infirmity thirty and eight years.

6 When Jesus saw him lie, and

knew that he had been now a long time *in that case,* he saith unto him, Wilt thou be made whole?

7 The impotent man answered him, Sir, I have no man, when the water is troubled, to put me into the pool: but while I am coming, another steppeth down before me.

8 Jesus saith unto him, ᴿRise, take up thy bed, and walk. Matt. 9:6

9 And immediately the man was made whole, and took up his bed, and walked: and ᴿon the same day was the sabbath.   9:14

10 The Jews therefore said unto him that was cured, It is the sabbath day: ᴿit is not lawful for thee to carry *thy* bed. Ex. 20:10; Neh. 13:19

11 He answered them, He that made me whole, the same said unto me, Take up thy bed, and walk.

12 Then asked they him, What man is that which said unto thee, Take up thy bed, and walk?

13 And he that was healed ᵀwist not who it was: for Jesus had conveyed himself away, a multitude being in *that* place.   *knew*

14 Afterward Jesus findeth him in the temple, and said unto him, Behold, thou art made whole: ᴿsin no more, lest a worse thing come unto thee. Matt. 12:45; [Mark 2:5]

15 The man departed, and told the Jews that it was Jesus, which had made him whole.

16 And therefore did the Jews persecute Jesus, and sought to slay him, because he had done these things on the sabbath day.

17 But Jesus answered them, ᴿMy Father worketh hitherto, and I work.   [9:4; 17:4]

18 Therefore the Jews ᴿsought the more to kill him, because he not only had broken the sabbath, but said also that God was his Father, ᴿmaking himself equal with God.   7:1, 19 · 10:30; Phil. 2:6

19 Then answered Jesus and said unto them, Verily, verily, I say unto you, ᴿThe Son can do nothing of himself, but what he seeth the Father do: for what things

soever he doeth, these also doeth the Son likewise.   8:28; 12:49; 14:10

20 For ᴿthe Father loveth the Son, and sheweth him all things that himself doeth: and he will shew him greater works than these, that ye may marvel.   3:35

21 For as the Father raiseth up the dead, and ᵀquickeneth *them;* even so the Son quickeneth whom he will.   *gives life to*

22 For the Father judgeth no man, but ᴿhath committed all judgment unto the Son: Matt. 11:27

23 That all *men* should honour the Son, even as they honour the Father. ᴿHe that honoureth not the Son honoureth not the Father which hath sent him.   1 John 2:23

24 Verily, verily, I say unto you, ᴿHe that heareth my word, and believeth on him that sent me, hath everlasting life, and shall not come into condemnation; but is passed from death unto life.   6:47

25 Verily, verily, I say unto you, The hour is coming, and now is, when ᴿthe dead shall hear the voice of the Son of God: and they that hear shall live.   [Eph. 2:1, 5]

26 For ᴿas the Father hath life in himself; so hath he given to the Son to have life in himself; Ps. 36:9

27 And ᴿhath given him authority to execute judgment also, because he is the Son of man.   9:39

28 Marvel not at this: for the hour is coming, in the which all that are in the graves shall ᴿhear his voice,   [1 Thess. 4:15–17]

29 And shall come forth; ᴿthey that have done good, unto the resurrection of life; and they that have done evil, unto the resurrection of damnation.   Dan. 12:2

30 I can of mine own self do nothing: as I hear, I judge: and my judgment is just; because I seek not mine own will, but the will of the Father which hath sent me.

31 ᴿIf I bear witness of myself, my witness is not true. 8:14; Rev. 3:14

32 ᴿThere is another that beareth witness of me; and I know that

the witness which he witnesseth of me is true.   [Matt. 3:17; 1 John 5:6]

33 Ye sent unto John, ^Rand he bare witness unto the truth.   [1:15]

34 But I receive not testimony from man: but these things I say, that ye might be saved.

35 He was a burning and a shining light: and ye were willing for a season to rejoice in his light.

36 But ^RI have greater witness than *that* of John: for the works which the Father hath given me to finish, the same ^Rworks that I do, bear witness of me, that the Father hath sent me.   1 John 5:9 · 9:16

37 And the Father himself, which hath sent me, ^Rhath borne witness of me. Ye have neither heard his voice at any time, ^Rnor seen his shape.   Matt. 3:17 · Deut. 4:12

38 And ye have not his word abiding in you: for whom he hath sent, him ye believe not.

39 ^RSearch the scriptures; for in them ye think ye have eternal life: and ^Rthey are they which testify of me.   Is. 8:20; 34:16 · Deut. 18:15, 18

40 ^RAnd ye will not come to me, that ye might have life.   [1:11; 3:19]

41 ^RI receive not honour from men.   v. 44; 7:18; 1 Thess. 2:6

42 But I know you, that ye have not the love of God in you.

43 I am come in my Father's name, and ye receive me not: if another shall come in his own name, him ye will receive.

44 ^RHow can ye believe, which receive honour one of another, and seek not the honour that *cometh* from God only?   12:43

45 Do not think that I will accuse you to the Father: ^Rthere is *one* that accuseth you, *even* Moses, in whom ye trust.   Rom. 2:12

46 For had ye believed Moses, ye would have believed me: ^Rfor he wrote of me.   Deut. 18:15, 18; Acts 26:22

47 But if ye believe ^Rnot his writings, how shall ye believe my words?   Luke 16:29, 31

6 After these things Jesus went over the sea of Galilee, which is *the sea* of ^RTi-be′-ri-as.   v. 23; 21:1

2 And a great multitude fol-

lowed him, because they saw his ^Tmiracles which he did on them that were ^Rdiseased. *signs* · Matt. 4:23

3 And Jesus went up into a mountain, and there he sat with his disciples.

4 ^RAnd the passover, a feast of the Jews, was ^Tnigh.   2:13 · *near*

5 When Jesus then lifted up *his* eyes, and saw a great company come unto him, he saith unto ^RPhilip, Whence shall we buy bread, that these may eat?   1:43

6 And this he said to ^Tprove him: for he himself knew what he would do.   *test*

7 Philip answered him, Two hundred pennyworth of bread is not sufficient for them, that every one of them may take a little.

8 One of his disciples, ^RAndrew, Simon Peter's brother, saith unto him,   1:40

9 There is a lad here, which hath five barley loaves, and two small fishes: ^Rbut what are they among so many?   2 Kin. 4:43

10 And Jesus said, Make the men sit down. Now there was much grass in the place. So the men sat down, in number about five thousand.

11 And Jesus took the loaves; and when he had given thanks, he distributed to the disciples, and the disciples to them that were set down; and likewise of the fishes as much as they would.

12 When they were filled, he said unto his disciples, Gather up the fragments that remain, that nothing be lost.

13 Therefore they gathered *them* together, and filled twelve baskets with the fragments of the five barley loaves, which remained over and above unto them that had eaten.

14 Then those men, when they had seen the miracle that Jesus did, said, This is of a truth ^Rthat prophet that should come into the world.   Deut. 18:15, 18; Acts 3:22; 7:37

15 When Jesus therefore perceived that they would come and take him by force, to make him a

Rking, he departed again into a mountain himself alone. [18:36]

16 RAnd when Teven was *now* come, his disciples went down unto the sea, Matt. 14:23 · *evening*

17 And entered into a ship, and went over the sea toward Ca-per′-na-um. And it was now dark, and Jesus Twas not come to them. *had*

18 And the sea arose by reason of a great wind that blew.

19 So when they had rowed about five and twenty or thirty furlongs, they see Jesus walking on the sea, and drawing nigh unto the ship: and they were afraid.

20 But he saith unto them, RIt is I; be not afraid. Is. 43:1, 2

21 Then they willingly received him into the ship: and immediately the ship was at the land whither they Twent. *were going*

22 The day following, when the people which stood on the other side of the sea saw that there was none other boat there, Tsave that one whereinto his disciples were entered, and that Jesus went not with his disciples into the boat, but *that* his disciples were gone away alone; *except*

23 (Howbeit there came other boats from Ti-be′-ri-as Tnigh unto the place where they did eat bread, after that the Lord had given thanks:) *near*

24 When the people therefore saw that Jesus was not there, neither his disciples, they also Ttook shipping, and came to Ca-per′-na-um, seeking for Jesus. *got into boats*

25 And when they had found him on the other side of the sea, they said unto him, Rabbi, when camest thou hither?

26 Jesus answered them and said, Verily, verily, I say unto you, Ye seek me, not because ye saw the miracles, but because ye did eat of the loaves, and were filled.

27 Labour not for the meat which perisheth, but Rfor that meat which endureth unto everlasting life, which the Son of man shall give unto you: for him hath God the Father sealed. 4:14

28 Then said they unto him, What shall we do, that we might work the works of God?

29 Jesus answered and said unto them, RThis is the work of God, that ye believe on him whom he hath sent. James 2:22; [1 John 3:23]

30 They said therefore unto him, RWhat sign shewest thou then, that we may see, and believe thee? what dost thou work? 1 Cor. 1:22

31 Our fathers did eat man′-na in the desert; as it is written, RHe gave them bread from heaven to eat. Ex. 16:4, 15; Neh. 9:15; Ps. 78:24

32 Then Jesus said unto them, Verily, verily, I say unto you, Moses gave you not that bread from heaven; but Rmy Father giveth you the true bread from heaven. 3:13, 16

33 For the bread of God is he which cometh down from heaven, and giveth life unto the world.

34 Then said they unto him, Lord, evermore give us this bread.

35 And Jesus said unto them, RI am the bread of life: Rhe that cometh to me shall never hunger; and he that believeth on me shall never thirst. vv. 48, 58 · 4:14; 7:37

36 RBut I said unto you, That ye also have seen me, and believe Rnot. vv. 26, 64; 15:24 · 10:26

37 RAll that the Father giveth me shall come to me; and Rhim that cometh to me I will in no wise cast out. v. 45 · [10:28, 29]; 1 John 2:19

38 For I came down from heaven, not to do mine own will, Rbut the will of him that sent me. 4:34

39 And this is the Father's will which hath sent me, Rthat of all which he hath given me I should lose nothing, but should raise it up again at the last day. 10:28; 17:12

40 And this is the will of him that sent me, Rthat every one which seeth the Son, and believeth on him, may have everlasting life: and I will raise him up at the last day. vv. 27, 47, 54; 3:15, 16; 4:14

41 The Jews then Tmurmured at him, because he said, I am the bread which came down from heaven. *grumbled*

42 And they said, ᴿIs not this Jesus, the son of Joseph, whose father and mother we know? how is it then that he saith, I came down from heaven?   Luke 4:22

43 Jesus therefore answered and said unto them, ᵀMurmur not among yourselves.   *Stop grumbling*

44 No man can come to me, except the Father which hath sent me ᴿdraw him: and I will raise him up at the last day.   [Phil. 1:29]

45 It is written in the prophets, And they shall be all taught of God. Every man therefore that hath heard, and hath learned of the Father, cometh unto me.

46 ᴿNot that any man hath seen the Father, save he which is of God, he hath seen the Father.   1:18

47 Verily, verily, I say unto you, ᴿHe that believeth on me hath everlasting life.   [3:16, 18]

48 I am that bread of life.

49 Your fathers did eat man'-na in the wilderness, and are dead.

50 This is the bread which cometh down from heaven, that a man may eat thereof, and not die.

51 I am the living bread which came down from heaven: if any man eat of this bread, he shall live for ever: and ᴿthe bread that I will give is my flesh, which I will give for the life of the world.   Heb. 10:5

52 The Jews therefore ᴿstroveᵀ among themselves, saying, How can this man give us *his* flesh to eat?   7:43; 9:16; 10:19 · *quarrelled*

53 Then Jesus said unto them, Verily, verily, I say unto you, Except ᴿye eat the flesh of the Son of man, and drink his blood, ye have no life in you.   Matt. 26:26

54 ᴿWhoso eateth my flesh, and drinketh my blood, hath eternal life; and I will raise him up at the last day.   vv. 27, 40; 4:14

55 For my flesh is meat indeed, and my blood is drink indeed.

56 He that eateth my flesh, and drinketh my blood, ᴿdwelleth in me, and I in him. [1 John 3:24; 4:15, 16]

57 As the living Father hath sent me, and I live by the Father: so he

that eateth me, even he shall live ᵀby me.   *because of*

58 ᴿThis is that bread which came down from heaven: not as your fathers did eat man'-na, and are dead: he that eateth of this bread shall live for ever.   vv. 49–51

59 These things said he in the synagogue, as he taught in Ca-per'-na-um.

60 ᴿMany therefore of his disciples, when they had heard *this*, said, This is an hard saying; who can ᵀhear it?   Matt. 11:6 · *understand*

61 When Jesus knew in himself that his disciples ᵀmurmured at it, he said unto them, Doth this offend you?   *grumbled*

62 ᴿ*What* and if ye shall see the Son of man ascend up where he was before?   3:13; Acts 1:9; Eph. 4:8

63 It is the spirit that quicken-eth; the flesh profiteth nothing: the words that I speak unto you, *they* are spirit, and *they* are life.

64 But ᴿthere are some of you that believe not. For ᴿJesus knew from the beginning who they were that believed not, and who should betray him.   v. 36 · 2:24, 25

65 And he said, Therefore ᴿsaid I unto you, that no man can come unto me, except it were given unto him of my Father.   vv. 37, 44, 45

66 ᴿFrom that *time* many of his disciples went ᵀback, and walked no more with him.   Luke 9:62 · *away*

67 Then said Jesus unto the twelve, Will ye also go away?

68 Then Simon Peter answered him, Lord, to whom shall we go? thou hast ᴿthe words of eternal life.   Acts 5:20

69 ᴿAnd we believe and are sure that thou art that Christ, the Son of the living God.   11:27; Mark 8:29

70 Jesus answered them, ᴿHave not I chosen you twelve, ᴿand one of you is a devil?   Luke 6:13 · [13:27]

71 He spake of ᴿJudas Is-car'-i-ot *the son* of Simon: for he it was that should betray him, being one of the twelve.   12:4; 13:2, 26

7 After these things Jesus walked in Galilee: for he would

not walk in ᵀJewry, because the Jews sought to kill him.   *Judea*

2 ᴿNow the Jews' feast of tabernacles was at hand.   Lev. 23:34

3 ᴿHis brethren therefore said unto him, Depart hence, and go into Ju-dae'-a, that thy disciples also may see the works that thou doest.   Matt. 12:46; Mark 3:21; Acts 1:14

4 For *there is* no man *that* doeth any thing in secret, ᵀand he himself seeketh to be known openly. If thou do these things, shew thyself to the world.   *while*

★ 5 For neither did his ᴿbrethren believe in him.   Matt. 12:46; 13:55

6 Then Jesus said unto them, ᴿMy time is not yet come: but your time is alway ready.   2:4; 8:20

7 ᴿThe world cannot hate you; but me it hateth, ᴿbecause I testify of it, that the works thereof are evil.   [15:19] · 3:19

8 Go ye up unto this feast: I go not up yet unto this feast; ᴿfor my time is not yet full come.   8:20

9 When he had said these words unto them, he ᵀabode *still* in Galilee.   *remained*

10 But when his brethren were gone up, then went he also up unto the feast, not openly, but as it were in secret.

11 Then the Jews sought him at the feast, and said, Where is he?

12 And ᴿthere was much murmuring among the people concerning him: for some said, He is a good man: others said, Nay; but he deceiveth the people.   9:16; 10:19

13 Howbeit no man spake openly of him for fear of the Jews.

★ 14 Now about the midst of the feast Jesus went up into the temple, and ᴿtaught.   Ps. 22:22; Matt. 4:23

15 And the Jews marvelled, saying, How knoweth this man letters, having never learned?

16 Jesus answered them, and said, ᴿMy doctrine is not mine, but his that sent me.   Deut. 18:15, 18, 19

17 ᴿIf any man will do his will, he shall know of the doctrine, whether it be of God, or *whether* I speak of myself.   3:21; 8:43

18 ᴿHe that speaketh of himself

seeketh his own glory: but he that ᴿseeketh his glory that sent him, the same is true, and ᴿno unrighteousness is in him.   5:41 · 8:50 · 8:46

19 ᴿDid not Moses give you the law, and *yet* none of you keepeth the law? ᴿWhy go ye about to kill me?   Acts 7:38 · Matt. 12:14

20 The people answered and said, ᴿThou hast a devil: who goeth about to kill thee?   8:48, 52

21 Jesus answered and said unto them, I have done one work, and ye all marvel.

22 ᴿMoses therefore gave unto you circumcision; (not because it is of Moses, ᴿbut of the fathers;) and ye on the sabbath day circumcise a man. Lev. 12:3 · Gen. 17:9–14

23 If a man on the sabbath day receive circumcision, that the law of Moses should not be broken; are ye angry at me, because ᴿI have made a man every whit whole on the sabbath day? 5:8, 9, 16

24 ᴿJudge not according to the appearance, but judge righteous judgment.   8:15; Prov. 24:23; James 2:1

25 Then said some of them of Jerusalem, Is not this he, whom they seek to ᴿkill?   5:18; 8:37, 40

26 But, lo, he speaketh boldly, and they say nothing unto him. ᴿDo the rulers know indeed that this is the very Christ?   v. 48

27 ᴿHowbeit we know this man whence he is: but when Christ cometh, no man knoweth whence he is.   Matt. 13:55; Mark 6:3; Luke 4:22

28 Then cried Jesus in the temple as he taught, saying, ᴿYe both know me, and ye know whence I am: and ᴿI am not come of myself, but he that sent me is true, ᴿwhom ye know not.   8:14 · 5:43 · 1:18; 8:55

29 But I know him: for I am from him, and he hath sent me.

30 Then ᴿthey sought to take him: but ᴿno man laid hands on him, because his hour was not yet come.   Mark 11:18 · Matt. 21:46

31 And ᴿmany of the people believed on him, and said, When Christ cometh, will he do more ᵀmiracles than these which this *man* hath done?   Matt. 12:23 · *signs*

32 The Pharisees heard that the people murmured such things concerning him; and the Pharisees and the chief priests sent officers to take him.

33 Then said Jesus unto them, ᴿYet a little while am I with you, and *then* I ᴿgo unto him that sent me.   13:33 · [Luke 24:51; Acts 1:9]

34 Ye ᴿshall seek me, and shall not find *me:* and where I am, *thither* ye cannot come.   Hos. 5:6

35 Then said the Jews among themselves, Whither will he go, that we shall not find him? will he go unto the dispersed among the Gentiles, and teach the Gentiles?

36 What *manner of* saying is this that he said,Ye shall seek me, and shall not find *me:* and where I am, *thither* ye cannot come?

37 ᴿIn the last day, that great *day* of the feast, Jesus stood and cried, saying, If any man thirst, let him come unto me, and drink. Lev. 23:36

38 ᴿHe that believeth on me, as the scripture hath said, ᴿout of his belly shall flow rivers of living water.   Deut. 18:15 · Is. 12:3; Rev. 22:17

39 (But this spake he of the Spirit, which they that believe on him should receive: for the Holy Ghost was not yet *given;* because that Jesus was not yet glorified.)

40 Many of the people therefore, when they heard this saying, said, Of a truth this is the Prophet.

41 Others said, This is ᴿthe Christ. But some said, Shall Christ come out of Galilee?   4:42

42 Hath not the scripture said, That Christ cometh of the seed of David, and out of the town of Beth'-le-hem, where David was?

43 So there was a division among the people because of him.

44 And ᴿsome of them would have taken him; but no man laid hands on him.   v. 30

45 Then came the officers to the chief priests and Pharisees; and they said unto them, Why have ye not brought him?

46 The officers answered, Never man spake like this man.

47 Then answered them the Pharisees, Are ye also deceived?

48 Have any of the rulers or of the Pharisees believed on him?

49 But this ᵀpeople who knoweth not the law are cursed. *crowd*

50 Nic-o-de'-mus saith unto them, (ᴿhe that came to Jesus by night, being one of them,)   19:39

51 ᴿDoth our law judge *any* man, before it hear him, and know what he doeth? Deut. 1:16, 17

52 They answered and said unto him, Art thou also of Galilee? Search, and look: for ᴿout of Galilee ariseth no prophet.   Matt. 4:15

53 And every man went unto his own house.

8 Jesus went unto the mount of Olives.

2 And early in the morning he came again into the temple, and all the people came unto him; and he sat down, and taught them.

3 And the scribes and Pharisees brought unto him a woman ᵀtaken in adultery; and when they had set her in the midst, *caught*

4 They say unto him, Master, this woman was taken in ᴿadultery, in the very act.   Ex. 20:14

5 Now Moses in the law commanded us, that such should be stoned: but what sayest thou?

6 This they said, ᵀtempting him, that they ᴿmight have to accuse him. But Jesus stooped down, and with *his* finger wrote on the ground, *as though he heard them not.*   *testing* · Matt. 22:15

7 So when they continued asking him, he ᵀlifted up himself, and said unto them, ᴿHe that is without sin among you, let him first cast a stone at her. *raised* · Deut. 17:7

8 And again he stooped down, and wrote on the ground.

9 And they which heard *it,* ᴿbeing convicted by *their own* conscience, went out one by one, beginning at the eldest, *even* unto the last: and Jesus was left alone, and the woman standing in the midst.   Rom. 2:22

10 When Jesus had lifted up himself, and saw none but the woman, he said unto her, Woman, where are those thine accusers? hath no man condemned thee?

11 She said, No man, Lord. And Jesus said unto her, RNeither do I condemn thee: go, and Rsin no more.   [3:17; Luke 9:56; 12:14] · [5:14]

12 Then spake Jesus again unto them, saying, RI am the light of the world: he that followeth me shall not walk in darkness, but shall have the light of life.   1:4; 9:5; Is. 9:2

13 The Pharisees therefore said unto him, RThou bearest record of thyself; thy record is not true.   5:31

14 Jesus answered and said unto them, Though I bear record of myself, yet my record is true: for I know whence I came, and whither I go; but ye cannot tell whence I come, and whither I go.

15 RYe judge after the flesh; RI judge no man.   7:24 · [3:17; 12:47; 18:36]

16 And yet if I judge, my judgment is true: for I am not alone, but I and the Father that sent me.

17 RIt is also written in your law, that the testimony of two men is true.   Matt. 18:16; 2 Cor. 13:1; Heb. 10:28

18 I am one that bear witness of myself, and Rthe Father that sent me beareth witness of me.   5:37

19 Then said they unto him, Where is thy Father? Jesus answered, RYe neither know me, nor my Father: Rif ye had known me, ye should have known my Father also.   16:3 · 14:7

20 These words spake Jesus in Rthe treasury, as he taught in the temple: and Rno man laid hands on him; for Rhis hour was not yet come.   Luke 21:1 · 2:4; 7:30 · 7:8

21 Then said Jesus again unto them, I go my way, and Rye shall seek me, and Rshall die in your Tsins: whither I go, ye cannot come.   7:34; 13:33 · v. 24 · Lit. sin

22 Then said the Jews, Will he kill himself? because he saith, Whither I go, ye cannot come.

23 And he said unto them, RYe are from beneath; I am from above: Rye are of this world; I am not of this world.   3:31 · 15:19; 17:16

24 RI said therefore unto you,

that ye shall die in your sins: for if ye believe not that I am he, ye shall die in your sins.   v. 21

25 Then said they unto him, Who art thou? And Jesus saith unto them, Even the same that I Rsaid unto you from the beginning.   4:26

26 I have many things to say and to judge of you: but Rhe that sent me is true; and RI speak to the world those things which I have heard of him.   7:28 · 3:32; 15:15

27 They understood not that he spake to them of the Father.

28 Then said Jesus unto them, When ye have lifted up the Son of man, then shall ye know that I am he, and that I do nothing of myself; but as my Father hath taught me, I speak these things.

29 And he that sent me is with me: Rthe Father hath not left me alone; Rfor I do always those things that please him.   16:32 · 4:34

30 As he spake these words, Rmany believed on him.   7:31; 10:42

31 Then said Jesus to those Jews which believed on him, If ye Rcontinue in my word, then are ye my disciples indeed;   [14:15, 23]

32 And ye shall know the Rtruth, and Rthe truth shall make you free.   [1:14, 17; 14:6] · [Rom. 6:14, 18, 22]

33 They answered him, We be Abraham's seed, and were never in bondage to any man: how sayest thou, Ye shall be made free?

34 Jesus answered them, Verily, verily, I say unto you, RWhosoever committeth sin is the Tservant of sin.   Prov. 5:22; Rom. 6:16; 2 Pet. 2:19 · slave

35 And Rthe servant abideth not in the house for ever: but the Son abideth ever.   Gen. 21:10; Gal. 4:30

36 RIf the Son therefore shall make you free, ye shall be free indeed.   [Rom. 8:2; 2 Cor. 3:17]; Gal. 5:1

37 I know that ye are Abraham's Tseed; but Rye seek to kill me, because my word hath no place in you.   descendants · 7:19

38 RI speak that which I have seen with my Father: and ye do that which ye have seen with your father.   [3:32; 5:19, 30; 14:10, 24]

39 They answered and said unto

him, RAbraham is our father. Jesus saith unto them, If ye were Abraham's children, ye would do the works of Abraham.   Matt. 3:9

40 RBut now ye seek to kill me, a man that hath told you the truth, Rwhich I have heard of God: this did not Abraham.   v. 37 · v. 26

41 Ye do the deeds of your father. Then said they to him, We be not born of fornication; Rwe have one Father, *even* God.   Deut. 32:6

42 Jesus said unto them, If God were your Father, ye would love me: Rfor I proceeded forth and came from God; neither came I of myself, but he sent me. 16:27; 17:8, 25

43 RWhy do ye not understand my speech? *even* because ye cannot hear my word.   [7:17]

44 Ye are of *your* father the devil, and the lusts of your father ye will do. He was a murderer from the beginning, and abode not in the truth, because there is no truth in him. When he speaketh a lie, he speaketh of his own: for he is a liar, and the father of it.

45 And because I tell *you* the truth, ye believe me not.

46 Which of you Tconvinceth me of sin? And if I say the truth, why do ye not believe me?   *convicts*

47 RHe that is of God heareth God's words: ye therefore hear *them* not, because ye are not of God.   10:26; Luke 8:15; 1 John 4:6

48 Then answered the Jews, and said unto him, Say we not well that thou art a Sa-mar'-i-tan, and Rhast a Tdevil?   7:20; 10:20 · *demon*

49 Jesus answered, I have not a devil; but I honour my Father, and Rye do dishonour me.   5:41

50 And RI seek not mine own glory: there is one that seeketh and judgeth.   5:41; 7:18; [Phil. 2:6-8]

51 Verily, verily, I say unto you, RIf a man keep my saying, he shall never see death.   5:24; 11:26

52 Then said the Jews unto him, Now we know that thou hast a devil. RAbraham is dead, and the prophets; and thou sayest, If a man keep my saying, he shall never taste of death.   Heb. 11:13

53 Art thou greater than our father Abraham, which is dead? and the prophets are dead: whom makest thou thyself?

54 Jesus answered, RIf I honour myself, my honour is nothing: Rit is my Father that honoureth me; of whom ye say, that he is your God: 5:31, 32 · 5:41; Acts 3:13

55 Yet ye have not known him; but I know him: and if I should say, I know him not, I shall be a liar like unto you: but I know him, and Rkeep his Tsaying. [15:10] · *word*

56 Your father Abraham Rrejoiced to see my day: and he saw *it*, and was glad.   Luke 10:24

57 Then said the Jews unto him, Thou art not yet fifty years old, and hast thou seen Abraham?

58 Jesus said unto them, Verily, verily, I say unto you, Before Abraham was, RI am.   Col. 1:17

59 Then Rtook they up stones to cast at him: but Jesus hid himself, and went out of the temple, Rgoing through the midst of them, and so passed by.   10:31; 11:8 · Luke 4:30

9 And as *Jesus* passed by, he saw a man which was blind from *his* birth.

2 And his disciples asked him, saying, TMaster, Rwho did sin, this man, or his parents, that he was born blind?   *Rabbi* · Luke 13:2; Acts 28:4

3 Jesus answered, Neither hath this man sinned, nor his parents: Rbut that the works of God should be made manifest in him.   11:4

4 I must work the works of him that sent me, while it is Rday: the night cometh, when no man can work.   11:9, 10; 12:35; Gal. 6:10

5 As long as I am in the world, RI am the light of the world.   [3:19]

6 When he had thus spoken, Rhe spat on the ground, and made clay of the Tspittle, and he anointed the eyes of the blind man with the clay,   Mark 7:33; 8:23 · *saliva*

7 And said unto him, Go, wash Rin the pool of Si-lo'-am, (which is by interpretation, Sent.) He went his way therefore, and washed, and came seeing.   Is. 8:6

8 The neighbours therefore,

and they which before had seen him that he was blind, said, Is not this he that sat and begged?

9 Some said, This is he: others *said,* He is like him: *but* he said, I am *he.*

10 Therefore said they unto him, How were thine eyes opened?

11 He answered and said, A man that is called Jesus made clay, and anointed mine eyes, and said unto me, Go to the pool of Si-lo'-am, and wash: and I went and washed, and I received sight.

12 Then said they unto him, Where is he? He said, I know not.

13 They brought to the Pharisees him that ᵀaforetime was blind.   *formerly*

14 And it was the sabbath day when Jesus made the clay, and opened his eyes.

15 Then again the Pharisees also asked him how he had received his sight. He said unto them, He put clay upon mine eyes, and I washed, and do see.

16 Therefore said some of the Pharisees, This man is not of God, because he keepeth not the sabbath day. Others said, ᴿHow can a man that is a sinner do such miracles? And ᴿthere was a division among them.   v. 33; 3:2 · 7:12, 43; 10:19

17 They say unto the blind man again, What sayest thou of him, that he hath opened thine eyes? He said, ᴿHe is a prophet.[4:19; 6:14]

18 But the Jews did not believe concerning him, that he had been blind, and received his sight, until they called the parents of him that had received his sight.

19 And they asked them, saying, Is this your son, who ye say was born blind? how then doth he now see?

20 His parents answered them and said, We know that this is our son, and that he was born blind:

21 But by what means he now seeth, we know not; or who hath opened his eyes, we know not: he is of age; ask him: he shall speak for himself.

22 These *words* spake his parents, because ᴿthey feared the Jews: for the Jews had agreed already, that if any man did confess that he was Christ, he ᴿshould be put out of the synagogue. 7:13 · 16:2

23 Therefore said his parents, He is of age; ask him.

24 Then again called they the man that was blind, and said unto him, Give God the praise: we know that this man is a sinner.

25 He answered and said, Whether he be a sinner *or no,* I know not: one thing I know, that, whereas I was blind, now I see.

26 Then said they to him again, What did he to thee? how opened he thine eyes?

27 He answered them, I have told you already, and ye did not hear: wherefore would ye hear *it* again? ᵀwill ye also be his disciples?   *do you also want to be*

28 Then they reviled him, and said, Thou art his disciple; but we are Moses' disciples.

29 We know that God spake unto Moses: *as for* this *fellow,* we know not from whence he is.

30 The man answered and said unto them, ᴿWhy herein is a marvellous thing, that ye know not from whence he is, and *yet* he hath opened mine eyes.   3:10

31 Now we know that God heareth not sinners: but if any man be a worshipper of God, and doeth his will, him he heareth.

32 Since the world began was it not heard that any man opened the eyes of one that was born blind.

33 ᴿIf this man were not of God, he could do nothing.   v. 16; 3:2

34 They answered and said unto him, ᴿThou wast altogether born in sins, and dost thou teach us? And they cast him out.   v. 2; Ps. 51:5

35 Jesus heard that they had cast him out; and when he had ᴿfound him, he said unto him, Dost thou ᴿbelieve on ᴿthe Son of God?   5:14 · 1:7; 16:31 · 10:36

36 He answered and said, Who is he, Lord, that I might believe on him?

37 And Jesus said unto him, Thou hast both seen him, and ᴿit is he that talketh with thee. 4:26
38 And he said, Lord, I believe. And he ᴿworshipped him. Matt. 8:2
39 And Jesus said, ᴿFor judgment I am come into this world, that they which see not might see; and that they which see might be made blind. [3:17; 5:22, 27; 12:47]
40 And *some* of the Pharisees which were with him heard these words, ᴿand said unto him, Are we blind also? [Rom. 2:19]
41 Jesus said unto them, ᴿIf ye were blind, ye should have no sin: but now ye say, We see; therefore your sin remaineth. 15:22, 24

10 Verily, verily, I say unto you, He that entereth not by the door into the sheepfold, but climbeth up some other way, the same is a thief and a robber.
2 But he that entereth in by the door is the shepherd of the sheep.
3 To him the porter openeth; and the sheep hear his voice: and he calleth his own sheep by ᴿname, and leadeth them out. 20:16
4 And when he putteth forth his own sheep, he goeth before them, and the sheep follow him: for they know his voice.
5 And a ᴿstranger will they not follow, but will flee from him: for they know not the voice of strangers. [2 Cor. 11:13–15]
6 This ᵀparable spake Jesus unto them: but they understood not what things they were which he spake unto them. *illustration*
7 Then said Jesus unto them again, Verily, verily, I say unto you, I am the door of the sheep.
8 All that ever came before me are thieves and robbers: but the sheep did not hear them.
9 ᴿI am the door: by me if any man enter in, he shall be saved, and shall go in and out, and find pasture. [14:6; Eph. 2:18]
10 The thief cometh not, ᵀbut for to steal, and to kill, and to destroy: I am come that they might have life, and that they might have *it* more abundantly. *except*

11 ᴿI am the good shepherd: the good shepherd giveth his life for the sheep. Is. 40:11; Ezek. 34:23
12 But he that is an hireling, and not the shepherd, whose own the sheep are not, seeth the wolf coming, and leaveth the sheep, and fleeth: and the wolf catcheth them, and scattereth the sheep.
13 The hireling fleeth, because he is an hireling, and careth not for the sheep.
14 I am the good shepherd, and ᴿknow my *sheep*, and ᴿam known of mine. 2 Tim. 2:19 · 2 Tim. 1:12
15 As the Father knoweth me, even so know I the Father: and I lay down my life for the sheep.
16 And other sheep I have, which are not of this fold: them also I must bring, and they shall hear my voice; and there shall be one ᵀfold, *and* one shepherd. *flock*
17 Therefore doth my Father ᴿlove me, because I lay down my life, that I might take it again. 5:20
18 No man taketh it from me, but I lay it down of myself. I ᴿhave power to lay it down, and I have power to take it again. ᴿThis commandment have I received of my Father. [2:19; 5:26] · [6:38; 14:31; 17:4]
19 ᴿThere was a division therefore again among the Jews for these sayings. 7:43; 9:16
20 And many of them said, ᴿHe hath a ᵀdevil, and is ᵀmad; why hear ye him? 7:20 · *demon* · *insane*
21 Others said, These are not the words of him that hath a devil. ᴿCan a devil ᴿopen the eyes of the blind? [Ex. 4:11] · 9:6, 7, 32, 33
22 And it was at Jerusalem the feast of the dedication, and it was winter.
23 And Jesus walked in the temple ᴿin Solomon's porch. Acts 3:11
24 Then came the Jews round about him, and said unto him, How long dost thou ᵀmake us to doubt? If thou be the Christ, tell us plainly. *keep us in suspense*
25 Jesus answered them, I told you, and ye believed not: the works that I do in my Father's name, they bear witness of me.

26 But ᴿye believe not, because ye are not of my sheep, as I said unto you.   [8:47]

27 ᴿMy sheep hear my voice, and I know them, and they follow me: vv. 4, 14

28 And I give unto them eternal life; and they shall never perish, neither shall any *man* ᵀpluck them out of my hand.   *snatch*

29 My Father, ᴿwhich gave *them* me, is greater than all; and no *man* is able to pluck *them* out of my Father's hand.   [17:2, 6, 12, 24]

30 I and *my* Father are one.

31 Then ᴿthe Jews took up stones again to stone him.   8:59

32 Jesus answered them, Many good works have I shewed you from my Father; for which of those works do ye stone me?

33 The Jews answered him, saying, For a good work we stone thee not; but for ᴿblasphemy; and because that thou, being a man, ᴿmakest thyself God.   5:18 · Matt. 9:3

34 Jesus answered them, ᴿIs it not written in your law, I said, Ye are gods?   Ps. 82:6

35 If he called them gods, unto whom the word of God came, and the scripture cannot be broken;

36 Say ye of him, ᴿwhom the Father hath sanctified, and ᴿsent into the world, Thou blasphemest; ᴿbecause I said, I am ᴿthe Son of God?   6:27 · 3:17 · 5:17, 18 · Luke 1:35

37 ᴿIf I do not the works of my Father, believe me not.   v. 25; 15:24

38 But if I do, though ye believe not me, ᴿbelieve the works: that ye may know, and believe, that the Father *is* in me, and I in him.   5:36

39 ᴿTherefore they sought again to take him: but he escaped out of their hand,   7:30, 44

40 And went away again beyond Jordan into the place ᴿwhere John at first baptized; and there he ᵀabode.   1:28 · *stayed*

41 And many resorted unto him, and said, John did no ᵀmiracle: but all things that John spake of this man were true.   *sign*

42 And many believed on him there.

11 Now a certain *man* was sick, *named* Laz'-a-rus, of Beth'-a-ny, the town of ᴿMary and her sister Martha.   Luke 10:38, 39

2 (ᴿIt was *that* Mary which anointed the Lord with ᵀointment, and wiped his feet with her hair, whose brother Laz'-a-rus was sick.)   Matt. 26:7 · *fragrant oil*

3 Therefore his sisters sent unto him, saying, Lord, behold, he whom thou lovest is sick.

4 When Jesus heard *that,* he said, This sickness is not unto death, but for the glory of God, that the Son of God might be glorified thereby.

5 Now Jesus loved Martha, and her sister, and Laz'-a-rus.

6 When he had heard therefore that he was sick, ᴿhe ᵀabode two days still in the same place where he was.   10:40 · *stayed*

7 Then after that saith he to *his* disciples, Let us go into Ju-dae'-a again.

8 *His* disciples say unto him, ᵀMaster, the Jews of late sought to ᴿstone thee; and goest thou thither again?   *Rabbi* · 8:59; 10:31

9 Jesus answered, Are there not twelve hours in the day? ᴿIf any man walk in the day, he stumbleth not, because he seeth the ᴿlight of this world.   9:4; 12:35 · Is. 9:2

10 But ᴿif a man walk in the night, he stumbleth, because there is no light in him.   12:35

11 These things said he: and after that he saith unto them, Our friend Laz'-a-rus ᴿsleepeth; but I go, that I may awake him out of sleep.   Matt. 9:24; Acts 7:60

12 Then said his disciples, Lord, if he sleep, he shall do well.

13 Howbeit Jesus spake of his death: but they thought that he had spoken of taking of rest in sleep.

14 Then said Jesus unto them plainly, Laz'-a-rus is dead.

15 And I am glad for your sakes that I was not there, to the intent ye may believe; nevertheless let us go unto him.

16 Then said ᴿThomas, which is

called Did'-y-mus, unto his fel-
lowdisciples, Let us also go, that
we may die with him.   Matt. 10:3
17 Then when Jesus came, he
found that he had *lain* in the
^Tgrave four days already.   *tomb*
18 Now Beth'-a-ny was ^Tnigh
unto Jerusalem, about fifteen furlongs off: *near*
19 And many of the Jews came
to Martha and Mary, to comfort
them concerning their brother.
20 Then Martha, as soon as she
heard that Jesus was coming,
went and met him: but Mary sat
still in the house.
21 Then said Martha unto Jesus,
Lord, if thou hadst been here, my
brother had not died.
22 But I know, that even now,
^Rwhatsoever thou wilt ask of God,
God will give *it* thee.   [v. 41; 9:31]
23 Jesus saith unto her, Thy
brother shall rise again.
24 Martha saith unto him, I
know that he shall rise again in
the resurrection at the last day.
25 Jesus said unto her, I am ^Rthe
resurrection, and the life: he that
believeth in me, though he were
dead, yet shall he live: 6:39, 40, 44
26 And whosoever liveth and
believeth in me shall never die.
Believest thou this?
27 She saith unto him, Yea, Lord:
^RI believe that thou art the Christ,
the Son of God, which should
come into the world.   4:42; 6:14, 69
28 And when she had so said,
she went her way, and called
Mary her sister secretly, saying,
The ^TMaster is come, and calleth
for thee.   *Teacher*
29 As soon as she heard *that*,
she arose quickly, and came unto
him.
30 Now Jesus was not yet come
into the town, but was in that
place where Martha met him.
31 ^RThe Jews then which were
with her in the house, and comforted her, when they saw Mary,
that she rose up ^Thastily and went
out, followed her, saying, She
goeth unto the grave to weep
there.   vv. 19, 33 · *quickly*

32 Then when Mary was come
where Jesus was, and saw him,
she ^Rfell down at his feet, saying
unto him, ^RLord, if thou hadst
been here, my brother had not
died.   Mark 5:22; 7:25; Rev. 1:17 · v. 21
33 When Jesus therefore saw
her weeping, and the Jews also
weeping which came with her, he
groaned in the spirit, and was
troubled,
34 And said, Where have ye laid
him? They said unto him, Lord,
come and see.
35 ^RJesus wept.   Luke 19:41
36 Then said the Jews, Behold
how he loved him!
37 And some of them said,
Could not this man, ^Rwhich
opened the eyes of the blind, have
caused that even this man should
not have died?   9:6, 7
38 Jesus therefore again groaning in himself cometh to the
^Tgrave. It was a cave, and a ^Rstone
lay upon it.   *tomb* · Matt. 27:60, 66
39 Jesus said, Take ye away the
stone. Martha, the sister of him
that was dead, saith unto him,
Lord, by this time he stinketh: for
he hath been *dead* four days.
40 Jesus saith unto her, Said
I not unto thee, that, if thou
wouldest believe, thou shouldest
^Rsee the glory of God?   [vv. 4, 23]
41 Then they took away the
stone *from the place* where the
dead was laid. And Jesus lifted up
his eyes, and said, Father, I thank
thee that thou hast heard me.
42 And I knew that thou hearest
me always: but ^Rbecause of the
people which stand by I said *it*,
that they may believe that thou
hast sent me.   12:30; 17:21
43 And when he thus had spoken, he cried with a loud voice,
Laz'-a-rus, come forth.
44 And he that was dead came
forth, bound hand and foot with
^Rgraveclothes: and ^Rhis face was
bound about with a napkin. Jesus
saith unto them, Loose him, and
let him go.   19:40 · 20:7
45 Then many of the Jews which
came to Mary, ^Rand had seen the

things which Jesus did, believed on him. 2:23; 10:42; 12:11, 18

46 But some of them went their ways to the Pharisees, and told them what things Jesus had done.

47 ᴿThen gathered the chief priests and the Pharisees a council, and said, What do we? for this man doeth many miracles. Ps. 2:2

48 If we let him thus alone, all *men* will believe on him: and the Romans shall come and take away both our place and nation.

49 And one of them, *named* ᴿCa′-ia-phas, being the high priest that same year, said unto them, Ye know nothing at all, Matt. 26:3

50 ᴿNor consider that it is expedient for us, that one man should die for the people, and that the whole nation perish not. 18:14

51 And this spake he not of himself: but being high priest that year, he prophesied that Jesus should die for that nation;

52 And not for that nation only, but that also he should gather together in one the children of God that were scattered abroad.

53 Then from that day forth they ᵀtook counsel together for to ᴿput him to death. *plotted to put · Matt. 26:4*

54 Jesus ᴿtherefore walked no more openly among the Jews; but went thence unto a country near to the wilderness, into a city called E′-phra-im, and there continued with his disciples. 4:1, 3; 7:1

55 ᴿAnd the Jews' passover was nigh at hand: and many went out of the country up to Jerusalem before the passover, to ᴿpurify themselves. 2:13; 5:1; 6:4 · Num. 9:10, 13

56 ᴿThen sought they for Jesus, and spake among themselves, as they stood in the temple, What think ye, that he will not come to the feast? 7:11

57 Now both the chief priests and the Pharisees had given a commandment, that, if any man knew where he were, he should ᵀshew *it*, that they might ᴿtakeᵀ him. *report · Matt. 26:14–16 · seize*

12 Then Jesus six days before the passover came to Beth′-a-ny, ᴿwhere Laz′-a-rus was which had been dead, whom he raised from the dead. 11:1, 43

2 ᴿThere they made him a supper; and Martha served: but Laz′-a-rus was one of them that sat at the table with him. Matt. 26:6

3 Then took Mary a pound of ointment of spikenard, very costly, and anointed the feet of Jesus, and wiped his feet with her hair: and the house was filled with the odour of the ointment.

4 Then saith one of his disciples, Judas Is-car′-i-ot, Simon's *son*, which should betray him,

5 Why was not this ᵀointment sold for three hundred pence, and given to the poor? *fragrant oil*

6 This he said, not that he cared for the poor; but because he was a thief, and ᴿhad the bag, and bare what was put therein. 13:29

7 Then said Jesus, Let her alone: ᵀagainst the day of my burying hath she kept this. *for*

8 For ᴿthe poor always ye have with you; but me ye have not always. Deut. 15:11; Matt. 26:11

9 Much people of the Jews therefore knew that he was there: and they came not for Jesus' sake only, but that they might see Laz′-a-rus also, ᴿwhom he had raised from the dead. 11:43, 44

10 ᴿBut the chief priests consulted that they might put Laz′-a-rus also to death; Luke 16:31

11 ᴿBecause that by reason of him many of the Jews went away, and believed on Jesus. v. 18; 11:45

12 ᴿOn the next day much people that were come to the feast, when they heard that Jesus was coming to Jerusalem, Matt. 21:4–9

13 Took branches of palm trees, ★ and went forth to meet him, and cried, Hosanna: ᴿBlessed *is* the King of Israel that cometh in the name of the Lord. Ps. 118:25, 26

14 ᴿAnd Jesus, when he had found a young ᵀass, sat thereon; as it is written, Matt. 21:7 · *donkey*

15 ᴿFear not, daughter of Si′-on: ★ behold, thy King cometh, sitting on an ass's colt. Is. 40:9; Zech. 9:9

16 These things ^Runderstood not his disciples at the first: ^Rbut when Jesus was glorified, ^Rthen remembered they that these things were written of him, and *that* they had done these things unto him. Luke 18:34 · v. 23; 7:39 · [14:26]

17 The people therefore that was with him when he called Laz'-a-rus out of his grave, and raised him from the dead, bare ^Trecord. *witness*

18 ^RFor this cause the people also met him, for that they heard that he had done this miracle. v. 11

19 The Pharisees therefore said among themselves, ^RPerceive ye how ye prevail nothing? behold, the world is gone after him. 11:47

20 And there ^Rwere certain Greeks among them that came up to worship at the feast: Acts 17:4

21 The same came therefore to Philip, which was of Beth-sa'-i-da of Galilee, and desired him, saying, Sir, we would see Jesus.

22 Philip cometh and telleth Andrew: and again Andrew and Philip tell Jesus.

23 And Jesus answered them, saying, ^RThe hour is come, that the Son of man should be glorified. 13:32; Matt. 26:18, 45; Acts 3:13

24 Verily, verily, I say unto you, ^RExcept a corn of wheat fall into the ground and die, it abideth alone: but if it die, it bringeth forth much fruit. 1 Cor. 15:36

25 ^RHe that loveth his life shall lose it; and he that hateth his life in this world shall keep it unto life eternal. Matt. 10:39; Mark 8:35; Luke 9:24

26 If any man serve me, let him ^Rfollow me; and ^Rwhere I am, there shall also my servant be: if any man serve me, him will *my* Father honour. [Matt. 16:24] · 14:3; 17:24

27 Now is my soul troubled; and what shall I say? Father, save me from this hour: ^Rbut for this cause came I unto this hour. 18:37

28 Father, glorify thy name. Then came there a voice from heaven, *saying,* I have both glorified *it,* and will glorify *it* again.

29 The people therefore, that stood by, and heard *it,* said that it

thundered: others said, An angel spake to him.

30 Jesus answered and said, ^RThis voice came not because of me, but for your sakes. 11:42

31 Now is the judgment of this world: now shall ^Rthe prince of this world be cast out. Matt. 12:29

32 And I, ^Rif I be lifted up from the earth, will draw ^Rall *men* unto me. 3:14; 8:28 · [Rom. 5:18; Heb. 2:9]

33 ^RThis he said, signifying what death he should die. 18:32; 21:19

34 The people answered him, ^RWe have heard out of the law that Christ abideth for ever: and how sayest thou, The Son of man must be lifted up? who is this Son of man? Ps. 89:36, 37; Is. 9:6, 7; Mic. 4:7

35 Then Jesus said unto them, Yet a little while is the light with you. ^RWalk while ye have the light, lest darkness come upon you: for ^Rhe that walketh in darkness knoweth not whither he goeth. [Gal. 6:10]; Eph. 5:8 · [1 John 2:9–11]

36 While ye have light, believe in the light, that ye may be ^Rthe children of light. These things spake Jesus, and departed, and did hide himself from them. 8:12

37 But though he had done so many ^Rmiracles before them, yet they believed not on him: 11:47

38 That the saying of E-sa'-ias the prophet might be fulfilled, which he spake, ^RLord, who hath believed our report? and to whom hath the arm of the Lord been revealed? Is. 53:1; Rom. 10:16

39 Therefore they could not believe, because that E-sa'-ias said again,

40 ^RHe hath blinded their eyes, ★ and hardened their heart; that they should not see with *their* eyes, nor understand with *their* heart, and be converted, and I should heal them. Is. 6:9, 10

41 ^RThese things said E-sa'-ias, when he saw his glory, and spake of him. Is. 6:1

42 Nevertheless among the chief rulers also many believed on him; but ^Rbecause of the Pharisees they did not ^Tconfess *him,* lest they

should be put out of the syna-
gogue: 7:13; 9:22 · *publicly acknowledge*
43 For they loved the praise of
men more than the praise of God.
44 Jesus cried and said, He that
believeth on me, believeth not on
me, but on him that sent me.
45 And ᴿhe that seeth me seeth
him that sent me.   [14:9]
46 ᴿI am come a light into the
world, that whosoever believeth
on me should not abide in darkness.   vv. 35, 36; 1:4, 5; 8:12
47 And if any man hear my
words, and believe not, I judge
him not: for I came not to judge
the world, but to save the world.
48 ᴿHe that rejecteth me, and
receiveth not my words, hath one
that judgeth him: the word that I
have spoken, the same shall judge
him in the last day.   [Luke 10:16]
49 For ᴿI have not spoken of
myself; but the Father which sent
me, he gave me a commandment,
ᴿwhat I should say, and what I
should speak.   8:38 · Deut. 18:18
50 And I know that his commandment is life everlasting:
whatsoever I speak therefore,
even as the Father said unto me,
so I ᴿspeak.   5:19; 8:28

13 Now ᴿbefore the feast of
the passover, when Jesus
knew that ᴿhis hour was come
that he should depart out of this
world unto the Father, having
loved his own which were in the
world, he ᴿloved them unto the
end.   Matt. 26:2 · 12:23; 17:1 · 15:9
2 And supper being ended, ᴿthe
devil having ᵀnow put into the
heart of Judas Is-car′-i-ot, Simon's
son, to betray him; Luke 22:3 · *already*
3 Jesus knowing ᴿthat the Fa-
ther had given all things into his
hands, and that he was come from
God, and went to God; [5:20–23; 17:2]
4 He riseth from supper, and
laid aside his garments; and took
a towel, and girded himself.
5 After that he poureth water
into a bason, and began to wash
the disciples' feet, and to wipe
them with the towel wherewith he
was girded.

6 Then cometh he to Simon
Peter: and Peter saith unto him,
Lord, dost thou wash my feet?
7 Jesus answered and said
unto him, What I do thou ᴿknowest not now; but thou shalt know
hereafter.   12:16; 16:12
8 Peter saith unto him, Thou
shalt never wash my feet. Jesus
answered him, If I wash thee not,
thou hast no part with me.
9 Simon Peter saith unto him,
Lord, not my feet only, but also
my hands and *my* head.
10 Jesus saith to him, He that is
washed needeth not save to wash
his feet, but is clean every whit:
and ᴿye are clean, but not all. [15:3]
11 For ᴿhe knew who ᵀshould
betray him; therefore said he, Ye
are not all clean.   6:64; 18:4 · *would*
12 So after he had washed their
feet, and had taken his garments,
and was set down again, he said
unto them, Know ye what I have
done to you?
13 Ye call me Master and Lord:
and ye say well; for so I am.
14 ᴿIf I then, *your* Lord and
Master, have washed your feet;
ᴿye also ought to wash one another's feet.   Luke 22:27 · [Gal. 6:1, 2]
15 For ᴿI have given you an
example, that ye should do as I
have done to you. Matt. 11:29; Phil. 2:5
16 Verily, verily, I say unto you,
ᴿThe servant is not greater than
his lord; neither he that is sent
greater than he that sent him.15:20
17 If ye know these things, happy are ye if ye do them.
18 I speak not of you all: I know   ★
whom I have chosen: but that the
ᴿscripture may be fulfilled, He
that eateth bread with me hath
lifted up his heel against me. 15:25
19 Now I tell you before it come,
that, when it is come to pass, ye
may believe that I am *he.*
20 ᴿVerily, verily, I say unto you,
He that receiveth whomsoever I
send receiveth me; and he that
receiveth me receiveth him that
sent me.   Luke 9:48; 10:16; Gal. 4:14
21 ᴿWhen Jesus had thus said,
ᴿhe was troubled in spirit, and tes-

tified, and said, Verily, verily, I say unto you, that one of you shall betray me.   Luke 22:21 · 12:27

22 Then the disciples looked one on another, ᵀdoubting of whom he spake.   *perplexed about*

23 Now there was ᵀleaning on Jesus' bosom one of his disciples, whom Jesus loved.   *reclining at*

24 Simon Peter therefore beckoned to him, that he should ask who it should be of whom he spake.

25 He then ᵀlying on Jesus' breast saith unto him, Lord, who is it?   *leaning back*

26 Jesus answered, He it is, to whom I shall give a sop, when I have dipped *it*. And when he had dipped the sop, he gave *it* to Judas Is-car'-i-ot, *the son* of Simon.

27 ᴿAnd after the sop Satan entered into him. Then said Jesus unto him, That thou doest, do quickly.   Luke 22:3

28 Now no man at the table knew for what ᵀintent he spake this unto him.   *reason*

29 For some *of them* thought, because ᴿJudas had the ᵀbag, that Jesus had said unto him, Buy *those things* that we have need of ᵀagainst the feast; or, that he should give something to the poor.   12:6 · *money box · for*

30 He then having received the ᵀsop went immediately out: and it was night.   *piece of bread*

31 Therefore, when he was gone out, Jesus said, ᴿNow is the Son of man glorified, and ᴿGod is glorified in him. 12:23; Acts 3:13 · [1 Pet. 4:11]

32 If God be glorified in him, God shall also glorify him in himself, and ᴿshall ᵀstraightway glorify him.   12:23 · *immediately*

33 Little children, yet a ᴿlittle while I am with you. Ye shall seek me: ᴿand as I said unto the Jews, Whither I go, ye cannot come; so now I say to you.   14:19 · [7:34; 8:21]

34 ᴿA new commandment I give unto you, That ye love one another; as I have loved you, that ye also love one another.   1 John 2:7

35 ᴿBy this shall all *men* know that ye are my disciples, if ye have love one to another.   1 John 2:5

36 Simon Peter said unto him, Lord, whither goest thou? Jesus answered him, Whither I go, thou canst not follow me now; but thou shalt follow me afterwards.

37 Peter said unto him, Lord, why cannot I follow thee now? I will ᴿlay down my life for thy sake.   Mark 14:29–31; Luke 22:33, 34

38 Jesus answered him, Wilt thou lay down thy life for my sake? Verily, verily, I say unto thee, The cock shall not crow, till thou hast denied me thrice.

14 Let ᴿnot your heart be troubled: ye believe in God, believe also in me.   [v. 27; 16:22, 24]

2 In my Father's house are many ᵀmansions: if *it were* not *so*, I would have told you. I go to prepare a place for you.   Lit. *dwellings*

3 And if I go and prepare a place for you, I will come again, and receive you unto myself; that where I am, *there* ye may be also.

4 And whither I go ye know, and the way ye know.

5 ᴿThomas saith unto him, Lord, we know not whither thou goest; and how can we know the way?   11:16; 20:24–29; 21:2; Matt. 10:3

6 Jesus saith unto him, I am the way, the truth, and the life: ᴿno man cometh unto the Father, ᴿbut by me.   1 Tim. 2:5 · [10:7–9; Acts 4:12]

7 ᴿIf ye had known me, ye should have known my Father also: and from henceforth ye know him, and have seen him. 8:19

8 Philip saith unto him, Lord, shew us the Father, and it ᵀsufficeth us.   *will satisfy*

9 Jesus saith unto him, Have I been so long time with you, and yet hast thou not known me, Philip? he that hath seen me hath seen the Father; and how sayest thou *then*, Shew us the Father?

10 Believest thou not that I am in the Father, and the Father in me? the words that I speak unto you I speak not of ᵀmyself: but the

Father that dwelleth in me, he doeth the works.   *my own* authority

11 Believe me that I *am* in the Father, and the Father in me: ^Ror else believe me for the very works' sake.   5:36; 10:38

12 ^RVerily, verily, I say unto you, He that believeth on me, the works that I do shall he do also; and greater *works* than these shall he do; because I go unto my Father.   Matt. 21:21; Mark 16:17

13 ^RAnd whatsoever ye shall ask in my name, that will I do, that the Father may be ^Rglorified in the Son.   [James 1:5–7; 1 John 3:22] · 13:31

14 If ye shall ask any thing in my name, I will do *it.*

15 ^RIf ye love me, keep my commandments.   1 John 5:3

16 And I will pray the Father, and ^Rhe shall give you another Comforter, that he may abide with you for ever;   [15:26; 20:22]; Acts 2:4, 33

17 *Even* ^Rthe Spirit of truth; whom the world cannot receive, because it seeth him not, neither knoweth him: but ye know him; for he dwelleth with you, and shall be in you.   [16:13; 1 John 4:6; 5:7]

18 I will not leave you ^Tcomfortless: I will come to you.   *orphans*

19 Yet a little while, and the world seeth me no more; but ^Rye see me: ^Rbecause I live, ye shall live also.   16:16, 22 · [Rom. 5:10]

20 At that day ye shall know that ^RI *am* in my Father, and ye in me, and I in you.   v. 11; 10:38

21 He that hath my commandments, and keepeth them, he it is that loveth me: and he that loveth me shall be loved of my Father, and I will love him, and will ^Tmanifest myself to him.   *reveal*

22 ^RJudas saith unto him, not Iscar'-i-ot, Lord, how is it that thou wilt manifest thyself unto us, and not unto the world?   Luke 6:16

23 Jesus answered and said unto him, If a man love me, he will keep my words: and my Father will love him, ^Rand we will come unto him, and make our abode with him.   2 Cor. 6:16; Eph. 3:17

24 He that loveth me not keep-

eth not my sayings: and ^Rthe word which ye hear is not mine, but the Father's which sent me.   5:19

25 These things have I spoken unto you, being *yet* present with you.

26 But the Comforter, *which is* the Holy Ghost, whom the Father will send in my name, he shall teach you all things, and bring all things to your remembrance, whatsoever I have said unto you.

27 ^RPeace I leave with you, my peace I give unto you: not as the world giveth, give I unto you. Let not your heart be troubled, neither let it be afraid.   Col. 3:15

28 Ye have heard how I said unto you, I go away, and come *again* unto you. If ye loved me, ye would rejoice, because I said, ^RI go unto the Father: for ^Rmy Father is greater than I.   16:16 · [5:18; Phil. 2:6]

29 And ^Rnow I have told you before it come to pass, that, when it is come to pass, ye might believe.   13:19

30 Hereafter I will not talk much with you: ^Rfor the prince of this world cometh, and hath ^Rnothing in me.   [12:31] · [2 Cor. 5:21; Heb. 4:15]

31 But that the world may know that I love the Father; and ^Ras the Father gave me commandment, even so I do. Arise, let us go hence.   10:18; Is. 50:5; Phil. 2:8

15 I am the true vine, and my Father is the husbandman.

2 ^REvery branch in me that beareth not fruit he taketh away: and every *branch* that beareth fruit, he purgeth it, that it may bring forth more fruit.   Matt. 15:13

3 ^RNow ye are clean through the word which I have spoken unto you.   [13:10; 17:17]; Eph. 5:26

4 ^RAbide in me, and I in you. As the branch cannot bear fruit of itself, except it abide in the vine; no more can ye, except ye abide in me.   17:23; Eph. 3:17; [Col. 1:23]

5 I am the vine, ye *are* the branches: He that abideth in me, and I in him, the same bringeth forth much fruit: for without me ye can do ^Rnothing.   2 Cor. 3:5

6 If a man abide not in me, ^Rhe is cast forth as a branch, and is withered; and men gather them, and cast *them* into the fire, and they are burned.   Matt. 3:10

7 If ye abide in me, and my words ^Rabide in you, ^Rye shall ask what ye will, and it shall be done ^Tunto you. 1 John 2:14 · 14:13; 16:23 · *for*

8 ^RHerein is my Father glorified, that ye bear much fruit; so shall ye be my disciples.   [Phil. 1:11]

9 As the Father hath ^Rloved me, so have I loved you: ^Tcontinue ye in my love.   5:20; 17:26 · *abide*

10 ^RIf ye keep my commandments, ye shall abide in my love; even as I have kept my Father's commandments, and abide in his love.   14:15

11 These things have I spoken unto you, that my joy might remain in you, and ^R*that* your joy might be full.   [16:24]; 1 John 1:4

12 ^RThis is my ^Rcommandment, That ye love one another, as I have loved you.   13:34 · Rom. 12:9

13 ^RGreater love hath no man than this, that a man lay down his life for his friends.   1 John 3:16

14 ^RYe are my friends, if ye do whatsoever I command you.   14:15

15 Henceforth I call you not servants; for the servant knoweth not what his lord doeth: but I have called you friends; for all things that I have heard of my Father I have made known unto you.

16 ^RYe have not chosen me, but I have chosen you, and ordained you, that ye should go and bring forth fruit, and *that* your fruit should remain: that whatsoever ye shall ask of the Father in my name, he may give it you.   6:70

17 These things I command you, that ye love one another.

18 ^RIf the world hate you, ye know that it hated me before *it hated* you.   7:7; 1 John 3:13

19 ^RIf ye were of the world, the world would love his own: but ^Rbecause ye are not of the world, but I have chosen you out of the world, therefore the world hateth you.   1 John 4:5 · 17:14

20 Remember the word that I said unto you, The servant is not greater than his lord. If they have persecuted me, they will also persecute you; if they have kept my saying, they will keep yours also.

21 But ^Rall these things will they do unto you for my name's sake, because they know not him that sent me.   Matt. 10:22; 24:9; [1 Pet. 4:14]

22 If I had not come and spoken unto them, they had not had sin: ^Rbut now they have no ^Tcloke for their sin. [Rom. 1:20; James 4:17] · *excuse*

23 ^RHe that hateth me hateth my Father also.   1 John 2:23

24 If I had not done among them ^Rthe works which none other man did, they had not had sin: but now have they both ^Rseen and hated both me and my Father.   3:2 · 14:9

25 But *this cometh to pass*, that the word might be fulfilled that is written in their law, ^RThey hated me without a cause.   Ps. 35:19; 69:4

26 But when the Comforter is come, whom I will send unto you from the Father, *even* the Spirit of truth, which proceedeth from the Father, he shall testify of me:

27 And ^Rye also shall bear witness, because ye have been with me from the beginning.   Luke 24:48

16 These things have I spoken unto you, that ye should not be ^Toffended.   *made to stumble*

2 They shall put you out of the synagogues: yea, the time cometh, that whosoever killeth you will think that he doeth God service.

3 And ^Rthese things will they do unto you, because they have not known the Father, nor me. 8:19

4 But these things have I told you, that when the time shall come, ye may remember that I told you of them. And these things I said not unto you at the beginning, because I was with you.

5 But now I go my way to him that sent me; and none of you asketh me, Whither goest thou?

6 But because I have said these things unto you, ^Rsorrow hath filled your heart.   Matt. 17:23

7 Nevertheless I tell you the

truth; It is ᵀexpedient for you that I go away: for if I go not away, the Comforter will not come unto you; but if I depart, I will send him unto you.   *advantageous*

8 And when he is ᴿcome, he will ᵀreprove the world of sin, and of righteousness, and of judgment: Acts 1:8; 2:1–4, 37 · *convict*

9 ᴿOf sin, because they believe not on me;   Acts 2:22

10 ᴿOf righteousness, ᴿbecause I go to my Father, and ye see me no more;   Acts 2:32 · 5:32

11 Of judgment, because the prince of this world is judged.

12 I have yet many things to say unto you, ᴿbut ye cannot bear them now.   Mark 4:33

13 Howbeit when he, ᴿthe Spirit of truth, is come, ᴿhe will guide you into all truth: for he shall not speak of himself; but whatsoever he shall hear, *that* shall he speak: and he will shew you things to come.   [14:17] · 14:26; Acts 11:28; Rev. 1:19

14 ᴿHe shall glorify me: for he shall receive ᵀof mine, and shall shew *it* unto you. 15:26 · *what is mine*

15 ᴿAll things that the Father hath are mine: therefore said I, that he shall take of mine, and shall shew *it* unto you. Matt. 11:27

16 A ᴿlittle while, and ye shall not see me: and again, a little while, and ye shall see me, because I go to the Father. 7:33; 12:35

17 Then said *some* of his disciples among themselves, What is this that he saith unto us, A little while, and ye shall not see me: and again, a little while, and ye shall see me: and, Because I go to the Father?

18 They said therefore, What is this that he saith, A little while? we cannot tell what he saith.

19 Now Jesus knew that they were desirous to ask him, and said unto them, Do ye enquire among yourselves of that I said, A little while, and ye shall not see me: and again, a little while, and ye shall see me?

20 Verily, verily, I say unto you, That ye shall weep and lament, but the world shall rejoice: and ye shall be sorrowful, but your sorrow shall be turned into joy.

21 ᴿA woman when she is in travail hath sorrow, because her hour is come: but as soon as she is delivered of the child, she remembereth no more the anguish, for joy that a man is born into the world.   Gen. 3:16; Is. 42:14; 1 Thess. 5:3

22 And ye now therefore have sorrow: but I will see you again, and your heart shall rejoice, and your joy no man taketh from you.

23 And in that day ye shall ask me nothing. ᴿVerily, verily, I say unto you, Whatsoever ye shall ask the Father in my name, he will give *it* you.   [14:13; 15:16]; Matt. 7:7

24 Hitherto have ye asked nothing in my name: ask, and ye shall receive, ᴿthat your joy may be ᴿfull.   17:13 · 15:11

25 These things have I spoken unto you in ᵀproverbs: but the time cometh, when I shall no more speak unto you in ᵀproverbs, but I shall shew you plainly of the Father.   *figurative language*

26 At that day ye shall ask in my name: and I say not unto you, that I will pray the Father for you:

27 ᴿFor the Father himself loveth you, because ye have loved me, and ᴿhave believed that I came out from God.   [14:21, 23] · 3:13

28 ᴿI came forth from the Father, and am come into the world: again, I leave the world, and go to the Father.   vv. 5, 10, 17; 13:1, 3

29 His disciples said unto him, Lo, now speakest thou plainly, and speakest no proverb.

30 Now are we sure that ᴿthou knowest all things, and needest not that any man should ask thee: by this ᴿwe believe that thou camest forth from God. 21:17 · 17:8

31 Jesus answered them, Do ye now believe?

32 ᴿBehold, the hour cometh, yea, is now come, that ye shall be scattered, ᴿevery man to his own, and shall leave me alone: and ᴿyet I am not alone, because the Father is with me.   Acts 8:1 · 20:10 · 8:29

33 These things I have spoken unto you, that in me ye might have peace. ᴿIn the world ye shall have tribulation: but be of good cheer; ᴿI have overcome the world. 2 Tim. 3:12 · Rom. 8:37; [1 John 4:4]

17 These words spake Jesus, and lifted up his eyes to heaven, and said, Father, the hour is come; glorify thy Son, that thy Son also may glorify thee:

2 As thou hast given him power over all flesh, that he should give eternal life to as many ᴿas thou hast given him.   6:37, 39

3 And this is life eternal, that they might know thee ᴿthe only true God, and Jesus Christ, whom thou hast sent.   1 Cor. 8:4; 1 Thess. 1:9

4 ᴿI have glorified thee on the earth: I have finished the work which thou gavest me to do.   13:31

5 And now, O Father, glorify thou me with thine own self with the glory ᴿwhich I had with thee before the world was.   1:1, 2; Phil. 2:6

6 I have manifested thy name unto the men ᴿwhich thou gavest me out of the world: thine they were, and thou gavest them me; and they have kept thy word.   6:37

7 Now they have known that all things whatsoever thou hast given me are of thee.

★ 8 For I have given unto them the words which thou gavest me; and they have received *them*, and have known surely that I came out from thee, and they have believed that thou didst send me.

9 I pray for them: ᴿI pray not for the world, but for them which thou hast given me; for they are thine.   [1 John 5:19]

10 And all mine are thine, and ᴿthine are mine; and I am glorified in them.   16:15

11 ᴿAnd now I am no more in the world, but these are in the world, and I come to thee. Holy Father, keep through thine own name those whom thou hast given me, that they may be one, as we *are*.   [Acts 1:9; Heb. 4:14; 9:24; 1 Pet. 3:22]

12 While I was with them in the world, I kept them in thy name: those that thou gavest me I have kept, and none of them is lost, but the son of perdition; that the scripture might be fulfilled.

13 And now come I to thee; and these things I speak in the world, that they might have my joy fulfilled in themselves.

14 I have given them thy word; and the world hath hated them, because they are not of the world, even as I am not of the world.

15 I pray not that thou shouldest take them out of the world, but ᴿthat thou shouldest keep them from the evil.   Gal. 1:4; 2 Thess. 3:3

16 They are not of the world, even as I am not of the world.

17 ᴿSanctify them through thy truth: thy word is truth.   [Eph. 5:26]

18 ᴿAs thou hast sent me into the world, even so have I also sent them into the world.   4:38; 20:21

19 And for their sakes I sanctify myself, that they also might be sanctified through the truth.

20 Neither pray I for these alone, but for them also which shall believe on me through their word;

21 ᴿThat they all may be one; as thou, Father, *art* in me, and I in thee, that they also may be one in us: that the world may believe that thou hast sent me.   [Gal. 3:28]

22 And the ᴿglory which thou gavest me I have given them; ᴿthat they may be one, even as we are one: 14:20; 1 John 1:3 · [2 Cor. 3:18]

23 I in them, and thou in me, that they may be made perfect in one; and that the world may know that thou hast sent me, and hast loved them, as thou hast loved me.

24 ᴿFather, I will that they also, whom thou hast given me, be with me where I am; that they may behold my glory, which thou hast given me: for thou lovedst me before the foundation of the world.   [12:26; 14:3; 1 Thess. 4:17]

25 O righteous Father, the world hath not known thee: but I have known thee, and these have known that thou hast sent me.

26 ᴿAnd I have declared unto them thy name, and will declare

it: that the love ^Rwherewith thou hast loved me may be in them, and I in them.   Ex. 34:5-7 · 15:9

18 When Jesus had spoken these words, ^Rhe went forth with his disciples over the brook Ce'-dron, where was a garden, into the which he entered, and his disciples.   Matt. 26:30, 36; Mark 14:26, 32

2 And Judas also, which betrayed him, knew the place: ^Rfor Jesus ofttimes resorted thither with his disciples.   Luke 21:37; 22:39

3 ^RJudas then, having received a band *of men* and officers from the chief priests and Pharisees, cometh thither with lanterns and torches and weapons.   Acts 1:16

4 Jesus therefore, ^Rknowing all things that should come upon him, went forth, and said unto them, Whom seek ye?   13:1, 3; 19:28

5 They answered him, Jesus of Nazareth. Jesus saith unto them, I am *he.* And Judas also, which ^Rbetrayed him, stood with them. 13:21

6 As soon then as he had said unto them, I am *he,* they went backward, and fell to the ground.

7 Then asked he them again, Whom seek ye? And they said, Jesus of Nazareth.

8 Jesus answered, I have told you that I am *he:* if therefore ye seek me, let these go their way:

9 That the saying might be fulfilled, which he spake, ^ROf them which thou gavest me have I lost none.   [6:39; 17:12]

10 ^RThen Simon Peter having a sword drew it, and smote the high priest's servant, and cut off his right ear. The servant's name was Mal'-chus.   Matt. 26:51; Mark 14:47

11 Then said Jesus unto Peter, Put up thy sword into the sheath: the cup which my Father hath given me, shall I not drink it?

12 Then the ^Tband and the captain and officers of the Jews took Jesus, and bound him,   *cohort*

13 And led him away to An'-nas first; for he was father in law to ^RCa'-ia-phas, which was the high priest that same year.   11:49, 51

14 Now Ca'-ia-phas was he,

which gave counsel to the Jews, that it was expedient that one man should die for the people.

15 ^RAnd Simon Peter followed Jesus, and *so did* ^Ranother disciple: that disciple was known unto the high priest, and went in with Jesus into the palace of the high priest.   Mark 14:54; Luke 22:54 · 20:2-5

16 ^RBut Peter stood at the door without. Then went out that other disciple, which was known unto the high priest, and spake unto her that kept the door, and brought in Peter.   Matt. 26:69

17 Then saith the damsel that kept the door unto Peter, Art not thou also *one* of this man's disciples? He saith, I am ^Rnot. Matt. 26:34

18 And the servants and officers stood there, who had made a fire of coals; for it was cold: and they warmed themselves: and Peter stood with them, and warmed himself.

19 The high priest then asked Jesus of his disciples, and of his doctrine.

20 Jesus answered him, ^RI spake openly to the world; I ever taught ^Rin the synagogue, and ^Rin the temple, whither the Jews always resort; and in secret have I said nothing.   8:26 · 6:59 · 7:14, 28

21 Why askest thou me? ask ^Rthem which heard me, what I have said unto them: behold, they know what I said.   Mark 12:37

22 And when he had thus spoken, one of the officers which stood by struck Jesus with the palm of his hand, saying, Answerest thou the high priest so?

23 Jesus answered him, If I have spoken evil, bear witness of the evil: but if well, why smitest thou me?

24 ^RNow An'-nas had sent him bound unto ^RCa'-ia-phas the high priest.   Luke 3:2; Acts 4:6 · 11:49

25 And Simon Peter stood and warmed himself. They said therefore unto him, Art not thou also *one* of his disciples? He denied *it,* and said, I am not.

26 One of the servants of the high

priest, being *his* kinsman whose ear Peter cut off, saith, Did not I see thee in the garden with him?

27 Peter then denied again: and immediately the cock crew.

28 ᴿThen led they Jesus from Ca'-ia-phas unto the hall of judgment: and it was early; ᴿand they themselves went not into the judgment hall, lest they should be defiled; but that they might eat the passover. Acts 3:13 · 11:55; Acts 11:3

29 Pilate then went out unto them, and said, What accusation bring ye against this man?

30 They answered and said unto him, If he were not a ᵀmalefactor, we would not have delivered him up unto thee.   *evildoer*

31 Then said Pilate unto them, Take ye him, and judge him according to your law. The Jews therefore said unto him, It is not lawful for us to put any man to death:

32 That the saying of Jesus might be fulfilled, which he spake, ᴿsignifying what death he should die.   3:14; 8:28; 12:32, 33

33 ᴿThen Pilate entered into the judgment hall again, and called Jesus, and said unto him, Art thou the King of the Jews?   Matt. 27:11

34 Jesus answered him, Sayest thou this thing of thyself, or did others tell it thee of me?

35 Pilate answered, Am I a Jew? Thine own nation and the chief priests have delivered thee unto me: what hast thou done?

36 ᴿJesus answered, ᴿMy kingdom is not of this world: if my kingdom were of this world, then would my servants fight, that I should not be delivered to the Jews: but now is my kingdom not from hence.   1 Tim. 6:13 · 6:15; 8:15

37 Pilate therefore said unto him, Art thou a king then? Jesus answered, Thou sayest that I am a king. To this end was I born, and for this cause came I into the world, that I should bear witness unto the truth. Every one that is of the truth ᴿheareth my voice.   8:47

38 Pilate saith unto him, What is truth? And when he had said this, he went out again unto the Jews, and saith unto them, ᴿI find in him no fault *at all*.   19:4, 6; 1 Pet. 2:22–24

39 ᴿBut ye have a custom, that I should release unto you one at the passover: will ye therefore that I release unto you the King of the Jews?   Matt. 27:15–26; Luke 23:17–25

40 ᴿThen cried they all again, ★ saying, Not this man, but Bar-ab'-bas. ᴿNow Bar-ab'-bas was a robber.   Is. 53:3; Acts 3:14 · Luke 23:19

19 Then ᴿPilate therefore took Jesus, and scourged *him*.   Matt. 20:19; 27:26; Mark 15:15

2 And the soldiers ᵀplatted a crown of thorns, and put *it* on his head, and they put on him a purple robe,   *twisted*

3 And said, Hail, King of the Jews! and they ᴿsmoteᵀ him with their hands.   Is. 50:6 · *struck*

4 Pilate therefore went forth again, and saith unto them, Behold, I bring him forth to you, ᴿthat ye may know that I find no fault in him.   Is. 53:9; 1 Pet. 2:22–24

5 Then came Jesus forth, wearing the crown of thorns, and the purple robe. And *Pilate* saith unto them, Behold the man!

6 When the chief priests therefore and officers saw him, they cried out, saying, Crucify *him*, crucify *him*. Pilate saith unto them, Take ye him, and crucify *him*: for I find no fault in him.

7 The Jews answered him, ᴿWe have a law, and by our law he ought to die, because he made himself the Son of God.   Lev. 24:16

8 When Pilate therefore heard that saying, he was the more afraid;

9 And went again into the ★ judgment hall, and saith unto Jesus, Whence art thou? ᴿBut Jesus gave him no answer.   Is. 53:7

10 Then saith Pilate unto him, Speakest thou not unto me? knowest thou not that I have ᵀpower to crucify thee, and have ᵀpower to release thee?   *authority*

11 Jesus answered, ᴿThou couldest have no power *at all* against

me, except it were given thee from above: therefore ᴿhe that delivered me unto thee hath the greater sin.   7:30 · 3:27; Rom. 13:1

12 And from thenceforth Pilate sought to release him: but the Jews cried out, saying, If thou let this man go, thou art not Caesar's friend: ᴿwhosoever maketh himself a king speaketh against Caesar.   18:33; Luke 23:2; Acts 17:7

13 ᴿWhen Pilate therefore heard that saying, he brought Jesus forth, and sat down in the judgment seat in a place that is called the Pavement, but in the Hebrew, Gab'-ba-tha.   Is. 51:12; Acts 4:19

14 And ᴿit was the preparation of the passover, and about the sixth hour: and he saith unto the Jews, Behold your King!   Matt. 27:62

15 But they cried out, Away with *him,* away with *him,* crucify him. Pilate saith unto them, Shall I crucify your King? The chief priests answered, ᴿWe have no king but Caesar.   [Gen. 49:10]

16 ᴿThen delivered he him therefore unto them to be crucified. And they took Jesus, and led *him* away.   Mark 15:15; Luke 23:24

17 And he bearing his cross ᴿwent forth into a place called *the place* of a skull, which is called in the Hebrew Gol'-go-tha: Heb. 13:12

★ 18 Where they crucified him, and two other with him, on either side one, and Jesus in the midst.

19 And Pilate wrote a title, and put *it* on the cross. And the writing was, JESUS OF NAZARETH THE KING OF THE JEWS.

20 This title then read many of the Jews: for the place where Jesus was crucified was ᵀnigh to the city: and it was written in Hebrew, *and* Greek, *and* Latin.   near

21 Then said the chief priests of the Jews to Pilate, Write not, The King of the Jews; but that he said, I am King of the Jews.

22 Pilate answered, What I have written I have written.

23 ᴿThen the soldiers, when they had crucified Jesus, took his garments, and made four parts, to every soldier a part; and also *his* ᵀcoat: now the ᵀcoat was without seam, woven from the top throughout.   Luke 23:34 · *tunic*

★ 24 They said therefore among themselves, Let us not rend it, but cast lots for it, whose it shall be: that the scripture might be fulfilled, which saith, ᴿThey parted my ᵀraiment among them, and for my ᵀvesture they did cast lots. These things therefore the soldiers did.   Ps. 22:18 · *garments · clothing*

25 ᴿNow there stood by the cross of Jesus his mother, and his mother's sister, Mary the *wife* of ᴿCle'-o-phas, and Mary Mag-da-le'-ne.   Luke 2:35; 23:49 · Luke 24:18

26 When Jesus therefore saw his mother, and ᴿthe disciple standing by, whom he loved, he saith unto his mother, Woman, behold thy son!   13:23; 20:2; 21:7, 20, 24

27 Then saith he to the disciple, Behold thy mother! And from that hour that disciple took her ᴿunto his own *home.*   1:11; 16:32; Acts 21:6

28 After this, Jesus knowing that all things were now accomplished, ᴿthat the scripture might be fulfilled, saith, I thirst.   Ps. 22:15

★ 29 Now there was set a vessel full of vinegar: and ᴿthey filled a spunge with vinegar, and put *it* upon hyssop, and put *it* to his mouth.   Ps. 69:21; Matt. 27:48, 50

30 When Jesus therefore had received the vinegar, he said, ᴿIt is finished: and he bowed his head, and gave up the ghost.   17:4

31 The Jews therefore, because it was the preparation, that the bodies should not remain upon the cross on the sabbath day, (for that sabbath day was an ᴿhigh day,) besought Pilate that their legs might be broken, and *that* they might be taken away.   Ex. 12:16

32 Then came the soldiers, and brake the legs of the first, and of the other which was crucified with him.

★ 33 But when they came to Jesus, and saw that he was dead already, they brake not his legs:

34 But one of the soldiers with

a spear pierced his side, and [T]forthwith [R]came there out blood and water. *immediately* · [1 John 5:6, 8]

35 And he that saw *it* bare record, and his record is [R]true: and he knoweth that he saith true, that ye might [R]believe. 21:24 · [20:31]

★ 36 For these things were done, [R]that the scripture should be fulfilled, A bone of him shall not be broken. [Ex. 12:46; Num. 9:12]; Ps. 34:20

★ 37 And again another scripture saith, [R]They shall look on him whom they pierced. Zech. 12:10; 13:6

38 And after this Joseph of Ar-i-ma-thae′-a, being a disciple of Jesus, but secretly [R]for fear of the Jews, besought Pilate that he might take away the body of Jesus: and Pilate gave *him* leave. He came therefore, and took the body of Jesus. [7:13; 9:22; 12:42]

39 And there came also [R]Nic-o-de′-mus, which at the first came to Jesus by night, and brought a mixture of myrrh and aloes, about an hundred pound *weight*. 7:50

40 Then took they the body of Jesus, and wound it in linen clothes with the spices, as the manner of the Jews is to bury.

41 Now in the place where he was crucified there was a garden; and in the garden a new [T]sepulchre, wherein was never man yet laid. *tomb*

42 [R]There laid they Jesus therefore because of the Jews' preparation *day*; for the sepulchre was nigh at hand. Is. 53:9; Matt. 26:12

20 The [R]first *day* of the week cometh Mary Mag-da-le′-ne early, when it was yet dark, unto the sepulchre, and seeth the [R]stone taken away from the sepulchre. Acts 20:7; 1 Cor. 16:2 · 11:38

2 Then she runneth, and cometh to Simon Peter, and to the [R]other disciple, whom Jesus loved, and saith unto them, They have taken away the Lord out of the sepulchre, and we know not where they have laid him. 21:23, 24

3 [R]Peter therefore went forth, and that other disciple, and came to the sepulchre. Luke 24:12

4 So they ran both together: and the other disciple did outrun Peter, and came first to the sepulchre.

5 And he stooping down, *and looking in*, saw [R]the linen clothes lying; yet went he not in. 19:40

6 Then cometh Simon Peter following him, and went into the sepulchre, and seeth the linen clothes lie;

7 And [R]the napkin, that was about his head, not lying with the linen clothes, but wrapped together in a place by itself. 11:44

8 Then went in also that [R]other disciple, which came first to the [T]sepulchre, and he saw, and believed. 21:23, 24 · *tomb*

9 For as yet they knew not the [R]scripture, that he must rise again from the dead. Ps. 16:10; Acts 2:25, 31

10 Then the disciples went away again unto their own home.

11 But Mary stood without at the sepulchre weeping: and as she wept, she stooped down, *and looked* into the sepulchre,

12 And seeth two angels in white sitting, the one at the head, and the other at the feet, where the body of Jesus had lain.

13 And they say unto her, Woman, why weepest thou? She saith unto them, Because they have taken away my Lord, and I know not where they have laid him.

14 [R]And when she had thus said, she turned herself back, and saw Jesus standing, and [R]knew not that it was Jesus. Matt. 28:9 · 21:4

15 Jesus saith unto her, Woman, why weepest thou? whom seekest thou? She, supposing him to be the gardener, saith unto him, Sir, if thou have borne him hence, tell me where thou hast laid him, and I will take him away.

16 Jesus saith unto her, [R]Mary. She turned herself, and saith unto him, Rab-bo′-ni; which is to say, [T]Master. 10:3 · *Teacher*

17 Jesus saith unto her, Touch me not; for I am not yet ascended to my Father: but go to my breth-

ren, and say unto them, I ascend unto my Father, and your Father; and *to* my God, and your God.

18 Mary Mag-da-le'-ne came and told the disciples that she had seen the Lord, and *that* he had spoken these things unto her.

19 Then the same day at evening, being the first *day* of the week, when the doors were shut where the disciples were assembled for ^Rfear of the Jews, came Jesus and stood in the midst, and saith unto them, ^RPeace *be* unto you.   9:22; 19:38 · 14:27; 16:16; Eph. 2:17

20 And when he had so said, he shewed unto them *his* hands and his side. Then were the disciples glad, when they saw the Lord.

21 Then said Jesus to them again, Peace *be* unto you: ^Ras *my* Father hath sent me, even so send I you.   17:18, 19; [2 Tim. 2:2]; Heb. 3:1

22 And when he had said this, he breathed on *them,* and saith unto them, Receive ye the Holy Ghost:

23 ^RWhose soever sins ye ^Tremit, they are remitted unto them; *and* whose soever *sins* ye retain, they are retained. Matt. 16:19; 18:18 · *forgive*

24 But Thomas, one of the twelve, called Did'-y-mus, was not with them when Jesus came.

25 The other disciples therefore said unto him, We have seen the Lord. But he said unto them, Except I shall see in his hands the print of the nails, and put my finger into the print of the nails, and thrust my hand into his side, I will not believe.

26 And after eight days again his disciples were within, and Thomas with them: *then* came Jesus, the doors being shut, and stood in the midst, and said, Peace *be* unto you.

★ 27 Then saith he to Thomas, Reach hither thy finger, and behold my hands; and ^Rreach hither thy hand, and thrust *it* into my side: and be not faithless, but believing. Zech. 12:10; 13:6; 1 John 1:1

28 And Thomas answered and said unto him, My Lord and my God.

29 Jesus saith unto him, Thomas, because thou hast seen me, thou hast believed: ^Rblessed *are* they that have not seen, and *yet* have believed.   2 Cor. 5:7; 1 Pet. 1:8

30 And ^Rmany other signs truly did Jesus in the presence of his disciples, which are not written in this book: 21:25

31 ^RBut these are written, that ye might believe that Jesus is the Christ, the Son of God; and that believing ye might have life through his name.   Luke 1:4

21 After these things Jesus shewed himself again to the disciples at the ^Rsea of Ti-be'-ri-as; and on this wise shewed he *himself.*   Matt. 26:32; Mark 14:28

2 There were together Simon Peter, and ^RThomas called Did'-y-mus, and ^RNa-than'-a-el of ^RCana in Galilee, and ^Rthe *sons* of Zeb'-e-dee, and two other of his disciples.   20:24 · 1:45–51 · 2:1 · Matt. 4:21

3 Simon Peter saith unto them, I ^Tgo a fishing. They say unto him, We also go with thee. They went forth, and entered into ^Ta ship immediately; and that night they caught nothing.   *am going* · Lit. *the*

4 But when the morning was now come, Jesus stood on the shore: but the disciples ^Rknew not that it was Jesus.   Luke 24:16

5 Then Jesus saith unto them, Children, have ye any ^Tmeat? They answered him, No.   *food*

6 And he said unto them, ^RCast the net on the right side of the ship, and ye shall find. They cast therefore, and now they were not able to draw it for the multitude of fishes.   Luke 5:4, 6, 7

7 Therefore ^Rthat disciple whom Jesus loved saith unto Peter, It is the Lord. Now when Simon Peter heard that it was the Lord, he girt *his* fisher's coat *unto him,* (for he was naked,) and did cast himself into the sea. 13:23; 20:2

8 And the other disciples came in a little ship; (for they were not far from land, but as it were two hundred cubits,) dragging the net with fishes.

9 As soon then as they were come to land, they saw a fire of coals there, and fish laid thereon, and bread.

10 Jesus saith unto them, Bring ^Tof the fish which ye have now caught.   *some of*

11 Simon Peter went up, and drew the net to land full of great fishes, an hundred and fifty and three: and for all there were so many, yet was not the net broken.

12 Jesus saith unto them, ^RCome and ^Tdine. And none of the disciples ^Tdurst ask him, Who art thou? knowing that it was the Lord.   Acts 10:41 · *eat breakfast · dared*

13 Jesus then cometh, and taketh bread, and giveth them, and fish likewise.

14 This is now ^Rthe third time that Jesus shewed himself to his disciples, after that he was risen from the dead.   20:19, 26

15 So when they had dined, Jesus saith to Simon Peter, Simon, *son* of Jo'-nas, lovest thou me more than these? He saith unto him, Yea, Lord; thou knowest that I love thee. He saith unto him, ^RFeed my lambs.   Acts 20:28; 1 Pet. 5:2

16 He saith to him again the second time, Simon, *son* of Jo'-nas, lovest thou me? He saith unto him, Yea, Lord; thou knowest that I love thee. ^RHe saith unto him, Feed my ^Rsheep.   1 Pet. 2:25 · Ps. 79:13

17 He saith unto him the third time, Simon, *son* of Jo'-nas, lovest thou me? Peter was grieved because he said unto him the third time, Lovest thou me? And he said unto him, Lord, ^Rthou knowest all things; thou knowest that I love

thee. Jesus saith unto him, Feed my sheep.   2:24, 25; 16:30

18 ^RVerily, verily, I say unto thee, When thou wast young, thou girdedst thyself, and walkedst whither thou wouldest: but when thou shalt be old, thou shalt stretch forth thy hands, and another shall gird thee, and carry *thee* whither thou wouldest not.   13:36; Acts 12:3, 4

19 This spake he, signifying by what death he should glorify God. And when he had spoken this, he saith unto him, ^RFollow me.   v. 22

20 Then Peter, turning about, seeth the disciple ^Rwhom Jesus loved following; ^Rwhich also leaned on his breast at supper, and said, Lord, which is he that betrayeth thee?   13:23; 20:2 · 13:25

21 Peter seeing him saith to Jesus, Lord, and ^Twhat *shall* this man *do*?   *what* about *this man*

22 Jesus saith unto him, If I will that he tarry till I come, what *is that* to thee? follow thou me.

23 Then went this saying abroad among the brethren, that that disciple should not die: yet Jesus said not unto him, He shall not die; but, If I will that he ^Ttarry till I come, what *is that* to thee?   *remain*

24 This is the disciple which ^Rtestifieth of these things, and wrote these things: and we know that his testimony is true.   19:35

25 ^RAnd there are also many other things which Jesus did, the which, if they should be written every one, ^RI suppose that even the world itself could not contain the books that should be written. A-men'.   20:30 · Amos 7:10

THE ACTS

of the Apostles

JESUS' last recorded words have come to be known as the Great Commission: "Ye shall be witnesses unto me both in Jerusalem, and in all Judea, and in Samaria, and unto the uttermost part of the earth" (1:8). The Book of Acts, written by Luke, is the story of the men and women who took that commission seriously and began to spread the news of a risen Savior to the most remote corners of the known world.

Each section of the book (1—7; 8—12; 13—28) focuses on a particular audience, a key personality, and a significant phase in the expansion of the gospel message.

As the second volume in a two-part work by Luke, this book probably had no separate title. But all available Greek manuscripts designate it by the title *Praxeis*, "Acts," or by an expanded title like "The Acts of the Apostles." *Praxeis* was commonly used in Greek literature to summarize the accomplishments of outstanding men. While the apostles are mentioned collectively at several points, this book really records the acts of Peter (1—12) and of Paul (13—28).

THE former treatise have I made, O ᴿThe-oph'-i-lus, of all that Jesus began both to do and teach,   Luke 1:3

2 ᴿUntil the day in which he was taken up, after that he through the Holy Ghost had given commandments unto the apostles whom he had chosen: vv. 9, 11, 22

3 ᴿTo whom also he shewed himself alive after his passion by many infallible proofs, being seen of them forty days, and speaking of the things pertaining to the kingdom of God: 1 Cor. 15:5-7

4 And, being assembled together with *them*, commanded them that they should not depart from Jerusalem, but wait for the promise of the Father, which, *saith he*, ye have heard of me.

5 ᴿFor John truly baptized with water; ᴿbut ye shall be baptized with the Holy Ghost not many days hence.   11:16 · [Joel 2:28]

6 When they therefore were come together, they asked of him, saying, Lord, wilt thou at this time restore again the kingdom to Israel?

7 And he said unto them, It is not for you to know the times or the seasons, which the Father hath put in his own power.

8 ᴿBut ye shall receive power, after that the Holy Ghost is come upon you: and ᴿye shall be witnesses unto me both in Jerusalem, and in all Ju-dae'-a, and in Sama'-ri-a, and unto the uttermost part of the earth.   [2:1, 4] · Luke 24:48

9 And when he had spoken these things, while they beheld, he was taken up; and a cloud received him out of their sight.

10 And while they looked stedfastly toward heaven as he went up, behold, two men stood by them ᴿin white apparel;   Luke 24:4

11 Which also said, Ye men of Galilee, why stand ye gazing up into heaven? this same Jesus, which is taken up from you into heaven, ᴿshall so come in like manner as ye have seen him go into heaven.   Luke 21:27; [John 14:3]

12 ᴿThen returned they unto Jerusalem from the mount called Olivet, which is from Jerusalem a sabbath day's journey.   Luke 24:52

13 And when they were come in, they went up ᴿinto an upper room, where abode both Peter, and James, and John, and Andrew, Philip, and Thomas, Bartholomew, and Matthew, James *the son* of Al-phae'-us, and Simon Ze-lo'-tes, and Judas *the brother* of James.   9:37, 39; 20:8; Luke 22:12

14 ᴿThese all continued with one accord in prayer and supplication, with the women, and Mary the mother of Jesus, and with ᴿhis brethren.   2:1, 46 · Matt. 13:55

15 And in those days Peter stood up in the midst of the disciples, and said, (the number ᴿof names together were about an hundred and twenty,)   Luke 22:32; Rev. 3:4

16 Men *and* brethren, this scripture must needs have been fulfilled, which the Holy Ghost by the mouth of David spake before concerning Judas, which was guide to them that took Jesus.

17 For ᴿhe was numbered with

us, and had obtained part of ᴿthis ministry.   Matt. 10:4 · v. 25

18 Now this man purchased a field with ᴿthe reward of iniquity; and falling headlong, he burst asunder in the midst, and all his bowels gushed out.   Luke 22:22

19 And it was known unto all the dwellers at Jerusalem; insomuch as that field is called in their ᵀproper tongue, A-cel′-da-ma, that is to say, The field of blood.   *own language*

★ 20 For it is written in the book of Psalms, ᴿLet his habitation be desolate, and let no man dwell therein: and ᴿhis bishoprick let another take.   Ps. 69:25 · Ps. 109:8

21 Wherefore of these men which have companied with us all the time that the Lord Jesus went in and out among us,

22 Beginning from the baptism of John, unto that same day that he was taken up from us, must one be ordained ᴿto be a witness with us of his resurrection.   2:32

23 And they appointed two, Joseph called Bar′-sa-bas, who was surnamed Justus, and Mat-thi′-as.

24 And they prayed, and said, Thou, Lord, which knowest the hearts of all *men*, shew whether of these two thou hast chosen,

25 That he may take part of this ministry and apostleship, from which Judas by transgression fell, that he might go to his own place.

26 And they ᵀgave forth their lots; and the lot fell upon Mat-thi′-as; and he was numbered with the eleven apostles.   *cast*

2 And when ᴿthe day of Pentecost was fully come, they were all with one ᵀaccord in one place.   20:16; 1 Cor. 16:8 · *purpose* or *mind*

2 And suddenly there came a sound from heaven as of a rushing mighty wind, and it filled all the house where they were sitting.

3 And there appeared unto them cloven tongues like as of fire, and it sat upon each of them.

4 And they were all filled with the Holy Ghost, and began ᴿto speak with other tongues, as the Spirit gave them utterance.   10:46

5 And there were dwelling at Jerusalem Jews, ᴿdevout men, out of every nation under heaven. 8:2

6 Now when this was noised abroad, the ᴿmultitude came together, and were confounded, because that every man heard them speak in his own language.   4:32

7 And they were all amazed and marvelled, saying one to another, Behold, are not all these which speak ᴿGal-i-lae′-ans?   1:11

8 And how hear we every man in our own ᵀtongue, wherein we were born?   *language* or *dialect*

9 Par′-thi-ans, and Medes, and E′-lam-ites, and the dwellers in Mes-o-po-ta′-mi-a, and in Ju-dae′-a, and ᴿCap-pa-do′-ci-a, in Pon′-tus, and Asia,   1 Pet. 1:1

10 Phryg′-i-a, and Pam-phyl′-i-a, in Egypt, and in the parts of Lib′-y-a about Cy-re′-ne, and ᵀstrangers of Rome, Jews and proselytes,   *visitors from*

11 Cretes and A-ra′-bi-ans, we do hear them speak in our tongues the wonderful works of God.

12 And they were all amazed, and were in doubt, saying one to another, What meaneth this?

13 Others mocking said, These men are full of new wine.

14 But Peter, standing up with the eleven, lifted up his voice, and said unto them, Ye men of Ju-dae′-a, and all *ye* that dwell at Jerusalem, be this known unto you, and hearken to my words:

15 For these are not drunken, as ye suppose, ᴿseeing it is *but* the third hour of the day.   1 Thess. 5:7

16 But this is that which was spoken by the prophet Jo′-el;

17 ᴿAnd it shall come to pass in the last days, saith God, ᴿI will pour out of my Spirit upon all flesh: and your sons and ᴿyour daughters shall prophesy, and your young men shall see visions, and your old men shall dream dreams: Joel 2:28–32 · 10:45 · 21:9

18 And on my servants and on

my handmaidens I will pour out in those days of my Spirit; ᴿand they shall prophesy: 21:4, 9

19 ᴿAnd I will shew wonders in heaven above, and signs in the earth beneath; blood, and fire, and vapour of smoke: Joel 2:30

20 ᴿThe sun shall be turned into darkness, and the moon into blood, before that great and notable day of the Lord come: Rev. 6:12

21 And it shall come to pass, *that* whosoever shall call on the name of the Lord shall be saved.

★ 22 Ye men of Israel, hear these words; Jesus of Nazareth, a man approved of God among you ᴿby miracles and wonders and signs, which God did by him in the midst of you, as ye yourselves also know: Is. 50:5; John 3:2; 5:6

23 Him, ᴿbeing delivered by the determinate counsel and foreknowledge of God, ye have taken, and by wicked hands have crucified and slain: Matt. 26:4; Luke 22:22

24 ᴿWhom God hath raised up, having loosed the pains of death: because it was not possible that he should be holden of it. Heb. 13:20

★ 25 For David speaketh concerning him, ᴿI foresaw the Lord always before my face, for he is on my right hand, that I should not be ᵀmoved: Ps. 16:8–11 · *shaken*

26 Therefore did my heart rejoice, and my tongue was glad; moreover also my flesh shall rest in hope:

27 Because thou wilt not leave my soul in ᵀhell, neither wilt thou suffer thine Holy One to see ᴿcorruption. Gr. *hades* · 13:30–37

28 Thou hast made known to me the ways of life; thou shalt make me full of joy ᵀwith thy countenance. *in thy presence*

29 Men *and* brethren, let me freely speak unto you ᴿof the patriarch David, that he is both dead and buried, and his sepulchre is with us unto this day. 13:36

★ 30 Therefore being a prophet, ᴿand knowing that God had sworn with an oath to him, that of the fruit of his loins, according to

the flesh, he would raise up Christ to sit on his throne; 2 Sam. 7:12

31 He seeing this before spake ★ of the resurrection of Christ, that his soul was not left in hell, neither his flesh did see corruption.

32 This Jesus hath God raised up, whereof we all are witnesses.

33 Therefore ᴿbeing by the right ★ hand of God exalted, and having received of the Father the promise of the Holy Ghost, he hath shed forth this, which ye now see and hear. 5:31; Ps. 68:18; Phil. 2:9

34 For David is not ascended ★ into the heavens: but he saith himself, The LORD said unto my Lord, Sit thou on my right hand,

35 Until I make thy foes thy footstool.

36 Therefore let all the house of Israel know assuredly, that God hath made that same Jesus, whom ye have crucified, both Lord and Christ.

37 Now when they heard *this,* ᴿthey were pricked in their heart, and said unto Peter and to the rest of the apostles, Men *and* brethren, what shall we do? Luke 3:10, 12, 14

38 Then Peter said unto them, ᴿRepent, and be baptized every one of you in the name of Jesus Christ for the ᵀremission of sins, and ye shall receive the gift of the Holy Ghost. Luke 24:47 · *forgiveness*

39 For the promise is unto you, and to your children, and ᴿto all that are afar off, *even* as many as the Lord our God shall call.11:15, 18

40 And with many other words did he testify and exhort, saying, Save yourselves from this ᵀuntoward generation. *crooked*

41 Then they that gladly received his word were baptized: and the same day there were added *unto them* about three thousand souls.

42 ᴿAnd they continued stedfastly in the apostles' doctrine and fellowship, and in breaking of bread, and in prayers. Rom. 12:12

43 And fear came upon every soul: and many wonders and signs were done by the apostles.

44 And all that believed were together, and ᴿhad all things common; 4:32, 34, 37; 5:2

45 And sold their possessions and goods, and parted them to all *men*, as every man had need.

46 And they, continuing daily with one accord in the temple, and breaking bread from house to house, did eat their meat with gladness and singleness of heart,

47 Praising God, and having favour with all the people. ᴿAnd the Lord added to the church daily such as should be saved. 5:14

3 Now Peter and John went up together ᴿinto the temple at the hour of prayer, ᴿ*being* the ninth *hour.* 2:46 · 10:30; Ps. 55:17; Matt. 27:45

2 And a certain man lame from his mother's womb was carried, whom they laid daily at the gate of the temple which is called Beautiful, ᴿto ask alms of them that entered into the temple; v. 10

3 Who seeing Peter and John about to go into the temple asked an alms.

4 And Peter, fastening his eyes upon him with John, said, Look on us.

5 And he gave heed unto them, expecting to receive something of them.

6 Then Peter said, Silver and gold have I none; but such as I have give I thee: ᴿIn the name of Jesus Christ of Nazareth rise up and walk. 4:10

7 And he took him by the right hand, and lifted *him* up: and immediately his feet and ancle bones received strength.

8 And he leaping up stood, and walked, and entered with them into the temple, walking, and leaping, and praising God.

9 ᴿAnd all the people saw him walking and praising God: 4:16, 21

10 And they knew that it was he which ᴿsat for alms at the Beautiful gate of the temple: and they were filled with wonder and amazement at that which had happened unto him. John 9:8

11 And as the lame man which was healed held Peter and John, all the people ran together unto them in the porch that is called Solomon's, greatly wondering.

12 And when Peter saw *it*, he answered unto the people, Ye men of Israel, why marvel ye at this? or why look ye so ᵀearnestly on us, as though by our own power or ᵀholiness we had made this man to walk? *intently · godliness*

13 ᴿThe God of Abraham, and of Isaac, and of Jacob, the God of our fathers, ᴿhath glorified his Son Jesus; whom ye delivered up, and denied him in the presence of Pilate, when he was determined to let *him* go. John 5:30 · Is. 49:3; John 7:39

14 But ye denied the Holy One and the Just, and desired a murderer to be granted unto you;

15 And killed the Prince of life, whom God hath raised from the dead; whereof we are witnesses.

16 ᴿAnd his name through faith in his name hath made this man strong, whom ye see and know: yea, the faith which is by him hath given him this perfect soundness in the presence of you all. 4:10; 14:9

17 And now, brethren, I ᵀwot that through ignorance ye did *it*, as *did* also your rulers. *know*

18 But those things, which God ★ before had shewed by the mouth of all his prophets, that Christ should suffer, he hath so fulfilled.

19 ᴿRepent ye therefore, and be converted, that your sins may be blotted out, when the times of refreshing shall come from the presence of the Lord; [2:38; 26:20]

20 And he shall send Jesus ☆ Christ, which before was preached unto you:

21 Whom the heaven must receive until the times of ᴿrestitution of all things, ᴿwhich God hath spoken by the mouth of all his holy prophets since the world began. Matt. 17:11; [Rom. 8:21] · Luke 1:70

22 For Moses truly said unto the ★ fathers, ᴿA prophet shall the Lord your God raise up unto you of your brethren, like unto me; him

shall ye hear in all things whatsoever he shall say unto you. 7:37

23 And it shall come to pass, *that* every soul, which will not hear that prophet, shall be destroyed from among the people.

24 Yea, and ᴿall the prophets from Samuel and those that follow after, as many as have spoken, have likewise foretold of these days. 2 Sam. 7:12; Luke 24:25

★ 25 Ye are the children of the prophets, and of the covenant which God made with our fathers, saying unto Abraham, ᴿAnd in thy seed shall all the kindreds of the earth be blessed. Gen. 12:3; 18:18; 22:18

26 Unto you first God, having raised up his Son Jesus, sent him to bless you, ᴿin turning away every one of you from his iniquities. Is. 42:1; Matt. 1:21

4 And as they spake unto the people, the priests, and the captain of the temple, and the Sad'-du-cees, came upon them,

2 Being ᵀgrieved that they taught the people, and preached through Jesus the resurrection from the dead. *greatly disturbed*

3 And they laid hands on them, and put *them* in ᵀhold unto the next day: for it was now ᵀeventide. *custody · evening*

4 Howbeit many of them which heard the word believed; and the number of the men was about five thousand.

5 And it came to pass on the morrow, that their rulers, and elders, and scribes,

6 And ᴿAn'-nas the high priest, and Ca'-ia-phas, and John, and Alexander, and as many as were of the ᵀkindred of the high priest, were gathered together at Jerusalem. Luke 3:2; John 11:49; 18:13 · *family*

7 And when they had set them in the midst, they asked, ᴿBy what power, or by what name, have ye done this? 7:27; Ex. 2:14; Matt. 21:23

8 ᴿThen Peter, filled with the Holy Ghost, said unto them, Ye rulers of the people, and elders of Israel, Luke 12:11, 12

9 If we this day ᵀbe examined of the good deed done to the ᵀimpotent man, by what means he is made whole; *are judged for · helpless*

10 Be it known unto you all, and to all the people of Israel, ᴿthat by the name of Jesus Christ of Nazareth, whom ye crucified, ᴿwhom God raised from the dead, *even* by him doth this man stand here before you whole. 2:22; 3:6, 16 · 2:24

11 ᴿThis is the stone which was ★ set at nought of you builders, which is become the head of the corner. Ps. 118:22; Is. 28:16; Matt. 21:42

12 Neither is there salvation in any other: for there is none other name under heaven given among men, whereby we must be saved.

13 Now when they saw the boldness of Peter and John, ᴿand perceived that they were unlearned and ignorant men, they marvelled; and they took knowledge of them, that they had been with Jesus. Matt. 11:25; [1 Cor. 1:27]

14 And beholding the man which was healed ᴿstanding with them, they could say nothing against it. 3:11

15 But when they had commanded them to go aside out of the council, they conferred among themselves,

16 Saying, ᴿWhat shall we do to these men? for that indeed a notable miracle hath been done by them *is* ᴿmanifest to all them that dwell in Jerusalem; and we cannot deny *it*. John 11:47 · 3:7–10

17 But that it spread no further among the people, let us ᵀstraitly threaten them, that they speak henceforth to no man in this name. *severely*

18 And they called them, and commanded them not to speak at all nor teach in the name of Jesus.

19 But Peter and John answered and said unto them, ᴿWhether it be right in the sight of God to hearken unto you more than unto God, judge ye. 5:29

20 ᴿFor we cannot but speak the things which ᴿwe have seen and heard. 1:8; 2:32 · 22:15; [1 John 1:1, 3]

21 So when they had further

threatened them, they let them go, finding nothing how they might punish them, ^Rbecause of the people: for all *men* glorified God for that which was done.   Luke 22:2

22 For the man was above forty years old, on whom this miracle of healing was shewed.

23 And being let go, they went to their own company, and reported all that the chief priests and elders had said unto them.

24 And when they heard that, they lifted up their voice to God with one accord, and said, Lord, ^Rthou *art* God, which hast made heaven, and earth, and the sea, and all that in them is: Ps. 146:6

★ 25 Who by the mouth of thy servant David hast said, ^RWhy did the heathen rage, and the people ^Timagine vain things?   Ps. 2:1, 2 · *plot*

26 The kings of the earth ^Tstood up, and the rulers were gathered together against the Lord, and against his Christ.   *took their stand*

27 For of a truth against thy holy child Jesus, ^Rwhom thou hast anointed, both Herod, and Pon'-tius Pilate, with the Gentiles, and the people of Israel, were gathered together,   Luke 4:18; John 10:36

28 ^RFor to do whatsoever thy hand and thy counsel determined before to be done.   2:23; 3:18

29 And now, Lord, behold their threatenings: and grant unto thy servants, ^Rthat with all boldness they may speak thy word,   9:27

30 By stretching forth thine hand to heal; ^Rand that signs and wonders may be done by the name of thy holy child Jesus.   5:12

31 And when they had prayed, the place was shaken where they were assembled together; and they were all filled with the Holy Ghost, ^Rand they spake the word of God with boldness.   v. 29

32 And the multitude of them that believed were of one heart and of one soul: neither said any of *them* that ought of the things which he possessed was his own; but they had all things common.

33 And with great power gave

the apostles witness of the resurrection of the Lord Jesus: and great grace was upon them all.

34 Neither was there any among them that lacked: ^Rfor as many as were possessors of lands or houses sold them, and brought the ^Tprices of the things that were sold,   2:45; [Matt. 19:21] · *proceeds*

35 ^RAnd laid *them* down at the apostles' feet: ^Rand distribution was made unto every man according as he had need.   5:2 · 2:45; 6:1

36 And Jo'-ses, who by the apostles was surnamed Barnabas, (which is, being interpreted, The son of consolation,) a Levite, *and* of the country of Cyprus,

37 ^RHaving land, sold *it*, and brought the money, and laid *it* at the apostles' feet.   vv. 34, 35; 5:1, 2

5 But a certain man named An-a-ni'-as, with Sap-phi'-ra his wife, sold a possession,

2 And kept back *part* of the price, his wife also being ^Tprivy *to it*, and brought a certain part, and laid *it* at the apostles' feet. *aware of*

3 ^RBut Peter said, An-a-ni'-as, why hath ^RSatan filled thine heart to lie to the Holy Ghost, and to keep back *part* of the price of the land?   Deut. 23:21 · Matt. 4:10; Luke 22:3

4 Whiles it remained, was it not thine own? and after it was sold, was it not in thine own power? why hast thou conceived this thing in thine heart? thou hast not lied unto men, but unto God.

5 And An-a-ni'-as hearing these words ^Rfell down, and ^Tgave up the ghost: and great fear came on all them that heard these things.   vv. 10, 11 · *breathed his last*

6 And the young men arose, ^Rwound him up, and carried *him* out, and buried *him*.   John 19:40

7 And it was about the space of three hours after, when his wife, not knowing what was done, came in.

8 And Peter answered unto her, Tell me whether ye sold the land for so much? And she said, Yea, for so much.

9 Then Peter said unto her,

How is it that ye have agreed together ^Rto ^Ttempt the Spirit of the Lord? behold, the feet of them which have buried thy husband *are* at the door, and shall carry thee out.   vv. 3, 4; Matt. 4:7 · *test*

10 ^RThen fell she down straightway at his feet, and yielded up the ghost: and the young men came in, and found her dead, and, carrying *her* forth, buried *her* by her husband.   v. 5; Ezek. 11:13

11 ^RAnd great fear came upon all the church, and upon as many as heard these things.   2:43; 19:17

12 And ^Rby the hands of the apostles were many signs and wonders wrought among the people; (and they were all with one accord in Solomon's porch.   2:43

13 And of the rest ^Tdurst no man join himself to them: ^Rbut the people magnified them. *dared* · 2:47; 4:21

14 And believers were the more added to the Lord, multitudes both of men and women.)

15 Insomuch that they brought forth the sick into the streets, and laid *them* on beds and couches, ^Rthat at the least the shadow of Peter passing by might overshadow some of them.   Matt. 9:21; 14:36

16 There came also a multitude *out* of the cities round about unto Jerusalem, bringing ^Rsick folks, and them which were vexed with unclean spirits: and they were healed every one.   Mark 16:17, 18

17 ^RThen the high priest rose up, and all they that were with him, (which is the sect of the Sad'-ducees,) and were filled with indignation,   4:1, 2, 6; Matt. 3:7

18 ^RAnd laid their hands on the apostles, and put them in the common prison.   4:3; 16:37; Luke 21:12

19 But the angel of the Lord by night opened the prison doors, and brought them forth, and said,

20 Go, stand and speak in the temple to the people ^Rall the words of this life.   [1 John 5:11]

21 And when they heard *that,* they entered into the temple early in the morning, and taught. ^RBut the high priest came, and they

that were with him, and called the council together, and all the ^Tsenate of the children of Israel, and sent to the prison to have them brought.   4:5, 6 · *council of elders*

22 But when the officers came, and found them not in the prison, they returned, and ^Ttold,   *reported*

23 Saying, The prison truly found we shut with all ^Tsafety, and the keepers standing ^Twithout before the doors: but when we had opened, we found no man within.   *security · outside*

24 Now when the high priest and ^Rthe captain of the temple and the chief priests heard these things, they doubted of them whereunto this would grow.   4:1

25 Then came one and told them, saying, Behold, the men whom ye put in prison are standing in the temple, and teaching the people.

26 Then went the captain with the officers, and brought them without violence: ^Rfor they feared the people, lest they should have been stoned.   Matt. 21:26

27 And when they had brought them, they set *them* before the council: and the high priest asked them,

28 Saying, ^RDid not we straitly command you that ye should not teach in this name? and, behold, ye have filled Jerusalem with your doctrine, ^Rand intend to bring this man's blood upon us.   4:17, 18 · 2:23

29 Then Peter and the *other* apostles answered and said, ^RWe ought to obey God rather than men.   4:19

30 ^RThe God of our fathers raised up Jesus, whom ye slew and hanged on a tree.   3:13, 15

31 Him hath God exalted with his right hand *to be* a Prince and a Saviour, for to give repentance to Israel, and forgiveness of sins.

32 And ^Rwe are his witnesses of these things; and *so is* also the Holy Ghost, whom God hath given to them that obey him. 15:28

33 When they heard *that,* they

were [R]cut *to the heart*, and took counsel to slay them.   2:37; 7:54

34 Then stood there up one in the council, a Pharisee, named Ga-ma'-li-el, a doctor of the law, had in reputation among all the people, and commanded to put the apostles forth a little space;

35 And said unto them, Ye men of Israel, take heed to yourselves what ye intend to do as [T]touching these men.   *regarding*

36 For before these days rose up Theu'-das, boasting himself to be somebody; to whom a number of men, about four hundred, joined themselves: who was slain; and all, as many as obeyed him, were scattered, and brought to nought.

37 After this man rose up Judas of Galilee in the days of the taxing, and drew away much people after him: he also perished; and all, *even* as many as obeyed him, were dispersed.

38 And now I say unto you, [T]Refrain from these men, and let them alone: for if this counsel or this work be of men, it will come to nought: *Keep away*

39 But if it be of God, ye cannot overthrow it; lest haply ye be found even to fight against God.

40 And to him they agreed: and when they had [R]called the apostles, [R]and beaten *them*, they commanded that they should not speak in the name of Jesus, and let them go. 4:18 · Matt. 10:17; Mark 13:9

41 And they departed from the presence of the council, [R]rejoicing that they were counted worthy to suffer shame for his name. Rom. 5:3

42 And daily in the temple, and in every house, they ceased not to teach and preach Jesus Christ.

6 And in those days, when the number of the disciples was multiplied, there arose a murmuring of the [R]Gre'-cians[T] against the Hebrews, because their widows were neglected [R]in the daily ministration.   9:29; 11:20 · *Hellenists* · 4:35

2 Then the twelve called the multitude of the disciples *unto them*, and said, It is not [T]reason

that we should leave the word of God, and serve tables.   *desirable*

3 Wherefore, brethren, [T]look ye out among you seven men of honest report, full of the Holy Ghost and wisdom, whom we may appoint over this business.   *seek*

4 But we [R]will give ourselves continually to prayer, and to the ministry of the word.   2:42

5 And the saying pleased the whole multitude: and they chose Stephen, [R]a man full of faith and of the Holy Ghost, and [R]Philip, and Proch'-o-rus, and Ni-ca'-nor, and Ti'-mon, and Par'-me-nas, and [R]Nic'-o-las a proselyte of An'-ti-och: 11:24 · 8:5, 26; 21:8 · Rev. 2:6, 15

6 Whom they set before the apostles: and [R]when they had prayed, [R]they laid *their* hands on them.   1:24 · Num. 8:10; 27:18; Deut. 34:9

7 And [R]the word of God [T]increased; and the number of the disciples multiplied in Jerusalem greatly; and a great company [R]of the priests were obedient to the faith.   12:24; Col. 1:6 · *spread* · John 12:42

8 And Stephen, full of faith and power, did great [R]wonders and miracles among the people.   2:43

9 Then there arose certain of the synagogue, which is called *the synagogue* of the [T]Lib'-er-tines, and Cy-re'-ni-ans, and Al-ex-an'-dri-ans, and of them of Ci-li'-ci-a and of Asia, disputing with Stephen.   *Freedmen*

10 And [R]they were not able to resist the wisdom and the spirit by which he spake. Ex. 4:12; Is. 54:17

11 Then they suborned men, which said, We have heard him speak blasphemous words against Moses, and *against* God.

12 And they stirred up the people, and the elders, and the scribes, and came upon *him*, and caught him, and brought *him* to the council,

13 And set up false witnesses, which said, This man ceaseth not to speak blasphemous words against this holy place, and the law:

14 [R]For we have heard him say,

that this Jesus of Nazareth shall destroy this place, and shall change the customs which Moses delivered us. 10:38; 25:8

15 And all that sat in the council, looking stedfastly on him, saw his face as it had been the face of an angel.

7 Then said the high priest, Are these things so?

2 And he said, [R]Men, brethren, and fathers, hearken; The [R]God of glory appeared unto our father Abraham, when he was in Mes-o-po-ta'-mi-a, before he dwelt in Char'-ran, 22:1 · Ps. 29:3; 1 Cor. 2:8

3 And said unto him, [R]Get thee out of thy country, and from thy kindred, and come into the land which I shall shew thee. Gen. 12:1

4 Then came he out of the land of the Chal-dae'-ans, and dwelt in Char'-ran: and from thence, when his father was [R]dead, he removed him into this land, wherein ye now dwell. Gen. 11:32

5 And he gave him none inheritance in it, no, not so much as to set his foot on: yet he promised that he would give it to him for a possession, and to his seed after him, when as yet he had no child.

6 And God spake on this wise, [R]That his seed should sojourn in a strange land; and that they should bring them into [R]bondage, and entreat them evil four hundred years. Gen. 47:11, 12 · Ex. 1:8–14

7 [R]And the nation to whom they shall be in bondage will I judge, said God: [R]and after that shall they come forth, and serve me in this place. Gen. 15:14 · Ex. 3:1

8 And he gave him the covenant of circumcision: and so Abraham begat Isaac, and circumcised him the eighth day; and Isaac begat Jacob; and Jacob begat the twelve patriarchs.

9 [R]And the patriarchs, moved with envy, sold Joseph into Egypt: but God was with him, Gen. 37:4, 11

10 And delivered him out of all his afflictions, [R]and gave him favour and wisdom in the sight of Pharaoh king of Egypt; and he

made him governor over Egypt and all his house. Gen. 41:38–44

11 [R]Now there came a [T]dearth over all the land of Egypt and Cha'-naan, and great affliction: and our fathers found no sustenance. Gen. 41:54; 42:5 · famine

12 [R]But when Jacob heard that there was corn in Egypt, he sent out our fathers first. Gen. 42:1, 2

13 And at the second time Joseph was made known to his brethren; and Joseph's kindred was made known unto Pharaoh.

14 [R]Then sent Joseph, and called his father Jacob to him, and [R]all his kindred, threescore and fifteen souls. Gen. 45:9, 27 · Gen. 46:26, 27

15 [R]So Jacob went down into Egypt, [R]and died, he, and our fathers, Gen. 46:1–7 · Gen. 49:33; Ex. 1:6

16 And were carried over into Sy'-chem, and laid in the sepulchre that Abraham bought for a sum of money of the sons of Em'-mor the father of Sy'-chem.

17 But when the time of the promise drew nigh, which God had sworn to Abraham, the people grew and multiplied in Egypt,

18 Till another king [R]arose, which knew not Joseph. Ex. 1:8

19 The same dealt [T]subtilly with our kindred, and evil entreated our fathers, so that they cast out their young children, to the end they might not live. treacherously

20 [R]In which time Moses was born, and was exceeding fair, and nourished up in his father's house three months: Ex. 2:1, 2

21 And [R]when he was [T]cast out, [R]Pharaoh's daughter took him up, and nourished him [T]for her own son. Ex. 2:3, 4 · set · Ex. 2:5–10 · as

22 And Moses was learned in all the wisdom of the Egyptians, and was [R]mighty in words and in deeds. Luke 24:19

23 [R]And when he was full forty years old, it came into his heart to visit his brethren the children of Israel. Ex. 2:11, 12; Heb. 11:24–26

24 And seeing one of them suffer wrong, he defended him, and

avenged him that was oppressed, and smote the Egyptian:

25 For he supposed his brethren would have understood how that God by his hand would deliver them: but they understood not.

26 And the next day he shewed himself unto them as they strove, and would have ^Tset them at one again, saying, Sirs, ye are brethren; why do ye wrong one to another?   *reconciled them*

27 But he that did his neighbour wrong thrust him away, saying, ^RWho made thee a ruler and a judge over us?   Luke 12:14; Ex. 2:14

28 Wilt thou kill me, as thou didst the Egyptian yesterday?

29 Then fled Moses at this saying, and was a stranger in the land of Ma'-di-an, where he ^Rbegat two sons.   Ex. 2:15, 21, 22

30 ^RAnd when forty years were expired, there appeared to him in the wilderness of mount Si'-na an angel of the Lord in a flame of fire in a bush.   Ex. 3:1–10; Is. 63:9

31 When Moses saw *it*, he ^Twondered at the sight: and as he drew near to behold *it*, the voice of the Lord came unto him,   *marvelled*

32 *Saying*, ^RI *am* the God of thy fathers, the God of Abraham, and the God of Isaac, and the God of Jacob. Then Moses trembled, and durst not behold.   Ex. 3:6, 15

33 ^RThen said the Lord to him, ^TPut off thy shoes from thy feet: for the place where thou standest is holy ground.   Ex. 3:5, 7, 8, 10 · *Take*

34 I have seen, I have seen the affliction of my people which is in Egypt, and I have heard their groaning, and am come down to deliver them. And now come, I will send thee into Egypt.

35 This Moses whom they refused, saying, ^RWho made thee a ruler and a judge? the same did God send *to be* a ruler and a deliverer ^Rby the hand of the angel which appeared to him in the bush.   Ex. 2:14 · Ex. 14:21

36 ^RHe brought them out, after that he had shewed wonders and signs in the land of Egypt, and in

the Red sea, and in the wilderness forty years. Ex. 12:41; 33:1; Deut. 6:21, 23

37 This is that Moses, which ★ said unto the children of Israel, ^RA prophet shall the Lord your God raise up unto you of your brethren, like unto me; ^Rhim shall ye hear.   3:22; Deut. 18:15, 18, 19 · Matt. 17:5

38 This is he, that was in the ^Tchurch in the wilderness with the angel which spake to him in the mount Si'-na, and *with* our fathers: who received the lively oracles to give unto us: *assembly*

39 To whom our fathers ^Rwould not obey, but thrust *him* from them, and in their hearts turned back again into Egypt,   Ps. 95:8–11

40 Saying unto Aaron, Make us gods to go before us: for *as for* this Moses, which brought us out of the land of Egypt, we ^Twot not what is become of him.   *know*

41 And they made a calf in those days, and offered sacrifice unto the idol, and rejoiced in the works of their own hands.

42 Then God turned, and gave them up to worship the host of heaven; as it is written in the book of the prophets, O ye house of Israel, have ye offered to me slain beasts and sacrifices *by the space of* forty years in the wilderness?

43 Yea, ye took up the tabernacle of Mo'-loch, and the star of your god Rem'-phan, figures which ye made to worship them: and ^RI will carry you away beyond Babylon.   2 Chr. 36:11–21; Jer. 25:9–12

44 Our fathers had the tabernacle of witness in the wilderness, as he had appointed, speaking unto Moses, ^Rthat he should make it according to the fashion that he had seen.   Ex. 25:40; [Heb. 8:5]

45 ^RWhich also our fathers that came after brought in with Jesus into the possession of the Gentiles, whom God drave out before the face of our fathers, unto the days of David;   Deut. 32:49; Josh. 3:14

46 Who found favour before God, and desired to find a tabernacle for the God of Jacob.

47 ^RBut Solomon built him an house. 1 Kin. 6:1–38; 8:20, 21; 2 Chr. 3:1–17

48 Howbeit the most High dwelleth not in temples made with hands; as saith the prophet,

49 Heaven *is* my throne, and earth *is* my footstool: what house will ye build me? saith the Lord: or what *is* the place of my rest?

50 Hath not my hand ^Rmade all these things?   Ps. 102:25

51 Ye ^Rstiffnecked and uncircumcised in heart and ears, ye do always resist the Holy Ghost: as your fathers *did*, so *do* ye.   Ex. 32:9

52 ^RWhich of the prophets have not your fathers persecuted? and they have slain them which shewed before of the coming of the Just One; of whom ye have been now the betrayers and murderers: 2 Chr. 36:16; Matt. 21:35; 23:35

53 ^RWho have received the law by the disposition of angels, and have not kept *it*.   Ex. 20:1; Deut. 33:2

54 ^RWhen they heard these things, they were ^Tcut to the heart, and they gnashed ^Ton him with *their* teeth.   5:33 · *furious · at*

55 But he, ^Rbeing full of the Holy Ghost, looked up stedfastly into heaven, and saw the glory of God, and Jesus standing on the right hand of God,   Matt. 5:8; 16:28; Mark 9:1

56 And said, Behold, ^RI see the heavens opened, and the ^RSon of man standing on the right hand of God.   Matt. 3:16 · Dan. 7:13

57 Then they cried out with a loud voice, and stopped their ears, and ran upon him with one accord,

58 And cast *him* out of the city, and stoned *him*: and ^Rthe witnesses laid down their clothes at a young man's feet, whose name was Saul.   22:20

59 And they stoned Stephen, calling upon *God*, and saying, Lord Jesus, receive my spirit.

60 And he kneeled down, and cried with a loud voice, ^RLord, lay not this sin to their charge. And when he had said this, he fell asleep.   Matt. 5:44; Luke 23:34

8 And Saul was consenting unto his death. And at that time there was a great persecution against the church which was at Jerusalem; and ^Rthey were all scattered abroad throughout the regions of Ju-dae'-a and Sa-ma'-ri-a, except the apostles.   John 16:2

2 And devout men carried Stephen *to his burial*, and made great lamentation over him.

3 As for Saul, he made havock of the church, entering into every house, and haling men and women committed *them* to prison.

4 Therefore they that were scattered abroad went every where preaching the word.

5 Then ^RPhilip went down to the city of Sa-ma'-ri-a, and preached Christ unto them.   6:5

6 And the ^Tpeople with one accord gave heed unto those things which Philip spake, hearing and seeing the miracles which he did.   *multitudes*

7 For unclean spirits, crying with loud voice, came out of many that were possessed *with them*: and many taken with palsies, and that were lame, were healed.

8 And there was great joy in that city.

9 But there was a certain man, called Simon, which beforetime in the same city ^Rused sorcery, and bewitched the people of Sa-ma'-ri-a, ^Rgiving out that himself was some great one: v. 11; 13:6 · 5:36

10 To whom they all gave heed, from the least to the greatest, saying, This man is the great power of God.

11 And to him they had regard, because that of long time he had bewitched them with sorceries.

12 But when they believed Philip ^Tpreaching the things ^Rconcerning the kingdom of God, and the name of Jesus Christ, they were baptized, both men and women.   *as he preached · v. 4; 1:3*

13 Then Simon himself believed also: and when he was baptized, he continued with Philip, and

wondered, beholding the miracles and signs which were done.

14 Now when the ᴿapostles which were at Jerusalem heard that Sa-ma'-ri-a had received the word of God, they sent unto them Peter and John: 5:12, 29, 40

15 Who, when they were come down, prayed for them, ᴿthat they might receive the Holy Ghost: 2:38

16 (For ᴿas yet he was fallen upon none of them: only ᴿthey were baptized in ᴿthe name of the Lord Jesus.)   19:2 · 2:38 · 10:48; 19:5

17 Then ᴿlaid they *their* hands on them, and they received the Holy Ghost.   6:6; 19:6; Heb. 6:2

18 And when Simon saw that through laying on of the apostles' hands the Holy Ghost was given, he offered them money,

19 Saying, Give me also this power, that on whomsoever I lay hands, he may receive the Holy Ghost.

20 But Peter said unto him, Thy money perish with thee, because ᴿthou hast thought that ᴿthe gift of God may be purchased with money.   [Matt. 10:8] · [2:38; 10:45; 11:17]

21 Thou hast neither part nor lot in this matter: for thy ᴿheart is not right in the sight of God.   Jer. 17:9

22 Repent therefore of this thy wickedness, and pray God, ᴿif perhaps the thought of thine heart may be forgiven thee.   2 Tim. 2:25

23 For I perceive that thou art in ᴿthe gall of bitterness, and ᵀ*in* the bond of iniquity.   Heb. 12:15 · *bound by*

24 Then answered Simon, and said, Pray ye to the Lord for me, that none of these things which ye have spoken come upon me.

25 And they, when they had testified and preached the word of the Lord, returned to Jerusalem, and preached the gospel in many villages of the Sa-mar'-i-tans.

26 And the angel of the Lord spake unto ᴿPhilip, saying, Arise, and go toward the south unto the way that goeth down from Je-rusalem unto Ga'-za, which is ᵀdesert.   6:5 · *deserted*

27 And he arose and went: and,

behold, ᴿa man of E-thi-o'-pi-a, an eunuch of great authority under Can-da'-ce queen of the E-thi-o'-pi-ans, who had the charge of all her treasure, and had come to Jerusalem for to worship,   Is. 56:3

28 Was returning, and sitting in his chariot read E-sa'-ias the prophet.

29 Then the Spirit said unto Philip, Go near, and join thyself to this chariot.

30 And Philip ran thither to *him*, and heard him read the prophet E-sa'-ias, and said, Understandest thou what thou readest?

31 And he said, How can I, except some man should guide me? And he ᵀdesired Philip that he would come up and sit with him.   *asked*

32 The place of the scripture ★ which he read was this, ᴿHe was led as a sheep to the slaughter; and like a lamb ᵀdumb before his shearer, ᴿso opened he not his mouth: Is. 53:7, 8 · *silent* · Matt. 26:62, 63

33 In his humiliation his judgment was taken away: and who shall declare his generation? for his life is taken from the earth.

34 And the eunuch answered Philip, and said, I pray thee, of whom speaketh the prophet this? of himself, or of some other man?

35 Then Philip opened his mouth, ᴿand began at the same scripture, and preached unto him Jesus.   17:2; 18:28; 28:23; Luke 24:27

36 And as they went on *their* way, they came unto a certain water: and the eunuch said, See, *here is* water; ᴿwhat doth hinder me to be baptized?   10:47; 16:33

37 And Philip said, If thou believest with all thine heart, thou mayest. And he answered and said, I believe that Jesus Christ is the Son of God.

38 And he commanded the chariot to stand still: and they went down both into the water, both Philip and the eunuch; and he baptized him.

39 And when they were come up out of the water, the Spirit of the

Lord caught away Philip, that the eunuch saw him no more: and he went on his way rejoicing.

40 But Philip was found at A-zo'-tus: and passing through he preached in all the cities, till he came to ᴿCaes-a-re'-a.   21:8

9 And ᴿSaul, yet breathing out threatenings and slaughter against the disciples of the Lord, went unto the high priest,   7:57

2 And ᵀdesired of him ᴿletters to Damascus to the synagogues, that if he found any of this way, whether they were men or women, he might bring them bound unto Jerusalem.   *asked* · 22:5

3 And ᴿas he journeyed, he came near Damascus: and suddenly there shined round about him a light from heaven: 26:12, 13

4 And he fell to the earth, and heard a voice saying unto him, Saul, Saul, ᴿwhy persecutest thou me?   [Matt. 25:40]

5 And he said, Who art thou, Lord? And the Lord said, I am Jesus whom thou persecutest: *it is* hard for thee to kick against the ᵀpricks.   *goads*

6 And he trembling and astonished said, Lord, what wilt thou have me to do? And the Lord *said* unto him, Arise, and go into the city, and it shall be told thee what thou must do.

7 And ᴿthe men which journeyed with him stood speechless, hearing a voice, but seeing no man.   [22:9; 26:13]; John 12:29

8 And Saul arose from the earth; and when his eyes were opened, he saw no man: but they led him by the hand, and brought *him* into Damascus.

9 And he was three days without sight, and neither did eat nor drink.

10 And there was a certain disciple at Damascus, ᴿnamed An-a-ni'-as; and to him said the Lord in a vision, An-a-ni'-as. And he said, Behold, I *am here*, Lord.   22:12

11 And the Lord *said* unto him, Arise, and go into the street which is called Straight, and enquire in

the house of Judas for *one* called Saul, ᴿof Tar'-sus: for, behold, he prayeth,   21:39; 22:3

12 And hath seen in a vision a man named An-a-ni'-as coming in, and putting *his* hand on him, that he might receive his sight.

13 Then An-a-ni'-as answered, Lord, I have heard by many of this man, how much evil he hath done to thy saints at Jerusalem:

14 And here he hath authority from the chief priests to bind all ᴿthat call on thy name.   7:59

15 But the Lord said unto him, Go thy way: for ᴿhe is a chosen vessel unto me, to bear my name before the Gentiles, and kings, and the children of Israel: 13:2

16 For ᴿI will shew him how great things he must suffer for my name's sake.   20:23; 2 Cor. 11:23–28

17 ᴿAnd An-a-ni'-as went his way, and entered into the house; and ᴿputting his hands on him said, Brother Saul, the Lord, *even* Jesus, that appeared unto thee in the way as thou camest, hath sent me, that thou mightest receive thy sight, and ᴿbe filled with the Holy Ghost.   22:12, 13 · 8:17 · 2:4; 4:31; 8:17

18 And immediately there fell from his eyes ᵀas it had been scales: and he received sight ᵀforthwith, and arose, and was baptized.   something *like* · *at once*

19 And when he had received ᵀmeat, he was strengthened. ᴿThen was Saul certain days with the disciples which were at Damascus.   *food* · 26:20

20 And straightway he preached Christ in the synagogues, that he is the Son of God.

21 But all that heard *him* were amazed, and said; ᴿIs not this he that destroyed them which called on this name in Jerusalem, and came hither for that intent, that he might bring them bound unto the chief priests?   8:3; Gal. 1:13, 23

22 But Saul increased the more in strength, and confounded the Jews which dwelt at Damascus, proving that this is very Christ.

23 And after that many days

were fulfilled, ᴿthe Jews took counsel to kill him: 23:12; 2 Cor. 11:26

24 ᴿBut their ᵀlaying await was known of Saul. And they watched the gates day and night to kill him.   2 Cor. 11:32 · *plot*

25 Then the disciples took him by night, and ᴿlet *him* down by the wall in a basket.   Josh. 2:15

26 And when Saul was come to Jerusalem, he assayed to join himself to the disciples: but they were all afraid of him, and believed not that he was a disciple.

27 ᴿBut Barnabas took him, and brought *him* to the apostles, and declared unto them how he had seen the Lord in the way, and that he had spoken to him, and how he had preached boldly at Damascus in the name of Jesus.   4:36; 13:2

28 And he was with them coming in and going out at Jerusalem.

29 And he spake boldly in the name of the Lord Jesus, and disputed against the Gre'-cians: but they went about to slay him.

30 *Which* when the brethren knew, they brought him down to Caes-a-re'-a, and sent him forth to Tar'-sus.

31 Then had the churches rest throughout all Ju-dae'-a and Galilee and Sa-ma'-ri-a, and were edified; and walking in the fear of the Lord, and in the comfort of the Holy Ghost, were multiplied.

32 And it came to pass, as Peter passed ᴿthroughout all *quarters*, he came down also to the saints which dwelt at Lyd'-da.   8:14

33 And there he found a certain man named Ae'-ne-as, which had kept his bed eight years, and was ᵀsick of the palsy.   *paralyzed*

34 And Peter said unto him, Ae'-ne-as, ᴿJesus Christ maketh thee whole: arise, and make thy bed. And he arose immediately. [3:6, 16]

35 And all that dwelt at Lyd'-da and Sa'-ron saw him, and ᴿturned to the Lord.   11:21; 15:19

36 Now there was at Jop'-pa a certain disciple named Tab'-i-tha, which by interpretation is called Dor'-cas: this woman was full ᴿof good works and almsdeeds which she did.   1 Tim. 2:10; Titus 3:8

37 And it came to pass in those days, that she was sick, and died: whom when they had washed, they laid *her* in ᴿan upper chamber.   v. 39; 1:13

38 And forasmuch as Lyd'-da was nigh to Jop'-pa, and the disciples had heard that Peter was there, they sent unto him two men, desiring *him* that he would not delay to come to them.

39 Then Peter arose and went with them. When he was come, they brought him into the upper chamber: and all the widows stood by him weeping, and shewing the ᵀcoats and garments which Dor'-cas made, while she was with them.   *tunics*

40 But Peter ᴿput them all forth, and kneeled down, and prayed; and turning *him* to the body ᴿsaid, Tab'-i-tha, arise. And she opened her eyes: and when she saw Peter, she sat up.   Matt. 9:25 · Mark 5:41, 42

41 And he gave her *his* hand, and lifted her up, and when he had called the saints and widows, presented her alive.

42 And it was known throughout all Jop'-pa; ᴿand many believed in the Lord.   John 11:45

43 And it came to pass, that he tarried many days in Jop'-pa with one ᴿSimon a tanner.   10:6

10 There was a certain man in ᴿCaes-a-re'-a called Cornelius, a centurion of the band called the Italian *band*,   8:40; 23:23

2 *A* devout *man*, and one that feared God with all his house, which gave much alms to the people, and prayed to God alway.

3 ᴿHe saw in a vision ᵀevidently about ᵀthe ninth hour of the day an angel of God coming in to him, and saying unto him, Cornelius. v. 30; 11:13 · *clearly* · 3:00 P.M.

4 And when he looked on him, he was afraid, and said, What is it, Lord? And he said unto him, Thy prayers and thine alms are come up for a memorial before God.

5 And now ᴿsend men to Jop'-

pa, and call for *one* Simon, whose surname is Peter: 11:13, 14

6 He lodgeth with one ^RSimon a tanner, whose house is by the sea side: ^Rhe shall tell thee what thou oughtest to do.   9:43 · 11:14

7 And when the angel which spake unto Cornelius was departed, he called two of his household servants, and a devout soldier of them that waited on him continually;

8 And when he had declared all *these* things unto them, he sent them to Jop'-pa.

9 On the ^Tmorrow, as they went on their journey, and drew nigh unto the city, ^RPeter went up upon the housetop to pray about ^Tthe sixth hour: *next day* · 11:5–14 · *Noon*

10 And he became very hungry, and would have eaten: but while they made ready, he fell into a trance,

11 And ^Rsaw heaven opened, and a certain vessel descending unto him, as it had been a great sheet knit at the four corners, and let down to the earth: Matt. 3:16

12 Wherein were all manner of fourfooted beasts of the earth, and wild beasts, and creeping things, and fowls of the air.

13 And there came a voice to him, Rise, Peter; kill, and eat.

14 But Peter said, Not so, Lord; for I have never eaten any thing that is common or unclean.

15 And the voice *spake* unto him again the second time, ^RWhat God hath cleansed, *that* call not thou common.   1 Cor. 10:25; [1 Tim. 4:4]

16 This was done ^Tthrice: and the vessel was received up again into heaven.   *three times*

17 Now while Peter ^Tdoubted in himself what this vision which he had seen should mean, behold, the men which were sent from Cornelius had made enquiry for Simon's house, and stood before the gate,   *wondered*

18 And called, and asked whether Simon, which was surnamed Peter, were lodged there.

19 While Peter thought on the vision, ^Rthe Spirit said unto him, Behold, three men seek thee. 11:12

20 Arise therefore, and get thee down, and go with them, doubting nothing: for I have sent them.

21 Then Peter went down to the men which were sent unto him from Cornelius; and said, Behold, I am he whom ye seek: what *is* the cause wherefore ye are come?

22 And they said, Cornelius the centurion, a just man, and one that feareth God, and ^Rof good report among all the nation of the Jews, was warned from God by an holy angel to send for thee into his house, and to hear words of thee.   22:12

23 Then called he them in, and lodged *them*. And on the morrow Peter went away with them, ^Rand certain brethren from Jop'-pa accompanied him.   v. 45; 11:12

24 And the morrow after they entered into Caes-a-re'-a. And Cornelius waited for them, and had called together his ^Tkinsmen and ^Tnear friends.   *relatives · close*

25 And as Peter was coming in, Cornelius met him, and fell down at his feet, and worshipped *him*.

26 But Peter ^Ttook him up, saying, ^RStand up; I myself also am a man.   *lifted* · 14:14, 15; Rev. 19:10; 22:8

27 And as he talked with him, he went in, and found many that were come together.

28 And he said unto them, Ye know how that it is an unlawful thing for a man that is a Jew to keep company, or come unto one of another nation; but God hath shewed me that I should not call any man common or unclean.

29 Therefore came I *unto you* without gainsaying, as soon as I was sent for: I ask therefore for what intent ye have sent for me?

30 And Cornelius said, Four days ago I was fasting until this hour; and at the ninth hour I prayed in my house, and, behold, ^Ra man stood before me ^Rin bright clothing,   1:10 · Matt. 28:3; Mark 16:5

31 And said, Cornelius, ^Rthy

prayer is heard, ^Rand thine alms are had in remembrance in the sight of God.   Dan. 10:12 · Heb. 6:10

32 Send therefore to Jop'-pa, and call hither Simon, whose surname is Peter; he is lodged in the house of *one* Simon a tanner by the sea side: who, when he cometh, shall speak unto thee.

33 Immediately therefore I sent to thee; and thou hast well done that thou art come. Now therefore are we all here present before God, to hear all things that are commanded thee of God.

34 Then Peter opened *his* mouth, and said, ^ROf a truth I perceive that God is no respecter of persons: Rom. 2:11; Gal. 2:6; Eph. 6:9

35 But in every nation he that feareth him, and worketh righteousness, is accepted with him.

36 The word which *God* sent unto the children of Israel, preaching peace by Jesus Christ: (^Rhe is Lord of all:)   Rom. 10:12

37 That word, *I say,* ye know, which was ^Tpublished throughout all Ju-dae'-a, and ^Rbegan from Galilee, after the baptism which John preached; *proclaimed* · Luke 4:14

38 How ^RGod anointed Jesus of Nazareth with the Holy Ghost and with power: who went about doing good, and healing all that were oppressed of the devil; for God was with him.   Is. 61:1–3

39 And we are ^Rwitnesses of all things which he did both in the land of the Jews, and in Jerusalem; whom they ^Rslew and hanged on a tree: 1:8 · 2:23

★ 40 Him God raised up the third day, and shewed him openly;

41 ^RNot to all the people, but unto witnesses chosen before of God, *even* to us, who did eat and drink with him after he rose from the dead.   [John 14:17, 19, 22; 15:27]

42 And he commanded us to preach unto the people, and to testify ^Rthat it is he which was ordained of God *to be* the Judge of quick and dead.   John 5:22, 27

43 ^RTo him give all the prophets witness, that through his name

whosoever believeth in him shall receive remission of sins.   [Is. 42:1]

44 While Peter yet spake these words, ^Rthe Holy Ghost fell on all them which heard the word.   4:31

45 And they of the circumcision which believed were astonished, as many as came with Peter, ^Rbecause that on the Gentiles also was poured out the gift of the Holy Ghost.   Is. 42:1, 6; 49:6; Luke 2:32

46 For they heard them speak with tongues, and magnify God. Then answered Peter,

47 Can any man forbid water, that these should not be baptized, which have received the Holy Ghost ^Ras well as we?   2:4; 11:17; 15:8

48 ^RAnd he commanded them to be baptized in the name of the Lord. Then prayed they him to tarry certain days.   1 Cor. 1:14–17

11 And the apostles and brethren that were in Ju-dae'-a heard that the Gentiles had also received the word of God.

2   And when Peter was come up to Jerusalem, ^Rthey that were of the circumcision ^Tcontended with him,   10:45 · *disputed*

3   Saying, ^RThou wentest in to men uncircumcised, ^Rand didst eat with them.   Matt. 9:11 · Gal. 2:12

4   But Peter ^Trehearsed *the matter* from the beginning, and expounded *it* ^Rby^T order unto them, saying,   *explained* · Luke 1:3 · *in*

5   ^RI was in the city of Jop'-pa praying: and in a trance I saw a vision, A certain vessel descend, as it had been a great sheet, let down from heaven by four corners; and it came even to me: 10:9

6   Upon the which when I had fastened mine eyes, I considered, and saw fourfooted beasts of the earth, and wild beasts, and creeping things, and fowls of the air.

7   And I heard a voice saying unto me, Arise, Peter; slay and eat.

8   But I said, Not so, Lord: for nothing common or unclean hath at any time entered into my mouth.

9   But the voice answered me

again from heaven, What God hath cleansed, *that* call not thou common.

10 And this was done three times: and all were drawn up again into heaven.

11 And, behold, immediately there were three men already come unto the house where I was, sent from Caes-a-re′-a unto me.

12 And ᴿthe Spirit bade me go with them, nothing doubting. Moreover these six brethren accompanied me, and we entered into the man's house: 10:19; 15:7

13 And he shewed us how he had seen an angel in his house, which stood and said unto him, Send men to Jop′-pa, and call for Simon, whose surname is Peter;

14 Who shall tell thee words, whereby thou and all thy house shall be saved.

15 And as I began to speak, the Holy Ghost fell on them, ᴿas on us at the beginning.   2:1-4; 15:7-9

16 Then remembered I the word of the Lord, how that he said, ᴿJohn indeed baptized with water; but ye shall be baptized with the Holy Ghost.   Matt. 3:11; Mark 1:8

17 ᴿForasmuch then as God gave them the like gift as *he did* unto us, who believed on the Lord Jesus Christ; ᴿwhat was I, that I could withstand God?   [15:8, 9] · 10:47

18 When they heard these things, they held their peace, and glorified God, saying, ᴿThen hath God also to the Gentiles granted repentance unto life.   Rom. 10:12, 13

19 ᴿNow they which were scattered abroad upon the persecution that arose about Stephen travelled as far as Phe-ni′-ce, and Cyprus, and An′-ti-och, preaching the word to none but unto the Jews only.   8:1, 4

20 And some of them were men of Cyprus and Cy-re′-ne, which, when they were come to An′-ti-och, spake unto ᴿthe Gre′-cians, preaching the Lord Jesus.   6:1; 9:29

21 And ᴿthe hand of the Lord was with them: and a great number believed, and ᴿturned unto the Lord.   2:47; Luke 1:66 · 9:35; 14:1

22 Then tidings of these things came unto the ears of the church which was in Jerusalem: and they sent forth ᴿBarnabas, that he should go as far as An′-ti-och.   4:36

23 Who, when he came, and had seen the grace of God, was glad, and ᴿexhorted them all, that with purpose of heart they would cleave unto the Lord.   13:43; 14:22

24 For he was a good man, and ᴿfull of the Holy Ghost and of faith: ᴿand much people was added unto the Lord.   6:5 · 5:14

25 Then departed Barnabas to ᴿTar′-sus, for to seek Saul: 9:11, 30

26 And when he had found him, he brought him unto An′-ti-och. And it came to pass, that a whole year they assembled themselves with the church, and taught much people. And the disciples were called Christians first in An′-ti-och.

27 And in these days came ᴿprophets from Jerusalem unto An′-ti-och.   2:17; 13:1; 15:32; 21:9

28 And there stood up one of them named ᴿAg′-a-bus, and signified by the Spirit that there should be great dearth throughout all the world: which came to pass in the days of ᴿClaudius Caesar.   21:10; John 16:13 · 18:2

29 Then the disciples, every man according to his ability, determined to send relief unto the brethren which dwelt in Ju-dae′-a:

30 ᴿWhich also they did, and sent it to the elders by the hands of Barnabas and Saul.   12:25

12 Now about that time Herod the king stretched forth *his* hands to ᵀvex certain of the church.   *harass*

2 And he killed James the brother of John with the sword.

3 And because he saw it pleased the Jews, he proceeded further to ᵀtake Peter also. (Then were ᴿthe days of unleavened bread.)   *seize* · 20:6; Ex. 12:15; 23:15

4 And ᴿwhen he had apprehended him, he put *him* in prison,

and delivered *him* to four quaternions of soldiers to keep him; intending after Easter to bring him forth to the people. John 21:18

5 Peter therefore was kept in prison: but prayer was made without ceasing of the church unto God for him.

6 And when Herod would have brought him forth, the same night Peter was sleeping between two soldiers, bound with two chains: and the ᵀkeepers before the door kept the prison.   *guards*

7 And, behold, the angel of the Lord came upon *him*, and a light shined in the prison: and he smote Peter on the side, and raised him up, saying, Arise up quickly. And his chains fell off from *his* hands.

8 And the angel said unto him, Gird thyself, and bind on thy sandals. And so he did. And he saith unto him, Cast thy garment about thee, and follow me.

9 And he went out, and followed him; and ᴿwistᵀ not that it was true which was done by the angel; but thought ᴿhe saw a vision.   Ps. 126:1 · *knew* · 10:3, 17; 11:5

10 When they were past the first and the second ward, they came unto the iron gate that leadeth unto the city; ᴿwhich opened to them of his own accord: and they went out, and passed on through one street; and forthwith the angel departed from him. 5:19; 16:26

11 And when Peter was come to himself, he said, Now I know of a surety, that the Lord hath sent his angel, and ᴿhath delivered me out of the hand of Herod, and *from* all the expectation of the people of the Jews.   2 Cor. 1:10; [2 Pet. 2:9]

12 And when he had considered *the thing*, he came to the house of Mary the mother of John, whose surname was Mark; where many were gathered together praying.

13 And as Peter knocked at the door of the gate, a damsel came to ᵀhearken, named Rhoda.   *answer*

14 And when she knew Peter's voice, she opened not the gate for gladness, but ran in, and told how Peter stood before the gate.

15 And they said unto her, Thou art mad. But she constantly affirmed that it was even so. Then said they, ᴿIt is his angel. Gen. 48:16

16 But Peter continued knocking: and when they had opened *the door*, and saw him, they were astonished.

17 But he, ᴿbeckoning unto them with the hand to hold their peace, declared unto them how the Lord had brought him out of the prison. And he said, Go shew these things unto James, and to the brethren. And he departed, and went into another place.   13:16

18 Now as soon as it was day, there was no small stir among the soldiers, what was become of Peter.

19 And when Herod had sought for him, and found him not, he examined the ᵀkeepers, and commanded that *they* should be put to death. And he went down from Ju-dae'-a to Caes-a-re'-a, and *there* abode.   *guards*

20 And Herod was highly displeased with them of Tyre and Si'-don: but they came with one accord to him, and, having made Blas'-tus the king's chamberlain their friend, desired peace; because their country was nourished by the king's *country.*

21 And upon a set day Herod, ᵀarrayed in royal apparel, sat upon his throne, and made an ᵀoration unto them.   *dressed · speech*

22 And the people ᵀgave a shout, *saying, It is* the voice of a god, and not of a man.   *kept shouting*

23 And immediately the angel of the Lord ᴿsmote him, because he gave not God the glory: and he was eaten of worms, and gave up the ghost. 1 Sam. 25:38; 2 Sam. 24:16, 17

24 But ᴿthe word of God grew and multiplied.   6:7; 19:20; Is. 55:11

25 And ᴿBarnabas and Saul returned from Jerusalem, when they had fulfilled *their* ministry,

and took with them John, whose surname was Mark.   11:30

13 Now there were ᴿin the church that was at An'-ti-och certain prophets and teachers; as ᴿBarnabas, and Simeon that was called Ni'-ger, and Lu'-cius of Cy-re'-ne, and Man'-a-en, which had been brought up with Herod the te'-trarch, and Saul.   14:26 · 11:22

2 As they ministered to the Lord, and fasted, the Holy Ghost said, ᴿSeparate me Barnabas and Saul for the work whereunto I have called them. 9:15; 22:21; Rom. 1:1

3 And when they had fasted and prayed, and laid *their* hands on them, they sent *them* away.

4 So they, being sent forth by the Holy Ghost, departed unto Se-leu'-ci-a; and from thence they sailed to ᴿCyprus.   4:36

5 And when they were at Sal'-a-mis, ᴿthey preached the word of God in the synagogues of the Jews: and they had also ᴿJohn to *their* minister.   [v. 46] · 12:25; 15:37

6 And when they had gone through the isle unto Pa'-phos, they found ᴿa certain sorcerer, a false prophet, a Jew, whose name *was* Bar–je'-sus: 8:9

7 Which was with the ᵀdeputy of the country, Ser'-gi-us Pau'-lus, a prudent man; who called for Barnabas and Saul, and desired to hear the word of God.   *proconsul*

8 But ᴿEl'-y-mas the sorcerer (for so is his name by interpretation) ᵀwithstood them, seeking to turn away the deputy from the faith.   Ex. 7:11; 2 Tim. 3:8 · *opposed*

9 Then Saul, (who also *is called* Paul,) ᴿfilled with the Holy Ghost, set his eyes on him,   2:4; 4:8

10 And said, O full of all subtilty and all mischief, ᴿ*thou* child of the devil, *thou* enemy of all righteousness, wilt thou not cease to pervert the right ways of the Lord? Matt. 13:38; John 8:44; [1 John 3:8]

11 And now, behold, ᴿthe hand of the Lord *is* upon thee, and thou shalt be blind, not seeing the sun for a season. And immediately

there fell on him a mist and a darkness; and he went about seeking some to lead him by the hand.   Ex. 9:3; Ps. 32:4; Heb. 10:31

12 Then the deputy, when he saw what was done, believed, being astonished at the ᵀdoctrine of the Lord.   *teaching*

13 Now when Paul and his company ᵀloosed from Pa'-phos, they came to Per'-ga in Pam-phyl'-i-a: and ᴿJohn departing from them returned to Jerusalem. *set sail* · 15:38

14 But when they departed from Per'-ga, they came to An'-ti-och in Pi-sid'-i-a, and ᴿwent into the synagogue on the sabbath day, and sat down.   16:13

15 And after the reading of the law and the prophets the rulers of the synagogue sent unto them, saying, Ye men *and* brethren, if ye have ᴿany word of exhortation for the people, say on.   Heb. 13:22

16 Then Paul stood up, and beckoning with *his* hand said, Men of Israel, and ᴿye that fear God, ᵀgive audience. 10:35 · *listen*

17 The God of this people of Israel ᴿchose our fathers, and exalted the people when they dwelt as strangers in the land of Egypt, and with an high arm brought he them out of it. Ex. 6:1, 6

18 And ᴿabout the time of forty years suffered he their manners in the wilderness.   Ex. 16:35

19 And when he had destroyed ᴿseven nations in the land of Cha'-naan, ᴿhe divided their land to them by lot.   Deut. 7:1 · Josh. 14:1, 2

20 And after that ᴿhe gave *unto them* judges about the space of four hundred and fifty years, until Samuel the prophet.   Judg. 2:16

21 ᴿAnd afterward they desired a king: and God gave unto them ᴿSaul the son of Cis, a man of the tribe of Benjamin, by the space of forty years. 1 Sam. 8:5 · 1 Sam. 10:20–24

22 And when he had removed him, ᴿhe raised up unto them David to be their king; to whom also he gave testimony, and said, I have found David the *son* of Jesse, ᴿa man after mine own

heart, which shall fulfil all my will. 1 Sam. 16:1, 12, 13 · 1 Sam. 13:14

★ 23 ᴿOf this man's seed hath God according to *his* promise raised unto Israel a Saviour, Jesus: Is. 11:1

24 ᴿWhen John had first preached before his coming the baptism of repentance to all the people of Israel.   Matt. 3:1; [Luke 3:3]

25 And as John fulfilled his course, he said, Whom think ye that I am? I am not *he*. But, behold, ᴿthere cometh one after me, whose shoes of *his* feet I am not worthy to loose.   John 1:20, 27

26 Men *and* brethren, children of the stock of Abraham, and ᴿwhosoever among you feareth God, ᴿto you is the word of this salvation sent.   Ps. 66:16 · Matt. 10:6

27 For they that dwell at Jerusalem, and their rulers, because they knew him not, nor yet the voices of the prophets which are read every sabbath day, they have fulfilled *them* in condemning *him*.

28 And though they found no cause of death *in him,* yet desired they Pilate that he should be slain.

29 And when they had fulfilled all that was written of him, they took *him* down from the tree, and laid *him* in a sepulchre.

30 ᴿBut God raised him from the dead: Ps. 16:10, 11; Hos. 6:2; Matt. 12:39, 40

31 And he was seen many days of them which came up with him from Galilee to Jerusalem, who are his witnesses unto the people.

32 And we declare unto you glad tidings, how that ᴿthe promise which was made unto the fathers,   [Gen. 3:15]

★ 33 God hath fulfilled the same unto us their children, in that he hath raised up Jesus again; as it is also written in the second psalm, ᴿThou art my Son, this day have I begotten thee.   Ps. 2:7; Heb. 1:5

★ 34 And as concerning that he raised him up from the dead, *now* no more to return to corruption, he said on this wise, I will give you the sure mercies of David.

★ 35 Wherefore he saith also in another *psalm,* ᴿThou shalt not

suffer thine Holy One to see corruption.   2:27; Ps. 16:10

36 For David, after he had served ᵀhis own generation by the will of God, ᴿfell on sleep, and was laid unto his fathers, and saw corruption: *in his* · 2:29

37 But he, whom God raised again, saw no ᵀcorruption.   *decay*

38 Be it known unto you therefore, men *and* brethren, that through this man is preached unto you the forgiveness of sins:

39 And ᴿby him all that believe are justified from all things, from which ye could not be justified by the law of Moses. [Is. 53:11; John 3:16]

40 Beware therefore, lest that come upon you, which is spoken of in the prophets;

41 ᴿBehold, ye despisers, and wonder, and perish: for I work a work in your days, a work which ye shall in no wise believe, though a man declare it unto you.   Hab. 1:5

42 And when the Jews were gone out of the synagogue, the Gentiles ᵀbesought that these words might be preached to them the next sabbath.   *begged*

43 Now when the congregation was broken up, many of the Jews and religious proselytes followed Paul and Barnabas: who, speaking to them, persuaded them to continue in the grace of God.

44 And the next sabbath day came almost the whole city together to hear the word of God.

45 But when the Jews saw the multitudes, they were filled with envy, and ᴿspake against those things which were spoken by Paul, contradicting and blaspheming.   18:6; 1 Pet. 4:4; Jude 10

46 Then Paul and Barnabas waxed bold, and said, ᴿIt was necessary that the word of God should first have been spoken to you: but ᴿseeing ye put it from you, and judge yourselves unworthy of everlasting life, lo, ᴿwe turn to the Gentiles. 3:26 · Rom. 10:19 · 18:6

47 For so hath the Lord commanded us, *saying,* I have set thee to be a light of the Gentiles, that ★

thou shouldest be for salvation unto the ends of the earth.

48 And when the Gentiles heard this, they were glad, and glorified the word of the Lord: ^Rand as many as were ordained to eternal life believed. [2:47]

49 And the word of the Lord was published throughout all the region.

50 But the Jews stirred up the devout and ^Thonourable women, and the chief men of the city, and ^Rraised persecution against Paul and Barnabas, and expelled them out of their coasts. *prominent · 7:52*

51 ^RBut they shook off the dust of their feet against them, and came unto I-co'-ni-um. Matt. 10:14

52 And the disciples were filled with joy, and with the Holy Ghost.

14 And it came to pass in I-co'-ni-um, that they went both together into the synagogue of the Jews, and so spake, that a great multitude both of the Jews and also of the Greeks believed.

2 But the unbelieving Jews stirred up the Gentiles, and made their ^Tminds ^Tevil affected against the brethren. Lit. *souls · bitter* or *angry*

3 Long time therefore abode they speaking boldly in the Lord, ^Rwhich gave testimony unto the word of his grace, and granted signs and ^Rwonders to be done by their hands. Mark 16:20; Heb. 2:4 · 5:12

4 But the multitude of the city was ^Rdivided: and part held with the Jews, and part with the ^Rapostles. Luke 12:51 · 13:2, 3

5 And when there was an assault made both of the Gentiles, and also of the Jews with their rulers, ^Rto ^Tuse *them* despitefully, and to stone them, 2 Tim. 3:11 · *abuse*

6 They were ware of *it*, and fled unto Lys'-tra and Der'-be, cities of Lyc-a-o'-ni-a, and unto the region that lieth round about:

7 And there they preached the gospel.

8 ^RAnd there sat a certain man at Lys'-tra, impotent in his feet, being a cripple from his mother's womb, who never had walked: 3:2

9 The same heard Paul speak: who ^Tstedfastly beholding him, and perceiving that he had faith to be healed, *intently observing*

10 Said with a loud voice, ^RStand upright on thy feet. And he leaped and walked. [Is. 35:6]

11 And when the people saw what Paul had done, they lifted up their voices, saying in the speech of Lyc-a-o'-ni-a, ^RThe gods are come down to us in the likeness of men. 8:10; 28:6

12 And they called Barnabas, Jupiter; and Paul, Mer-cu'-ri-us, because he was the chief speaker.

13 Then the priest of Jupiter, which was before their city, brought oxen and garlands unto the gates, ^Rand would have done sacrifice with the people. Dan. 2:46

14 *Which* when the apostles, Barnabas and Paul, heard *of*, they rent their clothes, and ran in among the people, crying out,

15 And saying, Sirs, why do ye these things? ^RWe also are men of like passions with you, and preach unto you that ye should turn from these vanities unto the living God, which made heaven, and earth, and the sea, and all things that are therein: James 5:17

16 ^RWho in times past suffered all nations to walk in their own ways. Ps. 81:12; Mic. 4:5; 1 Pet. 4:3

17 ^RNevertheless he left not himself without witness, in that he did good, and gave us rain from heaven, and fruitful seasons, filling our hearts with food and gladness. 17:24–27; Rom. 1:19, 20

18 And with these sayings scarce restrained they the people, that they had not done sacrifice unto them.

19 ^RAnd there came thither *certain* Jews from An'-ti-och and I-co'-ni-um, who persuaded the people, and, having stoned Paul, drew *him* out of the city, supposing he had been dead. 1 Thess. 2:14

20 Howbeit, as the disciples stood round about him, he rose up, and came into the city: and the

next day he departed with Barnabas to Der'-be.

21 And when they had preached the gospel to that city, ᴿand had taught many, they returned again to Lys'-tra, and *to* I-co'-ni-um, and An'-ti-och,   Matt. 28:19

22 Confirming the souls of the disciples, *and* exhorting them to continue in the faith, and that we must through much tribulation enter into the kingdom of God.

23 And when they had ordained them elders in every church, and had prayed with fasting, they commended them to the Lord, on whom they believed.

24 And after they had passed throughout Pi-sid'-i-a, they came to Pam-phyl'-i-a.

25 And when they had preached the word in Per'-ga, they went down into At-ta-li'-a:

26 And thence sailed to An'-ti-och, from whence they had been ᵀrecommended to the grace of God for the work which they fulfilled.   *commended*

27 And when they were come, and had gathered the church together, they rehearsed all that God had done with them, and how he had ᴿopened the door of faith unto the Gentiles.   1 Cor. 16:9

28 And there they abode long time with the disciples.

15 And ᴿcertain men which came down from Ju-dae'-a taught the brethren, *and said,* ᴿExcept ye be circumcised after the manner of Moses, ye cannot be saved.   Gal. 2:12 · Gal. 5:2; Phil. 3:2

2 When therefore Paul and Barnabas had no small dissension and ᵀdisputation with them, they determined that ᴿPaul and Barnabas, and certain other of them, should go up to Jerusalem unto the apostles and elders about this question.   *dispute* · Gal. 2:1

3 And being brought on their way by the church, they passed through Phe-ni'-ce and Sa-ma'-ri-a, declaring the conversion of the Gentiles: and they caused great joy unto all the brethren.

4 And when they were come to Jerusalem, they were received of the church, and *of* the apostles and elders, and they ᵀdeclared all things that God had done with them.   *reported*

5 But there rose up certain of the sect of the Pharisees which believed, saying, That it was ᵀneedful to circumcise them, and to command *them* to keep the law of Moses.   *necessary*

6 And the apostles and elders came together for to consider of this matter.

7 And when there had been much disputing, Peter rose up, and said unto them, ᴿMen *and* brethren, ye know how that a good while ago God made choice among us, that the Gentiles by my mouth should hear the word of the gospel, and believe.   10:20

8 And God, which knoweth the hearts, bare them witness, ᴿgiving them the Holy Ghost, even as *he did* unto us;   2:4; 10:44, 47

9 ᴿAnd put no difference between us and them, purifying their hearts by faith.   Rom. 10:12

10 Now therefore why tempt ye God, to put a yoke upon the neck of the disciples, which neither our fathers nor we were able to bear?

11 But we believe that through the grace of the Lord Jesus Christ we shall be saved, even as they.

12 Then all the multitude kept silence, and ᵀgave audience to Barnabas and Paul, declaring what miracles and wonders God had ᴿwrought among the Gentiles by them.   *listened* · 14:27

13 And after they had ᵀheld their peace, ᴿJames answered, saying, Men *and* brethren, hearken unto me: *stopped speaking* · 12:17

14 ᴿSimeon hath declared how God at the first did visit the Gentiles, to take out of them a people for his name.   2 Pet. 1:1

15 And to this agree the words of the prophets; as it is written,

16 ᴿAfter this I will return, and will build again the tabernacle of David, which is fallen down; and I

will build again the ruins thereof, and I will set it up: Amos 9:11, 12

17 That the residue of men might seek after the Lord, ^Tand all the Gentiles, upon whom my name is called, saith the Lord, who doeth all these things. *even*

18 Known unto God are all his works from the beginning of the world.

19 Wherefore ^Rmy sentence is, that we trouble not them, which from among the Gentiles ^Rare turned to God: 21:25 · 1 Thess. 1:9

20 But that we write unto them, that they abstain from pollutions of idols, and *from* fornication, ^Rand *from* things strangled, and *from* blood. Lev. 3:17; Deut. 12:16

21 For Moses of old time hath in every city them that preach him, ^Rbeing read in the synagogues every sabbath day. 2 Cor. 3:14

22 Then pleased it the apostles and elders, with the whole church, to send chosen men of their own company to An'-ti-och with Paul and Barnabas; *namely,* Judas surnamed ^RBar'-sa-bas, and Silas, chief men among the brethren: 1:23

23 And they wrote ^T*letters* by them after this manner; The apostles and elders and brethren *send* greeting unto the brethren which are of the Gentiles in An'-ti-och and Syria and Ci-li'-ci-a: this letter

24 Forasmuch as we have heard, that ^Rcertain which went out from us have troubled you with words, ^Rsubverting your souls, saying, *Ye must* be circumcised, and keep the law: to whom we gave no *such* commandment: Gal. 2:4 · Gal. 1:7; 5:10

25 It seemed good unto us, being assembled with one accord, to send chosen men unto you with our beloved Barnabas and Paul,

26 ^RMen that have hazarded their lives for the name of our Lord Jesus Christ. 13:50; 14:19

27 We have sent therefore Judas and Silas, who shall also tell *you* the same things by mouth.

28 For it seemed good to the Holy Ghost, and to us, to lay upon

you no greater burden than these necessary things;

29 ^RThat ye abstain from meats offered to idols, and from blood, and from things strangled, and from fornication: from which if ye keep yourselves, ye shall do well. Fare ye well. 21:25; Rev. 2:14, 20

30 So when they were ^Tdismissed, they came to An'-ti-och: and when they had gathered the multitude together, they delivered the epistle: *sent off*

31 *Which* when they had read, they rejoiced for the consolation.

32 And Judas and Silas, being ^Rprophets also themselves, exhorted the brethren with many words, and confirmed *them*. 11:27

33 And after they had tarried *there* ^Ta space, they were let ^Rgo in peace from the brethren unto the apostles. *for a time* · 1 Cor. 16:11

34 Notwithstanding it pleased Silas to abide there still.

35 ^RPaul also and Barnabas continued in An'-ti-och, teaching and preaching the word of the Lord, with many others also. 13:1

36 And some days after Paul said unto Barnabas, Let us go again and visit our brethren in every city where we have preached the word of the Lord, *and see* how they do.

37 And Barnabas determined to take with them ^RJohn, whose surname was Mark. 12:12, 25; Col. 4:10

38 But Paul thought not good to take him with them, ^Rwho departed from them from Pam-phyl'-i-a, and went not with them to the work. 13:13

39 And the contention was so sharp between them, that they departed asunder one from the other: and so Barnabas took Mark, and sailed unto Cyprus;

40 And Paul chose Silas, and departed, ^Rbeing recommended by the brethren unto the grace of God. 11:23; 14:26

41 And he went through Syria and Ci-li'-ci-a, ^Rconfirming^T the churches. 16:5 · *strengthening*

16 Then came he to Der'-be and Lys'-tra: and, behold, a certain disciple was there, named Ti-mo'-the-us, ᴿthe son of a certain woman, which was a Jewess, and believed; but his father *was* a Greek: 2 Tim. 1:5; 3:15

2 Which was well reported of by the brethren that were at Lys'-tra and I-co'-ni-um.

3 Him would Paul have to go forth with him; and ᴿtook and circumcised him because of the Jews which were in those quarters: for they knew all that his father was a Greek: [1 Cor. 9:20; Gal. 2:3; 5:2]

4 And as they went through the cities, they delivered them the decrees for to keep, that were ordained of the apostles and elders which were at Jerusalem.

5 And ᴿso were the churches established in the faith, and increased in number daily.   2:47

6 Now when they had gone throughout Phryg'-i-a and the region of ᴿGa-la'-ti-a, and were forbidden of the Holy Ghost to preach the word in Asia,   18:23

7 After they were come to My'-si-a, they ᵀassayed to go into Bi-thyn'-i-a: but the Spirit ᵀsuffered them not.   *tried · permitted*

8 And they passing by My'-si-a ᴿcame down to Tro'-as.   20:5

9 And a vision appeared to Paul in the night; There stood a man of Mac-e-do'-ni-a, and prayed him, saying, Come over into Mac-e-do'-ni-a, and help us.

10 And after he had seen the vision, immediately we endeavoured to go ᴿinto Mac-e-do'-ni-a, assuredly gathering that the Lord had called us for to preach the gospel unto them.   2 Cor. 2:13

11 Therefore ᵀloosing from Tro'-as, we came with a straight course to Sam-o-thra'-ci-a, and the next *day* to Ne-ap'-o-lis;   *sailing*

12 And from thence to ᴿPhi-lip'-pi, which is the chief city of that part of Mac-e-do'-ni-a, *and* a colony: and we were in that city abiding certain days.   20:6; Phil. 1:1

13 And on the sabbath we went out of the city by a river side, where prayer was ᵀwont to be made; and we sat down, and spake unto the women which ᵀresorted *thither.*   *customarily · met*

14 And a certain woman named Lyd'-i-a, a seller of purple, of the city of ᴿThy-a-ti'-ra, which worshipped God, heard *us:* whose heart the Lord opened, that she attended unto the things which were spoken of Paul.   Rev. 1:11; 2:18

15 And when she was baptized, and her household, she besought *us,* saying, If ye have judged me to be faithful to the Lord, come into my house, and abide *there.* And ᴿshe constrained us.   Luke 24:29

16 And it came to pass, as we went to prayer, a certain damsel ᴿpossessed with a spirit of divination met us, which brought her masters much gain by ᵀsoothsaying: Lev. 19:31; 20:6 · *fortune-telling*

17 The same followed Paul and us, and cried, saying, These men are the servants of the most high God, which shew unto us the way of salvation.

18 And this did she many days. But Paul, ᴿbeing grieved, turned and said to the spirit, I command thee in the name of Jesus Christ to come out of her. And he came out the same hour.   Mark 1:25, 34

19 And ᴿwhen her masters saw that the hope of their gains was gone, they caught Paul and Silas, and drew *them* into the marketplace unto the rulers,   19:25, 26

20 And brought them to the magistrates, saying, These men, being Jews, ᴿdo exceedingly trouble our city,   1 Kin. 18:17

21 And teach customs, which are not lawful for us to receive, neither to observe, being Romans.

22 And the multitude rose up together against them: and the magistrates rent off their clothes, and commanded to beat *them.*

23 And when they had laid many stripes upon them, they cast *them* into prison, charging the jailor to keep them ᵀsafely: *securely*

24 Who, having received such a

charge, thrust them into the inner prison, and ᵀmade their feet fast in the stocks. *fastened their feet in*

25 And at midnight Paul and Silas ᵀprayed, and sang praises unto God: and the prisoners heard them. *were praying and singing hymns*

26 ᴿAnd suddenly there was a great earthquake, so that the foundations of the prison were shaken: and immediately ᴿall the doors were opened, and every one's bands were loosed. 4:31 · 5:19

27 And the keeper of the prison awaking out of his sleep, and seeing the prison doors open, he drew out his sword, and would have killed himself, supposing that the prisoners had been fled.

28 But Paul cried with a loud voice, saying, Do thyself no harm: for we are all here.

29 Then he called for a light, and ᵀsprang in, and came trembling, and fell down before Paul and Silas, *ran*

30 And brought them out, and said, ᴿSirs, what must I do to be saved? 2:37; 9:6; 22:10; Luke 3:10

31 And they said, Believe on the Lord Jesus Christ, and thou shalt be saved, and thy house.

32 And they spake unto him the word of the Lord, and to all that were in his house.

33 And he took them the same hour of the night, and washed *their* stripes; and was baptized, he and all his, straightway.

34 And when he had brought them into his house, he set meat before them, and rejoiced, believing in God with all his house.

35 And when it was day, the magistrates sent the serjeants, saying, Let those men go.

36 And the keeper of the prison told this saying to Paul, The magistrates have sent to let you go: now therefore depart, and go in peace.

37 But Paul said unto them, They have beaten us openly uncondemned, being Romans, and have cast *us* into prison; and now do they thrust us out privily?

nay verily; but let them come themselves and fetch us out.

38 And the ᵀserjeants told these words unto the magistrates: and they feared, when they heard that they were Romans. Lit. *rodbearers*

39 And they came and besought them, and brought *them* out, and ᴿdesiredᵀ *them* to depart out of the city. Matt. 8:34 · *asked*

40 And they went out of the prison, ᴿand entered into *the house of* Lyd'-i-a: and when they had seen the brethren, they comforted them, and departed. v. 14

17 Now when they had passed through Am-phip'-o-lis and Ap-ol-lo'-ni-a, they came to ᴿThes-sa-lo-ni'-ca, where was a synagogue of the Jews: 1 Thess. 1:1

2 And Paul, as his manner was, went in unto them, and three sabbath days ᴿreasoned with them out of the scriptures, 1 Thess. 2:1–16

3 Opening and alleging, ᴿthat Christ must needs have suffered, and risen again from the dead; and that this Jesus, whom I preach unto you, is Christ. Gal. 3:1

4 And some of them believed, and consorted with Paul and ᴿSilas; and of the devout Greeks a great multitude, and of the chief women not a few. 15:22, 27, 32, 40

5 But the Jews which believed not, moved with ᴿenvy, took unto them certain lewd fellows of the baser sort, and gathered a company, and set all the city on an uproar, and assaulted the house of Ja'-son, and sought to bring them out to the people. 13:45

6 And when they found them not, they ᵀdrew Ja'-son and certain brethren unto the rulers of the city, crying, ᴿThese that have turned the world upside down are come hither also; *dragged* · [16:20]

7 Whom Ja'-son hath received: and these all do contrary to the decrees of Caesar, saying that there is another king, *one* Jesus.

8 And they troubled the people and the rulers of the city, when they heard these things.

9 And when they had taken

security of Ja′-son, and of the ᵀother, they let them go.   *rest*

10 And ᴿthe brethren immediately sent away Paul and Silas by night unto Be-re′-a: who coming *thither* went into the synagogue of the Jews.   v. 14; 9:25

11 These were more noble than those in Thes-sa-lo-ni′-ca, in that they received the word with all readiness of mind, and ᴿsearched the scriptures daily, whether those things were so.   Is. 34:16

12 Therefore many of them believed; also of honourable women which were Greeks, and of men, not a few.

13 But when the Jews of Thes-sa-lo-ni′-ca had knowledge that the word of God was preached of Paul at Be-re′-a, they came thither also, and stirred up the people.

14 And then immediately the brethren sent away Paul to go as it were to the sea: but Silas and Ti-mo′-the-us abode there still.

15 And they that conducted Paul brought him unto Athens: and ᴿreceiving a commandment unto Silas and Ti-mo′-the-us for to come to him with all speed, they departed.   18:5

16 Now while Paul waited for them at Athens, his spirit was stirred in him, when he saw the city wholly given to idolatry.

17 Therefore disputed he in the synagogue with the Jews, and with the ᵀdevout persons, and in the market daily with them that met with him.   Gentile *worshippers*

18 Then certain philosophers of the Ep-i-cu-re′-ans, and of the Sto′-icks, encountered him. And some said, What will this babbler say? other some, He seemeth to be a setter forth of strange gods: because he preached unto them Jesus, and the resurrection.

19 And they took him, and brought him unto Ar-e-op′-a-gus, saying, May we know what this new doctrine, whereof thou speakest, *is?*

20 For thou bringest certain strange things to our ears: we would know therefore what these things mean.

21 (For all the A-the′-ni-ans and ᵀstrangers which were there spent their time in nothing else, but either to tell, or to hear some new thing.)   *foreigners*

22 Then Paul stood in the midst of Mars′ hill, and said, Ye men of Athens, I perceive that in all things ye are too superstitious.

23 For as I passed by, and beheld your ᵀdevotions, I found an altar with this inscription, TO THE UNKNOWN GOD. Whom therefore ye ignorantly worship, him declare I unto you.   *objects of worship*

24 ᴿGod that made the world and all things therein, seeing that he is ᴿLord of heaven and earth, dwelleth not in temples made with hands;   14:15 · Matt. 11:25

25 Neither is worshipped with men's hands, as though he needed any thing, seeing he giveth to all life, and breath, and all things;

26 And hath made of one blood all nations of men for to dwell on all the face of the earth, and hath determined the times before appointed, and ᴿthe bounds of their habitation;   Deut. 32:8; Job 12:23

27 That they should seek the Lord, if haply they might feel after him, and find him, though he be not far from every one of us:

28 For in him we live, and move, and have our being; as certain also of your own poets have said, For we are also his offspring.

29 Forasmuch then as we are the offspring of God, we ought not to think that the Godhead is like unto gold, or silver, or stone, graven by art and man's device.

30 And ᴿthe times of this ignorance God winked at; but ᴿnow commandeth all men every where to repent: 14:16 · Luke 24:47

31 Because he hath appointed a day, in the which he will judge the world in righteousness by *that* man whom he hath ordained; *whereof* he hath given assurance unto all *men,* in that ᴿhe hath raised him from the dead.   2:24

32 And when they heard of the resurrection of the dead, some mocked: and others said, We will hear thee again of this *matter.*

33 So Paul departed from among them.

34 Howbeit certain men [T]clave unto him, and believed: among the which *was* Di-o-nys'-i-us the Ar-e-op'-a-gite, and a woman named Dam'-a-ris, and others with them. *joined*

18 After these things Paul departed from Athens, and came to Corinth;

2 And found a certain Jew named [R]Aq'-ui-la, born in Pon'-tus, lately come from Italy, with his wife Priscilla; (because that Claudius had commanded all Jews to depart from Rome:) and came unto them. 1 Cor. 16:19

3 And because he was of the same craft, he abode with them, [R]and wrought: for by their occupation they were tentmakers. 20:34

4 And he reasoned in the synagogue every sabbath, and persuaded the Jews and the Greeks.

5 And [R]when Silas and Ti-mo'-the-us were come from Mac-e-do'-ni-a, Paul was pressed in the spirit, and testified to the Jews *that* Jesus *was* Christ. 17:14, 15

6 And [R]when they opposed themselves, and blasphemed, [R]he shook *his* raiment, and said unto them, [R]Your blood *be* upon your own heads; I *am* clean: [R]from henceforth I will go unto the Gentiles. 13:45 · 13:51 · 20:26 · 28:28

7 And he departed thence, and entered into a certain *man's* house, named Justus, *one* that worshipped God, whose house joined hard to the synagogue.

8 [R]And Cris'-pus, the chief ruler of the synagogue, believed on the Lord with all his [T]house; and many of the Corinthians hearing believed, and were baptized. 1 Cor. 1:14 · *household*

9 Then [R]spake the Lord to Paul in the night by a vision, Be not afraid, but speak, and [T]hold not thy peace: 23:11 · *do not keep silent*

10 [R]For I am with thee, and no man shall [T]set on thee to hurt thee: for I have much people in this city. Jer. 1:18, 19 · *attack*

11 And he continued *there* a year and six months, teaching the word of God among them.

12 And when Gal'-li-o was the deputy of A-cha'-ia, the Jews [T]made insurrection with one accord against Paul, and brought him to the judgment seat, *rose up*

13 Saying, This *fellow* persuadeth men to worship God contrary to the law.

14 And when Paul was now about to open *his* mouth, Gal'-li-o said unto the Jews, If it were a matter of wrong or wicked lewdness, O *ye* Jews, reason would that I should bear with you:

15 But if it be a [R]question of words and names, and *of* your law, look ye *to it*; for I will be no judge of such *matters.* 23:29; 25:19

16 And he drave them from the judgment seat.

17 Then all the Greeks took [R]Sos'-the-nes, the chief ruler of the synagogue, and beat *him* before the judgment seat. And Gal'-li-o [T]cared for none of those things. 1 Cor. 1:1 · *took no notice*

18 And Paul *after this* tarried *there* yet a good while, and then took his leave of the brethren, and sailed thence into Syria, and with him Priscilla and Aq'-ui-la; having [R]shorn *his* head in Cen'-chre-a: for he had a vow. Num. 6:2, 5, 9, 18

19 And he came to Eph'-e-sus, and left them there: but he himself entered into the synagogue, and reasoned with the Jews.

20 When they [T]desired *him* to [T]tarry longer time with them, he consented not; *asked · stay a*

21 But bade them farewell, saying, [R]I must by all means keep this feast that cometh in Jerusalem: but I will return again unto you, [R]if God will. And he sailed from Eph'-e-sus. 19:21; 20:16 · James 4:15

22 And when he had landed at [R]Caes-a-re'-a, and gone up, and

[T]saluted the church, he went down to An'-ti-och.　　8:40 · *greeted*

23 And after he had spent some time *there*, he departed, and went over *all* the country of [R]Ga-la'-ti-a and Phryg'-i-a in order, strengthening all the disciples.　　Gal. 1:2

24 And a certain Jew named A-pol'-los, born at Alexandria, an eloquent man, *and* mighty in the scriptures, came to Eph'-e-sus.

25 This man was instructed in the way of the Lord; and being [R]fervent in the spirit, he spake and taught diligently the things of the Lord, [R]knowing only the baptism of John.　　Rom. 12:11 · 19:3; [Matt. 3:1–11]

26 And he began to speak boldly in the synagogue: whom when Aq'-ui-la and Priscilla had heard, they took him unto *them*, and [T]expounded unto him the way of God more perfectly.　　*explained*

27 And when he was disposed to pass into A-cha'-ia, the brethren wrote, exhorting the disciples to receive him: who, when he was come, helped them much which had believed through grace:

28 For he mightily [T]convinced the Jews, *and that* publickly, [R]shewing by the scriptures that Jesus was Christ.　　*refuted* · 9:22; 17:3

19 And it came to pass, that, while [R]A-pol'-los was at Corinth, Paul having passed through the upper coasts came to Eph'-e-sus: and finding certain disciples,　　1 Cor. 1:12; 3:5, 6; Titus 3:13

2 He said unto them, Have ye received the Holy Ghost since ye believed? And they said unto him, We have not so much as heard whether there be any Holy Ghost.

3 And he said unto them, Unto what then were ye baptized? And they said, Unto John's baptism.

4 Then said Paul, [R]John verily baptized with the baptism of repentance, saying unto the people, that they should believe on him which should come after him, that is, on Christ Jesus.　　Matt. 3:11

5 When they heard *this*, they were baptized [R]in the name of the Lord Jesus.　　8:12, 16; 10:48

6 And when Paul had laid *his* hands upon them, the Holy Ghost came on them; and [R]they spake with tongues, and prophesied.　2:4

7 And all the men were about twelve.

8 [R]And he went into the synagogue, and spake boldly for the space of three months, disputing and persuading the things concerning the kingdom of God.　17:2

9 But [R]when divers were hardened, and believed not, but spake evil of that way before the multitude, he departed from them, and separated the disciples, disputing daily in the school of one Ty-ran'-nus.　　2 Tim. 1:15; 2 Pet. 2:2; Jude 10

10 And [R]this continued by the space of two years; so that all they which dwelt in Asia heard the word of the Lord Jesus, both Jews and Greeks.　　20:31

11 And [R]God wrought special miracles by the hands of Paul: 14:3

12 [R]So that from his body were brought unto the sick handkerchiefs or aprons, and the diseases departed from them, and the evil spirits went out of them.　　5:15

13 Then certain of the vagabond Jews, exorcists, [R]took upon them to call over them which had evil spirits the name of the Lord Jesus, saying, We adjure you by Jesus whom Paul preacheth.　　Luke 9:49

14 And there were seven sons of *one* Sce'-va, a Jew, *and* chief of the priests, which did so.

15 And the evil spirit answered and said, Jesus I know, and Paul I know; but who are ye?

16 And the man in whom the evil spirit was leaped on them, and overcame them, and prevailed against them, so that they fled out of that house naked and wounded.

17 And this was known to all the Jews and Greeks also dwelling at Eph'-e-sus; and [R]fear fell on them all, and the name of the Lord Jesus was magnified. Luke 1:65; 7:16

18 And many that believed came, and confessed, and shewed their deeds.

19 Many of them also which used curious arts brought their books together, and burned them before all *men:* and they counted the price of them, and found *it* fifty thousand *pieces* of silver.

20 ᴿSo mightily grew the word of God and prevailed.　6:7; 12:24

21 ᴿAfter these things were ended, Paul ᴿpurposed in the spirit, when he had passed through Mac-e-do'-ni-a and A-cha'-ia, to go to Jerusalem, saying, After I have been there, I must also see Rome.　Gal. 2:1 · 20:22; 2 Cor. 1:16

22 So he sent into Mac-e-do'-ni-a two of them that ministered unto him, ᴿTi-mo'-the-us and E-ras'-tus; but he himself stayed in Asia for a season.　1 Tim. 1:2

23 And ᴿthe same time there arose no small stir about ᴿthatᵀ way.　2 Cor. 1:8 · 9:2 · *the Way*

24 For a certain *man* named De-me'-tri-us, a silversmith, which made silver shrines for ᵀDiana, brought ᴿno small ᵀgain unto the craftsmen; Gr. *Artemis* · 16:16, 19 · *profit*

25 Whom he called together with the workmen of ᵀlike occupation, and said, Sirs, ye know that by this ᵀcraft we have our wealth.　*similar* · *trade*

26 Moreover ye see and hear, that not alone at Eph'-e-sus, but almost throughout all Asia, this Paul hath persuaded and turned away much people, saying that ᴿthey be no gods, which are made with hands:　1 Cor. 8:4; 10:19; Rev. 9:20

27 So that not only this our craft is in danger to be set at nought; but also that the temple of the great goddess Diana should be despised, and her magnificence should be destroyed, whom all Asia and the world worshippeth.

28 And when they heard *these sayings,* they were full of wrath, and cried out, saying, Great *is* Diana of the E-phe'-sians.

29 And the whole city was filled with confusion: and having caught ᴿGa'-ius and Ar-is-tar'-chus, men of Mac-e-do'-ni-a,

Paul's companions in travel, they rushed with one accord into the theatre.　20:4; Rom. 16:23; 1 Cor. 1:14

30 And when Paul would have entered in unto the people, the disciples ᵀsuffered him not. *allowed*

31 And certain of the ᵀchief of Asia, which were his friends, sent unto him, ᵀdesiring *him* that he would not ᵀadventure himself into the theatre. *officials · pleading · venture*

32 Some therefore cried one thing, and some another: for the assembly was confused; and the ᵀmore part knew not wherefore they were come together. *majority*

33 And they drew Alexander out of the multitude, the Jews putting him forward. And ᴿAlexander beckoned with the hand, and would have made his defence unto the people. 1 Tim. 1:20; 2 Tim. 4:14

34 But when they knew that he was a Jew, all with one voice about the space of two hours cried out, Great *is* Diana of the E-phe'-sians.

35 And when the townclerk had ᵀappeased the people, he said, *Ye* men of Eph'-e-sus, what man is there that knoweth not how that the city of the E-phe'-sians is a worshipper of the great goddess Diana, and of the *image* which fell down from Jupiter? *quieted*

36 Seeing then that these things cannot be spoken against, ye ought to be quiet, and to do nothing rashly.

37 For ye have brought hither these men, which are neither robbers of ᵀchurches, nor yet blasphemers of your goddess. *temples*

38 Wherefore if De-me'-tri-us, and the craftsmen which are with him, have a matter against any man, the ᵀlaw is open, and there are ᵀdeputies: let them implead one another. *courts are · proconsuls*

39 But if ye enquire any thing concerning other matters, it shall be determined in a lawful assembly.

40 For we are in danger to be called in question for this day's uproar, there being no cause

whereby we may give an account of this concourse.

41 And when he had thus spoken, he dismissed the assembly.

20 And after the uproar was ceased, Paul called unto *him* the disciples, and embraced *them,* and ᴿdeparted for to go into Mac-e-do′-ni-a.   1 Cor. 16:5; 1 Tim. 1:3

2 And when he had gone over those parts, and had given them much ᵀexhortation, he came into ᴿGreece,   *encouragement* · 17:15; 18:1

3 And *there* abode three months. And when the Jews laid wait for him, as he was about to sail into Syria, he purposed to return through Mac-e-do′-ni-a.

4 And there accompanied him into Asia Sop′-a-ter of Be-re′-a; and of the Thes-sa-lo′-ni-ans, ᴿAr-is-tar′-chus and Se-cun′-dus; and Ga′-ius of Der′-be, and Ti-mo′-the-us; and of Asia, Tych′-i-cus and Troph′-i-mus.   19:29; Col. 4:10

5 These going before tarried for us at ᴿTro′-as.   2 Cor. 2:12

6 And we sailed away from Phi-lip′-pi after the days of unleavened bread, and came unto them ᴿto Tro′-as in five days; where we abode seven days.   16:8

7 And upon the first *day* of the week, when the disciples came together to break bread, Paul preached unto them, ready to depart on the morrow; and continued his speech until midnight.

8 And there were many lights ᴿin the upper chamber, where they were gathered together.   1:13

9 And there sat in a window a certain young man named Eu′-ty-chus, being fallen into a deep sleep: and as Paul was long preaching, he sunk down with sleep, and fell down from the third ᵀloft, and was taken up dead. *story*

10 And Paul went down, and ᴿfell on him, and embracing *him* said, Trouble not yourselves; for his life is in him.   1 Kin. 17:21

11 When he therefore was come up again, and had broken bread, and eaten, and talked a long while, even till break of day, so he departed.

12 And they brought the young man alive, and were not a little comforted.

13 And we went before to ship, and sailed unto As′-sos, there intending to take in Paul: for so had he ᵀappointed, ᵀminding himself to go afoot.   *ordered · intending*

14 And when he met with us at As′-sos, we took him in, and came to Mit-y-le′-ne.

15 And we sailed thence, and came the next *day* over against Chi′-os; and the next *day* we arrived at Sa′-mos, and tarried at Tro-gyl′-li-um; and the next *day* we came to Mi-le′-tus.

16 For Paul had determined to sail by Eph′-e-sus, because he would not spend the time in Asia: for ᴿhe hasted, if it were possible for him, to be at Jerusalem the day of Pentecost.   18:21; 19:21; 21:4

17 And from Mi-le′-tus he sent to Eph′-e-sus, and called the elders of the church.

18 And when they were come to him, he said unto them, Ye know, ᴿfrom the first day that I came into Asia, after what manner I have been with you at all ᵀseasons,   vv. 4, 16; 18:19; 19:1, 10 · *times*

19 Serving the Lord with all humility of mind, and with many tears, and ᵀtemptations, which befell me ᴿby the ᵀlying in wait of the Jews: *trials* · v. 3 · *plotting*

20 *And* how ᴿI kept back nothing that was profitable *unto you,* but have shewed you, and have taught you publickly, and from house to house,   v. 27

21 ᴿTestifying both to the Jews, and also to the Greeks, repentance toward God, and faith toward our Lord Jesus Christ. 18:5

22 And now, behold, ᴿI go bound in the spirit unto Jerusalem, not knowing the things that shall befall me there: 19:21

23 ᵀSave that ᴿthe Holy Ghost witnesseth in every city, saying that bonds and afflictions ᵀabide me.   *Except* · 21:4, 11 · *await*

24 But none of these things move me, neither count I my life dear unto myself, so that I might finish my course with joy, and the ministry, which I have received of the Lord Jesus, to testify the gospel of the grace of God.

25 And now, behold, I know that ye all, among whom I have gone preaching the kingdom of God, shall see my face no more.

26 Wherefore I take you to record this day, that I *am* ᴿpure from the blood of all *men*. 2 Cor. 7:2

27 For I have not shunned to declare unto you all ᴿthe counsel of God. Luke 7:30; John 15:15; Eph. 1:11

28 ᴿTake heed therefore unto yourselves, and to all the flock, over the which the Holy Ghost ᴿhath made you overseers, to ᵀfeed the church of God, which he hath purchased with his own blood. Luke 12:32 · 1 Cor. 12:28 · *shepherd*

29 For I know this, that after my departing ᴿshall ᵀgrievous wolves enter in among you, not sparing the flock. Ezek. 22:27; Matt. 7:15 · *savage*

30 Also ᴿof your own selves shall men arise, speaking perverse things, to draw away disciples after them. 1 Tim. 1:20; 2 Tim. 1:15

31 Therefore watch, and remember, that ᴿby the space of three years I ceased not to warn every one night and day with tears. 24:17

32 And now, brethren, I commend you to God, and ᴿto the word of his grace, which is able ᴿto build you up, and to give you an inheritance among all them which are sanctified. Heb. 13:9 · 9:31

33 I have coveted no man's silver, or gold, or apparel.

34 Yea, ye yourselves know, ᴿthat these hands have ministered unto my necessities, and to them that were with me. 18:3; 1 Thess. 2:9

35 I have shewed you all things, how that so labouring ye ought to support the weak, and to remember the words of the Lord Jesus, how he said, It is more blessed to give than to receive.

36 And when he had thus spo-

ken, he kneeled down, and prayed with them all.

37 And they all ᴿwept ᵀsore, and ᴿfell on Paul's neck, and kissed him,   21:13 · *freely* · Gen. 45:14

38 Sorrowing most of all for the words which he spake, that they should see his face no more. And they accompanied him unto the ship.

21 And it came to pass, that after we ᵀwere gotten from them, and had launched, we came with a straight course unto ᵀCo'-os, and the *day* following unto Rhodes, and from thence unto Pat'-a-ra: *had departed* · Or Cos

2 And finding a ship sailing over unto Phe-ni'-ci-a, we went aboard, and set ᵀforth.   *sail*

3 Now when we had discovered Cyprus, we left it on the left hand, and sailed into Syria, and landed at Tyre: for there the ship was to unlade her ᵀburden. *cargo*

4 And finding disciples, we ᵀtarried there seven days: ᴿwho said to Paul through the Spirit, that he should not go up to Jerusalem.   *stayed* · [v. 12; 20:23]

5 And when we had accomplished those days, we departed and went our way; and they all brought us on our way, with wives and children, till *we were* out of the city: and ᴿwe kneeled down on the shore, and prayed.   9:40; 20:36

6 And when we had taken our leave one of another, we took ship; and they returned ᴿhome again.   John 1:11

7 And when we had finished *our* ᵀcourse from Tyre, we came to Ptol-e-ma'-is, and ᵀsaluted the brethren, and ᵀabode with them one day.   *voyage · greeted · stayed*

8 And the next *day* we that were of Paul's company departed, and came unto ᴿCaes-a-re'-a: and we entered into the house of Philip ᴿthe evangelist, ᴿwhich was *one* of the seven; and abode with him.   8:40 · 8:5, 26 · 6:5

9 And the same man had four daughters, virgins, ᴿwhich did prophesy.   2:17; Joel 2:28

10 And as we ᵀtarried *there* many days, there came down from Ju-dae'-a a certain prophet, named ᴿAg'-a-bus.   *stayed* · 11:28

11 And when he was come unto us, he took Paul's ᵀgirdle, and bound his own hands and feet, and said, Thus saith the Holy Ghost, ᴿSo shall the Jews at Jerusalem bind the man that owneth this ᵀgirdle, and shall deliver *him* into the hands of the Gentiles.   *belt* · v. 33; 20:23; 22:25

12 And when we heard these things, both we, and they of that place, ᵀbesought him not to go up to Jerusalem.   *begged*

13 Then Paul answered, ᴿWhat mean ye to weep and to break mine heart? for I am ready not to be bound only, but also to die at Jerusalem for the name of the Lord Jesus.   20:24, 37

14 And when he would not be persuaded, we ceased, saying, The will of the Lord be done.

15 And after those days we ᵀtook up our carriages, and went up to Jerusalem.   *packed*

16 There went with us also *certain* of the disciples of Caes-a-re'-a, and brought with them one Mna'-son of Cyprus, an old disciple, with whom we should lodge.

17 ᴿAnd when we were come to Jerusalem, the brethren received us gladly.   15:4

18 And the *day* following Paul went in with us unto ᴿJames; and all the elders were present.   15:13

19 And when he had ᵀsaluted them, ᴿhe declared particularly what things God had wrought among the Gentiles ᴿby his ministry.   *greeted* · 15:4, 12 · 1:17

20 And when they heard *it*, they glorified the Lord, and said unto him, Thou seest, brother, how many thousands of Jews there are which believe; and they are all ᴿzealous of the law: Gal. 1:14

21 And they are informed of thee, that thou teachest all the Jews which are among the Gentiles to forsake Moses, saying that they ought not to circumcise

their children, neither to walk after the customs.

22 What is it therefore? the multitude must ᵀneeds come together: for they will hear that thou art come.   *certainly*

23 Do therefore this that we say to thee: We have four men which have a vow on them;

24 Them take, and purify thyself with them, and ᵀbe at charges with them, that they may ᴿshave *their* heads: and all may know that those things, whereof they were informed concerning thee, are nothing; but *that* thou thyself also walkest orderly, and keepest the law.   *pay their expenses* · 18:18

25 As touching the Gentiles which believe, ᴿwe have written *and* ᵀconcluded that they observe no such thing, save only that they keep themselves from *things* offered to idols, and from blood, and from strangled, and from fornication.   15:19, 20, 29 · *decided*

26 Then Paul took the men, and the next day purifying himself with them entered into the temple, to signify the accomplishment of the days of purification, until that an offering should be offered for every one of them.

27 And when the seven days were almost ended, ᴿthe Jews which were of Asia, when they saw him in the temple, stirred up all the people, and ᴿlaid hands on him,   20:19; 24:18 · 26:21

28 Crying out, Men of Israel, help: This is the man, ᴿthat teacheth all *men* every where against the people, and the law, and this place: and further brought Greeks also into the temple, and hath polluted this holy place.   6:13; 24:6

29 (For they had seen ᵀbefore with him in the city ᴿTroph'-i-mus an E-phe'-sian, whom they supposed that Paul had brought into the temple.)   *previously* · 20:4

30 And ᴿall the city was moved, and the people ran together: and they took Paul, and drew him out of the temple: and forthwith the doors were shut.   16:19; 26:21

31 And as they went about to kill him, tidings came unto the chief captain of the band, that all Jerusalem was in an uproar.

32 Who immediately took soldiers and centurions, and ran down unto them: and when they saw the chief captain and the soldiers, they left beating of Paul.

33 Then the ^Rchief captain came near, and took him, and commanded *him* to be bound with two chains; and demanded who he was, and what he had done. 24:7

34 And some cried one thing, some another, among the multitude: and when he could not know the certainty for the tumult, he commanded him to be carried into the ^Tcastle. *barracks*

35 And when he ^Tcame upon the stairs, so it was, that he was borne of the soldiers for the violence of the ^Tpeople. *reached · mob*

36 For the multitude of the people followed after, crying, ^RAway with him. Luke 23:18; John 19:15

37 And as Paul was to be led into the ^Tcastle, he said unto the ^Tchief captain, May I speak unto thee? Who said, Canst thou speak Greek? *barracks · commander*

38 ^RArt not thou that Egyptian, which before these days madest an uproar, and leddest out into the wilderness four thousand men that were murderers? 5:36

39 But Paul said, ^RI am a man *which am* a Jew of Tar'-sus, *a city* in Ci-li'-ci-a, a citizen of no mean city: and, I beseech thee, suffer me to speak unto the people. 9:11; 22:3

40 And when he had given him ^Tlicence, Paul stood on the stairs, and ^Rbeckoned with the hand unto the people. And when there was made a great silence, he spake unto *them* in the ^RHebrew tongue, saying, *permission · 12:17 · 22:2*

22 Men, ^Rbrethren, and fathers, hear ye my defence *which I make* now unto you. 7:2

2 (And when they heard that he spake in the ^RHebrew tongue to them, they kept the more silence: and he saith,) 21:40

3 ^RI am verily a man *which am* a Jew, born in Tar'-sus, *a city* in Ci-li'-ci-a, yet brought up in this city at the feet of Ga-ma'-li-el, *and* taught according to the perfect manner of the law of the fathers, and was zealous toward God, as ye all are this day. 21:39

4 ^RAnd I persecuted this way unto the death, binding and delivering into prisons both men and women. 8:3; 26:9-11; Phil. 3:6; 1 Tim. 1:13

5 As also the high priest doth bear me witness, and ^Rall the estate of the elders: ^Rfrom whom also I received letters unto the brethren, and went to Damascus, ^Rto bring them which were there bound unto Jerusalem, for to be punished. 23:14; 24:1; 25:15 · 4:5 · 9:2

6 And it came to pass, that, as I made my journey, and was come nigh unto Damascus about noon, suddenly there shone from heaven a great light round about me.

7 And I fell unto the ground, and heard a voice saying unto me, Saul, Saul, why persecutest thou me?

8 And I answered, Who art thou, Lord? And he said unto me, I am Jesus of Nazareth, whom thou persecutest.

9 And ^Rthey that were with me saw indeed the light, and were afraid; but they heard not the voice of him that spake to me. 9:7

10 And I said, What shall I do, Lord? And the Lord said unto me, Arise, and go into Damascus; and there it shall be told thee of all things which are appointed for thee to do.

11 And when I could not see for the glory of that light, being led by the hand of them that were with me, I came into Damascus.

12 And ^Rone An-a-ni'-as, a devout man according to the law, ^Rhaving a good report of all the Jews which dwelt *there*, 9:17 · 10:22

13 Came unto me, and stood, and said unto me, Brother Saul, receive thy sight. And the same hour I looked up upon him.

14 And he said, ^RThe God of our

fathers hath chosen thee, that thou shouldest know his will, and see that Just One, and shouldest hear the voice of his mouth.   3:13

15 ᴿFor thou shalt be his witness unto all men of ᴿwhat thou hast seen and heard.   23:11 · 4:20; 26:16

16 And now why tarriest thou? arise, and be baptized, ᴿand wash away thy sins, ᴿcalling on the name of the Lord.   2:38 · Rom. 10:13

17 And ᴿit came to pass, that, when I was come again to Jerusalem, even while I prayed in the temple, I was in a trance;   9:26; 26:20

18 And ᴿsaw him saying unto me, ᴿMake haste, and get thee quickly out of Jerusalem: for they will not receive thy testimony concerning me.   v. 14 · Matt. 10:14

19 And I said, Lord, ᴿthey know that I imprisoned and ᴿbeat in every synagogue them that believed on thee: v. 4; 8:3 · Matt. 10:17

20 And when the blood of thy martyr Stephen was shed, I also was standing by, and consenting unto his death, and kept the raiment of them that slew him.

21 And he said unto me, Depart: ᴿfor I will send thee far hence unto the Gentiles.   Rom. 1:5; 11:13

22 And they gave him audience unto this word, and *then* lifted up their voices, and said, ᴿAway with such a *fellow* from the earth: for it is not fit that he should live.   21:36

23 And as they cried out, and cast off *their* clothes, and threw dust into the air,

24 The chief captain commanded him to be brought into the castle, and ᵀbade that he should be examined by ᵀscourging; that he might know wherefore they cried so against him.   *said · whipping*

25 And as they bound him with thongs, Paul said unto the centurion that stood by, ᴿIs it lawful for you to scourge a man that is a Roman, and uncondemned?   16:37

26 When the centurion heard *that*, he went and told the ᵀchief captain, saying, Take heed what thou doest: for this man is a Roman.   *commander*

27 Then the chief captain came, and said unto him, Tell me, art thou a Roman? He said, Yea.

28 And the chief captain answered, With a great sum obtained I this freedom. And Paul said, But I was *free* born.

29 Then straightway they departed from him which should have examined him: and the chief captain also was afraid, after he knew that he was a Roman, and because he had bound him.

30 On the morrow, because he would have known the certainty ᵀwherefore he was accused of the Jews, he loosed him from *his* bands, and commanded the chief priests and all their council to appear, and brought Paul down, and set him before them.   *why*

23 And Paul, earnestly beholding the council, said, Men *and* brethren, ᴿI have lived in all good conscience before God until this day.   1 Cor. 4:4; Heb. 13:18

2 And the high priest An-a-ni'-as commanded them that stood by him to smite him on the mouth.

3 Then said Paul unto him, God shall smite thee, *thou* whited wall: for sittest thou to judge me after the law, and commandest me to be smitten contrary to the law?

4 And they that stood by said, Revilest thou God's high priest?

5 Then said Paul, I ᵀwist not, brethren, that he was the high priest: for it is written, ᴿThou shalt not speak evil of the ruler of thy people.   *knew · Ex. 22:28; Eccl. 10:20*

6 But when Paul perceived that the one part were Sad'-du-cees, and the other Pharisees, he cried out in the council, Men *and* brethren, ᴿI am a Pharisee, the son of a Pharisee: ᴿof the hope and resurrection of the dead I am called in question.   26:5 · 24:15, 21; 26:6

7 And when he had so said, there arose a dissension between the Pharisees and the Sad'-du-cees: and the multitude was divided.

8 ᴿFor the Sad'-du-cees say that there is no resurrection, neither

angel, nor spirit: but the Pharisees confess both.   Mark 12:18; Luke 20:27

9   And there arose a great cry: and the scribes *that were* of the Pharisees' part arose, and strove, saying, ᴿWe find no evil in this man: but if a spirit or an angel hath spoken to him, ᴿlet us not fight against God.   25:25; 26:31 · 5:39

10 And when there arose a great dissension, the ᵀchief captain, fearing lest Paul should have been pulled in pieces of them, commanded the soldiers to go down, and to take him by force from among them, and to bring *him* into the ᵀcastle.   *commander · barracks*

11 And the night following the Lord stood by him, and said, Be of good cheer, Paul: for as thou hast testified of me in ᴿJerusalem, so must thou bear witness also at ᴿRome.   21:18, 19; 22:1–21 · 28:16, 17, 23

12 And when it was day, ᴿcertain of the Jews banded together, and bound themselves under ᵀa curse, saying that they would neither eat nor drink till they had ᴿkilled Paul.   25:3 · *an oath* · 26:21; 27:42

13 And they were more than forty which had ᵀmade this conspiracy.   *formed*

14 And they came to the chief priests and ᴿelders, and said, We have bound ourselves under a great curse, that we will eat nothing until we have slain Paul. 4:5, 23

15 Now therefore ye with the council ᵀsignify to the chief captain that he bring him down unto you to morrow, as though ye would enquire something ᵀmore perfectly concerning him: and we, or ever he come near, are ready to kill him.   *suggest · further*

16 And when Paul's sister's son heard of their ᵀlying in wait, he went and entered into the ᵀcastle, and told Paul.   *ambush · barracks*

17 Then Paul called one of the centurions unto *him*, and said, Bring this young man unto the ᵀchief captain: for he hath a certain thing to tell him.   *commander*

18 So he took him, and brought *him* to the chief captain, and said,

Paul the prisoner called me unto *him*, and ᵀprayed me to bring this young man unto thee, who hath something to say unto thee.   *asked*

19 Then the chief captain took him by the hand, and went *with him* aside privately, and asked *him*, What is that thou hast to tell me?

20 And he said, ᴿThe Jews have agreed to ᵀdesire thee that thou wouldest bring down Paul to morrow into the council, as though they would enquire somewhat of him more ᵀperfectly. v. 12 · *ask · fully*

21 But do not thou yield unto them: for there lie in wait for him of them more than forty men, which have bound themselves with an oath, that they will neither eat nor drink till they have killed him: and now are they ready, looking for a promise from thee.

22 So the chief captain *then* let the young man depart, and charged *him, See thou* tell no man that thou hast ᵀshewed these things to me.   *revealed*

23 And he called unto *him* two centurions, saying, Make ready two hundred soldiers to go to Caes-a-re'-a, and horsemen ᵀthreescore and ten, and spearmen two hundred, at ᵀthe third hour of the night;   *seventy* · 9:00 P.M.

24 And provide *them* ᵀbeasts, that they may set Paul on, and bring *him* safe unto Felix the governor.   *mounts*

25 And he wrote a letter after this manner:

26 Claudius Lys'-i-as unto the most excellent governor Felix *sendeth* greeting.

27 This man was taken of the Jews, and should have been killed of them: then came I with an army, and rescued him, having understood that he was a Roman.

28 ᴿAnd when I would have known the cause wherefore they accused him, I brought him forth into their council: 22:30

29 Whom I perceived to be accused ᴿof questions of their law,

Rbut to have nothing laid to his charge worthy of death or of Tbonds. 18:15; 25:19 · 25:25; 26:31 · *chains*
30 And Rwhen it was told me how that the Jews laid wait for the man, I sent straightway to thee, and Rgave commandment to his accusers also to say before thee what *they had* against him. Farewell. v. 20 · 24:8; 25:6
31 Then the soldiers, as it was commanded them, took Paul, and brought *him* by night to An-tip'-a-tris.
32 On the morrow they left the horsemen to go with him, and returned to the Tcastle: *barracks*
33 Who, when they came to RCaes-a-re'-a, and delivered the Repistle to the governor, presented Paul also before him. 8:40 · vv. 26–30
34 And when the governor had read *the letter,* he asked of what province he was. And when he understood that *he was* of RCi-li'-ci-a; 6:9; 21:39
35 RI will hear thee, said he, when thine accusers are also come. And he commanded him to be kept in RHer'-od's judgment hall. 24:1, 10; 25:16 · Matt. 27:27

24 And after Rfive days RAn-a-ni'-as the high priest descended with the elders, and *with* a certain orator *named* Ter-tul'-lus, who informed the governor against Paul. 21:27 · 23:2, 30, 35; 25:2
2 And when he was called forth, Ter-tul'-lus began to accuse *him,* saying, Seeing that by thee we enjoy great Tquietness, and that very worthy deeds are done unto this nation by thy Tprovidence, *peace · foresight*
3 We accept *it* always, and in all places, most noble Felix, with all thankfulness.
4 Notwithstanding, that I be not further tedious unto thee, I pray thee that thou wouldest hear us of thy clemency a few words.
5 RFor we have found this man *a* pestilent *fellow,* and a mover of sedition among all the Jews throughout the world, and a ring-

leader of the sect of the Naza-renes: 6:13; 16:20; 17:6; 21:28; Luke 23:2
6 RWho also hath gone about to profane the temple: whom we took, and would have judged according to our law. 21:28
7 RBut the Tchief captain Lys'-i-as came *upon us,* and with great violence took *him* away out of our hands, 21:33; 23:10 · *commander*
8 RCommanding his accusers to come unto thee: by examining of whom thyself mayest take knowledge of all these things, whereof we accuse him. 23:30
9 And the Jews also assented, saying that these things were so.
10 Then Paul, after that the governor had Tbeckoned unto him to speak, answered, Forasmuch as I know that thou hast been of many years a judge unto this nation, I do the more cheerfully answer for myself: *nodded*
11 Because that thou mayest understand, that there are yet but twelve days since I went up to Jerusalem Rfor to worship. 21:15, 18
12 RAnd they neither found me in the temple disputing with any man, neither raising up the people, neither in the synagogues, nor in the city: 25:8; 28:17
13 Neither can they prove the things whereof they now accuse me.
14 But this I confess unto thee, that after Rthe way which they call heresy, so worship I the RGod of my fathers, believing all things which are written in Rthe law and in the prophets: 9:2 · 2 Tim. 1:3 · 26:22
15 And Rhave hope toward God, which they themselves also allow, Rthat there shall be a resurrection of the dead, both of the just and unjust. 23:6; 26:6, 7; 28:20 · [John 5:28, 29]
16 And Rherein do I exercise myself, to have always a conscience Tvoid of offence toward God, and *toward* men. 23:1 · *without*
17 Now after many years RI came to bring alms to my nation, and offerings. Rom. 15:25–28
18 RWhereupon certain Jews from Asia found me purified in

the temple, neither with multitude, nor with tumult. 21:27; 26:21

19 ^RWho ought to have been here before thee, and object, if they had ought against me. [23:30]

20 Or else let these same *here* say, if they have found any evil doing in me, while I stood before the council,

21 Except it be for this one voice, that I cried standing among them, ^RTouching the resurrection of the dead I am called in question by you this day. [v. 15; 23:6; 28:20]

22 And when Felix heard these things, having more perfect knowledge of *that* ^Rway, he deferred them, and said, When ^RLys'-i-as the chief captain shall come down, I will know the uttermost of your matter. 9:2; 18:26 · 23:26

23 And he commanded a centurion to keep Paul, and to let *him* have liberty, and ^Rthat he should forbid none of his acquaintance to minister or come unto him. 23:16

24 And after certain days, when Felix came with his wife Dru-sil'-la, which was a Jewess, he sent for Paul, and heard him concerning the ^Rfaith in Christ. [Rom. 10:9]

25 And as he reasoned of righteousness, temperance, and judgment to come, Felix trembled, and answered, Go thy way for this time; when I have a convenient ^Tseason, I will call for thee. *time*

26 He hoped also that money should have been given him of Paul, that he might loose him: wherefore he sent for him the oftener, and communed with him.

27 But after two years Por'-cius Festus came into Felix' room: and Felix, willing to shew the Jews a ^Tpleasure, left Paul bound. *favour*

25 Now when Festus was come into the province, after three days he ^Tascended from Caes-a-re'-a to Jerusalem. *went up*

2 Then the high priest and the chief of the Jews informed him against Paul, and besought him,

3 And desired favour against him, that he would send for him to Jerusalem, ^Rlaying wait in the way to kill him. 23:12, 15

4 But Festus answered, that Paul should be kept at Caes-a-re'-a, and that he himself would depart shortly *thither*.

5 Let them therefore, said he, which among you ^Tare able, go down with *me*, and accuse this man, ^Rif there be any wickedness in him. *have authority* · 18:14

6 And when he had ^Ttarried among them more than ten days, he went down unto Caes-a-re'-a; and the next day sitting on the judgment seat commanded Paul to be brought. *remained*

7 And when he was come, the Jews which came down from Jerusalem stood round about, ^Rand laid many and ^Tgrievous complaints against Paul, which they could not prove. 24:5, 13 · *serious*

8 While he answered for himself, ^RNeither against the law of the Jews, neither against the temple, nor yet against Caesar, have I offended any thing at all. 6:13; 24:12

9 But Festus, ^Rwilling to do the Jews a pleasure, answered Paul, and said, ^RWilt thou go up to Jerusalem, and there be judged of these things before me? 24:27 · v. 20

10 Then said Paul, I stand at Caesar's judgment seat, where I ought to be judged: to the Jews have I done no wrong, as thou very well knowest.

11 For if I be an offender, or have committed any thing worthy of death, I refuse not to die: but if there be none of these things whereof these accuse me, no man may deliver me unto them. ^RI appeal unto Caesar. 26:32; 28:19

12 Then Festus, when he had conferred with the council, answered, Hast thou appealed unto Caesar? unto Caesar shalt thou go.

13 And after certain days king A-grip'-pa and Ber-ni'-ce came unto Caes-a-re'-a to ^Tsalute Festus. *greet*

14 And when they had been there many days, Festus declared

Paul's cause unto the king, saying, [R]There is a certain man left [T]in bonds by Felix: 24:27 · *a prisoner*

15 [R]About whom, when I was at Jerusalem, the chief priests and the elders of the Jews informed *me*, desiring *to have* judgment against him. vv. 2, 3; 24:1

16 [R]To whom I answered, It is not the [T]manner of the Romans to deliver any man to die, before that he which is accused have the accusers face to face, and [T]have licence to answer for himself concerning the crime laid against him. vv. 4, 5 · *custom · has opportunity*

17 Therefore, when they were come hither, [R]without any delay on the morrow I sat on the judgment seat, and commanded the man to be brought forth. vv. 6, 10

18 Against whom when the accusers stood up, they brought none accusation of such things as I supposed:

19 [R]But had certain questions against him of their own [T]superstition, and of one Jesus, which was dead, whom Paul affirmed to be alive. 18:14, 15; 23:29 · *religion*

20 And because I [T]doubted of such manner of questions, I asked *him* whether he would go to Jerusalem, and there be judged of these matters. *was uncertain*

21 But when Paul had [R]appealed to be reserved unto the [T]hearing of Augustus, I commanded him to be kept till I might send him to Caesar. vv. 11, 12 · *decision*

22 Then [R]A-grip'-pa said unto Festus, I [T]would also hear the man myself. To morrow, said he, thou shalt hear him. 9:15 · *also would like to*

23 And on the morrow, when A-grip'-pa was come, and Ber-ni'-ce, with great pomp, and was entered into the [T]place of hearing, with the chief captains, and principal men of the city, at Festus' commandment [R]Paul was brought forth. *auditorium · 9:15*

24 And Festus said, King A-grip'-pa, and all men which are here present with us, ye see this man, about whom [R]all the multi-

tude of the Jews have dealt with me, both at Jerusalem, and *also* here, crying that he ought [R]not to live any longer. vv. 2, 3, 7 · 21:36; 22:22

25 But when I found that [R]he had committed nothing worthy of death, and that he himself hath appealed to Augustus, I have determined to send him. 23:9, 29

26 Of whom I have no certain thing to write unto my lord. Wherefore I have brought him forth before you, and specially before thee, O king A-grip'-pa, that, after examination had, I might have somewhat to write.

27 For it seemeth to me unreasonable to send a prisoner, and not withal to signify the crimes *laid* against him.

26 Then A-grip'-pa said unto Paul, Thou art permitted to speak for thyself. Then Paul stretched forth the hand, and answered for himself:

2 I think myself happy, king A-grip'-pa, because I shall answer for myself this day before thee touching all the things whereof I am [R]accused of the Jews: 21:28

3 Especially *because I know* thee to be expert in all customs and questions which are among the Jews: wherefore I beseech thee to hear me patiently.

4 My manner of life from my youth, which was at the first among mine own nation at Jerusalem, know all the Jews;

5 Which knew me from the beginning, if they would testify, that after the most straitest sect of our religion I lived a Pharisee.

6 And now I stand and am judged for the hope of the promise made of God unto our fathers:

7 Unto which *promise* our twelve tribes, [T]instantly serving God [R]day and night, [R]hope to come. For which hope's sake, king A-grip'-pa, I am accused of the Jews. *earnestly · 1 Thess. 3:10 · Phil. 3:11*

8 Why should it be thought a thing incredible with you, that God should raise the dead?

9 [R]I verily thought with myself,

that I ought to do many things contrary to the name of [R]Jesus of Nazareth.   1 Cor. 15:9 · 2:22; 10:38

10 [R]Which thing I also did in Jerusalem: and many of the saints did I shut up in prison, having received authority [R]from the chief priests; and when they were put to death, I gave my voice against *them*.   8:1–3; 9:13; Gal. 1:13 · 9:14

11 [R]And I punished them oft in every synagogue, and compelled *them* to blaspheme; and being exceedingly mad against them, I persecuted *them* even unto strange cities.   22:19; Matt. 10:17;

12 [R]Whereupon as I went to Damascus with authority and commission from the chief priests,   vv. 12–18; 9:3–8; 22:6–11

13 At midday, O king, I saw in the way a light from heaven, above the brightness of the sun, shining round about me and them which journeyed with me.

14 And when we were all fallen to the earth, I heard a voice speaking unto me, and saying in the Hebrew tongue, Saul, Saul, why persecutest thou me? *it is* hard for thee to kick against the pricks.

15 And I said, Who art thou, Lord? And he said, I am Jesus whom thou persecutest.

16 But rise, and stand upon thy feet: for I have appeared unto thee for this purpose, to make thee a minister and a witness both of these things which thou hast seen, and of those things in the which I will appear unto thee;

17 Delivering thee from the people, and *from* the Gentiles, [R]unto whom now I send thee,   22:21

18 To open their eyes, *and* to turn *them* from darkness to light, and *from* the power of Satan unto God, that they may receive forgiveness of sins, and inheritance among them which are [R]sanctified by faith that is in me.   20:32

19 Whereupon, O king A-grip′-pa, I was not disobedient unto the heavenly vision:

20 But [R]shewed first unto them of Damascus, and at Jerusalem,

and throughout all the coasts of Ju-dae′-a, and *then* to the Gentiles, that they should repent and turn to God, and do works meet for repentance.   9:19, 20, 22; 11:26

21 For these causes the Jews [T]caught me in the temple, and went about to kill *me*.   seized

22 Having therefore obtained help of God, I continue unto this day, witnessing both to small and great, saying none other things than those which the prophets and Moses did say should come:

23 [R]That Christ should suffer, *and* that he should be the first that should rise from the dead, and should shew light unto the people, and to the Gentiles.   Luke 24:26

24 And as he thus spake for himself, Festus said with a loud voice, Paul, [R]thou art beside thyself; much learning doth make thee mad.   2 Kin. 9:11; John 10:20

25 But he said, I am not mad, most noble Festus; but speak forth the words of truth and soberness.

26 For the king [R]knoweth of these things, before whom also I speak freely: for I am persuaded that none of these things are hidden from him; for this thing was not done in a corner.   v. 3

27 King A-grip′-pa, believest thou the prophets? I know that thou believest.

28 Then A-grip′-pa said unto Paul, Almost thou persuadest me to be a Christian.

29 And Paul said, I would to God, that not only thou, but also all that hear me this day, were both almost, and altogether such as I am, except these bonds.

30 And when he had thus spoken, the king rose up, and the governor, and Ber-ni′-ce, and they that sat with them:

31 And when they were gone aside, they talked between themselves, saying, [R]This man doeth nothing worthy of death or of [T]bonds.   23:9, 29; 25:25 · chains

32 Then said A-grip′-pa unto Festus, This man might have been

set at [R]liberty, [R]if he had not appealed unto Caesar.   28:18 · 25:11

27 And when [R]it was determined that we should sail into Italy, they delivered Paul and certain other prisoners unto *one* named Julius, a centurion of Augustus' band.   25:12, 25

2 And entering into a ship of Ad-ra-myt'-ti-um, we [T]launched, meaning to sail [T]by the coasts of Asia; *one* [R]Ar-is-tar'-chus, a Mac-e-do'-ni-an of Thes-sa-lo-ni'-ca, being with us.   *set sail · along · 19:29*

3 And the next *day* we touched at Si'-don. And Julius [R]courteously entreated Paul, and gave *him* liberty to go unto his friends to refresh himself.   24:23; 28:16

4 And when we had launched from thence, we sailed [T]under Cyprus, because the winds were contrary.   *under the shelter of*

5 And when we had sailed over the sea of Ci-li'-ci-a and Pam-phyl'-i-a, we came to My'-ra, *a city* of Ly'-ci-a.

6 And there the centurion found a ship of [R]Alexandria sailing into Italy; and he put us therein.   28:11

7 And when we had sailed slowly many days, and scarce were come over against Cni'-dus, the wind not suffering us, we sailed under [R]Crete, over against Sal-mo'-ne;   vv. 12, 21; 2:11; Titus 1:5, 12

8 And, [T]hardly passing it, came unto a place which is called The fair havens; nigh whereunto was the city *of* La-se'-a.   *with difficulty*

9 Now when much time was spent, and when sailing was now dangerous, [R]because the fast was now already past, Paul admonished *them*,   Lev. 16:29–31; 23:27–29

10 And said unto them, Sirs, I perceive that this voyage will be with [T]hurt and much [T]damage, not only of the [T]lading and ship, but also of our lives.   *disaster · loss · cargo*

11 Nevertheless the centurion believed the [T]master and the owner of the ship, more than those things which were spoken by Paul.   *pilot*

12 And because the haven was not [T]commodious to winter in, the more part advised to depart thence also, if by any means they might attain to Phe-ni'-ce, *and there* to winter; *which is* an haven of Crete, and lieth toward the south west and north west.   *suitable*

13 And when the south wind blew softly, supposing that they had obtained *their* purpose, loosing *thence*, they sailed close by Crete.

14 But not long after there arose against it a tempestuous wind, called Eu-roc'-ly-don.

15 And when the ship was caught, and could not bear up into the wind, we let *her* drive.

16 And running under a certain island which is called Clauda, we had much work to [T]come by the boat: *secure the ship's skiff*

17 Which when they had taken up, they used helps, undergirding the ship; and, fearing lest they should fall into the quicksands, strake sail, and so were driven.

18 And we being exceedingly tossed with a tempest, the next *day* they lightened the ship;

19 And the third *day* [R]we cast out with our own hands the tackling of the ship.   Jon. 1:5

20 And when neither sun nor stars in many days appeared, and no small tempest [T]lay on *us*, all hope that we should be saved was then taken away.   *beat*

21 But after long abstinence Paul stood forth in the midst of them, and said, Sirs, ye should have hearkened unto me, and not have loosed from Crete, and to have gained this harm and loss.

22 And now I [T]exhort you to [T]be of good cheer: for there shall be no loss of *any man's* life among you, but of the ship.   *urge · take heart*

23 [R]For there stood by me this night the angel of God, whose I am, and whom I serve,   18:9; 23:11

24 Saying, Fear not, Paul; thou must be brought before Caesar: and, lo, God hath given thee all them that sail with thee.

25 Wherefore, sirs, be of good cheer: for I believe God, that it shall be even as it was told me.

26 Howbeit [R]we must be cast upon a certain island.   28:1

27 But when the fourteenth night was come, as we were driven up and down in A'-dri-a, about midnight the shipmen [T]deemed that they drew near to some [T]country;   sensed · land

28 And sounded, and found *it* twenty fathoms: and when they had gone a little further, they sounded again, and found *it* fifteen fathoms.

29 Then fearing lest we should [T]have fallen upon rocks, they cast four anchors out of the stern, and wished for the day.   run aground

30 And as the [T]shipmen were about to flee out of the ship, when they had let down the [T]boat into the sea, under [T]colour as though they would have cast anchors out of the foreship,   sailors · skiff · pretense

31 Paul said to the centurion and to the soldiers, Except these abide in the ship, ye cannot be saved.

32 Then the soldiers cut off the ropes of the [T]boat, and let her fall off.   skiff

33 And while the day was coming on, Paul besought *them* all to take meat, saying, This day is the fourteenth day that ye have tarried and continued fasting, having [T]taken nothing.   eaten

34 Wherefore I pray you to take *some* meat: for this is for your [T]health: for [R]there shall not an hair fall from the head of any of you.   survival · 1 Kin. 1:52; [Matt. 10:30]

35 And when he had thus spoken, he took bread, and [R]gave thanks to God in presence of them all: and when he had broken *it*, he began to eat.   John 6:11; [1 Tim. 4:3, 4]

36 Then were they all [T]of good cheer, and they also took *some* [T]meat.   encouraged · food

37 And we were in all in the ship two hundred threescore and sixteen [R]souls.   7:14; Rom. 13:1; 1 Pet. 3:20

38 And when they had eaten enough, they lightened the ship, and cast out the wheat into the sea.

39 And when it was day, they [T]knew not the land: but they discovered a certain creek with a shore, into the which they were minded, if it were possible, to thrust in the ship.   did not recognize

40 And when they had taken up the anchors, they committed *themselves* unto the sea, and loosed the rudder bands, and hoised up the mainsail to the wind, and made toward shore.

41 And falling into a place where two seas met, [R]they ran the ship aground; and the forepart stuck fast, and remained unmoveable, but the hinder part was [T]broken with the violence of the waves.   2 Cor. 11:25 · being broken

42 And the soldiers' [T]counsel was to kill the prisoners, lest any of them should swim out, and escape.   plan

43 But the centurion, [T]willing to save Paul, kept them from *their* purpose; and commanded that they which could swim should cast *themselves* first *into the sea*, and get to land: wanting

44 And the rest, some on boards, and some on *broken pieces* of the ship. And so it came to pass, that they escaped all safe to land.

28 And when they were escaped, then they knew that [R]the island was called [T]Mel'-i-ta.   27:26 · Or *Malta*

2 And the barbarous people shewed us no little kindness: for they kindled a fire, and received us every one, because of the present rain, and because of the cold.

3 And when Paul had gathered a bundle of sticks, and laid *them* on the fire, there came a viper out of the heat, and fastened on his hand.

4 And when the barbarians saw the *venomous* beast hang on his hand, they said among themselves, No doubt this man is a murderer, whom, though he hath

escaped the sea, yet [T]vengeance [T]suffereth not to live. *justice · allows*

5 And he shook off the beast into the fire, and felt no harm.

6 Howbeit they looked when he should have swollen, or fallen down dead suddenly: but after they had looked a great while, and saw no harm come to him, they changed their minds, and [R]said that he was a god. 12:22; 14:11

7 In the same [T]quarters were possessions of the chief man of the island, whose name was Pub'-li-us; who received us, and lodged us three days courteously. *region*

8 And it came to pass, that the father of Pub'-li-us lay sick of a fever and of [T]a bloody flux: to whom Paul entered in, and prayed, and laid his hands on him, and healed him. *dysentery*

9 So when this was done, others also, which had diseases in the island, came, and were healed:

10 Who also honoured us with many honours; and when we departed, they laded *us* with such things as were necessary.

11 And after three months we departed in a ship of [R]Alexandria, which had wintered in the isle, whose [T]sign was Castor and Pol'-lux. 27:6 · *figurehead*

12 And landing at Syr'-a-cuse, we tarried *there* three days.

13 And from thence we [T]fetched a compass, and came to Rhe'-gi-um: and after one day the south wind blew, and we came the next day to Pu-te'-o-li: *circled around*

14 Where we found [R]brethren, and were [T]desired to tarry with them seven days: and so we went toward Rome. Rom. 1:8 · *invited to stay*

15 And from thence, when the brethren heard of us, they came to meet us as far as Ap'-pi-i for'-um, and The three [T]taverns: whom when Paul saw, he thanked God, and took courage. *Inns*

16 And when we came to Rome, the centurion delivered the prisoners to the captain of the guard: but [R]Paul was suffered to dwell by himself with a soldier that [T]kept him. 23:11; 24:25; 27:3 · *guarded*

17 And it came to pass, that after three days Paul called the chief of the Jews together: and when they were come together, he said unto them, Men *and* brethren, though I have committed nothing against the people, or customs of our fathers, yet was I delivered prisoner from Jerusalem into the hands of the Romans.

18 Who, [R]when they had examined me, would have let *me* go, because there was no cause of death in me. 22:24; 24:10; 25:8; 26:32

19 But when the Jews spake against *it*, I was constrained to appeal unto Caesar; not that I had ought to accuse my nation of.

20 For this cause therefore have I called for you, to see *you*, and to speak with *you*: because that for the hope of Israel I am bound with [R]this chain. Eph. 3:1; 4:1; 6:20; 2 Tim. 1:8

21 And they said unto him, We neither received letters out of Ju-dae'-a concerning thee, neither any of the brethren that came shewed or spake any [T]harm of thee. *evil*

22 But we desire to hear of thee what thou thinkest: for as concerning this sect, we know that every where it is spoken against.

23 And when they had appointed him a day, there came many to him into *his* lodging; [R]to whom he expounded and testified the kingdom of God, persuading them concerning Jesus, [R]both out of the law of Moses, and *out of* the prophets, from morning till evening. [17:3; 19:8]; Luke 24:27 · 26:6, 22

24 And [R]some believed the things which were spoken, and some believed not. 14:4; 19:9

25 And when they agreed not among themselves, they departed, after that Paul had spoken one word, Well spake the Holy Ghost by E-sa'-ias the prophet unto our fathers,

26 Saying, [R]Go unto this people, ★

and say, Hearing ye shall hear, and shall not understand; and seeing ye shall see, and not perceive: Is. 6:9, 10; Luke 8:10; John 12:40, 41

27 For the heart of this people is waxed gross, and their ears are dull of hearing, and their eyes have they closed; lest they should see with *their* eyes, and hear with *their* ears, and understand with *their* heart, and should be converted, and I should heal them.

★ 28 Be it known therefore unto you, that the salvation of God is sent ᴿunto the Gentiles, and *that* they will hear it. Luke 2:32; Rom. 11:11

29 And when he had said these words, the Jews departed, and had great ᵀreasoning among themselves.　　　　*dispute*

30 And Paul dwelt two whole years in his own ᵀhired house, and received all that came in unto him,　　　　*rented*

31 ᴿPreaching the kingdom of God, and teaching those things which concern the Lord Jesus Christ, with all confidence, no man forbidding him. 4:31; Eph. 6:19

The Epistle of Paul the Apostle to the

ROMANS

ROMANS, Paul's greatest work, is placed first among his thirteen epistles in the New Testament. While the four Gospels present the words and works of Jesus Christ, Romans explores the significance of His sacrificial death. Using a question-and-answer format, Paul records the most systematic presentation of doctrine in the Bible. Romans is more than a book of theology; it is also a book of practical exhortation. The good news of Jesus Christ is more than facts to be believed; it is also a life to be lived—a life of righteousness befitting the person, "justified freely by [God's] grace through the redemption that is in Christ Jesus" (3:24).

Although some manuscripts omit "in Rome" in 1:7, 15, the title *Pros Romaious,* "To the Romans," has been associated with the epistle almost from the beginning.

PAUL, a servant of Jesus Christ, called *to be* an apostle, separated unto the gospel of God,

2 (ᴿWhich he had promised ᵀafore ᴿby his prophets in the holy scriptures,) Acts 26:6 · *before* · Gal. 3:8

★ 3 Concerning his Son Jesus Christ our Lord, which was ᴿmade of the seed of David according to the flesh; Is. 9:7; Jer. 23:5; Gal. 4:4

★ 4 And ᴿdeclared *to be* the Son of God with power, according to the spirit of holiness, by the resurrection from the dead: Heb. 1:2

5 By whom ᴿwe have received grace and apostleship, for ᴿobedience to the faith among all nations, for his name: Eph. 3:8 · Acts 6:7

6 Among whom are ye also the called of Jesus Christ:

7 To all that be in Rome, beloved of God, ᴿcalled *to be* saints: ᴿGrace to you and peace from God our Father, and the Lord Jesus Christ. 1 Cor. 1:2, 24 · Num. 6:25

8 First, I thank my God through Jesus Christ for you all, that ᴿyour faith is spoken of throughout the whole world. 16:19; Acts 28:22

9 For God is my witness, whom I serve with my spirit in the gospel of his Son, that ᴿwithout ceasing I make mention of you always in my prayers; 1 Thess. 3:10

10 Making request, if by any means now at ᵀlength I might

have a prosperous journey by the will of God to come unto you. *last*

11 For I long to see you, that [R]I may impart unto you some spiritual gift, to the end ye may be established; 15:29

12 That is, that I may be [T]comforted together with you by [R]the mutual faith both of you and me. *encouraged · Titus 1:4*

13 Now I would not have you ignorant, brethren, that oftentimes I purposed to come unto you, (but was [T]let hitherto,) that I might have some [R]fruit among you also, even as among other Gentiles. *hindered · Phil. 4:17*

14 I am debtor both to the Greeks, and to the Barbarians; both to the wise, and to the unwise.

15 So, as much as in me is, I am ready to preach the gospel to you that are at Rome also.

16 For I am not ashamed of the gospel of Christ: for it is the power of God unto salvation to every one that believeth; to the Jew first, and also to the Greek.

17 For therein is the righteousness of God revealed from faith to faith: as it is written, [R]The just shall live by faith. Hab. 2:4; Gal. 3:11

18 [R]For the wrath of God is revealed from heaven against all ungodliness and unrighteousness of men, who [T]hold the truth in unrighteousness; [Acts 17:30] · *suppress*

19 Because [R]that which may be known of God is manifest in them; for [R]God hath shewed *it* unto them. [Acts 14:17; 17:24] · [John 1:9]

20 For [R]the invisible things of him from the creation of the world are clearly seen, being understood by the things that are made, *even* his eternal power and Godhead; so that they are without excuse: Job 12:7-9; Ps. 19:1-6; Jer. 5:22

21 Because that, when they knew God, they glorified *him* not as God, neither were thankful; but [R]became vain in their imaginations, and their foolish heart was darkened. 2 Kin. 17:15; Jer. 2:5; Eph. 4:17

22 [R]Professing themselves to be wise, they became fools, [1 Cor. 1:20]

23 And changed the glory of the [R]uncorruptible God into an image made like to corruptible man, and to birds, and fourfooted beasts, and creeping things. 1 Tim. 1:17

24 Wherefore God also gave them up to uncleanness through the lusts of their own hearts, to dishonour their own bodies [R]between themselves: Lev. 18:22

25 Who changed the truth of God [R]into a lie, and worshipped and served the creature more than the Creator, who is blessed for ever. A-men'. Is. 44:20; Jer. 10:14

26 For this cause God gave them up unto [R]vile affections: for even their women did change the natural use into that which is against nature: Lev. 18:22; Eph. 5:12

27 And likewise also the men, leaving the natural use of the woman, burned in their lust one toward another; men with men working that which is [T]unseemly, and receiving in themselves that [T]recompence of their error which was [T]meet. *shameful · penalty · due*

28 And even as they did not like to retain God in *their* knowledge, God gave them over to a [T]reprobate mind, to do those things which are not convenient; *debased*

29 Being filled with all unrighteousness, fornication, wickedness, covetousness, maliciousness; full of envy, murder, debate, deceit, malignity; whisperers,

30 Backbiters, haters of God, [T]despiteful, proud, boasters, inventors of evil things, disobedient to parents, *violent*

31 Without understanding, covenantbreakers, without natural affection, [T]implacable, unmerciful: *unforgiving*

32 Who [R]knowing the [T]judgment of God, that they which commit such things [R]are worthy of death, not only do the same, but have pleasure in them that do them. [2:2] · *righteous judgment* · [6:21]

2 Therefore thou art [R]inexcusable, O man, whosoever thou

art that judgest: Rfor wherein thou judgest another, thou condemnest thyself; for thou that judgest doest the same things.   [1:20] · [Matt. 7:1–5]

2 But we are sure that the judgment of God is according to truth against them which commit such things.

3 And thinkest thou this, O man, that judgest them which do such things, and doest the same, that thou shalt escape the judgment of God?

4 Or despisest thou the riches of his goodness and forbearance and longsuffering; Rnot knowing that the goodness of God leadeth thee to repentance?   [2 Pet. 3:9, 15]

5 But after thy hardness and impenitent heart treasurest up unto thyself wrath against the day of wrath and revelation of the righteous judgment of God;

6 Who will render to every man according to his deeds:

7 To them who by patient continuance in well doing seek for glory and honour and immortality, eternal life:

8 But unto them that are contentious, and Rdo not obey the truth, but obey unrighteousness, indignation and wrath,   [2 Thess. 1:8]

9 Tribulation and anguish, upon every soul of man that doeth evil, of the Jew Rfirst, and also of the Gentile;   1:16; Luke 12:47; Acts 3:26

10 RBut glory, honour, and peace, to every man that worketh good, to the Jew first, and also to the Gentile: v. 7; Heb. 2:7; [1 Pet. 1:7]

11 For Rthere is no respect of persons with God.   Acts 10:34

12 For as many as have sinned without law shall also perish without law: and as many as have sinned in the law shall be judged by the law;

13 (For not the hearers of the law are just before God, but the doers of the law shall be justified.

14 For when the Gentiles, which have not the law, do by nature the things contained in the law, these, having not the law, are a law unto themselves:

15 Which shew the Rwork of the law written in their hearts, their Rconscience also bearing witness, and their thoughts the mean while accusing or else excusing one another;)   1 Cor. 5:1 · Acts 24:25

16 In the day when God shall judge the secrets of men by Jesus Christ according to my gospel.

17 Behold, thou art called a Jew, and Rrestest in the law, and makest thy boast of God,   v. 23; 9:4

18 And Rknowest his will, and Rapprovest the things that are more excellent, being instructed out of the law;   Deut. 4:8 · Phil. 1:10

19 And Rart confident that thou thyself art a guide of the blind, a light of them which are in darkness,   Matt. 15:14; John 9:34

20 An instructor of the foolish, a teacher of babes, Rwhich hast the form of knowledge and of the truth in the law.   [2 Tim. 3:5]

21 Thou therefore which teachest another, teachest thou not thyself? thou that preachest a man should not steal, dost thou steal?

22 Thou that sayest a man should not commit adultery, dost thou commit adultery? thou that abhorrest idols, Rdost thou commit sacrilege?   Mal. 3:8

23 Thou that Rmakest thy boast of the law, through breaking the law dishonourest thou God?   9:4

24 For the name of God is blasphemed among the Gentiles through you, as it is written.

25 RFor circumcision verily profiteth, if thou keep the law: but if thou be a breaker of the law, thy circumcision is made uncircumcision.   Gen. 17:10–14; [Gal. 5:3]

26 Therefore if the uncircumcision keep the righteousness of the law, shall not his uncircumcision be counted for circumcision?

27 And shall not uncircumcision which is Tby nature, if Tit fulfil the law, Rjudge thee, who by the letter and circumcision dost transgress the law?   physical · he · Matt. 12:41

28 For Rhe is not a Jew, which is

one outwardly; neither *is that* circumcision, which is outward in the flesh: John 8:39; [Gal. 6:15]

29 But he *is* a Jew, which is one inwardly; and circumcision *is that* of the heart, in the spirit, *and* not in the letter; ^Rwhose praise *is* not of men, but of God. John 5:44

3 What advantage then hath the Jew? or what profit *is there* of circumcision?

2 Much every way: chiefly, because that ^Runto them were committed the oracles of God. Ps. 147:19

3 For what if some did not believe? shall their unbelief make the faith of God without effect?

4 God forbid: yea, let ^RGod be true, but ^Revery man a liar; as it is written, ^RThat thou mightest be justified in thy sayings, and mightest overcome when thou art judged. [John 3:33] · Ps. 62:9 · Ps. 51:4

5 But if our unrighteousness commend the righteousness of God, what shall we say? *Is* God unrighteous who taketh vengeance? (^RI speak as a man) 6:19

6 God forbid: for then how shall God judge the world?

7 For if the truth of God hath more abounded through my lie unto his glory; why yet am I also judged as a sinner?

8 And not *rather,* (as we be slanderously reported, and as some affirm that we say,) ^RLet us do evil, that good may come? whose damnation is just. 5:20

9 What then? are we better *than they?* No, in no wise: for we have before proved both Jews and Gentiles, that ^Rthey are all under sin; vv. 19, 23; 11:32; Gal. 3:22

10 As it is written, ^RThere is none righteous, no, not one: Ps. 14:3

11 There is none that understandeth, there is none that seeketh after God.

12 They are all gone out of the way, they are together become unprofitable; there is none that doeth good, no, not one.

13 ^RTheir throat *is* an open sepulchre; with their tongues they

have used deceit; the poison of asps *is* under their lips: Ps. 5:9

14 ^RWhose mouth *is* full of cursing and bitterness: Ps. 10:7

15 ^RTheir feet *are* swift to shed blood: Prov. 1:16; Is. 59:7, 8

16 Destruction and misery *are* in their ways:

17 And the way of peace have they not known:

18 ^RThere is no fear of God before their eyes. Ps. 36:1

19 Now we know that what things soever the law saith, it saith to them who are under the law: that ^Revery mouth may be stopped, and all the world may become guilty before God. Job 5:16

20 Therefore ^Rby the deeds of the law there shall no flesh be justified in his sight: for by the law *is* the knowledge of sin. Ps. 143:2

21 But now the righteousness of God without the law is manifested, ^Rbeing witnessed by the law and the prophets; John 5:46

22 Even the righteousness of God *which is* by faith of Jesus Christ unto all and upon all them that believe: for ^Rthere is no difference: 10:12; [Gal. 3:28; Col. 3:11]

23 For all have sinned, and come short of the glory of God;

24 Being justified freely ^Rby his grace through the redemption that is in Christ Jesus: [Eph. 2:8]

25 Whom God hath set forth ^R*to be* a propitiation through faith in his blood, to declare his righteousness for the remission of sins that are past, through the forbearance of God; Lev. 16:15

26 To declare, *I say,* at this time his righteousness: that he might be just, and the justifier of him which believeth in Jesus.

27 ^RWhere *is* boasting then? It is excluded. By what law? of works? Nay: but by the law of faith. 2:17

28 Therefore we conclude ^Rthat a man is justified by faith without the deeds of the law. Gal. 2:16

29 *Is* he the God of the Jews only? *is he* not also of the Gentiles? Yes, of the Gentiles also:

30 Seeing ^R*it is* one God, which

shall justify the circumcision by faith, and uncircumcision through faith. 10:12; [Gal. 3:8, 20]

31 Do we then make void the law through faith? God forbid: yea, we establish the law.

4 What shall we say then that Abraham our father, as pertaining to the flesh, hath found?

2 For if Abraham were [R]justified by works, he hath *whereof* to glory; but not before God. 3:20, 27

3 For what saith the scripture? [R]Abraham believed God, and it was counted unto him for righteousness. Gen. 15:6; Gal. 3:6; James 2:23

4 Now [R]to him that worketh is the reward not reckoned of grace, but of debt. 11:6

5 But to him that worketh not, but believeth on him that justifieth the ungodly, his faith is counted for righteousness.

6 Even as David also describeth the blessedness of the man, unto whom God imputeth righteousness without works,

7 *Saying,* [R]Blessed *are* they whose iniquities are forgiven, and whose sins are covered. Ps. 32:1, 2

8 Blessed *is* the man to whom the Lord will not impute sin.

9 *Cometh* this blessedness then upon the circumcision *only,* or upon the uncircumcision also? for we say that faith was [T]reckoned to Abraham for righteousness. *imputed*

10 How was it then reckoned? when he was in circumcision, or in uncircumcision? Not in circumcision, but in uncircumcision.

11 And he received the sign of circumcision, a seal of the righteousness of the faith which *he had yet* being uncircumcised: that he might be the father of all them that believe, though they be not circumcised; that righteousness might be imputed unto them also:

12 And the father of circumcision to them who are not of the circumcision only, but who also walk in the steps of that faith of our father Abraham,

which *he had* being *yet* uncircumcised.

13 For the promise, that he should be the heir of the world, *was* not to Abraham, or to his seed, through the law, but through the righteousness of faith.

14 For [R]if they which are of the law *be* heirs, faith is made void, and the promise made of none effect: Gal. 3:18

15 Because [R]the law worketh wrath: for where no law is, *there is* no transgression. 3:20

16 Therefore *it is* of faith, that *it might be* [R]by grace; [R]to the end the promise might be sure to all the seed; not to that only which is of the law, but to that also which is of the faith of Abraham; who is the father of us all, [3:24] · [Gal. 3:22]

17 (As it is written, I have made thee a father of many nations,) before him whom he believed, *even* God, who quickeneth the dead, and calleth those things which be not as though they were.

18 Who against hope believed in hope, that he might become the father of many nations, according to that which was spoken, [R]So shall thy seed be. Gen. 15:5

19 And being not weak in faith, he considered not his own body now dead, when he was about an hundred years old, neither yet the deadness of Sarah's womb:

20 He [T]staggered not at the promise of God through unbelief; but was [T]strong in faith, giving glory to God; *wavered · strengthened*

21 And being fully persuaded that, what he had promised, [R]he was able also to perform. Gen. 18:14

22 And therefore it was imputed to him for righteousness.

23 Now [R]it was not written for his sake alone, that it was imputed to him; 15:4; 1 Cor. 10:6

24 But for us also, to whom it shall be imputed, if we believe [R]on him that raised up Jesus our Lord from the dead; Acts 2:24

25 [R]Who was delivered for our offences, and [R]was raised again for our justification. Is. 53:4, 5 · [5:18]

5 Therefore being justified by faith, we have peace with God through our Lord Jesus Christ:

2 By whom also we have access by faith into this grace wherein we stand, and [R]rejoice in hope of the glory of God.   Heb. 3:6

3 And not only so, but [R]we glory in tribulations also: [R]knowing that tribulation worketh patience;   [Acts 5:41; 2 Cor. 12:9] · James 1:3

4 [R]And patience, experience; and experience, hope: Phil. 2:22

5 [R]And hope maketh not ashamed; [R]because the love of God is shed abroad in our hearts by the Holy Ghost which is given unto us.   Phil. 1:20 · 2 Cor. 1:22; Eph. 1:13

6 For when we were yet without strength, in due time [R]Christ died for the ungodly.   Is. 53:5

7 For scarcely for a righteous man will one die: yet [T]peradventure for a good man some would even dare to die.   perhaps

★ 8 But [R]God [T]commendeth his love toward us, in that, while we were yet sinners, Christ died for us.   [8:39; John 3:16; 15:13] · demonstrates

9 Much more then, being now justified by his blood, we shall be saved from wrath through him.

10 For [R]if, when we were enemies, [R]we were reconciled to God by the death of his Son, much more, being reconciled, we shall be saved by his life.   [8:32] · Col. 1:21

11 And not only so, but we also [R]joy in God through our Lord Jesus Christ, by whom we have now received the atonement.   [Gal. 4:9]

12 Wherefore, as [R]by one man sin entered into the world, and death by sin; and so death passed upon all men, for that all have sinned: [vv. 15–17]; Gen. 2:17; 3:6, 19

13 (For until the law sin was in the world: but [R]sin is not imputed when there is no law.   1 John 3:4

14 Nevertheless death reigned from Adam to Moses, even over them that had not sinned after the [T]similitude of Adam's transgression, who is the figure of him that was to come.   likeness

15 But not as the offence, so also is the free gift. For if through the offence of [T]one many be dead, much more the grace of God, and the gift by grace, which is by one man, Jesus Christ, hath abounded [R]unto many.   Adam · [Is. 53:11]

16 And not as it was by one that sinned, so is the gift: for the judgment was by one to condemnation, but the free gift is of many offences unto justification.

17 For if by one man's offence death reigned by [T]one; much more they which receive abundance of grace and of the gift of righteousness shall reign in life by one, Jesus Christ.)   the one

18 Therefore as by the offence ★ of one judgment came upon all men to condemnation; even so by the righteousness of one the free gift came [R]upon all men unto justification of life. Matt. 1:21; [John 12:32]

19 For as by one man's disobedience many were made sinners, so by the [R]obedience of one shall many be made righteous.   [Phil. 2:8]

20 Moreover [R]the law entered, that the offence might abound. But where sin abounded, grace did much more abound: John 15:22

21 That as sin hath reigned unto death, even so might grace reign through righteousness unto eternal life by Jesus Christ our Lord.

6 What shall we say then? [R]Shall we continue in sin, that grace may abound?   v. 15; 3:8

2 God forbid. How shall we, that are [R]dead to sin, live any longer therein? [Gal. 2:19; Col. 2:20; 3:3]

3 Know ye not, that [R]so many of us as were baptized into Jesus Christ [R]were baptized into his death? [Gal. 3:27]; Col. 2:12 · [1 Cor. 15:29]

4 Therefore we are [R]buried with him by baptism into death: that like as Christ was raised up from the dead by the glory of the Father, even so we also should walk in newness of life.   Col. 2:12

5 [R]For if we have been planted together in the likeness of his death, we shall be also in the likeness of his resurrection: 2 Cor. 4:10

6 Knowing this, that [R]our old

man is crucified with *him*, that the body of sin might be destroyed, that henceforth we should not serve sin.   Gal. 2:20; 5:24; 6:14

7 For ᴿhe that is dead is freed from sin.   1 Pet. 4:1

8 Now ᴿif we be dead with Christ, we believe that we shall also live with him: 2 Cor. 4:10

9 Knowing that ᴿChrist being raised from the dead dieth no more; death hath no more dominion over him.   Rev. 1:18

10 For in that he died, ᴿhe died unto sin once: but in that he liveth, he liveth unto God.   Heb. 9:27

11 Likewise reckon ye also yourselves to be ᴿdead indeed unto sin, but alive unto God through Jesus Christ our Lord.   [v. 2; 7:4, 6]

12 ᴿLet not sin therefore reign in your mortal body, that ye should obey it in the lusts thereof. Ps. 19:13

13 Neither yield ye your ᴿmembers *as* instruments of unrighteousness unto sin: but ᴿyield yourselves unto God, as those that are alive from the dead, and your members *as* instruments of righteousness unto God. 7:5; Col. 3:5 · 12:1

14 For sin shall not have dominion over you: for ye are not under the law, but under grace.

15 What then? shall we sin, because we are not under the law, but under grace? God forbid.

16 Know ye not, that ᴿto whom ye yield yourselves servants to obey, his servants ye are to whom ye obey; whether of sin unto death, or of obedience unto righteousness?   John 8:34; 2 Pet. 2:19

17 But God be thanked, that ye were the servants of sin, but ye have obeyed from the heart ᴿthat form of doctrine which was delivered you.   2 Tim. 1:13

18 Being then ᴿmade free from sin, ye became the servants of righteousness.   Gal. 5:1; 1 Pet. 2:16

19 I speak ᵀafter the manner of men because of the infirmity of your flesh: for as ye have yielded your members servants to uncleanness and to iniquity unto iniquity; even so now yield your members servants to righteousness unto holiness.   *in human* terms

20 For when ye were ᴿthe servants of sin, ye were free from righteousness.   John 8:34

21 ᴿWhat fruit had ye then in those things whereof ye are now ashamed? for ᴿthe end of those things *is* death.   7:5 · 1:32; Gal. 6:8

22 But now being made free from sin, and become servants to God, ye have your fruit unto holiness, and the end everlasting life.

23 For the wages of sin *is* death; but the gift of God *is* eternal life through Jesus Christ our Lord.

7 Know ye not, brethren, (for I speak to them that know the law,) how that the law hath dominion over a man as long as he liveth?

2 For ᴿthe woman which hath an husband is bound by the law to *her* husband so long as he liveth; but if the husband be dead, she is loosed from the law ᵀof *her* husband.   1 Cor. 7:39 · *concerning*

3 So then ᴿif, while *her* husband liveth, she be married to another man, she shall be called an adulteress: but if her husband be dead, she is free from that law; so that she is no adulteress, though she be married to another man.   [Matt. 5:32]

4 Wherefore, my brethren, ye also are become ᴿdead to the law by the body of Christ; that ye should be married to another, *even* to him who is raised from the dead, that we should bring forth fruit unto God.   Gal. 2:19; 5:18

5 For when we were in the flesh, the ᵀmotions of sins, which were ᵀby the law, ᴿdid work in our members ᴿto bring forth fruit unto death.   *passions · aroused by* · 6:13 · 6:21

6 But now we are delivered from the law, that being dead wherein we were held; that we should serve ᴿin newness of spirit, and not *in* the oldness of the letter.   2:29; 2 Cor. 3:6

7 What shall we say then? *Is* the law sin? God forbid. Nay, ᴿI had not known sin, but by the law:

for I had not known lust, except the law had said, ^RThou shalt not covet. 3:20 · Deut. 5:21; Acts 20:33
8 But ^Rsin, taking occasion by the commandment, wrought in me all manner of ^Tconcupiscence. For ^Rwithout the law sin *was* dead. 4:15 · *desire* · 1 Cor. 15:56
9 For I was alive without the law once: but when the commandment came, sin revived, and I died.
10 And the commandment, ^Rwhich *was ordained* to life, I found *to be* unto death. Gal. 3:12
11 For sin, taking occasion by the commandment, deceived me, and by it slew *me.*
12 Wherefore ^Rthe law *is* holy, and the commandment holy, and just, and good. Ps. 19:8
13 Was then that which is good made death unto me? God forbid. But sin, that it might appear sin, ^Tworking death in me by that which is good; that sin by the commandment might become exceeding sinful. *was producing*
14 For we know that the law is spiritual: but I am ^Tcarnal, ^Rsold under sin. *fleshly* · 6:16; 1 Kin. 21:20, 25
15 For that which I do I allow not: for ^Rwhat I would, that do I not; but what I hate, that do I. v. 19
16 If then I do that which I would not, I ^Tconsent unto the law that *it is* good. *agree with*
17 Now then it is no more I that do it, but sin that dwelleth in me.
18 For I know that ^Rin me (that is, in my flesh,) dwelleth no good thing: for to will is present with me; but *how* to perform that which is good I find not. [Gen. 6:5]
19 For the good that I ^Twould I do not: but the evil which I would not, that I do. *want to do*
20 Now if I do that I would not, it is no more I that do it, but sin that dwelleth in me.
21 I find then a law, that, when I ^Twould do good, evil is present with me. *want to do*
22 For I ^Rdelight in the law of God after the inward man: Ps. 1:2
23 But ^RI see another law in my

members, warring against the law of my mind, and bringing me into captivity to the law of sin which is in my members. James 4:1; 1 Pet. 2:11
24 O wretched man that I am! who shall deliver me ^Rfrom the body of this death? [1 Cor. 15:51, 52]
25 ^RI thank God through Jesus Christ our Lord. So then with the mind I myself serve the law of God; but with the flesh the law of sin. 1 Cor. 15:57
8 *There is* therefore now no condemnation to them which are in Christ Jesus, who walk not after the flesh, but after the Spirit.
2 For ^Rthe law of ^Rthe Spirit of life in Christ Jesus hath made me free from ^Rthe law of sin and death. 6:18, 22 · [1 Cor. 15:45] · 7:24, 25
3 For ^Rwhat the law could not do, in that it was weak through the flesh, ^RGod sending his own Son in the likeness of sinful flesh, and for sin, condemned sin in the flesh: Acts 13:39; [Heb. 7:18] · [Gal. 3:13]
4 That the righteousness of the law might be fulfilled in us, who ^Rwalk not after the flesh, but after the Spirit. Gal. 5:16, 25; Eph. 4:1; 5:2, 15
5 For they that are after the flesh do mind the things of the flesh; but they that are after the Spirit the things of the Spirit.
6 For ^Rto be carnally minded *is* death; but to be spiritually minded *is* life and peace. Gal. 6:8
7 Because ^Rthe carnal mind *is* enmity against God: for it is not subject to the law of God, ^Rneither indeed can be. James 4:4 · 1 Cor. 2:14
8 So then they that are in the flesh cannot please God.
9 But ye are not in the flesh, but in the Spirit, if so be that the Spirit of God dwell in you. Now if any man have not the Spirit of Christ, he is none of his.
10 And if Christ *be* in you, the body *is* dead because of sin; but the Spirit *is* life because of righteousness.
11 But if the Spirit of ^Rhim that raised up Jesus from the dead dwell in you, he that raised up Christ from the dead shall also

quicken your mortal bodies by his Spirit that dwelleth in you.   6:4

12 ᴿTherefore, brethren, we are debtors, not to the flesh, to live after the flesh.   [6:7, 14]

13 For if ye live after the flesh, ye shall die: but if ye through the Spirit do ᵀmortify the deeds of the body, ye shall live.   *put to death*

14 For ᴿas many as are led by the Spirit of God, they are the sons of God.   [Gal. 5:18]

15 For ᴿye have not received the spirit of bondage again to fear; but ye have received the ᴿSpirit of adoption, whereby we cry, Ab'-ba, Father.   [1 Cor. 2:12]; Heb. 2:15 · [Is. 56:5]

16 ᴿThe Spirit itself beareth witness with our spirit, that we are the children of God: Eph. 1:13

17 And if children, then ᴿheirs; heirs of God, and joint-heirs with Christ; ᴿif so be that we suffer with *him*, that we may be also glorified together.   Acts 26:18 · Phil. 1:29

18 For I reckon that ᴿthe sufferings of this present time *are* not worthy *to be compared* with the glory which shall be revealed in us.   2 Cor. 4:17; [1 Pet. 1:6; 4:13]

19 For the earnest expectation of the creature waiteth for the manifestation of the sons of God.

20 For the creature was made subject to vanity, not willingly, but by reason of him who hath subjected *the same* in hope,

21 Because the ᵀcreature itself also shall be delivered from the bondage of ᵀcorruption into the glorious ᴿliberty of the children of God.   *creation · decay* · Gal. 5:1, 13

22 For we know that the whole creation ᴿgroaneth and travaileth in pain together until now.   Jer. 12:4

23 And not only *they*, but ourselves also, which have the first-fruits of the Spirit, even we ourselves groan within ourselves, waiting for the adoption, *to wit*, the redemption of our body.

24 For we are saved by hope: but ᴿhope that is seen is not hope: for what a man seeth, why doth he yet hope for?   4:18; 2 Cor. 5:7; Heb. 11:1

25 But if we hope for that we see

not, *then* do we with ᵀpatience ᵀwait for *it*.   *perseverance · eagerly wait*

26 Likewise the Spirit also helpeth our ᵀinfirmities: for ᴿwe know not what we should pray for as we ought: but ᴿthe Spirit itself maketh intercession for us with groanings which cannot be uttered.   *weaknesses* · 2 Cor. 12:8 · Eph. 6:18

27 And ᴿhe that searcheth the hearts knoweth what *is* the mind of the Spirit, because he maketh intercession for the saints according to *the will* of God.   1 Chr. 28:9

28 And we know that all things work together for good to them that love God, to them ᴿwho are the called according to *his* purpose.   2 Tim. 1:9

29 For whom he did foreknow, he also did predestinate *to be* conformed to the image of his Son, that he might be the first-born among many brethren.

30 Moreover whom he did predestinate, them he also ᴿcalled: and whom he called, them he also justified: and whom he justified, them he also glorified.   1 Cor. 1:9

31 What shall we then say to these things? ᴿIf God *be* for us, who *can be* against us?   Num. 14:9

32 ᴿHe that spared not his own Son, but delivered him up for us all, how shall he not with him also freely give us all things?   5:6, 10

33 Who shall lay any thing to the charge of God's elect? ᴿIt *is* God that justifieth.   Is. 50:8, 9

34 Who *is* he that condemneth? *It is* Christ that died, yea rather, that is risen again, ᴿwho is even at the right hand of God, who also maketh intercession for us.   Col. 3:1

35 Who shall separate us from the love of Christ? *shall* tribulation, or distress, or persecution, or famine, or nakedness, or peril, or sword?

36 As it is written, ᴿFor thy sake we are killed all the day long; we are accounted as sheep for the slaughter.   Ps. 44:22; Acts 20:24; 1 Cor. 4:9

37 Nay, in all these things we are more than conquerors through him that loved us.

38 For I am persuaded, that neither death, nor life, nor angels, nor ᴿprincipalities, nor powers, nor things present, nor things to come,   [1 Cor. 15:24; Eph. 1:21; 1 Pet. 3:22]

39 Nor height, nor depth, nor any other creature, shall be able to separate us from the love of God, which is in Christ Jesus our Lord.

9 I ᴿsayᵀ the truth in Christ, I Tlie not, my conscience also bearing me witness in the Holy Ghost,   2 Cor. 1:23 · *tell* · *am not lying*

2 ᴿThat I have great ᵀheaviness and continual ᵀsorrow in my heart.   10:1 · *sorrow* · *grief*

3 For ᴿI could wish that myself were accursed from Christ for my brethren, my kinsmen according to the flesh: Ex. 32:32

4 Who are Israelites; to whom *pertaineth* the adoption, and the glory, and the covenants, and the giving of the law, and the service *of God*, and the promises;

5 ᴿWhose *are* the fathers, and of whom as concerning the flesh Christ *came*, who is over all, God blessed for ever. A-men'. Deut. 10:15

6 Not as though the word of God hath taken none effect. For ᴿthey *are* not all Israel, which are of Israel: [John 8:39; Gal. 6:16]

7 Neither, because they are the seed of Abraham, *are they* all children: but, In ᴿIsaac shall thy seed be called.   Gen. 21:12; Heb. 11:18

8 That is, They which are the children of the flesh, these *are* not the children of God: but ᴿthe children of the promise are counted ᵀfor the seed.   Gal. 4:28 · *as*

9 For this *is* the word of promise, ᴿAt this time will I come, and Sarah shall have a son.Gen. 18:10, 14

10 And not only *this;* but when Rebecca also had conceived by one, *even* by our father Isaac:

11 (For *the children* being not yet born, neither having done any good or evil, that the purpose of God according to election might stand, not of works, but of ᴿhim that calleth;)   [4:17; 8:28]

12 It was said unto her, The elder shall serve the younger.

13 As it is written, Jacob have I loved, but Esau have I hated.

14 What shall we say then? ᴿ*Is there* unrighteousness with God? ᵀGod forbid.   Deut. 32:4 · *Certainly not*

15 For he saith to Moses, I will have mercy on whom I will have mercy, and I will have compassion on whom I will have compassion.

16 So then *it is* not of him that willeth, nor of him that runneth, but of God that sheweth mercy.

17 For ᴿthe scripture saith unto Pharaoh, Even for this same purpose have I raised thee up, that I might shew my power in thee, and that my name might be declared throughout all the earth.   Gal. 3:8

18 Therefore hath he mercy on whom he will *have mercy,* and whom he will he ᴿhardeneth.   11:7

19 Thou wilt say then unto me, Why doth he yet find fault? For who hath resisted his will?

20 Nay but, O man, who art thou that repliest against God? ᴿShall the thing formed say to him that formed *it,* Why hast thou made me thus?   Is. 29:16; Jer. 18:6; 2 Tim. 2:20

21 Hath not the ᴿpotter power over the clay, of the same lump to make one vessel unto honour, and another unto dishonour? Prov. 16:4

22 *What* if God, ᵀwilling to shew *his* wrath, and to make his power known, endured with much longsuffering the vessels of wrath fitted to destruction: *wanting*

23 And that he might make known the riches of his glory on the vessels of mercy, which he had afore prepared unto glory,

24 Even us, whom he hath ᴿcalled, ᴿnot of the Jews only, but also of the Gentiles?   [8:28] · 3:29

25 As he saith also in O'-see, I will call them my people, which were not my people; and her beloved, which was not beloved.

26 And it shall come to pass, *that* in the place where it was said unto them, Ye *are* not my people; there shall they be called the ᵀchildren of the living God.   *sons*

27 E-sa'-ias also crieth concerning Israel, ^RThough the number of the children of Israel be as the sand of the sea, ^Ra remnant shall be saved: Is. 10:22, 23 · 11:5

28 For he will finish the work, and cut *it* short in righteousness: ^Rbecause a short work will the Lord make upon the earth. Is. 10:23

29 And as E-sa'-ias said before, ^RExcept the Lord of Sa-ba'-oth had left us a seed, ^Rwe had been as Sod'-o-ma, and been made like unto Go-mor'-rha.   Is. 1:9 · Is. 13:19

30 What shall we say then? ^RThat the Gentiles, which followed not after righteousness, have attained to righteousness, ^Reven the righteousness which is of faith.   4:11 · 1:17; 3:21; 10:6; [Gal. 2:16]

31 But Israel, ^Rwhich followed after the law of righteousness, ^Rhath not attained to the law of righteousness.   [10:2–4] · [Gal. 5:4]

32 ^TWherefore? Because *they sought it* not by faith, but as it were by the works of the law. For ^Rthey stumbled at that stumblingstone;   Why · [Luke 2:34; 1 Cor. 1:23]

★ 33 As it is written, ^RBehold, I lay in Si'-on a stumblingstone and rock of offence: and ^Rwhosoever believeth on him shall not be ashamed.   [Matt. 21:42; 1 Pet. 2:6–8] · 5:5

10 Brethren, my heart's desire and prayer to God for Israel is, that they might be saved.

2 For I bear them record ^Rthat they have a zeal of God, but not according to knowledge.   Gal. 1:14

3 For they being ignorant of ^RGod's righteousness, and going about to establish their own ^Rrighteousness, have not submitted themselves unto the righteousness of God.   [1:17] · [Phil. 3:9]

4 For ^RChrist *is* the end of the law for righteousness to every one that believeth. Matt. 5:17; [Gal. 3:24; 4:5]

5 For Moses describeth the righteousness which is of the law, ^RThat the man which doeth those things shall live by them.   Lev. 18:5

6 But the righteousness which is of faith speaketh on this wise, Say not in thine heart, Who shall ascend into heaven? (that is, to bring Christ down *from above*:)

7 Or, Who shall descend into the ^Tdeep? (that is, to bring up Christ again from the dead.) *abyss*

8 But what saith it? The word is ^Tnigh thee, *even* in thy mouth, and in thy heart: that is, the word of faith, which we preach;   *near*

9 That ^Rif thou shalt confess with thy mouth the Lord Jesus, and shalt believe in thine heart that God hath raised him from the dead, thou shalt be saved. Phil. 2:11

10 For with the heart man believeth unto righteousness; and with the mouth confession is made unto salvation.

11 For the scripture saith, ^RWho- ★ soever believeth on him shall not be ashamed.   9:33; Is. 28:16; Jer. 17:7

12 For ^Rthere is no difference between the Jew and the Greek: for the same Lord over all is rich unto all that call upon him.   Gal. 3:28

13 ^RFor whosoever shall call ^Rupon the name of the Lord shall be saved.   Joel 2:32; Acts 2:21 · Acts 9:14

14 How then shall they call on him in whom they have not believed? and how shall they believe in him of whom they have not heard? and how shall they hear ^Rwithout a preacher?   Acts 8:31

15 And how shall they preach, except they be sent? as it is written, ^RHow beautiful are the feet of them that preach the gospel of peace, and bring glad tidings of good things!   Is. 52:7; Nah. 1:15

16 But they have not all obeyed ★ the gospel. For E-sa'-ias saith, ^RLord, who hath believed our report?   Is. 53:1; John 12:38

17 So then faith *cometh* by hearing, and hearing by the word of God.

18 But I say, Have they not heard? Yes verily, their sound went into all the earth, and their words unto the ends of the world.

19 But I say, Did not Israel know? First Moses saith, ^RI will provoke you to jealousy by *them that are* no people, *and* by a foolish nation I will anger you.   11:11

20 But E-sa'-ias is very bold, and saith, ᴿI was found of them that sought me not; I was made manifest unto them that asked not after me.   9:30; Is. 65:1
21 But to Israel he saith, ᴿAll day long I have stretched forth my hands unto a disobedient and ᵀgainsaying people. Is. 65:2 · contrary

11 I say then, ᴿHath God cast away his people? God forbid. For ᴿI also am an Israelite, of the seed of Abraham, of the tribe of Benjamin.   Ps. 94:14 · 2 Cor. 11:22
2 God hath not cast away his people which he foreknew. Wot ye not what the scripture saith of E-li'-as? how he maketh intercession to God against Israel, saying,
3 ᴿLord, they have killed thy prophets, and digged down thine altars; and I am left alone, and they seek my life.   1 Kin. 19:10, 14
4 But what saith the answer of God unto him? ᴿI have reserved to myself seven thousand men, who have not bowed the knee to the image of Ba'-al.   1 Kin. 19:18
5 Even so then at this present time also there is a remnant according to the election of grace.
6 And if by grace, then is it no more of works: otherwise grace is no more grace. But if it be of works, then is it no more grace: otherwise work is no more work.
7 What then? ᴿIsrael hath not obtained that which he seeketh for; but the election hath obtained it, and the rest were blinded.   9:31
8 (According as it is written, ᴿGod hath given them the spirit of slumber, eyes that they should not see, and ears that they should not hear;) unto this day.   Is. 29:10, 13
★ 9 And David saith, ᴿLet their table be made a snare, and a trap, and a stumblingblock, and a recompence unto them: Ps. 69:22, 23
10 Let their eyes be darkened, that they may not see, and bow down their back alway.
11 I say then, Have they stumbled that they should fall? God forbid: but rather ᴿthrough their fall salvation is come unto the

Gentiles, for to provoke them to ᴿjealousy.   Is. 42:6, 7; Acts 28:28 · 10:19
12 Now if the ᵀfall of them be the riches of the world, and the ᵀdiminishing of them the riches of the Gentiles; how much more their fulness?   trespass · failure
13 For I speak to you Gentiles, inasmuch as ᴿI am the apostle of the Gentiles, I magnify mine office: Gal. 1:16; 2:7–9; Eph. 3:8
14 If by any means I may provoke to ᵀemulation them which are my flesh, and ᴿmight save some of them.   jealousy · 1 Cor. 9:22
15 For if the casting away of them be the reconciling of the world, what shall the receiving of them be, but life from the dead?
16 For if the firstfruit be holy, the lump is also holy: and if the root be holy, so are the branches.
17 And if ᴿsome of the branches be broken off, ᴿand thou, being a wild olive tree, wert graffed in among them, and with them partakest of the root and fatness of the olive tree;   [John 15:2] · Acts 2:39
18 ᴿBoast not against the branches. But if thou boast, thou bearest not the root, but the root thee.   [1 Cor. 10:12]
19 Thou wilt say then, The branches were broken off, that I might be graffed in.
20 Well; because of ᴿunbelief they were broken off, and thou standest by faith. Be not ᵀhighminded, but fear: Heb. 3:19 · haughty
21 For if God spared not the natural branches, take heed lest he also spare not thee.
22 Behold therefore the goodness and severity of God: on them which fell, severity; but toward thee, goodness, ᴿif thou continue in his goodness: otherwise thou also shalt be cut off.   1 Cor. 15:2
23 And they also, ᴿif they abide not still in unbelief, shall be graffed in: for God is able to graff them in again.   [2 Cor. 3:16]
24 For if thou wert cut out of the olive tree which is wild by nature, and wert graffed contrary to nature into a good olive tree: how

much more shall these, which be the natural *branches,* be graffed into their own olive tree?

25 For I would not, brethren, that ye should be ignorant of this mystery, lest ye should be wise in your own conceits; that [R]blindness in part is happened to Israel, [R]until the fulness of the Gentiles be come in. 2 Cor. 3:14 · John 10:16

☆ 26 And so all Israel shall be saved: as it is written, [R]There shall come out of Si'-on the Deliverer, and shall turn away ungodliness from Jacob: Ps. 14:7; Is. 59:20, 21

27 [R]For this *is* my covenant unto them, when I shall take away their sins. Is. 27:9; Heb. 8:12

28 As concerning the gospel, *they are* enemies for your sakes: but [T]as touching the election, *they are* [R]beloved for the fathers' sakes. *concerning the* · Deut. 7:8; 10:15

29 For the gifts and calling of God *are* without repentance.

30 For as ye [R]in times past have not believed God, yet have now obtained mercy through their unbelief: [Eph. 2:2]

31 Even so have these also now not [T]believed, that through [T]your mercy they also may obtain mercy. *obeyed* · *the mercy shown you*

32 For God hath concluded them [R]all in unbelief, that he might have mercy upon all. 3:9; [Gal. 3:22]

33 O the depth of the riches both of the wisdom and knowledge of God! how unsearchable *are* his judgments, and his ways past finding out!

34 For who hath known the [R]mind of the Lord? or who hath been his counsellor? 1 Cor. 2:16

35 [R]Or who hath first given to him, and it shall be [T]recompensed unto him again? Job 41:11 · *repaid*

36 For of him, and through him, and to him, *are* all things: to whom *be* glory for ever. A-men'.

12 I beseech you therefore, brethren, by the mercies of God, that ye present your bodies a [R]living sacrifice, holy, acceptable unto God, *which is* your reasonable service. Phil. 4:18; Heb. 10:18, 20

2 And [R]be not conformed to this world: but [R]be ye transformed by the renewing of your mind, that ye may prove what *is* that good, and acceptable, and perfect, will of God. 1 John 2:15 · Eph. 4:23

3 For I say, through the grace given unto me, to every man that is among you, not to think *of himself* more highly than he ought to think; but to think soberly, according as God hath dealt to every man the measure of faith.

4 For as we have many members in one body, and all members have not the same [T]office: *function*

5 So [R]we, *being* many, are one body in Christ, and every one members one of another. Gal. 3:28

6 Having then gifts differing according to the grace that is given to us, whether prophecy, *let us* [R]prophesy according to the proportion of faith; Acts 11:27

7 Or ministry, *let us wait* on *our* ministering: or [R]he that teacheth, on teaching; Eph. 4:11

8 Or he that exhorteth, on exhortation: he that giveth, *let him do it* with [T]simplicity; [R]he that ruleth, with diligence; he that sheweth mercy, [R]with cheerfulness. *liberality* · [Acts 20:28] · 2 Cor. 9:7

9 *Let* love be without dissimulation. Abhor that which is evil; cleave to that which is good.

10 *Be* kindly affectioned one to another with brotherly love; in honour preferring one another;

11 Not slothful in business; fervent in spirit; serving the Lord;

12 [R]Rejoicing in hope; [R]patient in tribulation; continuing instant in prayer; Luke 10:20 · Luke 21:19

13 [R]Distributing to the [T]necessity of saints; [R]given to hospitality. Heb. 13:16 · *needs* · 1 Tim. 3:2

14 [R]Bless them which persecute you: bless, and curse not. Luke 6:28

15 [R]Rejoice with them that do rejoice, and weep with them that weep. [1 Cor. 12:26]

16 [R]Be of the same mind one toward another. Mind not high things, but condescend to men of

low estate. Be not wise in your own conceits. 2 Cor. 13:11; 1 Pet. 3:8

17 [R]Recompense to no man evil for evil. Provide things honest in the sight of all men. 1 Pet. 3:9

18 If it be possible, as much as [T]lieth in you, [R]live peaceably with all men. depends on · Heb. 12:14

19 Dearly beloved, avenge not yourselves, but *rather* give place unto wrath: for it is written, [R]Vengeance *is* mine; I will repay, saith the Lord. Deut. 32:35; Ps. 94:1

20 [R]Therefore if thine enemy hunger, feed him; if he thirst, give him drink: for in so doing thou shalt heap coals of fire on his head. 2 Kin. 6:22; [Matt. 5:44]; Luke 6:27

21 Be not overcome of evil, but [R]overcome evil with good. vv. 1, 2

13 Let every soul be [R]subject unto the [T]higher powers. For there is no power but of God: the powers that be are ordained of God. Titus 3:1; 1 Pet. 2:13 · governing

2 Whosoever therefore resisteth [R]the [T]power, resisteth the ordinance of God: and they that resist shall receive to themselves [T]damnation. [Titus 3:1] · authority · judgment

3 For rulers are not a terror to good works, but to the evil. Wilt thou then not be afraid of the [T]power? [R]do that which is good, and thou shalt have praise of the same: authority · 1 Pet. 2:14

4 For he is the minister of God to thee for good. But if thou do that which is evil, be afraid; for he beareth not the sword in vain: for he is the minister of God, [T]a revenger to *execute* wrath upon him that doeth evil. an avenger

5 Wherefore *ye* must needs be subject, not only for wrath, [R]but also for conscience sake. Acts 24:16

6 For for this cause pay ye [T]tribute also: for they are God's ministers, attending continually upon this very thing. taxes

7 [R]Render therefore to all their dues: [T]tribute to whom [T]tribute *is due;* custom to whom custom; fear to whom fear; honour to whom honour. Mark 12:17; Luke 20:25 · tax

8 Owe no man any thing, but to

love one another: for [R]he that loveth another hath fulfilled the law. [Gal. 5:13, 14; 1 Tim. 1:5; James 2:8]

9 For this, Thou shalt not commit adultery, Thou shalt not kill, Thou shalt not steal, Thou shalt not bear false witness, Thou shalt not covet; and if *there be* any other commandment, it is briefly comprehended in this saying, namely, [R]Thou shalt love thy neighbour as thyself. Mark 12:31

10 Love worketh no ill to his neighbour: therefore [R]love *is* the fulfilling of the law. Gal. 5:14

11 And that, knowing the time, that now *it is* high time [R]to awake out of sleep: for now *is* our salvation nearer than when we believed. Mark 13:37; [1 Cor. 15:34]

12 The night is far spent, the day is at hand: let us therefore cast off the works of darkness, and let us put on the armour of light.

13 [R]Let us walk [T]honestly, as in the day; not in [T]rioting and drunkenness, not in chambering and wantonness, not in strife and envying. Phil. 4:8 · properly · revelry

14 But [R]put ye on the Lord Jesus Christ, and [R]make not provision for the flesh, to *fulfil* the lusts *thereof.* [Eph. 4:24] · [Gal. 5:16]; 1 Pet. 2:11

14 Him that [R]is weak in the faith receive ye, *but* not to doubtful disputations. [1 Cor. 8:9]

2 For one believeth that he [R]may eat all things: another, who is weak, eateth herbs. 1 Cor. 10:25

3 Let not him that eateth despise him that eateth not; and [R]let not him which eateth not judge him that eateth: for God hath received him. [Col. 2:16]

4 [R]Who art thou that judgest another man's servant? to his own master he standeth or falleth. Yea, he shall be holden up: for God is able to make him stand. 9:20

5 One man esteemeth one day above another: another esteemeth every day *alike.* Let every man be fully persuaded in his own mind.

6 He that [R]regardeth[T] the day, regardeth *it* unto the Lord; and he that [T]regardeth not the day, to

the Lord he doth not regard *it*. He that eateth, eateth to the Lord, for [R]he giveth God thanks; and he that eateth not, to the Lord he eateth not, and giveth God thanks. Gal. 4:10 · *observes* · [1 Cor. 10:31]

7 For none of us liveth to himself, and no man dieth to himself.

8 For whether we [R]live, we live unto the Lord; and whether we die, we die unto the Lord: whether we live therefore, or die, we are the Lord's.   2 Cor. 5:14, 15

9 For [R]to this end Christ both died, and rose, and revived, that he might be [R]Lord both of the dead and living. 2 Cor. 5:15 · Acts 10:36

10 But why dost thou judge thy brother? or why dost thou [T]set at nought thy brother? for [R]we shall all stand before the judgment seat of Christ.   *despise* · 2:16; 2 Cor. 5:10

☆ 11 For it is written, [R]*As I live*, saith the Lord, *every knee shall bow to me, and every tongue shall confess to God*. Is. 45:23; [Phil. 2:10, 11]

12 So then every one of us shall give account of himself to God.

13 Let us not therefore judge one another any more: but judge this rather, that [R]no man put a stumblingblock or an occasion to fall in *his* brother's way.   1 Cor. 8:9

14 I know, and am persuaded by the Lord Jesus, that *there is* nothing unclean of itself: but to him that esteemeth any thing to be unclean, to him *it is* unclean.

15 But if thy brother be grieved [T]with *thy* [T]meat, now walkest thou not charitably. [R]Destroy not him with thy [T]meat, for whom Christ died.   *by* · *food* · v. 20; 1 Cor. 8:11

16 [R]Let not then your good be evil spoken of: [12:17]

17 [R]For the kingdom of God is not [T]meat and drink; but righteousness, and [R]peace, and joy in the Holy Ghost. 1 Cor. 8:8 · *food* · [8:6]

18 For he that in these things serveth Christ [R]is acceptable to God, and approved of men. Phil. 4:8

19 [R]Let us therefore follow after the things which make for peace,

and things wherewith [R]one may edify another.   12:18 · 1 Cor. 14:12

20 For meat destroy not the work of God. All things indeed *are* pure; but *it is* evil for that man who eateth with offence.

21 *It is* good neither to eat [R]flesh, nor to drink wine, nor *any* thing whereby thy brother stumbleth, or is offended, or is made weak.   1 Cor. 8:13

22 Hast thou faith? have *it* to thyself before God. Happy *is* he that condemneth not himself in that thing which he alloweth.

23 And he that doubteth is [T]damned if he eat, because *he eateth* not of faith: for whatsoever *is* not of faith is sin.   *condemned*

15 We [R]then that are strong ought to bear the infirmities of the weak, and not to please ourselves.   [Gal. 6:1, 2]; 1 Thess. 5:14

2 [R]Let every one of us please *his* neighbour for *his* good to [T]edification.   2 Cor. 13:9 · *being built up*

3 For even Christ pleased not ★ himself; but, as it is written, The [R]reproaches of them that reproached thee fell on me.   Ps. 69:9

4 For [R]whatsoever things were written aforetime were written for our learning, that we through patience and comfort of the scriptures might have hope.   1 Cor. 10:11

5 [R]Now the God of patience and consolation grant you to be likeminded one toward another according to Christ Jesus: Phil. 1:27

6 That ye may [R]with one mind *and* one mouth glorify God, even the Father of our Lord Jesus Christ.   Acts 4:24

7 Wherefore [R]receive ye one another, [R]as Christ also received us to the glory of God.   14:1, 3 · 5:2

8 Now I say that [R]Jesus Christ was a minister of the circumcision for the truth of God, [R]to confirm the promises *made* unto the fathers: Acts 3:26 · [4:16]; 2 Cor. 1:20

9 And [R]that the Gentiles might glorify God for *his* mercy; as it is written, For this cause I will confess to thee among the Gentiles, and sing unto thy name. John 10:16

10 And again he saith, Rejoice, ye Gentiles, with his people.

11 And again, ^RPraise the Lord, all ye Gentiles; and laud him, all ye people. Ps. 117:1

★ 12 And again, E-sa′-ias saith, ^RThere shall be a root of Jesse, and he that shall rise to reign over the Gentiles; in him shall the Gentiles trust. Is. 11:1, 10

13 Now the God of hope fill you with all ^Rjoy and peace in believing, that ye may abound in hope, through the power of the Holy Ghost. 12:12; 14:17

14 And ^RI myself also am persuaded of you, my brethren, that ye also are full of goodness, filled with all knowledge, able also to admonish one another. 2 Pet. 1:12

15 Nevertheless, brethren, I have written the more boldly unto you in some sort, as putting you in mind, ^Rbecause of the grace that is given to me of God, 1:5; 12:3

16 That ^RI should be the minister of Jesus Christ to the Gentiles, ministering the gospel of God, that the offering up of the Gentiles might be acceptable, being sanctified by the Holy Ghost. 11:13

17 I have therefore ^Twhereof I may glory through Jesus Christ ^Rin those things which pertain to God. *reason to glory* · Heb. 2:17; 5:1

18 For I will not dare to speak of any of those things ^Rwhich Christ hath not wrought by me, to make the Gentiles obedient, by word and deed, Acts 15:12; 21:19; 2 Cor. 3:5

19 ^RThrough mighty signs and wonders, by the power of the Spirit of God; so that from Jerusalem, and round about unto Il-lyr′-i-cum, I have fully preached the gospel of Christ. Acts 19:11

20 Yea, so have I strived to preach the gospel, not where Christ was named, ^Rlest I should build upon another man's foundation: 1 Cor. 3:10; [2 Cor. 10:13, 15, 16]

☆ 21 But as it is written, ^RTo whom he was not spoken of, they shall see: and they that have not heard shall understand. Is. 52:15

22 For which cause also ^RI have

been much hindered from coming to you. 1:13; 1 Thess. 2:17, 18

23 But now having no more place in these parts, and ^Rhaving a great desire these many years to come unto you; Acts 19:21; 23:11

24 Whensoever I take my journey into Spain, I will come to you: for I trust to see you in my journey, ^Rand to be brought on my way thitherward by you, if first I be somewhat ^Rfilled with your *company*. Acts 15:3 · 1:12

25 But now I go unto Jerusalem to minister unto the saints.

26 For ^Rit hath pleased them of Mac-e-do′-ni-a and A-cha′-ia to make a certain contribution for the poor saints which are at Jerusalem. 1 Cor. 16:1; 2 Cor. 8:1–15

27 It hath pleased them verily; and their debtors they are. For ^Rif the Gentiles have been made partakers of their spiritual things, their duty is also to minister unto them in carnal things. 11:17

28 When therefore I have performed this, and have sealed to them ^Rthis fruit, I will come by you into Spain. Phil. 4:17

29 ^RAnd I am sure that, when I come unto you, I shall come in the fulness of the blessing of the gospel of Christ. [1:11]

30 Now I beseech you, brethren, for the Lord Jesus Christ's sake, and for the love of the Spirit, ^Rthat ye strive together with me in *your* prayers to God for me; Col. 4:12

31 That I may be delivered from them that do not believe in Ju-dae′-a; and that ^Rmy service which I *have* for Jerusalem may be accepted of the saints; 2 Cor. 8:4

32 ^RThat I may come unto you with joy by the will of God, and may with you be refreshed. 1:10

33 Now ^Rthe God of peace *be* with you all. A-men′. 16:20; Phil. 4:9

16 I commend unto you Phe′-be our sister, which is a servant of the church which is at ^RCen′-chre-a: Acts 18:18

2 ^RThat ye receive her in the Lord, as becometh saints, and that ye assist her in whatsoever busi-

ness she hath need of you: for she hath been a ᵀsuccourer of many, and of myself also. Phil. 2:29 · *helper*

3 Greet Priscilla and Aq′-ui-la my helpers in Christ Jesus:

4 Who have for my life ᵀlaid down their own necks: unto whom not only I give thanks, but also all the churches of the Gentiles. *risked*

5 Likewise greet ᴿthe church that is in their house. Salute my wellbeloved Ep-ae-ne′-tus, who is ᴿthe firstfruits of A-cha′-ia unto Christ. Col. 4:15; Philem. 2 · 1 Cor. 16:15

6 Greet Mary, who bestowed much labour on us.

7 Salute An-dro-ni′-cus and Ju′-ni-a, my kinsmen, and my fellowprisoners, who are of note among the apostles, who also ᴿwere in Christ before me. Gal. 1:22

8 Greet Am′-pli-as my beloved in the Lord.

9 Salute Ur′-bane, our helper in Christ, and Sta′-chys my beloved.

10 Salute A-pel′-les approved in Christ. Salute them which are of Ar-is-to-bu′-lus′ *household.*

11 Salute He-ro′-di-on my kinsman. Greet them that be of the *household* of Nar-cis′-sus, which are in the Lord.

12 Salute Try-phe′-na and Try-pho′-sa, who labour in the Lord. Salute the beloved Per′-sis, which laboured much in the Lord.

13 Salute Rufus chosen in the Lord, and his mother and mine.

14 Salute A-syn′-cri-tus, Phle′-gon, Her′-mas, Pat′-ro-bas, Her′-mes, and the brethren which are with them.

15 Salute Phi-lol′-o-gus, and Julia, Ne′-reus, and his sister, and O-lym′-pas, and all the saints which are with them.

16 ᴿSalute one another with an holy kiss. The churches of Christ salute you. 1 Cor. 16:20; 2 Cor. 13:12

17 Now I beseech you, brethren, ᵀmark them ᴿwhich cause divisions and offences contrary to the doctrine which ye have learned; and avoid them. *note* · [Acts 15:1]

18 For they that are such serve not our Lord Jesus Christ, but ᴿtheir own belly; and by good words and fair speeches deceive the hearts of the simple. Phil. 3:19

19 For ᴿyour obedience is ᵀcome abroad unto all *men.* I am glad therefore on your behalf: but yet I would have you ᴿwise unto that which is good, and simple concerning evil. 1:8 · *reported* · Matt. 10:16

20 And the God of peace shall bruise Satan under your feet shortly. The grace of our Lord Jesus Christ *be* with you. A-men′.

21 ᴿTi-mo′-the-us my workfellow, and Lu′-cius, and Ja′-son, and So-sip′-a-ter, my kinsmen, salute you. Acts 16:1; Heb. 13:23

22 I Ter′-tius, who wrote *this* epistle, salute you in the Lord.

23 ᴿGa′-ius mine host, and of the whole church, saluteth you. ᴿE-ras′tus the chamberlain of the city saluteth you, and Quar′-tus a brother. 1 Cor. 1:14 · Acts 19:22

24 The grace of our Lord Jesus Christ *be* with you all. A-men′.

25 Now to him that is of power to stablish you according to my gospel, and the preaching of Jesus Christ, according to the revelation of the mystery, which was kept secret since the world began,

26 But ᴿnow is made manifest, and by the scriptures of the prophets, according to the commandment of the everlasting God, made known to all nations for the obedience of faith: Eph. 1:9

27 To ᴿGod only wise, *be* glory through Jesus Christ for ever. A-men′. Jude 25

CORINTHIANS

CORINTH, the most important city in Greece during Paul's day, was a bustling hub of worldwide commerce, degraded culture, and idolatrous religion. There Paul founded a church (Acts 18:1–17), and two of his letters are addressed "Unto the church of God which is at Corinth" (1:2; 2 Cor. 1:1).

First Corinthians reveals the problems, pressures, and struggles of a church called out of a pagan society. Paul addresses a variety of problems in the lifestyle of the Corinthian church: factions, lawsuits, immorality, questionable practices, abuse of the Lord's Supper, and spiritual gifts. In addition to words of discipline, Paul shares words of counsel in answer to questions raised by the Corinthian believers.

The oldest recorded title of this epistle is *Pros Korinthious A*, in effect, the "First to the Corinthians." The *A* was no doubt a later addition to distinguish this book from Second Corinthians.

PAUL, ᴿcalled *to be* an apostle of Jesus Christ ᴿthrough the will of God, and ᴿSos'-the-nes *our* brother,   Rom. 1:1 · 2 Cor. 1:1 · Acts 18:17

2 Unto the church of God which is at Corinth, to them that are sanctified in Christ Jesus, ᴿcalled *to be* saints, with all that in every place call upon the name of Jesus Christ our Lord, both theirs and ours: Rom. 1:7; Eph. 4:1

3 Grace *be* unto you, and peace, from God our Father, and *from* the Lord Jesus Christ.

4 ᴿI thank my God always ᵀon your behalf, for the grace of God which is given you by Jesus Christ;   Rom. 1:8 · *concerning you*

5 That in every thing ye are enriched by him, ᴿin all utterance, and *in* all knowledge;   [12:8]

6 Even as the testimony of Christ was confirmed in you:

7 So that ye come behind in no gift; ᴿwaiting for the coming of our Lord Jesus Christ: Luke 17:30

8 ᴿWho shall also confirm you unto the end, *that ye may be* blameless in the day of our Lord Jesus Christ.   1 Thess. 3:13; 5:23

9 God *is* faithful, by whom ye were called unto the fellowship of his Son Jesus Christ our Lord.

10 Now I beseech you, brethren, by the name of our Lord Jesus Christ, ᴿthat ye all speak the same thing, and *that* there be no divisions among you; but *that* ye be perfectly joined together in the same mind and in the same judgment.   2 Cor. 13:11; 1 Pet. 3:8

11 For it hath been declared unto me of you, my brethren, by them *which are of the house* of Chlo'-e, that there are ᵀcontentions among you.   *quarrels*

12 Now this I say, that every one of you saith, I am of Paul; and I of ᴿA-pol'-los; and I of ᴿCe'-phas; and I of Christ.   Acts 18:24 · John 1:42

13 Is Christ divided? was Paul crucified for you? or were ye baptized in the name of Paul?

14 I thank God that I baptized ᴿnone of you, but ᴿCris'-pus and ᴿGa'-ius;   John 4:2 · Acts 18:8 · Rom. 16:23

15 Lest any should say that I had baptized in mine own name.

16 And I baptized also the household of ᴿSteph'-a-nas: besides, I know not whether I baptized any other.   16:15, 17

17 For Christ sent me not to baptize, but to preach the gospel: ᴿnot with wisdom of words, lest the cross of Christ should be made of none effect.   [2:1, 4, 13]

18 For the preaching of the cross is to them that perish foolishness; but unto us ᴿwhich are saved it is the ᴿpower of God.   [2:14; 15:2] · v. 24

19 For it is written, ᴿI will destroy the wisdom of the wise, and

will bring to nothing the understanding of the prudent.   Is. 29:14

20 Where *is* the wise? where *is* the scribe? where *is* the disputer of this world? hath not God made foolish the wisdom of this world?

21 For after that in the ᴿwisdom of God the world by wisdom knew not God, it pleased God by the foolishness of preaching to save them that believe.   Dan. 2:20

22 For the ᴿJews require a sign, and the Greeks seek after wisdom: Matt. 12:38; John 2:18; 4:48

23 But we preach Christ crucified, ᴿunto the Jews a stumblingblock, and unto the Greeks foolishness;   John 6:60; Gal. 5:11; [1 Pet. 2:8]

24 But unto them which are called, both Jews and Greeks, Christ the power of God, and ᴿthe wisdom of God.   Col. 2:3

25 Because the foolishness of God is wiser than men; and the weakness of God is stronger than men.

26 For ᵀye see your calling, brethren, how that ᴿnot many wise men after the flesh, not many mighty, not many noble, *are called*:   consider · John 7:48

27 But ᴿGod hath chosen the foolish things of the world to confound the wise; and God hath chosen the weak things of the world to confound the things which are mighty;   Ps. 8:2; Matt. 11:25

28 And ᵀbase things of the world, and things which are despised, hath God chosen, *yea*, and things which are not, to bring to nought things that are: insignificant

29 That no flesh should glory in his presence.

30 But of him are ye in Christ Jesus, who of God is made unto us wisdom, and righteousness, and sanctification, and redemption:

31 That, according as it is written, ᴿHe that glorieth, let him glory in the Lord.   2 Cor. 10:17

2 And I, brethren, when I came to you, came not with excellency of speech or of wisdom, declaring unto you the testimony of God.

2 For I determined not to know any thing among you, ᵀsave Jesus Christ, and him crucified.   except

3 And ᴿI was with you ᴿin weakness, and in fear, and in much trembling.   Acts 18:1 · [2 Cor. 4:7]

4 And my speech and my preaching ᴿ*was* not with enticing words of man's wisdom, ᴿbut in demonstration of the Spirit and of power: 2 Pet. 1:16 · 4:20; Rom. 15:19

5 That your faith should not stand in the wisdom of men, but in the ᴿpower of God.   Rom. 1:16

6 Howbeit we speak wisdom among them that are ᵀperfect: yet not the wisdom of this world, nor of the ᵀprinces of this ᵀworld, that come to nought: mature · rulers · age

7 But we speak the wisdom of God in a mystery, *even* the hidden *wisdom*, which God ordained before the world unto our glory:

8 Which none of the princes of this ᵀworld knew: for had they known *it*, they would not have crucified the Lord of glory.   age

9 But as it is written, Eye hath not seen, nor ear heard, neither have entered into the heart of man, the things which God hath prepared for them that love him.

10 But ᴿGod hath revealed *them* unto us by his Spirit: for the Spirit searcheth all things, yea, the deep things of God.   [Gal. 1:12; Eph. 3:3, 5]

11 For what man knoweth the things of a man, save the spirit of man which is in him? ᴿeven so the things of God knoweth no man, but the Spirit of God.   Rom. 11:33

12 Now we have received, not the spirit of the world, but the spirit which is of God; that we might know the things that are freely given to us of God.

13 Which things also we speak, not in the words which man's wisdom teacheth, but which the Holy Ghost teacheth; comparing spiritual things with spiritual.

14 ᴿBut the natural man receiveth not the things of the Spirit of God: for they are foolishness unto him: neither can he know *them*,

THE LIFE OF PETER

1 Born at Bethsaida, Peter was called from his fishing nets on the Sea of Galilee to become Jesus' disciple (John 1:44; Luke 5:1–11).

2 In the region of Caesarea Philippi, Peter acknowledged Jesus as Messiah, or the Christ (Matt. 16:13–16).

3 Peter, James, and John witnessed the transfiguration of Jesus on a mountain, perhaps Mt. Hermon, in this region (Matt. 17:1–9).

4 Peter denied Jesus three times on the night before His crucifixion in Jerusalem (Matt. 26:69–75).

5 After His resurrection, Jesus appeared to Peter and the other disciples in the Upper Room in Jerusalem (Luke 24:33–43).

6 A bold witness in the early church at Jerusalem (Acts 2:14–41), Peter broadened his witness to include the Gentiles following a vision on the rooftop of Simon the tanner in Joppa (10:9–23).

7 Beginning at Caesarea, Peter traveled through Judaea and Samaria, proclaiming Christ and witnessing to the Gentiles (Acts 10:24—11:18).

8 Peter made a bold appeal to the church leaders at Jerusalem to stop blocking Gentiles from coming into the faith (Acts 15:6–11). Yet on another occasion, at Antioch, Paul opposed Peter for distancing himself from Gentile Christians in order to save face with Jewish Christians (Gal. 2:11–14).

9 According to early church tradition, Peter was executed in Rome.

Mediterranean Sea

▲ Mt. Hermon

Caesarea Philippi

3

2

1 Bethsaida

Sea of Galilee

Caesarea **7**

Jordan River

6 Joppa

Jerusalem **4** **5**

Dead Sea

0   20   40
Miles

N

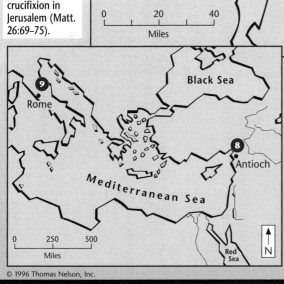

9 Rome

Black Sea

8 Antioch

Mediterranean Sea

0   250   500
Miles

Red Sea

N

© 1996 Thomas Nelson, Inc.

PAUL'S MISSIONARY

Come with Paul and Barnabas as they sail for the Island of Cyprus! After telling many people about Jesus, they travel to Pamphylia, and from there to the cities of Galatia—Derbe, Lystra, and Iconium, and to Antioch in Pisidia. Can you find these cities on the map? What happens to Paul in Derbe? (Acts 14:19) What does he do in all these places? (Acts 14:21–23)

On their second journey, Paul and Silas return to visit the new Christians in the churches they have started. But one of their most exciting adventures takes place in Macedonia (present-day Greece), where they go after they leave Galatia.

After being arrested in Philippi, Paul and Silas are beaten and put in a dungeon. (Acts 16:23, 24) While they are singing hymns in the prison at midnight, there is a miracle! What is it? (Acts 16:25, 26) The poor jailer is sure all the prisoners have escaped and is about to kill himself when Paul speaks up. What happens next? (Acts 16:29–33)

Paul sets out once more from Antioch to revisit the churches he has started in Galatia and Greece. (Acts 18:23) This time he goes on to Ephesus, where he stays for two years, teaching about Jesus and working miracles in His name.

Back home in Jerusalem, Paul's missionary work is interrupted when he is arrested in the temple on false charges. (Acts 21:30–33) He is held by Roman soldiers for many months before sailing to Rome to appeal to Caesar as a Roman citizen.

Adriatic
Sea

Rome
Three Inns
Appii Forum
ITALY

Rhegium

Sicily

Malta

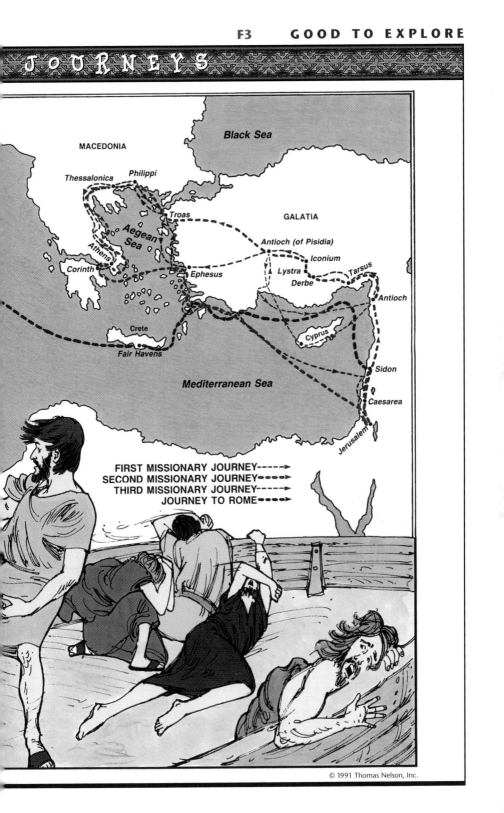

JOURNEYS

FIRST MISSIONARY JOURNEY ----▶
SECOND MISSIONARY JOURNEY ◼◼◼◼▶
THIRD MISSIONARY JOURNEY ----▶
JOURNEY TO ROME ◼◼◼◼▶

THE LIFE OF PAUL

❶ EARLY LIFE AND CONVERSION: Born in Tarsus; both a Jew and a Roman citizen (Acts 22:3); studied under the Jewish scholar Gamaliel at Jerusalem; persecuted the early Christians at Jerusalem (8:3); converted to Christianity through a vision of Christ on the road to Damascus (9:1–9).

❷ YEARS OF PREPARATION: After his conversion, Paul worked with the Christians in Damascus (Acts 9:22), the desert regions of Arabia (Gal. 1:17), and Jerusalem. Opposition from the Jewish leaders drove him to Tarsus (Acts 9:26–30), where he apparently worked for about ten years.

❸ EARLY WORK: Worked with Barnabas to reach Gentiles through the church at Antioch of Syria (Acts 11:19–26); on first missionary tour, visited island of Cyprus and the cities of Antioch of Pisidia, Iconium, Lystra, and Derbe (Acts 13; 14).

❹ LATER WORK: On second missionary tour, carried the gospel further west to the province of Macedonia and the cities of Philippi, Thessalonica, Berea, Athens, and Corinth (Acts 16—18); on third missionary tour, worked with churches at Ephesus, Troas, and Miletus (Acts 19; 20).

❺ TRIP TO ROME AND FINAL DAYS: Mobbed by Jewish zealots, Paul appealed his case to Rome (Acts 25); traveled by ship to Rome for a formal hearing (Acts 27); in Rome as a prisoner, he continued to proclaim the gospel (28:17–31); possibly died at Roman executioner's hand about A.D. 68.

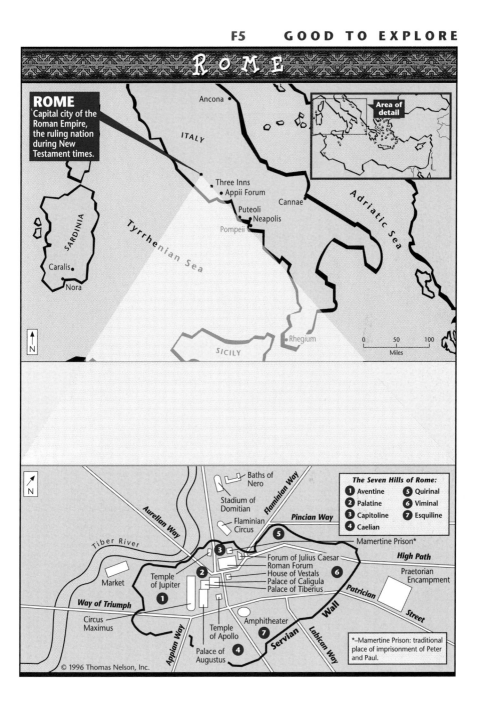

ROME

ROME
Capital city of the Roman Empire, the ruling nation during New Testament times.

Ancona

ITALY

Area of detail

Three Inns
Appii Forum
Cannae
Puteoli
Neapolis
Pompeii

SARDINIA

Tyrrhenian Sea

Adriatic Sea

Caralis
Nora

Rhegium

SICILY

N

0   50   100
Miles

The Seven Hills of Rome:
① Aventine   ⑤ Quirinal
② Palatine   ⑥ Viminal
③ Capitoline   ⑦ Esquiline
④ Caelian

Baths of Nero
Stadium of Domitian
Flaminian Circus

Flaminian Way
Pincian Way
Aurelian Way
Tiber River

Mamertine Prison*
High Path

Forum of Julius Caesar
Roman Forum
House of Vestals
Palace of Caligula
Palace of Tiberius

Praetorian Encampment

Temple of Jupiter
Market
①
②
③
⑤
⑥

Patrician
Street

Way of Triumph
Circus Maximus
Appian Way
Temple of Apollo
Amphitheater
⑦
④
Palace of Augustus

Servian
Wall
Labican Way

*–Mamertine Prison: traditional place of imprisonment of Peter and Paul.

© 1996 Thomas Nelson, Inc.

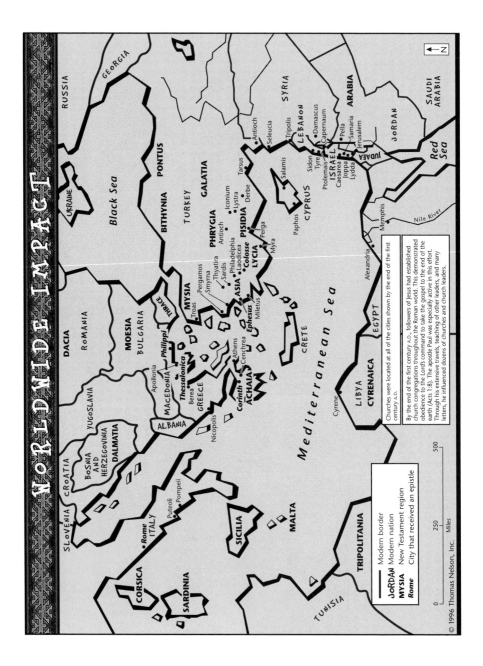

WORLDWIDE IMPACT

Churches were located at all of the cities shown by the end of the first century A.D.

By the end of the first century A.D., followers of Jesus had established church congregations throughout the Roman world. This demonstrated obedience to the Lord's command to take the gospel to the end of the earth (Acts 1:8). The apostle Paul was especially active in this effort. Through his extensive travels, teaching of other leaders, and many letters, he influenced dozens of churches and church leaders.

Modern border
JORDAN Modern nation
MYSIA New Testament region
Rome City that received an epistle

0   250   500
Miles

© 1996 Thomas Nelson, Inc.

THE LIFE OF JOHN

❶ John and his brother James met Jesus through the preaching of John the Baptist (John 1:35–37).

❷ Left his fishing nets on the Sea of Galilee to follow Jesus (Matt. 4:21, 22). He and brother James were called "the sons of thunder" (Mark 3:17).

❸ Traveled with Jesus during His public ministry; heard the teachings, saw the miracles, witnessed the Transfiguration (Matt. 17:1–9).

❹ Remained with Jesus during final week of His life; Triumphal Entry, rejection, Last Supper, Gethsemane, trial, and Crucifixion (John 19:25–27).

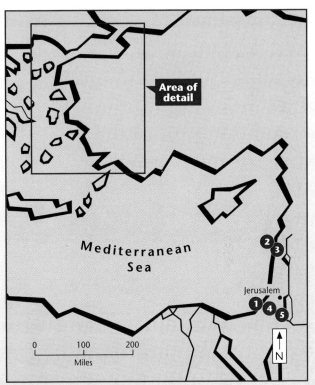

❺ Worked with Simon Peter as leader of early church in Jerusalem (Acts 3; 4); not heard from in Acts after death of his brother James (12:1, 2).

❻ John was banished for a time to the island of Patmos, where he wrote the Book of Revelation (Rev. 1:9).

❼ Tradition holds that John spent much of his later years in Ephesus, where he probably wrote the Gospel of John and the Letters of John.

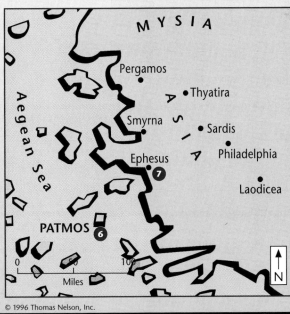

GENESIS AND REVELATION— THE FIRST AND LAST VOLUMES

The word "Bible" comes from the Greek word *biblos*, which means "book." The Bible is a complete book, unified in its theme and message. But it is also a collection of sixty-six books, a virtual library of God's Word to humanity. Genesis, the first book in the Bible, and Revelation, the last, help to define the collection, showing us the beginning and the end of history.

In Revelation 21, John reveals a new heaven and earth. In reading it, we can't help but look back to the beginnings of the world:

GENESIS	REVELATION
God creates the world.	God creates a new heaven and earth.
The devil introduces sin into the world.	The devil is defeated and destroyed; sin is done away with.
Humanity falls into sin.	God restores people to their original sinlessness.
The world is subjected to a curse.	The curse is removed.
People are separate from God.	People live with God forever.
People shed tears and know sorrow.	God wipes away every tear and removes sorrow.
People are barred from the tree of life.	People may eat freely from the tree of life.
Death enters the world.	Death is done away with and people live forever.
The languages of humanity are confused and the peoples scattered.	The peoples of the world are brought together before Christ and they sing His praises together.

because they are spiritually discerned. Matt. 16:23

15 But he that is spiritual judgeth all things, yet he himself is judged of no man.

16 [R]For who hath known the mind of the Lord, that he may instruct him? But we have the mind of Christ. Rom. 11:34

3 And I, brethren, could not speak unto you as unto spiritual, but as unto carnal, *even* as unto [R]babes in Christ. 2:6; Eph. 4:1

2 I have fed you with [R]milk, and not with meat: for hitherto ye were not able *to bear it,* neither yet now are ye able. Heb. 5:12

3 For ye are yet carnal: for whereas *there is* among you envying, and strife, and divisions, are ye not carnal, and walk as men?

4 For while one saith, I am of Paul; and another, I *am* of A-pol'-los; are ye not carnal?

5 Who then is Paul, and who *is* A-pol'-los, but [R]ministers by whom ye believed, even as the Lord gave to every man? Rom. 15:16

6 [R]I have planted, [R]A-pol'-los watered; [R]but God gave the increase. Acts 18:4 · 1:12 · [2 Cor. 3:5]

7 So then [R]neither is he that planteth any thing, neither he that watereth; but God that giveth the increase. 2 Cor. 12:11; [Gal. 6:3]

8 Now he that planteth and he that watereth are one: and every man shall receive his own reward according to his own labour.

9 For we are labourers together with God: ye are God's husbandry, *ye are* God's building.

10 [R]According to the grace of God which is given unto me, as a wise masterbuilder, I have laid [R]the foundation, and another buildeth thereon. But let every man take heed how he buildeth thereupon. Rom. 1:5 · 4:15

11 For other foundation can no man lay than [R]that is laid, [R]which is Jesus Christ. Is. 28:16 · Eph. 2:20

12 Now if any man build upon this foundation gold, silver, precious stones, wood, hay, stubble;

13 Every man's work shall be made manifest: for the day [R]shall declare it, because [R]it shall be revealed by fire; and the fire shall try every man's work of what sort it is. 1 Pet. 1:7 · Mal. 3:1–3; Luke 2:35

14 If any man's work [T]abide which he hath built thereupon, he shall receive a reward. *endures*

15 If any man's work shall be burned, he shall suffer loss: but he himself shall be saved; yet so as [T]by fire. *through*

16 [R]Know ye not that ye are the temple of God, and *that* the Spirit of God dwelleth in you? Rom. 8:9

17 If any man [T]defile the temple of God, him shall God destroy; for the temple of God is holy, which *temple* ye are. *destroys*

18 [R]Let no man deceive himself. If any man among you seemeth to be wise in this [T]world, let him become a fool, that he may be wise. Prov. 3:7 · *age*

19 For the wisdom of this world is foolishness with God. For it is written, [R]He taketh the wise in their own craftiness. Job 5:13

20 And again, [R]The Lord knoweth the thoughts of the wise, that they are [T]vain. Ps. 94:11 · *futile*

21 Therefore let no man glory in men. For all things are yours;

22 Whether Paul, or A-pol'-los, or Ce'-phas, or the world, or life, or death, or things present, or things to come; all are yours;

23 And [R]ye are Christ's; and Christ *is* God's. [Rom. 14:8]; 2 Cor. 10:7

4 Let a man so account of us, as of [R]the ministers of Christ, [R]and stewards of the mysteries of God. 2 Cor. 3:6; Col. 1:25 · Titus 1:7

2 Moreover it is required in stewards, that a man be found faithful.

3 But with me it is a very small thing that I should be judged of you, or of man's [T]judgment: yea, I judge not mine own self. Lit. *day*

4 For I know nothing [T]by myself; yet am I not hereby justified: but he that judgeth me is the Lord. *against*

5 [R]Therefore judge nothing before the time, until the Lord come,

who both will bring to ᴿlight the hidden things of darkness, and will make manifest the counsels of the hearts: and then shall every man have praise of God.   Rom. 2:1

6 And these things, brethren, I have ᵀin a figure transferred to myself and *to* A-pol'-los for your sakes; that ye might learn in us not to think *of men* above that which is written, that no one of you be ᵀpuffed up for one against another.   *figuratively · proud*

7 For who maketh thee to differ *from another?* and ᴿwhat hast thou that thou didst not receive? now if thou didst receive *it,* why dost thou glory, as if thou hadst not received *it?* John 3:27; Rom. 12:3, 6

8 Now ye are full, ᴿnow ye are rich, ye have reigned as kings without us: and I would to God ye did reign, that we also might reign with you.   Rev. 3:17

9 For I think that God hath set forth us the apostles last, as it were appointed to death: for we are made a spectacle unto the world, and to angels, and to men.

10 We *are* ᴿfools for Christ's sake, but ye *are* wise in Christ; ᴿwe *are* weak, but ye *are* strong; ye *are* honourable, but we *are* despised. Acts 17:18; 26:24 · 2:3; 2 Cor. 13:9

11 Even unto this present hour we both hunger, and thirst, and are naked, and are buffeted, and have no certain dwellingplace;

12 ᴿAnd labour, working with our own hands: ᴿbeing reviled, we bless; being persecuted, we suffer it: Acts 18:3; 20:34 · Matt. 5:44

13 Being defamed, we ᵀintreat: we are made as the filth of the world, *and are* the offscouring of all things unto this day.   *encourage*

14 I write not these things to shame you, but ᴿas my beloved sons I warn *you.*   2 Cor. 6:13; 12:14

15 For though ye have ten thousand instructers in Christ, yet *have ye* not many fathers: for ᴿin Christ Jesus I have begotten you through the gospel.   Gal. 4:19

16 Wherefore I beseech you, ᴿbe ye followers of me.   Phil. 3:17; 4:9

17 For this cause have I sent unto you Ti-mo'-the-us, ᴿwho is my beloved son, and faithful in the Lord, who shall bring you into remembrance of my ways which be in Christ, as I teach every where in every church. 1 Tim. 1:2, 18

18 Now some are puffed up, as though I would not come to you.

19 ᴿBut I will come to you shortly, if the Lord will, and will know, not the speech of them which are puffed up, but the power. 11:34; 16:5

20 For the kingdom of God *is* not in word, but in ᴿpower.   2:4

21 What will ye? shall I come unto you with a rod, or in love, and *in* the spirit of meekness?

5 It is reported commonly *that there is* fornication among you, and such fornication as is not so much as named among the Gentiles, that one should have his father's ᴿwife.   Deut. 22:30; 27:20

2 ᴿAnd ye are puffed up, and have not rather mourned, that he that hath done this deed might be taken away from among you.   4:18

3 ᴿFor I verily, as absent in body, but present in spirit, have judged already, as though I were present, *concerning* him that hath so done this deed,   1 Thess. 2:17

4 In the name of our Lord Jesus Christ, when ye are gathered together, and my spirit, with the power of our Lord Jesus Christ,

5 To deliver such an one unto Satan for the destruction of the flesh, that the spirit may be saved in the day of the Lord Jesus.

6 Your glorying *is* not good. Know ye not that ᴿa little leaven leaveneth the whole lump?   Gal. 5:9

7 Purge out therefore the old leaven, that ye may be a new lump, as ye are unleavened. For even ᴿChrist our ᴿpassover is sacrificed for us: Is. 53:7 · John 19:14

8 Therefore let us keep the feast, not with old leaven, neither with the leaven of malice and wickedness; but with the unleavened *bread* of sincerity and truth.

9 I wrote unto you in an epistle not to company with fornicators:

10 Yet not altogether with the fornicators of this world, or with the covetous, or extortioners, or with idolaters; for then must ye needs go out of the world.

11 But now I have written unto you not to keep company, ^Rif any man that is called a brother be a fornicator, or covetous, or an idolater, or a railer, or a drunkard, or an extortioner; with such an one ^Rno not to eat.   Matt. 18:17 · Gal. 2:12

12 For what have I to do ^Tto judge them also that are ^Twithout? do not ye judge them that are within?   with judging · outside

13 But them that are without God judgeth. Therefore ^Rput away from among yourselves that wicked person. v. 2; Deut. 13:5; 17:7, 12; 19:19

6 Dare any of you, having a matter against another, go to law before the unjust, and not before the ^Rsaints?   Matt. 19:28

2 Do ye not know that ^Rthe saints shall judge the world? and if the world shall be judged by you, are ye unworthy to judge the smallest matters?   Ps. 49:14

3 Know ye not that we shall judge angels? how much more things that pertain to this life?

4 If then ye have ^Tjudgments of things pertaining to this life, set them to judge who are least esteemed in the church.   courts

5 I speak to your shame. Is it so, that there is not a wise man among you? no, not one that shall be able to judge between his brethren?

6 But brother goeth to law with brother, and that before the unbelievers.

7 Now therefore there is utterly a fault among you, because ye go to law one with another. ^RWhy do ye not rather take wrong? why do ye not rather suffer yourselves to be defrauded?   [Prov. 20:22]

8 Nay, ye do wrong, and defraud, and that your brethren.

9 Know ye not that the unrighteous shall not inherit the kingdom of God? Be not deceived: ^Rneither fornicators, nor idolaters,

nor adulterers, nor effeminate, nor abusers of themselves with mankind,   Gal. 5:21; Eph. 5:5; 1 Tim. 1:9

10 Nor thieves, nor covetous, nor drunkards, nor revilers, nor extortioners, shall inherit the kingdom of God.

11 And such were ^Rsome of you: but ye are washed, but ye are sanctified, but ye are justified in the name of the Lord Jesus, and by the Spirit of our God. [Col. 3:5–7]

12 ^RAll things are lawful unto me, but all things are not ^Texpedient: all things are lawful for me, but I will not be brought under the power of any.   10:23 · helpful

13 Meats for the belly, and the belly for meats: but God shall destroy both it and them. Now the body is not for ^Rfornication, but for the Lord; and the Lord for the body.   5:1; Gal. 5:19; Eph. 5:3; Col. 3:5

14 And ^RGod hath both raised up the Lord, and will also raise up us by his own power.   2 Cor. 4:14

15 Know ye not that ^Ryour bodies are the members of Christ? shall I then take the members of Christ, and make them the members of an harlot? God forbid.12:27

16 What? know ye not that he which is joined to an harlot is one body? for ^Rtwo, saith he, shall be one flesh. Gen. 2:24; Matt. 19:5; Eph. 5:31

17 ^RBut he that is joined unto the Lord is one spirit. [Gal. 2:20]; Eph. 4:4

18 ^RFlee fornication. Every sin that a man doeth is without the body; but he that committeth fornication sinneth ^Ragainst his own body.   Rom. 6:12; Heb. 13:4 · Rom. 1:24

19 What? ^Rknow ye not that your body is the temple of the Holy Ghost which is in you, which ye have of God, ^Rand ye are not your own?   John 2:21 · Rom. 14:7

20 For ^Rye are bought with a price: therefore glorify God in your body, and in your spirit, which are God's.   7:23; Gal. 3:13

7 Now concerning the things whereof ye wrote unto me: ^RIt is good for a man not to touch a woman.   vv. 8, 26

2 Nevertheless, to avoid forni-

cation, let every man have his own wife, and let every woman have her own husband.

3 RLet the husband render unto the wife due Tbenevolence: and likewise also the wife unto the husband. Ex. 21:10 · *affection*

4 The wife hath not Tpower of her own body, but the husband: and likewise also the husband hath not power of his own body, but the wife. *authority over*

5 RDefraudT ye not one the other, except *it be* with consent for a time, that ye may give yourselves to fasting and prayer; and come together again, that RSatan tempt you not for your incontinency. Joel 2:16 · *Deprive* · 1 Thess. 3:5

6 But I speak this by permission, *and* not of commandment.

7 For RI would that all men were even as I myself. But every man hath his proper gift of God, one after this manner, and another after that. Acts 26:29

8 I say therefore to the unmarried and widows, RIt is good for them if they abide even as I. v. 26

9 But Rif they cannot contain, let them marry: for it is better to marry than to burn. 1 Tim. 5:14

10 And unto the married I command, *yet* not I, but the RLord, RLet not the wife depart from *her* husband: Mark 10:6–10 · [Matt. 5:32]

11 But and if she depart, let her remain unmarried, or be reconciled to *her* husband: and let not the husband put away *his* wife.

12 But to the rest speak I, not the Lord: If any brother hath a wife that believeth not, and she be pleased to dwell with him, let him not put her away.

13 And the woman which hath an husband that believeth not, and if he be pleased to dwell with her, let her not Tleave him. *divorce*

14 For the unbelieving husband is sanctified by the wife, and the unbelieving wife is sanctified by the husband: else Rwere your children unclean; but now are they holy. Ezra 9:2; Mal. 2:15

15 But if the unbelieving depart, let him depart. A brother or a sister is not under bondage in such *cases:* but God hath called us Rto peace. Rom. 12:18

16 For what knowest thou, O wife, whether thou shalt Rsave *thy* husband? or how knowest thou, O man, whether thou shalt save *thy* wife? Rom. 11:14; 1 Pet. 3:1

17 But as God hath distributed to every man, as the Lord hath called every one, so let him walk. And so ordain I in all churches.

18 Is any man called being circumcised? let him not become uncircumcised. Is any called in uncircumcision? Rlet him not be circumcised. Acts 15:1

19 RCircumcision is nothing, and uncircumcision is nothing, but the keeping of the commandments of God. [Gal. 3:28; 5:6; 6:15]

20 Let every man abide in the same calling wherein he was called.

21 Art thou called *being* a Tservant? care not for it: but if thou mayest be made free, use *it* rather. *slave*

22 For he that is called in the Lord, *being* a servant, is the Lord's freeman: likewise also he that is called, *being* free, is RChrist's servant. 1 Pet. 2:16

23 Ye are bought with a price; be not ye the servants of men.

24 Brethren, let every man, wherein he is called, therein abide with RGod. [Eph. 6:5–8; Col. 3:22–24]

25 Now concerning virgins I have no commandment of the Lord: yet I give my judgment, as one Rthat hath obtained mercy of the Lord to be faithful. 2 Cor. 4:1

26 I suppose therefore that this is good for the present distress, *I* say, Rthat *it is* good for a man so to be. vv. 1, 8

27 Art thou bound unto a wife? seek not to be loosed. Art thou loosed from a wife? seek not a wife.

28 But and if thou marry, thou hast not sinned; and if a virgin marry, she hath not sinned. Nev-

ertheless such shall have trouble in the flesh: but I spare you.

29 But ^Rthis I say, brethren, the time *is* short: it remaineth, that both they that have wives be as though they had none;   1 Pet. 4:7

30 And they that weep, as though they wept not; and they that rejoice, as though they rejoiced not; and they that buy, as though they possessed not;

31 And they that use this world, as not ^Rabusing *it:* for the fashion of this world passeth away.   9:18

32 But I would have you without ^Tcarefulness. ^RHe that is unmarried careth for the things that belong to the Lord, how he may please the Lord: concern · 1 Tim. 5:5

33 But he that is married careth for the things that are of the world, how he may please *his* wife.

34 There is difference *also* between a wife and a virgin. The unmarried woman ^Rcareth for the things of the Lord, that she may be holy both in body and in spirit: but she that is married careth for the things of the world, how she may please *her* husband. Luke 10:40

35 And this I speak for your own profit; not that I may ^Tcast a snare upon you, but for that which is ^Tcomely, and that ye may attend upon the Lord without distraction.   put a leash on · proper

36 But if any man think that he behaveth himself uncomely toward his virgin, if she pass the flower of *her* age, and need so require, let him do what he will, he sinneth not: let them marry.

37 Nevertheless he that standeth stedfast in his heart, having no necessity, but hath power over his own will, and hath so decreed in his heart that he will keep his virgin, doeth well.

38 ^RSo then he that giveth *her* in marriage doeth well; but he that giveth *her* not in marriage doeth better.   Heb. 13:4

39 ^RThe wife is bound by the law as long as her husband liveth; but if her husband be dead, she is at liberty to be married to whom she will; only in the Lord.   Rom. 7:2

40 But she is happier if she so abide, ^Rafter my judgment: and ^RI think also that I have the Spirit of God.   vv. 6, 25 · 1 Thess. 4:8

8 Now as touching things offered unto idols, we know that we all have knowledge. Knowledge puffeth up, but ^Tcharity ^Tedifieth.   love · builds up

2 And if any man think that he knoweth any thing, he knoweth nothing yet as he ought to know.

3 But if any man love God, the same is known of him.

4 As concerning therefore the eating of those things that are offered in sacrifice unto idols, we know that ^Ran idol *is* nothing in the world, and that *there is* none other God but one.   Is. 41:24

5 For though there be that are ^Rcalled gods, whether in heaven or in earth, (as there be gods many, and lords many,)   [John 10:34]

6 But to us *there is but* one God, the Father, of whom *are* all things, and we in him; and one Lord Jesus Christ, ^Rby whom *are* all things, and we by him.   John 1:3

7 Howbeit *there is* not in every man that knowledge: for some ^Rwith conscience of the idol unto this hour eat *it* as a thing offered unto an idol; and their conscience being weak is defiled.   [10:28]

8 But meat commendeth us not to God: for neither, if we eat, are we the better; neither, if we eat not, are we the worse.

9 But ^Rtake heed lest by any means this liberty of yours become ^Ra stumblingblock to them that are weak. Gal. 5:13 · Rom. 12:13, 21

10 For if any man see thee which hast knowledge sit at meat in the idol's temple, shall not ^Rthe conscience of him which is weak be emboldened to eat those things which are offered to idols;   10:28

11 And ^Rthrough thy knowledge shall the weak brother perish, for whom Christ died?   Rom. 14:15, 20

12 But ^Rwhen ye sin so against the brethren, and wound their

weak conscience, ye sin against Christ.   Matt. 25:40

13 Wherefore, if meat make my brother to offend, I will eat no flesh while the world standeth, lest I make my brother to offend.

9 Am I not an apostle? am I not free? have I not seen Jesus Christ our Lord? ^Rare not ye my work in the Lord?   3:6; 4:15

2 If I be not an apostle unto others, yet doubtless I am to you: for ^Rthe seal of mine apostleship are ye in the Lord.   2 Cor. 12:12

3 ^TMine answer to them that do examine me is this,   *My defence*

4 ^RHave we not ^Tpower to eat and to drink?   2 Thess. 3:8 · *right*

5 Have we not power to lead about a sister, a wife, as well as other apostles, and *as* ^Rthe ^Tbrethren of the Lord, and ^RCe'-phas?   Matt. 13:55 · *brothers* · Matt. 8:14

6 Or I only and Barnabas, ^Rhave not we ^Tpower to ^Tforbear working?   Acts 4:36 · *right* · *refrain from*

7 Who goeth a warfare any time at his own ^Tcharges? who planteth a vineyard, and eateth not of the fruit thereof? or who feedeth a flock, and eateth not of the milk of the flock?   *expense*

8 Say I these things as a man? or saith not the law the same also?

9 For it is written in the law of Moses, ^RThou shalt not muzzle the mouth of the ox that treadeth out the corn. Doth God take care for oxen?   Deut. 25:4; 1 Tim. 5:18

10 Or saith he *it* altogether for our sakes? For our sakes, no doubt, *this* is written: that he that ploweth should plow in hope; and that he that thresheth in hope should be partaker of his hope.

11 ^RIf we have sown unto you spiritual things, *is it* a great thing if we shall reap your ^Tcarnal things?   Rom. 15:27 · *material*

12 If others be partakers of *this* power over you, *are* not we rather? Nevertheless we have not used this power; but ^Tsuffer all things, lest we should hinder the gospel of Christ.   *endure*

13 Do ye not know that they which minister about holy things live *of the things* of the temple? and they which wait at the altar are partakers with the altar?

14 Even so hath the Lord ordained that they which preach the gospel should live of the gospel.

15 But ^RI have used none of these things: neither have I written these things, that it should be so done unto me: for ^R*it were* better for me to die, than that any man should make my glorying void.   Acts 18:3; 20:33 · 2 Cor. 11:10

16 For though I preach the gospel, I have nothing to glory of: for ^Rnecessity is laid upon me; yea, woe is unto me, if I preach not the gospel!   Acts 9:15; [Rom. 1:14]

17 For if I do this thing willingly, I have a reward: but if against my will, ^Ra dispensation *of the gospel* is committed unto me.   Eph. 3:2

18 What is my reward then? *Verily* that, ^Rwhen I preach the gospel, I may make the gospel of Christ without charge, that I ^Rabuse not my power in the gospel.   10:33 · v. 12; 7:31

19 For though I be free from all *men,* yet have ^RI made myself servant unto all, ^Rthat I might gain the more. Gal. 5:13 · Matt. 18:15; 1 Pet. 3:1

20 And unto the Jews I became as a Jew, that I might gain the Jews; to them that are under the law, as under the law, that I might gain them that are under the law;

21 ^RTo them that are without law, as without law, (being not without law to God, but under the law to Christ,) that I might gain them that are without law. [Gal. 2:3]

22 ^RTo the weak became I as weak, that I might gain the weak: ^RI am made all things to all *men,* ^Rthat I might by all means save some.   2 Cor. 11:29 · 10:33 · Rom. 11:14

23 And this I do for the gospel's sake, that I might be partaker thereof with *you.*

24 Know ye not that they which run in a race run all, but one

receiveth the prize? ^RSo run, that ye may obtain.   2 Tim. 4:7; Heb. 12:1

25 And every man that striveth for the mastery is temperate in all things. Now they *do it* to obtain a corruptible crown; but we ^Ran incorruptible.   2 Tim. 4:8; James 1:12

26 I therefore so run, ^Rnot as uncertainly; so fight I, not as one that beateth the air: 2 Tim. 2:5

27 ^RBut I keep under my body, and bring *it* into subjection: lest that by any means, when I have preached to others, I myself should be a castaway.   [Rom. 8:13]

10 Moreover, brethren, I would not that ye should be ignorant, how that all our fathers were under ^Rthe cloud, and all passed through the sea; Ex. 13:21, 22

2 And were all baptized unto Moses in the cloud and in the sea;

3 And did all eat the same ^Rspiritual ^Tmeat;   Deut. 8:3 · *food*

4 And did all drink the same spiritual drink: for they drank of that spiritual Rock that followed them: and that Rock was Christ.

5 But with many of them God was not well pleased: for they ^Rwere overthrown in the wilderness.   Num. 14:29, 37; Heb. 3:17; Jude 5

6 Now these things ^Twere our examples, to the intent we should not lust after evil things, as ^Rthey also lusted.   *became* · Num. 11:4, 34

7 Neither be ye idolaters, as *were* some of them; as it is written, The people sat down to eat and drink, and rose up to play.

8 ^RNeither let us commit fornication, as some of them committed, and ^Rfell in one day three and twenty thousand. Rev. 2:14 · Ps. 106:29

9 Neither let us tempt Christ, as some of them also tempted, and were destroyed of serpents.

10 Neither murmur ye, as ^Rsome of them also murmured, and were destroyed of the destroyer. Ex. 16:2

11 Now all these things happened unto them for ensamples: and they are written for our admonition, upon whom the ends of the ^Tworld are come.   *ages*

12 Wherefore let him that think-

eth he standeth take heed lest he fall.

13 There hath no temptation taken you but such as is common to man: but ^RGod *is* faithful, ^Rwho will not suffer you to be tempted above that ye are able; but will with the temptation also make a way to escape, that ye may be able to ^Tbear *it*.   1:9 · Ps. 125:3 · *endure*

14 Wherefore, my dearly beloved, ^Rflee from idolatry. 2 Cor. 6:17

15 I speak as to ^Rwise men; judge ye what I say.   8:1

16 ^RThe cup of blessing which we bless, is it not the communion of the blood of Christ? The bread which we break, is it not the communion of the body of Christ?   Matt. 26:26–28; Mark 14:23

17 For we *being* many are one bread, *and* one body: for we are all partakers of that one bread.

18 Behold ^RIsrael ^Rafter the flesh: ^Rare not they which eat of the sacrifices partakers of the altar?   Rom. 4:12 · Rom. 4:1 · Deut. 12:17

19 What say I then? ^Rthat the idol is any thing, or that which is offered in sacrifice to idols is any thing?   8:4

20 But *I say*, that the things which the Gentiles ^Rsacrifice, ^Rthey sacrifice to devils, and not to God: and I would not that ye should have fellowship with devils. Lev. 17:7 · Ps. 106:37; Gal. 4:8; Rev. 9:20

21 Ye cannot drink the cup of the Lord, and the cup of devils: ye cannot be partakers of the Lord's table, and of the table of devils.

22 Do we ^Rprovoke the Lord to jealousy? ^Rare we stronger than he?   Deut. 32:21 · Ezek. 22:14

23 All things are lawful for me, but all things are not ^Rexpedient: all things are lawful for me, but all things ^Tedify not. 6:12 · *do not build up*

24 Let no man seek his own, but every man another's *wealth*.

25 Whatsoever is sold in the shambles, *that* eat, asking no question for conscience sake:

26 For ^Rthe earth *is* the Lord's, and the fulness thereof.   Ps. 24:1

27 If any of them that believe

not bid you *to a feast,* and ye ᵀbe disposed to go; whatsoever is set before you, eat, asking no question for conscience sake.   *desire to*

28 But if any man say unto you, This is offered in sacrifice unto idols, eat not ᴿfor his sake that shewed it, and for conscience sake: for the earth *is* the Lord's, and the fulness thereof: [8:7, 10, 12]

29 Conscience, I say, not thine own, but of the other: for ᴿwhy is my liberty judged of another *man's* conscience?   [9:19]; Rom. 14:16

30 For if I by grace be a partaker, why am I evil spoken of for that for which I give thanks?

31 ᴿWhether therefore ye eat, or drink, or whatsoever ye do, do all to the glory of God.   Col. 3:17

32 Give none offence, neither to the Jews, nor to the Gentiles, nor to the church of God:

33 Even ᴿas I please all *men* in all *things,* not seeking mine own profit, but the *profit* of many, that they may be saved.   9:22; [Gal. 1:10]

11 Be ye followers of me, even as I also *am* of Christ.

2 Now I praise you, brethren, that ye remember me in all things, and ye keep the ᵀordinances, as I delivered *them* to you.   *traditions*

3 But I would have you know, that the head of every man is Christ; and ᴿthe head of the woman *is* the man; and the head of Christ *is* God.   Gen. 3:16; [Eph. 5:23]

4 Every man praying or prophesying, having *his* head covered, dishonoureth his head.

5 But every woman that prayeth or prophesieth with *her* head uncovered dishonoureth her head: for that is even all one as if she were ᴿshaven.   Deut. 21:12

6 For if the woman be not covered, let her also be shorn: but if it be ᴿa shame for a woman to be shorn or shaven, let her be covered.   Num. 5:18

7 For a man indeed ought not to cover *his* head, forasmuch as ᴿhe is the image and glory of God: but the woman is the glory of the man.   Gen. 1:26, 27; 5:1; 9:6; James 3:9

8 For the man is not of the woman; but the woman ᴿof the man.   Gen. 2:21–23; 1 Tim. 2:13

9 Neither was the man created for the woman; but the woman ᴿfor the man.   Gen. 2:18

10 For this cause ought the woman to have power on *her* head because of the angels.

11 Nevertheless ᴿneither is the man ᵀwithout the woman, neither the woman ᵀwithout the man, in the Lord.   [Gal. 3:28] · *independent of*

12 For as the woman *is* of the man, even so *is* the man also by the woman; but all things of God.

13 Judge in yourselves: is it ᵀcomely that a woman pray unto God uncovered?   *proper*

14 Doth not even nature itself teach you, that, if a man have long hair, it is a shame unto him?

15 But if a woman have long hair, it is a glory to her: for *her* hair is given her for a covering.

16 But ᴿif any man seem to be contentious, we have no such custom, ᴿneither the churches of God.   1 Tim. 6:4 · 7:17

17 Now in this that I declare *unto you* I praise *you* not, that ye come together not for the better, but for the worse.

18 For first of all, when ye come together in the church, ᴿI hear that there be divisions among you: and I partly believe it.   1:10–12

19 For there must be also ᵀheresies among you, ᴿthat they which are approved may be made manifest among you.   *factions* · [Deut. 13:3]

20 When ye come together therefore into one place, *this* is not to eat the Lord's supper.

21 For in eating every one taketh before *other* his own supper: and one is hungry, and ᴿanother is drunken.   2 Pet. 2:13; Jude 12

22 What? have ye not houses to eat and to drink in? or despise ye ᴿthe church of God, and shame them that have not? What shall I say to you? shall I praise you in this? I praise *you* not.   10:32

23 For I have received of the Lord that which also I delivered

unto you, ᴿThat the Lord Jesus the *same* night in which he was betrayed took bread: Matt. 26:26–28
24 And when he had given thanks, he brake *it*, and said, Take, eat: this is my body, which is broken for you: this do in remembrance of me.
25 After the same manner also *he took* the cup, ᵀwhen he had supped, saying, This cup is the new testament in my blood: this do ye, as oft as ye drink *it,* in remembrance of me.   *after supper*
26 For as often as ye eat this bread, and drink this cup, ye do ᵀshew the Lord's death ᴿtill he come.   *proclaim* · John 14:3; [Acts 1:11]
27 Wherefore whosoever shall eat ᴿthis bread, and drink *this* cup of the Lord, ᵀunworthily, shall be guilty of the body and blood of the Lord. [John 6:51] · *in an unworthy manner*
28 But let a man examine himself, and so let him eat of *that* bread, and drink of *that* cup.
29 For he that eateth and drinketh unworthily, eateth and drinketh damnation to himself, not discerning the Lord's body.
30 For this cause many *are* weak and sickly among you, and many ᵀsleep.   *Are dead*
31 For if we would judge ourselves, we should not be judged.
32 But when we are judged, ᴿwe are chastened of the Lord, that we should not be condemned with the world.   [Heb. 12:5–10; Rev. 3:19]
33 Wherefore, my brethren, when ye ᴿcome together to eat, ᵀtarry one for another.   14:26 · *wait*
34 And if any man hunger, let him eat at home; that ye come not together ᵀunto condemnation. And the rest will I set in order when I come.   *for judgment*

12 Now ᴿconcerning spiritual *gifts,* brethren, I would not have you ignorant.   v. 4; 14:1, 37
2 Ye know that ye were Gentiles, carried away unto these dumb idols, even as ye were led.
3 Wherefore I give you to understand, that no man speaking by the Spirit of God calleth Jesus

accursed: and ᴿ*that* no man can say that Jesus is the Lord, but by the Holy Ghost.   Matt. 16:17
4 Now ᴿthere are diversities of gifts, but the same Spirit.   v. 11
5 ᴿAnd there are differences of ᵀadministrations, but the same Lord.   Rom. 12:6 · *ministries*
6 And there are diversities of operations, but it is the same God ᴿwhich worketh all in all.   15:28
7 But the manifestation of the Spirit is given to every man to profit ᵀwithal.
8 For to one is given by the Spirit ᴿthe word of wisdom; to another ᴿthe word of knowledge by the same Spirit;   2:6, 7 · [2:11, 16]
9 ᴿTo another faith by the same Spirit; to another the gifts of healing by the same Spirit;   2 Cor. 4:13
10 ᴿTo another the working of miracles; to another ᴿprophecy; to another discerning of spirits; to another *divers* kinds of tongues; to another the interpretation of tongues: Mark 16:17 · Rom. 12:6
11 But all these worketh that one and the selfsame Spirit, ᴿdividing to every man severally ᴿas he will. Rom. 12:6; 2 Cor. 10:13 · [John 3:8]
12 For ᴿas the body is one, and hath many members, and all the members of that one body, being many, are one body: ᴿso also *is* Christ.   Rom. 12:4, 5; Eph. 4:4 · [Gal. 3:16]
13 For by one Spirit are we all baptized into one body, whether *we be* Jews or Gentiles, whether *we be* bond or free; and have been all made to drink into one Spirit.
14 For the body is not one member, but many.
15 If the foot shall say, Because I am not the hand, I am not of the body; is it therefore not of the body?
16 And if the ear shall say, Because I am not the eye, I am not of the body; is it therefore not of the body?
17 If the whole body *were* an eye, where *were* the hearing? If the whole *were* hearing, where *were* the smelling?
18 But now hath ᴿGod set the

members every one of them in the body, as it hath pleased him. v. 28

19 And if they were all one member, where *were* the body?

20 But now *are they* many members, yet but one body.

21 And the eye cannot say unto the hand, I have no need of thee: nor again the head to the feet, I have no need of you.

22 Nay, much more those members of the body, which seem to be more ᵀfeeble, are necessary: *weak*

23 And those *members* of the body, which we think to be less honourable, upon these we bestow more abundant honour; and our uncomely *parts* have more abundant comeliness.

24 For our ᵀcomely *parts* have no need: but God hath tempered the body together, having given more abundant honour to that *part* which lacked: *presentable*

25 That there should be no ᵀschism in the body; but *that* the members should have the same care one for another. *division*

26 And ᵀwhether one member suffer, all the members suffer with it; or one member be honoured, all the members rejoice with it. *if*

27 Now ᴿye are the body of Christ, and members in particular. Rom. 12:5; Eph. 1:23; 4:12; Col. 1:24

28 And ᴿGod hath set some in the church, first apostles, secondarily prophets, thirdly teachers, after that miracles, then gifts of healings, helps, governments, diversities of tongues. Eph. 4:11

29 *Are* all apostles? *are* all prophets? *are* all teachers? *are* all workers of miracles?

30 Have all the gifts of healing? do all speak with tongues? do all interpret?

31 But ᴿcovetᵀ earnestly the best gifts: and yet shew I unto you a more excellent way. 14:1, 39 · *desire*

13 Though I speak with the tongues of men and of angels, and have not ᵀcharity, I am become *as* sounding brass, or a ᵀtinkling cymbal. *love · clanging*

2 And though I have *the gift of* prophecy, and understand all mysteries, and all knowledge; and though I have all faith, so that I could remove mountains, and have not charity, I am nothing.

3 And ᴿthough I bestow all my goods to feed *the poor,* and though I give my body to be burned, and have not charity, it profiteth me nothing. Matt. 6:1, 2

4 Charity suffereth long, *and* is ᴿkind; charity ᴿenvieth not; charity vaunteth not itself, is not puffed up, Eph. 4:32 · Gal. 5:26

5 Doth not behave itself ᵀunseemly, ᴿseeketh not her own, is not easily provoked, thinketh no evil; *rudely · 10:24; Phil. 2:4*

6 ᴿRejoiceth not in iniquity, but rejoiceth in the truth; Rom. 1:32

7 ᴿBeareth all things, believeth all things, hopeth all things, endureth all things. Rom. 15:1; Gal. 6:2

8 ᵀCharity never faileth: but whether *there be* prophecies, they shall ᵀfail; whether *there be* tongues, they shall cease; whether *there be* knowledge, it shall ᵀvanish away. *Love · cease*

9 ᴿFor we know in part, and we prophesy in part. v. 12; 8:2

10 But when that which is ᵀperfect is come, then that which is in part shall be done away. *complete*

11 When I was a child, I spake as a child, I understood as a child, I thought as a child: but when I became a man, I put away childish things.

12 For ᴿnow we see through a glass, darkly; but then ᴿface to face: now I know in part; but then shall I know even as also I am known. James 1:23 · [1 John 3:2]

13 And now abideth faith, hope, ᵀcharity, these three; but the greatest of these *is* ᵀcharity. *love*

14 Follow after charity, and ᴿdesire spiritual *gifts,* but rather that ye may prophesy. 12:31

2 For he that ᴿspeaketh in an *unknown* tongue speaketh not unto men, but unto God: for no man understandeth *him;* howbeit in the spirit he speaketh mysteries. Acts 2:4; 10:46

3 But he that prophesieth speaketh unto men *to* ^Redification, and ^Rexhortation, and comfort.   Rom. 14:19; 15:2 · Titus 1:9; 2:15

4 He that speaketh in an *unknown* tongue edifieth himself; but he that prophesieth edifieth the church.

5 I would that ye all spake with tongues, but ^Trather that ye prophesied: for greater *is* he that prophesieth than he that speaketh with tongues, except he interpret, that the church may receive ^Tedifying.   *even more · building up*

6 Now, brethren, if I come unto you speaking with tongues, what shall I profit you, except I shall speak to you either by ^Rrevelation, or by knowledge, or by prophesying, or by doctrine?   v. 26; Eph. 1:17

7 And even things without life giving sound, whether pipe or harp, except they give a distinction in the sounds, how shall it be known what is piped or harped?

8 For if the trumpet give an uncertain sound, who shall prepare himself to the battle?

9 So likewise ye, except ye utter by the tongue words easy to be understood, how shall it be known what is spoken? for ye shall speak into the air.

10 There are, it may be, so many kinds of voices in the world, and none of them *is* without ^Tsignification.   *meaning*

11 Therefore if I know not the meaning of the voice, I shall be unto him that speaketh a ^Tbarbarian, and he that speaketh *shall be* a barbarian unto me.   *foreigner*

12 Even so ye, forasmuch as ye are zealous of spiritual *gifts*, seek that ye may excel to the edifying of the church.

13 Wherefore let him that speaketh in an *unknown* tongue pray that he may ^Rinterpret.   12:10

14 For if I pray in an *unknown* tongue, my spirit prayeth, but my understanding is unfruitful.

15 What is it then? I will pray with the spirit, and I will pray with the understanding also: I will sing with the spirit, and I will sing with the understanding also.

16 Else when thou shalt bless with the spirit, how shall he that occupieth the room of the unlearned say A-men' at thy giving of thanks, seeing he understandeth not what thou sayest?

17 For thou verily givest thanks well, but the other is not edified.

18 I thank my God, I speak with tongues more than ye all:

19 Yet in the church I had rather speak five words with my understanding, that *by my voice* I might teach others also, than ten thousand words in an *unknown* tongue.

20 Brethren, ^Rbe not children in understanding: howbeit in malice be ye children, but in understanding be men.   Rom. 16:19; Heb. 5:12, 13

21 In the law it is ^Rwritten, With *men of* other tongues and other lips will I speak unto this people; and yet for all that will they not hear me, saith the Lord.   Is. 28:11, 12

22 Wherefore tongues are for a ^Rsign, not to them that believe, but to them that believe not: but prophesying *serveth* not for them that believe not, but for them which believe.   Mark 16:17

23 If therefore the whole church be come together into one place, and all speak with tongues, and there come in *those that are* unlearned, or unbelievers, ^Rwill they not say that ye are mad?   Acts 2:13

24 But if all prophesy, and there come in one that believeth not, or *one* unlearned, he is convinced ^Tof all, he is judged ^Tof all: *by*

25 And thus are the secrets of his heart made manifest; and so falling down on *his* face he will worship God, and report ^Rthat God is in you of a truth.   Is. 45:14

26 How is it then, brethren? when ye come together, every one of you hath a psalm, hath a doctrine, hath a tongue, hath a revelation, hath an interpretation. Let all things be done unto edifying.

27 If any man speak in an *unknown* tongue, *let it be* by two, or

at the most *by* three, and *that* by course; and let one interpret.

28 But if there be no interpreter, let him keep silence in the church; and let him speak to himself, and to God.

29 Let the prophets speak two or three, and let the other judge.

30 If *any thing* be revealed to another that sitteth by, ᴿlet the first hold his peace. [1 Thess. 5:19, 20]

31 For ye may all prophesy one by one, that all may learn, and all may be ᵀcomforted.   *encouraged*

32 And the spirits of the prophets are subject to the prophets.

33 For God is not *the author* of ᵀconfusion, but of peace, as in all churches of the saints.   *disorder*

34 Let your women keep silence in the churches: for it is not permitted unto them to speak; but *they are commanded* to be under obedience, as also saith the law.

35 And if they will learn any thing, let them ask their husbands at home: for it is a shame for women to speak in the church.

36 What? came the word of God ᵀout from you? or came it unto you only?   *originally from*

37 ᴿIf any man think himself to be a prophet, or spiritual, let him acknowledge that the things that I write unto you are the commandments of the Lord.   2 Cor. 10:7

38 But if any man be ignorant, let him be ignorant.

39 Wherefore, brethren, ᴿcovet to prophesy, and forbid not to speak with tongues.   1 Thess. 5:20

40 ᴿLet all things be done decently and in order.   v. 33

15 Moreover, brethren, I declare unto you the gospel ᴿwhich I preached unto you, which also ye have received, and wherein ye stand;   Rom. 2:16

2 ᴿBy which also ye are saved, if ye keep in memory what I preached unto you, unless ye have believed in vain.   1:21; Rom. 1:16

★ 3 For I delivered unto you first of all that which I also received, how that Christ died for our sins according to the scriptures;

4 And that he was buried, and ★ that he rose again the third day according to the scriptures:

5 And that he was seen of ᵀCe'-phas, then of the twelve: Peter

6 After that, he was seen of above five hundred brethren at once; of whom the greater part remain unto this present, but some ᵀare fallen asleep.   Have died

7 After that, he was seen of James; then of all the apostles.

8 ᴿAnd last of all he was seen of me also, as of one born out of due time.   [Acts 9:3–8; 22:6–11; 26:12–18]

9 For I am the least of the apostles, that am not ᵀmeet to be called an apostle, because ᴿI persecuted the church of God.   *worthy* · Acts 8:3

10 But ᴿby the grace of God I am what I am: and his grace which *was bestowed* upon me was not in vain; but I laboured more abundantly than they all: ᴿyet not I, but the grace of God which was with me.   Eph. 3:7, 8 · Gal. 2:8; Phil. 2:13

11 Therefore whether *it were* I or they, so we preach, and so ye believed.

12 Now if Christ be preached that he rose from the dead, how say some among you that there is no resurrection of the dead?

13 But if there be no resurrection of the dead, ᴿthen is Christ not risen: [1 Thess. 4:14]

14 And if Christ be not risen, then *is* our preaching ᵀvain, and your faith *is* also vain.   *futile*

15 Yea, and we are found false witnesses of God; because ᴿwe have testified of God that he raised up Christ: whom he raised not up, if so be that the dead rise not.   Acts 2:24

16 For if the dead rise not, then is not Christ raised:

17 And if Christ be not raised, your faith *is* ᵀvain; ᴿye are yet in your sins.   *futile* · [Rom. 4:25]

18 Then they also which ᵀare fallen ᴿasleep in Christ are perished.   Have died · Job 14:12; Ps. 13:3

19 ᴿIf in this life only we have hope in Christ, we are of all men most miserable.   4:9; 2 Tim. 3:12

20 But now ᴿis Christ risen from the dead, *and* become the first-fruits of them that slept. 1 Pet. 1:3

21 For ᴿsince by man *came* death, by man *came* also the resurrection of the dead. Gen. 3:19

22 For as in Adam all die, even so in Christ shall all ᴿbe made alive. [John 5:28, 29]

23 But ᴿevery man in his own order: Christ the firstfruits; afterward they that are Christ's at his coming. [1 Thess. 4:15–17]

☆ 24 Then *cometh* the end, when he shall have delivered up the kingdom to God, even the Father; when he shall have put down all rule and all authority and power.

☆ 25 For he must reign, ᴿtill he hath put all enemies under his feet. Ps. 110:1; Matt. 22:44

☆ 26 ᴿThe last enemy *that* shall be destroyed *is* death. [Rev. 20:14; 21:4]

☆ 27 For he ᴿhath put all things under his feet. But when he saith all things are put under *him, it is* ᵀmanifest that he is excepted, which did put all things under him. Ps. 8:6 · *evident*

☆ 28 And when all things shall be subdued unto him, then ᴿshall the Son also himself be subject unto him that put all things under him, that God may be all in all. 3:23; 11:3

29 Else what shall they do which are baptized for the dead, if the dead rise not at all? why are they then baptized for the dead?

30 And ᴿwhy stand we in jeopardy every hour? 2 Cor. 11:26

31 I protest by your rejoicing which I have in Christ Jesus our Lord, ᴿI die daily. Rom. 8:36

32 If after the manner of men ᴿI have fought with beasts at Eph'-e-sus, what advantageth it me, if the dead rise not? let us eat and drink; for to morrow we die. 2 Cor. 1:8

33 Be not deceived: ᴿevil ᵀcommunications corrupt good ᵀmanners. [5:6] · *company corrupts · habits*

34 ᴿAwake to righteousness, and sin not; for some have not the knowledge of God: I speak *this* to your shame. Rom. 13:11

35 But some *man* will say, ᴿHow are the dead raised up? and with what body do they come? Ezek. 37:3

36 *Thou* fool, ᴿthat which thou sowest is not ᵀquickened, except it die: John 12:24 · *made alive*

37 And that which thou sowest, thou sowest not that body that shall be, but ᵀbare grain, ᵀit may chance of wheat, or of some other *grain:* *mere · perhaps wheat*

38 But God giveth it a body as it hath pleased him, and to every seed his own body.

39 All flesh *is* not the same flesh: but *there is* one *kind of* flesh of men, another flesh of beasts, another of fishes, *and* another of birds.

40 *There are* also ᵀcelestial bodies, and bodies ᵀterrestrial: but the glory of the celestial *is* one, and the *glory* of the terrestrial *is* another. *heavenly · earthly*

41 *There is* one glory of the sun, and another glory of the moon, and another glory of the stars: for *one* star differeth from *another* star in glory.

42 So also *is* the resurrection of the dead. It is sown in corruption; it is raised in incorruption:

43 ᴿIt is sown in dishonour; it is raised in glory: it is sown in weakness; it is raised in power: [Col. 3:4]

44 It is sown a natural body; it is raised a spiritual body. There is a natural body, and there is a spiritual body.

45 And so it is written, ᴿThe first man Adam was made a living soul; the last Adam *was made* a quickening spirit. Gen. 2:7

46 Howbeit that *was* not first which is spiritual, but that which is natural; and afterward that which is spiritual.

47 The first man *is* of the earth, earthy: the second man *is* the Lord ᴿfrom heaven. John 3:13

48 As *is* the earthy, such *are* they also that are earthy: ᴿand as *is* the heavenly, such *are* they also that are heavenly. Phil. 3:20

49 And ᴿas we have borne the image of the ᵀearthy, ᴿwe shall

also bear the image of the heavenly. Gen. 5:3 · man of dust · Rom. 8:29

50 Now this I say, brethren, that flesh and blood cannot inherit the kingdom of God; neither doth corruption inherit incorruption.

51 Behold, I shew you a mystery; We shall not all sleep, ^Rbut we shall all be changed, [Phil. 3:21]

52 In a moment, in the twinkling of an eye, at the last trump: ^Rfor the trumpet shall sound, and the dead shall be raised incorruptible, and we shall be changed. John 5:25

53 For this corruptible must put on incorruption, and ^Rthis mortal must put on immortality. 2 Cor. 5:4

54 So when this corruptible shall have put on incorruption, and this mortal shall have put on immortality, then shall be brought to pass the saying that is written, Death is swallowed up in victory.

55 O death, where is thy sting? O grave, where is thy victory?

56 The sting of death is sin; and the strength of sin is the law.

57 But thanks be to God, which giveth us ^Rthe victory through our Lord Jesus Christ. Rom. 8:37

58 Therefore, my beloved brethren, be ye stedfast, unmoveable, always abounding in the work of the Lord, forasmuch as ye know ^Rthat your labour is not in vain in the Lord. [3:8]

16 Now concerning the collection for the saints, as I have given ^Torder to the churches of Ga-la'-ti-a, even so do ye. orders

2 ^RUpon the first day of the week let every one of you lay by him in store, as God hath prospered him, that there be no gatherings when I come. Acts 20:7

3 And when I come, whomsoever ye shall approve by your letters, them will I send to bring your liberality unto Jerusalem.

4 And if it be meet that I go also, they shall go with me.

5 Now I will come unto you, ^Rwhen I shall pass through Mac-e-do'-ni-a: for I do pass through Mac-e-do'-ni-a. 2 Cor. 1:15, 16

6 And it may be that I will abide, yea, and winter with you, that ye may ^Tbring me on my journey whithersoever I go. send

7 For I will not see you now ^Tby the way; but I trust to ^Ttarry a while with you, ^Rif the Lord permit. on · stay · Acts 18:21; James 4:15

8 But I will tarry at Eph'-e-sus until ^RPentecost. Lev. 23:15–22

9 For ^Ra great door and effectual is opened unto me, and there are many adversaries. Acts 14:27

10 Now ^Rif Ti-mo'-the-us come, see that he may be with you without fear: for he worketh the work of the Lord, as I also do. Acts 19:22

11 ^RLet no man therefore despise him: but conduct him forth ^Rin peace, that he may come unto me: for I look for him with the brethren. 1 Tim. 4:12 · Acts 15:33

12 As touching our brother ^RA-pol'-los, I greatly desired him to come unto you with the brethren: but his will was not at all to come at this time; but he will come when he shall have convenient time. 1:12; 3:5; Acts 18:24

13 Watch ye, ^Rstand fast in the faith, ^Tquit you like men, be strong. 2 Thess. 2:15 · be brave

14 ^RLet all your things be done with ^Tcharity. [1 Pet. 4:8] · love

15 I beseech you, brethren, (ye know ^Rthe house of Steph'-a-nas, that it is ^Rthe firstfruits of A-cha'-ia, and that they have ^Taddicted themselves to the ministry of the saints,) 1:16 · Rom. 16:5 · devoted

16 That ye submit yourselves unto such, and to every one that helpeth with us, and laboureth.

17 I am glad of the coming of Steph'-a-nas and For-tu-na'-tus and A-cha'-i-cus: ^Rfor that which was lacking on your part they have supplied. 2 Cor. 11:9; Phil. 2:30

18 ^RFor they have refreshed my spirit and yours: therefore ^Racknowledge ye them that are such. Col. 4:8 · Phil. 2:29

19 The churches of Asia salute you. Aq'-ui-la and Priscilla salute you much in the Lord, with the church that is in their house.

20 All the brethren greet you. ᴿGreet ye one another with an holy kiss.   Rom. 16:16

21 ᴿThe salutation of *me* Paul with mine own hand.   Rom. 16:22

22 If any man love not the Lord Jesus Christ, ᴿlet him be An-ath'-e-ma Mar'-an-a'-tha.   Gal. 1:8, 9

23 ᴿThe grace of our Lord Jesus Christ *be* with you.   Rom. 16:20

24 My love *be* with you all in Christ Jesus. A-men'.

The Second Epistle of Paul the Apostle to the

CORINTHIANS

SINCE Paul's first letter, the Corinthian church had been swayed by false teachers who stirred the people against Paul. They claimed he was fickle, proud, unimpressive in appearance and speech, dishonest, and unqualified as an apostle of Jesus Christ. Paul sent Titus to Corinth to deal with these difficulties, and upon his return, rejoiced to hear of the Corinthians' change of heart. Paul wrote this letter to express his thanksgiving for the repentant majority and to appeal to the rebellious minority to accept his authority. Throughout the book he defends his conduct, character, and calling as an apostle of Jesus Christ.

To distinguish this epistle from First Corinthians, it was given the title *Pros Korinthious B*, the "Second to the Corinthians." The *A* and *B* were probably later additions to *Pros Korinthious*.

PAUL, an apostle of Jesus Christ by the will of God, and Timothy *our* brother, unto the church of God which is at Corinth, ᴿwith all the saints which are in all A-cha'-ia: Phil. 1:1; Col. 1:2

2 ᴿGrace *be* to you and peace from God our Father, and *from* the Lord Jesus Christ.   Rom. 1:7

3 ᴿBlessed *be* God, even the Father of our Lord Jesus Christ, the Father of mercies, and the God of all comfort;   Eph. 1:3; 1 Pet. 1:3

4 Who ᴿcomforteth us in all our tribulation, that we may be able to comfort them which are in any trouble, by the comfort wherewith we ourselves are comforted of God.   7:6, 7, 13; Is. 51:12; 66:13

5 For as the sufferings of Christ abound in us, so our consolation also aboundeth by Christ.

6 And whether we be afflicted, ᴿ*it is* for your consolation and salvation, which is effectual in the enduring of the same sufferings which we also suffer: or whether we be comforted, *it is* for your consolation and salvation.   4:15

7 And our hope of you *is* stedfast, knowing, that as ye are partakers of the sufferings, so *shall* ye *be* also of the consolation.

8 For we would not, brethren, have you ignorant of ᴿour trouble which came to us in Asia, that we were pressed out of measure, above strength, insomuch that we despaired even of life: Acts 19:23

9 But we had the sentence of death in ourselves, that we should ᴿnot trust in ourselves, but in God which raiseth the dead: Jer. 17:5, 7

10 ᴿWho delivered us from so great a death, and doth deliver: in whom we trust that he will yet deliver *us;*   [2 Pet. 2:9]

11 Ye also helping together by prayer for us, that ᴿfor the gift *bestowed* upon us by the means of many persons thanks may be given by many on our behalf.   4:15

12 For our rejoicing is this, the testimony of our conscience, that

in simplicity and godly sincerity, not with fleshly wisdom, but by the grace of God, we have had our conversation in the world, and more abundantly to you-ward.

13 For we write none other things unto you, than what ye read or ^Tacknowledge; and I trust ye shall ^Tacknowledge even to the end;   *understand*

14 As also ye have acknowledged us in part, that we are your rejoicing, even as ye also *are* ours in the day of the Lord Jesus.

15 And in this confidence ^RI was minded to come unto you before, that ye might have ^Ra second benefit;   1 Cor. 4:19 · Rom. 1:11; 15:29

16 And to pass by you into Mac-e-do'-ni-a, and ^Rto come again out of Mac-e-do'-ni-a unto you, and of you to be brought on my way toward Ju-dae'-a.   Acts 19:21

17 When I therefore was thus minded, did I use lightness? or the things that I purpose, do I purpose ^Raccording to the flesh, that with me there should be yea yea, and nay nay?   10:2; 11:18

18 But *as* God *is* ^Rtrue,^T our word toward you was not yea and nay.   1 John 5:20 · *faithful*

19 For the Son of God, Jesus Christ, who was preached among you by us, *even* by me and Sil-va'-nus and Ti-mo'-the-us, was not yea and nay, but in him was yea.

20 For all the promises of God in him *are* yea, and in him A-men', unto the glory of God by us.

21 Now he which stablisheth us with you in Christ, and ^Rhath anointed us, *is* God;   [1 John 2:20, 27]

22 Who hath also sealed us, and ^Rgiven the ^Tearnest of the Spirit in our hearts.   [Eph. 1:14] · *down payment*

23 Moreover ^RI call God for a record upon my soul, ^Rthat to spare you I came not as yet unto Corinth.   Gal. 1:20 · 1 Cor. 4:21

24 Not for ^Rthat we have dominion over your faith, but are helpers of your joy: for ^Rby faith ye stand.   1 Cor. 3:5 · Rom. 11:20; 1 Cor. 15:1

2 But I determined this with myself, ^Rthat I would not come again to you in heaviness.   1:23

2 For if I make you ^Rsorry,^T who is he then that maketh me glad, but the same which is made sorry by me?   7:8 · *sorrowful*

3 And I wrote this same unto you, lest, when I came, ^RI should have sorrow from them of whom I ought to rejoice; ^Rhaving confidence in you all, that my joy is *the joy* of you all.   12:21 · 8:22; Gal. 5:10

4 For out of much affliction and anguish of heart I wrote unto you with many tears; ^Rnot that ye should be grieved, but that ye might know the love which I have more abundantly unto you. [7:8, 12]

5 But if any have caused grief, he hath not ^Rgrieved me, but in part: that I may not ^Tovercharge you all.   Gal. 4:12 · *be too severe with*

6 Sufficient to such a man *is* this punishment, which *was inflicted* ^Rof many.   7:11; 1 Cor. 5:4, 5

7 ^RSo that contrariwise ye *ought* rather to forgive *him,* and comfort *him,* lest perhaps such a one should be swallowed up with overmuch sorrow.   Gal. 6:1; Eph. 4:32

8 Wherefore I beseech you that ye would ^Tconfirm *your* love toward him.   *reaffirm*

9 For to this end also did I write, that I might know the proof of you, whether ye be ^Robedient in all things.   7:15; 10:6

10 To whom ye forgive any thing, I *forgive* also: for if I forgave any thing, to whom I forgave *it,* for your sakes *forgave I it* in the ^Tperson of Christ;   *presence*

11 Lest Satan should get an advantage of us: for we are not ignorant of his devices.

12 Furthermore, ^Rwhen I came to Tro'-as to *preach* Christ's gospel, and a door was opened unto me of the Lord,   Acts 16:8

13 ^RI had no rest in my spirit, because I found not Titus my brother: but taking my leave of them, I went from thence into Mac-e-do'-ni-a.   Gal. 2:1, 3; 2 Tim. 4:10; Titus 1:4

14 Now thanks *be* unto God,

which always ^Tcauseth us to triumph in Christ, and maketh manifest the savour of his knowledge by us in every place.   *leads us in*

15 For we are unto God a sweet savour of Christ, in them that are saved, and in them that perish:

16 ^RTo the one *we are* the savour of death unto death; and to the other the savour of life unto life. And ^Rwho *is* sufficient for these things?   Luke 2:34 · [1 Cor. 15:10]

17 For we are not as many, which ^Rcorrupt the word of God: but as ^Rof sincerity, but as of God, in the sight of God speak we in Christ.   2 Pet. 2:3 · 1 Cor. 5:8; 1 Pet. 4:11

3 Do ^Rwe begin again to commend ourselves? or need we, as some *others*, epistles of commendation to you, or *letters* of commendation from you?   5:12; 10:12, 18

2 ^RYe are our epistle written in our hearts, known and read of all men: 1 Cor. 9:2

3 *Forasmuch as ye are* manifestly declared to be the epistle of Christ ^Rministered by us, written not with ink, but with the Spirit of the living God; not ^Rin tables of stone, but ^Rin fleshy tables of the heart.   1 Cor. 3:5 · Ex. 24:12; 31:18 · Ps. 40:8

4 And such trust have we through Christ to God-ward:

5 ^RNot that we are sufficient of ourselves to think any thing as of ourselves; but ^Rour sufficiency *is* of God;   [John 15:5] · 1 Cor. 15:10

6 Who also hath made us able ministers of the new ^Ttestament; not of the letter, but of the spirit: for ^Rthe letter killeth, but the spirit giveth life.   *covenant* · Gal. 3:10

7 But if the ministration of death, written *and* engraven in stones, was glorious, so that the children of Israel could not stedfastly behold the face of Moses for the glory of his countenance; which *glory* was to be done away:

8 How shall not ^Rthe ^Tministration of the spirit be ^Trather glorious?   [Gal. 3:5] · *ministry* · *more*

9 For if the ministration of condemnation *be* glory, much more

doth the ministration of righteousness exceed in glory.

10 For even that which was made glorious had no glory in this respect, ^Tby reason of the glory that excelleth.   *because*

11 For if that which is done away *was* glorious, much more that which remaineth *is* glorious.

12 Seeing then that we have such hope, ^Rwe use great ^Tplainness of speech: 7:4; Eph. 6:19 · *boldness*

13 And not as Moses, ^R*which* put a vail over his face, that the children of Israel could not stedfastly look to ^Rthe end of that which is abolished: Ex. 34:33–35 · Rom. 10:4

14 But their minds were blinded: for until this day remaineth the same vail untaken away in the reading of the old testament; which *vail* is done away in Christ.

15 But even unto this day, when Moses is read, the vail is upon their heart.

16 Nevertheless ^Rwhen ^Tit shall turn to the Lord, ^Rthe vail shall be taken away.   Ex. 34:34 · *one* · Is. 25:7

17 Now the Lord is that Spirit: and where the Spirit of the Lord *is*, there *is* ^Rliberty.   Gal. 5:1, 13

18 But we all, with open face beholding as in a glass the glory of the Lord, are changed into the same image from glory to glory, *even* as by the Spirit of the Lord.

4 Therefore seeing we have this ministry, as we have received mercy, we faint not;

2 But have renounced the hidden things of dishonesty, not walking in craftiness, nor ^Thandling the word of God deceitfully; but by manifestation of the truth ^Rcommending ourselves to every man's conscience in the sight of God.   *adulterating the word of God* · 5:11

3 But if our gospel be hid, it is hid to them that are ^Tlost: *perishing*

4 In whom ^Rthe god of this world hath blinded the minds of them which believe not, lest the light of the glorious gospel of Christ, who is the image of God, should shine unto them.   John 12:31

5 ^RFor we preach not ourselves,

but Christ Jesus the Lord; and
Rourselves your servants for Je-
sus' sake.   1 Cor. 1:13 · 1 Cor. 9:19
6 For God, Rwho commanded
the light to shine out of darkness,
hath Rshined in our hearts, to give
the light of the knowledge of the
glory of God in the face of Jesus
Christ.   Gen. 1:3 · Is. 9:2; 2 Pet. 1:19
7 But we have this treasure in
earthen vessels, Rthat the excellency of the power may be of God,
and not of us.   Judg. 7:2; 1 Cor. 2:5
8 We are Rtroubled on every
side, yet not distressed; we are
perplexed, but not in despair;   7:5
9 Persecuted, but not Rfor-
saken; Rcast down, but not destroyed;   Ps. 37:24 · Ps. 129:2; [Heb. 13:5]
10 Always bearing about in the
body the dying of the Lord Jesus,
that the life also of Jesus might be
made manifest in our body.
11 For we which live Rare alway
delivered unto death for Jesus'
sake, that the life also of Jesus
might be made manifest in our
mortal flesh.   Rom. 8:36
12 So then death worketh in us,
but life in you.
13 We having Rthe same spirit of
faith, according as it is written, RI
believed, and therefore have I
spoken; we also believe, and
therefore speak;   2 Pet. 1:1 · Ps. 116:10
14 Knowing that he which
raised up the Lord Jesus shall
raise up us also by Jesus, and
shall present us with you.
15 For Rall things are for your
sakes, that Rthe abundant grace
might through the thanksgiving
of many Tredound to the glory of
God.   Col. 1:24 · 1 Cor. 9:19 · abound
16 For which cause we faint not;
but though our outward man perish, yet the inward man is Rre-
newed day by day.   [Col. 3:10]
17 For our light affliction, which
is but for a moment, worketh for
us a far more exceeding and eternal weight of glory;
18 RWhile we look not at the
things which are seen, but at the
things which are not seen: for
the things which are seen are tem-

poral; but the things which are
not seen are eternal.   [5:7]; Rom. 8:24
5 For we know that if Rour
earthly house of this tabernacle were dissolved, we have a
building of God, an house Rnot
made with hands, eternal in the
heavens.   4:7 · Acts 7:48; Heb. 9:11, 24
2 For in this Rwe groan, ear-
nestly desiring to be clothed upon
with our house which is from
heaven: v. 4; Rom. 8:23
3 If so be that being clothed we
shall not be found naked.
4 For we that are in this Ttab-
ernacle do groan, being burdened:
not for that we would be un-
clothed, but Rclothed upon, that
mortality might be swallowed up
of life.   tent · 1 Cor. 15:53
5 Now he that hath wrought us
for the selfsame thing is God, who
also hath given unto us the Tear-
nest of the Spirit.   down payment
6 Therefore we are always confident, knowing that, whilst we
are at home in the body, we are
absent from the Lord:
7 (For Rwe walk by faith, not by
sight:)   Rom. 8:24; Heb. 11:1
8 We are confident, I say, and
Rwilling rather to be absent from
the body, and to be present with
the Lord.   Phil. 1:23
9 Wherefore we labour, that,
whether present or absent, we
may be accepted of him.
10 RFor we must all appear be-   ☆
fore the judgment seat of Christ;
Rthat every one may receive the
things done in his body, according
to that he hath done, whether it be
good or bad.   Rom. 2:16 · Gal. 6:7
11 Knowing therefore the terror
of the Lord, we persuade men; but
we are made manifest unto God;
and I trust also are made manifest
in your consciences.
12 For Rwe commend not ourselves again unto you, but
give you occasion to glory on
our behalf, that ye may have
somewhat to answer them which
glory in appearance, and not in
heart.   3:1
13 For whether we be beside

ourselves, *it is* to God: or whether we be sober, *it is* for your cause.

14 For the love of Christ constraineth us; because we thus judge, that ᴿif one died for all, then were all dead: [Gal. 2:20; Col. 3:3]

15 And *that* he died for all, ᴿthat they which live should not henceforth live unto themselves, but unto him which died for them, and rose again.　　[Rom. 6:11]

16 ᴿWherefore henceforth know we no man after the flesh: yea, though we have known Christ after the flesh, yet now henceforth know we *him* no more.　　10:3

17 Therefore if any man *be* in Christ, *he is* a new creature: old things are passed away; behold, all things are become new.

18 And all things *are* of God, ᴿwho hath reconciled us to himself by Jesus Christ, and hath given to us the ministry of reconciliation; Rom. 5:10; [Eph. 2:16; Col. 1:20]

19 ᵀTo wit, that ᴿGod was in Christ, reconciling the world unto himself, not imputing their trespasses unto them; and hath committed unto us the word of reconciliation.　　*That is* · [Rom. 3:24]

20 Now then we are ᴿambassadors for Christ, as though God did beseech us by us: we pray *you* in Christ's ᵀstead, be ye reconciled to God.　　Eph. 6:20 · *behalf*

★ 21 For ᴿhe hath made him *to be* sin for us, who knew no sin; that we might be made the righteousness of God in him.　　Is. 53:6, 9

6 We then, *as* ᴿworkers together *with him,* ᴿbeseech *you* also that ye receive not the grace of God in vain.　　1 Cor. 3:9 · 5:20

★ 2 (For he saith, ᴿI have heard thee in a time accepted, and in the day of salvation have I ᵀsuccoured thee: behold, now *is* the accepted time; behold, now *is* the day of salvation.)　　Is. 49:8 · *helped*

3 ᴿGiving no offence in any thing, that the ministry be not blamed:　　Rom. 14:13

4 But in all *things* approving ourselves as the ministers of God, in much patience, in afflic-

tions, in necessities, in distresses,

5 ᴿIn stripes, in imprisonments, in tumults, in labours, in ᵀwatchings, in fastings; 11:23 · *sleeplessness*

6 By pureness, by knowledge, by longsuffering, by kindness, by the Holy Ghost, by love ᵀunfeigned,　　Lit. *without hypocrisy*

7 ᴿBy the word of truth, by ᴿthe power of God, by ᴿthe armour of righteousness on the right hand and on the left,　7:14 · 1 Cor. 2:4 · 10:4

8 By honour and dishonour, by evil report and good report: as deceivers, and *yet* true;

9 As unknown, and *yet* well known; as dying, and, behold, we live; as chastened, and not killed;

10 As sorrowful, yet alway rejoicing; as poor, yet making many ᴿrich; as having nothing, and *yet* possessing all things. [8:9]

11 O *ye* Corinthians, our mouth ᵀis open unto you, ᴿour heart is enlarged.　　*has spoken freely* · 7:3

12 Ye are not ᵀstraitened in us, but ye are straitened in your own ᵀbowels.　　*restricted by* · *affections*

13 Now for a recompence in the same, (ᴿI speak as unto *my* children,) be ye also enlarged.　　4:14

14 ᴿBe ye not unequally yoked together with unbelievers: for ᴿwhat fellowship hath righteousness with unrighteousness? and what communion hath light with darkness?　　1 Cor. 5:9 · 1 John 1:6

15 And what ᵀconcord hath Christ with Be'-li-al? or what part hath he that believeth with an ᵀinfidel?　　*accord* · *unbeliever*

16 And what agreement hath the temple of God with idols? for ᴿye are the temple of the living God; as God hath said, I will dwell in them, and walk in *them*; and I will be their God, and they shall be my people.　　Eph. 2:21; [Heb. 3:6]

17 ᴿWherefore come out from among them, and be ye separate, saith the Lord, and touch not the unclean *thing*; and I will receive you,　　Num. 33:51–56; Is. 52:11; Rev. 18:4

18 ᴿAnd will be a Father unto you, and ye shall be my ᴿsons and

daughters, saith the Lord Almighty. [Rev. 21:7] · Phil. 2:15; 1 John 3:1

7 Having ᴿtherefore these promises, dearly beloved, let us cleanse ourselves from all filthiness of the flesh and spirit, perfecting holiness in the fear of God. [1 John 3:3]

2 Receive us; we have wronged no man, we have corrupted no man, we have defrauded no man.

3 I speak not *this* to condemn *you:* for ᴿI have said before, that ye are in our hearts to die and live with *you.* 6:11, 12

4 Great *is* my boldness of speech toward you, great *is* my glorying of you: ᴿI am filled with comfort, I am exceeding joyful in all our tribulation. Phil. 2:17; Col. 1:24

5 For, ᴿwhen we were come into Mac-e-do'-ni-a, our flesh had no rest, but ᴿwe were troubled on every side; without *were* fightings, within *were* fears. 2:13 · 4:8

6 Nevertheless ᴿGod, that comforteth those that are cast down, comforted us by ᴿthe coming of Titus; 1:3, 4; Is. 49:13 · v. 13; 2:13

7 And not by his coming only, but by the ᵀconsolation wherewith he was comforted in you, when he told us your earnest desire, your mourning, your ᵀfervent mind toward me; so that I rejoiced the more. *comfort · zeal for me*

8 For though I made you ᴿsorry with a letter, I do not ᵀrepent, ᴿthough I did repent: for I perceive that the same epistle hath made you sorry, though *it were* but for a season. 2:2 · *regret it* · 2:4

9 Now I rejoice, not that ye were made sorry, but that ye sorrowed to repentance: for ye were made sorry ᵀafter a godly manner, that ye might receive damage by us in nothing. *according to*

10 For godly sorrow worketh repentance to salvation not to be ᵀrepented of: but the sorrow of the world worketh death. *regretted*

11 For behold this selfsame thing, that ye sorrowed after a godly sort, what carefulness it wrought in you, yea, *what* clearing of yourselves, yea, *what* indignation, yea, *what* fear, yea, *what* vehement desire, yea, *what* zeal, yea, *what* ᵀrevenge! In all *things* ye have approved yourselves to be clear in this matter. *vindication*

12 Wherefore, though I wrote unto you, *I did it* not for his cause that had done the wrong, nor for his cause that suffered wrong, ᴿbut that our care for you in the sight of God might appear unto you. 2:4

13 Therefore we were comforted in your comfort: yea, and exceedingly the more joyed we for the joy of Titus, because his spirit was refreshed by you all.

14 For if I have boasted any thing to him of you, I am not ashamed; but as we spake all things to you in truth, even so our boasting, which I *made* before Titus, is found a truth.

15 And his inward affection is more abundant toward you, whilst he remembereth ᴿthe obedience of you all, how with fear and trembling ye received him. 2:9

16 I rejoice therefore that ᴿI have confidence in you in all *things.* 2:3; 8:22; 2 Thess. 3:4; Philem. 8, 21

8 Moreover, brethren, we ᵀdo you to wit of the grace of God bestowed on the churches of Mac-e-do'-ni-a; *make known to you*

2 How that in a great trial of affliction the abundance of their joy and ᴿtheir deep poverty abounded unto the riches of their liberality. Mark 12:44

3 For to *their* ᵀpower, I bear ᵀrecord, yea, and beyond *their* power *they were* willing of themselves; *ability · witness*

4 ᵀPraying us with much ᵀintreaty that we would receive the gift, and *take upon us* ᴿthe fellowship of the ministering to the saints. *Imploring · urgency* · Acts 11:29

5 And *this they did,* not as we hoped, but first gave their own selves to the Lord, and unto us by the ᴿwill of God. [Eph. 6:6]

6 Insomuch that ᴿwe ᵀdesired Titus, that as he had begun, so he

would also finish in you the same grace also. v. 17; 12:18 · *urged*

7 Therefore, as ^Rye abound in every *thing*, *in* faith, and ^Tutterance, and knowledge, and *in* all diligence, and *in* your love to us, *see* ^Rthat ye abound in this grace also. [1 Cor. 1:5; 12:13] · *speech* · 9:8

8 ^RI speak not by commandment, but by occasion of the forwardness of others, and to prove the sincerity of your love. 1 Cor. 7:6

9 For ye know the grace of our Lord Jesus Christ, ^Rthat, though he was rich, yet for your sakes he became poor, that ye through his poverty might be rich. Phil. 2:6, 7

10 And herein I give *my* advice: for ^Rthis is ^Texpedient for you, who have begun before, not only to do, but also to be ^Rforward a year ago. [Heb. 13:16] · *profitable* · 9:2

11 Now therefore perform the doing *of it;* that as *there was* a readiness to will, so *there may be* a ^Tperformance also out of that which ye have. *completion*

12 For ^Rif there be first a willing mind, *it is* accepted according to that a man hath, *and* not according to that he hath not. 9:7

13 For *I mean* not that other men be eased, and ye burdened:

14 But by an equality, *that* now at this time your abundance *may be a supply* for their ^Twant, that their abundance also may be *a supply* for your ^Twant: that there may be equality: *lack*

15 As it is written, ^RHe that *had gathered* much had nothing over; and he that *had gathered* little had no lack. Ex. 16:18

16 But thanks *be* to God, which put the same earnest care into the heart of Titus for you.

17 For indeed he accepted the exhortation; but being more ^Tforward, of his own accord he went unto you. *diligent*

18 And we have sent with him ^Rthe brother, whose praise *is* in the gospel throughout all the churches; 12:18; 1 Cor. 16:3

19 And not *that* only, but who was also chosen of the churches to travel with us with this grace, which is administered by us to the glory of the same Lord, and *declaration of* your ready mind:

20 Avoiding this, that no man should blame us in this ^Tabundance which is administered by us: *lavish gift*

21 Providing for honest things, not only in the sight of the Lord, but also in the sight of men.

22 And we have sent with them our brother, whom we have oftentimes proved diligent in many things, but now much more diligent, upon the great confidence which I *have* in you.

23 Whether *any do enquire of* Titus, *he is* my partner and fellowhelper concerning you: or our brethren *be enquired of, they are* ^Rthe messengers of the churches, *and* the glory of Christ. Phil. 2:25

24 Wherefore shew ye to them, and before the churches, the proof of your love, and of our ^Rboasting on your behalf. 7:4, 14; 9:2

9 For as touching ^Rthe ministering to the saints, it is superfluous for me to write to you: 8:4

2 For I know the ^Tforwardness of your mind, for which I boast of you to them of Mac-e-do'-ni-a, that A-cha'-ia was ready a ^Ryear ago; and your zeal hath provoked very many. *willingness* · 8:10

3 ^RYet have I sent the brethren, lest our boasting of you should be in vain in this behalf; that, as I said, ye may be ready: 8:6, 17

4 Lest haply if they of Mac-e-do'-ni-a come with me, and find you unprepared, we (that we say not, ye) should be ashamed in this same confident boasting.

5 Therefore I thought it necessary to exhort the brethren, that they would go before unto you, and make up beforehand your bounty, whereof ye had ^Tnotice before, that the same might be ready, as *a matter of* bounty, and not as *of* covetousness. *promised*

6 ^RBut this *I say,* He which soweth sparingly shall reap also sparingly; and he which soweth

bountifully shall reap also bountifully.   Prov. 11:24; 22:9; Gal. 6:7, 9

7 Every man according as he purposeth in his heart, *so let him give;* ᴿnot grudgingly, or of necessity: for ᴿGod loveth a cheerful giver.   Deut. 15:7 · [8:12]; Rom. 12:8

8 ᴿAnd God *is* able to make all grace abound toward you; that ye, always having all sufficiency in all *things,* may abound to every good work: [Prov. 11:24]

9 (As it is written, ᴿHe hath dispersed abroad; he hath given to the poor: his righteousness remaineth for ever.   Ps. 112:9

10 Now he that ministereth seed to the sower both minister bread for *your* food, and multiply your seed sown, and increase the fruits of your righteousness;)

11 Being enriched in every thing to all ᵀbountifulness, ᴿwhich causeth through us thanksgiving to God.   liberality · 1:11

12 For the administration of this service not only ᴿsupplieth the ᵀwant of the saints, but is ᵀabundant also by many thanksgivings unto God;   8:14 · needs · abounding

13 Whiles by the ᵀexperiment of this ministration they glorify God for your professed subjection unto the gospel of Christ, and for *your* liberal distribution unto them, and unto all *men;*   proof

14 And by their prayer for you, which long after you for the exceeding ᴿgrace of God in you.   8:1

15 Thanks *be* unto God ᴿfor his unspeakable gift.   [Rom. 6:23]

10 Now ᴿI Paul myself beseech you by the meekness and gentleness of Christ, ᴿwho in presence *am* ᵀbase among you, but being absent am bold toward you: Rom. 12:1 · 1 Thess. 2:7 · lowly

2 But I beseech *you,* ᴿthat I may not be bold when I am present with that confidence, wherewith I think to be bold against some, which think of us as if we walked according to the flesh.   13:2

3 For though we walk in the flesh, we do not war ᵀafter the flesh: according to

4 (ᴿFor the weapons of our warfare *are* not carnal, but mighty through God to the pulling down of strong holds;)   Eph. 6:13

5 ᴿCasting down imaginations, and every high thing that exalteth itself against the knowledge of God, and bringing into captivity every thought to the obedience of Christ;   1 Cor. 1:19

6 And having in a readiness to ᵀrevenge all disobedience, when your obedience is fulfilled.   punish

7 ᴿDo ye look on things after the outward appearance? If any man trust to himself that he is Christ's, let him of himself think this again, that, as he *is* Christ's, even so *are* we Christ's.   5:12

8 For though I should boast somewhat more ᴿof our authority, which the Lord hath given us for ᵀedification, and not for your destruction, ᴿI should not be ashamed: 13:10 · building up · 7:14

9 That I may not seem as if I would terrify you by letters.

10 For *his* letters, say they, *are* weighty and powerful; but ᴿhis bodily presence *is* weak, and *his* ᴿspeech contemptible.   12:7 · 11:6

11 Let such an one think this, that, such as we are in word by letters when we are absent, such *will we be* also in deed when we are present.

12 For we dare not make ourselves of the number, or compare ourselves with some that commend themselves: but they measuring themselves by themselves, and comparing themselves among themselves, are not wise.

13 ᴿBut we will not boast of things ᵀwithout *our* measure, but according to the measure of the ᵀrule which God hath distributed to us, a measure to reach even unto you.   v. 15 · beyond · province

14 For we stretch not ourselves beyond *our measure,* as though we reached not unto you: for we are come as far as to you also in *preaching* the gospel of Christ:

15 Not boasting of things without *our* measure, *that is,* of other

men's labours; but having hope, when your faith is increased, that we shall be enlarged by you according to our rule abundantly,

16 To preach the gospel in the *regions* beyond you, *and* not to boast in another man's line of things made ready to our hand.

17 ᴿBut he that glorieth, let him glory in the Lord.   Is. 65:16; 1 Cor. 1:31

18 For not he that commendeth himself is approved, but ᴿwhom the Lord commendeth.   Rom. 2:29

11 Would to God ye could bear with me a little in *my* folly: and indeed bear with me.

2 For I am ᴿjealous over you with godly jealousy: for I have espoused you to one husband, that I may present *you as a* chaste virgin to Christ.   Gal. 4:17

3 But I fear, lest by any means, as the serpent beguiled Eve through his subtilty, so your minds should be corrupted from the simplicity that is in Christ.

4 For if he that cometh preacheth another Jesus, whom we have not preached, or *if* ye receive another spirit, which ye have not received, or another gospel, which ye have not accepted, ye might well bear with *him*.

5 For I suppose ᴿI was not a whit behind the very chiefest apostles.   12:11; Gal. 2:6

6 But though *I be* rude in speech, yet not in knowledge; but we have been throughly made manifest among you in all things.

7 Have I committed an offence in abasing myself that ye might be exalted, because I have preached to you the gospel of God freely?

8 I robbed other churches, taking wages *of them*, to do you service.

9 And when I was present with you, and wanted, ᴿI was chargeable to no man: for that which was lacking to me ᴿthe brethren which came from Mac-e-do′-ni-a supplied: and in all *things* I have kept myself from being burdensome unto you, and *so* will I keep *myself*.   Acts 20:33 · Phil. 4:10

10 ᴿAs the truth of Christ is in me, ᴿno man shall stop me of this boasting in the regions of A-cha′-ia.   Rom. 1:9; 9:1; [Gal. 2:20] · 1 Cor. 9:15

11 Wherefore? ᴿbecause I love you not? God knoweth.   6:11; 12:15

12 But what I do, that I will do, ᴿthat I may cut off occasion from them which desire occasion; that wherein they glory, they may be found even as we.   1 Cor. 9:12

13 For such ᴿ*are* false apostles, ᴿdeceitful workers, transforming themselves into the apostles of Christ.   Rom. 16:18 · Phil. 3:2; Titus 1:10

14 And no marvel; for Satan himself is transformed into ᴿan angel of light.   Gal. 1:8

15 Therefore *it is* no great thing if his ministers also be transformed as the ministers of righteousness; ᴿwhose end shall be according to their works. [Phil. 3:19]

16 I say again, Let no man think me a fool; if otherwise, yet as a fool receive me, that I may boast myself a little.

17 That which I speak, ᴿI speak *it* not after the Lord, but as it were foolishly, in this confidence of boasting.   1 Cor. 7:6

18 Seeing that many glory after the flesh, I will glory also.

19 For ye suffer fools gladly, seeing ye *yourselves* are wise.

20 For ye suffer, ᴿif a man bring you into bondage, if a man devour *you*, if a man take *of you*, if a man exalt himself, if a man smite you on the face.   1:24; [Gal. 2:4; 4:3, 9; 5:1]

21 I speak as concerning ᵀreproach, ᴿas though we had been weak. Howbeit ᴿwhereinsoever any is bold, (I speak foolishly,) I am bold also.   *shame* · 10:10 · Phil. 3:4

22 Are they ᴿHebrews? so *am* I. Are they Israelites? so *am* I. Are they the seed of Abraham? so *am* I.   Acts 22:3; Rom. 11:1; Phil. 3:4–6

23 Are they ministers of Christ? (I speak as a fool) I *am* more; in labours more abundant, in stripes above measure, in prisons more frequent, ᴿin deaths oft.   1 Cor. 15:30

24 Of the Jews five times received I forty *stripes* save one.

25 Thrice was I beaten with rods, once was I stoned, thrice I suffered shipwreck, a night and a day I have been in the deep;

26 *In* journeyings often, *in* perils of waters, *in* perils of robbers, *in* perils by *mine own* countrymen, *in* perils by the heathen, *in* perils in the city, *in* perils in the wilderness, *in* perils in the sea, *in* perils among false brethren;

27 In weariness and [T]painfulness, in watchings often, in hunger and thirst, in fastings often, in cold and nakedness.　　*toil*

28 Beside those things that are without, that which cometh upon me daily, [R]the care of all the churches.　　Gal. 4:11; 1 Thess. 3:10

29 [R]Who is weak, and I am not weak? who is [T]offended, and I burn not? [1 Cor. 9:22] · *made to stumble*

30 If I must needs glory, [R]I will glory of the things which concern mine infirmities.　　[12:5, 9, 10]

31 [R]The God and Father of our Lord Jesus Christ, [R]which is blessed for evermore, knoweth that I lie not.　　Rom. 1:9 · Rom. 9:5

32 [R]In Damascus the governor under Ar'-e-tas the king kept the city of the Dam-a-scenes' with a garrison, desirous to apprehend me:　　Acts 9:19–25

33 And through a window in a basket was I let down by the wall, and escaped his hands.

12 It is not expedient for me doubtless to glory. I will come to [R]visions and [R]revelations of the Lord.　Acts 16:9; 18:9 · Acts 9:3–6

2 I knew a man in Christ above fourteen years ago, (whether in the body, I cannot tell; or whether out of the body, I cannot tell: God knoweth;) such an one [R]caught up to the third heaven.　　Acts 22:17

3 And I knew such a man, (whether in the body, or out of the body, I [T]cannot tell: God knoweth;)　　*do not know*

4 How that he was caught up into [R]paradise, and heard unspeakable words, which it is not lawful for a man to utter. [Rev. 2:7]

5 Of such an one will I glory:

yet of myself I will not [R]glory, but in mine infirmities.　　11:30

6 For though I would desire to glory, I shall not be a fool; for I will say the truth: but *now* I [T]forbear, lest any man should think of me above that which he seeth me *to be*, or *that* he heareth of me.　　*refrain*

7 And lest I should be exalted above measure through the abundance of the revelations, there was given to me a [R]thorn in the flesh, [R]the messenger of Satan to buffet me, lest I should be exalted above measure.　Gal. 4:13, 14 · Job 2:7

8 [R]For this thing I besought the Lord thrice, that it might depart from me.　　Deut. 3:23; Matt. 26:44

9 And he said unto me, My grace is sufficient for thee: for my [T]strength is made perfect in weakness. Most gladly therefore [R]will I rather glory in my [T]infirmities, that the power of Christ may rest upon me.　*power* · 11:30 · *weaknesses*

10 Therefore [R]I take pleasure in infirmities, in reproaches, in necessities, in persecutions, in distresses for Christ's sake: [R]for when I am weak, then am I strong.　　[Rom. 5:3; 8:35] · 13:4

11 I am become [R]a fool in glorying; ye have compelled me: for I ought to have been commended of you: for in nothing am I behind the very chiefest apostles, though I be nothing.　v. 6; 5:13; 11:1, 16

12 Truly the signs of an apostle were wrought among you in all [T]patience, in signs, and wonders, and mighty deeds.　　*perseverance*

13 For what is it wherein ye were inferior to other churches, except *it be* that I myself was not burdensome to you? forgive me this wrong.

14 [R]Behold, the third time I am ready to come to you; and I will not be burdensome to you: for [R]I seek not yours, but you: for the children ought not to lay up for the parents, but the parents for the children.　1:15; 13:1, 2 · Acts 20:33

15 And I will very gladly spend and be spent [R]for you; though the

more abundantly I love you, the less I be loved.　John 10:11; Rom. 9:3

16 But be it so, [R]I did not burden you: nevertheless, being crafty, I caught you with guile.　11:9

17 Did I [T]make a gain of you by any of them whom I sent unto you?　*take advantage*

18 I [T]desired Titus, and with *him* I sent a [R]brother. Did Titus make a gain of you? walked we not in the same spirit? *walked we* not in the same steps?　*urged* · 8:18

19 [R]Again, think ye that we excuse ourselves unto you? [R]we speak before God in Christ: but *we do* all things, dearly beloved, for your edifying.　5:12 · 11:31

20 For I fear, lest, when I come, I shall not find you such as I would, and *that* [R]I shall be found unto you such as ye would not: lest *there be* debates, envyings, wraths, strifes, backbitings, whisperings, swellings, tumults: 13:2, 10

21 *And* lest, when I come again, my God [R]will humble me among you, and *that* I shall [T]bewail many [R]which have sinned already, and have not repented of the uncleanness and [R]fornication and lasciviousness which they have committed.　2:1, 4 · *mourn* · v. 2 · 1 Cor. 5:1

13 This *is* [R]the third *time* I am coming to you. In the mouth of two or three witnesses shall every word be established.　12:14

2 [R]I told you before, and foretell you, as if I were present, the second time; and being absent now I write to them [R]which heretofore have sinned, and to all [T]other, that, if I come again, [R]I will not spare:　10:2 · 12:21 · *the rest* · 1:23

3 Since ye seek a proof of Christ [R]speaking in me, which to you-ward is not weak, but is mighty in you.　Matt. 10:20

4 [R]For though he was crucified through weakness, yet he liveth by the power of God. For we also are weak in him, but we shall live with him by the power of God toward you.　Phil. 2:7, 8; [1 Pet. 3:18]

5 Examine yourselves, whether ye be in the faith; prove your own selves. Know ye not your own selves, how that Jesus Christ is in you, except ye be reprobates?

6 But I trust that ye shall know that we are not reprobates.

7 Now I pray to God that ye do no evil; not that we should appear approved, but that ye should do that which is honest, though [R]we be as reprobates.　6:9

8 For we can do nothing against the truth, but for the truth.

9 For we are glad, [R]when we are weak, and ye are strong: and this also we wish, [R]*even* your perfection.　1 Cor. 4:10 · 1 Cor. 1:10; Eph. 4:12

10 [R]Therefore I write these things being absent, lest being present I should use sharpness, according to the power which the Lord hath given me to edification, and not to destruction.　1 Cor. 4:21

11 Finally, brethren, farewell. Be [T]perfect, [R]be of good comfort, be of one mind, live in peace; and the God of love and peace shall be with you.　*complete* · Rom. 12:16, 18

12 [R]Greet one another with an holy kiss.　Rom. 16:16

13 All the saints salute you.

14 The grace of the Lord Jesus Christ, and the love of God, and the communion of the Holy Ghost, *be* with you all. A-men'.

GALATIANS

THE Galatians, having launched their Christian experience by faith, seem content to leave their voyage of faith and chart a new course based on works—a course Paul finds disturbing. His letter to the Galatians is a vigorous attack against the gospel of works and a defense of the gospel of faith.

Paul begins by setting forth his credentials as an apostle with a message from God: blessing comes from God on the basis of faith, not law. The law declares men guilty and imprisons them; faith sets men free to enjoy liberty in Christ. But liberty is not license. Freedom in Christ means freedom to produce the fruits of righteousness through a Spirit-led lifestyle.

The book is called *Pros Galatas*, "To the Galatians," and it is the only letter of Paul that is specifically addressed to a number of churches ("unto the churches of Galatia," 1:2). The name *Galatians* was given to this Celtic people because they originally lived in Gaul before their migration to Asia Minor.

PAUL, an apostle, (not of men, neither by man, but ᴿby Jesus Christ, and God the Father, who raised him from the dead;) Acts 9:6

2 And all the brethren which are with me, unto the churches of Ga-la'-ti-a:

3 Grace *be* to you and peace from God the Father, and *from* our Lord Jesus Christ,

4 ᴿWho gave himself for our sins, that he might deliver us ᴿfrom this present evil ᵀworld, according to the will of God and our Father: [Matt. 20:28] · Heb. 2:5 · *age*

5 To whom *be* glory for ever and ever. A-men'.

6 I marvel that ye are so soon removed ᴿfrom him that called you into the grace of Christ unto another gospel: v. 15; 5:8; [Rom. 8:28]

7 ᴿWhich is not another; but there be some ᴿthat trouble you, and would ᴿpervert the gospel of Christ. 2 Cor. 11:4 · Acts 15:1 · 2 Cor. 2:17

8 But though ᴿwe, or an angel from heaven, preach any other gospel unto you than that which we have preached unto you, let him be accursed. 1 Cor. 16:22

9 As we said before, so say I now again, If any *man* preach any other gospel unto you ᴿthan that ye have received, let him be accursed. Deut. 4:2

10 For ᴿdo I now persuade men, or God? or do I seek to please men? for if I yet pleased men, I should not be the servant of Christ. [1 Cor. 10:33]; 1 Thess. 2:4

11 But I certify you, brethren, that the gospel which was preached of me is not after man.

12 For I neither received it of man, neither was I taught *it*, but by the revelation of Jesus Christ.

13 For ye have heard of my conversation in time past in the Jews' religion, how that ᴿbeyond measure I persecuted the church of God, and wasted it: Acts 9:1

14 And profited in the Jews' religion above many my equals in mine own nation, ᴿbeing more exceedingly zealous of the traditions of my fathers. Acts 26:9; Phil. 3:6

15 But when it pleased God, ᴿwho separated me from my mother's womb, and called *me* by his grace, Is. 49:1, 5; Jer. 1:5; Acts 9:15

16 To reveal his Son in me, that ᴿI might preach him among the heathen; immediately I conferred not with flesh and blood: Acts 9:15

17 Neither went I up to Jerusalem to them which were apostles before me; but I went into Arabia, and returned again unto Damascus.

18 Then after three years I went up to Jerusalem to see Peter, and abode with him fifteen days.

19 But ᴿother of the apostles saw I none, save ᴿJames the Lord's brother. 1 Cor. 9:5 · Matt. 13:55
20 Now the things which I write unto you, behold, before God, I lie not.
21 Afterwards I came into the regions of Syria and Ci-li'-ci-a;
22 And was unknown by face unto the churches of Ju-dae'-a which ᴿwere in Christ: Rom. 16:7
23 But they had heard only, That he which ᴿpersecuted us in times past now preacheth the faith which once he destroyed. Acts 8:3
24 And they ᴿglorified God in me. Acts 11:18

2 Then fourteen years ᵀafter ᴿI went up again to Jerusalem with Barnabas, and took Titus with *me* also. *later* · Acts 15:2
2 And I went up by revelation, and communicated unto them that gospel which I preach among the Gentiles, but privately to them which were of reputation, lest by any means ᴿI should run, or had run, in vain. 5:7; Phil. 2:16; 1 Thess. 3:5
3 But neither Titus, who was with me, being a Greek, was compelled to be circumcised:
4 And that because of false brethren unawares brought in, who came in privily to spy out our ᴿliberty which we have in Christ Jesus, that they might bring us into bondage: 3:25; 5:1, 13; [James 1:25]
5 To whom we gave place by subjection, no, not for an hour; that ᴿthe truth of the gospel might continue with you. [v. 14; 3:1]; Col. 1:5
6 But of these ᴿwho seemed to be somewhat, (whatsoever they were, it maketh no matter to me: ᴿGod accepteth no man's person:) for they who seemed *to be somewhat* in conference added nothing to me: v. 9; 6:3 · Acts 10:34; Rom. 2:11
7 But contrariwise, ᴿwhen they saw that the gospel of the uncircumcision was committed unto me, as *the gospel* of the circumcision *was* unto Peter; Acts 9:15; 13:46
8 (For he that wrought effectually in Peter to the apostleship of the ᴿcircumcision, ᴿthe same was

ᴿmighty in me toward the Gentiles:) 1 Pet. 1:1 · Acts 9:15 · [3:5]
9 And when James, ᵀCe'-phas, and John, who seemed to be pillars, perceived ᴿthe grace that was given unto me, they gave to me and Barnabas the right hands of fellowship; that we *should go* unto the heathen, and they unto the circumcision. Peter · Rom. 1:5
10 Only *they would* that we should remember the poor; ᴿthe same which I also was ᵀforward to do. Acts 11:30 · *eager*
11 ᴿBut when Peter was come to An'-ti-och, I ᵀwithstood him to the face, because he was to be blamed. Acts 15:35 · *opposed*
12 For before that certain came from James, ᴿhe did eat with the Gentiles: but when they were come, he withdrew and separated himself, fearing them which were of the circumcision. [Acts 10:28]
13 And the other Jews ᵀdissembled likewise with him; insomuch that Barnabas also was carried away with their ᵀdissimulation. *played the hypocrite · hypocrisy*
14 But when I saw that they walked not uprightly according to the truth of the gospel, I said unto Peter before *them* all, If thou, being a Jew, livest after the manner of Gentiles, and not as do the Jews, why compellest thou the Gentiles to live as do the Jews?
15 We *who are* Jews by nature, and not sinners of the Gentiles,
16 ᴿKnowing that a man is not justified by the works of the law, but ᴿby the faith of Jesus Christ, even we have believed in Jesus Christ, that we might be justified by the faith of Christ, and not by the works of the law: for ᴿby the works of the law shall no flesh be justified. 3:11 · Rom. 1:17 · Rom. 3:20
17 But if, while we seek to be justified by Christ, we ourselves also are found ᴿsinners, *is* therefore Christ the minister of sin? ᵀGod forbid. [1 John 3:8] · *Certainly not*
18 For if I build again the things which I destroyed, I make myself a transgressor.

19 For I ^Rthrough the law ^Ram dead to the law, that I might live unto God. Rom. 8:2 · 1 Cor. 9:20
20 I am ^Rcrucified with Christ: nevertheless I live; yet not I, but Christ liveth in me: and the life which I now live in the flesh ^RI live by the faith of the Son of God, ^Rwho loved me, and gave himself for me. [5:24; 6:14] · [Col. 3:1–4] · Eph. 5:2
21 I do not frustrate the grace of God: for ^Rif righteousness *come* by the law, then Christ ^Tis dead in vain. Heb. 7:11 · *died for nothing*

3 O foolish Ga-la'-tians, who hath bewitched you, that ye should not obey the truth, before whose eyes Jesus Christ hath been ^Tevidently set forth, crucified among you? *clearly*
2 This only ^Twould I learn of you, Received ye the Spirit by the works of the law, ^Ror by the hearing of faith? *I want to* · Rom. 10:16, 17
3 Are ye so foolish? ^Rhaving begun in the Spirit, are ye now made perfect by the flesh? [4:9]
4 Have ye suffered so many things in vain? if *it be* yet in vain.
5 He therefore that ministereth to you in the Spirit, and worketh miracles among you, *doeth he it* by the works of the law, or by the hearing of faith?
6 Even as ^RAbraham believed God, and it was accounted to him for righteousness. Gen. 15:6
7 Know ye therefore that ^Rthey which are of faith, the same are the children of Abraham. John 8:39
★ 8 And the scripture, foreseeing that God would justify the ^Theathen through faith, preached before the gospel unto Abraham, *saying,* ^RIn thee shall all nations be blessed. *nations* · Gen. 12:3; 18:18
9 So then they which be of faith are blessed with ^Tfaithful Abraham. *believing*
10 For as many as are of the works of the law are under the curse: for it is written, Cursed *is* every one that continueth not in all things which are written in the book of the law to do them.

11 But that no man is justified by the law in the sight of God, *it is* evident: for, ^RThe just shall live by faith. Hab. 2:4; Rom. 1:17; Heb. 10:38
12 And the law is not of faith: but, ^RThe man that doeth them shall live in them. Lev. 18:5; Rom. 10:5
13 Christ hath redeemed us from the curse of the law, being made a curse for us: for it is written, ^RCursed *is* every one that hangeth on a tree: Deut. 21:23
14 That the blessing of Abraham ★ might come on the ^RGentiles through Jesus Christ; that we might receive the promise of the Spirit through faith. Is. 42:1, 6
15 Brethren, I speak after the manner of men; ^RThough *it be* but a man's covenant, yet *if it be* confirmed, no man disannulleth, or addeth thereto. Heb. 9:17
16 Now to Abraham and his ★ seed were the promises made. He saith not, And to seeds, as of many; but as of ^Rone, And to thy seed, which is Christ. Gen. 12:7; 13:15
17 And this I say, *that* the covenant, that was confirmed before of God in Christ, the law, ^Rwhich was four hundred and thirty years after, cannot disannul, that it should make the promise of none effect. Gen. 15:13; Acts 7:6
18 For if ^Rthe inheritance *be* of the law, ^R*it is* no more of promise: but God gave *it* to Abraham by promise. [Rom. 8:17] · Rom. 4:14
19 Wherefore then *serveth* the law? ^RIt was added because of transgressions, till the ^Rseed should come to whom the promise was made; *and it was* ordained by angels in the hand ^Rof a mediator. John 15:22 · 4:4 · Ex. 20:19; Deut. 5:5
20 Now a mediator is not *a mediator* of one, but God is one.
21 *Is* the law then against the promises of God? ^TGod forbid: for if there had been a law given which could have given life, verily righteousness should have been by the law. *Certainly not*
22 But the scripture hath ^Tconcluded ^Rall under sin, ^Rthat the promise by faith of Jesus Christ

might be given to them that believe.   *confined* · Rom. 11:32 · Rom. 4:11
23 But before faith came, we were [T]kept under the law, [T]shut up unto the faith which should afterwards be revealed.   *guarded* · *confined*
24 Wherefore [R]the law was our schoolmaster *to bring us* unto Christ, [R]that we might be justified by faith.   Rom. 10:4 · Acts 13:39
25 But after that faith is come, we are no longer under a [T]schoolmaster.   *tutor*
26 For ye are all the children of God by faith in Christ Jesus.
27 For [R]as many of you as have been baptized into Christ [R]have put on Christ.   1 Cor. 10:2 · Rom. 10:12
28 [R]There is neither Jew nor Greek, there is neither bond nor free, there is neither male nor female: for ye are all [R]one in Christ Jesus.   Rom. 10:12; Col. 3:11 · John 17:11
★ 29 And if ye *be* Christ's, then are ye Abraham's seed, and [R]heirs according to the promise. Gen. 12:3

4 Now I say, *That* the heir, as long as he is a child, differeth nothing from a servant, though he be [T]lord of all;   *master*
2 But is under [T]tutors and governors until the time appointed of the father.   *guardians and stewards*
3 Even so we, when we were children, [R]were in bondage under the elements of the world: Col. 2:8
★ 4 But when the fulness of the time was come, God sent forth his Son, [R]made [R]of a woman, made under the law,   Rom. 1:3; 8:3 · Gen. 3:15
5 [R]To redeem them that were under the law, that we might receive the adoption of sons. [3:13]
6 And because ye are sons, God hath sent forth [R]the Spirit of his Son into your hearts, crying, Ab′-ba, Father. [Acts 16:7; Rom. 5:5; 8:9]
7 Wherefore thou art no more a servant, but a son; [R]and if a son, then an heir of God through Christ.   [Rom. 8:16, 17]
8 Howbeit then, [R]when ye knew not God, [R]ye did service unto them which by nature are no gods.   1 Thess. 4:5; 2 Thess. 1:8 · Rom. 1:25
9 But now, [R]after that ye have

known God, or rather are known of God, [R]how turn ye again to the weak and beggarly elements, whereunto ye desire again to be in bondage? [1 Cor. 8:3] · 3:1–3; Col. 2:20
10 Ye observe days, and months, and times, and years.
11 I am afraid [T]of you, [R]lest I have bestowed upon you labour in vain.   *for* · 1 Thess. 3:5
12 Brethren, I beseech you, be as I *am*; for I *am* as ye *are*; [R]ye have not injured me at all. 2 Cor. 2:5
13 Ye know how through infirmity of the flesh I preached the gospel unto you at the first.
14 And my [T]temptation which was in my flesh ye despised not, nor rejected; but received me as [T]an angel of God, [R]*even* as Christ Jesus.   *trial* · *a messenger* · [Luke 10:16]
15 Where is then the blessedness [T]ye spake of? for I bear you [T]record, that, if *it had been* possible, ye would have plucked out your own eyes, and have given them to me.   *you* enjoyed · *witness*
16 Am I therefore become your enemy, because I tell you the truth?
17 They zealously [T]affect you, *but* not well; yea, they would exclude you, that ye might [T]affect them.   *court* · *be zealous for them*
18 But *it is* good to be zealously affected always in *a* good *thing*, and not only when I am present with you.
19 [R]My little children, of whom I [T]travail in birth again until Christ be formed in you, 1 Cor. 4:15 · *labour*
20 I desire to be present with you now, and to change my [T]voice; for I [T]stand in doubt of you.   *tone* · *have doubts about*
21 Tell me, ye that desire to be under the law, do ye not hear the law?
22 For it is written, that Abraham had two sons, [R]the one by a bondmaid, [R]the other by a freewoman.   Gen. 16:15 · Gen. 21:2
23 But he *who was* of the bondwoman was born after the flesh; [R]but he of the freewoman *was* by promise.   Gen. 16:15; 17:15–19

24 Which things are ᵀan allegory: for these are the two covenants; the one from the mount Si'-nai, which gendereth to bondage, which is A'-gar.   *symbolic*

25 For this A'-gar is mount Si'-nai in Arabia, and answereth to Jerusalem which now is, and is in bondage with her children.

26 But ᴿJerusalem which is above is free, which is the mother of us all.   [Is. 2:2]

27 For it is written, ᴿRejoice, *thou* barren that bearest not; break forth and cry, thou that travailest not: for the desolate hath many more children than she which hath an husband.   Is. 54:1

28 Now we, brethren, as Isaac was, are the children of promise.

29 But as then ᴿhe that was born after the flesh persecuted him *that was born* after the Spirit, ᴿeven so *it is* now.   Gen. 21:9 · 5:11

30 Nevertheless what saith the scripture? Cast out the bondwoman and her son: for the son of the bondwoman shall not be heir with the son of the freewoman.

31 So then, brethren, we are not children of the bondwoman, but of the free.

5 Standᴿ fast therefore in the liberty wherewith Christ hath made us free, and be not entangled again with the ᴿyoke of bondage.   Phil. 4:1 · 2:4; Acts 15:10

2 Behold, I Paul say unto you, that ᴿif ye be circumcised, Christ shall profit you nothing.   Acts 15:1

3 For I testify again to every man that is circumcised, that he is a debtor to do the whole law.

4 ᴿChrist is become of no effect unto you, whosoever of you are justified by the law; ᴿye are fallen from grace.   [Rom. 9:31] · 2 Pet. 3:17

5 For we through the Spirit ᴿwaitᵀ for the hope of righteousness by faith.   Rom. 8:24 · *eagerly wait*

6 For ᴿin Jesus Christ neither circumcision availeth any thing, nor uncircumcision; but faith which worketh by love.   [1 Cor. 7:19]

7 Ye ᴿdid run well; who did hinder you that ye should not obey the truth?   1 Cor. 9:24

8 This persuasion *cometh* not of him that calleth you.

9 ᴿA little leaven leaveneth the whole lump.   1 Cor. 5:6

10 I have confidence in you ᵀthrough the Lord, that ye will be none otherwise minded: but he that troubleth you shall bear his judgment, whosoever he be.   Lit. *in*

11 And I, brethren, if I yet preach circumcision, why do I yet suffer persecution? then is the offence of the cross ceased.

12 I would they were even cut off ᴿwhich trouble you.   Acts 15:1, 2

13 For, brethren, ye have been called unto liberty; only ᴿ*use* not liberty for an ᴿoccasion to the flesh, but ᴿby love serve one another.   1 Cor. 8:9 · Rom. 6:1 · 1 Cor. 9:19

14 For ᴿall the law is fulfilled in one word, *even* in this; ᴿThou shalt love thy neighbour as thyself.   Matt. 7:12 · Lev. 19:18; Matt. 22:39

15 But if ye bite and devour one another, take heed that ye be not consumed one of another.

16 *This* I say then, ᴿWalk in the Spirit, and ye shall not fulfil the lust of the flesh.   Rom. 6:12

17 For ᴿthe flesh lusteth against the Spirit, and the Spirit against the flesh: and these are contrary the one to the other: ᴿso that ye cannot do the things that ye would.   Rom. 7:18, 22, 23; 8:5 · Rom. 7:15

18 But ᴿif ye be led of the Spirit, ye are not under the law.   [Rom. 6:14]

19 Now ᴿthe works of the flesh are manifest, which are *these*; Adultery, fornication, uncleanness, lasciviousness,   Rom. 1:26–31

20 Idolatry, witchcraft, hatred, variance, emulations, wrath, strife, seditions, heresies,

21 Envyings, murders, drunkenness, revellings, and such like: of the which I tell you before, as I have also told *you* in time past, that ᴿthey which do such things shall not inherit the kingdom of God.   1 Cor. 6:9, 10

22 But the fruit of the Spirit is

love, joy, peace, longsuffering, gentleness, goodness, faith,

23 Meekness, temperance: against such there is no law.

24 And they that are Christ's [R]have crucified the flesh with the affections and lusts.   Rom. 6:6

25 [R]If we live in the Spirit, let us also walk in the Spirit. [Rom. 8:4, 5]

26 [R]Let us not be desirous of vain glory, provoking one another, envying one another. Phil. 2:3

6 Brethren, if a man be [T]overtaken in a fault, ye which are spiritual, restore such an one in the spirit of [R]meekness; considering thyself, lest thou also be tempted. *caught* · Eph. 4:2

2 [R]Bear ye one another's burdens, and so fulfil [R]the law of Christ. 1 Thess. 5:14 · [James 2:8]

3 For [R]if a man think himself to be something, when he is nothing, he deceiveth himself. Rom. 12:3

4 But [R]let every man prove his own work, and then shall he have rejoicing in himself alone, and not in another. 1 Cor. 11:28

5 For [R]every man shall bear his own burden. [Rom. 2:6]

6 Let him that is taught in the word communicate unto him that teacheth in all good things.

7 Be not deceived; God is not mocked: for whatsoever a man soweth, that shall he also reap.

8 For he that soweth to his flesh shall of the flesh reap corruption; but he that soweth to the Spirit shall of the Spirit reap [R]life everlasting. [Rom. 6:8]

9 And [R]let us not be weary in well doing: for in due season we shall reap, if we faint not. 2 Cor. 4:1

10 [R]As we have therefore opportunity, let us do good unto all *men*, especially unto them who are of the household of faith. Prov. 3:27

11 Ye see [T]how large a letter I have written unto you with mine own hand. *with what large letters*

12 As many as desire to make a fair shew in the flesh, they constrain you to be circumcised; only lest they should suffer persecution for the cross of Christ.

13 For neither they themselves who are circumcised keep the law; but desire to have you circumcised, that they may glory in your flesh.

14 But God forbid that I should glory, save in the [R]cross of our Lord Jesus Christ, by whom the world is crucified unto me, and [R]I unto the world. [1 Cor. 1:18] · Col. 2:20

15 For [R]in Christ Jesus neither circumcision availeth any thing, nor uncircumcision, but a new creature. [Rom. 2:26, 28]; 1 Cor. 7:19

16 And as many as walk according to this rule, peace *be* on them, and mercy, and upon the Israel of God.

17 From henceforth let no man trouble me: for I bear in my body the marks of the Lord Jesus.

18 Brethren, the grace of our Lord Jesus Christ *be* with your spirit. A-men'.

The Epistle of Paul the Apostle to the

EPHESIANS

EPHESIANS is addressed to a group of believers who are rich beyond measure in Jesus Christ, yet living as beggars, and only because they are ignorant of their wealth. Paul begins by describing in chapters 1—3 the contents of the Christian's heavenly "bank account": adoption, acceptance, redemption, forgiveness, wisdom, inheritance, the seal of the Holy Spirit, life, grace, citizenship—in short, every spiritual blessing. In chapters 4—6 the Christian learns a spiritual walk rooted in his spiritual wealth. "For we are his workmanship, created in Christ Jesus [1—3] unto good works, . . . that we should walk in them [4—6]" (2:10).

The traditional title of this epistle is *Pros Ephesious*, "To the Ephesians." Many ancient manuscripts, however, omit *en Epheso*, "at Ephesus," in 1:1. This has led a number of scholars to challenge the traditional view that this message was directed specifically to the Ephesians. The encyclical theory proposes that it was a circular letter sent by Paul to the churches of Asia. It is argued that Ephesians is really a Christian treatise designed for general use: it involves no controversy and deals with no specific problems in any particular church. Some scholars accept an ancient tradition that Ephesians is Paul's letter to the Laodiceans (Col. 4:16), but there is no way to be sure. If Ephesians began as a circular letter, it eventually became associated with Ephesus, the foremost of the Asian churches. Another plausible option is that this epistle was directly addressed to the Ephesians, but written in such a way as to make it helpful for all the churches in Asia.

P AUL, an apostle of Jesus Christ by the will of God, to the saints which are at Eph´-e-sus, and to the faithful in Christ Jesus:

2 Grace *be* to you, and peace, from God our Father, and *from* the Lord Jesus Christ.

3 ᴿBlessed *be* the God and Father of our Lord Jesus Christ, who hath blessed us with all spiritual blessings in heavenly *places* in Christ: 2 Cor. 1:3

4 According as ᴿhe hath chosen us in him ᴿbefore the foundation of the world, that we should be holy and without blame before him in love: Rom. 8:28 · 1 Pet. 1:2

5 ᴿHaving predestinated us unto ᴿthe adoption of children by Jesus Christ to himself, ᴿaccording to the good pleasure of his will,   Acts 13:48 · John 1:12 · [1 Cor. 1:21]

6 To the praise of the glory of his grace, wherein he hath made us accepted in the beloved.

7 ᴿIn whom we have redemption through his blood, the forgiveness of sins, according to the riches of his grace;   [Heb. 9:12]

8 Wherein he hath abounded toward us in all wisdom and ᵀprudence;   *understanding*

9 Having made known unto us the mystery of his will, according to his good pleasure which he hath purposed in himself:

10 That in the dispensation of the fulness of times he might gather together in one ᴿall things in Christ, both which are in heaven, and which are on earth; *even* in him: 3:15; [Phil. 2:9; Col. 1:16, 20]

11 ᴿIn whom also we have obtained an inheritance, being predestinated according to ᴿthe purpose of him who worketh all things after the counsel of his own will: Rom. 8:17 · Is. 46:10

12 ᴿThat we should be to the praise of his glory, who first trusted in Christ.   2 Thess. 2:13

13 In whom ye also *trusted*, after that ye heard ᴿthe word of truth, the gospel of your salvation: in whom also after that ye believed, ye were sealed with that holy Spirit of promise,   John 1:17

14 ᴿWhich is the earnest of our inheritance until the redemption of the purchased possession, unto the praise of his glory.   2 Cor. 5:5

15 Wherefore I also, after I heard of your faith in the Lord Jesus, and love unto all the saints,

16 ᴿCease not to give thanks for you, making mention of you in my prayers;   Rom. 1:9

17 That ᴿthe God of our Lord Jesus Christ, the Father of glory, ᴿmay give unto you the spirit of wisdom and revelation in the knowledge of him: Rom. 15:6 · Col. 1:9

18 ᴿThe eyes of your under-

standing being enlightened; that ye may know what is ^Rthe hope of his calling, and what the riches of the glory of his inheritance in the saints,   2 Cor. 4:6; Heb. 6:4 · 2:12

19 And what *is* the exceeding greatness of his power to us-ward who believe, according to the working of his mighty power,

20 Which he wrought in Christ, when he raised him from the dead, and set *him* at his own right hand in the heavenly *places,*

21 Far above all principality, and power, and might, and dominion, and every name that is named, not only in this ^Tworld, but also in that which is to come: *age*

☆ 22 And ^Rhath put all *things* under his feet, and gave him ^R*to be* the head over all *things* to the church,   Ps. 8:6; 1 Cor. 15:27 · Heb. 2:7

23 Which is his body, the fulness of him that filleth all in all.

2 And ^Ryou *hath he quickened,* ^Rwho were dead in trespasses and sins;   v. 5; Col. 2:13 · 4:18

2 ^RWherein in time past ye walked according to the course of this world, according to the prince of the power of the air, the spirit that now worketh in the children of disobedience: Col. 1:21

3 ^RAmong whom also we all had our conversation in times past in ^Rthe lusts of our flesh, fulfilling the desires of the flesh and of the mind; and ^Rwere by nature the children of wrath, even as others.   1 Pet. 4:3 · Gal. 5:16 · [Ps. 51:5]

4 But God, ^Rwho is rich in mercy, for his great love wherewith he loved us,   Rom. 10:12

5 ^REven when we were dead in sins, hath ^Rquickened us together with Christ, (by grace ye are saved;)   Rom. 5:6, 8 · [Rom. 6:4, 5]

6 And hath raised *us* up together, and made *us* sit together in heavenly *places* in Christ Jesus:

7 That in the ages to come he might shew the exceeding riches of his grace in *his* kindness toward us through Christ Jesus.

8 For by grace are ye saved

through faith; and that not of yourselves: *it is* the gift of God:

9 Not of ^Rworks, lest any man should ^Rboast.   Rom. 11:6 · Rom. 3:27

10 For we are ^Rhis ^Tworkmanship, created in Christ Jesus ^Tunto good works, which God hath before ordained that we should walk in them.   Is. 19:25 · *creation · for*

11 Wherefore remember, that ye *being* in time past Gentiles in the flesh, who are called Uncircumcision by that which is called ^Rthe Circumcision in the flesh made by hands;   [Rom. 2:28; Col. 2:11]

12 That at that time ye were without Christ, being aliens from the commonwealth of Israel, and strangers from the covenants of promise, having no hope, and without God in the world:

13 But now in Christ Jesus ye who sometimes were far off are made nigh by the blood of Christ.

14 For he is our peace, who hath made both one, and hath broken down the middle wall of ^Tpartition *between us;*   *division* ★

15 Having abolished in his flesh the enmity, *even* the law of commandments *contained* in ordinances; for to ^Tmake in himself of ^Ttwain one ^Rnew man, *so* making peace;   *create · the two* · Gal. 6:15

16 And that he might ^Rreconcile both unto God in one body by the cross, ^Rhaving slain the enmity thereby: 2 Cor. 5:18 · [Rom. 6:6]

17 And came and preached peace to you which were afar off, and to them that were nigh.

18 For ^Rthrough him we both have access ^Rby one Spirit unto the Father.   John 10:9 · 1 Cor. 12:13

19 Now therefore ye are no more strangers and foreigners, but fellowcitizens with the saints, and of the household of God;

20 And are built upon the foundation of the ^Rapostles and prophets, Jesus Christ himself being the chief corner *stone;*   3:5; 1 Cor. 12:28 ★

21 In whom all the building fitly framed together groweth unto an holy temple in the Lord:

22 In whom ye also are builded together for an ^Rhabitation of God through the Spirit.   John 17:23

3 For this cause I Paul, the prisoner of Jesus Christ for you Gentiles,

2 If ye have heard of the dispensation of the grace of God which is given me to you-ward:

3 ^RHow that by revelation ^Rhe made known unto me the mystery; (as I wrote afore in few words, Acts 22:17, 21; 26:16 · Col. 1:26; 4:3

4 Whereby, when ye read, ye may understand my knowledge in the mystery of Christ)

5 Which in other ages was not made known unto the sons of men, as it is now revealed unto his holy apostles and prophets by the Spirit;

6 That the Gentiles ^Rshould be fellowheirs, and of the same body, and partakers of his promise in Christ by the gospel: Gal. 3:28, 29

7 ^RWhereof I was made a minister, ^Raccording to the gift of the grace of God given unto me by ^Rthe effectual working of his power.   Rom. 15:16 · Rom. 1:5 · Rom. 15:18

8 Unto me, who am less than the least of all saints, is this grace given, that I should preach among the Gentiles ^Rthe unsearchable riches of Christ;   [Col. 1:27; 2:2, 3]

9 And to make all *men* see what *is* the fellowship of the mystery, which from the beginning of the world hath been hid in God, who ^Rcreated all things by Jesus Christ: John 1:3; Col. 1:16; Heb. 1:2

10 ^RTo the intent that now unto the principalities and powers in heavenly *places* ^Rmight be known by the church the manifold wisdom of God,   1 Pet. 1:12 · 6:12; Col. 1:16

11 ^RAccording to the eternal purpose which he purposed in Christ Jesus our Lord: [1:4, 11]

12 In whom we have boldness and access ^Rwith confidence by the faith of him.   2 Cor. 3:4; Heb. 4:16

13 ^RWherefore I desire that ye faint not at my tribulations for you, which is your glory.   Phil. 1:14

14 For this cause I bow my knees unto the ^RFather of our Lord Jesus Christ,   1:3

15 Of whom the whole family in heaven and earth is named,

16 That he would grant you, ^Raccording to the riches of his glory, ^Rto be strengthened with might by his Spirit in the inner man;   [1:7; 2:4; Phil. 4:19] · Phil. 4:13

17 ^RThat Christ may dwell in your hearts by faith; that ye, being rooted and grounded in love, [2:22]

18 ^RMay be able to comprehend with all saints ^Rwhat *is* the ^Tbreadth, and length, and depth, and height;   1:18 · Rom. 8:39 · *width*

19 And to know the love of Christ, which passeth knowledge, that ye might be filled ^Rwith all the fulness of God.   1:23

20 Now ^Runto him that is able to do exceeding abundantly ^Rabove all that we ask or think, ^Raccording to the power that worketh in us,   Rom. 16:25 · 1 Cor. 2:9 · Col. 1:29

21 ^RUnto him *be* glory in the church by Christ Jesus throughout all ages, world without end. A-men'.   Rom. 11:36

4 I therefore, the prisoner of the Lord, beseech you that ye ^Rwalk worthy of the vocation wherewith ye are called,   2:10

2 With all lowliness and meekness, with longsuffering, forbearing one another in love;

3 Endeavouring to keep the unity of the Spirit ^Rin the bond of peace.   Col. 3:14

4 ^R*There is* one body, and one Spirit, even as ye are called in one hope of your calling;   Rom. 12:5

5 ^ROne Lord, ^Rone faith, ^Rone baptism, 1 Cor. 1:13 · Jude 3 · 1 Cor. 12:12

6 ^ROne God and Father of all, who *is* above all, and ^Rthrough all, and in you all.   1 Cor. 8:6 · Rom. 11:36

7 But unto every one of us is given grace according to the measure of the gift of Christ.

8 Wherefore he saith, ^RWhen ★ he ascended up on high, he led captivity captive, and gave gifts unto men.   Ps. 68:18; [Col. 2:15]

9 (^RNow that he ascended, what is it but that he also de-

scended first into the lower parts of the earth?   Luke 23:43; John 3:13

★ 10 He that descended is the same also ^Rthat ascended up far above all heavens, ^Rthat he might fill all things.)   Acts 1:9 · [1:23]

11 And ^The gave some, apostles; and some, prophets; and some, evangelists; and some, pastors and teachers;   *he himself*

12 For the perfecting of the saints, for the work of the ministry, ^Rfor the edifying of ^Rthe body of Christ: 1 Cor. 14:26 · Col. 1:24

13 Till we all come in the unity of the faith, ^Rand of the knowledge of the Son of God, unto ^Ra ^Tperfect man, unto the measure of the stature of the fulness of Christ: Col. 2:2 · Col. 1:28 · *mature*

14 That we *henceforth* be no more children, tossed to and fro, and carried about with every wind of doctrine, by the ^Tsleight of men, *and* cunning craftiness, ^Rwhereby they lie in wait to deceive;   *trickery* · Rom. 16:18

15 But speaking the truth in love, may grow up into him in all things, which is the ^Rhead, *even* Christ: 1:22

16 ^RFrom whom the whole body fitly joined together and ^Tcompacted by that which every joint supplieth, according to the ^Teffectual working in the measure of every part, maketh increase of the body unto the edifying of itself in love.   Col. 2:19 · *knit together* · *effective*

17 This I say therefore, and testify in the Lord, that ye henceforth ^Rwalk not as other Gentiles walk, in the vanity of their mind,   2:2

18 Having the understanding darkened, being alienated from the life of God through the ignorance that is in them, because of the blindness of their heart:

19 Who being past feeling ^Rhave given themselves over unto lasciviousness, to work all uncleanness with greediness.   1 Pet. 4:3

20 But ye have not so learned Christ;

21 If so be that ye have heard

him, and have been taught by him, as the truth is in Jesus:

22 That ye ^Rput off concerning the former conversation the old man, which is corrupt according to the deceitful lusts;   Col. 3:8

23 And ^Rbe renewed in the spirit of your mind;   [Rom. 12:2; Col. 3:10]

24 And that ye put on the new man, which after God is created in righteousness and true holiness.

25 Wherefore putting away lying, ^Rspeak every man truth with his neighbour: for we are members one of another.   v. 15; Col. 3:9

26 ^RBe ye angry, and sin not: let not the sun go down upon your wrath: Ps. 4:4; 37:8

27 ^RNeither give place to the devil.   [Rom. 12:19; James 4:7]; 1 Pet. 5:9

28 Let him that stole steal no more: but rather let him labour, working with *his* hands the thing which is good, that he may have to give to him that needeth.

29 ^RLet no corrupt communication proceed out of your mouth, but that which is good to the use of edifying, that it may minister grace unto the hearers.   5:4; Col. 3:8

30 And ^Rgrieve not the holy Spirit of God, whereby ye are sealed unto the day of redemption.   Is. 7:13

31 ^RLet all bitterness, and wrath, and anger, and clamour, and evil speaking, be put away from you, ^Rwith all malice: Col. 3:8, 19 · Titus 3:3

32 And be ye kind one to another, tenderhearted, forgiving one another, even as God for Christ's sake hath forgiven you.

5 Be ^Rye therefore followers of God, as dear children; Luke 6:36

2 And walk in love, ^Ras Christ also hath loved us, and hath given himself for us an offering and a sacrifice to God for a sweetsmelling ^Tsavour. Gal. 1:4; 1 John 3:16 · *aroma*

3 But fornication, and all ^Runcleanness, or covetousness, let it not be once named among you, as becometh saints;   Col. 3:5–7

4 ^RNeither filthiness, nor ^Rfoolish talking, nor jesting, which are

not convenient: but rather giving of thanks. Col. 3:8; James 1:21 · Titus 3:9

5 For this ye know, that no whoremonger, nor unclean person, nor covetous man, who is an idolater, hath any inheritance in the kingdom of Christ and of God.

6 Let no man deceive you with ᵀvain words: for because of these things cometh the wrath of God upon the ᵀchildren of disobedience.   empty · sons

7 Be not ye therefore ᴿpartakers with them.   1 Tim. 5:22

8 For ye were sometimes darkness, but now *are ye* light in the Lord: walk as children of light:

9 (For ᴿthe fruit of the Spirit *is* in all goodness and righteousness and truth;)   Gal. 5:22

10 ᴿProving what is acceptable unto the Lord.   [Rom. 12:1, 2]

11 And have ᴿno fellowship with the unfruitful works of darkness, but rather reprove *them*.   1 Cor. 5:9

12 ᴿFor it is a shame even to speak of those things which are done of them in secret.   Rom. 1:24

13 But ᴿall things that are reproved are made manifest by the light: for whatsoever doth make manifest is light.   [John 3:20, 21]

★ 14 Wherefore he saith, ᴿAwake thou that sleepest, and arise from the dead, and Christ shall give thee light.   [Is. 26:19; 60:1; Rom. 13:11]

15 ᴿSee then that ye walk ᵀcircumspectly, not as fools, but as wise,   Col. 4:5 · *carefully*

16 ᴿRedeeming the time, because the days are evil.   Col. 4:5

17 ᴿWherefore be ye not unwise, but ᴿunderstanding what the will of the Lord *is*.   Col. 4:5 · Col. 1:9

18 And ᴿbe not drunk with wine, wherein is excess; but be filled with the Spirit;   Rom. 13:13; 1 Cor. 5:11

19 Speaking to yourselves in psalms and hymns and spiritual songs, singing and making melody in your heart to the Lord;

20 ᴿGiving thanks always for all things unto God and the Father ᴿin the name of our Lord Jesus Christ;   Ps. 34:1 · [1 Pet. 2:5]

21 Submitting yourselves one to another in the fear of God.

22 Wives, ᴿsubmit yourselves unto your own husbands, as unto the Lord.   Col. 3:18—4:1; 1 Pet. 3:1-6

23 For the husband is the head of the wife, even as ᴿChrist is the head of the church: and he is the saviour of the body.   Col. 1:18

24 Therefore as the church is subject unto Christ, so *let* the wives *be* to their own husbands ᴿin every thing.   Titus 2:4, 5

25 Husbands, love your wives, even as Christ also loved the church, and gave himself for it;

26 That he might sanctify and cleanse it ᴿwith the washing of water ᴿby the word,   John 3:5 · [6:17]

27 That he might present it to himself a glorious church, ᴿnot having spot, or wrinkle, or any such thing; but that it should be holy and without blemish. Song 4:7

28 So ought men to love their wives as their own bodies. He that loveth his wife loveth himself.

29 For no man ever yet hated his own flesh; but nourisheth and cherisheth it, even as the Lord the church:

30 For ᴿwe are members of his body, of his flesh, and of his bones.   Gen. 2:23

31 For this cause shall a man leave his father and mother, and shall be joined unto his wife, and they two shall be one flesh.

32 This is a great mystery: but I speak concerning Christ and the church.

33 Nevertheless ᴿlet every one of you in particular so love his wife even as himself; and the wife *see* that she ᴿreverenceᵀ *her* husband.   Col. 3:19 · 1 Pet. 3:1, 6 · *respects*

6 Children, obey your parents in the Lord: for this is right.

2 ᴿHonour thy father and mother; which is the first commandment with promise; Ex. 20:12

3 That it may be well with thee, and thou mayest live long on the earth.

4 And, ᴿye fathers, provoke not your children to wrath: but ᴿbring

them up in the nurture and admonition of the Lord. Col. 3:21 · Ps. 78:4

5 ᴿServants, be obedient to them that are *your* masters according to the flesh, with fear and trembling, in singleness of your heart, as unto Christ; [1 Tim. 6:1]

6 ᴿNot with eyeservice, as menpleasers; but as the servants of Christ, doing the will of God from the heart; Col. 3:22

7 With good will doing service, as to the Lord, and not to men:

8 Knowing that whatsoever good thing any man doeth, the same shall he receive of the Lord, whether *he be* bond or free.

9 And, ye masters, do the same things unto them, forbearing threatening; knowing that your ᴿMaster also is in heaven; ᴿneither is there respect of persons with him. John 13:13; Col. 4:1 · Col. 3:25

10 Finally, my brethren, be strong in the Lord, and in the power of his might.

11 Put on the whole armour of God, that ye may be able to stand against the wiles of the devil.

12 For we wrestle not against flesh and blood, but against principalities, against powers, against the rulers of the darkness of this world, against spiritual wickedness in high *places*.

13 ᴿWherefore ᵀtake unto you the whole armour of God, that ye may be able to withstand ᴿin the evil day, and having done all, to stand. [2 Cor. 10:4] · *take up* · 5:16

14 Stand therefore, ᴿhaving your loins girt about with truth, and ᴿhaving on the breastplate of righteousness; 1 Pet. 1:13 · 1 Thess. 5:8

15 ᴿAnd your feet shod with the preparation of the gospel of peace; Is. 52:7; Rom. 10:15

16 Above all, taking ᴿthe shield of faith, wherewith ye shall be able to quench all the fiery darts of the ᵀwicked. 1 John 5:4 · *wicked one*

17 And take the helmet of salvation, and the sword of the Spirit, which is the word of God:

18 ᴿPraying always with all prayer and supplication in the Spirit, and watching thereunto with all perseverance and supplication for all saints; Col. 1:3; 4:2

19 And for me, that utterance may be given unto me, that I may open my mouth boldly, to make known the mystery of the gospel,

20 For which I am an ambassador in bonds: that therein I may speak boldly, as I ought to speak.

21 But that ye also may know my affairs, *and* how I do, ᴿTych'-i-cus, a beloved brother and faithful minister in the Lord, shall make known to you all things: Titus 3:12

22 Whom I have sent unto you for the same purpose, that ye might know our affairs, and *that* he might comfort your hearts.

23 Peace *be* to the brethren, and love with faith, from God the Father and the Lord Jesus Christ.

24 Grace *be* with all them that love our Lord Jesus Christ in sincerity. A-men'.

The Epistle of Paul the Apostle to the

PHILIPPIANS

PAUL writes a thank-you note to the believers at Philippi for their help in his hour of need, and he uses the occasion to send along some instruction on Christian unity. His central thought is simple: Only in Christ are real unity and joy possible. With Christ as your model of humility and service, you can enjoy a oneness of purpose, attitude, goal, and labor—a truth which Paul illustrates from his own life, and one the Philippians desperately need to hear.

Within their own ranks, fellow workers in the Philippian church are at odds, hindering the work in proclaiming new life in Christ. Because of this, Paul exhorts the church to "stand fast . . . be of the same mind . . . rejoice in the Lord alway . . . but in every thing by prayer and supplication with thanksgiving let your requests be made known . . . and the peace of God, which passeth all understanding, shall keep your hearts and minds through Christ Jesus" (4:1, 2, 4, 6, 7).

This epistle is called *Pros Philippesious*, "To the Philippians." The church at Philippi was the first church Paul founded in Macedonia.

P AUL and Ti-mo′-the-us, the servants of Jesus Christ, to all the saints in Christ Jesus which are at Phi-lip′-pi, with the ᵀbish-ops and deacons: *overseers*
2 Grace *be* unto you, and peace, from God our Father, and *from* the Lord Jesus Christ.
3 ᴿI thank my God upon every remembrance of you,   1 Cor. 1:4
4 Always in ᴿevery prayer of mine for you all making request with joy,   Eph. 1:16; 1 Thess. 1:2
5 ᴿFor your fellowship in the gospel from the first day until now;   [Rom. 12:13]
6 Being confident of this very thing, that he which hath begun a good work in you will perform *it* until the day of Jesus Christ:
7 Even as it is ᵀmeet for me to think this of you all, because I have you in my heart; inasmuch as both in my ᵀbonds, and in the defence and confirmation of the gospel, ye all are ᵀpartakers of my grace.   *right · chains · sharers*
8 For God is my record, how greatly I long after you all in the ᵀbowels of Jesus Christ.   *affection*
9 And this I pray, that your love may abound yet more and more in knowledge and *in* all ᵀjudg-ment;   *discernment*
10 That ye may approve things that are excellent; that ye may be sincere and without offence till the day of Christ;
11 Being filled with the fruits of righteousness, ᴿwhich are by Je-sus Christ, ᴿunto the glory and praise of God.   Col. 1:6 · John 15:8
12 But I would ye should under-stand, brethren, that the things *which happened* unto me have

ᵀfallen out rather unto the further-ance of the gospel;   *turned out*
13 So that my bonds in Christ are manifest ᴿin all the palace, and in all other *places;*   4:22
14 And ᵀmany of the brethren in the Lord, waxing confident by my bonds, are much more bold to speak the word without fear.   *most*
15 Some indeed preach Christ even of envy and strife; and some also of good will:
16 The one preach Christ of ᵀcontention, not sincerely, sup-posing to add affliction to my ᵀbonds: *selfish ambition · chains*
17 But the other of love, know-ing that I am ᵀset for the defence of the gospel.   *appointed*
18 What then? notwithstanding, every way, whether in pretence, or in truth, Christ is preached; and I therein do rejoice, yea, and will rejoice.
19 For I know that ᴿthis shall turn to my salvation through your prayer, and the supply of the Spirit of Jesus Christ,   Job 13:16
20 According to my earnest expectation and *my* hope, that in nothing I shall be ashamed, but *that* ᴿwith all boldness, as always, so now also Christ shall be mag-nified in my body, whether *it be* by life, or by death.   Eph. 6:19, 20
21 For to me to live *is* Christ, and to die *is* gain.
22 But if I live in the flesh, this *is* the fruit of my labour: yet what I shall choose I ᵀwot not.   *know*
23 For I am in a strait betwixt two, having a ᴿdesire to depart, and to be with Christ; which is far better: [2 Cor. 5:2, 8]; 2 Tim. 4:6

24 Nevertheless to abide in the flesh *is* more needful for you.

25 And having this confidence, I know that I shall abide and continue with you all for your [T]furtherance and joy of faith; *progress*

26 That your rejoicing may be more abundant in Jesus Christ for me by my coming to you again.

27 Only [R]let your conversation be as it becometh the gospel of Christ: that whether I come and see you, or else be absent, I may hear of your affairs, that ye stand fast in one spirit, [R]with one mind striving together for the faith of the gospel; Eph. 4:1 · 1 Cor. 1:10; Eph. 4:3

28 And in [T]nothing terrified by your adversaries: which is to them [T]an evident token of [T]perdition, but to you of salvation, and that of God. *no way · a proof · destruction*

29 For unto you it is given in the behalf of Christ, [R]not only to believe on him, but also to [R]suffer for his sake; Eph. 2:8 · [2 Tim. 3:12]

30 [R]Having the same conflict which ye saw in me, and now hear *to be* in me. Col. 1:29

2 If *there be* therefore any consolation in Christ, if any [T]comfort of love, if any fellowship of the Spirit, if any [R]bowels and mercies, *consolation ·* Col. 3:12

2 Fulfil ye my joy, that ye be likeminded, having the same love, *being* of one accord, of one mind.

3 *Let* nothing *be done* through strife or vainglory; but in lowliness of mind let each esteem other better than themselves.

4 [R]Look not every man on his own things, but every man also on the things of others. 1 Cor. 13:5

5 Let this mind be in you, which was also in Christ Jesus:

6 Who, [R]being in the form of God, thought it not robbery to be equal with God: 2 Cor. 4:4

7 But made himself of no reputation, and took upon him the form of a servant, and [R]was made in the likeness of men: Rom. 8:3

8 And being found in fashion as a man, he humbled himself,

and became obedient unto death, even the death of the cross.

9 [R]Wherefore God also [R]hath ★ highly exalted him, and [R]given him a name which is above every name: Heb. 2:9 · Acts 2:33 · Eph. 1:21

10 That at the name of Jesus every knee should bow, of *things* in heaven, and *things* in earth, and *things* under the earth;

11 And [R]*that* every tongue ☆ should confess that Jesus Christ *is* Lord, to the glory of God the Father. John 13:13; [Rom. 10:9; 14:9]

12 Wherefore, my beloved, [R]as ye have always obeyed, not as in my presence only, but now much more in my absence, [R]work out your own salvation with fear and trembling. 1:5, 6; 4:15 · 2 Pet. 1:10

13 For it is God which worketh in you both to will and to do [R]of *his* good pleasure. Eph. 1:5

14 Do all things without murmurings and [R]disputings: Rom. 14:1

15 That ye may be blameless and harmless, the sons of God, without [T]rebuke, in the midst of a crooked and perverse nation, among whom ye shine as [R]lights in the world; *fault ·* Matt. 5:15, 16

16 Holding forth the word of life; that I may rejoice in the day of Christ, that I have not run in vain, neither laboured in vain.

17 Yea, and if [R]I be offered upon the sacrifice [R]and service of your faith, [R]I joy, and rejoice with you all. 2 Tim. 4:6 · Rom. 15:16 · 2 Cor. 7:4

18 For the same cause also do ye joy, and rejoice with me.

19 But I trust in the Lord Jesus to send [R]Ti-mo'-the-us shortly unto you, that I also may be [T]of good comfort, when I know your state. Rom. 16:21 · *encouraged*

20 For I have no man [R]likeminded, who will naturally care for your state. 1 Cor. 16:10; 2 Tim. 3:10

21 For all seek their own, not the things which are Jesus Christ's.

22 But ye know the proof of him, that, as a son with the father, he hath served with me in the gospel.

23 Him therefore I hope to send

Tpresently, so soon as I shall see how it will go with me.   *at once*

24 But I trust in the Lord that I also myself shall come shortly.

25 Yet I supposed it necessary to send to you RE-paph-ro-di'-tus, my brother, and companion in labour, and Rfellowsoldier, Rbut your messenger, and he that ministered to my wants.   4:18 · Philem. 2 · John 13:16

26 RFor he longed after you all, and was Tfull of heaviness, because that ye had heard that he had been sick.   1:8 · *distressed*

27 For indeed he was sick nigh unto death: but God had mercy on him; and not on him only, but on me also, lest I should have sorrow upon sorrow.

28 I sent him therefore the more carefully, that, when ye see him again, ye may rejoice, and that I may be the less sorrowful.

29 Receive him therefore in the Lord with all gladness; and hold such in Treputation: *high esteem*

30 Because for the work of Christ he was nigh unto death, not regarding his life, Rto supply your lack of service toward me.   4:10

3 Finally, my brethren, rejoice in the Lord. To write the same things to you, to me indeed *is* not grievous, but for you *it is* safe.

2 RBeware of dogs, beware of Revil workers, Rbeware of the concision.   Gal. 5:15 · Ps. 119:115 · Rom. 2:28

3 For we are the circumcision, which worship God in the spirit, and rejoice in Christ Jesus, and have no confidence in the flesh.

4 Though RI might also have confidence in the flesh. If any other man thinketh that he hath whereof he might trust in the flesh, I more: 2 Cor. 5:16; 11:18

5 Circumcised the eighth day, of the stock of Israel, Rof the tribe of Benjamin, an Hebrew of the Hebrews; as touching the law, Ra Pharisee;   Rom. 11:1 · Acts 23:6

6 Concerning zeal, Rpersecuting the church; touching the righteousness which is in the law, blameless.   Acts 8:3; 22:4, 5; 26:9–11

7 But Rwhat things were gain to me, those I counted loss for Christ.   Matt. 13:44

8 Yea doubtless, and I count all things *but* loss Rfor the excellency of the knowledge of Christ Jesus my Lord: for whom I have suffered the loss of all things, and do count them *but* dung, that I may win Christ,   1 Cor. 2:2; [Eph. 4:13]

9 And be found in him, not having Rmine own righteousness, which is of the law, but Rthat which is through the faith of Christ, the righteousness which is of God by faith: Rom. 10:3 · Rom. 1:17

10 That I may know him, and the Rpower of his resurrection, and Rthe fellowship of his sufferings, being made conformable unto his death;   Eph. 1:19, 20 · 2 Cor. 1:5

11 If by any means I might RattainT unto the resurrection of the dead.   [1 Cor. 15:23] · Lit. *arrive at*

12 Not as though I had already Rattained, either were already Rperfect: but I follow after, if that I may apprehend that for which also I am apprehended of Christ Jesus.   [1 Tim. 6:12, 19] · Heb. 12:23

13 Brethren, I count not myself to have apprehended: but *this* one thing I *do*, Rforgetting those things which are behind, and Rreaching forth unto those things which are before,   Luke 9:62 · Heb. 6:1

14 I press toward the mark for the prize of the Thigh calling of God in Christ Jesus.   *upward*

15 Let us therefore, as many as be Rperfect,T be thus minded: and if in any thing ye be otherwise minded, God shall reveal even this unto you.   1 Cor. 2:6 · *mature*

16 Nevertheless, whereto we have already attained, let us walk Rby the same rule, let us mind the same thing.   Rom. 12:16; 15:5

17 Brethren, Rbe followers together of me, and mark them which walk so as Rye have us for an ensample.   4:9 · Titus 2:7, 8

18 (For many walk, of whom I have told you often, and now tell you even weeping, *that they are* Rthe enemies of the cross of Christ: Gal. 1:7

19 Whose end *is* destruction, whose God *is their* belly, and *whose* glory *is* in their shame, who mind earthly things.)

20 For ᴿour ᵀconversation is in heaven; from whence also we look for the Saviour, the Lord Jesus Christ: Eph. 2:6, 19 · *citizenship*

21 ᴿWho shall change our vile body, that it may be fashioned like unto his glorious body, according to the working whereby he is able even to subdue all things unto himself.   [1 Cor. 15:43–53]

4 Therefore, my brethren dearly beloved and longed for, my joy and crown, so ᴿstand fast in the Lord, *my* dearly beloved.   1:27

2 I beseech Eu-o'-di-as, and beseech Syn'-ty-che, ᴿthat they be of the same mind in the Lord.   2:2

3 And I intreat thee also, true ᵀyokefellow, help those women which ᴿlaboured with me in the gospel, with Clement also, and *with* other my fellowlabourers, whose names *are* in ᴿthe book of life.   *companion* · Rom. 16:3 · Luke 10:20

4 ᴿRejoice in the Lord alway: *and* again I say, Rejoice.   Rom. 12:12

5 Let your ᵀmoderation be known unto all men. ᴿThe Lord *is* at hand.   *gentleness* · 1 Cor. 16:22

6 ᴿBe ᵀcareful for nothing; but in every thing by prayer and supplication with thanksgiving let your requests be made known unto God.   Matt. 6:25; 1 Pet. 5:7 · *anxious*

7 And ᴿthe peace of God, which passeth all understanding, shall keep your hearts and minds through Christ Jesus.   Col. 3:15

8 Finally, brethren, whatsoever things are true, whatsoever things *are* ᵀhonest, whatsoever things *are* just, whatsoever things *are* pure, whatsoever things *are* lovely, whatsoever things *are* of good report; if *there be* any virtue, and if *there be* any praise, ᵀthink on these things.   *noble* · *meditate*

9 Those things, which ye have both learned, and received, and heard, and seen in me, do: and

ᴿthe God of peace shall be with you.   Rom. 15:33; Heb. 13:20

10 But I rejoiced in the Lord greatly, that now at the last ᴿyour care of me hath flourished again; wherein ye were also careful, but ye lacked opportunity.   2 Cor. 11:9

11 Not that I speak in respect of want: for I have learned, in whatsoever state I am, ᴿ*therewith* to be content.   2 Cor. 9:8; 1 Tim. 6:6, 8; Heb. 13:5

12 I know both how to be abased, and I know how to abound: every where and in all things I am instructed both to be full and to be hungry, both to abound and to suffer need.

13 I can do all things through Christ which strengtheneth me.

14 Notwithstanding ye have well done, that ye did ᵀcommunicate with my affliction.   *share in*

15 Now ye Phi-lip'-pi-ans know also, that in the beginning of the gospel, when I departed from Mac-e-do'-ni-a, no church communicated with me as concerning giving and receiving, but ye only.

16 For even in Thes-sa-lo-ni'-ca ye sent once and again unto my necessity.

17 Not because I ᵀdesire a gift: but I desire fruit that may abound to your account.   *seek*

18 But I have all, and abound: I am full, having received of E-paph-ro-di'-tus the things *which were sent* from you, an odour of a sweet smell, ᴿa sacrifice acceptable, wellpleasing to God.   Rom.12:1

19 But my God ᴿshall supply all your need according to his riches in glory by Christ Jesus.   2 Cor. 9:8

20 ᴿNow unto God and our Father *be* glory for ever and ever. A-men'.   Rom. 16:27

21 ᵀSalute every saint in Christ Jesus. The brethren ᴿwhich are with me greet you.   *Greet* · Gal. 1:2

22 All the saints ᵀsalute you, ᵀchiefly they that are of Caesar's household.   *greet* · *especially*

23 The grace of our Lord Jesus Christ *be* with you all. A-men'.

The Epistle of Paul the Apostle to the

COLOSSIANS

IF Ephesians can be labeled the epistle portraying the "church of Christ," then Colossians must surely be the "Christ of the church." Ephesians focuses on the body; Colossians focuses on the Head. Like Ephesians, the little Book of Colossians divides neatly in half with the first portion doctrinal (1 and 2) and the second practical (3 and 4). Paul's purpose is to show that Christ is preeminent—first and foremost in everything—and the Christian's life should reflect that priority. Because believers are rooted in Him, alive in Him, hidden in Him, and complete in Him, it is utterly inconsistent for them to live life without Him. Clothed in His love, with His peace ruling in their hearts, they are equipped to make Christ first in every area of life.

This epistle became known as *Pros Kolossaeis,* "To the Colossians," because of 1:2. Paul also wanted it to be read in the neighboring church at Laodicea (4:16).

PAUL, ^Ran apostle of Jesus Christ by the will of God, and Ti-mo'-the-us *our* brother,   Eph. 1:1
2 To the saints and faithful brethren in Christ which are at Co-los'-se: ^RGrace *be* unto you, and peace, from God our Father and the Lord Jesus Christ. Gal. 1:3
3 We give thanks to God and the Father of our Lord Jesus Christ, praying always for you,
4 Since we heard of your faith in Christ Jesus, and of the love *which ye have* to all the saints,
5 For the hope ^Rwhich is laid up for you in heaven, whereof ye heard before in the word of the truth of the gospel;   [1 Pet. 1:4]
6 Which is come unto you, as *it is* in all the world; and bringeth forth fruit, as *it doth* also in you, since the day ye heard *of it,* and knew the grace of God in truth:
7 As ye also learned of ^REp'-a-phras our dear fellowservant, who is for you ^Ra faithful minister of Christ;   4:12; Philem. 23 · 1 Cor. 4:1, 2
8 Who also declared unto us your ^Rlove in the Spirit.   Rom. 15:30
9 For this cause we also, since the day we heard *it,* do not cease to pray for you, and to desire that ye might be filled with the knowledge of his will in all wisdom and spiritual understanding;
10 ^RThat ye might walk worthy of the Lord ^Runto all pleasing,

being fruitful in every good work, and increasing in the knowledge of God;   Eph. 4:1; Phil. 1:27 · 1 Thess. 4:1
11 ^RStrengthened with all might, according to his glorious power, unto all patience and longsuffering with joyfulness;   [Eph. 3:16; 6:10]
12 Giving thanks unto the Father, which hath made us meet to be partakers of ^Rthe inheritance of the saints in light: Eph. 1:11
13 Who hath delivered us from ^Rthe power of darkness, ^Rand hath translated *us* into the kingdom of his dear Son: Eph. 6:12 · 2 Pet. 1:11
14 ^RIn whom we have redemption through his blood, *even* the forgiveness of sins: Eph. 1:7
15 Who is ^Rthe image of the invisible God, ^Rthe firstborn of every creature: Heb. 1:3 · Ps. 89:27
16 For ^Rby him were all things created, that are in heaven, and that are in earth, visible and invisible, whether *they be* thrones, or dominions, or principalities, or powers: all things were created by him, and for him: John 1:3; Heb. 1:2, 3
17 And he is before all things, and by him all things consist.
18 And ^Rhe is the head of the body, the church: who is the beginning, the firstborn from the dead; that in all *things* he might have the preeminence.   1 Cor. 11:3
19 For it pleased *the Father* that in him should all fulness dwell;

20 And, [R]having made peace through the blood of his cross, by him to reconcile all things unto himself; by him, *I say*, whether *they be* things in earth, or things in heaven. Rom. 5:1; Eph. 2:14

21 And you, that were sometime alienated and enemies in *your* mind by wicked works, yet now hath he [R]reconciled 2 Cor. 5:18, 19

22 In the body of his flesh through death, [R]to present you holy and unblameable and unreproveable in his sight: v. 28

23 If ye continue in the faith [R]grounded and settled, and *be* [R]not moved away from the hope of the gospel, which ye have heard, *and* which was preached to every creature which is under heaven; whereof I Paul am made a minister; 2:7 · [John 15:6]; 1 Cor. 15:58

24 Who now rejoice in my sufferings for you, and fill up that which is behind of the afflictions of Christ in my flesh for his body's sake, which is the church:

25 Whereof I am made a minister, according to the dispensation of God which is given to me for you, to fulfil the word of God;

26 *Even* [R]the mystery which hath been hid from ages and from generations, but now is made manifest to his saints: [1 Cor. 2:7]

27 [R]To whom God would make known what *is* the riches of the glory of this mystery among the Gentiles; which is Christ in you, the hope of glory: 2 Cor. 2:14

28 Whom we preach, [R]warning every man, and teaching every man in all wisdom; [R]that we may present every man perfect in Christ Jesus: Acts 20:20 · Eph. 5:27

29 Whereunto I also labour, striving according to his working, which worketh in me mightily.

2 For I would that ye knew what great [R]conflict I have for you, and *for* them at La-od-i-ce′-a, and *for* as many as have not seen my face in the flesh; Phil. 1:30

2 That their hearts might be [T]comforted, being knit together in love, and unto all riches of the full assurance of understanding, to the acknowledgement of the mystery of God, and of the Father, and of Christ; *encouraged*

3 [R]In whom are hid all the treasures of wisdom and knowledge. 1 Cor. 1:24, 30

4 And this I say, [R]lest any man should beguile you with enticing words. 2 Cor. 11:13; Eph. 4:14; 5:6

5 For [R]though I be absent in the flesh, yet am I with you in the spirit, joying and beholding your order, and the stedfastness of your faith in Christ. 1 Thess. 2:17

6 [R]As ye have therefore received Christ Jesus the Lord, *so* walk ye in him: 1 Thess. 4:1

7 [R]Rooted and built up in him, and stablished in the faith, as ye have been taught, abounding therein with thanksgiving. Eph. 2:21

8 Beware lest any man spoil you through philosophy and vain deceit, after the tradition of men, after the [R]rudiments of the world, and not after Christ. v. 20; Gal. 4:3

9 For [R]in him dwelleth all the fulness of the Godhead bodily. 1:19

10 And ye are complete in him, which is the [R]head of all principality and power: [Eph. 1:20, 21]

11 In whom also ye are circumcised with the circumcision made without hands, in [R]putting off the body of the sins of the flesh by the circumcision of Christ: 3:5; Rom. 6:6; 7:24; Gal. 5:24

12 Buried with him in baptism, wherein also ye are risen with *him* through [R]the faith of the operation of God, who hath raised him from the dead. Eph. 1:19, 20

13 And you, being dead in your sins and the uncircumcision of your flesh, hath he [T]quickened together with him, having forgiven you all trespasses; *made alive*

14 [R]Blotting out the handwriting of ordinances that was against us, which was contrary to us, and took it out of the way, nailing it to his cross; v. 20; [Eph. 2:15, 16]

15 *And* [R]having spoiled [R]principalities and powers, he made a

shew of them openly, triumphing over them in it. [Heb. 2:14] · Eph. 6:12

16 Let no man therefore judge you in meat, or in drink, or in respect of an holyday, or of the new moon, or of the sabbath *days:*

17 ᴿWhich are a shadow of things to come; but the ᵀbody *is* of Christ.   Heb. 8:5; 10:1 · *substance*

18 Let no man ᵀbeguile you of your reward in a voluntary humility and worshipping of angels, intruding into those things which he hath not seen, vainly puffed up by his fleshly mind,   *defraud*

19 And not holding ᴿthe Head, from which all the body by joints and ᵀbands having nourishment ministered, and knit together, ᴿincreaseth with the increase of God. Eph. 4:15 · *ligaments* · Eph. 1:23; 4:16

20 Wherefore if ye be ᴿdead with Christ from the rudiments of the world, ᴿwhy, as though living in the world, are ye subject to ordinances,   Rom. 6:2–5 · Gal. 4:3, 9

21 (ᴿTouch not; taste not; handle not;   1 Tim. 4:3

22 Which all are to perish with the using;) after the commandments and doctrines of men?

23 ᴿWhich things have indeed a shew of wisdom in will worship, and humility, and neglecting of the body; not in any honour to the satisfying of the flesh.   1 Tim. 4:8

★ **3** If ye then be ᴿrisen with Christ, seek those things which are above, where Christ sitteth on the right hand of God.   Eph. 2:6

2 Set your affection on things above, not on things on the earth.

3 ᴿFor ye are dead, and your life is hid with Christ in God. 2:20

4 When Christ, *who is* our life, shall appear, then shall ye also appear with him in glory.

5 Mortify therefore your members which are upon the earth; fornication, uncleanness, ᵀinordinate affection, evil ᵀconcupiscence, and covetousness, which is idolatry: *passion* · *desire*

6 ᴿFor which things' sake the wrath of God cometh on the children of disobedience: Eph. 5:6

7 In the which ye also walked some time, when ye lived in them.

8 ᴿBut now ye also put off all these; anger, wrath, malice, blasphemy, filthy communication out of your mouth.   Eph. 4:22; 1 Pet. 2:1

9 Lie not one to another, seeing that ye have put off the old man with his deeds;

10 And have put on the new *man,* which ᴿis renewed in knowledge after the image of him that created him: Rom. 12:2; 2 Cor. 4:16

11 Where there is neither ᴿGreek nor Jew, circumcision nor uncircumcision, Barbarian, Scyth'-i-an, bond *nor* free: ᴿbut Christ *is* all, and in all.   Gal. 3:27, 28 · Eph. 1:23

12 Put on therefore, as the elect of God, holy and beloved, bowels of mercies, kindness, humbleness of mind, meekness, longsuffering;

13 ᴿForbearingᵀ one another, and forgiving one another, if any man have a quarrel against any: even as Christ forgave you, so also *do* ye. [Mark 11:25] · *Bearing with*

14 And above all these things *put on* ᵀcharity, which is the ᴿbond of perfectness.   *love* · Eph. 4:3

15 And let the peace of God rule in your hearts, ᴿto the which also ye are called ᴿin one body; and be ye thankful.   1 Cor. 7:15 · Eph. 4:4

16 Let the word of Christ dwell in you richly in all wisdom; teaching and admonishing one another ᴿin psalms and hymns and spiritual songs, singing with grace in your hearts to the Lord.   Eph. 5:19

17 And whatsoever ye do in word or deed, *do* all in the name of the Lord Jesus, giving thanks to God and the Father by him.

18 ᴿWives, submit yourselves unto your own husbands, as it is fit in the Lord.   1 Pet. 3:1

19 Husbands, love *your* wives, and be not bitter against them.

20 Children, obey *your* parents ᴿin all things: for this is well pleasing unto the Lord.   Eph. 5:24

21 ᴿFathers, provoke not your children *to anger,* lest they be discouraged.   Eph. 6:4

22 ᴿServants, obey in all things

your masters according to the flesh; not with eyeservice, as menpleasers; but in singleness of heart, fearing God: Eph. 6:5; Titus 2:9

23 ᴿAnd whatsoever ye do, do *it* heartily, as to the Lord, and not unto men; [Eccl. 9:10]

24 ᴿKnowing that of the Lord ye shall receive the reward of the inheritance: ᴿfor ye serve the Lord Christ. Eph. 6:8 · 1 Cor. 7:22

25 But he that doeth wrong shall receive for the wrong which he hath done: and ᴿthere is no respect of persons. Rom. 2:11

4 Masters,ᴿ give unto *your* servants that which is just and ᵀequal; knowing that ye also have a Master in heaven. Eph. 6:9 · *fair*

2 ᴿContinue in prayer, and watch in the same ᴿwith thanksgiving; Luke 18:1 · 2:7

3 ᴿWithalᵀ praying also for us, that God would open unto us a door of utterance, to speak the mystery of Christ, for which I am also in bonds: Eph. 6:19 · *Meanwhile*

4 That I may make it manifest, as I ought to speak.

5 ᴿWalk in wisdom toward them that are ᵀwithout, redeeming the time. Eph. 5:15 · *outside*

6 Let your speech *be* alway ᴿwith grace, seasoned with salt, that ye may know how ye ought to answer every man. Eccl. 10:12

7 All my state shall Tych′-i-cus declare unto you, *who is* a beloved brother, and a faithful minister and fellowservant in the Lord:

8 ᴿWhom I have sent unto you for the same purpose, that he might know your estate, and comfort your hearts; Eph. 6:22

9 With ᴿO-nes′-i-mus, a faithful and beloved brother, who is *one* of you. They shall make known unto you all things which *are done* here. Philem. 10

10 ᴿAr-is-tar′-chus my fellowprisoner saluteth you, and ᴿMarcus, sister′s son to Barnabas, (touching whom ye received commandments: if he come unto you, receive him;) Acts 19:29 · Acts 15:37

11 And Jesus, which is called Justus, who are of the circumcision. These only *are my* fellow workers unto the kingdom of God, which have been a comfort unto me.

12 Ep′-a-phras, who is *one* of you, a servant of Christ, saluteth you, always ᴿlabouring fervently for you in prayers, that ye may stand ᴿperfect and complete in all the will of God. Rom. 15:30 · 1 Cor. 2:6

13 For I bear him ᵀrecord, that he hath a great zeal for you, and them *that are* in La-od-i-ce′-a, and them in Hi-e-rap′-o-lis. *witness*

14 ᴿLuke, the beloved physician, and De′-mas, greet you. 2 Tim. 4:11

15 ᵀSalute the brethren which are in La-od-i-ce′-a, and Nym′-phas, and ᴿthe church which is in his house. *Greet* · Rom. 16:5; 1 Cor. 16:19

16 And when ᴿthis epistle is read among you, cause that it be read also in the church of the La-od-i-ce′-ans; and that ye likewise read the *epistle* from La-od-i-ce′-a. 1 Thess. 5:27; 2 Thess. 3:14

17 And say to ᴿAr-chip′-pus, Take heed to ᴿthe ministry which thou hast received in the Lord, that thou fulfil it. Philem. 2 · 2 Tim. 4:5

18 The salutation by the hand of me Paul. Remember my bonds. Grace *be* with you. A-men′.

THESSALONIANS

PAUL has many pleasant memories of the days he spent with the infant Thessalonian church. Their faith, hope, love, and perseverance in the face of persecution are exemplary. Paul's labors as a spiritual parent to the fledgling church have been richly rewarded, and his affection is visible in every line of his letter.

Paul encourages them to excel in their newfound faith, to increase in their love for one another, and to rejoice, pray, and give thanks always. He closes his letter with instruction regarding the return of the Lord, whose advent signifies hope and comfort for believers both living and dead.

Because this is the first of Paul's two canonical letters to the church at Thessalonica, it received the title *Pros Thessalonikeis A,* the "First to the Thessalonians."

PAUL, and Sil-va'-nus, and Ti-mo'-the-us, unto the church of the Thes-sa-lo'-ni-ans *which is* in God the Father and *in* the Lord Jesus Christ: Grace *be* unto you, and peace, from God our Father, and the Lord Jesus Christ.

2 ᴿWe give thanks to God always for you all, making mention of you in our prayers; Rom. 1:8

3 Remembering without ceasing your work of faith, and labour of love, and patience of hope in our Lord Jesus Christ, in the sight of God and our Father;

4 Knowing, brethren beloved, ᴿyour election ᵀof God. Col. 3:12 · *by*

5 For our gospel came not unto you in word only, but also in power, and in the Holy Ghost, and in much assurance; as ye know what manner of men we were among you for your sake.

6 And ye became followers of us, and of the Lord, having received the word in much affliction, with joy of the Holy Ghost:

7 So that we were ensamples to all that believe in Mac-e-do'-ni-a and A-cha'-ia.

8 For from you ᴿsounded out the word of the Lord not only in Mac-e-do'-ni-a and A-cha'-ia, but also ᴿin every place your faith to God-ward is spread abroad; so that we need not to speak any thing. Rom. 10:18 · Rom. 1:8; 16:19

9 For they themselves ᵀshew of us ᴿwhat manner of entering in we had unto you, and how ye turned to God from idols to serve the living and true God; *declare* · 2:1

10 And to wait for his Son from heaven, whom he raised from the dead, *even* Jesus, which delivered us from the wrath to come.

2 For yourselves, brethren, know our ᵀentrance in unto you, that it was not in vain: *coming*

2 But even after that we had suffered before, and were shamefully entreated, as ye know, at Phi-lip'-pi, we were bold in our God to speak unto you the gospel of God with much contention.

3 ᴿFor our exhortation *was* not of ᵀdeceit, nor of uncleanness, nor in ᵀguile: 2 Cor. 7:2 · *error* · *deceit*

4 But as ᴿwe were allowed of God to be put in trust with the gospel, even so we speak; ᴿnot as pleasing men, but God, which trieth our hearts. 1 Cor. 7:25 · Gal. 1:10

5 For ᴿneither at any time used we flattering words, as ye know, nor a cloke of covetousness; ᴿGod *is* witness: 2 Cor. 2:17 · v. 10; Rom. 1:9

6 ᴿNor of men sought we glory, neither of you, nor *yet* of others, when ᴿwe might have been ᴿburdensome, as the apostles of Christ. 1 Tim. 5:17 · 1 Cor. 9:4 · 2 Cor. 11:9

7 But ᴿwe were gentle among you, even as a ᵀnurse cherisheth her children: 1 Cor. 2:3 · *nursing* mother

8 So being affectionately ᵀde-

sirous of you, we were [T]willing to have imparted unto you, not the gospel of God only, but also our own souls, because ye were dear unto us.   *longing for · well pleased*

9 For ye remember, brethren, our [R]labour and travail: for labouring night and day, because we would not be chargeable unto any of you, we preached unto you the gospel of God.   2 Thess. 3:7, 8

10 Ye *are* witnesses, and God *also,* how holily and justly and unblameably we behaved ourselves among you that believe:

11 As ye know how we exhorted and comforted and charged every one of you, as a father *doth* his children,

12 [R]That ye would walk worthy of God, who hath called you unto his kingdom and glory.   Eph. 4:1

13 For this cause also thank we God [R]without ceasing, because, when ye received the word of God which ye heard of us, ye received *it* not *as* the word of men, but as it is in truth, the word of God, which effectually worketh also in you that believe.   1:2, 3; Rom. 1:8

14 For ye, brethren, became [T]followers [R]of the churches of God which in Ju-dae'-a are in Christ Jesus: for [R]ye also have suffered like things of your own countrymen, even as they *have* of the Jews: *imitators · Gal. 1:22 · Acts 17:5*

15 [R]Who both killed the Lord Jesus, and their own prophets, and have persecuted us; and they please not God, and are contrary to all men: Luke 24:20; Acts 2:23

16 Forbidding us to speak to the Gentiles that they might be saved, [R]to fill up their sins alway: [R]for the wrath is come upon them to the uttermost.   Dan. 8:23 · Matt. 24:6

17 But we, brethren, being taken from you for a short time [R]in presence, not in heart, endeavoured the more abundantly to see your face with great desire.   1 Cor. 5:3

18 Wherefore we [T]would have come unto you, even I Paul, once and again; but [R]Satan hindered us.   *wanted to · Rom. 1:13; 15:22*

19 For what *is* our hope, or joy, or crown of rejoicing? *Are* not even ye in the presence of our Lord Jesus Christ at his coming?

20 For ye are our glory and joy.

3 Wherefore when we could no longer forbear, we thought it good to be left at Athens alone;

2 And sent [R]Ti-mo'-the-us, our brother, and minister of God, and our fellowlabourer in the gospel of Christ, to establish you, and to [T]comfort you concerning your faith: Rom. 16:21 · *encourage*

3 [R]That no man should be moved by these afflictions: for yourselves know that we are appointed thereunto.   Eph. 3:13

4 [R]For verily, when we were with you, we told you before that we should suffer tribulation; [T]even as it came to pass, and ye know.   Acts 20:24 · *just*

5 For this cause, when I could no longer forbear, I sent to know your faith, lest by some means the tempter have tempted you, and [R]our labour be in vain.   Gal. 2:2

6 [R]But now when Ti-mo'-the-us came from you unto us, and brought us good tidings of your faith and charity, and that ye have good remembrance of us always, desiring greatly to see us, [R]as we also *to see* you: Acts 18:5 · Phil. 1:8

7 Therefore, brethren, [R]we were comforted [T]over you in all our affliction and distress by your faith: 2 Cor. 1:4 · *concerning*

8 For now we live, if ye [R]stand fast in the Lord.   Phil. 4:1

9 For what thanks can we render to God again for you, for all the joy wherewith we joy for your sakes before our God;

10 Night and day praying exceedingly that we might see your face, and might perfect that which is lacking in your faith?

11 Now God himself and our Father, and our Lord Jesus Christ, [R]direct our way unto you.   Mark 1:3

12 And the Lord make you to increase and abound in love one toward another, and toward all *men,* even as we *do* toward you:

13 To the end he may stablish your hearts unblameable in holiness before God, even our Father, at the coming of our Lord Jesus Christ with all his saints.

4 Furthermore then we beseech you, brethren, and exhort *you* by the Lord Jesus, that as ye have received of us how ye ought to walk and to please God, *so* ye would abound more and more.

2　For ye know what commandments we gave you by the Lord Jesus.

3　For this is the will of God, *even* your sanctification, that ye should abstain from fornication:

4　^RThat every one of you should know how to possess his vessel in sanctification and honour;　　　　Rom. 6:19

5　^RNot in the lust of concupiscence, even as the Gentiles which know not God:　　　　Col. 3:5

6　That no *man* go beyond and defraud his brother in *any* matter: because that the Lord ^R*is* the avenger of all such, as we also have forewarned you and testified.　　　　2 Thess. 1:8

7　For God hath not called us unto uncleanness, ^Rbut unto holiness.　　　[Heb. 12:14]; 1 Pet. 1:14–16

8　^RHe therefore that despiseth, despiseth not man, but God, ^Rwho hath also given unto us his holy Spirit.　　　Luke 10:16 · 1 Cor. 2:10

9　But as touching brotherly love ye need not that I write unto you: for ye yourselves are taught of God to love one another.

10　And indeed ye do it toward all the brethren which are in all Mac-e-do'-ni-a: but we beseech you, brethren, ^Rthat ye increase more and more;　　　　3:12

11　And that ye study to be quiet, and ^Rto do your own business, and to work with your own hands, as we commanded you;　　　2 Thess. 3:11

12　That ye may walk honestly toward them that are without, and *that* ye may have lack of nothing.

13　But I would not have you to be ignorant, brethren, concerning them which are asleep, that ye

sorrow not, ^Reven as others which have no hope.　　　　Lev. 19:28

14　For ^Rif we believe that Jesus died and rose again, even so them also which sleep in Jesus will God bring with him.　　　　1 Cor. 15:13

15　For this we say unto you by the word of the Lord, that we which are alive *and* remain unto the coming of the Lord shall not prevent them which are asleep.

16　For the Lord himself shall descend from heaven with a shout, with the voice of the archangel, and with the trump of God: and the dead in Christ shall rise first:

17　Then we which are alive *and* remain shall be caught up together with them in the clouds, to meet the Lord in the air: and so shall we ever be with the Lord.

18　^RWherefore comfort one another with these words.　　　5:11

5 But of ^Rthe times and the seasons, brethren, ye have no need that I write unto you.　　Matt. 24:3

2　For yourselves know perfectly that the day of the Lord so cometh as a thief in the night.

3　For when they shall say, Peace and safety; then ^Rsudden destruction cometh upon them, as travail upon a woman with child; and they shall not escape. Is. 13:6–9

4　^RBut ye, brethren, are not in darkness, that that day should overtake you as a thief.　1 John 2:8

5　Ye are all ^Rthe ^Tchildren of light, and the ^Tchildren of the day: we are not of the night, nor of darkness.　　Eph. 5:8 · Lit. *sons*

6　^RTherefore let us not sleep, as *do* others; but ^Rlet us watch and be sober.　Matt. 25:5 · Matt. 25:13

7　For they that sleep sleep in the night; and they that be drunken are drunken in the night.

8　But let us, who are of the day, be sober, putting on the breastplate of faith and love; and for an helmet, the hope of salvation.

9　For God hath not appointed us to wrath, but to obtain salvation by our Lord Jesus Christ,

10　Who died for us, that,

whether we wake or sleep, we should live together with him.

11 Wherefore comfort yourselves together, and edify one another, even as also ye do.

12 And we beseech you, brethren, to know them which labour among you, and are over you in the Lord, and admonish you;

13 And to esteem them very highly in love for their work's sake. ᴿ*And* be at peace among yourselves.   Mark 9:50

14 Now we exhort you, brethren, warn them that are unruly, comfort the feebleminded, support the weak, be patient toward all *men.*

15 See that none render evil for evil unto any *man;* but ever follow that which is good, both among yourselves, and to all *men.*

16 ᴿRejoice evermore. [2 Cor. 6:10]

17 Pray without ceasing.

18 In every thing give thanks: for this is the will of God in Christ Jesus concerning you.

19 Quench not the Spirit.

20 Despise not prophesyings.

21 Prove all things; ᴿhold fast that which is good.   Phil. 4:8

22 Abstain from ᵀall appearance of evil.   *every form of*

23 And ᴿthe very God of peace ᴿsanctify you wholly; and *I pray* God your whole spirit and soul and body ᴿbe preserved blameless unto the coming of our Lord Jesus Christ.   Phil. 4:9 · 3:13 · 1 Cor. 1:8, 9

24 Faithful *is* he that calleth you, who also will ᴿdo *it.*   Phil. 1:6

25 Brethren, pray for us.

26 Greet all the brethren with an holy kiss.

27 I charge you by the Lord that this ᵀepistle be read unto all the holy brethren.   *letter*

28 The grace of our Lord Jesus Christ *be* with you. A-men'.

The Second Epistle of Paul the Apostle to the

THESSALONIANS

SINCE Paul's first letter, the seeds of false doctrine have been sown among the Thessalonians, causing them to waver in their faith. Paul removes these destructive seeds and again plants the seeds of truth. He begins by commending the believers on their faithfulness in the midst of persecution and encouraging them that present suffering will be repaid with future glory. Therefore, in the midst of persecution, expectation can be high.

Paul then deals with the central matter of his letter: a misunderstanding spawned by false teachers regarding the coming day of the Lord. Despite reports to the contrary, that Day has not yet come, and Paul recounts the events that must first take place. Laboring for the gospel, rather than lazy resignation, is the proper response.

As the second letter in Paul's Thessalonian correspondence, this was entitled *Pros Thessalonikeis B,* the "Second to the Thessalonians."

PAUL, and Sil-va'-nus, and Ti-mo'-the-us, unto the church of the Thes-sa-lo'-ni-ans in God our Father and the Lord Jesus Christ:

2 ᴿGrace unto you, and peace, from God our Father and the Lord Jesus Christ.   1 Cor. 1:3

3 We are bound to thank God always for you, brethren, as it is meet, because that your faith

groweth exceedingly, and the charity of every one of you all toward each other aboundeth;

4 So that ᴿwe ourselves glory in you in the churches of God ᴿfor your patience and faith in all your persecutions and tribulations that ye endure: [1 Thess. 2:19] · 1 Thess. 1:3

5 *Which is* ᴿa manifest token of the righteous judgment of God, that ye may be counted worthy of the kingdom of God, ᴿfor which ye also suffer: Phil. 1:28 · 1 Thess. 2:14

6 Seeing *it is* a righteous thing with God to recompense tribulation to them that trouble you;

7 And to you who are troubled rest with us, when ᴿthe Lord Jesus shall be revealed from heaven with his mighty angels,   Jude 14

8 In flaming fire taking vengeance on them that know not God, and that obey not the gospel of our Lord Jesus Christ:

9 ᴿWho shall be punished with everlasting destruction from the presence of the Lord, and from the glory of his power;   1 Thess. 5:3

10 When he shall come to be glorified in his saints, and to be admired in all them that believe (because our testimony among you was believed) in that day.

11 Wherefore also we pray always for you, that our God would count you worthy of *this* calling, and fulfil all the good pleasure of *his* goodness, and ᴿthe work of faith with power: 1 Thess. 1:3

12 ᴿThat the name of our Lord Jesus Christ may be glorified in you, and ye in him, according to the grace of our God and the Lord Jesus Christ.   [Col. 3:17]

2 Now we beseech you, brethren, by the coming of our Lord Jesus Christ, ᴿand *by* our gathering together unto him,   Matt. 24:31

2 ᴿThat ye be not soon shaken in mind, or be troubled, neither by spirit, nor by word, nor by letter as from us, as that the day of Christ is at hand.   Matt. 24:4

3 Let no man deceive you by any means: for *that day shall not come*, ᴿexcept there come a falling away first, and ᴿthat man of sin be revealed, the son of perdition; 1 Tim. 4:1 · v. 8; Dan. 7:25; Rev. 13:5

4 Who opposeth and ᴿexalteth himself ᴿabove all that is called God, or that is worshipped; so that he as God sitteth in the temple of God, shewing himself that he is God.   Is. 14:13, 14; Ezek. 28:2 · 1 Cor. 8:5

5 Remember ye not, that, when I was yet with you, I told you these things?

6 And now ye know what ᵀwithholdeth that he might be revealed in his time.   *is restraining*

7 For the mystery of iniquity doth already work: only he who now ᵀletteth *will let*, until he be taken out of the way.   *restrains*

8 And then shall that Wicked be revealed, whom the Lord shall consume ᴿwith the spirit of his mouth, and shall destroy with the brightness of his coming: Rev. 2:16

9 *Even him*, whose coming is ᴿafter the working of Satan with all power and ᴿsigns and lying wonders,   John 8:41 · Deut. 13:1

10 And with all deceivableness of unrighteousness in ᴿthem that perish; because they received not the love of the truth, that they might be saved.   2 Cor. 2:15

11 And for this cause God shall send them strong delusion, ᴿthat they should believe a lie: 1 Tim. 4:1

12 That they all might be ᵀdamned who believed not the truth, but ᴿhad pleasure in unrighteousness.   *condemned* · Rom. 1:32

13 But we are bound to give thanks alway to God for you, brethren beloved of the Lord, because God hath from the beginning chosen you to salvation through sanctification of the Spirit and belief of the truth:

14 Whereunto he called you by our gospel, to the obtaining of the glory of our Lord Jesus Christ.

15 Therefore, brethren, ᴿstand fast, and hold the traditions which ye have been taught, whether by word, or our epistle.   1 Cor. 16:13

16 Now our Lord Jesus Christ himself, and God, even our Father,

which hath loved us, and hath given *us* everlasting consolation and good hope through grace,

17 Comfort your hearts, ᴿand stablish you in every good word and work.   1 Cor. 1:8

3 Finally, brethren, pray for us, that the word of the Lord may have *free* course, and be glorified, even as *it is* with you:

2 And ᴿthat we may be delivered from unreasonable and wicked men: ᴿfor all *men* have not faith.   Rom. 15:31 · Acts 28:24

3 But ᴿthe Lord is faithful, who shall stablish you, and ᴿkeep *you* from evil.   1 Thess. 5:24 · John 17:15

4 And ᴿwe have confidence in the Lord touching you, that ye both do and will do the things which we command you. 2 Cor. 7:16

5 And the Lord direct your hearts into the love of God, and into the patient waiting for Christ.

6 Now we command you, brethren, in the name of our Lord Jesus Christ, ᴿthat ye withdraw yourselves ᴿfrom every brother that walketh disorderly, and not after the tradition which he received of us.   Rom. 16:17 · 1 Cor. 5:1

7 For yourselves know how ye ought to follow us: for we behaved not ourselves disorderly among you;

8 Neither did we eat any man's bread for nought; but wrought with ᴿlabour and travail night and day, that we might not be chargeable to any of you: 1 Thess. 2:9

9 Not because we have not power, but to make ourselves an ensample unto you to follow us.

10 For even when we were with you, this we commanded you, that if any would not work, neither should he eat.

11 For we hear that there are some which walk among you disorderly, working not at all, but are ᴿbusybodies.   1 Tim. 5:13; 1 Pet. 4:15

12 Now them that are such we command and exhort by our Lord Jesus Christ, ᴿthat with quietness they work, and eat their own bread.   Eph. 4:28; 1 Thess. 4:11, 12

13 But ye, brethren, ᴿbe not weary in well doing.   Gal. 6:9

14 And if any man obey not our word by this epistle, note that man, and have no company with him, that he may be ashamed.

15 ᴿYet count *him* not as an enemy, ᴿbut ᵀadmonish *him* as a brother.   Lev. 19:17 · Titus 3:10 · *warn*

16 Now the Lord of peace himself give you peace always by all means. The Lord *be* with you all.

17 The salutation of Paul with mine own hand, which is the token in every epistle: so I write.

18 The grace of our Lord Jesus Christ *be* with you all. A-men'.

The First Epistle of Paul the Apostle to

TIMOTHY

PAUL, the aged and experienced apostle, writes to the young pastor Timothy who is facing a heavy burden of responsibility in the church at Ephesus. The task is challenging: false doctrine must be erased, public worship safeguarded, and mature leadership developed. In addition to the conduct of the church, Paul talks pointedly about the conduct of the minister. Timothy must be on his guard lest his youthfulness become a liability, rather than an asset, to the gospel. He must be careful to avoid false teachers and greedy motives, pursuing instead righteousness, godliness, faith, love, perseverance, and the gentleness that befits a man of God.

The Greek title for this letter is *Pros Timotheon A*, the "First to Timothy." *Timothy* means "honoring God" or "honored by God," and probably was given to him by his mother Eunice.

PAUL, an apostle of Jesus Christ by the commandment of God our Saviour, and Lord Jesus Christ, *which is* our hope;

2 Unto Timothy, [R]*my* own son in the faith: Grace, mercy, *and* peace, from God our Father and Jesus Christ our Lord.　Acts 16:1, 2

3 As I besought thee to abide still at Eph'-e-sus, [R]when I went into Mac-e-do'-ni-a, that thou mightest charge some that they teach no other doctrine, Acts 20:1, 3

4 [R]Neither give heed to fables and endless genealogies, which [T]minister questions, rather than godly edifying which is in faith: *so do.*　6:3, 4; Titus 1:14 · *cause disputes*

5 Now the end of the commandment is charity out of a pure heart, and *of* a good conscience, and *of* faith unfeigned:

6 From which some having swerved have turned aside unto [R]vain[T] jangling;　6:4, 20 · *idle talk*

7 Desiring to be teachers of the law; understanding neither what they say, nor whereof they affirm.

8 But we know that the law *is* good, if a man use it lawfully;

9 Knowing this, that the law is not made for a righteous man, but for the lawless and disobedient, for the ungodly and for sinners, for unholy and profane, for murderers of fathers and murderers of mothers, for manslayers,

10 For whoremongers, for them that defile themselves with mankind, for [R]menstealers, for liars, for perjured persons, and if there be any other thing that is contrary to sound doctrine;　*kidnappers*

11 According to the glorious gospel of the blessed God, which was committed to my trust.

12 And I thank Christ Jesus our Lord, who hath enabled me, for that he counted me faithful, [R]putting me into the ministry;　Col. 1:25

13 [R]Who was before a blasphemer, and a persecutor, and [T]injurious: but I obtained mercy, because [R]I did *it* ignorantly in unbelief.　1 Cor. 15:9 · *insolent* · John 4:21

14 [R]And the grace of our Lord was exceeding abundant [R]with faith and love which is in Christ Jesus.　Rom. 5:20; 1 Cor. 3:10 · Titus 2:2

15 [R]This *is* a faithful saying, and ★ worthy of all acceptation, that [R]Christ Jesus came into the world to save sinners; of whom I am chief.　2 Tim. 2:11; Titus 3:8 · Matt. 9:13

16 Howbeit for this cause I obtained mercy, that in me first Jesus Christ might shew forth all longsuffering, for a pattern to them which should hereafter believe on him to life everlasting.

17 Now unto [R]the King eternal, immortal, invisible, the only wise God, *be* honour and glory for ever and ever. A-men'.　Ps. 10:16

18 This charge I commit unto thee, son Timothy, according to the prophecies which went before on thee, that thou by them mightest war a good warfare;

19 Holding faith, and a good conscience; which some having [T]put away concerning faith have [T]made shipwreck:　*rejected · suffered*

20 Of whom is Hy-me-nae'-us and Alexander; whom I have delivered unto Satan, that they may learn not to blaspheme.

2 I exhort therefore, that, first of all, supplications, prayers, intercessions, *and* giving of thanks, be made for all men;

2 For kings, and [R]*for* all that are in authority; that we may lead a quiet and peaceable life in all godliness and honesty.　[Rom. 13:1]

3 For this *is* [R]good and acceptable in the sight [R]of God our Saviour;　Rom. 12:2 · 2 Tim. 1:9

4 Who [T]will have all men to be saved, and to come unto the knowledge of the truth.　*desires to*

5 For *there is* one God, and one mediator between God and men, the man Christ Jesus;

6 Who gave himself a ransom for all, to be testified in due time.

7 [R]Whereunto I am ordained a preacher, and an apostle, (I speak the truth in Christ, *and* lie not;) a teacher of the Gentiles in faith and [T]verity.　2 Tim. 1:11 · *truth*

8 I will therefore that men pray

[R]every where, [R]lifting up holy hands, without wrath and doubting.   Luke 23:34 · Ps. 134:2

9 In like manner also, that [R]women adorn themselves in modest apparel, with [T]shamefacedness and sobriety; not with broided hair, or gold, or pearls, or costly array;   1 Pet. 3:3 · propriety

10 [R]But (which [T]becometh women professing godliness) with good works.   1 Pet. 3:4 · is proper for

11 Let the woman learn in silence with all subjection.

12 But I suffer not a woman to teach, nor to usurp authority over the man, but to be in silence.

13 For Adam was first formed, then Eve.

14 And Adam was not deceived, but the woman being deceived was in the transgression.

15 Notwithstanding she shall be saved in childbearing, if they continue in faith and [T]charity and holiness with sobriety.   love

3 This is a true saying, If a man desire the office of [T]a bishop, he desireth a good work.   overseer

2 A bishop then must be blameless, the husband of one wife, [T]vigilant, sober, of good behaviour, given to hospitality, [T]apt to teach;   temperate · able

3 Not [T]given to wine, [T]no striker, not greedy [T]of filthy lucre; but patient, not a brawler, not covetous;   addicted · not violent · for money

4 One that ruleth well his own house, having his children in subjection with all [T]gravity;   reverence

5 (For if a man know not how to rule his own house, how shall he take care of the church of God?)

6 Not a novice, lest being lifted up with pride he fall into the condemnation of the devil.

7 Moreover he must have a good report of them which are without; lest he fall into reproach and the snare of the devil.

8 Likewise must the deacons be grave, not doubletongued, [R]not given to much wine, not greedy of [T]filthy lucre;   Ezek. 44:21 · money

9 Holding the mystery of the faith in a pure conscience.

10 And let these also first be proved; then let them [T]use the office of a deacon, being found blameless.   serve as

11 Even so must their wives be [T]grave, not slanderers, sober, faithful in all things.   reverent

12 Let the deacons be the husbands of one wife, ruling their children and their own houses well.

13 For they that have used the office of a deacon well purchase to themselves a good [T]degree, and great boldness in the faith which is in Christ Jesus.   standing

14 These things write I unto thee, hoping to come unto thee shortly:

15 But if I tarry long, that thou mayest know how thou oughtest to [T]behave thyself in the house of God, which is the church of the living God, the pillar and [T]ground of the truth.   conduct · foundation

16 And without controversy great is the mystery of godliness: God was manifest in the flesh, justified in the Spirit, seen of angels, [R]preached unto the Gentiles, believed on in the world, [R]received up into glory.   Acts 10:34 · Luke 24:51

4 Now the Spirit speaketh expressly, that in the latter times some shall depart from the faith, giving heed [R]to seducing spirits, and doctrines of devils;   2 Tim. 3:13

2 [R]Speaking lies in hypocrisy; having their conscience [R]seared with a hot iron;   Matt. 7:15 · Eph. 4:19

3 Forbidding to marry, and commanding to abstain from [T]meats, which God hath created to be received with thanksgiving of them which believe and know the truth.   foods

4 For every creature of God is good, and nothing to be refused, if it be received with thanksgiving:

5 For it is sanctified by the word of God and prayer.

6 If thou put the brethren in remembrance of these things, thou shalt be a good minister of

Jesus Christ, ᴿnourished up in the words of faith and of good doctrine, whereunto thou hast ᵀattained.   2 Tim. 3:14 · *carefully followed*

7 But ᴿrefuse profane and old wives' fables, and exercise thyself *rather* unto godliness.   2 Tim. 2:16

8 For ᴿbodily exercise profiteth little: but godliness is profitable unto all things, ᴿhaving promise of the life that now is, and of that which is to come.   1 Cor. 8:8 · Ps. 37:9

9 This *is* a faithful saying and worthy of all acceptation.

10 For therefore we both labour and suffer reproach, because we trust in the living God, ᴿwho is the Saviour of all men, specially of those that believe.   Ps. 36:6

11 These things command and teach.

12 Let no man despise thy youth; but be thou an ᴿexample of the believers, in word, in ᵀconversation, in charity, in spirit, in faith, in purity.   Phil. 3:17; Titus 2:7 · *conduct*

13 Till I come, give attendance to reading, to exhortation, to ᵀdoctrine.   *teaching*

14 Neglect not the gift that is in thee, which was given thee by prophecy, with the laying on of the hands of the presbytery.

15 Meditate upon these things; give thyself wholly to them; that thy profiting may appear to all.

16 Take heed unto thyself, and unto the doctrine; continue in them: for in doing this thou shalt both save thyself, and them that hear thee.

5 Rebuke not an elder, but ᵀintreat *him* as a father; *and* the younger men as brethren;   *exhort*

2 The elder women as mothers; the younger as sisters, with all purity.

3 Honour widows that are widows indeed.

4 But if any widow have children or ᵀnephews, let them learn first to shew piety at home, and ᴿto ᵀrequite their parents: for that is good and acceptable before God.   *grandchildren* · Gen. 45:10 · *repay*

5 Now she that is a widow indeed, and desolate, trusteth in God, and continueth in supplications and prayers night and day.

6 But she that liveth in pleasure is dead while she liveth.

7 And these things ᵀgive in charge, that they may be blameless.   *command*

8 But if any provide not for his own, ᴿand specially for those of his own house, ᴿhe hath denied the faith, and is worse than an infidel.   Is. 58:7; 2 Cor. 12:14 · 2 Tim. 3:5

9 Let not a widow be taken into the number under threescore years old, having been the wife of one man,

10 Well reported of for good works; if she have brought up children, if she have lodged strangers, if she have washed the saints' feet, if she have relieved the afflicted, if she have diligently followed every good work.

11 But the younger widows ᵀrefuse: for when they have begun to ᵀwax wanton against Christ, they will marry;   Refuse to enroll · *grow*

12 Having damnation, because they have cast off their first faith.

13 And ᵀwithal they learn *to be* idle, wandering about from house to house; and not only idle, but ᵀtattlers also and busybodies, speaking things which they ought not.   *besides* · *gossips*

14 I will therefore that the younger women marry, bear children, ᵀguide the house, give none occasion to the adversary to speak reproachfully.   *manage*

15 For some are already turned aside after Satan.

16 If any man or woman that believeth have widows, let them ᵀrelieve them, and let not the church be ᵀcharged; that it may relieve them that are widows indeed.   *assist* · *burdened*

17 Let the elders that rule well be counted worthy of double honour, especially they who labour in the word and doctrine.

18 For the scripture saith, Thou shalt not muzzle the ox that tread-

eth out the corn. And, The labourer *is* worthy of his reward.

19 Against an elder receive not an accusation, but ᴿbefore two or three witnesses. Deut. 17:6; 19:15

20 Them that sin rebuke before all, that others also may fear.

21 I charge *thee* before God, and the Lord Jesus Christ, and the elect angels, that thou observe these things without ᵀpreferring ᴿone before another, doing nothing by partiality. *prejudice* · Deut. 1:17

22 Lay hands suddenly on no man, neither ᵀbe ᴿpartaker of other men's sins: keep thyself pure. *share in* · Eph. 5:6, 7; 2 John 11

23 Drink no longer water, but use a little wine for thy stomach's sake and thine often infirmities.

24 Some men's sins are ᴿopenᵀ beforehand, going before to judgment; and some *men* they follow after. Gal. 5:19-21 · *clearly evident*

25 Likewise also the good works *of some* are manifest beforehand; and they that are otherwise cannot be hid.

6 Let as many ᴿservants as are under the yoke count their own masters worthy of all honour, that the name of God and *his* doctrine be not blasphemed. Eph. 6:5; Titus 2:9

2 And they that have believing masters, let them not despise *them*, because they are brethren; but rather do *them* service, because they are faithful and beloved, partakers of the benefit. These things teach and exhort.

3 If any man teach otherwise, and consent not to wholesome words, *even* the words of our Lord Jesus Christ, and to the doctrine which is according to godliness;

4 He is proud, knowing nothing, but doting about questions and strifes of words, whereof cometh envy, strife, ᵀrailings, evil ᵀsurmisings, *reviling · suspicions*

5 Perverse disputings of men of corrupt minds, and destitute of the truth, supposing that gain is godliness: from ᴿsuch withdraw thyself. 2 Tim. 3:5

6 But godliness with ᴿcontentment is great gain. Phil. 4:11

7 For we brought nothing into *this* world, *and it is* ᴿcertain we can carry nothing out. Job 1:21

8 And having food and raiment let us be therewith content.

9 But they that ᵀwill be rich fall into temptation and a snare, and *into* many foolish and hurtful lusts, which drown men in destruction and perdition. *desire to be*

10 For the love of money is the root of ᵀall evil: which while some coveted after, they have erred from the faith, and pierced themselves through with many sorrows. *all* kinds of

11 But thou, O man of God, flee these things; and follow after righteousness, godliness, faith, love, patience, meekness.

12 Fight the good fight of faith, lay hold on eternal life, whereunto thou art also called, and hast ᵀprofessed a good profession before many witnesses. *confessed*

13 I give thee charge in the sight of God, who quickeneth all things, and *before* Christ Jesus, who before Pon'-tius Pilate witnessed a good confession;

14 That thou keep *this* commandment without spot, ᵀunrebukeable, until the appearing of our Lord Jesus Christ: *blameless*

15 Which in his times he shall ᵀshew, *who is* the blessed and only Potentate, the King of kings, and Lord of lords; *manifest*

16 Who only hath immortality, dwelling in the ᴿlight which no man can approach unto; ᴿwhom no man hath seen, nor can see: to whom *be* honour and power everlasting. A-men'. Dan. 2:22 · John 6:46

17 Charge them that are rich in this world, that they be not highminded, nor trust in uncertain ᴿriches, but in the living God, who giveth us richly all things ᴿto enjoy; Jer. 9:23; 48:7 · Eccl. 5:18, 19

18 That they do good, that they be rich in good works, ready to ᵀdistribute, willing to ᵀcommunicate; *give · share*

19 ᴿLaying up in store for themselves a good foundation against the time to come, that they may lay hold on eternal life. [Matt. 19:21]

20 O Timothy, ᴿkeep that which is committed to thy trust, ᴿavoid-

ing profane *and* vain babblings, and oppositions of science falsely so called: [2 Tim. 1:12, 14] · Titus 1:14

21 Which some professing have ᵀerred concerning the faith. Grace be with thee. A-men'.   *strayed*

The Second Epistle of Paul the Apostle to

TIMOTHY

PRISON is the last place from which to expect a letter of encouragement, but that is where Paul's second letter to Timothy originates. He begins by assuring Timothy of his continuing love and prayers, and reminds him of his spiritual heritage and responsibilities. Only the one who perseveres, whether as a soldier, athlete, farmer, or minister of Jesus Christ, will reap the reward. Paul warns Timothy that his teaching will come under attack as men desert the truth for ear-itching words (4:3). But Timothy has Paul's example to guide him and God's Word to fortify him as he faces growing opposition and glowing opportunities in the last days.

Paul's last epistle received the title *Pros Timotheon B,* the "Second to Timothy." When Paul's epistles were collected together the *B* was probably added to distinguish this letter from the first letter he wrote to Timothy.

PAUL, an apostle of Jesus Christ by the will of God, according to the ᴿpromise of life which is in Christ Jesus,   Titus 1:2

2 To Timothy, *my* dearly ᴿbeloved son: Grace, mercy, *and* peace, from God the Father and Christ Jesus our Lord.   1 Tim. 1:2

3 I thank God, whom I serve ᵀfrom *my* forefathers with pure conscience, that without ceasing I have remembrance of thee in my prayers night and day;   *as* did

4 Greatly desiring to see thee, being mindful of thy tears, that I may be filled with joy;

5 When I call to remembrance ᴿthe unfeigned faith that is in thee, which dwelt first in thy grandmother Lo'-is, and thy mother Eu-ni'-ce; and I am persuaded that in thee also.   1 Tim. 1:5; 4:6

6 Wherefore I put thee in remembrance ᴿthat thou stir up the gift of God, which is in thee by the putting on of my hands.   1 Tim. 4:14

7 For God hath not given us the

spirit of fear; but of power, and of love, and of a sound mind.

8 Be not thou therefore ashamed of ᴿthe testimony of our Lord, nor of me ᴿhis prisoner: but be thou partaker of the afflictions of the gospel according to the power of God;   1 Tim. 2:6 · Eph. 3:1

9 Who hath saved us, and called *us* with an holy calling, not according to our works, but ᴿaccording to his own purpose and grace, which was given us in Christ Jesus ᴿbefore the world began,   Rom. 8:28 · Eph. 1:4; Titus 1:2

10 But ᴿis now made manifest by the appearing of our Saviour Jesus Christ, who hath abolished death, and hath brought life and immortality to light through the gospel: Eph. 1:9

11 ᴿWhereunto I am appointed a preacher, and an apostle, and a teacher of the Gentiles.   Acts 9:15

12 For the which cause I also suffer these things: nevertheless I am not ashamed: ᴿfor I know

whom I have believed, and am persuaded that he is able to keep that which I have committed unto him against that day.   1 Pet. 4:19

13 ^RHold fast the form of ^Rsound words, which thou hast heard of me, in faith and love which is in Christ Jesus.   3:14; Titus 1:9 · 1 Tim. 6:3

14 That good thing which was committed unto thee keep by the Holy Ghost which dwelleth in us.

15 This thou knowest, that all they which are in Asia be turned away from me; of whom are Phy-gel'-lus and Her-mog'-e-nes.

16 The Lord give mercy unto the ^Rhouse of On-e-siph'-o-rus; for he ^Toft refreshed me, and was not ashamed of my chain: 4:19 · often

17 But, when he was in Rome, he sought me out very diligently, and found me.

18 The Lord grant unto him that he may find mercy of the Lord in that day: and in how many things he ministered unto me at Eph'-e-sus, thou knowest very well.

2 Thou therefore, ^Rmy son, ^Rbe strong in the grace that is in Christ Jesus.   1 Tim. 1:2 · Eph. 6:10

2 And the things that thou hast heard of me among many witnesses, the same commit thou to faithful men, who shall be able to teach others also.

3 Thou therefore ^Rendure hardness, ^Ras a good soldier of Jesus Christ.   4:5 · 1 Cor. 9:7; 1 Tim. 1:18

4 ^RNo man that warreth entangleth himself with the affairs of this life; that he may please him who hath chosen him to be a soldier.   [2 Pet. 2:20]

5 And if a man also strive for masteries, yet is he not crowned, except he ^Tstrive lawfully. competes

6 The ^Thusbandman that laboureth must be first partaker of the ^Tfruits.   farmer · crops

7 Consider what I say; and the Lord ^Rgive thee understanding in all things.   Prov. 2:6

8 Remember that Jesus Christ ^Rof the seed of David was raised from the dead ^Raccording to my gospel: Rom. 1:3, 4 · Rom. 2:16

9 Wherein I suffer trouble, as an evil doer, even unto bonds; but the word of God is not bound.

10 Therefore ^RI endure all things for the elect's sakes, ^Rthat they may also obtain the salvation which is in Christ Jesus with eternal glory.   Eph. 3:13 · 1 Thess. 5:9

11 It is a faithful saying: For ^Rif we be dead with him, we shall also live with him: Rom. 6:5, 8

12 ^RIf we suffer, we shall also reign with him: if we deny him, he also will deny us: [Rom. 5:17; 8:17]

13 If we believe not, yet he abideth faithful: he ^Rcannot deny himself.   Num. 23:19; Titus 1:2

14 Of these things put them in remembrance, charging them before the Lord that they strive not about words to no profit, but to the subverting of the hearers.

15 Study to shew thyself approved unto God, a workman that needeth not to be ashamed, rightly dividing the word of truth.

16 But shun profane and vain babblings: for they will increase unto more ungodliness.

17 And their word will eat as doth a canker: of whom is Hy-me-nae'-us and Phi-le'-tus;

18 Who concerning the truth have erred, saying that the resurrection is past already; and overthrow the faith of some.

19 Nevertheless the foundation of God standeth sure, having this seal, The Lord ^Rknoweth them that are his. And, Let every one that nameth the name of Christ depart from iniquity.   John 10:14, 27

20 But in a great house there are not only ^Rvessels of gold and of silver, but also of wood and of ^Tearth; and some to honour, and some to dishonour.   Rom. 9:21 · clay

21 If a man therefore purge himself from these, he shall be a vessel unto honour, sanctified, and meet for the master's use, and prepared unto every good work.

22 ^RFlee also youthful lusts: but ^Tfollow righteousness, faith, ^Tcharity, peace, with them that

call on the Lord out of a pure heart.   1 Tim. 6:11 · *pursue* · *love*

23 But foolish and unlearned questions avoid, knowing that they do [T]gender strifes.   *generate*

24 And the servant of the Lord must not strive; but be gentle unto all *men*, apt to teach, patient,

25 [R]In meekness instructing those that oppose themselves; if God peradventure will give them repentance to the acknowledging of the truth;   Gal. 6:1; Titus 3:2

26 And *that* they may recover themselves [R]out of the snare of the devil, who are taken captive by him [T]at his will.   1 Tim. 3:7 · *to do*

3 This know also, that [R]in the last days perilous times shall come.   1 Tim. 4:1; 2 Pet. 3:3; Jude 17, 18

2 For men shall be lovers of their own selves, [T]covetous, boasters, proud, blasphemers, disobedient to parents, unthankful, unholy,   *money lovers*

3 Without natural affection, [T]trucebreakers, false accusers, incontinent, fierce, despisers of those that are good,   *irreconcilable*

4 [R]Traitors, [T]heady, highminded, lovers of pleasures more than lovers of God;   2 Pet. 2:10 · *reckless*

5 [R]Having a form of godliness, but denying the power thereof: from such turn away.   Titus 1:16

6 For of this sort are they which creep into houses, and lead captive silly women laden with sins, led away with divers lusts,

7 Ever learning, and never able [R]to come to the knowledge of the truth.   1 Tim. 2:4

8 [R]Now as Jan'-nes and Jam'-bres withstood Moses, so do these also resist the truth: men of corrupt minds, reprobate concerning the faith.   Ex. 7:11, 12, 22; 8:7; 9:11

9 But they shall proceed no further: for their folly shall be manifest unto all *men*, as theirs also was.

10 [R]But thou hast fully known my doctrine, manner of life, purpose, faith, longsuffering, charity, patience,   Phil. 2:20, 22; 1 Tim. 4:6

11 Persecutions, afflictions,

which came unto me [R]at An'-ti-och, at I-co'-ni-um, at Lys'-tra; what persecutions I endured: but [R]out of *them* all the Lord delivered me.   Acts 13; 14 · Ps. 34:19

12 Yea, and [R]all that will live godly in Christ Jesus shall suffer persecution.   [Ps. 34:19]

13 But evil men and seducers shall wax worse and worse, deceiving, and being deceived.

14 But [R]continue thou in the things which thou hast learned and hast been assured of, knowing of whom thou hast learned *them*;   1:13; Titus 1:9

15 And that from a child thou hast known [R]the holy scriptures, which are able to make thee wise unto salvation through faith which is in Christ Jesus.   John 5:39

16 [R]All scripture *is* given by inspiration of God, [R]and *is* profitable for doctrine, for reproof, for correction, for instruction in righteousness: [2 Pet. 1:20] · Rom. 4:23; 15:4

17 [R]That the man of God may be perfect, [R]throughly furnished unto all good works.   1 Tim. 6:11 · 2:21

4 I [R]charge *thee* therefore before God, and the Lord Jesus Christ, [R]who shall judge the quick and the dead at his appearing and his kingdom;   1 Tim. 5:21 · Acts 10:42

2 Preach the word; be [T]instant in season, out of season; [R]reprove, rebuke, exhort with all longsuffering and doctrine.   *ready* · Titus 2:15

3 [R]For the time will come when they will not endure sound doctrine; but after their own lusts shall they heap to themselves teachers, having itching ears;   3:1

4 And they shall turn away *their* ears from the truth, and shall be turned unto fables.

5 But watch thou in all things, [R]endure afflictions, do the work of [R]an evangelist, make full proof of thy ministry.   1:8 · Acts 21:8

6 For [R]I am now ready to be offered, and the time of my departure is at hand.   Phil. 2:17

7 [R]I have fought a good fight, I have finished *my* course, I have kept the faith: Phil. 3:13, 14

8 Henceforth there is laid up for me a crown of righteousness, which the Lord, the righteous judge, shall give me at that day: and not to me only, but unto all them also that love his appearing.

9 Do thy diligence to come shortly unto me:

10 For De′-mas hath forsaken me, having loved this present world, and is departed unto Thes-sa-lo-ni′-ca; Cres′-cens to Ga-la′-ti-a, Titus unto Dal-ma′-ti-a.

11 Only Luke is with me. Take ᴿMark, and bring him with thee: for he is profitable to me for the ministry.   Acts 12:12, 25; 15:37–39

12 And ᴿTych′-i-cus have I sent to Eph′-e-sus.   Acts 20:4; Eph. 6:21, 22

13 The cloke that I left at Tro′-as with Carpus, when thou comest, bring *with thee*, and the books, *but* especially the parchments.

14 Alexander the coppersmith did me much evil: the Lord reward him according to his works:

15 Of whom ᵀbe thou ware also; for he hath greatly withstood our words.   *you beware*

16 At my first answer no man stood with me, but all *men* forsook me: *I pray God* that it may not be laid to their charge.

17 ᴿNotwithstanding the Lord stood with me, and strengthened me; ᴿthat by me the preaching might be fully known, and *that* all the Gentiles might hear: and I was delivered ᴿout of the mouth of the lion.   Acts 23:11 · Phil. 1:12 · Ps. 22:21

18 And the Lord shall deliver me from every evil work, and will preserve *me* unto his heavenly kingdom: ᴿto whom *be* glory for ever and ever. A-men′.   Rom. 11:36

19 Salute ᴿPris′-ca and Aq′-ui-la, and the household of ᴿOn-e-siph′-o-rus.   Acts 18:2; Rom. 16:3 · 1:16

20 ᴿE-ras′-tus abode at Corinth: but ᴿTroph′-i-mus have I left at Mi-le′-tum sick.   Rom. 16:23 · Acts 20:4

21 Do thy diligence to come before winter. Eu-bu′-lus greeteth thee, and Pu′-dens, and Li′-nus, and Claudia, and all the brethren.

22 The Lord Jesus Christ *be* with thy spirit. Grace *be* with you. A-men′.

The Epistle of Paul the Apostle to
TITUS

TITUS, a young pastor, faces the unenviable assignment of setting in order the church at Crete. Paul writes advising him to appoint elders, men of proven spiritual character in their homes and businesses, to oversee the work of the church. But elders are not the only individuals in the church who are required to excel spiritually. Men and women, young and old, each have their vital functions to fulfill in the church if they are to be living examples of the doctrine they profess. Throughout his letter to Titus, Paul stresses the necessary, practical working out of salvation in the daily lives of both the elders and the congregation. Good works are desirable and profitable for all believers.

This third Pastoral Epistle is simply titled *Pros Titon*, "To Titus." Ironically, this was also the name of the Roman general who destroyed Jerusalem in A.D. 70 and succeeded his father Vespasian as emperor.

PAUL a servant of God, and an apostle of Jesus Christ, according to the faith of God's elect, and the acknowledging of the truth which is after godliness;

2 In hope of eternal life, which God, that ᴿcannot lie, promised before the world began; Num. 23:19

3 But hath in due times manifested his word through preach-

ing, which is committed unto me according to the commandment of God our Saviour;

4 To ᴿTitus, *mine* own son after the common faith: Grace, mercy, *and* peace, from God the Father and the Lord Jesus Christ our Saviour. 2 Cor. 2:13; Gal. 2:3; 2 Tim. 4:10

5 For this cause left I thee in Crete, that thou shouldest ᴿset in order the things that are wanting, and ordain elders in every city, as I had appointed thee: 1 Cor. 11:34

6 If any be blameless, the husband of one wife, ᴿhaving faithful children not accused of ᵀriot or unruly. 1 Tim. 3:2–4 · *dissipation*

7 For ᵀa bishop must be blameless, as the steward of God; not selfwilled, not soon angry, not given to wine, no striker, not given to filthy lucre; *an overseer*

8 But a lover of hospitality, a lover of ᵀgood men, sober, just, holy, temperate; *what is good*

9 Holding fast the faithful word as he hath been taught, that he may be able by sound doctrine both to exhort and to convince ᵀthe gainsayers. *those who contradict*

10 For there are many unruly and vain talkers and deceivers, specially they of the circumcision:

11 Whose mouths must be stopped, who subvert whole houses, teaching things which they ought not, for filthy lucre's sake.

12 ᴿOne of themselves, *even* a prophet of their own, said, The Cre′-tians *are* alway liars, evil beasts, slow bellies. Acts 17:28

13 This witness is true. Wherefore rebuke them sharply, that they may be sound in the faith;

14 Not giving heed to Jewish fables, and commandments of men, that turn from the truth.

15 ᴿUnto the pure all things *are* pure: but unto them that are defiled and unbelieving *is* nothing pure; but even their mind and conscience is defiled. Rom. 14:14, 20

16 They profess that they ᴿknow God; but ᴿin works they deny *him*, being abominable, and disobedi-

ent, and unto every good work reprobate. 1 John 2:4 · [2 Tim. 3:5, 7]

2 But speak thou the things which become sound doctrine:

2 That the aged men be sober, ᵀgrave, temperate, sound in faith, in charity, in patience. *reverent*

3 The aged women likewise, that *they be* in behaviour as becometh holiness, not ᵀfalse accusers, not given to much wine, teachers of good things; *slanderers*

4 That they may ᵀteach the young women to be sober, to love their husbands, to love their children, *admonish*

5 *To be* discreet, chaste, keepers at home, good, obedient to their own husbands, that the word of God be not blasphemed.

6 Young men likewise exhort to be sober minded.

7 In all things shewing thyself a ᴿpattern of good works: in doctrine *shewing* uncorruptness, gravity, sincerity, Phil. 3:17; 1 Tim. 4:12

8 Sound speech, that cannot be condemned; that he that is of the contrary part may be ashamed, having no evil thing to say of you.

9 *Exhort* ᴿservants to be obedient unto their own masters, *and* to please *them* well in all *things*; not answering again; Eph. 6:5; 1 Tim. 6:1

10 Not ᵀpurloining, but shewing all good fidelity; that they may adorn the doctrine of God our Saviour in all things. *pilfering*

11 For ᴿthe grace of God that bringeth salvation hath appeared to all men, [Rom. 5:15]

12 Teaching us that, denying ungodliness and worldly lusts, we should live soberly, righteously, and godly, in this present world;

13 ᴿLooking for that blessed ᴿhope, and the glorious appearing of the great God and our Saviour Jesus Christ; 1 Cor. 1:7 · [Col. 3:4]

14 ᴿWho gave himself for us, ★ that he might redeem us from all iniquity, and purify unto himself a peculiar people, zealous of good works. Is. 53:12; Gal. 1:4

15 These things speak, and ex-

hort, and rebuke with all authority. Let no man despise thee.

3 Put them in mind to be subject to principalities and powers, to obey magistrates, [R]to be ready to every good work, Col. 1:10

2 To speak evil of no man, to be no brawlers, *but* gentle, shewing all meekness unto all men.

3 For [R]we ourselves also were sometimes foolish, disobedient, deceived, serving divers lusts and pleasures, living in malice and envy, hateful, *and* hating one another. 1 Cor. 6:11; 1 Pet. 4:3

4 But after that [R]the kindness and love of [R]God our Saviour toward man appeared, 2:11 · 1 Tim. 2:3

5 Not by works of righteousness which we have done, but according to his mercy he saved us, by the washing of regeneration, and renewing of the Holy Ghost;

6 [R]Which he [T]shed on us abundantly through Jesus Christ our Saviour; Ezek. 36:25 · *poured out*

7 That being justified by his grace, [R]we should be made heirs according to the hope of eternal life. Mark 10:17; [Rom. 8:17, 23, 24]

8 [R]*This is* a faithful saying, and these things I will that thou affirm constantly, that they which have believed in God might be careful to maintain good works. These things are good and profitable unto men. 1 Tim. 1:15

9 But avoid foolish questions, and genealogies, and contentions, and strivings about the law; for they are unprofitable and vain.

10 A man that is [T]an heretick after the first and second admonition [R]reject; *divisive* · Matt. 18:17

11 Knowing that he that is such is [T]subverted, and sinneth, being condemned of himself. *warped*

12 When I shall send Ar'-te-mas unto thee, or [R]Tych'-i-cus, be diligent to come unto me to Ni-cop'-o-lis: for I have determined there to winter. Eph. 6:21; Col. 4:7; 2 Tim. 4:12

13 Bring Ze'-nas the lawyer and [R]A-pol'-los on their journey diligently, that nothing be wanting unto them. Acts 18:24; 1 Cor. 16:12

14 And let ours also learn to maintain good works for [T]necessary uses, that they be not unfruitful. *urgent needs*

15 All that are with me [T]salute thee. Greet them that love us in the faith. Grace *be* with you all. A-men'. *greet*

The Epistle of Paul the Apostle to

PHILEMON

DOES Christian brotherly love really work, even in situations of extraordinary tension and difficulty? Will it work, for example, between a prominent slave owner and one of his runaway slaves? Paul has no doubt! He writes a "postcard" to Philemon, his beloved brother and fellow worker, on behalf of Onesimus—a deserter, thief, and formerly worthless slave, but now Philemon's brother in Christ. With much tact and tenderness, Paul asks Philemon to receive Onesimus back with the same gentleness with which he would receive Paul himself. Any debt Onesimus owes, Paul promises to make good. Knowing Philemon, Paul is confident that brotherly love and forgiveness will carry the day.

Since this letter is addressed to Philemon in verse 1, it becomes known as *Pros Philemona*, "To Philemon." Like First and Second Timothy and Titus, it is addressed to an individual, but unlike the Pastoral Epistles, Philemon is also addressed to a family and a church (v. 2).

PAUL, a prisoner of Jesus Christ, and Timothy *our* brother, unto Phi-le′-mon our dearly beloved, and fellowlabourer,

2 And to *our* beloved Ap′-phi-a, and [R]Ar-chip′-pus our fellowsoldier, and to the church in thy house: Col. 4:17

3 Grace to you, and peace, from God our Father and the Lord Jesus Christ.

4 [R]I thank my God, making mention of thee always in my prayers,   Eph. 1:16; 1 Thess. 1:2

5 Hearing of thy love and faith, which thou hast toward the Lord Jesus, and toward all saints;

6 That the communication of thy faith may become effectual [R]by the acknowledging of [R]every good thing which is in you in Christ Jesus.   Phil. 1:9 · [1 Thess. 5:18]

7 For we have great joy and [T]consolation in thy love, because the bowels of the saints are refreshed by thee, brother.   *comfort*

8 Wherefore, though I might be much bold in Christ to enjoin thee that which is [T]convenient,   *fitting*

9 Yet for love's sake I rather [T]beseech *thee*, being such an one as Paul the aged, and now also a prisoner of Jesus Christ.   *appeal to*

10 I beseech thee for my son [R]O-nes′-i-mus, whom I have begotten in my [T]bonds: Col. 4:9 · *chains*

11 Which in time past was to thee unprofitable, but now profitable to thee and to me:

12 Whom I have sent [T]again: thou therefore receive him, that is, mine own bowels: *back*

13 Whom I would have retained with me, that in thy [T]stead he might have ministered unto me in the bonds of the gospel: *behalf*

14 But without thy mind would I do nothing; that thy [T]benefit should not be as it were of necessity, but willingly.   *good deed*

15 For perhaps he therefore departed for a season, that thou shouldest receive him for ever;

16 Not now as a servant, but [T]above a servant, a brother beloved, specially to me, but how much more unto thee, both in the flesh, and in the Lord?   *more than*

17 If thou count me therefore a partner, receive him as myself.

18 If he hath wronged thee, or oweth *thee* [T]ought, put that on mine account;   *anything*

19 I Paul have written *it* with mine own [R]hand, I will repay *it*: albeit I do not say to thee how thou owest unto me even thine own self besides.   Gal. 6:11

20 Yea, brother, let me have joy of thee in the Lord: refresh my [T]bowels in the Lord.   *inward parts*

21 [R]Having confidence in thy obedience I wrote unto thee, knowing that thou wilt [T]also do more than I say.   2 Cor. 7:16 · *even*

22 But [T]withal prepare me also a lodging: for I trust that [R]through your prayers I shall be given unto you.   *meanwhile* · 2 Cor. 1:11

23 There [T]salute thee [R]Ep′-a-phras, my fellowprisoner in Christ Jesus;   *greet* · Col. 1:7; 4:12

24 Marcus, Ar-is-tar′-chus, De′-mas, Lucas, my fellowlabourers.

25 The grace of our Lord Jesus Christ *be* with your spirit. A-men′.

The Epistle of Paul the Apostle to the

HEBREWS

MANY Jewish believers, having stepped out of Judaism into Christianity, want to reverse their course in order to escape persecution by their countrymen. The writer of Hebrews exhorts them to "go on unto perfection" (6:1). His appeal is based on the superiority of Christ over the Judaic system. Christ is better than the angels, for they worship Him. He is better than Moses, for He created him. He is better than the Aaronic priesthood, for His sacrifice was once for all time. He is better than the law, for He mediates a better covenant. In short, there is more to be gained in Christ than to be lost in Judaism. Pressing on in Christ produces tested faith, self-discipline, and a visible love seen in good works.

Although the King James Version uses the title "The Epistle of Paul the Apostle to the Hebrews," there is no early manuscript evidence to support it. The oldest and most reliable title is simply *Pros Ebraious*, "To Hebrews."

GOD, who at sundry times and in divers manners spake in time past unto the fathers by the prophets,   Num. 12:6, 8; Joel 2:28
2 Hath in these last days spoken unto us by *his* Son, whom he hath appointed heir of all things, by whom also he made the ᵀworlds;   Or *ages*
★ 3 Who being the brightness of *his* glory, and the express image of his person, and upholding all things by the word of his power, when he had by himself purged our sins, sat down on the right hand of the Majesty on high;
4 Being made so much better than the angels, as ᴿhe hath by inheritance obtained a more excellent name than they. [Phil. 2:9, 10]
★ 5 For unto which of the angels said he at any time, ᴿThou art my Son, this day have I begotten thee? And again, ᴿI will be to him a Father, and he shall be to me a Son?   Ps. 2:7; Acts 13:33 · 2 Sam. 7:14
★ 6 And again, when he bringeth in the firstbegotten into the world, he saith, ᴿAnd let all the angels of God worship him. Deut. 32:43; Ps. 97:7
7 And of the angels he saith, Who maketh his angels spirits, and his ministers a flame of fire.
★ 8 But unto the Son *he saith*, ᴿThy throne, O God, *is* for ever and ever: ᵀa sceptre of righteousness *is* the sceptre of thy kingdom.   Ps. 45:6, 7 · A ruler's staff
★ 9 Thou hast loved righteousness, and hated iniquity; therefore God, *even* thy God, ᴿhath anointed thee with the oil of gladness above thy fellows.   Is. 61:1, 3
10 And, Thou, Lord, in the beginning hast laid the foundation

of the earth; and the heavens are the works of thine hands:
11 They shall perish; but thou remainest; and ᴿthey all shall wax old as doth a garment; Is. 50:9; 51:6
12 And as a vesture shalt thou fold them up, and they shall be changed: but thou art the ᴿsame, and thy years shall not fail. 13:8
13 But to which of the angels ★ said he at any time, ᴿSit on my right hand, until I make thine enemies thy footstool?   Ps. 110:1
14 ᴿAre they not all ministering spirits, sent forth to minister for them who shall be ᴿheirs of salvation?   Ps. 103:20; Dan. 7:10 · Rom. 8:17
2 Therefore we ought to give the more earnest heed to the things which we have heard, lest at any time we should ᵀlet *them* slip.   *drift away*
2 For if the word ᴿspoken by angels was stedfast, and ᴿevery transgression and disobedience received a just ᵀrecompence of reward;   Acts 7:53 · Num. 15:30 · *penalty*
3 ᴿHow shall we escape, if we neglect so great salvation; which at the first began to be spoken by the Lord, and was confirmed unto us by them that heard *him*;   10:28
4 God also bearing *them* witness, ᴿboth with signs and wonders, and with divers miracles, and gifts of the Holy Ghost, according to his own will?   Acts 2:22
5 For unto the angels hath he not put in subjection the world to come, whereof we speak.
6 But one in a certain place testified, saying, ᴿWhat is man, that thou art mindful of him? or the son of man, that thou ᵀvisitest him? Job 7:17; Ps. 8:4–6 · *take care of him*
7 Thou madest him a little

lower than the angels; thou crownedst him with glory and honour, and didst set him over the works of thy hands:

8 Thou hast put all things in subjection under his feet. For in that he put all in subjection under him, he left nothing *that is* not put under him. But now ᴿwe see not yet all things put under him. Ps. 8:6

9 But we see Jesus, who was made a little lower than the angels for the suffering of death, crowned with glory and honour; that he by the grace of God should taste death ᴿfor every man. Is. 53:12

10 For it became him, ᴿfor whom *are* all things, and by whom *are* all things, in bringing many sons unto glory, to make the ᵀcaptain of their salvation ᴿperfect through sufferings. Col. 1:16 · *author* · 5:8, 9; 7:28

11 For ᴿboth he that sanctifieth and they who are sanctified ᴿ*are* all of one: for which cause ᴿhe is not ashamed to call them brethren, 10:10 · Acts 17:26 · Matt. 28:10

★ 12 Saying, ᴿI will declare thy name unto my brethren, in the midst of the church will I sing praise unto thee. Ps. 22:22

★ 13 And again, ᴿI will put my trust in him. And again, ᴿBehold I and the children which God hath given me. 2 Sam. 22:3; Is. 8:17 · Is. 8:18

14 Forasmuch then as the children are partakers of flesh and blood, he also himself likewise took part of the same; ᴿthat through death he might destroy him that had the power of ᴿdeath, that is, the devil; Col. 2:15 · 2 Tim. 1:10

15 And deliver them who through fear of death were all their lifetime subject to bondage.

16 For verily he took not on *him the nature of* angels; but he took on *him* the seed of Abraham.

17 Wherefore in all things it behoved him ᴿto be made like unto *his* brethren, that he might be a merciful and faithful high priest in things *pertaining* to God, to make reconciliation for the sins of the people. v. 14; Phil. 2:7

18 ᴿFor in that he himself hath suffered being tempted, he is able to ᵀsuccour them that are tempted. [4:15, 16] · *aid*

3 Wherefore, holy brethren, partakers of the heavenly calling, consider the Apostle and High Priest of our ᵀprofession, Christ Jesus; *confession*

2 Who was faithful to him that appointed him, as also ᴿMoses *was faithful* in all his house. v. 5

3 For this *man* was counted worthy of more glory than Moses, inasmuch as ᴿhe who hath builded the house hath more honour than the house. Zech. 6:12, 13

4 For every house is builded by some *man;* but ᴿhe that built all things *is* God. [Eph. 2:10]

5 And Moses verily *was* faithful in all his house, as a servant, for a testimony of those things which were to be spoken after;

6 But Christ as ᴿa son over his own house; ᴿwhose house are we, if we hold fast the confidence and the rejoicing of the hope firm unto the end. Ps. 110:4 · 1 Tim. 3:15

7 Wherefore (as ᴿthe Holy Ghost saith, ᴿTo day if ye will hear his voice, Acts 1:16 · 4:7; Ps. 95:7–11

8 Harden not your hearts, as in the provocation, in the day of ᵀtemptation in the wilderness: *trial*

9 When your fathers ᵀtempted me, proved me, and saw my works forty years. *tested*

10 Wherefore I was ᵀgrieved with that generation, and said, They do alway ᵀerr in *their* heart; and they have not known my ways. *angry · go astray*

11 So I sware in my wrath, They shall not enter into my rest.)

12 Take heed, brethren, lest there be in any of you an evil heart of unbelief, in departing from the living God.

13 But exhort one another daily, while it is called To day; lest any of you be hardened through the deceitfulness of sin.

14 For we ᵀare made partakers of Christ, if we hold the beginning of our confidence stedfast unto the end; *have become*

15 While it is said, ^RTo day if ye will hear his voice, harden not your hearts, as in the ^Tprovocation.   Ps. 95:7, 8 · *rebellion*

16 ^RFor some, when they had heard, did ^Tprovoke: howbeit not all that came out of Egypt by Moses.   Deut. 1:35, 36, 38 · *rebel*

17 But with whom was he grieved forty years? *was it* not with them that had sinned, ^Rwhose ^Tcarcases fell in the wilderness?   Num. 14:22, 23 · *corpses*

18 And to whom sware he that they should not enter into his rest, but to them that believed not?

19 So we see that they could not enter in because of unbelief.

4 Let ^Rus therefore fear, lest, a promise being left *us* of entering into his rest, any of you should seem to come short of it.   2 Cor. 6:1

2 For unto us was the gospel preached, as well as unto them: but the word preached did not profit them, not being mixed with faith in them that heard *it*.

3 For we which have believed do enter into rest, as he said, ^RAs I have sworn in my wrath, if they shall enter into my rest: although the works were finished from the foundation of the world.   Ps. 95:11

4 For he spake in a certain place of the seventh *day* on this wise, And God did rest the seventh day from all his works.

5 And in this *place* again, If they shall enter into my rest.

6 Seeing therefore it remaineth that some must enter therein, and they to whom it was first preached entered not in because of ^Tunbelief: *disobedience*

7 Again, he limiteth a certain day, saying in David, To day, after so long a time; as it is said, ^RTo day if ye will hear his voice, harden not your hearts.   Ps. 95:7, 8

8 For if ^TJesus had given them rest, then would he not afterward have spoken of another day.   Joshua

9 There remaineth therefore a rest to the people of God.

10 For he that is entered into his rest, he also hath ceased from his own works, as God *did* from his.

11 ^RLet us ^Tlabour therefore to enter into that rest, lest any man fall after the same example of unbelief.   2 Pet. 1:10 · *be diligent*

12 For the word of God *is* ^Rquick, and powerful, and ^Rsharper than any twoedged sword, piercing even to the dividing asunder of soul and spirit, and of the joints and marrow, and *is* a discerner of the thoughts and intents of the heart.   Ps. 147:15 · Is. 49:2

13 ^RNeither is there any creature that is not manifest in his sight: but all things *are* naked and opened unto the eyes of him with whom we have to do.   Ps. 33:13–15

14 Seeing then that we have a great ^Rhigh priest, that is passed into the heavens, Jesus the Son of God, ^Rlet us hold fast *our* profession.   2:17; 7:26 · 10:23

15 For ^Rwe have not an high priest which cannot be touched with the feeling of our infirmities; but was in all points tempted like as *we are, yet* without sin.   Is. 53:3–5

16 ^RLet us therefore come boldly unto the throne of grace, that we may obtain mercy, and find grace to help in time of need.   [10:19, 22]

5 For every high priest taken from among men ^Ris ordained for men in things *pertaining* to God, that he may offer both gifts and sacrifices for sins: 2:17; 8:3

2 Who can have compassion on the ignorant, and on them that are ^Tout of the way; for that he himself also is compassed with ^Rinfirmity.   *going astray* · 7:28

3 And by reason hereof he ought, as for the people, so also for ^Rhimself, to offer for sins.   [7:27]

4 And no man taketh this honour unto himself, but he that is called of God, as *was* Aaron.

5 ^RSo also Christ glorified not ★ himself to be made an high priest; but he that said unto him, ^RThou art my Son, to day have I begotten thee.   John 8:54 · Ps. 2:7

6 As he saith also in another ★

place, Thou *art* a priest for ever after the order of Mel-chis'-e-dec.

7 Who in the days of his flesh, when he had offered up prayers and supplications with strong crying and tears unto him that was able to save him from death, and was heard in that he feared;

8 Though he were a Son, yet learned he ^Robedience by the things which he suffered;   Phil. 2:8

9 And ^Rbeing made perfect, he became the author of eternal salvation unto all them that obey him;   2:10

10 Called of God an high priest after the order of Mel-chis'-e-dec.

11 Of whom ^Rwe have many things to say, and hard to be uttered, seeing ye are ^Rdull of hearing.   [John 16:12] · [Matt. 13:15]

12 For when for the time ye ought to be teachers, ye have need that one teach you again which *be* the first principles of the ^Toracles of God; and are become such as have need of ^Rmilk, and not of strong meat.   *sayings* · 1 Cor. 3:1–3

13 For every one that useth milk *is* unskilful in the word of righteousness: for he is a babe.

14 But strong meat belongeth to them that are of full age, *even* those who by reason of use have their senses exercised ^Rto discern both good and evil.   Is. 7:15; Phil. 1:9

6 Therefore ^Rleaving the principles of the doctrine of Christ, let us go on unto perfection; not laying again the foundation of repentance from ^Rdead works, and of faith toward God, 5:12 · [9:14]

2 ^ROf the doctrine of baptisms, and of laying on of hands, and of resurrection of the dead, and of eternal judgment.   Acts 19:3–5

3 And this will we do, if God permit.

4 For *it is* impossible for those who were once enlightened, and have tasted of ^Rthe heavenly gift, and ^Rwere made partakers of the Holy Ghost,   [John 4:10]; Eph. 2:8 · 2:4

5 And have tasted the good word of God, and the powers of the ^Tworld to come,   *age*

6 If they shall fall away, to renew them again unto repentance; ^Rseeing they crucify to themselves the Son of God ^Tafresh, and put *him* to an open shame.   10:29 · *again*

7 For the earth which drinketh in the rain that cometh oft upon it, and bringeth forth herbs meet for them by whom it is dressed, ^Rreceiveth blessing from God: Ps. 65:10

8 ^RBut that which beareth thorns and briers *is* rejected, and *is* nigh unto ^Tcursing; whose end *is* to be burned.   Is. 5:6 · *being cursed*

9 But, beloved, we are ^Tpersuaded better things of you, and things that accompany salvation, though we thus speak.   *confident of*

10 For ^RGod *is* not unrighteous to forget ^Ryour work and labour of love, which ye have shewed toward his name, in that ye have ministered to the saints, and do minister.   Rom. 3:4 · 1 Thess. 1:3

11 And we desire that every one of you do shew the same diligence ^Rto the full assurance of hope unto the end: Col. 2:2

12 That ye be not ^Tslothful, but ^Tfollowers of them who through faith and patience ^Rinherit the promises.   *sluggish* · *imitators* · 10:36

13 For when God made promise to Abraham, because he could swear by no greater, ^Rhe sware by himself,   Gen. 22:16, 17; Luke 1:73

14 Saying, Surely blessing I will bless thee, and multiplying I will multiply thee.

15 And so, after he had patiently endured, he obtained the ^Rpromise.   Gen. 12:4; 21:5

16 For men verily swear by the greater: and ^Ran oath for confirmation *is* to them an end of all ^Tstrife.   Ex. 22:11 · *dispute*

17 Wherein God, willing more abundantly to shew unto the heirs of promise ^Rthe ^Timmutability of his counsel, confirmed *it* by an oath: Rom. 11:29 · *unchangeableness*

18 That by two immutable things, in which *it was* impossible for God to ^Rlie, we might have a strong consolation, who have fled

for refuge to lay hold upon the hope ᴿset before us: Titus 1:2 · 3:6

19 Which *hope* we have as an anchor of the soul, both sure and stedfast, ᴿand which entereth into that within the veil;   9:3, 7

20 ᴿWhither the forerunner is for us entered, *even* Jesus, made an high priest for ever after the order of Mel-chis′-e-dec.   [4:14]

7 For this ᴿMel-chis′-e-dec, king of Sa′-lem, priest of the most high God, who met Abraham returning from the slaughter of the kings, and blessed him; v. 6

2 To whom also Abraham gave a tenth part of all; first being by interpretation King of righteousness, and after that also King of Sa′-lem, which is, King of peace;

3 Without father, without mother, without descent, having neither beginning of days, nor end of life; but made like unto the Son of God; abideth a priest continually.

4 Now consider how great this man *was*, unto whom even the patriarch Abraham gave the tenth of the ᵀspoils.   *plunder*

5 And verily ᴿthey that are of the sons of Levi, who receive the office of the priesthood, have a commandment to take tithes of the people according to the law, that is, of their brethren, though they come out of the loins of Abraham: Num. 18:21–26; 2 Chr. 31:4

6 But he whose descent is not counted from them received tithes of Abraham, ᴿand blessed him that had the promises. Gen. 14:19, 20

7 And ᵀwithout all contradiction the less is blessed of the better.   *beyond*

8 And here men that die receive tithes; but there he *receiveth them*, ᴿof whom it is witnessed that he liveth.   5:6; 6:20; [Rev. 1:18]

9 And as I may so say, Levi also, who receiveth tithes, payed tithes ᵀin Abraham.   *through*

10 For he was yet in the loins of his father, when Mel-chis′-e-dec met him.

11 ᴿIf therefore ᵀperfection were by the Le-vit′-ic-al priesthood, (for

under it the people received the law,) what further need *was there* that another priest should rise after the order of Mel-chis′-e-dec, and not be called after the order of Aaron?   [Rom. 7:7–14] · *completion*

12 For the priesthood being changed, there is made of necessity a change also of the law.

13 For he of whom these things are spoken ᵀpertaineth to another tribe, of which no man gave attendance at the altar.   *belongs*

14 For *it is* evident that ᴿour ★ Lord sprang out of Juda; of which tribe Moses spake nothing concerning priesthood. Mic. 5:2; Matt. 1:3

15 And it is yet far more evident: for that after the ᵀsimilitude of Mel-chis′-e-dec there ariseth another priest,   *likeness*

16 Who ᵀis made, not after the law of a ᵀcarnal commandment, but after the power of an endless life.   *has come · fleshly*

17 For he testifieth, ᴿThou *art* a ★ priest for ever after the order of Mel-chis′-e-dec.   5:6; 6:20; Ps. 110:4;

18 For there is verily a disannulling of the commandment going before for the weakness and unprofitableness thereof.

19 For ᴿthe law made nothing perfect, but the bringing in of a better hope *did*; by the which we draw nigh unto God. Rom. 3:20; 7:7

20 And inasmuch as not without an oath *he was made priest*:

21 (For those priests were made ★ without an oath; but this with an oath by him that said unto him, The Lord sware and will not repent, Thou *art* a priest for ever after the order of Mel-chis′-e-dec:)

22 By so much was Jesus made a surety of a better testament.

23 And they truly were many priests, because they were not ᵀsuffered to continue by reason of death: *allowed*

24 But this *man*, because he continueth ever, hath an unchangeable priesthood.

25 Wherefore he is able also to save them to the uttermost that come unto God by him, seeing he

ever liveth ^Rto make intercession for them.   9:24; Rom. 8:34; 1 Tim. 2:5

26 For such an high priest became us, ^Rwho is holy, ^Tharmless, undefiled, separate from sinners, ^Rand made higher than the heavens;   [2 Cor. 5:21] · innocent · Eph. 1:20

27 Who needeth not daily, as those high priests, to offer up sacrifice, first for his ^Rown sins, and then for the people's: for this he did once, when he offered up himself.   5:3; Lev. 9:7; 16:6

28 For the law maketh men high priests which have infirmity; but the word of the oath, which was since the law, *maketh* the Son, who is consecrated for evermore.

8 Now of the things which we have spoken *this is* the sum: We have such an high priest, who is set on the right hand of the throne of the Majesty in the heavens;

2 A minister of the sanctuary, and of the true tabernacle, which the Lord pitched, and not man.

3 For ^Revery high priest is ordained to offer gifts and sacrifices: wherefore *it is* of necessity that this man have somewhat also to offer.   [Rom. 5:6, 8; Gal. 2:20; Eph. 5:2]

4 For if he were on earth, he should not be a priest, seeing that there are priests that offer gifts according to the law:

5 Who serve unto the example and ^Rshadow of heavenly things, as Moses was admonished of God when he was about to make the tabernacle: for, See, saith he, *that* thou make all things according to the pattern shewed to thee in the mount.   10:1; Col. 2:17

6 But now hath he obtained a more excellent ministry, by how much also he is the mediator of a better covenant, which was established upon better promises.

7 For if that ^Rfirst *covenant* had been faultless, then should no place have been sought for the second.   Ex. 3:8; 19:5

★ 8 For finding fault with them, he saith, ^RBehold, the days come, saith the Lord, when I will make a

new covenant with the house of Israel and with the house of Judah: Jer. 31:31–34

9 Not according to the covenant that I made with their fathers in the day when I took them by the hand to lead them out of the land of Egypt; because they continued not in my covenant, and I ^Tregarded them not, saith the Lord.   *disregarded them*

10 For this *is* the covenant that I will make with the house of Israel after those days, saith the ^RLord; I will put my laws into their mind, and write them in their hearts: and I will be to them a God, and they shall be to me a people: 10:16

11 And they shall not teach every man his neighbour, and every man his brother, saying, Know the Lord: for all shall know me, from the least to the greatest.

12 For I will be merciful to their unrighteousness, ^Rand their sins and their ^Tiniquities will I remember no more.   Rom. 11:27 · *lawless deeds*

13 ^RIn that he saith, A new *covenant*, he hath made the first old. Now that which decayeth and waxeth old *is* ready to vanish away.   1:11; [2 Cor. 5:17]

9 Then verily the first *covenant* had also ordinances of divine service, and a worldly sanctuary.

2 For there was a tabernacle made; the first, wherein *was* the ^Tcandlestick, and the table, and the shewbread; which is called the ^Tsanctuary.   *lampstand · holy place*

3 ^RAnd after the second veil, the tabernacle which is called the Holiest of all;   Ex. 26:31–35; 40:3

4 Which had the golden censer, and the ark of the covenant overlaid round about with gold, wherein *was* the golden pot that had man'-na, and Aaron's rod that budded, and ^Rthe tables of the covenant;   Ex. 25:16; 34:29; Deut. 10:2–5

5 And ^Rover it the cher'-u-bims of glory shadowing the mercyseat; of which we cannot now speak particularly.   Ex. 25:17, 20

6 Now when these things were thus ordained, the priests went

always into the first tabernacle, accomplishing the service of God.

7 But into the second went the high priest alone [R]once every year, not without blood, which he offered for [R]himself, and for the errors of the people: 10:3 · 5:3

8 The Holy Ghost this signifying, that [R]the way into the holiest of all was not yet made manifest, while as the first tabernacle was yet standing: [10:20; John 14:6]

9 Which was a figure for the time then present, in which were offered both gifts and sacrifices, [R]that could not make him that did the service perfect, as pertaining to the conscience; 7:19; [Gal. 3:21]

10 Which stood only in meats and drinks, and [T]divers washings, and carnal ordinances, imposed on them until the time of reformation. various baptisms

11 But Christ being come an high priest of [R]good things to come, by a greater and more perfect tabernacle, not made with hands, that is to say, not of this [T]building; [Eph. 1:3–11] · creation

12 Neither [R]by the blood of goats and calves, but [R]by his own blood he entered in once into the holy place, having obtained eternal redemption for us. 10:4 · Is. 53:12

13 For if [R]the blood of bulls and of goats, and [R]the ashes of an heifer sprinkling the unclean, sanctifieth to the purifying of the flesh: 10:4; Lev. 16:14, 15 · Num. 19:2

14 How much more shall the blood of Christ, who through the eternal Spirit offered himself without spot to God, [R]purge your conscience from dead works to serve the living God? 1 John 1:7

15 And for this cause [R]he is the mediator of the new [T]testament, that by means of death, for the redemption of the transgressions that were under the first testament, they which are called might receive the promise of eternal inheritance. Rom. 3:25 · covenant

16 For where a testament is, there must also of necessity be the death of the testator.

17 For [R]a testament is of force after men are dead: otherwise it is of no strength at all while the testator liveth. Gal. 3:15

18 [R]Whereupon [T]neither the first testament was dedicated without blood. Ex. 24:6 · not even

19 For when Moses had spoken every precept to all the people according to the law, [R]he took the blood of calves and of goats, with water, and scarlet wool, and hyssop, and sprinkled both the book, and all the people, Ex. 24:5, 6

20 Saying, This is the blood of the testament which God hath [T]enjoined unto you. commanded

21 Moreover [R]he sprinkled with blood both the tabernacle, and all the vessels of the ministry. Ex. 29:12

22 And almost all things are by the law purged with blood; and [R]without shedding of blood is no [T]remission. Lev. 17:11 · forgiveness

23 It was therefore necessary that [R]the patterns of things in the heavens should be [T]purified with these; but the heavenly things themselves with better sacrifices than these. 8:5 · cleansed

24 For [R]Christ is not entered into the holy places made with hands, which are the [T]figures of [R]the true; but into heaven itself, now [R]to appear in the presence of God for us: 6:20 · copies · 8:2 · Rom. 8:34

25 Nor yet that he should offer himself often, as [R]the high priest entereth into the holy place every year with blood of others; v. 7

26 For then must he often have suffered since the foundation of the world: but now once in the end of the [T]world hath he appeared to put away sin by the sacrifice of himself. ages

27 And as it is appointed unto men once to die, [R]but after this the judgment: [2 Cor. 5:10]; 1 John 4:17

28 So [R]Christ was once offered ★ to bear the sins of many; and unto them that look for him shall he appear the second time without sin unto salvation. Rom. 6:10

10 For the law having a [R]shadow of good things to

come, *and* not the very image of the things, ^Rcan never with those sacrifices which they offered year by year continually make the comers thereunto perfect.   8:5 · 7:19

2   For then would they not have ceased to be offered? because that the worshippers once ^Tpurged should have had no more conscience of sins.   *cleansed*

3   But in those *sacrifices there is* a remembrance again *made* of sins every year.

4   For ^R*it is* not possible that the blood of bulls and of goats should take away sins.   Mic. 6:6, 7

★   5   Wherefore when he cometh into the world, he saith, Sacrifice and offering thou wouldest not, but a body hast thou prepared me:

6   In burnt offerings and *sacrifices* for sin thou hast had no pleasure.

7   Then said I, Lo, I come (in the volume of the book it is written of me,) to do thy will, O God.

8   Above when he said, Sacrifice and offering and burnt offerings and *offering* for sin thou wouldest not, neither hadst pleasure *therein;* which are offered ^Tby the law;   *according to*

9   Then said he, Lo, I come to do thy will, O God. He taketh away the first, that he may establish the second.

10   ^RBy the which will we are sanctified ^Rthrough the offering of the body of Jesus Christ once *for all.*   John 17:19; [Eph. 5:26] · [9:12]

11   And every priest standeth daily ministering and offering oftentimes the same sacrifices, which can never take away sins:

★   12   ^RBut this man, after he had offered one sacrifice for sins for ever, sat down ^Ron the right hand of God;   1:3; Col. 3:1 · Ps. 110:1

★   13   From henceforth ^Texpecting ^Rtill his enemies be made his footstool.   *waiting* · 1:13

14   For by one offering he hath perfected for ever them that are sanctified.

15   *Whereof* the Holy Ghost also is a witness to us: for after that he had said before,

16   This *is* the covenant that I ★ will make with them after those days, saith the ^RLord, I will put my laws into their hearts, and in their minds will I write them;   Jer. 31:33

17   And their sins and iniquities ★ will I remember no more.

18   Now where ^Tremission of these *is, there is* no more offering for sin.   *forgiveness*

19   Having therefore, brethren, ^Rboldness to enter ^Rinto the holiest by the blood of Jesus,   4:16 · 9:8

20   By a new and ^Rliving way, which he hath consecrated for us, through the veil, that is to say, his flesh;   [7:24, 25]; John 14:6

21   And *having* an high priest over the house of God;

22   Let us ^Rdraw near with a true heart in full assurance of faith, having our hearts sprinkled from an evil conscience, and our bodies washed with pure water.   7:19

23   Let us hold fast the profession of *our* faith without wavering; (for ^Rhe *is* faithful that promised;)   1 Cor. 1:9; 10:13; 1 Thess. 5:24

24   And let us consider one another to ^Tprovoke unto love and to good works: *stir up*

25   Not forsaking the assembling of ourselves together, as the manner of some *is;* but exhorting *one another:* and so much the more, as ye see the day approaching.

26   For if we sin wilfully after that we have received the knowledge of the truth, there remaineth ^Rno more sacrifice for sins,   6:6

27   But a certain fearful looking for of judgment and ^Rfiery indignation, which shall devour the adversaries.   Zeph. 1:18

28   He that despised Moses' law died without mercy under two or three ^Rwitnesses: Deut. 17:2–6; 19:15

29   ^ROf how much sorer punishment, suppose ye, shall he be thought worthy, who hath trodden under foot the Son of God, and ^Rhath counted the blood of the covenant, wherewith he was sanctified, an unholy thing, and hath

T done despite unto the Spirit of grace? [2:3] · 1 Cor. 11:29 · *insulted*

30 For we know him that hath said, R Vengeance *belongeth* unto me, I will recompense, saith the Lord. And again, The Lord shall judge his people. Deut. 32:35, 36

31 *It is* a fearful thing to fall into the hands of the living God.

32 But R call to remembrance the former days, in which, after ye were illuminated, ye endured a great fight of afflictions; Gal. 3:4

33 Partly, whilst ye were made R a gazingstock both by reproaches and afflictions; and partly, whilst ye became companions of them that were so used. 1 Cor. 4:9

34 For ye had compassion of me in my bonds, and took joyfully the T spoiling of your goods, knowing in yourselves that ye have in heaven a better and an enduring T substance. *plundering · possession*

35 Cast not away therefore your confidence, R which hath great recompence of reward. Matt. 5:12

36 R For ye have need of T patience, that, after ye have done the will of God, ye might receive the promise. Luke 21:19 · *endurance*

☆ 37 For R yet a little while, and he that shall come will come, and will not T tarry. Luke 18:8 · *delay*

38 Now R the just shall live by faith: but if *any man* draw back, my soul shall have no pleasure in him. Hab. 2:3, 4; Rom. 1:17; Gal. 3:11

39 But we are not of them R who draw back unto T perdition; but of them that believe to the saving of the soul. 2 Pet. 2:20 · *destruction*

11 Now faith is the substance of things hoped for, the evidence R of things not seen. Rom. 8:24

2 For by it the elders obtained a good report.

3 Through faith we understand that the T worlds were framed by the word of God, so that things which are seen were not made of things which do appear. Or *ages*

4 By faith Abel offered unto God a more excellent sacrifice than Cain, by which he obtained witness that he was righteous,

God testifying of his gifts: and by it he being dead yet speaketh.

5 By faith E'-noch was translated that he should not see death; and was not found, because God had translated him: for before his translation he had this testimony, that he pleased God.

6 But without faith *it is* impossible to please *him*: for he that cometh to God must believe that he is, and *that* he is a rewarder of them that diligently seek him.

7 By faith R Noah, being warned of God of things not seen as yet, moved with fear, prepared an ark to the saving of his house; by the which he condemned the world, and became heir of the righteousness which is by faith. Gen. 6:13–22

8 By faith R Abraham, when he was called to go out into a place which he should after receive for an inheritance, obeyed; and he went out, not knowing whither he went. Gen. 12:1–4; Acts 7:2–4

9 By faith he sojourned in the land of promise, as *in* a strange country, dwelling in tabernacles with Isaac and Jacob, the heirs with him of the same promise:

10 For he looked for R a city which hath foundations, whose builder and maker *is* God. [12:22]

11 Through faith also R Sara herself received strength to conceive seed, and was delivered of a child when she was past age, because she judged him faithful who had promised. Gen. 17:19; 18:11–14; 21:1, 2

12 Therefore sprang there even of one, and him as good as dead, *so many* as the stars of the sky in multitude, and as the sand which is by the sea shore innumerable.

13 These all died in faith, not having received the R promises, but having seen them afar off, and were persuaded of *them,* and embraced *them,* and confessed that they were strangers and pilgrims on the earth. Gen. 12:7

14 For they that say such things R declare plainly that they seek a T country. 13:14 · *homeland*

15 And truly, if they had been

mindful of ᴿthat *country* from whence they came out, they might have had opportunity to have returned.   Gen. 11:31

16 But now they desire a better *country*, that is, an heavenly: wherefore God is not ashamed to be called their God: for he hath ᴿprepared for them a city. [Rev. 21:2]

17 By faith Abraham, when he was tried, offered up Isaac: and he that had received the promises offered up his only begotten *son,*

18 Of whom it was said, That in Isaac shall thy seed be called:

19 Accounting that God *was* able to raise *him* up, even from the dead; from whence also he received him in a figure.

20 By faith ᴿIsaac blessed Jacob and Esau concerning things to come.   Gen. 27:26–40

21 By faith Jacob, when he was a dying, ᴿblessed both the sons of Joseph; and worshipped, *leaning* upon the top of his staff. Gen. 48:1, 5

22 By faith ᴿJoseph, when he died, made mention of the departing of the children of Israel; and gave commandment concerning his bones. Gen. 50:24, 25; Ex. 13:19

23 By faith ᴿMoses, when he was born, was hid three months of his parents, because they saw *he was* a ᵀproper child; and they were not afraid of the king's commandment.   Ex. 2:1–3 · *beautiful*

24 By faith ᴿMoses, when he ᵀwas come to years, refused to be called the son of Pharaoh's daughter;   Ex. 2:11–15 · *came of age*

25 Choosing rather to suffer affliction with the people of God, than to enjoy the ᵀpleasures of sin for a season;   *passing pleasures of sin*

26 Esteeming ᴿthe reproach of Christ greater riches than the treasures in Egypt: for he ᵀhad respect unto the ᴿrecompence of the reward.   13:13 · *looked* · Rom. 8:18

27 By faith ᴿhe forsook Egypt, not fearing the wrath of the king: for he endured, as seeing him who is invisible.   Ex. 10:28

28 Through faith he kept the passover, and the sprinkling of blood, lest he that destroyed the firstborn should touch them.

29 By faith ᴿthey passed through the Red sea as by dry *land:* which the Egyptians assaying to do were drowned.   Ex. 14:22

30 By faith ᴿthe walls of Jericho fell down, after they were compassed about seven days. Josh. 6:20

31 By faith ᴿthe harlot Ra'-hab perished not with them that believed not, when she had received the spies with peace.   Josh. 2:9; 6:23

32 And what shall I more say? for the time would fail me to tell of Ged'-e-on, and *of* Ba'-rak, and *of* Samson, and *of* Jeph'-thae; *of* David also, and Samuel, and *of* the prophets:

33 Who through faith subdued kingdoms, wrought righteousness, obtained promises, ᴿstopped the mouths of lions,   Dan. 6:22

34 ᴿQuenched the violence of fire, escaped the edge of the sword, out of weakness were made strong, waxed valiant in fight, turned to flight the armies of the aliens.   Dan. 3:23–28

35 ᴿWomen received their dead raised to life again: and others were tortured, not accepting deliverance; that they might obtain a better resurrection: 1 Kin. 17:22

36 And others had trial of *cruel* mockings and scourgings, yea, moreover ᴿof bonds and imprisonment: 2 Chr. 18:26; Jer. 20:2; 37:15

37 ᴿThey were stoned, they were sawn asunder, were tempted, were slain with the sword: they wandered about in sheepskins and goatskins; being destitute, afflicted, tormented;   1 Kin. 21:13

38 (Of whom the world was not worthy:) they wandered in deserts, and *in* mountains, and *in* dens and caves of the earth.

39 And these all, having obtained a good report through faith, received not the promise:

40 God having provided some better thing for us, that they ᵀwithout us should not be ᴿmade ᵀperfect.   *apart from* · 5:9 · *complete*

12 Wherefore ᵀseeing we also are compassed about with so great a cloud of witnesses, ᴿlet us lay aside every weight, and the sin which doth so easily beset *us*, and let us run with patience the race that is set before us,   *since* · Col. 3:8

★ 2 Looking unto Jesus the author and finisher of *our* faith; who for the joy that was set before him endured the cross, despising the shame, and is set down at the right hand of the throne of God.

3 For consider him that endured such contradiction of sinners against himself, lest ye be wearied and faint in your minds.

4 Ye have not yet resisted unto blood, striving against sin.

5 And ye have forgotten the exhortation which speaketh unto you as unto ᵀchildren, ᴿMy son, despise not thou the chastening of the Lord, nor faint when thou art rebuked of him: *sons* · Job 5:17

6 For whom the Lord loveth he chasteneth, and scourgeth every son whom he receiveth.

7 If ye endure chastening, God dealeth with you as with sons; for what ᴿson is he whom the father chasteneth not?   Prov. 19:18; 23:13

8 But if ye be without chastisement, ᴿwhereof all are partakers, then are ye ᵀbastards, and not sons.   1 Pet. 5:9 · *illegitimate*

9 Furthermore we have had fathers of our flesh which corrected *us*, and we gave *them* ᵀreverence: shall we not much rather be in subjection unto ᴿthe Father of spirits, and live?   *respect* · [Job 12:10]

10 For they verily for a few days chastened *us* after their own pleasure; but he for *our* profit, ᴿthat *we* might be partakers of his holiness.   Lev. 11:44

11 Now no chastening for the present seemeth to be joyous, but grievous: nevertheless afterward it yieldeth the peaceable fruit of righteousness unto them which are ᵀexercised thereby.   *trained*

12 Wherefore ᴿliftᵀ up the hands which hang down, and the feeble knees;   Is. 35:3 · *strengthen*

13 And make straight paths for your feet, lest that which is lame be ᵀturned out of the way; but let it rather be healed.   Dislocated

14 ᴿFollow peace with all *men*, and holiness, without which no man shall see the Lord: Ps. 34:14

15 Looking diligently lest any man ᴿfail of the grace of God; lest any ᴿroot of bitterness springing up trouble *you*, and thereby many be defiled;   2 Cor. 6:1 · Deut. 29:18

16 Lest there *be* any fornicator, or ᵀprofane person, as Esau, ᴿwho for one morsel of ᵀmeat sold his birthright.   *godless* · Gen. 25:33 · *food*

17 For ye know how that afterward, when he would have inherited the blessing, he was ᴿrejected: for he found no place of repentance, though he sought it carefully with tears.   Gen. 27:30–40

18 For ye are not come unto ᴿthe mount that might be touched, and that burned with fire, nor unto blackness, and darkness, and tempest,   Ex. 19:12, 16; 20:18; Deut. 4:11

19 And the sound of a trumpet, and the voice of words; which *voice* they that heard ᴿintreated that the word should not be spoken to them any more: Ex. 20:18–26

20 (For they could not endure that which was commanded, And if so much as a beast touch the mountain, it shall be stoned, or thrust through with a dart:

21 And so terrible was the sight, *that* Moses said, ᴿI exceedingly fear and quake:)   Deut. 9:19

22 But ye are come unto mount Si′-on, and unto the city of the living God, the heavenly Jerusalem, and to an innumerable company of angels,

23 To the general assembly and church of the firstborn, which are written in heaven, and to God ᴿthe Judge of all, and to the spirits of just men made perfect,   Gen. 18:25

24 And to Jesus the mediator of the new covenant, and to the blood of sprinkling, that speaketh better things than *that of* Abel.

25 See that ye refuse not him that speaketh. For ᴿif they es-

caped not who refused him that spake on earth, much more *shall not* we *escape*, if we turn away from him that *speaketh* from heaven: 2:2, 3

26 Whose voice then shook the earth: but now he hath promised, saying, [R]Yet once more I shake not the earth only, but also heaven. Hag. 2:6

27 And this *word*, Yet once more, signifieth the [R]removing of those things that are shaken, as of things that are made, that those things which cannot be shaken may remain. [Rom. 8:19, 21]; 1 Cor. 7:31

28 Wherefore we receiving a kingdom which cannot be moved, let us have grace, whereby we may [R]serve God acceptably with reverence and godly fear: 13:15, 21

29 For [R]our God *is* a consuming fire. Ex. 24:17

13 Let [R]brotherly love continue. Rom. 12:10

2 Be not forgetful to entertain strangers: for thereby some have entertained angels unawares.

3 Remember them that are in bonds, as bound with them; *and* them which suffer adversity, as being yourselves also in the body.

4 Marriage *is* honourable in all, and the bed undefiled: [R]but whoremongers and adulterers God will judge. 1 Cor. 6:9; Gal. 5:19, 21

5 *Let your* conversation *be* without covetousness; *and be* content with such things as ye have: for he hath said, I will never leave thee, nor forsake thee.

6 So that we may boldly say, [R]The Lord *is* my helper, and I will not fear what man [T]shall do unto me. Ps. 27:1; 118:6 · *can*

7 Remember them which have the rule over you, who have spoken unto you the word of God: whose faith follow, considering the end of *their* conversation.

8 Jesus Christ the same yesterday, and to day, and for ever.

9 Be not carried about with [T]divers and strange doctrines. For *it is* a good thing that the heart be established with grace; not with [T]meats, which have not profited them that have been occupied therein. *various · foods*

10 We have an altar, whereof they have no right to eat which serve the tabernacle.

11 For the bodies of those beasts, whose blood is brought into the sanctuary by the high priest for sin, are burned [T]without the camp. *outside*

12 Wherefore Jesus also, that he might [T]sanctify the people with his own blood, suffered [T]without the gate. *set apart · outside*

13 Let us go forth therefore unto him [T]without the camp, bearing [R]his reproach. *outside ·* 1 Pet. 4:14

14 For here have we no continuing city, but we seek one to come.

15 [R]By him therefore let us offer [R]the sacrifice of praise to God continually, that is, [R]the fruit of *our* lips giving thanks to his name. Eph. 5:20 · Lev. 7:12 · Is. 57:19

16 But to do good and to [T]communicate forget not: for [R]with such sacrifices God is well pleased. *share ·* 2 Cor. 9:12; Phil. 4:18

17 [R]Obey them that have the rule over you, and submit yourselves: for they watch for your souls, as they that must give account, that they may do it with joy, and not with grief: for that *is* unprofitable for you. Phil. 2:29

18 Pray for us: for we trust we have a good conscience, in all things willing to live honestly.

19 But I beseech *you* the rather to do this, that I may be restored to you the sooner.

20 Now the God of peace, [R]that ★ brought again from the dead our Lord Jesus, that great shepherd of the sheep, through the blood of the everlasting covenant, Rom. 4:24

21 Make you [T]perfect in every good work to do his will, [R]working in you that which is wellpleasing in his sight, through Jesus Christ; to whom *be* glory for ever and ever. A-men'. *complete ·* Phil. 2:13

22 And I beseech you, brethren, [T]suffer the word of exhortation:

for I have written a letter unto you in few words.   *bear with*
23 Know ye that *our* brother Timothy is set at liberty; with whom, if he come shortly, I will see you.

24 [T]Salute all them that have the rule over you, and all the saints. They of Italy salute you.   *Greet*
25 Grace *be* with you all. A-men'.

The Epistle of

JAMES

FAITH without works cannot be called faith. "Faith without works is dead" (2:26), and a dead faith is worse than no faith at all. Faith must work; it must produce; it must be visible. Verbal faith is not enough; mental faith is insufficient. Faith must be there, but it must be more. It must inspire action. Throughout his epistle to Jewish believers, James integrates true faith and everyday practical experience by stressing that true faith must manifest itself in works of faith.

Faith endures trials. Trials come and go, but a strong faith will face them head-on and develop endurance. Faith understands temptations. It will not allow us to consent to our lust and slide into sin. Faith obeys the Word. It will not merely hear and not do. Faith produces doers. Faith harbors no prejudice. For James, faith and favoritism cannot coexist. Faith displays itself in works. Faith is more than mere words; it is more than knowledge; it is demonstrated by obedience; and it overtly responds to the promises of God. Faith controls the tongue. This small but immensely powerful part of the body must be held in check. Faith can do it. Faith acts wisely. It gives us the ability to choose wisdom that is heavenly and to shun wisdom that is earthly. Faith produces separation from the world and submission to God. It provides us with the ability to resist the Devil and humbly draw near to God. Finally, faith waits patiently for the coming of the Lord. Through trouble and trial it stifles complaining.

The name *Iakobos* (James) in 1:1 is the basis for the early title *Iakobou Epistole*, "Epistle of James." *Iakobos* is the Greek form of the Hebrew name Jacob, a Jewish name common in the first century.

JAMES, [R]a servant of God and of the Lord Jesus Christ, to the twelve tribes which are scattered abroad, greeting.   Acts 12:17
2 My brethren, [R]count it all joy [R]when ye fall into [T]divers temptations;   Acts 5:41 · 2 Pet. 1:6 · *various trials*
3 [R]Knowing *this*, that the [T]trying of your faith [T]worketh patience.   Rom. 5:3–5 · *testing* · *produces*
4 But let patience have *her* perfect work, that ye may be perfect and entire, wanting nothing.
5 [R]If any of you lack wisdom, let him ask of God, that giveth to

all *men* liberally, and upbraideth not; and it shall be given him. 3:17
6 But let him ask in faith, nothing wavering. For he that wavereth is like a wave of the sea driven with the wind and tossed.
7 For let not that man think that he shall receive any thing of the Lord.
8 [R]A double minded man *is* unstable in all his ways.   4:8
9 Let the brother of low degree rejoice in that he is exalted:
10 But the rich, in that he is

made low: because as the flower of the grass he shall pass away.

11 For the sun is no sooner risen with a burning heat, but it withereth the grass, and the flower thereof falleth, and the ᵀgrace of the fashion of it perisheth: so also shall the rich man fade away in his ways.   *beautiful appearance*

12 ᴿBlessed *is* the man that endureth temptation: for when he is tried, he shall receive the crown of life, which the Lord hath promised to them that love him.   5:11

13 Let no man say when he is tempted, I am tempted of God: for God cannot be tempted with evil, neither tempteth he any man:

14 But every man is tempted, when he is drawn away of his own ᵀlust, and enticed.   *desires*

15 Then ᴿwhen lust hath conceived, it bringeth forth sin: and sin, when it is finished, ᴿbringeth forth death.   Is. 59:4 · [Rom. 5:12; 6:23]

16 Do not ᵀerr, my beloved brethren.   *be deceived*

17 ᴿEvery good gift and every perfect gift is from above, and cometh down from the Father of lights, ᴿwith whom is no ᵀvariableness, neither shadow of turning.   John 3:27 · Num. 23:19 · *variation*

18 Of his own will begat he us with the ᴿword of truth, ᴿthat we should be a kind of firstfruits of his creatures.   2 Tim. 2:15 · Heb. 12:23

19 Wherefore, my beloved brethren, let every man be swift to hear, ᴿslow to speak, ᴿslow to wrath: Prov. 10:19 · Prov. 14:17; 16:32

20 For the wrath of man ᵀworketh not the righteousness of God.   *does not produce*

21 Wherefore lay apart all filthiness and ᵀsuperfluity of naughtiness, and receive with meekness the engrafted word, which is able to save your souls.   *abundance*

22 But ᴿbe ye doers of the word, and not hearers only, deceiving your own selves.   [2:14–20]

23 For ᴿif any be a hearer of the word, and not a doer, he is like unto a man beholding his natural face in a ᵀglass: Luke 6:47 · *mirror*

24 For he beholdeth himself, and goeth his way, and straightway forgetteth what manner of man he was.

25 But ᴿwhoso looketh into the perfect law of liberty, and continueth *therein*, he being not a forgetful hearer, but a doer of the work, this man shall be blessed in his deed.   Gal. 2:4; 6:2; 1 Pet. 2:16

26 If any man among you seem to be religious, and bridleth not his tongue, but deceiveth his own heart, this man's religion *is* vain.

27 Pure religion and undefiled before God and the Father is this, To visit the fatherless and widows in their affliction, *and* to keep himself unspotted from the world.

2 My brethren, have not the faith of our Lord Jesus Christ, ᴿ*the Lord* of glory, with respect of persons.   Acts 7:2; 1 Cor. 2:8

2 For if there come unto your assembly a man with a gold ring, in ᵀgoodly apparel, and there come in also a poor man in ᵀvile raiment;   *fine · filthy clothes*

3 And ye have respect to him that weareth the ᵀgay clothing, and say unto him, Sit thou here in a good place; and say to the poor, Stand thou there, or sit here ᵀunder my footstool: *fine · at*

4 Are ye not then partial in yourselves, and are become judges ᵀof evil thoughts?   *with*

5 Hearken, my beloved brethren, ᴿHath not God chosen the poor of this world ᴿrich in faith, and heirs of the kingdom which he hath promised to them that love him?   1 Cor. 1:27 · 1 Tim. 6:18

6 But ᴿye have despised the poor. Do not rich men oppress you, and draw you before the judgment seats?   1 Cor. 11:22

7 Do not they blaspheme that worthy name by the which ye are ᴿcalled?   Acts 11:26; 1 Pet. 4:16

8 If ye fulfil the royal law according to the scripture, ᴿThou shalt love thy neighbour as thyself, ye do well: Lev. 19:18

9 But if ye have respect to per-

sons, ye commit sin, and are ^Tconvinced of the law as ^Rtransgressors.   *convicted* · Deut. 1:17

10 For whosoever shall keep the whole law, and yet ^Roffend in one *point,* he is guilty of all.   Gal. 3:10

11 For he that said, Do not commit adultery, said also, Do not kill. Now if thou commit no adultery, yet if thou kill, thou art become a transgressor of the law.

12 So speak ye, and so do, as they that shall be judged by ^Rthe law of liberty.   1:25

13 For ^Rhe shall have judgment without mercy, that hath shewed no mercy; and mercy rejoiceth against judgment.   Job 22:6

14 ^RWhat *doth it* profit, my brethren, though a man say he hath faith, and have not works? can faith save him?   Matt. 21:28–32

15 If a brother or sister be naked, and destitute of daily food,

16 And ^Rone of you say unto them, Depart in peace, be *ye* warmed and filled; notwithstanding ye give them not those things which are needful to the body; what *doth it* profit? [1 John 3:17, 18]

17 Even so faith, if it hath not works, is dead, being alone.

18 Yea, a man may say, Thou hast faith, and I have works: ^Rshew me thy faith without thy works, ^Rand I will shew thee my faith by my works.   Col. 1:6 · 3:13

19 Thou believest that there is one God; thou doest well: the devils also believe, and tremble.

20 But ^Twilt thou know, O ^Tvain man, that faith without works is dead?   *do you want to know · foolish*

21 Was not Abraham our father justified by works, ^Rwhen he had offered Isaac his son upon the altar?   Gen. 22:9, 10, 12, 16–18

22 Seest thou how faith wrought with his works, and by ^Rworks was faith made perfect?   John 8:39

23 And the scripture was fulfilled which saith, Abraham believed God, and it was imputed unto him for righteousness: and he was called the Friend of God.

24 Ye see then how that by works a man is justified, and not by faith only.

25 Likewise also ^Rwas not Ra'-hab the harlot justified by works, when she had received the messengers, and had sent *them* out another way?   Heb. 11:31

26 For as the body without the spirit is dead, so faith without works is dead also.

3 My brethren, be not many ^Tmasters, knowing that we shall receive the ^Tgreater condemnation.   *teachers · stricter judgment*

2 For in many things we ^Toffend all. ^RIf any man offend not in word, the same *is* a perfect man, *and* able also to bridle the whole body.   *stumble* · Ps. 34:13

3 Behold, ^Rwe put bits in the horses' mouths, that they may obey us; and we turn about their whole body.   Ps. 32:9

4 Behold also the ships, which though *they be* so great, and *are* driven of fierce winds, yet are they turned about with a very small ^Thelm, whithersoever the ^Tgovernor listeth. *rudder · pilot wants*

5 Even so ^Rthe tongue is a little member, and boasteth great things. Behold, how great a matter a little fire kindleth!   Prov. 12:18

6 And the tongue *is* a fire, a world of iniquity: so is the tongue among our members, that it defileth the whole body, and setteth on fire the course of nature; and it is set on fire of ^Thell.   Gr. *gehenna*

7 For every kind of beasts, and of birds, and of serpents, and of things in the sea, is tamed, and hath been tamed of mankind:

8 But the tongue can no man tame; *it is* an unruly evil, ^Rfull of deadly poison.   Ps. 140:3; Rom. 3:13

9 Therewith bless we God, even the Father; and therewith curse we men, which are made after the similitude of God.

10 Out of the same mouth proceedeth blessing and cursing. My brethren, these things ought not so to be.

11 Doth a fountain send forth at

the same place sweet *water* and bitter?

12 Can the fig tree, my brethren, bear olive berries? either a vine, figs? so *can* no fountain both yield salt water and fresh.

13 Who *is* a wise man and endued with knowledge among you? let him shew out of a good ᵀconversation his works with meekness of wisdom.   *conduct*

14 But if ye have bitter envying and strife in your hearts, glory not, and lie not against the truth.

15 ᴿThis wisdom descendeth not from above, but *is* earthly, sensual, ᵀdevilish.   Phil. 3:19 · *demonic*

16 For ᴿwhere envying and strife *is*, there *is* confusion and every evil work.   1 Cor. 3:3

17 But the wisdom that is from above is first pure, then peaceable, gentle, *and* easy to be intreated, full of mercy and good fruits, ᴿwithout partiality, ᴿand without hypocrisy.   2:1 · 2 Cor. 6:6

18 ᴿAnd the fruit of righteousness is sown in peace of them that make peace.   [Gal. 6:8; Phil. 1:11]

4 From whence *come* wars and fightings among you? *come* *they* not hence, *even* of your lusts that war in your members?

2 Ye lust, and have not: ye kill, and ᵀdesire to have, and cannot obtain: ye fight and war, yet ye have not, because ye ask not. *covet*

3 Ye ask, and receive not, because ye ask amiss, that ye may consume *it* upon your lusts.

4 Ye adulterers and adulteresses, know ye not that the friendship of the world is enmity with God? ᴿwhosoever therefore will be a friend of the world is the enemy of God.   1 John 2:15 · Gal. 1:4

5 Do ye think that the scripture saith in vain, The spirit that dwelleth in us lusteth to envy?

6 But he giveth more grace. Wherefore he saith, ᴿGod resisteth the proud, but giveth grace unto the humble. Matt. 23:12; 1 Pet. 5:5

7 Submit yourselves therefore to God. ᴿResist the devil, and he will flee from you.   1 Pet. 5:8

8 Draw nigh to God, and he will draw nigh to you. Cleanse *your* hands, *ye* sinners; and purify *your* hearts, *ye* double minded.

9 ᴿBe afflicted, and mourn, and weep: let your laughter be turned to mourning, and *your* joy to ᵀheaviness.   Matt. 5:4 · *gloom*

10 ᴿHumble yourselves in the sight of the Lord, and he shall lift you up.   Luke 14:11; 18:14; 1 Pet. 5:6

11 ᴿSpeak not evil one of another, brethren. He that speaketh evil of *his* brother, and judgeth his brother, speaketh evil of the law, and judgeth the law: but if thou judge the law, thou art not a doer of the law, but a judge.   2 Cor. 12:20

12 There is one lawgiver, ᴿwho is able to save and to destroy: ᴿwho art thou that judgest another?   [Matt. 10:28] · Rom. 14:4

13 ᵀGo to now, ye that say, To day or to morrow we will go into such a city, and continue there a year, and buy and sell, and ᵀget gain: *Come now · make a profit*

14 Whereas ye know not what *shall be* on the morrow. For what *is* your life? ᴿIt is even a vapour, that appeareth for a little time, and then vanisheth away.   Job 7:7

15 For that ye *ought* to say, ᴿIf the Lord will, we shall live, and do this, or that.   Acts 18:21; 1 Cor. 4:19

16 But now ye ᵀrejoice in your ᵀboastings: ᴿall such rejoicing is evil.   *boast · arrogance · 1 Cor. 5:6*

17 Therefore ᴿto him that knoweth to do good, and doeth *it* not, to him it is sin.   John 9:41; 2 Pet. 2:21

5 Go to now, *ye* rich men, weep and howl for your miseries that shall come upon *you*.

2 Your ᴿriches are corrupted, and ᴿyour garments are motheaten.   Jer. 17:11; Matt. 6:19 · Job 13:28

3 Your gold and silver is ᵀcankered; and the rust of them shall be a witness against you, and shall eat your flesh as it were fire. Ye have heaped treasure together for the last days.   *corroded*

4 Behold, the hire of the labourers who have reaped down your fields, which is of you kept

back by fraud, crieth: and [R]the cries of them which have reaped are entered into the ears of the Lord of sabaoth. Ex. 2:23; Deut. 24:15

5 Ye have lived in pleasure on the earth, and been wanton; ye have [T]nourished your hearts, as in a day of slaughter.   *fattened*

6 Ye have condemned *and* killed the just; *and* he doth not resist you.

7 Be patient therefore, brethren, unto the coming of the Lord. Behold, the [T]husbandman waiteth for the precious fruit of the earth, and hath long patience for it, until he receive the early and latter rain.   *farmer*

8 Be ye also patient; [T]stablish your hearts: for the coming of the Lord draweth nigh.   *establish*

9 [T]Grudge not one against another, brethren, lest ye be condemned: behold, the judge standeth before the door.   *Grumble*

10 [R]Take, my brethren, the prophets, who have spoken in the name of the Lord, for an example of suffering affliction, and of [R]patience.   Matt. 5:12 · Heb. 10:36

11 Behold, [R]we count them happy which endure. Ye have heard of the patience of Job, and have seen the end of the Lord; that [R]the Lord is very [T]pitiful, and of tender mercy.   1:2 · Num. 14:18 · *compassionate*

12 But above all things, my brethren, [R]swear not, neither by heaven, neither by the earth, neither by any other oath: but let your yea be yea; and *your* nay, nay; lest ye fall into [T]condemnation.   Matt. 5:34–37 · *judgment*

13 Is any among you afflicted? let him [R]pray. Is any merry? let him sing psalms.   Ps. 50:14, 15

14 Is any sick among you? let him call for the elders of the church; and let them pray over him, [R]anointing him with oil in the name of the Lord: Mark 6:13; 16:18

15 And the prayer of faith shall save the sick, and the Lord shall raise him up; [R]and if he have committed sins, they shall be forgiven him.   Is. 33:24

16 Confess *your* faults one to another, and pray one for another, that ye may be healed. [R]The effectual fervent prayer of a righteous man availeth much.   Num. 11:2

17 E-li'-as was a man subject to like passions as we are, and [R]he prayed earnestly that it might not rain: and it rained not on the [T]earth by the space of three years and six months.   1 Kin. 17:1; 18:1 · *land*

18 And he prayed again, and the heaven gave rain, and the earth brought forth her fruit.

19 Brethren, if any of you do err from the truth, and one [R]convert him;   Matt. 18:15; Gal. 6:1

20 Let him know, that he which converteth the sinner from the error of his way [R]shall save a soul from death, and [R]shall hide a multitude of sins.   1 Cor. 1:21 · [1 Pet. 4:8]

The First Epistle of

PETER

PERSECUTION can cause either growth or bitterness in the Christian life. Response determines the result. In writing to Jewish believers struggling in the midst of persecution, Peter encourages them to conduct themselves courageously for the Person and program of Christ. Both their character and conduct must be above reproach. Having been born again to a living hope, they are to imitate the Holy One who has called them. The fruit of that character will be conduct rooted in submission: citizens to government, servants to masters, wives to husbands, husbands to wives, and Christians to one another. Only after submission is fully understood does Peter deal with the difficult area of suffering. The Christians are not to think it "strange concerning the fiery trial which is to try you, as though some strange thing happened unto you" (4:12), but are to rejoice as partakers of the suffering of Christ. That response to life is truly the climax of one's submission to the good hand of God.

This epistle begins with the phrase *Petros apostolos Iesou Christou,* "Peter, an apostle of Jesus Christ." This is the basis of the early title *Petrou A,* the "First of Peter."

PETER, an apostle of Jesus Christ, to the ᵀstrangers scattered throughout Pon'-tus, Ga-la'-ti-a, Cap-pa-do'-ci-a, Asia, and Bi-thyn'-i-a, *exiles of the dispersion in*

★ 2 ᴿElect according to the foreknowledge of God the Father, through sanctification of the Spirit, unto obedience and sprinkling of the blood of Jesus Christ: ᴿGrace unto you, and peace, be multiplied. Eph. 1:4 · Rom. 1:7

3 Blessed *be* the God and Father of our Lord Jesus Christ, which according to his abundant mercy ᴿhath begotten us again unto a ᵀlively hope ᴿby the resurrection of Jesus Christ from the dead, [John 3:3, 5] · *living* · 3:21

4 To an inheritance incorruptible, and undefiled, and that fadeth not away, ᴿreserved in heaven for you, Col. 1:5

5 ᴿWho are kept by the power of God through faith unto salvation ready to be revealed in the last time. John 10:28; [Phil. 4:7]

6 Wherein ye greatly rejoice, though now for a season, if need be, ye are ᵀin heaviness through manifold temptations: *distressed*

7 That the trial of your faith, being much more precious than of gold that perisheth, though it be tried with fire, might be found unto praise and honour and glory at the appearing of Jesus Christ:

8 ᴿWhom having not seen, ye love; ᴿin whom, though now ye see *him* not, yet believing, ye rejoice with joy unspeakable and full of glory: 1 John 4:20 · John 20:29

9 Receiving the end of your faith, *even* the salvation of *your* souls.

10 Of which salvation the prophets have enquired and searched diligently, who prophesied of the grace *that should come* unto you:

11 Searching what, or what manner of time ᴿthe Spirit of Christ which was in them did signify, when it testified beforehand the sufferings of Christ, and the glory that should follow. 2 Pet. 1:21

12 Unto whom it was revealed, that not unto themselves, but unto us they did minister the things, which are now reported unto you by them that have preached the gospel unto you with the Holy Ghost sent down from heaven; which things the ᴿangels desire to look into. Eph. 3:10

13 Wherefore gird up the loins of your mind, be sober, and hope to the end for the grace that is to be brought unto you at the revelation of Jesus Christ;

14 As obedient children, not ᴿfashioning yourselves according to the former lusts in your ignorance: 4:2; [Rom. 12:2]

15 ᴿBut as he which hath called you is holy, so be ye holy in all manner of conversation; [2 Cor. 7:1]

16 Because it is written, ᴿBe ye holy; for I am holy. Lev. 11:44, 45; 19:2

17 And if ye call on the Father, who without ᵀrespect of persons judgeth according to every man's work, pass the time of your sojourning *here* in fear: *partiality*

18 Forasmuch as ye know that ye were not redeemed with ᵀcorruptible things, *as* silver and gold, from your ᵀvain conversation *received* by tradition from your fathers; *perishable · aimless conduct*

19 But with the precious blood ★

of Christ, ^Ras of a lamb without blemish and without spot: Is. 53:7

20 Who verily was foreordained before the foundation of the world, but was ^Tmanifest ^Rin these last times for you,   *revealed* · Gal. 4:4

21 Who by him do believe in God, ^Rthat raised him up from the dead, and ^Rgave him glory; that your faith and hope might be in God.   Acts 2:24 · Acts 2:33

22 Seeing ye ^Rhave purified your souls in obeying the truth through the Spirit unto ^Tunfeigned ^Rlove of the brethren, *see that* ye love one another with a pure heart fervently: Acts 15:9 · *sincere* · John 13:34

23 Being born again, not of corruptible seed, but of incorruptible, ^Rby the word of God, which liveth and abideth for ever.   1 Thess. 2:13

24 For all flesh *is* as grass, and all the glory of man as the flower of grass. The grass withereth, and the flower thereof falleth away:

25 ^RBut the word of the Lord endureth for ever. ^RAnd this is the word which by the gospel is preached unto you. Is. 40:8 · [John 1:1]

2 Wherefore ^Rlaying aside all malice, and all guile, and hypocrisies, and envies, and all evil speakings,   Heb. 12:1

2   As newborn babes, desire the ^Tsincere ^Rmilk of the word, that ye may grow thereby: *pure* · 1 Cor. 3:2

3   If so be ye have ^Rtasted that the Lord *is* gracious.   Titus 3:4

4   To whom coming, *as unto* a living stone, ^Rdisallowed^T indeed of men, but chosen of God, *and* precious,   Ps. 118:22 · *rejected*

5   Ye also, as ^Tlively stones, ^Tare built up a spiritual house, an holy priesthood, to offer up spiritual sacrifices, acceptable to God by Jesus Christ.   *living* · *are being*

★ 6   Wherefore also it is contained in the scripture, ^RBehold, I lay in Sion a chief corner stone, elect, precious: and he that believeth on him shall not be confounded.   Is. 28:16; Rom. 9:32, 33; 10:11

★ 7   Unto you therefore which believe *he is* precious: but unto them which be disobedient, ^Rthe stone

which the builders disallowed, the same is made the head of the corner,   Ps. 118:22; Matt. 21:42; Luke 2:34

8   ^RAnd a stone of stumbling, ★ and a rock of offence, *even to them* which stumble at the word, being disobedient: whereunto also they were appointed.   Is. 8:14

9   But ye *are* a chosen generation, a royal priesthood, an holy nation, a peculiar people; that ye should shew forth the praises of him who hath called you out of ^Rdarkness into his marvellous light: Is. 9:2; 42:16; [Acts 26:18; 2 Cor. 4:6]

10 ^RWhich in time past *were* not a people, but *are* now the people of God: which had not obtained mercy, but now have obtained mercy. Hos. 1:9, 10; 2:23; Rom. 9:25; 10:19

11 Dearly beloved, I beseech *you* as strangers and pilgrims, abstain from fleshly lusts, ^Rwhich war against the soul;   James 4:1

12 ^RHaving your conversation honest among the Gentiles: that, whereas they speak against you as evildoers, ^Rthey may by *your* good works, which they shall behold, glorify God in the day of visitation.   Phil. 2:15; Titus 2:8 · John 13:31

13 ^RSubmit yourselves to every ^Tordinance of man for the Lord's sake: whether it be to the king, as supreme;   Matt. 22:21 · *institution*

14 Or unto governors, as unto them that are sent by him for the punishment of evildoers, and for the praise of them that do well.

15 For so is the will of God, that with well doing ye may put to silence the ignorance of foolish men:

16 As free, and not using *your* liberty for a cloke of maliciousness, but as the servants of God.

17 Honour all *men.* Love the brotherhood. Fear ^RGod. Honour the king.   Prov. 24:21

18 ^RServants, *be* subject to *your* masters with all fear; not only to the good and gentle, but also to the ^Tfroward.   Eph. 6:5–8 · *harsh*

19 For this *is* ^Rthankworthy,^T if a man for conscience toward God

endure grief, suffering wrongfully.   Matt. 5:10 · *commendable*

20 For ^Rwhat glory *is it*, if, when ye be buffeted for your faults, ye shall take it patiently? but if, when ye do well, and suffer *for it*, ye take it patiently, this *is* acceptable with God.   Luke 6:32–34

21 For ^Reven hereunto were ye called: because Christ also suffered for us, leaving us an example, that ye should follow his steps: Matt. 16:24; 1 Thess. 3:3, 4

★ 22 Who did no sin, neither was ^Tguile found in his mouth: *deceit*

★ 23 ^RWho, when he was reviled, reviled not again; when he suffered, he threatened not; but committed *himself* to him that judgeth righteously: 3:9; Is. 53:7; Heb. 12:3

★ 24 ^RWho his own self bare our sins in his own body on the tree, that we, being dead to sins, should live unto righteousness: by whose stripes ye were healed.   Is. 53:4, 11

★ 25 For ^Rye were as sheep going astray; but are now returned unto the Shepherd and ^TBishop of your souls.   Is. 53:5, 6 · *Overseer*

3 Likewise, ye wives, *be* in subjection to your own husbands; that, if any obey not the word, ^Rthey also may without the word be won by the ^Tconversation of the wives;   1 Cor. 7:16 · *conduct*

2 ^RWhile they behold your chaste conversation *coupled* with fear.   v. 6; 2:12

3 ^RWhose adorning let it not be that outward *adorning* of plaiting the hair, and of wearing of gold, or of putting on of apparel;   Is. 3:18

4 But *let it be* the hidden man of the heart, in that which is not corruptible, *even the ornament* of a meek and quiet spirit, which is in the sight of God of great price.

5 For after this manner in the old time the holy women also, who trusted in God, adorned themselves, being in subjection unto their own husbands:

6 Even as Sara obeyed Abraham, ^Rcalling him lord: whose daughters ye are, as long as ye do

well, and are not afraid with any ^Tamazement.   Gen. 18:12 · *terror*

7 Likewise, ye husbands, dwell with *them* according to knowledge, giving honour unto the wife, ^Ras unto the weaker vessel, and as being heirs together of the grace of life; ^Rthat your prayers be not hindered.   1 Cor. 12:23 · Job 42:8

8 Finally, *be ye* all of one mind, having compassion one of another, love as brethren, *be* ^Tpitiful, *be* courteous: *tenderhearted*

9 Not rendering evil for evil, or railing for railing: but contrariwise ^Rblessing; knowing that ye are thereunto called, that ye should inherit a blessing.   Matt. 5:44

10 For he that will love life, and see good days, ^Rlet him refrain his tongue from evil, and his lips that they speak no guile: James 1:26

11 Let him ^Teschew evil, and do good; let him seek peace, and ^Tensue it.   *turn away from · pursue*

12 For the eyes of the Lord *are* over the righteous, ^Rand his ears *are open* unto their prayers: but the face of the Lord *is* against them that do evil.   John 9:31

13 ^RAnd who *is* he that will harm you, if ye be followers of that which is good?   Prov. 16:7

14 ^RBut and if ye suffer for righteousness' sake, happy *are ye*: and be not afraid of their terror, neither be troubled;   James 1:12

15 But sanctify the Lord God in your hearts: and ^Rbe ready always to *give* an answer to every man that asketh you a reason of the ^Rhope that is in you with meekness and fear: Ps. 119:46 · [Titus 3:7]

16 ^RHaving a good conscience; that, whereas they speak evil of you, as of evildoers, they may be ashamed that falsely accuse your good conversation in Christ.   v. 21

17 For *it is* better, if the will of God be so, that ye suffer for well doing, than for evil doing.

18 For Christ also hath once suffered for sins, the just for the unjust, that he might bring us to God, being put to death in the

flesh, but ᵀquickened by the Spirit: *made alive*

19 By which also he went and preached unto the spirits in prison;

20 Which sometime were disobedient, when once the longsuffering of God waited in the days of Noah, while the ark was a preparing, wherein few, that is, eight souls were saved by water.

21 ᴿThe like figure whereunto *even* baptism doth also now save us ᴿ(not the putting away of the filth of the flesh, but the answer of a good conscience toward God,) by the resurrection of Jesus Christ: Acts 16:33; Eph. 5:26 · [Titus 3:5]

22 Who is gone into heaven, and is on the right hand of God; angels and authorities and powers being made subject unto him.

4 Forasmuch then as Christ hath suffered for us in the flesh, arm yourselves likewise with the same mind: for he that hath suffered in the flesh hath ceased from sin;

2 That he no longer should live the rest of *his* time in the flesh to the lusts of men, ᴿbut to the will of God.   John 1:13

3 For the time past of *our* life may suffice us to have wrought the will of the Gentiles, when we walked in ᵀlasciviousness, lusts, excess of wine, revellings, ᵀbanquetings, and abominable idolatries: *licentiousness · drinking parties*

4 Wherein they think it strange that ye run not with *them* to the same excess of ᵀriot, speaking evil of *you:*   *dissipation*

5 Who shall give account to him that is ready ᴿto judge the quick and the dead.   2 Tim. 4:1

6 For for this cause was the gospel preached also to them that are dead, that they might be judged according to men in the flesh, but ᴿlive according to God in the spirit.   [Rom. 8:9, 13]; Gal. 5:25

7 But ᴿthe end of all things is at hand: be ye therefore sober, and watch unto prayer.   1 John 2:18

8 And above all things have

fervent ᵀcharity among yourselves: for ᴿcharity shall cover the multitude of sins.   *love* · James 5:20

9 ᴿUse hospitality one to another without grudging.   1 Tim. 3:2

10 As every man hath received the gift, *even so* minister the same one to another, as good stewards of the manifold grace of God.

11 ᴿIf any man speak, *let him speak* as the oracles of God; if any man minister, *let him do it* as of the ability which God giveth: that God in all things may be glorified through Jesus Christ, to whom be praise and dominion for ever and ever. A-men'.   Eph. 4:29

12 Beloved, think it not strange concerning the fiery trial which is to try you, as though some strange thing happened unto you:

13 But rejoice, ᴿinasmuch as ye are partakers of Christ's sufferings; that, when his glory shall be revealed, ye may be glad also with exceeding joy.   James 1:2

14 If ye be reproached for the name of Christ, ᴿhappy *are ye;* for the spirit of glory and of God resteth upon you: on their part he is evil spoken of, ᴿbut on your part he is glorified.   Matt. 5:11 · Matt. 5:16

15 But let none of you suffer as a murderer, or *as* a thief, or *as* an evildoer, or as a ᵀbusybody in other men's matters.   *meddler*

16 Yet if *any man suffer* as a Christian, let him not be ashamed; but let him glorify God on this ᵀbehalf.   *matter*

17 For the time *is come* that judgment must begin at the house of God: and if *it* first *begin* at us, what shall the end *be* of them that obey not the gospel of God?

18 And if the righteous scarcely be saved, where shall the ungodly and the sinner appear?

19 Wherefore let them that suffer according to the will of God ᴿcommit the keeping of their souls *to him* in well doing, as unto a faithful Creator.   2 Tim. 1:12

5 The elders which are among you I exhort, who am also an elder, and a ᴿwitness of the suffer-

ings of Christ, and also a partaker of the ᴿglory that shall be revealed: Matt. 26:37 · Rom. 8:17, 18

2 Feed the flock of God which is among you, taking the oversight *thereof*, not by constraint, but willingly; not for ᵀfilthy lucre, but of a ready mind;   *dishonest gain*

3 Neither as ᴿbeing lords over *God's* heritage, but being ensamples to the flock.   Ezek. 34:4

4 And when ᴿthe chief Shepherd shall appear, ye shall receive ᴿa crown of glory that fadeth not away.   2:25; Heb. 13:20 · 2 Tim. 4:8

5 Likewise, ye younger, submit yourselves unto the elder. Yea, all *of you* be subject one to another, and be clothed with humility: for God resisteth the proud, and giveth grace to the humble.

6 Humble yourselves therefore under the mighty hand of God, that he may exalt you in due time:

7 Casting all your care upon him; for he careth for you.

8 Be sober, be vigilant; because your adversary the devil, as a roaring lion, walketh about, seeking whom he may devour:

9 Whom resist stedfast in the faith, knowing that the same afflictions are ᵀaccomplished in your brethren that are in the world.   *experienced by*

10 But the God of all grace, who hath called us unto his eternal glory by Christ Jesus, after that ye have suffered a while, make you perfect, ᵀstablish, strengthen, settle *you*.   *confirm*

11 To him *be* glory and dominion for ever and ever. A-men'.

12 By Sil'-va-nus, a faithful brother unto you, as I suppose, I have written briefly, exhorting, and testifying that this is the true grace of God wherein ye stand.

13 The *church that is* at Babylon, elected together with *you*, saluteth you; and *so doth* ᴿMarcus my son. Acts 12:12, 25; 15:37, 39; Col. 4:10

14 Greet ye one another with a kiss of ᵀcharity. Peace *be* with you all that are in Christ Jesus. A-men'.   *love*

The Second Epistle of

PETER

FIRST Peter deals with problems from the outside; Second Peter deals with problems from the inside. Peter writes to warn the believers about the false teachers who are peddling damaging doctrine. He begins by urging them to keep close watch on their personal lives. The Christian life demands diligence in pursuing moral excellence, knowledge, self-control, perseverance, godliness, brotherly kindness, and selfless love. By contrast, the false teachers are sensual, arrogant, greedy, and covetous. They scoff at the thought of future judgment and live their lives as if the present would be the pattern for the future. Peter reminds them that although God may be longsuffering in sending judgment, ultimately it will come. In view of that fact, believers should live lives of godliness, blamelessness, and steadfastness.

The statement of authorship in 1:1 is very clear: "Simon Peter, a servant and an apostle of Jesus Christ." To distinguish this epistle from the first by Peter it was given the Greek title *Petrou B*, the "Second of Peter."

SIMON Peter, a servant and an [R]apostle of Jesus Christ, to them that have obtained like precious faith with us through the righteousness of God and our Saviour Jesus Christ: Gal. 2:8

2 [R]Grace and peace be multiplied unto you [T]through the knowledge of God, and of Jesus our Lord,   Dan. 4:1 · *in*

3 According as his [R]divine power hath given unto us all things that *pertain* unto life and godliness, through the knowledge of him [R]that hath called us to glory and virtue: 1 Pet. 1:5 · 1 Pet. 5:10

4 Whereby are given unto us exceeding great and precious promises: that by these ye might be partakers of the divine nature, having escaped the corruption that is in the world through lust.

5 And beside this, [R]giving all diligence, add to your faith virtue; and to virtue knowledge;   3:18

6 And to knowledge temperance; and to temperance patience; and to patience godliness;

7 And to godliness brotherly kindness; and [R]to brotherly kindness [T]charity.   Gal. 6:10 · *love*

8 For if these things be in you, and abound, they make *you that ye shall* neither *be* [T]barren [R]nor unfruitful in the knowledge of our Lord Jesus Christ. *useless* · [John 15:2]

9 But he that lacketh these things is blind, and cannot see afar off, and hath forgotten that he was purged from his old sins.

10 Wherefore the rather, brethren, give diligence [R]to make your calling and election sure: for if ye do these things, ye shall never [T]fall: 2 Cor. 13:5; 1 John 3:19 · *stumble*

11 For so an entrance shall be [T]ministered unto you abundantly into the everlasting kingdom of our Lord and Saviour Jesus Christ.   *supplied*

12 Wherefore I will not be negligent to put you always in remembrance of these things, though ye know *them*, and be established in the present truth.

13 Yea, I think it [T]meet, [R]as long as I am in this tabernacle, [R]to stir you up by putting *you* in remembrance;   *is right* · [2 Cor. 5:1, 4] · 3:1

14 Knowing that shortly I must put off *this* my tabernacle, even as [R]our Lord Jesus Christ hath shewed me.   John 13:36; 21:18, 19

15 Moreover I will endeavour that ye may be able after my [T]decease to have these things always in remembrance.   *death*

16 For we have not followed cunningly devised fables, when we made known unto you the power and [R]coming of our Lord Jesus Christ, but were eyewitnesses of his majesty.   [1 Pet. 5:4]

17 For he received from God the Father honour and glory, when there came such a voice to him from the excellent glory, [R]This is my beloved Son, in whom I am well pleased.   Matt. 17:5; Mark 9:7

18 And this voice which came from heaven we heard, when we were with him in the holy mount.

19 We have also a more sure word of prophecy; whereunto ye do well that ye take heed, as unto a light that shineth in a dark place, until the day dawn, and the day star arise in your hearts:

20 Knowing this first, that no prophecy of the scripture is of any private [T]interpretation.   Or *origin*

21 For the prophecy came not in old time by the will of man: but holy men of God spake *as they were* moved by the Holy Ghost.

2 But there were false prophets also among the people, even as there shall be [R]false teachers among you, who privily shall bring in damnable heresies, even denying the Lord that bought them, and bring upon themselves swift destruction.   1 Tim. 4:1, 2

2 And many shall follow their [T]pernicious ways; by reason of whom the way of truth shall be evil spoken of.   *destructive*

3 And through covetousness shall they with feigned words make merchandise of you: whose

judgment now of a long time lingereth not, and their [T]damnation slumbereth not.   *destruction*

4 For if God spared not the angels that sinned, but cast *them* down to [T]hell, and delivered *them* into chains of darkness, to be reserved unto judgment;   Gr. *tartarus*

5 And spared not the old world, but saved Noah the eighth *person,* a preacher of righteousness, bringing in the flood upon the world of the ungodly;

6 And turning the cities of [R]Sodom and Go-mor'-rha into ashes condemned *them* with an overthrow, making *them* an ensample unto those that after should live ungodly;   Gen. 19:1–26

7 And [R]delivered just Lot, vexed with the filthy conversation of the wicked: Gen. 19:16, 29

8 (For that righteous man dwelling among them, [R]in seeing and hearing, vexed *his* righteous soul from day to day with *their* unlawful deeds;)   Ps. 119:139

9 [R]The Lord knoweth how to deliver the godly out of temptations, and to reserve the unjust unto the day of judgment to be punished: Ps. 34:15–19; 1 Cor. 10:13

10 But chiefly [R]them that walk after the flesh in the lust of uncleanness, and despise government. Presumptuous *are they,* selfwilled, they are not afraid to speak evil of dignities.   Jude 4, 7, 8

11 Whereas [R]angels, which are greater in power and might, bring not railing accusation against them before the Lord.   Jude 9

12 But these, [R]as natural brute beasts, made to be [T]taken and destroyed, speak evil of the things that they understand not; and shall utterly perish in their own corruption;   Jude 10 · *caught*

13 And shall receive the reward of unrighteousness, *as* they that count it pleasure to riot in the day time. [R]Spots *they are* and blemishes, sporting themselves with their own deceivings while they feast with you;   Jude 12

14 Having eyes full of adultery, and that cannot cease from sin; [T]beguiling unstable souls: [R]an heart they have [T]exercised with covetous practices; cursed children: *enticing* · Jude 11 · *trained*

15 Which have forsaken the right way, and are gone astray, following the way of [R]Ba'-laam *the son* of Bo'-sor, who loved the wages of unrighteousness; Rev. 2:14

16 But was rebuked for his iniquity: the dumb [T]ass speaking with man's voice [T]forbad the madness of the prophet.   *donkey · restrained*

17 These are wells without water, clouds that are carried with a tempest; to whom the mist of darkness is reserved for ever.

18 For when they speak great swelling *words* of vanity, they allure through the lusts of the flesh, *through much* wantonness, those that were clean escaped from them who live in error.

19 While they promise them liberty, they themselves are the servants of corruption: [R]for of whom a man is overcome, of the same is he brought in bondage.   John 8:34

20 For if after they [R]have escaped the pollutions of the world through the knowledge of the Lord and Saviour Jesus Christ, they are [R]again entangled therein, and overcome, the latter end is worse with them than the beginning. Matt. 12:45 · Luke 11:26; [Heb. 6:4–6]

21 For [R]it had been better for them not to have known the way of righteousness, than, after they have known *it,* to turn from the holy commandment delivered unto them.   Luke 12:47

22 But it is happened unto them according to the true proverb, [R]The dog [T]*is* turned to his own vomit again; and the sow that was washed to her wallowing in the mire.   Prov. 26:11 · *returns*

3 This second epistle, beloved, I now write unto you; in *both* which [R]I stir up your pure minds by way of remembrance: 1:13

2 That ye may be mindful of the words which were spoken before by the holy prophets, and

of the commandment of us the apostles of the Lord and Saviour: 3 Knowing this first, that there shall come in the last days ^Tscoffers, ^Rwalking ^Tafter their own lusts,   *mockers* · 2:10 · *according to*

4 And saying, Where is the promise of his coming? for since the fathers fell asleep, all things continue as *they were* from the beginning of the creation.

5 For this they willingly are ignorant of, that ^Rby the word of God the heavens were of old, and the earth standing out of the water and in the water: Gen. 1:6, 9

6 ^RWhereby the world that then was, being overflowed with water, perished: Gen. 7:11, 12, 21–23

7 But ^Rthe heavens and the earth, which are now, by the same word are kept in store, reserved unto ^Rfire against the day of judgment and perdition of ungodly men.   vv. 10, 12 · Matt. 25:41; [2 Thess. 1:8]

8 But, beloved, be not ignorant of this one thing, that one day *is* with the Lord as a thousand years, and ^Ra thousand years as one day.   Ps. 90:4

9 The Lord is not slack concerning his promise, as some men count slackness; but is longsuffering to us-ward, not willing that any should perish, but that all should come to repentance.

☆ 10 But the day of the Lord will come as a thief in the night; in the which ^Rthe heavens shall pass away with a great noise, and the elements shall melt with fervent heat, the earth also and the works that are therein shall be burned up.   Ps. 102:25, 26; Is. 51:6; Rev. 20:11

11 *Seeing* then *that* all these things shall be dissolved, what manner *of persons* ought ye to be ^Rin *all* holy ^Tconversation and godliness,   1 Pet. 1:15 · *conduct*

12 ^RLooking for and hasting unto the coming of the day of God, wherein the heavens being on fire shall ^Rbe dissolved, and the elements shall ^Rmelt with fervent heat?   Titus 2:13–15 · Ps. 50:3 · Is. 24:19

13 Nevertheless we, according to his promise, look for ^Rnew heavens and a new earth, wherein dwelleth righteousness.   Is. 65:17

14 Wherefore, beloved, seeing that ye look for such things, be diligent ^Rthat ye may be found of him in peace, without spot, and blameless.   1 Cor. 1:8; 15:58

15 And ^Taccount *that* ^Rthe long-suffering of our Lord *is* salvation; even as our beloved brother Paul also according to the wisdom given unto him hath written unto you;   Ps. 86:15; Rom. 2:4; 1 Pet. 3:20

16 As also in all *his* epistles, speaking in them of these things; in which are some things hard to be understood, which they that are unlearned and unstable wrest, as *they do* also the other scriptures, unto their own destruction.

17 Ye therefore, beloved, seeing ye know *these things* before, beware lest ye also, being led away with the error of the wicked, fall from your own stedfastness.

18 But grow in grace, and *in* the knowledge of our Lord and Saviour Jesus Christ. ^RTo him *be* glory both now and for ever. A-men'.   Rom. 11:36; 2 Tim. 4:18; Rev. 1:6

The First Epistle of

JOHN

GOD is light; God is love; and God is life. John is enjoying a delightful fellowship with that God of light, love, and life, and he desperately desires that his spiritual children enjoy the same fellowship.

God is light. Therefore, to engage in fellowship with Him we must walk in light and not in darkness. As we walk in the light, we will regularly confess our sins, allowing the blood of Christ to continually cleanse us. Two major roadblocks to hinder this walk will be falling in love with the world and falling for the alluring lies of false teachers.

God is love. Since we are His children we must walk in love. In fact, John says that if we do not love, we do not know God. Love is more than just words; it is actions. Love is giving, not getting. Biblical love is unconditional in its nature. Christ's love fulfilled those qualities and when that brand of love characterizes us, we will be free of self-condemnation and experience confidence before God.

God is life. Those who fellowship with Him must possess His quality of life. Spiritual life begins with spiritual birth which occurs through faith in Jesus Christ. Faith in Jesus Christ infuses us with God's life—eternal life.

Although the apostle John's name is not found in this book, it was given the title *Ioannou A*, the "First of John."

THAT which was from the beginning, which we have heard, which we have seen with our eyes, which we have looked upon, and ^Rour hands have handled, of the Word of life; Luke 24:39; John 20:27

2 (For ^Rthe life was manifested, and we have seen *it*, ^Rand bear witness, and shew unto you that eternal life, which was with the Father, and was manifested unto us;) John 1:4 · John 21:24

3 That which we have seen and heard declare we unto you, that ye also may have fellowship with us: and truly our fellowship *is* ^Rwith the Father, and with his Son Jesus Christ. 2:24; John 17:21; 1 Cor. 1:9

4 And these things write we unto you, ^Rthat your joy may be full. John 15:11; 16:24; 1 Pet. 1:8

5 ^RThis then is the message which we have heard of him, and declare unto you, that ^RGod is light, and in him is no darkness at all. John 1:19 · [1 Tim. 6:16]; James 1:17

6 ^RIf we say that we have fellowship with him, and walk in darkness, we lie, and do not the truth: [John 8:12]; 2 Cor. 6:14

7 But if we ^Rwalk in the light, as he is in the light, we have fellowship one with another, and the blood of Jesus Christ his Son cleanseth us from all sin. Is. 2:5

8 If we say that we have no sin, we deceive ourselves, and the truth is not in us.

9 If we ^Rconfess our sins, he is faithful and just to forgive us *our* sins, and to ^Rcleanse us from all unrighteousness. Ps. 32:5 · Ps. 51:2

10 If we say that we have not sinned, we ^Rmake him a liar, and his word is not in us. John 3:33

2 My little children, these things write I unto you, that ye sin not. And if any man sin, we have an advocate with the Father, Jesus Christ the righteous:

2 And ^Rhe is the propitiation for our sins: and not for our's only, but ^Ralso for *the sins of* the whole world. 4:10; Heb. 2:17 · John 1:29

3 And hereby we do know that we know him, if we keep his commandments.

4 He that saith, I know him, and keepeth not his commandments, is a ^Rliar, and the truth is not in him. Rom. 3:4

5 But ^Rwhoso keepeth his word, in him verily is the love of God perfected: hereby know we that we are in him. John 14:21, 23

6 ^RHe that saith he abideth in him ought himself also so to walk, even as he walked. John 15:4

7 Brethren, I write no new commandment unto you, but an old commandment which ye had from the beginning. The old commandment is the word which ye have heard from the beginning.

8 Again, ^Ra new commandment I write unto you, which thing is

true in him and in you: because the darkness is past, and the true light now shineth.   John 13:34; 15:12

9 ^RHe that saith he is in the light, and hateth his brother, is in darkness even until now.   3:14

10 He that loveth his brother abideth in the light, and ^Rthere is ^Tnone occasion of stumbling in him.   2 Pet. 1:10 · *no cause for*

11 But he that hateth his brother is in darkness, and ^Rwalketh in darkness, and knoweth not whither he goeth, because that darkness hath blinded his eyes.   1:6

12 I write unto you, little children, because your sins are forgiven you for his name's sake.

13 I write unto you, fathers, because ye have known him *that is* from the beginning. I write unto you, young men, because ye have overcome the wicked one. I write unto you, little children, because ye have known the Father.

14 I have written unto you, fathers, because ye have known him *that is* from the beginning. I have written unto you, young men, because ye are strong, and the word of God abideth in you, and ye have overcome the wicked one.

15 Love not the world, neither the things *that are* in the world. If any man love the world, the love of the Father is not in him.

16 For all that *is* in the world, the lust of the flesh, ^Rand the lust of the eyes, and the pride of life, is not of the Father, but is of the world.   [Eccl. 5:10, 11]

17 And ^Rthe world passeth away, and the lust thereof: but he that doeth the will of God abideth for ever.   1 Cor. 7:31; 1 Pet. 1:24

18 Little children, ^Rit is the last time: and as ye have heard that ^Ran'-ti-christ shall come, even now are there many an'-ti-christs; whereby we know that it is the last time.   1 Tim. 4:1 · 2 Thess. 2:3

19 They went out from us, but they were not of us; for ^Rif they had been of us, they would *no doubt* have continued with us: but *they went out*, ^Rthat they might be

made manifest that they were not all of us.   Matt. 24:24 · 1 Cor. 11:19

20 But ^Rye have an unction from the Holy One, and ye know all things.   v. 27; 2 Cor. 1:21; Heb. 1:9;

21 I have not written unto you because ye know not the truth, but because ye know it, and that no lie is of the truth.

22 ^RWho is a liar but he that denieth that ^RJesus is the Christ? He is an'-ti-christ, that denieth the Father and the Son.   2 John 7 · 4:3

23 Whosoever denieth the Son, the same hath not the ^RFather: [*but*] *he that acknowledgeth the Son hath the Father also.*   John 5:23

24 Let that therefore abide in you, ^Rwhich ye have heard from the beginning. If that which ye have heard from the beginning shall remain in you, ^Rye also shall continue in the Son, and in the Father.   2 John 6, 7 · John 14:23; 2 John 9

25 ^RAnd this is the promise that he hath promised us, *even* eternal life.   John 3:14–16; 6:40; 17:2, 3

26 These *things* have I written unto you concerning them that ^Tseduce you.   *try to deceive*

27 But the ^Ranointing which ye have received of him abideth in you, and ye need not that any man teach you: but as the same anointing teacheth you of all things, and is truth, and is no lie, and even as it hath taught you, ye shall abide in him.   v. 20

28 And now, little children, abide in him; that, when he shall appear, we may have ^Rconfidence, and not be ashamed before him at his coming.   3:21; 4:17; 5:14

29 ^RIf ye know that he is righteous, ye know that ^Revery one that doeth righteousness is born of him.   Acts 22:14 · 3:7, 10; John 7:18

3 Behold, ^Rwhat manner of love the Father hath bestowed upon us, that ^Rwe should be called the sons of God: therefore the world knoweth us not, because it knew him not.   [John 3:16] · [John 1:12]

2 Beloved, now are we the sons of God, and it doth not yet appear what we shall be: but we know

that, when he shall appear, [R]we shall be like him; for we shall see him as he is.   Rom. 8:29; 2 Pet. 1:4

3 [R]And every man that hath this hope in him purifieth himself, even as he is pure.   4:17

4 Whosoever committeth sin transgresseth also the law: for [R]sin is [T]the transgression of the law.   5:17; Rom. 4:15 · *lawlessness*

5 And ye know [R]that he was manifested to take away our sins; and in him is no sin.   v. 8; 1:2

6 Whosoever abideth in him sinneth not: whosoever sinneth hath not seen him, neither known him.

7 Little children, let no man deceive you: he that [T]doeth righteousness is righteous, even as he is righteous.   *practises*

8 He that committeth sin is of the devil; for the devil sinneth from the beginning. For this purpose the Son of God was manifested, [R]that he might destroy the works of the devil.   Luke 10:18

9 Whosoever is born of God doth not commit sin; for his seed remaineth in him: and he cannot sin, because he is born of God.

10 In this the children of God are manifest, and the children of the devil: whosoever doeth not righteousness is not of God, neither he that loveth not his brother.

11 For this is the message that ye heard from the beginning, that we should love one another.

12 Not as Cain, *who* was of that wicked one, and slew his brother. And wherefore slew he him? Because his own works were evil, and his brother's righteous.

13 Marvel not, my brethren, if [R]the world hate you.   [John 15:18]

14 We know that we have passed from death unto life, because we love the brethren. He that loveth not *his* brother abideth in death.

15 [R]Whosoever hateth his brother is a murderer: and ye know that no murderer hath eternal life abiding in him.   Matt. 5:21; John 8:44

16 Hereby perceive we the love of God, because he laid down his life for us: and we ought to lay down *our* lives for the brethren.

17 But whoso hath this world's good, and seeth his brother have need, and shutteth up his bowels *of compassion* from him, how dwelleth the love of God in him?

18 My little children, [R]let us not love in word, neither in tongue; but in deed and in truth.   Ezek. 33:31

19 And hereby we know that we are of the truth, and shall [T]assure our hearts before him.   *persuade*

20 [R]For if our heart condemn us, God is greater than our heart, and knoweth all things.   [1 Cor. 4:4, 5]

21 Beloved, if our heart condemn us not, [R]*then* have we confidence toward God.   [2:28; 5:14]

22 And [R]whatsoever we ask, we receive of him, because we keep his commandments, and do those things that are pleasing in his sight.   5:14, 15; Ps. 34:15; [John 15:7]

23 And this is his commandment, That we should believe on the name of his Son Jesus Christ, [R]and love one another, as he gave us commandment.   Matt. 22:39

24 And he that keepeth his commandments dwelleth in him, and he in him. And [R]hereby we know that he abideth in us, by the Spirit which he hath given us.   John 14:17

4 Beloved, believe not every spirit, but try the spirits whether they are of God: because [R]many false prophets are gone out into the world.   Matt. 24:5

2 Hereby know ye the Spirit of God: [R]Every spirit that confesseth that Jesus Christ is come in the flesh is of God: [Rom. 10:8–10]

3 And every spirit that confesseth not that Jesus Christ is come in the flesh is not of God: and this is that *spirit* of an′-ti-christ, whereof ye have heard that it should come; and even now already is it in the world.

4 Ye are of God, little children, and have overcome them: because greater is he that is in you, than [R]he that is in the world.   John 14:30

5 [R]They are of the world: there-

fore speak they of the world, and the world heareth them.   John 3:31

6 We are of God: he that knoweth God heareth us; he that is not of God heareth not us. Hereby know we the spirit of truth, and the spirit of error.

7 ^RBeloved, let us love one another: for love is of God; and every one that loveth is born of God, and knoweth God.   3:10, 11, 23

8 He that loveth not knoweth not God; for God is love.

9 ^RIn this was manifested the love of God toward us, because that God sent his only begotten ^RSon into the world, that we might live through him.   Rom. 5:8 · Is. 9:6, 7

10 Herein is love, ^Rnot that we loved God, but that he loved us, and sent his Son ^R*to be* the propitiation for our sins.   Titus 3:5 · 2:2

11 Beloved, if God so loved us, we ought also to love one another.

12 ^RNo man hath seen God at any time. If we love one another, God dwelleth in us, and his love is perfected in us.   John 1:18; 1 Tim. 6:16

13 ^RHereby know we that we dwell in him, and he in us, because he hath given us of his Spirit.   John 14:20

14 And ^Rwe have seen and do testify that ^Rthe Father sent the Son *to be* the Saviour of the world.   John 1:14 · John 3:17; 4:42

15 Whosoever shall confess that Jesus is the Son of God, God dwelleth in him, and he in God.

16 And we have known and believed the love that God hath to us. God is love; and he that dwelleth in love dwelleth in God, and God ^Rin him.   [John 14:23]

17 Herein is our love made perfect, that we may have boldness in the day of judgment: because as he is, so are we in this world.

18 There is no fear in love; but perfect love casteth out fear: because fear ^Thath torment. He that feareth is not made perfect in love.   *involves*

19 ^RWe love him, because he first loved us.   v. 10

20 If a man say, I love God, and hateth his brother, he is a liar: for he that loveth not his brother whom he hath seen, how can he love God whom he hath not seen?

21 And this commandment have we from him, That he who loveth God love his brother also.

5 Whosoever believeth that ^RJesus is the Christ is born of God: and every one that loveth him that begat loveth him also that is begotten of him.   2:22; 4:2, 15

2 By this we know that we love the children of God, when we love God, and ^Rkeep his commandments.   John 15:10; 2 John 6

3 ^RFor this is the love of God, that we keep his commandments: and ^Rhis commandments are not grievous.   John 14:15 · Matt. 11:30

4 For ^Rwhatsoever is born of God overcometh the world: and this is the victory that overcometh the world, *even* our faith. John 16:33

5 Who is he that overcometh the world, but he that believeth that Jesus is the Son of God?

6 This is he that came by water and blood, *even* Jesus Christ; not by water only, but by water and blood. ^RAnd it is the Spirit that beareth witness, because the Spirit is truth.   [John 14:17]

7 For there are three that bear ^Trecord in heaven, the Father, the Word, and the Holy Ghost: and these three are one.   *witness*

8 And there are three that bear witness in earth, ^Rthe spirit, and the water, and the blood: and these three agree in one. John 15:26

9 If we receive ^Rthe witness of men, the witness of God is greater: ^Rfor this is the witness of God which he hath testified of his Son.   John 5:34, 37; 8:17, 18 · John 5:32, 37

10 He that believeth on the Son of God hath the witness in himself: he that believeth not God ^Rhath made him a liar; because he believeth not the record that God gave of his Son.   John 3:18, 33

11 And this is the ^Trecord, that God hath given to us eternal life, and this life is in his Son. *testimony*

12 ^RHe that hath the Son hath

life; *and* he that hath not the Son of God hath not life.   [John 6:47]

13 These things have I written unto you that believe on the name of the Son of God; that ye may know that ye have eternal life, and that ye may believe on the name of the Son of God.

14 And this is the confidence that we have in him, that, ᴿif we ask any thing according to his will, he heareth us: [2:28; 3:21, 22]

15 And if we know that he hear us, whatsoever we ask, we know that we have the petitions that we ᵀdesired of him.   *asked*

16 If any man see his brother sin a sin *which is* not unto death, he shall ask, and ᴿhe shall give him life for them that sin not unto death. ᴿThere is a sin unto death:

ᴿI do not say that he shall pray for it.   Job 42:8 · [Matt. 12:31] · Jer. 7:16; 14:11

17 All unrighteousness is sin: and there is a sin not unto death.

18 We know that ᴿwhosoever is born of God sinneth not; but he that is begotten of God ᴿkeepeth himself, and that wicked one toucheth him not.   3:9 · James 1:27

19 *And* we know that we are of God, and ᴿthe whole world lieth in wickedness.   John 12:31; 17:15; Gal. 1:4

20 And we know that the ᴿSon of God is come, and hath given us an understanding, that we may know him that is true, *even* in his Son Jesus Christ. This is the true God, ᴿand eternal life.   4:2 · vv. 11, 12

21 Little children, keep yourselves from idols. A-men'.

The Second Epistle of
JOHN

"LET him that thinketh he standeth take heed lest he fall" (1 Cor. 10:12). These words of the apostle Paul could well stand as a subtitle for John's little epistle. The recipients, a chosen lady and her children, were obviously standing. They were walking in truth, remaining faithful to the commandments they had received from the Father. John is deeply pleased to be able to commend them. But he takes nothing for granted. Realizing that standing is just one step removed from falling, he hesitates not at all to issue a reminder: "love one another" (v. 5). The apostle admits that this is not new revelation, but he views it sufficiently important to repeat. Loving one another, he stresses, is equivalent to walking according to God's commandments.

John indicates, however, that this love must be discerning. It is not a naive, unthinking, open to anything and anyone kind of love. Biblical love is a matter of choice; it is dangerous and foolish to float through life with undiscerning love. False teachers abound who do not acknowledge Christ as having come in the flesh. It is false charity to open the door to false teaching. We must have fellowship with God. We must have fellowship with Christians. But we must not have fellowship with false teachers.

The "elder" of verse 1 has been traditionally identified with the apostle John, resulting in the Greek title *Ioannou B*, the "Second of John."

THE elder unto the ᵀelect lady and her children, whom I love in the truth; and not I only, but also all they that have known ᴿthe truth;   *chosen* · Col. 1:5

2 For the truth's sake, which ᵀdwelleth in us, and shall be with us for ever.   *abides*

3 ᴿGrace ᵀbe with you, mercy, *and* peace, from God the Father,

and from the Lord Jesus Christ, the Son of the Father, in truth and love. Rom. 1:7; 1 Tim. 1:2 · *will be*

4 I rejoiced greatly that I found of thy children walking in truth, as we have received a commandment from the Father.

5 And now I beseech thee, lady, not as though I wrote a new commandment unto thee, but that which we had from the beginning, that we love one another.

6 And this is love, that we walk after his commandments. This is the commandment, That, ^Ras ye have heard from the beginning, ye should walk in it. 1 John 2:24

7 For ^Rmany deceivers are entered into the world, who confess not that Jesus Christ is come in the flesh. This is a deceiver and an an'-ti-christ. 1 John 2:19; 4:1

8 ^RLook to yourselves, ^Rthat we lose not those things which we have wrought, but that we receive a full reward. Mark 13:9 · Gal. 3:4

9 ^RWhosoever transgresseth, and abideth not in the doctrine of Christ, hath not God. He that abideth in the doctrine of Christ, he hath both the Father and the Son. John 7:16; 8:31; 1 John 2:19, 23, 24

10 If there come any unto you, and bring ^Rnot this doctrine, receive him not into *your* house, neither bid him God speed: Titus 3:10

11 For he that ^Tbiddeth him God speed ^Tis partaker of his evil deeds. *greets him · shares in*

12 Having many things to write unto you, I would not *write* with paper and ink: but I trust to come unto you, and speak face to face, ^Rthat our joy may be full. John 17:13

13 ^RThe children of thy elect sister greet thee. A-men'. 1 Pet. 5:13

The Third Epistle of

JOHN

IN Third John the apostle encourages fellowship with Christian brothers. Following his expression of love for Gaius, John assures him of his prayers for his health and voices his joy over Gaius's persistent walk in truth and for the manner in which he shows hospitality and support for missionaries who have come to his church.

But not everyone in the church feels the same way. Diotrephes' heart is one hundred and eighty degrees removed from Gaius's heart. He is no longer living in love. Pride has taken precedence in his life. He has refused a letter John has written for the church, fearing that his authority might be superseded by that of the apostle. He also has accused John of evil words and refused to accept missionaries. He forbids others to do so and even expels them from the church if they disobey him. John uses this negative example as an opportunity to encourage Gaius to continue his hospitality. Demetrius has a good testimony and may even be one of those turned away by Diotrephes. He is widely known for his good character and his loyalty to the truth. Here he is well commended by John and stands as a positive example for Gaius.

The Greek titles of First, Second, and Third John are *Ioannou A, B,* and *G.* The *G* is gamma, the third letter of the Greek alphabet; *Ioannou G* means the "Third of John."

THE elder unto the wellbeloved Ga'-ius, ^Rwhom I love ^Tin the truth.   2 John 1 · Lit. *in truth*

2 Beloved, I ^Twish above all things that thou mayest prosper and be in health, even as thy soul prospereth.   *pray that in all things*

3 For I ^Rrejoiced greatly, when the brethren came and testified of the truth that is in thee, even as thou walkest in the truth.   2 John 4

4 I have no greater ^Rjoy than to hear that my children walk in truth.   1 Thess. 2:19, 20

5 Beloved, thou doest faithfully whatsoever thou doest ^Tto the brethren, and ^Tto strangers;   *for*

6 Which have borne witness of thy ^Tcharity before the church: whom if thou ^Tbring forward on their journey after a godly sort, thou shalt do well: *love · send*

7 Because that for his name's sake they went forth, ^Rtaking nothing of the Gentiles.   1 Cor. 9:12

8 We therefore ought to ^Rreceive such, that we might be fellowhelpers to the truth.   1 Pet. 4:9

9 I wrote unto the church: but Di-ot'-re-phes, who loveth to have the preeminence among them, receiveth us not.

10 Wherefore, if I come, I will remember his deeds which he doeth, prating against us with malicious words: and not content therewith, neither doth he himself receive the brethren, and forbiddeth them that would, and ^Tcasteth *them* out of the church.   *puts*

11 Beloved, ^Rfollow not that which is evil, but that which is good. He that doeth good is of God: but he that doeth evil hath not seen God.   1 Tim. 6:11; 2 Tim. 2:22

12 De-me'-tri-us ^Rhath good report of all *men*, and of the truth itself: yea, and we *also* bear record; ^Rand ye know that our record is true.   1 Tim. 3:7 · John 19:35

13 ^RI had many things to write, but I will not with ink and pen write unto thee: 2 John 12

14 But I trust I shall shortly see thee, and we shall speak face to face. Peace *be* to thee. *Our* friends ^Tsalute thee. Greet the friends by name.   *greet*

The Epistle of
JUDE

FIGHT! Contend! Do battle! When apostasy arises, when false teachers emerge, when the truth of God is attacked, it is time to fight for the faith. Only believers who are spiritually "in shape" can answer the summons. At the beginning of his letter Jude focuses on the believers' common salvation, but then feels compelled to challenge them to contend for the faith. The danger is real. False teachers have crept into the church turning God's grace into unbounded license to do as they please. Jude reminds such men of God's past dealings with unbelieving Israel, disobedient angels, and wicked Sodom and Gomorrah. In the face of such danger Christians should not be caught off guard. The challenge is great, but so is the God who is able to keep them from stumbling.

The Greek title *Iouda*, "Of Jude," comes from the name *Ioudas* which appears in verse 1. This name, which can be translated Jude or Judas, was popular in the first century because of Judas Maccabaeus (died 160 B.C.), a leader of the Jewish resistance against Syria during the Maccabean revolt.

JUDE, the servant of Jesus Christ, and brother of James, to them that are sanctified by God the Father, and ᴿpreserved in Jesus Christ, *and* called: John 17:1

2 Mercy unto you, and ᴿpeace, and love, be multiplied.   1 Pet. 1:2

3 Beloved, when I gave all diligence to write unto you ᴿof the common salvation, it was needful for me to write unto you, and exhort *you* that ᴿye should earnestly contend for the faith which was once delivered unto the saints.   Titus 1:4 · Phil. 1:27

4 For there are certain men crept in ᵀunawares, who were before of old ordained to this condemnation, ungodly men, turning the grace of our God into lasciviousness, and denying the only Lord God, and our Lord Jesus Christ.   *unnoticed*

5 I will therefore put you in remembrance, though ye once knew this, how that the Lord, having saved the people out of the land of Egypt, afterward destroyed them that believed not.

6 And the angels which kept not their ᵀfirst estate, but left their own habitation, he hath reserved in everlasting chains under darkness unto the judgment of the great day.   *proper domain*

7 Even as Sodom and Go-mor'-rha, and the cities about them in like manner, giving themselves over to fornication, and going after strange flesh, are set forth for an example, suffering the vengeance of eternal fire.

8 ᴿLikewise also these *filthy* dreamers defile the flesh, despise dominion, and ᴿspeak evil of dignities.   2 Pet. 2:10 · Ex. 22:28

9 Yet Mi'-cha-el the archangel, when contending with the devil he disputed about the body of Moses, durst not bring against him a railing accusation, but said, ᴿThe Lord rebuke thee.   Zech. 3:2

10 ᴿBut these speak evil of those things which they know not: but what they know naturally, as

brute beasts, in those things they corrupt themselves.   2 Pet. 2:12

11 Woe unto them! for they have gone in the way of Cain, and ᴿran greedily after the error of Ba'-laam for reward, and perished in the gainsaying of Co'-re.   Num. 31:16

12 These are spots in your feasts of charity, when they feast with you, feeding themselves without fear: clouds *they are* without water, carried about of winds; trees whose fruit withereth, without fruit, twice dead, plucked up by the roots;

13 ᴿRaging waves of the sea, foaming out their own shame; wandering stars, ᴿto whom is reserved the blackness of darkness for ever.   Is. 57:20 · 2 Pet. 2:17

14 And E'-noch also, the seventh ★ from Adam, prophesied of these, saying, Behold, the Lord cometh with ten thousands of his saints,

15 To execute judgment upon all, and to convince all that are ungodly among them of all their ungodly deeds which they have ungodly committed, and of all their ᴿhard *speeches* which ungodly sinners have spoken against him.   1 Sam. 2:3

16 These are murmurers, complainers, walking after their own lusts; and their ᴿmouth speaketh great swelling *words,* having men's persons in admiration because of advantage.   2 Pet. 2:18

17 ᴿBut, beloved, remember ye the words which were spoken before ᵀof the apostles of our Lord Jesus Christ;   2 Pet. 3:2 · *by*

18 How that they told you ᴿthere should be mockers in the last time, who should walk after their own ungodly lusts.   2 Tim. 3:1; 4:3

19 These be they who ᵀseparate themselves, ᵀsensual, having not the Spirit.   *cause divisions · worldly*

20 But ye, beloved, building up yourselves on your most holy faith, praying in the Holy Ghost,

21 Keep yourselves in the love

of God, [R]looking for the mercy of our Lord Jesus Christ unto eternal life.   Titus 2:13; Heb. 9:28; 2 Pet. 3:12

22 And of some have compassion, making a difference:

23 And others [R]save with fear, [R]pulling *them* out of the fire; hating even the garment spotted by the flesh.   Rom. 11:14 · Amos 4:11

24 [R]Now unto him that is able to keep you from [T]falling, and [R]to present *you* faultless before the presence of his glory with exceeding joy, [Eph. 3:20] · *stumbling* · Col. 1:22

25 To the only wise God our Saviour, *be* glory and majesty, dominion and power, both now and ever. A-men'.

THE REVELATION
of Jesus Christ

JUST as Genesis is the book of beginnings, Revelation is the book of consummation. In it, the divine program of redemption is brought to fruition, and the holy name of God is vindicated before all creation. Although there are numerous prophecies in the Gospels and Epistles, Revelation is the only New Testament book that focuses primarily on prophetic events. Its title means "unveiling" or "disclosure." Thus, the book is an unveiling of the character and program of God. Penned by John during his exile on the island of Patmos, Revelation centers around visions and symbols of the resurrected Christ, who alone has authority to judge the earth, to remake it, and to rule it in righteousness.

    The title of this book in the Greek text is *Apokalypsis Ioannou,* "Revelation of John." It is also known as the Apocalypse, a transliteration of the word *apokalypsis,* meaning "unveiling," "disclosure," or "revelation." Thus, the book is an unveiling of that which otherwise could not be known. A better title comes from the first verse: *Apokalypsis Iesou Christou,* "Revelation of Jesus Christ." This could be taken as a revelation which came from Christ or as a revelation which is about Christ—both are appropriate. Because of the unified contents of this book, it should not be called Revelations.

THE Revelation of Jesus Christ, which God gave unto him, to shew unto his servants things which must shortly come to pass; and he sent and signified *it* by his angel unto his servant John:

2 Who [T]bare record of the word of God, and of the testimony of Jesus Christ, and of all things [R]that he saw. *bore witness* · 1 John 1:1

3 [R]Blessed *is* he that readeth, and they that hear the words of this prophecy, and keep those things which are written therein: for [R]the time *is* at hand. 22:7 · 22:10

4 John to the seven churches which are in Asia: Grace *be* unto you, and peace, from him [R]which is, and [R]which was, and which is to come; [R]and from the seven Spirits which are before his throne; Ex. 3:14 · John 1:1 · 3:1; 4:5; 5:6

5 And from Jesus Christ, *who is* the faithful witness, *and* the [R]first begotten of the dead, and [R]the prince of the kings of the earth. Unto him that loved us, and washed us from our sins in his own blood, 1 Cor. 15:20 · 17:14

6 And hath [R]made us kings and

priests unto God and his Father; to him *be* glory and dominion for ever and ever. A-men'. I Pet. 2:5, 9

7 Behold, he cometh with clouds; and every eye shall see him, and ^Rthey *also* which pierced him: and all ^Tkindreds of the earth shall wail because of him. Even so, A-men'. John 19:37 · *the tribes*

8 ^RI am Alpha and Omega, the beginning and the ending, saith the Lord, ^Rwhich is, and which was, and which is to come, the ^RAlmighty. 21:6; 22:13 · 4:8; 11:17 · Is. 9:6

9 I John, who also am your brother, and ^Rcompanion in tribulation, and in the kingdom and patience of Jesus Christ, was in the isle that is called Pat'-mos, for the word of God, and for the testimony of Jesus Christ. Phil. 1:7

10 I was in the Spirit on the Lord's day, and heard behind me ^Ra great voice, as of a trumpet, 4:1

11 Saying, I am Alpha and Omega, the first and the last: and, What thou seest, write in a book, and send *it* unto the seven churches which are in Asia; unto Eph'-e-sus, and unto Smyrna, and unto Per'-ga-mos, and unto Thy-a-ti'-ra, and unto Sar'-dis, and unto Philadelphia, and unto La-od-i-ce'-a.

12 And I turned to see the voice that spake with me. And being turned, ^RI saw seven golden ^Tcandlesticks; 2:1; Zech. 4:2 · *lampstands*

13 And in the midst of the seven candlesticks ^R*one* like unto the Son of man, ^Rclothed with a garment down to the foot, and girt about the ^Tpaps with a golden ^Tgirdle. 14:14 · Dan. 10:5 · *chest · band*

14 His head and ^R*his* hairs *were* white like wool, as white as snow; and ^Rhis eyes *were* as a flame of fire; Dan. 7:9 · 2:18; 19:12; Dan. 10:6

15 ^RAnd his feet like unto fine brass, as if they burned in a furnace; and ^Rhis voice as the sound of many waters. Ezek. 1:7 · Ezek. 1:24

16 And he had in his right hand seven stars: and ^Rout of his mouth went a sharp twoedged sword:

and his countenance *was* as the sun shineth in his strength. 2:12, 16

17 And when I saw him, I fell at his feet as dead. And he laid his right hand upon me, saying unto me, Fear not; ^RI am the first and the last: 2:8; 22:13; Is. 41:4; 44:6; 48:12

18 *I am* he that liveth, and was dead; and, behold, I am alive for evermore, A-men'; and have the keys of ^Thell and of death. Gr. *hades*

19 Write the things which thou hast ^Rseen, and the things which are, ^Rand the things which shall be hereafter; vv. 9–18 · 4:1

20 The mystery of the seven stars which thou sawest in my right hand, and the seven golden candlesticks. The seven stars are ^Rthe ^Tangels of the seven churches: and ^Rthe seven candlesticks which thou sawest are the seven churches. 2:1 · *messengers* · Zech. 4:2

2 Unto the angel of the church of Eph'-e-sus write; These things saith ^Rhe that holdeth the seven stars in his right hand, who walketh in the midst of the seven golden candlesticks; 1:16

2 I know thy works, and thy labour, and thy patience, and how thou canst not bear them which are evil: and thou hast tried them which say they are apostles, and are not, and hast found them liars:

3 And hast ^Tborne, and hast patience, and for my name's sake hast laboured, and hast not ^Tfainted. *persevered · become weary*

4 Nevertheless I have *some-what* against thee, because thou hast left thy first love.

5 Remember therefore from whence thou art fallen, and repent, and do the first works; ^Ror else I will come unto thee quickly, and will remove thy ^Tcandlestick out of his place, ^Texcept thou repent. Matt. 21:41 · *lampstand · unless*

6 But this thou hast, that thou hatest the deeds of the Nic-o-la'-i-tanes, which I also hate.

7 ^RHe that hath an ear, let him hear what the Spirit saith unto the churches; To him that overcometh will I give ^Rto eat of the tree of life,

which is in the midst of the paradise of God.   Matt. 11:15 · [22:2, 14]

8 And unto the angel of the church in Smyrna write; These things saith ^Rthe first and the last, which was dead, and is alive;   1:8

9 I know thy works, and tribulation, and poverty, (but thou art ^Rrich) and *I know* the blasphemy of ^Rthem which say they are Jews, and are not, but *are* the synagogue of Satan.   Luke 12:21 · Rom. 2:17

10 ^RFear none of those things which thou shalt suffer: behold, the devil shall cast *some* of you into prison, that ye may be tried; and ye shall have tribulation ten days: ^Rbe thou faithful unto death, and I will give thee ^Ra crown of life.   Matt. 10:22 · Matt. 24:13 · James 1:12

11 ^RHe that hath an ear, let him hear what the Spirit saith unto the churches; He that overcometh shall not be hurt of ^Rthe second death.   13:9 · [20:6, 14; 21:8]

12 And to the angel of the church in Per′-ga-mos write; These things saith he which hath the sharp sword with two edges;

13 I know thy works, and where thou dwellest, *even* where Satan′s ^Tseat *is:* and thou holdest fast my name, and hast not denied my faith, even in those days wherein An′-ti-pas *was* my faithful martyr, who was slain among you, where Satan dwelleth.   *throne*

14 But I have a few things against thee, because thou hast there them that hold the doctrine of ^RBa′-laam, who taught Ba′-lac to cast a stumblingblock before the children of Israel, to eat things sacrificed unto idols, and to commit fornication.   Num. 31:16

15 So hast thou also them that hold the doctrine of the Nic-o-la′-i-tanes, which thing I hate.

16 Repent; or else I will come unto thee quickly, and ^Rwill fight against them with the sword of my mouth.   Is. 11:4; 2 Thess. 2:8

17 He that hath an ear, let him hear what the Spirit saith unto the churches; To him that overcometh will I give to eat of the hidden ^Rman′-na, and will give him a white stone, and in the stone ^Ra new name written, which no man knoweth saving he that receiveth *it.*   Ex. 16:33, 34; [John 6:49, 51] · Is. 56:5

18 And unto the ^Tangel of the church in Thy-a-ti′-ra write; These things saith the Son of God, ^Rwho hath his eyes like unto a flame of fire, and his feet *are* like fine brass;   *messenger* · 1:14, 15

19 ^RI know thy works, and ^Tcharity, and service, and faith, and thy ^Tpatience, and thy works; and the last *to be* more than the first.   v. 2 · *love* · *endurance*

20 Notwithstanding I have a few things against thee, because thou sufferest that woman Jez′-e-bel, which calleth herself a prophetess, to teach and to seduce my servants to commit fornication, and to eat things sacrificed unto idols.

21 And I gave her space ^Rto repent of her fornication; and she repented not.   9:20; 16:9, 11; Rom. 2:5

22 Behold, I will cast her into a ^Tbed, and them that commit adultery with her into great tribulation, ^Texcept they repent of their deeds.   *sickbed* · *unless*

23 And I will kill her children with death; and all the churches shall know that I am he which searcheth the reins and hearts: and I will give unto every one of you according to your works.

24 But unto you I say, and unto the rest in Thy-a-ti′-ra, as many as have not this doctrine, and which have not known the depths of Satan, as they speak; I will put upon you none other burden.

25 But ^Rthat which ye have *already* hold fast till I come.   3:11

26 And he that overcometh, and keepeth ^Rmy works unto the end, ^Rto him will I give power over the nations: [John 6:29] · [Matt. 19:28]

27 ^RAnd he shall rule them with a rod of iron; as the vessels of a potter shall they be broken to ^Tshivers: even as I received of my Father.   12:5; 19:15; Ps. 2:8, 9 · *pieces*

28 And I will give him ^Rthe morning star.   22:16; 2 Pet. 1:19

☆

29 He that hath an ear, let him hear what the Spirit saith unto the churches.

3 And unto the angel of the church in Sar'-dis write; These things saith he that [R]hath the seven Spirits of God, and the seven stars; I know thy works, that thou hast a name that thou livest, and art dead.   1:4, 16

2 Be watchful, and strengthen the things which remain, that are ready to die: for I have not found thy works perfect before God.

3 [R]Remember therefore how thou hast received and heard, and hold fast, and repent. If therefore thou shalt not watch, I will come on thee [R]as a thief, and thou shalt not know what hour I will come upon thee.   1 Tim. 6:20 · 1 Thess. 5:2

4 Thou hast [R]a few names even in Sar'-dis which have not defiled their garments; and they shall walk with me [R]in white: for they are worthy.   Acts 1:15 · 4:4; 6:11

5 He that overcometh, the same shall be clothed in white raiment; and I will not [R]blot out his name out of the book of life, but I will confess his name before my Father, and before his angels.[13:8]

6 [R]He that hath an ear, let him hear what the Spirit saith unto the churches.   2:7

★ 7 And to the angel of the church in Philadelphia write; These things saith he that is holy, he that is true, he that hath the key of David, [R]he that openeth, and no man shutteth; and shutteth, and no man openeth;   [1:18]

8 [R]I know thy works: behold, I have set before thee [R]an open door, and no man can shut it: for thou hast a little strength, and hast kept my word, and hast not denied my name.   v. 1 · 1 Cor. 16:9

9 Behold, I will make [R]them of the synagogue of Satan, which say they are Jews, and are not, but do lie; behold, [R]I will make them to come and worship before thy feet, and to know that I have loved thee.   2:9 · Is. 45:14; 49:23; 60:14

10 Because thou hast kept the word of my patience, [R]I also will keep thee from the hour of temptation, which shall come upon all the world, to try them that dwell upon the earth.   2 Tim. 2:12; 2 Pet. 2:9

11 Behold, I come quickly: [R]hold that fast which thou hast, that no man take [R]thy crown.   2:25 · [2:10]

12 Him that overcometh will I make a pillar in the temple of my God, and he shall go no more out: and [R]I will write upon him the name of my God, and the name of the city of my God, *which is* new Jerusalem, which [R]cometh down out of heaven from my God: [R]and *I will write upon him* my new name.   [14:1; 22:4] · 21:2 · [2:17; 22:4]

13 [R]He that hath an ear, let him hear what the Spirit saith unto the churches.   2:7

14 And unto the angel of the church of the La-od-i-ce'-ans write; [R]These things saith the A-men', the faithful and true witness, [R]the beginning of the creation of God;   2 Cor. 1:20 · [Col. 1:15]

15 [R]I know thy works, that thou art neither cold nor hot: I [T]would thou wert cold or hot.   v. 1 · *wish*

16 So then because thou art lukewarm, and neither cold nor hot, I will [T]spue thee out of my mouth.   *spit or vomit*

17 Because thou sayest, I am rich, and increased with goods, and have need of nothing; and knowest not that thou art wretched, and miserable, and poor, and blind, and naked:

18 I counsel thee [R]to buy of me gold tried in the fire, that thou mayest be rich; and white raiment, that thou mayest be clothed, and *that* the shame of thy nakedness do not appear; and anoint thine eyes with eyesalve, that thou mayest see.   Is. 55:1

19 As many as I love, I rebuke and [R]chasten: be zealous therefore, and repent.   [2 Cor. 11:32]

20 Behold, I stand at the door, and knock: [R]if any man hear my voice, and open the door, I will come in to him, and will sup with him, and he with me.   Luke 12:36, 37

21 To him that overcometh ᴿwill I grant to sit with me ᵀin my throne, even as I also overcame, and am set down with my Father ᵀin his throne.   [2:26; 20:4] · *on*

22 ᴿHe that hath an ear, let him hear what the Spirit saith unto the churches.   2:7

4 After this I looked, and, behold, a door *was* ᴿopened in heaven: and the first voice which I heard *was* as it were of a ᴿtrumpet talking with me; which said, Come up hither, and I will shew thee things which must be hereafter.   19:11; Ezek. 1:1 · 1:10

2 And immediately ᴿI was in the spirit: and, behold, ᴿa throne was set in heaven, and *one* sat on the throne.   1:10 · Is. 6:1; Ezek. 1:26

3 And he that sat was to look upon ᴿlike a jasper and a sardine stone: ᴿand *there was* a rainbow round about the throne, in sight like unto an emerald.   21:11 · 10:1

4 ᴿAnd round about the throne *were* four and twenty seats: and upon the seats I saw four and twenty elders sitting, clothed in white raiment; and they had on their heads crowns of gold.   11:16

5 And out of the throne proceeded ᴿlightnings and thunderings and voices: and *there were* seven lamps of fire burning before the throne, which are the seven Spirits of God. 8:5; 11:19; 16:18

6 And before the throne *there was* ᴿa sea of glass like unto crystal: and in the midst of the throne, and round about the throne, *were* four beasts full of eyes before and behind.   15:2; Ex. 38:8; Ezek. 1:22

7 ᴿAnd the first beast *was* like a lion, and the second beast like a calf, and the third beast had a face as a man, and the fourth beast *was* like a flying eagle.   Ezek. 1:10

8 And the four beasts had each of them ᴿsix wings about *him;* and *they were* full of eyes within: and they rest not day and night, saying, ᴿHoly, holy, holy, ᴿLord God Almighty, ᴿwhich was, and is, and is to come.   Is. 6:2 · Is. 6:3 · 1:8 · 1:4

9 And when those beasts give glory and honour and thanks to him that sat on the throne, ᴿwho liveth for ever and ever,   1:18

10 ᴿThe four and twenty elders fall down before him that sat on the throne, and worship him that liveth for ever and ever, and cast their crowns before the throne, saying,   5:8, 14; 7:11; 11:16; 19:4

11 ᴿThou art worthy, O Lord, to receive glory and honour and power: for thou hast created all things, and for ᴿthy pleasure they are and were created. 5:12 · Col. 1:16

5 And I saw in the right hand of him that sat on the throne ᴿa ᵀbook written within and on the backside, ᴿsealed with seven seals.   Ezek. 2:9, 10 · *scroll* · Dan. 12:4

2 And I saw a strong angel proclaiming with a loud voice, ᴿWho is worthy to open the book, and to loose the seals thereof?   v. 9; 4:11

3 And no man in heaven, nor in earth, neither under the earth, was able to open the ᵀbook, neither to look thereon.   *scroll*

4 And I wept much, because no man was found worthy to open and to read the book, neither to look thereon.

5 And one of the elders saith unto me, Weep not: behold, the Lion of the tribe of Juda, ᴿthe Root of David, hath ᴿprevailed to open the book, ᴿand to loose the seven seals thereof. 22:16 · 3:21 · 6:1

6 And I beheld, and, lo, in the midst of the throne and of the four beasts, and in the midst of the elders, stood ᴿa Lamb as it had been slain, having seven horns and ᴿseven eyes, which are ᴿthe seven Spirits of God sent forth into all the earth.   Is. 53:7 · Zech. 3:9 · 1:4; 3:1; 4:5

7 And he came and took the book out of the right hand ᴿof him that sat upon the throne.   4:2

8 And when he had taken the book, ᴿthe four beasts and four *and* twenty elders fell down before the Lamb, having every one of them harps, and golden vials full of ᵀodours, which are the prayers of saints. 4:8–10; 19:4 · *incense*

9 And they sung a new song,

saying, Thou art worthy to take the book, and to open the seals thereof: for thou wast slain, and hast redeemed us to God by thy blood out of every kindred, and tongue, and people, and nation;

10 And hast made us unto our God ᴿkings and priests: and we shall reign on the earth.   Ex. 19:6

11 And I beheld, and I heard the voice of many angels round about the throne and the ᵀbeasts and the elders: and the number of them was ten thousand times ten thousand, and thousands of thousands;   *living creatures*

★ 12 Saying with a loud voice, Worthy is the Lamb that was slain to receive power, and riches, and wisdom, and strength, and honour, and glory, and blessing.

13 And every creature which is in heaven, and on the earth, and under the earth, and such as are in the sea, and all that are in them, heard I saying, ᴿBlessing, and honour, and glory, and power, *be* unto him ᴿthat sitteth upon the throne, and unto the Lamb for ever and ever.   1 Pet. 4:11 · 4:2, 3; 6:16

14 And the four beasts said, A-men'. And the four *and* twenty elders fell down and worshipped him that liveth for ever and ever.

6 And ᴿI saw when the Lamb opened one of the seals, and I heard, as it were, the noise of thunder, ᴿone of the four beasts saying, Come and see.   Is. 53:7 · 4:7

2 And I saw, and behold a white horse: and he that sat on him had a bow; ᴿand a crown was given unto him: and he went forth conquering, and to conquer.   19:12

3 And when he had opened the second seal, ᴿI heard the second beast say, Come and see.   4:7

4 ᴿAnd there went out another horse *that was* red: and *power* was given to him that sat thereon to ᴿtake peace from the earth, and that they should kill one another: and there was given unto him a great sword.   Zech. 1:8; 6:2 · Matt. 24:6, 7

5 And when he had opened the third seal, ᴿI heard the third beast

say, Come and see. And I beheld, and lo ᴿa black horse; and he that sat on him had a pair of ᴿbalances in his hand.   4:7 · Zech. 6:2, 6 · Matt. 24:7

6 And I heard a voice in the midst of the four beasts say, A measure of wheat for a ᵀpenny, and three measures of barley for a penny; and ᴿsee thou hurt not the oil and the wine.   Gr. *denarius* · 7:3; 9:4

7 And when he had opened the fourth seal, ᴿI heard the voice of the fourth beast say, Come and see.   4:7

8 ᴿAnd I looked, and behold a pale horse: and his name that sat on him was Death, and Hell followed with him. And power was given unto them over the fourth part of the earth, ᴿto kill with sword, and with hunger, and with death, and with the beasts of the earth.   Zech. 6:3 · Ezek. 29:5; Matt. 24:9

9 And when he had opened the fifth seal, I saw under ᴿthe altar the souls of them that were slain ᴿfor the word of God, and for the testimony which they held: 8:3 · 1:2

10 And they cried with a loud voice, saying, ᴿHow long, O Lord, holy and true, dost thou not judge and avenge our blood on them that dwell on the earth?   Ps. 13:1–6

11 And ᴿwhite robes were given unto every one of them; and it was said unto them, that they should rest yet for a little season, until their fellowservants also and their brethren, that should be killed as they *were*, should be fulfilled.   7:9

12 And I beheld when he had opened the sixth seal, ᴿand, lo, there was a great earthquake; and ᴿthe sun became black as sackcloth of hair, and the moon became as blood;   8:5; 11:13 · Matt. 24:29

13 And the stars of heaven fell unto the earth, even as a fig tree casteth her untimely figs, when she is shaken of a mighty wind.

14 And the heaven departed as a scroll when it is rolled together; and every mountain and island were moved out of their places.

15 And the kings of the earth, and the great men, and the rich

men, and the chief captains, and the mighty men, and every bondman, and every free man, ᴿhid themselves in the dens and in the rocks of the mountains;　　19:18

16 ᴿAnd said to the mountains and rocks, Fall on us, and hide us from the face of him that ᴿsitteth on the throne, and from the wrath of the Lamb:　9:6; Luke 23:29, 30 · 20:11

17 For the great day of his wrath is come; ᴿand who shall be able to stand?　Is. 63:4; Jer. 30:7; Joel 1:15; 2:1, 11

7 And after these things I saw four angels standing on the four corners of the earth, ᴿholding the four winds of the earth, ᴿthat the wind should not blow on the earth, nor on the sea, nor on any tree.　Zech. 6:5; Matt. 24:31 · 8:7; 9:4

2 And I saw another angel ascending from the east, having the seal of the living God: and he cried with a loud voice to the four angels, to whom it was given to hurt the earth and the sea,

3 Saying, ᴿHurt not the earth, neither the sea, nor the trees, till we have sealed the servants of our God ᴿin their foreheads.　6:6 · 22:4

4 ᴿAnd I heard the number of them which were sealed: *and there were* sealed ᴿan hundred *and* forty *and* four thousand ᴿof all the tribes of the ᵀchildren of Israel.　9:16 · 14:1, 3 · Gen. 49:1–27 · Lit. *sons*

5 Of the tribe of Juda *were* sealed twelve thousand. Of the tribe of Reuben *were* sealed twelve thousand. Of the tribe of Gad *were* sealed twelve thousand.

6 Of the tribe of A'-ser *were* sealed twelve thousand. Of the tribe of Nep'-tha-lim *were* sealed twelve thousand. Of the tribe of Ma-nas'-ses *were* sealed twelve thousand.

7 Of the tribe of Simeon *were* sealed twelve thousand. Of the tribe of Levi *were* sealed twelve thousand. Of the tribe of Is'-sa-char *were* sealed twelve thousand.

8 Of the tribe of Zab'-u-lon *were* sealed twelve thousand. Of

the tribe of Joseph *were* sealed twelve thousand. Of the tribe of Benjamin *were* sealed twelve thousand.

9 After this I beheld, and, lo, ᴿa great multitude, which no man could number, ᴿof all nations, and kindreds, and people, and tongues, stood before the throne, and before the Lamb, ᴿclothed with white robes, and palms in their hands;　Rom. 11:25 · 5:9 · 3:5, 18; 4:4

10 And cried with a loud voice, saying, ᴿSalvation to our God ᴿwhich sitteth upon the throne, and unto the Lamb.　19:1; Ps. 3:8 · 5:13

11 ᴿAnd all the angels stood round about the throne, and *about* the elders and the four beasts, and fell before the throne on their faces, and ᴿworshipped God,　4:6 · 4:11; 5:9, 12, 14; 11:16

12 Saying, A-men': Blessing, and glory, and wisdom, and thanksgiving, and honour, and power, and might, *be* unto our God for ever and ever. A-men'.

13 And one of the elders answered, saying unto me, ᵀWhat are these which are arrayed in ᴿwhite robes? and whence came they?　*Who* · v. 9

14 And I said unto him, Sir, thou knowest. And he said to me, ᴿThese are they which came out of great tribulation, and have ᴿwashed their robes, and made them white in the blood of the Lamb.　6:9 · Zech. 3:3–5; [Heb. 9:14]

15 Therefore are they before the throne of God, and serve him day and night in his temple: and he that sitteth on the throne shall ᴿdwell among them.　21:3; Is. 4:5, 6

16 ᴿThey shall hunger no more, ☆ neither thirst any more; ᴿneither shall the sun light on them, nor any heat.　Ps. 121:5; Is. 49:10 · 21:4

17 For the Lamb which is in the ☆ midst of the throne ᴿshall feed them, and shall lead them unto living fountains of waters: ᴿand God shall wipe away all tears from their eyes.　Ps. 23:1 · 21:4

8 And ᴿwhen he had opened the seventh seal, there was

silence in heaven about the space of half an hour.   6:1

2 And I saw the seven angels which stood before God; and to them were given seven trumpets.

3 And another angel came and stood at the altar, having a golden censer; and there was given unto him much incense, that he should offer *it* with ^Rthe prayers of all saints upon the golden altar which was before the throne.   5:8

4 And the smoke of the incense, *which came* with the prayers of the saints, ascended up before God out of the angel's hand.

5 And the angel took the censer, and filled it with fire of the altar, and cast *it* into the earth: and ^Rthere were voices, and thunderings, ^Rand lightnings, and an earthquake.   11:19; 16:18; Ex. 19:16 · 4:5

6 And the seven angels which had the seven trumpets prepared themselves to sound.

7 The first angel sounded, ^Rand there followed hail and fire mingled with blood, and they were cast upon the earth: and the third part of trees was burnt up, and all green grass was burnt up.   Is. 28:2

8 And the second angel sounded, and as it were a great mountain burning with fire was cast into the sea: ^Rand the third part of the sea became blood;   11:6; 16:3

9 And the third part of the creatures which were in the sea, and had life, died; and the third part of the ships were destroyed.

10 And the third angel sounded, ^Rand there fell a great star from heaven, burning as it were a lamp, ^Rand it fell upon the third part of the rivers, and upon the fountains of waters;   6:13; 9:1 · 14:7; 16:4

11 ^RAnd the name of the star is called Wormwood: ^Rand the third part of the waters became wormwood; and many men died of the waters, because they were made bitter.   Ruth 1:20 · Ex. 15:23

12 ^RAnd the fourth angel sounded, and the third part of the sun was smitten, and the third part of the moon, and the third part of the

stars; so as the third part of them was darkened, and the day shone not for a third part of it, and the night likewise.   Is. 13:10; Matt. 24:29

13 And I beheld, and heard an angel flying through the midst of heaven, saying with a loud voice, Woe, woe, woe, to the inhabiters of the earth by reason of the other voices of the trumpet of the three angels, which are yet to sound!

9 ^Rand I saw a star fall from heaven unto the earth: and to him was given the key of ^Rthe bottomless pit.   8:10; Luke 10:18 · vv. 2, 11; 17:8

2 And he opened the bottomless pit; and there arose a smoke out of the pit, as the smoke of a great furnace; and the ^Rsun and the air were darkened by reason of the smoke of the pit.   Joel 2:2, 10

3 And there came out of the smoke locusts upon the earth: and unto them was given power, ^Ras the scorpions of the earth have power.   Ex. 10:4; Judg. 7:12

4 And it was commanded them ^Rthat they should not hurt ^Rthe grass of the earth, neither any green thing, neither any tree; but only those men which have not ^Rthe seal of God in their foreheads.   6:6 · 8:7 · Ex. 12:23; Ezek. 9:4

5 And to them it was given that they should not kill them, ^Rbut that they should be tormented five months: and their torment *was* as the torment of a scorpion, when he striketh a man.   [v. 10; 11:7]

6 And in those days ^Rshall men seek death, and shall not find it; and shall desire to die, and death shall flee from them.   Is. 2:19; Jer. 8:3

7 And ^Rthe shapes of the locusts *were* like unto horses prepared unto battle; and on their heads *were* as it were crowns like gold, ^Rand their faces *were* as the faces of men.   Joel 2:4 · Dan. 7:8

8 And they had hair as the hair of women, and ^Rtheir teeth were as *the teeth* of lions.   Joel 1:6

9 And they had breastplates, as it were breastplates of iron; and the sound of their wings *was* ^Ras

the sound of chariots of many horses running to battle.   Jer. 47:3

10 And they had tails like unto scorpions, and there were stings in their tails: and their power *was* to hurt men five months.

11 And they had a king over them, *which is* ᴿthe angel of the bottomless pit, whose name in the Hebrew tongue *is* A-bad'-don, but in the Greek tongue hath *his* name A-pol'-ly-on.   Eph. 2:2

12 ᴿOne woe is past; *and,* behold, there come two woes more hereafter.   8:13; 11:14

13 And the sixth angel sounded, and I heard a voice from the four horns of the ᴿgolden altar which is before God,   8:3

14 Saying to the sixth angel which had the trumpet, Loose the four angels which are bound ᴿin the great river Eu-phra'-tes.   16:12

15 And the four angels were loosed, which were prepared for ᵀan hour, and a day, and a month, and a year, for to slay the ᴿthird part of men.   *the* · v. 18; 8:7–9

16 And the number of the army of the horsemen *were* two hundred thousand thousand: ᴿand I heard the number of them.   7:4

17 And thus I saw the horses in the vision, and them that sat on them, having breastplates of fire, and of jacinth, and brimstone: ᴿand the heads of the horses *were* as the heads of lions; and out of their mouths issued fire and smoke and brimstone.   1 Chr. 12:8

18 By these three was the third part of men killed, by the fire, and by the smoke, and by the brimstone, which issued out of their mouths.

19 For their power is in their mouth, and in their tails: ᴿfor their tails *were* like unto serpents, and had heads, and with them they do hurt.   Is. 9:15

20 And the rest of the men which were not killed by these plagues yet repented not of the works of their hands, that they should not worship devils, ᴿand idols of gold, and silver, and

brass, and stone, and of wood: which neither can see, nor hear, nor walk: Ps. 135:15–17; Dan. 5:23

21 Neither repented they of their murders, ᴿnor of their sorceries, nor of their fornication, nor of their thefts.   21:8; 22:15

10 And I saw another mighty angel come down from heaven, clothed with a cloud: ᴿand a rainbow *was* upon his head, and his face *was* as it were the sun, and his feet as pillars of fire: 4:3

2 And he had in his hand a little book open: ᴿand he set his right foot upon the sea, and *his* left *foot* on the earth,   Ps. 95:5

3 And cried with a loud voice, as *when* a lion roareth: and when he had cried, ᴿseven thunders uttered their voices.   4:5; 8:5

4 And when the seven thunders had uttered their voices, I was about to write: and I heard a voice from heaven saying unto me, ᴿSeal up those things which the seven thunders uttered, and write them not. 22:10; Dan. 8:26; 12:4, 9

5 And the angel which I saw stand upon the sea and upon the earth ᴿlifted up his hand to heaven,   Ex. 6:8; Deut. 32:40; Dan. 12:7

6 And sware by him that liveth for ever and ever, who created heaven, and the things that therein are, and the earth, and the things that therein are, and the sea, and the things which are therein, ᴿthat there should be ᵀtime no longer: 16:17; Dan. 12:7 · *delay*

7 But ᴿin the days of the voice of the seventh angel, when he shall begin to sound, the mystery of God should be finished, as he hath declared to his servants the prophets.   11:15

8 And the voice which I heard from heaven spake unto me again, and said, Go *and* take the little book which is open in the hand of the angel which standeth upon the sea and upon the earth.

9 And I went unto the angel, and said unto him, Give me the little book. And he said unto me, Take *it,* and eat it up; and it shall

make thy belly bitter, but it shall be in thy mouth sweet as honey.

10 And I took the little book out of the angel's hand, and ate it up; ᴿand it was in my mouth sweet as honey: and as soon as I had eaten it, my belly was bitter.   Ezek. 3:3

11 And he said unto me, Thou must prophesy again before many peoples, and nations, and tongues, and kings.

11 And there was given me ᴿa reed like unto a rod: and the angel stood, saying, ᴿRise, and measure the temple of God, and the altar, and them that worship therein.   21:15; Zech. 2:1 · Num. 23:18

2 But the court which is without the temple leave out, and measure it not; for it is given unto the Gentiles: and the holy city shall they ᴿtread under foot ᴿforty and two months.   Dan. 8:10 · 12:6; 13:5

3 And I will give *power* unto my two ᴿwitnesses, and they shall prophesy ᴿa thousand two hundred *and* threescore days, clothed in sackcloth.   20:4 · 12:6

4 These are the ᴿtwo olive trees, and the two candlesticks standing before the God of the earth.   Ps. 52:8; Jer. 11:16; Zech. 4:2, 3

5 And if any man will hurt them, ᴿfire proceedeth out of their mouth, and devoureth their enemies: ᴿand if any man will hurt them, he must in this manner be killed.   Jer. 1:10; Hos. 6:5 · Num. 16:29

6 These ᴿhave power to shut heaven, that it rain not in the days of their prophecy: and have power over waters to turn them to blood, and to smite the earth with all plagues, as often as they will. 1 Kin. 17:1; Luke 4:25; [James 5:16, 17]

7 And when they shall have finished their testimony, ᴿthe beast that ascendeth ᴿout of the bottomless pit ᴿshall make war against them, and shall overcome them, and kill them.   17:8 · 9:1, 2 · 13:7

8 And their dead bodies *shall lie* in the street of ᴿthe great city, which spiritually is called Sodom and Egypt, ᴿwhere also our Lord was crucified.   14:8 · Heb. 13:12

9 ᴿAnd they of the people and kindreds and tongues and nations shall see their dead bodies three days and an half, ᴿand shall not suffer their dead bodies to be put in graves.   17:15 · 1 Kin. 13:22; Ps. 79:2, 3

10 ᴿAnd they that dwell upon the earth shall rejoice over them, and make merry, and shall send gifts one to another; because these two prophets tormented them that dwelt on the earth.   12:12

11 ᴿAnd after three days and an half the Spirit of life from God entered into them, and they stood upon their feet; and great fear fell upon them which saw them.   v. 9

12 And they heard a great voice from heaven saying unto them, Come up hither. And they ascended up to heaven ᴿin a cloud; and their enemies beheld them.   Is. 60:8

13 And the same hour ᴿwas there a great earthquake, ᴿand the tenth part of the city fell, and in the earthquake were slain of men seven thousand: and the remnant were affrighted, and gave glory to the God of heaven.   6:12; 8:5 · 16:19

14 ᴿThe second woe is past; *and,* behold, the third woe cometh quickly.   8:13; 9:12

15 And ᴿthe seventh angel sounded; and there were great voices in heaven, saying, The kingdoms of this world are become *the kingdoms* of our Lord, and of his Christ; and he shall reign for ever and ever.   8:2; 10:7

16 And ᴿthe four and twenty elders, which sat before God on their seats, fell upon their faces, and ᴿworshipped God,   4:4 · 4:11; 7:11

17 Saying, We give thee thanks, O Lord God Almighty, ᴿwhich art, and wast, and art to come; because thou hast taken to thee thy great power, and hast reigned. 16:5

18 And the nations were ᴿangry, and thy wrath is come, and the time of the ᴿdead, that they should be judged, and that thou shouldest give reward unto thy servants the prophets, and to the saints, and them that fear thy name, small and great; and shouldest

destroy them which destroy the earth.   Ps. 2:1 · [20:12, 13]; Dan. 7:10

19 And ᴿthe temple of God was opened in heaven, and there was seen in his temple the ark of his ᵀtestament: and ᴿthere were lightnings, and voices, and thunderings, and an earthquake, ᴿand great hail.   15:5, 8 · *covenant* · 8:5 · 16:21

12 And there appeared a great ᵀwonder in heaven; a woman clothed with the sun, and the moon under her feet, and upon her head a ᵀcrown of twelve stars: *sign · garland*

2 And she being with child cried, ᴿtravailing in birth, and pained to be delivered.   Is. 66:6–9

3 And there appeared another wonder in heaven; and behold ᴿa great red dragon, having seven heads and ten horns, and seven crowns upon his heads.   13:1; 17:3

4 And ᴿhis tail drew the third part ᴿof the stars of heaven, ᴿand did cast them to the earth: and the dragon stood before the woman which was ready to be delivered, for to devour her child as soon as it was born.   9:10, 19 · 8:7, 12 · Dan. 8:10

☆ 5 And she brought forth a man child, ᴿwho was to rule all nations with a rod of iron: and her child was caught up unto God, and *to* his throne.   19:15; Ps. 2:9; Is. 7:14; 9:6

6 And ᴿthe woman fled into the wilderness, where she hath a place prepared of God, that they should feed her there ᴿa thousand two hundred *and* ᵀthreescore days.   vv. 4, 14 · 11:3; 13:5 · *sixty*

7 And there was war in heaven: ᴿMi′-cha-el and his angels fought against the dragon; and the dragon fought and his angels,   Jude 9

8 And prevailed not; neither was ᵀtheir place found any more in heaven.   *a place found for them*

9 And the great dragon was cast out, that old serpent, called the Devil, and Satan, which deceiveth the whole world: he was cast out into the earth, and his angels were cast out with him.

10 And I heard a loud voice saying in heaven, ᴿNow is come salvation, and strength, and the kingdom of our God, and the power of his Christ: for the accuser of our brethren is cast down, ᴿwhich accused them before our God day and night.   11:15 · Job 1:9, 11

11 And ᴿthey overcame him by the blood of the Lamb, and by the word of their testimony; ᴿand they loved not their lives unto the death.   Rom. 16:20 · [2:10]; Luke 14:26

12 Therefore rejoice, ye heavens, and ye that dwell in them. ᴿWoe to the inhabiters of the earth and of the sea! for the devil is come down unto you, having great wrath, because he knoweth that he hath but a short time.   8:13

13 And when the dragon saw that he was cast unto the earth, he persecuted ᴿthe woman which brought forth the man *child.*   v. 5

14 ᴿAnd to the woman were given two wings of a great eagle, that she might fly into the wilderness, into her place, where she is nourished ᴿfor a time, and times, and half a time, from the face of the serpent.   Is. 40:31 · Dan. 7:25; 12:7

15 And the serpent ᴿcastᵀ out of his mouth ᵀwater as a flood after the woman, that he might cause her to be carried away of the flood.   Is. 59:19 · *spewed · a river of water*

16 And the earth helped the woman, and the earth opened her mouth, and swallowed up the flood which the dragon cast out of his mouth.

17 And the dragon was ᵀwroth with the woman, and went to make war with the remnant of her seed, which keep the commandments of God, and have the testimony of Jesus Christ.   *enraged*

13 And I stood upon the sand of the sea, and saw ᴿa beast rise up out of the sea, ᴿhaving seven heads and ten horns, and upon his horns ten crowns, and upon his heads the ᴿname of blasphemy.   Dan. 7:2, 7 · 12:3 · Dan. 7:8; 11:36

2 And the beast which I saw was like unto a leopard, and his feet were as *the feet* of a bear, and his mouth as the mouth of a lion:

and the ^Rdragon gave him his power, and his ^Tseat, and great authority. vv. 4, 12; 12:3, 9 · *throne*

3 And I saw one of his heads ^Ras ^Tit were wounded to death; and his deadly wound was healed: and ^Rall the world wondered after the beast. vv. 12, 14 · *if it had been* · 17:8

4 And they worshipped the dragon which gave power unto the beast: and they worshipped the beast, saying, ^RWho *is* like unto the beast? who is able to make war with him? 18:18; Ex. 15:11

5 And there was given unto him a mouth speaking great things and blasphemies; and power was given unto him to continue ^Rforty *and* two months. 11:2

6 And he opened his mouth in blasphemy against God, to blaspheme his name, ^Rand his tabernacle, and them that dwell in heaven. [John 1:14; Col. 2:9]

7 And it was given unto him ^Rto make war with the saints, and to overcome them: ^Rand power was given him over all kindreds, and tongues, and nations. 11:7 · 11:18

8 And all that dwell upon the earth shall worship him, whose names are not written in the book of life of the Lamb slain ^Rfrom the foundation of the world. 17:8

9 ^RIf any man have an ear, let him hear. 2:7

10 ^RHe that leadeth into captivity shall go into captivity: he that killeth with the sword must be killed with the sword. Here is the patience and the faith of the saints. Is. 33:1; Jer. 15:2; 43:11

11 And I beheld another beast ^Rcoming up out of the earth; and he had two horns like a lamb, and he spake as a dragon. 11:7

12 And he exerciseth all the power of the first beast before him, and causeth the earth and them which dwell therein to worship the first beast, ^Rwhose deadly wound was healed. vv. 3, 4

13 And he doeth great wonders, ^Rso that he maketh fire come down from heaven on the earth in the sight of men, 11:5; 20:9

14 And deceiveth them that dwell on the earth ^Rby *the means of* those miracles which he had power to do in the sight of the beast; saying to them that dwell on the earth, that they should make an image to the beast, which had the wound by a sword, ^Rand did live. 2 Thess. 2:9 · 2 Kin. 20:7

15 And he had power to give ^Tlife unto the image of the beast, that the image of the beast should both speak, ^Rand cause that as many as would not worship the image of the beast should be killed. *breath* · 16:2

16 And he causeth all, both small and great, rich and poor, free and bond, ^Rto receive a mark in their right hand, or in their foreheads: 7:3; 14:9; 20:4; Gal. 6:17

17 And that no man might buy or sell, save he that had the mark, or ^Rthe name of the beast, ^Ror the number of his name. 14:9–11 · 15:2

18 ^RHere is wisdom. Let him that hath ^Runderstanding count ^Rthe number of the beast: ^Rfor it is the number of a man; and his number *is* Six hundred threescore *and* six. 17:9 · [1 Cor. 2:14] · 15:2 · 21:17

14 And I looked, and, lo, a ^RLamb stood on the mount Si'-on, and with him an ^Rhundred forty *and* four thousand, having his Father's name ^Rwritten in their foreheads. 5:6 · 7:4 · 7:3; 22:4

2 And I heard a voice from heaven, ^Ras the voice of many waters, and as the voice of a great thunder: and I heard the voice of ^Rharpers harping with their harps: 1:15; 19:6 · 5:8

3 And they sung as it were a new song before the throne, and before the four beasts, and the elders: and no man could learn that song ^Rbut the hundred *and* forty *and* four thousand, which were redeemed from the earth. 5:9

4 These are they which were not defiled with women; for they are virgins. These are they which follow the Lamb whithersoever he goeth. These were redeemed from among men, *being*

the firstfruits unto God and to the Lamb.

5 And ᴿin their mouth was found no ᵀguile: for ᴿthey are without fault before the throne of God.   1 Pet. 2:22 · *deceit* · Eph. 5:27

6 And I saw another angel ᴿfly in the midst of heaven, having the everlasting gospel to preach unto them that dwell on the earth, ᴿand to every nation, and kindred, and tongue, and people,   8:13 · 13:7

7 Saying with a loud voice, ᴿFear God, and give glory to him; for the hour of his judgment is come: and worship him that made heaven, and earth, and the sea, and the fountains of waters.   11:18

8 And there followed another angel, saying, ᴿBabylon is fallen, is fallen, that great city, because ᴿshe made all nations drink of the wine of the wrath of her fornication.   18:2; Is. 21:9; Jer. 51:8 · 17:2

9 And the third angel followed them, saying with a loud voice, ᴿIf any man worship the beast and his image, and receive *his* mark in his forehead, or in his hand,   13:14

10 The same shall drink of the wine of the wrath of God, which is ᴿpoured out without mixture into ᴿthe cup of his indignation; and he shall be tormented with ᴿfire and brimstone in the presence of the holy angels, and in the presence of the Lamb: 18:6 · 16:19 · 19:20

11 And the smoke of their torment ascendeth up for ever and ever: and they have no rest day nor night, who worship the beast and his image, and whosoever receiveth the mark of his name.

12 ᴿHere is the patience of the saints: ᴿhere *are* they that keep the commandments of God, and the faith of Jesus.   13:10 · 12:17

13 And I heard a voice from heaven saying unto me, Write, Blessed *are* the dead which die in the Lord from henceforth: Yea, saith the Spirit, ᴿthat they may rest from their labours; and their works do follow them.   6:11

14 And I looked, and behold a white cloud, and upon the cloud *one* sat like unto the Son of man, having on his head a golden crown, and in his hand a sharp sickle.

15 And another angel ᴿcame out of the temple, crying with a loud voice to him that sat on the cloud, ᴿThrust in thy sickle, and reap: for the time is come for thee to reap; for the harvest ᴿof the earth is ripe.   16:17 · Joel 3:13 · Jer. 51:33

16 And he that sat on the cloud thrust in his sickle on the earth; and the earth was reaped.

17 And another angel came out of the temple which is in heaven, he also having a sharp sickle.

18 And another angel came out from the altar, ᴿwhich had power over fire; and cried with a loud cry to him that had the sharp sickle, saying, ᴿThrust in thy sharp sickle, and gather the clusters of the vine of the earth; for her grapes are fully ripe.   16:8 · Joel 3:13

19 And the angel thrust in his sickle into the earth, and gathered the vine of the earth, and cast *it* into ᴿthe great winepress of the wrath of God.   19:15; Is. 63:2

20 And ᴿthe winepress was trodden without the city, and blood came out of the winepress, ᴿeven unto the horse bridles, by the space of a thousand *and* six hundred furlongs.   19:15; Is. 63:3 · Is. 34:3

15 And I saw another sign in heaven, great and marvellous, seven angels having the seven last plagues; ᴿfor in them is filled up the wrath of God.   14:10

2 And I saw as it were ᴿa sea of glass mingled with fire: and them that had gotten the victory over the beast, ᴿand over his image, and over his mark, *and* over the ᴿnumber of his name, stand on the sea of glass, ᴿhaving the harps of God.   4:6 · 13:14, 15 · 13:17 · 5:8

3 And they sing the song of Moses the servant of God, and the song of the Lamb, saying, Great and marvellous *are* thy works, Lord God Almighty; just and true *are* thy ways, thou King of saints.

4 Who shall not fear thee, O

Lord, and glorify thy name? For *thou* only *art* ^Rholy: for ^Rall nations shall come and worship before thee; for thy judgments are made manifest.   4:8 · Ps. 86:9; Is. 66:23

5 And after that I looked, and, behold, ^Rthe temple of the tabernacle of the testimony in heaven was opened: Num. 1:50; Heb. 8:5

6 And the seven angels came out of the ^Ttemple, having the seven plagues, ^Rclothed in pure and white linen, and having their ^Tbreasts girded with golden ^Tgirdles.   *sanctuary* · Ex. 28:6 · *chests* · *bands*

7 ^RAnd one of the four beasts gave unto the seven angels seven golden ^Tvials full of the wrath of God, ^Rwho liveth for ever and ever.   4:6 · *bowls* · 1 Thess. 1:9

8 And the temple was filled with smoke from the glory of God, and from his power; and no man was able to enter into the temple, till the seven plagues of the seven angels were fulfilled.

16 And I heard a great voice out of the temple saying ^Rto the seven angels, Go your ways, and pour out the vials of the wrath of God upon the earth. 15:1

2 And the first went, and poured out his vial upon the earth; and there fell a ^Tnoisome and grievous sore upon the men which had the mark of the beast, and *upon* them which worshipped his image.   *foul and loathsome*

3 And the second angel poured out his vial upon the sea; and ^Rit became as the blood of a dead *man:* ^Rand every living ^Tsoul died in the sea.   Ex. 7:17–21 · 8:9 · *creature*

4 And the third angel poured out his vial ^Rupon the rivers and ^Tfountains of waters; and they became blood.   8:10 · *springs*

5 And I heard the angel of the waters say, ^RThou art righteous, O Lord, ^Rwhich art, and wast, and shalt be, because thou hast judged thus.   15:3, 4 · 1:4, 8

6 For they have shed the blood ^Rof saints and prophets, ^Rand thou hast given them blood to drink; for they are worthy.   11:18 · Is. 49:26

7 And I heard another out of the altar say, Even so, ^RLord God Almighty, ^Rtrue and righteous *are* thy judgments.   15:3 · 13:10; 19:2

8 And the fourth angel poured out his vial ^Rupon the sun; ^Rand power was given unto him to scorch men with fire. 8:12 · 9:17, 18

9 And men were scorched with great heat, and blasphemed the name of God, which hath power over these plagues: and they repented not to give him glory.

10 And the fifth angel poured out his vial ^Rupon the seat of the beast; ^Rand his kingdom was full of darkness; and they gnawed their tongues for pain, 13:2 · 8:12; 9:2

11 And blasphemed the God of heaven because of their pains and their sores, and repented not of their deeds.

12 And the sixth angel poured out his vial ^Rupon the great river Eu-phra'-tes; and the water thereof was dried up, ^Rthat the way of the kings of the east might be prepared.   9:14 · Is. 41:2, 25; 46:11

13 And I saw three unclean spirits like frogs *come* out of the mouth of the dragon, and out of the mouth of the beast, and out of the mouth of the false prophet.

14 For they are the spirits of devils, working miracles, *which* go forth unto the kings of the earth and of the whole world, to gather them to ^Rthe battle of that great day of God Almighty.   17:14

15 ^RBehold, I come as a thief. ☆ Blessed *is* he that watcheth, and keepeth his garments, ^Rlest he walk naked, and they see his shame. Matt. 24:43; Luke 12:39 · 2 Cor. 5:3

16 And he gathered them together into a place called in the Hebrew tongue Ar-ma-ged'-don.

17 And the seventh angel poured out his vial into the air; and there came a great voice out of the temple of heaven, from the throne, saying, ^RIt is done. 10:6; 21:6

18 And ^Rthere were voices, and thunders, and lightnings; ^Rand there was a great earthquake, such as was not since men were

upon the earth, so mighty an earthquake, *and* so great. 4:5 · 11:13

19 And ᴿthe great city was divided into three parts, and the cities of the nations fell: and ᴿgreat Babylon ᴿcame in remembrance before God, ᴿto give unto her the cup of the wine of the fierceness of his wrath. 14:8 · 17:5, 18 · 18:5 · 14:10

20 And ᴿevery island fled away, and the mountains were not found. 6:14; 20:11

21 And there fell upon men a great hail out of heaven, *every stone* about the weight of a talent: and men blasphemed God because of the plague of the hail; for the plague thereof was exceeding great.

17 And there came one of the seven angels which had the seven vials, and talked with me, saying unto me, Come hither; I will shew unto thee the judgment of ᴿthe great whore that sitteth upon many waters: Is. 1:21; Jer. 2:20

2 ᴿWith whom the kings of the earth have committed fornication, and the inhabitants of the earth have been made drunk with the wine of her fornication. 2:22; 18:3, 9

3 So he carried me away in the spirit ᴿinto the wilderness: and I saw a woman sit ᴿupon a scarlet coloured beast, full of ᴿnames of blasphemy, having seven heads and ten horns. 12:6, 14 · 12:3 · 13:1

4 And the woman ᴿwas arrayed in purple and scarlet colour, ᴿand decked with gold and precious stones and pearls, ᴿhaving a golden cup in her hand ᴿfull of abominations and filthiness of her fornication: 18:12, 16 · Dan. 11:38 · 18:6 · 14:8

5 And upon her forehead *was* a name written, ᴿMYSTERY, BABYLON THE GREAT, THE MOTHER OF HARLOTS AND ABOMINATIONS OF THE EARTH. 1:20; 2 Thess. 2:7

6 And I saw ᴿthe woman drunken ᴿwith the blood of the saints, and with the blood of ᴿthe martyrs of Jesus: and when I saw her, I wondered with great admiration. 18:24 · 13:15 · 6:9, 10

7 And the angel said unto me, Wherefore didst thou marvel? I will tell thee the mystery of the woman, and of the beast that carrieth her, which hath the seven heads and ten horns.

8 The beast that thou sawest was, and is not; and ᴿshall ascend out of the bottomless pit, and ᴿgo into perdition: and they that dwell on the earth ᴿshall wonder, ᴿwhose names were not written in the book of life from the foundation of the world, when they behold the beast that was, and is not, and yet is. 11:7 · 13:10 · 13:3 · 13:8

9 And ᴿhere *is* the mind which hath wisdom. ᴿThe seven heads are seven mountains, on which the woman sitteth. 13:18 · 13:1

10 And there are seven kings: five ᵀare fallen, and one is, *and* the other is not yet come; and when he cometh, he must ᴿcontinue a short ᵀspace. have · 13:5 · time

11 And the ᴿbeast that was, and is not, even he is the eighth, and is of the seven, and goeth into ᵀperdition. 13:3, 12, 14 · destruction

12 And ᴿthe ten horns which thou sawest are ten kings, which have received no kingdom as yet; but receive power as kings one hour with the beast. Dan. 7:20

13 These have one mind, and shall give their power and ᵀstrength unto the beast. authority

14 ᴿThese shall make war with the Lamb, and the Lamb shall ᴿovercome them: for he is Lord of lords, and King of kings: and they that are with him *are* called, and chosen, and faithful. 16:14 · 19:20

15 And he saith unto me, ᴿThe waters which thou sawest, where the whore sitteth, ᴿare peoples, and multitudes, and nations, and tongues. Is. 8:7; Jer. 47:2 · 13:7

16 And the ten horns which thou sawest upon the beast, ᴿthese shall hate the whore, and shall make her ᴿdesolate and naked, and shall eat her flesh, and burn her with fire. Jer. 50:41 · 18:17

17 ᴿFor God hath put in their hearts to fulfil his will, and to

agree, and give their kingdom unto the beast, until the words of God shall be fulfilled.   2 Thess. 2:11

18 And the woman which thou sawest ^Ris that great city, ^Rwhich reigneth over the kings of the earth.   11:8; 16:19 · 12:4

18 And ^Rafter these things I saw another angel come down from heaven, having great power; ^Rand the earth was lightened with his glory.   17:1 · Ezek. 43:2

2 And he cried mightily with a strong voice, saying, Babylon the great is fallen, is fallen, and ^Ris become the habitation of devils, and the hold of every foul spirit, and a cage of every unclean and hateful bird. Jer. 50:39; 51:37; Zeph. 2:14

3 For all nations have drunk of the wine of the wrath of her fornication, and the kings of the earth have committed fornication with her, and the merchants of the earth are waxed rich through the abundance of her delicacies.

4 And I heard another voice from heaven, saying, ^RCome out of her, my people, that ye be not partakers of her sins, and that ye receive not of her plagues. Is. 48:20

5 For her sins have reached unto heaven, and ^RGod hath remembered her iniquities.   16:19

6 Reward her even as she rewarded you, and double unto her double according to her works: ^Rin the cup which she hath filled ^Rfill to her double.   14:10 · 16:19

7 How much she hath glorified herself, and lived deliciously, so much torment and sorrow give her: for she saith in her heart, I sit a ^Rqueen, and am no widow, and shall see no sorrow.   Is. 47:7, 8

8 Therefore shall her plagues come ^Rin one day, death, and mourning, and famine; and ^Rshe shall be utterly burned with fire: ^Rfor strong is the Lord God who judgeth her.   Is. 47:9 · 17:16 · 11:17

9 And the kings of the earth, who have committed fornication and lived deliciously with her, ^Rshall bewail her, and lament for

her, ^Rwhen they shall see the smoke of her burning,   17:2 · 19:3

10 Standing afar off for the fear of her torment, saying, ^RAlas, alas that great city Babylon, that mighty city! ^Rfor in one hour is thy judgment come.   Is. 21:9 · vv. 17, 19

11 And ^Rthe merchants of the earth shall weep and mourn over her; for no man buyeth their merchandise any more: Ezek. 27:27–34

12 ^RThe merchandise of gold, and silver, and precious stones, and of pearls, and fine linen, and purple, and silk, and scarlet, and all thyine wood, and all manner vessels of ivory, and all manner vessels of most precious wood, and of brass, and iron, and marble,   17:4; Ezek. 27:12–22

13 And cinnamon, and odours, and ointments, and frankincense, and wine, and oil, and fine flour, and wheat, and beasts, and sheep, and horses, and chariots, and slaves, and souls of men.

14 And the fruits that thy soul ^Tlusted after are departed from thee, and all things which were dainty and goodly are departed from thee, and thou shalt find them no more at all.   *longed for*

15 The merchants of these things, which were made rich by her, shall stand afar off for the fear of her torment, weeping and wailing,

16 And saying, Alas, alas ^Rthat great city, ^Rthat was clothed in fine linen, and purple, and scarlet, and decked with gold, and precious stones, and pearls! 17:18 · 17:4

17 ^RFor in one hour so great riches is come to nought. And ^Revery shipmaster, and all the company in ships, and sailors, and as many as trade by sea, stood afar off,   v. 10 · Is. 23:14

18 ^RAnd cried when they saw the smoke of her burning, saying, ^RWhat *city is* like unto this great city!   Ezek. 27:30 · 13:4

19 And they cast dust on their heads, and cried, weeping and wailing, saying, Alas, alas that great city, wherein were made

rich all that had ships in the sea by reason of her costliness! for in one hour is she made desolate.

20 ᴿRejoice over her, *thou* heaven, and *ye* holy apostles and prophets; for ᴿGod hath avenged you on her. Is. 44:23; 49:13 · Luke 11:49

21 And a mighty angel took up a stone like a great millstone, and cast *it* into the sea, saying, Thus with violence shall that great city Babylon be thrown down, and shall be found no more at all.

22 And the voice of harpers, and musicians, and of pipers, and trumpeters, shall be heard no more at all in thee; and no craftsman, of whatsoever craft *he be*, shall be found any more in thee; and the sound of a millstone shall be heard no more at all in thee;

23 ᴿAnd the light of a candle shall shine no more at all in thee; and the voice of the bridegroom and of the bride shall be heard no more at all in thee: for thy merchants were the great men of the earth; for by thy sorceries were all nations deceived. Jer. 25:10

24 And ᴿin her was found the blood of prophets, and of saints, and of all that ᴿwere slain upon the earth. 16:6; 17:6 · Jer. 51:49

19 And after these things ᴿI heard a great voice of much people in heaven, saying, Al-le-lu'-ia; ᴿSalvation, and glory, and honour, and power, unto the Lord our God: 11:15; Jer. 51:48 · 4:11

2 For ᴿtrue and righteous *are* his judgments: for he hath judged the great whore, which did corrupt the earth with her fornication, and hath avenged the blood of his servants at her hand. 15:3

3 And again they said, Al-le-lu'-ia. ᴿAnd her smoke rose up for ever and ever. 14:11; Is. 34:10

4 And ᴿthe four and twenty elders and the four beasts fell down and worshipped God that sat on the throne, saying, ᴿA-men'; Al-le-lu'-ia. 4:4, 6 · 1 Chr. 16:36

5 And a voice came out of the throne, saying, Praise our God, all

ye his servants, and ye that fear him, ᴿboth small and great. 11:18

6 ᴿAnd I heard as it were the voice of a great multitude, and as the voice of many waters, and as the voice of mighty thunderings, saying, Al-le-lu'-ia: for the Lord God omnipotent reigneth. 1:15; 14:2

7 Let us be glad and rejoice, and give honour to him: for ᴿthe marriage of the Lamb is come, and his wife hath made herself ready. Luke 12:36; John 3:29; Eph. 5:23, 32

8 And ᴿto her was granted that she should be arrayed in fine linen, clean and white: ᴿfor the fine linen is the righteousness of saints. Ps. 45:13; Ezek. 16:10 · Ps. 132:9

9 And he saith unto me, Write, ᴿBlessed *are* they which are called unto the marriage supper of the Lamb. And he saith unto me, ᴿThese are the true sayings of God. Matt. 22:2; Luke 14:15 · 22:6

10 And I fell at his feet to worship him. And he said unto me, ᴿSee *thou do it* not: I am thy ᴿfellowservant, and of thy brethren ᴿthat have the testimony of Jesus: worship God: for the testimony of Jesus is the spirit of prophecy. Acts 10:26 · [Heb. 1:14] · 1 John 5:10

11 And I saw heaven opened, and behold ᴿa white horse; and he that sat upon him *was* called ᴿFaithful and True, and ᴿin righteousness he doth judge and make war. Ps. 45:3, 4 · 3:7, 14 · Ps. 96:13; Is. 11:4

12 ᴿHis eyes *were* as a flame of fire, and on his head *were* many crowns; ᴿand he had a name written, that no man knew, but he himself. 1:14; Dan. 10:6 · 2:17

13 And he *was* clothed with a ★ vesture dipped in blood: and his name is called The Word of God.

14 And the armies *which were* in heaven followed him upon white horses, ᴿclothed in fine linen, white and clean. Matt. 28:3

15 And ᴿout of his mouth goeth a sharp sword, that with it he should smite the nations: and he shall rule them with a rod of iron: and he treadeth the winepress of

the fierceness and wrath of Almighty God.   1:16; Is. 11:4; 2 Thess. 2:8

16 And ᴿhe hath on *his* vesture and on his thigh a name written, ᴿKING OF KINGS, AND LORD OF LORDS.   v. 12; 2:17 · Dan. 2:47

17 And I saw an angel standing in the sun; and he cried with a loud voice, saying to all the ᵀfowls that fly in the midst of heaven, ᴿCome and gather yourselves together unto the supper of the great God;   *birds* · 1 Sam. 17:44; Jer. 12:9

18 ᴿThat ye may eat the flesh of kings, and the flesh of captains, and the flesh of mighty men, and the flesh of horses, and of them that sit on them, and the flesh of all *men, both* free and ᵀbond, both small and great.   Ezek. 39:18–20 · *slave*

☆ 19 And I saw the beast, and the kings of the earth, and their armies, gathered together to make war against him that sat on the horse, and against his army.

20 ᴿAnd the beast was taken, and with him the false prophet that wrought miracles before him, with which he deceived them that had received the mark of the beast, and ᴿthem that worshipped his image. These both were cast alive into a lake of fire burning with brimstone.   16:13 · 13:8, 12, 13

21 And the remnant ᴿwere slain with the sword of him that sat upon the horse, which *sword* proceeded out of his mouth: ᴿand all the ᵀfowls ᴿwere filled with their flesh.   v. 15 · vv. 17, 18 · *birds* · 17:16

20 And I saw an angel come down from heaven, ᴿhaving the key of the bottomless pit and a great chain in his hand.   1:18; 9:1

2 And he laid hold on ᴿthe dragon, that old serpent, which is the Devil, and Satan, and bound him a thousand years,   2 Pet. 2:4

3 And cast him into the bottomless pit, and shut him up, and set a seal upon him, that he should deceive the nations no more, till the thousand years should be fulfilled: and after that he must be loosed a little season.

4 And I saw thrones, and they sat upon them, and judgment was given unto them: and *I saw* the souls of them that were beheaded for the witness of Jesus, and for the word of God, and which had not worshipped the beast, neither his image, neither had received *his* mark upon their foreheads, or in their hands; and they lived and ᴿreigned with Christ a thousand years.   Rom. 8:17; 2 Tim. 2:12

5 But the rest of the dead lived not again until the thousand years were finished. This *is* the first resurrection.

6 Blessed and holy *is* he that hath part in the first resurrection: on such the second death hath no power, but they shall be priests of God and of Christ, and shall reign with him a thousand years.

7 And when the thousand years are expired, Satan shall be loosed out of his prison,

8 And shall go out to deceive the nations which are in the four quarters of the earth, ᴿGog and Ma'-gog, to gather them together to battle: the number of whom *is* as the sand of the sea.   Ezek. 38:2

9 ᴿAnd they went up on the breadth of the earth, and compassed the camp of the saints about, and the beloved city: and fire came down from God out of heaven, and devoured them.   Is. 8:8

10 And the devil that deceived them was cast into the lake of fire and brimstone, ᴿwhere the beast and the false prophet *are*, and ᴿshall be tormented day and night for ever and ever.   19:20 · 14:10

11 And I saw a great white throne, and him that sat on it, from whose face the earth and the heaven fled away; and there was found no place for them.

12 And I saw the dead, small and great, stand before God; and the books were opened: and another book was opened, which is *the book* of life: and the dead were judged out of those things which were written in the books, ᴿaccording to their works.   2:23

13 And the sea gave up the dead

which were in it; ^Rand death and hell delivered up the dead which were in them: ^Rand they were judged every man according to their works. 1:18; 6:8; 21:4 · v. 12; 2:23

14 And ^Rdeath and hell were cast into the lake of fire. ^RThis is the second death. 1:18; 6:8; 21:4 · 21:8

15 And whosoever was not found written in the book of life was cast into the lake of fire.

21 And ^RI saw a new heaven and a new earth: ^Rfor the first heaven and the first earth were passed away; and there was no more sea. Is. 65:17; 66:22 · 20:11

2 And I John saw ^Rthe holy city, new Jerusalem, coming down from God out of heaven, prepared ^Ras a bride adorned for her husband. Is. 52:1; Heb. 11:10 · Is. 54:5

3 And I heard a great voice out of heaven saying, Behold, ^Rthe tabernacle of God *is* with men, and he will dwell with them, and they shall be his people, and God himself shall be with them, *and be* their God. Lev. 26:11; Ezek. 43:7

☆ 4 And God shall wipe away all tears from their eyes; and there shall be no more death, neither sorrow, nor crying, neither shall there be any more pain: for the former things are passed away.

5 And ^Rhe that sat upon the throne said, Behold, I make all things new. And he said unto me, Write: for ^Rthese words are true and faithful. 4:2, 9; 20:11 · 19:9; 22:6

6 And he said unto me, It is done. I am Alpha and Omega, the beginning and the end. I will give unto him that is athirst of the fountain of the water of life freely.

7 He that overcometh shall inherit all things; and I will be his God, and he shall be my son.

8 ^RBut the fearful, and unbelieving, and the abominable, and murderers, and whoremongers, and sorcerers, and idolaters, and all liars, shall have their part in ^Rthe lake which burneth with fire and brimstone: which is the second death. 1 Tim. 1:9; [Heb. 12:14] · 20:14

9 And there came unto me one of the seven angels which had the seven vials full of the seven last plagues, and talked with me, saying, Come hither, I will shew thee the bride, the Lamb's wife.

10 And he carried me away ^Rin the ^Tspirit to a great and high mountain, and shewed me ^Rthat great city, the holy Jerusalem, descending out of heaven from God, 1:10 · Or *Spirit* · Ezek. 48

11 Having the glory of God: and her light *was* like unto a stone most precious, even like a jasper stone, clear as crystal;

12 And had a wall great and high, *and* had ^Rtwelve gates, and at the gates twelve angels, and names written thereon, which are *the names* of the twelve tribes of the children of Israel: Ezek. 48:31–34

13 ^ROn the east three gates; on the north three gates; on the south three gates; and on the west three gates. Ezek. 48:31–34

14 And the wall of the city had twelve foundations, and ^Rin them the names of the twelve apostles of the Lamb. Matt. 16:18; Luke 22:29, 30

15 And he that talked with me ^Rhad a golden reed to measure the city, and the gates thereof, and the wall thereof. Ezek. 40:3; Zech. 2:1

16 And the city ^Tlieth foursquare, and the length is as large as the breadth: and he measured the city with the reed, twelve thousand furlongs. The length and the breadth and the height of it are equal. *is laid out as a square*

17 And he measured the wall thereof, an hundred *and* forty *and* four cubits, *according to* the measure of a man, that is, of the angel.

18 And the ^Tbuilding of the wall of it was *of* jasper: and the city *was* pure gold, like unto clear glass. *construction*

19 ^RAnd the foundations of the wall of the city *were* garnished with all manner of precious stones. The first foundation *was* jasper; the second, sapphire; the third, a chalcedony; the fourth, an emerald; Ex. 28:17–20; Is. 54:11

20 The fifth, sardonyx; the sixth, sardius; the seventh, ^Tchrysolyte; the eighth, beryl; the ninth, a topaz; the tenth, a chrysoprasus; the eleventh, a jacinth; the twelfth, an amethyst.   *chrysoprase*

21 And the twelve gates *were* twelve pearls; every several gate was of one pearl: ^Rand the street of the city *was* pure gold, as it were transparent glass.   22:2

☆ 22 And I saw no temple therein: for the Lord God Almighty and the Lamb are the temple of it.

☆ 23 ^RAnd the city had no need of the sun, neither of the moon, to shine in it: for the glory of God did lighten it, and the Lamb *is* the light thereof.   Is. 24:23; 60:19, 20

24 ^RAnd the nations of them which are saved shall walk in the light of it: and the kings of the earth do bring their glory and honour into it.   Is. 60:3, 5; 66:12

25 ^RAnd the gates of it shall not be shut at all by day: for there shall be no night there.   Is. 60:11

26 ^RAnd they shall bring the glory and honour of the nations into it.   v. 24

27 And ^Rthere shall in no wise enter into it any thing that defileth, neither *whatsoever* worketh abomination, or *maketh* a lie: but they which are written in the Lamb's book of life.   Is. 35:8

22 And he shewed me a pure river of water of life, clear as crystal, proceeding out of the throne of God and of the Lamb.

2 In the midst of the street of it, and on either side of the river, *was* there ^Rthe tree of life, which bare twelve *manner of* fruits, *and* yielded her fruit every month: and the leaves of the tree *were* for the healing of the nations. [vv. 14, 19; 2:7]

3 And there shall be no more curse: but the throne of God and of the Lamb shall be in it; and his ^Rservants shall serve him: 7:15

4 And ^Rthey shall see his face; and ^Rhis name *shall be* ^Tin their foreheads.   [1 John 3:2] · 14:1 · *on*

5 And there shall be no night there; and they need no candle, neither light of the sun; for the Lord God giveth them light: and they shall reign for ever and ever.

6 And he said unto me, ^RThese sayings *are* faithful and true: and the Lord God of the holy prophets ^Rsent his angel to shew unto his servants the things which must ^Rshortly be done. 19:9 · 1:1 · Heb. 10:37

7 ^RBehold, I come quickly: ^Rblessed *is* he that keepeth the sayings of the prophecy of this book.   [3:11] · 1:3

8 And I John saw these things, and heard *them*. And when I had heard and seen, ^RI fell down to worship before the feet of the angel which shewed me these things.   19:10

9 Then saith he unto me, ^RSee *thou do it* not: for I am thy fellowservant, and of thy brethren the prophets, and of them which keep the ^Tsayings of this book: worship God.   19:10 · *words*

10 ^RAnd he saith unto me, Seal not the ^Tsayings of the prophecy of this book: ^Rfor the time is at hand.   10:4; Dan. 8:26 · *words* · 1:3

11 He that is unjust, let him be unjust still: and he which is filthy, let him be filthy still: and he that is righteous, let him be righteous still: and he that is holy, let him be holy still.

12 And, behold, I come quickly; ☆ and ^Rmy reward *is* with me, ^Rto give every man according as his work shall be.   Is. 40:10; 62:11 · 20:12

13 ^RI am Alpha and Omega, the beginning and the end, the first and the last.   Is. 41:4

14 ^RBlessed *are* they that do his commandments, that they may have right ^Rto the tree of life, ^Rand may enter in through the gates into the city.   Dan. 12:12 · 2:7 · 21:27

15 For ^Rwithout *are* ^Rdogs, and sorcerers, and whoremongers, and murderers, and idolaters, and whosoever loveth and maketh a lie.   Matt. 8:12 · Deut. 23:18; Matt. 7:6

16 ^RI Jesus have sent mine angel

to testify unto you these things in the churches. [R]I am the root and the offspring of David, *and* the bright and morning star.   1:1 · 5:5

17 And the Spirit and [R]the bride say, Come. And let him that heareth say, Come. [R]And let him that is athirst come. And whosoever will, let him take the water of life freely.   [21:2, 9] · 21:6; Is. 55:1

18 For I testify unto every man that heareth the words of the prophecy of this book, [R]If any man shall add unto these things, God shall add unto him the plagues that are written in this book: Deut. 4:2; 12:32; Prov. 30:6

19 And if any man shall take away from the words of the book of this prophecy, [R]God shall take away his part out of the book of life, and out of the holy city, and *from* the things which are written in this book.   Ex. 32:33

20 He which testifieth these things saith, Surely I come quickly. A-men'. Even so, come, Lord Jesus.

21 The grace of our Lord Jesus Christ *be* with you all. A-men'.

CONCORDANCE

King James Version

A

ABASE
himself shall be *a* . . . . .Matt. 23:12
both how to be *a* . . . . .Phil. 4:12

ABIDE
shall *a* under the shadow . . . . . .Ps. 91:1
A in me, and I in you . . . . .John 15:4
a in my love . . . . .John 15:10
now *a* faith, hope . . . . .1 Cor. 13:13

ABLE
Believe ye that I am *a* . . . . . . .Matt. 9:28
a to separate us . . . . .Rom. 8:39
he is *a* to keep . . . . .2 Tim. 1:12
who shall be *a* to stand . . . . . . .Rev. 6:17

ABOMINATION
an *a* to the Lord . . . . .Prov. 15:8
the *a* of desolation . . . . .Matt. 24:15
worketh *a*, or maketh . . . . .Rev. 21:27

ABSTAIN
A from all . . . . .1 Thess. 5:22
a from fleshly lusts . . . . .1 Pet. 2:11

ABUNDANCE
a of his riches . . . . .Ps. 52:7
a of the heart . . . . .Matt. 12:34
of the *a* of the heart . . . . .Luke 6:45
in the *a* . . . . .Luke 12:15
a of the revelations . . . . .2 Cor. 12:7

ABUNDANT
a utter the memory . . . . .Ps. 145:7
for he will *a* pardon . . . . .Is. 55:7
have it more *a* . . . . .John 10:10
exceeding *a* above . . . . .Eph. 3:20

ACCEPT
No prophet is *a* . . . . .Luke 4:24
we may be *a* . . . . .2 Cor. 5:9
behold, now is the *a* time . . . . .2 Cor. 6:2

ACCEPTABLE
be *a* in thy sight, O Lord . . . . . .Ps. 19:14
holy, *a* unto God . . . . .Rom. 12:1

ACCESS
we have *a* by faith . . . . .Rom. 5:2

ACCORDING
a to his deeds . . . . .Rom. 2:6
a to his purpose . . . . .Rom. 8:28
See Titus 3:5; 1 Pet. 1:2

ACCOUNT
a of thy stewardship . . . . .Luke 16:2
shall give *a* . . . . .Rom. 14:12
that must give *a* . . . . .Heb. 13:17

ACKNOWLEDGE
I *a* my transgressions . . . . .Ps. 51:3
all thy ways *a* him . . . . .Prov. 3:6

ADMONISH
able also to *a* . . . . .Rom. 15:14
a one another . . . . .Col. 3:16
Lord, and *a* you . . . . .1 Thess. 5:12

ADMONITION
written for our *a* . . . . .1 Cor. 10:11
a of the Lord . . . . .Eph. 6:4

ADOPTION
the Spirit of *a* . . . . .Rom. 8:15
waiting for the *a* . . . . .Rom. 8:23

ADORN
women *a* themselves . . . . .1 Tim. 2:9
that outward *a* . . . . .1 Pet. 3:3
a for her husband . . . . .Rev. 21:2

ADVERSARY
Agree with thine *a* . . . . .Matt. 5:25
there are many *a* . . . . .1 Cor. 16:9
your *a* the devil . . . . .1 Pet. 5:8

ADVERSITY
born for *a* . . . . .Prov. 17:17
bread of *a* . . . . .Is. 30:20

ADVOCATE
an *a* with the Father . . . . .1 John 2:1

AFAR
you which were *a* off . . . . .Eph. 2:17
seen them *a* off . . . . .Heb. 11:13

AFFECTION
Be kindly *a* one . . . . .Rom. 12:10
crucified . . . with the *a* . . . . . . .Gal. 5:24
Set your *a* on things . . . . .Col. 3:2

AFFLICT
I have been *a* . . . . .Ps. 119:71
smitten of God, and *a* . . . . .Is. 53:4
relieved the *a* . . . . .1 Tim. 5:10
a, tormented . . . . .Heb. 11:37
Is any among you *a* . . . . .James 5:13

AFFLICTION
a of thine handmaid . . . . .1 Sam. 1:11
mine *a* and my pain . . . . .Ps. 25:18
In all their *a* . . . . .Is. 63:9
a or persecution . . . . .Mark 4:17
out of all his *a* . . . . .Acts 7:10
light *a*, which is . . . . .2 Cor. 4:17
a with the people . . . . .Heb. 11:25
widows in their *a* . . . . .James 1:27

AGES
That in the *a* to come . . . . .Eph. 2:7
throughout all *a* . . . . .Eph. 3:21

AGREE
two of you shall *a* . . . . .Matt. 18:19
these three *a* . . . . .1 John 5:8

AIR
the Lord in the *a* . . . . .1 Thess. 4:17

ALIENATED
a from the life . . . . .Eph. 4:18
that were sometime *a* . . . . .Col. 1:21

ALIVE
I kill, and I make *a* . . . . .Deut. 32:39
dead, and is *a* again . . . . . . .Luke 15:24
shewed himself *a* . . . . .Acts 1:3
but *a* unto . . . . .Rom. 6:11
we which are *a* . . . . .1 Thess. 4:15
I am *a* for evermore . . . . .Rev. 1:18

ALMIGHTY
is to come, the *A* . . . . .Rev. 1:8
holy, Lord God *A* . . . . .Rev. 4:8
O Lord God *A* . . . . .Rev. 11:17

ALMS
do not your *a* before men . . . . . .Matt. 6:1

ALWAY
I am with you *a* . . . . .Matt. 28:20

ALWAYS
spirit shall not *a* strive . . . . .Gen. 6:3
me ye have not *a* . . . . .Mark 14:7
the poor *a* ye have . . . . .John 12:8
in the Lord *a* . . . . .Phil. 4:4

AMBASSADOR
a for Christ . . . . .2 Cor. 5:20

AMEN
to everlasting, *A* . . . . .Ps. 41:13
glory, for ever, *A* . . . . .Matt. 6:13
saith the *A* . . . . .Rev. 3:14

ANGEL
a of the Lord . . . . .Ps. 34:7
shall give his *a* . . . . .Ps. 91:11
who hath sent his *a* . . . . .Dan. 3:28
are as the *a* which . . . . .Mark 12:25
there appeared an *a* . . . . . . .Luke 22:43
a went down . . . . .John 5:4
entertained *a* . . . . .Heb. 13:2
a desire to look . . . . .1 Pet. 1:12

ANGER
gracious, slow to *a* . . . . .Ps. 103:8
words stir up *a* . . . . .Prov. 15:1
and wrath, and *a* . . . . .Eph. 4:31
your children to *a* . . . . .Col. 3:21

ANGRY
God is *a* with the wicked . . . . . . .Ps. 7:11
an *a* countenance . . . . .Prov. 25:23
a with his brother . . . . .Matt. 5:22
Be ye *a*, and sin not . . . . .Eph. 4:26

ANOINTED (v.)
the Lord hath *a* me . . . . .Is. 61:1
hath *a* me to preach . . . . .Luke 4:18
a the feet of Jesus . . . . .John 12:3

ANOINTED (n.)
against the Lord's *a* . . . . .1 Sam. 26:9
Touch not mine *a* . . . . .Ps. 105:15
the Lord to his *a* . . . . .Is. 45:1

APPEAR
outwardly *a* righteous . . . . . . .Matt. 23:28
all *a* before the . . . . .2 Cor. 5:10
who is our life, shall *a* . . . . .Col. 3:4
the *a* of our Saviour . . . . .2 Tim. 1:10
that love his *a* . . . . .2 Tim. 4:8
for him shall he *a* . . . . .Heb. 9:28

ARCHANGEL
the voice of the *a* . . . . .1 Thess. 4:16
Michael the *a* . . . . .Jude 9

ARISE
Let God *a* . . . . .Ps. 68:1
children *a* up . . . . .Prov. 31:28
A, and take up . . . . .Mark 2:11
I will *a* and go . . . . .Luke 15:18
a from the dead . . . . .Eph. 5:14

ARMOUR
the *a* of light . . . . .Rom. 13:12
a of righteousness . . . . .2 Cor. 6:7
the whole *a* of God . . . . .Eph. 6:11

ASCEND
I will *a* into heaven . . . . .Is. 14:13
Son of man *a* up . . . . .John 6:62
shall *a* into heaven . . . . .Rom. 10:6

ASHAMED
let me never be *a* . . . . .Ps. 31:2
not *a* of the gospel . . . . .Rom. 1:16
a of the testimony . . . . .2 Tim. 1:8
needeth not to be *a* . . . . .2 Tim. 2:15
not *a* to be called . . . . .Heb. 11:16
let him not be *a* . . . . .1 Pet. 4:16

ASHES
which am but dust and *a* . . . . . .Gen. 18:27
and repent in dust and, *a* . . . . . .Job 42:6

ASK
A, and it shall be given . . . . .Matt. 7:7
to them that *a* him . . . . .Luke 11:13
abide in you, ye shall *a* . . . . . . .John 15:7
let him *a* of God . . . . .James 1:5
because ye *a* not . . . . .James 4:2
every man that *a* you . . . . .1 Pet. 3:15
if we *a* any thing . . . . .1 John 5:14

ASLEEP
some are fallen *a* . . . . .1 Cor. 15:6
them which are *a* . . . . .1 Thess. 4:13
the fathers fell *a* . . . . .2 Pet. 3:4

ASSURANCE
a of understanding . . . . .Col. 2:2
the full *a* of hope . . . . .Heb. 6:11
in full *a* of faith . . . . .Heb. 10:22

AUTHOR
God is not the *a* of . . . . .1 Cor. 14:33
the *a* and finisher . . . . .Heb. 12:2

AUTHORITY
as one having *a* . . . . .Matt. 7:29
as one that had *a* . . . . .Mark 1:22
all that are in *a* . . . . .1 Tim. 2:2
rebuke with all *a* . . . . .Titus 2:15
a and powers . . . . .1 Pet. 3:22

AVENGE
A me of mine . . . . .Luke 18:3
not God *a* his own . . . . .Luke 18:7

AVOID
a profane and vain . . . . .1 Tim. 6:20
But *a* foolish . . . . .Titus 3:9

AWAKE
a out of sleep . . . . .Rom. 13:11
A to righteousness . . . . .1 Cor. 15:34
A thou that sleepest . . . . .Eph. 5:14

B

BABE
mouth of *b* and sucklings . . . . .Ps. 8:2
the mouth of *b* . . . . .Matt. 21:16

BALM
Is there no *b* in Gilead . . . . .Jer. 8:22

BAPTISM
b that I am baptized with . . . . .Matt. 20:22
The *b* of John . . . . .Matt. 21:25
b of repentance . . . . .Mark 1:4
with the *b* of John . . . . .Luke 7:29
I have a *b* to be . . . . .Luke 12:50
buried with him by *b* . . . . .Rom. 6:4
one faith, one *b* . . . . .Eph. 4:5
with him in *b* . . . . .Col. 2:12
Of the doctrine of *b* . . . . .Heb. 6:2

BAPTIZE
I indeed *b* you . . . . .Matt. 3:11
I have need to be *b* . . . . .Matt. 3:14
believeth and is *b* . . . . .Mark 16:16
I *b* with water . . . . .John 1:26
he that sent me to *b* . . . . .John 1:33
Repent, and be *b* . . . . .Acts 2:38
b in the name . . . . .Acts 8:16
hinder me to be *b* . . . . .Acts 8:36
was *b*, he and all . . . . .Acts 16:33
believed, and were *b* . . . . .Acts 18:8
of us as were *b* . . . . .Rom. 6:3
all *b* into one body . . . . .1 Cor. 12:13
been *b* into Christ . . . . .Gal. 3:27

BEAR
not *b* false witness . . . . .Ex. 20:16
not worthy to *b* . . . . .Matt. 3:11
not *b* his cross . . . . .Luke 14:27
I am one that *b* witness . . . . . .John 8:18
also shall *b* witness . . . . .John 15:27
The Spirit itself *b* . . . . .Rom. 8:16
b the infirmities . . . . .Rom. 15:1
be able to *b* it . . . . .1 Cor. 10:13
B ye one another's . . . . .Gal. 6:2
for I *b* in my body . . . . .Gal. 6:17

offered to *b* the sins . . . . .Heb. 9:28
and *b* witness . . . . .1 John 1:2
b witness in earth . . . . .1 John 5:8

BEAST
fought with *b* . . . . .1 Cor. 15:32
as natural brute *b* . . . . .2 Pet. 2:12

BEAT
b their swords into . . . . .Is. 2:4
B your plowshares . . . . .Joel 3:10

BEAUTIFUL
b in his time . . . . .Eccl. 3:11
Thou art *b*, O my love . . . . .Song 6:4
which is called *B* . . . . .Acts 3:2
How *b* are the feet . . . . .Rom. 10:15

BEAUTY
the *b* of holiness . . . . .2 Chr. 20:21
the *b* of the Lord . . . . .Ps. 27:4
b is vain . . . . .Prov. 31:30

BEGINNING
In the *b* God created . . . . .Gen. 1:1
b of wisdom . . . . .Ps. 111:10
the *b* of knowledge . . . . .Prov. 1:7
Lord is the *b* . . . . .Prov. 9:10
the *b* was the Word . . . . .John 1:1
the *b* and the end . . . . .Rev. 21:6
See 1 Chr. 17:9; Prov. 8:22, 23

BEGOTTEN
his only *b* Son . . . . .John 3:16
b us again . . . . .1 Pet. 1:3
his only *b* Son . . . . .1 John 4:9

BEHOLD
b the upright . . . . .Ps. 37:37
b the face . . . . .Matt. 18:10
may *b* my glory . . . . .John 17:24

BELIEVE
b that ye receive them . . . . . .Mark 11:24
which for a while *b* . . . . .Luke 8:13
that *b* on his name . . . . .John 1:12
B thou this . . . . .John 11:26
ye *b* in God, *b* also . . . . .John 14:1
B on the Lord Jesus . . . . .Acts 16:31
whosoever *b* on him . . . . .Rom. 9:33
how shall they *b* . . . . .Rom. 10:14
given to them that *b* . . . . .Gal. 3:22
know whom I have *b* . . . . .2 Tim. 1:12
must *b* that he is . . . . .Heb. 11:6
devils also *b* . . . . .James 2:19

BELLY
upon thy *b* shalt thou go . . . . . .Gen. 3:14
out of his *b* shall . . . . .John 7:38
whose God is their *b* . . . . .Phil. 3:19

BELOVED
giveth his *b* sleep . . . . .Ps. 127:2
This is my *b* Son . . . . .Matt. 3:17
accepted in the *b* . . . . .Eph. 1:6
This is my *b* Son . . . . .2 Pet. 1:17

BETTER
obey is *b* than sacrifice . . . . .1 Sam. 15:22
lovingkindness is *b* than . . . . . . .Ps. 63:3

each esteem other *b* . . . . .Phil. 2:3
a *b* country . . . . .Heb. 11:16
For it had been *b* . . . . .2 Pet. 2:21

BEWARE
b of covetousness . . . . .Luke 12:15
b of evil workers . . . . .Phil. 3:2

BIND
b up the brokenhearted . . . . .Is. 61:1
shalt *b* on earth . . . . .Matt. 16:19

BISHOP
desire the office of *b* . . . . .1 Tim. 3:1
b must be blameless . . . . .Titus 1:7

BITTERNESS
Let all *b*, and wrath . . . . .Eph. 4:31
lest any root of *b* . . . . .Heb. 12:15

BLAME
be holy and without *b* . . . . .Eph. 1:4

BLAMELESS
be *b* in the day of . . . . .1 Cor. 1:8
that ye may be *b* . . . . .Phil. 2:15

BLASPHEME
b against the . . . . .Mark 3:29
name of God is *b* . . . . .Rom. 2:24

BLEMISH
holy and without *b* . . . . .Eph. 5:27
a lamb without *b* . . . . .1 Pet. 1:19

BLESS
The Lord *b* thee . . . . .Num. 6:24
B the Lord, O my soul . . . . .Ps. 103:1
B are the poor in . . . . .Matt. 5:3
more *b* to give than . . . . .Acts 20:35
for that *b* hope . . . . .Titus 2:13
B are the dead . . . . .Rev. 14:13

BLESSING
b of the Lord . . . . .Prov. 10:22
pour you out a *b* . . . . .Mal. 3:10
b and cursing . . . . .James 3:10
and glory, and *b* . . . . .Rev. 5:12

BLIND
their minds were *b* . . . . .2 Cor. 3:14
of this world hath *b* . . . . .2 Cor. 4:4
darkness hath *b* . . . . .1 John 2:11

BLINDNESS
because of *b* of their heart . . . . .Eph. 4:18

BLOOD
precious shall their *b* . . . . .Ps. 72:14
flesh and *b* . . . . .Matt. 16:17
His *b* be on us . . . . .Matt. 27:25
b of the new testament . . . . . .Mark 14:24
great drops of *b* . . . . .Luke 22:44
drinketh my *b* . . . . .John 6:54
justified by his *b* . . . . .Rom. 5:9
new testament in my *b* . . . . .1 Cor. 11:25
through his *b* . . . . .Eph. 1:7
without shedding of *b* . . . . . . .Heb. 9:22
precious *b* of Christ . . . . .1 Pet. 1:19
by the *b* of the Lamb . . . . .Rev. 12:11

BLOT
your sins may be *b* . . . . .Acts 3:19
I will not *b* out . . . . .Rev. 3:5

BOAST
B not thyself . . . . .Prov. 27:1
I may *b* myself . . . . .2 Cor. 11:16
lest any man should *b* . . . . . . .Eph. 2:9

BODY
b of sin might be . . . . .Rom. 6:6
present your *b* a living . . . . . .Rom. 12:1
many members in one *b* . . . . .Rom. 12:4
b is the temple . . . . .1 Cor. 6:19
I keep under my *b* . . . . .1 Cor. 9:27
give my *b* to be burned . . . . .1 Cor. 13:3
absent from the *b* . . . . .2 Cor. 5:8
I bear in my *b* . . . . .Gal. 6:17

BONE
the *b* which thou . . . . .Ps. 51:8
rottenness in his *b* . . . . .Prov. 12:4
of dead men's *b* . . . . .Matt. 23:27
hath not flesh and *b* . . . . . . .Luke 24:39

BOOK
name out of the *b* . . . . .Rev. 3:5
not written in the *b* . . . . .Rev. 13:8
another *b* was opened . . . . . .Rev. 20:12
the words of the *b* . . . . .Rev. 22:19

BORN
unto us a child is *b* . . . . .Is. 9:6
b King of the Jews . . . . .Matt. 2:2
For unto you is *b* . . . . .Luke 2:11
Except a man be *b* again . . . . .John 3:3
loveth is *b* of God . . . . .1 John 4:7
whatsoever is *b* of God . . . . . .1 John 5:4

BORNE
he hath *b* our griefs . . . . .Is. 53:4

BOSOM
Into Abraham's *b* . . . . .Luke 16:22
b of the Father . . . . .John 1:18
leaning on Jesus' *b* . . . . .John 13:23

BOUGHT
For ye are *b* . . . . .1 Cor. 6:20
Ye are *b* with a price . . . . . . .1 Cor. 7:23

BOW
every knee shall *b* . . . . .Is. 45:23
every knee shall *b* . . . . .Rom. 14:11

BRANCH
B shall grow out . . . . .Is. 11:1
David a righteous *B* . . . . .Jer. 23:5

BREAD
ravens brought him *b* . . . . . . .1 Kin. 17:6
Cast thy *b* upon . . . . .Eccl. 11:1
stones be made *b* . . . . .Matt. 4:3
shall not live by *b* . . . . .Matt. 4:4
this day our daily *b* . . . . .Matt. 6:11
I am the *b* of life . . . . .John 6:35
he took *b*, and gave . . . . .Acts 27:35
betrayed took *b* . . . . .1 Cor. 11:23

BREATH
into his nostrils the *b* . . . . .Gen. 2:7

BRIDE
prepared as a *b* . . . . .Rev. 21:2
the Spirit and the *b* . . . . .Rev. 22:17

BRIDEGROOM
to meet the *b* . . . . .Matt. 25:1
of the *b* voice . . . . .John 3:29

BRIMSTONE
Sodom and Gomorrah *b* . . . . .Gen. 19:24
with fire and *b* . . . . .Rev. 14:10

BRING
B ye all the tithes into the . . . . .Mal. 3:10
if thou *b* thy gift . . . . .Matt. 5:23
that it may *b* forth . . . . .John 15:2

BROKEN
b and a contrite heart . . . . .Ps. 51:17
bone shall not be *b* . . . . .John 19:36
b down the middle . . . . .Eph. 2:14

BROTHER
b is born for adversity . . . . . .Prov. 17:17
b offended is harder . . . . .Prov. 18:19

BROTHERLY
to another with *b* love . . . . . .Rom. 12:10
Let *b* love continue . . . . .Heb. 13:1

BRUISE
b for our iniquities . . . . .Is. 53:5

BUILD
labour in vain that *b* . . . . .Ps. 127:1
a time to *b* up . . . . .Eccl. 3:3
I will *b* my church . . . . .Matt. 16:18
if any man *b* upon . . . . .1 Cor. 3:12

BUILDER
stone which the *b* . . . . .1 Pet. 2:7
b and maker is God . . . . .Heb. 11:10

BUILDING
ye are God's *b* . . . . .1 Cor. 3:9
we have a *b* of God . . . . .2 Cor. 5:1
the *b* of the wall . . . . .Rev. 21:18

BURDEN
Cast thy *b* upon the Lord . . . . . .Ps. 55:22
my *b* is light . . . . .Matt. 11:30
one another's *b* . . . . .Gal. 6:2

BURN
and your lights *b* . . . . .Luke 12:35
did not our heart *b* . . . . .Luke 24:32
my body to be *b* . . . . .1 Cor. 13:3
b with brimstone . . . . .Rev. 19:20

BURY
dead *b* their dead . . . . .Luke 9:60
we are *b* with him . . . . .Rom. 6:4
he was *b* . . . . .1 Cor. 15:4
B with him in baptism . . . . .Col. 2:12

BUSINESS
diligent in his *b* . . . . .Prov. 22:29

about my Father's *b* . . . . .Luke 2:49
Not slothful in *b* . . . . .Rom. 12:11
to do your own *b* . . . . .1 Thess. 4:11

C

CALL
the hope of his *c* . . . . .Eph. 1:18
prize of the high *c* . . . . .Phil. 3:14
with a holy *c* . . . . .2 Tim. 1:9

CANDLE
lighted a *c* . . . . .Luke 8:16; 11:33

CARE
the *c* of this world . . . . .Matt. 13:22
and *c* of this life . . . . .Luke 21:34
Casting all your *c* . . . . .1 Pet. 5:7

CAREFUL
Be *c* for nothing . . . . .Phil. 4:6

CARNAL
c mind is enmity . . . . .Rom. 8:7
but as unto *c* . . . . .1 Cor. 3:1
weapons . . . are not *c* . . . . . . .2 Cor. 10:4

CAST
C thy burden upon . . . . .Ps. 55:22
in no wise *c* out . . . . .John 6:37
C all your care . . . . .1 Pet. 5:7
love *c* out fear . . . . .1 John 4:18

CAUGHT
be *c* up together . . . . .1 Thess. 4:17

CEASE
He maketh wars to *c* . . . . .Ps. 46:9
tongues, they shall *c* . . . . . . .1 Cor. 13:8
Pray without *c* . . . . .1 Thess. 5:17

CHANGE
I am the Lord, I *c* not . . . . .Mal. 3:6
we shall all be *c* . . . . .1 Cor. 15:51
c . . . from glory . . . . .2 Cor. 3:18

CHARITY
faith, *c* . . . . .2 Tim. 2:22
sound in faith, in *c* . . . . .Titus 2:2
brotherly kindness *c* . . . . .2 Pet. 1:7

CHASTEN
C thy son . . . . .Prov. 19:18
Lord loveth he *c* . . . . .Heb. 12:6
no *c* for the present . . . . .Heb. 12:11
I rebuke and *c* . . . . .Rev. 3:19

CHEER
be of good *c* . . . . .John 16:33
God loveth a *c* giver . . . . .2 Cor. 9:7

CHIEF
the *c* corner stone . . . . .Eph. 2:20

CHILD
a *c* is known by his . . . . .Prov. 20:11
Train up a *c* in the way . . . . . . .Prov. 22:6
What manner of *c* . . . . .Luke 1:66
When I was a *c* . . . . .1 Cor. 13:11

CHILDREN
Suffer little c . . . . .Matt. 19:14
we are the c of God . . . . .Rom. 8:16
no more c . . . . .Eph. 4:14
C, obey your parents . . . . .Eph. 6:1

CHOSEN
called, but few c . . . . .Matt. 20:16
c that good part . . . . .Luke 10:42
Ye have not c me . . . . .John 15:16
he is a c vessel . . . . .Acts 9:15
c the foolish things . . . . .1 Cor. 1:27
a c generation . . . . .1 Pet. 2:9

CHRIST
Thou art the C . . . . .Matt. 16:16
which is called C . . . . .John 4:25
in due time C died . . . . .Rom. 5:6
C liveth in me . . . . .Gal. 2:20
me to live is C . . . . .Phil. 1:21
Jesus is the C . . . . .1 John 2:22
of God and of C . . . . .Rev. 20:6

CHRISTIAN
were called C first . . . . .Acts 11:26
me to be a C . . . . .Acts 26:28
man suffer as a C . . . . .1 Pet. 4:16

CHURCH
added to the c daily . . . . .Acts 2:47
The c of Christ . . . . .Rom. 16:16
set some in the c . . . . .1 Cor. 12:28
also loved the c . . . . .Eph. 5:25
the body, the c . . . . .Col. 1:18
care of the c of God . . . . .1 Tim. 3:5

CIRCUMCISE
ye shall c the flesh . . . . .Gen. 17:11
Except ye be c . . . . .Acts 15:1

CIRCUMCISION
c nor uncircumcision . . . . .Col. 3:11

CITY
c of the living God . . . . .Heb. 12:22
the c of the nations . . . . .Rev. 16:19
the beloved c . . . . .Rev. 20:9

CLEAN
Create in me a c heart . . . . .Ps. 51:10
Wash you, make you c . . . . .Is. 1:16
canst make me c . . . . .Matt. 8:2
Ye are not all c . . . . .John 13:11
c through the word . . . . .John 15:3
linen, c and white . . . . .Rev. 19:8

CLEANSE
C your hands . . . . .James 4:8
to c us . . . . .1 John 1:9

CLOTHE
household are c . . . . .Prov. 31:21
if God so c . . . . .Matt. 6:30
Naked, and ye c me . . . . .Matt. 25:36
be c with humility . . . . .1 Pet. 5:5
c with a vesture . . . . .Rev. 19:13

CLOUD
by day in a pillar of a c . . . . . . .Ex. 13:21
in the c of heaven with . . . . . .Matt. 24:30

a c that overshadowed . . . . . . .Mark 9:7
in a c with power . . . . .Luke 21:27
caught up . . . in the c . . . . .1 Thess. 4:17
and behold a white c . . . . .Rev. 14:14

COLD
cup of c water . . . . .Matt. 10:42
many shall wax c . . . . .Matt. 24:12
in c and nakedness . . . . .2 Cor. 11:27
neither c nor hot . . . . .Rev. 3:15

COME
c ye to the waters . . . . .Is. 55:1
C unto me . . . . .Matt. 11:28
the Son of man is c . . . . .Matt. 18:11
compel them to c . . . . .Luke 14:23
I will c again . . . . .John 14:3
c, Lord Jesus . . . . .Rev. 22:20

COMFORT
staff they c me . . . . .Ps. 23:4
C ye, c ye my people . . . . .Is. 40:1
they shall be c . . . . .Matt. 5:4
able to c them . . . . .2 Cor. 1:4

COMFORTER
give you another C . . . . .John 14:16
when the C is come . . . . .John 15:26

COMMANDMENT
thy c are my delight . . . . .Ps. 119:143
A new c I give . . . . .John 13:34
first c with promise . . . . .Eph. 6:2
I write no new c . . . . .1 John 2:7

COMMIT
Thou shalt not c adultery . . . . . .Ex. 20:14
C thy way unto . . . . .Ps. 37:5
which I have c . . . . .2 Tim. 1:12

COMMUNICATION
let your c be, Yea . . . . .Matt. 5:37
What manner of c . . . . .Luke 24:17
evil c corrupt . . . . .1 Cor. 15:33
Let no corrupt c . . . . .Eph. 4:29

COMMUNION
c of the blood of Christ . . . . . .1 Cor. 10:16
c of the body of Christ . . . . . .1 Cor. 10:16
what c hath light . . . . .2 Cor. 6:14
c of the Holy Ghost . . . . .2 Cor. 13:14

COMPASSION
his c fail not . . . . .Lam. 3:22
he was moved with c . . . . .Matt. 9:36
Jesus, moved with c . . . . .Mark 1:41
saw him, and had c . . . . .Luke 15:20
will have c on whom . . . . .Rom. 9:15
one mind, having c . . . . .1 Pet. 3:8

COMPEL
c thee to go a mile . . . . .Matt. 5:41
c to bear his cross . . . . .Matt. 27:32
c them to come in . . . . .Luke 14:23

COMPREHEND
the darkness c it not . . . . .John 1:5
c with all saints . . . . .Eph. 3:18

CONDEMN
into the world to *c* . . . . .John 3:17
believeth not is *c* . . . . .John 3:18
Neither do I *c* thee . . . . .John 8:11
lest ye be *c* . . . . .James 5:9
if our heart *c* us . . . . .1 John 3:21

CONDEMNATION
shall not come into *c* . . . . .John 5:24
lest ye fall into *c* . . . . .James 5:12

CONFESS
c me before men . . . . .Matt. 10:32
c with thy mouth . . . . .Rom. 10:9
c that Jesus Christ . . . . .Phil. 2:11
C your faults . . . . .James 5:16
if we *c* our sins . . . . .1 John 1:9
c that Jesus is the . . . . .1 John 4:15

CONFESSION
mouth *c* is made . . . . .Rom. 10:10

CONFIDENCE
to put *c* in man . . . . .Ps. 118:8
Lord shall be thy *c* . . . . .Prov. 3:26
no *c* in the flesh . . . . .Phil. 3:3
this is the *c* that we . . . . .1 John 5:14

CONFIDENT
in this will I be *c* . . . . .Ps. 27:3
fool rageth, and is *c* . . . . .Prov. 14:16
we are always *c* . . . . .2 Cor. 5:6
c of this very thing . . . . .Phil. 1:6

CONFORM
c to the image of his Son . . . . .Rom. 8:29
not *c* to this world . . . . .Rom. 12:2
c unto his death . . . . .Phil. 3:10

CONQUER
we are more than *c* . . . . .Rom. 8:37
he went forth *c* . . . . .Rev. 6:2

CONSCIENCE
a good *c* . . . . .1 Tim. 1:5
faith, and a good *c* . . . . .1 Tim. 1:19
c seared with a hot iron . . . . . .1 Tim. 4:2

CONSIDER
When I *c* thy heavens. . . . . .Ps. 8:3
C the lilies of the . . . . .Matt. 6:28
c not the beam . . . . .Matt. 7:3
C the ravens . . . . .Luke 12:24

CONSUME
heed that ye be not *c* . . . . .Gal. 5:15
For our God is a *c* . . . . .Heb. 12:29
that ye may *c* it . . . . .James 4:3

CONTENT
therewith to be *c* . . . . .Phil. 4:11
godliness with *c* . . . . .1 Tim. 6:6
be *c* with such things . . . . .Heb. 13:5

CONTINUAL
praise shall *c* be . . . . .Ps. 34:1
Bind them *c* . . . . .Prov. 6:21
by her *c* coming . . . . .Luke 18:5
give ourselves *c* . . . . .Acts 6:4

CONTINUE
if ye *c* in my word . . . . .John 8:31
c ye in my love . . . . .John 15:9
Peter *c* knocking . . . . .Acts 12:16
to *c* in the grace . . . . .Acts 13:43
Shall we *c* in sin . . . . .Rom. 6:1
c instant in prayer . . . . .Rom. 12:2
If ye *c* in the faith . . . . .Col. 1:23
C in prayer, and watch . . . . .Col. 4:2
if they *c* in faith . . . . .1 Tim. 2:15
Let brotherly love *c* . . . . .Heb. 13:1

CONTRITE
a broken and a *c* heart . . . . . . .Ps. 51:17

CONVERSATION
ordereth his *c* aright . . . . .Ps. 50:23
our *c* is in heaven . . . . .Phil. 3:20
in *c*, in charity . . . . .1 Tim. 4:12
c be without . . . . .Heb. 13:5

CONVERT
perfect, *c* the soul . . . . .Ps. 19:7
Except ye be *c* . . . . .Matt. 18:3
they should be *c* . . . . .Mark 4:12
and be *c* . . . . .Acts 3:19

CORRECTION
rod of *c* shall drive . . . . .Prov. 22:15
for reproof, for *c* . . . . .2 Tim. 3:16

CORRUPT
and rust doth *c* . . . . .Matt. 6:19
a *c* tree bringeth forth . . . . . . .Matt. 7:17
communications *c* . . . . .1 Cor. 15:33
Let no *c* communication . . . . . .Eph. 4:29

COUNSEL
c of the ungodly . . . . .Ps. 1:1
The *c* of the Lord . . . . .Ps. 33:11
the *c* of the Lord . . . . .Prov. 19:21
took *c* together . . . . .John 11:53
all the *c* of God . . . . .Acts 20:27

COUNSELLOR
in the multitude of *c* . . . . .Prov. 15:22
called Wonderful, *C* . . . . .Is. 9:6

COUNT
is *c* wise . . . . .Prov. 17:28
and *c* the cost . . . . .Luke 14:28
I *c* loss for . . . . .Phil. 3:7
I *c* not myself . . . . .Phil. 3:13
may be *c* worthy . . . . .2 Thess. 1:5
he *c* me faithful . . . . .1 Tim. 1:12
c it all joy . . . . .James 1:2
as some men *c* . . . . .2 Pet. 3:9

COUNTENANCE
light of thy *c* . . . . .Ps. 44:3
maketh a cheerful *c* . . . . .Prov. 15:13
sharpeneth the *c* . . . . .Prov. 27:17
of a sad *c* . . . . .Matt. 6:16
c was like lightning . . . . .Matt. 28:3
his *c* was as the sun . . . . .Rev. 1:16

COURAGE
Be strong and of a good *c* . . . . .Deut. 31:6
be of good *c* . . . . .Ps. 27:14

COURSE
may have free c .... 2 Thess. 3:1
I have finished my c .... 2 Tim. 4:7
the c of nature .... James 3:6

COVENANT
c which God made .... Acts 3:25
glory, and the c .... Rom. 9:4
the c of promise .... Eph. 2:12
mediator of a better c .... Heb. 8:6

COVER
He shall c thee .... Ps. 91:4
love c all sins .... Prov. 10:12
He that c sins .... Prov. 28:13
whose sins are c .... Rom. 4:7
charity shall c .... 1 Pet. 4:8

COVET
Thou shalt not c .... Ex. 20:17
c earnestly .... 1 Cor. 12:31
while some c after .... 1 Tim. 6:10

COVETOUS
Thefts, c, wickedness .... Mark 7:22
beware of c .... Luke 12:15
c, nor drunkards .... 1 Cor. 6:10
all uncleanness, or c .... Eph. 5:3

CREATE
God c the heaven .... Gen. 1:1
So God c man in his .... Gen. 1:27
c for the woman .... 1 Cor. 11:9
c in Christ Jesus .... Eph. 2:10
were all things c .... Col. 1:16
for thou hast c .... Rev. 4:11

CREATOR
Remember now thy C .... Eccl. 12:1
more than the C .... Rom. 1:25
unto a faithful C .... 1 Pet. 4:19

CREATURE
gospel to every c .... Mark 16:15
nor any other c .... Rom. 8:39
but a new c .... Gal. 6:15
preached to every c .... Col. 1:23

CROSS
come down from the c ..... Matt. 27:40
take up the c .... Mark 10:21
come down from the c ..... Mark 15:30
take up his c daily .... Luke 9:23
the c of Christ .... 1 Cor. 1:17
glory, save in the c .... Gal. 6:14
the death of the c .... Phil. 2:8
endured the c .... Heb. 12:2

CROWN
woman is a c to her .... Prov. 12:4
children are the c .... Prov. 17:6
platted a c of thorns .... Matt. 27:29
a c of righteousness .... 2 Tim. 4:8
the c of life .... James 1:12
I will give thee a c .... Rev. 2:10
cast their c .... Rev. 4:10

CRUCIFY
C him, c him .... Luke 23:21
that our old man is c .... Rom. 6:6

Jesus Christ, and him c ...... 1 Cor. 2:2
I am c with Christ .... Gal. 2:20
have c the flesh .... Gal. 5:24

CRY
Doth not wisdom c .... Prov. 8:1
c day and night .... Luke 18:7
Jesus stood and c .... John 7:37
we c, Abba, Father .... Rom. 8:15

CUP
with oil, my c runneth ...... Ps. 23:5
c of cold water .... Matt. 10:42
let this c pass .... Matt. 26:39
give you a c .... Mark 9:41
And he took the c .... Mark 14:23
drink this c .... 1 Cor. 11:27

CURSE (n.)
ye are cursed with a c .... Mal. 3:9
ye c into .... Matt. 25:41
are under the c .... Gal. 3:10

CURSE (v.)
c God, and die .... Job 2:9
bless them that c .... Matt. 5:44
bless, and c not .... Rom. 12:14
C is every one .... Gal. 3:10
therewith c we men .... James 3:9

CUT
c it down .... Luke 13:7
c to the heart .... Acts 5:33
were even c off .... Gal. 5:12

D

DAILY
d loadeth us .... Ps. 68:19
our d bread .... Matt. 6:11
take up his cross d .... Luke 9:23
added to the church d ...... Acts 2:47
I die d .... 1 Cor. 15:31
destitute of d food .... James 2:15

DARKNESS
d be as the noon day .... Is. 58:10
d shall cover the earth ...... Is. 60:2
out into outer d .... Matt. 8:12
that sit in d .... Luke 1:79
d over all the earth .... Luke 23:44
d comprehended it not ...... John 1:5
loved d rather than .... John 3:19
from d to light .... Acts 26:18
hath light with d .... 2 Cor. 6:14
rulers of the d .... Eph. 6:12
the power of d .... Col. 1:13
out of d into .... 1 Pet. 2:9
in him is no d .... 1 John 1:5
and walk in d .... 1 John 1:6

DAY
For length of d .... Prov. 3:2
what a d may bring .... Prov. 27:1
Give us this d .... Matt. 6:11
d and hour knoweth .... Matt. 24:36
that d come .... Luke 21:34
again at the last d .... John 6:39
while it is d .... John 9:4
d of salvation .... 2 Cor. 6:2

the *d* of Jesus Christ . . . . .Phil. 1:6
d of the Lord . . . . .1 Thess. 5:2
d is with the Lord . . . . .2 Pet. 3:8

DAYSPRING
d from on high . . . . .Luke 1:78

DAY STAR
d arise in your hearts . . . . .1 Pet. 1:19

DEAD
let the *d* bury . . . . .Matt. 8:22
the *d* are raised up . . . . .Matt. 11:5
the damsel is not *d* . . . . .Mark 5:39
the rising from the *d* . . . . .Mark 9:10
For this my son was *d* . . . . . .Luke 15:24
though he were *d* . . . . .John 11:25
if we be *d* with Christ . . . . .Rom. 6:8
arise from the *d* . . . . .Eph. 5:14
firstborn from the *d* . . . . .Col. 1:18
And you, being *d* . . . . .Col. 2:13
d in Christ . . . . .1 Thess. 4:16
we be *d* with him . . . . .2 Tim. 2:11
being *d* yet speaketh . . . . .Heb. 11:4
again from the *d* . . . . .Heb. 13:20
being *d* to sins . . . . .1 Pet. 2:24
liveth, and was *d* . . . . .Rev. 1:18
and art *d* . . . . .Rev. 3:1

DEAF
shall the *d* hear . . . . .Is. 29:18
the *d* hear . . . . .Matt. 11:5
both the *d* to hear . . . . .Mark 7:37
dumb and *d* spirit . . . . .Mark 9:25

DEATH
the shadow of *d* . . . . .Ps. 23:4
in the shadow of *d* . . . . .Ps. 107:10
precious . . . is the *d* . . . . .Ps. 116:15
He will swallow up *d* . . . . .Is. 25:8
not taste of *d* . . . . .Matt. 16:28
sorrowful, even unto *d* . . . . . .Matt. 26:38
should not see *d* . . . . .Luke 2:26
from *d* unto life . . . . .John 5:24
shall never see *d* . . . . .John 8:51
by the *d* of his Son . . . . .Rom. 5:10
d by sin . . . . .Rom. 5:12
likeness of his *d* . . . . .Rom. 6:5
wages of sin is *d* . . . . .Rom. 6:23
law of sin and *d* . . . . .Rom. 8:2
O *d*, where is thy . . . . .1 Cor. 15:55
taste *d* for every man . . . . .Heb. 2:9
bringeth forth *d* . . . . .James 1:15
have passed from *d* . . . . .1 John 3:14
be thou faithful unto *d* . . . . . . .Rev. 2:10
be no more *d* . . . . .Rev. 21:4

DEBTOR
as we forgive our *d* . . . . .Matt. 6:12
I am *d* both . . . . .Rom. 1:14

DECEIT
Favour is *d* . . . . .Prov. 31:30
heart is *d* above . . . . .Jer. 17:9
the *d* of riches . . . . .Matt. 13:22
the *d* lusts . . . . .Eph. 4:22
vain *d*, after . . . . .Col. 2:8

DECEIVE
no man *d* you . . . . .Matt. 24:4

Be not *d* . . . . .1 Cor. 6:9
Be not *d*; God is not . . . . .Gal. 6:7
lie in wait to *d* . . . . .Eph. 4:14
d, and being *d* . . . . .2 Tim. 3:13
we *d* ourselves . . . . .1 John 1:8
let no man *d* you . . . . .1 John 3:7

DECENTLY
all things be done *d* . . . . .1 Cor. 14:40

DECLARE
heavens *d* the glory . . . . .Ps. 19:1
d thy faithfulness . . . . .Ps. 40:10
d thy mighty acts . . . . .Ps. 145:4
d unto you the counsel . . . . . .Acts 20:27
d to be the Son . . . . .Rom. 1:4
the day shall *d* it . . . . .1 Cor. 3:13

DEED
by the *d* of the law . . . . .Rom. 3:20
faith without the *d* . . . . .Rom. 3:28
the *d* of the body . . . . .Rom. 8:13
old man with his *d* . . . . .Col. 3:9
ye do in word or *d* . . . . .Col. 3:17
in *d* and in truth . . . . .1 John 3:18

DEFILE
would not *d* himself . . . . .Dan. 1:8
into the mouth *d* . . . . .Matt. 15:11
they *d* the man . . . . .Matt. 15:18
they should be *d* . . . . .John 18:28
d the temple . . . . .1 Cor. 3:17
being weak is *d* . . . . .1 Cor. 8:7
that *d* themselves . . . . .1 Tim. 1:10
thereby many be *d* . . . . .Heb. 12:15
which have not *d* . . . . .Rev. 3:4

DELIGHT (*n.*)
his *d* is in the law . . . . .Ps. 1:2
in whom is all my *d* . . . . .Ps. 16:3
thy law is my *d* . . . . .Ps. 119:77
I was daily his *d* . . . . .Prov. 8:30

DELIGHT (*v.*)
D thyself also . . . . .Ps. 37:4
thou *d* not in burnt . . . . .Ps. 51:16
I *d* in the law . . . . .Rom. 7:22

DELIVER
he shall *d* thee . . . . .Ps. 91:3
is able to *d* us . . . . .Dan. 3:17
d us from evil . . . . .Matt. 6:13
d from the bondage . . . . .Rom. 8:21
d unto *death* . . . . .2 Cor. 4:11
d me from . . . . .2 Tim. 4:18

DEN
a *d* of robbers . . . . .Jer. 7:11
the *d* of lions . . . . .Dan. 6:16
a *d* of thieves . . . . .Matt. 21:13

DENY
whosoever shall *d* . . . . .Matt. 10:33
let him *d* himself . . . . .Matt. 16:24
he cannot *d* himself . . . . .2 Tim. 2:13
in works they *d* him . . . . .Titus 1:16

DEPART
D from evil . . . . .Ps. 34:14
d from me . . . . .Matt. 7:23

desire to *d* ....Phil. 1:23
d from the faith ....1 Tim. 4:1

DESCEND
Spirit of God *d* ....Matt. 3:16
d from heaven ....1 Thess. 4:16
This wisdom *d* not ....James 3:15
d out of heaven ....Rev. 21:10

DESIRE (*n.*)
d of thine heart ....Ps. 37:4
satisfiest the *d* ....Ps. 145:16
d of the flesh ....Eph. 2:3
having a *d* to depart ....Phil. 1:23

DESIRE (*v.*)
More to be *d* ....Ps. 19:10
One thing have I *d* ....Ps. 27:4
that *d* life ....Ps. 34:12
If any *d* to be first ....Mark 9:35
ye *d*, when ye pray ....Mark 11:24
d spiritual gifts ....1 Cor. 14:1
as newborn babes *d* ....1 Pet. 2:2
petitions that we *d* ....1 John 5:15

DESPISE
thou wilt not *d* ....Ps. 51:17
fools *d* wisdom ....Prov. 1:7
He is *d* and rejected ....Is. 53:3
and *d* the other ....Matt. 6:24
d thou the riches ....Rom. 2:4
but we are *d* ....1 Cor. 4:10
D not prophesyings ......1 Thess. 5:20
Let no man *d* ....1 Tim. 4:12
Let no man *d* thee ....Titus 2:15
d the shame ....Heb. 12:2

DESTROY
the wicked will he *d* ....Ps. 145:20
not come to *d* ....Matt. 5:17
him that is able to *d* ....Matt. 10:28
I will *d* this temple ....Mark 14:58
save life, or *d* it ....Luke 6:9
d him ....Heb. 2:14
to save and to *d* ....James 4:12

DESTRUCTION
Pride goeth before *d* ....Prov. 16:18
that leadeth to *d* ....Matt. 7:13
Whose end is *d* ....Phil. 3:19
sudden *d* cometh ....1 Thess. 5:3
drown men in *d* ....1 Tim. 6:9
swift *d* ....2 Pet. 2:1

DEVIL
tempted of the *d* ....Matt. 4:1
prepared for the *d* ....Matt. 25:41
your father the *d* ....John 8:44
the *d* also believe ....James 2:19
Resist the *d* ....James 4:7
your adversary the *d* ....1 Pet. 5:8

DIE
thou shalt surely *d* ....Gen. 20:7
That which *d* of itself ....Lev. 22:8
d the common death ....Num. 16:29
let me *d* the death ....Num. 23:10
thou *d*, will I *d* ....Ruth 1:17
curse God, and *d* ....Job 2:9
worm shall not *d* ....Is. 66:24

let him *d* the death ....Matt. 15:4
shall never *d* ....John 11:26
will one *d* ....Rom. 5:7
It is Christ that *d* ....Rom. 8:34
no man *d* to himself ....Rom. 14:7
Christ both *d*, and rose ......Rom. 14:9
Christ *d* for our sins ....1 Cor. 15:3
I *d* daily ....1 Cor. 15:31
if one *d* for all ....2 Cor. 5:14
and to *d* is gain ....Phil. 1:21
that Jesus *d* ....1 Thess. 4:44
unto men once to *d* ....Heb. 9:27
These all *d* in faith ....Heb. 11:13

DINE
Come and *d* ....John 21:12

DIRECT
will I *d* my prayer ....Ps. 5:3
he shall *d* thy paths ....Prov. 3:6
the Lord *d* his steps ....Prov. 16:9
he *d* his way ....Prov. 21:29
d your hearts ....2 Thess. 3:5

DISCIPLE
his twelve *d* ....Matt. 10:1
The *d* is not above ....Matt. 10:24
tell his *d* that he is ....Matt. 28:7
His *d* came by night ....Matt. 28:13
Why do the *d* of John ....Mark 2:18
John also taught his *d* ....Luke 11:1
he cannot be my *d* ....Luke 14:26
are ye my *d* indeed ....John 8:31
to wash the *d* feet ....John 13:5
so shall ye be my *d* ....John 15:8
d whom Jesus loved ....John 21:7
d were called ....Acts 11:26

DISEASE
who healeth all thy *d* ....Ps. 103:3
it is an evil *d* ....Eccl. 6:2
The *d* have ye not ....Ezek. 34:4

DISHONOUR
another unto *d* ....Rom. 9:21
It is sown in *d* ....1 Cor. 15:43
and some to *d* ....2 Tim. 2:20

DISOBEDIENCE
by one man's *d* ....Rom. 5:19
the children of *d* ....Eph. 2:2
transgression and *d* ....Heb. 2:2

DISOBEDIENT
d to the wisdom ....Luke 1:17
d to parents ....Rom. 1:30
d to Parents ....2 Tim. 3:2
sometimes foolish, *d* ....Titus 3:3

DISORDERLY
behaved not ourselves *d* .....2 Thess. 3:7
walk among you *d* ....2 Thess. 3:11

DISSOLVE
things shall be *d* ....2 Pet. 3:11

DIVERS
D weights ....Prov. 20:10
with *d* diseases ....Matt. 4:24
in *d* places ....Matt. 24:7

DIVIDE (*cont.*)

earthquakes in *d* places ......Mark 13:8
sick with *d* diseases ....Luke 4:40
led away with *d* lusts ....1 Tim. 3:6

DIVIDE
D the living child ....1 Kin. 3:25
Every kingdom *d* ....Matt. 12:25
d to every man ....1 Cor. 12:11
rightly *d* the word ....2 Tim. 2:15
the *d* asunder of soul ....Heb. 4:12

DIVINE
of *d* service ....Heb. 9:1
as his *d* power hath ....2 Pet. 1:3
the *d* nature ....2 Pet. 1:4

DO
should *d* to you ....Matt. 7:12
this *d* in remembrance ......Luke 22:19
ye can *d* nothing ....John 15:5
I can *d* all things ....Phil. 4:13
and not a *d* ....James 1:23

DOCTRINE
form of *d* ....Rom. 6:17
every wind of *d* ....Eph. 4:14
abideth in the *d* ....2 John 9
See Deut. 32:2; Job 11:4

DOING
This is the Lord's *d* ....Ps. 118:23
shall find so *d* ....Matt. 24:46
went about *d* good ....Acts 10:38
not be weary in well *d* ....Gal. 6:9
d the will of God ....Eph. 6:6
suffer for well *d* ....1 Pet. 3:17
to him in well *d* ....1 Pet. 4:19

DOMINION
let them have *d* ....Gen. 1:26
have *d* over me ....Ps. 119:133
sin shall not have *d* ....Rom. 6:14
and *d*, and every name ....Eph. 1:21
they be thrones or *d* ....Col. 1:16

DOOR
on the upper *d* post ....Ex. 12:7
the *d* is the shepherd ....John 10:2
I am the *d* ....John 10:7, 9
opened the *d* of faith ....Acts 14:27
a great *d* ....1 Cor. 16:9
I stand at the *d* ....Rev. 3:20
behold, a *d* was opened ....Rev. 4:1

DOUBLE
and with a *d* heart ....Ps. 12:2
deacons not *d* tongued ....1 Tim. 3:8
worthy of *d* honour ....1 Tim. 5:17
a *d* minded man ....James 1:8

DOUBT
didst thou *d* ....Matt. 14:31
and *d* not ....Matt. 21:21
shall not *d* ....Mark 11:23
without wrath and *d* ....1 Tim. 2:8

DOVE
descending like a *d* ....Matt. 3:16

DRAGON
laid hold on the *d* ....Rev. 20:2
See Rev. 12:3; 13:2, 11; 16:13

DRAW
D me not away ....Ps. 28:3
redemption *d* nigh ....Luke 21:28
will *d* all men unto me ....John 12:32
when he is *d* away ....James 1:14

DREAM
old men shall *d* dreams ......Joel 2:28

DRINK (*n.*)
strong *d* is raging ....Prov. 20:1
ye gave me *d* ....Matt. 25:35
my blood is *d* indeed ....John 6:55
same spiritual *d* ....1 Cor. 10:4
in meat or in *d* ....Col. 2:16

DRINK (*v.*)
shall give to *d* ....Matt. 10:42
vinegar to *d* mingled ....Matt. 27:34
water to *d* ....Mark 9:41
Give me to *d* ....John 4:10
come unto me, and *d* ....John 7:37
nor to *d* wine ....Rom. 14:21
did all *d* the same ....1 Cor. 10:4
as oft as ye *d* it ....1 Cor. 11:25
to *d* into one Spirit ....1 Cor. 12:13

DRUNKARD
d and the glutton ....Prov. 23:21
hand of a *d* ....Prov. 26:9
nor *d*, nor revilers ....1 Cor. 6:10

DUMB
the tongue of the *d* ....Is. 35:6
as a sheep . . . is *d* ....Is. 53:7
blind, *d*, maimed ....Matt. 15:30
the *d* to speak ....Mark 7:37
hath a *d* spirit ....Mark 9:17
d before his shearer ....Acts 8:32

DUST
God formed man of the *d* .....Gen. 2:7
d shalt thou eat ....Gen. 3:14
d thou art ....Gen. 3:19
repent in *d* and ashes ....Job 42:6
that we are *d* ....Ps. 103:14
return to their *d* ....Ps. 104:29
d return to the earth ....Eccl. 12:7
d of your feet ....Matt. 10:14

DWELL
will *d* in the house ....Ps. 23:6
brethren to *d* together ....Ps. 133:1
but sin that *d* in me ....Rom. 7:17
d in your hearts ....Eph. 3:17
all fulness *d* ....Col. 1:19
word of Christ *d* ....Col. 3:16
d in the light ....1 Tim. 6:16
d righteousness ....2 Pet. 3:13

E

EAGLE
renewed like the *e* ....Ps. 103:5
with wings as *e* ....Is. 40:31
like a flying *e* ....Rev. 4:7

EAR
his *e* are open ....Ps. 34:15
their *e* ate dull ....Matt. 13:15
having *e*, hear ye not ....Mark 8:18
nor *e* heard ....1 Cor. 2:9
And if the *e* shall say ....1 Cor. 12:16
having itching *e* ....2 Tim. 4:3
e of the Lord ....James 5:4
his *e* are open ....1 Pet. 3:12

EARLY
e will I seek thee ....Ps. 63:1

EARNEST
the *e* expectation ....Rom. 8:19
covet *e* the best ....1 Cor. 12:31
the *e* of the Spirit ....2 Cor. 1:22
e of our inheritance ....Eph. 1:14

EARTH
shall inherit the *e* ....Ps. 37:11
though *e* be removed ....Ps. 46:2
let the *e* rejoice ....Ps. 97:1
the *e* shalt be full ....Is. 11:9
the ends of the *e* ....Is. 40:28
the *e* is my footstool ....Is. 66:1
e shall be filled ....Hab. 2:14
meek . . . inherit the *e* ......Matt. 5:5
treasures upon *e* ....Matt. 6:19
to send peace on *e* ....Matt. 10:34
shalt bind on *e* ....Matt. 16:19
shall agree on *e* ....Matt. 18:19
on *e* peace ....Luke 2:14
into all the *e* ....Rom. 10:18
in *e* vessels ....2 Cor. 4:7
things on the *e* ....Col. 3:2
who mind *e* things ....Phil. 3:19
pilgrims on the *e* ....Heb. 11:13
but is *e*, sensual ....James 3:15
e brought forth ....James 5:18
the *e* also ....2 Pet. 3:10
shall reign on the *e* ....Rev. 5:10
the *e* and heaven ....Rev. 20:11
heaven and a new *e* ....Rev. 21:1

EARTHQUAKE
e, and great noise...........Is. 29:6
e, in divers places ....Matt. 24:7
there was a great *e* ....Acts 16:26
lightnings, and an *e* ....Rev. 8:5

EAT
shall ye hot *e* ....Gen. 9:4
e of the fruit ....Prov. 1:31
come ye, buy, and *e* ....Is. 55:1
e with publicans ....Mark 2:16
dogs under the table *e* ....Mark 7:28
what ye shall *e* ....Luke 12:22
let us *e*, and be merry ....Luke 15:23
set before you, *e* ....1 Cor. 10:27
that *e* and drinketh ....1 Cor. 11:29
should he *e* ....2 Thess. 3:10
e of the tree of life ....Rev. 2:7

EDIFY
his good to *e* ....Rom. 15:2
charity *e* ....1 Cor. 8:1
speaketh unto men to *e* ......1 Cor. 14:3
all things *e* not ....1 Cor. 10:23
for the *e* of the body ....Eph. 4:12

ELDER
among the *e* of the ....Prov. 31:23
Let the *e* that rule ....1 Tim. 5:17
ordain *e* in every ....Titus 1:5
the *e* of the church ....James 5:14
unto the *e* ....1 Pet. 5:5

ELECT
gather together his *e* ....Matt. 24:31
God avenge his own *e* ....Luke 18:7
the charge of God's *e* ....Rom. 8:33
as the *e* of God ....Col. 3:12

ELECTION
of God according to *e* ....Rom. 9:11
calling and *e* sure ....2 Pet. 1:10

END
thy latter *e* should ....Job 8:7
the wicked come to an *e* ......Ps. 7:9
years shall have no *e* ....Ps. 102:27
the *e* thereof are ....Prov. 14:12
beginning to the *e* ....Eccl. 3:11
no *e* of all his labour.........Eccl. 4:8
there shall be no *e* ....Is. 9:7
endureth to the *e* ....Matt. 10:22
the *e* of the world ....Matt. 24:3
but the *e* shall not ....Mark 13:7
there shall be no *e* ....Luke 1:33
Whose *e* is ....Phil. 3:19
the *e* of your faith ....1 Pet. 1:9
e of all things ....1 Pet. 4:7
beginning and the *e* ....Rev. 21:6

ENDURE
weeping may *e* for a ....Ps. 30:5
goodness of God *e* ....Ps. 52:1
his truth *e* to all ....Ps. 100:5
thy mercy, O Lord, *e* ....Ps. 138:8
that *e* to the end ....Matt. 10:22
But he that shall *e* ....Matt. 24:13
e all things ....1 Cor. 13:7
they will not *e* sound ....2 Tim. 4:3
if ye *e* chastening ....Heb. 12:7
the man that *e* ....James 1:12
of the Lord *e* for ever ....1 Pet. 1:25

ENEMY
the presence of mine *e* ....Ps. 23:5
wiser than mine *e* ....Ps. 119:98
maketh even his *e* ....Prov. 16:7
if thine *e* be hungry ....Prov. 25:21
Love your *e*, bless ....Matt. 5:44
if when we were *e* ....Rom. 5:10
if thine *e* hunger ....Rom. 12:20
the *e* of the cross ....Phil. 3:18
not as an *e* ....2 Thess. 3:15
is the *e* of God ....James 4:4

ENTER
E into his gates with ....Ps. 100:4
e into thy closet ....Matt. 6:6
town ye shall *e* ....Matt. 10:11
thee to *e* into life ....Matt. 18:8
e thou into the joy ....Matt. 25:21
e into temptation ....Mark 14:38
e into his glory ....Luke 24:26
can he *e* the second ....John 3:4
e not by the door ....John 10:1

ENTREAT

sin *e* into the world ....Rom. 5:12
e into the heart ....1 Cor. 2:9

ENTREAT

E me not to leave ....Ruth 1:16

ENVY

Be thou not *e* ....Prov. 24:1
full of *e*, murder ....Rom. 1:29
not in strife and *e* ....Rom. 13:13
e, and strife ....1 Cor. 3:3
charity *e* not ....1 Cor. 13:4
E, murders ....Gal. 5:21
whereof cometh *e* ....1 Tim. 6:4
in malice and *e* ....Titus 3:3
lusteth to *e* ....James 4:5

EQUAL

hast made them *e* ....Matt. 20:12
e unto the angels ....Luke 20:36
e with God ....John 5:18
not robbery to be *e* ....Phil. 2:6
just and *e* ....Col. 4:1

ERR

do *e* from thy ....Ps. 119:21
do *e*, not knowing ....Matt. 22:29
ye not therefore *e* ....Mark 12:24
have *e* from ....1 Tim. 6:10
if any of you do *e* ....James 5:19

ERROR

e of his way ....James 5:20
e of the wicked ....2 Pet. 3:17
the spirit of *e* ....1 John 4:6

ESCAPE

shall not *e* ....Prov. 19:5
he *e* out of their ....John 10:39
they *e* all safe ....Acts 27:44
How shall we *e* ....Heb. 2:3
e the corruption ....2 Pet. 1:4

ETERNAL

may have *e* life ....Matt. 19:16
is in danger of *e* ....Mark 3:29
inherit *e* life ....Mark 10:17
but have *e* life ....John 3:15
ye have *e* life ....John 5:39
give unto them *e* life ....John 10:28
gift of God is *e* life ....Rom. 6:23
lay hold on *e* life ....1 Tim. 6:12
unto his *e* glory ....1 Pet. 5:10
even *e* life ....1 John 2:25
no murderer hath *e* life .....1 John 3:15
given to us *e* life ....1 John 5:11

EUNUCHS

there are some *e* ....Matt. 19:12
e of great authority ....Acts 8:27

EVERLASTING

even from *e* to *e* ....Ps. 90:2
lead me in the way *e* ....Ps. 139:24
Jehovah is *e* strength ....Is. 26:4
an *e* light ....Is. 60:19
cast into *e* fire ....Matt. 18:8
shall inherit *e* life ....Matt. 19:29
but have *e* life ....John 3:16
on him, may have *e* life .....John 6:40

EVERY

with *e* destruction ....2 Thess. 1:9
e consolation ....2 Thess. 2:16

E word of God is pure ......Prov. 30:5
e knee shall bow ....Rom. 14:11
e name that is named ......Eph. 1:21
above *e* name ....Phil. 2:9
lay aside *e* weight ....Heb. 12:1
E good gift ....James 1:17

EVIDENCE

the *e* of things ....Heb. 11:1

EVIL

Depart from *e* ....Ps. 34:14
depart from *e* ....Prov. 3:7
beholding the *e* ....Prov. 15:3
all manner of *e* ....Matt. 5:11
day is the *e* ....Matt. 6:34
If ye then, being *e* ....Matt. 7:11
deeds were *e* ....John 3:19
the *e* which I would ....Rom. 7:19
Abhor that which is *e* ......Rom. 12:9
overcome *e* with good ......Rom. 12:21
appearance of *e* ....1 Thess. 5:22
the root of all *e* ....1 Tim. 6:10

EXALT

let us *e* his name ....Ps. 34:3
E her, and she shall ....Prov. 4:8
Righteousness *e* ....Prov. 14:34
Every valley shall be *e* ......Is. 40:4
e himself ....Luke 14:11
if a man *e* himself ....2 Cor. 11:20
hath highly *e* him ....Phil. 2:9
that he may *e* you ....1 Pet. 5:6

EXAMINE

a man *e* himself ....1 Cor. 11:28
E yourselves ....2 Cor. 13:5

EXAMPLE

I have given you an *e* ....John 13:15
be thou an *e* ....1 Tim. 4:12
leaving us an *e* ....1 Pet. 2:21

EXCEEDING

with *e* great joy ....Matt. 2:10
an *e* high mountain ....Matt. 4:8
Rejoice, and be *e* glad ......Matt. 5:12
a far more *e* ....2 Cor. 4:17
the *e* greatness ....Eph. 1:19
e riches of his grace ....Eph. 2:7
able to do *e* abundantly ....Eph. 3:20

EXCELLENT

how *e* is thy name ....Ps. 8:1, 9
he hath done *e* things ......Is. 12:5
more *e* being ....Rom. 2:18
a more *e* way ....1 Cor. 12:31

EXCEPT

E ye be converted ....Matt 18:3
e ye repent ....Luke 13:3
E a man be born again ......John 3:3
e they be sent ....Rom. 10:15
e it die ....1 Cor. 15:36

EXPECTATION
his *e* shall perish ....Prov. 11:7
the earnest *e* ....Rom. 8:19
my earnest *e* ....Phil. 1:20

EXPEDIENT
It is *e* for you ....John 16:7
it was *e* that one man ....John 18:14

EYE
the *e* of the Lord ....2 Chr. 16:9
enlightening the *e* ....Ps. 19:8
the *e* of the Lord ....Ps. 33:18
the *e* of man ....Prov. 27:20
To open the blind *e* ....Is. 42:7
apple of thine *e* ....Lam. 2:18
e of the Lord ....Zech. 4:10
if thy right *e* ....Matt. 5:29
which opened the *e* ....John 11:37
E hath not seen ....1 Cor. 2:9
twinkling of an *e* ....1 Cor. 15:52
your own *e* ....Gal. 4:15
The *e* of your ....Eph. 1:18
e of the Lord ....1 Pet. 3:12
e of his majesty ....2 Pet. 1:16
the lust of the *e* ....John 2:16

EYESERVICE
Not with *e*, as menpleasers .....Eph. 6:6

F

FABLES
Neither give heed to *f* ....1 Tim. 1:4
cunningly devised *f* ....2 Pet. 1:16

FACE
f to the ground ....Neh. 8:6
Hide not thy *f* ....Ps. 27:9
Hide not thy *f* from me ....Ps. 102:2
f answereth to *f* ....Prov. 27:19
set my *f* like a flint ....Is. 50:7
sins have hid his *f* ....Is. 59:2
f did shine as the sun ......Matt. 17:2
f of my Father ....Matt. 18:10
but then *f* to *f* ....1 Cor. 13:12
all, with open *f* ....2 Cor. 3:18
withstood him to the *f* ....Gal. 2:11
his natural *f* ....James 1:23
from whose *f* ....Rev. 20:11

FADE
f as a leaf ....Is. 64:6
rich man *f* away ....James 1:11
that *f* not away ....1 Pet. 1:4
a crown of glory that *f* ......1 Pet. 5:4

FAIL
truth *f* ....Is. 59:15
his compassions *f* not ....Lam. 3:22
heavens that *f* not ....Luke 12:33
that thy faith *f* not ....Luke 22:32
Charity never *f* ....1 Cor. 13:8
thy years shall not *f* ....Heb. 1:12

FAINT
walk, and not *f* ....Is. 40:31

FAITH
O ye of little *f* ....Matt. 6:30

found so great *f* ....Matt. 8:10
f as a grain ....Matt. 17:20
if ye have *f* ....Matt. 21:21
have *f* in God ....Mark 11:22
Thy *f* hath saved thee ....Luke 7:50
Increase our *f* ....Luke 17:5
Holy Ghost and of *f* ....Acts 11:24
opened the door of *f* ....Acts 14:27
established in the *f* ....Acts 16:5
justified by *f* ....Rom. 3:28
we have access by *f* ....Rom. 5:2
the word of *f* ....Rom. 10:8
f cometh by hearing ....Rom. 10:17
the measure of *f* ....Rom. 12:3
though I have all *f* ....1 Cor. 13:2
And now abideth *f* ....1 Cor. 13:13
we walk by *f* ....2 Cor. 5:7
f of the Son ....Gal. 2:20
of the household of *f* ....Gal. 6:10
in your hearts by *f* ....Eph. 3:17
One Lord, one *f* ....Eph. 4:5
taking the shield of *f* ....Eph. 6:16
your work of *f* ....1 Thess. 1:3
and the work of *f* ....2 Thess. 1:11
he hath denied the *f* ....1 Tim. 5:8
erred from the *f* ....1 Tim. 6:10
the unfeigned *f* ....2 Tim. 1:5
I have kept the *f* ....2 Tim. 4:7
f is the substance ....Heb. 11:1
without *f* it is ....Heb. 11:6
These all died in *f* ....Heb. 11:13
finisher of our *f* ....Heb. 12:2
trying of your *f* ....James 1:3
let him ask in *f* ....James 1:6
f if it hath not works ....James 2:17
the prayer of *f* ....James 5:15

FAITHFUL
good and *f* servant ....Matt. 25:21
thou hast been *f* ....Luke 19:17
man be found *f* ....1 Cor. 4:2
F is he that ....1 Thess. 5:24
Lord is *f* ....2 Thess. 3:3
This is a *f* saying ....1 Tim. 1:15
thou to *f* man ....2 Tim. 2:2
It is a *f* saying ....2 Tim. 2:11
f that promised ....Heb. 10:23
judged him *f* ....Heb. 11:11
he is *f* ....1 John 1:9
be thou *f* unto death ....Rev. 2:10
true and *f* ....Rev. 21:5

FAITHFULNESS
great is thy *f* ....Lam. 3:23

FAITHLESS
O *f* generation ....Mark 9:19

FALL (n.)
haughty spirit before a *f* .....Prov. 16:18
great was the *f* ....Matt. 7:27

FALL (v.)
Though he *f* ....Ps. 37:24
A thousand shall *f* ....Ps. 91:7
shall *f* therein ....Prov. 26:27
f down and worship ....Matt. 4:9
f on the ground ....Matt. 10:29
they not both *f* ....Luke 6:39
Whosoever shall *f* ....Luke 20:18

heed lest he *f* ....1 Cor. 10:12
ye are *f* from grace ....Gal. 5:4
f into reproach ....1 Tim. 3:7
rich *f* into temptation ....1 Tim. 6:9
If they shall *f* away ....Heb. 6:6
when Ye *f* ....James 1:2
f into condemnation ....James 5:12

FALLING
my feet from *f* ....Ps. 56:13
a righteous man *f* ....Prov. 25:26
a *f* away first ....2 Thess. 2:3
keep you from *f* ....Jude 24

FALSE
Thou shalt not bear *f* ....Ex. 20:16
hate every *f* way ....Ps. 119:104
a *f* witness ....Prov. 6:19
A *f* balance ....Prov. 11:1
Beware of *f* prophets ....Matt. 7:15
many bare *f* witness ....Mark 14:56
by *f* accusation ....Luke 19:8
found *f* witnesses ....1 Cor. 15:15
are *f* apostles ....2 Cor. 11:13
f accusers ....2 Tim. 3:3
not *f* accusers ....Titus 2:3

FAMILY
all the *f* of the earth ....Gen. 28:14
f in heaven ....Eph. 3:15

FAMINE
there shall be *f* ....Matt. 24:7
f and troubles ....Mark 13:8

FAR
As *f* as the east ....Ps. 103:12
price is *f* above ....Prov. 31:10
a *f* more exceeding ....2 Cor. 4:17
F above all ....Eph. 1:21
which is *f* better ....Phil. 1:23

FAST
when ye *f* ....Matt. 6:16
thy disciples *f* not ....Matt. 9:14
f twice in the week ....Luke 18:12

FASTING
I humbled my soul with *f* .....Ps. 35:13
give yourselves to *f* ....1 Cor. 7:5

FATHER
A *f* of the fatherless ....Ps. 68:5
instruction of a *f* ....Prov. 4:1
maketh a glad *f* ....Prov. 10:1
thou art our *f* ....Is. 63:16
Our F which art ....Matt. 6:9
for your heavenly F ....Matt. 6:32
He that loveth *f* ....Matt. 10:37
in the name of the F ....Matt. 28:19
about my F business ....Luke 2:49
F, I have sinned ....Luke 15:21
F, forgive them ....Luke 23:34
F, into thy hands ....Luke 23:46
All that the F giveth ....John 6:37
the *f* of it ....John 8:44
I and my F are one ....John 10:30
unto the F, but by me ....John 14:6
And I will pray the F ....John 14:16
F, the hour is come ....John 17:1

we cry, Abba, F ....Rom. 8:15
One God and F of all ....Eph. 4:6
f, provoke not your ....Eph. 6:4
glory of God the F ....Phil. 2:11
it pleased the F ....Col. 1:19
F of lights ....James 1:17
an advocate with the F ....1 John 2:1
the love of the F ....1 John 2:15
of love the F hath ....1 John 3:1
the F, the Word ....1 John 5:7

FATHERLESS
the widow, and the *f* ....Mal. 3:5
To visit the *f* ....James 1:27

FAULTLESS
and to present you *f* ....Jude 24

FEAR (*n.*)
The *f* of the Lord is ....Ps. 19:9
The *f* of the Lord ....Ps. 111:10
not afraid of sudden *f* ....Prov. 3:25
f of the Lord ....Prov. 10:27
In the *f* of the Lord ....Prov. 14:26
of *f*, and not of peace ....Jer. 30:5
cried out for *f* ....Matt. 14:26
failing them for *f* ....Luke 21:26
but secretly for *f* ....John 19:38
f to whom *f* ....Rom. 13:7
with *f* and trembling ....Eph. 6:5
salvation with *f* ....Phil. 2:12
the spirit of *f* ....2 Tim. 1:7
moved with *f* ....Heb. 11:7

FEAR (*v.*)
I know that thou *f* God ....Gen. 22:12
I will *f* no evil ....Ps. 23:4
whom shall I *f* ....Ps. 27:1
f the Lord ....Ps. 34:9
not *f* what flesh ....Ps. 56:4
f the Lord ....Prov. 3:7
but a woman that *f* ....Prov. 31:30
F God, and keep his ....Eccl. 12:13
f him which is able ....Matt. 10:28
whom ye shall *f* ....Luke 12:5
F not, little flock ....Luke 12:32
again to *f* ....Rom. 8:15
I will not *f* what man ....Heb. 13:6
no *f* in love ....1 John 4:18

FEARFUL
It is a *f* thing ....Heb. 10:31

FEEBLE
not one *f* person ....Ps. 105:37
comfort the *f* ....1 Thess. 5:14
and the *f* knees ....Heb. 12:12

FEED
fools *f* on foolishness ....Prov. 15:14
the bear shall *f* ....Is. 11:7
and the lamb shall *f* ....Is. 65:25
F my lambs ....John 21:15
hunger, *f* him ....Rom. 12:20
F the flock ....1 Pet. 5:2

FEET
all things under his *f* ....Ps. 8:6
and my *f* from falling ....Ps. 116:8
a lamp unto my *f* ....Ps. 119:105

their *f* run to evil . . . . .Prov. 1:16
them under their *f* . . . . .Matt. 7:6
the dust of your *f* . . . . .Matt. 10:14
kissed his *f* . . . . .Luke 7:38
at the *f* of Jesus . . . . .Luke 8:35
my hands and my *f* . . . . .Luke 24:39
and wiped his *f* . . . . .John 11:2
wash the disciples' *f* . . . . .John 13:5
f are swift to shed . . . . .Rom. 3:15
beautiful are the *f* . . . . .Rom. 10:15
the head to the *f* . . . . .1 Cor. 12:21
all things under his *f* . . . . .Eph. 1:22
your *f* shod . . . . .Eph. 6:15

FELLOWSHIP
what *f* hath . . . . .2 Cor. 6:14
no *f* with the . . . . .Eph. 5:11
if any *f* of the Spirit . . . . .Phil. 2:1
the *f* of his . . . . .Phil. 3:10
we have *f* . . . . .1 John 1:7

FEMALE
and *f* created . . . . .Gen. 1:27
made them male and *f* . . . . . .Matt. 19:4

FERVENT
f in spirit . . . . .Rom. 12:11
f prayer of a . . . . .James 5:16
melt with *f* heat . . . . .2 Pet. 3:10

FEW
and *f* there be . . . . .Matt. 7:14
the labourers are *f* . . . . .Matt. 9:37
but *f* chosen . . . . .Matt. 20:16
faithful over a *f* . . . . .Matt. 25:21
a *f* small fishes . . . . .Mark 8:7

FIGHT
not *f* against God . . . . .Acts 23:9
F the good *f* of . . . . .1 Tim. 6:12
fought a good *f* . . . . .2 Tim. 4:7
come wars and *f* . . . . .James 4:1

FILL
the whole earth be *f* . . . . .Ps. 72:19
for they shall be *f* . . . . .Matt. 5:6
Elisabeth was *f* with . . . . .Luke 1:41
for ye shall be *f* . . . . .Luke 6:21
might be *f* with all . . . . .Eph. 3:19
be *f* with the Spirit . . . . .Eph. 5:18
f with the fruits . . . . .Phil. 1:11
be ye warmed and *f* . . . . .James 2:16

FIND
your sin will *f* you out . . . . . . .Num. 32:23
whoso *f* me, *f* life . . . . .Prov. 8:35
thy hand *f* to do . . . . .Eccl. 9:10
ye shall *f* rest . . . . .Jer. 6:16
seek, and ye shall *f* . . . . .Matt. 7:7
few there be that *f* it . . . . .Matt. 7:14
shall *f* it . . . . .Matt. 10:39
his ways past *f* out . . . . .Rom. 11:33
and *f* grace to help . . . . .Heb. 4:16

FINISH
have *f* the work . . . . .John 17:4
It is *f* .John 19:30
I have *f* my course . . . . .2 Tim. 4:7

author and *f* of our . . . . .Heb. 12:2
when it is *f* . . . . .James 1:15

FIRE
walkest through the *f* . . . . .Is. 43:2
and with *f* . . . . .Matt. 3:11
into a furnace of *f* . . . . .Matt. 13:42
into everlasting *f* . . . . .Matt. 18:8
cast them into the *f* . . . . .John 15:6
the tongue is a *f* . . . . .James 3:6
be tried with *f* . . . . .1 Pet. 1:7
into the lake of *f* . . . . .Rev. 20:10
with *f* and brimstone . . . . .Rev. 21:8

FIRMAMENT
Let there be a *f* . . . . .Gen. 1:6
the *f* sheweth his . . . . .Ps. 19:1

FIRST
seek ye *f* . . . . .Matt. 6:33
f cast out the beam . . . . .Matt. 7:5
man desire to be *f* . . . . .Mark 9:35
the *f* commandment . . . . .Mark 12:28
let him *f* cast a stone . . . . .John 8:7
Christians *f* in . . . . .Acts 11:26
the Jew *f* and also . . . . .Rom. 2:9
f commandment with . . . . .Eph. 6:2
the *f* from the dead . . . . .Col. 1:18
shall rise *f* . . . . .1 Thess. 4:16
a falling away *f* . . . . .2 Thess. 2:3
f principles of . . . . .Heb. 5:12
is *f* pure . . . . .James 3:17
he *f* loved us . . . . .1 John 4:19
left thy *f* love . . . . .Rev. 2:4
and do the *f* works . . . . .Rev. 2:5
f heaven and the *f* . . . . .Rev. 21:1

FLAME
tormented in this *f* . . . . .Luke 16:24

FLEE
The wicked *f* . . . . .Prov. 28:1
sighing shall *f* away . . . . .Is. 35:10
F also youthful . . . . .2 Tim. 2:22
he will *f* from you . . . . .James 4:7

FLESH
and they shall be one *f* . . . . . . .Gen. 2:24
f and blood hath . . . . .Matt. 16:17
shall be one *f* . . . . .Matt. 19:5
the *f* is weak . . . . .Matt. 26:41
not *f* and bones . . . . .Luke 24:39
Word was made *f* . . . . .John 1:14
power over all *f* . . . . .John 17:2
live after the *f* . . . . .Rom. 8:12
according to the *f* . . . . .Rom. 9:3
provision for the *f* . . . . .Rom. 13:14
a thorn in the *f* . . . . .2 Cor. 12:7
live in the *f* . . . . .Gal. 2:20
f lusteth . . . . .Gal. 5:17
soweth to his *f* . . . . .Gal. 6:8
two shall be one *f* . . . . .Eph. 5:31
wrestle not against *f* . . . . .Eph. 6:12
confidence in the *f* . . . . .Phil. 3:3
manifest in the *f* . . . . .1 Tim. 3:6
to death in the *f* . . . . .1 Pet. 3:18

FLESHLY
not with *f* wisdom . . . . .2 Cor. 1:12
from *f* lusts . . . . .1 Pet. 2:11

FLOURISH
righteous shall *f* ....Ps. 92:12
f as a branch ....Prov. 11:28

FLOWER
as the *f* of the field ....Is. 40:6

FOLLOW
mercy shall *f* me ....Ps. 23:6
unto them, *F* me ....Matt. 4:19
F after charity ....1 Cor. 14:1
I *f* after ....Phil. 3:12
ever *f* that ....1 Thess. 5:15
f after righteousness ....1 Tim. 6:11
f righteousness ....2 Tim. 2:22
F peace with all ....Heb. 12:14
that ye should *f* ....1 Pet. 2:21

FOOD
the tree was good for *f* ....Gen. 3:6
Man did eat angels' *f* ....Ps. 78:25
gathereth her *f* ....Prov. 6:8
bread for your *f* ....2 Cor. 9:10
having *f* and raiment ....1 Tim. 6:8
destitute of daily *f* ....James 2:15

FOOL
The *f* hath said ....Ps. 14:1
f despise wisdom ....Prov. 1:7
F make a mock at sin........Prov. 14:9
A *f* uttereth all ....Prov. 29:11
say, Thou *f* ....Matt. 5:22
they became *f* ....Rom. 1:22
We are *f* for Christ's ....1 Cor. 4:10
not as *f* ....Eph. 5:15

FOOLISH
f plucketh it down ....Prov. 14:1
A *f* son is a grief ....Prov. 17:25
five were *f* ....Matt. 25:2
f heart was darkened ....Rom. 1:21
nor *f* talking ....Eph. 5:4
f and hurtful lusts ....1 Tim. 6:9

FOOLISHNESS
F is bound ....Prov. 22:15
them that perish *f* ....1 Cor. 2:14
they are *f* unto him ....1 Cor. 2:14

FOOTSTOOL
and the earth is my *f* ....Is. 66:1
for it is his *f* ....Matt. 5:35
be made his *f* ....Heb. 10:13

FORBID
F him not.................Mark 9:39
f them not ....Mark 10:14

FOREKNOW
For whom he did *f* ....Rom. 8:29

FOREORDAINED
Who verily was *f* before ......1 Pet. 1:20

FORESEE
A prudent man *f* the evil ......Prov. 22:3
I *f* the Lord always ....Acts 2:25
f that God would ....Gal. 3:8

FORETELL
have likewise *f* ....Acts 3:4
and *f* you ....2 Cor. 13:2

FORGAVE
I *f* thee all that debt ....Matt. 18:32
he frankly *f* them ....Luke 7:42
even as Christ *f* you ....Col. 3:13

FORGET
and not *f* the works ....Ps. 78:7
I will not *f* thy word ....Ps. 119:16
My son, *f* not my law ....Prov. 3:1
And *f* the Lord thy ....Is. 51:13
Be not *f* to entertain ....Heb. 13:2
f what manner ....James 1:24

FORGIVE
Who *f* all ....Ps. 103:3
f us our debts ....Matt. 6:12
For if ye *f* men ....Matt. 6:14
power on earth to *f* sins .....Matt. 9:6
who can *f* sins ....Mark 2:7
f, if ye have ought ....Mark 11:25
and ye shall be *f* ....Luke 6:37
f us our sins ....Luke 11:4
Father, *f* them ....Luke 23:34
bath *f* you ....Eph. 4:32
f you all trespasses ....Col. 2:13
and just to *f* us ....1 John 1:9
your sins are *f* you ....1 John 2:12

FORGIVENESS
the *f* of sins ....Eph. 1:7

FORGOTTEN
hath *f* that he was ....2 Pet. 1:9

FORM (*n.*)
earth was without *f* ....Gen. 1:2
he hath no *f* ....Is. 53:2
the *f* of knowledge ....Rom. 2:20
the *f* of God ....Phil. 2:6
Having a *f* of godliness ......2 Tim. 3:5

FORM (*v.*)
I also am *f* out of ....Job 33:6
great God that *f* ....Prov. 26:10
the thing *f* say ....Rom. 9:20
Christ be *f* in you ....Gal. 4:19

FORMER
for the *f* things ....Rev. 21:4

FORNICATION
from *f*, and from ....Acts 15:20
But *f* ....Eph. 5:3
should abstain from *f* ....1 Thess. 4:3

FORSAKE
why hast thou *f* me ....Ps. 22:1
seen the righteous *f* ....Ps. 37:25
and *f* not the law ....Prov. 1:8
the wicked *f* his way ....Is. 55:7
every one that hath *f* ....Matt. 19:29
they *f* their nets ....Mark 1:18
they *f* all ....Luke 5:11
you that *f* not all ....Luke 14:33
but not *f* ....2 Cor. 4:9
nor *f* thee ....Heb. 13:5

FORTRESS
my strength, and my *f* . . . . .Jer. 16:19

FOUGHT
have *f* a good fight . . . . .2 Tim. 4:7

FOUND
while he may be *f* . . . . .Is. 55:6
not *f* so great faith . . . . .Matt. 8:10
f one pearl of great . . . . .Matt. 13:46
I have *f* my sheep . . . . .Luke 15:6
for I have *f* the piece . . . . .Luke 15:9
was lost, and is *f* . . . . .Luke 15:24
was guile *f* in his . . . . .1 Pet. 2:22

FOUNDATION
thou laid the *f* of . . . . .Ps. 102:25
the *f* on a rock . . . . .Luke 6:48
upon another man's *f* . . . . . . .Rom. 15:20
in him before the *f* . . . . .Eph. 1:4
the *f* of God . . . . .2 Tim. 2:19
a city which hath *f* . . . . .Heb. 11:10
the city had twelve *f* . . . . .Rev. 21:14

FOUNTAIN
is a *f* of life . . . . .Prov. 13:14
a *f* send forth . . . . .James 3:11
the *f* of the water . . . . .Rev. 21:6

FREE
f ye have received . . . . .Matt. 10:8
shall make you *f* . . . . .John 8:32
Being justified *f* . . . . .Rom. 3:24
so also is the *f* gift . . . . .Rom. 5:15
Being then made *f* . . . . .Rom. 6:18
f from the law of sin . . . . .Rom. 8:2
neither bond nor *f* . . . . .Gal. 3:28
the water of life *f* . . . . .Rev. 21:6

FRIEND
familiar *f* in whom I . . . . .Ps. 41:9
a *f* that sticketh closer . . . . . .Prov. 18:24
the wounds of a *f* . . . . .Prov. 27:6
his life for his *f* . . . . .John 15:13
the *F* of God . . . . .James 2:23
f of the world is the . . . . .James 4:5

FRUIT
the *f* of the womb . . . . .Ps. 127:3
know them by their *f* . . . . .Matt. 7:16
also beareth *f* . . . . .Matt. 13:23
bringeth forth *f* . . . . .Mark 4:28
bringeth forth much *f* . . . . . . .John 12:24
branch that beareth *f* . . . . .John 15:2
the *f* of the Spirit . . . . .Gal. 5:22
f of the Spirit is in . . . . .Eph. 5:9
peaceable *f* of . . . . .Heb. 12:11
the *f* of our lips . . . . .Heb. 13:15
of mercy and good *f* . . . . .James 3:17
yielded her *f* . . . . .Rev. 22:2

FULFIL
destroy, but to *f* . . . . .Matt. 5:17
things shall be *f* . . . . .Mark 13:4
the law might be *f* . . . . .Rom. 8:4
is *f* in one word . . . . .Gal. 5:14
so *f* the law of Christ . . . . .Gal. 6:2
f all the good . . . . .2 Thess. 1:11
If ye *f* the royal . . . . .James 2:8

FULL
f of grace and truth . . . . .John 1:14
Joy might be *f* . . . . .John 15:11
f of the Holy Ghost . . . . .Acts 6:3
f proof of thy ministry . . . . . . .2 Tim. 4:5
f of glory . . . . .1 Pet. 1:8
joy may be *f* . . . . .1 John 1:4

FULNESS
in thy presence is *f* of joy . . . . .Ps. 16:11
the *f* of the time . . . . .Gal. 4:4
filled with all the *f* . . . . .Eph. 3:19
should all *f* dwell . . . . .Col. 1:19
f of the Godhead bodily . . . . . . .Col. 2:9

G

GAIN
g the whole world . . . . .Matt. 16:26
and to die is *g* . . . . .Phil. 1:21
But what things were *g* . . . . . . .Phil. 3:7

GARDEN
God planted a *g* . . . . .Gen. 2:8

GARMENT
g of praise . . . . .Is. 61:3
the *g* of salvation . . . . .Is. 61:10
the hem of his *g* . . . . .Matt. 9:20
spread their *g* . . . . .Matt. 21:8
on a wedding *g* . . . . .Matt. 22:11
parted his *g* . . . . .Matt. 27:35
cast their *g* on him . . . . .Mark 11:7

GATE
Enter into his *g* . . . . .Ps. 100:4
known in the *g* . . . . .Prov. 31:23
for wide is the *g* . . . . .Matt. 7:13
the *g* of hell . . . . .Matt. 16:18
at the strait *g* . . . . .Luke 13:24
And the *g* of it . . . . .Rev. 21:25

GAVE
she *g* me of the tree . . . . .Gen. 3:12
Lord *g*, and the Lord . . . . .Job 1:21
g his only begotten . . . . .John 3:16
God *g* them over . . . . .Rom. 1:28
God *g* the increase . . . . .1 Cor. 3:6
he *g* some, apostles . . . . .Eph. 4:11
g himself for it . . . . .Eph. 5:25

GENERATION
from *g* to *g* . . . . .Is. 34:10
O *g* of vipers . . . . .Matt. 3:7
This *g* shall not pass . . . . .Matt. 24:34
O faithless *g* . . . . .Mark 9:19

GENTILES
apostle of the *G* . . . . .Rom. 11:13
walk not as other *G* . . . . .Eph. 4:17
teacher of the *G* . . . . .2 Tim. 1:11

GENTLE
we were *g* among you . . . . . . .1 Thess. 2:7
but be *g* unto all . . . . .2 Tim. 2:24
no brawlers, but *g* . . . . .Titus 3:2
g, and easy . . . . .James 3:17
the good and *g* . . . . .1 Pet. 2:18

GIFT

bring thy g. . . . . .Matt. 5:23
give good g . . . . .Matt. 7:11
the g of God . . . . .John 4:10
some spiritual g . . . . .Rom. 1:11
the g of God . . . . .Rom. 6:23
g differing according . . . . .Rom. 12:6
diversities of g . . . . .1 Cor. 12:4
the best g . . . . .1 Cor. 12:31
desire spiritual g . . . . .1 Cor. 14:1
his unspeakable g . . . . .2 Cor. 9:15
it is the g of God . . . . .Eph. 2:8
Neglect not the g . . . . .1 Tim. 4:14
stir up the g of God . . . . .2 Tim. 1:6
Every good g . . . . .James 1:17

GIVE

g thee the desires . . . . .Ps. 37:4
shall g his angels . . . . .Ps. 91:11
G to him that asketh . . . . .Matt. 5:42
G us this day . . . . .Matt. 6:11
will he g him a stone . . . . .Matt. 7:9
freely g .Matt. 10:8
G, and it shall . . . . .Luke 6:38
the Father g me . . . . .John 6:37
not as the world g . . . . .John 14:27
such as I have g . . . . .Acts 3:6
more blessed to g . . . . .Acts 20:35
also freely g us . . . . .Rom. 8:32
but rather g place . . . . .Rom. 12:19
g the increase . . . . .1 Cor. 3:7
so let him g . . . . .2 Cor. 9:7
and g him a name . . . . .Phil. 2:9
g us richly . . . . .1 Tim. 6:17
that g to all men . . . . .James 1:5
g more grace . . . . .James 4:6

GLAD

maketh g the heart . . . . .Ps. 104:15
I was g .Ps. 122:1
whereof we are g . . . . .Ps. 126:3
maketh a g father . . . . .Prov. 10:1
that g received . . . . .Acts 2:41

GLADNESS

put g in my heart . . . . .Ps. 4:7
g and singleness . . . . .Acts 2:46

GLORIFY

offereth praise g me . . . . .Ps. 50:23
and g your Father . . . . .Matt. 5:16
Son of God might be g . . . . .John 11:4
Herein is my Father g . . . . .John 15:8
he should g God . . . . .John 21:19
that we may be also g . . . . .Rom. 8:17
therefore g God . . . . .1 Cor. 6:20
g God in the day . . . . .1 Pet. 2:12

GLORIOUS

light of the g gospel . . . . .2 Cor. 4:4
to himself a g church . . . . .Eph. 5:27
like unto his g body . . . . .Phil. 3:21

GLORY

and the King of g . . . . .Ps. 24:7
give grace and g . . . . .Ps. 84:11
speak of the g . . . . .Ps. 145:11
the g of children . . . . .Prov. 17:6
is full of his g . . . . .Is. 6:3
the power, and the g . . . . .Matt. 6:13

his g was not . . . . .Matt. 6:29
with power and great g . . . . .Matt. 24:30
G to God . . . . .Luke 2:14
we beheld his g . . . . .John 1:14
come short of the g . . . . .Rom. 3:23
to whom be g . . . . .Rom. 11:36
the g of the Lord . . . . .2 Cor. 3:18
Unto him be g . . . . .Eph. 3:21
to his riches in g . . . . .Phil. 4:19
appear with him in g . . . . .Col. 3:4
received up into g . . . . .1 Tim. 3:16
full of g .1 Pet. 1:8
unto his eternal g . . . . .1 Pet. 5:10
received g and honour . . . . .Rev. 4:11
and honour, and g . . . . .Rev. 5:12
Blessing, and g . . . . .Rev. 7:12
the g of God . . . . .Rev. 21:23

GNASH

and g of teeth . . . . .Matt. 13:42, 50

GO

whither thou g . . . . .Ruth 1:16
to g a mile . . . . .Matt. 5:41
G ye therefore . . . . .Matt. 28:19
g unto my Father . . . . .John 14:12

GOD

and Noah walked with G . . . . .Gen. 6:9
G is not a man . . . . .Num. 23:19
My G, my G, why hast . . . . .Ps. 22:1
thou are the G . . . . .Is. 37:16
walk humbly with thy G . . . . .Mic. 6:8
is, G with us . . . . .Matt. 1:23
for there is one G . . . . .Mark 12:32
G is a Spirit . . . . .John 4:24
if G be for us . . . . .Rom. 8:31
G is not the author . . . . .1 Cor. 14:33
G is not mocked . . . . .Gal. 6:7
my G shall supply . . . . .Phil. 4:19
G was manifest . . . . .1 Tim. 3:16
that G is light . . . . .1 John 1:5
G is love . . . . .1 John 4:8
No man hath seen G . . . . .1 John 4:12
G shall wipe away . . . . .Rev. 21:4
I will be his G . . . . .Rev. 21:7

GODHEAD

fulness of the G bodily . . . . .Col. 2:9

GODLINESS

Having a form of g . . . . .2 Tim. 3:5
and to patience g . . . . .2 Pet. 1:6

GODLY

g sorrow worketh . . . . .2 Cor. 7:10
live g in Christ Jesus . . . . .2 Tim. 3:12
righteously, and g . . . . .Titus 2:12

GONE

sheep have g astray . . . . .Is. 53:6
They are all g . . . . .Rom. 3:12

GOOD (n.)

none that doeth g . . . . .Ps. 14:1
Withhold not g . . . . .Prov. 3:27
went about doing g . . . . .Acts 10:38
work together for g . . . . .Rom. 8:28

GOOD (*adj.*)
God saw that it was *g* . . . . .Gen. 1:10
g name is rather . . . . .Prov. 22:1
to give *g* gifts . . . . .Matt. 7:11
thou *g* and faithful . . . . .Matt. 25:21
g measure, pressed down . . . .Luke 6:38
chosen that *g* part . . . . .Luke 10:42
Why callest thou me *g* . . . . . .Luke 18:19
I am the *g* shepherd . . . . .John 10:11
prove what is that *g* . . . . .Rom. 12:2
to every *g* work . . . . .2 Cor. 9:8
in every *g* work . . . . .Col. 1:10
Fight the *g* . . . . .1 Tim. 6:12
zealous of *g* works . . . . .Titus 2:14

GOODNESS
Surely *g* and mercy . . . . .Ps. 23:6
the riches of his *g* . . . . .Rom. 2:4

GOSPEL
my sake and the *g* . . . . .Mark 8:35
ashamed of the *g* . . . . .Rom. 1:16
But if our *g* be hid . . . . .2 Cor. 4:3
preach any other *g* . . . . .Gal. 1:8

GOVERNMENT
the *g* shall be upon . . . . .Is. 9:6

GRACE
full of *g* and truth . . . . .John 1:14
G to you and peace . . . . .Rom. 1:7
freely by his *g* . . . . .Rom. 3:24
g did much more abound . . . .Rom. 5:20
but under *g* . . . . .Rom. 6:14
My *g* is sufficient . . . . .2 Cor. 12:9
by *g* ye are saved . . . . .Eph. 2:5
is this *g* given . . . . .Eph. 3:8
the throne of *g* . . . . .Heb. 4:16
But he giveth more *g* . . . . . . .James 4:6
and giveth *g* to . . . . .2 Pet. 5:5
grow in *g*, and in the . . . . .2 Pet. 3:18

GRACIOUS
thou art a *g* God . . . . .Jon. 4:2
the Lord is *g* . . . . .1 Pet. 2:3

GRAVE
be silent in the *g* . . . . .Ps. 31:27
the power of the *g* . . . . .Ps. 49:15
that are in the *g* . . . . .John 5:28
to the *g* to weep . . . . .John 11:31
O *g*, where is thy . . . . .1 Cor. 15:55

GREAT
make of thee a *g* nation . . . . . . .Gen. 12:2
for *g* is your . . . . .Matt. 5:12
one pearl of *g* price . . . . .Matt. 13:46
g is thy faith . . . . .Matt. 15:28
whosoever will be *g* . . . . .Matt. 20:26
so *g* salvation . . . . .Heb. 2:3

GREATER
g works than these . . . . .John 5:20
is *g* than all . . . . .John 10:29
The servant is not *g* . . . . .John 13:16
for my Father is *g* . . . . .John 14:28
G love hath no man . . . . .John 15:13
God is *g* than . . . . .1 John 3:20
because *g* is he that . . . . .1 John 4:4
I have no *g* joy . . . . .3 John 4

GREATEST
the *g* in the kingdom . . . . .Matt. 18:1

GRIEF
life is spent with *g* . . . . .Ps. 31:10
acquainted with *g* . . . . .Is. 53:3

GRIEVE
And *g* not the holy . . . . .Eph. 4:30

GROAN
g and travaileth . . . . .Rom. 8:22
in this we *g* . . . . .2 Cor. 5:2

GROUNDED
being rooted and *g* . . . . .Eph. 3:17

GROW
g unto an holy . . . . .Eph. 2:21
may *g* up into him . . . . .Eph. 4:15
g in grace . . . . .2 Pet. 3:18

GUIDE
g our feet into . . . . .Luke 1:79
he will *g* you . . . . .John 16:13

GUILE
in whom is no *g* . . . . .John 1:47
neither was *g* found . . . . .1 Pet. 2:22

GUILTY
become *g* before God . . . . . . .Rom. 3:19
shall be *g* of . . . . .1 Cor. 11:27
he is *g* of all . . . . .James 2:10

H

HAIR
the *h* of mine head . . . . .Ps. 40:12
make one *h* white . . . . .Matt. 5:36
the very *h* of your . . . . .Matt. 10:30
at thy right *h* . . . . .Ps. 16:41
the work of our *h* . . . . .Ps. 90:17
thy *h* findeth to do . . . . .Eccl. 9:10
the Lord's *h* is not . . . . .Is. 59:1
let not thy left *h* . . . . .Matt. 6:3
My time is at *h* . . . . .Matt. 26:18
thy *h* offend thee . . . . .Mark 9:43
The Lord is at *h* . . . . .Phil. 4:5
lifting up holy *h* . . . . .1 Tim. 2:8
h of the living God . . . . .Heb. 10:31
the end . . . is at *h* . . . . .1 Pet. 4:7

HAPPY
h shalt thou be . . . . .Ps. 128:2
H is that people . . . . .Ps. 144:15
h is every one . . . . .Prov. 3:18
h is he . . . . .Prov. 14:21
h are ye . . . . .John 13:17
we count them *h* . . . . .James 5:11

HARDEN
H not your heart . . . . .Ps. 95:8
he that *h* his heart . . . . .Prov. 28:14
and *h* their . . . . .John 12:40
h through the . . . . .Heb. 3:13

HARMLESS
wise as serpents, and *h* . . . . . .Matt. 10:16

HARVEST (cont.)
blameless and *h* . . . . .Phil. 2:15
who is holy, *h* . . . . .Heb. 7:26

HARVEST
the *h* is past . . . . .Jer. 8:20
The *h* truly is . . . . .Matt. 9:37
Lord of the *h* . . . . .Matt. 9:38
white already to *h* . . . . .John 4:35
the *h* of the earth . . . . .Rev. 14:15

HATE
and a time to *h* . . . . .Eccl. 3:8
to them that *h* you . . . . .Matt. 5:44
for either he will *h* . . . . .Matt. 6:24
men shall *h* you . . . . .Luke 6:22
and *h* not his father . . . . .Luke 14:26
h the light . . . . .John 3:20
h his own flesh . . . . .Eph. 5:29
h his brother . . . . .1 John 2:9
if the world *h* you . . . . .1 John 3:13

HAUGHTY
and an *h* spirit . . . . .Prov. 16:18
Proud and *h* scorner . . . . .Prov. 21:24

HEAD
Lift up your *h* . . . . .Ps. 24:7, 9
joy upon their *h* . . . . .Is. 35:10
lift up his *h* . . . . .Zech. 1:21
My *h* with oil . . . . .Luke 7:46
lift up your *h* . . . . .Luke 21:28
the *h* of every man . . . . .1 Cor. 11:3
gave him to be *h* . . . . .Eph. 1:22
the *h* of the body . . . . .Col. 1:18

HEAL
O Lord, *h* me . . . . .Ps. 6:2
h all thy diseases . . . . .Ps. 103:3
stripes we are *h* . . . . .Is. 53:5
and to *h* all manner . . . . .Matt. 10:1
H the sick . . . . .Matt. 10:8
h the brokenhearted . . . . .Luke 4:18
ye may be *h* . . . . .James 5:16
ye were *h* . . . . .1 Pet. 2:24

HEALING
h in his wings . . . . .Mal. 4:2
h all manner . . . . .Matt. 4:23
h of the nations . . . . .Rev. 22:2

HEAR
Lord will not *h* me . . . . .Ps. 66:18
whosoever *h* these . . . . .Matt. 7:24
the deaf *h* . . . . .Matt. 11:5
h ye him . . . . .Matt. 17:5
the deaf *h* . . . . .Luke 7:22
to *h* those things . . . . .Luke 10:24
h without a preacher . . . . .Rom. 10:14
that he *h* us . . . . .1 John 5:15
let him *h* . . . . .Rev. 2:7
if any man *h* my voice . . . . .Rev. 3:20

HEARD
h the word believed . . . . .Acts 4:4
we have seen and *h* . . . . .Acts 4:20
they have not *h* . . . . .Rom. 10:14
nor ear *h* . . . . .1 Cor. 2:9
received, and *h* . . . . .Phil. 4:9
by them that *h* . . . . .Heb. 2:3
which we have *h* . . . . .1 John 1:1

HEARER
and not *h* only . . . . .James 1:22

HEARING
The *h* ear . . . . .Prov. 20:12
h they hear not . . . . .Matt. 13:13
faith cometh by *h* . . . . .Rom. 10:17
ye are dull of *h* . . . . .Heb. 5:11

HEART
Lord looketh on the *h* . . . . . . .1 Sam. 16:7
and know my *h* . . . . .Ps. 139:23
Keep thy *h* . . . . .Prov. 4:23
thinketh in his *h* . . . . .Prov. 23:7
wise man's *h* . . . . .Eccl. 8:5
of a fearful *h* . . . . .Is. 35:4
sing for joy of *h* . . . . .Is. 65:14
The *h* is deceitful . . . . .Jer. 17:9
And rend your *h* . . . . .Joel 2:13
the pure in *h* . . . . .Matt. 5:8
there will your *h* be . . . . .Matt. 6:21
meek and lowly in *h* . . . . .Matt. 11:29
abundance of the *h* . . . . .Matt. 12:34
out of the *h* . . . . .Matt. 15:19
with all thy *h* . . . . .Matt. 22:37
with all thy *h* . . . . .Luke 10:27
Let not your *h* . . . . .John 14:1
For with the *h* . . . . .Rom. 10:10
into the *h* of man . . . . .1 Cor. 2:9
dwell in your *h* . . . . .Eph. 3:17
making melody in your *h* . . . . . .Eph. 5:19
from the *h* . . . . .Eph. 6:6
shall keep your *h* . . . . .Phil. 4:7
in singleness of *h* . . . . .Col. 3:22
intents of the *h* . . . . .Heb. 4:12
purify your *h* . . . . .James 4:8
hidden man of the *h* . . . . .1 Pet. 3:4
God in your *h* . . . . .1 Pet. 3:15

HEARTILY
whatsoever ye do, do it *h* . . . . . .Col. 3:23

HEATHEN
Why did the *h* rage . . . . .Acts 4:25

HEAVEN
When I consider thy *h* . . . . .Ps. 8:3
word is settled in *h* . . . . .Ps. 119:89
I create new *h* . . . . .Is. 65:17
Till *h* and earth pass . . . . .Matt. 5:18
H and earth shall . . . . .Matt. 24:35
he saw the *h* opened . . . . .Mark 1:10
angels which are in *h* . . . . .Mark 13:32
sinned against *h* . . . . .Luke 15:18
name under *h* given . . . . .Acts 4:12
eternal in the *h* . . . . .2 Cor. 5:1
conversation is in *h* . . . . .Phil. 3:20
are written in *h* . . . . .Heb. 12:23
I saw a new *h* . . . . .Rev. 21:1

HEAVENLY
a multitude of the *h* host . . . . . .Luke 2:13
your *h* Father . . . . .Luke 11:13
together in *h* places . . . . .Eph. 2:6
that is, an *h* . . . . .Heb. 11:16

HEIR
and *h* according . . . . .Gal. 3:29
should be made *h* . . . . .Titus 3:7

h of the righteousness . . . . . . .Heb. 11:7
h of the kingdom . . . . .James 2:5

HELL
if I make my bed in *h* . . . . .Ps. 139:8
his soul from *h* . . . . .Prov. 23:14
H and destruction . . . . .Prov. 27:20
danger of *h* fire . . . . .Matt. 5:22
be cast into *h* . . . . .Matt. 5:29
brought down to *h* . . . . .Matt. 11:23
and the gates of *h* . . . . .Matt. 16:18
cast into *h* fire . . . . .Matt. 18:9
in *h* he lift up . . . . .Luke 16:23
on fire of *h* . . . . .James 3:6
them down to *h* . . . . .2 Pet. 2:4

HELMET
the *h* of salvation . . . . .Eph. 6:17

HELP
will make him an *h* meet . . . . . .Gen. 2:18
a very present *h* . . . . .Ps. 46:1
whence cometh my *h* . . . . .Ps. 121:1
Our *h* is in the name . . . . .Ps. 124:8
h thou mine unbelief . . . . .Mark 9:24
find grace to *h* . . . . .Heb. 4:16

HID
Thy word have I *h* . . . . .Ps. 119:11
there is nothing *h* . . . . .Mark 4:22
the *h* wisdom . . . . .1 Cor. 2:7
if our gospel be *h* . . . . .2 Cor. 4:3
your life is *h* . . . . .Col. 3:3

HIDE
h me under the shadow . . . . . . .Ps. 17:8
the darkness *h* not . . . . .Ps. 139:12
be as an *h* place . . . . .Is. 32:2
shall *h* a multitude . . . . .James 5:20
h us from the face . . . . .Rev. 6:16

HIGH
the heaven is *h* . . . . .Ps. 103:11
He shall dwell on *h* . . . . .Is. 33:16
power from on *h* . . . . .Luke 24:49
Mind not *h* things . . . . .Rom. 12:16
it is *h* time . . . . .Rom. 13:11
h calling of God . . . . .Phil. 3:14

HIGHER
unto the *h* powers . . . . .Rom. 13:1
h than the heavens . . . . .Heb. 7:26

HIGHEST
the Son of the *H* . . . . .Luke 1:32
Glory to God in the *h* . . . . .Luke 2:14

HILL
dwell in thy holy *h* . . . . .Ps. 15:1
upon a thousand *h* . . . . .Ps. 50:10
eyes unto the *h* . . . . .Ps. 121:1
that is set on an *h* . . . . .Matt. 5:14

HOLD
h his peace . . . . .Prov. 11:12
H fast, that which . . . . .1 Thess. 5:21
H faith . . . . .1 Tim. 1:19
h fast the faithful . . . . .Titus 1:9
h fast our profession . . . . .Heb. 4:14
h fast my name . . . . .Rev. 2:13

HOLIEST
called the *H* of all . . . . .Heb. 9:3
into the *h* . . . . .Heb. 10:19

HOLINESS
H to the Lord . . . . .Ex. 28:36
in the beauty of *h* . . . . .1 Chr. 16:29
your fruit unto *h* . . . . .Rom. 6:22
perfecting *h* . . . . .2 Cor. 7:1
and true *h* . . . . .Eph. 4:24
unblameable in *h* . . . . .1 Thess. 3:13
but unto *h* . . . . .1 Thess. 4:7
as becometh *h* . . . . .Titus 2:3

HOLY
whereon thou standest is *h* . . . .Ex. 3:5
to keep it *h* . . . . .Ex. 20:8
be ye *h* . . . . .Lev. 20:7
h in all his works . . . . .Ps. 145:17
said, *H, h, h* . . . . .Is. 6:3
not that which is *h* . . . . .Matt. 7:6
against the *H* Ghost . . . . .Matt. 12:31
the *H* Ghost descended . . . . . . .Luke 3:22
H Ghost is come . . . . .Acts 1:8
receive the *H* Ghost . . . . .Acts 8:15
comfort of the *H* Ghost . . . . . . .Acts 9:31
a living sacrifice, *h* . . . . .Rom. 12:1
with an *h* kiss . . . . .Rom. 16:16
H Ghost teacheth . . . . .1 Cor. 2:13
temple of God is *h* . . . . .1 Cor. 3:17
unto an *h* temple . . . . .Eph. 2:21
it should be *h* . . . . .Eph. 5:27
h and beloved . . . . .Col. 3:12
all the *h* brethren . . . . .1 Thess. 5:27
lifting up *h* hands . . . . .1 Tim. 2:8
an *h* calling . . . . .2 Tim. 1:9
sober, just, *h* . . . . .Titus 1:8
renewing of the *H* Ghost . . . . . .Titus 3:5
called you is *h* . . . . .1 Pet. 1:15
an *h* priesthood . . . . .1 Pet. 2:5
an *h* nation . . . . .1 Pet. 2:9
saying, *H, h, h* . . . . .Rev. 4:8
the *h* Jerusalem . . . . .Rev. 21:10
he that is *h* . . . . .Rev. 22:11

HOME
their husbands at *h* . . . . .1 Cor. 14:35
shew piety at *h* . . . . .1 Tim. 5:4

HONEST
men of *h* report . . . . .Acts 6:3
h in the sight . . . . .Rom. 12:17
Let us walk *h* . . . . .Rom. 13:13
for *h* things . . . . .2 Cor. 8:21
things are *h* . . . . .Phil. 4:8

HONOUR (n.)
not without *h* . . . . .Matt. 13:57
hath no *h* in his . . . . .John 4:44
for glory and *h* . . . . .Rom. 2:7
in *h* preferring . . . . .Rom. 12:10
h to whom *h* . . . . .Rom. 13:7
worthy of double *h* . . . . .1 Tim. 5:17
some to *h* . . . . .2 Tim. 2:20
h unto the wife . . . . .1 Pet. 3:7
receive glory and *h* . . . . .Rev. 4:11

HONOUR (v.)
H thy father and thy . . . . .Ex. 20:12
H the Lord . . . . .Prov. 3:9

HOPE
that *h* not the Son . . . . .John 5:23
H all men . . . . .1 Pet. 2:17

HOPE (*n.*)
my *h* is in thee . . . . .Ps. 39:7
H deferred . . . . .Prov. 13:12
Rejoicing in *h* . . . . .Rom. 12:2
abideth faith, *h* . . . . .1 Cor. 13:13
h of eternal life . . . . .Titus 3:7

HOPE (*v.*)
h in the Lord . . . . .Ps. 31:24
and *h* to the end . . . . .1 Pet. 1:13

HOSPITALITY
given to *h* . . . . .1 Tim. 3:2
h one to another . . . . .1 Pet. 4:9

HOUR
of that day and *h* . . . . .Matt. 24:36
save me from this *h* . . . . .John 12:27
the *h* cometh . . . . .John 16:32

HOUSE
H and riches . . . . .Prov. 19:14
if a *h* be divided . . . . .Mark 3:25
upon that *h* . . . . .Luke 6:48
my Father's *h* . . . . .John 14:2
from *h* to, *h* . . . . .Acts 2:46
our earthly *h* . . . . .2 Cor. 5:1
those of his own *h* . . . . .1 Tim. 5:8

HOUSEHOLD
the *h* of faith . . . . .Gal. 6:10

HUMBLE
the *h* shall hear . . . . .Ps. 34:2
contrite and *h* spirit . . . . .Is. 57:15
therefore shall *h* . . . . .Matt. 18:4
that *h* himself shall . . . . .Luke 14:11
he *h* himself . . . . .Phil. 2:8
grace unto the *h* . . . . .James 4:6
H yourselves . . . . .1 Pet. 5:6

HUMBLY
to walk *h* with . . . . .Mic. 6:8

HUMILITY
and before honour is *h* . . . . . .Prov. 15:33
By *h* and the fear . . . . .Prov. 22:4

HUNGER
they which do *h* . . . . .Matt. 5:6
shall never *h* . . . . .John 6:35
If thine enemy *h* . . . . .Rom. 12:20
shall *h* no more . . . . .Rev. 7:16

HUNGRY
filled the *h* with good . . . . . . .Luke 1:53

HUSBAND
a crown to her *h* . . . . .Prov. 12:4
Her *h* is known . . . . .Prov. 31:23
shalt save thy *h* . . . . .1 Cor. 7:16
H, love your wives . . . . .Eph. 5:25
h of one wife . . . . .1 Tim. 3:12
love their *h* . . . . .Titus 2:4

HYMN
they had sung an *h* . . . . .Matt. 26:30
in psalms and *h* . . . . .Eph. 5:19

HYPOCRITE
be not, as the *h* . . . . .Matt. 6:16

I

IDLE
every *i* word . . . . .Matt. 12:36

IDOL
pollutions of *i* . . . . .Acts 15:20
an *i* is nothing . . . . .1 Cor. 8:4
to God from *i* . . . . .1 Thess. 1:9
yourselves from *i* . . . . .1 John 5:21

IGNORANCE
that through *i* ye did . . . . .Acts 3:17
i that is in them . . . . .Eph. 4:18
i of foolish men . . . . .1 Pet. 2:15

IGNORANT
unlearned and *i* men . . . . .Acts 4:13
For they being *i* . . . . .Rom. 10:3
if any man be *i* . . . . .1 Cor. 14:38

IMAGE
Let us make man in our *i* . . . . .Gen. 1:26
i of his Son . . . . .Rom. 8:29
same *i* from glory . . . . .2 Cor. 3:18

IMAGINATION
i of the thoughts . . . . .1 Chr. 28:9
i of his own heart . . . . .Jer. 23:17
vain in their *i* . . . . .Rom. 1:21

IMMORTALITY
mortal must put on *i* . . . . .1 Cor. 15:53

IMPOSSIBLE
With men this is *i* . . . . .Matt. 19:26
nothing shall be *i* . . . . .Luke 1:37

INCREASE (*n.*)
tithe all the *i* . . . . .Deut. 14:22
earth yield her *i* . . . . .Ps. 67:6
God gave the *i* . . . . .1 Cor. 3:6

INCREASE (*v.*)
Jesus *i* in wisdom . . . . .Luke 2:52
I our faith . . . . .Luke 17:5
word of God *i* . . . . .Acts 6:7
i with goods . . . . .Rev. 3:17

INFALLIBLE
by many *i* proofs . . . . .Acts 1:3

INFIRMITY
Himself took our *i* . . . . .Matt. 8:17

INHERIT
meek shall *i* . . . . .Ps. 37:11
i the kingdom . . . . .Matt. 25:34
i eternal life . . . . .Mark 10:17
shall not *i* . . . . .1 Cor. 6:9

INHERITANCE
earnest of our *i* . . . . .Eph. 1:14

INIQUITY
pardon mine *i* . . . . .Ps. 25:11
I was shapen in *i* . . . . .Ps. 51:5
forgiveth all thine *i* . . . . .Ps. 103:3
bruised for our *i* . . . . .Is. 53:5
i shall abound . . . . .Matt. 24:12
depart from *i* . . . . .2 Tim. 2:19
a world of *i* . . . . .James 3:6

INNOCENT
shall not be *i* . . . . .Prov. 28:20

INSPIRATION
by *i* of God . . . . .2 Tim. 3:16

INSTANT
continuing *i* in prayer . . . . . . .Rom. 12:12
be *i* in season . . . . .2 Tim. 4:2

INSTRUCTION
Whoso loveth *i* . . . . .Prov. 12:1
i in righteousness . . . . .2 Tim. 3:16

INTERCESSION
to make *i* for them . . . . .Heb. 7:25

INVISIBLE
For the *i* things of him . . . . . . .Rom. 1:20
image of the *i* God . . . . .Col. 1:15
immortal, *i* . . . . .1 Tim. 1:17

INWARD
after the *i* man . . . . .Rom. 7:22
i man is renewed . . . . .2 Cor. 4:16

J

JEALOUS
Lord thy God am a *j* God . . . . . .Ex. 20:5
am *j* over you . . . . .2 Cor. 11:2

JEALOUSY
For *j* is the . . . . .Prov. 6:34
the Lord to *j* . . . . .1 Cor. 10:22

JESUS
J the Son of God . . . . .Heb. 4:14
confess that J . . . . .1 John 4:15

JOIN
God hath *j* together . . . . .Matt. 19:16

JOY
the *j* of the Lord . . . . .Neh. 8:10
but *j* cometh . . . . .Ps. 30:5
j of thy salvation . . . . .Ps. 51:12
shall reap in *j* . . . . .Ps. 126:5
j shall be in heaven . . . . .Luke 15:7
j might be full . . . . .John 15:11
count it all *j* . . . . .James 1:2
with exceeding *j* . . . . .1 Pet. 4:13

JOYFUL
Make a *j* noise . . . . .Ps. 66:1

JUDGE (*n.*)
J of quick . . . . .Acts 10:42
the righteous *j* . . . . .2 Tim. 4:8
God the J of all . . . . .Heb. 12:23

JUDGE (*v.*)
J not .Matt. 7:1
Who art thou that *j* . . . . .Rom. 14:4

JUDGMENT
every work into *j* . . . . .Eccl. 12:14
danger of the *j* . . . . .Matt. 5:21
righteousness, and of *j* . . . . . . .John 16:8
j seat of Christ . . . . .Rom. 14:10
after this the *j* . . . . .Heb. 9:27

JUST
rain on the *j* . . . . .Matt. 5:45
of the *j* . . . . .Luke 14:14
j persons . . . . .Luke 15:7
j shall live by faith . . . . .Rom. 1:17
things are *j* . . . . .Phil. 4:8
Now the *j* shall . . . . .Heb. 10:38

JUSTIFY
that believe are *j* . . . . .Acts 13:39
shall no flesh be *j* . . . . .Rom. 3:20
being *j* by faith . . . . .Rom. 5:1
j by his blood . . . . .Rom. 5:9
not *j* by the works . . . . .Gal. 2:16
j in the Spirit . . . . .1 Tim. 3:16

K

KEEP
K me as the apple . . . . .Ps. 17:8
time to *k* . . . . .Eccl. 3:6
If a man *k* my saying . . . . .John 8:51
will *k* my words . . . . .John 14:23
shall *k* your hearts . . . . .Phil. 4:7
k thyself pure . . . . .1 Tim. 5:22
to *k* himself . . . . .James 1:27
k yourselves . . . . .1 John 5:21
k you from falling . . . . .Jude 24

KEEPER
my brother's *k* . . . . .Gen. 4:9
The Lord is thy *k* . . . . .Ps. 121:5

KEY
the *k* of the kingdom . . . . . . .Matt. 16:19
have the *k* of hell . . . . .Rev. 1:18

KILL
A time to *k* . . . . .Eccl. 3:3
that *k* the body . . . . .Luke 12:4
k all the day . . . . .Rom. 8:36

KIND
Charity . . . is *k* . . . . .1 Cor. 13:4

KING
Blessed be the K . . . . .Luke 19:38
unto the K eternal . . . . .1 Tim. 1:17
K of K, and Lord . . . . .1 Tim. 6:15
k and priests . . . . .Rev. 1:6

KINGDOM
For thine is the *k* . . . . .Matt. 6:13
us into the *k* . . . . .Col. 1:13
his heavenly *k* . . . . .2 Tim. 4:18
heirs of the *k* . . . . .James 2:5
the everlasting *k* . . . . .2 Pet. 1:11

KISS
the *k* of an enemy . . . . .Prov. 27:6
with an holy *k* . . . . .Rom. 16:16

KNEE
every *k* should bow . . . . .Phil. 2:10

KNOCK
k, and it shall be opened . . . . . .Matt. 7:7
at the door, and *k* . . . . .Rev. 3:20

KNOW
k that my redeemer . . . . .Job 19:25
k that I am God . . . . .Ps. 46:10
who can *k* it . . . . .Jer. 17:9
left hand *k* . . . . .Matt. 6:3
I *k* you not . . . . .Matt. 25:12
k my sheep . . . . .John 10:14
but thou shalt *k* . . . . .John 13:7
we *k* that all things . . . . .Rom. 8:28
we *k* in part . . . . .1 Cor. 13:9
to *k* the love . . . . .Eph. 3:19
for I *k* whom . . . . .2 Tim. 1:12
we *k* that . . . . .1 John 3:2
I *k* thy works . . . . .Rev. 2:2

KNOWLEDGE
K puffeth up . . . . .1 Cor. 8:1
k, it shall vanish . . . . .1 Cor. 13:8
which passeth *k* . . . . .Eph. 3:19
k of Christ Jesus . . . . .Phil. 3:8
k of the truth . . . . .1 Tim. 2:4

L

LABOUR (*n.*)
your *l* is not . . . . .1 Cor. 15:58
and *l* of love . . . . .1 Thess. 1:3
thy works, and thy *l* . . . . .Rev. 2:2
rest from their *l* . . . . .Rev. 14:13

LABOUR (*v.*)
Six days shalt thou *l* . . . . .Ex. 20:9
they *l* in vain . . . . .Ps. 127:1
all ye that *l* . . . . .Matt. 11:28
we are *l* together . . . . .1 Cor. 3:9

LAMB
the *L* of God . . . . .John 1:29, 36
l without blemish . . . . .1 Pet. 1:19
blood of the *L* . . . . .Rev. 12:11

LAST
first shall be *l* . . . . .Matt. 19:30

LAUGH
a time to *l* . . . . .Eccl. 3:4
your *l* be turned . . . . .James 4:9

LAW
thy *l* is my delight . . . . .Ps. 119:174
what the *l* could not do . . . . . . .Rom. 8:3
all the *l* is fulfilled . . . . .Gal. 5:14
fulfil the *l* of Christ . . . . .Gal. 6:2
l of liberty . . . . .James 1:25

LEAD
he *l* me beside . . . . .Ps. 23:2
and *l* me in the way . . . . .Ps. 139:24

And *l* us not . . . . .Matt. 6:13
may *l* a quiet . . . . .1 Tim. 2:2

LEAST
l in the kingdom . . . . .Luke 7:28
that which is *l* . . . . .Luke 16:10

LEAVE
l father and mother . . . . .Matt. 19:5
Peace I *l* with you . . . . .John 14:27
I will never *l* thee . . . . .Heb. 13:5

LIE
impossible for God to *l* . . . . . . .Heb. 6:18

LIFE
the breath of *l* . . . . .Gen. 2:7
the tree of *l* . . . . .Gen. 2:9
strength of my *l* . . . . .Ps. 27:1
findeth me findeth *l* . . . . .Prov. 8:35
thought for your *l* . . . . .Matt. 6:25
for a man's *l* . . . . .Luke 12:15
hath everlasting *l* . . . . .John 5:24
they might have *l* . . . . .John 10:10
I lay down my *l* . . . . .John 10:15
and the *l* . . . . .John 11:25
the truth, and the *l* . . . . .John 14:6
l which I now live . . . . .Gal. 2:20
For what is your *l* . . . . .James 4:14
the pride of *l* . . . . .1 John 2:16

LIGHT
The Lord is my *l* . . . . .Ps. 27:1
l unto my path . . . . .Ps. 119:105
Let your *l* so shine . . . . .Matt. 5:16
That was the true *L* . . . . .John 1:9
if we walk in the *l* . . . . .1 John 1:7
neither *l* of the sun . . . . .Rev. 22:5

LION
the den of *l* . . . . .Dan. 6:16
as a roaring *l* . . . . .1 Pet. 5:8

LIVE
not *l* by bread alone . . . . .Matt. 4:4
For in him we *l* . . . . .Acts 17:28
The just shall *l* . . . . .Rom. 1:17
If we *l* in the Spirit . . . . .Gal. 5:25
me to *l* is Christ . . . . .Phil. 1:21
I am he that *l* . . . . .Rev. 1:18

LIVING
man became a *l* soul . . . . .Gen. 2:7
given thee *l* water . . . . .John 4:10

LORD
The *L* our God . . . . .Deut. 6:4
God is the *L* . . . . .Ps. 33:12
saith unto me *L, L* . . . . .Matt. 7:21
One *L*, one faith . . . . .Eph. 4:5
L of peace . . . . .2 Thess. 3:16

LOSE
findeth his life shall *l* it . . . . . .Matt. 10:39
l his own soul . . . . .Matt. 16:26

LOST
that which was *l* . . . . .Matt. 18:11

LOVE (n.)
but *l* covereth . . . . .Prov. 10:12
where *l* is . . . . .Prov. 15:17
banner over me was *l* . . . . .Song 2:4
the *l* of many . . . . .Matt. 24:12
l one to another . . . . .John 13:35
Greater *l* hath no man . . . . . . .John 15:13
L worketh no ill . . . . .Rom. 13:10
And to know the *l* . . . . .Eph. 3:19
l of money . . . . .1 Tim. 6:10
no fear in *l* . . . . .1 John 4:18
left thy first *l* . . . . .Rev. 2:4

LOVE (v.)
l thy neighbour as thyself . . . . .Lev. 19:18
l the Lord thy God . . . . .Deut. 6:5
friend *l* at all times . . . . .Prov. 17:17
A time to *l* . . . . .Eccl. 3:8
L your enemies . . . . .Matt. 5:44
That ye *l* one another . . . . . . .John 15:12
l one another . . . . .1 John 4:7
We *l* him . . . . .1 John 4:19

LOVER
l of pleasures . . . . .2 Tim. 3:4
a *l* of hospitality . . . . .Titus 1:8

LOVINGKINDNESS
thy *l* is better . . . . .Ps. 63:3
To shew forth thy *l* . . . . .Ps. 92:2

LUST
of his own *l* . . . . .James 1:14
from fleshly *l* . . . . .1 Pet. 2:11

M

MAN
Let us make *m* in our . . . . .Gen. 1:26
No *m* can serve two . . . . .Matt. 6:24
No *m* hath seen God . . . . .John 1:18
outward *m* perish . . . . .2 Cor. 4:16
in fashion as a *m* . . . . .Phil. 2:8
the *m* Christ Jesus . . . . .1 Tim. 2:5

MARK
M the perfect man . . . . .Ps. 37:37
press toward the *m* . . . . .Phil. 3:14

MARRY
shall *m* her that is . . . . .Matt. 5:32
they neither *m* . . . . .Mark 12:25
I have *m* a wife . . . . .Luke 14:20

MARVELLOUS
m in our eyes . . . . .Ps. 118:23
his *m* light . . . . .1 Pet. 2:9

MASTER
can serve two *m* . . . . .Matt. 6:24
Ye call me *M* and Lord . . . . . .John 13:13
subject to your *m* . . . . .1 Pet. 2:18

MEAT
life more than *m* . . . . .Matt. 6:25
My *m* is to do . . . . .John 4:34
with thy *m* . . . . .Rom. 14:15
if *m* make my brother . . . . . . .1 Cor. 8:13

MEDITATE
his law doth he *m* . . . . .Ps. 1:2
I will *m* also . . . . .Ps. 77:12
m upon these . . . . .1 Tim. 4:15

MEEK
m shall inherit . . . . .Ps. 37:11
Blessed are the *m* . . . . .Matt. 5:5
for I am *m* . . . . .Matt. 11:29

MELODY
making *m* in your . . . . .Eph. 5:19

MEMBER
many *m* in one body . . . . .Rom. 12:4
the *m* of Christ . . . . .1 Cor. 6:15

MERCIFUL
God be *m* unto us . . . . .Ps. 67:1
Blessed are the *m* . . . . .Matt. 5:7
m to me a sinner . . . . .Luke 18:13

MERCY
goodness and *m* shall . . . . .Ps. 23:6
m endureth for ever . . . . .Ps. 136:1
m and truth . . . . .Prov. 16:6
they shall obtain *m* . . . . .Matt. 5:7
have *m* on whom . . . . .Rom. 9:15
by the *m* of God . . . . .Rom. 12:1
that we may obtain *m* . . . . .Heb. 4:16

MIGHT
with all thy *m* . . . . .Deut. 6:5
Not by *m* . . . . .Zech. 4:6

MIGHTY
Thou hast a *m* arm . . . . .Ps. 89:13
a rushing *m* wind . . . . .Acts 2:2

MILK
m and honey . . . . .Ex. 3:8
have need of *m* . . . . .Heb. 5:12
m of the word . . . . .1 Pet. 2:2

MIND
whose *m* is stayed . . . . .Is. 26:3
same *m* one toward . . . . .Rom. 12:16
Let this *m* be in you . . . . .Phil. 2:5
keep your hearts and *m* . . . . . . .Phil. 4:7
and of sound *m* . . . . .2 Tim. 1:7

MINISTER
ye *m* of his . . . . .Ps. 103:21
let him be your *m* . . . . .Matt. 20:26

MINISTRY
m of reconciliation . . . . .2 Cor. 5:18
proof of thy *m* . . . . .2 Tim. 4:5

MIRACLE
a *m* in my name . . . . .Mark 9:39
beginning of *m* . . . . .John 2:11
again the second *m* . . . . .John 4:54
John did no *m* . . . . .John 10:41

MOCK
God is not *m* . . . . .Gal. 6:7

MONEY
the love of *m* . . . . .1 Tim. 6:10

MORTAL
in your *m* body ....Rom. 6:12
this *m* must ....1 Cor. 15:53

MOTHER
Who is my *m* ....Matt. 12:48
and the *m* of Jesus ....John 2:1

MOURN
all that *m* ....Is. 61:2
they that *m* ....Matt. 5:4

MOUTH
Out of the *m* of babes ....Ps. 8:2
the *m* speaketh ....Matt. 12:34
the *m* confession ....Rom. 10:10

MULTITUDE
In the *m* of words ....Prov. 10:19
m of counsellors ....Prov. 11:14
cover a *m* of sins ....1 Pet. 4:8

MUZZLE
not *m* the mouth ....1 Cor. 9:9

MYSTERY
I shew you a *m* ....1 Cor. 15:51
This is a great *m* ....Eph. 5:32

N

NAKED
they were both *n* ....Gen. 2:25
N came I ....Job 1:21
N, and ye clothed ....Matt. 25:36
all things are *n* ....Heb. 4:13

NAME
A good *n* is rather ....Prov. 22:1
Hallowed be thy *n* ....Matt. 6:9
together in my *n* ....Matt. 18:20
shall ask in my *n* ....John 14:13
there is none other *n* ....Acts 4:12
at the *n* of Jesus ....Phil. 2:10
n of the Lord Jesus ....Col. 3:17

NATION
For *n* shall rise ....Matt. 24:7
perverse *n* ....Phil. 2:15

NATURAL
without *n* affection ....Rom. 1:31
But the *n* man ....1 Cor. 2:14
Without *n* affection ....2 Tim. 3:3

NAY
yea, yea, and *n*, *n* ....2 Cor. 1:17
and your *n*, *n* ....James 5:12

NEIGHBOUR
love thy *n* ....Matt. 19:19
And who is my *n* ....Luke 10:29

NEVER
are *n* satisfied ....Prov. 30:15
I *n* knew you ....Matt. 7:23
shall *n* thirst ....John 4:14
shall *n* hunger ....John 6:35
they shall *n* perish ....John 10:28
shall *n* die ....John 11:26

NEW
n faileth ....1 Cor. 13:8
will *n* leave thee ....Heb. 13:5

NEW
unto the Lord a *n* ....Ps. 96:1
n every morning ....Lam. 3:23
A *n* commandment ....John 13:34
he is a *n* creature ....2 Cor. 5:17
put on the *n* man ....Eph. 4:24
saw a *n* heaven ....Rev. 21:1

NEWNESS
should walk in *n* of life .....Rom. 6:4

NIGHT
the *n* cometh ....John 9:4
n is far spent ....Rom. 13:12
a thief in the *n* ....1 Thess. 5:2
be no *n* there ....Rev. 21:25

NOISE
Make a joyful *n* ....Ps. 66:1
with a great *n* ....2 Pet. 3:10

NUMBER
to *n* our days ....Ps. 90:12
no man could *n* ....Rev. 7:9

O

OBEY
to *o* is better ....1 Sam. 15:22
ought to *o* God ....Acts 5:29
o your parents ....Eph. 6:1
o in all things ....Col. 3:22
O them that ....Heb. 13:17

OBTAIN
that ye may *o* ....1 Cor. 9:24
to *o* salvation ....1 Thess. 5:9
that we may *o* mercy ....Heb. 4:16

OFFEND
A brother *o* ....Prov. 18:19
shall *o* one of these ....Matt. 18:6
eye *o* thee ....Matt. 18:9
yet *o* in one point ....James 2:10

OFFER
Whoso *o* praise ....Ps. 50:23
and *o* thy gift ....Matt. 5:24
o also the other ....Luke 6:29
o unto idols ....1 Cor. 8:1
and if I be *o* ....Phil. 2:17
o to bear the sins ....Heb. 9:28

ONE
and they shall be *o* flesh ....Gen. 2:24
I and my Father are *o* ......John 10:30
o in Christ Jesus ....Gal. 3:28
O Lord, *o* faith ....Eph. 4:5

OPEN
O thou mine eyes ....Ps. 119:18
is *o* unto me ....1 Cor. 16:9
o unto us a door ....Col. 4:3

ORDAIN
o twelve ....Mark 3:14
and *o* you ....John 15:16

o them elders . . . . .Acts 14:23
o of God . . . . .Rom. 13:1
o that we should . . . . .Eph. 2:10

ORDER
decently and in o . . . . .1 Cor. 14:40
set in o the things . . . . .Titus 1:5

ORDINANCE
the o of God . . . . .Rom. 13:2

OUGHT
O not Christ . . . . .Luke 24:26
men o to worship . . . . .John 4:20
o to obey God . . . . .Acts 5:29
pray for as we o . . . . .Rom. 8:26
o to be teachers . . . . .Heb. 5:12
these things o not . . . . .James 3:10

OUTWARD
appear beautiful o . . . . .Matt. 23:27
o in the flesh . . . . .Rom. 2:28
o man perish . . . . .2 Cor. 4:16

OVERCOME
I have o the world . . . . .John 16:33
Be not o of evil . . . . .Rom. 12:21
victory that o . . . . .1 John 5:4
To him that o . . . . .Rev. 2:7

P

PAIN
the p of hell . . . . .Ps. 116:3
the p of death . . . . .Acts 2:24

PARENTS
this man or his p . . . . .John 9:2
disobedient to p . . . . .Rom. 1:30
Children, obey your p . . . . .Eph. 6:1
disobedient to p . . . . .2 Tim. 3:2

PARTAKER
for we are all p . . . . .1 Cor. 10:17
p of the Holy Ghost . . . . .Heb. 6:4
p of Christ's . . . . .1 Pet. 4:13
might be p . . . . .2 Pet. 1:4

PASS
blood, I will p over you . . . . . .Ex. 12:13
cup p from me . . . . .Matt. 26:39
p all understanding . . . . .Phil. 4:7
the world p away . . . . .1 John 2:17

PATH
the p of life . . . . .Ps. 16:11
a light unto my p . . . . .Ps. 119:105
make his p straight . . . . .Matt. 3:3

PATIENCE
worketh p . . . . .Rom. 5:3
let us run with p . . . . .Heb. 12:1
faith worketh p . . . . .James 1:3
to p godliness . . . . .2 Pet. 1:6

PEACE
and a time of p . . . . .Eccl. 3:8
p been as a river . . . . .Is. 48:18
on earth p . . . . .Luke 2:14
P I leave with you . . . . .John 14:27

ye might have p . . . . .John 16:33
we have p with God . . . . .Rom. 5:1
the gospel of p . . . . .Rom. 10:15
For he is our p . . . . .Eph. 2:14
the p of God . . . . .Phil. 4:7
the p of God rule . . . . .Col. 3:15
Follow p with all men . . . . .Heb. 12:14

PEACEABLE
a quiet and p life . . . . .1 Tim. 2:2

PERFECT
law of the Lord is p . . . . .Ps. 19:7
Be ye therefore p . . . . .Matt. 5:48
acceptable, and p . . . . .Rom. 12:2
man of God may be p . . . . . . .2 Tim. 3:17
Make you p . . . . .Heb. 13:21
have her p work . . . . .James 1:4
p gift is from above . . . . .James 1:17

PERFECTION
go on unto p . . . . .Heb. 6:1

PERILOUS
p times shall come . . . . .2 Tim. 3:1

PERISH
ungodly shall p . . . . .Ps. 1:6
the wicked shall p . . . . .Ps. 37:20
that any should p . . . . .2 Pet. 3:9

PERSECUTE
and p you . . . . .Matt. 5:11
and p you . . . . .Matt. 5:44
Saul, why p thou me . . . . .Acts 9:4
P, but not forsaken . . . . .2 Cor. 4:9

PERSECUTION
p, distresses . . . . .2 Cor. 12:10
shall suffer p . . . . .2 Tim. 3:12

PERVERSE
crooked and p nation . . . . .Phil. 2:15

PERVERT
p the right ways . . . . .Acts 13:10
would p the gospel . . . . .Gal. 1:7

PIECE
thirty p of silver . . . . .Zech. 11:12

PIERCE
p my hands . . . . .Ps. 22:16
spear p his side . . . . .John 19:34

PILLAR
she became a p of salt . . . . . .Gen. 19:26

PIT
and cast him into some p . . . . .Gen. 37:20
out of a horrible p . . . . .Ps. 40:2
it fall into a p . . . . .Matt. 12:11
ox fallen into a p . . . . .Luke 14:5

PLACE
p whereon thou standest . . . . .Ex. 3:5
art my hiding p . . . . .Ps. 32:7
our dwelling p . . . . .Ps. 90:1
give p unto wrath . . . . .Rom. 12:19
p to the devil . . . . .Eph. 4:27

PLEASE
Whatsoever the Lord *p* . . . . .Ps. 135:6
When a man's ways *p* . . . . .Prov. 16:7
that which I *p* . . . . .Is. 55:11
to *p* ourselves . . . . .Rom. 15:1
it *p* God . . . . .1 Cor. 1:21
impossible to *p* him . . . . .Heb. 11:6

PLEASURE
hand there are *p* . . . . .Ps. 16:11
Do good in thy good *p* . . . . .Ps. 51:18
Lord taketh *p* . . . . .Ps. 147:11
p of this life . . . . .Luke 8:14
p in infirmities . . . . .2 Cor. 12:10
of his good *p* . . . . .Phil. 2:13
lovers of *p* . . . . .2 Tim. 3:4
enjoy the *p* of sin . . . . .Heb. 11:25

PLOWSHARES
swords into *p* . . . . .Is. 2:4
Beat your *p* . . . . .Joel 3:10

POOR
This *p* man cried . . . . .Ps. 34:6
The rich and *p* meet . . . . .Prov. 22:2
the *p* in spirit . . . . .Matt. 5:3
as *p*, yet making . . . . .2 Cor. 6:10
he became *p* . . . . .2 Cor. 8:9

POSSESS
p ye your souls . . . . .Luke 21:19

POSSIBLE
God all things are *p* . . . . .Matt. 19:26
things are *p* . . . . .Mark 9:23
are *p* with God . . . . .Luke 18:27

POUR
p you out a blessing . . . . .Mal. 3:10
p it on his head . . . . .Matt. 26:7
p out the . . . . .John 2:15
p out of my Spirit . . . . .Acts 2:17

POWER
p of thine hand . . . . .Prov. 3:27
p of the tongue . . . . .Prov. 18:21
p to the faint . . . . .Is. 40:29
nor by *p* . . . . .Zech. 4:6
kingdom, and the *p* . . . . .Matt. 6:13
All *p* is given . . . . .Matt. 28:18
p from on high . . . . .Luke 24:49
p to become . . . . .John 1:12
ye shall receive *p* . . . . .Acts 1:8
the *p* of his . . . . .Phil. 3:10
of *p*, and of love . . . . .2 Tim. 1:7
denying the *p* thereof . . . . .2 Tim. 3:5

POWERFUL
is quick, and *p* . . . . .Heb. 4:12

PRAISE (*n.*)
fearful in *p* . . . . .Ex. 15:11
p to thy name . . . . .Ps. 9:2
for *p* is comely . . . . .Ps. 33:1
his *p* glorious . . . . .Ps. 66:2
I will sing *p* . . . . .Ps. 104:33
garment of *p* . . . . .Is. 61:3
p of men . . . . .John 12:43
if there be any *p* . . . . .Phil. 4:8
sacrifice of *p* . . . . .Heb. 13:15

PRAISE (*v.*)
Shall the dust *p* thee . . . . .Ps. 30:9
shall yet *p* him . . . . .Ps. 42:5
my lips shall *p* thee . . . . .Ps. 63:3
p thy works . . . . .Ps. 145:4
another man *p* thee . . . . .Prov. 27:2
her own works *p* her . . . . .Prov. 31:31

PRAY
and *p*, and seek . . . . .2 Chr. 7:14
unto thee will I *p* . . . . .Ps. 5:2
at noon will I *p* . . . . .Ps. 55:17
therefore *p* ye . . . . .Matt. 6:9
mountain apart to *p* . . . . .Matt. 14:23
teach us to *p* . . . . .Luke 11:1
men ought always to *p* . . . . .Luke 18:1
we should *p* . . . . .Rom. 8:26
P without ceasing . . . . .1 Thess. 5:17
p one for another . . . . .James 5:16

PRAYER
p of the upright . . . . .Prov. 15:8
the house of *p* . . . . .Matt. 21:13
shall ask in *p* . . . . .Matt. 21:22
continually to *p* . . . . .Acts 6:4
the *p* of faith . . . . .James 5:15
p of a righteous man . . . . .James 5:16
the *p* of saints . . . . .Rev. 5:8

PREACH
p good tidings . . . . .Is. 61:1
Jesus began to *p* . . . . .Matt. 4:17
shall they *p* . . . . .Rom. 10:15
p of the cross . . . . .1 Cor. 1:18
of *p* to save . . . . .1 Cor. 1:21
have *p* to others . . . . .1 Cor. 9:27
is our *p* vain . . . . .1 Cor. 15:14
P the word . . . . .2 Tim. 4:2

PRECIOUS
P in the sight . . . . .Ps. 116:15
more *p* than rubies . . . . .Prov. 3:15
a *p* corner stone . . . . .Is. 28:16
more *p* than . . . . .1 Pet. 1:7
p blood of Christ . . . . .1 Pet. 1:19

PREDESTINATE
did *p* to be conformed . . . . .Rom. 8:29

PREPARE
P ye the way . . . . .Is. 40:3
p to meet thy God . . . . .Amos 4:12
p a great fish . . . . .Jon. 1:17
I go to *p* a place . . . . .John 14:2
hath *p* for them . . . . .1 Cor. 2:9

PRESENCE
I flee from thy *p* . . . . .Ps. 139:7

PRESENT
ye *p* your bodies . . . . .Rom. 12:1
may *p* every man . . . . .Col. 1:28
p you faultless . . . . .Jude 24

PRESS
measure, *p* down . . . . .Luke 6:38
p toward the mark . . . . .Phil. 3:14

PRICE
bought with a *p* . . . . .1 Cor. 6:20

PRIEST
kingdom of *p* ....Ex. 19:6
kings and *p* ....Rev. 5:10

PRIESTHOOD
an holy *p* ....1 Pet. 2:5
a royal *p* ....1 Pet. 2:9

PRINCE
confidence in *p* ....Ps. 118:9
a P and a Saviour ....Acts 5:31
p of the power ....Eph. 2:2

PRISON
opening of the *p* ....Is. 61:1
I was in *p* ....Matt. 25:36

PROCLAIM
p liberty ....Lev. 25:10
p the acceptable year ....Is. 61:2

PROFANE
p not my holy name ....Lev. 22:2
But shun *p* ....2 Tim. 2:16

PROFIT
what is a man *p* ....Matt. 16:26
shall *p* you nothing ....Gal. 5:2
exercise *p* little ....1 Tim. 4:8

PROFITABLE
godliness is *p* ....1 Tim. 4:8
is *p* for doctrine ....2 Tim. 3:16

PROMISE (n.)
all the *p* of God ....2 Cor. 1:20
are the children of *p* ....Gal. 4:28
p of the life ....1 Tim. 4:8
received the *p* ....Heb. 11:13
and precious *p* ....2 Pet. 1:4
p of his coming ....2 Pet. 3:4
concerning his *p* ....2 Pet. 3:9

PROMISE (v.)
what he had *p* ....Rom. 4:21
he is faithful that *p* ....Heb. 10:23
that he hath *p* us ....1 John 2:25

PROPHECY
whether there be *p* ....1 Cor. 13:8
the *p* came not ....2 Pet. 1:21
sayings of the *p* ....Rev. 22:7

PROPHESY
let us *p* according ....Rom. 12:6
we *p* in part ....1 Cor. 13:9
covet to *p* ....1 Cor. 14:39
Despise not *p* ....1 Thess. 5:20

PROPHET
Beware of false *p* ....Matt. 7:15
A *p* is not without ....Matt. 13:57
a greater *p* than John ....Luke 7:28
thou art a *p* ....John 4:19
a *p* hath no honour ....John 4:44
are all *p* ....1 Cor. 12:29
and some, *p* ....Eph. 4:11

PROPITIATION
p for our sins ....1 John 2:2

PROSPER
he doeth shall *p* ....Ps. 13
shall not *p* ....Prov. 28:13
thee shall *p* ....Is. 54:17
as God hath *p* him ....1 Cor. 16:2
as thy soul *p* ....3 John 2

PROUD
look and a *p* heart ....Ps. 101:5
A *p* look ....Prov. 6:17
is *p* in heart ....Prov. 16:5
and a *p* heart ....Prov. 21:4
God resisteth the *p* ....James 4:6

PROVE
p me, and saw ....Ps. 95:9
p me now herewith ....Mal. 3:10
p your own selves ....2 Cor. 13:5
P all things ....1 Thess. 5:21
tempted me, *p* me ....Heb. 3:9

PRUDENT
A *p* man concealeth ....Prov. 12:23
the *p* man looketh ....Prov. 14:15
and a *p* wife ....Prov. 19:14
the wise and *p* ....Matt. 11:25

PUNISHMENT
into everlasting *p* ....Matt. 25:46
Of how much sorer *p* ....Heb. 10:29
p of evildoers ....1 Pet. 2:14

PURCHASE
be *p* with money ....Acts 8:20
p with his own blood ....Acts 20:28
of the *p* possession ....Eph. 1:14

PURE
of the Lord is *p* ....Ps. 19:8
Thy word is very *p* ....Ps. 119:140
words of the *p* ....Prov. 15:26
things are *p* ....Phil. 4:8
with *p* conscience ....2 Tim. 1:3
P religion ....James 1:27
is first *p* ....James 3:17
even as he is *p* ....1 John 3:3
p river of water ....Rev. 22:1

PURGE
P me with hyssop ....Ps. 51:7
he *p* it ....John 15:2
p himself ....2 Tim. 2:21
p with blood ....Heb. 9:22

PURPOSE
p is established ....Prov. 20:18
according to his *p* ....Rom. 8:28
the eternal *p* ....Eph. 3:11

Q

QUENCH
fire is not *q* ....Mark 9:44
q all the ....Eph. 6:16
Q not the Spirit ....1 Thess. 5:19
Q the violence ....Heb. 11:34

QUICK
shall judge the *q* ....2 Tim. 4:1
word of God is *q* ....Heb. 4:12

QUICKEN
q thou me . . . . .Ps. 119:25
you hath he *q* . . . . .Eph. 2:1
hath *q* us together . . . . .Eph. 2:5
hath he *q* . . . . .Col. 2:13
q by the Spirit . . . . .1 Pet. 3:18

QUICKLY
Behold, I come *q* . . . . .Rev. 3:11

QUIET
be *q* from fear . . . . .Prov. 1:33
may lead a *q* . . . . .1 Tim. 2:2
and *q* spirit . . . . .1 Pet. 3:4

R

RACE
which run in a *r* . . . . .1 Cor. 9:24
r that is set . . . . .Heb. 12:1

RAIMENT
thought for *r* . . . . .Matt. 6:28
his *r* was white . . . . .Matt. 17:2
r became shining . . . . .Mark 9:3
food and *r* . . . . .1 Tim. 6:8
in vile *r* . . . . .James 2:2
and white *r* . . . . .Rev. 3:8

RAISE
r the dead . . . . .Matt. 10:8
be *r* again . . . . .Matt. 16:21
I will *r* it up . . . . .John 2:19
But God *r* him . . . . .Acts 13:30
r up Jesus . . . . .Rom. 8:11
is not Christ *r* . . . . .1 Cor. 15:16
is *r* in glory . . . . .1 Cor. 15:43
that he which *r* up . . . . .2 Cor. 4:14
when he *r* him . . . . .Eph. 1:20
hath *r* us up together . . . . .Eph. 2:6
shall *r* him up . . . . .James 5:15

RANSOM
nor give to God a *r* . . . . .Ps. 49:7
r of a man's life . . . . .Prov. 13:8
give his life a *r* . . . . .Matt. 20:28

REAP
shall *r* in joy . . . . .Ps. 126:5
r the whirlwind . . . . .Hos. 8:7
neither do they *r* . . . . .Matt. 6:26
r also sparingly . . . . .2 Cor. 9:6
that shall he also *r* . . . . .Gal. 6:7

REASON
let us *r* together . . . . .Is. 1:18
r among themselves . . . . .Matt. 16:7
What *r* ye . . . . .Luke 5:22

REBUKE
O Lord, *r* me not . . . . .Ps. 38:1
r a wise man . . . . .Prov. 9:8
He that *r* a man . . . . .Prov. 28:23
r the winds . . . . .Matt. 8:26
r the fever . . . . .Luke 4:39
thee, *r* him . . . . .Luke 17:3
R not an elder . . . . .1 Tim. 5:1
r, exhort with . . . . .2 Tim. 4:2
exhort, and *r* . . . . .Titus 2:15
art *r* of him . . . . .Heb. 12:5

RECEIVE
blind *r* their sight . . . . .Matt. 11:5
whoso shall *r* one . . . . .Matt. 18:5
believing, ye shall *r* . . . . .Matt. 21:22
R thy sight . . . . .Luke 18:42
own *r* him not . . . . .John 1:11
ask, and ye shall *r* . . . . .John 16:24
as Christ also *r* . . . . .Rom. 15:7
r his own reward . . . . .1 Cor. 3:8
r the things . . . . .2 Cor. 5:10
r Christ Jesus . . . . .Col. 2:6
r up into glory . . . . .1 Tim. 3:16
we *r* of him . . . . .1 John 3:22

RECOMPENSE
I will *r* evil . . . . .Prov. 20:22
R to no man . . . . .Rom. 12:17

REDEEM
Lord *r* the soul . . . . .Ps. 34:22
and *r* us . . . . .Ps. 44:26
God will *r* my soul . . . . .Ps. 49:15
Who *r* thy life . . . . .Ps. 103:4
Let the *r* . . . . .Ps. 107:2
that it cannot *r* . . . . .Is. 50:2
the *r* of the Lord . . . . .Is. 51:11
Christ hath *r* us . . . . .Gal. 3:13
To *r* them . . . . .Gal. 4:5
he might *r* us . . . . .Titus 2:14
not *r* with . . . . .1 Pet. 1:18
and hast *r* us . . . . .Rev. 5:9

REDEEMER
I know that my *r* liveth . . . . . . .Job 19:25
strength, and my *r* . . . . .Ps. 19:14

REDEMPTION
r draweth nigh . . . . .Luke 21:28
r of our body . . . . .Rom. 8:23
unto the day of *r* . . . . .Eph. 4:30

REFRESH
he *r* the soul . . . . .Prov. 25:13
the times of *r* . . . . .Acts 3:19

REGENERATION
the washing of *r* . . . . .Titus 3:5

REIGN
The Lord *r* . . . . .Ps. 93:1
The Lord *r* . . . . .Ps. 97:1
Thy God *r* . . . . .Is. 52:7
sin hath *r* unto death . . . . .Rom. 5:21
Let not sin therefore *r* . . . . .Rom. 6:12
For he must *r* . . . . .1 Cor. 15:25
also *r* with him . . . . .2 Tim. 2:12
r on the earth . . . . .Rev. 5:10
he shall *r* for ever . . . . .Rev. 11:15
God omnipotent *r* . . . . .Rev. 19:6

REJECT
despised and *r* of men . . . . .Is. 53:3
the builders *r* . . . . .Matt. 21:42
r of this generation . . . . .Luke 17:25

REJOICE
r in thy salvation . . . . .Ps. 9:14
shall *r* in him . . . . .Ps. 33:21
Let the heavens *r* . . . . .Ps. 96:11
let the earth *r* . . . . .Ps. 97:1

r with the wife . . . . .Prov. 5:18
my heart shall r . . . . .Prov. 23:15
r at his birth . . . . .Luke 1:14
in this r not . . . . .Luke 10:20
R with me . . . . .Luke 15:6
world shall r . . . . .John 16:20
your heart shall r . . . . .John 16:22
R with them . . . . .Rom. 12:15
R not in iniquity . . . . .1 Cor. 13:6
R in the Lord always . . . . .Phil. 4:4
R evermore . . . . .1 Thess. 5:16
ye r with joy . . . . .1 Pet. 1:8

REJOICING
come again with r . . . . .Ps. 126:6
R in hope . . . . .Rom. 12:2
yet always r . . . . .2 Cor. 6:10
or crown of r . . . . .1 Thess. 2:19

RELIGION
Pure r and undefiled . . . . . . .James 1:27

REMEMBER
R the sabbath day . . . . .Ex. 20:8
R now thy Creator . . . . .Eccl. 12:1
in wrath r mercy . . . . .Hab. 3:2
r me when thou comest . . . . .Luke 23:42
R without ceasing . . . . .1 Thess. 1:3
R therefore from . . . . .Rev. 2:5

REMEMBRANCE
this do in r . . . . .Luke 22:19
things to your r . . . . .John 14:26
do in r of me . . . . .1 Cor. 11:24
I have r of thee . . . . .2 Tim. 1:3

REMISSION
for the r of sins . . . . .Matt. 26:28
and r of sins . . . . .Luke 24:47

REND
And r your heart . . . . .Joel 2:13
turn again and r you . . . . .Matt. 7:6

RENDER
r to every man . . . . .Prov. 24:12
R to Caesar . . . . .Mark 12:17
R therefore to all . . . . .Rom. 13:7
r evil for evil . . . . .1 Thess. 5:15

RENEW
r a right spirit . . . . .Ps. 51:10
thy youth is r . . . . .Ps. 103:5
r their strength . . . . .Is. 40:31
r day by day . . . . .2 Cor. 4:16
is r in knowledge . . . . .Col. 3:10
to r them again . . . . .Heb. 6:6

REPAY
I will r thee . . . . .Luke 10:35
is mine; I will r . . . . .Rom. 12:19

REPENT
R ye: for the . . . . .Matt. 3:2
except ye r . . . . .Luke 13:3
one sinner that r . . . . .Luke 15:7
and if he r . . . . .Luke 17:3
R therefore of . . . . .Acts 8:22

REPENTANCE
fruits meet for r . . . . .Matt. 3:8
leadeth thee to r . . . . .Rom. 2:4
sorrow worketh r . . . . .2 Cor. 7:10
no place of r . . . . .Heb. 12:17

REPROVE
R not a scorner . . . . .Prov. 9:8
r hardeneth his neck . . . . .Prov. 29:1
shall r thee . . . . .Jer. 2:19
r the world of sin . . . . .John 16:8

REQUIRE
I r at thine hand . . . . .Ezek. 3:18
shall be much r . . . . .Luke 12:48

RESERVE
r in heaven . . . . .1 Pet. 1:4
r unto fire . . . . .2 Pet. 3:7

RESIST
God r the proud . . . . .James 4:6
R the devil . . . . .James 4:7

RESPECT
To have r of persons . . . . .Prov. 28:21
r to the Holy One . . . . .Is. 17:7
no r of persons . . . . .Rom. 2:11
in r of want . . . . .Phil. 4:11
no r of persons . . . . .Col. 3:25

REST (n.)
and I will give thee r . . . . .Ex. 33:14
Return unto thy r . . . . .Ps. 116:7
This is my r for ever . . . . .Ps. 132:14
returning and r . . . . .Is. 30:15
place of my r . . . . .Is. 66:1
r for your souls . . . . .Jer. 6:16
I will give you r . . . . .Matt. 11:28

REST (v.)
he r on the seventh day . . . . . .Gen. 2:2
R in the Lord . . . . .Ps. 37:7
and r a while . . . . .Mark 6:31
may r upon me . . . . .2 Cor. 12:9
they r not day . . . . .Rev. 4:8

RESTORE
He r my soul . . . . .Ps. 23:3
R unto me the joy . . . . .Ps. 51:12
I r him fourfold . . . . .Luke 19:8
r again the kingdom . . . . .Acts 1:6
r such an one . . . . .Gal. 6:1

RETURN
dust shalt thou r . . . . .Gen. 3:19
dog r to his vomit . . . . .Prov. 26:11
the ransomed . . . shall r . . . . . .Is. 35:10
r unto me void . . . . .Is. 55:11

REVEAL
A talebearer r . . . . .Prov. 11:13
blood hath not r . . . . .Matt. 16:17
Son of man is r . . . . .Luke 17:30
the Lord been r . . . . .John 12:38
God r from faith . . . . .Rom. 1:17
be r in us . . . . .Rom. 8:18
hath r them . . . . .1 Cor. 2:10
be r by fire . . . . .1 Cor. 3:13

that man of sin be *r* ....2 Thess. 2:3
ready to be *r* ....1 Pet. 1:5

REVELATION
visions and *r* ....2 Cor. 12:1
r of Jesus Christ ....Gal. 1:12

REVIVE
Wilt thou not *r* us again ....Ps. 85:6
to *r* the spirit ....Is. 57:15
will he *r* us ....Hos. 6:2
rose, and *r* ....Rom. 14:9

REWARD (*n.*)
there is great *r* ....Ps. 19:11
his *r* is with him ....Is. 40:10
for great is your *r* ....Matt. 5:12
ye have no *r* ....Matt. 6:1
r shall be great ....Luke 6:35
receive the *r* ....Col. 3:24
is worthy of his *r* ....1 Tim. 5:18

REWARD (*v.*)
r us according ....Ps. 103:10
r evil for good ....Prov. 17:13
Lord shall *r* thee ....Prov. 25:22
work shall be *r* ....Jer. 31:16

RICH
and maketh *r* ....1 Sam. 2:7
Both *r* and honour ....1 Chr. 29:12
not asked *r* ....2 Chr. 1:11
better than the *r* ....Ps. 37:16
r and honour ....Prov. 3:16
R profit not ....Prov. 11:4
deceitfulness of *r* ....Matt. 13:22
with cares and *r* ....Luke 8:14
not *r* toward God ....Luke 12:21
depth of the *r* ....Rom. 11:33
though he was *r* ....2 Cor. 8:9
r of his grace ....Eph. 1:7
who is *r* in mercy ....Eph. 2:4
the unsearchable *r* ....Eph. 3:8
that will be *r* ....1 Tim. 6:9
r in faith ....James 2:5
but thou art *r* ....Rev. 2:9
sayest, I am *r* ....Rev. 3:17

RIGHT
good and the *r* way ....1 Sam. 12:23
of the Lord are *r* ....Ps. 19:8
and renew a *r* spirit ....Ps. 51:10
judgments are *r* ....Ps. 119:75
way which seemeth *r* ....Prov. 14:12
Every way of a man is *r* ......Prov. 21:2
for this is *r* ....Eph. 6:1

RIGHTEOUS
The *r* cry ....Ps. 34:17
The *r* shall ....Prov. 10:30
to call the *r* ....Matt. 9:13
r shine forth ....Matt. 13:43
appear *r* unto men ....Matt. 23:28
r into life eternal ....Matt. 25:46
not to call the *r* ....Mark 2:17
both *r* before God ....Luke 1:6
There is none *r* ....Rom. 3:10
scarcely for a *r* man ....Rom. 5:7
many be made *r* ....Rom. 5:19
the *r* judge ....2 Tim. 4:8

that he was *r* ....Heb. 11:4
r scarcely be saved ....1 Pet. 4:18
Jesus Christ the *r* ....1 John 2:1
he that is *r* ....Rev. 22:11

RIGHTEOUSNESS
in the paths of *r* ....Ps. 23:3
declare his *r* ....Ps. 50:6
his *r* endureth ....Ps. 111:3
R exalteth a nation ....Prov. 14:34
and his *r* ....Is. 59:16
and all our *r* ....Is. 64:6
thirst after *r* ....Matt. 5:6
persecuted for *r* sake ....Matt. 5:10
therein is the *r* ....Rom. 1:17
r unto God ....Rom. 6:13
followed not after *r* ....Rom. 9:30
believeth unto *r* ....Rom. 10:10
the *r* of God ....2 Cor. 5:21
breastplate of *r* ....Eph. 6:14
not having mine own *r* ....Phil. 3:9
and follow after *r* ....1 Tim. 6:11
instruction in *r* ....2 Tim. 3:16
a crown of *r* ....2 Tim. 4:8
Not by works of *r* ....Titus 3:5
not the *r* of God ....James 1:20
should live unto *r* ....1 Pet. 2:24

RIGHTLY
r dividing the word ....2 Tim. 2:15

RISE
to *r* up early ....Ps. 127:2
She *r* also ....Prov. 31:15
glory of the Lord is *r* ....Is. 60:1
r on the evil ....Matt. 5:45
and *r* again ....Luke 2:34
third day *r* again ....Luke 24:7
The Lord is *r* indeed ....Luke 24:34
r from the dead ....1 Cor. 15:20
be *r* with Christ ....Col. 3:1
shall *r* first ....1 Thess. 4:16

RIVER
tree planted by the *r* ....Ps. 1:3
R of waters ....Ps. 119:136
shewed me a pure *r* ....Rev. 22:1

ROB
man *r* God ....Mal. 3:8
I *r* other churches ....2 Cor. 11:8

ROBBER
become a den of *r* ....Jer. 7:11
a thief and a *r* ....John 16:1
in perils of *r* ....2 Cor. 11:26

ROCK
He is the R ....Deut. 32:4
The Lord is my *r* ....2 Sam. 22:2
set me up upon a *r* ....Ps. 27:5
r and my fortress ....Ps. 31:3
my feet upon a *r* ....Ps. 40:2
upon this *r* ....Matt. 16:18
the mountains and *r* ....Rev. 6:16

ROOT
r shall be ....Is. 5:24
a *r* of Jesse ....Is. 11:10
r out of a dry ground ....Is. 53:2

ROSE

dried up from the *r* . . . . .Mark 11:20
r of all evil . . . . .1 Tim. 6:10
r of bitterness . . . . .Heb. 12:15
r and the offspring . . . . .Rev. 22:16

ROSE (n.)
I am the *r* of Sharon . . . . .Song 2:1
blossom as the *r* . . . . .Is. 35:1

ROSE (v.)
r from the dead . . . . .Luke 16:31
both died, and *r* . . . . .Rom. 14:9
that he *r* again . . . . .1 Cor. 15:4

RUN
shall *r* to and fro . . . . .Dan. 12:4
r in a race *r* all . . . . .1 Cor. 9:24
r with patience . . . . .Heb. 12:1

RUST
neither moth nor *r* . . . . .Matt. 6:20

S

SABBATH
s was made for man . . . . .Mark 2:27
of you on the *s* . . . . .Luke 13:15

SACKCLOTH
put off my *s* . . . . .Ps. 30:11
my clothing was *s* . . . . .Ps. 35:13
and put on *s* . . . . .Jon. 3:5

SACRIFICE
better than *s* . . . . .1 Sam. 15:22
s of joy .Ps. 27:6
desirest not *s* . . . . .Ps. 51:16
to the Lord than *s* . . . . .Prov. 21:3
offerings and *s* . . . . .Mark 12:33
bodies a living *s* . . . . .Rom. 12:1
and a *s* to God . . . . .Eph. 5:2
a more excellent *s* . . . . .Heb. 11:4
s of praise to God . . . . .Heb. 13:15
offer up spiritual *s* . . . . .1 Pet. 2:5

SAFETY
Peace and *s* . . . . .1 Thess. 5:3

SAINTS
O ye *s* of his . . . . .Ps. 30:4
souls of his *s* . . . . .Ps. 97:10
intercession for the *s* . . . . .Rom. 8:27
the necessity of *s* . . . . .Rom. 12:13
inheritance in the *s* . . . . .Eph. 1:18
perfecting of the *s* . . . . .Eph. 4:12
with all his *s* . . . . .1 Thess. 3:13
washed the *s* feet . . . . .1 Tim. 5:10

SAKE
for his name's *s* . . . . .Ps. 23:3
righteousness' *s* . . . . .Matt. 5:10
for Christ's *s* . . . . .1 Cor. 4:10
for their work's *s* . . . . .1 Thess. 5:13
thy stomach's *s* . . . . .1 Tim. 5:23
filthy lucre's *s* . . . . .Titus 1:11

SALVATION
shew forth . . . his *s* . . . . .1 Chr. 16:23
the *s* of the Lord . . . . .2 Chr. 20:17
God of my *s* . . . . .Ps. 25:5

my light and my *s* . . . . .Ps. 27:1
joy of thy *s* . . . . .Ps. 51:12
my rock and my *s* . . . . .Ps. 62:2, 6
is become my *s* . . . . .Ps. 118:14
Behold, God is my *s* . . . . .Is. 12:2
the garments of *s* . . . . .Is. 61:10
the *s* of the Lord . . . . .Lam. 3:26
shall see the *s* of God . . . . .Luke 3:6
is there *s* in any . . . . .Acts 4:12
power of God unto *s* . . . . .Rom. 1:16
now is the day of *s* . . . . .2 Cor. 6:2
the helmet of *s* . . . . .Eph. 6:17
work out your own *s* . . . . .Phil. 2:12
make thee wise unto *s* . . . . . . .2 Tim. 3:15
neglect so great *s* . . . . .Heb. 2:3
without sin unto *s* . . . . .Heb. 9:28
through faith unto *s* . . . . .1 Pet. 1:5

SAME
Be of the *s* mind . . . . .Rom. 12:16
Christ the *s* yesterday . . . . . . .Heb. 13:8

SANCTIFY
S ye a fast . . . . .Joel 1:14
S them through . . . . .John 17:17
but ye are *s* . . . . .1 Cor. 6:11
husband is *s* by the . . . . .1 Cor. 7:14
he might *s* and . . . . .Eph. 5:26
of peace *s* you wholly . . . . . . .1 Thess. 5:23
For it is *s* by the . . . . .1 Tim. 4:5
s, and meet for . . . . .2 Tim. 2:21
we are *s* through . . . . .Heb. 10:10
But *s* the Lord . . . . .1 Pet. 3:15

SATAN
Get thee behind me, *S* . . . . . . .Matt. 16:23
hath *S* filled thine . . . . .Acts 5:3
power of *S* unto God . . . . .Acts 26:18
messenger of *S* to . . . . .2 Cor. 12:7

SAVE
Lord *s* his anointed . . . . .Ps. 20:6
s such as be of a . . . . .Ps. 34:18
that it cannot *s* . . . . .Is. 59:1
and we are not *s* . . . . .Jer. 8:20
shall *s* his . . . . .Matt. 1:21
whosoever will *s* his . . . . .Matt. 16:25
is come to *s* that . . . . .Matt. 18:11
s thyself . . . . .Matt. 27:40
baptized shall be *s* . . . . .Mark 16:16
faith hath *s* thee . . . . .Luke 7:50
believe and be *s* . . . . .Luke 8:12
seek and to *s* that . . . . .Luke 19:10
he shall be *s* . . . . .John 10:9
the Lord shall be *s* . . . . .Acts 2:21
whereby we must be *s* . . . . . . .Acts 4:12
must I do to be *s* . . . . .Acts 16:30
us which are *s* . . . . .1 Cor. 1:18
preaching to *s* them . . . . .1 Cor. 1:21
y all means *s* some . . . . .1 Cor. 9:22
by grace are ye *s* . . . . .Eph. 2:8
the world to *s* sinners . . . . . . .1 Tim. 1:15
all men to be *s* . . . . .1 Tim. 2:4
s them to the uttermost . . . . . .Heb. 7:25
an ark to the *s* . . . . .Heb. 11:7
to *s* your souls . . . . .James 1:21
faith shall *s* the . . . . .James 5:15
s a soul from death . . . . .James 5:20
scarcely be *s* . . . . .1 Pet. 4:18

SAVIOUR
the S of all men ....1 Tim. 4:10
and our S Jesus Christ ......Titus 2:13
only wise God our S ....Jude 25

SEARCH
S me ... and know ....Ps. 139:23
Lord s the heart ....Jer. 17:10
Let us s and try our ways ....Lam. 3:40
he that s the hearts ....Rom. 8:27
for the Spirit s ....1 Cor. 2:10

SEASON
the times or the s ....Acts 1:7
of sin for a s ....Heb. 11:25

SECRET
our s sins ....Ps. 90:8
bread eaten in s ....Prov. 9:17
Father which is in s ....Matt. 6:6

SEE
when I s the blood ....Ex. 12:13
to s the goodness ....Ps. 27:13
they shall s God ....Matt. 5:8
blind, now I s ....John 9:25
s him as he is ....1 John 3:2

SEEK
will I s after ....Ps. 27:4
do good; s peace ....Ps. 34:14
early will I s thee ....Ps. 63:1
shall s me early ....Prov. 1:28
I will s it ....Prov. 23:35
ye shall s me ....Jer. 29:13
soul that s him ....Lam. 3:25
But s ye first ....Matt. 6:33
s, and ye shall find ....Matt. 7:7
s and to save ....Luke 19:10
s ye the living ....Luke 24:5
Ye shall s me ....John 7:34, 36
that s after God ....Rom. 3:11
s after wisdom ....1 Cor. 1:22
s not her own ....1 Cor. 13:5
s those things ....Col. 3:1
s whom he may devour ....1 Pet. 5:8

SEEN
s God at any time ....John 1:18
Eye hath not s ....1 Cor. 2:9
of things not s ....Heb. 11:1
Whom having not s ....1 Pet. 1:8

SEND
Here am I; s me ....Is. 6:8
s forth labourers ....Matt. 9:38
will s in my name ....John 14:26
God s his own Son ....Rom. 8:3

SEPARATE
he shall s them ....Matt. 25:32
shall s us ....Rom. 8:35

SERPENT
tongues like a s ....Ps. 140:3
it biteth like a s ....Prov. 23:32
give him a s ....Matt. 7:10
wise as s ....Matt. 10:16
lifted up the s ....John 3:14
old s, called ....Rev. 12:9

SERVANT
good and faithful s ....Matt. 25:21
S, be obedient ....Eph. 6:5
S, be subject ....1 Pet. 2:18

SERVE
whom ye will s ....Josh. 24:15
S the Lord with gladness .....Ps. 100:2
s two masters ....Matt. 6:24
should not s sin ....Rom. 6:6
s one another ....Gal. 5:13
for ye s the Lord ....Col. 3:24
idols to s ....1 Thess. 1:9

SHAME
despising the s ....Heb. 12:2

SHED
shall his blood be s ....Gen. 9:6
S for many for ....Matt. 26:28
is s abroad ....Rom. 5:5
without s of blood ....Heb. 9:22

SHEEP
as s which have no ....Num. 27:17
the s of his pasture ....Ps. 100:3
like s have gone ....Is. 53:6
to you in s clothing ....Matt. 7:15
shepherd of the s ....John 10:2
life for the s ....John 10:11
Feed my s ....John 21:16

SHEPHERD
The Lord is my s ....Ps. 23:1
his flock like a s ....Is. 40:11
I am the good s ....John 10:14

SHIELD
our help and our s ....Ps. 33:20
shall be thy s ....Ps. 91:4
the s of faith ....Eph. 6:16

SHINE
hath the light s ....Is. 9:2
Arise, s; for thy ....Is. 60:1
your light so s ....Matt. 5:16

SHOWER
there shall be s ....Ezek. 34:26

SICK
Is any s among ....James 5:14
shall save the s ....James 5:15

SICKNESS
and bare our s ....Matt. 8:17

SIGHT
received their s ....Matt. 11:5
good in thy s ....Matt. 11:26
blind he gave s ....Luke 7:21
the s of all men ....Rom. 12:17

SIN (n.)
from presumptuous s ....Ps. 19:13
sorry for my s ....Ps. 38:18
and my s is ever ....Ps. 51:3
with us after our s ....Ps. 103:10
but s is a reproach ....Prov. 14:34
He that is without s ....John 8:7

lay not this s . . . . Acts 7:60
wash away thy s . . . . Acts 22:16
where s abounded . . . . Rom. 5:20
wages of s is death . . . . Rom. 6:23
him to be s for . . . . 2 Cor. 5:21
bare our s in his . . . . 1 Pet. 2:24

SIN (v.)
I have s against . . . . Ex. 10:16
1 have s against . . . . Josh. 7:20
I have s . . . . 1 Sam. 15:24
I have s against . . . . 2 Sam. 12:13
the soul that s . . . . Ezek. 18:4
brother s against me . . . . . . Matt. 18:21
I have s against . . . . Luke 15:18, 21
go, and s no more . . . . John 8:11
s, and come short of . . . . Rom. 3:23
Be ye angry, and s . . . . Eph. 4:26
he cannot s . . . . 1 John 3:9

SINGING
s and making melody . . . . Eph. 5:19

SINNER
in the way of s . . . . Ps. 1:1
s shall be converted . . . . Ps. 51:13
if s entice thee . . . . Prov. 1:10
but s to repentance . . . . Matt. 9:13
heaven over one s . . . . Luke 15:7
merciful to me a s . . . . Luke 18:13
While we were yet s . . . . Rom. 5:8

SLACK
The Lord is not s . . . . 2 Pet. 3:9

SLAUGHTER
a lamb to the s . . . . Is. 53:7

SLAY
Though he s me . . . . Job 13:15

SLEEP (n.)
deep s from the Lord . . . . . 1 Sam. 26:12
giveth his beloved s . . . . Ps. 127:2
Yet a little s . . . . Prov. 6:10
were heavy with s . . . . Luke 9:32
awake out of s . . . . Rom. 13:11

SLEEP (v.)
neither slumber nor s . . . . Ps. 121:4
may rejoice, and s . . . . Jer. 51:39
We shall not all s . . . . 1 Cor. 15:51
Awake thou that s . . . . Eph. 5:14
which is in Jesus . . . . 1 Thess. 4:14
let us not s . . . . 1 Thess. 5:6

SLOW
s of speech . . . . Ex. 4:10
s to anger . . . . Ps. 103:8

SNARE
thee from the s of . . . . Ps. 91:3
the s of death . . . . Prov. 13:14
temptation and a s . . . . 1 Tim. 6:9
the s of the devil . . . . 2 Tim. 2:26

SNOW
be whiter than s . . . . Ps. 51:7
raiment white as s . . . . Matt. 28:3
exceeding white as s . . . . Mark 9:3

SON
A wise s maketh . . . . Prov. 10:1
foolish s is a grief . . . . Prov. 17:25
unto us a s is given . . . . Is. 9:6
spareth his own s . . . . Mal. 3:17
This is my beloved S . . . . Matt. 17:5
this Joseph's s . . . . Luke 4:22
begotten S of God . . . . John 3:18
S . . . make you free . . . . John 8:36
sending his own S . . . . Rom. 8:3
spared not his own S . . . . . . Rom. 8:32
the s of God . . . . Phil. 2:15
of his dear S . . . . Col. 1:13
Though he were a S . . . . Heb. 5:8
and scourgeth every s . . . . . . Heb. 12:6
He that hath the S . . . . 1 John 5:12

SONG
Sing unto him a new s . . . . Ps. 33:3
new s in my mouth . . . . Ps. 40:3
have been my s . . . . Ps. 119:54
unto the Lord a new s . . . . Is. 42:10
and spiritual s . . . . Eph. 5:19

SORROW
greatly multiply thy s . . . . Gen. 3:16
a man of s . . . . Is. 53:3
For godly s worketh . . . . 2 Cor. 7:10
that ye s not . . . . 1 Thess. 4:13

SOUL
man became a living s . . . . Gen. 2:7
my s thirsteth . . . . Ps. 63:1
the Lord, O my s . . . . Ps. 103:2
your s shall live . . . . Is. 55:3
the s that sinneth . . . . Ezek. 18:4
able to kill the s . . . . Matt. 10:28
exchange for his s . . . . Matt. 16:26
every s be subject . . . . Rom. 13:1
and s and body . . . . 1 Thess. 5:23
an anchor of the s . . . . Heb. 6:19
war against the s . . . . 1 Pet. 2:11
as thy s prospereth . . . . 3 John 2

SOUND
He layeth up s wisdom . . . . . . Prov. 2:7
A s heart . . . . Prov. 14:30
to s doctrine . . . . 1 Tim. 1:10
and of a s mind . . . . 2 Tim. 1:7

SOW
for they s not . . . . Matt. 6:26
whatsoever a man s . . . . Gal. 6:7

SPARE
s not his own Son . . . . Rom. 8:32

SPIRIT
and renew a right s . . . . Ps. 51:10
and a haughty s . . . . Prov. 16:18
be of a humble s . . . . Prov. 16:19
s of the Lord . . . . Is. 11:2
I will pour my s . . . . Is. 44:3
contrite and humble s . . . . . . Is. 57:15
S of the Lord God . . . . Is. 61:1
I will pour out my s . . . . Joel 2:28
s indeed is willing . . . . Matt. 26:41
God is a S . . . . John 4:24
the law of the S . . . . Rom. 8:2
S itself beareth . . . . Rom. 8:16

SPIRITUAL

S itself maketh . . . . .Rom. 8:26
the S of the Lord is . . . . .2 Cor. 3:17
fruit of the S . . . . .Gal. 5:22
grieve not the holy S . . . . .Eph. 4:30
Quench not the S . . . . .1 Thess. 5:19
of soul and s . . . . .Heb. 4:12
a meek and quiet s . . . . .1 Pet. 3:4
S and the bride say . . . . .Rev. 22:17

SPIRITUAL

unto you some s gift . . . . .Rom. 1:11
comparing s things . . . . .1 Cor. 2:13
hymns and s songs . . . . .Eph. 5:19

STAFF

thy s they comfort me . . . . .Ps. 23:4

STAND

Fear ye not, s still, and see . . . . .Ex. 14:13
nor s in the way . . . . .Ps. 1:1
shall not s . . . . .Ps. 1:5
or who shall s in . . . . .Ps. 24:3
hell shall not s . . . . .Is. 28:18
our God shall s . . . . .Is. 40:8
itself shall not s . . . . .Matt. 12:25
grace wherein we s . . . . .Rom. 5:2
s fast in the faith . . . . .1 Cor. 16:13
having done all, to s . . . . .Eph. 6:13
that ye s fast . . . . .Phil. 1:27
so s fast in the Lord . . . . .Phil. 4:1
I s at the door . . . . .Rev. 3:20
shall be able to s . . . . .Rev. 6:17
dead . . . s before God . . . . . . .Rev. 20:12

STILL

beside the s waters . . . . .Ps. 23:2
Be s, and know . . . . .Ps. 46:10
Peace, be s . . . . .Mark 4:39

STING

where is thy s . . . . .1 Cor. 15:55

STONE

foot against a s . . . . .Ps. 91:12
s which the builders . . . . .Ps. 118:22
cast a s at her . . . . .John 8:7

STORE

lay by him in s . . . . .1 Cor. 16:2
Laying up in s . . . . .1 Tim. 6:19

STRAIGHT

make thy way s . . . . .Ps. 5:8
shall be made s . . . . .Is. 40:4
make his paths s . . . . .Matt. 3:3
which is called S . . . . .Acts 9:11

STRANGER

I was a s . . . . .Matt. 25:35
ye are no more s . . . . .Eph. 2:19
they were s . . . . .Heb. 11:13

STRENGTH

The Lord is my s and song . . . . .Ex. 15:2
God is my s . . . . .2 Sam 22:33
Lord is the s . . . . .Ps. 27:1
The Lord is my s . . . . .Ps. 28:7
God is our refuge and s . . . . . . .Ps. 46:1
s and beauty . . . . .Ps. 96:6

my s and song . . . . .Ps. 118:14
he increaseth s . . . . .Is. 40:29

STRENGTHEN

and s thee . . . . .Ps. 20:2
to be s with might . . . . .Eph. 3:16
which s me . . . . .Phil. 4:13
S with all might . . . . .Col. 1:11

STRIPES

by whose s . . . . .1 Pet. 2:24

STRIVE

S not with a man . . . . .Prov. 3:30
S to enter . . . . .Luke 13:24

STRONG

rejoiceth as a s man . . . . .Ps. 19:5
The Lord s and mighty . . . . .Ps. 24:8
Lord is a s tower . . . . .Prov. 18:10
weak, but ye are s . . . . .1 Cor. 4:10

STUMBLE

shall s, and fall . . . . .Jer. 46:6
which s at the word . . . . .1 Pet. 2:8

SUBJECT

s to the law of God . . . . .Rom. 8:7
every soul be s . . . . .Rom. 13:1
s unto Christ . . . . .Eph. 5:24
s to like passions . . . . .James 5:17
all of you be s . . . . .1 Pet. 5:5

SUBMIT

Wives, s yourselves . . . . .Eph. 5:22
S yourselves . . . . .James 4:7

SUBSTANCE

with thy s . . . . .Prov. 3:9
faith is the s . . . . .Heb. 11:1

SUFFER

S little children . . . . .Matt. 19:14
Son of man must s . . . . .Mark 8:31
that Christ should s . . . . .Acts 3:18
we s with him . . . . .Rom. 8:17
one member s . . . . .1 Cor. 12:26
should s persecution . . . . .Gal. 6:12
shall s persecution . . . . .2 Tim. 3:12
to s affliction . . . . .Heb. 11:25
Christ also s . . . . .1 Pet. 2:21

SUFFICIENT

S unto the day . . . . .Matt. 6:34

SUN

a s and shield . . . . .Ps. 84:11
s shall not smite . . . . .Ps. 121:6
s to rise on . . . . .Matt. 5:45
shine forth as the s . . . . .Matt. 13:43
not the s go down . . . . .Eph. 4:26

SUPPLICATION

Lord hath heard my s . . . . .Ps. 6:9
all prayer and s . . . . .Eph. 6:18
s, prayers . . . . .1 Tim. 2:1

SUPPLY

s all your need . . . . .Phil. 4:19

SWALLOW
Death is s up in victory ......1 Cor. 15:54
be s up of life ....2 Cor. 5:4

SWORD
their tongue a sharp s ....Ps. 57:4
but a s ....Matt. 10:34
s of the Spirit ....Eph. 6:17
any twoedged s ....Heb. 4:12

T

TABERNACLE
who shall abide in thy t ....Ps. 15:1
a t that shall not ....Is. 33:20

TABLE
Thou preparest a t ....Ps. 23:5

TAKE
T no thought ....Matt. 6:25
T my yoke upon you ....Matt. 11:29
and said, T, eat ....Matt. 26:26
why t ye thought ....Luke 12:26

TASTE
O t and see ....Ps. 34:8
sweet ... unto my t ....Ps. 119:103
not t of death ....Matt. 16:28
should t death ....Heb. 2:9

TEACH
t them diligently ....Deut. 6:7
And ye shall t them ....Deut. 11:19
t me thy paths ....Ps. 25:4
T me thy way ....Ps. 27:11
I t transgressors ....Ps. 51:13
t us to number our ....Ps. 90:12
and t all nations ....Matt. 28:19
Lord, t us to pray ....Luke 11:1
Holy Ghost shall t ....Luke 12:12
he shall t you all ....John 14:26
ceased not to t ....Acts 5:42
and t every man ....Col. 1:28
to t others also ....2 Tim. 2:2
T us that ....Titus 2:12

TEACHER
than all my t ....Ps. 119:99
t come from God ....John 3:2
are all t ....1 Cor. 12:29
pastors and t ....Eph. 4:11
t of good things ....Titus 2:3

TEARS
They that sow in t ....Ps. 126:5
wipe away t ....Is. 25:8
wash his feet with t ....Luke 7:38
and with many t ....Acts 20:19
mindful of thy t ....2 Tim. 1:4

TEMPLE
in his t doth ....Ps. 29:9
train filled the t ....Is. 6:1
Destroy this t ....John 2:19
t of the living God ....2 Cor. 6:16

TEMPT
they t God ....Ps. 78:18
t the Lord thy God ....Matt. 4:7

to t the Spirit ....Acts 5:9
you to be t ....1 Cor. 10:13
lest thou also be t ....Gal. 6:1
suffered being t ....Heb. 2:18
was in all points t ....Heb. 4:15
say when he is t ....James 1:13

TENTH
I will surely give the t ......Gen. 28:22
the t shall be holy ....Lev. 27:32
it shall be a t ....Is. 6:13

TERROR
the t of death ....Ps. 55:4
for the t by night ....Ps. 91:5
the t of the Lord ....2 Cor. 5:11

TESTIMONY
Thy t are very sure ....Ps. 93:5
Thy t are wonderful ....Ps. 119:129
a t against them ....Matt. 10:18
to you for a t ....Luke 21:13
his t is true ....John 21:24
the t of God ....1 Cor. 2:1
ashamed of the t ....2 Tim. 1:8
had this t ....Heb. 11:5

THANKS
gave t likewise ....Luke 2:38
But t be to God ....1 Cor. 15:57
Giving t always ....Eph. 5:20

THANKSGIVING
supplication with t ....Phil. 4:6

THINK
he t in his heart ....Prov. 23:7
not to t of himself ....Rom. 12:3
if a man t himself ....Gal. 6:3
t on these things ....Phil. 4:8
that man t that he ....James 1:7

THIRST
Ho, every one that t ....Is. 55:1
t after righteousness ....Matt. 5:6
him shall never t ....John 4:14
If any man t, let him ....John 7:37
neither t any more ....Rev. 7:16

THOUGHT
and know my t ....Ps. 139:23
and thy t shall be ....Prov. 16:3
For my t are not your ....Is. 55:8
Take no t for your ....Matt. 6:25
take no t how or what ......Matt. 10:19
he knew their t ....Luke 6:8
t to the obedience ....2 Cor. 10:5
the t and intents of ....Heb. 4:12

THRONE
The heaven is my t ....Is. 66:1
the t of his glory ....Matt. 25:31
be t, or dominions ....Col. 1:16
the t of grace ....Heb. 4:16
sit with me in my t ....Rev. 3:21

TIDINGS
good t of great joy ....Luke 2:10

TIME
What *t* I am afraid ....Ps. 56:3
how short my *t* is ....Ps. 89:47
t to seek the Lord ....Hos. 10:12
high *t* to awake ....Rom. 13:11
the *t* is short ....1 Cor. 7:29
is the accepted *t* ....2 Cor. 6:2
Redeeming the *t* ....Eph. 5:16
in *t* of need ....Heb. 4:16
the *t* is at hand ....Rev. 1:3
should be *t* no longer ....Rev. 10:6

TOGETHER
exalt his name *t* ....Ps. 34:3
Can two walk *t* ....Amos 3:3
are gathered *t* ....Matt. 18:20
God hath joined *t* ....Matt. 19:6
work *t* for good ....Rom. 8:28
caught up *t* ....1 Thess. 4:17

TONGUE
Keep thy *t* from ....Ps. 34:13
A wholesome *t* is a ....Prov. 15:4
the power of the *t* ....Prov. 18:21
bridleth not his *t* ....James 1:26
the *t* is a fire ....James 3:6
his *t* from evil ....1 Pet. 3:10

TOOTH
Eye for eye, *t* for *t* ....Ex. 21:24

TRANSGRESSION
nor my *t* ....Ps. 25:7
blot out my *t* ....Ps. 51:1
blotteth out thy *t* ....Is. 43:25
wounded for our *t* ....Is. 53:5

TREASURE
thee his good *t* ....Deut. 28:12
where your *t* is ....Matt. 6:21
shalt have *t* in heaven ......Matt. 19:21

TREMBLE
earth *t*, and the ....Judg. 5:4
rejoice with *t* ....Ps. 2:11
earth saw, and *t* ....Ps. 97:4
t at thy presence ....Is. 64:2

TRESPASS
still in his *t* ....Ps. 68:21
forgive men their *t* ....Matt. 6:14
shall *t* against thee ....Matt. 18:15
If thy brother *t* ....Luke 17:3
who were dead in *t* ....Eph. 2:1
forgiven you all *t* ....Col. 2:13

TRIAL
great *t* of affliction ....2 Cor. 8:2

TRIBULATION
shall be great *t* ....Matt. 24:21
ye shall have *t* ....John 16:33
that *t* worketh patience ......Rom. 5:3
patient in *t* ....Rom. 12:12

TRIUMPH
enemies *t* over me ....Ps. 25:2
to *t* in Christ ....2 Cor. 2:14

TROUBLE
and full of *t* ....Job 14:1
in the time of *t* ....Ps. 27:5
present help in *t* ....Ps. 46:1
have *t* in the flesh ....1 Cor. 7:28

TRUE
Thy word is *t* ....Ps. 119:160
A *t* witness ....Prov. 14:25
that thou art *t* ....Matt. 22:16
the *t* Light ....John 1:9
I am the *t* vine ....John 15:1
the only *t* God ....John 17:3
things are *t* ....Phil. 4:8
with a *t* heart ....Heb. 10:22
him that is *t* ....1 John 5:20

TRUST
yet will I *t* in him ....Job 13:15
I *t* in thee ....Ps. 25:2
T in the Lord ....Ps. 37:3
in thee do I *t* ....Ps. 143:8
T in the Lord ....Prov. 3:5
let him *t* in the ....Is. 50:10
He *t* in God ....Matt. 27:43

TRUTH
thou desirest *t* ....Ps. 51:6
his *t* shall be thy ....Ps. 91:4
of grace and *t* ....John 1:14
know the *t* ....John 8:32
the *t*, and the life ....John 14:6
the Spirit of *t* ....John 16:13
thy word is *t* ....John 17:17
the *t* in love ....Eph. 4:15
the word of *t* ....2 Tim. 2:15
err from the *t* ....James 5:19

TRY
he hath *t* me ....Job 23:10
t the spirits ....1 John 4:1

TWINKLING
in the *t* of an eye ....1 Cor. 15:52

U

UNBLAMEABLE
to present you holy and *u* ......Col. 1:22
u in holiness ....1 Thess. 3:13

UNDEFILED
u before God ....James 1:27
incorruptible, and *u* ....1 Pet. 1:4

UNDERSTAND
that they might *u* ....Luke 24:45
There is none that *u* ....Rom. 3:11
u all mysteries ....1 Cor. 13:2
I *u* as a child ....1 Cor. 13:11

UNDERSTANDING
give me *u* ....Ps. 119:169
unto thine own *u* ....Prov. 3:5
Get wisdom, get *u* ....Prov. 4:5
and with all the *u* ....Mark 12:33
opened he their *u* ....Luke 24:45
passeth all *u* ....Phil. 4:7

UNFEIGNED
the *u* faith . . . . .2 Tim. 1:5
Spirit unto *u* love . . . . .1 Pet. 1:22

UNGODLINESS
from heaven against all *u*. . . . . .Rom. 1:18
shall turn away *u* . . . . .Rom. 11:26
unto more *u*. . . . . .2 Tim. 2:16
denying *u* . . . . .Titus 2:12

UNGODLY
counsel of the *u* . . . . .Ps. 1:1
died for the *u* . . . . .Rom. 5:6

UNHOLY
for *u* and profane . . . . .1 Tim. 1:9
unthankful, *u* . . . . .2 Tim. 3:2
an *u* thing . . . . .Heb. 10:29

UNITY
u of the Spirit . . . . .Eph. 4:3

UNJUST
and on the *u* . . . . .Matt. 5:45
of the just and *u* . . . . .Acts 24:15
just for the *u* . . . . .1 Pet. 3:18
He that is *u* . . . . .Rev. 22:11

UNMOVEABLE
be ye stedfast, *u* . . . . .1 Cor. 15:58

UNPUNISHED
wicked shall not be *u* . . . . . .Prov. 11:21
Ye shall not be *u* . . . . .Jer. 25:29

UNQUENCHABLE
with fire *u* . . . . .Luke 3:17

UNRIGHTEOUSNESS
hold the truth in *u* . . . . .Rom. 1:18
as instruments of *u* . . . . .Rom. 6:13
with *u* . . . . .2 Cor. 6:14
pleasure in *u* . . . . .2 Thess. 2:12
the reward of *u* . . . . .2 Pet. 2:13
from all *u* . . . . .1 John 1:9

UNSEARCHABLE
doeth great things and *u* . . . . . .Job 5:9
greatness is *u* . . . . .Ps. 145:3
how *u* are his . . . . .Rom. 11:31
u riches of Christ . . . . .Eph. 3:8

UNWORTHY
u of everlasting life . . . . .Acts 13:46
of the Lord, *u* . . . . .1 Cor. 11:27

UPHOLD
u me with thy free spirit . . . . . .Ps. 51:12
U me according . . . . .Ps. 119:116
u all that fall . . . . .Ps. 145:14
my servant, whom I *u* . . . . .Is. 42:1

UPRIGHT
the prayer of the *u* . . . . .Prov. 15:8

USE
despitefully *u* you . . . . .Matt. 5:44
u not vain repetitions . . . . .Matt. 6:7

V

VAIN
thy God in *v* . . . . .Ex. 20:7
imagine a *v* thing . . . . .Ps. 2:1
they labour in *v* . . . . .Ps. 127:1
beauty is *v* . . . . .Prov. 31:30
use not *v* repetitions . . . . .Matt. 6:7
have believed in *v* . . . . .1 Cor. 15:2
grace of God in *v* . . . . .2 Cor. 6:1
or had run, in *v* . . . . .Gal. 2:2
man's religion is *v* . . . . .James 1:26
v conversation . . . . .1 Pet. 1:18

VANISH
shall *v* away . . . . .Is. 51:6
it shall *v* . . . . .1 Cor. 13:8

VANITY
far from me *v* . . . . .Prov. 30:8
subject to *v* . . . . .Rom. 8:20
in the *v* of their . . . . .Eph. 4:17
swelling words of *v* . . . . .2 Pet. 2:18

VENGEANCE
To me belongeth *v* . . . . .Deut. 32:35
the day of *v* . . . . .Is. 61:2
the Lord's *v* . . . . .Jer. 51:6

VESSEL
he is a chosen *v* . . . . .Acts 9:15
shall be a *v* . . . . .2 Tim. 2:21
the weaker *v* . . . . .1 Pet. 3:7

VICTORY
the *v* that day . . . . .2 Sam. 19:2
gotten him the *v* . . . . .Ps. 98:1
the *v* that . . . . .1 John 5:4

VILE
unto *v* affections . . . . .Rom. 1:26
change our *v* body . . . . .Phil. 3:21

VIOLENCE
but *v* covereth . . . . .Prov. 10:6, 11
Do *v* to no man . . . . .Luke 3:14

VIRGIN
a *v* shall conceive . . . . .Is. 7:14
a *v* shall be with child . . . . . . .Matt. 1:23

VIRTUE
there be any *v* . . . . .Phil. 4:8
add to your faith *v* . . . . .2 Pet. 1:5

VIRTUOUS
v woman is a crown . . . . .Prov. 12:4
can find a *v* woman . . . . .Prov. 31:10
daughters have done *v* . . . . . .Prov. 31:29

VISION
there is no *v* . . . . .Prov. 29:18
seen a *v* of angels . . . . .Luke 24:23
the heavenly *v* . . . . .Acts 26:19

VISIT
sick, and ye *v* me . . . . .Matt. 25:36
To *v* the fatherless . . . . .James 1:27

VOICE
a still small *v* . . . . 1 Kin. 19:12
v of one crying . . . . Matt. 3:3
for they know his *v* . . . . John 10:4
v of the archangel . . . . 1 Thess. 4:16
if any man hear my *v* . . . . Rev. 3:20

W

WAGES
content with your *w* . . . . Luke 3:14
w of sin is death . . . . Rom. 6:23

WAIT
Lord, and *w* patiently . . . . Ps. 37:7
they that *w* . . . . Is. 40:31
quietly *w* for the . . . . Lam. 3:26
we with patience *w* . . . . Rom. 8:25
w for his Son . . . . 1 Thess. 1:10

WALK
I *w* through the valley . . . . Ps. 23:4
he that *w* uprightly . . . . Prov. 10:9
that *w* in darkness . . . . Is. 9:2
w in the light . . . . Is. 50:11
to *w* humbly . . . . Mic. 6:8
he *w* on the water . . . . Matt. 14:29
Rise up and *w* . . . . Luke 5:23
thy bed, and *w* . . . . John 5:8
not *w* in darkness . . . . John 8:12
w in newness of life . . . . Rom. 6:4
w not after the flesh . . . . Rom. 8:1, 4
For we *w* by faith . . . . 2 Cor. 5:7
in time past ye *w* . . . . Eph. 2:2
we should *w* in them. . . . . Eph. 2:10
w worthy of the vocation . . . . . . Eph. 4:1
w circumspectly . . . . Eph. 5:15
might *w* worthy . . . . Col. 1:10
w worthy of God . . . . 1 Thess. 2:12
w honestly toward . . . . 1 Thess. 4:12
w about, seeking . . . . 1 Pet. 5:8
we *w* in the light . . . . 1 John 1:7

WANT
my shepherd; I shall not *w* . . . . . . Ps. 23:1
Lord shall not *w* . . . . Ps. 34:10

WAR (*n.*)
maketh *w* to cease . . . . Ps. 46:9
a time of *w* . . . . Eccl. 3:8
of *w* and rumours of *w* . . . . . . Matt. 24:6
w against another . . . . Luke 14:31
w and fightings . . . . James 4:1
was *w* in heaven . . . . Rev. 12:7

WAR (*v.*)
w after the flesh . . . . 2 Cor. 10:3
w a good warfare . . . . 1 Tim. 1:18
No man that *w* . . . . 2 Tim. 2:4
w in your members . . . . James 4:1
w against the soul . . . . 1 Pet. 2:11

WASH
W me thoroughly . . . . Ps. 51:2
W you, make you clean . . . . Is. 1:16
w their stripes . . . . Acts 16:33
w away thy sins . . . . Acts 22:16
and have *w* their robes . . . . . . Rev. 7:14

WATCH
the Lord *w* between me . . . . . . Gen. 31:49
W therefore . . . . Matt. 24:42
W and pray . . . . Matt. 26:41
w unto prayer . . . . 1 Pet. 4:7

WATER
beside the still *w* . . . . Ps. 23:2
w to a thirsty soul . . . . Prov. 25:25
bread upon the *w* . . . . Eccl. 11:1
a well of living *w* . . . . Song 4:15
passeth through the *w* . . . . Is. 43:2
come ye to the *w* . . . . Is. 55:1
fountain of living *w* . . . . Jer. 2:13
baptize you with *w* . . . . Matt. 3:11
a cup of cold *w* . . . . Matt. 10:42
I baptize with *w* . . . . John 1:26
rivers of living *w* . . . . John 7:38
take the *w* of life . . . . Rev. 22:17

WAY
the right *w* . . . . 1 Sam. 12:23
his *w* is perfect . . . . 2 Sam. 22:31
he knoweth the *w* . . . . Job 23:10
w of the righteous . . . . Ps. 1:6
Teach me thy *w*, O Lord . . . . . . Ps. 27:11
Commit thy *w* . . . . Ps. 37:5
any wicked *w* in me . . . . Ps. 139:24
w acknowledge him . . . . Prov. 3:6
consider her *w* . . . . Prov. 6:6
a child in the *w* . . . . Prov. 22:6
w of the spirit . . . . Eccl. 11:5
teach us of his *w* . . . . Is. 2:3
are your *w* my *w* . . . . Is. 55:8
and broad is the *w* . . . . Matt. 7:13
w of God in truth . . . . Matt. 22:16
up some other *w* . . . . John 10:1
I am the *w*, the truth . . . . John 14:6
the *w* of salvation . . . . Acts 16:17
a more excellent *w* . . . . 1 Cor. 12:31
unstable in all his *w* . . . . James 1:8
w of righteousness . . . . 2 Pet. 2:21

WEAK
the flesh is *w* . . . . Matt. 26:41
the *w* things . . . . 1 Cor. 1:27
for when I am *w* . . . . 2 Cor. 12:10

WEALTH
W maketh many friends . . . . . . Prov. 19:4
we have our *w* . . . . Acts 19:25
one another's *w* . . . . 1 Cor. 10:24

WEAPON
No *w* that is formed . . . . Is. 54:17
w of our warfare . . . . 2 Cor. 10:4

WEARY
neither be *w* . . . . Prov. 3:11
cause the *w* to rest . . . . Is. 28:12
run, and not be *w* . . . . Is. 40:31
not *w* in well doing . . . . 2 Thess. 3:13

WEEPING
w may endure . . . . Ps. 30:5
be *w* and gnashing . . . . Matt. 8:12
at the sepulchre *w* . . . . John 20:11

WEIGHT
eternal *w* of glory ....2 Cor. 4:17
lay aside every *w* ....Heb. 12:1

WELL
is a *w* of life ....Prov. 10:11
w of living waters ....Song 4:15
a *w* of water ....John 4:14
w without water ....2 Pet. 2:17

WEPT
beheld the city, and *w* ....Luke 19:41
Jesus *w* ....John 11:35

WHATSOEVER
and *w* he doeth shall prosper .....Ps. 1:3
w ye would that men ....Matt. 7:12
w things are true ....Phil. 4:8

WHITE
be as *w* as snow ....Is. 1:18
not make one hair *w* ....Matt. 5:36
w already to harvest ....John 4:35
walk with me in *w* ....Rev. 3:4

WHITER
I shall be *w* than snow ....Ps. 51:7

WHOLE
the *w* duty of man ....Eccl. 12:13
gain the *w* world ....Matt. 16:26
They that are *w* ....Mark 2:17
w creation groaneth ....Rom. 8:22
Put on the *w* armour ....Eph. 6:11
keep the *w* law ....James 2:10
sins of the *w* world ....1 John 2:2

WICKED
w walk on every side ....Ps. 12:8
w shall fall by his ....Prov. 11:5
Let the *w* forsake ....Is. 55:7
that the *w* should die ....Ezek. 18:23
O thou *w* servant ....Matt. 18:32
that *w* person ....1 Cor. 5:13
fiery darts of the *w* ....Eph. 6:16
by *w* works ....Col. 1:21
then shall that *w* be ....2 Thess. 2:8

WICKEDNESS
w is an abomination ....Prov. 8:7
covetousness, *w* ....Mark 7:22
ravening and *w* ....Luke 11:39
w, covetousness ....Rom. 1:29
of malice and *w* ....1 Cor. 5:8
against spiritual *w* ....Eph. 6:12
world lieth in *w* ....1 John 5:19

WIFE
Whoso findeth a *w* ....Prov. 18:22
and a prudent *w* ....Prov. 19:14
I have married a *w* ....Luke 14:20
Remember Lot's *w* ....Luke 17:32
the head of the *w* ....Eph. 5:23

WILL
I *w*; be thou clean ....Matt. 8:3
w of him that sent me ....John 4:34
for to *w* is present ....Rom. 7:18
both to *w* and to do ....Phil. 2:13
whosoever *w* ....Rev. 22:17

WILLING
spirit indeed is *w* ....Matt. 26:41
first a *w* mind ....2 Cor. 8:12
not *w* that any ....2 Pet. 3:9

WIND
shall inherit the *w* ....Prov. 11:29
they have sown the *w* ....Hos. 8:7
The *w* bloweth where ....John 3:8
every *w* of doctrine ....Eph. 4:14

WINGS
shadow of thy *w* ....Ps. 36:7
in the shadow of thy *w* ....Ps. 57:1
and under his *w* ....Ps. 91:4
mount up with *w* ....Is. 40:31
healing in his *w* ....Mal. 4:2

WISDOM
W is the principal ....Prov. 4:7
better is it to get *w* ....Prov. 16:16
w of this world ....1 Cor. 3:19
his will in all *w* ....Col. 1:9
Walk in *w* toward them ....Col. 4:5
any of you lack *w* ....James 1:5
w that is from above ....James 3:17
and *w*, and strength ....Rev. 5:12
Here is *w* ....Rev. 13:18

WISE
desired to make one *w* ....Gen. 3:6
making *w* the simple ....Ps. 19:7
w man will hear ....Prov. 1:5
consider ... and be *w* ....Prov. 6:6
winneth souls is *w* ....Prov. 11:30
be ye therefore *w* ....Matt. 10:16
both to the *w* ....Rom. 1:14
Be not *w* in your own ......Rom. 12:16
ye are *w* in Christ ....1 Cor. 4:10
to make thee *w* ....2 Tim. 3:15

WITHER
his leaf also shall not *w* ....Ps. 1:3
the grass *w* ....1 Pet. 1:24
trees whose fruit *w* ....Jude 12

WITHHOLD
W not good from them ......Prov. 3:27
W not correction ....Prov. 23:13

WITHOUT
Wisdom crieth *w* ....Prov. 1:20
toward them that are *w* ......Col. 4:5

WITNESS
as a faithful *w* ....Ps. 89:37
w will not lie ....Prov. 14:5
true and faithful *w* ....Jer. 42:5
the world for a *w* ....Matt. 24:14
same came for a *w* ....John 1:7
have greater *w* than ....John 5:36

WOMAN
A foolish *w* is ....Prov. 9:13
virtuous *w* is a crown ....Prov. 12:4
Every wise *w* buildeth ....Prov. 14:1
find a virtuous *w* ....Prov. 31:10
on a *w* to lust ....Matt. 5:28
w, great is thy faith ....Matt. 15:28
W, behold thy son ....John 19:26

not to touch a *w* ....1 Cor. 7:1
but the *w* is the glory ....1 Cor. 11:7

WOMEN
that are born of *w* ....Matt. 11:11
w shall be grinding ....Matt. 24:41
art thou among *w* ....Luke 1:28
w keep silence ....1 Cor. 14:34
w adorn themselves ....1 Tim. 2:9

WONDERFUL
thy love to me was *w* ....2 Sam. 1:26
things too *w* for me ....Job 42:3
knowledge is too *w* ....Ps. 139:6
name shall be called *W* ....Is. 9:6

WORD
the *w* of truth ....Ps. 119:43
a *w* fitly spoken ....Prov. 25:11
every idle *w* that men ......Matt. 12:36
w shall not pass away ....Matt. 24:35
w of eternal life ....John 6:68
Let the *w* of Christ ....Col. 3:16
unto you in *w* ....1 Thess. 1:5
with these *w* ....1 Thess. 4:18
dividing the *w* ....2 Tim. 2:15
Preach the *w* ....2 Tim. 4:2
the *w* of God is quick ....Heb. 4:12
doers of the *w* ....James 1:22
by the *w* of God ....1 Pet. 1:23
milk of the *w* ....1 Pet. 2:2
if any obey not the *w* ....1 Pet. 3:1
of the *W* of life ....1 John 1:1
whoso keepeth his *w* ....1 John 2:5
let us not love in *w* ....1 John 3:18
w of the book ....Rev. 22:19

WORK (*n.*)
w of thy fingers ....Ps. 8:3
for his wonderful *w* ....Ps. 107:8
her own *w* praise her ....Prov. 31:31
know their *w* ....Is. 66:18
ye after their *w* ....Matt. 23:3
do no mighty *w* ....Mark 6:5
shew him greater *w* ....John 5:20
the *w* that I do ....John 14:12
destroy not the *w* ....Rom. 14:20
man's *w* shall be ....1 Cor. 3:13
by the *w* of the law ....Gal. 2:16
Not of *w*, lest any ....Eph. 2:9
by *w* of righteousness ....Titus 3:5
faith without thy *w* ....James 2:18
w of the devil ....1 John 3:8
I know thy *w* ....Rev. 3:8
and their *w* do follow ....Rev. 14:13

WORK (*v.*)
for I will *w* ....Hab. 1:5
when no man can *w* ....John 9:4
tribulation *w* patience ....Rom. 5:3
all things *w* together ....Rom. 8:28
spirit that now *w* ....Eph. 2:2
to the power that *w* ....Eph. 3:20
w out your own ....Phil. 2:12
and to *w* with ....1 Thess. 4:11
if any would not *w* ....2 Thess. 3:10
faith *w* patience ....James 1:3

WORKMAN
a *w* that needeth ....2 Tim. 2:15

WORKMANSHIP
we are his *w* ....Eph. 2:10

WORLD
the light of the *w* ....Matt. 5:14
The field is the *w* ....Matt. 13:38
gain the whole *w* ....Matt. 16:26
w should be taxed ....Luke 2:1
if he gain the whole *w* ....Luke 9:25
He was in the *w* ....John 1:10
For God so loved the *w* ......John 3:16
light unto the *w* ....John 8:12
I am the light of the *w* ....John 8:12
not as the *w* giveth ....John 14:27
If the *w* hate you ....John 15:18
In the *w* ye shall ....John 16:33
conformed to this *w* ....Rom. 12:2
the god of this *w* ....2 Cor. 4:4
the present evil *w* ....Gal. 1:4
course of this *w* ....Eph. 2:2
from the *w* ....James 1:27
a *w* of iniquity ....James 3:6
the friendship of the *w* ......James 4:4
Love not the *w* ....1 John 2:15
the *w* knoweth us not ....1 John 3:1
if the *w* hate you ....1 John 3:13
Saviour of the *w* ....1 John 4:14

WORM
w shall not die ....Is. 66:24
their *w* dieth not ....Mark 9:44

WORSE
of that man is *w* ....Matt. 12:45
last error shall be *w* ....Matt. 27:64
shall wax *w* and *w* ....2 Tim. 3:13

WORSHIP
let us *w* and bow down ....Ps. 95:6
fall down and *w* me ....Matt. 4:9
men ought to *w* ....John 4:20

WORTHY
shoes I am not *w* ....Matt. 3:11
for the workman is *w* ....Matt. 10:10
am no more *w* ....Luke 15:19
time are not *w* ....Rom. 8:18
that ye walk *w* ....Eph. 4:1
walk *w* of the Lord ....Col. 1:10

WOUND
he was *w* for ....Is. 53:5

WRATH
the *w* of man ....Ps. 76:10
a fool's *w* is heavier ....Prov. 27:3
in *w* remember mercy ....Hab. 3:2
from the *w* to come ....Matt. 3:7
your children to *w* ....Eph. 6:4
appointed us to *w* ....1 Thess. 5:9
without *w* and ....1 Tim. 2:8

WRESTLE
there *w* a man with him ......Gen. 32:24
w not against flesh ....Eph. 6:12

WRETCHED
O *w* man that I am ....Rom. 7:24

WRITE

thou shalt *w* them . . . . Deut. 6:9
w it in their hearts . . . . Jer. 31:33

WRITTEN

are *w* in heaven . . . . Luke 10:20
they are *w* for . . . . 1 Cor. 10:11
w in our hearts . . . . 2 Cor. 3:2

Y

YEAR

For a thousand *y* . . . . Ps. 90:4
y shall have no end . . . . Ps. 102:27
y of the Lord . . . . Is. 61:2
let it alone this *y* . . . . Luke 13:8
a thousand *y* . . . . Rev. 20:2

YESTERDAY

years . . . . are but as *y* . . . . Ps. 90:4
same *y*, and to day . . . . Heb. 13:8

YET

y will I trust in him . . . . Job 13:15
end shall not be *y* . . . . Mark 13:7
hour is not *y* come . . . . John 2:4
y shall he live . . . . John 11:25
y without strength . . . . Rom. 5:6
y in your sins . . . . 1 Cor. 15:17
y not I, but Christ . . . . Gal. 2:20
y without sin . . . . Heb. 4:15
not *y* appear . . . . 1 John 3:2

YOKE

Take my *y* upon you . . . . Matt. 11:29
y together with . . . . 2 Cor. 6:14
the *y* of bondage . . . . Gal. 5:1
are under the *y* . . . . 1 Tim. 6:1

YOUTH

the sins of my *y* . . . . Ps. 25:7
wife of thy *y* . . . . Prov. 5:18
days of thy *y* . . . . Eccl. 12:1
from my *y* up . . . . Matt. 19:20
despise thy *y* . . . . 1 Tim. 4:12

Illustrated Word List

This illustrated word list will help you to find the meanings of some of the words used in your Bible. It will also help you find a key passage using that word. The verse references give you the name of the Bible book, then the chapter, and then the verse or verses. Thus, Luke 24:30–51 would be Luke, chapter 24, verses 30 through 51. See the abbreviations of the Bible books listed below.

If you need additional verses for a word, look the word up in the Concordance in this Bible and see if that word appears in more verses as well.

Abbreviations for the Books of the Bible

Acts	Acts	Judges	Judg.
Amos	Amos	1 Kings	1 Kin.
1 Chronicles	1 Chr.	2 Kings	2 Kin.
2 Chronicles	2 Chr.	Lamentations	Lam.
Colossians	Col.	Leviticus	Lev.
1 Corinthians	1 Cor.	Luke	Luke
2 Corinthians	2 Cor.	Malachi	Mal.
Daniel	Dan.	Mark	Mark
Deuteronomy	Deut.	Matthew	Matt.
Ecclesiastes	Eccl.	Micah	Mic.
Ephesians	Eph.	Nahum	Nah.
Esther	Esth.	Nehemiah	Neh.
Exodus	Ex.	Numbers	Num.
Ezekiel	Ezek.	Obadiah	Obad.
Ezra	Ezra	1 Peter	1 Pet.
Galatians	Gal.	2 Peter	2 Pet.
Genesis	Gen.	Philippians	Phil.
Habakkuk	Hab.	Philemon	Philem.
Haggai	Hag.	Proverbs	Prov.
Hebrews	Heb.	Psalms	Ps.
Hosea	Hos.	Revelation	Rev.
Isaiah	Is.	Romans	Rom.
James	James	Ruth	Ruth
Jeremiah	Jer.	1 Samuel	1 Sam.
Job	Job	2 Samuel	2 Sam.
Joel	Joel	Song of Solomon	Song
John (Gospel)	John	1 Thessalonians	1 Thess.
1 John	1 John	2 Thessalonians	2 Thess.
2 John	2 John	1 Timothy	1 Tim.
3 John	3 John	2 Timothy	2 Tim.
Jonah	Jon.	Titus	Titus
Joshua	Josh.	Zechariah	Zech.
Jude	Jude	Zephaniah	Zeph.

A

Aaron The older brother of Moses (Ex. 6:20; 7:7); the spokesman for Moses (Ex. 7:1); brings on plagues with his rod (Ex. 7:10—8:17); from him are descended the class of priests in Israel (Ex. 29:9).

Abba Aramaic for "Father" (Rom. 8:15).

Abed-nego Babylonian name of one of Daniel's companions (Dan. 1:7; 3:16).

Abel Son of Adam; murdered by his brother Cain (Gen. 4:2ff). He is described as righteous (Matt. 23:35). In Hebrews 11:4 he stands at the head of the heroes of faith.

abhor 1. To despise, hate (Ps. 119:163). 2. To shrink from (Job 42:6).

abide To endure (John 15:4).

abject One cast aside (Ps. 35:15).

abomination Something loathsome or disgusting (Prov. 8:7).

Abraham; Abram Israel's first great patriarch or leader. Through faith in God's promise to make of him a great nation, he is led from Ur to Canaan (Gen. 11:31—15:7). God makes a covenant with him (Gen. 15:7-21); God tests Abraham's faith (Gen. 22:1-19). He stands as the father of all the faithful (Gal. 3:7).

abroad Outside (Jer. 6:11).

Absalom Son of David and Maacah; turned the people against his father; was defeated and then slain by Joab, to the great sorrow of David (2 Sam. 3:3; 13:20—19:10).

acquaint To come to terms with (Job 22:21).

Adam The first man, from whom all mankind descends. Created on the same day as the animals, he is particularly blessed by God (Gen. 1:27, 28). He and Eve were driven from the Garden of Eden because of their disobedience (Gen. 3:1-24).

addicted Devoted (1 Cor. 16:15).

adultery Unchastity; unfaithfulness to one's husband or wife (Ex. 20:14).

adventure To go, venture (Acts 19:31).

advertise To inform (Ruth 4:4).

advise To tell, inform (1 Kin. 12:6).

advisement Consultation (1 Chr. 12:19).

advocate One who speaks in defense of another. Christ is so called (1 John 2:1).

affinity A marriage alliance (1 Kin. 3:1).

affliction Distress; pain; adversity (Gen. 31:42).

aforehand In advance (Mark 14:8).

aforetime Formerly (Is. 52:4).

agone Ago (1 Sam. 30:13).

Agrippa King of Judea before whom Paul appeared to plead his defense (Acts 25:13—26:32).

Ahab An evil king of the northern kingdom of Israel in the time of Elijah; married Jezebel, a Sidonian princess, which caused religious turmoil; robbed Naboth of his vineyard and then caused his death (1 Kin. 16:29—22:40).

affliction

Ahasuerus The name of two kings in the Old Testament. 1. A king of Persia and the husband of the Jewess, Esther (Esth. 1:2, 19; 2:16, 17). Through her guardian, Mordecai, Esther was able to save her people, Israel, from an evil plan. 2. A king of the Medes and the father of Darius (Dan. 9:1).

Ahaz A name which means "he has grasped." 1. A wicked king of Judah who worshiped idols on the "high places" and even offered one of his own sons on an altar (2 Kin. 16:3, 4); refused to listen to the prophet Isaiah when he encouraged the king to call on God instead of seeking foreign aid against the army of Syria (Is. 7:1–16); heard the wonderful announcement of the promised Messiah. Hosea and Micah also prophesied during the reign of Ahaz (Hos. 1:1; Mic. 1:1). 2. A descendant of King Saul, the son of Micah and the father of Jehoadah (1 Chr. 8:35, 36; 9:42).

albeit But, although (Ezek. 13:7).

alien A foreigner (Ex. 18:3).

allege To mention as a source of authority (Acts 17:3).

Alleluia Hallelujah; "Praise the Lord" (Rev. 19:1, 3, 4, 6).

Almighty, the God, as being all powerful (Gen. 17:1).

Alpha and Omega The first and last letters of the Greek alphabet; hence, "the First and the Last." Applied to God and to Christ (Rev. 1:8, 11; 21:6; 22:13).

altar Table of sacrifice (Gen. 8:20).

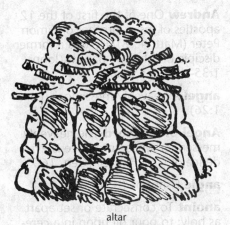

altar

Am Exist; be. The reply to Moses' question for the name of the Deity (or God), "I AM THAT I AM" (Ex. 3:14), indicates that the Lord makes Himself present as He wills.

ambassage Group sent on a mission (Luke 14:32).

Amen Verily; so be it (Matt. 6:13; Rev. 3:14).

amerce To punish by a fine (Deut. 22:19).

Amos A prophet of Israel; the first to proclaim that God is the ruler of the whole universe; foretold the downfall of the northern kingdom. The OT Book of Amos is the third of the 12 Minor Prophets.

Ananias 1. A Christian of Jerusalem who lost his life for lying and attempting to hold back part of the price of property he had sold (Acts 5:1–10). 2. A Christian of Damascus who received Paul into Christian fellowship (Acts 9:10–17). 3. A Jewish high priest before whom Paul was tried in Jerusalem (Acts 23:2).

Ancient of Days The judge in Daniel's vision; probably intended to be God Himself (Dan. 7:9, 13, 22).

Andrew One of the first of the 12 apostles of Jesus; brother of Simon Peter (Matt. 4:18). He was a former disciple of John the Baptist (John 1:35–40). *See* Simon.

angel A heavenly messenger (Luke 1:26).

Angel of the Lord The heavenly messenger whose presence is evidence of God Himself (Gen. 16:7).

angle Fishhook (Is. 19:8).

anoint To consecrate or set apart as holy; to pour oil upon in a ceremony (Ex. 28:41).

anon Immediately (Mark 1:30).

answer A reply (Prov. 15:1).

ant An insect (Prov. 6:6).

antichrist Opponent or enemy of Christ (1 John 2:22).

Antioch 1. In Syria; the name "Christian" was first used here (Acts 11:26). 2. In Pisidia; visited by Paul and Barnabas (Acts 13:14–52).

anxious Worried; careful (Phil. 4:6).

Apollos A well-educated Jew and a follower of John the Baptist; knew the Old Testament well and taught others (Acts 18:24–28); learned of the Holy Spirit from Aquila and Priscilla in Ephesus; preached in Corinth (1 Cor. 1:12). Some teachers think Apollos wrote the Letter to the Hebrews.

apostle One of the 12 disciples chosen by Jesus (Matt. 10:2–4) or certain other early Christian leaders (Acts 14:14).

apothecary Perfume maker (Neh. 3:8).

apple A fruit (Deut. 32:10).

Aquila A Jew who lived in Rome with his wife Priscilla until the emperor ordered all Jewish people to leave; moved to Corinth where he worked as a tentmaker with Paul (Acts 18:1–3); traveled with Paul to Syria (Acts 18:18, 19).

Arabia; Arabians The NW part of the large peninsula in SW Asia; scene of many biblical events. The peoples of the area were nomads or wanderers.

Arameans A Semitic people, traditionally descendants of Shem, the oldest son of Noah (Gen. 10:1, 22, 23). They were nomads, wandering along the W side of the Syrian desert.

Ararat The mountain on which the ark came to rest after the Flood (Gen. 8:4); the land of Ararat is Armenia.

archangel An angel of the highest order (1 Thess. 4:16).

ark A floating vessel; ship (Gen. 6:14—8:19).

ark of the testimony The chest which held the two stone tablets on which were inscribed the Ten

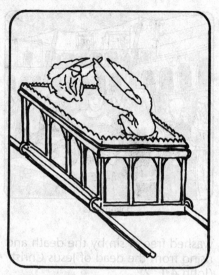

ark of the testimony

Commandments (Ex. 25:10–22). Also called the ark of the covenant (1 Kin. 8:6).

Armageddon The name means "mountain of Megiddo." The large valley of Jezreel or Plain of Esdraelon near the ancient fortified city of Megiddo in northern Israel. According to prophecy, this is the place where the last battle of this age will be fought between the forces of good and evil.

armhole Armpit (Jer. 38:12).

Artaxerxes The name of two Persian kings: the first, mentioned in Ezra 7 and Nehemiah 2; 13; his grandson, the second, may have been the builder of the palace described in Esther 1:5, 6.

Ascension The return of the risen Christ to heaven (Luke 24:51) on the fortieth day after the Resurrection.

Ascents, Song of A title given to each of Psalms 120—134; probably so called because of their use in a procession ascending to the temple or for pilgrims going up to Jerusalem.

Asher The eighth son of Jacob, the second by Zilpah (Gen. 30:12ff); one of the 12 tribes of Israel.

Asherah The wife of the Canaanite god, Baal. Asherah often refers to a wooden pole that stood near Canaanite high places of worship ("grove"). Gideon was ordered by the Lord to destroy the wooden image beside the altar (Judg. 6:25).

Asia A Roman province in the western part of what we call Asia Minor (Acts 16:6).

ask To request (Matt. 7:7).

assay To attempt, try (Job 4:2).

asswage To grow less (Job 16:5).

Assyria A kingdom between the Tigris and Euphrates Rivers in Mesopotamia; ruled over the ancient world from the 9th to the 7th centuries B.C. (before Christ). After defeating the northern kingdom of Israel in 722 B.C., the Assyrians captured and carried away thousands of Israelites to their country. In 701 B.C., Assyria attacked the southern kingdom of Judah, but did not succeed because a plague from the "Angel of the Lord" struck down the soldiers (2 Kin. 19:35). Thousands died, and Jerusalem, the capital, was saved. (Find out more about Assyria in the Book of Jonah and in Is. 10:5, Ezek. 16:28, and Hos. 8:9.)

Athens The capital city of the ancient Greeks as well as the modern capital, located on the southern coast of Attica; center of Greek art, architecture, literature, and politics during the golden age of Grecian history. The world's most famous building—the Parthenon—stands here in ruins. During his second missionary journey, the apostle Paul preached his famous sermon on Areopagus, Mars' Hill (Acts 17:15—18:1).

Atonement, Day of An annual fast day of the Jews. Ordained in the Law as a day of humbling oneself and making amends for sins (Lev. 23:27).

attent Attentive (2 Chr. 6:40).

bakemeats

B

Baal One of the fertility gods of Canaan. There were many local Baals. Elijah met the prophets of Baal in a contest (1 Kin. 18:1–40).

Babel Hebrew form of the name "Babylon," capital of Babylonia; site of the Tower of Babel (Gen. 11:1–9).

babes Infants; small children (Ps. 8:2).

Babylon An ancient walled city, once the capital of the Babylonian Empire, located between the Tigris and Euphrates Rivers. In 586 B.C., the leading citizens of Judah were taken captive by King Nebuchadnezzar and brought to Babylon where they stayed for 70 years during the period called the Exile (see the books of Isaiah, Jeremiah, Ezekiel, and Daniel). Here were the famous hanging gardens and, nearby, the Tower of Babel (Gen. 11:1–9).

bakemeats Foods made by a baker (Gen. 40:17).

baptism A ceremony in which one enters the church family. It is a way of showing that you have been washed free of sin by the death and rising from the dead of Jesus Christ (John 4:1, 2)

Barabbas A robber held in prison by the Roman authorities at the time of Jesus' trial; Pilate freed him and condemned Jesus to death (Matt. 27:20–26).

Barnabas Meaning "son of consolation," the name given by the apostles to Joses or Joseph, a Levite of Cyprus, who accompanied Paul on his first missionary journey (Acts 13:1–13).

Bartholomew One of the 12 apostles of Jesus (Matt. 10:3).

Baruch Jeremiah's scribe, or secretary (Jer. 36:4ff).

bath A liquid measure equal to the dry measure ephah (Ezek. 45:10, 11); about six gallons.

Bath-sheba The wife of Uriah, the Hittite, and King David (2 Sam. 11; 12:24); the woman with whom David sinned. David had her husband, Uriah, killed in battle. Then David married her and she became the mother of Solomon, who ruled after David's death.

beam A piece of timber (Matt. 7:5).

beard The growth of hair on the lower part of a man's face. The Hebrews were forbidden to cut the edges of their beards (Lev. 19:27). The shaving off of beards was an indignity (2 Sam. 10:4, 5).

beard

beast Animal (used for all living things other than man, as a general term); in the Book of Revelation the word is used of both "heavenly" beasts and "beasts from the bottomless pit."

Beatitudes The blessings listed by Jesus in the Sermon on the Mount (Matt. 5:3–12).

Beelzebub The prince of demons whom Jesus refers to as Satan (Matt. 12:26, 27).

beginning Outset; start (Gen. 1:1).

begotten Having been brought into being (John 1:18).

Benjamin The youngest son of Jacob. His mother, Rachel, died at his birth (Gen. 35:18). Especially beloved by his father and by Joseph, his only full brother (Gen. 42:4; 45:22). Ancestor of the tribe of Benjamin, the smallest of the 12 tribes of Israel.

besom Broom (Is. 14:23).

bestead Pressed; distressed (Is. 8:21).

Bethany A small village on the E slope of the Mount of Olives, about one and one-half mi. E of Jerusalem. From here Jesus made His triumphal entry into Jerusalem (Mark 11:1–11); the home of Simon the leper (Matt. 26:6); home of Lazarus, Mary, and Martha (John 11:1–44); site of Jesus' final parting from His disciples (Luke 24:50, 51).

Beth-el City 14 mi. N of Jerusalem. Near here Abraham built an altar (Gen. 12:8); here Jacob's name was changed to Israel (Gen. 35:10–15).

Bethlehem A very old town about six mi. SSW of Jerusalem; the birthplace of Jesus (Matt. 2:1–16); also associated with David (1 Sam. 16:1–13).

betimes Early (Gen. 26:31).

bird A winged creature (Gen. 7:14).

birthright Privilege of the firstborn son of a family (Gen. 25:34).

bishop Overseer (church leader) or pastor (1 Tim. 3:2).

blain Blister; sore (Ex. 9.9).

blood The life-giving fluid of the body. In the OT it is regarded as the seat of life; but since shed blood signifies death, the word is used of both life and death (Lev. 7:26).

Boaz A wealthy Bethlehemite who married Ruth (Ruth 2:1—4:22).

body The physical human being or animal. The church is called "the body of Christ" as the living spiritual community of which Christ is the head and all believers are members. At the Lord's Supper, Jesus broke bread to represent His body given in sacrifice for sinners (Matt. 26:26).

bolled Budding (Ex. 9:31).

boss Embossed knob or stud (Job 15:26).

Booths, Feast of *See* Feast of Tabernacles.

booties Plural of booty; spoils of war (Hab. 2:7).

botch A boil (Deut. 28:27).

bowels Inward parts; deep feelings (Lam. 1:20).

bray 1. Sound of a donkey's cry (Job 6:5). 2. To grind (Prov. 27:22).

bread A food made of a dough of flour or meal and water and baked; sustenance in general. Often used in offerings by OT peoples. In the NT, also used in reference to the coming of the kingdom of God or to Jesus Himself (John 6:35).

bread, breaking of Since the earliest form of the Lord's Supper involved the "breaking of bread," the term has been used for worship in general (Acts 2:42).

bread from heaven The food—manna—miraculously provided by God for the Israelites in their wanderings through the wilderness (Ps. 105:40).

brigandine Lightweight armor (Jer. 46:4).

brother A male relative of the same parents; a close associate (Prov. 18:24).

bruit Rumor; report (Nah. 3:19).

buckler Small, round shield (Ps. 18:30).

bushel The container for holding a dry measure (Matt. 5:15).

brigandine

C

Cain Son of Adam; murdered his brother Abel (Gen. 4:2ff); used as an example (or type) for wicked men (1 John 3:12).

Calvary From the Latin word meaning "skull." A place outside the second wall of Jerusalem where Jesus was crucified (Luke 23:33). Since Jerusalem has been destroyed and rebuilt so many times, no one knows for sure where this event took place, but there are at least two opinions: (1) A spot under the Church of the Holy Sepulcher; (2) "Gordon's Calvary," named for General Charles Gordon, a British soldier and explorer. The Hebrew name for the place where Jesus was crucified is *Golgotha* (Matt. 27:33).

camel A large animal of desert areas (Matt. 19:24).

Canaan; Canaanites 1. The fourth son of Ham and grandson of Noah (Gen. 9:18–27). 2. The region along the Mediterranean Sea known as the Promised Land—the land given by God to Abraham and the Children of Israel; known as Israel today; the land bridge between three continents—Africa, Europe, and Asia. Because of its position, this narrow strip of land has always been very important to invading armies as well as to traders.

cankered Rusted (James 5:3).

cankerworm A kind of locust (Nah. 3:15).

Capernaum A city on the NW shore of the Sea of Galilee. Jesus lived there (Mark 2:1); home of Peter and Andrew (Matt. 8:5).

Carmel, Mount A mountain range in northern Palestine, Israel; stretches SE from the Mediterranean Sea about thirteen miles. Here Elijah held his famous contest with the priests of Baal (1 Kin. 18:19, 20).

chambering Sexual excesses (Rom. 13:13).

champaign A plain (Deut. 11:30).

chapiter The head or upper part of a column (2 Kin. 25:17).

chapmen Traders (2 Chr. 9:14).

cheek The side of the face (Matt. 5:39).

cherubims Winged creatures, statues of which were fixed to the mercy seat of the ark of the testimo-

ny. Two cherubims carved from olive wood were placed within the inner room of the temple (Ex. 25:18).

child A young person—boy or girl (Is. 9:6).

child

children Young persons—boys or girls (Matt. 18:3).

choler Anger (Dan. 8:7).

Christians Followers of Christ (Acts 11:26).

Christmas The holiday on December 25 which celebrates the birth of Jesus Christ.

church The people of God; those destined to inherit the kingdom of God. Also, any local group of believers (Eph. 5:23).

clean Free from defilement or dirt. Under the Hebrew law certain animals are declared clean and others unclean (Lev. 11:1–47).

cloud A visible mass of water particles in the air above the earth (Ex. 13:21).

clout A rag (Jer. 38:11).

clouted Patched (Josh. 9:5).

coat An outer garment (Gen. 37:3; Luke 9:3).

cockatrice Poisonous serpent (Is. 11:8).

cockatrice

college The second section (2 Kin. 22:14).

collops Thick folds (of flesh) (Job 15:27).

Colosse; Colossians A city in Asia Minor. Paul wrote an epistle to the Christians of this city.

Comforter The Holy Spirit; the intercessor promised by Christ to help and guide believers (John 14:26).

commandment Any of the Ten Commandments or laws given to Moses by God at Mount Sinai (Ex. 20:1–17); other OT laws (Matt. 19:17).

concupiscence Strong desire (Col. 3:5).

confection Compounds of spices (Ex. 30:35).

confectionary Perfumer (1 Sam. 8:13).

confess To admit to a fault or sin, particularly as a sign of repentance (Mark 1:5); to acknowledge God's redeeming acts and openly acknowledge that Jesus is the Messiah, Lord, and Son of God (Matt. 16:16).

confound Put to shame (1 Cor. 1:27).

congregation An assembly; gathering (Ps. 1:5).

contrariwise On the contrary (1 Pet. 3:9).

conversant Living (Josh. 8:35).

converted Changed, as one's religion or belief (Matt. 18:3).

Corinth Most important trade city of ancient Greece (Acts 18:1); situated on the Isthmus of Corinth, a narrow strip of land between the Aegean and Ionian Seas. Today a deep canal saves scores of miles of sea travel. Corinth was a very wealthy and wicked city in Paul's day. He did establish a strong church here to which he wrote letters—1 and 2 Corinthians.

Cornelius A Roman soldier stationed in Caesarea who was the first recorded Gentile convert to Christianity (Acts 10:1–33). Even before his conversion, he was a God-fearing man who believed in the Jewish teaching of one God (monotheism) and opposed the worship of idols. The apostle Peter took part in Cornelius's conversion.

counsellor An adviser or teacher. Counsellors seem to have been court officials of the Israelite kings (1 Chr. 27:33). The coming Messiah is so called (Is. 9:6).

countervail Make up for (Esth. 7:4).

covenant A binding agreement. The great covenant between God and Israel was made at Sinai (Ex. 24:3–8); the stone tablets on which the Ten Commandments were engraved were called "the tables of the covenant" (Deut. 9:11). The chest in which these tablets were placed was called the "ark of the covenant" (Deut. 31:26). The new covenant came into being through the blood of Christ (Mark 14:24).

cracknel Cake (1 Kin. 14:3).

creation The act of God in making heaven and earth and bringing forth all life; the whole universe (Gen. 1:1—2:25).

creator; Creator The maker; originator; hence, **Creator:** God; the Lord (Is. 40:28).

creature Any living thing that God has made (Gen. 2:19).

creeping thing Reptile (Gen. 1:26).

cross An upright post with crossbeam on which victims of execution were nailed; used by the Romans. A symbol of Christianity (Matt. 10:38).

crown A headdress of gold, precious stones, etc; a wreath encircling the head (Prov. 16:31; Matt. 27:29).

Crucifixion, the Jesus' execution on the Cross by the Romans at the instigation of the Jewish leaders (Matt. 27).

crucify To put to death by fastening to a cross (Matt. 20:19).

Crucifixion, the

cubit A measure of length of about 18 inches (Matt. 6:27).

cumber To clutter up (Luke 13:7).

cup A vessel from which to drink (Ps. 23:5).

curse To call on God to punish (Gen. 12:3).

Cyrus The powerful king of Persia (559–530 B.C.), sometimes called "Cyrus the Great." In 538 B.C., he wrote a law that allowed the Jewish captives in Babylon to return to their homeland in Jerusalem; praised in the OT as God's "shepherd" and "anointed" (Is. 44:28; 45:1); encouraged the rebuilding of the temple. God often uses nonbelievers in working out His plans for His people. (Find out more about Cyrus in Ezra and Daniel.)

D

Dagon The chief god of the Philistines. Samson destroyed the temple of Dagon and killed hundreds of Philistines when he pulled down the supporting pillars (Judg. 16:23–30). When Samuel was a young man and Eli was still serving as priest in Israel, the Philistines defeated the army of Israel and captured the ark of the covenant and took it to the temple of Dagon in Ashdod (1 Sam. 5:2–7).

Damascus A very ancient city, capital of Syria; in OT times the capital of the Aramean kingdom. Site of Saul's conversion (Acts 9:1–22).

Dan The fifth son of Jacob, born of Bilhah (Gen. 30:1–6); one of the 12 tribes of Israel.

dance To move in rhythm, usually to the sound of music (Eccl. 3:4).

Daniel The Jewish prophet at the Babylonian court about whom the OT Book of Daniel is written. Interpreted dreams (Dan. 2:1–45) and the handwriting on the wall (5:17–30); saved by God from the lions (6:16–24).

David The second and greatest king over Israel; youngest son of Jesse (1 Sam. 17:12); killed Goliath (1 Sam. 17:41–50); friend of Jonathan (1 Sam. 19:1—20:42); a fugitive from Saul's wrath (1 Sam. 21—27; 30); king of Judah (2 Sam. 1:1—5:5); king of Israel (2 Sam. 3:6—1 Kin. 2:11); names his son Solomon to succeed him (1 Kin. 1:11—2:12).

day The time between sunrise and sunset; a period of 24 hours (Gen. 1:5).

day of the Lord In the OT, the day when God punishes evil (Amos 5:18–20); a day of universal disaster (Is. 2). In the NT, the day of the Last Judgment and the end of the world (1 Cor. 5:5).

daysman Mediator (Job 9:33).

deacon A servant or minister; an officer of a local church who assists the minister or priest (Phil. 1:1).

Dead Sea The salt lake at the mouth of the Jordan River. One of its biblical names was "Salt Sea" (Gen. 14:3).

dearth Famine (Gen. 41:54).

death The condition of being without life; the act of dying. Symbol of the final state of the unsaved (John 8:51), and of the power that rules over man in the age of sin (Rom. 5:14).

Deborah 1. Rebekah's nurse and companion (Gen. 35:8). 2. An early "judge" of Israel; aroused the scattered tribes to opposition to Canaanite oppression; Song of Deborah (Judg. 5:2–31) celebrates her achievement.

debts Obligations; anything owed to another (Matt. 6:12).

Dedication, Feast of An eight-day festival observing the victories of Judas Maccabaeus and the purification and rededication of the temple (John 10:22). Also called Feast of Lights; Hanukkah; Chanukah.

Delilah A woman from the Valley of Sorek; betrayed Samson to the Philistines (Judg. 16:4–22).

deliverer, the In five OT passages (2 Sam. 22:2; Ps. 18:2; 40:17; 70:5; 144:2) God is referred to as "the deliverer"; but even though Christ is the instrument of God's deliverance of mankind from sin, the NT does not use the word except when Paul repeats Is. 59:20, using "Deliverer" instead of "Redeemer" (Rom. 11:26).

den Lair; cave of a wild animal (Dan. 6:7).

denounce Proclaim (Deut. 30:18).

detestable Abominable; loathsome; disgusting (Ezek. 5:11).

Deuteronomy The fifth book of the Law in the OT; teaches that God's laws are given for our own good—to help us stay close to Him in attitude and action. The name means "second law" or the second time the Law was given. (Look up Ex. 20:1–17 for the first giving of the Law.)

devil A demon or evil spirit (Matt. 4:24).

Devil The chief demon, Satan (Matt. 4:1–11).

die Perish; lose life (Gen. 2:17).

disannul Cancel; make of no effect (Is. 14:27).

disciple A learner; a follower, particularly one who follows Jesus Christ (Matt. 10:1).

discomfit Defeat (Ex. 17:13).

Dispersion The widespread settlement of Jewish people outside of Palestine from the time of the Exile through the following centuries.

disquietness Anxiety (Ps. 38:8).

divers Some (Mark 8:3).

doctrine Teaching or instruction, particularly that of Jesus or the apostles concerning God's will (John 7:16).

door Entranceway (Ex. 12:23).

dote Act foolishly (Jer. 50:36).

doxology A hymn, usually in a set formula, for expressing praise to God (Luke 2:14).

dreadful Awesome; feared; terrible (Mal. 4:5).

door

duke Leader, chief (Gen. 36:15).

dure To last, stay on (Matt. 13:21).

dust Fine, dry, powdery earth (Gen. 2:7).

E

earnest Money paid to seal an agreement; a pledge, or guarantee (2 Cor. 1:22; Eph. 1:14).

earth The planet on which we live; the soil (Gen. 1:1).

Easter A Christian festival celebrating the Resurrection of Jesus; on a Sunday between March 22 and April 25.

Ebal, Mount A mountain in N Israel opposite Mount Gerizim (Deut. 11:29). It became known as the Mount of Cursing when Joshua read the curses of the Law. People on the mountain cried out with an "Amen!" When he read the blessings, people on nearby Mount

Gerizim responded in the same way. These two mountains marked the center of the land of the Samaritans in the OT. *See* Gerizim, Mount.

Eden, Garden of A garden of trees planted by the Lord (Gen. 2:8) in which Adam and Eve first lived; actual site unknown; symbolically identified with Paradise.

Edom; Edomites A country to the E and S of Israel; its people had a close relationship to the Israelites, being descendants of Esau.

Egypt A land in NE Africa. Temporary home of Abraham (Gen. 12:10–20); Joseph sold "into Egypt" (Gen. 37:28, 36); Israel in bondage (Ex. 1:1—12:36); the Exodus (Ex. 12:37—14:31); Jesus taken there (Matt. 2:13).

Egypt

Elah, Valley of A narrow valley surrounded by low hills, SW of Jerusalem, where David killed Goliath (1 Sam. 17:2; 21:9).

elders Seniors; among the Jews, the old and mature men who were civil and religious leaders; in the Christian church, leaders of the local church (Ex. 24:9).

Eli The priest of Shiloh to whom the boy Samuel was brought (1 Sam. 1—4).

Elijah A prophet from Tishbe to Gilead in the northern kingdom; fed by ravens (1 Kin. 17:6); performs miracles (1 Kin. 17:14–24; 20:30; 2 Kin. 1:10–12; 2:8); taken up by a whirlwind into heaven (2 Kin. 2:11). Malachi prophesies his return before the day of the Lord (Mal. 4:5). In NT times, some thought Jesus to be Elijah (Matt. 16:14); others thought John the Baptist to be Elijah (John 1:21). At the Transfiguration, Elijah appears with Moses (Matt. 17:3, 4).

Elisabeth Wife of the priest, Zacharias, and mother of John the Baptist (Luke 1:5–66).

Elisha A prophet; disciple and successor to Elijah; performed many miracles (2 Kin. 2:14–24; 3:16–20; 4:2–7); contact with his bones revives a dead man (2 Kin. 13:20, 21).

Elohim One of the names of God; the other is Yahweh. Elohim appears first in Gen. 1:1 and is plural, meaning to Christians—"Trinity"—not three gods. The abbreviated form, El, is found in many biblical names—Beth-*el*, Ezeki*el*, Dani*el*, *El*isabeth.

Emmanuel *See* Immanuel.

Emmaus A village in Judaea, probably NW of Jerusalem, where Jesus revealed Himself to two disciples on the road after His resurrection from the grave (Luke 24:13–29).

emulation Jealousy (Gal. 5:20).

enemies Foes; opponents (Ps. 23:5).

engine Military machine (2 Chr. 26:15).

enter To go or come into (Ps. 100:4).

ephah A dry measure equal to the liquid measure bath; estimated as three-eighths to two-thirds of a bushel (Ezek. 45:10).

Ephesus; Ephesians A seaport in the Roman province of Asia; visited by Paul on his second and third journeys. Paul's NT Epistle to the Ephesians seems to be a general letter to the churches of Asia Minor.

Ephraim The younger son of Joseph; adopted by Jacob (Gen. 48:1ff); ancestor of one of the most powerful of the 12 tribes of Israel.

epistle Letter; specifically those letters written by the apostles that are included in the NT. **Pastoral Epistles:** The NT books of 1 and 2 Timothy and Titus, which are written in the name of Paul as the chief pastor of the churches. **General (Catholic) Epistles:** The NT books of James, 1 and 2 Peter, 1, 2, and 3 John, and Jude.

Esau Son of Isaac and Rebekah who traded his birthright to his younger twin brother Jacob for a bowl of pottage (Gen. 25:22–34; 27; 33:1–16).

eschew Avoid (1 Pet. 3:11).

espoused Engaged (Matt. 1:18).

estate Condition (Ezek. 16:55).

Esther A Jewess of Shushan who became Ahasuerus's queen and uncovered a plot to kill all the Jews, later commemorated, or remembered, by the Jewish festival of Purim. The Book of Esther tells the story.

Euphrates Means "that which waters." The longest river in W Asia and one of the two major rivers in Mesopotamia; begins in the mountains of Turkey and runs down to the Persian Gulf, almost two thousand miles away. The ruins of many ancient cities, including Babylon, Nippur, and Ur of the Chaldees, are located along this river in Iraq.

Eve The first woman; wife of Adam (Gen. 2:21–25); tempted by the serpent (Gen. 3:1–5).

everlasting Eternal; never ending (Is. 40:28).

evil Wickedness; talking about someone in a way that would purposely hurt them (Matt. 6:13).

Exile, the A period during which most of the people of Judah and Jerusalem were forced to live in Babylonia.

Exodus The going out of Israel from Egypt as recorded in the second book of the OT. It includes the deliverance from slavery, the wandering through the wilderness, the covenant with the Lord at Mount Sinai, and the provision of the tabernacle and ark of the covenant.

Ezekiel A major Jewish prophet; author of the OT Book of Ezekiel; one of the captives of the Babylonian exile. Vision of God (Ezek. 1:4–28); parable of the two eagles and the vine (Ezek. 17:1–24); the fall of Jerusalem (Ezek. 24:1–27); various prophecies about other nations (Ezek. 25—32).

Ezra A priest and scribe; supposed author of the Book of Ezra, which details the first return of the Israelites from Babylon and the rebuilding of the temple.

F

face The front of the head; the surface or top side; frequently used to indicate the presence of God. Among the Hebrews, "seeking the face of God" referred to attendance at public worship (Ps. 27:8).

fain Gladly (Luke 15:16).

faith Belief or trust in someone or something. Among Christians, belief in the Holy Trinity (Rom. 4:5).

Fall, the A sinking into sin; the disobedience of Adam and Eve in the Garden of Eden, which allowed sin to enter the world (Gen. 3).

falsehood Lying (Ps. 4:2).

familiars Close friends (Jer. 20:10).

fashion Plan (1 Kin. 6:38).

fast To go without food (Matt. 6:16).

father The male parent or ancestor. In the OT, used of God as the One who made a covenant with the people of Israel (Is. 64:8).

Father The First Person of the Holy Trinity (Matt. 5:16).

fear To dread; to be afraid of; to be anxious (Ps. 23:4).

fear of the LORD The term used in the OT for "religion" (Deut. 6:2). In the NT, "those who fear the Lord" are the faithful (Luke 1:50) or converts to Judaism (Acts 10:2).

feast A festival; in ancient Israel associated with occasions of religious joy. Those mentioned in the Bible: 1. **Passover and Feast of Unleavened Bread** (Ex. 12:1–30). 2. **Feast of Weeks or Pentecost** (Deut. 16:9–12). 3. **Feast of Tabernacles** (Lev. 23:34–36). 4. **Purim** (Esth. 9:20–28). 5. **Feast of the Dedication or Feast of Lights** (John 10:22).

feebleminded Discouraged (1 Thess. 5:14).

fellowship Companionship; a group of persons with a common interest. Among Christians, the common bond is their faith in Christ, particularly in partaking of the Lord's Supper (Phil. 2:1).

fight Struggle against; do battle (1 Tim. 6:12).

firmament Sky; heavens (Ps. 19:1).

First and the Last, the A title used by Isaiah (Is. 41:4) to give us the idea of God's everlasting sovereignty and eternal power and majesty. The same title is used in Revelation (1:11, 17; 2:8; 22:13) implying God's sovereign lordship shown in Jesus Christ.

firstborn, firstfruits The eldest; the earliest fruits harvested. The consecration of the first of the male children, of animals, and of fruits was an important part of the religion of Israel (Ex. 12:29).

flagon Raisin cake (Song 2:5).

flesh The soft part of the human body; all mankind (Is. 40:6).

Flood, the The covering of the earth with water because of man's wickedness. Noah's family and the animals of the earth are saved in an ark (Gen. 6:1—8:19).

fool A silly or unwise person (Prov. 1:7).

foolish Silly; unwise. Parables of Jesus deal with: foolish and wise virgins (Matt. 25:1–13) and a foolish rich man (Luke 12:16–21).

Flood, the

forgive To pardon; show mercy to (Matt. 6:12).

fountain The source, as the spring from which water flows. The Lord is called "the fountain of living waters" (Jer. 2:13) and the "fountain of life" (Ps. 36:9).

frame Manage (Judg. 12:6).

frankincense A fragrant incense (Matt. 2:11).

fret Eaten away (Lev. 13:55).

friend An associate whom one likes (Prov. 17:17).

furbish To polish (Ezek. 21:10).

G

Gabriel An angel of high rank (Luke 1:19).

Gad The seventh son of Jacob; born of Leah's maid Zilpah (Gen. 30:10, 11); ancestor of Gad, one of the 12 tribes of Israel.

Galatia; Galatians A region and Roman province in Asia Minor. Paul, in the NT Epistle to the Galatians, tells of his own conversion.

Galilee A region of N Palestine, including the Sea of Galilee on the E side. Jesus' active ministry was almost entirely within its borders.

Galilee, Sea of The larger of the two freshwater lakes on the Jordan River system. Site of miracles: the great catch of fish (Luke 5:1–11); Jesus stills the sea (Matt. 8:23–26); Jesus walks on the sea (Matt. 14:25–27). Also called "Chinnereth" (Num. 34:11); "Chinneroth" (Josh. 12:3); "Gennesaret" (Luke 5:1); and "Tiberias" (John 6:1).

Gamaliel A famous member of the Jewish Sanhedrin and a teacher of the Law; taught Paul in Tarsus (Acts 22:3); advised the Sanhedrin in Jerusalem to treat well the apostles of the young Christian church. His approach was simple: If Jesus was a false prophet, Christianity would soon fail. If the movement was of

God, "You cannot overthrow it!" (Acts 5:39).

gate Doorway (Ps. 100:4).

Gaza One of the five principal cities of the Philistines, located along the southern Mediterranean coast of Israel, on the great caravan route between Mesopotamia and Egypt. Philip preached to the Ethiopian eunuch on the road to Gaza and baptized him (Acts 8:26–40).

gender To breed (Lev. 19:19).

Gerizim, Mount A mountain in N Israel, close to Mount Ebal in the district of Samaria. The main north-south road through central Palestine ran between these mountains. Jacob's Well, where Jesus talked with the Samaritan woman, is situated at the foot of Mount Gerizim (John 4:14). *See* Ebal, Mount.

Gethsemane A garden on the Mount of Olives where Jesus prayed and where He was betrayed by Judas (Matt. 26:36).

Gideon A prophet of Israel especially favored by the Lord with revelations and unusual powers (Judg. 6:11—8:35).

Gilead A rugged, mountainous region E of the Jordan. Possibly also a city (Judg. 10:17) and a tribe (Judg. 5:17).

Gilgal The name of several places in the OT, one of them a city of the tribe of Benjamin, near Jericho; site of the first encampment of the Israelites after crossing the Jordan (Josh. 3; 4); there Saul was made king (1 Sam. 11:14, 15).

gin Trap or snare (Ps. 141:9).

give To bestow; hand over to another (Acts 20:35).

giver One who bestows or gives (2 Cor. 9:7).

glad tidings Good news; the gospel (Luke 1:19).

glass Mirror (Job 37:18).

glistering Gleaming; shining (1 Chr. 29:2).

glory of the Lord The word *glory* is sometimes used to represent the presence of "God" (Ex. 33:22). In the OT, used of the fiery presence at Sinai (Ex. 24:16, 17) and of the radiance that filled the tabernacle (Ex. 40:34). In the NT, used of the divine Presence (Mark 8:38), and of the quality of Jesus' appearance in His transfiguration (Luke 9:29–32), and of Jesus' second coming (Matt. 25:31).

gnat A tiny insect (Matt. 23:24).

God, kingdom of *See* kingdom of God; heaven, kingdom of.

gods Idols (Ex. 20:3)

Golden Gate The eastern gate of Jerusalem, sometimes called the Gate Beautiful on the Temple Mount, directly across the Kidron Valley from the Garden of Gethsemane where Judas betrayed Jesus. According to prophecy, this gate will be opened when the Messiah, Jesus, returns the second time.

Golden Rule A commandment given by Jesus in the Sermon on the Mount (Matt. 7:12).

Golgotha Place where Jesus was crucified (Matt. 27:33, 35).

Goliath A Philistine giant about 9½ to 11 feet tall; from a family of giants called the Anakim, who lived in Gath (Num. 13:33). David, while still a young man, killed Goliath

Goliath

with a stone from his sling (1 Sam. 17:4–51).

Gomer A prostitute whom God told the prophet Hosea to marry as a lesson to Israel about their relationship to Him. Hosea's forgiveness of his wife symbolized God's forgiving love toward Israel (Hos. 1:2; 14:1–4).

Gomorrah One of the two cities destroyed by the Lord because of their wickedness (Gen. 19:24–28).

good Virtuous; honorable (Matt. 19:17).

Good Friday The Friday before Easter; the anniversary of the Crucifixion of Jesus.

Goshen A fertile part of the Nile delta in N Egypt, given to the family of Joseph by Pharaoh because of the famine in Israel (Gen. 45:10–13).

gospel Good news; glad tidings. Hence, the teachings of Jesus and of the apostles. The NT books of Matthew, Mark, Luke, and John are called the Gospels (Luke 4:18).

grace OT usage: "favor" in the expression "found grace in the eyes of" (Gen. 6:8). In NT usage: "the

unmerited and abundant gift of God's love and favor to man," particularly made effective in Jesus Christ for the Christian. Used by Paul as an opening and farewell greeting (Rom. 16:24).

grisled Gray; spotted (Gen. 31:10).

H

Habakkuk A prophet of Judah; the OT book which bears his name is the eighth of the 12 Minor Prophets.

habergeon Coat of mail; armor (2 Chr. 26:14).

Hagar The Egyptian servant of Sarah, Abraham's wife; mother of Abraham's son, Ishmael (Gen. 16:1–16). When Sarah was very old, God gave her a son, Isaac, who became the father of the Jewish nation. Hagar's son Ishmael, his half brother, became the father of the Arab nation. The two nations cannot get along to this day.

Haggai A Jewish prophet who lived at the same time as Zechariah; the tenth of the 12 Minor Prophets of the OT.

Hallelujah "Praise the Lord" (not used in the KJV). *See* Alleluia.

hallowed Made sacred; consecrated (Matt. 6:9).

hands, laying on of A symbolic ritual: 1. Of divine blessing (Matt. 19:13–15), sometimes accompanied by the gift of the Holy Spirit (Acts 19:6). 2. Of divine healing (Mark 7:32). 3. Of consecration of a man for a specific office (Acts 13:2, 3; 1 Tim. 4:14).

4. Of dedication of an animal as for sacrifice (Lev. 16:21).

Hannah The wife of Elkanah and mother of Samuel. For many years, Hannah prayed for a child, promising God that she would dedicate him to the Lord's service. Samuel, who became a great judge, priest, and prophet, was God's answer to her prayers (1 Sam. 1:11–17, 22).

Hanukkah Hebrew word for "dedication." *See* Feast of Dedication.

hap Chance (Ruth 2:3).

haply Perchance, perhaps (Mark 11:13).

Haran A city of N Mesopotamia, on one of the main trade routes between Babylon and the Mediterranean Sea; home of Abraham and his father Terah (Gen. 11:31, 32; 12:4, 5); home of Jacob and his wives, Leah and Rachel (Gen. 28:10; 29:4–6).

harp A stringed musical instrument (1 Sam. 16:23).

haughty Overbearing; proud (Prov. 16:18).

Hazael A Syrian official whom the prophet Elijah anointed king of Syria at God's command (1 Kin. 19:15); sent by Ben-hadad, king of Syria, to the prophet Elisha to ask whether the king would recover from an illness; assassinated Ben-hadad and took the throne (2 Kin. 8:7–15); fought against God's people when the Lord's anger "was kindled against Israel" (2 Kin. 13:3).

heart The physical organ thought of as being the seat of the affections (Ps. 51:17).

heaven A term sometimes used for "God" (Luke 15:18).

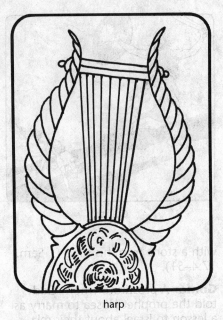

harp

heaven; heavens 1. The sky; the space in which the sun, the moon, and the stars move; the firmament (Gen. 1:8). 2. The place where God, the risen Christ, the angels, and the saints reside; the future home of the redeemed (Is. 65:17).

heaven, kingdom of Used throughout the Gospel of Matthew for "kingdom of God" (Matt. 3:2).

heavenly host *See* host, heavenly.

Hebrews The descendants of Eber (Gen. 10:21); sometimes used interchangeably with "Israelites."

Hebron An ancient city in the mountains of Judah, 19 mi. S of Jerusalem. Here Abraham purchased a cave for a family burial place (Gen. 23:1–20). David's capital city for the first seven and one-half years of his reign (2 Sam. 2:1—5:5).

help meet Companion (Gen. 2:18).

helve Wooden handle of a tool (Deut. 19:5).

heresy False doctrine or teaching which denies the truth about God or Jesus Christ. In 2 Corinthians, Paul spoke against "false apostles" and "deceitful workers" who claimed to be "apostles of Christ" (2 Cor. 11:13); in 1 John, the writer also condemned a group known as the gnostics, who denied that Jesus was the Son of God (1 John 2:22).

Hermon, Mount "Sacred mountain." The highest mountain in the area (9,232 feet), which marks the N boundary of Canaan; the major source of the Jordan River because of its melting snows and glaciers. Some scholars think Jesus' transfiguration took place near Caesarea Philippi, at the southern base of Mount Hermon.

Hermon, Mount

Herod 1. Ruler of Jewish Palestine under Rome (37–4 B.C.); sent the wise men to search out the infant Jesus (Matt. 2:1–9). 2. **Herod Antipas:** Tetrarch of Galilee (4 B.C.–A.D. 39); put John the Baptist to death (Matt. 14:1–12).

Hezekiah The name of four persons in the OT, one of whom was king of Judah (715–687 B.C.; 2 Kin. 18—20).

highminded Proud, haughty (Rom. 11:20).

Hinnom, Valley of A deep, narrow, curving valley at the south end of Jerusalem (Josh. 18:16), used as a garbage dump where waste and dead animals were burned.

Hiram A king of Tyre and friend of both David and Solomon (2 Sam. 5:11); furnished cedar wood from the famous Cedars of Lebanon and workmen to help David build his palace; sent supplies and skilled laborers to help Solomon build the temple in Jerusalem.

Hittites A people of the ancient world who lived in Asia Minor between 1900 and 1200 B.C.; spread into N Syria and later into the land promised Abraham; had to be driven out when Israel conquered Canaan under Joshua (Ex. 3:8). The most famous Hittite was Uriah, the husband of Bath-sheba. David had Uriah killed in battle so he could marry Bath-sheba.

holpen Past participle of "help" (Luke 1:54).

Holy Spirit *See* Spirit, Holy.

Holy Trinity *See* Trinity.

Holy Week The week before Easter.

honour To esteem; to give respect (Ex. 20:12).

Horeb, Mount A sacred mountain (Ex. 3:1) which may be the same mountain as Mount Sinai.

Hosea A prophet of Israel; the first of the 12 Minor Prophets of the OT.

host, heavenly 1. The celestial bodies—the sun, moon, and stars (Deut. 4:19). 2. The mighty army in God's service, including the angels (Luke 2:13).

Hosts, LORD of God, first as leader of the armies of Israel (1 Sam. 17:45), then as leader of the "heavenly host" (Is. 47:4).

hough To hamstring, or cut the tendons in the back of the foot (Josh. 11:6).

house 1. A dwelling place (Ex. 20:17). 2. A family group; a nation (Matt. 12:25).

husbandman Farmer (Zech. 13:5).

husks Pods (Luke 15:16).

hypocrite A person who pretends to be what he or she is not. In the Greek theater of NT times, a hypocrite was an actor who wore a mask and played a part on the stage. **hypocrisy** Jesus spoke against the hypocrisy of many persons who opposed Him, especially the scribes and Pharisees, who tried to give the appearance of being godly, but were actually blind to the truth of God (Matt. 23:28, 29).

I

idol A false god; an image or figure regarded as an object of worship (Lev. 19:4).

image A likeness; an idol (Ex. 20:4).

Immanuel A Hebrew name meaning "God with Us," used by Isaiah in foretelling the birth of the Messiah (Is. 7:14).

implead To sue or bring charges against (Acts 19:38).

impotent Helpless (John 5:3).

Incarnation The taking by God of human characteristics in the Person of Jesus; God's presence on earth.

incontinency Lack of self-control (1 Cor. 7:5).

incontinent Without self-control (2 Tim. 3:3).

indite Express freely (Ps. 45:1).

inerrancy Free from error (John 17:17).

iniquity Sin; wickedness; see sin (Ps. 25:11).

injurious Abusive (1 Tim. 1:13).

inquisition Inquiry (Deut. 19:18).

intercession A plea on behalf of another; for example, Christ's prayer for His followers (John 17:6–26).

intermeddle Mix, mingle (Prov. 14:10).

inwards Internal organs (Ex. 29:17).

Isaac The son of Abraham and Sarah, and half brother of Ishmael; by his wife Rebekah he was the father of Jacob and Esau (Gen. 21:1–12).

Isaiah A prophet of Israel; the first book of the OT Major Prophets.

Ishmael The name of six persons in the OT, one of them Abraham's son by Hagar (Gen. 16).

Israel The name that Jacob received after his mysterious struggle at Jabbok (Gen. 32:22–30); also the name of the whole people descended from him. After the separation into two kingdoms under Jeroboam, the name was confined to the northern kingdom of the ten tribes.

Israelites A name applied to Israel (the people); also called "Hebrews," mostly by foreigners, as was the name "Jews"; the latter arose at the time when Judah, after the fall of the northern kingdom, represented the entire people.

Issachar The ninth son of Jacob, the fifth by Leah (Gen. 30:17, 18); ancestor of the tribe of Issachar.

J

Jacob Son of Isaac and Rebekah; younger twin brother of Esau; father of the people of Israel. Gained by trickery the blessing meant for Esau; married Leah and Rachel, the daughters of his uncle Laban; received the name Israel; finally found refuge in Egypt with his favorite son, Joseph (Gen. 25:21—49:33).

Jacob's Well An ancient well near Shechem and Mount Ebal and Gerizim in central Palestine; dug by hand and crude tools; site of a conversation between Jesus and a Samaritan woman, in which He told her how to find "living water" (John 4:5–10).

James The name of several persons in the NT. 1. "The Elder," son of Zebedee and brother of John; one of the 12 apostles; martyred under Herod Agrippa (Matt. 4:21). 2. The son of Alphaeus, also one of the 12 apostles (Matt. 10:3). 3. One of the sons of Mary; known as "the Less" (Mark 15:40). Tradition regards James (3) to be the same person as James (2). 4. The father of Judas (Luke 6:16). 5. "The brother of the Lord"; a pillar of the church at Jerusalem; called "James the Just"; traditionally the author of the Epistle of James (Matt. 13:55).

jangling Useless talk or discussion (1 Tim. 1:6).

jealous Envious; suspicious; full of zeal. When used of God, jealousy describes either His anger against His unfaithful people or His zeal to protect His persecuted people (Ex. 20:5).

Jehovah The LORD; God. Used by some Bible translators for the name of the covenant God of Israel (Ex. 6:3).

Jephthah A warrior of Gilead; sacrificed his daughter in fulfillment of a vow (Judg. 11:1—12:7).

Jeremiah The name of ten persons in the OT, one of them the prophet Jeremiah (c. 626–580 B.C.). His prophecies, visions, and life story are narrated in the second book of the OT Major Prophets, which bears his name. The almond rod and the boiling pot (1:11–19); the potter's wheel (18:2–10); the good and bad figs (24); Baruch records Jeremiah's prophecies (36:4–32).

Jericho An ancient city at the S end of the Jordan Valley; the fall of the city is told in Joshua 6:1–25.

Jeroboam 1. The first king of Israel (c. 922–901 B.C.); son of Nebat (1 Kin. 11:26—14:20). 2. King of Israel (c. 786–747 B.C.); son and successor of Joash (2 Kin. 14:23–29).

Jerusalem The chief city of Palestine; most sacred city of both Jews and Christians; mentioned under one name or another (Shalem; Salem; City of David; Moriah; Jebus; Zion; Ariel) in about 40 of the 66 books of the Bible. David captured the city (2 Sam. 5:6–9) and made it his capital; brought the ark of the testimony to the city (2 Sam. 6:1–17). Solomon built the temple and other buildings there (1 Kin. 5—7). Captured by Nebuchadnezzar (Jer. 39); rebuilt by

Ezra and Nehemiah. Several events in the life of Jesus occurred there: His presentation in the temple (Luke 2:22–38); the cleansing of the temple (John 2:13–25); the conversation with Nicodemus (John 2:23; 3:1–21); and the events of the last week of His life (Matt. 21—28).

Jesse Son of Obed; grandson of Boaz and Ruth; father of David (1 Sam. 16:1–13; 17:12ff).

Jesus Christ The personal name of the One whose title gave its name to the Christian faith. Since "Jesus" was a fairly common name in the first century, distinguishing phrases were used when referring to Him (Jesus of Nazareth; Jesus, Son of David; Christ Jesus; the Messiah Jesus; and Jesus Christ). The four Gospels (the NT books of Matthew, Mark, Luke, and John) detail His life and ministry.

Job Chief character in the OT Book of Job; unknown otherwise.

Joel The name of several persons in the OT, including the prophet, son of Pethuel, author of the second book of the 12 Minor Prophets.

John The name of five persons in the NT, among them: 1. **John the apostle:** A son of Zebedee, brother of James (Matt. 4:21); sometimes called "the beloved disciple" and "Saint John"; traditional author of the Fourth Gospel, the three epistles of John, and the Book of Revelation. 2. **John the Baptist:** The son of Elisabeth and Zacharias (Luke 1:5–25, 57–66); a prophet, called the forerunner of Jesus (John 1:15–28); baptized Jesus (Matt. 3:13–17); imprisoned by Herod and beheaded (Matt. 14:3–12). 3. **John Mark:** *See* Mark.

Jonah The name of two persons of the OT, one of whom was the prophet about whom the fifth book of the 12 Minor Prophets is written. Swallowed by a great fish (Jon. 1:17—2:10).

Jonah

Jonathan The name of 15 persons in the OT, one of whom was the oldest son of Saul; David's friend (1 Sam. 13:2; 14:1–45; 19:1–7; 20).

Jordan The chief river of Palestine, flowing from the slopes of Mount Hermon through Lake Huleh and the Sea of Galilee to the Dead Sea. The waters were miraculously stopped for the Israelites to pass (Josh. 3:14—4:24). Jesus was baptized there (Matt. 3:13).

Jordan

Joseph: Joses The name of 14 persons in the Bible, among them:

1. The son of Jacob and Rachel (Gen. 30:22–24); his coat of many colors (Gen. 37:3); sold into Egypt by his brothers (Gen. 37:18–36); imprisoned on false accusations (Gen. 39:7–23); interpreted Pharaoh's dreams, thus gaining favor (Gen. 41:1–36); as administrator of Egypt (Gen. 41:37—50:26); his brothers come to him for food (Gen. 42—45). 2. The husband of Mary mother of Jesus; resident of Nazareth; descendant of David (Matt. 1:16–25). 3. **Joseph of Arimathaea:** A member of the Sanhedrin; buried the body of Jesus on his own property (Matt. 27:57–60).

Joshua; Jeshua The name of several persons in the OT, the most important being Joshua, son of Nun, the main character in the Book of Joshua. This book tells the story of Joshua who became the leader of the Israelites after Moses died. His miraculous crossing of the Jordan (Josh. 3:14—4:24); conquest of Jericho (Josh. 6:1–21).

Josiah One of the few good kings of Judah; son of Amon and grandson of Manasseh (2 Kin. 21:23—23:30); became king at the age of 8; found the Book of the Law while the house of the Lord was being repaired (2 Chr. 34:14); read the Book to the people of Judah (2 Chr. 34:29–32), resulting in repentance and change.

jot The least bit; smallest letter (Matt. 5:18).

Judaea An area of SW Palestine; formerly called Judah.

Judah The fourth son of Jacob, by Leah (Gen. 29:31, 35); ancestor of the tribe of Judah.

Judas The name of six persons in the NT, including: 1. A brother of Jesus (Matt. 13:55). *See* Jude, The General Epistle of. 2. **Judas Iscariot** One of the 12 apostles; the betrayer of Jesus (Matt. 26:20–25, 47–50). 3. The brother of James; one of the 12 apostles (Luke 6:16). *See* Thaddaeus. 4. **Judas Barsabas** A Jewish Christian (Acts 15:22, 27, 32).

Jude, The General Epistle of This NT letter designates its author as a "servant of Jesus Christ, and brother of James." *See* Judas (1).

judge To decide; form an opinion (Matt. 7:1).

judge One who forms an opinion. In the OT Book of Judges, one chosen by God to save the people from foreign oppressors (or enemies); a military leader with power to make laws and power to take care of national affairs and to make sure laws are obeyed (Ex. 2:14).

Judge God; Christ (Gen. 18:25).

justified The way sinful human beings are made acceptable to a holy God. Christianity is different from all other religions because of its teaching of being justified by grace (Rom. 3:24)—an act of love from God to undeserving sinners. We can have grace and be justified when we believe and have faith that Jesus died on the cross to save us from our sins (Rom. 3:25–30; 4:3, 5, 9; John 6:28, 29).

keeper One who guards or takes care of someone or something (Gen. 4:9).

kerchief Veil (Ezek. 13:18).

kick against the pricks Useless resistance (Acts 9:5).

kidneys The best of (Deut. 32:14).

Kidron Valley A very important valley E of the walls of Jerusalem and extending all the way to the Dead Sea; site of Nehemiah's inspection of the broken-down walls of Jerusalem (Neh. 2:13–15); site of a common burial ground (2 Kin. 23:6); dumping ground for ashes of idols (1 Kin. 15:13); Jesus crossed the valley to go to the Garden of Gethsemane to pray just before He was arrested and crucified (John 18:1).

king A chief ruler; among ancient peoples, a religious leader often held to be divine. God and Jesus Christ are called "King" (Ps. 5:2; 1 Tim. 6:15).

kingdom of God The eternal sovereignty or kingly rule of God, manifested in its acceptance by men on earth and the hope for the future; the central theme of Jesus' teaching. The phrase does not occur in the OT, but the idea is present in "Your kingdom," "My kingdom," etc., which are also sometimes used in the NT. "Kingdom of heaven" is used in Matthew's gospel; "kingdom of his dear Son" (Col. 1:13); "kingdom of our Lord and Saviour Jesus Christ" (2 Pet. 1:11).

knop Ornamental knob (Ex. 25:31).

L

Laban Brother of Rebekah and father-in-law of Jacob; lived near Haran where Abraham once lived; instrumental in two important marriages—Isaac to Rebekah (Gen. 24) and Jacob to Leah and Rachel (Gen. 29).

ladder A framework of uprights and crosspieces on which one may go up or down. Jacob dreams of a ladder to heaven (Gen. 28:12).

lade Load; weigh down (Luke 11:46).

lamb The young of a sheep, commonly used as the sacrificial animal of the Passover (Is. 53:7).

Lamb (of God) Christ, whose sacrificial death removed the sins of the world. By extension of "lamb" as the most common victim of OT sacrifices, particularly the "Passover." Christ, our Passover (John 1:29, 36; 1 Cor. 5:7).

lampstand Particularly the seven-branched lampstand of the tabernacle and the temple, and the symbolic one of Revelation (Ex. 25:31; Rev. 1:12).

lampstand

lasciviousness Unbridled passions (Eph. 4:19).

Last Supper The last meal eaten by Jesus with His disciples, on the night before His crucifixion.

laver A basin in which priests washed their hands for purification purposes while serving at the altar of the tabernacle or temple; made by Moses so Aaron and the priests could wash their hands and feet before offering sacrifices (Ex. 30:18–21). Ten brass (bronze) lavers, decorated with lions, oxen, and cherubim, were made by Hiram for Solomon's temple (1 Kin. 7:27–39).

law Rules of conduct or behavior; particularly rules given by God to Moses by which the Israelites were to live and which were defined in the Pentateuch, the Law of Moses (Ps. 19:7).

Lazarus 1. The beggar in a parable told by Jesus (Luke 16:19–31). 2. A friend of Jesus; brother of Martha and Mary (John 11:1–44; 12:1–11).

Leah Oldest daughter of Laban; Jacob's first wife to whom were born six of his sons (Gen. 29:16—30:21).

leaven Yeast or other fermenting agent used to make bread rise. It was forbidden to the Israelites in all offerings made with fire (Lev. 2:11; 6:17) and at the Passover (Ex. 12:17–19).

Lebanon A nation just N of Israel (ancient Phoenicia in Bible times); named for the snow-capped range of mountains running the entire length of the country; has been conquered by the Egyptians, Assyrians, Persians, Greeks, Romans, Arabs, and Turks; famous for the Cedars of Lebanon, the wood of which was used in Solomon's tem-ple and palace. Well-known cities include Byblos, from which we get the word "Bible," Sidon, and Tyre (Gen. 10:19; Matt. 15:21–28; Mark 7:24–31).

Lent The forty weekdays that come before Easter; a period of fasting and repentance in Christian churches.

leopard A wild animal of the cat family (Is. 11:6).

Levi; Levites Third son of Jacob and Leah (Gen. 29:31, 34); ancestor of the tribe of Levites, who were charged with the care of the taber-nacle and the temple.

Leviticus The third book of the OT; it deals mainly with the priests and their duties.

libertines Freed men (former slaves) (Acts 6:9).

lieutenant A provincial ruler (Ezra 8:36).

life The union of body and soul. Christ is called the "Prince of life" (Acts 3:15).

Lights, Feast of *See* Dedication, Feast of.

lilies Flowering plants that grow from bulbs (Matt. 6:28).

log A measure of oil—approximate-ly half a pint (Lev. 14:10).

longsuffering Slow to anger (Ex. 34:6).

lord One who has authority over persons or things; hence, **Lord:** God, as the supreme authority; Jesus, as leader during His ministry and as the Son of God. When large and small capitals are used for Lord, the original Hebrew reads YHWH (Deut. 6:4).

Lord of Hosts *See* Hosts, Lord of.

Lord's Day Sunday (Rev. 1:10).

Lord's Prayer The prayer, taught by Jesus to His disciples, that begins "Our Father" (Matt. 6:9–13; Luke 11:2–4).

Lord's Supper 1. Holy Communion (1 Cor. 11:20). 2. Last Supper.

lost Mislaid; not to be found (Luke 15:8–10).

Lot The nephew of Abraham who came with him to Canaan (Gen. 11:27—13:12). Saved from Sodom's destruction (Gen. 19:1–38). His wife was turned into a pillar of salt (Gen. 19:26).

love A deep affection; devotion (Prov. 10:12).

lucre Dishonest gain (1 Sam. 8:3).

Luke Author of the Book of Luke and the Acts of the Apostles; a Gentile, the only non-Jewish writer of a NT book; a laborer with the apostle Paul, who accompanied him on parts of the second and third missionary journeys and the journey to Rome (2 Tim. 4:11; Philem. 24); a physician by profession (Col. 4:14).

lunatick A person who has seizures (Matt. 4:24).

Lydia A prosperous businesswoman from the city of Thyatira in W Asia Minor (Turkey), a seller of purple cloth; lived in Philippi in N Greece, where she heard Paul preach about Jesus and became the first convert to Christianity in Europe (Acts 16:14, 15, 40).

Lystra A city of Lycaonia in central Asia Minor (Turkey); home of Timothy (Acts 16:1, 2). Paul preached and healed here on his first and second missionary jour-

neys, was stoned and left for dead (Acts 14:6–21; 2 Tim. 3:11).

M

Macedonia A mountainous country N of Greece, which Paul visited on his missionary journeys after receiving his "Macedonian call" (Acts 16:9); at Philippi, the first European convert to Christianity was Lydia, a businesswoman (Acts 16:14, 15, 40). Philip II of Macedon, father of Alexander the Great, established his capital at Philippi and made Macedon internationally important.

Machpelah The name of a field, a cave, and the surrounding land that Abraham bought as a burial place for his wife, Sarah, from Ephron the Hittite. Abraham, Sarah, Isaac, Rebekah, Jacob, and Leah are all buried in this cave (Gen. 49:31; 50:13). The modern city of Hebron was built around this site, now covered by a large Muslim mosque.

Magi The wise men who came to worship the infant Jesus (Matt. 2:1–12); because they offered three gifts, it is often assumed that there were three Magi.

maker One who brings into being; creator; **Maker:** God (Heb. 11:10).

Malachi An OT prophet, author of the last book of the OT, one of the 12 Minor Prophets.

mammon Money or riches (Matt. 6:24).

man A male human being; the whole human race (Num. 23:19).

Manasseh 1. Joseph's eldest son, born in Egypt (Gen. 41:50, 51). Like his younger brother, Ephraim, Manasseh was half Hebrew and half

Egyptian. Both of Joseph's sons were "adopted" by Jacob and became two of the heads of the tribes of Israel. 2. King of Judah (2 Kin. 21:1–18); reigned longer than any of the Israelite kings, but was the most wicked; rebuilt the altars to idols that had been destroyed by King Hezekiah and even sacrificed his own son to the heathen god Molech; deported to Babylon where he repented (2 Chr. 33:11–13); tried to introduce reforms when he returned, but was opposed by his wicked son Amon, who succeeded him.

mar To damage beyond repair (Jer. 13:9).

mark A sign (Gen. 4:15).

Mark; John Mark Son of Mary of Jerusalem; companion of Paul and other early Christian missionaries; the traditional author of the Second Gospel (Acts 12:12, 25; 15:37).

marriage The union of one man and one woman. Explained by Jesus (Mark 10:6–9).

martyr A witness. Because the early Christians often suffered for their faith, the word soon came to mean one who suffered or died because of his witness to Christ. The apostle Paul called Stephen a martyr (Acts 22:20); the Book of Revelation mentions "the martyrs of Jesus" (Rev. 17:6).

Mary The name of seven persons in the NT, among them: 1. The mother of Jesus (Matt. 1:16, 18–25). 2. **Mary Magdalene:** A Galilean follower of Jesus (Matt. 27:55, 56, 61; Mark 15:40, 47; 16:1). 3. The sister of Martha and Lazarus (Luke 10:38–42). 4. The mother of James "the Less" (Matt. 27:55, 56, 61).

martyr

5. The mother of John Mark (Acts 12:12).

master A male person in authority; one who controls someone or something; owner (Luke 16:13).

Matthew One of the 12 apostles; called "Levi the son of Alphaeus" in Mark 2:14; traditional author of the First Gospel.

maul A heavy metal club (Prov. 25:18).

maw An animal's stomach (Deut. 18:3).

measure A certain amount; capacity (Luke 6:38).

mediator One who acts as a go-between in making an agreement between two people or two groups. Moses is so called (Gal. 3:19) in making the covenant at Sinai. Christ is called the "one mediator between God and men" (1 Tim. 2:5).

meditate To study; contemplate, think about (Ps. 1:2).

meek Humble; gentle (Matt. 5:5).

Megiddo A fortified, walled city at the foot of the Carmel mountain range in N Israel, overlooking the Valley of Jezreel where the last battle between good and evil will be fought (Rev. 16:16); a chariot city for Kings Solomon and Ahab; site of many important OT battles. Megiddo is another name for Armageddon.

Melchizedek A king of Salem (Jerusalem) and priest of the Most High God (Gen. 14:18–20; Heb. 5:6–11); appeared and disappeared somewhat mysteriously in the Book of Genesis; bestowed a blessing on Abraham and praised God for giving him a victory in battle. Melchizedek is seen as a type (symbolic figure) of Christ in both Psalm 110 and the Book of Hebrews.

"Mene, Mene, Tekel, Upharsin" Means "numbered, numbered, weighed, and divided." An inscription that appeared on the wall of the palace of King Belshazzar in Babylon, written by a mysterious hand during a feast (Dan. 5:1–29). The king ordered that the gold vessels taken from the temple of Jerusalem be brought in for the guests to use in eating and drinking. When the words appeared on the wall, Daniel was called in to interpret. Daniel told the king that God had weighed him on the scales of righteousness, and he did not measure up. The kingdom would be divided between his enemies, the Medes and the Persians. That very night, Belshazzar was killed and his kingdom fell.

Mephibosheth A son of Jonathan and grandson of King Saul; only five years old when his father and grandfather were killed on Mount Gilboa in the Battle of Jezreel (2 Sam. 4:4); dropped by his nurse and crippled for the rest of his life (2 Sam. 4:4); treated kindly by King David because of an agreement

made between the king and his father, Jonathan (2 Sam. 9:7–13).

merciful Forgiving; unwilling to punish (Ps. 67:1).

mercy Forgiveness or kindness, particularly to a wrongdoer (Ezra 3:11).

mercy seat Literally, "covering." The lid of the ark of the testimony, from above which God spoke to His people (Ex. 25:22).

merry Joyous; happy (Prov. 15:13).

Meshach The Babylonian name of one of Daniel's friends (Dan. 1:7; 3:12).

Mesopotamia "Land between the rivers." A region between the Tigris and Euphrates Rivers in the modern countries of Iraq and Iran; the "cradle of civilization"; traditional site of the Garden of Eden; Ur of the Chaldees is located in the S part of the region (Acts 7:2).

Messiah Literally, "anointed one"; one sent by God to save others. In Hebrew belief, the coming savior of the Jewish people; in Christianity, Jesus.

mete Measure (Ex. 16:18).

meteyard A measurement of length (Lev. 19:35).

Methuselah Noah's grandfather; lived for 969 years, the oldest person mentioned in the Bible (Gen. 5:27).

Micah A Judean prophet, who lived at the same time as Isaiah, whose prophecies appear in the OT Book of Micah, the sixth of the 12 Minor Prophets.

mighty Powerful; very strong (Luke 24:19).

minish Reduce (Ex. 5:19).

ministry God's service (Acts 6:4).

miracle An event that exceeds the known laws of nature and science. Usually an act of God done through humans. The OT miracles include:

ten plagues of Egypt (Ex. 7:14—12:30)
parting of the Red Sea (Ex. 14:21–31)
feeding with bread from heaven (Ex. 16:14–35)
walls of Jericho fall (Josh. 6:1–21)
strength of Samson (Judg. 14:1—16:30)
Elijah taken by a whirlwind (2 Kin. 2:11)
Elisha reviving a dead child (2 Kin. 4:18–37)
three men saved from fiery furnace (Dan. 3:19–27)
Daniel saved from lions (Dan. 6:16–23)
Jonah saved (Jon. 1:10—2:10)

The NT miracles of Jesus include:

the leper cured (Matt. 8:2, 3; Mark 1:40–42; Luke 5:12, 13)
centurion's servant healed (Matt. 8:5–13; Luke 7:1–10)
the storm stilled (Matt. 8:23–26; Mark 4:35–39; Luke 8:22–24)
devils entered into swine (Matt. 8:28–32; Mark 5:1–13; Luke 8:26–32)
feeding the 5,000 (Matt. 14:15–21; Mark 6:35–44; Luke 9:10–17; John 6:1–14)
Jesus walks on the sea (Matt. 14:25–27; Mark 6:48–51; John 6:19–21)
ten lepers cleansed (Luke 17:11–19)
Lazarus raised from dead (John 11:38–44)

Other NT miracles include:

the gift of tongues (Acts 2:4–11)
Peter restores Tabitha (Dorcas) (Acts 9:36–41)

Peter's release from prison (Acts 12:5–10)

mite A copper coin of small value (Mark 12:42).

money Riches; coins (1 Tim. 6:10).

money changers Bankers who exchanged one nation's currency (or money) for another, often charging too much for this service. Twice, Jesus found them in the temple, made a whip of cords, and drove them out, along with those who sold oxen, sheep, and doves (John 2:13–16; Matt. 21:12, 13). Jesus said, "Make not my Father's house an house of merchandise" (John 2:16).

money changers

Mordecai The Jewish hero of the OT Book of Esther; Esther's older cousin and guardian.

Moses The great deliverer and law-giver of Israel; born during the oppression of the Israelites in Egypt (Ex. 1:22—2:2); brought up in Pharaoh's house (Ex. 2:5–10); fled to Midian where he lived 40 years (Ex. 2:15–25); called by God from the burning bush (Ex. 3:2–5) to deliver the Israelites; after performing ten miracles of plagues (Ex. 7:14—12:30), he got Pharaoh's consent to take the Israelites from Egypt; led them 40 years through the wilderness; received the Ten Commandments from God (Ex. 20). The OT books of Exodus, Leviticus, Numbers, and Deuteronomy detail his life and deeds.

Most High, the A name used of God (Dan. 4:25).

most holy place The innermost room of the temple or tabernacle in which the ark of the testimony was kept.

mother Female parent (Ex. 20:12).

Mount of Olives A ridge of hills E of Jerusalem, where Jesus was betrayed by Judas on the night before His crucifixion; site of Jesus' triumphal entry into Jerusalem, when He wept over the city because the people would not believe (Luke 19:37–41); traditional location of the tomb of Mary, Jesus' mother; site of Jesus' ascension (Matt. 28:16).

mourn To grieve for (Matt. 5:4).

munition A defensive fortress (Is. 33:16).

murder To kill; cause the death of (Matt. 19:18).

muse Think about (Ps. 143:5).

myrrh An aromatic, resinous substance used in incense and perfumes (Matt. 2:11).

N

Naaman Commander of the Syrian army, who was "a great man with his master [Ben-hadad, king of

Syria] . . . but he was a leper" (2 Kin. 5:1–27); served by a young Israelite girl who had been captured on one of Syria's frequent raids of Israel; encouraged to see the prophet Elisha, who could heal his leprosy; finally, following Elisha's instructions, dipped himself seven times in the Jordan River and was healed; became a worshiper of God.

Nahum A prophet. His prophecies are given in the OT Book of Nahum, the seventh of the 12 Minor Prophets.

name The word by which a person, place, or thing is called (Ex. 20:7).

Naomi The mother-in-law of Ruth, the Moabitess. After her husband and two sons died, Naomi returned to Bethlehem with her daughter-in-law Ruth, who insisted on going with her (Ruth 1:16, 17). Ruth became an ancestor of Jesus Christ when she married her kinsman, Boaz (Ruth 4:21, 22; Matt. 1:5).

Naphtali The sixth son of Jacob, the second born of Bilhah (Gen. 30:7, 8); ancestor of one of the 12 tribes of Israel.

narrow Not wide; small in width (Matt. 7:14).

Nathan A prophet during the reign of David and Solomon; told David that he would not be the one to build the temple at Jerusalem (1 Chr. 17:1–15); confronted David after he had Uriah killed in battle so he could marry Uriah's wife, Bathsheba (2 Sam. 12:9–15).

nation A group of people under one government or sharing the same history (Gen. 12:2).

Nazareth The town in Lower Galilee where Jesus was brought up (Luke 2:39, 51).

Nazarite A person who took a vow to be separated from the world and completely dedicated to God (Num. 6:1–8). They promised not to touch strong drink, not to shave or cut their hair (Samson), not to touch or go near a dead body, not even to bury a relative (Num. 6:5–12; Prov. 20:1; Eph. 5:17, 18).

Nebuchadnezzar King of Babylonia (605–562 B.C.).

neesing Sneezing (Job 41:18).

Nehemiah The name of three persons in the OT, one of whom was the rebuilder of Jerusalem after the Babylonian Exile. The Book of Nehemiah tells his story.

neighbor A person who lives near another (Matt. 19:19).

Nicodemus A wealthy, well-educated, and well-respected Pharisee and member of the Sanhedrin, who probably became a disciple of Jesus; visited Jesus at night to learn more about His teachings (John 3:1–8; 7:50). On this visit Jesus told him he must be "born again" (John 3:7); later gave him the Gospel in one verse: John 3:16. Nicodemus defended Jesus before the Sanhedrin; purchased a hundred pounds of spices to be placed between the folds of the cloth in which Jesus was buried (John 19:39).

night The period of darkness between sunset and sunrise (Gen. 1:5).

Nineveh One of the oldest and greatest cities of Mesopotamia; capital of Assyria; destroyed 612 B.C. (Gen. 10:11, 12; 2 Kin. 19:36; Is. 37:37; Jon. 1:2; 4:11; Nah. 1:1; 2:8; 3:7).

Nisan The name given, after the captivity lasting 70 years, to the former month of Abib—the first month of the Jewish sacred year (Esth. 3:7).

nitre Soda (Prov. 25:20).

Noah The ninth descendant of Adam; the survivor, with his family, of the Great Flood (Gen. 6—9).

noisome Hurtful (Rev. 16:2).

nought, set at Reject as worthless (Mark 9:12).

O

Obadiah The name of 11 persons in the OT, none of whom can be assumed to be the author of the Book of Obadiah, the shortest OT book and fourth of the 12 Minor Prophets.

occurrent Happening (1 Kin. 5:4).

offering Something given in worship. In the OT we find offerings of: 1. **grain:** Made up of unleavened bread, cakes, wafers, or grain mixed with salt and, except when a sin offering, with olive oil (Lev. 2:1–16; 5:11; 6:14–23). Sometimes accepted from the poor as a sin offering in place of the burnt offering (Lev. 5:11–13). 2. **drink:** Made up of wine and used with the grain and burnt offerings, except in the sin and trespass offerings (Num. 6:17; 15:5, 10). 3. **animals,** or **sacrifice:** Cattle, sheep, and goats that were free from blemish (flaws) (Lev. 1:3). These were used with: a. The **burnt offering** in which a male lamb, ram, goat, bull, dove, or pigeon was entirely burned up on the altar (Lev. 1). b. The **sin offering** in which a bull, a male or female goat, a female lamb, a dove,

offering

or a pigeon was given (Lev. 4).
c. The **trespass offering** in which
a ram or lamb was used (Lev. 5:6,
15). d. The **peace offering,**
including the giving of thanks (Lev.
7:12–15), the payment of a vow
(Lev. 7:16–20), and the voluntary or
freewill offering (Lev. 7:16–20); for
these any animal without blemish,
male or female, could be used,
except birds (Lev. 3). In sacrifices,
the term "wave offering" is used of
those parts dedicated to the Lord
by the rite of "waving" (Lev.
7:30–34); and the term "heave
offering" is used of those parts
taken away and set apart for the
Lord (Lev. 7:14).

oil Any of several greasy liquids that
can be burned (Ps. 23:5).

**Olives, Mount of; Olivet, mount
called** A mountain E of Jerusalem
(2 Sam. 15:30; Zech. 14:4). Closely
associated with the last days in the
life of Jesus (in the four Gospels and
Acts 1:12).

ordain 1. To appoint, consecrate,
or set apart as for the ministry (Acts
14:23). 2. To establish (1 Chr. 17:9)

ouches Settings (Ex. 28:11).

outlandish Foreign (Neh. 13:26).

outwent Went faster than (Mark
6:33).

P

Palestine The Greek and Roman
name for Canaan; modern usage
applies the name to the territory
allotted to the 12 tribes of Israel.

palmerworm The chewing locust
(Joel 1:4).

Palm Sunday The Sunday before
Easter; commemorates the tri-
umphal entry of Jesus into Jerusalem
(John 12:12, 13).

parable A short story teaching a
moral lesson. Parables in the NT
include:

lamp under a bushel (Matt.
5:14–16)
unshrunk cloth on an old garment
(Luke 5:36–39)
tares (weeds) among wheat (Matt.
13:24–30)
the mustard seed (Mark 4:30–32)
lost sheep (Luke 15:4–7)
laborers in a vineyard (Matt. 20:1–16)
wise and foolish virgins (Matt.
25:1–13)

parable; lost sheep

the talents (Matt. 25:14–30)
two debtors (Luke 7:41–50)
good Samaritan (Luke 10:30–37)
prodigal son (Luke 15:11–32)
Pharisee and publican (tax collector)
(Luke 18:9–14)
shepherd and the sheep (John
10:1–30)

Passover 1. A seven-day Jewish festival held in March or April, remembering the slaying of the firstborn
just before the Israelites were freed
from slavery in Egypt (Ex. 12); combined with the Feast of Unleavened
Bread, which is held in honor of the
actual flight from Egypt (Ex.
13:3–16). 2. The sacrificial lamb of
the Passover (Ex. 12:11, 21, 27).
Paul refers to Christ as the Passover
lamb (1 Cor. 5:7).

Pastoral Epistles The epistles to
Timothy and Titus are so called
because they deal chiefly with direc-
tions about the work of the pastor
of a church.

pasture Grassy land where cattle
and sheep graze (Ps. 23:2).

Patmos, Isle of A small, rocky,
irregularly shaped island off the
western coast of Asia Minor or modern Turkey; used by the Romans to
hold exiled criminals, one of whom
was the apostle John, who received
messages from the Lord, which
became the Book of Revelation (Rev.
1:9–11).

Paul As Saul, the son of Hebrew
parents, he persecuted the followers
of Jesus (Acts 8:3; Gal. 1:13).
Miraculously converted (Acts 9:1ff);
his name changed to Paul (Acts
13:9); he became the leading missionary of early Christianity. His life
is detailed in the NT Book of Acts.
He founded many churches in Asia
Minor and Greece and carried on

extensive correspondence with
them.

peace Freedom from turmoil and
war (Eccl. 3:8).

peeled Rubbed bare (Ezek. 29:18).

peep Cheep (Is. 10:14).

Pentecost A Jewish festival on the
fiftieth day after Passover; also
called Feast of Weeks (Lev. 23:15,
16). Observed by the Christian
church as the day on which the gift
of the Holy Spirit was given to the
church (Acts 2:1).

peradventure Perhaps (2 Kin.
2:16).

perish To die; to be destroyed
(John 3:16).

Peter; Simon Peter A fisherman
on the Sea of Galilee who was
called with his brother Andrew by
Jesus (Matt. 4:18–20). He became
the "first" of the 12 apostles (Matt.
10:2) and sometimes spoke for all
the disciples. Jesus changed his
name from Simon to Peter (Matt.
16:18; Mark 3:16; Luke 6:14; John
1:42). His mother-in-law healed by
Jesus (Matt. 8:14, 15); his confession that Jesus is the Christ (Luke
9:20); his denial of Jesus (Luke
22:54–62). The author of two NT
epistles.

Pharaoh A title used as a name of,
or added at the beginning of a
name of, the king of Egypt. Joseph
interprets Pharaoh's dream (Gen.
41:1–36); the Pharaoh of the
Exodus (Ex. 7—14).

Pharisee A member of a strict
Jewish sect, holding the Mosaic Law
(laws given to Moses) and their own
traditions as binding. The parable of
the Pharisee and the publican (Luke
18:9–14).

Pharaoh

Philemon A Christian of Colosse to whom the NT Epistle to Philemon was written by Paul. In the letter Paul asks Philemon to pardon (forgive) Onesimus, a runaway slave whom Paul has converted.

Philip The name of four persons in the NT, among them: 1. The apostle (Matt. 10:3; Acts 1:13). 2. The evangelist (Acts 6:5; 8:5–40; 21:8).

Philippi; Philippians A city of Macedonia where Paul founded his first Christian congregation in Europe. The NT Epistle to the Philippians was written by Paul to the church there.

Philistines The people who lived along the S coast of Palestine; often at war with the Israelites. Goliath was a champion of the Philistines (1 Sam. 17:23–51).

Phoenicia A country W of the Lebanon range and Galilee on the coast of the Mediterranean Sea (Acts 11:19; 15:3; 21:2); its chief cities were Tyre and Sidon.

physician A medical doctor (Matt. 9:12).

Pilate; Pontius Pilate The Roman governor of Judaea (A.D. 26–36); the judge in the trial and execution of Jesus (Luke 23:1–25; John 18:28—19:16).

pillar An upright column (Ex. 13:21).

pilled Stripped off the bark (Gen. 30:38).

plank A log; a piece of timber (1 Kin. 6:15).

plowing To break up and turn over earth with a farm implement in order to prepare for planting (Luke 17:7).

plowing

plowshare The cutting blade of a plow (Is. 2:4).

poll 1. Head (Num. 3:47). 2. Cut off the hair (Ezek. 44:20).

pommel Bowl-shaped ornament (2 Chr. 4:12).

poor Needy; having little or no goods or money (Matt. 26:11).

post Messenger; runner (Jer. 51:31).

pransing Galloping (Judg. 5:22).

prayer Words addressed to God (Mark 11:17).

pride Conceit; vanity (Prov. 16:18).

priest A minister. Aaron and his sons, of the tribe of Levi, were appointed to the priesthood at Sinai; the office became hereditary and restricted to that family (Ex. 28:1; 40:12–15).

prince One who has authority or influence; a ruler; hence, **Prince:** the Messiah; Christ (Is. 9:6).

privily Secretly (Matt. 1:19).

privy Share in the knowledge (Acts 5:2).

prodigal Wasteful. The parable of the prodigal son is given in Luke 15:11–32.

prophet A man called by God to be His spokesman (Deut. 18:18).

propitiation God's merciful removal of the guilt and penalty of sin because of Christ's perfect sacrifice of Himself in our place (Rom. 3:25).

proverb; Proverbs, the Book of A short, meaningful saying about the nature of man and life. Proverbs in the Bible, most of which were written down by Solomon (1 Kin. 4:32), help to explain God's truths for wise and godly living.

psalm; Psalms, the Book of The hymnbook of the Bible—a collection of prayers, poems, and hymns that focus the worshiper's thoughts on God in praise; the longest (150 psalms) book in the Bible. Subjects include God and His creation, war, worship, wisdom, sin and evil, judgment, justice, and the coming of the Messiah. Psalms are grouped by subject—thanksgiving, repentance, praise, confession, messianic, as well as psalms to be sung by pilgrims as they traveled to Jerusalem.

psaltery Lyre (Ps. 57:8).

publican One who collects taxes for a fee (Matt. 10:3; Luke 19:2).

purge Purify (Ps. 51:7).

Purim A Jewish festival celebrating the deliverance of the Hebrew people from massacre (Esth. 9:20–28).

purtenance Inner parts (Ex. 12:9).

quaternion A group of four (Acts 12:4).

quick Alive (Acts 10:42).

quicken Revive; make alive (Eph. 2:5).

R

Rabbi Master; teacher (John 1:38).

Rabbi

Rachel The younger daughter of Laban; Jacob's second wife; mother of Joseph and Benjamin (Gen. 29:1—31:35; 35:16–19).

Rebekah Wife of Isaac; mother of Esau and Jacob (Gen. 24:10–67; 25:20–26).

reconciliation Brought into balance or a right and peaceful relationship with God (2 Cor. 5:19).

redeemer One who buys back, rescues (as from sin), or ransoms. Jesus is called "the Redeemer," through His sacrificial death (Is. 59:20).

Red Sea; Sea of Reeds The body of water between Arabia and Africa; the miraculous parting of the sea (Ex. 14:21–31) enabled the Israelites to escape the Egyptians.

rehearse Declare; recite (Judg. 5:11).

remember To bring to mind again (Ex. 20:8).

repent To feel regret; to change one's mind about (Luke 13:3).

reprobate Disqualified; rejected (2 Tim. 3:8).

resurrection A rising from the dead; a return to life; hence, **Resurrection:** The rising of Christ from the dead (Matt. 28; Mark 16; Luke 24; John 20).

Reuben; Reubenites The firstborn son of Jacob, by Leah (Gen. 29:32); the ancestor of the tribe of Reuben.

revelation The making known of something previously concealed or hidden (Eph. 1:17).

reward To give payment for something done; used particularly of God's blessing upon the obedient and His punishment of the wicked (Luke 6:23).

rich Wealthy; having money or property (Prov. 23:4).

riches Wealth; property; material goods (Prov. 27:24).

riddance Removal (Lev. 23:22).

righteous One who does what is right; a virtuous person (Ps. 1:6).

righteousness Virtue; right action; particularly, conformity (obedience) to God's will (Matt. 5:6).

ringstraked Having bands of color around the body (Gen. 30:35).

rock A mass of stone; anything hard like a rock (Ps. 31:3).

Rock The Lord (Ps. 18:2).

Rome; Romans The capital of the Roman Empire; Christianity probably came to Rome early in the apostolic age. Paul wrote the NT Epistle to the Romans to the Christian community there.

rooster Adult, male chicken (Matt. 26:34, 75).

Ruth A Moabite woman who became an ancestress of David through her second marriage, to Boaz. Her story of devotion is told in the OT Book of Ruth.

S

sabbath The day of rest ordained by God. Among Jews, the seventh day, Saturday (Ex. 20:8); among Christians, the first day of the week (Sunday), the day of divine worship (1 Cor. 16:2).

sackbut A bass trumpet, similar to a trombone (Dan. 3:5).

sackcloth and ashes Wearing rough clothing and scattered with ashes as a sign of mourning (Esth. 4:3).

sacrifice An offering, usually of the life of a person or an animal, made to God (Mark 12:33).

Sadducees The socially prominent or aristocratic party of the Jews at the time of Christ. They cooperated with the Roman officials so that they would be popular with those in power.

safeguard Safekeeping (1 Sam. 22:23).

salt A seasoning; a preservative (Matt. 5:13).

salvation Deliverance from evil, danger, or trouble; God's gift, through Christ, to save men's souls (Luke 3:6).

Samaria; Samaritans The capital city of the northern kingdom, Israel. Also the name of the territory near the city. The term "Samaritan" is usually applied to a member of a religious sect living in that area. The parable of the good Samaritan told by Jesus (Luke 10:30–37).

Samson A hero of the tribe of Dan, noted for his great strength (Judg. 13—16).

Samuel The last "judge" of Israel; a prophet of the eleventh century B.C. The two OT books of Samuel record his life and deeds and the history of Israel through the reigns of Saul and David. The Lord calls Samuel (1 Sam. 3); Samuel anoints David (1 Sam. 16:11–13).

sanctify To set apart as holy; to consecrate to religious use; to make holy (Gen. 2:3).

sanctuary A building or place set apart for religious worship; in the OT, the tabernacle (Ex. 25:8) or the temple (1 Chr. 22:19).

Sanhedrin A council or assembly, the highest ruling body and court of justice among the Jewish people in the time of Jesus; headed by the high priest of Israel; composed of 71 members, among whom were Joseph of Arimathaea (Mark 15:43), Gamaliel, Paul's teacher (Acts 5:34), Nicodemus (John 3:1; 7:50), the high priests, Annas and Caiaphas (Luke 3:2), and Ananias (Acts 23:2); given limited authority over certain religious, civil, and criminal matters involving foreign nations that dominated Israel at various times in its history.

Sarah; Sarai The wife of Abraham; mother of Isaac, the child promised to her by God (Gen. 17:15–21; 18:1–15).

sardine A red precious stone (Rev. 4:3).

Satan The Devil; the adversary or enemy of God and Christ (Mark 1:13).

Saul Son of Kish, of the tribe of Benjamin; first king over Israel. The prophet Samuel anoints him to be king (1 Sam. 10:1); he disobeys the Lord (1 Sam. 15); David enters his service (1 Sam. 16:14–23); he tries to kill David (1 Sam. 19:9, 10); David spares his life (1 Sam. 26:6–24).

Saul of Tarsus *See* Paul.

Saviour Literally, "one who saves or delivers"; Christ, as the One who delivers us from the sins of this life and through whom salvation is obtained; God, as the deliverer of the Israelites from oppression and as the redeemer of all peoples (John 4:42).

scall A scab on the head (Lev. 13:32).

scrip Pouch; small bag (1 Sam. 17:40).

scripture; Scriptures, the Any writing, particularly that of a sacred nature; hence, the Bible. Also "Scriptures"; "Holy Scripture"; "Holy Scriptures" (John 5:39).

seek To search for; to try to find (Matt. 7:7).

selfsame The very same (Gen. 7:13).

Sermon on the Mount Name given to a talk by Jesus while teaching His disciples in the hill country of Galilee early in His ministry (Matt. 5:3—7:27). It includes a series of blessings, the Beatitudes (5:3–12); the Lord's Prayer (6:9–13); and the Golden Rule (7:12). A similar sermon in Luke 6:17–49 is called the "Sermon on the Plain."

serpent A snake; in biblical usage, many times a synonym for "Satan" (2 Cor. 11:3).

sever To set apart; separate (Lev. 20:26).

Shadrach The Babylonian name of one of Daniel's companions (Dan. 1:7; 3:12).

shambles Meat market (1 Cor. 10:25).

shamefacedness Modesty (1 Tim. 2:9).

shapen Created; formed (Ps. 51:5).

Sheba, queen of A queen, probably Arabian, who came to test Solomon's wisdom (1 Kin. 10:1–13; 2 Chr. 9:1–12).

Shem The eldest son of Noah who stands as the ancestor of the Semites generally and of the Hebrews specifically (Gen. 5:32; 9:18–27; 10:21–31; Luke 3:36).

shepherd One who herds and takes care of sheep; by extension, the ruler or king of a people. The

Lord is the shepherd of Israel; Christ is the Good Shepherd (John 10:7–18).

shew 1. Show (Luke 20:47). 2. To proclaim (1 Cor. 11:26).

shoe's latchet Thong or strap to fasten a sandal (John 1:27).

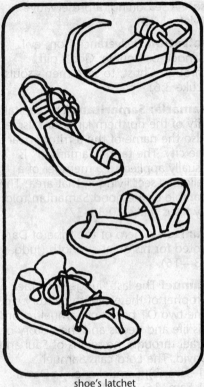

shoe's latchet

Silas; Silvanus One of the earliest of the apostolic missionaries, associated with both Paul (Acts 16:19ff; 1 Thess. 1:1; 2:1, 2) and Peter (1 Pet. 5:12).

Siloam, Pool of A storage pool and tunnel that provided a water supply for the people of Jerusalem, fed by the Gihon Spring; dug through solid rock in the time of King Hezekiah of Judah (2 Chr.

32:30). Water still flows through the tunnel to this day.

silverling A piece of silver (Is. 7:23).

Simeon The name of six persons in the Bible, including: 1. The second son of Jacob, by Leah (Gen. 29:33); ancestor of the tribe of Simeon. 2. A devout man who blessed the infant Jesus when His parents presented Him in the temple (Luke 2:25–35).

similitude Likeness; form (Num. 12:8).

Simon The name of nine persons in the NT, including: 1. **Simon Peter:** *See* Peter (Matt. 16:17). 2. **Simon the Zealot:** Also one of the 12 apostles (Luke 6:15). 3. **Simon the Pharisee,** in whose home Jesus was anointed by the sinful woman (Luke 7:36–50). 4. **Simon the leper,** in whose home Jesus was anointed by Mary (Mark 14:3–9). 5. **Simon of Cyrene,** who was forced to carry Jesus' cross (Matt. 27:32). 6. **Simon the sorcerer,** who offered money to Peter and John for the power of the Holy Spirit (Acts 8:9–24).

sin An offense or disobedience against God (as Adam and Eve in the Garden of Eden); deliberate defiance; wickedness; iniquity; ungodliness (John 1:29).

Sinai, Mount The name of a peninsula, a wilderness, and a mountain. 1. The barren, triangular-shaped peninsula stands between Egypt and Israel. 2. In the wilderness, there are no flowing streams or rivers, only wadis (dry stream-beds, which carry off the occasional rains). 3. The traditional mountain where Moses received the Ten Commandments (Ex. 19:3–20) is in the Sinai range and is called Jebel Musa, the mountain of Moses.

Sinai, Mount

When the Israelites camped there, it was called Sinai (Ex. 19:11), or sometimes called Horeb (Ex. 3:1).

sinful Wicked; full of iniquity (Is. 1:4).

sinner One who commits an offense against God (Ps. 1:1).

sith Since (Ezek. 35:6).

sleight Trickery (Eph. 4:14).

Sodom One of the two cities destroyed by the Lord because of their wickedness (Gen. 19:24–28).

Solomon Son of David and Bath-sheba; third king of Israel; under his reign the kingdom reached its high-est point of wealth and power; noted for his wisdom (1 Kin. 3:16–28) and his gift of expressing himself. The OT books of Proverbs, Ecclesiastes, and Song of Solomon, and Psalms 72 and 127 are attrib-uted to him. He built the temple (1 Kin. 6; 7); was visited by the queen of Sheba (1 Kin. 10:1–13).

son A male child or man as related to his parents; a male descendant (Prov. 10:1).

Son; Son of God The Second Person of the Trinity; Christ (Matt. 3:17; Mark 1:11; Luke 9:35).

son of man Any human being (Ps. 8:4); the prophet Ezekiel (used throughout the OT Book of Ezekiel); in the Gospels, Jesus uses "Son of Man" as a name for Himself, particularly in the passages relating to His second coming.

sons of God Angels (Job 1:6; Dan. 3:25); any human beings, as created in God's image (Hos. 1:10); Christians (Rom. 8:14).

sottish Foolish; stupid (Jer. 4:22).

soul The life principle of a human being; the immortal element of man; the spirit; the living individual (Matt. 16:26).

sow To plant (Luke 12:24).

space A period of time (Ezra 9:8).

spirit That part of person's being thought of as the center of life, the will, thinking, feeling; that part of man that survives death (Ps. 31:5).

Spirit, Holy The Third Person of the Trinity; that divine Spirit, referred to in the OT as "Spirit of the LORD" or "Spirit of God," through which men receive power, particularly effective through Jesus Christ in bringing men into fellowship with God (Eph. 1:13). Also translated "Holy Ghost" rather than "Holy Spirit."

Spirit of the Lord; Spirit of God; Holy Spirit The divine source of all life; a special manifestation of God's divine Presence (Gen. 1:2).

spitefully Shamefully (Matt. 22:6).

spoil Plunder (Ex. 3:22).

stablish Establish (1 Chr. 17:12).

stagger Walk unevenly (Job 12:25).

stead 1. Place (1 Chr. 5:22). 2. On behalf of (2 Cor. 5:20).

Stephen The first Christian martyr; one of the seven men chosen by the apostles for the special "service of tables"; his death was the signal for a general persecution of the Christians (Acts 6:1—8:3).

stew A thick soup (Gen. 25:29–34).

steward A manager of a household or of property; used of Christians, particularly ministers, as guardians of the affairs of God (1 Cor. 4:1).

stomacher An ornamental covering for the stomach and chest (Is. 3:24).

stone A rock; a hard mineral (Matt. 24:2).

straiten Restrict (2 Cor. 6:12).

straitly 1. Tightly (Josh. 6:1); 2. Strictly (Matt. 9:30).

strawed Scattered (Ex. 32:20).

stuff Belongings (Josh. 7:11).

subscribe Sign (Jer. 32:10).

suburbs Pasturelands (Num. 35:7).

succour Help (2 Sam. 8:5).

sufficient Enough; ample (Matt. 6:34).

Supper, Last See Last Supper.

Supper, Lord's See Lord's Supper.

surfeiting Overindulging (Luke 21:34).

swear To declare or promise under oath (Matt. 5:34).

sword A sharp-bladed weapon with a hilt or handle (Heb. 4:12).

synagogue A building where Jewish religious services and schools and other meetings are held (Acts 13:5).

T

tabering Beating (Nah. 2:7).

tabernacle Literally, "tent of meeting"; the portable shelter used by the Israelites as a place of worship (Ex. 25:9).

Tabernacles, Feast of One of the three great joyous festivals of the Jewish year; held in autumn at the end of the harvest; celebrates a renewal of the covenant and recalls the wilderness pilgrimage (Ex. 23:16; Lev. 23:34–36; Deut. 16:13–15). Also called "Feast of Booths" (Lev. 23:42); "the Feast of Ingathering" (Ex. 23:16).

tables Flat stones bearing inscriptions (Ex. 31:18).

tabret Tambourine; small drum (Gen. 31:27).

tache Clasp (Ex. 26:6).

talent A unit of money or of weight. Parable of the talents (Matt. 25:14–30).

target A light shield (2 Chr. 14:8).

Tarsus The birthplace of Saul, who, after his conversion, was called Paul (Acts 9:11; 22:3); chief city of Cilicia, a province in SW Asia Minor or modern Turkey; located on the banks of the Cydnus River, about ten miles from the Mediterranean Sea; a learning center of the world. "I am a man which am a Jew of Tarsus, a city in Cilicia, a citizen of no mean city," declared Paul (Acts 21:39).

Teacher Title, used of Jesus during His ministry (John 13:13).

temper Mix; combine (Ex. 29:2).

temperance Self-control (2 Pet. 1:6).

temple A building for the worship of a deity or god; hence, the temple at Jerusalem. *See* 1 Kin. 5—8 for a description of Solomon's temple.

temple

temptation An attempt to get someone to do something wrong; a test of character (Matt. 6:13).

temptations of Jesus Satan's attempts to get Jesus to sin. *See* Matthew 4:1–11; Luke 4:1–13.

Ten Commandments The ten laws given by God to Moses on Mount Sinai (Ex. 20:1–17).

testimony In OT: the divine law, especially the Ten Commandments; in NT: witness (John 21:24).

Thaddaeus One of the 12 apostles of Jesus (Mark 3:18); also called Lebbaeus (Matt. 10:3) and probably Judas. *See* Judas (3).

thereunto To it, for it (Ex. 32:8).

Thessalonica; Thessalonians An important city of Macedonia where Paul and his helpers founded an early Christian church. The two NT epistles to the Thessalonians were among the earliest written by Paul.

thitherward In that direction (Jer. 50:5).

Thomas One of the 12 apostles; his unbelief in Jesus' resurrection gained him the name "doubting

Thomas" (Matt. 10:3; Mark 3:18; Luke 6:15; John 11:16; Acts 1:13).

thought Anxiety (Matt. 6:28).

Timothy A trusted companion and assistant of Paul, from the early part of Paul's second missionary journey. According to tradition the two epistles to Timothy were written near the close of Paul's life.

tithe The tenth part of one's income paid to support God's work (Lev. 27:30–32).

title An inscribed monument or tomb (2 Kin. 23:17).

tittle Any small stroke in writing (Luke 16:17).

Titus A Gentile Christian associate of Paul (2 Cor. 7:5–7); according to Titus 1:4, 5, Paul wrote the letter bearing his name in order to encourage him in his work in the churches of Crete.

tomb A place of burial (Matt. 23:27).

tomb

Torah Guidance or direction from God to His people for living the covenant relationship—a total way of life; in earlier times, a term referring directly to the first five books of Moses, but came to mean both the hearing and doing of the Law (Deut. 32:46). Later, the Hebrew OT included the books of wisdom and prophets, and this entire collection became known as the Torah.

Transfiguration Jesus' glorious and radiant change in appearance; witnessed by three disciples (Matt. 17:1–9; Mark 9:2–10; Luke 9:28–36).

transgression A sin; disobedience or rebellion against God's will (Rom. 5:14).

treatise Narrative (Acts 1:1).

tribute 1. Tax paid to "buy" peace and security (Num. 31:40). 2. Forced labor (Gen. 49:15).

Trinity The doctrine or belief held by most Christians that there are three divine Persons (Father, Son, and Holy Spirit) united in the one Supreme Divine Being, God. NT teachings (Matt. 12:32; 28:19; Luke 12:10; Acts 2:33; 1 Cor. 12:4–6; 2 Cor. 13:14) support this doctrine.

trow Think; believe (Luke 17:9).

trust To have or put confidence in someone or something (Prov. 3:5).

truth A proven sincerity, fact; righteousness (John 8:32).

turtle Turtledove (Song 2:12).

tutor Guardian (Gal. 4:2).

twain Two (Matt. 19:5).

Tyropoeon Valley A small valley in the city of Jerusalem, which divides hill Ophel, the original City of

David, from the Western Hill, or Upper City.

U

unawares Unexpectedly (Luke 21:34).

uncomely Unpresentable (1 Cor. 12:23).

unction Anointing (1 John 2:20).

unleavened bread Bread baked from unfermented dough, or dough without yeast or "leaven" (Gen. 19:3; Josh. 5:11; 1 Sam. 28:24); the flat bread used in the Passover celebration and the priestly rituals, recalling the Exodus, when the Hebrews left Egypt so quickly that they had no time to wait for the bread to rise (Ex. 12:8, 15–20, 34, 39; 13:6, 7).

unsavoury Tasteless (Job 6:6).

upholden Upheld (Prov. 20:28).

Ur An ancient city on the Euphrates, called "Ur of the Chaldees"; home of Abraham (Gen. 11:28).

usury Lending money at interest (Deut. 23:20).

utter Reveal (Josh. 2:14).

Uzziah The name of three persons in the OT, one of them a king of Judah (c. 783–742 B.C.).

V

vainglory Idle boasting (Phil. 2:3).

vanity Futility; emptiness (Eccl. 1:2).

vex Harass (Num. 20:15).

vexation Troubling (Is. 65:14).

vile Disgusting; worthless (Judg. 19:24).

viper A poisonous snake (Matt. 12:34).

visage Face; appearance (Dan. 3:19).

vision Something seen other than by ordinary sight, as in a dream. God's revelations to the prophets were usually by visions (Dan. 2:19).

voice A sound uttered through the mouth as in speaking (1 Kin. 19:12).

volume Scroll; roll (Ps. 40:7).

W

wages The payment for services (Rom. 6:23).

walk To move by stepping (Ps. 23:4).

want To lack or need (*not* in the sense of "to desire") (Ps. 23:1).

war Fighting with weapons between large groups (Matt. 24:6).

ware Aware; wary (Acts 14:6).

wash To clean with water or other liquid (Luke 7:38).

waster One who destroys (Prov. 18:9).

water The colorless liquid that falls as rain (Mark 1:8).

wax Grow (2 Chr. 24:15).

way The direction; path; man's way of living (Prov. 22:6).

Weeks, Feast of Seven weeks after Passover (Lev. 23:15–21; Deut. 16:9–12). Also called Feast of Harvest (Ex. 23:16). *See* Pentecost.

whit Bit; part (1 Sam. 3:18).

whited sepulchre Whitewashed tomb (Matt. 23:27).

will Desire; something wished (Matt. 6:10).

wine The fermented juice of fruits (Prov. 20:1).

winebibber Heavy drinker of wine (Prov. 23:20).

wise Having good judgment (Prov. 1:5).

wist Knew (Luke 2:49).

wit Learn; know (Gen. 24:21).

witness Someone or something that bears testimony to the truthfulness of a statement or to the occurrence of a happening (Matt. 24:14).

word A spoken sound having meaning (Ex. 20:1).

Word; Word of God; word of the Lord God's revealed will; the Holy Scriptures (Luke 8:21).

Word; Word of God; word of the Lord

Word; Word of God A title of Christ (John 1:1; Rev. 19:13).

work 1. Labor; effort (Gen. 2:2). 2. To labor; to toil (Rom. 8:28).

works Deeds; efforts (Matt. 16:27).

world The earth; the universe (Ps. 50:12).

worry Be or become anxious (Matt. 6:34).

worship To honor; to show reverence for (Matt. 4:10; Luke 4:8).

wot Know (Rom. 11:2).

wrath Great anger, especially God's punishment of sin (1 Thess. 1:10).

wrest Twist; distort (Ps. 56:5).

Y

Yahweh The covenant God of Israel, YHWH in the original Hebrew. According to Jewish custom, because of reverence the divine name was not to be spoken, so the Hebrew words for Lord and God were substituted. Whenever the words LORD and GOD appear in large and small capital letters, the original Hebrew reads YHWH.

yesternight Last night (Gen. 31:29).

Z

Zacchaeus Chief publican (tax collector) of Jericho at the time of one of Jesus' visits (Luke 19:2–8).

Zealot A term used to designate the more radical Jewish rebels against foreign, particularly Roman, rule; one motivated by zeal for the Jewish law.

Zebedee The father of the apostles James and John (Matt. 4:21).

Zebulun The tenth son of Jacob, the sixth by Leah (Gen. 30:19, 20); ancestor of the tribe of Zebulun.

Zechariah; Zacharias The name of 33 persons in the Bible, including: 1. Son of the priest Jehoiada (2 Chr. 24:20, 21). 2. One of the OT Minor Prophets, who lived at the same time as Haggai; urged the rebuilding of the temple (Ezra 5:1; 6:14; Zech. 1:1, 7; 7:1, 8). 3. The father of John the Baptist (Luke 1:5–67; 3:2).

Zedekiah The name of three persons in the OT, including the last king of Judah (c. 597–587 B.C.). Also called Mattaniah.

Zephaniah The name of four persons in the OT, including a prophet during the time of Josiah; his prophecies appear in the OT Book of Zephaniah, the ninth of the 12 Minor Prophets.

Zion; Sion Originally the name of the fortified hill of pre-Israelite Jerusalem; poetically extended to refer to the religious capital of Israel.

God's Word is Good to Keep

"Thy word have I hid in mine heart, that I might not sin against thee."
—Psalm 119:11

God's Word is the most important book we have. This Book helps us understand how God wants us to live: what is right and what is wrong, how we are to treat each other, how we can know God and walk in obedience, and so much more. In "God's Word Is Good to Keep," you will begin the life-long process of putting portions of God's Word in your mind and heart so they will always be with you. God will bring these verses that you've memorized to your mind as you make choices and decisions throughout your life . . . helping you to live wisely. Having God's Word in your heart will help you grow into a strong and mature child of God.

The Books of the Bible [Track 1]

One of the first steps in keeping God's Word is to learn the order of the books of the Bible so that you can begin to find verses and passage with ease.

Old Testament Books

Genesis	Ecclesiastes
Exodus	Song of Solomon
Leviticus	Isaiah
Numbers	Jeremiah
Deuteronomy	Lamentations
Joshua	Ezekiel
Judges	Daniel
Ruth	Hosea
1 Samuel	Joel
2 Samuel	Amos
1 Kings	Obadiah
2 Kings	Jonah
1 Chronicles	Micah
2 Chronicles	Nahum
Ezra	Habakkuk
Nehemiah	Zephaniah
Esther	Haggai
Job	Zechariah
Psalms	Malachi
Proverbs	

New Testament Books

Matthew	1 Timothy
Mark	2 Timothy
Luke	Titus
John	Philemon
Acts	Hebrews
Romans	James
1 Corinthians	1 Peter
2 Corinthians	2 Peter
Galatians	1 John
Ephesians	2 John
Philippians	3 John
Colossians	Jude
1 Thessalonians	Revelation
2 Thessalonians	

Verses to Remember [Track 2]

The entire Bible was written and preserved for your instruction and guidance. God wants you to have answers and help as you live your life. The following verses are a beginning point for allowing God's Word to fill your mind and heart. Try memorizing one new verse each day and reviewing the verses you've already learned, so that God's Word will begin to be in your mind all day, every day.

Day	Reference	Verse	Date Learned
1	Exodus 20:12	¹²Honour thy father and thy mother: that thy days may be long upon the land which the LORD thy God giveth thee.	
2	Leviticus 19:18	¹⁸Thou shalt not avenge, nor bear any grudge against the children of thy people, but thou shalt love thy neighbour as thyself: I am the LORD.	
3	Numbers 6:24–26	²⁴The LORD bless thee, and keep thee: ²⁵The LORD make his face shine upon thee, and be gracious unto thee: ²⁶The LORD lift up his countenance upon thee, and give thee peace.	
4	Deuteronomy 6:5	⁵And thou shalt love the LORD thy God with all thine heart, and with all thy soul, and with all thy might.	

Day	Reference	Verse	Date Learned
5	Joshua 24:15	[15]And if it seem evil unto you to serve the LORD, choose you this day whom ye will serve; whether the gods which your fathers served that were on the other side of the flood, or the gods of the Amorites, in whose land ye dwell: but as for me and my house, we will serve the LORD.	
6	2 Chronicles 16:9	[9]For the eyes of the LORD run to and fro throughout the whole earth, to shew himself strong in the behalf of them whose heart is perfect toward him. Herein thou hast done foolishly: therefore from henceforth thou shalt have wars.	
7	Psalm 27:14	[14]Wait on the LORD: be of good courage, and he shall strengthen thine heart: wait, I say, on the LORD.	
8	Psalm 32:1	[1]Blessed is he whose transgression is forgiven, whose sin is covered.	
9	Psalm 34:18	[18]The LORD is nigh unto them that are of a broken heart; and saveth such as be of a contrite spirit.	
10	Psalm 37:5	[5]Commit thy way unto the LORD; trust also in him; and he shall bring it to pass.	
11	Psalm 46:1	[1]God is our refuge and strength, a very present help in trouble.	
12	Psalm 106:1	[1]Praise ye the LORD. O give thanks unto the LORD; for he is good: for his mercy endureth for ever.	
13	Psalm 119:11	[11]Thy word have I hid in mine heart, that I might not sin against thee.	
14	Psalm 139:23, 24	[23]Search me, O God, and know my heart: try me, and know my thoughts: [24]And see if there be any wicked way in me, and lead me in the way everlasting.	
15	Psalm 145:8	[8]The LORD is gracious, and full of compassion; slow to anger, and of great mercy.	
16	Proverbs 3:11, 12	[11]My son, despise not the chastening of the LORD; neither be weary of his correction: [12]For whom the LORD loveth he correcteth; even as a father the son in whom he delighteth.	
17	Proverbs 4:13	[13]Take fast hold of instruction; let her not go: keep her; for she is thy life.	
18	Proverbs 15:1	[1]A soft answer turneth away wrath: but grievous words stir up anger.	

Day	Reference	Verse	Date Learned
19	Proverbs 17:17	¹⁷A friend loveth at all times, and a brother is born for adversity.	
20	Proverbs 29:25	²⁵The fear of man bringeth a snare: but whoso putteth his trust in the LORD shall be safe.	
21	Ecclesiastes 1:9	⁹The thing that hath been, it is that which shall be; and that which is done is that which shall be done: and there is no new thing under the sun.	
22	Isaiah 40:31	³¹But they that wait upon the LORD shall renew their strength; they shall mount up with wings as eagles; they shall run, and not be weary; and they shall walk, and not faint.	
23	Micah 6:8	⁸He hath shewed thee, O man, what is good; and what doth the LORD require of thee, but to do justly, and to love mercy, and to walk humbly with thy God?	
24	Matthew 5:6	⁶Blessed are they which do hunger and thirst after righteousness: for they shall be filled.	
25	Matthew 5:9	⁹Blessed are the peacemakers: for they shall be called the children of God.	
26	Matthew 6:33	³³But seek ye first the kingdom of God, and his righteousness; and all these things shall be added unto you.	
27	Matthew 7:7	⁷Ask, and it shall be given you; seek, and ye shall find; knock, and it shall be opened unto you.	
28	Matthew 11:28	²⁸Come unto me, all ye that labour and are heavy laden, and I will give you rest.	
29	Mark 10:14	¹⁴But when Jesus saw it, he was much displeased, and said unto them, Suffer the little children to come unto me, and forbid them not: for of such is the kingdom of God.	
30	Luke 6:31	³¹And as ye would that men should do to you, do ye also to them likewise.	
31	Luke 11:28	²⁸But he said, Yea rather, blessed are they that hear the word of God, and keep it.	
32	John 1:12	¹²But as many as received him, to them gave he power to become the sons of God, even to them that believe on his name.	

Day	Reference	Verse	Date Learned
33	John 3:16, 17	[16]For God so loved the world, that he gave his only begotten Son, that whosoever believeth in him should not perish, but have everlasting life. [17]For God sent not his Son into the world to condemn the world; but that the world through him might be saved.	
34	John 13:34, 35	[34]A new commandment I give unto you, That ye love one another; as I have loved you, that ye also love one another. [35]By this shall all men know that ye are my disciples, if ye have love one to another.	
35	John 14:6	[6]Jesus sayeth unto him, I am the way, the truth, and the life; no man cometh unto the Father, but by me.	
36	Acts 20:35	[35]I have shewed you all things, how that so labouring ye ought to support the weak, and to remember the words of the Lord Jesus, how he said, It is more blessed to give than to receive.	
37	1 Corinthians 10:13	[13]There hath no temptation taken you but such as is common to man: but God is faithful, who will not suffer you to be tempted above that ye are able; but will with the temptation also make a way to escape, that ye may be able to bear it.	
38	2 Corinthians 4:8	[8]We are troubled on every side, yet not distressed; we are perplexed, but not in despair.	
39	Galatians 6:9	[9]And let us not be weary in well doing: for in due season we shall reap, if we faint not.	
40	Ephesians 4:2	[2]With all lowliness and meekness, with longsuffering, forbearing one another in love.	
41	Ephesians 4:31, 32	[31]Let all bitterness, and wrath, and anger, and clamour, and evil speaking, be put away from you, with all malice: [32]And be ye kind one to another, tenderhearted, forgiving one another, even as God for Christ's sake hath forgiven you.	
42	Ephesians 6:10	[10]Finally, my brethren, be strong in the Lord, and in the power of his might.	
43	Philippians 4:4	[4]Rejoice in the Lord alway: and again I say, Rejoice.	
44	Philippians 4:6	[6]Be careful for nothing; but in every thing by prayer and supplication with thanksgiving let your requests be made known unto God.	

Day	Reference	Verse	Date Learned
45	Philippians 4:13	[13]I can do all things through Christ which strengtheneth me.	
46	Colossians 3:17	[17]And whatsoever ye do in word or deed, do all in the name of the Lord Jesus, giving thanks to God and the Father by him.	
47	1 Timothy 6:12	[12]Fight the good fight of faith, lay hold on eternal life, whereunto thou art also called, and hast professed a good profession before many witnesses.	
48	James 1:12	[12]Blessed is the man that endureth temptation: for when he is tried, he shall receive the crown of life, which the Lord hath promised to them that love him.	
49	1 Peter 5:7	[7]Casting all your care upon him; for he careth for you.	
50	1 John 1:9	[9]If we confess our sins, he is faithful and just to forgive us our sins, and to cleanse us from all unrighteousness.	
51	1 John 3:7	[7]Little children, let no man deceive you: he that doeth righteousness is righteous, even as he is righteous.	
52	Revelation 1:8	[8]I am Alpha and Omega, the beginning and the ending, saith the Lord, which is, and which was, and which is to come, the Almighty.	

Passages to Remember [Track 3]

The next step in hiding God's Word in your heart is to commit passages of Scripture to memory. Here are some selected passages for you to study. As you read God's Word on your own, mark passages from your personal reading and add them to your list of passages to remember.

Day	Passage	Date Learned
1	Exodus 20:3–10	
2	Exodus 20:11–17	
3	Deuteronomy 6:4–9	
4	Joshua 24:14, 15	
5	Psalm 19:7–14	
6	Psalm 37:23–31	
7	Psalm 40:1–8	
8	Psalm 91:1–16	
9	Proverbs 3:1–8	
10	Proverbs 8:12–21	
11	Proverbs 16:1–9	
12	Proverbs 31:10–31	
13	Isaiah 6:8–11	
14	Isaiah 40:25–31	
15	Matthew 5:1–10	
16	Matthew 5:11–16	
17	Matthew 6:9–13	
18	Matthew 6:19–24	
19	Matthew 7:7–11	
20	Matthew 28:1–8	
21	Matthew 28:18–20	
22	Luke 2:1–10	
23	Luke 2:11–20	
24	Luke 6:13–16	
25	John 1:1–5	
26	John 14:1–7	
27	John 15:1–5	
28	John 15:6–11	

Day	Passage	Date Learned
29	Acts 2:1–4	
30	Romans Road: 3:23; 5:8; 10:9; 10:10; 10:13	
31	Romans 5:1–10	
32	Romans 8:28–33	
33	Romans 8:34–39	
34	2 Corinthians 5:17–21	
35	Galatians 5:22, 23	
36	Galatians 6:1–10	
37	Ephesians 2:4–10	
38	Ephesians 4:1–4	
39	Ephesians 4:25–32	
40	Ephesians 6:1–3	
41	Ephesians 6:10–18	
42	Ephesians 6:13–17	
43	Philippians 2:4–11	
44	Philippians 4:4–8	
45	Philippians 4:9–13	
46	Colossians 3:12–17	
47	1 Thessalonians 4:13–18	
48	1 Timothy 2:1–3	
49	1 Timothy 4:12–16	
50	2 Timothy 3:14–17	
51	James 1:1–8	
52	1 Peter 1:18, 19	

chapters to Remember [Track 4]

The following chapters are also good portions of Scripture to hide in your heart. Try learning one chapter each month for 12 months, continuing to review what you've already committed to memory. When you've mastered these twelve chapters, begin on some of your own favorite chapters.

Day	Chapter	Date Learned
1	Psalm 1	
2	Psalm 19	
3	Psalm 23	
4	Psalm 46	
5	Psalm 98	
6	Psalm 100	
7	Psalm 121	
8	Isaiah 53	
9	Romans 12	
10	1 Corinthians 13	
11	Ephesians 2	
12	Hebrews 11	

God's Word is Good to Pray

Talking with God is one of the most important parts of the Christian life. Prayer is how we can tell God about our deepest thoughts and desires. It is also a good way to listen to the direction and encouragement of God's Spirit. In our times of prayer, God can bring Bible verses to our minds in order to help us grow in the Lord. Prayer is also a time when God tells us about sins that need to be confessed (admitted to Him). He helps us see areas of our lives where we need to improve and please Him more. There are many prayers recorded in the Bible to help us understand how to pray and for what we should pray. Let's take a look at some of those.

Prayers of the Bible

Abijah's army—for victory	*2 Chronicles 13:14*
Abraham—for a son	*Genesis 15:1–6*
Abraham—for Ishmael	*Genesis 17:18–21*
Abraham—for Sodom	*Genesis 18:20–32*
Abraham—for Abimelech	*Genesis 20:17*
Abraham's servant—for guidance	*Genesis 24:12–52*
Asa—for victory	*2 Chronicles 14:11*
Cain—for mercy	*Genesis 4:13–15*
Centurion—for his servant	*Matthew 8:5–13*
Christians—for Peter	*Acts 12:5–12*
Christians—for kings in authority	*1 Timothy 2:1, 2*
Corinthians—for Paul	*2 Corinthians 1:9–11*
Cornelius—for enlightenment	*Acts 10:1–33*
Criminal—for salvation	*Luke 23:42, 43*
Daniel—for the Jews	*Daniel 9:3–19*
Daniel—for knowledge	*Daniel 2:17–23*
David—for blessing	*2 Samuel 7:18–29*
David—for help	*1 Samuel 23:10–13*

David—for guidance	*2 Samuel 2:1*
David—for grace	*Psalm 25:16*
David—for justice	*Psalm 9:17–20*
Disciples—for boldness	*Acts 4:24–31*
Elijah—for drought and rain	*James 5:17, 18*
Elijah—for the raising to life of the widow's son	*1 Kings 17:20–23*
Elijah—for triumph over Baal	*1 Kings 18:36–38*
Elijah—for death	*1 Kings 19:4*
Elisha—for blindness and sight	*2 Kings 6:17–23*
Ezekiel—for undefilement	*Ezekiel 4:12–15*
Ezra—for the sins of the people	*Ezra 9:6–15*
Gideon—for proof of his call	*Judges 6:36–40*
Habakkuk—for deliverance	*Habakkuk 3:1–19*
Habakkuk—for justice	*Habakkuk 1:1–4*
Hagar—for consolation	*Genesis 21:14–20*
Hannah—for a son	*1 Samuel 1:10–17*
Hezekiah—for deliverance	*2 Kings 19:15–19*
Hezekiah—for health	*2 Kings 20:1–11*
Holy Spirit—for Christians	*Romans 8:26, 27*
Isaac—for children	*Genesis 25:21, 24–26*
Israelites—for deliverance	*Exodus 2:23–25; 3:7–10*
Jabez—for prosperity	*1 Chronicles 4:10*
Jacob—all night	*Genesis 32:24–30*
Jacob—for deliverance from Esau	*Genesis 32:9–12*
Jehoahaz—for victory	*2 Kings 13:1–5*
Jehoshaphat—for protection	*2 Chronicles 20:5–12, 27*
Jehoshaphat—for victory	*2 Chronicles 18:31*
Jeremiah—for Judah	*Jeremiah 42:1–6*
Jeremiah—for mercy	*Jeremiah 14:7–10*

Jesus—Lord's Prayer	*Matthew 6:9–13*
Jesus—praise for revelation to babes	*Matthew 11:25, 26*
Jesus—at Lazarus's tomb	*John 11:41, 42*
Jesus—for the Father's glory	*John 12:28*
Jesus—for the church	*John 17:1–26*
Jesus—for deliverance	*Matthew 26:39, 42, 44*
Jesus—for forgiveness for others	*Luke 23:34*
Jesus—in submission	*Luke 23:46*
Jewish people—for safe journey	*Ezra 8:21, 23*
Jonah—for deliverance from the fish	*Jonah 2:1–10*
Joshua—for help and mercy	*Joshua 7:6–9*
Leper—for healing	*Matthew 8:2, 3*
Manasseh—for deliverance	*2 Chronicles 33:12, 13*
Manoah—for guidance	*Judges 13:8–15*
Mary—praise for being the mother of the Messiah	*Luke 1:46–55*
Miriam—praise for victory	*Exodus 15:20, 21*
Moses—for Pharaoh	*Exodus 8:9–13*
Moses—for water	*Exodus 15:24, 25*
Moses—for Israel	*Exodus 32:31–35*
Moses—for Miriam	*Numbers 12:11–14*
Moses—that he might see the Promised Land	*Deuteronomy 3:23–25; 34:1–4*
Moses—for a successor	*Numbers 27:15–17*
Nehemiah—for the Jewish people	*Nehemiah 1:4–11*
Paul—for the healing of Publius's father	*Acts 28:8*
Paul—for the Ephesians	*Ephesians 3:14–21*
Paul—for grace	*2 Corinthians 12:8, 9*
People of Judah—for a covenant	*2 Chronicles 15:12–15*
Peter—for the raising of Tabitha (Dorcas)	*Acts 9:40*

Priests—for blessing	*2 Chronicles 30:27*
Publican (tax collector)—for mercy	*Luke 18:13*
Rebekah—for understanding	*Genesis 25:22, 23*
Reubenites—for victory	*1 Chronicles 5:18–20*
Samson—for water	*Judges 15:18, 19*
Samson—for strength	*Judges 16:29, 30*
Samuel—for Israel	*1 Samuel 7:5–12*
Solomon—for wisdom	*1 Kings 3:6–14*
Zacharias—for a son	*Luke 1:13*

How Your Parents and Friends Can Pray for You

Prayer Request	Scripture Promise
1. That you would come to know Jesus as your personal Savior and Lord and that you would live a faithful, committed Christian life.	1 Corinthians 1:4–9; Galatians 1:3–5; Ephesians 1:3–14; 3:14–21; Philippians 1:3–11; 2 Timothy 1:3–7
2. That you would feel safe and loved.	Psalm 91:10–12; John 17:14–17; Romans 8:35–39
3. That you would be a good example to others and that your life would be Christlike.	Ephesians 6:1–4; 1 Thessalonians 1:2–10; 2 Thessalonians 1:3–8; Philemon 4–7
4. That you would learn to have the "mind of Christ"—begin to think the way Jesus would have you to think.	Philippians 2:5–11; Colossians 1:3–12
5. That you would understand right and wrong and that you would make right choices in your life.	Proverbs 20:11; 28:13; Philippians 1:9, 10
6. That you would be safe from evil.	Proverbs 4:14, 15; Galatians 5:16; Ephesians 6:11; James 4:7–9

Prayer Request	Scripture Promise
7. That you would have a good understanding of God's truth and that God would protect you from false teachers and false teaching.	Matthew 7:15; Colossians 2:8
8. That you would make good choices and wise decisions.	Proverbs 3:5, 6; Romans 12:1, 2; 1 Corinthians 10:13, 31; Philippians 3:12–14
9. That you would have realistic, God-pleasing goals and dreams for your life.	Psalm 32:8; 138:8; 143:8–10; Proverbs 4:20–27
10. That you would make wise, godly friendships.	Proverbs 13:20; 22:24, 25
11. That God would provide for you a godly husband or wife and a strong marriage.	2 Corinthians 6:14; Ephesians 5:22, 23, 25–29
12. That you would use your time wisely and trust God.	Proverbs 16:9; Philippians 4:6
13. That you would develop good work habits and that your work would please God.	Colossians 3:23; 2 Timothy 2:15
14. That you would use your money wisely.	Mark 12:41–44; 2 Thessalonians 3:7–10

Prayer Journal

You may use the following pages to record your praises, confessions, and prayer requests as you spend time in prayer and grow in your relationship with God. Remember, when you take time out to talk with God, He will begin to teach you and to answer the prayers of your heart. Don't forget to write down in these journal pages when and how God's answered you!

_____

_____

_____

_____

_____

_____

_____

_____

_____

_____

_____

_____

_____

_____

_____

_____

_____

_____

_____

_____

_____

Prayer Journal

_____

_____

_____

_____

_____

_____

_____

_____

_____

_____

_____

_____

_____

_____

_____

_____

_____

_____

_____

_____

_____

_____

_____

_____

Prayer Journal

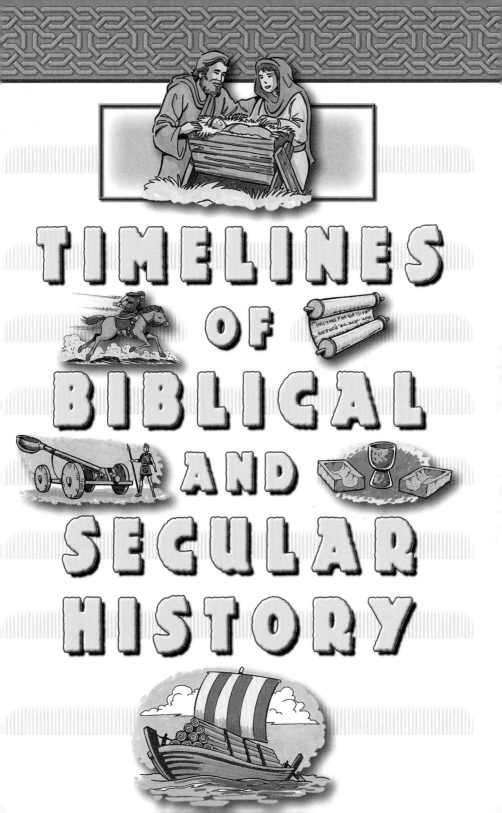

TIMELINES OF BIBLICAL AND SECULAR HISTORY

2000 TO 1500 B.C.

BIBLICAL HISTORY

Abram (Abraham) born (c. 2166 B.C.):
The patriarch Abram, later named Abraham, is born in Ur, located in southern Babylonia. His wife, Sarai (later named Sarah), is born about ten years later.

Abram moves to Canaan and later to Egypt (c. 2091 B.C.):
At God's command, Abram travels with his family from Ur to Haran and then to Canaan. Later they go to Egypt because of severe famine in the land. (Dates are based on early Exodus dating.)

Ishmael and Isaac born (c. 2080–2066 B.C.):
Back in Canaan, Abraham begets a son, Ishmael, by Sarah's slave Hagar with Sarah's approval. But later, Isaac is born to Abraham and Sarah when Abraham is over 100 and Sarah is in her 90s.

Sodom and Gomorrah destroyed (c. 2066 B.C.):
God destroys these cities south of the Dead Sea because of their extreme depravity. The wife of Abraham's nephew Lot turns to a pillar of salt when she looks back at the burning cities.

Jacob born (c. 2006 B.C.):
Twins Jacob and Esau are born to Rebekah.

Jacob fathers twelve sons (c. 1950–1920 B.C.):
With two wives and two concubines, Jacob fathers the twelve sons who would beget the tribes of Israel: Reuben, Simeon, Levi, Judah, Dan, Naphtali, Gad, Asher, Issachar, Zebulun, Joseph (whose sons Ephraim and Manasseh would become tribes), and Benjamin. There is also a daughter, Dinah.

Joseph sold into slavery and taken to Egypt (c. 1890 B.C.):
Joseph's brothers, jealous of their father's favor for Joseph, sell him into slavery. He is taken to Egypt, where he later becomes a trusted official second only to Pharaoh.

SECULAR HISTORY

2500 B.C.

The Great Pyramid at Giza demonstrates the architectural precision and advancement of the Egyptian Old Kingdom (c. 2550 B.C.).

2250 B.C.

Egyptians make copper pipes and use oars to propel large boats (c. 2450–2400 B.C.).

2150 B.C.

The Bronze Age is underway, with bronze in general use in Egypt (c. 2160 B.C.).

2000 B.C.

Mathematicians discover the Pythagorean Theorem (c. 1900 B.C.).

$$(5^2 = 4^2 + 3^2)$$

1900 B.C.

Astronomy and musical notation are developed in Babylon (c. 1800 B.C.).

1800 B.C.

Earliest evidence of spoked wheels (c. 1779 B.C.).

1500 B.C.

Phoenicians develop a consonantal alphabet (c. 1700 B.C.).

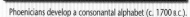

1500 TO 1200 B.C.

BIBLICAL HISTORY

Moses born and taken into Pharaoh's household (c. 1526 B.C.):
Moses' mother hides her baby to save him from Pharaoh's command that all Hebrew baby boys should be killed. Pharaoh's daughter finds Moses and raises him as her own.

Moses leads the Israelites out of Egypt (c. 1446 B.C.):
Having fled from Egypt 40 years earlier, Moses returns at God's command to free his people from slavery. Pharaoh refuses, God sends plagues on the Egyptians, and the Israelites leave Egypt. God parts the Red Sea for them and they enter the Sinai Peninsula. (Dated according to the early date for the Exodus.)

The Israelites enter the Promised Land (c. 1406 B.C.):
After God gives the Law to Moses at Mount Sinai, the people refuse to enter the Promised Land and God makes them travel in the wilderness for 40 years. Finally, a new generation led by Joshua crosses the Jordan River and enters the land.

The wall of Jericho falls (c. 1406 B.C.):
The Israelites are able to conquer the walled city of Jericho when God makes its wall fall so the Israelites can end their siege of the city. Rahab the harlot, who helped the Israelites, is spared with her family.

The sun stands still for Joshua (c. 1405 B.C.):
In a battle with the Amorites, Joshua pursues them to Gibeon, but he needs more time to defeat them. So God causes the sun to stand still, extending the hours of daylight for Joshua to complete his victory.

SECULAR HISTORY

Horses are in use in Nubia in southern Egypt (c. 1660 B.C.).

The Hittites and the Egyptians are using chariots (c. 1600 B.C.).

The New Kingdom is in power in Egypt; Pharaoh moves to Memphis (c. 1500 B.C.).

Massive volcanic eruption on the Aegean island of Thera (c. 1470 B.C.).

Earliest Egyptian shadow clock (c. 1450 B.C.).

Mycenaean Greeks invade Crete, destroying the palace at Knossos (c. 1400 B.C.).

Fire in the palace at Ugarit destroys royal archives (c.1360 B.C.).

1500 B.C.
1450 B.C.
1400 B.C.
1350 B.C.
1300 B.C.
1250 B.C.
1200 B.C.

1200 TO 930 B.C.

BIBLICAL HISTORY

For an extended time following Joshua's death, the Israelites are ruled by judges.

Deborah defeats Sisera (c. 1125 B.C.):
The judge Deborah and her general Barak battle the Canaanite king Sisera and are victorious. Deborah composes her famous victory song.

Samson defeats the Philistines (c. 1120 B.C.):
The judge Samson is tricked by Delilah and captured by the Philistines and blinded, but he brings down their temple on them as his strength returns, sacrificing his own life in the process.

Eli serves as priest and judge (c. 1100 B.C.):
Eli is priest at Shiloh. His sons are unworthy, but young Samuel is brought up under Eli's care and becomes Israel's leading prophet.

Saul becomes Israel's first king (c. 1050 B.C.):
The people demand a king like the other nations have, so against his judgment the prophet Samuel anoints Saul, a Benjamite, to be king.

David is king of Israel (c. 1010–970 B.C.):
Saul proves unworthy, so God has Samuel anoint David to be king. David slays Goliath. Later, Saul turns on David and they become enemies. Saul dies in battle, and David becomes the great king of a united kingdom.

Solomon is king of Israel (c. 970–930 B.C.):
The son of David and Bathsheba, Solomon comes to the throne as his father's successor. He gets to build the temple in Jerusalem that had been planned by David. Solomon is known for his wealth and his wisdom.

SECULAR HISTORY

The Iron Age begins with the rise of iron technology (c. 1200 B.C.).

Troy falls to the Greeks (c. 1200 B.C.).

Lumber trade by sea between Lebanon and Egypt thrives (c. 1100 B.C.).

The temple of Hera is constructed at Olympia in Greece (c. 975 B.C.).

Assyrians make armor with iron scales (c. 950 B.C.).

1200 B.C.
1150 B.C.
1100 B.C.
1050 B.C.
1000 B.C.
950 B.C.
900 B.C.

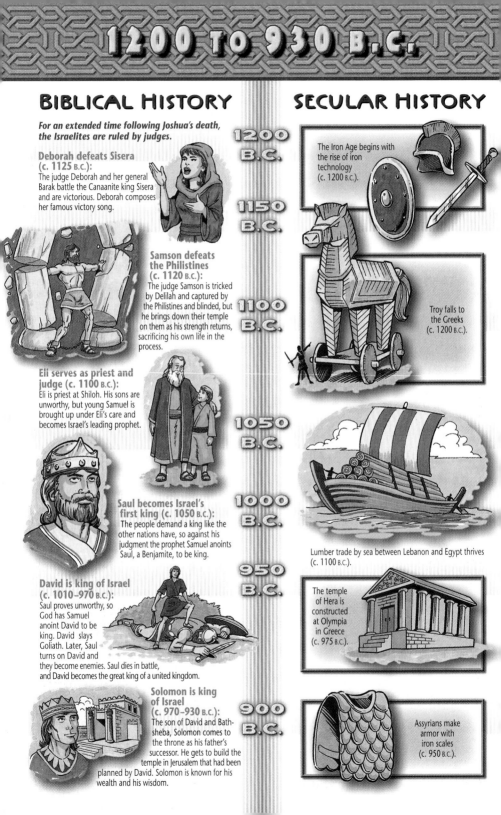

930 TO 586 B.C.

BIBLICAL HISTORY

Rehoboam and Jeroboam divide the kingdom (c. 930 B.C.):
After Solomon's death, his son Rehoboam alienates his supporters and gets to be king only of the southern kingdom of Judah. Jeroboam sets up a rival kingdom in the north, known as Israel.

Ahab and Jezebel (874–853 B.C.):
King Ahab of Israel is influenced badly by his Phoenician princess wife Jezebel, a Baal-worshiper. Ahab builds shrines to the Phoenician god and brings many of his false priests to Israel. Corruption reigns.

Elijah and Elisha (c. 870–835 B.C.):
The prophet Elijah stands against the Baal worship in Ahab's Israel. He works miracles and finally is taken to heaven without dying, in a chariot of fire. Elijah's protégé Elisha takes over for him after he leaves. Elisha travels throughout Israel and also works many miracles.

Isaiah (c. 740–680 B.C.):
The greatest of the writing prophets, Isaiah has been called "the fifth evangelist," because his book refers in so many ways to the coming Messiah. Isaiah pronounces judgments on surrounding nations for opposing God, and warns his own.

Israel falls to the Assyrians (722 B.C.):
The mighty armies of Assyria conquer the northern kingdom of Israel. Most of the Israelites are deported to Assyria and other groups are brought in to repopulate the land. The southern kingdom of Judah is miraculously spared, but they have to pay tribute.

Josiah's reforms (c. 622 B.C.):
The Book of the Law is found and king Josiah leads a revival of godly worship in Judah. The Passover is kept again.

Judah falls to the Babylonians (586 B.C.):
The southern kingdom of Judah is conquered by the forces of Babylonian king Nebuchadnezzar and the Jewish people are taken into exile in Babylon.

SECULAR HISTORY

Phoenicians establish trading colonies as far away as Spain (c. 900 B.C.).

Ashurnasirpal II of Assyria has a military campaign every year of his reign (883–859 B.C.).

The royal inscription called the Moabite Stone is made (850 B.C.).

The city of Carthage in northern Africa is founded (c. 825 B.C.).

Athletic contests begin at Olympia (776 B.C.).

Homer's *Iliad* and *Odyssey* descend from oral tradition (c. 750 B.C.).

Greeks start making clay objects using molds (c. 650 B.C.).

The Hanging Gardens of Babylon are built (c. 594 B.C.).

Timeline
950 B.C.
850 B.C.
750 B.C.
650 B.C.
550 B.C.

BIBLICAL HISTORY

SECULAR HISTORY

Ezekiel sees visions of the future (c. 573 B.C.):
The prophet Ezekiel, in exile in Babylon with his people, sees visions of their future restoration and a magnificent new temple.

600 B.C.

Greeks use saws for cutting (c. 575 B.C.).

Cyrus allows the Jews to rebuild the temple (538–515 B.C.):
Cyrus the Persian's defeat of Babylon brings in a ruler with some religious tolerance. The Jews are given the go-ahead to return and build a new temple in Jerusalem, which they eventually do under Zerubbabel's leadership.

500 B.C.

Anaximander proposes a mathematical model of the universe (555 B.C.).

Cambyses of Persia builds a naval fleet with Ionians and Phoenicians (530–522 B.C.).

400 B.C.

Ezra and Nehemiah return to Jerusalem (c. 458–445 B.C.):
Ezra and Nehemiah lead additional returns to Jerusalem under the reign of the Persian king Artaxerxes. Nehemiah leads a project to rebuild the wall of Jerusalem.

Persians begin a royal mounted messenger service (500 B.C.).

300 B.C.

The conquests of Alexander the Great (336–323 B.C.):
Alexander of Macedon's conquered empire covers a huge portion of the ancient world by the time he dies of illness in Babylon at age 32. Greek culture becomes dominant for centuries to come.

Greek philosophers Socrates (469–399 B.C.), Plato (428–347 B.C.), and Aristotle (384–322 B.C.).

Overshot waterwheel used in the marketplace of Athens (c. 450 B.C.).

200 B.C.

Invention of the screw (c. 400 B.C.).

Maccabeans and Hasmoneans (166–64 B.C.):
Alexander's successors the Seleucids are defeated by a revolt led by Jewish leader Judas Maccabeus. He and his family restore home rule to the Jews in Judaea, followed by their successors the Hasmoneans.

100 B.C.

Macedonian armies use catapults for shooting arrows (323 B.C.).

30 B.C.

Third Punic War, Rome v. Carthage (149–146 B.C.).

Pompey takes control of Palestine (63 B.C.):
Rule by Rome begins in the Holy Land when the Roman general Pompey captures Jerusalem.

Julius Caesar is assassinated by Brutus and Cassius (44 B.C.).

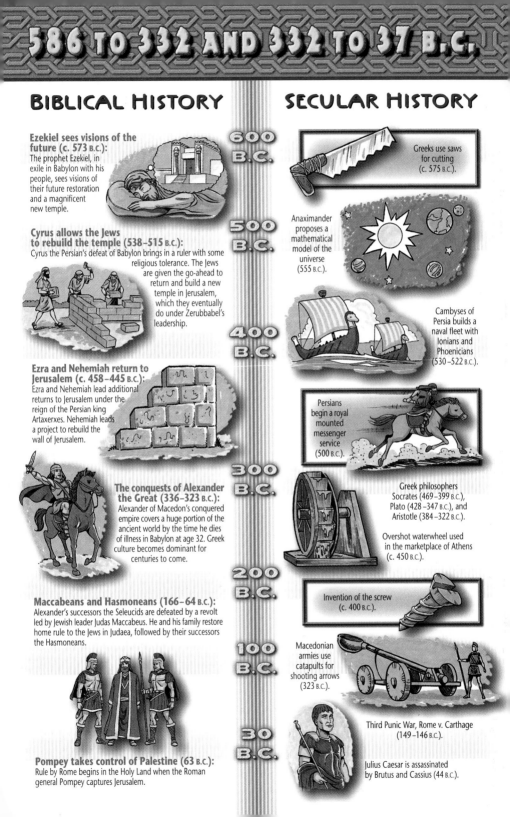

37 B.C. TO A.D. 30

BIBLICAL HISTORY

Herod the Great's reign (37–4 B.C.): Not really a Jew, but an Idumean, Herod serves as Rome's puppet king in Judaea. He begins a new temple in 19 B.C. He attempts to deceive the Magi at the time of Jesus' birth, and orders the "massacre of the innocents."

Jesus is born (c. 5 B.C.); Mary gives birth to the Son of God in a humble stable in Bethlehem.

Jesus astonishes teachers in the temple (c. A.D. 7): At age 12, the missing Jesus is found by Mary and Joseph as He amazes the teachers in the temple in Jerusalem with His wisdom and insights.

Tiberius becomes emperor of Rome (A.D. 14): Tiberius Caesar, adopted son and successor to Augustus, rules the Roman Empire during the time of the ministry of Christ. He sends Pontius Pilate to be procurator, Rome's appointed ruler, in Judaea.

John the Baptist baptizes Jesus (c. A.D. 26): Christ's cousin John is baptizing people in the River Jordan for repentance and remission of sins. Jesus is without sin, but He submits to John's baptism "to fulfil all righteousness," and His public ministry begins.

Crucifixion and resurrection of Jesus (A.D. 30): The crowd's cries of "Hosanna!" on Palm Sunday turn to "Crucify!" less than a week later. The Son of God is led to His death on a cross at Calvary—then He rises again on the third day.

SECULAR HISTORY

35 B.C.

Defeated by Octavian (Augustus), the Roman leader Mark Antony and Egyptian queen Cleopatra commit suicide (30 B.C.).

20 B.C.

Veterans of two Roman legions colonize Berytus (Beirut) (15 B.C.).

MEDITERRANEAN SEA · LEBANON · BEIRUT

10 B.C.

Augustus revives the priesthood of Jupiter in Rome (11 B.C.).

Herod Antipas puts on a gladiator display at Caesarea (10 B.C.).

Herod the Great executes his sons Alexander and Aristobulus (7 B.C.).

A.D. 10

Caesar Augustus dies and the Senate of Rome declares him a god (A.D. 14).

A.D. 20

Syria and Judaea petition Rome to lower their taxes (A.D. 17).

The emperor Tiberius begins his retirement on the Isle of Capri (A.D. 26).

A.D. 30

A.D. 30 TO 100

BIBLICAL HISTORY

Pentecost (A.D. 30):
After Christ ascends to heaven, His followers are filled with the Holy Spirit as they assemble together in Jerusalem. Beginning at Jerusalem and spreading from there, they are empowered to share the gospel.

Saul is converted (A.D. 34):
Saul, a zealous Pharisee bent on persecuting the young church, is converted to faith in Christ when the risen Savior appears to him on the road to Damascus.

Paul's first missionary journey (A.D. 46):
Saul, renamed Paul, goes on his first journey to preach the gospel with Barnabas. They travel through Cyprus and several towns in Asia Minor.

Paul preaches on Mars Hill in Athens (A.D. 50):
On his second missionary journey, Paul tells Athenians that their "unknown god" is none other than the one true God who sent His Son Jesus and raised Him from the dead.

Paul is sent to Rome (A.D. 57–59):
Paul is arrested in Jerusalem and takes his fourth journey, this time as a prisoner. After surviving shipwreck, he gets his wish to visit Rome. He shares his faith there in chains and eventually is executed under the persecutions of the emperor Nero (c. A.D. 67).

The Romans destroy Jerusalem (A.D. 69–70):
Judaea rebels against Rome, and Rome sends armies under the command of Titus who set up a siege of Jerusalem. After a valiant defense, the city is taken and the temple is destroyed.

John is exiled on Patmos (c. A.D. 95):
John sees visions of Christ's future glorious triumph and writes the Book of Revelation while exiled on the island of Patmos off the western coast of Asia Minor.

SECULAR HISTORY

Pontius Pilate is recalled to Rome for misconduct (A.D. 36).

The emperor Caligula orders his statue to be placed in the temple, and Herod Agrippa persuades him not to (A.D. 40).

Caligula is assassinated (A.D. 41).

Famine, as predicted by the prophet Agabus (A.D. 44–48).

The emperor Nero compels senators to fight in the stadium (A.D. 57).

Nero orders his own mother to be put to death (A.D. 59).

Rome burns and Nero blames the Christians (A.D. 64).

Masada, the last Jewish stronghold, falls to the Romans and its defenders commit suicide (A.D. 74).

The volcano Vesuvius erupts, burying Pompeii and Herculaneum (A.D. 79).

The Council of Jamnia meets and begins to settle the canon of the Hebrew Scriptures (A.D. 90).

A.D. 30
A.D. 50
A.D. 70
A.D. 85
A.D. 100

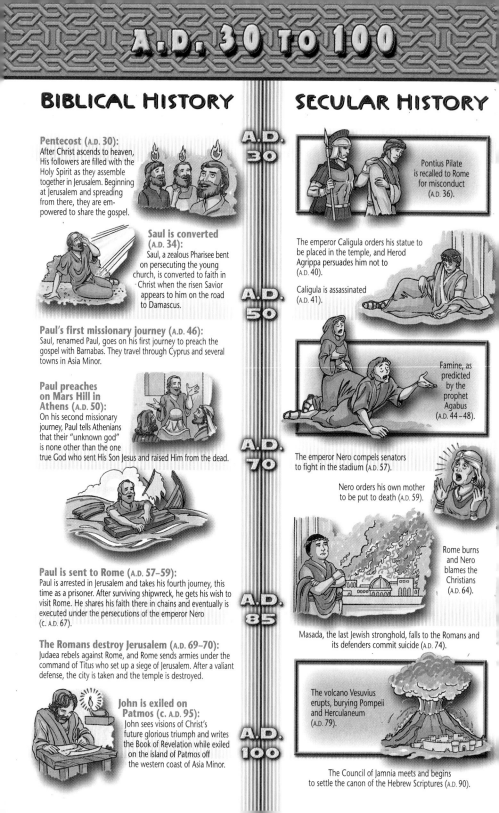